Y0-AKN-680

Bookman's Price Index

ISSN 0068-0141

Bookman's Price Index

VOLUME 99

A Guide to the Values of
Rare and Other Out of Print Books

Edited by
Anne F. McGrath

GALE
CENGAGE Learning

Farmington Hills, Mich • San Francisco • New York • Waterville, Maine
Meriden, Conn • Mason, Ohio • Chicago

GALE
CENGAGE Learning

Bookman's Price Index, Vol. 99
Anne F. McGrath

Product Management: Michele LeMeau

Project Editor: Kristin B. Mallegg

Manufacturing: Rita Wimberley

© 2014 Gale, Cengage Learning
WCN: 01-100-101

ALL RIGHTS RESERVED. No part of this work covered by the copyright herein may be reproduced, transmitted, stored, or used in any form or by any means graphic, electronic, or mechanical, including but not limited to photocopying, recording, scanning, digitizing, taping, Web distribution, information networks, or information storage and retrieval systems, except as permitted under Section 107 or 108 of the 1976 United States Copyright Act, without the prior written permission of the publisher.

This publication is a creative work fully protected by all applicable copyright laws, as well as by misappropriation, trade secret, unfair competition, and other applicable laws. The authors and editors of this work have added value to the underlying factual material herein through one or more of the following: unique and original selection, coordination, expression, arrangement, and classification of the information.

For product information and technology assistance, contact us at
Gale Customer Support, 1-800-877-4253.
For permission to use material from this text or product,
submit all requests online at www.cengage.com/permissions.
Further permissions questions can be emailed to
permissionrequest@cengage.com

While every effort has been made to ensure the reliability of the information presented in this publication, Gale, a part of Cengage Learning, does not guarantee the accuracy of the data contained herein. Gale accepts no payment for listing; and inclusion in the publication of any organization, agency, institution, publication, service, or individual does not imply endorsement of the editors or publisher. Errors brought to the attention of the publisher and verified to the satisfaction of the publisher will be

EDITORIAL DATA PRIVACY POLICY
Does this product contain information about you as an individual? If so, for more information about how to access or correct that information or about our data privacy policies please see our Privacy Statement at www.gale.cengage.com

Gale
27500 Drake Rd.
Farmington Hills, MI 48331-3535

LIBRARY OF CONGRESS CATALOG CARD NUMBER 64-008723

ISBN-13: 978-1-5730-2853-0
ISSN 0068-0141

Printed in the United States of America
1 2 3 4 5 6 7 18 17 16 15 14

Contents

Introduction vii
Dealers Represented in This Volume 1
Bookman's Price Index 9
Association Copies 841
Fine Bindings 1081
Fore-edge Paintings 1133

Introduction

Bookman's Price Index, established in 1964, is published two to four times each year as an index to both the prices and availability of antiquarian books in the United States, Canada, and the British Isles. Each issue of *BPI* reports the prices and availability of over 12,000 different antiquarian books. Thus, in the course of an average calendar year, *BPI* reports the prices and availability of about 25,000 antiquarian books that are important to readers in the North Atlantic portion of the English-speaking community.

Definition of Antiquarian Books

An antiquarian book is one that is, or has been, traded on the antiquarian book market. It is, or was, traded there because it is important (or in demand) and scarce.

Importance, in the case of antiquarian books, is national. American, Canadian, and British readers buy and sell the artifacts of their own literature and history, science and art as well as a select number of books that document the Continental and Classical origins of certain aspects of their cultures. There are special enthusiasms, too, such as children's books, sporting books, and books that are important principally for their physical beauty; but even the books of these special enthusiasms reflect the national preoccupations of English-speaking readers.

Scarcity means that the number of copies of any book that might come onto the market is measured, at most, in scores, and that only a dozen or a half-dozen, at most, come onto the market during any calendar year.

Lots of important books are not scarce, and lots of scarce books are not important. And, despite the word *antiquarian*, age is no guarantee of either scarcity or importance. Conversely, many books that are less than a generation old bring a handsome price on the market.

The antiquarian books that do appear on the North Atlantic market are a small percentage of the world's entire antiquarian book market, and, necessarily, they are the tiniest fraction of the total number of books published over the centuries.

Despite their thin ranks and scant number, antiquarian books are usually not outrageously expensive. They often range in price from $50 to $500, with most clustering between $100 and $200, and precious few enjoying four-figure prominence.

Prices Reported in *BPI*

The prices reported in *Bookman's Price Index* each year are established by some 100-200 antiquarian booksellers in the United States, Canada, and the British Isles. Usually, about 50 of these booksellers are represented in any one volume of *BPI*. By drawing information from a large number of antiquarian booksellers across English-speaking North America, as well as the British Isles, *BPI* is able to report broad, consistent, and reliable market patterns in the whole North Atlantic English-speaking community.

Within the ranks of the antiquarian booksellers whose prices are reported in *BPI*, the group most interesting is the specialist dealers, whose stock is limited to books in a single subject such as law, or psychiatry, or maritime studies, or horticulture. Such specialists provide readers of *BPI* with information that is not easily available elsewhere.

The prices that all of these antiquarian booksellers report are retail prices that they have established on the basis of their working experience and familiarity with current market conditions, including supply and demand and the effect upon price of the general physical condition of a book, as well as such extraordinary factors as the presence of important autographs.

The willingness of the various antiquarian booksellers to publish their prices in direct comparison with the prices of all other antiquarian booksellers serves as a general indication of the reliability of the prices reported in *BPI* as well as the probity of the antiquarian booksellers. These prices are public market prices, not private deals.

Availability of Books in *BPI*

Every one of the books in *Bookman's Price Index* was recently available in one of the shops of the antiquarian booksellers whose catalogs are included in this volume of *BPI*. It was upon the basis of a hands-on appraisal of each book that an antiquarian bookseller established its price. Thus, the prices reported in *BPI* are actual prices for specific books rather than approximate prices for probable or possible books.

While a particular book may no longer be in the shop of the antiquarian bookseller who established its price, the fact that the book stood on the shelf there recently means that the book is still to be found on the market and that the antiquarian bookseller who established its price may have access to another copy of the same book, or that a different antiquarian bookseller may price another copy of the book in the following issue of *BPI*. Thus, by reporting prices of actual books and their real availability, *Bookman's Price Index* serves as an index to the general market availability of a particular antiquarian book.

Conversely, *BPI* is an index to the absence of certain antiquarian books from the market: books not priced in *BPI* may be presumed to be generally unavailable on the antiquarian book market. *BPI* makes no effort to predict what such unavailable books might be worth if they were perhaps to someday come on the market; *BPI* reports only what is going on in the market, not what might go on.

For example, if a reader were to search the six most recent issues of *BPI* for the price of the first edition of Edgar Allan Poe's *Tamerlane,* he might not find it and could safely conclude that a first edition of *Tamerlane* was not generally available during the past two years or so. If, on the other hand, the same reader were to make a similar search for a first edition of *The Stand* by Poe's spiritual son Stephen King, he might discover that *The Stand* has been found in the shops from time to time and that it is worth about $1600 for a signed first edition, or between $200 and $400 for an unsigned first, depending on condition.

The Importance of Condition

Condition is critical in antiquarian books as in any other antiquarian artifact. The condition of all of the books priced in *Bookman's Price Index* is stated in elaborate detail because it is impossible to understand or justify the price of any antiquarian book without full knowledge of its condition.

Arrangement of *BPI*

The books priced in *Bookman's Price Index* are arranged in a single main alphabet according to the name of the author: in cases of personal authorship, the author's last name; in cases of books produced by corporate bodies such as governments of countries or states, the name of that corporation; in cases of anonymous books, the title; and in cases of anonymous classics such as the *Arabian Nights,* by customary title.

All names of authors, or titles, are standardized according to the usage of American libraries, thus gathering all works by an author.

The works of an author are arranged under his or her name in alphabetical sequence according to the first word of the title, excepting initial articles. However, editions of an author's collected works are listed, out of alphabetical sequence, at the end of the list of his or her individual works.

Different editions of a single work are arranged according to date of publication, with the earlier preceding the later even though this sequence sometimes disrupts alphabetical regularity. In such cases, the editor has sought to consult the reader's convenience rather than any rigid consistency.

The reasons for the occasional disruption of alphabetical regularity are two: the first is that in reporting prices, antiquarian booksellers sometimes refer to a book elliptically, leaving unknown the complete title. The second reason is that certain books change title without changing substance. The most obvious example of this particular editorial problem is the Bible. Title pages of Bibles can begin with such words as Complete, Holy, Sacred, New, Authorized, and so on: it is still the same book. Therefore all English Bibles appear, under the heading BIBLES – ENGLISH, in chronological order. Following the title of each book is its imprint: the place and date of publication and the name of the publisher (or the name of the printer in cases of certain books produced prior to the late eighteenth century).

Description of the Condition of Books

Following the author, title, and imprint of each book is a thorough description of the physical condition of the book, insofar as the bookseller has provided this information. While antiquarian booksellers do not always apply a standard formula in describing the condition of a book, they generally include, as appropriate, most of the following details:

Edition. *BPI* reports which edition of a book is being priced when this information is critical, as in cases when several editions were published in one year. If an edition was published in more than one issue, or state, *BPI* distinguishes among them and identifies them either by the order in which they appeared, or by the physical peculiarities that characterize them. When necessary, *BPI* even describes those obscure details, called "points," that are used to distinguish among issues or states. The points are often minute and consist of such details as one misspelled word buried in the text. Finally, *BPI* identifies limited editions, stating the number of copies in the press run and, if necessary, the types of paper used and the specific number assigned to the book being priced.

Physical Size. *BPI* describes the height and the bulk of each book when this information is available. Height is usually described in the traditional language of the antiquarian book trade: folio, for a tall book; quarto (4to) for a medium-size book; and octavo (8vo) or duodecimo (12mo) for a smaller book. Miniature books are usually described in inches top to bottom and left to right. The bulk of a book is described by stating its pagination, a custom that operates to assure the reader that the book in question is complete.

Illustrations. Since many antiquarian books are more valuable for their illustrations than for their text, *BPI* describes such illustrations carefully, sometimes in considerable detail, as in the case of a book with hand-colored plates.

Binding. All bindings are described fully as to the material used, be it paper, cloth or leather, and even as to the type and color of the material and the time at which it was applied. ("Contemporary tan calf" means that a binding of cattle hide was made for the book contemporaneously with its printing.) Decorations of the binding are also described, and in the cases of twentieth century books, the presence or absence of the dust jacket is always noted.

Authors' Signatures. These are always cited, as they have a significant effect on the price of a book.

General Physical Condition, Specific Flaws, and Relative Scarcity. Usually, *BPI* provides some advice on the general condition of a book by stating that its condition is good, very good, or fine. Additionally, specific flaws are usually listed; some of them are significant, as in the case of a missing leaf or a worn binding, while others are very minor, as in the case of a worm hole in an ancient tome.

Availability. Frequently *BPI* will point out that certain books are of unusual scarcity or rarity. As all antiquarian books are by definition scarce, a special remark that a book is uncommonly scarce should be noted carefully.

Prices. Following the description, *BPI* gives the price of the book along with the name of the antiquarian bookseller who established the price and provided the physical description. Accompanying the antiquarian bookseller's name is the number of the catalog in which he published the price and description of the book, plus the item number of the book in the catalog. The addresses of the antiquarian booksellers whose prices are reported in *BPI* are listed following this Introduction, in the section entitled Dealers Represented in This Volume.

Association Copies, Fine Bindings, and Fore-edge Paintings

Following the main section of *Bookman's Price Index* are three small sections of association copies of books, books in fine bindings, and books decorated with fore-edge paintings. The books in these three sections take on additional interest and value because of features peculiar to them that are not found in other copies of the same books. Their value, or some portion of it, derives from factors not inherent in the text and not identifiable through the name of the author, thereby requiring that they be isolated so that readers can search them out according to the factors that create, or influence, their worth: association, binding or fore-edge painting.

All books priced and described in one of the special sections are also priced and described in the main section of *BPI*, thus permitting the reader to compare an ordinary copy of a book with one that enjoys added attraction because of a unique feature.

Association Copies. Certain antiquarian books acquire added value because of their association with a prominent owner. For instance, an ordinary eighteenth century book would take on enormous extra worth if it had once belonged to George Washington. Association copies of books priced in the special section of *BPI* are arranged according to the name of the person with whom the book was associated rather than according to the name of the author. (The same book is listed in the main body of *BPI* under the name of the author.)

Fine Bindings. Some books are valuable because custom bindings were applied to them alone, and not to other copies of the same book. In the Fine Bindings section of *BPI*, books are gathered under the name of the binder, when known, and then listed according to author. (Each of the books so listed is also listed under the name of the author in the main section of *BPI*.)

Fore-edge Paintings. Fore-edge paintings are original watercolor drawings upon the vertical edges of the leaves of a book. The book is laid flat with the front cover open so that the vertical edges of the leaves slant a little when the painting is applied; when the book is closed, the painting is not visible. These unusual examples of book decoration are gathered in the Fore-edge section under the year of publication of the book, and then arranged according to the name of the author. Generally, fore-edge paintings are not signed and dated, and it is often difficult, if not impossible, to be sure a fore-edge painting was executed in the year of publication of the book. When there is conclusive evidence as to the name of the artist and the date of a fore-edge painting, the book is listed under the year in which the painting was executed. (All books listed in the Fore-edge section are also listed in the main section of *BPI* under the name of the author.)

Errors in *BPI*

The multiple volumes of *BPI* that appear each year combine to include millions of letters and numerals. The editor makes every effort to get them all right, and she asks the reader to be understanding about an occasional typo.

Suggestions Are Welcome

Comments on the *Bookman's Price Index* series and suggestions for corrections and improvements are always welcome. Please contact:

Editor, *Bookman's Price Index*
Gale
27500 Drake Rd.
Farmington Hills, MI 48331-3535
Phone: 248-699-GALE
Toll-free: 800-877-GALE

Antiquarian Book Dealers in Volume 99

Charles Agvent
291 Linden Road
Mertztown PA 19539
USA

Telephone: (610) 682-4750
e-mail: info@charlesagvent.com
http://www.charlesagvent.com
Contact: Charles Agvent

Aleph-Bet Books, Inc.
85 Old Mill River Road
Pound Ridge NY 10576
USA

Telephone: (914) 764-7410
Fax: (914) 764-1356
e-mail: helen@alephbet.com
http://www.alephbet.com
Contact: Helen & Marc Younger
Specialties: Children's & illustrated books for the collector, first editions, pop-ups, picture books, fairy tales and more.

Argonaut Book Shop
786-792 Sutter Street
San Francisco CA 94109
USA

Telephone: (415) 474-9067
Fax: (415) 474-2537
e-mail: argonautSF@PacBell.net
http://www.argonautbookshop.com

Barnaby Rudge Booksellers
1445 Glenneyre Street
Laguna Beach CA 92651
USA

Telephone: (866) 840-5900; (949) 497-4079
Fax: (949) 376-3111
e-mail: info@barnabyrudge.com
http://www.barnabyrudge.com
Contact: Edward S. Postal
Specialties: Antiquarian, Children's & Illustrated Books, Early Printed Books, Bibles

Beasley Books
1533 W. Oakdale
Chicago IL 60657
USA

Telephone: (773) 472-4528
Fax: (773) 472-7857
e-mail: beasley@beasleybooks.com
http://www.beasleybooks.com
Contact: Paul and Beth Garon; hours by appointment.
Specialties: Modern first editiions, black literature, jazz & blues, radicalism, psychoanalysis.

Between The Covers Rare Books, Inc.
112 Nicholson Road
Gloucester City NJ 08030
USA

Telephone: (856) 456-8008
Fax: (856) 456-7675
e-mail: mail@betweenthecovers.com
http://www.betweenthecovers.com
Contact: Tom Congalton, Heidi Congalton, Gwen Waring, Jessica Luminoso, Dan Gregory, Jennifer Gregory

Blackwell's Rare Books
48-51 Broad Street
Oxford OX1 3BQ
England

Telephone: 01865 333555
Fax: 01865 794143
e-mail: rarebooks@blackwell.co.uk
http://www.rarebooks.blackwell.co.uk

J & S L Bonham
Flat 14
84 Westbourne Terrace
London W2 6QE
England

Telephone: 20 7402 7064
Fax: 20 7402 0955
e-mail: bonbooks@dial.pipex.com
http://www.bonbooks.dial.pipex.com

David Brass Rare Books, Inc.
PO Box 9029
Calabasas CA   91372
USA

Telephone: (818) 222-4103
e-mail: info@davidbrassrareabooks.com
http://www.davidbrassrarebooks.com
Specialties: Children's Books, Color-Plate Books, Early Printed Books, Fine Bindings, Illustrated Books, Literature, Original Artwork, Private Press Books

The Brick Row Book Shop
49 Geary Street #230
San Francisco CA   94108
USA

Telephone: (415) 398-0414
Fax: (415) 398-0435
e-mail: book@brickrow.com
http://www.brickrow.com
Specialties: First Editions, Rare Books and Manuscripts of 17th, 18th & 19th Century English and American Literature

By the Book, LC ABAA-ILAB
1045 East Camelback Road
Phoenix AZ   85014
USA

Telephone: (602) 222-8806
Fax: (480) 596-1672
e-mail: bythebooklc@qwestoffice.net
http://bythebooklc.com
Specialties: Art, Children's China/Japan/Korea, History of Ideas, Literature, Medicine, Science &Technology, Signed Books

L. W. Currey, Inc.
203 Water Street
Elizabethtown NY   12932
USA

Telephone: (518) 873-6477
http://www.lwcurrey.com
Contact: Lloyd Currey
Specialties: Popular fiction, with emphasis on science fiction and fantasy literature from the earliest times to end of the twentieth century.

Dumont Maps & Books Of The West
314 McKenzie Street
P.O. Box 10250
Santa Fe NM   87501
USA

Telephone: (505) 988-1076
Fax: (505) 986-6114
e-mail: info@dumontbooks.com
http://www.dumontbooks.com

Joseph J. Felcone Inc.
P.O. Box 366
Princeton NJ   08542
USA

Telephone: (609) 924-0539
Fax: (609) 924-9078
e-mail: info@felcone.com
http://www.felcone.com

Gemini Fine Books & Arts, Ltd.
917 Oakwood Terrace
Hinsdale IL   60521
USA

Telephone: (630) 986-1478
Fax: (630) 986-8992
e-mail: art@geminibooks.com
http://www.geminibooks.com
Specialties: Art Reference Books, French Symbolism, Art Nouveau and Art Deco, German Expressionism, Modern Illustrated Books (Livres D'artistes)

James Tait Goodrich
Antiquarian Books And Manuscripts
125 Tweed Boulevard
Grandview-on-Hudson NY   10960
USA

Telephone: (845) 359-0242
Fax: (845) 359-0142
e-mail: goodrich@aecom.yu.edu
Contact: James T. Goodrich
Specialties: Medicine, science, medical instruments, Pre-Columbian artifacts.

Heritage Book Shop, LLC
9024 Burton Way
Beverly Hills CA 90211
USA

Telephone: (310) 659-3674
Fax: (310) 659-4872
e-mail: books@heritagebookshop.com
http://www.heritagebookshop.com
Contact: Ben Weinstein
Specialties: Illustrated Books, Bindings, Literature, Manuscripts, Early Printed Books, First Editions

Jeff Hirsch Books
39850 N. Dilleys Rd.
Wadsworth IL 60083
USA

Telephone: (847) 662-2665
e-mail: mail@jhbooks.com
http://www.jhbooks.com
Contact: Jeff or Susan Hirsch
Specialties: 20th Century Photography, Art Monographs, Drama, Modern Literary Firsts, Poetry, Signed Books, Broadsides

Ian Hodgkins & Co. Ltd.
47 Lansdown
Stroud
Gloucestershire GL5 1BN
England

Telephone: 44 (0) 1453 755 233
Fax: 44 (0) 1453 755 233
e-mail: inquiries@ianhodgkins.com
http://www.ianhodgkins.com
Contact: Tony Yablon, Ian Hoy, Simon Weager

R. F. G. Hollett And Son
6 Finkle Street
Sedbergh
Cumbria LA10 5BZ
England

Telephone: 44 0 15396 20298
Fax: 44 0 15396 21396
e-mail: hollett@sedburgh.demon.co.uk
http://www.holletts-rarebooks.co.uk
Contact: C. G. Hollett
Specialties: Fine, rare and collectable books of all kinds.

C P Hyland
Rosscarbery
Co. Cork
Ireland

Telephone: 023 48063
Fax: 023 48658
e-mail: calbux@gmail.com
http://www.rossbarbery.ie/cphyland
Contact: Cal and Joan Hyland

James S. Jaffe Rare Books Llc
790 Madison Ave
Suite 605
New York NY 10065
USA

Telephone: (212) 988-8042
Fax: (212) 988-8044
e-mail: jamesjaffe@earthlink.net
http://www.jamessjafferarebooks.com
Contact: James Jaffe, Ingrid Lin, Mark Lowe
Specialties: Rare books, literary first editions, poetry, livres d'artistes, association copies, letters and manuscripts, archives.

Jarndyce Antiquarian Booksellers
46, Great Russell Street
Bloomsbury
London WC1B 3PA
England

Telephone: 020 7631 4220
Fax: 020 7631 1882
e-mail: books@jarndyce.co.uk
http://www.jarndyce.co.uk
Contact: Brian Lake, Janet Nassau
Specialties: Specialty: 18th and particularly 19th century English literature and history; Dickens.

Priscilla Juvelis, Inc.
11 Goose Fair
Kennebunkport ME 04046
USA

Telephone: (207) 967-0909
e-mail: pf@juvelisbooks.com
http://www.juvelisbooks.com
Contact: Priscilla Juvelis
Specialties: Book Arts, Literary First Editions

Kaaterskill Books
PO Box 122
East Jewett NY   12424
USA

Telephone: (518) 589-0555
Fax: (518) 589-0555
e-mail: books@katerskillbooks.com
http://www.kaaterskillbooks.com
Contact: Joan Kutcher, Charles Kutcher
Specialties: Americana, Latin Americana, Asia, Art, Books on Books, History, Literature, Religion

The Kelmscott Bookshop
34 W 25th Street
Baltimore MD   21218
USA

Telephone: (410) 235-6810
Fax: (410) 366-9446
e-mail: info@kellmscottbookshop.com
http://www.kelmscottbookshop.com
Specialties: Artists' Books, Book Arts, Pre-Raphaelites, Private and Fine Press, Victorian British Literature, William Morris

Leather Stalking Books
107 Bartlett Road
Cooperstown NY   13326
USA

Telephone: (607) 547-5748
e-mail: info@leatherstalkingbooks.com
http://www.leatherstalkingbooks.com
Contact: Bill & Vi Elsey
Specialties: Mystery and detective fiction; baseball

Ken Lopez, Bookseller
51 Huntington Rd.
Hadley MA   01035
USA

Telephone: (413) 584-4827
Fax: (413) 584-2045
e-mail: klopez@well.com
http://www.lopezbooks.com
Specialties: Modern literary first editions, literature of the 1960's, Vietnam War, native American literature, nature writing.

M & S Rare Books.Inc.
P.O. Box 2594
East Side Station
Providence RI   02906
USA

Telephone: (401) 421-1050
Fax: (401) 272-0831
e-mail: dsiegel@msrarebooks.com
http://www.msrarebooks.com
Contact: Daniel G. Siegel
Specialties: Office hours by appointment

Maggs Bros Ltd.
10 Berkeley Square
London W1J 6AA
England

Telephone: 00 44 207 4937160
Fax: 00 44 207 4992007
e-mail: enquiries@maggs.com
http://www.maggs.com

Marlborough Rare Books Ltd.
144-146 New Bond Street
London W1S 2TR
England

Telephone: 020 7493 6993
Fax: 020 7499 2479
e-mail: sales@mrb-books.co.uk
Contact: Jonathan Gestetner
Specialties: Art & architecture, English literature, early books on fine and applied arts, garden design, history of London.

Mordida Books
P.O. Box 79322
Houston TX   77279
USA

Telephone: (713) 783-7535
e-mail: rwilson@mordida.com
http://www.mordida.com

Howard S. Mott, Inc.
P. O. Box 309
170 South Main Street
Sheffield MA 01257
USA

Telephone: (413) 229-2019
Fax: (413) 229-8553
e-mail: mottinc@vgernet.net
Contact: Donald N. Mott
Specialties: Americana, English & American literature, unusual imprints, West Indies, historical manuscripts.

Oak Knoll Books
310 Delaware Street
New Castle DE 19720
USA

Telephone: (302) 328-7232
Fax: (302) 328-7274
e-mail: oakknoll@oakknoll.com
http://www.oakknoll.com
Specialties: Bibliography, book collecting, book design, book illustration, book selling, bookbinding, bookplates, fine press books, forgery, libraries, literary criticism, papermaking, printing history, publishing, typography, writing & calligraphy.

Phillip J. Pirages
Fine Books And Manuscripts
P.O. Box 504
2205 Nut Tree Lane
McMinnville OR 97128
USA

Telephone: (503) 472-0476; (800) 962-6666
Fax: (503) 472-5029
e-mail: pirages@onlinemac.com
http://www.pirages.com
Contact: Phil Pirages
Specialties: Early printing, bindings, illuminated manuscripts, illustrated books, private press books.

Ken Sanders Rare Books
268 South 200 East
Salt Lake City UT 84111
USA

Telephone: (801) 521-3819
Fax: (801) 521-2606
e-mail: books@dreamgarden.com
http://www.kensandersbooks.com
Specialties: Modern first editions, literature of the American west, Edward Abbey, Wallace Stegner, B. Traven, poetry & small presses, western explorations, voyages & travels, Powell, Wheeler, Hayden & King, USGS, Railroad Surveys, Western Americana, Native Americana & Literature, Maps & Atlases, Utah & the Mormons.

Schooner Books Ltd.
5378 Inglis Street
Halifax NS
  B3H 1J5
Canada

Telephone: (902) 423-8419
Fax: (902) 423-8503
e-mail: SchoonerBooks@schoonerbooks.com
http://www.SchoonerBooks.com
Specialties: Second hand and rare books, antique maps & prints.

Second Life Books, Inc.
P.O. Box 242
55 Quarry Road
Lanesborough MA 01237
USA

Telephone: (413) 447-8010
Fax: (413) 499-1540
e-mail: info@secondlifebooks.com
http://www.secondlifebooks.com

Ed Smith Books
14283 Sunrise Dr NE
Bainbridge Island WA 98110
USA

Telephone: (206) 201-3231
e-mail: info@edsbooks.com
http://www.edsbooks.com

Ken Spelman Rare Books
70 Micklegate
York YO1 6LF
England

Telephone: 01904 624414
Fax: 01904 626276
e-mail: ask@kenspelman.com
http://www.kenspelman.com

Unsworths Booksellers Ltd.
Crownleigh House, The Street
Botesdale IP22 1BS
England

Telephone: +44 (0) 1379 898389
Fax: +44 (0) 7802 875469
e-mail: books@unsworths.com
http://www.unsworths.com
Contact: Charlie Unsworth, Leo Cadogan
Specialties: Scholarly and Antiquarian books on the humanities, especially Classics and History.

Jeff Weber Rare Books
P.O. Box 3368
Glendale CA 91221-0368
USA

Telephone: (323) 344-9332
Fax: (323) 344-9267
e-mail: info@WeberRareBooks.com
Contact: Jeff Weber, Linda Weber

Bookman's Price Index

A

Aardema, Verna *Why Mosquitoes Buzz in People's Ears.* New York: Dial Press, 1975. Stated first edition, first issue dust jacket without medal and with original issue glassine, with original issue glassine dust jacket protector, with program from Caldecott/Newbery Dinner signed by Leo and Diane Dillon laid in, near fine, in near fine dust jacket with front flap clipped with price intact, mild soil and edge wear, 4to.   By the Book, L. C.   36 - 28   2013 $600

Aardema, Verna *Why Mosquitoes Buzz in People's Ears.* New York: Dial Press, 1975. Stated first printing, square 4to., pictorial cloth with touch of fading on edge, else fine in near fine dust jacket (no award medal, not price clipped), illustrations by Leo and Diane Dillon, this copy signed by the Dillons.   Aleph-Bet Books, Inc.   105 - 83   2013 $875

Abbey, Edward *Abbey's Road.* New York: E. P. Dutton, 1979. First edition, 8vo., signed and inscribed by author, near fine in like dust jacket with short closed tears.   By the Book, L. C. 38 - 75   2013 $650

Abbey, Edward *Desert Solitaire.* New York: McGraw Hill, 1968. First edition, drawings by Peter Parnall, fine, clean copy, touch of foxing to top edge, nearly fine dust jacket with light toning at spine.   Ed Smith Books   78 - 1   2013 $850

Abbey, Edward *Fire on the Mountain.* New York: Dial, 1962. First edition, fine in fine dust jacket with merest suggestion of rubbing at corners and folds.   Ken Lopez Bookseller   159 - 1   2013 $1500

Abbey, Edward *The Thunderbird. Volume VI Number I.* Albuquerque: University of New Mexico Oct., 1950. 34 pages, 19cm., light blue stapled wrappers near fine, minor sunning to extremities of covers, rare.   Ken Sanders Rare Books   45 - 42   2013 $500

Abbey, Edward *The Thunderbird. Volume VI Number 3.* Albuquerque: University of New Mexico March, 1951. Yellow stapled wrappers, 34 pages, 19cm., near fine, very subtle bowing to covers.   Ken Sanders Rare Books   45 - 43   2013 $2500

Abbot Hall Art Gallery *Lady Anne Clifford 1590-1676.* Kendal: Abbot Hall Art Gallery, 1976. Original wrappers, pages 56, 8 plates.   R. F. G. Hollett & Son   Lake District and Cumbria - 65   2013   £30

Abbott, T. K. *Catalogue of the Fifteenth Century Books in the Library of Trinity College, Dublin and Marsh's Library, Dublin and a Few from Other Collections.* 1905. First edition, 3 color and 8 black and white illustrations, cloth, very good.   C. P. Hyland   261 - 39   2013   £100

ABC Book. New York: Doubleday Page, 1923. Limited to 100 copies signed by artist, folio, printed on handmade paper illustrations by C. B. Falls, folio, boards with color pictorial paste-on, paper spine replaced and tips worn, otherwise tight and fine, exceedingly rare.   Aleph-Bet Books, Inc.   105 - 250   2013 $8750

ABC Dogs. New York: Wilfred Funk, 1940. First edition, folio, cloth backed pictorial boards, tips worn and few faint marks on cover, else very good+, illustrations in color on every page, this copy signed by Clara Tice with charming 3 inch drawing of Scottie dog.   Aleph-Bet Books, Inc. 104 - 5   2013 $1500

ABC for the Little Ones. London: Nister, n.d circa, 1890. 4to., cloth backed pictorial boards, some soil and wear to covers, else very good, illustrations on every page.   Aleph-Bet Books, Inc.   104 - 18   2013 $225

ABC of Happy Playtime. N.P.: McLoughlin, 1927. Large 4to., pictorial linen, very good to fine, illustrations in bright color on every page by Dorothy Hope Smith.   Aleph-Bet Books, Inc. 104 - 10   2013 $150

ABC Work Book. Racine: Whitman, 1936. Square 4to., cloth backed pictorial card covers, fine and unused, 24 illustrated pages, 36 pages of tracing paper and 36 pages of colored construction paper, by tracing and cutting out the letters and objects and then pasting them on a large sheet, the child creates his own ABC poster, scarce and nice unused condition.   Aleph-Bet Books, Inc.   105 - 15   2013 $200

Abe, Kobo *The Little Elephant is Dead.* Abe Kobo Studio, 1979. First edition, wrappers, fine, quite hard to find.   Beasley Books   2013 - 2013 $50

Abecedaire des Enfants. Paris: Fonteney et Peltier, n.d. circa, 1840. 12mo., 71 pages, pictorial boards, slightest bit of rubbing, else near fine, 26 lovely hand colored engravings by M. E. Blanchard, each letter has half page color illustration.   Aleph-Bet Books, Inc.   105 - 8   2013 $875

Abercrombie, John *The Culture and Discipline of the Mind. Addressed to the Young.* Edinburgh: William Whyte and Co., 1837. Fifth edition, 12mo., original gilt lettered pebble grain cloth, little unevenly faded.   Ken Spelman Books Ltd.   75 - 100   2013   £20

Abercrombie, John   1726-1806 *Every Man His Own Gardener.* printed for W. Griffin... 17(6)7., First edition, clean tear to one leaf almost right across but without loss, occasional minor staining, 12mo., contemporary calf, double gilt fillets on sides, spine gilt ruled in compartments, red lettering piece, lettering piece chipped, some wear and joints cracking though firm, good.   Blackwell's Rare Books Sciences - 1   2013   £950

Abraham, Ashley P. *Beautiful Lakeland.* Keswick: G. P. Abraham, 1926. 4to., original wrappers with pictorial onlay, side sewn with cord, yapp edges at head and foot little chipped, 32 full page monogravure illustrations by G. A. Abraham.   R. F. G. Hollett & Son   Lake District & Cumbria - 1   2013   £30

Abraham, George D. *Motor Ways at Home and Abroad.* London: Methuen, 1928. First edition, modern half straight grained morocco.   R. F. G. Hollett & Son   Lake District & Cumbria - 2   2013   £65

Abraham, George D. *Motor Ways in Lakeland.* London: Methuen & Co., 1913. First edition, original cloth, gilt, spine trifle faded, few slight mark, 24 illustrations and map on front endpapers.   R. F. G. Hollett & Son   Lake District & Cumbria - 3   2013   £45

Abram, David *The Spell of the Sensuous: Perception and Language in a More than Human World.* New York: Pantheon Books, 1996. First edition, fine in fine dust jacket.   Between the Covers Rare Books, Inc.   Philosophy - 118597   2013 $65

Abrams, Albert *Spondylotherapy: Spinal Concussion and the Application of Other Methods in the Spine in the Treatment of Disease.* San Francisco: Philopolis Press, 1910. First edition, 243 x 162mm, xvii, 400 pages, 97 figures, white cloth, spine dust soiled, lightly rubbed, ownership signatures, very good.   Jeff Weber Rare Books   172 - 1   2013 $400

Abrams, Max *The Book of Django.* Los Angeles: the author, 1973. First edition, paperback, spiral bound, 188 pages, illustrations, small 4to., very good+ with two separate sets of corrections laid in.   Beasley Books   2013 - 2013 $100

Abse, Dannie *O. Jones, O. Jones.* London: Hutchinson, 1970. First edition, 8vo., original grey cloth, dust jacket, inscribed by author for David Gibson, near fine.   Maggs Bros. Ltd.   1460 - 1   2013   £50

Abse, Dannie *A Poet in the Family.* London: Hutchinson, 1974. First edition, 8vo., original brick red cloth, dust jacket, signed by author, fine.   Maggs Bros. Ltd.   1460 - 2   2013   £25

Abse, Dannie *Way Out in the Centre.* London: Hutchinson, 1981. First edition, 8vo., original black cloth, dust jacket, inscribed by author for Roy Fuller, near fine.   Maggs Bros. Ltd.   1460 - 3   2013   £75

Academie Royale De Chirurgie, Paris *Recueil des Pieces qui ont Concouru pur le Prix de l'Academie Royale de Chirurgie.* Paris: Delaguette, 1753. 1757. 1759. 1778, 4to., 4 volumes, engraved frontispiece in volume 1 and 2, uniformly bound in contemporary full brown mottled calf, gilt paneled spines, joints starting on 2 volumes, all edges red, binding wear and rubbing, lower spine panel on volume 4 lacking, otherwise overall very nice, tight set.   James Tait Goodrich   75 - 1   2013 $1500

An Account of the Constitution and Present State of Great Britain, Together with a View of Its Trade, Policy and Interest, Respecting Other Nations... London: printed for J. Newbery, 1759. First edition, 18mo. engraved frontispiece, engraved titlepage, 7 engraved plates, second paper flaw to B5 touching several letters, some light browning, contemporary sheep, gilt ruled borders, expertly rebacked, raised and gilt banded spine, corners rubbed.   Jarndyce Antiquarian Booksellers   CCIV - 42   2013   £150

Account of the County Stock Levied Raised by the County of Cumberland and of Other Sums Carried to the Credit Thereof for the Year Ending at the Easter Quarter Sessions 1849. Carlisle: C. Thurnam, 1849. Disboumd as issued, pages 42, outer leaves trifle creased and dusty, very scarce.   R. F. G. Hollett & Son   Lake District & Cumbria - 4   2013   £75

An Account of the Dispensary for Administering... Medicines to the Poor in the City and County of Cork. Flyn: 1788. 39 pages, disbound, very closely trimmed.   C. P. Hyland   261 - 262   2013   £250

Account of the Proposed Canal from Worcester to Providence. Containing the Report of the Engineer: together with some Remarks on Inland Navigation. Providence: printed by John Miller, Journal Office, 1825. 8vo., 16 pages, recent marbled wrappers, title rather heavily foxed, text less so, otherwise very good.   M & S Rare Books, Inc.   95 - 29   2013 $275

Accum, Friedrich Christian *A Treatise on the Art of Brewing...* London: Longman, Hurst, Rees, Orme & Brown, 1821. Second edition, engraved copperplate frontispiece and title, 1 engraved plate and 2 folding tables, 8vo., original boards, printed paper label on spine, joints cracked but firm, slight staining of boards, good.   Blackwell's Rare Books Sciences - 2   2013   £750

Acker, Kathy *Pussy, King of the Pirates.* New York: Grove, 1996. First edition, review copy, full page inscription by author to Greg Gatenby, founding Artistic Director of Toronto's International Festival of Authors, Gatenby's signature on half title, fine in fine dust jacket with publisher's press release laid in.   Ken Lopez Bookseller   159 - 3   2013 $350

Ackerley, J. R. *My Dog Tulip.* London: Secker & Warburg, 1956. First edition, 8vo., original brown cloth, dust jacket, loosely inserted 2 page ALS from author to T. C. Worsley dated 17/7/58, excellent copy in slightly rubbed and foxed dust jacket.   Maggs Bros. Ltd.   1460 - 4   2013   £500

Ackermann, Rudolph *The History of the Colleges of Winchester, Eton and Westminster.* London: printed for and published by R. Ackermann, 1816. First edition, large quarto, 48 hand colored plates, text watermarked 1812, plates watermarked 1812 and 1816, bound circa 1950 (by Sangorski & Sutcliffe) for C. J. Sawyer in full red crushed levant morocco, decoratively tooled in gilt, occasional very light offsetting from plates to text, "Eton College" with small light stain to inner margin of recto of leaf G1 (page 41) and very slight browning to recto of leaf K1 (page 65), excellent copy with early watermarks, very attractive binding.   David Brass Rare Books, Inc.   Holiday 2012 Chapter Two - DB 00331   2013 $4500

Ackermann, Rudolph *A History of the University of Oxford, Its Colleges Halls and Public Buildings.* London: R. Ackermann, 1814. First edition, early state of plates, 2 volumes, large quarto, 114 plates, all hand colored aquatints or stipple engravings, bound without half titles and arrangement of plates leaf, all plates watermarked no later than 1814, contemporary three quarter maroon morocco, very nice, extremely attractive binding.   David Brass Rare Books, Inc.   Holiday 2012 Chapter Two - DB 01868   2013 $6500

Ackermann, Rudolph *Swiss Views.* London: Ackermann's Repository, 1819. 5 hand colored aquatints.   J. & S. L. Bonham Antiquarian Booksellers   Europe - 7655   2013   £80

Acton, Harold *The Bourbons of Naples. (and) The Last Bourbons of Naples.* London: Methuen, 1956-1961. First editions, 2 volumes, 8vo., original blue cloth, dust jackets excellent copies, jackets slightly rubbed, inscribed by author to Noel Blakiston.   Maggs Bros. Ltd.   1460 - 5   2013   £650

Acton, Harold *Memoirs of an Aesthete 1939-1969.* New York: Viking Press, 1971. First US edition, 8vo., original cloth backed purple boards, dust jacket, inscribed by author, loosely inserted APS by author, near fine.   Maggs Bros. Ltd.   1460 - 7   2013   £200

Acton, Harold *Three Extraordinary Ambassadors.* London: Thames and Hudson, 1983. First edition, 8vo., original grey cloth, gilt, dust jacket, inscribed by author for A. L. Rowse, with occasional marginal stress marks, near fine in slightly marked dust jacket.   Maggs Bros. Ltd.   1460 - 6   2013   £150

Adams, Andy *The Log of a Cowboy.* Boston and New York: Houghton Mifflin & Co., 1903. First edition, first state without a map and without mention of map in list of illustrations, beautiful copy, 12mo., original pictorial cloth, pages 387, some offset from jacket flaps which have become separated in interim, this copy otherwise fine, quarter blue morocco slipcase, 1903 bookplate of Hervey E. Burr, future Conn. banker.   Howard S. Mott Inc.   262 - 2   2013 $1000

Adams, Ansel *Camera and Lens.* Hastings on Hudson: Morgan & Morgan, 1970. First revised edition, 304 pages, 147 photo reproductions and 25 diagrams, red cloth, very fine, pictorial dust jacket.   Argonaut Book Shop   Recent Acquisitions June 2013 - 2   2013 $75

Adams, Ansel *Death Valley.* Redwood City: 5 Associates, 1970. Fourth edition, photo reproductions in black and white and color, maps by Edith Hamlin, peach cloth, very fine, pictorial dust jacket.   Argonaut Book Shop   Recent Acquisitions June 2013 - 8   2013 $75

Adams, Ansel *My Camera in Yosemite Valley.* Boston: Virginia Adams, Yosemite National Park and Houghton Mifflin, 1949. 70 pages, inscribed by Adams for Dennis Deal, Carmel 4-18-84, 24 full page photos, soft covers bound with white spiral comb which is broken in several places, front cover present but detached, edges of both covers worn, minor staining to rear cover, light rubbing to covers, interior clean and bright on glossy paper.   The Kelmscott Bookshop   7 - 91   2013 $450

Adams, Ansel *The Pageant of History and the Panorama of Today in Northern California.* San Francisco: American Trust Corp., 1954. First edition, signed by Adams and dated May 25th 1980, soft covers with clear plastic spiral comb which has broken in several places but continues to hold pages together, few scuff marks to covers and minor wear to edges, this copy is ex-library from Carmel Valley Manor with unobtrusive stamp on dedication page, only library marking, unpaginated.   The Kelmscott Bookshop   7 - 92   2013 $450

Adams, Ansel *The Portfolios of Ansel Adams.* Boston: New York Graphic Society, 1977. First edition, 90 full page photos, previous owner's inscription, else vey fine, pictorial dust jacket.   Argonaut Book Shop   Recent Acquisitions June 2013 - 3   2013 $125

Adams, Ansel *Sierra Nevada: the John Muir Trail.* Berkeley: Archetype Press, 1938. First edition, large folio, 202 (1) pages plus 50 tipped-in fine screen halftones from photos by Adams, white cloth lettered in black on spine and front cover, spine slightly darkened, front cover much less so, rear cover with slight darkening or fading and with small spot to lower edge, overall fine and bright, clean, signed by Adams, with his presentation inscription.   Argonaut Book Shop   Recent Acquisitions June 2013 - 4   2013 $9500

Adams, Ansel *Taos Pueblo.* Boston: New York Graphic Society, 1977. Facsimile or rare 1930 edition, number 822 of 950 copies signed by Adams, folio, 12 full page fine screen duotone photo plates, titlepage printed and decorated in black and orange, design by Valenti Angelo, bound by Vincent Mullins in half tan Niger leather with orange linen covered boards, title stamped in blind on front cover, marbled ends, very fine, as new with matching slipcase.   Argonaut Book Shop   Recent Acquisitions June 2013 - 7   2013 $3000

Adams, Ansel *The Tetons and the Yellowstone.* Redwood City: 5 Associates, 1970. First edition, 4to., 95 pages, black and white photos, map, gilt lettered blue cloth, very fine, pictorial dust jacket.   Argonaut Book Shop   Recent Acquisitions June 2013 - 9   2013 $125

Adams, Ansel *Yosemite Valley.* Redwood City: 5 Associates, 1967. First edition, third printing, quarto 45 photo reproductions in black and white, light green cloth, very fine, pictorial dust jacket.   Argonaut Book Shop   Recent Acquisitions June 2013 - 6   2013 $75

Adams, C. L. *Congaree Sketches: Scenes from Negro Life in the Swamps of the Congaree...*   Chapel Hill: University of North Carolina Press, 1927. First edition, boards little soiled, near fine in like dust jacket with some toning and small stains, particularly on rear panel, attractive copy.   Between the Covers Rare Books, Inc.   165 - 39   2013 $150

Adams, Charlotte *Boys at Home.* London: Routledge, 1857. New edition, original red blindstamped cloth gilt extra, pages 414, 8 full page tissue guarded woodcuts by John Gilbert, nice, bright copy, contemporary school prize inscription Wesleyan School, Ulverston presented to John Briggs, Christmas 1857.   R. F. G. Hollett & Son   Children's Books - 1   2013   £45

Adams, E. A. *Yearbook and Historical Guide to the African Methodist Episcopal Church.* Columbia: Bureau of Research and History, 1955. First edition, 344 pages, green wrappers, modest wear, very good plus, uncommon.   Between the Covers Rare Books, Inc.   165 - 38   2013 $175

Adams, Henry 1836-1918 *Democracy.* London: Macmillan and Co., 1882. First English edition, 8vo., 280 pages, contemporary pebbled green cloth, trial binding?, very scarce.   M & S Rare Books, Inc.   95 - 1   2013 $200

Adams, Herbert *The Secret of Bogey House.* London: Methuen, 1924. First edition, tiny wear on top edge fron cover, otherwise fine, without dust jacket.   Mordida Books 81 - 1   2013 $450

Adams, John *Message from the President of the United States Inclcsing (sic) a Letter and Sundry Documents, from the Governor of the State of Pennsylvania, Respecting the Arrival in the Ports of the United States...*   Philadelphia: printed by Joseph Gales, 1798. 8vo., small hole in title (far from any text), little foxing, disbound, good.   Blackwell's Rare Books   172 - 3   2013   £500

Adams, John *Mines of the Lake District Fells.* Dalesman Books, 1988. First edition, original pictorial wrappers, pages 160, numerous maps and diagrams.   R. F. G. Hollett & Son   Lake District & Cumbria - 7   2013   £25

Adams, John *The Sketches of the History, Genius, Disposition, Accomplishments, Employments, Customs, Virtues and Vices of the Fair Sex...*   Boston: Bumstead, 1807. Second US edition, pages 6-300, 8vo., leather, somewhat browned, hinges tender, little insect damage to last few leaves, cover scuffed, somewhat worn at edges, and spine, otherwise very good.   Second Life Books Inc. 182 - 1   2013 $700

Adams, John Quincy *Message from the President of the United States, Relative to the Disposition of the Africans Landed at Key West from a Stranded Spanish Vessel.* Washington: Printed by Gales & Seaton, 1828. First edition, 4to., original printed self wrappers, (5) pages, disbound, oval stamp of NY Society Library on titlepage, very good.   The Brick Row Book Shop   Miscellany Fifty-Nine - 1   2013 $200

Adams, Randolph G. *Who Uses a Library of Rare Books.* New York: Columbia University Press, 1941. Second printing, 185 x 125mm., 20 pages, original printed wrappers, near fine, scarce.   Jeff Weber Rare Books   171 - 1   2013 $75

Adams, Richard *The Plague Dogs.* Allen Lane, 1977. First edition, original cloth, gilt, dust jacket, pages 461, illustrations and diagrams by A. Wainwright.   R. F. G. Hollett & Son   Lake District & Cumbria - 8   2013   £50

Adams, Richard *Watership Down.* London: Penguin Books, 1976. First illustrated edition, large 8vo., original cloth backed boards, dust jacket, slipcase, inscribed by author to his editor, John Guest, further signed on dedication page by dedicatee, the author's daughter, Rosamund Adams, near fine in dust jacket, edges lightly browned. Maggs Bros. Ltd. 1460 - 8 2013 £675

Adams, Samuel Hopkins *Average Jones.* Indianapolis: Bobbs Merrill Co., 1911. First edition, owner's name front pastedown, painted spine lettering nicely readable, trifle soiled, near fine. Between the Covers Rare Books, Inc. Mystery & Detective Fiction - 304611 2013 $250

Adams, William Henry Davenport 1828-1891 *Famous Regiments of the British Army: Their Origin and Services.* 1974. 320 pages, illustrations, cloth. C. P. Hyland 261 - 2 2013 £32

Addison, Joseph 1672-1719 *The Free-Holder; or Political Essays.* London: printed for D. Midwinter, 1732. Fifth edition, 12mo., some foxing, lacking front free endpaper, contemporary sprinkled calf, double gilt ruled borders, raised and gilt banded spine, red morocco label, hinges cracked but firm, some insect damage to spine. Jarndyce Antiquarian Booksellers CCIV - 34 2013 £45

Addison, Joseph 1672-1719 *Plays.* London: printed for J. Tonson, 1735. First collected edition, titles printed in red and black, general title with small woodcut vignette, those to the plays with woodcut medallion portrait of Shakespeare, 2 engraved plates, some foxing and browning, 12mo., disbound, signature of Mary Cowper dated 1735, purchase price (4/6) on flyleaf, sound. Blackwell's Rare Books B174 - 1 2013 £400

Addison, Joseph 1672-1719 *The Works of.* Birmingham: printed by John Baskerville, 1761. 4 volumes, without the very scarce "Directions to the Binder" leaf in volume i (which carried instruction that it be cut out) but with 7 plates in volume ii (probably not printed by Baskerville, and sometimes missing), frontispiece and titlepage of volume I browned, little browning elsewhere, occasional foxing, mostly sparse but heavier on few gatherings, 4to., contemporary red morocco, single gilt fillet borders on sides, upper covers with arms of Joshua Hutchinson blocked in gilt at centre, gilt rules around raised bands on spines, gilt edges, lower edges of boards with waterstain of varying height (not affecting textblock), not exceeding 1 inch, engraved Hutchinson bookplate inside front cover, later bookplate opposite Henry J. B. Clements, good. Blackwell's Rare Books B174 - 2 2013 £1200

An Address to the People of the United States Adopted at a Conference of Colored Citizens Held at Columbia, SC July 20-21 1876. Columbia: 1876. First edition, 8vo., 13 pages, original printed wrappers. M & S Rare Books, Inc. 95 - 138 2013 $1750

Adler, Jacob *The Fantastic Life of Walter Murray Gibson, Hawaii's Minister of Everything.* Honolulu: University of Hawaii Press, 1986. First edition, review copy, frontispiece, numerous photos, reproductions, map, black cloth, fine with pictorial dust jacket (tiny tear to top edge), review copy, review slip laid in, scarce. Argonaut Book Shop Summer 2013 - 2 2013 $90

Adoff, Arnold *Black is Brown is Tan.* New York: Harper & Row, 1973. First edition, illustrations by Emily McCully, fine in pictorial boards and fine dust jacket with single short tear, inscribed by author. Between the Covers Rare Books, Inc. 165 - 104 2013 $125

Adolphus, John *Biographical Memoirs of the French Revolution.* London: printed for T. Cadell, 1799. First edition, 2 volumes, half title to volume II, 8vo., some occasional foxing, manuscript table of contents, handsome copy in full contemporary calf, gilt decorated spines, gilt flowerheads, decorative bands, volume numbers set within gilt shields. Jarndyce Antiquarian Booksellers CCIV - 35 2013 £350

Adomeit, Ruth E. *Miniature Book Collector. Volume I Nos. 1-4; Volume 2, Nos. 1-4 Complete, plus index.* Worcester: Achille J. St. Onge, 1960-1963. Complete run, 10.1 x 8.5 cm., later full leather with original paper wrappers bound in, 16 16, 16, 16, 72, 40 pages, from the collection of Donn W. Sanford. Oak Knoll Books 303 - 3 2013 $350

Adomeit, Ruth E. *Three Centuries of Thumb Bibles: a Checklist.* New York: Garlard Publishing, 1980. First edition, 8vo., cloth, xl, 390 pages, from the collection of Donn W. Sanford. Oak Knoll Books 303 - 4 2013 $152

Adorno, T. W. *The Authoritarian Personality.* New York: Harper, 1950. Reprint, dear fine in very good with dust jacket slightly sunned at spine and with short edge tears. Beasley Books 2013 - 2013 $50

Adra *Legends of Lakeland.* Scarborough: S. W. Theakston, 1881. Small 4to., original red cloth gilt over bevelled boards, few slight marks, edges of first and last leaves little spotted. R. F. G. Hollett & Son Lake District & Cumbria - 9 2013 £85

Advertising Arts and Crafts. Volume I. New York: Lee & Kirby, 1924. First National edition, volume 1 only, 8vo., 415 pages, color and black and white illustrations, navy blue cloth, blue stamped paper spine label, lightly rubbed, hinges starting, very good, scarce. Jeff Weber Rare Books 171 - 7 2013 $60

Advice to Sabbath School Children. Northampton: John Metcalf, 1838. 16mo., wrappers, old tape stain on cover, 24 pages with woodcuts, good. Barnaby Rudge Booksellers Children 2013 - 021224 2013 $55

Aeschylus *The Agamemnon of Aeschyus.* London: Faber and Faber, 1936. Proof copy, 8vo., original lilac wrappers, loosely inserted is a publisher's compliments slip declaring the proposed publication date as 29th October, covers slightly faded on spine and some worming to rear covers, excellent condition internally. Maggs Bros. Ltd. 1442 - 206   2013   £175

Aeschylus *The Agamemnon of Aeschyus.* New York: Harcourt Brace and Co., 1937. First edition translated by Louis MacNeice, 71 pages, tight close to near fine copy in beige cloth with small ownership signature, minor poet, on front pastedown, in very good price clipped dust jacket that is very lightly soiled. Jeff Hirsch Books   Fall 2013 - 129272   2013 $60

Aeschylus *The Oresteia.* printed by A. Colish, 1961. 453/1500 copies, printed in black and maroon, signed by artist Michael Ayrton and 8 photogravure plates in grey and maroon by him, large 4to., original quarter red leatherette, gilt lettered brown cloth label, brown linen cloth sides, large gilt "O" on front cover, board slipcase with printed label, fine. Blackwell's Rare Books   B174 - 358   2013   £50

Aeschylus *Tragoediae VII.* Geneva: Henrici Stephani, 1557. First complete edition, some toning and spotting, lower corner tip of first few leaves worn, title little creased from bookplate, 4to., contemporary calf, expertly rebacked preserving old label and endpapers, corners repaired, bookplate and stamp of Trinity College Cambridge ('sold'), good. Blackwell's Rare Books   172 - 5   2013   £2250

Aesopus *Aesop's Fables.* London: Collins clear-type Press, n.d. 1920's, 4to., original pictorial boards, spine covered with adhesive film, corners worn and rounded, edges rubbed, unpaginated, 4 colored plates and line drawings. R. F. G. Hollett & Son   Children's Books - 522   2013   £25

Aesopus *Les Fables d'Esope Phrygien.* Rouen: Chez Jean & David Berthelin, 1659. Few leaves with small tears or closely trimmed with minor loss, illustrations, old vellum spine with gilt stamped label, lacking leaf X#, including etching 69, light to moderate foxing, some soiling. Joseph J. Felcone Inc.   Books Printed before 1701 - 1   2013 $400

Aesopus *The Fables of Aesop and Others.* London: Chatto & Windus, 1875. 4to., hand colored frontispiece, illustrated title, hand colored plates, original green pictorial cloth, blocked in gilt, slightly rubbed, embossed stamp of W. H. Smith, very good. Jarndyce Antiquarian Booksellers   CCV - 20   2013   £180

Aesopus *The Fables of Aesop.* London: Hodder and Stoughton, 1909. Limited to 750 numbered copies, signed by artist, 25 magnificent tipped in color plates by Edward Detmold, lettered paper guards, scarce in such nice clean condition, thick folio, white gilt pictorial cloth, gilt top, bookplate removed from blank endpaper, else fine. Aleph-Bet Books, Inc.   104 - 154   2013 $2750

Aesopus *Aesop's Fables.* Art Society Press (UK) Kings College, 1957. Limited to 300 copies, 4to., spiral backed decorative card covers, near fine, 7 striking color woodcuts, plus pictorial titlepage. Aleph-Bet Books, Inc.   105 - 19   2013 $200

An Affecting History of the Captivity and Suffering of Mrs. Mary Velnet an Italian Lady. Boston: William Crary, 1804? First edition, 12mo., 164 pages, woodcut frontispiece, contemporary leather backed paper covered boards, front outer hinge cracked, sound, half of front endpaper lacking, perforated library stamp on title, barely noticeable, very nice. M & S Rare Books, Inc.   95 - 9   2013 $575

African Orphan - boy. New York: American Tract Society, 1852. First edition, 16mo., 16 pages plus wrappers, 3 woodcuts, very good. Barnaby Rudge Booksellers   Children 2013 - 021221   2013 $50

Agee, James *A Way of Seeing.* Durham: Duke University Press, 1989. third edition, 20 additional photos by Helen Levitt, near fine in blue cloth boards with gilt title to spine, very slight fading to edges of boards, interior very clean overall although previous owner has penned in check marks along top margins of several pages, very good dust jacket, very minor wear to edges of jacket, 86 pages. The Kelmscott Bookshop   7 - 94   2013 $300

Agg, John *The General-Post Bag; or News!* London: J. Johnston, 1814. First edition, half title, uncut in original blue boards, little marked, drab spine defective, slight worming to endpapers and first four pages, Renier booklabel. Jarndyce Antiquarian Booksellers   CCIII - 334   2013   £50

Agg, John *The General-Post Bag; or News! Foreign and Domestic.* London: J. Johnston, 1814. Second edition, half title, uncut in original drab boards, rubbed, slightly later roan spine defective, booklabels of C. J. Peacock and the Reniers. Jarndyce Antiquarian Booksellers   CCIII - 335   2013   £35

Agnes, Sister *The Story of Kendal.* Kendal: Westmorland Gazette, 1947. First edition, original cloth dust jacket little chipped and worn, price clipped, 10 plates by John Watton, scarce. R. F. G. Hollett & Son   Lake District & Cumbria - 10   2013   £45

Agnew, Georgette *Let's Pretend.* London: J. Saville, 1927. Limited to only 156 numbered copies, signed by author and artist (150 for sale), 4to., vellum backed cloth, fine in publisher's slipcase with limitation number on spine, few neat mends to case, uncommon, illustrations by E. H. Shepard. Aleph-Bet Books, Inc.   104 - 534   2013 $1275

Ahmed, Hannibal El-Mustafa *Introduction to Pan-Africanism: a Philosophy/Ideology for African Americans.* Atlanta: Hannibal Ahmed, 1970. First edition, mimeographed sheets stapled in upper left corner, small stain on front page, else about fine, scarce.   Between the Covers Rare Books, Inc.   165 - 41   2013 $225

Aiding and Abetting.   Marlborough: Libanus Press, 1981. One of 385 copies printed on Velin Arches paper, color printed illustrations by 32 modern artists, 8vo., original lime green cloth backed pink boards, backstrip gilt lettered, front cover printed in purple, patterned pink endpapers, board slipcase, fine.   Blackwell's Rare Books   B174 - 357   2013   £75

Aiken, James W.   *High School Football and How to Win Games.*   Toledo: Wilkinson Sloat Printing Co., 1928. First edition, green cloth with white painted decoration, small owner name to front pastedown, approximately top one third of front fly torn away, presumably by someone removing another owner name, else nice, lightly worn, very good or better, very scarce.   Between the Covers Rare Books, Inc.   Football Books - 64817   2013 $315

Aiken, John   *Nightly Deadshade.*   London: Macmillan, 1971. First edition, near fine in like dust jacket, signed and inscribed by author, laid in are several pieces of correspondence from John Aiken to book's previous owner.   Leather Stalking Books   October 2013 - 2013 $150

Aiken, John   *A View of the Life, Travels and Philanthropic Labours of the Late John Howard.*   Boston: J. White & Others, 1794. First American edition, 12mo., full leather, good copy, joints repaired crudely.   Barnaby Rudge Booksellers   Biography 2013 - 021295   2013 $75

Aikin, John   *Evenings at Home.*   Darton & Co. n.d c., 1850. Original cloth gilt, little rubbed, pages 355, all edges gilt, engraved frontispiece and title, edges rather damp-stained, joints cracked.   R. F. G. Hollett & Son   Children's Books - 5   2013   £35

Aikin, John   *The Natural History of the Year.*   London: printed for J. Johnson, 1805. Third edition, engraved folding plate, 12mo., small paper flaw to F3 touching several letters, full contemporary sprinkled calf, gilt decorated spine, red morocco label, very slight cracks to ends of hinges, some offset browning from turn-ins, attractive copy.   Jarndyce Antiquarian Booksellers   CCIV - 36   2013   £75

Aikin, John   *A View of the Character and Public Services of the Late John Howard, Esq.*   London: J. Johnson, 1792. First edition, small 8vo., 248 pages, frontispiece, original drab boards, black stamped spine title uncut, spine neatly replaced, ink signature on titlepage, notation in same hand on page 195, fine.   Jeff Weber Rare Books   172 - 143   2013 $500

Ainslee, Kathleen   *Catharine Susan and Me Goes Abroad.* London & New York: Castell & Stokes, n.d., 1906. 12mo., stiff pictorial card covers, lacks ties, else very good+, full page chromolithographs.   Aleph-Bet Books, Inc.   104 - 26   2013 $275

Ainslie, R. St. J.   *Sedbergh School Songs.*   Leeds: Richard Jackson, 1896. Deluxe edition, tall 8vo., original vellum gilt boards little warped and slightly spotted as usual, all edges gilt, illustrations by author, scarce.   R. F. G. Hollett & Son   Lake District & Cumbria - 12   2013   £85

Ainslie, R. St. J.   *Sedbergh School Songs.*   Leeds: Richard Jackson, 1896. First edition, original pictorial blue cloth gilt, pages 104, all edges gilt, illustrations by author, scarce.   R. F. G. Hollett & Son   Lake District & Cumbria - 11   2013   £65

Ainslie, R. St. J.   *Sedbergh School Songs.*   Sedbergh: Jackson & son, n.d. circa, 1900. Large 8vo., original green cloth gilt binding, old school arms and motto in gilt roundel on upper board, unpaginated, scarce.   R. F. G. Hollett & Son   Lake District & Cumbria - 14   2013   £75

Ainslie, R. St. J.   *Sedbergh School Songs.*   Sedbergh: Jackson & Sons, n.d. circa, 1910. Large 8vo., original brown cloth gilt, school arms and motto in gilt on upper board, unpaginated, scarce.   R. F. G. Hollett & Son   Lake District & Cumbria - 13   2013   £75

Ainsworth, Ed   *The Cowboy in Art.*   New York: World Pub. Co., 1968. First edition, quarto, photos, reproductions, drawings, brown cloth, gilt, very fine with pictorial dust jacket.   Argonaut Book Shop   Recent Acquisitions June 2013 - 12   2013 $60

Ainsworth, Ed   *Painters of the Desert.*   Palm Desert: Desert Magazine, 1960. First edition, large quarto, 111 pages, reproductions form drawings, paintings, with portraits, orange cloth, very fine with dust jacket (some extremity rubbing and chipping to head of spine), long presentation inscription signed by author, also signed by Chuck Shelton, also signed by five of the thirteen artists.   Argonaut Book Shop   Recent Acquisitions June 2013 - 13   2013 $400

Airey, Frederick Wilkin Iago   *Pidgin Inglis Tails and Others.*   Shanghai: Hong Kong: Singapore: Yokohama: Kelly & Walsh Ltd., 1906. First edition, 12mo., illustrations, original pictorial cloth (little soiled).   Howard S. Mott Inc. 262 - 5   2013 $285

Akeley, Mary L. Jobe   *The Wilderness Lives Again.*   New York: Dodd Mead, 1940. First edition, 8vo., xiv, 411 pages, very good+ minimal sun spine, soil to covers and edges in very good+ price clipped dust jacket with short closed tears, internal tape, mild soil and creases.   By the Book, L. C. 36 - 82   2013 $300

Akenside, Mark   1721-1770   *Poems of Mark Akenside, M.D.*   London: printed by W. Bowyer and J. Nichols and sold by J. Dodsley, 1772.   First of this edition, 4to., mezzotint frontispiece, frontispiece foxed, little foxing elsewhere, contemporary sprinkled calf, spine gilt in compartments, red morocco label, rebacked preserving original spine and corners, repaired by Chris Weston, old leather somewhat scratched and rubbed, evidence of oval bookplate removed from pastedown.   Unsworths Antiquarian Booksellers   28 - 61   2013   £200

Akerman, J. Y.   *Tales of Other Days.*   London: Effingham, 1830.   8vo., early half leather and marbled boards, leather slightly rubbed, else very good+, 6 full page woodcuts and vignette on title.   Aleph-Bet Books, Inc.   105 - 158   2013 $300

Akin, Emma   *Gifts.*   Oklahoma City: Harlow Pub., 1938.   8vo., red cloth, titlepage creased, else fine, silhouettes and photos, very scarce, nice.   Aleph-Bet Books, Inc.   104 - 81   2013 $500

Al-Kindi   *Oeuvres Philosophiques et Scientifiques d'al-Kindi.*   Leiden: New York & Koln: E. J. Brill, 1997.   Volume I, 8vo., xiii, 776 pages, navy cloth, gilt stamped cover and spine titles, dust jacket, fine.   Jeff Weber Rare Books   169 - 2   2013 $175

Albee, Edward   *A Delicate Balance.*   New York: Atheneum, 1966.   First edition, signed by author as well as six members of the original cast, Jessica Tandy, Hume Cronyn, Rosemary Murphy, Carmen Matthews, Henderson Forsythe and Marian Seldes, fine in nearly fine dust jacket.   Ed Smith Books   78 - 3   2013 $750

Albee, Edward   *Who's Afraid of Virginia Woolf?*   New York: Atheneum, 1962.   First edition, fine in nearly fine, crisp dust jacket (faint crease to front flap).   Ed Smith Books   78 - 2   2013 $600

Albert Schloss's Bijou Almanacs 1839-1843.   London: Nattali & Maurice, 1969.   Limited to 150 numbered copies, 4to., 19, (33) pages with plate, 4to., quarter vellum, paper covered boards, title gilt stamped on spine, dust jacket, impressions tissue guard, dust jacket chipped along edges, from the collection of Donn W. Sanford.   Oak Knoll Books   303 - 2   2013 $125

Albert Schloss's Bijou Almanacs 1839-1843.   London: Nattali & Maurice, 1969.   Limited to 150 numbered copies, one of 25 copies, nos. 1-25 include a full set of impressions direct from plates, of which this copy is such, 4to., quarter vellum, paper covered boards, title gilt stamped on spine, dust jacket, 19, (33) pages, with plates, impressions tissue guarded, dust jacket torn at front bottom along spine and along back bottom, pencilled notation on front pastedown about this special limited edition; from the collection of Donn W. Sanford.   Oak Knoll Books   303 - 1   2013 $325

Alberti, Salomon   *Historia Plearunque Partium Humani Corposris.*   Wittenberg: Zacharias Lehman, 1583.   Small 8vo., 18th century burgundy paste boards (faded), armorial crest on boards, old owner's stamp on title, text browned and foxed, dampstaining affecting margins of final 8 leaves, title vignette engraving, numerous woodcuts, plus 4 full page engravings (one lightly shaved at top), plus 3 folding anatomical sheets, text annotated in parts by early hand, very rare.   James Tait Goodrich   75 - 2   2013 $12,500

The Albion Hotel, Duke St., Barrow and Several Cottages and Houses at Barrow-in-Furness and Marton near Dalton-in-Furness to be sold at The Imperial Hotel 13th May 1891.   Barrow-in-Furness: Lowden & Postlethwaite, 1891.   Folio, 4 pages, folded, small plan, hand colored in outline.   R. F. G. Hollett & Son   Lake District & Cumbria - 84   2013   £25

Album Contemporain: Collection de Dessins et Croquis des Meilleurs Artistes de Notre Epoque.   Paris: Au Siege de la Societe Iconographique, 1873.   First edition, 2 pages of text, 25 hors texte lithographs and engravings after drawings, all prints signed in plate, foxing ranging from none to moderate, bound in original burgundy buckram, very minor old repairs at front hinge and spine, corners with slight wear, unobtrusive soiling on covers, small French ownership stamp, overall very good, extremely rare.   Gemini Fine Books & Arts., Ltd.   Art Reference & Illustrated Books - 2013 $1500

Album Lefevre-Utile: les Contemporains Celebres.   Paris: Octave Beauchamp circa, 1905.   Large 4to., cloth spine, painted wooden covers with circular cut-out into which is inserted a carved medallion of Sarah Bernhardt by Mucha, fine, photos, color decorations by Orazi and Fraikin and other illustrations by Vogel, this copy does not have extra plates after each illustration, lovely and lavish art nouveau book.   Aleph-Bet Books, Inc.   104 - 372   2013 $575

Alciphron   *Alciphron's Epistles..*   London: G. G. J. and J. Robinson; Leigh and Sotheby and R. Faulder, 1791.   First English translation, half title with errata, first few leaves browned, some toning and spotting elsewhere, 8vo., modern quarter calf with marbled boards, smooth backstrip with maroon label between gilt fillet, touch scuffed, good.   Blackwell's Rare Books   172 - 6   2013   £70

Alcoholics Anonymous. The Story of How Many Thousands of Men and Women Have Recovered from Alcoholism.   New York: Works Pub., 1946.   First edition, 10th printing, octavo, publisher's original blue cloth with blindstamped cover and gilt spine, original dust jacket, some chipping and wear to jacket, cloth very slightly rubbed on corners, previous owner's inscription (as usual) to front free endpaper, still very good, better than usually seen.   Heritage Book Shop   Holiday Catalogue 2012 - 1   2013 $1750

Alcoholics Anonymous. The Story of How Many Thousands of Men and Women Have Recovered from Alcoholism. New York: Works Publ Inc., 1950. First edition, 13th printing, 8vo., viii, 400 pages, signed, inscribed and dated by Bill Wilson using his full name, mild toning to endpapers mild sun to spine, near fine in very good++ original dust jacket (with mild scuffs, minimal edge wear, unobtrusive tape dust jacket verso, in custom cloth covered clamshell box gilt, gilt lettering on clamshell cover and spine labels. By the Book, L. C.   36 - 79   2013 $8500

Alcoholics Anonymous. The Story of How Many Thousands of Men and Women Have Recovered from Alcoholism. New York: Works Pub., 1950. First edition, 13th printing, very good++, minimal cover edge wear, mild soil page edges in very good+ dust jacket with short closed tears, soil and edge wear, spine gilt lettering bright, housed in custom made red and black cloth covered clamshell box with gilt lettering on black leather title labels, 8vo., 400 pages. By the Book, L. C.   36 - 1   2013 $750

Alcoholics Anonymous. The Story of How Many Thousands of Men and Women Have Recovered from Alcoholism. New York: Alcoholics Anonymous Pub. Co., 1955. Second edition, first printing, first issue, (with "realy" on p. xx, line 6 and "6000 groups" on p. 16), mild spotting to endpapers, 8vo., xxx, 575 pages, minimal cover edge wear, very good++ in very good original dust jacket with edge wear, sun spine, .5 x 1.5 inch chip to crown of dust jacket spine, no lettering affected, taping on dust jacket verso, signed and inscribed by Bill W(ilson). By the Book, L. C.   36 - 78   2013 $5000

Alcott, Amos Bronson   *Conversations with Children on the Gospels.* Boston: James Munroe & Co., 1836-1837. First edition, 2 volumes, partly unopened in original purple cloth, largely faded to brown, very good.   Jarndyce Antiquarian Booksellers   CCV - 1   2013   £280

Alcott, Louisa May   1832-1888   *The Candy Country.* Boston: Little Brown, 1900. First separate edition, 8vo., tan cloth stamped in pink, green and gilt, offsetting on endpaper, else fine in dust jacket (chipped), 3 halftone plates and one pen and ink drawing done for this edition, rare in dust jacket.   Aleph-Bet Books, Inc.   104 - 29   2013 $350

Alcott, Louisa May   1832-1888   *A Christmas Dream.* Boston: Little Brown, 1901. First separate edition, 8vo., green pictorial cloth stamped in red, green, white and gilt, 3 half tone plates by H. Ireland and 2 pen and inks done for this edition.   Aleph-Bet Books, Inc.   104 - 30   2013 $250

Alcott, Louisa May   1832-1888   *A Hole in the Wall.* Boston: Little Brown, 1899. first separate edition, 8vo., yellow cloth stamped in black, green and gilt, 62 pages + (1) page ad, fine in dust jacket (chipped), 4 halftone plates, incredible copy, rare in dust jacket.   Aleph-Bet Books, Inc.   105 - 21   2013 $350

Alcott, Louisa May   1832-1888   *Horn of Plenty of Home Poems and Pictures.* Boston: William F. Gill and Co., 1876. 4to., green cloth with elaborate gilt and black pictorial cover and spine, all edges gilt, 191 pages, fine, beautiful Victorian gift book, profusely illustrated with fine full page and smaller woodcuts, beautiful copy.   Aleph-Bet Books, Inc.   105 - 22   2013 $200

Alcott, Louisa May   1832-1888   *Jo's Boys.* Boston: Roberts Brothers, 1886. First edition, first state, 12mo., dark green cloth, fine, beautiful copy.   Aleph-Bet Books, Inc.   104 - 27   2013 $475

Alcott, Louisa May   1832-1888   *May Flowers.* Boston: Little Brown, 1899. First separate edition, 8vo., tan cloth stamped in black and gold, fine in dust jacket, 4 half tone plates.   Aleph-Bet Books, Inc.   105 - 24   2013 $350

Alcott, Louisa May   1832-1888   *National Elgin Watch Company's Illustrated Almanac for 1875.* Chicago: Elgin National Watch Co., 1875. First printing, pictorial wrappers, slight bit of cover soil, else fine, 5 full page and 13 half page wood engravings by Church, scarce, rarely found in such nice condition.   Aleph-Bet Books, Inc.   105 - 25   2013 $300

Alcott, Louisa May   1832-1888   *An Old Fashioned Girl.* Boston: Roberts Brothers, 1870. First edition, second printing, 12mo., terra cotta cloth, occasional internal soil, binding slightly leaning, soil on spine affecting few letters, really nice, clean copy, 4 black and white plates, nice copy.   Aleph-Bet Books, Inc.   104 - 28   2013 $475

Alcott, Louisa May   1832-1888   *"Old Fashioned Thanksgiving." in St. Nicholas Magazine.* New York: Century Co. Volume 9 part 1 Nov. 1881-May 1882, 4to., bound volume of the 6 issues, three quarter leather and cloth, near fine, black and white illustrations.   Aleph-Bet Books, Inc.   104 - 31   2013 $500

Alcott, Louisa May   1832-1888   *Our Famous Women.* Hartford: A. D. Worthington & Co., 1884. (1883). first edition, Thick 8vo., 715 pages, brown cloth, extensive gilt decorations on cover and spine, near fine, sold by subscription, portraits, full page engravings by T. W. Williams, nice.   Aleph-Bet Books, Inc.   105 - 26   2013 $400

Alcott, Louisa May 1832-1888 *Rose in Bloom. A Sequel to "Eight Cousins".* Boston: Roberts Brothers, 1876. First edition, first state with last signature in 4, with no "S" in "illustration" on titlepage, period after "illustration" is clean, noted only in first printing copies, 12mo., blue blindstamped cloth, some cover soil, hinges neatly strengthened, 1 signature beginning, occasional soil, really overall very good, illustrated with an extra illustrated titlepage, scarce.   Aleph-Bet Books, Inc.   105 - 27   2013 $550

Alden, Timothy *A Collection of American Epitaphs and Inscriptions with Occasional Notes Pentade I.* New York: 1814. First edition of volumes 2-5, Volumes I-V (all), 18mo., engraved portraits, original tree calf, all rebacked with labels, new back cover volume I, two portraits lacking.   M & S Rare Books, Inc.   95 - 7   2013 $450

Alden, W. L. *Among the Freaks.* London: Longmans Green & Co., 1896. Half title, frontispiece and illustrations, original decorated turquoise cloth, slightly rubbed, signature of S. Musgrave on half title.   Jarndyce Antiquarian Booksellers   CCV - 2   2013   £150

Aldin, Cecil *Bunnyborough.* Eyre & Spottiswoode, 1946. Large 8vo., 14 fine color plates and numerous line drawings by Aldin, original yellow cloth, dust jacket, few creases, closed tears, small chips.   R. F. G. Hollett & Son   Children's Books - 6   2013   £75

Aldin, Cecil *Jack and Jill.* London: Henry Frowde and Hodder & Stoughton, n.d., 1914. Large square 4to., original cloth backed pictorial boards, sometime neatly rebacked to match, corners trifle worn, unpaginated 24 color plates and pictorial endpapers, few marks to blank flyleaf, short tear to lower corner of half title repaired, otherwise excellent, clean and sound, rare.   R. F. G. Hollett & Son   Children's Books - 8   2013   £450

Aldin, Cecil *Mac.* New York: Hodder & Stoughton, n.d. circa, 1912. First US edition, 4to., cloth backed pictorial boards, 24 color plates, pictorial titlepage, excellent copy, rare in this condition.   Aleph-Bet Books, Inc.   105 - 31   2013 $850

Aldin, Cecil *Merry Puppy Book.* London: Henry Frowde & Hodder & Stoughton, n.d. circa, 1913. First edition, 4to., cloth backed pictorial boards, slightest bit of edge rubbing, fine and bright, 36 full page color illustrations plus numerous black and whites, rare.   Aleph-Bet Books, Inc.   104 - 32   2013 $1200

Aldin, Cecil *Pickles.* London & New York: n.d. 1909, 4to., cloth backed pictorial boards, light corner stain on 2 pages of text, rear free endpaper, edges worn, overall very good, 24 fabulous color plates on heavy green paper, blue pictorial endpapers, very scarce.   Aleph-Bet Books, Inc.   104 - 33   2013 $850

Aldin, Cecil *Puppy Dog Frolics.* London: & Glasgow: Collins Clear Type Press, n.d. circa, 1930. Folio, cloth backed pictorial boards, tips rubbed, rear cover soil, very good++, printed on coated paper, 16 full page color illustrations, 2 illustrations in black and white, charming pictorial border on every page, rare.   Aleph-Bet Books, Inc.   104 - 34   2013 $975

Aldin, Cecil *The Romance of the Road.* London: and New York: Eyre and Spottiswoode & Charles Scribner, 1928. First trade edition, Folio, black cloth, white lettering, top edge gilt, slight rubbing to spine ends and tips, very good++, printed on high quality paper, with a profusion of 2-color and black and white illustrations, tipped in color plates.   Aleph-Bet Books, Inc.   105 - 29   2013 $500

Aldin, Cecil *Rough and Tumble.* Oxford University Press, n.d., circa, 1910. Original cloth backed pictorial boards, backstrip trifle soiled and frayed, corners lightly rounded, title and 24 color plates, label removed from pastedown, otherwise excellent clean and sound copy.   R. F. G. Hollett & Son   Children's Books - 7   2013   £350

The Aldine Poets. London: printed by Charles Whittingham for William Pickering, 1830-1845. Complete series, 53 volumes, 24 frontispiece portraits, especially pretty polished light brown calf, attractively gilt by Zaehnsdorf, stamp signed, covers with gilt double fillet border and gilt Aldine/Pickering anchor centerpiece, raised bands, spines gilt in compartments with scrolling foliate cornerpieces and loping stem centerpiece, surrounded by diamond frame of circlets and tiny stars, each spine with red and green titling label (at bottom) a red date label, elaborately gilt turn-ins, marbled endpapers, all edges gilt, spines uniformly faded to darker brown, a number of small nicks or tiny scuffs to backstrips, slight offsetting from engraved frontispieces, but fine and in many ways an amazing set, joints and remarkably bright covers almost entirely without wear and text pristine.   Phillip J. Pirages   61 - 134   2013 $7800

Aldiss, Brian W. *The Airs of Earth.* London: Faber & Faber, 1963. First edition, fine in fine dust jacket, as new.   Between the Covers Rare Books, Inc.   Sci-Fi, Fantasy & Horror - 316309   2013 $75

Aldiss, Brian W. *Intangibles Inc. & Other Stories.* London: Faber and Faber, 1969. First edition, 8vo., original red cloth, dust jacket, near fine in dust jacket, inscribed by author for Kingsley Amis.   Maggs Bros. Ltd.   1460 - 11   2013   £175

Aldiss, Brian W. *Report on Probability A.* London: Faber & Faber, 1968. First edition, 8vo., original red dust cloth, dust jacket, excellent copy, some light staining to dust jacket spine, inscribed by author.   Maggs Bros. Ltd.   1460 - 10   2013   £50

Aldrich, Thomas Bailey 1836-1907 *Marjorie Daw.* Boston & New York: Houghton Mifflin, 1908. First edition, Large 8vo. red gilt decorated cloth, top edge gilt, owner inscription on endpaper, very fine in dust jacket with publisher's box, name on box, else very good-fine, illustrations by John Cecil Clay with lovely color illustrations, printed on heavy coated paper, rare. Aleph-Bet Books, Inc. 105 - 34 2013 $250

Alec-Tweedie, Mrs. *Tight Corners of My Adventurous Life.* Hutchinson, 1933. First edition, 8vo., 315 page, 33 plates, original red cloth. J. & S. L. Bonham Antiquarian Booksellers Europe - 9603 2013 £30

Alembert, Jean Le Rond D' *Miscellaneous Pieces in Literature, History and Philosophy.* printed for C Henderson, 1764. First edition in English, uniformly slightly browned, few spots and stains, last leaf torn at upper inner corner (caused by adhesion of free endpaper), 8vo., modern marbled boards stamp of Lynn Free Public Library, accession number in ink , few 19th century pencil notes, good. Blackwell's Rare Books B174 - 3 2013 £1800

The Alesculapian. Brooklyn: 1909. 280 pages, Volume one of the series, ex-library in buckram, binding worn and rubbed but tight, front flyleaf loose, internally very good. James Tait Goodrich S74 - 180 2013 $150

Alexander, Bob *John H. Behan, Sacrificed Sheriff.* Silver City: High Lonesome Books, 2002. First edition, one of 500 copies signed by author, vintage photo portraits and views, grey cloth, very fine, spine faded pictorial dust jacket. Argonaut Book Shop Summer 2013 - 3 2013 $60

Alexander, James Bradun *The Lunarian Professor and His Remarkable Revelations Concerning the Earth, the Moon and Mars Together with an Account of the Cruise of the Sally Ann.* Minneapolis: 1909. First edition, octavo, original red cloth, front and rear panels ruled in blind, spine panel stamped in gold. L. W. Currey, Inc. Fall Sampler Sept. 2013 - 146446 2013 $3500

Alexander, James Edward *Travels to the Seat of War in the East, through Russia and the Crimea in 1829.* London: Henry Colburn and Richard Bentley, 1830. First edition, frontispiece, 11 aquatint plates, 2 engraved plates, 8vo., period half calf over marbled boards, five raised bands ruled in gilt black morocco spine labels, some scattered foxing, mainly to initial leaves and map, spine mildly rubbed, otherwise near fine. Kaaterskill Books 16 - 1 2013 $950

Alexander, Michael *The Reluctant Legionnaire.* Hart Davis, 1956. First edition, 196 pages, original cloth, dust jacket, extremities rather chipped and stained. R. F. G. Hollett & Son Africana - 1 2013 £30

Alexander, the Coppersmith *Remarks Upon the Religion...* 1974. Reprint of 1737 original, octavo, cloth, original dust jacket, near fine. C. P. Hyland 261 - 5 2013 £60

Alexander, William *Picturesque Representations of the Dress and Manners of the Russians.* London: printed for John Murray by W. Bulmer and Co., 1814. First edition, small 4to., 64 hand colored plates, three quarter later navy blue pebbled morocco over blue cloth boards, four raised bands with gilt links, four medallions, titles in gilt, recent endpapers, minor foxing to titlepage, else fine. Kaaterskill Books 16 - 2 2013 $1500

Alexie, Sherman *Indian Killer.* New York: Atlantic Monthly Press, 1996. First edition, inscribed by author to Greg Gatenby, with Gatenby's signature, fine in fine dust jacket. Ken Lopez Bookseller 159 - 146 2013 $250

Alford, Sterling G. *Famous First Blacks.* New York/ Washington: Vantage/Alford Publications, 1974. First edition, corners little bumped, else near fine in very good dust jacket (rubbed and price clipped with crease on spine), inscribed by author. Between the Covers Rare Books, Inc. 165 - 42 2013 $125

Algarotti, Francesco *Sir Isaac Newton's Philosophy Explain'd for the Use of the Ladies.* London: printed for E. Cave at St. John's-gate and sold also by Messrs Bindley (and others), 1739. 2 volumes, 12mo., some even browning, old waterstaining to endpapers in volume 1, full contemporary mottled calf, double gilt ruled borders, gilt panelled spines, little rubbed, lacking labels, slight wear double gilt ruled borders, gilt panelled spines, little rubbed, lacking labels, slight wear to foot of spine volume II, early ownership name Cath: Williams on front endpapers. Jarndyce Antiquarian Booksellers CCIV - 216 2013 £580

Algeo, Sara M. *The Story of a Sub-Pioneer.* Providence: Snow and Farnham, 1925. First edition, 1/1000 numbered copies, 8vo., 318 pages, 91 half tones, author's presentation, maroon cloth, stamped in gilt, ex-library with stamps, bookplate and spine label, front hinge little tender, else very good. Second Life Books Inc. 182 - 2 2013 $75

Algren, Nelson *The Last Carousel.* New York: Putnam, 1973. First edition, inscribed by author with felt tip pen, fine in fine dust jacket, 435 pages. Beasley Books 2013 - 2013 $100

Algren, Nelson *The Man With the Golden Arm.* Garden City: Doubleday & Co., 1949. First edition, 8vo., original pale brown cloth, inscribed by author for Simone de Beauvoir, excellent copy, very slightly rubbed at extremities. Maggs Bros. Ltd. 1460 - 12 2013 £650

Algren, Nelson *The Man with the Golden Arm.* New York: Pocket Books, 1951. First paperback printing, wrappers, issued in dust jacket with imprint of Cardinal C-31, book near fine, very slight soiling and dust jacket very good with tiny chip at head of spine, rear jacket flap still adhered to rear wrapper of book, as issued, front dust jacket flap now free, some splitting at folds of dust jacket, 16mo., 454 pages.   Beasley Books   2013 - 2013 $65

Algren, Nelson *A Walk on the Wild Side.* New York: Farrar Straus & Cudahy, 1956. First edition, signed by author on bookplate tipped to f.e.p. (with consequent rippling), otherwise near fine in very good+ dust jacket with mild wear at top edge, 8vo., 346 pages.   Beasley Books   2013 - 2013 $100

Algren, Nelson *Who Lost an American?* New York: Macmillan, 1963. First edition, fine in close to fine dust jacket, signed by author, 337 pages.   Beasley Books   2013 - 2013 $60

Alken, Henry *Ideas, Accidental and Incidental to Hunting and Other Sports...* London: Thomas M'Lean, n.d., 1826-1830. First edition, early issue, plates dated 1826-1830 and watermarked 1831-32, upright folio, letterpress title and 42 hand colored etchings, full forest green crushed morocco by Riviere or Sangorski & Sutcliffe (circa 1940), occasional mild spots to margins not affecting imagery, neat professional repair to closed margin tear on plate #6, otherwise beautiful copy.   David Brass Rare Books, Inc.   Holiday 2012 Chapter Two - DB 02149   2013 $16,500

All About Little Boy Blue. New York: Cupples & Leon, 1924. First edition, 24mo., 8 color plates, paper covered boards, very good.   Barnaby Rudge Booksellers   Children 2013 - 021338 2013 $75

The All About Story Book. New York: Cupples and Leon, 1929. First collected edition, frontispiece, illustrated titlepage, many color text illustrations by John B. Gruelle, orange cloth with black titling to front cover, white endpapers, fine in very slightly torn dust jacket.   Ian Hodgkins & Co. Ltd.   134 - 48   2013   £110

All About the Night Before Christmas. New York: Cupples & Leon, 1918. First edition, illustrations by Gladys Hall, paper covered boards, very good in like dust jacket, 24mo., beautiful copy, previous owner's erased inscription, small closed tear to top front of dust jacket, 8 color plates and many black and white illustrations.   Barnaby Rudge Booksellers   Children 2013 - 021337   2013 $150

Allbutt, Henry Arthur *Di froy's handbukh...* R. Forder, 1897. First Yiddish edition, 8vo., wrappers, some minor soiling and wear, good.   Blackwell's Rare Books   172 - 7   2013   £1500

Allen, Betty *Menehune Alphabet Book.* Honolulu: Paradise of the Pacific, 1949. 14 stiff card pages ring bound on top edge, one leaf reinforced at rings, else very good, charming and scarce.   Aleph-Bet Books, Inc.   104 - 7   2013 $300

Allen, C. R. *Illustrated Historical Atlas of Pictou County, Nova Scotia.* Belleville: Mika Publishing, 1975. Limited to 500 numbered copies, this #32, blue cloth with gilt to front cover, folio, maps, small white spots to front cover and wear to edges, interior very good.   Schooner Books Ltd.   105 - 51   2013 $125

Allen, C. R. *Illustrated Historical Atlas of Pictou County Nova Scotia.* Philadelphia: J. H. Meacham & Co., printed F. Bourquin, 1879. folio, brown cloth with gilt to front cover and leather spine, maps, views, 2 loose folding maps, cloth scuffed with hinges separated at front and back and spine very worn, interior good with minor foxing and dampstaining to paper edges, separate maps have creases and minor tears to edges.   Schooner Books Ltd.   101 - 84   2013 $475

Allen, Daphne *Birth of the Opal: a Child's Fancies.* London: George Allen, 1913. First edition, 4to., boards, color plate on cover, fine condition in slightly worn dust jacket, 12 lovely tipped-in color plates, full page half tones and delicate line illustrations, including pictorial endpapers.   Aleph-Bet Books, Inc.   105 - 234   2013 $425

Allen, Grant *An African Millionaire: Episodes in the Life of the Illustrious Colonel Clay.* London: Grant Richard, 1897. First edition, corners slightly bumped and endpapers little browned, handsome, near fine.   Between the Covers Rare Books, Inc.   Mystery & Detective Fiction - 46889   2013 $700

Allen, Grant *Michael's Crag.* New York: Rand McNally & Co., 1893. First American edition, over 350 marginal illustrations in silhouette by Francis Carruthers Gould and Alec Carruthers Gould, blue-green cloth decorated in red and gold, contemporary gift inscription, some modest fading to spine, very good or better.   Between the Covers Rare Books, Inc.   Mystery & Detective Fiction - 288177   2013 $65

Allen, Jerome *National System of Map Drawing Adapted to Monteith & McNally's System of Geographies.* New York: 1870. 16 pages, maps, original printed wrappers, quarto, light wear to wrapper, else clean and near fine, many pages of maps - all blank save for outlines - are nicely hand colored.   Dumont Maps & Books of the West   125 - 27   2013 $150

Allen, Phoebe *The Old Galleries of Cumbria and Early Wool Trade.* Kendal: Abbot Hall Art Gallery, 1984. First edition, 4to., original wrappers, 56 pages, illustrations, color frontispiece, scarce.   R. F. G. Hollett & Son   Lake District & Cumbria - 16   2013   £25

Allen, R. E. *Studies in Presocoratic Philosophy. volume II.* Atlantic Highlands: Humanities Press, 1975. 8vo., red cloth, gilt stamped spine title, dust jacket, ownership signature, fine.   Jeff Weber Rare Books   169 - 5   2013 $90

Allen, Richard *A Souvenir of Newstead Abbey, Formerly the Home of Lord Byron.* Nottingham: Richard Allen, 1874. First edition, 4to., frontispiece, photos, final ad leaf, original green cloth, bevelled boards, attractively blocked in black and gilt, slight rubbing, gift inscription May 1878, very good, bright copy.   Jarndyce Antiquarian Booksellers   CCIII - 336   2013   £65

Allen, Thomas *Pacific Railroad Commenced. Addressed.... to Board of Directors of the Pacific Railroad Company at their First Meeting Jan. 31 1850.* St. Louis: Republican Office, 1850. First edition, 8vo., 46 pages recent cloth covered boards, foxed but very good.   M & S Rare Books, Inc.   95 - 279   2013 $2500

Allen, Walter *The Music of Fletcher Henderson.* Highland Park: the author, 1974. Blue cloth, second printing, very good+.   Beasley Books   2013 - 2013 $100

Allestree, Richard *The Art of Contentment.* Oxford: at the Theatre, 1675. First edition, 8vo., original speckled calf, spine elaborately gilt, gilt lettered, raised bands, front hinge starting at top, very small chip out of top of spine, original owner's signature Albinia Foorthe 1675.   Howard S. Mott Inc.   262 - 6   2013 $500

Alley, George *Observations on the Hydrargyria or that Vesicular Disease, Arising from the Exhibition of Mercury.* London: Longman, Hurst, Rees and Orme, 1810. xx, 103 pages, 3 hand colored plates of skin lesions, 4to., new quarter calf and marbled boards.   James Tait Goodrich   75 - 4   2013 $850

Alley, Ronald *Francis Bacon. Catalogue Raisonne.* London: Thames and Hudson, 1964. First edition, 4to., 292 pages, 27 color plates and 260 monochrome plates, near fine, in very good++ dust jacket with mild edge wear.   By the Book, L. C.   36 - 8   2013 $700

Alleyne, James *Every Man His Own Doctor; or a New English Dispensatory in four parts.* printed for Thomas Astley, 1733? First edition?, possibly lacking prelim ad leaf, little staining from use, piece torn from corner of first flyleaf at front, last gathering little proud, 8vo., contemporary calf, spine gilt ruled in compartments, red lettering piece, spine chipped at either end, corners slightly worn, armorial bookplate of Seton of Mounie, sound.   Blackwell's Rare Books   Sciences - 4   2013   £250

Allibone, S. Austin *A Critical Dictionary of English Literature and British and American Authors.... (with) A Supplement to Albion's Critical Dictionary...*   Philadelphia: J. B. Lippincott, 1886-1898. 5 volumes, large 8vo., green cloth, gilt stamped spines, extremities rubbed, some volumes waterstained, some hinges cracked but still strong, bookplates of Burndy Library.   Jeff Weber Rare Books   169 - 4   2013 $275

Allingham, Margery *Cargo of Eagles.* London: Chatto & Windus, 1968. First edition, fine in dust jacket.   Mordida Books   81 - 5   2013 $85

Allingham, Margery *The Oaken Heart.* Garden City: Doubleday Doran, 1941. First American edition, very good in dust jacket with chips at spine ends and along top edges of front and back panels.   Mordida Books   81 - 3   2013 $100

Allingham, Margery *Tether's End.* Garden City: Doubleday, 1958. First American edition, fine in dust jacket.   Mordida Books   81 - 4   2013 $65

Allison, K. J. *The History of the County of York East Riding.* Oxford University Press, 1968-1989. 5 volumes, very good in dust jackets, one jacket little worn.   Ken Spelman Books Ltd.   73 - 174   2013   £300

Allison, Robert *Lectures and Addresses.* Arthur L. Humphreys, 1913. First edition, 250 pages, large 8vo., original green cloth gilt, scarce.   R. F. G. Hollett & Son   Lake District & Cumbria - 18   2013   £45

Allom, Thomas *Westmorland, Cumberland, Durham and Northumberland Illustrated.* F. Fisher etc., n.d., 1832. 4to., old half calf gilt, marbled boards, edges little rubbed and neatly recased, 220 pages, all edges gilt, complete with vignette on title, 215 steel engraved plates, little occasional browning and spotting, but very good.   R. F. G. Hollett & Son   Lake District & Cumbria - 21   2013   £450

Allom, Thomas *Westmorland, Cumberland, Durham and Northumberland Illustrated.* Fisher Son and Co., 1832. 4to., old half calf, gilt, patterned cloth boards, foot of spine trifle defective, pages 220, title vignette and 215 steel engraved plates, scattered light spotting, very good, sound, clean copy.   R. F. G. Hollett & Son   Lake District & Cumbria - 20   2013   £450

Allom, Thomas *Westmorland, Cumberland, Durham and Northumberland Illustrated.* H. Fisher, R. Fisher and P. Jackson, 1832. 4to., old diced calf gilt, hinges rubbed, edges little worn and scraped, 220 pages, vignette on title and 214 tissue guarded steel engraved plates, little occasional browning and spotting but very good, sound copy. R. F. G. Hollett & Son   Lake District & Cumbria - 19   2013   £450

Allsop, Thomas *Letters Conversations and Recollections of S. T. Coleridge.* London: Edward Moxon, 1836. First edition, 2 volumes, half titles, pencil notes in text volume I, original dark green cloth, paper label volume I chipped and missing entirely volume II, spines faded and slightly worn at heads and tails, inscribed to G. H. B. Coleridge by W. King. Mar 14 1944.   Jarndyce Antiquarian Booksellers   CCIII - 557   2013   £85

Allsop, Thomas *Letters Conversations and Recollections of S. T. Coleridge.* London: Edward Moxon, 1836. Second edition, half title, original dark green cloth by Westleys, spine little worn at head, booklabel of John Johnson.   Jarndyce Antiquarian Booksellers   CCIII - 558   2013   £40

Allsop, Thomas *Letters Conversations and Recollections of S. T. Coleridge.* London: Frederick Farrah, 1864. Third edition, half title, original purple cloth, bevelled boards, spine faded to brown, still very good.   Jarndyce Antiquarian Booksellers   CCIII - 559   2013   £50

Almond, Linda Stevens *Peter Rabbit & Jack the Jumper.* Philadelphia: Henry Altemus, 1922. First edition, frontispiece, 28 color illustrations, red cloth backed purple boards, color pictorial onlay, front cover within green decorated titling to front cover and backstrip, green and white illustrated endpapers, 5 1/2 x 4 inches, boards faded and slight wear to corner tips, name to free endpaper and small ink number top title and recto frontispiece, very good.   Ian Hodgkins & Co. Ltd.   134 - 6   2013   £45

Almond, Linda Stevens *Peter Rabbit & Little White Rabbit.* Philadelphia: Henry Altemus, 1923. First edition, frontispiece and color illustrations, 5 3/8 x 4 inches, red cloth backed purple boards, color illustration pasted front cover, green titling, black titling, blue and white pictorial endpapers, some fading to edges of covers and slight rubbing onlay, endpapers cracked at hinges with small nameplate pastedown, name to free endpaper, some marks to contents and bottom corner few pages creased, still good copy.   Ian Hodgkins & Co. Ltd.   134 - 7   2013   £42

Almond, Linda Stevens *Peter Rabbit & the Little Boy.* Philadelphia: Henry Altemus, 1922. First edition, frontispiece and color illustrations, red cloth backed purple boards, color illustration pasted front cover, fine in dust jacket, name to free endpaper.   Ian Hodgkins & Co. Ltd.   134 - 10   2013   £65

Almond, Linda Stevens *Peter Rabbit & the Old Witch Woman.* Philadelphia: Henry Altemus, 1923. First edition, frontispiece and color illustrations, red cloth backed purple boards, color illustration pasted front cover, slight fading to covers, name to endpapers and odd slight mark, very good in soiled and slightly worn dust jacket.   Ian Hodgkins & Co. Ltd.   134 - 11   2013   £65

Almond, Linda Stevens *Peter Rabbit & The Tinybits.* Altemus, 1924. First edition, frontispiece and 24 color illustrations from original drawings by Margaret Hoopes, red cloth backed purple boards, decorated front cover with color illustration pasted on, some fading to covers and very slight wear top and bottom backstrip, very good.   Ian Hodgkins & Co. Ltd.   134 - 12   2013   £48

Almond, Linda Stevens *Peter Rabbit & the Two Terrible Foxes.* Philadelphia: Henry Altemus, 1925. First edition, frontispiece and color illustrations Bess Goe Willis, red cloth backed purple boards color illustration pasted front cover, slight fading around edges rear cover, small ink number top title and recto frontispiece, very nice.   Ian Hodgkins & Co. Ltd.   134 - 13 2013   £48

Almond, Linda Stevens *Peter Rabbit Goes A-Visiting.* Philadelphia: Henry Altemus, 1921. First edition, frontispiece and color illustrations, red cloth backed purple boards, color illustration pasted front cover, boards faded, 2 inch split lower front hinge, 4 pages with crease from printing fault, 4 pages with marks to margins and other odd mark to contents, still good.   Ian Hodgkins & Co. Ltd.   134 - 15   2013   £38

Almond, Linda Stevens *Peter Rabbit Went A-Fishing.* Philadelphia: Henry Altemus, 1923. First edition, frontispiece and color illustrations by Margaret Campbell Hoopes, 64 pages, red cloth backed purple boards, color illustration pasted front cover, edges of covers with very slight fading and small ink number top title, very good.   Ian Hodgkins & Co. Ltd.   134 - 31   2013   £48

Almond, Linda Stevens *Peter Rabbit, Jack-The Jumper and Little White Rabbit.* Philadelphia: Henry Altemus, 1923. First edition, 28 color illustrations, red cloth backed purple boards, color illustration pasted front cover, some fading bottom backstrip and edges of boards, slight wear at corner tips, some finger soiling to contents, very good, scarce.   Ian Hodgkins & Co. Ltd.   134 - 16   2013   £48

Almond, Linda Stevens *Peter Rabbit's Birthday.* Philadelphia: Henry Altemus, 1921. First edition, 28 color illustrations, red cloth backed purple boards, color illustrated front cover, edges covers very slightly faded, name free endpaper, small ink number top title and recto frontispiece, slight soiling last blank, very good.   Ian Hodgkins & Co. Ltd.   134 - 19   2013   £45

Almond, Linda Stevens *Peter Rabbit's Easter.* Philadelphia: Henry Altemus, 1921. First edition, frontispiece and color illustrations, red cloth backed purple boards, color illustration pasted front cover, very nice in lightly soiled dust jacket.   Ian Hodgkins & Co. Ltd.   134 - 21   2013   £60

Almond, Linda Stevens *Peter Rabbit's Holiday.* Philadelphia: Henry Altemus, 1927. First edition, 30 color illustrations, red cloth backed purple boards, color illustration pasted front cover, usual light fading to edges of boards, name to free endpapers and slight odd mark to fore edge, very good.   Ian Hodgkins & Co. Ltd.   134 - 22   2013   £48

Almond, Linda Stevens *When Peter Rabbit Went to School.* Philadelphia: Henry Altemus, 1921. First edition, 27 color illustrations, red cloth backed purple boards, color illustration pasted front cover, slight fading to edges covers and corner tips with slight wear, ink number top title and recto frontispiece, very good.   Ian Hodgkins & Co. Ltd.   134 - 32   2013   £45

Alphabet Book. Akron: Saalfield, 1934. Folio, pictorial wrappers, light edgewear, bright color illustrations on each page.   Aleph-Bet Books, Inc.   104 - 1   2013 $100

Alphabet of History. London: Cowan and Standring, n.d. circa, 1845. 4to., pictorial wrappers, neat spine repair and covers dusty, very good, pictorial cover plus 4 very fine full page hand colored pages, each divided into 6 sections, each section has captioned illustration.   Aleph-Bet Books, Inc.   105 - 6   2013 $875

Alsop, Richard *The Echo.* New York: Noah Bailey, 1807. First edition, 8vo., 8 engraved plates, full contemporary calf, some browning and foxing, but very good.   M & S Rare Books, Inc.   95 - 6   2013 $425

Altgeld, John P. *Reasons for Pardoning Fielden, Neebe & Schwab the Haymarket Anarchists.* Chicago: 1893. First edition, 12mo., 63 pages, self wrappers, cover and rear wrapper separate (lacks corner of last page).   Second Life Books Inc.   183 - 2   2013 $50

Ambler, Eric *The Ability to Kill.* London: Bodley Head, 1963. First edition, second issue with James Hanratty essay, fine in dust jacket.   Mordida Books   81 - 7   2013 $85

Ambler, Eric *The Intercom Conspiracy.* New York: Atheneum, 1969. First edition, fine in dust jacket.   Mordida Books   81 - 8   2013 $65

Ambler, Eric *Passage of Arms.* New York: Alfred A. Knopf, 1960. First American edition, fine in advance copy dust jacket which is darkened at spine and chipped at top of spine and along top edge of front panel.   Mordida Books   81 - 6   2013 $75

The American Boy's Book of Sports and Games... New York: Dick & Fitzgerald, 1864. Thick 8vo., 600 pages, brown cloth stamped in black, green and gold, bright, tight, very good+ with minor condition issues (slight fraying to spine ends, front hinge not weak but slight wear and slight lean), great copy.   Aleph-Bet Books, Inc.   105 - 57   2013 $900

American Colonization Society *Report of the Naval Committee to the House of Representatives August 1850 in Favor of the Establishment of a Line of Mail Steamships to the Western Coast of Africa...* Washington: Gideon & Co., 1850. First edition, 8vo., 79 pages, original printed wrappers, front wrapper soiled, otherwise fine.   M & S Rare Books, Inc.   95 - 76   2013 $200

American Federation of Labor History, Encyclopedia, Reference Book. Washington: American Federation of Labor, 1919. First edition, hardcover, 320 pages, very good with few clumsily glued prelims.   Beasley Books   2013 - 2013 $50

The American Socialist. Oneida: 1876-1879. Volume I-V, folio.   M & S Rare Books, Inc.   95 - 274   2013 $2000

The American Stage of Today. New York: P. F. Collier, 1910. First edition, folio, black cloth backed boards.   Barnaby Rudge Booksellers   Biography 2013 - 021465   2013 $75

Ames, Mrs. Ernest *Maid's Progress.* London: Grant Richards, 1901. 4to., cloth backed pictorial boards, some edge rubbing and light soil, very good+, full page color illustrations.   Aleph-Bet Books, Inc.   105 - 35   2013 $475

Amic, Yolande *L'Opaline Francaise au XIXe Siecle.* Pais: Librairie Grund, 1952. First edition, no. 631 of 1500 copies, 188 pages + plates, 48 plates, 24 in text figures, 4to., cloth, near fine with light browning along edges.   Kaaterskill Books   16 - 21   2013 $350

Amini, Johari *Let's Go Some Where.* Chicago: Third World Press, 1970. First edition, stapled wrappers, fine.   Between the Covers Rare Books, Inc.   165 - 43   2013 $100

Amis, Kingsley *A Frame of Mind.* Reading: printed at the School of Art, University of Reading, 1953. First edition, one of 150 numbered copies, this unnumbered but penned "Proof" copy, 8vo., original printed cream wrappers over card, with less than usual darkening to covers, very faint stain to front cover, fore edge, good.   Blackwell's Rare Books   172 - 157   2013   £275

Amis, Lola Jones *3 Plays: Helen, The Other Side of the Wall; The Place of Wrath.* New York: Exposition Press, 1965. First edition, fine in fine dust jacket, very lightly rubbed, scarce. Between the Covers Rare Books, Inc. 165 - 44   2013 $175

Amis, Martin *Invasion of the Space Invaders.* Hutchinson, 1982. First edition, printed on art paper, numerous color printed illustrations, a number of full or double page, imperial 8vo., original illustrated gloss card wrappers, fine. Blackwell's Rare Books 172 - 158 2013 £150

Ammons, A. R. *Ommateum with Doxology.* Philadelphia: Dorrance & Co., 1955. First edition, one of 300 copies of which only 100 were bound, small 8vo., original salmon cloth, dust jacket, very fine, essentially as new. James S. Jaffe Rare Books Fall 2013 - 1 2013 $3500

Amory, Thomas *The Life of John Bucle, Esq.* London: printed for T. Becket and P. A. Dehondt and T. Cadell, 1770. New edition, 4 volumes, 12mo., few minor spots, late 19th/early 20th century sprinkled and polished tan calf by Riviere, rebacked to style by Chris Weston, board edges slightly rubbed, ink ownership inscription 'B. Gaskell' with 'Thomas House' added in volume 4, armorial bookplate of Charles George Milnes Gaskell. Unsworths Antiquarian Booksellers 28 - 62 2013 £300

Ampere, Andre Marie *Expose des Nouvelles Decouvertes sur l'Electricite et le Magnetisme...* Paris: Mequignon-Marvis, 1822. First edition, numerous woodcut diagrams and illustrations in text, 8vo., drab wrappers, good. Blackwell's Rare Books Sciences - 5 2013 £1800

Amundsen, Roald *The South Pole. An Account of the Norwegian Antarctic Expedition in the 'Fram' 1910-1912.* London: 1912. First English edition, 2 volumes, 21 maps and charts, 136 illustrations, 8vo., original red cloth, gilt, with Norwegian flag on backs and upper cover, very good. Maggs Bros. Ltd. 1467 - 132 2013 £3750

Amundsen, Roald *The South Pole, An Account of the Norwegian Antarctic Expedition in the "Fram" 1910-1912.* London/New York: John Murray/Lee Keedick, 1925. 2 volumes in one as issue, 8vo., xxxv, 392, map; vi, 438, index 439-449 pages, signed and inscribed by author, rare thus, very good++ in original blue cloth gilt lettered spine, spine mildly sunned, mild toning to pages, binding tight, all illustrations present as called for, volume I frontispiece plus 4 illustrations and map, volume II with 7 illustrations. By the Book, L. C. 36 - 83 2013 $4000

Anacreon *Teij Odae. Ab Henrico Stephano Luce & Latinate...* Paris: Apud Henricum Stephanum, 1554. Editio princeps, browned in places, Henri Estienne's name censored n title with early ink, 8vo., modern quarter vellum, pasteboard boards, backstrip plain, small booklabel of Elizabeth Armstrong, good. Blackwell's Rare Books 172 - 8 2013 £1600

Anacreon *Odae et Fragmenta, Graece et Latine...* Utrecht: Apud Guilielmum Kroon, 1732. 4to., light toning and few spots, contemporary Dutch calf, boards panelled in blind with central blind lozenge, backstrip with five raised bands, second compartment dyed dark and gilt lettered, rest plain, front joint rubbed, corners slightly worn, pastedowns lifted and boards bowed slightly, shelfmark inked to front board, good. Blackwell's Rare Books 172 - 9 2013 £175

Anacreon *Teiou Mele: Praefixo Commentario quo Poetae Genus...* Parma: Bodoni, 1791. One of 150 copies, 16mo. in 4's, 2 engraved portraits, text i Greek, commentaries in Latin, very occasional marginal foxing, small marginal tear to page 91, contemporary vellum, spine gilt with black morocco labels, all edges gilt, upper joint split but neatly repaired with vellum, lower joint starting, binding little soiled, particularly at spine, labels slightly chipped, armorial bookplate of John Wells Esq. to front pastedown, with small Greek inscription, armorial bookplate of Gul. D. Geddes. Unsworths Antiquarian Booksellers 28 - 1 2013 £600

Anagnostakis, Andreas *Essai sur l'Exploration de la Retine et des Milieux de l'Oeil sur le Vivant...* Paris: Rignoux, 1854. First edition, 8vo., 2 folding wood engraved plates, modern quarter maroon morocco, marbled boards, gilt ruled covers, brown leather spine label, gilt spine, library rubber stamp on verso of plate I, fine, bookplate of Jerry F. Donin, rare. Jeff Weber Rare Books 172 - 6 2013 $2000

Analavage, Robert *The Lessons of Laurel: Grass-Roots Organizing in the South.* Louisville: SCEF Press/Southern Conference Educational Fund Press, 1970. First edition, quarto, stapled wrappers, 12 pages, illustrations, slightly soiled, else near fine. Between the Covers Rare Books, Inc. 165 - 45 2013 $275

Ancillon, Charles *Eunuchism Display'd.* London: printed for E. Curll, 1718. First edition, 12mo., some slight browning and foxing, very good, handsomely bound in recent full panelled calf, ornate gilt panelled spine, red morocco label. Jarndyce Antiquarian Booksellers CCIV - 40 2013 £580

Andersen, Hans Christian 1805-1875 *Fairy Tales.* London: Sampson Low Marston, Low and Searle, 1872. First edition, 4to., brownish maroon cloth, extensively illustrated in black and gold, beveled edges, all edges gilt, spine ends inconspicuously strengthened and slight cover soil, near fine, 12 magnificent large full page chromolithographs by E. V. Boyle, done in rich colors, very scarce.   Aleph-Bet Books, Inc.   104 - 88   2013 $3250

Andersen, Hans Christian 1805-1875 *Fairy Tales and Stories.* New York: Century, 1900. First US edition, large 4to., red pictorial cloth stamped in gold, 524 pages, spine extremes frayed and light shelfwear, very good+, full and partial page drawings by Hans Tegner.   Aleph-Bet Books, Inc.   105 - 36   2013 $400

Andersen, Hans Christian 1805-1875 *Hans Andersen's Fairy Tales.* London: Raphael Tuck, n.d. circa, 1902. 4to., blue cloth stamped in gold, all edges gilt, spine end frayed, else near fine, black and white drawings by S. Jacobs, 8 chromolithographed plates by E. J. Andrews.   Aleph-Bet Books, Inc.   104 - 35   2013 $350

Andersen, Hans Christian 1805-1875 *Hans Andersen's Fairy Tales.* Blackie & Son, n.d c., 1914. 4to., original pictorial boards, unpaginated, 14 color plates, numerous line drawings by Helen Stratton, some full page, little light fingering in places.   R. F. G. Hollett & Son   Children's Books - 579   2013   £75

Andersen, Hans Christian 1805-1875 *Andersen's Fairy Stories.* London: Collins Clear Type Press, n.d. circa, 1915. 4to., blue cloth stamped in gold, pictorial paste-on, slight bit of wear, near fine, 8 beautiful color plates and numerous full and partial page line illustrations and pictorial endpapers.   Aleph-Bet Books, Inc.   104 - 36   2013 $400

Andersen, Hans Christian 1805-1875 *Andersen's Fairy Tales.* New York: Cupples & Leon, 1923. 4to., blue cloth gilt, color pictorial paste-on, 180 pages, very good+, 3 color plates with a profusion of black and whites.   Aleph-Bet Books, Inc.   104 - 377   2013 $200

Andersen, Hans Christian 1805-1875 *Andersen's Fairy Tales.* New York: Cupples & Leon, 1923. 4to., blue gilt cloth, color pictorial paste-on, 180 pages, fine and bright, 3 beautiful color plates and profusion of black and whites throughout text, beautiful copy.   Aleph-Bet Books, Inc.   105 - 418   2013 $275

Andersen, Hans Christian 1805-1875 *Fairy Tales by Hans Andersen.* New York: George Doran, 1924. First US trade edition, large 4to., black cloth with elaborate silver pictorial paste-on, as new in publisher's box, few neat repairs to box, illustrations by Kay Nielsen with 12 beautiful tipped in color plates plus many full page back and whites to accompany 16 fairy tales, great copy, rare in box.   Aleph-Bet Books, Inc.   104 - 390   2013 $1875

Andersen, Hans Christian 1805-1875 *Fairy Tales by Hans Andersen.* New York: George H. Doran, 1924. First US trade edition, large 4to., black cloth with elaborate silver pictorial cover and spine, spine faded, else near fine, illustrations by Kay Nielsen with 12 beautiful tipped in color plates, plus many full page black and whites to accompany 16 fairy tales.   Aleph-Bet Books, Inc.   105 - 429   2013 $950

Andersen, Hans Christian 1805-1875 *Fairy Tales.* Philadelphia: David McKay Co., 1932. First American trade edition, large octavo, 12 full page color illustrations and 59 black and white drawings by Arthur Rackham, publisher's rose red cloth, original color pictorial dust jacket, publisher's box, very near fine to mint dust jacket, fine copy.   David Brass Rare Books, Inc.   Holiday 2012 Chapter One - DB 01894   2013 $1150

Andersen, Hans Christian 1805-1875 *Fairy Tales.* London: Harrap, 1932. One of 25 copies, of a total limited edition of 525 copies (of which 500 were for sale), this marked presentation in Rackham's hand and signed by Rackham, with original drawing by Rackham on integral blank, 4to., publisher's special full green morocco with triple gilt fillet border and pictoral gold design on front cover after Rackham, spine slightly toned, else fine, 12 beautiful color plates, pictorial endpapers and 59 wonderful black and whites.   Aleph-Bet Books, Inc.   105 - 491   2013 $22,000

Andersen, Hans Christian 1805-1875 *Hans Andersen's Fairy stories. Bookano Series.*   Strand Publications, n.d., 1938. Large 8vo., original pictorial boards, spine little creased, unpaginated with tinted endpapers, color frontispiece and title, 4 fine colored pop-ups and black and white drawings, inscription dated 1949 on front endpapers, else in good crisp, unused condition.   R. F. G. Hollett & Son Children's Books - 226   2013   £120

Andersen, Hans Christian 1805-1875 *Hans Andersen's Fairy Tales.* London: Hodder & Stoughton, 1981. Facsimile edition, large 8vo., original cloth, gilt extra, glassine wrapper, 16 color plates, line drawings.   R. F. G. Hollett & Son   Children's Books - 517   2013   £45

Andersen, Hans Christian 1805-1875 *Hans Christian Andersen Fairy Tales.* New York: Holt Rinehart, 1981. First edition, limited to 350 numbered copies, signed by Michael Hague with large and detailed original drawing, with his beautiful color plates, cloth, pictorial paste-on, fine in slipcase.   Aleph-Bet Books, Inc.   104 - 271   2013 $300

Andersen, Hans Christian 1805-1875 *Hans Andersen's Fairy Tales.* London: Hodder & Stoughton for Boots the Chemist, n.d., 1913. First edition, 4to., original plum cloth gilt, upper board very slightly differentially faded, 16 tipped in color plates and illustrated with line drawings, few spots to fore-edge, otherwise fine.   R. F. G. Hollett & Son Children's Books - 516   2013   £175

Andersen, Hans Christian 1805-1875 *The Garden of Paradise and Other Stories.* London: Heinemann, 1923. First edition, large 8vo., original green cloth gilt, pictorial onlay, trifle rubbed and scratched, 10 plates, head and tailpieces, top corners slightly bumped, uncommon.   R. F. G. Hollett & Son   Children's Books - 625   2013   £45

Andersen, Hans Christian 1805-1875 *The Improvisatore; or Life in Italy.* London: Richard Bentley, 1847. Early edition, Engraved frontispiece, 8vo., good in contemporary dark green half calf, marbled boards, later red morocco labels, some occasional foxing and bound without final ad leaf.   Ken Spelman Books Ltd.   75 - 114   2013   £95

Andersen, Hans Christian 1805-1875 *Stories from Hans Andersen.* Hodder and Stoughton, n.d. 1920's, Original cloth gilt, pictorial dust jacket, pages 195, 14 tipped in color plates, light spotting to edges and few leaves, otherwise fine in lovely dust jacket.   R. F. G. Hollett & Son   Children's Books - 177   2013   £250

Andersen, Hans Christian 1805-1875 *The Swineherd.* New York: Alfred A. Knopf, n.d., 10 full page color plates by Einar Nrman, decorated endpapers, square 4to., original pictorial boards, head of spine trifle bruised.   R. F. G. Hollett & Son   Children's Books - 10   2013   £75

Andersen, Hans Christian 1805-1875 *Tales for the Young.* London: James Burns, 1847. 12mo., green cloth, blindstamped, normal light wear, very good, 3 engraved plates by Dalziel Brothers.   Aleph-Bet Books, Inc.   105 - 37   2013 $400

Andersen, Hans Christian 1805-1875 *Thumbelina.* Holiday House, 1939. Limited to 1200 copies, hand colored, square 16mo., cloth backed decorative boards, fine condition, illustrations by Hilda Scott with lovely hand colored illustrations, designed by Helen Gentry.   Aleph-Bet Books, Inc.   105 - 38   2013 $200

Andersen, Hans Christian 1805-1875 *Het Leelijke Jonge Eendje. (The Ugly Duckling).* Amsterdam: C. M. Van Gogh, 1893. Number 1 proof copy, inscribed by Hoytema, limitation page has 2 extra mounted color plates, limitation leaf and ownership leaf, both inscribed by Hoytema, 31 large color plates mounted on heavy paper by Theo Van Hoytema, cloth backed pictorial boards, covers soiled and edges rubbed, else very good+.   Aleph-Bet Books, Inc.   105 - 328   2013 $3500

Andersen, Hans Christian 1805-1875 *The Ugly Duckling.* New York: Macmillan, August, 1927. First edition, square 12mo., pictorial boards, fine in very good+ dust jacket with light soil, color illustrations.   Aleph-Bet Books, Inc.   105 - 302   2013 $275

Anderson, Edward *Thieves Like Us.* New York: Frederick A. Stokes, 1937. First edition, fine in very good plus example of dust jacket with some modest chipping on rear panel, tiny nicks at spine ends, some rubbing and closed tear on front panel, exceptionally scarce in dust jacket.   Between the Covers Rare Books, Inc.   Mystery & Detective Fiction - 87132   2013 $6500

Anderson, Elbert *The Skylight and the Dark Room...* Philadelphia: Benerman & Wilson, 1872. First edition, 4to., illustrations, 12 photos laid down on 5 plates, 14 pages ads, original pictorial green cloth, bevelled boards, very good.   Jarndyce Antiquarian Booksellers   CCV - 4   2013   £2800

Anderson, George *The Art of Skating.* London: Horace Cox, 1880. Fourth edition, 191 x 127mm., original green cloth over thin flexible boards, upper cover with stylized gilt titling around central illustration of skates, flat unlettered spine, with 9 full page illustrations, 7 of them diagrams and the other two showing a very still figure gliding on the ice in top hat, as well as five diagrams in text, front free endleaf with ink ownership inscription of Dorothea L. S. Murray, Jan. 1887; lower corner of rear cover with faint diagonal crease, hinge open at page 66, but very fine of an insubstantial book, binding solid and with surprisingly few signs of wear, text very clean and fresh.   Phillip J. Pirages   63 - 440   2013 $325

Anderson, Isabel *Great Sea Horse.* Boston: Little Brown, Dec., 1909. Limited to 300 copies on handmade paper, 4to., gilt pictorial vellum, top edge gilt, slightest of cover soil and dimpling on spine, else fine, 24 magnificent tipped in color plates by John Elliott, color endpapers.   Aleph-Bet Books, Inc.   104 - 210   2013 $600

Anderson, James 1739-1808 *An Account of the Present State of the Hebrides and Western Coasts of Scotland...* Edinburgh: printed (by Mundell & Wilson) for G. Robinson, London and C. Elliot, Edinburgh, 1785. First edition, large folding map, 1 engraved plate and folding table, map torn an repaired with small patch missing from engraved text to right, split in folding table also neatly repaired, 8vo., contemporary tree calf, red lettering piece on spine, slightly worn, armorial bookplate inside front cover of Seton of Mounie, descendant of author, good.   Blackwell's Rare Books   Sciences - 6   2013   £400

Anderson, James 1739-1808 *Essays Relating to Agriculture and Rural Affairs.* London: printed for G. G. and J. Robinson and for Bell and Bradfute (sic), Edinburgh (volume iii: Edinburgh: printed for Bell & Bradfute, 1796), 1797. Fourth edition, volume first (-third) editions, 3 engraved plates, page of woodcuts in volume i, 18 engraved plates and page of woodcuts in volume ii, and a page of woodcuts in volume iii, some foxing and browning, 8vo., contemporary tan calf, gilt rules on either side of raised bands on spine, red lettering pieces, bit worn, especially spine ends, of the raised bands on spine, red lettering pieces, bit worn, especially spine ends, ownership inscription T. Hutchinson in volumes i and iii, armorial bookplates in all volumes of William Hutchinson of Eggleston (Teesdale, Co. Durham) and above it the later bookplate of Seton of Mounie, sound. Blackwell's Rare Books   Sciences - 7   2013   £300

Anderson, James 1739-1808 *Works.* Edinburgh and London: various publishers, 1776-1800. Volumes II-IV, a total f 23 monographs, pamphlets, prospecti &c, manuscript titlepage in volume II, few plates, occasional minor foxing and browning, 3 leaves in volume II scorched with loss to outer margins (not affecting text), half Russia c. 1800 spines gilt and blind tooled with gilt wheatsheaf and pair of agricultural tools in each compartment, lettered direct "Anderson's Works", marbled edges, joints and corners skillfully repaired, first volume in volumes ii and iii with bookstamp of George Anderson designed by John Anderson, each volume with armorial bookplate of Alexander David Seton of Mounie, with pencil Mounie Castle shelfmark.   Blackwell's Rare Books   172 - 11   2013   £8500

Anderson, John *Catalogue of Early Belfast Printed Books 1694-1830.* 1890. New and enlarged edition, 52 pages, octavo, wrappers, illustrations.   C. P. Hyland   261 - 41   2013   £75

Anderson, John Redwood *White the Fates Allow.* Beckenham: The Bee & Blackthorn Press, 1962. First edition, number 1 of 10 special copies, 8vo., original white cloth, dust jacket, inscribed by author for his wife Gwyneth, near fine, jacket spine little faded.   Maggs Bros. Ltd. 1460 - 13   2013   £150

Anderson, Kent *Night Dogs.* Tucson: Dennis McMillan, 1996. First edition, this copy signed by author and by James Crumley (provided introduction), also signed by publisher Dennis McMillan and by Michael Kellner, who designed dust jacket, fine in fine dust jacket inscribed by Anderson for Terrill Lee Lankford, with note from Lankford laid in.   Ken Lopez Bookseller   159 - 6   2013 $550

Anderson, Poul *Brain Wave.* Melbourne: London: Toronto: William Heinemann Ltd., 1955. First British and first hardcover edition, octavo, boards.   L. W. Currey, Inc. Fall Sampler Sept. 2013 - 146080   2013 $750

Anderson, R. C. *Canoeing and Camping Adventures...* London: C. Gilbert-Wood, 1910. First edition, 8vo., pages x, 192, map, diagrams, original blue decorative cloth, spine faded.   J. & S. L. Bonham Antiquarian Booksellers Europe - 6992   2013   £65

Anderson, Rasmus B. *The Flatey Book and Recently Discovered Vatican Manuscripts Concerning America as Early as the Tenth Century.* London: Norrena Society, 1906. 176 pages, 4to., original decorative green and brown cloth, front cover stamped and lettered silver.   James Tait Goodrich   S74 - 213   2013 $495

Anderson, Robert *Ballads in the Cumberland Dialect.* Wigton: E. Rook, 1815. Modern half levant morocco, gilt. R. F. G. Hollett & Son   Lake District & Cumbria - 23   2013 £85

Anderson, Robert *Ballads in the Cumberland Dialect Chiefly by R. Anderson...* Wigton: printed by R. Hetherton, 1808. Second edition, original printed boards, printed backstrip little defective neatly recased, untrimmed, frontispiece. R. F. G. Hollett & Son   Lake District & Cumbria - 24   2013 £120

Anderson, Robert *Ballads in the Cumberland Dialect.* Wigton: printed by R. Hetherton, 1808. Second edition, modern cloth, gilt, untrimmed, interleaved with engraved frontispiece, prelims rather browned, some fingering in places.   R. F. G. Hollett & Son   Lake District & Cumbria - 26   2013   £85

Anderson, Robert *Ballads in the Cumberland Dialect.* Carlisle: H. K. Snowden, 1828. Original printed boards, worn, spine chipped at head, untrimmed, engraved title foxed, front flyleaf removed.   R. F. G. Hollett & Son   Lake District & Cumbria - 25   2013   £35

Anderson, Robert *Ballads in the Cumberland Dialect.* Carlisle: B. Stewart, 1864. 12mo., original blindstamped cloth, gilt.   R. F. G. Hollett & Son   Lake District & Cumbria - 27   2013 £25

Anderson, Robert *Cumberland Ballads.* Carlisle: G. & T. Howard, 1881. Small 8vo., contemporary quarter morocco gilt, hinges rather rubbed.   R. F. G. Hollett & Son   Lake District & Cumbria - 30   2013   £30

Anderson, Robert *Poetical Works...* Carlisle: printed and sold by B. Scott, 1820. First edition, 2 volumes, uncut in original blue boards, carefully rebacked, dusted and little rubbed, signature of Jane Strong 1835, volume I. Jarndyce Antiquarian Booksellers   CCIII - 628   2013 £350

Anderson, Rufus *The Hawaiian Islands: Their Progress and Condition Under Missionary Labors.* Boston: Gould & Lincoln, 1864. First edition, tall 12mo., frontispiece, folding map, 14 illustrations, original brown blindstamped cloth, spine ends neatly restored, bookplate of Charles Atwood Kofoid, fine. Jeff Weber Rare Books 171 - 157 2013 $150

Anderson, William *Blanche the Huguenot.* London: Nathaniel Cooke, 1853. First edition, 8vo., original blind and gilt stamped green cloth, frontispiece, extra engraved title, 6 plates. Howard S. Mott Inc. 262 - 8 2013 $175

Anderson, William *Glimpses of Natural Science and Art for the Young.* Gall & Inglis n.d., 1853. Small 8vo., original green decorated cloth, gilt, all edges gilt, 3 woodcut plates, one leaf refixed, upper joint cracked, prize label on flyleaf. R. F. G. Hollett & Son Children's Books - 12 2013 £35

Anderson, Winslow *Mineral Springs and Health Resorts.* San Francisco: Bancroft Co., 1892. First edition, 2nd printing, Tall 8vo., 67 wood engraved illustrations, brick pictorial cloth stamped in black and gold, gilt lettered spine, owner's name, light dampstain to portion of fore-edge and top edge of first 20 leaves, covers slightly bowed, else fine. Argonaut Book Shop Recent Acquisitions June 2013 - 14 2013 $350

Andersson, Charles John *Notes on the Birds of Damara Land and the Adjacent Countries of South-West Africe.* John van Voorst, 1872. First edition, original green blind panelled cloth, gilt, spine slightly worn and scraped at head ad foot, frontispiece map, 4 lithographed plates, presentation from editor, J. H. Gurney to his friend Jules Verraux (1807-1873), engraved bookplates on endpapers of David Simson of Ickleford. R. F. G. Hollett & Son Africana - 2 2013 £450

Andreae, Christopher *Lines of Country: an Atlas of Railway and Waterway History in Canada.* Ontario: Boston Mills Press, 1997. Black cloth, black and white illustration to front cover, publisher's wrap to back cover, half title, 39 full page color maps and 560 archival and contemporary photos, maps and drawings, 12.25 x 16.25 inches, very good book and wrap. Schooner Books Ltd. 105 - 136 2013 $100

Andrews, H. C. *The Heathery; or a Monograph of Genus Erica.* London: Richard Taylor, 1806. Volume 3 only of 6, 50 beautiful hand colored plates, modern brown three quarter morocco, 8vo., fine. Barnaby Rudge Booksellers Natural History 2013 - 019846 2013 $495

Andrews, R. McCants *John Merrick: a Biographical Sketch.* Durham: Seeman Printery, 1920. First edition, red cloth, gilt 229 pages, owner stamp inked out on front fly, some modest and scattered erosion to cloth, very good plus. Between the Covers Rare Books, Inc. 165 - 46 2013 $150

Andrews, Ralph W. *Redwood Classic.* Seattle: Superior Pub. Co., 1958. First edition, quarto, 174 pages, photos, gray cloth lettered in red, owner's neat inscription on end, fine with pictorial dust jacket. Argonaut Book Shop Recent Acquisitions June 2013 - 15 2013 $60

Andrews, Roy Chapman *On the Trail of Ancient Man.* New York: Putnam, 1926. First edition, 8vo., xxiv, 375 pages, signed and inscribed by author to John D. Rockefeller, with bookplate of Abbey Aldrich Rockefeller and John D., very good++, top edge gilt, mild cover edge wear, in good+ dust jacket with pieces missing along top edge. By the Book, L. C. 36 - 84 2013 $2500

Andrews, Stephen Pearl 1812-1886 *The Basic Outline of Universology.* New York: Dion Thomas, 1872. First edition, thick 8vo., original cloth, very good. M & S Rare Books, Inc. 95 - 8 2013 $950

Andrews, William *North Country Poets.* London: Simpkin Marshall & Co., 1888. First edition, original cloth, gilt. R. F. G. Hollett & Son Lake District & Cumbria - 31 2013 £45

Andrews, William J. H. *The Quest for Longitude.* Cambridge: Collection of Historical Scientific Instruments, Harvard University, 1996. First edition, quarto, profusely illustrated with color plates, photos, reproductions, drawings, maps, full cloth, very fine with pictorial dust jacket. Argonaut Book Shop Recent Acquisitions June 2013 - 16 2013 $125

Andrews, William Loring *Sextodecimos et Infra.* New York: Charles Scribner's Sons, 1899. First edition, limited to 152 copies, this one of 140 printed on English handmade plate paper by Gilliss Press, 8vo., 27 illustrations of miniature books, 14 of which are in full color, stiff paper wrappers, outer dust jacket, extremely scarce, small tears along bottom and top of hinges of dust jacket, from the library of De Witt Miller with his ink inscription, also from the library of noted miniature collector Kathryn Rickard with her bookplate, with additional bookplate on front free endpaper, number in ink in corner of front free endpaper, paper slipcase not present, scarce; from the collection of Donn W. Sanford. Oak Knoll Books 303 - 7 2013 $450

Andry De Bois Regard, Nicolas *An Account of the Breeding of Worms in Human Bodies...* London: printed for H. Rhodes, 1701. First edition in English, 8vo., 1 folding plate and 4 smaller plates, first and last pages with small adherences from old endpapers in gutter, few short marginal tears, one touching two characters with no loss, light toning and some minor spotting, 20th century russet morocco, spine in five compartments with two gilt lettered direct, just touch of sunning to spine, small stamps of Birmingham Medical Institute to titlepage and each of the plates, bookplate noting volume's presentation by Dr. Blackall to upper pastedown.   Unsworths Antiquarian Booksellers   28 - 63   2013   £800

Angeli, Margurite *The Door in the Wall.* Garden City: Doubleday & Co., 1949. Stated first edition, 8vo., blue cloth, fine in dust jacket with closed tear and small chip at corner, 2 full page color illustrations and many full and partial page black and whites, laid in is handwritten note to a fan done on promotional piece from publisher, this copy also inscribed by De Angeli.   Aleph-Bet Books, Inc.   104 - 141   2013 $650

Angell, Roger *The Summer Game.* New York: Viking, 1972. First edition, fine in price cl ipped dust jacket with few creases on fron flap.   Beasley Books   2013 - 2013 $50

Angelou, Maya *I Know Why the Caged Bird Sings.* New York: Random House, 1969. Fifth edition, 8vo., original black cloth, near fine in dust jacket, inscribed by author for Julian Jebb.   Maggs Bros. Ltd.   1460 - 14   2013   £250

The Anglo-Boer War 1899-1900. Cape Town: Dennis Edwards & Co., 1901. Oblong 4to., original pictorial cloth gilt, extremities little worn, illustrations.   R. F. G. Hollett & Son   Africana - 21   2013   £75

Animals and Their Little Ones. London: Dean's Rag Book Co. Ltd. n.d. circa, 1914. 8vo., pictorial cloth, 14 pages, as new, charming color illustrations on each page by Stanley Berkeley.   Aleph-Bet Books, Inc.   104 - 126   2013 $250

Anker, Jean *Bird Books and Bird Art: an Outline of Literary History...* The Hague: Dr. W. Junk B.V., Anatiquariaat Junk B.V., 1979. 4to., frontispiece, 12 plates, gilt stamped green cloth, corners worn, very good.   Jeff Weber Rare Books   171 - 3   2013 $85

Anley, Charlotte *Influence: Moral Tale for Young People.* London: I. B. Seeley and Son, 1824. Second edition, half titles, very good, contemporary half calf, double gilt bands to spine and black morocco labels, 12mo., contemporary name of Mr. Fothergill at head of each titlepage, one gathering just little pround in binding.   Ken Spelman Books Ltd.   75 - 84   2013   £220

Anouilh, Jean *Pieces Brillantes. L'Invitation au Chateau.* Paris: Les Editions de la Table Ronde, 1960. Later edition, 8vo., original cloth, pictorial label on upper cover, excellent copy, cloth unevenly browned with some pale soiling to tail of spine, inscribed by author for Lady Onslow (Nina Sturdee).   Maggs Bros. Ltd.   1460 - 15   2013   £150

Anquetil, Louis Pierre *Compendio de la Historia de Espana.* Madrid: Imprenta real, 1806. Corrected edition, 8vo., 54 engravings, three quarter polished calf over marbled boards, five raised bands, 4 compartments decorated gilt, brown morocco labels, 3 of four boards detached, edges worn, rear board volume I worn through, otherwise contents quite clean, images sharp, gift from Pedro de Alcantara Alvarez de Toledo and Salm-Salm, to Sr Charles Richard Vaughan, with ALS from Alvarez de Toledo to Vaughan.   Kaaterskill Books   16 - 77   2013 $500

Ansell, W. F. H. *Mammals of Northern Rhodesia.* Lusaka: Government Printer, 1960. First edition, 7 color plates, 19 figures 17 maps, original red cloth, presentation copy, inscribed by author.   R. F. G. Hollett & Son   Africana - 3   2013   £25

Ansted, Daivd Thomas *The Gold-Seeker's Manual.* London: John Van Voort, 1849. Second edition, 8vo., original cloth, paper labels to spine and upper board, some minor staining, library stamp to title, near fine, inscribed by author for Clara Ansted.   Maggs Bros. Ltd.   1467 - 117   2013   £1250

Anstey, Christopher *The New Bath Guide; or Memoirs of the B-N-R-D Family.* London: for J. Dodsley, 1773. Ninth edition, engraved frontispiece, full contemporary mottled calf, gilt panelled spine, red morocco label, slight crack to upper joint.   Ken Spelman Books Ltd.   75 - 33   2013   £40

Anstey, F. *The Tinted Venus: a Historical Romance.* Bristol: J. W. Arrowsmith, 1885. First edition, 12m., brown cloth stamped in black and gilt, corners slightly bumped and little rubbed, fresh and bright, near fine.   Between the Covers Rare Books, Inc.   Sci-Fi, Fantasy & Horror - 82647   2013 $200

Anstey, John *The Pleader's Guide, a Didactic Poem, in two parts...* London: T. Cadell & W. Davies, 1808. New edition, contemporary full scarlet roan, gilt spine and borders, spine dulled, leading hinge beginning to split at tail, all edges gilt, good plus.   Jarndyce Antiquarian Booksellers   CCIII - 632   2013   £70

Anthony, Joseph *Casanova Jones.* New York: Century, 1930. First edition, illustrations by Willy Pogany, fine in price clipped, very good plus dust jacket with couple of very small chips at corners.   Between the Covers Rare Books, Inc.   Cocktails, Etc. - 57347   2013 $225

Anthony, Piers *The Ring.* London: MacDonald Science Fiction, 1969. First British and first hardcover edition, octavo, boards.   L. W. Currey, Inc. Utopian Literature: Recent Acquisitions (April 2013) - 139943   2013 $100

Anthony, Susan B. *An Account of the Proceedings on the Trial of Susan B. Anthony, on the Charge of Illegal Voting at the Presidential Election in Nov. 1872...* Rochester: Daily Democrat and Chronicle Book Print, 1874. First edition, inscribed by Anthony in barely visible pencil on front wrappers, laid in news account of appearance by Anthony at the invitation of the Grand Rapids trade assembly to the workingmen on Work and Wages; 8vo., original drab gray blue front wrapper, printed in black, lightly soiled, spine missing about 1 1/4 inch at either end, corners of wrapper chipped, later professional restoration, housed in custom made cloth clamshell box.   Priscilla Juvelis - Rare Books   55 - 1   2013 $4000

The Antiquarian Casket... Scarborough: published by John Cole, 1829. 8vo., 8 pages, 3 lithograph plates, original red printed wrappers, little rubbed, but good copy, scarce.   Ken Spelman Books Ltd.   73 - 151   2013 $45

Anton Ramirez, Braulio *Diccionario de Bibliografia Agronomica y de Toda Clase de Escritos Relacionados con la Agricultura.* Madrid: Impr. y Estereot de M. Rivadeneyra, 1865. First edition, 4to., later black cloth, very good, rebound copy, endpapers foxed, else contents near fine, bookplate of Bibliograph Library of William P. Wreden.   Kaaterskill Books   16 - 76   2013 $400

Antoninus, Brother 1912-1994 *The Last Crusade.* Berkeley: Oyez, 1969. First edition, one of 165 numbered copies signed by author (of a total edition of 180), fine in original dust jacket, as issued.   Ed Smith Books   78 - 14   2013 $200

Antoninus, Brother 1912-1994 *The Masks of Drought.* Santa Barbara: Black Sparrow Press, 1980. First edition, one of 250 numbered copies, signed by poet, fine in fine glassine dust jacket, as issued.   Ed Smith Books   78 - 15   2013 $75

The Apache Scout. Volumes IX through XXIV, 1931-1946. Various paginations, totaling 1416 pages, illustrations, 2 volumes bound in buckram, issues from 8 to 16 pages, photos.   Dumont Maps & Books of the West   125 - 29   2013 $250

Apocalypse de Saint Jean. Monaco: Club International de Bibliophile Jaspard, Polus & Cie, 1959. First and only edition, limited to 255 copies, this being number 45, folio, numerous loose gathering housed in original rives paper wrappers and folder, 142 pages with 15 original lithographs, each with tissue guard, loose gatherings as issued housed in original Rives wrappers and folder, front of folder lettered in black and red, occasional finger smudging, otherwise about fine, chemise and custom cloth clamshell.   Heritage Book Shop   Holiday Catalogue 2012 - 149 2013 $4500

Apollinaris, Bp. of Laodicea *Metaphrasis tou Psalterous dia Stichon Heroikon.* Excudebat Georgius Bishop, 1590. First printing in England, ownership embossment to titlepage causing small hole affecting two characters, intermittent light dampmark to fore-edge, 8vo., contemporary blind ruled sheep, rebacked preserving original spine, few other tidy repairs, hinges lined with printed binder's waste, bookplate of Shirburn Castle, good.   Blackwell's Rare Books   172 - 26   2013   £900

Apollonius Rhodius *Argonautica (in Greek).* Florence: Laurentius Francisci de Alopon, 1496. Editio princeps, 235 x 165mm., 18th century vellum, double blind rule border on covers, spine with 4 raised bands, handmade paste papers, edges sprinkled red and brown, small wormhole in text from v5 to end, occasionally affecting a few letters, intermittent light foxing, overall exceptional copy, housed in custom full brown calf clamshell, gilt stamped on spine.   Heritage Book Shop   50th Anniversary Catalogue - 1   2013 $35,000

Apperley, Charles James   1777-1843 *The Life of a Sportsman.* London: Rudolph Ackerman, 1842. First edition, first issue, with plates at pages 13, 14, 15 and 55, mounted, fine, bound without 8 pages of ads at end, large 8vo., full red morocco, front hinge expertly and almost imperceptibly repaired, upper and lower covers gilt ruled, elaborately gilt decorated spine and inner dentelles, raised bands, top edge gilt by Riviere & Son, handsome copy, cloth slipcase.   Howard S. Mott Inc.   262 - 9   2013 $2650

Appianus *De Civilibus Romanoru Bellis Historiarum Libri Quinque.* Paris: Michaelis Vascosani, 1538. Woodcut on title (repeated on second title), woodcut initials, old vellum, tiny blank piece at bottom of titlepage neatly replaced, neat early repairs at foot of title and in fore-edges of last several leaves, browning of text, nice.   Joseph J. Felcone Inc. Books Printed before 1701 - 3   2013 $1400

Appleton's General Guide to the United States and Canada... New York: 1892. 2 volumes, maps and illustrations, extremities slightly rubbed, couple of corners bumped, one map loose, short tears at gutter of some maps, very good set in blue cloth, gilt lettering bright, particularly nice set, complete and complete with matching dates.   Dumont Maps & Books of the West   122 - 41   2013 $350

Apuleius *Lucii Apulei Madaurensis Platonici Philosophi Opera Interpretatione et Notis Illustravit Julianus Floridus...* Parisiis: apud Fredericum Leonard, 1688. First edition edited by Julien Fleury, 2 volumes, 4to., elaborate engraved frontispiece, title vignette, woodcut coat of arms, engraving, woodcut diagram, original full rose vellum, rubbed but in excellent condition, printed library marks on titles, ownership signature of Rev. Edgell Wyatt Edgell, Rome 1854, very good.   Jeff Weber Rare Books   171 - 4   2013 $350

Apuleuis *Cupid and Psyches.* London: Nonesuch Press, 1923. Number 370 of 525 copies, 60 pages set within decorative border, 8vo., very good in original linen backed patterned paper boards, matching slipcase which is just little worn, bookplate.   Ken Spelman Books Ltd.   75 - 168   2013   £35

Arabian Nights *Adventures of Sinbad the Sailor.* London: Bancroft, 1960. Oblong 4to., cloth backed pictorial boards, slight rubbing, very good+, 2 fine pop-up pages with moveable mechanisms as well.   Aleph-Bet Books, Inc.   105 - 465   2013 $200

Arabian Nights *Aladdin or the Wonderful Lamp.* New York: McLoughlin Bros. n.d. circa, 1865. 12mo., pictorial wrappers, highlighted in gold and mounted on linen, small spot on upper margin of front cover and inside front cover, else near fine, 8 brightly colored half page illustrations.   Aleph-Bet Books, Inc.   105 - 20   2013 $275

Arabian Nights *Aladdin or the Wonderful Lamp.* New York: McLoughlin Bros., 1895. 4to., stiff pictorial wrappers die cut in shape of Aladdin, small edge repair on back cover, else very good, 6 fine full page chromolithographs and line illustrations on text pages.   Aleph-Bet Books, Inc.   105 - 538   2013 $225

Arabian Nights *Aladdin and the Wonderful Lamp.* New York: Macmillan, 1935. First edition, 4to., cloth, edges slightly faded, else very good+ in chipped and frayed dust jacket, full page and partial page color illustrations by Elizabeth Mackinstry.   Aleph-Bet Books, Inc.   104 - 333   2013 $200

Arabian Nights *The Arabian Nights. (with) Supplemental Nights.* Benares: privately printed for the Kamashastra Society, 1885-1888. First edition, 16 volumes, large 8vo., original cloth, spines of supplement little faded, some expert repairs to spines, lovely copy.   Maggs Bros. Ltd.   1467 - 27   2013   £5000

Arabian Nights *New Arabian Nights' Entertainments...* London: Henry Colburn, 1829. Second edition, 6 plates, good set bound in original linen cloth with paper labels, some foxing, mainly to endpapers, pastedowns and frontispieces, 3 volumes.   Ken Spelman Books Ltd.   75 - 92   2013   £120

Arabian Nights *Sinbad the Sailor and Other Stories from the Arabian Nights.* London: Hodder & Stoughton, n.d., 1914. First edition, limited to 500 numbered copies, signed by artist, this #19, thick large 4to., full vellum with elaborate gilt decorations on cover and spine, top edge gilt other edges untrimmed, most minimal cover soil, fine, ties renewed, illustrations by Edmund Dulac with 23 tipped in color plates on gilt decorated mounts with lettered guards and with gilt decorations and borders on text pages, outstanding copy, very scarce.   Aleph-Bet Books, Inc.   104 - 183   2013 $6500

Aragon, Louis *La Diane Francaise.* Paris: Editions Pierre Seghers, 1945. First trade edition, 8vo., later blue cloth, excellent copy, spine slightly faded and marked, inscribed by author to poet Frances Cornford.   Maggs Bros. Ltd.   1460 - 16   2013   £750

Aragon, Louis *Fernand Leger: Mes Voyages.* Paris: Francais Reunis, 1960. First edition, one of 250 numbered copies (total edition of 281) with 28 original lithographs by Leger, 10 in color, folio, 220 pages, loose leaves in lithographed paper portfolio, publisher's boards chemise and slipcase, in excellent condition.   Gemini Fine Books & Arts., Ltd.   Art Reference & Illustrated Books - 2013 $2400

Aratus *The Skies and Weather-Forecasts of Aratus.* London: Macmillan & Co., 1880. Small 8vo., vii, 71 pages, original blue cloth, gilt stamped cover and spine titles, extremities rubbed, very good.   Jeff Weber Rare Books   169 - 11   2013 $75

Arblay, Frances Burney D' 1752-1840 *Diary and Letters.* London: Henry Colbrun, 1842. First collected edition, 7 volumes, very good, contemporary half red calf, gilt spines, morocco labels.   Ken Spelman Books Ltd.   75 - 109   2013   £295

Arblay, Frances Burney D' 1752-1840 *Evelina; or a Young Lady's Entrance into the World.* London: printed by S. Wright Gracechurch Street for and sold by the Booksellers, circa, 1820. New edition, 12mo., signature of Frances Danbey 1820, full contemporary tree calf, neatly rebacked retaining original gilt decorated spines, corners repaired.   Jarndyce Antiquarian Booksellers   CCIV - 80   2013   £65

Arbus, Doon *The Sixties.* New York: Random House, 1999. First edition, photos by Richard Avedon, fine in very good dust jacket with few edge tears, signed and inscribed by Avedon and additionally signed by Arbus, uncommon signed by both.   Jeff Hirsch Books   Fall 2013 - 129140   2013 $500

Arbuthnet, John *An Examination of Dr. Woodward's Account of the Deluge, &c.* London: printed for G. Bateman, 1697. 84 pages, small 8vo., recently rebound by Bernard Middleton, period style English binding, text with some light foxing.   James Tait Goodrich   75 - 11   2013 $850

Archer, Annie *Family Omnibus.* Kendal: privately printed by Titus Wilson for the author, n.d. Circa, 1960. Original blue cloth gilt, illustrations.   R. F. G. Hollett & Son   Lake District & Cumbria - 34   2013   £35

Archer, Jan *The Flap Jack.* London: Treherne, n.d. circa, 1909. Second edition, square 16mo., 99 pages, pictorial tan cloth, very slight cover soil else tight and very good+, pictorial tan cloth, very slight cover soil, else tight and very good+, printed on heavy paper on one side of page, each page of text faces charming full page color illustration. Aleph-Bet Books, Inc.   104 - 290   2013 $45-

Archimedes *De Iis quae Vehuntur in Aqua Libri Duo. (bound with) Commandino (Federico) Liber de centro Gravitatis Solidorum.* Bologna: Alexander Benacius, 1565. First edition, 2 works in one volume, fine large historiated woodcut initials, numerous geometrical diagrams in text, contemporary limp vellum, later black morocco spine label, Bute bookplate, very good, scarce in contemporary binding. Blackwell's Rare Books   Sciences - 8   2013   £5850

Architectural and Archaeological Society of Durham and Northumberland *Transactions volume II 1869-1879.* Durham: Andrews and Co., 1883. Old half morocco, gilt with raised bands, 15 photo plates and 4 folding plans and plates, some little stained.   R. F. G. Hollett & Son   Lake District & Cumbria - 35   2013   £75

The Architecture and Landscape Gardening of the Exposition. San Francisco: Paul Elder, 1915. First edition, 8vo., 202 pages, untrimmed, near fine, contemporary name on endpaper, 96 tipped in sepia half tone plates. Second Life Books Inc.   183 - 285   2013 $50

Ardley, Patricia B. *The Adventures of Mr. Horace Hedgehog.* Collins, 1935. First edition, oblong 4to., original cloth backed pictorial pink boards, trifle dusty, pages 56 with 6 full page color plates and numerous line drawings by E. C. Ardley, occasional spot and mark, very nice copy.   R. F. G. Hollett & Son   Children's Books - 28   2013   £45

Ardley, Patricia B. *Mr. and Mrs. Hedgehog.* London: Collins, 1936. First edition, oblong 4to., original cloth backed pictorial boards, dust jacket (few short closed edge tears), pages 55, 6 full page color plates and numerous line drawings, lovely, clean copy.   R. F. G. Hollett & Son   Children's Books - 29   2013   £85

Argonaut Stories. San Francisco: Payot, Upham & Co., 1906. First edition, square 12mo., flexible canvas boards with printed paper overlays on front board and spine, contemporary bookplate (name partly effaced), some chips to edges of paper onlays, particularly on spine, about very good, fragile volume.   Between the Covers Rare Books, Inc.   Sci-Fi, Fantasy & Horror - 298619   2013 $400

Argosy Book Stores *The Negro & Slavery.* New York: Argosy Book Stores, circa, 1955? Stapled mimeographed folio leaves, (24) pages, folded once horizontally, paper browned, small tears on fold of first leaf, last leaf pulled through staples, very good, fragile.   Between the Covers Rare Books, Inc.   165 - 85   2013 $125

Aringhi, Paolo *Triumphus Poenitentiae sive Selectae Poenitentim Mortes ex Variis Probatisque Historiarum Monumentis...* Romae: typis Philippi Mariae Mancini, 1670. 4to., original full vellum, some minor worming at gutter, generally fine, rubber ownership stamp of St. Joseph's Retreat, Highgate Hill, London, signature of M. Math. Buspell?, rare.   Jeff Weber Rare Books   171 - 5   2013 $750

Aristophanes *The Comedies of Aristophanes.* London: R. Clavel, 1695. 8vo., some dustiness, volume rebound in unsympathetic quarter morocco, marbled boards, poor gilt label, Thomas Gent's copy, he bought a defective copy, lacking the first gathering, and has made his own pen and ink titlepage to which he signs his name dated 1770.   Ken Spelman Books Ltd.   73 - 6   2013   £495

Aristotle, Pseud. *Aristotle's Last Legacy...* printed for C. Hitch and L. Hawes S. Crowder and Co. and H. Woodgate and S. books and C. Ware, 1761. Wood engraved frontispiece, trimmed close at fore-edge with loss of few individual letters on page 11, minor dampstaining at beginning and end, 12mo., original sheep, lower joint cracked, though stitching sound, worn at extremities, slightly defective at foot of spine, very good.   Blackwell's Rare Books   172 - 12   2013   £800

Aristotle, Pseud. *Aristotle's Complete Masterpiece, in Three Parts.* London: i.e. Boston: printed and sold for Zechariah Feeling (i.e. Zechariah Fowle?), 1766. Thirteenth edition, frontispiece, 7 in text woodcuts, illustrations, 8vo., contemporary sheep, hinges partly cracked but firm, very good, complete copy, some foxing and general use as well as few very short joined marginal tears, with no loss.   Howard S. Mott Inc.   262 - 133   2013 $12,500

Aristotle, Pseud. *The Works of Aristotle, the Famous Philosopher.* printed by Plummer & Brewis for Miller, Law & Cater, circa, 1810. with 8 woodcut illustrations in text, occasional minor spotting, last few leaves creased, one gathering little sprung, original sheep, spine gilt ruled in compartments, red lettering piece, cracks in joints but binding firm, spine slightly defective at foot, corner slightly worn, good.   Blackwell's Rare Books   Sciences - 9   2013   £450

Aristotles *Opera Omnia, Graece et Latine. Doctissimorum Virorum Interpretatione.* Paris: Billaine, Pieget, Leonard via Jacobea, 1654. 4 volumes, folio, worming to volume II at pages 81-137 and pages 511-end and volume Iv pages 219-253, mostly marginal or between lines of text but worsening sporadically and then affecting some letters, small hole in one leaf in volume IV affecting a few characters on page 11, slightly toned, occasional light staining, short closed tears and small chips from blank margins (one leaf in volume III with larger flaw still clear of text), ms. notes at end of index in volume I, dark brown contemporary calf, gilt titles to spines, edges sprinkled red, all volumes quite worn and pitted with peeling and areas of surface loss, endcaps torn with some loss, all hinges cracked though boards remain attached, endpapers rumpled, bookplates to each front pastedown showing an S and R entwined beneath a crown, each obscuring an earlier bookplate, old bookseller's pencil note.   Unsworths Antiquarian Booksellers   28 - 3   2013   £600

The Arkham Sampler. Sauk City: Arkham House, 1949. Four issues, Winter, Spring, Summer and Fall 1949, each issue with stamp of horror writer Stanley Wiater inside front cover, titles and dates handwritten on spines, Winter issue has chip to lower spine, all issues wearing at spine folds and have bit of bleedthrough at staples, still very good, each issue had print run of 1200 copies, scarce now.   Ken Lopez Bookseller   159 - 8   2013 $200

Arkwright His Counterblast to an Effusion Entitled: Panflet on the Four Basic Dialects of Pig-Latin. Tujunga (Los Angeles): William M. Cheney, 1951. 7.7 x 5cm., stiff paper wrappers, label on front wrapper, from the collection of Donn W. Sanford.   Oak Knoll Books   303 - 94   2013 $150

Arlen, Michael *Men Dislike Women. A Romance.* New York: Doubleday Doran and Co., 1931. First edition, 8vo., original cloth, very good, cloth little soiled, lettering to spine faded, inscribed by author for Hilary Charles.   Maggs Bros. Ltd.   1460 - 17   2013   £50

Arlen, Michael *These Charming People: Being a Tapestry of the Fortunes, Follies, Adventures, Gallantries and General Activities...* New York: George H. Doran, 1924. First American edition, very near fine in very good dust jacket with some shallow chips and tears at upper extremities, nicely inscribed by author for Samuel Shipman.   Between the Covers Rare Books, Inc.   Sci-Fi, Fantasy & Horror - 94877   2013 $250

Arlott, John *Clausentum.* London: Jonathan Cape, 1946. First edition, 8vo. original turquoise boards, dust jacket, excellent copy, jacket lightly browned and with slight wear towards edges, inscribed by author for George Rostrevor-Hamilton.   Maggs Bros. Ltd.   1460 - 18   2013   £125

Armengaud, Jacques Eugene *The Engineer and Machinist's Drawing-Book: a Complete Course of Instruction for the Practical Engineer...* Glasgow (printed): Edinburgh: London: and New York: Blackie and Son, 1855. With additional engraved title and 71 leaves of plates (2 pairs forming double-page plates, both pages numbered), one hand colored, 2 plates with clean tears, one browned, first two leaves creased, few minor stains, folio, contemporary half brown morocco little worn, cloth bubbled on upper cover, original owner's name in gilt at foot of spine (H. Patchett), sound.   Blackwell's Rare Books   172 - 14   2013   £170

Armisted, Wilson *Tales and Legends of the English Lakes.* London: Simpkin, Marshall & Co., 1891. First edition, original blue cloth, uncut, front endpapers little spotted.   R. F. G. Hollett & Son   Lake District & Cumbria - 36   2013   £45

Armitage, Merle *The Art of Edward Weston.* New York: E. Weyhe, 1932. Limited to 550 copies, signed by Weston, this being 287, small folio, 39 black and white plates, each plate with facing description page, frontispiece by Brett Weston, original quarter white over black boards, front board and spine lettered in black, black endpapers, spine with some professional repairs, no new material, spine bit darkened, corners and edges bit rubbed and bumped, boards with few scratches, plates 13-24 bit sprung, overall very good and internally quite clean.   Heritage Book Shop Holiday Catalogue 2012 - 159   2013 $3000

Armitt, Mary L. *The Church of Grasmere: a History.* Kendal: Titus Wilson, 1912. First edition, uncut, frontispiece and 30 illustrations and maps, original blue cloth, trifle rubbed, spine faded.   R. F. G. Hollett & Son   Lake District & Cumbria - 38   2013   £30

Armitt, Mary L. *Studies of Lakeland Birds.* Ambleside: George Middleton, 1901. 12mo., original stiff wrappers, scarce.   R. F. G. Hollett & Son   Lake District & Cumbria - 37   2013   £30

Armour, W. S. *Facing the Irish Question.* 1935. First edition, 8vo., cloth, good.   C. P. Hyland   261 - 900   2013   £27

Armstrong, A. M. *The Place-Names of Cumberland.* Cambridge: Cambridge University Press, 1950-1952. First edition, 3 volumes, original cloth, gilt, 565 pages, map in rear pocket final volume.   R. F. G. Hollett & Son   Lake District & Cumbria - 40   2013   £150

Armstrong, Anthony *The Strange Case of Mr. Pelham.* Garden City: Doubleday Crime Club, 1957. First American edition, fine in lightly rubbed, near fine dust jacket.   Between the Covers Rare Books, Inc.   Mystery & Detective Fiction - 278060   2013 $65

Armstrong, Edmund John *Essays and Sketches.* London: Longmans, 1877. First edition, half title with small tear in upper margin due to careless opening, 2 pages ads, original dark green cloth, bevelled boards, little rubbed, very good, signed presentation from editor, George Francis Armstrong to his cousins. Jarndyce Antiquarian Booksellers CCIII - 634 2013 £45

Armstrong, Edward A. *Birds of the Grey Wind.* 1944. Second edition, 46 photos, text illustrations, 8vo., cloth, dust jacket worn, very good. C. P. Hyland 261 - 901 2013 £33

Armstrong, John 1709-1799 *The Art of Preserving Health.* London: printed for A. Millar, 1744. Rare first edition, Tall large paper copy, tall 4to., blue levant morocco with lavish gilt tooling and borders and centerpieces, spine gilt in compartments and red burgundy label, all edges gilt, fine presentation binding, previous owners bookplates, including W. N. Elliot, Graham Pollard,. James Tait Goodrich 75 - 12 2013 $995

Armstrong, John J. *An Oration Delivered at Jamaica, Long Island, Fourth of July 1865.* Jamaica, L.I.: L. I. Democrat Print, 1865. First edition, tan printed wrappers trifle soiled, couple of small spots on wrappers and bottom of first couple of leaves, near fine. Between the Covers Rare Books, Inc. New York City - 285576 2013 $300

Arnason, H. H. *Robert Motherwell.* New York: Harry N. Abrams, 1977. First edition, 251 pages, over 300 color and black and white illustrations, close to near fine and tight copy with some minor wear and with near fine wraparound band. Jeff Hirsch Books Fall 2013 - 129139 2013 $125

Arnaud, Noel *Critique offprint, being Arnaud's Review of Christophe Colomb by Francois Caradec.* Revue generale des publications francaises, et etrangeres Juillet, 1957. First edition, 8vo., 8 pages, original wrappers, fine, inscribed by author. Maggs Bros. Ltd. 1460 - 19 2013 £500

Arndt, Karl J. R. *A Documentary History of the Indiana Decade of the Harmony Society.* Indianapolis: Indiana Historical Society, 1975-1978. First edition, wrappers, 2 volumes, near fine. Beasley Books 2013 - 2013 $65

Arneberg, Halfdan *Norsk Folkekunst, Mannsarbeid.* Oslo: Fabritius & Sonners Florlag, 1951. 4to., 110 plates, illustrations, tan cloth, green stamped cover emblem and spine title, dust jacket stained, very good. Jeff Weber Rare Books 171 - 6 2013 $80

Arnesen, Con *Voices of Cumbria.* Kendal: Westmorland Gazette, 1987. First edition, large 8vo., original cloth, gilt, dust jacket, 16 color plates, 18 illustrations and pen and ink drawings by Ann Southward, stamped "Westmorland Gazette Office Copy" on flyleaf and title. R. F. G. Hollett & Son Lake District & Cumbria - 42 2013 £25

Arnold Forster, Hugh Oakley *In a Conning Tower; or How I Took H.M.S. "Majestic" into action.* London: Paris & Melbourne: Cassell Co. Ltd., 1891. First edition, octavo, five full page illustrations, original stiff pictorial gray paper wrappers, printed in black with black cloth spine, edges stained black. L. W. Currey, Inc. Fall Sampler Sept. 2013 - 144374 2013 $150

Arnold, Matthew 1812-1888 *Mixed Essays.* London: Smith, Elder & Co., 1879. First edition, 8vo., original blue cloth, lettered in gilt, inscribed by author, covers damp-stained, otherwise very good. Maggs Bros. Ltd. 1460 - 21 2013 £275

Arnold, Matthew 1812-1888 *Poems.* London: Longman, Brown, Green, Longmans & Roberts, 1857. Third edition, 8vo., original green cloth, excellent copy, rebacked with original spine laid down, top edge little soiled. Maggs Bros. Ltd. 1460 - 20 2013 £275

Arnold, Mattie Lenal *My First Twenty-Four Poems.* Memphis: The Author/Johnson Printery, 1939. First edition, 24mo., frontispiece, (24) pages, printed green wrappers, rear wrapper lacking, front wrapper detached and spotted, fair, internally very good, rare. Between the Covers Rare Books, Inc. 165 - 6 2013 $750

Arnot, Fred S. *Garenganze; or Seven Years Pioneer Mission Work in Central Africa.* James E. Hawkins, 1889. Original pictorial cloth gilt, extremities trifle worn, light crease across upper board, 19 illustrations, 2 text maps, large folding map, endpapers lightly foxed, crack on front pastedown repaired. R. F. G. Hollett & Son Africana - 4 2013 £50

Arnould, M., Pseud. *La Mort du Capitaine Cook a son Troisieme Voyage au Nouveau Monde.* Paris: Chez Lagrange, 1788. First edition, 8vo., contemporary calf, gilt little rubbed, headcap chipped, last leaf browned, but still entirely legible, rare. Maggs Bros. Ltd. 1467 - 70 2013 £12,500

Arp, Hans *Behaarte Herzen 1923-1926, Konige vor der Sintflut 1952-1953.* Frankfurt: Meta Verlag, 1953. Number 94 of 100 copies, tipped in full page original black and white woodcut, one original woodcut laid in loose, superb woodcut signed by Arp, 52 pages, pictorial paper over boards, tiny bump at lower corner, else fine. Gemini Fine Books & Arts., Ltd. Art Reference & Illustrated Books - 2013 $1200

Arredondo, Antonio De *Arredondo's Historical Proof of Spain's Title to Georgia.* Berkeley: University of California Press, 1925. First edition, 10 photo plates and maps, some folding, publisher's navy blue cloth, gilt, very fine and bright copy, very scarce. Argonaut Book Shop Summer 2013 - 24 2013 $300

Art Work of Utah. Chicago: W. H. Parish, 1896. 12 parts, quarto, publisher's tan wrappers, printed titles and decorations on front panels, all parts very good or better, over 70 full page photos, uncommon. Ken Sanders Rare Books 45 - 1 2013 $1000

Arter, Jared Maurice *Echoes from a Pioneer Life.* Atlanta: A. B. Caldwell Pub. Co., 1922. First edition, small octavo, 126 pages, photos, text wire stitched and bound in publisher's green cloth stamped in black, staples oxidized a tad, rear hinge appears to have been repaired (or perhaps slightly misbound), still sound, very good, better, very scarce. Between the Covers Rare Books, Inc. 165 - 9 2013 $950

Artizan Club *A Treatise on the Steam Engine in Its Application of Mines, Mills, Steam Navigation and Railways.* London: Long, Brown Green and Longmans, 1846. First edition, 285 x 215mm., very pleasing recent retrospective full calf, raised bands, red morocco label, 349 wood engravings in text, 30 engraved plates, titlepage little soiled, two plates with short tears at margin or fold (not affecting images), another plate with two inch brown stain to tail edge, occasional minor foxing, smudges or thumbing, otherwise clean and fresh, unworn binding. Phillip J. Pirages 63 - 448 2013 $450

Arwaker, Edmund *The Vision: a Pindaric Ode.* London: by J. Playford for Henry Playford, 1685. Second edition, folio, (2), 6 pages, title within mourning rules, modern leatherette. Joseph J. Felcone Inc. English and American Literature to 1800 - 1 2013 $550

Arzt, Leopold *Die Haut- und Geschlechiskrankheiten.* Berlin & Vienna: Urban & Schwarzenberg, 1934-1935. 5 volumes, 1597 illustrations and 85 colored plates, tall 8vo., original red roan back linen boards, spines bit scuffed, otherwise very clean, very good set. James Tait Goodrich S74 - 16 2013 $1395

Arzt, Leopold *Die Haut- und Geschlechiskrankheiten.* Vienna: Urban & Schwarzengerg, 1934-1935. 5 volumes, with 1597 illustrations and 85 colored plates tall 8vo., original red roan back linen boards spines bit scuffed, otherwise very clean and very good set. James Tait Goodrich 75 - 13 2013 $1295

Asbjornsen, Peter *East of the Sun and West of the Moon.* London: Hodder & Stoughton, 1914. Limited to only 500 numbered copies, signed by artist, large 4to., full vellum stamped in blue and gold, top edge gilt, light cover soil and rubbing, else very good+, pictorial endpapers, 25 magnificent tipped in colored plates with lettered guards as well as numerous black and whites, all by Kay Nielsen, rare. Aleph-Bet Books, Inc. 105 - 428 2013 $12,750

Asbury, Herbert *The Barbary Coast. An Informal History of the San Francisco Underworld.* New York: Knopf, 1933. First edition, scarce thus, prints and photos, dark blue cloth backed pictorial boards, spine decorated and lettered in orange, fine. Argonaut Book Shop Summer 2013 - 6 2013 $90

Asbury, Herbert *The Gangs of New York.* New York: Alfred A. Knopf, 1928. First edition, small bookplate, neat owner's name on front fly, else tight, fine copy without dust jacket, seldom found in this condition. Between the Covers Rare Books, Inc. New York City - 185539 2013 $500

Ash, Alan *Conditioned for Space.* London and Melbourne: Ward, Lock & Co., 1955. First edition, small octavo, dark green cloth spine panel stamped in white. L. W. Currey, Inc. Fall Sampler Sept. 2013 - 146263 2013 $250

Ash, Lee *Subject Collections: a Guide to Special Book Collections and Subject Emphases as Reported by University, College, Public and Special Libraries and Museums in the United States and Canada.* New York and London: R. and R. Bowker, 1985. Sixth edition, 2 volumes, 4to., blue cloth, white and gilt stamped cover and spine titles, near fine. Jeff Weber Rare Books 171 - 8 2013 $50

Ashbery, John *Locus Solus.* France: Locus Solus, 1960-1962. First edition, regular issue being the second (trimmed state of the first volume), 4 volumes, 8vo. original printed wrappers, fine set, artist Nell Blaine's set with her ownership signature. James S. Jaffe Rare Books Fall 2013 - 12 2013 $1250

Ashbery, John *The Tennis Court Oath. A Book of Poems.* Middletown: Wesleyan University Press, 1962. First edition, one of only 750 copies, 8vo., original cloth, dust jacket, fine in fine dust jacket, presentation copy inscribed by author for artist Nell Blaine. James S. Jaffe Rare Books Fall 2013 - 10 2013 $2500

Ashbury, John *A Wave.* New York: Viking, 1984. First edition, fine in fine dust jacket. Beasley Books 2013 - 2013 $50

Asher, Michael *Impossible Journey.* Viking, 1988. First edition, original cloth, gilt, dust jacket, 301 pages, 78 illustrations. R. F. G. Hollett & Son Africana - 5 2013 £30

Ashford, Daisy *The Young Visiters, or Mr. Salteena's Plan.* London: Chatto & Windus, 1919. Reprint, 8vo., frontispiece and one facsimile, original marbled boards, black cloth, printed paper label, signed by author and inscribed by actress Edyth Goodall and one Agnes Strang, worn along edges of boards and lettering piece, otherwise very good. Maggs Bros. Ltd. 1460 - 23 2013 £75

Ashley, Doris *Children's Stories from French Fairy Tales.* London and Paris: Raphael Tuck & Philadelphia: David McKay, n.d. circa, 1920. 4to., blue cloth stamped in gold, as new in dust jacket with spider web design and publisher's box (flap repair), 12 wonderful color plates plus many black and white plates in text, beautiful copy, rare in box. Aleph-Bet Books, Inc. 105 - 45 2013 $800

Ashton, Herbert *The Locked Room: a Comedy Mystery in three Acts.* New York: Samuel French, 1934. First edition, fine in soft covers with nicks at top of spine and small corner-chips on back cover. Mordida Books 81 - 19 2013 $125

Asimov, Isaac 1920-1992 *The Best of Isaac Asimov.* London: Sidgwick & Jackson, 1973. First edition, slightest bump to bottom corners, fine in fine dust jacket, beautiful copy. Between the Covers Rare Books, Inc. Sci-Fi, Fantasy & Horror - 322235 2013 $100

Asimov, Isaac 1920-1992 *David Starr: Space Ranger.* Boston: Gregg Press, 1978. First edition thus, near fine in near fine dust jacket. Leather Stalking Books October 2013 - 2013 $60

Asimov, Isaac 1920-1992 *Election Day 2084: a Science Fiction Anthology on the Politics of the Future.* Buffalo: Prometheus Books, 1984. First edition, octavo, cloth. L. W. Currey, Inc. Utopian Literature: Recent Acquisitions (April 2013) - 139116 2013 $75

Asimov, Isaac 1920-1992 *How Did We Find Out About DNA?* New York: Walker, 1985. First edition, 8vo., fine in near fine dust jacket, price clipped. By the Book, L. C. 37 - 3 2013 $300

Asimov, Isaac 1920-1992 *Pebble in the Sky.* Garden City: Doubleday, 1950. First edition, page edges slightly tanned, still fine in near fine dust jacket with slight rubbing to corners of spine ends, thin paper jacket usually found well worn. Between the Covers Rare Books, Inc. Sci-Fi, Fantasy & Horror - 58823 2013 $1750

Asimov, Isaac 1920-1992 *The Union Club Murders.* Garden City: Doubleday, 1983. First edition, paperback original Avon no. T-287, near fine in wrappers. Mordida Books 81 - 13 2013 $65

Asimov, Isaac 1920-1992 *The Universe.* New York: Walker and Co., 1966. Second printing, near fine, age darkening to edges and endpapers in very good++ dust jacket with mild soil and edge wear, 8vo., 308 page, signed and inscribed by author. By the Book, L. C. 36 - 95 2013 $300

Asquith, Cynthia *The Black Cap: New Stories of Murder & Mystery.* London: Hutchinson, 1928. First edition, some slight fading along cover edges, offsetting on endpapers and some scattered spotting on top of page edges, otherwise very good in dust jacket with closed tear at base of spine and attendant internal tape mends that have been removed and small stain on front panel. Mordida Books 81 - 9 2013 $500

Asquith, Cynthia *The Flying Carpet.* Partridge and Co., n.d., 1926. 4to. original cloth, lower board little soiled, 4 tipped in color plates, monochrome illustrations, flyleaves rather browned, few spots to fore edge, 2 early Attwell postcards loosely inserted. R. F. G. Hollett & Son Children's Books - 32 2013 £40

Asquith, Cynthia *The Second Ghost Book.* London: James Barrie, 1952. First edition, octavo, cloth. L. W. Currey, Inc. Fall Sampler Sept. 2013 - 146489 2013 $250

Asquith, Cynthia *She Walks in Beauty.* London: William Heinemann, 1934. First edition, 8vo., original blue cloth, excellent copy, spine slightly faded, inscribed by author to Rex Whistler with pencil drawing, possibly by Whistler. Maggs Bros. Ltd. 1460 - 24 2013 £175

Assarino, Luca *Raguagli Del Regno d'Amore Cipro.* In Venetia: per li Turrini, 1646. 12mo., old waterstain visible on original coarse grain paper wrappers, not intrusive in text, hand lettered backstrip, slightly worn with loss. Jarndyce Antiquarian Booksellers CCIV - 1 2013 £420

Associated Students of the University of New Mexico *Annual.* Albuquerque: University of New Mexico, 1951. 304 pages, quarto, silver grained boards, near fine, includes 3 photos of Edward Abbey. Ken Sanders Rare Books 45 - 41 2013 $250

Astley, Thomas *A New General Collection of Voyages and Travels.* London: 1745. 4 volumes, 232 engraved maps and plates, 18th century speckled calf, fine. Maggs Bros. Ltd. 1467 - 18 2013 £5000

Athale, Bhikadev Vasudev *A Marathi-English Dictionary.* Bombay: printed at the Asiatic Printing Press, 1871. Only edition, 12mo., modern cloth, 230 pages, ownership stamp on title B(ijay) C(handra) Mazumdar (1861-1942), title backed with loss of one letter, last leaf repaired at bottom with tape, with no loss. Howard S. Mott Inc. 262 - 11 2013 $250

Atherton, Gertrude *The Splendid Idle Forties.* Kentfield: Allen Press, 1960. Limited to 150 copies, folio, 110 pages, hand colored titlepage and chapter headings, red printed running heads, Venetian Fortuny floral pattern cloth boards, printed paper spine label, publisher's prospectus laid in. Jeff Weber Rare Books 171 - 2 2013 $400

Atkins, Ringrose *The Rude Stone Monuments of Our Own and Other Lands: a Lecture.* Waterford: 1896. 51 pages, 10 photos, original wrapper under protected card covers, latter with Robert Day's catalogue label, very good. C. P. Hyland 261 - 14 2013 £60

Atkins, Thomas B. *Selections from the Public Documents of the Province of Nova Scotia.* Halifax: Charles Annand pub., 1869. 8vo., original green cloth boards with gilt title to spine, wear to edges of binding, tear to top of spine and small nick to bottom, inner hinge cracks and wear to outer edges of text, folding facsimile document has few tears to folds and under edges. Schooner Books Ltd. 101 - 83 2013 $150

Atkinson, George *Rambles and Scrambles in Lakeland.* London: Warne, 1933. First edition, original cloth, dust jacket, pictorial onlay (small piece lost from spine), 20 illustrations by E. H. Atkinson. R. F. G. Hollett & Son Lake District & Cumbria - 45 2013 £25

Atkinson, George *The Worthies of Westmorland...* J. Robinson, 1849. First edition, 2 volumes, original blindstamped red cloth gilt, steel engraved frontispiece, excellent, sound set. R. F. G. Hollett & Son Lake District & Cumbria - 47 2013 £140

Atkinson, J. C. *Forty Years in a Moorland Parish: Reminiscences and Researches on Danby in Cleveland.* London: Macmillan, 1891. Reprint, 8vo, pages xvi, 471, illustrations, maps, original green cloth. J. & S. L. Bonham Antiquarian Booksellers Europe - 5074 2013 £65

Atkinson, J. C. *Playhours and Half-Holidays.* London: Macmillan, 1900. Original green cloth, gilt, rather worn and marked, illustrations by Coleman, prize label on flyleaf, joints cracked. R. F. G. Hollett & Son Children's Books - 33 2013 £25

Atkinson, M. E. *Challenge to Adventure.* London: John Lane Bodley Head, 1943. First reprint, original cloth, dust jacket edges little worn, few closed tears, pages 288, illustrations by Stuart Tresilian. R. F. G. Hollett & Son Children's Books - 34 2013 £30

Atkinson, Rev. Christopher *The Emigrant's Guide to New Brunswick, British North America.* Berwick upon Tweed: Printed at the Warder Office, 1842. Original cloth, paper label on spine, frontispiece, folding map at rear, small 8vo., slip tipped in stating there is no errata slip, some staining to prelim leaves, but generally very good. Schooner Books Ltd. 104 - 1 2013 $375

Atkinson, William *A Candid Inquiry into the Democratic Schemes of the Dissenters, During These Troublesome Times.* Bradford: R. Sedgwick, 1801. First edition, 36 pages, some early notes on titlepage, final two leaves marked and 'withdrawn', stamp at head of first leaf of text, disbound. Ken Spelman Books Ltd. 75 - 51 2013 £50

Attwell, Mabel Lucie *Lucie Attwell's Annual.* Dean and Son, 1973. Small 4to., original glazed pictorial boards, pages 94, color and two-tone illustrations, child's name and address on cover spread, otherwise fine. R. F. G. Hollett & Son Children's Books - 35 2013 £30

Attwell, Mabel Lucie *Lucie Boo-Boos At School.* Dundee: London: Montreal: Valentine, n.d. circa, 1921. Not a first edition, 12mo., boards, pictorial paste-on, near fine, 8 color plates, many green line illustrations, pictorial endpapers, very scarce. Aleph-Bet Books, Inc. 105 - 44 2013 $500

Attwell, Mabel Lucie *Mabel Lucy Attwell's Story Book.* Dean and Son, n.d. 1960'2, Large 8vo., original glazed pictorial boards, lower corners trifle bruised, 29 pages, color illustrations. R. F. G. Hollett & Son Children's Books - 38 2013 £30

Aubrey, John *Wiltshire the Topographical Collections...* Wilthshire Archaeological and Natural History Society by Henry Bull, 1862. First edition, etched frontispiece, engraved portrait, 44 plates and 3 folding family trees, plate offset onto last page, 4to. original morocco grain brown cloth, blindstamped borders on both boards, gilt titled on upper board and spine, short tear at foot of spine, very good. Blackwell's Rare Books B174 - 158 2013 £300

Aucassin et Nicolette *Aucassin and Nicolette.* London: Andrew Melrose, 1914. Limited edition, 4to., parchment backed boards, top edge gilt, 138 pages, some cover soil, very good+, illustrations by Eileen Lawrence Smith with 3 beautiful tipped in color plates and 14 other black and white plates, printed on fine paper, printed on fine paper. Aleph-Bet Books, Inc. 105 - 47 2013 $275

Auden, Wystan Hugh 1907-1973 *The Dyer's Hand and Other Essays.* New York: Random House, 1962. First edition, 8vo., original green cloth, dust jacket, inscribed by author for Louis Kronenberger, excellent copy in slightly chipped dust jacket.   Maggs Bros. Ltd.   1460 - 27   2013   £375

Auden, Wystan Hugh 1907-1973 *Homage to Clio.* London: Faber, 1960. First English edition, crown 8vo., pages 96, original mauve cloth, backstrip gilt lettered, free endpapers lightly browned in part, dust jacket, near fine. Blackwell's Rare Books   B174 - 163   2013   £70

Auden, Wystan Hugh 1907-1973 *New Year Letter.* London: Faber and Faber, 1941. First edition, 8vo., original cream cloth, one of 2000 copies, very good, cloth stained on back cover and tail of spine, inscribed by T. S. Eliot for Michael Tipett.   Maggs Bros. Ltd.   1460 - 269   2013   £750

Auden, Wystan Hugh 1907-1973 *Poems.* London: Faber, 1930. First edition, pages 80, 8vo., original printed pale blue wrappers over card, little soiled, covers sunned on and around area of backstrip, some flaking with loss to wrappers in area of backstrip, untrimmed, inscribed by author.   Blackwell's Rare Books   B174 - 164   2013   £1700

Auden, Wystan Hugh 1907-1973 *Collected Shorter Poems 1930-1944.* London: Faber & Faber, 1950. First edition, 8vo., original blue cloth, spine very slightly faded, as is top inch of lower cover, inscribed by author for Yvonne Hamilton.   Maggs Bros. Ltd.   1460 - 26   2013   £300

Auden, Wystan Hugh 1907-1973 *The Poet's Tongue. An Anthology.* London: G. Bell, 1935. First edition, 8vo., original blue cloth, dust jacket, inscribed by author for Cecil Beaton, excellent copy in slightly rubbed dust jacket.   Maggs Bros. Ltd.   1460 - 25   2013   £675

Audiberti, Jacques *Lagune Herissee.* Paris: Societe des Cent Une, 1958. First Carzou edition, number 44 of 145 copies (total edition) signed by Jean Carzou and President & VP of Societe on justification page, 20 original color lithographs, including 16 full page, each with tissue guard, lithos and 169 text leaves printed on Arches a la Forme, handmade paper, each leaf watermarked 'Arches', except for front cover litho, which contains an extra suite of 20 full page lithos in tones of black and one refusee litho, with additional justification page for the suite, numbered 8/8 and signed by Jean Carzou in pen, lithos not signed, unique copy in signed Master binding by Simone Fontanes, full tan calf, beautiful mosaic design of gilt and black engraved lines with onlaid painted strips of leather, on both front and back panels, spine with lettering gilt and black, integrating covers' design, endleaves made of fine suede, all edges gilt, original wrappers preserved and bound in, contained in matching half leather chemise and leather trimmed slipcase, overall size 32.5 x 25.5 x 5.5. cm, very slight age toning to spine, otherwise in new condition, from the library of Jean Jacobs with his small bookplate.   Gemini Fine Books & Arts., Ltd. Art Reference & Illustrated Books - 2013 $1300

Audubon, John James 1785-1851 *The Birds of America from Drawings Made in the United States and their Territories.* New York: Philadelphia: J. J. Audubon/J. B. Chevalier, 1840-1844. First Royal octavo edition, 7 volumes, late 19th century marbled paper over boards with recent rebacking and recornering in green morocco leather, spine with five gilt ruled compartments, three with pictorial elements, complete with 500 hand colored lithographic plates, text and plates fine, volumes trimmed, few plates closely, overall very handsome set.   By the Book, L. C.   38 - 1   2013 $62,500

Audubon, John James 1785-1851 *Audubon Society Elephant Folio Audubon's Birds of America.* New York: Abbeville Press, 1984. First edition, #421 of limited edition of 2500 signed by both authors, signed, baby elephant folio, full leather fine.   Barnaby Rudge Booksellers   Natural History 2013 - 021252   2013 $275

Audubon, John James 1785-1851 *Original Water-Color Paintings by James Audubon for The Birds of America.* New York: American Heritage Pub., 1966. First edition, folio, 2 volumes, over 400 color plates, brown buckram, fine, slipcase repaired at one end.   Barnaby Rudge Booksellers Natural History 2013 - 021253   2013 $95

Auel, Jean M. *The Clan of the Cave Bear.* New York: Crown, 1980. First edition, fine in fine, but price clipped dust jacket.   Beasley Books   2013 - 2013 $65

Auenbrugger, L. *Experimentum Nascens de Remedio Specifico sub Signo Specifico in Mania Virorum.* Wien: Kurzbock, 1776. Engraved title vignete, lacks portrait, full calf, rebacked spine.   James Tait Goodrich   S74 - 18   2013 $1250

Augustine Aurelius, Saint, Bp. of Hippo *The Confessions and Letters.* Wm. B. Eerdmans, 1974. 8 volumes, very good in original cloth.   Ken Spelman Books Ltd.   75 - 187   2013   £95

Aulnoy, Marie Catherine Lejumel De Barnville, Comtesse D' *D'aulnoy's Fairy Tales.* Philadelphia: McKay, 1923. First Tenggren edition, 4to., blue cloth, pictorial paste-on, top edge gilt, 457 pages, cover plate slightly rubbed, some light shelfwear, very good, illustrations by Gustaf Tenggren, with pictorial endpapers, cover plate, pictorial titlepage plus 8 beautiful color plates.   Aleph-Bet Books, Inc.   105 - 556   2013 $225

Aungerville, Richard   1281-1345 *Philobiblon.* Zuilichem: Catharijne Press, 1992. Experimental miniature book limited to only 25 unnumbered copies, 5.8 x 4.1 cm., stiff paper wrappers, 2 illustrations, from the collection of Donn W. Sanford.   Oak Knoll Books   303 - 77   2013 $150

Aunt Kitty's Nursery Rhymes. New York: Hurd & Houghton, n.d. circa, 1865. 12mo., pictorial wrappers, some foxing, very good, printed on linen, 10 nice half page color illustrations.   Aleph-Bet Books, Inc.   105 - 405   2013 $200

Aunt Lely's Picture Alphabet. New York: McLoughlin Bros. 30 Beekman St. n.d. circa, 1865. 12mo., pictorial wrappers, margin soil on few pages, very good+, each leaf with fine three quarter page engraving with large red letter superimposed on the picture, signed W. G. Mason, scarce.   Aleph-Bet Books, Inc.   104 - 11   2013 $500

Aunt Louisa   *Aunt Louisa's Birthday Gift Book...* London: Frederick Warne & Co. n.d. circa, 1869. Large square 8vo., original pictorial and decorated brown cloth gilt, little stained and faded, extremities slightly worn, neatly recased, 23 (ex 24) full page colored plates.   R. F. G. Hollett & Son   Children's Books - 706   2013   £180

Auntie's Little Rhyme Book: No. 3 of Old Nursery Rhymes. Philadelphia & London: McKay & Augener, n.d. circa, 1920. Oblong 12mo., pictorial boards, very fine in dust jacket (shows some wear), illustrations by H. W. Le Mair with 10 lovely full page color illustrations plus pictorial cover.   Aleph-Bet Books, Inc.   105 - 361   2013 $325

Ausonius, Decimus Magnus   *Opera.* Biponti: Ex Typographia Societatis, 1785. 8vo, dark brown calf with brown paste paper boards, vellum label to spine, edges colored red, small loss to head-cap, joint and edges worn, boards scuffed but internally clean and still very good, bookplate to front pastedown and inkstamp to f.f.e.p., both reading 'Ex Libris Studentatus Prov. Sti. Ludovici", inkstamp of library code and oval inkstamp from Redemptorist Library of St. Alphonsus Church, New Orleans, also an illegible embossed library stamp.   Unsworths Antiquarian Booksellers   28 - 4   2013   £40

Austen, Jane   1775-1817 *Emma: a Novel.* London: John Murray, 1816. First edition, 3 volumes, 12mo., nick to upper margin of title, volume I, bound without half titles, contemporary half brown calf, gilt bands, compartments in blind, light brown morocco labels, some slight rubbing to extremities, but very nice, inscription "Elizabeth Anne Sandford with affectionate love from her Aunt, Anne Anderton, Wake Green Dec. 29, 1869".   Jarndyce Antiquarian Booksellers   CCV - 12   2013   £15,000

Austen, Jane   1775-1817 *Sense and Sensibility: a Novel.* London: printed for the author, C. Roworth & published by T. Egerton, 1813. Second edition, 3 volumes, half titles, some minor paper flaws, mostly marginal but occasionally within text touching a single letter, some light spotting, overall nice, clean copy, contemporary half brown calf, marbled boards, expertly rebacked in matching calf, ruled and decorated in gilt, red morocco labels, handsome copy.   Jarndyce Antiquarian Booksellers   CCV - 13   2013   £7800

Auster, Paul   *Autobiography of the Eye.* Portland: printed at the Beaverdam Press for Charles Seluzicki, 1993. First edition, one of 35 copies, 8vo., photographic frontispiece by Karin Welch tipped-in, original string tied French-fold unprinted wrappers, printed paper label, publisher's envelope, fine, rare.   James S. Jaffe Rare Books   Fall 2013 - 13   2013 $850

Austin, Alfred   *Lamia's Winter Quarters.* London: A. & C. Black, 1907. First edition, No. 192 of 250 deluxe editions copies, signed by author, quarto, pages 164, original ivory decorative cloth, spine faded, cloth cockled.   J. & S. L. Bonham Antiquarian Booksellers   Europe - 6159   2013   £70

Austin, Alfred   *A Vindication of Lord Byron.* London: Chapman & Hall, 1869. First edition, facsimile, slightly spotted, original cream wrappers, spine chipped at head and tail, otherwise very good, 67 pages.   Jarndyce Antiquarian Booksellers   CCIII - 351   2013   £125

Austin, Alfred   *A Vindication of Lord Byron.* London: Chapman & Hall, 1869. Second edition, disbound, inserted into dusted paper wrapper from parcel addressed to Doris Langley Moore, from the Bookshop, Wells, 9 pages.   Jarndyce Antiquarian Booksellers   CCIII - 352   2013   £60

Austin, Mary   *The Land of Little Rain.* Boston: Houghton Mifflin and Co., 1903. First edition, square octavo, illustrations and border decorations by C. Boyd Smith, original dark olive ribbed cloth, front cover pictorially stamped in black, gray and green and ruled and lettered gilt within blind panel spine ruled and lettered gilt, top edge gilt and near fine in rare pictorial dust jacket, some minor chipping to spine extremities, and edges of jacket, inside of jacket with some tape repairs, mainly along flap folds.   Heritage Book Shop   Holiday Catalogue 2012 - 6   2013 $1750

Austin, Sarah *Characteristics of Goethe from the German of Falk, Von Muller &c.* London: Effingham Wilson, 1833. First English edition, contemporary dark green half calf, red labels, slightly rubbed, nice set.   Jarndyce Antiquarian Booksellers   CCV - 113   2013   £180

Avallone, Michael *Violence in Velvet.* London: W. H. Allen, 1958. First English edition, fine in attractive very good plus dust jacket with 1.25" tear on front panel and light edgewear, scarce.   Between the Covers Rare Books, Inc.   Mystery & Detective Fiction - 76575   2013 $200

Ave Maria. Budapest or Italy: circa, 1970. 10 x 11mm., 6 unnumbered leaves, 3 of them blank, charming burgundy calf, upper cover with head of the Madonna tooled in gilt, flat spine with gilt bands, black pebble grain morocco slipcase, nestled in fabric inside a 32 x 34mm., metal box with latch, cross printed on first leaf, simple engraving of the Madonna's head on second, tiny scratch to head of spine, otherwise fine specimen.   Phillip J. Pirages   63 - 340   2013 $250

Avedon, Richard *The American West.* New York: Harry N. Abrams, 1985. First edition, light very near fine in photo illustrated cloth boards, near fine glassine jacket, clean copy, portraits.   Jeff Hirsch Books   Fall 2013 - 129147   2013 $225

Avedon, Richard *Portraits.* New York: Farrar Straus and Giroux, 1976. First edition, black and white photos, fine in very near fine, price clipped dust jacket, very nice.   Jeff Hirsch Books Fall 2013 - 129225   2013 $200

Averill, Esther *Adventures of Jack Ninepins.* New York: Harper Bros., 1944. Stated first edition, illustrations by Averill, from the library of Bertha Mahoney Miller with her bookplate, small 4to., cloth, fine in frayed dust jacket.   Aleph-Bet Books, Inc.   104 - 45   2013 $150

Avery, C. Louise *Masterpieces of European Porcelain: a Catalogue of a Special Exhibition March 18- May 15 1949.* New York: printed by Marchbanks Press for The Metropolitan Museum of Art, 1949. One of 2000 copies, 290 x 222mm., attractive crimson crushed morocco by James MacDonald Co. of NY (stamp signed), covers with single gilt fillet border, upper cover with initials "F.W." in lower right corner, raised bands flanked by gilt rules, small gilt fleuron at head and tail of spine, vertical titling, densely gilt turn-ins, marbled endpapers; with 32 black and white photos; tipped to front pastedown is handwritten note to Mr. Wickes from Francis Henry Taylor, director of Metropolitan Museum, presenting this book in gratitude for Wickes' support of the Exhibition; couple of small marks to covers, but very fine with virtually no signs of use.   Phillip J. Pirages   63 - 492   2013 $150

Avery, Gillian *Nineteenth Century Children.* London: Hodder and Stoughton, 1965. First edition, original cloth, gilt, dust jacket, pages 260, 16 pages of plates, uncommon.   R. F. G. Hollett & Son   Children's Books - 39   2013   £35

Avery, Samuel P. *A Short List of Microscopic Books in the Library of the Grolier Club Mostly Presented by Samuel P. Avery.* New York: Grolier Club, 1911. First edition, 16mo., paper wrappers, well preserved, from the collection of Donn W. Sanford.   Oak Knoll Books   303 - 6   2013 $75

Axe, Ruth Frey *The Published Writings of Henry R. Wagner.* New Haven: William Reese, 1988. First edition, one of 500 copies, 73 pages, frontispiece, orange cloth, spine, maroon boards, gilt lettering, very fine.   Argonaut Book Shop   Recent Acquisitions June 2013 - 299   2013 $75

Axsom, Richard H. *The Prints of Ellsworth Kelly: a Catalogue Raisonne 1949-1985.* New York & Ann Arbor: Hudson Hills Press in association with the American Federation of Arts, 1987. First edition, 201 pages, numerous color and black and white illustrations, tight, near fine copy in wrappers.   Jeff Hirsch Books   Fall 2013 - 129174   2013 $50

Axton, Mae Boren *Country Singers as I Know Em.* Austin: Sweet Pub., 1973. First edition, fine, bit sunned dust jacket, with publication data on stickers on titlepage and pastedown.   Beasley Books   2013 - 2013 $65

Ayckbourn, Alan *The Norman Conquests. A Trilogy of Plays.* London: Chatto & Windus, 1975. First edition, 8vo., original blue cloth, inscribed by author, bumped on top corners, otherwise near fine in slightly browned dust jacket.   Maggs Bros. Ltd.   1460 - 29   2013   £125

Ayliffe, John *The Antient and Present State of the University of Oxford.* London: E Curll, 1714. First edition, 2 volumes, contemporary brown panelled calf, joints cracked, lacks labels, clean and crisp.   J. & S. L. Bonham Antiquarian Booksellers   Europe - 8723   2013   £300

Ayres, Philip *Cupids Addresse to the Ladies.* London: Sold by R. Bently in Covent Garden, S. Tidmarch..., 1683. frontispiece, 44 emblematic plates and engraved verse in Latin, English, Italian and French, 8vo., several plates bound in incorrect order, some occasional browning mainly to fore-edges, 19th century tree calf, hinges repaired, new red morocco label, spine and board edges rubbed, corners little worn, bookplate of Baron de Spon.   Jarndyce Antiquarian Booksellers   CCIV - 2   2013   £2500

Ayscu, Edward *A Historie Contayning the Warres, Treaties, Marriages and Other Occurents Betweene England and Scotland from King William the Conqueror...*   London: G. Eld., 1697.   8vo, lacks blank leaf A1, substantial loss to page 135 (misnumbered as p. 133), missing portion painstakingly supplied in manuscript on handmade paper and tipped in, endpapers somewhat rumpled and little torn but otherwise nice and bright inside, contemporary limp vellum, ink to spine, yapp edges, vellum little yellowed and marked, some staining and remnants of ties to lower wrapper.
Unsworths Antiquarian Booksellers   28 - 66   2013   £650

B

B., A. O. *Story of the Kings of Judah and Israel.* Edinburgh: William P. Nimmo, 1868. Third edition, small square 8vo., original green pictorial cloth gilt, extra, all edges gilt, chromolithographed frontispiece and additional title, lovely copy, very scarce. R. F. G. Hollett & Son Children's Books - 40 2013 £120

B., H. *More Beasts for Worse Children.* Edward Arnold, n.d., 1897. First edition, oblong 4to., original cloth backed pictorial boards, little rubbed, corners slightly worn drawings in style of Edward Lear. R. F. G. Hollett & Son Children's Books - 595 2013 £65

Baas, J. H. *Outlines of the History of Medicine and the Medical Profession.* New York: Vail, 1889. First English edition, 1173 pages, original cloth, inner hinges just starting to split, light rubbing, otherwise good, tight copy, translator's presentation from H. E. Handerson to Dr. G. H. Monks. James Tait Goodrich 75 - 14 2013 $495

Babbage, Charles 1792-1871 *On the Economy of Machinery and Manufactures.* London: Charles Knight, 1832. (1833). Third edition, titlepage, vignette slightly spotted, original purple wavy grained cloth, spine lettered gilt with gilt border, boards slightly marked, spine faded to brown, embossed stamp of Castle Archdale, Irvinestown, very good. Jarndyce Antiquarian Booksellers CCV - 14 2013 £450

Babcock, Dwight V. *Murder for Hannah.* London: Robert Hale, 1941. First English edition, some light spotting on page edges and fading on covers otherwise fine in lightly soiled dust jacket. Mordida Books 81 - 15 2013 $150

The Babes in the Woods. London: Blackie, n.d. circa, 1915. 4to., cloth backed boards, very good 12 fine color plates, 3 full page line illustrations and pictorial endpapers by Frank Adams. Aleph-Bet Books, Inc. 104 - 25 2013 $200

Baby Bunting ABC. New York: McLoughlin Bros. Inc. circa, 1915. 4to., pictorial wrappers, fine, 3-color illustration on each page. Aleph-Bet Books, Inc. 104 - 16 2013 $125

Baby's Book. London: Raphael Tuck, n.d. circa, 1920. 4to., cloth backed pictorial boards, edges rubbed, else very good, pages mounted on thick boards, pictorial titlepage, decorative border around each page of text and 16 fine full page color illustrations by Mabel Lucy Attwell, scarce. Aleph-Bet Books, Inc. 104 - 44 2013 $850

Baby's Book. New York: Simon & Schuster, 1942. First printing of Little Golden Book #10, illustrations in color by Bob Smith, rare in dust jacket, blue spine, fine in near fine dust jacket with just touch of fraying. Aleph-Bet Books, Inc. 105 - 278 2013 $1200

Baby's Primer. Boston: D. Lothrop Co., 1885. First edition, 8vo., wrappers, good+, restapled. Barnaby Rudge Booksellers Children 2013 - 021613 2013 $50

Baby's Record. London: George Harrap, 1928. Most likely first cloth edition, 4to., pink moire stamped in gold and blue, top edge gilt, 63 pages, few entries erased, otherwise fine in publisher's pictorial box, 6 beautiful color plates and lovely line illustrations by Anne Anderson, superb, rare. Aleph-Bet Books, Inc. 105 - 39 2013 $600

Bach, Friedrich Teja *Constantin Brancusi 1978-1957.* Philadelphia: and Cambridge: Philadelphia Museum of Art and MIT Press, 1995. First edition, numerous color and black and white illustrations, numerous photos, very near fine in very near fine dust jacket. Jeff Hirsch Books Fall 2013 - 129128 2013 $200

Backman, Phil *Bluenose.* Toronto: McClelland & Stewart, 1965. Quarto, cloth in dust jacket, pages 112, half title, black and white photo illustrations, dust jacket with wear and few small nicks and tears to edges, small portion of jacket torn from top edge and this is small tear to top of spine of dust jacket, signed by Angus J. Walters, Sydney C. Oland & Don Oland, Ellsworth L. Coggins, Brian and Phil Backman and another unreadable signature. Schooner Books Ltd. 105 - 50 2013 $75

Backus, Anna Jean *Through Bonds of Love: in the Shadow of the Mountain Meadows Massacre.* Orem: AJB Distributing, 1998. Limited edition, number 29 of 20 signed copies, 235 pages, octavo, red leatherette, very good. Ken Sanders Rare Books 45 - 2 2013 $100

Bacon, D. *The New York Judicial Repository for November 1818.* New York: Gould and Banks, 1818. First edition, stitched printed wrappers, untrimmed, small tears at margins, large but very faint dampstain throughout text, nice, very good, scarce. Between the Covers Rare Books, Inc. New York City - 296303 2013 $375

Bacon, Francis Viscount St. Albans 1561-1626 *De Dignitate & Augmentis Scientiarum Libri IX.* Leiden: Apud Franciscum Moyardum & Adrianum Wijngaerde, 1645. Pocket edition, 12mo., engraved titlepage, some light spotting, occasional underlining, contemporary vellum boards, long sides overlapping spine lettered in ink, soiled, early manuscript table of contents.   Unsworths Antiquarian Booksellers   28 - 68   2013   £350

Bacon, Francis Viscount St. Albans 1561-1626 *Essays, Moral, Economical and Political.* London: Printed for J. Johnson (and others), 1807. 8 woodcut plates, frontispiece, some offsetting from frontispiece, little marked, occasional light browning, full contemporary diced calf, double gilt ruled borders, gilt tooled spine, bookplate of Sarah Phillott, attractive.   Jarndyce Antiquarian Booksellers CCIV - 51   2013   £75

Bacon, Francis Viscount St. Albans 1561-1626 *Bacon's Essays with annotations by Richard Whately.* London: John W. Parker and Son, 1857. Third edition, octavo, 22cm., full calf stamped in blind with elaborate gilt tooling on spine and red morocco spine label, marbled endpapers, all edges marbled, near fine with slight rubbing and some, tiny scuffs on rear board, else handsome, fine copy. Between the Covers Rare Books, Inc.   Philosophy - 285818   2013 $150

Bacon, Francis Viscount St. Albans 1561-1626 *Letters, Speeches, Charges, Advices &c. of Francis Bacon...* London: printed for Andrew Millar, 1763. 8vo., very good, clean copy, full contemporary diced calf, triple gilt bands. Jarndyce Antiquarian Booksellers   CCIV - 52   2013   £120

Bacon, Francis Viscount St. Albans 1561-1626 *(Novum Organum) Francisci de Verulamio, Summi Angliae: Cancellari Instauratio Magna...* London: 1620. First edition, 2nd issue with cancel colophon/errata leaf e4, small folio, copper engraved titlepage, numerous historiated initials and head and tailpieces, contemporary vellum over boards, retaining most of original vellum, spine title written in manuscript, marginal repair to first blank, corners renewed on titlepage, marginal wormholes repaired, occasional slight foxing, otherwise very good.   Heritage Book Shop   50th Anniversary Catalogue - 3   2013 $20,000

Bacon, Francis Viscount St. Albans 1561-1626 *Of Gardens.* London: Hacon and Ricketts (Eragny Press), 1902. One of 226 copies, although not called for, this copy signed by designer, Lucien Pissaro, celadon green paper decorated with orange and green plant design, ivory paper spine title and author and decorative leaf devices on front panel, two neat ex-libris on front pastedown, offsetting to both endpapers, small amount of foxing to 4 blank pages at rear, bit of darkening and soiling to binding, generally very good, printed on Vale type in three colors, green, orange and black, double page wood engraved opening page spread and circular device of Eragny Press at end plus colophon with three irises; frontispiece engraved by Lucien Pissarro and double border and initial letters designed by Pissarro and engraved by Esther Pissaro,.   Priscilla Juvelis - Rare Books   55 - 6   2013 $1050

Bacon, Francis Viscount St. Albans 1561-1626 *Sylva Sylvarum, sive Hist. Naturalis et Novus Atlas.* Amsterdam: Apud Ludovicum Elzevirium, 1648. Pocket edition, 12mo., engraved titlepage, some light browning, contemporary vellum boards, spine lettered ink, bit soiled, front flyleaf excised, old ownership inscription foot of titlepage (partially rubbed on), from the collection, but without any signs of ownership, of Ferdinand Tonnies (1855-1936).   Unsworths Antiquarian Booksellers   28 - 69   2013   £350

Bacon, Francis Viscount St. Albans 1561-1626 *The Twoo Bookes of Francis Bacon, of the Proficience and Advancement of Learning, Divine and Humane.* London: for Henri Thomes, 1605. First edition, 4to., lacks final blank 3H2 and, as always, the rare two leaves of errata at end, late 18th century half calf and marbled boards, (extremities of boards worn), very skilfully and imperceptively rebacked retaining entire original spine, small worm trail in bottom margin of quires 2D-2F, occasional minor marginalia in early hand, else lovely copy, early signature of Row'd Weatherald and signature of Horatio Carlyon, 1861, Sachs bookplate and modern leather book label, calf backed clamshell box.   Joseph J. Felcone Inc.   Books Printed before 1701 - 5   2013 $7500

Bacon, Francis Viscount St. Albans 1561-1626 *The Twoo Bookes of Francis Bacon. Of the Proficience and Advancement of Learning, Divine and Humane.* London: printed for Henrie Tomes, 1605. First edition, 2 parts in one small quarto volume, complete with final blank leaf, but without two extra leaves of errata found only in very few copies, decorative woodcut initials, 19th century quarter brown morocco over brown cloth, spine decoratively stamped and lettered gilt, all edges gilt, text professionally washed, so vey clean, overall very good, few minute marginal stains.   Heritage Book Shop   50th Anniversary Catalogue - 4   2013 $6000

Bacon, Francis Viscount St. Albans 1561-1626 *The Two Bookes of Sr. Francis Bacon. Of the Proficience and Advancement of Learning, Divine and Humane to the King.* London: printed for William Washington, 1629. Second edition, small quarto, contemporary paneled calf, newer morocco spine labels, original endpapers, edges sprinkled red, boards with some scuffing, corners and edges chipped and rubbed head of spine chipped, outer hinges starting, still firm, some offsetting to endpapers, few old pencil marks in margins and on titlepage, one instance of old ink marginalia, light dampstain across upper half of some leaves, mostly in rear, altogether very good.   Heritage Book Shop   Holiday Catalogue 2012 - 7   2013 $1750

Bacon, Francis Viscount St. Albans 1561-1626 *The Works of Francis Bacon.* Boston: Brown and Taggard, 1861. 8vo., frontispieces, original triple ruled pebbled brown cloth, gilt stamped spines, mild edgewear, some spine heads torn, few inner hinges repaired, bookplates of John F. McGee, very good.   Jeff Weber Rare Books   169 - 24   2013 $650

Bacon, Marion *Life at Vassar. Seventy-Five Years in Pictures.* Poughkeepsie: Vassar Coop Bookshop, 1940. First edition, 4to., 141 illustrations, tan cloth, printed in red, cover, edges somwhat soiled, else very good, tight copy. Second Life Books Inc.   183 - 13   2013 $85

Bacon, Mary *Winged Thoughts.* London: Longman & Co., 1851. First edition, scarce, chromolithographs by Owen Jones, book highly decorated with gilt dentelles, all edges gilt, gilt name of bird with design on verso of its illustration, very light aging to margins of some pages and offsetting to gilt design on verso of eagle illustration, but in very good condition, brown leather with relivio, highly embossed title and design to front and rear covers, some scuffing and rebacked, still very nice, lovely endpapers, printed on silk, unpaginated.   The Kelmscott Bookshop   7 - 68   2013 $900

Bacon, Peggy *The Terrible Nuisance and Other Tales.* New York: Junior Literary Guild, 1931. First edition, near fine in very good dust jacket, illustrations by author. Leather Stalking Books   October 2013 - 2013 $50

Bacon's Oxford Railway ABC Guide and Visitors' Handbook No. 167. November 1927. Oxford: Bacon, 1927. Text, ads within letterpress printed double border, numerous photos, square 16mo., original printed cream wrappers, very good.   Blackwell's Rare Books   B174 - 111   2013   £30

Badius Ascensius, Jodocus 1462-1535 *Nauis Stultifere Collectanea.* Paris: J. Badius Ascensius for himself and the de Marnef Brothers 1 July, 1513. 4to., 108 leaves, title printed in red and black, 114 text woodcuts, woodcut initials, de Marnef pelican device on title, contemporary vellum, with yapp edges, 19th century parchment straps, clasps (one broken) and endpapers, first and last few leaves soiled and darkened with early repairs to blank corners, few other early repairs including one on m2 affecting woodcut, minor dampstain at upper blank edge of several leaves, few woodcuts partly colored, good, sound copy.   Joseph J. Felcone Inc. Books Printed before 1701 - 6   2013 $8000

Baer, Morley *Light Years: The Photographs of Morley Baer.* Carmel: Photography West Graphics Inc., 1988. First edition, beautifully printed, black and white photos, 51 plates, very good plus, some slight bumping to bottom corners, very good plus, price clipped dust jacket, usual fading, signed by Baer.   Jeff Hirsch Books   Fall 2013 - 129177   2013 $125

Baer, Warren *The Duke of Sacramento.* San Francisco: Grabhorn Press, 1934. One of 550 copies, 78 pages, printed in red and black, illustrations by Arvilla Parker, cloth backed boards, paper spine label, lightest of offsetting to free ends, but very fine with plain dust jacket.   Argonaut Book Shop   Summer 2013 - 7   2013 $60

Bagby, George *The Corpse with the Purple Thighs.* New York: Doubleday Crime Club, 1939. First edition, fine in dust jacket with some tiny wear at spine ends and at corners.   Mordida Books   81 - 16   2013 $200

Bage, Robert *Man As He Is.* London: printed for William Lane, at the Minerva Press, Leadenhall Street, 1792. First edition, 12mo., half titles, original paper flaw to leading edge volume III E2 not affecting text, old pen strokes volume IV, page 122, some foxing and occasional browning to text, contemporary quarter calf, marbled boards, vellum tips, gilt banded spines, red morocco labels, spines rubbed, each spine has faint shelf number blindstamped at head with contemporary ownership name of Mary Lyon.   Jarndyce Antiquarian Booksellers   CCIV - 53   2013   £2500

Bagley, Will *With Golden Visions Bright Before Them...* Norman: Arthur H. Clark Co., 2012. Collector's edition, octavo, 464 pages, decorative suede like cloth, fine, signed by author, limited to 55 copies, this copy #3.   Ken Sanders Rare Books   45 - 34   2013 $150

Bagnold, Enid *The Loved and Envied.* London: Heinemann, 1951. First edition, 8vo., original black cloth, dust jacket, inscribed by author for Gerald Hart, near fine in slightly nicked dust jacket, rear inner flap price clipped. Maggs Bros. Ltd.   1460 - 30   2013   £100

Bagot, Annette *'All Things Is Well Here'. Letters from Hugh James of Levens to James Grahme 1692-95.* Kendal: Titus Wilson, 1988. First hardback edition, original cloth gilt, dust jacket, 3 plates, 3 figures.   R. F. G. Hollett & Son   Lake District & Cumbria - 55   2013   £30

Bagot, Josceline *Colonel James Grahme of Levens.* Kendal: T. Wilson, 1886. First edition, original parchment, few marks, 4 plates, scarce, gift inscriptions.   R. F. G. Hollett & Son   Lake District & Cumbria - 57   2013   £95

Bailer, Adele *Hei Von Allerlei.* Leipzig: Ferdinand Hirt & Sohn, 1924. 13 x 10 1/4 inches, cloth backed white pictorial boards, small scrape on cover, else near fine, magnificent silhouettes by Bailer,.   Aleph-Bet Books, Inc.   105 - 272   2013 $650

Bailey, H. C. *Black Land White Land: a Reggie Fortune Novel.* Garden City: Doubleday Doran/Crime Club, 1927. First American edition, very faint ring on front board, else near fine in fine dust jacket.   Between the Covers Rare Books, Inc.   Mystery & Detective Fiction - 316641   2013 $200

Bailey, H. C. *Dead Man's Effects.* London: Macdonald, 1945. First English edition, fine in dust jacket.   Mordida Books   81 - 19   2013 $125

Bailey, H. C. *Meet Mr. Fortune.* Garden City: Doubleday Crime Club, 1942. First edition, fine in price clipped dust jacket with some fading on spine and scattered nicks along edges.   Mordida Books   81 - 19   2013 $125

Bailey, H. C. *Mr. Clunk's Text.* Garden City: Doubleday Crime Club, 1939. First American edition, fine in dust jacket, some light stains on back panel and tiny wear at base of spine.   Mordida Books   81 - 18   2013 $100

Bailey, Hamilton *Demonstrations of Physical Signs in Clinical Surgery.* Bristol: John Wright and Sons, 1933. Fourth edition, 8vo., 335 illustrations, original gilt stamped black cloth, extremities worn, especially at spine ends, signed and inscribed by author for H. E. Alexander in ink at half title, very good.   Jeff Weber Rare Books   172 - 9   2013 $75

Bailey, Lynn R. *Supplying the Mining World: the Mining Equipment Manufacturers of San Francisco, 1850-1900.* Tucson: Westernlore Press, 1996. First edition, Quarto, 133 pages, numerous engravings, halftone portraits from photos, red cloth, very fine, pictorial dust jacket.   Argonaut Book Shop   Recent Acquisitions June 2013 - 18   2013 $75

Bailey, Nathan *Dictionarium Rusticum, Urbanicum & Botanicum; or a Dictionary of Husbandry...*   London: printed for James and John Knapton, 1726. 2 engraved plates, repair and little worn along leading edge, numerous woodcuts in text, 8vo., contemporary panelled calf, raised bands, hinges slightly cracked but very firm, some wear, contemporary name Harbin on each front endpaper.   Jarndyce Antiquarian Booksellers   CCIV - 54   2013   £580

Bailey, Pearl *Talking to Myself.* New York: Harcourt Brace Jovanovich, 1971. First edition, slightest fading to very edges of boards, some spotting to fore edge, very good in like dust jacket with single short tear, inscribed by author, rubber stamped "Gift of Pearl Bailey".   Between the Covers Rare Books, Inc.   165 - 229   2013 $75

Bailey, Percival *A Classification of the Tumors of the Glioma Group on a Histogenetic Basis with a Correlated Study on Prognosis.*   Philadelphia: J. B. Lippincott, 1926. 108 illustrations, original red cloth, very nice, internally fine.   James Tait Goodrich   75 - 71   2013 $395

Bailey, Percival *Tumors Arising from the Blood Vessels of the Brain.* London: Bailliere, Tindall & Cox, 1928. One of 1000 copies, first English edition, 219 pages, original red cloth, light wear, otherwise clean, tight copy, signature of "CP Symmonds".   James Tait Goodrich   S74 - 62   2013 $495

Bailey, Thomas *Hand-book to Newstead Abbey.* London: Simpkin, Marshall & Co., 1855. 2 plates, frontispiece, 9 pages ads, original printed yellow wrappers, printed in black, elaborate embossed floral borders, small scratch on front wrapper, slightly dusted, booklabel of Alex Bridge, very good.   Jarndyce Antiquarian Booksellers   CCIII - 343   2013   £125

Baillarger, J. *Recherches sur l'Anatomie, La Physioologie et la Pathologie du Systeme Nerveus.* Paris: Masson, 1872. 19th century quarter black polished calf and marbled boards, light text foxing, overall clean, tight copy.   James Tait Goodrich   75 - 15   2013 $695

Baillie-Grohman, W. A. *Sport in the Alps; in the Past and Present, an Account of the Chase of the Chamois, Red-Deer, Bouquetin, Roe-Deer, Capercaillie and Black Cock...* London: Adam and Charles Black, 1896. First edition, 8vo., pages xv, 356, frontispiece, 17 plates, text illustrations, early 20th century brown half calf, joints little rubbed.   J. & S. L. Bonham Antiquariam Booksellers   Europe - 8000   2013   £75

Baillie, Joanna *(Works - A Collection of Plays in Four Volumes).* London: T. Cadell, Longman, 1802-1812. Volume 1 4th edition, volume 2 second edition, volume 3 first edition; first edition of Miscellaneous Plays, (Series of Plays in 3 volumes), Miscellaneous Plays 1 volume, together 4 volumes, uniform contemporary full brown calf, borders in blind, gilt spines, very good, bright. Jarndyce Antiquarian Booksellers CCV - 15 2013 £400

Baillie, Matthew *A Series of Engravings, Accompanied with Explanations which Are Intended to Illustrate the Morbid Anatomy of Some of the Most Important Parts of the Human Body. (with) The Morbid Anatomy of Some of the Most Important Parts of the Human Body.* London: printed by W. Bulmer and Co., 1812. Second edition. London: printed for J. Johnson, 1797. Second edition, 228 pages, folio, 73 full page engraved plates, recent half polished calf and marbled boards, some light foxing, else very good; 2nd work 8vo., 140 pages, contemporary half morocco, light marginal dampstaining, some text foxing. James Tait Goodrich 75 - 16 2013 $2495

Baillou, Guillaume De *Opera Omnia Medica.* Venetiis: apud Angelum Jeremiam, 1734-1736. First collected edition, 4 volumes, 8vo., half titles each volume with separate titlepage, headpieces, tailpieces, historiated initials, volume 1 with engraved portrait of author, headpieces, tailpieces, historiated initials, volume I page 161 torn, volume III browned and waterstained, volume IV foxing top marking browned, early quarter red morocco, marbled boards, spine, boards and edges heavily scuffed, spine mostly lacking, joints cracked but holding firm, paper spine label with ms. inventory numbers, untrimmed, very good. Jeff Weber Rare Books 172 - 10 2013 $800

Bain, Willard *Informed Sources (Day East Received).* San Francisco: The Communication Co., 1967. Second printing, stated Manuscript Editions Number One, quarto, mimeographed in stapled wrappers, rear wrapper, little of last leaf of two laced from insect damage, good copy. Between the Covers Rare Books, Inc. Sci-Fi, Fantasy & Horror - 291205 2013 $400

Baines, Edward *A Companion to the Lakes of Cumberland, Westmoreland and Lancashire...* London: Hurst, Chance and Co., 1829. First edition, original cloth, paper spine label, boards rather marked, spine faded and joints cracked but firm, lacks folding map, errata slip tipped in, Edward Hailstone's copy with his label, very scare. R. F. G. Hollett & Son Lake District & Cumbria - 60 2013 £150

Baines, Edward *A Companion to the Lakes of Cumberland, Westmoreland and Lancashire...* London: Hurst, Chance & Co., 1829. First edition, early 20th century three quarter levant morocco gilt, top edge gilt, linen backed folding map, hand colored in outline, errata slip tipped in, few scattered spots, very scarce, from the Appleby Castle Library with monogram of Lord Hothfield. R. F. G. Hollett & Son Lake District & Cumbria - 61 2013 £250

Baines, Edward *A Companion to the Lakes of Cumberland, Westmoreland and Lancashire...* London: Simpkin and Marshall, 1830. Second edition, Original boards with spine label, patchily faded, corners little bumped and spine rather rucked at head, complete with hand colored folding map, armorial bookplate of Edward Conder, Terry Bank, Co. Westmorland. R. F. G. Hollett & Son Lake District & Cumbria - 59 2013 £150

Baines, Thomas *The Gold Regions of South Eastern Africa Rhodesia Reprint Library Volume One.* Bulawayo: Books of Rhodesia, 1974. Original pictorial green cloth, gilt, dust jacket rather worn and dampstained, tinted plates, folding facsimile and large folding map in rear pocket. R. F. G. Hollett & Son Africana - 6 2013 £30

Baird, Charles W. *History of the Huguenot Emigration to America.* New York: Dodd Mead, 1885. First edition, 8vo., 15 maps and plates, original cloth, library label on front cover, hinge loose in volume I, tear to blank portion of map in volume one. Second Life Books Inc. 183 - 14 2013 $135

Baird, Henry M. *The Huguenots and Henry of Navarre with Maps.* New York: Scribner's Sons, 1886. First edition, 8vo. 2 volumes, folding map at rear of each volume, stamped brown cloth, library on cover of each book, hinge tender in volume 2, otherwise very good, clean set. Second Life Books Inc. 183 - 15 2013 $135

Baird, Jonathan *Day Job.* Boston: Allen & Osborne, 1998. First edition, inscribed by author to another writer, fine in pictorial boards and elastic seal without dust jacket, as issued. Ken Lopez Bookseller 159 - 10 2013 $75

Baird, W. David *A Creek Warrior for the Confederacy.* Norman: University of Oklahoma Press, 1988. First edition, 2 maps, numerous portraits and photos, red cloth, very fine, pictorial dust jacket. Argonaut Book Shop Summer 2013 - 8 2013 $75

Baj, Enrico *La Cravate Ne Vaut Pas Une Medaille.* Geneva: Rousseau, 1972. First edition, one of 160 copies (total edition 200 copies), signed and numbered 87 on colophon by Baj, original Lego constructed art-object pasted to front of slipcase, about 40 loose sheets with large number of original color lithographs and silkscreens, many of them with collage, with another full page collage laid in loose at back, all fine in publisher's carton chemise, folding portfolio case and slipcase, overall size 40 x 40cm., lego collage numbered and signed by artist, plastic tie collage is replica of Pollock's "tie" from 1969, the art and book object is in excellent condition. Gemini Fine Books & Arts., Ltd. Art Reference & Illustrated Books - 2013 $3000

Baker, E. C. Stuart *Mishi the Man-Eater and Other Tales of Big Game.* H. F. and G. Witherby, 1928. First edition, 222 pages, ad leaf, frontispiece and 3 plates, very good in original red cloth, gilt lettered spine just little sunned, inscription dated 1929, very slight dent to rear board. Ken Spelman Books Ltd. 75 - 174 2013 £75

Baker, Henry *Employment for the Microscope.* London: printed for R. and J. Dodsley, 1764. Second edition, folding engraved frontispiece, 17 folding three quarter, slightly browned, little offsetting from plates, 8vo., mid 20th century half green straight grained morocco, top edge gilt, otherwise uncut, bookplate of microscope collector Schuitema Meier, good. Blackwell's Rare Books Sciences - 10 2013 £500

Baker, Henry *The Microscope Made Easy.* London: printed for R. Dodsley, 1744. Third edition, 8vo., blank lower corner o E6 torn, light browning, contemporary calf, gilt ruled borders, raised bands, early paper spine label, hinges little cracked but firm, covers rather rubbed, some crazing to surface leather, foot of spine worn, small and unusual bookplate of Maurice Wynne. Jarndyce Antiquarian Booksellers CCIV - 55 2013 £220

Baker, John *The Christian House, Built by Truth on a Rock.* London: printed for the author and sold by W. Williams, 1820. 20 pages, disbound, illustrations, slight waterstaining. Jarndyce Antiquarian Booksellers CCV - 16 2013 £85

Baker, Josephine *La Tribu Arc-en-Ciel.* Neterland: Mulder & Zoon, Oper Mundi, Paris, 1957. 4to., pictorial cloth, ink scribbling on 2 pages, else very good, inscribed by Baker and tipped in photo signed by her. Aleph-Bet Books, Inc. 104 - 74 2013 $1600

Baker, Nicholson *Vox.* New York: Random House, 1992. Advance reading copy, signed by author, slight bump to spine base, else fine in wrappers enclosed in publisher's plain brown paper wrapper. Ken Lopez Bookseller 159 - 11 2013 $100

Baker, Piet D. *The Young Stork's Baedeker, Travel Guide with Lexicon.* Zuilichem: Catharijne Press, 1998. Limited to 190 copies, this one of 15 lettered copies bound thus and has the second volume which is not in original edition, 6.7 x 4.2 cm., paper covered boards, slipcase, illustrations, including foldout map, bound by Luce Thurkow, from the collection of Donn W. Sanford. Oak Knoll Books 303 - 75 2013 $275

Baker, Richard *A Chronicle of the Kings of England.* London: for H. Sawbridge, B. Tooke and T. Sawbridge, 1684. folio, portrait, engraved title, contemporary calf, very worn at extremities, neatly rebacked, later endpapers, overall foxing and soiling. Joseph J. Felcone Inc. Books Printed before 1701 - 7 2013 $450

Baker, Roy, Pseud. *Penal Battalion.* London: Sampson Low, Marston & Co. n.d., 1934. Original black cloth, gilt, spine little faded and with slight crease, very scarce. R. F. G. Hollett & Son Africana - 8 2013 £85

Baker, Samuel White *The Albert N'Yanza, Great Basin of the Nile and Explorations of the Nile Sources.* Macmillan, 1879. New edition, modern half calf gilt, map and 33 illustrations, scattered spotting. R. F. G. Hollett & Son Africana - 9 2013 £85

Baker, Samuel White *The Albert N'Yanza. Great Basin of the Nile and Explorations of the Nile Sources.* Sidgwick & Jackson, 1962. 2 volumes, original cloth, gilt, dust jackets, numerous maps, illustrations, excellent facsimile. R. F. G. Hollett & Son Africana - 10 2013 £50

Baker, Samuel White *Cyprus; as I Saw It in 1879.* Macmillan, 1879. First edition, 8vo., pages xx, 501, ads, frontispiece, contemporary green full polished calf, light fading at top of lower cover, otherwise fine. J. & S. L. Bonham Antiquarian Booksellers Europe - 9736 2013 £700

Baker, Thomas *The Geometrical Key; or Gate of Equations Unlocked...* printed by J. Playford for R. Clavel, 1684. First edition, 2 tables, 1 folding and 10 folding engraved plates, parallel Latin and English, small 4to., contemporary polished calf, spine gilt with fleuron in each compartment, lettered direct, old paper covering of lettering defective, joints cracked, minor wear, very good. Blackwell's Rare Books Sciences - 11 2013 £850

Bakst, Leon *L'Oeuvre...Pour la Belle au Bois Dormant.* Paris: de Brunoff, 1922. 241/500 copies signed by Bakst and de Brunoff, 54 color printed plates by Leon Bakst, each pasted to cream card, captioned tissue guard present with each plate, 2 smaller color printed plates by Bakst also pasted in on title and contents pages, also with lithographed plate portraying Bakst by Pablo Picasso, plates, folio, original cream wrappers, backstrip and front cover with gilt lettering and typographical designs untrimmed, (original?) tissue jacket with few tears, fine. Blackwell's Rare Books B174 - 165 2013 £1350

Balabanoff, Angelica *My Life as a Rebel.* New York: Harper and Bros., 1938. Fourth US edition, large 8vo., original grey cloth, near fine, inscribed by author. Maggs Bros. Ltd. 1460 - 31 2013 £125

Baldelli, Francesco *Di Polidoro Virgilio Da Vrbino de Gli Invetori Delle Cose, Libri Otto.* In Florenza: per Filippo Givnti, 1692. 4to., rebound by Bernard Middleton in contemporary style full panel English calf, endpapers renewed, first 8 leaves washed, title browned, text foxed in parts, overall very good, clean, crisp copy, Sir Kenelm Digby's copy with his gold signature and signature of John Shipton. James Tait Goodrich 75 - 17 2013 $1495

Baldwin, James *Blues for Mister Charlie: a Play.*   New York: Dial Press, 1964.   First edition, fine in very near fine dust jacket with two short tears on front panel, especially nice copy, usually found well worn.   Between the Covers Rare Books, Inc.   165 - 58   2013 $150

Baldwin, James *The Evidence of Things Not Seen.*   New York: HRW, 1985.   First edition, review copy, signed by author, faint foxing to top edge, else fine in fine, price clipped dust jacket, review slip taped to front endpaper.   Ken Lopez Bookseller   159 - 14   2013 $300

Baldwin, James *The Fire Next Time.*   New York: Dial press, 1963.   First edition, signed by author, owner signature to first blank, small date (Feb. '63) to verso of first blank, also small blindstamps of previous owner to prelims and small sticker removal shadow front flyleaf, none of these things add up to make this less than near fine, in very good dust jacket with minor rubbing and edge wear.   Ken Lopez Bookseller   159 - 12   2013 $300

Baldwin, James *Giovanni's Room.*   New York: Dial Press, 1956-1957.   Second printing, slight wear to boards, very good in fair only dust jacket with chips and wear, warmly inscribed by author, scarce thus.   Between the Covers Rare Books, Inc.   165 - 12   2013 $850

Baldwin, James *Going to Meet the Man.*   New York: Dial Press, 1965.   First edition, fine in fine dust jacket, touch of rubbing, beautiful copy seldom found thus.   Between the Covers Rare Books, Inc.   165 - 13   2013 $400

Baldwin, James *If Beale Street Could Talk.*   New York: Dial Pres, 1974.   First edition, advance review copy with slip laid in, fine in fine dust jacket.   Between the Covers Rare Books, Inc.   165 - 60   2013 $150

Baldwin, James *Jimmy's Blues: Selected Poems.*   London: Michael Joseph Ltd., 1983.   First edition, fine in fine dust jacket.   Between the Covers Rare Books, Inc.   165 - 61   2013 $125

Baldwin, James *One Day When I Was Lost.*   New York: Dial, 1973.   First American edition, signed by author on half title, owner signature to first blank, foxing to edge, otherwise fine in very near fine, price clipped dust jacket.   Ken Lopez Bookseller   159 - 13   2013 $450

Baldwin, James *One Day When I Was Lost...*   New York: Dial Press, 1973.   First American edition, fine in fine dust jacket with two small tears, superior copy, scarce.   Between the Covers Rare Books, Inc.   165 - 59   2013 $175

Baldwin, James *Speeches from Soledad Brothers Rally, Central Hall Westminster 20/4/71.*   London: Friends of Soledad/Notting Hill Press ltd., 1975.   First edition, stapled red printed wrappers, photos, fine.   Between the Covers Rare Books, Inc.   165 - 63   2013 $125

Baldwin, James *Tell Me How Long the Train's Been Gone.*   New York: Dial Press, 1968.   First edition, fine in fine dust jacket, lovely copy, uncommon thus.   Between the Covers Rare Books, Inc.   165 - 14   2013 $300

Baldwin, Roger Sherman *An Examination of the 'Remarks' on Considerations Suggested by the Establishment of a Second College in Connecticut.*   Hartford: Peter B. Gleason, 1825.   First edition, 8vo., 26 pages, sewn as issued, uncut.   M & S Rare Books, Inc.   95 - 81   2013 $200

Baldwin, William Charles *African Hunting and Adventure from Natal to the Zambesi Including Lake Ngamie and Kalahari Deset &c from 1852 to 1860.*   London: Richard Bentley, 1863.   Second edition, modern half calf, gilt with raised bands and spine label, 6 tinted plates by Wolf, frontispiece, folding map, little worn in folds, numerous text figures.   R. F. G. Hollett & Son   Africana - 11   2013   £250

Balfour-Browne, E. M. C. *Solway Tides and Other Tales.*   Dumfries: Robert Dinwiddie, 1928.   First edition, small 8vo., original cloth backed boards, spine little torn at head and foot, pages 188, frontispiece and few line drawings by V. R. Balfour-Browne.   R. F. G. Hollett & Son   Lake District & Cumbria - 62   2013   £30

Ball, James Moore *Andreas Vesalius the Reformer of Anatomy.*   St. Louis: Medical Science Press, 1910.   Frontispiece, portrait, 140 pages, numerous illustrations, tall 4to., original stiff printed wrappers, wrappers worn and chipped along edges, some taping along hinges pages uncut and unopened, spine worn and some of the labeling missing, internally tall uncut copy.   James Tait Goodrich   S74 - 231   2013 $135

Ballance, Charles *Some Points in the Surgery of the Brain and Its Membranes. (with) Essays on the Surgery of the Temporal Bones.*   London: Macmillan, 1907.   xv, 405 pages, illustrations, original cloth worn and rubbed, especially along fore-edges, internally very good, author's presentation with penned note in ink on front flyleaf, for R(obert) B(entley) Todd; xxiv, 223 pages, 75 plates, xiii, (255)-612 pages, 50 plates, partially colored, tall 4to., 2 volumes, original publishers green cloth, recased, new endpapers renewed, cloth bit rubbed, couple of signatures loosening, some marginalia from early owner.   James Tait Goodrich   S74 - 19   2013 $3500

Ballantyne, R. M. *The Gorilla Hunters.* T. Nelson and Sons, 1870. Early edition, original blindstamped green cloth, gilt, hinges rubbed and little frayed, woodcut title and plates, slightly shaken, but very good. R. F. G. Hollett & Son Children's Books - 42 2013 £65

Ballantyne, R. M. *The Gorilla Hunters.* T. Nelson & Sons, 1870. Early edition, original blindstamped green cloth, gilt, hinges rubbed and little frayed, woodcut title and plates, slightly shaken, but very good, early edition. R. F. G. Hollett & Son Africana - 12 2013 £65

Ballantyne, R. M. *The Kitten Pilgrims or Great Battles and Grand Victories.* James Nisbet, n.d circa, 1897. Original pictorial red cloth, gilt, rather soiled, spine little faded, rear panel damped in places, 9 full page illustrations and numerous text drawings, some fingering in places, front joint cracking, scarce. R. F. G. Hollett & Son Children's Books - 43 2013 £75

Ballantyne, R. M. *The Young Fur-Traders: or Snowflakes and Sunbeams from the Far North.* T. Nelson and Sons, 1882. flyleaves browned, scattered foxing, rear joint cracked, later binder's cloth with leather label, little soiled. R. F. G. Hollett & Son Children's Books - 41 2013 £30

Ballard, J. G. *Crash.* New York: Farrar, Straus & Giroux, 1973. First American edition, fine in fine dust jacket with just touch of usual darkening to edges of white jacket. Between the Covers Rare Books, Inc. Sci-Fi, Fantasy & Horror - 306400 2013 $175

Ballard, J. G. *Empire of the Sun.* London: Gollancz, 1984. First edition, signed by author, small owner signature, near fine in very near fine dust jacket with two tiny indents to rear panel, jacket is first issue, with only two comments on rear panel by Graham Greene and Angela Carter, rather thin six. Ken Lopez Bookseller 159 - 15 2013 $500

Ballard, J. G. *Hello America.* New York: Carroll & Graf, 1988. First American edition, fine in fine dust jacket, signed by author. Between the Covers Rare Books, Inc. Sci-Fi, Fantasy & Horror - 306404 2013 $125

Ballard, J. G. *Vermilion Sands.* London: Jonathan Cape, 1971. First hardcover edition, fine in fine dust jacket, bright, beautiful copy. Between the Covers Rare Books, Inc. Sci-Fi, Fantasy & Horror - 291404 2013 $600

Ballou, Adin *Liberty Chimes.* Providence: Ladies' Anti-Slavery Society, 1845. First edition, 12mo., contemporary boards, rebacked. M & S Rare Books, Inc. 95 - 13 2013 $225

Balzac, Honore De *L'Oeuvre de Balzac...* Le Club Francais du Livre, 1966. 8vo., 16 volumes, original gilt limp morocco with author's name reading across the top of the spines in gilt when volumes are in correct order, some slight rubbing. Ken Spelman Books Ltd. 75 - 184 2013 £120

Bancroft, Hubert Howe 1832-1918 *California Pastoral 1769-1848.* San Francisco: History Company, 1888. First edition, 808 pages, publisher's maroon cloth, gilt lettered spine, slight rubbing to extremities, minor half inch stain to extreme fore-edge of first five leaves, but fine, tight copy, clean. Argonaut Book Shop Summer 2013 - 9 2013 $150

Bancroft, Hubert Howe 1832-1918 *History of Alaska 1730-1885.* San Francisco: 1885. 775 pages, folding map, rebound in sturdy cloth, library stamps, dampstain on bottom and fore edge but no adhesion, good usable copy. Dumont Maps & Books of the West 125 - 40 2013 $50

Bancroft, Hubert Howe 1832-1918 *History of the Life of Leland Stanford: a Character Study.* Oakland: Biobooks, 1952. First edition, one of 750 copies, portraits, half red leatherette, red cloth sides, spine lettered in silver, upper portion of front board lightly faded, else fine. Argonaut Book Shop Recent Acquisitions June 2013 - 19 2013 $75

Bancroft, Hubert Howe 1832-1918 *The Zamorano Index to History of California.* Los Angeles: University of Southern California, 1985. First edition, 2 volumes, 8vo., gray cloth with gilt lettered spines. By the Book, L. C. 36 - 62 2013 $200

Bancroft, Laura *Prince Mud Turtle.* Chicago: Reilly & Britton, 1906. First edition, 8vo., pictorial cloth, 61 pages, slightest bit of edge soil, else fine, rare, illustrations in color by Maginel Wright Enright. Aleph-Bet Books, Inc. 105 - 70 2013 $875

The Bank Case. A Report in the Cases of the Bank of South Carolina and the Bank of Charleston Upon Scire Facias to Vacate with the Final Agrument and Determination Thereof in the Court for the Correction and Errors of South Carolina, in the Years 1842 and 1843. Charleston: W. Riley, Nov., 1844. First edition, large 8vo., full contemporary sheep, leather label on spine, light foxing, very good, inscribed in ink "Hon. A. P. Butler//with respects of the Atty. Genl./Jan. 1845", beneath that signed in ink "M. C. Butler 1857". M & S Rare Books, Inc. 95 - 350 2013 $1500

Bank, Ted *Birthplace of the Winds.* Robert Hale, 1957. First edition, original cloth, gilt, dust jacket trifle worn, 25 illustrations. R. F. G. Hollett & Son Polar Exploration - 1 2013 £30

Banks, A. G. *H. W. Schneider of Barrow and Bowness.* Kendal: Titus Wilson, 1984. First edition, original cloth, gilt, dust jacket, price clipped, lower panel little defective, 45 illustrations, 5 maps.   R. F. G. Hollett & Son   Lake District & Cumbria - 63   2013   £30

Banks, Iain *Against a Dark Background.* Orbit, 1993. First edition, 8vo., original black boards, backstrip blocked in silver, dust jacket, fine, inscribed by author.   Blackwell's Rare Books   B174 - 166   2013   £80

Banks, Iain *The Bridge.* London: Macmillan, 1986. First edition, octavo, boards.   L. W. Currey, Inc.   Fall Sampler Sept. 2013 - 146440   2013 $250

Banks, Iain *The Player of Games.* London: Macmillan, 1988. First edition, octavo, boards. L. W. Currey, Inc.   Fall Sampler Sept. 2013 - 145402   2013 $250

Banks, Lynne Reid *The L-Shaped Room.* London: Chatto & Windus, 1960. First edition, 8vo., original blue green cloth, dust jacket, inscribed by author, fine in price clipped dust jacket, slightly marked at head of spine.   Maggs Bros. Ltd.   1460 - 32   2013   £250

Banks, W., & Son *Views of the English Lakes.* Windermere: J. Garnett, n.d., Oblong 8vo., original brown cloth gilt over bevelled boards, extremities trifle frayed, all edges gilt, wood engraved title and 26 tissue guarded engraved vignettes by Banks of Edinburgh, nice, clean set, plates printed on heavy paper.   R. F. G. Hollett & Son   Lake District & Cumbria - 64   2013   £175

Bannerman, Helen *Jumbo Sambo.* Philadelphia: Stokes, various dates, 1942. First edition, 8vo., cloth, fine in very good dust jacket frayed at spine ends, original color lithos, very scarce.   Aleph-Bet Books, Inc.   104 - 46   2013 $750

Bannerman, Helen *The Story of Little Black Mingo.* New York: Frederick A Stokes, 1902. First American edition, 18mo., 142 pages, printed on facing pages, extensively illustrated in color with frontispiece, original cloth backed decorated paper covered boards, several hinges neatly reinforced with small strips of paper, most of paper off back cover, somewhat shaken but complete.   M & S Rare Books, Inc.   95 - 178   2013 $350

Bannerman, Helen *The Story of Little Black Quibba.* New York: Stokes Sept., 1903. First US edition, 16mo., cloth backed pictorial boards, edges rubbed and light finger soil, else clean, tight, full color illustrations.   Aleph-Bet Books, Inc.   104 - 47   2013 $850

Bannerman, Helen *The Story of Little Black Sambo.* London: Grant Richards, 1899. First edition, 16mo., green cloth, very good, 27 full page illustrations, original pale green cloth lettered and stamped in dark green with ruled borders and vertical stripes, minor rubbing to cloth and some very light internal spotting, very small (approximately 2mm.) marginal chip to page 11, not affecting text, housed in green full morocco clamshell case with gilt lettering on spine, very scarce.   Barnaby Rudge Booksellers   Children 2013 - 201043   2013 $4650

Bannerman, Helen *The Story of Little Black Sambo.* New York: Frederick A. Stokes, n.d. circa, 1901. 16mo., gold cloth spine, pictorial covers lettered in black, oval pictorial paste-on, fine in original dust jacket printed in green (frayed, small pieces off corners), printed on one side of paper with each page of text facing a full page color illustration, exceedingly rare in dust jacket.   Aleph-Bet Books, Inc.   105 - 50   2013 $1400

Bannerman, Helen *The Little Black Sambo Story Book.* New York: Platt & Munk, 1935. 4to., blue pictorial cloth, fine in frayed dust jacket, illustrations in color.   Aleph-Bet Books, Inc. 105 - 52   2013 $450

Bannerman, Helen *Little Black Sambo.*   N.P.: Duenewald Printing Corporation, 1949. Reprint, plastic comb has been replaced with ties, paper covered boards, with four animation, corners bumped, tables on animations thumbed but intact, all animations in working order, else very good or better.   Between the Covers Rare Books, Inc.   165 - 105   2013 $150

Bannerman, Helen *Story of Little White Squibba.* London: Chatto & Windus, 1966. First edition, 16mo., pictorial boards, 64 pages, fine in dust jacket, illustrations by author.   Aleph-Bet Books, Inc.   105 - 51   2013 $200

Bannister, Saxe *Some Revelations in Irish History of Old Elements of Creed and Class Conciliation in Ireland.*   New York: 1970. Reprint, 8vo., cloth, very good.   C. P. Hyland 261 - 780   2013   £45

Banta, N. Moore *The Brownie Primer.* Chicago: Flanagan, 1905. 8vo. pictorial cloth, 98 pages, some finger soil on covers and margins else very good, charming color illustrations by Alpha Banta Benson.   Aleph-Bet Books, Inc.   105 - 155   2013 $200

Banville, John *The Book of Evidence.* London: Secker & Warburg, 1989. First edition, 8vo., original black cloth, dust jacket, fine, pasted on front free endpaper is cream printed book label "The Sunday Times presents 1989 Booker Prize Shortlist Signed Editions. The Book of Evidence by John Banville, Secker & Warburg" signed by author below this.   Maggs Bros. Ltd. 1442 - 2   2013   £60

Banville, John *Conversation in the Mountains.* Loughcrew: The Gallery Press, 2008. Limited to 400 numbered copies printed on Rives Artist and signed by author, large 8vo., original brown linen opaque acetate dust jacket, fine in dust jacket.   Maggs Bros. Ltd.   1442 - 7   2013   £100

Banville, John *First Light.* London: Bridgewater Press, 2006. One of 26 lettered copies, 8vo., original quarter pale green cloth, marbled paper boards, lettered gilt on spine, fine.   Maggs Bros. Ltd.   1442 - 6   2013   £175

Banville, John *Love in the Wars.* Loughcrew: Gallery Press, 2005. One of approximately 300 copies, 8vo., original black cloth, dust jacket, fine.   Maggs Bros. Ltd.   1442 - 3   2013   £50

Banville, John *The Sea.* Oxford: Joe McCann, 2005. One of 46 numbered copies signed by author, 40 only for sale, from total edition of 56 (48 copies only for sale), 8vo., original blue Ratchford cloth, letterpress printed moulmade paper labels by the Evergreen Press, sewn by hand and bound by Fine Bindery, fine in clear acetate dust jacket.   Maggs Bros. Ltd.   1442 - 5   2013   £250

Banville, John *The Sea.* London: Picador, 2005. First edition, original blue cloth, dust jacket, signed by author, fine dust jacket.   Maggs Bros. Ltd.   1442 - 4   2013   £75

Baraka, Amiri Imamu *Afrikan Revolution: a Poems.* Newark: Jihad Pub. Co., 1969. First edition, 24mo., stapled wrappers, fine, signed by author.   Between the Covers Rare Books, Inc.   165 - 69   2013 $150

Baraka, Amiri Imamu *Bumpy: a Bopera.* Newark: Amiri Baraka, 1987. First edition (or typescript), five leaves, photo mechanically reproduced on rectos only, stapled in upper left hand corner, little toning and spotting on first leaf, else fine, housed in blue folder with "Bumpy" hand lettered on front cover by author in green marker, signed by author and dated 1995.   Between the Covers Rare Books, Inc.   165 - 16   2013 $4500

Baraka, Amiri Imamu *The Dead Lecturer.* New York: Grove Press, 1964. First edition, fine in near fine dust jacket with some slight indentations from writing on front panel, scarce in this condition.   Between the Covers Rare Books, Inc.   165 - 65   2013 $85

Baraka, Amiri Imamu *The Dutchman and the Slave.* New York: William Morrow, 1964. First edition, fine in fine dust jacket with "Off Broadway Winner Award" sticker, publisher's card laid in.   Between the Covers Rare Books, Inc.   165 - 67   2013 $200

Baraka, Amiri Imamu *Four Black Revolutionary Plays.* Indianapolis: Bobbs Merrill, 1969. First edition, about fine in rubbed, very good or better dust jacket, scarce hardcover issue.   Between the Covers Rare Books, Inc.   165 - 68   2013 $125

Baraka, Amiri Imamu *Preface to a Twenty Volume Suicide Note...* New York: Totem/Corinth, 1961. First edition, first issue, stapled decorated wrappers, English price sticker on front wrapper, else fine.   Between the Covers Rare Books, Inc.   165 - 64   2013 $125

Baraka, Amiri Imamu *The System of Dante's Hell.* New York: Grove Press, 1965. First edition, fine in fine dust jacket, beautiful copy.   Between the Covers Rare Books, Inc.   165 - 66   2013 $85

Baraka, Amiri Imamu *Transbluesency: the Selected Poems of... 1961-1995.* New York: Marsilio Pub., 1995. Uncorrected proof, printed wrappers, fine.   Between the Covers Rare Books, Inc.   165 - 70   2013 $100

Barba, Alvaro Alondo *The Second Book of the Art of Mettals; Wherein is Taught the Common Way of Refining Silver by Quicksilver with some New Rules Added for the Better Performance of the Same.* London: S. Mearne, 1674. First English edition, 12mo., plate, recently bound in brown quarter calf.   J. & S. L. Bonham Antiquarian Booksellers   Europe - 8229   2013   £390

Barbauld, Anna Laetitia 1743-1825 *Works.* London: Longman &c, 1825. First edition, 2 volumes, frontispiece volume I slightly spotted, contemporary half maroon calf largely faded to brown, spines lettered and with compartments in gilt, slight rubbing to corners and heads & tails of spines, signatures of Sarah Frances Talbot, 1840, good plus tight copy.   Jarndyce Antiquarian Booksellers   CCIII - 636   2013   £180

Barber, John B. *Lakeland Passes.* Ulverston: James Atkinson, n.d., 1927. First edition, original pictorial wrappers, 56 pages, 12 illustrations.   R. F. G. Hollett & Son   Lake District & Cumbria - 65   2013   £25

Barber, Samuel *Beneath Helvellyn's Shade.* London: Elliot Stock, 1892. First edition, original pictorial red cloth gilt, spine and edges rather faded, scarce, colored lithograph folding plan loosely inserted.   R. F. G. Hollett & Son   Lake District & Cumbria - 66   2013   £85

Barber, Thomas *Picturesque Illustrations of the Isle of Wight.* London: Simpkin & Marshall, n.d., 1835. First edition, 8vo., pages 110, folding map, 40 plates, some occasional foxing, 19th century half calf, spine lightly rubbed, small waterstain top corner titlepage.   J. & S. L. Bonham Antiquarian Booksellers   Europe - 9608   2013   £200

Barber, Thomas Gerrard *Byron and Where He is Buried.* Hucknall: Henry Morley & Sons, 1939. First edition, half title, frontispiece, plates, unopened in original red cloth, very good, signed by author.   Jarndyce Antiquarian Booksellers CCIII - 344   2013   £25

Barbier, Antoine Alexandre *Dictionnaire des Ouvrages Anonymes.* Mansfield Centre: Martino Pub., 1999. 5 volumes bound in 4, publisher's gray buckram titling in gilt on spine, new, 3 volumes still in publisher's wrapping.   Phillip J. Pirages   63 - 389   2013 $275

Barbusse, Henri *Le Feu.* Paris: Ernest Flammarion, n.d. circa, 1920. Three hundred and twentieth thousand, 8vo., modern quarter brown morocco, original wrappers bound in, inscribed by author for Friderike Maria Winternitz Zweig, excellent copy, original wrappers lightly soiled, rubbing to head and tail of spine, pages browned, last few pages stamped through in bottom corner, not affecting foot.   Maggs Bros. Ltd.   1460 - 33   2013   £1000

Barcia, Jose Fernandez *Andanzas.* Gijon: Imp. El Noroeste, 1924. First edition, warmly inscribed by author for Enrique Naranjo in pencil, small 8vo., paper wrappers, spine creased, front wrapper soiled, small tear to bottom edge, chip to top corner, owner's rubber stamp, fore-edge curled, corners dog eared in first dozen leaves, otherwise contents very good.   Kaaterskill Books   16 - 78   2013 $450

Barcia, Jose Fernandez *Sonatina Gijonesa.* Madrid: Talleres Espasa Calpe, 1929. First edition, small 8vo., paper wrappers worn, small chips to edges, some minor sunning, spine cocked, still very good, very scare, inscribed by author to Enrique Naranjo.   Kaaterskill Books   16 - 79   2013 $500

Barckley, Richard *A Discourse of the Felicitie of Man or His Summum Bonum.* London: William Ponsonby, 1598. First edition, small quarto, woodcut device on leaf facing title and on final leaf, old worn and mottled calf, rebacked and restored, later endpapers, morocco lettering piece, spine bit rubbed, tiny wormhole at gutter near center, neat marginal ink annotations, occasional pencil notes or underlining, bookplate of A. E. Housman, 19th century signatures to recto of first leaf, rare.   Heritage Book Shop   50th Anniversary Catalogue - 6   2013 $10,000

Barclay, John *Argenis.* Leiden: ex officina Elzeviriana, 1630. 24mo., printing flaw on one leaf affecting couple of characters (a strand of hair having stuck to the page 629), first and last pages with slight loss from inside margins (from adherence to endpapers), otherwise just touch of light spotting, later vellum boards, red morocco labels to spine, somewhat soiled.   Unsworths Antiquarian Booksellers   28 - 71   2013   £125

Barclay, Robert *Theologiae Vere Christianae Apologia.* Amsterdam: Jacob Claus for Benjamin Clark, London, Isaac van Neer (Rotterdam) and Heinrich Betkey (Frankfurt, 1676. First edition, rare, 4to., contemporary sprinkled calf blind fillet around covers and run twice along spine, gilt sawtooth roll on board edges, spine with gilt fillet above and bellow each cord, old paper ms. title label, hinges split but held securely by cords, corners bumped and tips worn through, spine with very faint white-ish cast internally slight dampstain at top margin, some slight, sporadic foxing and browning, edges of endpapers discolored from leather turn-ins, very good.   Joseph J. Felcone Inc.   Books Printed before 1701 - 8   2013 $8000

Bardin, John Franklin *The Case Against Butterfly.* New York: Scribners, 1951. First edition, fine in dust jacket. Mordida Books   81 - 21   2013 $85

Bardon, Jonathan *A History of Ulster.* Belfast: Blackstaff Press, 1992. Number 154 of 250 numbered copies signed by author, large 8vo., original green cloth, lettered gilt on spine, color plate illustration blocked on to upper cover, fine in matching slipcase.   Maggs Bros. Ltd.   1442 - 10   2013 £150

Bardwell, Thomas *The Practice of Painting and Perspective Made Easy.* printed by S. Richardson, for the author, and sold by him... and by A. Millar... R. and J. Dodsley... and J. and J. Rivington, 1756. First edition, 6 engraved plates, author's bold signature on title verso as guarantee of authenticity, few ink corrections to text (in author's hand?), few light marginal stains, modern half calf, good.   Blackwell's Rare Books   172 - 18   2013   £950

Baretti, Joseph   1719-1789 *A Journey from London to Genoa.* London: T. Davies, 1770. First edition, 4 volumes in 2, volume I waterstained in margins, full brown contemporary calf, joints cracked, spines and corners rubbed, some light scuffing, new labels, light browning to prelims.   J. & S. L. Bonham Antiquarian Booksellers   Europe - 8522   2013 £550

Barham, Richard Harris   1788-1845 *The Ingoldsby Legends or Mirth & Marvels.* London: J. M. Dent & Co., 1898. First Rackham edition, 200 x 137mm., frontispiece, titlepage with green ornamental border, numerous black and white illustrations and 13 color plates, all by Arthur Rackham, very attractive contemporary Arts & Crafts style binding of russet Niger goatskin, lavishly gilt, covers with central panel of gilt ruled squares within wide frame of flowers and foliage, raised bands, spine compartments densely gilt with tooling repeating cover frame design, gilt turn-ins, top edge gilt, other edges gilded on the rough, slight and even darkening to spine, covers with minor soiling, title and frontispiece rather foxed, text with hint of browning at edges, very attractive copy, animated gilt of binding still bright, leather with only insignificant wear, text almost entirely bright, clean and fresh.   Phillip J. Pirages   61 - 99   2013 $1500

Baring-Gould, William S. *The Annotated Mother Goose.* New York: Bramhall House, 1962. 4to., original cloth backed boards, dust jacket, pages 349, illustrations, historical woodcuts.   R. F. G. Hollett & Son   Children's Books - 45   2013   £30

Baring, Maurice *Forget-me-Not and Lily of the Valley.* Dublin: Campio Press, 1960. First edition, large 8vo., original green cloth, pictorial onlay, dust jacket little stained, long vertical closed tear repaired on reverse, text printed in blue, color text illustrations.   R. F. G. Hollett & Son   Children's Books - 44   2013   £65

Baring, Maurice *Selected Poems.* London: Heinemann, 1930. First edition, 8vo., excellent copy, original green cloth, inscribed by author for Elisabeth Bergner.   Maggs Bros. Ltd.   1460 - 35   2013   £125

Baring, Maurice *Tinker's Leave.* London: Heinemann, 1927. First edition, large 8vo., original brown cloth dust jacket, very good, jacket spine browned and chipped at head and tail, inscribed by author for James Agate 1948 August 19.   Maggs Bros. Ltd.   1460 - 34   2013   £175

Barker, Cicely Mary *Flower Songs of the Seasons with Music.* New York: Dodge Pub., 1930. First American edition, 4to., 12 tipped in color plates, Christmas inscription dated 1932 verso of frontispiece with card tipped in, grey cloth, very good.   Barnaby Rudge Booksellers   Children 2013 - 019362   2013 $85

Barker, Cicely Mary *Summer Songs with Music...* Blackie & Son, n.d., 1927. Large 8vo., original cloth backed boards, pictorial onlay, corners little bruised, unpaginated, 12 tipped in plates, flyleaves lightly spotted, pencilled list of flowers, otherwise very good.   R. F. G. Hollett & Son   Children's Books - 46   2013   £80

Barker, Cicely Mary *Summer Songs with Music.* London: Blackie & Son, 1929. 4to., 12 tipped in color plates, green cloth backed boards, very good, illustrations by Cicely Mary Barker.   Barnaby Rudge Booksellers   Children 2013 - 021427   2013 $95

Barker, Clive *Cabal.* New York: Poseidon Press, 1988. Uncorrected proof of the first American edition, lightly faded spine and small crease in bottom front corner, else fine in wrappers.   Between the Covers Rare Books, Inc.   Sci-Fi, Fantasy & Horror - 309705   2013 $100

Barker, George *At Thurgarton Church. A Poem with Drawings.* London: Trigram Press, 1969. First edition, number 61 of 100 copies signed by author, 8vo., original burgundy buckram, fine.   Maggs Bros. Ltd.   1460 - 37   2013   £50

Barker, George *Calamiterror.* London: Faber and Faber, 1937. First edition, 8vo., original green cloth, dust jacket, near fine in slightly rubbed dust jacket, small closed tear at head of spine, inscribed by author for Jerry Rowe.   Maggs Bros. Ltd.   1460 - 36   2013   £50

Barker, George *Dreams of a Summer Night.* London: Faber and Faber, 1966. First edition, very near fine in very good plus dust jacket with small tear and bit of wear to top of spine, signed and inscribed by Barker on titlepage, uncommon thus.   Jeff Hirsch Books   Fall 2013 - 129161   2013 $65

Barker, George *In Memory of David Archer.* London: Faber and Faber, 1973. First edition, 8vo., original black cloth, dust jacket, inscribed by author, fine.   Maggs Bros. Ltd.   1460 - 38   2013   £50

Barker, Lewellyns F. *A Case of Circumscribed Unilateral and Elective Sensory Paralysis.* Baltimore: Phys. Lab. at University of Leipzig, 1896. First edition, 8vo., original printed wrappers, very good.   James Tait Goodrich   S74 - 20   2013 $495

Barkhouse, Joyce *The Lorenzen Collection.* Halifax: Ventures Ltd., 1985. 222 x 16cm., color illustrated card covers, 40 color plates, very good.   Schooner Books Ltd.   102 - 41   2013 $95

Barkly, Fanny Alexandra *Among Boers and Basutos. The Story of Our Life on the Frontier.* London: Remington, 1894. Second edition, original olive brown cloth, blocked to black, lettered gilt, very good.   Jarndyce Antiquarian Booksellers   CCV - 17   2013   £150

Barlow, James *One Half of the World.* London: Cassell & Co., 1957. First edition, octavo, boards.   L. W. Currey, Inc.   Uptopian Literature: Recent Acquisitions (April 2013) - 139856   2013 $150

Barlow, Leila Mae *Across the Years: Memoirs.* Montgomery: Paragon Press, 1959. First edition, 84 pages, presentation stamp from author's daughter on front fly, else fine in fine dust jacket, very scarce.   Between the Covers Rare Books, Inc.   165 - 72   2013 $225

Barnard, George *The Theory and Practice of Landscape Painting in Water Colours.* London: William S. Orr, 1855. Large 8vo., 26 plates, 43 woodcuts, index, occasional light foxing, especially verso plates, decorative blindstamped brown cloth, gilt stamped front cover and spine extremities lightly worn, rare hinge cracked, bookplate of Agness A. Parkin, titlepage signature of John Dawson, very good. Jeff Weber Rare Books   171 - 12   2013 $200

Barnard, M. R. *Sport in Norway and Where to Find It, Together with a Short Account of the Vegetable Productions of the Country.* London: Chapman & Hall, 1864. First edition, 8vo., pages xvi, 334, ads, frontispiece, stains on both covers. J. & S. L. Bonham Antiquarian Booksellers Europe - 8346   2013   £100

Barnes, Arthur K. *Interplanetary Hunter.* New York: Gnome Press, 1956. First edition, pages toned, else fine in fine dust jacket, with small price sticker on front panel, bright. Between the Covers Rare Books, Inc. Sci-Fi, Fantasy & Horror - 3020255   2013 $65

Barnes, Djuna *The Book of Repulsive Women * Rhymes and 5 Drawings.* New York: Guido Bruno, 1915. First edition, 4to., original printed orange wrappers, stapled as issued, (24) pages, unopened, wrappers little dust soiled, fine. The Brick Row Book Shop   Miscellany Fifty-Nine - 6   2013 $750

Barnes, F. *Barrow and District.* Barrow-in-Furness: Barrow Printing Co., 1978. Second edition, original pictorial wrappers, pages 126, illustrations. R. F. G. Hollett & Son   Lake District & Cumbria - 67   2013   £25

Barnes, F. *Handlist of Newspapers Published in Cumberland, Westmorland, and North Lancashire.* Kendal: Titus Wilson, 1951. Original wrappers, 16 page, loosely inserted is Wilson's "Key Days in History of Newspapers in Cumbria", 8 pages, folded and stapled. R. F. G. Hollett & Son   Lake District & Cumbria - 68   2013   £25

Barnes, Julian *Before She Met Me.* London: Jonathan Cape, 1982. First edition, signed by author, fine in fine dust jacket. Ed Smith Books   78 - 4   2013 $150

Barnes, Julian *Flaubert's Parrot.* London: Cape, 1984. First edition, 8vo., original pale green boards, with tail corners just trifle bumped, backstrip gilt lettered, dust jacket, near fine. Blackwell's Rare Books   B174 - 167   2013   £200

Barnes, Julian *Flaubert's Parrot.* New York: Knopf, 1985. First American edition, fine in fine dust jacket. Ed Smith Books   78 - 5   2013 $100

Barnes, Julian *The Lemon Table.* London: Jonathan Cape, 2004. First edition, 8vo., original brown cloth, dust jacket, inscribed by author for Beryl Bainbridge, fine in dust jacket. Maggs Bros. Ltd.   1460 - 39   2013   £150

Barnes, Julian *Metroland.* London: Jonathan Cape, 1980. First edition, signed by author in 1985, fine in fine dust jacket with wraparound band announcing title as winner of Somerset Maugham Award laid in, nice, copy, uncommon signed. Ken Lopez Bookseller   159 - 16   2013 $475

Barnes, William *The Settlement and Early History of Albany.* Albany: J. Munsell, 1864. First edition, contemporary quarter calf and marbled paper covered boards, contemporary ownership signature, spine chipped at crown, erosion and wear to spine, front fly detached, but present, old library mark on rear pastedown, tight, good copy. Between the Covers Rare Books, Inc.   New York City - 292451   2013 $65

Barnum, H. I. *The American Farrier; Containing a Minute Account of the Formation of Every Part of the Horse...* Philadelphia: Uriah Hunt, 1832. First edition, frontispiece, illustration, full contemporary calf with brown morocco spine label, front joint split, edgewear, some loss at foot, good copy only. Between the Covers Rare Books, Inc.   Horses, Horsemanship, Horse Racing, Etc. - 288578   2013 $300

Baron, Peter *The Round Table Murders.* New York: Macaulay, 1931. First American edition, fine in fine dust jacket with very slight wear at extremities, superb copy. Between the Covers Rare Books, Inc.   Mystery & Detective Fiction - 465793   2013 $315

Baron, Stanley *Brewed in America. The History of Beer and Ale in the United States.* Boston: Little Brown, 1962. First edition, numerous photos and reproductions throughout, brown cloth, very fine with very good dust jacket. Argonaut Book Shop   Summer 2013 - 10   2013 $60

Barrett, Joseph O. *History of Old Abe the Live War Eagle of the Eighth Regiment Wisconsin Volunteers.* Chicago: Alfred L. Sewell, 1865. First edition, 8vo., 71 pages, map and 2 colored plates, original printed wrappers, spine chipped. M & S Rare Books, Inc.   95 - 65   2013 $300

Barrett, Marvin *The Jazz Age.* New York: G. P. Putnam's Sons, 1959. First edition, quarto, picture edition, boards bit soiled, good or better, without dust jacket, Ralph Ellison's copy with his ownership signature. Between the Covers Rare Books, Inc.   165 - 322   2013 $500

Barrett, Walter *The Old Merchants of New York City.* New York: Carleton, 1863. First edition, publisher's brown cloth titled gilt, bookplate, small tear at crown, gilt little tarnished, still nice, near fine, scarce. Between the Covers Rare Books, Inc.   New York City - 294009   2013 $150

Barrie, James Matthew 1860-1937 *The Admirable Crichton.* London: Hodder & Stoughton, n.d., 1914. First edition, large thick 4to., red cloth with elaborate gilt pictorial cover nearly as new, 20 beautiful tipped in color plates with pictorial, lettered guards plus few line illustrations by Hugh Thomson, ornate binding pristine. Aleph-Bet Books, Inc.   104 - 554 2013 $300

Barrie, James Matthew 1860-1937 *Courage.* London: Hodder and Stoughton, 1922.   First edition, large 8vo., original cream cloth, covers rubbed, rear endpaper damaged, otherwise very good, inscribed by author to J. Wallett Waller.   Maggs Bros. Ltd.   1460 - 42   2013   £250

Barrie, James Matthew 1860-1937 *The Little White Bird.* London: Hodder and Stoughton, 1902.   First edition, 8vo., original black cloth, excellent copy, some foxing to page edges and endpapers, spine lightly faded, inscribed by author for Addison Bright.   Maggs Bros. Ltd.   1460 - 41   2013   £450

Barrie, James Matthew 1860-1937 *Peter Pan in Kensington Gardens.* New York: Scribner, Dec., 1906.   First American edition, 126 pages, mint, large 4to., green gilt pictorial cloth, 50 magnificent color plates by Arthur Rackham with tissue guards, black and white drawing on title, beautiful copy.   Aleph-Bet Books, Inc.   104 - 473   2013 $1500

Barrie, James Matthew 1860-1937 *Peter and Wendy.* New York: Scribners, 1911.   First US edition, 8vo., green gilt pictorial cloth, fine+ in nice dust jacket (archvial repair at folds, small chip at at top of spine), 12 beautifully detailed black and white plates and pictorial titlepage, beautiful copy, rare in dust jacket.   Aleph-Bet Books, Inc.   105 - 55   2013 $3500

Barrie, James Matthew 1860-1937 *Peter Pan in Kensington Gardens.* London: Hodder & Stoughton, n.d., 1912.   Deluxe edition, one of 50 (?) copies, large quarto, 50 mounted color plates by Arthur Rackham, finely bound by Zaehnsdorf in full red morocco pictorially stamped and lettered gilt to match, original 1906 cover stamping, excellent.   David Brass Rare Books, Inc.   Holiday 2012 Chapter One - Db 00581   2013 $3800

Barrie, James Matthew 1860-1937 *Peter Pan I Wendy.* Barcelona: Editorial Joventut, n.d. circa, 1930.   Oblong 4to., pictorial board panels folded accordion style, some cover soil, very good+, each side of the 12 panels illustrated in color by A. Salo, 3 tab operated moveable pages, rare.   Aleph-Bet Books, Inc.   104 - 48   2013 $1200

Barrie, James Matthew 1860-1937 *Quality Street.* London: Hodder & Stoughton, 1913.   One of 1000 numbered copies, one of 1000 numbered copies, 4to., 198 pages, 22 plates, signed by artist, Hugh Thomson, full vellum boards, stamped in gilt, boards little warped, otherwise fine.   Second Life Books Inc.   183 - 17   2013 $450

Barrie, James Matthew 1860-1937 *Tommy and Grizel.* London: Cassell, 1900.   First edition, 8vo., original blue cloth, inscribed by author for Addison Bright Nov. 1 1900, excellent copy, some light foxing, spine lightly faded.   Maggs Bros. Ltd.   1460 - 40   2013   £450

Barrow Naturalists' Field Club *Annual Report and Proceedings. third Year volume 3.*   Barrow: Barrow Times, 1879.   Original pink wrappers.   R. F. G. Hollett & Son   Lake District & Cumbria - 75   2013   £40

Barrow Naturalists' Field Club *Annual Report and Proceedings. For 24th and 25th Years ended 25th March 1901.*   Barrow: J. Milner, 1901.   Original wrappers, rather chipped, 130 page, illustrations.   R. F. G. Hollett & Son   Lake District & Cumbria - 76   2013   £25

Barrow Naturalists' Field Club *Annual Reports and Proceedings for the 27th and 28th Years ended 25th March 1904. Volume XVII.*   Barrow: News and Mail, 1909.   Modern cloth gilt, pages 288, numerous illustrations, folding plans.   R. F. G. Hollett & Son   Lake District & Cumbria - 83   2013   £75

Barrow Naturalists' Field Club *Annual Report and Proceedings. for 29th and 30th Years ended 25th March 1906.*   Barrow: Barrow News and Mail, 1907.   Original wrappers, corners chipped and worn, spine faded, illustrations, scattered spotting.   R. F. G. Hollett & Son   Lake District & Cumbria - 77   2013   £35

Barrow Naturalists' Field Club *Annual Report and Proceedings for 31st-34th Years ended 25th March 1910.* Barrow: Barrow News and Mail, 1913.   Original wrappers, edges chipped and worn, pages 158, illustrations.   R. F. G. Hollett & Son   Lake District & Cumbria - 78   2013   £35

Barrow Naturalists' Field Club and Photographic Society *Proceedings for the 76th to the 80th years ended 31st March 1956. Volume VIII new series.*   1956.   4 plates, original wrappers, staples little rusted.   R. F. G. Hollett & Son   Lake District & Cumbria - 73   2013   £25

Barrow, John 1764-1848 *Mountain Ascents in Cumberland and Westmorland.* London: Sampson Low, 1886.   First edition, modern cloth gilt, woodcut frontispiece, little soiled, stained on reverse, 15 woodcut text illustrations and folding map, some foxing and fingering, few annotations and one deletion, sound, scarce.   R. F. G. Hollett & Son   Lake District & Cumbria - 71   2013   £150

Barrow, John 1764-1848 *A Tour Round Ireland through the Sea-Cast Counties in the Autumn of 1835.*   1835.   First edition, 7 plates (discolored, 3 misplaced), 2 maps, 8vo., modern cloth.   C. P. Hyland   261 - 20   2013   £250

Barrow, S. *A Popular Dictionary of fact and Knowledge for the Use of Schools and Students.*   Poole and Edwards, 1827.   Original green roan gilt, rather rubbed and scraped, text woodcuts, 1 or 2 illustrations with added hand coloring, scattered foxing or browning.   R. F. G. Hollett & Son   Children's Books - 47   2013   £45

Barry, P. *By Bride and Blackwater: Poems, Stories...* Lee Press, 1944. 168 pages, wrappers repaired, piece torn from top of titlepage and damage to margins on 3 leaves but no text loss, good.   C. P. Hyland   261 - 22   2013   £35

Barry, P. *Thye Cork Accent.* N.P.: n.p., n.d. circa, 1950. 8vo., 179 pages, wrappers, good.   C. P. Hyland   261 - 25   2013   £35

Barry, Sebastian *The Pinkening Boy.* Oxford: Joel McCann, 2004. First edition, limited to 65 copies signed by author, from a total edition of 85, 8vo., original brown cloth, printed paper labels on spine and upper cover, blue endpapers, hand bound by Fine Bindery in Northamptonshire, fine in clear acetate dust jacket.   Maggs Bros. Ltd.   1442 - 8   2013   £50

Barry, Sebastian *Tales of Ballycumber.* First edition, limited to 40 copies signed by author, from a total edition of 52, 8vo., original green cloth, 150gsm archival paper with paper labels on spine and upper cover with red endpapers reproducing the author's drawing of the stage design for the play, hand bound by Fine Book Bindery.   Maggs Bros. Ltd.   1442 - 9   2013   £75

Barry, Sebastian *Tales of Ballycumber.* Oxford: Four Candles Press, 2009. First edition, 10/40 copies of an edition of 52 copies, signed author, foolscap 8vo., original lime green linen, printed backstrip and front cover labels inset, endpapers reproduce the author's original sketch for a stage set in the play, glassine dust jacket, fine.   Blackwell's Rare Books   B174 - 168   2013   £55

Barry, Tom *Guerilla Days in Ireland.* Mercier, 1955. Octavo, 223 pages, illustrations, maps, dust jacket, very good.   C. P. Hyland   261 - 26   2013   £35

Barske, Charlotte *King Cotton.* Poughkeepsie: Artists and Writers Guild, 1938. folio, pictorial wrappers, covers frayed on edges, else very good, color lithos by George Wright, in rear of book are 2 sheets of 18 smaller photos, reader is instructed to build a small theater and to use the pictures as a movie.   Aleph-Bet Books, Inc.   104 - 75   2013 $150

Bart, Harriet *Rondo Library. A Miscellany of Visual Poetry.* St. Paul: Mnemnonic Press and Hermetic Press, 2006. Artist's book, one of 40 copies, each signed and numbered by artist, text on 175 gsm Somerset paper, page size single sheet 24 1/8 x 38 5/8 inches, folded 4 times lengthwise resulting in 6 pages, each about 6 1'2 inches wide, silver gilt paper that is cover weight Stardream Apollo silver, printed in black on front and back panels, text sheet affixed to inside front cover, loose at end so that it pulls out and can stand as accordion-fold 'sculpture', wrap-around band of white paper 2 inches wide, printed in back, closed with silver sticker with silver card 9 1/2 x 6 3/8 inches folded in half with further details on origin of this work, fine, handsome and visually intriguing piece.   Priscilla Juvelis - Rare Books   56 - 1   2013 $650

Barth, Karl *Wolfgang Amadeus Mozart.* Grand Rapids: Eerdmans, 1986. First edition thus, with 6 page foreword by John Updike, inscribed by Updike for Cyril and Sylvia Wismar, only issued in wrappers, faint fore edge spots to front cover, else fine.   Ken Lopez Bookseller   159 - 204   2013 $150

Barthelemy, Jean Jacques *Carite et Polydore.* Lausanne: et a Paris: chez les marchands de noueautes, 1796. 12mo., fine wide margined copy, contemporary quarter continental calf, marbled boards, vellum tips, gilt banded spine, red morocco label, slight insect damage to marbled boards.   Jarndyce Antiquarian Booksellers   CCIV - 56   2013   £125

Bartholomew, Charles *Mechanical Toys.* Hamlyn, 1979. First edition, 4to., original cloth, gilt, dust jacket, top edge little creased, price clipped, pages 156, illustrations.   R. F. G. Hollett & Son   Children's Books - 48   2013   £25

Bartlett, Charles W. *Cruising Directions Newfoundland with some Material on the Labrador. Volume I.* Boston: Cruising Club of America, 1974. 8vo., green flexible cloth ring binding with gilt to front cover and spine, unpaginated (over 200 pages), hand drawn maps and 1 black and white illustration, covers bent due to binding and one page has top corner cut out affecting small map, previous owners name and address on second page.   Schooner Books Ltd.   105 - 24 2013 $55

Bartlett, J. S. *The Physician's Pocket Synopsis; Affording a Concise View of the Symptoms and Treatment of the Medical and Surgical Diseases Incident to the Human Frame...* Boston: Monroe and Francis, 1822. First edition, 16mo., 396 pages, contemporary flexible red morocco, edges stamped with gilt.   M & S Rare Books, Inc.   95 - 14   2013 $225

Bartlett, John Russell 1805-1886 *Dictionary of Americanisms. A Glossary of Words and Phrases Usually Regarded as Peculiar to the United States.* Boston and London: Little Brown and Co. and Trubner, 1859. Second edition, brown cloth, gilt stamped spine title, extremities faded, spine ends chipped, previous owner's bookplate, ink stamp, good.   Jeff Weber Rare Books   171 - 13   2013 $50

Bartlett, John Russell 1805-1886 *Personal Narrative of Explorations and Incidents in Texas, New Mexico, California Sonora and Chihuahua, Connected During the Years 1850, '51 and '53.* Chicago: Rio Grande Press, 1965. Facsimile reprint of rare 1854 first edition, 2 volumes, 3 folding maps, frontispieces, 110 illustrations, brown leatherette, very fine set.   Argonaut Book Shop   Summer 2013 - 11   2013 $175

Bartlett, Robert A. *The Last Voyage of the Karluk Flagship of Vilhjalmar Stefansson's Canadian Arctic Expedition of 1913-1916...* Boston: Small Maynard, 1916. First edition, blue cloth with gilt titles and vignette on front, half title, frontispiece, 2 maps and 23 black and white photo illustrations, 8vo., small front inner hinge crack otherwise good, author's presentation copy.   Schooner Books Ltd.   101 - 20   2013 $200

Bartlett, Vernon *No Man's Land.* London: George Allen and Unwin, 1930. First edition, 8vo., original black cloth, dust jacket, inscribed by author for Francis and Joe Farjeon, excellent copy, jacket faded on spine and creased and worn at head.   Maggs Bros. Ltd.   1460 - 44   2013   £50

Barto, A. *Pesn O Stroike. (Song of Construction).* Moscow: Ogiz, Molodai Gvardia, 1932. 8vo., pictorial wrappers, spine and edge mends, very good, illustrations by Tatiana Mavrino.   Aleph-Bet Books, Inc.   104 - 506   2013 $600

Bartoli, Pietro Santi 1635-1700 *Le Antiche Lucerne Sepolcrali Figurate Raccolte dalle Caue Sotterranee e Grotte di Roma.* Roma: Nella Stamperia di Gio. Francesco Buagni, 1691. First edition, 4to., engraved section titlepages for each of the 3 parts, 116 full page engraved plates, full modern antique style speckled calf, blindstamped covers, raised bands, gilt stamped calf spine label, fine.   Jeff Weber Rare Books   171 - 14   2013 $2750

Barton, Bernard *Selections from the Poems and Letters.* London: Hall, Virtue & Co., 1850. Second edition, frontispiece, plates, unopened in original light blue cloth, spine slightly faded, small booklabel of John Sparrow, very good.   Jarndyce Antiquarian Booksellers   CCIII - 638   2013   £40

Barwick, Peter *The Life of the Reverend Dr. John Barwick.* London: printed by J. Bettneham, 1724. First English edition, large paper copy, 8vo., portrait frontispieces, contemporary Cambridge, style panelled calf, spine gilt in compartments, orange morocco label extremities rubbed, spine darkened, joints split but boards still attached, endcaps worn, "James Affleck" book label, contemporary inscription "Eliz. Dolben" and above "James Affleck, 20th century provenance note by Peter G. Binnall.   Unsworths Antiquarian Booksellers   28 - 72   2013   £200

Basham, William R. *The Croonian Lectures for 1864 Delivered Before the President and Fellows of the Royal College of Physicians of England.* London: John Churchill, 1864. 6 plates, original brown cloth, worn, spine chipped, top 1 inch lacking, ex-library with spine label and bookplate, pages unopened and internally very good.   James Tait Goodrich   S74 - 22   2013 $125

Bashford, Herbert *A Man Unafraid. The Story of John Charles Fremont.* San Francisco: Hart Wagner Publishing Co., 1927. First edition, 406 pages, tinted frontispiece, 19 plates, 2 tipped-in color illustrations, gilt lettered green cloth, almost imperceptible dampstain to outer cover at foot of spine, minor offsetting to front endpaper, fine.   Argonaut Book Shop   Summer 2013 - 114   2013 $90

Basile, Giovanni Battista *Stories from the Pentamerone.* London: Macmillan and Co., 1911. Edition deluxe, limited to 150 copies, quarto, 32 tipped in color plates, original vellum boards, alter yellow silk ties, original blue paper dust jacket, chemise and blue full morocco slipcase, very fine, in incredibly scarce dust jacket with vellum unusually clean and bright, this copy finest we have ever seen.   David Brass Rare Books, Inc.   Holiday 2012 Chapter One - DB 02166   2013 $3500

Baskin, Lisa Unger *The Gehenna Press - the Work of Fifty Years 1942-1992. The Catalogue of an Exhibition Curated by Lisa Unger Baskin...* Amherst: Bridwell Library, Southern Methodist University & Gehenna Press, 1992. First edition, one of a limited edition of 2000, this copy signed by Leonard Baskin, large 8vo., 238 pages, illustrations in black and white and color, printed wrappers, very good, tight copy.   Second Life Books Inc.   183 - 18   2013 $200

Bassereau, P. I. A. *Traite Affections de la Peau Symptomatiques De La Syphillis.* Paris: Chez J. B. Bailliere, 1852. Half title, text foxed and browned in parts, 8vo., contemporary quarter brown calf, burgundy linen boards, light rubbing, else very good.   James Tait Goodrich   S74 - 23   2013 $595

Basta, Giorgio *Le Gouvernement de la Cavalerie Legere.* Rouen: Jean Berthelin, 1616. Early French translation, folio, engraved titlepage with lower margin removed, 11 double page copperplate engravings, lacking 2 pages following ad before regular numbering begins, lacking plate between pages 20-21, faint dampstaining top corners of page 73-end, contemporary vellum, holograph paper spine label, piece missing lower spine, light soiled, very good, very rare.   Jeff Weber Rare Books   171 - 16   2013 $600

Basterfield, George *Mountain Lure.* Kendal: Titus Wilson, 1947. First edition, original cloth, dust jacket, edges very worn and chipped, 6 plates.   R. F. G. Hollett & Son   Lake District & Cumbria - 85   2013   £65

Batchelor, John M. *A Strange People.* New York: J. S. Ogilvie..., 1888. First edition, octavo, original terra cotta wrappers printed in black.   L. W. Currey, Inc.   Utopian Literature: Recent Acquisitions (April 2013) - 138053   2013 $1000

Bateman, Gerald Cooper *A Countryman's Calendar.* Ditchling, Sussex: Saint Dominic's Press, 1927. 4 wood engravings by David Jones and 12 other engravings, pages 32, foolscap 8vo., original cream wrappers, with one of the Jones engravings blocked on front cover beneath printed title, spine tail trifle defective, cover edges little dull, untrimmed, good.   Blackwell's Rare Books   B174 - 378   2013   £135

Bates, Arthenia J. *Seeds Beneath the Snow.* New York: Greenwich Book Pub., 1969. First edition, fine in lightly rubbed and chipped, very good dust jacket, signed by author.   Between the Covers Rare Books, Inc.   165 - 78   2013 $125

Bates, Craig D. *Tradition and Innovation: a Basket History of the Indians of the Yosemite-Mono Lake Region.* Yosemite National Park: Yosemite Association, 1990. First edition, one of 2000 copies, square 4to., duotones, dark grey cloth, very fine, pictorial dust jacket.   Argonaut Book Shop   Recent Acquisitions June 2013 - 20   2013 $150

Bates, Herbert Ernest 1905-1974 *Catherine Foster.* London: Jonathan Cape, 1929. First edition, 8vo., original green cloth, dust jacket, excellent copy in slightly rubbed dust jacket, creased at head and tail of spine, inscribed by author to dedicatee, Edward Garnett.   Maggs Bros. Ltd.   1460 - 47   2013   £1500

Bates, Herbert Ernest 1905-1974 *Edward Garnett.* London: Max Parrish, 1950. First edition, small 8vo., original brown cloth, dust jacket, offset foxing to endpapers, else excellent copy in worn, creased and lightly soiled and nicked dust jacket, inscribed by author to photographer Douglas Glass, 1/58.   Maggs Bros. Ltd.   1460 - 49   2013   £100

Bates, Herbert Ernest 1905-1974 *Flowers and Faces.* Golden Cockerel Press, 1935. First edition, 192/319 copies of an edition of 325, printed on Batchelor handmade paper and signed by author, 4 superb full page wood engravings and wood engraved floral topped by sun to titlepage, royal 8vo., original quarter dark green crushed morocco, gilt lettered backstrip trifle faded, marbled cloth sides, bookplate, top edge gilt, others untrimmed, very good.   Blackwell's Rare Books   B174 - 338   2013   £500

Bates, Herbert Ernest 1905-1974 *A German Idyll.* Waltham St. Lawrence: The Golden Cockerel Press, 1932. First edition, number 218 of 307 copies signed by author, small 4to., original quarter red leather, patterned cloth, lettered gilt on spine, fine, inscribed by dedicatee, Karl (Charles) Lahr for F. G. Robinson, wood engravings by Lynton Lamb.   Maggs Bros. Ltd.   1460 - 48   2013   £300

Bates, Herbert Ernest 1905-1974 *The Seasons and the Gardener.* Cambridge: University Press, 1945. Large 8vo. original cloth backed pictorial boards, matching dust jacket (trifling wear to extremities), drawings by C. F. Tunnicliffe.   R. F. G. Hollett & Son   Children's Books - 611   2013   £35

Bates, Herbert Ernest 1905-1974 *The Seekers.* London: John and Edward Bumpus, 1926. First edition, one of an unknown edition for presentation, this copy signed by author, 8vo., original grey paper boards, gilt, near fine in tissue dust jacket, slightly torn.   Maggs Bros. Ltd.   1460 - 46   2013   £100

Bates, Herbert Ernest 1905-1974 *The Seekers.* London: John and Edward Bumpus, 1926. First edition, 8vo., original grey paper boards, gilt, inscribed by author for S. Pena, near fine, remains of tissue dust jacket in rear.   Maggs Bros. Ltd.   1460 - 45   2013   £75

Bates, Herbert Ernest 1905-1974 *Summer in Salandar.* Boston: Little Brown, 1957. First US edition, 8vo., original yellow cloth, near fine, inscribed by author for Elizabeth Hamilton.   Maggs Bros. Ltd.   1460 - 50   2013   £100

Bates, Joseph D. *Spinning for Salt Water Game Fish.* Boston: Little Brown and Co., 1957. First edition, fine in very good dust jacket with crease on spine and short tears, author Ralph Ellison's copy with his ownership signature.   Between the Covers Rare Books, Inc.   165 - 19   2013 $350

Bateson, William *Materials for the Study of Variation Treated with Special Regard to Discontinuity in the Origin Species.* London: Macmillan, 1894. First edition, 8vo., 204 illustrations, very good+ in original green cloth, gilt lettered spine, mild cover edge wear, foxing to edges, foxing first and last few pages.   By the Book, L. C.   37 - 6   2013 $600

Bateson, William *Mendel's Principles of Heredity.* Cambridge: Cambridge University Press, 1909. First edition, very good+, rebacked with original spine laid down and new endpapers, cover with edgewear, scuffs to covers, age darkening to titlepage, soil to last page, 8vo.   By the Book, L. C. 37 - 36 2013 $200

Bateson, William *On Gameric Series Involving Reduplication of Certain Terms.* Cambridge: Cambridge University Press, 1911. Offprint from Journal of Genetics Volume I No. 4, Dec. 9, 1911, Small 4to., fine in printed wrappers.   By the Book, L. C. 37 - 5 2013 $250

Battersby & Co. Auction *Catalogue of the Valuable, Antique, and Interesting Contents of Kilkenny Castle November 1935.* November, 1935. 2nd issue, photos, entry ticket, errata slip, original stiff wrappers, slightly dusty, almost pristine.   C. P. Hyland 261 - 121 2013 £65

Battie, William *A Treatise on Madness.* London: printed for J. Whiston and B. White, 1758. vii, 99 pages, rebound in half calf by Sangorski & Sutcliffe, endpapers renewed with binding, text foxed in parts, lower right blank portion of leaf B4 missing.   James Tait Goodrich 75 - 19 2013 $2250

Batty, Robert *German Scenery from Drawings Made in 1820.* London: Rodwell & Martin, 1825. First edition, quarto, 61 steel engravings, vignette on titlepage, original purple decorative straight grained morocco, all edges gilt, joints rubbed, light foxing to prelims, very good.   J. & S. L. Bonham Antiquarian Booksellers Europe - 8850 2013 £700

Batty, Robert *Hanoverian and Saxon Scenery from Drawings by Batty.* London: Robert Jennings, 1829. First edition, quarto, pages iv, 120, frontispiece (small tear in margin), vignette on titlepage, 60 steel engraved plates, original brown morocco, gilt decorated, raised bands, joints and corners rubbed.   J. & S. L. Bonham Antiquarian Booksellers Europe - 8827 2013 £950

Batty, Robert *Scenery of the Rhine, Belgium and Holland.* London: Robert Jennings, 1826. First edition, quarto, frontispiece, vignette on titlepage, 60 steel engraved plates, some occasional light foxing in margins, original purple morocco, gilt decoration, raised bands, joints and corners rubbed, inner joint cracked.   J. & S. L. Bonham Antiquarian Booksellers Europe - 8828 2013 £550

Baudelaire, Charles *Les Fleurs du Mal.* Paris: 1857. First edition, first printing with six suppressed poems, in second state wrappers, with back wrapper announcing "Les Fleurs du Mal", octavo, title printed in red and black, original light yellow printed wrappers, uncut as published, perfectly pure without spots, some professional restoration to spine, front wrapper with small crease along fore-edge and half title, also bit creased, beautiful copy in glassine dust jacket with custom full morocco clamshell.   Heritage Book Shop Holiday Catalogue 2012 - 8 2013 $35,000

Baudelaire, Charles *Les Fleurs du Mal.* Paris: Le Circle du Livre Precieux, 1964. First Fini edition, one of 480 copies (total edition 500), 24 color lithographs by Leonor Fini, all full page, circa 300 pages, loose leaves in wrapper folder and very handsomely designed cloth chemise and slipcase, oveall size 18 x 13.5 page size 435 X320mm.), practically new condition.   Gemini Fine Books & Arts., Ltd. Art Reference & Illustrated Books - 2013 $1500

Baudelaire, Charles *La Spleen de Paris, 41 Poemes.* Paris: Les Cent Une, 1963. First Jansem edition, number LXXIX (79) of 140 exemplars on velin d'Arches (total edition 140, signed by Jean Jansem, Club's President and VP, 15 original hors texte color lithographs by Jansem, about 170 pages, loose leaves, publisher's wrappers, boards chemise and slipcase, new condition.   Gemini Fine Books & Arts., Ltd. Art Reference & Illustrated Books - 2013 $1600

Baudouin, Benoit *B. Balduinus De Calceo Antiquo et Jul Nigronus De Caliga Veterum...* Amsterdam: Andreae Frisii, 1667. 12mo., engraved plates, lacking 7 folding plates, later vellum, titlepage torn and backed affecting engraved vignette, some dampstaining, imperfect.   Joseph J. Felcone Inc. Books Printed before 1701 - 9 2013 $600

Baughan, Peter E. *North of Leeds. The Leeds-Settle-Carlisle Line and Its Branches.* Roundhouse Books, 1966. First edition, thick 8vo., original cloth, gilt, dust jacket extremities little chipped, pages 500 with 58 illustrations and 4 maps, excellent copy.   R. F. G. Hollett & Son Lake District & Cumbria - 88 2013 £50

Baum, Lyman Frank *Baum's American Fairy Tales.* Indianapolis: Bobbs Merrill, 1908. First edition thus, small 4to., blue cloth, pictorial paste-on, cover plate ever so slightly soiled, else fine and bright, 16 color plates by George Kerr.   Aleph-Bet Books, Inc. 104 - 58 2013 $800

Baum, Lyman Frank *Baum's Juvenile Speaker.* Chicago: Reilly & Britton, 1910. 4to., tan cloth pictorially stamped in red black and silver, 196 pages + ads, fine, illustrations by John Neill and Maginel Wright-Enright in black and white, beautiful, rare.   Aleph-Bet Books, Inc. 105 - 72 2013 $950

Baum, Lyman Frank *Baum's Own Book for Children.* Chicago: Reilly & Britton, 1912. 4to., cloth backed pictorial boards, 196 pages, edges and corners rubbed and soil on a few pages, else very good, illustrations in black and white by John R. Neill and Enright, scarce. Aleph-Bet Books, Inc. 105 - 71 2013 $750

Baum, Lyman Frank *Boy Fortune Hunters in Panama.* Chicago: Reilly & Britton, 1908. First edition, first printing, 8vo., brown cloth stamped in black, cream and white, 310 pages, very good-fine, 4 color plates by Howard Heath, rare. Aleph-Bet Books, Inc. 104 - 57 2013 $1200

Baum, Lyman Frank *Dorothy and the Wizard of Oz.* Chicago: Reilly & Britton, 1908. First edition, first state, in primary binding with longer spine imprint, 4to., blue cloth, pictorial paste-on with gold background, spine stamped in black and silver with all upper case imprint, ads through John Dough slight edge and cover rubbing, else near fine and bright with metallic background at cover plate in nice shape, illustrations by J. R. Neill with 16 captioned color plates, beautiful copy. Aleph-Bet Books, Inc. 105 - 60 2013 $2500

Baum, Lyman Frank *The Emerald City of Oz.* Chicago: Reilly & Britton, 1910. First edition, first state, H-G, VI.1, 4to., dark blue cloth, pictorial paste-on, slightest bit of cover rubbing, very occasional margin soil, fine and bright, illustrations by J. R. Neill with cover plate, 2 color pictorial endpapers, 16 color plates plus many black and whites in text, beautiful copy, rare dark blue binding. Aleph-Bet Books, Inc. 105 - 61 2013 $2000

Baum, Lyman Frank *Fortune Hunters in Alaska.* Chicago: Reilly & Britton, 1908. First edition, first printing, 8vo., brown cloth, stamped in black and white, 271 pages, cloth at head of spine repaired, tiny part of bottom corner of some pages worn off, else very good, 3 half tone plates by Howard Heath. Aleph-Bet Books, Inc. 105 - 68 2013 $700

Baum, Lyman Frank *John Dough and the Cherub.* Chicago: Reilly & Britton, 1906. First edition, first state, without correction line 10 on page 275 (cage instead of cave), 4to., tan cloth stamped in red, black and brown on front and in black on rear, 40 full page color illustrations, 20 color pictorial chapter heads, 100 black and whites plus pictorial endpapers and title by J. R. Neill, super rare with dust jacket. Aleph-Bet Books, Inc. 105 - 67 2013 $8500

Baum, Lyman Frank *The Marvelous Land of Oz.* Chicago: Reilly & Britton, 1904. First edition first state, in B binding with red cloth titled in dark blue on spine panel in blue and silver on front cover, 4to., red pictorial cloth, 6 tiny margin mends, front hinge slightly rubbed but not weak, occasional margin soil and slight cover soil, else fine and bright, numerous full and partial page black and whites, 16 full page color plates on glossy stock by J. R. Neill and photo pictorial endpapers, beautiful copy, rare. Aleph-Bet Books, Inc. 104 - 51 2013 $12,500

Baum, Lyman Frank *Ozma and the Little Wizard.* Chicago: Reilly & Lee, n.d. circa, 1932. 8vo., pictorial wrappers, near fine, illustrations by J. R. Neill with 8 color plates plus black and whites. Aleph-Bet Books, Inc. 105 - 66 2013 $275

Baum, Lyman Frank *Ozma of Oz.* Chicago: Reilly & Britton, 1907. First edition, first state, binding state A, including pictorial endpapers, pictorial rear cover front ad listing only John Dough and Land of Oz, 4to., tan pictorial cloth, slightest bit of cover soil and rubbing to spine ends, else fine and beautiful, pictorial endpapers, lovely copy, rare first state. Aleph-Bet Books, Inc. 105 - 62 2013 $2500

Baum, Lyman Frank *Patchwork Girl of Oz.* Chicago: Reilly & Britton, 1913. First edition (H/G VII) but "c" in chap 3 on p. 35 does not overlap text, 4to., green pictorial cloth, tiny snag at base of spine and name erased from title edge, else very fine and bright, illustrations by J. R. Neill, rare in this condition. Aleph-Bet Books, Inc. 104 - 52 2013 $1800

Baum, Lyman Frank *The Road to Oz.* Chicago: Reilly & Britton, 1909. First edition, first state with paper colors in order, earliest copy with no type damage on page 34, 121, caption and numeral on page 129, 8vo., green pictorial cloth stamped in black, green, tan and red, fine, bright copy, owner inscription, no color plates as issued, pictorial endpapers and a profusion of black and whites by J. R. Neill, beautiful, bright copy. Aleph-Bet Books, Inc. 105 - 63 2013 $3000

Baum, Lyman Frank *Scarecrow and the Tin Wood-Man.* Chicago: Reilly & Lee, n.d. circa, 1932. 8vo., pictorial wrappers, near fine, illustrations by J. R. Neill with 8 color plates plus black and whites. Aleph-Bet Books, Inc. 105 - 65 2013 $250

Baum, Lyman Frank *The Scarecrow of Oz.* Chicago: Reilly & Britton, 1915. First edition, first state in first state dust jacket with ads listing this title last, 4to., green cloth, pictorial paste-on, mint in dust jacket with slight chipping at spine ends restored, else very good+, illustrations by John Neill with 12 color plates, pictorial endpapers and black and whites throughout, magnificent copy, rare in this condition in wrapper. Aleph-Bet Books, Inc. 105 - 59 2013 $10,000

Baum, Lyman Frank *The Wizard of Oz.* New York: Holt, 1982. 4to., pictorial boards mint in dust jacket, illustrations by Michael Hague, with color illustrations, signed by Hague with wonderful drawing of an Oz character. Aleph-Bet Books, Inc. 105 - 64 2013 $325

Baum, Lyman Frank *The Woggle-Bug Book.* Chicago: Reilly & Britton, 1905. First edition, secondary binding, folio, green cloth spine, stiff pictorial card covers with yellow stippled background and title in yellow on rear cover, (48) pages, covers soiled, small portion of front bottom corner restored, corner of title little frayed, else internally very good, clean, overall very good, illustrations by Ike Morgan, large fragile book. Aleph-Bet Books, Inc. 104 - 56 2013 $3000

Baum, Lyman Frank *The Wonderful Wizard of Oz.* Chicago: Geo. M. Hill Co., 1900. First edition, second state of text and second state of plates, quarto, 24 color plates, 24 color plates, original light green cloth pictorially stamped and lettered in fred and darker green (variant C), pristine, housed in velvet lined green cloth clamshell case, inscribed for Lyman from Aunt Maud, 1901. David Brass Rare Books, Inc. Holiday 2012 Chapter One - DB00967 2013 $29,500

Baum, Lyman Frank *The Wonderful Wizard of Oz.* Chicago: George M. Hill, 1900. First edition, 2nd state, large 8vo., pale green cloth stamped in red and green, color illustrations by W. W. Denslow, remarkable, beautiful, clean copy. Aleph-Bet Books, Inc. 104 - 50 2013 $32,500

Baumagin, Susan Jo *Dreaming Cows, the Paintings, Murals and Drawings of Betty Laduke Celebrating Heifer International.* Little Rock: Heifer International, 2009. First edition, fine in fine dust jacket, 4to., 171 pages. Beasley Books 2013 - 2013 $100

Bawden, Edward *Hold Fast by Your Teeth.* London: Routledge & Kegan Paul, 1963. 4to., original pictorial boards, matching dust jacket, illustrations in color, scattered spots to endpapers, half title and fore-edge, otherwise very good. R. F. G. Hollett & Son Children's Books - 49 2013 £250

Bawtry, Peck W. *A Topographical History and Description of Bawtry and Thorne, with the Villages Adjacent.* Doncaster: printed for the author, 1813. With Supplement. One of 100 copies signed by author 1814, folding frontispiece map, 9 plates, some browning and light foxing, but good copy bound in recent half calf, marbled boards, rare supplement uncut and rather browned, bound in recent boards, printed paper label. Ken Spelman Books Ltd. 73 - 61 2013 £220

Bax, Clifford *The Beauty of Women.* 1946. First edition, 95 pages, 16 plates, 8vo., cloth, very good. C. P. Hyland 261 - 27 2013 £30

Baxter, Lucy E. *The Cathedral Builders. The Story of a Great Masonic Guild.* London: Sampson Low, Marston and Co., 1899. 8vo., 83 illustrations, red cloth, gilt design to upper board, top edge gilt, fore-edge uncut, spotting, odd pencil mark, mild discoloration to some plates, browning to titlepage and endpapers, boards somewhat worn and soiled in places, despite minor faults, mostly clean and entirely firm copy. Unsworths Antiquarian Booksellers 28 - 145 2013 £50

Baxter, Richard *A Call to the Unconverted to Turn and Live...* North Allerton: printed by J. Langdale, 1802. New edition, very good, full contemporary unlettered sheep, blind ruled borders, slight chip to foot of spine, scarce. Ken Spelman Books Ltd. 75 - 55 2013 £75

Bayer, Oliver Weld *An Eye for an Eye.* Garden City: Doubleday Crime Club, 1945. First edition, fine in dust jacket. Mordida Books 81 - 29 2013 $65

Bayles, W. Harrison *Old Taverns of New York.* New York: Frank Allaben Genealogical Co., 1915. First edition, publisher's red buckram, gilt, 489 pages, illustrations, bookplate, corners little bumped, else near fine. Between the Covers Rare Books, Inc. New York City - 302503 2013 $150

Bayley, Nathan *English and Latine Exercises for School-Boys.* Boston: printed by T. Fleet for the Booksellers, 1720. First American edition, 12mo., contemporary calf over boards, rebacked, text browned but very good. M & S Rare Books, Inc. 95 - 180 2013 $3750

Bayley, Nicola *One Old Oxford Ox.* London: Cape, 1977. First edition thus, large 8vo., pages not numbered, illustrations in color, pictorial paper over boards, cover slightly faded at spine, otherwise nice, Vivien Green's book from the estate of Graham Greene. Second Life Books Inc. 183 - 19 2013 $75

Baynes, E. S. A. *Revised Catalogue of Irish Macrolepidoptera.* 1964. 8vo., cloth, very good. C. P. Hyland 261 - 905 2013 £23

Beach, Charles A. *Too Good for Anything; or a Waif of the World.* London: Frederick Warne & Co., circa, 1900. Half title, original light brown cloth, slightly rubbed, very good. Jarndyce Antiquarian Booksellers CCV - 18 2013 £50

Beamish, C. T. M. *Beamish, a Genealogical Study of a Family in County Cork and Elsewhere.* 1950. First edition, 275 pages, ex-libris Horace E. Jones, with his informative annotations, cloth, very good. C. P. Hyland 261 - 372 2013 £175

Beamish, Richard Pigott *Pedigrees of the Families of Beamish, Heise, King Robertson and Masson.* Cork: for private circulation, 1892. First edition, 44 pages, original red morocco (distressed), text very good.   C. P. Hyland 261 - 373   2013   £105

Bear, Greg *Anvil of Stars.* London: Century a Legend Book, 1992. First edition, one of 200 copies, fine in illustrated boards and slipcase, signed by author, from the library of Bruce Kahn.   Between the Covers Rare Books, Inc.   Sci-Fi, Fantasy & Horror - 311553   2013 $80

Bear, Ted *My Life Story.* New York: S. Gabriel, n.d. circa, 1930. 4to. cloth backed pictorial boards, edges rubbed, very good+, full page color illustrations and in line, cover with die-cut bear head that reader can lift up.   Aleph-Bet Books, Inc.   105 - 76   2013 $250

Beard, Adelia Belle *The Beard Animals.* New York: Frederick Stokes, 1914. Large oblong 4to., cloth backed pictorial boards, slight edgewear and cover rubbing, else very good+ and unused, every other page features a life sized drawing.   Aleph-Bet Books, Inc.   105 - 433   2013 $200

Beard, Geoffrey *Lake District.* Ian Allan, 1982. Large 4to., original cloth, gilt, dust jacket, pages 110, illustrations in color.   R. F. G. Hollett & Son   Lake District & Cumbria - 90   2013   £25

Beard, Lina *American Girl's Handy Book.* New York: Scribners, 1898. 8vo., green decorated cloth, very good, very clean and bright, 559 pages plus ads.   Barnaby Rudge Booksellers   Children 2013 - 021321   2013 $110

Bearden, Romare *A History of African-American Artists from 1792 to the Present.* New York: Pantheon, 1993. First edition, thick quarto, fine in fine dust jacket.   Between the Covers Rare Books, Inc.   165 - 53   2013 $65

Beardsley, Alice *Turn-Around Book.* Indianapolis: Bobbs Merrill, 1914. Small 4to., green cloth, pictorial paste-on, some soil, very good, printed on heavy coated paper on rectos only, full page illustration with caption.   Aleph-Bet Books, Inc.   104 - 386   2013 $450

Beardsley, Aubrey Vincent   1872-1898 *Four Plates Issued to Accompany the Works of Edgar Allan Poe.* Chicago: Stone and Kimball, 1895. First edition, circa 10 copies, 4 plates, each printed on Japan Paper, 20.3 x 13 cm, Beardsley's name pencilled at foot of each plate by later owner, foolscape 8vo. original white parchment folder with white cloth flaps, covers illustrated overall with repeat gilt blocked pattern to design by Fran Hazenplug, covers dust soiled, bookplate on inside of folder, good, rare. Blackwell's Rare Books   B174 - 169   2013   £1000

Beardsley, Aubrey Vincent   1872-1898 *An Issue of Five Drawings Illustrative of Juvenal and Lucien.* London?: Book-Dandies for private circulation, n.d., 1906 or after. 1 of 50 copies, first edition, 2 copies of each plate, one printed in black and the other in red, they are loose in original blue wrappers, spine of wrapper split, otherwise very good, some light foxing to margins of few plates but also in very good condition, housed in handsome blue cloth box with title and illustrator to leather label on spine.   The Kelmscott Bookshop   7 - 69   2013 $850

Beardsley, Aubrey Vincent   1872-1898 *Sous La Colline. (Under the Hill).* Paris: H. Floury, Editeur, 1908. 1 of 1000 copies, first French edition, 13 illustrations by Beardsley and 2 portraits of him, all protected by tissue guards, bound in modern black half calf with marbled paper covered boards, foxing to frontispiece and last few pages, affecting last illustration, otherwise very good.   The Kelmscott Bookshop   7 - 69   2013 $275

Bearss, Edwin C. *Fort Smith Little Gibraltar on the Arkansas.* Norman: University of Oklahoma Press, 1969. First edition, 16 illustrations, 3 maps, dark tan cloth, very fine with dust jacket.   Argonaut Book Shop   Summer 2013 - 12   2013 $60

Bearss, Edwin C. *History Basic Data. Redwood National Park, Del Norte and Humboldt Counties, California.* N.P.: Division of History, Office of Archeology and Historic Preservation, 1969. First edition, 4to., 41 plates from photos and maps, illustrations, original pictorial stiff red wrappers, extremities faded, corners slightly bumped, overall fine.   Argonaut Book Shop   Recent Acquisitions June 2013 - 21   2013 $75

Beaton, Cecil *Cecil Beaton's Diaries 1948-1955. The Strenuous Years.* London: Weidenfeld and Nicolson, 1973. First edition, 8vo., original red cloth, dust jacket, excellent copy, jacket spine faded, worn at extremities, inscribed by author for Douglas Glass, loosely inserted is short ALS from Beaton to Glass.   Maggs Bros. Ltd.   1460 - 56   2013   £200

Beaton, Cecil *Far East.* London: B. T. Batsford, 1945. First edition, large 8vo., original orange cloth, lettered in yellow, near fine, spine faded, inscribed by author for James Pope-Hennessy, neat bookplate of recipient.   Maggs Bros. Ltd.   1460 - 52   2013   £350

Beaton, Cecil *My Royal Past.* London: B. T. Batsford, 1939. First edition, 4to., original orange brown cloth, dust jacket, excellent copy in dust jacket, chipped at extremities and browned on spine inscribed by author for Winifred Ashton.   Maggs Bros. Ltd.   1460 - 51   2013   £250

Beaton, Cecil *Photobiography.* London: Odhams Press, 1951. First edition, 4to., original cream cloth, covers rubbed and stained, otherwise very good, detached dust jacket loosely inserted at rear, inscribed by Beaton for Douglas Glass 1952.   Maggs Bros. Ltd.   1460 - 54   2013   £200

Beatson, Robert *An Essay on the Comparative Advantages of Vertical and Horizontal Wind Mills...* London: printed for Messrs. I and J. Taylor, 1798. 2 engraved folding plates, 8vo., titlepage little dusted, disbound and partially unopened.   Jarndyce Antiquarian Booksellers   CCIV - 58   2013   £480

Beattie, David Johnstone *Prince Charlie and the Borderland.* Carlisle: Charles Thurnam & Sons, 1928. First edition, original cloth, gilt, spine trifle faded, 25 plates, rather scarce.   R. F. G. Hollett & Son   Lake District & Cumbria - 91   2013   £50

Beattie, James   1735-1803 *An Essay on the Nature and Immutability of Truth, in Opposition to Sophistry and Sceptisim.* London: printed for J. Mawman, 1807. Seventh edition, 8vo, some light spotting in places, contemporary straight grain dark blue morocco, spine divided by gilt rules, small central tools in compartments, boards bordered with greek key roll, marbled endpapers, all edges gilt, corners and pages bit rubbed, boards unevenly sunned, contemporary ownership inscription "Ann Gladstone/Liverpool/1808" at head of titlepage, plain printed booklabel "Fasque" on front pastedown.   Unsworths Antiquarian Booksellers   28 - 146   2013   £125

Beattie, James   1735-1803 *An Essay on the Nature and Immutability of Truth in Opposition to Sophistry and Scepticism.* Andrew Wilson, Camden Town, St. Pancrass, 1811. Stereotype edition, 8vo., slight foxing, very good, contemporary half calf, marbled boards, double gilt banded spine, red morocco label, attractive.   Jarndyce Antiquarian Booksellers   CCIV - 59   2013   £75

Beattie, William   1793-1875 *The Danube with Beauties of the Bosphorous.* London: Virtue, n.d., 1840. 1845. First edition, quarto, frontispiece, map, steel engravings (clean with protective tissues), vignette on titlepage, contemporary red calf, raised bands, all edges gilt, handsome.   J. & S. L. Bonham Antiquarian Booksellers   Europe - 9917   2013   £650

Beattie, William   1793-1875 *Life and Letters of Thomas Campbell.* London: Edward Moxon, 1849. First edition, 3 volumes, half titles, frontispieces slightly dampstained, foxing in prelims, small tear in outer margin of half title volume I, without loss, slightly later half brown cloth, labels of Norfolk & Norwich Library, good plus.   Jarndyce Antiquarian Booksellers   CCIII - 473   2013   £100

Beattie, William   1793-1875 *Life and Letters of Thomas Campbell.* London: Hall, Virtue and Co., 1850. Second edition, 3 volumes, half titles, frontispieces, 8 page catalog volume I, uncut in original dark blue/green cloth, blocked in blind, slightly marked, corners slightly bumped, inner hinges cracking in places, contemporary owner's inscription, nice set.   Jarndyce Antiquarian Booksellers   CCIII - 474   2013   £100

Beattie, William   1793-1875 *The Waldenses; or Protestant Valleys of Piedmont and Dauphiny, and the Bar de la Roche....* London: Geo. Virtue, 1838. First edition, quarto, folding map, 70 plates, original dark green, small wear to head of spine, small nick on fore-edge, waterstaining in corner of first few pages.   J. & S. L. Bonham Antiquarian Booksellers   Europe - 9692   2013   £300

Beaufort, Jean De *Le Tresor des Tresors de France...* Paris?: 1615. First edition, extremely rare quarto format, this copy dedicated to King Louis XIII and specially bound for him in full vellum entirely covered with gilt stamped fleur-de-lys on both covers, gilt heart within larger central fleur-de-lys, triple fillet gilt borders, gilt floral corner ornaments, fleurs-de-lys on spine, housed in custom brown calf clamshell stamped with fleur de lys on front and back, gilt stamped on spine.   Heritage Book Shop   50th Anniversary Catalogue - 8   2013 $37,500

Beaumarchais, Pierre Augustin Caron De *Le Folle Journee, ou Le Mariage de Figaro.* Paris: Chez Ruault Librarie, Pres. le Theatre, 1785. First edition, first issue, octavo, five plates after Saint Quentin, half title present, 19th century full green morocco by Petit, triple gilt ruled borders, spine gilt in compartments and with central flower devices, gilt spine lettering, gilt board edges and turn-ins, densely gilt burgundy morocco doublures, marbled endpapers, all edges gilt, morocco edged slipcase, sumptuous presentation for this scarce title.   Heritage Book Shop   Holiday Catalogue 2012 - 10   2013 $2000

Beaumont, Albanis *Travels through the Rhaetian Alps in the Year MDCCLXXXVI from Italy to Germany through the Tyrol.* London: C. Clarke, 1792. First edition, folio, 10 uncolored sepia aquatint plates, contemporary half calf marbled boards, spine rubbed, small loss to head, internally very good, crisp copy with clean plates.   J. & S. L. Bonham Antiquarian Booksellers Europe - 8734   2013   £1850

Beaumont, Cyril Winthrop *Sea Magic.* London: John Lane, Bodley Head, 1928. First edition, original cloth backed decorated boards, frontispiece, and text illustration in colors, flyleaves trifle browned.   R. F. G. Hollett & Son Children's Books - 438   2013   £30

Beaumont, Roberts *Colour in Woven Design.* Chiswick Press for Whittaker and Co. and George Bell & sons, 1890. First edition, inscribed by author, 8vo., original cloth, very good, inscribed to Mons. Waddington, secretary of Jury in class 77 Paris Exhibition 1900 with author's compliments. Blackwell's Rare Books   Sciences - 118   2013   £60

The Beauties of the Anti-Jacobin: or Weekly Examiner; Containing Very Article of Permanent Utility in that Valuable and Highly Esteemed Paper, Literary and Political. London: printed by J. Plymsell, 1799. 12mo., old brown mark to pages 161-172, some slight foxing, 19th century half calf, marbled boards, spine rubbed, lacking label, ownership inscription of Geoffrey Tillotson, 1932.   Jarndyce Antiquarian Booksellers   CCIV - 50   2013   £45

The Beauties of English Poetry... Paris: Sold by Vergani and Favre, 1800-18001. 12mo., little foxing at either end, occasional minor browning and dampstaining, contemporary calf, rebacked, sides crackled, sound, very rare. Blackwell's Rare Books   B174 - 4   2013   £550

Beck, Louis J. *New York's Chinatown: an Historical Presentation of Its People and Places.* New York: Bohemia Pub. Co., 1898. First edition, black boards decorated an titled in silver, crossed opium pipes on spine, hinges restored, soiling to front fly, boards little lightly rubbed, else nice, very good, uncommon.   Between the Covers Rare Books, Inc.   New York City - 291462   2013 $300

Beck, Thomas Alcock *Annales Furnesienses. History and Antiquities of the Abbey of Furness.* London: Payne and Foss, M. A. Nattali; s. Soulby, 1844. First and only edition (250 copies), large 4to. contemporary full pebble grain morocco gilt by Murray's Nottingham Book Company with their ticket, monogram of JTS intertwined (John Tricks Spalding) in black and red leathers, decorated in gilt on upper board, all edges gilt, engraved title, printed title in red and black 3 lithographed facsimiles, 1 engraved plan, 18 fine tissue guarded steel engraved plates, 3 tinted lithographs, 11 text woodcuts, scattered foxing, mainly to flyleaves and half title.   R. F. G. Hollett & Son   Lake District & Cumbria - 93   2013   £595

Beck, Thomas Alcock *Annales Furnesienses. History and Antiquities of the Abbey of Furness.* Payne and Foss, M. A. Nattali and Ulverston: S. Soulby, 1844. First and only edition (250 copies), large 4to., contemporary full pebble grain morocco gilt over heavy bevelled boards, boards panelled and decorated gilt cathedral style, spine with 5 raised bands and contrasting label, panels decorated overall in blind, few slight old scuffs to boards, all edges gilt and gauffered, engraved title, printed title in red and black, 3 lithographed facsimiles, 1 engraved plan, 18 fine tissue guarded steel engraved plates, 3 tinted lithographs and 11 text woodcuts, occasional spot to plates.   R. F. G. Hollett & Son   Lake District & Cumbria - 92   2013   £650

Becker, Robert H. *Designs on the Lands, Disenos of California Ranchos and Their Makers.* San Francisco: Book Club of California, 1969. First edition, one of 500 copies, oblong folio, 180 pages, 64 maps, tan suede spine, cloth covered boards, slight fading to rear board, spine slightly spotted and with minor repair, else fine.   Argonaut Book Shop   Recent Acquisitions June 2013 - 22   2013 $350

Becket, David *His Book of Bookplates.* Edinburgh: Schulze, 1906. 3 pages, octavo, 24 plates (unopened), wrappers (rear damaged), very good.   C. P. Hyland   261 - 49   2013   £50

Beckett, Hazel Williams *Growing Up in Dallas.* Austin: 1985. One of 500 copies, illustrations, map endpapers, near fine in plain dust jacket.   Dumont Maps & Books of the West   122 - 42   2013 $75

Beckett, J. C. *The Anglo Irish Tradition.* Faber, 1976. First edition, octavo, 159 pages, cloth, dust jacket, very good.   C. P. Hyland   261 - 30   2013   £30

Beckett, Samuel   1906-1989 *All that Fall.* London: Faber and Faber, 1957. First edition, 8vo., original pictorial wrappers, chipped at head and tail of spine, otherwise very good, inscribed by author to cousin, John.   Maggs Bros. Ltd.   1460 - 62   2013   £1200

Beckett, Samuel   1906-1989 *The Beckett Country Samuel Beckett's Ireland.* Dublin/London: Black Cat Press in association with Faber and Faber, 1986. First edition, number 210 of 250 copies, signed by author, oblong 4to., original full grey goatskin, hand bound by Antiquarian Bookcrafts of Dublin with larch tree emblem after a drawing by Robert Ballagh, embossed in gold on upper and lower covers, furze yellow ater silk endpapers, all edges gilt, fine in matching slipcase.   Maggs Bros. Ltd.   1442 - 20   2013   £3500

Beckett, Samuel   1906-1989 *Comedie et Actes Divers.* Paris: Les Editions de Minuit, 1966. First edition, 8vo., original white wrappers lettered in black and blue, covers slightly rubbed, otherwise excellent copy in protective folding box, inscribed by author for cousin John Beckett and wife Vera. Maggs Bros. Ltd.   1460 - 65   2013   £1200

Beckett, Samuel   1906-1989 *Compagnie.* Paris: Editions de Minuit, 1980. First edition, foolscap 8vo., original printed white wrappers, fine, Kay Boyle's copy with her signature, inscribed for her by author, parcel address label written by Beckett, loosely inserted in book.   Blackwell's Rare Books   172 - 161   2013   £750

Beckett, Samuel 1906-1989 *Company.* Iowa City: Iowa Center for the Book ath the University of Iowa, 1983. First edition thus, one of only 52 press numbered copies (entire edition), signed by author and artist, printed by hand on Arches cover paper, folio, 13 full page etchings by Dellas Henke, quarter black morocco, black morocco fore-tips, paste paper over boards, speckled endpapers by Bill Anthony, fine in publisher's slipcase, which is slightly sunned at edges, rare. James S. Jaffe Rare Books Fall 2013 - 15 2013 $10,000

Beckett, Samuel 1906-1989 *Fin de Partie, Suivi de Acte sans paroles. (Endgame).* Paris: Les Editions de Minuit, 1957. First edition, first issue on 'grand papier', published Jan. 30 1957, one of 50 copies on 'velin pur fil du marais', this being number 13, 8vo., original printed wrappers, immaculate unopened copy, rare issue, preserved in folding linen box with leather spine. James S. Jaffe Rare Books Fall 2013 - 14 2013 $12,500

Beckett, Samuel 1906-1989 *Fin de Partie Suivi de Acte sans Paroles.* Paris: Les Editions de Minuit, 1957. First edition, 8vo., original white wrappers, lettered black and blue, fore and bottom edges uncut, all over little browned, inscribed by author for Henri et Josette Hayden, very good. Maggs Bros. Ltd. 1442 - 15 2013 £1750

Beckett, Samuel 1906-1989 *First Love.* London: Calder and Boyars, 1973. First edition, 8vo., original pink cloth, dust jacket with fading to spine, fine, inscribed by author for John Beckett and Ruth David. Maggs Bros. Ltd. 1460 - 66 2013 £1200

Beckett, Samuel 1906-1989 *Fizzles/Foirades.* London: Petersburg Press, 1976. First English edition, artist's book limited signed edition, one of 250 copies, each with 33 original etchings by Jasper Johns (26 lift-ground aquatints, most with etching, soft-ground-etching, drypoint, screenprint and/ or photogravure), 5 etchings, 1 soft ground etching and 1 aquatint, 31 in black, 2 (endpapers) in color and 1 lithograph (box lining) in color, signed by author and artist, all on handmade paper by Richard de Bas, watermarked with initials of Beckett and signature of Johns, 62 unnumbered folios (including endpapers and excluding binding support leaves), bound by Rudolf Riser in Cologne, as issued, in paper wrappers, accordion fold around support leaves with colored etchings as endpapers, housed in tan cloth clamshell box with Johns' colored etchings in green, purple and orange laid down in inside trays with distinctive purple silk pull visible when box closed, set in 16pt. Caslon Old Face and handprinted by Frequent and Bawdier in Paris. Priscilla Juvelis - Rare Books 55 - 12 2013 $35,000

Beckett, Samuel 1906-1989 *Hommage a Jack B. Yeats.* Dublin: Locus Solus, 1988. Limited to 54 copies, first separate printing, 16mo., original white wrappers, fine. Maggs Bros. Ltd. 1442 - 21 2013 £75

Beckett, Samuel 1906-1989 *How It Is.* London: John Calder, 1964. First edition, 8vo., original grey cloth, dust jacket, excellent copy, inscribed by author to cousin John Beckett and wife Vera, with John's ownership signature. Maggs Bros. Ltd. 1460 - 63 2013 £1200

Beckett, Samuel 1906-1989 *How It Is.* London: John Calder, 1964. First edition, number 4 of 100 copies signed by author, series A in full vellum, near fine in matching slipcase. Maggs Bros. Ltd. 1460 - 64 2013 £950

Beckett, Samuel 1906-1989 *Ill Seen Ill Said.* New York: Grove Press, 1981. First edition, 8vo., original quarter cream cloth, near fine, inscribed by author for John Beckett and Ruth David. Maggs Bros. Ltd. 1460 - 67 2013 £1000

Beckett, Samuel 1906-1989 *Ill Seen, Ill Said.* Northridge: Lord John Press, 1982. One of an unknown number of copies, described in colophon as presentation copy, from declared edition of 325 copies signed by author, 8vo., original quarter black leather, marbled paper boards, lettered gilt on spine and printed on Bugrabutten mouldmade paper. Maggs Bros. Ltd. 1442 - 19 2013 £750

Beckett, Samuel 1906-1989 *Mal vu Mal dit.* Paris: Editions de Minuit, 1981. First edition, 80 pages, foolscap 8vo., original printed white wrappers, near fine, inscribed by author for Kay Boyle. Blackwell's Rare Books 172 - 162 2013 £700

Beckett, Samuel 1906-1989 *Malone Meurt.* Paris: Les Editions de Minuit, 1951. First edition, small 8vo., original white wrappers, printed in black and blue, inscribed by author, one of 3000 printed slightly creased on covers, otherwise excellent. Maggs Bros. Ltd. 1442 - 11 2013 £500

Beckett, Samuel 1906-1989 *Malone Dies.* New York: Grove Press, 1956. First US edition, 8vo., wrapper issue, very good in protective folding box, inscribed by author to cousin John Beckett and wife Vera. Maggs Bros. Ltd. 1460 - 61 2013 £1000

Beckett, Samuel 1906-1989 *Nohow On.* New York: Limited Editions Club, 1989. One of 550 copies all on Magnani and Arches paper, each signed by author and artist, Robert Ryman, page size 7 1/4 x 10 3/4 inches, bound by Carol Joyce in full black nigerian Oasis goatskin leather with spine and front board stamped in 22 carat gold leaf, housed in custom made black Italian cotton cloth over boards, clamshell box with inside of box lined in grey suede, and label stamped in gilt on black morocco label inset into spine, fine, typeset in English Monotype Bodoni at Golgonooza Letterfoundry, text printed at Shagbark Press, etching printed on Arches at Wingate Studio and Renaissance Press. Priscilla Juvelis - Rare Books 56 - 2 2013 $4500

Beckett, Samuel   1906-1989   *Nouvelles et Textes pour Rien.*   Paris: Les Editions de Minuit, 1955.   One of 1000 numbered copies, first edition, 8vo., original white wrappers, lettered in black and blue, spine browned, fore and bottom edges uncut, inscribed by author for Henri et Josette Hayden, covers slightly browned, otherwise very good.   Maggs Bros. Ltd.   1442 - 13   2013   £1000

Beckett, Samuel   1906-1989   *Nouvelles et Textes pour Rien.*   Paris: Les Editions de Minuit, 1955.   First edition, number 46 of 50 numbered hors commerce on Velin from total edition of 1185, 8vo., original white wrappers, lettered in black and blue, chipped at heel of spine and rubbed overall, otherwise very good in protective folding box, inscribed by author to cousin John Becket and wife Vera.   Maggs Bros. Ltd.   1460 - 60   2013   £1500

Beckett, Samuel   1906-1989   *Pour Finir Encore et Autres Foirades.*   Paris: Editions de Minuit, 1976.   First edition, 16mo., original printed white wrappers, near fine, inscribed by author for Kay Boyle.   Blackwell's Rare Books   172 - 163   2013   £600

Beckett, Samuel   1906-1989   *Sample.*   London: Faber and Faber, 1962.   First edition, 8vo., original wrappers, signed by author, fine.   Maggs Bros. Ltd.   1442 - 16   2013   £200

Beckett, Samuel   1906-1989   *Sans.*   Paris: Editions de Minuit, 1969.   First edition, XLVIII/100 copies, foolscap 8vo., original printed white wrappers, untrimmed, fine, inscribed by author for Kay Boyle.   Blackwell's Rare Books   172 - 164   2013   £800

Beckett, Samuel   1906-1989   *That Time.*   London: Faber, 1976.   First edition, 16mo., original printed wrappers, front cover with image of Beckett, near fine, inscribed by author for Kay Boyle.   Blackwell's Rare Books   172 - 165   2013   £650

Beckett, Samuel   1906-1989   *En Attendant Godot. (Waiting for Godot).*   Paris: Les Editions de Minuit, 1952.   One of 2500 copies printed on 17th Oct. 1952, 8vo., original white wrappers, printed in black and blue, glassine dust jacket, faint creases to spine and one word underlined in text, otherwise near fine.   Maggs Bros. Ltd.   1442 - 12   2013   £2500

Beckett, Samuel   1906-1989   *En Attendant Godot.*   Paris: Les Editions de Minuit, 1952.   First edition, 8vo., original white wrappers printed in black and blue, very good with inch or so lost from tail of spine, wrappers touch rubbed at extremities, inscribed by author to his cousin John Beckett and wife Vera.   Maggs Bros. Ltd.   1460 - 58   2013   £5000

Beckett, Samuel   1906-1989   *Waiting for Godot.*   London: Faber, 1956.   First English edition, with publisher's note concerning textual changes tipped in, foolscap 8vo., original yellow cloth, backstrip blocked in red, free endpapers browned in part as usual, owner's signature on front free endpaper, neatly price clipped dust jacket with backstrip panel very lightly browned and trifle frayed at head and tail, very good.   Blackwell's Rare Books   172 - 166   2013   £435

Beckett, Samuel   1906-1989   *Waiting for Godot.*   London: Faber and Faber, 1956.   First edition in English, 8vo., original fawn cloth, lettered in red, dust jacket, first issue with jacket price of '9s 6d' and publisher's ads for their James Joyce titles, publisher's note tipped in, ownership of actor Julian Curry with his signature, usual offsetting to endpapers, otherwise excellent copy in dust jacket, slightly creased and rubbed at extremities.   Maggs Bros. Ltd.   1442 - 14   2013   £300

Beckett, Samuel   1906-1989   *En Attendant Godot.*   Paris: Les Editions de Minuit, 1960.   Reprint, small 8vo., original wrappers slightly creased at edges, otherwise excellent copy in protective folding box, inscribed by author.   Maggs Bros. Ltd.   1460 - 50   2013   £7250

Beckett, Samuel   1906-1989   *Watt.*   Paris: Editions de Minuit, 1968.   Limited First edition in French, number 63 of 92 copies reserved for La Librairie des editions (189) total, of preferred edition with Beckett's translation, small quarto, original ivory printed wrappers, printed in black on front cover and spine, uncut and unopened, original glassine, glassine lightly browned, housed in custom half morocco clamshell box, exceedingly scarce, fine.   Heritage Book Shop   Holiday Catalogue 2012 - 11   2013 $1000

Beckett, Samuel   1906-1989   *Watt. Roman.*   Paris: Les Editions de Minuit, 1968.   First French edition, 8vo., very good in original white wrappers, lettered in black and blue, spine little sunned, very good, inscribed by author for Henri et Josette (Hayden).   Maggs Bros. Ltd.   1442 - 18   2013   £1000

Beckett, Samuel   1906-1989   *Worstward Ho.*   London: Calder and Boyars, 1983.   First edition, 8vo., original green cloth, fine in dust jacket with fading to spine, inscribed by author for John Beckett and Ruth David.   Maggs Bros. Ltd.   1460 - 67   2013   £1000

Beckford, William   1760-1844   *Italy with Sketches of Spain and Portugal.*   London: Richard Bentley, 1834.   First edition, 2 volumes, 8vo., original purple cloth, spines rubbed, joints split.   J. & S. L. Bonham Antiquarian Booksellers   Europe - 9096   2013   £120

Beckford, William   1760-1844   *Recollections of an Excursion to the Monasteries of Alcobaca and Batalha.* London: Richard Bentley, 1835.   First edition, frontispiece, bound without half title, contemporary half black calf, spine gilt in compartments, brown leather label, corners and hinges slightly rubbed, armorial label of Weston Library, good plus.   Jarndyce Antiquarian Booksellers   CCIII - 641   2013   £350

Beckford, William   1760-1844   *Vathek: an Arabian Tale.* London: William Tegg, 1868.   New edition, frontispiece, vignette title, plates, 8 pages ads, 32 page catalog, original green cloth, attractively blocked in black and gilt, lettered in red and gilt, very slight rubbing, owner's inscription Dec. 1869, very good.   Jarndyce Antiquarian Booksellers   CCIII - 640   2013   £30

Beckwourth, James P.   *The Life and Adventures of James P. Beckwourth, Mountaineer, Scout and Pioneer and Chief of the Crow Nation of Indians.*   New York: Harper & Bros., 1856.   First edition, small octavo, frontispiece, 12 engraved plates, publisher's blindstamped red cloth, gilt lettered spine, contemporary owner's name on blank end, spine badly faded with slight damage, short one inch split to upper front hinge, bookplate removed from inner over, overall very good, without usual heavy foxing and wear, very scarce. Argonaut Book Shop   Recent Acquisitions June 2013 - 23   2013 $450

Beddoes, Thomas   1760-1808   *Hygeia or Essays Moral and Medical on the Causes Affecting the Personal State of Our Middling and Affluent Classes.*   Bristol: J. Mills for R. Phillips, 1802-1803.   First edition, 8vo., new buff flyleaves, some light waterstaining to margin of last few leaves of volume II, modern half tan calf, over marbled boards, gilt stamped spines with raised bands and black leather, gilt stamped labels, ink stamp at top and bottom of volume II titlepage ink stamp of T. Bardon, rare.   Jeff Weber Rare Books   172 - 13   2013 $1350

Beddoes, Thomas Lovell   1803-1849   *The Bride's Tragedy.*   London: F. C. & J. Rivington, 1822.   First edition, 2 pages ads, nicely bound in later half vellum, dark green leather label, Nowell-Smith booklabels.   Jarndyce Antiquarian Booksellers   CCIII - 642   2013   £120

Bedell, E. W.   *An Account of Hornsea, in Holderness, in the East Riding of Yorkshire.*   Hull: William Stephenson, 1848.   8vo., 5 lithograph views on 4 plates by Monkhouse after drawings by Bevan, very good in 19th century full vellum, gilt decorated spine, black label, scarce.   Ken Spelman Books Ltd.   73 - 88   2013   £120

Bedier, Joseph   *La Chanson de Roland.*   Paris: Societe Ippocrate & Ses Amis, 1932.   First Daragnes edition, number 49 of 135 examples, none were for sale, 29 original woodcuts with pochoir in very bright colors, printed on "Hollande" handmade paper, justification page signed in ink by artist and publisher, about 200 leaves, unique copy bound by master binder Therese Monsey signed by her, full red morocco with an Art Deco motif in gilt with onlaid mosaic of colored leathers, all edges gilt, handsome suede endleaves, original wrappers bound in, fit in chemise and slipcase by binder, overall 34 x 25cm., excellent condition. Gemini Fine Books & Arts., Ltd.   Art Reference & Illustrated Books - 2013 $2900

Bedier, Joseph   *The Romance of Tristan and Iseult.* London: George Allen, 1903.   Edition d'Art, one of 300 copies, this #152, 310 x 213mm., color vignette on half title, decorative design on limitations page, color frame on titlepage and color illustrations by Robert Engels, 6 of them full page, splendid contemporary green morocco, exuberantly and extravagantly gilt and inlaid by Sir Edward Sullivan (signed with monogram "ES" on lower board), front cover with wide scallop-edges gilt frame filled with leafy gilt stems terminating in inlaid orange tulips in middle of each side, diamond cornerpieces of maroon morocco accented with small morocco daisies and gilt tools of each side, diamond cornerpieces of maroon morocco accented with small morocco daisies and gilt tools, upper third of central panel with very prominent densely gilt oval wreath with inlaid pink roses and leafy stems, all on stippled background, spray of inlaid pink and gilt lilies in corners above wreath, lower two thirds of panel featuring a particularly striking design incorporating nine long stemmed gilt lilies with inlaid pink blossoms emanating from base filled with flowering gilt vines and heart tools on stippled ground, lower cover with similar but simpler designs, including a vertically oriented version of large oval wreath, present here at upper left and four long stemmed lilies at lower right, flat spine densely gilt, lower two thirds with two long stemmed tulips rising from rectangular base filled with inlaid flowering vines on stippled ground, upper quarter with gilt and inlaid lily growing downward from a similar base (covers and spine with total of 52 larger floral inlays in all), gilt and inlaid turn-ins repeating these design elements, all edges gilt, one corner somewhat rubbed, spine slightly and evenly sunned, hint of splaying to boards, rear turn-in with one inlaid morocco circle partly gone, few shallow marks on back cover, binding lustrous, scarcely worn and altogether dazzling, offsetting from turn-ins onto free endleaves (as typical), text with hint of browning at edges, isolated minor thumbing, marginal stains, or other trivial imperfections, fresh, smooth copy internally. Phillip J. Pirages   61 - 128   2013 $3500

Bedouin, Jean Louis   *Andre Breton. Une etude par Jean-Louis Bedouin.*   Paris: Editions Pierre Seghers, 1950. First edition, square 12mo., original wrappers, preserved in folding box, inscribed by author for Carlos Williams, very good, worn at extremities, spine faded.   Maggs Bros. Ltd. 1460 - 137   2013   £450

Beeding, Francis *The Hidden Kingdom.* Boston: Little Brown and Co., 1927. First edition, octavo, original black cloth, front and spine panels stamped in blue-green. L. W. Currey, Inc. Fall Sampler Sept. 2013 - 146416 2013 $250

Beedome, Thomas *Select Poems, Divine and Humanae.* London: Nonesuch Press, 1928. 552/1250 copies, printed on Van Gelder handmade paper, typographical border to titlepage, foolscap 8vo., original limp white parchment, backstrip and front cover blocked in gilt, pigskin thongs, untrimmed, board slipcase, fine. Blackwell's Rare Books B174 - 365 2013 £90

Beerbohm, Max 1872-1956 *A Book of Caricatures.* London: Methuen, 1907. First edition, folio, each caricature protected by tissue guard, original red cloth backed red cloth boards, spine printed paper label on front cover and gilt title and author to spine, spine has few split boards faded and rubbed, with bumping to corners, foxing to endpapers but plates clean, very good. The Kelmscott Bookshop 7 - 72 2013 $750

Beerbohm, Max 1872-1956 *Mainly on the Air.* London: Heinemann, 1946. First edition, 8vo., original red cloth, near fine, inscribed by author, loosely inserted c. 60 word als to recipient. Maggs Bros. Ltd. 1460 - 70 2013 £275

Beerbohm, Max 1872-1956 *The Works of Max Beerbohm.* London: William Heinemann, 1922. One of 780 copies signed by author, First volume only of the collected edition, 8vo., original red cloth, printed label on spine, spine faded, endpapers browned, bookplate to front pastedown, excellent copy. Maggs Bros. Ltd. 1460 - 69 2013 £200

Beerbohm, Max 1872-1956 *Zuleika Dobson or an Oxford Love Story.* Oxford: Shakespeare Head Press, 1975. 580/750 copies signed by artist, 2 color printed plates, reproductions of 5 pencil character sketches by Beerbohm within prelims, initial letter at beginning of each chapter and shoulder titles printed in dark cerise, titlepage printed in black and cerise, small folio, original quarter Oxford blue morocco, gilt lettered backstrip with gilt blocked Lancaster drawing "Bullington" blue and white vertically striped sides, bookplate, top edge gilt, blue cotton marker, near fine. Blackwell's Rare Books 172 - 306 2013 £225

Beeton, S. O. *Beeton's Famous Voyages, Brigand Adventures, Tales of the Battlefield, Life and Nature.* London: Ward, Lock and Tyler, n.d., 1873. Thick 8vo., original blindstamped cloth, gilt, neatly recased, frontispiece (repaired in gutter on reverse) and numerous text woodcuts. R. F. G. Hollett & Son Children's Books - 54 2013 £85

Begbie, Harold *Great Men.* London: Grant Richards, 1901. 4to, 51 pages, cloth backed pictorial boards, some cover soil, else very good and clean, full page color illustrations by F. Carruthers Gould. Aleph-Bet Books, Inc. 105 - 522 2013 $200

Begg, James *The Proposed Disestablishment of Protestantism in Ireland...* Edinburgh: 1868. First edition, octavo, 32 pages, including one page of ads, modern wrappers, very good. C. P. Hyland 261 - 31 2013 £50

Begley, Louis *Wartime Lies.* New York: Knopf, 1991. First edition, signed by author, fine in fine dust jacket. Ed Smith Books 78 - 6 2013 $175

Behan, Brendan *The Quare Fellow.* London: Methuen, 1956. First edition, original black cloth, dust jacket slightly nicked and creased at head and tail of spine and at corners, near fine, inscribed by author to artist Arnold Rosin. Maggs Bros. Ltd. 1460 - 71 2013 £1800

Behan, Dominic *Teems of Times and Happy Returns.* London: Heinemann, 1961. First edition, 8vo., original purple cloth, dust jacket, near fine, jacket slightly nicked, creased at head and tail of spine and corners, inscribed by Behan 7th Dec. 1961. Maggs Bros. Ltd. 1460 - 73 2013 £100

Behn, Aphra 1640-1689 *All the Histories and Novels Written by the Late Ingenious Mrs. Behn... Together with the History of the Life and Memoirs of Mrs. Behn.* London: for R. Wellington, 1705. Fifth edition, contemporary panelled calf, very skillfully rebacked in period style tear through several line of text on S2 repaired, several other minor largely marginal tears neatly repaired and blank corners replaced, marginal staining on last few leaves, very good. Joseph J. Felcone Inc. English and American Literature to 1800 - 2 2013 $2800

Behn, Aphra 1640-1689 *The Fair Jilt or The Amours of Prince Tarquin and Miranda.* London: printed and sold by C. Sympson and J. Miller between, 1750-1770. Second edition, small hole in inner margin of first leaf, not affecting text, rust hole in inner margin of first leaf, not affecting text, rust hole in another leaf with loss of couple of letters, last leaf little browned, mainly in margins, 8vo., 20th century full simulated ocelot fur (actual skin being rabbit), ownership inscription along inner margin of titlepage partially erased (producing small hole mentioned above), very good. Blackwell's Rare Books 172 - 19 2013 £1500

Behrend, Arthur *Unlucky for Some.* London: Eyre & Spottiswoode, 1955. First edition, original cloth, gilt, dust jacket, pages 190, presentation copy from author for A(rthur) Duxbury June 1958, with APC from author loosely inserted. R. F. G. Hollett & Son Lake District & Cumbria - 96 2013 £30

Behrman, S. N. *Brief Moment.* New York: Farrar & Rinehart Inc., 1931. First edition, inscribed by Behrman to Dame Nellie Burton, Berhman's landlady when he stayed in London, red cloth with title and author in black on front cover and spine, interior bright and clean, some light spotting to fore edge, jacket has small tears to top and bottom of spine, near fine, very good dust jacket.   The Kelmscott Bookshop   7 - 85   2013 $300

Belcher, Henry *Illustrations of the Scenery on the Line of the Whitby and Pickering Railway in the North Eastern Part of Yorkshire.* London: Longman, Rees, 1836. Large 8vo., errata slip, frontispiece, engraved titlepage and 11 plates, some slight foxing, but very good in original gilt lettered cloth, foot of spine neatly repaired.   Ken Spelman Books Ltd.   73 - 166   2013   £140

Bell, Adrian *Sunrise to Sunset.* London: John Lane, Bodley Head, 1944. First edition, original cloth, rather marked, nice, clean copy, rather scare.   R. F. G. Hollett & Son   Lake District & Cumbria - 97   2013   £30

Bell, Arthur G. *Nuremberg.* London: A. & C. Black, 1905. First edition, 8vo., top edge gilt, original blue decorative cloth.   J. & S. L. Bonham Antiquarian Booksellers   Europe - 6261   2013   £45

Bell, Charles   1774-1842 *The Anatomy and Philosophy of Expression as Connected in the Fine Arts.* London: John Murray, 1844. Third edition, half morocco and pebbled boards, gilt paneled spine, rubbed and worn, illustrations, plus 2 tipped in illustrations hand drawn by Bell, inscribed by author's wife, Marion for friend Alexander Snow.   James Tait Goodrich   75 - 21   2013 $9500

Bell, Charles   1774-1842 *The Anatomy and Physiology of the Human Body.* New York: Collins, 1827. Fifth American edition, 2 volumes, 4to., 9 plates, tables foxed, browned, original tree calf, gilt spine, red leather spine label, rubbed, ownership signature of Samuel Tredwell, very good.   Jeff Weber Rare Books   172 - 15   2013 $900

Bell, Charles   1774-1842 *The Anatomy of the Brain, Explained in a Series of Engravings.* London: T. N. Longman & O. Rees, 1802. 4to., 12 engraved plates, 11 are hand colored, original boards, new backing in linen and corners repaired, original paper label on front board, text uncut, large margins, some light foxing and browning, otherwise clean, tall handsome copy in original boards, with ALS by Bell dated July 29 1836.   James Tait Goodrich   75 - 20   2013 $5950

Bell, Charles   1774-1842 *The Hand: Its Mechanism and Vital Endowments as Evincing Design.* London: William Pickering, 1833. Second edition, 8vo., illustrations, lacks half title, modern blue cloth, red leather spine label, head of spine expertly repaired, spine faded, label rubbed, ownership signature of Charles A. Carton, ownership rubber stamp of Bellis on title, fine.   Jeff Weber Rare Books   172 - 19   2013 $750

Bell, Charles   1774-1842 *Illustrations of the Great Operations of Surgery, Trepan, Hernia, Amputation, Aneurism and Lithotomy.* London: Longman, Hurst, Rees, Orme and Brown, 1821. First edition, first issue with "Hurst and date in imprint, and Bell's title not mentioning the University of London, 20 surgical plates, of which 17 are hand colored, oblong 4to., recent quarter calf and marbled boards, some light offsetting, occasional spotting on plates, overall very good.   James Tait Goodrich   S74 - 27   2013 $5500

Bell, Charles   1774-1842 *Institutes of Surgery; Arranged in the Order of the Lectures Delivered in the University of Edinburgh.* Edinburgh: Adam and Charles Black; London: Longman, Orme, Brown, Green & Longmans, 1838. First edition, 2 volumes, 12mo., original green cloth, printed paper spine labels, rubbed, volume II faded, ownership signatures of I. M. Brandon 1839, very good.   Jeff Weber Rare Books   172 - 18   2013 $375

Bell, Charles   1774-1842 *Letters Concerning the Diseases of the Urethra.* Boston: W. Wells & T. B. Wait; Philadelphia: Edward Earle, 1811. First American edition, small 4to., 6 engraved plates, untrimmed, last 2 plates moderately foxed, original printed boards, extremities and spine chipped, bookplate of Robert A. Chase, very good, very rare in original printed boards, laid in new blue cloth drop back box, black calf spine label.   Jeff Weber Rare Books   172 - 20   2013 $600

Bell, Charles   1774-1842 *The Nervous System of the Human Body.* Washington: Duff, Green, 1833. First American edition, 8vo., 9 engraved plates, contemporary half tan calf and marbled boards, text foxed, clean, tight copy.   James Tait Goodrich   S74 - 26   2013 $795

Bell, Charles   1774-1842 *Observations on Injuries of the Spine and of the Thigh Bone in Two Lectures Delivered in the School of Great Windmill Street.* London: printed for Thomas Tegg, 1824. First edition, 4to., 9 engraved plates, with plate 9 bound in as frontispiece, light offsetting associated with plates marginal waterstains, quarter red buckram, boards, gilt spine, cover soil, blindstamp of Presbyterian Hospital, Ludlow Library, Philadelphia, ownership signature of Charles A. Carton, very good, unopened, rare.   Jeff Weber Rare Books   172 - 21   2013 $1200

Bell, Charles 1774-1842 *A Series of Engravings, Explaining the Course of the Nerves.* London: Longman, Hurst, Rees Orme & Brown, 1816. Second edition, 4to., 9 engraved plates, light foxing, modern half calf over marbled boards, gilt stamped spine title, fine, choice copy.   Jeff Weber Rare Books   172 - 22   2013 $1200

Bell, Christine *Saint.* Englewood: Pineapple Press, 1985. First edition, signed by author in 1992, with 3 page original story by Bell in form of letter, book has foxing to endpages and page edges, near fine in like dust jacket foxed on verso, letter/story is a dot matrix printout folded in thirds and signed by Bell.   Ken Lopez Bookseller   159 - 17   2013 $350

Bell, Clive *The Legend of Monte Della Siblilla or Le Paradis de la Reine Sibille.* Richmond: printed and published by Leonard and Virginia Woolf at the Hogarth Press, 1923. First edition, 4to., original pictorial boards, excellent copy, inscribed by author, loosely inserted is 18 line poem in author's holograph with title.   Maggs Bros. Ltd.   1460 - 74   2013   £500

Bell, J. Bowyer *The Secret Army: a History of the IRA 1916-1970.* 1970. 8vo., illustrations., cloth, dust jacket, near fine.   C. P. Hyland   261 - 909   2013   £34

Bell, John 1763-1820 *The Anatomy and Physiology of the Human Body.* New York: Collins, 1817-1822. Complete set, mixed set, volumes I and II third American edition, volume III fourth American edition, 3 volumes, small 4to., 35 engraved plates, foxed, browned, volume III heavily, occasional ink marginalia, volumes I and II, offsetting from plates and figures, occasional marginal waterstaining, original tree calf, gilt spine, brown leather spine labels, rebacked, preserving original spines, rubbed, ownership signatures of George Eagen, Cranford, Montgomery, New York, N.D. 1837 and William H. Mann, John Mann and Arthur H. Mann Jr., Baltimore, very good.   Jeff Weber Rare Books   172 - 23   2013 $750

Bell, John 1763-1820 *The Principles of Surgery.* Edinburgh: T. Cadell Jun & Davies, 1801. 1806, 3 parts bound as two, numerous illustrations, some folding, some hand colored, drawn by Bell, 4to., three quarter calf.   James Tait Goodrich   75 - 24   2013 $3500

Bell, Julian *Winter Movement and Other Poems.* London: Chatto & Windus, 1930. First edition, 8vo., original brown cloth, printed paper label, signed by author, label browned and little worn along one edge, cloth lightly soiled otherwise excellent.   Maggs Bros. Ltd.   1460 - 75   2013   £75

Bell, Lady *The Singing Circle.* London: Longmans, Green and Co., 1911. Large 8vo., original blue cloth gilt, pictorial onlay, trifle stained at fore-edge, color illustrations.   R. F. G. Hollett & Son   Children's Books - 92   2013   £25

Bell, Louise Price *Kitchen Fun.* Cleveland: Harter, 1932. First edition?, with H114 on cover, small 4to., 28 pages, pictorial cover by Jessie Wilcox Smith, illustrations, covers bent, affecting paper on pastedowns, some foxed, inscription "Alice from Mother/Christmas 1934", good, clean copy.   Second Life Books Inc.   183 - 20   2013 $50

Bell, Madison Smartt *L'Amoure en Ronde" in Camping d'Amour No. 2.* Brussels: Fondation Europeene pour la Sculpture, 1997. One of 500 numbered copies, fine in stapled wrappers, scarce, attractively illustrated.   Ken Lopez Bookseller   159 - 18   2013 $150

Bell, Walter Dalrymple Maitland 1800-1851 *The Wanderings of an Elephant Hunter.* Neville Spearman & The Holland Press, 1958. Facsimile edition, original cloth, gilt, dust jacket spine very slightly browned, 87 illustrations, small label removed, top edges trifle dusty.   R. F. G. Hollett & Son   Africana - 15   2013   £65

Bell, William A. *New Tracks in North America.* Albuquerque: 1965. Reprint of 1869 First edition, Folding map, illustrations, near fine in dust jacket.   Dumont Maps & Books of the West   125 - 41   2013 $85

Bell, William Gardner *Will James. the Life and Works of a Lone Cowboy.* Flagstaff: Northland Press, 1987. First edition, quarto, xx, 130 pages, color frontispiece, 13 color plates, 68 reproductions, numerous photos, brown cloth, lettered in gilt, very fine with pictorial dust jacket.   Argonaut Book Shop   Recent Acquisitions June 2013 - 155   2013 $150

Bell, Winthrop *The "Foreign Protestants" and the Setting of Nova Scotia.* Toronto: University of Toronto Press, 1961. First edition, red cloth with gilt to spine in dust jacket, half title, maps and black and white photos illustrations, 10 x 7 inches, large 8vo., very good, dust jacket sunned along spine and edges, generally very good.   Schooner Books Ltd.   105 - 54   2013 $125

Bellagatta, Antonio *Le Disavventure Della Medicina Cagionate da' Pregiudizj della Falsa Emulzione....* Milan: Heirs of Domenico Bellagatta, 1743. First edition, 2 parts in one volume, continuously paginated, some foxing and dampstaining, original carta rustica, spine partly defective, sound, rare.   Blackwell's Rare Books   Sciences - 12   2013   £650

Bellairs, George *Death Brings in the New Year.* New York: Macmillan, 1950. First American edition, foxing to endpapers and jacket flaps, else fine in near fine dust jacket with slight wear at extremities, Advance Review copy with slip and publisher's publicity material laid in.   Between the Covers Rare Books, Inc.   Mystery & Detective Fiction - 285382   2013 $200

Bellamy, Edward *Looking Backward 2000-1887.* Boston: Houghton Mifflin, 1926. Riverside Library, 8vo., pages 337, very good in publisher's cloth, stain on hinge of rear endpaper, inscribed by author's wife, Emma for Walter James Henry, also inscribed by his daughter Marian Bellamy Ernshaw Oct. 24 1935, laid in is 9 x 6 inch handbill advertising talk given by Marion and Emma Bellamy at the Seattle Civic Auditorium, scarce.   Second Life Books Inc.   183 - 21   2013 $300

Bellin, J. Nicolas *Description des Debouquemens qui Sont au Nord de l'"isle de Saint Domingue.* Versailles: Dept. de Marin, 1773. Second edition, engraved title and 34 plates, including 11 folding charts, 4to., fine contemporary French mottled calf, marbled endpapers, clean and bright copy, scarce.   Maggs Bros. Ltd.   1467 - 109   2013   £4450

Bellmer, Hans *Die Puppe.* Berlin: Gehrdt Verlag, 1962. First edition, one of 2000 copies, softcover, 15 tipped in color plates, fine in very near fine plastic jacket, fresh copy.   Jeff Hirsch Books   Fall 2013 - 129101   2013 $450

Belloc, Hilaire 1870-1953 *Essays of a Catholic Layman in England.* London: Sheed & Ward, 1931. First edition, 8vo., original blue cloth, excellent copy, spine faded, closed tear to head of cloth of spine, inscribed by author for Charlotte Balfour.   Maggs Bros. Ltd.   1460 - 77   2013   £200

Belloc, Hilaire 1870-1953 *Esto Perpetua.* London: Duckworth, 1911. Original blue cloth gilt, tipped in color frontispiece and line drawings in text, scarce.   R. F. G. Hollett & Son   Africana - 16   2013   £50

Belloc, Hilaire 1870-1953 *Europe and the Faith.* London: Constable, 1920. First edition, large 8vo., original blue cloth, inscribed by author 8th Sept. 1920 for Charlotte Balfour, excellent copy, spine faded.   Maggs Bros. Ltd.   1460 - 76   2013   £350

Belloc, Hilaire 1870-1953 *New Cautionary Tales.* London: Duckworth, 1930. First edition, Small 4to., cloth backed pictorial boards, 79 pages, faint crease in some pages, else fine in chipped dust jacket, illustrations in line by Bentley.   Aleph-Bet Books, Inc.   105 - 77   2013 $275

Bellow, Saul *Herzog.* London: Weidenfeld and Nicolson, 1965. First UK edition, 8vo., original black cloth, excellent copy, dust jacket slightly rubbed and chipped, inscribed by author.   Maggs Bros. Ltd.   1460 - 78   2013   £275

Bellow, Saul *Him with His Foot in His Mouth.* New York: Harper & Row, 1984. First edition, inscribed by author to Chicago author John Frederick Nims and his wife, Bonnie Larkin Nims, offsetting to rear endpages where two articles about Bellow were laid in, also laid in is copy of typed review of the book by Chicago bookseller Stuart Brent.   Ken Lopez Bookseller   159 - 19   2013 $500

Bellow, Saul *Something to Remember Me By.* New York: Albondocani Press, 1991. First edition, one of 350 numbered copies signed by author, total edition of 376, publisher's prospectus laid in, fine in fine acetate dust jacket.   Ed Smith Books   75 - 2A   2013 $225

Bellow, Saul *Something to Remember Me By.* New York: Albondocani Press, 1991. First edition one of 26 lettered copies signed by author, total edition of 376, publisher's prospectus laid in, fine in acetate dust jacket as issued.   Ed Smith Books   75 - 2   2013 $750

Bellow, Saul *The Victim.* New York: Vanguard, 1947. First edition, signed by author, very good in black cloth boards, blue title to spine, minor wear to corners and spine ends, very light evidence of minor dampstain to rear board, signed by previous owner, browning to both gutters, otherwise clean, good, light blue dust jacket with white title to spine and front panel, several large chips to top edge of dust jacket, few small chips to bottom edge, browning to spine and panel and subtle dampstaining to rear panel, 294 pages.   The Kelmscott Bookshop   7 - 96   2013 $500

Beloe, Edward Milligen *Our Churches: King's Lynn, Norfolk.* Cambridge: Macmillan and Bowes, 1900. 4to., 70 plates, brown cloth, paper label to spine, endcaps creased, boards very slightly marked, splitting a little near p. 28 but binding sound, ownership inscription of R. C. Coulton.   Unsworths Antiquarian Booksellers   28 - 147   2013   £200

Bembo, Pietro 1470-1547 *Rime Di M. Pietro Bembo.* Venice: Giovanni Antonio & Fratelli da Sabbio, 1530. First edition, 2 parts in one small quarto, 58 of 60 leaves, lacking initial and final blanks, separate collation for each part, contemporary mottled calf, spine decoratively gilt, edges stained red, top joint cracked but cords strong, some spine restoration and old leather repairs to edges, old ink signature on (A2), former owner's color penciled initials, occasional soiling and light marginal dampstains, few repairs in gutters, overall very good with magnificent broad margins, quarter morocco clamshell case.   Heritage Book Shop   50th Anniversary Catalogue - 9   2013 $8000

Bemelmans, Ludwig *Madeline's Christmas.* New York: 1956. First edition, pictorial wrappers, original pictorial envelope, rear flap repaired, toned where originally attached to magazine, color illustrations, fragile, very scarce, especially with envelope.   Aleph-Bet Books, Inc.   104 - 67   2013 $400

Bemelmans, Ludwig *Madeline's Rescue.* New York: Viking, 1953. First edition, folio, cloth, 56 pages, fine in very good+ dust jacket with small chip at head of spine, color illustrations by author, nice.   Aleph-Bet Books, Inc.   104 - 68   2013 $1000

Bemelmans, Ludwig *Madeline's Rescue.* New York: Viking, 1953. First edition, folio, cloth, 56 pages, fine in dust jacket lightly frayed at spine ends, illustrations in color, rare.   Aleph-Bet Books, Inc.   105 - 79   2013 $1200

Bemelmans, Ludwig *Sunshine.* New York: Simon & Schuster, 1950. First edition, folio, boards, near fine, dust jacket worn on spine, color pictorial endpapers, color illustrations on every page.   Aleph-Bet Books, Inc.   104 - 69   2013 $250

Bemelmans, Ludwig *True Love Story.* no publishing information, 1950. 8 1/8 x 3 inches, stapled pictorial wrappers, light cover soil and corners nipped on last leaf, else very good+, printed on one side of paper, each leaf with full page color illustration, rare.   Aleph-Bet Books, Inc.   105 - 78   2013 $600

Benard, Claude *Lecons des Anesthesiques et sur l'Asphysie.* Paris: J. B. Bailliere et fils, 1875. First edition, 8vo., 7 text figures, modern quarter black morocco over marbled boards, raised bands, gilt stamped spine title, original paper wrappers bound in, bookplate of Andras Gedeon, fine.   Jeff Weber Rare Books   172 - 24   2013 $700

Bence-Jones, M. *Burke's Guide to Country Houses. Volume I Ireland.* 1978. First edition, 8vo., profusely illustrated, cloth, dust jacket, near fine.   C. P. Hyland   261 - 32   2013   £55

Bence-Jones, M. *Twilight of the Ascendancy.* 1987. First edition, cloth, 8vo., dust jacket, near fine.   C. P. Hyland   261 - 33   2013   £35

Benci, Spinello *Storia di Montepulciano... Dedicata al Sereniss. Principe Giovancarlo di Toscana...* Florence: Amador Massi, 1646. Second edition, 4to., engraved titlepage coat of arms, full page woodcut portrait, errata, woodcut initials, headpieces and tailpieces, light foxing to final 2 pages, 19th century quarter vellum over marbled paper backed boards, gilt stamped leather spine label, label worn, bookplate of Bernadine Murphy, booklabel at spine's foot, fine.   Jeff Weber Rare Books   171 - 22   2013 $1000

Benezet, Anthony *Some Historical Account of Guinea...* London: J. Phillips, 1788. New edition, half title, very good, large uncut copy, recent quarter calf, marbled boards.   Ken Spelman Books Ltd.   75 - 42   2013   £595

Benjamin, Asher *The Country Builder's Assistant....* Greenfield: John Denio, 1805. Fourth and final edition, 8vo., (35 of 36) pages, frontispiece and 36 numbered plates, two folded, contemporary calf, leather label, unrepaired and unsophisticated, some browning and offsetting but very nice, 2 folding plates have slight damage (some short breaks in folds), but complete, unfortunately plate 18 present in duplicate and plate 16 is lacking, never having been bound in, one descriptive leaf of text is lacking.   M & S Rare Books, Inc.   95 - 18   2013 $6000

Bennet, William *Songs of Solitude.* Glasgow: W. R. M'Phun, 1831. First edition, contemporary half black calf, spine with raised gilt bands and blind devices, black leather label little rubbed, ownership inscription of Alex Donald.   Jarndyce Antiquarian Booksellers   CCIII - 643   2013   £75

Bennett, Alan *Habeas Corpus.* London: Faber and Faber, 1973. First edition, 8vo., original grey cloth, inscribed by author for Ian Gray, excellent copy in dust jacket, rubbed at edges with 2cm. chunk missing from lower spine.   Maggs Bros. Ltd.   1460 - 79   2013   £350

Bennett, Arnold   1867-1931 *Mediterranean Scenes: Rome-Greece-Constantinople.* London: Cassell, 1928. First edition, number 789 of 1000 copies, large 8vo., pages 84, 40 illustrations, original cloth, covers faded and flecked.   J. & S. L. Bonham Antiquarian Booksellers   Europe - 2683   2013   £65

Bennett, Arnold   1867-1931 *The Old Wives' Tale.* London: Hodder & Stoughton, 1912. First edition, 8vo., original blue cloth, inscribed by author for Hugh Walpole, with his armorial bookplate, excellent copy.   Maggs Bros. Ltd.   1460 - 81   2013   £1200

Bennett, Arnold   1867-1931 *Riceyman Steps.* London: Cassell, 1923. First edition, 8vo., original pale green cloth, excellent copy, dust jacket rubbed and nicked

dust jacket, long closed tear at outer edge, inscribed by author to Andre Gide.   Maggs Bros. Ltd.   1460 - 83   2013   £1850

Bennett, Arnold   1867-1931 *These Twain.* London: Methuen, 1916. First edition, 8vo., original blue cloth, excellent copy, inscribed by author 5/1/16 for Edward Garnett.   Maggs Bros. Ltd.   1460 - 82   2013   £750

Bennett, Arnold   1867-1931 *The Truth About an Author.* New York: George H. Doran, 1911. New edition, 8vo., original cream cloth, printed paper label on spine, inscribed by author for Duff (Alistair Tayler - sic), excellent copy, loosely inserted is ALS to Duff from John Drinkwater.   Maggs Bros. Ltd.   1460 - 80   2013   £350

Bennett, Arnold 1867-1931 *Venus Rising from the Sea.* London: Cassell, 1931. First edition, 177/350 copies, printed on handmade paper and signed by artist, 12 full page stencilled line drawings by E. McKnight Kauffer, imperial 8vo., original pale grey linen, lightly sunned backstrip and front cover lettered and with line design in dark grey, owner's name on front free endpaper, untrimmed, lightly worn, board slipcase with printed label, fine.   Blackwell's Rare Books   172 - 218   2013   £200

Bennett, C. J. B. *The Galweys of Iota.* 1909. First edition, 4 photos, 166 pages, cloth, very good.   C. P. Hyland   261 - 389   2013   £105

Bennett, Charles Henry *London People; Sketched from Life.* London: Smith, Elder and Co., 1863. 4to., half title, frontispiece and plates, some spotting, original blue cloth, bevelled boards, slightly rubbed and dulled, armorial bookplate of Horace Noble Pym, all edges gilt.   Jarndyce Antiquarian Booksellers   CCV - 19   2013   £150

Bennett, Frederick Debell *Narrative of a Whaling Voyage Round the Globe from the Year 1833 to 1836.* London: 1840. First edition, 2 volumes, folding map and 2 aquatint frontispiece, 8vo., original cloth, rebacked, original spines laid down, prelims trifle foxed, contemporary annotations in pencil to volume two, increasingly rare.   Maggs Bros. Ltd.   1467 - 71   2013   £2500

Bennett, Joan *Pigtails of Ah Lee Ben Loo.* New York and London: Longmans Green, 1928. First edition, 4to., 200 comical silhouettes, orange cloth, titlepage.   Barnaby Rudge Booksellers Children 2013 - 020586   2013 $50

Bennett, Melba Berry *Robinson Jeffers and the Sea.* San Francisco: Gelber, Lilienthal, 1936. First edition, one of 300 copies, frontispiece, facsimile, 7 pages of photos, printed throughout in red and black, dark green morocco spine, orange boards decorated in yellow and green spine ends slightly faded, light offsetting to free ends, else very fine.   Argonaut Book Shop   Summer 2013 - 172   2013 $400

Bennett, Rodney *Widgery Wink and His New Friends.* London: University of London Press, 1945. First edition, large 8vo., original pages 124 color frontispiece and line drawings by Frank Rogers, few colored by hand, semicircular piece chewed out of bottom margin of first 58 pages.   R. F. G. Hollett & Son   Children's Books - 55   2013   £30

Bennett, William Harper *Catholic Footsteps in Old New York: a Chronicle of Catholicity in the City of New York from 1524 to 1808.* New York: Schwartz, Kirwin and Fauss, 1909. First edition, small gift inscription, else fine bright copy.   Between the Covers Rare Books, Inc.   New York City - 286040   2013 $150

Benson, Allan L. *A Way to Prevent War.* Girard Appeal to Reason, 1915. First edition, blue cloth stamped gilt, fine.   Beasley Books   2013 - 2013 $65

Benson, C. E. *Crag and Hound in Lakeland.* London: Hurst and Blackett, 1902. First edition, original cloth, gilt, 28 illustrations.   R. F. G. Hollett & Son   Lake District & Cumbria - 101   2013   £60

Benson, E. F. *The Angel of Pain.* London: Heinemann, 1906. First edition, owner name, some foxing to fore edge and scattered throughout text, top corners bumped, little soiling to boards, attractive, very good, lacking rare dust jacket.   Between the Covers Rare Books, Inc.   Sci-Fi, Fantasy & Horror - 56671   2013 $450

Benson, E. F. *The Babe B. A. Being the Uneventful History of a Young Gentleman at Cambridge University.* Putnam, 1897. First edition, frontispiece and 5 other photographic plates, frontispiece tissue foxed, hinges weak, foolscap 8vo., original maroon straight grain morocco cloth slightly stained, faded backstrip gilt lettered, front cover lettered in blue with crest stamped in Cambridge blue and gilt at its centre, owner's name, rough trimmed, good.   Blackwell's Rare Books   B174 - 171   2013   £60

Benson, E. F. *Ravens' Brood.* New York: Doubleday Doran and Co., 1934. First American edition, very slightly cocked else fine in very good dust jacket with small chips near foot and modest chip to rear panel, very scarce.   Between the Covers Rare Books, Inc.   Sci-Fi, Fantasy & Horror - 89161   2013 $600

Benson, E. F. *Visible and Invisible.* New York: Doran, 1924. First American edition, fine in attractive very good plus dust jacket with some small chips internally repaired with brown paper, very scarce in jacket.   Between the Covers Rare Books, Inc.   Sci-Fi, Fantasy & Horror - 42400   2013 $950

Benson, Raymond *High Time to Kill.* London: Hodder & Stoughton, 1999. First edition, 8vo., original black boards backstrip gilt lettered, dust jacket, fine, signed by author.   Blackwell's Rare Books   B174 - 203   2013   £125

Benson, Raymond *The World Is Not Enough 07.* London: Hodder & Stoughton, 1999. First edition, signed by author, very fine in dust jacket.   Mordida Books   81 - 179   2013 $150

Benson, Therese *Death Wears a Mask.* New York: Harper & Bros., 1935. First edition, fine in striking, about fine dust jacket with couple of short tears and one flap professionally reattached.   Between the Covers Rare Books, Inc.   Mystery & Detective Fiction - 46710   2013 $280

Benson, Thomas Park *"As I Return to Yesteryear".* Owen Sound, Ontario: privately published by Fleming Folding Cartons, 1981. Second printing, original pictorial wrappers, 13 pages of illustrations, stapled in single thick section, scare.   R. F. G. Hollett & Son   Lake District & Cumbria - 102   2013   £50

Bent, Samuel A. *Short Sayings of Great Men with Historical and Explanatory Notes.* Boston: James R. Osgood, 1882. Second edition, original cloth, wear to extremities, shaken, else very good, recent protective custom made folding cloth box, Mark Twain's personal copy signed S. L. Clemens Hartford 1885, with marginal and interlinear pencil annotations in four places.   James Tait Goodrich   75 - 206   2013 $7995

Bentham, Jeremy   1748-1832 *Bentham's Radical Reform Bill; with Extracts from the Reasons.* London: E. Wilson, 1819. Half title, recently bound in half calf, new endpapers. Jarndyce Antiquarian Booksellers   CCV - 21   2013   £450

Bentham, Jeremy   1748-1832 *Plan of Parliamentary Reform, in the Form of a Catechism...* London: R. Hunter, 1817. First edition, rebound in marbled boards, black cloth spine, black morocco label "from the author" trimmed through at head of titlepage, stamps of Tate Central Library, very good.   Jarndyce Antiquarian Booksellers   CCV - 22   2013   £750

Bentley, Edmund Clerihew *Trent's Own Case.* London: Constable, 1936. First edition, 8vo., original orange cloth lettered in blue, lightly browned on spine, otherwise excellent copy, inscribed by author.   Maggs Bros. Ltd.   1460 - 85   2013   £375

Berardis, Vincenzo *Italy and Ireland in the Middle Ages.* 1950. First edition, octavo, cloth, illustrations, dust jacket torn, very good.   C. P. Hyland   261 - 34   2013   £45

Berdmore, Thomas *A Treatise on the Disorders and Deformities of the Teeth and Gums.* London: printed for the author, 1768. First edition, early quarter calf and marbled boards, later rebacking saving original spine, binding worn, final leaf in facsimile, 3 three of the front prelims have tears in margins, one just affecting catch word.   James Tait Goodrich   75 - 77   2013 $2500

Berendt, John *Midnight in the Garden of Good and Evil.* New York: Random House, 1994. First edition, advance reading copy, wrappers, 8 x 9 inches, fine, inscribed by author.   Beasley Books   2013 - 2013 $50

Berengario Da Carpi, Giacomo *Tractatus de Fractura Calve sive Cranel.* Bologna: Hieronymus de Benedictis 10 Dec., 1518. Roman type, title in gothic, anatomical woodcut on title, some early pen hatch strokes, 21 woodcut illustrations, 2 large woodcut initials numerous other smaller initials, early contemporary vellum, worn in parts and dusty, another work was bound in at front and removed at an early date.   James Tait Goodrich   75 - 26   2013 $12,500

Beresford, Elisabeth *The Wandering Wombles.* London: Ernest Benn, 1970. First edition, original cloth, gilt, dust jacket, pages 182, illustrations by Oliver Chadwick, fine. R. F. G. Hollett & Son   Children's Books - 56   2013   £95

Beresford, Elisabeth *The Wombles at Work.* London: Ernest Benn, 1973. First edition, original cloth gilt, dust jacket price clipped, 192 pages, illustrations by Margaret Gordon, fine.   R. F. G. Hollett & Son   Children's Books - 57   2013   £85

Berezniak, Leon A. *The Theatrical Counselor.* Chicago: Cooper Syndicate, 1923. First edition, gilt stamped black covers, uncommon work, near fine.   Beasley Books   2013 - 2013 $100

Berg, Charles *The Unconscious Significance of Hair.* London: George Allen & Unwin, 1951. First edition, trifle sunned at crown, else fine in age toned and modestly spine tanned, very good dust jacket.   Between the Covers Rare Books, Inc.   Psychology & Psychiatry - 97035   2013 $75

Berkeley, Anthony *Trial and Error.* Garden City: Doubleday, 1937. First edition, advance copy in perfect bound beige wrappers with publisher's letter printed on front cover, little flaking at spine crown and light corner crease to front (top) corner and few pages, tight solid, very good copy. Ed Smith Books   75 - 3   2013 $350

Berkeley, George, Bp. of Cloyne   1685-1793 *The Analyst; or a Discourse Addressed to an Infidel Mathematician.* London: printed for J. Tonson, 1734. First edition, 8vo., some browning, top corner of some leaves lightly creased recent functional half black calf, marbled boards, gilt lettered spine.   Jarndyce Antiquarian Booksellers   CCIV - 60   2013   £3800

Berkeley, George, Bp. of Cloyne   1685-1793 *Three Dialogues Between Hylas and Philonous.* London: printed for William and John Innys, 1725. Second edition, without 4-leaf gathering of ads at end, washed, several corners repaired (notably last leaf), small contemporary inscription to titlepage, 8vo., modern (not new) half calf, yellow edges by Bayntun sound.   Blackwell's Rare Books   172 - 20   2013   £1200

Berkeley, M. *Naval Alphabet.* London: A. & C. Black, n.d. circa, 1915. 4to., cloth, pictorial paste-on, light rubbing, very good+, full page color plates, pictorial border, illustrations by J. H. Hartley. Aleph-Bet Books, Inc. 105 - 13 2013 $400

Berman, Ed *Ten of the Best British Short Plays.* London: Inter-Action Imprint, 1979. First edition, this copy signed by Tom Stoppard, contributor, fine in fine, crisp dust jacket. Ed Smith Books 78 - 65 2013 $125

Berman, Wallace *Radio/Aether Series 1966/1974.* Los Angeles: Gemini G.E.L., 1974. First edition, limited to 50 copies with 10 artist's proofs, signed by Berman on titlepage, portfolio of 13 two-color offset lithographs, each photographed from original Verifax collage and printed on starwhite cover mounted on Gemini rag-board, in original screen printed fabric covered box, very fine. James S. Jaffe Rare Books Fall 2013 - 7 2013 $12,500

Bernard, Claude *Lecons de Physiologie Operatoire.* Paris: J. B. Balliere et Fils, 1879. First edition, 8vo., xvi, 624 pages, 116 illustrations, original printed wrappers, extremities lightly chipped, spine splitting, front cover ownership signature. Jeff Weber Rare Books 169 - 26 2013 $175

Bernard, Claude *Lecons sur la Pathologye et la Pathologie du Systeme Nerveux.* Paris: J. B. Bailliere, 1858. First edition, 2 volumes, 8vo., 65 woodcuts and illustrations, original printed wrappers, modern quarter gilt stamped black leather over marbled paper backed boards folding cases, matching slipcase, wrappers carefully repaired, spines slightly rubbed, fine. Jeff Weber Rare Books 172 - 26 2013 $1250

Bernard, Claude *Lecons sur la Physiologie et la Pathologie de Systeme Nerveux.* Paris: J. B. Bailliere et Fils, 1858. First edition, 2 volumes, 8vo., lightly foxed, 12 figures, contemporary cloth backed marbled boards, cloth corners, gilt spine, rubbed, fore edge bumped on volume I, very good, ownership signature of O. J. Raeder. Jeff Weber Rare Books 172 - 25 2013 $750

Bernard, Claude *Lecons sur les Proprieties Physiologiques et les Alterations Pathologiques des Liquides de L'Organisme.* Paris: Bailliere et fils, 1859. First edition, 2 volumes, 8vo., illustrations, foxed, modern black cloth, gilt spine, fine. Jeff Weber Rare Books 172 - 27 2013 $300

Bernard, Theos *Penthouse of the Gods.* New York: Charles Scribner's, 1939. First edition, signed and inscribed by author in year of publication, near fine in black cloth with gilt lettering and photo of Lhasa Palace tipped on front board as issued, front endpapers with offsetting from prior news clippings, very good dust jacket with 2 inch piece missing base of dust jacket spine, mild edge wear, 8vo., xii, 342 pages, with four issues of magazine "Family Circle" included, with 6 x 4 inch photo of author, and publicity brochure from W. Colson Leigh. By the Book, L. C. 36 - 87 2013 $1000

Berne, Jacques *Le Flux Meme: Seize Poemes de Jacques Berne Illustres par Jean Dubuffet.* Paris: Editions St. Germain des Pres, 1976. First edition, number 7 of 50 copies (total edition 70 + several HC copies), numbered and signed by author and artist, 26 original color serigraphs by Jean Dubuffet, 64 loose leaves in wrapper folder cloth chemise and slipcase, in new condition, overall size 13.25 x 10.25 inches. Gemini Fine Books & Arts., Ltd. Art Reference & Illustrated Books - 2013 $2500

Berners, Gerald Hugh *First Childhood.* London: Constable, 1934. First edition, 8vo., rebound in blue cloth, printed lettering piece to spine, inscribed by author. Maggs Bros. Ltd. 1460 - 88 2013 £250

Berners, Lord *A Distant Prospect, a Sequel to First Childhood.* London: Constable, 1945. First edition, 8vo., original blue cloth, dust jacket, inscribed by author to Violet Trefusis, near fine in dust jacket. Maggs Bros. Ltd. 1460 - 89 2013 £650

Bernstein, Morey *The Search for Bridey Murphy.* Garden City: Doubleday and Co., 1965. Stated new edition, near fine in very good dust jacket with modest chip at crown, with rubbing and small tears, inscribed by subject of the book, Virginia Morrow as "Bridey". Between the Covers Rare Books, Inc. Psychology & Psychiatry - 394851 2013 $100

Berrigan, Ted *In the Nam What Can Happen?* New York: Granary Books, 1997. First edition, limited to 70 copies, printed letterpress from magnesium plates on Rives 300 gm paper by Philip Gallo at Hermetic Press, signed by artist, of which 50 copies were for sale, square 4to., loose sheets in clear plastic slipcase, as new. James S. Jaffe Rare Books Fall 2013 - 20 2013 $1000

Berrigan, Ted *Memorial Day. A Collaboration by Ted Berrigan and Anne Waldman.* New York: Poetry Project, 1971. First edition, mimeographed, signed on first leaf of blue India paper by author with address and date "242 W 14th Fri. 8.30", presentation copy inscribed by author for Bernadette Mayer, fine. James S. Jaffe Rare Books Fall 2013 - 17 2013 $1500

Berrigan, Ted *The Morning Line.* Santa Barbara: Am Here Books/Immediate Editions, 1982. First edition, mimeographed, special issue, with manuscript poem by Berrigan bound in at back, in this copy, the two separated stapled sheets of paper holding the manuscript poem are separated from book, owing to fact that they evidently were not placed in a plastic binder as intended, manuscript poem "Old Moon" is signed by Berrigan, hand colored cover design signed by Tom Clark, fine.   James S. Jaffe Rare Books   Fall 2013 - 19   2013 $2500

Berrigan, Ted *Nothing for You.* Lenox: Angel Hair Books, 1977. First edition, limited to 1000 copies, 8vo., frontispiece by George Schneeman, original pictorial wrappers, author's copy inscribed on colopon page "Copy #1", advance copy sent to me by publisher for George and me to approve or demand re-printing. Rec'd Feb. 16th, 1978 and approved. Ted Berrigan. (an updated copy**) (**see corrections)", signed and annotated as well on same page by George Schneeman, this copy bears Berrigan's annotations, Berrigan has signed and dated frontispiece and added dedications to 8 of the poems, significantly revised poem "Kirsten" and signed one poem in full, fine.   James S. Jaffe Rare Books   Fall 2013 - 18   2013 $4500

Berrigan, Ted *Some Things.* New York: no publisher, circa, 1964. First edition, 4to., drawings by Joe Brainard, loose mimeograph sheets laid into plain paper folder, one of probably fewer than 100 copies printed, signed by Berrigan, Ron Padgett and Joe Brainard, (presumably) as usual, Brainard has signed twice, fine.   James S. Jaffe Rare Books   Fall 2013 - 21   2013 $1250

Berrigan, Ted *The Sonnets.* New York: Lorenz & Ellen Gude, 1964. First edition, mimeographed, limited to 300 numbered copies (plus an unspecified number of unnumbered copies), on colophon page, in place for number in statement, Berrigan has written the number '1' and signed his name, although not called for, this copy signed by Berrigan on titlepage, 4to., original stapled wrappers creased at lower right corner, covers worn and lightly soiled, otherwise very good.   James S. Jaffe Rare Books   Fall 2013 - 16   2013 $6500

Berry, Frank *Whittington. Memories of a Cotswold Village.* Andoversford: Whittington Press, 1982. 43/350 copies, printed on cream Glastonbury Laid paper and signed by author, 10 tipped in plates from photos, 5 capitals in text and title printed in orange, crown 8vo. original quarter dark brown cloth, printed label, patterned white boards, endpaper map engraved by Miriam Macgregory, untrimmed, fine. Blackwell's Rare Books   172 - 310   2013   £60

Berry, Geoffrey *Across Northern Hills.* Kendal: Westmorland Gazette, 1975. First edition, square 8vo. original cloth gilt, dust jacket, 122 photos, 10 maps, inscribed by author, scarce.   R. F. G. Hollett & Son   Lake District & Cumbria - 104   2013   £45

Berry, Geoffrey *The Lake District a Century of Conservation.* Edinburgh: John Bartholomew & Son, 1980. First edition, large 8vo., original cloth, gilt, dust jacket, 114 plates.   R. F. G. Hollett & Son   Lake District & Cumbria - 103   2013   £30

Berry, Wendell *Findings (Poems).* Iowa City: Prairie Press, 1969. First edition, 8vo., 63 pages, fine in dust jacket.   Second Life Books Inc.   183 - 29   2013 $300

Berry, Wendell *The Gift of Gravity, Illustrated by Timothy Engelland.* Deerfield/Dublin: Deerfield Press/Gallery Press, 1979. First edition, limited to 300 copies, signed, fine in dust jacket with closed tear to rear of dust jacket, brown endpapers with, some offsetting from dust jacket, spine title printed in upper and lower case letters dust jacket state 2 with title on spine in upper cover and lower case letters. Second Life Books Inc.   183 - 30   2013 $225

Berry, Wendell *The Landscape of Harmony Two Essays on Wilderness & Community...* London: Five Seasons Press, 1987. First edition, issued in an edition of 1000 copies, 8vo., pages 80, printed wrappers, near fine. Second Life Books Inc.   183 - 31   2013 $75

Berry, Wendell *The Long Legged Horse.* New York: Harcourt, 1969. First edition, 8vo., contemporary inscription on endpaper, otherwise fine in dust jacket (little soiled). Second Life Books Inc.   183 - 32   2013 $275

Berry, Wendell *The Memory of Old Jack.* New York: Harcourt Barce, 1974. First edition, 8vo., fine in frontispiece.   Second Life Books Inc.   183 - 34   2013 $165

Berry, Wendell *Nathan Coutler, a Novel.* Boston: Houghton Mifflin, 1960. First edition, endpapers little foxed, little wear at extremities of dust jacket spine, waterstain at bottom of spine of dust jacket, book near fine, scarce.   Second Life Books Inc.   183 - 35   2013 $300

Berry, Wendell *New Collected Poems.* Berkeley: Counterpoint, 2012. First edition, 8vo., fine in dust jacket. Second Life Books Inc.   183 - 35   2013 $300

Berry, Wendell *A Place on Earth.* New York: Harcourt Brace, 1967. First edition, 8vo., just about fine in fine dust jacket.   Second Life Books Inc.   183 - 37   2013 $500

Berry, Wendell *Collected Poems 1957-1982.* Berkeley: North Point Press, 1985. First edition, 8vo., 268 pages, fine in dust jacket, inscribed by author March 3 1987. Second Life Books Inc.   183 - 28   2013 $250

Berry, Wendell *The Rise.* Lexington: University of Kentucky Library Press, 1968. First edition, one of 100 numbered copies, signed by author, large 8vo., 16 pages, drab green-gray boards with white label on spine, very slightly rubbed at top of spine, couple of light soiling marks on covers, about fine, rare.   Second Life Books Inc.   183 - 39   2013 $350

Berry, Wendell *Three Memorial Poems.* Berkeley: Sand Dollar, 1977. First edition. 1/100 numbered and signed copies, 8vo., cloth, fine in little nicked original tissue, with one inch closed tear.   Second Life Books Inc.   183 - 40   2013 $150

Berry, Wendell *The Unforseen Wilderness.* Lexington: University Press of Kentucky, 1971. First edition, 1/1500 copies of a total edition of 3000, white cloth (covers little bowed), flat spine in little soiled dust jacket, very good.   Second Life Books Inc.   183 - 42   2013 $150

Berryman, John *Stephen Crane. The American Men of Letters Series.* New York: William Sloane Associates, 1950. First edition, 8vo., original cloth, dust jacket, inscribed by author to his teacher Mark Van Doren and Dorothy, fine, dust jacket neatly reinforced on verso of couple of places along flap folds.   James S. Jaffe Rare Books Fall 2013 - 23   2013 $5000

Bert, Paul *Recherches Experimentales sur l'Influence que les Modifications dans la Pression Barometrique Exercent sur les Phenomenes de la vie.* Paris: G. Masson, 1874. First edition in book form, 6 plates, 8vo., contemporary styled quarter morocco, marbled boards, fine.   Jeff Weber Rare Books   172 - 28   2013 $1200

Berton, Ralph *Remebering Bix.* New York: Harper, 1974. First edition, fine in fine dust jacket.   Beasley Books   2013 - 2013 $50

Bertrand, Philippus *Tractatus Tres de Justitia et Jure Ad Supplementum Theologiae Moralis Christianae Rev. Adm. D. Laurentii Neesen.* Liege: ex officina typographica Gerardi Grison, 1684. 4to., final leaf loose but present, two gatherings rather foxed, occasional underlining and pencil marks in text, contemporary sprinkled calf, spine in five compartments with raised bands, second gilt lettered direct, rest with gilt decoration, rubbed at extremities, some wear to edges.   Unsworths Antiquarian Booksellers   28 - 73   2013   £150

Besant, Walter *The Inner House.* Bristol: J. W. Arrowsmith 11 Quay Street, London: Simpkin, Marshall and Co., 1886. small octavo, original brown cloth, front panel stamped in black, spine panel stamped in gold, rear panel stamped in blind, black coated endpapers.   L. W. Currey, Inc.   Fall Sampler Sept. 2013 - 146182   2013 $1500

Beskow, Elsa *Peter's Voyage.* New York: Knopf, 1931. First US edition, square 4to., cloth backed pictorial boards, faint edge stain on boards, else fine in stained and frayed dust jacket, illustrations in color on every page by author.   Aleph-Bet Books, Inc.   104 - 70   2013 $250

Besnard, Peter *Observations on the Promotion of the Cultivation of Hemp and Flax... in the South of Ireland.* 1816. First edition, octavo, 26, 16 pages, disbound, light foxing.   C. P. Hyland   261 - 38   2013   £350

Best, Lloyd *Black Power and National Reconstruction: Proposals Following the February Revolution.* San Francisco: Tapia/Vanguard Pub. Co. Ltd. circa, 1970. First edition, folded sheets, 8 pages, soiled and little worn, very good,.   Between the Covers Rare Books, Inc.   165 - 79   2013 $150

Bestall, Alfred *Adventures of Rupert.* Daily Express Annual, 1950. First edition, pages 120, color illustrations, original pictorial boards, spine complete but creased and taped down, inscription on ownership page.   R. F. G. Hollett & Son   Children's Books - 58   2013   £85

Bestall, Alfred *More Adventures of Rupert.* Daily Express, 1947. First edition, small 4to., original pictorial wrappers, hinges trifle rubbed, 120 pages, illustrations in color, very nice, clean, sound copy.   R. F. G. Hollett & Son   Children's Books - 59   2013   £220

Bestall, Alfred *The New Rupert Book.* Daily Express, 1938. First edition, small 4to., original cloth backed boards, corners little bumped, 126 pages, illustrations in red and black, faint spots to title, small inked tiks to contents leaf, last leaf and lower pastedown trifle marked.   R. F. G. Hollett & Son   Children's Books - 60   2013   £350

Bestall, Alfred *A New Rupert Book.* Daily Express, 1945. First edition, small 4to., original pictorial wrappers, extremities faintly rubbed, illustrations in color, lovely clean unmarked copy.   R. F. G. Hollett & Son   Children's Books - 61   2013   £350

Bestall, Alfred *The New Rupert Book.* Daily Express, 1946. First edition, small 4to., original pictorial wrappers, extremities little rubbed, pages 120, illustrations in color, ownership box page filled in, very good, clean copy.   R. F. G. Hollett & Son   Children's Books - 62   2013   £140

Bestall, Alfred *The New Rupert Book.* Daily Express, 1946. First edition, small 4to., original pictorial boards, head and foot of spine, trifle worn, illustrations in color, ownership box page filled in, very good, clean, very nice, clean.   R. F. G. Hollett & Son   Children's Books - 63   2013   £120

Bestall, Alfred *The Rupert Book.* Daily Express, 1948. Small 4to., original pictorial wrappers, extremities little worn, 120 pages, illustrations in color, inscription on ownership box page, very good. R. F. G. Hollett & Son Children's Books - 65 2013 £120

Bestall, Alfred *Rupert.* Daily Express, 1949. First edition, small 4to., original pictorial wrappers, extremities little rubbed, pages 120, illustrations in color, name in ownership box, few light patches of browning to last leaf but very nice, sound copy. R. F. G. Hollett & Son Children's Books - 64 2013 £175

Bester, Alfred *The Computer Connection.* New York: Berkeley/G. P. Putnam's Sons, 1975. First edition, fine in fine dust jacket, virtually as new. Between the Covers Rare Books, Inc. Sci-Fi, Fantasy & Horror - 31993 2013 $100

Bester, Alfred *The Stars My Destination.* New York: Signet Book Pub. by the New American Library, 1957. First US edition, small octavo, pictorial wrappers. L. W. Currey, Inc. Fall Sampler Sept. 2013 - 146479 2013 $100

Betham-Edwards, Miss *Holidays in Eastern France.* London: Hurst & Blackett, 1879. First edition, 8vo., pages x, 328, ads, frontispiece, original red cloth, spine faded. J. & S. L. Bonham Antiquarian Booksellers Europe - 8495 2013 £30

Betham, Matilda *Elegies and Other Small Poems.* Ipswich: printed by W. Burrell, 1797. Half title discarded, lightly spotted, few leaves with small chips from blank margins, 2 early inscriptions (A. H. Cole - cropped) and (cropped 'to C. E. Adams 1810'), 12mo., slightly later half sprinkled calf, marbled boards, spine divided by sextuple gilt fillets, red morocco lettering piece, other compartments infilled with wave pallets or with central decorative gilt stamp, somewhat rubbed, good. Blackwell's Rare Books 172 - 22 2013 £700

Bethune, John Drinkwater 1762-1844 *A History of the Late Siege of Gibraltar.* London: 1786. Second edition, printed on thick paper, extra large folding frontispiece, 4 large folding engraved maps, engraved vignette to title and 6 fine folding engraved views printed in sepia, 4to., extremely fine contemporary tree calf, spine richly gilt in compartments with red morocco label and Macclesfield library plates, discreet Macclesfield crest blindstamped to title and maps, magnificent copy on thick paper. Maggs Bros. Ltd. 1467 - 39 2013 £2250

Betjeman, John 1906-1984 *Altar and Pew. Church of England Verse.* London: Edward Hulton, 1959. First edition, small 8vo., original wrappers, inscribed by author, later owner's signature, otherwise near fine. Maggs Bros. Ltd. 1460 - 96 2013 £175

Betjeman, John 1906-1984 *Church Poems.* London: John Murray, 1980. First edition, 8vo., original green cloth, dust jacket, first state with various printing omissions, fading to spine, otherwise near fine in dust jacket, inscribed by author. Maggs Bros. Ltd. 1460 - 102 2013 £120

Betjeman, John 1906-1984 *High and Low.* London: John Murray, 1966. First reprint, original yellow cloth, 8vo., near fine in excellent dust jacket (spine faded with some signs of wear at folds), inscribed by author. Maggs Bros. Ltd. 1460 - 98 2013 £150

Betjeman, John 1906-1984 *Murray's Buckinghamshire Guide.* London: John Murray, 1948. First edition, 4to., original red cloth, dust jacket, rubbed, somewhat torn at extremities, with modicum of loss, excellent copy, inscribed by John Piper to Stella and Eric Newton. Maggs Bros. Ltd. 1460 - 92 2013 £250

Betjeman, John 1906-1984 *Murray's Buckinghamshire Guide.* London: John Murray, 1948. First edition, 4to., original red cloth, dust jacket, inscribed by author for W. H. Auden, excellent copy in rubbed price clipped dust jacket, chipped at extremities. Maggs Bros. Ltd. 1460 - 91 2013 £1250

Betjeman, John 1906-1984 *An Oxford University Chest.* London: John Miles, 1938. First edition, 4to., original dark blue cloth, lettered gilt, marbled boards, top edge gilt, illustrations in line and half tone by L. Moholy-Nagy, Osbert Lancaster, Edward Bradley, et al, excellent copy, inscribed to the widow of the artist Richard Wyndham, Greta by author. Maggs Bros. Ltd. 1460 - 90 2013 £350

Betjeman, John 1906-1984 *Poems in the Porch.* London: SPCK, 1955. Later edition, 8vo., original cream illustrated wrappers, lettered in red, signed by artist, covers dusty and browning, otherwise near fine, illustrations by John Piper. Maggs Bros. Ltd. 1460 - 94 2013 £75

Betjeman, John 1906-1984 *A Ring of Bells. Poems of...* London: John Murray, 1967. Second edition, 8vo., original wrappers, near fine, inscribed by author. Maggs Bros. Ltd. 1460 - 99 2013 £100

Betjeman, John 1906-1984 *Shropshire. A Shell Guide.* London: Faber and Faber, 1951. First edition, 4to., original yellow cloth, dust jacket, inscribed by Betjeman to his secretary Jill Elizabeth Duncan Menzies, very good, jacket reinforced with tape in such a way that jacket can not be removed. Maggs Bros. Ltd. 1460 - 93 2013 £1250

Betjeman, John 1906-1984 *Summoned by Bells.* London: John Murray, 1960. First edition, 4to., original green cloth, near fine in price clipped dust jacket, inscribed by author to his secretary with large drawing. Maggs Bros. Ltd. 1460 - 97 2013 £1250

Betjeman, John 1906-1984 *Summoned by Bells.* London: John Murray, 1969. First reprint, 4to., original green cloth, dust jacket, inscribed by author for A. L. Rowse with holograph drawing of coat of arms with words "one & all 1975", with Rowse's familiar initials across the join of the front endpapers and his manuscript annotations throughout, excellent copy in price clipped and nicked dust jacket, faded to white on spine.   Maggs Bros. Ltd.   1460 - 100   2013   £200

Betjeman, John 1906-1984 *The Illustrated Summond by Bells.* London: John Murray, 1989. First edition, 4to., original green cloth, near fine in price clipped dust jacket, with original watercolor by artist and inscribed by him "Hugh Casson Nov. 1991".   Maggs Bros. Ltd.   1460 - 104   2013   £750

Betjeman, John 1906-1984 *Victorian and Edwardian London from Old Photographs.* London: B. T. Batsford, 1970. Reprint, 4to., original pale blue brown cloth dust jacket, near fine in slightly rubbed dust jacket, creased at extremities, inscribed by author to Stewart.   Maggs Bros. Ltd.   1460 - 101   2013   £150

Betrand, Louis *Histoire de Napoleon.* Tours: Alfred Mame, n.d. circa, 1930. 4to., cloth backed pictorial boards, fine, 16 full page richly colored illustrations plus 60 pen and inks.   Aleph-Bet Books, Inc.   104 - 223   2013 $275

Bettelheim, Bruno *Educational News and Editorial Comment; German Schools Revisited.* Chicago: n.d., Offprint from Elementary School Journal, near fine with few wrinkles.   Beasley Books   2013 - 2013 $65

Bettelheim, Bruno *Mental Health and Current Mores.* 1952. Offprint from Journal of Orthopsychiatry XXII Jan. 1952, Near fine, soiled rear wrapper (blank).   Beasley Books   2013 - 2013 $65

Bettelheim, Bruno *A Psychiatric School.* 1949. Offprint from Quarterly Journal of Child Behavior I Jan 149, signed by author, fine.   Beasley Books   2013 - 2013 $65

Bettelheim, Bruno *Violence: a Neglected Mode of Behavior.* Philadelphia: 1966. Offrprint from Annals of American Academy of Political and Social Science 364 March 1966, near fine with old folds, signed by author.   Beasley Books   2013 - 2013 $65

Beverley, Robert *The History of Virginia in Four Parts.* London: Fayram & Clarke, 1722. 8vo., ,engraved half title and 14 engraved plates, early 19th century russia repaired.   Maggs Bros. Ltd.   1467 - 118   2013   £2750

Bew, Charles *Opinions on the Causes and Effects of the Disease Denominated Tic Douloureux: Deduced from Practical Observations of it Supposed Origin...*   Brighton: W. Leppard for Underwood in London and Cordwell and Tuppen, Brighton, 1824. First edition, 8vo., folding lithographic frontispiece and 2 lithograph plates, text lightly brown, jear joint starting, binding bit rubbed, deep blue Brighton Regency gilt morocco by P. Taylor, gilt panels and fleur-de-lys on front and back boards, spine gilt in compartments, all edges gilt, very rare first edition, dedicatee copy with signed presentation note to Duke of Clarence.   James Tait Goodrich   75 - 26   2013 $3750

Bewick, Elizabeth *Comfort Me with Apples and Other Poems.* Biddenden, Kent: Florin Press, 1987. 32/135 copies, printed on very pleasant mouldmade paper and signed by author and artist, 8 superb wood engravings by Graham Williams, title printed in apple grain, prospectus loosely inserted, tall 8vo, original cream linen with overall pattern of green sprays surrounded by red dots, green leather label, card slipcase, fine.   Blackwell's Rare Books   B174 - 335   2013   £90

Bewick, Thomas 1753-1828 *The Fables of Aesop and Others with Designs on Wood by Thomas Bewick.* Newcastle: printed by E. Walker for T. Bewick and Son, 1818. One of 500 copies on imperial paper, Large paper copy, 188 wood engraved headpieces, 136 other vignettes and tailpieces, royal 8vo., bound without prelim thumb mark receipt, very clean copy, slightly later half russia, sugar paper boards, raised and gilt bands, spine rubbed and slightly chipped at head, some wear to corners.   Jarndyce Antiquarian Booksellers   CCIV - 61   2013   £350

Bewick, Thomas 1753-1828 *The Fables of Aesopus and Others.* Newcastle: printed by E. Walker for T. Bewick and Son, 1818. First edition, Royal paper copy with his thumbmark receipt tipped in before title, but sometime folded with offset of oval portrait at top, occasional minor spotting, large 8vo., original boards, rebacked, short split at foot of upper joint, corners slightly worn, very good.   Blackwell's Rare Books   172 - 23   2013   £850

Bewick, Thomas 1753-1828 *The Fables of Aesop and Others, with Designs on Wood.* Newcastle: 1823. Second edition, xxiv, 376 pages, 188 woodcut headpieces to fables and 136 engraved vignettes, tail pieces and other decorations, with thumb mark receipt, numbered and priced by hand with Bewick's signature in facsimile, very good, late 19th century full calf, gilt ruled borders, gilt spine with red morocco label, top edge gilt.   Ken Spelman Books Ltd.   75 - 83   2013   £350

Bewick, Thomas 1753-1828 *The History of British Birds.* Newcastle: by Edward Walker, 1821. Seventh edition of Land Birds and fifth edition of Water Birds, with the first edition of the supplements with additional figures to both volumes, contemporary dark blue gilt, calf, red morocco labels, royal 8vo.   Ken Spelman Books Ltd.   75 - 81   2013   £220

Bewick, Thomas   1753-1828 *A Memoir.* Newcastle: Robert Ward, 1862.   First edition, 8vo., frontispiece, titlepage vignette and numerous illustrations, near fine in original gilt cloth.   Ken Spelman Books Ltd.   75 - 128   2013   £100

Bewick, Thomas   1753-1828 *Vignettes from Birds, Quadrupeds and Fables.*   Chicago: Black Cat Press, 1971.   Limited to 200 copies, 6.8 x 5.5 cm., leather, author's surname gilt stamped on spine, full name gilt stamped on front board, unpaginated, included is one of the actual Bewick wood blocks that was used to print illustration on page 8, also includes letter dated May 25 2004 from Bill Hesterberg of Hesterberg Press of Evanston to Donn Sanford, loose pages 5 and 8 of text laid in.   Oak Knoll Books   303 - 50   2013 $750

Bewick, Thomas   1753-1828 *Vignettes from Birds, Quadrupeds and Fables.*   Chicago: Black Cat Press, 1971.   Limited to 200 copies, 6.8 x 5.5cm., full leather, author's surname gilt stamped on spine, full name gilt stamped on front board, unpaginated, illustrations printed from original woodblocks by R. Hunter Middleton, from the collection of Donn W. Sanford.   Oak Knoll Books   303 - 49   2013 $275

Beyer, Hartmann   *Quaestiones Novae in Libellum de Saphaera Ioannis de Sacrobusto, in Gratiam Studiosae Iuuent Utis Collectae.*   Frankfurt: Petrus Brubach, 1549.   First edition, woodcut printer's device of a Janus head on title, another version on recto of last leaf within cartouche, 4 woodcut initials, one repeat of very poor quality, 2 diagrams in text, uniformly slightly browned, few spots and stains, defects in outer margin of 3 leaves at end repaired with loss of 2 or 3 letters verso of one leaf, some dog-ears, extensively annotated in contemporary hand, small 8vo. plain modern calf, sound.   Blackwell's Rare Books   B174 - 8   2013   £800

Beyle, Marie Henri   1783-1842 *Maxims of Love.*   London: Arthur L. Humphreys, 1906.   167 x 130mm., 2 p.l., 201 pages, very attractive contemporary hunter green crushed morocco for Hatchards, stamp signed on front turn-in, covers with simple gilt Arts & Crafts style frame, gilt titling on upper cover, raised bands, spines gilt in double ruled compartments with gilt dot in each corner, titling in gilt, 3 compartments with gilt dot in each corner, titling gilt in three compartments, gilt ruled turn-ins, top edge gilt, text in French and English, bookplate of Victoria Sackville, occasional pencilled marginalia, spine uniformly a couple of shades darker, mild offsetting from turn-ins, otherwise fine, especially clean inside and out.   Phillip J. Pirages   63 - 413   2013 $550

Bible Stories: with Colored Pictures..   Dean & Son, n.d. circa 1860's, Tall 8vo., original blindstamped blue cloth gilt, little worn and stained, neatly rebacked to match, 120 hand colored woodcuts, pastedowns little damaged and repaired, new front flyleaf, few edge repairs in places.   R. F. G. Hollett & Son   Children's Books - 13   2013   £250

Bible. Dutch - 1477   *Bibla Neerlandica.*   Delft: Jacob Jacobszoen van der Meer and Mauricius Yemantszoen 10 Jan., 1477.   Lacking first leaf (prologue) text on folio 213v in corrected state with text consequently a line short, small woodcut shield (arms of Delft) at colophon and the twin shields of printers printed in red, rubricated throughout, 12 line initial to Genesis with interlocking red, blue and yellow with tracery in red, other book initials in brown, few marginal notes in early hand, first leaf weak at inner margin, one leaf rehinged and short in fore-margin, two leaves with clean tears, crossing text but without significant loss, somewhat crudely repaired, some soiling and staining here and there, occasionally a heavier wax stain, in one case with loss of a letter, last leaf cut down at inner margin, just touching letters and laid down, folio, 18th century ivory vellum, yapp edges lettered in ink at top of spine, slightly soiled, patch at foot of spine, bookplate, c. 1900 of South African lawyer Eugene Nielen Marais (1871-1936), good.   Blackwell's Rare Books   172 - 28   2013   £30,000

Bible. English - 1589   *Text of the Nevv Testament of Iesus Christ, Translated out of the Vulgar Latine...*   London: by the Deputies of Christophr Barkr, 1589.   First Fulke edition, title within elaborate woodcut border, titlepage rehinged with 2 short closed tears just entering printed areas, titlepage bit browned around edges, rest of volume also to a lesser degree, single wormhole in lower margin of last dozen leaves, ownership inscription of David Jones at foot of title dated Jany 17th 1772, folio, recent calf backed boards, gilt lettered on spine, original sprinkled edges, crack at head of upper joint, shelfmark in red ink in outer margin, good, tall copy.   Blackwell's Rare Books   172 - 25   2013   £4000

Bible. English - 1754   *The Psalms of David... (bound with) Translations and Paraphrases.*   Aberdeen: printed and sold by F. Douglass and W. Murray, 1754.   One gathering in Psalms slightly sprung and its last leaf detached, lower outer corner of one leaf in second part torn away with loss of three or four words and parts of a number of letters, minor staining towards end, 12mo., contemporary Scottish (?Aberdeen), black morocco, gilt roll tooled borders on sides, spine gilt in compartments, signature of Lady Grant on title.   Blackwell's Rare Books   B174 - 12   2013   £475

Bible. English - 1780   *The Bible in Miniuture (sic), or a Concise History of the Old and New Testaments.*   printed for F. Newbery, 1780.   2 engraved titlepages and 14 plates some spotting and thumbing, 64mo., contemporary plain calf, rubbed, corner tips worn, front joint cracking but sound, vertical crease to front board and text block slightly warped, ownership inscription "S Smart Her Book 1797", sound, unsophisticated copy.   Blackwell's Rare Books   B174 - 9   2013 £450

Bible. English - 1790 *The Holy Bible Containing the Old Testament and the New...*   printed for Scatcherd & Whitaker, 1790. Engraved frontispiece and titlepage, trimmed removing footnotes (as intended), a number of early ms. annotations and citations in margins (some cropped), binder's blanks at front and rear largely filled with lists, birth records, notes, etc., 12mo., slightly later dark calf gilt, sometime fully covered in dark red roan to from a wallet style binding, flap tucking under strap on bottom board, front board decoratively (but faintly) stamped in blind, marbled endpapers, all edges gilt, very good.   Blackwell's Rare Books   172 - 24   2013   £250

Bible. English - 1827 *The Comprehensive Bible containing the Old and New Testaments.* London: printed for Samuel Bagster, 1827. 330 x 250mm., excellent contemporary black pebble grain morocco, handsomely gilt, covers with floral frame enclosing central panel featuring scrolling cornerpiece compartments and, at center, intricate elongated ornament, wide raised bands with multiple gilt rules and floral endpieces, spine panels tooled gilt, floral and leaf ornaments, gilt titling and turn-ins, all edges gilt (neat older repairs to head and tail of joints); with bustling modern fore-edge painting by Martin Frost, showing flotilla of vessels on Thames with St. Paul's Cathedral in background; large gilt presentation bookplate "Tribute of Respect from Teachers of Mosely Street Sabbath School, Manchester, to their kind and generous friend James Kershaw, Esq. June 28 1838", joints little worn, corners and extremities bit rubbed, one tiny gouge to upper cover, otherwise fine, ornate binding entirely solid and generally well preserved and text exceptionally clean, fresh and smooth.   Phillip J. Pirages   61 - 56   2013 $3500

Bible. English - 1846 *The Illuminated Bible containing the old and New Testaments.* New York: Harper & Bros., 1846. First edition, very thick large 4to., full contemporary gilt tooled black morocco, all edges gilt, edges and spine cords rubbed, very sound in fine condition.   M & S Rare Books, Inc.   95 - 20   2013 $1000

Bible. English - 1846 *The Illuminated Bible, containing the Old and New Testaments...* New York: Harper & Bros., 1846. First edition, very thick large 4to., full contemporary gilt tooled, red morocco, all edges gilt, scuffed hinges quite rubbed, but sound.   M & S Rare Books, Inc.   95 - 19   2013 $750

Bible. English - 1896 *The Holy Bible.* Glasgow: David Bryce and Son, n.d, but, 1896. 4.5 x 3.3 cm., with frontispiece and illustrations, pocket on back pastedown for magnifying glass, no indication of that in this copy, original leather, title stamped on spine, frontispiece and titlepage folded, from the collection of Donn W. Sanford.   Oak Knoll Books   303 - 74   2013 $400

Bible. English - 1897 *The Song of Solomon.* London: printed by William Clowes and Sons for Guild of Women Binders, circa, 1897. One of 100 copies on Japanese paper, this copy #13, 290 x 220mm., 1 p.l., 16 pages plus illustrations, with 12 pleasing plates by H. Granville Fell on Japanese paper, made from pencil drawings, as well as 4 different illustrated titles and vignette closing leaf, immaculate copy, superb contemporary dark blue morocco, elegantly gilt by Guild of Women Binders (stamp signed), covers tooled in Art Nouveau design featuring a large central anthemium of flowers rising on long stem from stippled base, this central ornament flanked by three long stemmed irises on either side, flat spine with vertical gilt titling, single fillet and small circles, matching blue morocco doublures tooled with with particularly attractive complex central oval ornament encompassing considerable stippling and 20 large stylized flowers on curvilinear stems, vellum free endleaves with gilt hearts at corners, top edge gilt, fine matching folding morocco box, lined with pale blue suede gilt titling on its spine.   Phillip J. Pirages   61 - 108   2013 $3500

Bible. English - 1903 *The English Bible.* Hammersmith: Doves Press, 1903-1905. One of 500 copies, printed on handmade paper by T.J. Cobden-Sanderson and Emery Walker, five volumes, folio, printed in red and black, beautiful full blue morocco by Doves Bindery, boards with triple gilt rule, spines lettered and stamped in gilt, gilt dentelles with floral corner devices, all edges gilt, very minimal foxing and "Genesis" leaf very clean, small split to inner hinge of volume 1 when opened wide, bit of offsetting to endpapers from dentelles, previous owner's bookplate on front pastedown on each volume, near fine, housed in morocco tipped cloth slipcase.   Heritage Book Shop Holiday Catalogue 2012 - 46   2013 $35,000

Bible. English - 1910 *The New Testament of Our Lord and Saviour Jesus Christ.* London: Oxford University Press, circa, 1910. 8vo., limp black morocco, 'Antarctic Expedition Terra Nova 1910' gilt to upper cover, inscribed by A. R. Falconer, Sailor's Missionary Dunedin, for Captain Robert Falcon Scott.   Maggs Bros. Ltd.   1467 - 141   2013   £6000

Bible. English - 1924 *The Apocrypha Reprinted According to the Authorised Version 1611.* London: Nonesuch Press, 1924. One of 1250 copies, copper plates by Stephen Gooden, 4to., near fine.   Ken Spelman Books Ltd.   75 - 170   2013   £70

Bible. English - 1932 *The Wisdom of Jesus, the Son of Sirach, Commonly called Ecclesiasticus.* Chelsea: printed by C. H. St. J. Hornby at the Ashendene Press, 1932. One of 328 copies on Batchelor handmade paper with bugle watermark, out of a total edition of 353, folio, printed in black and red in Subiaco type, initials supplied by hand in blue and green by Graily Hewitt and his two assistants, Ida Henstock and Helen Hinkley; original limp orange vellum with matching silk ties, spine lettered gilt, original marbled board slipcase, vellum spine lightly sunned, 2 previous owner's bookplates, otherwise near fine.   Heritage Book Shop Holiday Catalogue 2012 - 3   2013 $3000

Bible. English - 1985 *The Song of Songs by Solomon.* Ultrecht: Catharijne Press, 1985. Limited to 167 copies, this one of 150 numbered trade copies, 6.2 x 4.3cm. paper coverd boards stamped in gilt, design and initials by Bram de Does, copperplate engraving by Bertril Schmull and binding and hand coloring by Luce Thurkow, engraving signed and numbered in pencil, large initial letters hand colored, miniature bookplate of Kathryn Rickard, from the collection of Donn W. Sanford. Oak Knoll Books 303 - 88 2013 $125

Bible. English - 1989 *The First Book of Moses, called Genesis. The King James Version.* New York: Limited Editions Club, 1989. First edition, one of 400 copies signed by artist, this being number 360, silkscreens by Jacob Lawrence on Whatman paper, large folio, publisher's blue cloth, lettered gilt on front, publisher's black cloth clamshell with leather label, publisher's newsletter laid in, fine. Heritage Book Shop Holiday Catalogue 2012 - 12 2013 $5500

Bible. French - 1947 *Cantique des Cantiques. (Song of Songs).* Paris: Editions du Livre de Plantin, 1947. First Lobel-Riche edition, number 96 of 100 copies on rives (total edition 200), numbered and initialled ink by artist on justification page, 21 drypoint etchings by Almery Lobel-Riche, printed by manuel Robbe, 13 x 10 inches, about 70 pages in French, all leaves loose in publisher's wrappers and handsome cloth folding box, by Ann Repp, very good. Gemini Fine Books & Arts., Ltd. Art Reference & Illustrated Books - 2013 $1300

Bible. Greek - 1658 *Novum Testamentum Editio nova...* Amsterdam: Ex Officina Elzeviriana, 1658. 24mo., area of adhesion between 2 leaves affecting few words on 3 pages, headline occasionally shaved, some dust soiling and light spotting, particularly to titlepage, 19th century vellum boards, spine lettered gilt, somewhat dust soiled, front joint cracking but sound, ownership inscriptions of John Clark dated 1837 and William Cleminson (gifted by Clark to initial blank later genealogical ownership note tipped to verso of flyleaf), sound. Blackwell's Rare Books B174 - 19 2013 £250

Bible. Hawaiian - 1843 *Ke Kauoha hou a kakou Hake e ola'i a Iesu Kristo. (New Testament in Hawaiian).* Honolulu: Na na Misionari Mea i pai, 1843. First separate dudecimo edition, 12mo., contemporary sheep, rebacked to style, edges speckled brown, boards rubbed and bumped, some dampstaining throughout, especially to front endpapers through page 27, some browning and foxing to various signatures, overall very good. Heritage Book Shop Holiday Catalogue 2012 - 13 2013 $1000

Bible. Hieroglyphic - 1796 *A New Hieroglyphical Bible for the Amusement and Instruction of Children.* New York: printed for and published by the Booksellers, 1796. 18mo., 144 pages, extensively illustrated, recent cloth backed boards, engraved titlepage, lacks frontispiece, small replacement at inner margin, top of titlepage just affecting the "H", corners frayed on a number of early leaves, text browned, sound. M & S Rare Books, Inc. 95 - 179 2013 $1250

Bible. Italian - 1566 *Prima parte del Nuouo Testamento...* Venice: colophon: Bartolomeo Rubini, 1566. 2 volumes, woodcut vignette on title, some headlines cropped, last page slightly affected by prior adhesion of flyleaf with loss of couple of letters, 16mo., 18th century French mottled calf, spines gilt in compartments, twin red lettering pieces, upper one on volume i lacking, upper joint of both volumes cracked but cords still firm, worm at extremities, good, scarce. Blackwell's Rare Books B174 - 11 2013 £850

Bible. Latin - 1921 *A Noble Fragment. Being a Leaf of the Gutenberg Bible 1450-1455.* New York: Gabriel Wells, 1921. Limited to 600 copies, folio, actual leaf 393 x 287mm., (6) pages text, titlepage and on initial letter printed in red, original unwatermarked paper leaf from Gutenberg Bible tipped in, black gothic letter, rubricated in red, headlines, chapter numbers and two large initial letters supplied in red and blue, original full black blindstamped morocco by Stikeman & Co., front cover lettered gilt, gilt turn-ins, grey endpapers, head and foot of spine very lightly worn, leaf in this copy very clean except for minor foxing at edges, ink still very black and crisp, remarkably fresh and lovely example. Heritage Book Shop 50th Anniversary Catalogue - 10 2013 $100,000

Bible. Latin - 1961 *(Bible).* Paterson and New York: Pageant Books, 1961. Limited to 1000 copies, gorgeous facsimile of the Gutenberg Bible, Folio, not paginated, text printed by lithography and illuminations by sheet-fed gravure on rag-paper made especially for this book, color illuminations uncial letters and decorations, all edges gilt, hand bound in full gilt stamped deep red morocco, five raised spine bands, fine,. Jeff Weber Rare Books 171 - 151 2013 $3000

Bible. Polyglot - 1672 *Georgii Pasoris Manvale Novi Testamenti...* Amstelodami: ex Officina Elzeviriana, 1672. Reissue of text of Elzeivr editions of 1654 and 1664, 12mo., text in Greek and Latin, engraved titlepage, head and tailpieces and initials, endpapers and pastedowns dusted, original paper flaw to blank lower margin of V6, contemporary calf, gilt panelled spine with label, head and tail of spine slightly worn, label "Man Vale Pasoris". Jarndyce Antiquarian Booksellers CCIV - 3 2013 £350

Biblio. Eugene: Aster, 1996-1998. Volume One Nos. 1-12 (1996) Volume Two Nos. 1-4, 6-12 (1997). Volume Three Nos. 1-4 (1998); together 27 issues, illustrations, original printed wrappers, near fine. Jeff Weber Rare Books 171 - 27 2013 $100

Bichat, Francois Xavier *Anatomie Generale Appliquee a la Physiologie et a la Medecine.* Paris: Brosson & Gabon, 1812. Second edition, 4 volumes, 8vo., 2 folding charts, contemporary quarter calf over marbled boards, gilt stamped spine panels and titles, light insect damage to spine volume 4, very good.   Jeff Weber Rare Books   172 - 29   2013 $650

Bichat, Francois Xavier *Oeuvres Chirurgicale ou Expose de la Doctrine et de la Pratique.* Paris: Chez Mequignon, 1801. Second edition, folding plates, engraved portrait, marginal repairs to titles and prelims just affecting text, bound in later quarter calf and linen boards, uncut and unopened.   James Tait Goodrich   S74 - 28   2013 $695

Bickersteth, E. *Domestic Portraiture; or the Successful Application of Religious Principle in the Education of a Family, Exemplified in the Memoirs of Three of the Deceased Children of the Rev. Leigh Richmond.* R. B. Seeley and W. Burnside, 1833. First edition, very good, contemporary half calf, marbled boards, blind and gilt stamped spine, binder's ticket of H. Whitmore 109 Market Street, Manchester.   Ken Spelman Books Ltd.   75 - 94   2013   £50

Bicknell, Peter *The Illustrated Wordsworth's Guide to the Lakes.* Webb & Bower, 1984. First edition, 4to., original cloth, gilt, dust jacket, pages 208, illustrations in color and monochrome.   R. F. G. Hollett & Son   Lake District & Cumbria - 109   2013   £35

Bicknell, Peter *The Picturesque Scenery of the Lake District 1752-1855.* Cambridge: Smith Settle for the Book Collector, 1987. Original wrappers, 36 plates.   R. F. G. Hollett & Son   Lake District & Cumbria - 108   2013   £30

Bicknell, Peter *The Picturesque Scenery of the Lake District 1752-1855.* Winchester: St. Paul's Bibliographies, 1990. First edition, 4to., original cloth, gilt, dust jacket, 12 pages of plates and other illustrations.   R. F. G. Hollett & Son   Lake District & Cumbria - 107   2013   £45

Biddle, Anthony J. *Drexel Shantytown Sketches.* Philadelphia: Drexel Biddle, 1897. First edition, fine but for lightly sunned spine.   Beasley Books   2013 - 2013 $100

Bidlake, John *A Familiar Introduction to the Study of Geography...* London: John Murray, 1808. Fourth edition, contemporary drab wrappers, rather soiled and chipped, corners creased, title lightly dampstained, little dusty in places, scarce.   R. F. G. Hollett & Son   Children's Books - 66   2013   £65

Bidlake, John *The Poetical Works.* London: J. Murray, and J. Harding, 1804. Second edition, half title, frontispiece damp marked, final ad leaf, later half brown cloth imitating leather.   Jarndyce Antiquarian Booksellers   CCIII - 644   2013   £50

Bidwell, John *A Bibliophile's Los Angeles.* Los Angeles: William Andrews Clark Memorial Library, 1985. Limited to 350 copies, 8vo., vii, 186 pages, folding frontispiece, 2 color title (printed in blue and black), index, quarter beige cloth with patterned paper sides, printed paper spine label, fine.   Jeff Weber Rare Books   171 - 30   2013 $90

Bidwell, John *Echoes of the Post: an Account of the First Emigrant Train to California, Fremont in the Conquest of California, the Discovery of Gold and Early Reminiscences.* Chico: Chico Advertiser, 1914. Thin 12mo., photos, publisher's green printed wrappers, first endpaper lightly toned with tiny repair to lower edge, else fine, without usual trashing of spine, somewhat flimsy, but adequate box.   Argonaut Book Shop   Summer 2013 - 14   2013 $175

Bidwell, John *Fine Papers at the Oxford University Press.* Andoversford: Whittington Press, 1999. 27/235 copies printed on Zerkall mouldmade paper with book's title, flytitles and large initial letters printed in brown, 2 plates of photographic reproductions, 40 examples of handmade papers from Oxford Unviersity Press collection, each tipped to black backing paper, examples of papers on backing paper, folio, original quarter lime green cloth, matching cloth fore-edges, backstrip gilt lettered, lime green boards, untrimmed, cloth and boards slipcase, fine.   Blackwell's Rare Books   172 - 311   2013   £350

Bidwell, John *A Journey to California.* San Francisco: John Henry Nash, 1937. Third edition, one of 600 copies, quarto, linen backed boards, paper spine label, very fine and bright, dust jacket (paper label on jacket spine).   Argonaut Book Shop   Summer 2013 - 15   2013 $150

Bidwell, Paul *Hadrian's Wall 1989-1999.* Carlisle: CWAAS and Soc. Antiquaries Newcastle-Upon-tyne, 1999. Original glazed pictorial boards, 67 plates and plans, map and text illustrations.   R. F. G. Hollett & Son   Lake District & Cumbria - 110   2013   £30

Bierce, Ambrose 1842-1914 *Fantastic Fables.* New York and London: G. P. Putnam's Sons, Knickerbocker Press, 1899. First edition, first state, 4 pages ads, original light yellow pictorial cloth, spine slightly dulled, nice, crisp copy.   Jarndyce Antiquarian Booksellers   CCV - 24   2013   £180

Bierkowski, Ludwig Jospeph *Erklerung der Anatomisch-Chirurgische Nebst Beschrelbung der Chirurgischen Opeationen Nach den Methoden von V. Grasfe,Klug und Rust.* Berlin: verlag von Friedr. Aug Herbig, 1827. First editions, 3 volumes, with two 8vo. text volumes and large atlas (with 55 lithograph plates, 45 of them partially hand colored), in addition 3 further outline plates, some light text foxing and browning, ink stain affecting outer margins of several leaves in atlas, faint library stamps on front endpapers and titlepage of both text volumes, two text volumes bound in early quarter calf and marbled boards with gilt spine and red leather labels, folio atlas bound in early quarter calf and marbled boards with paper label on front board, spine and corners have later repair, very nice and likely mixed set.   James Tait Goodrich   75 - 27   2013 $3950

Big Book. Boston: Houghton Mifflin circa, 1940. large size folio, spiral bound in blue boards, 19 1/2 x 24 1/2 inches with easel on rear cover that allows book to be propped up for display, 32 pages, edges rubbed, else very good, printed on heavy card stock and wonderfully illustrated in bright colors in typical 40's style, rare.   Aleph-Bet Books, Inc.   104 - 159   2013 $850

Big Book: the New Our Big Book: Cathedral Edition. Chicago: Scott Foresman, 1951.   Black cloth 19 x 26 inches, slight rubbing, very good-fine, pages 3-26 are present, each page has wonderful full color illustrations, rare.   Aleph-Bet Books, Inc.   104 - 155   2013 $1850

Bigelow, Henry *Insensibility During Surgical Operations Produced by Inhalation.* Boston: Medical and Surgical Journal, First separate edition, 8vo., unbound, stitched as issued in protective case, pages browned, text from page 317.   James Tait Goodrich   75 - 29   2013 $2500

Biggers, Earl Derr *Behind that Curtain.* Indianapolis: Bobbs Merrill, 1928. Later edition, without the bow and arrow symbol on copyright page, fine in very good dust jacket with tow inch piece missing from back panel, chipping at spine ends and several short closed tears.   Mordida Books   81 - 32   2013 $150

Biggers, Earl Derr *Charlie Carries On.* Indianapolis: Bobbs Merrill, 1930. First edition, name on front endpaper, otherwise near fine in dust jacket with closed tear on back panel and crease along edge of spine.   Mordida Books   81 - 33   2013 $700

Biggers, Earl Derr *The Chinese Parrot.* New York: Grosset & Dunlap, n.d., Reprint edition, three very small holes along joint of red cover, otherwise fine in bright unfaded dust jacket with some scattered rubbing on spine and a short closed tear, exceptional.   Mordida Books   81 - 31   2013 $200

Biggers, Earl Derr *Seven Keys to Baldpate.* New York: Grosset & Dunlap, n.d., Reprint edition, small labels removed from front endpapers and pages darkened, otherwise near fine in dust jacket with several short closed tears and minor fraying at top of spine.   Mordida Books   81 - 30   2013 $65

Biggers, Earl Derr *Seven Keys to Baldpate.* Indianapolis: Bobbs Merrill, 1913. First edition, lacking scarce dust jacket.   Between the Covers Rare Books, Inc.   Mystery & Detective Fiction - 82782   2013 $200

Biggs, Charlotte *A Residence in France During the Years 1792, 1793, 1794 and 1795...* London: printed for T. N. Longman, 1797. Third edition, 2 volumes, 8vo., some occasional foxing, handsome, full contemporary calf, gilt decorated spines, gilt flowerheads, decorative bands, volume numbers set within gilt shields.   Jarndyce Antiquarian Booksellers   CCIV - 62   2013   £380

Biggs, Michael *A Gaelic Alphabet.* Dublin: Dolmen Press, 1960. Number 114 of 300 numbered copies, tall 8vo., original wrappers, excellent.   Maggs Bros. Ltd.   1442 - 62   2013   £85

Bigland, John *Letters on Natural History.* James Cundee, 1810. Second edition, old tree calf, edges little worn, nicely rebacked to match with leather spine label, frontispiece, 100 illustrations on 51 plates, few small patches of browning, excellent copy.   R. F. G. Hollett & Son   Children's Books - 67   2013   £140

Bigmore, E. C. *A Bibliography of Printing with Notes and Illustrations.* London: Bernard Quartich, 1880-1886. small 4to., 3 volumes in 1, two color title (printed in red and black), illustrations, original brown leather (signed by Bennett, NY), professionally rebacked by Bruce Levy, gilt stamped spine title with raised spine bands, top edge gilt, some marginal checkmarks, bookplates of Marcus Crahan and the Zamorano Club (gift of Crahan), signature P. R. Lee Jr. (1939), near fine, choice copy.   Jeff Weber Rare Books   171 - 31   2013 $750

Billings, Robert William *Architectural Illustrations, History and Description of Carlisle Cathedral.* Thomas and William Boone and R. W. Billings, 1840. First edition, 4to., original black blind ruled cloth, gilt, 45 steel engraved plates on stiff cream paper and vignette on title, exceptionally clean and bright.   R. F. G. Hollett & Son   Lake District & Cumbria - 111   2013   £275

Billroth, Christian Albert Theodor *Uber des Lehren und Lernen der Medicinischen Wissenschaften an den Universitaten der Deutschen Nation...* Wien: von Carl Gerold's Sohn, 1876. First edition, 8vo., 5 foldout tables at rear, full gilt stamped brown cloth, neatly repaired, internally very good, fine.   Jeff Weber Rare Books   172 - 31   2013 $600

Billroth, Theodor *Untersuchungen uber de Entwicklung der Blutgefasse Nebst Beobacktungen aus der Koniglichen Chirurgischen Universitats zu Berlin.* Berlin: George Reimer, 1856. 81 pages, 5 engraved plates which are partly hand colored, original linen backed boards, text lightly foxed, uncut, unopened, rare, some light wear and rubbing to boards. James Tait Goodrich S74 - 29 2013 $495

Bilz, Friedrich Eduard *In Hundert Jahren reich Illustrierter Romain.* Leipzig und Dresden-Radebeul: F. E. Bilz, 1907. First edition, octavo, 188 illustrations, original grey cloth, stamped in black, pictorial paper onlays affixed to front and to rear panels. L. W. Currey, Inc. Utopian Literature: Recent Acquisitions (April 2013) - 139583 2013 $1250

Bingham, Clifton *ABC Surprise Book.* London: Nister, n.d. circa, 1890. Small 4to., cloth backed pictorial boards, light tip wear and tabs strengthened, else very good and in working order, each verso has four five line rhymes, facing each text page is tab operated slatted moveable page, 4 letters of alphabet are stationary and as the slat is pulled, pictures for each letter dissolve into new images for the specific letter, six moveables in all, rare. Aleph-Bet Books, Inc. 105 - 14 2013 $1400

Bingham, Clifton *All Sorts of Comical Cats.* London: Nister, 1902. Small 4to., cloth backed pictorial boards, covers lightly soiled and bottom of inner hinge bumped, else very good+, illustrations by Louis Wain with fabulous mounted chromolithographed frontispiece plus marvelous 2 color and line illustrations, very scarce. Aleph-Bet Books, Inc. 104 - 581 2013 $700

Bingham, Clifton *Animals School Treat.* London: Dean, n.d. circa, 1910. 4to., pictorial cloth, some soil, one page reinforced at spine, overall very good, 24 pages of fabulous color illustrations, rare. Aleph-Bet Books, Inc. 105 - 32 2013 $1250

Bingham, Clifton *The Fairy Picture Book.* London: Nister cica, 1895. Square 4to., cloth backed pictorial boards, few margin mends, else fine in original pictorial dust jacket, with 7 round mechanical plates, by pulling a ribbon the picture on top dissolves to reveal new picture below, illustrations particularly beautiful, enclosed within chromolithographed borders, illustrations by E. S. Hardy, fine, scarce. Aleph-Bet Books, Inc. 104 - 366 2013 $3500

Bingham, Clifton *Fur Coats and Father Frocks.* London: Ernest Nister, n.d., 4to., original cloth backed pictorial glazed boards, little worn and scratched, 24 full page color plates, text illustrations, joints cracked. R. F. G. Hollett & Son Children's Books - 69 2013 £85

Bingham, Clifton *Jumbo Crusoe.* London & New York: Nister & Dutton, n.d. circa, 1900. 4to., cloth backed pictorial boards, some cover scratching else very good+, 12 full page chromolithographs, pictorial endpapers plus many full and partial page line illustrations all by G. H. Thompson, quite scarce. Aleph-Bet Books, Inc. 104 - 150 2013 $1500

Bingham, Clifton *Magic Moments.* Ernest Nister, circa, 1900. First edition, pen and ink illustrations by Florence Hardy, 7 revolving plates, plates all in fine state and complete with cotton pulls used to reveal circular picture and overlay in each plate, text leaves browned at edges and trifle brittle, title illustration by E. Nister, 4to., original pale blue cloth backed boards, pale blue boards, front cover with title and delightfully illustrated overall, inner joints strengthened, floral endpapers, very good. Blackwell's Rare Books 172 - 104 2013 £500

Bingham, Clifton *Mixed Pickles.* London: Tuck, n.d. circa, 1910. 4to., green pictorial cloth soiled with spine neatly repaired else very good+ to very good, illustrations by Louis Wain. Aleph-Bet Books, Inc. 105 - 583 2013 $600

Bingham, Clifton *More Jingles, Jokes and Funny Folks.* New York: McLoughlin, n.d. circa, 1910. 4to., pictorial wrappers, small mend on cover margin, else very good+, illustrations by Louis Wain, very scarce. Aleph-Bet Books, Inc. 104 - 582 2013 $400

Bingham, Clifton *Proverbs Old Newly Told.* London: Raphael Tuck, n.d. circa, 1900. Folio, cloth backed pictorial boards, 2 archival margin mends, some cover rubbing and paper toning, very good, 12 full page chromolithographs, black and white illustrations. Aleph-Bet Books, Inc. 105 - 456 2013 $400

Bingham, Frances Lydia *Short Poems, Religious and Sentimental.* Bolton-le-Moors: Henry Bradbury, 1848. Second edition, original red limp cloth wrappers, front wrapper lettered gilt, slightly marked, small repair to head of spine, contemporary owner's signature Eliza G. James, all edges gilt, good plus. Jarndyce Antiquarian Booksellers CCIII - 645 2013 £75

Bingham, Roger *The Chronicles of Milnthorpe.* Milnthorpe: Cicerone Press, 1987. First edition, original cloth, gilt, dust jacket, 467 pages, illustrations. R. F. G. Hollett & Son Lake District & Cumbria - 112 2013 £25

Bingham, Roger *The Church at Heversham.* Milnthorpe: privately published, 1984. First edition, original cloth, gilt, dust jacket, pages 160, illustrations, signed by author, fine, scarce. R. F. G. Hollett & Son Lake District & Cumbria - 113 2013 £60

Bingham, Roger *Memories of Hevershamm.* Milnthorpe: privately published, 2007. First edition (1000 copies only), square 8vo., original pictorial wrappers, pages 136, profusely illustrated, 8 pages in color.   R. F. G. Hollett & Son   Lake District & Cumbria - 115   2013   £25

Binns, Joseph *Exercises, Instructive and Entertaining in false English...* Leeds: printed by Edward Baines, for T. Binns and sold by J. Johnson, D. Ogilvy and Crosby and Co. and Vernot and Hood, London, 1803. 12mo., pages viii, 111, original sheep, little worn, contemporary ownership inscription of Elizabeth Dent dated 1805, good.   Blackwell's Rare Books   172 - 29   2013   £350

Binyon, Laurence 1859-1943 *The Winnowing Fan: Poems on the Great War.* London: Elkin Matthews, 1914. First edition, 8vo., original grey wrappers, uncut, inscribed by author to Mrs. Tate April 1915, covers unevenly browned, half title marked, otherwise excellent in protective folding box.   Maggs Bros. Ltd.   1460 - 105   2013   £75

Biographical memoirs and Anecdotes of the Celebrated Mary Anne Clarke, Giving and Original and Impartial Account of Her Amours... Hull: printed by D. Innes, 1809. 32 pages, frontispiece, recent green cloth, some old waterstaining.   Ken Spelman Books Ltd.   73 - 98   2013   £120

Bion *(Bion and Moschus) Opera.* Londini: T. Bensley, 1795. Large paper copy, 8vo., occasional spotting, little toning to edges of front and rear blanks, tan sheep very slightly diced, spine gilt, gilt dentelles, marbled edges and endpapers upper joint cracked but board still firmly attached, lower joint starting, loss to endcaps, spine and edges rubbed, corner tips worn, name Gulielmus (William) M. Blencowe in gilt to upper board and 'Honoris Causu" similarly gilt to lower board.   Unsworths Antiquarian Booksellers   28 - 5   2013   £125

Birch, Peter *St. Kieran's College, Kilkenny.* 1951. First edition, 8vo., illustrations, cloth, dust jacket, very good, ex-institutional library with stamps.   C. P. Hyland   261 - 910   2013   £40

Birchall, J. *The Admonitory Task Book.* Manchester: J. Gleave, 1819. Original roan backed marbled boards, woodcut tailpiece, scarce, paper label, hinges cracking.   R. F. G. Hollett & Son Children's Books - 70   2013   £180

Bird, Robert *Lakeland Gardens.* London: Ward Lock, 1994. First edition, small 4to., original cloth, gilt, dust jacket, 160 pages, illustrations in color.   R. F. G. Hollett & Son   Lake District & Cumbria - 117   2013   £25

Bird, Robert Montgomery *Nick of the Woods, or Jibbenainosay.* Philadelphia: Carey, Lea and Blanchard, 1837. First edition, 12mo., original blue green cloth printed paper labels on spines, moderate foxing, covers lightly spotted but unworn, very good.   M & S Rare Books, Inc.   95 - 21   2013 $500

Bird, Will R. *The Two Jacks: the Amazing Adventures of Major Jack M. Veness and Major Jack L. Fairweather.* Toronto: Ryerson Press, 1954. First edition, green cloth with gilt to spine in dust jacket, half title, 22 black and white photo illustrations, 8vo., previous owner's bookplate on front endpaper, otherwise very good, dust jacket chipped and worn with small pieces missing form lower spine, signed by author and Jack Veness and Jack Fairweather.   Schooner Books Ltd.   105 - 56   2013 $75

Birdwood, James *Heart's Ease in Heart Trouble: or A Sovereign Remedy Against All Trouble of Heart that Christ's Disciples are Subject to...* London: printed for W. Johnston at the Golden Ball in Ludgate Street, 1762. 12mo., frontispiece, original hessian cloth, very good, signature of Ann Ashmore Mr. 14 1836.   Jarndyce Antiquarian Booksellers   CCV - 25   2013   £200

Birkett, H. F. *The Book of Overton.* J. and E. Bumpus Ltd., 1928. First edition, original cloth, paper spine label, spine trifle rubbed and faded, large bookplate.   R. F. G. Hollett & Son   Lake District & Cumbria - 118   2013   £30

Birkett, H. F. *The Story of Ulverston.* Kendal: Titus Wilson, 1949. First edition, large 8vo., original cloth, gilt, 12 plates.   R. F. G. Hollett & Son   Lake District & Cumbria - 120   2013   £65

Birney, James G. *The American Churches, the Bulwarks of American Slavery.* London: Thomas Ward and Co., 1840. First edition, 8vo., recent wrappers, label.   M & S Rare Books, Inc.   95 - 22   2013 $325

Birrell, Augustine *Obiter Dicta.* London: Elliott Stock, 1884. First edition, inscribed by author for friend Margaret Muir, very good, original green cloth with gilt title and small rectangle gilt design to front cover, spine faded and some bumping to spine and corners, interior pages clean with slight pulling away of rear hinge, nice, scarce, 234 pages.   The Kelmscott Bookshop   7 - 97   2013 $350

Bishop, Elizabeth *Poems: North & South - a Cold Spring.* Boston: Houghton Mifflin, 1955. First edition, one of 2000 copies printed, 8vo., original blue cloth, dust jacket, presentation copy inscribed by author for Brazilian poet Joao Cabral de Melo Neto, Dec. 18th 1955, pencil annotations to poems on table of contents page, representing a numerical tally of the number of words and lines, head of spine bit frayed, otherwise very good in dust jacket with some shallow chipping and light foxing to spine, extremely rare. James S. Jaffe Rare Books   Fall 2013 - 24   2013 $4500

Bishop, Hal *Romantic Landscape. the Wood Engravings of Raymond Hawthorne.* Exeter: Bishop Books, printed by Libanus Press, 1999. One of 120 numbered copies, of an edition of 140, printed on Zerkall mouldmade paper, this unnumbered and instead, inscribed "Presentation copy. To Richard at Christmas 1999" with 11 wood engravings, each displayed on separate page, titlepage printed in black and green, royal 8vo., original plain cream sewn card, dust jacket, fine. Blackwell's Rare Books   172 - 296   2013   £45

Bishop, R. *American Decorative Arts. 360 Years of Creative Design.* New York: Abrams, 1982. First edition, folio, fine in near fine dust jacket with few invisible scratches. Beasley Books   2013 - 2013 $50

Black and White Budget. Volume I. No. 1 - Volume II No. 24. Nov. 1899 - 24 March 1900. W. J. P. Monckton, 1900. 2 volumes in 1, 4to., publisher's green cloth gilt, upper board blindstamped with floral design, extremities trifle rubbed, profusely illustrated with photos, flyleaves spotted or browned, otherwise excellent. R. F. G. Hollett & Son   Africana - 20   2013   £85

Black, R. D. Collison *Economic Thought and the Irish Question 1817-1870.* Cambridge: University Press, 1960. First edition, cloth, 8vo., ex-library, covers dull, else very good. C. P. Hyland   261 - 126   2013   £45

Blackburn, Henry *Artistic Travel in Normandy, Brittany, the Pyrenees, Spain and Algeria.* London: Sampson Low, 1892. First edition, 8vo., pages xiii, 320, ads, numerous illustrations, original blue decorative cloth. J. & S. L. Bonham Antiquarian Booksellers   Europe - 8400   2013   £75

Blackford, Audrey *The Royal Queen Elizabeth Miller...* New York: Greenwich Book Pub., 1961. First edition, endpapers trifle foxed, else fine in good plus dust jacket with fading light dampstaining and some tears along edge of spine, inscribed by author, very scarce.   Between the Covers Rare Books, Inc.   165 - 82   2013 $200

Blackie's Popular Nursery Stories. Blackie and Son, n.d., 1921. Small 4to., original cloth backed pictorial boards, edges little worn, unpaginated, 23 full page color plates, numerous drawings, pencilled line on front flyleaves and erasures on first endpapers, otherwise nice, sound copy. R. F. G. Hollett & Son   Children's Books - 264   2013   £35

Blackmore, Richard **1654-1729** *Prince Arthur.* London: printed for J. Tonson, 1714. 12mo, dusted, some foxing, tear across Q2 without loss and repaired, full contemporary calf, blindstamped tulips to corners, raised bands, red morocco label, upper board only loosely attached, following hinge cracked, wear to head of spine. Jarndyce Antiquarian Booksellers   CCIV - 63   2013   £40

Blackmore, Richard **1654-1729** *A Treatise of Consumptions and Other Distempers Belonging to the Breast and Lungs.* London: John Pemberton, 1724. First edition, 8vo., original full polished calf, five raised spine bands, white spine library number, leather worn and discolored, spine ends chipped, top right front corner and lower spine edges torn, bookplate remnants, rear pastedown glue spots, bookplate of Dr. Morris Parker, formerly of Chicago Medical School, titlepage signature of David Hay(?), holograph table of contents at free endpaper, small recipe at rear free endpaper, very good, rare.   Jeff Weber Rare Books   172 - 32 2013 $1850

Blackmore, Richard Doddridge **1825-1900** *Lorna Done.* London: Sampson Low, 1890. 34th edition, 8vo, original pictorial cloth, staining to lower edge, extremities worn, otherwise very good, inscribed by author Aug. 1891.   Maggs Bros. Ltd.   1460 - 106   2013   £100

Blackmore, Richard Doddridge **1825-1900** *Lorna Doone.* London: Sampson Low, Son & Marston, 1869. First edition, one of only 500 printed, 3 small octavo volumes, bound circa 1960 by Bayntun-Riviere in full red morocco, few minor tears and some occasional minor foxing or soiling, laid in is ALS from author to James Payn, Teddington, Dec. 3rd 1877 thanking him for his assistance in publishing of his works, excellent copy.   David Brass Rare Books, Inc. Holiday 2012 Chapter Five - DB 00726   2013 $6500

Blackmur, R. P. *The Good European and Other Poems.* Cummington: Cummington Press, 1947. First edition, copy 233 of 270 printed on Etruria paper, from a total edition of 310, close to near fine, some minor abrasions to rear board and some other slight wear without dust jacket as issued, signed by author.   Jeff Hirsch Books   Fall 2013 - 129350   2013 $150

Black's Economical Guide to the English Lakes. Edinburgh: Adam and Charles Black, 1859. Small 8vo., original green blindstamped limp cloth gilt, fore-edge of upper board rather damped, 3 maps, title vignette and 3 woodcut plates. R. F. G. Hollett & Son   Lake District & Cumbria - 122   2013   £65

Black's Guide to Killarney and South of Ireland. 1871. Frontispiece, 8vo., original green cloth with bright gilt lettering and design, very good.   C. P. Hyland   261 - 127   2013   £60

Blackwell, Elizabeth *The Laws of Life, With Special Reference to the Physical Education of Girls.* New York: George P. Putnam, 1852. First edition, first book by America's first female doctor, original grey-green blind-stamped cloth, all edges stained red, spine sunned to green (as usual with this cloth), small professional repair at bottom of spine resulting in loss of part of "P" and all of "U" and "T" in publisher's name, original owner's name in pencil, "Robert Porter" dated 1852, name in pencil repeated on page 63, else fine, lovely copy, scarce. Priscilla Juvelis - Rare Books 55 - 3 2013 $15,000

Blackwell, Thomas *An Enquiry into the Life and Writings of Homer.* London: printed for J. Oswald in the year, 1736. Second edition, 8vo., engraved frontispiece, folding engraved map, lightly spotted in places, corner of one leaf torn just touching page number, contemporary sprinkled and polished calf, spine divided by gilt rules, edges sprinkled red, lightly rubbed, slightly worn at endcaps and corners, few small scrapes to boards, armorial bookplate of William Hammond Esqr. of East Kent, contemporary inscription "Will= Hammond" at upper forecorner of titlepage. Unsworths Antiquarian Booksellers 28 - 6 2013 £125

Blackwood, Algernon *A Prisoner in Fairyland.* London: Macmillan, 1925. Reprint, 8vo., original green cloth, excellent copy, inscribed by author to Florence Edwards. Maggs Bros. Ltd. 1460 - 107 2013 £75

Blackwood, Algernon *Tales of the Uncanny and Supernatural.* London: Peter Nevill, 1949. First edition, large 8vo., original green cloth, dust jacket, excellent copy in dust jacket, inscribed by author. Maggs Bros. Ltd. 1460 - 108 2013 £450

Blaine, Nell *Nell Blaine Sketchbook.* New York: The Arts Publisher, 1986. First edition, one of 100 copies, original tipped in frontispiece etching "Flowers" numbered and signed by Blaine, out of a total edition of 726 copies numbered and signed by artist, this copy additionally inscribed by Blaine to "A.L.", 4to., illustrations in color and black and white, original two-toned cloth, matching publisher's slipcase, printed at Marderstieg's Stamperia Valdonega, Verona, on Tintoretto paper, etching was printed at the Center Street Studio, Gloucester, laid in are invitation to publication party at Metropolitan Museum of Art on April 9, 1986, similar card noting where the book was printed, and a color reproduction of Blaine's painting "Summer Interior with Open Book 1986" from the "Collection of Mr. and Mrs. A. L. Aydelott", presumably the person to whom this copy is inscribed, slipcase lightly soiled, otherwise fine, far scarcer than limitation would suggest. James S. Jaffe Rare Books Fall 2013 - 11 2013 $1500

Blake, James *Jim Blake's Tour from Conave to London.* Dublin: printed for private distribution by M. H. Gill, 1867. 4to., half title, plates with photos onlaid, odd spot, original green cloth, slightly rubbed and dulled, leading inner hinge affected by slight adhesion, all edges gilt, 9 plates, 24 pages. Jarndyce Antiquarian Booksellers CCV - 26 2013 £250

Blake, Joyce *The Story of Carlisle.* Carlisle: Education Committee, 1958. First edition, original cloth, lettered in silver, illustrations by Colin Allen. R. F. G. Hollett & Son Lake District & Cumbria - 126 2013 £25

Blake, Peter *Alphabets.* Nottingham: DE Editions, 2010. First edition, 68/100 copies (of an edition of 600), signed by Peter Blake with signed numbered print by Blake, in red card folder, loosely inserted in book, over 200 pages of color reproductions of photos of artist's work and including 2 folding leaves, 4to., original crimson cloth, backstrip longitudinally gilt lettered, printed front cover label within gilt frame, cotton marker, matching board slipcase and label, fine. Blackwell's Rare Books B174 - 172 2013 £500

Blake, William 1757-1827 *The Poems. Comprising Songs of Innocence and Experience together with Poetical Sketches...* London: Basil Montagu Pickering, 1874. Original maroon cloth, borders in blind, spine lettered gilt, spine faded and slightly rubbed at head and tail, good plus. Jarndyce Antiquarian Booksellers CCIII - 5 2013 £150

Blake, William 1757-1827 *The Poetical Sketches.* Basil Montagu Pickering, 1868. Uncut in original brown cloth boards damp affected, spine little worn at head and tail, paper label slightly chipped, good, sound copy, signed Minnie Cook 3873. Jarndyce Antiquarian Booksellers CCIII - 2 2013 £90

Blake, William 1757-1827 *Poetical Sketches.* London: Basil Montagu Pickering, 1868. Uncut in original brown cloth, spine slightly faded, paper label defective, good plus. Jarndyce Antiquarian Booksellers CCIII - 1 2013 £110

Blake, William 1757-1827 *Poetical Sketches.* London: Ballantyne Press, 1899. Half title, illustrations, uncut, original pale blue boards, paper label on spine defective, spine little dulled and slightly chipped at head, booklabel of Decherd Turner. Jarndyce Antiquarian Booksellers CCIII - 3 2013 £85

Blake, William 1757-1827 *The Poetical Works of William Blake.* London: Oxford University Press, 1913. Frontispiece, plates, original green cloth, blocked in blind and gilt, lettered in gilt, very good. Jarndyce Antiquarian Booksellers CCIII - 6 2013 £125

Blake, William   1757-1827 *Songs of Innocence and Experience.* London: Pickering, 1866. Vellum, gilt decorated, all edges gilt, monogram on front cover FAF, inscribed Eleanor Alicia O'Brien with Anne Martineau's afft. love Nov. 1866 and F. G. Arnold-Forster from R. V. O'Brien Aug. 1891, New Hall, and Flora Vere O'Brien Sept. 19, 1921, very good.   C. P. Hyland   261 - 187   2013   £105

Blake, William   1757-1827 *Songs of Innocence and Experience with other Poems.* London: Basil Montagu Pickering, Chiswick Press, 1866. Half title, uncut in original plain brown cloth, paper label slightly chipped, repairs to following hinge, armorial bookplate of Horace Pym. Jarndyce Antiquarian Booksellers   CCIII - 4   2013   £120

Blake, William   1757-1827 *Songs of Innocence.* London: Medici Society, 1927. First edition, 4to., cloth, 42 pages, fine in chipped dust jacket, 12 magnificent color plates and a profusion of lovely black and whites, beautiful copy.   Aleph-Bet Books, Inc.   104 - 85   2013 $275

Blake, William   1757-1827 *Songs of Innocence & Experience.* 21st, Publishers of Fine Art Photography, 2004. First Witkin edition, number 59 (LIX) of 75 deluxe copies (85 if to count the 10 artist's proofs that were for sale, with separate original platinum print, signed in pencil by artist, contained in separate portfolio and book, numbered and signed by the artist, Joel-Peter Witkin, printed on Arches 100 per cent cotton rag paper, 171 pages, 62 high quality monochrome plates, hand bound in cloth and contained in handsomely designed folding box, overall size 15 x 14 inches, new.   Gemini Fine Books & Arts., Ltd.   Art Reference & Illustrated Books - 2013 $1400

Blakeley, Phyllis R. *Glimpses of Halifax.* Belleville: Mika Pub., 1973. Facsimile edition, 8vo, cloth, photos, very good.   Schooner Books Ltd.   105 - 55   2013 $55

Blanchard, Amy *Bonny Bairns.* New York: Worthington, 1888. 4to., cloth backed pictorial boards, 48 pages, edges slightly rubbed, else very good+, full and partial page chromolithographs by Ida Waugh.   Aleph-Bet Books, Inc.   105 - 585   2013 $400

Blanchard, Amy *Ida Waugh's Alphabet Book.* Philadelphia: Lippincott, 1888. 4to., cloth backed pictorial boards, some cover soil and edge wear, very good, printed on heavy paper on rectos only, each leaf has alphabet pictorial border, line illustrations for each letter, rare.   Aleph-Bet Books, Inc.   104 - 24   2013 $650

Blanchard, Amy *My Own Dolly.* London: Griffith & Farrar and New York: E. P. Dutton & Co., 1882. First edition, original cloth backed pictorial boards, edges very worn and damaged by damp, 15 fine chromolithograph plates, all pages with red single rule border, fore-edges of first 3 pages dampstained, margins of plate little marked.   R. F. G. Hollett & Son   Children's Books - 73   2013   £65

Blanco, Francisco Manuel *Flora de Filipinas.* Manila: Impr. de St. Thomas, 1837. First edition, 4to., lacking final leaf of errata (should be 2ff. last a blank), waterstains first and last leaves torn and repaired, last leaves loose (also with some loss), original gilt stamped brown tree calf with red and black calf spine labels, rubbed, good, rare on market, bookplate of Howard Sprague Reed and ownership inscription Jaime Barrachina y Almeda, Madrid 1929.   Jeff Weber Rare Books   172 - 33   2013 $1600

Bland, John Salkeld *The Vale of Lyvennet.* Kendal: Titus Wilson, 1910. First (only) edition, original blue cloth gilt, spine little faded and rubbed, pages xi, 90, frontispiece portrait and illustrations from drawings by author, flyleaves lightly browned, otherwise very good, extremely scarce title.   R. F. G. Hollett & Son   Lake District & Cumbria - 127   2013   £180

Blandin, Philippe Frederic *Taite d'Anatomie Topographique ou Anatomie des Regions du Corps Humains.* Paris: Auger Mequignon, 1826. Paris: Germet Bailliere, 1834. First edition of text, second edition of atlas, 2 volumes, 8vo. text and folio atlas, with half titles, 20 partially colored lithographed plates, light soiling and dampstaining, text in contemporary quarter calf with marbled boards, atlas in original printed boards which has recently been rebacked in original style.   James Tait Goodrich   75 - 31   2013 $1450

Blanford, W. T. *Observations on the Geology and Zoology of Abyssinia, Made During the Progress of the British Expedition to that Country in 1867-68.* Macmillan, 1870. First edition, large 8vo., original blind panelled green cloth, extremities little worn and frayed, partly unopened, 2 extending tinted lithographs and 8 lithographs, 4 woodcuts and 9 vignettes, joints tender, little occasional dustiness, but very good.   R. F. G. Hollett & Son   Africana - 18   2013   £650

Blanshard, Frances *Portraits of Wordsworth.* London: Allen & Unwin, 1959. First edition, original cloth, gilt, dust jacket, 208 pages, 48 pages of collotype plates.   R. F. G. Hollett & Son   Lake District & Cumbria - 128   2013   £40

Blashford-Snell, John *In the Steps of Stanley.* Hutchinson, 1975. Original cloth, gilt, dust jacket, maps and illustrations, few spots on front endpapers, signed by author, 5 first day covers from Zaire River Expedition 1974-1975 loosely inserted.   R. F. G. Hollett & Son   Africana - 19   2013   £35

Blasingame, Ike *Dakota Cowboy. My Life in the Old Days.* New York: G. P. Putnam's Sons, 1958. First edition, 317 pages, drawings by John Mariani, endpaper amps, light brown cloth, gilt, very fine with pictorial dust jacket.   Argonaut Book Shop   Summer 2013 - 18   2013 $175

Blatty, William Peter *The Exorcist.* New York: Harper & Row, 1971. First edition, very good+ i near fine dust jacket, attractive copy, small bruise top edge of rear board, few spots of foxing on lower and fore edges of text block, dust jacket has very minor wear at extremities, small chip at head of spine. Leather Stalking Books   October 2013 - 2013 $200

Blayney, Major-General Lord *Narrative of a Force Journey through Spain and France as a Prisoner of War in the Year 1810 to 1814.* London: E. Kerby, 1814. First edition, 2 volumes, 8vo., frontispieces, contemporary brown half calf, ink stain to margin of titlepage, good set.   J. & S. L. Bonham Antiquariam Booksellers   Europe - 8433   2013   £400

Blessington, Marguerite Power Farmer Gardiner, Countess of 1789-1849 *Conversations de Lord Byron, avec la Comtesse de Blessington) (Conversations of Lord Byron with the Countess of Blessington).* Bruxelles: J. P. Meline, 1833. First edition, half title, slightly spotted, contemporary half diced calf, green leather label, very slight rubbing, label of Bibliotheque du Chateau d'Oplieux, very good.   Jarndyce Antiquarian Booksellers   CCIII - 346 2013   £120

Blessington, Marguerite Power Farmer Gardiner, Countess of 1789-1849 *Conversations of Lord Byron with the Countess of Blessington.* London: for Henry Colburn by R. Bentley, 1834. First English edition, tall 8vo., frontispiece slightly spotted, uncut in original purple cloth, unevenly faded to brown, spine recased, black paper label chipped, booklabels of H. Pinnock and John Johnson. Jarndyce Antiquarian Booksellers   CCIII - 347   2013   £125

Bleuler, Eugen *Textbook of Psychiatry.* privately printed, n.d., Reprint, fully bound in blue gray leather with gilt stamping, raised bands, ribbon marker, marbled paper endpapers, all edges gilt, quite fine.   Beasley Books   2013 - 2013 $100

Blezard, Ernest *The Birds of Lakeland.* Arbroath: Buncle, 1943. Original cloth, 6 plates.   R. F. G. Hollett & Son   Lake District & Cumbria - 129   2013   £30

Blezard, Ernest *Lakeland Natural History.* Arbroath: T. Buncle & Co., 1946. Original gilt cloth, 3 illustrations and 2 maps in rear pocket.   R. F. G. Hollett & Son   Lake District & Cumbria - 131   2013   £40

Bligh, William 1754-1817 *Voyage a la Mer du Sud, Entrepris par Ordre de S. M. Britannique pour introduire aux Indes Occidentales...* Paris: chez Garnery, Buisson, Desenne & Blanchon, 1792. Early French edition, 8vo., 2 folding maps, 1 folding engraved plate, minor repair to titlepage, original plain wrappers, ms. paper spine label, printer's cartonnage used as part of the wrapper, very good.   Jeff Weber Rare Books   171 - 35   2013 $1750

Blish, James *The Devil's Day.* New York: Baen, 1971. First hardcover edition, fine in fine dust jacket.   Between the Covers Rare Books, Inc.   Sci-Fi, Fantasy & Horror - 320718   2013 $50

Blish, James *Titan's Daughter.* London: White Lion, 1975. First edition, fine in fine dust jacket.   Leather Stalking Books   October 2013 - 2013 $75

Bloch, Robert *The Early Fears.* Minneapolis: Fedogan ^& Bremer, 1994. Limited edition, #54 of 100 copies signed by author and artist, Jon Arfstrom, fine in fine dust jacket with fine slipcase.   Between the Covers Rare Books, Inc.   Sci-Fi, Fantasy & Horror - 285694   2013 $450

Bloch, Robert *Psycho.* New York: Simon and Schuster, 1959. First edition, pages with usual uniform browning, else fine in near fine dust jacket with slight rubbing and wear, very nice.   Between the Covers Rare Books, Inc. Mystery & Detective Fiction - 59836   2013 $1650

Bloch, Robert *Screams.* San Rafael: Underwood Miller, 1969. First edition, one of 300 numbered copies signed by Bloch, fine in dust jacket with tiny rubbing on spine with slipcase.   Mordida Books   81 - 36   2013 $125

Bloch, Robert *The Skull of the Marquis de Sade.* London: Robert Hale, 1975. First hardcover edition, fine in dust jacket.   Mordida Books   81 - 34   2013 $130

Block, Lawrence *After Hours.* Albuquerque: University of New Mexico, 1995. Limited edition, one of 350 numbered copies signed by Block and Ernie Bulow, very fine in dust jacket.   Mordida Books   81 - 41   2013 $75

Block, Lawrence *Even the Wicked.* London: Orion, 1996. First edition, publisher's bookplate signed by Block laid in, very fine in dust jacket.   Mordida Books   81 - 38 2013 $300

Block, Lawrence *Random Walk. A Novel for a New Age.* New York: Tor, 1988. First edition, fine in fine dust jacket, signed by Block, beautiful copy.   Between the Covers Rare Books, Inc.   Sci-Fi, Fantasy & Horror - 311011   2013 $85

Block, Lawrence *Ronald Rabbit Is a Dirty Old Man.* New York: Bernard Geis Associates, 1971. First edition, fine, slight spine soiled, else fine in dust jacket, signed by Block. Between the Covers Rare Books, Inc.   Mystery & Detective Fiction - 310978   2013 $400

Block, Lawrence *The Scoreless Thai.* Boston: Subterranean, 2000. First hardcover edition, signed by author, very fine in dust jacket.   Mordida Books   81 - 40 2013 $100

Block, Lawrence *Spin Me a Web: Lawrence Block on Writing Fiction.* Cincinnati: Writer's Digest, 1988. First edition, signed by author, fine in dust jacket. Mordida Books 81 - 38 2013 $75

Block, Lawrence *Writing the Novel: from Plot to Print.* Cincinnati: Writer's Digest, 1979. First edition, fine in dust jacket. Mordida Books 81 - 37 2013 $100

Bloomfield, Robert *The Banks of the Wye: a Poem.* London: printed for the author, Vernor, Hood & Sharpe &c, 1811. First edition, engraved frontispiece, final ad leaf, uncut in original drab boards, fairly recently respined with tan calf, inscribed by author for Dr. J. Judkins. Jarndyce Antiquarian Booksellers CCIII - 26 2013 £185

Bloomfield, Robert *The Banks of the Wye: a Poem in Four Books.* (bound with) *May Day with the Muses.* (with) *Hazelwood-Hall: a Village Drama.* London: B. & B. Crosby & Co., 1813. London: printed for the author, 1822. London: Baldwin, Cradock & Joy, 1823. 2nd edition, first edition and first edition respectively, 3 volumes in 1, first with frontispiece and plate, slightly darkened, in functional green binder's cloth, paper label, good plus, pasted on initial blank, engraved bookplate of Bloomfield, dated 1813. Jarndyce Antiquarian Booksellers CCIII - 13 2013 £150

Bloomfield, Robert *The Banks of the Wye: a Poem.* B. & B. Crosby & Co., 1813. Second edition, engraved frontispiece and plate, full contemporary calf, gilt borders and dentelles, spine rather worn, poor copy, armorial bookplate of Robert Washington Oates, Renier booklabel. Jarndyce Antiquarian Booksellers CCIII - 27 2013 £30

Bloomfield, Robert *The Farmer's Boy: a Rural Poem.* London: Vernor and Hood, 1801. Fifth edition, frontispiece, plates, occasional pencil underlining in text, contemporary half speckled calf, gilt spine, red leather label, rubbed and worn, inner hinges cracking, contemporary signature on title, sound copy. Jarndyce Antiquarian Booksellers CCIII - 18 2013 £30

Bloomfield, Robert *The Farmer's Boy: aa Rural Poem.* London: Vernor, Hood & Sharpe, 1806. Ninth edition, half title, frontispiece, plates, illustrations, contemporary half calf, gilt devices, spine slightly darkened, small split in tail of following hinge, owner's signature on half title Feb. 1807. Jarndyce Antiquarian Booksellers CCIII - 19 2013 £40

Bloomfield, Robert *The Farmer's Boy: a Rural Poem.* London: Longman, 1827. Fifteenth edition, half title, engraved title and plates after R. Westall, some spotting, slightly later half calf, gilt bands, brown leather label, signed "Fanny Tetley" in contemporary hand, Renier booklabel, very good. Jarndyce Antiquarian Booksellers CCIII - 20 2013 £30

Bloomfield, Robert *The Farmer's Boy, Rural Tales, Ballads, Songs and Wild Flowers.* London: Joseph Smith, circa, 1841. 32mo., engraved frontispiece and title, occasional woodcuts in text, original olive green vertical grained cloth, gilt spine, bands blocked with intricate swirling borders, gift inscription on leading f.e.p. "Miss Dowling, presented by her friend Mr. Abbott Sept 26th 1848", very good. Jarndyce Antiquarian Booksellers CCIII - 16 2013 £45

Bloomfield, Robert *The Farmer's Boy: Rural Tales, Ballads, Songs and Wild Flowers.* London: T. J. Allman, 1862. 32mo., engraved frontispiece and title, printed title, final ad leaf, one or two gatherings slightly proud, original pebble grained dark pink cloth, borders in blind, gilt spine and central vignette on front board, worn, all edges gilt, sound. Jarndyce Antiquarian Booksellers CCIII - 17 2013 £25

Bloomfield, Robert *May Day with the Muses.* London: printed for the author &c. for Baldwin, Cradock & Joy, 1822. First edition, 12mo., illustrations, uncut in contemporary pale blue boards, drab spine, paper label, gift inscription to Catherine Sharpe 1822, later inscription in blue ink on leading f.e.p., very good. Jarndyce Antiquarian Booksellers CCIII - 28 2013 £125

Bloomfield, Robert *Poems.* London: John Van Noorst, 1845. Handsomely bound in full contemporary calf, gilt spine borders and dentelles, green leather labels with very slight rubbing, small monogram booklabel of W. M. W. ,Bookseller's ticket, Pawsye of Ipswich, very good. Jarndyce Antiquarian Booksellers CCIII - 12 2013 £85

Bloomfield, Robert *Rural Tales, Ballads and Songs.* (bound with) *Wild Flowers; of Pastoral and Local Poetry.* (bound with) *The Farmer's Boy: a Rural Poem.* London: Vernor, Hood and Sharpe, Poultry, 1811. London: Longman etc., 1816. London: Longman &c. 1837. Seventh and fifteenth edition, 3 volumes in 1, contemporary half green calf, spine gilt in compartments, maroon leather label, armorial bookplate of Henry Hickman Barnes, with his name crossed through and that of Arthur Swinbourne added, Barnes' name has been struck through where present, very good. Jarndyce Antiquarian Booksellers CCIII - 14 2013 £75

Bloomfield, Robert *Rural Tales, Ballads and Songs.* London: Longman &c., 1820. Ninth edition, illustrations, 4 neatly colored by previous owner, some internal marking, full contemporary green calf, gilt spine, gilt and blind borders, Renier booklabel, very good, school prize inscription Bromely Seminary 1826. Jarndyce Antiquarian Booksellers CCIII - 21 2013 £30

Bloomfield, Robert *Wild Flowers; or Pastoral and Local Poetry.* London: Vernor, Hood & Sharpe, 1806. First edition, frontispiece and plates, some light offsetting, following f.e.p., edges chipped, contemporary full tree calf, gilt spine, black leather label, head and tail of spine little worn, slight rubbing to hinges, news cutting on leading pastedown, contemporary inscription.   Jarndyce Antiquarian Booksellers   CCIII - 22   2013   £65

Bloomfield, Robert *Wild Flowers; or Pastoral and Local Poetry.* London: Longman &c, 1819. New edition, frontispiece and plates, uncut in original blue boards, drab spine titled in ink chipped, Renier booklabel.   Jarndyce Antiquarian Booksellers   CCIII - 23   2013   £35

Bloomfield, Robert *(Wild Flowers). The Horkey: a Ballad.* London: Macmillan, 1882. 4to., half title, illustrations by George Cruikshank, half title, color printed throughout, original pictorial boards, slightly rubbed at edges and corners, green cloth spine bit dulled and slightly damp marked, 48 pages.   Jarndyce Antiquarian Booksellers   CCIII - 25   2013   £35

Bloomfield, Robert *(Wild Flowers). The Horkey: a Ballad.* London: Macmillan, 1882. 4to., half title, color printed with incorrect register for blue on some leaves, original pictorial boards, rubbed at edges and corners, blue cloth spine dulled, f.e.p.'s slightly spotted and creased, 48 pages, illustrations by George Cruikshank.   Jarndyce Antiquarian Booksellers   CCIII - 24   2013   £45

Blosius, Franciscus Ludovicus *Igniarium Divini Amoris Seu Precationes Piae ex Operibus.* Antverpiae: ex Officina Platiniana Balthasaris Moreti, 1635. Engraved titlepage vignette, full page engraving, woodcut initials, 12mo., some occasional light browning, top edge gilt and front endpaper dusted, recent marbled boards, parchment spine, red morocco label.   Jarndyce Antiquarian Booksellers   CCIV - 4   2013   £250

Blount, Charles *The Oracles of Reason... in Several Letters to Mr. Hobbs and Other Persons of Eminent Quality and Learning.* London: printed, 1693. First edition, 12mo., full modern calf, new endpapers, red leather label, gilt lettering, ink signature of Joseph Trapp dated 1724, paper browned, one signature trimmed little close in top margin, shaving some page numbers, front free endpaper, little stained from removal of pastedown bookseller's description, very good.   The Brick Row Book Shop   Miscellany Fifty-Nine - 13   2013 $1750

Blumberg, Fannie *Rowena Teena Tot and the Runaway Turkey.* Chicago: Whitman, 1936. First edition, 4to., cloth, 32 pages some cover soil, very good+, illustrations by Mary Grosjean.   Aleph-Bet Books, Inc.   104 - 76   2013 $225

Blumenback, Johann Friedrich *Introdvctio in Historiam Medicinae Litterariam.* Goettingae: Apud Jo. Christ Dieterich, 1786. 8vo., recent quarter tan morocco and linen boards, raised bands, nicely tooled spine, tall well margined, uncut copy, paper toned and foxing in parts, author's presentation copy with note "From the author" in brown ink.   James Tait Goodrich   75 - 32   2013 $795

Blumenthal, Walter Hart *Book Gluttons and Book Gourmets.* Chicago: Black Cat Press, 1961. Limited to 300 copies, 6.7 x 5.3cm., full leather, 84, (1) pages, from the collection of Donn W. Sanford.   Oak Knoll Books   303 - 51   2013 $150

Blumenthal, Walter Hart *Formats and Foibles, a few Books Which Might Be Called Curious.* Worcester: Achille J. St. Onge, 1956. Limited to 300 copies, 6 x 4.9 cm., printed on Barcham Green's handmade paper, bound by Sangorski & Sutcliffe, full red morocco, all edges gilt, from the collection of Donn W. Sanford.   Oak Knoll Books   303 - 26   2013 $175

Blunden, Edmund *De Bello Germanico. A Fragment of Trench History.* Hawstead: G. A. Blunden, 1930. First edition, limited to 250 copies, 8vo., original grey boards, paper label on spine, paper label browned and nicked, otherwise excellent copy, enclosed within protective box, inscribed by author for Jack Morpugo 22 April 1953.   Maggs Bros. Ltd.   1460 - 114   2013   £275

Blunden, Edmund *English Poems.* Thavies Inn: Richard Cobden Sanderson, 1925. First edition, tall 8vo., original red cloth, dust jacket, excellent copy in browned and slightly nicked dust jacket, enclosures in excellent state, inscribed by author Sep. 9 1926 for C. G. Oxley Brennan, and further APS c. 65 words.   Maggs Bros. Ltd.   1460 - 112   2013   £175

Blunden, Edmund *The Face of England. A Series of Occasional Sketches.* London: Longmans, Green and Co., 1932. First edition, small 8vo., original green cloth, dust jacket, fading to spine, otherwise excellent copy, inscribed by author for Sylva Norman, with pencilled correction in author's holograph on page 141.   Maggs Bros. Ltd.   1460 - 117   2013   £400

Blunden, Edmund *Halfway House. A Miscellany of New Poems.* London: Cobden Sanderson, 1932. First edition, 8vo., original brown cloth, printed paper label on spine, inscribed by author, inked address on rear endpaper, cloth slightly marked on lower board, otherwise excellent.   Maggs Bros. Ltd.   1460 - 118   2013   £90

Blunden, Edmund *In Summer. The Rotunda of the Bishop of Derry.* London: privately printed for Terence Fytton Armstrong, 1931. First edition, 8vo., original grey boards, lettered in pale green, acetate dust jacket slightly torn, near fine, inscribed by author for A. F. Webling, rector of Stansfield in Suffolk. Maggs Bros. Ltd. 1460 - 115 2013 £125

Blunden, Edmund *Poems of Many Years.* London: Collins, 1957. First edition, 8vo., original dark pink cloth, inscribed by author for Sylva, loosely inserted are clippings from news reviews of book, excellent copy in thoroughly browned dust jacket. Maggs Bros. Ltd. 1460 - 120 2013 £300

Blunden, Edmund *A Selection of this Poetry and Prose.* London: Rupert Hart-Davis, 1950. First edition, 8vo., original green cloth, fine in dust jacket browned on spine, inscribed by author for Sylva 1 Nov. 1950. Maggs Bros. Ltd. 1460 - 119 2013 £300

Blunden, Edmund *Undertones of War.* London: Richard Cobden Sanderson, 1929. Seventh impression, 8vo., original black cloth, author has inscribed the poem How Sleep the Brave on front free endpaper and written beneath "William Collins was the Expeditionary Force in Flanders 1745-1746 with Edmund Blunden's best wishes to all those who came from Ireland into Flanders in 1914-1918 May 15 1930", excellent copy. Maggs Bros. Ltd. 1460 - 113 2013 £500

Blunden, Edmund *The Waggoner and Other Poems.* London: Sidgwick & Jackson, 1920. Second impression, 8vo., original burgundy cloth, printed paper label on spine inscribed in unknown pencilled hand "To a fine critic 28 June 1921. F.P." and inscribed below by author, recipient is Frederick Page, loosely inserted ALS to Page from Blunden and short ALS to Page from Wilfrid Meynell, faded on spine, label rubbed, otherwise excellent copy, enclosures in presentable order. Maggs Bros. Ltd. 1460 - 111 2013 £180

Blundeville, Thomas *M. Blundeuile His Exercises, Containing Eight Treatises...* imprinted by William Stansby, 1613. Fourth edition, woodcuts on section titles, numerous woodcuts in text, some with volvelles, 4 folding tables (3 unattached), map, 2 diagrams cropped, one by about 5mm, the other just touched, one signature of gathering Q shaved, few rust holes with minor loss, square 8vo., early 17th century calf, blind ruled borders on sides, double blind fillets towards spines, spine gilt in compartments, red lettering piece, marbled edges, sides rubbed, spine defective at either end, loss of gilt, Macclesfield copy with bookplate and blindstamp. Blackwell's Rare Books Sciences - 13 2013 £5000

Blunt, Wilfrid Scawen *A New Pilgrimage and Other Poems.* 1889. First edition, 8vo., cloth, top edge gilt, very good. C. P. Hyland 261 - 129 2013 £50

Blunt, Wilfrid Scawen *A New Pilgrimage and Other Poems.* 1889. First edition, 8vo., cloth, very good, ownership inscription by Historian H. W. C. Davis, top edge gilt. C. P. Hyland 261 - 130 2013 £75

Blunt, Wilfrid Scawen *Poems.* New York: 1923. First edition, 8vo., quarter cloth, very good. C. P. Hyland 261 - 131 2013 £32

Blunt, Wilfrid Scawen *The Poetical Works of Wilfrid Scawen Blunt.* London: Macmillan, 1914. 2 volumes, original dark blue cloth, excellent set, spine of second volume slightly faded, inscribed by author for Adah Russell, loosely inserted are two small photos of Blunt in Arab dress and manuscript poem in his hand dated Aug. 5 1900. Maggs Bros. Ltd. 1460 - 121 2013 £650

Blyth, R. H. *Senryu. Japanese Satirical Verses.* Japan: Hokuseido Press, 1949. First edition, 8vo., profusely illustrated by Sobun Taniwaki with black and white drawings and color plates with printed tissue guards, including foldout color frontispiece, near fine, minimal foxing to edge, in very good dust jacket with small pieces, tape, 2 inch piece missing from dust jacket spine lower tip. By the Book, L. C. 38 - 58 2013 $300

Blythe, Ronald *First Friends. Paul and Bunty, John and Christine - and Carrington.* Denby Dale: Fleece Press, 1997. One of 300 copies on Zerkall mouldmade paper in black and red, numerous tipped in reproductions of work by them in monochrome and color, also with line drawings by artists, small folio, original orange quarter orange linen, printed label, pale blue boards, repeated design overall in darker blue, untrimmed, linen and boards slipcase, fine. Blackwell's Rare Books 172 - 274 2013 £300

Blyton, Enid *Bom Goes to the Circus.* Brockhampton Press, 1961. First edition, oblong 12mo., original cloth backed pictorial wrappers, some surface damage to upper panel, 2 illustrations per page by R. Paul-Hoye, some early leaves little dented. R. F. G. Hollett & Son Children's Books - 75 2013 £25

Blyton, Enid *Clicky and the Flying Horse.* Brockhampton Press, 1957. First edition, oblong 12mo., original cloth backed pictorial wrappers, little soiled, rebacked, 2 illustrations per page printed in red and black by Molly Brett, few leaves little creased. R. F. G. Hollett & Son Children's Books - 76 2013 £25

Blyton, Enid *Mary Mouse Goest to the Fair.* Brockhampton Press, 1958. First edition, oblong 12mo., original cloth backed pictorial wrappers little soiled, 2 illustrations peer page printed in red and black, odd mark and crease. R. F. G. Hollett & Son Children's Books - 78 2013 £25

Boaden, James *An Inquiry into the Authenticity of Various Pictures and Prints....* London: printed for Robert Triphook, 1824. First edition, scarce large paper copy, with 5 mounted India proofs, tipped in at end is copy of a printed letter from portrait painter Abraham to C. U. Kingston of Ashbourne, Birmingham, March 24h 1847, 4to., later half red morocco, marbled boards, front hinge repaired, spine gilt raised bands, half title, title, 5 plates, tipped in sheet, top edge gilt, fore and bottom edges uncut, fine.   Howard S. Mott Inc.   262 - 18   2013 $400

Boardman, John *Geomorphology of the Lake District: a Field Guide.* Oxford: Environmental Change Unit, 1997. First edition, original wrappers, illustrations.   R. F. G. Hollett & Son   Lake District & Cumbria - 132   2013   £25

Boccaccio, Giovanni   1313-1375 *Decameron. The Model of Wit, Mirth, Eloquence and Conversation Framed in Ten Days of an Hundred Curious Pieces.* Oxford: Shakepeare Head Press, 1934-1935. 15/325 sets (of an edition of 328), printed in double column on Batchelor handmade paper, in black and blue, large historiated capitals also printed in blue, superb wood engravings, including beautifully executed borders to titlepage, small folio, original mid blue hermitage calf a trifle edge rubbed, smooth backstrips gilt lettered, blue, green and tan marbled endpapers, top edge gilt on rough, others untrimmed, near fine.   Blackwell's Rare Books   B174 - 384   2013   £850

Boccaccio, Giovanni   1313-1375 *The Modell of Wit, Mirth, Eloquence and Conversation. (bound with) The Decameron.* London: Isaac Jaggard, 1625. 1620. Second edition in English of volume I, first English edition of volume II,, 2 volumes, folio, bound in one, without prelim blank leaf of volume II, often omitted in rebound copies, each titlepage with elaborate woodcut border, 98 woodcut illustrations, numerous woodcut initials, head and tailpieces, 19th century brown calf antique, neatly rebacked, covers ruled and decorated in blind, gilt corner pieces, spine gilt decorated in compartments with red morocco lettering label, marbled endpapers, edges stained red, extremities very lightly rubbed, text washed and pressed with some residual staining, light browning and soiling, title of part one shorter at fore-edge as in some copies, few marginal tears neatly repaired, overall fine and fresh, custom quarter brown morocco clamshell case.   Heritage Book Shop   50th Anniversary Catalogue - 11   2013 $12,500

Boelter, Homer H. *Portfolio of Hopi Kachinas.* Hollywood: Homer H. Boelter, 1969. Number 528 of 1000 numbered copies signed by author, folio, 16 full page chromolithograph plates, numerous text drawings in color and black and white, decorative endpapers, pale green cloth decoratively stamped and lettered in metallic green, plus extra suite of 16 loose folio color plates in light cardboard portfolio, housed in matching pale green slipcase, very fine.   Argonaut Book Shop   Recent Acquisitions June 2013 - 25   2013 $325

Boerhaave, Hermann *Atrocis Nec Descripti Prius Morbi Historia (bound with) Atrocis, Rarissimique Morbi Historia Altera.* Leyden: Ex Officina Boutestentiana, 1724. Leyden: Apud Samulem Luchtmans & Theodorum Haak, 1728, Title skilfully laid down on old paper, top outer blank corner lacking, recent binding of quarter calf and marbled boards, clean, crisp copy, on first title is penned " E. Libris Gulilelmi Hillary" (William Hillary).   James Tait Goodrich   75 - 34   2013 $1950

Boerhaave, Hermann *Praelectiones Academicae in Proprias Institutiones rei medicae...* Naples: Sumptibus Dom,inci Terres ex typographia Josephi Raymundi, 1754-1755. 7 volumes, title of volume i printed in red and black, each titlepage with woodcut vignette, two small burn holes in B2 of volume vi with loss of few letters, some very minor marginal dampstaining and occasional light foxing, 4to., original carta rustica, front inner hinge volume i little weak, slight soiling, contemporary signature on each title of Michael Boette, very good.   Blackwell's Rare Books   172 - 30   2013   £1500

Boethius *De Consolatione Philosophiae Libri Quinque Recensuit..* Paris: Sumptibus Lamy, 1783. Engraved frontispiece, large but faint dampmark towards rear, one leaf with few ink splashed, Belgian convent library stamp to title, 12mo., contemporary red crushed morocco, boards bordered with triple gilt fillet, spine divided by gilt roll, central urn tools in compartments, lettered gilt direct, all edges gilt, marbled endpapers, some marks and surface damage to leather, edges and corners bit worn, spine darkened, sound.   Blackwell's Rare Books 172 - 31   2013   £100

Bogg, Edmund *A Thousand Miles of Wandering Along the Roman Wall, the Old Border Region.* Leeds: Edmund Bogg and James Miles, 1898. First edition, 4to., original green cloth, 180 illustrations, nice.   R. F. G. Hollett & Son   Lake District & Cumbria - 134   2013   £45

Bogg, Edmund *Two Thousand Miles of Wandering in the Border Country, Lakeland and Ribblesdale.* Leeds: the author; York; John Sampson, 1898. Large 4to. original half morocco gilt with raised bands, 350 illustrations, joints cracked but sound, blind ownership stamps on flyleaves, handsome copy.   R. F. G. Hollett & Son   Lake District & Cumbria - 135   2013   £175

Bogue, Thomas *A Treatise on the Structure, Color and Preservation of the Human Hair.* Philadelphia: J. Perry, 1841. First edition, 16mo., 107 pages, frontispiece, 2 plates, original cloth, spine chipped.   M & S Rare Books, Inc.   95 - 137   2013 $750

Boileau, Pierre *Spells of Evil.* London: Hamish Hamilton, 1961. First English edition, fine in price clipped near fine dust jacket.   Between the Covers Rare Books, Inc. Mystery & Detective Fiction - 287264   2013 $65

Boileau, Pierre *The Woman Who Was No More.* New York: Rinehart & Co., 1954. First American edition, page edges very slightly browned, still fine in fine dust jacket, exceptionally uncommon title.   Between the Covers Rare Books, Inc.   Mystery & Detective Fiction - 89160   2013 $3500

Boileau, Thomas *Choice Cuts.* New York: Dutton, 1966. First American edition, page edges lightly foxed and little mottling to boards, very good plus in near fine dust jacket with some rubbing to spinal extremities.   Between the Covers Rare Books, Inc.   Sci-Fi, Fantasy & Horror - 17119   2013 $140

Bois, Yve-Alain *Ellsworth Kelly: the Years in France 1948-1954.* Washington: & Munich: National Gallery of Art/Prestel, 1992. First edition, 208 pages, 222 illustrations with 106 in color, fine in fine dust jacket.   Jeff Hirsch Books Fall 2013 - 129172   2013 $150

Bois, Yve-Alain *Ellsworth Kelly: the Early Drawings 1948-1955.* Cambridge: Winterthur: Harvard University Art Museums/Kunstmuseum Winterthur, 1999. Second printing, 263 pages, large oblong softcover, over 180 color illustrations, tight, near fine copy in wrappers.   Jeff Hirsch Books   Fall 2013 - 129716   2013 $50

Boisguilbert, Pierre Le Pesant De *Le France Ruinee Souls le Regne de Louis XIV.* Cologne: Pierre Marteau, 1696. Early printing, small 12mo., 214 pages, frontispiece, lacks folding map (apparently as issued for this copy), 20th century olive boards, green morocco gilt stamped spine label, fine, rare.   Jeff Weber Rare Books   171 - 38   2013 $375

Boissonnas, Edith *Limbe.* Paris: Ales (PAB), 1959. First edition, number 37 of 50 copies on Arches (total edition 59), signed by PAB and Andre Masson, 2 original hors texte etchings with drypoint by Andre Masson, printed on celluloid, loose leaves in publisher's wrappers, custom folding box by Ann Repp, overall size 26 x 20 x 3cm., excellent condition. Gemini Fine Books & Arts., Ltd.   Art Reference & Illustrated Books - 2013 $2500

Boland, Eavan *Limitations.* New York: Center for Books Arts, 2000. Limited to 25 copies in this binding, from a total of 100 copies signed by author, narrow 4to., printed letterpress on Iyo glazed handmade Japanese paper hand sewn in khadi natural black covers, indigo and azure endpapers with title and colophon calligraphy by Malachi McCormick, near fine.   Maggs Bros. Ltd.   1442 - 27   2013   £200

Boland, Eavan *New Territory.* Dublin: Allen Figgis and Co., 1967. First edition, 8vo., original grey cloth, dust jacket, excellent copy in dust jacket, rubbed at edges with small piece missing from upper left corner.   Maggs Bros. Ltd. 1442 - 25   2013   £200

Boland, Eavan *The War Horse.* London: Gollancz, 1975. First edition, 8vo. original wrappers, from the library of Richard Murphy, signed by him, excellent copy.   Maggs Bros. Ltd.   1442 - 26   2013   £50

Bolger, Dermot *Leinster Street Ghosts.* Dublin: Raven Arts, 1989. First edition, signed by author, one of 50 copies, 8vo., original brown cloth, fine in dust jacket.   Maggs Bros. Ltd.   1442 - 31   2013   £125

Bolger, Dermot *Never a Dull Moment.* Dublin: Raven Arts, 1978. First edition, slim 8vo., original wrappers, from the library of Richard Murphy, inscribed by author, covers slightly foxed, otherwise near fine.   Maggs Bros. Ltd. 1442 - 29   2013   £125

Bolger, Dermot *No Waiting America.* Dublin: Raven Arts, 1982. First edition, 8vo., original wrappers, fading to spine, else near fine, from the library of Richard Murphy, inscribed by author.   Maggs Bros. Ltd.   1442 - 30   2013   £100

Bolingbroke, Henry St. John, 1st Viscount   1678-1751 *Letters on the Study and Use of History.* London: printed for A. Millar, 1752. 2 volumes in 1, half titles, engraved portrait has been mounted to from a frontispiece, 8vo., clean copy, contemporary tree calf, spine attractively decorated in gilt, red morocco label, armorial bookplate of William Waddington with ownership inscription, contemporary ms. notes to margins of pages 182-183, slightly trimmed in binding.   Jarndyce Antiquarian Booksellers   CCIV - 64   2013   £250

Bolingbroke, Henry St. John, 1st Viscount   1678-1751 *Letters on the Study and Use of History.* London: printed for T. Cadell, 1779. New edition, 8vo., some occasional foxing, several marginal notes in contemporary hand, full contemporary calf, gilt banded spine, head and tail slightly chipped, armorial bookplate of Francis, Duke of Bedford, Oakley House, recent bookplate of Thomas Duffy. Jarndyce Antiquarian Booksellers   CCIV - 65   2013   £40

Bolton, Herbert Eugene   1870-1953 *Anza's California Expeditions.* Berkeley: University of California Press, 1930. First edition, signed by author in volume 1, 5 volumes, approximately 500 pages per volume, 14 maps, 106 plates, 47 facsimiles, navy blue cloth, gilt lettered spines, printed description tipped to endpaper of volume 1, very fine.   Argonaut Book Shop   Recent Acquisitions June 2013 - 26   2013 $1000

Bolton, Herbert Eugene   1870-1953 *Anza's California Expeditions.* New York: Russell and Russell, 1966. Reprint edition, 14 maps, some folding, 106 plates, 47 facsimiles, navy blue cloth, gilt, very fine set.   Argonaut Book Shop   Summer 2013 - 19   2013 $400

Bolton, Herbert Eugene   1870-1953 *Font's Complete Diary.* Berkeley: University of California Press, 1931. First separate edition, 34 illustrations, folding map, navy blue cloth, gilt, very fine.   Argonaut Book Shop   Recent Acquisitions June 2013 - 28   2013 $250

Bolton, Herbert Eugene   1870-1953 *Font's Complete Diary. A Chronicle of the Founding of San Francisco.* Berkeley: University of California Press, 1931. First separate edition, first printing, beautiful copy, 34 illustrations, folding map, navy blue cloth, gilt, very fine with printed and decorated dust jacket (minor tear to lower edge).   Argonaut Book Shop   Summer 2013 - 25   2013 $275

Bolton, Herbert Eugene   1870-1953 *Fray Juan Crespi: Missionary Explorer on the Pacific Coast 1769-1774.* Berkeley: University of California Press, 1926. First edition, 402 pages, frontispiece, 10 maps and plates, navy blue cloth.   Argonaut Book Shop   Summer 2013 - 20   2013 $275

Bolton, Herbert Eugene   1870-1953 *Outpost of Empire. The Story of the Founding of San Francisco.* New York: Alfred A. Knopf, 1931. First separate edition, 66 illustrations, 11 maps, navy cloth, owner's name on end, spine very so slightly faded, fine.   Argonaut Book Shop Summer 2013 - 21   2013 $175

Bolton, Herbert Eugene   1870-1953 *Outpost of Empire.* New York: Alfred A. Knopf, 1939. Second printing, 66 illustrations, 11 maps, one folding map with short gutter tear, red cloth, spine ends very slightly darkened, fine, worn printed dust jacket.   Argonaut Book Shop   Summer 2013 - 22   2013 $125

Bolton, Herbert Eugene   1870-1953 *Pacific Coast Pioneer.* Berkeley: the author, 1927. First sepatate edition, frontispiece, 7 plates, navy blue cloth, gilt, very fine, presentation signed by author.   Argonaut Book Shop   Recent Acquisitions June 2013 - 27   2013 $200

Bolton, Herbert Eugene   1870-1953 *Rim of Christendom: a Biography of Eusebio Francisco Kino, Pacific Coast Pioneer.* New York: 1936. First edition, xiv, 644 pages, illustrations, 8 folding maps, no dust jacket, previous owner's discrete initials, else very good, clean copy.   Dumont Maps & Books of the West   124 - 47   2013 $65

Bolton, Herbert Eugene   1870-1953 *Rim of Christendom.* New York: Macmillan, 1936. First edition, 644 pages, 25 plates, 3 facsimiles, 8 folding maps, dark blue green cloth, very fine, bright.   Argonaut Book Shop   Summer 2013 - 23   2013 $225

Bolton, Herbert Eugene   1870-1953 *Rim of Christendom.* New York: Russell & Russell, 1960. Second edition, 25 plates, 54 photo illustrations, 3 facsimiles, 8 maps, medium blue cloth gilt, very fine, with lightly worn pictorial jacket.   Argonaut Book Shop   Summer 2013 - 179   2013 $150

Bolton, John *Geological Fragments Collected Principally from Rambles Among the Rocks of Furness and Cartmel.* London: Whittaker & Co. and Ulverston: D. Atkinson, 1869. First edition, original blindstamped cloth gilt, 5 plates, few spots to frontispiece, scarce original edition.   R. F. G. Hollett & Son   Lake District & Cumbria - 137   2013   £95

Bolton, John *Geological Fragments Collected Principally from Rambles Among the Rocks of Furness and Cartmel.* Beckermet: Michael Moon, 1978. Limited edition (600 copies), original cloth gilt, dust jacket, 5 plates.   R. F. G. Hollett & Son   Lake District & Cumbria - 136 2013   £35

Bombal, Susana *Green Wings.* Buenos Aires: Ediciones Losange, 1959. First edition, 8vo., original green wrappers, inscribed by author to Margot Fonteyn, near fine, just slightly rubbed at extremities.   Maggs Bros. Ltd.   1460 - 122   2013   £100

Bonaparte-Wyse, William C. *Vox Clamantis or Letters on the Land League.* 1880. First collected edition, iv, 59 pages, octavo, modern wrappers, very good.   C. P. Hyland 261 - 139   2013   £150

Bonaparte, Napoleon *Maximes de Napoleon.* London: Arthur L. Humphreys, 1903. 164 x 127mm., appealing russet crushed morocco, covers with gilt rule border and blind tooled three leaf extensions from raised bands, spine gilt in compartments with either an "N" and coronet or bee centerpiece, turn-ins with multiple gilt rules, all edges gilt, engraved bookplate of Victoria Sackville West, just hint of rubbing to joints, scattered freckling, dark spots on boards, minor offsetting on free endpapers from turn-ins, isolated spots of foxing or faint marginal stains, otherwise excellent copy, clean, fresh , bright in binding with very few signs of wear.   Phillip J. Pirages   63 - 418   2013 $200

Bond, Edward *Saved.* London: Methuen, 1966. First edition, original wrappers, near fine, inscribed by author for actor Richard Butler, loosely inserted is Christmas card, also inscribed by author.   Maggs Bros. Ltd.   1460 - 123   2013   £175

Bond, Edward *The Sea.* London: Methuen, 1973. First edition, small 8vo., original black cloth, fine in dust jacket, inscribed by author to Alan Webb, the actor.   Maggs Bros. Ltd.   1460 - 124   2013   £200

Bond, Gladys Baker *Seven Little Stories on Big Subjects.* New York: Anti Defamation League, 1955. 7 volumes, 12mo., pictorial wrappers, neat owner name on covers and box, else fine in original pictorial box (slightly soiled), complete set of 7 rare booklets, each illustrated by Maurice Sendak.   Aleph-Bet Books, Inc.   104 - 517   2013 $4500

Bondy, Louis W. *Small is Beautiful.* Morro Bay: Miniature Book Society, 1987. Limited to 400 copies, printed at Tabula Rasa Press, 6.5 x 6 cm., cloth with gilt lettering on front cover and gilt design on spine, signed by author and by Francis Weber, from the collection of Donn W. Sanford.   Oak Knoll Books   303 - 5   2013 $150

Bone, Gavin *Anglo-Saxon Poetry.* Oxford: Clarendon Press, 1944. First reprint, 8vo., original cream cloth, excellent copy, inscribed by Muirhead and Gertrude Bone to A. S. F. Gow.   Maggs Bros. Ltd.   1460 - 125   2013   £50

Bonet, Honore *L'Apparition de Jehan de Meun ou le Songe Du Prieur De Salon.* Paris: Imprime par Crapelet pur la Societe des Bibliophiles Francais, 1845. One of 170 copies on velllum (this copy #7 printed for M. Le Comte e La Bedoyere, member of the Societe des Bibliophiles) (another 100 copies on issued on paper), recent fine white pigskin, decorated in blind to a Medieval style by Courtland Benson, housed in titled custom made morocco backed folding cloth box, 10 engraved plates, morocco bookplate of Comte H. De La Bedoyere and engraved bookplate of Marcellus Schlimovich, embossed library stamp of Dr. Detlef Mauss; half title with ink library stamp of Sociedad Hebraica Argentina, fine, especially clean and bright internally, only most trivial imperfections in new retrospective binding.   Phillip J. Pirages   63 - 477   2013 $3500

Bonet, Theophile *Sepulchretum: sive Anatomia Practica Ex Cadaveribus Morb Denatis.* Geneva: Gramer & Pearchon, 1700. 3 volumes in 2, engraved portrait, folio, handsome contemporary blindstamped vellum with morocco lettering pieces, arabesque designs on front boards, bindings showing wear and soiling, some toning and minor worming.   James Tait Goodrich   75 - 33   2013 $2495

Bonhams. The Contents of Birket Houses, Cumbria... Bonhams: Montpellier Galleries, 1984. Large 8vo., original wrappers, pages 106, well illustrated, partly in color.   R. F. G. Hollett & Son   Lake District & Cumbria - 52   2013   £25

Bonnobergers, Ludwig *Betbuechlein.* Vienna: K. K. Hofibliothek, 1912. 32mo., bound in buff cloth with interwoven silver threads, edges gilt, with two indented circles on each edge housed in scooped out compartment at back of a parent volume, boards of miniature facsimile volume partly detached at spine, boards of larger volume lightly scuffed at edges, from the collection of Donn W. Sanford.   Oak Knoll Books   303 - 63   2013 $850

Bonsall, Brian *Sir James Lowther and Cumberland and Westmorland Elections 1754-1775.* Manchester: University Press, 1960. First edition, original cloth, gilt, dust jacket price clipped.   R. F. G. Hollett & Son   Lake District & Cumbria - 138   2013   £45

Bonsor, N. R. P. *North Atlantic Seaway: an Illustrated History of the Passenger Series Linking the Old World with the New. Volumes I and II.* Jersey & Channel Islands: Brookside, 1978. 2 volumes, 237 x 158mm., illustrations, blue cloth, dust jacket, very good.   Jeff Weber Rare Books   169 - 35   2013 $60

Bontemps, Arna *Anyplace but Here.* New York: Hill and Wang, 1966. First edition, small stain on rear board, else fine in slightly spine faded, very good dust jacket, full page inscription from Jack Conroy.   Between the Covers Rare Books, Inc.   165 - 84   2013 $150

Bontemps, Arna *Personals.* London: Paul Breman, 1963. First edition, one of 250 numbered copies, wrappers as issued, some modest foxing on front wrapper, thus very good.   Between the Covers Rare Books, Inc.   165 - 83   2013 $200

The Book of Trades or Library of the Useful Arts. Tabart and Co., 1810. Fourth edition, part I, 12mo., original roan backed boards gilt, rather worn, 23 copper engraved plates, few plates little browned, otherwise very nice.   R. F. G. Hollett & Son   Children's Books - 14   2013   £120

The Book of Oz Cooper. An Appreciation of Oswald Bruce Cooper. Chicago: Society of Typographic Arts, 1949. First edition, 4to., very good+ with tiny spot on front board.   Beasley Books   2013 - 2013 $100

The Book of Garden Management... London: Ward Lock, 1890. Large 8vo. maroon cloth, hinges repaired, colored plate, 600 engravings on wood, good.   Barnaby Rudge Booksellers   Natural History 2013 - 020509   2013 $50

Book of Model Fire Engines. New York: Grosset & Dunlap, 1951. Oblong folio, spine paper repaired else very good+, although never used, at some time a few small non essential pieces have detached themselves and are not present, 10 large pages of colored die cut pieces to be used to assemble authentic scale models of fire engines and fire house, quite hard to find in unpunched condition.   Aleph-Bet Books, Inc.   105 - 254   2013 $350

Book of Mormon *Book of Mormon: An Account Written by the Hand of Mormon...* Paljyra: E. B. Grandin, 1830. First edition, 588 pages, octavo, original brown calf boards with gilt rules on backstrip, completely unsophisticated copy, which has hand no repair or restoration work, contemporary name "Manchester" in ink on rear pastedown, label on backstrip missing, usual foxing, name "Enoch Knight" stamped in small ink twice on front free endsheet. Ken Sanders Rare Books 45 - 17 2013 $90,000

Book of Mormon *Le Livre De Mormon Recit Ecrit De La Main de Mormon...* Paris: Imprimerie De Marc Ducloux et Compagnie... circa, 1854. Second printing, 519 pages, duodecimo, black pebbled cloth with gilt bands and title on backstrip decorative endsheets and pastedowns, very good, corners bumped and rubbed, cloth splitting at hinges between boards and backstrip. Ken Sanders Rare Books 45 - 20 2013 $6000

Book of Something to Do. Rhymes & Stories. New York: United Art Pub. Co., 1916. oblong folio, cloth backed pictorial boards, fine and unused and complete with 72 pictorial stamps in unopened glassine envelopes, interspersed throughout text are blank rectangles in center of which the reader is to affix the corresponding 72 color pictorial stamps, very rare in such nice unused condition. Aleph-Bet Books, Inc. 104 - 392 2013 $750

Boone, James Shergold *The Oxford Spy: a Dialogue in Verse. (bound with) Dialogue the Fourth. (with) Dialogue the Fifth.* Oxford: Munday & Slatter, 1818. 1818. 1819. Second edition, first edition, first edition, 3 volumes in 1, expertly bound in drab boards, paper label, very good. Jarndyce Antiquarian Booksellers CCIII - 646 2013 £85

Boone, James Shergold *The Oxford Spy in Four Dialogues.* Oxford: Munday & Slatter, 1819. Fourth edition, uncut in original pale blue boards, drab spine, paper label, slight wear to hinges, 3 small marks on front board, otherwise very good as issued. Jarndyce Antiquarian Booksellers CCIII - 647 2013 £65

Booth, George *The Primitive Methodist Hymnal with Accompanying Tunes.* Edwin Dalton, 1889. Original full black calf, gilt, spine and hinges cracked, rather stripped at head and foot. R. F. G. Hollett & Son Wesleyan Methodism - 57 2013 £25

Booth, Joseph *An Address to the Public on the Polygraphic Art, or the Copying or Multiplying Pictures in Oil Colours....* London: printed at the Logographic Press for the Proprietors, 1787? First edition, 8vo., very good, disbound. Jarndyce Antiquarian Booksellers CCIV - 67 2013 £500

Booth, Mary L. *History of the City of New York, From Its Earliest Settlement to the Present Time.* New York: W. R. C. Clark & Meeker, 1860. First edition, half leather and marbled paper covered boards and marbled page edges, contemporary owner's name and faint dampstain affecting first few prelim pages, else near fine, handsome copy. Between the Covers Rare Books, Inc. New York City - 286282 2013 $275

Borden, Mary *The Forbidden Zone.* London: Heinemann, 1929. First edition, 8vo., original black cloth, dust jacket, excellent copy, jacket slightly rubbed and browned at spine, inscribed by author to Commander Fletcher. Maggs Bros. Ltd. 1460 - 126 2013 £125

Bordeu, Theophile De *Recherches Antomiques sur la Position des Glandes et sur leur Action.* Paris: Chez G. F. Quillau, 1751. First edition, 12mo., titlepage vignette, headpieces, decorative initials, tailpieces, new imprint slip pasted over original imprint partially removed, contemporary full mottled calf, raised bands, gilt spine, all edges red, marbled endleaves, leather scuffed, joints starting, spine ends chipped, very good. Jeff Weber Rare Books 172 - 35 2013 $400

Borein, Edward *Ed Borein's West.* Santa Barbara: The Schauer Printing Studio Inc., 1952. First edition, quarto, mounted color frontispiece, profusely illustrated, tan cloth lettered in black, fine with pictorial dust jacket. Argonaut Book Shop Recent Acquisitions June 2013 - 30 2013 $125

Borelli, G. A. *De Motu Animalium, Pars Parma (et Secunda).* Leiden: P. vander Aa, 1710. 2 volumes bound in one, early calf boards with later rebacking, covers worn, inner hinges repaired, title margins worn, two title stamps, 4to., frontispiece, 19 folded engraved copperplates, couple of plate fore-edges bit worn. James Tait Goodrich S74 - 31 2013 $1750

Boreman, Thomas *The Gigantick History of the Two Famous Giants and Other Cuiriosities in Guildhall, London.* London: printed for Tho. Boreman, 1740. Second edition, 64mo., woodcut frontispiece, full page woodcut illustrations, decorative tailpieces, gathered in eights, some slight browning but very good, contemporary quarter calf, embossed floral boards, lacking hinge cracked but firm, corners little rounded, early name of Miss Blackwell on inner front board. Jarndyce Antiquarian Booksellers CCIV - 68 2013 £1500

Borges, Jorge Luis *El Aleph.* Buenos Aires: Ediciones Dos Amigos, 1997. One fo 25 copies, each copy unique, all printed on cream velin d-Arches paper, etchings and aquatints by Gabriela Aberastury, this copy one of publisher's copies, unnumbered but signed in white pencil by artist, printer, Rubin Lapolla and one of the publishers, Samuel Cesar Pauli, page size 13 1/4 x 10 inches, 176 pages, each page an original print and many times several different print processes, bound loose in original black wrappers and Hebrew letter (aleph) engraved in silver gilt on front panel and spine, housed in grey cloth over boards clamshell box with original etching on front of box, title printed in black on spine, box bit dinged at edges, book fine.   Priscilla Juvelis - Rare Books   56 - 7   2013 $35,000

Borges, Jorge Luis *Ficciones.* New York: Limited Editions Club, 1984. Limited to numbered copies signed by sol Lewitt, square 4to., full black cowhide, fine in slipcase, Monthly Newsletter laid in, 22 geometric illustrations by Sol Lewitt, strikingly beautiful.   Aleph-Bet Books, Inc.   104 - 324   2013 $650

Borges, Jorge Luis *La Hermana de Eloisa.* Buenos Aires: E. N. E. Editorial, 1955. First edition, 8vo., original orange and black wrappers, preserved in folding box, signed by author, near fine.   Maggs Bros. Ltd.   1460 - 127   2013   £600

Borget, Auguste *La Chine et les Chinois.* Paris: Goupil and Vibert, 1842. First edition, lithograph title, 32 sepia tinted lithograph plates on 25 sheets, imperial folio, recently bound in half calf.   Maggs Bros. Ltd.   1467 - 49   2013   £2800

Borghini, Vincenzio *Discorsi di Monsignore Don Vincenzio Borghini.* Florence: Filippo & Jacopo Giunti, 1584-1585. First edition, 2 volumes, 4to., 8 engraved plates on 7 sheets, 5 folding with blank Rr8 in volume I, added titlepage (volume II), some minor staining, light foxing, occasional browning, original full vellum with manuscript spine titles and additional inscriptions on both front covers, cover stain with some light wear, early ownership inscription (1597), bookplate of Bernadine Murphy, very good.   Jeff Weber Rare Books   171 - 48   2013 $1600

Borland, R. *Border Raids and Reivers.* Dalbeattie: Thomas Fraser, 1910. Second edition, Original cloth, gilt, rather faded, excellent copy.   R. F. G. Hollett & Son   Lake District & Cumbria - 139   2013   £50

Borlase, William *Observations on the Antiquities Historical and Monumental of the County of Cornwall.* Oxford: W. Jackson, 1754. First edition, folio, 25 engraved plates, including foldout map, engraved head and tailpieces, list of subscribers, titlepage slightly creased with repair to bottom edge, closed tear from bottom of page 31 touching text but with no loss, little blue ink transfer to map, occasional light staining and spotting, contemporary dark brown calf, rather conspicuously rebacked, lower joint cracking, upper corners crudely repaired, leather patch repair to fore-edge, extremities worn, endpapers replaced, 'Surry Institution" in gilt to centre of upper board.   Unsworths Antiquarian Booksellers   28 - 74   2013   £500

Born, Max *Atomic Physics.* London: Blackie and Son, 1935. First edition in English, 8vo., xii, 352 (4 ads), signed and inscribed by author for Hern Goldhaber, very good+ in original black cloth, mild foxing to endpapers, mild wear to upper spine tip, rare signed.   By the Book, L. C.   36 - 96   2013 $1000

Bosanquet, R. C., Mrs. *Days in Attica.* London: Methuen, 1914. First edition, 8vo., pages xiv, 348, ads, color frontispiece, illustrations, plans, original red cloth, small split at head of spine, joint rubbed.   J. & S. L. Bonham Antiquarian Booksellers   Europe - 3844   2013   £35

Bosqui, Edward *Grapes and Grape Vines of California.* New York: Harcourt Brace Jovanovich, 1981. Second facsimile printing (slightly reduced), folio, 10 full color plates after original color drawings by Hannah Millard, facsimile title, maroon cloth, large printed title label on front cover, fine with slightly darkened printed mylar jacket.   Argonaut Book Shop   Recent Acquisitions June 2013 - 35   2013 $90

Bosshart, J. *Neben der Heerstrasse.* Zurich: 1923. First edition, 8 x 5.7 inches, 434 page, 26 original woodcuts by Ernst Ludwig Kirchner, board covers with minor imperfections, internally clean, publisher's dust jacket with original color woodcuts on spine and both panels, latter with expertly repaired tiny corner chips, colors still bright and crisp, overall very good, extremely rare complete dust jacket.   Gemini Fine Books & Arts., Ltd.   Art Reference & Illustrated Books - 2013 $1500

Boswell, James   1740-1795 *The Life of Samuel Johnson.* New York: Heritage Press, 1963. 8vo., 3 volumes, brown cloth, very good+.   Barnaby Rudge Booksellers   Biography 2013 - 021036   2013 $50

Bosworth, Joseph *An Anglo-Saxon Dictionary. (with) An Anglo-Saxon Dictionary: Supplement.* Oxford University Press, 1973. Reprint, 2 volumes, 4to., red cloth, wear and light markings to boards and spine, primarily at extremities, slight wear to lower corners of volume I, minor browning and dustiness to edges, very good, volume I lacks dust jacket, volume II jacket with several tears to edges, creasing and wear, otherwise very good, ownership inscription of M. Collins to both volumes.   Unsworths Antiquarian Booksellers   28 - 149   2013   £160

Bottomley, Samuel *The Second Message from "Mars" The Gold Standard It's Relation to Business, Labor and World Peace.* Providence: Martian Pub. Co., 1925. First edition, octavo, original textured gray green wrappers printed in gold, side stapled.   L. W. Currey, Inc.   Utopian Literature: Recent Acquisitions (April 2013) - 141606   2013 $250

Bouch, C. M. L. *The Lake Counties 1500-1830.* Manchester: University Press, 1961. First edition, original cloth, gilt, dust jacket, 3 plates and 3 plans, scarce.   R. F. G. Hollett & Son   Lake District & Cumbria - 145   2013   £75

Bouch, C. M. L. *The Manor and Advowson of Great Orton from 1639.* Kendal: Titus Wilson, 1940. Original wrappers, 2 plates, 2 folding pedigree.   R. F. G. Hollett & Son   Lake District & Cumbria - 142   2013   £25

Bouch, C. M. L. *Prelates and People of the Lake Counties.* Kendal: Titus Wilson, 1948. First edition, original cloth, 9 illustrations and map, the copy of Frank Parrott, Kirkby Stephen historian with presentation card to him tipped to flyleaf.   R. F. G. Hollett & Son   Lake District & Cumbria - 153   2013   £50

Bouch, C. M. L. *Sidelights on Old Appleby.* reprinted from CWAAS Trans NS Vol. LI, 1951. Original printed wrappers, staples little rusted.   R. F. G. Hollett & Son   Lake District & Cumbria - 144   2013   £25

Boucher, Anthony *The Case of the Seven of Calvary.* New York: Simon and Schuster, 1937. First edition, little spotting on top edge, else near fine in rubbed about very good dust jacket with some internally repaired nicks and tears.   Between the Covers Rare Books, Inc.   Mystery & Detective Fiction - 87804   2013 $375

Boudinot, Elias *A Star in the West, or a Humble Attempt to Discover the Long Lost Ten Tribes of Israel.* Trenton: 1816. First edition, 8vo., 4, 312 pages, contemporary calf, browning as usual, hinges cracking, but sound.   M & S Rare Books, Inc.   95 - 176   2013 $625

Bougainville, Louis De *A Voyage Round the World...* London: J. Nourse, 1772. First English edition, 4to., plus folding plate and 5 folding charts, contemporary calf, beautifully rebacked by Aquarius.   Maggs Bros. Ltd.   1467 - 72   2013   £4500

Boulanger, Nicolas Antoine *The Origin and Progress of Despotism in the Oriental and Other Empires of Africa, Europe and America.* Amsterdam: printed in the year, 1764. First English edition, Pages 185-192 misbound but present, contemporary calf, sometime rebacked retaining spine and red morocco label, bookplate of "Prodesse quam conspici".   Jarndyce Antiquarian Booksellers   CCIV - 69   2013   £250

Boulle, Pierre *The Bridge on the River Kwai.* London: Secker and Warburg, 1954. First edition, 8vo., original black cloth, excellent copy in slightly rubbed and chipped dust jacket, inscribed by translator, Xan Fielding for his wife Daphne.   Maggs Bros. Ltd.   1460 - 283   2013   £375

Boulton, David *Early Friends in Dent.* Dent: Dales Historical Monographs, 1986. First edition, original cloth, gilt, spine little faded as usual, illustration, map, signed by author, very scarce.   R. F. G. Hollett & Son   Lake District & Cumbria - 146   2013   £75

Boumphrey, R. S. *An Armorial for Westmorland and Lonsdale.* Kendal: Titus Wilson, 1975. Limited de luxe edition, no. 30 of 35 copies, signed, original full crimson calf gilt, arms in gilt on boards, frontispiece, 4 plates and 5 pages arms, Whittington Hall copy with bookplate of Brian dated Enid Greenwood.   R. F. G. Hollett & Son   Lake District & Cumbria - 150   2013   £150

Boumphrey, R. S. *Armorial for Westmorland and Lonsdale.* Lake District Museum Trust and CWAAS, 1975. Original crimson rexine gilt, frontispiece and 5 pages illustrations, inscribed by Roy Hudleston for his cousin Cayton Hall and dated Ambleside 1 Sept. 1976.   R. F. G. Hollett & Son   Lake District & Cumbria - 149   2013   £65

Boumphrey, R. S. *Kirkby Lonsdale Armorial.* Kendal: Titus Wilson, 1971. Original wrappers.   R. F. G. Hollett & Son   Lake District & Cumbria - 148   2013   £25

The Bounding Billow: Published in the Interests of American Men-o'-Warsmen. Manila: on board the USFS Olympia June, 1898. Rare shipboard printing, Volume I, No. 5, colored illustration to title, smal 4to., inscription, small tear to titlepage not effecting text.   Maggs Bros. Ltd.   1467 - 128   2013   £750

Bourgoing, Jean Francois *Atlas pour Servir au Tableau de L'Espagne Moderne.* Levrault, 1803. First edition, quarto, folding map, 3 plans, plates, some folding, some light waterstaining mainly in margins and prelims, contemporary full speckled calf, atlas complete but lacks the 3 volumes of text.   J. & S. L. Bonham Antiquarian Booksellers   Europe - 9543   2013   £600

Bourgoing, Jean Francois *Travels in Spain.* London: G. G. J. and J. Robinson, 1789. First English edition, 3 volumes, 8vo., pages xii, 472; 558; 503, folding map, 11 plates, contemporary brown half calf, spines rubbed, small wear to head and tail of spines.   J. & S. L. Bonham Antiquarian Booksellers   Europe - 9743   2013   £950

Bourgoing, Jean Francois *Voyage Du Ci-Devant Duc Du Chatelet en Portugal...* Paris: F. Buisson, n.d., 1799. First edition, 2 volumes, 8vo., folding frontispiece, folding map, contemporary brown full calf, joints rubbed, small loss of leather at base of spines, internally clean.   J. & S. L. Bonham Antiquarian Booksellers   Europe - 8417   2013   £450

Bourne, Henry *The History of Newcastle Upon Tyne...* Newcastle upon Tyne: printed and sold by John White, 1736. First edition, engraved folding map mounted on linen, decorative head and tailpieces and initial letters, folio, fine, clean, large copy bound by F. Bedford in 19th century gilt panelled calf, spine gilt decorated in 6 compartments, gilt dentelles, marbled endpapers, expert repairs to hinges and corners, the Huth library copy with oval gilt morocco label and armorial bookplate of Viscount Ridley, all edges gilt.   Jarndyce Antiquarian Booksellers   CCV - 27   2013   £1200

Bourrit, Marc Theodore *Description des Cols ou Passages des Alpes.* Geneve: chez G. J. Manget, 1803. First edition, 2 volumes in 1, half titles, 4 engraved plates, large uncut copy, some waterstaining to front pastedown and endpaper, otherwise very clean, original glazed boards, later calf spine.   Jarndyce Antiquarian Booksellers   CCIV - 70   2013   £1500

Boutet De Monvel, M. *Joan of Arc.* New York: Century, 1926. 4to., green and gilt decorative gold, slight soil, very good-fine, rich color illustrations on every page, printed on coated paper.   Aleph-Bet Books, Inc.   105 - 90   2013 $225

Bova, Ben *The Star Conquerors.* Philadelphia: Toronto: John C. Winston Co., 1959. First edition, octavo, cloth.   L. W. Currey, Inc.   Fall Sampler Sept. 2013 - 146540   2013 $1500

Bove, Emmanuel *Le Crime d'une Nuit.* Paris: Yves Riviere editeur, 1973-1974. First Van Velde edition, one of 75 examples (total edition 108) on velin d'Arches paper, 5 original color lithographs, each fully signed and numbered in pencil by Bram Van Velde, reportedly some copies contained lithos that were initialled, not signed, 46 leaves, loose in wrapper, boards chemise and slipcase, overall size 13.5 x 11 inches, excellent condition.   Gemini Fine Books & Arts., Ltd. Art Reference & Illustrated Books - 2013 $2400

Bovill, E. W. *Missions to the Niger. Second Series. Nos. CXXII, CXXVIII, CXXIX and XCCC.* Cambridge University Press for the Hakluyt Society, 1964-1966. 4 volumes, original cloth, gilt, dust jackets (spines evenly faded), 37 plates, 24 maps and charts, several text illustrations, fine set.   R. F. G. Hollett & Son   Africana - 23   2013   £150

Bowden, John *Norway; Its People, Products and Institutions.* London: Chapman & Hall, 1867. First edition, 8vo., 250 pages, later blue cloth.   J. & S. L. Bonham Antiquarian Booksellers   Europe - 8456   2013   £80

Bowdle, Stanley E. *Speech of... Delegate from Hamilton County on Woman Suffrage before the Ohio Constitutional Convention.* Cincinnati: Cincinnati and Hamilton County Association Opposed to Woman Suffrage, circa, 1912. 8vo., self wrappers, (8) pages, fine, rare.   Second Life Books Inc.   182 - 26   2013 $75

Bowen, Elizabeth *Collected Impressions.* 1950. First edition, 8vo., cloth, good.   C. P. Hyland   261 - 141   2013   £28

Bowers, Newton L. *Actuarial Mathematics.* Society of Actuaries, 1997. Third printing of second edition, fine in fine dust jacket, 4to.   Beasley Books   2013 - 2013 $100

Bowes Lyon, Lilian *Collected Poems.* London: Jonathan Cape, 1948. First edition, 8vo., original blue cloth, excellent copy, spine slightly faded, inscribed by author for Elizabeth Bowen.   Maggs Bros. Ltd.   1460 - 128   2013   £125

Bowles, Jane *Two Serious Ladies.* London: Peter Owen, 1965. First British edition, inscribed by author for George (possibly George Cukor, the director, fine in very good to near fine dust jacket with usual light rubbing to front panel and moderate soiling to white back panel.   Ed Smith Books   75 - 5   2013 $1850

Bowles, John *The Retrospect; or a Collection of Tracts, Published at Various Periods of the War...* London: printed for T. N. Longman, 1798. 19th century half morocco, spine neatly repaired at head and tail, family copy, signature of George Bowles Junr., Jan. 1852 on titlepage.   Ken Spelman Books Ltd.   75 - 49   2013   £120

Bowles, Paul *Their Heads Are Green Their Hands are Blue.* London: Peter Owen, 1985. Second British edition, inscribed by author for Mary Robbins, fine in very near fine dust jacket with small nick to rear panel. Ken Lopez Bookseller 159 - 22 2013 $175

Bowles, Paul *The Thicket of Spring. Poems 1926-1969.* Los Angeles: Black Sparrow Press, 1972. First edition, large 8vo., original wrappers, fine in protective folding box, inscribed by author for Angus. Maggs Bros. Ltd. 1460 - 129 2013 £125

Bowles, William Lisle *A Final Defence of the Rights of Patronage in Deans and Chapters...* London: John Murray, 1838. Second impression, disbound. Jarndyce Antiquarian Booksellers CCIII - 39 2013 £110

Bowles, William Lisle *Hermes Britannicus.* London: J. B. Nichols & Son, 1828. First edition, disbound, inscribed on title Arch Deacon Macdonald, some corrections in ink, possibly authorial, few marginal notes in another hand. Jarndyce Antiquarian Booksellers CCIII - 37 2013 £125

Bowles, William Lisle *Illustrations of those Stupendous Monuments of Celtic Antiquity Avebury and Silbury and Their Mysterious Origin Traced.* Caine: printed and sold by William Baily, 1827. Disbound. Jarndyce Antiquarian Booksellers CCIII - 36 2013 £120

Bowles, William Lisle *Letters to Lord Byron on a Question of Poetical Criticism.* London: Hurst, Robinson, 1822. Second edition, drab printed boards, spine little faded, very good. Jarndyce Antiquarian Booksellers CCIII - 285 2013 £120

Bowles, William Lisle *The Missionary: a Poems.* London: John Murray, 1813. Second edition, full contemporary dark blue morocco, gilt and blind spine and borders, gilt dentelles, spine slightly rubbed, slight wear to head small booklabel of John Sparrow, all edges gilt, inscribed "from the author..." Latin ownership and note, armorial bookplate of George Downing Bowles, of Fawley, Southampton. Jarndyce Antiquarian Booksellers CCIII - 34 2013 £150

Bowles, William Lisle *The Plain Bible and the Protestant Church in England, with reflections on Some Important Subjects of existing Religious Controversy.* Bath: Richard Cruttwell, 1818. First edition, large 8vo., uncut in contemporary blue boards, drab spine, paper label, corners slightly knocked, very good, as issued, presentation from author, signature and small armorial roundel of John Scott, first Earl of Eldon. Jarndyce Antiquarian Booksellers CCIII - 35 2013 £150

Bowles, William Lisle *(Collection) Poems. (with) Sonnets and Other Poems.* London: T. Cadell Jun. and W. Davies, 1801. 1802. First edition, eighth edition, plates, frontispiece an plates, 2 volumes, attractively bound in slightly later full blue calf, gilt spines, borders and dentelles, maroon leather labels, author's name on spine, slightly rubbed and faded, small booklabels of John Sparrow, all edges gilt, handsome. Jarndyce Antiquarian Booksellers CCIII - 31 2013 £280

Bowles, William Lisle *Some Account of the Last Days of William Chillingworth...with Remarks on the Character of Cromwell...* Salisbury: W. B. Broche & Co., 1836. Errata slip, spotted, disbound. Jarndyce Antiquarian Booksellers CCIII - 38 2013 £95

Bowles, William Lisle *Sonnets, written chiefly on Picturesque Spots, During a Tour.* Bath: printed and sold by R. Cruttwell &c, 1789. Second edition, 4to., half title, early sewn repair to small tear, final leaf slightly spotted, disbound. Jarndyce Antiquarian Booksellers CCIII - 32 2013 £150

Bowles, William Lisle *Sonnets with other Poems.* Bath: printed by R. Cruttwell and sold by C. Dilly, Poultry, London, 1794. Third edition, half title, contemporary full calf, gilt spine, border and dentelles, dark green leather label, bit rubbed, hinges little worn, one or two small splits, possibly author's copy with armorial bookplate "Revd. Mr. Bowles", also small booklabel of Charles Wells and gift inscription "Anna Maria Pinney 1835. From S. M. Booth", blindstamped and labels of Birkbeck College Library. Jarndyce Antiquarian Booksellers CCIII - 33 2013 £150

Bowles, William Lisle *Two Letters to the Right Honourable Lord Byron in answer to His Lordship"s Letter to **********, More Particularly on the Question, Whether Poetry be More Immediately Indebted to What is Sublime or Beautiful in the Works of Nature...* London: John Murray, 1821. Second edition, 67 pages, slightly spotted, disbound. Jarndyce Antiquarian Booksellers CCIII - 284 2013 £60

Bowness, Alan *Victor Pasmore. A Catalogue Raisonne of the Paintings, Constructions and Graphics 1926-1979.* New York: Rizzoli, 1980. First American edition, original color lithographs "The Pool of Narcissus" no. 49 of 100 laid in and "Untitled" no. 249 of 400 (the book jacket), 4to., 342 pages, with 249 plates, fine in fine dust jacket with minimal soil, jacket covered by original printed acetate protector. By the Book, L. C. 36 - 26 2013 $1750

Box of ABC Books. Keosha: Samuel Lowe, 1944. 5 books in pictorial box, box flaps repaired, else fine, illustrations. Aleph-Bet Books, Inc. 104 - 3 2013 $200

Box, Edgar *Death Likes It Hot.* London: Heinemann, 1955. First English edition, signed by Box/Vidal, fine in dust jacket with small punch tear on spine, nicks at spine ends and small chips at corners. Mordida Books 81 - 43 2013 $200

Boyce, D. G. *Nationalism in Ireland.* Johns Hopkins University Press, 1982. First edition, octavo, dust jacket, cloth, fine.   C. P. Hyland   261 - 146   2013   £35

Boycotting in the County of Cork. Cork Defence Union, 1886. (39) pages, 8vo., lacks rear wrapper.   C. P. Hyland   261 - 235   2013   £50

Boyd, Ernest A. *The Contemporary Drama of Ireland.* 1917. First US edition, 8vo., cloth, very good, ex-institutional library with stamps.   C. P. Hyland   261 - 913   2013   £38

Boyd, William Harland *A Centennial Bibliography on the History of Kern County, California.* Bakersfield: Kern County Historical Society, 1966. First edition, orange cloth lettered in black, bookplate on blank flyleaf, fine in dust jacket.   Argonaut Book Shop   Recent Acquisitions June 2013 - 37   2013 $60

Boyd, William Harland *Stagecoach Heyday in the San Joaquin Valley 1853-18876.* Bakersfield: Kern County Historical Society, 1983. First edition, signed by author, numerous views and portraits from photos, maps, facsimiles, dark blue cloth gilt, very fine with dust jacket.   Argonaut Book Shop   Recent Acquisitions June 2013 - 36   2013 $60

Boyer, Abel *Boyer's Royal Dictionary Abridged.* London: printed for Messrs, Bathurst, Pote, Rivingtons, Owen, Buckland, Longman (and 23 others), 1786. Sixteenth edition, one folding table, some light spotting, 8vo., contemporary sheep rebacked preserving original morocco lettering piece, corners repaired, hinges neatly relined, old leather marked, bookplate of Scawen Blunt (probably Francis, father of poet Wilfrid), good.   Blackwell's Rare Books   B174 - 14   2013   £300

Boyer, Rick *Billingsgate Shoal.* Boston: Houghton Mifflin, 1982. First edition, fine in price clipped dust jacket with tiny wear to lower corners.   Mordida Books   81 - 45   2013 $75

Boylan, Grace *Our Little Hawaiian Kiddies. Volume 4 of Kids of Many Colors.* New York: Hurst, 1901. Small 4to., pictorial cloth, some holes in spine paper, else fine, color illustrations by Ike Morgan.   Aleph-Bet Books, Inc.   104 - 87   2013 $200

Boyle, J. R. *Memoirs of the Life of Master John Shawe, Sometime Vicar of Rotherham, Minister of St. Mary's, Lecturer of Holy Trinity Church and Master of the Charterhouse at Kingston-upon-Hull.* Hull: M. C. Peck and Son, 1882. Half title, 4to., very good, original blind-stamped and gilt lettered cloth.   Ken Spelman Books Ltd.   73 - 102   2013   £80

Boyle, Kay *American Citizen Naturalized in Leadville, Colorado.* New York: Simon and Schuster, 1944. First edition, 8vo., 16 pages, printed wrappers, fine.   Second Life Books Inc.   182 - 27   2013 $65

Boyle, Kay *Being Geniuses Together 1920-1930.* Garden City: Doubleday, 1968. First US edition, inscribed by Boyle to bookseller David Magg in year of publication, near fine in very good+ with dust jacket with wear at top edge, large 8vo., 392 pages.   Beasley Books   2013 - 2013 $100

Boyle, Robert   1627-1691 *Certain Physiological Essays and Other Tracts.* London: Henry Herringman, 1669. Second edition, small quarto, contemporary panelled calf, rebacked and recornered to style, spine elaborately tooled in gilt, red morocco spine label lettered gilt, titlepage bit soiled, some toning and foxing, mainly to endpapers, signature Y with paper flaw at bottom edge of each leaf, not affecting text, overall very good.   Heritage Book Shop   Holiday Catalogue 2012 - 18   2013 $2850

Boyle, Robert   1627-1691 *An Essay of the Great Effects of Even Languid and Unheeded Motion.* London: By M. Flesher for Richard Davis, 1685. First edition with first state titlepage (without Boyle's name), 8vo., neat modern calf antique, retaining original front flyleaf with signature of Mr. Jocelyn, light dust soiling of first few leaves, else fine, clean copy.   Joseph J. Felcone Inc.   Books Printed before 1701 - 12   2013 $2800

Boyle, Robert   1627-1691 *Experiments, Notes &c. about Mechanical Origine or Production of Divers Particular Qualities...* E. Flesher for R. Davis, bookseller in Oxford, 1676. First edition, 2nd issue (same as the 1675 first issue apart from cancel title, remains of cancelled title visible), 11 parts in one volume, without blank leaf B8 but with the other three, closed tear ot blank margin of second leaf, little dampstaining in margins of few leaves, tiny hole caused by paper fault in one leaf, not affecting text, little bit of spotting here and there, various paginations, small 8vo., contemporary calf, skillfully rebacked with original spine laid on, later spine label, contemporary signature of John Stratford, Balliol College, 1681.   Blackwell's Rare Books   Sciences - 15   2013   £4800

Boyle, Robert 1627-1691 *The Sceptical Chymist or Chymico Physical Doubts and Paradoxes.* London: J. Caldwell for J. Crooke, 1661. First edition, octavo, second titlepage printed in red and black and bound as title, type ornament headbands and woodcut initials, contemporary English speckled calf, boards with double rule blind borders, spine ruled in compartments, red speckled edges, occasional light spotting or marking, few leaves trimmed at head touching number, light marginal worming on second title and A-C, touching text on few leaves, lacking first title, small paper flaws on Y6-8 and Z1, lacking final 3 postliminary leaves and final blank (as this final signature is comprised of printer's notes it is entirely possible that early issues were bound without it; this combination is often seen); binding little rubbed and scuffed, small skillful repairs to board edges, skilfully rejointed, but overall, lovely copy. Heritage Book Shop Holiday Catalogue 2012 - 19 2013 $55

Boyle, Robert 1627-1691 *The Sceptical Chymist of Chymico-Physical Doubts and Paradoxes...to which in this edition are subjoyn'd Divers Experiments and Notes about the Producibleness of Cymical Principles.* Oxford: printed by Henry Hall for Richard Davis and B. Took, 1680. Second edition of first work and first edition of Eperiments, 8vo., some browning, confined to three gatherings in first part, more general in second, few ink or rust spots, contemporary English calf, double gilt fillets on sides, gilt fleurons in corners, surface of covers crackled, rebacked and recornered, old staple holes to upper board from a chained library, old ink notes to front flyleaf and name of author at top of titlepage written in old hand, Sion College library stamp and release stamp (dated 1938), good. Blackwell's Rare Books Sciences - 16 2013 £12,000

Boyle, Robert 1627-1691 *Tracts... the Cosmicall Qualities of Things. Cosmicall Supsitions. The Temperature of Subterraneall Regions. The Temperature of the Submarine Regions. The Bottom of the Sea.* (bound with) *Tracts Consisting of Observations about the Saltness of the Sea...* Oxford: printed by W. H. for Ric. Davis, 1670. printed for E. Flesher for R. Davis, bookseller in Oxford, 1674, i,e, 1673. First edition, first issue, without blank H8 as usual; first edition of second work, last gathering in Subterraneall Regions somewhat soiled and last 2 leaves with clean tears across text, latter laid down, some dampstaining, oddly distributed; second work with bit of marginal worming at end and just touching 3 letters and some dampstaining at end, 8vo., bound in contemporary panelled calf, rebacked, preserving original spine, sound. Blackwell's Rare Books Sciences - 14 2013 £9000

Boyle, T. Coraghessan *Descent of Man.* Boston: Little Brown, 1979. First edition, inscribed by author, recipient's signature, fine in rubbed, near fine, price clipped dust jacket. Ken Lopez Bookseller 159 - 24 2013 $375

The Boys Book of Trades and Tools Used in Them Comprsing Brickmaker, Mason, Plasterer, etc... London and New York: George Routledge circa, 1870. 316 pages, 8vo., green cloth stamped in black and gilt, very good, tight copy. Second Life Books Inc. 183 - 4 2013 $125

Boys, Edward *Narrative of a Captivity and Adventures in France and Flanders Between the Years 1803 and 1809.* London: printed for Richard Long, 1827. 8vo., frontispiece, folding colored lithograph plan, 3 lithograph plates, woodcut in text, 8vo., some foxing, later 19th century half roan, gilt banded and lettered spine, little rubbed, signature of A. R. Winington-Ingram, 1885, few pencil underlinings in text. Jarndyce Antiquarian Booksellers CCIV - 71 2013 £150

Brace, Charles Loring *The Dangerous Classes of New York and Twenty Years' Work Among Them.* New York: Wynkoop & Hallenbeck, 1872. First edition, red brown boards, bookplate and owner's name on front endpapers, trifle rubbed, just about fine, uncommon in this condition. Between the Covers Rare Books, Inc. New York City - 291465 2013 $200

Brachelius, Adolphus *Histroria Nostri Temporis, dat is Geschiedenis Onses Tijts Door Adolphus Brachelius...* Tot Nymegen: voor Andries van Hoogenhuyse, 1659. Second edition, small 8vo., engraved extra title and 98 (of 101?) portraits, later calf stamped in blind over beveled wood boards, four raised bands, metal clasps, very good, clasps lacking locks, some soiling to titlepage and endpapers, few minor tears, few leaves at end with small loss to upper forecorners not affecting text small ink stain on fore edge, text and portraits quite sharp. Kaaterskill Books 16 - 84 2013 $500

Bradbury, Malcolm *The History of Man.* Boston: Houghton Mifflin, 1976. First US edition, 8vo., original black cloth, near fine in dust jacket lightly faded on spine, inscribed by author to photographer Terence Donovan. Maggs Bros. Ltd. 1460 - 130 2013 £250

Bradbury, Ray *The Anthem Sprinters and other Antics.* New York: Dial Press, 1963. First edition, hardcover issue, fine in price clipped, near fine dust jacket with bit of modest spine fading, very uncommon. Between the Covers Rare Books, Inc. Sci-Fi, Fantasy & Horror - 93038 2013 $475

Bradbury, Ray *Fahrenheit 451.* New York: Ballantine, 1953. First edition, binding state D (no established priority), slight rubbing to spine ends, tiny tear to edge of one leaf in text, else fine in lightly soiled, very good plus dust jacket with shallow chip at crown, some of the usual fading red '451' on spine, signed by author. Between the Covers Rare Books, Inc. Sci-Fi, Fantasy & Horror - 64489 2013 $4500

Bradbury, Ray *Fahrenheit 451.* New York: Ballantine Books, 1953. First edition, 8vo., original red cloth, browned on spine, otherwise excellent, inscribed by author for director John Huston Aug. 19 1953. Maggs Bros. Ltd. 1460 - 131 2013 £2500

Bradbury, Ray *The Golden Apples of the Sun.* Garden City: Doubleday & Co., 1953. First edition, 8vo., original grey buckram, yellow lettering to spine, near fine, little rubbed at extremities, inscribed by author for director John Huston. Maggs Bros. Ltd. 1460 - 132 2013 £500

Bradbury, Ray *The Halloween Tree.* Colorado Springs: Gauntlet Press, 2005. Limited edition, #507 of 750 numbered copies, assembled by Donn Albright, signed by author, bookplate of Stanley Wiater, fine in fine dust jacket. Ken Lopez Bookseller 159 - 26 2013 $450

Bradbury, Ray *It Came from Outer Space.* Colorado Springs: Gauntlet Publications, 2004. Limited edition, #174 of 750 numbered copies, signed by author, bookplate of writer Stanley Wiater, fine in fine dust jacket. Ken Lopez Bookseller 159 - 25 2013 $150

Bradbury, Ray *Long After Midnight.* New York: Knopf, 1976. First edition, fine in dust jacket with crease tear on back panel. Mordida Books 81 - 46 2013 $125

Bradbury, Ray *The Martian Chronicles.* Garden City: Doubleday & Co., 1950. First edition, octavo, cloth. L. W. Currey, Inc. Utopian Literature: Recent Acquisitions (April 2013) - 140698 2013 $6500

Bradbury, Ray *The Martian Chronicles.* New York: Time Incorporated, 1963. First printing of this edition, octavo, pictorial wrappers. L. W. Currey, Inc. Utopian Literature: Recent Acquisitions (April 2013) - 140278 2013 $100

Bradbury, Robert C. *Antique United States Miniature Books 1690-1900.* North Clarendon: Microbibliophile, 2001. Limited to 1000 copies, 8vo., 13 pages fo illustrations, cloth, dust jacket, from the collection of Donn W. Sanford. Oak Knoll Books 303 - 8 2013 $150

Bradbury, Robert C. *Twentieth Century United States Miniature Books.* North Clarendon: Microbibliophile, 2000. Limited to 1000 copies, 8vo., cloth, dust jacket, 16 pages of illustrations, from the collection of Donn W. Sanford. Oak Knoll Books 303 - 9 2013 $75

Bradby, Christopher *Well on the Road.* G. Bell and Sons, 1935. First edition, small 4to., original cloth backed pictorial boards, spine little faded at head and foot, matching dust jacket (pieces missing from one corner and head of backstrip, lower panel rather torn and creased, lower two inches of backstrip missing), illustrations in line by Edward Bawden, excellent copy, remarkably rare. R. F. G. Hollett & Son Children's Books - 50 2013 £350

Bradford, John *John Bradford's Historical Notes on Kentucky from the Western Miscellany.* San Francisco: Grabhorn Press, 1932. One of 500 copies, small octavo, 212 pages, folding map plus vignettes, tan pictorial boards, red paper spine label, very fine. Argonaut Book Shop Summer 2013 - 29 2013 $175

Bradford, William *Bradford's History "Of Plimoth Plantation" from the Original Manuscript.* Boston: Wright & Potter, 1901. First edition, 8vo., 555 pages, illustrations, blue cloth, name on endpaper, fine. Second Life Books Inc. 183 - 51 2013 $95

Bradley, A. G. *Highways and Byways in the Lake District.* London: Macmillan, 1901. First edition, original cloth, gilt, hinges cracking and trifle chipped at head, few small spots, top edge gilt, illustrations by Joseph Pennell. R. F. G. Hollett & Son Lake District & Cumbria - 152 2013 £40

Bradley, Helen *And Miss Carter Wore Pink.* London: Cape, 1971. First edition, oblong 4to., original cloth gilt, dust jacket price clipped, illustrations in color. R. F. G. Hollett & Son Lake District & Cumbria - 153 2013 £40

Bradley, Helen *"In the Beginning" said Great Aunt Jane.* Cape, 1974. First edition, oblong 4to., original cloth, gilt, dust jacket, 32 pages, illustrations in color. R. F. G. Hollett & Son Lake District & Cumbria - 154 2013 £50

Bradley, Helen *Miss Carter Came with Us.* Cape, 1973. Oblong 4to., original cloth, gilt, dust jacket, 31 pages, illustrations in color. R. F. G. Hollett & Son Lake District & Cumbria - 157 2013 £65

Bradley, Helen *Miss Carter Came with Us.* London: Cape, 1973. Oblong 4to., original cloth, gilt, dust jacket, pages 32, illustrations in color, presentation copy inscribed from the artist with small drawing of a fly. R. F. G. Hollett & Son Lake District & Cumbria - 156 2013 £150

Bradley, Helen *Miss Carter Came With Us.* Cape, 1973. Signed limited edition, number 83 of 2000 copies, oblong 4to., original cloth, gilt, slipcase, trifle scratched, illustrations in color, bound in Red Bridge book cloth Textis 69 with matching case. R. F. G. Hollett & Son Lake District & Cumbria - 155 2013 £250

Bradley, Richard *Interpreting the Axe Trade.* Cambridge University Press, 1993. First edition, 24 plates, numerous figures, original cloth, gilt, dust jacket. R. F. G. Hollett & Son Lake District & Cumbria - 158 2013 £40

Bradlow, Edna *Thomas Bowler of the Cape of Good Hope.* Cape Town and Amsterdam: A. A. Balkema, 1955. First edition, no. 1340 of 2000 copies, 4to., original cloth, gilt, dust jacket with color plate tipped on (laid down, lacking lower panel and part of backstrip), pages 248 with 137 tipped in plates.   R. F. G. Hollett & Son   Africana - 24   2013   £120

Bradstreet, Anne *The Works of Anne Bradstreet in Prose and Verse.* Charlestown: Abram E. Cutter, 1867. First edition, small 4to., frontispiece, original cloth, spine laid down, new paper label, new editions.   M & S Rare Books, Inc.   95 - 35   2013 $475

Brady, A. J. *Gone to Glory Land.* Cork: Pursell, 1902. (28) pages, photo portrait, very good, cloth.   C. P. Hyland   261 - 472   2013   £45

Brady, Anne *The Bookmaker.* Dublin: National Print Museum, 2008. First illustrated edition, limited to 250 numbered copies signed by author, large 8vo., original black cloth, lettered and blocked in silver, printed letterpress on 170gsm mouldmade Zerkall, numerous black and white illustrations, drawings, fine, decorated endpapers.   Maggs Bros. Ltd.   1442 - 68   2013   £125

Brady, John *Clavis Calendaria, or a Compendious Analysis of the Calendar...*   London: printed for the author and sold by Longman (and others), 1812. 8vo., wood engraved frontispiece, 7 engravings in text, few leaves, little dusted, some foxing to titlepages, contemporary half calf, marbled boards, gilt banded spine, red morocco labels, gilt volume numbers within circular flower head frames, hinges rubbed, spines little dry, one headcap slightly chipped, armorial bookplate of Ralph Creyke Marton.   Jarndyce Antiquarian Booksellers   CCIV - 72   2013   £125

Brady, N. *A New Version of the Psalms of David, Fitted to the Tunes Used in the Churches.* Edinburgh: printed by Adrian Watkins, 1757. 8vo., with initial imprimatur leaf, full contemporary reverse calf with handsome red morocco label to upper board, "T. E. Headlam, Gateshead, 1770".   Ken Spelman Books Ltd.   75 - 30   2013   £120

Braga, Theophilo *Bibliographia Camoniana.* Lisboa: Impr de Christovao A. Rodrigues, 1880. First edition, no. 153 of 325 copies, signed by author, 4to., half morocco over marbled boards, raised bands, 6 compartments decorated in gilt, marbled endpapers, very good, spine ends worn, fore edge scuffed, owner's stamp on titlepage.   Kaaterskill Books   16 - 12   2013 $1000

Bragdon, Elspeth *The New Adventures of Peter Rabbit.* Ohio: Artcraft Paper Products, n.d. circa, 1950. illustrations by Laura Schmeing, with 5 spring-up 3 dimensional color pictures with color pictorial background and text beneath printed on thick card, pages 10, color illustrations thick card covers, titling on front in blue and in white on backstrip, slight rubbing to hinges, very nice.   Ian Hodgkins & Co. Ltd.   134 - 34   2013   £70

Bragg, Melvyn *Land of the Lakes.* London: Secker and Warburg, 1983. First edition, large 8vo., original cloth, gilt, dust jacket, pages 248, illustrations, partly in color.   R. F. G. Hollett & Son   Lake District & Cumbria - 159   2013   £30

Bragg, Melvyn *Speak for England.* New York: Alfred A. Knopf, 1977. First US edition, large 8vo., original cloth backed boards gilt, dust jacket trifle worn, neat repairs to reverse, 32 pages of plates and plan.   R. F. G. Hollett & Son   Lake District & Cumbria - 160   2013   £30

Braidwood, James *On the Construction of Fire-Engines and Apparatus...*   Edinburgh: sold by Bell & Bradfute and Oliver & Boyd, 1830. First edition, double frontispiece tipped in on stub, folding plates, uncut in recent half brown calf by Philip Dusel, gilt spine signed M. Braidwood 1.2.22 on recto of front. additional inscription "City road 14.12.69" with signature of J. Grant in similar hand, handsome copy.   Jarndyce Antiquarian Booksellers   CCV - 28   2013   £2250

Braine, John *Room at the Top.* London: Eyre & Spottiswoode, 1957. Fifth impression, 8vo., original green cloth, dust jacket, previous owner's name and date, otherwise excellent copy in dust jacket, nicked at edges, inscribed by author.   Maggs Bros. Ltd.   1460 - 133   2013   £75

Braine, Sheila *To Tell the King the Sky is Falling.* Blackie & Son n.d. circa, 1897. First edition, original green pictorial cloth, gilt, all edges gilt, illustrations by Alice Woodward.   R. F. G. Hollett & Son   Children's Books - 79   2013   £50

Braithwaite, G. E. *Generoso Germine Gemmo.* Kendal: Titus Wilson, 1965. Tall 8vo., original stiff wrappers, edges trifle browned, 17 illustrations, family trees, excellent copy.   R. F. G. Hollett & Son   Lake District & Cumbria - 163   2013   £85

Braithwaite, George Foster *The Salmonidae of Westmorland, Angling Reminiscences and Leaves from an Angler's Notebook.* Kendal: Atkinson and Pollitt, 1884. First edition, original cloth, gilt, trifle damped, neatly recased, 4 illustrations, presentation copy inscribed by author for Rt. Hon. F. Stanley, very scarce.   R. F. G. Hollett & Son   Lake District & Cumbria - 164   2013   £180

Braithwaite, J. Bevan *J. Bevan Braithwaite.* London: Hodder & Stoughton, 1909. First edition, original blue cloth, gilt, untrimmed, 19 illustrations, scattered spotting, inscribed by D. B. Braithwaite for Alexander Dunlop. R. F. G. Hollett & Son   Lake District & Cumbria - 166   2013   £40

Braithwaite, J. W. *Guide to Kirkby Stephen.* Kirkby Stephen: J. W. Braithwaite, 1938. Original red pictorial wrappers, rather soiled and worn and rebacked with black tape, 10 plates on pink paper, 5 pages of local ads, little used, scarce. R. F. G. Hollett & Son   Lake District & Cumbria - 167   2013   £65

Braithwaite, M. *Many Happy Returns.* privately published, 1949. Original blue stiff wrappers little faded and soiled, 12 illustrations, very scarce. R. F. G. Hollett & Son   Lake District & Cumbria - 168   2013   £65

Bramsen, John *Letters of a Prussian Traveller...* London: Henry Colburn, 1818. First edition, 2 volumes, 8vo., contemporary brown full polished calf, recently rebacked, internally crisp, scarce. J. & S. L. Bonham Antiquarian Booksellers   Europe - 8715   2013   £1250

Bramston, James *The Art of Politicks.* London: printed for Lawton Gilliver, 1729. Variant issue of first edition, 8vo., frontispiece, few light spots, small abrasion to title affecting one letter of imprint, recent quarter calf by Chris Weston, paste paper boards red morocco label lettered vertically. Unsworths Antiquarian Booksellers   28 - 75   2013   £125

Bramwell, Byron *Intracranial Tumors.* Edinburgh: Young J. Pentland, 1888. First edition, Original green cloth, worn and rubbed, remnants of paper label on spine, portion of half, including text, has been cut away, internally very good. James Tait Goodrich   75 - 35   2013 $495

Branch, William *Life, a Poem in Three Books...* Richmond: from the Franklin Press, W. W. Gray, Printer, 1819. First edition, 12mo., contemporary quarter calf spine, drab paper boards, red leather label, gilt rules and lettering, leaf of errata present, edges little rubbed margin torn on one leaf, not touching text, light foxing, very good. The Brick Row Book Shop   Miscellany Fifty-Nine - 4   2013 $275

Brand, Christianna *Nurse Matilda.* Brockhampton Press, 1964. First edition, 40 illustrations in text by Edward Ardizzone, 16mo., 128 pages, original mid green bards, backstrip and front cover with overall gilt lettering and designs by Ardizzone, pink cotton marker, fine. Blackwell's Rare Books   B174 - 161   2013   £55

Brande, Barbara *The Slave's Appeal.* Chicago: H. M. Higgins, 1863. First edition, folio, title and 3 pages of text, disbound, small inner marginal tear, scattered foxing. M & S Rare Books, Inc.   95 - 346   2013 $3500

Brande, Dorothea *Most Beautiful Lady.* New York: Farrar & Rinehart, 1935. First edition, 8vo., original red cloth, pages 342, excellent, very good pictorial dust jacket, not price clipped. Howard S. Mott Inc.   262 - 22   2013 $100

Brandelius, Jerilyn Lee *Grateful Dead Family Album.* New York: Warner Books, 1989. First edition, 4to., "Grateful Dead All Area Access" sticker laid down to jacket, this copy signed by band members Jerry Garcia, Mickey Hart and Bob Bralove, as well as road crew members "Ram Rod" Shurtliff, Bill "Kid" Candelario, Steve Parish and Robbie Taylor, among others, hundreds of photos. Ed Smith Books   78 - 23   2013 $1250

Brandes, Ray *Troopers West: Military & Indian Affairs on the American Frontier.* San Diego: 1970. xii, 206 pages, illustrations, near fine in slightly soiled dust jacket, illustrations by Ted DeGrazia. Dumont Maps & Books of the West   124 - 48   2013 $85

Brandt, Bill *Camera in London. Masters of the Camera Series.* Focal Press, 1948. First edition, 61 full page reproductions of photos by Brandt, folding plate of technical detail 90 pages, 8vo. original yellow and white boards, front cover illustrating photographic self portrait with printing in black and white, small piece torn from tail of backstrip, good. Blackwell's Rare Books   B174 - 173   2013   £200

Brant, Sebastian *(Ship of Fools) Stultifero Nauis, Quo Omnium Moralium Narratur Stultitio Odmodum Vtilis & Necessaria ab Omnibus ad Suam...* London: in Paules Church: John Cawood, 1570. Second edition, folio in sixes, printed in black letter, 116 woodcuts, full 17th century calf, rebacked with original spine laid down, red calf spine label, lettered in gilt, all edges speckled red, newer endpapers, bit of rubbing to boards and edges, occasional marginal dampstaining, overall very good. Heritage Book Shop 50th Anniversary Catalogue - 5   2013 $40,000

Brassey, Thomas, Lord *Gleanings . I. A. Christmas Card for 1899.* Melbourne: printed for private circulation by Sands & McDougall Ltd., 1899. One volume only, of two, pleasing contemporary crimson crushed morocco for Hatchards of Piccadilly (stamp signed), covers with gilt rule border, raised bands, spine compartments with central gilt lily, gilt ruled turn-ins, marbled endpapers, all edges gilt, bookplate of V(ictoria) SackvilleWest, hint of uniform darkening to spine just slightest wear to joints and extremities, several pages with marginal pencil markings, but never any words, otherwise fine, especially fresh and clean inside and out. Phillip J. Pirages   63 - 414   2013 $150

Brathwaite, Edward *Rights of Passage.* London: Oxford University Press, 1967. First edition, fine in fine dust jacket, very scarce. Between the Covers Rare Books, Inc.   165 - 20   2013 $300

Brathwaite, Richard   1588-1673   *Barnabae Itinerarium, or Barnabee's Journal.*   J. Harding, 1818.   Seventh edition, Later cloth, printed spine label, pages 204, engraved frontispiece by Will Marshall, 7 engraved plates, old taped repairs to some hinges and torn leaf, engraved armorial bookplate of William Brooke, A.M.   R. F. G. Hollett & Son   Lake District & Cumbria - 169   2013   £120

Brathwaite, Richard   1588-1673   *Drunken Barnaby's Four Journeys to the North of England.*   printed for S. Illidge, 1723.   Third edition, small 8vo., old polished calf gilt with new spine label, engraved frontispiece and typographical head and tailpieces, inscription, lacks five plates called for in this edition.   R. F. G. Hollett & Son   Lake District & Cumbria - 171   2013   £75

Brathwaite, Richard   1588-1673   *Drunken Barnaby's Four Journeys to the North of England.*   T. & J. Allman, 1822.   New edition, modern half calf gilt, 4 lithographed plates by D. Dighton.   R. F. G. Hollett & Son   Lake District & Cumbria - 170   2013   £95

Brathwaite, Richard   1588-1673   *Essaies vpon the Five Senses...*   printed by E. G. for Richard Whittaker, 1620.   First edition, rare, cut close with loss of tips of first line of title and several headlines and touching one sidenote (no loss of sense), bit browned, more especially around edges and in terminal leaves which are slightly frayed (no loss).   Blackwell's Rare Books   B174 - 15   2013   £4000

Braun, Lilian Jackson   *The Cat Who Ate Danish Modern.*   New York: E. P. Dutton, 1967.   First edition, previous owner's booklabel, else fine in modestly soiled, very good or better, price clipped dust jacket.   Between the Covers Rare Books, Inc.   Mystery & Detective Fiction - 292970   2013 $200

Braun, Lionel H.   *Fanny Hill's Cook Book.*   New York: Taplinger, 1971.   First American edition, illustrations by Brian Forbes fine in near fine dust jacket with some rubbing and tiny tears, scarce in nice condition.   Between the Covers Rare Books, Inc.   Cocktails, Etc. - 29567   2013 $125

Braune, Christian Wilhelm   *Topographisch Anatomischer Atlas Nach Durchschnitten an Gefrorenen Cadavern.*   Leipzig: Veit, 1875.   Second edition, imperial folio, 31 color plates, 1 with short tear professionally repaired, small early rubber stamp verso each plate, handsome modern parchment backed marbled boards, early titlepage rubber stamp, very good, extremely rare.   Jeff Weber Rare Books   172 - 41   2013 $2000

Brautigan, Richard   *Dreaming of Babylon.*   New York: Delacorte, 1977.   First edition, very fine in dust jacket.   Mordida Books   81 - 48   2013 $100

Brautigan, Richard   *Willard and His Bowling Trophies.*   New York: Simon & Schuster, 1975.   First edition, very fine in dust jacket.   Mordida Books   81 - 47   2013 $100

Brawley, Benjamin   *The Negro Genius: a New Appraisal of the Achievement of the American Negro in Literature and the Fine Arts.*   New York: Dodd, Mead & Co., 1937.   First edition, frontispiece, many photos, very light rubbing, fine copy lacking uncommon dust jacket.   Between the Covers Rare Books, Inc.   165 - 88   2013 $300

Bray, Anna Eliza   *Life of Thomas Stothard, R. A.*   London: John Murray, 1851.   First edition, 216 x 171mm., excellent contemporary dark green morocco, handsomely gilt by James Toovey (stamp signed), covers with French fillet border, raised bands, heavily gilt spine compartments featuring scrolling cornerpieces and large ad intricate floral centerpiece, turn-ins densely gilt with botanical tools, marbled endpapers, all edges gilt, frontispiece, engraved titlepage frame and more than 50 illustrations in text; spine evenly faded to pleasing olive brown, covers with just touch of fading and soiling, handful of pages with extensive freckled foxing, trivial to minor foxing in much of the rest of the text, still extremely fresh, scarcely worn and very attractive binding.   Phillip J. Pirages   63 - 451   2013 $550

Brayley, Edward Wedlake   1773-1854   *Views in Suffolk, Norfolk and Northamptonshire.*   London: Vernor, Hood & Sharpe, 1806.   First edition, engraved frontispiece and title, printed title, 13 full page engravings, contemporary half calf, spine with devices in blind, lacking label, following board little rubbed, label carefully removed from leading pastedown.   Jarndyce Antiquarian Booksellers   CCIII - 29   2013   £40

Brazil, Angela   *The Leader of the Lower School.*   Blackie & Son n.d.,   Original blue cloth, dust jacket trifle worn and creased, 4 plates, prize label dated 1945.   R. F. G. Hollett & Son   Children's Books - 80   2013   £25

Brazil, Angela   *The Little Green School.*   Blackie and Son, n.d., 1931.   First edition, original cloth lettered in blue and decorated in green, little marked, spine slightly darkened, 6 plates by Frank Wiles, small inscription.   R. F. G. Hollett & Son   Children's Books - 81   2013   £65

Brazil, Angela   *The Luckiest Girl in the School.*   Blackie and Son, n.d. circa, 1925.   Original pictorial brown cloth, 6 plates, flyleaves browned, small scratch to illustrations leaf.   R. F. G. Hollett & Son   Children's Books - 82   2013   £30

Brazil, Angela   *A Pair of School Girls.*   Blackie & Son, n.d. 1920's,   Original sage green pictorial cloth, few slight marks to lower boards, 4 plates, half title little browned.   R. F. G. Hollett & Son   Children's Books - 83   2013   £30

Brazil, Angela   *The School by the Sea.*   Blackie and son, n.d. circa, 1925.   Original pictorial pale blue cloth, 4 plates.   R. F. G. Hollett & Son   Children's Books - 84   2013   £30

Breasted, James Henry *Egypt through the Stereoscope...* New York: Underwood & Underwood, 1905. 6 pages ads, original brown cloth, with pocket (unusually) on outside of back board containing 19 maps on 17 plates, mostly folding, with ink numbers and some annotations, in slightly torn brown wrappers, near fine.   Jarndyce Antiquarian Booksellers   CCV - 29   2013   £68

Breay, John *Light in the Dales.* Norwich: Canterbury Press, 1996. First (only) edition, original pictorial wrappers.   R. F. G. Hollett & Son   Lake District & Cumbria - 173   2013   £40

Brecht, Bertolt *Poems on the Theatre.* Northwood: Scorpion Press, 1961. First edition, 8vo., original wrappers, inscribed by John and Anna Berger for Basil (probably Basil Bunting), near fine.   Maggs Bros. Ltd.   1460 - 86   2013   £200

Breeze, David J. *Hadrian's Wall.* Allen Lane, 1976. First edition, original cloth, gilt, dust jacket, 29 plates, 45 text figures and maps, 14 tables.   R. F. G. Hollett & Son   Lake District & Cumbria - 175   2013   £25

Breeze, David J. *The Northern Frontiers of Roman Britain.* Batsford Academic and Educational, 1982. First edition, original cloth, gilt, dust jacket, 19 plates, 40 maps and diagrams.   R. F. G. Hollett & Son   Lake District & Cumbria - 174   2013   £25

Breham, Edward *Treatise on the Structure, Formation and Various Diseases of the Teeth and Gums...* Edinburgh: printed by Mundell Doig and Stevenson, 1810. First edition, frontispiece, stab holes along fore-edge of plate, very minor staining to parts of fore-edge of plate, very minor staining to parts of fore edges, 8vo., original paper wrappers, pink spine, blue covers, slightly soiled and foxed, label skillfully removed from upper cover, good.   Blackwell's Rare Books   Sciences - 17   2013   £1100

Bremer, Walther *Ireland's Place in Prehistoric and Early Historic Europe.* 1928. First edition, 8vo., 38 pages, wrappers worn, text and illustrations, very good.   C. P. Hyland   261 - 914   2013   £32

Bremner, Benjamin *Memories of Long Ago, Being a Series of Sketches Pertaining to Charlottetown in the Past.* Charlottetown: Irwin Printing Co. Ltd., 1930. First edition, 8vo., card covers string tied, gilt on cover, frontispiece, black and white photo, 16 glossy illustrations, other illustrations, spine and edges chipped, interior very good, signed.   Schooner Books Ltd.   104 - 137   2013 $55

Brendel, Johann Philipp *Consilia Medica Celeberrimorum Quorundam Germaniae Medicorum.* Frankfurt am Main: ex Bibliopolio Palthenlano, 1615. 4to., early 17th century full calf, surface worming on front board, text browned, ex-libris of Samuel X. Radbill with his bookplate, bookstamp of Melk Benedictine Monastery.   James Tait Goodrich   S74 - 33   2013 $495

Brennan, Martin *The Boyne Valley Vision.* Dolmen, 1980. First edition, 8vo., cloth, illustrations, dust jacket, very good, ex-institutional library with stamps.   C. P. Hyland   261 - 916   2013   £40

Brentano, Robyn *112 Workship/112 Green Street.* New York: New York University Press, 1981. First edition, 385 pages, numerous illustrations, clean, very near fine in very good plus dust jacket with a number of small edge tears and some minor wear, very nice.   Jeff Hirsch Books   Fall 2013 - 129453   2013 $150

Brenton, Howard *Diving for Pearls.* London: Nick Hern Books, 1989. First edition, 8vo., original black cloth, fine in dust jacket, inscribed by author for Tariq Ali.   Maggs Bros. Ltd.   1460 - 135   2013   £175

Brenton, Howard *Greenland.* London: Methuen, 1988. First edition, 8vo., original wrappers, inscribed by author for cast member, Larry Lamb, near fine.   Maggs Bros. Ltd.   1460 - 134   2013   £120

Brera, Valriano Luigi *Classificazione delle Malattie Secondo i Principi di Brown Esposta in una Tavola.* Venice: no printer or publisher, 1799. First edition, large folding engraved table at end, title with tear at lower inner margin not affecting text, little spotting, pages 47 (1 ads), 8vo., uncut in contemporary patterned paper over carta rustica, surface wear to spine, good.   Blackwell's Rare Books   Sciences - 18   2013   £450

Breslauer, Bernard H. *Bibliography: Its History and Development.* New York: Grolier Club, 1984. Limited to 600 copies, 8vo., 223 pages, 2-color illustrations, green cloth, gilt stamped cover emblem and spine title, fine, scarce.   Jeff Weber Rare Books   171 - 49   2013 $165

Bret, Antoine *Ninon De Lenclos.* London: Arthur L. Humphreys, 1904. 214 x 154mm., attractive contemporary russet morocco in Arts and Crafts style, covers with frame of plain gilt rules and oak leaves and dots at intersections of lines, gilt titling on upper cover, raised bands, spine gilt in double ruled compartments with three large gilt dots at each corner connected by lines of tiny dots, gilt ruled turn-ins, all edges gilt, engraved bookplate of Victoria Sackville West, with best wishes from Bob Capel Xmas 1904, black and white photo portrait of Ninon de Lenclos tipped onto verso of half title, with identifying inscription in Victoria Sackville-West's hand, spine bit sunned, little mild soiling at boards, extremities lightly rubbed, hint of moisture here and there to tail edge margin, otherwise excellent, binding sound, text unusually bright clean and fresh.   Phillip J. Pirages   63 - 417   2013 $250

Breton, Andre *Poemes.* Paris: Gallimard, 1948. First edition, 8vo., original wrappers preserved in folding box, near fine, inscribed by author for A. G. Antonini.   Maggs Bros. Ltd.   1460 - 136   2013   £350

Brett, Edward M. *The British Auxiliary Legion in the First Carlist War 1835-8.* Four Courts, 2005. First edition, 8vo., illustrations, cloth, dust jacket, near fine.   C. P. Hyland   261 - 152   2013   £35

Brett, Simon *The Detection Collection.* Gladestry: Scorpion Press, 2005. First edition, one of 16 lettered copies (this being C), fine in quarter leather with raised bands, marbled boards and fine acetate dust jacket, signed by editor, Claire Francis, Robert Goddard, John Harvey, Reginald Hill, P. D. James, H. R. F. Keatin, Michael Ridpath, Margaret Yorke, Robert Barnard, Lindsey Davis and Colin Dexter, includes signatures of Boris Akunin and Michael Johnson, from the library of Bruce Kahn.   Between the Covers Rare Books, Inc.   Mystery & Detective Fiction - 312104   2013 $400

Brewer, J. M. *The Beauties of Ireland.* 1825-1826. 2 volumes, large paper (10 inches tall), octavo, 24 plates from Petre originals, original cloth backed marbled boards, many plates have rice paper guards, but there is some foxing. C. P. Hyland   261 - 153   2013   £750

Brewer, William Henry *Such a Landscape!* Yosemite: Yosemite Association, Sequoia Nat. Hist. Assoc., 1987. First edition, number 347 of 500 numbered copies, signed by Alsup, square quarto, 124 pages, frontispiece, 39 plates, half cloth, boards, fine.   Argonaut Book Shop   Recent Acquisitions June 2013 - 39   2013 $225

Brewer, William Henry *Up and Down California in 1860-1864.* New Haven: Yale University Press, 1931. First edition, 2nd printing, frontispiece, 1 folding map, numerous plates, old prints and photos, dark blue cloth, gilt, owner's neat signature on end, very fine.   Argonaut Book Shop   Recent Acquisitions June 2013 - 41   2013 $160

Brewer, William Henry *Up and Down California in 1860-1864.* New Haven: Yale University Press, 1931. First edition, 2nd printing, frontispiece, 1 folding map, numerous plates from drawings, old prints and photos, dark blue cloth, gilt, fine with darkened and lightly worn pictorial dust jacket.   Argonaut Book Shop   Recent Acquisitions June 2013 - 40   2013 $175

Brewster, David *The Edinburgh Encyclopaedia.* Philadelphia: Joseph Parker, 1832. First American edition, 4to., 18 volumes, 531 full page plates plus 5 portraits, 11 maps, large view, 2 double page maps which are numbered in the plates, uniformly bound in simulated leather spine over boards with spine labels pasted on, plates all bound at back of each volume, some browning.   Barnaby Rudge Booksellers   Natural History 2013 - 02126   2013 $1950

Brewster, Margaret Maria *Household Economy.* Edinburgh: Thomas Constable and Co., circa, 1858. Second edition, half title, 8vo., very good in original blind-stamped and gilt lettered limp brown cloth, very scarce. Ken Spelman Books Ltd.   75 - 122   2013   £100

Brick, Kay A. *The Powder Puff Derby Commemorative Album.* North Little Rock: Heritage Pub., 1974. 4to., 176 pages, copiously illustrated with photos, maps, cartoons, paper wrappers, ex-library, stamps, labels, pocket, date slip, very good, tight copy.   Second Life Books Inc.   182 - 29   2013 $75

The Bridal Night, Attributed to Lord Byron, together with two other Poems. London: privately printed, circa, 1930. One of 500 privately printed copies, original plain orange card wrappers, bound into marbled boards, red cloth spine, very good.   Jarndyce Antiquarian Booksellers   CCIII - 342   2013   £120

Bridges, Robert *New Verse Written in 1921, with Other Poems of that Year and a few Earlier Pieces.* Oxford: at the Clarendon Press, 1925. First edition, number 81 of 100 signed by author, 8vo., original white vellum backed boards, lettered gilt, dust jacket, unusually fine.   Maggs Bros. Ltd.   1460 - 139   2013   £100

Bridgman, Betty *Lullaby for Eggs.* New York: Macmillan, 1955. Stated first edition, square 8vo., cloth, near fine in slightly worn dust jacket, pastel illustrations by Elizabeth Jones.   Aleph-Bet Books, Inc.   104 - 303   2013 $200

Briggs, John *The Lonsdale Magazine, or Provincial Repository...* Kendal: J. Briggs, 1820-1822. 3 volumes, early 20th century three quarter scarlet morocco gilt with flattened raised bands, all edges gilt, 27 aquatint plates, 1 folding table, 1 engraved plate and several text illustrations, upper margins of aquatints little cropped, but most handsome clean set, from the Appleby Castle Library with monogram of Lord Hothfield.   R. F. G. Hollett & Son   Lake District & Cumbria - 178   2013   £650

Briggs, John *The Lonsdale Magazine, or Provincial Repository...* Kendal: J. Briggs, 1820-1822. 3 volumes, modern half levant morocco gilt with contrasting raised bands (volume 2 slightly taller than others and differing trifle in leather), 27 aquatint plates, 1 hand colored map, 1 folding table, 1 engraved plate and text illustrations, 2 plates in volume 2 poorly tinted in red, staining the opposing leaves, little light browning in places, but very good, sound set. R. F. G. Hollett & Son Lake District & Cumbria - 177 2013 £395

Briggs, John *The Remains of John Briggs...* Kirkby Lonsdale: printed and sold by Arthur Foster, 1825. First edition, old half calf gilt, neatly recased, original backstrip cracked but laid down, pages 408, half title and subscriber list, excellent copy, near contemporary inscription of Henrietta Harrison dated April 1826. R. F. G. Hollett & Son Lake District & Cumbria - 176 2013 £395

Briggs, Raymond *Fungus the Bogeyman.* Puffin Books, 2002. Folio, original black boards, color printed illustrations, dust jacket, fine. Blackwell's Rare Books B174 - 174 2013 £30

Briggs, Raymond *Ivor the Invisible.* Channel 4 Books, 2001. First edition, color printed illustrations and endpapers, 4to., 40 pages, original mid blue boards, backstrip blocked in silver, dust jacket, fine, signed by Briggs. Blackwell's Rare Books B174 - 175 2013 £45

Briggs, Raymond *The Man.* MacRae Books, 1992. First edition, color printed illustrations, folio, (64) pages, original white boards, illustrated overall, cover lettering printed in black, dust jacket, fine. Blackwell's Rare Books B174 - 176 2013 £45

Briggs, Raymond *Ug. Boy Genius of the Stone Age and His Search for Soft Trousers.* Cape, 2001. First edition, color printed illustrations, folio, (32) pages, original grey boards illustrated overall, cover lettering printed in black, dust jacket, fine, signed by Briggs. Blackwell's Rare Books B174 - 177 2013 £45

Brigham, Amariah *An Inquiry Concerning the Diseases and Functions of the Brain. The Spinal Cord, and The Nerves.* New York: George Alard, 1840. Original cloth, 1 inch portion of inferior spine defective, some foxing, overall good, clean, tight copy, rare. James Tait Goodrich S74 - 35 2013 $495

Bright, Richard *Reports of Medical Cases, Selected with a View of Illustrating the Symptoms and Cure of Diseases by a Reference in Morbid Anatomy.* London: Richard Taylor for Longman et al, 1827-1831. 4to., 3 volumes, recent half calf and marbled boards, 54 plates (47 hand colored aquatints and 7 uncolored lithographs), lacking half titles with errata leaf in volume 2/1, with light dampstaining at end of volume 2/2 affecting last several plates, institutional stamps on titles, some text leaves, some plates on recto. James Tait Goodrich 75 - 36 2013 $29,500

Bright, Timothy *A Treatise of Melancholie.* London: imprinted...by Thomas Vautrollier, 1586. First edition, small octavo, this copy includes original leaf O8, which was intended to be canceled, woodcut printer's device on title, bound by Lakeside Bindery in full antique style calf, covers panelled in gilt, smooth spine decoratively tooled and lettered gilt, edges stained red, lower margin of title and following leaf renewed with some loss to few letters of imprint on title, title soiled slightly, bottom edge of lower margin frayed slightly in prelims, short internal tear to A4 crossing text, few other minor marginal flaws or repairs, some faint dampstaining, very good, extremely rare, from the library of Haskell Norman, with his bookplate. Heritage Book Shop 50th Anniversary Catalogue - 13 2013 $25,000

Brin, David *Startide Rising.* West Bloomfield: Phantasia Press, 1985. First hardcover edition, octavo, cloth. L. W. Currey, Inc. Fall Sampler Sept. 2013 - 145084 2013 $225

Brine, Mary *Little People.* Boston: Lothrop, 1898. 4to., cloth backed pictorial boards, edges rubbed, else very good+. illustrations by Paul King with 6 fine chromolithographed plates. Aleph-Bet Books, Inc. 105 - 332 2013 $350

Brinkley, Douglas *Kurt Vonnegut's Apocalypse Blues.* Ann Arbor: State Street Press, 2007. Advance reading copy, with a photo copy of Brinkley's original typescript, typescript with some editorial changes in unknown hand and is near fine, the advance reading copy is fine in wrappers. Ken Lopez Bookseller 159 - 208 2013 $750

Brinton, Daniel G. *American Hero-Myths.* Philadelphia: Watts, 1882. First edition, 8vo., green cloth stamped in gilt, very good, tight copy. Second Life Books Inc. 183 - 54 2013 $165

Brissenden, Paul *The IWW a Study of American Syndicalism.* New York: Columbia University, 1919. First edition, very good, name obliterated on front page, name on titlepage, hinge going very slightly at first few prelims, hardcover. Beasley Books 2013 - 2013 $50

Bristed, John *America and Her Resources; or a View of the Agricultural, Commercial, Manufacturing, Financial, Political, Literary, Moral and Religious Capacity...* London: printed for Henry Colburn, 1818. 8vo., slight foxing to titlepage, some minor marks, near contemporary half calf, gilt banded spine, slightly chipped black morocco label, head of spine very slightly worn, later but not recent endpapers and pastedowns, early signature at head of titlepage. Jarndyce Antiquarian Booksellers CCIV - 73 2013 £220

Britaine, William De *Humane Prudence, or the Art by Which a Man May Raise Himself and His Fortune to Grandeur.* London: Richard Sare at Gray's Inn Gate in Holborn, 1697. Seventh edition, 12mo., small paper flaw on F3 slightly touching few letters, contemporary speckled calf, excellently rebacked, various inscriptions on endpapers. Jarndyce Antiquarian Booksellers CCV - 30 2013 £250

British Quadrupeds. Religious Tract Society, n.d. circa, 1850. New edition, square 12mo., original blindstamped cloth, all edges gilt, 24 hand colored woodcut vignette plates, trifle shaken. R. F. G. Hollett & Son Children's Books - 86 2013 £85

The British Florist; or Lady's Journal of Horticulture. London: Henry G. Bohn, 1846. First edition, 8vo., 14 hand colored plates, rebound in modern green cloth, volume 4 only, of 6, very good, bookplate of Edward Bury. Barnaby Rudge Booksellers Natural History 2013 - 020458 2013 $110

Brittain, Vera *In the Steps of John Bunyan.* London: Rich and Cowan, 1950. First edition, 8vo., original black cloth, excellent copy, inscribed by author June 1950. Maggs Bros. Ltd. 1460 - 140 2013 £50

Broad-Sheet Ballads Being a Collection of Irish Popular Songs. Dublin: Maunsel, 1913. First edition, frontispiece, 16mo., original mid green cloth, backstrip and front cover gilt lettered, faint endpaper browning, rough trimmed, very good. Blackwell's Rare Books 172 - 173 2013 £50

Broad, Lewis *The Tale of Ming the Giant Panda.* John F. Shaw, n.d., 1940. First edition, square 8vo., original pictorial wrappers (little dusty), pages 30 with map and photo illustrations, very scarce. R. F. G. Hollett & Son Children's Books - 87 2013 £50

Broca, Paul *Memoires D'Anthropologie.* Paris: C. Reinwald, 1871-1877. Volumes 1-3 (of 5), original green line, edges uncut, light foxing, else very good, numerous engravings, quite scarce if not rare. James Tait Goodrich S74 - 38 2013 $2750

Brock, Alan St. H. *A History of Fireworks.* London, et al: George G. Harrap, 1949. First edition, 8vo., 280 pages, 40 plates, including frontispiece, text illustrations, dark blue cloth, gilt stamped spine, dust jacket worn, Burndy bookplate, very good, signed by Cyril Stanley Smith. Jeff Weber Rare Books 169 - 44 2013 $125

Brock, Carey, Mrs. *The Rectory and the Manor.* London: Seeley, Jackson & Halliday, 1866. Fifth thousand, frontispiece, original green cloth, prize inscription on leading f.e.p., fine. Jarndyce Antiquarian Booksellers CCV - 33 2013 £40

Brockbank, Elisabeth *Richard Hubberthorne of Yealand, Yeoman, Soldier, Quaker 1628-1662.* Friends Book Centre, 1929. Limited edition, signed, original cloth, gilt, pages 168, illustrations by author, tipped-in colored frontispiece, 1 plate and 4 tipped in plates from blocks cut by James Jackson of Yealand after designs by author, inscribed by author, little spotting in places. R. F. G. Hollett & Son Lake District & Cumbria - 179 2013 £45

Brockbank, Elisabeth *Richard Hubberthorne of Yealand, Yeoman, Soldier, Quaker 1628-1662.* Friends Book Centre, 1929. First edition, original boards, pictorial onlay to upper board, 168 pages, illustrations by author, blocks cut by James Jackson of Yealand, map to front endpapers, rather scarce. R. F. G. Hollett & Son Lake District & Cumbria - 180 2013 £45

Brockedon, William 1787-1854 *Road-Book from London to Naples.* London: John Murray, 1835. First edition, frontispiece, additional engraved title, plates, contemporary half vellum, spine decorated in gilt, green morocco label, slightly dulled and marked, but very good, attractive copy. Jarndyce Antiquarian Booksellers CCV - 34 2013 £380

Brockett, L. P. *Our Western Empire; or the New West Beyond the Mississippi.* San Francisco: 1882. 1312 pages, maps and illustrations, brown cloth with black and gilt illustration, large text block is sagging and tips of extremities show tiny bit of rubbing, otherwise beautiful, near fine. Dumont Maps & Books of the West 125 - 42 2013 $300

Brockett, Paul *Bibliography of Aeronautics.* Washington: Smithsonian Institution, 1910. First edition, 8vo., xiv, 940 pages, printed wrappers, worn, small front cover library blindstamp, very good, Burndy bookplate. Jeff Weber Rare Books 169 - 45 2013 $75

Brockway, Thomas *The Gospel Tragedy; an Epic Poem.* Worcester: James R. Hutchins, 1795. First edition, frontispiece, bit browned and spotted, pronounced waterstaining at either end, text corrected in 3 places, 8vo., original tree sheep, worn and scraped in places, cracks in joints but cords holding, contemporary signature at head of title "Silvester Gilbert", sound. Blackwell's Rare Books B174 - 17 2013 £450

Brockwell, Charles *The Natural and Political History of Portugal...* London: T. Warne, 1726. First edition, 8vo., frontispiece, 2 folding maps, 2 plates, 16 pages browned, contemporary brown full panelled calf, recently rebacked, clean, crisp copy.   J. & S. L. Bonham Antiquarian Booksellers   Europe - 8905   2013   £1250

Brodhurst-Hill, Evelyn *So This is Kenya!* Blackie & Son, 1936. First edition, original cloth, dust jacket price clipped, foot of spine defective, 16 plates and map.   R. F. G. Hollett & Son   Africana - 25   2013   £30

Brodhurst, Bernard E. *The Deformities of the Human Body; a System of Orthopaedic Surgery Being a Course of Lectures Delivered at St. George's Hospital.* London: J. & A. Churchill, 1871. First edition, 8vo., original blind and gilt stamped maroon cloth, rebacked, preserving original spine, unopened, gift copy, inscribed by author on half title, ex-library, rare.   Jeff Weber Rare Books   172 - 42   2013 $850

Brodsky, Joseph *"Elegy for John Donne".* No place: but Lawrence, Kansas: reprinted from The Russian Review Volume 24 No. 4, October, 1965. First separate edition, offprint, 8vo., printed self wrappers, light use, otherwise fine, rare, signed presentation from author for Peter Viereck, inscribed by translator, George Kline for Viereck.   James S. Jaffe Rare Books   Fall 2013 - 28   2013 $2250

Brodsky, Joseph *Verses on the Winter Campaign 1980.* London: Anvil Press Poetry, 1981. First edition, one of 200 copies signed by Brodsky and by Translator, Alan Myers (out of a total edition of 500), 12mo., original unprinted wrappers, dust jacket, fine, presentation copy inscribed by author to poet Mark Strand, with Brodsky's corrections.   James S. Jaffe Rare Books   Fall 2013 - 29   2013 $1250

Brody, Catherine Tyler *Checklist: Stone House Press Books & Ephemera 1978-1988.* New York: New York Public Library & Stone House Press, 1989. Limited, numbered edition of 200, signed by Brody and printer, 8vo., 113 pages, title engraving, 24 illustrations, quarter maroon cloth with patterned paper boards, gilt stamped spine title, fine.   Jeff Weber Rare Books   171 - 51   2013 $75

Brogger, W. C. *Fridtjof Nansen 1861-1893.* London: Longmans Green and Co., 1896. First English edition, original pictorial cloth, silvered, spine and top edges little faded, neatly recased, 8 plates, 3 maps, numerous text illustrations, scarce.   R. F. G. Hollett & Son   Polar Exploration - 2   2013   £150

Bromfield, William *The Schemers; or the City Match.* London: printed for I. Pridden, 1755. 8vo., small hole at foot of H1 slightly affecting a catchword, final leaf torn, old repair on blank verso, titlepage dusted, disbound.   Jarndyce Antiquarian Booksellers   CCIV - 74   2013   £150

Bronowski, J. *The Ascent of Man.* London: BBC, 1973. First edition, 4to., original brown cloth, near fine in dust jacket, inscribed by author for Graham Spiers, 1 Nv. 1973, loosely inserted are two black and white photos of author and another depicting an artist's head and shoulders study of him, also inserted are programme for a tribute service, 2 obit clippings and invitation to the preview of BBC programme of the same name.   Maggs Bros. Ltd.   1460 - 141   2013   £75

Bronte, Charlotte 1816-1855 *Jane Eyre.* London: Smith, Elder & Co., 1847. First edition, 3 volumes, octavo, with half titles as called for but without 32 page publisher catalog (dated Oct. 1847) in volume 1 and without inset catalog fly title dated June 1847 and the inset leaf on thicker paper advertising the Calcutta Review, many copies lack these two haphazardly inserted elements, the Richard Manney copy (Sotheby's NY 1991) and presentation copy of Pierpont Morgan Library, rebound in half blue morocco over blue cloth, spines ruled and lettered gilt, top edges gilt, marbled endpapers, 2 previous owner's bookplates to each volume, old bookseller description tipped in to front free endpaper volume I, some light foxing to blanks and half titles of each volume, also some light foxing to fore-edge of text block, bit of light marginal soiling, overall very nice, housed in slipcase.   Heritage Book Shop   Holiday Catalogue 2012 - 20   2013 $35,000

Bronte, Charlotte 1816-1855 *Villette.* London: Smith, Elder and Co., 1853. First edition, 3 volumes, 12 page catalog (Jan. 1853) volume I, colophon leaf volume III, pale yellow endpapers, small marginal tear to pages 209.210 volume 1, and pages 79/80 and 196 volume II, original dark brown cloth by Westley's and Co., boards blocked in blind, spines blocked in blind and lettered in gilt, some small expert repairs to hinges and tail of volume 1, small pencil inscription of J. J. Brigg, very good.   Jarndyce Antiquarian Booksellers   CCV - 34   2013   £380

Bronte, Emily 1818-1848 *Wuthering Heights.* New York: Limited Editions Club, 1993. First edition one of 300 copies signed by artist, this being number 249, with 15 lithographs by Balthus, folio, printed on Arches paper, publisher's full tan leather, lettered in brown on front board, spine very lightly toned, housed in full cloth felt lined clamshell, with leather spine label, about fine, publisher's newsletter laid in.   Heritage Book Shop   Holiday Catalogue 2012 - 21   2013 $6000

Bronte, The Sisters *Life and Works of Charlotte Bronte and her sisters.* London: Smith, Elder & Co., 1879. 7 volumes, 8vo. contemporary half morocco, gilt panelled spines, marbled boards and edges, some rubbing to corners and head and tail of spines.   Ken Spelman Books Ltd.   75 - 140   2013   £325

Bronte, The Sisters *The Novels of...* Edinburgh: John Grant, 1907. 12 volumes, 8vo., titlepages printed in red and black, frontispiece portraits, numerous plates throughout, dark green three quarter calf and green cloth, spine gilt in compartments, top edge gilt, by Bayntun of Bath, hinge of volume little tender, fine. Second Life Books Inc. 183 - 55 2013 $2000

Brook, Richard *A New Family Herbal; or a History and Description of all the British and Foreign Plants...* Huddersfield: printed and published by Richard Book, 1851? Fourth edition, 21 hand colored plates and two plain, little bit of soiling consistent with use, errata slip tipped in opposite page 87, 12mo., contemporary half calf, gilt ruled compartments on backstrip and lettered direct, bit rubbed, good. Blackwell's Rare Books Sciences - 19 2013 £350

Brooke-Hunt, Violet *Lord Roberts.* James Nisbet & Co., 1901. Full tree calf prize binding, frontispiece. R. F. G. Hollett & Son Children's Books - 90 2013 £45

Brooke, Frances *The Excursion, a Novel.* London: printed for T. Cadell, 1785. Second edition, rare, lightly spotted, occasional browning, 12mo., contemporary half green roan, marbled boards, spines lettered gilt and divided by gilt fillet, rubbed, backstrips darkened, bookplate of antiques dealer Stephen Pitt Hatherell Long and early ownership inscription of John Mansel, good. Blackwell's Rare Books 172 - 35 2013 £600

Brooke, Frances *Histoire de Julie Maneville; ou Lettres...* Paris: Chez Duchesne, 1764. 2 volumes, half titles, 12mo., slight paper flaw to leading blank edge of two leaves volume I, uncut and unpressed in original marbled paper wrappers, handwritten title and shelf labels on each spine, chipped at head and tail, contemporary signature B. A. Desalus and later stamps on titlepages. Jarndyce Antiquarian Booksellers CCIV - 75 2013 £250

Brooke, Henry *The Fool of Quality; or the History of Henry Earl of Moreland.* London: printed for Edward Johnston, 1777. 12mo., some offset browning on endpapers and pastedowns, paper flaw to leading edge of D1 volume IV, gatherings D & E in volume IV rather heavily foxed, contemporary full sprinkled calf, hinges cracked, slight wear to head and tail of spines, lacks all labels and volume numbers, ownership inscription of Eliza Giffard, Nerquis, Flintshire 1807. Jarndyce Antiquarian Booksellers CCIV - 76 2013 £125

Brooke, Henry *Juliet Grenville; or the History of the Human Heart.* printed for G. Robinson, 1774. First edition, lightly spotted, occasional browning, 12mo., contemporary half green roan, marbled boards, spines lettered in gilt, and divided by gilt fillet, (volume iii mistakenly labelled as volume i and vice versa), rubbed, backstrips darkened, slight wear to headcaps, bookplate of antiques dealer Stephen Pitt Hatherell Long and early ownership inscription of John Mansel, good. Blackwell's Rare Books 172 - 36 2013 £900

Brooke, Henry *Twelve Planispheres, forming a Guide to the Stars for Every Night of the Year.* Taylor & Walton, 1841. Re-issue, 12 engraved plates, folded and mounted on linen guards, slightly foxed, few smudges of ink or color, pages mounted on linen guards, 8vo., modern half calf, good. Blackwell's Rare Books Sciences - 20 2013 £450

Brooke, J. M. S. *The Transcript of the Registers of the United Parishes of S. Mary Woolnoth and S. Mary Woolchurch Haw, in the City of London...* Bowles and Son, 1886. Only 300 copies printed, Large 8vo., frontispiece, plate, rubricated throughout, very good in full contemporary red morocco bevelled boards, all edges gilt, some light rubbing, armorial bookplates of Sir George and Sir James Whitehead. Ken Spelman Books Ltd. 75 - 145 2013 £75

Brooke, Richard *Brookes' General Gazetteer Abridged.* printed for B. Law, C. Dilly, J. Johnson, G. and G. Robinson......, 1799. Small 8vo., 6 folding engraved maps, frontispiece slightly soiled, creased and with portion missing from upper outer corner with small loss to engraved surface, small 8vo., original sturdy green morocco backed marbled boards, vellum corners, worn at extremities, loss of most of vellum front corners, sound. Blackwell's Rare Books Sciences - 21 2013 £350

Brooke, Rupert 1887-1915 *Poems.* London: Sidgwick & Jackson, 1911. First edition, minimal faint foxing to prelims, pages viii, 88, foolscap 8vo., original dark blue cloth, printed label just touch chipped, Simon Nowell's copy with his booklabel, very good. Blackwell's Rare Books B174 - 178 2013 £550

Brooke, Rupert 1887-1915 *Rugby School Prize Compositions 1905.* Rugby: printed by A. J. Lawrence printer to the school, 1905. First edition, 8vo., original blue wrappers, pages loose, otherwise excellent copy, author's own copy signed by him below his winning entry, cover bears his further holograph. Maggs Bros. Ltd. 1460 - 142 2013 £3500

Brooks, Douglas S. *The Oakland Waterfront 1850-1940.* Berkeley: John F. Kennedy University, 1983. First edition, quarto, printed on rectos only, frontispiece, 45 mounted photos, maps, very fine. Argonaut Book Shop Summer 2013 - 30 2013 $75

Brooks, George Alexander *Peerless Laymen in the African Methodist Episcopal Zion Church Volume I.* State College: Hines Printing Co., 1974. First edition, gray cloth, 148 pages, photos, slight soiling, just about fine, issued without dust jacket. Between the Covers Rare Books, Inc. 165 - 89   2013 $225

Brooks, Gwendolyn *(Contributor) Meine Dunklen Hande: Moderen Negerlyrik... (My Dark Hands: Contemporary Negro Poetry).* Munchen: Nymphenburger Verlagshandlng, 1953. Second edition, text in English and German, boards little bowed, pages 50-51 little offset from publisher's response card, else near fine in near fine dust jacket, with letter laid in to Gwendolyn Brooks (whose poems are included in anthology). Between the Covers Rare Books, Inc. 165 - 91   2013 $125

Brooks, Gwendolyn *The Tiger Who Wore White Gloves of What You are You Are.* Chicago: Third World Press, 1974. Second printing, illustrations by Timothy Jones, oblong small quarto, stapled wrappers, trifle rubbed, else fine, inscribed by author. Between the Covers Rare Books, Inc.   165 - 106   2013 $100

Brooks, J. Barlow *Lancashire Bred.* Oxford: privately published, n.d. c., 1942-1951. First edition, 2 volumes, original blue cloth gilt, 4 illustrations in volume 2.   R. F. G. Hollett & Son   Wesleyan Methodism - 3   2013   £35

Brooks, Walter *Freddy and Simon the Dictator.* New York: Knopf, 1956. Stated first edition, 8vo., cloth, fine in frayed dust jacket with some neat mends, illustrations in black and white by Kurt Wiese, nice, very uncommon. Aleph-Bet Books, Inc.   104 - 89   2013 $375

Brooks, Walter R. *New York: an Intimate Guide.* New York: Alfred A. Knopf, 1931. First edition, just about fine, lacking dust jacket, very uncommon. Between the Covers Rare Books, Inc.   New York City - 286256   2013 $150

Broom, Walter William *Abraham Lincoln's Character.* New York: Macmillan, 1906. First edition, 2nd printing, titlepage tipped in, 8vo., original slate blue vertically ribbed cloth (little faded), stamped in white, gold and blue-black, 8 color plates by Charles Livingston Bull (including frontispiece),.   Howard S. Mott Inc.   262 - 91   2013 $100

Brotherton, I. N. *"Jack" Annals of Stanislaus County - River Towns and Ferries.* Santa Cruz: Western Tanager Press, 1982. First edition, quarto, photos, maps, brick cloth lettered in white, very fine with pictorial dust jacket. Argonaut Book Shop   Summer 2013 - 31   2013 $60

Brotherton, I. N. *Twenty Years The History of Estanislao Chapter No. 58, Ancient and Honorable Order of E. Clampus Vitus 1958-1978.* Modesto: Southern Mines Press, 1979. First edition, limited edition, very scarce, quarto, numerous photos, map, stiff red wrappers printed in black, fine.   Argonaut Book Shop   Summer 2013 - 90   2013 $150

Brough, John Cargill *The Fairy Tales of Science.* Griffith and Farran, 1866. Second edition, small 8vo., original blue cloth, gilt, hinges rather worn, all edges gilt, 16 woodcut plates by Charles H. Bennett.   R. F. G. Hollett & Son Children's Books - 91   2013   £130

Brough, Robert B. *The Life of Sir John Falstaff.* London: Longman, Brown, Green, Longmans and Roberts, 1858. First edition in book form, pages xx, 196 + 20 etched plates, including frontispiece and 1 in text illustration, tall 8vo., full crushed blue morocco (original pictorial gilt cloth, front cover bound in), upper and lower covers ruled, spine and dentelles elaborately gilt, raised bands by Stikeman & Co., cloth slipcase.   Howard S. Mott Inc.   262 - 19   2013 $275

Brougham and Vaux, Henry Peter Brougham, 1st Baron 1778-1868 *Extract of the Review of Lord Byron's Hours of Idleness, from the Edinburgh Review No. XXII.* London: printed for Wilton & Son, 1820. Some spotting, contemporary half dark blue calf, gilt spine, spine little dulled and slightly rubbed at head and tail, bookplates of Gilbert Compton Elliot & Alex Bridge, all edges gilt, nice, scarce. Jarndyce Antiquarian Booksellers   CCIII - 115   2013   £450

Broughton, Rhoda *Dear Faustina.* London: Richard Bentley and Son, 1897. First edition, original cloth with blindstamped design to front and rear covers and gilt title and author to spine, very good plus with slight bumping to corners, interior very good, few small brown spots to fore edge and light offsetting to front free endpaper, 400 pages, plus 31 pages of ads.   The Kelmscott Bookshop   7 - 98   2013 $250

Brower, David *Manual of Ski Mountaineering.* San Francisco: Sierra Club, 1962. Third edition, small octavo, photos and drawings, blue pictorial cloth stamped in silver, very fine with pictorial dust jacket.   Argonaut Book Shop Recent Acquisitions June 2013 - 42   2013 $60

Brown-Sequard, Charles Edouard *Course of Lectures of the Physiology and Pathology of the Central Nervous System Delivered at the Royal College of Surgeons of England in May 1858.* Philadelphia: Collins, 1860. 276 pages, 3 engraved plates, original boards, recently rebacked.   James Tait Goodrich   S74 - 39   2013 $1295

Brown-Sequard, Charles Edouard *Notice sur les Travaux Originancx...* Paris: Victor Masson et Fils, 1863. First edition, 8vo., lightly foxed, original printed wrappers, soiled, extremities rubbed, inscribed by author for Dr. Percival Wright, very good. Jeff Weber Rare Books 172 - 44 2013 $800

The Brown American November 1936. Philadelphia: Research Institute of the Bureau on Negro Affiars, 1936. Volume I number 6, stapled photographic wrappers, illustrations in sepia from photos, front wrapper nearly detached, light dampstain to upper right hand margin throughout, presentable, good copy. Between the Covers Rare Books, Inc. 165 - 267 2013 $125

Brown, A. Gordon *South African Heritage.* Cape Town & Pretoria: 1965. Large 8vo., original boards, gilt, dust jacket, edges little chipped and creased, illustrations in color and tints. R. F. G. Hollett & Son Africana - 169 2013 £25

Brown, A. Gordon *South and East African Year Book & Guide.* London: Sampson Low Marston & Co., 1947. Thick 8vo., original pictorial cloth with rounded corners, small white shelf numbers to foot of spine, colored maps, excellent copy, ex-libris of Brendan Viscount Bracken of Christchurch. R. F. G. Hollett & Son Africana - 170 2013 £65

Brown, Abbie Farwell *The Lonesomest Doll.* New York: Houghton Mifflin, 1928. First edition, illustrations by Arthur Rackham, octavo, titlepage, frontispiece and 2 full page illustrations in rose and greenish-blue, 26 black and white drawings by Arthur Rackham, original tan pictorially stamped cloth, remarkably fresh, clean and exceptionally fine, text printed on poor and brittle paper. David Brass Rare Books, Inc. Holiday 2012 Chapter One - DB 01580 2013 $1450

Brown, Christy *Down all the Days.* London: Secker & Warburg, 1970. First edition, 8vo., original maroon cloth, dust jacket price clipped, little worn at extremities, otherwise very good, pasted on front free endpaper is slip of paper bearing author's signature. Maggs Bros. Ltd. 1442 - 33 2013 £150

Brown, Christy *My Left Foot.* London: Secker & Warburg, 1954. First edition, 8vo., original maroon cloth, dust jacket, excellent copy in dust jacket, little chipped at head and tail of spine, inscribed by author for Ismay Philips 30/5/56 and inscribed below this by his mother Bridget Brown, half title and rear endpaper contain 31 signatures of unknown personages. Maggs Bros. Ltd. 1460 - 144 2013 £275

Brown, Christy *Of Snails and Skylarks.* London: Secker & Warburg, 1977. First edition, original brown cloth, excellent copy in dust jacket, chipped and rubbed, inscribed by author for friend Harris Weston Jan. 1978, tipped in is TLS from author to same, recipient's bookplate. Maggs Bros. Ltd. 1460 - 145 2013 £350

Brown, Dan *The Da Vinci Code.* New York: Doubleday, 2003. First edition, first issue with 'skitoma' on page 243, line 25, very fine in dust jacket. Mordida Books 81 - 49 2013 $400

Brown, Fred H. *One Dollar's Worth.* Chicago: Fred H. Brown, 1893. octavo, flyleaf at front, inserted frontispiece plus numerous vignette drawings, original black cloth, front and spine panels stamped in silver. L. W. Currey, Inc. Fall Sampler Sept. 2013 - 146184 2013 $750

Brown, Fredric *The Case of the Dancing Sandwiches.* New York: E. P. Dutton, 1949. First edition, paperback original, little darkening to pages, very slight wear, near fine in wrappers, uncommon, especially in this condition. Between the Covers Rare Books, Inc. Mystery & Detective Fiction - 92463 2013 $375

Brown, Fredric *The Far Cry.* New York: Dutton, 1951. First edition, fine in dust jacket with tiny rub at base of spine, exceptional copy. Mordida Books 81 - 50 2013 $400

Brown, Fredric *The Freak Show Murders.* Belen: Dennis McMillan, 1985. First edition, one of 350 numbered copies signed by author of introduction, Richard Lupoff, very fine in dust jacket. Mordida Books 81 - 53 2013 $150

Brown, Fredric *Knock Three-One-Two.* New York: Dutton, 1959. First edition, very fine in dust jacket. Mordida Books 81 - 52 2013 $400

Brown, Fredric *The Office.* New York: Dutton, 1958. First edition, fine in dust jacket with some slight spine fading. Mordida Books 81 - 51 2013 $250

Brown, Fredric *Space on My Hands.* Chicago: Shasta, 1951. First edition, trifle foxd on endpaper, else fine in lightly rubbed and spine tanned, very good dust jacket, signed by author. Between the Covers Rare Books, Inc. Sci-Fi, Fantasy & Horror - 88803 2013 $400

Brown, Fredric *The Wench is Dead.* New York: Dutton, 1955. First edition, small tape shadow on each pastedown, else near fine in attractive, very good or better dust jacket with faint stain to bottom of front flap and some subtle rubbing at bottom of front panel. Between the Covers Rare Books, Inc. Mystery & Detective Fiction - 46672 2013 $315

Brown, George H. *On Foot Round Settle.* Settle: J. W. Lambert, 1896. 8vo., 246 pages, half title, folding map, 8 plates, good copy in original dark blue gilt lettered cloth, slight wear to head and tail of spine, some underlining to one page, tear to map without loss.   Ken Spelman Books Ltd.   73 - 158   2013   £25

Brown, Henry McLauren *Mineral King Country: Visalia to Mount Whitney.* Fresno: Pioneer Pub. Co., 1988. First edition, signed by author, oblong octavo, photos, maps, reproductions, dark green leatherette gilt, very fine.   Argonaut Book Shop   Recent Acquisitions June 2013 - 45   2013 $60

Brown, Isaac Baker *On the Curability of Certain Forms of Insanity, Epilepsy, Catalepsy and Hysteria in Females.* London: Robert Hardwicke, 1866. 8vo., 20th century half navy blue morocco over marbled boards, marbled endpapers, spine lettered vertically gilt, very slightly rubbed at corners.   Unsworths Antiquarian Booksellers   28 - 150   2013   £300

Brown, J. *Tourist Rambles in the Northern and Midland Counties. Second Series.* London: Simpkin, Marhsall and Co. and York: J. Sampson and E. H. Pickering, 1885. Deluxe edition with additional plates, original green cloth gilt extra by Potter & Son of York, little rubbed and marked in places, all edges gilt, 7 photo plates, scattered spots to prelims, scarce.   R. F. G. Hollett & Son   Lake District & Cumbria - 185   2013   £150

Brown, J. H. *Spectropia; or, Surprising Spectral Illusions.* Griffith and Farran and Hl & C. Treacher, Brighton, 1865. Fourth edition, 6 diagrams in text, 16 plates, all but 3 hand colored, hint of foxing page 11, 4to., original cloth backed pictorial boards, slightly worn, good.   Blackwell's Rare Books   Sciences - 22   2013   £500

Brown, J. Walter *Carlisle. Three Acts.* Carlisle: Charles Thurnam, 1904-1912. 3 tracts, original cloth gilt, trifle rubbed, folding town plan, plate and 2 pages of music, original wrappers bound in.   R. F. G. Hollett & Son   Lake District & Cumbria - 186   2013   £45

Brown, J. Walter *Round Carlisle Cross.* Carlisle: Cumberland News, 1951. First edition, 9 volumes, original cloth, gilt, little marked, dust jacket rather creased and chipped, 9 plates.   R. F. G. Hollett & Son   Lake District & Cumbria - 187   2013   £30

Brown, John *An Estimate of the Manners and Principles of the Times.* London: printed for L. Davis and C. Reymers, Printers to the Royal Society, 1757. 8vo., pages 221, iii), some foxing in places, 19th century marbled paper boards, later backed to sheep, front board lightly scuffed.   Unsworths Antiquarian Booksellers   28 - 76   2013   £95

Brown, John *Testimonies of Capt. John Brown at Harper's Ferry, with his address to the Court (cover title).* New York: American Anti-Slavery Society, 1860. First edition, 8vo., self wrappers, stitched as issued, 16 pages, wrappers slightly browned, fine.   The Brick Row Book Shop   Miscellany Fifty-Nine - 2   2013 $400

Brown, John Henry *Early Days of San Francisco, California.* Oakland: Biobooks, 1949. Limited to 500 copies, color plate, folding map and index, two-tone cloth, spine label, very fine.   Argonaut Book Shop   Summer 2013 - 33   2013 $50

Brown, John Henry *Reminiscences and Incidents of Early Days of San Francisco (1845-1850).* San Francisco: Grabhorn Press, 1933. Reprint of 1886 first edition, chapter heading illustrations, folding map in rear, tan cloth spine, marbled boards, printed paper labels, very fine.   Argonaut Book Shop   Summer 2013 - 32   2013 $125

Brown, Leslie *Birds of the African Bush.* Collins, 1975. First edition, folio, original leather effect green cloth, gilt, dust jacket creased tear and few small nicks to foot of upper panel, unpaginated, 14 full page color plates and numerous other illustrations.   R. F. G. Hollett & Son   Africana - 66   2013   £45

Brown, Leslie *Birds of the African Waterside.* Collins, 1979. First edition, folio, original cloth, gilt, dust jacket, unpaginated, 24 full page color plates and numerous other illustrations, endpapers little spotted.   R. F. G. Hollett & Son   Africana - 67   2013   £30

Brown, Lloyd *The Story of Maps.* Boston: Little Brown and Co., 1949. First edition, 82 maps and diagrams, green cloth decorated in red, lettered gilt, slight rubbing to spine ends, fine with pictorial dust jacket (quite worn, protected with acetate).   Argonaut Book Shop   Recent Acquisitions June 2013 - 46   2013 $75

Brown, Marcia *Once a Mouse.* New York: Charles Scribner's Sons, 1961. Squarish 4to., durable pictorial cloth, fine in dust jacket (no medal, price intact), color woodcuts, scarce, this copy inscribed by author.   Aleph-Bet Books, Inc.   104 - 90   2013 $1500

Brown, Margaret Wise *A Child's Good Night Book.* New York: Scott, 1950. First edition thus, 4to., pictorial boards, fine in dust jacket (mild rubbing and slight fraying at spine ends, otherwise very good+), illustrations by Jean Charlot.   Aleph-Bet Books, Inc.   105 - 95   2013 $650

Brown, Margaret Wise *Little Chicken.* New York: Harper Bros., 1943. 10-43 I-S. Stated first edition, oblong 8vo., cloth, 2 faint, small brown marks on endpapers, else fine in dust jacket, lovely color illustrations by Leonard Weisgard, rare in first edition with jacket.   Aleph-Bet Books, Inc.   105 - 96   2013 $850

Brown, Margaret Wise *The Little Cowboy.* New York: William Scott, 1948. First edition, 4to., pictorial boards, fine in dust jacket with few closed tears and spine chip, really very nice, illustrations in color by Slobodkina. Aleph-Bet Books, Inc. 104 - 92 2013 $400

Brown, Margaret Wise *The Little Fireman.* New York: William Scott, 1946. First edition thus, 4to., pictorial boards, faint foxing on cover, else near fine in nice dust jacket with 3 closed tears and light soil, illustrations by Esphyr Slobodkina. Aleph-Bet Books, Inc. 105 - 97 2013 $425

Brown, Margaret Wise *Little Fur Family.* New York: Harper Bros., 1946. First edition, 16mo., bound in real fur, complete with pictorial box with circular cut-out in bear's stomach through which fur protrudes, book fine, box lightly browned with some mends and rubbing, illustrations by Garth Williams with full and partial page color illustrations. Aleph-Bet Books, Inc. 104 - 93 2013 $1000

Brown, Margaret Wise *Pussycat's Christmas.* New York: Thomas Crowell, 1949. First edition, square small 4to., cloth, fine in dust jacket, jacket very good, not price clipped, few chips, lovely full page and smaller color lithographs by Helen Stone, scarce. Aleph-Bet Books, Inc. 104 - 94 2013 $375

Brown, Margaret Wise *Red Light Green Light.* New York: Doubleday and Co., 1944. Stated first edition, oblong 4to., cloth backed pictorial boards, fine in very good+ dust jacket with 2 closed edge tears, illustrations in color on every page by Leonard Weisgard, extremely scarce. Aleph-Bet Books, Inc. 105 - 98 2013 $650

Brown, Margaret Wise *Where Have You Been?* New York: Crowell, 1952. First edition, oblong 16mo., cloth fine in price clipped dust jacket, illustrations by Barbara Cooney with delicately detailed and charming black and red illustrations, quite scarce. Aleph-Bet Books, Inc. 105 - 99 2013 $600

Brown, Mark H. *Before Barbed Wire. L. A. Huffman, Photographer on Horseback.* New York: Henry Holt and Co., 1956. First edition, quarto, 124 photos, endpaper map, black cloth stamped in green, fine, lightly rubbed pictorial dust jacket. Argonaut Book Shop Recent Acquisitions June 2013 - 47 2013 $80

Brown, Mark H. *The Frontier Years: L. A. Huffman, Photographer of the Plains.* New York: Henry Holt, 1955. First edition, 4to., 272 pages, 125 photos, endpaper map, fine, slightly chipped dust jacket. Argonaut Book Shop Recent Acquisitions June 2013 - 48 2013 $80

Brown, Mattye Jeanette *The Reign of Terror.* New York: Vantage Press, 1962. First edition, pages browned, else fine in very good plus dust jacket with modest triangular chip on front panel. Between the Covers Rare Books, Inc. 165 - 93 2013 $100

Brown, Palmer *Cheerful.* New York: Harper Bros., 1957. First edition, 12mo., plain cloth, fine in dust jacket with small chip at base of spine, exquisite color and line drawings, this copy signed by Brown with small sketch, very scarce, especially signed. Aleph-Bet Books, Inc. 105 - 100 2013 $475

Brown, Paul *Draw Horses: It's Fun and It's Easy.* New York: Charles Scribner's Sons, 1949. First edition, printed paper covered boards, fine in very good or better dust jacket with small chips and tears. Between the Covers Rare Books, Inc. Horses, Horsemanship, Horse Racing, Etc. - 291518 2013 $150

Brown, Q. E., Mrs. *God and the Rising Negro.* N.P.: Mrs. Q. E. Brown, 1960. First edition, wire stitched text block bound into black faux morocco wrappers printed in silver, 140, (4) pages, couple of creases on wrappers, very good or better. Between the Covers Rare Books, Inc. 165 - 21 2013 $650

Brown, R. P. *Edward Wilson of Nether Levens (1557-1653) and his Kin.* Kendal: Titus Wilson, 1930. Original printed wrappers, 7 folding or extending pedigrees. R. F. G. Hollett & Son Lake District & Cumbria - 193 2013 £45

Brown, Robert "Remarks on the Structure and Affinities of Cephalotus." in *The London, Edinburgh and Dublin Philosophical Magazine and Journal of Science Third Series volume 1 No. 4, October 1832.* Entire issue, unopened, original printed wrappers, 2 small stains near top of spine, otherwise fine. Blackwell's Rare Books Sciences - 22 2013 £400

Brown, Robert *The Story of Africa.* Cassell, 1892-1895. 4 volumes in 2, 4to., modern cloth with paper spine labels, illustrations, text in double columns, excellent set. R. F. G. Hollett & Son Africana - 27 2013 £125

Brown, Stephen J. *Ireland in Fiction.* IUP, 1959. 8vo., cloth, very good. C. P. Hyland 261 - 156 2013 £40

Brown, Stephen J. *Poetry of Irish History.* New York: Stokes, 1927. 8vo., ex-public library, rebound, good. C. P. Hyland 261 - 157 2013 £35

Brown, Sterling *The Negro in American Fiction.* Washington: Associates in Negro Folk Education, 1937. First edition, wrapper issue, 209 pages, very top of the paper at crown lacking, else near fine, inscribed by author for Stanton Wormley, who was president of Howard University.   Between the Covers Rare Books, Inc.   165 - 27   2013 $650

Brown, Thomas *Lectures on the Philosophy of the Human Mind.* Philadelphia: John Grigg, 1824.   3 volumes, fully bound in brown leather with gilt stamped spines, very good- with some boards rubbed and marked.   Beasley Books 2013 - 2013 $100

Brown, Thomas *The Paradise of Coquettes, a Poem.* Edinburgh: printed by George Ramsay & Co. for Archibald Constable & co., 1817.   Second edition, half title, final ad leaf, uncut in blue boards, spine chipped at head and tail, hinges and corners worn, Renier booklabel, good, solid copy.   Jarndyce Antiquarian Booksellers   CCIII - 648 2013   £40

Brown, Virginia *Catalogus Translationum et Commentariorum: Mediaeval and Renaissance.* Washington: Catholic University of America Press, 1992. 8vo., gilt stamped black buckram, Burndy Library bookplate, fine.   Jeff Weber Rare Books   171 - 52   2013 $60

Brown, Walter C. *Laughing Death.* Philadelphia: J. B. Lippincott, 1932.   First edition, fine in attractive near fine dust jacket with discreet creased tear at edge of crown. Between the Covers Rare Books, Inc.   Mystery & Detective Fiction - 277218   2013 $275

Brown, William Wells *A Lecture Delivered before the Female Anti-Slavery Society of Salem at Lyceum Hall Nov. 14 1847.* Boston: Anti-Slavery Society, 1847.   First edition, 16mo., 22 pages, sewn, original self wrappers soiled, very good.   M & S Rare Books, Inc.   95 - 39   2013 $1750

Browne, A. D. *A Pictorial History of the Queen's College of Saint Margaret and Saint Bernard Commonly Called Queens' College Cambridge 1448-1948.*   printed for the College, 1951.   One of 750 copies, 24 pages, frontispiece, 137 plates and plan, very good, folio half morocco, raised bands, gilt lettered spine, top edge gilt, corners little bumped, bookplate.   Ken Spelman Books Ltd.   75 - 179 2013   £95

Browne, Howard *Warrior of the Dawn.* Chicago: Reilly & Lee, 1943.   First edition, attractive bookplate, else fine in very good dust jacket with small chips and tears at extremities, inscribed by author at an alter date, very uncommon signed.   Between the Covers Rare Books, Inc.   Sci-Fi, Fantasy & Horror - 37198   2013 $157

Browne, Janet *Charles Darwin Voyaging Volume I. of a Biography.*   New York: Alfred A. Knopf, 1995.   First edition, thick 8vo., frontispiece, quarter gilt stamped gold cloth over gilt stamped yellow paper backed boards, dust jacket with small nick to corner, otherwise fine.   Jeff Weber Rare Books   169 - 87   2013 $200

Browne, John Ross   1821-1875   *Relacion de los Debates de la Convecuib de California, Sobre la Formacion de la Constitucion de Estado en Setiembre y Octubre de 1849.* Nueva York: Imprenta de S. W. Benedict, 1851.   First edition, Spanish issue, publisher's blindstamped brown cloth, gilt, portion of front free endpaper lacking, but exceptionally clean, without normal foxing.   Argonaut Book Shop Recent Acquisitions June 2013 - 49   2013 $750

Browne, Thomas   1605-1682   *Pseudodoxia Epidemica...* London: Miller, 1650.   Second edition, small folio in fours, contemporary English paneled calf, later rebacking in calf with renewed endpapers, top front corner repaired, title laid down and rather marked, last blank with some contemporary calculations in brown ink, errata correct in early hand, occasional foxing and marginal marking, page numbers of page 266 and page 271 transposed which is typical, leaves Qq2 and Qq3 transposed, good overall, from the library of Alfred W. Franklin, co-founder of Osler Club.   James Tait Goodrich   S74 - 36   2013 $1295

Browne, Thomas   1605-1682   *Religio Medici.*   London: Andrew Crooke, 1642.   Engraved frontispiece, 159 pages, upper inner corner of titlepage repaired, few catchwords cropped, tiny repaired worm track in last gathering affecting few letters, rich, modern crushed morocco, all edges gilt, protective quarter calf slipcase, rare.   James Tait Goodrich 75 - 37   2013 $7500

Browne, Thomas   1605-1682   *Urne Buriall and the Garden of Cyrus.*   Cassell, 1932.   212/215 copies printed on Barcham Green handmade paper, 32 stencilled collotypes, by Paul Nash, small folio original cream vellum by Sangorski & Sutcliffe, backstrip gilt lettered, large dark brown crushed morocco, front cover inlay incorporating a Design by Paul Nash comprising two cream vellum inlays and interrelated gilt urn and lattice work design, rear cover repeating gilt front cover urn and lattice-work design and incorporates two dark brown crushed morocco inlays, gilt edges, brown cloth, slipcase, fine.   Blackwell's Rare Books 172 - 222   2013   £6000

Browning, Elizabeth Barrett 1806-1861 *Aurora Leigh.* London: Chapman and Hall, 1859. Fourth edition, presentation copy from author to William Allingham, dated Paris October 1858 on slip of paper glued to verso of titlepage, Allingham's pencil notes on about 15 pages, mostly detailing differences between text and that of 1857 first edition, original green cloth with blindstamp design to covers and gilt title and author to spine, spine ends and corners bumped and spine faded, otherwise very good, interior pages clean except for some foxing and offsetting to front endpaper, very good, 403 pages.   The Kelmscott Bookshop 7 - 88 2013 $3850

Browning, Elizabeth Barrett 1806-1861 *He Giveth His Beloved Sleep.* Boston: Lee and Shepard, 1880. First edition, small 4to., green cloth backed boards, very good, small torn, black and white illustrations, color cover illustration by Maud Humphrey, truley scarce, all edges gilt. Barnaby Rudge Booksellers Poetry 2013 - 021140   2013 $125

Browning, Elizabeth Barrett 1806-1861 *Poems.* London: Chapman & Hall, 1862. Fifth edition, original blue wavy grain cloth, spines slightly faded unevenly, but nice set, slightly later pencil inscription.   Jarndyce Antiquarian Booksellers CCV - 36 2013 £125

Browning, Elizabeth Barrett 1806-1861 *The Seraphim and Other Poems.* London: Saunders & Otley, 1838. First edition, 8vo., original embossed brown cloth, spine lettered and decorated in gilt, slightly worn at head of spine and rubbed overall, otherwise excellent copy in protective slipcase lettered gilt on spine at edges, near fine in slightly rubbed dust jacket, inscribed by author to her governess Mrs. Orme.   Maggs Bros. Ltd. 1460 - 147 2013 £3000

Browning, Elizabeth Barrett 1806-1861 *Sonnets from the Portuguese.* New York: printed at the Club's Printing Office, 1948. 60/1500 copies, signed by artist, large capital to each sonnet printed in gold with surrounding decoration to each initial printed in blue and red, all to design by Valenti Angelo, folio, original blue canvas, faded backstrip gilt lettered, Browning's initials gilt blocked on front cover, matching canvas slipcase with some fading, good. Blackwell's Rare Books B174 - 360 2013 £50

Browning, Robert 1812-1889 *The Pied Piper of Hamelin.* Harry Quilter, 1898. First edition, small folio, original green decorated cloth gilt, edges little rubbed, 28 leaves interleaved with tissues, printed throughout in fine and intricate detail, illustrations by Harry Quilter. R. F. G. Hollett & Son Children's Books - 491 2013 £150

Browning, Robert 1812-1889 *The Pied Piper of Hamelin.* SPCK, n.d. circa, 1910. First edition, small folio, original cloth backed pictorial boards, edges little worn, illustrations in color, trifle loose, but very good, clean copy, scarce. R. F. G. Hollett & Son Children's Books - 624 2013 £150

Browning, Robert 1812-1889 *Pied Piper of Hamelin.* Chicago: Whitman, 1927. 4to., maroon gilt cloth, pictorial paste-on, very fine in pictorial dust jacket and original pictorial publisher's box (flap repaired), color illustrations on nearly every page, outstanding copy rare in wrapper and box.   Aleph-Bet Books, Inc. 104 - 95 2013 $350

Browning, Robert 1812-1889 *Pied Piper of Hamelin.* New York: Macmillan, Aug., 1927. First edition, square small 8vo., pictorial boards, owner inscription on copyright page, else fine in lightly soiled and frayed dust jacket, beautifully illustrated in bold colors by G. M. Richards.   Aleph-Bet Books, Inc. 104 - 96 2013 $275

Browning, Robert 1812-1889 *Poems.* London: Chapman & Hall, 1849. New edition, 8vo., original brown bevelled cloth, inscribed by author for Frederic Leighton Aug. 2 56, with Leighton's distinctive bookplate by Robert Anning Bell, worn at extremities, otherwise excellent set in quarter blue leather slipcase, lettered in gilt.   Maggs Bros. Ltd. 1460 - 146 2013 £3000

Browning, Robert 1812-1889 *Poems.* London: George Bell & sons, 1904. 205 x 138mm., excellent contemporary brick red crushed morocco for Hatchards of Piccadily (stamp signed), covers with unusual asymmetrical frame combining geometrical gilt rules with twisting black strapwork, central panel with two interlocked circles, one containing a "V", the other and "S", and both surmounted by a coronet, raised bands, spine with simple gilt ruled compartments, turn-ins with gilt fillets, marbled endpapers, top edge gilt, numerous head and tailpieces, vignettes in text, 21 full page wood engravings by Byram Shaw; bookplate of Victoria Sackville-West, black and white photo of Browning tipped onto verso of front free endpaper, labelled apparently in Lady Sackville's hand, slight wear to joints, just breath of foxing in couple of places, otherwise fresh and clean, inside and out. Phillip J. Pirages 63 - 412 2013 $550

Browning, Robert 1812-1889 *The Poetical Works.* London: Smith, Elder & Co., 1888-1894. First complete edition, one of 250 copies on handmade paper, 17 volumes, 235 x 159mm, excellent contemporary purple morocco (stamped "Knickerbocker Press" on rear turn-in), front covers with flourish or gilt monogram (perhaps "G") at center, wide raised bands, spine panels with gilt titling, very broad turn-ins with simple gilt ruling, violet watered silk pastedowns and free endleaves, morocco hinges, edges untrimmed and all but 3 volumes unopened, frontispiece in five volumes, large paper copy, spines uniformly faded to pleasing chestnut brown, shadow of a silk place marker on two pages, otherwise extremely fine set with almost no wear to bindings, text nearly pristine.   Phillip J. Pirages 61 - 96 2013 $3600

Browning, Robert 1812-1889 *The Ring and the Book.* London: Smith Elder, 1868-1869. First edition, 4 volumes, 8vo., occasional light scattered foxing to free endleaves, original black stamped green cloth, gilt stamped spines by Harrison in quarter gilt stamped calf over blue cloth slipcase, volume 3 rear hinge cracked with light front pastedown soiling, volumes 1 and 2 hinges cracked, Robert Browning's signature tipped in volume I opposite titlepage, ownership signatures of W. J. Settle, Sherborne, Dorset Feb. 21 1869 and F. Rowlandson, ownership signatures of E. M. Forster volume 2, attractive, very good copy.   Jeff Weber Rare Books   171 - 53   2013 $4000

Browning, Robert 1812-1889 *Some Poems by Robert Browning.* Ergany Press, 1904. One of 215 copies on paper (an additional 11 copies printed on vellum), 210 x 134mm., 64 pages, (3) leaves, lovey wood engraved color frontispiece, large decorative initials and device at end, all by Lucien and Esther Pissarro, very fine handsomely gilt and inlaid cordovan crushed morocco by Zaehnsdorf (signed on front turn-in), covers ruled in gilt, inlaid olive green morocco frame decorated with gilt scrolling foliation and inlaid pink morocco roses, raised bands, spine compartments similarly decorated with gilt and inlays, turn-ins gilt with inner toothed roll, ruled borders and foliation, top edge gilt, original paper covers bound in rear, bookplate of John Whiting Friel and Helen Otillie Friel, area under frontispiece with ink inscription dated 1905, now very faded (presumably after an attempt to wash it out?), printed in black and red, very few leaves with quite minor foxing but (setting aside inscription on frontispiece), very fine in splendid binding, especially fresh, bright inside and out.   Phillip J. Pirages   61 - 130   2013 $3500

Bruccoli, Matthew J. *Kenneth Millar/Ross MacDonald: a Checklist.* Detroit: Gale Research, 1971. First edition, very fine, without dust jacket as issued.   Mordida Books   81 - 342   2013 $90

Bruccoli, Matthew J. *Ross MacDonald: a Bibliography.* Pittsburgh: University of Pittsburg, 1983. First edition, very fine, without dust jacket as issued.   Mordida Books   81 - 346   2013 $100

Bruce, J. Collingwood *Handbook to the Roman Wall.* Newcastle upon Tyne: Andrew Reid & Co., 1957. Eleventh edition, original cloth, dust jacket, numerous illustrations and 12 maps, ex-libris of Leonard Cottrell on flyleaf.   R. F. G. Hollett & Son   Lake District & Cumbria - 196   2013   £25

Bruce, Robert *Custer's Last Battle.* New York: 1927. 40 pages, maps and illustrations, original printed wrappers, large magazine format, slight wear and soil to wrappers, else fine, signature of Elizabeth Bacon Custer.   Dumont Maps & Books of the West   124 - 50   2013 $125

Bruchac, Joseph *Translator's Son.* Merrick: Cross Cultural Communications, 1980. First edition, inscribed by author to his parents, fine in wrappers.   Ken Lopez Bookseller   159 - 147   2013 $250

Bruele, Gualtherus *Praxis Medicinae; or the Physicians Practice.* London: printed by John Norton of William Subares, 1639. Second edition, 4to., contemporary calf, rebacked, pastedowns renewed, no endpapers, title soiled and right lower portion repaired, some dampstaining affecting upper outer corners of second half, rare.   James Tait Goodrich   75 - 38   2013 $1395

Bruen, Ken *The Devil.* New York: Mysterious Bookshop, 2010. First edition, limited to 126 signed copies, this no. 88, signed by Bruen, as new in like glassine dust jacket.   By the Book, L. C.   36 - 39   2013 $115

Bruman, Pieter *Poetae Latini Minores.* Leidae: apud Conradum Wishoff et Danielem Goeduael, 1731. 2 volumes, 4to., additional engraved allegorical title to volume I, titlepages in red and intermittent light foxing, later half vellum, purple cloth covered boards, red morocco labels to spines, labels slightly chipped at edges and spines, slightly grubby, boards little rubbed, 'Toehampton' and library codes handwritten on prelim blank of each volume, small red inkstamp reading 'Athenaeum Library Duplicate' to each titlepage, crossed through in volume i.   Unsworths Antiquarian Booksellers   28 - 23   2013   £450

Brundell, Barry *Pierre Gassendi: from Aristotelianism to a New Natural Philosophy.* Dordrecht, et al: D. Reidel Pub., 1987. 8vo., blue cloth, gilt stamped spine title, dust jacket, ownership signature, fine.   Jeff Weber Rare Books   169 - 153   2013 $95

Bruner, Charlotte H. *Reverberations: Black Poets There and Here.* Ames: Iowa State Univ. Research Foundation, 1977. First edition, perfectbound illustrated wrappers, little wear to edges of wrappers, very good or better, nicely inscribed by editor Charlotte H. Bruner, scarce.   Between the Covers Rare Books, Inc.   165 - 49   2013 $125

Brunhammer, Yvonne *Andre Arbus. Architecte-Decorateur des Annees 40.* Paris: Editions Norma, 1996. First edition, 399 pages, color and black and white plates, 4to., blind embossed maroon morocco, gilt spine letters, silk bookmark, faint rubbing to rear board, else fine in original raw cardboard slipcase.   Kaaterskill Books   16 - 9   2013 $500

Brunhoff, Jean De 1899-1937 *Le Roi Babar.* Paris: Jardins des Modes/Conde Nast, 1933. First edition, folio, cloth backed pictorial boards, slight bit of cover scratching, else very good+, color illustrations.   Aleph-Bet Books, Inc.   104 - 142   2013 $700

Brunhoff, Jean De 1899-1937 *The Story of Babar, the Little Elephant.* London: Methuen, 1939. Fourth UK edition, folio, original cloth backed pictorial boards, edges and corners little worn, illustrations in color, few scattered marks, but very good.   R. F. G. Hollett & Son   Children's Books - 159   2013   £150

Brunhoff, Jean De 1899-1937 *Les Vacances de Zephir.* Paris: Hachette, 1936. First edition, French text, numerous color printed illustrations, pages (40), folio, original pale yellow cloth backed boards illustrated overall, edges of boards lightly rubbed, just little more at corners, very good.   Blackwell's Rare Books   B174 - 179   2013   £250

Brunhoff, Jean De 1899-1937 *Le Voyage de Babar.* Paris: Jardin des Modes, 1932. First edition, folio, cloth backed pictorial boards, light cover scratching a usual, margin soil on few pages, very good+ and tight.   Aleph-Bet Books, Inc.   104 - 143   2013 $700

Brunhoff, Jean De 1899-1937 *Zephir's Holidays.* New York: Random House, 1937. First edition, folio, cloth backed pictorial boards, slight rubbing, near fine in edge frayed and chipped dust jacket, color illustrations.   Aleph-Bet Books, Inc.   104 - 144   2013 $600

Brunhoff, Laurent De *Babar and the Professor.* New York: Random House, 1957. First English language edition, small 4to., glazed pictorial boards, fine in dust jacket, wonderful color lithos.   Aleph-Bet Books, Inc.   105 - 166   2013 $200

Brunhoff, Laurent De *Babar Comes to America.* New York: Random House, 1965. First American edition, 4to., glazed pictorial boards, fine in slightly worn dust jacket, correct price and no ads for later titles, wonderful color illustrations, quite scarce.   Aleph-Bet Books, Inc.   104 - 145   2013 $400

Brunhoff, Laurent De *Babar's Cousin That Rascal Arthur.* New York: Random House, 1948. First American edition, 4to., printed paper over boards, illustrations in color name in pencil on black, imprint on rear black partially crossed out, cover scuffed at corners and ends of spine, rubbed along edges of boards, front hinge loose, otherwise good.   Second Life Books Inc.   183 - 58   2013 $125

Brunhoff, Laurent De *Babar's Museum of Art.* New York: Abrams, 2003. First edition, inscribed by Brunhoff, fine in fine dust jacket, 4to., 44 pages.   Beasley Books   2013 - 2013 $60

Brunhoff, Laurent De *Babar's Picnic.* New York: Random House, 1949. First edition, folio, cloth backed pictorial boards, near fine, color illustrations.   Aleph-Bet Books, Inc.   105 - 164   2013 $425

Brunhoff, Laurent De *Bonhome and the Huge Beast.* New York: Pantheon, 1974. First edition, first printing (correct code), 4to., pictorial boards, some natural darkening in gutters from binding glue, else very good+ in chipped dust jacket, this copy signed by author with small sketch, full page color illustrations.   Aleph-Bet Books, Inc.   104 - 146   2013 $400

Brunner, John *Double, Double.* London: Sidgwick & Jackson, 1971. First English and first hardcover edition, fine in fine dust jacket.   Between the Covers Rare Books, Inc.   Sci-Fi, Fantasy & Horror - 316138   2013 $100

Brunner, John *Stand of Zanzibar.* Garden City: Doubleday & Co., 1968. First edition, large 8vo., cloth.   L. W. Currey, Inc.   Utopian Literature: Recent Acquisitions (April 2013) - 138768   2013 $650

Brunner, John *Timescoop.* London: Sidgwick & Jackson, 1972. First English and First hardcover edition, fine in fine dust jacket, beautiful unread copy.   Between the Covers Rare Books, Inc.   Sci-Fi, Fantasy & Horror - 316531   2013 $100

Brunner, John *Total Eclipse.* Garden City: Doubleday and Co., 1975. First edition, fine in fine dust jacket and uncommon thus.   Between the Covers Rare Books, Inc.   Sci-Fi, Fantasy & Horror - 316125   2013 $75

Brunner, John *The Whole Man.* New York: Walker & Co., 1969. First US hardcover edition, octavo, boards.   L. W. Currey, Inc.   Utopian Literature: Recent Acquisitions (April 2013) - 138852   2013 $150

Brunot, Francois *Traite de la Science des Nombres...* Paris: Claude Jambert, 1723. First edition, signed as usual by author at end of the Avis for authentification, bit browned, some dampstaining in upper corner, 8vo., contemporary mottled calf, spine gilt in compartments, red lettering piece, bit rubbed and worn, manuscript corrections to last two lines of table of arithmetical progression on last page and few letters in text below made good in ink, ownership inscription, sound, rare.   Blackwell's Rare Books   Sciences - 24   2013   £650

Brunskill, R. W. *Vernacular Architecture of the Lake Counties.* London: Faber, 1974. First edition, original cloth, gilt, dust jacket, pages 164, illustrations, scarce.   R. F. G. Hollett & Son   Lake District & Cumbria - 199   2013   £75

Brunskill, R. W. *Vernacular Architecture of the Lake Counties.* London: Faber, 1978. First softback edition, original pictorial wrappers, pages 164, illustrations.   R. F. G. Hollett & Son   Lake District & Cumbria - 197   2013   £35

Brussel, Nicolas *Nouvel Examen de l'Usage General des Fiefs en France Pendant le XI le XII le XIII & le XIVe. Siecle pour servir a l'Intelligence des Plus Anciens Titres du Domaine de la Couronne.* Paris: C. Purd'homme et C. Robustel, 1727. First edition, 4to., 2 volumes, full speckled calf, spine with five raised bands, 2 morocco lettering pieces, one red, one green, four compartments heavily decorated gilt, marbled endpapers, all edges stained red, very good, joints rubbed, corners worn with minor loss, volume I with one inch split to lower joint and shallow chips to spine ends, small insect hole on front board, but has not penetrated, edges of free endpapers and blanks stained, otherwise leaves quite clean with odd bit of foxing.   Kaaterskill Books 16 - 31   2013 $900

Bryant, Louise *Six Red Months in Russia...* London: Heinemann, 1919. Half title, frontispiece, 15 plates, facsimile documents, original maroon cloth, ownership inscription, very good.   Jarndyce Antiquarian Booksellers   CCV - 37   2013   £60

Bryant, William Cullen 1794-1878 *A New Library of Poetry and Song.* New York: J. B. Ford and Co., 1876-1878? 2 volumes, full gilt and blindstamped brown, Turkey morocco, silk moire endpapers, inner gilt dentelles, 20 steel portraits, 20 engravings on wood, 20 ornamental titles in silhouette (with on verso, 20 manuscripts and autograph facsimiles), all edges gilt, handsome copy, lovely gift book, issued in 21 parts and bound.   Howard S. Mott Inc.   262 - 23 2013 $300

Bryce, James *Impressions of South Africa.* Macmillan, 1900. Modern half levant morocco gilt, folding colored map, scattered light spotting.   R. F. G. Hollett & Son   Africana - 28   2013   £75

Brydges, Egerton *Letters on the Character and Poetical Genius of Lord Byron.* London: Longman &c, 1824. First edition, unobtrusive tear on title repaired with archival tape on verso, contemporary half purple calf, black leather label, slight rubbing, spine faded to brown, armorial bookplate of Dr. Nathaniel Rogers and with "Dr. Rogers" stamped in gilt at tail of spine, Doris Langley Moore's copy with few pencil notes by her.   Jarndyce Antiquarian Booksellers   CCIII - 349   2013   £250

Brydges, Egerton *Letters on the Character and Poetical Genius of Lord Byron.* London: &c, 1824. First edition, handsome full contemporary morocco, gilt spine and borders, pale green leather label, spine little rubbed, early bookseller's ticket, Newby of Cambridge.   Jarndyce Antiquarian Booksellers   CCIII - 348   2013   £320

Brydges, Samuel Egerton *The Autobiography, Times, Opinions and Contemporares.* London: Cochrane & M'Crone, 1834. First edition, 2 volumes, half titles, frontispiece portraits little foxed, titles in red and black, contemporary half maroon morocco, gilt spines, marbled boards, edges and endpapers, slight rubbing, bookplates of John Sparrow with few pencil notes by him, very good.   Jarndyce Antiquarian Booksellers   CCIII - 43   2013   £150

Brydges, Samuel Egerton *Coningsby, a Tragic Tale.* Paris & Geneve: J. J. Paschoud; London: Rob. Triphook, 1819. First edition, half title, few marks in text, full contemporary maroon calf, gilt spine, slightly faded, gilt borders, old booklabel defaced, later booklabel of John Sparrow.   Jarndyce Antiquarian Booksellers   CCIII - 42   2013   £450

Brydges, Samuel Egerton *Imaginative Biography.* London: Saunders & Otley, 1834. First edition, 2 volumes, contemporary half red calf gilt spines, black labels, spines slightly darkened, small booklabels of John Sparrow, good plus.   Jarndyce Antiquarian Booksellers   CCIII - 45   2013   £185

Brydges, Samuel Egerton *The Ruminator.* London: Longman &c., 1813. First edition, later blue binder's cloth, small booklabels of Ian Jack, very good.   Jarndyce Antiquarian Booksellers   CCIII - 41   2013   £95

Brydges, Samuel Egerton *Sonnets and Other Poems.* London: B. & J. White, 1795. New edition, contemporary full tree calf, spine with bands and devices in gilt, dark green leather label, gilt wearing from spine, corners and hinges little rubbed, ownership inscription of Lady Frances Benson, gift inscription of Miss Louisa Brown, Nov. 1836.   Jarndyce Antiquarian Booksellers   CCIII - 40   2013   £125

Brydone, Patrick *A Tour Through Sicily and Malta: in a Series of Letters to William Beckford....* Strahan, T. Cadell, 1775. Second edition, 2 volumes in 1, 8vo., folding engraved map in volume 2, contemporary brown calf, joints rubbed.   J. & S. L. Bonham Antiquarian Booksellers   Europe - 9605   2013   £220

Brydson, A. P. *Sidelights on Mediaeval Windermere.* Kendal: Titus Wilson, 1911. First edition, original green cloth, lower hinge little rubbed, 107 pages, illustrations.   R. F. G. Hollett & Son   Lake District & Cumbria - 200   2013   £45

Buchan, John 1875-1940 *John Macnab.* London: Hodder & Stoughton, 1925. First edition, half title, frontispiece, original light blue cloth, rubbed and worn, signed presentation from author for Isaac Foot.   Jarndyce Antiquarian Booksellers   CCV - 38   2013   £150

Buchan, John 1875-1940 *The Long Traverse.* London: Hodder & Stoughton, 1941. First edition, original blue cloth, spine patchily stained white, dust jacket worn and chipped, 5 plates by J. Morton Sale. R. F. G. Hollett & Son Children's Books - 93 2013 £45

Buchan, John 1875-1940 *The Magic Walking-Stick.* London: Hodder & Stoughton, 1932. First edition, 8vo., original blue cloth, signed by author, rebacked with original spine laid down, otherwise very good. Maggs Bros. Ltd. 1460 - 148 2013 £250

Buchan, John 1875-1940 *Sick Heart River.* London: Hodder & Stoughton, 1941. First edition, some spotting on front cover, otherwise very good in price clipped dust jacket with internal tape mends and spotting on back panel. Mordida Books 81 - 54 2013 $85

Buchan, John 1875-1940 *The Thirty Nine Steps.* Edinburgh & London: William Blackwood, 1915. First edition, half title, 2 pages ads, slight marginal browning, binding slightly cracked but still firm at pages 192-3, original light blue cloth, spine slightly faded and little rubbed, contemporary ownership inscription, bookplate of Christopher Clark Geest, nice. Jarndyce Antiquarian Booksellers CCV - 39 2013 £600

Buchan, William 1729-1805 *Domestic Medicine or the Family Physician.* Edinburgh: Balfour et al, 1769. First edition, 8vo., contemporary full calf, spine worn, some light soiling, occasional minor dampstaining in lower margins, rare. James Tait Goodrich S74 - 37 2013 $1295

Buchanan, John *Albert: a Poem in Two Cantos; Hilda; and other Poems.* London: Baldwin & Cradock, 1831. Second edition, inscription torn from head of dedication, attractive full contemporary purple calf, gilt spine and elaborate borders and dentelles, slight fading and marking, all edges gilt, very good. Jarndyce Antiquarian Booksellers CCIII - 649 2013 £60

Buchanan, Joseph R. *Sketches of Buchanan's Discoveries in Neurology.* Louisville: J. Eliot and Co.'s Power Press, 1842. First edition, 8vo., 120 pages, removed. M & S Rare Books, Inc. 95 - 41 2013 $350

Buck, Pearl S. *China in Black and White.* New York: John Day Co., 1945. First edition, small 4to., 95 pages, near fine, minimal cover edgewear in very good, price clipped dust jacket with chips, short closed tears, soil and stains. By the Book, L. C. 36 - 88 2013 $180

Buck, Pearl S. *To My Daughters, with Love.* New York: John Day Co., 1967. First edition, 8vo., 250 pages, scarce, signed by author, near fine in very good++ price clipped dust jacket with minimal sun spine, scuffs. By the Book, L. C. 36 - 40 2013 $150

Buckbee, Edna Bryan *The Saga of Old Tuolumne.* New York: Press of the Pioneers, 1935. First edition, Frontispiece, plus 18 photos, original gilt lettered red cloth, very fine and bright, pictorial dust jacket. Argonaut Book Shop Summer 2013 - 36 2013 $250

Buckbee, Edna Bryan *The Saga of Old Twolumne.* New York: Press of the Pioneers, 1935. First edition, number 109 of 200 copies signed by author, this special edition with colophon leaf, signed, at rear, frontispiece, 18 photos, original gilt lettered red cloth, very slight fading to extreme spine ends, but very fine, bright copy, pictorial dust jacket (very minor chipping at spine ends), protected by glassine cover. Argonaut Book Shop Summer 2013 - 37 2013 $300

Bucke, Charles *The Philosophy of Nature; or the Influence of Scenery on the Mind and Heart.* London: John Murray, 1813. First edition, 2 volumes, half titles, contemporary full maroon calf, gilt spines, borders and dentelles, slightly marked, spines faded and hinges, little rubbed, small repair at tail of spine volume I, contemporary signature of W. Walker, very good. Jarndyce Antiquarian Booksellers CCIII - 650 2013 £250

Buckland Wright, John *Baigneuses.* Denby Dale: Fleece Press, 1995. One of 204 copies (of an edition of 240), prelims printed in black and blue, frontispiece and 23 other wood engravings on rectos of 21 leaves, wood engraved tailpiece, reproductions of 2 photos, 2 wood engraved plates printed in green and cream and black and blue, 2 further large black and white wood engraved plates copperplates engraving and color reproductions of 2 oil paintings all by Buckland Wright and tipped in, 8vo., original quarter cream vellum, backstrip gilt lettered, pink and blue marbled white boards, untrimmed, one corner bumped on fawn cloth solander box with printed label, very good. Blackwell's Rare Books 172 - 275 2013 £400

Buckland Wright, John *Surreal Times.* Denby Dale: Fleece Press, 2000. One of 210 copies (of an edition of 266), printed in black with sub-titles printed in orange on Magnani mouldmade paper, 27 engravings, 13 tipped in plates, a further 14 in text, all by John Buckland Wright, reproduction of photo tipped in, folio, original quarter cinnamon linen cloth, backstrip gilt lettered on black ground, repeat pattern of Buckland Wright's initials in yellow on cream boards, untrimmed, matching cloth and board slipcase, fine. Blackwell's Rare Books 172 - 276 2013 £240

Buckland, Francis Trevelyan *Log-Book of a Fisherman and Zoologist.* London: Chapman & Hall, 1875. First edition, wood engraved frontispiece, 3 plates, illustrations in text, some full page, endpapers through-set on to outside of flyleaves, 8vo., original green cloth, slightly darkened and worn, neat repair to front inner hinge and spine ends, inscribed by author to friend Henry Lee of the Brighton aquarium, good. Blackwell's Rare Books 172 - 37 2013 £300

Buckley, J. M. *Oats or Wild Oats? Common-sense for Young Men.* New York: Harper & Brothers, 1885. First edition, 8vo., maroon cloth, very scarce, original cloth with some rubbing to extremities, otherwise sound.   Barnaby Rudge Booksellers   Children 2013 - 021142   2013 $110

Buckley, M. B. *The Life and Writings of Rev. Arthur O'Leary.* 1868. First edition, 8vo., original blind embossed green cloth, gilt titled, portrait, good.   C. P. Hyland   261 - 659   2013   £30

Buckley, Stella *John Buckley 1865-1944.* Kendal: Titus Wilson, 1946. First edition, later green cloth gilt, frontispiece.   R. F. G. Hollett & Son   Lake District & Cumbria - 201   2013   £25

Bucknall, Thomas Skip Dyot *The Orchardist; or a System of Close Pruning....* London: printed for G. Nicol, 1797. Uncut, wide margins, disbound.   Jarndyce Antiquarian Booksellers   CCIV - 77   2013   £220

Buckton, Alice Mary *The Burden of Engela: a Ballad-Epic.* London: Methuen & Co., 1904. Second edition, half title, 40 page catalog but with pages 3-36 removed, original blue cloth, attractively decorated in gilt, slightly marked, very good.   Jarndyce Antiquarian Booksellers   CCV - 40   2013   £30

Budworth, Joseph *A Fortnight's Ramble to the Lakes in Westmoreland, Lancashire and Cumberland.* Upper Basildon: Preston Pub., 1990. Original pictorial stiff wrappers, 2 portraits.   R. F. G. Hollett & Son   Lake District & Cumbria - 203   2013   £30

Bukowski, Charles *Beerspit Night and Cursing: the Correspondence of Charles Bukowski and Sheri Martinelli 1960-1967.* Santa Rosa: Black Sparrow Press, 2001. First edition, #37 of 526 numbered and lettered copies with color serigraph by Bukowski, pictorial boards, fine in fine glassine dust jacket.   Charles Agvent   Charles Bukowski - 6   2013 $75

Bukowski, Charles *Bone Palace Ballet: New Poems.* Santa Rosa: Black Sparrow Press, 1997. First edition, #131 of 426 numbered copies, pictorial boards by Earle Gray, with original color serigraph by author, fine in fine glassine dust jacket.   Charles Agvent   Charles Bukowski - 7   2013 $125

Bukowski, Charles *Bukowski Photographs 1977-1991.* Hollywood: Buckskin Press, 1993. First edition, folio, #22 of only 74 signed copies, signed by author and photographer, Michael Montfort, handbound by Earle Gray in white boards with color photo of Bukowski on front cover, tipped-in photos, fine.   Charles Agvent   Charles Bukowski - 38   2013 $1000

Bukowski, Charles *Darkness and Ice.* Arctic Circle: Burn Again Press, 1990. First edition, #9 of only 50 numbered copies signed by author, light gray-green boards, 8 x 11 inches, printed paper labels on front cover and spine, laid in is one page prospectus for book, fine.   Charles Agvent   Charles Bukowski - 10   2013 $1250

Bukowski, Charles *Dear Mr. Bukowski.* Augsburg: Maro Verlag, 1979. Facsimile reprint edition, includes facsimile envelope addressed to author at 69 Cachinnation Row, Catatonia City, along with folded letter and 10 silk screened cards that answer the question of what Bukoski's typical day is like, illustrations by author, fine.   Charles Agvent   Charles Bukowski - 12   2013 $250

Bukowski, Charles *Fire Station.* Santa Barbara: Capricorn Press, 1970. First edition, pictorial boards, one of only 100 hardcover copies, fine in fine glassine dust jacket, lacking scarce red tissue dust jacket, if it ever had it.   Charles Agvent   Charles Bukowski - 14   2013 $850

Bukowski, Charles *Fire Station.* Santa Barbara: Capricorn Press, 1970. First trade edition, 8vo., fine, original decorated wrappers, light sun at spine, contemporary presentation inscription from author for Herbert Graf, drawing by author.   Ed Smith Books   75 - 10   2013 $850

Bukowski, Charles *Ham on Rye.* Santa Barbara: Black Sparrow Press, 1982. First edition, one of 350 numbered copies (#28) signed by author, cloth and boards, acetate dust jacket, fine.   Ed Smith Books   75 - 9   2013 $850

Bukowski, Charles *Horsemeat.* Santa Barbara: Black Sparrow Press, 1982. First edition, #76 of 125 copies signed by author and photographer on colophon page, folio handbound by Earle Gray in pictorial boards with color photo of Bukowski on front cover, tipped in color photos by Michael Montfort, fine.   Charles Agvent   Charles Bukowski - 39   2013 $1500

Bukowski, Charles *Love is a Dog From Hell.* Santa Barbara: Black Sparrow Press, 1977. First edition, #251 of 300 numbered copies, signed by author, pictorial boards, fine in fine glassine dust jacket.   Charles Agvent   Charles Bukowski - 17   2013 $500

Bukowski, Charles *The Night Torn Mad with Footsteps: New Poems.* Santa Rosa: Black Sparrow Press, 2000. First edition, copy 1 of 26 lettered copies from a total of 176 handbound copies, fine in fine white paper dust jacket.   Charles Agvent   Charles Bukowski - 20   2013 $75

Bukowski, Charles *The Night Torn Mad with Footsteps: New Poems.* Santa Rosa: Black Sparrow Press, 2001. First edition, #57 of 526 numbered and lettered copies, handbound by Earle Gray in pictorial boards, and containing original serigraph print by Bukowski, in addition there were 100 hardcover copies and an unspecified edition in wrappers, fine in fine glassine dust jacket.   Charles Agvent   Charles Bukowski - 18   2013 $75

Bukowski, Charles *The Night Torn Mad with Footsteps.* Santa Rosa: Black Sparrow Press, 2001. First edition, #57 of 526 numbered and lettered copies handbound by Earle Gray and containing an original serigraph print by Bukowski, in addition there were 1000 hardcover copies and un unspecified edition in wrappers, fine in fine glassine dust jacket.   Charles Agvent Charles Bukowski - 19   2013 $125

Bukowski, Charles *Not Quite Bernadette.* Compton: Greybeard Press, 1990. First edition, #50 of only 75 copies signed by author and artist, large folio, full blue denim clamshell style, book and binding designed and produced for Greybeard Press by noted book artist Joe D'Ambrosio, text on leaves of various abstract shapes, 9 mezzotints by James Johnson, each signed, numbered and titled in pencil in lower margin, rare, spectacular production.   Charles Agvent   Charles Bukowski - 37   2013 $3500

Bukowski, Charles *Open All Night: New Poems.* Santa Rosa: Black Sparrow Press, 2000. First edition, #195 of 426 numbered copies, hand bound in pictorial boards by Earle Gray, with original color serigraph by author, fine in fine glassine.   Charles Agvent   Charles Bukowski - 21   2013 $125

Bukowski, Charles *Reach for the Sun: Selected Letters 1978-1984. Volume 3.* Santa Rosa: Black Sparrow Press, 1999. First edition, one of 750 hardcover copies in addition to 376 numbered and lettered copies, unspecified edition in wrappers, small faint stain to bulked fore-edge of text, just about fine in fine glassine dust jacket.   Charles Agvent   Charles Bukowski - 24   2013 $60

Bukowski, Charles *Run with the Hunted. A Charles Bukowski Reader.* New York: Harper Collins, 1993. First edition, #55 of 326 numbered and lettered copies signed by author with additional drawing by Bukowski, near fine in near fine glassine dust jacket.   Charles Agvent   Charles Bukowski - 25   2013 $300

Bukowski, Charles *Screams from the Balcony. Selected Letters 1960-1970.* Santa Rosa: Black Sparrow Press, 1993. First edition, pictorial boards, new, still in shrinkwrap.   Charles Agvent   Charles Bukowski - 26   2013 $60

Bukowski, Charles *This.* Andernach: Burn Again Press, 1990. First edition, #41 of only 50 numbered copies signed by author, fine, light green boards with printed paper labels on front cover and spine.   Charles Agvent   Charles Bukowski - 29   2013 $1250

Bukowski, Charles *A Visitor Complains of My Disenfranchise.* Los Angeles: Illuminati, 1987. First edition, published in an edition of 225 copies, stiff wrappers with small knob (made of metal) on front cover so that opening the book is like opening a door, narrow 8vo., although not called for, this copy signed by author, fine.   Ed Smith Books   75 - 12   2013 $500

Bukowski, Charles *War All the Time: Poems 198-1984.* Santa Barbara: Black Sparrow Press, 1987. first edition, 2nd printing, reading copy but for the unsigned fancy dark blue leather binding on it and with inset on front cover using various color leathers, near fine.   Charles Agvent   Charles Bukowski - 30   2013 $150

Bukowski, Charles *What Matters Most is How Well You Walk through fire.* Santa Rosa: Black Sparrow Press, 1999. First edition, one of 750 trade copies in an addition of 426 numbered and lettered copies and an unspecified edition in wrappers, fine in fine glassine dust jacket.   Charles Agvent   Charles Bukowski - 33   2013 $60

Bukowski, Charles *You Kissed Lilly.* Santa Barbara: Black Sparrow Press, 1978. First edition, pictorial boards, corduroy spine, copy 21 of 200 numbered copies signed by author from total edition of 275, fine in very good, lightly soiled white dust jacket.   Charles Agvent   Charles Bukowski - 35   2013 $500

Bulfin, William *Rambles in Eirinn.* 1915. 8vo., cloth, very good.   C. P. Hyland   261 - 159 2013   £35

Buliard, Roger P. *Inuk.* London: Macmillan, 1953. First edition, original cloth, gilt, 8 pages of plates.   R. F. G. Hollett & Son   Polar Exploration - 3   2013   £25

Buller, Walter Lawry *A History of the Birds of New Zealand.* London: John Van Voorst, 1873. First edition, frontispiece, 35 fine hand colored lithographs, 4to., half calf, spine gilt bookplate, lovely copy, the Foljambe copy bearing bookplate of Cecil Foljambe, first early of Liverpool.   Maggs Bros. Ltd.   1467 - 73   2013   £7500

Bulmer, Kenneth *Empire of Chaos.* London: Panther Books... Published by Hamilton & Co.,, Stafford), Ltd., 1953. First edition, octavo, cloth.   L. W. Currey, Inc.   Fall Sampler Sept. 2013 - 146473   2013 $125

Bulmer, T., & Co. *History and Directory of West Cumberland 1901.* Whitehaven: Michael Moon, 1994. Facsimile edition, original pictorial wrappers, frontispiece. R. F. G. Hollett & Son   Lake District & Cumbria - 205   2013   £25

Bulmer, T., & Co. *History, Topography and Directory of East Cumberland...* Manchester: T. Bulmer & Co., 1884. First edition, original blue cloth, gilt, hinges rather rubbed, two stains to lower board, large folding colored map (rather creased and torn in places but complete), engraved bird's-eye view of Carlisle Grammar School on rear pastedown. R. F. G. Hollett & Son   Lake District & Cumbria - 215   2013   £85

Bulmer, T., & Co. *History, Topography and Directory of East Cumberland...* Manchester: T. Bulmer & Co., 1884. Second edition, old binder's cloth, gilt, spine lettering faded. R. F. G. Hollett & Son   Lake District & Cumbria - 208   2013   £65

Bulmer, T., & Co. *History, Topography and Directory of Furness & Cartmel with Part of the Western or Egremont Division of Cumberland.* Preston: T. Snape, n.d., Second edition, original cloth, gilt, extremities little worn, head of spine rather frayed and pulled, folding pedigree (little torn) and folding map loosely inserted.   R. F. G. Hollett & Son   Lake District & Cumbria - 206   2013   £95

Bulmer, T., & Co. *History, Topography and Directory of Furness & Cartmel comprising Its History and Archaeology, Physical and Geological Features...* Preston: T. Snape, n.d., Second edition, original half calf, gilt, few slight old scraps, folding pedigree (trifle torn).   R. F. G. Hollett & Son   Lake District & Cumbria - 207   2013   £110

Bulmer, T., & Co. *History, Topography and Directory of Westmorland.* Manchester: T. Bulmer & Co., 1885. Original blue cloth, gilt, extremities rather worn, joints cracked (front joint taped), includes final unpaginated decorative ad leaf for James Douglas, Kendal grocer, which is often lacking.   R. F. G. Hollett & Son   Lake District & Cumbria - 212   2013   £160

Bulmer, T., & Co. *History, Topography and Directory of Westmorland.* Preston: T. Snape & Co., n.d., 1906. Original red cloth gilt, neatly recased, few edges little chipped and repaired.   R. F. G. Hollett & Son   Lake District & Cumbria - 211   2013   £120

Bulpin, T. V. *Discovering Southern Africa.* Muizenberg: Discovering Southern Africa Productions, 1992. Fifth edition, original pictorial boards, extremities trifle rubbed, colored ads.   R. F. G. Hollett & Son   Africana - 171   2013   £25

Bunce, Daniel *Language of the Aboriginies of Victoria, and other Australian Districts...* Melbourne: Daniel Harrison, 1851. First edition, 12mo., contemporary black moire cloth, lovely copy.   Maggs Bros. Ltd.   1467 - 74   2013   £1500

The Bunker Hill Songster. New York: Wm. H. Murphy, 2 3/4 x 4 3/8 inches, 34 pages, woodcuts, paper wrappers, cover slightly soiled, nice.   Second Life Books Inc.   183 - 6   2013 $50

Bunker, Edward *The Animal Factory.* New York: Viking, 1977. First edition, fine in fine dust jacket.   Between the Covers Rare Books, Inc.   Mystery & Detective Fiction - 79044   2013 $200

Bunting, Basil *Loquitur.* Fulcrum Press, 1965. First edition, one of 200 copies (of an edition of 1000) printed on Glastonbury laid paper, pages 80, imperial 8vo., original black cloth, backstrip gilt lettered, dust jacket, very good. Blackwell's Rare Books   B174 - 181   2013   £200

Bunting, Basil *What the Chairman Told Tom.* Cambridge: Pym Randall Press, 1967. First edition, 160/200 copies (of an edition of 226), signed by author, foolscap 8vo., original printed grey sewn wrappers, single diagonal crease to front covers, near fine.   Blackwell's Rare Books   B174 - 182   2013   £70

Bunyan, John   1628-1688 *A Book for Boys and Girls; or Country Rhymes for Children.* London: Elliot Stock, 1889. 1889, Large paper copy, top edge gilt, untrimmed, handsome copy, large square 8vo., later quarter levant morocco gilt by Stoakley of Cambridge (but unsigned).   R. F. G. Hollett & Son   Children's Books - 94   2013   £120

Bunyan, John   1628-1688 *The Holy City; or the New Jerusalem. (bound with) Come and Welcome to Jesus Christ.* London: 1665. 1750. First edition and tenth edition respectively, small octavo, 2nd work with woodcut portrait, engraved frontispiece and 2 woodcut illustrations, 18th century sprinkled calf, smooth spine ruled in gilt and lettered in blind, head of spine little chipped, slightly shaved occasionally affecting catchwords in 'Come and Welcome', small portion torn from upper inner margin of first two leaves If "The Holy City" affecting first word of title, occasional light spotting or staining, early ink ownership inscription of William March, few additional early ink annotations and underlining, very good, rare, housed in cloth clamshell case, from the libraries of R. L. Harmsworth and George Goyder with his armorial bookplate.   Heritage Book Shop   50th Anniversary Catalogue - 14   2013 $22,500

Bunyan, John 1628-1688 *The Pilgrim's Progress from this World to that Which is to Come.* London: printed for Nathanael Ponder, 1682. Eighth edition, 12mo., frontispiece, 2 full page woodcuts, early 19th century blind tooled sheep, spine blindstamped in compartments and with gilt spine lettering, brown endpapers, some wear to upper spine with small crack, marginal notes trimmed in few places, old rust mark to pages 88-89, some browning, overall very good, very rare. Heritage Book Shop Holiday Catalogue 2012 - 22 2013 $40,000

Bunyan, John 1628-1688 *The Pilgrim's Progress from this World to that Which is to Come. (with)....the second part...third part.* London: printed by A. W. for J. Clarke, 1727. London: printed for J. Clarke, 1728. London: Printed for A. Bettesworth, 1722. First combined edition, 22nd edition of part 1, 14th edition of part 2 and 10th edition of part 3, 3 parts in one 12mo. volume, woodcut frontispieces, 14 other woodcuts in part one, included in pagination, contemporary paneled sheep professionally rebacked, boards tooled in blind, spine with red morocco spine label, lettered gilt, edges of boards bit bumped and chipped, few signatures sprung, however binding tight, few pages have been trimmed close on fore-edge, previous owner's bookplate and old ink inscription, overall very good. Heritage Book Shop Holiday Catalogue 2012 - 23 2013 $5000

Bunyan, John 1628-1688 *The Pilgrim's Progress from this World to that Which is to Come Delivered Under the Similitude of a Dream.* London: Faber, 1947. First edition, original cloth, gilt, dust jacket head of spine chipped, other extremities trifle frayed, price clipped, illustrations. R. F. G. Hollett & Son Children's Books - 27 2013 £50

Burbank, Luther *Luther Burbank. His Methods and Discoveries and Their Practical Application.* New York and London: Luther Burbank Press, 1914-1915. First edition, 8vo., 12 volumes, 1260 color photo prints, original red cloth with oval photo of Burbank inset on front cover, little staining on 2 volumes, slight waterstaining in one volume, top of one volume slightly gnawed, very good. M & S Rare Books, Inc. 95 - 42 2013 $600

Burgess, Anthony *A Clockwork Orange.* London: Heinemann, 1962. First edition, crown 8vo., original first issue black boards, backstrip gilt lettered, first issue dust jacket rubbed at head of lightly faded backstrip panel with two short tears, very good. Blackwell's Rare Books 172 - 167 2013 £2000

Burgess, Anthony *Tremor of Intent.* London: Heinemann, 1966. First edition, crown 8vo., original black boards, backstrip gilt lettered, lightly rubbed dust jacket, near fine. Blackwell's Rare Books B174 - 183 2013 £85

Burgess, Anthony *The Wanting Seed.* London: Heinemann, 1965. First reprint, 8vo., original black cloth dust jacket, inscribed by author, excellent copy in slightly rubbed dust jacket. Maggs Bros. Ltd. 1460 - 150 2013 £175

Burgess, Gelett 1866-1951 *Blue Goops and Red.* New York: Frederick Stokes Oct., 1909. First edition, 4to., green, red and blue pictorial cloth, 81 pages, slightest of cover soil, else near fine, movable flap book as well, illustrations. Aleph-Bet Books, Inc. 104 - 97 2013 $875

Burgess, Gelett 1866-1951 *Gelett Burgess Behind the Scenes. Glimpses of fin de Siecle San Francisco.* San Francisco: Book Club of California, 1968. First edition thus, one of 400 copies, small quarto, 130 pages, woodcut decorations by Shirley Barker, photos, cloth backed decorated boards, paper spine label bookplate, else very fine. Argonaut Book Shop Summer 2013 - 38 2013 $100

Burgess, Gelett 1866-1951 *Goop Tales Alphabetically Told.* New York: Frederick Stokes, 1904. 4to., blue pictorial cloth, small spot on rear cover and margin soil on last 2 pages, else near fine, illustrations. Aleph-Bet Books, Inc. 104 - 98 2013 $850

Burgess, Gelett 1866-1951 *Goops and How to Be Them.* New York: Frederick A. Stokes, 1900. First edition, 4to., original pictorial red cloth, excellent, Mildred Greenhill/H. Bradley Martin copy. Howard S. Mott Inc. 262 - 24 2013 $300

Burgess, Gelett 1866-1951 *The Lark. Book the First Nos. 1 to 12. May 1895 to April 1896. Book the Second Nos. 13 to 24 May 1896 to April 1897.* San Francisco: William Doxey, 1896-1897. First edition, 2nd issue with Doxey imprint, 2 volumes, original colored pictorial cloth, uncut, excellent copy, ex-libris of Estelle Doheny in each volume. Howard S. Mott Inc. 262 - 26 2013 $400

Burgess, Gelett 1866-1951 *The Lively City O'Ligg.* New York: Frederick A. Stokes, 1899. First American edition, 8vo., 53 illustrations by, with 6 of 8 color plates, text page 75 torn with some loss, maroon cloth, very good, custom clamshell bx. Barnaby Rudge Booksellers Children 2013 - 018038 2013 $65

Burgess, Gelett 1866-1951 *The Purple Cow!* San Francisco: William Doxey, 1895. First edition, first issue printed on both sides of each leaf on rough paper, 12mo., original pictorial self wrapper, 8 leaves (including wrappers), stapled, uncut as issued, folding case, signed by author, one short marginal slit in front wrapper, else fine, Carroll Wilson's copy. Howard S. Mott Inc. 262 - 25 2013 $400

Burgess, John *Bishop of the Lake Counties. Letters of Samuel Wadegrave Volume I 1860-1864.* Carlisle: privately published by author, 1985. printed in very limited edition, 4to., original blue wrappers, gilt lettered, pages of plates, map and family tree. R. F. G. Hollett & Son Lake District & Cumbria - 237 2013 £75

Burgess, John *Bishop of the Lake Counties. Letters of Samuel Wadegrave. 1860-1869.* Carlisle: privately published by author, 1985-1987. 4 volumes 4to., original wrappers, gilt lettered by hand, numerous photocopied plates, map and family tree, printed rectos only, author's own unique set with his original annotated color photos throughout in volume 3. R. F. G. Hollett & Son Lake District & Cumbria - 238 2013 £350

Burgess, John *Carlisle Cathedral.* Carlisle: privately published by author, 1988. Printed in a very limited edition, Original cloth backed acetate wrappers, photo copied plates, all printed on rectos, text cyclostyled. R. F. G. Hollett & Son Lake District & Cumbria - 216 2013 £35

Burgess, John *The Castles of Cumbria. Volume I: Carlisle and North Cumbria.* Carlisle: privately published by author, n.d. circa, 1988. Very limited edition, 4to., original cloth backed acetate wrappers, photocopied plates, all printed on rectos, text cyclostyled. R. F. G. Hollett & Son Lake District & Cumbria - 217 2013 £40

Burgess, John *Cumbrian Castles.* Carlisle: privately published by author, 1988. Printed in very limited edition, 4to., original cloth backed acetate wrappers, photocopied plates, all printed on rectos, text cyclostyled. R. F. G. Hollett & Son Lake District & Cumbria - 218 2013 £50

Burgess, John *Cumbrian Churches the Architectural Heritage of Cumbrian Places of Worship.* Carlisle: privately published by the author, 1988. printed in very limited edition, oblong folio, original cloth backed acetate wrappers, all printed on rectos, text cyclostyled. R. F. G. Hollett & Son Lake District & Cumbria - 219 2013 £120

Burgess, John *The Georgian Heritage of North West England.* Carlisle: privately published by author, 1989. Printed in very limited edition, original cloth backed acetate wrappers, all printed on rectos, text cyclostyled, photocopied plates. R. F. G. Hollett & Son Lake District & Cumbria - 220 2013 £50

Burgess, John *The Heritage of North West England in the Seventeenth Century.* Carlisle: privately published by author, 1990. printed in very limited edition, original cloth backed acetate wrappers, all printed on rectos, text cyclostyled, photocopied plates. R. F. G. Hollett & Son Lake District & Cumbria - 221 2013 £65

Burgess, John *The Historic Ports of North West England.* Carlisle: privately published by author, 1989. original cloth backed acetate wrappers, all printed on rectos, text cyclostyled, photocopied plates. R. F. G. Hollett & Son Lake District & Cumbria - 222 2013 £75

Burgess, John *A History of Cumbrian Methodism.* Kendal: Titus Wilson, 1980. Original wrappers, one of a few superior copies folded into sections and sewn by publisher, most were perfect bound (glued) and tend to fall apart after use. R. F. G. Hollett & Son Wesleyan Methodism - 53 2013 £25

Burgess, John *A History of Keswick.* Carlisle: privately published by author, 1989. printed in very limited edition, 4to., original cloth backed acetate wrappers, all printed on rectos, text cyclostyled, photocopied plates. R. F. G. Hollett & Son Lake District & Cumbria - 226 2013 £50

Burgess, John *A History of Penrith.* Carlisle: privately published by author, 1989. printed in very limited edition, original cloth backed acetate wrappers, all printed on rectos, text cyclostyled, 20 photocopied plates, gift inscription on title (non-authorial). R. F. G. Hollett & Son Lake District & Cumbria - 227 2013 £45

Burgess, John *Methodist Ministers in Cumbria.* Carlisle: Wesley Historical Society, 1977. 2 volumes, tall 4to., side stapled, cyclostyled. R. F. G. Hollett & Son Lake District & Cumbria - 229 2013 £25

Burgess, John *Methodist Ministers in Cumbria.* Carlisle: The Wesley Historical Society, 1977. 2 volumes, tall 4to., side stapled, cyclostyled. R. F. G. Hollett & Son Wesleyan Methodism - 4 2013 £25

Burgess, John *The Monasteries of Cumbria.* Carlisle: privately published by author, 1987. 4 volumes, oblong folio, original cloth backed stiff blue card, lettered in red, unpaginated, each volume with cyclostyled text, plus same size facsimiles of relevant historical publications and plates, all printed recto only. R. F. G. Hollett & Son Lake District & Cumbria - 230 2013 £75

Burgess, John *The Nobility of North West England.* Carlisle: privately published by author, 1989. Printed in a very limited edition, original cloth backed acetate wrappers, photocopies plates, all printed on rectos, text cyclostyled. R. F. G. Hollett & Son Lake District & Cumbria - 231 2013 £75

Burgess, John *Pagan Cumbria.* Carlisle: privately published by author, 1987. printed in very limited edition, original clothbacked acetate wrappers, photocopied plates, printed on rectos, text cyclostyled. R. F. G. Hollett & Son Lake District & Cumbria - 232 2013 £75

Burgess, John *A Portrait of Carlisle 1780-1930.* Carlisle: privately published by author, 1991. Printed in very limited edition, original cloth backed acetate wrappers, photocopied plates, all printed on rectos, text cyclostyled. R. F. G. Hollett & Son   Lake District & Cumbria - 233   2013   £50

Burgess, John *The Roman Heritage in North west England.* Carlisle: privately published by author, 1989. printed in very limited edition, 4to., original cloth backed acetate wrappers, photocopied, plates, all printed on rectos, text cyclostyled.   R. F. G. Hollett & Son   Lake District & Cumbria - 235   2013   £65

Burgess, John *The Victorian Heritage of North West England.* Carlisle: privately published by author, 1989. printed in very limited edition, 4to., original cloth backed acetate wrappers, photocopied, plates, all printed on rectos, text cyclostyled.   R. F. G. Hollett & Son   Lake District & Cumbria - 235   2013   £65

Burgess, John *Westmorland. A Guide.* Carlisle: privately published by author, 2000. Printed in very limited edition, 4to. 4to., original cloth backed acetate wrappers, photocopied, plates, all printed on rectos, text cyclostyled. R. F. G. Hollett & Son   Lake District & Cumbria - 236   2013   £50

Burgess, Larry E. *Zamorano Select.* Los Angeles: Zamorano Club, 2010. First edition, one of 350 numbered copies, this copy signed by all four compilers, Larry Burgess, Bill Donohoo, Alan Jutzi and Gordon J. Van De Water, 18 black and white plates, 8 tipped in color plates, black cloth stamped in gold and red, very fine.   Argonaut Book Shop   Recent Acquisitions June 2013 - 327   2013 $150

Burgess, Thornton *Aunt Sally's Friends in Fur in the Woodhouse Night Club.* Boston: Little Brown, 1955. Stated first edition, 8vo., cloth, fine in slightly worn dust jacket, 34 half tones, rare, uncommon.   Aleph-Bet Books, Inc.   105 - 103   2013 $350

Burgess, Thornton *The Bedtime Story Calendar.* Chicago: Volland, 1915. 5 1/2 x 11 inches, (54) pages, slight soil on covers of calendar, else near fine in original pictorial box, box flaps replaced, printed on rectos only, illustrations in blue and black, very scarce.   Aleph-Bet Books, Inc.   104 - 99   2013 $600

Burgess, Thornton *Blacky the Crow.* Boston: Little Brown, April, 1922. First edition, 8vo., blue cloth, pictorial paste on near fine, illustrations by Harrison Cady with 8 color plates.   Aleph-Bet Books, Inc.   104 - 100   2013 $225

Burgess, Thornton *Blacky the Crow.* London: John Lane Bodley Head, 1933. First edition, original green cloth, pictorial onlay, little rubbed, 8 color plates by Harrison Cady.   R. F. G. Hollett & Son   Children's Books - 95   2013   £45

Burgess, Thornton *Grandfather Frog Gets a Ride.* Boston: Whitman, 1927. 8vo., 29 pages, pictorial boards, near fine, illustrations by Harrison Cady in bold color on every page.   Aleph-Bet Books, Inc.   105 - 104   2013 $150

Burgess, Thornton *Jerry Muskrat at Home.* Boston: Little Brown, Sept., 1926. First edition, 8vo., green cloth, pictorial paste-on some soil on endpapers, else very good+, illustrations by Harrison Cady with 8 color plates.   Aleph-Bet Books, Inc.   105 - 105   2013 $225

Burgess, Thornton *Lightfoot the Deer.* Boston: Little Brown, April, 1921. First edition, 8vo., blue cloth, slight wear to spine extremes, else very good-fine, 8 color plates by Harrison Cady.   Aleph-Bet Books, Inc.   105 - 106   2013 $175

Burgess, Thornton *Little Joe Otter.* Boston: Little Brown, Oct., 1925. First edition, 8vo., green cloth, pictorial paste-on, slight edgewear to 3 pages, else near fine, illustrations by Harrison Cady, with 8 great color plates, this copy inscribed by author dated 1925.   Aleph-Bet Books, Inc.   104 - 101   2013 $450

Burghope, George *Autarchy; or the Art of Self-Government, in a Moral Essay.* London: printed for Dorman Newman at the King's Arms in the Poultry, 1691. 8vo., small paper flaws to margins of D, F1 & G6 corner of H3 torn with loss not affecting text, old waterstaining and browning, contemporary calf, raised bands, original label, the hinges, board edges, head and tail of spine neatly repaired, 18th century names on front endpaper and inner board & verso of titlepage, 2 leaves of handwritten 18th century verse at end.   Jarndyce Antiquarian Booksellers   CCIV - 5   2013   £350

Burke, Bill *Portraits by Bill Burke.* New York: Ecco Press, 1987. First edition, signed in full by Raymond Carver and inscribed by him for James and Norma Ray, June 1988, fine in near fine dust jacket.   Ed Smith Books   75 - 14   2013 $750

Burke, Edmund 1729-1797 *A Philosophical Enquiry into the Origin of Our Ideas of the Sublime and Beautiful.* London: printed for R. and J. Dodsley, 1757. First edition, limited to 500 copies, octavo, bound without half title, contemporary calf, early ink inscription of John Digby Jr. and armorial bookplate of John Hamilton Siree, very good.   Heritage Book Shop   50th Anniversary Catalogue - 17   2013 $3500;

Burke, Edmund   1729-1797 *A Philosophical Enquiry into the Origin of Our Ideas of the Sublime and Beautiful.* London: printed for J. Dodsley, 1767. 8vo., some occasional foxing and light browning, full contemporary calf, gilt panelled spine, red morocco label, leading hinge cracked but firm, slight insect damage, spine chipped at head, 18th century armorial bookplate of Rev. Chas. Bishop, with name A. R. Winnington-Ingram 1880 who has underlined many sections of text in pencil and added several marginal notes to his reading.   Jarndyce Antiquarian Booksellers   CCIV - 78   2013   £125

Burke, Edmund   1729-1797 *Reflections on the Revolution in France and on the Proceedings in Certain Societies in London Relative to that Event...*   London: printed for J. Dodsley, 1790. First edition, first issue, 19th century half sheep over marbled boards, original bluish-gray drab wrappers bound in to front and back, some wear at corners and joints, spine bit scuffed, some occasional pale spotting along top edge, overall very nice, octavo, the copy of William Lee, Bart (presentation inscription) and of Archibald Philip Primrose, 5th Earl of Rosebery, ALS to Rosebery from John Morley tipped in, small Rosebery/Durdans blindstamp on titlepage and page 99, gift inscription, armorial bookplate.   Heritage Book Shop   50th Anniversary Catalogue - 16   2013 $15,000

Burke, Edmund   1729-1797 *Reflections on the Revolution in France and on the Proceedings in Certain Societies in London Relative to that Event.*   London: printed for J. Dodsley, 1790. Seventh edition, uncut in original pale blue boards, drab swine, spine little darkened and slightly chipped, corners slightly knocked, following board bit marked, small label and signature of Douglas Grant, good plus, internally clean.   Jarndyce Antiquarian Booksellers   CCIII - 651   2013   £250

Burke, Edmund   1729-1797 *The Works of.* Bohn, 1889. Volumes 4, 5 (of 6), original cloth, very good.   C. P. Hyland   261 - 159   2013   £35

Burke, J. Bernard *Genealogical and Heraldic Dictionary of the landed Gentry of (G.B. & I).*   1860. First edition in 1 volume, 1405 pages = 4 pages ads, modern cloth, good.   C. P. Hyland   261 - 375   2013   £60

Burke, J. Bernard *Vicissitudes of Families.*   1860. Fourth edition, 3 volumes, some wear to original cloth, text very good.   C. P. Hyland   261 - 378   2013   £60

Burke, J. Bernard *A Visitation of Seats and Arms of the Noblemen and Gentlemen of Great Britain Part II.* Colburn, 1852. 16 engravings, plates, titlepage and indices for volume 1 in original printed stiff wrappers, good.   C. P. Hyland   261 - 380   2013   £90

Burke, James Lee *Heartwood.* New Orleans: B. E. Trice, 1999. First edition, one of 150 numbered and specially bound copies signed by author, very fine in slipcase, without dust jacket.   Mordida Books   81 - 55   2013 $150

Burke, James Lee *Lay Down My Sword and Shield.* New York: Crowell, 1971. First edition, fine in near fine dust jacket with three short tears, two of them trifling and third along edge of spine little rubbed, scarce.   Between the Covers Rare Books, Inc.   Mystery & Detective Fiction - 51883   2013 $1500

Burke, James Lee *Sunset Limited.* New York: Doubleday, 1998. First edition, inscribed by author for author Vine Deloria, Jr., minor browning to boards, else fine in fine dust jacket.   Ken Lopez Bookseller   159 - 28   2013 $250

Burke's... Peerage, Baronetage & Knightage.   1938. 96th edition, 8vo., cloth, flyleaf and titlepage loose, binding shaky, else good.   C. P. Hyland   261 - 376   2013   £70

Burkett, Mary E. *Read's Point of View.* Windermere: Skiddaw Press, 1995. First edition, large 8vo., original cloth, gilt, dust jacket, 16 colored plates and 40 black and white illustrations, inscribed by author, prospectus sheet loosely inserted.   R. F. G. Hollett & Son   Lake District & Cumbria - 242   2013   £30

Burkett, Mary E. *William Green of Ambleside. A Lake District Artist (1760-1823).* Kendal: Abbot Hall Art Gallery, 1984. First edition, large 8vo., original cloth, gilt, dust jacket with Lakeland Book of the Year Award 1984 wraparound band, illustrations.   R. F. G. Hollett & Son   Lake District & Cumbria - 240   2013   £25

Burlington Fine Arts Club *Exhibition of Bookbindings.* London: printed for the Burlington Fine Arts Club, 1891. First edition, frontispiece and CXIII (i.e. 114) plates, each with guard sheet and descriptive letterpress, folio, modern brown cloth, original titles from front board laid down, near fine.   Kaaterskill Books   16 - 6   2013 $1250

Burman, J. L. *Cango. The Story of the Cango Caves of South Africa.* Cape Town: Maskew Miller, 1960. Second edition, small vo., original boards, dust jacket rather rough tear repaired on reverse of upper panel, color frontispiece, 14 illustrations and plans on endpapers.   R. F. G. Hollett & Son   Africana - 31   2013   £50

Burne-Jones, Edward *The Flower Book.* Reproduced by Henri Piazza et Cie for the Fine Art Society, 1905. First edition, 221/300 copies, 38 color plates, half title, titlepage and prelim leaves printed in red and green, remainder of text printed in green except for the 4 page facsimile list of flowers made by Burne-Jones at rear which is printed in black, printed rectos only (except for half title/limitation leaf and facsimile list), very slight spotting, page bearing Plate X and verso of its title leaf opposite browned, large 4to., contemporary crushed dark green morocco in Cockerell style by W. H. Smith Bindery, flat spine divided by wide low raised bands, gilt lettered direct in second compartment and at foot, remaining compartments with gilt single line border and three gilt dots at corners, repeated on sides, upper spine gilt lettered, gilt single fillet on board edges, grey endpapers, top edge gilt, others uncut, one corner with small snag, preserved in its original fleece lined green cloth drop-down folding box with metal catch, lettered gilt on upper side, box rebacked and showing bit of wear and tear, but performing its function splendidly, good.   Blackwell's Rare Books   B174 - 18   2013   £7500

Burnet, Gilbert, Bp. of Salisbury   1643-1715 *The Abridgement of Bishop Burnet's History of His Own Times.* London: printed and sold by J. Smith, 1724. First edition, variant with page 440 correctly numbered, engraved frontispiece and woodcut vignette on titlepage, 8vo., some foxing and dusting, frontispiece foxed, expertly bound in recent quarter sprinkled calf, marbled boards, vellum tips, raised and gilt banded spine, red morocco label.   Jarndyce Antiquarian Booksellers   CCIV - 79   2013   £185

Burnet, Gilbert, Bp. of Salisbury   1643-1715 *A Exhortation to Peace and Union. A Sermon at St. Lawrence-Jury at the Election of Lord Mayor of London on the 29th of September 1681.* London: printed for Richard Chiswell, 1681. Small 4to., first and last leaves bit soiled, faint damp mark to upper cover, recent quarter calf by Chris Weston, paste paper boards, red morocco label lettered vertically, contemporary but not Burnet's ink inscription.   Unsworths Antiquarian Booksellers   28 - 77   2013   £95

Burnet, Gilbert, Bp. of Salisbury   1643-1715 *A Relation of a Conference, Held about Religion at London the Third of April 1676.* London: printed and are to be sold by Moses Pitt, 1676. First edition, 8vo., prelim imprimatur leaf and final ad leaf, ink splashes to A4 recto of pages 12-13, one marginal note identifying an anonymous name in text, full contemporary calf, raised bands, rubbed, hinges cracked, head and tail of spine worn, early paper label chipped, handwritten shelf label flap, armorial bookplate of W. Wynne, signature of G. Wynne on title, Edw. Solme (?) struck through.   Jarndyce Antiquarian Booksellers   CCIV - 6   2013   £150

Burnet, Gilbert, Bp. of Salisbury   1643-1715 *Some Letters, containing an Account of What Seemed Most Remarkable in Travelling through Switzerland, Italy, Some Parts of Germany, &c. in the Years 1685 and 1686.* Rotterdam: printed by Abraham Acher, 1687. 12mo., prelim ad leaf, but without final blank, rust hole to F3 slightly affecting 3 letters, some early marginal notes, slight dustiness and browning, recent quarter calf marbled boards, gilt banded spine, blind tooled flower device, red morocco label.   Jarndyce Antiquarian Booksellers   CCIV - 7   2013   £250

Burnet, Richard *A Word to the Members of the Mechanic's Institutes.* Devonport: printed for J. Johns, 1826. First edition, 6 engraved plates by George Banks, slip regarding original binding attached to titlepage, first two leaves reinforced at gutter and brittle at top, some browning and foxing, especially towards end, plates close trimmed with slight loss to one at fore-edge, accession number in biro at foot of title, very scarce.   Blackwell's Rare Books   172 - 38   2013   £600

Burnett, Frances Hodgson *Giovanni and the Other.* New York: Charles Scribner & Co., 1892. First edition, small 4to., green cloth, very good, spine faded, spots on front endpaper, inscribed by author Dec. 1892.   Barnaby Rudge Booksellers   Children 2013 - 021651   2013 $295

Burnett, Frances Hodgson *Little Lord Fauntleroy.* Leipzig: Bernhard Tauchnitz, 1887. Copyright edition, 12mo., original decorated cloth, gilt.   R. F. G. Hollett & Son   Children's Books - 96   2013   £40

Burnett, Frances Hodgson *Secret Garden.* New York: Stokes Aug., 1911. First edition, 8vo., blue gilt cloth, 375 pages, top edge gilt, slightest of rubbing, else near fine.   Aleph-Bet Books, Inc.   104 - 102   2013 $1750

Burnett, W. R. *Good-Bye, Chicago 1928: End of an Era.* New York: St. Martin's Press, 1981. First edition, 8vo., 175 pages, signed by author, fine in fine dust jacket.   By the Book, L. C.   36 - 41   2013 $250

Burney, Charles *The Present State of Music in France and Italy.* (with) *The Present State of Music in Germany and the Netherlands.* London: printed for T. Becket, J. Robson and G. Robinson, 1773-1775. Second editions, 3 volumes, some scattered foxing in volume I of Germany, 8vo., contemporary tree calf, rebacked, contrast

ing lettering pieces, evidence of scorching around edges, corners worn, sound.   Blackwell's Rare Books   B174 - 18   2013   £900

Burney, James *A Chronological History of the Discoveries in the South Sea or Pacific Ocean.* London: 1803-1817. First edition, 5 volumes, 28 engraved maps, 16 of which are folding, some with usual offsetting, 13 engraved plates, 4to., early cloth, backs trifle soiled with old morocco labels, excellent set.   Maggs Bros. Ltd.   1467 - 75   2013   £11,000

Burns, Robert   1759-1796   *An Address to the Deil.. with Explanatory Notes.* London: James Gilbert, 1830.   First edition, engraved portrait and title plates, 8 page catalog, odd spot, minor dampstains to lower inner margins of plates, original printed wrappers, slightly dusted, bound into 19th century maroon cloth, slight rubbing, very good.   Jarndyce Antiquarian Booksellers   CCIII - 52   2013   £85

Burns, Robert   1759-1796   *An Address to the Deil.. with Explanatory Notes.* London: James Gilbert, 1832.   11 first rate engravings on wood, engraved frontispiece and title, plates, odd spot, original pink printed wrappers, slightly dusted, spine partly defective, contemporary plain booklabel of Edwin Yarnold, all edges gilt, good plus.   Jarndyce Antiquarian Booksellers   CCIII - 53   2013   £65

Burns, Robert   1759-1796   *Fac-simile of Burns' celebrated poem entitled the Jolly Beggars.*   Glasgow: James Lumsden & Son, 1823.   First edition, half title text on rectos only, edges dusted and little chipped, original purple limp cloth, wrappers, paper label, spine neatly repaired, little faded & rubbed.   Jarndyce Antiquarian Booksellers   CCIII - 50   2013   £75

Burns, Robert   1759-1796   *Fac-simile of Burns' celebrated poem entitled the Jolly Beggars.*   Glasgow: James Lumsden & Son, Edinburgh: W. & A. K. Johnston, 1838. 4to., engraved frontispiece, some staining and spotting, contemporary tartan card wrappers, drab spine, blue label printed in gilt, bit rubbed and slightly dusted, printed ticket to Burns Centenary Dinner pasted to leading pastedown, all edges gilt, tipped into prelims are several letters relating to purchase of original manuscript of Jolly Beggars.   Jarndyce Antiquarian Booksellers   CCIII - 51   2013   £120

Burns, Robert   1759-1796   *Poems, Chiefly in the Scottish Dialect.* Edinburgh: printed for the author and sold by William Creech, 1787.   Second edition, half title, frontispiece, uncut in later full scarlet rushed morocco by Riviere & Son, gilt spine, border and dentelles, top edge gilt, very good, close to fine.   Jarndyce Antiquarian Booksellers   CCIII - 48   2013   £3800

Burns, Robert   1759-1796   *Poems, Chiefly in the Scottish Dialect.* London: printed for a. Strahan and T. Cadell,, in the Strand, and W. Creech Edinburgh, 1787.   Third edition, frontispiece, bound without half title, contemporary half calf, marbled boards, spine with raised and gilt bands, red morocco label, very slightly rubbed, slight wear to marbled paper on edges of following board, very good, clean copy in attractive contemporary binding, this copy was bought for 6s by Mr. D. Stacy of Hackney, London who adds his name to subscriber list.   Jarndyce Antiquarian Booksellers   CCIII - 49   2013   £1600

Burns, Robert   1759-1796   *Poems, Chiefly in the Scottish Dialect.* Glasgow: John Smith & Son, 1929.   Facsimile of 1789 Kilmarnock edition, uncut, mostly unopened in original pale blue wrappers, very good in original pale blue printed slipcase, knocked at head, spine label chipped.   Jarndyce Antiquarian Booksellers   CCIII - 47   2013   £65

Burns, Robert   1759-1796   *The Entire Works of Robert Burns...*   London: Andrew Moffat, 1842.   Seventh diamond edition, 4 volumes in one, frontispiece and engraved title 1822-1888e (1841), printed title, plates by Stewart, odd spot, lacking leading f.e.p., one gathering slightly proud, original dark blue cloth, blocked in blind, gilt spine, slightly dulled.   Jarndyce Antiquarian Booksellers   CCIII - 46   2013   £40

Burns, Robert   1759-1796   *The Complete Works of Robert Burns.*   London: Virtue and Co., 1870.   three quarter leather, extra engraved titlepage plus over 50 steel engravings, very good.   Barnaby Rudge Booksellers Poetry 2013 - 020692   2013 $70

Burr, David H.   *The Steamboat, Stage and Canal Register... for the Year 1832.*   New York: D. H. Burr, 1832. First edition, 18mo., 32 pages, large colored folding map, original calf, breaks in few folds, considerable foxing.   M & S Rare Books, Inc.   95 - 256   2013 $450

Burroughs, Edgar Rice   1875-1950   *Carson of Venus.* Tarzana: Edgar Rice Burroughs Inc., 1939.   First edition, fine in slightly spine faded, near fine dust jacket, inscribed by author to noted collector.   Between the Covers Rare Books, Inc.   Sci-Fi, Fantasy & Horror - 96878   2013 $2750

Burroughs, Edgar Rice   1875-1950   *Land of Terror.* Tarzana: Edgar Rice Burroughs, 1944.   First edition, pages 320, crown 8vo., original light blue cloth, backstrip and front cover with lettering blocked in orange, fore edges rough trimmed, fading to backstrip panel of dust jacket which is edge rubbed and with minor internal tape strengthening to folds at heads and tails, good.   Blackwell's Rare Books B174 - 184   2013   £250

Burroughs, Edgar Rice 1875-1950 *Tales of Three Planets.* New York: Canaveral Press, 1964. First edition, octavo, illustrations by Roy Krenkel, blue cloth variant binding. L. W. Currey, Inc. Fall Sampler Sept. 2013 - 144852 2013 $350

Burroughs, Edgar Rice 1875-1950 *Tarzan and the Jewels of Opar.* Chicago: A. C. McClurg, 1918. First edition, 8vo., original blue cloth, spine faded, otherwise excellent copy, inscribed by author to his brother-in-law Edward Gilbert. Maggs Bros. Ltd. 1460 - 151 2013 £350

Burroughs, William *The Dead Star.* San Francisco: City Lights, 1969. First edition, narrow 8vo., signed by author, oddly bound with two covers, outer covers rubbed, otherwise excellent copy in protective box. Maggs Bros. Ltd. 1460 - 152 2013 £250

Burroughs, William *The Letters of William Burroughs 1945-1959.* New York: Viking, 1993. First edition, wrappers, advance uncorrected proofs, fine. Beasley Books 2013 - 2013 $50

Burrowes, J. F. *The Piano-Forte Primer; Containing the Rudiments of Music...* Published (and sold wholesale only) by author, 1841. Twenty fourth edition, half title, musical notation, original cloth, engraved paper label on upper cover, spine little sunned and some slight foxing. Ken Spelman Books Ltd. 75 - 108 2013 £45

Burrows, E. H. *Captain Owen of the African Survey.* Rotterdam: A. A. Balkema, 1979. First edition, large 8vo., original cloth, gilt, dust jacket little rubbed in folds, 42 illustrations, and two family trees. R. F. G. Hollett & Son Africana - 32 2013 £30

Burrus, Ernest J. *Kino and Manje, Explorers of Sonora and Arizona.* Rome and St. Louis: Jesuit Historical Intstitute, 1971. First edition, thick 8vo., 4 facsimiles, large folding map in rear, navy blue cloth, gilt, fine. Argonaut Book Shop Summer 2013 - 180 2013 $250

Bursill, Henry *Hand Shadows to be Thrown Upon the Wall.* Griffith and Farran, 1859. 4to., modern cloth backed boards, 18 hand colored plates, attractive copy, coloring probably later, but nicely done. R. F. G. Hollett & Son Children's Books - 97 2013 £95

Bursill, Henry *Hand Shadows to be Thrown Upon the Wall.* Griffith and Farran, 1860. Fourth edition, 4to., modern three quarter levant morocco by N. A. Hyman, pages 4, with 1 hand colored plates, attractive copy, coloring probably late but well done. R. F. G. Hollett & Son Children's Books - 98 2013 £120

Burt, Kendal *The One that Got Away.* Collins and Michael Joseph, 1956. First edition, original black cloth, dust jacket (little worn and chipped), 18 plates, 6 maps. R. F. G. Hollett & Son Lake District & Cumbria - 244 2013 £35

Burt, Struthers *Powder River. Let'er Buck.* New York: Farrar & Rinehart, 1938. First edition, red cloth, contemporary owner's neat name and address, dated 1938, fine, pictorial dust jacket printed in black, yellow and red (slight chipping to extremities). Argonaut Book Shop Summer 2013 - 39 2013 $175

The Burton Legends. London: John R. Day, 1876. Illustrated with teetotal cuts, original printed paper boards, neatly rebacked, slightly bubbled by damp. Jarndyce Antiquarian Booksellers CCV - 6 2013 £85

Burton, John Hill *Life and Correspondence of David Hume from the Papers Bequeathed by His Nephew to the Royal Society of Edinburgh and other Original Sources.* Edinburgh: William Tote, 1846. First edition, 2 volumes, octavo, complete with both half titles, both engraved portraits and two folding facsimiles, full tan calf with gilt ruled and tooled borders, spine compartments richly gilt with central gilt urn devices, red and black morocco gilt labels, gilt board edges and turn-ins, marbled endpapers, top edge gilt, excellent set. Heritage Book Shop 50th Anniversary Catalogue - 54 2013 $1250

Burton, Richard Francis 1821-1890 *Explorations of the Highlands of Brazil..,.* London: 1869. First edition, first issue, 2 volumes, folding map, pictorial half titles and frontispieces, 8vo., original green pictorial cloth, gilt, faultless copy apart from remnants of small paper labels on backs. Maggs Bros. Ltd. 1467 - 104 2013 £5250

Burton, Richard Francis 1821-1890 *First Footsteps in East Africa or an Exploration of Harar.* Time Life Books, 1984. Facsimile edition, 2 volumes, original full padded leather, stamped in red and gilt, all edges gilt, 13 color plates and yellow silk bookmarks, prospectus and bookplate loosely inserted, fine set. R. F. G. Hollett & Son Africana - 33 2013 £45

Burton, Richard Francis 1821-1890 *Julnar the Sea Born and Her Son King Badr Basim of Persia.* Belfast: Crannog Press, 1975. First edition, one of 100 numbered copies, 6 single page and 8 other line block and linocut illustrations, large 8vo., original green hessian wrappers, printed paper label, fine. Maggs Bros. Ltd. 1442 - Crannog 2013 £75

Burton, Richard Francis 1821-1890 *The Kasidah of Haji Abdu El-Yezdi.* Philadelphia: David McKay, 1931. First edition, 4to., black cloth stamped in silver, pictorial paste-on, mint in publisher's box (stain on bottom of box), illustrations by Pogany with 12 stunning gravure plates, scarce in box. Aleph-Bet Books, Inc. 105 - 460 2013 $350

Burton, Richard Francis 1821-1890 *The Tale of Abu Kir and Abu Sir.* Belfast: Crannog Press, 1974. First edition, one of 100 numbered copies, large 8vo., original brown hessian wrappers, printed paper label, with four single page and one double page and 8 other line block and linocut illustrations by publisher Margaret McCord, fine.   Maggs Bros. Ltd. 1442 - Crannog 2013 £75

Burton, Richard Francis 1821-1890 *To the Gold Coast for Gold.* London: 1883. First edition, 2 volumes, octavo, 2 folding, colored maps in volume 1 and colored frontispiece in volume II, original red cloth, stamped in black and gilt on boards, spines lettered gilt and stamped in black, black coated endpapers, spines slightly rubbed and sunned, top edges bit foxed, minimal and invisible restoration to inner hinges, bookplate of John Ralph Willis, prominent collector of Rare Africana, each volume with previous owner's ink signature and date of 1888 on front free endpapers, on same page in same hand is written "Valley Forge Historical Society & Washington Memorial Library, Valley Forge", very good, handsome set.   Heritage Book Shop   Holiday Catalogue 2012 - 24 2013 $5500

Burton, Robert 1577-1640 *The Anatomy of Melancholy.* Oxford: John Lichfield and James for Henry Cripps, 1621. First edition, Lacks last 4 leaves, 4to., 18th century polished sheep, gilt ruled edges, gilt paneled spine with raised bands, rebacked saving original boards and spine, text has marginal dampstaining through first half of volume, scattered stains elsewhere, worming and few rust holes in blank outer margins, title soiled with inscriptions on recto and verso and blank upper margin has been re-edged and restored. James Tait Goodrich   S74 - 40   2013 $7500

Burton, Robert 1577-1640 *The Anatomy of Melancholy.* Oxford: Printed by John Lichfield and James Short for Henry Cripps, 1624. Second folio edition, full ruled 18th century calf, early rebacking with panels and tooling on spine, lower right corner of title (blank area repaired) light foxing and browning throughout, otherwise very good, tight, allegorical engraved title, rare. James Tait Goodrich 75 - 39 2013 $5000

Burton, Thomas *The History and Antiquities of the Parish of Hemingborough.* Sampson Bros., 1888. 8vo., frontispiece, folding tables, very good in original gilt lettered brown cloth.   Ken Spelman Books Ltd. 73 - 86 2013 £60

Burton, Thomas *The History of Hemingborough.* Sampson Bros., 1888. Large paper copy, frontispiece, folding tables and plates, original dark green roan backed boards, joints and head and tail of spine rubbed, later bookplate.   Ken Spelman Books Ltd. 73 - 85 2013 £60

Burton, Virginia Lee *Katy and the Big Snow.* Boston: Houghton Mifflin, 1943. First edition, first printing, oblong 4to., pictorial cloth, slightest bit of edge wear, else near fine in dust jacket (good-very good with some soil, several neat mends, edge restoration, price intact), rare, color illustrations.   Aleph-Bet Books, Inc.   105 - 109   2013 $2850

Burton, Virginia Lee *Mike Mulligan and His Steam Shovel.* Boston: Houghton Mifflin, 1939. First edition, first printing, oblong 4to., slight cover soil, else near fine in bright, price clipped dust jacket with no tears but with paper rubbed bit roughly in a narrow 1 inch section along spine and covers, this copy inscribed by Burton thanking the owner for his help,

rare, special copy.   Aleph-Bet Books, Inc.   105 - 107   2013 $8500

Bury, Thomas Talbot *Six Coloured Views on the Liverpool and Manchester Railway...* London: published by R. Ackermann and sold by R. Ackermann June, 1831. First edition, large quarto, 7 hand colored aquatint plates, plate 7 watermarked 1827, plate 7 watermarked 1831, all plates dated Feby. 1831, original quarter calf backed printed drab wrappers with printed ads on inside front and inside outside back, exceptional copy, slightly larger than Abbey's, custom made half brown morocco clamshell case.   David Brass Rare Books, Inc.   Holiday 2012 Chapter Two - DB 01695 2013 $4500

Bush, Christopher *The Perfect Murder Case.* Garden City: Doubleday Crime Club, 1929. First American edition, fine in dust jacket.   Mordida Books 81 - 57 2013 $500

Bush, James *The Choice; or Lines on the Beatitudes Square.* London: R. Saywell; Cockermouth: Bailey & Sons and Carlisle: C. Thurnam, 1841. First edition, square 8vo., full polished calf gilt, edges rubbed, pages 102, engraved frontispiece of Buttermere Chapel (foxed), scattered foxing in places, scarce, presentation copy inscribed by author to Mrs. Joshua Stanger. R. F. G. Hollett & Son   Lake District & Cumbria - 246 2013 £75

Bushnell, Horace *Woman Suffrage; Reform Against Nature.* New York: Scribner, 1869. First edition, 8vo., 184 pages + ads, publisher's green cloth, lacks half inch of cloth at bottom of spine, small piece at top, ex-libris with labels on front pastedowns and pocket in rear, couple of small stamps, good.   Second Life Books Inc. 182 - 33 2013 $125

Buswell, John *An Historical Account of the Knights of the Most Noble Order of the Garter from Its First Institution in the Year MCCCL to the Present Time.* London: R. Griffiths and T. Payne, 1757. First edition, 8vo., three quarter leather, truly scarce, bound in original marbled covers over leather spine, joints very weak, inside clean and crisp.   Barnaby Rudge Booksellers Biography 2013 - 021310 2013 $525

Bute, John Stuart Earl of *The Tabular Distribution of British Plants. Part I. containing the Genera (only).* printed by J. Davis, 1787. Oblong 8vo., original quarter calf, worn at extremities, headcap defective, boards slightly soiled, good, very rare. Blackwell's Rare Books 172 - 39 2013 £1500

Butler, Blanche *Puppy Dog Number Book for Tiny Tots.* Akron: Saalfield, 1939. Folio, stiff wrappers, slight wear to cover and pages, else very good, illustrations by Grace Mallon. Aleph-Bet Books, Inc. 105 - 190 2013 $125

Butler, Charles *The Historical Memoirs of the Church of France, in the Reigns of Lewis the Fourteenth.* London: T. Cadell and W. Davies, 1810. First edition, frontispiece, contemporary full speckled calf, gilt spine, borders and dentelles, red, green and black leather labels, armorial bookplate of John Trotter Brockett, very good. Jarndyce Antiquarian Booksellers CCIII - 652 2013 £110

Butler, David M. *Quaker Meeting Houses of the Lake Counties.* Friends Historical Society, 1978. First softback edition, small 4to., original pictorial stiff wrappers, illustrations. R. F. G. Hollett & Son Lake District & Cumbria - 247 2013 £30

Butler, David M. *Summer Houses of Kendal.* Kendal: Abbot Hall Art Gallery, 1982. First edition, small 4to., original pictorial wrappers, pages 22, illustrations. R. F. G. Hollett & Son Lake District & Cumbria - 248 2013 £25

Butler, Frederick *The Farmer's Manual: Being a Plain Practical Treatise on the Art of Husbandry...* Weathersfield: published by the author, 1821. 8vo., text toned and foxed with some waterstaining, still clearly legible, original quarter brown calf over marbled paper backed boards, pieces missing at corners and spine head, front cover torn, binding heavily worn, ownership signature of Edwin B. Ripley, a Connecticut farmer, rare, as is. Jeff Weber Rare Books 169 - 50 2013 $75

Butler, George *Butterfly Babies.* Chicago: Magill Weinsheimer, 1917. 16mo., pictorial boards, light soil and spine rubbing, very good+. Aleph-Bet Books, Inc. 104 - 202 2013 $250

Butler, Robert Olen *Alleys of Eden.* New York: Horizon, 1981. First edition, signed by author, inscribed by him in 1982, five photocopied pages of publicity material laid in, 2 pages of review excerpts from 21 sources and 3 pages of published reviews, faint offsetting to pastedowns, foxing to top edge of text block, near fine in very good, lightly foxed dust jacket with shallow chipping to spine ends, small pull to rear panel, small bookstore stamp there. Ken Lopez Bookseller 159 - 29 2013 $250

Butler, Samuel 1612-1680 *Hudibras.* London: printed or C. Bathurst et al, 1772. Third edition, 2 volumes, 8vo., frontispiece ad 9 engraved plates after Hogarth, + 7 engraved plates after Hogarth, light toning, plates little foxed, contemporary sprinkled tan calf, spines gilt in compartments, red and green morocco labels, edges speckled, joints and corners repaired, old leather darkened, scratched at extremities, contemporary armorial bookplate of Thomas Webb/Hoston. Unsworths Antiquarian Booksellers 28 - 78 2013 £120

Butler, Samuel 1835-1902 *Ex Voto.* London: Trubner & Co., 1888. First edition, inscribed by author to T(homas) Ballard, close friend of author, very good, bumping and small chips to cloth on corners, interior clean and tight, several illustrations from photos, 277 pages, 3 pages ads, very nice. The Kelmscott Bookshop 7 - 130 2013 $450

Butler, W. F. *The Wild North Land...* London: Sampson Low etc, 1874. Fifth edition, full soft blue polished calf gilt, raised bands, spine label, little scratched and faded, woodcut frontispiece, folding map, 15 woodcut plates. R. F. G. Hollett & Son Polar Exploration - 4 2013 £75

Butterworth, Benjamin *The Growth of Industrial Art.* Washington: Government Printing Office, 1892. Second edition, 510 x 410mm., 2 p.l., 200 pages, publisher's black cloth (faded) gilt titling on upper cover, flat spine, with 200 pages of illustrations, head and tail of spine and upper corner of front cover with remnants of small paper labels, titlepage with library blindstamped seal and ink de-accession stamp; extremities rather rubbed, boards bit soiled, spine with three horizontal cracks and two one-inch patches of missing cloth, cloth at head of spine fraying occasional minor smudges, otherwise excellent copy, text and illustrations clean and fresh, binding solid despite defects. Phillip J. Pirages 63 - 259 2013 $400

Buxton, Thomas Fowell *The African Slave Trade and Its Remedy.* London: John Murray, 1840. 14 page prospectus, folding map, original brown publisher's cloth, blocked in blind, spine lettered gilt, armorial Downshire bookplate, very good. Jarndyce Antiquarian Booksellers CCV - 42 2013 £450

By the Seaside. London: Dean's Rag Book Co. Ltd. n.d. circa, 1915. 8vo., pictorial cloth. as new, charming color illustrations on every page. Aleph-Bet Books, Inc. 105 - 139 2013 $275

Bynington, Margaret F. *Homestead: the Households of a Mill Town.* New York: Charities Publication Committee, 1910. First edition, 8vo., 292 pages, foldout photo frontispiece (panorama), green cloth (little dust soiled), very good tight copy, from the library of reformer Florence Kelley (1859-1932). Second Life Books Inc. 182 - 35 2013 $375

Byrd, Richard Evelyn *Little America: Aerial Exploration the Antarctic and the Flight to the South Pole.* G. P. Putnam's Sons, 1931. First English edition, large 8vo., original cloth, gilt, few spots to spine, 74 illustrations and maps.   R. F. G. Hollett & Son   Polar Exploration - 5   2013   £45

Byrd, William *The Westover Manuscripts...* Petersburg: Edmund and Julian C. Ruffin, 1841. First edition, large 8vo., contemporary cloth backed plain boards, most of spine cloth gone, sound, considerably foxed.   M & S Rare Books, Inc.   95 - 45   2013 $1750

Byrne, Francis J. *Irish Kings and High-Kings.* 1973. First edition, 8vo., 341 pages, maps, illustrations, cloth, dust jacket, very good.   C. P. Hyland   261 - 166   2013   £50

Byrne, Miriam *The Would Be Witch.* New York: Frederick Stokes, 1906. First edition, green cloth, very good+, 12mo., beautiful copy, previous owner's inscription dated 1907, 8 illustrations, including frontispiece.   Barnaby Rudge Booksellers   Children 2013 - 021406   2013 $50

Byrom, John *Miscellaneous Poems.* Leeds: printed by and for James Nichols, 1814. 2 volumes, engraved frontispiece, lightly foxed, 8vo., untrimmed, original boards, spines with paper labels, somewhat soiled and rubbed, good.   Blackwell's Rare Books   B174 - 20   2013   £80

Byron Painted by His Compeers; or all About Lord Byron, from His Marriage to His Death as Given in the Various Newspapers of His Day... London: Samuel Palmer, 1869. Original dark green cloth, bevelled boards, front board lettered in gilt within attractive gilt roundel, very good, tight copy, Doris Langley Moore's copy with few pencil notes by her.   Jarndyce Antiquarian Booksellers   CCIII - 340   2013   £150

Byron, George Gordon Noel, 6th Baron 1788-1824 *The Age of Bronze, or Carmen Secualre et Annus Haud Mirabilis.* London: printed for John Hunt, 1823. First edition, disbound, lacking half title, signature of Henry Talbot, very good.   Jarndyce Antiquarian Booksellers   CCIII - 310   2013   £120

Byron, George Gordon Noel, 6th Baron 1788-1824 *The Age of Bronze, or Carmen Secualre et Annus Haud Mirabilis.* London: John Hunt, 1823. Second edition, half title, few minor internal marks, disbound.   Jarndyce Antiquarian Booksellers   CCIII - 311   2013   £50

Byron, George Gordon Noel, 6th Baron 1788-1824 *The Age of Bronze, or Carmen Secualre et Annus Haud Mirabilis.* London: printed or John Hunt, 1823. Third edition, half title, uncut in original brown wrappers, paper label to front wrapper, dusted, edges little chipped, spine worn, booklabel and signature of Alex Bridge.   Jarndyce Antiquarian Booksellers   CCIII - 312   2013   £60

Byron, George Gordon Noel, 6th Baron 1788-1824 *The Beauties of Byron.* London: printed by T. Davison for Thomas Tegg &c, circa, 1833? 12mo., half title, frontispiece, full contemporary calf, spine gilt in compartments, gilt and blind borders, spine slightly chipped at head, small split to tail of following hinge, slight rubbing, contemporary owner's inscription on initial blank.   Jarndyce Antiquarian Booksellers   CCIII - 98   2013   £60

Byron, George Gordon Noel, 6th Baron 1788-1824 *Beppo, a Venetian Story.* London: John Murray, 1818. Either Second or third edition, edition statement carefully erased from titlepage to give impression of a first, bound without half title, later half calf.   Jarndyce Antiquarian Booksellers   CCIII - 243   2013   £50

Byron, George Gordon Noel, 6th Baron 1788-1824 *Beppo, a Venetian Story.* London: John Muurray, 1818. First edition, bound without half title and final blank, contemporary half calf, gilt spine, slightly rubbed, small chip at head of spine, bookseller's ticket T. James & Co., Southampton, good plus copy, scarce.   Jarndyce Antiquarian Booksellers   CCIII - 242   2013   £750

Byron, George Gordon Noel, 6th Baron 1788-1824 *Beppo, a Venetian Story.* London: John Murray, 1818. Fifth edition, half title, little spotted, disbound, booklabel and signature of Alex Bridge.   Jarndyce Antiquarian Booksellers   CCIII - 244   2013   £30

Byron, George Gordon Noel, 6th Baron 1788-1824 *Beppo and Don Juan.* London: John Murray, 1853. 2 volumes, original plain brown cloth, spines lettered in gilt, very good.   Jarndyce Antiquarian Booksellers   CCIII - 103   2013   £35

Byron, George Gordon Noel, 6th Baron 1788-1824 *The Bride of Abydos.* London: John Murray, 1813. Third edition, disbound.   Jarndyce Antiquarian Booksellers   CCIII - 172   2013   £35

Byron, George Gordon Noel, 6th Baron 1788-1824 *The Bride of Abydos.* London: John Murray, 1813. Fifth edition, slightly spotted, disbound, ownership inscription Enniskillen, all edges gilt.   Jarndyce Antiquarian Booksellers   CCIII - 173   2013   £25

Byron, George Gordon Noel, 6th Baron 1788-1824 *Byroniana. The Opinions of Lord Byron on Men, Manners and Things...* London: Hamilton, Adams & Co., 1834. 16mo., engraved frontispiece, slightly later purple binder's cloth, spine little faded, armorial bookplate and signature of Lord Carlingford, 1875.   Jarndyce Antiquarian Booksellers   CCIII - 99   2013   £200

Byron, George Gordon Noel, 6th Baron   1788-1824
Byron's Letters and Journals.   London: John Murray, 1973-1978.   First edition, 11 volumes, half titles, frontispiece, original red cloth, very good in dust jackets.   Jarndyce Antiquarian Booksellers   CCIII - 331   2013   £350

Byron, George Gordon Noel, 6th Baron   1788-1824
Cain; a Mystery.   London: printed by H. Gray, 1822.   12mo., contemporary full calf, gilt spine, rubbed, spine chipped at tail with slight loss.   Jarndyce Antiquarian Booksellers   CCIII - 305   2013   £85

Byron, George Gordon Noel, 6th Baron   1788-1824
Cain; a Mystery.   London: printed by H. Gray, 1822.   Uncut in original drab boards, brown cloth spine little worn and slightly chipped at head, contemporary signature of John Chatto, booklabel and signature of Alex Bridge.   Jarndyce Antiquarian Booksellers   CCIII - 304   2013   £120

Byron, George Gordon Noel, 6th Baron   1788-1824
Cain; a Mystery.   London: printed & published by W. Dugdale, 1826.   Early piracy, 12mo., disbound, 63 pages.   Jarndyce Antiquarian Booksellers   CCIII - 306   2013   £50

Byron, George Gordon Noel, 6th Baron   1788-1824
Childe Harold's Pilgrimage.   London: John Murray, 1815.   Ninth edition, 16 page catalog (Nov. 1815) uncut in original blue boards, drab spine, paper label, spine chipped with some loss at at head and tail, corners slightly rubbed, armorial bookplate and signature of William Hibbs Bevan.   Jarndyce Antiquarian Booksellers   CCIII - 140   2013   £110

Byron, George Gordon Noel, 6th Baron   1788-1824
Childe Harold's Pilgrimage.   London: John Murray, 1815.   Tenth edition, 4 page catalog (Jan. 1818) but without facsimile leaf and no sign of removal, uncut in original drab boards, paper label, spine slightly rubbed at head and tail, name crossed out in ink on upper board, booklabel of Erling Kehlet-Hansen, very good.   Jarndyce Antiquarian Booksellers   CCIII - 141   2013   £50

Byron, George Gordon Noel, 6th Baron   1788-1824
Childe Harold's Pilgrimage.   London: John Murray, 1816.   First edition, 2nd issue, half title 8 pages ads (No. 1816), edges little dusted, uncut in original drab wrappers, spine weakening and slightly chipped, small label and ink spot on front wrapper, ownership inscription of Charles Gibbon on initial blank and title, good plus.   Jarndyce Antiquarian Booksellers   CCIII - 142   2013   £150

Byron, George Gordon Noel, 6th Baron   1788-1824
Childe Harold's Pilgrimage.   London: W. Dugdale, Russell Court, 1825.   12mo., disbound.   Jarndyce Antiquarian Booksellers   CCIII - 134   2013   £50

Byron, George Gordon Noel, 6th Baron   1788-1824
Childe Harold's Pilgrimage.   Paris: n.p., 1827.   Pirated edition, 24mo., frontispiece, contemporary half calf, black leather label, little rubbed and worn, spine chipped at tail.   Jarndyce Antiquarian Booksellers   CCIII - 135   2013   £45

Byron, George Gordon Noel, 6th Baron   1788-1824
Childe Harolds Pilgrimsfaard.   Stockholm: Johan Horberg, 1832.   First Swedish edition, mostly unopened, uncut in original plain blue wrappers, near fine.   Jarndyce Antiquarian Booksellers   CCIII - 136   2013   £200

Byron, George Gordon Noel, 6th Baron   1788-1824
Childe Harold's Pilgrimage.   New York: Charles Grattan, circa, 1840.   171 pages, half title, frontispiece, original olive green cloth, gilt, spine slightly rubbed, ownership inscription on titlepage, 1861 and occasional pencil underlining, attractive copy.   Jarndyce Antiquarian Booksellers   CCIII - 137   2013   £45

Byron, George Gordon Noel, 6th Baron   1788-1824
Childe Harold's Pilgrimage.   London: John Murray, 1855.   4to., half title, unopened in original glazed pale green printed boards by Edmonds & Remnants, pink cloth spine, corners little worn, otherwise, very good.   Jarndyce Antiquarian Booksellers   CCIII - 138   2013   £65

Byron, George Gordon Noel, 6th Baron   1788-1824
Childe Harold's Pilgrimage. with Childe Harold's Pilgrimage. Canto the third.   London: John Murray, 1814-1816.   Seventh edition and First edition, 2nd issue, respectively, half titles, disbound, all edges gilt.   Jarndyce Antiquarian Booksellers   CCIII - 139   2013   £150

Byron, George Gordon Noel, 6th Baron   1788-1824
Childe Harold's Pilgrimage. Canto the Third.   London: John Murray, 1816.   First edition, 2nd issue, 2nd variant, half title, 4 pages ads (Dec. 1816), uncut in original drab wrappers, spine slightly chipped at tail, leading hinge splitting, good plus as originally issued in later blue cloth folder, armorial bookplate of Chadwyck-Healey, loosely inserted is letter dated 1930 in original envelope from T. J. Wise to Oliver Nowell Chadwyck-Healey.   Jarndyce Antiquarian Booksellers   CCIII - 144   2013   £350

Byron, George Gordon Noel, 6th Baron   1788-1824
Childe Harold's Pilgrimage Canto the Third.   London: John Murray, 1816.   First edition, 2nd issue, slightly damp marked in lower margin, disbound.   Jarndyce Antiquarian Booksellers   CCIII - 143   2013   £35

Byron, George Gordon Noel, 6th Baron   1788-1824
Childe Harold's Pilgrimage. Canto the Third. with Canto the Fourth.   London: John Murray, 1818.   First edition, 2nd issue and first edition, 4th issue, 2 volumes in 1, half title, contemporary full calf, spine and borders blocked in blind, bit rubbed and marked, leading hinge repaired at tail, front board with evidence of old repair.   Jarndyce Antiquarian Booksellers   CCIII - 145   2013   £180

Byron, George Gordon Noel, 6th Baron   1788-1824
Childe Harold's Pilgrimage. canto the Fourth. with Beppo, a Venetian Story. with Monody on the Derath of R. B. Sheridan.   London: John Murray, 1818. London: R. B. Sheridan, 1817. First edition, 2nd issue, sixth edition, new edition respectively, 3 volumes in 1, full contemporary calf, gilt spine with black bands, brown leather label titled "Lord Byron's Poems", gilt borders and dentelles, slight rubbing, hinges little worn, presentation inscription to Doris Langley Moore.   Jarndyce Antiquarian Booksellers   CCIII - 89   2013   £65

Byron, George Gordon Noel, 6th Baron   1788-1824
Childe Harold's Pilgrimage. Canto the Fourth.   London: John Murray, 1818. First edition, 2nd issue, 4 page inserted ads, preceding title, final ad leaf and 12 page catalog on smaller size pale blue paper, uncut in original drab boards, paper label, following hinge slightly worn, neat repairs at head and tail of spine, small bookseller's ticket, C. Chapple, Pall Mall, good plus copy.   Jarndyce Antiquarian Booksellers   CCIII - 146   2013   £150

Byron, George Gordon Noel, 6th Baron   1788-1824
Childe Harold's Pilgrimage. Canto the Fourth.   London: John Murray, 1818. First edition, 2nd issue, disbound, some light foxing, ownership inscription of A. Fraget (?) Dartmouth.   Jarndyce Antiquarian Booksellers   CCIII - 147   2013   £50

Byron, George Gordon Noel, 6th Baron   1788-1824
Childe Harold's Pilgrimage. Canto the Fourth.   London: John Murray, 1818. First edition, 4th issue, 12 page catalog preceding title, final ad leaf, uncut in original pale blue boards, paper label, small ink stain on front board, spine and hinges little worn, armorial bookplate of Chadwyck-Healey, good copy, custom made blue morocco and cloth slipcase by Riviere & son.   Jarndyce Antiquarian Booksellers   CCIII - 148   2013   £300

Byron, George Gordon Noel, 6th Baron   1788-1824
Choice Works of Lord Byron. The Giaour, Bride of Abydos, The Corsair, Lara, Childe Harold (Canto I and II) with Miscellaneous Poems and Life of the Author.   London: Thomas Allman, 1844. 32mo., frontispiece, engraved title, original dark green cloth, slightly rubbed, slight wear to head of spine, armorial bookplate of Fitzpatrick of Grantstown Manor.   Jarndyce Antiquarian Booksellers   CCIII - 102   2013   £35

Byron, George Gordon Noel, 6th Baron   1788-1824
Correspondence of Lord Byron, with a Friend, Including His Letters to his Mother... in 1809, 1810 and 1811...   Paris: A. & W. Galignani, 1825. 2 volumes, half titles, browned, contemporary half dark green calf, slightly rubbed, Renier booklabels.   Jarndyce Antiquarian Booksellers   CCIII - 321   2013   £60

Byron, George Gordon Noel, 6th Baron   1788-1824
Correspondence. Chiefly with Lady Melbourne, Mr. Hobhouse, The Hon. Douglas Kinnaird, and P. B. Shelley.   London: John Murray, 1922. Reprint, 2 volumes, half titles, frontispiece, plates, pastedowns strengthened at edges with tape, original dark green cloth, spines little dulled and slightly worn at head and tail, Doris Langley Moore's copy with her signature and bookplates and extensive annotations in her hand.   Jarndyce Antiquarian Booksellers   CCIII - 326   2013   £75

Byron, George Gordon Noel, 6th Baron   1788-1824
Correspondence. Chiefly with Lady Melbourne, Mr. Hobhouse, The Hon. Douglas Kinnaird, and P. B. Shelley.   London: John Murray, 1922. Reprint, 2 volumes, half titles, frontispiece portrait, plates, fore-edges slightly spotted, original dark green cloth, very good in slightly torn dust jackets.   Jarndyce Antiquarian Booksellers   CCIII - 327   2013   £30

Byron, George Gordon Noel, 6th Baron   1788-1824   *The Corsair, a Tale.*   London: John Murray, 1814. First edition, 2nd issue, half title, name neatly erased from title, disbound.   Jarndyce Antiquarian Booksellers   CCIII - 182   2013   £50

Byron, George Gordon Noel, 6th Baron   1788-1824   *The Corsair, a Tale.*   London: John Murray, 1814. First edition, first issue, disbound, all edges gilt.   Jarndyce Antiquarian Booksellers   CCIII - 181   2013   £120

Byron, George Gordon Noel, 6th Baron   1788-1824   *The Corsair, a Tale.*   London: John Murray, 1814. Second edition, third issue, 2nd variant, half title, contemporary half black calf, vellum corners, marbled boards, slightly rubbed, very good.   Jarndyce Antiquarian Booksellers   CCIII - 173   2013   £35

Byron, George Gordon Noel, 6th Baron   1788-1824   *The Corsair, a Tale.*   London: John Murray, 1814. Fourth edition, 3rd issue, 2nd variant, without half title, disbound.   Jarndyce Antiquarian Booksellers   CCIII - 185   2013   £30

Byron, George Gordon Noel, 6th Baron   1788-1824   *The Corsair, a Tale.*   London: John Murray, 1814. Fourth edition, first issue, half title, 8 page catalog, later drab wrappers, spine with two small repaired tears, ink title, booklabel of Alex Bridge and ownership inscription of Charles Strachey, very good.   Jarndyce Antiquarian Booksellers   CCIII - 184   2013   £30

Byron, George Gordon Noel, 6th Baron   1788-1824   *The Corsair, a Tale.*   London: John Murray, 1815. Ninth edition, disbound.   Jarndyce Antiquarian Booksellers   CCIII - 187   2013   £25

Byron, George Gordon Noel, 6th Baron   1788-1824   *The Deformed Transformed. (bound with) The Island, or Christian and His Comrades.*   London: printed for J. & H. L. Hunt, 1824. London: John Hunt, 1823. Second edition and third edition, 2 volumes in 1, half titles, contemporary half calf, gilt spine, rubbed, corners and spine little worn, booklabel ad signature of Alex Bridge, library label of Harry Matthews.   Jarndyce Antiquarian Booksellers   CCIII - 319   2013   £180

Byron, George Gordon Noel, 6th Baron   1788-1824   *The Deformed Transformed: a Drama.*   London: J. Dicks, circa, 1875. New edition, illustrations, original cream pictorial wrappers, slightly dusted.   Jarndyce Antiquarian Booksellers   CCIII - 320   2013   £25

Byron, George Gordon Noel, 6th Baron   1788-1824   *Don Juan. (Cantos I & II).*   London: J. Onwhyn, 1819. Early piracy, contemporary brown boards, corners and hinges bit rubbed, spine chipped at head, good plus.   Jarndyce Antiquarian Booksellers   CCIII - 253   2013   £120

Byron, George Gordon Noel, 6th Baron   1788-1824   *Don Juan. (Cantos I & II).*   London: Thomas Davison, 1819. First edition, 4to., half title, uncut in original drab boards, expertly rebacked with appropriate drab spine, paper label, very good.   Jarndyce Antiquarian Booksellers   CCIII - 250   2013   £650

Byron, George Gordon Noel, 6th Baron   1788-1824   *Don Juan. (Cantos I & II).*   London: Thomas Davison, 1819. First edition, 4to., half title, corner of titlepage expertly repaired where ownership details removed, slight spotting, slightly later half dark green calf decorated in gilt and blind, maroon leather label, few careful repairs to hinges, good plus.   Jarndyce Antiquarian Booksellers   CCIII - 252   2013   £550

Byron, George Gordon Noel, 6th Baron   1788-1824   *Don Juan. (Cantos I & II).*   London: Thomas Davison, 1819. First edition, 4to., half title, slightly spotted, expertly rebound in appropriate drab boards, paper label, very good.   Jarndyce Antiquarian Booksellers   CCIII - 251   2013   £500

Byron, George Gordon Noel, 6th Baron   1788-1824   *Don Juan. (Cantos I & II).*   London: Thomas Davison, 1819. Second edition, Slight spotting, disbound.   Jarndyce Antiquarian Booksellers   CCIII - 254   2013   £50

Byron, George Gordon Noel, 6th Baron   1788-1824   *Don Juan. (Cantos I & II).*   London: Thomas Davison, 1820. New edition, disbound.   Jarndyce Antiquarian Booksellers   CCIII - 256   2013   £30

Byron, George Gordon Noel, 6th Baron   1788-1824   *Don Juan. (Cantos I & II).*   London: Thomas Davison, 1820. Half title, uncut, original drab boards, paper label, spine slightly dulled, but very good, well preserved.   Jarndyce Antiquarian Booksellers   CCIII - 255   2013   £150

Byron, George Gordon Noel, 6th Baron   1788-1824   *Don Juan. (Cantos I to V).*   London: printed by G. Smeeton, 1821? Color frontispiece bound in at page 207, engraved title, printed title, 5 other hand colored plates by I. R. Cruikshank, small tear in outer margin page 101/102 not affecting text, few internal marks, later full tree calf, gilt spine and borders, black leather label, marbled endpapers, slightly rubbed, lacking title label, armorial bookplate of C. Robert Bignold, very good, scarce.   Jarndyce Antiquarian Booksellers   CCIII - 265   2013   £280

Byron, George Gordon Noel, 6th Baron   1788-1824   *Don Juan. (Cantos I to V).*   Benbow, printer and publisher 1822, 1824. 12mo., frontispiece and title (122), printed title (1824) with Sudbury imprint), slight browning, uncut in original drab boards, paper label, rubbed, spine cracked and little darkened, booklabel and signature of Alex Bridge.   Jarndyce Antiquarian Booksellers   CCIII - 266   2013   £90

Byron, George Gordon Noel, 6th Baron   1788-1824   *Don Juan. (Cantos III, IV & V).*   London: printed for Sherwin & Co., 1821. Pirated edition, uncut in original brown wrappers, very neatly rebacked, contemporary ownership inscription of Daniel Davies, very good in later brown cloth slipcase.   Jarndyce Antiquarian Booksellers   CCIII - 259   2013   £120

Byron, George Gordon Noel, 6th Baron   1788-1824   *Don Juan. (Cantos III, IV & V).*   London: Thomas Davison, 1821. First edition, half title, spotted, uncut in later pale blue boards, retaining original paper label, tail of spine strengthened, very good, small paper edition.   Jarndyce Antiquarian Booksellers   CCIII - 258   2013   £110

Byron, George Gordon Noel, 6th Baron   1788-1824   *Don Juan. (Cantos III, IV & V).*   London: Thomas Davison, 1821. First edition, half title, uncut in original drab boards, paper label, spine little worn, little chipped at head, evidence of booklabel removal, large paper edition.   Jarndyce Antiquarian Booksellers   CCIII - 257   2013   £300

Byron, George Gordon Noel, 6th Baron   1788-1824   *Don Juan. (Cantos VI, VII & VIII).*   London: John Hunt, 1823. First edition, final ad leaf, uncut in original pale blue boards, paper label, spine dulled and chipped at head and tail, else nice, tight, small paper edition.   Jarndyce Antiquarian Booksellers   CCIII - 260   2013   £150

Byron, George Gordon Noel, 6th Baron   1788-1824
Don Juan. (Cantos IX, X, and XI). London: John Hunt, 1823. First edition, 4 pages ads (Sept. 1823), uncut in original drab boards, paper label, spine dulled and slightly rubbed at head and tail, very good, small paper edition.   Jarndyce Antiquarian Booksellers   CCIII - 261   2013   £150

Byron, George Gordon Noel, 6th Baron   1788-1824
Don Juan. (Cantos IX, X, and XI). London: John Hunt, 1823. First edition, 4 pages ads (Sept. 1823), unopened, uncut in original pale blue boards, blue glazed paper spine paper label, spine defective, small bookseller's ticket, John Stacy, Norwich.   Jarndyce Antiquarian Booksellers   CCIII - 262   2013   £50

Byron, George Gordon Noel, 6th Baron   1788-1824
Don Juan. (Cantos XII, XIII & XIV). London: John Hunt, 1823. First edition, 12 page catalog (Oct. 1823), uncut, original pale blue boards, paper label, spine slightly dulled and with some minor careful repairs at head, small paper edition.   Jarndyce Antiquarian Booksellers   CCIII - 263   2013   £150

Byron, George Gordon Noel, 6th Baron   1788-1824
Don Juan. (Cantos XV & XVI). London: John and H. L. Hunt, 1824. First edition, final ad leaf, errata slip, uncut in original drab boards, paper label, spine rubbed and chipped at head and tail, slightly damp marked, small paper edition.   Jarndyce Antiquarian Booksellers   CCIII - 264   2013   £150

Byron, George Gordon Noel, 6th Baron   1788-1824
Don Juan. printed by Thomas Davison, 1820-1821. John Hunt, 1823-1824. First editions of volumes ii-vi, later printing of volume i, 6 volumes, all foolscap octavo, small paper issue, all complete with half titles and ads where called for, foxed and lightly browned, volume ii with faint dampmark in lower margin, 12mo., modern pale blue paper boards, printed spine labels, sound.   Blackwell's Rare Books   172 - 40   2013   £400

Byron, George Gordon Noel, 6th Baron   1788-1824
Don Juan: in sixteen cantos. London: William Clark, 1826. First one volume edition, Complete in 1 volume frontispiece, slightly spotted, contemporary full green calf, borders in blind and gilt, spine with raised gilt bands, brown leather label, good plus.   Jarndyce Antiquarian Booksellers   CCIII - 267   2013   £125

Byron, George Gordon Noel, 6th Baron   1788-1824
Don Juan complete; English Bards and Scotch Reviewers; Hours of Idleness; The Waltz and all the Other Minor Poems. London: J. F. Dove, 1827. 12mo., frontispiece and title, printed title, slight dampstaining towards end of text block, contemporary full black calf, slightly rubbed, very good.   Jarndyce Antiquarian Booksellers   CCIII - 95   2013   £50

Byron, George Gordon Noel, 6th Baron   1788-1824
Don Juan; Hours of Idleness; English Bards and Scotch Reviewers; The Waltz and Other Poems. London: J. F. Dove, 1828. 2 volumes, 24mo., frontispiece, contemporary half maroon calf, spines attractively blocked in gilt and blind, maroon leather labels, slight rubbing, good plus.   Jarndyce Antiquarian Booksellers   CCIII - 96   2013   £65

Byron, George Gordon Noel, 6th Baron   1788-1824
Don Juan: in sixteen cantos. N.P.: (London: printed for the booksellers). circa, 1833. Pirated edition, Original dark brown cloth, slightly dulled, spine little worn with careful repairs at head and tail, endpapers replaced.   Jarndyce Antiquarian Booksellers   CCIII - 268   2013   £45

Byron, George Gordon Noel, 6th Baron   1788-1824
Don Juan: in sixteen cantos. London: Charles Daly, 1839. 16mo., engraved frontispiece and title, original dark brown cloth, slightly damp affected & rubbed, signatures on endpapers, all edges gilt.   Jarndyce Antiquarian Booksellers   CCIII - 269   2013   £65

Byron, George Gordon Noel, 6th Baron   1788-1824
Don Juan: in sixteen cantos. London: T. Allman, 1841. 12mo., uncut in original dark blue cloth, spine very slightly rubbed, overall very good.   Jarndyce Antiquarian Booksellers   CCIII - 270   2013   £65

Byron, George Gordon Noel, 6th Baron   1788-1824
English Bards and Scotch Reviewers. London: James Cawthorn, First edition, first issue, half title, few blank leaves bound in at end, some minor internal marks, uncut in 19th century full dark blue morocco, slightly rubbed, booklabels of Alexander McGrigor & Alex Bridge, top edge gilt.   Jarndyce Antiquarian Booksellers   CCIII - 116   2013   £450

Byron, George Gordon Noel, 6th Baron   1788-1824
English Bards and Scotch Reviewers, a Satire. London: James Cawthorn, 1809. Spurious issue of first edition, 12mo., half title, uncut in original drab printed boards, slightly marked, hinges splitting, corners strengthened, good, Renier booklabel.   Jarndyce Antiquarian Booksellers   CCIII - 117   2013   £150

Byron, George Gordon Noel, 6th Baron   1788-1824
English Bards and Scotch Reviewers. London: James Cawthorn, 1809. Second edition, half title, final ad leaf, contemporary full tan calf by F. Bedford, gilt spine, borders and dentelles, green leather label, spine slightly rubbed, leading hinge repaired, armorial bookplate of Laurence Currie and Alex Bridge booklabel, all edges gilt, good plus.   Jarndyce Antiquarian Booksellers   CCIII - 118   2013   £220

Byron, George Gordon Noel, 6th Baron   1788-1824
English Bards and Scotch Reviewers.   London: James Cawthorn, 1809.   Second edition, half title, final ad leaf, contemporary half speckled calf, armorial bookplate of George Moffatt & later Nowell-Smith booklabels, very good.   Jarndyce Antiquarian Booksellers   CCIII - 119   2013   £200

Byron, George Gordon Noel, 6th Baron   1788-1824
English Bards and Scotch Reviewers.   London: James Cawthorn, 1810.   Third edition, half title, 3 pages ads, lower part of leading pastedown torn away, uncut in original blue boards, early strengthening to spine with cream paper, ink title, ownership inscription of J. Stackhouse, small booklabel of John Sparrow, very good.   Jarndyce Antiquarian Booksellers   CCIII - 120   2013   £150

Byron, George Gordon Noel, 6th Baron   1788-1824
English Bards and Scotch Reviewers.   London: James Cawthorn, 1810.   Fourth edition, without half title and final ad leaf, contemporary half calf, expertly rebacked with green label, nice bright copy.   Jarndyce Antiquarian Booksellers   CCIII - 129   2013   £60

Byron, George Gordon Noel, 6th Baron   1788-1824
English Bards and Scotch Reviewers.   London: James Cawthorn, 1810.   Fourth edition, half title, 3 pages ads, uncut in original pink boards, lacking spine, front board detached, bit marked, leading pastedown with Renier booklabel, previous owner's notes, poor copy.   Jarndyce Antiquarian Booksellers   CCIII - 130   2013   £35

Byron, George Gordon Noel, 6th Baron   1788-1824
English Bards and Scotch Reviewers.   London: printed for James Cawthorn and Sharpe and Hailes, 1811.   Fourth edition, complete with half title, printed on stiff paper, watermarked 'J. Whatman/1805', 8vo., contemporary blue straight grained morocco, single gilt fillet on sides, spine gilt with lyre in each compartment, lettered gilt direct in one compartment, armorial bookplate of Thomas Harrison on top of what may be another bookplate on inside front cover, excellent, elegant copy.   Blackwell's Rare Books   B174 - 21   2013   £300

Byron, George Gordon Noel, 6th Baron   1788-1824
English Bards and Scotch Reviewers.   London: James Cawthorn, 1812.   Third edition, half title, 3 pages ads, interleaved with blanks, edges slightly affected by damp, maroon floral cloth circa 1830, spine lettered in gilt, faded to brown, booklabel of Alex Bridge.   Jarndyce Antiquarian Booksellers   CCIII - 121   2013   £60

Byron, George Gordon Noel, 6th Baron   1788-1824
English Bards and Scotch Reviewers.   London: James Cawthorn, 1816.   Fifth spurious fourth edition, bound without half title or final ad leaf, interspersed with leaves from unidentified edition of English Bards, bound in at corresponding pages and at end, profusely illustrated with 87 portraits and views, contemporary full green grained morocco by Dawson & Lewis of Soho, boards attractively blocked in gilt, spine gilt in compartments, gilt dentelles, leading hinge very slightly rubbed, armorial bookplate of Charles Tennant, all edges gilt, very good, handsome.   Jarndyce Antiquarian Booksellers   CCIII - 131   2013   £480

Byron, George Gordon Noel, 6th Baron   1788-1824
English Bards and Scotch Reviewers.   London: James Cawthorn, 1817.   Third edition, half title, 3 pages ads, contemporary half red calf, slightly rubbed, booklabel of Alex Bridge.   Jarndyce Antiquarian Booksellers   CCIII - 122   2013   £65

Byron, George Gordon Noel, 6th Baron   1788-1824
English Bards and Scotch Reviewers.   London: James Cawthorn, 1817.   Mixture of fourth and fifth third edition, half title, 3 pages ads, unopened, uncut in contemporary drab boards, pale green paper spine, head and tail of spine slightly chipped, booklabel of Alex Bridge, good plus.   Jarndyce Antiquarian Booksellers   CCIII - 123   2013   £65

Byron, George Gordon Noel, 6th Baron   1788-1824
English Bards and Scotch Reviewers.   London: James Cawthorn, 1818.   Third edition, uncut in original pale blue boards, faded purple spine strip, paper label, small ink stain on front board, very good, bookplate of Alex Bridge.   Jarndyce Antiquarian Booksellers   CCIII - 127   2013   £75

Byron, George Gordon Noel, 6th Baron   1788-1824
English Bards and Scotch Reviewers.   London: James Cawthorn, 1818.   Eighth spurious third edition, without half title, contemporary half black calf, gilt spine, bit rubbed, booklabel of Alex Bridge.   Jarndyce Antiquarian Booksellers   CCIII - 126   2013   £60

Byron, George Gordon Noel, 6th Baron   1788-1824
English Bards and Scotch Reviewers.   London: James Cawthorn, 1818.   Sixth spurious third edition, half title, 1 page following ad contemporary full tan calf gilt spine, hinges weak, lacking spine label, booklabel of Alex Bridge, offsetting to leading f.e.p. from previous owner's bookplate.   Jarndyce Antiquarian Booksellers   CCIII - 124   2013   £45

Byron, George Gordon Noel, 6th Baron   1788-1824
English Bards and Scotch Reviewers.   London: James Cawthorn, 1818.   Seventh spurious third edition, half title, 3 pages ads, uncut in original drab boards, boards & prelims damp marked, spine chipped at head and tail, bookplate of Alex Bridge.   Jarndyce Antiquarian Booksellers   CCIII - 125   2013   £45

Byron, George Gordon Noel, 6th Baron 1788-1824
Fare Thee Well! A Sketch. &s. Napoleon's Farewell. On the Star of the Legion of Honour and an Ode. London: Sherwood, Neely & Jones, 1816. First edition of this pirated collection, Stabbed as issued, slightly spotted, disbound. Jarndyce Antiquarian Booksellers   CCIII - 214   2013   £150

Byron, George Gordon Noel, 6th Baron 1788-1824 *The Rare Quarto Edition of Lord Byron's "Fugitive Pieces" (1806).* Nottingham: printed for private circulation, Derry & sons, 1919. Frontispiece, plates, uncut in original white boards, white cloth spine, lettered in black, little dusted, bookplate and signature of Alex Bridge, good plus. Jarndyce Antiquarian Booksellers   CCIII - 107   2013   £60

Byron, George Gordon Noel, 6th Baron 1788-1824
Fugitive Pieces. New York: Columbia University Press, 1933. Half title, original brown cloth, very good, signature and booklabel of Alex Bridge.   Jarndyce Antiquarian Booksellers   CCIII - 108   2013   £60

Byron, George Gordon Noel, 6th Baron 1788-1824 *The Genuine Rejected Addresses, Presented to the Committee of Management for Drury Lane Theatre.* London: printed and sold by B. McMillan, 1812. First edition, first issue, contemporary half calf, excellently rebacked, very good. Jarndyce Antiquarian Booksellers   CCIII - 151   2013   £320

Byron, George Gordon Noel, 6th Baron 1788-1824 *The Giaour, a Fragment of a Turkish Tale. (bound with) The Bride of Abydos.* London: printed by T. Davison for John Murray, 1813. Sixth and fourth edition, first work with half title and final ad leaf, first few pages dampstained, second work without half title, 2 volumes in 1, contemporary half calf, spine and maroon label chipped, front board becoming detached, booklabels of John Mair and Alex Bridge. Jarndyce Antiquarian Booksellers   CCIII - 165   2013   £50

Byron, George Gordon Noel, 6th Baron 1788-1824 *The Giaour, a Fragment of a Turkish Tale.* London: printed by T. Davison for John Murray, 1813. First edition, 2nd issue, half title, contemporary full tan calf, gilt spine, borders and dentelles, maroon and green leather labels, small chip to head of spine, hinges little worn, all edges gilt.   Jarndyce Antiquarian Booksellers   CCIII - 163   2013   £180

Byron, George Gordon Noel, 6th Baron 1788-1824 *The Giaour, a Fragment of a Turkish Tale.* London: printed by T. Davison for John Murray, 1813. First edition, 2nd issue, half title, unopened, original drab wrappers, front wrapper slightly marked, spine beginning to split at tail, good plus in later purple cloth folder.   Jarndyce Antiquarian Booksellers   CCIII - 162   2013   £450

Byron, George Gordon Noel, 6th Baron 1788-1824 *The Giaour, a Fragment of a Turkish Tale.* London: printed by T. Davison for John Murray, 1813. Fifth edition, half title slightly marked, lacking final ad leaf, later brown binder's cloth, initialled "O.I." in gilt.   Jarndyce Antiquarian Booksellers   CCIII - 164   2013   £25

Byron, George Gordon Noel, 6th Baron 1788-1824 *The Giaour, a Fragment of a Turkish Tale.* London: printed by T. Davison for John Murray, 1813. Eighth edition, half title, slightly spotted, later marbled wrappers, spine slightly dulled and with small chip at tail, ownership inscription of Mrs. Crampton on half title, booklabel of Alex Bridge.   Jarndyce Antiquarian Booksellers   CCIII - 166   2013   £30

Byron, George Gordon Noel, 6th Baron 1788-1824 *The Giaour, a Fragment of a Turkish Tale.* London: printed by J. Davison for John Murray, 1814. Tenth edition, without half title, sympathetically bound in later drab boards, paper label, very good.   Jarndyce Antiquarian Booksellers   CCIII - 168   2013   £25

Byron, George Gordon Noel, 6th Baron 1788-1824 *Il Giauro, Frammento di Novella Turca. (The Giaour, a Fragment of a Turkish Tale).* Ginevra: G. J. Paschoud, 1818. Geneva edition, Half title, verso of final leaf of text dusted, contemporary half calf, spine with floral devices in gilt, slightly rubbed, good plus.   Jarndyce Antiquarian Booksellers   CCIII - 170   2013   £150

Byron, George Gordon Noel, 6th Baron 1788-1824 *The Giaour, a Fragment of a Turkish Tale.* London: printed and published by W. Dugdale, 1825. 12mo., disbound. Jarndyce Antiquarian Booksellers   CCIII - 171   2013   £30

Byron, George Gordon Noel, 6th Baron 1788-1824
Hebrew Melodies. London: John Murray, 1815. First edition, half title, disbound, all edges gilt.   Jarndyce Antiquarian Booksellers   CCIII - 205   2013   £120

Byron, George Gordon Noel, 6th Baron 1788-1824
(Hebrew Melodies) Fugitive Pieces and Reminiscences. London: Whittaker, Treacher and Co., 1829. 12 page catalog, odd spot, uncut in original drab boards, green cloth spine, paper label, slightly chipped, hinges splitting in places, boards with some surface wear, booklabel of Alex Bridge.   Jarndyce Antiquarian Booksellers   CCIII - 206   2013   £480

Byron, George Gordon Noel, 6th Baron 1788-1824
(Hebrew Melodies) Fugitive Pieces and Reminiscences. London: Whittaker, Treacher & Son, 1829. Half title, 12 page catalog, handsomely bound in later half tan calf by G. H. May of London, spine with raised bands and devices gilt, armorial bookplate of Gilbert Compton Elliot, top edge gilt, very good, handsome.   Jarndyce Antiquarian Booksellers   CCIII - 207   2013   £480

Byron, George Gordon Noel, 6th Baron 1788-1824 *His Very Self and Voice: Collected Conversations of Lord Byron.* New York: Macmillan, 1954. First edition, half title, original maroon cloth, dusted and torn dust jacket, Doris Langley Moore's copy with her pencil notes.   Jarndyce Antiquarian Booksellers   CCIII - 106   2013   £30

Byron, George Gordon Noel, 6th Baron 1788-1824 *Hours of Idleness, a Series of Poems. (bound with) English Bards and Scotch Reviewers: a Satire.* Newark: S. & J. Ridge, 1807. London: James Cawthorn, 1816. First edition 2nd issue and fourth edition respectively, bound without half title, 2 volumes in 1, slightly later full calf, gilt and blind spine and borders, very good, handsome copy.   Jarndyce Antiquarian Booksellers   CCIII - 110   2013   £650

Byron, George Gordon Noel, 6th Baron 1788-1824 *Hours of Idleness: a Series of Poems.* Newark: S. & J. Ridge, 1807. First edition, first issue, half title, uncut in full calf by F. Bedford, expertly rebacked retaining gilt spine and dentelles, dark green morocco label, armorial booklabel of Cardiff Castle, top edge gilt, very good, handsome.   Jarndyce Antiquarian Booksellers   CCIII - 109   2013   £1850

Byron, George Gordon Noel, 6th Baron 1788-1824 *Hours of Idleness.* Newark: S. & J. Ridge, 1807. First edition, 2nd issue, without half title, slightly later full calf, spine gilt in compartments, blind borders, red and green leather labels, slight rubbing, very good.   Jarndyce Antiquarian Booksellers   CCIII - 111   2013   £600

Byron, George Gordon Noel, 6th Baron 1788-1824 *Hours of Idleness: a Series of Poems.* Paris: Galignani, 1819. 12mo., half title, disbound.   Jarndyce Antiquarian Booksellers   CCIII - 114   2013   £60

Byron, George Gordon Noel, 6th Baron 1788-1824 *The Island, or Christian and His Comrades.* London: printed for John Hunt, 1823. Second edition, occasional unobtrusive pencil annotations in contemporary hand, contemporary half calf carefully rebacked, corners slightly rubbed, ownership inscription W. P. de Bathe 1824, nice, scarce.   Jarndyce Antiquarian Booksellers   CCIII - 313   2013   £150

Byron, George Gordon Noel, 6th Baron 1788-1824 *The Lament of Tasso.* London: John Murray, 1817. Third edition, slightly damp marked at head, disbound.   Jarndyce Antiquarian Booksellers   CCIII - 234   2013   £25

Byron, George Gordon Noel, 6th Baron 1788-1824 *The Lament of Tasso. To which is added Prometheus.* London: printed & published by W. Dugdale, 1825. Pirated edition, 12mo., disbound.   Jarndyce Antiquarian Booksellers   CCIII - 236   2013   £40

Byron, George Gordon Noel, 6th Baron 1788-1824 *Lara, a Tale. Jacqueline, a Tale.* London: printed for J. Murray, by T. Davison, 1814. First edition, 4th variant, lacking half title, some old tape repairs, contemporary half calf, black leather label chipped, leading hinge defective, spine chipped at head and tail, corners worn.   Jarndyce Antiquarian Booksellers   CCIII - 196   2013   £180

Byron, George Gordon Noel, 6th Baron 1788-1824 *Lara, a Tale. Jacqueline, a Tale.* London: printed for J. Murray by T. Davison, 1814. First edition, first variant, original half dark green sheep, spine chipped at head and tail, hinges and corners rubbed and worn, Renier booklabel, contemporary booklabel and signature of Marianne Ford, good, sound copy.   Jarndyce Antiquarian Booksellers   CCIII - 195   2013   £65

Byron, George Gordon Noel, 6th Baron 1788-1824 *Lara, a Tale.* London: John Murray, 1814. Fourth edition, half title, 8 pages ads, uncut in original grey wrappers, slight dampstaining along inner margin, very good, iv, 72 pages. Jarndyce Antiquarian Booksellers   CCIII - 198   2013   £200

Byron, George Gordon Noel, 6th Baron 1788-1824 *Lara, a tale.* London: John Murray, 1814. Fourth edition first issue, text complete, lacking final imprint leaf pages 71/72, disbound.   Jarndyce Antiquarian Booksellers   CCIII - 199   2013   £35

Byron, George Gordon Noel, 6th Baron 1788-1824 *Lara, a Tale.* London: John Murray, 1815. Fifth edition, half title, slight browning sympathetic later drab boards, booklabel and signature of Alex Bridge, very good.   Jarndyce Antiquarian Booksellers   CCIII - 201   2013   £35

Byron, George Gordon Noel, 6th Baron 1788-1824 *Lara, a tale. (bound with) Hebrew Melodies.* London: John Murray, 1815. Fifth edition and First edition, first issue, 2 volumes in 1 half titles, contemporary half calf, gilt spine, black leather labels, small chip at tail of spine, hinges bit worn, some repairs, armorial bookplate, signed "Wodehouse, Kimberly 1838".   Jarndyce Antiquarian Booksellers   CCIII - 202   2013   £75

Byron, George Gordon Noel, 6th Baron 1788-1824 *Lara, a Tale.* London: John Murray, 1817. Fifth edition, half title, final leaf, disbound.   Jarndyce Antiquarian Booksellers   CCIII - 203   2013   £25

Byron, George Gordon Noel, 6th Baron 1788-1824 *Lara, a Tale.* London: printed and published by W. Dugdale, 1824. 52 pages, 12mo., disbound.   Jarndyce Antiquarian Booksellers   CCIII - 204   2013   £45

Byron, George Gordon Noel, 6th Baron   1788-1824
Letters and Journals of Lord Byron; With Notices of His Life. London: John Murray, 1830.   First edition, 2 volumes, large 4to., half title volume I, engraved frontispiece and errata leaf volume II, text slightly spotted, contemporary full calf, black leather labels, borders in blind, rubbed, corners worn, remains of sellotape on endpapers, sometime rebacked, hinges volume 1 slightly weakening, from the library of Doris Langley Moore.   Jarndyce Antiquarian Booksellers   CCIII - 323   2013   £250

Byron, George Gordon Noel, 6th Baron   1788-1824
Letters and Journals of Lord Byron with Notices of His Life. London: John Murray, 1830.   First edition, 4 volumes, large 4to., half titles, frontispiece, portraits, plates, additional titlepage volume I, occasional light spotting and offsetting, contemporary half red morocco by Tout, little rubbed, spine and corner of volumes III and IV slightly worn, very good, attractive.   Jarndyce Antiquarian Booksellers   CCIII - 322   2013   £580

Byron, George Gordon Noel, 6th Baron   1788-1824
Letters and Journals of Lord Byron; With Notices of His Life. London: John Murray, 1833.   Third edition, 3 volumes, frontispiece volumes I and III, plates, volume II and III lacking titlepages, volume II lacking frontispiece, expertly recased in original sand grained purple cloth, spines lettered gilt, borders in blind, spines uniformly faded to brown, slightly marked, "From Hugh Walpole's library with his bookplate, formerly the copy of John Ruskin with his bookplate and marginal notes.   Jarndyce Antiquarian Booksellers   CCIII - 324   2013   £850

Byron, George Gordon Noel, 6th Baron   1788-1824   *The Liberal. Verse and Prose from Due South.*   London: printed by and for John Hunt, 1822.   (1823). Second edition, 2 volumes, rebound in 20th century half tan calf, red and black labels, Leigh' Hunts name only on spines, very good. Jarndyce Antiquarian Booksellers   CCIII - 308   2013   £320

Byron, George Gordon Noel, 6th Baron   1788-1824
Lord Byron's Farewell to England, with three other poems, viz. Ode to St. Helena. To My Daughter, on the Morning of her Birth and To the Lily of France.   London: J. Johnston, 1816.   Contemporary drab wrappers, spine carefully repaired.   Jarndyce Antiquarian Booksellers   CCIII - 215   2013   £150

Byron, George Gordon Noel, 6th Baron   1788-1824
Manfred, a Dramatic Poem.   London: John Murray, 1817. First edition, third issue, half title, later pale blue boards, very good.   Jarndyce Antiquarian Booksellers   CCIII - 238   2013   £150

Byron, George Gordon Noel, 6th Baron   1788-1824
Manfred, a Dramatic Poem.   London: John Murray, 1817. First edition, half title, 4 page catalog (June 1817), uncut in original drab wrappers, tail of spine slightly worn, early label of Coddenham Book Society and its details in next ms. on front wrapper 1817, very good in custom made red cloth box.   Jarndyce Antiquarian Booksellers   CCIII - 237   2013   £450

Byron, George Gordon Noel, 6th Baron   1788-1824
Manfred, a Dramatic Poem.   London: John Murray, 1817. First edition, third issue, demi 8vo., bound in drab publisher's paper wrappers (separate), untrimmed, little foxed, but very good.   Second Life Books Inc.   183 - 62   2013 $350

Byron, George Gordon Noel, 6th Baron   1788-1824
Manfred, a Dramatic Poem.   London: John Murray, 1817. Second edition, half title, little dampmarked, later blue wrappers.   Jarndyce Antiquarian Booksellers   CCIII - 239   2013   £25

Byron, George Gordon Noel, 6th Baron   1788-1824
Manfred, a Dramatic Poem.   London: J. Dicks, circa, 1880. New edition, final ad leaf, sewn as issued in original pink printed wrappers, edges with one or two tiny chips, otherwise very good.   Jarndyce Antiquarian Booksellers   CCIII - 240   2013   £30

Byron, George Gordon Noel, 6th Baron   1788-1824
Marino Faliero, Doge of Venice. The Prophecy of Dante, a Poem.   Paris: A. & W. Galignani, 1821.   12mo., half title, sympathetic later drab wrappers.   Jarndyce Antiquarian Booksellers   CCIII - 293   2013   £25

Byron, George Gordon Noel, 6th Baron   1788-1824
Marino Faliero, Doge of Venice. The Prophecy of Dante, a Poem.   London: John Murray, 1821.   First edition, 2nd issue, half title, final ad leaf, uncut in original drab boards, paper label, hinges and head and tail of spine little worn, one corner slightly creased, booklabel and signature of Alex Bridge, nice copy.   Jarndyce Antiquarian Booksellers   CCIII - 290   2013   £250

Byron, George Gordon Noel, 6th Baron   1788-1824
Marino Faliero, Doge of Venice. The Prophecy of Dante, a Poem.   London: John Murray, 1821.   First edition, first issue, slight spotting, disbound.   Jarndyce Antiquarian Booksellers   CCIII - 289   2013   £75

Byron, George Gordon Noel, 6th Baron   1788-1824
Marino Faliero, Doge of Venice. The Prophecy of Dante, a Poem.   London: John Murray, 1821.   First edition, 2nd issue, half title, slightly spotted, contemporary full purple calf, elaborately blocked in blind on boards, gilt spine, borders and dentelles, little rubbed, some wear to spine, all edges gilt, attractive.   Jarndyce Antiquarian Booksellers   CCIII - 291   2013   £85

Byron, George Gordon Noel, 6th Baron 1788-1824
Marino Faliero, Doge of Venice. The Prophecy of Dante, a Poem. London: John Murray, 1821. First edition, 2nd issue, variant A, half title, small repair, disbound, ownership inscription G. B. Wharton, 1821.   Jarndyce Antiquarian Booksellers   CCIII - 292   2013   £35

Byron, George Gordon Noel, 6th Baron 1788-1824
Marino Faliero, Doge of Venice. The Prophecy of Dante, a Poem. London: John Murray, 1821. First edition,, first issue, half title, uncut in original pale blue boards, drab spine, paper label, small nick in front board, hinge little worn, armorial bookplate of J.G.B., booklabel of Alex Bridge, good plus.   Jarndyce Antiquarian Booksellers   CCIII - 288   2013   £150

Byron, George Gordon Noel, 6th Baron 1788-1824
Marino Faliero, Doge of Venice. The Prophecy of Dante, a Poem. London: John Murray, 1823. Third edition, half title, uncut in original pink boards, paper label, marked, spine little worn and chipped at ends, label partially removed from tail of spine, booklabel and signature of Alex Bridge.   Jarndyce Antiquarian Booksellers   CCIII - 294   2013   £85

Byron, George Gordon Noel, 6th Baron 1788-1824
Marino Faliero, Doge of Venice. The Prophecy of Dante, a Poem. London: printed and published by W. Dugdale, 1826. Contemporary full calf, recently neatly rebacked leading f.e.p. replaced, Renier booklabel.   Jarndyce Antiquarian Booksellers   CCIII - 295   2013   £110

Byron, George Gordon Noel, 6th Baron 1788-1824
Marino Faliero, Doge of Venice. with Sardanaplus. The Two Foscari. Cain. London: John Murray, 1821. First edition, first issue and First edition, 2 volumes in 1, full calf, black leather label titled "Byron's Plays", rubbed, some marks, spine later rebacked.   Jarndyce Antiquarian Booksellers   CCIII - 90   2013   £45

Byron, George Gordon Noel, 6th Baron 1788-1824
Marino Faliero, Doge of Venice. The Prophecy of Dante, a Poem. London: John Murray, 1821. First edition first issue, half title, final ad leaf, uncut in slightly later tan calf by G. H. May of London, spine with raised bands and gilt devices, armorial bookplate of Gilbert Compton Elliot, top edge gilt, very handsome, neatly tipped into prelims are 3 printed playbills, in excellent condition.   Jarndyce Antiquarian Booksellers   CCIII - 286   2013   £1800

Byron, George Gordon Noel, 6th Baron 1788-1824
Mazeppa, a Poem. London: John Murray, 1819. First edition, 2nd issue, half title, final ad leaf and 8 page catalog & July 1819, spotted, uncut in original drab wrappers, spine little chipped, contemporary ownership inscription, booklabel and signature of Alex Bridge.   Jarndyce Antiquarian Booksellers   CCIII - 246   2013   £350

Byron, George Gordon Noel, 6th Baron 1788-1824
Mazeppa, a Poem. London: John Murray, 1819. First edition, 2nd issue, half title, final ad leaf, disbound.   Jarndyce Antiquarian Booksellers   CCIII - 247   2013   £65

Byron, George Gordon Noel, 6th Baron 1788-1824
Mazeppa, a Poem. London: W. Dugdale, 23 Russell Court, 1824. First English pirated edition, 12mo., disbound.   Jarndyce Antiquarian Booksellers   CCIII - 248   2013   £40

Byron, George Gordon Noel, 6th Baron 1788-1824 *The Miscellaneous Works.* London: Hunt & Clarke, 1830. 2 volumes in one as issued, uncut and partially unopened in original brown boards, green cloth spine, paper label chipped, slightly marked, spine dulled but very good as originally issued, booklabel of Alex Bridge.   Jarndyce Antiquarian Booksellers   CCIII - 97   2013   £125

Byron, George Gordon Noel, 6th Baron 1788-1824
Monody on the Death of the Right Honourable R. B. Sheridan... London: John Murray, 1816. First edition, third issue, disbound.   Jarndyce Antiquarian Booksellers   CCIII - 232   2013   £100

Byron, George Gordon Noel, 6th Baron 1788-1824
Monody on the Death of the Right Honourable R. B. Sheridan... London: John Murray, 1816. First edition, first issue, half title, disbound, little foxed, Renier signature.   Jarndyce Antiquarian Booksellers   CCIII - 231   2013 £180

Byron, George Gordon Noel, 6th Baron 1788-1824
Monody on the Death of the Right Honourable R. B. Sheridan... London: John Murray, 1817. New edition, half title, later drab boards, booklabel and signature of Alex Bridge, very good.   Jarndyce Antiquarian Booksellers   CCIII - 233   2013   £25

Byron, George Gordon Noel, 6th Baron 1788-1824
Ode to Napoleon Bonaparte. London: John Murray, 1814. Eighth edition, half title, final ad leaf, disbound.   Jarndyce Antiquarian Booksellers   CCIII - 192   2013   £25

Byron, George Gordon Noel, 6th Baron 1788-1824
Ode to Napoleon Bonaparte. London: John Murray, 1814. First edition, lacking half title as usual, final ad leaf, disbound, all edges gilt.   Jarndyce Antiquarian Booksellers   CCIII - 190   2013   £250

Byron, George Gordon Noel, 6th Baron 1788-1824
Ode to Napoleon Bonaparte. London: printed for John Murray by W. Bulmer & Co., 1814. First edition, lacking half title as usual, final ad leaf, disbound, all edges gilt.   Jarndyce Antiquarian Booksellers   CCIII - 190   2013   £250

Byron, George Gordon Noel, 6th Baron   1788-1824
Ode to Napoleon Bonaparte.   London: printed for John Murray by W. Bulmer and Co., 1814.   First edition, retains often missing half title, final ad leaf, slight spotting to prelims, handsomely bound in full royal blue crushed morocco by Riviere & Son, gilt spine, borders and dentelles, armorial bookplate of Chadwyck-Healey, very good, attractive copy.   Jarndyce Antiquarian Booksellers   CCIII - 189   2013   £850

Byron, George Gordon Noel, 6th Baron   1788-1824
Ode to Napoleon Bonaparte.   London: John Murray, 1814.   Fourth edition, half title, disbound, booklabel & signature of Alex Bridge.   Jarndyce Antiquarian Booksellers   CCIII - 191   2013   £30

Byron, George Gordon Noel, 6th Baron   1788-1824
Ode to Napoleon Bonaparte.   London: John Murray, 1815.   Eleventh edition, half title, final ad leaf, slightly browned, disbound, booklabel of Alex Bridge.   Jarndyce Antiquarian Booksellers   CCIII - 193   2013   £25

Byron, George Gordon Noel, 6th Baron   1788-1824
Poems.   London: John Murray, 1816.   First edition, 2nd issue, disbound, very good.   Jarndyce Antiquarian Booksellers   CCIII - 223   2013   £60

Byron, George Gordon Noel, 6th Baron   1788-1824
Poems. containing The Giaour; Bride of Abydos; The Corsair; Lara.   London: C. Daly, circa, 1840.   32mo., frontispiece, engraved title, 6 pages ads, original dark blue cloth, blocked and lettered in gilt, all edges gilt, very good, attractive little volume.   Jarndyce Antiquarian Booksellers   CCIII - 101   2013   £40

Byron, George Gordon Noel, 6th Baron   1788-1824
Poems On His Domestic Circumstances &c &c.   London: W. Hone &c, 1816.   Thirteenth edition, frontispiece, disbound.   Jarndyce Antiquarian Booksellers   CCIII - 221   2013   £50

Byron, George Gordon Noel, 6th Baron   1788-1824
Poems On His Domestic Circumstances. I. Fare Thee Well!. II. A Sketch from Private Life. With the Star of Legion of Honour and Other Poems.   London: H. Hone, 1816.   First edition, half title, slight spotting, disbound, scarce.   Jarndyce Antiquarian Booksellers   CCIII - 216   2013   £250

Byron, George Gordon Noel, 6th Baron   1788-1824
Poems On His Domestic Circumstances. &c &c. With the Star of the Legion of Honour and Four Other Poems.   London: printed for W. Hone, 1816.   Second edition, title slightly browned, later drab wrappers, booklabel and signature of Alex Bridge.   Jarndyce Antiquarian Booksellers   CCIII - 217   2013   £65

Byron, George Gordon Noel, 6th Baron   1788-1824
Poems On His Domestic Circumstances &c &c. With His Memoirs and Portrait.   London: printed for W. Hone, 1816.   Eighth edition, frontispiece slightly stained at head, disbound.   Jarndyce Antiquarian Booksellers   CCIII - 218   2013   £120

Byron, George Gordon Noel, 6th Baron   1788-1824
Poems On His Domestic Circumstances. &c &c. With the Star of the Legion of Honour and Other Poems.   London: printed for R. Edwards, 1816.   Ninth edition, frontispiece with slight offsetting, 4 page initial blanks embellished with 3 ms. poems copied from Byron in black ink, disbound, rare.   Jarndyce Antiquarian Booksellers   CCIII - 219   2013   £125

Byron, George Gordon Noel, 6th Baron   1788-1824
Poems On His Domestic Circumstances &c &c. With His Memoirs and Portrait.   London: W. Hone &c., 1816.   Ninth edition, frontispiece, some light spotting, slight offsetting, disbound, booklabel and signature of Alex Bridge.   Jarndyce Antiquarian Booksellers   CCIII - 220   2013   £40

Byron, George Gordon Noel, 6th Baron   1788-1824
Poems On His Domestic Circumstances &c &c. With His Memoirs and Portrait.   London: W. Hone &c., 1817.   Twenty-second edition, disbound.   Jarndyce Antiquarian Booksellers   CCIII - 222   2013   £30

Byron, George Gordon Noel, 6th Baron   1788-1824
Poems Original and Translated.   Newark: printed and sold by S. & J Ridge, 1808.   (1811 or 1812). Second edition, issued without half title, frontispiece, contemporary half calf, at some time rebacked with brown morocco, corners rubbed and worn, booklabel and signature of Alex Bridge.   Jarndyce Antiquarian Booksellers   CCIII - 113   2013   £150

Byron, George Gordon Noel, 6th Baron   1788-1824
Poems Original and Translated.   Newark: printed and sold by S. and J. Ridge, 1808.   Second edition, half title, frontispiece, few minor internal marks, full brown morocco by Bayntun, gilt spine, borders and dentelles, bookplate and signature of Alex Bridge, top edge gilt, very good, attractive.   Jarndyce Antiquarian Booksellers   CCIII - 112   2013   £500

Byron, George Gordon Noel, 6th Baron   1788-1824
Poems with his Memoirs.   London: Jones & Co., 1825.   Frontispiece, slightly damp marked, name cut from title head of title and corner of frontispiece repaired prelims little spotted, contemporary half calf, rubbed, tail of spine slightly chipped.   Jarndyce Antiquarian Booksellers   CCIII - 93   2013   £50

Byron, George Gordon Noel, 6th Baron   1788-1824
Poems with His Memoirs.   London: Jones & Co., 1826. 32mo., frontispiece, 2 pages ads, original purple moire, patterned silk cloth, black paper label, slightly bumped, slight fading to spine Renier and Robert Washington Oates booklabels, all edges gilt, very good.   Jarndyce Antiquarian Booksellers   CCIII - 94   2013   £50

Byron, George Gordon Noel, 6th Baron   1788-1824   *The Poetical Works.*   London: John Murray, 1854. Tall 8vo., frontispiece and engraved title, dedication leaf from John Murray to Sir Robert Peel, facsimiles, 32 page catalog (Jan. 1854), original pink cloth by Edmonds & Remnants, little marked, spine faded and with repairs to following hinge signed "Gunning Symons 1854" to leading f.e.p., fairly good copy.   Jarndyce Antiquarian Booksellers   CCIII - 81   2013   £45

Byron, George Gordon Noel, 6th Baron   1788-1824   *The Poetical Works.*   London: John Murray, 1855-1856.   New edition, 6 volumes, half titles, frontispiece, 32 page catalog (Feb. 1871 volume VI, original pink cloth by Remnant & Edmonds, few slight marks, spines fading to brown, nice crisp set.   Jarndyce Antiquarian Booksellers   CCIII - 82   2013   £120

Byron, George Gordon Noel, 6th Baron   1788-1824
Poetical Works.   London: Henry Frowde, Oxford University Press, 1910.   Oxford edition, half title, frontispiece, contemporary half tan crushed morocco by Bickers & Son, ruled in gilt, armorial bookplate of Cordell William Firebrace, top edge gilt, very good in fine binding.   Jarndyce Antiquarian Booksellers   CCIII - 84   2013   £120

Byron, George Gordon Noel, 6th Baron   1788-1824
Poetical Works.   London: Oxford University Press, Humphrey Milford, 1935.   Oxford edition, half title, frontispiece, contemporary half dark blue calf by Bickers & Son, front board blocked with school crest in gilt, spine slightly faded, Newcastle Grammar school prize label 1935-1936, top edge gilt, very good. Jarndyce Antiquarian Booksellers CCIII - 85   2013   £35

Byron, George Gordon Noel, 6th Baron   1788-1824   *The Prisoner of Chillon and Other Poems. (with) The Corsair, a Tale. (with) Beppo a Venetian Story. (with) Letter to **** *******.*   London: John Murray, 1816. 1815. 1818. 1821, 4 volumes in 1, contemporary half purple calf, gilt spine faded to brown, very good, ms. notes by Cecil Price loosely inserted.   Jarndyce Antiquarian Booksellers   CCIII - 88   2013   £125

Byron, George Gordon Noel, 6th Baron   1788-1824   *The Prisoner of Chillon.*   London: John Murray, 1816.   First edition, without half title or final ad leaf, disbound.   Jarndyce Antiquarian Booksellers   CCIII - 227   2013   £40

Byron, George Gordon Noel, 6th Baron   1788-1824   *The Prisoner of Chillon.*   London: John Murray, 1816.   First edition, first issue, half title with watermark, final ad leaf and 4 pages ads, uncut in original drab wrappers, bound into later half tan calf, armorial bookplate of Gilbert Compton Elliot, very good.   Jarndyce Antiquarian Booksellers   CCIII - 226   2013   £350

Byron, George Gordon Noel, 6th Baron   1788-1824   *The Prisoner of Chillon.*   London: John Murray, 1816.   First edition, first issue, half title, final ad leaf and 4 pages ads (Nov. 1816), uncut in original drab wrappers, tiny nick at head of spine, but still exceptionally well preserved as originally issued in later maroon cloth folder.   Jarndyce Antiquarian Booksellers   CCIII - 225   2013   £1200

Byron, George Gordon Noel, 6th Baron   1788-1824   *The Prisoner of Chillon.*   Lausanne: 1818.   Disbound, ownership inscription of Richard May.   Jarndyce Antiquarian Booksellers   CCIII - 228   2013   £85

Byron, George Gordon Noel, 6th Baron   1788-1824
Prophecy of Dante.   Paris: A. & W. Galignani, 1821.   First separate edition?, 12mo., half title, disbound.   Jarndyce Antiquarian Booksellers   CCIII - 296   2013   £45

Byron, George Gordon Noel, 6th Baron   1788-1824
Sardanapalus, a Tragedy. The Two Foscari, a Tragedy. Cain. A Mystery.   London: John Murray, 1821.   First edition, variant A, half title, uncut in original drab boards, paper label, slightly rubbed, neatly rebacked retaining original spine strip, good plus.   Jarndyce Antiquarian Booksellers CCIII - 297   2013   £85

Byron, George Gordon Noel, 6th Baron   1788-1824
Sardanapalus, a Tragedy. The Two Foscari, a Tragedy. Cain. A Mystery.   London: John Murray, 1821.   First edition, variant B, half title, slight damp marking in prelims, contemporary full olive green calf, spine gilt in compartments, gilt and blind borders, boards blocked in blind with star design maroon leather label chipped spine faded to brown and little worn, small split to head of leading hinge. Jarndyce Antiquarian Booksellers   CCIII - 300   2013   £90

Byron, George Gordon Noel, 6th Baron   1788-1824
Sardanapalus, a Tragedy. The Two Foscari, a Tragedy. Cain. A Mystery.   London: John Murray, 1821.   First edition, variant B, half title, uncut, in original glazed purple cloth, paper label, very slightly chipped, spine slightly faded and with small repaired nick at head, very good.   Jarndyce Antiquarian Booksellers   CCIII - 299   2013   £200

Byron, George Gordon Noel, 6th Baron   1788-1824
Sardanapalus.   London: John Murray, 1823.   First separate edition, uncut in original blue boards, drab spine and paper label slightly chipped, hinges slightly cracked, armorial bookplate of Prof. W. Blair-Bell, Renier booklabel. Jarndyce Antiquarian Booksellers   CCIII - 301   2013   £35

Byron, George Gordon Noel, 6th Baron   1788-1824
Lord Byron's Historical Tragedy of Sardanapalus. Manchester: John Heywood, 1877? 5 pages ads, original buff wrappers, printed in red and black, slightly marked, spine chipped, booklabel and signature of Alex Bridge.   Jarndyce Antiquarian Booksellers   CCIII - 302   2013   £120

Byron, George Gordon Noel, 6th Baron   1788-1824 *The Select Poems of Lord Byron. Hours of Idleness, English Bards & Scotch Reviewers, Cain , a Mystery, Bride of Abydos and Other Interesting Pieces.*   Wakefield: William Nicholson & Sons, circa, 1880. 32mo., half title, frontispiece, final ad leaf, original dark green cloth, blocked and lettered in black and gilt, front board slightly creased, later booklabel of Allston A. Kisby.   Jarndyce Antiquarian Booksellers   CCIII - 105   2013   £30

Byron, George Gordon Noel, 6th Baron   1788-1824 *The Siege of Corinth. A Poem. Parisina. A Poem.*   London: John Murray, 1816. First edition, later pale green cloth, brown leather label, very good.   Jarndyce Antiquarian Booksellers   CCIII - 210   2013   £45

Byron, George Gordon Noel, 6th Baron   1788-1824 *The Siege of Corinth. A Poem. Parisina. A Poem.*   London: John Murray, 1816. First edition, half title, 2 additional plates by Richard Westall 1819, plates slightly spotted, disbound, all edges gilt.   Jarndyce Antiquarian Booksellers   CCIII - 209   2013   £30

Byron, George Gordon Noel, 6th Baron   1788-1824 *The Siege of Corinth. A Poem. Parisina. A Poem.*   London: John Murray, 1816. First edition, half title, 4 pages ads, recent brown wrappers, very good.   Jarndyce Antiquarian Booksellers   CCIII - 208   2013   £35

Byron, George Gordon Noel, 6th Baron   1788-1824 *The Siege of Corinth. A Poem. Parisina. A Poem.*   London: John Murray, 1816. Second edition, lacking half title, disbound.   Jarndyce Antiquarian Booksellers   CCIII - 211   2013   £25

Byron, George Gordon Noel, 6th Baron   1788-1824 *The Siege of Corinth. A Poem. Parisina. A Poem.*   London: John Murray, 1818. Fourth edition, ad on verso of final leaf, disbound, all edges gilt.   Jarndyce Antiquarian Booksellers   CCIII - 212   2013   £45

Byron, George Gordon Noel, 6th Baron   1788-1824 *The Siege of Corinth. A Poem.*   London: printed and published by W. Dugdale, 1826. 12mo, disbound.   Jarndyce Antiquarian Booksellers   CCIII - 213   2013   £40

Byron, George Gordon Noel, 6th Baron   1788-1824
Waltz.   London: W. Clark, 1821. Pirated edition, Uncut in original pale blue wrappers, very good, exceptionally well preserved.   Jarndyce Antiquarian Booksellers   CCIII - 159   2013   £280

Byron, George Gordon Noel, 6th Baron   1788-1824
Waltz; an Apostrophic Hymn.   London: W. Clark, 1821. Excellently rebound in half calf, marbled boards, brown label, very good, attractive copy.   Jarndyce Antiquarian Booksellers   CCIII - 160   2013   £280

Byron, George Gordon Noel, 6th Baron   1788-1824
Waltz: an Apostrophic Hymn.   London: W. Clark, 1821. Excellently rebound in half calf, marbled boards, brown label, very good, attractive copy.   Jarndyce Antiquarian Booksellers   CCIII - 160   2013   £280

Byron, George Gordon Noel, 6th Baron   1788-1824
Waltz: an Apostrophic Hymn.   London: W. Clark, 1821. Disbound, all edges gilt.   Jarndyce Antiquarian Booksellers   CCIII - 161   2013   £150

Byron, George Gordon Noel, 6th Baron   1788-1824
Werner, a Tragedy.   London: John Murray, 1823. first edition, 2nd issue, disbound contemporary ownership inscription of Henry Talbot.   Jarndyce Antiquarian Booksellers   CCIII - 317   2013   £60

Byron, George Gordon Noel, 6th Baron   1788-1824
Werner, a Tragedy.   London: John Murray, 1823. First edition, first issue, 7 page catalog (Nov. 1822), unopened in original drab wrappers, small ink mark on front wrapper, spine slightly rubbed, very good, as originally issued in custom made blue cloth box.   Jarndyce Antiquarian Booksellers   CCIII - 314   2013   £450

Byron, George Gordon Noel, 6th Baron   1788-1824
Werner, a Tragedy.   London: John Murray, 1823. First edition, 2nd issue, half title, expertly rebound in half tan calf, gilt spines, olive green leather label, very good, handsome copy.   Jarndyce Antiquarian Booksellers   CCIII - 316   2013   £250

Byron, George Gordon Noel, 6th Baron   1788-1824
Werner, a Tragedy.   London: John Murray, 1823. First edition, first issue, 7 page catalog (Nov. 1822), recent grey wrappers, very good.   Jarndyce Antiquarian Booksellers   CCIII - 315   2013   £250

Byron, George Gordon Noel, 6th Baron   1788-1824 *The Works.*   London: John Murray, 1815. 4 volumes, some light foxing in prelims, slightly later half purple calf by J. Seacome of Chester, spines ruled gilt, black leather labels, spines uniformly faded, very slight rubbing, nice set.   Jarndyce Antiquarian Booksellers   CCIII - 69   2013   £420

Byron, George Gordon Noel, 6th Baron   1788-1824 *The Works.*   London: John Murray, 1821. 5 volumes, half titles, contemporary full green grained calf, gilt spines borders and dentelles, spines uniformly darkened and little rubbed at heads and tails, good plus set.   Jarndyce Antiquarian Booksellers   CCIII - 71   2013   £180

Byron, George Gordon Noel, 6th Baron 1788-1824 *The Works.* London: John Murray, 1823-1825. 6 volumes, volume 1, slight spotting and browning in prelims, contemporary full dark blue grained calf, spine gilt in compartments, gilt borders and dentelles, occasional rubbing, fading to purple in places, each volume signed Mrs. Kirklees in contemporary hand, good plu.   Jarndyce Antiquarian Booksellers   CCIII - 72   2013   £750

Byron, George Gordon Noel, 6th Baron 1788-1824 *The Works.* London: John Murray, 1830. 4 volumes, 16mo., frontispieces, uncut and partially unopened in original drab boards, maroon cloth spines, paper labels, spines little faded and labels slightly rubbed, overall very good.   Jarndyce Antiquarian Booksellers   CCIII - 73   2013   £150

Byron, George Gordon Noel, 6th Baron 1788-1824 *The Works. (with) Don Juan.* London: John Murray, 1831. London: Thomas Davison, 18218., 6 volumes and 2 volumes respectively, uniformly bound in contemporary full dark olive green morocco, gilt spines, borders in gilt and blind, volume I with slight rubbing to front board, volume I all edges gilt, very good.   Jarndyce Antiquarian Booksellers   CCIII - 75   2013   £350

Byron, George Gordon Noel, 6th Baron 1788-1824 *The Works.* London: John Murray, 1831. 6 volumes, small 8vo., frontispieces, some damp marking, contemporary half black calf, front board volume I with crease, else nice.   Jarndyce Antiquarian Booksellers   CCIII - 74   2013   £120

Byron, George Gordon Noel, 6th Baron 1788-1824 *The Works... with His Letters and Journals and His Life.* London: John Murray, 1832-1833. 17 volumes, half titles (not in volumes I, IX), frontispieces and titles, illustrations, small repair to half title volume III, original dark green moire cloth, green paper label volume I, gilt, little rubbed and bumped, slightly marked armorial bookplates of William Henry Charlton.   Jarndyce Antiquarian Booksellers   CCIII - 76   2013   £480

Byron, George Gordon Noel, 6th Baron 1788-1824 *The Works.* London: John Murray, 1833. 17 volumes, engraved frontispieces and vignette titles, printed titles, slightly later full dark green morocco, spines lettered in gilt, some spines very slightly faded, each volume with dust jacket gift inscription to Matilda Butcher from her sister, all edges gilt, very good, bright.   Jarndyce Antiquarian Booksellers   CCIII - 77   2013   £620

Byron, George Gordon Noel, 6th Baron 1788-1824 *Oeuvres de Lord Byron.* Paris: Furne, 1836. 6 volumes, half titles, plates, slightly damp affected, slight worming in volume IV, contemporary full tree calf, blocked in blind ad gilt, black and orange labels, slightly rubbed, attractive.   Jarndyce Antiquarian Booksellers   CCIII - 79   2013   £280

Byron, George Gordon Noel, 6th Baron 1788-1824 *The Works...* Paris: Baudry's European Library and A. & W. Galignani, 1837. Tall 8vo., 4 page inserted ads preceding half title, frontispiece, vignette title, facsimiles, some light foxing, uncut in continental marbled boards, green cloth spine, paper label, slightly dulled, corners slightly bumped, good plus.   Jarndyce Antiquarian Booksellers   CCIII - 80   2013   £85

Byron, George Gordon Noel, 6th Baron 1788-1824 *The Works.* London: John Murray, 1853. 12mo., 8 volumes, fine set in contemporary half red calf, ornate gilt panelled spines, marbled boards and edges.   Ken Spelman Books Ltd.   75 - 118   2013   £295

Byron, George Gordon Noel, 6th Baron 1788-1824 *The Works - Poetry - Letters & Journals.* London: John Murray, 1899-1904. 13 volumes, half titles, plates, uncut in original blue cloth, decorated and lettered gilt, boards creased in places, some spines little dulled, volume III with library stamps and shelf marks, volume VI with booklabel of E. H. Williams, top edge gilt, good plus, made up set.   Jarndyce Antiquarian Booksellers   CCIII - 83   2013   £250

Byron, Henry James *Mazeppa! A Burlesque Extravaganza in One Act.* London: Thomas Hailes Lacy, 1860? Disbound.   Jarndyce Antiquarian Booksellers   CCIII - 249   2013   £35

Byron, May *Cecil Aldin's Happy Family Humpty and Dumpty.* London: Henry Frowde, 1912. Paper covered boards, good copy, square 8vo., inscription dated 1913, color illustrations, front joint little ragged and paper covering front inside hinge separating.   Barnaby Rudge Booksellers Children 2013 - 014159   2013 $95

Byron, May *The Chunkies at the Seaside.* Springfield: McLoughlin Bros., n.d. circa, 1920. 4to., pictorial boards, pictorial paste-on, slight rubbing, very good to fine, illustrations by Chloe Preson, with 8 great color plates, black and whites in text and pictorial endpapers, scarce.   Aleph-Bet Books, Inc.   104 - 459   2013 $500

Byron, Robert *First Russia Then Tibet.* London: Macmillan & Co. Ltd., 1933. First edition, 328 pages, numerous black and white images, about good in green cloth with attractive bookplate on front pastedown, some slanting to spine, minor bumping to corners, some splitting to back rear hinge and some minor soiling to boards as well, no dust jacket, still very presentable copy.   Jeff Hirsch Books   Fall 2013 - 129511   2013 $75

C

Cabala; Sive Sacra. Mysteries of State Government: in Letters of Illustrious Persons, and Great Agents; in the Reigns of Henry the Eighth, Queen Elizabeth, K. James and the Late King Charles... London: printed for G. Bedel and T. Collins..., 1654. First edition, small 8vo., cloth, general titlepage and titlepage to part 2 in red and black, from the library of William R. Williams, NY 1856 and William R. Street, 1845; spine label scuffed, owner's name on top edge of first blank and title, first titlepage and last page of index mounted, rare marginalia, damp spotting to lower margin of last half of second part, few last leaves soiled at top edge, overall still solid.   Kaaterskill Books   16 - 4   2013 $475

Cabell, James Branch *Gallantry.*   New York: Harper Bros., Oct., 1907. First edition, 8vo., grey cloth with elaborate silver gold and white decoration, top edge gilt, fine, illustrations by Howard Pyle, nice.   Aleph-Bet Books, Inc.   104 - 463   2013 $200

Cabet, Etienne *Voyage et Aventures de Lord Villiam Corisdall en Icorie.*   Paris: Hippolyte Souverain, 1840. (1839). First edition, 2 volumes, modern half morocco, marbled sides, gilt lettering to spine by Lobstein-Laurenchet, repair to "Tables des Chapitres" of volume I, without loss of text.   Heritage Book Shop   50th Anniversary Catalogue - 18   2013 $10,000

The Cabinet of Useful Arts and Manufactures...   Dublin: printed by Thomas Courtney, 1821.   10 full page woodcuts, few dogears, modicum of soiling, pages 180, 12mo., original tree sheep, gilt lettered library classification on spine. splits in joints and spine defective at foot, inscription inside front cover, "Great Ness lending Library. Presented by R. A. Slang Esq. 1858", good.   Blackwell's Rare Books   Sciences - 65   2013   £450

Cady, Harrison *Harrison Cady Animal Book.*   Racine: Whitman, 1928. 4to., linen like flexbile pictorial wrappers, slight cover soil, else very good+, brightly colored illustrations on each page.   Aleph-Bet Books, Inc.   104 - 103   2013 $300

Cady, Harrison *Harrison Cady Picture Book.*   Racine: Whitman, 1928. 4to., stiff pictorial wrappers, name erased in margin, else very good+, brightly colored illustrations.   Aleph-Bet Books, Inc.   104 - 104   2013 $300

Cady, Harrison *Ol' Mr. Bear's Honey Hunt.*   Racine: Whitman, 1928. 4to., linen like pictorial wrappers, some cover soil and spine wear, very good, illustrations.   Aleph-Bet Books, Inc.   104 - 105   2013 $200

Cady, Harrison *Peter Rabbit Picture, Story, Painting, Crayon Book. Series B-1.*   New York: John Eggers, 1923. Oblong 8vo., stiff full color pictorial wrappers, fine and unused, 2 full color illustrations and 8 full page black and whites designed to be colored, rare.   Aleph-Bet Books, Inc.   104 - 107   2013 $400

Cady, Harrison *Peter Rabbit Picture, Story, Painting, Crayon Book. Series B-2.*   New York: John Eggars, 1923. Oblong 8vo., stiff full color pictorial wrappers, fine and unused, 2 full page full color illustrations, 8 full page black and whites designed to be colored, rare.   Aleph-Bet Books, Inc.   104 - 108   2013 $400

Cady, Harrison *Peter Rabbit Picture, Story, Painting, Crayon Book. Series B-3.*   New York: John Eggars, 1923. Oblong 8vo., stiff full color pictorial wrappers, fine, unused, 2 full page full color illustrations, , 8 full page black and white's designed to be colored, rare.   Aleph-Bet Books, Inc.   104 - 110   2013 $400

Cady, Harrison *Peter Rabbit Picture, Story, Painting, Crayon Book. Series B-4.*   New York: John Eggers, 1922. Oblong 8vo., stiff full color pictorial wrappers fine and unused, 2 full page full color illustrations and 8 full page black and whites designed to be colored, rare.   Aleph-Bet Books, Inc.   104 - 109   2013 $400

Cahier, Charles *Nouveaux Melanges D'Archeologie d'Histoire et de Litterature sur le Moyen Age par les Auteurs de la Monographie des Virtraux de Bourges...*   Paris: Firmin Didot Freres, 1874-1877. First edition, 4 volumes, folio, 32 copper plates and 1212 wood engravings, quarter bound red morocco over marbled paper covered boards, raised bands, gilt rules, gilt titles, top edge gilt, marbled endpapers, spines and boards rubbed, extremities worn with loss of paper to corners of two boards, some minor splits at hinges, scattered foxing, bindings tight, leaves crisp, overall very good, sound set.   Kaaterskill Books   16 - 10   2013 $650

Caidin, Martin *Cyborg; Operation Nuke: High Crystal.*   New York: Arbor House, 1972. 1973. 1974. First editions, 3 volumes, each volume fine in fine dust jacket with very slightest of wear, second work is Advance Review copy with slip laid in, all volumes very uncommon in fine condition.   Between the Covers Rare Books, Inc.   Sci-Fi, Fantasy & Horror - 403967   2013 $1250

Caillois, Roger *Un Mannequin sur la Trottoir. Remarques au Pinceau.*   Paris: Yves Riviere, 1974. First edition, one of 450 copies, signed on colophon page by Alechinsky and Caillois, 5 color plates, 14 in text drawings, 4to., loose folded leaves, as issued in chemise and illustrated slipcase, fine in lightly rubbed chemise and very good soiled slipcase.   Kaaterskill Books   16 - 11   2013 $650

Cain, James M. *Jealous Woman.* London: Robert Hale, 1955. First English edition, fine in bright, very near fine dust jacket with tiny nick and couple of short tears, lovely, fresh copy. Between the Covers Rare Books, Inc. Mystery & Detective Fiction - 57185   2013 $400

Cain, James M. *The Postman Always Rings Twice.* New York: Otto Penzler, 1996. Facsimile edition, very fine in original shrinkwrap. Mordida Books   81 - 58   2013 $100

Caine, Caesar *Capella de Gerardegile or the Story of a Cumberland Chapelry (Garrigill).* Halthwistle: R. M. Saint, 1908. Limited edition no. 120, original cloth, gilt, 16 plates and map, 4 text illustrations, excellent sound copy, scarce. R. F. G. Hollett & Son   Lake District & Cumbria - 249   2013   £275

Caine, Hall *Recollections of Rossetti.* London: Cassell and Co., 1928. First edition, 8vo., original red cloth gilt, inscribed by author to Hannen Swaffer, journalist, very good with some water damage to top corners, otherwise just little rubbed and darkened in places. Maggs Bros. Ltd.   1460 - 154   2013   £175

Caine, Hall *The Woman of Knockaloe. A Parable.* London: Cassell and Co., 1923. First edition, 8vo., original black cloth, gilt, excellent copy, extremities rubbed, first and last gathering lightly foxed, loosely inserted ALS from author to Mr. Anderson dated 24th May 1928. Maggs Bros. Ltd. 1460 - 153   2013   £100

Caird, James *The Irish Land Question.* 1869. Second edition, 32 pages, modern wrappers, very good. C. P. Hyland   261 - 168   2013   £80

Caldecott, Randolph *Caldecott's Picture Book.* London: George Routledge, n.d. circa, 1885. 12mo., pictorial cloth, all edges gilt, covers naturally discolored, else fine, illustrations in color and brown line, rare. Aleph-Bet Books, Inc. 104 - 111   2013 $400

Caldecott, Randolph *The Panjandrum Picture Book.* Warne & Co., n.d. circa, 1900. Oblong 8vo., original pictorial cloth, 24 full page color illustrations and line drawings. R. F. G. Hollett & Son   Children's Books - 102   2013   £45

Caldecott, Randolph *Picture Books.* London: George Routledge, n.d., 2 volumes, square 8vo. and oblong 8vo., contemporary half crimson roan gilt, rubbed and scraped, one corner very defective and chewed, the first volume contains 6 picture books, with original wrappers bound in, the second volume contains 8 titles, all bound without wrappers, all illustrations in color, first few titles in second volume with some chewed damage to top corners. R. F. G. Hollett & Son   Children's Books - 103   2013   £150

Caldecott, Randolph *R. Caldecott's Picture Book No. 3...* London: Frederick Warne and Co. n.d., Original pictorial boards, little rubbed and soiled, rebacked to match, 88 pages with full page colored plates and sepia illustrations, few slight finger marks in places. R. F. G. Hollett & Son Children's Books - 105   2013   £65

Caldecott, Randolph *R. Caldecott's Second Collection of Pictures and Songs.* London: Frederick Warne and Co. n.d., Oblong large 8vo., original pictorial cloth gilt, over bevelled boards, dust jacket (edges little torn and chipped, piece missing from head of spine), numerous color printed plates, short closed tear to one leaf, scarce in wrapper. R. F. G. Hollett & Son   Children's Books - 106   2013   £150

Caldecott, Randolph *Sing a Song of Sixpence.* London: Frederick Warne & co. n.d., Square 8vo., original pictorial wrappers trifle soiled, 8 full page color illustrations and line drawings. R. F. G. Hollett & Son   Children's Books - 108 2013   £25

Caldwell, Charles *An Eulogium of Caspar Wistar, Professor of Anatomy...* Philadelphia: Thomas Dobson and Son, 1818. First edition, 8vo., 28 pages, removed, whip stitched along bottom edge, sheets toned. M & S Rare Books, Inc.   95 - 46   2013 $150

Caldwell, Erskine Preston   1903-1987 *The Bastard.* New York: Heron Press, 1929. First edition, one of 1100 copies, lacking clear acetate dust jacket, fine but for light sunning to edges. Beasley Books   2013 - 2013 $50

Caldwell, Erskine Preston   1903-1987 *God's Little Acre.* New York: Viking, 1933. First edition, tiny books tore label to rear pastedown and small rectangle of offsetting to front flyleaf, still fine in fine dust jacket with just minuscule corner nicks, beautiful copy, from the Bruce Kahn collection. Ken Lopez Bookseller   159 - 30   2013 $4500

Caldwell, Erskine Preston   1903-1987 *The Sacrilege of Alan Kent.* Portland: Falmouth Book House, 1936. Copy #23 of 300 numbered copies, signed by author, red boards and vellum spine, wood engravings by Russell Frizzell, fine in near fine slipcase, scarce. Ken Lopez Bookseller   159 - 31   2013 $375

California. A Guide to the Golden State. New York: Hastings House, 1939. First edition, many photos and maps, including large folding map in rear pocket, light green cloth, lettered in dark green, fine. Argonaut Book Shop Summer 2013 - 4   2013 $90

California Brand Book - 1977. Sacramento: State of California, Dept. of Food and Agriculture, Bur. of Livestock Identification, 1977. Thick quarto, 2 maps, gray cloth lettered in black on spine and front cover, fine. Argonaut Book Shop   Recent Acquisitions June 2013 - 50   2013 $90

California Historical Society *Index to California Historical Society Quarterly. Volume One to Forty 1922-1961. (with) Volumes Forty-One to Fifty Four 1962-1975.* San Francisco: California Historical Society, 1965. 1977, First edition, 2 volumes, printed wrappers, vertical crease to front cover of second volume, else fine set.   Argonaut Book Shop   Recent Acquisitions June 2013 - 51   2013 $125

California. Department of Public Works - 1947 *Report to the California Toll Bridge Authority Covering Preliminary Studies for an Additional Bridge Between San Francisco and the East Bay Metropolitan Area.* Sacramento: California Dept. of Public Works, January 31, 1947. First edition, light soiling to wrappers, fine, complete copy, very scarce.   Argonaut Book Shop   Summer 2013 - 80   2013 $450

California. Department of Water Resources *California State Water Project Atlas.* Sacramento: California Department of Water Resources, 1999. First edition, small folio, color photos, maps, graphs, technical drawings, charts, blue cloth, gilt, very fine, pictorial dust jacket lightly rubbed at spine ends.   Argonaut Book Shop   Recent Acquisitions June 2013 - 55   2013 $275

California. Insurance Commission *Second Annual Report of the Insurance Commissioner for the State of California (Year Ending Dec. 31, 1869).* Sacramento: D. W. Gelwicks, State Printer, 1870. First edition thus, 361 pages, plus index, handsomely bound in modern three quarter brown calf, marbled sides, original presentation label affixed to front cover, head of spine with slight wear, titlepage bit darkened, else fine, original presentation label affixed to front cover, printed in gold on black leather "J.B. Scotchler, President Merchants' Mutual Marine Ins. Co.".   Argonaut Book Shop   Recent Acquisitions June 2013 - 52   2013 $150

California. Laws, Statutes, etc. *Public Land Laws Providing for the Sale and Management of Lands Belonging to the State of California.* Sacramento: D. W. Gelwicks, State Printer, 1870. First edition, 36 pages, light blue wrappers printed in black, very minor wear to spine ends, fine, clean copy.   Argonaut Book Shop   Recent Acquisitions June 2013 - 53   2013 $125

The Californian. Summer 1935. (Volume 3 number 2). Pomona: Hyman Bradofsky, Summer, 1935. Octavo, decorated wrappers, stapled.   L. W. Currey, Inc.   Fall Sampler Sept. 2013 - 146567   2013 $225

Calkin, John B. *The Geography and History of Nova Scotia with a General Outline of Geography.* Halifax: A. & W. Mackinlay, 1859. Small 8vo., brown pressed cloth with blindstamps, boards detached and badly repaired, with scotch tape, interior badly dampstained, otherwise very good.   Schooner Books Ltd.   104 - 45   2013 $175

Calkin, John B. *A History and Geography of Nova Scotia.* Halifax: A. & W. Mackinlay, 1878. Small 8vo., brown cloth with blindstamped design to front and back cover, some wear to edges of covers and foxing to prelim leaves.   Schooner Books Ltd.   105 - 59   2013 $50

Callwell, Charles *The History of the Royal Artillery from the Indian Mutiny to the Great War.* Woolwich: printed at the Royal Artillery Institution, 1931. First edition, 3 volumes plus portfolio of maps, very good, original gilt lettered blue cloth, spine of volume III little faded, although not inscribed, this came from the library of co-author John Headlam.   Ken Spelman Books Ltd.   75 - 175   2013   £180

Calmeil, Louis Florentin *De La Paralysi Consideree chez Les Alieneis Recherches Faites dans le Service de Feu M. Royer-Collard et de M. Esquirol.* Paris & London: J. B. Bailliere, 1826. First edition, 8vo., errata, contemporary quarter calf over marbled boards, gilt ruled spine, gilt stamped black morocco spine label, extremities rubbed, corners bumped, hinges worn at foot of spine, very good.   Jeff Weber Rare Books   172 - 49   2013 $900

Calmet, Augustin *An Historical, Critical, Geographical, Chronological and Etymological Dictionary of the Holy Bible.* London: printed for J. J. and P. Knapton, 1732. First English edition, engraved frontispiece and 162 engraved plates, titlepages in red and black one plate in volume ii with closed tear (through part of image, c. 14 cm. long, but with no loss), several plates with small handling tears in blank margins or at folds, 2 plates in volume ii slightly proud and with fore-edges worn as a result, some browning and spotting, folio, modern calf, spines with six raised bands, dark red morocco lettering pieces, compartments, new endpapers, good.   Blackwell's Rare Books   B174 - 22   2013   £1200

Calmette, A. *La Vaccination Preventive Contre la Tuberculose...* Paris: Masson, 1927. 250 pages + ads, photo plates, 8vo., original publisher's printed brown wrappers, uncut, unopened, near fine.   James Tait Goodrich   S74 - 41   2013 $395

Calt, Stephen *King of the Delta Blues, the Life and Music of Charlie Patton.* Newton: Rock Chapel Press, 1988. First edition, wrappers, near fine but for little wrinkling to upper right corner of front wrapper, 8vo., 341 pages.   Beasley Books   2013 - 2013 $100

Calvary Cemetery, New York *Rules and Regulations of Calvary Cemetery, New York.* New York: Broun, Green & Adams, printers, 1889. First edition?, printed self wrappers, 16, (2) pages, little nicking at fore edge but nice, very good or better.   Between the Covers Rare Books, Inc. New York City - 285007   2013 $200

Calverley, William Slater *Notes on the Early Sculptured Crosses, Shrines and Monuments in the Present Diocese.* Kendal: T. Wilson, 1899. Original brown cloth gilt, portrait and numerous plates and illustrations, flyleaves browned, scarce.   R. F. G. Hollett & Son   Lake District & Cumbria - 250   2013   £95

Calvert, Albert F. *South West Africa During the German Occupation 1884-1914.* London: T. Werner Laurie, 1916. Second edition, original blue cloth, gilt, rather marked and stained, spine faded and frayed at head and foot, plates and maps, tissue guarded color frontispiece, flyleaves and last few leaves of text rather foxed, scarce.   R. F. G. Hollett & Son   Africana - 34   2013   £65

Calvert, W. R. *Wild Life on Moor and Fell.* London: Hodder & Stoughton, 1937. First edition, tall 8vo., original cloth, edges faded in places, dust jacket (spine darkened, edges worn and chipped), pages 230 with fine woodcut illustrations by Winifred M. Thridgould.   R. F. G. Hollett & Son   Lake District & Cumbria - 251   2013   £40

Calvino, Italo *The Path to the Nest of Spiders.* London: Collins, 1956. First English edition, pages 192, foolscap 8vo., original black boards, backstrip gilt lettered, edges lightly spotted, dust jacket with backstrip panel faded, few very short tears, very good, copy for review with publisher's printed review request slip loosley inserted.   Blackwell's Rare Books   B174 - 185   2013   £250

Cambridge, Richard Owen *An Account of the War in India, Between the English and French...* London: printed for T. Jeffreys, 1761. 4to., directions to binder, 4 maps, 9 folding plans, 6 engraved plates, with additional plan, not called for in list of plates, 4to., some light foxing, offsetting of text on to one plate, minor worming to a few blank upper margins of final 'proceedings', full contemporary marbled calf, raised and gilt banded spine, red morocco label, slight wear to hinges and edge of label.   Jarndyce Antiquarian Booksellers   CCV - 43   2013   £680

Cambridge, Richard Owen *The Scribleriad: an Heroic Poems.* London: printed for R. Dodsley and sold by M. Cooper, 1751. First edition, 4to., engraved frontispiece and another 6 engraved plates, foxed and toned in places, one section title with horizontal closed tear through imprint (no loss), two omitted lines in Book IV with publisher's offering a cancellans, supplied in MS by early owner, marbled calf, boards bordered with decorative gilt rule, rebacked and recornered to style by Chris Weston, old leather bit scratched.   Unsworths Antiquarian Booksellers   28 - 79   2013   £250

Cameron, Agnes Deans *The New North.* D. Appleton & Co., 1910. First edition, large 8vo., original pictorial cloth, gilt, extremities trifle rubbed, illustrations.   R. F. G. Hollett & Son   Polar Exploration - 6   2013   £75

Cameron, Lucy Lyttleton Butt *The Broken Doll.* Houlston and Wright, circa, 1860. Woodcut frontispiece (printed on inside front cover), vignette on title, 6 woodcut illustrations in text, verso of last leaf (blank), slightly discolored, pages 45, including front wrapper, 16mo., original printed wrappers, good.   Blackwell's Rare Books   B174 - 24   2013   £90

Cameron, Lucy Lyttleton Butt *The Three Flower-Pots.* Houlston and Sons circa, 1860. New edition, woodcut frontispiece printed on inside front wrapper and 6 woodcuts in text, bit of foxing in gutter at centre of booklet, pages 30 (pagination including front wrapper), 16mo., original printed wrappers, good.   Blackwell's Rare Books   B174 - 23   2013   £80

Camos, Narciso *Jardin de Maria, Planatdo en el Principiado de Cataluna.* Gerona: Por Joseph Bro. Impressor, 1772. Small 8vo., 24 pages, full page wood engraving, 2 small vignettes, full vellum, boards soiled and slightly warped, few leaves darkened, pencil notations on free rear endpaper, overall very good.   Kaaterskill Books   16 - 14   2013 $1500

Camp, Charles *Muggins. The Cow Horse.* Long Beach: Charles Camp; Denver: The Welch Haffener Printing Co., 1928. First edition, privately printed by author, very scarce, photo illustrations, stiff peach wrapper, label on front cover, printed in peach and black, publisher's numbered small sticker to inner rear cover, some fading to top edge of rear cover and spine, else fine.   Argonaut Book Shop   Summer 2013 - 40   2013 $375

Campbell, Archibald *Reports Upon the Survey of the Boundary Between the Territory of the United States and the Possessions of Great Britain.* Washington: 1878. 624 pages, 18 full page plates, 10 folding maps, recased with original spine and boards, new endpapers, internally clean and very good.   Dumont Maps & Books of the West   122 - 47   2013 $450

Campbell, Duncan *Nova Scotia, In Its Historical Mercantile and Industrial Relations.* Montreal: John Lovell, 1873. First edition, full black calf with gilt and raised bands to spine, gilt Nova Scotia coat of arms to front cover, red title label on spine, 21.6 x 14cm., calf scuffed and top and bottom of spine.   Schooner Books Ltd.   102 - 44   2013 $100

Campbell, Helen *Wah Sing Our Little Chinese Friend.* Philadelphia: David McKay, 1906. 8vo., pictorial cloth, bookplate removed front endpaper, else fine and bright.   Aleph-Bet Books, Inc.   105 - 128   2013 $125

Campbell, Hubert J. *Another Space - Another Time.* London: Panther Books..., 1953. First edition, octavo, cloth.   L. W. Currey, Inc.   Fall Sampler Sept. 2013 - 146472   2013 $125

Campbell, Ivar *Poems. With Memoir by Guy Ridley.* London: A. L. Humphreys, 1917. First edition, 8vo., original brown cloth, lettered gilt, untrimmed, near fine, inscribed by author's mother, Sybil Campbell for Duff Cooper.   Maggs Bros. Ltd.   1460 - 155   2013   £125

Campbell, John Francis   1822-1888 *Popular Tales of the West Highlands Orally Collected...* 1860-1862. First editions, original gilt decorated cloth, needs attention, frontispiece to volume 3 with guard, 4 volumes, text very good.   C. P. Hyland   261 - 921   2013   £200

Campbell, John Francis   1822-1888 *A Short American Tramp in the Fall of 1864.* Edinburgh: Edmonston and Douglas, 1865. Original maroon cloth, gilt to spine, half title, index, frontispiece, map, illustrated titlepage, numerous tables, 8vo., cloth slightly worn and sunned.   Schooner Books Ltd.   104 - 13   2013 $125

Campbell, John W. *Invaders from the Infinite.* Reading: Fantasy, 1961. Limited to 112 signed copies, very good++, minimal sun spine, soil to edges, without dust jacket as issued, 8vo.   By the Book, L. C.   38 - 76   2013 $900

Campbell, John W. *Islands of Space.* Reading: Fantasy, 1956. Limited to 500 signed copies, this no. 300, signed by author, fine, small 8vo., fine dust jacket.   By the Book, L. C.   38 - 77   2013 $700

Campbell, Joseph *The Mountainy Singer.* 1909. First edition, 4to., cloth, crack about 2 inches on outside of hinge, else very good.   C. P. Hyland   261 - 922   2013   £45

Campbell, Joseph *The Mountainy Singer.* Boston: 1919. First US edition, 4to., cloth, very good.   C. P. Hyland   261 - 923   2013   £45

Campbell, Neil *Shadow & Sun, a Nautical Memoir.* Cape Town: circa, 1947. First edition, 8vo., cloth, photos, very good.   C. P. Hyland   261 - 924   2013   £45

Campbell, Reau *Campbell's New Revised Complete Guide and Descriptive Book of Mexico.* City of Mexico: Sonora News Co., 1899. First edition, 8vo., pages 351, large foldout map, maroon cloth, stamped in gilt, illustrations, near fine, edges of leaves stained red.   Second Life Books Inc.   183 - 63   2013 $65

Campbell, Ruth *Small Fry and Winged Horse.* Chicago: Volland, 1927. Stated first edition, 8vo., cloth backed pictorial boards, fine in dust jacket with few pieces off edges, illustrations by Gustaf Tenggren, quite scarce, especially in dust jacket.   Aleph-Bet Books, Inc.   104 - 552   2013 $375

Campbell, Ruth *The Turtle Whose Snap Unfastened.* Chicago: Volland, 1927. No additional printings, 8vo., pictorial boards, slight tip rubbing, else near fine, illustrations by Ve Elizabeth Cadie wit bold color illustrations.   Aleph-Bet Books, Inc.   105 - 578   2013 $200

Campbell, Thomas   1733-1795 *Dr. (Thomas) Campbell's Diary of a Visit to England.*   1947. First edition, portrait, 8vo., cloth, dust jacket, near fine.   C. P. Hyland   261 - 926   2013   £34

Campbell, Thomas   1733-1795 *A Philosophical Survey of the South of Ireland...* Dublin: 1778. First edition, 6 plates, full calf, rebacked, good.   C. P. Hyland   261 - 170   2013   £400

Campbell, Thomas   1733-1795 *A Philosophical Survey of the South of Ireland...* Dublin: Watkinson, et al, 1778. First Dublin edition, 3 plates, xvi, 478 pages, full contemporary calf, hinges cracked, text good.   C. P. Hyland   261 - 169   2013   £250

Campbell, Thomas   1777-1844 *Frederick the Great and His Times.* Philadelphia: Lea & Blanchard, 1842. First American edition, 2 volumes, some light spotting, original vertical grained cloth, spines lettered gilt, very slight rubbing, very good.   Jarndyce Antiquarian Booksellers   CCIII - 472   2013   £35

Campbell, Thomas   1777-1844 *Gertrude of Wyoming: a Pennsylvanian Tale and Other Poems.* London: T. Bensley published for the author by Longman, Hurst, Rees and Orme, 1809. First edition, 4to., lacks ads and errata slip, half gilt stamped green calf, extremities worn, bookplate of Auchincruive, very good.   Jeff Weber Rare Books   171 - 60   2013 $125

Campbell, Thomas   1777-1844 *Gertrude of Wyoming: a Pennsylvania Tale. And Other Poems.* London: Longman, Hurst, Rees & Orme, 1809. First edition, 4to., contemporary half dark blue calf by J. Carss & Co. of Glasgow, spine gilt in compartments, maroon leather label, hinges and corners little rubbed, contemporary gift inscription, bookseller's ticket J. Carss & Co. Glasgow.   Jarndyce Antiquarian Booksellers   CCIII - 464   2013   £120

Campbell, Thomas   1777-1844 *Gertrude of Wyoming: a Pennsylvania Tale. And Other Poems.* London: Longman, Hurst, Rees & Orme, 1809. First edition, 4to., errata slip, 16 page catalog (Dec. 1808), uncut 8vo. sheets bound in 4to., uncut in original blue boards, edges little rubbed, inner hinges cracking, signed "Kindersley" in contemporary hand, good plus.   Jarndyce Antiquarian Booksellers   CCIII - 463   2013   £150

Campbell, Thomas   1777-1844   *Gertrude of Wyoming: a Pennsylvania Tale. And Other Poems.*   London: Longman, 1810.   Second edition, uncut in original pale blue boards, paper label, marked and chipped at edges, spine cracked and partly defective overall decent copy as originally issued.   Jarndyce Antiquarian Booksellers   CCIII - 465   2013   £35

Campbell, Thomas   1777-1844   *Gertrude of Wyoming: a Pennsylvania Tale. And Other Poems.*   London: Longman, 1810.   Second edition, uncut in original pale blue boards, paper label, marked and chipped at edges, spine cracked and partly defective, overall decent copy as originally issued.   Jarndyce Antiquarian Booksellers   CCIII - 465   2013   £35

Campbell, Thomas   1777-1844   *Gertrude of Wyoming: a Pennsylvania Tale. And Other Poems.*   London: Longman &c, 1814.   Fifth edition, slightly spotted, 4 page catalog, contemporary full diced calf gilt spine and borders, black leather label, hinges little worn, armorial booklabel of James Hodson, label and signature of Charles Rossier, San Francisco 1942.   Jarndyce Antiquarian Booksellers   CCIII - 466   2013   £35

Campbell, Thomas   1777-1844   *Gertrude of Wyoming: a Pennsylvania Tale. And Other Poems.*   London: Longman, 1821.   Eighth edition, engraved title (1822) and printed title (1821), plates, half title removed, slightly later full dark pink calf, gilt spine, borders and dentelles, black leather label, spine slightly faded but still, very good, attractive.   Jarndyce Antiquarian Booksellers   CCIII - 467   2013   £35

Campbell, Thomas   1777-1844   *The Pleasures of Hope, with Other Poems.*   Edinburgh: printed for Mundell & Son, 1805.   Eighth edition, half title, 4 plates by Burney, some browning and offsetting, full scarlet morocco, gilt spine, borders and dentelles, spine dulled and little rubbed, all edges gilt.   Jarndyce Antiquarian Booksellers   CCIII - 459   2013   £30

Campbell, Thomas   1777-1844   *The Pleasures of Hope, with Other Poems.*   Edinburgh: Mundell, Doig & Stevenson &c, 1808.   Frontispiece and 3 plates by Burney, 2 pages ads, slight browning, later marbled wrappers, very good.   Jarndyce Antiquarian Booksellers   CCIII - 461   2013   £30

Campbell, Thomas   1777-1844   *The Pleasures of Hope, with Other Poems.*   Edinburgh: Mundell, Doig & Stevenson &c., 1808.   4 plates by Burney, 18 page catalog, contemporary full tree calf, gilt spine, borders and dentelles, red leather label, slightly rubbed, handsome copy.   Jarndyce Antiquarian Booksellers   CCIII - 460   2013   £35

Campbell, Thomas   1777-1844   *The Pleasures of Hope, with Other Poems.*   Edinburgh: printed for Mundell, Doig & Stevenson &c, 1810.   Plates dated 1808, contemporary full mottled calf, gilt spine, borders and dentelles, black label, bit rubbed, hinges slightly worn but holding, inscription to Ellen Carlyle the gift of her Aunt Bowers Augs. 2nd 1813.   Jarndyce Antiquarian Booksellers   CCIII - 462   2013   £25

Campbell, Thomas   1777-1844   *The Poetical Works of Thomas Campbell.*   New York: Wiley & Putnam, 1841.   24mo., 2 volumes in one, all edges gilt, full red leather, gilt decorations on covers and spine, very good.   Barnaby Rudge Booksellers   Poetry 2013 - 020495   2013 $65

Campbell, Thomas   1777-1844   *The Poetical Works.*   London: Edward Moxon, 1846.   8 page catalog (March 1 1847) preceding half title, frontispiece slightly spotted, illustrations, original dark brown cloth, floral borders in blind, one corner and head of spine very slightly worn, otherwise very good.   Jarndyce Antiquarian Booksellers   CCIII - 453   2013   £25

Campbell, Thomas   1777-1844   *The Poetical Works.*   London: Edward Moxon, 1854.   Half title, frontispiece, illustrations, contemporary full green morocco, gilt spine borders and dentelles, slightly rubbed, spine little darkened, armorial booklabel of

Viscount Newry and neat gift inscription "Newry from A. F. Birch. Eton Election 1858", all edges gilt, attractive copy.   Jarndyce Antiquarian Booksellers   CCIII - 454   2013   £45

Campbell, Thomas   1777-1844   *The Poetical Works.*   London: Routledge &c, 1864.   New edition, illustrations by John Gilbert, half title, frontispiece, plates, original red cloth, bevelled boards, heavily embossed and decorated in gilt, spine slightly dulled, gift inscription 1864, all edges gilt, very good.   Jarndyce Antiquarian Booksellers   CCIII - 456   2013   £35

Campbell, Thomas   1777-1844   *The Poetical Works.*   London: Edward Moxon, 1864.   New edition, half title, frontispiece, contemporary half dark green calf, brown leather label, slightly rubbed, signature of M. M. Walker, 1860.   Jarndyce Antiquarian Booksellers   CCIII - 455   2013   £35

Campbell, Thomas   1777-1844   *The Poetical Works.*   London: George Routledge & Sons, 1871.   New edition, half title, frontispiece, plates, 4 pages ads may 1871, original green cloth, bevelled boards, attractively blocked in red, black and gilt, ownership inscription April 1883, all edges gilt, very good, bright.   Jarndyce Antiquarian Booksellers   CCIII - 457   2013   £25

Campbell, Thomas 1777-1844 *The Poetical Works.* London: George Bell & Sons, 1875. Frontispiece, contemporary full olive brown morocco by Maclehose of Glasgow, corners and hinges very slightly rubbed, all edges gilt, very good, attractive copy. Jarndyce Antiquarian Booksellers CCIII - 458   2013   £120

Campbell, Thomas 1777-1844 *The Scenic Annual of MDCCCXXXVIII.* London: George Virtue, 1838. First edition, 4to., cloth, 36 engraved plates, gilt lightly rubbed, else very good+, occasional foxing. Kaaterskill Books   16 - 15   2013 $350

Campbell, Thomas 1777-1844 *Specimens of the British Poets: with Biographical and Critical Notices...* London: John Murray, 1819. First edition, 7 volumes, slightly later half calf, red and green labels, gilt, slight marking, very good, attractive set. Jarndyce Antiquarian Booksellers CCIII - 468   2013   £520

Campbell, Thomas 1777-1844 *Specimens of the British Poets: with Biographical and Critical Notices...* London: John Murray, 1845. New edition, half title, engraved frontispiece and title (1841), printed title (1845), uncut in original green cloth, lettered and decorated gilt, small repairs to inner hinges, ownership stamp of Mary M. Hinds, with unusual stamped coat of arms on leading pastedown, very good. Jarndyce Antiquarian Booksellers   CCIII - 469   2013   £50

Campbell, Thomas 1777-1844 *Theodric: a Domestic Tale, and Other Poems.* London: Longman, 1824. First edition, half title, text largely erased, lacking leading f.e.p., spotted, uncut in original drab boards, paper label chipped, spine worn with some old repairs, bookplate of C. Arthur Vansittart of Pontifical Zouaves, fairly good copy. Jarndyce Antiquarian Booksellers   CCIII - 470   2013   £35

Campbell, Thomas 1777-1844 *Theodric: a Domestic Tale, and Other Poems.* London: Longman &c, 1824. Second edition, half title, uncut, original drab boards, paper label chipped, slight wear to spine and corners, good plus. Jarndyce Antiquarian Booksellers   CCIII - 471   2013   £40

Campbell, Tony *The Earliest Printed Maps 1472-1500.* Berkeley: University of California Press, 1987. First American edition, quarto, double page color frontispiece, 68 black and white reproductions, tables, charts, brown cloth, gilt, tiny chip to upper corner of jacket, else very fine, pictorial dust jacket. Argonaut Book Shop   Recent Acquisitions June 2013 - 56   2013 $125

Campe, J. H. *Columbus; or the Discovery of America.* Cradock and Joy, 1811. New edition, contemporary tree calf gilt, edges and hinges darkened, upper hinge cracked and repaired, folding map. R. F. G. Hollett & Son Children's Books - 113   2013   £65

Camper, Petrus *Optical Dissertation on Vision 1746.* Nieuwkoop: B. de Graaf, 1962. 8vo., 31 pages, frontispiece, illustrations, cream marbled gilt stamped paper backed boards, folding archival case, Burndy Library bookplate, fine. Jeff Weber Rare Books   172 - 47   2013 $75

Campion, J. S. *On Foot in Spain; a Walk from the Bay of Biscay to the Mediterranean.* London: Chapman & Hall, 1879. Second edition, 8vo., 6 photographic plates, marginal light foxing to some plates, contemporary brown half calf. J. & S. L. Bonham Antiquarian Booksellers   Europe - 8157   2013   £120

Cancillon, Richard *Essai sur la Nature du Commerce ed General.* Londres: chez Fletcher Gyles (but probably Paris), 1755. First edition, octavo, half title and final "Table des Chapitres", contemporary French mottled calf, red morocco spine label, spine gilt in compartments, marbled endpapers, red edges, fine, housed in custom full brown calf, clamshell, decoratively tooled in gilt o spine. Heritage Book Shop   50th Anniversary Catalogue - 19   2013 $45,000

Cangiamila, Francesco Emmanuale *Abregi de l'Embryologie Sacree ou Teraite des Devoirs des Pretres des Medecins des Chirurgiens...* Paris: Nyon, 1766. Second edition, 12mo., headpieces, tailpieces, 3 engraved plates, contemporary mottled calf, raised bands, gilt spine, red leather spine label, red edges, marbled endleaves, rubbed, head of spine chipped, hinge starting, Crainz rubber stamp, very good. Jeff Weber Rare Books   172 - 51   2013 $450

Caniff, Milton *Terry and the Pirates in Shipwrecked.* Chicago: Pleasure Books, 1935. Square 4to., pictorial boards, business name stamped on cover, else fine, 3 great color-pop-ups and black and whites, scarce. Aleph-Bet Books, Inc.   104 - 435   2013 $475

Canney, Margaret *University of London Library. Catalogue of the Goldsmiths' Library of Economic Literature.* Cambridge: Cambridge University Press, 1970. First edition, oversize 8vo., frontispiece, dark green cloth, gilt stamped cover emblem and spine title, ownership signature of Owen Chadwick, fine. Jeff Weber Rare Books   171 - 61   2013   £135

Cannon, David Wadsworth *Black Labor Chant and Other Poems.* New York: The National Council on Religion in Higher Education (Assoc. Press), 1939. First edition, boards with hand decorated paper label, presumably decorated by previous owner, slight chipping to edges of boards, good plus. Between the Covers Rare Books, Inc.   165 - 97   2013 $150

Cannon, Walter B. *The Wisdom of the Body.* New York: W. Norton, 1939. Revised edition, signed, inscribed and dated by author, very good++ with mild toning spine in very good+ dust jacket with mild soil, sun darkening to spine, edge wear, 8vo., scarce signed work. By the Book, L. C. 38 - 40 2013 $500

Canny, Nicholas *The Elizabethan Conquest of Ireland.* 1976. First edition, cloth, dust jacket, fine. C. P. Hyland 261 - 171 2013 £85

Cape, Thomas *Brief Sketches Descriptive of Bridlington-Quay and the Most Striking Objects of interest at Bridlington & Flamborough, with a Map of the Coast and District.* Bridlington-Quay: 1877. Folding map, original lemon-yellow printed wrappers which are slightly dusty, but good, scarce guide. Ken Spelman Books Ltd. 73 - 64 2013 £45

Capek, Karel *Krakatit. Roman.* Praha: Aventinum, 1924. First edition, octavo, titlepage printed in red and black, original decorated buff wrappers, printed in brown and black, all edges untrimmed. L. W. Currey, Inc. Fall Sampler Sept. 2013 - 144791 2013 $2250

Capek, Karel *R U R Rossum's Universal Robots: Kolektivni Drama.* Praha: Aventinum, 1920. First edition, octavo, original decorated lavender wrappers, printed in brown and black, all edges untrimmed. L. W. Currey, Inc. Utopian Literature: Recent Acquisitions (April 2013) - 138580 2013 $5000

Capek, Karel *R U R Rossum's Universal Robots: Kolektivni Drama.* Praha: Aventium, 1920. First edition, octavo, original decorated lavender wrappers, printed in brown and black, all edges untrimmed. L. W. Currey, Inc. Fall Sampler Sept. 2013 - 144771 2013 $3500

Capek, Karel *R U R (Rossum's Universal Robots) A Fantastic Melodrama.* Garden City: Doubleday, Page & Co., 1923. First edition in English, octavo, titlepage printed in orange and black, original orange cloth, front and spine panels stamped in black,. L. W. Currey, Inc. Fall Sampler Sept. 2013 - 146478 2013 $350

Capek, Karel *R U R (Rossum's Universal Robots).* London: Humphrey Milford/Oxford University Press, 1923. First British edition, small octavo, original printed black wrappers. L. W. Currey, Inc. Utopian Literature: Recent Acquisitions (April 2013) - 138579 2013 $1500

Capek, Karel *R.U.R. (Robots Universales de Reason).* Buenos Aires: Ediciones Drusa, 1957. First Argentine edition and first in Spanish, self wrappers, beautiful copy. Between the Covers Rare Books, Inc. Sci-Fi, Fantasy & Horror - 85078 2013 $250

Capek, Karel *War with the Newts.* New York: Putnam, 1973. First American edition, slight spotting to boards, very good plus in moderately worn, about very good dust jacket with three modest chips and some overall soiling and wear. Between the Covers Rare Books, Inc. Sci-Fi, Fantasy & Horror - 54270 2013 $500

Capivaccio, Girolamo *Practica Medicina seu Methodus Cognoscendorum... Studio et Opera...* Frankfurt: Palthenius for Peter Fischer, 1594. Title in red and black, 4to. dated and initialed binding in original vellum pigskin over wood boards, original brass clasps intact and working, initialed on front board "I H B" dated on lower panel "1594" which is year of printing, binding elaborately tooled with arabesque and filigree panels, spine with raised bands and hand lettered titles, fine contemporary binding, some light wear and discoloration of vellum, clasps intact and working. James Tait Goodrich 75 - 40 2013 $3950

Capote, Truman 1924-1985 *The Grass Harp.* London: Heinemann, 1952. First UK edition, 8vo., original brown cloth, inscribed by author for Yvonne Hamilton, with her ownership signature, excellent copy. Maggs Bros. Ltd. 1460 - 157 2013 £2500

Capote, Truman 1924-1985 *In Cold Blood.* New York: Random House, 1965. Third printing, 8vo. original burgundy cloth, hinge cracked at half title, otherwise excellent copy in torn and chipped dust jacket, housed in protective box, with indistinct presentation inscription from author. Maggs Bros. Ltd. 1460 - 159 2013 £1250

Capote, Truman 1924-1985 *Music for Chameleons.* New York: Random House, 1980. First trade edition, signed by author and also signed by book's dedicatee, Tennessee Williams, marvelous association, foxing to top and front edges, else near fine in like dust jacket (price clipped). Ed Smith Books 75 - 13 2013 $2500

Capote, Truman 1924-1985 *Other Voices Other Rooms.* London: Heinemann, 1948. First UK edition, 8vo., original brown cloth, excellent copy, inscribed by author for Yvonne Hamilton, with her ownership signature. Maggs Bros. Ltd. 1460 - 156 2013 £2000

Capper, Samuel James *The Shores and Cities of the Boden See; Rambles in 1879 and 1880.* London: de la Rue, 1881. First edition, 8vo., 2 maps, 22 plates, top edge gilt, original red decorative cloth, slightly. J. & S. L. Bonham Antiquarian Booksellers Europe - 6616 2013 £250

Caradoc, of Llancarvan *The History of Wales Comprehending the Lives and Succession of the Princes of Wales, from Cadwalader...* London: B. M. Clark for the author and R. Clavell, 1697. Contemporary calf, rebacked in period style, later endpapers, very nice. Joseph J. Felcone Inc. Books Printed before 1701 - 88 2013 $450

Carco, Francis *Auguste Brouet. Jesus-la-Caille.* Paris: Editions de l'Estampe, 1925. From a total edition of 272 copies, this example is from the edition of 50 copies on Madagascar handmade paper with 30 original etchings, 10 of them full page by Auguste Brouet, 11 x 8.5 inches, 225 pages, bound in outstanding Art Deco binding by Soudee, signed by the master binder, full dark blue morocco with geometric mosaic of silver, burgundy, brown and beige leather onlays, both covers, plain spine with burgundy onlay stamped in black, original wrappers preserved and bound in, top edge gilt, double endleaves of silk and hand painted heavy stock, housed in quarter morocco chemise with gilt on spine, matching slipcase, very handsome.   Gemini Fine Books & Arts., Ltd.   Art Reference & Illustrated Books - 2013 $2995

Card, Orson Scott *Ender's Game.* New York: Tor, 1985. First edition, octavo, boards.   L. W. Currey, Inc.   Fall Sampler Sept. 2013 - 145059   2013 $2250

Cardano, Girolamo   1501-1576 *De Utilitate ex Adversis Capienda Libri IIII.* Basle: colopone: Henrich Petri, 1561. First edition, title in roman, text in italic type, one woodcut diagram in text, woodcut printer's device at end, little bit browned, more so at end but not seriously, few dog ears at end, 8vo., contemporary vellum over wooden boards, pair of later dark green morocco lettering pieces on spine (chipped), library stamp on title, good.   Blackwell's Rare Books   Sciences - 25   2013   £1500

Carey, Fleming *Alibi. April 1934 (Volume 1 Number 4).* New York: Magazines Inc. April, 1934. Octavo, pictorial wrappers.   L. W. Currey, Inc.   Fall Sampler Sept. 2013 - 146563   2013 $350

Carey, Peter *The Fat Man in History.* London: Faber, 1980. First English edition, crown 8vo., pages 1883, original light blue boards, backstrip blocked in silver, dust jacket, fine.   Blackwell's Rare Books   B174 - 186   2013   £100

Carin, Frank *The New Adventures of Peter Rabbit. Comic No. 16.* New York: Avon Periodicals Feb., 1953. First edition, full color strip cartoon stories, 36 pages, including covers, wrappers, very nice, fresh copy.   Ian Hodgkins & Co. Ltd.   134 - 35   2013   £30

Carlberg, David M. *Essentials of Bacterial and Viral Genetics.* Springfield: Charles C. Thomas, 1976. First edition, 8vo., photos, figures, green cloth, dust jacket, fine.   Jeff Weber Rare Books   172 - 53   2013 $325

Carleton, James Henry *An Excursion to the Ruins of Abo Quarra and Gran Quivira in New Mexico.* Washington: 1855. With a Copy of the Santa Fe" 1965 edition, 2 volumes, first volume in original stamped boards, some loss of cloth at top of spine, well foxed, but completely legible and with a sound binding, second volume near fine in like dust jacket.   Dumont Maps & Books of the West   124 - 53   2013 $95

Carlisle Natural History Society *Transactions.* Carlisle: The Society, 1909-1928. Volumes 1-4, original wrappers, spine of first volume faded and chipped, excellent run, scarce.   R. F. G. Hollett & Son   Lake District & Cumbria - 256   2013   £120

Carlisle, Earl of *Diary in Turkish and Greek Waters.* London: Longman, Brown, Green, 1854. Second edition, 8vo., buff cloth, rebacked.   J. & S. L. Bonham Antiquarian Booksellers Europe - 5723   2013   £75

Carlisle. Council *City of Carlisle. Proceedings of the Council and of the Several Committees of the Council from the 9th Day of November 1894 to the 9th Day of November 1895.* Carlisle: The Council, 1895. Original full roan, gilt, large folding lithographed plan (slightly torn), numerous tables.   R. F. G. Hollett & Son   Lake District & Cumbria - 253   2013   £35

Carlson, Natalie Savage *Family Under the Bridge.* New York: Harper & Bros., 1958. Large 8vo., pictorial cloth, fine in dust jacket (near fine with few tiny chips, no award seal, not price clipped), illustrations by Garth Williams with 12 full page black and white lithos including pictorial title and frontispiece spread.   Aleph-Bet Books, Inc.   105 - 578   2013 $150

Carlson, Stan *The Minnesota Huddle: a Pictorial Publication Devoted in Its Entirety to Football at the University of Minnesota.* Minneapolis: Stan Carlson, 1936. Volume I, mildly creased, thus very good plus in lightly rubbed wrappers.   Between the Covers Rare Books, Inc.   Football Books - 71520   2013 $125

Carlyle, Joseph Dacre *Specimens of Arabian Poetry, from the Earliest Time to the Extinction of the Khaliphat, with some account of the Authors.* London: T. Cadell & W. Davies, 1810. Second edition, half title, engraved music, contemporary full speckled calf, gilt spine, little rubbed, slight wear to leading hinge, overall very good.   Jarndyce Antiquarian Booksellers   CCIII - 653   2013   £350

Carlyle, Thomas   1795-1881 *Chartism.* London: James Fraser, 1840. First edition, 12mo., 1 pages ads, original black cloth, bordered and decorated in blind, spine unlettered gilt, very slight rubbing at head and tail of spine, very good.   Jarndyce Antiquarian Booksellers   CCV - 46   2013   £150

Carlyle, Thomas   1795-1881 *The French Revolution.* London: James Fraser, 1837. First edition, 3 volumes, octavo, with half titles and integral ad leaf in volume II, uncut, publisher's brown boards, expertly rebacked to style and with original printed spine labels laid down, some expectable rubbing to boards, still remarkable copy, very difficult to find in original boards and complete, housed in blue cloth clamshell case with red morocco gilt spine label.   Heritage Book Shop   Holiday Catalogue 2012 - 25   2013 $5000

Carlyle, Thomas 1795-1881 *The Life of Friedrich Schiller.* London: printed for Taylor & Hessey, 1825. First edition, Frontispiece, errata slip preceding text, lower outer margin pages 351/352 torn not affecting text, contemporary half calf, marbled boards, black morocco label, little rubbed, contemporary signature.   Jarndyce Antiquarian Booksellers   CCV - 241   2013   £150

Carmichael, Richard *An Essay on Venereal Diseases and the Uses and Abuses of Mercury in their Treatment.* Philadelphia: Judah Dobson and A. Sherman, 1825. Second American edition, 4to., uncut, 5 color plates, modern green library buckram, gilt stamped spine title, ex-library bookplates, early signature of Ch. H. Steele (?), very good.   Jeff Weber Rare Books   172 - 52   2013 $400

Carmody, Francis J. *Physiologus. The Very Ancient Book of Beasts, Plants and Stones.*   San Francisco: Book Club of California, 1953. One of 325 copies, small quarto, (76) pages, hand colored title engraving, 53 hand colored text engravings, hand colored initials, all by Mallette Dean, white parchment binding. spine darkened, covers lightly stained from publisher's glue (as usual), else fine.   Argonaut Book Shop   Summer 2013 - 42   2013 $325

Carnap, Rudolf *Logical Foundations of Probability.* Chicago: University of Chicago Press, 1951. Second printing, 8vo., red cloth, gilt lettered spine, minimal sun to spine, cover edge wear, signed and inscribed by author.   By the Book, L. C.   38 - 24   2013 $750

Carnap, Rudolf *Philosophy and Logical Syntax.* London: Kegan Paul, Trench, Trubner, 1935. First edition, signed and inscribed by author for educator and philosopher, Arthur Schilpp, very good, red spine and cream colored printed boards, paper spine label Schilpp's bookplate, mild sun and scuff to spine, cover edges worn, 16mo., 100 pages.   By the Book, L. C.   38 - 25   2013 $500

Carnarvon, Henry John George Herbert, 3rd Earl of *The Moor.* London: Charles Knight, 1825. First edition, final errata leaf, slight spotting, contemporary half dark blue calf, gilt, spine, slightly rubbed, signature of P. Champion, Old Broad Street, booksellers ticket Joseph Capes, Flleet St.   Jarndyce Antiquarian Booksellers   CCIII - 654   2013   £35

Carnarvon, Henry John George Herbert, 3rd Earl of *Portugal and Gallicia; with a Review of the Social and Political State of the Basques Provinces and a few Remarks on Recent Events in Spain.* London: John Murray, 1837. First edition, 2 volumes, 8vo., contemporary black half calf, raised bands, very good.   J. & S. L. Bonham Antiquarian Booksellers   Europe - 8396 2013   £320

Carnegie, Andrew *James Watt.* Edinburgh: Oliphant Anderson & Ferrier, n.d., First edition, original red cloth, spine faded on spine, otherwise near fine, inscribed by author to Arthur Irons. Maggs Bros. Ltd.   1460 - 162   2013   £350

Carney, James *The Irish Bardic Poet.* Dolmen Press, 1967. First edition, wrappers, 8vo., dust jacket, very good.   C. P. Hyland   261 - 928   2013   £32

Carnot, Lazare Niola Marguerite *Geometrie de Position.* Paris: Imprimerie Crapelet for J. B. M. Duprat An XI, 1803. First edition, 18 folding engraved plates, few gatherings browned, tiny holes in first 4 leaves touching but not effacing text in places, 4to., contemporary half calf, little worn, signature of an artillery officer on title, good.   Blackwell's Rare Books   Sciences - 26   2013   £500

Carpenter, Edward *Angels' Wings: a Series of Essays on Art and Its Relation to Life.* London: Swan Sonnenschein, 1908. Third edition, half title, frontispiece, plates, original dark blue cloth, spine dulled, very good.   Jarndyce Antiquarian Booksellers   CCV - 49   2013   £50

Carpenter, Edward *The Drama of Love and Death: a Study of Human Evolution and Transfiguration.* London: George Allen, 1912. Second edition, half title, 2 pages ads, original blue gray cloth, lettered in gilt, top edge gilt, very good.   Jarndyce Antiquarian Booksellers   CCV - 50   2013   £40

Carpenter, John *When Little boys Sings.* Chicago: McClurg, Oct. 29th, 1904. First edition, oblong folio, patterned cloth, spine slightly soiled, else fine, printed on coated paper, wonderful color illustrations.   Aleph-Bet Books, Inc.   104 - 427   2013 $400

Carpenter, Joseph Edward *Penny Readings in Prose and Verse.* London: Frederick Warne & Co., 1865. 4 pages ads, ads on endpapers, original orange cloth, lettered in black, spine dulled and slightly faded, slightly rubbed.   Jarndyce Antiquarian Booksellers   CCV - 51   2013   £45

Carpenter, Joseph Edward *Penny Readings in Prose and Verse.* London: Warne & Co., 1867. 4 pages ads, ads on endpapers, original orange cloth, lettered in black, slightly rubbed and dulled.   Jarndyce Antiquarian Booksellers   CCV - 52   2013   £50

Carpenter, William *The People"s Book; Comprising their Chartered Rights and Practical Wrongs.* London: W. Strange, 1831. 12mo., recently rebound in drab boards, plain brown cloth spine.   Jarndyce Antiquarian Booksellers   CCV - 53   2013   £150

Carr, Daniel *Gifts of the Leaves with Prints from the Ova Series by Julia Ferrari.* Ashuelot: Trois Fontaines, Golgonooza Letter Foundry, 1997. One of 26 lettered 'de tete' copies, from a total issue of 109 (26 lettered copies, 80 numbered copies, 3 Artist's proof copies), all on Arches paper, each signed and numbered or lettered by author and type designer, punch cutter and printer, Dan Carr, and artist, Julia Ferrari, the lettered copy has unique colored monotype by Richard de Bas paper as the frontispiece of book, a copper strike from the hand cut punches bound into custom made clamshell box, housing book and 4 etchings, page size 12 1/2 x 9 1/4 inches, 74 pages, bound by Julia Ferrari, handmade tan/brown pastepaper over boards housed in black cloth clamshell box with copper strike from hand cut punches inlaid into inside, front panel of box, pastepaper spine label, new. Priscilla Juvelis - Rare Books 56 - 12 2013 $3500

Carr, Daniel *Gifts of the Leaves with Prints from the Ova Series by Julia Ferrari.* Ashuelot: Trois Fontaines (Golgonooza Letter Foundry), 1997. One of 80 regular copies, from a total issue of 109 (26 lettered copies, 80 numbered copies, 3 Artist's proof copies), all on Arches paper, each signed and numbered or lettered by author and type designer, punch cutter and printer, Dan Carr, and artist, Julia Ferrari, bound by Julia Ferrari, in green pastepaper over boards. Priscilla Juvelis - Rare Books 56 - 13 2013 $1500

Carr, Harry *Prairie Feathers.* San Diego: Ash Ranch Press, 1988. Limited to 26 numbered copies and deluxe lettered edition of 26, signed by printer, this is the deluxe copy, 5.7 x 6.4cm., leather, title and author gilt stamping on spine faded, beadwork on front board, edges uncut, slipcase, spine gilt stamped, from the collection of Donn W. Sanford. Oak Knoll Books 303 - 36 2013 $375

Carr, J. L. *A Month in the Country.* Cornucopia Press, 1990. One of 300 numbered copies signed by author and Ronald Blythe, titlepage printed in black and red, royal 8vo., original mid green cloth, printed backstrip and front cover labels, top edge gilt, glassine jacket, new. Blackwell's Rare Books 172 - 168 2013 £140

Carr, John *The Stranger in Ireland or Tour in the Southern & Western Parts of that Country in the Year 1805.* 1806. First edition, 15 aquatints, tinted map, full calf (worn), text good. C. P. Hyland 261 - 172 2013 £750

Carr, John Dickson *Death-Watch.* New York: Harpers, 1935. First edition, fine without dust jacket. Mordida Books 81 - 60 2013 $185

Carr, John Dickson *It Walks by Night.* New York: Harpers, 1930. First edition, scrape at base of front pastedown and small holes on front endpaper and first prelims, otherwise very good, without dust jacket. Mordida Books 81 - 59 2013 $150

Carr, Richard *The Classical Scholar's Guide...* London: printed for the author by John Richardson and Kirkby Lonsdale: Arthur Foster, 1832. First edition, original cloth backed boards with paper spine label, little soiled, bound in 6s with some 4-, 5- and 8-leaf sections and little erratic pagination in places, endpapers lightly spotted, few edges and inner margins little stained, but very good unsophisticated untrimmed copy. R. F. G. Hollett & Son Lake District & Cumbria - 258 2013 £125

Carranco, Lynwood *Steam in the Redwoods.* Caldwell: The Caxton Printers, 1988. First edition, 4to., x, 224 pages, profusely illustrated with photos, maps, drawings, etc., very fine, pictorial dust jacket, very scarce. Argonaut Book Shop Recent Acquisitions June 2013 - 57 2013 $150

Carrick, T. W. *History of Wigton (Cumberland) from its Origin to the Close of the Nineteenth Century.* Carlisle: Charles Thurnam, 1949. First edition, original cloth, gilt, dust jacket little chipped and creased, stained on reverse, illustrations, presentation copy inscribed by author dated 25 Sept. 1952, very good, scarce. R. F. G. Hollett & Son Lake District & Cumbria - 259 2013 £120

Carrighar, Sally *Moonlight at Midday.* London: Michael Joseph, 1959. First edition, original cloth, gilt, dust jacket trifle worn, 48 illustrations, flyleaves little browned. R. F. G. Hollett & Son Polar Exploration - 7 2013 £25

Carroll, William Henry *A Practical Index, or Digest of Statutes...33rd, 35th, 37th, 43rd & 45th Years of King George III for the Regulation of Contested Elections in Ireland.* Barlow, 1810. Suede fold-over travelling binding, pocket-size, very good. C. P. Hyland 261 - 183 2013 £100

Carruth, Hayden *Aura. A Poem...* West Burke: Janus Press, 1977. First edition, tall folio, in printed handmade paper folder, enclosed in linen folding box with printed paper label on spine, limited to only 50 copies, this copy press lettered especially 'for Michael Boylen and inscribed by Claire Van Vliet in pencil for Bruce Hubbard', a folded paperwork landscape by CVV and Kathryn and Howard Clark enclosed in folded paper wrapper on which text is printed, unfolded wrapper measures 14 3/4 x 30 inches, front and back panels measure 14 3/4 x 8 1/2 inches, text flaps measure 14 3/4 x 16 3/4 inches; there is a half inch spine, unfolded paperwork measures 15 x 47 inches, folded in half and each half is accordion folded into three panels, the two central panels measure 15 x 8 inches, four outer panels measure 15 x 7 3/4 inches, edition of 50 unsigned, press numbered copies, housed in clamshell box covered and lined with natural linen with sides of dull red-orange Seta cloth, very fine, rare. James S. Jaffe Rare Books Fall 2013 - 76 2013 $4500

Carson, Ciaran *Letters from the Alphabet.* Oldcastle: Gallery Press, 1995. One of 75 numbered copies, signed by author (reserved for patrons and friends of the press) from a total edition of 500, 8vo., original black cloth, blocked gilt on upper board and spine, dust jacket, fine. Maggs Bros. Ltd. 1442 - 35 2013 £100

Carson, James H. *Recollections of the California Mines.* Oakland: Biobooks, 1950. One of 750 copies printed by Saul & Lillian Marks, x, 113 pages, wood engravings by Henry Shire, large folding map, pictorial endpapers, two-tone cloth, lettered gilt on spine, spine ends show light rubbing, light offsetting to endpapers, else fine. Argonaut Book Shop Recent Acquisitions June 2013 - 58 2013 $90

Carson, Rachel *Silent Spring.* Boston: Houghton Mifflin, 1962. First edition, drawings by Lois and Louis Darling, dark blue-green cloth, gilt, very fine with dust jacket (slight wear to head of jacket spine and one top corner, slight rub marks to lower margin), very scarce in this condition. Argonaut Book Shop Summer 2013 - 44 2013 $750

Carson, Rachel *Silent Spring.* Boston: Houghton Mifflin, 1968. First edition, 8vo., original cloth, pages 368, signed by author, very good, unclipped dust jacket, morocco backed cloth slipcase. Howard S. Mott Inc. 262 - 29 2013 $2000

Carter, Angela *The Bloody Chamber and Other Adult Tales.* New York: Harper & Row, 1979. First American edition, inscribed by author to the promoter of Toronto Literary Festival and dated 1984 at the Harbourfront festival, fine in fine, price clipped dust jacket, books signed by Carter relatively uncommon. Ken Lopez Bookseller 159 - 34 2013 $350

Carter, Angela *Nights at the Circus.* London: Hogarth Press/Chatto & Windus, 1984. First edition, large 8vo., original red cloth, dust jacket, fine, dust jacket slightly faded on spine, inscribed by author to Salman Rushdie and his first wife Clarissa Luard. Maggs Bros. Ltd. 1460 - 163 2013 £450

Carter, Charlotte *Sheltered Life.* New York: Angel Hair Books, 1975. One of 350 copies, scarce, quarto, stapled illustrated wrappers, cover illustrations after portrait of author by Raphael Soyer, slightly age toned, very near fine. Between the Covers Rare Books, Inc. 165 - 98 2013 $150

Carter, George Goldsmith *Red Charger.* London: Constable, 1950. Original blue cloth lettered in red, illustrations by R. P. Bagnall-Oakley. R. F. G. Hollett & Son Polar Exploration - 8 2013 £35

Carter, Howard *The Tomb of King Tut-ankh-amen Discovered by the Late Earls of Carnarvon and Howard Carter.* London: Cassell, 1930. 1927. 1933. First edition, 3 volumes, numerous photo plates, large 8vo., fine pictorial cloth, gilt, volume I slightly shaken, otherwise fine, very rare. Maggs Bros. Ltd. 1467 - 28 2013 £5850

Carter, Jane Foster *If the Walls Could Talk Colusa's Architectural Heritage.* Colusa: Heritage Preservation Committee, 1988. First edition, quarto, black and white photos, blue cloth, gilt, very fine, pictorial dust jacket, presentation inscription, signed by author. Argonaut Book Shop Recent Acquisitions June 2013 - 59 2013 $275

Carter, John 1905-1975 *Printing and the Mind of Man.* Munich: Karl Pressler, 1983. Second edition, 4to., red buckram, printed paper title labels, dust jacket, front jacket hole, jacket spine head torn, near fine in good jacket. Jeff Weber Rare Books 171 - 64 2013 $150

Carter, Leon J. *Black Windsongs.* London: Mitre Press, 1973. First edition, fine in lightly worn, near fine dust jacket, inscribed by author's mother, Lillie Bland Carter. Between the Covers Rare Books, Inc. 165 - 99 2013 $225

Carter, Lillie Mae *Black Thoughts: Forty-Two Poems.* London: Mitre Press, 1971. First edition, 56 pages, author's address label on front pastedown, slight soiling to boards, else fine in near fine dust jacket, very nicely, inscribed by author to Alice Dunnigan, first female correspondent for Congress and the White House. Between the Covers Rare Books, Inc. 165 - 100 2013 $125

Carter, Susannah *The Frugal Housewife; or Complete Woman Cook.* Philadelphia: 1796. 16mo., 132 pages, 2 plates, 1 table, contemporary quarter calf and marbled boards, front cover detached. M & S Rare Books, Inc. 95 - 88 2013 $1750

Carter, Thomas Fortescue *A Narrative of the Boer War: Its Causes and Results.* Remington & Co., 1883. First edition, modern half blue levant morocco gilt, little faint spotting to prelims. R. F. G. Hollett & Son Africana - 36 2013 £85

Carter, Yolanda *Amistad Courier, a Newsletter About Miniature Books.* Austin: Yolanda Carter of Amistad press, 1984. Reprint, contains all 24 issues, includes 9 supplements, 5 x 11 inch unbound sheets in 9.75 x 11.75 inch three ring notebook with plastic covered boards, from the collection of Donn W. Sanford. Oak Knoll Books 303 - 12 2013 $125

Cartey, Wilfred *Red Rain.* New York: Emerson Hall, 1977. First edition, octavo, 79 pages, wrappers, very slightly worn, about fine. Between the Covers Rare Books, Inc. 165 - 101 2013 $125

Carton, James *Twice Married.* London: Griffith, Farran, Okeden & Welsh, 1886. Half title, original red cloth, very good. Jarndyce Antiquarian Booksellers CCV - 57 2013 £75

Cartwright, David Edgar *Tides: a Scientific History.* Cambridge: Cambridge University Press, 1999. First edition, tall 8vo., xii, 292 pages, frontispiece, illustrations, figures, black cloth, silver stamped spine, dust jacket, Burndy bookplate, fine, rare in cloth with jacket. Jeff Weber Rare Books 169 - 56 2013 $100

Cartwright, William *Comedies, Tragi-Comedies with other Poems.* London: for Humphrey Moseley, 1651. 8vo., engraved portrait, 5 section titles, with duplicates leaves U1-3 as usual, blank f4 present, b2 folded an untrimmed to preserve shoulder notes, modern calf very skillfully executed in 17th century style, title and dedication leaf and few running heads slightly cropped by binder's knife, one note to binder cropped, very nice, Arthur Spingarn's copy, rebound, with his bookplate and collation notes laid in. Joseph J. Felcone Inc. English and American Literature to 1800 - 4 2013 $2400

Caruana, A. A. *Recent Discoveries at Notabile.* Malta: GPO, 1881. First edition, 11 original mounted photos by Formosa, small folio, very good, original decorative red cloth, head and tail slightly worn, titled in gilt on upper board, 23 pages. Maggs Bros. Ltd. 1467 - 35 2013 £675

Carver, George Washington *Bulletin No. 3: Fertilizer Experiments in Cotton.* Tuskegee: Tuskegee Inst. Steam Print, 1900. First edition, stapled printed wrappers, 16 pages, photos, slight offsetting and very small chip on front wrapper, else near fine. Between the Covers Rare Books, Inc. 165 - 102 2013 $450

Carver, Raymond *Cathedral.* New York: Knopf, 1983. First edition, signed by author on titlepage, fine in fine dust jacket. Ed Smith Books 75 - 15 2013 $350

Carver, Raymond *Furious Seasons and Other Stories.* Santa Barbara: Capra Press, 1977. First edition, octavo, pictorial wrappers. L. W. Currey, Inc. Fall Sampler Sept. 2013 - 146383 2013 $150

Carver, Raymond *Where Water Comes Together with Other Water.* New York: Random House, 1985. First edition, signed by author on titlepage, laid in is press release about book printed on cardstock with Random House letterhead 5 1/4 x 8 1/4 inches, fine in fine dust jacket. Ed Smith Books 75 - 17 2013 $250

Carver, Raymond *Where I'm Calling From.* New York: Atlantic Monthly, 1988. First edition, deluxe issue, one of 250 numbered copies signed by Carver, cloth, publisher's matching slipcase (issued without dust jacket), fine. Ed Smith Books 75 - 16 2013 $250

Carver, Raymond *Will You Please Be quiet, Please?* New York: McGraw Hill, 1976. First edition, signed by author, trifling spotting to top stain, still fine in fine dust jacket, beautiful copy, from the Bruce Kahn collection. Ken Lopez Bookseller 159 - 35 2013 $5000

Cary, John *Cary's New and Correct English Atlas.* London: printed for John Cary... Jan. 1st, 1793. 47 engraved maps, hand colored in outline, each map with accompanying leaf of text, apart from general map and two West Riding of Yorkshire maps, 4to., front endpaper creased, some occasional foxing to original tissue guards, contemporary tree calf, well rebacked, gilt bands retaining original red morocco label, corners neatly repaired. Jarndyce Antiquarian Booksellers CCIV - 83 2013 £680

Casaide, Seamus O. *A Guide to Old Waterford Newspapers.* Waterford: 1917. 30, 2 pages ads, wrappers, very good. C. P. Hyland 261 - 90 2013 £50

Casaide, Seamus O. *A Typographical Gazetteer of Ireland.* Dublin: 1923. 8vo., 49 pages, wrappers, very good. C. P. Hyland 261 - 91 2013 £40

Casanova De Seingalt, Girolamo 1725-1798 *Memoirs of Jacques Casanova De Seignalt.* London: Navare Society, 1922. 2 volumes, 8vo., beautifully bound in white cloth with gilt titles and decorations, very scarce dust jackets have some minor chipping, 2 portraits and 10 photogravures, dust jacket very good. Barnaby Rudge Booksellers Biography 2013 - 020665 2013 $95

Casey, Juanita *Azerbaijan!* Godshill: Millersford Press, 2008. Number 33 of 50 copies signed by author, large 8vo., original red cloth, lettered gilt. Maggs Bros. Ltd. 1442 - 34 2013 £120

Casserly, Gordon *The Monkey God.* New York: Sears Pub. Co., 1929. First American edition, bookplate, little soiling to boards, very good plus, near fine dust jacket with little age toning and not very noticeable erasures on rear panel, very attractive. Between the Covers Rare Books, Inc. Sci-Fi, Fantasy & Horror - 38877 2013 $275

Castaenda, Pedro De *The Journey of Francisco Vazquez de Coronado 1540-1542 as told by...* San Francisco: Grabhorn Press, 1933. One of 500 copies, illustrations by Arvilla Parker, initials throughout printed in red-orange, yellow tan linen, lettered in red orange on spine very fine, uncut, elusive plain dust jacket. Argonaut Book Shop Summer 2013 - 45 2013 $350

Castellan, A. L. *Letters on Italy.* London: Richard Phillips, 1820. First UK edition, 8vo., pages 108, 7 illustrations, recent gray boards.   J. & S. L. Bonham Antiquarian Booksellers   Europe - 6331   2013   £55

Castlehaven, Mervyn Touchet, Earl of *The Case of Sodomy in the Tryal of Mervin Lord Audley, Earl of Castlehaven for Committing a Rape...*   London: printed for E. Curll, Second edition, 40 pages, half title, 8vo., recent half calf, marbled boards, gilt lettered spine.   Jarndyce Antiquarian Booksellers   CCIV - 85   2013   £750

Castletown, Lord   *"EGO" Random Records of Sport, Service & Travel in Many Lands.* Murray, 1923. First edition, lacks front flyleaf, else good, 8vo., cloth.   C. P. Hyland   261 - 176   2013   £30

Castro, Rodrigo De   *De Universa Mulielbrium Morborum Medicina, Novo & Antehac.... (bound with) Medicus-Politicus sive de Officiis Medico-Politicis Tractatus, Quatuor Distinctus Libris.* Hamburg: Apud Zachariam Hertelium, 1662. Fourth edition, 4to., folding plate, titlepage in red and black, browned, some foxing and spotting, few marginal paper flaws (one leaf with blank corner torn away), slightly later vellum boards, spine lettered, long sides overlapping, dust soiled, gilt stamp of Birmingham Medicall Institute to spine, small stamp to title of Birmingham Medical Institute. Unsworths Antiquarian Booksellers   28 - 80   2013   £650

A Catalogue of Books, Ancient and Modern, Lately Selected in London and Paris... Boston: Charles C. Little and James Brown, 1842. First edition, 8vo., original printed brown wrappers, 162 pages + 24 page publisher's catalog, wrappers little soiled and worn, dampstain on rear wrapper, with little loss to wrapper, but not to any text, very good, rare. The Brick Row Book Shop   Miscellany Fifty-Nine - 3   2013 $425

Catalogue of Shropshire Sheep, Coach Horses and Short Horn Cattle at Woodside Farm, Property of A. O. Fox, Oregon, Dane County, Wisconsin. Madison: Democrat Printing Co., 1890. Stapled illustrated wrappers, 34, (2) pages, full page illustrations and 2 foldout illustrations, front wrapper soiled, staples oxidized and bled through on inner hinges of few pages, handsome.   Between the Covers Rare Books, Inc.   Horses, Horsemanship, Horse Racing, Etc. - 83873   2013 $275

Catalogue of Trotting and Pacing Horses Property of Campbell Brown, Ewell Farm, Spring Hill, Maury County Tenn. Nashville: Brandon Printing Co., 1888. 68 pages, printed yellow ribbed wrappers, overprinted in red, small chips and modest stains on wrappers, spine restored, near very good, scarce.   Between the Covers Rare Books, Inc. Horses, Horsemanship, Horse Racing, Etc. - 45628   2013 $350

A Catechism of Christian Doctrine. Ditchling, Sussex: Saint Dominic's Press, 1931. 95/500 copies, printed on Batchelor handmade paper, very well executed decorative wood engraved border to every page of text by Philip Hagreen, pages 110, foolscap 8vo., original black leatherette backed fawn cloth sides backstrip gilt lettered, front cover with design by Hagreen blocked in black in centre, faintly browned free endpapers, untrimmed, fine. Blackwell's Rare Books   B174 - 377   2013   £275

Cather, Willa Sibert   1873-1947 *Death Comes for the Archbishop.* New York: Alfred A. Knopf, 1927. First edition, one of 175 copies on Borzoi all rag paper, this being number 81, signed by author, octavo, titlepage and half title verso printed with blue border, publisher's quarter green cloth over marbled paper boards, black leather spine label lettered in gilt, edges uncut, mostly unopened, very light amount of sunning to spine, front board lightly rubbed, very good.   Heritage Book Shop   Holiday Catalogue 2012 - 27   2013 $2750

Cather, Willa Sibert   1873-1947 *A Lost Lady.* Boston: Houghton Mifflin, 1938. First edition thus, #7 of the Autograph Edition, this copy marked "Publisher's Copy" on colophon page, not signed by author, blue and beige cloth with spine label in decorated light green dust jacket that is taller than book, fine in very good jacket.   Ed Smith Books   75 - 20   2013 $100

Catholic Prayers and Hymns in the Tinneh Language. (bound with) Tinneh Indian Catechism of Christian Doctrine. Holy Cross Mission Kosoreffski, Alaska: Indian Boys' Press, 1897. Square 16mo., original limp floral cloth.   Maggs Bros. Ltd.   1467 - 131   2013   £750

Catholic Church. Liturgy & Ritual *Beatae Mariae Virginis Officium.* Venice: G. B. Pasquali, 1740. 12mo., engraved throughout, pages (lx), 427, (4), text engraved by Angela Baroni, engraved frontispiece, 15 full page illustrations, title vignette and 20 tailpieces all by Marco Pitteri after Giovanni Battista Piazzetta; contemporary Italian (Venetian?) binding of full dark red morocco gilt, spine gilt in 5 compartments with leaf and flower tool decorations, narrow roll tool borders of interlinked leaves, enclosing contrasting onlaid borders of dark olive morocco to sides enclosing floriated tool decorations to central panels with further oval olive morocco onlay forming centre piece which is overtooled in gilt with arched bands and sprouting pomegranates to top and bottom, gilt edges, light green silk doublures.   Marlborough Rare Books Ltd.   218 - 112   2013   £2500

Cats, Jacob *Moral Emblems with Aphorisms, Adages and Proverbs of All Ages and Nations.* London: Longman, Green Longman and Roberts, 1860. First edition with these illustrations, 275 x 195mm., xvi, 239, (1) pages, allegorical frontispiece, 60 large tondo emblems and 60 tailpieces by John Leighton and others after Adriaen van de Venne; fine contemporary green straight grain morocco handsomely gilt, covers framed by multiple rules and wide, ornate dentelle, the whole enclosing detailed Greek urn centerpiece, raised bands, spine densely gilt in compartments featuring many small botanical and floral tools, gilt turn-ins, all edges gilt, presentation "Wilhelmina Colquhoun Jones/1863/with Charlotte Harriet Jones/love and best wishes", spine darkened to olive brown (as almost always with green morocco), just faintest hint of wear to joints, occasional minor foxing or staining, extremely attractive, very decorative contemporary binding bright and scarcely worn and text very fresh and showing no signs of use.   Phillip J. Pirages   63 - 315   2013 $750

Catt, Carrie Chapman *Woman Suffrage by Federal Constitutional Amendment.* New York: National Woman Suffrage Library, 1917. 8vo., 100 pages, dark blue cloth stamped in gilt, ex-library with bookplate and stamps, owner's name on flyleaf, cover somewhat scuffed at edges and ends of spine, otherwise very good.   Second Life Books Inc.   182 - 37   2013 $95

Catullus, Gaius Valerius *Catullus, Tibullus, Propertius Cum C. Galli Fragmentis.* Amstaeledami sic: Apud Isbrandum Haring, 1686. 16mo., engraved titlepage, paper flaw to lower outer corner P2 touching couple of letters, full contemporary panelled calf, blindstamped cornerpiece decoration, raised bands, blind ruled spine, leading hinge cracked but firm, nice, early signature of Sam Pytts on prelim blank, later bookplate "Pytt's book Room at Kyre". Jarndyce Antiquarian Booksellers   CCIV - 8   2013   £180

Catullus, Gaius Valerius *(Catullus, Tibullus, Propertius) (Opera).* Lyon: Seb. Gryphius, 1548. 16mo., woodcut printer's device to titlepage an some woodcut initials to text, occasional underlining and marginal marks in sepia ink, handwritten note in grey ink to r.f.e.p. verso, small drop of candle wax to text at pages 30-31 observing only a few letters, little dampstaining to rear endpapers and browning to prelims, recently pleasantly rebound to period style in dark brown calf with blind ruled border ad five raised bands, black morocco and gilt label to spine, ink library stamp of Student Library, St. Peters' College, Jersey City to f.f.ep. verso, ink date stamp to June 5th 1944 and pencilled library notes to page 3.   Unsworths Antiquarian Booksellers   28 - 7   2013   £450

Cauchy, Augustin Louis *"Memoire sur les Integrales Definieis." (and) "Memoire sur la Theorie de la Propagation des Ondes a la Surface d'Un Fluide Pesant." in Memoires Presente par Divers Savans a l'Academie Royale des Sciences de l'Institut de France...* Paris: Imprimerie Royal, 1827. First editions, General title slightly soiled and slightly dampstained, few spots here and there and occasional patch of light browning, 4to., uncut and unopened in original paper wrappers, slightly worn with spine partly defective at head and tail.   Blackwell's Rare Books   Sciences - 27   2013   £1200

Caulfeild, S. F. A. *Encyclopedia of Victorian Needlework.* New York: Dover Publications, 1972. First Dover edition, 2 volumes, quarto, extensively illustrated in black and white, original printed wrappers bound in full blue cloth over boards, covers elaborately decorated in multi-colored needlework, floral patterns in red, yellow, purple and green thread, spines and front boards lettered in gilt, original wrappers bound in, housed in red cloth slipcase.   Heritage Book Shop   Holiday Catalogue 2012 - 56   2013 $850

Caulfield, Richard *The Council Book of the Corporation of the City of Cork from 1609 to 1643 and from 1690-1800.* Guildford: 1876. Octavo, full blue leather, although not signed, looks like the style (Guy's (Cork), sadly front hinge cracked, but text tight as a tick, with marbled edges, very good.   C. P. Hyland   261 - 178   2013   £400

Caulibus, Johannes De *The Mirrour of the Blessed Lyf of Jesu Christ.* Oxford: at the Clarendon Press, Henry Frowde, 1908. Occasional fox spot, pencil note in margin of introduction, 4to., original quarter line, printed paper label, pale blue paper boards, couple of tiny marks and merest touch of wear to forecorners, prospectus (creased at top) loosely inserted very good, inscribed by editor, Lawrence Powell for Ethelywn Steane.   Blackwell's Rare Books B174 - 27   2013   £100

Caunter, Hobart *Eastern Legends and Romances.* London: Henry G. Bohn, 1846. Engraved frontispiece and title, 20 engravings from drawings by W. Daniel, contemporary dark green morocco by Westley, Son & Jarvis, attractively blocked with Oriental Goddess design in gilt and black, spine dated 1839, little rubbed, all edges gilt. Jarndyce Antiquarian Booksellers   CCIII - 657   2013   £85

Causley, Charles *Jack the Treacle Eater.* Macmillan, 1987. First edition, illustrations by Charles Keeping, majority colored and a number full page, small folio, original mid brown boards, backstrip gilt lettered, dust jacket, fine. Blackwell's Rare Books   172 - 169   2013   £30

Cavafy, Constantine P. *Poiemata (1908-1914).* Alexandria: Kasimath & Iona (Print Shop), circa, 1920. First edition, tall 8vo., 29 numbered pages printed rectos only, table of contents, beige printed wrappers, very fine in half morocco folding box, presentation copy from author to Christopher Nomikos.   James S. Jaffe Rare Books   Fall 2013 - 30   2013 $25,000

Cavafy, Constantine P. *Poiemata (1916-1918).* Alexandria: Kasimath & Iona, 1927-1932. First edition, 8vo., original printed wrappers, faint spotting to few leaves, generally in very good condition, some leaves mounted on stubs in original grey blue sewn wrappers with title printed in green on front cover, spine discolored, one or two chips to edges, small tear to front hinge, chronological listing of poems (1916-1918) loosely inserted, preserved in folding cloth case.   James S. Jaffe Rare Books   Fall 2013 - 31   2013 $4500

Cavalli, Ella Kimball   *The Seasons in Silhouette.*   New York: Juvenile Mag. Pub. Co., 1931. First edition, square 4to., cloth backed boards, pictorial paste-on, faint tape ghost on titlepage and endpaper, else near fine, printed on french-fold rag paper, full page silhouette illustrations by Marion Merrill, quite lovely.   Aleph-Bet Books, Inc.   105 - 457   2013 $200

Caverhill, Learmont & Co. Ltd.   *1925 General Catalogue No. 24 Caverhill, Learmont & Co. 451 St. Peter Street, Montreal Wholesale Hardware.*   Montreal: published by Southern Press, 1925.   Quarto, blue cloth with white lettering, color illustrations, 6 color ads, numerous black and white illustrations, wear to edges of their binding, interior very good.   Schooner Books Ltd. 102 - 119   2013 $95

Caxton, William   *Ars Moriendi that is to Saye the Craft for to Deye for the Helthe of Mannes Sowle.*   London and Oxford: Bernard Quaritch and Clarendon Press, 1891. Facsimile, 8vo. original grey printed wrappers bound in, tan morocco, blind tooled title to spine and upper board, boards very slightly marked, endpapers little discolored, ownership to titlepage verso.   Unsworths Antiquarian Booksellers   28 - 151   2013   £125

Cecily Parsley's Nursery Rhymes.   London: Warne, 1922. First edition, frontispiece and 14 other color printed plates by author, pages 54, 16mo., original pink boards trifle finger soiled, backstrip longitudinally lettered in white, front cover lettered in white and with rectangular color printed label onlaid depicting a rabbit hurrying down a burrow with a laden wheelbarrow, color printed pictorial endpapers as called for, good.   Blackwell's Rare Books   B174 - 279   2013   £300

Celli, Rose   *Album Magique.*   Paris: Flammarion, 1950. 4to., flexible pictorial card covers, near fine, with anaglyph glasses, each page of text faces full page 2-color illustration printed in red and blue, which cannot be clearly seen, when child wears 'glasses' they can see 2 pictures, one in red and one in blue, illustrations by Nathalie Parain and Helene Guertik, rare.   Aleph-Bet Books, Inc.   105 - 450   2013 $275

Celli, Rose   *Baba Yaga.*   New York: Artists & Writers Guild, 1935.   Folio, flexible card covers, small piece of corner nipped and slight edge wear, else very good, color lithographs by Parain.   Aleph-Bet Books, Inc.   104 - 404   2013 $225

Celsus, Aulus Cornelius   *Celsus on the True Doctrine: a Discourse Against the Christians.*   New York & Oxford: Oxford University Press, 1987.   8vo., xiii, 146 pages, maroon cloth, gilt stamped spine title, ownership signature, fine, rare in cloth.   Jeff Weber Rare Books   169 - 58   2013 $60

Celsus, Aulus Cornelius   *De Medicina Libri Octo.* Lugduni Batavorum: Apud John. Arn. Langerak, 1746. 8vo., frontispiece, title in red and black, headpieces, tailpieces, floriated initials, engraved portrait, 2 engraved figures, early quarter red vellum, vellum corners, marbled boards, ms. spine title, vellum along hinges and spine, split, inner hinges cracked, gutter waterstained, entirely untrimmed, very good.   Jeff Weber Rare Books   172 - 55   2013 $325

Cendrars, Blaise   *Panama of The Adventures of My Seven Uncles.*   New York: Harper, 1931. First edition, one of 300 copies printed on Utopian Laid paper, numbered and signed by author and artist, small 4to., pages 156, set in Linotype Bodoni and printed from original types, illustrations reproduced by the photogelatine process by four color separation, by John dos Passos, plain paper wrappers with illustrated paper dust jacket, some toning to cover, lacks top half inch of spine with some wear at bottom, very good.   Second Life Books Inc.   183 - 65   2013 $450

Census of Fifteenth Century Books Owned in America. New York: 1919.   xxiv, 245 pages, cloth, leather spine label, covers dust soiled ad bit grubby.   Joseph J. Felcone Inc. Books Printed before 1701 - 54   2013 $60

Centenary Record of the Christian Brothers, Our Lady's Mount, Cork 1811-1911.   Guy's Cork, 1911.   (206) pages, photos, ads, original card covers, good.   C. P. Hyland   261 - 185   2013   £65

Central Park Association   *The Central Park.*   New York: Thomas Seltzer, 1926.   First edition, very good with little browning and tiny chip to title sticker on spine and bump to head of spine.   Between the Covers Rare Books, Inc. New York City - 294029   2013 $75

Certani, Giacomo *La Santita Prodigiosa Vita di S. Brigida Ibernese...* Bologna: Eredi di Antonio Pisarri, 1695. Small 4to., modern antique style engraved plates calf, marbled boards, rare, fine.   Jeff Weber Rare Books   171 - 66   2013 $750

Cervantes Saavedra, Miguel De   1547-1616 *Comedias y Entremeses de Miguel De Cervantes Saavedra...*   Madrid: Antonio Marin, 1749. 2 books in one volume, engraved head and tailpieces, occasional foxing, contemporary full vellum, ms. spine title, lightly soiled, small chip on spine, very good.   Jeff Weber Rare Books   171 - 67   2013 $1275

Cervantes Saavedra, Miguel De   1547-1616 *The Life and Exploits of the Ingenious Gentleman Don Quixote de la Mancha.*   London: printed for J. and R. Tonson, 1749. Second edition, 2 volumes, engraved frontispiece, 23 engraved plates, 8vo., some light browning, expertly rebacked in matching style, raised and gilt banded spines, red morocco labels, armorial bookplate of John Hallifax, Esq., Kenilworth on inner front boards, 19th century bookplate of J. Blackwood Greenshields.   Jarndyce Antiquarian Booksellers   CCIV - 86   2013   £1500

Cervantes Saavedra, Miguel de   1547-1616 *El Ingenioso Hidalgo Don Quixote de la Mancha.*   Madrid: Joachin Ibarra, 1780. Magnificent Academy Edition, 4 volumes, large quarto, engraved titles, engraved two page map of Spain with Cervantes' wanderings shown in red, 43 vignettes, 13 decoratively engraved initial letters and one inserted portrait, 31 engraved plates, contemporary full sprinkled calf, rebacked, preserving original spines, spine decoratively gilt stamped with green morocco spine labels, lettered gilt, covers ruled gilt, marbled endpapers, previous owner's bookplate, corners bumped, extremities bit rubbed, overall very good, clean copy.   Heritage Book Shop   50th Anniversary Catalogue - 20   2013 $25,000

Cervantes Saavedra, Miguel De   1547-1616 *The Adventures of the Renowned Don Quixote de la Mancha.* Glasgow: printed by and for Chapman and Lang, 1803. 4 volumes, 8vo., half titles, frontispieces, some offsetting from plates, otherwise very clean, handsome contemporary polished tree calf, ornate gilt decorated spines, black morocco label, volume numbers in gilt ovals.   Jarndyce Antiquarian Booksellers   CCIV - 87   2013   £950

Cervantes Saavedra, Miguel De   1547-1616 *Life and Exploits of Don Quixote de la Manca.*   Exeter: J. & B. Williams, 1828. 18mo., 4 volumes, frontispieces in each volume and vignette 1827 titlepages, contemporary green morocco, rubbed, spines worn, some hinges weak.   M & S Rare Books, Inc.   95 - 54   2013 $225

Cervantes Saavedra, Miguel De   1547-1616 *Don Quixote de la Mancha.* London: Henry G. Bohn, 1842. 2 volumes, 8vo., frontispiece, engraved titlepage to each volume, 23 full page illustrations, numerous further illustrations in text, publisher's purple cloth, gilt to spine and upper board, spines and top board edges faded, endcaps creased and little torn, boards scuffed, corners slightly bumped, lower hinge volume II cracking, endpapers foxed but otherwise clean internally, very good, bookplate of Samuel Joshua Cooper.   Unsworths Antiquarian Booksellers   28 - 152   2013   £180

Cervantes Saavedra, Miguel De   1547-1616 *Don Quixote De La Mancha.*   London: Charles Daly, 1842. 8vo., 2 parts bound in single volume, frontispiece and engraved titlepage pus 30 engraved plates, all by Sir John Gilbert, full calf (rubbed and scuffed , front cover separate), nice, clean copy, this copy belonged to English journalist George Augustus Sala with his ownership signature at top of titlepage in his neat hand.   Second Life Books Inc.   183 - 66   2013 $95

Cervantes Saavedra, Miguel De   1547-1616 *The Ingenious Gentleman Don Quixote De La Mancha Chapter VIII.* 's-Hertogenbosch: Catharijne Press, 2001. Limited to 170 copies, of which this is one of the 20 lettered copies bound thus with an extra wood engraving, printed in a different color, 7 x 4.2cm., paper covered boards, slipcase, illustrations on both covers, 47 pages, frontispiece numbered and signed by the artist Gerard Gaudaen, bound by Luce Thurkow, from the collection of Donn W. Sanford.   Oak Knoll Books   303 - 76   2013 $300

Cervantes Saavedra, Miguel De   1547-1616 *La Gitanilla: the Little Gypsie.* London: printed for D. Midwinter... and B. Lintott... and sold by J. Morphew, 1709. First edition in English, woodcut vignette on title and one engraved plate, half title discarded, slightly browned, slightly soiled in places, 12mo., original calf, corners worn, rebacked, new endpapers, good.   Blackwell's Rare Books   B174 - 29   2013   £4000

Cervantes Saavedra, Miguel Del   1547-1616 *Don Quixote De La Mancha.* London: T. M'Lean, 1819. 4 volumes, half titles, color plates, contemporary half dark blue calf, raised bands, elaborate gilt compartments, slightly rubbed, very attractive.   Jarndyce Antiquarian Booksellers   CCV - 58   2013   £950

Cesalpino, Andrea *Quaestionum Peripateticarum Lib. V. Daemonum Investigatio Peripatetica. Quaestionum Medicorum Libri II.* Venetiis: Giunta, 1593. Second edition, 8vo., woodcut printer's device on title, several woodcut figures, contemporary ink notations on front endpaper, contemporary full vellum, manuscript spine title, spine lightly chipped, early ink stamp on titlepage and final leaf, bookplate of Andras Gedeon, very good, quite scarce.   Jeff Weber Rare Books   172 - 57   2013 $9500

Ceuleers, Jan *Man Ray 1890-1976.* Antwerp: Ronnie Van de Velde Gallery, 1994. First deluxe edition, number 78 of 200 copies, cloth folder with double leaf and 2 photographic plates and justification, also in this folder 2 loose original photos after Man Ray, each numbered in pencil with stamps "an Ray/Paris" and "Tirage original realise par Pierre Gassmann" verso, over 300 pages and about 300 monochrome plates by Man Ray, cloth with all edges gilt in dust jacket, the 2 items housed in solander case with leather spine and gilt lettering, front of case with plexiglas window display a 'trompe-l'oeil' replica of "Pechage" an assemblage by Man Ray from 1969, case is fit in slipcase, overall size 35 x 29 x 7 cm., as new. Gemini Fine Books & Arts., Ltd. Art Reference & Illustrated Books - 2013 $1500

Chabon, Michael *Werewolves in their Youth.* New York: Random House, 1999. First edition, fine in fine dust jacket. Leather Stalking Books October 2013 - 2013 $50

Chabuah Mission Hospital *The Memsahib's Cook Book.* Dibrugarh: printed by the Borroah Press, circa, 1935. Original grey wrappers, slight dampstain to front wrapper, spine worn with slight loss. Jarndyce Antiquarian Booksellers CCV - 59 2013 £120

Chagall, Marc *The Jerusalem Windows.* New York: George Braziller, 1962. First US edition, hardcover, 2 original color lithographs, fine in fine price clipped dust jacket in very near fine glassine jacket and in close to near fine example of scarce cardboard slipcase, sharp copy. Jeff Hirsch Books Fall 2013 - 12119 2013 $1500

Chalfant, W. A. *The Story of Inyo.* Chicago: the Author, 1922. First edition, very scarce thus, errata slip tipped-in to inner rear cover, folding frontispiece map, red cloth, cover extremities lightly rubbed, spine and upper rear cover bit faded, spotting to rear cover, very good. Argonaut Book Shop Recent Acquisitions June 2013 - 62 2013 $75

Challinor, Raymond *A Radical Lawyer in Victorian England...* Tauris, 1990. First edition, 8vo., illustrations, cloth, dust jacket, very good. C. P. Hyland 261 - 746 2013 £35

Chalmers, Claudine *Paul Frenzeny's Chinatown Sketches.* San Francisco: Book Club of California, 2012. First edition, one of 425 copies, one of 425 copies, folio, 19 wood engravings, decorative boards, silk brocade spine, very fine, original 4 page announcement laid in. Argonaut Book Shop Recent Acquisitions June 2013 - 63 2013 $225

Chalmers, George *The Life of Mary Queen of Scots.* London: John Murray, 1822. Second edition, first printing of the third part, 3 volumes, 216 x 140mm., pleasant 19th century salmon pink polished half calf, raised bands, spines ornately gilt in compartments with volute cornerpieces framing decorative pineapple centerpiece surrounded by small tools, each spine with two olive green morocco titling labels, marbled sides and endpapers, top edge gilt, medallions on title and endpages, 3 frontispiece portraits, 4 folding plates, spines sunned to soft terra cotta, extremities just little rubbed, one board with tiny scratches, leaves slightly toned and with minor offsetting one plate with small tears along two folds, still excellent set, text clean and fresh, attractive bindings with virtually no wear to joints. Phillip J. Pirages 63 - 330 2013 $450

Chamberlain, B. H. *Japanese Fairy Tales.* Tokyo: Kobunsha and London: Griffith and Farran, circa, 1900. 16 books, printed on crepe paper, from wood blocks, printed french fold and all in fine condition, rare set, uniformly bound in 4 volumes in contemporary moire, rubbed on joints and lacks sheet on one volume, else very good+. Aleph-Bet Books, Inc. 104 - 295 2013 $1500

Chamberlain, George Agnew *The Silver Cord.* New York: G. P. Putnam's Sons, 1927. First edition, small, nearly invisible dampstain on edge of couple of leaves, else fine in very near fine dust jacket, nicely inscribed by author for W. A. Dusenburg, scarce. Between the Covers Rare Books, Inc. Mystery & Detective Fiction - 295502 2013 $450

Chamberlain, Samuel *Tudor Homes of England with Some Examples from Later Periods by...* New York: Architectural Book Pub. Co., 1929. First edition, large folio, pages 246, fine in dust jacket (little soiled and stained). Second Life Books Inc. 183 - 67 2013 $250

Chambers, Ernest J. *A Regimental History of the Forty-Third Regiment Active Militia of Canada "The Duke of Cornwall's Own Rifles.* Ottawa: E. L. Ruddy, 1903. Quarto, quarter leather with cloth boards, patterned endpapers, pages 82, 12 pages ads, photo illustrations, spine poorly repaired with electrical tape, covers scuffed, interior very good. Schooner Books Ltd. 104 - 144 2013 $75

Chambers, R. *The Book of Days: a Miscellany of Popular Antiquities in Connection with the Calendar Including Anecdote, Biography and History....* London & Edinburgh: W. & R. Chambers, 1869. 2 volumes, large 8vo., titlepage engraving by John Leighton, hundreds of illustrations, light foxing, original full crimson blind and gilt stamped morocco, five raised bands with black and gilt compartments, all edges speckled, ex-church library bookplate, very good. Jeff Weber Rare Books 171 - 68 2013 $250

Chambers, Robert William *The Green Mouse.* New York and London: D. Appleton and Co., 1910. First edition, first printing with code '(1)" at base of page 281, octavo, six inserted plates and illustrations by Edmund Frederick as well as numerous black and white vignettes in text, original green cloth, front and spine panels, stamped in white and blind, pictorial paper inlay on front panel.   L. W. Currey, Inc. Fall Sampler Sept. 2013 - 146061   2013 $650

Chambers, Robert William *The King in Yellow.* Chicago: New York: F. Tennyson Neely, 1895. First edition, first issue, green cloth with no inserted frontispiece, moderately worn, very good copy with light wear at crown, little rubbing and soiling and small tears to some prelim pages, Ellen Glasgow's copy, inscribed by her to her sister Rebe Gordon Glasgow July 1896.   Between the Covers Rare Books, Inc. Sci-Fi, Fantasy & Horror - 47612   2013 $700

Chambers, Robert William *The King in Yellow.* New York: London: D. Appleton Century Co., 1938. Memorial edition, first printing with code '(1)' on page (274), original red cloth, front and spine panels stamped in gold and black. L. W. Currey, Inc. Fall Sampler Sept. 2013 - 146044   2013 $150

Champion, F. W. *The Jungle in Sunlight and Shadow.* London: Chatto & Windus, n.d., First edition, large 8vo., library cloth, gilt, 96 plates, lower joint cracked.   R. F. G. Hollett & Son Africana - 37   2013   £35

Champion, Joseph *Bowles's Elegant Set of Copies in German Text.* London: printed for Carington Bowles in St. Paul's Church Yard, circa 176-?-1780?, First edition, oblong 12mo., original plain wrappers, title + 14 copper engraved leaves, minor foxing, moderately so at front.   Howard S. Mott Inc. 262 - 27   2013 $500

Champneys, Arthur C. *Irish Ecclesiastical Architecture with Some Notice of Similar on Related Work in England, Scotland &...* 1910. First edition, 8vo., 114 plates, cloth, good, ex- Prinknash Abbey.   C. P. Hyland 261 - 180   2013   £275

Chancellor, F. B. *Around Eden.* Appleby: Whitehead, 1954. First edition, original cloth, dust jacket, trifle spotted, pages 159, scarce.   R. F. G. Hollett & Son Lake District & Cumbria - 262   2013   £60

Chancellor, John *The Dark God.* New York: Century, 1928. First American edition, fine in dust jacket with tiny wear at corners and several tiny tears.   Mordida Books 81 - 61   2013 $200

Chandler, John Greene *The Remarkable History of Chicken Little.* Boston: A. & D. Bromer, 1979. Limited to 85 numbered copies of which 50 are for sale,, 3.1 x 2.5cm., marbled paper covered boards, paper cover label (24) pages, printed letterpress by Darrell Hyder with hand colored initial letter miniature bookplate of Kalman Levitan, from the collection of Donn W. Sanford.   Oak Knoll Books 303 - 67   2013 $175

Chandler, Raymond   1886-1959   *Farewell, My Lovely.* New York: Alfred A. Knopf, 1940. First edition, lightly rubbed, near fine in very good dust jacket with chip on front panel, some rubbing and short tears ad faint, barely visible stain, completely devoid of restoration, repair and sophistications.   Between the Covers Rare Books, Inc. Mystery & Detective Fiction - 107062   2013 $4800

Chandler, Raymond   1886-1959   *The Finger Man and Other Stories.* New York: Avon, 1946. First edition, paperback original, name and address on titlepage, otherwise very good in wrappers.   Mordida Books 81 - 63   2013 $150

Chandler, Raymond   1886-1959   *Five Sinister Characters.* New York: Avon, 1945. First edition of a paperback original, 8vo., original colored pictorial wrappers, inconspicuous vertical crease in front wrapper, printed on cheap paper which has browned.   Howard S. Mott Inc. 262 - 31   2013 $125

Chandler, Raymond   1886-1959   *Killer in the Rain.* London: Hamish Hamilton, 1964. First edition, some light spotting on top of page edges, otherwise fine.   Mordida Books 81 - 69   2013 $500

Chandler, Raymond   1886-1959   *Killer in the Rain.* Boston: Houghton Mifflin, 1964. First American edition, fine in dust jacket with several short closed tears and some scattered rubbing. Mordida Books 81 - 70   2013 $350

Chandler, Raymond   1886-1959   *The Lady in the Lake.* London: and Melbourne: Hamish Hamilton, 1946. First Australian edition, page edges browned, some offsetting from jacket on front board, else about fine in very attractive, very good plus dust jacket with couple of small chips at folds, some slight tanning of spine lettering, tiny chip at foot, exceptionally scarce.   Between the Covers Rare Books, Inc. Mystery & Detective Fiction - 67135   2013 $2750

Chandler, Raymond   1886-1959   *The Little Sister.* New York: Otto Penzler, 1996. Facsimile of 1949 edition, very fine in dust jacket, original shrinkwrap.   Mordida Books 81 - 64   2013 $100

Chandler, Raymond 1886-1959 *The Long Goodbye.* Boston: Houghton Mifflin, 1954. First American edition, bookplate, fine in near fine dust jacket with creases top corner of front panel, tiny wear at spine ends and at corners, scattered wear along spine fold, short closed tear.   Mordida Books   81 - 66   2013 $850

Chandler, Raymond 1886-1959 *Playback.* London: Hamilton, 1958. First edition, some darkening on endpapers, otherwise fine in dust jacket with some slight spine fading and tiny wear at base of spine.   Mordida Books   81 - 67   2013 $300

Chandler, Raymond 1886-1959 *Raymond Chandler Speaking.* London: Hamish Hamilton, 1962. First edition, fine in dust jacket with lightly soiled back panel slightly faded spine and tiny wear at corners.   Mordida Books   81 - 68   2013 $125

Chandler, Raymond 1886-1959 *The Simple Art of Murder.* Boston: Houghton Mifflin, 1950. First edition, bookplate on front pastedown, fine in dust jacket with some spine fading, short closed tear and tiny wear at corners. Mordida Books   81 - 65   2013 $1250

Chang, Iris *The Chinese in America.* New York: Viking Press, 2003. First edition, 8vo., fine, in fine dust jacket, signed by author and dated year of publication.   By the Book, L. C.   38 - 59   2013 $250

Channing, Mark *The Poisoned Mountain.* Philadelphia: J. B. Lippincott, 1936. First American edition, fine in nice, near fine dust jacket with couple of nominal shallow nicks and tears, bright, attractive copy, very scarce in jacket. Between the Covers Rare Books, Inc.   Sci-Fi, Fantasy & Horror - 87167   2013 $350

Channing, Walter *A Treatise on Etherization in Childbirth.* Boston: 1848. First edition, 400 pages, original cloth with horizontal cracks across backstrip, boards partly detached, contemporary morocco bookplate of Austin Flint, M.D., library notes this copy was donated by Flint.   James Tait Goodrich   75 - 42   2013 $995

Chapelin, R. A. *Poetry of the Hart; or Thoughts from the Soul: Together with Verses on Various Subjects.*   St. John: J. & A. McMillan, 1872. 8vo., decorative purple cloth covered boards with gilt to spine and front cover, half title, 8vo., cloth badly stained, interior very good.   Schooner Books Ltd.   101 - 9   2013 $85

Chaplow, R. *The Geology and Hydrogeology of the Sellafield Area.* Geological Society, 1996. Large 8vo., original wrappers, pages 107, illustrations in color.   R. F. G. Hollett & Son   Lake District & Cumbria - 263   2013   £30

Chapman, Arthur *The Pony Express.*   New York: A. L. Burt, 1932. Reprint, large bookplate from a distinguished collection of Western Americana, else fine in almost fine dust jacket, sharp.   Between the Covers Rare Books, Inc. Horses, Horsemanship, Horse Racing, Etc. - 52109   2013 $85

Chapman, Frederic *Proverbs Improved.*   London: John Lane, n.d., 1901. 24 color pictures, oblong small 8vo., original pictorial glazed boards, edges trifle cracked in places, 24 delicately colored full page plates by Grace May.   R. F. G. Hollett & Son   Children's Books - 380   2013   £75

Chapman, Guy *A Passionate Prodigality: Fragments of Autobiography.* London: Ivor Nicholson & Watson, 1933. First edition, 8vo., original cloth, presentation copy inscribed by Chapman, bearing two ownership signatures of A. J. Gridley, book is signed by 26 people, presumably members of the Royal Fusiliers, on copyright page, dedication page, the contents page, the first sectional titlepage and rear free endpaper, spine cocked and creased, otherwise very good, correction in pencil on page 71, changing "Gerrard" to "Goddard".   James S. Jaffe Rare Books   Fall 2013 - 153 2013 $3000

Chapman, James *Pictures of African Travel.*   Cape Town: J(osepeh) Kirkman, Hour Street, n.d. circa, 1865.   20 stereoscope photos, each image measuring approximately 70 x 75mm on card measuring 73 x 180mm., title and captioned on verso.   Maggs Bros. Ltd.   1467 - 19   2013   £4400

Chapman, John *Chloroform and other Anaesthetics: Theiry History and Use During Childbirth.*   Williams and Norgate: (colophon:) London: Savill and Edwards, 1859. Outer leaves slightly browned, sometime folded, lacking titlepage, 8vo., modern drab boards, good.   Blackwell's Rare Books   Sciences - 28   2013   £250

Chapman, John Jay *Causes and Consequences.*   New York: Charles Scribner's Sons, 1898. First edition, 12mo., original cloth, faded.   M & S Rare Books, Inc.   95 - 56 2013 $150

Chapone, Hester *Letters on the Improvement of the Mind.* Dublin: printed for J. Exshaw, 1773. 2 volumes in 1 with continuous pagination, 12mo., full contemporary sheep, gilt label, slight wear to head of spine.   Ken Spelman Books Ltd.   75 - 34   2013   £160

Chapone, Hester *Letters on the Improvement of the Mind, Addressed to a Young Lady.*   London: published for the proprietors and printed and sold by H. and G. Mozley, Market Place, Gainsbro, 1800.   12mo., signed in sixes, browned, tears to H3 and H4 without loss, contemporary sheep, double gilt banded spine, red morocco label, following hinge little cracked, wear to foot of spine and corners, contemporary signature of Johanna Maria Lindberg and underneath this Hannah Maria.   Jarndyce Antiquarian Booksellers   CCIV - 88   2013   £50

Chappe D'Auteroche, Jean Baptiste   1728-1769 *The 1769 Transit of Venus...*   Los Angeles: Natural History Museum of Los Angeles County, 1982.   Limited to 500 copies, 8vo., 185 pages, full page illustrations, reddish brown cloth, gilt stamped spine title, fine.   Jeff Weber Rare Books   171 - 71   2013 $65

Chapuis, Alfred   *Automata: a Historical and Technological Study.*   New York: Central Book Co., 1958.   4to., cloth, slight wear, near fine, profusely illustrated with photos and color plates.   Aleph-Bet Books, Inc.   104 - 557   2013 $275

Char, Rene   *Dent Prompte.*   Paris: Galerie Lucie Weill/Au Pont des Arts, 1969.   First Max Ernst edition, one of 2420 examples on Arches wove paper (total edition of 290), signed by Ernst and Chart, 10 full page color lithographs, loose leaves in wrapper folder with additional color lithograph (signed in place) on front cover, housed in publisher's cloth portfolio case, internally fine, box with imperfections, overall size circa 19.5 x 16 inches.   Gemini Fine Books & Arts., Ltd.   Art Reference & Illustrated Books - 2013 $2500

Char, Rene   *Poemes et Prose Choisis de Rene Char.*   Paris: Gallimard, 1957.   First edition, 8vo., original wrappers, preserved in folding case, inscribed by author for Ted Roethke, wrappers slightly soiled, otherwise excellent.   Maggs Bros. Ltd.   1460 - 165   2013   £450

Charcot, J. M.   *Lecons Maladies de Systeme Nerveux Faites a La Salpetriere.*   Paris: V. Adrien Delahaye, 1875-1877.   2 volumes, original bindings though volume 2 has more wear and loss of spine labeling, partially unopened set, text foxing, some soiling, numerous text illustrations and engravings, inscribed by author, rare thus.   James Tait Goodrich   75 - 41   2013 $1500

Charcot, J. M.   *Lectures on Localization of Diseases of the Brain Delivered at the Faculty of Medicine, Paris 1875.*   New York: William Wood, 1878.   45 text illustrations, original green cloth, clean tight copy.   James Tait Goodrich   S74 - 42   2013 $495

Charles-Roux, Edmonde   *To Forget Palermo.*   New York: Delacorte, 1968.   First American edition, fine n very near fine dust jacket with couple of very short tears and little soiling.   Between the Covers Rare Books, Inc.   Mystery & Detective Fiction - 32571   2013 $60

Charles I, King of Great Britain   *Articles of Peace Between Charles...with John the 4. King of Portugal, Algerres &c.*   London: for J. Harrison, 1642.   4to., (8) pages, removed, some soiling.   Joseph J. Felcone Inc.   Books Printed before 1701 - 15   2013 $100

Charles I, King of Great Britain   *His Majesties Letter and Declaration to the Sheriffes and City of London Jan. 17 1642.*   Oxford: by Leonard Lichfield Jan. 18, 1642.   4to., (2), 6 pages, modern cloth.   Joseph J. Felcone Inc.   Books Printed before 1701 - 16   2013 $325

Charles II, King of Great Britain   *Articles of Peace, Commerce & Alliance, Between the Crowns of Great Britain and Spain, Concluded in a Treaty at Madrid.*   In the Savoy: by the assigns of John Bill and Christopher Barker, 1667.   4to., 32 pages, modern cloth.   Joseph J. Felcone Inc.   Books Printed before 1701 - 17   2013 $250

Charles II, King of Great Britain   *His Majesties Gracious Speech to both Houses of Parliament... the 21st of Octo. 1680.*   London: by John Bill, Thomas Newcomb and Henry Hills, 1680.   Folio, 7 pages, modern cloth.   Joseph J. Felcone Inc.   Books Printed before 1701 - 18   2013 $300

Charles II, King of Great Britain   *His Majesties Gracious Speech, Together with the Lord Chancellors to both Houses of Parliament... the 23d of May 1678.*   London: by John Bill, Christopher Barker, Thomas Newcomb and Henry Ills, 1678.   First edition, folio, 19 pages, modern bookplate, titlepage with some stains and early repair costing part of imprint.   Joseph J. Felcone Inc.   Books Printed before 1701 - 19   2013 $300

Charles Johnson: the Novelist as Philosopher.   Jackson: University Press of Mississipi, 2007.   First edition, fine in fine dust jacket, warmly inscribed by author for Nicholas Delbanco.   Between the Covers Rare Books, Inc.   165 - 185   2013 $200

Charlton, D. E. A.   *The Art of Packaging.*   New York: Studio, 1938.   First edition, hardcover, 127 pages, numerous black and white images, about very good in green cloth boards and with front flap of dust jacket present but rest of jacket missing, good reference copy.   Jeff Hirsch Books   Fall 2013 - 129218   2013 $75

Charlton, Lionel   *The History of Whitby and of Whitby Abbey.*   York: printed by A. Ward, 1779.   4to., large folding frontispiece plan, 3 plates, large uncut copy, 4to., 19th century half red morocco marbled boards, raised and gilt banded spine, some slight rubbing to head and tail of spine, minor foxing, good, clean copy.   Ken Spelman Books Ltd.   73 - 165   2013   £220

Charriere, Henri   *Papillon.*   Hart Davis, 1970.   First English edition, 568 pages, 8vo., original mid brown boards, backstrip gilt lettered, endpaper maps, dust jacket, near fine.   Blackwell's Rare Books   B174 - 188   2013   £200

Charteris, Leslie *The Ace of Knaves.* London: Hodder & Stoughton, 1937. First edition, 8vo., original pale blue cloth, inscribed by author, spine very slightly faded, otherwise excellent copy.   Maggs Bros. Ltd.   1460 - 166   2013   £450

Charteris, Leslie *The Avenging Saint.* Garden City: Doubleday Crime Club, 1931. First American edition, previous owner's stamps on endpapers and spotting on top of page edges, else fine, bright copy, without dust jacket.   Mordida Books   81 - 73   2013 $75

Charteris, Leslie *Call for the Saint.* Garden City: Doubleday Crime Club, 1948. First edition, pages darkened, otherwise fine in dust jacket with some slight spine fading, couple of short closed tears and tiny wear at corners.   Mordida Books   81 - 75   2013 $200

Charteris, Leslie *The Last Hero.* London: Hodder & Stoughton, 1930. First edition, spine soiled, otherwise very good without dust jacket.   Mordida Books   81 - 72   2013 $250

Charteris, Leslie *The Saint on Guard.* Garden City: Doubleday Crime Club, 1944. First edition, pages slightly darkened, otherwise fine in dust jacket with slightly faded and rubbed spine.   Mordida Books   81 - 74   2013 $300

Charteris, Leslie *The Saint on the Spanish Main.* Garden City: Doubleday Crime Club, 1955. First edition, some darkening on endpapers and small light stain top of spine, otherwise near fine in very good dust jacket with closed three inch tear on front panel that has had internal tape repair removed but has bled through, couple of other internal tape repairs with tape removed, some wear along folds, inscribed by author for Grace Campbell.   Mordida Books   81 - 76   2013 $350

Charteris, Leslie *The Saint to the Rescue.* Garden City: Doubleday Crime Club, 1959. First edition, page edges slightly darkened otherwise near fine in dust jacket with faint stain on front panel, short closed tear, minor wear at spine ends.   Mordida Books   81 - 78   2013 $100

Charteris, Leslie *Senor Saint.* Garden City: Doubleday Crime Club, 1958. First edition, fine in lightly soiled dust jacket with short closed tear.   Mordida Books   81 - 77   2013 $125

Chase, Samuel *The Answer and Pleas of Samuel Chase, One of the Associate Justices of the Supreme Court of the United States to the articles of Impeachment Delivered Against Him...* Washington City: William Duane & Son, 1805. First edition, 8vo. 84 pages, removed, title browned and foxed.   M & S Rare Books, Inc.   95 - 87   2013 $875

Chassaignac, M. E. *Lecons sur la Tracheotomie.* Paris: Chez J. B. Bailliere, 1855. Half title, title, 120 pages, 8 text engravings, recent plain wrappers, light foxing, engravings, author's presentation.   James Tait Goodrich   75 - 43   2013 $495

Chasseguet-Smirgel, Janine *Creativity and Perversion.* New York and London: W. W. Norton and Co., 1985. First British edition, pages little browned, else fine in fine dust jacket.   Between the Covers Rare Books, Inc.   Psychology & Psychiatry - 97033   2013 $65

Chassepol, Francois De *The History of the Grand Visiers, Mahomet and Achmet Coprogli of the Three Last Grand Signiors, their Sultana's and Chief Favourites...* printed for H. Brome, 1677. First edition in English, engraved frontispiece, worming in lower margins, on few occasions affecting a letter or two, small 8vo., original sheep, blind ruled borders on sides, corner ornaments, compartments blind ruled on spine, worn at extremities, but sound.   Blackwell's Rare Books   B174 - 30   2013   £1250

Chateaux Forts. Paris: Flammarion, 1950. Square 4to., stiff pictorial wrappers, fine and unused, 12 lovely full page illustrations in silhouette with thick frames around edges all printed in blue, each illustration represents a different aspect of a French Chateau to be used as a design for a stained glass window, full page illustrations, rare.   Aleph-Bet Books, Inc.   105 - 451   2013 $225

Chatterbox 1921. Wells, Gardner, Darton & Co., 1921. Small 8vo., original cloth backed pictorial boards, little worn, color frontispiece and numerous illustrations, joints cracking.   R. F. G. Hollett & Son   Children's Books - 125   2013   £30

Chatterton, Thomas 1752-1770 *Miscellanies in Prose and Verse.* London: printed for G. Kearsley, 1778. First edition, half title, engraved frontispiece, small tear in lower margin of title, nicely bound in 19th century half calf, spine with devices in blind, slightly rubbed.   Jarndyce Antiquarian Booksellers   CCIII - 658   2013   £180

Chatterton, Thomas 1752-1770 *Poems, Supposed to Have Been Written at Bristol, by Thomas Rowley and Others in the Fifteenth Century.* London: for T. Payne and Son, 1777. First edition, 2nd state, with leaf c4 a cancel, plate of purported Rowley manuscript facsimile, contemporary calf, rebacked in morocco, tiny hole in blank margin of G3, corners very worn with board exposed, armorial bookplate of Richard Edgcumbe.   Joseph J. Felcone Inc.   English and American Literature to 1800 - 5   2013 $750

Chaucer, Geoffrey   1340-1400   *The Canterbury Tales of Chaucer Modernis'd by Several Hands.*   London: printed for J. and R. Tonson, 1741.   3 volumes, 8vo., bound without frontispiece, full contemporary sprinkled calf, raised and gilt banded spines, red morocco labels, some wear to tail volume I and III, armorial bookplate of William Waddington, attractive set.   Jarndyce Antiquarian Booksellers   CCIV - 89   2013   £380

Chaucer, Geoffrey   1340-1400   *The Canterbury Tales of Geoffrey Chaucer, together with a Version in Modern English verse.*   New York: Covici Friede, 1930.   One of 75 deluxe copies, printed on Crane's Old Book paper at the Stratford Press, specially bound and accompanied by a separate set of five panoramic sheets of Kent's full plate woodcuts, each signed by him in lower right margin, out of an edition of 999, signed by artist, 2 volumes, folio, five panorama sheets with additional woodcuts in two colors of five Canterbury Pilgrims on each sheet, 25 woodcuts in 2 colors of Canterbury Pilgrims as well as numerous head and tailpieces, by Rockwell Kent, full tan pigskin, boards and spines stamped and lettered in blind, top edge gilt, others uncut, the additional five sheets lightly folded and chemised, all three housed together in brown cloth slipcase, exceptionally fine with no chipping or fading.   Heritage Book Shop Holiday Catalogue 2012 - 30   2013 $5000

Chaucer, Geoffrey   1340-1400   *The Ellesmere Manuscript of Chaucer's Canterbury Tales.*   Cambridge: D. S. Brewer, 1989.   Working facsimile, 4to., red cloth, black label with gilt lettering to spine, head and tail of spine slightly bumped, upper edge little dust soiled, very good.   Unsworths Antiquarian Booksellers   28 - 153   2013   £175

Chaucer, Geoffrey   1340-1400   *Troilus and Criseyde.*   Cambridge: D. S. Brewer, 1978.   Only 300 copies printed, 4to., brown cloth, black label with gilt lettering, little bruised to upper edge, very good.   Unsworths Antiquarian Booksellers   28 - 154   2013   £175

Chaucer, Geoffrey   1340-1400   *The Workes of Geffray Chaucer...*   London: printed by Thomas Godfray, 1532.   First collected edition, folio in sixes, black letter, 48 lines plus headline, double columns, several sets of decorated initials and lombards used as initials, few capital spaces with guides, 15 woodcuts in Canterbury Tales, handsomely bound by Riviere & Son, decoratively panelled in blind, spine in six, compartments with five raised bands, gilt lettered in two compartments and decoratively tooled in blind in remaining four, board edges and turn-ins ruled in blind, all edges gilt, few early ink annotations, house in custom full brown morocco clamshell.   Heritage Book Shop   50th Anniversary Catalogue - 21   2013 $100,000

Chaucer, Geoffrey   1340-1400   *The Workes of Geffrey Chaucer.*   London: imprinted by Jhon Kyngston for Jhon Wight, 1561.   Fifth collected edition, first issue, 22 woodblocks in "The Prologues" taken from blocks used by Caxton in his second edition of Canterbury Tales, folio, 22 woodcuts of Pilgrims in "the Prologues" and woodcut of a knight on a horse at head of "The Knightes Tale", large and small historiated and decorative initials and ther ornaments, black letter, 56 lines, double columns; late 19th century crimson morocco by Riviere, covers with gilt and toll tool border enclosing a central olive wreath and elaborate cornerpieces composed of scroll work and spreading olive branches, remaining field seme with cinquefoils, spine in seven compartments with six raised bands, lettered in gilt in two compartments, rest decoratively tooled in gilt with repeated olive leaf motif, board edges and turn-ins decoratively tooled in gilt, all edges gilt, marbled endpapers, pastedowns with decorative gilt tooling, title creased and lightly soiled with small repair in outer blank margin, lower corner of second leaf renewed, affecting catchword on recto and two letters on verso, closed tear through lower half of divisional title to "Canterbury Tales", closed tear to A2 of "The Prologues" affecting 8 lines of text in first column and another closed tear at lower margin, F2 with small paper repair to margin and closed tear just touching text 2U2 with paper fault affecting one word in bottom line of text on recto and verso, few additional small marginal tears or repairs, not affecting text, occasional early ink underlining and markings, early ink signature of James Reo (faded) on title, wonderful copy, from the library of C. W. Dyson Perrins and William Foyle, with their bookplates.   Heritage Book Shop   50th Anniversary Catalogue - 22   2013 $65,000

Chaucer, Geoffrey   1340-1400   *The Workes of Our Ancient and Learned English Poet, Geoffrey Chaucer.*   London: by Adam Islip, 1602.   Folio, title surrounded by woodcut border, lacking initial blank as always, and errata leaf 3U8, copperplate portrait of Chaucer woodcuts of Chaucer's arms and of the knight woodcut initials black letter, late 19th century dark brown morocco, blind panel on covers, edges gilt, small worm track in margin of first several gatherings, two very minor repaired tears, one blank corner torn away, very clean, attractive copy, 1882 gift inscription.   Joseph J. Felcone Inc.   English and American Literature to 1800 - 6   2013 $9000

Chaucer, Geoffrey   1340-1400   *The Works of Our Ancient, Learned and Excellent English Poet...*   London: 1687.   Eighth edition and third edition, folio in fours, frontispiece, large woodcut arms of Chaucer on divisional title to the Works, black letter, signature c1 is signed 'd', full modern calf, boards ruled in blind and tooled in blind floral pattern, spine stamped and ruled in gilt, original brown morocco spine label, lettered gilt, all edges brown, newer endpapers, bottom half of fore-edge and text block with dampstain throughout, it occasionally creeps into lower quarter of text, bit of toning to leaves, overall very good.   Heritage Book Shop   Holiday Catalogue 2012 - 29   2013 $2500

Chaucer, Geoffrey 1340-1400 *The Works.* London: printed for Bernard Lintot, 1721. First Urry edition, engraved frontispiece, fine portrait of Chaucer, title vignette and 27 excellent headpiece vignettes of pilgrims, just little light browning, folio, 19th century diced Russia, boards panelled and framed in blind, gilt roll tool border, neatly rebacked preserving original spine, decorated in gilt and blind, corners renewed, old leather somewhat scratched and rubbed around edges, bookplate of R. St. John Mathews and pencil inscription of J. Henry Stormont dated 1901 to endpapers good.   Blackwell's Rare Books   B174 - 31   2013   £1200

Chaucer, Geoffrey 1340-1400 *The Works of...* Hammersmith: Kelmscott Press, 1896. One of 425 copies on paper, out of a total edition of 438, folio, 87 woodcut illustrations after Sir Edward Burne-Jones, woodcut titlepage, 14 variously repeated woodcut borders, 18 variously repeated woodcut frames around illustrations, 26 nine-line woodcut initial words, numerous three, six and ten line woodcut initial letters and woodcut printer's device, printed in black and red in Chaucer type, original holland backed blue paper boards, printed paper label on spine, spine and label very lightly browned, with little chipping to label, occasional light foxing or spotting on fore-edge, otherwise fine, bookplate of John Charrington, full brown morocco slipcase.   Heritage Book Shop   Holiday Catalogue 2012 - 91   2013 $85,000

Cheatham, Kitty *A Nursery Garland.* New York: G. Schrimmer, 1917. First edition, large 4to., red cloth backed boards, very good.   Barnaby Rudge Booksellers   Children 2013 - 015136   2013 $55

Cheever, George B. *Protest Against the Robbery of the Colored Race by the Proposed Amendement of the Constitution.* New York: 1866. First edition, 12mo., 44 pages, sewn as issued, some wrinkling.   M & S Rare Books, Inc.   95 - 58   2013 $525

Cheever, Henry T. *The Whale and His Captors; or the Whaleman's Adventures and the Whales Biography...* Thomas Nelson and Sons, 1855. 12mo., original blind-stamped blue cloth gilt extra, all edges gilt, tinted lithograph frontispiece and title, prize label on pastedown.   R. F. G. Hollett & Son   Children's Books - 127   2013   £85

Chemant, M. Dubois De *A Dissertation on Artificial Teeth in General.* London: printed by J. Barker, 1797. 8vo., 36 pages, disbound, lacking two plates.   Jarndyce Antiquarian Booksellers   CCIV - 90   2013   £75

Chen, Julie *Memento.* Berkeley: Flying Fish Press, 2012. Artist's book, one of 50 copies all on Kitakata paper, each signed and numbered on colophon by Chen, page size 1 9/16 x 2 1/8 x 5/16 inches, 36 pages, 10 of which are foldouts, bound sewn into tan and gold silk over boards brocade, persimmon linen spine, oval cut-out faced with Mylar on front panel revealing title on blue/green striped Kitakata paper, housed in copper locket which can be worn (silk cord with attachment loop enclosed), locket fabricated by Christina Kemp based on design by Julie Chen, locket size 1 7/8 x 2 7/16 x 3/4 inches, locket opens on one side with peg clasp to house book, title visible for a 'porthole' type opening on front, on reverse, box opens as a triptych, 'porthole' type opening on this side reveals words taken from preambles of constitutions of US and Iraq, when opened, photos of a bookseller's stall on Al-Mutanabbi Street in Baghdad prior to bombing in 2007 surround the words, locket containing the book housed in brown silk over boards clamshell box, edged with same brocade used in locket and book binding, box opens to reveal richly padded presentation box for locket and silk cord for wearing it, colophon pulls out from front of box with brown gros-grain ribbon.   Priscilla Juvelis - Rare Books   56 - 11   2013 $1575

Cheney, Ednah *The Children's Friend.* Boston: L. Prang & Co., 1888. First edition, oblong 4to., pictorial cloth, fine, chromolithographed frontispiece and line illustrations by Lizbeth B. Comins, beautiful copy.   Aleph-Bet Books, Inc.   105 - 23   2013 $350

Chermside, R. S. *Artist and Craftsman.* Cambridge: Macmillan and Co., 1860. 8vo., very good in contemporary dark green half calf, marbled boards, raised and gilt banded spine with black gilt label, slight mark to final page and some light foxing to few leaves, armorial bookplate of the Somerhill Library, scarce.   Ken Spelman Books Ltd.   75 - 126   2013   £65

Chernow, Burt *Milton Avery. The Drawings of Milton Avery.* New York: Taplinger Pub. Co., 1984. First edition, illustrations, very near fine dust jacket with some minor fading.   Jeff Hirsch Books   Fall 2013 - 129200   2013 $65

Cherry, John Law *Life and Remains of John Clare, the "Northamptonshire Peasant Poet".* London: Frederick Warne & Co., 1873. First edition, frontispiece and illustrations by Birket Foster, 4 pages ads, original dark green cloth, borders blocked in blind, spine lettered gilt, spine slightly rubbed, good plus.   Jarndyce Antiquarian Booksellers   CCIII - 487   2013   £110

Chesbro, George C. *The Beasts of Valhalla.* New York: Valhalla, 1985. First edition, very fine in dust jacket.   Mordida Books   81 - 80   2013 $150

Chesbro, George C. *Shadow of a Broken Man.* New York: Simon & Schuster, 1977. First edition, page edges slightly darkened, otherwise fine in dust jacket.   Mordida Books   81 - 79   2013 $100

Chesley, Hervey E. *Adventuring with Old Timers; Trails Travelled, Tales Told.* Midland: 1979. xv, 184 pages, illustrations, dust jacket has short tears and minor loss, book very slightly cocked with some soiling to edges, overall very good.   Dumont Maps & Books of the West   122 - 49   2013 $65

Chesney, Francis Rawdon *Reports on the Navigation of the Euphrates.* London: 1833. First edition, folding map and folding diagram, folio, contemporary calf, gilt, worn, original upper wrapper bound in, presentation "W. P. Andrew Esq. from the author", rare.   Maggs Bros. Ltd.   1467 - 29   2013   £3000

Chester, George Randolph *Young Wallingford.* Indianapolis: Bobbs Merrill, 1910. First edition, some light foxing on top of page edges and shelfwear along bottom cover edges, otherwise fine in blue cloth covered boards with gold stamped titles and decorations.   Mordida Books   81 - 81   2013 $85

Chesterfield, Philip Dormer Stanhope, 4th Earl of   1694-1773 *Letters Written by the Late Right Honourable Philip Dormer Stanhope, Earl of Chesterfield, to his son, Philip Stanhope, Esq.... Together with Several Other Pieces on Various Subjects.* London: printed for J. Dodsley, 1774. 4 volumes, engraved frontispiece, 8vo., slight tear to leading edge O6 volume III, some occasional foxing and light browning only affecting a few leaves, attractive 19th century half green morocco, marbled boards, small gilt floral device on spines.   Jarndyce Antiquarian Booksellers   CCIV - 91   2013   £280

Chesterfield, Philip Dormer Stanhope, 4th Earl of   1694-1773 *Letters Written... to His Son, Philip Stanhope Esq...* London: printed for J. Dodsley, 1774. First edition, first state (erratum on page 55 of volume i uncorrected), 2 volumes, frontispiece volume i, bound without errata leaf in volume ii (but with blank leaf of matching paper in its place) some light foxing, embossment of Grendon Hall 1850 (the belonging to Sir George Chetwynd, 3rd Baronet), 4to., modern biscuit calf, spines gilt with red morocco lettering pieces, circular red morocco numbering pieces on green morocco grounds, new endpapers, preserving old bookplates of William Frederick, 2nd Duke of Gloucester and Edinburgh, manuscript letter loosely inserted, very good.   Blackwell's Rare Books   B174 - 146   2013   £900

Chesterfield, Philip Dormer Stanhope, 4th Earl of   1694-1773 *Lord Chesterfield's Advice to His Son, On Men and Manners.* Paris: printed for Vergani, 1800? 12mo., titlepage browned, slight tears to blank gutter margin, some age toning, contemporary mottled sheep, gilt spine, black gilt label, leading hinge cracked but firm, spine slightly rubbed and chipped at head and tail.   Jarndyce Antiquarian Booksellers   CCIV - 92   2013   £120

Chesterton, Gilbert Keith   1874-1936 *The Ballad of St. Barbara and Other Verses.* London: Cecil Palmer, 1922. First edition, tall 8vo., original quarter black cloth, patterned paper boards, lettered in gilt, lightly rubbed, otherwise excellent, inscribed by author.   Maggs Bros. Ltd.   1460 - 167   2013   £150

Chesterton, Gilbert Keith   1874-1936 *Four Faultless Felons.* London: Cassell, 1930. First edition, fine in very good dust jacket with slight chipping at spinal extremities, particularly at foot, exceptionally scarce in jacket.   Between the Covers Rare Books, Inc.   Mystery & Detective Fiction - 47323   2013 $1500

Chesterton, Gilbert Keith   1874-1936 *Four Faultless Felons.* London: Cassell, 1930. First edition, foolscap 8vo., original black cloth, backstrip gilt lettered, pale yellow dust jacket in fine state, overall unusually fine.   Blackwell's Rare Books   172 - 170   2013   £1000

Chesterton, Gilbert Keith   1874-1936 *The Innocence of Father Brown.* London: Cassell, 1911. First edition, frontispiece with tissue guard, 7 other plates by Sidney Seymour Lucas, crown 8vo., original red cloth, backstrip and front cover gilt lettered, light free endpaper browning, gift inscription on front free endpaper dated "Christmas 1911", light fox spotting to edges, but far better than normally met with, very good.   Blackwell's Rare Books   172 - 171   2013   £500

Chesterton, Gilbert Keith   1874-1936 *The Man Who Knew Too Much and Other Stories.* London: Cassell and Co., 1922. First edition, fine in very attractive, near fine dust jacket with shallow chipping at top of spine, lovely copy, very scarce.   Between the Covers Rare Books, Inc.   Mystery & Detective Fiction - 59854   2013 $6000

Chesterton, Gilbert Keith   1874-1936 *Peace, War and Adventure...* London: Longman, 1853. 2 volumes in 1, 2 pages ads, some occasional light spotting, original orange cloth with imprint of Bickers & Bush, publisher's ad laid down, but still loose in identical printed cloth on back board, very nice,.   Jarndyce Antiquarian Booksellers   CCV - 60   2013   £350

Chew, Samuel C. *Byron in England: His Fame and After-Fame.* London: John Murray, 1924. First edition, half title, frontispiece, 6 pages ads, original green cloth, repaired tears at head of spine, traces of cellophane wrappers attached to endpapers, bookplate of Doris Langley Moore and signature "Centenary week" April 1924.   Jarndyce Antiquarian Booksellers   CCIII - 359   2013   £60

Cheyne, George   1671-1743 *An Essay on Health and Long Life.* London: George Strahan, 1724. First edition, contemporary full English paneled calf, front blank lacking (removed).   James Tait Goodrich   75 - 45   2013 $595

Cheyne, George 1671-1743 *An Essay on Health and Long Life.* Philadelphia: 1814. First American edition, contemporary full mottled tree calf, contents browned, light rubbing to spine, else very good.   James Tait Goodrich   75 - 44   2013 $1500

Cheyne, John *An Essay on Hydocephalus Acutus or Dropsy of the Brain.* Philadelphia: 1814. First American edition, contemporary paper backed blue sugar boards, uncut and unopened, contents browned, very nice unsophisticated copy.   James Tait Goodrich   S74 - 43   2013 $1500

Cheyne, John *An Essay on Hydrocephalus Acutus or Dropsy of the Britain.* Philadelphia: 1814. First American edition, contemporary full mottled tree calf, contents browned, light rubbing to spine, else very good.   James Tait Goodrich   75 - 44   2013 $1500

Cheyne, John *Essays on Hydrocephalus Acutus or Water in the Brain.* Dublin: Hodges & McArthur et al, 1819. Second Dublin edition, 8vo., unopened, lightly foxed, original paper boards, printed spine label, spine neatly repaired, fine, rare.   Jeff Weber Rare Books   172 - 58   2013 $750

Cheyney, Peter *Dark Hero.* London: Collins, 1946. First edition, one of 250 numbered copies, signed by author and additionally inscribed by him to Freddy Phillips? 8vo., original purple cloth, excellent copy, dust jacket little nicked and worn at extremities.   Maggs Bros. Ltd. 1460 - 169   2013   £75

Cheyney, Peter *I'll Say She Does!* Collins, 1945. First edition, foolscap 8vo., pages 192, original lemon yellow cloth, backstrip blocked in green dust jacket, little rubbed and with few short tears, very good.   Blackwell's Rare Books   B174 - 188   2013   £70

Cheyney, Peter *Sinister Errand.* London: Collins, 1945. First edition, 8vo., original yellow cloth, excellent copy, some light soiling to cloth, inscribed by author to Mrs. Thea O'Brien 14/11/45.   Maggs Bros. Ltd.   1460 - 168   2013   £50

Chicken Little and Little Half Chick. New York: Macmillan Aug., 1927. First edition, 12mo., pictorial boards, light cover soil and edge rubbing, very good, illustrations by Berta and Elmer Hader.   Aleph-Bet Books, Inc.   104 - 269   2013 $200

Child, Dennis *Painters in the Northern Counties of England and Wales.* Leeds: privately published by author, 2002. Second edition, 2 parts, 4to., original cloth, gilt, dust jacket.   R. F. G. Hollett & Son   Lake District & Cumbria - 267   2013   £35

Child, Julia *Julia Child.* New York: Alfred A. Knopf, 1978. First edition, clean very near fine in close to near fine, price clipped dust jacket with few small edge tears and some very slight wear, signed by Julia and Paul Child, very nice.   Jeff Hirsch Books   Fall 2013 - 129480   2013 $400

Child, Lydia Maria Francis 1802-1880 *Correspondence Between Lydia Maria Child and Gov. Wise and Mrs. Mason of Virginia.* Boston: published by the American Anti-Slavery Society, 1860. First edition, 8vo., original printed self wrappers, stitched as issued, 28 pages, wrappers little soiled, small chip in margin of rear wrapper, very good.   The Brick Row Book Shop   Miscellany Fifty-Nine - 7   2013 $500

Child, Lydia Maria Francis 1802-1880 *The Family Nurse; or Companion of the Frugal Housewife.* Boston: Charles J. Hendee, 1837. First edition, 8vo., original blind-stamped brown cloth, rebacked with new printed paper label, gilt lettering to upper board, edges somewhat worn, text moderately foxed, very good.   The Brick Row Book Shop   Miscellany Fifty-Nine - 8   2013 $600

Child, Lydia Maria Francis 1802-1880 *Letters from New York.* New York and Boston: Charles S. Francis and Co. and James Munroe & Co., 1843. First edition, bookplate, contemporary gift inscription, chipping at edges of spine, good or better.   Between the Covers Rare Books, Inc.   New York City - 285606   2013 $250

The Children in the Wood Restored by Honestas, the Hermit of the Forest ... Banbury: printed by J. G. Rusher, circa, 1820. 11 woodcuts, just slightly dusty, 16 pages, 16mo., unopened and folded as issued, near fine.   Blackwell's Rare Books   172 - 81   2013   £100

The Children's Fancy Dress Ball. London: E. Nister, First edition, 64mo., wrappers, rare, very small bookplate, 12 pages, 4 chromolithographs.   Barnaby Rudge Booksellers   Children 2013 - 021413   2013 $175

The Child's Companion and Juvenile Instructor. Religious Tract Society, 1859-1865. Small 8vo., a collection of 32 numbers in original printed wrappers, upper panels with decorative borders, first wrapper missing, last chipped, numerous full page and other text illustrations.   R. F. G. Hollett & Son   Children's Books - 128   2013   £75

The Child's Delight. Philadelphia: Sunshine, n.d. circa, 1890. Large 4to., blue pictorial cloth, some cover soil and slight soil on one page, else very good, illustrations by Childe Hassam, Boz, J.G. Francis plus 3 fine fullpage chromolithographs.   Aleph-Bet Books, Inc.   104 - 568   2013 $225

The Child's Instructor, or Picture Alphabet. Glasgow: Lumsden & Son, circa, 1812. 24mo., (30) pages, plain brown wrapper, top edge gilded and some wear to spine paper, else fne, 27 woodcuts.   Aleph-Bet Books, Inc.   105 - 3   2013 $400

Chilvers, Hedley A.   *The Seven Wonders of Southern Africa.*   Johannesburg: South African Railways and Habours Administration, 1929.   First edition, original cloth, gilt, rather rubbed and stained, 18 color plates by C. E. Peers, maps on endpapers, front joint cracked.   R. F. G. Hollett & Son   Africana - 38   2013   £30

Chin, Henin   *Official Chinatown Guide Book for Visitors & New Yorkers.*   New York: Henin & Co., 1939.   First edition, illustrated yellow wrappers, 96 pages, very near fine.   Between the Covers Rare Books, Inc.   New York City - 286279   2013 $250

Chisholm, Louey   *The Golden Staircase.*   T. C. & E. C. Jack, n.d. circa, 1906.   Large 8vo., original decorated cream cloth, gilt extra, top edge gilt, 16 color plates, flyleaves little browned.   R. F. G. Hollett & Son   Children's Books - 568   2013   £75

Chittenden, Hiram Martin   *The American Fur Trade of the Far West.*   Stanford: Academic Reprints, 1954.   2 volumes, 10 plates, fine set with pictorial dust jackets (short tear to top edge of one jacket).   Argonaut Book Shop   Summer 2013 - 46   2013 $150

Choulant, Ludwig   *History and Bibliography of Anatomic Illustration.*   New York: Hafner Reprints, 1962.   8vo., original binding, dust jacket, nice.   James Tait Goodrich   S74 - 45   2013 $75

Chrimes, Mike   *The Civil Engineering of Canals and Railways Before 1850.*   Aldershot, et al: Ashgate, 1997.   Volume 7, 8vo., illustrations, tables, red cloth, gilt stamped cover and spine titles, Burndy bookplate, fine.   Jeff Weber Rare Books   169 - 65   2013 $100

Christen, Sydney M.   *The Story of an Artist's Life.*   1910.   First edition, 61 black and white and 62 color plates, cover damp marked, text and plates very good.   C. P. Hyland   261 - 184   2013   £32

The Christian Examiner and General Review Volume XVI and Volume XVII.   Boston: Charles Bowen, 1834-1835.   First edition, 2 volumes bound in one, contemporary half leather and marbled paper covered boards, modest edge wear, handsome, very good or better.   Between the Covers Rare Books, Inc.   165 - 336   2013 $400

Christian Miscellany , and Family Visiter for the Year 1847. Volume II.   John Mason, 1847.   Old half calf, little worn, text woodcuts.   R. F. G. Hollett & Son   Wesleyan Methodism - 43   2013   £45

Christian Miscellany, and Family Visiter for the Year 1850. Volume V.   John Mason, 1850.   Original blindstamped green cloth gilt, lower board little damped, frontispiece and text woodcuts, little soiling, slightly loose.   R. F. G. Hollett & Son   Wesleyan Methodism - 45   2013   £30

Christian Miscellany, and Family Visiter for the Year 1867. Second Series. Volume XIII.   Wesleyan Conference Office, 1867.   Original blindstamped green cloth gilt, 384 pages, colored Kronheim print frontispiece and text woodcuts.   R. F. G. Hollett & Son   Wesleyan Methodism - 44   2013   £45

Christian, Anne Hait   *The Search for Holmes, Robson, Hind, Steele and Graham Families of Cumberland and Northumberland, England.*   California: La Jolla, 1984.   Privately printed limited edition no. 53 of 1033 copies, small 4to., original blue cloth gilt, 75 illustrations, chart, presentation copy inscribed by author for Lorna Carleton.   R. F. G. Hollett & Son   Lake District & Cumbria - 268   2013   £65

Christie, Agatha   1891-1976   *The Body in the Library.*   London: Collins Crime Club, 1942.   First edition, bookseller's small label, spine slightly faded and lightly soiled, otherwise near fine in very good restored dust jacket, which has been entirely backed with plain white paper.   Mordida Books   81 - 85   2013 $450

Christie, Agatha   1891-1976   *Death Comes as the End.*   London: Collins Crime Club, 1945.   First English edition, near fine in very good, slightly darkened dust jacket with internal tape mend, nicks at spine ends, wear along folds.   Mordida Books   81 - 87   2013 $200

Christie, Agatha   1891-1976   *The Hollow.*   London: Collins Crime Club, 1946.   First edition, small faded area top of spine, otherwise near fine in very good price clipped dust jacket with faded spine, chipping at spine ends, wear along folds.   Mordida Books   81 - 88   2013 $100

Christie, Agatha   1891-1976   *The Labours of Hercules.*   London: Collins Crime Club, 1947.   First edition, some tiny fading top of spine, otherwise fine in very good dust jacket with chip at top of spine, light wear at spine ends and war at corners of front panel.   Mordida Books   81 - 89   2013 $200

Christie, Agatha   1891-1976   *The Mystery of the Blue Train.*   New York: Dodd, Mead & Co., 1928.   First American edition, very faint and small stain at edge of front board, near fine in near fine dust jacket with slight spine sunning and little soiling, very nice.   Between the Covers Rare Books, Inc.   Mystery & Detective Fiction - 88262   2013 $2500

Christie, Agatha 1891-1976 *N or M?*   London: Collins, 1941. First edition, pages 192, foolscap 8vo., original orange cloth, backstrip lettered in black, very presentable, bright, price clipped dust jacket, backstrip panel faded to grey-pink, very good.   Blackwell's Rare Books   B174 - 190   2013   £800

Christie, Agatha 1891-1976 *Passenger to Frankfurt.* London: published for the Crime Club by Collins, 1970. First edition, 8vo., original red cloth, near fine in price clipped dust jacket, slightly faded on spine, inscribed by author.   Maggs Bros. Ltd.   1460 - 170   2013   £300

Christie, Agatha 1891-1976 *The Secret of Chimneys.* London: John Lane, Bodley Head, 1925. First edition, spine darkened, covers soiled and page edges darkened and soiled otherwise very good, without dust jacket. Mordida Books   81 - 83   2013 $400

Christie, Agatha 1891-1976 *The Seven Dials Mystery.* London: Collins, 1929. First edition, stamp on titlepage and spine lightly faded, otherwise very good without dust jacket.   Mordida Books   81 - 84   2013 $300

Christie, Agatha 1891-1976 *Towards Zero.* London: Collins Crime Club, 1944. First edition, name on front endpaper, otherwise near fine in price clipped dust jacket with darkened spine and nicks at corners.   Mordida Books   81 - 86   2013 $250

Christie, Agatha 1891-1976 *Unfinished Portrait.* Garden City: Doubleday Doran, 1934. First American edition, neat contemporary owners name, corners slightly bumped, else fine in fine dust jacket with couple of tiny nicks, no fading to delicate pink color on jacket, lovely copy, very scarce.   Between the Covers Rare Books, Inc. Mystery & Detective Fiction - 33090   2013 $2000

Christie, Manson & Woods *Catalouge of the Collection of Pictures, Works of Art and Decorative Objects, the Property of His Grace the Duke of Hamilton, K.T... Saturday June 17, Monday June 19, 1882 and the Following Day.* London: Christie, Manson & Woods, 1882. First edition, 77 monochrome carbon print photographic plates, 8vo., cloth, scarce, especially in such beautiful condition in such a fine binding, near fine copy.   Kaaterskill Books   16 - 3   2013 $750

Christina, Queen of Sweden *Pensees De Christine, Reine de Suede.*   Stockholm: P. A. Norstedt & Soners Forlag, 1906. One of 42 copies (this #42), 195 x 129mm., original dark blue calf, upper cover with elegant gilt floral frame, floral cornerpieces and royal arms at center lower cover with entwined "RS", flat spine with gilt titling and coat of arms, gilt turn-ins, marbled endpapers, all edges gilt, front pastedown with engraved bookplate of Victoria Sackville, Knole, occasional pencilled underlinings, spine somewhat faded, joints and extremities rather rubbed, half a dozen small scratches to spine, top inch of rear board bit faded, once handsome binding still sound, very fine internally. Phillip J. Pirages   63 - 415   2013 $400

Christmas ABC.   Akron: Saalfield, 1910. Narrow folio, printed cloth, some light normal soil very good+, illustrations. Aleph-Bet Books, Inc.   105 - 4   2013 $250

Christmas Tales of Flanders.   New York: Dodd Mead, 1917. First edition, 4to., blue gilt pictorial cloth, fine, 12 magnificent tissue guarded color plates and a profusion of 2-color and black and white illustrations by Jean De Bosschere.   Aleph-Bet Books, Inc.   105 - 163   2013 $250

Christopher, Anne *Petunia Be Keerful.*   Racine: Whitman Pub. Co., 1934. First edition, illustrations by Inez Hogan, paper covered boards, former owner's name and date, near fine.   Between the Covers Rare Books, Inc.   165 - 107 2013 $200

Christopher, John *The Long Winter.* New York: Simon and Schuster, 1962. First American edition, pages little browned, else fine in fine dust jacket, beautiful, unread copy. Between the Covers Rare Books, Inc.   Sci-Fi, Fantasy & Horror - 316509   2013 $150

Christopher, John *The Long Winter.* New York: Simon & Schuster, 1962. Second American edition, pages little browned, else fine in fine dust jacket, small ink price on front flap, beautiful, unread copy.   Between the Covers Rare Books, Inc.   Sci-Fi, Fantasy & Horror - 316511   2013 $50

Christopher, John *Sweeney's Island.* New York: Simon and Schuster, 1964. First American edition, fine in fine dust jacket, beautiful, unread copy.   Between the Covers Rare Books, Inc.   Sci-Fi, Fantasy & Horror - 316589   2013 $100

Chronicles of America Series. New Haven: 1921. Complete set as of the time of publication, 50 volumes, small octavo, each 175 to 300 pages, most with frontispiece and folding map, little dusty, occasional fading, else very good.   Dumont Maps & Books of the West   124 - 54 2013 $225

Chronicles of England. (and) Description of Britain. London: Wynkyn de Worde, 1515. Seventh edition, 2 parts in 1 volume, folio, 172 (of 192) leaves, lacking first 6 leaves (gathering Aa) containing the full page woodcut arms of England and the table and blank, leaves bb8 and D4, 12 leaves (a1-16, C4-C6, and D1-D3) supplied in pen facsimile (19th century or earlier) and two leaves (S2 and S5) supplied from another copy, large woodcut of city in landscape, 22 (of 24) woodcut illustrations, 8 (of 10) woodcut diagrams, woodcut printer's device on bb7 verso, lacking woodcut printer's device, decorative woodcut and lombard initials, black letter, 44 lines plus headline, double columns; 19th century embossed and blindstamped calf over bevelled boards, expertly rebacked, original spine laid down, spine decoratively tooled in blind, all edges gilt, marbled endpapers, leaves d2-36 remargined, several leaves strengthened in margin, several leaves with marginal repairs, some resulting in few letters being supplied in pen facsimile, occasional stain and soiling, armorial bookplate on front pastedown, few early ink annotations, good copy, exceptionally scarce book.   Heritage Book Shop   50th Anniversary Catalogue - 83   2013 $42,500

The Church of Ireland and the Present Crisis. Report of the Special Meeting of the General Synod March 23rd 1886. 8vo., 62 pages, wrappers, very good.   C. P. Hyland   261 - 936   2013   £29

Chukovskii, K.   *Mukha Tsokotooka. (The Chattering Fly).* 1933.   First edition, Small 4to., pictorial wrappers, corner creased, else very good, black and white illustrations by V. Konashevich.   Aleph-Bet Books, Inc.   104 - 504   2013 $1500

Church of England. Book of Common Prayer   *The Booke of Common Prayer and Administration of the Sacraments and Other Rites and Ceremonies of the Church of England.*   London: by Robert Barker, printer to the Kings most excellent Majesty, 1634.   4to., very good, 19th century quarter calf, pebble grain cloth boards, armorial bookplate of A. C. Gloucester, with near contemporary name Rog. Blaq in blank space at foot of titlepage border with few manuscript emendations to text, verse numbers noted at head of titlepage.   Ken Spelman Books Ltd.   75 - 2   2013   £350

Church of England. Book of Common Prayer   *The Book of Common Prayer and Administration of the Sacraments... (bound with) The Whole Book of Psalms, Collected into English Metre by Thomas Sternhold, John Hopkins and others...*   London: printed by Thomas Baskett..., 1741. London: printed by A. Wilde for the Company of Stationers, 1752, First titlepage little dusted, old marginal repair to first leaf of Veni Creator, bound in elaborate early 19th century straight grained dull blue morocco gilt borders surrounding a central panel, decorations formed from small ornamental devices, leaves circles, floral sprays, gilt decorated spine, following hinge cracked but firm, all edges gilt.   Jarndyce Antiquarian Booksellers   CCIV - 101   2013   £150

Church of Ireland   *General Synod Revision Committee Report 1873.*   Dublin: 1873.   With loose inserts, 8vo., cloth, very good.   C. P. Hyland   261 - 937   2013   £50

Church, E. M.   *Sir Richard Church in Italy and Greece...*   London: Wm. Blackwood, 1895.   First edition, 8vo., pages x, 356, frontispiece, original red decorative cloth, gilt vignette on upper cover, corners bumped.   J. & S. L. Bonham Antiquarian Booksellers   Europe - 8814   2013   £65

Churchill, Winston   1620-1688   *Divi Britannici being a Remark Upon the Lives of all the Kings of This Isle...*   London: printed by Tho. Roycroft, 1675.   Folio, small wormhole in text from page 77 onwards, often touching a letter never affecting sense, gatherings e and d bound in reverse order, lightly browned, occasional spotting, watermark traced in pencil on verso of titlepage, contemporary speckled calf, crackled and rubbed, now rebacked and recornered with reverse calf, printed paper label to spine, new f.f.e.p., ownership inscriptions of Charlotte Bull (19th century) and John Woodford of Pembroke College, Oxford (18th century) to titlepage.   Unsworths Antiquarian Booksellers   28 - 83   2013   £750

Ciardi, John   *The King Who Saved.*   Philadelphia and New York: Lippincott, 1965.   First edition ($2.95 price), Oblong 12mo. cloth, fine in slightly soiled dust jacket, signed by Gorey.   Aleph-Bet Books, Inc.   105 - 284   2013 $200

Cicero, Marcus Tullius   *Cato Maior de Senectute. Cato the Elder on Old Age.*   San Francisco: Greenwood Press, 2001.   Special limited edition, one of 250 copies signed by printer, Jack Wenrer Stauffacher, 2 color printing (printed in blue and black), paper wrappers, printed dust jacket, fine. Jeff Weber Rare Books   171 - 73   2013 $85

Cicero, Marcus Tullius   *The Dream of Scipio.*   London: Fortune Press, 1927.   Number 24 of 525 copies, 48 pages, frontispiece in 2 states, small 4to., deluxe binding of full japanese vellum, gilt lettered spine, some slight marking to covers, mainly on rear board.   Ken Spelman Books Ltd.   75 - 171   2013   £60

Cicero, Marcus Tullius   *Hoc i Volumine Continentur M. Tulii Ciceronis Epistolarum Familiarum Libri Sexdecim...*   Venice: Simonem Bivilaqua Papiensem, 1495.   Frequent small woodcut decorative initials, small wormhole in last 6 leaves (affecting a couple of characters on last 2), few tiny wormholes in first 10 or so leaves (mostly marginal but not just touching a character on some leaves), first and last few leaves soiled, little dampmarking at end, small stains and ink blots elsewhere, light browning in places, old ownership inscriptions gently washed from title, folio, early 18th century vellum, rebacked preserving original spine with lettering piece (bit chipped), marbled endpapers, little simple gilt decoration, boards lightly soiled and bowing slightly sound. Blackwell's Rare Books   172 - 42   2013   £4500

Cicero, Marcus Tullius *Here Begynneth the Prohemye Upon the Reducynge Both Out of Latyn as of Frensshe in to Our Englyssh Tongue of the Polytque Book....* Westminster: William Caxton, 1481. Editio princeps in English, 2 parts in one folio volume, complete but for two blanks 1 and 72 and retaining blank 11, complex and ornate Flemish lettre batarde for the text, bold English block letter for some proper names (type 3), rubricated, capitals painted red and red underscores and paragraph marks, 271 x 192, modern blind tooled reddish goatskin to antique style, clasps and catches by Bernard Middleton, old red edges, this copy is fine, presented to Sion College by Lord Berkeley, excellent copy.   Heritage Book Shop   50th Anniversary Catalogue - 24   2013 $1,250,000

Cicero, Marcus Tullius *Letters to Atticus.* Cambridge: University Press, 1965-1970. 8vo., 7 volumes, very good set in dust jackets, scarce.   Ken Spelman Books Ltd.   75 - 186   2013   £280

Cicero, Marcus Tullius *De Officis Paradoxa De Amicitia De Senectute; De Somno Scipionis...* Venice: Filippo di Pietro, 1480. Small folio, 90 leaves, including prelim blank, 36 lines in Roman type, some passages in Greek, first initial painted in blue with ornamental penwork, initials painted somewhat flamboyantly in red, rubricated; modern maroon morocco by Doves Binder Charles McLeish for William Morris, from the library of Morris, spine lettered gilt, five raised bands, gilt board edges and turn-ins, all edges gilt, few light spots and stains, numerous contemporary and 16th century marginalia, bookplates, overall very good, housed in brown cloth open ended slipcase.   Heritage Book Shop 50th Anniversary Catalogue - 23   2013 $15,000

Cicero, Marcus Tullius *Tully's Offices in Three Books.* London: printed for R. Bentley, 1688. Fourth edition, engraved titlepage, one page neatly repaired without loss and some near contemporary marginal notes indicating chapters, full contemporary sheep, expert repairs to head and tail of spine, corners worn.   Ken Spelman Books Ltd. 75 - 10   2013   £140

Cicero, Marcus Tullius *Opera Rhetorica.* Paris: Venundantur cu(m) Ceteris ab Ioanne Paruo & Iodoco Badio, 1511. Editio princeps, 4 volumes bound in 2, fine woodcut titlepages printed in red and black decorative initial letters, some worming just touching few letters and leading edge of titlepage to volume 1 frayed with slight loss, clean tear without loss to second titlepage, with some neat contemporary marginal notes, handsomely bound in 18th century full panelled calf, raised bands, black morocco labels, corners expertly repaired, armorial bookplate of Robert Maxwell of Finnebrogue on the verso of titlepages.   Ken Spelman Books Ltd.   75 - 1   2013   £950

Cicero, Marcus Tullius *(Opera). Orationes, Epistolarum ad Atticum, Philosophicorum.* Strasbourg: Impensis Iosiae Rihelii & Iacobi Dupuys, 1581. 5 volumes only (form a 9 volume set of the works), 8vo., toned and sometimes spotted, fifth volume with staining to first half, third volume with occasional early ink notes, uniformly bound in contemporary pigskin dyed yellow, boards with blind rolled borders and central portrait stamp, all edges red and gauffered, intials 'APA' stamped in black to front board, ownership inscription of A. P. Alvin (1801) and Andreae Petri Aubogiensis (i. e. Andreas Petrus of Arboga in Sweden) dated 1591.   Unsworths Antiquarian Booksellers   28 - 8   2013   £625

Cicero, Marcus Tullius *Opera, cum Optimis Examplaribus Accurate Collata.* Leiden: Elzevir, 1642. 10 volumes, 12mo., engraved portrait plate, engraved titlepage to volume i printer's device to all other titlepages, repeated pagination of page 229-238 in volume IX as called for, light intermittent browning, few marginal notes, including pencil marks to volume VII, few closed tears not affecting text, volume IV with some worming to lower margin, recent tidy but somewhat utilitarian brown half calf with red labels to spines, little marked, top edges dusty.   Unsworths Antiquarian Booksellers   28 - 9   2013   £750

Cinderella *Cinderella.* Hamburg: Gustav W. Seitz, circa, 1860. 16mo., pictorial wrappers die-cut in shape of Cinderella, fine, color lithographs on each page with text in middle, rare.   Aleph-Bet Books, Inc.   104 - 527   2013 $800

Cinderella *Cinderella or the Little Glass Slipper.* New York: MacLoughlin Bros., n.d. circa, 1865. 12mo., pictorial wrappers highlighted in gold, mounted on linen, fine, beautiful copy.   Aleph-Bet Books, Inc.   105 - 241   2013 $300

Cinderella *Cinderella and the Little Glass Slipper.* New York: White & Allen, 1889. 4to., cloth backed pictorial boards, covers scuffed, else very good+, 10 magnificent full page chromolithographs plus 14 partial page illustrations. Aleph-Bet Books, Inc.   104 - 205   2013 $250

Cinderella *Cinderella.* London: William Heinemann: Philadelphia: J. B. Lippincott, 1919. One of 850 copies signed, this #417, one of 525 on English hand made paper, 286 x 229, illustrations by Arthur Rackham, very attractive red three quarter morocco (stamp signed "Putnams" along front turn-in), raised bands, spine handsomely gilt in compartments formed by plain and decorative rules, quatrefoil centerpiece surrounded by densely scrolling cornerpieces, sides and endleaves of rose colored linen, top edge gilt, with one color plates and silhouette illustrations, tiny portion of one spine band and of leather at head of spine worn away, very slight hints of wear to corners and joints, faint offsetting from illustrations (never severe, but more noticeable in those opening with facing illustrations, otherwise excellent copy.   Phillip J. Pirages   63 - 377   2013 $1250

Cinderella *Cinderella.* New York: Scribner, 1954. A. First edition, first printing, 4to., cloth, corner slightly worn, else fine in very good dust jacket (not price clipped, no award seal, small chips off spine ends), illustrations in color by Marcia Brown, this copy signed by Brown. Aleph-Bet Books, Inc.   104 - 91   2013 $1500

Cinderella *Cinderella and other Tales.* New York: Blue Ribbon, 1933. Thick 4to., pictorial boards, spine creased and slightly cocked, else very good+, illustrations by Harold Lentz, including 4 fabulous double page color pop-ups, very scarce.   Aleph-Bet Books, Inc.   104 - 433   2013 $750

Cinderella *Cinderella or the Little Glass Slipper.* New York: McLoughlin Bros., 1896. Small 4to., wrappers, 3 full page and 1 double page chromolithograph plus cover illustrations, rear cover creased.   Barnaby Rudge Booksellers   Children 2013 - 021675   2013 $125

Cinderella *The Interesting Story of Cinderella and Her Glass Slipper.* Banbury: printed by J. G. Rusher, circa, 1820. 8 woodcuts (one signed 'J.G'), just slightly dusty, pages 16, 16mo., unopened and folded as issued, near fine.   Blackwell's Rare Books   172 - 80   2013   £100

Circumnavigation of the Globe and Progress of Discovery in the Pacific Ocean. London: T. Nelson and Sons, 1852. Prize label of Huddersfield Mechanics Institution relaid on pastedown, original blindstamped cloth, gilt extra, rather soiled and spine darkened, neatly recased, engraved title and 5 engraved plates (rather browned) numerous text woodcuts.   R. F. G. Hollett & Son   Polar Exploration - 10   2013   £65

Circus in Hanky Town. No place: Hermann Hadf. Co., n.d. circa, 1948. Pictorial card covers with string ties, covers slightly sunned, else fine, 6 pages brightly illustrated, each with cut-out containing color embroidered handkerchief.   Aleph-Bet Books, Inc.   105 - 307   2013 $600

Claassen, Harold *The History of Professional Football.* Englewood Cliffs: Prentice Hall, 1963. First edition, quarto, fine in near fine, slightly rubbed dust jacket, spine sunned.   Between the Covers Rare Books, Inc.   Football Books - 74757   2013 $85

Clair, Jean *Lost Paradise. Symbolist Europe.* Montreal: Museum of Fine Arts, 1995. First edition, 4to., near fine with small bump to rear joint, like dust jacket.   Beasley Books   2013 - 2013 $100

Claire, William *Voyages: a National Literary Magazine.* Washington: 1967-1973. Complete run, Volume I # 1, Fall 1967 to Volume 5, numbers 1-4 1973, 9 volumes.   Second Life Books Inc.   183 - 71   2013 $350

Clap, Thomas *An Essay on the Nature and Foundation of Moral Virtue and Obligation...* New Haven: B. Mecom, 1765. First edition, 12mo., decorated with several attractive woodcut head and tailpieces, contemporary plain blue wrappers, slight foxing, but very crisp copy.   M & S Rare Books, Inc.   95 - 298   2013 $550

Clapham, Richard *The Book of the Otter.* Heath Cranton, 1922. First edition, original blue cloth gilt, 13 plates.   R. F. G. Hollett & Son   Lake District & Cumbria - 269   2013   £60

Clapham, Richard *Rough Shooting for the Man of Moderate Means.* Heath Cranton, 1922. First edition, original cloth, gilt, 17 illustrations, front flyleaf removed.   R. F. G. Hollett & Son   Lake District & Cumbria - 271   2013   £35

Clapham, Richard *Sport on Fell, Beck & Tarn.* Heath Cranton, 1924. First edition, original cloth gilt, 164 pages, illustrations.   R. F. G. Hollett & Son   Lake District & Cumbria - 272   2013   £40

Clappe, Louise Amelia Knapp Smith 1819-1906   *The Shirley Letters from California Mines in 1851-51.* San Francisco: Thomas C. Russell, 1922. First book edition, hand-set type, 8 full page hand colored plates, gray boards, tan coarse Irish linen backstrip, printed paper spine label, top edge gilt, spine lightly worn at spine ends and outer rear hinge, bookplate, very good, internally fine, numbered and signed by publisher with his ink notation "Gilt", indicating top edges gilt, this number 94 of 200 special hand numbered copies on Buff California Bond-Paper, out of a total edition of 450.   Argonaut Book Shop   Recent Acquisitions June 2013 - 257   2013 $750

Clappe, Louise Amelia Knapp Smith 1819-1906   *California in 1851. The Letters of Dame Shirley.* San Francisco: Grabhorn Press, 1933. First edition thus, one of 500 copies, 8vo. 2 volumes, bound in cloth backed gray boards, fine set.   Second Life Books Inc.   183 - 72   2013 $95

Clar, C. Raymond *Quarterdecks and Spanish Grants.* Felton: Glenwood Publishers, 1971. First edition, small quarto, illustrations, facsimiles, portraits, plates, maps, blue cloth, fine with lightly rubbed pictorial dust jacket.   Argonaut Book Shop   Summer 2013 - 47   2013 $50

Clare, John 1754-1832   *Poems Descriptive of Rural Life and Scenery.* London: Taylor & Hessey & E. Drury, Stamford, 1820. First edition, half title, 6 line errata slip following contents leaf, 10 pages ads, uncut in original drab boards, paper label, spine little dulled and with wear to hinges, head and tail.   Jarndyce Antiquarian Booksellers   CCIII - 477   2013   £900

Clare, John 1754-1832 *Poems Descriptive of Rural Life and Scenery.* London: Taylor & Hessey & E. Drury Stamford, 1820. First edition, 6 line errata slip following contents leaf, slight spotting to title, expertly & sympathtically rebound in half tan calf, vellum tipped corners, spine ruled gilt, maroon leather label, very good.   Jarndyce Antiquarian Booksellers   CCIII - 478   2013   £1200

Clare, John 1754-1832 *The Rural Muse.* London: Whittaker & Co., 1835. First edition, inserted ad leaf preceding frontispiece and vignette title, occasional spot, original dark green floral patterned cloth, paper label, following board slightly creased at head and with signs of repair to sall split at head of following hinge, overall very good. Jarndyce Antiquarian Booksellers   CCIII - 484   2013   £750

Clare, John 1754-1832 *The Shepherd's Calendar; with Village Stories and other Poems.* London: published for John Taylor by James Duncan, 1827. First edition, half title, engraved frontispiece, cancel title, contemporary full dark blue textured calf, gilt spine and borders, maroon leather labels, excellently rebacked very good.   Jarndyce Antiquarian Booksellers   CCIII - 483   2013   £580

Clare, John 1754-1832 *The Shepherd's Calendar; with Village Stories, and Other Poems.* London: published for John Taylor, Waterloo Place by James Duncan, Paternoster Row and sold by J. A. Hessey 93 Fleet Street, 1827. First edition, 2 pages publisher's ads at back, presentation copy inscribed by author to Mrs. Bellairs, April 30 1827, spine perished, boards somewhat soiled, gatherings bit loose, otherwise good copy with rare inscription, Bradley Martin copy preserved in folding cloth box.   James S. Jaffe Rare Books   Fall 2013 - 32   2013 $8500

Clare, John 1754-1832 *The Village Minstrel and Other Poems.* (with) *Poems Descriptive of Rural Life and Scenery.* London: Taylor & Hessey, 1821. Stamford: E. Drury, 1821. First edition and fourth edition, uniformly bound as "Clare's Poems" in contemporary full purple panelled calf, gilt spines, small chip at head of leading hinge volume 1, hinges and edges little worn, fading to brown in places, contemporary ownership inscription of W. Dawson Kent and armorial bookplates of John A. G. Gere.   Jarndyce Antiquarian Booksellers   CCIII - 480   2013   £850

Clare, John 1754-1832 *The Village Minstrel and Other Poems.* London: Taylor & Hessey, 1821. First edition, 2 volumes, half titles, frontispiece, volume 1, 4 pages ads volume 2, nicely bound in late 19th century half calf, red leather labels, new endpapers, contemporary signature of Mrs. Gallard, very good.   Jarndyce Antiquarian Booksellers   CCIII - 481   2013   £600

Clare, John 1754-1832 *The Village Minstrel and Other Poems.* London: Taylor & Hessey, 1821. First edition, 2 volumes in 1, frontispiece volume 1, contemporary half calf, gilt spine carefully repaired at head and hinges, maroon leather label, armorial bookplate of Richard Oskatel Latham. Jarndyce Antiquarian Booksellers   CCIII - 482   2013   £450

Clare, Tom *Archaeological Sites of the Lake District.* Moorland Publishing, 1981. First edition, original cloth, gilt, dust jacket, pages 159, illustrations.   R. F. G. Hollett & Son   Lake District & Cumbria - 273   2013   £25

Clarendon, Edward Hyde, Earl of *The Life of Edward Earl of Clarendon, Lord High Chancellor of England.* Oxford: at the Clarendon Printing House, 1761. 3 volumes, 8vo., very clean and attractive copy, 19th century half calf, marbled boards, wide multi-ruled gilt bands, gilt monogram, "AJ" at head of each spine.   Jarndyce Antiquarian Booksellers   CCIV - 93   2013   £320

Clark, Ann *Ridge Porcupine.* U.S. Office of Indian Affairs, 1940. 1941 on titlepage, Oblong 4to., cloth backed pictorial wrappers, 42 pages, slight soil, very good, lovely illustrations by Andrew Standing Soldier.   Aleph-Bet Books, Inc.   105 - 335   2013 $125

Clark, Ann Nolan *Looking for Something.* New York: Viking, 1952. First edition, 8vo., cloth, fine in slightly worn dust jacket, beautifully illustrated in color by Leo Politi, special copy with watercolor of burro and embellished inscription.   Aleph-Bet Books, Inc.   104 - 432   2013 $400

Clark, David R. *W. B. Yeats and the Theatre of Desolate Reality.* Dublin: Dolmen Press, 1964. Proof copy, 8vo., original sand wrappers. excellent.   Maggs Bros. Ltd.   1442 - 63   2013   £150

Clark, Jeff *Sun on 6.* Calais: Z Press, 2000. First edition, one of 26 lettered copies signed by Clark, with tipped in original linocut in black, grey and beige, numbered and signed by Jasper Johns in pencil, there were an additional (200 unsigned copies, without linocut), sewn in original wrappers with label on front cover, overall size 9.75 x 6.75 inches, set in Bembo type printed on handmade papers, as new.   Gemini Fine Books & Arts., Ltd.   Art Reference & Illustrated Books - 2013 $3000

Clark, John Willis *The Life and Letters of the Rev. Adam Sedgwick, LL.D....* Cambridge: University Press, 1890. First edition, 2 volumes, large 8vo., original brown cloth gilt, spines little frayed at head and foot, 1 cm. hole to backstrip of volume 2, 2 frontispiece portraits, 2 colored geological maps and other plates and illustrations, one joint cracked. R. F. G. Hollett & Son   Lake District & Cumbria - 275   2013   £180

Clark, John Willis *The Life and Letters of The Rev. Adam Sedgwick, LL.D...* Gregg International Pub., 1970. Facsimile edition, 2 volumes, original cloth, gilt, 2 frontispiece portraits, 2 folding maps and other plates and illustrations. R. F. G. Hollett & Son Lake District & Cumbria - 276 2013 £75

Clark, Kenneth *The Nude. A Study of Ideal Art.* London: John Murray, 1956. First edition, small 4to., original red cloth, excellent copy, inscribed by John Betjeman to his wife Penelope Chetwoad. Maggs Bros. Ltd. 1460 - 95 2013 £500

Clark, Larry *Tulsa.* New York: Self published, 1971. First edition, black cloth covered boards with silver title to spine, black dust jacket with photo illustration to front panel, minor wear to jacket along edges and light rubbing to rear panel, previous owner signature, otherwise interior very clean and bright, unpaginated. The Kelmscott Bookshop 7 - 90 2013 $350

Clark, LaVerne Harrell *They Sang for Horses: The Impact of the Horse on Navajo and Apache Folklore.* Tucson: University of Arizona, 1966. First edition, quarto, illustrations by De Grazia, fine in fine dust jacket. Between the Covers Rare Books, Inc. Horses, Horsemanship, Horse Racing, Etc. - 53269 2013 $125

Clark, Mary Senior *Sing a Song of Sixpence Another Lost Legend.* Boston: Geo. H. Ellis, 1902. First edition, 8vo., blue cloth, 8 illustrations by Lear, extremities worn, very good. Barnaby Rudge Booksellers Children 2013 - 021494 2013 $50

Clark, Robert *Poems on Golf.* Edinburgh: printed (by Robert Clark) for private circulation, 1867. First edition, 8vo., fine armorial binding of full dark green horizontal ribbed 19th century crushed morocco by Zaehnsdorf (original green cloth covers and spine bound in), gilt Lion rampant in center of both covers, around each of which are 24 gilt thistle badges, spine gilt, raised bands, light green silk moire endpapers and free halves of endpapers, large gilt stamped heraldic devices of Robert Tyndall Hamilton Bruce, all edges gilt, fine copies as here are rarely found. Howard S. Mott Inc. 262 - 63 2013 $4000

Clark, Stephen *The Lake View Saga 1837-1974.* Chicago: Lake View Trust & Savings Bank, 1974. First edition, fine, blue cloth stamped in silver, issued without dust jacket, original wrappers bound in, 4to., 80 pages. Beasley Books 2013 - 2013 $65

Clark, Sterling B. F. *How Many Miles from St. Jo? the Log of Sterling B. F. Clark a Forty Niner.* San Francisco: privately printed, 1929. First edition, 12mo., 56 pages, illustrations, maroon cloth backed boards, pictorial pastedown on front cover, fine. Argonaut Book Shop Summer 2013 - 48 2013 $60

Clark, Sue Ainslie *Making both Ends Meet: The Income and Outlay of New York Working Girls.* New York: Macmillan, 1911. First edition, 8vo., 270 pages, nice, frontispiece photo, from the library of reformer Florence Kelley (1859-1932), inscribed by Edith Wyatt to Kelley. Second Life Books Inc. 182 - 41 2013 $65

Clark, Willard *Recuerdos de Santa Fe 1928-1943.* Santa Fe: 1990. frontispiece, block prints, no dust jacket issued, brown leatherette with printed title block, boards lightly soiled, spot title block, internally bright and near fine, inscribed by author to previous owner. Dumont Maps & Books of the West 124 - 55 2013 $95

Clark, Willene B. *Beasts and Birds of the Middle Ages: the Bestiary and Its Legacy.* Philadelphia: University of Pennsylvania Press, 1989. 8vo., x, 224 pages, red cloth, gilt stamped spine title, dust jacket, ownership signature, fine. Jeff Weber Rare Books 169 - 69 2013 $60

Clark, William *Ladies' Society Book for Promoting the Early Education of Negro Children.* London: Edward Sutter, 1833. Folio, 6 aquatints, 20th century morocco, title gilt in upper board, 128 tipped onto stubbs, last leaf in facsimile, rare. Maggs Bros. Ltd. 1467 - 3 2013 £2200

Clarke, A. V. *Cybernetic Controller.* London: Panther Books printed in Great Britain and pub. by Hamilton & Co., 1952. First edition, octavo, pictorial wrappers. L. W. Currey, Inc. Uptopian Literature: Recent Acquisitions (April 2013) - 139088 2013 $100

Clarke, Arthur C. *Against the Fall of Night.* New York: Gnome Press, 1953. First edition, octavo, boards. L. W. Currey, Inc. Utopian Literature: Recent Acquisitions (April 2013) - 140794 2013 $250

Clarke, Arthur C. *Against the Fall of Night.* New York: Gnome Press Inc., 1953. First edition, octavo, boards. L. W. Currey, Inc. Utopian Literature: Recent Acquisitions (April 2013) - 140044 2013 $1500

Clarke, Arthur C. *Astounding Days: a Science Fictional Autobiography.* London: Victor Gollancz, 1989. First edition, fine in fine dust jacket, signed by author, additionally inscribed by him on titlepage to his protege and one time secretary and longtime friend Ian Macauley, splendid association copy. Between the Covers Rare Books, Inc. Sci-Fi, Fantasy & Horror - 312490 2013 $850

Clarke, Arthur C. *Childhood's End.* New York: Ballantine Books, 1953. First edition, octavo, cloth. L. W. Currey, Inc. Utopian Literature: Recent Acquisitions (April 2013) - 138776 2013 $1000

Clarke, Arthur C. *A Fall of Moondust.* New York: Harcourt Brace and World, 1961. First edition, modest edgewear, nice, very good in near very good dust jacket with some wear and tear, mild stain on rear panel, nicely inscribed by author.   Between the Covers Rare Books, Inc. Sci-Fi, Fantasy & Horror - 63764   2013 $750

Clarke, Arthur C. *The Fountains of Paradise.* London: Victor Gollancz, 1979. First edition, octavo, boards.   L. W. Currey, Inc.   Fall Sampler Sept. 2013 - 145511   2013 $450

Clarke, Arthur C. *Rendezvous with Rama.* New York: Harcourt Brace Jovanovich, 1973. First US edition, octavo, cloth.   L. W. Currey, Inc.   Fall Sampler Sept. 2013 - 145518   2013 $100

Clarke, Austin   1896-1974   *The Bright Temptation.* London: George Allen & Unwin, 1932. First edition, 8vo., original green cloth, dust jacket (browned on spine and rubbed at head and tail of spine), excellent copy.   Maggs Bros. Ltd.   1442 - 37   2013   £225

Clarke, Austin   1896-1974   *Flight to Africa.* Dublin: Dolmen Press, 1963. Proof copy, original beige wrappers printed in brown, yapp edges slightly creased, otherwise near fine, form the library of Richard Murphy, signed by him.   Maggs Bros. Ltd.   1442 - 38   2013   £125

Clarke, Austin   1896-1974   *The Sun Dances at Easter.* 1952. First edition, lack front flyleaf and half title, good.   C. P. Hyland   261 - 190   2013   £75

Clarke, Desmond M.   *Occult Powers and Hypotheses: Cartesian Natural Philosophy Under Louis XIV.* Oxford: Clarendon Press, 1989. 8vo., 265 pages, navy cloth, gilt stamped spine title, dust jacket, ownership signature, fine.   Jeff Weber Rare Books   169 - 71   2013 $75

Clarke, Dwight L.   *Stephen Watts Kearny: Solider of the West.* Norman: University of Oklahoma Press, 1961. First edition, xv, 448 pages, numerous illustrations, map, gray cloth, fine.   Argonaut Book Shop   Summer 2013 - 49   2013 $60

Clarke, Edward Daniel   *The Life and Remains of the Rev. Edward Daniel Clarke, LLD.* London: printed for George Cowie and Co., 1824. First edition, 4to., some foxing to frontispiece, titlepage and subscriber list, contemporary sprinkled calf, gilt ruled border, attractive gilt decorated spine, red morocco label, expert repairs to hinges, corners and head and tail of spine, armorial bookplate of William Harrison.   Jarndyce Antiquarian Booksellers   CCIV - 94   2013   £380

Clarke, Edwin   *The Human Brain and Spinal Cord.* Berkeley: University of California Press, 1968. 925 pages, large thick 8vo., original cloth, worn and torn dust jacket present.   James Tait Goodrich   75 - 49   2013 $225

Clarke, Edwin   *An Illustrated History of Brain Function.* UC Press, 1972. 154 pages, numerous illustrations, 4to. in dust jacket with some light wear, signed by Kenneth Dewhurst.   James Tait Goodrich   75 - 48   2013 $225

Clarke, Edwin   *Nineteenth Century Origins of Neuroscientific Concepts.* Los Angeles: 1987. 593 pages, rubberstamp ownership markings, very good, original binding.   James Tait Goodrich   S74 - 46   2013 $85

Clarke, H. L.   *History of Sedbergh School 1525-1925.* Sedbergh: Jackson & Son, 1925. Variant, possibly remainder binding of chocolate brown cloth gilt, top edge gilt, plan and graph.   R. F. G. Hollett & Son   Lake District & Cumbria - 278   2013   £45

Clarke, H. L.   *History of Sedbergh School 1525-1925.* Sedbergh: Jackson & Son, 1925. First (limp) edition, original printed wrappers with yapp edges, pages 224 uncut and partly unopened, with plan and graph.   R. F. G. Hollett & Son   Lake District & Cumbria - 277   2013   £35

Clarke, H. L.   *History of Sedbergh School 1525-1925.* Sedbergh: Jackson & Son, 1925. First edition, in standard original brown buckram gilt, top edge gilt, plan, graph, flyleaves little spotted.   R. F. G. Hollett & Son   Lake District & Cumbria - 279   2013   £45

Clarke, James   *History of Cricket in Kendal from 1836 to 1905.* Kendal: printed by Thompson Brothers, 1906. First edition, original green cloth gilt, illustrations, first few leaves little crinkled in gutters, scarce.   R. F. G. Hollett & Son   Lake District & Cumbria - 280   2013   £75

Clarke, James   *History of Football in Kendal from 1871 to 1908.* Kendal: printed by Thompson Brothers, 1908. First (only) edition, original green cloth gilt, spine lettered in blind, numerous plates and portraits, 2 sections shaken rather loose and edges little chipped, otherwise very good, very scarce.   R. F. G. Hollett & Son   Lake District & Cumbria - 281   2013   £95

Clarke, James   *A Survey of the Lakes of Cumberland, Westmorland and Lancashire...* printed for the author, 1789. Second edition, tall folio full diced calf gilt with gilt rule borders, edges rather worn, rebacked in polished calf gilt, one small scrape, 11 large folding plans and maps, few small creases or repairs to back of maps as usual, excellent uncut, clean and sound copy, maps tipped on to guards for easier opening, several printed on heavy paper, armorial bookplate of John Towneley (relaid).   R. F. G. Hollett & Son   Lake District & Cumbria - 282   2013   £1500

Clarke, James I. C. *My Life and Memories.* London: 1926. First edition, illustrations, cloth, very good.   C. P. Hyland   261 - 191   2013   £35

Clarke, John *An Essay Upon the Education of Youth in Grammar Schools.* printed for Arthur Bettesworth, 1730. Second edition, minor staining from turn-ins affecting first few leaves at either end, tiny bit of worming in lower margins of last few leaves, 12mo., contemporary panelled sheep, plain spine, minor wear to extremities.   Blackwell's Rare Books   B174 - 33   2013   £550

Clarke, John *An Introduction to the Making of Latin.* printed by M. Brown for J. and C. Rivington etc., 1787. Twenty fifth edition, contemporary sheep, lacks front flyleaf, juvenile scribbling to pastedowns, title little soiled, few spots and stains.   R. F. G. Hollett & Son   Children's Books - 129   2013   £40

Clarke, Joseph Wilkinson *Mr. John MacKenzyes Narrative of the Siege of London-Derry a False Libel, in Defence of Dr. George Walker...* R. Simpson, 1690. First edition, 2 + 18 pages, original marbled paper wrappers, good, very rare.   C. P. Hyland   261 - 192   2013   £750

Clarke, Judith *Penrith.* Eden District Council, n.d. circa, 2000. First edition, tall 4to., original pictorial boards, matching dust jacket, pages 160, illustrations in color and tint.   R. F. G. Hollett & Son   Lake District & Cumbria - 284   2013   £25

Clarke, Lewis *Narrative of the Sufferings of Lewis Clarke, during a Captivity of the Sufferings of Lewis Clarke, During a Captivity of more than Twenty-five Years...* Boston: David H. Ela, 1845. First edition, 8vo., 108 pages, frontispiece, original printed wrappers, slight fraying to wrappers, in two part slipcase, very fare in original wrappers.   M & S Rare Books, Inc.   95 - 24   2013 $1250

Clarke, Mary Anne *The Rival Princes or a Faithful Narrative of Facts Relating to Mrs. Clarke's Political Acquaintance with Col. Wardle...* London: printed for the author, 1810. First edition, 8vo., bound with half titles, three quarter morocco and marbled boards (little rubbed), very good, frontispiece, signed by author.   Second Life Books Inc.   183 - 74   2013 $300

Clarke, Samuel 1675-1729 *A Collection of Papers, Which Passed Between the Late Learned Mr. Leibnitz and Dr. Clarke in the Years 1715 and 1716.* London: James Knapton, 1717. First edition, 8vo., headpieces, decorative initials, tailpieces, 2 figures, occasional spotting, contemporary paneled calf, raised bands, blindstamped spine title, outer hinge starting, early 19th century engraving of lady mounted on front pastedown, ownership signature of Robert Orr, very good.   Jeff Weber Rare Books   169 - 68   2013 $1300

Clarke, Thomas *Specimens of the Dialects of Westmorland.* Kendal: Atkinson & Pollitt, 1879. Small 8vo., original printed wrappers, little worn, 52 pages.   R. F. G. Hollett & Son   Lake District & Cumbria - 286   2013   £30

Clarke, Thomas *Specimens of the Dialects of Westmorland.* Kendal: Atkinson & Pollitt, 1887. 3 parts in 1, binder's cloth, pages 52, 52, 48.   R. F. G. Hollett & Son   Lake District & Cumbria - 285   2013   £65

Clarke, Thomas *Specimens of the Dialects of Westmorland. Part the Third.* Kendal: Atkinson & Pollitt, 1924. Original printed wrappers, 48 pages.   R. F. G. Hollett & Son   Lake District & Cumbria - 287   2013   £25

Clarkson, Christopher *The History of Richmond...* Richmond: T. Bowman, 1814. 8vo., 436 pages, frontispiece, 3 plates, very good, full contemporary calf, gilt, spine little rubbed, some slight foxing, scarce.   Ken Spelman Books Ltd.   73 - 140   2013   £160

Clarkson, Thomas *Thoughts on the Necessity of Improving the Condition of the Slaves in the British Colonies, with a View to Their Ultimate Emancipation.* London: Richard Taylor, 1823. First edition, 8vo., removed, stamp on verso of title, else very good.   M & S Rare Books, Inc.   95 - 73   2013 $225

Classics Written by the Goddess of Mercy. Tokyo: National Treasure, n.d., 9.4 x 3.8cm., scroll, housed in wooden box bound with ribbon, unpaginated, from the collection of Donn W. Sanford.   Oak Knoll Books   303 - 97   2013 $250

Clater, Francis *Every Man His Own Farrier; or the Whole Art of Farriery Lid Open...* Newark: printed by and for A. Tomlinson, 1803. Fifteenth edition, half title, 8vo., some light foxing, later 19th century half calf, marbled boards, bookplate removed from pastedown.   Jarndyce Antiquarian Booksellers   CCIV - 95   2013   £125

Claudianus, Claudius *Quae Exstant.* Ludguni Batavorum: Ex Officina Elzeviriana, 1650. 12mo., titlepage engraved, lightly browned, some spotting, one or two marginal ink notes, contemporary vellum boards, long sides overlapping, a bit soiled, Monogram stamp to margin of titlepage, 19th century note to front endpaper.   Unsworths Antiquarian Booksellers   28 - 10   2013   £150

Clay, John *My Life on the Range.* Norman: University of Oklahoma Press, 1962. New edition, first printing, frontispiece, 17 photos on 15 plates, tan cloth, very fine, pictorial dust jacket.   Argonaut Book Shop   Summer 2013 - 50   2013 $175

Clayton, J. W. *The Sunny South; an Autumn in Spain and Majoraca.* London: Hurst and Blackett, 1869. First edition, 8vo., pages xii, 332, frontispiece, original purple cloth, spine sunned, very clean internally. J. & S. L. Bonham Antiquarian Booksellers Europe - 9735 2013 £220

Clearwater, Rudi Fuchs *Julian Schnabel. Versions of Chuck and Other Words.* Derneburg: 2007. First edition, 4to, 206 pages, fine, in fine dust jacket, inscribed and dated by Schanbel. By the Book, L. C. 36 - 22 2013 $400

Cleaver, Eldridge *Soul on Ice.* New York: Ramparts/McGraw Hill, 1968. First edition, fine in very near fine dust jacket with two very short tears, Advance review copy with slip laid in. Between the Covers Rare Books, Inc. 165 - 115 2013 $200

Cleland, Robert Glass *The Irvine Ranch of Orange County 1810-1950.* San Marino: Huntington Library, 1952. First edition, 15 photo plates, gilt lettered brown cloth, fine with printed dust jacket. Argonaut Book Shop Recent Acquisitions June 2013 - 64 2013 $60

Clemens, Samuel Langhorne 1835-1910 *Adventures of Huckleberry Finn.* New York: Charles L. Webster & Co., 1885. First American edition, later issue with page 13, illustration captioned "Him and another Man" correctly listed at page 87, on page 57, eleventh line from bottom reads "with the saw"; on page 155, the final "5" extends below line of figures that precede it and frontispiece is Blanck's third state with imprint of the Photo-Gravure Company, octavo, frontispiece inserted, text illustrations by C. W. Kemble, original green cloth, pictorial stamped and lettered in black and gilt on front cover and spine, gilt exceptionally bright, top edge of spine bit frayed, corners lightly bumped, some light staining to fore-edge, overall very good. Heritage Book Shop Holiday Catalogue 2012 - 151 2013 $1250

Clemens, Samuel Langhorne 1835-1910 *Adventures of Huckleberry Finn.* New York: Charles L. Webster and Co., 1885. First American edition, later issue, octavo, frontispiece with tissue guard, wood engraved text illustrations, original dark green cloth pictorially stamped and lettered gilt and black, original pale peach endpapers, at one time there was a slip of paper inserted between frontispiece and frontispiece portrait which has left faint brown mark in gutter, affecting tissue guard for portrait and frontispiece, otherwise as fine a copy as you could wish for, absolutely bright and fresh, quarter green morocco clamshell case. David Brass Rare Books, Inc. Holiday 2012 Chapter Five - DB 00568 2013 $9500

Clemens, Samuel Langhorne 1835-1910 *The Adventures of Tom Sawyer.* Hartford: American Pub. Co., 1876. First American edition, first printing on wove paper with half title and frontispiece printed on separate leaves, 8vo., original gilt and black decorated blue cloth, quarter inch repairs top and bottom of spine, inner hinges strengthened, minor soiling, couple of small stains and corners, frontispiece, minor stains on pages 107-111, morocco backed cloth slipcase. Howard S. Mott Inc. 262 - 34 2013 $5000

Clemens, Samuel Langhorne 1835-1910 *A Double Barrelled Detective Story.* New York: Harper, 1902. First edition, one of 7 plates missing, spine slightly darkened, small stain on back cover otherwise near fine in red cloth covered boards with gilt top page edges. Mordida Books 81 - 522 2013 $250

Clemens, Samuel Langhorne 1835-1910 *The Innocents Abroad by Mark Twain.* Hartford: American Pub. Co., 1869. First edition, third issue, 8vo., 2 frontispieces, 14 inserted plates, publisher's black cloth, small chip of gilt missing from title on spine, front hinge slightly tender, some soiling to front flyleaf (small pinprick in front endpaper), quite nice, clean copy. Second Life Books Inc. 183 - 76 2013 $750

Clemens, Samuel Langhorne 1835-1910 *Love Letters of Mark Twain.* New York: Harper and Brothers, 1949. Stated first edition, tall 8vo., 374 pages, black cloth, as new in green dust jacket, photo frontispiece, beautiful copy. Aleph-Bet Books, Inc. 105 - 568 2013 $5000

Clemens, Samuel Langhorne 1835-1910 *Mark Twain Compliments the President's Wife.* Boston: Anne & David Bromer, 1984. Limited to 200 numbered copies signed by printer, this one of 150 trade copies, 5. x 4.6 cm., brown cloth, paper cover label inset onto front cover, printed letterpress by Rez' Lignen at his Poote Press, from the collection of Donn W. Sanford. Oak Knoll Books 303 - 68 2013 $100

Clemens, Samuel Langhorne 1835-1910 *Nicodemus Dodge.* San Diego: Ash Ranch Press, 1989. Limited to 52 copies, 26 black bonded leather, gold stamped and numbered, deluxe edition of 26 bound in special printed and goldstamped paper over boards with blue bonded leather spine and slipcase, and matching endpapers, signed by publisher, Don Hildreth, this is a deluxe copy, from the collection of Donn W. Sanford. Oak Knoll Books 303 - 40 2013 $275

Clemens, Samuel Langhorne 1835-1910 *Roughing It.* Hartford: American Pub. Co., 1872. First edition, 2nd state, 8vo., double frontispiece, interleaved with tissue guard, 6 additional leaves of full page plates, text illustrations, black cloth with buff endpapers, small chip out of cloth on spine, couple of small nicks, hinges loose, but clean. Second Life Books Inc. 183 - 77 2013 $750

Clemens, Samuel Langhorne 1835-1910 *"1601" or Conversation at the Social Fireside as It Was in the Time of the Tudors.*   Chicago: Black Cat Press, 1962.   Limited to 400 copies, only 100 bound, of which this copy is thus, 4.9 x 6.9 cm., leather, title gilt stamped on spine and front board, gilt stamped decorative border on front board, decorated endpapers, edges gilt, frontispiece and titlepage decoration engraved on wood by Ben Albert Benson, from the collection of Donn W. Sanford.   Oak Knoll Books   303 - 57   2013 $200

Clement, Hal *Intuit.* Cambridge: The NESFA Press, 1987.   First edition trade issue, fine in fine dust jacket, Between the Covers Rare Books, Inc.   Sci-Fi, Fantasy & Horror - 316299   2013 $50

Cleveland, John *The Idol of the Clownes or Insurrection of Wat the Tyler, with His Priests Baal and Straw...*   London: printed in the year, 1654.   Second edition, small 8vo., (12), 154 pages, full polished calf, spine gilt, edges gilt, by Riviere, without final blank L4, front cover cleanly detached, few very tiny repairs.   Joseph J. Felcone Inc.   English and American Literature to 1800 - 7   2013 $1200

Cleveland, Norman *The Morleys - Young Upstarts on the Southwest Frontier.*   Albuquerque: Calvin Horn, 1971.   First edition, 19 vintage photos, map endpapers, red cloth, very fine, slightly chipped pictorial dust jacket, presentation inscription signed by author.   Argonaut Book Shop   Summer 2013 - 51   2013 $75

Clevenger, S. V. *Spinal Concussion: Surgically Considered as a Cause of Spinal Injury and Neurologically Restricted to Certain Symptom Group...*   Philadelphia: Davis, 1889.   Cloth bit worn, binding tight, internally clean, plates.   James Tait Goodrich   S74 - 47   2013 $495

Clifford, Charles *How to Lower Ships' Boats.*   London: Charles Wilson, 1858.   Fifth thousand, plates, 4 pages endorsements, original dark blue cloth, slightly rubbed and dulled, signs of label removed from leading f.e.p., with folded advertising sheet, Saving Life at Sea, loosely inserted.   Jarndyce Antiquarian Booksellers   CCV - 61   2013   £280

Clifford, D. J. H. *The Diaries of Lady Anne Clifford.*   Alan Sutton, 1990.   Original cloth gilt, dust jacket, 25 plates, 2 tables and map.   R. F. G. Hollett & Son   Lake District & Cumbria - 291   2013   £25

Clifton, Lucille *Good Times.*   New York: Random House, 1969.   First edition, fine in slightly age toned, near fine dust jacket.   Between the Covers Rare Books, Inc.   165 - 116   2013 $85

Cline, Gloria Griffin *Exploring the Great Basin.*   Norman: University of Oklahoma Press, 1963.   First edition, 7 photo reproductions of early maps, 5 text maps, 9 plates and portraits, rust cloth, very fine, pictorial dust jacket, presentation inscription signed by author.   Argonaut Book Shop   Summer 2013 - 52   2013 $60

Clinton, George *Memoirs of the Life and Writings of Lord Byron.*   London: James Robins & Co., 1826.   Frontispiece, plates, few internal spots, contemporary half dark green morocco, spine gilt in compartments, leading hinge weak and repaired with archival tape, little rubbed, armorial bookplate of William E. Ffennell.   Jarndyce Antiquarian Booksellers   CCIII - 361   2013   £120

Clinton, George *Memoirs of the Life and Writings of Lord Byron.*   London: James Robins & Co., 1828.   Reprint, frontispiece, engraved title dated 1824 and plates with some browning and staining, marks in text, contemporary black straight grained morocco, decorated spine, dark green labels, slightly rubbed, signed "W.B. 1831", Renier and earlier booklabels.   Jarndyce Antiquarian Booksellers   CCIII - 362   2013   £80

Clinton, Jane Grey *Happy Hours in an Irish Home.*   Edinburgh: privately printed by William Brown Ltd., 1938.   First edition, large 8vo., original cream cloth lettered gilt, near fine, tipped on is typed label "Hotel Royal Westminster, Menton, France. With love from the author.".   Maggs Bros. Ltd.   1442 - 39   2013   £150

Clive-Bayley, A. M. *Vignettes from Finland.*   London: Sampson Low, 1895.   First edition, 8vo., pages viii, 302, original blue decorative cloth.   J. & S. L. Bonham Antiquarian Booksellers   Europe - 6263   2013   £65

Cloquet, Jules Germain *Manuel d'Anatomie Descriptive du Corps Humain.*   Paris: Chez Bechet Jeune, 1831.   Plate volume only of plates 152 to 300, (text volume and first plate volume not present), tall folio in late 19th century, quarter calf and marbled boards, spine defective with boards off and missing portions of spine, plates have some foxing and browning but overall good to very good internally.   James Tait Goodrich   75 - 50   2013 $595

Close, Chuck *Keith/Six Drawings/1979.*   New York: Lapp Princess Press, 1979.   First edition, softcover, Leporello style book with 12 black and white illustrated panels, very near fine copy in wrappers.   Jeff Hirsch Books   Fall 2013 - 129222   2013 $75

Cloud, C. Carey *The Tale of Peter Rabbit.*   New York: Blue Ribbon Press, 1934.   First edition, 26 full page and black and white illustrations + double page color pop-up picture, 58 pages, color pictorial blue boards, red and black titling, 5 x 3 1/2 inches, extremities little worn, very good, rare.   Ian Hodgkins & Co. Ltd.   134 - 39   2013   £350

Clough, Arthur Hugh *Poems.* Cambridge: Macmillan, 1862. First collected edition, 8vo., original green honeycomb cloth, gilt, minor wear to extremities, good, inscribed by author for Rev'd. R. P. Graves.   Blackwell's Rare Books B174 - 34   2013   £450

Clowes, John *The True Ground of the Present National Danger.* Chester: Printed by C. W. Leadbeater, 1798. 12mo., some soiling, fore-edges browned and slightly browned and slightly frayed.   Blackwell's Rare Books B174 - 35   2013   £400

Clysmic King of Table Waters Booze Book. Waukesha: Cylsmic, n.d., 1910-1919. First edition, 12mo., 32 pages, silk cord tied embossed wrappers, front wrapper and titlepage printed in multiple covers, two short tears at front wrapper, else near fine.   Between the Covers Rare Books, Inc. Cocktails, Etc. - 301607   2013 $300

Coale, Josiah *The Books and Divers Epistles of the Faithful Servant of the Lord Josiah Coale.* London: printed in the year, 1671. First edition, 4to., complete as issued, contemporary calf, neatly rebacked and recornered, later (but old) endpapers, modern bookplate.   Joseph J. Felcone Inc. Books Printed before 1701 - 22   2013 $3000

Coates, James *Bridlington-Quay, a Descriptive Poem.* Scarborough: printed for the author by G. Broadrick, 1813. sewn as issued in original cream wrappers, front wrapper doubles as folding frontispiece map, little fragile but good example of scarce item.   Jarndyce Antiquarian Booksellers CCIII - 660   2013   £125

Coats, James Monro *Diary of a Holiday spent in India, Burmah and Ceylon in the Winter of 1901-1902.* Glasgow: J. Coats privately printed by McCorquodale & Co., 1902. First edition, 8vo., limp tan cloth, 27 black and white photos, compliments card tipped to signed by author, very good, crease to lower corner of front board, boards lightly soiled, light foxing on only few leaves, else contents and plates clean.   Kaaterskill Books   16 - 49   2013 $725

Coatsworth, Elizabeth *The Cat Who Went to Heaven.* New York: Macmillan, 1930. First edition, first printing, 4to., cloth, near fine in dust jacket (mended on back with light stain on joints), illustrations by Lynd Ward, quite scarce in jacket.   Aleph-Bet Books, Inc.   104 - 583   2013 $700

Cobb, Belton *Double Detection.* London: Longmans Green, 1945. First edition, fine in dust jacket with several short closed tears.   Mordida Books   81 - 90   2013 $150

Cobb, Irvin S. *Poindexter, Colored.* New York: George H. Doran, 1922. First edition, fine in near fine dust jacket, spine faded and with faint stain on rear panel, scarce in jacket.   Between the Covers Rare Books, Inc.   165 - 26 2013 $350

Cobbe, Frances Power *Darwinism in Morals and Other Essays.* Williams & Norgate, 1872. First edition of this collection, slightly foxed at either end, 8vo., original smooth green cloth, spine gilt lettered, trifle worn at extremities, inner hinges strained, inscription "Mrs. Waller from Nora, Christmas 1872", good.   Blackwell's Rare Books Sciences - 30   2013   £275

Cobbett, William *Cobbett's Oppression!!* London: printed and published by T. Gillet & sold by Sherwood, Neely & Jones, 1809. 8vo., evidence of original stab holes, some browning, early 20th century cloth, armorial bookplate of Lord Esher and later signature of Michael Foot.   Jarndyce Antiquarian Booksellers   CCIV - 96   2013   £225

Cobbett, William *Democratic Principles Illustrated by Example. Part the First.* London: printed for J. Wright, 1798. Eighth edition, 12mo., outer pages and some leading edges browned, disbound.   Jarndyce Antiquarian Booksellers   CCIV - 97   2013   £75

Cobbett, William *A New Year's Gift to the Democrats; or Observations on a Pamphlet, entitled "A Vindication of Mr. Randolph's Resignation".* Philadelphia: published by Thomas Bradford, 1796. Second edition, some tanning and foxing, early 20th century linen backed boards, armorial bookplate of Lord Esher & later signature of Michael Foot. Jarndyce Antiquarian Booksellers   CCIV - 98   2013   £280

Cobbett, William *Rural Rides in the Counties of Surrey, Kent.* London: William Cobbett, 1830. First edition, 12mo., plate, 12 pages ads, original brown drab boards, carefully rebacked in contemporary pebble grained blue cloth, neat new paper label, contemporary signature in brown ink of George Young of Staines.   Jarndyce Antiquarian Booksellers   CCV - 62   2013   £850

Cobden, Sanderson, Thomas James 1840-1922 *Credo.* London: printed at the Doves Press, 1908. One of 250 copies printed on paper, an additional 12 copies were printed on vellum, contemporary full crushed morocco by Doves Bindery, lettered in gilt on front board and spine, very slightly dulled, otherwise handsome copy, unidentified leather booklabel on leading pastedown, small paper label printed with '63' on following f.e.p., all edges gilt.   Jarndyce Antiquarian Booksellers   CCV - 63   2013   £320

Coblentz, Stanton A. *After 12,000 Years.* Los Angeles: Fantasy Pub. Co., 1950. Uncorrected proof, very short tear on half title, else fine in unprinted wrappers, fine dust jacket, unusually crisp copy and scarce in this format. Between the Covers Rare Books, Inc.   Sci-Fi, Fantasy & Horror - 30511   2013 $400

Coburn, Alvin Langdon *London.* London: New York: Duckworth & Co./Brentano's, 1909. First edition, near fine, original leather backed grey boards, gilt lettering on front board, binding edgewear, 20 hand pulled gravures tipped on heavy grey paper as issued, tipped-on photogravures, scarce, with ALS by Coburn laid in.   By the Book, L. C. 38 - 3   2013 $15,000

Coburn, Alvin Langdon *Men of Mark.* London: New York: Duckworth & Co./Mitchell Kinnerley, 1913. First edition, first printing, 4to., 30 pages, 33 tipped in photogravure plates, each with tissue guard, very good++, original quarter linen cloth covered board binding with gilt lettering front cover, cover mildly soiled, owner inscription, darkening to endpapers due to laid in invitation, laid in is invitation to 1912 exhibition at Blanchard Gallery in LA, scarce.   By the Book, L. C.   36 - 7   2013 $5500

Cockburn, James Pattison *Swiss Scenery.* London: Rodwell & Martin, 1820. First edition, quarto, 200 pages, vignette on titlepage and page 200, 60 steel engravings, original green decorative morocco, gilt, joints and corners rubbed, light foxing to prelims, good.   J. & S. L. Bonham Antiquarian Booksellers   Europe - 8851   2013   £550

Cockburn, W. *Profluvia Ventris; or the Nature and Causes of the Loosenesses Plainly Discovered Their Symptoms and Sorts Evidently Settled, the Maxims for Curing...* London: R. Barker, 1701. 12mo., full contemporary paneled calf, skillfully rebacked in calf by Bernard Middleton with new label.   James Tait Goodrich   75 - 53   2013 $495

Cocker, Edward *The Young Clerk's Tutor.* London: William Battersby, 1700. Fourteenth edition, small 8vo., 4 plates, titlepage edges chipped with some lower edge loss, 20th century full dark brown calf, gilt stamped red leather spine labels, extremities faintly rubbed, titlepage ownership signature, good in near fine binding.   Jeff Weber Rare Books   171 - 74   2013 $175

Cockroft, Barry *The Dale that Died.* London: J. M. Dent, 1975. First (only) edition, square 8vo., original cloth gilt, dust jacket, extremities trifle worn, pages 128, illustrations, excellent copy, scarce.   R. F. G. Hollett & Son   Lake District & Cumbria - 295   2013   £100

Cocktail Recipes compiled for Waldorf Liquor Store 111 Montgomery Street San Francisco. San Francisco: Waldorf Liquor Store, n.d., circa, 1948. 12mo., 28 pages, stapled printed wrappers, one pencil check mark in text.   Between the Covers Rare Books, Inc.   Cocktails, Etc. - 312641   2013 $85

Cocteau, Jean *The Eagle Has Two Heads.* London: Vision, 1948. First edition thus, 8vo., original black cloth, dust jacket, near fine, jacket has few small nicks and signs of wear at extremities, inscribed by author.   Maggs Bros. Ltd.   1460 - 174   2013   £500

Cocteau, Jean *Morceaux Choisis. Poemes.* Paris: Librarie Gallimard, 1932. First edition, 8vo., original wrappers, cheap paper browned, otherwise excellent copy in chipped glassine dust jacket, housed in cloth folding box with two leather labels on spine, lettered gilt, inscribed by author for Clive with ink sketch of female face.   Maggs Bros. Ltd.   1460 - 171   2013   £600

Cocteau, Jean *Opium. the Diary of a Cure.* London: Peter Owen, 1957. First edition in English, 8vo., original brown cloth, lettered in gilt, inscribed by author with blue ink sketch of a face, excellent copy.   Maggs Bros. Ltd.   1460 - 175   2013   £500

Cocteau, Jean *Portraits - Souvenir 1900-1914.* Paris: Editions Bernard Grasset, 1935. Reprint, 8vo. original wrappers, near fine in protective folding box, lettered, inscribed by author for Sarah Bernhardt.   Maggs Bros. Ltd.   1460 - 172   2013   £500

Cocteau, Jean *Souvenir de Jean Giraudoux.* Paris: Jacques Haumont, 1946. First edition, one of 1000 numbered copies, 8vo., original wrappers, acetate dust jacket, preserved in folding box, inscribed by author, fine.   Maggs Bros. Ltd.   1460 - 173   2013   £300

Codex Argenteus. Uppsala: Bibliothecae R. Univ. Upsaliensis, n.d. but, 1959. 3.5 x 3cm., silver case with clasps, text loosely inserted, unpaginated, from the collection of Donn W. Sanford.   Oak Knoll Books   303 - 98   2013 $350

Codman & Shurtleff *Catalogue of Dental Furniture Instruments, Implements and Materials for Sale by Codman & Shurtleff...* Boston: 1870. First edition, 8vo., original green cloth, errata, folding plate, nearly fine.   Howard S. Mott Inc.   262 - 148   2013 $500

Coe, Charles Francis *The River Pirate.* New York: G. P. Putnam's Sons, 1928. First edition, small tear on front fly, else fine in good dust jacket with chip at crown and other chips and tears.   Between the Covers Rare Books, Inc.   Mystery & Detective Fiction - 287032   2013 $200

Coe, Jonathan *What a Carve Up!* Viking, 1994. Uncorrected advance proofs, crown 8vo., original pink and grey wrappers, printed in blue and white, near fine.   Blackwell's Rare Books   B174 - 191   2013   £235

Coel, Margaret *Day of Rest.* Clarkston: Mission Viejo: A.S.A.P., First edition, one of 26 lettered copies, signed by author, C. J. Box who wrote introduction and Phil Parks, the artist, fine in purple cloth with paper label and fine plastic slipcase, from the library of Bruce Kahn.   Between the Covers Rare Books, Inc.   Mystery & Detective Fiction - 312263   2013 $250

Coel, Margaret *Dead End.* Royal Oak: Mission Viejo: ASAP, 1997. Of a total of 186 copies, this number 22 of 150 numbered copies, signed by author, artist, Phil Parks and Jamie Doss who provided introduction, inscription by author in Arapaho, color photo frontispiece of Coel tipped in, illustrations by Parks tipped in, minor rubbing to cover graphic and very small spine has bump, near fine, without dust jacket as issued. Ken Lopez Bookseller 159 - 148 2013 $150

Coel, Margaret *The Eagle Catcher.* Boulder: Boulder University Press of Colorado, 1995. First edition, first printing of 2000 copies, fine in fine dust jacket, signed, laid in promotional bookmark and postcard, both signed by author. Leather Stalking Books October 2013 - 2013 $175

Coelho, Paulo *Alchemist.* New York: Harper San Francisco, 1993. First American edition, advance reading copy, author's name misspelled "Coehlo" on front cover, fine in illustrated self wrappers. Ken Lopez Bookseller 159 - 38 2013 $500

Coetzee, J. M. *Age of Iron.* New York: Random House, 1990. Uncorrected proof of first US edition, inscribed by author, recipient's signature and date on first blank, hint of bump at spine base, very near fine in wrappers. Ken Lopez Bookseller 159 - 43 2013 $450

Coetzee, J. M. *Boyhood.* New York: Viking, 1997. First American edition, inscribed by author, recipient's signature on half title, fine in fine dust jacket. Ken Lopez Bookseller 159 - 45 2013 $350

Coetzee, J. M. *Doubling the Point.* Cambridge: Harvard University Press, 1992. Simultaneous softcover issue, inscribed by author, recipient's name and date on half title, front cover lightly splayed, near fine in wrappers,. Ken Lopez Bookseller 159 - 44 2013 $300

Coetzee, J. M. *Dusklands.* Johannesburg: Raven Press, 1974. First edition, original cloth, gilt, dust jacket, very slight creasing to lower panel, short edge tear to final leaf, else near fine, very scarce. R. F. G. Hollett & Son Africana - 39 2013 £450

Coetzee, J. M. *Elizabeth Costello.* New York: Viking, 2003. First American edition, signed by author, blue cloth backed paper covered boards with white title to spine, fine blue illustrated dust jacket with orange title to spine, 233 pages. The Kelmscott Bookshop 7 - 100 2013 $250

Coetzee, J. M. *Foe.* Toronto: Stoddard, 1986. First Canadian edition, signed by author, owner signature, stamp "Review Copy - Not for Resale", fine in near fine dust jacket with lamination peeling at top edge of front panel, review slip laid in. Ken Lopez Bookseller 159 - 41 2013 $300

Coetzee, J. M. *Life and Times of Michael K.* New York: Viking, 1984. First American edition, review copy, signed by author beneath owner signature, 3 small dots to fore edge of one page, else fine in fine dust jacket with review slip and author photo laid in, uncommon advance copy. Ken Lopez Bookseller 159 - 40 2013 $400

Coetzee, J. M. *The Lives of Animals.* Princeton: Princeton University Press, 1999. First edition, inscribed by author, recipient's dated signature on endpaper, fine in fine dust jacket, uncommon signed. Ken Lopez Bookseller 159 - 46 2013 $350

Coetzee, J. M. *A Land Apart. A South African Reader.* London: Faber and Faber, 1986. Uncorrected proof copy, signed by Coetzee and co-editor Andre Brink, owner signature, near fine in wrappers, uncommon proof, rare. Ken Lopez Bookseller 159 - 48 2013 $500

Coetzee, J. M. *Stranger Shores. Essays 1986-1999.* London: Secker & Warburg, 2001. First edition, inscribed by author, recipient's signature, fine in fine dust jacket. Ken Lopez Bookseller 159 - 47 2013 $375

Coetzee, J. M. *Waiting for the Barbarians.* New York: Penguin, 1982. First American edition, review copy, inscribed by author in 1994, recipient's signature, several small cover creases, near fine in wrappers, publicity letter from Penguin Books Canada laid in, uncommon advance copy. Ken Lopez Bookseller 159 - 39 2013 $500

Coetzee, J. M. *White Writing. On the Culture of Letters in South Africa.* New Haven: Yale University Press, 1988. First edition, inscribed by author, recipient's dated signature, fine in very near fine dust jacket with bit of spine fading, uncommon book, especially signed. Ken Lopez Bookseller 159 - 42 2013 $500

Coffin, Charles Carleton *The Seat of Empire.* Boston: 1871. vii, 232 pages, (11 pages ads), large folding map, slight wear to extremities and fraying of cloth on top of spine, else very good, some separations on folds of map and repaired tear, but complete and bright. Dumont Maps & Books of the West 122 - 48 2013 $120

Cogan, Sara G. *The Jews of San Francisco and the Greater Bay Area 1849-1919.* Berkeley: Western Jewish History Center, 1973. First edition, one of 500 copies, frontispiece, light blue cloth, gilt, very fine. Argonaut Book Shop Summer 2013 - 53 2013 $75

Cogan, Sara G. *Pioneer Jews of the California Mother Lode 1849-1880.* Berkeley: Western Jewish History Center, 1968. First edition, frontispiece, black cloth, gilt, bookplate, very fine. Argonaut Book Shop Summer 2013 - 54 2013 $75

Cogan, Thomas *The Haven of Health, Chiefly Made for the Comfort of Students and Consequently for All Those that Have a Care of their Health, Amplified Upon Fine Words of Hippocrates...* London: printed by Melch. Bradwood for John Norton, 1605. 4to., later 19th century cat's Paw calf, text foxed in parts with some staining on title, also a couple of index leaves, also have some brown staining, final leaf is photo facsimile done nicely on old paper.   James Tait Goodrich   75 - 54   2013 $1895

Cogniard, Hippolyte *Byron a l'Ecole d'Harrow, Episode Mele de Couplets...* Paris: J. Breaute, 1834. 24mo., contemporary full green marbled morocco, wheat sheaf device of Lord Houghton in gilt on upper board, armorial booklabel of Marquis of Crewe, all edges gilt, very good, attractive copy.   Jarndyce Antiquarian Booksellers   CCIII - 364   2013   £450

Cohen, Bernard I. *Introduction to Newton's "Principia".* Cambridge: University Press, 1971. Large 8vo., 16 plates, navy blue cloth, gilt stamped spine, dust jacket, Burndy Library bookplate, fine.   Jeff Weber Rare Books   169 - 320   2013 $100

Cohen, Ira *7 Marvels.* Kathmandu: Bardo Matrix, 1975. Limited edition, small 4to., softcover, loose sheets in folder with pocket, woodblock prints, on rice paper, very good.   Beasley Books   2013 - 2013 $100

Cohen, Octavius Roy *Jim Hanvey Detective.* New York: Dodd, Mead and Co., 1923. First edition, 12mo., original green cloth, slightly cocked and little rubbed, 283 pages, mildly browned, inscribed in pencil "For Dannay 10/1/42 sorry it is read out of shape. J.S" in Fred Dannay's hand.   Howard S. Mott Inc.   262 - 33   2013 $150

Cohen, Paul E. *Mapping the West. America's Westward Movement 1524-1890.* New York: Rizzoli International Pub., 2002. First edition, quarto, 208 pages, color reproductions, brown cloth, embossed and gilt lettered, very fine, pictorial dust jacket.   Argonaut Book Shop   Recent Acquisitions June 2013 - 66   2013 $75

Cohodas, Nadine *Spinning Blues into Gold the Chess Records.* New York: St. Martin's Press, 2000. First edition, inscribed by author, fine in fine dust jacket, 8vo, 358 pages.   Beasley Books   2013 - 2013 $60

Cohoe *A Cheyenne Sketchbook.* Norman: University of Oklahoma Press, 1964. First edition, two-tone cloth, very fine, pictorial dust jacket.   Argonaut Book Shop   Summer 2013 - 55   2013 $50

Coke, Edward *The Compleate Copy-Holder Wherein is Contained a Learned Discourse of the Antiquity and Nature of Manors and Copy-holds...* London: for Matthew Walbanck and Richard Best, 1644. Second edition, neat modern full calf, period style, worm trail toward end of text but confined largely to margin, margins close on titlepage, but ample, else very good.   Joseph J. Felcone Inc.   Books Printed before 1701 - 23   2013 $750

Colden, Cadwallader D. *Memoir... at the Celebration of the Completion of the New York Canals. (and) Appendix... (and) Narrative of the Festivities Observed in Honor of the Completion of the Grand Erie Canal...* New York: W. A. Davis, 1825. 1826. 1825. First edition, 4to., maps, lithographic plates, portraits, complete old marbled boards, rebacked, presentation inscription from Recorder of NY, Richard Riker.   M & S Rare Books, Inc.   95 - 258   2013 $2250

Cole, F. J. *Early Theories of Sexual Generation.* Oxford: Oxford University Press, 1930. First edition, very good+, mild cover edge war, minimal scuffs and stains to covers, small owner bookplate to front pastedown, minimal foxing to edges and endpapers, 8vo.   By the Book, L. C.   37 - 11   2013 $250

Cole, J. A. *Prince of Spies, Henri Le Caron.* London: Faber, 1984. First edition, 221 pages, 8vo., cloth, dust jacket, mint.   C. P. Hyland   261 - 547   2013   £35

Cole, Richard L. *The Cole Family of Carbery.* Bell & Logan, 1943. 24 pages, 1 page typescript tipped in o blank endpaper bringing family up to date to 1st Jan. 1956, very good.   C. P. Hyland   261 - 383   2013   £75

Cole, Robert William *The Struggle for Empire: a Story of the Year 2236.* London: Elliot Stock, 1900. First edition, octavo, original dark olive green cloth, front and spine panels stamped in gold, black coated endpapers, all edges untrimmed.   L. W. Currey, Inc.   Utopian Literature: Recent Acquisitions (April 2013) - 139557   2013 $4500

Coleman, McAlister *Eugene V. Debs. A Man Unafraid.* New York: Greenberg, 1930. First edition, owner's name, joints tender (repaired?), very good.   Beasley Books   2013 - 2013 $65

Coleman, R. W. *An Open Letter to the Negro Baptist of the United States of America.* N.P.: The author, circa, 1920. First edition, 32 pages, stapled wrappers, old library stamps, one signature mis-stapled with resultant overhang of a few pages with small tears to edges, very good.   Between the Covers Rare Books, Inc.   165 - 117   2013 $125

Coleman, Satis N. *The Gingerbread Man and Other Songs of Children's Story Book Friends.* John Day Co., 1931. 7 3/4 x 10 3/4 inches, 71 pages, illustrations, buff boards with some wear top and bottom of backstrip and covers lightly soiled, contents slightly shaken, very good. Ian Hodgkins & Co. Ltd. 134 - 53 2013 £45

Coleridge, Hartley *Biographia Borealis; or Lives of Distinguished Northerns.* London: Whitaker, Treacher & Co., 1833. First edition, frontispiece, plates, contemporary half maroon morocco, spine slightly faded, little rubbed, bookplate of Charles Birch Crisp, good plus. Jarndyce Antiquarian Booksellers CCIII - 591 2013 £90

Coleridge, Hartley *Lives of Northern Worthies.* London: Edward Moxon, 1852. New edition, 3 volumes, half titles, final ad leaves, original olive green cloth, boards little marked, spines faded to brown, volume I worn at head. Jarndyce Antiquarian Booksellers CCIII - 592 2013 £95

Coleridge, Mary Elizabeth *Fancy's Following.* Oxford: Daniel Press, 1896. First edition, number 88 of 125 copies, contemporary dark blue crushed morocco, blocked in gilt, signature of L. H. G. Noble on leading blank, top edge gilt, very good. Jarndyce Antiquarian Booksellers CCV - 64 2013 £250

Coleridge, Samuel Taylor 1772-1834 *Aids to Reflection in the Formation of a Manly Character on the Several grounds of Prudence, Morality and Religion...* London: Hurst, Chance & Co., 1831. Second edition, half title, 2 pages ads, uncut in original drab boards, corners bumped, spine and paper label defective, signature of Edward Vansittart Neale on title. Jarndyce Antiquarian Booksellers CCIII - 544 2013 £100

Coleridge, Samuel Taylor 1772-1834 *Aids to Reflection in the Formation of a Manly Character on the Several grounds of Prudence, Morality and Religion...* London: William Pickering, 1836. Third edition, 16 page small format catalog preceding half title, few spots in prelims, original blue cloth, paper label, slightly rubbed, nice, signatures of Robert Vigne and Peter Mann. Jarndyce Antiquarian Booksellers CCIII - 545 2013 £60

Coleridge, Samuel Taylor 1772-1834 *Aids to Reflection in the Formation of a Manly Character on the Several Grounds of Prudence, Morality and Religion...* London: William Pickering, 1836. Third edition, half title, handsomely rebound in quarter calf, red and green labels, new endpapers, very good. Jarndyce Antiquarian Booksellers CCIII - 546 2013 £60

Coleridge, Samuel Taylor 1772-1834 *Aids to Reflection in the Formation of a Manly Character on the Several Grounds of Prudence, Morality and Religion...* London: William Pickering, 1839. Fourth edition, Half title, contemporary plain maroon morocco by Hayday, slightly rubbed, signature of T. K. Leighton, 1842, all edges gilt. Jarndyce Antiquarian Booksellers CCIII - 547 2013 £50

Coleridge, Samuel Taylor 1772-1834 *Aids to Reflection...* London: William Pickering, 1848. Sixth edition, 2 volumes, half titles, slightly later full calf, gilt spines, borders, dentelles, red and green label, gilt monograms on front boards, booklabels of George Milne obscuring previous owner's bookplate, all edges gilt, very good, handsome. Jarndyce Antiquarian Booksellers CCIII - 548 2013 £75

Coleridge, Samuel Taylor 1772-1834 *Aids to Reflection...* London: Edward Moxon, 1854. Seventh edition, half title, contemporary full brown impressed calf, tan and brown leather labels, gilt borders, hinges slightly rubbed, spine dulled and slightly chipped at head. Jarndyce Antiquarian Booksellers CCIII - 549 2013 £45

Coleridge, Samuel Taylor 1772-1834 *The Ancient Mariner and Other Poems.* London: Charles Tilt, 1836. Half title, frontispiece, 2 pages ads, original red watered silk, front board blocked and lettered in gilt, little dulled, spine slightly worn at head and tail, contemporary gift inscription, all edges gilt. Jarndyce Antiquarian Booksellers CCIII - 514 2013 £75

Coleridge, Samuel Taylor 1772-1834 *Biographia Literaria; or Biographical Sketches of My Literary Life and Opinions.* New York: Leavitt, Lord & Co.; Boston: Crocker & Brewster, 1834. Second American edition, 2 volumes in 1, as issued, in original pale blue boards, paper label, pink cloth spine faded and slightly rubbed, signature of A. K. Putnam. Jarndyce Antiquarian Booksellers CCIII - 536 2013 £110

Coleridge, Samuel Taylor 1772-1834 *Biographia Literaria; or Biographical Sketches of My Literary Life and Opinions.* London: William Pickering, 1847. Second edition, 2 volumes, half titles, preceded by 8 page catalog Jana. 1852 volume I, unopened in original brown cloth, spines chipped at head, armorial bookplates by Joseph Jones. Jarndyce Antiquarian Booksellers CCIII - 537 2013 £60

Coleridge, Samuel Taylor 1772-1834 *Biographia Literaria; or Biographical Sketches of My Literary Life and Opinions and Two Lay Sermons.* London: Bell and Daldy, 1870. New edition, original red cloth, bevelled boards, generally darkened. Jarndyce Antiquarian Booksellers CCIII - 538 2013 £25

Coleridge, Samuel Taylor 1772-1834 *Christabel; Kubla Khan, a Vision; the Pains of Sleep.* London: John Murray, 1816. First edition, half title, expertly bound in appropriate quarter calf, marbled boards, vellum tipped corners, dark green leather label, very good, handsome.   Jarndyce Antiquarian Booksellers   CCIII - 529   2013   £2000

Coleridge, Samuel Taylor 1772-1834 *Christabel; Kubla Khan, a Vision; the Pains of Sleep.* London: printed for John Murray by William Bulmer & Co., 1816. Second edition, half title, slight spotting in prelims, attractively bound in mid 19th century royal blue wavy grained cloth, blocked with crown and wheat sheaf design in silver, spine carefully replaced with plain blue cloth, slightly dulled and rubbed, good plus.   Jarndyce Antiquarian Booksellers   CCIII - 530   2013   £500

Coleridge, Samuel Taylor 1772-1834 *Christabel; Kubla Khan, a Vision; the Pains of Sleep.* London: Sampson, Low Son & Marston, 1878. New edition, half title, title printed in red and black, original blue cloth blocked in black, lettered gilt, spine dulled boards affected by damp and slightly marked, all edges gilt.   Jarndyce Antiquarian Booksellers   CCIII - 531   2013   £40

Coleridge, Samuel Taylor 1772-1834 *Christabel: Kubla Khan, a Vision; the Pains of Sleep.* London: John Murray, 1816. First edition, half title, handsomely bound in full scarlet morocco, gilt borders and dentelles, all edges gilt, very good, attractive.   Jarndyce Antiquarian Booksellers   CCIII - 528   2013   £2500

Coleridge, Samuel Taylor 1772-1834 *Conciones Ad Populum. Or Addresses to the People.* n.p.: 1795. Name cut from head of titlepage, neatly repaired with appropriate paper, contemporary half calf, spine rubbed and little worn at head and tail, good, sound copy, extremely scarce.   Jarndyce Antiquarian Booksellers   CCIII - 501   2013   £1500

Coleridge, Samuel Taylor 1772-1834 *Confessions of an Inquiring Spirit.* London: William Pickering, 1840. First edition, half title, contemporary half black morocco by Hayday, slightly rubbed, top edge gilt, signature and bookplate of Alexander W. Gillman and of Peter Mann 1951.   Jarndyce Antiquarian Booksellers   CCIII - 562   2013   £180

Coleridge, Samuel Taylor 1772-1834 *Confessions of an Inquiring Spirit.* London: William Pickering, 1840. First edition, ad leaf preceding half title, original dark blue cloth, paper label slightly chipped, spine slightly faded, leading hinge cracking, bookplate of Joseph Jones, booksellers ticket, C. Ambery Manchester.   Jarndyce Antiquarian Booksellers   CCIII - 563   2013   £75

Coleridge, Samuel Taylor 1772-1834 *Confessions of an Inquiring Spirit.* Boston: James Munroe & Co., 1841. First American edition, half title, some spotting and unobtrusive dampstaining, recent quarter dark green calf, very good.   Jarndyce Antiquarian Booksellers   CCIII - 564   2013   £60

Coleridge, Samuel Taylor 1772-1834 *Confessions of an Inquiring Spirit.* London: William Pickering, 1849. Second edition, 4 pages ads, lacking leading f.e.p., original dark blue cloth, paper label browned and slightly chipped, edges little damp marked.   Jarndyce Antiquarian Booksellers   CCIII - 565   2013   £70

Coleridge, Samuel Taylor 1772-1834 *The Devil's Walk; a Poem.* London: Marsh & Miller, 1830. First edition, 2nd issue, frontispiece and illustrations by Robert Cruikshank, 3 pages ads, slightly spotted, original drab printed wrappers, spine partially defective, slightly and marked, decent copy.   Jarndyce Antiquarian Booksellers   CCIII - 552   2013   £280

Coleridge, Samuel Taylor 1772-1834 *The Devil's Walk; a Poem.* London: Marsh & Miller, 1830. First edition, First issue, frontispiece and illustrations by Robert Cruikshank, ad on verso of final leaf, contemporary half dark green calf, marbled boards, little rubbed, hinges carefully strengthened, internally very clean.   Jarndyce Antiquarian Booksellers   CCIII - 551   2013   £220

Coleridge, Samuel Taylor 1772-1834 *The Devil's Walk; a Poem.* London: Marsh & Miller, 1830. First edition, first issue, frontispiece and illustrations by Robert Cruikshank, 3 pages ad, engravings on wood, original drab printed wrappers, lacking majority of spine, otherwise very good, first state with blank leaf in place of page 21-22, cancelled in later issues.   Jarndyce Antiquarian Booksellers   CCIII - 550   2013   £280

Coleridge, Samuel Taylor 1772-1834 *The Dramatic Works.* London: Edward Moxon, 1852. First separate edition, half title, frontispiece slightly spotted, contemporary full grained calf, light and dark brown leather labels, single ruled gilt borders, slightly rubbed, small chip at head of spine.   Jarndyce Antiquarian Booksellers   CCIII - 494   2013   £50

Coleridge, Samuel Taylor 1772-1834 *Hints Towards the Formation of a More Comprehensive Theory of Life.* London: John Churchill, 1848. First edition, half title, postscript leaf, original vertical grained purple cloth, blocked in blind, fading to brown and slightly rubbed, signature of Gilbert Chilcot on title, very good, scarce.   Jarndyce Antiquarian Booksellers   CCIII - 566   2013   £180

Coleridge, Samuel Taylor 1772-1834 *Lay Sermons...* London: Edward Moxon, 1852. Third edition, 8 page catalog (Jan. 1852) preceding half title, original brown cloth, very good.   Jarndyce Antiquarian Booksellers   CCIII - 534   2013   £50

Coleridge, Samuel Taylor 1772-1834 *Lay Sermons.* London: Routledge & Kegan Paul, 1972. Half title, frontispiece, plates, original grey cloth, bevelled boards, very good in dust jacket.   Jarndyce Antiquarian Booksellers   CCIII - 535   2013   £50

Coleridge, Samuel Taylor 1772-1834 *Letters from the Lake Poets.* printed for private circulation, West Newman and Co., 1889. First edition, half title, uncut in original olive green cloth, spine lettered in gilt, unevenly faded, otherwise very good.   Jarndyce Antiquarian Booksellers   CCIII - 575   2013   £40

Coleridge, Samuel Taylor 1772-1834 *Collected Letters.* Oxford: Clarendon Press, 1956-1971. First edition, 6 volumes, half titles, frontispieces volumes I, III & V, plates, original maroon cloth, all volumes very good in slightly worn dust jackets, volumes III-VI in clear protective wrappers.   Jarndyce Antiquarian Booksellers   CCIII - 574   2013   £480

Coleridge, Samuel Taylor 1772-1834 *The Literary Remains.* London: William Pickering, 1836-1839. First edition, 4 volumes, half titles, corrigenda slip volume I, slight foxing in prelims volume I caused by loosely inserted engraved portrait, original dark blue cloth, paper labels slightly rubbed.   Jarndyce Antiquarian Booksellers   CCIII - 560   2013   £280

Coleridge, Samuel Taylor 1772-1834 *The Literary Remains.* London: William Pickering, 1836-1839. First edition, 4 volumes, half title volumes II, III and IV, errata slip volume II, occasional mark, small tear to volume I repaired on verso with tape, rebound in 20th century half maroon morocco, very good, signature of Peter Mann, London.   Jarndyce Antiquarian Booksellers   CCIII - 561   2013   £200

Coleridge, Samuel Taylor 1772-1834 *Miscellanies, Aesthetic and Literary: to which is added, the Theory of Life.* London: George Bell & Sons, 1885. First edition, half title, with signature of George R. Noyes 1900, rebound in 19th century quarter dark blue calf, new endpapers, very good.   Jarndyce Antiquarian Booksellers   CCIII - 573   2013   £50

Coleridge, Samuel Taylor 1772-1834 *Notes and Lectures Upon Shakespeare and Some of the Old Poets and Dramatists with Other Literary Remains.* London: William Pickering, 1849. First edition, 2 volumes, original purple cloth, paper labels browned, spines fading to brown and slightly rubbed at heads and tails, armorial bookplates of Joseph James.   Jarndyce Antiquarian Booksellers   CCIII - 567   2013   £75

Coleridge, Samuel Taylor 1772-1834 *Notes on the English Divines.* London: Edward Moxon, 1853. First edition, 2 volumes, half titles, mostly unopened in original bright green pebble grained cloth by Bone and Son, blocked in blind, spines lettered gilt, slightly rubbed, later booklabels, very good.   Jarndyce Antiquarian Booksellers   CCIII - 569   2013   £85

Coleridge, Samuel Taylor 1772-1834 *Notes, Theological, Political and Miscellaneous.*   London: Edward Moxon, 1853. First edition, half title, largely unopened in original vertical grained olive brown cloth, boards and spine bands blocked in blind, little rubbed, endpapers replaced.   Jarndyce Antiquarian Booksellers   CCIII - 570   2013   £65

Coleridge, Samuel Taylor 1772-1834 *Notes, Theological, Political and Miscellaneous.*   London: Edward Moxon, 1853. First edition, 8 page catalog (Nov. 1853), largely unopened in original olive green wavy grained cloth, boards and spine bands blocked in blind, slightly rubbed at head and tail.   Jarndyce Antiquarian Booksellers   CCIII - 571   2013   £75

Coleridge, Samuel Taylor 1772-1834 *Omniana; or Horae Otiosiores.* London: Longman &c., 1812. First edition, 2 volumes, odd spot, small tear from corner of leading f.e.p., contemporary full diced calf, excellent rebacked, slightly rubbed, booklabels of Kathleen Coburn, neat signatures of M. E. Hawkins.   Jarndyce Antiquarian Booksellers   CCIII - 524   2013   £200

Coleridge, Samuel Taylor 1772-1834 *Omniana; or Horae Otiosiores.* Fontwell, Sussex: Centaur Press, 1969. Original dark blue cloth, near fine in price clipped dust jacket.   Jarndyce Antiquarian Booksellers   CCIII - 525   2013   £30

Coleridge, Samuel Taylor 1772-1834 *On the Constitution of Church and State, According to the Idea of Each, with Aid Towards a Right Judgment on the Late Catholic Bill...*   London: Hurst, Chance and Co., 1830. Second edition, contemporary full calf, gilt, little rubbed, very good, inscribed by author for Rev. (Hugh)James Rose, presentation to Henry John Rose by Coleridge.   Jarndyce Antiquarian Booksellers   CCIII - 553   2013   £2000

Coleridge, Samuel Taylor 1772-1834 *On the Constitution of Church and State...* London: William Pickering, 1839. Second edition, half title, some browning in prelims, contemporary full calf, spine gilt in compartments, dark brown leather label, little rubbed, Carlingford armorial bookplate with his signature as Chichester Fortescue, Oxford 1849.   Jarndyce Antiquarian Booksellers   CCIII - 554   2013   £60

Coleridge, Samuel Taylor 1772-1834 *On the Constitution of Church and State...* London: Edward Moxon, 1852. Fourth edition, half title, original dark blue cloth, bevelled boards, front and spine marked, spine slightly dulled.   Jarndyce Antiquarian Booksellers   CCIII - 555   2013   £30

Coleridge, Samuel Taylor 1772-1834 *Osorio: a Tragedy.* London: John Pearson, 1873. First edition, half title, contemporary full tan calf by Bickers & Son, gilt spine, borders and dentelles, maroon and green leather labels, spine slightly chipped at head, hinges rubbed, armorial bookplate of Adeleine Puxley, all edges gilt, fine binding using poor leather, good plus.   Jarndyce Antiquarian Booksellers   CCIII - 527   2013   £85

Coleridge, Samuel Taylor 1772-1834 *Poems.* Bristol: printed by N. Biggs for J. Cottle, and Robinsons, London, 1797. Second edition, expertly rebound in full dark brow speckled calf, red label, very good, handsome.   Jarndyce Antiquarian Booksellers   CCIII - 504   2013   £950

Coleridge, Samuel Taylor 1772-1834 *Poems.* Bristol: printed by N. Biggs for J. Cottle and Robinsons, London, 1797. Second edition, first 3 leaves of prelims and little dusted with minimal worm damage, final leaf pages 278/279 facsimile replacement, slightly later half dark blue calf, marbled boards, spine gilt in compartments, slightly rubbed.   Jarndyce Antiquarian Booksellers   CCIII - 505   2013   £280

Coleridge, Samuel Taylor 1772-1834 *The Poems.* London: Edward Moxon, 1870. New edition, frontispiece slightly damp marked, light spotting in prelims, contemporary full green morocco, slightly rubbed, Eton prize label, 1872, all edges gilt.   Jarndyce Antiquarian Booksellers   CCIII - 496   2013   £35

Coleridge, Samuel Taylor 1772-1834 *The Poems.* London: Bell & Daldy, 1873. half title, frontispiece slightly spotted, original dark green cloth, bevelled boards, spine darkened and slightly rubbed.   Jarndyce Antiquarian Booksellers   CCIII - 497   2013   £25

Coleridge, Samuel Taylor 1772-1834 *Coleridge's Poems.* Westminster: Archibald Constable & Co., 1899. One of 250 copies, half title, ad slip, uncut in original blue cloth, paper label slightly chipped, little dulled.   Jarndyce Antiquarian Booksellers   CCIII - 506   2013   £35

Coleridge, Samuel Taylor 1772-1834 *The Poetical Works.* London: William Pickering, Reprint of 1834 edition, 3 volumes, 16 page catalog in volume 1, original dark blue cloth, paper labels, spine little faded and slightly marked, G. Hamilton booklabels, nice.   Jarndyce Antiquarian Booksellers   CCIII - 492   2013   £90

Coleridge, Samuel Taylor 1772-1834 *The Poetical and Dramatic Works.* London: William Pickering, 1847. 3 volumes, half titles, 4 pages ads volume I, original purple cloth, paper labels slightly rubbed, spines faded with small hole in volume 1.   Jarndyce Antiquarian Booksellers   CCIII - 493   2013   £85

Coleridge, Samuel Taylor 1772-1834 *The Poetical Works.* London: Macmillan & Co., 1893. Half title, frontispiece uncut in original green cloth, following board slightly marked, spine very lightly dulled, signed "A Stradbroke 1894", very good.   Jarndyce Antiquarian Booksellers   CCIII - 499   2013   £30

Coleridge, Samuel Taylor 1772-1834 *Remorse, a Tragedy.* London: printed for W. Pople, 1813. Second edition, handsomely bound in later quarter calf, vellum tipped corners, maroon leather label, very good.   Jarndyce Antiquarian Booksellers   CCIII - 526   2013   £200

Coleridge, Samuel Taylor 1772-1834 *The Rime of the Ancient Mariner.* London: Harrap, 1910. First edition, folio, green gilt pictorial cloth, top edge gilt, others trimmed, small faded area top rear corner, barely visible, else fine in dust jacket (few edge chips), illustrations by Willy Pogany, rare in dust jacket.   Aleph-Bet Books, Inc.   104 - 430   2013 $1400

Coleridge, Samuel Taylor 1772-1834 *The Rime of the Ancient Mariner.* London: George G. Harrap & Co., 1910. First edition with these illustrations, 321 x 235mm., extremely pleasing green crushed morocco gilt, covers with double gilt fillet border, upper cover with inset color plate from book within a printed paper frame, raised bands, spine compartments with leafy gilt frames, marbled endpapers, top edge gilt, other edges rough trimmed, animated color titlepage, ornate boarders framing text, 13 full page illustrations, 20 mounted color plates, all by Willy Pogany; little (natural?) variation in green of morocco, couple of trivial scuffs or nicks to leather, two plates with corner creases but quite excellent copy, binding essentially unworn, interior fresh and clean.   Phillip J. Pirages   63 - 369   2013 $950

Coleridge, Samuel Taylor 1772-1834 *Seven Lectures on Shakespeare and Milton.* London: Chapman and Hall, 1856. First edition, half title, original purple pebble grained cloth by Burn, borders in blind, unevenly faded with slight wear at head of spine.   Jarndyce Antiquarian Booksellers   CCIII - 572   2013   £65

Coleridge, Samuel Taylor 1772-1834 *Shakespeare, Ben Jonson, Beaumont and Fletcher. Notes and Lectures.* Liverpool: Edward Howell, 1881. New edition, half title, final ad leaf, original brown cloth, very slight wear to head and tail of spine.   Jarndyce Antiquarian Booksellers   CCIII - 568   2013   £50

Coleridge, Samuel Taylor   1772-1834   *Sibylline Leaves: a Collection of Poems.*   London: Rest Fenner, 1817.   First edition, half title, expertly rebacked in half calf, spine ruled and with devices in gilt, red leather label, very good.   Jarndyce Antiquarian Booksellers   CCIII - 540   2013   £650

Coleridge, Samuel Taylor   1772-1834   *Specimens of the Table Talk.*   London: John Murray, 1836.   Second edition, frontispiece, slightly damp marked in lower margin, original dark pink cloth, spine fading to brown and little ink spotted, good plus, signature of A. Atherton.   Jarndyce Antiquarian Booksellers   CCIII - 556   2013   £40

Coleridge, Samuel Taylor   1772-1834   *The Statesman's Manual; or the Bible the Best Guide to Political Skill and Foresight... (with) "Blessed are ye that sow beside all Waters!".*   London: Gale & Fenner, 1816.   1817. First editions, some minor internal marks, 2 volumes in 1, 20th century dark green calf, new endpapers, very good.   Jarndyce Antiquarian Booksellers   CCIII - 533   2013   £250

Coleridge, Samuel Taylor   1772-1834   *The Watchman. No. 1-10, Tuesday March 1 1796-Friday May 13 1796.*   Bristol: published by author, pages 291/2 chipped at edges with some loss of text but carefully repaired with appropriate paper, contemporary half calf expertly rebacked, signatures and bookplate of Mary Wood, overall very good, scarce.   Jarndyce Antiquarian Booksellers   CCIII - 502   2013   £3500

Coleridge, Samuel Taylor   1772-1834   *Zapolya: a Christmas Tale.*   London: Rest Fenner, 1817.   First edition, half title, disbound.   Jarndyce Antiquarian Booksellers   CCIII - 542   2013   £180

Coleridge, Samuel Taylor   1772-1834   *Zapolya: a Christmas Tale, in two parts.*   London: Rest Fenner, 1817.   First edition, first 2 leaves, slightly damp marked at head, nicely bound in later tan quarter calf, marbled boards.   Jarndyce Antiquarian Booksellers   CCIII - 541   2013   £250

Coleridge, Sara   *Phantasmion, a Fairy Tale.*   London: Henry S. King & Co., 1874.   Second edition, 3 pages ads + 39 page catalog (Feb. 1874), some spotting in prelims, original green cloth, bevelled boards, lettered in gilt, slightly rubbed, inner hinges slightly cracking.   Jarndyce Antiquarian Booksellers   CCIII - 595   2013   £110

Coleridge, Sara   *Phantasmion.*   London: William Pickering, 1837.   First edition, one of 250 copies, half title, 4 pages ads, untrimmed in slightly later blue binder's cloth, maroon leather label, small split at head of following hinge, upper corners slightly knocked, good plus.   Jarndyce Antiquarian Booksellers   CCIII - 594   2013   £400

Coleridge, Sara   *Phantasmion.*   C. Whittingham for William Pickering, 1837.   First edition, inscribed presentation from Mrs. H. N. Coleridge for Miss Theodosia Hinckes, , loosely inserted ALS by author to Mrs. Lonsdale, (pencil inscription "Given me by John Sparrow"), 8vo., flyleaves little spotted, through setting slightly on to half title, few areas of minor spotting, contemporary pebble grained green morocco, double blind ruled borders on sides with corner ornaments, thick blind rules on either side of raised bands on spine, lettered direct in gilt, gilt edges by Hayday, mostly faded to brown, little rubbed, short split at head of lower joint, good.   Blackwell's Rare Books   172 - 43   2013   £3500

Coles, Benjamin   *A Memoir on the Subject of the Wheat and Flour of the State of New York.*   New York: Kirk and Mercein, 1820.   First edition, 8vo., 46 pages, text illustration and folding plate, removed.   M & S Rare Books, Inc.   95 - 387   2013 $225

Coles, Manning   *The Far Traveller.*   London: Hodder & Stoughton, 1957.   First edition, near fine in dust jacket with internal tape mends, nicks at spine ends, some staining along flap folds and lightly darkened spine.   Mordida Books   81 - 95   2013 $75

Coles, Manning   *The Fifth Man.*   London: Hodder & Stoughton, 1946.   First edition, some tiny light spotting on page edges, otherwise fine in dust jacket with tiny wear at corners.   Mordida Books   81 - 93   2013 $75

Coles, Manning   *A Knife for the Juggler.*   London: Hodder & Stoughton, 1964.   First edition, some light spotting on top of page edges, otherwise fine in dust jacket with couple of tiny tears.   Mordida Books   81 - 96   2013 $65

Coles, Manning   *The Man in the Green Hat.*   London: Hodder & Stoughton, 1955.   First edition, Goldstone bookplate, some light stains on endpapers, otherwise fine in dust jacket with internal tape mend at base of spine and one on back panel which have bled through, some light rubbing to spine.   Mordida Books   81 - 94   2013 $65

Colette, Sidonie Gabrielle   1873-1954   *Cheri. Roman.*   Paris: Artheme Fayard, 1920.   First edition, 8vo., original yellow wrappers, acetate dust jacket, near fine, slight wear to foot of spine, one short closed tear at top edge of upper cover, inscribed by author for Leon Deffoux.   Maggs Bros. Ltd.   1460 - 176   2013   £500

Colette, Sidonie Gabrielle   1873-1954   *Claudine's en va.*   Monte Carlo: Editions Du Livre, 1946.   Later edition, one of 3000 copies, this copy unnumbered, 8vo., original wrappers, acetate dust jacket preserved in folding box, near fine, dust jacket just little chipped at head and tail of spine, inscribed by the artist, Christian Berard for Cecil Beaton.   Maggs Bros. Ltd.   1460 - 53   2013   £175

Colish, Marcia L. *The Stoic Tradition from Antiquity to the Early Middle Ages.* Leiden: E. J. Brill, 1985. Volumes I and II, 8vo., navy cloth, gilt stamped cover and spine titles, dust jacket, ownership signature, fine, rare in cloth.   Jeff Weber Rare Books   169 - 73   2013 $300

A Collection of Memorials Concerning Divers Deceased Ministers and others of the People Called Quakers, in Pennsylvania, New Jersey and Parts Adjacent... Philadelphia: Joseph Cruikshank, 1787. First edition, 8vo., 8, 439 pages, contemporary calf, spine and back cover only, lacks front endpapers.   M & S Rare Books, Inc.   95 - 307   2013 $450

A Collection of Poems on Religious and Moral Subjects. Elizabeth Town: printed by Shepard Kollock for Cornelius Davis, New York, 1797. Contemporary mottled sheep, short crack at bottom of upper hinge, occasional minor stains, but very good.   Joseph J. Felcone Inc.   English and American Literature to 1800 - 9   2013 $350

Collier, John *His Monkey Wife or Married to a Chimp.* New York: Appleton, 1931. First American edition, fine in fine dust jacket with little rubbing and nominal tear.   Between the Covers Rare Books, Inc.   Sci-Fi, Fantasy & Horror - 32615   2013 $500

Collin, Paul Ries *Calling Bridge.* Oxford University Press, 1976. First edition, original cloth gilt, dust jacket by Harold Jones, drawings.   R. F. G. Hollett & Son   Children's Books - 311   2013   £35

Collingwood, C. S. *Memoirs of Bernard Gilpin, Parson of Houghton-le-Spring and Apostle of the North.* London: Simpkin, Marshall and Co. and Sunderland: Hills & Co., 1884. First edition, original cloth, upper hinge repaired, head and foot of spine trifle worn, 3 tissue guarded photo plates, verso of first leaf of preface little dusty, scarce.   R. F. G. Hollett & Son   Lake District & Cumbria - 296   2013   £75

Collingwood, W. G. *Coniston Tales.* Ulverston: Wm. Holmes, 1899. First edition, original printed patterned boards, spine rather darkened, frontispiece and decorated title, labels removed from ront endpapers.   R. F. G. Hollett & Son   Lake District & Cumbria - 297   2013   £75

Collingwood, W. G. *Dutch Agnes Her Valentine. Being the Journal of the Curate of Coniston 1616-1623.* Kendal: Titus Wilson, 1910. First edition, library cloth, flyleaf removed, library stamps on title.   R. F. G. Hollett & Son   Lake District & Cumbria - 298   2013   £25

Collingwood, W. G. *Elizabethan Keswick. Extracts from the Original Account Books 1564-1577...* Kendal: Titus Wilson, 1912. First edition, modern quarter calf gilt with Spanish marbled boards, untrimmed 11 text illustrations, title lightly spotted.   R. F. G. Hollett & Son   Lake District & Cumbria - 300   2013   £120

Collingwood, W. G. *Elizabethan Keswick. Extracts from the Original Account Books 1564-1577...* Kendal: Titus Wilson, 1912. First edition, original printed wrappers, few text illustrations, fine, very scarce.   R. F. G. Hollett & Son   Lake District & Cumbria - 299   2013   £120

Collingwood, W. G. *The Memoirs of Sir Daniel Fleming.* Kendal: Titus Wilson, 1928. Original wrappers, portrait, Kendal Grammar School bookplate, very nice, clean copy.   R. F. G. Hollett & Son   Lake District & Cumbria - 305   2013   £75

Collingwood, W. G. *Thorstein of the Mere: a Saga of the Northmen in Lakeland...* London: Heinemann, 1931. Reissue in new format, original cloth, gilt pages (x), 298, frontispiece.   R. F. G. Hollett & Son   Lake District & Cumbria - 304   2013   £25

Collins, Joseph *The Treatment of Diseases of the Nervous System.* New York: William Wood, 1900. xiv, 609 pages, 23 text engravings, errata leaf tipped in, original green cloth, rubbed, some bubbling of cloth on boards, front fore edge worn, dirt smudge on title.   James Tait Goodrich   75 - 51   2013 $295

Collins, William   1721-1759 *The Poetical Works of Mr. William Collins.* London: for T. Becket and P. A. DeHondt, 1765. First collected edition, final blank M6, contemporary calf, spine gilt in compartments, covers sprinkled with stencil in interlacing bordered pattern within a gilt fillet, edges sprinkled blue green, marbled endpapers, extremities worn, crown of spine chipped away, respectable copy, fine internally, armorial bookplate of Richd. Cox.   Joseph J. Felcone Inc.   English and American Literature to 1800 - 10   2013 $1000

Collins, William   1721-1759 *The Poetical Works.* London: printed by T. Bensley for E. Harding, 1798. 20 engravings within text, light browning in places, 8vo., contemporary flame calf, spine divided by gilt rolls, black morocco lettering piece n second compartment, remainder with central lyre tools, marbled endpapers, bit rubbed and marked, good.   Blackwell's Rare Books   B174 - 36   2013   £100

Collins, William Wilkie   1824-1889 *Little Novels.* London: Chatto & Windus, 1890. Frontispiece, 32 page (catalog) Sept. 1891, original green cloth, slight damp mark to for-edges, slightly rubbed, very good.   Jarndyce Antiquarian Booksellers   CCV - 67   2013   £120

Collins, William Wilkie 1824-1889 *La Pierre de Lune. (The Moonstone).* Paris: Librairie Hachette & Cie, 1872. First French edition, 2 volumes, half titles, contemporary half red morocco, gilt spines, corners slightly bumped, contemporary signatures on leading f.e.p. and bookseller's tickets on leading pastedowns, very good.   Jarndyce Antiquarian Booksellers   CCV - 68   2013   £450

Collins, William Wilkie 1824-1889 *Sans Nom. (No Name).* Paris: J. Hetzel, 1863. First French edition, 2 volumes, contemporary half red pebble grained calf, marbled boards, very good.   Jarndyce Antiquarian Booksellers   CCV - 69   2013   £150

Colman, George 1732-1794 *Broad Grins...* London: T. Cadell and W. Davies, 1804. Second edition, half title, slightly spotted, disbound.   Jarndyce Antiquarian Booksellers   CCIII - 661   2013   £40

Colman, George 1732-1794 *Broad Grins...* London: T. Cadell & W. Davies, 1809. Fourth edition, engraved title, woodcuts, contemporary full red grained calf, gilt spine and borders, little rubbed, and worn and slight worming at head of leading hinge, Marquess of Headfort's armorial bookplate, all edges gilt, good, sound.   Jarndyce Antiquarian Booksellers   CCIII - 662 2013   £40

Colman, George 1732-1794 *Broad Grins...* London: Chatto and Windus, 1871. Original purple cloth, blocked and lettered gilt, slightly dulled, spine faded, very good.   Jarndyce Antiquarian Booksellers   CCIII - 663   2013   £35

Colman, George 1732-1794 *The History of Mr. John Decastro and His brother Bat, Commonly called Old Crab.* London: T. Egerton, 1815. First edition, 4 volumes, half titles, very slight marginal worming in first few leaves volume II, uncut in later blue binder's cloth, purple labels, very good.   Jarndyce Antiquarian Booksellers   CCIII - 665   2013   £250

Colman, George 1762-1834 *My Night Gown and Slippers; or Tales in Verse.* London: printed to T. Cadell Jun. and W. Davies, 1797. 4to., lacking half title, tear without loss to inner margins, some foxing, address to reader cropped along leading edge with some loss to letters, disbound.   Jarndyce Antiquarian Booksellers   CCIV - 100   2013   £40

Colman, Julia *The Child's Anti-Slavery Book...* New York: Carlton & Porter, 1859. 12mo., brown blindstamped cloth, some foxing and spine ends worn, very good, 10 engravings, 8 plates and 2 in-text, very scarce.   Aleph-Bet Books, Inc.   104 - 78   2013 $1450

Colnett, J. *A Voyage to the South Atlantic and Round Cape Horn to the Pacific Ocean for the Purpose of Extending the Spearmaceti Whale Fisheries and Other Objects of Commerce, by Ascertaining the Ports, Bays, Harbours and Anchoring Berths.* London: 1798. First edition, frontispiece, 6 folding maps, 2 engraved plates, diagrammatic plate slightly cropped at upper margin, 4to., smart early 19th century half calf, black morocco label to spine, gilt, small piece replaced at foot of spine.   Maggs Bros. Ltd.   1467 - 76   2013   £11,000

Colombo, Realdo *De Re Anatomica Libri XV.* Paris: Wechel, 1572. Second Paris edition, woodcut printer's device on title and at end, small hole n title and at end, small hole in title crudely patched, 8vo., contemporary vellum over boards, bit soiled and worn, lacking ties, recased, notes on inside cover legible through Japanese tissue paper reinforcement, extensive contemporary annotations on endleaves and in text, good.   Blackwell's Rare Books   Sciences - 32   2013   £3500

Colombo, Realdo *De re Anatomica Libri XV...* Frankfurt am Main: Joannes Wechel, 1590. Fourth edition, 8vo., contemporary vellum, title in red and black, some browning of text, title spotted and minor repairs to upper blank portion, early signature.   James Tait Goodrich   75 - 59   2013 $1495

Colquhoun, John Campbell *Scattered Leaves of Biography.* London: William Macintosh, 1864. First edition, 4 pages ads, some internal marks, original dark brown cloth, bevelled boards, slightly rubbed, spine slightly dulled, gift inscription, 1885.   Jarndyce Antiquarian Booksellers   CCIII - 666   2013   £50

Colquhoun, Patrick 1745-1820 *A Treatise on the Police of the Metropolis.... (with) A Treatise on the Commerce and Police of the River Thames...* London: printed by H. Fry for C. Dilly/London: printed for Joseph Mawman, successor to Mr. Dilly, H. Baldwin & Son, 1797-1800. First edition, 2 volumes, folding map and table, matching full tree calf, elaborately gilt spines, red labels, slight rubbing, very good, clean, handsome copies.   Jarndyce Antiquarian Booksellers   CCV - 261   2013   £750

Colquhoun, Patrick 1745-1820 *Treatise on Wealth, Power and Resources of the British Empire, in Every Quarter of the World, Including the East Indies.* London: printed for Joseph Mawman, 1815. Second edition, 4to., slight indentations to opening leaves, uncut in original brown paper boards, paper label, slightly rubbed in places, label with small repair, armorial bookplate of MacLean of Ardgour, signed on leading f.e.p. by Auls (?) MacLean, 1822, very nice in original binding, from the library of the clan of MacLean.   Jarndyce Antiquarian Booksellers CCV - 71   2013   £480

Colton, Charles Caleb *Hypocrisy.* London: Taylor & Hessey, 1812.   Later 2 pages ads (June 1823), uncut in original drab boards, paper label darkened, slightly rubbed at head of spine, stamped, " A. J. above coronet design at head of introduction", Renier booklabel, good plus.   Jarndyce Antiquarian Booksellers   CCIII - 668   2013   £120

Colton, Charles Caleb *Hypocrisy.* Tiverton: printed & sold by T. Smith, 1812.   First edition, uncut in original boards which have been at an early date, covered with half vellum and marbled paper, later label with ink title, corners knocked, edges little worn.   Jarndyce Antiquarian Booksellers   CCIII - 667   2013   £140

Colton, Charles Caleb *Lacon; or Many Things in Few Words; Addressed to Those Who Think. (with) Remarks Critical and Moral on Talents of Lord Byron and the Tendencies of Don Juan. With The Conflagration of Moscow: a Poem.* London: Longman, 1823. 1819. 1822, 4 volumes in one, bound in full diced calf, gilt spine, black leather labels, slightly rubbed, front hinge replaced.   Jarndyce Antiquarian Booksellers   CCIII - 365   2013   £75

Colton, Charles Caleb *Lacon; or Many Things in Few Words; Addressed to Those Who Think. (with) Remarks Critical and Moral on Talents of Lord Byron and the Tendencies of Don Juan. With The Conflagration of Moscow: a Poem.* London: Longman, 1825. 1819. 1822. New edition, 4 volumes in 1, contemporary half red morocco, marbled boards, hinges and corners rubbed, armorial bookplate of Joseph Jones.   Jarndyce Antiquarian Booksellers   CCIII - 367   2013   £75

Colton, Charles Caleb *Modern Antiquity and Other Poems.* London: B. B. King, 1835.   First edition, disbound.   Jarndyce Antiquarian Booksellers   CCIII - 669   2013   £75

Colton, Charles Caleb *Remarks Critical and Moral on the Talents of Lord Byron and the Tendencies of Don Juan.* London: printed for the author, 1819.   First edition, handsomely rebound in later half calf, marbled boards, scarlet leather label, very good, clean.   Jarndyce Antiquarian Booksellers   CCIII - 279   2013   £480

Colum, Mary *Our Friend James Joyce.* New York: Doubleday, 1958.   First edition, 8vo., 239 pages, little faded, spine and couple of minor cover nicks, inscribed by Padraic Colum.   Second Life Books Inc.   183 - 80   2013 $75

Colum, Padraic 1881-1972 *Castle Conquer.* New York: 1923.   First edition, 8vo., cloth, very good.   C. P. Hyland   261 - 941   2013   £28

Colum, Padraic 1881-1972 *A Half Day's Ride or Estates in Corsica.* New York: 1932.   First edition, 8vo., cloth, good, ex-institutional library with stamps.   C. P. Hyland   261 - 942   2013   £30

Colum, Padraic 1881-1972 *The Land: A Play in 3 Acts.* 1905.   Second edition, wrappers worn, text good, 8vo., ex-institutional library with stamps.   C. P. Hyland   261 - 940   2013   £32

Colum, Padraic 1881-1972 *The Collected Poems of...* New York: 1956.   Quarter cloth, 8vo., very good.   C. P. Hyland   261 - 944   2013   £30

Colum, Padraic 1881-1972 *The Poet's Circuit. Collected Poems of Ireland.* 1960.   First edition, 8vo. cloth, very good.   C. P. Hyland   261 - 943   2013   £32

Columbus, Christopher *The Log of Christopher Columbus.* Camden: International Marine Pub. Co., 1987.   First edition, oblong octavo, maps, photos, facsimiles, drawings, red cloth, very fine, pictorial dust jacket.   Argonaut Book Shop   Recent Acquisitions June 2013 - 67   2013 $60

Columbus, Christopher *Oceanica Claffis.* Zuilichem: Catharijne Press, n.d.,   Limited to 190 copies, this one of 15 lettered copies bound thus, printed from zinc blocks by Arie van Diemen in Amsterdam on old Dutch paper, 6..5 x 4.7cm., full brown leather stamped in blind and with metal clasp, enclosed in clamshell box with leather spine and paper cover containing reproduction of the Columbus letter, (26) pages, reproductions of woodcut illustrations, from the collection of Donn W. Sanford.   Oak Knoll Books   303 - 79   2013 $350

Colvil, Samuel *The Whigs Supplication or the Scotch-Hudibra.* Glasgow: printed by Robert Urie, 1751.   8vo., pages 164, lightly spotted and browned, recent dark brown half calf, marbled boards, spine with two raised bands, middle compartment lettered vertically in gilt, 18th century armorial bookplate of "Geo. Jas. Campbell Esqr./of Treesbank, relaid on front pastedown, above in the paper ex-libris of J. L. Weir.   Unsworths Antiquarian Booksellers   28 - 84   2013   £125

Combe, William 1742-1823 *The Three Tours of Dr. Syntax: In Search of the Picturesque, In Search of Consolation, in Search of a Wife.* London: R. Ackermann's Repository of Arts, 1812. 1820. 1821. First editions in book form, 3 separately published volumes, very handsome gilt decorated early 20th century dark blue crushed morocco by Riviere & Son (stamp signed), cover with French fillet border, spines lavishly and elegantly gilt in compartments with flower filled cornucopia centerpiece surrounded by small tools and volute cornerpieces, inner gilt dentelles, top edge gilt, other edges untrimmed, one woodcut illustration, one engraved tailpiece and 80 artfully hand colored aquatint plates by Thomas Rowlandson, engraved armorial bookplate of John Taylor Reynolds; spines uniformly more black than blue, four of the covers with just hint of soiling, most plates with variable offsetting (usually faint but noticeable in half dozen cases), other trivial imperfections, extremely desirable set, strong impressions and good coloring of first edition plates, spacious margins, lovely bindings, lustrous and virtually unworn. Phillip J. Pirages 63 - 409 2013 $4500

Come and Go in Fairyland! London: Nister, n.d., circa, 1890. Oblong 4to., cloth backed pictorial boards, some cover rubbing and normal wear, very good, 5 beautiful mechanical plates that feature rarely seen mechanism, 2 slender ribbons attached to each side of plate, as the ribbon is pulled, part of the illustrations revolves 180 degrees to reveal another illustration below, rare. Aleph-Bet Books, Inc. 104 - 365 2013 $2750

Commack, Key *A Spartan Primer.* New York: Duffield, 1913. 4to., cloth backed pictorial boards, some cover soil and tips rubbed, very good, full page color illustrations by Grace Drayton, extremely scarce. Aleph-Bet Books, Inc. 105 - 5 2013 $650

The Compleat Wizzard; Being a Collection of Authentic and Entertaining Narratives of the Real Existence and Appearance of Ghosts, Demons and Spectres... London: printed for T. Evans, 1770. 8vo., name or note roughly erased from foot of page 74 with some thinning to paper and one small hole shaving a letter, some browning in first four leaves, occasional foxing, slight old waterstaining to few lower margins, marginal notes on two pages in early hand, one noting an alias and letters IM and date added within decorative initial to account of John Mompesson, the Invisible Drummer, 19th century half calf, marbled boards, rebacked retaining original spine and label, corners worn, bookplate removed. Jarndyce Antiquarian Booksellers CCIV - 43 2013 £4800

Compton Burney, Ivy 1892-1969 *Brothers and Sisters.* London: Heath Cranton, 1929. First edition, 8vo., 239 pages, red cloth in red printed dust jacket (wear at fore edge and bottom of spine), spine faded, mended internally, very good, scarce. Second Life Books Inc. 183 - 81 2013 $350

Compton, David Guy *The Steel Crocodile.* New York: Ace Publishing Corp., 1970. Unpaged galleys of the first edition, folio, loose sheets printed rectos only. L. W. Currey, Inc. Utopian Literature: Recent Acquisitions (April 2013) - 140294 2013 $250

Compton, R. H. *Our South African Flora.* Johannesburg: circa, 1941. Original cloth backed pictorial boards, pages 100, 4 full page plates, 100 cigarette card text plate, tipped in, all in full color. R. F. G. Hollett & Son Africana - 41 2013 £40

Comstock, Francis Adams *A Gothic Vision. F. L. Griggs and His Work.* Boston: Boston Public Library, 1966. Number 429/600 copies, illustrations, very good in original gilt lettered black cloth, slight vertical crease to cloth on upper board, 4to. Ken Spelman Books Ltd. 75 - 185 2013 £60

Comstock, Sarah *Old Roads from the Heart of New York.* New York: G. P. Putnam's sons, 1915. First edition, very good, without dust jacket with foldout maps. Between the Covers Rare Books, Inc. New York City - 286041 2013 $75

Comyn, James *Irish at Law.* 1981. First edition, 8vo., quarter cloth, very good. C. P. Hyland 261 - 944 2013 £30

Conard, Howard Louis *"Uncle Dick" Wootton: the Pioneer Frontiersman of the Rocky Mountain Region.* Chicago: 1890. 474 pages, illustrations, original illustrated boards, very good, boards unevenly faded and pages browned, binding intact, all of the many illustrations present. Dumont Maps & Books of the West 124 - 57 2013 $350

Concanen, Matthew *The Flower-Piece.* London: printed for J. Walthoe, 1731. First edition, little browned in places, 2 leaves crinkled, 12mo., contemporary speckled calf, double gilt fillet borders on sides, spine gilt in compartments, red lettering piece spine worn at head and tail, slightly darkened, upper joint cracked but cords firm, 18th century armorial bookplate of Sir Atwill Lake, with that of Sr John J. Scott Douglas (engraved by Lizars) superimposed, good. Blackwell's Rare Books B174 - 38 2013 £350

A Concise History of Birmingham... Birmingham: R. Jabet, 1808. Fourth edition, pages xviii, 78, folding map, 3 plates, original grey boards, spine worn. J. & S. L. Bonham Antiquarian Booksellers Europe - 7280 2013 £60

Conder, Josiah *The Associate Minstrels.* London: printed by George Ellerton for Thomas Conder published by his father, Thomas, 1810. Engraved frontispiece and little spotted, final ad leaf, contemporary half maroon calf, dark green label, spine and corners rubbed and faded, good plus. Jarndyce Antiquarian Booksellers CCIII - 671 2013 £75

Condit, Carl W. *The Port of New York: a History of the Rail and Terminal System from the Grand Central Electrification to the Present.* Chicago: University of Chicago Press, 1981. 8vo., map frontispiece, 49 illustrations, 10 tables, silver stamped light brown cloth, bookplate, fine.   Jeff Weber Rare Books   171 - 76   2013 $100

Condon, T. *Gilla Hugh or the Patriot Monk.* Cork: 1864. First edition, cover dull, some foxing in text, else good, signed presentation from author to Thomas A. O'Callaghan, later Bishop of Cork April 7th 1864.   C. P. Hyland   261 - 201   2013   £65

Condorcet, Marie Jean Antoine Nicolas de Caritat, Marquis De   1743-1794 *Outlines of an Historical View of the progress of the Human Mind...* London: printed for J. Johnson, 1795. First English edition, 8vo., half title, some offset browning from turn-ins on pastedowns and endpapers, some occasional light foxing, pencil notes on following endpapers, contemporary calf, black morocco label, double gilt rules spine, slightly rubbed anf marked.   Jarndyce Antiquarian Booksellers   CCV - 73   2013   £950

Cone, Helen *Bonnie Little People.* New York: Stokes, 1890. Folio, cloth backed pictorial boards, light cover soil, edge of frontispiece creased, very good+, printed on rectos only, 6 magnificent full page chromolithographs, rare. Aleph-Bet Books, Inc.   105 - 331   2013 $1200

Confederate Victories in the Southwest: Prelude to Defeat. (with) Union Army Operations in the Southwest: Final Victory. Albuquerque: 1961. 2 volumes, 201 pages, maps, 152 pages, folding map, dust jacket lightly soiled and spines faded, minor loss, tears and price clipped on dust jacket of volume I, else clean and very good.   Dumont Maps & Books of the West   124 - 69   2013 $135

The Confession of Adam Horn, Alias Andrew Hellman, Embodying Particulars of His Life... Baltimore: printed by James Young, 1843. 8vo., 29 pages, disbound, browned and foxed, edges chipped.   M & S Rare Books, Inc.   95 - 243   2013 $150

Connell, Evan *Son of the Morning Star.* San Francisco: North Point, 1984. First edition, long galleys 6 1/4 x 13 3/4 inches x 1 1/2 inch, original plain beige perfect bound wrappers, signed on titlepage by author with his holograph corrections throughout, near fine, solid copy.   Ed Smith Books   78 - 7   2013 $950

Connell, Mary *Help is on the Way (Poems).* Reinhardt, 1986. First edition, line drawings by author, crown 8vo., original light blue card wrappers printed in black, red and white, fine, inscribed by Grahame Greene for Yvonne Coletta.   Blackwell's Rare Books   172 - 190   2013   £1500

Connelly, John *The Killing Kind.* London: Hodder & Stoughton, 2001. First edition, signed by author, very fine in dust jacket.   Mordida Books   81 - 104   2013 $75

Connelly, Michael *Chasing the Dime.* New York: Little Brown, 2002. First edition, signed by author, very fine in dust jacket.   Mordida Books   81 - 99   2013 $60

Connelly, Michael *The Poet.* Boston: Little Brown, 1995. First edition, fine in fine dust jacket, signed by author. Between the Covers Rare Books, Inc.   Mystery & Detective Fiction - 311214   2013 $50

Connelly, Michael *Trunk Music.* Boston: Little Brown, 1997. First edition, very fine in dust jacket.   Mordida Books   81 - 97   2013 $65

Connington, J. J. *The Castleford Conundrum.* London: Hodder and Stoughton, 1932. First edition, 8vo., original blue cloth, pages 350, very good, slightly cocked and rubbed, edges little foxed.   Howard S. Mott Inc.   262 - 35   2013 $150

The Connoisseur. printed for J. Johnson, 1808. 3 volumes, 12mo., very good, contemporary half black roan, marbled boards, gilt ruled and lettered spines.   Ken Spelman Books Ltd.   75 - 59   2013   £120

Connolly, Cyril   1903-1974 *The Condemned Playground. Essays 1927-1944.* London: Routledge, 1945. First edition, 8vo., frontispiece by Augustus John, original black cloth, dust jacket nicked at extremities, near fine, inscribed by author for Noel Blakiston.   Maggs Bros. Ltd.   1460 - 185   2013   £750

Connolly, Cyril   1903-1974 *Enemies of Promise.* London: George Routledge, 1938. First edition, large 8vo., original blue cloth, inscribed by author, excellent copy. Maggs Bros. Ltd.   1460 - 179   2013   £650

Connolly, Cyril   1903-1974 *Enemies of Promise.* London: George Routledge, 1938. First edition, large 8vo., original blue cloth, dust jacket browned and slightly creased and nicked at edges, excellent copy, inscribed by author to Noel Blakiston.   Maggs Bros. Ltd.   1460 - 178   2013 £1250

Connolly, Cyril   1903-1974 *The Golden Horizon.* London: Weidenfeld & Nicolson, 1953. First edition, large 8vo., original blue cloth, excellent copy in dust jacket chipped and creased at edges.   Maggs Bros. Ltd.   1460 - 187   2013   £500

Connolly, Cyril 1903-1974 *The Missing Diplomats.* London: Queen Anne Press, 1952. First edition, 8vo., original wrappers with printed paper label on upper board, dust jacket, near fine, inscribed by author.   Maggs Bros. Ltd. 1460 - 186   2013   £500

Connolly, Cyril 1903-1974 *Previous Convictions.* New York: Harper and Row, 1963. First US edition, 8vo., original blue cloth, near fine, inscribed by author.   Maggs Bros. Ltd. 1460 - 189   2013   £375

Connolly, Cyril 1903-1974 *Previous Convictions.* London: Hamish Hamilton, 1963. First edition, large 8vo., original blue cloth, near fine in dust jacket slightly browned on spine, inscribed by author for Yvonne Hamilton.   Maggs Bros. Ltd. 1460 - 188   2013   £450

Connolly, Cyril 1903-1974 *The Unquiet Grave.* London: Horizon, 1944. First edition, 8vo., original wrappers, inscribed by author for Noel Blakiston, with further 45 word note beneath, slightly chipped, otherwise near fine in protective box.   Maggs Bros. Ltd. 1460 - 182   2013   £750

Connolly, Cyril 1903-1974 *The Unquiet Grave.* London: Horizon, 1944. First edition, one of 1000 copies, 8vo., original wrappers bound in full Oxford blue calf, lettered gilt within compartments, slightly rubbed, otherwise near fine, inscribed by author for Caresse Crosby, presentation binding.   Maggs Bros. Ltd. 1460 - 181   2013   £750

Conover, Richard Grover *As True as Sea Serpents.* New York: Knickerbocker Press, 1928. First edition, fine in very near fine dust jacket that is trifle faded at spine and has couple of tiny tears, very scarce, especially so in dust jacket.   Between the Covers Rare Books, Inc.   Sci-Fi, Fantasy & Horror - 62520   2013 $450

Conrad, Joseph 1857-1924 *Almayer's Folly. A Story of an Eastern River.* London: Fisher Unwin, 1895. First edition, first state, with titlepage printed in black and red, prelims, final leaves and endpaper lightly foxed, pages 272, crown 8vo., original mid green fine ribbed cloth, backstrip gilt lettered within gilt boxes, front inner hinge skilfully repaired, bookplate (or some other piece of paper), formerly attached at corners to front free endpaper, top edge gilt, others untrimmed, preserved in navy blue fleece lined folding box, lining foxed very good.   Blackwell's Rare Books B174 - 192   2013   £2500

Conrad, Joseph 1857-1924 *Heart of Darkness.* Paris: Editions d'Art Edoaurd Pelletan, 1910. First Steinlen edition, number 221 of 267 copies on wove Marais paper (total edition 340) signed by publisher in ink on justification page, 252 original black and white lithographs, by Theophile Alexandre Steinlen, 366 pages, bound by Rene Kieffer in exceptionally handsome Art Deco dark green full polished morocco with mosaic of inlaid maroon leathers and embossed gilt decorations on both covers and spine, latter with 4 embossed bands, dentelles, matching design, framing decorative silk centerpiece, matching front endleaf, additional endleaves of decorative green with silver and gilt paper, top edge gilt, original wrappers and backstrip preserved and bound in, contained in matching morocco trimmed slipcase, binding signed by Kieffer, publisher subscription ads bound in at end, overall size 27 x 21, pristine condition.   Gemini Fine Books & Arts., Ltd.   Art Reference & Illustrated Books - 2013 $2900

Conrad, Joseph 1857-1924 *Laughing Anne. One Day More. Two Plays.* New York: Doubleday Page and Co., 1925. first US edition, 8vo., original dark blue cloth, spine and upper cover lettered gilt, inscribed by author's widow Jessie for R. B. Cunninghame Graham, excellent copy.   Maggs Bros. Ltd. 1460 - 192   2013   £450

Conrad, Joseph 1857-1924 *The Rescue.* London: J. M. Dent & Sons Ltd., 1920. First edition, 8vo., original green cloth inscribed by author for Robert Cunninghame Graham, excellent copy.   Maggs Bros. Ltd. 1460 - 190   2013   £6500

Conrad, Joseph 1857-1924 *The Rover.* London: T. Fisher & Unwin, 1924. Fourth impression, 8vo., original green vertically ribbed cloth, spine and upper cover lettered in gilt, good copy, little waterstaining at foot of front cover, inscribed by author for H. P. C. Hare.   Maggs Bros. Ltd. 1460 - 191   2013   £500

Conrad, Joseph 1857-1924 *Some Reminiscences.* Eveleigh Nash, 1912. First edition, pages 238, crown 8vo., original dark blue fine grain cloth, backstrip and front cover gilt lettered and decorated, covers bordered in blind, untrimmed, red cloth chemise and gilt lettered quarter maroon morocco and red cloth slipcase, fine.   Blackwell's Rare Books 172 - 174   2013   £750

Conrad, Joseph 1857-1924 *Tales of Hearsay.* London: T. Fisher Unwin, 1925. First edition, 8vo., original dark green cloth, spine and upper cover lettered in gilt, excellent copy, spine dulled, inscribed from R. B. Cunninghame Graham (provided preface).   Maggs Bros. Ltd. 1460 - 193   2013   £250

Conrad, Joseph 1857-1924 *Typhoon and Other Stories.* London: William Heinemann, 1903. First English edition, initial ad leaf, uncut in original grey cloth blocked and lettered in gilt, slight rubbing, inscription on leafing f.e.p. "G. Pembroke 17th June 1903", very good.   Jarndyce Antiquarian Booksellers   CCV - 74   2013   £380

Conrad, Joseph 1857-1924 *The Works.* Garden City: Doubleday Page & Co., 1920-1926. One of 735 copies signed by Conrad, 22 volumes, "Sun-dial edition", frontispiece, fine and especially flamboyant lilac morocco, elaborately gilt, by Stikeman, covers panelled with single, double gilt fillets and intricate scrolling foliate cornerpieces, raised bands, spine attractively gilt in ruled compartments with marine ornaments (seashell or anchor) as centerpiece and with scrolling cornerpieces, crimson morocco doublures, front doublures with central panel of blue morocco, wide turn-ins with alternating floral tools, doublures decorated with wavy gilt lines and (at corners) floral bouquets, blue central panels with large gilt sailing vessel at middle, watered silk endleaves, morocco hinges, all edges gilt; with APS signed by author tipped in, also signature of Richard Curle, written next to his printed name as dedicatee of volume 16, spines uniformly faded to even chestnut brown, hint of rubbing to handful of joints and corners (only), one opening in one volume with marginal spots, quite handsome set in fine condition, text virtually pristine, covers bright and wear to leather entirely minor.   Phillip J. Pirages   61 - 122   2013 $15,000

Conrad, Joseph 1857-1924 *(Works).* Gresham, 1925-1928. Medallion edition, 22 volumes, frontispiece in each volume, 8vo., original blue cloth, backstrips lettered and decorated in gilt, front covers with Conrad's bust embossed in gilt at centres, free endpapers faintly browned as usual, near fine.   Blackwell's Rare Books   B174 - 193   2013   £800

Conroy, Pat *The Great Santini.* Boston: Houghton Mifflin, 1976. First edition, 8vo., original red cloth, dust jacket, signed by author and by his father Donald Conroy, near fine in dust jacket.   Maggs Bros. Ltd.   1460 - 194   2013   £350

Considerations Suggested by the Establishment of a Second College in Connecticut. Hartford: P. B. Gleason and Co., 1824. First edition, 8vo., 36 pages, removed, uncut, spine bit rough, sheets lightly toned else very good, wide margined copy.   M & S Rare Books, Inc.   95 - 83   2013 $100

Conspiracy to Murder: a Tool of Repression. New York: Committee to defend the Panthers, 1970. First edition?, 4 pages, stapled yellow paper, soiled, small tears and chips in margins, about very good.   Between the Covers Rare Books, Inc.   165 - 80   2013 $65

Constable, Henry *Poems and Sonnets.* Vale Press, 1897. One of 210 copies, printed on Arnold handmade paper in Vale type, wood engraved border and initial letters designed by Charles Ricketts, crown 8vo., original quarter grey boards foxed, printed label on darkened backstrip, grey boards with repeated pink printed pattern, free endpapers browned as usual, untrimmed, good.   Blackwell's Rare Books   B174 - 394   2013   £185

Constantine, Storm *Hermetech.* London: Headline, 1991. First edition, octavo, boards.   L. W. Currey, Inc. Utopian Literature: Recent Acquisitions (April 2013) - 140644   2013 $65

Cook, Eliza *Diamond Dust.* London: F. Putman, 1865. First edition, half title, 8 pages ads, original sand grained green cloth, bevelled boards, blocked and lettered gilt, inscription from author for Misses Constable.   Jarndyce Antiquarian Booksellers   CCV - 75   2013   £85

Cook, James *A Voyage Towards the South Pole and Round the World Performed in His Majesty's Ships the Resolution and Adventure in the Years 1772, 1773, 1774 and 1775.* London: W. Strahan and T. Cadell, 1777. First edition, 3 volumes, (2 volumes 4to. plus folio atlas), text with folding letterpress table, atlas with engraved portrait, engraved folding map, 62 engraved plates, maps and chart, text expertly bound to style in 18th century russia over contemporary marbled paper covered boards, spines uniform to text, rare, with plates unfolded, uncut and edge bound in separate folio atlas.   Maggs Bros. Ltd.   1467 - 77   2013   £15,000

Cook, Tennessee Celeste, Lady 1845-1923 *Constitutional Equality a Right of Woman, In Consideration of the Various Relations Which She Sustains as a Necessary Part of the Body of Society and Humanity...* New York: Woodhull & Claflin, 1871. First edition, 8vo., pages 148, frontispiece, green cloth stamped in gilt little foxing on front and rear leaves, cover scuffed, little soiled, little worn at edges, otherwise very good, scarce.   Second Life Books Inc.   182 - 40   2013 $500

Cook, Tennessee Celeste, Lady 1845-1923 *Constitutional Equality a Right of Woman; or a Consideration of the Various Relations Which She Sustains as a Necessary part of the Body of Society and Humanity.* New York: Woodhull, Claflin & Co., 1871. First edition, 8vo., original cloth, few chips to spine, bookplate removed from inside front cover, inner front joint starting.   M & S Rare Books, Inc.   95 - 72   2013 $750

Cook, Theodore Andrea *The Water-Colour Drawings of J. M. W. Turner, R.A. in the National Gallery.* London: Cassell and Co., 1904. Limited edition (No. 217 of 1200 copies), folio, original cloth gilt folder with line ties, 5 plates plus 88 color plates set into mounts, top edge gilt, all loose in folder as issued, scarce, presentation copy from Canon Hardwick Rawnsley for his wife Edith. R. F. G. Hollett & Son   Lake District & Cumbria - 308   2013   £450

Cook, Thomas H. *The Orchids.* Boston: Houghton Mifflin, 1982. First edition, signed by author, very fine in dust jacket.   Mordida Books   81 - 105   2013 $90

Cook, Walter *Peggy's Travels.* Blackie and Son, n.d., 1908. 4to., original cloth backed pictorial boards, pictorial title, 16 full page color plates and numerous line drawings and pictorial endpapers, prize label on pastedown, very nice, fresh, scarce title.   R. F. G. Hollett & Son   Children's Books - 133   2013   £140

Cook, Walter *Peggy's Travels.* New York and Boston: H. M. Caldwell, 1908. First American edition, 4to., very good, 16 color plates by Alice Cook, repaired closed tear to one plate, minor foxing but plates clean and bright, red cloth backed boards.   Barnaby Rudge Booksellers   Children 2013 - 021010   2013 $70

Cook, Warren L. *Flood Tide of Empire: Spain and the Pacific Northwest 1543-1819.* New Haven: Yale University Press, 1973. First edition, 20 pages illustrations, folding map in rear pocket, black cloth, gilt, very fine, pictorial dust jacket.   Argonaut Book Shop   Recent Acquisitions June 2013 - 69   2013 $90

Cooke, Alexander *A Present for a Papist; or the Life and Death of Pope John from Her Birth to Her Death.* London: printed for and sold by Olive Payne, 1740. Reissue, Frontispiece, later half calf, rubbed.   Jarndyce Antiquarian Booksellers   CCIV - 102   2013   £150

Cooke, Edmund Vance *The Biography of Our Baby.* New York: Dodge, 1906. 4to., white gilt and pictorial cloth, very fine and unused in original box, illustrations by Bessie Collins Pease, with 20 color illustrations.   Aleph-Bet Books, Inc.   104 - 411   2013 $450

Cooke, John Estes *Tamawaca Folks.* Macatawa: Tamawaca Press, 1907. First edition, 8vo., green cloth stamped in blue and white, 185 pages, fine, quite scarce, beautiful.   Aleph-Bet Books, Inc.   105 - 69   2013 $2500

Cooke, M. C. *British Fungi.* 1884. 166 pages, 20 color plates, good, cloth, owner inscribed by Hugh Allingham.   C. P. Hyland   261 - 6   2013   £40

Cooke, M. C. *Rambles Among the Wild Flowers.* London: T. Nelson & Sons, 1898. 8vo., 5 parts in one volume, 10 color plates, 42 wild flowers and 286 engravings, blue gilt binding, very good.   Barnaby Rudge Booksellers   Natural History 2013 - 020490   2013 $75

Cooke, Miles *An Exact Table of Fees, of all the Courts at Westminster as the Same Were, by Orders of the Several Courts Carefully Corrected and Diligently Examin'd...* London: Assigns of Richard & Edward Atkyns for John Walthoe, 1694. Very rare, 8vo., publisher's ads, table of contents pages (iii-iv) missing a piece, half 20th century calf over original calf boards, gilt stamped black leather spine label, rubbed, bookseller label, very fare.   Jeff Weber Rare Books   171 - 77   2013 $200

Coombe, William *The History of the Abbey Church of St. Peter's Westminster in Antiquities and Monuments.* London: printed for R. Ackermann by L. Harrison & J. C. Leigh, 1812. First edition, 2 volumes, folio, color frontispiece and plates, some offsetting and foxing, but largely nice, clean copy, full contemporary calf, tooled in blind and marbled edges, slightly rubbed and well rebacked with gilt raised bands, red and brown morocco labels, armorial bookplates of Charles Langton Massingherd.   Jarndyce Antiquarian Booksellers   CCV - 76   2013   £750

Cooney, Barbara *Chanticleer and the Fox.* New York: Crowell, 1958. First edition, first printing, fine in dust jacket (not price clipped, no seal, slight fraying at spine ends, else very good+), brightly illustrated in color by Barbara Cooney, this copy signed by Cooney.   Aleph-Bet Books, Inc.   104 - 130   2013 $800

Cooper, Ambrose *The Complete Distiller.* printed for P. Vaillant, 1757. First edition, folding engraved plate, slight offsetting on plate, tendency to browning, 8vo., contemporary calf, rebacked preserving original spine, corners worn, ownership inscription on title of Joseph Leay, Feb. 26th 1822 on title, pencil scribblings on verso of half title in same hand, armorial bookplate of one of the Barons Caher, good.   Blackwell's Rare Books   Sciences - 36   2013   £950

Cooper, Diana *The Rainbow Comes and Goes; The Light of Common Day; Trumpets from the Steep.* London: Rupert Hart-Davis, 1958-1960. First editions, 3 volumes, 8vo., original cloth, dust jackets, inscribed by author to Violet Trefusis, excellent, jackets of first and last volumes show light signs of wear.   Maggs Bros. Ltd.   1460 - 197   2013   £250

Cooper, Duff *Operation Heartbreak.* London: Rupert Hart Davis, 1950. First edition, 8vo. original black cloth, inscribed by author, some very light foxing, otherwise excellent copy.   Maggs Bros. Ltd.   1460 - 196   2013   £150

Cooper, Duff *The Toast of the Immortal Memory of Quintus Horatius Flaccus Proposed at the Annual Banquet of the Horatian Society on 22nd Nov. 1937.* N.P.: privately printed, 1937. Limited to 100 copies, inscribed by author for Osbert, 8vo., original wrappers, excellent copy, wrappers lightly soiled. Maggs Bros. Ltd. 1460 - 195 2013 £175

Cooper, Elizabeth *The Muses Library; or a Series of English Poetry, from the Saxons to the reign of King Charles II.* London: printed for J. Wilcox, 1737. First edition, 216 x 140mm., xvi, 400 pages, titlepage with volume number obscured by early ink hatching, especially attractive caramel-colored morocco handsomely gilt by Zaehnsdorf (signed on front turn-in) covers framed in gilt with border and inner panel of French fillets as well as fleuron tool cornerpieces, raised bands, spine densely gilt in compartments with stippled scrolling cornerpieces, center panel with an ornament featuring 8 points and French fillet border as well as small floral centerpiece, elaborately gilt turn-ins, marbled endpapers, top edge gilt, other edges untrimmed, boards with hint of soiling, occasional very light foxing, two leaves at rear with faint dampstain in upper fore margin, one leaf with small, neatly repaired marginal tear, other trivial imperfections, excellent copy, untrimmed text bright, clean and fresh, handsome binding lustrous and generally very pleasing. Phillip J. Pirages 61 - 129 2013 $1250

Cooper, Erwin *Aqueduct Empire: a Guide to Water in California, Its Turbulent History and Its Management Today.* Glendale: Arthur H. Clark Co., 1968. First edition, one of 2589 copies, 439 pages, photo plates, folding map, very fine, pictorial dust jacket. Argonaut Book Shop Recent Acquisitions June 2013 - 70 2013 $125

Cooper, James Fenimore 1789-1851 *The History of the Navy of the United States of America.* Paris: A. and W. Galignani & Co., 1839. 8vo., 2 volumes, frontispiece, map, 2 half titles, contemporary calf backed cloth, rubbing of spines, foxing, several ex-library stamps on titles, otherwise very good and sound. M & S Rare Books, Inc. 95 - 91 2013 $275

Cooper, James Fenimore 1789-1851 *The Last of the Mohicans.* London: John Miller, 1826. First English edition, with half titles in volumes 2 and 3 as issued, 3 volumes, octavo, contemporary half dark green calf over marbled boards, excellent copy, custom made half green morocco, fleece lined clamshell case. David Brass Rare Books, Inc. Holiday 2012 Chapter Five - DB 02130 2013 $4500

Cooper, James Fenimore 1789-1851 *The Pioneers; or the Sources of the Susquehanna...* New York: Charles Wiley, 1823. First edition, 12mo., contemporary calf, date deleted from imprint in volume I, some cuts in last leaves volume II, sound copy, lacks front endleaves. M & S Rare Books, Inc. 95 - 92 2013 $325

Cooper, James Fenimore 1789-1851 *The Pioneers, or the Sources of the Susquehanna.* New York: Charles Wiley, 1823. first edition first printing of volume I, first state of volume II, 2 volumes, 12mo., original drab boards, uncut, boards detached, most of paper gone from one spine, portions of printed paper labels intact. M & S Rare Books, Inc. 95 - 90 2013 $1250

Cooper, John *Detective Fiction: the Collector's Guide.* Aldershot: Scolar, 1994. Second edition, very fine in dust jacket. Mordida Books 81 - 444 2013 $85

Cooper, John Gilbert *Letters Concerning Taste.* London: printed for R. and J. Dodsley, 1757. Third edition, half title, frontispiece by Grignion, very good in contemporary calf, expertly rebacked with corners repaired, some occasional browning and light foxing, ownership name of Catherine Nevile Thorney 1809. Ken Spelman Books Ltd. 75 - 22 2013 £395

Cooper, M. P. *Minerals of the English Lake District: Caldbeck Fells.* Natural History Museum, 1990. First edition, 4to., original pictorial wrappers, illustrations in color. R. F. G. Hollett & Son Lake District & Cumbria - 312 2013 £25

Cooper, T. P. *A Guide to the Guildhall of the City of York.* York: The Corporation of the City, 1909. 8vo., frontispiece, decorative titlepage and plates by E. Ridsdale Tate, very good in original wrappers, very slight wear to head and tail of backstrip, presentation copy from author. Ken Spelman Books Ltd. 73 - 51 2013 £25

Cooper, W. Heaton *The Hills of Lakeland.* London: Warne, 1938. First edition, small 4to., original cloth, gilt, dust jacket little worn, price clipped, 16 colored plates, colored label on flyleaf. R. F. G. Hollett & Son Lake District & Cumbria - 313 2013 £65

Cooper, W. Heaton *The Hills of Lakeland.* Kendal: Frank Peters, 1984. Third edition, small 4to., original cloth, gilt, dust jacket, 16 colored plates. R. F. G. Hollett & Son Lake District & Cumbria - 314 2013 £40

Cooper, W. Heaton *The Lakes.* London: Frederick Warne and Co., 1966. First edition, 4to., original pictorial cloth, dust jacket, 17 colored plates and 64 drawings by author, 1979 brochure for Heaton Cooper's Log House, Ambleside loosely inserted, signed. R. F. G. Hollett & Son Lake District & Cumbria - 315 2013 £75

Cooper, W. Heaton *Mountain Painter.* Kendal: Frank Peters, 1984. First edition, large 8vo., original cloth, gilt, dust jacket with little spotting to upper panel, illustrations in color. R. F. G. Hollett & Son Lake District & Cumbria - 316 2013 £65

Cooper, W. Heaton *The Tarns of Lakeland.* London: Frederick Warne and Co., 1960. First edition, small 4to, original cloth, gilt, dust jacket, 16 colored plates, signed. R. F. G. Hollett & Son Lake District & Cumbria - 317 2013 £95

Cooper, William A. *Thank God for a Song: a Novel of Negro Church Life in the Rural South.* New York: Exposition Press, 1962. First edition, fine in spine faded, else fine dust jacket with little rubbing and couple of tiny tears, very scarce. Between the Covers Rare Books, Inc. 165 - 118 2013 $175

Coover, Robert *The Origin of the Brunists.* New York: Putnam, 1966. First edition, signed by author, very good plus to near fine in near fine, clean dust jacket. Ed Smith Books 75 - 21 2013 $175

Cope, Wendy *Making Cocoa for Kingsley Amis.* London: Faber & Faber, 1986. First edition, wrapper edition, 8vo., original wrappers, spine faded, otherwise near fine, inscribed by author. Maggs Bros. Ltd. 1460 - 198 2013 £50

Cope, Zachary *The Diagnosis of the Acute Abdomen in Rhyme.* London: H. K. Lewis, 1955. Third edition, very good++ with mild sun spine, tinted endpapers, foxing to edges, 12mo., binding tight. By the Book, L. C. 38 - 46 2013 $300

Copeland, Charles *The Black Cat Book.* London: Blackie & Son, n.d., 1905. 4to., pictorial paper covered boards, slight rubbing, spine wear, near fine, illustrations by Charles Robinson, with full page red and black silhouettes and with black silhouettes on every page of text, rare in such nice condition. Aleph-Bet Books, Inc. 104 - 489 2013 $1200

Coppard, Alfred Edward 1878-1957 *The Hundredth Story of A. E. Coppard.* Waltham St. Lawrence: Golden Cockerel Press, 1931. Limited to 1000 copies, quarter morocco, some wear on spine, else very good. C. P. Hyland 261 - 446 2013 £105

Corcoran, Thomas *Celtica: Series Pro Scholis Classicis Nova.* Dublin: circa, 1930. 8vo., (35) pages, folding map, 2 photos, wrappers, good. C. P. Hyland 261 - 950 2013 £27

Corcoran, Thomas *Education Systems in Ireland from the Close of the Middle Ages.* 1928. First edition, quarter cloth, 8vo., very good. C. P. Hyland 261 - 948 2013 £52

Corelli, Marie *The Strange Visitation of Josiah McNason.* London: George Newnes Ltd., 1904. First edition, large octavo, 10 full page pen and ink drawings by H. Millar, rebound in plain blue wrappers with substantially complete remains of original pictorial front wrapper laid down on front panel. L. W. Currey, Inc. Christmas Themed Books - 129539 2013 $350

Corelli, Marie *Vendetta! or the Story of One Forgotten.* London: Richard Bentley & Son, 1891. New edition, 8vo., original black cloth, inscribed by author to Italian opera singer Adelina Patti, excellent copy, head and tail of spine lightly rubbed. Maggs Bros. Ltd. 1460 - 199 2013 £125

The Cork & Fermoy and Waterford & Wexford Railway Act 1890. 1890. 8vo., iii 62 pages, disbound. C. P. Hyland 261 - 263 2013 £75

Cork and Munster Trades' Directory. 1910. Folding map, 158, 58 pages, original cloth, dull and used, text very good. C. P. Hyland 261 - 226 2013 £40

Cork and Munster Trades' Directory. 1939. 8vo., Cork city map, original cloth, very good. C. P. Hyland 261 - 227 2013 £35

Cork Agricultural Society *Summer Show Catalogue July 7th & 7th 1904.* 1904. 206 pages, original wrappers, 8vo., well used copy. C. P. Hyland 261 - 259 2013 £35

Cork Agricultural Society *Three Prize Essays on Dairy Management.* Purcell, 1879. v, 61 pages, original printed wrappers, pencil marks occasionally, else good. C. P. Hyland 261 - 258 2013 £105

Cork Historical & Archaeological Society *Journal of... Volume I, First series.* 1892. Card binding Guy's used for such sets, needs some attention, text clean. C. P. Hyland 261 - 694 2013 £35

Cork Historical & Archaeological Society *Journal of... Nos. 217 Jan. 1968- 247, 1983.* 1968-1983. 24 issues, original wrappers, very good. C. P. Hyland 261 - 696 2013 £250

Cork Industrial Development Association *14th Annual Report.* Shandon Printing Works, 1916. On irish made paper with Irish made ink, 64 pages, wrappers, with typed letter from the Committee to a Tralee businessman, very good. C. P. Hyland 261 - 228 2013 £30

Cork Industrial Development Association. *2nd Annual Exhibition.* Eagle Printing Works: Nov. 20th - Dec. 2nd, 1905. 8vo., on Irish made paper with Irish made ink, 92 pages, disbound. C. P. Hyland 261 - 223 2013 £45

Cork International Exhibition 1902 *Fine Art Catalogue.* 66 pages, original wrappers, 8vo., very good.   C. P. Hyland   261 - 219   2013   £45

Cork International Exhibition 1902 *Official Guide.* Folding plan, 8vo., original wrappers, very good.   C. P. Hyland   261 - 220   2013   £45

Corkery, Daniel *I Bhreasail: a Book of yris.* 1921. First edition, quarter cloth, 8vo., very good.   C. P. Hyland   261 - 953   2013   £32

Corkery, Daniel *The Stormy Hills.* 1929. First edition, 8vo., cloth, very good.   C. P. Hyland   261 - 265   2013   £30

Corkran, Alice *The Baim's Annual for 1885-1886 (Volume I).* Field & Tuer, 1885. Small 8vo., original blue paper covered boards, diamond shaped paper labels (spine label title darkened and chipped), corners rather worn, spine rubbed, uncut, frontispiece aquatint by William Luker and 5 pages of music, scarce.   R. F. G. Hollett & Son   Children's Books - 135   2013   £85

Corkran, Alice *Down the Snow Stairs; or from good-Night to Good-Morning.* Blackett & Son, n.d., 1887. First edition, original brown cloth gilt, one corner little bruised, all edges gilt, 6 woodcut illustrations by Gordon Browne.   R. F. G. Hollett & Son   Children's Books - 134   2013   £50

Corner, Miss *All Good Things come from God; or Frank and His Mamma.* London: Dean and Son, n.d., 1855 on rear, 16mo., pictorial wrappers, corner rear cover repaired, else very good, 14 nice hand colored engravings.   Aleph-Bet Books, Inc.   105 - 225   2013 $125

Corner, Miss *Careless James; or the Box of Toys.* London: Dean and Son, n.d., 1855 code on rear, 16mo., pictorial wrappers, near fine, 14 hand colored engravings.   Aleph-Bet Books, Inc.   105 - 224   2013 $200

Corner, Miss *Good Man of the Mill.* London: Dean and Son, n.d., 1855. 16mo., pictorial wrappers, corner cover soil, else very good+, 10 hand colored engravings.   Aleph-Bet Books, Inc.   105 - 223   2013 $150

Corner, Miss *Little Plays for Little People. Series the First.* Dean & Son, n.d., First edition, original blue cloth, gilt over bevelled boards with oval central chromolithograph on upper board, extremities little rubbed, all edges gilt, woodcut illustrations, upper joint cracked, few spots, armorial bookplate of Hugh Cecil, Earl of Lonsdale.   R. F. G. Hollett & Son   Children's Books - 149   2013   £95

Corning, James Leonard *Brain Exhaustion with some Preliminary Considerations on Cerebral Dynamics.* New York: D. Appleton, 1884. Original green cloth, corners bumped, small spine label at top of spine, stamp on titlepage, internally very good.   James Tait Goodrich S74 - 49   2013 $395

Cornwell, Patricia D. *All That Remains.* London: Little Brown, 1992. First edition, very fine in dust jacket.   Mordida Books   81 - 111   2013 $125

Cornwell, Patricia D. *The Body Farm.* New York: Scribners, 1994. First edition, signed by author, very fine in dust jacket.   Mordida Books   81 - 112   2013 $100

Correy, Lee *Rocket Man.* New York: Henry Holt, 1955. First edition, small, light stain on front board and couple of tiny spots on titlepage, else near fine in very good or better dust jacket with tiny nicks and tear, mostly confined to spine ends on rear panel, signed by author and additionally inscribed by him in 1957.   Between the Covers Rare Books, Inc.   Sci-Fi, Fantasy & Horror - 98243   2013 $400

Corri, Haydn *Hindustanee. Serenading Song...* Dublin: William Power, 1818. Folio, engraved music, titlepage attractively lettered in italics, publisher's stamp at base of title, contemporary signature "Mary J. Taylor" on page 3, disbound, 7 pages.   Jarndyce Antiquarian Booksellers   CCIII - 368   2013   £60

Cort, Louise Allison *Isamu Noguchi and Modern Japanese Ceramics: a Close Embrace of the Earth.* Washington: & Berkeley: Arthur M. Sackler Gallery, Smithsonian Institution in association with the University of California Press, 2003. First edition, 219 pages, numerous color and black and white illustrations, very near fine copy in near fine dust jacket with tiny tear to top of spine.   Jeff Hirsch Books   Fall 2013 - 129117   2013 $50

Corte, Corneille De *De Clavis Dominicis Liber.* Antwerp: Andreae Frisii, 1670. 12mo., with final blank H6, engraved fore-title, engraved vignette on titlepage, 16 engravings by Arnold Loemans, contemporary vellum, very good, bookplate.   Joseph J. Felcone Inc.   Books Printed before 1701 - 24   2013 $400

Cosgrove, H. S. *The Swarts Ruin: a Typical Mimbres Site in Southwestern New Mexico.* Cambridge: 1932. xxiii, 178 pages, plus 236 plates and 3 folding site plans, rebound in cloth, some pencil underlining, else very good.   Dumont Maps & Books of the West   124 - 58   2013 $135

Cosmpolitan, A. *Miss Columbia's Public School or Will It Blow Over.* New York: Francis B. Velt, 1871. 8vo., brown cloth stamped in gold edge faded, else very good+, 72 illustrations, scarce.   Aleph-Bet Books, Inc.   104 - 373   2013 $325

Costello, Con *In Quest of an Heir: Life... John Butler, Catholic Bishop of Cloyne.* 1978. First edition, 175 pages, cloth, 8vo., dust jacket, Castle Hacket bookplate, else fine. C. P. Hyland 261 - 164 2013 £30

Costello, Louisa Stuart *A Summer Amongst the Bocages and the Vines.* London: Richard Bentley, 1840. First edition, 2 volume, 8vo., 4 lithographic plates, 8 text illustrations, some foxing to plates, original green blindstamped cloth, spines faded. J. & S. L. Bonham Antiquarian Booksellers Europe - 8725 2013 £250

Cosway, Richard *Catalogue of a Collection of Miniatures by Richard Cosway...* N.P.: for private circulation only, 1883. Limited edition, limitation not stated, folio, (32)ff., frontispiece, 26 full page mounted original photographic plates, original half brown morocco, marbled boards, morocco corners, raised bands, gilt spine title, all edges gilt, bound by J. Leighton, Brewer St. (stamp on front flyleaf), inscribed "With Mr. Edward Joseph's Kindest regards New York 22 Dec. (18)83", bookplate of John Nolty, fine, rare. Jeff Weber Rare Books 171 - 78 2013 $750

Cota, Claudio Manoel Da *Orbas de Claudio Manoel de Costa Arcade Ultramarino Chamado Glauceste Saturnio.* Coimra: Luiz Seco Ferreira, 1768. First edition, 16mo., contemporary calf, moderately worn, inked inscription, very good, very rare. Maggs Bros. Ltd. 1467 - 103 2013 £1500

Cotes, Roger *Hydrostatical and Pneumatical Lectures.* London: printed for J. Nurse, 1775. Third edition, 8vo., 5 folding plates, bit of light spotting to titlepage, contemporary sprinkled calf, orange morocco label to spine, touch worn around edges, neat repairs to spine ends and front joint, ownership inscription of J. Fleming Oriel College, Oxford dated 1775. Unsworths Antiquarian Booksellers 28 - 85 2013 £300

Cottingham, E. R. *Pedigree of Bowen of Court House.* 1927. First edition, large 4to., 36 pages, 2 folding pedigrees, cloth, very good, inscribed by Aubrey Toppin. C. P. Hyland 261 - 374 2013 £75

Cottle, Joseph *Early Recollections, Chiefly Relating to the Late Samuel Coleridge, During His Long Residence in Bristol.* London: Longman, Rees & Co., 1837. First edition, 2 volumes, half titles, frontispieces, plates, contemporary full tan calf by Bickers & Son, gilt spines, borders and dentelles, maroon & brown leather labels, heads of spines chipped with some loss, hinges cracking, armorial booklabel of Adelaine Puxley, all edges gilt, fine binding using poor leather, good plus. Jarndyce Antiquarian Booksellers CCIII - 580 2013 £125

Cottle, Joseph *Reminiscences of Samuel Taylor Coleridge and Robert Southey.* London: Houlston & Stoneman, 1847. First edition, half title, frontispiece, plates, bound without final ad leaf, plates slightly spotted, contemporary half calf, little rubbed, lacking title label, booklabel of J. W. Hornbuckle, good, sound copy. Jarndyce Antiquarian Booksellers CCIII - 581 2013 £125

Cottle, Joseph *Reminiscences of Samuel Taylor Coleridge and Robert Southey.* London: Houlston & Stoneman, 1848. Second edition, half title, frontispiece, plates, smartly bound in later 20th century maroon cloth, paper label, very good. Jarndyce Antiquarian Booksellers CCIII - 582 2013 £90

Cotton, Charles *Poems on Several Occasions.* printed for Tho. Basset, Will. Hensmann and Tho. fox, 1689. First edition, little browned and stained in places, one leaf dust stained in fore-margin and frail at foot, rust hole in one leaf in blank area, 8vo., contemporary panelled calf, rebacked preserving most of the original spine, gilt almost entirely faded away, red lettering piece, contemporary initials EJL on flyleaf, inscription of John Amson dated 1722 on title and also on flyleaf, later armorial bookplate of E. and F. Bolton, good. Blackwell's Rare Books B174 - 39 2013 £650

Cotton, Henry *Editions of the Bible and Parts Thereof, in English from the Year MDV to MDCCCL.* Oxford: Oxford University Press, 1852. Second edition, 4to., small title vignette, index, original brown cloth, printed paper spine label, spine ends chipped, label chipped, inner hinges bit cracked, good, inscribed "From the Author". Jeff Weber Rare Books 171 - 81 2013 $120

Cotton, Robert *Cottoni Posthuma.* London: printed by Francis Leach, 1651. 8vo., slight browning, titlepage little dusted, one small rust hole, contemporary calf, neatly rebacked, not recently, corners slightly worn, inscription, ex-library Car. Weston 1761, earlier name at head of titlepage. Jarndyce Antiquarian Booksellers CCIV - 9 2013 £225

Cotugno, Domenico *De Ischiade Nervosa Commentarias.* Vienna: apud Rudolphum Graffer, 1770. One engraved plate, 8vo., modern boards. James Tait Goodrich 75 - 56 2013 $750

Cotugno, Domenico *Onori Funeri Resi all Memoria del Cavaliere Domenico Cotugion il Di 17 Febbraro de 1823 nel Collegio Medico-Cerusico Eretio Nell'Ospedale degl'Incunabili.* Naples: A. Nobile, 1823. Engraved portrait, red gilt boards, rare. James Tait Goodrich 75 - 57 2013 $850

Coulson, Frederick Raymond *Darwin on Trial at the Old Baily (&) Judicial Scandals and Errors.* London: University Press, 19...(sic), First edition but probably later printing with titlepage dated "19..", 2 parts in 1, as issued, 8vo., original blindstamped maroon cloth, gilt lettering, five pages of publisher's terminal ads, cloth, slightly rubbed, fine.   The Brick Row Book Shop   Miscellany Fifty-Nine - 11   2013 $250

Counselor, Jim *Wild, Woolly and Wonderful.* Vantage Press: 1954. Review copy slip tipped in, vi, 392 pages, green cloth some foxing on top of text block, else very good in dust jacket with foxing, edgewear and minor loss, quite scarce.   Dumont Maps & Books of the West   124 - 60   2013 $150

The County & City of Cork Almanac for 1849. Jackson, 100 pages, disbound, good.   C. P. Hyland   261 - 208   2013   £50

Courlander, Harold *The Fire on the Mountain and Other Ethiopian Stories.* New York: Henry Holt, 1950. First edition, fine in lightly soiled, very good dust jacket with pencilled number on front panel, faint sticker shadow on spine and light general wear, illustrations, nicely inscribed by author and artist, Robert Kane, to same recipient.   Between the Covers Rare Books, Inc.   165 - 121   2013 $150

Courlander, Harold *Negro Folk Muis, USA.* London: Jazz Book Club, 1966. First English edition, foxing on top edge, still fine in fine dust jacket, beautiful copy, scarce.   Between the Covers Rare Books, Inc.   165 - 120   2013 $75

Courlander, Harold *Terrapin's Pot of Sense.* New York: Holt, Rinehart and Winston, 1961. Third printing, illustrations by Elton Fax, near owner name, else fine in very good dust jacket (foxed with bit of shallow nicking at spine), very scarce, illustrations.   Between the Covers Rare Books, Inc.   165 - 119   2013 $225

Court De Gebelin, Antoine *Histoire Naturelle de La Parole.* Paris: 1776. First separate edition, (2), 400 pages, frontispiece, folding engraved table plus fine colored mezzotint plate, 8vo., contemporary full tan polished calf, raised bands, no spine label, front joint cracked.   James Tait Goodrich   S74 - 52   2013 $1500

Court De Gebelin, Antoine *Histoire Naturelle de la Parole ou Precis de l'Origine du Langage & De La Grammaire Universelle.* Paris: Chez L'Auteur, 1776. First separate edition, frontispiece, woodcut titlepage vignette, headpieces, tailpieces, 1 engraved folding plate, 1 engraved colored folding plate, modern calf, original marbled boards, gilt spine, fine.   Jeff Weber Rare Books   172 - 59   2013 $950

Courtenay, William J. *Covenant and Causality in Medieval Thought: Studies in Philosophy, Theology and Economic Practice.* London: Variorum Reprint, 1984. 8vo., xi, 350 pages, blue cloth, gilt stamped cover and spine title, ownership signature, fine.   Jeff Weber Rare Books   169 - 78   2013 $100

Coutler, Lane *Navajo Saddle Blankets: Textiles to Ride in the American West.* Santa Fe: 2002. 144 pages, illustrations, near fine in like dust jacket, uncommon in hardcover.   Dumont Maps & Books of the West   124 - 59   2013 $125

Couture. The Great Designers. New York: Stewart, Tabori & Chang, 1985. Second edition, fine in fine dust jacket.   Beasley Books   2013 - 2013 $50

Coventry, Andreas *Dissertatio Medico Inauguralis de Scarlatina Cynanchica.* Edinburgi: apud Balfour et Smellie Academiae Typographos, 1783. 8vo., touch of faint dust soiling, contemporary tree calf, spine gilt in compartments with tree of life, marbled endpapers, all edges gilt, rebacked and recornered preserving original spine by Chris Weston, old spine bit chipped, pencil MS note (modern).   Unsworths Antiquarian Booksellers   28 - 86   2013   £200

Cowan, Robert Ernest *A Bibliography of the History of California 1510-1930.* Los Angeles: 1964. Reprint, 4 volumes bound in 1, original three quarter green cloth, marbled sides, paper spine label, fine.   Argonaut Book Shop   Recent Acquisitions June 2013 - 71   2013 $200

Cowan, Robert Granniss *Ranchos of California. A List of Spanish Concessions 1775-1822 and Mexican Grants 1822-1846.* Los Angeles: Historical Society of Southern California, 1977. Facsimile of 1956 printing, endpaper maps, green cloth gilt, small spot to front cover, fine.   Argonaut Book Shop   Recent Acquisitions June 2013 - 72   2013 $60

Coward, Noel 1899-1973 *Poems by Hernia Whittlebot.* Waddington, 1923. first edition, 'errata slip' tipped in, owner's gift inscription, 4to., original fawn stapled wrappers, front cover printed in black, rear cover with publisher's name also in black, near fine, scarce.   Blackwell's Rare Books   172 - 175   2013   £300

Coward, Noel 1899-1973 *Quadrille.* London: Heinemann, 1952. First edition, 8vo., 116 pages, signed by 17 members of the English cast and producer Jack Wilson and by Lynn Fontann and Alfred Lunt, inscribed by author to Dorothy Sands (Octavia in NY production).   Second Life Books Inc.   183 - 83   2013 $500

Cowboy Tom's Round-up Book. New York: Bibl-Lang., 1933. First edition, wrappers, 64 pages, folio, very good.   Beasley Books   2013 - 2013 $50

Cowell, Joe *Thirty Years Passed Among the Players in England and America Interspersed with Anecdotes and Reminiscences of a Variety of persons, Directly or Indirectly Connected with the Drama During the Theatrical Life of Joe Cowell, Comedian.* New York: Harper & Bros., 1844. First edition, 8vo., 2 parts in 1 volume, lacks wrappers, else very good.   M & S Rare Books, Inc.   95 - 364   2013 $225

Cowell, John *Nomothetes. The Interpreter Containing the Genuine Signification of Such Obscure words and terms...* London: printed by J. Streater, 1672. First edition, 300 pages, half title and final blank, folio, small tear to margin M2, corner torn of dd1, slight worming to blank inner margins clear of text, full contemporary blind ruled calf, raised bands, very good, early signatures to front endpaper.   Jarndyce Antiquarian Booksellers   CCIV - 10   2013   £1250

Cowen, William Joyce *They Gave Him a Gun.* New York: Harrison Smith and Robert Haas, 1936. First edition, fine in attractive, very good plus dust jacket with small nicks at corners, nicely inscribed by author to his daughter Antonia Joyce Cowen, Jan. 27 1936.   Between the Covers Rare Books, Inc.   Mystery & Detective Fiction - 97568   2013 $1500

Cowham, Hilda *Mother Goose's Rag Book.* Dean's Rag Book Co. n.d., early 20th century, square 8vo., original red cloth, stitched spine, color printed cloth, sometime washed and rather faded, little frayed at head and foot.   R. F. G. Hollett & Son   Children's Books - 136   2013   £50

Cowley, Abraham   1618-1667 *Poems: viz. I. Miscellanies. II. The Mistress, or Love Verses. III. Pindarique Odes. And IV. Davideis, or a Sacred Poem of the Troubles of David.* London: for Humphrey Moseley, 1656. First collected edition, contemporary panelled calf, edges gilt, very skillfully rebacked to style, later endpapers, occasional minor spots and repaired marginal tears, 3L2, soiled and with paper defect costing several letters, lovely, early signature of Edmund Henry Marshall, "Ex Libris George Bernard Shaw" on front endpaper.   Joseph J. Felcone Inc.   English and American Literature to 1800 - 11   2013 $2500

Cowley, Abraham   1618-1667 *The Works of Mr. Abraham.* London: printed for J. Tonson, Charles Haper, 1710-1711. Ninth edition, 3 volumes, 8vo., frontispiece, 17 engraved plates, frontispiece, 9 engraved plates, frontispiece and 4 engraved plates, lightly browned, little minor spotting, contemporary calf, plain spine with red morocco labels, boards bordered in blind, edges sprinkled red, rubbed at extremities, neatly conserved by Chris Weston replacing original labels, f.f.e.p. removed from first volume, early ink ownership inscription "Anne Pitt and large armorial bookplate John Borthwick/Crookston".   Unsworths Antiquarian Booksellers   28 - 87   2013   £225

Cowley, Malcolm *Writers at Work: the Paris Review Interviews.* New York: Viking Press, 1948. First edition, 8vo., fine in fine, bright dust jacket (trifle rubbed at spine extremities).   Ed Smith Books   75 - 55   2013 $75

Cowling, Tom Pierce *Little Songs: a Book of Poems.* London: Henry Frowde Hodder & Stoughton, n.d. circa, 1915. Large 4to., cloth backed boards, pictorial paste-on, corners rubbed, else fine, color plate frontispiece, 2 full page black and whites and numerous other line illustrations by Edward Gorey on other text pages.   Aleph-Bet Books, Inc.   105 - 286   2013 $125

Cowper, Henry Swainson *Hawkshead....* Bemrose and Sons, 1899. First edition, large 8vo., original buckram gilt over bevelled boards, little rubbed and faded, top edge gilt, 2 colored folding maps and 32 illustrations, lower joints just cracking, but very good, scarce.   R. F. G. Hollett & Son   Lake District & Cumbria - 322   2013   £240

Cowper, Henry Swainson *The Hill of the Graves.* London: Methuen, 1897. First edition, original green cloth gilt, 898 illustrations, folding plan, large folding map, few spots to prelims, presentation copy inscribed by author to Hawkshead Institute, with his armorial bookplate and Institute library labels.   R. F. G. Hollett & Son   Africana - 42   2013   £75

Cowper, Henry Swainson *Robert Kitchin, Mayor of Bristol: a Native of Kendal.* Kendal: Titus Wilson, 1920. Reprint, original wrappers, portrait, extending pedigree, presentation copy from author for C. R(oy) H(udleston).   R. F. G. Hollett & Son   Lake District & Cumbria - 323   2013   £30

Cowper, William   1666-1709 *Myotomia Reformata or an Anatomical Treatise on the Muscles of the Human Body...* London: printed for Robert Knaplock and William and John Innys, 1724. First folio edition, fine engraved frontispiece, title in red and black, plates and tables but lacking one plate and one table, which appear to be having never been bound in, printer has designated a number of elegant head and tailpieces along historiated initials with anatomical themes, 58 (of 60) copperplates, tall folio, presentation style calf, gilt tooled panelled spine with large functional brass clasps on fore edges, printed on heavy stock, well margined paper, calf showing some wear, some outerskin loss on boards, joints firm.   James Tait Goodrich   75 - 58   2013 $2450

Cowper, William   1731-1800 *Poems.* printed for J. Johnson, 1787. Third edition, 2 volumes, signature B of volume ii in first state, occasional minor foxing, 8vo., contemporary polished calf, gilt rule compartments on spines, green lettering and numbering pieces, latter being oval, circular label of Trinity College Library on upper covers, traces of sellotape at foot of spines, slightly worn, good.   Blackwell's Rare Books   B174 - 40   2013   £250

Cowper, William 1731-1800 *Poems.* London: printed for J. Johnson, 1793. Fifth edition, 2 volumes, contemporary tree calf, spines ruled gilt, later red morocco labels, numbered direct, unobtrusive repairs to hinges, leading f.e.p. volume I inscribed "Richard Forster French 1739 the gift of Mrs. Nicholas", later bookplate of F. L. Edwards, nice copy.   Jarndyce Antiquarian Booksellers   CCIII - 611   2013   £150

Cowper, William 1731-1800 *Poems.* London: Tilt & Bogue, 1841. 2 volumes, half titles, illustrations, final ad leaf volume I, original royal blue cloth, attractively blocked in blind and gilt, spines slightly dulled and very slightly rubbed at heads and tails, very good.   Jarndyce Antiquarian Booksellers   CCIII - 612   2013   £35

Cowper, William 1731-1800 *Poetical Works of William Cowper.* Edinburgh: James Nichol, 1854. 8vo., 2 volumes, three quarter leather, very good.   Barnaby Rudge Booksellers   Poetry 2013 - 020049   2013 $60

Cox, Edward Godfrey   *A Reference Guide to the Literature.*   Seattle: University of Washington, 1935-1949. First printing, 3 volumes, large 8vo., printed wrappers, wrappers and spine worn (with pieces missing on volumes I and II), volume I front cover detached, volume II rear cover missing, Burndy bookplates rubber stamps and markings of MIT libraries.   Jeff Weber Rare Books   169 - 80   2013 $100

Cox, George   *Back Gowns & Red Coats, or Oxford in 1834.* London: James Ridgway & Sons, 1834. Part I first edition, pages II-VI second edition, Parts I-VI, half titles, contemporary half red morocco, slightly rubbed, armorial bookplate of George S. Munn, good plus.   Jarndyce Antiquarian Booksellers   CCIII - 672   2013   £80

Cox, J. Charles   *Cumberland and Westmorland.*   George Allen & Co., 1913. First edition, small 8vo., original decorated cloth, 14 plates, 14 text illustrations, maps on endpapers.   R. F. G. Hollett & Son   Lake District & Cumbria - 326   2013   £25

Cox, J. Stevens   *Monographs on the Life of Thomas Hardy.*   Beaminster: Dorset & elsewhere: Stevens Cox, the Toucan Press, 1962-1971. 72 volumes, 12mo., original wrappers, stapled as issued, numerous illustrations, uniformly very good, from the Gary Lepper Collection of Thomas Hardy.   The Brick Row Book Shop   Bulletin Nine - 101   2013 $850

Cox, Morris   *The Curtain.* London: Gogmagog Press, 1960. Copy 19 of 26 copies numbered and signed in ink by author, 10 double page reverse-offset prints, printed on cream wove cartridge paper, bound in black cloth boards with white stripes, acetate dust jacket, very fine.   James S. Jaffe Rare Books   Fall 2013 - 58   2013 $1750

Cox, Morris   *From a London Suburb.*   London: Gogmagog Press, 1975. Copy number 2 of 24 copies, numbered and signed by author on colophon, double page spread titlepage reverse offset print from lace and four reverse/direct offset prints on colored papers, Corrie Guy's copy printed on Japanese handmade Yamato-Chiri and Mingei papers, bound in green silk boards with acetate dust jacket, laid in is long TLS 1 page 4to. 28 Nov. 1975 from author to Guyt, very fine.   James S. Jaffe Rare Books   Fall 2013 - 60   2013 $1250

Cox, Morris   *From a London Suburb. Poems.*   Gogmagog Press, 1975. 20/24 copies, printed on Japanese Yamato-chiri fawn handmade paper double leaves, signed by author, 4 double page reverse/direct offset prints in various colours, final print and titlepage both repeated at end of book, double page titlepage, text printed in black and blue and with decorative border to head and tail reproduced from lace, tall foolscap 8vo., original blue silk, printed label, tail edges untrimmed, fine.   Blackwell's Rare Books   172 - 286   2013   £500

Cox, Morris   *An Impression of Winter: A Landscape Panorama, An Impression of Spring; A Landscape Panorama; An Impression of Summer: A Landscape Panorama; & An Impression of Autumn: A Landscape Panorama.* London: Gogmagog Press, 1966. First editions, limited to 100 copies printed on Japanese Hosho paper and signed by artist, 4 volumes, 8vo., each volume illustrated with 3 embossed reverse/direct offset prints joined in continuous strip, bound in Ingres paper boards, printed with monotypes, acetate dust jackets, very fine set.   James S. Jaffe Rare Books   Fall 2013 - 59   2013 $4000

Cox, Morris   *Magogomagog. Being Random Examples of the Innumerable, Incredible Ideas & Guises of Gog, Ma, Gogma & Magog.*   Gogmagog Press, 1973. 2/75 copies, printed on yellow Japanese Mingei handmade paper for text and white Hosho handmade paper for illustrations, signed by author, 9 full page linocuts printed in black on blue ground, text printed in black and titlepage in brown, green and yellow, small folio, original quarter white vellum, backstrip blocked in black and red, blue and brown silks interwoven with gold thread, glassine jacket, fine, this copy specially bound for Corrie Guyt, card from Cox loosely inserted. Blackwell's Rare Books   172 - 287   2013   £700

Cox, Morris   *A Mystique of Mummers.* London: Gogmagog Press, 1983. First edition, copy number 6 of only 12 sets printed in black, with each linocut individually titles and signed and dated by artist/publisher, in quarter cloth solander box with cork lining, printed label on spine, by Gemma O'Connor and monoprint covers on Japanese paper by Cox, 20 colored elimination linocuts, 12 14 x 17 inches, 22 loose sheets, plus list of plates and 2 sheets of notes pasted inside front and back of box, very fine. James S. Jaffe Rare Books   Fall 2013 - 57   2013 $8500

Cox, Morris *The Whirligig and Other Poems.* London: Routledge & Kegan Paul, 1954. First edition, crown 8vo., original red boards, backstrip blocked in silver, exuberant Cox design to dust jacket which has short tears, small hole and internal tape stains, very good. Blackwell's Rare Books   172 - 288   2013   £250

Cox, Morris *Young Legs Eleven.* Gogmagog Press, 1976. 21/25 copies printed on outer pages of Japanese handmade paper double leaves, signed by author, 4 double page reverse/direct offset prints from linocuts in black and blue, grey green or pink, 3 of the 4 repeated, also with double page titlepage (repeated) with design printed in black and green and its letterpress in black and red, tall foolscap 8vo., original grey green silk, printed label tail edges untrimmed, fine, loosely inserted leaf 'all my unpublished poetry to date..'. Blackwell's Rare Books   172 - 289   2013   £500

Cox, Palmer *The Brownies. Their Book.* New York: Century Co., 1887. First edition, second state with DeVinne device 2 1/2" from bottom of copyright page instead of directly below date), 4to., glazed pictorial boards, paper at front joint partially split in 2 places (no loss of paper, not wak), spine ends a bit worn, else lovely copy in pictorial dust jacket (few chips), illustrations on every page. Aleph-Bet Books, Inc.   105 - 154   2013 $1750

Cox, Palmer *The Brownies. Their Book.* New York: Century Co., 1887. First edition, first issue with DeVinne seal immediately below copyright notice, 4to., original light green glazed pictorial colored boards, minor wear at spine tips, fine condition, original dust jacket although browned, chipped at extremities and with inner folds having old tape repairs, remarkably good condition, morocco backed cloth slipcase. Howard S. Mott Inc.   262 - 36   2013 $1350

Cox, Palmer *The Brownies Around the World.* New York: Century Co., 1894. First edition, 4to., glazed pictorial boards, edges and extremes lightly rubbed, first 2 leaves with scattered foxing, else near fine in original pictorial dust jacket (chip off front panel and soiled). Aleph-Bet Books, Inc.   104 - 132   2013 $975

Cox, Palmer *The Brownies at Home.* London: Century Co., 1893. First edition, 4to., glazed pictorial boards, light edge and corner wear, very good++. illustrations on every page. Aleph-Bet Books, Inc.   105 - 153   2013 $400

Cox, Palmer *Brownies at Home.* London: T. Fisher Unwin, 1893. First UK edition, 4to., pictorial cloth, all edges gilt slight cover soil, else near fine, with a profusion of illustrations, beautiful copy. Aleph-Bet Books, Inc.   105 - 152   2013 $500

Coxe, Daniel *A Description of the English Province of Carolana by the Spaniards called Florida and by the French La Louisiane.* St. Louis: Churchill and Harris, 1840. First American edition, 8vo., large folding engraved map, modern buckram, folds of map weak and one entirely broken, map complete. M & S Rare Books, Inc.   95 - 126   2013 $600

Coxe, George Harmon *Four Frightened Women.* New York: Knopf, 1939. First edition, fine in very good dust jacket with chip at top of darkened spine and some scattered nicks on front panel. Mordida Books   81 - 113   2013 $135

Coy, Owen C. *A Pictorial History of California.* Berkeley: University of California Press, 1925. First edition, oblong 4to., 261 full page plates, publisher's gray-green cloth, gilt, remnants from semi-removed bookplate on inner cover, cloth lightly rubbed at extremities, spine lightly faded, very good, internally fine and clean, scarce. Argonaut Book Shop   Recent Acquisitions June 2013 - 73   2013 $325

Coy, Owen C. *A Pictorial History of California.* Berkeley: University of California Press, 1925. First edition, oblong 4to., 261 full page plates, publisher's loose sheets, never bound, broken slipcase. Argonaut Book Shop   Recent Acquisitions June 2013 - 74   2013 $225

Cozzens, F. S. *Acadia or a Month with the Blue Noses.* New York: Derby & Jackson, 1859. 8vo., brown pressed cloth boards, gilt title to spine, 2 lithographs, cloth sunned and worn, some foxing to lithographs. Schooner Books Ltd.   105 - 63   2013 $65

Cozzens, Issachar *A Geological History of Manhattan or New York Island, Together with a Map of the Island.* New York: W. E. Dean, Printer & Publisher, 1843. First edition, 114 pages, foldout map and 8 hand colored plates, publisher's brown cloth decorated in blind, titled in gilt, bookplate, small split in top joint, corners bumped and rubbed and dampstains in text, still handsome, near very good, inscribed in pencil by author's daughter 1898. Between the Covers Rare Books, Inc.   New York City - 299806   2013 $500

Crabbe, George *Life of the Rev. George Crabbe by his Son.* London: John Murray, 1838. New edition, frontispiece, plates engraved by Finden after Stanfield, slightly spotted, contemporary full olive green calf, attractively blocked in gilt, dark green leather label, slight rubbing, very good. Jarndyce Antiquarian Booksellers   CCIII - 626   2013   £65

Crabbe, George *Tales of the Hall.* London: John Murray, 1820. 12mo., 3 volumes in full black leather with gilt decorations, all edges gilt, engraved throughout, very good. Barnaby Rudge Booksellers   Poetry 2013 - 020993   2013 $125

Crabbe, George 1754-1832 *The Borough: a Poem in Twenty-Four Letters.* London: J. Hatchard, 1810. First edition, half title, 4 pages ads little spotted, contemporary full tree calf, black leather label, expertly rebacked, armorial bookplate of Charles first Viscount of Eversley. Jarndyce Antiquarian Booksellers CCIII - 624 2013 £150

Crabbe, George 1754-1832 *Poems.* London: J. Hatchard, 1808. Second edition, half title, contemporary full diced calf, gilt borders, dentelles and central monogram, bit rubbed and marked, small chip at tail of spine, prize label of Holy Trinity College Dublin & gift inscription on title, good plus. Jarndyce Antiquarian Booksellers CCIII - 620 2013 £65

Crabbe, George 1754-1832 *Poems.* London: printed for J. Hatchard, 1808. Third edition, half title, 2 pages ads, neatly rebound in grey boards, paper label, very good. Jarndyce Antiquarian Booksellers CCIII - 621 2013 £50

Crabbe, George 1754-1832 *Poems.* London: printed for J. Hatchard, 1810. Fifth edition, 2 volumes, half titles, contemporary full vellum, gilt spines, borders and dentelles, red leather labels, little dulled, inscription of Octavia Cholmely 1854, later booklabel of John Baker in volume II, all edges gilt. Jarndyce Antiquarian Booksellers CCIII - 622 2013 £65

Crabbe, George 1754-1832 *Poems. Containing The Library, The Village, The Newspaper, The Parish Register, The Borough.* London: John James Chidley, 1846. New edition, frontispiece and engraved title, printed title, contemporary dark blue morocco, decorated in gilt, leading hinges slightly rubbed, beginning to split at tail, armorial bookplate of Rev. John Henry Ellis & Ellis family inscription, all edges gilt, attractive copy. Jarndyce Antiquarian Booksellers CCIII - 623 2013 £40

Crabbe, George 1754-1832 *The Poetical Works, with Letters and Journals and His Life by His Son.* London: John Murray, 1834-1835. 8 volumes, frontispiece and engraved titles, 2 pages ads volumes I and IV, 3 pages ads volume V, original light brown cloth, odd mark, very good. Jarndyce Antiquarian Booksellers CCIII - 618 2013 £150

Crabbe, George 1754-1832 *Tales.* London: J. Hatchard, 1812. First edition, half title, contemporary full diced calf, gilt borders, dentelles and central monogram, bit rubbed and marked, head of leading hinge beginning to split, prize label of Holy Trinity College Dublin and gift inscription on title. Jarndyce Antiquarian Booksellers CCIII - 625 2013 £90

Crabb's New Book of Trades... London: printed and published by T. Crabb (also J. Bysh, C. Penny, R. Hill & Lingley and Belch, n.d. circa, 1815. 12mo., leather spine, marbled boards, spine repaired with parts of original laid down, tight and very good, 12 very fine full page engravings, rare. Aleph-Bet Books, Inc. 105 - 220 2013 $1200

Craddock, Harry *The Savoy Cocktail Book...* New York: Richard R. Smith, 1930. First American edition, illustrations by Gilbert Rumbold, former owner's attractive bookplate, neat gift inscription, both on front fly, bit of usual edgewear to foil over boards, still nicer than usual, near fine, without dust jacket as issued. Between the Covers Rare Books, Inc. Cocktails, Etc. - 98114 2013 $700

Cragg, R. Balderston *Legendary Rambles: Ingleton & Lonsdale.* Skipton: privately published by author, n.d. circa, 1890. First edition, original green cloth, 10 illustrations and floral patterned endpapers, from Appleby Castle Library with monogram of Lord Hothfield, very scarce. R. F. G. Hollett & Son Lake District & Cumbria - 331 2013 £120

Craig, Maurice *Irish Bookbindings 1600-1800.* London: Cassell & Co., 1954. First edition, 4to., original blue cloth lettered in gilt, excellent copy. Maggs Bros. Ltd. 1442 - 41 2013 £150

Craighead, Meinrad *The Mother's Birds. Images for a Death and a Birth.* Worcester: Stanbrook Abbey Press, 1976. XXV/XXX special copies (of an edition of 235 copies), printed on Chatham handmade paper and signed by author and printer, 20 full page reproductions of charcoal drawings by author, 4to., original black morocco by George Percival, backstrip gilt lettered there is large circle blind tooled in front cover and correspondingly large square to rear cover, De Wint coffee mouldmade paper endpapers, untrimmed, boards slipcase, fine. Blackwell's Rare Books B174 - 386 2013 £285

Craighead, Meinrad *The Mother's Birds.* Stanbrook Abbey Press, 1976. 170/240 copies signed by author and printer, 42 pages, 20 illustrations, 4to., near fine in original cream card covers, bookplate. Ken Spelman Books Ltd. 75 - 188 2013 £65

Crais, Robert *Lullaby Town.* New York: Bantam, 1992. First edition, fine in dust jacket with very slightly faded spine. Mordida Books 81 - 114 2013 $450

Cramer, G. *Henry Moore: Catalogue of Graphic Work 1931-1984.* Geneva: G. & P. Cramer, 1973-1986. One of 200 deluxe copies, each of the 4 volumes numbered and signed by Henry Moore, 13 x 10 x 2 inches, in total, 1660 pages 749 pages, 444 in color, cloth in dust jacket and cloth slipcases, excellent condition. Gemini Fine Books & Arts., Ltd. Art Reference & Illustrated Books - 2013 $1350

Cramer, J. A. *The Second Book of the Travels of Nicander Nucius of Corcyra.* London: Camden Society, 1841. First edition, small quarto, original dark green blindstamped cloth. J. & S. L. Bonham Antiquarian Booksellers Europe - 9233 2013 £50

Cramer, Zadock *The Navigator: Containing Directions for Navigating the Monongahela, Allegheny, Ohio and Mississippi Rivers....* Pittsburgh: printed and published by Cramer, Spar & Eichbaum, 1811. Seventh edition, 12mo., numerous maps, contemporary calf backed marbled boards, rubbed, remarkably fine, very clean, crisp internally, which is very unusual for this work. M & S Rare Books, Inc. 95 - 253 2013 $15,000

Crane, Thomas *Abroad.* Marcus Ward & Co., 1882. Square 8vo., original cloth backed pictorial boards, corners worn, edges rubbed, pages 56, illustrations in color, occasional spot or mark. R. F. G. Hollett & Son Children's Books - 137 2013 £120

Crane, Thomas *At Home.* Marcus Ward & Co. n.d. circa, 1882. Large square 8vo., original cloth backed pictorial boards, edges worn and corners rounded, illustrations in color, front flyleaf removed, few slight scribbles in places. R. F. G. Hollett & Son Children's Books - 140 2013 £65

Crane, Thomas *London Town.* Marcus Ward & Co., 1883. First edition, square 8vo., original cloth backed pictorial boards, corners worn, edges rather rubbed, illustrations in color, couple of short edge tears, very scarce. R. F. G. Hollett & Son Children's Books - 139 2013 £120

Crane, Walter *The Baby's Bouquet.* Routledge, n.d., 1878. First edition, square 8vo., original cloth backed decorated glazed boards, little soiled edges slightly rubbed, pages 56, illustrations in color, flyleaves spotted. R. F. G. Hollett & Son Children's Books - 141 2013 £65

Crane, Walter *The Baby's Own Aesop.* London: George Routledge, 1887. First edition, square 8vo., original decorated glazed boards, little scratched, edges and corners rather worn, pages 56 with color illustrations and decorations, good clean copy. R. F. G. Hollett & Son Children's Books - 143 2013 £120

Crane, Walter *The Baby's Opera.* Frederick Warne and Co. n.d. circa, 1900. Square 8vo., original cloth backed pictorial boards, corners rather worn, little wear to edges, otherwise bright and clean, pages 56, illustrations, inscription dated 1927. R. F. G. Hollett & Son Children's Books - 142 2013 £85

Crane, Walter *Eight Illustrations to Shakespeare's Two Gentlemen of Verona.* London: J. M. Dent & Boston: Copeland & Day, 1894. Limited to 650 numbered copies signed yb Crane and Dallas who printed the plates, folio, loose as issued, housed in two-color cloth box decorated in gold, some wear to front joint of box, else fine, 8 beautiful art nouveau plates, executed on tissue that matted with lettered tissue guards, great copy. Aleph-Bet Books, Inc. 104 - 134 2013 $850

Crane, Walter *The First of May: a Fairy Masque.* London: Henry Sotheran, 1881. Limited to only 300 numbered india proof copies signed by Crane, oblong folio, leather spine, color pictorial fairy motif paste-on with gilt art nouveau design, some rubbing, foxing in margins, lacks ties, very good+ limited to only 300 numbered India proof copies signed by author, 57 folio sheets, each with delicate photogravures, lovely, rare. Aleph-Bet Books, Inc. 104 - 133 2013 $1850

Crane, Walter *Pan-Pipes. A book of Old Songs, Newly Arranged...* London: George Routledge and Sons, 1883. First edition, oblong 4to., original cloth backed decorated boards, few small frayed snags to backstrip, lower corners slightly worn, printed in colors throughout, very good. R. F. G. Hollett & Son Children's Books - 145 2013 £220

Crane, Walter *Queen Summer or the Journey of the Lily and the Rose.* London: Cassell & Co., 1891. First edition, large tall 8vo., original cloth backed decorated boards, edges rather worn and corners rounded, neatly rebacked, printed in color on french-folded sheets, bottom third of rear flyleaf replaced in very good facsimile. R. F. G. Hollett & Son Children's Books - 144 2013 £175

Cranworth, Lord *Kenya Chronicles.* London: Macmillan, 1939. First edition, original brown cloth gilt, 24 plates, gift inscription, multiple signatures, else very good. R. F. G. Hollett & Son Africana - 44 2013 £75

Cranworth, Lord *Profit and Sport in British East Africa.* Macmillan, 1919. Second edition, original cloth, gilt, spine lettering dulled, edges of boards frayed in places, colored frontispiece, 3 plates, 2 maps. R. F. G. Hollett & Son Africana - 43 2013 £120

Crawford, Dan *Back to the Long Grass.* London: Hodder and Stoughton, n.d. early 1920's, Original cloth, gilt, pages 376, with 33 illustrations and 3 maps. R. F. G. Hollett & Son Africana - 45 2013 £45

Crawford, Francis Marion *Don Orsino.* London: Macmillan and New York, 1892. First UK edition, 8vo., 3 volumes, hinges loose, may be lacking a flyleaf, red mark on cover bound in blue/gray cloth, binding little loose in volume 3, good set. Second Life Books Inc. 183 - 84 2013 $325

Crawford, Francis Marion *Saint Ilario.* London: Macmillan, 1889. First edition, 3 volumes, 8vo, blue cloth, rear hinge loose in volume 3, spine faded bookplates, very good. Second Life Books Inc. 183 - 85 2013 $300

Crawford, Francis Marion *Saracinesca.* Edinburgh & London: Blackwood, 1887. First edition, 8vo., 3 volumes, salmon brown cloth, front hinge loose in volume I, not the 'olive' called for BAL, names clipped from each title, very good set. Second Life Books Inc. 183 - 86 2013 $350

Crawford, Lucy *The History of the White Mountains from the First Settlement of Upper Coos and Peguaket...* Portland: Hoyt, Fogg & Donham, 1883. Second edition, 8vo., pages 230, rubbed publisher's cloth, good, tight copy. Second Life Books Inc. 183 - 87 2013 $100

Crawley, Peter *A Mormon Fifty. An Exhibition in the Harold B. Lee Library in Conjunction with the Annual Conference of the Mormon History Association.* Provo: Friends of the Brigham Young University Library, 1984. printed wrappers, fine, scarce. Jeff Weber Rare Books 171 - 83 2013 $50

Craxton Smith, A. *Gun Dogs; their Training, working and management.* London: Seeley Service, 1932. First edition, 8vo., pages 114, illustrations, original yellow cloth, dust jacket. J. & S. L. Bonham Antiquarian Booksellers Europe - 7777 2013 £30

Creasey, John *Death of a Racehorse.* London: Hodder & Stoughton, 1959. First edition, 8vo., original red cloth, dust jacket very lightly soiled, excellent copy, inscribed by author. Maggs Bros. Ltd. 1460 - 200 2013 £75

Creasey, John *A Mask for the Toff.* New York: Walker, n.d., 1966. First American edition, cocked and slightly bumped at spinal extremities, near fine in near fine dust jacket with moderate soiling to rear panel. Between the Covers Rare Books, Inc. Mystery & Detective Fiction - 145553 2013 $60

Crebillon, C. P. J. De *Le Sopha.* Paris: Le Vasseur, 1935. First Icart edition, one of 440 copies on Rives, from a total edition of 517, 23 original color etchings by Louis Icart, 21 of them full page, very handsome full scarlet morocco, unsigned with 5 bands, gilt on top edge and spine, moire silk endleaves, original wrappers bound in, matching slipcase, excellent condition, beautiful copy. Gemini Fine Books & Arts., Ltd. Art Reference & Illustrated Books - 2013 $2900

Creeley, Robert *A Day Book.* Berlin: Graphis, 1972. First edition, edition de tete, one of only 25 roman numeraled copies signed by author and artist, elephant folio, 44 leaves, 14 original graphics by R. B. Kitaj, original full blue and green decorated leather, in publisher's full blue leather slipcase, fine. James S. Jaffe Rare Books Fall 2013 - 34 2013 $7500

Creeley, Robert *Words.* Rochester: Perishable Press, 1965. first edition, one of 30 copies printed (entire edition), this copy signed by author, 4to., original brown boards, plain unprinted dust jacket, top of spine lightly bumped, otherwise fine, in lightly soiled dust jacket,. James S. Jaffe Rare Books Fall 2013 - 33 2013 $4000

Creighton, Mandell *Carlisle.* London: Longmans, Green and Co., 1889. Second edition, original cloth gilt, spine little faded, 2 folding maps. R. F. G. Hollett & Son Lake District & Cumbria - 332 2013 £25

Creswick, Paul *The Turning Wheel.* London: Heath Cranton Ltd., 1928. First edition, bookstore stamp, couple of tiny spots and rubbed spots on boards, still near fine, in about very good dust jacket, with top edge of rear flap fold slightly eroded, nicely inscribed by author for Mr. and Mrs. Robert H. Smith July 22 1929, rare in jacket,. Between the Covers Rare Books, Inc. Sci-Fi, Fantasy & Horror - 84793 2013 $1500

Crews, Donald *Freight Train.* New York: Greenwillow, 1978. First edition, first printing with number code 1-10, oblong 4to., pictorial cloth, fine in dust jacket with award seal, illustrations in color by Donald Crews, this copy inscribed and dated 1979 by Crews who has also added some smoke coming from the picture of the train on endpaper, first printings are scarce, signed copies even more so. Aleph-Bet Books, Inc. 105 - 82 2013 $325

Crichton, Alexander *The Land o' the Leal.* Peterhead: P. Scroge Ltd., 1919. Third edition, frontispiece, original dark green cloth, slightly loose. Jarndyce Antiquarian Booksellers CCIII - 57 2013 £25

Crichton, Michael *Binary.* New York: Alfred A. Knopf, 1972. First edition, fine in dust jacket. Mordida Books 81 - 122 2013 $85

Crichton, Michael *Jasper Johns.* New York: Abrams/Whitney, 1977. First edition, 68 color plates and over 100 other plates, fine in very near fine dust jacket. Jeff Hirsch Books Fall 2013 - 129110 2013 $150

Crick, Francis *What Mad Pursuit.* New York: Basic Books, 1988. Fourth printing, 8vo., very good++, original printed wrappers, mild toning to page edges, minimal soil to covers and edges. By the Book, L. C. 37 - 12 2013 $300

Cripps, George R. *About Furs.* Liverpool: Willmer Bros. c., 1897. Original wrappers (edges worn), 83 pages, 2 colored maps, slightly loose, very scarce. R. F. G. Hollett & Son Polar Exploration - 11 2013 £50

Crisp, Quentin *The Naked Civil Servant.* London: Jonathan Cape, 1968. First edition, 8vo., cloth, dust jacket lightly browned, fine, inscribed by author to David Enders. Maggs Bros. Ltd. 1460 - 201 2013 £250

Criswick, James *A Walk Round Dorchester: an Account of Every Thing Worth the Observation of the Traveller and Antiquairy...* Dorchester: J. Criswick, 1820. Frontispiece, folding map, uncut, original drab boards, pink marbled paper spine, paper label, spine little dulled with some slight rubbing, very good. Jarndyce Antiquarian Booksellers CCV - 78 2013 £250

Critchley, MacDonald *The Divine Banquet of the Brain and Other Essays.* New York: Raven Press, 1979. 269 pages, near fine in original cloth. James Tait Goodrich 75 - 62 2013 $75

Crite Allan Rohan *Three Spirituals from Earth to Heaven.* Cambridge: Harvard University Press, 1948. First edition, fine in price clipped, very good plus dust jacket with four modest tears and small chip at base of spine, illustrations, inscribed by artist with drawing. Between the Covers Rare Books, Inc. 165 - 7 2013 $1750

Croce, Giovanni Andrea Della *Chirvrggiae Vniversalis Opus Absolutum Ioannis Andreae.* Venetiis: Apud Robertum Meiettum, 1596. First edition of the complete Latin edition, title printed in red and black, numerous woodcut illustrations, and almost 500 illustrations, later vellum, rebacked, some marginal worming, light dampstaining, overall very good. James Tait Goodrich 75 - 60 2013 $6750

Crofts, Charley *Memoirs of Charley Crofts.* Cork: Edwards & Savage, 1829. First edition, 177 pages, quarter cloth, some staining on text, binding firm, scarce. C. P. Hyland 261 - 270 2013 £95

Croker, E. J. O'B. *Retrospective Lessons on Railway Strikes.* London and Guy, Cork, 1898. First edition, vi, 205, xv pages, photos, 8vo., cloth, errata slip, very good. C. P. Hyland 261 - 271 2013 £125

Croker, Thomas Crofton *Killarney Legends.* circa, 1869. 8vo., 5 plates, original pictorial cloth, lacks front fly, else good. C. P. Hyland 261 - 273 2013 £30

Croker, Thomas Crofton *Researches in the South of Ireland.* 1824. First edition, 393 pages, 17 plates (some staining), original quarter cloth (binding tight), ms. note on front flyleaf, else text generally good. C. P. Hyland 261 - 272 2013 £200

Croly, David G. *Miscegenation: the Theory of the Blending of the Races...* London: Trubner & Co., 1864. First English edition, 16mo., 91 pages, original cloth, rubbed, front endpaper nearly loose, slightly shaken. M & S Rare Books, Inc. 95 - 98 2013 $375

Croly, George *Salathiel the Immortal: a History.* London: David Bryce, 1856. New edition, half title, contemporary signature of M. T. Saunders, Wilmington Hall, odd spot, original purple cloth, slightly marked, spine faded to brown, good plus. Jarndyce Antiquarian Booksellers CCIII - 673 2013 £35

Croly, Jenniee *The History of the Woman's Club Movement in America.* New York: Henry G. Allen, 1898. First edition, 4to., pages xi, 1184, photos, maroon cloth, stamped in gilt, front hinge tender, rear starting, cover little worn at corners and ends of spine, very good. Second Life Books Inc. 183 - 88 2013 $225

Crone, John *Henry Bradshaw, His Life and Work.* Three Candles, 1931. 16 pages, octavo, wrappers (dusty), text good, "with the Author's Compts.". C. P. Hyland 261 - 50 2013 £35

Crosby, Caresse *Portfolio IV. (Complete)* Rome. Washington: Black Sun Press, 1946. First edition, folio, bond in paper portfolio, as issued, very good+. Ed Smith Books 75 - 4 2013 $250

A Cross Section. The Society of Wood Engravers in 1988. Fleece Press, 1988. One of 218 copies (of an edition of 225), printed on Zerkall mouldmade paper and illustrating a wide range of engraver's work of the period, wood engraved titlepage, reproduction of photo portrait of Stanley Lawrence tipped in, 42 wood engravings, imperial 8vo., original quarter fawn cloth, backstrip printed in mauve, pale blue grey boards with repeated wood engraved pattern by Edwina Ellis, rough trimmed, cloth slipcase, fine. Blackwell's Rare Books 172 - 273 2013 £250

Cross, Andrew B. *Priest's Prisons for Women or a Consideration of the Question, whether Unmarried Foreign Priests ought to be Permitted to erect Prisons, Into which, Under Pretence of Religion, to Seduce or Entrap...* Baltimore: Sherwood & Co., 1854. First edition, 8vo., 47 pages, becoming disbound, titlepage loose, early wear staining and browning to title leaf, corner missing from title, affecting letter of imprint, very rare. M & S Rare Books, Inc. 95 - 396 2013 $225

Cross, Henry P. *Peter Rabbit.* New York: J. Fischer & Bro., copyright, 1924. performance copyright 1929, 10 3/4 x 7 inches, wrappers with some browning, 2 inch split top backstrip and slight wear to bottom, tear bottom front cover and cover with tiny mark, pencil notes page 1, very good. Ian Hodgkins & Co. Ltd. 134 - 65 2013 £38

Cross, Tom Peete *Motif-Index of Early Irish Literature.* Bloomington: circa, 1952. xx, 537 pages, wrappers, very good. C. P. Hyland 261 - 274 2013 £150

Crosse, John *An Account of the Grand Musical Festival held in September 1823 in the Cathedral Church of York...* York: John Wolstenholme, 1825. 4to., 3 hand colored plates, hand colored frontispiece, folding plan, large wide margined copy, contemporary half calf, marbled boards, most handsomely rebacked with broad decorative gilt bands and blind ruled compartments, black morocco label.   Ken Spelman Books Ltd.   73 - 197   2013   £360

Crossland, J. Brian *Looking at Whitehaven.* Whitehaven: Borough Council, 1971. First edition, large 8vo., original cloth, gilt, dust jacket, 99 illustrations.   R. F. G. Hollett & Son   Lake District & Cumbria - 340   2013   £30

Crothers, Samuel Mcchord *The Children of Dickens.* New York: Scribners, 1925. First edition, near fine in like dust jacket, 8vo., 259 pages.   By the Book, L. C.   36 - 30   2013 $300

Crowe, Catherine *Susan Hopley or the Adventures of a Maid Servant.* Edinburgh: William Tait &c, 1842. Half title, frontispiece, contemporary half brown calf, hinges slightly splitting, Renier booklabel, nice, clean copy.   Jarndyce Antiquarian Booksellers   CCV - 79   2013   £120

Crowinshield, Frank *Manners for the Metropolis: an Entrance Key to the Fantastic Life of the 400.* New York: D. Appleton and Co., 1910. Fifth printing, decorations by Louis Fancher, printed paper covered boards, bookplate, little soiling, at least very good copy, exceptionally scarce.   Between the Covers Rare Books, Inc.   New York City - 279292   2013 $400

Croxall, Samuel *The Fables of Aesop with Instructive Applications.* Halifax: William Milner, 1844. 12mo., original blindstamped cloth gilt, extending frontispiece and over 100 woodcut illustrations.   R. F. G. Hollett & Son   Children's Books - 150   2013   £65

Crozier, Gladys Beattie *Children's Games and Children's Parties.* Routledge, 1913. Original pictorial cloth gilt, top edge gilt, photo text illustrations, flyleaves spotted.   R. F. G. Hollett & Son   Children's Books - 151   2013   £45

CRS Report for Congress: Historically Black Colleges and Universities and African-American Participation in Higher Education. Washington: Congressional Research Service/ Library of Congress, 1989. First edition, quarto, stapled self wrappers, 74 pages, couple of smudges on front wrapper, else very near fine.   Between the Covers Rare Books, Inc.   165 - 140   2013 $75

Cruikshank, George *The Bachelor's Own Book.* London: D. Bogue, 1844. First edition, colored state, intermediate issue with misspelling "Persuit" on title corrected, but "Amusememt" not corrected, oblong 8vo., full crushed red morocco by Riviere & Son, original colored front wrapper bound in, spine gilt, inner gilt dentelles, title leaf + 24 colored etchings on 12 leaves, evidence of removed bookplate, else fine.   Howard S. Mott Inc.   262 - 37   2013 $600

Cruikshank, George *Cruikshank Fairy Book.* New York: G. P. Putnam, 1897. Tall 8vo., blue cloth, 216 pages, all edges gilt, elaborate gilt pictorial covers and spine, signed by FBS, margin repair on page with list of illustrations, occasional finger mark, very good+, 40 black and white plates.   Aleph-Bet Books, Inc.   104 - 136   2013 $350

Cruikshank, George *Forty Illustrations of Lord Byron...* James Robins & Co., 1825. Facsimile, illustrations, 4 pages ads, slight damp marking in first few leaves, sewn as issued in original brown wrappers, dusted and slightly worn at spine and edges.   Jarndyce Antiquarian Booksellers   CCIII - 363   2013   £350

Cruikshank, George *Phrenological Illustrations or an Artist's View of the Craniological System of Doctors Gall and Spurzheim.* London: printed by George Cruikshank, 1825. 6 hand colored engraved leaves, oblong 4to. in half red morocco, some wear to spine, final leaf with some brown staining not affecting plates, rare.   James Tait Goodrich   S74 - 53   2013 $1595

Crumley, James *Bordersnakes.* Tucson: Dennis McMillan, 1996. First edition, one of 300 numbered copies signed by author, very fine in slipcase.   Mordida Books   81 - 126   2013 $200

Crumley, James *The Final Country.* Tucson: Dennis McMillan, 2001. First edition, one of 400 numbered copies signed by author, very fine in dust jacket with slipcase.   Mordida Books   81 - 127   2013 $125

Crumley, James *The Last Good Kiss.* New York: Random House, 1978. First edition, very fine in dust jacket.   Mordida Books   81 - 123   2013 $125

Crumley, James *The Mexican Tree Duck.* Bristol: Scorpion, 1993. Limited edition, one of 75 numbered copies, bound in quarter leather with marbled boards, signed by author, very fine in acetate dust jacket with nick at top of spine.   Mordida Books   81 - 125   2013 $250

Cruveilheir, J. *Anatomie Patholgique du Corps Humain.* Paris: Bailliere, Fascicles from the first edition, tall folio in 3 volumes, contemporary quarter calf that have been recently rebacked in new calf, text with foxing and browning, this set uncut, one of the fascicles has original printed cover present, rest were issues single items, rarely seen in this state.   James Tait Goodrich   75 - 63   2013 $3250

Cuala Press *A Woman's Reliquary.* Churchtown: Cuala Press, 1916. One of 300 copies, 8vo., original quarter linen over pale cream boards, spine and upper board lettered in black, small rectangular ticket of binder "Galwey & Co. Eustace St. Dublin" at foot of front pastedown, offsetting to endpapers and boards slightly marked, otherwise near fine.   Maggs Bros. Ltd.   1442 - 42   2013   £250

Cubbin, Thomas *The Wreck of the Serica.* Dropmore Press, 1950. First edition, 41/270 copies (of an edition of 300 copies) on Hodgkinson's handmade paper, 7 color wood engravings by John Worsley, including 3 full page, imperial 8vo., original mid blue buckram, backstrip and front cover gilt blocked, untrimmed, dust jacket with internal tape repairs, good.   Blackwell's Rare Books   B174 - 329   2013   £50

Cullen, Countee *The Ballad of the Brown Girl.* New York: Harper & Bros., 1927. First trade edition, illustrations and decorations by Charles Cullen, fine in original unpriced dust jacket, chipped.   Between the Covers Rare Books, Inc.   165 - 125   2013 $125

Cullen, Countee *Caroling Dusk: an Anthology of Verse by Negro Poets.* New York: Harper, 1927. First edition, fine in attractive, about very good dust jacket a bit spine tanned and with some modest chipping at extremities, mostly to rear panel.   Between the Covers Rare Books, Inc.   165 - 50   2013 $450

Cullen, Countee *Color.* New York: Harper and Brothers, 1925. First edition, contemporary owner name, corners bit rubbed and worn, very good, lacking the dust jacket. Between the Covers Rare Books, Inc.   165 - 27   2013 $350

Cullen, Countee *The Medea and Some Poems.* New York: Harper and Bros., 1935. First edition, small owner label on front pastedown, else fine in lightly soiled, very good dust jacket with couple of tears on front panel. Between the Covers Rare Books, Inc.   165 - 126   2013 $150

Cullen, Luke *Insurgent Wicklow, 1798.* 1948. Second edition, 133 pages, very good, dust jacket over wrapper. C. P. Hyland   261 - 278   2013   £30

Cullen, Luke *Princes and Pirates, The Dublin Chamber of of Commerce 1783-1983.* 1983. First edition, 126 pages, cloth, illustrations, dust jacket, fine.   C. P. Hyland   261 - 277   2013   £25

Culley, John H. *Cattle, Horses & Men of the Western Range.* Los Angeles: 1940. First edition, xvi, 337 pages, illustrations, hinges just starting, light soil, else very good. Dumont Maps & Books of the West   122 - 50   2013 $95

Culpepper, Galen *The Antidote; or Cure for Radicals with a Recipe for 'Sculls that Cannot Teach and Will Not Learn'.* London: Baldwin and Co., 1819. Half title, apology slip, disbound.   Jarndyce Antiquarian Booksellers   CCV - 80   2013   £55

Culpepper, Nicolas *Culpeper's English Physician and Complete Herbal to Which are now First Added Upwards of One Hundred Additional Herbs...* London: printed for the author, 1793. Tall 4to., 40 numbered plates, 2 unnumbered plates, engraved frontispiece, contemporary quarter calf and marbled boards, spine worn and chipped especially about head and tail, front joint just starting, internally clean, botanical plates hand colored and anatomical plates in sepia tone.   James Tait Goodrich   75 - 64   2013 $1450

Cumberland Association for the Advancement of Literature and Science *Transactions.* Keswick: R. Bailey and Carlisle: G. & T. Coward, 1876-1893. 17 volumes in 4, modern half levant morocco gilt with raised bands and contrasting spine labels, together with separate volume of copies of contents page of each volume, modern stiff wrappers, illustrations, original wrappers bound in, fine, complete set in handsome binding.   R. F. G. Hollett & Son   Lake District & Cumbria - 345   2013   £550

Cumberland Association for the Advancement of Literature and Science *Transactions. Parts 1-3.* Keswick: R. Bailey and Carlisle: G. and T. Coward, 1876-1878. Modern half calf gilt, illustrations, original wrappers bound in.   R. F. G. Hollett & Son   Lake District & Cumbria - 347   2013   £95

Cumberland Association for the Advancement of Literature and Science *Transactions No. VIII.* Carlisle: G. & T. Coward, 1883. Original wrappers, neatly rebacked and wrappers laid on to matching card, presentation copy from J. Postlethwaite to H. E. Quilter.   R. F. G. Hollett & Son   Lake District & Cumbria - 346   2013   £35

Cumbria Federation of Women's Institutes *Cumbria Within Living Memory.* Newbury: Countryside Books, 1994. Original wrappers, pages 255, map and drawings, inscribed.   R. F. G. Hollett & Son   Lake District & Cumbria - 352   2013   £25

Cumbria Parish Registers *Brough: the Registers of Brough Under Stainmore 1556-1812.* Kendal: Titus Wilson for the Society, 1923-1924. 2 volumes, original printed wrappers, uncut, partially unopened, excellent set, extremely scarce.   R. F. G. Hollett & Son   Lake District & Cumbria - 353   2013   £250

Cumbria Parish Registers *Kendal: The Registers of Kendal. Part I Westmorland 1558-1587.* Kendal: Titus Wilson for the society, 1921. Original printed wrappers, frontispiece, 98 pages.   R. F. G. Hollett & Son   Lake District & Cumbria - 356   2013   £75

Cumbria Parish Registers *Kendal: The Registers of Kendal, Westmorland Part I-IV, Index of Parts III and IV.* Kendal: Titus Wilson for the Society, 1921-1973. 5 volumes, original printed wrappers, fine, complete set.   R. F. G. Hollett & Son   Lake District & Cumbria - 355   2013   £300

Cumbria Parish Registers *Kendal: The Registers of Kendal. Part III.* Kendal: Titus Wilson, 1952. Original wrappers, 217 pages.   R. F. G. Hollett & Son   Lake District & Cumbria - 357   2013   £75

Cumbria Parish Registers *Kendal: The Registers of Kendal. Part IV.* Kendal: Titus Wilson, 1960. Original wrappers, 386 pages.   R. F. G. Hollett & Son   Lake District & Cumbria - 358   2013   £65

Cumbria Parish Registers *Lamplugh: The Registers of Lamplugh 581-1812.* Penrith: Herald Printing Co., 1933. 216 pages, original printed wrappers.   R. F. G. Hollett & Son   Lake District & Cumbria - 359   2013   £75

Cumbria Parish Registers *Penrith: The Registers of St. Andrews Parish Church, Penrith, Volumes I-V.* Penrith: privately printed for the Parish Register Section, CWAAS, 1938-1942. 5 volumes, original printed wrappers, head of spine volume 1 little creased, otherwise excellent set.   R. F. G. Hollett & Son   Lake District & Cumbria - 360   2013   £350

Cumbria Parish Registers *Sedbergh: the Registers of the Parish Church of Sedbergh, Co. York 1594-1800.* Sedbergh: Jackson and Son, 1911. 4 volumes, modern boards, very good sound set, extremely scarce.   R. F. G. Hollett & Son   Lake District & Cumbria - 361   2013   £350

Cumbria Parish Registers *Skelton: The Registers of the Parish Church of Skelton, Cumberland 1580-1812.* Kendal: Titus Wilson, 1918. Original printed wrappers, frontispiece.   R. F. G. Hollett & Son   Lake District & Cumbria - 362   2013   £85

Cumbria Parish Registers *Stanwix: the Marriage Register of Stanwix.* W. P W. Phillimore & Co., n.d., 56 pages, original cloth, paper label, endpapers little spotted, inscribed on label "Transcriber's Copy" (C. W. Ruston-Harrison).   R. F. G. Hollett & Son   Lake District & Cumbria - 363   2013   £85

Cumbria Parish Registers *Ulverston: The Registers of Ulverston Parish Church.* Ulverston: James Atkinson, 1886. First edition, number 120 of c. 200 wets, disbound set of original parts, some original wrappers preserved, title and introductory leaf present in good modern facsimile, rather dishevelled but very good complete working set.   R. F. G. Hollett & Son   Lake District & Cumbria - 365   2013   £250

Cumbria Parish Registers *Ulverston: The Registers of Ulverston Parish Church.* Ulverston: James Atkinson, 1886. First (only) edition, very thick large 8vo., publisher's half black morocco gilt, raised bands, all edges and endpapers marbled, armorial bookplate of H. N. Clarke, handsome copy, extremely scarce.   R. F. G. Hollett & Son   Lake District & Cumbria - 364   2013   £850

Cumbria Religious History Society *Bulletin.* Carlisle: 1980-1993. Broken run, nos. 1-8, 10-13, 20, 23 and special 10th anniversary edition, scarce, together 14 numbers, original wrappers, mostly side stapled, mostly 16 to 50 pages each, cyclostyled, few duplicates included.   R. F. G. Hollett & Son   Lake District & Cumbria - 366   2013   £40

Cumbrian Railways Association *The Midland's Settle & Carlisle Distance Diagrams.* Grange-over-Sands: Cumbrian Railways Association, 1992. 4to., original wrappers, maps, diagrams.   R. F. G. Hollett & Son   Lake District & Cumbria - 367   2013   £25

Cummings, Edward Estlin *Eimi.* New York: Covic Friede, 1933. First edition, limited to 1381 numbered copies, signed by author, one extremely slight lower corner tap, else fine in fine dust jacket, very attractive, seldom found with jacket at all, let alone in near perfect condition.   Ken Lopez Bookseller   159 - 49   2013 $1500

Cummings, Edward Estlin *Eimi.* New York: Covic Friede, 1933. First edition, one of 1381 copies signed by author, 8vo., original yellow cloth, excellent copy.   Maggs Bros. Ltd.   1460 - 202   2013   £300

Cummings, Edward Estlin *50 Poems.* New York: Duell, Sloan and Pearce, 1940. First edition, 88/150 copies, crown 8vo., original fawn cloth, backstrip gilt lettered, gilt lettered large maroon leather label on front cover, yellowing to endpaper gutters, untrimmed, glassine-jacket, matching cloth slipcase and leather label, unusually nice, near fine, signed by author.   Blackwell's Rare Books   172 - 176   2013   £1000

Cummings, Edward Estlin *Tulips and Chimneys.* New York: Thomas Seltzer, 1923. First edition, 8vo., original canvas backed boards, printed paper label, fine in extremely rare dust jacket, which has some minor soiling, some edge wear (not affecting any of the lettering) and two inch closed tear in front panel in dust jacket.   James S. Jaffe Rare Books   Fall 2013 - 35   2013 $7500

Cummings, Richard O. *The American Ice Harvests: a Historical Study in Technology 1800-1918.* Berkeley: University of California Press, 1949. 8vo, gilt stmped red cloth, dust jacket verso reinforced with cellophane tape, mild staining to back edge, though generally very good, rare.   Jeff Weber Rare Books   171 - 87   2013   £125

Cummins, Robert C. *Unusual Medical Cases. A Cork Physician's Memories.* Cork: University Press, 1962. First edition, 118 pages, wrappers, very good. C. P. Hyland 261 - 282 2013 £50

Cunard, Nancy *Nous Gens d'Espagne.* Imprimerie Labu: Perpignan, 1949. First edition, one of 500 numbered copies signed by author, this one additionally inscribed by author, 4to., original wrappers preserved in folding box, excellent copy, wrappers unevenly browned, lightly foxed. Maggs Bros. Ltd. 1460 - 203 2013 £250

Cundall, H. M. *Kate Greenaway Pictures from Original presented by her to John Ruskin and Other Personal Friends.* Warne, 1921. First edition, 4to., original two-tone cloth gilt over bevelled boards, dust jacket rather worn, pages 11, uncut, tissue guarded portrait frontispiece and 17 tipped in tissue guarded color plates, fine. R. F. G. Hollett & Son Children's Books - 152 2013 £350

Cunn, Samuel *A New Treatise of the Construction and Use of the Sector.* printed for John Wilcox and Thomas Heath, Mathematical Instrument Maker, 1729. First edition, engraved frontispiece, large folding engraved plate, diagrams in text, bit browned, closed tear in folding plate, not affecting engraved surface, 8vo., contemporary panelled calf, rebacked, ownership inscription of E. G. Smith, Caius College Cambridge, 1814, sound. Blackwell's Rare Books Sciences - 39 2013 £950

Cunningham, A B. *Death Rides a Sorrel Horse.* New York: E. P. Dutton, 1946. First edition, very slight sunning to boards, still about fine in fresh and attractive, near fine dust jacket with some modest wear, mostly at spine ends, inscribed by author to John Mulholland. Between the Covers Rare Books, Inc. Mystery & Detective Fiction - 65848 2013 $275

Cunningham, Allan *Biographical and Critical History of the British Literature of the last Fifty Years.* Paris: Baudry's Foreign Library, 1834. First edition, half title, corner neatly cut from leading f.e.p., uncut in contemporary continental marbled boards, blue cloth spine, paper label partly defective, corners worn, French armorial bookplate, good plus, scarce. Jarndyce Antiquarian Booksellers CCIII - 675 2013 £120

Cunningham, Allan *Paul Jones: a Romance.* Edinburgh: Oliver & Boyd, 1826. First edition, 3 volumes, half titles removed, slightly spotted, contemporary half calf, red leather labels, slightly rubbed, booklabels of R. G. Taylor. Jarndyce Antiquarian Booksellers CCIII - 674 2013 £380

Cunningham, Brysson *A Treatise on the Principles and Practice of Dock Engineering.* Charles Griffin, 1904. First edition, 34 folding plates and 468 illustrations in text, 86 pages ads, half title, large 8vo., good, slightly rubbed original blue gilt decorated cloth. Ken Spelman Books Ltd. 75 - 156 2013 £85

Cunynghame, Arthur Augustus Thurlow *Travels in the Eastern Caucasus on the Caspian and Black Seas.* London: John Murray, 1872. First edition, illustrated frontispiece and 26 other illustrations and maps, 8vo., green cloth, decorative gilt to front, spine gilt. Maggs Bros. Ltd. 1467 - 36 2013 £750

The Curious Book of Clampus or Gumshaniana. Yerba Buena: issued from the Hall of Comparative Ovations, 1935. first edition, copy number '2' of 200 copies, color illustrations, green-gray boards, printed paper labels on front cover and spine, description from Newbegin's Book Shop tipped-in at front, slight offsetting to front end, spine label slightly darkened, else very fine. Argonaut Book Shop Summer 2013 - 91 2013 $200

Curley, James M. *I'd Do It Again.* 1957. 8vo. illustrations, light stains on cover, text good, cloth. C. P. Hyland 261 - 280 2013 £30

Curnock, Nemehian *The Journal of the Rev. John Wesley, A. M.* Robert Culley, 1909. Standard edition, 8 volumes, original half roan gilt, little worn, few slight nicks and scuffs, numerous plates, maps, etc., excellent sound set. R. F. G. Hollett & Son Wesleyan Methodism - 6 2013 £250

Currie, Barton W. *Officer 666.* New York: H. K. Fly, 1912. First edition, very good with lettering and board edges lightly rubbed, without dust jacket as issued, with four color plate illustrations and endpapers. Between the Covers Rare Books, Inc. Mystery & Detective Fiction - 74229 2013 $65

Curry, Eugene *Cath Mhuighe Leana Or the Battle of Magh Leana. Together with Tocmarc Momera, or the Courtship of Momera.* Dublin: Celtic Society, 1855. First edition thus, 8vo., some foxing, mainly to prelims, publisher's olive cloth decorated in blind bit faded with bumping to corners and edges, nick to headcap, edges uncut, as issued and slightly dusty, bookplate of Bibliotheca Lindesiana, Irish Archaeological and Celtic Society leaflet loosely inserted. Unsworths Antiquarian Booksellers 28 - 155 2013 £125

Curry, Neil *Norman Nicholson.* Carlisle: Northern Lights, 2001. First edition, original wrappers, 20 pages, fine. R. F. G. Hollett & Son Lake District & Cumbria - 368 2013 £20

Curry, Patrick *Astrology, Science and Society: Historical Essays.* Wolfeboro: Boydell Press, 1987. 8vo. ix, 302 pages, navy cloth, silver stamped spine title, dust jacket, ownership signature, fine.   Jeff Weber Rare Books   169 - 83   2013 $175

Curtin, L. S. M. *Healing Herbs of the Upper Rio Grande.* Santa Fe: 1947. First edition, x, 281 pages, illustrations, owners' names, beautiful, right dust jacket designed by Merle Armitage, many page number and spelling corrections, also deletions and additions of reference citations and even an addition of information in text.   Dumont Maps & Books of the West   125 - 44   2013 $95

Curtis, Edmund *A History of Ireland.*   1937.   Third edition, 8vo., cloth, cover dull, text very good, ownership inscription by Anne Yeats.   C. P. Hyland   261 - 958   2013   £32

Curtis, George William *Nile Notes of a Howadji.*   New York: Harper, 1851. First American edition, 8vo., black cloth stamped in gilt, nicked at extremities of spine, some minor foxing and staining, little musty smell, good copy.   Second Life Books Inc.   183 - 93   2013 $250

Curwen, John F. *The Ancient Parish of Heversham with Milnthorpe...* Kendal: Titus Wilson & Son, 1930. First (only) Edition, original cloth, patchily faded as usual, 7 plates and illustrations, scarce.   R. F. G. Hollett & Son   Lake District & Cumbria - 369   2013   £120

Curwen, John F. *The Castles and Fortified Towers of Cumberland, Westmorland and Lancashire North-of-the Sands....* Kendal: Titus Wilson, 1913. Thick 8vo., original brown cloth gilt, neatly recased, boards rather marked, 80 plates, illustrations and plans, very good, extremely scarce.   R. F. G. Hollett & Son   Lake District & Cumbria - 373   2013   £450

Curwen, John F. *Heversham Church.* Kendal: Titus Wilson, 1925. Original wrappers, 2 plates, 6 plans in text, some pencilled annotation.   R. F. G. Hollett & Son   Lake District & Cumbria - 377   2013   £30

Curwen, John F. *A History of the Ancient House of Curwen of Workington in Cumberland...* Kendal: Titus Wilson and Son, 1928. First (only) edition, 4to., original red cloth gilt, spine rather faded, frontispiece arms, 25 plates, map, text plans, illustrations, pedigrees, extremely scarce.   R. F. G. Hollett & Son   Lake District & Cumbria - 378   2013   £450

Curwen, John F. *Kirkbie-Kendall.* Kendal: T. Wilson, 1900. First edition, small 4to., modern half green levant morocco gilt raised bands, contrasting spine label, gilt roundel from original binding relaid on upper board, illustrations, handsome, very scarce.   R. F. G. Hollett & Son   Lake District & Cumbria - 379   2013   £250

Curwen, John F. *Kirkbie-Kendall.* Kendal: T. Wilson, 1900. First edition, small 4to., original green cloth, gilt, rather rubbed and marked in places, pages 455, illustrations throughout, joints neatly repaired, very scarce.   R. F. G. Hollett & Son   Lake District & Cumbria - 380   2013   £180

Curwen, John F. *The Later Records Relating to North Westmorland or the Barony of Appleby.* Kendal: Titus Wilson, 1932. Original ribbed green cloth, gilt, frontispiece, fine, unopened, scarce.   R. F. G. Hollett & Son   Lake District & Cumbria - 385   2013   £150

Curwen, John F. *Records Relating to the Barony of Kendale.* Kendal: Titus Wilson, 1923. Volume I, original green ribbed cloth, gilt, slight wear to extremities, untrimmed, map, 2 facsimiles, very good, extremely scarce.   R. F. G. Hollett & Son   Lake District & Cumbria - 382   2013   £180

Curwen, John F. *Records Relating to the Barony of Kendale.* Kendal: Titus Wilson, 1998. Facsimile edition, Volume I, original green cloth, gilt, map, 2 facsimiles.   R. F. G. Hollett & Son   Lake District & Cumbria - 381   2013   £30

Curzon, Colin *The Body in the Barrage Balloon or Who Killed the Corpse?* New York: Macmillan Co., 1942. First American edition, fine in near fine dust jacket with little rubbing at foot.   Between the Covers Rare Books, Inc.   Mystery & Detective Fiction - 286502   2013 $200

Cusack, Mary F. *A History of the City and County of Cork.* 1875. First edition, 8vo., 586 pages, folding map, illustrations, binding needs attention, text good.   C. P. Hyland   261 - 285   2013   £100

Cusack, Mary F. *A History of the Kingdom of Kerry.* 1871. First edition, 8vo., colored map, 1 plate, many text illustrations, cloth.   C. P. Hyland   261 - 284   2013   £190

Cushing, Harvey Williams   1869-1939 *A Bio-Bibliography of Andreas Vesalius.* New York: Scuhman, 1943. Limited edition of 800 copies,, 228 pages, numerous illustrations, quarter green morocco and linen boards with armorial crest of Vesalius on front board, very nice, clean copy, minimal wear.   James Tait Goodrich   75 - 213   2013 $850

Cushing, Harvey Williams   1869-1939 *The Chiasmal Syndrome of Primary Optic Atrophy and Bitemporal Field Defects in Adult Patients with a Normal Sella Turcia.* Leiden: 1929.   offprint, 76 text illustrations, photos and tables, original green printed wrappers, placed in recent pamphlet board.   James Tait Goodrich   S74 - 65   2013 $175

Cushing, Harvey Williams   1869-1939   *Electro-Surgery as an Aid to the Removal of Intracranial Tumors.*   Offprint from Surgery, Gynecology and Obstetrics Dec., 1925. Numerous illustrations, photos, 4to., blue printed publisher's wrappers, some wear to wrapper, bit dusty.   James Tait Goodrich   75 - 74   2013 $250

Cushing, Harvey Williams   1869-1939   *From a Surgeon's Journal 1915-1918.*   Boston: Little Brown, 1936. First edition, 534 pages, light cloth wear and corners bumped, else very good, clean.   James Tait Goodrich   S74 - 59   2013 $75

Cushing, Harvey Williams   1869-1939   *From a Surgeon's Journal 1915-1918.*   Boston: Little Brown, 1936. First edition, deluxe issue signed by author, 8vo., frontispiece foxed, 34 illustrations, gilt stamped navy blue cloth, signed by previous owner Lowering Hathaway 1936, very good.   Jeff Weber Rare Books   172 - 61   2013 $2000

Cushing, Harvey Williams   1869-1939   *Instruction in Operative Medicine.*   Offprint from Johns Hopkins Hospital Bulletin, 1906. 2 diagram illustrations, plates, some soiling and foxing on front wrapper, early writing on first leaf, signed inscribed presentation copy from author for Prof. N. Steward.   James Tait Goodrich   S74 - 63   2013 $1750

Cushing, Harvey Williams   1869-1939   *The Life of Sir William Osler.*   Oxford University Press, 1925. First edition, first impression, 2 volumes, blue cloth showing some rubbing and wear, one dust jacket present frayed, signed presentation copy from author, uncommon thus.   James Tait Goodrich   75 - 68   2013 $1750

Cushing, Harvey Williams   1869-1939   *The Life of Sir William Osler.*   Oxford University Press, 1925. First impression, nice in blue cloth, some light wear to cloth, near fine internally, ownership inscription of Alfred Franklin on front flyleaf, with rare "Corrigenda and Addenda to the Life of Sir William Osler" issued by Cushing August 1936, penned in brown ink at top "Alfred Franklin with regards HC", with TLS from Cushing to Alfred Franklin May 20 1937.   James Tait Goodrich   75 - 161   2013 $2995

Cushing, Harvey Williams   1869-1939   *Manual of Neurosurgery.*   Washington: GPO, 1919. Expanded edition, Recent full black pebbled cloth, internally very good.   James Tait Goodrich   S74 - 55   2013 $395

Cushing, Harvey Williams   1869-1939   *Manual of Neurosurgery.*   Washington: GPO, 1919. Expanded edition, 492 pages, numerous text illustrations, original full leather, some wear and rubbing, joints starting, very good.   James Tait Goodrich   S74 - 43   2013 $450

Cushing, Harvey Williams   1869-1939   *The Medical Career and Other Papers.*   Boston: Little Brown, 1940. First edition, 8vo., 302 pages, green cloth, printed paper labels, spine label slightly soiled, bookplate (foxed) of Cobb Pilcher (light offsetting), very good.   Jeff Weber Rare Books   172 - 63   2013 $95

Cushing, Harvey Williams   1869-1939   *Meningiomas: Their Classification, Regional Behavior, Life History and Surgical End Results.*   Springfield: Charles C. Thomas, 1938. First edition, 8vo., frontispiece, illustrations, original navy blue cloth, gilt stamped spine, dust jacket, spine faded, jacket spine ends chipped, ownership signature of Dr. Murl E. Kinal, bookplate of Harry B. Friedman, very good in like dust jacket.   Jeff Weber Rare Books   172 - 67   2013 $1500

Cushing, Harvey Williams   1869-1939   *Papers Relating to the Pituitary Body, Hypothalmus and Parasympathetic Nervous System.*   Springfield: Thomas, 1932. 234 pages, original green publisher's cloth.   James Tait Goodrich   S74 - 58   2013 $395

Cushing, Harvey Williams   1869-1939   *Papers Relating to the Pituitary Body, Hypothalamus and Parasympathetic Nervous System.*   Springfield & Baltimore: Charles C. Thomas, 1932. 8vo., 99 figures, 2 color plates, 2 charts, 4 tables, green blind and gilt stamped cloth, rubbed, corners showing, ink ownership signature of J. Richard Baringer, Oct. 1961, very good.   Jeff Weber Rare Books   172 - 64   2013 $300

Cushing, Harvey Williams   1869-1939   *The Pituitary Body and Its Disorders: Clinical States produced by the Disorders of the Hypophysus Cerebri.*   Philadelphia and London: J. B. Lippincott, 1912. First edition, first issue, being one of 2000 copies, 8vo., color frontispiece, 319 illustrations, large foldout plate after page 166, burgundy cloth with faded gilt stamped spine, ownership in ink handwriting of Robert Coleman Dean, extremities worn, corners showing, very good.   Jeff Weber Rare Books   172 - 65   2013 $650

Cushing, Harvey Williams   1869-1939   *The Pituitary Body and Its Disorders...*   Philadelphia: 1912. First edition, 2nd impression with Moseley Professor in title, original cloth, very light wear, overall very clean and bright.   James Tait Goodrich   S74 - 57   2013 $395

Cushing, Harvey Williams   1869-1939   *The Pituitary Body and Its Disorders. Clinical States Produced by Disorders of the Hypophysis Cerebri.*   Philadelphia: 1912. First edition, first impression, original cloth, some light wear, head and tail of spine rubbed, overall very good.   James Tait Goodrich   S74 - 56   2013 $495

Cushing, Harvey Williams   1869-1939   *Selected Papers on Neurosurgery.*   New Haven: 1969.   669 pages, near fine, in worn dust jacket, nice association, from the library of William Sweet, M.D. with his bookplate and name rubber-stamped on flyleaf.   James Tait Goodrich   S74 - 68   2013 $175

Cushing, Harvey Williams   1869-1939   *Studies in Intracranial Physiology and Surgery. The Third Circulation. The Hypophysis. the Gliomas. The Cameron Prize Lectures.*   Oxford University Press, 1926.   Original cloth, spine slightly sunned, small stain on front board, very good, tight copy.   James Tait Goodrich   75 - 73   2013 $495

Cushing, Harvey Williams   1869-1939   *Tumors Arising from the Blood Vessels of the Brain.*   London: Bailliere Tindall & Cox, 1928.   First English edition, original red cloth, light wear otherwise clean, tight copy, signature of C. P. Symmonds, English neurologist.   James Tait Goodrich   75 - 72   2013 $495

Cushing, Harvey Williams   1869-1939   *Tumors of the Nervus Acusticus and the Syndrome of the Cerebellopontile Angle.*   Philadelphia: W. B. Saunders, 1917.   First edition, 8vo., 262 figures, original double ruled green cloth, gilt stamped spine, extremities lightly rubbed, bookplate of Harry B. Friedman, rare, very good.   Jeff Weber Rare Books   172 - 66   2013   £800

Cushman, Karen   *Midwife's Apprentice.*   New York: Clarion, 1995.   First edition, first printing, 8vo., cloth, as new in like dust jacket, with no award medal, color dust jacket by Trina Schart Hyman, warmly inscribed by author and Hyman as well, scarce edition and with both signatures.   Aleph-Bet Books, Inc.   104 - 137   2013 $450

Cussler, Clive   *Pacific Vortex!*   Mission Viejo: James Cahill, 2000.   Limited edition, one of 300 nuumbered copies signed by author and dust jacket artist, David Monette, very fine in dust jacket with slipcase.   Mordida Books   81 - 127   2013 $400

Cutt, M. Nancy   *Mrs. Sherwood and Her Books for Children.*   Oxford University Press, 1974. First edition, small 8vo., original cloth, gilt, dust jacket price clipped, portrait ad facsimile reproduction, fine.   R. F. G. Hollett & Son Children's Books - 153   2013   £30

Cutter, Donald C.   *The California Coast.*   Norman: University of Oklahoma Press, 1969.   278 pages, photos, facsimiles, cloth backed boards, very fine with dust jacket.   Argonaut Book Shop   Summer 2013 - 62   2013 $50

Cutter, Donald C.   *California in 1792. A Spanish Naval Visit.*   Norman: University of Oklahoma Press, 1990.   First edition thus, 18 reproductions from old prints and manuscripts, blue cloth, very fine, pictorial dust jacket.   Argonaut Book Shop   Summer 2013 - 63   2013 $50

Cutter, Donald C.   *Malaspina in California.*   San Francisco: John Howell Books, 1960.   First edition, limited to 1000 copies, quarto, 96 pages, frontispiece map, 18 plates, 2 folding tables, gilt lettered and decorated tan cloth, very minor dampstain to extreme bottom of front board, slight bubbling to cloth a upper front corner, else fine.   Argonaut Book Shop   Summer 2013 - 64   2013 $90

Cyprian, Saint, Bp. of Carthage   *S. Cacilii Cyprianai Opera Recognita & Illustrata a Joanne Fello...*   Amstelodami: apud Joannem Ludovicum de Lorme, 1700.   Tall quarto, engraved illustrations on title, full page engraved plate, original full blindstamped vellum, black manuscript spine title, joints splitting, head and tail of spine chipped or missing, untouched, good+.   Jeff Weber Rare Books   171 - 89   2013 $500

Czarnowski, Lucile K.   *Dances of Early California Days.*   Palo Alto: Pacific Books, 1950.   First edition, 3 plates, quarto, numerous music scores, dance-step diagrams, detailed instructions, notes, light blue cloth, spine bit darkened, upper corners lightly jammed, small spot, near fine, internally fine and clean.   Argonaut Book Shop   Summer 2013 - 65   2013 $75

D

D'Ambrosio, Joseph J. *Birds in Paradise.* Los Angeles: Woman's Graphic Center & Joseph D'Ambrosio, 1984. Limited to 50 numbered copies, 10 artist proofs, this copy an artist proof, 8vo., black and gold trimmed leather frame style binding with original illustrations beneath glass at front and rear, black felt lined slipcase, slipcase pivotal hinge, no longer functional (separated), else fine, signed by author, ALS from D'Ambrosio to Wally and Rose Marie Dawes laid in, rare. Jeff Weber Rare Books 171 - 91 2013 $1500

D'Ambrosio, Joseph J. *Daisies Never Tell.* Sherman Oaks: Joseph J. D'Ambrosio, 1982. Limited edition, # 14 of 50 numbered copies, 8vo., prelims feature cut-out flowers and fan-fold action element, dark green cowhide with 2 glass windows showing folded paper daisies from pages within, housed in green paper clamshell slipcase lined in green felt, box worn at spine edges, else fine, signed by author. Jeff Weber Rare Books 171 - 90 2013 $850

D'Ambrosio, Joseph J. *Nineteen Years and Counting: a Reptrospective Bibliography 1969 to 1988.* Arizona: Joseph J. D'Ambrosio, 1989. Limited to 75 numbered copies and 10 artist proofs, 8vo., 129 pages, decorative title and preface, 60 photographic tipped in plates, gray leather backed metal hinged boards, polished copper overlay in gray cloth chemise (signed) edged in marbled paper backed boards, signed and inscribed from author to Rose Marie and Wally Dawes, titlepage signed and with holograph "A.P." (for Artist Proof), fine. Jeff Weber Rare Books 171 - 92 2013 $500

D'Ambrosio, Joseph J. *The Twilight of Orthodoxy in New England.* Northridge: Santa Susana Press, 1987. Limited to 60 copies, of which this is an artist's proof, 8vo., 65 pages, die cut titlepage flame device, 3 original graphic drawings, each signed by artist and marked "A.P." for Artist proof, binding designed to be both a binding and dropback box, with metal hinges and quarter black calf over marbled paper backed boards featuring upper front cover cut-out showing blazing golden fire, small marbled paper dot on spine, scarce, fine. Jeff Weber Rare Books 171 - 94 2013 $400

D'Ambrosio, Joseph J. *You Dress "Funny": an Experience.* No location given: Joseph D'Ambrosio, 1970. Limited to 100 copies, this is an artist's proof, 8vo., 44ff., printed using a variety of papers and textures, including tracing paper, newsprint, silver foil, gold foil, machine copy paper, black construction paper and clear acetate with serigraphic graphics, quarter brown cloth over silver cloth, screwed holed binder, brown cloth gently rubbed, author later had many copies rebound in silver cloth over boards, this this copy in earlier format, signed by author, from the collection of Wally Dawes. Jeff Weber Rare Books 171 - 93 2013 $500

D'Arcy, Charles F. *Adventures of a Bishop.* 1934. First edition, 8vo., cloth, good. C. P. Hyland 261 - 959 2013 £29

D'Aulaire, Ingri *Norse Gods and Giants.* New York: Doubleday, 1967. First edition, large 4to., cloth, fine in lightly frayed dust jacket, beautifully illustrated. Aleph-Bet Books, Inc. 105 - 162 2013 $275

D'Obsonville, Foucher *Philosophic Essays on the Manners of Various Foreign Animals: With Observations on the Laws and Customs of Several Eastern Nations.* printed for John Johnson, 1784. First edition, little browned or foxed in places, 8vo. near contemporary flyleaves watermarked 1797, tree calf, separate contrasting lettering pieces on spine few abrasions, cracks (or worming) at head of spine, armorial bookplate inside front cover of John Campbell of Orange Bay, Jamaica, very good. Blackwell's Rare Books 172 - 45 2013 £750

D., Margaret *Al-Anon's Favorite Forum Editorials.* New York: Al-Anon Family Group, 1970. Stated first edition, 8vo., xx, 268 pages; near fine with mild wear to cover edges and with inscriptions and signatures on endpapers, signed and inscribed by Margaret D. and signed by Lois (Wilson), and by other members of AA and Al-Anon, very good+ dust jacket with mild sun edgewear. By the Book, L. C. 36 - 81 2013 $1500

Dabbs, Edith M. *Face of an Island: Leigh Richmond Miner's Photographs of Saint Helena Island.* New York: Grossman Publishers, 1971. Second edition, large square quarto, near fine in age toned and faintly splash marked, very good dust jacket with several chips and tears. Between the Covers Rare Books, Inc. 165 - 236 2013 $150

Dacier, Andre *The Life of Pythagoras with his Symbols and Golden Verses. Together with the Life of Hierocles...* London: printed for Jacob Tonson within Grays-Inn Lane, 1707. First English translation, 8vo., some browning to titlepage, early name written down leading margin, expertly bound in recent quarter sprinkled calf, marbled boards, vellum tips, raised and gilt banded spine, red morocco label, bookplate of Henry Bowlby. Jarndyce Antiquarian Booksellers CCIV - 103 2013 £280

Dacus, J. *Annals of the Great Strikes in the United States.* Chicago: L. T. Palmer, 1877. First edition, very good-, worn copy, hardcover.   Beasley Books   2013 - 2013 $50

Dahl, Edward H. *Sphaerae Mundi. Early Globes at the Stewart Museum.* McGill-Queen's University Press, 2000. First English language edition, large quarto, 204 pages, profusely illustrated with color plates and illustrations, black boards, very fine, pictorial dust jacket.   Argonaut Book Shop   Recent Acquisitions June 2013 - 76   2013 $90

Dahl, Roald *Charlie and the Chocolate Factory.* New York: Alfred A. Knopf, 1964. True first edition, first issue with 6 lines of printing information (instead f five) on final page, octavo, black and white text illustrations, original red cloth with covers stamped in blind, spine stamped and lettered in gilt, top edge stained chocolate, mustard endpapers, original color pictorial dust jacket (spine very slightly sunned, few small chips and some small professionally repaired closed tears, shallow crease to bottom right corner to bottom middle of jacket), overall near fine in very good dust jacket.   Heritage Book Shop   Holiday Catalogue 2012 - 33   2013 $2750

Dahl, Roald *Charlie and the Chocolate Factory.* New York: Alfred A. Knopf, 1964. True first edition, first issue, with 6 lines of printing information (instead of five) in colophon, octavo, black and white text illustrations, original red cloth, fine, original first issue color pictorial dust jacket, jacket mildly soiled and with few light creases and tiny closed tears, overall excellent.   David Brass Rare Books, Inc. Holiday 2012 Chapter One - DB01597   2013 $6500

Dahl, Roald *James and the Giant Peach.* New York: Knopf, 1961. 4to., red cloth, 119 pages, fine in near fine dust jacket, slightly worn at top of spine, beautifully illustrated by Nancy Burkert, signed by author, super copy in excellent condition, rare with signature.   Aleph-Bet Books, Inc. 105 - 161   2013 $13,500

Dahl, Roald *My Uncle Oswald.* London: Michael Joseph, 1979. First edition, original cloth, gilt, dust jacket price clipped.   R. F. G. Hollett & Son   Children's Books - 155   2013   £45

Dahl, Roald *Switch Bitch.* London: Michael Joseph, 1974. First edition, 8vo., original blue cloth, fine in price clipped dust jacket, inscribed by author to Bryan Forbes. Maggs Bros. Ltd.   1460 - 204   2013   £375

Daiken, Leslie *World of Toys.* Lambarde Press, 1963. First edition, original cloth, gilt, dust jacket, 49 plates.   R. F. G. Hollett & Son   Children's Books - 156   2013   £25

Daily Express *Rupert Adventure Book No. 49.* Oldbourne Books, 1963. Large 8vo., original pictorial wrappers, little childish writing on upper panel, extremities slightly rubbed, illustrations in color.   R. F. G. Hollett & Son Children's Books - 157   2013   £65

Daire, George John *The Rime of the New Made Baccalere.* Oxford: printed and published by J. Vincent, 1841. First edition, 31 pages, 4 pages following ads, sewn as issued in drab printed wrappers, little spotted, spine partially defective, corners slightly chipped.   Jarndyce Antiquarian Booksellers   CCIII - 515   2013   £120

Daisy Dell Farm ABC.   New York: and London: Raphael Tuck & Sons, 1900. First edition, 8vo., 8 pages plus wrappers, one small spot on cover, very good.   Barnaby Rudge Booksellers   Children 2013 - 021662   2013 $65

Dale, Ivan R. *Kenya Trees and Shrubs.* Nairobi: Buchanan's Kenya Estates & Hatchards, 1961. First edition, large thick 8vo., original black cloth, gilt, 31 colored plates by Joy Adamson, 80 plates, 110 figures.   R. F. G. Hollett & Son   Africana - 47   2013   £75

Dale, Nellie *The Dale Readers. Book 1.* London: George Philip & Son, 1902. New pictures by Walter Crane, original cloth, little rubbed and soiled, pages 94, with 4 full page color plates and color printed illustrations scattered through text, some fingering, but good, sound copy.   R. F. Hollett & Son   Children's Books - 146   2013   £45

Dales, Richard C. *Robert Grosseteste Hexaemeron.* London: Oxford University Press, 1982. 8vo., navy cloth, gilt stamped spine title, dust jacket, presentation inscription from editor, fine, rare in cloth with jacket.   Jeff Weber Rare Books   169 - 176   2013 $175

Daley, Robert *Only a Game.* New York: New American Library, 1967. First edition, fine in near fine dust jacket with lightly tanned spine, inscribed by author.   Between the Covers Rare Books, Inc.   Football Books - 355773   2013 $150

Dalkeith, Ferguson Summerville *How I Cured My Craving for Drink, by One who Twice Suffered from Delirium Tremens.* Glasgow: James Hedderwick & sons, n.d., 1885. First edition, 16mo., stitched paper wrappers, quite uncommon, removed from larger volume, spine and rear wrapper lacking, front wrapper scuffed, contents very good. Kaaterskill Books   16 - 19   2013 $250

Dallas, Paul V. *The Lost Planet.* Philadelphia: Toronto: John C. Winston, 1956. First edition, octavo, cloth. L. W. Currey, Inc.   Fall Sampler Sept. 2013 - 146542   2013 $250

Dallas, Robert Charles *Recollections of the Life of Lord Byron, from the Year 1808 to the end of 1814...* London: Charles Knight, 1824. First edition, contemporary half maroon calf, slightly rubbed, very good, bookplate of Viscount Hood, very good. Jarndyce Antiquarian Booksellers CCIII - 370 2013 £250

Dallas, Robert Charles *Recollections of the Life of Lord Byron, from the Year 1808 to the end of 1814...* London: printed for Charles Knight, 1824. First edition, half title, frontispiece, facsimile letter, few internal spots, uncut in original drab boards, paper label, spine little chipped at head, booklabels of Alastair Forbes & Alex Bridge. Jarndyce Antiquarian Booksellers CCIII - 369 2013 £280

Dallas, Robert Charles *Recollections of the Life of Lord Byron, from the Year 1808 to the end of 1814...* Philadelphia: A. Small, H. C. Carey & I. Lea, 1825. First American edition, spotted, slightly later three quarter olive green morocco, spine gilt in compartments, spine faded to brown, top edge gilt, very good. Jarndyce Antiquarian Booksellers CCIII - 371 2013 £225

Dalrymple, William *Travels through Spain and Portugal in 1774....* London: J. Almon, 1777. First edition, small quarto, 187 pages, folding map (small loss at base), frontispiece, contemporary brown quarter calf, rebacked using original red morocco label, covers rubbed, ink stain to titlepage, otherwise crisp. J. & S. L. Bonham Antiquarian Booksellers Europe - 9665 2013 £380

Dalton, J. P. *Sarsfield at Limerick and Other Poems.* Cork: Guys, 1898. 47 pages, original stiff card covers (spine broken), text clean. C. P. Hyland 261 - 287 2013 £40

Dalton, Richard *Remarks on Prints, that Were Published in the Year 1781...* London: printed by J. Nichols, 1790. 8vo., half title, frontispiece, 8vo., uncut, disbound. Jarndyce Antiquarian Booksellers CCIV - 104 2013 £550

Daly, Carroll John *The Amateur Murderer.* New York: Ives Washburn, 1933. First edition, owner's small name stamp twice on front endpapers, spine nominally toned, near fine, lacking dust jacket, scarce. Between the Covers Rare Books, Inc. Mystery & Detective Fiction - 319851 2013 $400

Daly, Carroll John *Emperor of Evil.* New York: Frederick A. Stokes, 1937. First edition, advance review copy with publisher's slip tipped in, near fine, lacking dust jacket, scarce. Between the Covers Rare Books, Inc. Mystery & Detective Fiction - 319832 2013 $200

Daly, Carroll John *Mr. Strang.* New York: Frederick A. Stokes, 1936. First edition, ex-private-lending library copy, tape shadows to boards, shadows and remnants from old jacket protector to endpapers and flaps, small hole to first few leaves, no stamps or ownership marks, else good in good dust jacket with some shallow chipping. Between the Covers Rare Books, Inc. Mystery & Detective Fiction - 56173 2013 $450

Daly, Sean *Cork: a City in Crisis.* Tower Books, 1978. First edition, 8vo., cloth, dust jacket, light foxing on prelims, else near fine. C. P. Hyland 261 - 288 2013 £50

Daly, Sean *Ireland and the First International.* 1984. First edition, xi, 233 pages, illustrations, wrappers, signed presentation, fine. C. P. Hyland 261 - 289 2013 £40

Dalziel, The Brothers *Dalziel's Bible Gallery.* London: George Routledge & Sons, 1881. Folio, half title, India proof plates, binding cracking in places, some plates loose, original parchment covered boards, decorated in red and gilt, very good. Jarndyce Antiquarian Booksellers CCV - 81 2013 £1500

Dana, Charles A. *The Life of Ulysses S. Grant.* Springfield: Gurdon Bill & Co., 1868. First edition, 8vo., frontispiece, blindstamped full calf, leaves little toned and minor foxing, marking around frontispiece some browned, very good. Second Life Books Inc. 183 - 96 2013 $150

Dana, Juan Francsico *The Blond Ranchero Memories of Juan Francisco Dana.* Los Angeles: Dawson's Book Shop, 1960. First edition, one of 500 copies, extremely scarce, 133 pages, 5 plates from old photos, portrait sketch, 2 facsimiles, light brown cloth, gilt, very fine. Argonaut Book Shop Recent Acquisitions June 2013 - 66 2013 $150

Dana, Julian *The Man Who Built San Francisco. A Study of Ralston's Journey with Banenrs.* New York: Macmillan, 1936. First edition, signed by author, illustrations, gray cloth, very fine with slightly chipped pictorial dust jacket, signed by author. Argonaut Book Shop Summer 2013 - 68 2013 $75

Dana, Julian *Sutter of California. A Biography.* New York: Press of the Pioneers, 1934. First edition, signed by author, illustrations, map, red pictorial cloth, gilt, some offsetting to front ends, very fine with torn pictorial dust jacket (protected with plastic cover). Argonaut Book Shop Summer 2013 - 69 2013 $75

Dana, Richard Henry 1815-1882 *To Cuba and Back: a Vacation Voyage.* Boston: 1859. 288, 16 pages, original cloth, spine faded, owner's name on f.f.e.p., quarter inch loss of cloth at top of spine, else clean and very good. Dumont Maps & Books of the West 125 - 45 2013 $150

Dana, Richard Henry   1815-1882   *To Cuba and Back.* Boston: Ticknor and Fields, 1859.   First edition, 8vo., may ad, blue cloth stamped in blind and gilt, little dusty on endpapers, very good, tight, early ownership signature of Addison Child, May 1859.   Second Life Books Inc.   183 - 97   2013 $450

Dana, Richard Henry   1815-1882   *Two Years before the Mast.* New York: Harper and Bros., 1840. First edition, first state with dot over the "I" in the word "in", first line of copyright notice and by the unbroken running head on page 9, first state of binding with Harper's Family Library listed as 105 titles only, 12mo., original printed tan muslin, pages 483, full black morocco pull-off case with inner chemise, aside from stain on spine, fine, entirely without foxing, bookplate of Albert G. Brice (1830-1912), evidence at top of spine of removal of his small label with short mark, with short ANS from author June 9 1866 to William H. Cary Esq., NY, Cary was partner in Cary, Howard, Sanger & Co. of NY. Howard S. Mott Inc.   262 - 39   2013 $6000

Dana, Richard Henry   1815-1882   *Two Years Before the Mast: a Personal Narrative of Life at Sea.*   San Francisco: printed for Random House, 1936.   One of 1000 copies, 14 plates, handset Oxford type, half white sheep over cloth boards, spine lettered in dark brown, very fine and clean copy with printed gold dust jacket (slight chipping at spine ends).   Argonaut Book Shop   Summer 2013 - 71   2013 $250

Dandy, Walter   *Benign Tumors in the Third Ventricle of the Brain: Diagnosis and Treatment.*   Springfield: 1933.   171 pages, numerous illustrations, very good, original dust jacket which is quite scarce, plates.   James Tait Goodrich   S74 - 69   2013 $495

Dandy, Walter   *Benign Tumors in the Third Ventricle of the Brain: Diagnosis and Treatment.*   Springfield: 1933.   171 pages, numerous illustrations, original red cloth, spine sunned, else very good, tight copy.   James Tait Goodrich   S74 - 70   2013 $275

Dandy, Walter   *Benign Tumors in the Third Ventricle of the Brain: Diagnosis and Treatment.*   Springfield: 1933.   171 pages, numerous illustrations, very good, original dust jacket, quite scarce.   James Tait Goodrich   75 - 75   2013 $495

Dandy, Walter   *Benign, Encapsulated Tumors n the Lateral Ventricles of the Brain. Diagnosis and Treatment.* Baltimore: Williams and Wilkins, 1934.   Near fine, original blue cloth, head and tail of spine showing some light wear, ownership stamp on front board.   James Tait Goodrich   75 - 76   2013 $495

Dandy, Walter   *Intracranial Arterial Aneurysms.*   Ithaca: Comstock, 1947.   Third printing, 8vo., 6 folding charts, blue cloth, gilt stamped spine, extremities rubbed, ownership rubberstamps and signature of Bland Wilson Cannon, M.D., with related original signature, scarce, very good.   Jeff Weber Rare Books   172 - 69   2013 $125

Dandy, Walter J.   *Orbita Tumors Results Following the Transcranial Operative Attack.*   New York: Oscar Priest, 1941.   First edition, With Hafner Pub. Co. cancel stamp, 168 pages, 100 illustrations, original cloth, light wear, else very good, tight copy.   James Tait Goodrich   S74 - 71   2013 $350

Dane, Clemence   *Tradition and Hugh Walpole.*   London: Heinemann, 1930.   First edition, original cloth, gilt, dust jacket, 250 pages, edges rather spotted.   R. F. G. Hollett & Son   Lake District and Cumbria - 3   2013 $25

Dane, Clemence   *Will Shakespeare.*   London: William Heinemann, 1921. First edition, 8vo., original red cloth, inscribed by Clemence Dane for Graham Greene, excellent copy, bookplate "Raymond Greene from H. Graham Greene Dec. 21".   Maggs Bros. Ltd.   1460 - 370   2013   £600

Dane, Joel Y.   *The Christmas Tree Murders.*   New York: Doubleday, Doran and Co., for the Crime Club, 1938.   First edition, bottom corners bumped, thus near fine in very good dust jacket with small chip o front flap, not effecting text or price, modest edgewear.   Between the Covers Rare Books, Inc.   Mystery & Detective Fiction - 316127   2013 $350

Daniel Boone: Les Aventures d'un Chasseur Americain Parmi Les Peaux-Rouges.   Paris: Domino Press, 1931.   One of only 25 numbered copies in French, signed by artist, with extra suite of illustrations printed without text, folio, loose as issued in color pictorial folder, fine, protective glassine wrapper which does have some wear, text printed on high quality Velin D'Arches paper, beautiful, richly colored lithographs by Fedor Rojankovsky.   Aleph-Bet Books, Inc.   104 - 494   2013 $2500

Daniel, James   *The Shipowners' and Shipmasters' Directory to the Port Charger Testament.*   London: Mrs. James Taylor, 1869.   Enlarged, improved edition, original wavy grain green cloth, paper label, few nicks, very good. Jarndyce Antiquarian Booksellers   CCV - 82   2013   £120

Daniel, Samuel   *The Collection of the History of England.* London: Simon Waterson, 1626.   Folio, imprimatur leaf between A2 and 13 and is frequently lacking, title within ornamental border, modern half blue morocco, cloth slipcase, leaves K3-4 in early pen facsimile, several smal tears repaired and now turning a bit brown, corner of M5 replaced costing a few letters of marginal notes, dampstain at top margin.   Joseph J. Felcone Inc.   Books Printed before 1701 - 26   2013 $900

Daniel, William *My Memories of the Century Club 1919-1958.* New York: privately printed for Members of the Century Association, 1959. First edition, fine in original near fine, unprinted glassine dust jacket, warmly inscribed by author.   Between the Covers Rare Books, Inc.   165 - 128   2013 $125

Daniel, William B. *Rural Sports.* London: Longman Hurst, Rees, Orme and Brown, 1812. New edition, 4 volumes including supplement, 76 full page plates, double page table and one hand colored plate, some light foxing, otherwise very good, clean, tight set, wide margins, three quarter tan calf and marbled boards.   Second Life Books Inc.   183 - 98   2013 $1600

Danielewski, Mark Z. *House of Leaves.* New York: Pantheon, 2000. Uncorrected proof copy (which states '2nd edition' on titlepage, but has 'first edition' and full number line on copyright page), fine in blue wrappers, reportedly one of 293 copies.   Ken Lopez Bookseller   159 - 52   2013 $375

Dankers, Jaspar *Journal of a Voyage to New York and a Tour in Several of the American Colonies in 1679-80.* Brooklyn: published by the Society, 1867. First edition, 440 pages, 12 plates, publisher's cloth and paper covered boards, bookplate, tiny owner's name rebacked with leather spine label gilt, new endpapers, very good or better. Between the Covers Rare Books, Inc.   New York City - 299779   2013 $150

Dann, A. G. *George Webster, D. D. A Memoir.* Dublin: McGee, 1892. 8vo., frontispiece, cloth, come marks on cover, else very good.   C. P. Hyland   261 - 865   2013   £35

Dante Alighieri   1265-1321 *La Divina Commedia....* Venice: Antonia Zatta, 1757. First collected edition, 4 volumes bound in five, quarto, frontispiece, engraved dedication and 111 engraved plates, numerous engraved and head and tailpieces and folding table, title to volume I printed in red and black, contemporary Italian half sheep over paper boards decorated in red and green to a floral pattern, spine with gilt lettering direct, red sprinkled edges, very fresh, crisp copy.   Heritage Book Shop   50th Anniversary Catalogue - 25   2013 $17,500

Dante Alighieri   1265-1321 *The Divine Comedy of Dante Aligheri.* New York: Bruce Rogers and the Press of A. Colish, 1955. Limited to 300 numbered copies, this copy unnumbered, folio, illustrations from designs by Botticelli, original full brick morocco, boards decoratively stamped in gilt with corner devices, spine lettered in gilt, top edge gilt, others uncut, original plain paper dust jacket, with two copies of publisher's prospectus laid in, beautiful about fine copy in black cloth slipcase.   Heritage Book Shop   Holiday Catalogue 2012 - 127   2013 $1250

Dante Alighieri   1265-1321 *The Divine Comedy.* New York: Bruce Rogers & Press of A. Colish, 1955. One of 300 numbered copies (this unnumbered),, beautifully printed on handmade paper, occasional light foxing, foolscap 8vo., contemporary black morocco backstrip with five raised bands, each band with gilt ornamentation and double gilt rules above and below, acorn device gilt blocked in compartments, front cover lettered with acorn ornament beneath all in gilt, double gilt rule border to sides, original vellum wrappers preserved at front and end, lavish ornamentation to inner dentelles, red marbled endpapers, booklabel, top edge gilt, others untrimmed, fine, rare.   Blackwell's Rare Books   172 - 271   2013   £1700

Darling, F. Fraser *The Seasons & The Fisherman.* Cambridge: University Press, 1942. Large 8vo., original pictorial boards, dust jacket (closed edge tear at foot of spine), 50 drawings in black and white by C. F. Tunnicliffe.   R. F. G. Hollett & Son   Children's Books - 613   2013   £35

Darlington, C. D. *The Little Universe of Man.* London: George Allen & Unwin, 1978. First edition, 8vo., 307 pages, near fine, in very good++ dust jacket with mild sun spine.   By the Book, L. C.   37 - 13   2013 $125

Darrow, Clarence Seward   1857-1938 *Farmington.* Chicago: A. C. McClurg, 1904. First edition, very good, hardcover.   Beasley Books   2013 - 2013 $100

Darwin, Bernard *Every Idle Dream.* London: Collins, 1948. First edition, signed by author, 8vo., 254 pages, very good++ in like dust jacket with mild foxing and edgewear. By the Book, L. C.   36 - 70   2013 $1000

Darwin, Charles Robert   1809-1882 *The Descent of Man in Relation to Sex.* London: John Murray, 1871. First edition, first issue, first word on page 297 of volume 1 is 'transmitted' with added note tipped in volume II on pages (ix-x), and 25 errata verso of title leaf to volume II, 2 octavo volumes, 76 woodcut text illustrations, original green cloth stamped in blind on covers, spines lettered in gilt with ornamental rules at head and tail of spines, black endpapers, contemporary booksellers ticket to Wm. Henry Greer of Belfast on upper left corner front pastedown, very little wear to extremities and corners, mild fraying to tail volume II, overall exceptionally attractive, covers and spines bright, text clean, housed in green cloth slipcase.   Heritage Book Shop   50th Anniversary Catalogue - 26   2013 $8,500

Darwin, Charles Robert 1809-1882 *Dobor Plciowy. Przetlomacy z Angielskie go za Uopowaznieniem Autora Ludwik Maklowski.* Lwow (Lviv): Ksiegarna Polska, 1875-1876. First edition in Polish, 2 volumes in 1, illustrations in text, front free endpaper loose, occasional minor foxing, slightly browned around edges, 8vo., original cloth backed boards, rebacked and recornered in grey cloth matching original (of which there have been traces), duplicate stamp of the Jagellonium at end, bold signature at foot of first title of Boleslav Rembowski, sound.   Blackwell's Rare Books Sciences - 41   2013   £2200

Darwin, Charles Robert 1809-1882 *The Effects of Cross and Self Fertilization in the Vegetable Kingdom.* London: John Murray, 1876. First edition, original green cloth, gilt lettered spine, very good++, mild cover edge wear, creases to f.f.e.p., hinges archivally and subtly strengthened, 8vo., 3 line errata slip.   By the Book, L. C.   37 - 14   2013 $1000

Darwin, Charles Robert 1809-1882 *The Formation of Vegetable Mould, through the Action fo Worms...* London: John Murray, 1881. Second thousand, 8vo., very good+, original green cloth, gilt lettering to spine, hinges archivally and subtly strengthened, scuffs to covers, cover edge wear, cover corners bumped, scattered foxing, few pages uncut.   By the Book, L. C.   37 - 15   2013 $500

Darwin, Charles Robert 1809-1882 *Journal of Researches into the Natural History and Geology of the Countries Visited During the Voyage of HMS Beagle...* London: John Murray, 1870. 8vo., very good ex-library in later half brown leather and red cloth, raised bands, rebacked, gilt lettering on red leather title label spine, library sticker, library stamps, no other library markings, cover edge wear, stains and scuffs to covers.   By the Book, L. C.   37 - 18   2013 $250

Darwin, Charles Robert 1809-1882 *Journal of Researches into the Natural History and Geology of the Countries Visited During the Voyage of HMS Beagle...* New York: D. Appleton, 1871. First American one volume edition, 8vo., very good++ in original brown cloth with gilt lettering to spine, mild cover edge wear, owner bookplate to front pastedown, lower corner of titlepage missing and repaired.   By the Book, L. C.   37 - 16   2013 $400

Darwin, Charles Robert 1809-1882 *Journal of Researches into the Natural History and Geology of the Countries Visited During the Voyage of HMS Beagle...* London: John Murray, 1884. Sixteenth thousand, 8vo., original green cloth with gilt lettered spine, mild scuffs and edgewear to spine and covers, foxing, hinges archivally repaired, bookseller label.   By the Book, L. C.   37 - 19   2013 $125

Darwin, Charles Robert 1809-1882 *Journal of Researches into the Natural History and Geology of the Countries Visited During the Voyage of HMS Beagle...* London: John Murray, 1897. 8vo., very good+ in original green cloth with gilt lettered spine and gilt illustration to front cover, mild scuff to spine, minimal cover edge wear, cover corners bumped foxing to endpapers.   By the Book, L. C.   37 - 17   2013 $125

Darwin, Charles Robert 1809-1882 *Narrative of the Surveying Voyages of His Majesty's Ships Adventure and Beagle, Between the Years 1826 and 1836.* London: Henry Colburn, 1839. First edition, first issue of volume III, 2 folding maps, half title, contemporary diced calf (probably a gift binding) neatly rebacked, marbled endpapers and edges, armorial bookplate of Hensleigh C. Wedgwood, inscribed by author to same (his brother-in-law), endpapers little foxed and soiled, otherwise exceptional association and attractive looking copy in custom full brown morocco clamshell case, gilt stamped.   Heritage Book Shop   50th Anniversary Catalogue - 27   2013 $100,000

Darwin, Charles Robert 1809-1882 *On the Origin of Species by means of Natural Selection or the Preservation of Favoured Races in the Struggle for Life.* London: John Murray, 1859. First edition, first issue, octavo, one folding diagram, original green cloth decoratively stamped in blind on covers, hinges expertly repaired, spine decorated and lettered in gilt (Freeman variant 'a'), extremities and corners slightly rubbed, binder's ticket of Edmonds & Remnants of London on back pastedown, contemporary bookplate of John Clerk with his signature dated "Jun 1859" and Roberto Salinas Price bookplate, overall very good, housed in full green morocco clamshell case.   Heritage Book Shop   50th Anniversary Catalogue - 28   2013 $160,000

Darwin, Charles Robert 1809-1882 *On the Origin of Species by Means of Natural Selection...* London: John Murray, 1869. Fifth edition, 10th thousand, 8vo., very good+, modern half leather marbled board, edges previously trimmed without text loss, titlepage edges chipped, soiled with faint library stamp, no other writing or markings, mild scattered foxing, folding plate.   By the Book, L. C.   37 - 21   2013 $1250

Darwin, Charles Robert 1809-1882 *On the Various Contrivances by Which British and Foreign Orchids are Fertilised by Insects and on the Good Effects of Intercrossing.* London: John Murray, 1862. First edition, original plum cloth with vertical lines, Freeman variant 'a', ad dated Dec. 1861, bound by Edmonds & Remnants, with their ticket, publisher's blindstamp "Presented by Mr. Murray" on titlepage, this often indicated a copy sent on request of Darwin to a friend or colleague, volume rebacked with remnants of original sunned spine laid down, minimal cover edge wear, scuffs to front pastedown, scattered foxing, 8vo., very good.   By the Book, L. C.   37 - 22   2013 $2750

Darwin, Charles Robert 1809-1882 *The Various Contrivances by Which Orchids are Fertilised by Insects.* London: John Murray, 1890. Second edition, 5th thousand, very good+, original green cloth, gilt lettered spine, mild scuffs to spine, cover corners bumped, endpapers dampstained, minimal scattered foxing, 8vo, catalog at rear dated 1891. By the Book, L. C. 37 - 24 2013 $400

Darwin, Charles Robert 1809-1882 *The Origin of Species by Means of Natural Selection...* London: John Murray, 1861. Third edition, seventh thousand, folding chart, half title present, edges of text lightly browned, soiled at foot of titlepage, 8vo., original wavy grain green cloth by Edmonds & Remnants, with their ticket, extremities rubbed, backstrip gilt lettered direct, sides blind paneled with stamped border, chalked brown endpapers, hinges strengthened, neat repairs to head and tail of spine, good. Blackwell's Rare Books 172 - 46 2013 £3850

Darwin, Charles Robert 1809-1882 *The Origin of Species by mean of natural selection...* London: John Murray, 1894. 45th thousand, contemporary ownership inscription at head of title, endpapers slightly foxed, 8vo., original cloth, blind blocked borders ons ides, spine gilt lettered, excellent, almost pristine copy. Blackwell's Rare Books   Sciences - 42 2013 £600

Darwin, Charles Robert 1809-1882 *Origin of Certain Instincts. in Nature No. 179 Volume 7, Thursday April 3, 1873.* London: Macmillan, 1873. Entire issue offered, very good++, self wrappers with minimal scattered foxing, disbound but spine intact and no writing or other markings, 4to. By the Book, L. C. 37 - 23 2013 $275

Darwin, Charles Robert 1809-1882 *The Variation of Animals and Plants Under Domestication.* New York: Orange Judd, 1868. First American edition, 2 volumes, complete set, original green cloth with gilt lettered spines, binding tight, mild edge wear and scuffs to covers, scattered foxing, four inch piece missing from bottom of ad page rear volume II, 8vo. By the Book, L. C. 37 - 25 2013 $290

Darwin, Charles Robert 1809-1882 *Works.* New York: D. Appleton and Co., 1896. Authorized edition, 15 volumes, folding plates, illustrations, interior pages very clean, margins slightly browned, modern brown cloth, gilt titles to spines, many pages unopened, each volume with bookplate of Valentine Everit Macy and Edith Carpenter Macy, chairman of Girl Scouts, very good. The Kelmscott Bookshop 7 - 131 2013 $1250

Darwin, Francis *The Life and Letters of Charles Darwin...* London: John Murray, 1887. Fifth thousand revised, 3 volumes, 8vo., original green cloth, gilt lettered spines, volume I recased with new endpapers, evidence of label removed from upper boards of each volume, cover corners bumped, minimal foxing edges and endpapers, minimal cover edge wear. By the Book, L. C. 37 - 10 2013 $250

Dary, David *Kanzana 1854-1900: a Selected Bibliography of Books, Pamphlets and Ephemera of Kansas.* Lawrence: 1986. Limited to 250 numbered and signed copies, xii, 294 pages, illustrations, issued without dust jacket, near fine, very well done. Dumont Maps & Books of the West 122 - 51 2013 $100

Dary, David *Kanzana 1854-1900: a Selected Bibliography of Books, Pamphlets and Ephemera of Kansas.* London: 1986. limited to 250 numbered copies, signed by author, illustrations, near fine. Dumont Maps & Books of the West 125 - 46 2013 $95

Dashwood, Richard Lewes *Chiploquorgan; or Life by the Camp Fire in the Dominion of Canada and Newfoundland.* London: Simpkin Marshall, 1872. New edition, brown cloth, gold title and vignette on front board, half title, frontispiece, 8vo., cloth worn with spine torn along top interior good. Schooner Books Ltd. 104 - 15 2013 $125

Daudet, Alphonse *Tartarin of Tarascon.* printed by Richard W. Ellis, The Georgian Press, 1930. 253/1500 sets, 2 volumes, signed by artist, several illustrations from sketches by W. A. Dwiggins, 16mo., original pale grey, black cloth backed boards, backstrips gilt lettered and decorated, boards with overall decorative pattern in green and pink untrimmed, dust soiled board slipcase with printed label, very good, Ruari McLean's copy with his booklabel. Blackwell's Rare Books B174 - 361 2013 £150

Daugherty, James *Poor Richard.* New York: Viking Press, 1941. First edition, large 8vo., signed by Daughtery, orange cloth, spine faded, very small tear at very bottom of spine, illustrations. Barnaby Rudge Booksellers Children 2013 - 020819 2013 $65

Daunt, John *Some Account of the Family of Daunt.* 1881. First edition, 34 pages, 2 plates pasted in blank pages, text good binding shaky, cloth. C. P. Hyland 261 - 384 2013 £65

Daunt, W. J. O'Neill *Catechism of the History of Ireland.* 1874. 8vo., cloth, good, signed by author 19th May 1876. C. P. Hyland 261 - 290 2013 £65

Daunt, W. J. O'Neill *A Life Spent for Ireland; Being Selections from... Journals of... Late W. J. O'Neill Daunt.* 1896. First edition, portrait, some foxing, 8vo., stiff line wrappers, good. C. P. Hyland 261 - 291 2013 £55

Daunt, W. J. O'Neill *A Life Spent for Ireland; Being Selections from... Journals of... Late W. J. O'Neill Daunt.* IUP, 1972. First issue, 8vo., portrait, cloth, dust jacket, near fine. C. P. Hyland 261 - 292 2013 £40

Dau's New York Social Blue Book 1930. New York: Dau's Blue Books, 1930. First edition, very good with minimal pen notations on few pages without a dust jacket, 682 pages, scarce. Between the Covers Rare Books, Inc. New York City - 308720   2013 $275

Davenant, William   1606-1668   *The Works of Sr. William Davenant Kt...* London: by T. N. for Henry Herringman, 1673. First collected edition, folio, portrait, turn of the century red levant morocco, gilt arabesque centerpiece on covers, all edges gilt, by Riviere, very skillfully rebacked, though the new leather at joints and on cords has uniformly faded, unusually fine, fresh, wide margined copy with fine impression of the portrait, leather tipped fleece lined slipcase, edges rubbed, bookplates of Duke of Beaufort, E. F. Leo, A. E. Newton.   Joseph J. Felcone Inc.   English and American Literature to 1800 - 12   2013 $2200

Davenant, William   1606-1668   *The Works of Sr. William Davenant...* London: by T. N. for Henry Herringman, 1673. First collected edition, folio, portrait, turn of the century red levant morocco, gilt arabesque centerpiece on covers, all edges gilt, by Riviere, very skillfully rebacked, though new leather at joints and on cords has uniformly faded, unusually fine, fresh, wide margined copy, with fine impression of the portrait, leather tipped fleece lined slipcase (edges rubbed), the Duke of Beaufort, E. F. Leo and A. E. Newton copy with their bookplates.   Joseph J. Felcone Inc.   Books Printed before 1701 - 27   2013 $2200

Davenport, Cyril   *Thomas Berthelet, Royal Printer and Bookbinder to Henry VIII, King of England...*   Chicago: Caxton Club, 1901. Limited to 252 copies on handmade paper, 4to., 95 pages, 18 full page tissue guarded plates, 6 color text engravings, original quarter red cloth over grey paper boards, printed paper spine label, ink presentation gift inscription, bookplate of St. Mary of the Woods College Library, fine.   Jeff Weber Rare Books   171 - 24   2013 $395

Davenport, W.   *A Week in Holland.*   London: Sinclair, Haymarket, 1905. volumes I and II, oblong 8vo., 2 calligraphic titles and 90 Platinum prints measuring from 48 x 72mm. to 75 x 104mm., some occasional foxing, contemporary crushed full ed morocco by Sinclair of Haymarket, London, ruled and lettered in gilt, inner dentelles, ornamented in gilt, all edges gilt, mottled red endpapers,.   Marlborough Rare Books Ltd.   218 - 80   2013   £250

Davidoff, Leo   *Brain Tumors their Pathology, Symptomology, Diagnosis and Progress.*   Utrica: State Hospital Press, 1931. Separate offprint, 158 pages, original printed green wrappers.   James Tait Goodrich   S74 - 75   2013 $150

Davidoff, Leo   *The Normal Encephalogram.*   Philadelphia: Lea & Febiger, 1946. Second edition, 1155 engravings, 240 pages, original green cloth very clean tight copy, author's presentation to Gill Rose.   James Tait Goodrich   S74 - 73   2013 $175

Davidson, Bruce   *Bruce Davidson Photographs.*   New York: Agrinde, 1978. First edition, oblong 4to., wrappers, very good+.   Beasley Books   2013 - 2013 $100

Davidson, Bruce   *East 100th Street.*   Los Angeles: St. Ann's Press, 2003. First edition thus, limited to 3000 copies, this copy additionally signed, 4to., cream colored cloth with paste-on black and white photo to front cover, original acetate dust jacket, fine.   By the Book, L. C.   36 - 17   2013 $300

Davidson, Bruce   *Time of Change. Bruce Davidson Civil Rights Photographs 1961-1965.*   Los Angeles: St. Ann's Press, 2002. Limited to 4500 copies, this copy additionally signed, 4to., 144 pages + afterword, mild soil to edges, black cloth with black and white paste-on photo illustration on front cover, original acetate dust jacket with mild scuffs and edge wear, fine.   By the Book, L. C.   36 - 18   2013 $200

Davidson, Harold G.   *Edward Borein, Cowboy Artist: The Life and Works of John Edward Borein 1872-1945.*   Garden City: Doubleday & co., 1974. First trade edition, quarto, 189 pages, reproductions of drawings and etchings, photos and paintings, maroon cloth, gilt, very fine with pictorial dust jacket.   Argonaut Book Shop   Recent Acquisitions June 2013 - 31   2013 $90

Davidson, J. W.   *Peter Dillon of Vanikoro.*   1975. First edition, 8vo., cloth, dust jacket, fine.   C. P. Hyland   261 - 960   2013   £32

Davidson, John   *The Great Men and a Practical Novelist.*   London: Ward & Downey, 1891. Scarce first edition, 4 illustrations by E. J. Ellis, original red cloth with attractive embossed floral design on front and back covers, gilt author and title to spine.   The Kelmscott Bookshop   7 - 102   2013 $250

Davidson, John   *Smith: a Tragedy.*   Glasgow: Frederick W. Wilson and Brother, 1888. First edition, 300 copies printed, scarce presentation, inscribed by author to Mrs. John A. Cramb, original parchment wrappers which are browned and lightly soiled, otherwise very good, interior pages clean and bright, very light rippling caused by tight signatures, enclosed in red cloth folder, which is inserted into red cloth slipcase with quarter leather spine, gilt title, author, date and "presentation copy" to spine, 82 pages, including publisher catalog.   The Kelmscott Bookshop   7 - 101   2013 $850

Davidson, Laura *Culinaria.* Boston: 2009. Artist's book, one of 10 copies only, all on magnani pecia paper, each signed and numbered by artist in pencil, page size 5 x 6 inches, 20 pages, bound by artist in stainless steel with red and green floral print retro fabric recalling vintage apron or kitchen curtains on spine, copper grommets with brass spatula ingeniously held on by magnets decorating front panel, endpapers are original linoleum prints in pink and white check, with forks, knives, spoons and measuring cups within checks, book comprised of 10 dry points with ink wash of well designed and useful kitchen tools, such as egg beater, strainer, scoop, whisk and masher, etc.   Priscilla Juvelis - Rare Books   56 - 6   2013 $1250

Davidson, Levette *Rocky Mountain Tales.* Norman: University of Oklahoma Press, 1947. First edition, 8 illustrations by Shelly, green cloth, very fine, pictorial dust jacket, slight rubbing to head of jacket spine.   Argonaut Book Shop   Summer 2013 - 73   2013 $60

Davidson, Lionel *The Chelsea Murders.* London: Cape, 1978. First edition, pages darkened, otherwise fine in price clipped dust jacket with publisher's price sticker.   Mordida Books   81 - 131   2013 $65

Davidson, Lionel *A Long Way to Shiloh.* London: Gollancz, 1966. First edition, lower corners slightly bumped, otherwise fine in price clipped dust jacket with closed tear on back panel and small chips at corners.   Mordida Books   81 - 129   2013 $75

Davidson, Lionel *Making Good Again.* London: Cape, 1968. First edition, corner creasing on front endpaper, otherwise fine in dust jacket with couple of short closed tears.   Mordida Books   81 - 130   2013 $100

Davies-Shiel, Mike *Watermills of Cumbria.* Dalesman Publications, 1978. First edition, original pictorial stiff wrappers, pages 120, over 50 plans and diagrams, half title price clipped, scarce.   R. F. G. Hollett & Son   Lake District and Cumbria - 12   2013   £45

Davies, Hunter *Wainwright. The Biography.* London: Michael Joseph, 1995. First edition, original cloth, gilt, dust jacket, well illustrated.   R. F. G. Hollett & Son   Lake District and Cumbria - 5   2013   £40

Davies, Hunter *A Walk Around the Lakes.* London: Weidenfeld and Nicolson, 1979. First edition, original cloth, gilt, dust jacket, 21 illustrations and line drawing by Wainwright, scarce.   R. F. G. Hollett & Son   Lake District and Cumbria - 7   2013   £60

Davies, Hunter *William Wordsworth. A Biography.* London: Weidenfeld & Nicolson, 1980. First edition, original cloth, gilt, dust jacket, pages xiii, 367, 26 plates, signed by author.   R. F. G. Hollett & Son   Lake District and Cumbria - 8   2013   £35

Davies, John *Orchestra or a Poeme of Dauncing (1596).* Wembley Hill: Stanton Press, 1922. 68/175 copies printed on handmade paper and signed by printer Richard Stanton Lambert, numerous wood engravings by Elinor Lambert, 4to., original quarter pale grey linen corners little worn, printed label, pale blue boards, free endpapers browned, bookplate, untrimmed, good.   Blackwell's Rare Books   B174 - 390   2013   £50

Davies, K. G. *Northern Quebec and Labrador Journals and Correspondence 1819-1835.* London: Hudson's Bay Record Society, 1963. Limited edition, 8vo., black cloth boards, gilt to front and spine with dust jacket, half title, index, 2 folding maps in rear pocket, very good in like dust jacket.   Schooner Books Ltd.   105 - 27   2013 $75

Davies, Richard *An Account of the Convincement, Exercises, Services and Travels of the Ancient Servant of the Lord...* Newtown: Gregynog Press, 1928. 52/150 copies (of an edition of 175 copies, printed on Batchelor handmade paper, press device on title printed in red, crown 8vo., original dark blue bevel edged buckram, faded backstrip and front cover gilt lettered and ruled bookplate, untrimmed, very good.   Blackwell's Rare Books   B174 - 345   2013   £150

Davies, Robertson *Tempest-Tost.* Toronto: Clarke, Irwin & Co., 1951. First edition, 8vo., original turquoise cloth, excellent copy in slightly rubbed dust jacket, signed by author, having crossed through his printed name.   Maggs Bros. Ltd.   1460 - 205   2013   £150

Davies, W. J. K. *The Ravenglass & Eskdale Railway.* David & Charles, 1968. First edition, original cloth, gilt, dust jacket (faded), pages 204, color frontispiece, 51 illustrations and 18 text drawings and facsimiles.   R. F. G. Hollett & Son   Lake District and Cumbria - 10   2013   £35

Davies, W. J. K. *The Ravenglass & Eskdale Railway.* Newton Abbot: David & Charles, 1981. Second edition, original cloth, gilt, dust jacket, pages 204, color frontispiece, 51 illustrations and 18 text drawings and facsimiles.   R. F. G. Hollett & Son   Lake District and Cumbria - 11   2013   £30

Davies, William *Extracts from the Journal of Rev. William Davies.* Llanidloes: Wesleyan Printing Office, 1835. First edition, 78 pages, 8vo., later cloth, very good.   Maggs Bros. Ltd.   1467 - 20   2013   £1250

Davis, Angela Y. *If They Come in the Morning: Voices of Reistance.* New York: Third Press, 1971. First edition, fine in lightly rubbed, otherwise fine dust jacket.   Between the Covers Rare Books, Inc.   165 - 129   2013 $100

Davis, Audrey *Bloodletting Instruments in the National Museum of History and Technology.* Washington: Smithsonian Institution Press, 1979. First edition, tall 8vo., v, 103 pages, illustrations, printed wrappers, lightly rubbed, spine sunned, else near fine, Burndy bookplate. Jeff Weber Rare Books 169 - 90 2013 $220

Davis, Bob *Tree Toad.* Philadelphia: Stokes, 1942. First edition, 8vo., 276 pages, cloth, fine, illustrations in line, color dust jacket by Robert McCloskey, frontispiece by Charles Dana Gibson. Aleph-Bet Books, Inc. 105 - 376 2013 $400

Davis, Cynthia *Where Water is King.* Willows: Glenn-Colusa Irrigation District, 1984. First edition, quarto, iv, 149 pages, profusely illustrated from vintage photos, reproductions, maps, brown cloth gilt, very fine, very scarce. Argonaut Book Shop Recent Acquisitions June 2013 - 78 2013 $175

Davis, George *Coming Home.* New York: Random House, 1971. First edition, small owner name on front fly, page edges little browned, else near fine in like dust jacket with short tear on rear panel, uncommon. Between the Covers Rare Books, Inc. 165 - 130 2013 $75

Davis, John *Udgorn Seion neu Seren y Saint yn Cynnwy Egwyddorion...* Merthyr Tydfil: Argraffwyd, Cyhoeddwyd, ac Ar Werth Gan J. Davis, 1849. First edition, 240 pages, 17cm., contemporary three quarter leather over marbled boards, backstrip professionally rebacked with original gilt stamped backstrip laid over, boards rubbed, minor discoloring to rear of text block. Ken Sanders Rare Books 45 - 22 2013 $750

Davis, N. *Carthage and Her Remains: Being an Account of the Excavations and Researches on the Site of the Phoenician Metropolis in Africa and Other Adjacent Places.* London: Richard Bentley, 1861. First edition, large 8vo., original blindstamped cloth gilt, rather faded, head of spine little frayed in places, gilt stamp of Dunblain Academy on upper board, all edges gilt, with half title, 1 folding map (repaired on reverse), 31 plates, several text woodcuts, prize label. R. F. G. Hollett & Son Africana - 48 2013 £195

Davis, R. V. *Geology of Cumbria.* Dalesman Books, 1977. First edition, original pictorial wrappers, pages 80, diagrams. R. F. G. Hollett & Son Lake District and Cumbria - 13 2013 £25

Davis, Richard C. *Encyclopedia of American Forest and Conservation History.* New York: Macmillan, 1983. First edition, 2 volumes, quarto, photos, maps, green cloth, gilt, very fine set. Argonaut Book Shop Summer 2013 - 74 2013 $90

Davis, Tenney L. *Chymia: Annual Studies in the History of Chemistry. Nos. 1-12.* Philadelphia: University of Pennsylvania Press, 1948-1967. 8vo., frontispieces, illustrations, blue cloth (nos. 1-4), green cloth (no. 7), red cloth (nos. 8 & 12), black cloth (no. 9), grey cloth (no. 10), yellow cloth (no. 11), gilt stamped spines, dust jackets, nos. 1-4 lacking jackets, rubber stamps, near fine, Burndy Library bookplates. Jeff Weber Rare Books 169 - 91 2013 $850

Davis, William *A Complete Treatise of Land Surveying by the Chain, Corss and Offset Staffs Only.* London: printed for the author, 1798. 8vo., 6 folding plates, numerous diagrams in text, slight foxing, mainly to leading edges and plates, contemporary half calf marbled boards, gilt morocco label, expert repairs to hinges and corners, spine repaired, contemporary signature of J. Brooke and of William Wilson, Tilsey. Jarndyce Antiquarian Booksellers CCIV - 105 2013 £320

Davis, William Heath 1822-1909 *Seventy-Five Years in California.* San Francisco: John Howell Books, 1929. First trade edition, one of 2000 copies, 2 color plates, 41 black and white illustrations, facsimile newspaper, offsetting from newspaper as usual, publisher's blue-grey cloth, slightest of rubbing to spine ends, very fine, bright copy. Argonaut Book Shop Summer 2013 - 75 2013 $200

Davis, William Heath 1822-1909 *Seventy-Five Years in California.* San Francisco: John Howell Books, 1967. Third edition, color frontispiece, 19 plates, gilt lettered yellow cloth, very fine, pictorial dust jacket. Argonaut Book Shop Summer 2013 - 76 2013 $75

Davis, Winfield J. *History of Political Conventions in California 1849-1892.* Sacramento: California State Library, 1893. First edition, handsomely bound in new dark brown cloth, leather spine label, errata slip, very fine,. Argonaut Book Shop Recent Acquisitions June 2013 - 80 2013 $325

Davy, Humphry 1778-1829 *Elements of Agricultural Chemistry in a Course of Lectures for the Board of Agriculture.* London: Longman et al, 1813. First edition, 4to., 10 plates, one folding, original linen backed boards, rebacked, untrimmed, nice wide margins, some offsetting to titlepage, some light waterstaining. Second Life Books Inc. 183 - 99 2013 $600

Davy, John *The Angler in the Lake District...* London: Longman Brown, etc., 1857. First edition, original decorated green cloth, gilt, spine trifle faded, cloth on boards slightly bubbled, presentation copy "From the author" rear joint cracking, otherwise very nice, scarce. R. F. G. Hollett & Son Lake District and Cumbria - 14 2013 £150

Dawkins, Richard *The Ancestor's Tale.* Boston: Houghton Mifflin, 2004. First edition, fine in fine dust jacket, 8vo., scarce book signed by author.   By the Book, L. C. 37 - 26   2013 $175

Dawson, Andrew *Lives of Philadelphia Engineers: Capital Class and Resolution 1830-1890.* Aldershot: Ashgate, 2004. 8vo., 5 tables, 2 charts, 20 figures, pictorial backed boards, Burndy library bookplate, fine.   Jeff Weber Rare Books   169 - 92   2013 $75

Dawson, E. C. *James Hannington First Bishop of Eastern Equatorial Africa.* London: Seeley and Co., 1896. Thirty-seventh thousand, full calf gilt prize binding, extremities trifle rubbed, frontispiece, map, text illustrations, scattered foxing, upper hinge just cracking.   R. F. G. Hollett & Son   Africana - 49   2013   £45

Dawson, Nicholas *Narrative of Nicholas 'Cheyenne' Dawson (Overland to California in '41 & '49 and Texas in '51.* San Francisco: Grabhorn Press, 1933. Second edition, cloth backed decorated boards, very fine and bright. Argonaut Book Shop   Summer 2013 - 77   2013 $125

Dawson, S. J. *Report on the Exploration of the Country Between Lake Superior and the Red River Settlement.* N.P.: 1968. approximately 150 pages, 5 folding maps, 3 folding tables,.   Dumont Maps & Books of the West   125 - 47   2013 $75

Day Lewis, Cecil *Country Comets.* London: Martin Hopkinson, 1928. First edition, small 8vo., rebound in pale green boards, printed paper label, excellent copy, pages lightly browned and foxed, inscribed by author for friend Wilfrid Cowley.   Maggs Bros. Ltd.   1460 - 206   2013   £125

Day Lewis, Cecil *The Gate and Other Poems.* London: Jonathan Cape, 1962. First edition, 8vo., original green cloth, excellent copy with just a few spots of browning to dust jacket and light foxing to page edges, inscribed by author to poet Laurence Whistler.   Maggs Bros. Ltd.   1460 - 208   2013   £75

Day Lewis, Cecil *A Penknife in My Heart.* New York: Harper & Bros., 1958. First US edition, 8vo., original grey cloth, red spine, dust jacket, excellent copy, one small piercing to spine, dust jacket browned at spine, inscribed by author for S. F. Ireland.   Maggs Bros. Ltd.   1460 - 207   2013   £200

Day Lewis, Cecil *The Room and Other Poems.* London: Jonathan Cape, 1965. First edition, original cloth backed boards, near fine in dust jacket, inscribed by author. Maggs Bros. Ltd.   1460 - 210   2013   £50

Day, Geoffrey *How Trains Work.* Hutchinson, n.d., 1952. Oblong 8vo., original pictorial colored card wrappers (one lower corner slightly creased), illustrations in color, scarce. R. F. G. Hollett & Son   Children's Books - 158   2013   £45

Day, J. G F. *The Cathedrals of the Church of Ireland.* 1932. First edition, illustrations, cloth, very good, signed presentation from Godfrey Ossory.   C. P. Hyland   261 - 296   2013   £38

Day, John *Memoir of the Honble Elizabeth Aldworth.* 1914. 22 pages, color and black and white photos, original cloth (faded), some dust marking to text, else good.   C. P. Hyland   261 - 298   2013   £75

Day, John *Memoir of the Honble Elizabeth Aldworth.* 1941. Third edition, leatherette, illustrations, near fine.   C. P. Hyland   261 - 299   2013   £60

Day, Lal Behari *Folk Tales of Bengal.* London: Macmillan, 1912. First edition, thick 4to., fine in rare dust jacket (chipped on rear, else very good), 32 magnificent full page color plates with lettered tissue guards, brilliant copy, beautiful book, rare in dust jacket.   Aleph-Bet Books, Inc. 104 - 237   2013 $900

Day, Thomas   1748-1789 *The History of Sanford and Merton.* printed for J. Wallis, 1790. 6 engraved plates, G2-3 (with plate in between) reinforced at inner margin, slight loss of text on latter near the plate made good in ink on recto, 2 other leaves towards end guarded (no loss), few spots here and there, front hinge strained, frontispiece separated from titlepage, 12mo., original green vellum backed marbled boards, earl (crude) hand lettered label on spine, rubbed and slightly worn, short tear at foot of spine, sound, rear.   Blackwell's Rare Books   B174 - 42   2013   £750

Day, Thomas   1748-1789 *The History of Sandford and Merton.* Whitehall: printed for William Young, Philadelphia, 1798. Seventh edition, 12mo., 3 volumes in 1, contemporary sheep, front hinge split, rear beginning to crack, gathering G foxed, scattered foxing elsewhere, small piece torn from blank margin of 2P5, just touching letter or two, contemporary signature of John Hough.   Joseph J. Felcone Inc. English and American Literature to 1800 - 18   2013 $900

Day, Thomas   1748-1789   *A History of Sandford and Merton.*   London: F. and C. Rivington et al, 1815. Abridged edition, 8vo., frontispiece, lacks 12 pages of publisher's ads, very good internally, tan marbled sheep, somewhat worn, upper joint cracking, spine and edges rubbed, ownership inscription of Master Charles Knight dated Aug. 16th 1821, with scrap of paper (presumably part of the packaging in which he received it) addressed to same loosely inserted, frontispiece with inscription "C. H. Knight's present to his daughter Fanny. Leamington Jan. 7th 1850" and beneath this ownership inscription of Jack Marshall dated 1887.   Unsworths Antiquarian Booksellers   28 - 156   2013   £30

Day, Wesley   *On to me Now.*   N.P.: self published, n.d., Quarto, near fine in claspbound wrappers, inscribed by author to Pauline Kael, former New Yorker film critic.   Ken Lopez Bookseller   159 - 174   2013 $200

Dayes, Edward   *A Picturesque Tour through the Principal Parts of Yorkshire and Derbyshire...*   John Nichols and Son, 1825. Second edition, large 8vo., 14 engraved plates, very good in later 19th century half calf, morocco cloth boards, raised and gilt banded spine with small gilt floral devices, top edge gilt.   Ken Spelman Books Ltd.   73 - 168   2013   £160

Daysh, G. H. J.   *Cumberland and With Special Reference to the West Cumberland Area.*   Whitehaven: Cumberland Development Council, 1951. Second edition, small 4to., original cloth, gilt, 11 maps, 11 figures maps and sections, 3 plates and 21 photos.   R. F. G. Hollett & Son   Lake District and Cumbria - 18   2013   £35

De Bernieres, Louis   *The Troublesome Offspring of Cardinal Guzman.*   London: Secker & Warburg, 1992. First edition, fine in black cloth over boards with silver spine lettering, fine dust jacket.   Ed Smith Books   78 - 12   2013 $300

De Bernieres, Louis   *The War of Don Emmanuel's Nether Parts.*   London: Secker & Warburg, 1990. First edition, fine in black cloth over boards with gold spine lettering, fine dust jacket.   Ed Smith Books   78 - 10   2013 $150

De Blacam, Aodh   *The Druid's Cave: a Tale of Mystery & Adventure for Young People of Seven to Seventy.*   1920. First edition, George Monk illustrations, 8vo., cloth, very good.   C. P. Hyland   261 - 963   2013   £30

De Blacam, Aodh   *First Book of Irish Literature.*   circa, 1935. First and only edition, 8vo., cloth, dust jacket, near fine.   C. P. Hyland   261 - 339   2013   £38

De Blacam, Aodh   *From a Gaelic Outpost.*   1921. First edition, quarter cloth (pictorial boards), 8vo., very good, from an institutional library with stamps.   C. P. Hyland   261 - 964   2013   £34

De Breffny, Brian   *The Churches and Abbeys of Ireland.*   1976. First edition, color and black and white illustrations, 8vo., cloth, dust jacket, fine.   C. P. Hyland   261 - 965   2013   £65

De Breffny, Brian   *The Irish World.*   New York: 1977. First edition, color and black and white illustrations, 8vo., cloth, dust jacket, fine.   C. P. Hyland   261 - 966   2013   £45

De Breffny, Brian   *The Irish World.*   1978.   8vo., color and black and white illustrations, cloth, dust jacket, fine.   C. P. Hyland   261 - 967   2013   £45

De Brisay, Mathers   *History of the County of Lunenburg.*   Belleville: Mika Studio, 1980. Facsimile edition, 8vo., frontispiece, numerous black and white photo illustrations, red cloth, some shelfwear to edges and news clipping about Bluenose on last flyleaf.   Schooner Books Ltd.   101 - 87   2013 $50

De Burca, Seamus   *Brendan Behan. A Memoir.*   Dublin: P. J. Bourke, 1985. First Irish edition, limited to 1000 copies, 8vo. original wrappers, near fine, inscribed by author.   Maggs Bros. Ltd.   1460 - 72   2013   £50

De Burca, Seamus   *The Soldier's Song. The Story of Peadar Kearney.*   Dublin: P. J. Bourke, 1957. First edition, small 8vo., original burgundy cloth, excellent copy in dust jacket slightly torn on front panel, inscribed by author to publisher Timothy O'Keefe.   Maggs Bros. Ltd.   1442 - 357   2013   £150

De Camp, L. Sprague   *Divide and Rule.*   Reading: Fantasy Press, 1948. First edition, octavo, cloth.   L. W. Currey, Inc.   Utopian Literature: Recent Acquisitions (April 2013) - 140817   2013 $250

De Camp, L. Sprague   *The Wheels of If and Other Science Fiction.*   Chicago: Shasta Pub., 1948. First edition, octavo, cloth.   L. W. Currey, Inc.   Fall Sampler Sept. 2013 - 145618   2013 $250

De Camp, Sprague   *The Conan Reader.*   Baltimore: Mirage, 1968. First edition, one of 1500 numbered copies, fine in lightly rubbed, just about fine dust jacket.   Between the Covers Rare Books, Inc.   Sci-Fi, Fantasy & Horror - 319868   2013 $85

De Camp, Sprague   *The Conan Swordbook.*   Baltimore: Mirage, 1969. First edition, fine in fine dust jacket with one tiny scrape on rear flap, one of approximately 1500 numbered copies, beautiful copy.   Between the Covers Rare Books, Inc.   Sci-Fi, Fantasy & Horror - 319893   2013 $95

De Flers, Robert *Ilsee, Princesse de Tripoli.* Paris: Editions d'art H. Piazza & Cie, Editeurs, 1897. First edition, one of 10 copies on Japon with original watercolor, which refers to page 80, with penciled noted, plus original hand watercolored plate for page 33 and another hand colored plate for page 116 and hors texte plate for Part III and subsequent 3 pages, plus 3 extra suites as called for in the colophon 1) suite of colored lithographs on Chine before the letter, 2) suite of plates in black and white on Chine and 3) suite of the cancelled plates on Chine, by Alphonse Mucha, one folio missing from cancelled suite and 4 folios missing from suite on Chine in black and white, else very nearly fine with only handful of tiny blemishes on additional suites with book itself mint; total edition consists of 252 copies; bound by Donald Glaister, full green morocco cloth, gilt tooling on front panel surrounded a raised blind panel, suuggesting the page design of the book with text block surrounded by design and art, raised rectangle highlighted in red, gilt tooling surrounding panel suggesting the intricate at nouveau page design, spine smooth with title stamped in gold, design repeated on back panel, gold silk doublures, yellow and green silk headbands, top edge smooth gilt, other edges rough gilt, original wrappers bound in, housed in custom made clamshell box of green paper over boards, special pull out tray to hold extra suites, as well as original colored drawing and hand colored drawings for original binding design by Donald Glaister, binding signed on rear turn-in in blind with signature gold dot, illustrated with 132 colored lithographs by Mucha, four of which are heightened in silver, with warm greens and browns predominating the colored lithographs, 10 initial letters in color, tailpieces and flourishes.   Priscilla Juvelis - Rare Books   55 - 19   2013 $38,000

De Genestux, Magdeleine *Mickey et Le Prince Malalapatte. (Mickey Mouse in King Arthur's Court).* Paris: Hachette, 1935. 4to., pictorial boards, edges rubbed, else near fine in frayed dust jacket, color endpapers, 4 fabulous color pop-ups, full page and smaller black and whites.   Aleph-Bet Books, Inc.   105 - 472   2013 $1500

De Kekkawe, Richard *The Register of Richard De Kellawe, Lord Palatine and Bishop of Durham 1311-1316.* London: Longman & Co., 1873. 4 volumes, very good set in contemporary quarter morocco, gilt lettered spines, presentation label to St. Benedict's Abbey, Fort Augustus.   Ken Spelman Books Ltd.   75 - 137   2013   £125

De Knight, Freda *A Date with a Dish: a Cook Book of American Negro Recipes.* New York: Hermitage, 1948. Second printing, fine in fine dust jacket, beautiful copy.   Between the Covers Rare Books, Inc.   165 - 122   2013 $150

De Kruif, Paul *Life Among the Doctors.* New York: Harcourt Brace, 1949. 8vo., beige cloth, ownership signature of Philip S. Hench, Rochester, Minn., with his purchase slip, very good+.   Jeff Weber Rare Books   172 - 75   2013 $50

De La Mare, Walter   1873-1956 *A Child's Day a Book of Rhymes.* London: Constable & Co., 1912. First edition, paper over boards, good, 4to., 24 tipped in photos in excellent condition, good, cover soiled with scratches to photo and corners worn.   Barnaby Rudge Booksellers   Children 2013 - 020325   2013 $50

De La Mare, Walter   1873-1956 *Down-Adown-Derby.* London: Constable, 1922. First edition, 4to., blue gilt cloth, fine in pictorial dust jacket sunned, illustrations by Dorothy Lathrop with 3 color plates and beautiful black and whites.   Aleph-Bet Books, Inc.   105 - 357   2013 $400

De La Mare, Walter   1873-1956 *The Fleeting and Other Poems.* London: Constable, 1933. First edition, 8vo., original green cloth, spine faded, otherwise excellent, inscribed by author to T. W. Slater.   Maggs Bros. Ltd.   1460 - 216   2013   £60

De La Mare, Walter   1873-1956 *On the Edge.* London: Faber and Faber, 1930. First edition, one of 300 numbered copies signed by author, this one additional inscribed to J. N. Hart, tall 8vo., original red cloth, excellent copy, wood engravings by Elizabeth Rivers.   Maggs Bros. Ltd. 1460 - 213   2013   £150

De La Mare, Walter   1873-1956 *On the Edge.* London: Faber and Faber, 1930. First edition, 8vo., original blue cloth, gilt, endpapers foxed, spine faded, cloth little scuffed and marked, otherwise very good, wood engravings by Elizabeth Rivers, inscribed by author for poet Emile Cammaerts.   Maggs Bros. Ltd.   1460 - 214   2013   £100

De La Mare, Walter   1873-1956 *On the Edge.* London: Faber and Faber, 1947. New edition, 8vo., original blue cloth, price clipped by publishers with new printed price, otherwise near fine in dust jacket, slightly nicked at head and tail of spine, inscribed by author for Ernest Rasdale.   Maggs Bros. Ltd.   1460 - 217   2013   £50

De La Mare, Walter   1873-1956 *Peacock Pie.* London: Constable, 1913. Second impression, 8vo., original blue cloth, near fine inscribed by author for Paula Shuster.   Maggs Bros. Ltd.   1460 - 211   2013   £150

De La Mare, Walter   1873-1956 *Poems for Children.* London: Constable, 1930. First edition, original blue cloth, gilt.   R. F. G. Hollett & Son   Children's Books - 160   2013   £30

De La Mare, Walter   1873-1956 *Collected Poems.* London: Faber and Faber, 1951. Tenth impression, 8vo., original green cloth, excellent copy, offset browning to endpapers, dust jacket has few nicks and closed tears around head and tail of spine, inscribed by author.   Maggs Bros. Ltd.   1460 - 218   2013   £125

De La Mare, Walter 1873-1956 *Private View.* London: Faber and Faber, 1953. First edition, 8vo., original blue cloth, excellent copy, dust jacket slightly worn at head of spine, inscribed by author. Maggs Bros. Ltd. 1460 - 219 2013 £60

De La Mare, Walter 1873-1956 *A Snowdrop.* London: Faber and Faber, 1929. First edition one of 500 numbered copies, signed by author, tall 8vo., original green boards, excellent copy, extremities very slightly worn. Maggs Bros. Ltd. 1460 - 212 2013 £50

De La Mare, Walter 1873-1956 *Songs of Childhood.* London: Longmans, Green and Co., 1902. First edition, 8vo., frontispiece after Richard Doyle, original half parchment and pale blue linen over boards, top edge gilt, dust jacket, author's own copy, signed by poet and inscribed below to his nurse and companion of many years, Sister Nathalie Saxton, backstrip lightly rubbed along joints, otherwise fine in dust jacket with very small chip out of bottom spine panel and offsetting from two small old cello-tape repairs at bottom spine and bottom front flap fold, preserved in half morocco slipcase, booklabel of J. O. Edwards, beautiful and distinguished association copy, in extremely rare jacket. James S. Jaffe Rare Books Fall 2013 - 37 2013 $12,500

De La Mare, Walter 1873-1956 *Songs of Childhood.* London: Longmans Green, 1902. First edition, 12mo., blue cloth stamped in gold, parchment spine, top edge gilt, other edges uncut, 106 pages, some light soil, else near fine, gravure frontispiece by Richard Doyle,. Aleph-Bet Books, Inc. 104 - 147 2013 $1200

De La Mare, Walter 1873-1956 *This Year: Next Year.* London: Faber, 1937. First edition, large 8vo., original pictorial boards, foot of spine and lower corners, rather worn, illustrations in color, front flyleaf trifle spotted, scarce. R. F. G. Hollett & Son Children's Books - 312 2013 £140

De La Mare, Walter 1873-1956 *To Lucy.* London: Faber & Faber, 1931. First edition, limited to 275 copies signed by author, tall 8 vo., original yellow boards, some wear to extremities otherwise excellent. Maggs Bros. Ltd. 1460 - 215 2013 £50

De La Ramee, Louise 1839-1908 *Two Offenders.* London: Chatto & Windus, 1893. First edition, presentation copy in author's presentation binding, to Sir Philip and Lady Currie, cream cloth with gilt ruling and design to front cover, boards smudged and show other signs of handling, small red spot on front board that may be ink, spine browned and slightly chipped, interior has light foxing to some pages and slight loosening of few signatures, although text block tight, all edges gilt, very good, 254 pages. The Kelmscott Bookshop 7 - 125 2013 $750

De La Ramee, Louise 1839-1908 *In a Winter City; a Sketch.* London: Chatto & Windus, 1882. New edition, initial ad leaf, 32 page catalog (Oct. 1882), 'yellowback', original printed boards, slightly dulled, very good. Jarndyce Antiquarian Booksellers CCV - 218 2013 £50

De La Ree, Gerry *Virgil Finlay.* West Kingston: Donald M. Grant, 1971. First edition, small quarto, fine in near fine age toned dust jacket with small tear to front and rear. Between the Covers Rare Books, Inc. Sci-Fi, Fantasy & Horror - 318033 2013 $50

De Lalande, Joseph *The Art of Papermaking.* Sixmilebridge: Ashling Press, 1976. 211/355 copies (of an edition of 405 copies), signed by Ian O'Casey and printed on mouldmade paper, handmade paper for illustrations and endpapers made by Ian O'Casey with 14 facsimile engraved plates, one folded, printed on blue handmade papers, folio, original half tan calf, lettering to backstrip and decorative borders to sides all gilt blocked, brown canvas sides, light green marbled endpapers, untrimmed, fine. Blackwell's Rare Books 172 - 266 2013 £400

De Leon, Solon *The American Labor Who's Who.* New York: Hanford Press, 1925. First edition, hardcover, very good. Beasley Books 2013 - 2013 $50

De Leon, T. C. *The Rock of the Rye.* Mobile: Gossip Printing Co., 1888. First edition, square 12mo., 34 pages, original printed wrappers, some chipping. M & S Rare Books, Inc. 95 - 99 2013 $125

De Lespinasse, Mlle. *Letters.* London: William Heinemann, 1903. 8vo., 342 pages, half title, frontispiece, very good in dark blue half morocco by Bayntun, top edge gilt, spine in 6 compartments with gilt floral device. Ken Spelman Books Ltd. 75 - 155 2013 £50

De Lillo, Don *White Noise.* New York: Viking, 1985. First edition, inscribed by author in 1991, recipient's signature, fine in fine, price clipped dust jacket, probably clipped by publisher to accommodate sale in Canada, as nice a copy as seen. Ken Lopez Bookseller 159 - 53 2013 $500

De Lucia, David F. *The David De Lucia Chess Library.* New York: David F. De Lucia, 1990. Limited to 250 copies, 4to., iii, 71 pages, printed wrappers, fine. Jeff Weber Rare Books 171 - 70 2013 $175

De Morgan, Mary *On a Pincushion and Other Fairy Tales.* London: T. Fisher Unwin, n.d. circa, 1907. Fifth impression, Original decorated brown cloth gilt, frontispiece and numerous text illustrations and decoration, 2 inscriptions on flyleaf. R. F. G. Hollett & Son Children's Books - 161 2013 £120

De Morgan, William *Alice-for-Short. A Dichronism.* London: William Heinemann, 1907. First edition, 8vo., original green cloth very slightly soiled and spine faded, otherwise very good, inscribed by author to Maisie Dowson. Maggs Bros. Ltd. 1460 - 220 2013 £150

De Quincey, Thomas 1785-1859 *Autobiographical Sketches.* Edinburgh: James Hogg, 1853. First edition, inscribed by author for Mary Augusta Widnell, 8vo., crudely rebound in black morocco with recent gift inscription, excellent copy. Maggs Bros. Ltd. 1460 - 221 2013 £600

De Quincey, Thomas 1785-1859 *The Works of...* Edinburgh: Adam and Charles Black, MDCCCLXVIII, Reprinted 1883. Fourth edition, 16 volumes, plates, illustrations, 8vo., contemporary half dark brown morocco, spines gilt in compartments, marbled edges, matching boards, spines faded, good. Blackwell's Rare Books B174 - 43 2013 £800

De Segur, Alexandre Joseph Pierre, Viscount *Women their Condition and Influence in Society.* London: printed by C. Whittingham for T. N. Longman, 1803. First English edition, 3 volumes, small 8vo., somewhat foxed, original boards, untrimmed, spines and fore tips chipped, lacks paper on spines, one board detached, very good set in original state, with ownership signature (last name only) in each volume of US diplomat and Congressman, Samuel Sitgreaves, scarce. Second Life Books Inc. 182 - 51 2013 $1800

De Selincourt, E. *Journals of Dorothy Wordsworth.* Macmillan, 1941. First edition, 2 volumes, original cloth gilt, dust jackets (trifle frayed at head of spines), 11 plates and 7 maps, excellent set. R. F. G. Hollett & Son Lake District and Cumbria - 19 2013 £140

De Selincourt, E. *The Letters of William and Dorothy Wordsworth.* Oxford University Press, 1935-1939. 6 volumes, original cloth, gilt, spines trifle faded, 2 facsimiles and map in first volume, excellent sound, clean set, all but one volume with bookplate of Aida Foster, who ran stage and drama school and agency in London. R. F. G. Hollett & Son Lake District and Cumbria - 21 2013 £275

De Selincourt, E. *The Letters of William and Dorothy Wordsworth.* Oxford University Press, 1935-1939. 6 volumes, original cloth, gilt, dust jackets trifle worn, 2 facsimiles and map in first volume, excellent clean and sound set. R. F. G. Hollett & Son Lake District and Cumbria - 20 2013 £350

De Selincourt, E. *The Letters of William and Dorothy Wordsworth. III. The Middle Years, Part 2 1812-1860.* Oxford: Clarendon Press, 1970. Revised edition, original cloth, gilt, frontispiece, roundel library stamp on title. R. F. G. Hollett & Son Lake District and Cumbria - 22 2013 £60

De Shields, James T. *Border Wars of Texas... Matt Bradley, Revising Editor and Publisher.* Tioga: Herald Col., 1912. First edition, 8vo., 400 pages, dozens of plates, original pictorial cloth, very bright, fine. M & S Rare Books, Inc. 95 - 360 2013 $400

De Stael Holstein, Auguste Louis, Baron De *Letters on England.* Treuttel and Wurtz, Treuttel, Jun. and Richter, 1825. 8vo., frontispiece, little bit of foxing to either end, frontispiece offset onto titlepage, 8vo., contemporary half green calf, spine gilt, black lettering piece, spine darkened, very good. Blackwell's Rare Books 172 - 47 2013 £175

De Vries, Leonard *Flowers of Delight Culled from the Osborne Collection of Early Children's Books.* Dennis Dobson, 1965. First edition, 4to., original pictorial cloth gilt, dust jacket, over 700 illustrations. R. F. G. Hollett & Son Children's Books - 162 2013 £45

De Windt, Harry *Finland As It Is.* London: John Murray, 1901. First edition, 8vo., 316 pages folding map, frontispiece with tissue guard, illustrations, slight foxing to edges and endpapers, original blue cloth, gilt and red vignette, spine rubbed. J. & S. L. Bonham Antiquarian Booksellers Europe - 4359 2013 £65

Deacon, Margaret *Scientists and the Sea 1650-1900: a Study of Marine Science.* Aldershot: and Brookfield: Ashgate, 1997. Second edition, 8vo., xl, 459 pages, illustrations, aqua cloth, silver stamped spine, dust jacket, fine, Burndy bookplate. Jeff Weber Rare Books 169 - 94 2013 $90

Deacon, Samuel *On the Choice of a Wife.* Leicester: 1836. 109 pages, half title, frontispiece, good in contemporary dark green half morocco, gilt spine, corners and head and tail of spine rubbed. Ken Spelman Books Ltd. 75 - 99 2013 £95

Deacon's Synchronological Chart, Pictorial and Descriptive of University History... no printer, circa, 1901. 4 pages of text printed in red and black with diagram and an image of key, concertina 14 section color printed charts, text leaves loose (as issued), text leaves little dust soiled at edges, charts hinged with linen, last pasted inside back cover first backed with green marbled paper matching front pastedown, folio, original green crocodile skin cloth, lettered in gilt on upper cover, bit worn in places with little water damage to edges, withal good copy. Blackwell's Rare Books Sciences - 43 2013 £350

Dean, John *The Gray Substance of the Medulla Oblongata and Traperzium.* Washington: Smithsonian Institution, 1864, issued c., 1870. 4to., 16 plates, later quarter calf, gilt spine, raised bands, marbled boards, original printed wrappers, bound inside, corners bumped, original front wrapper worn and soiled, with corners rebuilt, else fine. Jeff Weber Rare Books 172 - 71 2013 $900

Deane, Seamus *The Field Day Anthology of Irish Writing.* Derry: Field Day Pub., 1991. First editions, 4to., original blue cloth, lettered gilt, fine set in matching slipcase, from the library of Richard Murphy.   Maggs Bros. Ltd.   1442 - 59   2013   £250

Deane, Seamus *Gradual Wars.* Shannon: Irish University Press, 1972. First edition, 8vo., original wrappers, from the library of Richard Murphy, signed by him, near fine. Maggs Bros. Ltd.   1442 - 56   2013   £100

Deane, Seamus *History Lessons.* Dublin: Gallery Press, 1983. First edition, 8vo., original black cloth, near fine in dust jacket, from the library of Richard Murphy, signed by him on front endpaper.   Maggs Bros. Ltd.   1442 - 58   2013   £125

Deane, Seamus *Rumours.* Dublin: Dolmen Press, 1977. First edition, 8vo., original wrappers, inscribed by author on titlepage, for Ian Steepe, fine.   Maggs Bros. Ltd.   1442 - 57   2013   £90

Dean's Postal Toy Book. Just a Tot. Dean's Pickaninny Series I. Dean, circa, 1900. Sole edition, titlepage, pages 4/5 and final page (8) all with color printed illustrations, pages 2/3 and 6/7 with line drawings (printed in blue), 16mo., (8) pages, original stapled wrappers, front cover design as a postcard for address and stamp and with glue-tipped fore-edge (inside rear cover was set aside for messages), rear cover with further colour printed illustration, fine.   Blackwell's Rare Books   172 - 305   2013   £100

Dearden, James S. *The Professor. Arthur Severn's Memoir of John Ruskin.* London: Allen & Unwin, 1967. First edition, original cloth, gilt, dust jacket, 9 illustrations. R. F. G. Hollett & Son   Lake District and Cumbria - 24 2013   £25

Dearden, James S. *Ruskin & Coniston.* Covent Garden Press, 1971. Limited, signed edition, number 81 of 100 copies, 4to., original quarter calf gilt with yellow cloth boards, portrait, 23 plates, scarce.   R. F. G. Hollett & Son   Lake District and Cumbria - 23   2013   £120

Dearden, Seton *A Nest of Corsairs.* London: John Murray, 1976. First edition, original cloth, gilt, dust jacket, price clipped, 15 illustrations and 2 maps.   R. F. G. Hollett & Son   Africana - 52   2013   £25

Deaver, Jeffery Wilds *Mistress of Justice.* New York: Doubleday, 1992. First edition, signed by author, very fine in dust jacket.   Mordida Books   81 - 132   2013 $300

Deaver, John Blair *A Treatise on Appendicitis.* Philadelphia: P. Blakiston, 1896. First edition, 8vo., 4 figures, 32 plates, red cloth, beveled edges, gilt spine, fine, clean copy.   Jeff Weber Rare Books   172 - 72   2013 $400

Debow, Samuel P. *Who's who in Religious, Fraternal, Social, Civic and Commercial Life on the Pacific Coast. State of Washington.*   Seattle: The Searchlight Pub. Co., 1926-1927. First edition, gray cloth stamped in gilt, 235 pages, copiously illustrated from photos, very light edge-wear, small stain on rear board, near fine, very scarce. Between the Covers Rare Books, Inc.   165 - 29   2013 $1250

Debrett's Peerage, Baronetage, Knightage. 1881. 34 pages, 2 photos pasted on blank pages, text good, cloth shaky.   C. P. Hyland   261 - 385   2013   £50

Debus, Allen G. *Chemistry, Alchemy and the New Philosophy 1550-1700: Studies in the History of Science and Medicine.* London: Variorum Reprints, 1987. 8vo., xii, 320 pages, blue cloth, gilt stamped cover and spine titles, ownership signature, fine.   Jeff Weber Rare Books   169 - 95   2013 $75

A Declaration and Vindication of the Lord Mayor, Aldermen and Commons of the City of London in Common Councell Assembled. London: by James Flesher, 1660. 4to., (2), 26 pages, text partly in black letter, modern cloth, bottom margin of title torn with loss of part of date.   Joseph J. Felcone Inc.   Books Printed before 1701 - 28   2013 $300

Decorative Style 1880-1940. Seacaucus: Chartwell, 1986. First edition, hardcover, 2 books, slipcase, both fine in fine dust jackets.   Beasley Books   2013 - 2013 $50

Deduction of the Title to Harlem Commons and Abstract of the Title of Dudley Selden. New York: De Puy, Holmes & Co., 1872. First edition, contemporary flexible cloth boards, (73) pages, tipped in is small broadside for rare bookseller RD Cooke dated July 1886 tipped to front pastedown, bottom corner little bumped, tiny tears to edges of few pages, very good.   Between the Covers Rare Books, Inc. New York City - 302585   2013 $500

Deeping, Warwick *Sorrell and Son.* London: Cassell & Co., 1925. First edition, 8vo., original red cloth, spine slightly faded, excellent copy, inscribed by author for A Crichton.   Maggs Bros. Ltd.   1460 - 223   2013   £75

Deevy, Mary B. *Medieval Ring Brooches in Ireland.* 1998. First edition, Color and black and white illustrations, 8vo., cloth, dust jacket, mint.   C. P. Hyland   261 - 340   2013   £30

A Defence of the Rights of the Dock Company at Kingston upon Hull. Hull: 1787. Half title with manuscript note "wrote by David Hartley, William & George Hammond", very good, stitched as issued, but with signs of at some stage having been disbound, preserved in recent marbled paper wrappers, 8vo.   Ken Spelman Books Ltd.   73 - 93   2013   £120

Deffeyes, Kenneth S.   *Hubbert's Peak. The Impending World Oil Shortage.*   Princeton: Princeton University Press, 2001. First edition, photos, diagrams, maps, graphs, blue cloth, very fine, as new, pictorial dust jacket.   Argonaut Book Shop   Recent Acquisitions June 2013 - 81   2013 $75

Defoe, Benjamin Norton   *A Complete History of the Wars in Italy.*   London: printed for W. Mears, 1734. Engraved folding map bound as frontispiece, 8vo., some slight worming to blank lower margin from page 253, single hole to page 301 then slightly more noticeable, handsome full contemporary calf, gilt panelled spine, red morocco label, free endpapers pasted down on boards.   Jarndyce Antiquarian Booksellers   CCIV - 106   2013   £580

Defoe, Daniel   *The Dyet of Poland, a Satyr.*   printed at Dantzick, 1705. 4to. some light spotting and browning, few small expert paper repairs, bound by Riviere in full crushed red morocco, elaborate gilt borders and dentelles, raised bands, gilt compartments, armorial bookplate of William Henry Smith, Viscount Hambleden, all edges gilt, very good, handsome.   Jarndyce Antiquarian Booksellers   CCIV - 107   2013   £850

Defoe, Daniel   *A Journal of the Plague Year...*   London: printed for E. Nutt at the Royal Exchange, J. Roberts... A. Dodd... and J. Graves, 1722. First edition, 8vo., half title lacking, some light spotting or soiling throughout, mostly in margins, title and following leaf reinforced at gutter, contemporary calf, rebacked with black leather spine labels, chain rule surround, modern endleaves, corners worn, very rare.   Jeff Weber Rare Books   172 - 73   2013 $6000

Defoe, Daniel   *A Journal of the Plague Year.*   Thomas Tegg & Son, 1835. New edition, superb copy, small 8vo. later 19th century full polished calf with ornate gilt panelled spine, red morocco label, top edge gilt.   Ken Spelman Books Ltd.   75 - 98   2013   £120

Defoe, Daniel   *The Life and Adventures of Robinson Crusoe.*   printed for C. Cooke, 1793. First Cooke edition, 3 volumes, 6 engraved plates (3 each in volumes i and ii, none in iii), woodcut device on titlepages and woodcut tailpiece, last page of volume ii with two small sections of text adhering to flyleaf, 12mo., original tree sheep, gilt ruled compartments on spine, red lettering piece on volume iii, missing from i and ii, numbered gilt direct, joints cracked, corners worn, ownership inscription of F. Royse dated 1793, fair.   Blackwell's Rare Books   B174 - 44   2013   £250

Defoe, Daniel   *Life and Surprising Adventures of Robinson Crusoe.*   London: printed by T. Cadell and W. Davies, 1820. 2 volumes, original full calf bound by Riviere with gilt rules on covers and extensive gilt tooling on spines in compartments, gilt dentelles, top edge gilt, inconspicuous professional strengthening of joints, near fine set, most minimum of spotting, illustrations by Thomas Stothard with 48 exquisite copper engraved plates, which includes complete second set of plates on India paper before lettering,.   Aleph-Bet Books, Inc.   104 - 148   2013 $2850

Defoe, Daniel   *Robinson Crusoe.*   New York: McLoughlin Bros. circa, 1870. 4to., pictorial wrappers, some spine wear and soil, very good, very fine chromolithographs.   Aleph-Bet Books, Inc.   104 - 149   2013 $200

Defoe, Daniel   *Robinson Crusoe.*   New York: Cosmopolitan, 1920. First edition, 4to., royal blue gilt cloth, pictorial paste-on, nearly as new, top edge plain not gilt illustrations by N. C. Wyeth, signed and dated by artist, great copy, very scarce with signature.   Aleph-Bet Books, Inc.   105 - 598   2013 $3500

Defoe, Daniel   *The Wonderful Life and Most Surprizing Adventures of Robinson Crusoe of York, Mariner...*   printed for J. Fuller at the Bible and Dove, Ave Maria Lane, circa, 1750. Woodcut frontispiece, 20 woodcuts in text, frontispiece pasted to inside front cover, little worming touching some letters but without loss of sense, uniformly slightly browned, stitching weak, pages 144, 12mo., contemporary sail cloth, slightly worn, sound.   Blackwell's Rare Books   172 - 48   2013   £1500

Dehan, Richard   *Off Sandy Hook and Other Stories.*   New York: Frederick A. Stokes Co., 1915. First edition, near fine in good plus white, yellow and blue dust jacket, nice copy, scarce.   Between the Covers Rare Books, Inc.   Sci-Fi, Fantasy & Horror - 85025   2013 $225

Deighton, Len   *An Expensive Place to Die.*   London: Jonathan Cape, 1967. First edition, 8vo., original black Linson boards, dust jacket, near fine, dust jacket with inserted folder of facsimile documents, sometimes missing, inscribed by author.   Maggs Bros. Ltd.   1460 - 224   2013   £250

Deighton, Len   *An Expensive Place to Die.*   London: Cape, 1967. First edition, crown 8vo., pages 254, original black boards backstrip gilt lettered, dust jacket trifle edge rubbed, lightly faded, backstrip panel very fine, the "In Transit Docket" folder an documents loosely inserted.   Blackwell's Rare Books   B174 - 194   2013   £75

Deighton, Len   *Twinkle, Twinkle Little Spy.*   London: Jonathan Cape, 1976. First edition, 8vo., original black cloth, dust jacket, near fine, inscribed by author for Alan with A J. P. Taylor's bookplate.   Maggs Bros. Ltd.   1460 - 225   2013   £150

Dejerine, Joseph Jules *Clinique des Maladies du Systeme Nerveus Iecon Inaugurale.* Paris: Masson, 1911. 46 pages, original wrappers and bound into black linen cloth typed label on front board, author's presentation with rubber stamp, given to Hospice De La Salpetriere.   James Tait Goodrich   S74 - 77   2013 $495

Dejerine, Joseph Jules *Maladies de la Moelle Epiniere.* Paris: Librairie J. B. Bailliere et Fils, 1909. 420 text images and figures, tall thick octavo, quarter linen backed marbled boards, original printed wrappers bound in, uncut, near fine, rubbing to binding, internally fine.   James Tait Goodrich   S74 - 76   2013 $596

Dejong, Meindert *The House of Sixty Fathers.* New York: Harper Bros., 1956. First edition, 8vo., cloth, fine in fine dust jacket, illustrations in black and white by Maurice Sendak.   Aleph-Bet Books, Inc.   105 - 529   2013 $500

Dejong, Meindert *Shadrach.* Lutterworth Press, 1957. First UK edition, original cloth, dust jacket spine rather faded, edges rubbed and frayed, pages 182, line drawings by Maurice Sendak.   R. F. G. Hollett & Son   Children's Books - 541   2013   £60

Delamotte, F. *A Primer of the Art of Illumination for the Use of Beginners...* Lockwood, 1874. Printed in black and red, 20 chromolithographed plates of initial letters, 20 plates of examples, small 4to., original bevel edged maroon cloth, plain backstrip faded, sides with blindstamped double line border and fleur-de-lys cornerpieces, upper side elaborately gilt blocked with title and passion flowers, yellow chalked endpapers, gilt edges, Vivian Ridler's copy with his embossed address on front free endpaper.   Blackwell's Rare Books   B174 - 45   2013   £200

Delano, Alonzo *Alonzo Delano's Pen-Knife Sketches or chips of the Old Block.* San Francisco: Grabhorn Press, 1934. Reprint, one of 500 copies, frontispiece, 20 headpieces and four full page drawings in color by Charles Nahl, blue green boards, tan spine, printed paper spine label, colored drawing and title by Charles Nahl on front cover, very fine and bright copy, with elusive plain peach dust jacket, scarce in this condition.   Argonaut Book Shop   Summer 2013 - 78   2013 $150

Delano, Alonzo *A Sojourn with Royalty and Other Sketches.* San Francisco: George Fields, 1936. First book edition, one of 500 copies, small octavo, illustrations by Charles Lindstrom, seven initials in sepia, 8 headpieces and titlepage illustration in color, orange pictorial boards, tan cloth spine, orange spine label printed in black, very light offsetting to ends from jacket flaps but very fine and bright copy with plain gold dust jacket.   Argonaut Book Shop   Summer 2013 - 79   2013 $90

Delany, Samuel Ray *The Einstein Intersection.* Hanover: Wesleyan University Press/University Press of New England, 1998. First printing thus, signed and inscribed by Delany, fine in fine dust jacket, xii, 135 pages, 8vo.   By the Book, L. C.   36 - 42   2013 $200

Delany, Samuel Ray *Nova.* Garden City: Doubleday and Co., 1968. First edition, octavo, cloth.   L. W. Currey, Inc. Fall Sampler Sept. 2013 - 145623   2013 $250

Deleuze, Gilles *Expressionism in Philosophy: Spinoza.* New York: Zone Books, 1990. First edition, remnants of a price sticker on front pastedown, else fine in fine, lightly bumped dust jacket.   Between the Covers Rare Books, Inc.   Philosophy - 103786   2013 $60

Delille, Jacques *L'Homme des Champs ou les Georgiques Francoises... (with) Dithyrame sur l'Immoralite de l'ame, Suivi du Passage du st. Gothard...* Basel: Chez Jacques Decker, 1800. Paris: chez giguet et Michaud, 1802. First editions, 4 plates, dampstaining throughout at tail of gutter margin, some browning; engraved frontispiece, 12mo., bound together in contemporary dark blue straight grain morocco, smooth backstrip divided by double gilt rules, second compartment gilt lettered direct, single gilt rule on sides, gilt ball roll on board edges and turn-ins, marbled endpapers, all edges gilt, touch of rubbing to joints, very good, bookplate of Sir Gore Ouseley, Baronet.   Blackwell's Rare Books   172 - 49   2013   £150

Dell, Henry *The Spouter; or the Double Revenge.* London: printed for and sold by S. Crowder, 1756. 8vo., titlepage and final leaf dusted, latter torn without loss, disbound.   Jarndyce Antiquarian Booksellers   CCIV - 108   2013   £180

Delord, Taxile *Les Fleurs Animees.* Paris: Garnier Freres, 1867. New edition, with plates retouched for engraving and coloring by M. Maubert, 2 volumes, 4to., publisher's green leather spine and cloth, all edges gilt, 339, 324 pages, light cover rubbing, faint corner stain on first few leaves of volume one, else tight, clean very good+ set, 50 magnificent hand colored plates, 2 hand colored titlepages, each page depicting J. J. Grandville's flowers, also includes many smaller black and white engravings.   Aleph-Bet Books, Inc.   105 - 287   2013 $2000

Demby, William *The Catacombs.* New York: Pantheon, 1965. First edition, fine in near fine dust jacket with few tiny tears at foot, inscribed by author in year of publication, especially fresh and bright.   Between the Covers Rare Books, Inc.   165 - 132   2013 $125

Deming, Therese *Indians in Winter Camp.* Chicago: Laidlaw, 1931. 8vo., pictorial cloth, 126 pages, fine, 14 full page and 76 partial page color illustrations, beautiful copy.   Aleph-Bet Books, Inc.   105 - 333   2013 $225

Democratic Expositor and United States Journal for the Country. Washington: 1845-1846. 8vo., uncut and unopened as issued, Volume I, #4, 15-23, 26, 28, some soiling and wear, but good.   M & S Rare Books, Inc. 95 - 360   2013 $650

Dempsey, G. Dryddlane *The Practical Railway Engineer.* London: John Weale, 1847. First edition, 286 x 220mm., excellent recent retrospective grained calf, raised bands, red morocco label, 50 double page copper engravings showing railway plans, equipment and environmental contexts, handwritten card "Stationery Engine Minoris Terminus Blackwall Railway" mounted on front pastedown, plates little browned at edges, about half of them with minor foxing (more conspicuous on final 2 plate), occasional minor smudges, thumbing or short marginal tears, otherwise really excellent copy, internally quite fresh and in unworn, attractive binding.   Phillip J. Pirages   63 - 385   2013 $950

Denby, Edwin *Aerial. A Collection of Poetry. Aerial Images by Yvonne Jacquette.* New York: Eyelight Press, 1981. One of 26 lettered copies signed by most contributors on tipped in sheet, 4to., illustrated, original pictorial wrappers, fine.   James S. Jaffe Rare Books   Fall 2013 - 4   2013 $850

Denham, John *Poems and Translations with the Sophy: a Tragedy.* London: printed for Jacob Tonson, 1719. Sixth edition, plate reported by one library is not bound in here, rebacked, contemporary mottled calf.   Jarndyce Antiquarian Booksellers   CCIV - 109   2013   £50

Denham, John *Poems and Translations.* Glasgow: printed by Robert and Andrew Foulis, 1771. 12mo., some browning to title and half title, latter with tear to lower outer corner, title and facing page to 'Sophy' both have old brown stain recent marbled paper wrappers.   Jarndyce Antiquarian Booksellers   CCIV - 130   2013   £25

Denison, Charles *Sheet Anchor Volume 2 #1 - Volume 3 #24, Jan. 6 1844 - December 20 1845.* Boston: Jonathan Howe, 1844-1845. Folio, 48 issues, contemporary calf backed marbled boards, some browning, early staining, but very good.   M & S Rare Books, Inc. 95 - 295   2013 $425

Dennis, George *A Summer in Andalucia.* London: Richard Bentley, 1839. First edition, 2 volumes, 8vo., 2 sepia frontispieces (waterstaining to margin of frontispiece volume II), original black blindstamped cloth, small splits in joints of both volumes.   J. & S. L. Bonham Antiquarian Booksellers   Europe - 9732   2013   £2000

Dennis, John *The Pioneer of Progress; or the Early Closing Movement in Relation to the Saturday Half-Holiday and Early Payment of Wages.* Hamilton, Adams & Co., 1860. First edition, 8vo., original cloth, near fine.   Ken Spelman Books Ltd.   75 - 125   2013   £75

Dennis, John *The Usefulness of th Stage, to the Happiness of mankind, to Government and to Religion.* London: printed for Rich. Parker, 1698. Errata list on last page, some marginal waterstains on few leaves, final leaf slightly brittle, attractively rebound in quarter speckled calf, marbled boards, unobtrusive stamps of Hampstead Public Libraries.   Jarndyce Antiquarian Booksellers   CCV - 65   2013   £225

Denslow, W. W. *Denslow's One Ring Circus and Other Stories.* Chicago: Donahue, Dillingham, 1903. 4to., cloth, pictorial paste-on, cloth slightly worn in two aeas in gutter, else near fine, 6 picture books, boldly and wonderfully illustrated in full color throughout, quite scarce.   Aleph-Bet Books, Inc.   104 - 152   2013 $950

Denslow, W. W. *Denslow's Mother Goose.* New York: McClure Phillips Co., 1901. First edition, 2nd issue, 4to., cloth backed pictorial boards, (96) pages, edges and covers rubbed, else clean, tight and very good+ in original pictorial dust jacket (chipped at corner folds, missing 1 1/2" piece off spine with some other chipping but overall very good), this is the Schiller auction copy, with large Denslow signature plus Denslow has drawn his characteristic seahorse facing titlepage.   Aleph-Bet Books, Inc.   105 - 168   2013 $8000

Denslow, W. W. *Denslow's Humpty Dumpty and Other Stories.* New York: Dillingham, 1903. 4to., green pictorial wrappers, 16 pages, including covers, covers dusty else, very good+, illustrations by Denslow, very scarce.   Aleph-Bet Books, Inc.   104 - 151   2013 $475

Denson, Alan *Printed Writings by George W. Russell (A. E.).* Evanston: 1961. First edition, 8vo., cloth, dust jacket, fine.   C. P. Hyland   261 - 761   2013   £65

Denton, Thomas *A Perambulation of Cumberland 1687-1688...* Boydell Press, 2003. First edition, original cloth, gilt, dust jacket, frontispiece.   R. F. G. Hollett & Son   Lake District and Cumbria - 27   2013   £65

Denwood, Ernest Russell *Oor Mak O'Toak. An Anthology of Lakeland Dialect Poems 1747-1946.* Carlisle: Charles Thurnam and Sons, 1946. First edition, original blue cloth, 167 pages.   R. F. G. Hollett & Son   Lake District and Cumbria - 28   2013   £30

Denwood, J. M. *Red Ike.* London: Hutchinson & Co., n.d., 1931. First edition, original cloth, dust jacket little worn, pages 288.   R. F. G. Hollett & Son   Lake District and Cumbria - 29   2013   £35

Denwood, M. *A Lafter O'Farleys in t' Dialect o' Lakeland.* Carlisle: Charles Thurnam and Sons, 1950. First edition, original cloth, gilt dust jacket little worn and chipped, price clipped.   R. F. G. Hollett & Son   Lake District and Cumbria - 30   2013   £30

Derbec, Etienne *A French Journalist in the California Gold Rush.* Georgetown: Talisman Press, 1964. First English translation, quarto, 258 pages, frontispiece, illustrations, gray-green cloth very fine, soiled dust jacket.   Argonaut Book Shop   Recent Acquisitions June 2013 - 84   2013 $90

Derby, George H. *Musical Review Extraordinary.* Bohemian Grove: Silverado Squatters, 1960. First edition thus, printed in red and black titlepage vignette, printed wrappers, very fine. Argonaut Book Shop   Recent Acquisitions June 2013 - 87   2013 $75

Derby, George H. *Phoenixiana: or Sketches and Burlesques.* New York: D. Appleton & Co., 1856. First edition, frontispiece, publisher's original brown embossed cloth, gilt illustration on upper cover (repeated in blind on lower cover), gilt pictorial spine, spine gilt slightly dulled, fine, tight, very scarce.   Argonaut Book Shop   Recent Acquisitions June 2013 - 85   2013 $350

Derby, George H. *Phoenixiana: or Sketches and Burlesques.* San Francisco: Grabhorn Press, 1937. One of 550 copies, 240 pages, illustrations, facsimile sketches, cloth backed pictorial boards, paper spine label, fine. Argonaut Book Shop   Recent Acquisitions June 2013 - 86   2013 $150

Derby, George H. *The Squibob Papers.* New York: Carleton, 1865. First edition, frontispiece 11 plates, 17 text illustrations, publisher's brown cloth, light wear and chipping to head of spine, corners slightly jammed, slight foxing, fading to spine, overall fine, internally fine with very little of the usual heavy foxing, original owner's dated signature W. G. Howell July 18 1865.   Argonaut Book Shop   Recent Acquisitions June 2013 - 88   2013 $150

Derham, William 1657-1735 *Astro-Theology; or a Demonstration of the Being and Attributes of God, from a Survey of the Heavens.* London: printed for W. Innys, 1715. 8vo., 3 folding copper engraved plates, titlepage little dusted, first gathering slightly browned, full contemporary panelled calf, raised bands, red morocco label, small paper shelf number at head of spine, hinges cracked, head and tail of spine slightly rubbed, contemporary booklabel of Tho. Jowling, A.M. Rect de Alcester 19th century armorial bookplate of W. Wynne.   Jarndyce Antiquarian Booksellers   CCIV - 111   2013   £280

Derham, William 1657-1735 *Astro-Theology.* London: Printed for J. Richardson, 1758. Ninth edition, 8vo., 3 folding copper engraved plates, offset browning on endpapers and titlepage, one plate rather foxed, contemporary sprinkled calf, double gilt ruled borders, expertly rebacked, raised and gilt banded spine, red morocco labels, corners neatly repaired, early signature of Wm. J. Staines, ownership name of Walter Crouch, Wanstead.   Jarndyce Antiquarian Booksellers   CCIV - 112   2013   £250

Dering, E. H. *Memoirs of Lady Georgiana Chatterton.* London: Hurst & Blackett, 1878. First edition, cloth, errata slip, some foxing on early & late leaves, original green cloth with gilt titling, good.   C. P. Hyland   261 - 183   2013   £120

Derleth, August *The Casebook of Solar Pons.* Sauk City: Mycroft & Moran, 1965. First edition, fine in dust jacket.   Mordida Books   81 - 139   2013 $165

Derleth, August *In Re: Sherlock Holmes.* Sauk City: Mycroft & Moran, 1945. First edition, fine in dust jacket.   Mordida Books   81 - 135   2013 $200

Derleth, August *Mischief in the Lane.* New York: Scribners, 1944. First edition, inscribed by author, fine in dust jacket.   Mordida Books   81 - 134   2013 $350

Derleth, August *The Night Side: Masterpieces of the Strange and Terrible.* New York: Toronto: Rinehart & Co. Inc., 1947. First edition, octavo, illustrations by Lee Brown Coye, cloth, with 'R' monogram on copyright page.   L. W. Currey, Inc.   Fall Sampler Sept. 2013 - 146551   2013 $150

Derleth, August *100 Books by August Derleth.* Sauk City: Arkham House, 1962. First edition, wrappers, tiny owner name on bottom page edge, wrappers bit rubbed, else near fine, briefly inscribed by Derleth, one of 1025 copies.   Between the Covers Rare Books, Inc.   Sci-Fi, Fantasy & Horror - 89341   2013 $200

Derleth, August *The Reminiscences of Solar Pons.* Sauk City: Mycroft & Moran, 1961. First edition, fine in dust jacket.   Mordida Books   81 - 138   2013 $140

Derleth, August *The Return of Solar Pons.* Sauk City: Mycroft & Moran, 1958. First edition, fine in dust jacket.   Mordida Books   81 - 137   2013 $175

Derleth, August *Sentence Deferred.* New York: Scribners, 1939. First edition, fine in dust jacket with tiny wear at corners and base of spine.   Mordida Books   81 - 133   2013 $350

Derleth, August *Three Problems for Solar Pons.* Sauk City: Mycroft & Moran, 1952. First edition, fine in dust jacket with tiny wear at spine corners.   Mordida Books   81 - 136   2013 $300

Derleth, August *Three Problems for Solar Pons.* Sauk City: Mycroft and Moran, 1952. First edition, fine in near fine dust jacket with little rubbing and short tear on front panel.   Between the Covers Rare Books, Inc.   Mystery & Detective Fiction - 29213   2013 $275

Desaint, C. *Hand Book of medicine by Revd. C. Desaint.* Bangalore: printed at the Catholic Mission Press, 1884. 328 pages, original linen back printed boards, some wear with light soiling of front board, uncommon. James Tait Goodrich   75 - 79   2013 $495

Descartes, Rene *Renati Des Cartes Meditationes de Prima Philosophia in Quibus Dei Existentia & Animae Humanae a Corproe Distinctio Demonstrantur...(bound with) Passiones Animae per Renatum Des Cartes; Gallice ab Ipso Conscriptae...* Amstelodami: apud Ludovicum Elzevirium, 1650. Tertia edition of second work, first Latin edition of first work of second w, printer's device, initials and head and tailpieces, small 4to., contemporary vellum, spine titles in manuscript, 4to., vellum soiled worn at lower fore edge, spotted, seminary library bookplate on front pastedown, faint fragment of label on rear free endpapers lacking, pastedowns soiled and split, first blank with three sets of annotations, all in different hands, first two dozen leaves or so with medium brown circular stains starting at under 4 centimeters and becoming progressively smaller and fainter, until extinguished at G3, just touching (though not obscuring) last few letters of text on corner of last lines, odd short and faint underline on perhaps a dozen pages, still good. Kaaterskill Books   16 - 25   2013 $1500

Descartes, Rene *Le Monde ou Traite de la Lumiere.* New York: Abaris Books, 1979. 8vo., xxvi, 224 pages, green cloth, gilt stamped cover and spine title, ownership signature, very good, scarce. Jeff Weber Rare Books   169 - 104   2013 $200

Descartes, Rene *Les Passions de L'Ame.* Paris: Chez Henry Le Gras, 1649. First edition, rare, expertly rebacked in brown calf, original leather boards and original marbled endpages, minor wear to corners and edges with slight bumping and few small chips to leather, interior very clean overall with small sporadic spots of foxing, woodcut initials and tailpieces, full gilt edges, very good, xlviii + 286 pages. The Kelmscott Bookshop   7 - 132   2013 $15,000

Descot, Pierre Jules *Dissertation sur les Affections Locales Des Nerfs...* Paris: chez Ms. Delaunay, 1825. Half title, engraved folding facsimile leaf as front leaf, contemporary quarter blue gilt leather spine, marbled boards some light foxing, near fine. James Tait Goodrich   75 - 80   2013 $795

A Description of Stonehenge, Abiry &c. in Wiltshire. Salisbury: printed and sold by Collins and Johnson, sold also by J. Wilkie, London, 1776. First edition, 6 woodcut plates on leaves which form part of gatherings, but not included in pagination, 12mo., original mottled sheep, doubl gilt fillet borders on sides, rebacked preserving most of original lettering piece lettered ('STONE/HINGE'), armorial bookplate inside front cover of James Comerford, placed over another good. Blackwell's Rare Books   172 - 135   2013   £750

A Description of the Grand Musical Festival, Held in the City of York, September the 23rd (-26th) 1823... York: Henry Cobb, 1823. 8vo., 4 engraved plates, half title, very good, uncut inl original boards, neatly rebacked, handsome 19th century armorial bookplate of Thomas Bowman Whytehead, of Fulford York, later name at head and front endpaper, scarce. Ken Spelman Books Ltd.   73 - 196   2013   £160

Descriptive Particulars of rhe Fee-Simple Estate of the Earl of Shannon. 1842. 23 pages, 2 maps, lithograph, very good, cloth. C. P. Hyland   261 - 775   2013   £95

Descriptive Particulars of the Fee-Simple Estate of the Earl of Shannon. 1852. 23 pages, 3 maps, lithograph, cloth, very good. C. P. Hyland   261 - 775   2013   £95

Desmaizeaux, Pierre *An Historical and Critical Account of the Life and Writings of the ever Memorable Mr. John Hales, Fellow of Eton College...* London: printed for R. Robinson, 1719. 8vo., light browning, recent black pebble grained cloth, new endpapers and pastedowns, inner hinges reinforced with cloth tape. Jarndyce Antiquarian Booksellers CCIV - 113   2013   £125

Desmarres, Louis Auguste *Traite Theorique et Pratique des Maladies Des Yeux.* Paris: Germer Bailliere, 1847. Half title, viii, 940 pages, 78 figures and illustrations in text, contemporary quarter green roan and patterned boards, some light rubbing to binding, light foxing in text, otherwise very good. James Tait Goodrich   S74 - 78   2013 $595

Detmold, E. J. *The Book of Baby Birds.* London: Henry Frowde, circa, 1912. 4to., 19 fine colored plates, very good, clean, original linen backed decorative boards, slight knock to fore edge of one board in unusually good state, inscription dated Xmas 1912. Ken Spelman Books Ltd.   75 - 163   2013   £120

Detmold, E. J. *Book of Baby Birds.* London: Humphrey Milford/Oxford University Press, n.d., 1919. First edition, 4to., cloth backed boards, pictorial paste-on, 120 pages, fine in dust jacket, illustrations by Detmold with 19 magnificent mounted color plates, uncommon title, great copy. Aleph-Bet Books, Inc.   105 - 173   2013 $950

Detmold, E. J. *The Book of Baby Dogs.* London: Henry Frowde, n.d. circa, 1925. 4to., cloth backed boards, round pictorial paste-on, 120 pages, corners rubbed, else cean, tight and very good+, illustrations by Detmold, with 19 mounted color plates, scarce. Aleph-Bet Books, Inc.   105 - 170   2013 $425

Deutsch, Felix *The Clinical Interview.* New York: IUP, 1955. First edition, 2 volumes, volume 1 near fine, lacking dust jacket, volume 2 fine in sunned and slightly worn dust jacket. Beasley Books   2013 - 2013 $50

Devlin, Denis *The Complete Poems Of.* University Review Volume III No. 5, 8vo., wrappers, very good.   C. P. Hyland   261 - 196   2013   £40

Dewees, William P. *A Treatise on the Physical and Medical Treatment of Children.* Philadelphia: 1826. Second edition, contemporary calf, foxing and some late staining, small black corner lacking on title, very good.   M & S Rare Books, Inc.   95 - 100   2013 $350

Dewey, Thomas B. *Hue and Cry.* New York: Jefferson House, 1944. First edition, fine in price clipped dust jacket with nicks at spine ends, short internal tape repair and couple of short closed tears.   Mordida Books   81 - 149   2013 $135

Dexter, Colin *The Dead of Jericho.* London: Macmillan, 1981. First edition, full page plan of Jericho, pages 224, crown 8vo., original black boards, backstrip gilt lettered, lightly faded backstrip panel to dust jacket, near fine, inscribed by author.   Blackwell's Rare Books   B174 - 195   2013   £435

Dexter, Colin *The Daughters of Cain.* New York: Crown Publishers, 1994. First American edition, fine in fine dust jacket, signed by author.   Between the Covers Rare Books, Inc.   Mystery & Detective Fiction - 293562   2013 $65

Dexter, Colin *Death is Now My Neighbour.* London: Macmillan, 1996. First edition, crown 8vo., original black boards, backstrip gilt lettered, blue cotton marker, dust jacket, fine, signed by author.   Blackwell's Rare Books   172 - 177   2013   £45

Dexter, Colin *The Jewel that Was Ours.* Macmillan, 1991. First edition, full page plan, 8vo., original blue boards, backstrip gilt lettered, lightly faded backstrip panel to dust jacket, near fine, inscribed by author.   Blackwell's Rare Books   172 - 178   2013   £100

Dexter, Colin *Last Bus to Woodstock.* London: Macmillan, 1975. First edition, 8vo., original brown cloth, dust jacket, inscribed by author, pages browned as ever, few small nicks and one inch long closed tear to edge of dust jacket.   Maggs Bros. Ltd.   1460 - 226   2013   £750

Dexter, Colin *Last Bus to Woodstock.* Macmillan, 1975. First edition, text browned as usual crown 8vo., original mid brown boards, covers with puncture holes caused by sharp instrument, backstrip lettered in black, top stain little spotted, dust jacket with fraying to head of backstrip panel and extreme heads of flap folds, with author's gift inscription. Blackwell's Rare Books   B174 - 196   2013   £500

Dexter, Colin *The Remorseful Day.* London: Macmillan, 1999. Second impression, 8vo. original black cloth, dust jacket, near fine, inscribed by author to David MacKenzie. Maggs Bros. Ltd.   1460 - 227   2013   £125

Dexter, Colin *The Remorseful Day.* London: Macmillan, 1999. First edition, 8vo., original black boards, backstrip gilt lettered, dust jacket, fine, signed by author.   Blackwell's Rare Books   172 - 179   2013   £60

Dexter, Colin *The Riddle of the Third Mile.* Macmillan, 1983. First edition, unusually faint browning to poor quality paper, 224 pages, foolscap 8vo., original grey boards, backstrip lettered in silver, faint foxing to dust jacket flaps, near fine.   Blackwell's Rare Books   B174 - 197   2013   £200

Dexter, Colin *Service of all the Dead.* Macmillan, 1979. First edition, crown 8vo., 256 pages, original pale blue boards, backstrip lettered in silver, dust jacket, very good, inscribed by author.   Blackwell's Rare Books   B174 - 198   2013   £385

Dexter, Colin *The Way through the Woods.* Macmillan, 1992. First edition, full page and double page plans, 8vo., original mid green boards, backstrip gilt lettered, dust jacket, fine, signed by author.   Blackwell's Rare Books   172 - 180   2013   £55

Dexter, Colin *The Wench is Dead.* Macmillan, 1989. First edition, full page map, crown 8vo., original mid brown boards, backstrip gilt lettered, dust jacket, fine, inscribed by author.   Blackwell's Rare Books   B174 - 199   2013   £120

Di Peso, Charles C. *Casas Grandes, a Fallen Trading Center of the Gran Chichimeca.* Flagstaff: 1974. First edition, 8 volumes, near fine.   Dumont Maps & Books of the West   122 - 52   2013 $750

The Diary of a Sky Pilot... Johnson Johnson, n.d., 1916. First edition, original pictorial cloth, spine little faded, text drawings, very scarce.   R. F. G. Hollett & Son   Wesleyan Methodism - 1 2013   £30

Dibble, Sheldon *History of the Sandwich Islands.* Lahainaluna: Press of the Mission Seminary, 1843. First edition, 2nd issue, this copy one of 100 copies in sheets, of the 600 copies printed which were forwarded to Boston, bound there and distributed, 12mo., original gilt lettered black cloth blocked in blind (1/8" spine extremities worn, almost imperceptible 1 1/2 inch repair to lower outer hinge and corners little rubbed), large folding map, fine copy of folding engraved map (some offsetting), 3 small old stamps of "Foreign Mission Board S(outhern) B(aptist) C(onvention), Richmond, Virginia, excellent copy in morocco backed cloth folding case. Howard S. Mott Inc. 262 - 40 2013 $6750

Dibdin, James C. *The Annals of the Edinburgh Stage, with an Account of the Rise and Progress of Dramatic Writing in Scotland.* Edinburgh: Richard Cameron, 1888. First edition, 257 x 197mm., tipped-on errata slip, later (recent?) maroon crushed half morocco over scarlet straight grain cloth, raised bands, spine panels with intricate gilt central lozenge and two black labels, marbled endpapers, top edge gilt, other edges rough trimmed, significant portions of leaves, unopened, buckram reinforcement applied without great skill to hinge after the free endpaper at front and back, 7 illustrations mostly portraits one facsimile reproduction of playbill, very light soil to covers, trivial imperfections internally but excellent copy, binding quite solid and bright, text very clean and fresh, rare. Phillip J. Pirages 63 - 465 2013 $450

Dibdin, Thomas Frognall 1776-1847 *Bibliotheca Spenceriana or a Descriptive Catalogue of the Books Printed in the Fifteenth Century.* (with) *Supplement ot the Bibliotheca Spenceriana.* (with) *Ades Althorpianae; or an Account of the Mansion, Books and Picturess at Althorp.* (with) *A Descriptive Catalogue of the Books Printed in the Fifteenth Century, Lately forming Part of the Library of the Duke Di Cassano Serra, and Now the Property of George John Earl Spencer.* London: for the author by Shakespeare Press, 1814-1815. 1822-1823., 7 volumes, 4to., engraved plates, hundreds of facsimiles of early woodcuts and type, some printed in color, modern full tan morocco, richly gilt, covers with central arms and cornerpieces within a two-line fillet, board edges and turn-ins gilt, spines fully gilt in compartments, some engraved plates foxed and few dampstained, offsetting from text illustrations, gathering M in v. 4 heavily foxed, else very good in very fine, fresh bindings. Joseph J. Felcone Inc. Books Printed before 1701 - 29 2013 $2800

Dibner, Bern *The Atlantic Cable.* Norwalk: Burndy, 1959. 4to., numerous illustrations, original stiff printed wrappers. James Tait Goodrich S74 - 79 2013 $75

Dicey, A. V. *A Leap in the Dark.* 1911. 8vo., good, cloth. C. P. Hyland 261 - 971 2013 £27

Dick Whittington and His Cat. New York: Scribner, 1950. A. First edition, 4to., pictorial cloth, fine in nice dust jacket with few small edge chips, wonderful linoleum cuts by Marcia Brown, this copy inscribed by Brown. Aleph-Bet Books, Inc. 105 - 94 2013 $600

Dick, Kay *Ivy and Stevie. Ivy Compton-Burnett and Stevie Smith. Conversations and Reflections.* London: Duckworth, 1971. First edition, 8vo., original black cloth, dust jacket, inscribed by author for Dr. Anthony Ston? and signed again by author on titlepage, excellent copy. Maggs Bros. Ltd. 1460 - 228 2013 £50

Dick, Philip K. *The Broken Bubble.* New York: Ultramarine, 1988. First edition, limited issue, one of 26 lettered copies bound by Denis Gouey (of a total edition of 150), signed by Tim Powers and James Blaylock, full morocco, fine, this is Tim Powers' copy designated "AC1" (for "Author's Copy #1" with letter from publisher laid in to Powers sending his copies. Between the Covers Rare Books, Inc. Sci-Fi, Fantasy & Horror - 88045 2013 $1850

Dick, Philip K. *The Man Who Japed.* London: Eyre Methuen, 1978. First English edition, cheap pages little browned, still fine in fine dust jacket, scarce. Between the Covers Rare Books, Inc. Sci-Fi, Fantasy & Horror - 53033 2013 $350

Dick, Philip K. *Martian Time-Slip.* London: New English Library, 1976. First hardcover edition, octavo, boards. L. W. Currey, Inc. Fall Sampler Sept. 2013 - 144767 2013 $350

Dick, Philip K. *Now Wait for Last Year.* Garden City: Doubleday, 1966. Stated first edition, very good++, 8vo., mild foxing to edges and endpapers, near fine dust jacket with edge wear. By the Book, L. C. 38 - 78 2013 $225

Dick, Philip K. *Now Wait for Last Year.* Garden City: Doubleday & Co., 1966. First edition, octavo, cloth. L. W. Currey, Inc. Utopian Literature: Recent Acquisitions (April 2013) - 138771 2013 $350

Dick, R. A. *The Ghost and Mrs. Muir.* London: George G. Harrap, 1947. First English edition, little foxing to endpapers, else fine in fine dust jacket. Between the Covers Rare Books, Inc. Sci-Fi, Fantasy & Horror - 284622 2013 $1200

Dickason, Graham *Irish Settlers to the Cape: The Clanwilliam 1820. Settlers from Cork Harbour.* Cape Town: 1973. First edition, 113 pages, maps and illustrations, dust jacket, very good. C. P. Hyland 261 - 342 2013 £60

Dickens, Charles 1812-1870 *The Adventures of Oliver Twist or the Parish Boy's Progress.* London: published for the author by Bradbury and Evans, 1846. First edition, very rare 10 monthly parts issue, octavo, 24 plates, collates complete, all wrappers correct and complete as well, some of the parts professionally rebacked, or with other small neat repairs, part VII front wrapper has been extended in bottom margin, but still bit short, front wrapper of part V and back wrapper of part VII trimmed, bit short on bottom margin, back wrapper of part X slightly soiled, usual rubbing and foxing to parts, period ownership inscription on front wrapper of parts IV, VI and VIII, still handsome, blue quarter morocco and chemise.   Heritage Book Shop   Holiday Catalogue 2012 - 39   2013 $30,000

Dickens, Charles 1812-1870 *The Battle of Life.* London: Bradbury & Evans, 1846. First edition, half title, frontispiece, vignette titlepage is fourth and usual state, with angel holding banner and with no publisher's imprint, some slight wear to head and tail of spine and rear joint, very good in bright original red gilt cloth.   Ken Spelman Books Ltd.   75 - 112   2013   £75

Dickens, Charles 1812-1870 *Christmas Books.* London: Chapman and Hall, 1852. First English collected edition, frontispiece final ad leaf, ads on endpapers, original olive green cloth, blocked in blind, spine blocked and lettered in gilt, armorial bookplate of John Browne, small bookseller's ticket, G. Mann, very good, close to fine copy.   Jarndyce Antiquarian Booksellers   CCV - 83   2013   £400

Dickens, Charles 1812-1870 *A Christmas Carol.* London: Chapman & Hall, 1843. First edition, first issue with red and blue titlepage dated 1843 Stave I as first chapter heading, half title printed in blue and with green endpapers, gilt wreath on front cover 15mm at closest point to blindstamping in left, small 8vo., original vertical ribbed brown cloth, gilt wreath on front cover, few minor spots, 4 hand colored plates, all edges gilt, couple of minor spots of wear on spine and corners little rubbed, as are green endpapers, as often, not pristine, but superior copy, morocco backed cloth slipcase.   Howard S. Mott Inc.   262 - 41   2013 $14,000

Dickens, Charles 1812-1870 *A Christmas Carol...* London: William Heinemann, 1915. Limited to 525 numbered copies, signed by artist, large quarto, 12 color plates and 20 black and white drawings by Arthur Rackham, original vellum over boards pictorially stamped and lettered gilt, original yellow silk ties, gray and white pictorial endpapers, very bright, near fine.   David Brass Rare Books, Inc.   Holiday 2012 Chapter One - DB 02096   2013 $3850

Dickens, Charles 1812-1870 *David Copperfield.* London: Bradbury & Evans, 1850. First edition, half title, frontispiece, vignette title, plates by Phiz, some plates browned, generally quite clean, contemporary half dark green calf, spine decorated in gilt, black leather label, bit rubbed, signed F. E. Stevens in contemporary hand on printed title, loose armorial bookplate of Arthur Earl of Castlestewart.   Jarndyce Antiquarian Booksellers   CCV - 85   2013   £450

Dickens, Charles 1812-1870 *Dombey and Sons.* New York: Wiley and Putnam, 1846-1848. First American edition, in original parts, 20 parts in 19, each part with 2 engraved plates, with the exception of part1, as it states on bottom of front wrapper, "the illustrations for this Number will be given with the Next", each numbers states this on bottom of wrapper, original grey-brown printed wrappers, some soiling and staining to wrappers, many wrappers chipped along edges and spines, number xix-xx with back wrapper crudely repaired along back joint, pages foxed as usual for American stock, overall very good, housed in quarter blue morocco clamshell. Heritage Book Shop   Holiday Catalogue 2012 - 41   2013 $6000

Dickens, Charles 1812-1870 *Dombey and Son.* London: Bradbury and Evans, 1848. First edition in book form, mixed early issue, with page 324 'captin' for 'captain' and in titlepage vignette Captain Cuttle's book is on his left hand, half title, frontispiece, 38 plates, 12 line errata slip, 8vo., very good, clean, almost completely free of foxing, 19th century half red morocco, raised gilt bands, marbled endpapers.   Ken Spelman Books Ltd.   75 - 115   2013   £220

Dickens, Charles 1812-1870 *Dombey and Son.* London: Bradbury & Evans, 1848. First edition in book form, first state following all points in Smith, the Kenyon Starling - William Self copy, octavo, publisher's variant binding of moderate green fine diaper grain cloth, original pale yellow coated endpapers, spine very faded, corners very slightly bumped, just tiny amount of board show through, otherwise binding as fresh as one could possibly wish for, chemised in half green morocco slipcase, Self bookplate on chemise.   David Brass Rare Books, Inc.   Holiday 2012 Chapter Five - DB 01693   2013 $11,500

Dickens, Charles 1812-1870 *Great Expectations.* London: Chapman and Hall, 1861. Volume I second impression, volume II fourth impression, volume 3 first impression, 3 volumes, later inserted half title volume I, engraved title and plates by Pailthorpe, occasional light browning in prelims, slightly later full brown crushed morocco by Riviere, spines gilt in compartments, gilt borders and dentelles, armorial bookplates of William H. R. Saunders, top edge gilt, very good, handsome.   Jarndyce Antiquarian Booksellers   CCV - 86   2013   £4500

Dickens, Charles   1812-1870   *Hard Times. for These Times.* London: Bradbury & Evans, 1854. First edition, half title, original olive green cloth, spine lettered i gilt with 'price 5/-', spine faded, slight rubbing, otherwise very good, cloth slipcase.   Jarndyce Antiquarian Booksellers   CCV - 87   2013   £1750

Dickens, Charles   1812-1870   *The Haunted Man and the Ghost's Bargain.* Leipzig: Bernhard Tauchnitz Jun., 1848. First European edition, small octavo, 19th century three quarter black calf and marbled boards, spine panel tooled in gold and blind, brown leather title label affixed to spine panel, cream endpapers.   L. W. Currey, Inc.   Christmas Themed Books - 90316   2013 $250

Dickens, Charles   1812-1870   *Little Dorrit.* London: Bradbury and Evans, 1857. First bookform edition, frontispiece and title and 38 etched plates by Phiz, plates generally somewhat spotted, as usual with dampstains in lower outer corners (plates only, not text), 8vo., contemporary half green calf, spine richly gilt, red lettering piece, minor shelfwear, contemporary ownership inscription of C. J. Hallam, early 20th century M. A. Hallam below this and below this inscription of Dorrit W. Fountain, Christmas 1922, good. Blackwell's Rare Books   B174 - 46   2013   £300

Dickens, Charles   1812-1870   *Mr. Pickwick: Pages from Pickwick Papers.* London: Hodder & Stoughton, n.d. circa, 1910. First edition, large 4to., red cloth stamped in gold and black, 174 pages, few fox spots, else nearly as new in publisher's box, box flaps repaired, illustrations by Frank Reynolds with 25 tipped in color plates with lettered guards. Aleph-Bet Books, Inc.   104 - 485   2013 $500

Dickens, Charles   1812-1870   *Nicholas Nickleby.* London: Chapman & Hall, 1839. First edition, half title, frontispiece, 39 plates by Phiz, uncut in later full olive green crushed morocco by Riviere & Son, gilt spine, borders and dentelles, front wrapper to part XIV bound in at end, armorial bookplate of John Nevill Cross, top edge gilt, very good, handsome copy.   Jarndyce Antiquarian Booksellers   CCV - 88   2013   £850

Dickens, Charles   1812-1870   *The Old Curiosity Shop.* London: Hodder & Stoughton, n.d. circa, 1913. Thick 4to., pictorial cloth, nearly as new in publisher's box with mounted color plate, illustrations by Frank Reynolds, with mounted color plate, and 20 beautiful richly colored tipped in color plates, amazing copy, rare in box.   Aleph-Bet Books, Inc. 105 - 500   2013 $500

Dickens, Charles   1812-1870   *Our Mutual Friend.* London: Chapman & Hall, 1865. First edition, 2 volumes, octavo, 40 engraved plates, including frontispieces by Marcus Stone, 20 in each volume, original purplish-brown sand-grain cloth, stamped in blind, spines decoratively stamped and lettered gilt, endpapers coated pale yellow, top of spines lightly frayed, front hinges volume 1 and both inner hinges volume II with hairline crack, small repair to inner hinge of volume II, small embossed bookseller's label on front free endpaper of each volume, superior copy, usually found in remainder bindings or rebound, cloth slipcase. Heritage Book Shop   Holiday Catalogue 2012 - 42   2013 $9500

Dickens, Charles   1812-1870   *The Personal History of David Copperfield...* London: Bradbury & Evans (May 1849-November 1850), 1850. First edition in original monthly parts, 20 numbers bound in 19, first issue, with all points in Hatton & Cleaver, octavo, with all called for ads, and with all samples present, and all slips, Part II possesses an unrecorded extra two page catalogue of miscellaneous books from Dalton, original blue printed pictorial wrappers, expert restoration to some backstrips, near fine set, rarely seen in this condition, chemised in green half straight grain morocco slipcase, rare.   David Brass Rare Books, Inc. Holiday 2012 Chapter Five - DB 01244   2013 $12,500

Dickens, Charles   1812-1870   *The Posthumous Papers of the Pickwick Club.* London: Chapman and Hall, April, 1836. - November 1837, 20 parts in 19, 8vo., original pictorial wrappers, 43 plates, very good, attractive set, mixed issues as usual, some parts almost imperceptibly respined, inconsequential marginal light soiling of first part, otherwise wrappers quite clean, internally clean and with very good plates, only few of which are little browned, quarter green morocco slipcase.   Howard S. Mott Inc.   262 - 43   2013 $6000

Dickens, Charles   1812-1870   *The Posthumous Papers of the Pickwick Club.* London: Chapman & Hall, 1837. First edition in book form, mixed issue, thick 8vo., 43 illustrations including frontispiece and vignette titlepage, 7 plates by Seymouor and remaining ones by Phiz, with marginal note on page 9 that was suppressed in later issues; contemporary half brown calf over marbled boards, green morocco spine label, lettered in gilt, spine stamped and ruled in gilt, marbled endpapers, all edges marbled, small news clipping tipped in on half title, not affecting text, previous owner's old ink signature on half title, some of the plates bit foxed, text quite clean, overall very handsome in contemporary binding. Heritage Book Shop   Holiday Catalogue 2012 - 43   2013 $1250

Dickens, Charles   1812-1870   *The Posthumous Papers of the Pickwick Club.*   London: Chapman and Hall, 1837. First edition in book form, mixed issue with 'S. Veller' on page 342, line 5; 'his friends' correct on page 400, line 21 and 'f' in 'of' imperfect in headline on page 432, frontispiece and half title and 41 plates in early states, with page locations but without titles or imprints, some foxing to plates and blank corner of one plate repaired, 19th century half morocco, marbled boards, decorative gilt bands, some slight rubbing to joints and corners, but good copy.   Ken Spelman Books Ltd.   75 - 101   2013   £220

Dickens, Charles   1812-1870   *The Posthumous Papers of the Pickwick Club.*   London: Macmillan and Co., 1886. Jubilee Edition, 2 volumes, octavo, illustrations extra illustrated, 94 plates, stamped on rear flyleaves of each volume "Extra illustrated by A. W. Waters", bound circa 1925 by Bayntun of Bath in three quarter blue morocco, fine.   David Brass Rare Books, Inc.   Holiday 2012 Chapter Five - DB 00561   2013 $1800

Dickens, Charles   1812-1870   *Posthumous Papers of the Pickwick Club.*   New York: George D. Sproul, 1902. Autograph Variorum Edition, 6 volumes, signed original frontispiece, finely bound by Whitman Bennett, frontispiece and plates, descriptive tissue guards, frontispiece in volumes I, III and V on India paper mounted, signed by artist, Harry Furniss, three quarter burgundy leather and marbled boards, gilt ruled and spine divided into six compartments with "CD: cipher in third, gilt lettering ad design spines, top edges gilt, marbled endpapers, mild cover edgewear, owner name, small 4to.   By the Book, L. C.   36 - 43   2013 $750

Dickens, Charles   1812-1870   *Sketches of Young Couples, Young Ladies, Young Gentlemen.*   London: Cassell, Petter & Galpin, 1869. Frontispiece and plates, 2 pages ads, original green pictorial cloth, bevelled boards, very good.   Jarndyce Antiquarian Booksellers   CCV - 89   2013   £120

Dickens, Charles   1812-1870   *The Story of Little Dombey.*   London: Bradbury and Evans, 1858. Small 8vo., later but not recent half cloth, marbled boards, morocco label, original green printed wrappers have been bound in and are in very good condition, half title, but bound without final ad leaf.   Ken Spelman Books Ltd.   75 - 123   2013   £50

Dickens, Charles   1812-1870   *A Tale of Two Cities.*   Philadelphia: T. B. Peterson and Bros., 1859. First one volume US edition, 33 full page illustrations from designs by John McLenan, publisher's original brown cloth with blind-stamped decoration and ruling to front and rear covers, gilt title and small illustrations of man to spine, rebacked, original spine laid down, edges and corners of boards worn with few small chips to book cloth, cloth somewhat mottled on front cover, book otherwise very good, interior very clean with just few spots of foxing, gutters in center of book have pulled away slightly from book having been opened flat, gift inscription dated 1861, 211 pages, 12 pages ads.   The Kelmscott Bookshop   7 - 103   2013 $575

Dickens, Charles   1812-1870   *A Tale of Two Cities.*   London: Chapman & Hall, 1859. First edition, first issue, frontispiece, additional engraved title and plates, page number 213 misprinted 113, original red cloth, spine lettered in gilt, neatly recased, little rubbed, nice, bright copy, original cloth, bookplates of George Henry Virtue (son of publisher George C. Virtue, in cloth slipcase.   Jarndyce Antiquarian Booksellers   CCV - 90   2013   £5200

Dickens, Charles   1812-1870   *The Works.*   London: Chapman & Hall, 1879. 30 volumes, illustrations, green cloth, stamped in black on covers and gilt on spines, very good, clean set.   Second Life Books Inc.   183 - 105   2013 $700

Dickens, Charles   1812-1870   *The Nonesuch Dickens.*   Bloomsbury: Nonesuch Press, 1937-1938. One of 877 sets, large 8vo, 23 volumes + box with original steel plate, original variously colored buckram, black leather labels, top edge gilt, others uncut, except for wanting volume II of the 2 volume "Collected Papers" a complete set, including the steel plate and Nonesuch Dickensiana, printed on handmade paper, large 8vo., 23 volumes, box with original steel plate, the steel plate engraved by Phiz from Martin Chuzzlewit, accompanied by printed pull from the plate and letter of authenticity signed by Arthur Waugh, excellent set with occasional minor soiling, few spines slightly faded, extreme corners of two leather labels slightly clipped.   Howard S. Mott Inc.   262 - 42   2013 $8500

Dickens, Charles   1812-1870   *The Complete Works and Letters, together with the "Prospectus Volume", The Nonesuch Dickens.*   London: 1937-1938. 138/877 sets, 24 volumes, illustrations printed from original steel plates or woodblocks (with the exception of few woodblocks which had split, those being reproduced from electrotyped facsimile or photo reproductions, royal 8vo., original vari colored buckram, uniform black leather labels, fading or darkening to few backstrips as usual, Prospectus in blue linen, gilt lettered as issued, top edge gilt, on rough others untrimmed, near fine.   Blackwell's Rare Books   172 - 302   2013   £900

Dickenson, J.   *God's Protecting Providence, Man's Surest Help and Defence in Times of the Greatest Difficulty and Most Eminent Danger.*   London: T. Sowle, 1700. Second edition, small 8vo., late 19th century speckled calf, red morocco label to spine, rare.   Maggs Bros. Ltd.   1467 - 119   2013   £16,000

Dickeson, Montroville Wilson   *The American Numismatic Manual of the Currency or Money of the Aborigines and Colonial, State and United States Coins.*   Philadelphia: J. B. Lippincott, 1865. Third edition, small 4to., 271 pages, 20 plates, frontispiece, contemporary three quarter leather and marbled boards, fine, quite unusual thus.   M & S Rare Books, Inc.   95 - 270   2013 $475

Dickinson, Goldsworthy Lowes *Poems.* N.P.: privately Printed at Chiswick Press, 1896. First edition, 8vo., original printed blue-gray wrappers (68) pages, untrimmed, pictorial title, inscribed "R.A. Furness from the author June 20", wrappers worn and somewhat chipped around top edges, very good, uncommon.   The Brick Row Book Shop   Miscellany Fifty-Nine - 14   2013 $150

Dickinson, J. C. *The Land of Cartmel.* Kendal: Titus Wilson, 1980. First edition, large 8vo., original cloth, gilt, dust jacket, 16 plates and 5 text figures, presentation copy, inscribed by author.   R. F. G. Hollett & Son   Lake District and Cumbria - 31   2013   £40

Dickinson, William *Cumbriana or Fragments of Cumbrian Life.* London: Whittaker and Co. and Whitehaen: Callender and Dixon, 1875. First edition, later cloth gilt, lower joint cracked.   R. F. G. Hollett & Son   Lake District and Cumbria - 37   2013   £35

Dickson, Carter *Behind the Crimson Blind.* London: William Heinemann, 1952. First English edition, page edges slightly darkened, otherwise fine in very good dust jacket, wear at corners and several short closed tears.   Mordida Books   81 - 147   2013 $60

Dickson, Carter *The Cavalier's Cup.* New York: Morrow, 1953. First edition, fine in very good dust jacket with wrinkling on back panel, nicks and tears on spine ends, wear at corners and several short closed tears.   Mordida Books   81 - 148   2013 $75

Dickson, Carter *He Wouldn't Kill Patience.* New York: Morrow, 1944. First edition, bookplate, top edges lightly soiled and small scrapes on spine otherwise fine in dust jacket with some tiny closed tears and light wear at spine ends and along folds.   Mordida Books   81 - 145   2013 $200

Dickson, Carter *My Late Wives.* New York: Morrow, 1946. First edition, fine in dust jacket with tiny fraying at spine ends and wear at corners.   Mordida Books   81 - 146   2013 $250

Dickson, George S. *A Nursery Geography.* Thomas Nelson and Sons, n.d., Revised edition, large 8vo., original pictorial boards, 20 color plates and numerous drawings by George Morrow.   R. F. G. Hollett & Son   Children's Books - 164   2013   £25

Dickson, John Carr *Fear is the Same.* London: William Heinemann, 1956. First edition, some scuffing to boards, foxing to fore edge and edges of pages, near very good in attractive, near fine dust jacket, nicely inscribed by author to Bruce Montgomery, real name of mystery writer Edmund Crispin, nice association.   Between the Covers Rare Books, Inc.   Mystery & Detective Fiction - 94111   2013 $1500

Dictys Cretensis *Historia Troiana.* Messina: Guilelmus Schonberger, 1498. First combined edition, small quarto, 79 leaves (of 80, lacking final blank), woodcut initials with profuse branch-work and floral decoration, printer's device on verso of last leaf, 19th century calf, previous owner's bookplate, near fine in custom full calf clamshell, gilt stamped on spine.   Heritage Book Shop   50th Anniversary Catalogue - 29   2013 $28,500

Diderot, Denis *Encyclopedie, ou Dictionnaire Raisonne des Sciences, des Arts et des Metiers, par une Societe des Gens de Lettres.* (with) *Recueil de Planches sur les Sciences les Arts Liberaux, et les Arts Mechaniques avec Leur Explication...* (with) *Supplement a l'Encyclopedie...* (with) *Table Analytique et Raisonne des Matieres Contenues Dans les XXXIII volumes in-folio du Dictionnaire des Sciences....* Paris: 1751-1780. First edition, complete in 35 volumes, over 2000 engraved plates, contemporary French mottled calf over speckled boards, red and green morocco spine labels, spines richly decorated gilt, bookplate of Bibliotheque de Mr. Leon Muller-Saint-Mande in each volume, minimal wear to bindings, superb copy in attractive contemporary binding.   Heritage Book Shop   50th Anniversary Catalogue - 30   2013 $75,000

Dieffenbach, Johann Friedrich *Ueber die Durchschneidung der Sebnen und Muskeln.* Berlin: Albert Forstner, 1841. First edition, 8vo., 20 lithographed plates, occasional foxing, original brown cloth backed boards, printed paper spine label, extremities worn, bookplate of Dr. Fr. Bonhoff, rare.   Jeff Weber Rare Books   172 - 78   2013 $1250

Diehl, Edna Groff *Vegetable and Fruit Children.* Chicago: Whitman, 1923. 12mo., blue cloth, pictorial paste-on, very good+ in torn and chipped dust jacket, charmingly illustrated in color by Vera Stone.   Aleph-Bet Books, Inc.   104 - 42   2013 $175

Diemerbroeck, Isbrand De *The Anatomy of Human Bodies.* London: printed for W. Whitwood, 1694. Reissue of first English edition, Folio, 16 engraved plates, full contemporary paneled calf, later rebacking, corners renewed.   James Tait Goodrich   75 - 81   2013 $3500

Diereville, N. De *Relation du Voyage du Prot Royal de l'Acadie ou de la Nouvelle France.* Amsterdam: Pierre Humbert, 1710. Second edition, 12mo., contemporary calf, back gilt, fine, engraved frontispiece, title printed in red and black.   Maggs Bros. Ltd.   1467 - 105   2013   £1650

Digby, Kenelm   1603-1665 *A Choice Collection of Rare Chymical Secrets and Experiments in Philosophy.* London: printed for the publisher, 1682. Second issue, 3 plates, one of which is in facsimile, plate skillfully done on old paper, early contemporary English panel calf with skilful rebacking by Middleton.   James Tait Goodrich   75 - 82   2013 $1500

Digby, Kenelm 1603-1665 *A Late Discourse Made in a Solemne Assembly of Nobles and Learned Men of Montpellier in France.* London: printed by R. Lowndes, 1658. Second edition in English, 12mo., full contemporary calf, later skillful rebacking in calf, spine label faded, corners bumped.   James Tait Goodrich   75 - 83   2013 $795

Digby, Kenelm 1603-1665 *Theatrum Sympatheticum in quo Sympathiae Actiones Variae, Singulares & Admirandae tam Macro-quam Microosmicae Exhibentur & Mechanice.* Nuremberg: J. A. & W. Endter, 1660. First edition in Latin, 12mo., contemporary vellum with yapped edges, double page allegorical frontispiece.   James Tait Goodrich   75 - 84   2013 $1750

Dillon, E. J. *The Eclipse of Russia.* London: J. M. Dent, 1918. First edition, 8vo., pages 420, original green cloth, slight rubbing to head of spine, clean internally.   J. & S. L. Bonham Antiquarian Booksellers   Europe - 8847   2013   £45

Dillon, Ellis *The Voyage of Mael Duin.* London: Faber, 1969. First edition, 29 pages, color and black and white illustrations by Alan Howard, 8vo., cloth, dust jacket.   C. P. Hyland   261 - 343   2013   £32

Dillon, John *The Truth About the Mitchelstown Massacre.* 1887. 30 pages, 8vo., disbound, good.   C. P. Hyland   261 - 345   2013   £40

Dillon, Myles *The Archaism of Irish Tradition: Rhys Lecture 1947.* 1947. First edition, 20 pages, wrappers, 8vo., good.   C. P. Hyland   261 - 972   2013   £30

Dillon, Richard *Napa Valley Heyday.* San Francisco: Book Club of California, 2004. First edition, one of 450 copies, 43 vintage photos by Charles Turrill, large folding map in color laid in at rear, full natural linen, pictorial inset on front cover, printed paper spine label, very fine.   Argonaut Book Shop   Recent Acquisitions June 2013 - 92   2013 $250

Dilnot, George *Sister Satan.* Boston and New York: Houghton Mifflin Co., 1933. First edition, fine in fine photographic dust jacket with couple of short tears, lovely copy.   Between the Covers Rare Books, Inc.   Mystery & Detective Fiction - 313746   2013 $275

Dinesen, Isak 1885-1962 *Anecdotes of Destiny.* New York: Random House, 1958. First edition, first printing, signed by author as Karen Blixen dated 1959, octavo, publisher's cream cloth, spine lettered and stamped in brown and black, top edge black, spine bit darkened, original price clipped dust jacket slightly chipped along top edge, else near fine.   Heritage Book Shop   Holiday Catalogue 2012 - 44   2013 $1000

Dinesen, Isak 1885-1962 *Last Tales.* London: Putnam, 1957. First edition, 8vo., original black cloth, spine lettered gilt, attractive dust jacket, few light marks to cloth, dust jacket little marked and slightly worn at head and tail of spine, inscribed by author for Violet Trefusis.   Maggs Bros. Ltd.   1460 - 229   2013   £1000

Dinkins, Pauline E *African Folk Tales.* Nashville: Sunday School Pub. Board, 1933. First edition, (48) pages, quarto, quarter canvas and printed stiff paper covered wrappers, 16 full page color illustrations, slight smudges on wrappers, very scarce.   Between the Covers Rare Books, Inc.   165 - 23   2013 $2750

Diodorus Siculus *Bibliothecae Historicae Libri qui Supersunt.* Amstelodami: Jacob Westten, 1746. 2 volumes, folio, 2 plates, engraved allegorical frontispiece and engraved portrait, both to volume 1, titlepages in red and black with engraved vignettes, text in Greek and Latin, some light browning, contemporary vellum, red labels to spines, blindstamped centerpieces and borders with gilt Athenaeum stamps to upper boards and tails of spines, both volumes rebacked in vellum, some loss to endcaps, vellum somewhat darkened in places, Athenaeum Library bookplate to each volume.   Unsworths Antiquarian Booksellers   28 - 12   2013   £600

Diogenes, Laertius *Diogene Laertio Delle vite e Sententie de' Filosofi Illvstri. (The Lives and Opinions of Eminent Philosophers).* Vinegia: Appresso D. Farri, 1567. Octavo, 15cm., woodcut title vignette and initial, owner's name, good copy in near contemporary full vellum, some chipping to crown and foot of spine, some age toning, scattered light staining to text pages, scarce.   Between the Covers Rare Books, Inc.   Philosophy - 329335   2013 $550

Diogenes, Pseud. *The Royal Eclippse; Or Delicate Facts Exhibiting the Secret Memoirs of Squire George and His Wife.* London: printed by D. N. Shury for J. F. Hughes, 1807. Second edition, half title, 12mo., 8 pages ads, 24 page catalog (Jan. 1807) on smaller paper, uncut in original blue boards, slightly dulled, spine little chipped, but overall good plus.   Jarndyce Antiquarian Booksellers   CCIII - 656   2013   £65

Dionysius Areopagiticus *Opera (quae quidem extent) Omnia, Quintuplici Translatione Versa & Commentariis.* Cologne: ex officina Haeredum Ioannis Quentel, 1556. 2 small wormholes in blank margins at beginning and end, some minor browning and light soiling, folio, contemporary blind stamped pigskin, two brass clasps on pigskin mount, scattering of wormholes to boards, some light staining one corner damaged, no flyleaves, good.   Blackwell's Rare Books   B174 - 47   2013   £900

Directori de la Vistita del General del Principat de Catalunya y Comptats de Rossello y Cerdanya... Barcelona: en casa de Rafel (sic) Figuero, 1698. Woodcut arms on title, tear in last leaf passing through one letter on recto (verso blank) without loss, lacking initial blank, square 8vo., contemporary limp vellum, remains of ties little soiled, rear endleaf partially torn away, contemporary ownership inscription "Del Fran(cis)co Aparici", very good.   Blackwell's Rare Books   B174 - 26   2013   £1500

Directory of Directors in the City of New York 1929-1930. New York: Directory of Directors Company, 1929. Red cloth, gilt, 1235 pages, worm hole in last fifty or so leaves, otherwise sound and tight, good copy, uncommon.   Between the Covers Rare Books, Inc.   New York City - 292108   2013 $275

Disch, Thomas M.   *Ringtime.*   West Branch: Toothpaste Press, 1982. First edition, one of 100 numbered copies specially bound and signed by Disch and artist, Ann Mikolowski, quarter cloth and decorated paper over boards, fine.   Between the Covers Rare Books, Inc.   Sci-Fi, Fantasy & Horror - 312229   2013 $85

Disney, Walt   *The Cinderella Magic Wand Book.*   Dean & Son, 1950. Oblong small 4to., original cloth backed pictorial boards, corners worn and edges rubbed, 6 color plates and numerous black and white illustrations, with magic spectacles in front pocket, 2 examples included.   R. F. G. Hollett & Son   Children's Books - 165   2013   £95

Disney, Walt   *Father Noah's Ark.*   Birn Brothers, circa, 1939. Oblong small 8vo., original pictorial boards, very slight rubbing to extremities, lovely bright colors, full page black and white illustrations, front joint just splitting at foot, otherwise very nice, clean copy.   R. F. G. Hollett & Son   Children's Books - 166   2013   £85

Disney, Walt   *Mickey Mouse Fire Brigade.*   Racine: Whitman, 1936. 4to., pictorial boards, fine in pictorial dust jacket slightly frayed, full page red, pink and black and white illustrations, plus pictorial endpapers and many partial page color and black and whites, beautiful copy, very scarce.   Aleph-Bet Books, Inc.   104 - 161   2013 $875

Disney, Walt   *Mickey Mouse in Giantland.*   Philadelphia: McKay, 1934. 8vo., red cloth, pictorial paste on, 45 pages, small scrape on cover, inconspicuous mend on one page, else very good+, full color illustrations on every page plus pictorial endpapers, beautiful copy.   Aleph-Bet Books, Inc.   105 - 181   2013 $450

Disney, Walt   *Mickey Mouse on Tour.*   London: Birn Bros., n.d. circa, 1936. 4to., pictorial board, near fine, great color covers, nearly full page illustrations on every page done in red and black, red stipple background.   Aleph-Bet Books, Inc.   105 - 182   2013 $350

Disney, Walt   *Mickey Mouse Story Book.*   Philadelphia: McKay, 1931. 8vo., variant binding in cloth backed stiff pictorial card covers, 62 pages, near fine and bright, illustrations in black and white on every page with small figure of Mickey in corner of every page that appears to move when pages are flipped, nice.   Aleph-Bet Books, Inc.   104 - 162   2013 $400

Disney, Walt   *Mickey en las Carreras. (Mickey Mouse Waddle Book).*   Barcelona: Editorial Molina, 1935. Segunda edition, 4to., pictorial boards, fine in slightly worn dust jacket, this copy is original and intact and includes 4 Waddle figures unpunched and pictorial band that goes around cover, original printed pictorial instruction envelope contains the ramp and the brass fasteners, stamped "Archive" on instruction envelope, undoubtedly publisher's file copy, illustrated with color endpapers, 12 bright full color illustrations and many black and whites, of utmost rarity.   Aleph-Bet Books, Inc.   104 - 160   2013 $8750

Disney, Walt   *Pinocchio.*   New York: House, 1939. First Disney edition, 4to., cloth backed glazed pictorial boards, fine in fine dust jacket, vibrant color lithographs in black and white from Disney motion pictures, fine copies in dust jacket are scarce.   Aleph-Bet Books, Inc.   105 - 193   2013 $350

Disney, Walt   *The Pop-Up Mickey Mouse.*   New York: Blue Ribbon, 1933. 8vo., pictorial boards, fine, pop-ups, many half page black and white illustrations in text, nice.   Aleph-Bet Books, Inc.   105 - 473   2013 $1200

Disney, Walt   *Sketch Book (of Snow White and the Seven Dwarfs).*   London: Collins, 1938. First edition, 4to., tan cloth, fine in dust jacket with 3 small chips on edges, 2 pieces out of spine, one of which wraps around to top of front cover removing top part of 2 letters, this copy signed and dated by Disney, 12 beautiful tipped in color plates, lettered tissue guards, many drawings.   Aleph-Bet Books, Inc.   104 - 164   2013 $6000

Disney, Walt   *Snow White and the Seven Dwarfs.*   Collins, n.d., 1939. First edition, large 4to., original cloth backed pictorial boards, edges little browned in places, pages 80, illustrations in color and monochrome, front joint starting, very nice, clean copy.   R. F. G. Hollett & Son   Children's Books - 167   2013   £150

Disney, Walt   *Three Little Pigs. (and) The Big Bad Wolf and Little Red Riding Hood.*   New York: Blue Ribbon, 1933-1934. 4to., pictorial boards, tips rubbed, else very good, 2 books in one, illustrated with great covers, color endpapers, full page color illustrations, many full page and smaller black and whites.   Aleph-Bet Books, Inc.   104 - 165   2013 $475

Disney, Walt *Walt Disney Annual.* Racine: Whitman, 1937. Folio, pictorial boards, 123 pages, paper aging and some wear to extremis, else fine in slightly chipped dust jacket, 8 color plates and large half page black and whites on almost every page of text, very rare. Aleph-Bet Books, Inc. 104 - 166 2013 $1500

Disney, Walt *Walt Disney's Circus.* New York: Simon & Schuster, 1944. First edition, 4to., pictorial boards, near fine in slightly worn dust jacket, full color illustrations, including 12 pages with felt appliques incorporated into illustrations (plus felt on dust jacket), nice. Aleph-Bet Books, Inc. 105 - 184 2013 $250

Disney, Walt *Walt Disney's Country Cousin.* Philadelphia: McKay, 1937. Square 4to., pictorial boards, tail of spine chipped and edges rubbed, else very good in frayed dust jacket, great color illustrations, quite scarce. Aleph-Bet Books, Inc. 104 - 167 2013 $250

Disney, Walt *Walt Disney's Famous Dwarfs.* Racine: Whitman, 1938. Stiff pictorial wrappers, slight edge wear, very good+, illustrations on every page. Aleph-Bet Books, Inc. 105 - 187 2013 $275

Disney, Walt *Walt Disney's Thumper.* New York: Grosset & Dunlap, 1942. Small 4to., pictorial boards fine in very good dust jacket with tape repairs on verso, color lithos, uncommon. Aleph-Bet Books, Inc. 105 - 185 2013 $150

Disney, Walt *Who's Afraid of the Big Bad Wolf/Three Little Pits.* Philadelphia: McKay, 1933. 8vo., cloth backed stiff pictorial card covers, 31 pages, near fine, large full page black and whites, nice. Aleph-Bet Books, Inc. 105 - 186 2013 $350

Disney, Walt *Winter Draws on - Meet the Spandules.* Prepared by the Safety Education Division, Flight Control Command of the US Army Air Forces, 1943. Oblong 16mo., pictorial wrappers, some cover soil, very good+, 3-color lithos. Aleph-Bet Books, Inc. 104 - 168 2013 $850

Disraeli, Benjamin 1804-1881 *Alroy. Ixion in Heaven. The Infernal Marriage. Popanilla.* London: Longmans, circa, 1878. New edition, half title, 8 page catalog, yellowback, original printed boards, slightly rubbed and dulled, very good. Jarndyce Antiquarian Booksellers CCV - 91 2013 £75

Disraeli, Benjamin 1804-1881 *Venetia.* London: Longmans, Green and Co. circa, 1875. New edition, half title, 3 pages ads, ads on endpapers, original yellow pictorial boards, slightly darkened and rubbed, hinges little worn, overall good. Jarndyce Antiquarian Booksellers CCIII - 374 2013 £35

Disraeli, Benjamin 1804-1881 *Vivian Grey.* London: Henry Colburn, 1833. 5 volumes bound in 4, contemporary half purple brown calf, black labels, slightly rubbed, very good, attractive. Jarndyce Antiquarian Booksellers CCIII - 372 2013 £250

Disston, Harry *Riding Rhymes for Young Riders.* New York: Bond Wheelwright, 1951. First edition, large 4to., red cloth last page opened roughly, else very good in frayed dust jacket, with a profusion of illustrations by Paul Brown, uncommon. Aleph-Bet Books, Inc. 105 - 101 2013 $375

The Distilleries Considered, in Their Connection with the Agriculture, Commerce and Revenue of Britain.. Edinburgh: printed for Mundell & Son, 1797. 8vo., titlepage dusted, some light browning, uncut and partially unopened, disbound. Jarndyce Antiquarian Booksellers CCIV - 263 2013 £580

Distrunell, W. C. *Disturnell's Strangers' Guide to San Francisco and Vicinity.* San Francisco: W. C. Disturnell, 1883. First edition, 12mo., numerous ads, including endpapers, blind and gilt stamped dark blue cloth, mild rubbing to spine ends and extremities, but fine, clean copy. Argonaut Book Shop Summer 2013 - 83 2013 $900

Divall, Colin *Suburbanizing the Masses: Public Transport and Urban Development in Historical Perspective.* Aldershot and Burlington: Ashgate, 2003. First edition, 8vo., xvi, 319 pages, figures, tables, pictorial boards, Burndy bookplate, fine. Jeff Weber Rare Books 169 - 120 2013 $150

The Diverting History of John Gilpin. London: George Routledge, n.d. circa, 1885. Square 12mo., stiff pictorial wrappers, all edges gilt, slight rubbing, else fine, illustrations in color and brown line, engraved and printed by Edmund Evans, rare miniature edition. Aleph-Bet Books, Inc. 105 - 110 2013 $200

Divine, David *Hadrian's Wall.* Barnes and Noble, 1995. Original cloth, gilt, dust jacket, 16 plates, 5 diagrams, map. R. F. G. Hollett & Son Lake District and Cumbria - 38 2013 £25

Divine, David *The North-West Frontier of Rome.* MacDonald, 1969. Original cloth, gilt, dust jacket, 16 plates, 5 diagrams and map, ex-libris of Leonard Cottrell. R. F. G. Hollett & Son Lake District and Cumbria - 39 2013 £25

Dix, E. R. McC. *Books... Printed in Waterford in the 18th Century.* Waterford: 1916. Octavo, 19 pages, wrappers, very good. C. P. Hyland 261 - 59 2013 £40

Dix, E. R. McC. *Irish Printers, Booksellers & Stationers 1726-1775.* 1932. Offprint, (58) pages, wrappers, mint. C. P. Hyland 261 - 44 2013 £40

Dix, E. R. McC. *List of Books, Pamphlets Printed in Limerick to 1800.* Limerick: Guy, 1907. Octavo, 32 pages, wrappers, signed presentation copy, very good. C. P. Hyland 261 - 58 2013 £60

Dix, E. R. McC. *List of Books, Pamphlets...Printed in Drogheda... to 1800.* Dundalk: 1911. Octavo, 24 pages, wrappers, very good. C. P. Hyland 261 - 60 2013 £40

Dix, E. R. McC. *List of Books, Pamphlet...Printed in Monaghan... in 18th Century.* Dundalk: 1911. Octavo, 30 pages, wrappers, very good. C. P. Hyland 261 - 61 2013 £50

Dix, John *Local Legends and Rambling Rhymes.* Bristol: George Davey, 1839. First edition, 12mo., frontispiece, additional engraved title, plates, some slight spotting and foxing, original brown pictorial cloth, blocked in gilt, slightly marked, spine slightly faded, very good. Jarndyce Antiquarian Booksellers CCV - 92 2013 £220

Dixon, Joshua *The Literary Life of William Brownrigg...* London: Longman & Rees etc. and Whitehaven: A Dunn, 1801. First edition, original blue boards, paper spine label, very rubbed, very scarce, excellent, uncut, unsophisticated copy from the library of J. (Fred) Hughes of Kendal, local historian, with his label. R. F. G. Hollett & Son Lake District and Cumbria - 40 2013 £375

Doberer, K. K. *The Goldmakers. 10,000 Years of Alchemy.* London: and Brussels, 1948. First edition, 8vo., 24 illustrations, blue cloth, gilt stamped spine title, dust jacket, fine. Jeff Weber Rare Books 171 - 106 2013 $85

Dobie, James Frank 1888-1964 *Apache Gold & Yaqui Silver.* Boston: Little Brown, 1939. Reprint, 8vo., illustrations, first signature shaky, gilt stamped rust cloth, front cover Apache head pictorial, dust jacket chipped top front corner missing, signed and inscribed from author to Elwood Payne in ink, near fine in good jacket. Jeff Weber Rare Books 171 - 105 2013 $165

Dobofsky, Maurice *Everybody's Football.* Washington: American Pub. Co., 1947. First edition, 88 pages, stapled wrappers, just about fine, inscribed by one of the co-authors, scarce. Between the Covers Rare Books, Inc. Football Books - 292283 2013 $200

Dobson, Matthew *A Medical Commentary on Fixed Air.* London: T. Cadell, 1785. Second edition, 2 parts in 1 volume, small 8vo., titlepage browned, withdrawal stamp of Wellcome Library, modern half straight grain morocco over marbled boards, gilt stamped decoration on covers, raised bands on spine, gilt stamped title and decoration on spine, beautiful copy. Jeff Weber Rare Books 172 - 80 2013 $450

Dobyns, Stephen *Saratoga Longshot.* New York: Atheneum, 1976. First edition, fine in near fine dust jacket, excellent copy, jacket with one short, closed tear in rear panel. Leather Stalking Books October 2013 - 2013 $95

Dobyns, Stephen *Saratoga Swimmer.* New York: Atheneum, 1981. First edition, advance review copy with review slip laid in, very fine in dust jacket. Mordida Books 81 - 149 2013 $75

Doctor Comicus or the Frolics of Fortune. London: B. Blake, 1825? 210 x 133mm., without printed titlepage, very attractive light tan smooth calf by Sangorski & Sutcliffe/Zaehnsdorf (stamp signed), corners bordered with French fillet and fleuron cornerpieces, raised bands, spine gilt in compartments featuring decorative bands, scrolling cornerpieces, fleuron centerpiece and small tools, maroon morocco labels, gilt inner dentelles, marbled endpapers, all edges gilt, 12 plates, all colored by hand, bookplate of Robert Marceau, engraved title and two plates little foxed, 3 plates slightly trimmed at fore edge without apparent loss, few leaves with light marginal foxing or soiling, otherwise excellent copy, plates bright and well preserved, leaves clean and fresh, sympathetic binding mint. Phillip J. Pirages 63 - 460 2013 $400

Doctorow, E. L. *Billy Bathgate.* Franklin Center: Franklin Library, 1989. First edition, one of unspecified number of copies printed and signed for members of First Edition Society, fine, signed on tipped in page, blue leather with raised bands, gilt decoration and titles and gilt edges, without dust jacket. Leather Stalking Books October 2013 - 2013 $60

Doctorow, E. L. *Drinks Before Dinner.* New York: Random House, 1979. First edition, finein fine dust jacket, inscribed by author for Ray Carver. Ken Lopez Bookseller 159 - 55 2013 $350

Doctorow, E. L. *Ragtime.* Taiwan: Piracy, 1975. First edition, inscribed by author, recipient's signature with inscription, near fine in fear fine dust jacket, scarce. Ken Lopez Bookseller 159 - 54 2013 $450

Doctorow, E. L. *World's Fair.* New York: Random House, 1985. Advance reading copy, shot from word processed typescript and reproducing holograph corrections and changes in text, inscribed by author in year of publication, recipient's name and date on front flyleaf, stray pen mark to fore edge, near fine in wrappers, together with a copy of the first trade edition, signed by author, again, recipient's name ad date, with slight splaying to boards, bit of color fading near spine, near fine in fine dust jacket with shallow crease to crown.   Ken Lopez Bookseller   159 - 56   2013 $500

Dodd, Anna Bowman   *Falaise The Town of the Conqueror.* Boston: Little Brown, 1900. First edition, 8vo., xiv, 280 blue cloth, pictorial stamping in gilt, top edge gilt, from the library of Florence Kelley, long inscription by author from another author, B. Van Vorsh, cover slightly spotted and little scuffed at edges and sides of spine, otherwise.   Second Life Books Inc.   183 - 106   2013 $85

Dodd, James Solas   *An Essay Towards a Natural History of the Herring.* London: printed for T. Vincent, 1752. First edition, 8vo., contemporary calf, double gilt fillet borders on sides, spine gilt ruled in compartments later green paper label, lettering in ink faded, slightly worn, contemporary ownership inscription of P. Bartley with note of the price (5s), armorial bookplate of Alexander David Seton of Mounie Castle, with pencil Mounie shelfmark inside front cover, good.   Blackwell's Rare Books   Sciences - 44   2013   £400

Dodd, William   *The Beauties of History of Pictures of Vittue and Vice.* London: printed by T. Maiden ... for Vernor and Hood; E. Newbery (and others), 1800. Third edition, frontispiece by Thomas Sothard, 12mo., titlepage vignette and wood engraved vignettes, some even browning, leading edge of titlepage little dusted, contemporary calf, spine rubbed, corners bumped, leading hinge neatly repaired, early ownership name of Ann Smith.   Jarndyce Antiquarian Booksellers   CCIV - 114   2013   £75

Doddridge, Philip   *The Rise and Progress of Religion in the Soul.* Chelsea: printed by Jaques and Thomas and sold by Goadby and Berry, circa, 1797. Fore-margin cut close, but without loss, 16mo., original sheep, black lettering piece to spine, lacking upper cover, lower cover nearly detached, spine worn and defective at head.   Blackwell's Rare Books   B174 - 48   2013   £500

Dodge, Mary Elizabeth Mapes   *Hans Brinker; or the Silver Skates.* New York: James O'Kane, 1866. First edition, 12mo., original green cloth, expertly rebacked, old back laid down, hinges reinforced, inserted frontispiece, 3 inserted plates, very good with narrow ink stain at upper blank margins of first 30 pages, early gift inscription, morocco backed slipcase.   Howard S. Mott Inc.   262 - 44   2013 $500

Dodgson, Charles Lutwdige   1832-1898   *Alice's Adventures in Wonderland.* London: Macmillan & co., 1866. First edition, 8vo., early full polished blue calf with triple gilt rules by Riviere with original covers and spine bound in at rear, spine has raised bands in 6 compartments with gold flower design, all edges gilt, gilt dentelles, fine, 42 illustrations by John Tenniel, remainder of the unacceptable first issue sheets were sent to New York and bound by Appleton, with new titlepage, tipped in to this copy is quirky 2 sided letter by author using his characteristic purple ink, dated Feb. 8 1888.   Aleph-Bet Books, Inc.   104 - 113   2013 $12,500

Dodgson, Charles Lutwdige   1832-1898   *Alice in Wonderland.* Paris: Black Sun Press, 1930. Limited to only 350 copies, printed on Rives paper, oblong 4to., white wrappers, 114 pages, covers and flyleaves lightly foxed, else fine in original slipcase and chemise (case scuffed and soiled some), illustrations by Marie Laurencin with 6 magnificent color plates, quite scarce.   Aleph-Bet Books, Inc.   104 - 114   2013 $4000

Dodgson, Charles Lutwdige   1832-1898   *Alice in Wonderland.* New York: Grosset & Dun, 1957. Folio, white pictorial boards, 110 pages, fine in slightly worn dust jacket, illustrations by Maraja with wonderful full page color illustrations.   Aleph-Bet Books, Inc.   104 - 115   2013 $250

Dodgson, Charles Lutwidge   1832-1898   *Alice's Adventures in Wonderland. (with) Through the Looking Glass and What Alice Found There.* London: 1866. 1872. First published edition, with inverted 's' on last line of contents page, first edition of second work, octavo, 42 illustrations by John Tenniel, including frontispiece, original cloth bound in at end, octavo, misprint "wade" instead of 'wabe' on page 21, 51 illustrations by John Tenniel including frontispiece, one page publisher's ads, with original cloth binding bound in at end; the two volumes uniformly bound by Bayntun-Riviere in red calf, boards ruled in gilt, gilt dentelles, all edges gilt, stamped and lettered in gilt, spines stamped and lettered in gilt with blue and green spine label on each volume, marbled endpapers, volume 1 with minor professional repairs to outer hinges, three quarter inch closed tear professionally repaired to outer margin of k3 of volume 1, bit of very light spotting on few pages, otherwise extremely nice set, housed in red cloth slipcase.   Heritage Book Shop   Holiday Catalogue 2012 - 26   2013 $12,500

Dodgson, Charles Lutwidge   1832-1898   *Alice's Adventures in Wonderland.* New York: D. Appleton, 1866. First NY edition, from sheets of true first English (suppressed) edition of 1865, small quarto, original red cloth, small crack on front joint expertly and almost invisibly closed, minimal wear to spine extremities, overall, housed in chemise with red morocco case.   David Brass Rare Books, Inc.   Holiday 2012 Chapter Five - DB02022   2013 $14,500

Dodgson, Charles Lutwidge 1832-1898 *Le Avventure D'Alice Nel Paese Delle Meraviglie.* London: Macmillan, 1872. First edition, 8vo., red cloth, top edge gilt, near fine, illustrations by John Tenniel, beautiful copy.   Aleph-Bet Books, Inc.   105 - 111   2013 $2500

Dodgson, Charles Lutwidge 1832-1898 *Le Avventure d'Alice nel Paese delle Meraviglie.* Turin: Ermanno Loescher, 1872. First Italian edition, half title, frontispiece, illustrations, duplicate title loosely inserted at end, original orange cloth, slightly rubbed, small repair to head of spine, all edges gilt, nice.   Jarndyce Antiquarian Booksellers   CCV - 55   2013   £1250

Dodgson, Charles Lutwidge 1832-1898 *Alice's Adventures in Wonderland.* London: Macmillan, 1886. 78th thousand, half title, frontispiece, illustrations, 1 page catalog, occasional pencil marks, later half red morocco, gilt compartments, contemporary gift inscription on half title, top edge gilt, nice.   Jarndyce Antiquarian Booksellers   CCV - 54   2013   £450

Dodgson, Charles Lutwidge 1832-1898 *Adventures D'Alice Au Pays Des Merveilles. (Alice's Adventures in Wonderland).* Paris: Hachette, 1907. One of only 20 copies printed on vellum, large 4to., full vellum discolored on corners of both covers, else fine, 13 large, fabulous tipped in color plates by Arthur Rackham with guards, numerous full page and in-text illustrations in line and pictorial endpapers, rare and special copy, this copy has an extra printed presentation page reading "Exemplaire Reserve Pour Madame Judith Gautier" (daughter of Theophile).   Aleph-Bet Books, Inc.   105 - 490   2013 $7500

Dodgson, Charles Lutwidge 1832-1898 *Alice's Adventures in Wonderland.* New York: Duffield/London: Chatto & Windus, 1908. First American edition with these illustrations, 8vo., rose colored cloth stamped in white, pictorial paste-on, 166 pages, corner stain on edge of few leaves, else very good+, illustrations by Millicent Sowerby, 12 beautiful color plates, plus illustrated chapter heads in line, extremely scarce.   Aleph-Bet Books, Inc.   104 - 116   2013 $450

Dodgson, Charles Lutwidge 1832-1898 *Alice through the Looking Glass and What Alice found there.* London: Macmillan, 1920. Original green pictorial cloth, gilt, few slight marks, 50 illustrations by John Tenniel, half title rather browned.   R. F. G. Hollett & Son   Children's Books - 115   2013   £25

Dodgson, Charles Lutwidge 1832-1898 *Alice in Wonderland and through the Looking Glass.* New York: Grosset & Dunlap, n.d. circa, 1925. 8vo., brown cloth, color photo paste-on, very good, 8 photo plates.   Aleph-Bet Books, Inc.   105 - 115   2013 $175

Dodgson, Charles Lutwidge 1832-1898 *Alice in Wonderland.* London: Raphael Tuck, n.d. circa, 1935. 8vo., cloth backed pictorial boards, some cover scratching and edgewear, very good+, illustrations by A. L. Bowley with 2 color plates, numerous black and white, marvelous double page color panorama pop-up.   Aleph-Bet Books, Inc.   105 - 116   2013 $500

Dodgson, Charles Lutwidge 1832-1898 *Alice's Adventures in Wonderland and through the Looking Glass.* Zephyr Books, 1946. First edition, original printed wrappers, hinges trifle rubbed, head of spine little chipped and creased, illustrations by Mervyn Peake.   R. F. G. Hollett & Son   Children's Books - 443   2013   £120

Dodgson, Charles Lutwidge 1832-1898 *Alice's Adventures in Wonderland.* New York: Maecdenas Press-Random House, 1969. One of 2500 numbered portfolios, printed on Mandeure paper, signed by artist, Salvador Dali, on titlepage, this being 307, large folio, original color frontispiece etching plus 12 full page color illustrations, each with original remarque, title printed in orange and black, loose as issued, publisher's brown cloth portfolio lettered gilt on front cover, fine, housed in publisher's quarter orange leather over linen clamshell case with leather and ivory clasps, about fine.   Heritage Book Shop   Holiday Catalogue 2012 - 35   2013 $8500

Dodgson, Charles Lutwidge 1832-1898 *Alice's Adventures in Wonderland.* West Hatfield: Pennyroyal Press, 1982. Limited to 350 numbered copies signed by Barry Moser, 75 wood engravings and additional suite of plates, each one signed by Moser, printed on handmade paper in red and black, this is stunning edition, folio, publisher's half purple morocco lettered in gold, marbled boards, bound by Gray Parrot, fine, additional suite of plates in cloth chemise, all housed in purple morocco backed and linen clamshell box (just touch of fading).   Aleph-Bet Books, Inc.   105 - 112   2013 $3500

Dodgson, Charles Lutwidge 1832-1898 *Eight or Nine Wise Words about Letter-Writing. (with) The Wonderland Postage Stamp Case.* Oxford: Emberlin and Son, 1890. First edition, presentation copies "Wise Words" inscribed on first page to Mabel Burton 'from the author, July 10, 1890', stamp case inscribed inside "M.B. from C.L.D. ap. 4 1890", 24mo., "Wise Words" stitched as issued, lightly spotted and with slight wear to spine ends, stamp case lightly foxed and with outer color printed cotton lined paper sleeve, very good.   Blackwell's Rare Books   172 - 41   2013   £4000

Dodgson, Charles Lutwidge 1832-1898 *Further Nonsense Verse and Prose.* New York: D. Appleton, 1926. First US edition, 4to., black cloth, fine in fine dust jacket, illustrations by H. M. Bateman in line, photos.   Aleph-Bet Books, Inc.   105 - 118   2013 $225

Dodgson, Charles Lutwidge   1832-1898   *The Game of Logic.*   London: Macmillan and Co., 1887.   Second edition, one of only 500 copies, 8vo., original scarlet cloth, gilt frontispiece, plans, envelope containing printed plan and full complement of nine counters, four red and five gray, slightly faded on spine and rubbed at head and tail of spine, front endpapers cracked at hinge, otherwise excellent copy, envelope slightly foxed, inscribed by author Feb. 19th 1894 for Helen M. Egerton.   Maggs Bros. Ltd.   1460 - 233   2013   £950

Dodgson, Charles Lutwidge   1832-1898   *The Game of Logic.*   London: Macmillan and Co., 1887.   Second edition, 8vo., original scarlet cloth, gilt, frontispiece pattern, other plans, envelope containing printed plan, two grey and one red counter (from five and four respectively), browned on spine and slightly worn at head and tail of spine, otherwise excellent copy, as is envelope, inscribed by author Mar 20 1894 for Ethel Mallam.   Maggs Bros. Ltd.   1460 - 234   2013   £950

Dodgson, Charles Lutwidge   1832-1898   *The Hunting of the Snark.*   London: Macmillan, 1876.   First edition, small 8vo., original red cloth, gilt decoration, all edges gilt, slightly bumped at head and tail of spine, otherwise excellent, this is the special presentation binding, 100 were bound thus, inscribed on dary of publication Mar 29 1876 for Jane Heaton Cunyngham Clark.   Maggs Bros. Ltd.   1460 - 231   2013   £3500

Dodgson, Charles Lutwidge   1832-1898   *The Hunting of the Snark.*   London: Dempsey, 1975.   Illustrations by Ralph Steadman, fine in near fine, price clipped dust jacket with some fading to edges and spine, signed by Steadman with drawing dated in year of publication.   Ken Lopez Bookseller   159 - 180   2013 $150

Dodgson, Charles Lutwidge   1832-1898   *The Hunting of the Snark. and All the Snarks. The Illustrated Editions of the Hunting of the Snarks.*   Oxford: Artists' Choice Edition/Ink Parrot Press, 2006.   First work is limited to 220 copies, of which 36 are case bound with set of handcolored prints produced by Anne Cathcart under artist's supervision, this copy XX/XXXVI in black cloth spine and printed blue-green paper covered boards with gilt lettered spine, set in Joanna, printed on Zerkall paper and bound by Chris Hicks; second work signed by Dr. Selwyn Goodacre, as new hardback, limited to 220 copies, this #89 set in Joanna, printed on Mohawk Tomahawk paper and bound by Chris Hicks, in as new dust jacket, 3 hand colored etchings, pencil signed by John Vernon Lord in separate folder and prospectus for the book and prospectus for Inky Parrot Press, housed in fine blue green paper covered slipcase with black and white paste-on illustrations, 4to.   By the Book, L. C.   36 - 29   2013 $750

Dodgson, Charles Lutwidge   1832-1898   *Sylvie and Bruno.*   London: Macmillan and Co., 1889.   First edition, 8vo., 46 illustrations by Harry Furniss original scarlet cloth, gilt, edges gilt, spine faded and rebacked, frontispiece and Magic Locket engraving colored by previous owner, otherwise very good, inscribed by author for May Nicholson May 26 1896.   Maggs Bros. Ltd.   1460 - 235   2013   £750

Dodgson, Charles Lutwidge   1832-1898   *Sylvie and Bruno Concluded.*   Macmillan, 1893.   First edition, original red cloth gilt, dust jacket spine little darkened, trifle frayed at head and foot, few light marks to front panel, one fold cracked and repaired on reverse, all edges gilt, with 46 illustrations by Harry Furniss, lovely crisp and clean in rare wrapper.   R. F. G. Hollett & Son   Children's Books - 120   2013   £450

Dodgson, Charles Lutwidge   1832-1898   *Sylvie and Bruno Concluded.*   Macmillan, 1893.   First edition, original red cloth, gilt little marked and darkened, all edges gilt, 46 illustrations by Harry Furniss.   R. F. G. Hollett & Son   Children's Books - 118   2013   £85

Dodgson, Charles Lutwidge   1832-1898   *Sylvie and Bruno.*   London: Macmillan and Co. 1889, but, 1898.   People's edition, Original green pictorial cloth, spine trifle rubbed, 46 illustrations by Harry Furniss, endpapers rather spotted.   R. F. G. Hollett & Son   Children's Books - 116   2013   £45

Dodgson, Charles Lutwidge   1832-1898   *Sylvie and Bruno Concluded.*   Macmillan and Co., 1898.   People's edition, original pictorial green cloth, 46 illustrations by Harry Furniss.   R. F. G. Hollett & Son   Children's Books - 119   2013   £30

Dodgson, Charles Lutwidge   1832-1898   *Sylvie and Bruno.*   Macmillan and Co., 1922.   Original green pictorial cloth, corner of upper board rather creased and bumped, 46 illustrations by Harry Furniss, endpapers rather spotted.   R. F. G. Hollett & Son   Children's Books - 117   2013   £25

Dodgson, Charles Lutwidge   1832-1898   *Through the Looking Glass and What Alice Found There.*   New York and London: Macmillan and Co., 1872.   First American edition, with misprint, 8vo., 6 leaves, 224 pages, contemporary brown cloth, stamped at top in gilt with title only, slight damage to outer hinges and trifle bit of staining on front cover, text foxed, tight, sound and very good with reddish salmon endleaves.   M & S Rare Books, Inc.   95 - 104   2013 $950

Dodgson, Charles Lutwidge   1832-1898   *Through the Looking Glass and What Alice Found There.*   Macmillan and Co., 1872.   First edition, First issue with 'wade' o page 21, frontispiece, with tissue guard, some light spotting, 8vo., original red cloth, boards and backstrip blocked in gilt, all edges gilt, binder's ticket, slightly soiled, spine bit darkened, two small repairs to rear joint, spine ends bumped, good.   Blackwell's Rare Books   B174 - 25   2013   £1200

Dodgson, Charles Lutwidge 1832-1898 *Through the Looking Glass and What Alice Found There.* New York: and London: Macmillan, 1883. Second edition (fiftieth thousand), 8vo., 224 pages + ads, blue cloth stamped in black and gilt, little fading and rubbing, very good, tight copy. Second Life Books Inc.   183 - 64   2013 $65

Dodgson, Charles Lutwidge 1832-1898 *Through the Looking Glass and What Alice Found There.* London: Macmillan and Co., 1887. 57th thousand, 8vo., original red cloth, 50 illustrations by Tenniel, slightly faded on spine, otherwise near fine, inscribed by author for Margaret Noel Jeune.   Maggs Bros. Ltd.   1460 - 232   2013   £750

Dodgson, Charles Lutwidge 1832-1898 *Through the Looking-Glass and What Alice Found There.* (bound with) *Alice's Adventures in Wonderland.* London: Macmillan, 1898-1899. 2 volumes in 1, large 8vo., old binder's cloth gilt, trifle bubbled, 92 illustrations by Joh Tenniel.   R. F. G. Hollett & Son   Children's Books - 121   2013   £35

Dodgson, Charles Lutwidge 1832-1898 *Through the Looking Glass and What Alice Found There.* New York: Harper & Bros. Oct., 1902. First edition with these illustrations, 8vo, white imitation vellum boards, gilt decoration, fine in original green cloth backed wrapper stamped in gold (green wrapper slightly faded, else fine), illustrations by Peter Newell with gravure frontispiece, with facsimile signature, plus 40 full page plates, beautiful pictorial border on each page of text, wonderful copy.   Aleph-Bet Books, Inc.   105 - 114   2013 $650

Dodgson, Charles Lutwidge 1832-1898 *Through the Looking Glass and What Alice Found There.* West Hatfield: Pennyroyal Press, 1982. Limited to 350 copies signed by Barry Moser, illustrated by him with 92 wood engravings, including additional suite of illustrations, each one signed by Moser, printed on handmade paper in red and black, folio, publisher's half morocco lettered in gold and decorative paper boards, bound by Gray Parrot, fine, with additional suite of plates in cloth chemise, all housed in morocco backed and linen clamshell box (with slightest touch of fading).   Aleph-Bet Books, Inc.   105 - 113   2013 $4000

Dodgson, Charles Lutwidge 1832-1898 *Through the Looking Glass and What Alice Found There.* Artist's Choice Editions, 2011. One of 322 numbered copies (of an edition of 420) signed by artist, printed on Mohawk cook-white paper in black and blue, title, chapter and shoulder titles printed in red, illustrations, almost all in color, a number full page, by John Vernon Lord, pages 144, small folio, original green cloth backed boards, backstrip gilt lettered, front board illustrated overall in color, rear board with large black and white design, black design of chequerboard on orange endpapers, new.   Blackwell's Rare Books   172 - 262   2013   £98

Dods, Marcus *The Bunker at the Fifth.* Edinburgh and Glasgow: William Hodge & Co., 1927. First edition, black cloth titled in red, illustrations, owner name on front fly, foxing on fore-edge that encroaches a little on some pages, else near fine lacking dust jacket.   Between the Covers Rare Books, Inc.   Mystery & Detective Fiction - 98477   2013 $1500

Dodsley, Robert 1703-1764 *A Collection of Poems in Six Volumes.* London: for R. and J. Dodsley, 1763. 6 volume, 2 engraved plates, engraved title vignettes and headpieces, half titles present, contemporary mottled calf, spines gilt, red and black spine labels, bindings moderately rubbed at extremities, few hinges cracking but secure, very attractive set, armorial bookplates of James Perrot and Admiral Duff, latter dated 1858.   Joseph J. Felcone Inc.   English and American Literature to 1800 - 8   2013 $500

Dodsley, Robert 1703-1764 *A Collection of Poems by Several Hands.* London: J. Dodsley, 1766. 6 volumes, engraved plate of music in volume iv, half titles present, small oval engraving on each titlepage, 8vo., contemporary sprinkled calf, backstrips with raised bands, red morocco lettering pieces in second compartments, small gilt tool in centre of remaining compartments, touch of wear to one or two headcaps, very good.   Blackwell's Rare Books   B174 - 49   2013   £600

Dodsley, Robert 1703-1764 *The Economy of Human Life.* London: printed for William Lane at the Minerva Press, 1799. Engraved frontispiece, 24mo., some minor browning to endpapers, slight offsetting from frontispiece, contemporary sheep, expertly rebacked, gilt banded spine, corners little worn, contemporary ownership name of D. Constable.   Jarndyce Antiquarian Booksellers   CCIV - 116   2013   £150

Dodsley, Robert 1703-1764 *The Economy of Human Life.* London: printed for William Lane at the Minerva Press, 1799. 24mo., frontispiece, some minor browning to endpapers, slight offsetting from frontispiece, contemporary sheep expertly rebacked, gilt banded spine, corners little worn, contemporary ownership name of D. Constable.   Jarndyce Antiquarian Booksellers   CCIV - 115   2013   £125

Dodsley, Robert 1703-1764 *The Toy-Shop; or Sentimental Preceptor. Designed for Instruction and Amusement.* Middlebury: published by H. Richardson, Copeland & Allen, 1819. 18mo., 34 pages, original printed wrappers (stained), text quite browned and foxed.   M & S Rare Books, Inc.   95 - 378   2013 $100

Doesticks, Q. K. Philander *The Witches of New York as Encountered by.* New York: Rudd & Carleton, 1859. Second edition, octavo, publisher's brown cloth gilt, stamped in blind, bookplate, old fire company library bookplate, erosion to cloth, particularly near crown, good copy. Between the Covers Rare Books, Inc. New York City - 292304 2013 $475

Doggett's New York Business Directory for 1846 & 1847. New York: John Doggett Jr., 1846. Map that served as frontispiece torn away leaving only small remnant, contemporary brown cloth, gilt, staining to cloth, fair only. Between the Covers Rare Books, Inc. New York City - 300856 2013 $300

The Doggy ABC. London: Thomas Nelson, 1920. Large 4to., 14 pages of illustrations, illustrated boards, good+. Barnaby Rudge Booksellers Children 2013 - 019719 2013 $50

Doherty, Hugh *The Discovery; or the Mysterious Separation of Hugh Doherty, Esq. and Ann His Wife.* London: sold at no. 12, Temple Place &c, 1807. Third edition, 12mo., illustrations, slight spotting and occasional small marginal tears, contemporary marbled boards, later tan calf spine, gilt ands and compartments, maroon morocco label, signature of author Hugh Doherty on title, very slightly trimmed through, additional signature of J. Wolus, Rysbrooke, 1878, recent bookplate of Peter Haining. Jarndyce Antiquarian Booksellers CCV - 93 2013 £580

Dolaeus, J. *Encyclopaedia Chirugica Rationalis.* Venetiis: Apud Ioannem Iacobum Hertz, 1690. Appears to be the second issue, 4to., 2 tall volumes, engraved title in red and black, frontispiece, modern quarter calf and cloth boards, some text browning and foxing, light dampstain in parts. James Tait Goodrich S74 - 91 2013 $750

Dolan, Liam *Land War and Eviction in Derryveagh 1840-1865.* Dundalk: 1980. Limited to 600 copies, 217 pages, cloth, illustrations, very good. C. P. Hyland 261 - 349 2013 £100

Dolben, Digby Mackworth *The Poems of Digby Mackworth Dolben.* London: Oxford University Press, 1911. First edition, inscribed by editor, Robert Bridges 'sent to the Times for review RB", rare (prospectus with manuscript note by Bridges) and errata leaflets inserted, original linen backed grey boards, spine label browned and bit worn, cloth on spine browned as are top edges of boards, offsetting to endpapers, else very clean, very good. The Kelmscott Bookshop 7 - 194 2013 $450

Dolbey, George W. *The Architectural Expression of Methodism.* Epworth Press, 1964. First edition, original cloth, gilt dust jacket price clipped, 24 pages of plates and plans, edges lightly spotted, presentation copy, inscribed by author, signed on title, uncommon. R. F. G. Hollett & Son Wesleyan Methodism - 7 2013 £45

Dolbier, Maurice *Jenny the Bus that Nobody Loved.* New York: Random House, 1944. First edition, 4to., pictorial boards, slight wear to spine ends, else near fine in dust jacket (few small mends on back of dust jacket, slight wear at folds else very good, not price clipped, illustrations by Tibor Gergely with color lithos or black and white lithos. Aleph-Bet Books, Inc. 105 - 267 2013 $200

Dollfus, Charles *Histoire de l'Aeronautique.* Paris: L'Illustration, 1932. First edition, 126 color and 1656 black and white plates, photos, plans, diagrams and maps, very good or better, boards rubbed, minor wear at extremities. Kaaterskill Books 16 - 26 2013 $500

Dolly's Library. London: Nister, n.d. circa, 1895. 24mo., cloth backed pictorial boards, as new in original publisher's box (slightly worn), 6 miniature books, 4 fine full page chromolithographs plus many in-text illustrations, rare in box. Aleph-Bet Books, Inc. 104 - 569 2013 $1200

Don Juan, a Poem by the Late Lord Byron and Forming Part of the Private Journal of His Lordship, Supposed to Have Been Entirely Destroyed by Thos. Moore. London: printed for the booksellers (Alencon: Imprimerie Veuve Felix Guy & Cie) 1866, circa, 1890. Half title, leaves roughly opened, ordinary paper edition original pink printed front wrapper, back wrapper sympathetically replaced, dusted and slightly chipped. Jarndyce Antiquarian Booksellers CCIII - 273 2013 £90

Don Juan, a Poem by the Late Lord Byron and Forming Part of the Private Journal of His Lordship, Supposed to Have Been Entirely Destroyed by Thos. Moore. London: Fortune Press, 1934. Number 868 of 1000 copies, half title, title in red and black, uncut in original plain black cloth, very good. Jarndyce Antiquarian Booksellers CCIII - 274 2013 £75

Don Juan: with a Biographical Account of Lord Byron and His Family; Anecdotes of His Lordship's Travels and Residence in Greece, at Genev &c. London: William Wright, 1819. First edition, half title, 3 pages ads, lacking frontispiece and with mention of it inked out on titlepage, some internal marks and slight dampstaining to last few pages, uncut in original boards, early spine replacement with appropriate pink paper, rubbed and marked, booklabel and signature of Alex Bridge. Jarndyce Antiquarian Booksellers CCIII - 272 2013 £250

Donahey, William *Teenie Weenie Land.* Chicago: Beckley Cardy, 1923. 8vo., pictorial cloth, 128 pages, fine, clean and bright, illustrations in color, extremely scarce in such fine condition. Aleph-Bet Books, Inc. 104 - 178 2013 $375

Donahey, William *Teenie Weenie Town.* New York: Whittlesey House, 1942. First edition, 4to., red cloth, pictorial paste-on, (72) pages, fine in slightly worn dust jacket, color pictorial endpapers, 10 full page color illustrations plus many black and whites. Aleph-Bet Books, Inc. 104 - 176 2013 $425

Donahey, William *The Teenie Weenies.* Chicago: Beckley-Cardy, 1917. 8vo., pictorial cloth, 128 pages, fine, clean and bright, illustrations in color, extremely scarce in such fine condition. Aleph-Bet Books, Inc. 104 - 177 2013 $375

Donaldson, Scott *Archibald MacLeish. An American Life.* Boston: Houghton Mifflin, 1992. First edition, large 8vo., 622 pages, illustrations, fine in dust jacket, inscribed by author to poet and editor, Bil Claire. Second Life Books Inc. 183 - 256 2013 $125

Donaldson, William *Gemini. The Initial 5 parts. Spring 1957-Spring 1958.* Sole editions, 4to., original printed white wrappers, near fine, scarce. Blackwell's Rare Books 172 - 185 2013 £150

Donders, Franciscus Cornelius *Astigmatisme en Cilindrische Glazen.* Amsterdam: C. C. Van der Post, 1862. First edition, 8vo., 15 figures, tables, light browning and spotting, modern half cloth, cloth corners, marbled boards, decorative endleaves, bookplate of Haskell Norman, very good. Jeff Weber Rare Books 172 - 81 2013 $500

Donne, John 1571-1631 *Biathantos (in Greek).* London: printed by John Dawson, 1644. First edition, first issue, small quarto, lacking initial blank, as often, contemporary calf, rebacked, red morocco label, some scuffing, housed in custom full brown morocco clamshell, gilt stamped on spine, small ink spot on titlepage, small burn through Q4 affecting few letters, generally quite clean and fresh, very nicely margined, small split along spine, near fine overall, from collection of Robert S. Pirie of Hamilton, Mass., previous owner's bookplate. Heritage Book Shop 50th Anniversary Catalogue - 31 2013 $8500

Donne, John 1571-1631 *Poems by J. Donne.* London: printed by M. F(lesher) for John Marriot, 1633. First edition, small quarto, this copy contains page 273 in corrected state (with running title and 33 lines of text), and bound without first blank leaf, but retaining last, two inserted leaves bound immediately after titlepage, 18th century mottled calf, neatly rebacked to style, minimal wear to extremities, trimmed close, though not affecting text, very lightly browned, bookplate of Robert S. Pirie, excellent, very fresh copy, custom quarter morocco clamshell. Heritage Book Shop 50th Anniversary Catalogue - 32 2013 $55,000

Donne, John 1571-1631 *Poems, &c. With Elegies on the Author's Death.* London: printed by T. N. for Henry Herringman, 1669. Fifth edition, complete with initial and terminal blanks, some dampstaining in later half of volume, contemporary calf, double blind ruled borders on sides, ornamental corner pieces, binder's flyleaf at end of early 16th century text printed in red and black, bearing contemporary (1669), signature of William Stanell, rebacked, cover crackled, bookplate of archaeologist John William Brailsford. Blackwell's Rare Books B174 - 50 2013 £3250

Donne, John 1571-1631 *Pseudo-Martyr: Wherein Out of Certain Propositions and Gradations...* London: printed by W. Stansby for Walter Burre,, 1610. 392 pages, 4to., 18th century half calf and marbled boards, black leather label, gilt rules and lettering, 2 often missing leaves following Table of the Chapters, containing ad to reader and errata; ink signature "Sam Foley/1689" in upper margin of titlepage, below is earlier signature that has been marked through, apparently by Foley, and is not decipherable by ordinary means, minor wear to binding including some rubbing to joints, few minor waterstains and occasional foxing, some line borders trimmed by binder in upper margin, as usual with this book, still unusually large, fresh and attractive copy. The Brick Row Book Shop Miscellany Fifty-Nine - 15 2013 $27,500

Donne, John 1571-1631 *Sermon of Valediction at His Going into Germany Preached at Lincoln's Inn April 18 1619.* Nonesuch Press, 1932. 35/750 copies, printed in Fell types on Auvergne handmade paper, typographic border to titlepage printed in red, usual foxing and browning to text, small folio, original (unusually clean), white boards with yapp edges, backstrip lettered in black and front cover stamped in blind to 17th century design, untrimmed, near fine. Blackwell's Rare Books B174 - 366 2013 £145

Donoghue, Denis *The Third Boice: Modern British & American Verse Drama.* Princeton: 1959. First edition, 8vo., cloth, dust jacket, very good. C. P. Hyland 261 - 976 2013 £29

Donovan, Arthur J. *Fatso: Football When Men Where Really Men.* New York: William Morrow and Co., 1987. First edition, fine in very slightly rubbed, otherwise fine, price clipped dust jacket, signed by author. Between the Covers Rare Books, Inc. Football Books - 327915 2013 $250

Doran, Adelaide Le Mert *Pieces of Eight Channel Islands: A Bibliographical Guide and Source Book.* Glendale: Arthur H. Clark Co., 1980. First edition, one of 1586 copies, 340 pages, illustrations and maps, light green cloth, very fine. Argonaut Book Shop Recent Acquisitions June 2013 - 93 2013 $125

Doran, F. S. A. *Their Majesties Servants; or Annals of the English Stage.* 1897. People's edition, 8vo., original cloth, dull, rear hinge worn, text and plates very good. C. P. Hyland 261 - 978 2013 £32

Dorgeles, Roland *Vacances Forcees.* Paris: Editions Vialetay, 1956. First edition, one of several deluxe copies "nominatif" (Marcelle Blanchet), produced for collaborators on book, from total edition of 233, printed on Rives wove paper, signed in ink by Dorgeles, Jacques Beltrand and the publisher, on justification page, 24 original color woodcuts, including 23 in texte, engraved by Beltrand after original watercolors by Raoul Dufy + a suite of 23 hors texte woodcuts on thin Japon paper in separate folder, woodcuts are color decompositions of one plate + a suite of 22 hors texte color decomposition woodcuts on Rives wove paper + one 'etat incomplet' woodcut, also in separate folder, also included is publisher's ad brochure, this exemplar inscribed to Marcelle Blanchet and signed by Beltrand, book's designer, page size 13 x 10 inches, overall size 14 x 1.5 x 3 inches, 224 pages, all sheets loose, as issued in wrapper portfolio, all housed in boards chemise and slipcase, unusually fine. Gemini Fine Books & Arts., Ltd. Art Reference & Illustrated Books - 2013 $3000

Dorman, Richard L. *D & R G W: Durango to Alamosa and Salida; Rocky Mountain Railroads. Volume II.* Santa Fe: 2005. Styled 'Collector's Edition", but not signed or numbered, 174 pages, illustrations, light shelfwear, else near fine, photos. Dumont Maps & Books of the West 124 - 61 2013 $75

Dorr, Rheta Childe *What Eight Million Women Want.* Boston: Small Maynard, 1910. First edition, 8vo., 339 pages, black cloth stamped in gilt, illustrations, ex-library with stamps and bookplate, cover someowhat scuffed at edges, front flyleaf missing, but very good, tight copy. Second Life Books Inc. 182 - 56 2013 $50

Dorrance, Ethel Smith *Damned: the Intimate Story of a Girl.* New York: Macaulay, 1923. First edition, pencil signature, small stain on top edge, light wear, very good plus in very good with two tears, small chip and some overall age toning. Between the Covers Rare Books, Inc. Sci-Fi, Fantasy & Horror - 55544 2013 $200

Dos Passos, John 1896-1970 *Henry and William, Ford & Hearst, Or Tin Lizzie and the Poor Little Rich Boy...* San Francisco: printed by Sherwood and Katharine Grover, 1940. First separate edition, one of only 35 copies, 4to., original tan linen cloth and printed paper label, fine. The Brick Row Book Shop Miscellany Fifty-Nine - 16 2013 $450

Dos Passos, John 1896-1970 *One Man's Initiation.* London: George, Allen & Unwin, 1920. First edition, 2nd state, with handwritten signed postcard from author laid in, in original envelope addressed to John S. Mayfield also laid in, very good in blue cloth boards, black title to spine and front board, fading to spine although title remains bright, offsetting to first and last couple of pages and remnants a sticker on rear pastedown, otherwise interior very clean, very good, 128 pages. The Kelmscott Bookshop 7 - 107 2013 $1300

Doudney, Sarah *Thistle-Down.* Marcus Ward & Co. n.d. circa, 1893. Original cloth backed pictorial boards, pages 32, full page color frontispiece and chromolithographed vignettes, patterned endpapers, nice, fresh copy. R. F. G. Hollett & Son Children's Books - 170 2013 £35

Dougall, John *The Self Instructor; or Young Man's Companion.* Halifax: William Milner, 1850. Original blind-stamped crimson cloth, gilt, pictorial gilt spine, little marked and neatly recased, frontispiece and title, 3 folding maps, new endpapers. R. F. G. Hollett & Son Children's Books - 171 2013 £85

Douglas, Gavin *The Poetical Works of...* Edinburgh: William Paterson, 1874. First edition, 4 volumes, 8vo., contemporary polished calf by Andrew Grieve of Edinburgh, sides gilt panelled with pairs of double fillets with fleurons in corners, spines gilt in compartments, twin red lettering pieces, top edge gilt, others uncut and unopened, spines trifle faded, fore edges lightly spotted, excellent, beautiful copy. Blackwell's Rare Books B174 - 51 2013 £600

Douglas, Gawin *A Description of May.* London: printed for J. Whitson and B. White, 1752. Second edition, 4to., outer leaves dusted, creasing to lower corner of top edge gilt, slight marginal wear to final leaf, faint waterstaining to final four leaves, some lower corners turned in, stitched as issued, with thread missing form upper section, early paper slip pasted at head of titlepage with number '140'. Jarndyce Antiquarian Booksellers CCIV - 117 2013 £120

Douglas, George M. *Lands Forlorn: the Story of an Expedition to Hearne's Coppermine River.* New York: 1914. xv, 285 pages, illustrations, 2 folding maps, some wear to extremities, else exceptionally clean, near fine copy. Dumont Maps & Books of the West 122 - 53 2013 $400

Douglas, James *Myographiae Comparatae Specimen; or a Comparative Description of All the Muscles in a Man...* London and Edinburgh: printed by A. Donaldson and J. Reed for Alexander Donaldson, 1763. Early edition, recased, small 4to., first and last leaves with minor marginal worming, rebacked, preserving original calf boards, extremities with minor nicks, early ink ownership signature of William Benser(?) (or Penrose), very good, rare. Jeff Weber Rare Books 172 - 82 2013 $1000

Douglas, Lloyd C. *Precious Jeopardy.* Boston and New York: Houghton Mifflin Co., 1933. First edition, octavo, 64 pages, inserted frontispiece, titlepage printed in blue and black, original decorated blue cloth stamped in gold. L. W. Currey, Inc. Christmas Themed Books - 134383 2013 $75

Douglas, Lord Alfred *The Autobiography of Lord Alfred Douglas.* London: Martin Secker, 1929. Second impression, 8vo., original blue cloth, inscribed by author, extremities worn, few marks to cloth, otherwise very good. Maggs Bros. Ltd. 1460 - 238 2013 £175

Douglas, Lord Alfred *The City of the Soul.* London: Grant Richards, 1899. First edition, inscribed by author to artist, William Rothenstein, original vellum backed blue-grey boards with faded gilt title to spine, spine slightly darkened and boards show minor signs of handling, previous owner affixed something to corners of front and rear endpapers with tape and tape has left residue on those pages, tape mark slightly overlaps Rothenstein's name but does not affect its legibility, typical offsetting to endpapers, Rothenstien bookplate, very good, 110 pages, 2 pages ads. The Kelmscott Bookshop 7 - 105 2013 $3250

Douglas, Lord Alfred *The City of the Soul.* London: Grant Richards, 1899. First edition, original Japanese vellum backed blue paper boards, lettered in gilt, near fine, boards just little browned, inscribed by author June 1899 for Edward Strangman. Maggs Bros. Ltd. 1460 - 237 2013 £500

Douglas, Lord Alfred *My Friendship with Oscar Wilde being the Autobiography of Lord Alfred Douglas.* New York: Coventry House, 1932. One of 100 numbered copies, signed by author, from a total edition of 1000, 8vo., original buckram spine and patterned boards, dust jacket nicked and rubbed, excellent copy. Maggs Bros. Ltd. 1460 - 239 2013 £500

Douglas, Norman 1868-1952 *Old Calabria.* London: Martin Secker, 1930. Fifth printing, 8vo., original green cloth, very good, spine faded, some soiling to back cover, endpapers browned, inscribed by author below his drawing of an owl for Ian Parsons. Maggs Bros. Ltd. 1460 - 240 2013 £300

Douglas, Norman 1868-1952 *Paneros. Some Words on Aphrodisiacs and the Like.* privately printed for subscribers by G. Orioli, Lungarno, Dec., 1930. First edition, out of series copy of the stated 250 numbered and signed copies, 8vo,., original decorated and 'vermiculated' gold cloth boards, black leather spine label, inscribed by publisher Pino Orioli for Nancy Cunard, then passed on to her principal assistant Winifred Henderson by author, with Henderson's bookplate, extremities slightly rubbed, otherwise excellent. Maggs Bros. Ltd. 1460 - 242 2013 £750

Douglas, Robert *Sophie Arnould.* Paris: C. H. Carrington, 1898. One of 425 copies, this #8, 238 x 154mm., titlepage vignette, engraved vignettes at beginning and end of text, allegorical frontispiece and 3 full page plates by Adolphe Lalauze, very pretty contemporary tan crushed morocco, gilt and inlaid, covers with border of leafy tools and French fillets, central panel formed by a delicate frame of plain and dotted rules punctuated by leafy ornaments, cornerpieces of inlaid black morocco inside wreath of gilt leaves topped by tulip, central panel with palmette and garland cornerpieces accented with floral tools, upper cover with gilt titling at center, flat spine gilt in one long compartment with multiple ruled frame and central inlaid black morocco dot with floral extensions terminating at head and tail with ornate leaf design, lavishly gilt wide inner dentelles, marbled endpapers, all edges gilt, original slightly browned printed paper wrappers bound in, elaborate - apparently original - pen, ink and wash scenic bookplate of Victoria Sackville-West with handwritten note (by her?) tipped in at front stating bookplate design was based on Lalauze's frontispiece (as is apparent), thin cracks alongside top inch of joints, otherwise only trivial defects, very attractive, luxurious paper clean, fresh and bright, margins very wide, handsome binding lustrous and generally well preserved. Phillip J. Pirages 61 - 110 2013 $1250

Douglas, Ronald *The Irish Book: a Miscellany.* 1936. First edition, 8vo., cloth, good, from an institutional library with stamps. C. P. Hyland 261 - 979 2013 £35

Douglass, Frederick *Narrative of the Life of Frederick Douglass, an American Slave.* Boston: Anti-Slavery Office, 1845. First edition, 12mo., 16, 125 pages, frontispiece, original cloth, slight wear to corners, bright copy, occasional foxing, remarkably nice. M & S Rare Books, Inc. 95 - 105 2013 $4500

Douthit, Mary Osborn *The Souvenir of Western Women.* Portland: 1905. Large 8vo., pages 200, illustrations, paper wrappers, partially unopened, ex-library with labels, bookplate, cover somewhat worn and edges slightly chipped, small tear in margin of pages 161-164, otherwise very good, tight, rare. Second Life Books Inc. 183 - 107 2013 $125

Dove, Rita *Through the Ivory Gate.* New York: Vintage Books, 1993. First Vintage Books, wrappers, warmly inscribed by Dove to fellow author, Nicholas Delbanco. Between the Covers Rare Books, Inc. 165 - 133 2013 $75

Dowden, Edward *Poems.* London: Henry S. King & Co., 1876. First edition, 8vo., original green cloth, decorated in gilt and black, excellent copy, extremities rubbed, inscribed by author for Mrs. Rae, inscription in another hand on front free endpaper has been effaced leaving only 'from A.M.'. Maggs Bros. Ltd. 1460 - 243 2013 £100

Dower, Kenneth Gandar *The Spotted Lion.* London: Heinemann, 1937. First edition, original brown cloth, gilt, 27 plates, folding map. R. F. G. Hollett & Son Africana - 54 2013 £30

Downey, David G. *Militant Methodism.* Cincinnati: The Methodist Book Concern, n.d., 1913. First edition, pages 379, few spots to fore-edge, original maroon cloth, gilt. R. F. G. Hollett & Son Wesleyan Methodism - 8 2013 £25

Downing, Andrew Jackson *A Treatise on the Theory and Practice of Landscape Gardening.* New York: Orange Judd, 1859. Eighth edition, 8vo., 576 pages, frontispiece, 6 additional steel engravings, 39 of wood, and six on stone, later calf backed marbled boards, new endpapers, little marginal waterstaining to first 50 pages, overall very good, tight, clean copy. Second Life Books Inc. 183 - 108 2013 $275

Dowsing, William *Rambles in Switzerland with Reminiscences of the Great St. Bernard, Mont Blanc, and the Bernese Alps.* Kingston: Upton Hull & London, 1869. 140 pages, 8vo., original plum cloth, gilt, uncommon. Maggs Bros. Ltd. 1467 - 38 2013 £250

Dowty, Aglen A. *(Don Juan). Jon Duan.* London: Weldon & Co. circa, 1874. 4to., illustrations, original color printed wrappers, spine defective, very good, bright, disbound. Jarndyce Antiquarian Booksellers CCIII - 277 2013 £65

Doyle, Arthur Conan 1859-1930 *The Adventures of Sherlock Holmes. (with) The Memoirs of Sherlock Holmes.* London: George Newnes, 1892. First edition, first impression; Londo: George Newnes, 1894. First edition, (with no name on street sign in The Strand Library device on front cover and misprint "Violent Hunter" for "Violet Hunter" on page 317), large octavo, 104 illustrations by Sidney Paget, original light blue cloth over beveled boards, front cover and spine blocked and lettered gilt and black, all edges gilt, gray flower and leaf endpapers, front hinge expertly and almost invisibly repaired, edges, head and tail of spine and corners bit rubbed and bumped, spine lightly sunned and rubbed, some light offsetting to free endpapers, minor foxing, previous owner's old ink inscription dated 1893 on half title, overall very good; "Memoirs" - large 8vo., 90 illustrations including frontispiece, original dark blue cloth over beveled boards, front cover and spine blocked and lettered gilt and black, all edges gilt, gold feather patterned endpapers, binding slightly cocked, edges, head and tail of spine and corners bit rubbed and bumped, previous owner's ink signature, overall very nice, both volumes housed in open-end slipcase. Heritage Book Shop Holiday Catalogue 2012 - 47 2013 $4500

Doyle, Arthur Conan 1859-1930 *The Case for Spirit Photography.* New York: Doran, 1923. First American edition, photos, slight browning to first opening of text, 8vo., original light brown cloth, lettered in black on upper cover, with mounted photographic image, backstrip also lettered in black, endpapers lightly foxed, tail edges rough trimmed, dust jacket defective at head of backstrip panel with loss of 10 letters and partial loss of 3 more, very good. Blackwell's Rare Books B174 - 201 2013 £500

Doyle, Arthur Conan 1859-1930 *A Case of Identity.* Kokie: Black Cat Press, 1984. Limited to 249 copies, signed by producer, 6.1 x 4.5 cm., leather, title gilt stamped on spine, decoration gilt stamped on front cover, marbled endpapers, miniature bookplate of Kathryn Rickard, from the collection of Donn W. Sanford. Oak Knoll Books 303 - 52 2013 $125

Doyle, Arthur Conan 1859-1930 *A Case of Identity.* Sacramento: Press of Arden Park, 1987. Limited to 120 numbered copies signed by Budd Westreich, 5.8 x 7.2 cm., cloth, title gilt stamped on spine, dust jacket, illustrations in text and on endpapers, with miniature bookplate of Kathryn Rickard, from the collection of Donn W. Sanford. Oak Knoll Books 303 - 34 2013 $100

Doyle, Arthur Conan 1859-1930 *Dangerous Work.* British Library, 2012. First edition, 80/150 copies, 4to., original quarter grey cloth, backstrip gilt lettered, board sides with facsimile overall of boards of original diary, cloth slipcase, new. Blackwell's Rare Books B174 - 200 2013 £150

Doyle, Arthur Conan 1859-1930 *The Great Boer War.* London: Smith Elder and Co., 1903. Complete edition, 19th impression, 8vo., original blue cloth, very good, little faded on spine, endpapers foxed, inscribed by author for I. E. Player July 30th 1906, loosely inserted ALS to Player from author. Maggs Bros. Ltd. 1460 - 246 2013 £450

Doyle, Arthur Conan 1859-1930 *The History of Spiritualism.* London: Cassell, 1926. First edition, 16 plates, foxing to prelims and final few leaves, 8vo., original mid blue cloth with dampstaining only to the very tips of the lower fore-corners of the cover, backstrips gilt lettered, good. Blackwell's Rare Books Sciences - 45 2013 £400

Doyle, Arthur Conan 1859-1930 *The Hound of the Baskervilles.* London: George Newnes, 1902. First edition in book form, small octavo, 16 plates by Sidney Paget, original scarlet cloth, spine slightly faded, otherwise excellent copy, gilt bright and fresh, full morocco clamshell box. David Brass Rare Books, Inc. Holiday 2012 Chapter Five - DB 00348 2013 $5500

Doyle, Arthur Conan 1859-1930 *The Hound of the Baskervilles.* London: George Newnes, 1902. First edition, first issue in book form, with 'you' for 'your' on page 13, line 3, small octavo, 16 black and white plates, including frontispiece by Sidney Paget, original scarlet cloth decoratively stamped in gilt and black (in a design by Alfred Garth Jones) and lettered gilt on front cover and decoratively stamped and lettered gilt on spine, bit of wrinkling to cloth, spine bit darkened cloth bit rubbed, bit of foxing to endpapers and edges of text block, few instances of brown stains to text, mainly to pages 68/69 and 74/75, housed in marbled paper slipcase, overall very good. Heritage Book Shop Holiday Catalogue 2012 - 48 2013 $2000

Doyle, Arthur Conan 1859-1930 *The Memoirs of Sherlock Holmes.* New York: A. L. Burt Co., 1894. First US edition, 8vo., original pictorial cloth, front free endpaper missing, spine slightly faded, with inked inscription in another hand, but very good, inscribed by author. Maggs Bros. Ltd. 1460 - 244 2013 £1250

Doyle, Arthur Conan 1859-1930 *The Memoirs of Sherlock Holmes.* London: Smith, Elder & Co., 1912. New edition, 8vo., original red cloth lettered in gilt, bookplate of Victoria Sackville of Knole and neat inscription to her by author, excellent copy. Maggs Bros. Ltd. 1460 - 245 2013 £750

Doyle, Arthur Conan 1859-1930 *The Poems of Arthur Conan Doyle.* London: John Murray, 1922. Collected edition, 8vo., original blue cloth, very good, lettering to spine faded and some evidence of paper having been stuck onto back pastedown and removed, inscribed by author Xmas 1922 to Mrs. English. Maggs Bros. Ltd. 1460 - 248 2013 £500

Doyle, Arthur Conan 1859-1930 *The Red-Headed League.* Sacramento: Press of Arden Park, 1985. Limited to 120 copies signed by Budd Westreich, 5.8 x 7.2 cm., cloth, title gilt stamped on spine, dust jacket, illustrated endpapers, illustrations, from the collection of Donn W. Sanford, miniature bookplate of Kathryn Rickard. Oak Knoll Books 303 - 35 2013 $100

Doyle, Arthur Conan 1859-1930 *A Scandal in Bohemia.* Skokie: Black Cat Press, 1984. Limited to 240 copies signed by producer, 6.1 x 4.5 cm., cloth, title stamped on spine, decoration gilt stamped on front cover, binding by Lariviere, miniature bookplate of Kathryn Rickard, from the collection of Donn W. Sanford. Oak Knoll Books 303 - 53 2013 $125

Doyle, Arthur Conan 1859-1930 *The Sign of Four.* London: Spencer Blackett, 1890. First edition in book form, second issue with foot of spine reading 'Griffith Farran & Cos. Standard Library", octavo, frontispiece by Charles Kerr with tissue guard, with numeral '138' on contents page incomplete and reading '13', as usual and with 'wished' appearing as 'w shed' on page 56, line 16; original dark red fine ribbed cloth blocked in black with front cover and spine lettered in gilt, all edges uncut, dark brown coated endpapers, minimal wear to spine extremities, pinhole in cloth of spine and corners bit bumped and rubbed, front inner hinge repaired with some new paper, overall very nice. Heritage Book Shop Holiday Catalogue 2012 - 49 2013 $7500

Doyle, Arthur Conan 1859-1930 *The Stark Munro Letters.* London: Longmans Green and Co., 1909. New impression, 8vo., original brown cloth, frontispiece by Alice Barber Stephens, pictorial titlepage, excellent copy, spine slightly faded, inscribed by author to Lady Sackville, Victoria Sackville-West. Maggs Bros. Ltd. 1460 - 247 2013 £850

Doyle, Arthur Conan 1859-1930 *Tales of Long Ago.* London: John Murray, 1922. First edition, small 8vo., later half red calf, some wear to extremities, otherwise excellent copy, inscribed by author for Abraham Wallace, with Doyle's visiting card loosely inserted. Maggs Bros. Ltd. 1460 - 249 2013 £750

Doyle, Arthur Conan 1859-1930 *The Valley of Fear.* New York: George H. Doran, 1914. True first edition, octavo, 7 full page illustrations by Keller, including frontispiece, publisher's red cloth with gilt spine and cover lettering, rare original dust jacket, couple of small scrapes to front board, jacket chipped and with short tears at edges, rubbed along joint and fore-edge margin, spine of dust jacket foxed, foxing and browning to endpapers, previous owner's embossed book mark on front free endpaper, bright, fine, very good dust jacket. Heritage Book Shop Holiday Catalogue 2012 - 50 2013 $10,000

Doyle, Arthur Conan 1859-1930 *White Company.* New York: Cosmopolitan Book Co., 1922. First Wyeth edition, 4to., maroon gilt cloth, pictorial paste-on, top edge gilt, very fine in white paper dust jacket (quarter size piece off mid spine), 3 small chips off bottom edges, else very good, illustrations by N. C. Wyeth, rare in such nice dust jacket. Aleph-Bet Books, Inc. 104 - 596 2013 $1350

Doyle, Richard 1824-1883 *In Fairy Land.* London: Longmans, Green Reader & Dyer, 1870. Large folio, green gilt cloth, all edges gilt, 31 pages, free endpapers replaced with matching paper, 1 tiny mend in title, else near fine, 16 color engraved plates, graet copy. Aleph-Bet Books, Inc. 104 - 179 2013 $3600

Doyle, Richard   1824-1883   *Jack the Giant Killer.*   London: Eyre & Spottiswoode, 1888.   (printed on cover), 4to., pictorial cloth, beveled edges, minimal soil, near fine, large full color illustrations enclosed within ruled border.   Aleph-Bet Books, Inc.   105 - 200   2013 $450

Doyle, Richard   1824-1883   *Journal Kept by Richard Doyle in the Year 1840.*   London: Smith, Elder, 1885.   4to., tan pictorial cloth, all edges gilt, 152 pages, covers uniformly soiled, else very good, mounted frontispiece portrait of Doyle with numerous illustrations throughout text.   Aleph-Bet Books, Inc.   105 - 201   2013 $300

Dozy, Reinhart   *Spanish Islam: a History of the Moslems in Spain.*   London: Chatto & Windus, 1913.   First English edition, large 8vo., folding map, frontispiece, original red cloth, spine slightly faded, else very good.   J. & S. L. Bonham Antiquarian Booksellers   Europe - 8501   2013   £150

Drachmann, A. G.   *The Mechanical Technology of Greek and Roman Antiquity.*   Copenhagen: and London: Munksgaard University of Wisconsin Press & Hafner, 1963. 8vo., 218 pages, orange cloth, black stamped spine title, dust jacket, ownership signatures, fine.   Jeff Weber Rare Books   169 - 199   2013 $70

Drake, Daniel   *An Inaugural Discourse on Medical Education: Delivered at the Opening of the Medical College of Ohio in Cincinnati 11 Nov. 1820.*   New York: Henry Schuman, 1951.   First edition thus, reprint limited to 500 copies, now quite scarce, fine, signed and inscribed by Emmet Field Horine (provided introduction).   Leather Stalking Books   October 2013 - 2013 $100

Drake, Francis   1540-1596   *Eboracum; or the History and Antiquities of the City of York.*   W. Bowyer for the author, 1736.   Lacking one plate of monumental inscriptions, otherwise complete, very good, clean copy in full contemporary calf, gilt spine, morocco label, joints and corners worn, some wear to spine, folio.   Ken Spelman Books Ltd.   73 - 3   2013   £420

Drake, Francis   1540-1596   *Eboracum; or the History and Antiquities of the City of York, from its Original to Present Times...*   London: W. Bowyer for the author, 1736.   60 engraved plates, 53 engravings in letterpress, very clean, large copy, contemporary sprinkled calf, gilt ruled borders, expertly rebacked in matching style, raised and gilt banded spine with handsome red morocco label, folio, inscribed "Richard Wood of Red Lyon Square and of Hollin Hall near Rippon in the County of York Esqr. 1778" with pen and ink crest beneath, later pencil note referencing a page in text that refers to the Wood family.   Ken Spelman Books Ltd. 73 - 2   2013   £850

Drake, Samuel G.   *Indian Captivities or Life in the Wigwam...*   Auburn: Derby and Miller, 1850.   First edition, 200 x 125mm., 367, (5) pages, publisher's green buckram, flat spine with gilt titling and large indian stamped in gilt on lower half, frontispiece, 3 full page illustrations and 6 vignettes in text; front free endpaper with pencilled ownership signature of F. D. Woodwell and ink inscription of C. H. Woodwell; extremities rubbed, cloth bit faded (with gilt not as bright as it once was), titlepage somewhat foxed, occasional minor foxing elsewhere, one gathering little loose, otherwise excellent copy, clean and fresh in solid original binding.   Phillip J. Pirages   63 - 258   2013 $350

Draper, B. H.   *The Juvenile Naturalist; or Walks in the Country...*   Henry G. Bohn, 1845.   Small square 8vo., original blindstamped cloth gilt, head of spine rather torn, all edges gilt, frontispiece and numerous woodcut text vignettes, new endpapers, first few leaves rather dampstained.   R. F. G. Hollett & Son   Children's Books - 172   2013   £30

Draper, Theodore   *American Communism and Soviet Russia.*   New York: Viking, 1960.   First edition, near fine with bookplate and little soiling, very light used dust jacket.   Beasley Books   2013 - 2013 $65

A Dream of Fair Women.   Indianapolis: Bobbs Merrill Oct., 1907.   First edition, 4to., tan cloth, pictorial paste-on, nearly as new, original blue ribbon, glassine wrapper and pictorial box, box worn on flaps, printed on heavy coated paper, illustrated with 20 full page color illustrations.   Aleph-Bet Books, Inc.   104 - 214   2013 $850

Dressler, Albert   *California's Pioneer Artist, Ernest Narjoi, a Brief Resume of the Career of a Versatile Genius.*   San Francisco: Albert Dressler, 1936.   First edition, of a total of 150 copies, this number 15 of 15 reserved for private distribution, presentation inscription from author for Bill Gilman, 2 tipped in reproductions, printed gold wrappers, fine.   Argonaut Book Shop   Summer 2013 - 249   2013 $90

Drew, Edward   *The Sludge.*   New York: Vantage Press, 1988.   First edition, fine in dust jacket (trifle rubbed, otherwise fine).   Between the Covers Rare Books, Inc.   Sci-Fi, Fantasy & Horror - 295983   2013 $250

Drew, Frederic   *The Jummoo and Kashmir Territories.*   London: 1875.   First edition, large folding map (in front pocket), 6 further folding maps (on 5 sheets), 7 folding profiles (on 2 sheets), frontispiece and 4 Woodbury type photographic plates, further illustrations, large 8vo., original cloth, rebacked, old spine laid down, small stamp on margin of title, 1 map with tear at fold, xv, 568 pages, presentation inscription from author for his brother Henry Drew.   Maggs Bros. Ltd.   1467 - 50   2013   £900

Drexel, Jeremias *Gymnasium Patientiae.* Coloniae: Agrippinae (i.e. Cologne, but Actually Amsterdam: Apud Cornelium ab Egmond (i.e. Blaeu), 1632. 16mo., engraved plates, contemporary vellum with yapp edges, spine moderately soiled, else very good.   Joseph J. Felcone Inc. Books Printed before 1701 - 30   2013 $300

Dreyfus, John *Italic Quartet.* Cambridge: printed at the University printing House, 1966. One of 500 copies, printed on Saunders' handmade paper, 10 illustrations and facsimiles, including 9 collotypes, royal 8vo., original beige cloth, lightly rubbed backstrip gilt lettered on brown ground, overall art nouveau design of rose buds in light and dark brown with intertwining dark brown links, slipcase, near fine. Blackwell's Rare Books   B174 - 322   2013   £140

Driggs, Frank *Black Beauty, White Heat. A Pictorial History of Classic Jazz 1920-1950.* New York: Morrow, 1982. First edition, 4to., fine in very lightly used dust jacket with tiny tears at few folds.   Beasley Books   2013 - 2013 $60

Drinkwater, John 1882-1937 *Cromwell and Other Poems.* London: David Nutt, 1913. First edition, inscribed by author for Agnes Murray, 8vo., original red cloth, spine little faded, very good.   Maggs Bros. Ltd.   1460 - 250   2013   £75

Drinkwater, John 1882-1937 *Shakespeare.* London: Duckworth, 1933. Second impression, 12mo., original red cloth, excellent copy, spine little darkened, some rubbing to edges of spine, inscribed by author for Ivor Brown.   Maggs Bros. Ltd.   1460 - 252   2013   £50

Drinkwater, John 1882-1937 *The Storm.* published by author at the Birmingham Repertory Theatre, 1915. First edition, 12mo., original green wrappers, fine, inscribed by author for John Masefield, with Masefield's bookplate. Maggs Bros. Ltd.   1460 - 251   2013   £100

Drummond, Henry *Tropical Africa.* London: Hoddger & Stoughton, 1889. Third edition, original cloth, gilt, rather darkened, head of spine trifle frayed, 6 folding colored maps, full page and text illustrations.   R. F. G. Hollett & Son   Africana - 55   2013   £35

Dryden, John 1631-1700 *Fables Ancient and Modern.* London: printed for Jacob Tonson, 1700. First edition, folio, tiny burnhole in one leaf (clear of text), two pinprick wormholes in lower margin of first half (few times stretching slightly but never near text), some light browning in places, few tiny stains, contemporary Cambridge style panelled calf, rebacked in different shade, corners repaired, few old scratches to old leather, hinges neatly relined, beginnings of early manuscript index, early ownership inscriptions of John Weekes and P. Towhouse?   Unsworths Antiquarian Booksellers   28 - 89   2013   £500

Du Bois, W. E. B. *The College-Bred Negro: Report of a Social Study Made Under the Direction of Atlanta University...* Atlanta: Atlanta University Press, 1900. First edition, octavo, printed blue wrappers trifle soiled with slight erosion of paper on unprinted spine, near fine.   Between the Covers Rare Books, Inc.   165 - 31   2013 $1000

Du Bois, W. E. B. *The Crises. A Record of the Darker Races. Volume 24 No. 4 Whole Number 142.* New York: NAACP August, 1922. 8vo., pages 147-190 + ads, original pictorial wrappers, front separate, lacking rear wrapper, some nicked and stained, good, rare, from the library of consumer advocate Florence Kelley, rare.   Second Life Books Inc.   183 - 114   2013 $175

Du Bois, W. E. B. *The Crises. A Record of the Darker Races. Volume 24 No. 5 Whole number 143.* New York: NAACP, Sept., 1922. 8vo., original pictorial wrappers, some nicked and stained, date stamp top of front cover, from the library of Florence Kelley, rare.   Second Life Books Inc.   183 - 113   2013 $200

Du Bois, W. E. B. *Dark Princess: a Romance.* New York: Harcourt Brace and Co., 1928. First edition, signed by author, bookplate of "The Wrights" on front pastedown, tiny bit of wear at crown, near fine, signed by author, exceptionally uncommon thus, lacking rare dust jacket.   Between the Covers Rare Books, Inc.   165 - 32   2013 $5000

Du Bois, William Pene *Giant Otto (and) Otto at Sea.* New York: Viking, 1936. First edition, 2 books, square 8vo., pictorial boards, light cover soil, else near fine in dust jackets in original pictorial box, quite rare in original box. Aleph-Bet Books, Inc.   104 - 180   2013 $1600

Du Chaillu, Paul B. *The Land of the Midnight Sun Summer and Winter Journeys through Sweden, Norway, Lapland and Northern Finland.* New York: Harper, 1882. First edition, 2 volumes, 8vo., copiously illustrated with engravings and map in pocket in rear volume 1, publisher's original sea blue cloth elaborately decorated with pictorial overall designs in gilt and red on upper covers and spines, covers wrinkled, otherwise very good.   Second Life Books Inc.   183 - 109   2013 $450

Du Chaillu, Paul B. *Stories of the Gorilla Country Narrated for Young People.* New York: Harper & Brothers, 1868. First edition, 8vo., green cloth with elaborate gilt spine and cover, 292 pages + ads, fine, tipped in charming 4 page handwritten letter from Du Chaillu dated 1868. Aleph-Bet Books, Inc.   104 - 181   2013 $1100

Du Chaillu, Paul B. *The Viking Age.* London: John Murray, 1889. First UK edition, 2 volumes, 8vo., frontispiece, illustrations, original red decorative cloth, spines little faded, otherwise good and clean.   J. & S. L. Bonham Antiquarian Booksellers   Europe - 9878   2013   £75

Du Laruens, Henri Joseph *Le Compere Mathieu ou les Bigarrures de l'Esprit Humain.* Paris: Chez Andre An IX, 1801. 4 volumes, most attractive set, contemporary calf backed marbled boards, gilt decorated spines, red and black morocco labels, some light foxing, scarce.   Ken Spelman Books Ltd.   75 - 52   2013   £160

Du Maurier, Daphne *Jamaica Inn.* London: Gollancz, 1936. First edition, original blue cloth, signed by author, slight foxing, otherwise excellent in browned dust jacket slightly worn at extremities, few marks on upper cover.   Maggs Bros. Ltd.   1460 - 253   2013   £8500

Du Maurier, Daphne *My Cousin Rachel.* London: Gollanxz, 1951. First edition, 8vo., original red cloth, very good, dust jacket torn at head and tail of spine, inscribed by author.   Maggs Bros. Ltd.   1460 - 254   2013   £1200

Du Maurier, Daphne *The Scapegoat.* London: Gollancz, 1957. First edition, 8vo., original red cloth, near fine, dust jacket slightly browned on spine, inscribed by author for Maurice Chevalier, August 1958.   Maggs Bros. Ltd.   1460 - 255   2013   £2250

Du Moulin, Pierre *The Antibarbarian; or a Treatise Concerning an Unknowne Tongue.* printed by George Miller for George Edwards, 1630. Lacking initial and two terminal blanks though the ante-penultimate present, titlepage little soiled and fragment of doeskin cord adhering and partially obscuring one letter, small 8vo., textblock sometime rather ruthlessly over stitched and all but loose in its original limp vellum, contemporary ownership inscription "John Clarkson His Book", soiled.   Blackwell's Rare Books   B174 - 52   2013   £900

Du Plessis, I. D. I *The Cape Malays.* Cape Town: Maskew Miller, 1944. First edition, original cloth, dust jacket rather chipped, spine spotted, 20 plates, scattered foxing.   R. F. G. Hollett & Son   Africana - 56   2013   £30

Du Verney, Joseph Guichard *Tractatus de Organo Auditus, Continens Structuarm Usum et Morbos Omnium auris Partium.* Nuremberg: Johann Zieger, 1684. First edition in Latin, 4to., (12), 48 pages, with 16 engraved folding plates, 19th century paper wrappers, plate 16 neatly backed, title very lightly soiled, else very good, Joseph Friedrich Blumenbach's copy with his signature, fine morocco backed clamshell box.   Joseph J. Felcone Inc.   Books Printed before 1701 - 67   2013 $4800

Dube, Annemarie *Erich Heckel: Das Graphische Werk.* New York/Berlin: Rathenau, 1964-1965. First edition, number 23 of 50 deluxe copies, 1/50 with 6 signed prints, 3 volumes, 12.9.5 inches, 74 pages, 1017 illustrations, 2 original woodcuts, 1 original etching, 1 original lithograph, all 6 original graphics are hors text and individually signed in pencil by Heckel, fine in cloth and slipcases, very rare.   Gemini Fine Books & Arts., Ltd.   Art Reference & Illustrated Books - 2013 $3000

Dublin Brigade Review. 1939. 8vo., 124 pages, modern cloth, very good.   C. P. Hyland   261 - 351   2013   £125

Dublin, Louis I. *Health and Wealth.* New York: Harper, 1928. First edition, 8vo., author's presentation to his daughter on blank, red leather, stamped in gilt, top edge gilt, marbled endpapers, edges little worn, otherwise very good, tight copy.   Second Life Books Inc.   183 - 110   2013 $75

Dublin, Louis I. *Twenty Five Years of Health Progress.* New York: Metropolitan Life, 1937. First edition, large 8vo., charts and graphs, blue cloth, stamped in gilt, cover little bumped at corners and somewhat scuffed, top edges little soiled, otherwise very good, tight copy.   Second Life Books Inc.   183 - 111   2013 $50

Dubouquet, Amelie *Le Dictionnaire Aux Mille Images.* Saint Saulve: no publisher, 1935. First edition, Narrow 8vo., cloth backed pictorial boards, some cover soil, else very good+, 1000 pictures in all, quite scarce.   Aleph-Bet Books, Inc.   105 - 10   2013 $400

Duche, Jacob *Observations on a Variety of Subjects, Literary, Moral and Religious in a Series of Original Letters.* Philadelphia: John Dunlap, 1774. First edition, 12mo., contemporary calf, rebacked corners rubbed, new leather label, errata, this copy belonged to Samuel Chase, signer from Maryland, of the Declaration of Independence, later Supreme Court justice, occasional staining.   Howard S. Mott Inc.   262 - 46   2013 $2750

Duck, Stephen *Poems on Several Occasions.* London: printed for W. Bickerton, 1737. Second edition, 8vo., engraved frontispiece, touch of minor spotting, contemporary sprinkled calf, unlettered spine divided by gilt rules, slight wear to headcap, boards scratched and rear board stained white, contemporary ink ownership inscription Thos. Packwood/E. Libris 1748 and later ink inscription 1811/ Sophia Killner her/Book. Southam Febry 19.   Unsworths Antiquarian Booksellers   28 - 90   2013   £250

Ducret, E. *Les Gamineries Punies.* Paris: Nouvelle Librarie de la Jeunesse, n.d. circa, 1899. First French edition, folio, cloth backed pictorial boards, light cover soil, tab end chipped else near fine, illustrations by Lothar Meggendorfer, with 6 slatted transformation plates, also illustrated in line on text pages by Meggendorfer.   Aleph-Bet Books, Inc.   105 - 382   2013 $3500

Ducuing, Jean *Phlebites Thromboses et Emboliespost Operatoires.* Paris: Masson, 1939. 478 pages, original half red polished calf and marbled boards, raised bands, light sunning to spine, otherwise very good.   James Tait Goodrich   S74 - 92   2013 $450

Dufferin and Ava, Harriot Georgina Blackwood, Marchioness *My Canadian Journal 1872-1878.* Appleton, 1891. First American edition, illustrations, frontispiece, 9 black and white sketches, folding map, original cloth, little rubbed. Second Life Books Inc. 182 - 63 2013 $125

Dufferin, Lord *Narrative of a Journey From Oxford to Skibbereen During the Year of the Irish Famine.* Oxford: Parker, 1847. First edition, 27 pages, disbound. C. P. Hyland 261 - 352 2013 £150

Dufferin, Lord *Narrative of a Journey From Oxford to Skibbereen During the Year of the Irish Famine.* Oxford: Parker, 1847. Third edition, 27 pages, frontispiece, modern plain wrapper, very good. C. P. Hyland 261 - 353 2013 £250

Duffus, R. L. *Mastering a Metropolis: Planning the Future of the New York Region.* New York: Harper & Bros., 1930. First edition, very near fine in attractive good or better dust jacket with shallow chipping, mostly on front panel. Between the Covers Rare Books, Inc. New York City - 293420 2013 $100

Duffy, Carol Ann *Thrown Voices.* London: Turret Books, 1984. First edition, limited to 1000 copies, small 8vo., original pale blue wrappers, near fine, inscribed by author. Maggs Bros. Ltd. 1460 - 256 2013 £75

Duganne, Augustine *Bianca.* New York: Samuel French, 1854? First edition, 100 pages, 8vo., original pictorial wrappers, some fraying and chipping, very good. M & S Rare Books, Inc. 95 - 107 2013 $400

Dugdale, Florence *Book of Baby Beasts.* London: Hodder & Stoughton, n.d., 1911. 4to., cloth backed boards, pictorial paste-on (120) pages, tips slightly worn else near fine, uncommon, 19 wonderful color plates, quite scarce. Aleph-Bet Books, Inc. 105 - 171 2013 $550

Dugdale, William 1605-1686 *Monasticum Anglicanum or the History of the Ancient Abbies and Other Monasteries, Hospitals, Cathedral and Collegiate Churches in England and Wales...* London: printed for Sam Keble, 1693. Folio, browned and foxed, each leaf mounted on tissue in gutter, a number of closed tears, repaired, modern half vellum, brown buckram boards, leather label (much rubbed), recent ownership inscription. Unsworths Antiquarian Booksellers 28 - 91 2013 £450

Dugmore, Arthur Radclyffe *Camera Adventures in the African Wilds.* London: Heinemann, 1913. 4to., original cloth, gilt, spine trifle marked, 104 illustrations, flyleaves browned, pastedowns little spotted. R. F. G. Hollett & Son Africana - 57 2013 £30

Dugmore, Arthur Radclyffe *The Wonderland of Big Game.* Arrowsmith, 1925. First edition, large 8vo., original cloth, gilt, 288 pages, 8 monochrome plates, 52 photos and map. R. F. G. Hollett & Son Africana - 58 2013 £75

Duhamel, Georges *Memorial de la Guerre Blanche.* Paris: Mercure de France, 1939. First edition, 8vo., original yellow wrappers preserved in folding cloth box, wrappers worn, hinges cracking, spine darkened, good copy, inscribed by author for Alfred Kerr. Maggs Bros. Ltd. 1460 - 258 2013 £175

Duhamel, Georges *Le Prince Jaffar.* Paris: Mecure de France, 1924. Second edition, 8vo. original yellow wrappers, preserved in marbled paper dust jacket with manuscript lettering piece to spine and folding cloth box, slightly scuffed at extremities, otherwise excellent, inscribed by author for Roger Fry. Maggs Bros. Ltd. 1460 - 257 2013 £450

Duhem, Pierre *Le Systeme du Monde: Histoire des Doctrines Cosmologiques de Platon a Copernic.* Paris: Libraire Schientifique A. Hermann et Fils, 1913-1959. First edition, 10 volumes, 8vo., figures, text clean and bright, original blue printed wrappers, bound in beautiful quarter gilt stamped red morocco over marbled paper backed boards, leather and corners gently rubbed, paper labels, Carnegie Institution of Washington Solar Observatory blindstamps at f.f.e.p.'s, very good. Jeff Weber Rare Books 169 - 128 2013 $750

Duigenan, Patrick *A Fair Representation of the Present Political State of Ireland.* Milliken, 1800. Genuine edition, 8vo., modern wrappers, very good. C. P. Hyland 261 - 354 2013 £120

Dujardin, Francois *Histoire de Chirurgie Depuis son Origine Jusqu'a nos Jours.* Paris: L'Imprimerie Royale, 1774. First editions, 2 4to. volumes, 4 copper engraved plates, new modern full brown calf, gilt paneled spines with raised bands, label in red leather, all edges marbled. James Tait Goodrich S74 - 93 2013 $1495

Duke-Elder, Stewart *System of Ophthalmology.* St. Louis & London: C. V. Mosby Co. & Henry Kimpton, 1958-1976. Complete set, mixture of St. Louis and London issues, 19 volumes, 8vo., 250 color plates, 350 text figures, blue cloth (15 volumes) and red cloth (4 volumes), dust jackets (3 volumes), signatures and embossed stamps of Bert Potts, very good. Jeff Weber Rare Books 172 - 83 2013 $800

Dulac, Edmund *Edmund Dulac's Fairy Book. Fairy Tales of the Allied Nations.* London: Hodder & Stoughton, n.d., 1916. Limited to 350 numbered copies, signed by artist, large quarto, 15 color plates, mounted on Japanese vellum, original white cloth pictorially stamped, minimal browning to endpapers, fine. David Brass Rare Books, Inc. Holiday 2012 Chapter One - DB 02168 2013 $2250

Dulcken, H. W. *Domestic Animals and Their Habits.* Ward, Lock & Tyler, 1865. Folio, original cloth backed pictorial boards, edges little worn, scrapes to lower board, 12 superb hand colored double page plates, joints cracked and little shaken, but very good.   R. F. G. Hollett & Son   Children's Books - 178   2013   £350

Dumas, Alexandre   1802-1870   *Chateau Rouge; or the Reign of Terror.* London: Routledge, Warnes & Routledge, 1859. 6 page catalog, original yellow printed paper covered boards, slightly rubbed with wear to leading hinge, good plus.   Jarndyce Antiquarian Booksellers   CCV - 95   2013   £85

Dumas, Alexandre   1802-1870   *The Count of Monte Cristo.* London: 1846. First edition in English in book form, 20 woodcut plates, including frontispieces, however frontispiece to volume 1 has been bound between pages 2 and 3) by M. Valentin, late 19th century/early 20th century full speckled calf, almost invisibly rebacked to style, boards double ruled gilt, spines stamped in gilt, spines each with red and black morocco spine labels, lettered gilt, gilt dentelles, marbled endpapers, top edge gilt, few very small spots of foxing in text, few plates with some minor toning to fore edge, not affecting illustration, few pages have been opened bit rough, previous owner's signature to each volume, dated 1889, same owner's old notes final blank volume 1, dated 1923, overall very good.   Heritage Book Shop   Holiday Catalogue 2012 - 51   2013 $10,000

Dumas, Alexandre   1802-1870   *La Dame De Monsoreau.* Boston: Little Brown and Co., 1889. First edition thus, 2 volumes, 8vo., top edge gilt, maroon cloth, spine and front cover elaborately stamped in gilt, very good.   Second Life Books Inc.   183 - 117   2013 $125

Dumas, Alexandre   1802-1870   *A Gil Blas in California.* Los Angeles: Primavera Press, 1933. First English translation, one of 500 copies, folding wood-block map and 20 wood-block illustrations by Paul Landacre, notes, gray cloth, printed paper spine label, very fine and bright with worn pictorial dust jacket.   Argonaut Book Shop   Summer 2013 - 87   2013 $150

Dumas, Charles Louis   *Doctrine Generale des Maladies Chroniques...* Paris: chez Deterville, 1812. 8vo., quarter brown roan leather, rubbed and worn along spine, green patterned boards, text lightly toned, overall very good tight copy, signed copyright with Dumas signature.   James Tait Goodrich   S74 - 94   2013 $275

Dumas, Charles Louis   *Principes de Physiologie ou Intruduction a la Science Experimentale, Philosophique et Medicale de l'Homme Vivant...* Paris: Chez Mequignon Marvis Libraire, 1806. Second edition, 4 volumes, 8vo., 1 folding engraved plate, modern quarter tan calf, marbled paper over boards, former library stamp on titlepage, otherwise fine, scarce.   Jeff Weber Rare Books   172 - 84   2013 $750

Dumont, Pierre Joseph   *Narrative of Thirty-Four Years Slavery and Travels in Africa.* London: Sir Richard Phillips & Co., 1819. 42 pages, frontispiece, uncut, disbound, from the library of Anne and Fernand Renier.   Jarndyce Antiquarian Booksellers   CCV - 96   2013   £120

Cuna De Daiquiri Cocktail. Havana: Artes Graficas, S. A., 1939. printed wrappers, 4.5 x 6 inches, 63, (1) pages, faint dampstain on edge of rear wrapper and on last leaf, few small stains on facing pages 24-25, very good.   Between the Covers Rare Books, Inc.   Cocktails, Etc. - 284332   2013 $250

Dunbar, Paul Laurence   *A Cabin Tale.* San Francisco: Julian Richardson Associates, 1969. First separate edition, stapled wrappers, 28 pages, slight offsetting to wrappers and old tiny ink price on first leaf, else about fine, very scarce.   Between the Covers Rare Books, Inc.   165 - 138   2013 $125

Dunbar, Paul Laurence   *Candle-Lightin- Time.* New York: Dodd, Mead & Co., 1901. First edition, photos, small contemporary bookplate and some offsetting to flyleaves from jacket flaps, else fine in good plus example of rare dust jacket with several chips at extremities, superb copy, fragile jacket.   Between the Covers Rare Books, Inc.   165 - 36   2013 $2000

Dunbar, Paul Laurence   *Chris'mus is A'comin' & Other Poems.* New York: Dodd, Mead and Co., 1907. Reprint of 1905 first edition, with different designs on front wrapper and titlepage and with decorated initial letter of text in green, stiff wrappers, neat gift inscription, tiny tears to wrappers, tiny stain to edge of one page still fine in rare, original unprinted glassine dust jacket with mild wear, lovely copy, exceptionally uncommon.   Between the Covers Rare Books, Inc.   165 - 135   2013 $250

Dunbar, Paul Laurence   *Folks from Dixie.* New York: Dodd, Mead, 1898. First edition, 8vo., cloth, 263 pages, top edge gilt, near fine, illustrations by E. W. Kemble with 2 color plates and 6 black and white plates.   Aleph-Bet Books, Inc.   104 - 77   2013 $350

Dunbar, Paul Laurence   *Lyrics of Lowly Life.* London: Chapman & Hall, 1897. First British edition, half title, frontispiece, occasional pencil underlining, original dark grey cloth, news clipping laid down on leading pastedown, inscription "Helen R. C. Ostling with love from Irene, Xmas 1905", all edges gilt, near fine.   Jarndyce Antiquarian Booksellers   CCV - 98   2013   £180

Dunbar, Paul Laurence   *Majors and Minors.* Toledo: Hadley & Hadley, 1895. First edition, tan cloth with unbevelled boards, titled gilt on front board frontispiece, fragile front endpaper detached but present, hinges slightly started and some foxing to boards, else very good, rare.   Between the Covers Rare Books, Inc.   165 - 35   2013 $1250

Dunbar, Paul Laurence *Oak and Ivy.* Dayton: Press of the United Brethren Pub. House, 1893. First edition, red cloth titled in gilt, professionally and pretty much seamlessly recased, little spotting to boards, couple of older professional paper repairs on couple of leaves, still handsome and very presentable copy, rare, lovely copy. Between the Covers Rare Books, Inc. 165 - 33 2013 $4000

Dunbar, Paul Laurence *Oak and Ivy.* Dayton: Press of the United Brethren Pub. House, 1893. First edition, blue cloth titled gilt, professionally recased, hinges strengthened, few modest and older professional paper repairs o few leaves, still handsome and presentable copy. Between the Covers Rare Books, Inc. 165 - 34 2013 $3000

Dunbar, Paul Laurence *The Complete Poems of Paul Laurence Dunbar.* New York: Dodd, Mead & Co., 1913. First edition, contemporary owner name, else very good or better with some light wear at extremities, lacking rare dust jacket. Between the Covers Rare Books, Inc. 165 - 136 2013 $200

Dunbar, Paul Laurence *The Uncalled.* New York: Dodd, Mead & Co., 1898. first edition, binding B, with author's first name spelled correctly, bit cocked, else very good or better with lettering and decoration largely unrubbed. Between the Covers Rare Books, Inc. 165 - 134 2013 $300

Dunbar, Paul Laurence *When Malindy Sings.* New York: Dodd Mead & Co., 1903. First edition, frontispiece and photo illustrations, professionally recased, two moderate stains on rear board, else very good in very good plus, supplied example of the rare dust jacket with couple of very small chips and in internally repaired text, housed in custom half leather and marbled paper clamshell case, inscribed by author for Dr. William "Buf" Burns, physician from Dayton. Between the Covers Rare Books, Inc. 165 - 37 2013 $4500

Duncan, Isadora *My Life.* New York: Boni & Liveright, 1927. Limited edition, number 445 of 650 copies, 24 black and white photos (2 by Arnold Genthe), one of the 'presentation copies' published as a limited edition, very good, black cloth boards with red leather label titled gilt on spine, light rubbing to boards, wear to spine ends, few small chips tot title label, clean and bright, 359 pages. The Kelmscott Bookshop 7 - 110 2013 $250

Duncan, Robert *Caesar's Gate: Poems 1949-1950.* Palma de Majorca: Divers Press, 1955. First edition, one of 10 copies with original collage by Jess and original manuscript poems by Duncan, signed by poet and artist, the entire edition consisted of 213 copies of which 200 were regular copies for regular circulation and 13 special copies marked A to C and 1 to 10, this number 8, 8vo., illustrations, original pictorial white wrappers, marbled paper slipcase with pictorial label on front, printed label on spine, very fine in slipcase, preserved in folding cloth chemise. James S. Jaffe Rare Books Fall 2013 - 40 2013 $15,000

Duncan, Robert *Faust Foutu. Act One (-Act Four).* San Francisco: privately printed by author, 1953. One of 100 copies printed, 4to., loose mimeographed sheets, this copy accompanied by large manila envelope addressed by Mary Fabilli to Robert Duncan in Stinson Beach, fine, rare. James S. Jaffe Rare Books Fall 2013 - 39 2013 $2500

Duncan, Robert *Letters.* Highlands: Jargon Society, 1958. First edition, 4to., five drawings by author, quarter leather and marbled boards, deluxe issue, specially bound with hand decorations by poet, one of 15 copies with original watercolor painting by Duncan as frontispiece, out of the issue of 60 copies, printed on Shogun paper, specially bound and signed by Duncan and including original pen and ink drawing by Duncan on endpapers, out of a total edition of 510, watercolor in this copy initialled by RD, leather spine very slightly scuffed as usual, otherwise fine, rarest form. James S. Jaffe Rare Books Fall 2013 - 41 2013 $4000

Duncan, Robert *Medea at Kolchis. The Maiden Head.* Berkeley: Oyez, 1965. First edition, hardbound issue, one of 28 numbered copies, signed by author, out of a total edition of 500, although not called for, this copy also signed by Graham Mackintosh, book's designer and printer, 8vo., original unprinted linen over boards, dust jacket, the second dust jacket with same design (as first) but printed on white enameled stock, with design of first jacket embossed on front cover, covers slightly splayed, otherwise fine. James S. Jaffe Rare Books Fall 2013 - 43 2013 $1250

Duncan, Robert *Poems 1948-49.* Berkeley: Miscellany Editions, 1949. First edition, second (expurgated) state, 8vo., original printed wrappers, usual, but in this instance very faint, discoloration to poor quality paper wrappers, still fine, presentation copy from author to his mother. James S. Jaffe Rare Books Fall 2013 - 38 2013 $2500

Duncan, Robert *Six Prose Pieces.* Rochester: Perishable Press Ltd., 1966. First edition, special issue, one of only 15 copies printed on handmade paper made by Walter Hamady, the printer/publisher, signed by Duncan, out of a total edition of 70 copies, illustrations by author, unbound folded & gathered signatures, natural linen cloth chemise, facsimile signature printed in red, matching slipcase, presentation copy from author inscribed and signed in full by Duncan for Hamady, slipcase very slightly soiled otherwise fine, scarce.   James S. Jaffe Rare Books   Fall 2013 - 44   2013 $6000

Duncan, Robert *A Song from the Structures of Rime Ringing as the Poet Paul Celan Sings.* Malakoff, France: Chutes: Orange Export Ltd., 1977. First edition, one of 9 copies printed by hand by Emmanuel Hocquard, numbered and signed by Duncan, oblong small 8vo., loose sheets in original printed folder, glassine dust jacket, very fine, Duncan's rarest book, folding cloth box.   James S. Jaffe Rare Books   Fall 2013 - 47   2013 $7500

Duncan, Robert *Writing Writing.* Portland: Trask House, 1971. First Trask House edition (1000 copies printed), large 8vo., original stapled printed wrappers, presentation copy inscribed by Duncan to book's publisher Carlos Reyes, April 1971, accompanied by TLS from Duncan to Reyes, 1 page, Feb. 25 1971, accompanied by one quarto sheet of original pen and ink drawings by Duncan captioned "two studies for the Epilogos drawings for Henry and Adele/RD/ June 1967" in Duncan's holograph, handmade 1970 Christmas card, 14 line greeting in Duncan's holograph with original crayon design initialed by Duncan with original mailing envelope and handmade 1971 New Year's card, in both Duncan's and Jess' hand, folded from mailing, otherwise fine.   James S. Jaffe Rare Books   Fall 2013 - 46   2013 $2500

Duncan, Robert *The Years as Catches. First Poems (1939-1946).* Berkeley: Oyez, 1966. First edition, deluxe hardbound issue, one of 30 numbered and signed hors commerce copies with original endpaper decorations by author (out of 200 copies comprising the hardbound issue), 8vo., pictorial boards, dust jacket, very fine.   James S. Jaffe Rare Books   Fall 2013 - 45   2013 $2250

Duncanson, Andrew *The Saint's Duty and Britain's Safety.* Glasgow: printed by A. Duncan and R. Chapman, 1794. First edition, trifle browned, 8vo., 33 pages, modern marbled wrappers, 3 manuscript marginal annotations (cropped), good, rare.   Blackwell's Rare Books   B174 - 53   2013   £250

Duncanson, John Victor *Rawdon and Douglas: Two Loyalist Townships in Nova Scotia.* Belleville: Mika Pub., 1989. 8vo., blue cloth boards, gilt titles to front and spine, half title, numerous maps and illustrations, very good, dust jacket slightly worn along edges generally very good.   Schooner Books Ltd.   101 - 89   2013 $95

Duncon, John *The Holy Life and Death of the Lady Letice, Vi-Countess Falkland.* London: Richard Royston, 1653. third edition, 12mo., frontispiece slightly offset to titlepage, little worming near gutter, occasional light spotting, contemporary blind tooled calf, marbled endpapers, calf crackled, bit chipped, small loss to front board, old inconspicuous repairs to spine, several ownership inscriptions to initial blanks, first illegible "S. Sparke a gift of M.S. 1798?" "Sarah Sparke 1798 to her niece (?) M. Amery.   Unsworths Antiquarian Booksellers   28 - 92   2013   £400

Dunderdale, J. W. *Kendal Brown.* Kendal: Helm Press, 2003. First edition, original pictorial wrappers, 174 pages, illustrations, signed by editor, Anne Bonney on titlepage.   R. F. G. Hollett & Son   Lake District and Cumbria - 50   2013   £25

Dundonald, Archibald Cochrane, 9th Earl of *A Treatise Shewing the Intimate Connection that Subsists Between Agriculture and Chemistry.* printed for the author and sold by R. Edwards, March, 1795. First edition, printed on blueish paper, inscribed "From the author" ad below this signature of J(John) Scott, first Lord Eldon, Chancellor of Exchequer, with his small circular armorial bookplate inside front cover, inside front cover inscribed 'Eldon' 4to., uncut in original drab board, little soiling an wear, spine defective little at head and foot, very good.   Blackwell's Rare Books   Sciences - 31   2013   £450

Dunham, Curtis *The Golden Goblin.* Indianapolis: Bobbs Merrill, Sept., 1906. First edition, 8 color plates by George Kerr, every page illustrated with text being superimposed upon illustrations, scarce, 4to., grey pictorial boards, slight wear, near fine.   Aleph-Bet Books, Inc.   104 - 60   2013 $600

Dunham, I. N. *The DNA Sequence of Human Chromosome 22.* Offprint from Nature Volume 402, 2 Dec., 1999. fine in original printed wrappers.   By the Book, L. C.   37 - 28   2013 $300

Dunlap, William *History of the New Netherlands, Province of New York and State of New York to the Adoption of the Federal Constitution.* New York: printed for the author by Carter and Thorp, 1839. First edition, 2 volumes, publisher's cloth, gilt, considerable dampstaining to text and boards, fair copy only.   Between the Covers Rare Books, Inc. New York City - 297297   2013 $150

Dunn, Dorothy *American Indian Painting of the Southwest and Plains Area.* Albuquerque: 1968. 429 pages, illustrations, clean, near fine, bright dust jacket, beautiful copy, 15 illustrations, 33 in full color.   Dumont Maps & Books of the West   124 - 62   2013 $150

Dunne, J. *Orders, Rules, Regulations and Instructions framed and Issued for the Government and Guidance of the Cumberland and Westmorland County Police Under the Acts 2 and 3...* Carlisle: Charles Thurnam & Sons, 1857. Original diced roan, upper hinge cracked, folding table and 12 page 12mo leaflet on abstracts relating to cruelty to animals (RSPCA 1857) printed on yellow paper, tipped in at end, little scattered fingering and spotting, joints strengthened with tape, but very good, extremely scarce. R. F. G. Hollett & Son Lake District and Cumbria - 51 2013 £350

Dunnett, Dorothy *Match for a Murderer.* Boston: Houghton Mifflin, 1971. First edition, fine in fine dust jacket, beautiful copy. Between the Covers Rare Books, Inc. Mystery & Detective Fiction - 316194 2013 $350

Dunsany, Edward John Moreton Drax Plunkett 1878-1957 *The Gods of Pegana.* London: Elkin Mathews, 1905. First edition, square 8vo., original quarter cloth, grey boards, excellent. Maggs Bros. Ltd. 1442 - 72 2013 £100

Dunsany, Edward John Moreton Drax Plunkett 1878-1957 *Guerrilla.* 1944. First US edition, 8vo., cloth, very good. C. P. Hyland 261 - 983 2013 £32

Dunsany, Edward John Moreton Drax Plunkett 1878-1957 *The King of Elfland's Daughter.* London/New York: G. P. Putnam's, 1924. Number 66 of 250 copies signed by author and artist, 4to., original quarter vellum, excellent. Maggs Bros. Ltd. 1442 - 73 2013 £375

Dunsany, Edward John Moreton Drax Plunkett 1878-1957 *The Last Revolution.* London: New York: Melbourne: Sydney; Cape Town: Jarrolds Pub., 1951. First edition, octavo, cloth. L. W. Currey, Inc. Uptopian Literature: Recent Acquisitions (April 2013) - 140876 2013 $150

Dunsany, Edward John Moreton Drax Plunkett 1878-1957 *The Old Folk of the Centuries.* London: Elkin Matthews, 1930. First edition, 8vo., original quarter cloth, marbled paper boards, number 861 of 1000 copies, this being one of 50 copies for presentation, boards scuffed, spine dusty, otherwise very good, inscribed by author for Pansy Longford who married Henry Lamb. Maggs Bros. Ltd. 1460 - 259 2013 £500

Dunsany, Edward John Moreton Drax Plunkett 1878-1957 *Plays of Gods & Men.* London: 1917. Dublin printed, first edition, 8vo., portrait, quarter cloth, good. C. P. Hyland 261 - 982 2013 £27

Dupin, Charles *Developpements de Geometrie, avec des Applications a la Stabilite das Vaisseaux, aux Deblais et Remblais au Defilement a l'optique etc....* Paris: the widow Courcier, 1813. First edition, 11 engraved plates, slight browning in places, 4to., uncut and unopened in original speckled boards, pastedowns from a double columned religious work, spine darkened and lacking label, good. Blackwell's Rare Books Sciences - 46 2013 £650

Duplaix, Lily *Pedro, Nina and Perrito.* New York: Harper Bros., 1939. First edition, large 4to., cloth backed pictorial boards, tiny mend on edge of endpaper, else fine in very good with piece off spine, color lithographs by Barbara Latham, scarce in jacket. Aleph-Bet Books, Inc. 105 - 355 2013 $250

Dupuytren, Guillaume *Lecons Orales de Clinique Chirurgicale.* Paris: Germer Bailliere, 1839. 1839, 6 volumes, bound in later marbled boards, rebacked with plain brown linen, no labels, from the collection of Dr. Willard Parker and his signature on front fly of each volume, library stamp on titles, no external markings. James Tait Goodrich 75 - 86 2013 $1495

Dupuytren, Guillaume *Lectures on Clinical Surgery Delivered in the Hotel Dieu of Paris.* Washington: Duff Green, 1835. 548 pages, with content leave bound in back, original full brown calf, light rubbing and joints cracked but solid, rubber library stamp on title, remnants of call number on spine, text foxed in parts. James Tait Goodrich S74 - 95 2013 $150

Durant, Frederick C. *Worlds Beyond the Art of Chesley Bonestell.* Norfolk: Virginia Beach: Donning, 1983. First edition, limited to 300 copies, this no. 103, 4to., 133 pages, fine in original matching slipcase, signed by Bonestell on tipped in bookplate. By the Book, L. C. 36 - 101 2013 $475

Durcan, Paul *Jumping the Tracks with Angela.* Dublin: Raven Arts Press/ Carcanet New Press, 1983. First edition, 8vo., original sand cloth, dust jacket, signed by author, near fine, slightly rubbed dust jacket. Maggs Bros. Ltd. 1442 - 76 2013 £250

Durcan, Paul *O Westport in the Light of Asia Minor.* Dun Laoghaire: Anna Livia Books, 1975. First edition, 8vo., original wrappers, near fine, from the library of Richard Murphy, inscribed by author to Murphy. Maggs Bros. Ltd. 1442 - 74 2013 £450

Duret, Theodore *(Henri de Toulouse)-Lautrec.* Paris: Bernheim Jeune, 1920. First edition, one of 100 deluxe copies, printed entirely on Japon paper (total edition 200), 124 pages, 38 full page heliogravure plates + 1 original etching, + 1 original color lithograph, both are strong impressions, very clean and bright, half calf janseniste binding by Gruel, signed by the Master binder, original wrappers bound in, top edge gilt, front hinge strengthened, otherwise in excellent condition.   Gemini Fine Books & Arts., Ltd.   Art Reference & Illustrated Books - 2013 $1500

Duret, Theodore   *Histoire d'Edouard Manet et de Son Oeuvre.*   Paris: Floury, 1902.   First edition, limited to 600 copies, 27 x 21cm., 307 pages, profusely illustrated, with 2 original drypoint etchings plus 21 full page engravings by Beltrand after Manet, several of them pochoir colored, three quarter blue morocco, title gilt on spine, original wrappers bound in, unusually clean, excellent condition, some very minor creasing on few tissue guards.   Gemini Fine Books & Arts., Ltd.   Art Reference & Illustrated Books - 2013 $2500

Durham, David L.   *California's Geographic Names: a Gazetteer of Historic and Modern names of the State.*   Fresno: World Dancer Press, 1998.   First edition, thick quarto, 1680 pages, pictorial boards, spine with vertical wrinkle, fine.   Argonaut Book Shop   Recent Acquisitions June 2013 - 96   2013 $225

Durham, Mary Edith   *Twenty Years of Balkan Tangle.*   London: George Allen, 1920.   First edition, 8vo., 295 pages, original blue cloth, spine faded, presentation copy "Miss Saunders from the old fellow student Xmas 1933". J. & S. L. Bonham Antiquarian Booksellers   Europe - 8149 2013   £220

Durrell, Gerald   *A Zoo in My Luggage.*   Rupert Hart-Davis, 1960.   First edition, original blue cloth, dust jacket spine trifle faded, closed at tear at head, illustrations by Ralph Thompson.   R. F. G. Hollett & Son   Africana - 59   2013   £75

Durrell, Lawrence   1912-1990   *The Alexandria Quartet.*   London: Faber & Faber, 1962.   Limited to 500 signed copies, this no. 119, signed by author, 8vo., fine, orange cloth with gilt lettered spine, top edge gilt, fine clear plastic dust jacket and very good+ diamond patterned paper covered slipcase with scuffs and wear.   By the Book, L. C.   38 - 79   2013 $1100

Durrell, Lawrence   1912-1990   *Balthazar.*   New York: E. P. Dutton and Co., 1958.   First US edition, signed by author, very good in black cloth boards with gilt title to spine, very good in pink dust jacket with white title to spine and front panel, slight fading to spine panel of jacket, 2 short closed tears, few small chips to head of jacket spine, 250 pages.   The Kelmscott Bookshop   7 - 108   2013 $650

Durrell, Lawrence   1912-1990   *Caesar's Vast Ghost.*   Arcade, 1990.   First US edition, large 8vo., pages xiv, 210, illustrations, original blue cloth, very good.   J. & S. L. Bonham Antiquarian Booksellers   Europe - 9851   2013 £30

Durrell, Lawrence   1912-1990   *Sicilian Carousel.*   London: Faber, 1977.   First edition, 8vo., 223 pages, map, illustrations, original red cloth, dust jacket, very good.   J. & S. L. Bonham Antiquarian Booksellers   Europe - 9824 2013   £40

Durrell, Lawrence   1912-1990   *Livia or Buried Alive.*   London: Faber & Faber, 1978.   First edition, fine in near fine dust jacket, signed by author, 8vo, 265 pages. Beasley Books   2013 - 2013 $60

Durrell, Lawrence   1912-1990   *The Plant Magic Man.*   Santa Barbara: Capra Press, 1973.   First edition, number 9 of 200 hardcover copies, numbered and signed by author, 8vo., 25 pages, fine.   Beasley Books   2013 - 2013 $60

Durrell, Lawrence   1912-1990   *Reflections on a Marine Venus.*   London: Faber, 1953.   First edition, 8vo., pages 198, illustrations, original green cloth, dust jacket, small loss at head of spine, otherwise very good and clean.   J. & S. L. Bonham Antiquarian Booksellers   Europe - 9834   2013 £70

Duruy, Victor   *History of Rome and of the Roman People, from Its Origin to the Invasion of the Barbarians and Fall of the Empire.*   Boston: Dana Estes and Charles E. Lauriat, 1884-18887.   One of 250 copies, edition de grand luxe, printed on Imperial Japanese vellum, this #247, 292 x 203mm., pleasing contemporary rose colored crushed half morocco, raised bands, spines gilt in double ruled compartments, marbled sides and endpapers, top edge gilt, over 300 engravings, 100 maps and plans, numerous chromolithographs printed on coated stock, one joint with short thin crack at head and tail, 2 spines with small faint area of discoloration from leather preservative, additional insignificant defects, otherwise quite fine, attractive bindings showing very little war, interiors consistently smooth, clean and fresh. Phillip J. Pirages   63 - 406   2013 $2800

Dutch Windmills.   Zuilichem: Catharijne Press, 1993. Limited to 199 copies, of which this is one of 175 numbered copies, 6 x 4.7 cm., brown paper covered boards, paper spine label, picture of a windmill mounted on front cover, illustrations, from the collection of Donn W. Sanford.   Oak Knoll Books   303 - 78   2013 $100

Dutens, Louis   *Journal of Travels Made through the Principal Cities of Europe.*   London: J. Wallis, 1782.   First UK edition, 8vo., contemporary brown half calf, original marbled boards, spine rubbed, joints cracked, internally clean, rare.   J. & S. L. Bonham Antiquarian Booksellers   Europe - 8397   2013   £450

Dutton, Clarence Edward *Tertiary History of the Grand Canon with Atlas to Accompany the Monograph on the Tertiary History of the Grand Canon District.* Washington: USGPO, Julius Bien & Co., Lith., NY, 1882. First edition, monograph 264 pages, quarto, atlas with 23 sheets, 12 color maps, 10 color views, folio, complete fine, monograph and atlas have been beautifully rebound in three quarter black leather over tan canvas boards, green leather labels on both backstrips. Ken Sanders Rare Books 45 - 35 2013 $10,000

Dutton, E. A. T. *Kenya Mountain.* Cape, 1930. Second edition, small 4to., original buckram gilt, slightly stained, discolored in plates, frontispiece, 55 plates, 3 sketch maps and large folding map, flyleaves little browned. R. F. G. Hollett & Son Africana - 60 2013 £150

Duvosin, Roger *Two Lonely Ducks.* New York: Knopf, 1955. First edition, oblong 4to., pictorial cloth, fine in dust jacket, color and line illustrations. Aleph-Bet Books, Inc. 104 - 190 2013 $125

Dwight, Theodore *The Father's Book or Suggestions for Government and Instruction of Young Children on Principles Appropriate to a Christian Country.* Springfield: Meriam, 1835. Second edition, 12mo., engraved frontispiece, contemporary embossed cloth, covers faded, very good, tight copy, contemporary name of Granby Mass. farmer and diarist Holland Montague. Second Life Books Inc. 182 - 64 2013 $150

Dwight, Theodore *The Father's Book; or Suggestions for the Government and Instruction of Young Children...* Springfield: Meriam, 1835. Second edition, 12mo., frontispiece, contemporary embossed cloth, covers faded, very good, tight, contemporary name on endpaper and titlepage of Granby Mass farmer and diarist Holland Montague. Second Life Books Inc. 183 - 118 2013 $150

Dwyer, James A. *The Dominicans of Cork City and County.* 1896. First edition, xi, 243 pages, cloth, dust jacket, near fine. C. P. Hyland 261 - 356 2013 £35

Dwyer, Philip *The Siege of Londonderry in 1689.* 1893. First edition, illustrations, ex-library, half morocco, very good. C. P. Hyland 261 - 844 2013 £160

Dyer, Thomas H. *The Ruins of Pompeii; a Series of Eighteen Photographic Views...* London: Bell & Daldy, 1867. First edition, quarto, 108 pages, 18 original photos. J. & S. L. Bonham Antiquarian Booksellers Europe - 3986 2013 £300

Dykes, Jeff C. *Western High Spots. Reading and Collecting Guides.* Flagstaff: Northland Press, 1977. First collected edition, large octavo, original gray-blue cloth lettered in silver, very fine with spine faded printed dust jacket, signed by author. Argonaut Book Shop Summer 2013 - 88 2013 $150

E

Eachard, John *Mr. Hobb's State of Nature Considered... (bound with) The Grounds and Occasions of the Contempt of the Clergy and Religion... (bound with) Some Observations Upon the Answer to an Enquiry into the Grounds and Occasions of the Contempt of the Clergy.* London: Printed for E. Blagrave, 1696. Fourth edition, 8vo., contemporary mottled calf, blind ruled borders, expertly rebacked in matching style, some browning, slight wear to foot of front endpaper, 19th century armorial bookplate of Richardson of Pitfour, Bart.   Jarndyce Antiquarian Booksellers   CCIV - 11   2013   £380

Eagle, Mary Kavanaugh Oldham *The Congress of Women Held in the Woman's Building, World's Columbian Exposition, Chicago USA 1893.* Chicago: Smedley, 1895. Official edition, large 8vo., pages 824, frontispiece, olive cloth stamped in gilt, ex-library with bookplate and stamps, one hinge tender, cover scuffed, spotted, little bumped at corners, very good.   Second Life Books Inc.   182 - 65   2013 $125

Earle, John *The Alfred Jewel.* Oxford: Clarendon Press, 1901. 8vo., foldout map and 6 further plates ad called for, some in color, illustrations in text, orange cloth, gilt title to spine and upper board, top edge gilt, other edges uncut, spine sunned and somewhat stained, boards little scuffed, endpapers darkened, still very good.   Unsworths Antiquarian Booksellers   28 - 157   2013   £75

Earle, John *Microcosmography or a Piece of the World Discover'd in Essays and Characters.* London: printed by E. Say, 1732. 12mo., top corner of titlepage excised (clear of text), lightly browned throughout, some light staining, contemporary sprinkled sheep, title lettered gilt to front board, sometime rebacked, later vertical red morocco label to spine, somewhat rubbed and scratched, fore edges bit worn, smaller bookplate of Lytton Strachey.   Unsworths Antiquarian Booksellers   28 - 93   2013   £200

Earman, John *Philosophical Problems of Serial Publications in Psychology 1850-1950.* Pittsburgh: University Pittsburgh Press, 1993. First edition, fine, issued without dust jacket.   Beasley Books   2013 - 2013 $60

An Earnest Address to the Worthy Independent Freeholders of the County of York and to the Respectable Citizens of the Ancient and Loyal City of York. York: Printed for and sold by T. Wilson, 1769. 8vo., disbound.   Jarndyce Antiquarian Booksellers   CCIV - 190   2013   £225

Eastman, Sophie E. *In Old South Hadley.* Chicago: Blakely Pub. Co., 1912. First edition, 8vo., illustrations, spine little wrinkled but very good, clean, ownership signature of professor Cornelia M. Clapp.   Second Life Books Inc.   183 - 119   2013 $75

The Easy A.B.C. Book and Child's First Reader. J. J. Gilbertson, printer 85, Walmgate, York, circa, 1850. 16 pages, alphabets and 12 woodcuts, original pale green printed wrappers, some browning to the paper and corners chipped, but good, scarce.   Ken Spelman Books Ltd.   73 - 28   2013   £45

An Easy Introduction to the Game of Chess; Containing One Hundred Examples of Games... Philadelphia: M. Carey, September, 1817. New edition, 8vo., 282 pages, contemporary boards, spine broken, uncut, lacking folding plate.   M & S Rare Books, Inc.   95 - 59   2013 $350

Eaton, Arthur Wentworth Hamilton *The History of Kings County Nova Scotia Heart of the Acadian Land.* Salem: Salem Press Co., 1910. First edition, green cloth and gilt title to spine, half title, index, 8vo., some light wear to edges, generally very good.   Schooner Books Ltd.   102 - 55   2013 $175

Eaton, Seymour *The Bear Detectives Teddy B. and Teddy G.* Philadelphia: Edward Stern, 1909. 4to., mostly in black and white drawings, few in color, several colored by young owner, gray paper over boards, cloth spine and paper picture pasted on front, hinges tender, covers somewhat worn, good.   Second Life Books Inc.   183 - 120   2013 $300

Eaton, Seymour *More About Teddy B and Teddy G, The Roosevelt Bears.* Philadelphia: Edward Stern, 1907. First edition, 4to., over 200 black an white in text illustrations, 15 color plates, few drawings colored by former owner, brown paper over boards, color picture pasted on front cover worn, few pages loose, good.   Second Life Books Inc.   183 - 121   2013 $300

Eaton, Seymour *The Roosevelt Bears Abroad.* New York: Stern, 1908. First edition, 4to., cloth backed pictorial boards, fine in original cloth very chipped, frayed and worn, illustrations by R. K. Culver with 15 color plates plus many black and whites.   Aleph-Bet Books, Inc.   104 - 196   2013 $950

Eaton, Seymour *The Roosevelt Bears Abroad.* New York: Barse & Hopkins, 1908. First edition, 4to., 153 pages, many drawings, few color plates, some drawings colored by former owner, dark gray paper over boards, cloth spine and color picture pasted on front, cover worn at edges, very good.   Second Life Books Inc.   183 - 122   2013 $300

Eavenson, Howard N. *Map Maker and Indian Traders.* Pittsburgh: 1949. One of 300 numbered copies, 2 folding maps, spine faded, extremities rubbed, previous owner's address sticker to f.f.e.p., else very good. Dumont Maps & Books of the West   125 - 48   2013 $120

Eberhart, Richard *Song and Idea.* London: Chatto & Windus, 1940. First edition, tall 8vo., original ochre cloth backed patterned boards, excellent copy, some fading to spine, inscribed by author for Trekkie and Ian Parsons. Maggs Bros. Ltd.   1460 - 261   2013   £150

Ebina, Masao *Illustrations for Genji Monogatari in 54 Wood-cut Prints.* Tokyo: Yonekichi Yamada, 1953. 54 wood block prints, complete set, prints measure 9.x x 13 inches and are matted, each has tissue guard, plates fine with vibrant color, mats and text sheets mildly toned, all 54 plates and text loose as issued in original mildly worn cloth covered folding box with bone closures, box has tipped on label with title in Japanese. By the Book, L. C.   36 - 90   2013 $3500

Eccentric Biography; or, Memoirs of Remarkable Female Characters, Ancient and Modern. Worcester: Isiah Thomas for Homan, 1804. First American edition, 12mo., pages viii, 9-338, calf, front and rear covers almost separated, sides scuffed, spine worn. Second Life Books Inc.   182 - 8   2013 $350

Eccleston, Robert *Overland to California on the Southwest Trail 1849. Diary of...* Los Angeles: University of California Press, 1950. First edition, one of 750 copies, quite scarce, frontispiece, 2 folding maps, rust cloth, gilt, very fine, pictorial dust jacket (spine slightly faded). Argonaut Book Shop   Summer 2013 - 89   2013 $225

Eckenstein, Lina *Comparative Studies in Nursery Rhymes.* London: Duckworth, 1906. First edition, original green cloth, gilt, scarce. R. F. G. Hollett & Son   Children's Books - 179   2013   £40

Eckfeldt, Jacob *A Manual of Gold and Silver Coins of all Nations, Struck within the Past Quarter Century...* Philadelphia: Assay Office of the Mint, 1842. First edition, 4to., engraved title and 13 plates, contemporary three quarter leather, marbled sides, some browning and blindstamps verso of plates but inconspicuous very nice. M & S Rare Books, Inc.   95 - 108   2013 $3000

Eco, Umberto *The Name of the Rose.* New York: HBJ, 1983. Advance reading copy of the first American edition, advance reading copy, inscribed by author, recipient's name and address on half title, very good in wrappers, very scarce, more so signed. Ken Lopez Bookseller   159 - 57   2013 $1000

Eddings, David (The Belgariad): *Pawn of Prophecy, Queen of Sorcery, Magician's Gambit, Castle of Wizardry, Enchanters' End Game.* London: Century, 1983-1985. First editions, 5 volumes, very slight aging to cheap paper pages, still easily fine in fine dust jackets, lovely and uniform set. Between the Covers Rare Books, Inc.   Sci-Fi, Fantasy & Horror - 97965   2013 $3000

Eddy, William A. *F. D. R. Meets Ibn Saud.* New York: American Friends of the Middle East Inc., 1954. First edition, near fine, signed twice and inscribed to Harry (Henry R.) Labouisse American diplomat, very scarce. Leather Stalking Books   October 2013 - 2013 $1500

Eden, Frederick Morton *The State of the Poor; or an History of the Labouring Classes in England, from the Conquest to the Present Period...* London: printed by I. J. Davis, for B. & J. White..., 1797. First edition, 3 volumes, quarto, bound without half titles, but with "Directions to Binder" leaf at end of volume III, which is often lacking, errata leaf to volume 1 bound before the preface, folding table facing page viii of appendix (in volume III), contemporary calf, neatly rebacked to style, covers with decorative gilt border, spines decoratively tooled in gilt in compartments, with red and green morocco gilt lettering labels, board edges and turn-ins decoratively tooled in gilt, some light foxing and minor soiling, 1.5 inch crack to bottom of outer front hinge volume I, corners bit bumped, short tear to outer margin f 3U3 in volume 1, not affecting text, from the library of William A. Foyle, with his red morocco bookplate, excellent copy. Heritage Book Shop   Holiday Catalogue 2012 - 52   2013 $13,500

Edgcumbe, Rose *Anna Freud: a View of Development, Disturbance and Therapeutic Techniques.* London: Routledge, 2000. First edition, decorated boards, corners little bumped, else near fine. Between the Covers Rare Books, Inc.   Psychology & Psychiatry - 92831   2013 $75

Edgeworth, Maria   1768-1849   *Memoir of Richard L. Edgeworth Begun by Himself & Concluded by His Daughter Maria.* 1969. Facsimile of first edition of 1820, 2 volumes, 8vo., dust jacket, cloth, very good. C. P. Hyland   261 - 359   2013   £60

Edgeworth, Maria   1768-1849   *Tales and Novels.* London: Baldwin & Cradock, 1832-1833. 18 volumes, frontispiece and vignette titlepage, volumes 2-18 in the more usual reddish brown cloth with gilt decorated spine (in good condition), volume 1 in alternative publisher's binding, grey buckram with gilt titling and blind impress decorations with owner inscription on vignette titlepage and some foxing to frontispiece. C. P. Hyland   261 - 358   2013   £315

Edgeworth, Maria   1769-1849   *Castle Rackrent.* London: printed for J. Johnson by J. Crowder, 1800. First edition, 8vo., near contemporary half calf, marbled boards, half title, lettered in gilt, worn at extremities, else excellent. Maggs Bros. Ltd.   1442 - 78   2013   £1500

Edlefsen, David *The Mystery of the Magic Box: an Open and Shut Case.* Anchorage: Anchorage Museum of History and Art, n.d. but, 1995. Square miniature, 8.5 x 8.5cm., text housed in paper covered box, laid in insert signed "Ed", color illustrations with descriptive text, from the collection of Donn W. Sanford.   Oak Knoll Books   303 - 33   2013 $125

Edmondes, Clement *Observations Upon Caesars Comentaries.* London: Math(ew) Lownes, 1609. Second edition, 2nd issue, with imprint added to engraved titlepage, small folio, engraved frontispiece, and 12 engraved folding plates, embellished with numerous decorative wood engraved head an tailpieces and initials, 18th century speckled calf with double rule border on covers, spine decoratively gilt tooled in compartments with maroon morocco lettering label, all edges sprinkled red, joints, corners little rubbed, armorial bookplate, unidentified, overall, very good, clean, scarce.   Heritage Book Shop   50th Anniversary Catalogue - 33   2013 $2750

Edrehi, M. *An Historical Account of the Ten Tribes, Settled Beyond the River Sambayton in the East with many Other Curious Matter Relating to the State of the Israelties.* London: printed for the author, 1836. First edition, 8vo., 290 pages, index, portrait and folding plate, original cloth, crudely rebacked.   M & S Rare Books, Inc.   95 - 174   2013 $200

Edwards, E. I. *Desert Harvest.* Los Angeles: Westernlore Press, 1962. First edition, one of 600 copies, 128 pages, illustrations, blind embossed cloth, gilt, very fine, pictorial dust jacket, presentation inscription signed by author to fellow author, W. W. Robinson.   Argonaut Book Shop   Recent Acquisitions June 2013 - 97   2013 $175

Edwards, E. I. *Desert Treasure. A Bibliography.* Los Angeles: the author, 1948. First edition, tan cloth, gilt, very fine.   Argonaut Book Shop   Recent Acquisitions June 2013 - 98   2013 $90

Edwards, Edward *A Sermon Preached in Wrexham Church Nov. 3 1799, being the Sunday after the Interment of Thomas Joines, Esq..* Wrexham: printed by John Painter, 1800. 8vo., half title discarded, some light dust soiling, extracted from bound volume, stab holes also visible.   Blackwell's Rare Books   172 - 51   2013   £300

Edwards, George Wharton *Sundry Rhymes from the Days of Our Grandmothers.* New York: A. D. F. Randolph & Co., 1888. First edition, folio blue leather backed boards, good+, gilt decorations and title on cover, few pages with small closed tears, some smudges.   Barnaby Rudge Booksellers   Poetry 2013 - 019344   2013 $50

Edwards, Jonathan *Dissertation Concerning Liberty and Necessity.* Worcester: 1797. First edition, 8vo., 23 pages plus errata leaf, rubbed contemporary calf, chipped at extremities of spine, endpapers soiled, text block little browned, very good, inscribed by Rev. Sam'l Austin of Worcester, Oct. 15 1806 for Joseph Goffes.   Second Life Books Inc.   183 - 123   2013 $300

Edwards, Jonathan *History of Redemption... with the Life and Experience of the Author.* New York: printed by T. and J. Swords for the editor, 1793. 8vo., engraved portrait, later three quarter leather and cloth, some foxing.   M & S Rare Books, Inc.   95 - 115   2013 $225

Edwards, Llewellyn Nathaniel *A Record of History and Evolution of Early American Bridges.* Orono: University Press, 1959. 8vo., frontispiece, 54 illustrations on 36 pages of plates, gilt stamped textured navy cloth, rubbed, Burndy bookplate, pencil and ink note with signature, very good.   Jeff Weber Rare Books   171 - 112   2013 $85

Edwards, Paul *Wyndham Lewis Painter and Writer.* New Haven: Yale University Press for the Paul Mellon Centre for Studies in British Art, 2000. First edition, fine in fine dust jacket but for small corner crease on front wrapper small 4to., 576 pages.   Beasley Books   2013 - 2013 $60

Edwards, R. D. *Ireland and the Italian Risorgimento: 3 Lectures.* Italian Institute, 1960. First edition, 92 pages, wrappers, publisher's presentation, very good.   C. P. Hyland   261 - 360   2013   £30

Edwards, Richard *The Paradise of Dainty Devices...* London: printed (by T. Bensley) for Robert Triphook, 1810. 4to., prelim and final leaves foxed, otherwise very good, clean, 19th century diced calf, blind and gilt ruled borders, gilt panelled spine, red morocco label, slight crack to head of leading hinge, all edges gilt.   Jarndyce Antiquarian Booksellers   CCIV - 120   2013   £250

Edwards, Thomas *Canons of Criticism and Glossary; the Trial of the Letter (Upsilon) alias Y, and Sonnets.* London: printed for C. Bathurst, 1758. 8vo. toned and bit spotted, contemporary speckled calf, spine gilt in compartments with raised bands, red morocco label, marbled edges and endpapers, rubbed, slight wear to headcap, contemporary ink inscription 'North Side/Case 7 Shelf 7 No. 10" on rectangular paper label on front pastedown, pencil annotation on first plain flyleaf states 'from the library of Lord Lisburne".   Unsworths Antiquarian Booksellers   28 - 94   2013   £95

Edwards, W. F. *De L'Influence des Agents Physiques sur la Vie.* Paris: Chez Crochard Libraire, 1824. Errata leaf and one folding engraved plate, recent quarter linen backed boards, original (?) leather label laid down on spine, 2 later rubber stamps of owners on title, well margined, uncut and partially unopened, text foxing and browning, otherwise very good.   James Tait Goodrich   S74 - 98   2013 $495

Edwards, William *Art of Boxing and Science of Self-Defense, Together with a Manual of Training.* New York: Excelsior Pub. House, cop., 1888. First edition, 12mo., original cloth backed pictorially yellow cloth, hinges cracked, corners rubbed, very good.   Howard S. Mott Inc.   262 - 21   2013 $375

Edwords, Clarence *Bohemian San Francisco: Its Restaurants and Their Most Famous Recipies, the Elegant Art of Dining.* San Francisco: Paul Elder, 1914. First edition, tipped in frontispiece, index, printed throughout in orange and black, tan cloth lettered in black, glue remnants on inner cover from removed bookplate, else very fine with very elusive decorated dust jacket printed in black and gold (minor chip to head of spine).   Argonaut Book Shop Summer 2013 - 93   2013 $250

Edwords, Clarence *Bohemian San Francisco: Its Restaurants and Their Most Famous Recipes, the Elegant Art of Dining.* San Francisco: Paul Elder, 1914. First edition, tipped-in frontispiece, printed in orange and black tan cloth lettered in black contemporary owner's name, slight rubbing to spine ends, fine, contemporary owner's name "Helen M. Wadsworth/San Francisco, California/1920".   Argonaut Book Shop   Summer 2013 - 94   2013 $175

Eeles, Francis *The Parish Church of St. Kentigern, Crosthwaite.* Carlisle: Charles Thurnam and Sons, 1953. First edition, small 8vo., original cloth, gilt, dust jacket head of spine trifle worn, 23 illustrations.   R. F. G. Hollett & Son Lake District and Cumbria - 54   2013   £30

Egan, Howard T. *Gassendi's View of Knowledge: a Study of the Epistemological Basis of His Logic.* New York & London: University Press of American, 1964. 8vo., printed wrappers, ownership signature on titlepage, fine.   Jeff Weber Rare Books   169 - 157   2013 $75

Egan, P. M. *Illustrated Guide to the City & County of Kilkenny.* 1885. 12 views on 6 plates, cover stained and worn, text good, 8vo., cloth.   C. P. Hyland   261 - 361   2013   £200

Egan, Thomas J. *History of the Halifax Volunteer Battalion and Volunteer Companies 1859-1887.* Halifax: A. & W. Mackinlay, 1888. Small 8vo., decorated cloth boards, gilt titles to front and spine, frontispiece and other illustrations, cloth worn and badly stained, interior good.   Schooner Books Ltd.   105 - 69   2013 $150

Egenhoff, Elisabeth L. *Fabricas, a Collection of Pictures and Statements on the Mineral Materials Used in Building in California Prior to 1850.* San Francisco: Division of Mines, 1952. First edition, 189 pages, profusely illustrated from old drawings, prints, photos and maps, stiff turqoise wrappers, very fine.   Argonaut Book Shop   Recent Acquisitions June 2013 - 100   2013 $60

Eggenhofer, Nick *Horses, Horses, Always Horses: the Life and Art of Nick Eggenhofer.* Cody: Rustler Printing, 1981. First edition, fine in near fine dust jacket with some rubbing, signed by author.   Between the Covers Rare Books, Inc.   Horses, Horsemanship, Horse Racing, Etc. - 52815   2013 $200

Eggers, Dave *A Hologram for the King.* San Francisco: McSweeney's, 2011. Advance copy, in the form of bound typescript, scarce, 339 pages, velobound with acetate cover, fine,.   Ken Lopez Bookseller   159 - 58   2013 $350

Eggleston, Edward *The Mystery of Metropolisville.* New York: Judd, 1873. First edition, corner torn from front endpaper and pages darkened, otherwise very good in soiled cloth covered boards.   Mordida Books   81 - 158   2013 $100

Ehrsam, Theodore G. *Major Byron: the Incredible Career of a Literary Forger.* New York: Charles S. Boesen; and London: John Murray, 1951. First edition, half title, frontispiece, plates, original dark green cloth, very good in slightly worn dust jacket.   Jarndyce Antiquarian Booksellers   CCIII - 378   2013   £25

Eidlitz, Walther *Zodiak.* New York: Harper & Brothers, 1931. First American edition, bookplate and light abrasion to top of a few pages, else fine in near fine dust jacket with tiny nick at crown and few short tears, this copy inscribed by author to Dorothy Day, founder of the Catholic Worker Movement.   Between the Covers Rare Books, Inc.   Sci-Fi, Fantasy & Horror - 58258   2013 $850

Einstein, Izzy *Prohibition Agent No. 1.* New York: Frederick A. Stokes, 1932. First edition, some rubbing to edges of cloth, else near fine in near fine dust jacket with tiny nicks and little spine fading.   Between the Covers Rare Books, Inc.   Cocktails, Etc. - 320478   2013 $850

Eiseley, Loren *The Firmament of Time.* New York: Atheneum, 1960. First edition, fine in fine dust jacket, single very short tear on front panel, signed by author.   Between the Covers Rare Books, Inc.   Philosophy - 91274   2013 $500

Eisenhower, Dwight David *Mandate for Change 1953-1956. The White House Years.* Garden City: Doubleday, 1963. First edition, signed, 55 illustrations, 9 maps, gilt stamped half red leather over red cloth, 5 raised spinal bands, leather very worn, hinges starting (especially front hinge), signed by author in ink on removable tipped in note card, good.   Jeff Weber Rare Books   171 - 114   2013 $150

Eisenmann, G. H. *Tabulae Anatomicae Quatuor Uteri Duplicis Observationum Rariorum Sistentes.* Strasburg: Konig, 1752. First edition, text lightly foxed and browned in parts, 2 engraved plates, some faint stamps in text and plates, early quarter calf and marbled boards. James Tait Goodrich S74 - 195 2013 $1295

El Cid *Chronica del Famoso Cavallero Cid Ruy Diez Campeador.* Burgos: Philippe de Junta y Juan Baptista Varesio, 1593. Folio, 318 pages, frontispiece in red and black, woodcut coat of arms, old vellum, gently washed and sized, usual page spotting, here absent, text generally fresh and clean, titlepage has some restoration, affecting three letters, very well margined, overall very good, appropriate old binding. Heritage Book Shop 50th Anniversary Catalogue - 34 2013 $10,000

Elder, William *A Memoir of Henry C. Carey Read Before the Historical Society of Pennsylvania.* Philadelphia: Henry Carey Baird Co., 1880. First edition, 8vo., pages 39, brown cloth stamped in black, blind and gilt, small scrape on front cover, otherwise very good, presentation from Wm. E. Ringwalt April 2 '84 for William D. Kelley, from the library of Florence Kelley. Second Life Books Inc. 183 - 124 2013 $65

Eldredge, Zoeth Skinner *The Beginnings of San Francisco from the Expedition of Anza 1774 to the Cty Charter of April 15 1850.* San Francisco: by the author, 1912. First edition, 2 volumes, 837 pages, numerous illustrations, portraits, maps, spines faded as usual, minor rubbing to spine ends, very good set. Argonaut Book Shop Recent Acquisitions June 2013 - 101 2013 $150

Eldridge, Eleanor *Memoirs of...* Providence: Albro, 1828. First edition, 12mo., 128 pages, cloth backed boards, some foxed and soiled, portrait, some stained and foxed, very good, very scarce, notes in pencil "Mrs. E. Choate/from her affecionate/ aunt A. Baker/ New Bedford/ Jan 22nd/ 1939/ I purchased this book/ of Eleanor herself". Second Life Books Inc. 183 - 442 2013 $600

Elias, E. L. *The Book of Polar Exploration.* Harrap, 1928. First edition, original striking pictorial cloth, matching dust jacket rather rubbed, numerous plates, illustrations, maps on endpapers, fore edge and prelim leaves little foxed. R. F. G. Hollett & Son Children's Books - 180 2013 £75

Eliot, George, Pseud. 1819-1880 *Felix Holt the Radical.* London: William Blackwood and Sons, 1866. First edition, 3 volumes, octavo, half title in volume I and III, original reddish brown sand grain cloth with blindstamped borders on covers and spines stamped and lettered gilt (Carter's "B" binding), mostly unopened, pale yellow endpapers, light toning to half title volume I, exceptionally bright, clean set, cloth chemise and quarter green morocco slipcase. Heritage Book Shop Holiday Catalogue 2012 - 54 2013 $3500

Eliot, George, Pseud. 1819-1880 *The Legend of Jubal and Other Poems.* Berlin: Albert Cohn, printed by Stephen Geibel & Co., Altenbourg, 1874. Contemporary half red sheep by Birdsall & Son, dark green leather label, ownership inscription June 1887. Jarndyce Antiquarian Booksellers CCV - 99 2013 £175

Eliot, George, Pseud. 1819-1880 *The Mill on the Floss.* London: Blackwood, 1860. First edition, 3 volumes, 8vo., bound with half titles in each volume, brown cloth, blindstamped and printed gilt on spines, occasional foxing and soil on some leaves, half title mended in volume I, covers somewhat soiled and worn at edges, good set, labels removed from covers of each volume. Second Life Books Inc. 183 - 129 2013 $950

Eliot, George, Pseud. 1819-1880 *The Novels.* William Blackwood and Sons, circa, 1880. 8 titles in 7 volumes, contemporary half calf, gilt spines with red and dark green morocco labels marbled boards, some rubbing to spines and corners. Ken Spelman Books Ltd. 75 - 142 2013 £120

Eliot, George, Pseud. 1819-1880 *Romola.* London: Smith Elder and Co., 1880. One of 1000 copies (this being #57), 2 volumes, 265 x 180mm., remarkable contemporary honey brown crushed morocco by Fazakerley (stamp signed on front turn-in), upper cover of one volume with ornate gilt monogram of "MMK", the other front cover with monogram of "NDK", spines with raised bands and gilt titling, splendid brown morocco doublures elaborately tooled in gilt featuring scalloped French fillet frame incorporating large floral cornerpieces and enclosing exuberantly swirling flowering vines emerging from a Greek urn at foot, brown watered silk endleaves, edges gilt and ornately gauffered in bold strapwork pattern on stippled ground, each volume with 3 lovely and delicate fore-edge paintings the ones at head and tail of each fore-edge being lozenge-shaped views (measuring approximately 25 x 30 mm across) and larger rectangular painting at center (measuring approximately 80 x 45mm), all depicting finely painted scenes from book; 24 engraved plates, mounted plates after Sir Frederick Leighton, plus 13 smaller engravings mounted in text as called for, flyleaf of each volume with lovely calligraphic manuscript inscription of quote from book, half title of volume 1 with ink ownership inscription of Jean Stewart Russell dated 1902; spine faintly and evenly sunned, plates bit spotted (from mounting glue?), otherwise superb copy, text clean, fresh and bright, margins especially ample, bindings lustrous and unworn, fore edges richly painted and glittering with particularly bright gold. Phillip J. Pirages 61 - 78 2013 $16,000

Eliot, Thomas Stearns 1888-1965 *Animula.* London: Faber and Faber, 1929. First edition, one of 400 copies signed by author, tall 8vo., original yellow boards, excellent copy. Maggs Bros. Ltd. 1460 - 265 2013 £375

Eliot, Thomas Stearns 1888-1965 *The Cocktail Party.* London: Faber and Faber, 1950. First edition, 8vo., original green cloth, excellent copy in slightly nicked dust jacket, browned on spine, presentation copy inscribed by author for M. C. D'Arcy 6.iii.50. Maggs Bros. Ltd. 1460 - 272 2013 £2000

Eliot, Thomas Stearns 1888-1965 *The Dry Salvages.* London: Faber, 1941. First edition, pages 16, 8vo., original printed pale blue grey stapled wrappers, spine faded, untrimmed, good, Anne Ridler's copy gifted to her by Eliot. Blackwell's Rare Books B174 - 202 2013 £3500

Eliot, Thomas Stearns 1888-1965 *The Dry Salvages.* London: Faber, 1941. First edition, 8vo., original printed pale blue-grey stapled wrappers faded at edges, with two short tears to head of rear cover, untrimmed, partly unopened, good, signed by author on piece of paper excised from letter tippled to titlepage beneath his printed name. Blackwell's Rare Books 172 - 181 2013 £2500

Eliot, Thomas Stearns 1888-1965 *For Lancelot Andrewes. Essays on Style and Order.* London: Faber & Gwyer, 1928. Second impression, 8vo., original blue cloth, printed paper label on spine, inscribed by author for Barbara Rothschild, excellent copy. Maggs Bros. Ltd. 1460 - 263 2013 £600

Eliot, Thomas Stearns 1888-1965 *Four Quartets.* London: Faber and Faber, 1944. First UK edition, 8vo., original tan cloth, near fine, slightly marked dust jacket with slight wear to extremities, preserved in folding box, inscribed by author for Sarah Gertrude Millin Jan. 1950. Maggs Bros. Ltd. 1460 - 271 2013 £2500

Eliot, Thomas Stearns 1888-1965 *Four Quartets.* printed at the Officina Bodoni for Faber, 1960. 140/290 copies, signed by author, printed on Magnani paper using Dante typeface, small folio, original quarter cream vellum, backstrip gilt lettered, green and yellow Putois marbled boards, top edge gilt, others untrimmed, matching marbled board slipcase, rubbed and defective as usual, near fine. Blackwell's Rare Books B174 - 370 2013 £2700

Eliot, Thomas Stearns 1888-1965 *Little Gidding.* London: Faber & Faber, 1942. First edition, wrappers, close to fine with barest tiny bump at fore-edge corners, first state with sewn binding (rather than later staples), 8vo., 16 pages. Beasley Books 2013 - 2013 $60

Eliot, Thomas Stearns 1888-1965 *Marina.* London: Faber and Faber, 1930. First edition, drawings by E. McKnight Kauffer, original wrappers, preserved in folding box, inscribed by author for Ramon Fernandez, one squarish hole 'punched' through from front to back, but closed without loss, otherwise excellent copy. Maggs Bros. Ltd. 1460 - 266 2013 £650

Eliot, Thomas Stearns 1888-1965 *Old Possum's Book of Practical Cats.* London: Faber and Faber, 1939. First edition, 8vo., pictorial cloth, fine in pictorial dust jacket with small chip off spine, illustrations by Nicolas Bentley. Aleph-Bet Books, Inc. 104 - 199 2013 $1350

Eliot, Thomas Stearns 1888-1965 *The Rock.* London: Faber and Faber, 1934. Second impression, 8vo., original grey board, spine slightly browned, otherwise excellent copy, inscribed by author for Miss Gwyneth Thurburn. Maggs Bros. Ltd. 1460 - 268 2013 £450

Eliot, Thomas Stearns 1888-1965 *A Song for Simeon.* London: Faber and Gwyer, 1928. First edition, 8vo., original pale blue wrappers, wrappers split at spine, now loose, otherwise excellent, inscribed by author for John Gould Fletcher. Maggs Bros. Ltd. 1460 - 264 2013 £900

Eliot, Thomas Stearns 1888-1965 *Triumphal March.* London: Faber and Faber, 1931. First edition, 8vo., original grey wrappers, fine, inscribed by author for Ramon Fernandez. Maggs Bros. Ltd. 1460 - 267 2013 £650

Eliot, Thomas Stearns 1888-1965 *The Waste Land.* New York: Boni and Liveright, 1922. First edition, first issue, limited to 1000 numbered copies, this being number 134, small octavo, original flexible black cloth boards lettered gilt on front cover and spine, uncut, spine very lightly sunned, some very light rubbing to boards, small dampstain on fore-edge of pages 15-26, overall nice. Heritage Book Shop Holiday Catalogue 2012 - 55 2013 $8500

Elkins, Aaron *Fellowship of Fear.* New York: Walker, 1982. First edition, very good with glue stains on pastedowns where dust jacket protector once adhered, slightly cocked, otherwise no ex-library signs in near dust jacket. Beasley Books 2013 - 2013 $100

Elkus, Richard J. *Alamos: a Philosophy In Living.* San Francisco: Grabhorn Press, 1965. One of 487 copies, numbered and signed by author/photographer and by both Grabhorn brothers, folio, 64 pages 24 tipped in glossy photo plates, handset type printed on all-rag handmade paper, half brown embossed suede over hand dyed orange, brown and yellow striped Mexican cloth, very minor shelf rubbing to suede bottom edge of covers, but very fine. Argonaut Book Shop Recent Acquisitions June 2013 - 103 2013 $375

Ellin, Stanley *The Blessington Method and Other Strange Tales.* New York: Random House, 1964. First edition, small spot on fore-edge and on bottom of page edges, otherwise fine in dust jacket with some light wear at spine ends. Mordida Books 81 - 161 2013 $65

Ellin, Stanley *The Eighth Circle.* New York: Random House, 1958. First edition, pages darkened as usual and name on front endpaper, otherwise near fine in unfaded dust jacket. Mordida Books 81 - 159 2013 $250

Ellin, Stanley *The Panama Portrait.* New York: Random House, 1962. First edition, inscribed by author August 1962, fine in dust jacket with darkened spine. Mordida Books 81 - 161 2013 $65

Elliot, S. R. *Scarlet to Green a History of Intelligence in the Canadian Army 1903-1963.* Ottawa: Canadian Intelligence and Security Association, 1981. 8vo., cloth, dust jacket, half title, color frontispiece, black and white illustrations, very good, dust jacket has some light wear, otherwise very good. Schooner Books Ltd. 102 - 109 2013 $125

Elliott, G. H. *Catalogue of the Reference Department Belfast Free Public Library.* 1896. First edition, 480 pages, octavo, cloth, fine. C. P. Hyland 261 - 63 2013 £75

Elliott, Mary *Confidential Memoirs...* William Darton, 1821. First edition, small 8vo., modern half calf gilt, 4 steel engraved plates, few spots and marks, excellent copy, scarce. R. F. G. Hollett & Son Children's Books - 181 2013 £150

Elliott, Maud Howe *Art and Handicraft in the Woman's Building of the World's Columbian Exposition Chicago 1893.* Paris: Goupil, 1893. Official edition, large 8vo., 287 pages, profusely illustrated, yellow cloth, very decorative stamping in silver and gilt, all edges gilt, ex-library with bookplate and stamp, cover somewhat scuffed, soiled, little worn at corners and ends of spine, hinges tender, few soil marks in interior, else very good. Second Life Books Inc. 182 - 69 2013 $85

Elliott, O. L. *"The Mississippi Girl".* Toledo: The Author/West Toledo Pub. Co., 1947. First edition, little rubbed, near fine in lightly chipped, very good or better dust jacket, pencil name and address of author on front flap, in his hand? Between the Covers Rare Books, Inc. 165 - 141 2013 $125

Ellis, Daniel *An Inquiry into the Changes Induced on Atmospheric Air, by the Germination of Seeds, the Vegetation of Plants and the Respiration of Animals. (bound with) Further Inquires into the changes Induced on Atmospheric Air.* Edinburgh: William Creech, 1807. Edinburgh: W. Blackwood, 1811. First edition, 2 volumes in 1, 8vo., signature and date on half title, penciled marginal notes, signature and date on half title, pencilled marginal notes, original brown tree calf, rebacked, gilt stamped spine title, new front free endpaper, corners and edges showing. Jeff Weber Rare Books 172 - 85 2013 $500

Ellis, George *Specimens of Early English Metrical Romances Chiefly Written During the Early Part of the Fourteenth Century.* London: printed for Longman, Hurst, Rees, Orme and Brown, 1811. Second edition, 3 volumes, 8vo., touch of minor spotting, contemporary polished tan calf, spines gilt in compartments with raised band, orange and green morocco labels, one with slight loss, neat repairs by Chris Weston, little rubbed around edges, armorial bookplate of Somerhill Library. Unsworths Antiquarian Booksellers 28 - 158 2013 £180

Ellis, George F. *Bell Ranch as I Knew It.* Kansas City: 1973. One of a numbered limited edition of 250, signed by author, Mrs. Ellis, Donald Orunduff and Robert Lougheed, 163 pages, illustrations, map endpapers, large map in rear pocket, lacking printed called for in limitation, near fine in slightly shelfworn slipcase. Dumont Maps & Books of the West 122 - 54 2013 $150

Ellis, George F. *Bell Ranch as I Knew It.* Kansas City: 1973. Trade edition, 163 pages, illustrations, map endpapers, dust jacket spine faded, couple of short tears, else clean and very good. Dumont Maps & Books of the West 122 - 55 2013 $100

Ellis, Henry Havelock 1859-1939 *Affirmations.* London: Constable and Co., 1915. Second edition with new preface, 8vo., original black cloth, gilt, spine faded, otherwise excellent copy, inscribed by author to the Ellis Club, with John Quinn's bookplate. Maggs Bros. Ltd. 1460 - 274 2013 £150

Ellis, Henry Havelock 1859-1939 *Concerning Jude the Obscure.* London: Ulysses Bookshop, 1931. First edition, number 14 of 185 numbered copies signed by Ellis, 4to., original gray cloth, salmon paper boards, printed in black on upper board, untrimmed, fine in original glassine wrapper, from the Gary Lepper Collection of Thomas Hardy. The Brick Row Book Shop Bulletin Nine - 91 2013 $125

Ellis, Henry Havelock 1859-1939 *Little Essays of Love and Virtue.* London: A. & C. Black, 1922. First edition, 8vo., original green cloth, inscribed by author for Dr. Marie Stopes, with a number of her pencilled underlinings and emphases, with 3 textual holograph remarks, excellent copy. Maggs Bros. Ltd. 1460 - 275 2013 £500

Ellis, Henry Havelock 1859-1939 *My Confessional.* London: John Lane, The Bodley Head, 1934. First edition, 8vo., original green cloth, spine little faded, otherwise excellent copy, inscribed by author for Hugh de Selincourt. Maggs Bros. Ltd. 1460 - 276 2013 £250

Ellis, Mattie *Bell Ranch Wagon Work.* Conchas Dam: 1984. 76 pages, illustrations, folding map laid in, soft cover with light rubbing, else very good, photos, signed by both Ellis and co-author, Mark Wood, (although handwriting looks suspiciously similar), scarce. Dumont Maps & Books of the West 122 - 57 2013 $65

Ellis, Peter Beresford *The Rising of the Moon.* London: Methuen, 1987. First edition, 637 pages, cloth, very good, dust jacket.   C. P. Hyland   261 - 363   2013   £30

Ellis, Robert *The Travellers' Hand-Book to Copenhagen and Its Environs by Anglicanus.* Copenhagen: Steen ad Son, 1853. First edition, 8vo., 8 lithographs, folding map, original brown cloth, library label on upper cover but no stamps in text, very good, clean.   J. & S. L. Bonham Antiquarian Booksellers   Europe - 8105   2013   £100

Ellis, William *Philo-socrates. Part V. Among the Boys.* London: Smith, Elder & Co., 1863. Original light brown printed paper wrappers, hinges slightly splitting with some repair to head of leading hinge, inscription from author for Caroline Lindley.   Jarndyce Antiquarian Booksellers   CCV - 100   2013   £150

Ellison, Ralph *Invisible Man.* New York: Random House, 1952. First edition, near fine with spine lettering rubbed as usual in moderately worn, very good dust jacket with some internal tissue strengthening to joints.   Between the Covers Rare Books, Inc.   165 - 301   2013 $1250

Ellmann, Richard *James Joyce's Tower.* 1969. First edition, 8vo., illustrations, wrappers, very good.   C. P. Hyland   261 - 519   2013   £40

Ellwood, T. *The Landnama Book of Iceland...* Kendal: T. Wilson, 1894. First edition, original blue cloth, gilt extremities trifle rubbed, pages xvii 69, very scarce.   R. F. G. Hollett & Son   Lake District and Cumbria - 56   2013   £150

Elphin Lloyd Jones (a Memoir). Newtown: Gregynog Press, March, 1929. printed on Japanese vellum, 3 wood engravings by R. A. Maynard, 8 page facsimile printed in blue and red, initial page of text printed in black and red, latter in Greek types, pages 16, royal 8vo., original pale blue boards, front cover with design in dark blue, spine and half of rear cover faded, untrimmed, good.   Blackwell's Rare Books   B174 - 347   2013   £85

Elson-Gray *More Dick and Jane Stories.* Chicago: Scott Foresman, 1934. 8vo., pictorial wrappers, 48 pages, near fine, illustrations in color on every page, scarce.   Aleph-Bet Books, Inc.   105 - 177   2013 $300

Elting, Mary *Sailors, Fliers and Marines.* New York: Doubleday Doran, 1943. Stated first edition, 8vo., cloth backed pictorial boards, tips rubbed, else fine in worn dust jacket with smallish pieces off corners, illustrations in color.   Aleph-Bet Books, Inc.   104 - 590   2013 $125

Elton, Ben *Popcorn.* London: Simon and Schuster, 1996. First edition, very fine in dust jacket.   Mordida Books   81 - 163   2013 $75

Eluard, Paul *Au Rendez-vous Allemand.* Paris: Les Editions de Minuit, 1945. Nouvelle edition, 8vo., later red morocco, original wrappers bound in, morocco slightly discolored with few marks, inscribed by author for Carmen Gandarillas.   Maggs Bros. Ltd.   1460 - 277   2013   £450

Elwood, Roger *The Many Worlds of Poul Anderson.* Radnor: Chilton Book Co., 1974. Stated first edition, 8vo., 324 pages, fine in near fine dust jacket with mild chip.   By the Book, L. C.   36 - 54   2013 $250

Elze, Karl *Lord Byron, a Biography.* London: John Murray, 1872. First English edition, half title, frontispiece, folding facsimile, original brown cloth, rubbed, spine little darkened and slightly worn at head and tail, leading inner hinge slightly cracking, bookplate of Arthur Wright.   Jarndyce Antiquarian Booksellers   CCIII - 380   2013   £50

Emanuel, Walter *The Zoo. A Scamper.* Alston Rivers, 1904. First edition, small 4to., original pictorial boards, little fingered and neatly rebacked, 12 plates, in brown black and white, numerous line drawings, new endpapers, light crayoning to one small drawing, but very good.   R. F. G. Hollett & Son   Children's Books - 268   2013   £65

Emanuels, George *Walnut Creek Arroyo de las Nueces.* Walnut Creek: Diablo Books, 1984. First edition, frontispiece, illustrations from photos, map, map endpapers, gilt lettered and decorated black cloth, very fine.   Argonaut Book Shop   Summer 2013 - 96   2013 $75

Emerson, Caroline D. *Old New York for Young Yorkers.* New York: E. P. Dutton, 1932. First edition, illustrations by Alida Conover, covers with bit of soiling, thus near fine in very good plus dust jacket with chips and edge tears, uncommon in dust jacket.   Between the Covers Rare Books, Inc.   New York City - 69167   2013 $100

Emerson, Ralph Waldo   1803-1882 *An April Day. A Poem Recited at Concord at the Celebration of the One Hundred and twenty-Fifth Anniversary of Concord Fight April 19th 1900.* Cambridge: Riverside Press, 1900. First edition, 8vo., contemporary cloth backed boards, original wrappers bound in, excellent copy, inscribed by author to C. R. Ashbee.   Maggs Bros. Ltd.   1460 - 279   2013   £375

Emerson, Ralph Waldo   1803-1882 *Henry Thoreau as Remembered by a Young Friend.* Boston and New York: Houghton Mifflin, 1917. First edition, 8vo., 152 pages, bound in green cloth stamped in gilt, top edge gilt, fine, frontispiece.   Second Life Books Inc.   183 - 127   2013 $135

Emerson, Ralph Waldo 1803-1882 *Representative Men: Seven Lectures.* Boston: Phillips, Smapson and Co., 1850. First edition, 8vo., original brown cloth, gilt, preserved in folding box, inscribed by author for Professor Guglielmo Gajani, excellent copy, endpapers lightly browned and foxed, cloth worn at head and tail of spine.   Maggs Bros. Ltd.   1460 - 280   2013   £3500

Emery, Carlyle *Twinkie Town Tales Book No. 2.* St. Louis: Hamilton Brown Co., 1927. 8vo., pictorial boards, slight spine wear, very good+, illustrations by Arthur Henderson in bright colors, very scarce, beautiful.   Aleph-Bet Books, Inc.   105 - 239   2013 $350

Emhardt, William Chauncey *Religion in Soviet Russia: Anarchy.* Milwaukee: Morehouse, 1929. First edition, near fine, owner's inscription, very good dust jacket, uncommon.   Beasley Books   2013 - 2013 $100

Emori, Nahiko *Chashitsu (Rooms for Tea-Ceremony).* Tokyo: Asahi Shimbunsha, 1949. First edition, 4to., fine in very good+ dust jacket with edge wear, closed tears, creases, tiny chips, book and dust jacket in original mildly worn red board folder with original ties and paste-on paper labels, 200+ photos and drawings.   By the Book, L. C.   38 - 60   2013 $650

Ende, Michael *Jim Button and Luke the Engine Driver.* London: Harrap, 1963. First edition, original green cloth, spine trifle faded, dust jacket edges trifle worn and creased, backstrip worn at head and foot with little loss and repaired, illustrations by Maurice S. Dodd, few spots to edges, but very good, rare edition.   R. F. G. Hollett & Son   Children's Books - 182 2013   £650

Endore, Guy *Methinks the Lady.* New York: Duell, Sloan and Pearce, 1945. First edition, about fine in good dust jacket with considerable rubbing and small tears.   Between the Covers Rare Books, Inc.   Mystery & Detective Fiction - 98488   2013 $275

Engberg, Siri *Edward Ruscha: Editions 1959-1999: Catalogue Raisonne.* Minneapolis: Walker Art Center, 1990. 2 volumes, grey covered boards with white title to spine and front cover, except for tiny chip on rear cover volume 2 books near fine, interior pages pristine, housed in black cloth slipcase covered by color wrappers, showing light wear, volume I 127 pages, volume 2, 155 pages.   The Kelmscott Bookshop   7 - 89   2013 $250

Engelbrecht, Martin *Fancy Ball.* Augsburg: n.d. circa, 1780. 6 hand colored panels each 7 7/8 x 6 3/8 inches, high in fine condition, each panel has cut-out hand colored scenes which, when viewed at spaced intervals, provide a three dimensional view of an elaborate party held inside a castle.   Aleph-Bet Books, Inc.   105 - 448   2013 $3000

Engelbreit, Mary *Book.* San Diego: Ash Ranch Press, 1990. Limited to 100 copies, 24 with jewelled onlay on front board, of which this copy is one, 5 x 3 cm., leather, jewelled onlay on front board, title gilt stamped on spine, marbled endpapers, from the collection of Donn W. Sanford.   Oak Knoll Books   303 - 37   2013 $100

Engen, Rodney K. *Kate Greenaway.* Academy Editions, 1976. First edition, 4to., original cloth, gilt, dust jacket, pages 68, illustrations, 4 color plates.   R. F. G. Hollett & Son   Children's Books - 183   2013   £25

England, George Allan *Pod, Bender & Co.* New York: McBride, 1916. First edition, slight offsetting to endpapers from flaps, else about fine in attractive, very good or better dust jacket with some old internal brown paper repairs and some negligible and very shallow chipping, signed by author in pencil, exceptionally scarce in jacket, or signed.   Between the Covers Rare Books, Inc.   Mystery & Detective Fiction - 46824   2013 $1250

England, George Allan *Vikings of the Ice. Being the Log of a Tenderfoot on the Great Newfoundland Sea Hunt.* New York: Doubleday Page, 1924. 8vo., half title, frontispiece, map and 89 black and white photo illustrations, cloth with paper label to spine, cloth slightly worn.   Schooner Books Ltd.   101 - 27   2013 $65

England, Thomas R. *The Life of the Rev. Arthur O'Leary.* London: Longman, 1822. First edition, 8vo., portrait, half leather (worn), text good.   C. P. Hyland   261 - 657   2013   £45

England, Thomas R. *A Short Memoir of an Antique Medal Lately Found Friars' Walk Near the City of Cork.* 1819. First edition, 20th century boards, very good.   C. P. Hyland   261 - 364   2013   £65

English Lake Country. no publisher, circa, 1910. Oblong 4to., original cloth backed boards, gilt, edges worn, 6 stiff card leaves on linen guards bearing 34 photographic illustrations, some with additional inset illustrations, all titled within illustrations, rather loose.   R. F. G. Hollett & Son   Lake District and Cumbria - 59   2013   £25

The English Lakes. Nelson's Hand-Books for Tourists. T. Nelson and Sons, 1859. Original blindstamped cloth, gilt, trifle rubbed, 24 color printed plates in blue and purple.   R. F. G. Hollett & Son   Lake District and Cumbria - 60   2013   £140

English Lyrics. London: printed at the Chiswick Press for Kegan Paul, Trench & Co., 1883. First edition, one of 50 large paper copies, this #32, 206 x 130mm., fine turn-of-the-century Hazel brown crushed morocco, very elaborately gilt by Zaehnsdorf (stamp signed on front turn-in, oval blind-stamp on rear pastedown), covers richly gilt with very wide floral border featuring many tendrils and small tools, border enclosing panel filled with alternating rows of floral sprigs and leaves (tiny stars in between), raised bands, spine compartments gilt with either floral bouquet or rows of leaves and flowers, densely gilt turn-ins, gray silk endleaves, top edge gilt, other edges untrimmed, armorial bookplate of Mary Louise Curtis Bok, half title with pencilled note "Wedding present to M.L.C./from Charles Scribner October 1896", (spine just slightly sunned toward a darker brown, front joint and very top and bottom of back joint little worn, with flaking and thin cracks, but no looseness), corners slightly rubbed, still especially attractive with lovely binding with glistening covers and beautifully printed text pristine. Phillip J. Pirages   63 - 65   2013 $1250

English, Arthur   *The Vanished Race.*   Montreal: Editions Edouard Garand, 1927. Small 8vo., cloth, spine with marbled boards, half title, edges worn, otherwise good. Schooner Books Ltd.   101 - 28   2013 $60

Enright, Elizabeth   *The Sea is All Around.*   New York: Farrar Rinehart, 1940. First edition, 4to., cloth, fine in very good+ dust jacket, 6 full page color lithos plus numerous black and whites, quite scarce.   Aleph-Bet Books, Inc.   105 - 227   2013 $250

Entwistle, Mary   *The Call Drum: African Stories and Studies for Primary Children.*   New York: Friendship Press, 1928. First edition (Teachers Edition), cloth and paper covered boards with paper spine label, folding illustrations tipped to rear pastedown as issued, lightly rubbed at extremities, near fine without dust jacket, scarce.   Between the Covers Rare Books, Inc.   165 - 108   2013 $150

Epictetus   *The Discourses of Epictetus.*   London: George Bell and Sons, 1902. Limited to 250 copies, printed at the Chiwcik Press on handmade paper, 2 volumes, 282, 265 pages, 24cm., full tan morocco with gilt 17th century French period design on front boards, gilt fillet on turn-ins, gilt spine title, raised bands, marbled endpapers, both volumes very good, wear to back joints, board edges and spine, front joints cracked but snug, text pages clean and tight, ex-library with just one small inventory stamp on back of each titlepage with 'canceled" neatly stamped upon it, small bookplate, very handsome.   Between the Covers Rare Books, Inc.   Philosophy - 339479   2013 $200

Epictetus   *The Golden Sayings of Epictetus with Hymn of Cleanthes.*   London: Macmillan and Co., 1920. Reprint, 16.5cm., near fine in three quarter morocco, gilt spine title, raised bands and marbled endpapers, front joint cracked, still snug and strong, with light wear to back joint and board edges, else fine.   Between the Covers Rare Books, Inc.   Philosophy - 105299   2013 $100

Epworth and Its Surroundings. The Home of the Wesleys.   Epworth: Epworth Bells Printing Works, n.d., Second edition, Oblong 8vo., original green ribbed pictorial cloth, gilt, 24 plates, frontispiece, pictorial title.   R. F. G. Hollett & Son   Wesleyan Methodism - 2   2013   £35

Equiano, Olaudah   *The Interesting Narrative of the Life of Olaudah Equiano or Gustavus Vassa, the African.*   Dublin: printed for and sold by the author, 1791. Fourth edition, frontispiece, 8vo., some foxing and browning to a number of gatherings, old marginal waterstain to frontispiece, inksplash to tissue guard, full contemporary calf, gilt banded spine, red morocco label, rather rubbed, spine little chipped at tail, wear to lower following hinge, with slightly later name of C. W. Dillon on inner board, possibly a relation of Irish subscriber Richard Dillon.   Jarndyce Antiquarian Booksellers   CCIV - 123   2013   £480

Erasmus, Desiderius 1466-1536   *Adagiorum D. Erasmi Roterodami Epitome.*   Amsterdam: Ludovicum Elzevirium, 1650. First Elzevir edition, 12mo., old calf, titlepage in red and black with Minerva vignette, title somewhat soiled, else very nice.   Joseph J. Felcone Inc.   Books Printed before 1701 - 37   2013 $600

Erasmus, Desiderius 1466-1536   *Eloge De La Folie D'Erasme.*   Paris: Librarie Des Bibliophiles, 1876. Third edition, number 266 of 500 copies on Holland paper, original wrappers sewn in, 83 black and white gravures, small 4to., three quarter red morocco over red marbled boards, raised bands, gilt titles, marbled endpapers, very good plus or better, tight, clean copy, just bit of wear at extremities, handsome copy, somewhat uncommon Charles Fairfax Murray bookplate.   Kaaterskill Books   16 - 28   2013 $300

Erckmann, Emile   *The Outbreak of the Great French Revolution; Related by a Peasant of Lorraine.*   London: Richard Bentley & Son, 1871. First English edition, 3 volumes, lacking following f.e.p. volume III, original red cloth decorated in black, little dulled and marked, hinges & extremities slightly rubbed, W. H. Smith embossed stamp in volume I.   Jarndyce Antiquarian Booksellers   CCV - 101   2013   £350

Erdmuthe Sophia, Margaravin   *Sondervbahre Kirchen-Staat-nd Welt-Sachen.*   Nuremberg: Wolfgang Moritz Endter, 1689. 12mo., portrait, engraved fore-title, 2 folding tables, contemporary vellum, fine.   Joseph J. Felcone Inc.   Books Printed before 1701 - 38   2013 $475

Erdrich, Louise   *The Game of Silence.*   New York: Harper Collins, 2005. Advance reading copy, signed by author, fine in wrappers, especially scarce signed.   Ken Lopez Bookseller   159 - 149   2013 $150

Erichsen, Hugo *Medical Rhymes, a Collection of Rhymes of ye Anciente Time...* St. Louis: J. H. Cambers, 1884. 8vo., frontispiece, many fine illustrations, original brown publisher's blind and gilt stamped cloth, spine ends and corners worn, good, manuscript sheet written by Philip S. Hench and blank memo sheet with his printed name, with manuscript sheet where Hench has written out an anonymous poem. Jeff Weber Rare Books   172 - 88   2013 $95

Ernest, Edward *Alphablock Books.* New York: Grosset and Dunlap, 1943. 26 miniature books, housed in publisher's pictorial box measuring 9 1'2 inches square, books fine, box slightly dusty, else near fine, illustrations by Lee Morss. Aleph-Bet Books, Inc.   104 - 20   2013 $450

Ernst, Max *Max Ernst Ne Peint Plus!...* Nice & Venice: Galerie Chave, 1973. First edition, number 16 of 80 impressions, total edition, 198, 2 original lithographs, 18 color photo lithographs+ one on cover, all hors-texte and hand mounted on separate leaves, the 2 lithographs were printed in colors on Japon nacre and hand mounted on separate sheets of Arches, each of the the 2 lithos individually numbered and signed in pencil by Ernst, 13.5 x 10 inches, 50 pages (unpaginated), excellent copy in board covers, protective glassine and slipcase.   Gemini Fine Books & Arts., Ltd.   Art Reference & Illustrated Books - 2013 $2500

Erskine, John *The Principles of the Law of Scotland: In the Order of Sir George Mackenzie's Institutions of the Law.* Edinburgh: printed by Hamilton, Balfour and Neill, 1754. First edition, little light browning, contemporary sprinkled calf, spine with five raised bands between gilt fillets, red morocco lettering piece in second compartment, rest with small central gilt tools, just bit rubbed, armorial bookplate of Carmichael of Eastend, very good.   Blackwell's Rare Books   172 - 52   2013   £850

Erskine, William *Epistle from Lady Grange to Edward D-, Esq.* London: printed for Cadell & Davies, 1798. First edition, 4to., lacking half title, expertly bound in recent quarter calf, marbled boards, vellum tips, gilt banded spine, red morocco label.   Jarndyce Antiquarian Booksellers   CCIV - 124   2013   £350

Escobar, Juan De *Romancero a Historia del Muy Valeroso Cavallero El cid Ruy Diaz en Lenguge Antiguo.* Cadiz: Pedro Ortiz, 1702. Second Cadiz edition, woodcut printer's device on title, top of gutter of one opening torn by intrusive sewing, entering text but without loss paper flaw in one leaf affecting 3 or 4 letters on either side, slight ocasional browning or soiling, fairly tightly sewn, long 12mo., recased in original vellum, lettered ink on spine, marbled edges, armorial bookplate, inside front cover of George Jacob Bosanquet, good.   Blackwell's Rare Books   172 - 53   2013   £650

Eshleman, Clayton *The Chavin Illumination.* Lima: 1965. First edition, copy 50 of 100, very near fine in string tied wrappers, very good plus dust jacket with some creasing to top edge near spine, signed by Eshleman on limitation page, additionally inscribed by him for poet Ronald Johnson. Jeff Hirsch Books   Fall 2013 - 129345   2013 $75

Eskimo Cut-Outs. Racine: Whitman, 1938. Oblong 4to., stiff wrappers, very good+, unused, 6 pages of die-cut color figures that reader can punch out to assemble on Eskimo igloo village.   Aleph-Bet Books, Inc.   104 - 589   2013 $225

Estaing, Charles Hector, Comte D' *Exrait du Journal d'u Officcier de la Marine de l'Escadre de M. Le Comte D'Estaing.* Paris: 1782. First edition, first state, 8vo., modern quarter blue cloth, marbled boards, original grey wrappers bound in, frontispiece, engraved portrait with vignette facing page (1), uncut, partially unopened, fine, original wrappers bound in, blank leading margins of 4 leaves at end, one corner of front wrapper slightly ragged.   Howard S. Mott Inc.   262 - 47   2013 $1000

Esten, Cornelius *Warning to Youth from a Fellow Youth, who Died When He was Near 23 Years Old....* Providence?: 1769? First edition?, 8o., 24 pages, self wrappers? sewn, sheets browned, outer couple of leaves stained, top margin cropped, shaving some page numbers, two very faint library stamps on margins of first page, decent copy in spite of flaws.   M & S Rare Books, Inc.   95 - 329   2013 $500

Estienne, Charles   1504-1564 *De Dissectione Partium Corporis Humani Libri Tres.* Paris: Apud Simonem Colinaeum, 1545. First edition, 202 leaves with 62 full page woodcut illustrations printed from 56 blocks, skillful repairs to blank margin of title, some browning and staining of text, nicely rebound in full pigskin done in period style with panels and arabesque and filigrees in panels, spine with raised bands and blind tooling, quite handsome modern binding.   James Tait Goodrich   75 - 88   2013 $45,000

Estienne, Charles   1504-1564 *Les Figures et Portraicts des Parties du Corps Humain.* Paris: Jacques Kervet, 1575. Folio, 61 full page woodcuts, 8 smaller woodcuts, Kerver's unicorn device on title, few marginal repairs, one horizontal tear repaired, fine modern paneled calf done in period style, rare.   James Tait Goodrich   75 - 89   2013 $45,000

Estienne, Henri 1528-1598 *Traicte de la Conformite du Langage Francois avec le Grec, Divise en Trio Liures dont les Deux Premiers Traictent des Manieres de Parler Conformes le Troisieme...* Paris: Robert Estienne, 1569. First Paris edition, small 8vo., all edges gilt, Zaehnsdorf style full brown morocco, blind ruled covers and spine, gilt stamped ornaments, raised bands, gilt stamped title, gilt stamped turn-ins, 19th century leather armorial bookplate of Marigues de Champ-Repus, fine. Jeff Weber Rare Books 171 - 118   2013 $2500

Ettinger, Nathalie *Africa and Asia: Mapping Two Continents.* Aldus Books and Jupiter Books, 1973. Original cloth, gilt, dust jacket with little edgewear, pages 488, illustrations in color. R. F. G. Hollett & Son Africana - 61   2013   £25

Euaclaire, Sally *The New Color Photography.* New York: Abbeville Press, 1981. First edition, 287 pages, 166 color plates, tight, near fine in wrappers with some very slight wear, very nice. Jeff Hirsch Books Fall 2013 - 129170 2013 $75

Euclides *Geometricorum Elementorum Libri XV.* Paris: Henri Estienne, 7 January, 1516-1517. Sixth edition, Roman types with numerous woodcut geometrical diagrams in margins, fine crible initials in a variety of styles and sizes, titlepage soiled and cut down and mounted on old paper, one diagram just cropped at its extreme outer corner, folio, 19th century half brown calf by Hatton of Manchester, marbled edges, original order for the binder loosely inserted (in fact calling for half Russia), the Macclesfield copy with bookplate but no blindstamps and annotated by John Collins, preserved in cloth folding box, good. Blackwell's Rare Books Sciences - 48   2013   £15,000

Euclides *The Elements of Geometrie of the Most Aunciente Philosopher ...* London: imprinted... by John Daye, 1570. First edition, with all 37 overslips, folio, with folding letterpress "Groundplat" or table accompanying John Dee's preface, title within allegorical woodcut border showing, at top, woodcut geometrical diagrams, woodcut portrait of John Day on colophon leaf, decorative woodcut head and tailpieces and initials, early full brown calf neatly rebacked and restored to style, ruled in gilt and blind, boards with central gilt device, gilt spine bands, compartments blind paneled with central oval gilt devices, title neatly restored in margins and bit soiled, folding plate with few closed tears, expertly and neatly repaired, some minor marginal dampstaining and light soiling, boards with few scuffs and scratches, overall excellent copy, very clean overall and on strong paper. Heritage Book Shop Holiday Catalogue 2012 - 57   2013 $100,000

Euripides *Opera Omnia.* London: Richard Priestley, 1821. 9 volumes, 8vo., text in Greek with Latin footnotes, printer's list in volume vi, triangular closed tear to page ix in volume vii (no loss of text) sporadic foxing, occasional light pencil annotations, half vellum, marbled paper boards and endpapers, black morocco label to spine, edges red, boards rubbed, edges worn with occasional small bumps but still very good, armorial bookplate of Aston Walker to each front pastedown, various library tickets and inkstamps from London Borough of Southwark Special Collection to prelims, pencilled ownership inscription of M. R. Barker to half title. Unsworths Antiquarian Booksellers 28 - 13   2013   £300

Eusebius *Chronicon.* Venice: Erhard Ratdolt 13 September, 1483. Second edition, small quarto, printed in red and black, two large and fourteen smaller white on black floriated woodcut initials, near contemporary binding of limp vellum lettered in manuscript on spine, minor worming to spine and to outer blank margin of several gatherings, very minor dampstaining to inner blank margin of final third of volume, several early ink annotations on final blank leaf and in margins, bookplates, exceptionally nice, very fine and bright, housed in custom green cloth clamshell case. Heritage Book Shop 50th Anniversary Catalogue - 35 2013 $15,000

Eustachius, Bartolomeo *Explicatio Tabulae Anatomocarum.* Leidae Batavorum: Apud J A. Langerak, J. & H. Verbeek, 1744. First edition edited by B. S. Albinus, 47 engraved plates, folio, full antique style English panel calf, gilt edges, raised bands, gilt armorial tooling of spine, internally some dampstaining and foxing. James Tait Goodrich 75 - 90   2013 $3250

Eustachius, Bartolomeo *Opuscula Anatomica...* Leiden: 1707. Second edition, 3 volumes bound in 1, contemporary worn vellum, title in red and black, hand lettered spines, inner hinges split but tight, some light dampstaining and few mildew spots, tear to lower edge of spine, ownership plate and gift note of the British physician and physicist Joseph Hodgson, very rare. James Tait Goodrich S74 - 106 2013 $3500

Eustachius, Bartolomeo *Tabulae Anatomicae Clarissimi Viri Bartolomaei Eustachii quas e Tenbris Tandem vindicatas et Claeentis Papae XI.* Romae: Sumptibus Laurentii & Thomae Pagliarini bibliopol sub signo Palladis..., 1728. Folio, titlepage slightly browned and foxed, traces of old watermarking to some lower edges, only intrusive on final few leaves of index and following endpapers, few occasional marks but generally in good clean condition, contemporary calf, excellently rebacked, red morocco label. Jarndyce Antiquarian Booksellers CCIV - 126   2013   £2800

Eustathius Makrembolites *De Ismeniae et Ismenes Amoribus Libri XI.*   Paris: Summptibus Hieronymi Drouart, 1617.   Editio princeps of the Greek text, lower corner dampstained throughout, browned in places, annotations washed from second leaf resulting in few small paper repairs, one text leaf recto annotated in early Italian hand and blank corner verso skilfully reinforced, 8vo., 18th century Italian vellum, spine lettered in gilt on yellow dyed background, all edges yellow, bit soiled, later ink biblio-critical note, sound.   Blackwell's Rare Books   172 - 54   2013   £600

Evans, Albert S.   *La California. Sketches of Life in the Golden State.*   San Francisco: A. L. Bancroft, 1874.   First edition, second printing, 379 pages, 25 full page woodcut plates from original drawings by Ernest Narjot, publisher's patterned violet cloth stamped in black and gold, spine faded to brown, some spotting to covers, very good, internally very fine.   Argonaut Book Shop   Summer 2013 - 98   2013 $300

Evans, C. S.   *Cinderella. Retold by....*   London: William Heinemann, 1919.   Edition deluxe, one of 325 copies on Japanese vellum, out of a total edition of 850 numbered copies, signed by artist, this being number 233, quarto, mounted color frontispiece with color pictorial board and tissue guard, 3 double page silhouette illustrations with color, 14 single page silhouettes and 36 silhouette text illustrations by Arthur Rackham, black and white titlepage and color illustrations; original quarter vellum, ruled in gilt over white boards, front cover and spine lettered and pictorially stamped in gilt, top edge gilt, green and white pictorial endpapers, some minor wear to corners and board edges, closed tear partially through "Heinemann" on spine, with no loss of text, boards bit sunned at extremities, very good.   Heritage Book Shop   Holiday Catalogue 2012 - 126   2013 $2000

Evans, Edward R. G. R.   *South with Scott.*   London: Collins, 1924.   Original pictorial cloth, trifle worn, illustrations, 1 plate little worn and chipped.   R. F. G. Hollett & Son   Polar Exploration - 13   2013   £25

Evans, Eva Knox   *Key Corner.*   New York: G. P. Putnam's Sons, 1938.   First edition, illustrations by Erick Berry, some modest, light dampstaining, mostly on rear board, else very good, lacking dust jacket, briefly inscribed by author.   Between the Covers Rare Books, Inc.   165 - 147   2013 $125

Evans, Eva Knox   *Ten Ring Circus Books.*   New York: Capital Pub., 1949.   10 miniature books in simulated ten, housed in oblong pictorial card case simulating a circus ten, case and all books illustrated in color by Richard M. Powers, excellent condition.   Aleph-Bet Books, Inc.   104 - 124   2013 $200

Evans, Francis *Furness and Furness Abbey; or a Companion through the Lancashire Part of the Lake District.*   Ulverston: D. Atkinson, 1842.   First edition, original blind-stamped cloth gilt, spine rather cracked but sound, 3 engraved plates, plan and hand colored map.   R. F. G. Hollett & Son   Lake District and Cumbria - 63   2013   £175

Evans, J. B.   *Some Facts About Suffrage Leaders a Cause is No Stronger than Its Leaders.*   Montgomery: Brown Publishing circa, 1920.   First edition, rare, 14 x 8 1/2 inches.   Second Life Books Inc.   182 - 72   2013 $400

Evans, Joan   *Pattern. A Study of Ornament in Western Europe from 1180-1900.*   Oxford: Clarendon Press, 1931.   2 volumes, 4to., blue cloth, gilt to spine and upper board, spines and edges dusty, endcaps creased, endpapers little discolored by very good, small slip letterpress printed "With the author's compliments" loosely inserted.   Unsworths Antiquarian Booksellers   28 - 161   2013   £90

Evans, Myfanwy   *Diggory Goest to the Never-Never.*   Collins, 1937.   First edition, 4to., original pictorial boards, matching dust jacket, edges little worn and faded, illustrations, front flyleaf lightly spotted, very nice, scarce.   R. F. G. Hollett & Son   Children's Books - 594   2013   £75

Evans, Nathaniel   *Poems on Sever Occasions with some other Compositions.*   Philadelphia: John Dunlap, 1772.   First and only contemporary edition, contemporary calf, very skillfully rebacked in period style, usual foxing, nicest copy we have seen, late 19th century booklabel of A. G. Odenbaugh.   Joseph J. Felcone Inc.   English and American Literature to 1800 - 13   2013 $750

Evans, Robert Maunsell   *Poems with a Memoir.*   Cork: Purcell, 1892.   First edition, viii, 38 pages, cloth, 8vo., very good.   C. P. Hyland   261 - 367   2013   £45

Evans, Valerie   *We that are Left. Remember New Brunswickers in the Air Force.*   Saint John: 250 RCAF (Saint John) Wing, Air Force Association of Canada, 2002.   Quarto, blue cloth, pages xvi, illustrations, very good in dust jacket.   Schooner Books Ltd.   105 - 126   2013 $65

Evans, Walker   *Walker Evans American Photographs.*   New York: Museum of Modern Art, 1962.   Second edition, very good in black cloth boards with gilt title to spine, few speckles to boards and minor foxing to fore edge, else clean, in off-white illustrated dust jacket with black title to spine and front panel, jacket has few small chips to edges and minor dampstaining, foxing and toning along edges, 195 pages.   The Kelmscott Bookshop   7 - 93   2013 $375

Evelyn, John 1620-1706 *Diary of John Evelyn.* London: Bickers & Son, 1879. three quarter leather, very good, 4to., 4 volumes complete, raised bands and gilt titles, some joints rubbed.   Barnaby Rudge Booksellers   Biography 2013 - 021567   2013 $175

Evelyn, John 1620-1706 *Fumifugium; or the Inconvenience of the Aer and Smoake of London Dissipated Together with Some Remedies Humbly Proposed by John Evelyn...* Chelsea: Swan Press, 1930. 16/100 copies (of an edition of 110), printed on handmade paper, 54, 32m., original quarter cream cloth, printed label, grey boards, endpapers browned, untrimmed, dust jacket lightly soiled, near fine.   Blackwell's Rare Books   B174 - 393   2013   £100

Evelyn, John 1620-1706 *Kalendarium Hortense; or the Gard'ners Almanac, Directing What He Is to Do Monthly Throughout the Year.* London: printed for T. Sawbridge in Little Britain, 1683. 12mo., little old waterstaining, visible on upper margin of some leaves, not intrusive, occasional minor foxing, full contemporary calf, blind ruled central panel enclosing a lozenge, raised bands, unlettered spine, spine little chipped at head & tail.   Jarndyce Antiquarian Booksellers   CCIV - 12   2013   £680

Evenson, Brian *Altmann's Tongue. Stories and a Novella.* New York: Knopf, 1994. First edition, proof of author's first book, red printed wrappers as issued, sticker ghost, fine.   Ed Smith Books   75 - 26   2013 $150

Everett-Green, E. *After Worcester.* Thomas Nelson, 1901. First edition, original red cloth, gilt over bevelled boards, little marked and spine trifle dulled, top edge gilt, pictorial title and 5 illustrations.   R. F. G. Hollett & Son Children's Books - 187   2013   £35

Everett, Percival *Aulus.* Sag Harbor: The Permanent Press, 1990. First edition, fine in fine dust jacket but for crease on front flap, nicely inscribed by author for Nicholas Delbanco.   Between the Covers Rare Books, Inc.   165 - 143   2013 $75

Everts, Truman C. *Thirty-Seven Days of Peril.* San Francisco: Edwin & Robert Grabhorn and James McDonald, 1923. One of 375 copies, frontispiece and title decoration by Joseph Sinel, light green cloth, gilt brown boards, very fine, uncut, plain dust jacket.   Argonaut Book Shop Summer 2013 - 99   2013 $225

Everybody, Valentine *A Run through the South of Ireland.* Cork: O'Brien, 1852. First edition, 8 plates, vii, 55 pages, folding map, lacks front wrapper, shaky, clean.   C. P. Hyland   261 - 368   2013   £95

Evison, Jonathan *West of Here.* Chapel Hill: Algonquin, 2011. First edition, one of 100 numbered copies signed by author, fine in fine wooden slipcase with inserts, as issued.   Ed Smith Books   75 - 27   2013 $150

Ewbank, Jane *The Life and Works of William Carus Wilson 1791-1859.* Kendal: Titus Wilson, 1960. First (only) edition, original wrappers, portrait and folding pedigree, ex-library with stamps and labels on wrapper and back of frontispiece, scarce.   R. F. G. Hollett & Son   Lake District and Cumbria - 64   2013   £50

Ewell, Thomas *Statement of Improvements in the Theory and Practice of the Science of Medicine.* Philadelphia: printed for the author, 1819. First edition, 8vo., 168 pages, original two toned boards uncut, binding in excellent condition, boards and sheets lightly to moderately stained.   M & S Rare Books, Inc.   95 - 121   2013 $375

Ewing, Juliana Horatia *Jackanapes.* New York: Oxford University, 1948. First edition, fine, very good+ price clipped dust jacket with mild chips, short closed tears, soil, small piece missing dust jacket spine tip, 61 pages, 8vo., illustrations by Tasha Tudor.   By the Book, L. C.   36 - 37   2013 $250

Ewing, Juliana Horatia *Jackanapes. Daddy Darwin's Dovecot. Lob Lie-by-the-Fire.* SPCK, n.d., Collected edition, large 8vo. original pictorial cloth, gilt extremities minimally rubbed, 184 pages, illustrations by Randolph Caldecott.   R. F. G. Hollett & Son   Children's Books - 110   2013   £60

Excerpta Lyrica. Rugby: Crossley and Billington, 1866. First edition, 8vo., pages 16, Greek text, moderate foxing, original plain wrappers, foxed, worn with some loss to extremities, ownership inscription of H. Lee Warner and his light pencil notes to wrapper and few places in text, scarce.   Unsworths Antiquarian Booksellers   28 - 2   2013   £30

Exquemeling, J. *The History of the Bucaniers in America.* London: D. Winter, 1741. Fourth English edition, 2 volumes, 12mo., very attractive contemporary speckled calf, morocco label to spines.   Maggs Bros. Ltd.   1467 - 110   2013   £1600

F

Faber, Basil *Thesaurus Eruditionis Scbolasticae; Sive Supellex Instructissima Dictionum, Verborum, Phrasium, Adagiorum...* Lipsae & Francofurti: Sumptibus Johannis Fritzschii, 1680. Early edition, folio in 6s, large copperplate engraved frontispiece, title with ownership signature of L. L. Hinsch, original full blindstamped vellum, joints repaired, recent front endleaves, very good.   Jeff Weber Rare Books   171 - 119   2013 $1500

Fable, Leonard *The Gingerbread Man.* George G. Harrap, n.d., 1915. First English edition, large 8vo., original cloth backed boards with pictorial onlay, little worn, title in red and black with line drawing and 8 double page color plates by Willy Pogany, text on reverse, rather loose, scarce.   R. F. G. Hollett & Son   Children's Books - 469   2013   £75

Fable, Lionel *The Children at the Pole.* London: George G. Harrap & Co. n.d. circa, 1914. First edition thus, square 12mo., original pictorial boards, little rubbed, corners rather worn and bumped, 14 page panorama, 16 color plates by Willy Pogany, with text below, main text on reverse together with double page map (with added hand coloring - childish but well done), opening accordion style, odd slight finger mark but generally nice, clean and sound, very scarce.   R. F. G. Hollett & Son   Polar Exploration - 49   2013   £180

Fabricius Ab Aquapendente, Hieronymus *Opera Chirurgica.* Padua: typis Mathaei de Cadorinis, 1666. Double page surgical plates, modern half vellum, occasional browning, some dampstaining, lower outer corners restored in first half of volume.   James Tait Goodrich   75 - 91   2013 $1450

Fabricius Ab Aquapendente, Hieronymus *Opera Omnia Anatomica et Physiolgica cum Praefarune Bernardi Stegfried Albuni.* Leiden: Apud Johannem van Kereckhem, 1738. Half title, frontispiece, 61 engraved plates, folio, 18th century french gilt calf with gilt spine and raised bands, some rubbing with bumped corners, internally fine, clean, crisp copy.   James Tait Goodrich   75 - 92   2013 $7995

Fabricius, Andreas *Harmonia Confessionis Augustanae, Doctrinae Evangelicae Cosensum Declarans.* Cologne: Maternus Cholinus, 1573. Woodcut printer's device on title, uniformly slightly browned, folio, contemporary calf, two frames of triple blind rule fillets on sides, gilt fleurons at corners, large central gilt stamped emdallion, 18th century pigskin covering spine and extending some 2 cm. onto boards, remains of green silk ties, corners worn, some worming at top of inner hinge, good.   Blackwell's Rare Books   172 - 55   2013   £950

Fabulas de Iriarte. Barcelona: Casa Editorial Araluce, 1933. Large 4to., cloth backed pictorial boards, slight bit of cover rubbing, else near fine, illustrations on every page by Asha.   Aleph-Bet Books, Inc.   105 - 233   2013 $750

Facetiae Facetiarum hoc est Joco-Seriorum Fasciculus, Exhibens Varia Variorum Auctorum Scripta non tam Lectu Iucunda and Iocosa Amoena... Francofurti: ad Moenum, 1615. 16mo., contemporary calf with raised bands, gilt spine, edges stained red, titlepage printed in red and black, some mid 17th century listings of the book being offered for sale on front blank, from the library of J. B. Hazard, contemporary ownership signature.   Second Life Books Inc.   183 - 136   2013 $950

Fages, Pedro *A Historical, Political and Natural Description of California by... Soldier of Spain.* Berkeley: University of California Press, 1937. First English translation, small octavo, xi, 83 pages, folding facsimile map, green cloth, some light rubbing to corners, slightly more so to spine ends, very good.   Argonaut Book Shop   Recent Acquisitions June 2013 - 105   2013 $90

Faggett, Harry Lee *Lines to a Little Lady: From Someone Who Begs to Be Remembered.* Philadelphia: and Ardmore: Dorrance, 1977. First edition, fine in lightly rubbed, about fine dust jacket, very nicely inscribed by author to his best friend, very scarce.   Between the Covers Rare Books, Inc.   165 - 144   2013 $150

Fahrenheit, Daniel Gabriel *"Experimenta Circa Gradum Coloris." in Philosophical Transactions Volume XXIII no. 381.* London: printed for W. and J. Innys, 1724. Disbound, some very light foxing, housed in quarter morocco clamshell.   Heritage Book Shop   Holiday Catalogue 2012 - 58   2013 $3500

The Fair One with Golden Locks. Edinburgh: Oliver & Boyd, 1840. First edition, 16mo., 34 pages plus wrappers, good, 9 woodcuts.   Barnaby Rudge Booksellers   Children 2013 - 021316   2013 $55

Fairbairn, William Alexander *Some Game Birds of West Africa.* Oliver & Boyd, 1952. First edition, original cloth, gilt, short scrape to upper hinge, dust jacket torn and defective, 9 colored plates by P. M. Sumner.   R. F. G. Hollett & Son   Africana - 62   2013   £30

Fairbank's Juvenile History of the United States. Chicago: Fairbank Co., 1911. First edition, oblong 8vo., pictorial wrappers, 56 pages, slight cover soil, else near fine, 27 wonderful full page color illustrations by W. W. Denslow.   Aleph-Bet Books, Inc.   104 - 153   2013 $300

Fairbridge, Dorothea *Gardens of South Africa.* A. & C. Black, 1924. First edition, one of only 250 copies with the Black imprint at foot of spine, remainder of the 300 copies had South African imprint, original decorated green cloth gilt, 16 color plates, scattered foxing, scarce.   R. F. G. Hollett & Son   Africana - 63   2013   £65

Fairchild, David *Book of Monsters.* Washington: National Geographic Society, 1914. First edition, maroon cloth, very good, 4to., portraits, 226 pages with photos, extremities worn.   Barnaby Rudge Booksellers   Natural History 2013 - 021257   2013 $75

Fairfield, Asa Merrill *Fairfield's Pioneer History of Lassen County, California...* San Francisco: H. S. Crocker for the author, 1916. First edition, 4 plates, folding map, pictorial maroon cloth, gilt decorated and lettered, top edge gilt, spine faded, small unobtrusive dent to front cover, near spine, else fine.   Argonaut Book Shop   Summer 2013 - 190   2013 $175

Fairlie, Gerard *Bulldog Drummond Attacks.* London: Hodder & Stoughton, 1939. First edition, some darkening on endpapers and scattered light spotting on fore-edge otherwise near fine in lightly soiled dust jacket with slightly darkened spine and internal tape mends.   Mordida Books   81 - 164   2013 $250

Fairlie, Gerard *Captain Bulldog Drummond.* London: Hodder & Stoughton, 1945. First edition, some scattered spotting on page edges, otherwise fine in dust jacket.   Mordida Books   81 - 165   2013 $65

Fairmont, Ethel *The Lovely Garden.* Chicago: Volland, 1919. First edition, 8vo. pictorial boards, fine in pictorial box, illustrations by John Rae with lovely full page color illustrations, rare title.   Aleph-Bet Books, Inc.   104 - 574   2013 $350

Fairmont, Ethel *Rhymes for Kindly Children.* Chicago: Volland, 1916. Later edition, 8vo., pictorial boards, small spine mend, else fine in pictorial box, illustrations by Johnny Gruelle with pictorial endpapers plus many full page and in-text color illustrations, very scarce, beautiful copy.   Aleph-Bet Books, Inc.   104 - 262   2013 $500

The Fairy Book. Crest Series. Thomas Nelson and Sons, n.d. early 1920's, 4to., original pictorial boards, upper panel rather stained, 6 color plates and line drawings.   R. F. G. Hollett & Son   Children's Books - 412   2013   £35

The Fairy Favour. London: E. Tringham, Henry Wass, J. Merry and L. Tomlinson, May 13th, 1791. 4 panels 3 x 7 1/2 inches when folded, slight browning and slight edge splitting at folds with archival reinforcement else near fine condition, custom morocco backed folding box, 4 large sections, each folded over at top and bottom divided in middle, each section has 4 fine hand colored engraved illustrations and by lifting flaps, reader reveals the continuation of story and new illustrations below.   Aleph-Bet Books, Inc.   105 - 309   2013 $15,500

Falconar, Maria *Poems by Maria and Harriet Falconar. (bound with) Poems on Slavery by Maria Falconar aged 17 and Harriet Falconar aged 14.* London: printed for J. Johnson/printed for Messrs Egertons... Mr. Murray ... and Mr. J. Johnson, 1788. First edition of each work, 2 volumes bound together, 12mo., contemporary or early full calf, spine decorated in blind and gilt red morocco spine, label gilt, possibly or perhaps more probably a presentation binding, boards crudely touched up, front joints starting but firm, light dampstain on edge of first few leaves, externally good copy, internally about fine, ownership name of Caroline Falconar and signed "From the authors" in unknown hand but likely one of the authors.   Between the Covers Rare Books, Inc.   165 - 302   2013 $8500

Falconer, Hugh *Merrie Carlisle and Poems of Tradition.* Carlisle: Chas. Thurnam, 1913. First edition, original cloth gilt, 126 pages, 15 illustrations, inscribed to Herbert Smith from J. M. Denwood (dialect author of Cockermouth) and dated Sept. 1920 and with postcard of Balloch Castle loosely inserted, with note by Denwood on reverse.   R. F. G. Hollett & Son   Lake District and Cumbria - 72   2013   £25

Falconer, Lanoe *Cecilia de Noel.* London: Macmillan & Co., 1891. First edition, scarce, very good, original dark blue cloth boards, light bumping to corners and chipping to spine, interior pages clean with some splitting to signatures but text block holding, 197 pages, 44 page classified catalog.   The Kelmscott Bookshop   7 - 109   2013 $300

Falconer, William *The Shipwreck.* London: John Sharpe, 1822. Full leather, very good, small 8vo., attractive full leather with gilt and blind decorations, joints and corners rubbed, 2 black morocco spine labels, previous owner's signatures, extra engraved titlepage and 5 sub titlepages, all with engraved vignettes and all with dampstains down right edge, rest of book clean.   Barnaby Rudge Booksellers   Poetry 2013 - 019998   2013 $60

Falkiner, Caesar Litton *Essays Relating to Ireland.* 1909. First edition, cloth, author's bookplate on half title, very good.   C. P. Hyland   261 - 369   2013   £60

Fall, Anna Christy *The Tragedy of a Widow's Third.* Boston: Fox, 1898. First edition, small 8vo., 117 pages, illustrations by Vesper L. George, author's presentation on flyleaf dated 1925, brown cloth, top edge gilt, ex-library with stamps and bookplate, cover little scuffed at edges, else very good, right copy.   Second Life Books Inc.   182 - 74   2013 $85

Fallon, Peter *The First Ten Years. Dublin Arts Festival Poetry.* Dublin: Dublin Arts Festival, 1979. First edition, 8vo., original black cloth, dust jacket, photographic portraits, slightly bumped at head of spine, otherwise fine.   Maggs Bros. Ltd.   1442 - 93   2013   £75

Family of Farish of Cumberland Formerly of Dumfriesshire. (Corrected to 31st December 1901). Privately printed, 1902. Modern wrappers, scarce.   R. F. G. Hollett & Son   Lake District and Cumbria - 73   2013   £30

Fanthorpe, Robert Lionel *Space-Borne.* London: John Spencer & Co. n.d., 1959. First edition, small octavo, pictorial wrappers.   L. W. Currey, Inc.   Fall Sampler Sept. 2013 - 144144   2013 $100

Faraday, M. A. *The Westmorland Protestation Returns 1641/2.* Kendal: Titus Wilson, 1971. First edition, original wrappers, pages 86.   R. F. G. Hollett & Son   Lake District and Cumbria - 74   2013   £30

Farago, Ladislas *Abyssinia on the Eve.* Putnam, 1935. First reprint, original blue cloth gilt, extremities, rubbed, maps on endpapers, well illustrated, nice and clean internally.   R. F. G. Hollett & Son   Africana - 64   2013   £25

Farington, Joseph   1747-1821 *The Farington Diary July 13th 1793 to Dec. 30th 1821.* 1923-1928. 8 volumes, 8vo., cloth, hinge worn on volume I, dust jacket on volumes 2 and 5-8, very good.   C. P. Hyland   261 - 418   2013   £225

Farington, Joseph   1747-1821 *Lake Views.* From Views of the Lakes, etc.,, 1816. Oblong folio, old cloth, so titled in gilt, 30 steel engraved plates after drawings by Barington, without title, front flyleaf little creased and worn, but very nice, clean collection plates.   R. F. G. Hollett & Son   Lake District and Cumbria - 75   2013   £750

Farish, Thomas Edwin *The Gold Hunters of California.* Chicago: M. A. Donohue, 1904. First edition, 246 pages, frontispiece and 12 illustrations, light green pictorial cloth decorated and stamped in red on gold background and black, spine slightly darkened, minor rubbing to spine ends, else fine, signed by J. R. Knowland, owner of Oakland Tribune, very scarce.   Argonaut Book Shop   Summer 2013 - 100   2013 $250

Farjeon, Eleanor *Cherrystones.* London: Michael Joseph, 1942. First edition, 8vo., original yellow decorated cloth, dust jacket, excellent copy, dust jacket browned and nicked, price clipped, inscribed by author with drawing.   Maggs Bros. Ltd.   1460 - 281   2013   £125

Farley, Walter *The Horse-Tamer.* New York: Random House, 1958. First edition, cheap paper somewhat browned, else fine in very near fine dust jacket with touch of rubbing.   Between the Covers Rare Books, Inc.   Horses, Horsemanship, Horse Racing, Etc. - 68342   2013 $85

Farm Cut-Outs. Racine: Whitman, 1938. Oblong 4to., stiff wrappers, folded accordion style, fine and unused, 6 pages of color figures that reader can cut-out to assemble into farm.   Aleph-Bet Books, Inc.   105 - 591   2013 $200

Farmer, Philip Jose *The Alley God.* London: Sidgwick and Jackson, 1970. First edition, signed and inscribed by Farmer, near fine in very good++ dust jacket with mild soil, mild edge wear, 176 pages, small 8vo.   By the Book, L. C.   36 - 46   2013 $325

Farmer, Philip Jose *Dayworld.* New York: G P Putnams Sons, 1985. First edition, fine in dust jacket with just hint of age toning on rear panel, else fine, white label with author's signature laid in.   Between the Covers Rare Books, Inc.   Sci-Fi, Fantasy & Horror - 320725   2013 $60

Farmer, Philip Jose *Doc Savage: His Apocalyptic Life.* Garden City: Doubleday, 1973. First edition, pages edges slightly darkened and spotted, otherwise fine in dust jacket.   Mordida Books   81 - 445   2013 $75

Farmer, Philip Jose *The Green Odyssey.* New York: Ballantine Books, 1957. First edition, vertical creases on cheap cardboard boards, else about fine in fresh, near fine dust jacket with some very modest wear, exceptionally uncommon.   Between the Covers Rare Books, Inc.   Sci-Fi, Fantasy & Horror - 71918   2013 $4500

Farmer, Philip Jose *The Image of the Beast: an Exorcism (Ritual 1).* Los Angeles: Essex House, 1968. First edition, paperback original, bump to upper right corner, light stress creases to spine, else near fine.   Between the Covers Rare Books, Inc.   Sci-Fi, Fantasy & Horror - 2232   2013 $140

Farnham, Eliza W. *Woman and Her Era.* New York: Davis, 1864. First edition, 8vo., 318, 466 + ads, publisher's cloth, stamped in gilt on spine, blind on cover (wear to fore edge of cover of both volumes, some chips to spine cloth and tips to volume two, lacks some of the cloth at extremities of spine and along hinges), tear to fore edge of leaves of index and final matter of volume 2, without affecting letterpress, ex-library with small labels at top of spine and stamp on upper corner of each titlepage, good clean set, contemporary ownership signatures on end paper of each volume, rare.   Second Life Books Inc.   182 - 77   2013 $1600

Farnham, Eliza W. *Woman and Her Era.* New York: Plumb, 1865. Second edition, 8vo., pages 318, 466 + ad, publisher's cloth, lacks some of the cloth at extremities of spine, couple of pieces at lower hinges and on tips, nice and clean inside, rare.   Second Life Books Inc.   182 - 76   2013 $1200

Farnsworth, Oliver   *The Cincinnati Directory, Containing the Names, Profession and Occupation of the Inhabitants of the town....*   Cincinnati: Pub. by Oliver Farnsworth, Oct., 1819. First edition, 8vo., large engraved folding map (short tear at gutter), some wrinkling, original printed boards (with ads on back), foxed, uncut, spine rubbed and lightly chipped, covers virtually unrubbed, lacks back endpaper, outer front hinge cracking but sound.   M & S Rare Books, Inc.   95 - 272   2013 $2500

Farquhar, Francis P.   *History of the Sierra Nevada.* Berkeley: University of California Press, 1965.   First edition, quarto, 276 pages, frontispiece in color, drawings, photos, maps, silver decorated blue cloth, spine lettered gilt, slight offsetting (as usual) to endpapers, tiny ownership sticker, fine, pictorial dust jacket.   Argonaut Book Shop   Recent Acquisitions June 2013 - 107   2013 $90

Farrar, Frederic W.   *St. Winifred's or the World of School.* Edinburgh: A. & C. Black, 1887. Sixteenth edition, original brown pictorial cloth, gilt, all edges gilt, tissue guarded frontispiece and title vignette, front joint cracked, else attractive copy.   R. F. G. Hollett & Son   Children's Books - 195   2013   £30

Farrelly, M. J.   *The Settlement After the War in South Africa.*   Macmillan and Co., 1900. First edition, original cloth, gilt, edge of lower board little damped, library stamps, small tears to title through careless opening.   R. F. G. Hollett & Son   Africana - 65   2013   £30

Farrer, Richard R.   *A Tour in Greece.*   Edinburgh: Blackwood, 1882. First edition, 8vo., 27 plates, 216 pages, original orange decorative cloth, spine lightly rubbed. J. & S. L. Bonham Antiquarian Booksellers   Europe - 6254   2013   £140

Farrington, Thomas   *A Life of the Honble. Robert Boyle, F. R. S...*   1917. 8vo., 24 pages, cloth, very good, signed presentation from author.   C. P. Hyland   261 - 149   2013   £45

Farrow, G. E.   *The Wallypug of Why.*   London: Hutchinson, 1895. First edition, 8vo., green cloth, extensive pictorial cover, all edges gilt, near fine, illustrations by Harry Furniss, vignettes by his daughter Dorothy, scarce.   Aleph-Bet Books, Inc.   105 - 120   2013 $300

The Fast Express.   Chicago: Donohue, 1911.   Folio, pictorial wrappers, slight edgewear to covers, few tiny mends, else very good+, 10 full page chromolithographs and numerous in-text chromolithographs.   Aleph-Bet Books, Inc.   105 - 562   2013 $250

Father Tuck's Mechanical Animals.   London: Raphael Tuck circa, 1905.   Series II Wild & Tame Animals, Housed in original pictorial box (10 1/2 x 7 inches), 8 large chromolithographed animal figures, box flaps strengthened, else very good and all animals are in fine condition, animals are hinged with paper joints capable of being placed in hundreds of different positions and are double side, fantastic mechanical animals.   Aleph-Bet Books, Inc.   105 - 409   2013 $900

Father Tuck's Rocking Animals.   London, et al: Raphael Tuck, n.d. circa, 1905.   Housed in original pictorial box are 10 large chromolithographed animal figures, box has some wear but is sound and very good, animals are fine with minor repair to tiger's ear.   Aleph-Bet Books, Inc.   105 - 410   2013 $900

Faulconer, Albert   *Foundations of Anesthesiology.* Springfield: Charles C. Thomas, 1965.   First edition, large 8vo., numerous illustrations and tables, beige cloth, dust jackets chipped, ownership rubber stamps, very good.   Jeff Weber Rare Books   172 - 87   2013 $300

Faulkner, William Harrison   1897-1962   *Big Woods.* New York: Random House, 1955. First edition, 8vo., small stain on covers from remnants of scotch tape, otherwise nice, clean in unclipped dust jacket.   Second Life Books Inc.   183 - 132   2013 $400

Faulkner, William Harrison   1897-1962   *Faulkner on Love: a Letter to Marjorie Lyons.*   Fargo: Merrykit Press, 1974. First edition, one of 100 (of 110) copies, 8vo., original printed red wrappers, five pages and double page photographically reproduced letter, fine.   The Brick Row Book Shop   Miscellany Fifty-Nine - 21   2013 $275

Faulkner, William Harrison 1897-1962 *The Hamlet.* New York: Random House, 1940. First edition, limited issue, number 203 of 250 numbered copies, signed by author, 8vo., half blue green cloth and patterned paper boards, gilt lettering, all edges gilt, pictorial title, boards little worn and soiled at edges, patterned paper slightly foxed, very good. The Brick Row Book Shop Miscellany Fifty-Nine - 22 2013 $3250

Faulkner, William Harrison 1897-1962 *The Hamlet.* New York: Random House, 1940. First issue, fine in very near fine, price clipped, first issue dust jacket with hint of rubbing to front spine fold and short closed tear on rear panel, beautiful copy, from the Bruce Kahn collection. Ken Lopez Bookseller 159 - 59 2013 $7500

Faulkner, William Harrison 1897-1962 *Pylon.* New York: Harrison Smith and Robert Haas Inc, 1935. First edition, 2nd printing, signed by author, very good, original blue cloth boards, black title to spine, very slight fading to spine and top edges of boards, interior clean and bright, very good price clipped dust jacket with off-white title to blue spine panel few small chips to spine ends, hinges and corners of jacket, 315 pages. The Kelmscott Bookshop 7 - 111 2013 $1100

Faulkner, William Harrison 1897-1962 *Salmagundi...and a Poem.* Milwaukee: Casanova Press, 1932. First edition, limited to 525 copies, original printed wrappers, uncut, tipped in frontispiece, fine, rubbed and cracked publisher's box. Second Life Books Inc. 183 - 133 2013 $600

Faulkner, William Harrison 1897-1962 *William Faulkner's Letters to Malcolm Franklin.* Irving: published by the Society for the Study of Traditional Culture, 1976. First edition, one of only 40 copies, Special advance printing, 4to., printed self wrappers, stapled as issued (16) pages, fine. The Brick Row Book Shop Miscellany Fifty-Nine - 23 2013 $500

Faust, Frederick *The Night Flower.* New York: Macaulay Co., 1936. First edition, bookplate, else near fine in good dust jacket with small chips at spine ends and staining on rear panel. Between the Covers Rare Books, Inc. Mystery & Detective Fiction - 287746 2013 $200

Favorsky, V. *Miniature Woodcuts.* Leningrad: Aurora Art Pub., 1979. 6 x 7 cm., cloth, title gilt stamped on spine, initial gilt stamped on front boards, slipcase, unpaginated, 3 volumes, illustrations in black and white, inscribed on dust jacket to Margaret and Ward Schori, bottom and top of slipcase missing, slipcase worn at edges, from the collection of Donn W. Sanford. Oak Knoll Books 303 - 42 2013 $225

Fawcett, E. Douglas *Hartmann the Anarchist; or the Doom of the Great City.* London: Edward Arnold, 1893. First edition, apparently American issue with "MacMillan & Co." spine imprint and with 2 page Arnold catalogue inserted after text, pictorial cloth, illustrations by Fred T. Jane, large contemporary ownership stamp of Midwestern newspaper, spine ends very slightly frayed, very good or little better. Between the Covers Rare Books, Inc. Sci-Fi, Fantasy & Horror - 54736 2013 $200

Fawkes, Richard *Dion Boucicault, a Biography.* Quartet, 1979. First edition, 8vo., illustrations, cloth, dust jacket, near fine. C. P. Hyland 261 - 140 2013 £35

Fawley, Wilbur *Shuddering Castle.* New York: Green Circle Books, 1936. First edition, some spotting to boards, very good in like dust jacket, price clipped with few tiny nicks and modest tears. Between the Covers Rare Books, Inc. Sci-Fi, Fantasy & Horror - 68391 2013 $225

Fay, Theodore S. *Views in New York and Its Environs from Accurate Characteristic & Picturesque Drawings...with Historical, Topographical and Critical Illustrations.* New York: Peabody Co., 1831-1834. First edition, 4to., 50 pages text, 11 full page plates, but without vignette titlepage, 6 parts of 8, old boards, detached, but present, colored folding map, tissues foxed, affecting plates, text very clean. M & S Rare Books, Inc. 95 - 260 2013 $825

Fearing, Kenneth *The Big Clock.* London (Sydney): The Bodley Head in Association with the Australasian Pub. Co., 1947. First Australian edition, fine near fine dust jacket, but for shallow chips at foot of thin spine, uncommon edition. Between the Covers Rare Books, Inc. Mystery & Detective Fiction - 76225 2013 $200

Fearn, John Russell *Creature from the Black Lagoon.* London: Dragon Pub. Limited, n.d., 1954. First edition, octavo, boards. L. W. Currey, Inc. Fall Sampler Sept. 2013 - 143513 2013 $1500

Fearn, John Russell *The Red Insects.* London: Scion Ltd., 1951. First edition, octavo, pictorial wrappers. L. W. Currey, Inc. Fall Sampler Sept. 2013 - 143730 2013 $150

Fearnside, William *Eight Picturesque Views on the Thames and Medway.* London: published by Tombleson & Comp. circa 1830's, 283 x 222mm., 2 p.l., iv, 84 pages, contemporary moss green moire cloth by Cleaver (binder's ticket), flat spine, original brown morocco label, engraved dedication, engraved title with vignette, folding panoramic map (frequently missing), 79 steel engravings, corners and head of spine little bumped, rear joint starting at head, label chipped at lower edge, two small water spots to front board, persistent minor foxing to plates, as usual (noticeable on four, but never offensive), otherwise excellent, fresh, strong plate-marks, ample margins and sound binding (map without usual extra creases and entirely smooth and clean). Phillip J. Pirages   63 - 470   2013 $1250

Feather, Leonard *The Encyclopedia Yearbook of Jazz.* New York: Horizon, 1956. First edition, fine in very good dust jacket with tears.   Beasley Books   2013 - 2013 $50

Feather, Leonard *The New Encyclopedia of Jazz.* New York: Horizon, 1960. First printing of the revised edition, fine, offsetting on f.e.p. from clippings, near fine dust jacket but for few clear tape reinforcements.   Beasley Books   2013 - 2013 $50

Feather, Leonard *The New Yearbook of Jazz. Volume III of the Encyclopedia of Jazz Series.* New York: Horizon, 1958. First edition, minor spotting to spine, otherwise fine in lightly used dust jacket, uncommon.   Beasley Books   2013 - 2013 $50

The Federalist. New York: Printed and sold by George F. Hopkins, 1802. Second edition, rare, 2 volumes, octavo, contemporary tree calf, professional, near invisible restoration to head and tail of spines, corners little worn, still very handsome set, individually chemised in half brown morocco clamshell case, exceptionally rare in contemporary binding.   David Brass Rare Books, Inc.   Holiday 2012 Chapter Five - DB 01694   2013 $24,500

Fell & Rock Climbing Club *Borrowdale. Rock Climbing Guides to the English Lake District, Second Series.* Fell and Rock Climbing Club of the English Lake Distrit, 1953. First edition thus, small 8vo., original cloth, spine lettering trifle faded, illustrations by W. Heaton Cooper, uncommon. R. F. G. Hollett & Son   Lake District and Cumbria - 84   2013   £30

Fell & Rock Climbing Club *Borrowdale. Rock-Climbing Guides to the English Lake District, Second Series.* Fell and Rock Climbing Club of the English Lake District, 1966. Small 8vo., original cloth, spine lettering, little faded, illustrations by W. Heaton Cooper, very nice, clean copy, uncommon.   R. F. G. Hollett & Son   Lake District and Cumbria - 83   2013   £35

Fell & Rock Climbing Club *Climbs on Great Gable: Rock Climbing in Borrowdale.* Fell & Rock Climbing Club, 1925. First edition, original stiff red leather effect wrappers, little cockled and marked, illustrations, rather used and worn in places, one page rather soiled, half of page 51/2 torn away, some annotations, scarce.   R. F. G. Hollett & Son   Lake District and Cumbria - 95   2013   £30

Fell & Rock Climbing Club *Climbs on the Scawfell Group.* Fell & Rock Climbing Club, 1924. First edition, original stiff red leather effect wrappers, illustrations, one section loose, scarce.   R. F. G. Hollett & Son   Lake District and Cumbria - 94   2013   £60

Fell & Rock Climbing Club *Doe Crags and Climbs Around Coniston.* Barrow-in-Furness: for the Fell & Rock Climbing Club of the English lake District, 1922. Original limp red leather effect cloth cover over red printed wrappers, illustrations, top of back inner wrappers faded, contemporary postcard of Dow Crag with mss. key to various ascents in hand of E. L. Burrows both loosely inserted, scarce, Burrows' copy.   R. F. G. Hollett & Son   Lake District and Cumbria - 92   2013   £60

Fell & Rock Climbing Club *Dow Crag and Other Climbs.* Fell & Rock Climbing Club, 1957. Small 8vo., original cloth, illustrations by W. Heaton Cooper, uncommon.   R. F. G. Hollett & Son   Lake District and Cumbria - 89   2013   £30

Fell & Rock Climbing Club *Great Gable, Borrowdale, Buttermere. Climbing Guides to the English Lake District.* Fell & Rock Climbing Club of the English Lake District, 1937. Small 8vo., original cloth, illustrations by W. Heaton Cooper.   R. F. G. Hollett & Son   Lake District and Cumbria - 82   2013   £30

Fell & Rock Climbing Club *Great Gable, Green Gable, Kirkfell, Yewbarrow, Buckbarrow.* Fell & Rock Climbing Club, 1948. Small 8vo., original cloth, little soiled, illustrations by W. Heaton Cooper, uncommon.   R. F. G. Hollett & Son   Lake District and Cumbria - 86   2013   £35

Fell & Rock Climbing Club *Great Gable Green Gable, Kirkfell, Yewbarrow, Buckbarrow. Rock-Climbing Guides to the English Lake District. Second Series.* Fell & Rock Climbing Club, 1958. Small 8vo., original cloth, illustrations by W. Heaton Cooper, uncommon.   R. F. G. Hollett & Son   Lake District and Cumbria - 85   2013   £30

Fell & Rock Climbing Club *Pillar Rock and Neighbouring Climbs.* Fell & Rock Climbing Club, 1923. First edition, original limp red leather effect cloth, illustrations by H. J. Doughty, very good, scarce.   R. F. G. Hollett & Son   Lake District and Cumbria - 93   2013   £65

Fell, Alfred *The Early Iron Industry of Furness and District...*   Ulverston: Hume Kitchin, 1908.   Signed, limited edition, number 136 of 157 copies, thick large 8vo., modern full black levant morocco gilt with gilt ruled boards and gilt bordered raised bands, uncut and 20 illustrations, collotypes, drawings etc. and 2 maps, complete with errata slip, few spots, excellent copy, exceptionally scarce.   R. F. G. Hollett & Son   Lake District and Cumbria - 77   2013   £450

Fell, Alfred   *A Furness Military Chronicle.*   Ulverston: Kitch & Co., 1937.   First (only) edition, tall 8vo., original green cloth gilt, spine and front board lightly faded, uncut, frontispiece, very nice, lean copy, original ALS from publisher's dated 1944 offering a copy of the book, loosely inserted, very scarce.   R. F. G. Hollett & Son   Lake District and Cumbria - 79   2013   £350

Fell, Clare   *Early Settlement in the Lake Counties.*   Clapham: Dalesman Books, 1972.   First edition, original pictorial wrappers, 94 pages, illustrations.   R. F. G. Hollett & Son   Lake District and Cumbria - 81   2013   £25

Fellowes, Edmund H.   *The Tenbury Letters.*   Golden Cockerel Press, 1942.   288/300 copies printed on Arnold mouldmade paper, 7 full page facsimiles of letters, foolscap 8vo., original crimson buckram, lettering on backstrip, Cockerel press device on front cover, all gilt blocked, top edge gilt, others untrimmed, fine.   Blackwell's Rare Books   B174 - 342   2013   £85

Fellowes, William Dorset   *Melancholy Loss of the Lady Hobart Packet, which Struck on an Island of Ice in the Atlantic Ocean June 28 1803...*   London: printed for Thomas Tegg, 1805.   Folding mezzotint frontispiece, refolded, browned on verso, disbound, good.   Blackwell's Rare Books   B174 - 139   2013   £250

Fendrick, Virginia Shannon   *American Revolutionary Soldier of Franklin County Pennsylvania.*   Chambersburg: Historical Works Committee, Franklin County Capter DAR, 1969.   First edition, small 4to., near fine, 332 pages.   Beasley Books   2013 - 2013 $100

Fenelon, Francois Salignac De La Mothe, Abp.   1651-1715   *The Adventures of Telemachus, the Son of Ulysses.*   London: printed for W. Innys and R. Munby et al, 1735.   2 volumes, 8vo, 13 engraved full page illustrations and foldout map, half title in volume two, 1 inch square piece missing from upper corner of titlepage of each volume not affecting any letterpress, remnant of bookplate on one endpaper, bookplate on another, little rubbed contemporary mottled calf, very good, clean.   Second Life Books Inc.   183 - 266   2013 $350

Fenelon, Francois Salignac De La Mothe, Abp.   1651-1715   *A Demonstration of the Existence of God...*   Printed for John Murray, successor to Mr. Sandby, 1769.   Third edition, or second edition, second issue, 12mo., original sheep, rebacked preserving original spine, corners worn, good.   Blackwell's Rare Books   172 - 56   2013   £850

Fenn, Eleanor   *The Rational Dame; or Hints Towards Supplying Prattle for Children.*   printed and sold by J. Marshall and Co., n.d., 1790?   Second edition, rare, original marbled boards, sometime rebacked in green sheep, rather worn, half title, frontispiece, 9 engraved plates, lacks 2 leaves (pages 53-56, replaced with blanks), some tears repaired in places, rather loose.   R. F. G. Hollett & Son   Children's Books - 196   2013   £750

Fenn, G. Manille   *The Silver Canyon - a Tale of the Western Plains.*   London: Sampson Low, Marston, 1894.   First edition, 8vo., blue gilt binding, previous owner's inscription dated 1895, illustrations, very good.   Barnaby Rudge Booksellers   Children 2013 - 021449   2013 $75

Fenn, John   *Original Letters Written During the Reigns of Henry VI, Edward I and Richard III by Various Persons of Rank or Consequence... with Notes Historical and Explanatory, and Authenticated by Engravings of Autographs...*   London: printed for G. G. J. and J. Robinson, 1787.   1789.   1823.   Volumes I-II second editions with additions and corrections, volumes III-V first editions, 4to., all plates called for, including some hand colored and 1 folding pedigree chart (repaired), Volume I and III titlepages reinforced at fore edge, volume II plates quite foxed, little occasional offsetting, contemporary tan calf, skilfully rebacked in slightly lighter calf with blind tooling, gilt and red and black morocco labels to spines, corners repaired, endpapers sympathetically replaced, armorial bookplate of Earls of Dartrey (family name Dawson), relaid to each front pastedown, bookplate of Adrian Bullock, Sherringham, Norfolk dated 1987, to each front and rear pastedown, recent note transcribing Paston family gravestone inscriptions loosely inserted.   Unsworths Antiquarian Booksellers   28 - 119   2013   £1250

Fenn, William Wilithew   *Half Hours of Blind Man's Holiday or Summer and Winter Sketches in Black and White.*   London: Sampson Low, Marston, Searle & Rivington, 1878.   First edition, octavo, 2 volumes, original dark green cloth, front and rear panels stamped in blind, spine panels stamped in gold, all edges untrimmed, gray coated endpapers.   L. W. Currey, Inc.   Fall Sampler Sept. 2013 - 146254   2013 $450

Fenner, B.   *Fenner's Complete Forumlary Containing Original and Select Working Forumlas...*   New York: Westfield, 1894.   Tenth edition, 1509 pages, thick 8vo., full contemporary sheep, binding lightly rubbed, front joint just started, text toned, overall good, tight copy.   James Tait Goodrich   S74 - 110   2013 $75

Fenner, B. *Fenner's Working Formulae.* New York: Westfield, 1886. Second edition, 528 pages, original sheep, some wear.   James Tait Goodrich   S74 - 107   2013 $125

Fenner's Hand-Book of the United States Pharmacopoeia. Westfield: 1894. Seventh Revision, 221 pages, original calf burgundy boards, both off and spine label lacking.   James Tait Goodrich   S74 - 108   2013 $65

Fenning, Daniel   *The British Youth's Instructor; or a New and Easy Guide to Practical Arithmetic.*   printed for S. Crowder, 1762. Fourth edition, old speckled calf, little scraped, front fllyleaf removed.   R. F. G. Hollett & Son   Children's Books - 198   2013   £85

Fenning, Daniel   *The Ready Reckoner; or Trader's Most Useful Assistant in Buying and Selling all Sorts of Commodities...*   London: printed for S. Crowder, 1788. Ninth edition, 12mo., E3 torn without loss, some occasional browning, few old ink splashes, one gathering little proud, contemporary calf, hinges cracked but firm, old signature at foot of ad on titlepage verso.   Jarndyce Antiquarian Booksellers   CCIV - 127   2013   £65

Fenning, Hugh   *The Undoing of the Friars of Ireland.* Louvain: 1972. First edition, wrappers, near fine, 8vo.   C. P. Hyland   261 - 421   2013   £60

Fenton, Elijah   *Marianne. A Tragedy.*   London: printed for J. Tonson, 1723. First edition, Little dusted, faint old waterstain to some leading edges, disbound.   Jarndyce Antiquarian Booksellers   CCIV - 128   2013   £35

Ferber, Edna   *Stage Door, a Play.*   New York: Doubleday Doran, 1936. First edition, 8vo., 230 pages, 8vo., , fine, slightly worn dust jacket, scarce in jacket.   Second Life Books Inc.   183 - 134   2013 $300

Ferchl, Fritz   *A Pictorial History of Chemistry.*   London: William Heinemann, 1939. First edition in English, 8vo., viii, 214 pages, illustrations, navy cloth, gilt stamped spine title, near fine, Burndy bookplate.   Jeff Weber Rare Books   169 - 138   2013 $95

Ferguson, Adam   *An Essay on the History of Civil Society.* Edinburgh: 1767. First edition, quarto, contemporary full calf, gilt spine with raised bands and red morocco label, edges sprinkled red, joints cracked and tender, edges of boards rubbed, few light pencilled annotations, very good crisp copy, red cloth clamshell.   Heritage Book Shop   50th Anniversary Catalogue - 36   2013 $7500

Ferguson, Adam   *An Essay on the History of Civil Society.* London: printed for T. Cadell, 1782. 8vo., bit of faint foxing, contemporary marbled calf, spine gilt in compartments, red morocco label, marbled endpapers, edges yellow, rebacked and recornered, preserving original spine. Unsworths Antiquarian Booksellers   28 - 95   2013   £200

Ferguson, James   1710-1776   *Astronomy Explained Upon Sir Isaac Newton's Principles and made Easy to Those Who Have not Studied Mathematics.*   London: printed for and sold by author, 1757. Second edition, small 4to., 283 pages + index, very good in full contemporary calf with gilt lettering on red leather spine label, complete with 13 folding copper plate engravings and folding frontispiece, from the library of F. R. S. Murdoch Mackenzie, with his signature, scuffs, edgewear to spine and covers, owner bookplate, scattered foxing and soil.   By the Book, L. C.   36 - 98   2013 $2000

Ferguson, James   1710-1776   *Lectures on Select Subjects in Mechanics, Hydrostatics, Hydraulics, Pneumatics and Optics.*   London: printed for W. Strahan, 1776. Fifth edition, 13 folding engraved plates, 8vo., bound without half title, leading edge of one plate, little browned and chipped, expertly bound in recent quarter sprinkled calf, marbled boards, vellum tips, raised and gilt banded spine, red morocco label, signature on title of J. Dugmore. Jarndyce Antiquarian Booksellers   CCIV - 129   2013   £350

Ferguson, R. S.   *An Accompt of the Most Considerable Estates and Families in the County of Cumberland, from the Conquest unto the Beginning of the Reign of K. James (the first) by John Denton, of Cardew.*   Kendal: T. Wilson, 1887. Original printed wrappers, rather soiled and heavily chipped, edges defective, rebacked in cloth, little loose, scarce.   R. F. G. Hollett & Son   Lake District and Cumbria - 106   2013   £95

Ferguson, R. S.   *The Booke off Recorde or Register (of Kirkbie Kendall).*   Kendal: T. Wilson, 1892. First edition, original brown cloth, gilt, front joint cracked.   R. F. G. Hollett & Son   Lake District and Cumbria - 107   2013   £150

Ferguson, R. S.   *The Boke off Recorde or Register (of Kirkbie Kendall).*   Kendal: for the CWAAS, 2001. Facsimile edition, original cloth, gilt.   R. F. G. Hollett & Son   Lake District and Cumbria - 108   2013   £35

Ferguson, R. S.   *Cumberland and Westmorland M.P.'s (sic) from the restoration to the Reform Bill of 1867 (1660-1867).*   London: Bell and Daldy, and Carlisle; Thurnam, 1871. First edition, original cloth, gilt over bevelled boards, little faded, handsomely rebacked in matching levant morocco, raised bands, contrasting double spine labels, frontispiece, very good, scarce.   R. F. G. Hollett & Son   Lake District and Cumbria - 96   2013   £175

Ferguson, R. S. *Early Cumberland and Westmorland Friends.* F. Bowyer Kitto, 1871. First edition, original brown cloth, gilt, 208 pages, front flyleaf removed, scattered spotting or browning, little shaken, scarce.   R. F. G. Hollett & Son   Lake District and Cumbria - 97   2013   £85

Ferguson, R. S. *A History of Cumberland.* London: Elliot Stock, 1890. First edition, original two-tone cloth gilt, untrimmed.   R. F. G. Hollett & Son   Lake District and Cumbria - 98   2013   £65

Ferguson, R. S. *A History of Westmorland.* London: Elliot Stock, 1894. First edition deluxe issue, original quarter black roan, gilt, uncut, printed on thick laid paper.   R. F. G. Hollett & Son   Lake District and Cumbria - 99   2013   £65

Ferguson, R. S. *A History of Westmorland.* London: Elliot Stock, 1894. First edition, proof copy, original stiff glazed wrappers, side sewn, pages 312, scattered spotting, author's own proof copy, with his armorial bookplate and neat corrections to text throughout in his hand, annotated 'revised 7.5.94'.   R. F. G. Hollett & Son   Lake District and Cumbria - 100   2013   £95

Ferguson, R. S. *A History of Westmorland.* London: Elliot Stock, 1894. First edition, original two-tone cloth, gilt, pages 312, uncut.   R. F. G. Hollett & Son   Lake District and Cumbria - 101   2013   £50

Ferguson, R. S. *Miscellany Accounts of the Diocese of Carlisle with the Terriers Delivered in to Me at my Primary Visitation, by William Nicolson, late Bishop of Carlisle.* London: George Bell and Carlisle: C. Thurnam & Sons, 1877.   R. F. G. Hollett & Son   Lake District and Cumbria - 109   2013   £130

Ferguson, R. S. *Old Church Plate in the Diocese of Carlisle with Makers and Marks.* Carlisle: C. Thurnam, 1882. First edition, original brown cloth, gilt, neatly recased, 29 lithographed plates and 7 text woodcuts.   R. F. G. Hollett & Son   Lake District and Cumbria - 110   2013   £150

Ferguson, R. S. *On a Massive Timber Platform of Early Date Uncovered at Carlisle and on Sundry Relics Found in Connection Therewith.* Archaeological Journal, 1892. Old plain wrappers, trifle chipped, 5 plates, 2 page ALS to author from William Phillips of Carlisle, loosely inserted.   R. F. G. Hollett & Son   Lake District and Cumbria - 103   2013   £25

Ferguson, R. S. *The Royal Charters of the City of Carlisle, Printed at the Expense of the Mayor and Corporation.* London: Elliot Stock; Carlisle: C. Thurnam; Kendal: T. Wilson, 1894. Original brown cloth, gilt, 5 folding maps, 2 large colored lithographs, small library stamps on title and backs of plates, very scarce.   R. F. G. Hollett & Son   Lake District and Cumbria - 111   2013   £180

Ferguson, R. S. *Some Municipal Records of the City of Carlisle...* Carlisle: C. Thurnam & Sons, 1887. Original brown cloth, gilt, pages 340, extending frontispiece, 2 colored lithographs and 9 illustrations, very scarce.   R. F. G. Hollett & Son   Lake District and Cumbria - 115   2013   £180

Ferguson, R. S. *Testamenta Karleolensia.* Kendal: T. Wilson, 1893. Original brown cloth, gilt.   R. F. G. Hollett & Son   Lake District and Cumbria - 105   2013   £50

Fergusson, C. Bruce *Place-Names and Places of Nova Scotia.* Halifax: 1967. Red cloth, pages 751, folding maps, 8vo., cloth split at edges of spine, otherwise good.   Schooner Books Ltd.   102 - 101   2013 $75

Fergusson, C. Bruce *Place-Names and Places of Nova Scotia.* Belleville: Mika Pub., 1982. Third printing, 8vo., red simulated leather, folding maps, very good.   Schooner Books Ltd.   105 - 71   2013 $75

Ferlinghetti, Lawrence *Literary San Francisco. A Pictorial History from Its Beginnings to the Present Day.* San Francisco: City Lights Books & Harper & Row, 1980. First edition, 4to., profusely illustrated from photos, green cloth gilt, very fine, pictorial dust jacket.   Argonaut Book Shop   Summer 2013 - 101   2013 $90

Fermor, Patrick Leigh *Mani: Travels in the Southern Peloponnese.* London: John Murray, 1958. First edition, 8vo., illustrations, original red decorative cloth, wrap round band, dust jacket with "Book Society Choice" wrap round band.   J. & S. L. Bonham Antiquarian Booksellers   Europe - 9830   2013   £120

Fermor, Patrick Leigh *Roumeli: Travels in Northern Greece.* London: John Murray, 1966. First edition, 8vo., 248 pages, illustrations, original blue decorative cloth, dust jacket, near fine.   J. & S. L. Bonham Antiquarian Booksellers   Europe - 9829   2013   £140

Fernett, Gene *Swing Out, Great Negro Dance Bands.* Midland: Pendell, 1970. First edition, 4to., fine in dust jacket, rubbed, many photos.   Beasley Books   2013 - 2013 $50

Ferrier, Alexandre *La Russie.* Bruxelles: Societe belge Librairie, Haumann & Cie, 1841. First edition, 214 pages, 10 engraved plates, 2 in text drawings, 2 folding maps, 16mo., quarter morocco over marbled boards, 4 raised bands, ruled in gilt, 4 compartments with gilt florets, gilt title, marbled endpapers, quite uncommon, very good, spine rubbed, corners worn, scattered foxing, nearly invisible repair at fold on small map, mostly marginal.   Kaaterskill Books   16 - 30   2013 $750

Ferrier, Auger *A Learned Astronomical Discourse of the Iudgement of Natiuiies.* printed at the widow Charlewoods House, for Edwarde White, 1593. First edition in English, title within elaborate woodcut border, without final blank, title bit browned and stained, weak area causing short vertical split with loss of couple of letter, hole in inside border with slight less of engraved surface, text slightly browned, dampstain at head, headline of table shaved, last couple of leaves frayed in fore margin, ink trials on verso of last leaf seeping through three small holes, two of which touch letters, small 4to, later sheep rebacked, fore edges worn, early ownership inscription, later bookplate of Jay Gould (railway magnate) and at end that of his daughter, sound.   Blackwell's Rare Books   Sciences - 49   2013   £4000

Ferrier, David *The Croonian Lectures on Cerebral Localisation.* London: Smith Elder and Co., 1890. 152 pages, 35 text figures, original green publisher cloth, ex-library, blacked out spine label, bookplate removed, binding bit worn, outer hinges just starting, internally clean and tight.   James Tait Goodrich   S74 - 113   2013 $495

Ferrier, David *The Functions of the Brain.* London: Smith Elder, 1876. First edition in later cloth, xv, 523 pages, numerous text illustrations.   James Tait Goodrich   S74 - 111   2013 $1500

Ferrier, David *The Functions of the Brain.* London: Smith, Elder, 1876. First edition, 8vo., 62 figures, page 57 marked in red ink, pages 311-12 outlined in pencil and cut away, remounted in its original place, previous owner making pencil marks in text questioning elements of text , pages 61-64 cut at gutter, original double ruled black and gilt stamped green cloth, extremities lightly worn, rear free endleaf ink notation, generally very good.   Jeff Weber Rare Books   172 - 89   2013 $750

Ferrier, David *The Functions of the Brain.* London: Smith Elder, 1886. Second edition, xvii, 498 pages, numerous illustrations, original cloth, light rubbing, internally fine.   James Tait Goodrich   S74 - 112   2013 $695

Ferrier, David *The Localisation of Cerebral Disease being the Gulstonian Lectures of the Royal College of Physicians for 1878.* London: Smith, Elder and Co., 1878. 142 pages, 58 text figures, original green publisher's cloth, mild cloth wear, else very good, tight copy.   James Tait Goodrich   75 - 93   2013 $495

Ferrier, David *On Tabes Dorsalis. The Lumieian Lecture. Delivered before the Royal College of Physicians, London, March 1906.* Text illustrations, original green publisher's cloth, lacking blank front flyleaf, light text toning, otherwise very good plus.   James Tait Goodrich   S74 - 114   2013 $395

Ferrier, Susan *Destiny; or the Chief's Daughter.* Edinburgh: printed for Robert Cadell, 1831. First edition, 3 volumes, 8vo., lightly foxed and spotted, contemporary polished half calf with marbled boards, rebacked to style by Chris Weston, boards scuffed, contemporary ink ownership inscription of David Anderson of St. Germains.   Unsworths Antiquarian Booksellers   28 - 162   2013   £180

Ferrier, William Warren *Origin and Development of the University of California.* Berkeley: The Sather Gate Book Shop, 1930. First edition, frontispiece, map, navy blue cloth, gilt, very fine.   Argonaut Book Shop   Summer 2013 - 102   2013 $75

Ferris, William *Local Color: a Sense of Place in Folk Art.* New York: McGraw Hill, 1982. First edition, paperback issue, very near fine in wrappers, inscribed by author for Ralph Ellison.   Between the Covers Rare Books, Inc.   165 - 149   2013 $200

Feuchtwanger, Lion *La Guerre des Juifs.* Paris: Albin Michel, 1933. First French edition, 8vo., original yellow wrappers, very good, spine darkened and little worn at head and tail, inscribed by Mrs. Elcock by author.   Maggs Bros. Ltd.   1460 - 282   2013   £500

A Few Beverage Recipes and How to Mix Them. Meridan: International Silver Company, 1928. First edition, 24mo., (24) pages, stapled decorated wrappers, few tiny holes on front wrapper, scattered foxing and some soiling to a couple of pages, very good.   Between the Covers Rare Books, Inc.   Cocktails, Etc. - 321215   2013 $125

A Few Cursory Observations Addressed to the Protestants of Ireland... Cork: Barry Drew, 1835. 14 pages, modern quarter cloth, very scarce.   C. P. Hyland   261 - 254   2013   £75

Fewkes, Jesse Walter *Hopi Katcinas Drawn by Native Artists.* Chicago: Rio Grande Press, 1969. Second printing, quarto, 190 pages, color plates, beige leatherette stamped in red and green, gilt lettering, very fine.   Argonaut Book Shop   Recent Acquisitions June 2013 - 108   2013 $75

Feynman, Richard *Elementary Particles and the Laws of Physics.* Cambridge: Cambridge University, 1987. First edition, small 8vo., x, 110 pages, signed by Steven Weinberg, small 8vo., x, 110 pages, fine in near fine dust jacket.   By the Book, L. C.   36 - 97   2013 $500

Ffinch, Michael *The Beckwalker and Other Poems.* Latimer New Dimensions, 1977. First limp edition, signed by author, original pictorial wrappers, pages 53.   R. F. G. Hollett & Son   Lake District and Cumbria - 118   2013   £25

Ffinch, Michael *Portrait of Kendal and the Kent Valley.* London: Robert Hale, 1983. First edition, original cloth, gilt, dust jacket, 30 illustrations and map.   R. F. G. Hollett & Son   Lake District and Cumbria - 120   2013   £25

Ffinch, Michael *Portrait of Penrith and the East Fellside.* Robert Hale, 1985. First edition, 3o illustrations, original cloth, gilt, dust jacket.   R. F. G. Hollett & Son   Lake District and Cumbria - 121   2013   £25

Ffinch, Michael *Portrait of the Howgills and the Upper Eden Valley.* Robert Hale, 1982. First edition, original cloth, gilt, dust jacket, 220 pages, 35 illustrations and map, fine.   R. F. G. Hollett & Son   Lake District and Cumbria - 122   2013   £35

Ffinch, Michael *Selected Poems.* Kendal: Titus Wilson, 1979. First edition, original card wrappers, rather faded and marked, scarce.   R. F. G. Hollett & Son   Lake District and Cumbria - 123   2013   £25

Ffinch, Michael *Simon's Garden.* Kendal: Titus Wilson, 1981. First edition, tall 4to., original red stiff wrappers, unpaginated, woodcuts by Durer.   R. F. G. Hollett & Son   Lake District and Cumbria - 124   2013   £30

Ffinch, Michael *Voices Round a Star and Other Poems.* London: Latimer Press, 1970. First edition, copy 4 from an edition of 50 printed on Glastonbury Antiqe laid Paper and specially bound in buckram, fine in fine dust jacket, signed by Ffinch, 59 pages.   Jeff Hirsch Books   Fall 2013 - 129390   2013 $65

Ffinch, Michael *Voices Round a Star and Other Poems.* Latimer Press, 1970. First edition, original cloth, gilt, dust jacket, mint, signed by author.   R. F. G. Hollett & Son   Lake District and Cumbria - 125   2013   £30

Ffinch, Michael *Westmorland Poems.* Kendal: Titus Wilson, 1980. First edition, small 4to., original pictorial wrappers, 40 pages, illustrations by Caroline Metcalfe-Gibson.   R. F. G. Hollett & Son   Lake District and Cumbria - 126   2013   £25

Fforde, Jasper *Lost in a Good Book.* London: Hodder & Stoughton, 2002. First edition, fine in fine dust jacket, signed by author.   Between the Covers Rare Books, Inc.   Mystery & Detective Fiction - 306960   2013 $60

Fiddes, Richard *The Life of Cardinal Wolsey.* London: printed for John Barber, 1724. First edition, folio, 7 copper plate engravings, one in text engraving, cloth, very good or better copy, modern rebinding, leaves very bright, small chip to lower margin of frontispiece, else plates sharp and clean, overall contents near fine.   Kaaterskill Books   16 - 32   2013 $450

Field, E. M., Mrs. *The Child and His Book.* Wells Gardner, Darton & Co. n.d., 1891. Original green pictorial cloth, gilt, frontispiece, front joint trifle tender, else excellent.   R. F. G. Hollett & Son   Children's Books - 199   2013   £65

Field, Eugene *Gingham Dog and the Calico Cat; The Duel and Other Child Verses.* Newark: Charles Graham, 1926. Folio, cloth backed pictorial boards, slight bit of edgewear, else fne, beautiful full page color illustrations.   Aleph-Bet Books, Inc.   104 - 212   2013 $275

Field, Eugene *Wynken Blynken and Nod and other Child Verses.* Newark: Chas. Graham, 1925. Folio, cloth backed pictorial boards (32) pages, edges slightly rubbed, else very good-fine, part of dust jacket laid in, illustrations. Aleph-Bet Books, Inc.   104 - 213   2013 $275

Field, F. J. *An Armorial for Cumberland.* Kendal: Titus Wilson, 1937. First edition, original brown cloth gilt, 18 illustrations, fine.   R. F. G. Hollett & Son   Lake District and Cumbria - 127   2013   £175

Field, James *A Devout Soldier.* circa, 1870. First edition, original cloth damp marked, mounted photo portrait 12 illustrations (lacks map), text dust marked, else good.   C. P. Hyland   261 - 423   2013   £60

Field, Matthew C. *Prairie and Mountain Sketches.* Norman: University of Oklahoma Press, 1957. First edition, sketches by author and from watercolors by Alfred Jacob Miller, brown cloth decorated in dark green, very fine, pictorial dust jacket, minor tear to upper edge of jacket. Argonaut Book Shop   Summer 2013 - 103   2013 $50

Field, Michael, Pseud. *Stephania: a Trialogue.* London: Elkin Mathews & John Lane, 1892. One of 250 copies, 197 x 146mm., 6 p.l., 100 pages, 4 leaves colophon and ads, titlepage with full woodcut border filled with intertwined pine branches and mistletoe, colophon with pine cone device, exceptionally attractive modelled goatskin by Mrs. Annie MacDonald of the Guild of Women Binders, front cover with large lobed frames, its upper corners enclosing binder's initial and date (1897), lower corners with daffodil blooms, large central panel showing an elaborately detailed scene featuring a woman with long, flowing hair entreating god mercury in his signature winged hat and sandals, two figures surmounted by imperial brown through which twines a sprig of mistletoe (design that appears in woodcut frame on titlepage), lower cover showing woman kneeling by man reclining on a couch, this scene enclosed in an oval beaded frame, flat spine with modelled title flanked by pine cone device at head and tail, green watered silk pastedowns, framed by unusual turn-ins decorated with gilt vines and calf circles painted green and blue, leather hinges, top edge gilt, others edges untrimmed, verso of front flyleaf with engraved bookplate of Charles Williston McAlpin, extra paper title labels tipped onto rear blank, 2 tiny red (ink?) marks to upper cover, inevitable offsetting from turn-ins to endpapers, once detached front flyleaf tipped onto front free endpaper, other trivial defects, still very attractive copy, binding lustrious and scarcely worn and leaves fresh and clean. Phillip J. Pirages 61 - 106 2013 $4500

Fielding, Henry 1707-1754 *An Enquiry into the Causes of the Late Increase of Robbers, &c...* London: printed for A. Millar, 1751. First edition, 8vo., full brown calf by Whitman Bennett of NY, with shelfmark "Lauderdale Law" in contemporary hand, presumably Earl of Lauderdale. Howard S. Mott Inc. 262 - 49 2013 $750

Fielding, Henry 1707-1754 *The History of the Adventures of Joseph Andrews and His Friend Mr. Abraham Andrews.* London: printed for John Bell, 1775. 12mo., half title, expert repair to small tear at head of titlepage, some occasional browning and foxing, corner of D4 torn with slight loss of text, near contemporary mottled calf boards, neatly rebacked, raised and gilt banded spine, red morocco label, corners repaired, new endpapers and pastedowns. Jarndyce Antiquarian Booksellers CCIV - 130 2013 £225

Fielding, Henry 1707-1754 *The Adventures of Joseph Andrews and His Friend Mr. Abraham Andrews...* London: printed for J. Murray... and J. Sibbald, Edinburgh, 1792. 8vo., 8 etched plates, contemporary calf with rope twist gilt borders, expertly rebacked retaining original gilt decorated spine and labels, spine rubbed, labels slightly chipped, armorial bookplate of John Thomas Stanley Esq. of Alderley. Jarndyce Antiquarian Booksellers CCIV - 131 2013 £280

Fielding, Henry 1707-1754 *The History of Tom Jones, a Foundling.* London: printed for A. Millar, 1749. Second edition, 12mo., small tear to inner margin volume II, B2, occasional browning in some gatherings, volumes I and III bound without final blank leaves, recent half calf, marbled boards, raised bands, black morocco labels. Jarndyce Antiquarian Booksellers CCIV - 132 2013 £750

Fielding, Henry 1707-1754 *The History of Tom Jones, a Foundling.* Philadelphia: Birch and Small, 1810. Second complete American edition?, 16mo., contemporary calf, leather labels, one cover worn, some foxing, one name torn from corner of title volume I, but very nice. M & S Rare Books, Inc. 95 - 122 2013 $300

Fielding, Henry 1707-1754 *The Works of...with a life of the Author.* London: Strahan, 1783. 11 of 12 volumes, missing volume (8) has been supplied from 1771 Martin & Wotherspoon, Edinburgh issue, each of the Strahan volumes has frontispiece, full contemporary calf (some wear), text good. C. P. Hyland 261 - 894 2013 £250

Fielding, Sarah *L'Orpheline Angloise, ou Histoire du Charlotte Summers...* Londres (i.e. Paris): et se trouse a Paris chez Rollin fils Quay des Augustins, Chez Praut fils Quay de Conti, 1751. 4 volumes, 12mo., engraved frontispiece and frontispiece to each volume, woodcut headpieces and initial letters, very good, clean set, full contemporary mottled calf, ornate gilt panelles spines decorated with small gilt floral devices, gilt morocco labels, slight chip to head of volume III, otherwise in near fine condition, bookplate Bibliothucca Blomiana. Jarndyce Antiquarian Booksellers CCIV - 134 2013 £280

Fiennes, Ranulph *To the Tends of the Earth.* B.C.A., 1983. Original cloth, gilt, dust jacket, 24 pages of colored plates, 10 pages on endpapers, card signed and dated by author, loosely inserted. R. F. G. Hollett & Son Polar Exploration - 15 2013 £30

Film Culture Issue 45 - Summer 1967. New York: Film Culture, 1967. First edition, film still images from Warhol, clean and tight, very near fine in wrappers. Jeff Hirsch Books Fall 2013 - 129106 2013 $450

Fincham, J. R. S. *Genetic Complementation.* New York: Benjamin, 1966. First edition, 8vo., signed by author, near fine, foxing to edges, very good dust jacket (sun to spine, mild edgewear, foxing to rear). By the Book, L. C. 37 - 30 2013 $600

Findlay, Frederick Roderick Noble *Big Game Shotting and Travel in South East Africa.* London: T. Fisher Unwin, 1903. First edition, original buckram gilt over bevelled boards, spine rather faded, top edge gilt, folding map and numerous illustrations, flyleaves little browned, otherwise excellent copy. R. F. G. Hollett & Son Africana - 69 2013 £350

Fine Arts Festival, Talladega College, Talladega Alabama. Kent: Institute for African American Affairs, Kent State University, 1975. Stapled decorated wrappers, (20) pages, modest horizontal crease on front wrapper, else very good plus, although not otherwise indicated, from the library of Gwendolyn Brooks. Between the Covers Rare Books, Inc. 165 - 92 2013 $75

Finglass, Esther *The Recluse; or History of Lady Gertrude Lesby.* Dublin: printed for P. Wogan, P. Byrne, J. Moore and J. Halpen, 1789. First Irish edition, 12mo., some offset browning to endpapers and pastedowns, otherwise very good, clean copy, full contemporary tree calf, double gilt bands, red morocco label, book block edges stained, green suggesting an Irish binding. Jarndyce Antiquarian Booksellers CCIV - 135 2013 £2500

Fini, Franesco *The Oscar Peterson Discography.* Imola: Fini Editions, 1992. First edition, illustrations, fine, hardcover. Beasley Books 2013 - 2013 $100

Finlay, George Irving *Colorado Springs: a Guide Book Describing the Rock Formations in the Vicinity of Colorado Springs.* Colorado Springs: 1906. 61 pages, 42 plates, map, errata slip tipped in, spine little faded, slight wear to extremities, owner's name, else bright and very good. Dumont Maps & Books of the West 122 - 57 2013 $65

Finlay, Michael *The Mining and Related Tokens of West Cumberland.* Wetheral: privately published by Plains Book, 2006. Signed, limited edition, number 187 of 500 copies, pages vii, 196, 275 illustrations, original cloth, gilt, splendid work. R. F. G. Hollett & Son Lake District and Cumbria - 128 2013 £50

Finney, Jack *Assault on a Queen.* New York: Simon and Schuster, 1959. First edition, fine in lightly rubbed, very good plus dust jacket with nick at corners. Between the Covers Rare Books, Inc. Mystery & Detective Fiction - 85197 2013 $200

Finny's Royal Cork, Almanack for 1831. J. Connor, 8vo., 96 pages, original wrappers repaired, good. C. P. Hyland 261 - 206 2013 £75

The Firelight Book of Nursery Stories. Blackie & Son, n.d., 1924. Small 4to., original cloth backed pictorial boards, edges little rubbed, 7 full page color plates and numerous drawings by John Hassall, nice, clean and sound copy. R. F. G. Hollett & Son Children's Books - 265 2013 £45

The First Book of Records of the Town of Southampton with Other Ancient Documents of Historic Value. Sag Harbor: John H. Hunt, Book and Job Printer, 1874. First edition, half diced leather with leather spine label gilt and paper covered boards, 177 pages, hairline crack to front joint, stain o rear board, else tight and attractive, very good, exceptionally uncommon. Between the Covers Rare Books, Inc. New York City - 285388 2013 $2500

Fischl, Eric *Portraits. Mary Boone Gallery 6 May - 26 June 1999.* Mary Boone Gallery, 1999. First edition, small 4to., 44 pages, near fine, signed by Fischl. By the Book, L. C. 36 - 19 2013 $135

Fish, Robert L. *The Bridge that Went Nowhere.* New York: Putnam, 1968. First edition, fine in lightly worn, very good dust jacket with couple of nicks and short tears at extremities, inscribed by author to fellow mystery writer, Clayton and Kate Rawson, splendid association. Between the Covers Rare Books, Inc. Mystery & Detective Fiction - 34366 2013 $475

Fishbein, Morris *The Medical Follies.* New York: Boni & Liveright, 1925. Fourth printing, 8vo., lacks front free endpaper, original reddish brown cloth, gilt, signed and inscribed by author, signed for Philip Hench by author, very good. Jeff Weber Rare Books 172 - 90 2013 $100

Fisher, Anne *The Pleasing Instructor...* Newcastle upon Tyne: printed for Thomas Slack, 1756. Second edition, Contemporary full calf, rather rubbed, head of spine chipped, title printed in red and black, front flyleaf removed. R. F. G. Hollett & Son Children's Books - 200 2013 £275

Fisher, Anne *The Pleasing Instructor or Entertaining Moralist...* London: G. G. J. & J. Robinson, 1785. New edition, old sheep, rather rubbed, hinges cracking, few surface defects, vignette and 3 engraved plates, front flyleaf removed, armorial bookplate of Isaac Greenwood, signed by him and dated 1788 on title. R. F. G. Hollett & Son Children's Books - 201 2013 £180

Fisher, George *The Instructor or Young Man's Best Companion..* printed for A. Millar, W. Cadell and W. Cater, 1794. Engraved frontispiece, one folding engraved plate, inscription "Thomas Allanson's Book, Hutton, 1804", woodcut illustrations in text, bit of spotting, staining and thumbing, 12mo., original calf in contemporary covering of fine suede, curiously sewn together over inside front covers, good. Blackwell's Rare Books 172 - 57 2013 £400

Fisher, Harrison *Harrison Fisher Girls.* New York: Dodd Mead, 1914. 12 large and beautiful tipped in color plates, in text illustrations, pictorial endpapers, magnificent copy, very scarce, 4to., cloth backed boards stamped in gold, pictorial paste-on, top edge gilt, edge of frontispiece slightly creased, else new in original glassine and publisher's box. Aleph-Bet Books, Inc. 104 - 215 2013 $1850

Fisher, Roy *Collected Poems 1968.* London: Fulcrum Press, 1969. First edition, copy 34 from an edition of 100 copies, very good plus with some foxing to page edges, particularly top edge in very near fine dust jacket and glassine, signed by Fisher on limitation page.   Jeff Hirsch Books   Fall 2013 - 129349   2013 $60

Fisher, Ruth B. *On the Borders of Pigmy Land.* Marshall Brothers, n.d. circa, 1910. Fifth edition, original green pictorial cloth, rather rubbed, 32 plates, including frontispiece.   R. F. G. Hollett & Son   Africana - 70   2013   £35

Fisher, Samuel *Unity and Equality in the Kingdom of God Stated and Demonstrated from the Plain Testimony of the Holy Spirit in the Scriptures...* Norwich: printed by Stevenson and Matchett, 1797. 8vo., title and final leaf soiled, small paper flaw each (affecting two letters in quotation on title), little spotting elsewhere, modern blue sugar paper wrappers, good.   Blackwell's Rare Books   172 - 58   2013   £75

Fisher, St. John *Sermon Against Luther.* Pepler & Sewell St. Dominic's Press, Ditchling, Sussex, 1935. One of 30 copies printed on handmade paper, small wood engraving of Luther by Edward Walters, after Holbein, 16mo., original quarter cream canvas, spine sunned, printed front cover label, pale grey boards with little handling soiling, corners rubbed, small glue stain left following bookplate removal, untrimmed, good, inscribed by Michael Sewell 23 March 1936 for Vincent Maxwell.   Blackwell's Rare Books   B174 - 379   2013   £120

Fiske, John *Tobacco and Alcohol.* New York: Leypodlt & Holt, 1869. First edition, small octavo, purple cloth gilt, contemporary pencil owner name on titlepage, corners little bumped, else fine.   Between the Covers Rare Books, Inc.   Cocktails, Etc. - 82650   2013 $200

Fiske, Turbese Lummis *Charles F. Lummis. The Man and His West.* Norman: University of Oklahoma Press, 1975. First edition, number 98 of 200 copies, signed by Keith Lummis, quarto, frontispiece, profusely illustrated from photos, facsimiles and reproductions, beige buckram printed in red and black, fine in pictorial dust jacket.   Argonaut Book Shop   Summer 2013 - 213   2013 $90

Fitz-Florian's Alphabet; or Lyrical Fables for Children Grown Up. London: J. J. Stockdale, 1819. Second edition, full contemporary calf, gilt borders and dentelles, slightly marked and bit rubbed, contemporary gift inscription to Elizabeth Luke, Renier booklabel.   Jarndyce Antiquarian Booksellers   CCIII - 631   2013   £75

Fitzgerald, Brian *The Anglo-Irish: 3 Representative Types, Cork, Ormonde, Swift 1602-1745.* 1952. First edition, 8vo., cloth, cover faded, text very good.   C. P. Hyland   261 - 426   2013   £30

Fitzgerald, Francis Scott Key   1896-1940 *All the Sad Young Men.* New York: Charles Scribner's Sons, 1926. First edition, first issue with Scribner seal in copyright page and unbroken type on page 38, 90 and 248, dark green cloth lettered gilt on spine, lettered in blind on front cover, spine gilt slightly dulled, very nice, quite scarce issue.   Argonaut Book Shop   Recent Acquisitions June 2013 - 109   2013 $1250

Fitzgerald, Francis Scott Key   1896-1940 *The Great Gatsby.* New York: Charles Scribner's Sons, 1925. First edition, first printing, with "chatter" on page 60, line 16, "northern" on page 119, line 22, "it's" on page 165, line 16, "away" on page 165, line 29, "Sick in tired" on page 205, lines 9-16 and "Union Street station" on page 211, lines 7-8, octavo, original dark green linen like grain cloth with front cover lettered in blind and spine ruled and lettered in gilt, top edge trimmed, others uncut, gilt on spine very bright and not rubbed, previous owner's pencil inscription dated 1925, about fine.   Heritage Book Shop   Holiday Catalogue 2012 - 59   2013 $5000

Fitzgerald, Francis Scott Key   1896-1940 *The Great Gatsby.* New York: Charles Scribner, 1925. First edition, 8vo., original black cloth, covers rubbed and edges bumped, otherwise very good, Clifford Odets' copy with his personal rubber stamp on front pastedown and name blindstamped on front free endpaper.   Maggs Bros. Ltd.   1460 - 284   2013   £4500

Fitzgerald, Francis Scott Key   1896-1940 *Safety First. A Musical Comedy in Two Acts.* Cincinnati: Princeton University Triangle Club John Church Co., 1916. First edition, 4to., 99 pages, very good in original color printed flexible thin boards with considerable scuffs, vertical crease to boards with considerable scuffs, vertical crease to boards and text page, full page ANS about Fitzgerald dated Sept. 11 1975 by W. I. Harris, who wrote some of the music and appeared in the play, his initials misprinted as "E" rather than "W H", he corrected that on cast list, custom beige linen covered chemise contained in quarter leather, matching linen covered slipcase with leather spine labels and gilt lettering.   By the Book, L. C.   38 - 81   2013 $2000

Fitzgerald, John *The Cork Remembrancer.* Cork: J. Sullivan, 1783. Textualy complete but some amateur repairs and one modern ms. note (verso of titlepage), full calf, worn, extreme rarity.   C. P. Hyland   261 - 428   2013   £450

Fitzgerald, John *Echoes of Ninety-Eight.* Cork: 1898. First edition, portrait, cloth, 8vo., all edges gilt, very good.   C. P. Hyland   261 - 429   2013   £40

Fitzgerald, Penelope *The Beginning of Spring.* London: Collins, 1988. First edition, fine in fine, crisp jacket with new publisher price sticker over printed price at bottom of front flap.   Ed Smith Books   78 - 17   2013 $100

Fitzgerald, Penelope *Offshore.* London: Collins, 1979. First edition, near fine, little foxing to edges in very good dust jacket that would be fine except for snag at top of rear panel. Ed Smith Books 78 - 16 2013 $100

Fitzgerald, Pitt *Joey and Gigi.* Los Angeles: Wagner Co., 1965. First edition in English, square 8vo., illustrated boards, very good. Barnaby Rudge Booksellers Children 2013 - 021605 2013 $50

Fitzgerald, Redmond *Cry Blood Cry Erin.* Barrie & Rockliff, 1966. First edition, 8vo., profusely illustrated, cloth, dust jacket, very good. C. P. Hyland 261 - 430 2013 £50

Fitzgibbon, Gerald *Ireland in 1868. The Battle-Field for English Party Strife.* 1868. First edition, 8vo., cloth, cover worn, text very good. C. P. Hyland 261 - 431 2013 £32

Fitzgibbon, Mary Rose *Lakeland Scene.* London: Chapman and Hall, 1948. First edition, original cloth, gilt, dust jacket rather worn, 16 plates. R. F. G. Hollett & Son Lake District and Cumbria - 130 2013 £30

Fitzhugh, George *Cannibals All - Or Slaves without Masters.* Richmond: A. Morris, 1857. First edition, 8vo., 379 pages, original cloth, rebacked. M & S Rare Books, Inc. 95 - 123 2013 $575

Fitzpatrick, Berchmans *The Souvenier of Canon Sheehan.* 1914. First edition, xii, 157 pages, cloth, portrait, very good, scarce. C. P. Hyland 261 - 779 2013 £35

Fitzpatrick, H. M. *The Forests of Ireland...from Early Times Until the Present.* 1966. First edition, 8vo., photos, maps, cloth, very good. C. P. Hyland 261 - 433 2013 £40

Fitzpatrick, J. P. *The Transvaal from Within.* London: Heinemann, 1899. Fifth impression, original cloth, gilt, one corner trifle bumped, flyleaves little spotted. R. F. G. Hollett & Son Africana - 71 2013 £50

Fitzsimons, F. W. *The Natural History of South Africa - Mammals.* Longmans, Green and Co., 1919. 4 volumes, original cloth, gilt, illustrations, edges lightly spotted, very good. R. F. G. Hollett & Son Africana - 73 2013 £175

5 Little Pigs. New York: McLoughlin Bros., 1890. First edition, 8vo., 12 pages, including wrappers on linen, chromolithograph illustrations, tiny tear to very top right corner of front wrapper. Barnaby Rudge Booksellers Children 2013 - 021660 2013 $85

Flack, Marjorie *Angus and the Cat.* New York: Doubleday Doran, 1931. Stated first edition, oblong 8vo., pictorial boards, fine in dust jacket with rectangular pieces off blank edge of dust jacket flap, bold color illustrations on every page. Aleph-Bet Books, Inc. 104 - 216 2013 $850

Flake, Lester W. *Tales from Oz.* N.P. n.d. circa: 1985, 110 pages, hardcover, illustrations. Dumont Maps & Books of the West 125 - 49 2013 $50

Flamsteed, John *Atlas Celeste de Flamsteed..* Paris: F. G. Deschamps et Chez l'Auteur, 1776. Stated second edition, 8vo., 30 plates, contemporary calf with mild edgewear, prelims with mild foxing, plates and text quite clean and fresh. By the Book, L. C. 38 - 50 2013 $6000

Flanagan, Thomas *The Year of the French.* London: Macmillan, 1979. First UK edition, 8vo., original green cloth, dust jacket, near fine, jacket nicked and browned, from the library of Richard Murphy, inscribed by author for Murphy. Maggs Bros. Ltd. 1442 - 80 2013 £75

Flanner, Janet *Men and Monuments.* New York: Harper and Brother, 1957. First edition, 8vo., original black cloth over boards, inscribed by author for Russell Page, excellent copy unevenly faded, lettering rubbed and faded. Maggs Bros. Ltd. 1460 - 285 2013 £150

Flanner, Janet *Paris Journal 1944-1965 and Paris Journal Volume two. 1965-1971.* New York: Atheneum, 1965. 1971. First edition, second volume is review copy with review slip, author photo and promotional page laid in, but for some faint sunning to jacket of second volume, each volume fine in fine dust jacket, inscribed by author in first volume in 1974. Ken Lopez Bookseller 159 - 62 2013 $500

Flatlands, Gravesend, New Utrecht, Bushwick. Brooklyn: Brooklyn Eagle, 1946. First editions, 4 booklets, near fine in wrappers. Between the Covers Rare Books, Inc. New York City - 293315 2013 $225

Flatman, Thomas *Poems and Songs.* London: printed for Benjamin Tooke at the Ship in St. Paul's church-yard, 1682. 8vo., frontispiece, small mark to foot of frontispiece, minor tear to foot of titlepage, slight browning, bound without prelim blank but with two final errata and ad leaves, manuscript correction from errata on page 101, bound by Riviere and son in full dark red crushed morocco gilt, ruled border, elaborate gilt decorated spine, inner gilt cornerpiece decoration, marbled endpapers, slight rubbing to board edges, corners little bruised, contemporary signature at head of titlepage, bookplates of E. M. Cox and John Drinkwater, latter adding bibliographical pencil note to leading endpaper, all edges gilt, variant with M74 and the ad, in a different setting, beginning on verso. Jarndyce Antiquarian Booksellers CCV - 102 2013 £620

Flaubert, Gustave 1821-1880 *Flaubert & Louise: Letters and Impressions.* San Francisco: Pacific Editions & Limestone Press, 1988. One of 18 copies only, each numbered and signed by artist/publisher, all on BFK Rives paper, 5 original monotypes by Charles Hobson, each presented with 5 letterpress printed texts, printed in Baskerville and Baskerville italic at Limestone Press, assembled in 18 portfolios, loose as issued in blue cloth with white labels on spine and front cover by Klaus Rotzcher, quite scarce. Priscilla Juvelis - Rare Books   55 - 20   2013 $3000

Flaubert, Gustave 1821-1880 *Madame Bovary, Moeurs de Province.* Paris: Michel Levy Freres, Libraires Editeurs, 1857. First edition, 2 volumes, dedication leaf, volume I, half titles, with original wrappers cut down and laid on to green paper, bound before half titles, near contemporary quarter blue cloth, light brown morocco labels, marbled boards, leading inner hinge slightly cracking, with unidentified armorial bookplate on leading pastedowns and armorial bookplate of Charles George Milnes Gaskell, very good. Jarndyce Antiquarian Booksellers   CCV - 103   2013   £2800

Flaubert, Gustave 1821-1880 *Madame Bovary.* Paris: Michel Levy Freres, Libraires Editeurs, 1857. First edition, first issue, with misspelling "Senart" on dedication leaf, 2 volumes, 12mo., Dec. 1587 catalog laid in at back volume 1, original pale green printed wrappers and glassine jackets, all edges uncut, only lightest of wear and foxing, both volumes chemised together in a quarter red morocco slipcase, spine of slipcase lettered in gilt, overall, very attractive copy in original state. Heritage Book Shop   Holiday Catalogue 2012 - 60   2013 $15,000

Flaubert, Gustave 1821-1880 *Un Coeur Simple.* London: Eragny Press Hacon and Ricketts, 1901. One of 226 copies, all on Arnold handmade paper, 116 pages, including colophon and printer's device, drab boards with linen spine, white paper label printed in black with author and title and leaf flourishes on front panel, offsetting at endpapers, tips bit rubbed, bit of faint foxing to end blanks, still near fine, printed in Vale type with wood engraved frontispiece designed and cut by Lucien Pissarro and decorative borders and initial letters designed by him and cut by Esther Pissaro. Priscilla Juvelis - Rare Books   55 - 7   2013 $800

Flaxman, John *Anatomical Studies of the Bones and Muscles for the Use of Artists.* London: M. A. Nattali, 1833. First edition, royal folio, 22 plates, frontispiece, pencil sketches to verso of pages 20 and 21, some plates little offset, occasional spotting, some browning to last few leaves at fore-edge, contemporary red cloth, gilt title to upper board and "V.R.", monogram to lower board, binding inkstained, endcaps and corners frayed, joints worn, small embossed stamp reading Department of Science and Art - Reward. Unsworths Antiquarian Booksellers   28 - 163   2013   £400

Flecker, James Elroy *The King of Alsander.* London: Max Goschen, 1914. First edition, first issue, red cloth lettered in white and gilt, very slight fading at spine, very good or better. Between the Covers Rare Books, Inc. Sci-Fi, Fantasy & Horror - 314696   2013 $150

Fleischman, Sid *The Whipping Boy.* New York: Greenwillow, 1987. Stated first edition, 8vo., cloth, fine in as new dust jacket, no price clipped, no award seal, light rubbing on tips, illustrations by Peter Sis. Aleph-Bet Books, Inc.   104 - 217   2013 $250

Fleischmann's Mixer's Manual. New York: Fleischmann Distilling Corp. n.d. circa, 1948. 12mo., 16 pages, stapled color printed wrappers, illustrations in color from drawings, liquor store stamp on rear wrapper, else fine. Between the Covers Rare Books, Inc. Cocktails, Etc. - 312652   2013 $100

Fleming, Alexander *On the Antibacterial Action of Cultures of a Pencillium with Special Reference to Their Use in the Isolation of B. Influenza. in British Journal of Experimental Biology 10:226-236 1929.* Entire issue offered, 4to., later cloth. James Tait Goodrich   75 - 95   2013 $5000

Fleming, Alexander *On the Antibacterial Action of Cultures of a Penicillium with Special Reference to their Use in the Isolation of B. Influenza.* London: 1929, i.e., 1944. Second separate printing, one of 250 copies, quarto, 12 pages, self wrappers stapled as issued, folding red cloth case, fine. Heritage Book Shop   Holiday Catalogue 2012 - 62   2013 $5000

Fleming, Daniel *Description of the County of Westmoreland.* London: Bernard Quaritch and Kendal: T. Wilson, 1882. Original printed wrappers, 42 pages, endpapers very spotted. R. F. G. Hollett & Son   Lake District and Cumbria - 45   2013   £35

Fleming, E. McClurg *R. R. Bowker: Militant Liberal.* Norman: University of Oklahoma Press, 1952. First edition, numerous photo portraits and group shoots, brick cloth, gilt, very fine with pictorial dust jacket (small smudge to rear of jacket). Argonaut Book Shop   Summer 2013 - 104   2013 $50

Fleming, Ian Lancaster 1908-1964 *Casino Royale.* New York: Macmillan, 1954. First American edition, fine in dust jacket with tiny wear at spine ends and some very slight spine fading. Mordida Books   81 - 169   2013 $2000

Fleming, Ian Lancaster 1908-1964 *Doctor No.* New York: Macmillan, 1958. First American edition, some offsetting on endpapers, fine in near fine dust jacket with small chips and wear at corners and some scattered very light wear along folds. Mordida Books   81 - 170   2013 $450

Fleming, Ian Lancaster 1908-1964 *James Bond in Facsimile.* Shelton: First Edition Library, 1990. Facsimile editions, 14 volumes, all as new in slipcases with 8 of the 14 still shrinkwrapped.   Mordida Books   81 - 178   2013 $2500

Fleming, Ian Lancaster 1908-1964 *The Man with the Golden Gun.* London: Cape, 1965. First edition, small scrape on front endpaper, otherwise fine in dust jacket.   Mordida Books   81 - 177   2013 $350

Fleming, Ian Lancaster 1908-1964 *The Man with the Golden Gun.* London: Cape, 1965. First edition, crown 8vo., original black boards, backstrip gilt lettered, dust jacket with very faintest edge rubbing, near fine.   Blackwell's Rare Books   172 - 182   2013   £200

Fleming, Ian Lancaster 1908-1964 *On Her Majesty's Secret Service.* London: Cape, 1963. First edition, fine in price clipped dust jacket with small spot on front pane and light soiling on back panel.   Mordida Books   81 - 172   2013 $650

Fleming, Ian Lancaster 1908-1964 *The Spy who Loved Me.* London: Jonathan Cape, 1962. First edition, double page black and white illustration, black cloth patterned paper over boards, front board stamped in silver and blind in shape of a dagger, spine lettered in silver, red endpapers, top edge of text block foxed, binding slightly skewed, spine of book with light crease down center, dust jacket spine darkened, light edgewear to jacket, mainly at creases and spine extremities, inside of jacket with some small tape reinforcements, overall very good.   Heritage Book Shop Holiday Catalogue 2012 - 61   2013 $1000

Fleming, Ian Lancaster 1908-1964 *The Spy Who Loved Me.* London: Cape, 1962. First edition, double page illustration, crown 8vo., original grey boards, backstrip gilt lettered in silver and dagger design on front cover blocked in blind and silver, edges and rear panel of dust jacket lightly foxed, very good.   Blackwell's Rare Books   172 - 183   2013   £500

Fleming, Ian Lancaster 1908-1964 *Thrilling Cities.* London: Jonathan Cape, 1963. First edition, fine in with small light burn mark on back panel.   Mordida Books   81 - 174   2013 $150

Fleming, Ian Lancaster 1908-1964 *Thunderball.* London: Cape, 1962. First edition, bookplate, tiny spot on top of page edges, otherwise fine in dust jacket with tear on back panel and tiny wear at base of spine.   Mordida Books   81 - 171   2013 $900

Fleming, Ian Lancaster 1908-1964 *You Only Live Twice.* London: Jonathan Cape, 1964. First edition, first state without month on copyright page, lower corners slightly bumped and some very light spotting on page edges, otherwise fine in price clipped dust jacket with tiny wear at corners.   Mordida Books   81 - 175   2013 $400

Fleming, Ian Lancaster 1908-1964 *You Only Live Twice.* London: Jonathan Cape, 1964. First edition, 2nd state with "March 1964" on copyright page, some light staining on page edges, otherwise fine in dust jacket with tiny wear at corners and some slight darkening.   Mordida Books   81 - 176   2013 $200

Fleming, L. T. *The Flemings & Reeves of Co. Cork.* circa, 1970. 4to., 38 pages, wrappers.   C. P. Hyland   261 - 387   2013   £35

Fleming, Lionel *Head or Harp.* Barrie: 1965. First edition, 8vo. cloth, dust jacket, very good.   C. P. Hyland   261 - 435   2013   £35

Fletcher, E. M. *Youngsters in Yorkshire.*   A. Brown & Sons, n.d., Original blue cloth, extremities little rubbed, 21 plates, map on front endpapers.   R. F. G. Hollett & Son Children's Books - 202   2013   £25

Fletcher, J. S. *Cobweb Castle.* New York: Alfred A. Knopf, 1928. First edition, fine in about very good dust jacket with several small chips and some fading atop front panel, scarce in jacket.   Between the Covers Rare Books, Inc.   Mystery & Detective Fiction - 316312   2013 $200

Fletcher, William Younger 1830-1913 *English Bookbindings in the British Museum Illustrations of Sixty-Three Examples Selected on Account of Their Beauty of Historical Interest with Introduction...* London: Kegan Paul, Trench, Trubner & Co. Ltd., 1895. Limited numbered edition of 500 copies, large 4to., 66 chromolithographic plates, occasional light foxing, original silver blue moire cloth, gilt stamped cover and spine titles, corners bumped, spine ends worn, rear inner hinge cracked, very good.   Jeff Weber Rare Books   171 - 121   2013 $500

Flint, Timothy *Francis Berrigan, or the Mexican Patriot.* Boston: Cummings, Hilliard and Co., 1826. First edition, 12mo., 2 volumes, original tan paper covered boards, printed paper labels, uncut, front covers detached, spines chipped and worn, slight loss of text on labels, text foxed (mostly moderate but some heavy), clamshell box.   M & S Rare Books, Inc.   95 - 124   2013 $1750

Flint, William Russell 1880-1969 *Drawings.* London: Collins, 1950. First edition, 134 plates (a number printed to two or more colors), folio, original purple cloth, backstrip and front cover gilt lettered, dust jacket rubbed, very good, signed by W. Russell Flint on half title.   Blackwell's Rare Books   B174 - 205   2013   £400

Flip Flop Face. Los Angeles: Jack Built, 1957. 4to., spiral backed pictorial boards, some wear at spirals, very good, each page divided into 3 sections (slices), printed in color on both sides of paper, scarce. Aleph-Bet Books, Inc. 105 - 412   2013 $275

Flipper, Henry O. *The Colored Cadet at West Point. Autobiography of Lieut. Henry Ossian Flipper USA...* New York: Homer Lee & Co., 1878. First edition, 8vo., 322 pages, recent calf backed cloth, lacks frontispiece, faint library stamp on title, very nice. M & S Rare Books, Inc. 95 - 125   2013 $600

The Florence Miscellany. Florence: (privately) printed for G(aetano) Cam.(biagi)..., 1785. 224 pages, 3 leaves of engraved music within pagination, 8vo., some light foxing, mainly to prelims, bound in 20th century full light brown morocco in period style by Philip Dusel, gilt spine and dentelles, near contemporary signature of Eliz. Harvey. Jarndyce Antiquarian Booksellers   CCIV - 230   2013   £2600

Florenz, Karl *Poetical Greetings from the Far East.* T. Hasegawa, 1897? printed on double leaves of crepe paper wrappers, sewn as issued, front cover slightly creased, with original illustrated folding card box and fasteners, slightly rubbed and dulled, very nice. Jarndyce Antiquarian Booksellers   CCV - 104   2013   £180

Florian, Jean Pierre Claris De   1755-1794 *Theatre de M. de Florian.* Paris: De L'Imprimerie de Didot Jeune, 1791. Quatrieme edition, 12 engraved plates, little light foxing, 12mo., contemporary tan straight grained morocco, boards with decorative gilt border, spines divided by double gilt fillets, second and fourth compartments gilt lettered direct, rest with central gilt flowers surrounded by small tools in blind, purple watered silk endpapers, edges gilt, few tiny marks, near fine. Blackwell's Rare Books   B174 - 56   2013   £300

Florilegium, a Collection of Flower initials designed by Maurice Dubrene. Utrecht: Catharijne Press, 1988. Limited to 168 copies,, this one of the 15 lettered copies bound thus and having initial heightened in gold, full color floral alphabet, 6.2 x 4 cm., full green suede with brown leather cover label, enclosed in slipcase with leather pull-off spine covering, not paginated, from the collection of Donn W. Sanford. Oak Knoll Books   303 - 81   2013 $450

Flourens, Pierre *Theorie Experimentale de la Formation des Os.* Paris: Chez J. B. Bailliere, 1847. Half title, title, 164 pages, 7 folding engraved plates, one colored, uncut, original publisher's printed wrappers, light foxing. James Tait Goodrich   75 - 94   2013 $995

Flowers from Shakespeare's Garden. London: Cassell, 1906. 4to., cloth backed pictorial boards, some edge wear, very good++, printed on frenchfold paper, each leaf features magnificent full page color portrayal (by Walter Crane) of a humanized flower with reference to Shakespeare play. Aleph-Bet Books, Inc.   105 - 156   2013 $600

Flowers for Busy Bees to Light On. Philadelphia: American Sunday School Union, n.d. circa, 1864. 4to., green cloth stamped in gold, 16 leaves printed both sides, slight wear to spine extremes, else very good+, 16 very fine engraved plates plus color engraved titlepage. Aleph-Bet Books, Inc. 104 - 192   2013 $225

Floyd-Jones, Elbert *St. Mary's Church in the Highlands Cold Spring-on-the-Hudson.* Poughkeepsie: Frank B. Howard, 1920. First edition, front hinge tender, else near fine, one of 200 copies. Between the Covers Rare Books, Inc. New York City - 285887   2013 $275

Fludd, Robert *Philosophia Moysaica.* Gouda: Petrus Rammazenius, 1638. Folio, engraved titlepage vignette (repeated in second part), woodcut text illustrations, panelled sprinkled calf, mixed paper stocks, some gatherings lightly browned, some very lightly foxed, lovely, fresh, near fine. Joseph J. Felcone Inc.   Books Printed before 1701 - 39   2013 $8000

Flynn, Gillian *Gone Girl.* New York: Crown, 2012. First edition, fine in fine dust jacket, signed by author. Ken Lopez Bookseller   159 - 63   2013 $75

Foden, Giles *The Last King of Scotland.* London: Faber & Faber, 1998. First edition, paperback original, fine copy, perfect bound in original illustrated wrappers in fine dust jacket. Ed Smith Books   78 - 18   2013 $75

Fodere, Francois Emmanuel *Traite de Medecine Legale et d'Hygene Publique ou de Police de Sante...* Paris: Mame, 1813. Second edition, 6 volumes, frontispiece, 2 folding tables, foxed, early quarter red morocco, morocco corners, gilt spine, rubbed, ownership signature of P. Forget, bookseller's ticket, very good, beautifully bound set. Jeff Weber Rare Books   172 - 92   2013 $1500

Folk Style No. 3, 8. November, 1958-1961. First edition, 6 issues, good to very good. Beasley Books   2013 - 2013 $50

Fontaine, James *Memoirs of a Huguenot Family.* RTS, circa, 1875. 8vo., cloth, corner torn from titlepage, no loss, else good. C. P. Hyland   261 - 388   2013   £85

Fontana, Felice *Dei Moti Dell'Iride.* Lucca: Jacopo Giusti, 1765. First edition, 8vo., signature D browned, original boards, ms. spine title, stained, spine with minor damage, top rear corner chipped, bookplate of Jerry Donin, housed in modern brown cloth drop-back box, brown leather spine label, gilt spine, very good.   Jeff Weber Rare Books   172 - 94   2013 $575

Fontenelle, Bernard Le Bovier De *The History of Oracles and Cheats of the Pagan Priests.* London: printed in the year, 1688. 8vo., small paper flaw to E4 touching several letters, blank margin of #6 and L3 repaired, some browning, contemporary calf, double gilt ruled borders, gilt panelled spine, red morocco label, expert repairs to hinges and corners, contemporary inscription "Ex-libris Sarah Howson (?)" struck through.   Jarndyce Antiquarian Booksellers   CCIV - 13   2013   £620

Foote, Samuel *A Trip to Calais; a Medley Maritime Sketch...* printed for the author and sold by J. Bew, 1775. First edition, somewhat browned, 8 leaves reinforced at inner margins, 8vo., modern calf backed boards, signature of John Munnings at head of title.   Blackwell's Rare Books   B174 - 57   2013   £750

Footner, Hulbert *The Almost Perfect Murder: a Case Book of Madame Storey.* Philadelphia: J. B. Lippincott, 1937. First edition, near fine with light fading to boards, in good plus dust jacket with rubbing, few small, internally repaired tears, couple of small chips, scarce in dust jacket. Between the Covers Rare Books, Inc.   Mystery & Detective Fiction - 84979   2013 $375

For Form of Prayers for the Feast of the New-Year According to the Custom of the German & Polish Jews. Vienna: Schlesinger (Budapest, printed), 1900. 8vo., pages 46, 60, 200, 160 20, celluloid with bone and brass edges, upper cover with silver gilt and fabric inlays, all edges gilt, edges worn, one clasp missing.   Marlborough Rare Books Ltd.   218 - 89   2013   £150

Forbes, Edwin *Life Studies of the Great Army.* New York: Henry J. Johnson, 1876. First edition, elephant folio, original cloth portfolio, very worn, descriptive sheet of title and plates pasted inside front over, mounts generally foxed, plates occasionally foxed, but very bright, chipping to few mount margins, overall fine, each of the 40 copperplate etchings signed in pencil by Forbes.   M & S Rare Books, Inc.   95 - 67   2013 $6500

Forbes, Eric G. *Greenwich Observatory; the Royal Observatory of Greenwich and Herstmonceux 1675-1975.* London: Taylor & Francis, 1975. Volumes 1-3, 130 figures, 8vo., gilt stamped navy blue cloth, rubber stamps verso titlepages, rear bookplates, fine.   Jeff Weber Rare Books   169 - 143   2013 $280

Forbes, Hugh *Four Lectures Upon Recent Events in Italy Delivered in New York University... March 1851.* New York: printed for the author by D. Fanshaw, 1851. First edition, 12mo., 110 pages, original printed wrappers, front wrapper nearly loose, some minor wear and chipping, library bookplate, faint stain across lower portion of title.   M & S Rare Books, Inc.   95 - 40   2013 $750

Forbes, James *Oriental Memoirs.* London: printed for the author by T. Bensley, published by White, Cochrane and Co., 1813. First edition, 4 volumes, large quarto, half titles present, frontispiece and 93 full plate plates, contemporary full tan calf, covers very lightly diced, boards triple ruled in gilt with gilt stamped floral devices at corners, spines stamped and lettered gilt in compartments, edges and turn-ins ruled in gilt, all edges gilt, marbled endpapers, outer hinges bit rubbed, 2 previous owner's old bookplates, 1 inch closed tear to lower margin of plate "A Hindoo Family" from volume I, not affecting engraving, the "cobra" plate in volume 1 trimmed close at top, some minor foxing and toning throughout, mainly to frontispiece portrait, overall very nice. Heritage Book Shop   Holiday Catalogue 2012 - 63   2013 $8000

Forbes, John *Sight-Seeing in Germany and the Tyrol in the Autumn of 1855.* London: Smith, Elder, 1856. First edition, 8vo. folding map, tinted frontispiece, original purple cloth skillfully rebacked with new endpapers, spine faded. J. & S. L. Bonham Antiquarian Booksellers   Europe - 3944   2013   £110

Forbes, R. B. *Shipwreck by Lightning.* Boston: Sleeper & Rogers, 1853. First edition, tall 8vo., original cloth, ends of spine chipped, corners bumped, very sound.   M & S Rare Books, Inc.   95 - 247   2013 $225

Forbes, Rosita *From Red Sea to Blue Nile.* New York: Lee Furman, 1935. Large 8vo., original light green cloth, hinges neatly repaired, 59 plates.   R. F. G. Hollett & Son Africana - 74   2013   £25

Ford, Edsel *Love is the House It Lives In.* Fort Smith: Homestead House, 1965. First edition, stapled stiff unprinted card wrappers, fine in fine dust jacket, inscribed by author to poet Gwendolyn Brooks, laid in is printed slip for ordering additional copies on verso of which Ford has penned a brief note, signed to Brooks.   Between the Covers Rare Books, Inc.   165 - 151   2013 $175

Ford, Ford Madox 1873-1939 *A Mirror to France.* London: Duckworth, 1926. First edition, 8vo., original green cloth, cloth little soiled, spine and edges faded, very good, inscribed to Caroline Tate (wife of Allen Tate), cloth little soiled, spine and edges faded, very good.   Maggs Bros. Ltd.   1460 - 286   2013   £750

Ford, Ford Madox   1873-1939   *New York is Not America.* London: Duckworth, 1927.   First edition, 8vo., original green cloth, dust jacket, excellent copy in slightly nicked dust jacket, inscribed by author for Irita van Doren, editor of NY Herald Tribune.   Maggs Bros. Ltd.   1460 - 287   2013   £750

Ford, Ford Madox   1873-1939   *The Spirit of the People.* Alston Rivers, 1907.   First edition, light foxing to initial and final text leaves, crown 8vo., original maroon cloth, lightly faded backstrip and front cover, all gilt blocked, top edge gilt, others rough trimmed, good.   Blackwell's Rare Books   172 - 184   2013   £250

Ford, Julia Ellsworth   *Snickerty Nick.*   New York: Moffat Yard & Co., 1919.   First edition, quarto, 3 full page color plates and 10 full page black and white drawings by Arthur Rackham, original light blue cloth, original pictorial dust jacket, few small closed tears, otherwise fine.   David Brass Rare Books, Inc.   Holiday 2012 Chapter One - DB 01502   2013 $1250

Ford, Richard   *A Piece of My Heart.*   London: Collins Harvill, 1987.   First British edition, inscribed by author to Irish memoirist Nuala O'Faolain and her partner John Low-Beer, couple of small, stray marks to edge of text block, still fine in fine dust jacket, good literary association.   Ken Lopez Bookseller   159 - 64   2013 $250

Ford, Richard   *Women with Men.*   New Orleans: B. E. Trice, 1997.   Limited edition, true first edition, this copy has printed on colophon "Gary Fisketjon's Copy" and shares its design with lettered issue, quarterbound in leather, signed by Ford, fine in fine slipcase, presentation issue.   Ken Lopez Bookseller   159 - 65   2013 $750

Ford, William   *A Description of Scenery in the Lake District Intended as a Guide to Strangers.*   Carlisle: Charles Thurnam, 1840.   Second edition, original patterned cloth gilt, engraved paper label with view of waterfall on upper panel, spine trifle faded, 3 double page hand colored maps, panoramic view, extending table, few small pencil scribbles in margins, lacks folding map (as frequently occurs).   R. F. G. Hollett & Son   Lake District and Cumbria - 132   2013   £145

Ford, Worthington Chauncey   *George Washington.*   New York: Goupil & Co. and Charles Scribner's sons, 1900.   One of 200 copies of "Edition de Luxe", 2 volumes, 267 x 203mm., 88 full page plates, as well as 32 tailpieces, chapter initials in black and red; attractive green crushed morocco, covers with two-line gilt frame, raised bands, gilt framed compartments and gilt titling, red morocco doublures surrounded by inch wide green morocco turn-ins with four gilt fillets, watered silk endleaves, top edges gilt, other edges untrimmed, large paper copy, hint of wear to joints and extremities, spines mildly faded to olive green, spine of second volume with just slightly irregular fading, still fine, bindings solid and pleasing, text and plates virtually pristine; bookplate of William P. Olds laid in at front of each volume.   Phillip J. Pirages   63 - 487   2013 $1500

Forde, C. M.   *Mrs. O.*   New York: 1958.   First edition, 8vo., cloth, dust jacket, very good.   C. P. Hyland   261 - 436   2013   £35

Forder, John   *Hill Shepherd.*   Kendal: Frank Peters, 1989.   First edition, oblong 4to., original pictorial boards, dust jacket, pages 157, illustrations in color, inscribed to Arthur (Raistrick) from authors.   R. F. G. Hollett & Son   Lake District and Cumbria - 133   2013   £50

Foreman, Grant   *A Pathfinder in the Southwest. The Itinerary of Lieutenant A. W. Whipple.*   Norman: University of Oklahoma Press, 1941.   first edition thus, 279 pages, 7 color plates, large folding map, brick cloth, spine slightly faded, else fine.   Argonaut Book Shop   Recent Acquisitions June 2013 - 110   2013 $90

Foreman, Michael   *After the War Was Over.*   Arcade Pub., 1996.   First US edition, oblong large 8vo., original cloth, dust jacket, illustrations in color, fine.   R. F. G. Hollett & Son   Children's Books - 205   2013   £35

Forester, Cecil Scott   1899-1966   *Brown on Resolution.* London: Bodley Head, 1929.   First edition, 8vo., original blue cloth, dust jacket, near fine, jacket just slightly nicked at extremities, inscribed by author "With compliments from C. S. Forester".   Maggs Bros. Ltd.   1460 - 288   2013   £2750

Forester, Cecil Scott   1899-1966   *Colours Including a Ship of the Line.*   Joseph: The Book Society, 1938.   First edition issued for The Book Society one day prior to the trade publication of 'Flying Colours', pages 290, foolscap 8vo., original mid green cloth, backstrip and front cover blocked in silver, dust jacket, fine, with Book Society bookplate, signed by author at bottom of dust jacket.   Blackwell's Rare Books   B174 - 206   2013   £1500

Forester, Cecil Scott 1899-1966 *The Happy Return.* London: Joseph, 1937. First edition, pages 288, foolscap 8vo., original mid green cloth, faded backstrip blocked in silver, dust jacket in nice save fore vertical crease to backstrip panel where it has been tucked within book for safekeeping, near fine, signed by C. S. Forester.   Blackwell's Rare Books   B174 - 207   2013   £1250

Forester, Cecil Scott 1899-1966 *Lord Hornblower.* New York: Grosset Dunlap, 1946. 8vo., 322 pages, very good+, dust jacket with chips, soil, short closed tears, scarce, signed by author.   By the Book, L. C.   36 - 47   2013 $500

Forester, Cecil Scott 1899-1966 *Mr. Midshipman Hornblower.* London: Michael Joseph, 1950. First edition, 8vo. original green cloth, dust jacket, near fine in price clipped dust jacket, edges little rubbed, inscribed by author.   Maggs Bros. Ltd.   1460 - 289   2013   £750

The Frog who Would a Wooing Go. London: Blackie, circa, 1920. Folio, cloth backed pictorial boards, covers with some soil and edges rubbed, very good, 12 glorious full page color illustrations, text bellow and with 3 illustrations in line.   Aleph-Bet Books, Inc.   105 - 18   2013 $225

Forgue, Norman W. *Bibliography of Miniature Books and Ephemera 1961-1977.* Chicago: Skokie: Black Cat Press, 1977. Limited to 240 copies, 2 volumes, leather, title gilt stamped on spine, press mark gilt stamped on front board, decorated endpapers, marbled slipcase, from the collection of Donn W. Sanford.   Oak Knoll Books   303 - 54   2013 $125

Forman, S. E. *The Woman Voter's Manual.* New York: Century, 1920. Small 8 vo., black cloth, ex-library with bookplate and stamps, cover slightly scuffed and bumped at edges, otherwise very good, tight copy.   Second Life Books Inc.   182 - 82   2013 $75

Formey, Jean Henri Samuel *A Concise History of Philosophy and Philosophers.* London: printed for F. Newbery at the Crown in Pater Noster Row, 1766. 12mo., titlepage slightly foxed, very nice, handsomely bound in recent quarter sprinkled calf, raised and gilt banded spine, red gilt label, marbled boards, vellum corner pieces.   Jarndyce Antiquarian Booksellers   CCV - 105   2013   £420

Forrest, Helen *I Had the Craziest Dream.* New York: Coward, McCann & Geoghegan, 1982. First edition, near fine in near fine dust jacket, 307 pages.   Beasley Books   2013 - 2013 $60

Forrest, Mary *Women of the South Distinguished in Literature Illustrated with Portraits on Steel.* Detroit: Woman's Publ. Co., 1913. First edition, 8vo., green cloth, hinges barely beginning tender, cover somewhat rubbed and slightly worn at corners, otherwise very good tight.   Second Life Books Inc.   182 - 83   2013 $125

Forssman, Werner *Experiments on Myself: Memoirs of a Surgeon in Germany.* New York: St. Martin's Press, 1974. First Edition in English, 8vo., pastedowns lightly foxed, gilt stamped black cloth, dust jacket torn, scarce, very good.   Jeff Weber Rare Books   172 - 95   2013 $275

Forster, Edward Morgan 1879-1970 *Abinger Harvest.* London: Edward Arnold, 1936. First edition, first issue, 8vo., original blue cloth, gilt, signed by author and inscribed to Forster's aunt by his friend Rosalie Alford from Joe Ackerley, excellent copy, some slight wear to extremities.   Maggs Bros. Ltd.   1460 - 293   2013   £600

Forster, Edward Morgan 1879-1970 *Howards End.* London: Edward Arnold, 1929. Uniform edition, first reprint, 8vo., original red cloth, excellent copy, inscribed by author for Mrs. Grace Morrow 13-6-31.   Maggs Bros. Ltd.   1460 - 292   2013   £275

Forster, Edward Morgan 1879-1970 *The Longest Journey.* London: Edward Arnold, 1937. Uniform edition, first reprint, 8vo., original red cloth, inscribed by author for Rose Macaulay, excellent copy.   Maggs Bros. Ltd.   1460 - 294   2013   £350

Forster, Edward Morgan 1879-1970 *A Passage to India.* London: Edward Arnold, 1926. Uniform edition, first reprint, 8vo., original red cloth, excellent copy, inscribed by author.   Maggs Bros. Ltd.   1460 - 291   2013   £350

Forster, Edward Morgan 1879-1970 *Pharos and Pharillon.* Surrey: Leonard and Virginia Woolf at the Hogarth Press, 1923. First edition, 8vo., original blue cloth backed patterned board boards, printed paper label on spine, extremities and spine label slightly browned, otherwise excellent, inscribed by author for Phyllis Shuttleworth 16-5-23.   Maggs Bros. Ltd.   1460 - 290   2013   £2500

Forster, Edward Morgan 1879-1970 *Virginia Woolf. The Rede Lecture 1941.* Cambridge: at the University Press, 1942. First edition, 8vo., original cream wrappers, near fine, inscribed by author for Marie Stopes, near fine.   Maggs Bros. Ltd.   1460 - 295   2013   £950

Forster, George *A Voyage Round the World in His Britanic Majesty's Sloop, Resolution, Commanded by Captain James Cook, during the Years 1772, 3, 4, and 5.* London: 1777. First edition, 2 volumes, large folding engraved map, 4to., fine in contemporary pale calf, yellow and green morocco labels to spine, lovely copy from Northern Lightboard Trust with its distinctive gilt stamp to both spines.   Maggs Bros. Ltd.   1467 - 78   2013   £6500

Forster, John R. *Travels through Sicily and that Part of Italy Formerly Called Magna Graecia and a Tour through Egypt...* Edward and Charles Dilly, 1773. First English edition, 8vo., contemporary brown full calf, joints rubbed and cracked, spine faded with small loss at head and tail corners rubbed, wear to front cover.   J. & S. L. Bonham Antiquarian Booksellers   Europe - 9655   2013   £550

Forster, Joseph *Studies in Red and Black.* London: Ward & Downy, 1896. First edition, 8vo., original pictorial black cloth stamped in red and gold, uncut, very good, some foxing and browning.   Howard S. Mott Inc.   262 - 50   2013 $75

Forster, Westgarth *A Treatise on a Section of the Strata, from Newcastle-upon-Tyne, to the Mountains of Cross Fell, in Cumberland.* Alston: printed for the author at the Geological Press and sold by John Pattinson, etc., 1821. 12mo., original boards, corners worn, attractively rebacked in pigskin with green lettering piece, uncut, 12 plates, mostly folding or extending and including 3 colored plates of sections, large folding table of superposition of strata, 12 hand colored pages of sections of strata and 8 further hand colored woodcuts, little scattered browning, excellent wide margined copy, rare, with 12mo. ad leaf, tipped in before title, text woodcuts are not usually found colored, armorial bookplates of William Henry Brockett and Edward Joicey of Whinney House.   R. F. G. Hollett & Son   Lake District and Cumbria - 136   2013   £650

Forsyth, Frederick *The Biafra Story; the Making of an African Legend.* Severn House, 1983. First hardback edition, original cloth, gilt, dust jacket, map.   R. F. G. Hollett & Son   Africana - 75   2013   £120

Forsyth, Frederick *No Comebacks and Other Stories.* Helsinki: Eurographica, 1986. First edition thus, one of 350 copies boldly signed by author, this being copy #15, fine, perfect bound in stiff paper wrappers, as issued, in stiff brown printed dust jacket.   Ed Smith Books   78 - 19   2013 $75

Fortescue, J. W. *The Story of a Red-Deer.* London: Macmillan, 1925. First illustrated edition, large 8vo., original green cloth, 24 plates.   R. F. G. Hollett & Son   Children's Books - 30   2013   £35

45 Wood-Engravers. Wakefield: printed at the Whittington Press for Simon Lawrence, 1982. 259/335 copies (of an edition of 350), printed on Zerkall mouldmade paper, 45 wood engravings, each printed on recto of a leaf, further engraving above Colophon, title colophon and name beneath each engraving printed in brown, imperial 8vo., original quarter dark green cloth, backstrip gilt lettered, mid green marbled boards, untrimmed, board slipcase a touch faded, fine.   Blackwell's Rare Books   172 - 308   2013   £275

46 Great Drinks from New York and Restaurants at the World's Fair. St. Louis: Southern Comfort, 1964. 12mo., stapled illustrated wrappers (8) pages, illustrations in color from drawings and photos, tiny tear on rear wrapper, else fine.   Between the Covers Rare Books, Inc. Cocktails, Etc. - 312620   2013 $50

Foskett, Daphne *John Harden of Brathay Hall 1772-1847.* Kendal: Abbot Hall Art Gallery, 1974. Large 8vo., original cloth gilt, dust jacket, 33 monochrome plates , 5 color plates.   R. F. G. Hollett & Son   Lake District and Cumbria - 137   2013   £30

Foster, Alan Dean *Star Wars: From the Adventures of Luke Skywalker.* New York: Ballantine Books, 1977. First printing of the first trade hardcover edition, octavo, cloth.   L. W. Currey, Inc.   Utopian Literature: Recent Acquisitions (April 2013) - 141284   2013 $250

Foster, Coram *Rear Admiral Byrd and the Polar Expeditions with an Account of His Life and Achievements.* New York: A. L. Burt and Co., 1930. First edition, original cloth, 16 plates.   R. F. G. Hollett & Son   Polar Exploration - 16   2013   £30

Foster, Lemuel H. *The Legal Rights of Women.* Detroit: Woman's Pub. Co., 1913. First edition, 8vo., green cloth, hinges beginning tender, cover slightly worn at corners and ends of spine, edges little soiled, otherwise very good.   Second Life Books Inc.   182 - 84   2013 $65

Foster, Marcia Lane *Let's Do It.* Collins, 1938. First edition, 4to., original cloth, dust jacket (piece chipped from top edge), 4 color plates and numerous drawings after chalk sketches.   R. F. G. Hollett & Son   Children's Books - 207   2013   £35

Foster, Michael *Hornby Dublo Trains.* New Cavendish Books, 1991. Oblong 4to., original cloth gilt, dust jacket, 632 photos and diagrams.   R. F. G. Hollett & Son   Children's Books - 208   2013   £40

Foster, Myles *A Day in a Child's Life.* London: Engraved and printed by Edmund Evans, n.d., 1881. First edition, quarto, color printed wood engraved text illustrations, most accompanied with musical notations, original light green glazed pictorial boards with green cloth backstrip, beveled edges, original printed dust jacket, exceptionally clean, near fine.   David Brass Rare Books, Inc.   Holiday 2012 Chapter One - DB 01404   2013 $1100

Foster, Myles *A Day in a Child's Life.* London: George Routledge & Sons, 1881. First edition, 4to., casing loose, extremities worn, illustrations by Kate Greenaway, about good condition.   Barnaby Rudge Booksellers   Children 2013 - 013499   2013 $85

Fothergill, John *The Fothergill Omnibus.* London: Eyre and Spottiswoode, 1931. First edition, one of 250 numbered copies, signed by contributors, 8vo., original green maroon, gilt, spine and edges faded, otherwise excellent copy.   Maggs Bros. Ltd.   1460 - 296   2013   £275

The Four First Rules of Arithmetic. n.p. sold by J.. Satcherd and J. Whitaker, 1787? Only edition, various contemporary calculations, pen trials, inkblots &c consistent with classroom use, stain of paper clip affecting top of first 3 leaves, pages 62, 8vo., original drab card wrappers, bit worn and stained, good.   Blackwell's Rare Books   172 - 13   2013   £750

The Four Gospels of the Lord Jesus Christ According to the Authorized Version of King James I. Wellingborough: September Press, 1988. 14/80 copies of an edition of 600 printed on Saunders' mouldmade paper, afterword printed using monotype Gill Sans Light on Mohawk Superfine Smooth Softwhite paper, supplemented with reproductions of 4 photos, folio, original tan morocco by Zaehnsdorf, gilt lettered black morocco label, "Cockerel" press device blindstamped on front, single gilt rule inner borders, top edge gilt, rough trimmed, felt lined black cloth, slipcase, fine.   Blackwell's Rare Books   B174 - 337   2013   £1500

Fouracre, P. *The New Cambridge Medieval History.* Cambridge: Cambridge University Press, 2005. 1995. 1999. 2000. 1999. 2004. 2004. 1998, Volumes I-VII, (volume IV in 2 parts), together 8 volumes, 8vo., maps and illustrations, dark red cloth with title labels to spine, few slight marks but near fine, dust jackets with occasional creasing to edges and light scratches but very good.   Unsworths Antiquarian Booksellers   28 - 164   2013   £600

Fournet, Jules *Recherches Cliniques sur L'Auscultation der Organs Respiratoires et sur La Premiere Periode de la Phthisie Pulmonaire.* Paris: Chez J. S. Chaude, 1839. Folding table and one plate, 2 parts bound in one volume, 8vo., contemporary quarter brown roan with marbled boards, some rubbing but tight, light text foxing and toning of paper.   James Tait Goodrich   S74 - 115   2013 $495

Fournier, Alfred *Les Affections Parasyphiliti Affectionsques.* Reuff: circa, 1894. 375 pages, full burgundy polished calf, all edges gilt, some light wear, else very good.   James Tait Goodrich   S74 - 116   2013 $895

Fournier, Edmund E. *An English Irish Dictionary & Phrase Book.* 1903. First edition, 8vo., cloth, needs recasing, owner inscribed by Mary Hutton, text clean.   C. P. Hyland 261 - 439   2013   £75

The Fourth Yorkshire Grand Musical Festival held on the 8th, 9th, 10th and 11th Days of September 1835 in York Minster. York: printed by B. Wikeley & Wm. Sotheran, Petergate, 1835. 2 plates on green tinted paper, plate of facsimile signatures, very good in contemporary half calf, marbled boards, expertly rebacked, scarce, name on front endpaper.   Ken Spelman Books Ltd.   73 - 198   2013 £160

Fowler, O. S. *Maternity; or the Bearing and Nursing of Children.* New York: Fowler and Wells, 1856. Small 8vo., original printed wrappers, light wear, some spotty foxing, well preserved, contemporary blindstamp of Tewksbury & Brother, Booksellers and Stationers, Museum Building.   M & S Rare Books, Inc.   95 - 394   2013 $150

Fowles, John *Ourika.* Austin: W. Thomas Taylor, 1977. First edition, limited to 500 copies signed by author at foot of page 64, 4to., original quarter blue morocco, marbled paper boards, lettered in gilt, printed at the Bird and Bull Press on Green's Hayle paper, inscribed by author for Karel Reisz, near fine, spine little sunned.   Maggs Bros. Ltd.   1460 - 297   2013   £650

Fox, George Henry *Photographic Atlas of the Diseases of the Skin.* New York: Treat, 1880. First edition, 48 plates and 102 pages, tall 4to., original half brown morocco and pebbled boards, spine and corners rubbed and bumped, some bubbling of cloth on boards, spine scuffed, overall good tight copy.   James Tait Goodrich   75 - 78   2013 $795

Fox, John *Little Shepherd of Kingdom Come.* New York: Charles Scribner's Sons, 1931. (1931 A). First edition, 4to., black cloth, pictorial paste-on, 322 pages owner name, bookplate, else fine in original box, mounted color plate (flap repaired), illustrations by N. C. Wyeth, scarce in box.   Aleph-Bet Books, Inc.   104 - 598   2013 $1200

Fox, John *Little Shepherd of Kingdom Come.* New York: Scribner, 1931. First edition, 4to., black cloth, pictorial paste-on, 322 pages, fine in dust jacket with original box with mounted color plate (flaps of top replaced), illustrations by N. C. Wyeth, super copy.   Aleph-Bet Books, Inc.   105 - 595   2013 $1200

Fox, Lue *North-west Fox or Fox from the North-West Passage.* S.R. Publishers, Ltd. Johnson Reprint Corp, 1965. Facsimile of 1635 edition, blue cloth, plain dust jacket, pages 273, frontispiece and folding map, 8vo., very good, dust jacket with previous owner's stamp on end flap, generally very good.   Schooner Books Ltd.   105 - 146   2013 $200

Foxe, John *The Lives of the Primitive Martyrs from the Birth of Our Blessed Saviour, to the Reign of Queen Mary I with the Life of Mr. John Fox. (with) The Book of Martyrs.* London: printed and sold by H. Trapp no. 1, Pater Noster Row, 1776? London: publish'd as the act directs Octr. 125h, 1776. First edition thus, 2 volumes in 1, folio, first book with half title, frontispiece and frontispiece portrait, second book with frontispiece and engraved title, additional 38 engraved plates, contemporary full brown calf, rebacked to style, spine stamped in blind, red morocco spine label lettered in gilt, all edges brown, newer endpapers, fair amount of foxing, toning and offsetting throughout, some pages bit brittle with marginal chipping, not affecting text, worming to bottom margin of leaves 6L-7M, not affecting text, leaf B2 of "Lives" bound out of place, behind C2, overall very good.   Heritage Book Shop   Holiday Catalogue 2012 - 65   2013 $1500

Francatelli, Charles *The Modern Cook: a Practical Guide to the Culinary Art in All Its Branches.* Richard Bentley, Twenty eighth edition, frontispiece and text illustrations, very good in original diced dark green cloth, gilt lettered spine, slight ink mark to edge of book block towards end, just visible on some index pages, some wear to rear joint.   Ken Spelman Books Ltd.   75 - 144   2013   £35

France, Anatole *Honey-Bee.* London: John Lane/the Bodley Head, 1911. First edition, illustrations by Florence Lundburg, 4to., original pictorial red cloth blocked in gilt, black and brown, top edge gilt, others untrimmed, inscribed by author to his English translator, Mrs. John Lane, rear hinge cracked, otherwise excellent copy.   Maggs Bros. Ltd.   1460 - 298   2013   £350

Francessco D'Assisi, Saint 1182-1226 *Un Mazzetto Scelto d Certi Fioretti del Glorioso Poverello di Cristo San Francesco di Assisi Insieme Col Cantico al Sole del Medesimo.* Ashendene Press, 1904. One of 125 copies (of an edition of 150), printed on Batchelor 'Hammer and Anvil' handmade paper, chapter headings, large initial letters and shoulder titles all printed in red, 10 wood engravings by Charles Gere, few gatherings stressed, folio, original cream linen backed light blue boards, printed label, title printed in black on front cover, untrimmed, near fine.   Blackwell's Rare Books   172 - 265   2013   £1200

Franchere, Gabriel *Adventure at Astoria 1810-1814.* Norman: University of Oklahoma Press, 1967. First edition thus, illustrations, double page map, gray cloth, very fine, pictorial dust jacket.   Argonaut Book Shop   Summer 2013 - 106   2013 $50

Franchini, Giovanni *Antiquioritatis Franciscanae Conventualibus Adjudicatae Apologema Oradea.* Romania: Typis Seminarii Csakiani per Michaelem Beckskereki, 1747. 12mo., small wormhole to first 4 leaves and patch of worming to last 4 leaves touching three characters in each place (no less of sense), foxed, 20th century half cloth, boards covered in marbled paper (substantially defective), spine gilt, textured endpapers, old stamp to rear pastedown, sound, very rare.   Blackwell's Rare Books   B174 - 58   2013   £200

Francis, Dick *Blood Sport.* New York: Harper, 1968. First American edition, fine in dust jacket with some slight spine fading.   Mordida Books   81 - 187   2013 $150

Francis, Dick *Bolt.* London: Michael Joseph, 1986. First edition, fine in dust jacket.   Mordida Books   81 - 196   2013 $65

Francis, Dick *Bonecrack.* London: Michael Joseph, 1971. First edition, fine in dust jacket with some light staining on inner flaps.   Mordida Books   81 - 189   2013 $200

Francis, Dick *Dead Cert.* London: Michael Joseph, 1964. Fourth edition, signed by author, tiny spot on for-edge, otherwise fine in dust jacket.   Mordida Books   81 - 181   2013 $400

Francis, Dick *Flying Finish.* New York: Harper, 1967. First American edition, fine in dust jacket.   Mordida Books   81 - 188   2013 $175

Francis, Dick *For Kicks.* London: Michael Joseph, 1965. First edition, very good in price clipped dust jacket with three quarter inch pieces missing at spine ends, chips at corners and several closed tears.   Mordida Books   81 - 184   2013 $200

Francis, Dick *High Stakes.* London: Michael Joseph, 1975. First edition, 'Xmas 1975' written on front endpaper, otherwise fine in price clipped dust jacket.   Mordida Books   81 - 193   2013 $100

Francis, Dick *Hot Money.* New York: G. P. Putnam's Sons, 1988. First edition, signed by author, fine in fine dust jacket.   Between the Covers Rare Books, Inc.   Horses, Horsemanship, Horse Racing, Etc. - 331102   2013 $100

Francis, Dick *In the Frame.* London: Michael Joseph, 1976. First edition, inscription and dated on front endpaper, otherwise fine in dust jacket.   Mordida Books   81 - 194   2013 $90

Francis, Dick *Knock Down.* London: Michael Joseph, 1974. First edition, very fine in dust jacket. Mordida Books 81-192 2013 $150

Francis, Dick *Nerve.* New York: Harper, 1964. First American edition, fine in very good rubbed, price clipped dust jacket with wrinkled back panel and tiny fraying at spine ends. Mordida Books 81-183 2013 $200

Francis, Dick *Nerve.* London: Michael Joseph, 1964. First edition, some scattered tiny spotting on page edges, otherwise fine in dust jacket with some very slight spine fading and some scattered stains on back panel. Mordida Books 81-182 2013 $1000

Francis, Dick *Odds Against.* London: Michael Joseph, 1965. First edition, some light spotting on top of page edges, otherwise fine in dust jacket with some light soiling on back panel. Mordida Books 81-185 2013 $500

Francis, Dick *Odds Against.* New York: Harper, 1966. First American edition, fine in dust jacket. Mordida Books 81-186 2013 $250

Francis, Dick *Risk.* London: Michael Joseph, 1977. First edition, fine in price clipped dust jacket. Mordida Books 81-195 2013 $100

Francis, Dick *Slay-Ride.* London: Michael Joseph, 1973. First edition, fine in price clipped dust jacket with slightly faded spine. Mordida Books 81-191 2013 $100

Francis, Dick *Smokescreen.* London: Michael Joseph, 1972. First edition, fine in dust jacket. Mordida Books 81-190 2013 $200

Francis, Dick *Under Orders.* London: Michael Joseph, 2006. First edition, very fine in dust jacket. Mordida Books 81-197 2013 $60

Francis, Edward William *Characters and Caricatures.* Charlottesville: John S. Francis, 2010. Limited to 42 copies, oblong 8vo., silver stamped black cloth, dust jacket, illustrations, TLS 10/24/2010 from author to rare book dealer Jeff Weber laid in, mint. Jeff Weber Rare Books 171-123 2013 $75

Francis, John W. *Old New York or Reminiscences of the Past Sixty Years.* New York: W. J. Widdleton, 1865. Copy number 7 of 100 numbered large paper copies, 4to pages, rebound in older blue cloth with leather spine label, little foxing on first couple of leaves, else near fine. Between the Covers Rare Books, Inc. New York City - 286288 2013 $250

Franco, Gaspare a Reis *Elysius Iucundarum Quaestionum Campus Omnium Literarum Amoeissima Varietate Refertus.* Brussels: Francisci Vivien, 1661. First edition, 4to., half title, elaborate titlepage, pages 219 and 223 have marginal ink drawing of a 'hand' pointing to text, contemporary white pigskin, elaborate stamped decorations, five raised spinal bands, black stamped spine title, manuscript spine title, paper spine label added, pigskin clasps missing, corners worn, slightly soiled, spine rubbed, front hinge cracked, four tiny rear cover holes, ownership signatures, very good, rare. Jeff Weber Rare Books 172-96 2013 $1800

Frank, Anne *Diary of a Young Girl.* West Hatfield: Pennyroyal Press with Jewish Heritage Pub., 1985. Limited to 350 numbered copies, signed by artist, Joseph Goldyne and designer Barry Moser, with additional suite of etchings, each signed in pencil by artist, folio, 10 color etchings by Joseph Goldyne, each signed in pencil by artist, plates with tissue guards, printed by Harold McGrath in gray and rose in Bembo on Mohawk Letterpress, etchings printed by R. C. Townsend Inc. on gray Arches, engraved tailpiece on endgrain boxwood, publisher's full gray morocco by Harcourt Bindery, front cover and spine ruled and lettered in blind, fine, with the additional suite of ten color etchings in quarter gray morocco portfolio, both items housed in publisher's linen slipcase, fine set. Heritage Book Shop Holiday Catalogue 2012 - 114 2013 $2750

Frank, George *Ryedale and North Yorkshire Antiquities.* York: Sampson Bros., 1888. First edition, large 8 vo, half title, text engravings, original dark red cloth, gilt lettered, spine rubbed and some old waterstaining in lower edges, but not intrusive. Ken Spelman Books Ltd. 73-170 2013 £25

Frank, Waldo *Chalk Face.* New York: Boni and Liveright, 1924. First edition, small price on front pastedown and trifle spotted on boards, else near fine in good dust jacket with few chips, modestly on front panel, some old and unnecessary internal repairs. Between the Covers Rare Books, Inc. Sci-Fi, Fantasy & Horror - 87534 2013 $600

Frantz, Joe B. *The American Cowboy. The Myth and the Reality.* Norman: University of Oklahoma Press, 1955. First edition, 16 vintage photos, light tan cloth, very fine with lightly rubbed pictorial dust jacket. Argonaut Book Shop Summer 2013 - 107 2013 $60

Franzen, Jonathan *How to be Alone.* New York: FSG, 2002. First edition, signed by author, fine in mildly rubbed, else fine dust jacket, uncommon signed. Ken Lopez Bookseller 159-66 2013 $125

Franzen, Jonathan *My Father's Brain.* printed at the Libanus Press for the Belmont Press, 2002. First edition, M/26 copies (of an edition of 226), signed by author, frontispiece, crown 8vo., original quarter blue morocco, backstrip gilt lettered, light blue boards, design in brown and printing in black on front cover, cloth slipcase, fine. Blackwell's Rare Books B174 - 208 2013 £200

Fraser, Claud Lovat 1890-1921 *Sixteen Songs Originally for 6d.* Oldham: Incline Press, 1996. 14/30 copies (of an edition of 150), being one of those hand colored by printers, signed by Graham Moss and Jane Audas, and screen printer Tony Grimes, 16 illustrations by Lovat Fraser, 16mo., original pale green wrappers, covers printed in black and purple, rough trimmed, fine. Blackwell's Rare Books B174 - 355 2013 £75

Fraser, George MacDonald *The Steel Bonnets.* Barrie and Jenkins, 1971. First edition, large 8vo., original cloth, gilt, dust jacket, edges trifle rubbed, 19 illustrations, maps on endpapers, plan and large folding map at end, few light stains to fore edge. R. F. G. Hollett & Son Lake District and Cumbria - 138 2013 £225

Fraser, George MacDonald *The Steel Bonnets.* History Book Club, 1972. Large 8vo., original cloth, gilt, dust jacket (torn, chipped and rather creased), 19 illustrations, maps on endpapers, plan and large folding map at end. R. F. G. Hollett & Son Lake District and Cumbria - 139 2013 £45

Fraser, James George *The Golden Bough.* London: Macmillan and Co., 1923. Abridged edition, frontispiece, 8vo., original blue cloth, decorated in gilt, inscribed by author for Kate and Mabel Chaplin, excellent copy, spine very slightly faded, extremities lightly rubbed. Maggs Bros. Ltd. 1460 - 299 2013 £250

Fraunce, Abraham *The Lawiers Logike...* London: by William How for Thomas Gubbin and T. Newman, 1588. First edition, 4to., folding table, title within type ornament border, woodcut initials, mixed black letter and roman, full red gilt panelled morocco, edges gilt by Bedford, first two leaves lightly washed, short closed tear on table, blank corner of 2K4 replaced, else fine clean copy, armorial bookplate of Sir Edwin Priaulx and booklabel of Abel E. Berland. Joseph J. Felcone Inc. Books Printed before 1701 - 40 2013 $8000

Frazer, James *The Golden Bough.* London: Macmillan, 1890. First edition, 2 volumes, octavo, original fine diaper green cloth with elaborate botanical gilt stamping on covers, spines lettered gilt, black endpapers, excellent copy. Heritage Book Shop Holiday Catalogue 2012 - 66 2013 $3750

Frazer, Lilly *The Singing Wood.* A. & C. Black, 1931. First edition, original pictorial blue cloth, dust jacket with closed edge tear, color frontispiece, line drawings. R. F. G. Hollett & Son Children's Books - 88 2013 £35

Frazetta, Frank *At the Earth's Core and Pellucidar.* Evergreen: Opar Press, 1968. Portfolio of plates, cover sheet and 16 unbound printed plates of drawings for a proposed edition of At the Earth's Core and Pellucidar, housed in original printed envelope with cardboard backer, plates, scarce. Between the Covers Rare Books, Inc. Sci-Fi, Fantasy & Horror - 300749 2013 $400

Freart, Roland *A Parallel of the Antient Architecture with the Modern, in a Collection of Ten Principal Authors Who Have Written Upon the Five Orders...* London: printed by T. W. for D. Brown, 1723. Third edition, folio, titlepage misbound before general dedication leaf, folio, some old waterstaining along leading edge, mainly towards end, oval stamp of Bingham Public Lbrary, Cirencester at foot of titlepage, verso of final page and foot of some additional pages, 18th &19th century signatures at head of titlepage, contemporary panelled calf, neatly attacked, corners repaired. Jarndyce Antiquarian Booksellers CCIV - 136 2013 £950

Fredericks, J. Paget *Miss Pert's Christmas Tree.* New York: Macmillan, 1929. First edition, folio, cloth, near fine, full page color illustrations, detailed black and whites, this copy signed by author. Aleph-Bet Books, Inc. 105 - 137 2013 $125

Freedman, Alfred *Comprehensive Textbook of Psychiatry.* Baltimore: Williams & Wilkins, 1975. Second edition, 2 volumes, hardcover, slipcase, very good+. Beasley Books 2013 - 2013 $50

Freedman, Barnett *Real Farmhouse Cheese.* Milk Marketing Board, 1949. First edition, 8 lithographs by Freedman, printed in black and green or yellow, pages 16, folio, original sewn linen wrappers over card with design, overall in grey, green and yellow by Freedman, trifle rubbed at heads and tails of fold, near fine, scarce, Philip Ardizzone's copy (son of Edward) with his signature. Blackwell's Rare Books B174 - 209 2013 £450

Freeman, Bud *You Don't Look like a Musician.* Detroit: Balamp, 1974. First edition, fine in lightly suede and lightly soiled dust jacket. Beasley Books 2013 - 2013 $50

Freeman, Don *Dandelion.* New York: Viking Press, 1964. First edition, oblong 4to., pictorial cloth, fine in dust jacket (chip on spine and few closed tears), full page multicolor drawing of Dandelion inscribed by author, great copy. Aleph-Bet Books, Inc. 104 - 221 2013 $1200

Freeman, Don *The Guard Mouse.* New York: Viking Press, 1967. First edition, 4to., pictorial cloth, fine in very good+ dust jacket with few marks on bottom margin, color illustrations by Freeman.   Aleph-Bet Books, Inc.   104 - 222   2013 $300

Freeman, James W. *Prose and Poetry of the Live Stock Industry of the United States.* New York: Antiquarian Press, 1959. Facsimile reprint of very rare 1905 edition, thick quarto, 757 pages, photos, old prints, etc., half cowhide and gilt stamped buckram, spine lettered gilt, very fine with slipcase.   Argonaut Book Shop   Recent Acquisitions June 2013 - 111   2013 $350

Freeman, Leila Crocheron *Nip and Tuck.* New York: Sears, 1926. Large 4to., cloth pictorial paste-on, 157 pages, slight cover soil, else very good+, 8 great color plates, numerous text illustrations, nice.   Aleph-Bet Books, Inc.   104 - 200   2013 $225

Freeman, Lewis R. *The Colorado River: Yesterday, to-Day and To-morrow.* New York: 1923. First edition, xix, 451 pages, illustrations map, folding profile, errata slip, blue boards, little dusty on top, spine slightly faded, intermittent dampstain to bottom edge, else very good and largely unopened, lengthy inscription by author.   Dumont Maps & Books of the West   125 - 50   2013 $75

Freeman, R. Austin *A Savant's Vendetta.* London: Arthur Pearson, 1920. First English edition, cheap paper browned, small spot on front board, very good or better, inscribed by author for P. M. Stone, scarce, very seldom found and never signed or inscribed.   Between the Covers Rare Books, Inc.   Mystery & Detective Fiction - 54833   2013 $2500

Freeman, Walter *Psychosurgery. Intelligence, Emotion and Social Behavior Following Prefontal Labotomy for mental Disorders.*   Springfield & Baltimore: Charles C. Thomas, 1942. First edition, 8vo., original blue cloth, gilt stamped spine, spine end bit rubbed, small '150' painted at foot of spine, rubber stamps of Semmes-Murphy Clinic in Memphis, bottom edge as well and Dr. E. C. (Dutch) Schultz, titlepage with red rubber stamp, very good.   Jeff Weber Rare Books   172 - 97   2013 $500

Freeman, Walter *Psychosurgery. Intelligence Emotion and Social Behavior Following Prefrontal Lobotomy for Mental Conditions.* Springfield: Thomas, 1942. 337 pages, text illustrations, original cloth, dust jacket bit worn, else very good plus, presentation copy from James Watts for Bill Sweet.   James Tait Goodrich   S74 - 117   2013 $350

Freemasons. Grand Lodge of Tennessee *Annual Proceedings of the M(ost) W(orshipful) Grand Lodge of the State of Tennessee held in... Nashville on the First Monday in octo., A. L. 5867...*   Nashville: printed at the Southern Methodist Pub. House, 1867. First edition, 8vo., original printed wrappers, little dust soiled, spine with some loss, internally some marginal browning and few stains, corners curled &c., faint pencil signature on front wrapper, not quite very good but entirely sound.   M & S Rare Books, Inc.   95 - 359   2013 $150

Frees, Harry *Circus Day at Catnip Center.* Chicago: Manning, 1932. 4to., stiff pictorial card covers, owner name on top edge of cover, else very good+, 2-color pictorial borders, scarce.   Aleph-Bet Books, Inc.   105 - 453   2013 $250

Freiburg Im Breisgau *Nuwe Strattrechten und Statuten der Statt Fryburg im Pryszgow Gelegen.* Basle: Adam Petri, 1520. Folio, 2 large Holbein woodcuts, illustrations repeated a second time, modern full calf, light old ink stain in bottom blank margin of two leaves, scattered foxing on few leaves, else clean.   Joseph J. Felcone Inc.   Books Printed before 1701 - 41   2013 $5500

Freind, John *Opera Omnia Medica.* London: Typis Johannis Wright, 1733. First collected edition, folio, frontispiece, small rusthole in one leaf (5B2) affecting two characters, prelims dusty and spotted with few silked repairs in black margins, some light spotting and soiling elsewhere but text generally quite clean, contemporary mottled sheep, edges worn and chipped, rebacked with calf, spine in seven compartments, raised bands, two gilt lettered direct, new endpapers, small stamp of Birmingham Medical Institute.   Unsworths Antiquarian Booksellers   28 - 96   2013   £400

Fremont, Jessie Benton *Mother Lode Narratives.* Ashland: Lewis Osborne, 1970. First edition, one of 650 numbered copies, 12mo., text illustrations, map ends, cloth backed decorated boards, gilt lettered spine, owner's address sticker on half titlepage, very fine.   Argonaut Book Shop   Summer 2013 - 108   2013 $75

Fremont, John Charles 1813-1890 *The Expeditions of John Charles Fremont.* London: University of Illinois Press, 1970. First edition, very scarce when found complete and in such fine condition, 3 volumes in 4 plus map portfolio, 5 folding maps in 11 sections in matching double slipcase, illustrations from plates, 5 folding maps, very fine set with dust jackets.   Argonaut Book Shop   Summer 2013 - 110   2013 $750

Fremont, John Charles 1813-1890 *Geographical Memoir Upon Upper California...* Washington: Wendell and Van Benthuysen, 1848. First edition, Senate issue, thin octavo, 67 pages, early cloth backed marbled boards, preserving original pale green front wrapper with title printed in black, subtle and small library embossed stamp on title leaf, overall, remarkably condition for such a fragile item, fine. Argonaut Book Shop   Recent Acquisitions June 2013 - 112   2013 $350

Fremont, John Charles 1813-1890 *Geographical Memoir Upon Upper California in Illustration of His Map of Oregon and California.* Washington: Wendell and Van Benthuysen, 1848. First edition, Senate issue, thin octavo, 67 pages, early cloth backed marbled boards preserving original pale green front wrapper with title printed in black, subtle and small library embossed stamp on title leaf, overall in remarkable condition, fine.   Argonaut Book Shop Summer 2013 - 111   2013 $350

Fremont, John Charles 1813-1890 *Geographical Memoir Upon Upper California in Illustration of His Map of Oregon and California.* San Francisco: Book Club of California, 1964.   One of 425 copies, portrait, large folding map in rear pocket, decorated boards, very fine.   Argonaut Book Shop   Summer 2013 - 112   2013 $150

Fremont, John Charles 1813-1890 *Memoirs of My Life...* Chicago and New York: Belford, Clarke & Co., 1887. First edition, thick quarto, frontispiece, 80 plates, wood engravings, photogravures, etc., 1 chromolithograph and 7 maps, publisher's pictorial cloth stamped in various colors, small bookplate on inner cover, just hint of rubbing to spine ends, front and rear inner hinges expertly and beautifully reinforced, very fine, from the library of Herbert McLean Evans with his small oval bookplate, quite scarce in this condition.   Argonaut Book Shop   Recent Acquisitions June 2013 - 114   2013 $1250

Fremont, John Charles 1813-1890 *Report of the Exploring Expedition to the Rocky Maoutnains in the Year 1842 and to Oregon and North California in the Years 1843-'44.* Washington: Gales and Seaton, 1845. First edition, 693 pages, 4 maps, 22 lithographed plates, large Preuss map not present, blindstamped brown cloth, gilt, expertly recased, preserving original cloth, new endpapers, occasional light foxing, few minor exceptions, plates bright and clean, beautifully preserved in original cloth, collated complete, with short contemporary presentation signed by Hon. C(harles) G(ordon) Atherton (1804-1853).   Argonaut Book Shop   Recent Acquisitions June 2013 - 115   2013 $2500

French, Thomas *The Psychogenic Factors in Bronchial Asthma.* National Research Council, 1941. First edition, issued in two paperback volumes, near fine but for external library stamps and notation "File Copy" stamped on one cover.   Beasley Books   2013 - 2013 $65

Freneau, Philip *Poems Written Between the Years 1768 & 1794...* Monmouth: printed at the presss of the author, at Mount Pleasant, near Middletown Point, 1795. Only edition, contemporary sheep, many gatherings variously foxed or browned, as always with this book, else unusually nice, contemporary signatures of Geo. J. Warner and slightly later Susan Nichols. Joseph J. Felcone Inc.   English and American Literature to 1800 - 14   2013 $1200

Frenkel-Brunswick, Else *Motivation and Behavior.* Genetic Psych Monograph 26, 1942. First edition, paperback wrappers, very good+ with title inked on spines and half inch chip at head of spine, this copy inscribed by author for Robert Redfield.   Beasley Books   2013 - 2013 $65

Frere, John Hookham *The Monks and the Giants.* London: John Murray, 1821. Fourth edition, half title, uncut, original blue boards, drab spine, paper label and spine chipped, inscribed to revd. Thomas Price by Henry Bartle Frere, brother of author.   Jarndyce Antiquarian Booksellers   CCIII - 382   2013   £65

Frere, John Hookham *The Monks and the Giants.* Bath: printed by H. E. Carrington, 1842. Half title, uncut in original brown wrappers, spine excellently rebacked, booklabel of John Sparrow, very good.   Jarndyce Antiquarian Booksellers   CCIII - 383   2013   £50

Freuchen, Peter *Arctic Adventure.* London: Heinemann, 1936. First edition, large 8vo., original cloth, trifle rubbed and bubbled in places, pages 405 66 illustrations and maps, occasional spotting, piece cut from corner of flyleaf.   R. F. G. Hollett & Son   Polar Exploration - 18   2013   £45

Freuchen, Peter *It's Adventure.* London: Heinemann, 1938. First edition, large 8vo., original cloth, gilt, 33 illustrations, 2 maps.   R. F. G. Hollett & Son   Polar Exploration - 20   2013   £45

Freud, Sigmund 1856-1939 *Massenpsychologie und Ich-Analyse. (Group Psychology and the Analysis of Ego).* Leipzig: Internationaler Psychoanalytischer Verlag, 1921. First edition, small chip to front fly, age toning to endpapers, else near fine.   Between the Covers Rare Books, Inc.   Psychology & Psychiatry - 297240   2013 $250

Freud, Sigmund 1856-1939 *Die Traumdeutung. (The Interpretation of Dreams).* Leipzig: Franz Deuticke, 1909. Second edition, good with soiling and wear along edges, without dust jacket as issued, ownership signature of J. C. Flugel.   Between the Covers Rare Books, Inc.   Psychology & Psychiatry - 274302   2013 $500

Freud, Sigmund 1856-1939 *Zur Auffassung der Aphasien.* Leipzig: & Vienna, 1891. First edition, Original printed wrappers, lacking top portion of spine strip, uncut and unopened, particularly nice, unsophisticated copy.   James Tait Goodrich   75 - 96   2013 $7500

Freud, Tom Seidmann *Kinga O Mnogikh Prekrasnykh Predmetakh.* Berlin: Peregrin, 1923. 4to., cloth backed pictorial boards, rebacked with some cover and occasional mild text spotting, very good+, 16 hand colored full page illustrations printed on one side of paper only, rare.   Aleph-Bet Books, Inc.   105 - 258   2013 $4750

Freyer, Kurt *Mikrobiblion: Das Buch Von Den Kleinen Buchern.* Berlin: Horodisch & Marx, 1929. Limited to 426 numbered copies, 10.5 x 7.3 cm., full parchment, title hand lettered on front board, fore-edge uncut, text in German, with miniature bookplate of Kathryn Rickard, from the collection of Donn W. Sanford.   Oak Knoll Books   303 - 15   2013 $550

Friedenwald, Harry *The Jews and Medicine Essays.* Baltimore: Johns Hopkins, 1944. 2 volumes, original dust jacket.   James Tait Goodrich   S74 - 118   2013 $150

Friedlander, Lee *Cray at Chippewa Falls.* Minneapolis: Cray Research, 1987. First edition, very fine in cloth with paper label on front cover, issued without dust jacket, fine copy of the prospectus, very fresh.   Jeff Hirsch Books   Fall 2013 - 129138   2013 $450

Friedlander, Lee *Like a One-Eyed Cat Photographs 1956-1987.* New York: Abrams, 1989. Horizontal 4to., 119 pages, yellow cloth, nice in little chipped and scuffed dust jacket, 153 black and white plates.   Second Life Books Inc.   183 - 135   2013 $150

Friedman, Milton *A Theory of the Consumption Function.* Princeton: Princeton University, 1957. First edition, very good++, original blue cloth, owner name, minimal foxing to edges, minimal cover edge wear, 8vo., scarce.   By the Book, L. C.   38 - 14   2013 $1000

Friel, Brian *Aristocrats.* Dublin: Gallery Press, 1980. First edition, 8vo., original black cloth, dust jacket, fine in slightly dusty jacket, Faber and Faber file copy with pencilled note on titlepage "Not for setting".   Maggs Bros. Ltd.   1442 - 81   2013   £75

Friel, Brian *Dancing at Lughnasa.* London: Faber & Faber, 1990. First edition, inscribed by author June '90 for Tom and Gita (Paulin), cheap paper slightly browned as usual, otherwise fine.   Maggs Bros. Ltd.   1460 - 302   2013   £450

Friel, Brian *Fathers and Sons.* London: Faber and Faber, 1987. First edition, 8vo., original wrappers, cheap paper slightly browned as usual, otherwise fine, inscribed by author Aug. 87 for Gita and Tom (Paulin).   Maggs Bros. Ltd.   1460 - 301   2013   £275

Friel, Brian *Give Me Your Answer, Do!* Loughcrew: Gallery Press, 1994. First edition, 8vo., original black cloth fine in dust jacket slightly faded on spine and bleeding on to lower cover, inscribed by author in month of publication March 97 for Tom and Gita Paulin.   Maggs Bros. Ltd.   1460 - 307   2013   £300

Friel, Brian *The Home Place.* Loughcrew: The Gallery Press, 2005. First edition, 8vo., original black cloth, fine in dust jacket, inscribed by author for Tom and Gita Paulin.   Maggs Bros. Ltd.   1460 - 312   2013   £300

Friel, Brian *The London Vertigo.* Loughcrew: Gallery Press, 1990. First edition, original black cloth, dust jacket, fine, dust jacket with fading on spine, bleeding over to covers, inscribed by author for Tom and Gita Paulin.   Maggs Bros. Ltd.   1460 - 303   2013   £250

Friel, Brian *Molly Sweeney.* Loughcrew: Gallery Press, 1994. First edition, 8vo., original black cloth, dust jacket, fine in dust jacket slightly nicked at head of spine with very minor fading to spine, inscribed by author 18 Aug 94 for Tom and Gita (Paulin).   Maggs Bros. Ltd.   1460 - 306   2013   £300

Friel, Brian *A Month in the Country. After Turgenev.* Loughcrew: Gallery Press, 1992. First edition, 8vo., original black cloth, fine in dust jacket, inscribed by author for Tom and Gita Paulin.   Maggs Bros. Ltd.   1460 - 304   2013   £300

Friel, Brian *Performances.* Loughcrew: The Gallery Press, 2003. First edition, 8vo., original black cloth, fine in dust jacket, inscribed by author for Tom and Gita Paulin Oct. '03.   Maggs Bros. Ltd.   1460 - 311   2013   £300

Friel, Brian *Selected Plays.* London: Faber and Faber, 1984. First edition, 8vo., original black cloth, dust jacket, inscribed by author to Tom Paulin and his wife Gita, cheap paper browning as usual and slightly faded on spine, otherwise near fine in dust jacket.   Maggs Bros. Ltd.   1460 - 300   2013   £375

Friel, Brian *Three Plays After. The Yalta Game. The Bear and Afterplay.* Loughcrew: The Gallery Press, 2002. First edition, 8vo., original black cloth, dust jacket, fine, jacket slightly nicked on upper cover, inscribed by author March '02 for Tom and Gita Paulin.   Maggs Bros. Ltd.   1460 - 310   2013   £300

Friel, Brian *To Let.* London: William Heinemann, 1921. First edition, 8vo., original pale green cloth, spine and upper cover lettered in gilt, spine darkened, pages browned, some very faint soiling to lower cover, otherwise very good, inscribed by author for Morley Roberts.   Maggs Bros. Ltd.   1460 - 316   2013   £50

Friel, Brian *Uncle Vanya.* Loughcrew: Gallery Press, 1998. First edition, 8vo., original black cloth, fine, dust jacket with slightest of fading on spine, inscribed by author Oct. 98 for Tom and Gita Paulin.   Maggs Bros. Ltd.   1460 - 308   2013   £300

Friel, Brian *Wonderful Tennessee.* Loughcrew: Gallery Press, 1993. First edition, 8vo., original black cloth, fine, dust jacket slightly nicked at head of spine and with very minor fading to spine, inscribed by author June 30 '93 for Tom and Gita (Paulin).   Maggs Bros. Ltd.   1460 - 305   2013   £300

Friel, Brian *The Yalta Game.* Loughcrew: Gallery Press, 2001. First edition, 8vo., original black cloth, fine in dust jacket, inscribed by author Oct. '01 for Tom and Gita Paulin.   Maggs Bros. Ltd.   1460 - 309   2013   £300

The Friend, a Series of Essays...   London: Rest Fenner, 1818. New edition, half titles, 3 volumes, some spotting, few small library stamps, rebound in quarter maroon calf, endpapers replaced.   Jarndyce Antiquarian Booksellers   CCIII - 517   2013   £250

The Friend, a Series of Essays...   London: William Pickering, 1837. Third edition, 3 volumes, half titles, 16 page catalog and final ad leaf volume I, pencil notes, original blue cloth, paper labels, spines and paper labels rubbed and little worn, Peter Mann's copy with his signature.   Jarndyce Antiquarian Booksellers   CCIII - 518   2013   £95

The Friend, a Series of Essays...   London: William Pickering, 1844. Fourth edition, 3 volumes, half titles, final ad leaf volume I, blindstamps of Royal Museum Library, small tear page 353 volume III without loss, attractively rebound in dark blue quarter calf, new endpapers.   Jarndyce Antiquarian Booksellers   CCIII - 519   2013   £150

The Friend, a Series of Essays...   London: William Pickering, 1850. Fifth edition, 3 volumes, half titles, contemporary full calf by Bickers & Son, gilt spines, borders and dentelles, maroon and green leather labels, spine volume III darkened and rebacked with small repair to head, armorial booklabels of Adeleine Puxley, all edges gilt, attractive, if slightly worn copy.   Jarndyce Antiquarian Booksellers   CCIII - 520   2013   £110

The Friend, a Series of Essays...   London: Bell and Daldy, 1865. Half title obscured by booklabel, portrait, initial and final catalogs including endpapers, original uniform green cloth, two booklabels, one of C. J. Peacock, ownership inscription of Peter Mann, very good.   Jarndyce Antiquarian Booksellers   CCIII - 521   2013   £30

The Friend. London: Routledge, 1969. 2 volumes, half titles, frontispiece, volume I, facsimile volume II, original grey cloth, bevelled boards, very good in dust jackets and original slipcase.   Jarndyce Antiquarian Booksellers   CCIII - 523   2013   £60

Frikell, Wiljalba *The Magician's Own Book.* London: John Camden Hotten, 1871. First edition, initial ad leaf, half title, frontispiece, illustrations, 30 pages ads, original pictorial blue cloth, slightly rubbed.   Jarndyce Antiquarian Booksellers   CCV - 106   2013   £150

Frith, Francis *Francis Frith in Egypt and Palestine: A Victorian Photographer Abroad.*   Princeton and Oxford: Princeton University Press, 2004. First printing, 4to., 239 pages, frontispiece, 75 duotone plates, 10 black and white plates, quarter brown cloth over pictorial paper backed boards gilt stamped spine, dust jacket, bookplate of Burndy library, fine.   Jeff Weber Rare Books   169 - 144   2013 $75

Fritz, Emanuel *California Coast Redwood.*   San Francisco: Foundation for American Resource Management, 1957. First edition, cloth very fine.   Argonaut Book Shop Recent Acquisitions June 2013 - 117   2013 $150

Frizot, Michel *A New History of Photography.*   Koln: Konemann, 1998. First edition, 4to., fine in fine dust jacket.   Beasley Books   2013 - 2013 $100

Frog Who Would a Wooin Go.   Boston: Brown, Taggard & Chase, 1858. 12mo., (32) pages pictorial wrappers, spine repaired and margins trimmed, else fine, 14 half page and one full page hand colored engravings, sold together with a worn but complete and untrimmed.   Aleph-Bet Books, Inc.   105 - 259   2013 $300

Frohlich, Karl *Karl Frohlich's Frolicks with Scissors and Pen.*   London: Joseph Myers & Co., 1860. First edition, 2 illustrated rhymes on rectos only, some slight marking, original red cloth decorated in blind and gilt, slightly dulled and rubbed, bookseller's ticket of E. C. Purin, all edges gilt, nice in custom made double slipcase, slightly faded blue morocco spine.   Jarndyce Antiquarian Booksellers   CCV - 107   2013   £280

Froissart, John *The Boy's Froissart.* London: Sampson Low, n.d., Full dark green calf, gilt prize binding, little used, 12 plates, prize label of Wisbech Barton School dated 1883.   R. F. G. Hollett & Son   Children's Books - 350   2013   £30

From the Bottom Up.   N.P.: date, pub. by Mutual Broadcasting Co. circa, 1945. Folio, pictorial boards, edges and covers rubbed some, else very good+, 4 large great pop-ups, illustrations by Scott Johnston.   Aleph-Bet Books, Inc.   104 - 446   2013 $2000

Frost, Charles *Notices Relative to the Early History of the Town and Port of Hull.* J. B. Nichols, 1827. First edition, double page plan, 6 plates, 2 pedigrees, very good, clean copy, full contemporary diced calf with blindstamped and gilt ruled borders, raised and gilt banded spine, morocco label, marbled edges and endpapers. Ken Spelman Books Ltd. 73 - 99 2013 £95

Frost, Robert Lee 1874-1963 *A Boy's Will.* London: David Nutt, 1913. First edition, first issue in earliest binding (Crane's Binding A), of approximately 1000 copies, fewer than 350 were issued by Nutt, even fewer copies were bound in first binding of bronze cloth before April 1, 1913, small 8vo., original bronze brown pebbled cloth, very fine, preserved in half morocco folding box. James S. Jaffe Rare Books Fall 2013 - 50 2013 $12,500

Frost, Robert Lee 1874-1963 *A Boy's Will.* London: David Nutt, 1913. First edition, 2nd issue, binding D, small 8vo., near fine, original printed wrappers with mild soil to covers, minimal foxing to edges. By the Book, L. C. 38 - 83 2013 $1250

Frost, Robert Lee 1874-1963 *A Masque of Reason.* New York: Henry Holt, 1945. First trade edition, fine in very good, unclipped dust jacket, signed by author, 8vo., original cloth. Howard S. Mott Inc. 262 - 51 2013 $250

Frost, Robert Lee 1874-1963 *New Hampshire. A Poem with Notes and Graces Notes.* New York: Henry Holt & Co., 1923. First edition, one of 350 numbered copies signed by author, large 8vo., original gilt decorated black cloth, top edge gilt, , woodcuts by J. J. Lankes, small ink signature stamp, tiny bookseller's label, otherwise fine, bright copy, rare in fine condition. James S. Jaffe Rare Books Fall 2013 - 52 2013 $2250

Frost, Robert Lee 1874-1963 *New Hampshire.* Hanover: New Dresden Press, 1955. First separate edition, one of 750 copies, signed by author, 12mo., original cloth backed boards, fore and bottom edges uncut, fine in original semi-transparent unprinted rough white Japanese paper. Howard S. Mott Inc. 262 - 52 2013 $450

Frost, Robert Lee 1874-1963 *North of Boston.* London: David Nutt, 1914. First edition, first issue, binding "A", one of 350 copies, occasional light foxing, two leaves little carelessly opened and very slight rubbing to corners, excellent copy, morocco backed cloth slipcase. Howard S. Mott Inc. 262 - 2013 $1750

Frost, Robert Lee 1874-1963 *North of Boston.* London: David Nutt, 1914. First edition, one of 350 copies bound in coarse green linen out of a total edition of 1000, fine, preserved in black cloth slipcase and chemise, presentation copy inscribed by author for Earle Bernheimer. James S. Jaffe Rare Books Fall 2013 - 51 2013 $15,000

Frost, Robert Lee 1874-1963 *Collected Poems.* New York: Henry Holt and Co., 1930. First trade edition, after limited signed edition of 1000 copies, one of 3870 printed, 8vo., frontispiece by Doris Ulmann, original cloth, dust jacket, very fine, jacket price clipped. James S. Jaffe Rare Books Fall 2013 - 54 2013 $500

Frost, Robert Lee 1874-1963 *Collected Poems.* New York: Random House, 1930. First edition, limited to 1000 copies, signed by Frost, tall 8vo., original buckram with leather label on spine, top edge gilt, some slight discoloration along outer hinges, offsetting to endpapers as usual, otherwise unusually fine unopened copy, scarce. James S. Jaffe Rare Books Fall 2013 - 53 2013 $2500

Frost, Robert Lee 1874-1963 *Complete Poems of Robert Frost.* New York: Henry Holt, 1949. First edition, limited to 500 numbered copies, signed by author, thick 8vo., portrait, original buckram, glassine dust jacket with few small chips and creases. James S. Jaffe Rare Books Fall 2013 - 55 2013 $2500

Frost, Robert Lee 1874-1963 *Complete Poems of Robert Frost.* New York: Henry Holt and Co., 1949. First US edition, 8vo., original green cloth, rubbed and soiled but very good, inscribed by author for Douglas Glass, Oct. 1953, with few manuscript poem in Glass's hand on back endpapers. Maggs Bros. Ltd. 1460 - 313 2013 £1500

Frost, Robert Lee 1874-1963 *Selected Poems.* London: Penguin Books, 1955. First edition thus, 8vo., original wrappers, preserved in folding box, pages browned, wrappers torn and worn, good copy, inscribed by author of Douglas Glass May 1957. Maggs Bros. Ltd. 1460 - 314 2013 £450

Frost, Robert Lee 1874-1963 *A Wishing Well.* New York: Spiral Press, 1959. First edition, one of 100 copies used as a Christmas Greeting by Leda and Stanley Burnshaw, from an 10,760 copies printed, wrappers, fine. Beasley Books 2013 - 2013 $50

Frost, Robert Lee 1874-1963 *You Came Too.* New York: Henry Holt, 1959. First edition, 8vo., original cloth, fine in very good dust jacket, signed by author and by editor, Hyde Cox. Howard S. Mott Inc. 262 - 53 2013 $850

Fryer, Alfred *Tales from the Harz Mountains.* London: David Nutt, 1908. 4to., green gilt cloth, very good+, charming illustrations by Alice Ogders, this is presentation copy from author, inscribed and with 2 handwritten letters from author. Aleph-Bet Books, Inc. 105 - 243 2013 $200

Fryer, Jane Eayre *The Mary Frances Book or Adventures Among the Kitchen People.* Philadelphia: John C. Winston, 1912. 4to., blue cloth, pictorial paste-on, near fine, color frontispiece plus a profusion of color and line illustrations. Aleph-Bet Books, Inc.   104 - 226   2013 $450

Fryer, John *A New Account of East-India and Persia, in Eight Letters.* London: R(obert) R(oberts) for Ri(chard) Chiswell, 1698. First edition, folio, calf ruled and decorated in blind, five raised bands, compartments heavily decorated in gilt, red morocco lettering piece, all to period style, engraved frontispiece, 5 engraved plates and 3 maps, one printed overslip, title in red and black, woodcut illustrations in text, small puncture on one leaf at Oo, not affecting text, leaves at Pp and Pp4 browned, few minor shallow stains on fore margins of some later leaves, very faint institutional stamp on margins of few leaves, otherwise leaves clean, impressions sharp and overall near fine, exceptionally handsome binding.   Kaaterskill Books   16 - 36   2013 $3750

Fuchs, Adalbert *Atlas of the Histopathology of the Eye.* Leipzig and Vienna: Franz Denticke, 1924-1927. First edition in English, 2 volumes, original black cloth, first volume with defective spine and binding splitting, volume one has 191 illustrations on 44 color plates, volume two has 108 illustrations contained in 32 color plates.   James Tait Goodrich   S74 - 199   2013 $150

Fuchs, Vivian *The Crossing of Antarctica.* London: Cassell, 1958. First edition, original cloth, gilt numerous illustrations.   R. F. G. Hollett & Son   Polar Exploration - 21   2013   £25

Fuller, Andrew C. *A Reprint of Legal Notes on Motoring as Published from Time to Time in the Official Journal of the Royal Automobile Club of South Africa.* Cape Town: Edina Press, 1949. Original half calf gilt, 412 pages.   R. F. G. Hollett & Son   Africana - 76   2013   £45

Fuller, Thomas *Pharmacopoeia Domestica; or the Family Dispensatory.* printers to the Royal Society, 1739. First edition in English, frontispiece, woodcut head and tailpieces, occasional minor spotting, minor worming in ad leaves, 8vo., contemporary calf double gilt fillets on sides, rebacked (not recently), new spine richly gilt, new endpapers, corners slightly worn, preserved in red morocco backed slip-pin case, good.   Blackwell's Rare Books   Sciences - 51   2013   £750

Fulton, John Farquhar *Grace Revere Osler. Her Influence on Men of Medicine.* Offprint from Bulletin of the History of Medicine, 1949. Original printed wrappers, penned presentation note from Lady Osler's sister, Susan Revere Chapin.   James Tait Goodrich   S74 - 122   2013 $225

Fulton, John Farquhar *Harvey Cushing: A Biography.* Springfield: Charles C. Thomas, 1946. 8vo., frontispiece, figures, blue cloth, gilt stamped spine, spine faded, extremities worn, especially at spine ends, signed and inscribed by Cushing's wife, Katherine Crowell Cushing to Dr. Frank Glenn, her signature seldom seen, good.   Jeff Weber Rare Books   172 - 68   2013 $450

Fulton, John Farquhar *Harvey Cushing. A Biography.* Springfield: 1946. First edition, nice, cloth, dust jacket present with light wear, internally very good.   James Tait Goodrich   S74 - 61   2013 $95

Fulton, Robert *Torpedo War and Submarine Explosions.* New York: William Elliott, 1810. First edition, oblong folio, with all five plates, first two leaves (blank and title) bit short, as issued in marbled wrappers, old, faint crease to center, some occasional light foxing, overall very good, clean copy, rare.   Heritage Book Shop   Holiday Catalogue 2012 - 67   2013 $12.500

Funfzehn Ansichten der Neuen St. Gotthards-Strasse Vom St. Gotthard-Hospiz bis Lugano. Zurich: for Heinrich Fussli, 1833. 238 305mm., original green paper wrappers, very good recent buckram folding case with morocco label on upper cover, 15 very fine hand colored aquatints of scenic swiss views by Josef Meinrad Kalin and Jakob Suter, paper wrapper chipped at head and tail of spine, intermittent faint freckled foxing to text, otherwise fine copy of fragile item, with clean, fresh text bright, richly colored plate.   Phillip J. Pirages   63 - 459   2013 $15,000

Funk, Wilfred *If You Drink.* New York: Wilfred Funk, 1941. First edition, slight foxing to endpapers, near fine in fresh and bright, very near fine dust jacket with faint crease on rear panel, signed by author and dated 1942.   Between the Covers Rare Books, Inc.   Cocktails, Etc. - 273281   2013 $350

Furious Flower: a Revolution in African American Poetry. Charlottesville: Virginia Foundation for the Humanities, 1994. First edition, one of 300 numbered copies, quarto, 33 loose sheets in printed folder, fine in original shrinkwrap which has been opened at top.   Between the Covers Rare Books, Inc.   165 - 48   2013 $100

Furlong, Charles Wellington *Let 'er Buck. A Story of the Passing of the Old West.* New York: G. P. Putnam's Sons, 1921. First edition, scarce thus, 35 photo plates, text drawings, full dark blue cloth, photo pastedown on front cover, lettering in gilt, one upper corner slightly bent, fine.   Argonaut Book Shop   Summer 2013 - 121   2013 $150

Furness Year Book. Sixth Annual. Ulverston: H. W. Mackereth, 1899. Original cloth, gilt, extremities trifle rubbed and faded, folding map, numerous illustrations, very good.   R. F. G. Hollett & Son   Lake District and Cumbria - 143   2013   £140

Furness Year Book. Eighth Annual.   Ulverston: H. W. Mackereth, 1901.   Original printed cloth gilt, little bubbled and faded, double page map, numerous illustrations.   R. F. G. Hollett & Son   Lake District and Cumbria - 144   2013   £100

Furness Year Book. Fourteenth Annual.   Ulverston: W. Holmes, 1907.   271 pages, folding map, numerous portraits, illustrations, original cloth backed printed boards, upper board, little stained at head, staples rather rusted, otherwise excellent.   R. F. G. Hollett & Son   Lake District and Cumbria - 145   2013   £75

Furness Year Book. Fifteenth Annual.   Ulverston: W. Holmes, 1908.   original cloth backed printed boards, upper board trifle stained, 279 pages, folding maps, portraits, illustrations, joints just cracking, otherwise excellent.   R. F. G. Hollett & Son   Lake District and Cumbria - 146   2013   £75

Furness Year Book: Sixteenth Annual.   Ulverston: W. Holmes, 1909.   12 portraits and illustrations, numerous local ads, original cloth backed printed boards, rather soiled, folding map.   R. F. G. Hollett & Son   Lake District and Cumbria - 147   2013   £75

Furness, Alfred   *The English Lakes.*   Allen and Unwin, 1948.   First edition, 4to., original cloth, gilt, trifle marked and spine faded, 75 half tone plates.   R. F. G. Hollett & Son   Lake District and Cumbria - 141   2013   £25

Furness, William   *History of Penrith from the Earliest Record to the Present Time.*   Penrith: William Furness, 1894.   First edition, original patterned brown cloth, gilt, all edges gilt, frontispiece, numerous illustrations, one section little shaken, but very good.   R. F. G. Hollett & Son   Lake District and Cumbria - 142   2013   £150

Furnival, Benjamin   *Windsor of the North.*   Ross Features International, 1999.   First edition, original pictorial wrappers, 50 illustrations.   R. F. G. Hollett & Son   Lake District and Cumbria - 148   2013   £20

Fyfe, Christopher   *Freetown. A Symposium.*   Freetown: Sierra Leone University Press, 1968. First edition, original cloth, gilt, dust jacket, plates, 12 maps, large folding town plan.   R. F. G. Hollett & Son   Africana - 77   2013   £45

Fyfield, Frances   *Blind Date.*   London: Bantam Press, 1998.   First edition, fine in fine dust jacket, signed by author, from the library of Bruce Kahn.   Between the Covers Rare Books, Inc. Mystery & Detective Fiction - 302195   2013 $65

Fyleman, Rose   *Fifty-one New Nursery Rhymes.*   London: Methuen & Co., 1931.   First edition, oblong 4to., original cloth backed pictorial boards, corners little bumped, illustrations in colors by Dorothy Nurroughes.   R. F. G. Hollett & Son   Children's Books - 210   2013   £40

Fyleman, Rose   *Quipic the Hedgehog.*   London: Allen & Unwin, n.d 1940's,   Fifth impression, large square 8vo., original pictorial boards with flaps, pages 36, illustrations, partly lithographed colors.   R. F. G. Hollett & Son   Children's Books - 212   2013   £25

Fyleman, Rose   *The Rainbow Cat and other Stories.*   London: Methuen, 1922.   First edition, original orange cloth gilt, top margins little dusty, scarce.   R. F. G. Hollett & Son   Children's Books - 211   2013   £50

Fyleman, Rose   *The Sunny Book.*   Oxford University Press, n.d., 1918.   First edition, original embossed pictorial boards, top edge gilt of upper board dusty, head of backstrip torn and bruised, 12 full page color plates by Millicent Sowerby.   R. F. G. Hollett & Son   Children's Books - 559   2013   £95

G

Gabelkhover, Oswald *Artzneybuch Darinen...* Frankfurt am Main: Nicolaus Hoffmann for Johann Jacob Porsch and Johann Berner, 1610. 2 parts in 1 volume, 4to., fine blind tooled pigskin with concentric ornamental and historiated rolls surrounding Holy Monogram on covers, brass catches and clasps present and intact, text browned in parts, early owners' signatures on title. James Tait Goodrich S74 - 123 2013 $2500

Gadesby, Richard *A New and Easy Introduction to Geography, by Way of Question and Answer...* printed for the author and sold by S. Bladon, 1783. Second edition, 12mo., folding engraved plates, short tear in plate, little foxing, original sheep, spine gilt ruled, minor wear, good. Blackwell's Rare Books 172 - 59 2013 £650

Gag, Wanda *Gone is Gone.* New York: Coward McCann, 1935. First edition, 12mo., green cloth, fine in lightly soiled and worn dust jacket, illustrations by Gag with color frontispiece and black and whites on every page. Aleph-Bet Books, Inc. 104 - 228 2013 $450

Gage, Thomas *Thomas Gage's Travels in the New World.* Norman: University of Oklahoma Press, 1958. Drawings, photos, mas, green cloth, very fine, dust jacket. Argonaut Book Shop Summer 2013 - 122 2013 $60

Gail, Otto Willi *By Rocket to the Moon: the Story of Hans Hardt's Miraculous Flight.* New York: Sears Pub. Co. Inc., 1931. First edition English, octavo, 8 inserted plates with illustrations by R. V. Grunberg, original pictorial black cloth, front and spine panels stamped in red, top edge stained red, other edges untrimmed. L. W. Currey, Inc. Fall Sampler Sept. 2013 - 146506 2013 $1500

Gaiman, Neil *American.* Ossining: Hill House, 2003. First edition, limited to 750 numbered and 52 lettered, signed copies, this no. 286, signed by Gaiman, small 4to., 529 pages, purple satin with printed paper spine label and paste-on paper illustration front cover, matching purple satin covered slipcase. By the Book, L. C. 36 - 49 2013 $400

Gaines, Ernest J. *The Autobiography of Miss Jane Pittman.* New York: Dial Press, 1971. First edition, fine in fine dust jacket with tiny creased tear on front panel, nicely inscribed by author in year of publication, very nice, although not marked in any way, this copy from the collection of Bruce Kahn. Between the Covers Rare Books, Inc. 165 - 303 2013 $600

Gaines, Ernest J. *A Lesson Before Dying.* New York: Alfred A. Knopf, 1993. Uncorrected proof, crease on front cover, else fine in pictorial wrappers. Between the Covers Rare Books, Inc. 165 - 153 2013 $85

Gaines, Ernest J. *A Lesson Before Dying.* New York: Alfred A. Knopf, 1993. First edition, fine in very lightly worn, but still fine dust jacket, ownership signature of author Nicholas Delbanco. Between the Covers Rare Books, Inc. 165 - 154 2013 $85

Gale, Elizabeth *Circus Babies.* Chicago: Rand McNally, 1930. Square 4to., cloth, 100 pages, fine, full page and partial page color illustrations by John Dukes. Aleph-Bet Books, Inc. 104 - 123 2013 $200

Gale, John *The Missouri Expedition 1818-1820. The Journal of Surgeon John Gale with Related Documents.* Norman: University of Oklahoma Press, 1969. First edition, 10 photo illustrations, 3 maps, turquoise cloth, gilt very fine, pictorial dust jacket. Argonaut Book Shop Summer 2013 - 123 2013 $60

Gale, Norman *Songs for Little People.* London: Constable, 1896. First edition, original pictorial light brown rubbed cloth, gilt, corners trifle bruised, top edge gilt, tissue guard pictorial title in yellow and black and black and white drawings, scarce. R. F. G. Hollett & Son Children's Books - 214 2013 £140

Gale, Thomas *Opuscula Mythologica, Ethica et Physica.* Cantabrigiae: ex officina J. Hayes.... Joann. Creed biblioplae Cantab., 1671. Very good, full contemporary mottled calf, raised bands with old paper label on spine, each of the 10 parts with separate titlepage and pagination, 8vo.,. Ken Spelman Books Ltd. 75 - 4 2013 £495

Galen *Epitome Galeni Pergame ni Opervm.* Basileae: apud Mich. Ifingrinium anno, 1551. Small folio, full rich contemporary calf skillfully rebacked with original spine tastefully laid down, from the library of Nicolas Marchant with his signature and stamp on title, some early signatures, gilt armorial crest on front board of two lions facing crowned staff, ruled boards, gilt emblems in each corner, raised tooled bands on spine, text with light marginal dampstaining, early underlining of text with contemporary marginalia throughout, early ownership signature of Rene Minault, 1702. James Tait Goodrich 75 - 97 2013 $2950

Galen *In Hippocratis Librum de Humoribus Commentarii Tres Ejusdem Reliquum Sexti Commentarii in Sextum De Vulgaribus Morbis...* Venetiis: Apud Vincenzo Valgrisium, 1562. 12mo., old vellum, pastedowns bit wormed, early marginal annotations, some text underlining. James Tait Goodrich 75 - 100 2013 $295

Galen *Methodi Medendi id est de Morbis Curandis Libri Quatuordecim Denuo Magna Diligentia Martini Grigorii Recogniti... (with) De Curandi Ratione per Sanguinis Missionem.* Paris: C. Chevallon, 1538. Paris: C. Wechel, 1539, 2 works in 1 volume, elegant printer on each title leaf, calf over oak boards, worn, raised bands, armorial gilt stamps on boards, with ruling of calf, spine worn with chipping, rear board has some mild worming, text lightly foxed, some marginal dampstaining, contemporary ownership signature. James Tait Goodrich S74 - 125 2013 $2450

Galerie Duret *Exposition Henri Matisse Galerie Druet 114 rue de Faubourg Saint Honore du 19 amrs au 17 Avril 1906.* Paris: Imprimerie A. Laine 10..., 1906. 8vo., pages (8), on cream paper, 3 illustrations, including cover, slightly soiled, stapled as issued. Marlborough Rare Books Ltd. 218 - 102 2013 £750

Galilei, Galileo *Dialog uber die Beiden Hauptsachlichsten Weltsystem...* Leipzig: B. G. Teubner, 1891. First German edition, 8vo., lxxix, 586 pages, original half brown morocco over marbled boards, gilt stamped, red leather spine label, raised bands, joints rubbed, ownership signature, very good. Jeff Weber Rare Books 169 - 146 2013 $800

Galilei, Galileo *Dialogo... Sopra i due Massimi Sistemi del Mondo Tolemaico e Copernicano...* Florence: Per Gio: Batista Landini, 1632. First edition, quarto, bound without final blank leaf, printed correction slip pasted in margin of versos of F6 (p. 92), engraved title, fourth state, with artist's signature present, sized and mounted (no loss whatsoever), woodcut diagrams in text, woodcut printer's device on title, late 18th century quarter dark red roan over marbled boards, vellum tips, smooth spine decoratively tooled and lettered gilt, some light foxing and browning to few gatherings, few marginal paper flaws, front joint starting, bookplate of Albert May Todd, with one other armorial bookplate, excellent and very tall copy, many leaves uncut, quarter red morocco clamshell, gilt stamped. Heritage Book Shop 50th Anniversary Catalogue - 38 2013 $95,000

Gallagher, Frank *The Indivisible Island: History of the Partition of Ireland.* London: Gollancz, 1957. First edition, cloth, dust jacket, near fine. C. P. Hyland 261 - 441 2013 £32

Gallatin, A. E. *Gaston Lachaise. Sixteen Reproductions in Collotype of the Sculptor's Work.* New York: E. P. Dutton & Co., 1924. First edition, limited to 400 copies, 4to., photogravures from photos by Charles Sheeler, original cloth backed boards, printed labels, glassine dust jacket, very fine, unopened copy in somewhat worn and chipped glassine dust jacket, inscribed by Lachaise to friend and patron Scofield Thayer, with Thayer bookplate laid in. James S. Jaffe Rare Books Fall 2013 - 8 2013 $1750

Gallenga, Antonio *A Summer Tour in Russia.* London: Chapman & Hall, 1882. First edition, half title, folding map, final ad leaf, 2 lines of annotation in different hand, original dark olive green cloth, slight rubbing, lending library label on pastedown, contemporary signature of Malcolm McCon, nice. Jarndyce Antiquarian Booksellers CCV - 109 2013 £150

Gallwey, Hubert *The Wall Family in Ireland 1170-1970.* Leinster Leader, 1970. First edition, 8vo., cloth, illustrations, dust jacket, very good. C. P. Hyland 261 - 847 2013 £200

Galsworthy, John 1867-1933 *A Commentary.* London: Richards Press, 1930. First limited edition, one of 275 numbered copies, signed by author, 8vo., original red cloth, excellent copy. Maggs Bros. Ltd. 1460 - 320 2013 £50

Galsworthy, John 1867-1933 *The Inn of Tranquility. Studies and Essays.* London: William Heinemann, 1912. First edition, 8vo., original green cloth, inscribed by author, excellent copy, endpapers lightly browned, spine faded, little shelf worn, tape residue to rear pastedown. Maggs Bros. Ltd. 1460 - 315 2013 £100

Galsworthy, John 1867-1933 *Loyalties. A Drama in three acts.* London: Duckworth, 1922. First edition, small 8vo., original green cloth, excellent copy, spine faded, few marks to cloth, inscribed by author in 1923. Maggs Bros. Ltd. 1460 - 317 2013 £50

Galsworthy, John 1867-1933 *Loyalties. A Drama in three Acts.* London: Duckworth, 1930. First illustrated edition, one of 315 numbered and signed copies, 4to., original buff buckram, very good dust jacket with few nicks and closed tears at edges, word 'signed' handwritten in ink on spine, an excellent copy, spine browned, inscribed by author for Frank Pepper. Maggs Bros. Ltd. 1460 - 321 2013 £75

Galsworthy, John 1867-1933 *A Modern Comedy.* London: William Heinemann Ltd., 1929. First collected edition, one of 1030 copies, signed and numbered by author, folding family tree as frontispiece, 8vo., original stiff vellum, gilt, near fine, previous owner's bookplate. Maggs Bros. Ltd. 1460 - 319 2013 £75

Galsworthy, John 1867-1933 *Two Forsyte Interludes. A Silent Wooing. Passers By.* London: William Heinemann, 1927. First edition, one of 525 numbered copies signed by author, 8vo., original quarter black cloth, patterned paper boards, dust jacket slightly nicked, excellent copy. Maggs Bros. Ltd. 1460 - 318 2013 £50

Galt, John 1779-1839 *The Life of Lord Byron.* London: Henry Colburn, 1830. First edition, 2 pages ads preceding series title, engraved frontispiece and title, plate, slightly spotted, original glazed purple cloth faded to brown, black label, marked, Renier booklabel, good, sound. Jarndyce Antiquarian Booksellers CCIII - 384 2013 £125

Galt, John 1779-1839 *The Life of Lord Byron.* London: Henry Colburn & Richard Bentley, 1830. First edition, engraved title, engraved frontispiece and title, plate, contemporary half calf, following hinge splitting and repaired, some worm damage to leather on boards, contemporary owner's inscription to series title. Jarndyce Antiquarian Booksellers CCIII - 385 2013 £110

Galt, John 1779-1839 *Sir Andrew Wylie, of that Ilk.* Edinburgh: printed for William Blackwood, 1822. 3 volumes, 8vo., lightly browned, contemporary straight grained half green morocco with marbled boards, spine in compartments with central gilt tools, lettered and numbered in gilt direct, edges marbled, spines gently sunned, armorial bookplate of William, Duke of Bedford, Edinburgh, signed binding by Feaston, with his circular red ticket on front pastedown. Unsworths Antiquarian Booksellers 28 - 165 2013 £180

Galton, Francis 1822-1911 *Typical Laws of Heredity.* London: Royal Institution of Great Britain, 1877. Offprint from Royal Institution of Great Britain, Weekly Meeting, Friday Feb. 9 1877, 8vo., 20 pages, near fine in self wrappers. By the Book, L. C. 37 - 33 2013 $225

Galvin, John *The Etchings of Edward Borein. A Catalogue of His Work.* San Francisco: John Howell Books, 1971. First edition, frontispiece, 318 black and white reproductions, brown cloth, gilt, very fine with dust jacket. Argonaut Book Shop Recent Acquisitions June 2013 - 32 2013 $125

Galvin, Patrick *Man on the Porch.* London: Martin Britan & O'Keefe, 1979. First edition, 8vo., original grey cloth dust jacket, fine. Maggs Bros. Ltd. 1442 - 82 2013 £35

Galway, George *Six Short Stories.* Belfast: Crannog Press, 1978. One of only 10 copies in this binding, from total edition of 100 copies, first edition, large 8vo., original quarter black morocco with green silk cloth, lettered in relief, illustrations, fine. Maggs Bros. Ltd. 1442 - Crannog 2013 £400

Galway, George *Six Short Stories.* Belfast: Crannog Press, 1978. First edition, one of 90 copies in this binding from total edition of 100 numbered copies, fine, large 8vo., original quarter dark blue cloth over decorated paper, printed paper label on spine. Maggs Bros. Ltd. 1442 - Crannog 2013 £100

Gamba, Peter *A Narrative of Lord Byron's Last Journey to Greece.* London: John Murray, 1825. First edition, half title, 2 folding facsimiles, uncut in original pale blue boards, drab spine, paper label, corners bumped, spine little worn and chipped, with loss at tail, Marquess of Headfort's armorial bookplate, good plus. Jarndyce Antiquarian Booksellers CCIII - 386 2013 £220

Gambles, Robert *The Story of the Lakeland Dales.* Phillimore, 1997. First edition, large 8vo., original cloth, gilt, dust jacket, 17 color plates, 47 illustrations, 15 maps, review copy, typescript note from publisher loosely inserted. R. F. G. Hollett & Son Lake District and Cumbria - 149 2013 £25

Gannij, Joan Levine *The Cruelty of Loveless Love.* New York: Kunst Editions, 2001. First edition, copy # 11 of 35 copies for sale from a total edition of 65, photos and text by Gannij, 12 leaves printed rectos only and 18 paper folders each containing mounted monochrome photo with letterpress poem on facing page, folio, houed in burgundy satin covered clamshell case 12 1/4 x 14 3/4 inches, with photo inset of Charles Bukowski, fine in fine black cardboard slipcase in original shipping bag. Charles Agvent Charles Bukowski - 83 2013 $1000

Garband, John *The Grand Inquest, or a Full and Perfect Answer to Several Reasons.* London: for James Vade, 1680. first of three editions, 4to., wanting either prelim blank or half title, modern buckram. Joseph J. Felcone Inc. Books Printed before 1701 - 43 2013 $325

Garber, Daniel *The Cambridge History of Seventeenth Century Philosophy.* Cambridge: Cambridge University Press, 1998. 8vo., 2 volumes, navy cloth, gilt stamped spine title, dust jacket, fine. Jeff Weber Rare Books 169 - 151 2013 $90

Garces, Francisco *A Record of Travels in Arizona and California.* San Francisco: John Howell Books, 1965. Second edition in English, first printing, one of 1250 copies, colored frontispiece, folio, 5 plates, 2 folding maps, text illustrations, decorative cloth, very fine. Argonaut Book Shop Recent Acquisitions June 2013 - 119 2013 $75

Garcia-Marquez, Gabriel 1928- *One Hundred Years of Solitude.* New York: Limited Editions Club, 1982. First edition, 1/2000 copies, large 8vo., 348 pages, with additional original lithograph, bound in natural straw colored Chinese silk with gilt stamped spine of top grain aniline leather, text and drawings printed at Stinehour Press, 8 oil paintings reproduced by Seaboard Lithograph Corp. in New York and original lithograph hand painted on Rives paper at Blackburn Studio, bound by Robert Burlen & Son, signed by Ferrer, Reid and Rabassa, fine in original slipcase, LEC Monthly Letter laid in. Second Life Books Inc. 183 - 259 2013 $250

Garcia-Marquez, Gabriel 1928- *Cien Anos de Soledad. (One Hundred Years of Solitude).* Santafe de Bogata: Editorial Norna, 1997. Limited to 500 copies, bound in calf, this No. LXXVI of 100 (C) copies numbered in roman numerals and signed by author, the remaining 400 leather bound copies are unsigned, Thirtieth Anniversary edition, 8vo., fine in original calf with raised bands, gilt lettered, marbled endpapers, original board slipcase.   By the Book, L. C.   38 - 85   2013 $2000

Gardiner, Robert *Frigates of the Napoleonic Wars.* Annapolis: Naval Institue Press, 2000. First edition, 4to., 208 pages, frontispiece, illustrations, tables, navy paper boards, gilt stamped spine, dust jacket bookplate of Burndy library, fine.   Jeff Weber Rare Books   169 - 154   2013 $85

Gardner, E. *Ballads and Songs of Southern Michigan.* Ann Arbor: University Michigan Press, 1939. First edition, fine in lightly used dust jacket, uncommon, especially in jacket.   Beasley Books   2013 - 2013 $100

Gardner, Erle Stanley *The Case of the Black-Eyed Blonde.* New York: Morrow, 1944. First edition, bookplate, fine in dust jacket.   Mordida Books   81 - `99   2013 $250

Gardner, Erle Stanley *The Case of the Drowsy Mosquito.* New York: Morrow, 1943. First edition, fine in very good dust jacket with chipped and frayed spine ends, wear and nicks along edges and at corners, couple of closed tears. Mordida Books   81 - 198   2013 $125

Gardner, Erle Stanley *The Case of the Gold Diggers Purse.* New York: Morrow, 1945. First edition, date, otherwise fine in dust jacket with some tiny wear at corners. Mordida Books   81 - 200   2013 $200

Gardner, Erle Stanley *The Case of the Hesitant Hostess.* New York: William Morrow, 1953. First edition, bookplate, else very near fine in rubbed, but very good dust jacket with small nicks and tears.   Between the Covers Rare Books, Inc.   Mystery & Detective Fiction - 94506   2013 $65

Gardner, Erle Stanley *The Case of the Lazy Love.* New York: Morrow, 1947. First edition, fine in fine dust jacket with chip at top corner of spine.   Mordida Books   81 - 201   2013 $165

Gardner, Erle Stanley *The Case of the Spurious Spinster.* New York: William Morrow, 1961. First edition, bookplate, else fine in dust jacket with tiny tear.   Between the Covers Rare Books, Inc.   Mystery & Detective Fiction - 94538   2013 $65

Gardner, Erle Stanley *Neighborhood Frontiers.* William Morrow, 1954. First edition, 8vo., original blue cloth, very good, dust jacket chipped with some notable loss to head of spine, rear endpapers unevenly browned, inscribed by author.   Maggs Bros. Ltd.   1460 - 323   2013   £150

Gardner, Erle Stanley *Traps Need Fresh Bait.* New York: William Morrow, 1967. First edition, near fine, minimal cover edge wear, stray pen mark edge, very good++ dust jacket with mild soil, 8vo., 216 pages, signed and inscribed by Gardner.   By the Book, L. C.   36 - 45   2013 $400

Gardner, Erle Stanley *The World of Water: exploring the Sacramento Delta.* New York: Morrow, 1965. First edition, spine lettering, little foxing, also on spine, very good, lacking dust jacket, inscribed by author.   Between the Covers Rare Books, Inc.   Mystery & Detective Fiction - 38622   2013 $275

Gardner, George E. *Ed Case Studies in Childhood Emotional Disabilities I and II.* New York: American Ortho. Assn., 1953-1956. First edition, 2 volumes, near fine but for dulling to one spine and tape shadows on endpapers of one volume, hardcover.   Beasley Books   2013 - 2013 $50

Gardner, John *License Renewed.* New York: Marek, 1981. First American edition, inscribed by author, very fine in dust jacket, with publisher's press release folder, all very fine.   Mordida Books   81 - 180   2013 $150

Gardner, John *Win, Lose or Die.* London: Hodder & Stoughton, 1989. First edition, 8vo., 224 pages, original mid blue boards, backstrip gilt lettered dust jacket, fine. Blackwell's Rare Books   B174 - 204   2013   £80

Garengeot, Rene Jacques Croissant De *Traite des Operations de Chirurgie.* Paris: Rue Jacques chez Huart, 1731. Second edition, engraved plates, small 8vo., 3 volumes, fine contemporary French polished tree calf, gilt compartment spines, tooled gilt panels, all edges red, some marginal dampstaining and light rubbing, near fine.   James Tait Goodrich   75 - 102   2013 $3000

Garfield, Brian *Fear in a Handful of Dust.* New York: Dutton, 1978. First edition, fine in dust jacket, inscribed by author.   Mordida Books   81 - 203   2013 $60

Garfield, James A. *Investigation into the Causes of the Gold Panic. Report of the Majority of the Committee on Banking and Currency March 1, 1870.* Washington: House of Representatives, 1870. 487 pages, cloth, spine little faded, boards spotted, scattered foxing, overall very good. Dumont Maps & Books of the West   125 - 51   2013 $100

Garland, Hamlin 1860-1940 *Prairie Folks.* Chicago: F. J. Schulte, 1893. First edition, 8vo., 255 pages, original printed wrappers, spine chipped, wrappers somewhat weary, very scarce in wrappers. M & S Rare Books, Inc. 95 - 128 2013 $150

Garland, Hamlin 1860-1940 *The Shadow World.* New York: Harper, 1908. First edition, fine in attractive, very near fine dust jacket, scarce in jacket. Between the Covers Rare Books, Inc. Sci-Fi, Fantasy & Horror - 42399 2013 $850

Garn *Tommy on the Train.* Akron: Saalfield, 1946. Oblong 4to., cloth backed spiral boards, slight edgewear, else very good-fine in worn and torn dust jacket, 4 tab operated moveable plates and color and black and white illustrations by Zaffo. Aleph-Bet Books, Inc. 104 - 371 2013 $200

Garner, Elvira *Way Down in Tennessee.* New York: Julian Messner, 1941. First edition, 4to., cloth, fine in frayed dust jacket with small pieces off spine ends, illustrations by author in color and black and white. Aleph-Bet Books, Inc. 105 - 88 2013 $200

Garnet, Henry *A True and Perfect Relation of the Proceedings at the Severall Arraignments of the Late Most Barbarous Traits.* London: by Robert Barker, 1606. First edition, first issue, 4to., coat-of arms verso of titlepage, woodcut initials and type ornaments, without final blank 3F4, titlepage slightly browned, some occasional cropping to upper margin shaving some running heads, near contemporary note at foot of Q3 verso, few later marginal pencil marks, expertly bound in recent full calf, gilt ruled borders, raised and gilt banded spine, small gilt device in each compartment. Jarndyce Antiquarian Booksellers CCIV - 14 2013 £1500

Garnett, David *A Man in the Zoo.* London: Chatto & Windus, 1924. First edition, 8vo., original patterned cloth, some pages foxed, otherwise near fine in dust jacket, inscribed by author for Stephen Tomkin. Maggs Bros. Ltd. 1460 - 324 2013 £150

Garnett, Louise Ayres *Rhyming Ring.* Chicago: Rand Mcnally, 1919. 4to., cloth backed pictorial boards, tips rubbed and slight cover soil, 64 pages, very good+, pictorial endpapers, 7 color plates, 7 black and white plates, many text illustrations by Hope Dunlap. Aleph-Bet Books, Inc. 104 - 189 2013 $400

Garrard, Lewis H. *Wah-to-Yah and the Taos Trail: Prairie Travel and Scalp Dances.* San Francisco: Grabhorn Press, 1936. Second edition, limited to 550 copies, illustrations in color, cloth backed decorated boards, paper spine label, facsimile of Josiah Gregg map tipped in at front endpaper, very fine and bright copy. Argonaut Book Shop Summer 2013 - 125 2013 $250

Garratt, Evelyn R. *Free to Serve.* London: RTS, 1881. Half title, frontispiece, vignette title, illustrations, 16 page catalog, original green cloth, pictorially blocked in black, silver and gilt, lettered in black and gilt, owner's inscription May 1882, very good bright. Jarndyce Antiquarian Booksellers CCV - 110 2013 £35

Garrett, Phineas *One Hundred Choice Selections...A Repository of Readings, Recitations and Declamations...* Philadelphia and Chicago: P. Garrett & Co., 1877. First edition, 8vo., original printed yellow wrappers, 180 pages + 10 pages of publisher's terminal ads, from the library of George Barr McCutcheon with his bookplate tipped in, wrappers little worn and stained, very good, enclosed in cloth slipcase. The Brick Row Book Shop Miscellany Fifty-Nine - 27 2013 $750

Garrison, Wiliam Lloyd *Sonnets and Other Poems.* Boston: Oliver Johnson, 1843. First edition, 16mo., 96 pages, original cloth, some browning, near fine, this copy inscribed in ink by publisher, to his sister. M & S Rare Books, Inc. 95 - 120 2013 $600

Garston, Guy *The Champagne Mystery.* London: Muller, 1935. First edition, very good in dust jacket. Mordida Books 81 - 204 2013 $100

Garth, Samuel *The Poetical Works.* Glasgow: printed by Robert and Andrew Foulis, 1775. Folio, 12mo., contents leaf bound in at beginning, some light browning to first and final leaves, recent marbled paper wrappers. Jarndyce Antiquarian Booksellers CCIV - 138 2013 £30

Garth, Samuel *The Works of...* Dublin: Printed for Thomas Ewing, 1769. First edition, small 8vo., contemporary calf, finely rebacked, gilt decorated borders, leather label, tipped in errata, copper engraved portrait, several large copper engraved head and tailpieces, titlepage in red and black. Howard S. Mott Inc. 262 - 59 2013 $300

Garton, Ray *Live Girls.* London: MacDonald, 1987. First English and First hardcover edition, fine in fine dust jacket, as new. Between the Covers Rare Books, Inc. Sci-Fi, Fantasy & Horror - 13182 2013 $175

Gary, Romain *The Colours of the Day.* London: Michael Joseph, 1953. First edition, 8vo., original black cloth, dust jacket, near fine, jacket just little worn at head and tail of spine, inscribed by author to fellow diplomat, Mons. et Madam Francois Coulet. Maggs Bros. Ltd. 1460 - 325 2013 £175

Gascoigne, George *The Pleasauntest Workes of George Gascoigne, Esqyre.* London: printed by Abell Ieffes, 1587. First edition with this title and designated third edition, with scarce variant title with word 'pleasauntest' rather than 'VVhole', small quarto, pages 111-122 and 129-142 of locasta remargined and supplied from a copy of the first edition of Gascoigne's Works, A Hundredth Sundrie Flowres (1573), pages from Supposes are remargined along top and bottom edge as well as fore-edge, pages from locasta remargined along bottom edges, leaves B-H4, I2 supplied from a copy of the first edition of the Steele Glas (1576), leaves S4 (of the Steele Glas) and (Y)5 and A-B8 (of the Complaint of Philomene) shorter and supplied from another copy of this edition of Gascoigne's works, very rare on the market, early 2th century mottled calf by W. Pratt, gilt double rule border on covers with floral corner ornaments, gilt spine, tooled in compartments, red morocco spine labels, gilt board edges and inner dentelles, marbled endpapers, all edges gilt, joints almost invisibly repaired, few leaves with neat paper repairs, few leaves closely trimmed affecting some printed marginalia, very nice, rare, housed in quarter brown calf clamshell case.   Heritage Book Shop   50th Anniversary Catalogue - 40   2013 $30,000

Gash, Jonathan *The Judas Pair.* New York: Harper & Row, 1977. First American edition, fine in modestly rubbed, plus dust jacket, pleasing copy.   Between the Covers Rare Books, Inc. Mystery & Detective Fiction - 78805   2013 $200

Gask, Lilian *Babes of the Wild.* London: Harrap, 1917. First edition, tall 8vo., original cloth backed glazed pictorial boards, edges little worn and soiled, pages 160, 4 color plates by Wilma Nickson, endpapers rather spotted.   R. F. G. Hollett & Son   Children's Books - 1215   2013   £30

Gaskell, Elizabeth Cleghorn   1810-1865 *Cranford.* London: Macmillan, 1891. First reprint, 8vo., original green cloth, excellent copy, cloth just little marked and scuffed, inscribed by Lady Augusta Gregory for Arabella Waithman, Dec. 25 1981.   Maggs Bros. Ltd.   1460 - 379   2013   £250

Gaskell, Ernest *Westmorland and Cumberland Leaders.* Queenhithe Printing & Publishing Co., n.d. circa, 1910. 4to., original half morocco gilt, spine trifle faded, all edges gilt, unpaginated, scarce.   R. F. G. Hollett & Son   Lake District and Cumbria - 153   2013   £180

Gaskell, Philip *John Baskerville: a Bibliography.* Cambridge: Cambridge University Press, 1959. First edition, 4to., 12 plates, facsimile of type specimen placed in rear pocket, maroon cloth, gilt stamped black spine label, dust jacket lightly chipped, previous owner bookplate (John Howell Books), very good.   Jeff Weber Rare Books   171 - 15   2013 $65

Gaskin, Arthur, Mrs. *A Tale of Six Little Travellers.* London: H. R. Allenson, n.d. circa, 1900. 16mo., red boards, pictorial paste-on, (59) pages + 1 page ads some wear to paper on joints, else very good+, printed on coated paper, text hand lettered in large font, 25 full page color illustrations by Mrs. Gaskin.   Aleph-Bet Books, Inc.   105 - 263   2013 $350

Gaskin, Catherine *The Property of a Gentleman.*   Collins, 1974. First edition, original cloth, gilt, dust jacket, 348 pages, presentation copy inscribed by author.   R. F. G. Hollett & Son   Lake District and Cumbria - 154   2013   £25

Gaskin, Ruth L. *A Good Heart and a Light Hand: Ruth L Gaskin's Collection of Traditional Recipes.* Annandale: The Turnpike Press, 1968. First edition, spiral bound pictorial boards, illustrations by Porge Buck, neat owner name, fine, without dust jacket as issued.   Between the Covers Rare Books, Inc.   165 - 123   2013 $75

Gasset, Jose Ortega Y *The Revolt of the Masses.* London: George Allen and Unwin, 1932. First edition in English, 8vo., original black cloth, with ownership inscription "A. C. F. Beales" below which is inscribed "from J. R. Carey the translator", loosely inserted TLS in Spanish from author to Carey, excellent copy.   Maggs Bros. Ltd.   1460 - 326   2013   £350

Gatti De Gamond, Zoe Charlotte *Fourier et Son System.* Paris: Administration de Librairie, 1840. Fourth edition, 12mo., contemporary calf backed boards, initial signature printed on lower grade paper and browned, very good, just minor foxing.   Second Life Books Inc.   183 - 139   2013 $350

Gatty, Margaret Scott   1809-1873 *The Book of Sun-Dials.* London: George Bell and Sons, 1900. Fourth edition, folio, frontispiece, additional 8 photographic and engraved plates, numerous black and white illustrations, plates with tissue guards, beautifully bound by Worrall Birmingham in full green morocco, boards double ruled in gilt, single ruled in blind with corner ornaments, spine elaborately stamped and lettered in gilt, gilt dentelles, marbled endpapers, top edge gilt, some toning to tissue guards, about fine.   Heritage Book Shop   Holiday Catalogue 2012 - 68   2013 $1250

Gatty, Margaret Scott   1809-1873 *Parables from Nature.* George Bell and Sons, 1884-1885. 2 volumes, small 8vo., original green cloth, gilt, 2 woodcut frontispieces, some spotting to fore-edges, one joint cracked.   R. F. G. Hollett & Son   Children's Books - 218   2013   £50

Gatty, Margaret Scott   1809-1873 *Parables from Nature.* London: George Bell and Sons, 1896. Original decorated green cloth, trifle rubbed and soiled, all edges, numerous woodcut plates.   R. F. G. Hollett & Son   Children's Books - 217   2013   £75

Gautier, Jean Jacques *Une Femme Prisonniere.* Paris: Editions Bernard Grasset, 1968. First edition, original wrappers, fine, inscribed by author for Gillian Sutro. Maggs Bros. Ltd.   1460 - 327   2013   £350

Gawsworth, John *Backwaters. Excursions in the Shades.* London: Denis Archer, 1932. First US edition, 8vo., original cloth, dust jacket, near fine, inscribed by author, signed on half title "Don Coralle".   Maggs Bros. Ltd.   1460 - 329   2013   £650

Gay, Amorous *Love's Perpetual Almanack, According to the Astronomical Observations of Cupid, Calculated for the Meridian of the Heart.* London: printed for T. C. and Sold by J. Roberts near the Oxford Arms in Warwick Lane, 1721. 12mo., paper poor and rather browned apart from gatherings K. L & N, old mark to upper inch of leading edge of top edge gilt, small marginal paper flaw to E1, tear to P1 without loss, early 20th century sprinkled calf, red morocco label. Jarndyce Antiquarian Booksellers   CCIV - 139   2013   £1800

Gay, John   1685-1732 *Fables by John Gay, with a Life of the Author...* London: by Darton & Harvey for E. & C. Rivington et al, 1793. xvi, 256 pages, plates, full calf, richly gilt, all edges gilt by Bayntun, hinges split but held by cords, else lovely copy, cloth slipcase.   Joseph J. Felcone Inc.   English and American Literature to 1800 - 15   2013 $250

Gay, John   1685-1732 *Poems on Several Occasions.* Glasgow: printed by Robert and Andrew Foulis, 1770. 2 volumes in 1, 12mo., pages toned, contemporary polished tan sheep, spine divided by gilt rules, compartment with gilt centre and corner tools, red morocco label, marbled endpapers, slight rubbing, rear joint cracking, minor chipping to spine ends.   Unsworths Antiquarian Booksellers   28 - 97   2013   £65

Gaze, Harold *The Billiabonga Bird.* Melbourne: Auckland: Christchurch: Dunedin and Wellington and London: Whitcombe & Tombs Ltd., 1919. 4to., wrappers, color plate on cover, string tie, light foxing, few marks on rear cover, very good-fine copy, illustrated by Gaze with 2 tipped in color plates plus color plate on cover repeated in text, 1 tipped in black and white plate and 8 pen and ink drawings in text.   Aleph-Bet Books, Inc.   104 - 230   2013 $1850

Gaze, Harold *Chew-um-Blewg-um.* Melbourne: Whitcombe & Tombs Ltd., 1919. 4to., wrappers, color plate on cover, string tie, faint corner stain on cover, else near fine, 2 tipped in color plates plus color plate on cover repeated in text, 1 tipped in black and white plate and 8 pen and ink drawings in text, great copy, rare.   Aleph-Bet Books, Inc.   105 - 265   2013 $1850

Gaze, Harold *The Enchanted Fish.* Melbourne: Aukland: Christchurh: Dunedin and Wellington and London: Whitcombe & Tombs Limited, n.d., 1921. 8vo., wrappers, color plate on cover, slight edge wear, owner name on verso of first page, near fine, 3 color plates plus color plate on cover repeated in text, 3 full page pen and inks plus several smaller text illustrations, rare.   Aleph-Bet Books, Inc.   105 - 266   2013 $650

Gaze, Harold *The Merry Piper.* Boston: Little Brown, 1925. First US edition, 4to., 247 pages, yellow pictorial cloth, slight soil, very good-fine, pictorial endpapers and 8 gorgeous color plates.   Aleph-Bet Books, Inc.   104 - 231   2013 $250

Gaze, Harold *The Simple Jaggajay.* Melbourne: Aukland: Christchurch: Dunedin and Wellington and London: Whitcombe & Tombs Ltd., 1919. 4to., wrappers, color plate on cover, string ties, mend on title, slight bit of foxing, near fine, 2 tipped in color plates plus color plate on cover repeated in text, 1 tipped in black and white plate and 8 pen and ink drawings in text.   Aleph-Bet Books, Inc.   105 - 264   2013 $1850

Geddes, Michael *The Council of Trent, Plainly Discover'd Not to Have Been a free Assembly by a Collection of Letters and Papers of the Learned Dr. Vargas...* London: printed for B. Barker at the White Hart, 1714. 8vo., some foxing and browning to endpapers and pastedowns, full contemporary calf, double gilt ruled borders, gilt compartments, red morocco label, leading hinge cracked but firm, slightly chipped to head of spine, armorial bookplate of John Campbell, Esq. of Stackpole Court in the County of Pembroke.   Jarndyce Antiquarian Booksellers   CCIV - 140   2013   £125

Geddes, R. Stanley *Burlington Blue Grey a History of the Slate Quarries, Kirkby-in-Furness.* Kirkby-in-Furness: privately published, 1975. First limited edition, original cloth, gilt, dust jacket, pages 320, 67 illustrations, 2 maps, 4 folding sections and 19 diagrams.   R. F. G. Hollett & Son Lake District and Cumbria - 156   2013   £40

Gee, Edward *A Second Letter to father Lewis Sabran, Jesuite, in Answer to His Reply.* London: for Henry Mortlock, 1688. 4to., 16 pages, removed.   Joseph J. Felcone Inc.   Books Printed before 1701 - 44   2013 $90

Gee, John *Bunnie Bear.* Gordon Volland, 1928. Second printing, square 8vo., pictorial boards, fine in original box, illustrations by Gee, very scarce.   Aleph-Bet Books, Inc.   104 - 571   2013 $350

Geiger, Maynard *Franciscan Missionaries in Hispanic California 1769-1848.* San Marino: Huntington Library, 1969. First edition, brown cloth, bookplate, fine in lightly chipped dust jacket.   Argonaut Book Shop   Summer 2013 - 126   2013 $60

Geiger, Maynard *The Life and Times of Fray Junipero Serra, O. F.M. or the Man Who Never Turned Back.* Washington: Academy of American Franciscan History, 1959. First edition, 2 volumes, frontispiece in each volume 11 plates, 6 maps, dark blue cloth, gilt, "Review copy" stamps on front end, half title and titlepage of each volume, else very fine set.   Argonaut Book Shop   Recent Acquisitions June 2013 - 256   2013 $150

Geil, William Edgar *A Yankee in Pigmy Land.* London: Hodder and Stoughton, 1905. First edition, original pictorial cloth gilt, lettering on front board rather faded, spine darkened, lower board rather marked, 125 illustrations, flyleaves browned, scattered spotting, presentation copy, inscribed by Rev. H. Bissett.   R. F. G. Hollett & Son   Africana - 78   2013   £50

Geisel, Theodor Seuss   1904-1994 *The Cat in the Hat.* New York: Random House, 1957. First edition, first issue, octavo, color illustrations, original color pictorial endpapers, near fine, in rare original first issue color pictorial dust jacket with "200/200" on front flap and with no mention of "Beginner Books" series on rear panel, jacket with bare minimum rubbing at folds.   David Brass Rare Books, Inc.   Holiday 2012 Chapter One - DB 00381   2013 $5500

Geisel, Theodor Seuss   1904-1994 *The Cat in the Hat comes Back.* Beginner Books, Random House, 1958. Stated first printing, small 4to., glazed pictorial boards, near fine in lighty worn dust jacket, illustrations in color on every page.   Aleph-Bet Books, Inc.   104 - 524   2013 $500

Geisel, Theodor Seuss   1904-1994 *The Cat in the Hat Comes Back.* Random House, 1958. First edition, original glazed pictorial boards, little worn, few scratches, illustrations in color, child's inscription.   R. F. G. Hollett & Son   Children's Books - 552   2013   £50

Geisel, Theodor Seuss   1904-1994 *Dr. Seuss's ABC.* New York: Random House, 1963. First edition, 8vo., glazed pictorial boards, 63 pages, very good-fine in very good dust jacket with some soiling and with price intact, full color illustrations.   Aleph-Bet Books, Inc.   104 - 523   2013 $850

Geisel, Theodor Seuss   1904-1994 *Dr. Suess's ABC.* New York: Random House, 1963. First edition, 8vo., glazed pictorial boards, 63 pages, very good-fine in very good dust jacket with some soiling and with price intact, full color illustrations.   Aleph-Bet Books, Inc.   104 - 522   2013 $650

Geisel, Theodor Seuss   1904-1994 *Dr. Seuss's Sleep Book.* New York: Random House, 1962. First edition, 4to., fine in slightly worn dust jacket with small chip on front panel, full color illustrations, scarce.   Aleph-Bet Books, Inc.   104 - 522   2013 $650

Geisel, Theodor Seuss   1904-1994 *The 500 Hats of Bartholomew Cubbins.* New York: Vanguard, 1938. First edition, with correct endpaper configuration, large 4to, cloth backed pictorial boards, fine in dust jacket with correct $1.50 price (jacket frayed at spine ends and has few closed tears), otherwise beautiful example of jacket, illustrations in black and white, rare in excellent condition.   Aleph-Bet Books, Inc.   105 - 532   2013 $6500

Geisel, Theodor Seuss   1904-1994 *The Foot Book.* New York: Random House, 1968. First edition, 8vo., glazed boards, fine dust jacket slightly frayed, else very good, rare, illustrations in color.   Aleph-Bet Books, Inc.   105 - 533   2013 $1250

Geisel, Theodor Seuss   1904-1994 *How the Grinch Stole Christmas.* New York: Random House, 1957. First edition, first printing, quarto, illustrations in black and red, original illustrated glossy paper boards, pictorial endpapers, price clipped dust jacket, previous owner's small signature neatly inked out on front free endpaper and half title, jacket spine and corners with some chipping and rubbing, small crease marks along extremities of jacket, overall near fine, very good dust jacket.   Heritage Book Shop   Holiday Catalogue 2012 - 130   2013 $850

Geisel, Theodor Seuss   1904-1994 *I Had Trouble Getting to Solla Sollew.* New York: Random House, 1965. First edition (correct price and ads), 8vo., glazed pictorial boards, fine in dust jacket with closed tear on rear panel, illustrations in color by B. Tobey.   Aleph-Bet Books, Inc.   105 - 534   2013 $750

Geisel, Theodor Seuss   1904-1994 *I Wish That I Had Duck Feet.* New York: Random House/Beginner, 1965. First edition (correct price and ads), 8vo., glazed pictorial boards, fine in dust jacket with closed tear on rear panel, illustrations in color by B. Tobey.   Aleph-Bet Books, Inc.   105 - 535   2013 $1500

Geisel, Theodor Seuss   1904-1994 *If I Ran the Zoo.* New York: Random, 1950. First edition, folio, red glazed pictorial boards, fine in near fine dust jacket with price intact, exceedingly scarce.   Aleph-Bet Books, Inc.   104 - 521   2013 $2500

Geisel, Theodor Seuss   1904-1994 *Marvin K. Mooney Will You Please Go Now.* New York: Random House, 1972. First edition in curious variant first edition dust jacket that has no printed price at all and has 2025 on rear cover, instead of ISBN#, 8vo., name on endpaper, else fine in dust jacket with few closed tears, very scarce.   Aleph-Bet Books, Inc.   104 - 525   2013 $1750

Geisel, Theodor Seuss 1904-1994 *Secrets of the Deep. (and) Secrets of the Deep Volume II.* Standard Oil Essomarine, 1935-1936. 2 volumes, 8vo., pictorial wrappers, 34 pages, small margin mend and crease to volume 2, else both very good, both volumes inscribed by Seuss, quite rare. Aleph-Bet Books, Inc. 104 - 526 2013 $2700

Geisel, Theodor Seuss 1904-1994 *The Seven Lady Godivas.* New York: Random House, 1939. First edition, first printing, octavo, printed and illustrated in red and black, inscribed by author, original pink cloth, front board decoratively stamped in red with coat of arms, spine lettered in red, pictorial endpapers, original publisher's pictorial dust jacket with price of $1.75, inner hinges of book slightly toned, dust jacket slightly chipped at spine extremities and corners, closed two inch tear at fold of front flap, bit of darkening to jacket spine and edges, overall very good, clean. Heritage Book Shop Holiday Catalogue 2012 - 131 2013 $2000

Geisel, Theodor Seuss 1904-1994 *Ten Apples Up in Top!* New York: Random House, 1961. First edition, first printing, illustrations by Ray McKie, 8vo., glazed pictorial boards, fine in very good+ dust jacket that is slightly rubbed at spine ends. Aleph-Bet Books, Inc. 105 - 536 2013 $1500

Geissler, Rudolf *Little Max.* Seeley, Jackson and Halliday, 1869. 4to., 15 engravings, original brown cloth gilt, recased, 15 tinted illustrated pages, new endpapers. R. F. G. Hollett & Son Children's Books - 219 2013 £75

Gelber, Louis Jack *Medico-Legal Text on Traumatic Inquiries.* Newark: Soney and Sage, 1938. 8vo., xiii, 482 pages, frontispiece, plates, double ruled black cloth, 4 raised spine bands, gilt stamped red leather spine labels, top corners gently bumped, bookseller label, rare, very good. Jeff Weber Rare Books 172 - 106 2013 $75

Gellibrand, Henry *A Discourse Mathematical on the Variation of the Magnetical Needle.* Berlin: A. Asher, 1897. Facsimile reprint of 1635 London edition, 8vo., diagrams and charts, half green cloth over green paper backed boards, gilt stamped spine, bookplate of Burndy Library and previous owner, near fine. Jeff Weber Rare Books 169 - 160 2013 $50

Gellius, Aulus *Noctes Atticae.* Venice: Ioannes Gryphius, 1550. 8vo., (64), 591, (1) pages, elaborate woodcut initials, neat modern vellum, near fine. Joseph J. Felcone Inc. Books Printed before 1701 - 45 2013 $800

Gems of the Cork Poets. Barter, 1883. xvi, 510 pages, suede binding on boards by Kingsnorth, 9 Cook Street Cork, good. C. P. Hyland 261 - 255 2013 £75

Genealogical Notes of the O'Briens of Kilcor. privately printed, 1887. 14 pages, very good, 8vo., 4 ALS's to W. A. Coppinger. C. P. Hyland 261 - 404 2013 £100

Geneja, Stephen Conrad *The Cruiser Uganda One War-Many Conflicts. the First Documented and Eyewitness Account of Canada's Only Cruiser in World War Two...* Ontario: Tyendinaga Pub., 1994. Large 8vo., blue cloth, map endpapers in dust jacket, black and white illustrations, maps, previous owner's inscription, otherwise very good, dust jacket very good. Schooner Books Ltd. 105 - 127 2013 $75

General Motors Corp. *Futurama.* N.P.: General Motors Corp., 1940. Probably first and only?) edition, oblong octavo, pages (1-24), black and white photos, pictorial self wrappers, stapled. L. W. Currey, Inc. Uptopian Literature: Recent Acquisitions (April 2013) - 139857 2013 $75

General Rules and Special Rules to be Observed by the Owner Agents, Underground-Viewers, Deputies, Enginewright and Work-People of Benjamin Huntsman, Esq. Sheffield, Manor Castle and Handsworth Colleries, Sheffield. Wakefield: Alfred W. Stanfield, circa, 1870. 8vo. 20 pages, very good, original printed wrappers, scarce. Ken Spelman Books Ltd. 73 - 159 2013 £25

General Society of Mechanics and Tradesmen of the City of New York *One Hundred and Fourth Annual Report of the...* New York: Henry Bessey Printer, 1890. Pale pink printed wrappers, ink check mark and some creases on front wrapper, very good, complimentary slip from Society's Secretary tipped in. Between the Covers Rare Books, Inc. New York City - 291550 2013 $65

Genlis, Stephanie Felicite Ducrest De Saint Aubin, Madame De 1746-1830 *De L'Influence des Femems sur La Litterature Francaise.* Paris: Maraden, 1811. First edition, 8vo., contemporary calf backed boards, spine gilt, some modest stains to half title, very good. Second Life Books Inc. 183 - 102 2013 $475

Gent, Thomas *Annales Regioduni Hullini; or the Entertaining History of the Royal and Beautiful Town of Kingston-upon-Hull.* York: Printing Office, near the Star-in Stone-Gate, 1735. Folding frontispiece and 3 plates, 100 woodcuts in text, lacks 2 plates and frontispiece and one plate in good facsimile, 8vo., very good, early 19th century half calf, raised and gilt banded spine, marbled boards. Ken Spelman Books Ltd. 73 - 92 2013 £120

Gent, Thomas *Annales Regioduni Hullini; or the Entertaining History of the Royal and Beautiful Town of Kignston-upon-Hull.* Printing Officer near the Star in Stone-Gate, York, 1735. 8vo., folding frontispiece and 5 plates, 100 woodcut illustrations in text, unusually good, clean copy, late 19th century full vellum, gilt ruled boards, red and black gilt labels to spine, some age toning to velum. Ken Spelman Books Ltd. 73 - 91 2013 £395

Gent, Thomas *The Antient and Modern History of the Loyal Town of Rippon.* Printing Officer over against the Star in Stone-Gate, York, 1733. 8vo., lacks titlepage, folding frontispiece, 2 plates, but with the woodcuts in text, very good, clean, 19th century half calf, marbled boards. Ken Spelman Books Ltd. 73 - 141 2013 £120

Gent, Thomas *The Life of Mr. Thomas Gent, printer of York...* C. Adlard for Thomas Thrope, 1832. First edition, frontispiece, 8vo., very good, original cloth, expertly rebacked retaining original paper label, scarce. Ken Spelman Books Ltd. 73 - 22 2013 £95

Geoghegan, A. G. *The Monks of Kilcea & Other Poems.* 1861. First edition, with 2 page ALS from poet to D J. O'Donoghue, dated 17 Dec. 1888, confirming authorship, 348 pages, original cloth, very good. C. P. Hyland 261 - 443 2013 £150

George Washington University *Analytical Guide and Indexes to the Coloured American Magazine 1900-1909.* Westport: Greenwood Press, 1974. First edition, 2 volumes, very slight wear, fine, issued without dust jackets, very scarce. Between the Covers Rare Books, Inc. 165 - 155 2013 $200

George, Jean Craighead *Julie of the Wovles.* New York: Harper Row, 1972. Stated first edition, 8vo., pictorial boards, fine in slightly worn dust jacket, illustrations by John Schoenherr, scarce. Aleph-Bet Books, Inc. 104 - 232 2013 $250

Gerard, John *The Herball or General Historie of Plantes.* London: by Adam Islip, Joice Norton and Richard Whitakers, 1633. First printing of the second and best edition, folio, engraved title, over 2500 woodcuts, early 19th century panelled calf, neatly rebacked retaining original fully gilt spine, title lightly soiled but complete and free of any repair, blank fore and bottom edges of A4-5 neatly extended, few marginal tears neatly closed, intermittent faint dampstain in top margin becoming bit more noticeable toward end of text, marginal repair to 741 (index) costing several page numbers, blank lower corner of 7B5 replaced, very good, most attractive without extensive repairing and sophistication that nearly always comes with early English herbals, ownership inscription and cost dated 1634. Joseph J. Felcone Inc. Books Printed before 1701 - 46 2013 $8000

Gerhardi, William *Futility. A Novel on Russian Themes.* London: Duckworth, 1927. 16mo., original blue cloth, gilt lettered faded backstrip, good. Blackwell's Rare Books 172 - 186 2013 £100

Gerhardi, William *Jazz and Jasper.* London: Duckworth, 1928. First edition, 8vo., original pink cloth, spine faded and marked, endpapers browned, very good, inscribed by author. Maggs Bros. Ltd. 1460 - 331 2013 £75

Gerhardi, William *My Wife's the Least of It.* London: Faber and Faber, 1938. First edition, 8vo., original tan cloth, excellent copy, inscribed by author for Barbara. Maggs Bros. Ltd. 1460 - 333 2013 £150

Gerhardi, William *Pretty Creatures.* London: Ernest Best, 1927. First edition, 8vo., original black cloth little soiled, spine faded, otherwise very good, inscribed by author for Yvonne and Luigino Franchetti. Maggs Bros. Ltd. 1460 - 330 2013 £250

Gerhardi, William *Resurrection.* London: Cassell, 1934. First edition, original green cloth, front endpapers and first gathering lightly foxed, excellent copy, inscribed by author for John Arlott. Maggs Bros. Ltd. 1460 - 332 2013 £150

Gerhardt, Charles *Traite de Chimie Organique.* Paris: Fermin Didot Freres, 1853-1856. First edition, 4 volumes, 8vo., contemporary quarter green morocco, marbled boards, gilt spine, marbled endleaves, former owner added to volume 1 a carte de viste photographic portrait of Gerhardt (albumen print) taken by Ch. Winter of Strasbourg, also inserted is 2 page ALs dated Jan. 1883 from Gerhardt's son to unidentified correspondent, bookplates of Haskell Norman, fine. Jeff Weber Rare Books 172 - 104 2013 $800

Gerlot, Guillaume Joseph *Relation Nouvelle d'un Voyage de Constantinople.* Paris: Pierre Rocolet, 1680. First edition, 13 plans and views, 10 of which are folding and including spectacular panorama, four further costume engravings in text, contemporary calf, nicely rebacked, nice, tight copy. Maggs Bros. Ltd. 1467 - 41 2013 £5500

Gernsack, Hugo *Science and Invention August 1923. Volume 11 number 4.* Jamaica, NY: Experimenter Pub. Co. Inc. August, 1923. Large octavo, pictorial wrappers. L. W. Currey, Inc. Fall Sampler Sept. 2013 - 146579 2013 $1000

Gerry, Vance *Jazz Instruments; Weather Bird Press Picture Portfoio.* Pasadena: Weather Bird Press, 2003. Limited edition of 50 copies only, 12 sheets, 31 x 48cm., final sheet is a glossary of names and nicknames of mentioned musicians, fine. Jeff Weber Rare Books 171 - 130 2013 $2850

Gersaint, E. F. *Catalogue Raisonne d'une Collection Considerable de Diverses Curiosites en tous genres...* Paris: 1744. Frontispiece, 12mo., fine French contemporary marbled calf, spine richly gilt in compartments, occasional annotations to margins in fine hand. Maggs Bros. Ltd. 1467 - 40 2013 £2400

Gersh, Stephen *Platonism in Late Antiquity.* Notre Dame: University of Notre Dame Press, 1992. 8vo., xiv, 258 pages, grey cloth, red stamped cover and spine titles, ownership signature, fine, rare.   Jeff Weber Rare Books   169 - 162   2013 $125

Gershe, Leonard *Butterflies are Free.* New York: Random House, 1970. First edition, review copy with review slip laid in, fine in fine dust jacket, from the library of film critic Pauline Kael.   Ken Lopez Bookseller   159 - 68   2013 $125

Gershonson, M. *Vysoko Vverkh Gluboko Vniz. (Up High and Deep Below).* Ogiz: Malidaya Gvardya, 1932. 12mo., pictorial wrappers, very good+. color illustrations by A. Brei.   Aleph-Bet Books, Inc.   105 - 512   2013 $500

Gerstaecker, F. *The Young Gold-Digger; or a Boy's Adventures in the Gold Regions.* London: Routledge, Warne and Routledge, 1860. First English edition, small 8vo., full calf, gilt blind ruled prize binding, 4 woodcut illustrations, little spotting in places.   R. F. G. Hollett & Son   Children's Books - 220   2013   £30

Gesner, Konrad   1516-1565 *Thierbuch das Ist. Ausfuhriche Beschreibung und Lebendige ja Auch Eigentliche Contrafactur und Abmahlung aller Vierfluffigen Thieren... (bound with) Fischbuch, das ist, Aussfuhrliche Beschreibung und Lebendige Conterfacture Aller unnd Jeden Fischen von dem Kleinstein Fischlein...* Heidelberg: Durch Johan Lancellot in Verlegung Andreae Cambier, 1606. Franckfurt am meyn: Dutch Johann Saur in Verlegung Robert Amblers Erben, 1598, (344) pages, numerous illustrations, title has two early paper repairs involving bottom outer blank margin and top right corner with repair just affecting the lettering, text foxed and browned in parts; title in red and black, five leaves of prelims and index, (404) pages, text foxed and browned, final leaf has been mounted, numerous illustrations, folio format, bound in contemporary full alum pigskin, elaborately blind tooled boards over wood, arabesque designs on boards with floral panels, original clasps still present, binding soiled with age, inner front hinge weak, first signature just starting.   James Tait Goodrich   75 - 104   2013 $7500

Gesner, Konrad   1516-1565 *Tigurini Historiae Animalium Liber III. Qui est Piscium & Aquatilium Animanium Natura.* Tigvri: Apvd Christoph Froschouerum, 1558. First edition, Titlepage vignette, over 900 woodcuts, title and dedication leaf repaired in outer blank margin, some of the page headings shaved by binder, preface and index leaves have early remargining of lower blank margin, some marginal dampstaining and early marginal annotations, page 1043 has publishing defect in page where during printing inner third of page was torn out, this leaf followed by two blank leaves that were not printed on though text is complete, bound in late 17th century full polished calf, raised bands, red burgundy title label, raised bands, binding bit rough but tight, front joint in lower quarter is missing small piece of leather, joint just starting to split.   James Tait Goodrich   75 - 105   2013 $5000

Gessner, Abraham *A Practical Treatise on Coal, Petroleum and Other Distilled Oils.* New York: Bailliere Brothers, 1865. Second edition, 8vo., 181 pages, lithographic frontispiece, original cloth, some splits in outer spine, very good.   M & S Rare Books, Inc.   95 - 132   2013 $750

Geston, Mark Symington *Lords of the Starship.* London: Michael Joseph, 1971. First British and first hardcover edition, octavo, boards.   L. W. Currey, Inc.   Utopian Literature: Recent Acquisitions (April 2013) - 141857   2013 $200

Gheon, Henri *Jeux et Miracles pour la Peuple Fidele.* Paris: Editions de la revue des Jeunes, 1922. First edition, later cloth, red morocco label to spine, original wrappers bound in, cloth slightly spotted, otherwise excellent, inscribed by author for Andre Ruyters.   Maggs Bros. Ltd.   1460 - 334   2013   £275

Giancol, Anthony *The Three Racketeers.* New York: Vantage Press, 1955. First edition, spine lettering rubbed, else fine in near fine dust jacket with couple of words written on spine, but not too obtrusively, and tiny chip, very scarce.   Between the Covers Rare Books, Inc.   Mystery & Detective Fiction - 84976   2013 $200

Giants of the Railroad. Collins, n.d. late 1930's, Oblong large 8vo., original pictorial colored card wrappers, illustrations, nice, very scarce.   R. F. G. Hollett & Son   Children's Books - 419   2013   £45

Gibbings, Robert *A True Tale of Love in Tonga.* London: Faber and Faber, 1935. First edition, 8vo., original green cloth spine, decorated yellow boards, excellent copy, inscribed by author.   Maggs Bros. Ltd.   1460 - 335   2013   £75

Gibbon, Edward 1737-1794 *The History of the Decline and Fall of the Roman Empire.* London: A. Strahan and T. Cadell, 1776-1788. First edition, 6 volumes, quarto, engraved portrait of Gibbon by Hall after Reynolds, not usually found, 3 engraved folding maps, with all half titles and errata leaves in volumes I, II, II and VI, volume I is in second state with leaves X4, a4 and b2 not being cancels, with errata corrected, in volume III page 177 is correctly numbered, and "Honorious" is left uncorrected on page 179, line 18, engraved portrait of Gibbon was issued separately in 1780, contemporary mottled calf, gilt spines with centre gilt tool in four compartments, extremities rubbed, all volumes attractively and uniformly rebacked, occasional light foxing and browning, few leaves with short tears, generally very good.   Heritage Book Shop   50th Anniversary Catalogue - 42   2013 $25,000

Gibbon, Edward 1737-1794 *Gibbon's History of the Decline and Fall of the Roman Empire.* London: printed for G. Kearsley, 1789. First abridged edition, 2 volumes, 8vo., contemporary tree calf, rebacked and rehinged with new endpapers, old backs laid down, corners repaired, edges rubbed, leather labels, wanting half titles and terminal ad leaf in each volume, still very good, with 1941 ownership signature of Richard Charlton MacKenzie.   Howard S. Mott Inc.   262 - 61   2013 $750

Gibbon, Edward 1737-1794 *The History of the Decline and Fall of the Roman Empire.* London: printed by G. Woodfall, 1807. New edition, 12 volumes, frontispiece in volume I, half titles, 8vo., some foxing, some pages browned, contemporary continental dark blue green glazed paper boards, gilt ruled and lettered spines, some slight rubbing to heads and tails of spines and board edges, minor abrasion to several areas on backstrips.   Jarndyce Antiquarian Booksellers   CCIV - 141   2013   £420

Gibbons, Floyd *The Red Napoleon.* New York: Cape and Smith, 1929. First edition, darkening in gutters, as always seems the case, else fine in bright, near fine dust jacket with small chip on rear panel, tipped to front pastedown is card signed by Gibbons, exceptionally uncommon in this condition.   Between the Covers Rare Books, Inc.   Sci-Fi, Fantasy & Horror - 56941   2013 $700

Gibbs, C. Armstrong *Lakeland Limericks.* Kendal: Titus Wilson & Son, 1942. Second edition, original cloth backed boards, edges trifle bumped, 39 pages, drawings in sepia throughout.   R. F. G. Hollett & Son   Lake District and Cumbria - 169   2013   £25

Gibbs, Ed *Have a Drink! (Or How to Drink).* N.P.: Ed Gibbs, 1955. First edition, stated special limited edition, this copy unnumbered, quarto, 122 pages, illustrated wrappers by Edward Bawden, some modest soiling to wrappers, else near fine, inscribed by Gibbs in 1958.   Between the Covers Rare Books, Inc.   Cocktails, Etc. - 314919   2013 $125

Gibbs, Josiah Willard *Elementary Principles in Statistical Mechanics Developed with Especial Reference to the Rational Foundation of Thermodynamics.* New York & London: Charles Scribner's Sons & Edward Wrnold, 1902. First edition, 8vo., original blue cloth, gilt stamped spine title and cover ornament, ex-library bookplate "Chief Astronomer" and ink stamp, possibly the copy of William Frederick King (1854-1916 chief astronomer), fine.   Jeff Weber Rare Books   169 - 159   2013 $1500

Gibbs, May *Gumnut Babies.* Sydney: Angus Robertson, n.d., 1916. Tall 8vo., brown wrappers, brown string ties, color paste-on, 28 leaves, near fine, 2 color plates (color plate on cover, color frontispiece) and 11 sepia plates, scarce.   Aleph-Bet Books, Inc.   105 - 274   2013 $350

Gibson, A. L. *Another Alice Book, Please!* London: John Castle, 1924. First edition, 171 pages, 8vo., red cloth, illustrations in black and white by H. R. Millar, very good+.   Aleph-Bet Books, Inc.   105 - 119   2013 $125

Gibson, Alexander Craig *The Folk-Speech of Cumberland and Some Districts Adjacent.* London: John Russell Smith and Carlisle: G. & T. Coward, 1869. First edition, original maroon cloth gilt, spine trifle faded, scattered spotting.   R. F. G. Hollett & Son   Lake District and Cumbria - 170   2013   £45

Gibson, C. B. *The History of the County and City of Cork.* 1861. First edition, 2 volumes, map, signed presentation copy to his daughter, Dorinda, in Guy's special red morocco binding, gilt embossed, all edges gilt, lacks signature 31 (pages 72-89) of volume 2, else very good.   C. P. Hyland   261 - 447   2013   £750

Gibson, Eva Katherine *The Wise Witch.* Chicago: Robert Smith, 1901. 4to., blue pictorial cloth, fine, color illustrations on every page.   Aleph-Bet Books, Inc.   104 - 61   2013 $300

Gibson, James R. *Otter Skins, Boston Ships and China Good. The Maritime Fur Trade of the Northwest Coast 1785-1841.* Seattle: University of Washinton Press, 1992. First edition, color frontispiece, text illustrations, maps, map endpapers, tables, black cloth, gilt, very fine, pictorial dust jacket.   Argonaut Book Shop   Recent Acquisitions June 2013 - 120   2013 $125

Gibson, Richard *Mirror for Magistrates.* London: Anthony Blond, 1958. First edition, octavo, 172 pages, very good, some age toning and scattered light stains to endpapers, else near fine in near fine dust jacket with some light soiling to top edge and light age toing to inside panel, inscribed by author for writer Peter Taylor.   Between the Covers Rare Books, Inc.   165 - 157   2013 $650

Gibson, Thomas *Legends and Historical Notes on Places in the East and West Wards.* Manchester: John Heywood, 1877. First edition, small 8vo., original red cloth gilt, 2 extra leaves inserted before the title with cuttings laid in. R. F. G. Hollett & Son   Lake District and Cumbria - 171   2013   £75

Gibson, Thomas *Legends and Historical Notes on Places of North Westmoreland.* London: Unwin Brothers and Appleby; J. Whitehead and Son, 1887. First edition, original decorated cloth gilt, spine little darkened and worn, lively full page woodcut drawings by Unwin brothers, including fine frontispiece, scarce. R. F. G. Hollett & Son   Lake District and Cumbria - 172   2013   £150

Gibson, Walter B. *Looks that Kill.* New York: Atlas, 1948. First edition, pages edges darkened, otherwise fine in wrappers. Mordida Books   81 - 205   2013 $100

Gibson, Wilfrid *Challenge.* London: Oxford University Press, 1942. First edition, 8vo., original red wrappers, near fine, protective folding box, inscribe by author to Stephen Gwynn. Maggs Bros. Ltd.   1460 - 337   2013   £125

Gibson, Wilfrid *Islands. Poems, 1930-1932.* London: Macmillan and Co., 1932. First edition, 8vo., original green cloth, darkened at spine and edges, dust jacket in two pieces, having split at lower hinge, little chipped at edges, very good, inscribed by author for J. Redwood Anderson. Maggs Bros. Ltd.   1460 - 336   2013   £100

Gibson, William *Count Zero.* London: Gollancz, 1986. First edition, fine, tight, unread copy in fine, fresh dust jacket. Ed Smith Books   75 - 29   2013 $175

Gibson, William *Count Zero.* London: Victor Gollancz Ltd., 1986. First edition, ocatvo, boards. L. W. Currey, Inc.   Utopian Literature: Recent Acquisitions (April 2013) - 141858   2013 $250

Gibson, William *Neuromancer.* London: Victor Gollancz Ltd., 1984. First British edition and first hardcover edition, octavo, boards. L. W. Currey, Inc.   Utopian Literature: Recent Acquisitions (April 2013) - 140924   2013 $2250

Gide, Andre   1869-1951 *Journal des Faux-Monnayeurs.* Paris: Gallimard, 1938. Twenty-fifth edition, 8vo., original wrappers, acetate dust jacket, preserved in folding box, good copy, wrappers little worn at extremities, dust jacket chipped and worn, inscribed by author for Alexandre Bachrach. Maggs Bros. Ltd.   1460 - 339   2013   £500

Gide, Andre   1869-1951 *Le Retour de L'Enfant Prodique.* Paris: Nouvelle Revue Francaise, 1912. First edition, 8vo., original wrappers bound in to half red leather, slight fading to spine, otherwise near fine, inscribed by author for Arnold Bennett. Maggs Bros. Ltd.   1460 - 338   2013   £3000

Gieson, Judith Van *The Stole Blue: a Claire Reyneir Mystery.* Albuquerque: University of New Mexico Press, 2000. First edition, fine in fine dust jacket, signed by author, from the library of Bruce Kahn. Between the Covers Rare Books, Inc.   Mystery & Detective Fiction - 304603   2013 $60

Giffen, Helen S. *Casas & Courtyards Historic Adobe Houses of California.* Oakland: Biobooks, 1955. First edition, limited to 600 copies, quite scarce, 153 pages, color frontispiece, 65 photos, two-tone cloth, gilt, lower corner very slightly jammed, but fine. Argonaut Book Shop   Summer 2013 - 127   2013 $75

Giffen, Helen S. *Trail-Blazing Pioneer. Colonel Joseph Ballinger Chiles.* San Francisco: John Howell Books, 1969. First edition, limited to 750 copies by Lawton and Alfred Kennedy, 100 pages, frontispiece, 6 plates, red cloth, gilt, very fine, bright copy, pictorial dust jacket. Argonaut Book Shop   Summer 2013 - 128   2013 $90

Gifford, John *The Maeviad.* London: printed for the author, 1785. First edition, 4to., without half title, some light foxing, disbound. Jarndyce Antiquarian Booksellers   CCIV - 143   2013   £50

The Gift of Affection: a Christmas and New Year's Present. New York: Leavitt & Allen N. 379 Broadway, n.d. circa 1856, or after, First edition, octavo, five inserted plates with steel engravings plus decorative presentation page printed in gold, red and green, original decorated red leather, front spine and rear panels stamped in gold and blind, all edges gilt, caoted endpapers. L. W. Currey, Inc.   Christmas Themed Books - 112217   2013 $100

Giger, H. R. *Species Design.* Beverly Hills: Morpheus International, 1995. First edition, one of 350 specially bound copies, with original lithograph bound in which is numbered and signed by Giger, photos, drawings, full color paintings, publisher's slipcase, fine. Ed Smith Books   75 - 30   2013 $300

Ginger and Brownie. Racine: Whitman, 1936. 4to., stiff pictorial wrappers, paper slightly browned, else very good-fine, 3 color double page pop-ups, scarce, illustrated in two color and black and whites. Aleph-Bet Books, Inc.   104 - 441   2013 $200

Gila, Roque Antonio *Sermon Funebre de el Excmo Senor Don Jaime Miguel de Guzman &c Marques de la Mina &c Grande de Espana de Primera Clase.* Barcelona: Thomas Piferer, 1767. First edition, frontispiece, later blanks bound in, small 8vo., later full mottled calf, gilt titles, 4 raised bands, very good, minor wear at spine ends, light foxing and faint dampstain on few leaves, scarce. Kaaterskill Books 16 - 39 2013 $500

Gilbert, Anthony *The Murder of Mrs. Davenport.* New York: Dial, 1928. First American edition, very good in very fine, as new dust jacket. Mordida Books 81 - 206 2013 $150

Gilbert, Anthony *No Dust in the Attic.* London: Collins Crime Club, 1962. First edition, fine in dust jacket, internal tape mend and lightly soiled back panel. Mordida Books 81 - 207 2013 $75

Gilbert, Christopher *Furniture at Temple Newsam and Lotherton Hall.* National Art Collections Fund and Leeds Art Collections Fund, 1978. 1998., 3 volumes, profusely illustrated, original cloth, dust jackets. Marlborough Rare Books Ltd. 218 - 63 2013 £175

Gilbert, John T. *Documents Relating to Ireland 1795-1804.* IUP, 1970. Facsimile, 8vo., cloth, dust jacket, very good. C. P. Hyland 261 - 448 2013 £110

Gilbert, Michael *The Ninety-Second Tiger.* London: Hodder & Stoughton, 1973. First edition, little dampstaining to top edge, else fine in fine dust jacket (touch of rubbing at crown). Between the Covers Rare Books, Inc. Mystery & Detective Fiction - 61652 2013 $65

Gilbert, William *The Magic Mirror.* London: Maclaren Co., 1907. Small 4to., purple cloth with elaborate art nouveau binding highlighted in gold, pictorial paste-on, top edge gilt, 233 pages, award bookplate on endpaper, near fine, 20 color plates by John Menzies. Aleph-Bet Books, Inc. 105 - 246 2013 $350

Gilbert, William Schwenck 1836-1911 *A Colossal Idea.* London and New York: Putnam, 1932. First edition, one of a limited number of copies issued with the illustrations hand colored, signed by artist, Townley Searle, small 8vo., 62 pages, blue cloth, very nice, tight copy. Second Life Books Inc. 183 - 140 2013 $650

Gilbert, William Schwenck 1836-1911 *Yeomen of the Guard O the Merryman and His Maid.* London: Macmillan, 1929. First edition, large 8vo., red gilt cloth, fine in slightly chipped dust jacket, illustrations by Russell Flint with 8 beautiful color plates, many line illustrations by C. E. Brock. Aleph-Bet Books, Inc. 105 - 256 2013 $250

Gilchrist, Alexander *Life of William Blake.* London and Cambridge: Macmillan, 1863. First edition, 2 volumes, half titles, frontispieces, plates, illustrations, original maroon cloth by Burn & Co., blocked and lettered gilt, corners slightly worn, spines faded, booklabels of Walter Hirst very good, clean and attractive copy. Jarndyce Antiquarian Booksellers CCIII - 10 2013 £320

Gilchrist, Ellen *In the Land of Dreamy Dreams.* Fayetteville: University of Arkansas Press, 1981. Hardover issue, there were 1000 copies issued in wrappers, review copy, inscribed by author, this copy belonged to Ray Roberts, Gilchrist's editor at Little Brown, fine in fine dust jacket with review slip laid in, excellent association copy, uncommon first book. Ken Lopez Bookseller 159 - 69 2013 $1500

Gilder, William H. *Ice-Pack and Tundra.* London: Sampson Low, 1883. First edition, original green pictorial cloth gilt, rather marked, spine very discolored, hinges and corners worn and frayed, 48 illustrations and 3 maps, 1 extending and colored in outline, rather spotted, library stamp on title and armorial bookplate on pastedown. R. F. G. Hollett & Son Polar Exploration - 22 2013 £120

Giles, Henry *Illustrations of Genius in Some Relation to Culture and Society.* Boston: Ticknor and Fields, 1854. First edition, 8vo., original brown embossed cloth, lettered in gilt, excellent copy inscribed by publisher for Thomas De Quincy. Maggs Bros. Ltd. 1460 - 222 2013 £325

Giles, Herbert A. *Strange Stories from a Chinese Studio.* London: T. Werner Laurie, 1916. Third edition, slight foxing to fore edge and endpapers, else fine in spine sunned, near fine dust jacket with very shallow chip at crown, very scarce in jacket. Between the Covers Rare Books, Inc. Sci-Fi, Fantasy & Horror - 97747 2013 $450

Gilkey, Gordon W. *Officially Approved Etchings - New York World's Fair "Building the Word of Tomorrow".* New York: Charles Scribner's, 1939. First edition, quarto, blue cloth with gilt pictorial device on front board, fine in slightly soiled, still fine dust jacket, text and 54 page illustrations by Gilkey, very scarce in jacket. Between the Covers Rare Books, Inc. New York City - 92612 2013 $850

Gill, Eric 1882-1940 *Art & Prudence.* Golden Cockerel Press, 1928. First edition, 481/500 copies, printed on Kelmscott handmade paper, 2 full page copperplate engravings and wood engraved title vignette by author, foolscap 8vo., original orange buckram, fading to gilt lettered backstrip, untrimmed, dust jacket, near fine. Blackwell's Rare Books B174 - 339 2013 £300

Gill, Eric 1882-1940 *Art Nonsense and Other Essays.* London: Cassell, 1929. First edition, 34/100 copies signed by Gill, printed on large handmade paper, wood engraved title vignette by Gill, royal 8vo., original maroon bevel edged buckram, backstrip gilt lettered, usual faint free endpaper browning, top edge gilt, others untrimmed, fine. Blackwell's Rare Books B174 - 210 2013 £500

Gill, Eric 1882-1940 *Beauty Looks After Herself.* London: Sheed & Ward, 1933. First edition, 8vo., original black cloth, dust jacket, Eric Gill's own copy with his bookplate and pencilled initials, excellent copy in chipped and browned dust jacket. Maggs Bros. Ltd. 1460 - 340 2013 £350

Gill, Eric 1882-1940 *Clothing Without Cloth.* Waltham St. Lawrence: Golden Cockerell Press, 1931. First edition, 1/500 copies, 8vo., 4 wood engravings, red cloth, faded for inch along top, top edge gilt, nice, tight copy. Second Life Books Inc. 183 - 145 2013 $300

Gill, Eric 1882-1940 *Engraved Work.* HMSO Victoria & Albert Museum, 1963. sole edition, numerous reproductions, 4to., original printed pale grey wrappers, backstrip and edges somewhat browned, good. Blackwell's Rare Books 172 - 187 2013 £30

Gill, Eric 1882-1940 *Songs without Clothes, being a Dissertation on the Song of Solomon and Such-Like Songs...* Ditchling, Sussex: Saint Dominic's Press, 1921. First edition, one of 240 copies, printed on Batchelor handmade paper, the 'c' in McNabb on titlepage not 'skied', 16mo., original quarter white linen, plain grey brown boards, light browning to free endpapers, trimmed plain (original?) dust jacket, Evan Gill's copy with his letterpress bookplate. Blackwell's Rare Books B174 - 380 2013 £250

Gill, Stephen *William Wordsworth.* Oxford University Press, 1989. First edition, original cloth, gilt, dust jacket, 20 plates, map. R. F. G. Hollett & Son Lake District and Cumbria - 173 2013 £35

Gillam, J. P. *The Roman Bath-House at Bewcastle, Cumbria.* Alan Sutton for The Cumberland and Westmorland Antiquarian and Archaeological Society, 1993. 4to., original pictorial wrappers, 12 plates, 24 illustrations, 3 tables. R. F. G. Hollett & Son Lake District and Cumbria - 174 2013 £25

Gillespie, T. H. A. *A Book of King Penguins.* London: Herbert Jenkins, 1932. First edition, original cloth, gilt, dust jacket, faded, rather chipped 60 illustrations, scarce. R. F. G. Hollett & Son Polar Exploration - 23 2013 £45

Gillette, William *The Painful Predicament of Sherlock Holmes.* Chicago: Abramson, 1955. First edition, fine without dust jacket, as issued, with publisher's flyer announcing publication. Mordida Books 81 - 151 2013 $85

Gilliam, E. W. *Uncle Sam and the Negro in 1920.* Lynchburg: J. P. Bell Co., 1906. First edition, red cloth gilt, 469 pages, frontispiece and two illustrations, owner name on front fly, spine gilt little dull and modest rubbing at spinal extremities, still fresh, very near fine. Between the Covers Rare Books, Inc. Sci-Fi, Fantasy & Horror - 86132 2013 $650

Gillies, John *Memoirs of the Life of Rev. George Whitefield, M. A. Late Chaplain to the Right Hon. The Countess of Huntingdon...* printed for Edward and Charles Dilly, 1772. First edition, contemporary calf, little rubbed, corners bumped, upper hinge splitting at foot, engraved portrait frontispiece, title little dusty, light stain to top edges of first few leaves, upper joint cracked, rare. R. F. G. Hollett & Son Wesleyan Methodism - 10 2013 £650

Gillies, Robert Pearse *Tales of a Voyager to the Arctic Ocean.* London: Henry Colburn, 1826. First edition, 3 volumes, 12mo., internal tear to leading blank, volume 1, marginal tear to pages 23/24, volume I not affecting text, contemporary full brown calf, gilt spine, black morocco labels, some neat repair to hinges and to label of volume II, signs of labels removed from leading pastedowns, attractive. Jarndyce Antiquarian Booksellers CCV - 111 2013 £850

Gillman, Alexander W. *The Gillmans of Highgate with Letters from Samuel Taylor Coleridge.* London: Elliot Stock, 1895. 4to., half title, plates, 2 final ad leaves, original dark green cloth, bevelled boards, blocked and lettered gilt, all edges gilt, very good, bright copy. Jarndyce Antiquarian Booksellers CCIII - 584 2013 £185

Gillman, Alexander W. *Searches into the History of the Gilman or Gilman Family.* 1895. First edition, photos, 8vo., original green cloth, very good. C. P. Hyland 261 - 390 2013 £200

Gillman, James *The Life of Samuel Taylor Coleridge.* London: William Pickering, 1838. First edition, cancel title, final errata leaf, browned, uncut in original dark brown cloth, recased retaining original spine, corners slightly bumped, little rubbed, contemporary signature of James Braid on title. Jarndyce Antiquarian Booksellers CCIII - 585 2013 £125

Gillon, John Fergie *Rules and Examples by Which Theoretical and Practical Arithmetic are Made Easy.* York: E. Hawkin, printer..., 1869. 12mo., 20 pages, including wrappers, near fine, original lemon yellow printed wrappers, tables printed on rear wrapper. Ken Spelman Books Ltd. 73 - 39 2013 £120

Gilman, Alfred *Proteins and Regulation of Adenylyl Cyclase.* Stockholm: Nobel Foundation, 1994. First separate printing, offprint, signed dated and inscribed by Gilman, fine, 8vo., 180 pages, original red printed wrappers.   By the Book, L. C.   37 - 34   2013 $225

Gilman, Charlotte Perkins *Concerning Children.* Boston: Small Maynard, 1900. First edition, 8vo., 298 pages, blue cloth stamped in green and gold, signed MLP, spine rubbed and soiled, very good, rare.   Second Life Books Inc.   183 - 141A   2013 $1500

Gilman, Charlotte Perkins *Concerning Children.* Boston: Small & Maynard, 1900. First edition, 8vo., 298 pages, blue cloth, stamped in green and gold,.   Second Life Books Inc.   183 - 141A   2013 $400

Gilman, Charlotte Perkins *Gems of Art for the Home and Fireside.* Providence: J. & A. & R. A. Reid, 1890. Second edition, 4to., 102 pages, grey cloth stamped in gilt and black, 50 black and white plates, rare.   Second Life Books Inc.   183 - 141   2013 $1500

Gilman, Charlotte Perkins *In This Our World.* Boston: Small Maynard, 1914. Fifth edition, 12mo., 217 pages, frontispiece, uncut, blue cloth stamped in gilt, top edge gilt, contemporary ownership signature, couple of small ticks in table of contents, one closed marginal tear, else very good.   Second Life Books Inc.   183 - 141B   2013 $200

Gilman, Charlotte Perkins *Women and Economics, a Study of the Economic Relation Between Men and Women as a Factor in Social Evolution.* Boston: Small Maynard, 1900. Third edition, 8vo., maroon cloth, ex-library with stamps and bookplate, owner's name on flyleaf, hinges tender, few pencil marks in margins, cover spotted and little worn at corners and ends of spine, otherwise very good.   Second Life Books Inc.   182 - 90   2013 $75

Gilmour, Margaret *Ameliaranne Gives a Concert.* London: Harrap, 1949. Original cloth backed pictorial boards, illustrations in color and black and white by Susan Pearse, small mark on front flyleaf.   R. F. G. Hollett & Son   Children's Books - 448   2013   £25

Gilpin, Joshua *Twenty-One Discourses Delivered in the Parish Church of Wrockwardine, in the County of Salop.* London: John Hatchard and Son, 1827. First edition, 219 x 133mm., appealing contemporary red straight grain morocco, covers with gilt ruled border and small sunburst cornerpieces, raised bands flanked by plain and decorative gilt rules, turn-ins with decorative gilt roll, marbled endpapers, all edges gilt, front joint very expertly renewed, very accomplished fore-edge painting of West Gate, Canterbury, flyleaf facing titlepage with faint but readable offset of the (backward) text of a previously tipped in presentation letter from author, corners bit bruised, spine little dried, leather slightly marked and soiled, expertly repaired binding sound and attractive, lustrous covers, 2 inch horizontal tear to front endpaper, top edge gilt bit soiled, text remarkably clean, bright and fresh.   Phillip J. Pirages   63 - 187   2013 $1250

Gilpin, Sidney *The Songs and Ballads of Cumberland and the Lake Country with Biographical Sketches...* London: John Russell Smith and Carlisle: G. and T. Coward, 1874. Second edition, original green cloth, gilt, spine rather marked and cockeled.   R. F. G. Hollett & Son   Lake District and Cumbria - 176   2013   £35

Gilpin, William *Observations on the Mountains and Lakes of Cumberland and Westmorland.* Richmond Pub. Co., 1973. Facsimile edition, 30 plates, original cloth, gilt, library labels on front endpapers and stamp to back of title.   R. F. G. Hollett & Son   Lake District and Cumbria - 177   2013   £45

Gilson, Julius P. *Catalogue of the Additions to the Manuscripts in the British Museum 1896-1910.* 1912. First edition, cloth, octavo, very good.   C. P. Hyland   261 - 66   2013   £100

Gingerbread Boy. New York: Dutton, 1943. 8vo., spiral backed boards, light edge wear, very good+, 6 fine moveable plates and with other color illustrations by Julian Wehr.   Aleph-Bet Books, Inc.   104 - 370   2013 $200

Ginsberg, Allen *Howl and Other Poems.* San Francisco: City Lights Books, 1958. Sixth printing, small 8vo., original wrappers, signed by author, rubbed and browned on covers, otherwise very good, housed in protective box, replicating design of cover.   Maggs Bros. Ltd.   1460 - 341   2013   £250

Ginsberg, Allen *Howl for Carl Solomon.* New York: Gotham Book Mart, circa, 1979. First edition, 2nd issue, 17 single 27.8 x 21.5 cm. sheets printed on recto only, stapled as issued, Gotham Book Mart ink stamp at foot of titlepage, fine.   The Brick Row Book Shop   Miscellany Fifty-Nine - 26   2013 $1500

Ginsberg, Allen *Reality Sandwiches.* San Francisco: City Lights Books, 1985. Fifteenth printing, small 8vo., original wrappers, excellent copy housed in protective folding box, inscribed by author with holograph drawing. Maggs Bros. Ltd. 1460 - 342 2013 £200

Ginsberg, Debra *Blind Submission: a Novel.* New York: Shaye Areheart Books, 2006. First edition, fine in fine dust jacket, signed by author, from the library of Bruce Kahn. Between the Covers Rare Books, Inc. Mystery & Detective Fiction - 304512 2013 $60

Giordano, Raymond V. *The Antiquarian Scientist: Antiquarian Science, Medicine and Instruments. Catalog 10, 12-14, 16-18.* Amesbury: Antiquarian Scientist, 1981-1986. 7 volumes, 8vo., most volumes with holograph pencil or ink date to front cover, original printed wrappers, very good. Jeff Weber Rare Books 169 - 165 2013 $75

Giraldi, Giglio Gregorio *L. G. Gyraldi... Opera Omnia Dvobvs Tomis Distincta Complectentina Historiam de Deis Gentivm...* Lugduni Batavorum: Hackium Boutesteyn, Vivie, Vander AA & Luchtmans, 1696. First collected edition, 2 works in one volume, each with separate titlepages, large 4to., full page engraved additional title, engraved printer's device on titlepage, titlepage in red and black, 2 double page engravings, 7 full page engravings, plates engraved by John Aveele after Drawings by F. Boitard, short tear on 2N2 without loss, original dark calf, raised bands, gilt stamped compartments on spine, black gilt stamped morocco spine, title label, neatly rebacked preserving covers and spine, signature of J. Fazakerley, very good. Jeff Weber Rare Books 171 - 138 2013 $4500

Giraud, S. Louis *Bookano Stories Potpourri Edition.* London: Strand, n.d. circa, 1940. 8vo., pictorial boards, fine, color endpapers and other color illustrations, 5 wonderful double page pop-ups full of color and detail, particularly nice. Aleph-Bet Books, Inc. 105 - 471 2013 $4000

Giraud, S. Louis *Bookano Stories No. 2.* London: Strand, 1935. 4to., pictorial boards, some wear to paper on spine, else very good+, 5 very fine full color double paged pop-ups, color and black and white illustrations. Aleph-Bet Books, Inc. 105 - 469 2013 $350

Giraud, S. Louis *Bookano Stories No. 3.* London: Strand, n.d. circa, 1936. 4to., pictorial boards, slight spine wear, near fine, 6 double page color pop-ups, illustrations in color and black and white. Aleph-Bet Books, Inc. 104 - 436 2013 $450

Giraud, S. Louis *Bookano Stories. Series No. 4.* Strand Publications, n.d., 1937. Color frontispiece, 5 double page full color popups, line drawings, excellent copy, original pictorial boards, few creased to spine, little wear to extremities. R. F. G. Hollett & Son Children's Books - 223 2013 £150

Giraud, S. Louis *Bookano Stories No. 4.* London: Strand, n.d. circa, 1937. 8vo., pictorial boards, slight rubbing, near fine, 5 action packed double page color pop-ups, color and black and whites, beautiful copy. Aleph-Bet Books, Inc. 105 - 470 2013 $350

Giraud, S. Louis *Bookano Stories No. 5.* London: Strand, n.d. circa, 1938. 8vo., pictorial boards, fine and bright, 5 particularly wonderful doublepage color pop-ups, illustrations throughout, beautiful copy. Aleph-Bet Books, Inc. 104 - 439 2013 $425

Giraud, S. Louis *Bookano Stories No. 6.* London: Strand, n.d., 1939. 4to., pictorial boards, near fine, 5 particularly wonderful double page color pop-ups, illustrations in color and black and white. Aleph-Bet Books, Inc. 104 - 437 2013 $400

Giraud, S. Louis *Bookano Stories No. 11.* London: Strand, n.d. circa, 1942. 4to., pictorial boards, fine, color endpapers and other color illustrations and featuring 5 wonderful double page pop-ups full of color. Aleph-Bet Books, Inc. 105 - 468 2013 $375

Giraud, S. Louis *Bookano Stories Series No. 12.* Strand Publications, n.d. 1930's, Original pictorial boards, extremities trifle rubbed and bruised, unpaginated, 5 double page full color pop-ups, color and black and white illustrations in text, very rare. R. F. G. Hollett & Son Children's Books - 222 2013 £180

Giraud, S. Louis *Bookano Stories. Series 13.* Strand Publications, n.d. 1940s, Large 8vo., original pictorial boards, spine creased and little worn, color endpapers, color frontispiece and title, 5 fine color pop-ups and black and white drawings, inked name to head of title, otherwise good, crisp, unused condition. R. F. G. Hollett & Son Children's Books - 225 2013 £85

Giraud, S. Louis *Bookano Stories with Pictures that Spring Up in Model Form #15.* London: Strand Publications, 1945. 8vo., illustrated boards, very good, 5 pop-ups in excellent condition, previous owners name on titlepage, small piece of paper from spine missing one page has been colored. Barnaby Rudge Booksellers Children 2013 - 021709 2013 $125

Giraud, S. Louis *Bookano Stories No. 17.* London: Strand, n.d., 1948. 8vo., pictorial boards, fine and bright, 5 wonderful double page color pop-ups, rarely found so clean. Aleph-Bet Books, Inc. 104 - 438 2013 $425

Giraud, S. Louis *Daily Express Children's Annual.* Lane Publication, 1930. Original pictorial boards, spine rather creased, pages 95, 6 fine pop-ups all in excellent order. R. F. G. Hollett & Son Children's Books - 224 2013 £175

Giraud, S. Louis *The Story of Jesus.* Strand Publications, n.d. circa, 1930. Large 8vo., original cloth, inset on upper board, hinges trifle rubbed, color endpapers and 8 fine color pop-ups, one short tear, otherwise in good crisp unused condition.   R. F. G. Hollett & Son   Children's Books - 227   2013   £85

Giraudoux, Jean *Fugues sur Siegfried.* Paris: Aux Editions Lapina, 1930. First edition, of the total edition of 100 copies, this one of 19 deluxe examples (de tete) printed on Vieux Japon paper, with 60 pages of text in French, etching by G. Gorvel and 4 original full page etchings by Jean Emile Laboureur, each of the 5 etchings signed in plate, also containing separate wrapper folder with 3 additional suites of 3 progressive states of each of the 5 etchings, all horstexte, 10 of them signed in plate, circa 8 x 6 inches, book in original publisher's wrappers with pictorial dust jacket, housed in original slipcase, most pages unopened, few very minor fox marks at very edge of pages, but overall in excellent condition, some published ephemera laid in, very rare.   Gemini Fine Books & Arts., Ltd.   Art Reference & Illustrated Books - 2013 $1400

Girdner, John H. *Newyorkitis.* New York: Grafton Press, 1901. First edition, blue cloth decorated with image of NY skyline, white spine lettering bit rubbed, else bright, near fine, uncommon.   Between the Covers Rare Books, Inc.   New York City - 286266   2013 $225

Girvin, Brenda *Good Queen Bess 1533-1603.* David Nutt, n.d. circa, 1907. First edition, oblong 4to., original pictorial boards, rather dusty and marked, edges worn, unpaginated, 23 full page colored plates with title guard with pictorial border by John Hassall, and accompanying text leaf, front joint cracked, flyleaf replaced, half title frayed at fore-edge, few edge tears, rear endpapers, rather browned.   R. F. G. Hollett & Son   Children's Books - 269   2013   £65

Girvin, Brenda *Round Fairyland with Alice and the White Rabbit.* Wells, Gardner, Darton, 1916. First edition, 16 plates by Dorothy Furniss, frontispiece tissue guard present, little light, mainly marginal, foxing, crown 8vo., original light green cloth, backstrip and front cover lettered in brown and white and with four color designs overall by Furness, gift inscription dated Xmas 1916, very good.   Blackwell's Rare Books   B174 - 187   2013   £160

Girvin, Ernest Alexander *Domestic Duels or Evening Talks on the Woman Question.* San Francisco: Bronson, 1898. First edition, 8vo., 277 pages, gray cloth stamped in green and gilt, hinge little tender, but very good, scarce.   Second Life Books Inc.   182 - 91   2013 $300

Gisborne, Thomas *An Enquiry into the Dutie of Men in the Higher and Middle Classes of Society in Great Britain...* London: printed for B. and J. White, Fleet Street, 1797. Fourth edition, 2 volumes, half titles, 8vo., full contemporary calf, raised and gilt banded spines, red morocco labels, slight wear to following hinge volume I, spines rubbed, 19th century note on inner front board, Ebberston Library No. 84 in later hand, gift from Mrs. Baker.   Jarndyce Antiquarian Booksellers   CCIV - 144   2013   £200

Gissing, George *The Emancipated.* London: Richard Bentley & Son, 1890. First edition, 3 volumes, original olive brown smooth cloth, spines lettered in gilt, grey paper covered boards, printed with pattern in brown, corners slightly browned, otherwise very good.   Jarndyce Antiquarian Booksellers   CCV - 112   2013   £600

Gissing, George *Sleeping Fires.* London: T. Fisher Unwin, 1895. First edition, tall 12mo., recently bound in pale brown calf, burgundy label lettered gilt on spine, terminal 10 pages of ads, inscribed by author for Miss Clara Collet Dec. 1895, and signed in full on titlepage, excellent copy.   Maggs Bros. Ltd.   1460 - 343   2013   £1250

Gittings, Robert *Dorothy Wordsworth.* Oxford: Clarendon Press, 1985. First edition, original cloth gilt, dust jacket, 12 plates.   R. F. G. Hollett & Son   Lake District and Cumbria - 178   2013   £25

Gladstone, W. E. *The Irish Question.* NPA, 1886. Authorised Cheap edition, 32 pages, modern wrappers, very good.   C. P. Hyland   261 - 449   2013   £40

Glaister, Geoffrey Ashall *Glossary of the Book.* London: George Allen and Unwin, 1960. First edition, signed letter from author to LA bookseller Jeff Weber, 8vo., frontispiece, plates, text illustrations, quarter maroon cloth with gray cloth sides, gilt stamped cover illustrations and spine title, dust jacket bit worn and spotted, very good.   Jeff Weber Rare Books   171 - 139   2013 $150

A Glance at New York: Embracing the City Government, Theaters, Hotels, Churches... New York: A. Greene, 1837. First edition, 12mo., contemporary quarter morocco gilt, unprinted paper covered boards, later bookplate and two earlier names, including that of Harriet Ann Chapman, joints rubbed and worn, front hinge little tender, still reasonably tight, just about very good.   Between the Covers Rare Books, Inc.   New York City - 300867   2013 $350

Glancy, Diane *Traveling On.* Tulsa: Hadassah Press, 1980. First edition, near fine in wrappers, inscribed by author, approximately a dozen corrections to text in author's hand.   Ken Lopez Bookseller   159 - 150   2013 $1500

Glanville's Guide to South Africa, Including Cape Colony; The Diamond-Fields, Bechuanaland, Transvaal, The Goldfields, Natal and The Orange Free State... London: 1890. Tenth edition, original cloth, gilt, very dampstained with pictorial onlay of a Union line ship to upper board, flyleaves browned, joints tender, very scarce, map was issued separately and as usual is not present. R. F. G. Hollett & Son Africana - 80 2013 £120

Glas, George *The History of the Discovery and Conquest of the Canary Islands...* London: R. & J. Dodsley and T. Durham, 1764. First edition, quarto, folding engraved map, 3 charts on 2 pages, foxing to 10 pages, 19th century brown half calf, rebacked using original backstrip, spine rubbed, foxing to prelims. J. & S. L. Bonham Antiquarian Booksellers Europe - 9486 2013 £480

Glaser, Elizabeth *For Our Children.* Walt Disney, 1991. First edition, 4to., cloth backed boards, new in dust jacket, illustrations. Aleph-Bet Books, Inc. 105 - 571 2013 $125

The Glasgow Almanack for 1789. Glasgow: printed by J. Mennons, 1789. 12mo., some occasional browning, mainly marginal offsetting from binding, original wallet style calf binding, blind ruled borders, part of original ties attached to flap, blindstamped "G" on spine, official tax stamp dated 1788 on titlepage, few contemporary notes on inner boards. Jarndyce Antiquarian Booksellers CCIV - 37 2013 £185

Glasse, Hannah *The Art of Cookery Made Plain and Easy.* Alexandria: Cottom and Stewart, 1805. First American edition, 16mo., contemporary calf, leather label, some wear, slightly shaken, lacking endleaves, very scarce. M & S Rare Books, Inc. 95 - 89 2013 $1500

Glasson, Naomi *Gordon's Jet Flight.* New York: Golden, 1961. 8vo., illustrations in color on every page by Mel Crawford, including 2 pages of die-cut pieces to be used to assemble American Airlines 707 Astrojet, completely unused and in wonderful condition, rare. Aleph-Bet Books, Inc. 104 - 238 2013 $275

Gleave, Tom *They Fell in the Battle A Roll of Honour of the Battle of Britain 10 July - 31 October 1940.* London: Royal Air Force Museum printed by Rampant Lions Press, 1980. First edition, limited to 80 signed copies, this #42, signed by Prince Philip, near fine in specially dyed goatskin binding with cross device stamped in gilt on front board and titles gilt on spine, top edge gilt, mild sun spine, printed on Arches Velin mould made paper, binding by Morrell in original blue cloth covered slipcase as issued, mildly sunned, folio. By the Book, L. C. 36 - 2 2013 $1250

Glen, A. R. *Under the Pole Star. The Oxford University Arctic Expedition 1935-1936.* London: Methuen, 1937. First edition, flyleaves spotted, small 4to., original blue cloth, gilt, little marked and faded, 48 plates, 18 maps, 4 diagrams. R. F. G. Hollett & Son Polar Exploration - 24 2013 £75

Glibota, Ante *Chicago. 150 Years of Architecture.* Paris: Paris Art Center, 1985. First edition, 4to., lovely bi-lingual presentation, nearly 400 pages, fine in very good+ dust jacket with few short tears. Beasley Books 2013 - 2013 $65

Glines, Carroll V. *Doolitte's Tokyo Raiders.* New York: Arno Press, 1980. Reprint, 8vo., illustrations, gilt stamped blue cloth, signed and inscribed by James Doolittle to Larry Seyferth in ink, near fine. Jeff Weber Rare Books 171 - 107 2013 $75

Glisson, Francis *De Rachitide sive Morbo Puerili qui Volgo The Rickets Dicitur Tractatus... Adscitis in Operis Societatem Georgio Bate & Ahasuero Regemortero Medicinae Quoque Doctoribus...* London: G. Du-gard for L. Sadler & R. Beaumont, 1650. First edition, 8vo., woodcut illustrations, contemporary speckled calf, sides ruled in blind brown leather spine stamped spine label, prelim leaf signed "A" (otherwise blank), armorial bookplate of Honorable Sir William Irby of Boston, Lincolnshire, splendid copy. Jeff Weber Rare Books 172 - 107 2013 $15,000

Gloag, John *To-morrow's Yesterday.* London: George Allen & Unwin, 1932. First edition, light dampstain at spine, little soiling and bumping to edges of boards, about very good in like dust jacket with light overall swear, scarce in dust jacket. Between the Covers Rare Books, Inc. Sci-Fi, Fantasy & Horror - 85422 2013 $350

Glover, Richard *Leonidas, a Poem.* London: printed for R. Dodsley, 1737. 4to., just touch of faint spotting, contemporary mottled and polished calf, edges sprinkled red, rebacked and recornered with original spine preserved, old leather little scratched, square paper label, corners clipped, printed "Lf" on front pastedown. Unsworths Antiquarian Booksellers 28 - 100 2013 £200

Glover, Richard *Leonidas; a Poem.* Dublin: printed for H. Saunders, 1763. Sixth edition, 12mo., contemporary sprinkled calf, red morocco lettering piece to spine, darkened around edges, joints cracking but strong, sound, scarce. Blackwell's Rare Books 172 - 61 2013 £100

Gluge, G. *Anatomisch-Mikroscopische Untersuchungen zur Allgemeinen und Speziellen Pathologie.* Leipzig: Jena Mauke, 1839-1841. First edition, 2 volumes bound in 1, half calf, bit rubbed and corners bumped, front joint cracked, text browned and foxed in parts, plates in color. James Tait Goodrich S74 - 127 2013 $795

Gmelin, Leopold *Hand-book of Chemistry.* London: Cavendish Society, 1848-1872. 8vo., 19 volumes, multiple paginations, some foxing, original green publisher's cloth, gilt stamped cover emblems and spine titles, top edge gilt, extremities worn, many of volumes' hinges cracked, good, rare. Jeff Weber Rare Books 169 - 161 2013 $850

Gobineau, Arthur, Comte De *Les Pleiades.* Stockholm: Jos. Muller & Cie, 1874. First edition, 412 pages, 12mo., three quarter calf over marbled boards, five raised bands ruled in gilt, morocco lettering piece, five compartments with gilt flowers and decorations, all edges marbled, marbled endpapers, very good, spine and boards rubbed, owner's bookplate, scattered foxing, heavier to blanks and first and last few leaves. Kaaterskill Books 16 - 35 2013 $600

Goble, Paul *Girl Who Loved Wild Horses.* Scarsdale: Bradbury Press, 1978. First edition, 4to., cloth, fine in very good dust jacket (one closed tear with seal), full and partial page drawings by Goble. Aleph-Bet Books, Inc. 105 - 276 2013 $375

Goddard, H. Orpen *The Orpen Family...* for private circulation, 1930. 8vo., cloth, very good, photo of Monksgrange & specimen leaves, interesting copy with 2 ALS's to C. P. Curran. C. P. Hyland 261 - 406 2013 £450

Godden, Rumer *The Tale of the Tales.* London: Frederick Warne, 1971. First edition, 4to., original cloth, gilt, dust jacket, illustrations in color. R. F. G. Hollett & Son Children's Books - 229 2013 £45

Godden, Rumer *The Tale of the Tales. The Beatrix Potter Ballet.* London: Frederick Warne, 1971. First edition, 4to., original cloth, gilt, dust jacket, 208 pages, illustrations in color. R. F. G. Hollett & Son Lake District and Cumbria - 180 2013 £45

Godfrey, J. H. *Jugoslavia.* London: Naval Intelligence, 1944. First edition, 8vo., numerous maps (2 in slipcase), illustrations, plans, original tan cloth. J. & S. L. Bonham Antiquarian Booksellers Europe - 7176 2013 £40

Godwin, William 1756-1836 *Caleb Williams.* London: Henry Colburn and Richard Bentley, 1831. 12mo., complete in one volume, frontispiece, engraved titlepage, very good in contemporary black half calf, marbled boards, gilt banded spine with morocco label. Ken Spelman Books Ltd. 75 - 93 2013 £50

Godwin, William 1756-1836 *An Enquiry Concerning Political Justice and Its Influence on General Virtue and Happiness..* London: G. G. J. and J. Robinson, 1793. 2 volumes, quarto, 19th century polished calf, spines tooled gilt in compartments and lettered gilt on burgundy morocco label, raised bands, gilt turn-ins, marbled endpapers, all edges trimmed, half titles slightly soiled, each with ink signature of former owner and one short marginal tear, margins of few leaves very lightly foxed, otherwise very good, clean and fresh. Heritage Book Shop 50th Anniversary Catalogue - 43 2013 $10,000

Godwin, William 1756-1836 *Life of Geoffrey Chaucer the Early English Poet...* London: printed by T. Davison for Richard Phillips, 1804. Second edition, 4 volumes, 8vo., frontispieces, lightly browned and foxed, titles bit dusty, contemporary plum half calf with marbled boards, edges sprinkled brown, marbled endpapers, rebacked to style by Chris Weston, boards scuffed, armorial bookplate of John Wickham Flower/Park III/Croydon. Unsworths Antiquarian Booksellers 28 - 166 2013 £400

Godwin, William 1756-1836 *Life of Geoffrey Chaucer, Including Memoirs of John of Gaunt, Duke of Lancaster.* London: printed by T. Davison for Richard Phillips, 1804. Second edition, 4 volumes, frontispiece portraits, 8vo., fine set, bound in full contemporary diced calf, gilt borders triple gilt banded spine. Jarndyce Antiquarian Booksellers CCIV - 145 2013 £380

Godwin, William 1756-1836 *Thoughts of Man, His Nature, Productions and Discoveries.* London: Effingman Wilson, 1831. First edition, tall 8vo., contemporary three quarter calf and marbled boards, spine chipped and banged, lacks some of the lower label, old bookseller label on endpaper, some offsetting, some toning to titlepage, very good, lacks ad in front and rear. Second Life Books Inc. 183 - 144 2013 $950

Goethe, Johann Wolfgang Von 1749-1832 *Eventyret: Das Marchen. (Fairy Tales).* Kobenhavn: Forlaget Kronos, 1949. Limited to 350 numbed copies, 4to., 63 pages, loose as issued in decorative boards and slipcase, fine, 2 full page and one almost full page black and white by Kay Nielsen, in his typical style, rare. Aleph-Bet Books, Inc. 104 - 389 2013 $1500

Goethe, Johann Wolfgang Von 1749-1832 *Faust.* Stuttgart & Tubingen: J. G. Cotta, 1854-1858. 2 volumes in one, folio, 19 full page steel engravings, woodcuts, scattered foxing throughout some plates heavily foxed, original full morocco, with gorgeous gilt stamped decorations in style of Seibertz, initials "E.S." in stylized botanical decorations, professionally restored, marvelous original binding,. Jeff Weber Rare Books 171 - 140 2013 $2000

Goetzmann, William H. *Army Exploration in the American West 1803-1863.* New Haven: 1959. First edition, xx, 509 pages, illustrations, maps plus 5 folding maps in rear pocket, publisher's slip indicating this is review copy laid in, dust jacket somewhat soiled, edge wear and short repaired tears, else clean and very good. Dumont Maps & Books of the West 122 - 59 2013 $85

Goetzmann, William H. *Army Explorations in the American West 1803-1863.* New Haven: 1959. First edition, xx, 509 pages, illustrations, five folding maps in back pocket, modest previous owner's name stamp on f.f.e.p., dust jacket and book otherwise bright and near fine, book clean and very good. Dumont Maps & Books of the West 125 - 52 2013 $75

Gogarty, Oliver St. John 1878-1957 *As I Was Going Down Sackville Street.* London: Rich & Cowan, 1937. First reprint, 8vo., original green cloth, this book was the subject of famous Dublin legal suit taken against the author by the brothers William and Harry Sinclair who felt that they had been libelled in the book, ownership copy of the presiding judge in the case, Mr. Justice Hanna with his inked signature and clipping tipped-in to rear with account of opening of the trial from The Irish Times June 8 1937.   Maggs Bros. Ltd.   1460 - 345   2013   £450

The Gold Rush and Other Stories... Long Beach: Applezaba Press, 1989. First edition, one of 50 numbered copies signed by Gerald Locklin, white hardbound book with bar scene on front cover, issued without dust jacket, 176 pages, near fine.   Ed Smith Books   75 - 8   2013 $125

Gold, Glen David *Carter Beats the Devil.* London: Sceptre, 2001. First edition, signed by author, 563 pages, fine in dust jacket.   Ed Smith Books   78 - 21   2013 $100

Goldberg, Arnold *Misunderstanding Freud.* New York: Other Press, 2004. First edition, fine in near fine dust jacket.   Beasley Books   2013 - 2013 $65

Goldberg, Benjamin *The Mirror and Man.* Charlottesville: University Press of Virginia, 1985. First edition, 8vo., xii 260 pages, 38 illustrations, grey cloth with white paper boards, silver stamped spine title, dust jacket, Burndy bookplate.   Jeff Weber Rare Books   169 - 167   2013 $115

Golding, Harry *Bully Boy: The Story of a Bulldog and His Friend Jock.* New York: Platt and Peck, n.d. circa, 1910. 12mo., pictorial boards, 96 pages, fine, 27 wonderful color plates by Arthur Cooke.   Aleph-Bet Books, Inc.   104 - 170   2013 $250

Golding, Harry *Bully Boy: the Story of a Bulldog and his Friend Jock.* London: Ward Lock & Co. n.d. circa, 1931. 12mo., original pictorial boards, spine stripped, edges rather rubbed, 16 illustrations in color and 8 in black and white by Arthur Cooke, front joint cracked, scarce.   R. F. G. Hollett & Son   Children's Books - 230   2013   £45

Golding, Harry *Wonder Book.* London: Ward, Lock & Co., 1924. Nineteenth year of issue, small 4to., original cloth backed pictorial boards, corners rounded, edges rubbed, pages 264, illustrations, 12 color plates.   R. F. G. Hollett & Son   Children's Books - 231   2013   £30

Golding, Harry *Zoo Days.* London: Ward Lock, 1919. 8vo., 48 color plates, cloth, pictorial paste-on, 344 pages, some foxing and rubbing to joints, very good, illustrations by Margaret Tarrant.   Aleph-Bet Books, Inc.   104 - 550   2013 $225

Golding, Louis *Magnolia Street.* London: Victor Gollancz, 1932. First edition, 8vo., original black cloth, excellent copy, dust jacket nicked and browned, inscribed by author for Marion Ryan.   Maggs Bros. Ltd.   1460 - 347   2013   £175

Golding, Louis *Sicilian Noon.* London: Chatto and Windus, 1925. First edition, 8vo., original black cloth, excellent copy, inscribed by author for Dick Ellis.   Maggs Bros. Ltd.   1460 - 346   2013   £120

Golding, Louis *Sorrow of War. Poems.* London: Methuen, 1919. First edition, 16mo., original grey boards, printed label trifle chipped, on darkened backstrip, tail edges untrimmed, good.   Blackwell's Rare Books   B174 - 211   2013   £70

Golding, William 1911-1993 *The Inheritors.* London: Faber and Faber, 1955. First edition, 8vo., original blue cloth, dust jacket, excellent copy in slightly browned dust jacket, worn at head and tail of spine, inscribed by author with ownership signature of Faber's publishing director, Charles Monteith above.   Maggs Bros. Ltd.   1460 - 348   2013   £1500

Golding, William 1911-1993 *The Pyramid.* New York: Harcourt Brace and World, 1967. First American edition, signed by author, owner signature, near fine, very good dust jacket internally tape mended at crown, scarce signed.   Ken Lopez Bookseller   159 - 73   2013 $250

Golding, William 1911-1993 *The Pyramid.* London: Faber & Faber, 1967. First edition, signed by author, owner signature and date on front flyleaf, mildly cocked, near fine in very good dust jacket with some minor staining to rear panel and verso, uncommon book signed.   Ken Lopez Bookseller   159 - 72   2013 $350

Goldman, William *Soldier in the Rain.* New York: Atheneum, 1960. First edition, inscribed by author, small mark (remainder?) lower edge of text block, near fine in very good, rubbed and price clipped dust jacket with couple of internally tape mended edge tears.   Ken Lopez Bookseller   159 - 74   2013 $175

Goldmark, Josephine *Fatigue and Efficiency a Study in Industry.* New York: Charities Publication Committee, 1912. First edition, 8vo., 591 pages, little rubbed drab green cloth, hinges little tender, very good, from the library of reformer Florence Kelley (1859-1932) presentation copy from author to Kelley.   Second Life Books Inc.   182 - 94   2013 $325

Goldsmith, J. *Geography, on a Popular Plan.* printed for Richard Phillips, 1806. New edition, 60 copperplates, modern full polished calf, gilt, 41 maps and woodcut plates (ex 60), map of England torn with some loss, some wear and fingering, despite being sadly defective.   R. F. G. Hollett & Son   Children's Books - 232   2013   £120

Goldsmith, J. *A Grammar of General Geography.* London: Longmans, Green Reader and Dyer, n.d. late 1860's, Original cloth gilt, head of spine chipped, engraved frontispiece, volvelle title vignette, 11 folding maps, 12 engraved plates and text woodcuts.   R. F. G. Hollett & Son   Children's Books - 233   2013   £140

Goldsmith, Martin M. *The Miraculous Fish of Domingo Gonzales.* New York: W. W. Norton, 1950. First edition, illustrations by William de la Torre, small bookstore label on front fly and old tape shadows on pastedowns where previous owner had affixed the flaps, else fine in attractive, very good dust jacket that has been laminated, with corresponding shadows on flaps and has suffered some modest fading at extremities, very scarce.   Between the Covers Rare Books, Inc.   Mystery & Detective Fiction - 74357   2013 $1500

Goldsmith, Oliver   1730-1774 *The History of Little Goody Twoshoes, Otherwise Called Mrs. Margery Twohsoes...* Worcester: Isaiah Thomas, 1787. First Worcester edition, 3.8 x 2.5 inches, 35 woodcuts, frontispiece is not present in this copy, old rebacked contemporary paper covered boards, without endleaves, some foxing, very sound.   M & S Rare Books, Inc.   95 - 135   2013 $3250

Goldsmith, Oliver   1730-1774 *Mrs. Mary Blaize.* London: George Routledge & Sons, n.d. circa, 1885. Oblong 8vo. original pictorial wrappers, pages 24, 6 full page color illustrations and line drawings by Randolph Caldecott.   R. F. G. Hollett & Son   Children's Books - 112   2013   £30

Goldsmith, Oliver   1730-1774 *The Poems of Oliver Goldsmith.* London: George Routledge and Co., 1859. 8vo., color illustrations, gilt borders and decorative titlepieces in text foxed, one leaf more so and also showing few small handling tears, discoloration from ribbon bookmark to pages 60-61, green and orange morocco, heavily embossed and decorated in black and gilt, bevelled edges, all edges gilt, neatly rebacked, spine sunned, boards little scuffed, hinges splitting, still very good, gift inscription reading 'Meggie with her Husband's love March 27th 1859", small label of R. Davies, bookseller...Birmingham.   Unsworths Antiquarian Booksellers   28 - 167   2013   £95

Goldsmith, Oliver   1730-1774 *The Poems of Oliver Goldsmith.* London and New York: George Routledge, 1877. Very good, small 4to., all edges gilt, color illustrations, some light foxing, very good.   Barnaby Rudge Booksellers   Poetry 2013 - 020491   2013 $65

Goldsmith, Oliver   1730-1774 *The Poetical and Prose Works of Oliver Goldsmith.* Edinburgh: Gall and Inglis, 1880. 12mo., full red leather with gilt decorations on covers and spine, all edges gilt, extra engraved titlepage, some foxing, few full page engravings.   Barnaby Rudge Booksellers   Poetry 2013 - 020424   2013 $80

Goldsmith, Oliver   1730-1774 *The Poetical Works of....* New York: and London: White & Allen, 1889. First edition, #15 of 200 copies, of which 100 were for America (large paper edition with India proofs), 4to., untrimmed, signed by publisher, small stains at corners of proofs, from glue attaching them to leaves, elaborately stamped covers, leather spine labels chipped, nice, clean copy.   Second Life Books Inc.   183 - 146   2013 $200

Goldsmith, Oliver   1730-1774 *The Vicar of Wakefield.* New York: printed by James Oram for Christian Brown, 1803. First American illustrated edition, first NY edition in any form, excellent copy, 2 volumes in 1, 12mo., contemporary tree calf, rebacked, old back laid down, corners rubbed, leather label, pages 252 + 4 wood engraved plates by Anderson, early oval hand decorated bookplate of Ellen Thompson, very good.   Howard S. Mott Inc.   262 - 62   2013 $650

Goldsmith, Oliver   1730-1774 *The Vicar of Wakefield.* London: 1886. Large 8vo., 114 color illustrations, modern full autumn morocco, boards quadruple, gilt ruled, spine decoratively stamped in gilt in compartments and lettered gilt, top edge gilt, gilt dentelles, green watered silk endpapers, previous owner's bookplate, few tiny scratches to back board, otherwise about fine.   Heritage Book Shop   Holiday Catalogue 2012 - 121   2013 $450

Goldsmith, Oliver   1730-1774 *The Vicar of Wakefield.* London/New York: Macmillan, 1922. Reprint, 8vo., finely bound by Riviere in brown leather with cottage motif on front cover and steaming bowl with clay pipe on rear cover, all edges gilt, gilt ruled turn-ins, spine creased at joints, generally clean and sound, fine etched bookplate for Beatrice E. Smith, signed by "H. Martyn", handsome copy, illustrations by Hugh Thomson.   Ed Smith Books   75 - 32   2013 $375

Goldsmith, Oliver   1730-1774 *The Vicar of Wakefield.* London: Harrap, 1929. Limited to 575 copies for England, numbered and signed by artist, 4to., full gilt vellum, top edge gilt, bottom front cover slightly toned, else fine in publisher's box (stain on lid of box), 12 very lovely color plates plus text black and whites and pictorial endpapers, laid in is 4 page prospectus for the book and color plate, great copy.   Aleph-Bet Books, Inc.   104 - 479   2013 $2500

Goldsmith, Oliver   1730-1774 *Vicar of Wakefield.* London: Harrap, 1929. First edition, 4to., gilt cloth, top edge gilt, very fine in dust jacket (slightly worn), illustrations by Arthur Rackham, beautiful copy.   Aleph-Bet Books, Inc.   104 - 480   2013 $250

Goldsmith, Oliver   1730-1774   *The Vicar of Wakefield.* Philadelphia: Davd McKay Co., 1929.   One of 775 copies signed by artist, including 575 for England (ours being #95 of 200 copies for America), 267 x 206mm., illustrations by Arthur Rackham, very attractive red three quarter morocco stamp signed "Putnams" along front turn-in, raised bands, spine handsomely gilt in compartments formed by plain and decorative rules, quatrefoil centerpiece surrounded by densely scrolling cornerpieces, sides and endleaves or rose colored linen, top edge gilt, other edges untrimmed and mostly unopened, 12 color plates by Rackham, front board with insignificant small, round spot to cloth, very fine, unusually bright and clean inside and out, almost no signs of use.   Phillip J. Pirages   63 - 378   2013 $2900

Goldsmith, Oliver   1730-1774   *Vicar of Wakefield.* London: Harrap, 1929.   First edition, 4to., gilt cloth, top edge gilt, endpaper foxed, light wear, very good+, illustrations by Arthur Rackham with cover design, pictorial endpapers, 12 color plates plus 22 black and whites, this copy has large half page drawing signed and dated Nov. 1929 by Rackham special copy.   Aleph-Bet Books, Inc.   105 - 498   2013 $2200

Goldsmith, Oliver   1794-1861   *The Rising Village and Other Poems.*   Saint John: Mc'Millan, printed by Henry Chubb, Market Square, 1834.   12mo., original dark brow silk with gilt title to spine, spine has outer hinge cracks with small loss of silk cover and bottom of spine is loose, interior very good with half title, small bookplate of Nova Scotia collector Wilfred Roebuck, Truro, Nova Scotia, with small news clipping, book review, attached to first flyleaf.   Schooner Books Ltd.   101 - 11   2013 $1250

Goldstein, Bernard R.   *Theory and Observation in Ancient and Medieval Astronomy.*   London: Variorum Reprints, 1985.   8vo., xi, 348 pages, blue cloth, gilt stamped cover and spine titles, ownership signature, fine, rare.   Jeff Weber Rare Books   169 - 168   2013 $100

Goldsworthy, Andy   *Stone.*   New York: Harry N. Abrams, 1994.   First edition, signed by Goldsworthy, fine, 4to., 120 pages, fine dust jacket.   By the Book, L. C.   36 - 9   2013 $400

Gollancz, Victor   *Russia and Ourselves.*   London: Victor Gollancz, 1941.   First edition, 8vo. original blue cloth, spine faded, rust staining and small hole to front flap from a staple, closed tear to head of spine, rust staining to front pastedown, otherwise very good, inscribed by author for Ivor.   Maggs Bros. Ltd.   1460 - 349   2013   £100

Golownin, Vasilii Mikhailovich   *Recollections of Japan, Comprising a Particular Account of the Religion, Language, Government, Laws and Manners of the People with Observations...*   London: printed for Henry Colburn, 1819.   First edition, 8vo., later 19th century half calf, marbled boards, with red leather spine label, gilt lettering, rare, particularly in this condition.   By the Book, L. C.   38 - 62   2013 $1800

Gomeldon, Jane   *The Medley.*   Newcastle: printed by J. White and T. Saint, 1766.   220 pages, frontispiece, 8vo., offsetting from frontispiece, occasional foxing, 19th century half calf, marbled boards, leading hinge cracked but firm, spine rubbed, bookplate of Sir Henry Hay Makdougall, Bart, of Makerstoun.   Jarndyce Antiquarian Booksellers   CCIV - 146   2013   £520

Goncourt, Edmond   *La Femme Ali Dix-Huitieme Siecle.* Paris: Bibliotheque-Charpentier, 1903.   183 x 116mm., pleasing contemporary green morocco, covers with double gilt rule border, upper over with gilt titling, spine gilt in compartments with central floral spring and curling floral vine cornerpieces, turn-ins densely gilt, snakeskin patterned green endpapers, all edges gilt, engraved bookplate of Victoria Sackville West, spine uniformly sunned to pleasing light brown, leaves somewhat browned because of inferior paper stock, few tear of no consequence, one repaired, otherwise excellent, few signs of use.   Phillip J. Pirages   63 - 416   2013 $175

Gooch-Iglehart, Fanny Chambers   *The Boy Captive of the Texas Mier Expedition.*   N.P.: 1909.   Revised, illustrated paper over boards, extremities rubbed with some loss at tips, one plate loose, scattered foxing, previous owner's name stamp in several places, binding sound.   Dumont Maps & Books of the West   122 - 60   2013 $75

Good Old Catherine Prescott and the Boy of Dundee. Philadelphia: American Sunday School Union, 1870.   First edition, 24mo., cloth backed boards, very rare, green cloth backed marbled boards, frontispiece, very good.   Barnaby Rudge Booksellers   Children 2013 - 021392   2013 $55

Goodall, Armitage   *Place-Names of South-West Yorkshire.* Cambridge: 1913.   Half title, 8vo., very good on original gilt lettered red cloth.   Ken Spelman Books Ltd.   73 - 172   2013   £30

Goodman, Allegra   *Total Immersion. Stories.*   New York: Harper & Row, 1989.   First edition, fine in dust jacket.   Ed Smith Books   78 - 22   2013 $150

Goodman, George J.   *Retracing Major Stephen H. Long's 1820 Expedition.*   Norman: University of Oklahoma Press, 1995.   First edition, 26 illustrations, 6 maps, green cloth, very fine with pictorial dust jacket.   Argonaut Book Shop Summer 2013 - 129   2013 $60

Goodman, Murray *My Greatest Day in Football.* New York: A. S. Barnes, 1948. First edition, near fine, rubbing to spine ends, very good, creased dust jacket with chip to head of spine. Between the Covers Rare Books, Inc. Football Books - 35286   2013 $100

Goodman, Philip *Franklin Street.* New York: Alfred A. Knopf, 1942. Second printing, fine in lovely, near fine dust jacket with some tanning on rear panel, very scarce in jacket. Between the Covers Rare Books, Inc.   165 - 62   2013 $200

Goodrich, Abraham *A River Claim. Letters from the California Gold Fields, 1857.* El Cajon: Nineteen Hundred Press, 2007. First edition, one of 115 numbered copies, 4 wood engravings by James Horton, map ends, bound by John Robinson at the Tortoise Press in half Nigerian goatskin, marbled boards, very fine.   Argonaut Book Shop Recent Acquisitions June 2013 - 122   2013 $125

Goodrich, Mary *The Palace Hotel.* San Francisco: Crandall Press, 1930. First edition, thin octavo, photos and drawings, gray cloth backed boards, light tan boards, title on front cover in gold, bottom edges of covers slightly rubbed, very fine.   Argonaut Book Shop   Summer 2013 - 265   2013 $125

Goodrich, Samuel Griswold   1793-1860 *Atlas of Modern Maps and Geographical Tables...* Darton and Clark, 1844. 4to., double page engraved and hand colored map and 8 on single sheets, bit dog-eared, some foxing and browning in maps, pages 20, 4to., loose (gutta percha perished) in original cloth, blindstamped frame borders on sides, lettered in gilt on upper cover, within gilt cartouche, slightly faded, ownership inscription on title of Thomas Griffin (1832-1874), used copy, still tolerably good.   Blackwell's Rare Books 172 - 110   2013   £250

Goodrich, Samuel Griswold   1793-1860 *The Child's Botany.* Boston: S. G. Goodrich, 1828. First edition, scattered light foxing, small square 8vo., original black sheep backed green boards, rubbed, chipped at head and foot of spine, 6 plates, including frontispiece early female ownership signature in pencil.   Howard S. Mott Inc.   262 - 64   2013 $350

Goodrich, Samuel Griswold   1793-1860 *Peter Parley's Visit to London During the Coronation of Queen Victoria.* London: Charles Tilt, 1838. 12mo., original cloth, gilt extra, neatly recased with new endpapers, pictorial title and 6 hand colored plates, scarce.   R. F. G. Hollett & Son Children's Books - 234   2013   £175

Goodrich, Samuel Griswold   1793-1860 *The Token and Atlantic Souvenir: a Christmas and New Year's Present.* Boston: published by Charles Bowen, 1873. First edition, 12mo., inserted plates, full embossed black leather, all edges gilt, decorated endpapers.   L. W. Currey, Inc. Christmas Themed Books - 137494   2013 $150

Goodsir, Robert Anstruther *An Arctic Voyage to Baffin's Bay and Lancaster Sound, In Search of Friends with John Franklin.* Plaistow & Sutton Coldfield: Arctic Press, 1996. Facsimile of 1850 edition, small 8vo., blue cloth, pages 152, frontispiece, folding map, fine.   Schooner Books Ltd.   105 - 148   2013 $50

Goodwin, W. L. D. *Geology and Minerals of New Brunswick.* Gardenvale: Industrial and Educational Pub. Co., 1928. Limp maroon with gilt title to front cover, 2 folding maps in rear pocket, 7 x 5 inches, folio, wear to edges of cover.   Schooner Books Ltd.   101 - 14   2013 $125

Gordimer, Nadine *The Black Interpreters. Notes on African Writing.* Johannesburg: Spro-cas/Ravan, 1973. First edition, 8vo., original pictorial wrappers with just few marks, excellent copy, signed by author.   Maggs Bros. Ltd. 1460 - 352   2013   £100

Gordimer, Nadine *The Lying Days.* London: Victor Gollancz, 1953. Second impression, 8vo., original red cloth, excellent copy, spine slightly faded, inscribed by author for Erica Kreutzberger.   Maggs Bros. Ltd.   1460 - 530   2013   £100

Gordimer, Nadine *My Son's Story.* London: Bloomsbury, 1990. First edition, fine in fine dust jacket, signed on titlepage.   Leather Stalking Books   October 2013 - 2013 $75

Gordimer, Nadine *A World of Strangers.* New York: Simon and Schuster, 1958. First US edition, 8vo., original quarter blue cloth, near fine, inscribed by author for Brigitte and Bu.   Maggs Bros. Ltd.   1460 - 351   2013   £150

Gordon, Adam Lindsay *Bush Ballads and Galloping Rhymes.* Melbourne: Clarson, Massina and Co., 1870. First edition, 8vo., original burgundy cloth, lettered gilt, inscribed by author for Lindsay Gordon, wear to head and tail of spine, otherwise very good.   Maggs Bros. Ltd.   1460 - 353   2013   £375

Gordon, Cosmo *Life and Genius of Lord Byron.* London: Knight and Lacey, 1824. First edition, frontispiece very slightly browned, engraved title, odd internal mark, uncut in slightly later blue morocco by J. Larkins, spine slightly faded, Renier signature and booklabel.   Jarndyce Antiquarian Booksellers   CCIII - 387   2013   £220

Gordon, Elizabeth *Loraine and the Little People of Spring.* Chicago: Rand McNally, 1918. First edition, 8vo., nice, color plates, 2 small light stains on back cover, brown cloth, very good, illustrations by Ella Dolbear Lee.   Barnaby Rudge Booksellers   Children 2013 - 021395   2013 $85

Gordon, Elizabeth *Loraine and the Little People of Summer.* Chicago: Rand McNally, 1920. First edition, 8vo., green pictorial boards, 64 pages, fine, illustrations by James McCracken.   Aleph-Bet Books, Inc.   104 - 203   2013 $200

Gordon, Elizabeth *Really So Stories.* Chicago: Volland, 1924. 4to., cloth backed pictorial boards, as new in original pictorial box (flaps repaired), illustrations in color by John Rae, beautiful copy.   Aleph-Bet Books, Inc.   104 - 575   2013 $300

Gordon, Elizabeth *Tale of Johnny Mouse.* Chicago: Volland, 1920. Later printing, 8vo., pictorial boards, near fine in pictorial box (flaps repaired), beautifully illustrated by Maginel Wright Enright, very scarce.   Aleph-Bet Books, Inc.   104 - 572   2013 $300

Gordon, Elizabeth *The Turned Into's.* Chicago: Volland, 1920. First edition, no additional printings, 8vo., pictorial boards, fine in original box (with light soil and some repair on flaps), illustrations by Janet Laura Scott with pictorial endpapers, plus many full page and in text bold and beautiful color illustrations, Volland ad laid in, nice, scarce.   Aleph-Bet Books, Inc.   104 - 578   2013 $350

Gordon, Elizabeth *Two Teddy Bears in Toyland.* New York: Dodd, Mead, Sept., 1907. First edition, oblong 4to., cloth backed pictorial boards, light cover soil and some edge and tip wear, very good+, printed on coated paper, photo illustrated pictures, rare, nice copy.   Aleph-Bet Books, Inc.   105 - 73   2013 $1500

Gordon, Elizabeth *What We Saw at Madame World's Fair.* San Francisco: Samuel Levinson, 1915. First edition, pink cloth, very good, 4to., drawings by Bertha Corbett and tipped in color photos, 86 pages.   Barnaby Rudge Booksellers   Children 2013 - 021379   2013 $65

Gordon, Elizabeth *Wild Flower Children...* Chicago: Volland, 1918. no additional printings, 4to., green pictorial boards, slight tip wear, else near fine in original box (flaps repaired), illustrations by Janet Laura Scott with pictorial endpapers plus color illustrations, excellent copy, very scarce.   Aleph-Bet Books, Inc.   105 - 579   2013 $500

Gordon, Ian *The Burden of Guilt.* New York: Simon and Schuster, 1951. First edition, limerick written in ink and signed by author, fine in dust jacket.   Mordida Books   81 - 209   2013 $65

Gordon, James *History of the Rebellion in Ireland in the Year 1798...* London: printed by J. D. Dewick, Aldersgate Street for T. Hurst, 1803. Second edition, 8vo., titlepage little dusted with splash at foot, lower blank corners of B1, I1 & Cc2 torn, contemporary mottled calf, gilt spine, red morocco label, hinges slightly cracked, corners bumped, spine little rubbed, label of W. Andrews, Jun. Bookseller 91 Redcliffe Street, Bristol.   Jarndyce Antiquarian Booksellers   CCIV - 147   2013   £280

Gordon, James *History of Ireland from the Earliest times to the Union.* London: 1806. Volume 2 (of 2), 8vo., contemporary half calf (worn), binding tight, text good.   C. P. Hyland   261 - 451   2013   £30

Gordon, M. A. *Early History of North West England Volume I (all published).* Kentmere: Henry Marshall, 1963. First edition, original cloth, gilt, dust jacket little worn, pages 193, illustrations.   R. F. G. Hollett & Son   Lake District and Cumbria - 181   2013   £30

Gordon, Rex *The Paw of God.* London: Anthony Gibbs Library 33 Limited, 1967. First British and first hardcover edition, octavo, boards.   L. W. Currey, Inc.   Fall Sampler Sept. 2013 - 146413   2013 $250

Gordon, Seton *Amid Snowy Wastes.* London: Cassell and Co., 1922. First edition, original cloth, gilt, neatly recased and cloth re-laid, numerous illustrations and 2 maps.   R. F. G. Hollett & Son   Polar Exploration - 25   2013   £95

Gordon, W. J. *Perseus The Gorgon Slayer.* London: Sampson Low, n.d., Large 8vo., original cloth backed decorated colored boards, little marked and used, edges slightly bumped, 16 stiff leaves, illustrations and decorations in colors, neatly recased.   R. F. G. Hollett & Son   Children's Books - 235   2013   £65

Gore-Booth, Eva *The Perilous Light.* London: Erskine MacDonald, 1915. First edition, 8vo., original blue yapp wrappers, lightly faded on spine, otherwise excellent.   Maggs Bros. Ltd.   1442 - 83   2013   £100

Gore, J. Howard *A Bibliography of Geodesy.* Washington: GPO, 1889. Dark brown cloth, gilt stamped cover and spine titles, edges worn, very good, rare.   Jeff Weber Rare Books   171 - 141   2013 $75

Gorer, Geoffrey *The Revolutionary Ideas of the Marquis de Sade.* London: Wishart and Co., 1934. First edition, 8vo., original cream cloth worn at extremities and little soiled, but very good, inscribed by author for Frances, tipped in ALS from author to photographer Douglas Glass.   Maggs Bros. Ltd.   1460 - 354   2013   £75

Gorey, Edward *The Blue Aspic.* New York: Meredith Press, 1968. Stated first edition, Oblong 8vo., pictorial boards, fine in very good+ dust jacket, small old mend on verso, full page drawings by Gorey. Aleph-Bet Books, Inc. 104 - 245   2013 $250

Gorey, Edward *The Haunted Tea Cosy.* New York: Harcourt Brace & Co., 1997. First edition (abcde code), 7 1/2 inch square, pictorial boards, fine in fine dust jacket, full page color illustrations, this copy signed by Gorey with label mounted on half title. Aleph-Bet Books, Inc. 105 - 282   2013 $200

Gorey, Edward *The Haunted Tea Cosy.* New York: Harcourt Brace & Co., 1997. First edition, first printing, abcde code, full page color illustrations, 7 12 inch square, pictorial boards, as new in like dust jacket, signed and dated by Gorey. Aleph-Bet Books, Inc. 104 - 244   2013 $225

Gorey, Edward *Q. R. V.* Boston: Anne & David Bromer, 1989. Limited to 400 numbered copies signed by Gorey, 3.2 x 3.8 cm., decorated paper covered boards, paper cover label, 29 Gorey illustrations in black and white, bound by Barbara Blumenthal, from the collection of Donn W. Sanford. Oak Knoll Books   303 - 69   2013 $725

Gorey, Edward *The Utter Zoo.* New York: Hawthorn, 1967. Third printing of reprint edition, 16mo., minimal cover edge wear, fine hardback. By the Book, L. C.   36 - 31   2013 $160

Gorey, Edward *Vinegar Works.* New York: Simon & Schuster, 1963. Stated first printings, 3 books, pictorial boards housed in pictorial slipcase, 7 1/4 x 7 inches, edges of slipcase rubbed, else very good, books very good, worn on spine,. Aleph-Bet Books, Inc. 105 - 283   2013 $300

Goring, C. R. *Micrographia: Containing Practical Essays on Reflecting, Solar, Oxy Hydrogen Gas Microscopies, Micrometers; Eye-pieces &c.* Whittaker and Co., 1837. First edition, folding engraved frontispiece, 2 engraved plates and one full page illustration, 8vo., original boards, surface cracks at joints, contemporary signature of Michael Carmichael at head of title and his arms stencilled inside front cover, bookplate of D. J. Schuitema Meier, very good. Blackwell's Rare Books   Sciences - 52   2013   £400

Gorki, Maxim *Reminiscences of Leonid Andreyev.* London: William Heinemann, 1922. First edition in English, 8vo., original black cloth, excellent copy, slightly foxed, cover rubbed and worn at head and tail of spine, inscribed by author for Ida. Maggs Bros. Ltd.   1460 - 355   2013   £500

Gorman, R. H. *All Kings of Kids.* Chicago: Thompson & Thomas, 1907. Small 4to., stiff pictorial wrappers, light normal wear, very good, two of the pages are cut into slots that the reader can combine, move and change to form over 120 pictures, interchanging faces and costumes of children. Aleph-Bet Books, Inc.   104 - 367   2013 $225

Gorter, Johannes De *Cirugia Expurgada.* Madrid: Pedro Marin, 1780. First Spanish edition, 8vo., errata, headpieces, decorative initials, tailpieces, indexes, materia medica, 3 engraved folding plates, top and fore edges of prelims and titlepage waterstained, first 100 pages of text waterstained (gradually lessens), occasional light foxing, modern full Spanish tree calf, raised bands, maroon leather spine label, gilt spine, all edges red, new endleaves, ms. notation on title, ownership mark, very good, bookplate of Jerry F. Donin.   Jeff Weber Rare Books   172 - 108   2013 $900

Gorter, Johannes De *Medicina Dogmatica tres Morbos Particularies Delirium, Vertignem et Tussim....* Harderovici: Apud Gulielmum Brikine, 1741. Title, small 4to, half vellum, marbled patterned boards, very good, clean copy internally, signed by author.   James Tait Goodrich   S74 - 128   2013 $495

Gortner, Willis A. *Ancient Rock Carvings of the Central Sierra. The North Fork Indian Petroglyphs.* Woodside: Portola Press, 1984. First edition, 4to., profusely illustrated with reproductions, some photos, site map, orange wrappers printed in black, spine lightly faded, else very fine. Argonaut Book Shop   Summer 2013 - 130   2013 $90

Gosse, Edmund 1849-1928 *Ibsen. Literary Lives Series.* London: Hodder and Stoughton, 1907. First edition, 8vo., original blindstamped red cloth, inscribed by author for Henry James, very good, spine faded, marked and in one place pierced, cloth in general little soiled. Maggs Bros. Ltd.   1460 - 356   2013   £600

Gosse, P. H. *Natural History - Birds.* SPCK, 1849. First edition, small 8vo., original blindstamped cloth, gilt, spine mellowed, woodcuts.   R. F. G. Hollett & Son   Children's Books - 236   2013   £85

Gotch, Phyllis *Romance of a Boo-Bird Chick.* London: R. Brimley Johnson, 1903. 8vo., pictorial boards, 60 pages, spine ends worn, edges of boards discolored, else very good printed on one side of paper, each page with bold full color plate (15 in all). Aleph-Bet Books, Inc.   105 - 285   2013 $200

Gottlieb, Gerald *Early Children's Books and their Illustration.* Boston: David Godine, 1975. First edition, folio, 263 pages, color and black and white illustrations, red cloth.   Barnaby Rudge Booksellers   Children 2013 - 021389   2013 $50

Gottling, Johann Friedrich August *Almanach, Oder Taschen-Buch fur Scheiderkunstler und Apothekar auf das Jahr 1785-1786. (bound with) Vollstandiges Register uber den Almanach oder Taschen Buch fur Scheidekunstler und Apotheke der Jahre 1780-(85).* Weimar: Hofmann, 1785-1786. First edition, 2 volumes, engraved vignette on titlepages, one folding engraved plate and large folding table at end table outreaching ordinary pages and consequently bit ragged at extreme edge; pages xvi, 208; (xxxii), 191, (1), small 8vo.; second title ff. 40, some black chemical staining obscuring text on few leaves, bound together in slightly later English half calf, red morocco lettering piece (in English), rather rubbed and bit warped, joints splitting, sound, rare. Blackwell's Rare Books   Sciences - 53   2013   £875

Goudy, Frederic W. *The Story of the Village Type by Its Designer.* New York: Press of the Woolly Whale, 1933. First edition, one of 450 copies on Arnold unbleached hand made paper for members of the AIGA, of an edition of 650, pencil ownership signature of John Clyde Oswald, fine in chipped glassine jacket and soiled slipcase, 8vo., original cloth backed boards, paper labels, uncut.   Howard S. Mott Inc.   262 - 65   2013 $100

Gouge, Thomas *Gwyddorion y grefydd Gristianogol, Wedi eu Hegluro i Ddealltwriaeth y Gwaelaf, Ai Cymmwy o tuag at Hyffordd Buchedd Dda.* Tho. Dawks, 1679. First edition, dampstained in lower margins with some consequent fraying to lower edge, loss of few letters, others trimmed, original sheep, double gilt fillets on sides, corners worn, rebacked (little crudely), contrasting lettering pieces (title mis-transcribed and date wrong), new endpapers, succession of early Welsh signatures, girls and boys, one dated 1711, scattered through the book, sound, rare.   Blackwell's Rare Books   B174 - 156   2013   £1200

Gough, J. W. *John Locke's Political Philosophy: Eight Studies.* Oxford: Clarendon Press, 1950. First edition, small label from London bookseller Blackwell's near fine, without dust jacket, Graham Greene's ownership signature, which has been lightly struck through with another name beneath it.   Between the Covers Rare Books, Inc.   Philosophy - 328306   2013 $350

Goulart, Ron *Groucho Marx, Private Eye.* New York: St. Martin's Press, 1999. First edition, near fine in like dust jacket, signed with charming full page color drawing by Goulart and dated in year of publication.   Jeff Hirsch Books Fall 2013 - 129503   2013 $50

Gould, G. M. *Anomalies and Curiosities of Medicine Being an Encyclopedic Collection of Rare and Extraordinary Cases...* Philadelphia: W. B. Saunders, 1897. Likely second issue as copyright is listed at 1896, 968 pages, numerous text illustrations and plates, ex-library in later library buckram, title dusty and with tape marks, overall good. James Tait Goodrich   75 - 106   2013 $175

Gould, Heywood *Cocktail.* New York: St. Martins, 1984. First edition, fine in fine black dust jacket with touch of rubbing and tiny tear on rear panel, exceptionally uncommon. Between the Covers Rare Books, Inc.   Cocktails, Etc. - 71197   2013 $350

Gould, Nat *A Great Surprise.* London: John Long, 1922. First edition, endpapers little foxed, green spine slightly faded, still about fine in attractive, very good or better dust jacket with modest stain at crown, scarce in jacket. Between the Covers Rare Books, Inc.   Horses, Horsemanship, Horse Racing, Etc. - 76729   2013 $275

Goulden, Shirley *Tales from Japan.* London: W. H. Allen, 1961. Folio, original pictorial boards, rather worn and soiled, neatly rebacked, color illustrations by Benvenuti.   R. F. G. Hollett & Son   Children's Books - 237   2013   £65

Gove, Mary Sargeant Nichols *Mary Lyndon or Revelations of a Life.* New York: Stringer and Townsend, 1855. First edition, 8vo., recased and partially rebacked with spine laid down, very good, tight, clean copy, scarce. Second Life Books Inc.   183 - 47   2013 $650

Gowers, William Richard *The Diagnosis of Diseases of the Spinal Cord.* London: 1881. Second edition, viii, 486 pages, illustrations, original binding.   James Tait Goodrich   S74 - 132 2013 $395

Gowers, William Richard *The Diagnosis of Diseases of the Brain and Spinal Cord.* New York: William Wood, 1885. First American edition, original red cloth, text illustrations.   James Tait Goodrich   S74 - 133   2013 $395

Gowers, William Richard *Lectures on the Diagnosis of Diseases of the Brain Delivered at the University College Hospital.* London: J. and A. Churchill, 1885. First edition, original green cloth, nice tight copy with minimal cloth wear. James Tait Goodrich   S74 - 129   2013 $850

Gowers, William Richard *Lectures on the Diagnosis of Diseases of the Brain Delivered at the University College Hospital.* Philadelphia: B. Blakiston, 1887. Second American edition, 8vo., original blindstamped olive green cloth gilt spine, rubbed, ex-library bookplate and rubber stamp, very good.   Jeff Weber Rare Books   172 - 109 2013 $365

Gowers, William Richard *A Manual on Diseases of the Nervous System.* London: J. and A. Churchill, 1886-1888. First edition, original green cloth, cloth wear, very good. James Tait Goodrich   S74 - 130   2013 $1500

Gowers, William Richard *A Manual of Diseases of the Nervous System.* London: J. and A. Churchill, 1886-1888. First edition, original green cloth with wear, internally very good.   James Tait Goodrich   75 - 108   2013 $1500

Goyder, David G. *My Battle for Life The Autobiography of a Phrenologist.* London: Simpkin Marshall, 1857. First edition, large 12mo., 604 pages, bound in publisher's original blue cloth, very good.   Barnaby Rudge Booksellers   Biography 2013 - 020571   2013 $150

Graber, G. *Zurich and Environs.* Zurich: Official General Inquiry Office, 1917. Small 8vo., pages 80, illustrations by C. Conradin, large folded map, printed wrappers, from the library of reformer Florence Kelley (1859-1932) with her light signature and holograph notes, some staining, good.   Second Life Books Inc.   182 - 137   2013 $75

Grabham, Michael   *The Garden Interests of Madeira.* London: Wm. Clowes, 1926. First edition, 8vo., 100 pages, illustrations, original green cloth, small crease mark on upper cover.   J. & S. L. Bonham Antiquarian Booksellers   Europe - 8960   2013   £35

Grabhorn, Jane Bissell   *California Gold Rush Miscellany.* San Francisco: Grabhorn Press, 1934. First edition, one of 550 copies, quarto, colored frontispiece, 16 plates and facsimiles, 2 folding maps, original gilt decorated burgundy boards, red cloth spine, leather label on spine, very fine.   Argonaut Book Shop   Summer 2013 - 131   2013 $125

Grace, William   *Trial of William Grace, Capt. of Queen's Co. Regt. of Militia for Breach of Promise of Marriage to Mary Anne McCarthy of Killarney... at Tralee Assizes March 27th 1816.* Cork: J. O'Conor, 28 pages, modern wrappers, titlepage dusty, else good.   C. P. Hyland 261 - 455   2013   £125

Gracq, Julien   *Un Balcon en Foret.* Toulon: Bibliophile de Provence Publisher, First Singier edition, number 64 (LXIV) of 160 copies on pure fil de Lana paper, issued for members of the club (total edition was 455), 21 original lithographs in colors, + 40 original small woodcuts by Gustave Singier, Box of the editor and 2 supplements, size of lithographs about 35 x 25cm., 187 pages, loose as issued in publisher's wrappers, cloth chemise and slipcase, folder with two additional brochure, overall excellent condition, box sized 14.5 x 10.25 inches.   Gemini Fine Books & Arts., Ltd.   Art Reference & Illustrated Books - 2013 $1250

Graefe, Friedrich Wilhelm Ernst Albrecht Von   *Symptomenlehre der Augnmuskellahmungen.* Berlin: Hermann Peters, 1867. First edition, 8vo., contemporary quarter black morocco, morocco corners, brown boards, gilt spine, gilt filigree covers, lightly rubbed, bookplate and rubber stamps of Bernard Samuels Library, NY Eye and Ear Infirmary, bookplate of Haskell Norman, another ownership signature, fine.   Jeff Weber Rare Books   172 - 110   2013 $1333

Graefe, Friedrich Wilhelm Ernst Albrect Von   *Symptomenlehre der Augenmuskellabmungen.* Berlin: Hermann Peters, 1867. First edition, 8vo., modern quarter dark red morocco, marbled boards, black leather spine label, gilt spine, new endleaves, bookplate of Jerry Donin, fine.   Jeff Weber Rare Books   172 - 112   2013 $800

Graff, John Franklin   *"Graybeards" Colorado; or Notes on the Centennial State.* Philadelphia: 1882. 90 pages, printed boards, boards and extremities rubbed, else clean and very good.   Dumont Maps & Books of the West   124 - 6   2013 $95

Graffman, Gary   *I Really Should Be Practicing: Reflections on the Pleasures and Perils of Playing the Piano in Public.* Garden City: Doubleday, 1981. 8vo., quarter gilt stamped navy blue cloth over beige paper backed boards, dust jacket, jacket spine ends chipped, signed and inscribed from author to Todds in ink, very good.   Jeff Weber Rare Books   171 - 144   2013 $70

Grafton, Anthony   *Commerce with the Classics: Ancient Books & Renaissance Readers.*   Ann Arbor: University of Michigan Press, 2000. 8vo., plates, gilt stamped black cloth, dust jacket, fine, Burndy bookplate.   Jeff Weber Rare Books   171 - 145   2013 $50

Grafton, C. W.   *The Rat Began to Gnaw the Rope.* New York: Farrar & Rinehart, 1943. First edition, fine in near fine dust jacket with short crease tears at spine ends, nicks at corners and along edges and tears along flap-folds.   Mordida Books   81 - 210   2013 $350

Grafton, Sue   *"A" is for Alibi.* New York: Holt Rinehart Winston, 1982. First edition, signed by author, very fine in dust jacket.   Mordida Books   81 - 211   2013 $2500

Grafton, Sue   *"A" is for Alibi.* London: Macmillan, 1986. First English edition, very fine in dust jacket.   Mordida Books   81 - 212   2013 $500

Grafton, Sue   *"B" is for Burglar.* New York: Holt Rinehart Winston, 1985. First edition, inscribed by author, library labels removed from endpapers and library stamp on copyright page where small label has been removed, otherwise fine in dust jacket.   Mordida Books   81 - 213   2013 $150

Grafton, Sue   *"B" is for Burglar.* London: Macmillan, 1986. First English edition, signed by author, pages slightly darkened, otherwise fine in dust jacket.   Mordida Books   81 - 214   2013 $300

Grafton, Sue   *"C" is for Corpse.* New York: Holt, 1986. First edition, signed by author, very fine in dust jacket.   Mordida Books   81 - 215   2013 $750

Grafton, Sue *"C" is for Corpse.* New York: Holt Rinehart Winston, 1986. First edition, uncorrected proof, signed by author, fine in wrappers. Mordida Books 81 - 215 2013 $150

Grafton, Sue *"D" is for Deadbeat.* New York: Holt, 1987. First edition, signed by author, very fine in dust jacket. Mordida Books 81 - 217 2013 $350

Grafton, Sue *"F" is for Fugitive.* New York: Holt, 1989. First edition, inscribed by author, fine in dust jacket. Mordida Books 81 - 218 2013 $75

Grafton, Sue *Keziah Dane.* New York: Macmillan, 1967. Stated first edition, 220 pages, 8vo., cloth, soil on endpaper, else fine in dust jacket that is wrinkled on bottom of front panel. Aleph-Bet Books, Inc. 104 - 246 2013 $450

Graham, Caroline *The Envy of the Stranger.* London: Century, 1984. First edition, fine in price clipped dust jacket. Mordida Books 81 - 220 2013 $185

Graham, Caroline *Fire Dance.* London: Severn House, 1995. first hardcover edition, very fine in dust jacket. Mordida Books 81 - 222 2013 $75

Graham, Caroline *Murder at Maddingly Grange.* London: Mysterious Press, 1990. First edition, fine in dust jacket. Mordida Books 81 - 221 2013 $90

Graham, Duff *How Peter Rabbit Went to Sea.* Philadelphia: Henry Altemus, 1917. First edition, frontispiece and 28 color illustrations, orange cloth backed brown boards, color illustration pasted front cover, yellow titling and decorated front cover, red titling backstrip, plain endpapers, 5 3/28 x 4 inches, some fading/light soiling to backstrip, rear endpapers repaired at hinge, very good. Ian Hodgkins & Co. Ltd. 134 - 5 2013 £48

Graham, Duff *Peter Rabbit at the Farm.* Philadelphia: Henry Altemus, 1917. First edition, 30 color illustrations, yellow cloth backed blue boards, color illustration pasted front cover, rear cover slightly marked, very good, scarce variant. Ian Hodgkins & Co. Ltd. 134 - 14 2013 £60

Graham, Duff *Peter Rabbit's Christmas.* Philadelphia: Henry Altemus, 1917. First edition, 30 color illustrations, red cloth backed purple boards, color illustration pasted front cover, some discoloration to edges covers and corner tips worn, nameplate pastedown, endpapers cracked at hinges, some soiling few marks to contents, but very good. Ian Hodgkins & Co. Ltd. 134 - 20 2013 £42

Graham, Edson *Souvenir Views Land of Evangline Nova Scotia, Canada.* Wolfville: Pub. by Edson Graham, Photographer, 1930. 15.9 x 24m., card covers bound with silk string and gilt title to front cover, 12 sepia photos with tissue guards and tiles in lower margin, covers worn with few small stains, sepia photos very good. Schooner Books Ltd. 101 - 93 2013 $75

Graham, Frank *Old Inns and Taverns of Lakeland. (Second Series).* Newcastle: V. Graham, 1963. First edition, original wrappers, 47 pages, illustrations, photos. R. F. G. Hollett & Son Lake District and Cumbria - 183 2013 £20

Graham, Frank *Picturesque Lakeland One Hundred Years Ago.* Newcastle upon Tyne: Frank Graham, 1969. 4to., original cloth, gilt, rubbed, 80 pages, illustrations. R. F. G. Hollett & Son Lake District and Cumbria - 184 2013 £20

Graham, Henry *The New Coinage.* Civil Service Printing & Publishing Co., 1878. 152 pages, original black cloth gilt, rather bubbled and stained by damp, endpapers rather cockled and stained, presentation with author's compliments for Hy. W. Schneider Dec. 26th 1878. R. F. G. Hollett & Son Lake District and Cumbria - 185 2013 £75

Graham, Stephen *New York Nights.* New York: George H. Doran Co., 1927. First edition, illustrations by Kurt Wiese, little soiling to boards, else near fine in rubbed, good dust jacket with some modest chips mostly on front panel. Between the Covers Rare Books, Inc. New York City - 95819 2013 $275

Graham, T. H. B. *The Barony of Gilsland.* Kendal: Titus Wilson, 1934. Original brown cloth, gilt. R. F. G. Hollett & Son Lake District and Cumbria - 186 2013 £120

Grahame, Kenneth 1859-1932 *Dream Days.* London: John Lane Bodley Head, n.d., First edition thus, Original pictorial green cloth, extremities rubbed, 9 photogravures by Maxfield Parrish, joints cracked. R. F. G. Hollett & Son Children's Books - 238 2013 £35

Grahame, Kenneth 1859-1932 *The Dream Days.* London: John Lane Bodley Head, 1930. Limited to 275 copies signed by author and artist, large paper edition, tall 8vo., vellum backed marbled boards, slight tip rubbing, else near fine, printed on special rag paper and illustrations by E. H. Shepard with beautiful black and whites. Aleph-Bet Books, Inc. 104 - 248 2013 $800

Grahame, Kenneth 1859-1932 *The Golden Age.* London and New York: John Lane/Bodley Head, 1900. First edition, 8vo., deep red cloth with elaborate gilt design, top edge gilt, near fine, with illustrations by Maxfield Parrish, with 19 beautiful black and white plates plus pictorial tailpieces. Aleph-Bet Books, Inc. 105 - 443 2013 $400

Grahame, Kenneth 1859-1932 *The Golden Age.* London: John Lane, Bodley Head, 1915. 4to., original pictorial cloth, 19 color plates.   R. F. G. Hollett & Son   Children's Books - 185   2013   £75

Grahame, Kenneth 1859-1932 *The Reluctant Dragon.* New York: Holt Rinehart Winston, 1983. Limited to 350 copies signed by Hauge, 4to., cloth, new in slipcase with original mailer, full and partial page color illustrations by Michael Hague.   Aleph-Bet Books, Inc.   105 - 303   2013 $425

Grahame, Kenneth 1859-1932 *The Wind in the Willows.* London: Methuen, 1922. Twelfth edition, original blind-stamped cloth, gilt extra, corners little bumped and extremities slightly frayed, pages 302, uncut, frontispiece by Graham Robertson, joints just cracking.   R. F. G. Hollett & Son   Children's Books - 249   2013   £75

Grahame, Kenneth 1859-1932 *The Wind in the Willows.* London: Methuen, 1923. Fifteenth century, original blind-stamped cloth gilt extra, extremities trifle rubbed, uncut, frontispiece, light spotting to flyleaves, nice.   R. F. G. Hollett & Son   Children's Books - 241   2013   £75

Grahame, Kenneth 1859-1932 *The Wind in the Willows.* New York: Scribner, 1925. (1913), 8vo., blue pictorial cloth, 351 pages, fine in original box with color plate on cover, illustrations by Nancy Barnhart with great pictorial endpapers and 12 color plates, rare in box.   Aleph-Bet Books, Inc.   104 - 247   2013 $375

Grahame, Kenneth 1859-1932 *The Wind in the Willows.* London: 1931. First edition illustrated by E. H. Shepard, limited to 200 numbered copies on handmade paper, signed by author and artist, small quarto, text illustrations, folding map at end, original quarter green buckram over gray boards, printed paper label on spine, all edges uncut, additional printed paper label bound in at end, minimal foxing to spine label, fine, original cream colored printed dust jacket, housed in cloth clamshell case.   Heritage Book Shop 50th Anniversary Catalogue - 44   2013 $12,500

Grahame, Kenneth 1859-1932 *The Wind in the Willows.* New York: Limited Editions Club printed at the Walpole Printing Office Under the Direction of Bruce Rogers, 1940. First Rackham edition, 1103.2020 copies signed by Rogers, 16 color printed plates by Arthur Rackham, each pasted to white card within a grey frame and with grey printed caption, titlepage printed in black and brown and with a Rackham vignette printed in grey, chapter numerals also printed in brown, 4to., original quarter russet morocco, backstrip gilt lettered, marbled light brown boards, top edge, others rough trimmed, later tan cloth slipcase.   Blackwell's Rare Books B174 - 283   2013   £1200

Grahame, Kenneth 1859-1932 *Wind in the Willows.* New York: Heritage Press, 1940. First trade edition of Rackham's last work, 4to., red cloth spine with blue cloth covers, 190 pages, spine faded, else fine in lightly soiled dust jacket and pictorial slipcase (somewhat soiled with light wear), 12 color plates and 15 pen and ink drawings by Arthur Rackham.   Aleph-Bet Books, Inc.   104 - 481   2013 $750

Grahame, Kenneth 1859-1932 *The Wind in the Willows.* London: Folio Society, 1995. Large 8vo., original pictorial watered silk gilt, slipcase, pages 206, illustrations in color by James Lynch.   R. F. G. Hollett & Son   Children's Books - 239   2013   £35

Grainger, James *The Sugar-Cane: a Poem.* London: printed and sold by the Booksellers, 1766. Second edition, half title, engraved frontispiece, 8vo., slight foxing to some pages, front endpaper little loose, contemporary mottled calf, gilt, borders and spine, hinges cracked, spine rubbed and chipped, lacking label, armorial bookplate of William Rhodes James.   Jarndyce Antiquarian Booksellers   CCIV - 148   2013   £280

Granados Y Galvez, Joseph Joaquin *Tardes Americanas: Gobierno Gentil y Catalico....* Mexico: en la nueva Imprenta Matritense de D. Felipe de Zuniga y Ontiveros, 1778. First edition, small quarto, (72), 540 pages, engraved arms at head of dedication and three engraved plates, contemporary vellum with leather loop and toggle fastening, spine lettered in manuscript, front hinge cracked but cords still strong, some light foxing and occasional thumb soiling, worm track on leaves, affecting few words, two of the plates shaved little close at fore edge, very good, rare.   Heritage Book Shop 50th Anniversary Catalogue - 39   2013 $4500

Grande, George K. *Canadians on Radar Royal Canadian Air Force 140-1945.* Ottawa: Canadian Radar History Project, n.d., 2000. Quarto, blue buckram with gilt insignia and titles, photo illustrations on endpapers, sections individually paginated, photo illustrations.   Schooner Books Ltd. 105 - 128   2013 $150

Grandville, J. J. *Les Metamorphoses Du Jour...* Paris: Garnier Freres, 1869. Nouvele edition, 4to., contemporary period quarter leather, pebbled cloth, slight wear to top of spine, some rubbing, all edges gilt, very good++, with none of the extensive foxing that often occurs with this book, beautiful copy.   Aleph-Bet Books, Inc.   105 - 288   2013 $2500

Grange & District Red Book. Sixty-fifth year of issue. Grange-over-Sands: J. Wadsworth, 1969. Original red wrappers, pages 136.   R. F. G. Hollett & Son   Lake District and Cumbria - 187   2013   £25

Gransden, Antonia *Historical Writing in England.* London: Routledge & Kegan Paul, 1974. 1982. First editions, 8vo., blue cloth, top edges blue, dust jackets, that of volume I price clipped with fading to spine as usual, very good, scarce as a set.   Unsworths Antiquarian Booksellers 28 - 168   2013   £175

Grant, Anne *Memoirs of an American Lady: with Sketches of Manners and Scenery in America...* London: Longman et al, 1808. First edition, 12mo., 2 volumes, 19th century half calf, lacks half inch triangle of leather near bottom of spine of volume one, hole (half inch triangle) in blank portion of inner margin of titlepage of volume 1), very nice, clean copy, contemporary bookplate of Anne Isabella Kevill, repair to leather on spine of volume two, little rubbed, very good. Second Life Books Inc.   183 - 150A   2013 $700

Grant, Anne *Poems on Various Subjects.* Edinburgh: printed for the author by J. Moir, 1803. First edition, 8vo., pages 447, contemporary leather, rebacked with library name on spine and library bookplate on endpaper, very good.   Second Life Books Inc.   183 - 150   2013 $350

Grant, Edward *Mathematics and Its Applications to Science and Natural Philosophy in the Middle Ages...* Cambridge et al: Cambridge University Press, 1987. 8vo., xii, 337 pages, navy cloth, gilt stamped cover and spine titles, signature of David C. Lindberg (contributing author's copy), fine.   Jeff Weber Rare Books   169 - 70   2013 $125

Grant, Edward *A Source Book in Medieval Science.* Cambridge: Harvard University Press, 1974. 8vo., xvii, 864 pages, black cloth, gilt stamped spine title, extremities rubbed, inscribed by author, very good.   Jeff Weber Rare Books   169 - 169   2013 $175

Grant, Edward *Studies in Medieval Science and Natural Philosophy.* London: Variorum Reprints, 1981. 8vo., iv, 378 pages, blue cloth, gilt stamped cover and spine titles, presentation copy from author to David Lindberg, fine.   Jeff Weber Rare Books   169 - 170   2013 $100

Grant, Gordon *Ship Ahoy: a Construction Book for Fireside Sailors.* Garden City: Doubleday Doran, 1934. Stated first edition, Oblong large folio, spiral backed thick cardboard covers, some edge rubbing and slight soil, else very good+ and completely unused, full color illustrations, rare.   Aleph-Bet Books, Inc.   105 - 432   2013 $850

Grant, James *Jack Chaloner; or the Fighting Forty-Third.* London: George Routledge & Sons, 1883. First edition, half title, inserted 4 page W.H. Smith ads tipped in between following endpapers, 'yellowback', original yellow pictorial boards, little rubbed, corners worn, contemporary pencil inscription, very good.   Jarndyce Antiquarian Booksellers CCV - 117   2013   £125

Grant, James Edward *The Green Shadow.* New York: Hartney Press, 1935. First edition, fine in lightly worn, near fine and very attractive dust jacket, with few short tears and some rubbing, jacket with tops and bottoms of flaps extended, folded inward and glued (as issued).   Between the Covers Rare Books, Inc.   Mystery & Detective Fiction - 39295   2013 $2000

Grant, Joseph D. *Redwoods and reminiscences.* San Francisco: Save the Redwoods League, 1973. First edition, color frontispiece, photos, brown pictorial cloth, gilt, fine.   Argonaut Book Shop   Recent Acquisitions June 2013 - 123   2013 $60

Grant, Maxwell *Norgil: More Tales of Prestigitection.* New York: Mysterious Press, 1979. First edition, one of 250 numbered copies signed by Gibson and Grant, very fine in dust jacket with slipcase.   Mordida Books   81 - 224   2013 $125

Grant, Maxwell *Norgil the Magician.* New York: Mysterious Press, `977. First edition, one of 250 numbered copies signed by Gibson and Grant, very fine in dust jacket with slipcase.   Mordida Books   81 - 223   2013 $200

Grant, Maxwell *The Shadow and the Voice of Murder from the Private Annals of the Shadow.* Los Angeles: Bantam Publications, 1940. First edition, small octavo, 2 volumes, printed wrappers and pictorial wrappers.   L. W. Currey, Inc. Fall Sampler Sept. 2013 - 146559   2013 $1500

Grant, Robert *Jack Hall: the School Days of an American Boy.* Boston: Jordan Marsh and Co., 1888. First edition, 8vo., green pictorial cloth stamped in black, 394 pages, slightest bit of cover soil, else near fine, full page black and whites by F. G. Attwood, scarce.   Aleph-Bet Books, Inc. 105 - 289   2013 $225

Granville, A. B. *The Spas of Germany.* London: Henry Colburn, 1839. Second edition, 8vo., 5 maps, 13 plates, illustrations, original red blindstamped cloth, head of spine has small tear, corners bumped, internally clean, good.   J. & S. L. Bonham Antiquarian Booksellers   Europe - 9609 2013   £150

Grascombe, Samuel *Considerations upon the Second Canon in the Book entituled Constitutions and Canons Ecclesiastical &c.* London: printed in the year, 1693. 4to., 32 pages, removed, considerable browning.   Joseph J. Felcone Inc.   Books Printed before 1701 - 47   2013 $90

Gratacap, L. P. *The Evacuation of England: the Twist in the Gulf Stream.* New York: Brentanos, 1908. First edition, corners very slightly bumped, still easily fine, very scarce.   Between the Covers Rare Books, Inc.   Sci-Fi, Fantasy & Horror - 54760   2013 $300

Gratacap, L. P. *The New Northland.* New York: Thomas Benton, 1915. First edition, 16 designs by Albert Operti, slight foxing to fore edge, corners slightly rubbed, very small spot on spine, still very near fine, attractive copy. Between the Covers Rare Books, Inc. Sci-Fi, Fantasy & Horror - 54733 2013 $200

Graves, Robert 1895-1985 *Antigua, Penny, Puce.* Deya Majorca: Seizin Press, Constable, 1936. First edition, with misprints as called for, on pages 100, 103 and 293, crown 8vo., original maroon cloth, backstrip lettered in white, bookplate, dust jacket, revised issue with front flap a cancel and price 7/6, a trifle frayed at head of backstrip panel, very good. Blackwell's Rare Books 172 - 188 2013 £350

Graves, Robert 1895-1985 *At the Gate.* London: Privately printed, Bertram Rota, 1974. First edition, one of 536 copies, 500 of which are numbered and signed by poet, fine in fine dust jacket, 8vo., 47 pages. Beasley Books 2013 - 2013 $100

Graves, Robert 1895-1985 *I, Claudius.* London: Arthur Baker, 1934. First edition, very good, black cloth boards with gilt title to spine, light spotting to boards and light wear to edges, previous owner's bookplate and note in pencil, offsetting from article that is no longer present on front endpaper and front flap of jacket, minor foxing to endpapers, foldout family tree at rear of book, blue illustrated dust jacket with white title to spine and front panel, jacket is in 3 pieces with small chips to spine ends, edges and hinges, browning to spine of jacket, nice despite noted wear, 494 pages. The Kelmscott Bookshop 7 - 112 2013 $1200

Graves, Robert 1895-1985 *Impenetrability or the Proper Habit of English.* London: published by Leonard & Virginia Woolf at Hogarth Press, 1926. First edition, small 8vo., original pale blue-green boards lettered in black, inscribed by author for Mary with pencilled ownership inscription of Mary Ellidge, browned at edges as ever, otherwise excellent. Maggs Bros. Ltd. 1460 - 360 2013 £1500

Graves, Robert 1895-1985 *The Isles of Unwisdom.* Cassell, 1950. First English edition, double page map, foolscap 8vo., original black cloth, backstrip gilt lettered, light edge spotting, dust jacket with backstrip panel trifle sunned and with internal sellotape repair at head, very good, inscribed by author for Charles (Morgenstern). Blackwell's Rare Books 172 - 189 2013 £500

Graves, Robert 1895-1985 *John Kemp's Wager; a Ballad Opera.* Oxford: Blackwell, 1925. First edition, 21/100 copies, printed on Kelmscott handmade paper and signed by author, 16mo., original white vellum backed cream boards with overall repeat pattern in green, backstrip gilt lettered, tail corners rubbed, book label of Simon Nowell-Smith, untrimmed and partly unopened, very good. Blackwell's Rare Books B174 - 212 2013 £500

Graves, Robert 1895-1985 *Mock Beggar Hall.* Hogarth Press, 1924. First edition, occasional faing foxing to prelim and final few leaves, 4to., original dark grey boards, imposing overall front cover design by William Nicholson and printed in black, Simon Nowell-Smith, untrimmed, fine. Blackwell's Rare Books B174 - 213 2013 £500

Graves, Robert 1895-1985 *More Poems 1961.* London: Cassell, 1961. First edition, 8vo., original maroon cloth, near fine, dust jacket torn at head and tail of spine, inscribed by author for John Crensman May 26 1961. Maggs Bros. Ltd. 1460 - 364 2013 £150

Graves, Robert 1895-1985 *Over the Brazier.* London: Poetry Bookshop, 1916. Second edition, 8vo., original wrappers worn and slightly nicked, otherwise very good, protected within folding slipcase, author's copy with his armorial bookplate which bears the gift inscription from him to Aubrey Farra, there are substantial manuscript revisions by Graves to two of the poems. Maggs Bros. Ltd. 1460 - 358 2013 £1500

Graves, Robert 1895-1985 *The Owl: a Miscellany No. 1. May 1919.* London: Martin Secker, 1919. First edition, one of 24 special copies signed by man contributors, few signatures pasted in as issued, including Max Beerbohm, Randolph Caldecott, John Galsworthy, Graves Thomas Hardy and others, folio, illustrations, original pictorial wrappers, very good, preserved in half morocco folding box. James S. Jaffe Rare Books Fall 2013 - 2 2013 $1750

Graves, Robert 1895-1985 *Poems 1929.* Seizin Press, 1929. First edition, 76/225 copies, printed on Batchelor handmade paper and signed by author foolscap 8vo., original apple green buckram, faded backstrip gilt lettered, faint band of fading also to head of rear cover, browned free endpapers, booklabel of Simon Nowell-Smith and bookplate of Oliver Brett, First Viscount Esher, very good. Blackwell's Rare Books B174 - 214 2013 £300

Graves, Robert 1895-1985 *Poems and Satires. 1951.* London: Cassell, 1951. First edition, 8vo., original green cloth, dust jacket, signed by author, fine in dust jacket. Maggs Bros. Ltd. 1460 - 363 2013 £150

Graves, Robert 1895-1985 *Poems. 1968-1970.* London: Cassell, 1970. First edition, 8vo., original green cloth, signed by author, near fine in price clipped dust jacket. Maggs Bros. Ltd. 1460 - 365 2013 £150

Graves, Robert 1895-1985 *Sergeant Lamb's America.* New York: Random House, 1940. First edition, large 8vo., original red cloth, dust jacket, excellent copy in dust jacket, torn at head of spine and missing couple of inches or so from lower spine, inscribed by author. Maggs Bros. Ltd. 1460 - 362 2013 £200

Graves, Robert 1895-1985 *Ten Poems More.* Paris: Hours Press, 1930. First edition, 98/200 copies signed by author, small folio original green morocco backed boards, backstrip gilt lettered, illustrated monochrome boards reproducing a photographic montage by Len Lye, booklabel of Simon Nowell-Smith, untrimmed, fine.   Blackwell's Rare Books   B174 - 215   2013   £300

Graves, Robert 1895-1985 *Treasure Box.* London: Chiswick Press, 1919. First edition, 8vo., original blue unprinted wrappers, excellent copy in protective over sized folding box, leather label, lettered in gilt, inscribed by author and Nancy Nicholson for Robert Graves, inherited by his son Alec Waugh who gave it to Cyril Connolly at Christmas 1967.   Maggs Bros. Ltd.   1460 - 359   2013   £1750

Gray, Asa *Darwiniana: Essays and Reviews Pertaining to Darwinism.* New York: D. Appleton, 1876. First edition, original green cloth gilt lettered spine and front cover, gift inscription, small bookstore stamp, mild cover edge wear, spine sunned, gilt dulled, 8vo.   By the Book, L. C.   37 - 35   2013 $500

Gray, Christopher *Fifth Avenue 1911 from Start to Finish in Historic Block-by-Block Photographs.* Mineola: Dover Publications, 1995. First edition, near fine in wrappers.   Between the Covers Rare Books, Inc.   New York City - 286153   2013 $150

Gray, Hilary *Cumbria. Lake District Life.* Pelham Books, 1991. First edition, 184 pages, illustrations, original cloth, gilt, dust jacket.   R. F. G. Hollett & Son   Lake District and Cumbria - 193   2013   £25

Gray, Thomas 1716-1771 *An Elegy Wrote in a Country Church Yard.* London: for R. Dodsley and sold by M. Cooper, 1751. First edition, 4to., 11 pages, full black crushed levant morocco by Zaehnsdorf (very lightly rubbed at extremities), fine with no loss of punched-through types, bookplates.   Joseph J. Felcone Inc.   English and American Literature to 1800 - 16   2013 $15,000

Gray, Thomas 1716-1771 *Odes. (with) An Elegy Writte in a Country Church Yard.* London: printed at Strawberry Hill Press for R. and J. Dodsley, 1757. London: printed for R. Dodsley, 1751. First and fourth edition., 2 works bound together, engraved vignette on title, mild dampstain in upper margins, few spots, 21 pages; titlepage with few small stains, dampstain continuing from previous work, pages 11, 4to., 20th century calf, blind tooled Greek key borders on sides with ornaments in corners, longitudinal red morocco lettering piece on spine, upper cover darkened at upper inner corner, few minor scratches on sides, spine slightly worn, good.   Blackwell's Rare Books   B174 - 52   2013   £1000

Gray, Thomas 1716-1771 *Poems by Mr. Gray.* Glasgow: printed by Robert and Andrew Foulis, 1768. First Glasgow edition, 4to., large uncut copy, some dusting to endpapers and pastedowns, original grey stiff sugar paper wrappers, neatly rebacked.   Jarndyce Antiquarian Booksellers   CCIV - 149   2013   £750

Gray, Thomas 1716-1771 *Poems.* privately printed for Eton College Medici Society, 1946. Presentation leaf, near fine in full vellum, gilt crest on upper board, large 8vo. bookplate.   Ken Spelman Books Ltd.   75 - 178   2013   £30

Gray, Thomas 1716-1771 *The Works...* London: Vernor Hood and Sharp, 1807. Third edition, 2 volumes, frontispiece, text clean, foxing to frontispiece and titlepages, contemporary calf, gilt spines and borders, joints expertly repaired, corners bumped.   Ken Spelman Books Ltd.   75 - 57   2013   £50

Gray, Thomas 1716-1771 *The Works of Thomas Gray.* London: for Harding, Triphook and Lepard, 1825. New edition, 8vo., 2 volumes, frontispiece, full contemporary scarlet calf, decorative gilt spines, red and olive green gilt morocco labels, marbled edges and endpapers, some offsetting from frontispiece, slight foxing.   Ken Spelman Books Ltd.   75 - 88   2013   £120

Gray, William *New Before We Read.* Chicago: Scott Foresman, 1951. Teacher's edition, oblong large 4to., pictorial wrappers, tiny mend in corner of cover and light cover soil, very good+, full color and in line illustrations.   Aleph-Bet Books, Inc.   105 - 178   2013 $325

Gray, William *The New Fun with Dick and Jane.* Chicago: et al Scott, Foresman and Co., n.d., 1956. 8vo., pictorial cloth, 160 pages, some soil, very good, illustrations in color.   Aleph-Bet Books, Inc.   104 - 156   2013 $250

Gray, William *The New Pre-Primers (on cover).* Chicago: et al, Scott Foresman and Co., 1951. Teacher's edition, 8vo., pictorial cloth, school stamp on endpapers and slight rubbing, very good, illustrations in color by Eleanor Campbell, scarce.   Aleph-Bet Books, Inc.   104 - 157   2013 $450

Gray, William *We Look and See.* Chicago: Scott Foresman, 1946-1947. 8vo., cloth backed pictorial wrappers, fine, illustrations in color by Eleanor Campbell.   Aleph-Bet Books, Inc.   105 - 180   2013 $300

Great Britain. Army. Cavalry - 1797 *Instructions and Regulations for the Formations and Movements of the Cavalry.* printed for the War Office, by T. Egerton, 1797. 16 folding engraved plates, title slightly soiled, minor dust staining, 8vo., uncut, dust soiling to deckled edges, original boards, bit worn, soiled, upper hinge cracked, cords holding, spine defective at head and tail, sound.   Blackwell's Rare Books   B174 - 63   2013   £1100

Great Britain. Historical Manuscripts Commission - 1890 *The Manuscripts of S. H. Le Fleming Esq. of Rydal Hall. Twelfth Report.* London: HMSO, 1890. Large paper edition, tall 4to., contemporary full tan calf, gilt, spine with 5 raised bands, elegantly gilt panelled and scarlet lettering piece trifle rubbed and scratched, few early leaves little torn in lower margin, small piece lost from margin, little scattered foxing, otherwise handsome copy.   R. F. G. Hollett & Son   Lake District and Cumbria - 259   2013   £180

Great Britain. Historical Manuscripts Commission - 1890 *The Manuscripts of S. H. Le Fleming, Esq. of Rydal Hall. Twelfth Report, Appendix Part VII.* London: HMSO, 1890. Tall 8vo., modern half levant morocco, original printed wrappers (neatly repaired) bound in.   R. F. G. Hollett & Son   Lake District and Cumbria - 258   2013   £150

Great Britain. Historical Manuscripts Commission - 1890 *The Manuscripts of S. H. Le Fleming Esq. of Rydal Hall. Twelfth Report. Part VII.* London: HMSO, 1890. Tall 8vo., contemporary binder's cloth, gilt, modern slipcase, pages iv, 474, signature of G. O. Trevelyan.   R. F. G. Hollett & Son   Lake District and Cumbria - 260   2013   £120

Great Britain. Historical Manuscripts Commission *The Manuscripts of S. H. Le Fleming Esq. of Rydal Hall. Twelfth Report, Appendix Part VII.* London: HMSO, 1890. Tall 8vo., old binder's cloth, gilt, hinges little rubbed, some staining to final leaves, C. Roy Hudleston's copy.   R. F. G. Hollett & Son   Lake District and Cumbria - 261   2013   £95

Great Britain. Historical Manuscripts Commission *The Manuscripts of the Earl of Westmorland, Captain Stewart, Lord Stafford, Lord Muncaster and Others Fourth Report, Appendix Part IV.* London: HMSO, 1885. Tall 8vo., original printed wrappers, little dusty, pages 660, some wormholes to last few pages.   R. F. G. Hollett & Son   Lake District and Cumbria - 262   2013   £95

Great Britain. Laws, Statutes, Etc. - 1689 *Anno Regni Gulielmi et Mariae, Regi & Reginae Anglae Scotiae, Franciase & Hiberniae, Primo. On the Sixteenth Day of December Anno Dom. 1689.* printed by Charles Bill and Thomas Newcomb, 1689. First edition, royal arms on title and sectional titles, with variants between them, mainly Black Letter, poorly printed either over or under inked in places, some leaves browned, bit spotted, extensive pen trials in fore-margin of one page, various other signs of use, folio, contemporary calf, blind ruled borders on sides with fleuron at each corner, rubbed and with few ink or other stains, split at top of upper joint, front inner hinge split but cords holding, front flyleaf almost detached, various contemporary annotations &c.   Blackwell's Rare Books   172 - 2   2013   £7500

Great Britain. Parliament - 1648 *A Declaration of the Parliament of England, Concerning a Paper Subscribed by the Commissioners of Scotland Dated 24 Feb. 1649/50.* London: for Edward Husband Feb. 27, 1648. Folio, modern cloth.   Joseph J. Felcone Inc.   Books Printed before 1701 - 33   2013 $175

Great Britain. Parliament - 1653 *An Ordinance for Alteration of Several Names and Forms Heretofore Used in Courts, Writs, Grants... in the Courts of Law.* London: by Henry Hills, 1653. Folio, pages 9-15, modern cloth.   Joseph J. Felcone Inc.   Books Printed before 1701 - 34   2013 $175

Great Britain. Parliament - 1657 *An Act for the Attainder of the Rebels in Ireland. At the Parliament Begun at Westminster the 17th Day of September 1656.* London: Henry Hills and John Field, 1657. Folio, (2), 24 pages + final blank G2, modern boards, leather spine label, light dampstain in margins of few leaves.   Joseph J. Felcone Inc.   Books Printed before 1701 - 31   2013 $250

Great Britain. Parliament - 1680 *A True Copy of the Journal Book of the Last Parliament...* London: printed in the year, 1680. 8vo., text complete despite erratic pagination, front and rear blanks wanting, modern utilitarian cloth (covers warped), text very browned and margins very brittle, complete but good at best.   Joseph J. Felcone Inc.   Books Printed before 1701 - 73   2013 $90

Great Britain. Parliament. House of Commons - 1681 *The Debates in the House of Commons Assembled at Oxford the Twenty First of March 1680.* London: for R. Baldwin, 1681. Folio, 20 pages, modern cloth.   Joseph J. Felcone Inc.   Books Printed before 1701 - 32   2013 $250

Great Britain. Parliament. House of Commons - 1681 *The Proceedings of the Honourable House of Commons, Who Met at Oxford, March 21 1680/1.* London: for John Peacock, 1681. Folio, modern cloth, title trifle dusty.   Joseph J. Felcone Inc.   Books Printed before 1701 - 35   2013 $300

Great Britain. Parliament. House of Commons - 1791 *An Abstract of the Evidence Delivered Before a Select Committee of the House of Commons in the Years 1790 and 1791....* London: printed by James Phillips, 1791. First edition, folding plate, with 2 inch tear not affecting image and map, uncut in original drab boards, paper spine, slightly chipped paper label, spine slightly creased with few small nicks, very good in original binding.   Jarndyce Antiquarian Booksellers   CCV - 139   2013   £3200

Great Britain. Parliament. House of Commons - 1828 *Report of the Select Committee on Anatomy, Ordered, by the House of Commons, to be Printed 22 July 1828.* London: 1828. First edition, 160 pages, small folio, recently bound in quarter calf and marbled boards.   James Tait Goodrich   75 - 5   2013 $600

Great Britain. Royal Navy - 1790 *A List of the Flag-Offices of His Majesty's Fleet; with the Dates of their First Commissions, as Admirals, Vice-Admirals, Rear Admirals and Captains.* London: 1790. 8vo., original red morocco, gilt roll tooled borders on sides, flat spine gilt in compartments, lacking lettering piece, little worn and few abrasions, engraved armorial bookplate of Sir Thomas Pasley inside front cover, pencil signature of another Pasley on flyleaf, good. Blackwell's Rare Books B174 - 64 2013 £900

Great Britain. Treaties, etc. - 1795 *Treaty of Defensive Alliance Between His Britannick Majesty and the Empress of Russia. Signed at St. Petersburgh the 18th of Feb. 1795.* London: printed by Edward Johnston, 1795. 16 pages, parallel French and English text, 4to., disbound. Jarndyce Antiquarian Booksellers CCIV - 259 2013 £85

Great Britain. War Office - 1783 *A List of the Officers of the Army (with an alphabetical index).* London: 1783. First edition, 8vo., contemporary calf, hinges cracked, corners rubbed, inscribed "With Mr. Bethell Cox's Compliments". Howard S. Mott Inc. 262 - 7 2013 $950

Greater Cork International Exhibition 1903 *Official Catalogue.* 132 pages, map, silk bound, ex-library Baron Barrymore (one of the Vice Presidents), spine faded, else very good. C. P. Hyland 261 - 221 2013 £95

Thre Greek Portrait. an Anthology of English Verse Translations from the Greek Poets. Nonesuch Press, 1934. 85/425 copies, printed on Pannekoek paper using Fleischman Greek and Lutetia types, creasing to 3 plates by Mariette Lydis as is to be expected, typographical design on titlepage printed in blue, small folio, original cream linen with two small areas of dust soiling, tail corners rubbed, lettering on backstrip and design by Lydis on front cover all blocked in blue, pale blue endpapers, top edge gilt on rough, others untrimmed, original glassine jacket (defective) with card flaps, very good. Blackwell's Rare Books B174 - 364 2013 £135

Green, Elsa Goodwin *Raiders and Rebels in South Africa.* George Newnes, 1898. First edition, original pictorial brown cloth gilt, 14 illustrations, some dampstaining in places, prize inscription, scarce. R. F. G. Hollett & Son Africana - 81 2013 £85

Green, Floride *Some Personal Recollections of Lillie Hitchcock Coit - 5.* San Francisco: Grabhrn Press, 1935. Limited to 4t0 copies, quarto, portraits and facsimile letters, printed in red and black, handset type, orange boards, black cloth spine, orange paper spine label printed in black, very fine, bright. Argonaut Book Shop Summer 2013 - 132 2013 $125

Green, Henry 1905-1973 *Nothing.* London: Hogarth Press, 1950. First edition, 8vo., original red cloth, near fine in dust jacket, chipped at extremities, inscribed by author for Olivia Manning. Maggs Bros. Ltd. 1460 - 367 2013 £4000

Green, Henry 1905-1973 *Pack My Bag.* London: Hogarth Press, 1940. First edition, original red cloth, dust jacket, inscribed by author to book's publisher, John Lehmann, near fine in dust jacket, little browned on spine. Maggs Bros. Ltd. 1460 - 366 2013 £6000

Green, J. F. N. *The Age of the Chief Intrusions of the Lake District.* Geologists' Association, 1917. Original wrappers, pages 30, 2 extending color lithograph maps, presentation copy inscribed Dr. Newell Arbor, with author's compliments. R. F. G. Hollett & Son Lake District and Cumbria - 196 2013 £30

Green, J. F. N. *The Older Palaeozoic Succession of the Duddon Estuary.* privately printed, 1913. 24 pages, 3 maps, inscribed by author, original wrappers, scarce. R. F. G. Hollett & Son Lake District and Cumbria - 199 2013 £30

Green, J. F. N. *The Structure of the Eastern Part of the Lake District.* Geologists' Association, 1915. Reprinted from Proceedings of Geological Association volume XXVI, 4 illustrations, large extding color lithograph of sections, large folding colored , presentation copy from author for Dr. Newell Arbor, lithograh map of the area loosely inserted, original wrappers. R. F. G. Hollett & Son Lake District and Cumbria - 200 2013 £30

Green, Roger Lancelyn *Modem Fairy Stories.* London: J. M. Dent, 1955. 8vo., 270 pages, pictorial cloth, fine in dust jacket, very good+ but lightly worn at spine ends, illustrations by E. H. Shepard with 8 color plates and many black and whites. Aleph-Bet Books, Inc. 104 - 535 2013 $125

Green, Thomas *The Case of Capt. Tho. Green, Commander of the Ship Worcester and His Crew Tried and Condemned for Pyracy & Murther in the High Court of Admiralty Scotland.* London: John Nutt, 1705. First edition, small 4to., recent half calf, spine gilt, small tear to titlepage expertly repaired with no loss of text, cloth slipcase, 30 pages. Maggs Bros. Ltd. 1467 - 51 2013 £3000

Green, William *A Description of a Series of Sixty Small Prints Etched By William Green of Ambleside...* Ambleside: published by William Green, 1814. Oblong large 8vo., modern plain wrappers with lettering piece, a collection of 58 (ex 60) soft-ground etched prints, lacking final two prints, first print rather soiled and edges chipped and repaired, last print damp stained, otherwise in nice clean state, engravings in uncolored and untinted state, without title or text.   R. F. G. Hollett & Son   Lake District and Cumbria - 201   2013   £450

Green, William *The Tourist's New Guide Containing a Description of the Lakes, Mountains, and Scenery, in Cumberland, Westmorland and Lancashire.* Kendal: R. Lough and Co., 1819. First edition, 2 volumes, modern full levant morocco, gilt with raised bands and contrasting spine labels, boards panelled with blind rules, 2 half titles, folding map (neatly repaired) full complement of 36 plates by Green, contemporary mss. index to plates added at end of each volume, few items added to printed index, titlepage of first volume little soiled, otherwise excellent, complete set.   R. F. G. Hollett & Son   Lake District and Cumbria - 204   2013   £1500

Green, William *The Tourist's New Guide, containing a Description of the Lakes, Mountains and Scenery, in Cumberland, Westmorland and Lanchashire...* Kendal: R. Lough and Co., 1819. First edition, 2 volumes, old black half gilt, volume 1 lacks folding map, preface (pages v-xii), index (iii-viii) and errata leaf, volume 2 lacks half title, errata leaf and 2 aquatints (Isle of Windermere and Derwentwater), little spotting in places, small edge tear neatly repaired, good, sound set, rarely found complete, labels of Ravenstonedale Reading Room and Library on each pastedown.   R. F. G. Hollett & Son   Lake District and Cumbria - 202   2013   £850

Green, William *The Tourist's New Guide Containing a Description of the Lakes, Mountains, and Scenery, in Cumberland, Westmorland and Lancashire.* Kendal: R. Lough and Co., etc., 1819. First edition, 2 volumes in 1, old half red morocco gilt, little worn, with second half title, only 4 engraved plates, one section bound out of order, mss. copy of inscription n Green's tombstone in Grasmere churchyard on final blank; from the library of William Grayson of Simonswood (Liverpool).   R. F. G. Hollett & Son   Lake District and Cumbria - 203   2013   £350

Greenaway, Kate 1846-1901   *Almanack for 1884.* London: George Routledge, 1883. First edition, 16mo., stiff wrappers, very good+, illustrations.   Barnaby Rudge Booksellers   Children 2013 - 021632   2013 $75

Greenaway, Kate 1846-1901   *Almanack for 1884.* London: George Routledge & Sons, 1884. First edition, large 12mo., original cream pictorial stiff wrappers, trifle soiled and creased, illustrations in color.   R. F. G. Hollett & Son   Children's Books - 242   2013   £175

Greenaway, Kate 1846-1901   *Almanack for 1887.* London: George Routledge & Sons, 1886. First edition, scarce variant, 24mo., publisher's hand painted cream parchment card, original yellow ribbon tie, original glassine dust jacket, scalloped edges to wrappers, some ink offsetting onto (blank) lower cover, otherwise fine, few copies bound in this manor.   David Brass Rare Books, Inc.   Holiday 2012 Chapter One - DB 02171   2013 $750

Greenaway, Kate 1846-1901   *Almanack for 1886.* London: George Routledge & Sons, 1886. First edition, 12mo., original publisher's special binding of cream imitation pigskin with green printed borders to boards and gilt design by Greenaway on upper board, all edges gilt, color illustrations with orange endpapers, near fine.   R. F. G. Hollett & Son   Children's Books - 243   2013   £350

Greenaway, Kate 1846-1901   *Almanack for 1887.* London: George Routledge & Sons, 1887. First edition, oblong 12mo., original yellow cloth backed glazed pale yellow pictorial boards, trifle soiled, two tiny edge chips, color illustrations, pale blue-green endpapers, corners minimally bruised, but attractive copy.   R. F. G. Hollett & Son   Children's Books - 244   2013   £220

Greenaway, Kate 1846-1901   *Almanack for 1888.* London: George Routledge & Sons, 1888. First edition, 12mo., original blue cloth backed glazed dark yellow pictorial boards, illustrations in color, olivine edges and endpapers, corners minimally bruised, but fine.   R. F. G. Hollett & Son   Children's Books - 245   2013   £350

Greenaway, Kate 1846-1901   *Almanack for 1892.* London: Routledge, 1892. 32mo., blue spine, pictorial boards with gold background, few spots on half title, else near fine, illustrations in color on every page.   Aleph-Bet Books, Inc.   104 - 252   2013 $225

Greenaway, Kate 1846-1901   *Almanack for 1893.* London: Routledge, 1893. 16mo., yellow cloth spine, glazed pictorial boards, all edges green, blue endpapers, near fine, illustrations in color by Kate Greenaway.   Aleph-Bet Books, Inc.   104 - 253   2013 $250

Greenaway, Kate 1846-1901   *Almanack for 1894.* London: Routledge, 1894. 32mo., orange cloth spine, glazed pictorial boards, blue endpapers, slight bit of cover soil, very good+, illustrations in color.   Aleph-Bet Books, Inc.   104 - 254   2013 $225

Greenaway, Kate 1846-1901   *Kate Greenaway's Almanack for 1895. Publisher's Proofs.* London: George Routledge & Sons, 1894. 24mo., publisher's proofs, untrimmed, with leaves of varying size, with Rewards of Merit set of tiny cards (4) by Emma Hardy in the style of Greenaway, publisher's salmon endleaves as wrappers, very fine, housed in quarter morocco clamshell box.   David Brass Rare Books, Inc.   Holiday 2012 Chapter One - DB 02170   2013 $1500

Greenaway, Kate 1846-1901 *Almanack for 1895.* London: George Routledge & Sons, 1895. First edition, 12mo., original special binding of cream imitation pigskin, boards panelled with triple green rules and gilt design by Greenaway on upper board, upper hinge just cracking, all edges gilt, illustrations in color with olivine endpapers, near fine.   R. F. G. Hollett & Son   Children's Books - 246   2013   £450

Greenaway, Kate 1846-1901 *Almanack for 1925.* London: Warne, 1925. Oblong 16mo., cloth backed glazed pictorial boards, slightest of cover soil, near fine, in printed glassine wrapper (chipped), 12 beautiful color illustrations.   Aleph-Bet Books, Inc.   104 - 255   2013 $250

Greenaway, Kate 1846-1901 *Calendar of the Seasons 1881.* Marcus Ward & Co., 1881. First edition, 12mo., 4 page booklet, now separated into 4 leaves, printed in colors on both sides, tiny stab holes from original sewing just visible, two sides little darkened.   R. F. G. Hollett & Son   Children's Books - 247   2013   £175

Greenaway, Kate 1846-1901 *A Day in a Child's Life.* London: George Routledge and Sons, n.d., Square small 4to., original cloth backed glazed and bevelled boards, edges little rubbed, plates 30, illustrations in color, occasional finger mark, but very nice.   R. F. G. Hollett & Son   Children's Books - 248   2013   £180

Greenaway, Kate 1846-1901 *Greenaways Children.* Akron: Saalfield, 1907. 12mo., cloth, few pencil marks and some soil, very good, illustrations in color on every page after Greenaway, scarce.   Aleph-Bet Books, Inc.   105 - 292   2013 $200

Greenaway, Kate 1846-1901 *Kate Greenaway's Birthday Book for Children.* London & New York: George Routledge and Sons, n.d., 1880. First edition, 32mo., 12 color plates, 370 small black and white interleaved illustrations, original beige pictorial cloth, beveled edges, publishers scarce, unprinted blue dust jacket (chipped and in two pieces), bit of soiling to cloth, otherwise internally clean.   David Brass Rare Books, Inc.   Holiday 2012 Chapter One - DB01755   2013 $650

Greenaway, Kate 1846-1901 *Language of Flowers.* London: George Routledge and Sons, 1888. First edition, square large 12mo., publisher's special binding of imitation cream pigskin gilt, boards panelled with triple rule, gilt on upper and in blind on lower board, small nick to spine, lower hinge just cracking in places, all edges gilt, illustrations and printed in color, very nice.   R. F. G. Hollett & Son   Children's Books - 249   2013   £350

Greenaway, Kate 1846-1901 *Marigold Garden.* London: Routledge, n.d., 1885. First edition, 4to., original cloth backed glazed boards, corners rather worn, illustrations in color, short tear to final leaf.   R. F. G. Hollett & Son   Children's Books - 250   2013   £140

Greenaway, Kate 1846-1901 *Marigold Garden.* London: George Routledge and Sons, n.d., 1885. First edition, first issue, quarto, over 50 colored illustrations, many full page, original green glazed pictorial boards, brown cloth backstrip, corners very slightly rubbed, otherwise fine, Estelle Doheny copy, original woodblock for on page 54, both items housed together in custom quarter tan calf over marbled boards clamshell case.   David Brass Rare Books, Inc.   Holiday 2012 Chapter One - DB 02024   2013 $3250

Greenaway, Kate 1846-1901 *Mother Goose or the Old Nursery Rhymes.* London and New York: George Routledge and Sons, 1881. First edition, first issue, binding A, octavo, 48 color illustrations, including frontispiece, original pictorial wrappers of glazed yellow paper with vignette of girl in pink dress holding umbrella and bouquet of roses surrounded by green garland of ivy and fine black line with red shading, whole duplicated on rear wrapper, paper spine experptly and invisibly strengthened, fine, housed in felt lined half green morocco clamshell case, rarest of all bindings of her Mother Goose.   David Brass Rare Books, Inc.   Holiday 2012 Chapter One - DB 02172   2013 $1850

Greenaway, Kate 1846-1901 *Under the Window.* London: Routledge, n.d., 1879. First edition, large square 8vo., original glazed pictorial boards, few faint scratches, illustrations in color, lovely clean and fresh.   R. F. G. Hollett & Son   Children's Books - 251   2013   £275

Greene, George Dawes *The Caveman's Valentine.* New York: Warner, 1994. First edition, signed by author, very fine in dust jacket.   Mordida Books   81 - 225   2013 $65

Greene, Graham 1904-1981 *A Burnt-Out Case.* London: Heinemann, 1961. First edition, fine in price clipped dust jacket with short closed tear.   Mordida Books   81 - 227   2013 $150

Greene, Graham 1904-1981 *Doctor Fischer of Geneva or the Bomb Party.* New York: Simon and Schuster, 1980. Deluxe limited edition, number 429 of 500 copies, signed by author, first American edition, near fine in black cloth boards with gilt title to spine, slight fading to spine, interior pristine, near fine black cloth slipcase, minor edge wear, 156 pages.   The Kelmscott Bookshop   7 - 113   2013 $350

Greene, Graham 1904-1981 *It's a Battlefield.* London: Heinemann, 1934. First edition, tape shadows to endpages, cracked at rear hinge, text block shaken, very good in very good second issue dust jacket (3/6 price) with rubbing and minor wear to edges and golds, short tear to front flap fold, tape strengthening to edges on verso, extremely scarce in dust jacket at all.   Ken Lopez Bookseller   159 - 75   2013 $3500

Greene, Graham 1904-1981 *It's a Battlefield.* Garden City: Doubleday Doran, 1934. First American edition, page edges darkened, otherwise fine in very good dust jacket with chipping at spine ends and at corners, several tiny closed tears and light wear along edges and folds. Mordida Books 81 - 226 2013 $500

Greene, Graham 1904-1981 *The Little Fire Engine.* Max Parrish, 1950. First edition, oblong large 8vo., original pictorial boards, spine little worn, hinges cracking, but repaired, one lower corner trifle bruised, illustrations in color by Dorothy Craigie. R. F. G. Hollett & Son Children's Books - 254 2013 £250

Greene, Graham 1904-1981 *Lord Rochester's Monkey, Being the Life of John Wilmot, Second Earl of Rochester.* London: Bodley Head, 1974. First edition, 4to., original brown cloth, dust jacket, near fine, jacket little worn at head and tail of spine, inscribed by author to his wife Vivien. Maggs Bros. Ltd. 1460 - 376 2013 £2250

Greene, Graham 1904-1981 *The Man Within.* London: Heinemann, 1929. Second impression, 8vo., excellent copy, original black cloth, lettered gilt, inscribed by author, loosely inserted is inside flap of dust jacket. Maggs Bros. Ltd. 1460 - 371 2013 £750

Greene, Graham 1904-1981 *The Potting Shed.* London: William Heinemann, 1958. First edition, small 8vo., original blue cloth, inscribed by author for Fr. Simpson, near fine in dust jacket. Maggs Bros. Ltd. 1460 - 374 2013 £750

Greene, Graham 1904-1981 *The Power and the Glory.* London: Heinemann, 1945. 8vo., original green cloth, excellent copy, cloth rubbed at extremities, inscribed by author to journalist Negley Farson. Maggs Bros. Ltd. 1460 - 473 2013 £450

Greene, Graham 1904-1981 *The Third Man and the Fallen Idol.* London: William Heinemann, 1950. First edition, 8vo., original black cloth, inscribed by author, very good, upper hinge splitting, spine little worn. Maggs Bros. Ltd. 1460 - 373 2013 £300

Greene, Graham 1904-1981 *Travels with my Aunt.* London: Bodley Head, 1969. First edition, 8vo., original dark green cloth, excellent copy, dust jacket unevenly browned along top and on spine, original dark green cloth, dust jacket, inscribed by author for Brigid Brophy. Maggs Bros. Ltd. 1460 - 375 2013 £750

Greene, Julia *Make-Believe Gift box.* Make: New York, Cupples & Leon 1917. Oblong 12mo., fine in box (soiled with strengthening), with 4 books, full page color illustrations and text illustrations in blue, lovely set. Aleph-Bet Books, Inc. 105 - 91 2013 $275

Greenfield, Eloise *Honey, I Love and Other Love Poems.* New York: Crowell, 1978. First edition, illustrations by the Dillons, fine in near fine, price clipped dust jacket with tiny tear and sticker shadow on front flap. Between the Covers Rare Books, Inc. 165 - 159 2013 $65

Greenland, Powell *Hydraulic Mining in California. A Tarnished Legacy.* Spokane: Arthur H. Clark Col., 2001. First edition, one of 756 copies, 320 pages, maps and illustrations, light brown cloth, very fine. Argonaut Book Shop Summer 2013 - 133 2013 $60

Greenwood, Frederick *Margaret Denzil's History.* London: Smith, Elder & Co., 1864. First edition, 2 volumes, original green sand grained cloth, boards blocked in lind, spine decorated and lettered in gilt, apart from two slightly loose gatherings in volume I fine, 2 pages ads in both volumes. Jarndyce Antiquarian Booksellers CCV - 118 2013 £750

Greenwood, Isaac *Arithmetick Vulgar and Decimal...* Boston: S. Kneeland and T. Green for T. Hancock, 1729. First edition, 8vo., both contents leaves lacking, contemporary calf, raised bands on spine, very good, small pieces lacking from two leaves, affecting small number of words, early leaves trimmed, close in outer margins, just touching lat letters down the leaves, some ink spotting at top of first page of introduction and word "Advertisement" written beneath the same printed word, very sound. M & S Rare Books, Inc. 95 - 110 2013 $4500

Greenwood, James *The London Vocabulary, English and Latin.* London: R. Baldwin, 1807. Twenty-third edition, 26 woodcuts, good, clean copy, contemporary sheep, neatly rebacked and corners repaired. Ken Spelman Books Ltd. 75 - 58 2013 £140

Greenwood, James *The Philadelphia Vocabulary.* Philadelphia: Carey and Co., 1787. First American edition, 16mo., old calf, crudely rebacked, inner front hinge crudely repaired, some leaves printed faintly, light foxing, small pieces lacking from front endleaf, ink signatures on title. M & S Rare Books, Inc. 95 - 181 2013 $1750

Greenwood, Jeremy *Omega Cuts.* Woodbridge, Suffolk: Wood Lea Press, 1998. First edition, one of 450 copies (of an edition of 555), numerous reproductions of wood engravings by members of the Omega Workshop, including number of tipped in color printed plates, also with 3 pages of reproductions of photos of woodblocks title printed in pale grey, pages 150, folio, original cream canvas, backstrip and front cover with designs blocked in gilt and maroon, cloth and board slipcase, fine. Blackwell's Rare Books B174 - 373 2013 £150

Greenwood, Robert *The California Outlaw, Tiburcio Vasquez.* Los Gatos: Talisman Press, 1960. First edition, one of 975 copies, 296 pages, illustrations, portraits, facsimiles, etc., cloth backed boards, very fine, dust jacket. Argonaut Book Shop   Summer 2013 - 134   2013 $125

Greenwood, Thomas *The London Vocabulary, English and Latin.* London: printed for J. F. and C. Rivington, 1785. Nineteenth edition, 12mo., 26 woodcut illustrations, some offset browning to endpapers and pastedowns, contemporary sheep, upper board detached, head and tail of spine worn, some abrasions to boards.   Jarndyce Antiquarian Booksellers   CCIV - 150   2013   £75

Greenwood, W. *The Redmans of Levens and Harewood.* Kendal: Titus Wilson, 1905. First large paper issue, 4to., original crimson cloth gilt, little marked and neatly recased, 12 pedigrees and 30 plates, flyleaves rather spotted, presentation copy from author to Miss Redmayne, 7th March 1908.   R. F. G. Hollett & Son   Lake District and Cumbria - 206   2013   £275

Greer, Robert *The Devil's Hatband.* New York: Mysterious Press, 1996. First edition, signed by author, very fine in dust jacket.   Mordida Books   81 - 228   2013 $65

Greever, William S. *The Bonanza West. The Story of the Western Mining Rushes 1848-1900.* Norman: University of Oklahoma Press, 1963. First edition, photographs, old engravings, maps, etc., brown cloth, gilt, very fine, pictorial dust jacket.   Argonaut Book Shop   Summer 2013 - 135   2013 $60

Gregorius Nazianzenus *Opera.* Paris: Typis Regiis apud Claudium Morellum, 1609. First complete collected edition, 2 volumes, folio, lightly browned, titlepages slight dust soiled, contemporary Oxford calf, spine ruled in blind, board panelled in blind with foliage panelled roll and with initials RW, printed endpapers from a 16th century edition of Mesue, edges red, small paper labels to spines, little rubbed and scratched, labels worn, ties removed, headcap of volume 2 defective, both volumes with ink inscription 'Brentley Library '.   Unsworths Antiquarian Booksellers   28 - 14   2013   £1200

Gregory, Benjamin *The Life of Frederick James Jobson, D.D.* T. Woolmer, 1884. First edition, original cloth, gilt, spine and edges worn and marked, engraved frontispiece, scarce.   R. F. G. Hollett & Son   Wesleyan Methodism - 58   2013   £65

Gregory, David *Elements of Catoptrics and Dioptrics.* London: printed for E. Curll, 1735. Second English edition, 4 folding engraved plates, 3 signed by John Senex, plates refolded, first little frayed and browned in fore margin, little browning here and there, 8vo., contemporary speckled calf, double gilt fillets on sides and on either side of raised bands on spine, red lettering piece, crack in joints, headcaps chipped, corners slightly worn, good.   Blackwell's Rare Books   Sciences - 54   2013   £1750

Gregory, Isabella Augusta Perse   1859-1932 *The A Book of Saints and Wonders Put Down Her by Lady Gregory According to the Old Writings and Memoir of the People of Ireland.* Dundrum: Dun Emer Press, 1906. First edition, limited to 200 copies, 8vo., original linen backed boards, printed label on spine, spine browned, excellent copy, from the library of Richard Murphy inscribed: "Richard Murphy bought from Hodges Figgis & Co. in Dublin c. 1946-47".   Maggs Bros. Ltd.   1442 - 70   2013   £250

Gregory, Isabella Augusta Perse   1859-1932 *The Golden Apple.* London: John Murray, 1916. First edition, 8vo., original green cloth, inscribed by author for Seamus and Iris, near fine in dust jacket chipped at head and tail of spine with some minor loss.   Maggs Bros. Ltd.   1460 - 380   2013   £450

Gregory, Isabella Augusta Perse   1859-1932 *Hugh Lane's Life and Achievement.* London: John Murray, 1921. First edition, 8vo., original dark grey cloth, printed paper label, inscribed by author March 21 '26 for Rt. Hon. L. S. Amery, spine label browned, otherwise excellent.   Maggs Bros. Ltd.   1460 - 381   2013   £300

Gregory, Isabella Augusta Perse   1859-1932 *The Kiltartan History Book.* London: T. Fisher Unwin, 1926. First UK edition, small 8vo., original red cloth, lettered gilt, near fine, inscribed by author for Lyle Donaghy.   Maggs Bros. Ltd.   1460 - 382   2013   £500

Gregory, Isabella Augusta Perse   1859-1932 *The Kiltartan Poetry Book.* Dundrum: Dun Emer Press, 1918. First edition, limited to 400 copies, 8vo., original linen backed boards, printed label on spine, covers marked and browned, very good, inscribed by Murphy "Richard Murphy I bought this book from Willie Figgis....Hodges Figgis & Co. in Dublin, c. 1946-47".   Maggs Bros. Ltd.   1442 - 71   2013   £200

Gregory, John *A Comparative View of the State and Faculties of Man with those of the Animal World.* London: printed for J. Dodsley, 1785. New edition, 8vo., contemporary tree calf, minor wear, leather label, half title, large armorial bookplate of Robert R. Livingston.   Howard S. Mott Inc.   262 - 68   2013 $200

Gregory, Vere R. T. *The House of Gregory.* 1943. First edition, illustrations, 8vo., quarter cloth, dust jacket, very good.   C. P. Hyland   261 - 392   2013   £34

Grenfell, Anne *Le Petit Nord or Annals of a Labrador Harbour.* Boston and New York: Houghton Mifflin, 1920. 8vo., quarter cloth and paper covered boards in dust jacket, half title, 25 illustrations from drawings by Dr. Wilfred Grenfell, very good, jacket has some tape repair to inside, generally good.   Schooner Books Ltd.   101 - 30   2013 $75

Grenfell, Wilfred *A Labrador Doctor.* London: Hodder and Stoughton, n.d., 1919. First edition, original cloth, gilt, trifle worn, 28 illustrations.   R. F. G. Hollett & Son   Polar Exploration - 26   2013   £75

Grenfell, Wilfred *A Labrador Doctor.* London: Hodder and Stoughton, n.d., 1919. First edition, modern half green levant morocco gilt with spine label, 28 illustrations, handsome copy.   R. F. G. Hollett & Son   Polar Exploration - 27   2013   £120

Grenfell, Wilfred *Labrador Looks at the Orient Notes of Travel in the Near and Far East.* Boston and New York: Houghton Mifflin, 1928. 8vo., red cloth slightly stained, illustrations, author's presentation with original pen and ink drawing.   Schooner Books Ltd.   105 - 31   2013 $175

Grenfell, Wilfred *The Story of a Labrador Doctor.* London: Hodder and Stoughton, n.d. circa, 1935. Original blue cloth, pages 300, 6 plates, signed by author.   R. F. G. Hollett & Son Polar Exploration - 28   2013   £35

Greville, Violet *Creatures of Clay.* London: George Routledge and Sons, 1885. Yellowback in original printed boards, spine worn but sound, with original artwork by Greville for the front cover of this book, 16 x 23cm., pen and ink on card with printer's instructions in pencil on verso,.   Jarndyce Antiquarian Booksellers   CCV - 9   2013   £180

Grey, Harry *Call Me Duke.* New York: Crown, 1955. First edition, light wear, near fine in attractive very good dust jacket with some rubbing and large but very faint dampstain on rear panel, exceptionally scarce.   Between the Covers Rare Books, Inc.   Mystery & Detective Fiction - 75101   2013 $1500

Grey, Sydney *Story-Land.* Religious Tract Society, n.d., Large 8vo., original glazed pictorial board, rebacked in cloth, corners worn, 32 illustrations by Robert Barnes, little light and occasional fingering.   R. F. G. Hollett & Son Children's Books - 255   2013   £45

Grey, Zane   1872-1939 *The Trail Driver.* New York and London: Harper & Bros., 1936. First edition, octavo, publisher's dust jacket, from author's library with blindstamp, full blue cloth stamped and lettered in yellow on front board and spine, book about fine, jacket with few specks of chipping and with some minor creasing on front panel, inside of jacket with bit of browning, not affecting front, overall very good to fine.   Heritage Book Shop   Holiday Catalogue 2012 - 70   2013 $1000

Grey, Zane   1872-1939 *The Vanishing American.* New York: Harper, 1925. First edition, 8vo., very good++ with mild cover edge wear, offsetting to endpapers, very good+ price clipped dust jacket with edgewear, mild soil, small corner chips, signed, inscribed and dated by author to his sister, Ida.   By the Book, L. C.   38 - 34   2013 $1750

Griersn, Francis *Modern Mysticism and Other Essays.* London: George Allen, 1899. First edition, 12mo., original green cloth, gilt lettering, cloth waterstained, very good, from Thomas Hardy's library with his posthumous Max Gate bookplate and his signature, tipped to front free endpaper is printed presentation slip from publisher, George Allen, from the Gary Lepper Collection of Thomas Hardy.   The Brick Row Book Shop   Bulletin Nine - 43   2013 $750

Griffin, A. Harry *Adventuring in Lakeland.* Robert Hale, 1980. First edition, original cloth, gilt, dust jacket, pages 189, with 40 illustrations, fine, scarce.   R. F. G. Hollett & Son   Lake District and Cumbria - 208   2013   £50

Griffin, A. Harry *Freeman of the Hills.* Robert Hale, 1978. First edition, original cloth, gilt, dust jacket, photos by Geoffre Berry, scarce.   R. F. G. Hollett & Son   Lake District and Cumbria - 209   2013   £60

Griffin, A. Harry *In Mountain Lakeland.* Preston: Guardian Press, 1963. Second impression, original cloth, gilt, dust jacket, upper edges worn and frayed, head of spine chipped, pages 216, numerous illustrations.   R. F. G. Hollett & Son   Lake District and Cumbria - 210   2013   £40

Griffin, A. Harry *Inside the Real Lakeland.* Preston: Guardian Press, 1961. First edition, original cloth, gilt, dust jacket rather worn, 240 pages, illustrations.   R. F. G. Hollett & Son   Lake District and Cumbria - 211   2013   £40

Griffin, A. Harry *A Lakeland Notebook.* Robert Hale, 1975. First edition, original cloth, gilt, dust jacket price clipped, 203 pages, photos by Geoffrey Berry, scarce.   R. F. G. Hollett & Son   Lake District and Cumbria - 212   2013   £50

Griffin, A. Harry *Long Days in the Hills.* Robert Hale, 1974. First edition, original cloth, gilt, dust jacket closed tears repaired on reverse, 188 pages, 46 illustrations, scarce. R. F. G. Hollett & Son Lake District and Cumbria - 213 2013 £50

Griffin, A. Harry *Pageant of Lakeland.* London: Robert Hale, 1966. First edition, 188 pages, 46 illustrations, scarce, original cloth, gilt, dust jacket (closed tears repaired on reverse). R. F. G. Hollett & Son Lake District and Cumbria - 214 2013 £25

Griffin, A. Harry *The Roof of England.* Robert Hale, 1968. First edition, original cloth, gilt, dust jacket (title lettering on spine and trifle faded), 192 pages, illustrations, Norman Nicholson's copy with his bookplate, scarce. R. F. G. Hollett & Son Lake District and Cumbria - 215 2013 £45

Griffin, A. Harry *Still the Real Lakeland.* Robert Hale, 1970. First edition, original cloth, gilt, dust jacket, 192 pages, color frontispiece and numerous illustrations. R. F. G. Hollett & Son Lake District and Cumbria - 216 2013 £50

Griffin, Gregory *The Microcosm a Periodical Work.* Windsor: C. Knight, 1809. Fourth edition, 2 volumes, fine and most attractive copy, full contemporary straight grain plum morocco, broad gilt foliate, ornate gilt spines. Ken Spelman Books Ltd. 75 - 60 2013 £120

Griffis, William Elliot *The Japanese Nation in Evolution.* New York: Thomas Y. Crowell, 1907. First edition, small 8vo., xii, 408 pages, very good in original red cloth, top edge gilt, gilt lettering spine and cover, mild sun to spine, foxing to endpapers, rear hinge archivally repaired, inscribed by author for Rev. John Batchelor. By the Book, L. C. 36 - 89 2013 $250

Griffith, Nicola *Slow River.* New York: Ballantine Books, 1995. First edition, octavo, cloth backed boards. L. W. Currey, Inc. Fall Sampler Sept. 2013 - 146396 2013 $100

Griffiths, Major Arthur *Ford's Folly, Ltd.* London: Macqueen, 1900. First edition, near fine in brown pictorial cloth covered boards. Mordida Books 81 - 230 2013 $180

Grigg, Richard *Report Upon the Conditions and Prospects of British Trade in Newfoundland (at top of title) Trade with Newfoundland.* London: HMSO, Darling & Son, 1908. Quarto, 48 pages, blue paper wrappers, quarto, wrappers torn along spine but still attached. Schooner Books Ltd. 102 - 23 2013 $75

Grildrig, Quinbus Flestrin *Readings from Dean Swift His Tale of a Tub.* 1836. First edition, 6 Richard Cruikshank illustrations, original quarter cloth, stiff printed wrappers, fair to good. C. P. Hyland 261 - 808 2013 £60

Grimble, A. *Shooting and Salmon Fishing.* London: Chapman & Hall, 1892. First edition, 8vo., pages xi, 259, illustrations, original blue cloth, occasional light foxing. J. & S. L. Bonham Antiquarian Booksellers Europe - 3964 2013 £85

Grimes, Martha *The Anodyne Necklace.* Boston: Little Brown, 1983. First edition, fine in dust jacket. Mordida Books 81 - 232 2013 $100

Grimes, Martha *The Dirty Duck.* Boston: Little Brown, 1984. First edition, fine in dust jacket. Mordida Books 81 - 234 2013 $75

Grimes, Martha *The Old Silent.* Boston: Little Brown, 1989. First edition, signed by author, very fine in dust jacket. Mordida Books 81 - 235 2013 $65

Grimes, Nikki *For Our Children.* N.P.: the author, 1971. First edition, stapled photographic self wrappers, (8) pages, fine. Between the Covers Rare Books, Inc. 165 - 160 2013 $250

Grimeston, Edward *A Generall Historie of the Netherlands...* London: A. Islip and G. Eld., 1609. First edition, 2nd issue, folio, engraved titlepage with historiated border, many near full page illustrations in text, paper flaw resulting in small hole to first leaf, little marginal worming to first few leaves, tiny burn holes to pages 111, 117 and 597 affecting a few letters, occasional light ink smudges to margins, few slight creases, contemporary dark brown calf, gilt border and centerpiece, sympathetically rebacked with parts of original spine retained and some gilt reapplied to style, evidence of clasps though none remain, bookplate of Adrian Bullock, Sherringham, Norfolk 1988, recently handwritten list of illustrations. Unsworths Antiquarian Booksellers 28 - 101 2013 £1250

Grimm, the Brothers *Fairy Tales of the Brothers Grimm.* New York: Doubleday Page, 1909. First American edition with Rackham illustrations, thick 4to., suede backed pictorial boards, stamped in black and gold, 325 pages, edges and corners rubbed, else near fine, pictorial endpapers, 40 tipped in color plates with lettered tissue guards and 55 black and white illustrations by Arthur Rackham, particularly scarce in American edition. Aleph-Bet Books, Inc. 104 - 468 2013 $2500

Grimm, The Brothers *Fairy Tales of the Brothers Grimm.* London: Constable, 1909. Limited to only 750 copies signed by artist, large thick 4to., 325 pages, full vellum, gilt decorations, top edge gilt, except for few small spots of natural discoloration of vellum, some browning on front endpaper, near fine, with vellum clean and with silk ties, 40 tipped-in color plates by Arthur Rackham with guards plus a profusion of full page and smaller black and whites.   Aleph-Bet Books, Inc.   104 - 467   2013 $11,000

Grimm, The Brothers *The Fairy Tales of the Brothers Grimm.* London: Constable and Co. Ltd., 1909. One of 750 copies signed by artist, Arthur Rackham, this #732, 292 x 235mm., very attractive red three quarter morocco (stamp signed Putnams), raised bands, spine handsomely gilt in compartments formed by plain and decorative rules, quatrefoil centerpiece surrounded by densely scrolling cornerpieces, sides and endleaves of rose colored linen, top edge gilt (front joint and headcap very expertly repaired by Courtland Benson), titlepage with pictorial frame, numerous black and white illustrations in text, 10 full page black and white illustrations, 40 color plates by Arthur Rackham, mounted on cream stock and protected by lettered tissue guards, cover with faint minor soiling, just hint of wear to corners, small corner tear to one plate, 2 tissue guards with minor creasing or chipped edges, otherwise fine, handsome binding, text and plates clean and fresh, bright.   Phillip J. Pirages   63 - 379   2013 $4500

Grimm, The Brothers *German Popular Stories.* London: published by C. Baldwyn, 1823. James Robbins and Co., London and Joseph Robins Junr. and Co., Dublin, 1826. First English edition, first issue without umlaut on the word "Marchen" on first pictorial titlepage, with half titles, but without final blank leaf in volume II, 2 volumes, full brown morocco by Bartlett & Co. Boston, 12 etched plates by George Cruikshank, printed in sepia, including pictorial title, 10 etched plates by Cruikshank, printed in black, including pictorial title, all edges gilt, fine, minor browning on few leaves, morocco backed slipcase.   Howard S. Mott Inc.   262 - 69   2013 $11,500

Grimm, The Brothers *Grimm's Animal Stories.* New York: Duffield, 1909. First edition, 4to., green cloth, pictorial paste-on, some margin finger soil, photo on endpaper, else very good+, illustrations by John Rae, including 9 color plates plus many silhouettes and black and whites, very uncommon edition.   Aleph-Bet Books, Inc.   104 - 256   2013 $475

Grimm, The Brothers *Grimm's Tales.* New York: Oxford University Press, 1954. 8vo., cloth, 144 pages, fine in dust jacket, illustrations in color, from the library of Bertha Mahoney Miller with her bookplate.   Aleph-Bet Books, Inc.   105 - 294   2013 $250

Grimm, The Brothers *Hansel and Grethel & Snow White and Rose Red.* Chicago: Reilly and Britton, 1908. 12mo., 58 pages, red cloth stamped in yellow and black, round pictorial paste-on, fine, 8 full page color illustrations, few smaller illustrations and pictorial endpapers, great.   Aleph-Bet Books, Inc.   105 - 419   2013 $275

Grimm, The Brothers *Hansel & Gretel.* London: Constable & Co., 1920. First separate edition, quarto, 20 mounted color plates and 28 black and white drawings in text by Arthur Rackham, little within pictorial border, original dark blue cloth pictorially stamped and lettered gilt on front cover and spine, top edge stained blue, free endpapers slightly browned from pastedown glue, tiny bookseller's label on front pastedown, fine in very scarce original tan paper dust jacket printed in dark blue, front panel matching gilt stamping on front cover of book and back panel with publisher's ads (jacket spine very slightly darkened).   David Brass Rare Books, Inc.   Holiday 2012 Chapter One - DB 02093   2013 $1250

Grimm, The Brothers *Household Tales.* London: Eyre & Spottiswoode, 1946. First edition, original yellow cloth, dust jacket very worn and chipped, double page color title, 5 color plates, numerous black and white illustrations by Mervyn Peake.   R. F. G. Hollett & Son   Children's Books - 447   2013   £65

Grimm, The Brothers *The Juniper Tree and Other tales from Grimm.* London: Bodley Head, 1974. First UK edition, 2 volumes, small 8vo., original cloth gilt, dust jackets, slipcase, 2 tiny nicks at top edge of one wrapper, otherwise fine, crisp set.   R. F. G. Hollett & Son   Children's Books - 540   2013   £95

Grimm, The Brothers *Bruderchen Und Schwesterchen. (Little Brother and Little Sister).* Mainz: Jos. Scholz n.d. circa, 1910. 4to., cloth backed pictorial boards, some rubbing, very good, illustrations by Franz Muller-Munster with 8 very beautiful full page color illustrations, plus other line illustrations.   Aleph-Bet Books, Inc.   105 - 293   2013 $200

Grimm, The Brothers *Little Brother & Little Sister.* London: Constable, 1917. Limited to only 525 numbered copies, signed by Rackham, complete with additional signed color plate in envelope! Folio, grey cloth with pictorial label stamped in gold, top edge gilt, slight bit of rubbing and slight rubbing of spine ends, else fine, illustrations by Arthur Rackham, 13 beautiful tipped-in color plates, plus pictorial endpapers and 43 black and whites, exceptional copy. Aleph-Bet Books, Inc.   104 - 469   2013 $7500

Grimm, Wilhelm *Dear Mili.* New York: Farrar Straus & Giroux, 1988. Stated first edition, oblong 4to., cloth, as new in like dust jacket, magnificent, rich and detailed full page color illustrations by Maurice Sendak, this copy inscribed by Sendak.   Aleph-Bet Books, Inc.   104 - 514   2013 $125

Grinstein, Alexander *The Index of Psychoanalytic Writings I-X.* New York: IUP, 1956. First edition, 10 volumes, fine in very good+ to near fine dust jackets. Beasley Books   2013 - 2013 $100

Grinstein, Alexander *The Index of Psychoanalytic Writings I-V.* New York: IUP, 1956-1960. First edition, 5 volumes, hardcover, fine in very good to near fine dust jackets.   Beasley Books   2013 - 2013 $100

Grinstein, Alexander *The Index of Psychoanalytic Writings. Volumes 10; 14.* New York: IUP, 1971-1975. First edition, nice set, mostly without dust jackets.   Beasley Books   2013 - 2013 $100

Grisham, John *Bleachers.* New York: Doubleday, 2003. First edition, limited to 350 copies signed by author, fine in fine glassine dust jacket with fine slipcase, still sealed in shrinkwrap, although not marked in any way, this from the collection of Bruce Kahn.   Between the Covers Rare Books, Inc.   Football Books - 328538   2013 $250

Grisham, John *A Time to Kill.* Garden City: Doubleday, 1993. Limited edition, one of 350 numbered copies, full leather, fine in unprinted fine dust jacket, fine slipcase, signed by author.   Between the Covers Rare Books, Inc.   Mystery & Detective Fiction - 103804   2013 $3500

Groening, Matt *Life in Hell. Bonus Fun-Fest Holiday Treat #3.* Los Angeles: Self published, 1983. Limited edition, one of 100 numbered copies, rare edition, slight edge sunning, still fine in stapled wrappers.   Ken Lopez Bookseller   159 - 76   2013 $750

Groner, Augusta *Mene Tekel: A Tale of Strange Happenings.* New York: Duffield, 1912. First American edition and first edition in English, fine with white painted spine lettering unrubbed, in nice, very good example of exceptionally scarce dust jacket with shallow loss at crown (affecting no lettering), some overall age toning and several internal repairs.   Between the Covers Rare Books, Inc.   Sci-Fi, Fantasy & Horror - 88547   2013 $1250

Gronovius, Johann Friederich *Bibliotheca Regni Animalis Atique Lapidei seu Recensio Auctorum et Librorum qui de Regno Animali et Lapideo.* Leiden: for the author, 1760. First edition, some foxing, dampstaining towards end, chiefly in lower margins, few ink smudges, 4to., contemporary or slightly later half calf, rebacked, corners worn, presentation copy with numerous manuscript notes (few slightly trimmed), inscribed by author for Mortren Thrane Brunnich 1737-1827, Danish zoologist, good.   Blackwell's Rare Books   172 - 64   2013   £1750

Gronow, Rees Howell *The Reminiscences and Recollections of Captain Gronow...* London: printed by Ballantyne and Co. for C. Nimmo, 1889. One of 870 copies printed for England and America with 25 plates in two states (this copy #22), 268 x 169mm., 2 volumes, 50 plates (comprising 25 images, each in two states; one proofs before letters done on plate paper, the other on Whatman paper titled and hand colored), as called for, a large paper copy; extremely handsome red crushed morocco, ornately gilt by Zaehnsdorf (stamp-signed on front turn-ins and with special oval gilt stamp on rear pastedowns), cover with wide filigree frame with massed densely scrolling fleurons, raised bands, unevenly spaced in the continental style, forming five compartments, second and two small bottom compartments with titling, top and elongated middle compartment decorated with intricate gilt in same way as boards, broad inner gilt dentelles, marbled endpapers (with thickly gilt lining between dentelles and pastedowns), top edge gilt, other edges untrimmed, engraved bookplate of John Raymond Danson, couple of very faint scratches on back cover volume II, just hint of rubbing at top and bottom of lower joint of same volume, especially fine in gloriously decorated morocco, text virtually pristine and bindings extremely lustrous and scarce worn.   Phillip J. Pirages   63 - 66   2013 $1900

Groot, William De *De Principiis Juris Naturalis Enchiridion.* Cantabrigiae: Joannes Hayes, 1673. 8vo., early full calf, heavily rubbed, spine foot torn and missing a piece, joints reinforced with kozo rice paper, signature of Ja. Garden (professor of divinity, King's College) 1688, rare, good.   Jeff Weber Rare Books   171 - 147   2013 $125

Grose, Francis   1731-1791 *A Classical Dictionary of the Vulgar Tongue.* London: Hooper and Co., 1796. Third edition, small ink blot to pages (35-8) affecting few words, contemporary tan calf, gilt title to spine, neatly rebacked with original spine retained, top corners little worn, endpapers very slightly mottled, armorial bookplate of Frances Mary Richardson Currer, pencilled bookseller's notes.   Unsworths Antiquarian Booksellers   28 - 102   2013   £450

Gross, Charles *Bibliography of British Municipal History.* 1966. Octavo, cloth, dust jacket, very good.   C. P. Hyland   261 - 67   2013   £32

Grosseteste, Robert *Episcopi Lincolniensis. Commentarius in VIII libros Physicorum Aristotelis.* Boulder: University of Colorado Press, 1963. 8vo., navy cloth, gilt stamped spine title, dust jacket, ownership signature, fine.   Jeff Weber Rare Books   169 - 173   2013 $100

Grossmith, George *Diary of a Nobody.* Bristol: J. W. Arrowsmith, 1892. First edition, 2nd issue, 8vo., original brown cloth, decorated in blue and black, with ALS from George Grossmith to Sir Henry Lucy dated Oct. 16th 1899, slightly rubbed, otherwise excellent.   Maggs Bros. Ltd.   1460 - 383   2013   £750

Grotius, Hugo 1583-1645 *Apologeticus Eorum qui Hollandiae Westfrisiaeque & Vicinis Quibusdam Nationibus ex Legibus Praefuerunt ante Mutationem quae Evit anno MDCXVIII.* Paris: 1665, 12mo., touch of minor spotting, contemporary vellum boards, spine lettered ink, slightly soiled, pastedowns lifted.   Unsworths Antiquarian Booksellers   28 - 103   2013   £300

Grotius, Hugo 1583-1645 *Poemata Omnia.* Leyden: Apud Hieronymum de Vogel, 1645. 12mo., engraved title, contemporary vellum, spine bit soiled with remnants of paper label, endpapers with few minor tears, internally clean with light age toning just noticeable around edges of pages, small piece torn from fore-edge of K1, just grazing two letters.   Joseph J. Felcone Inc.   Books Printed before 1701 - 48   2013 $325

Grover, Eulalie *Mother Goose.* Chicago: Volland, 1915. First edition, folio, blue gilt cloth, pictorial paste-on, fine in original box (box flaps repaired, else very good+), magnificently illustrated by Frederick Richardson.   Aleph-Bet Books, Inc.   104 - 362   2013 $1200

Grover, Eulalie *Sunbonnet Babies in Italy.* Chicago: Rand McNally, 1922. First edition, 8vo., pictorial cloth, small mend on one page, else fine, illustrations by Bertha Corbett Melcher and James McKracken with pictorial endpapers and lovely color illustrations, signed by Grover.   Aleph-Bet Books, Inc.   104 - 257   2013 $400

Groves, Jay *Fireball at the Lake: a Story of Encounter with Another World.* New York: Exposition Press, 1967. First edition, little spotting on front boar, else near fine in good dust jacket with long tear and sticker remnant, both on front panel, very scarce.   Between the Covers Rare Books, Inc.   Sci-Fi, Fantasy & Horror - 301459   2013 $225

Grubb, Davis *The Night of the Hunter.* New York: Harper & Bros., 1955. First edition, near fine in like dust jacket, exceptional, unread copy with one minutely bumped corner and small closed triangular tear in rear panel of dust jacket, otherwise fine.   Leather Stalking Books   October 2013 - 2013 $450

Gruber, Frank *The Hungry Dog.* New York: Farrar & Rinehart, 1941. First edition, fine in very near fine dust jacket with few tiny nicks at extremities, very scarce.   Between the Covers Rare Books, Inc.   Mystery & Detective Fiction - 55491   2013 $450

Gruber, Frank *The Silver Jackass.* New York: Reynal Hitchcock, 1941. First edition, fine in very good dust jacket with scraping on front panel, light wear at spine ends and several short closed tears.   Mordida Books   81 - 237   2013 $200

Gruelle, Johnny *All About Cinderella.* New York: Cupples & Leon, 1816. 12mo., beautiful copy, 8 color plates, many black and white illustrations by Gruelle, scarce dust jacket has small closed tear at top of spine, paper covered boards, very good, previous owner's inscription.   Barnaby Rudge Booksellers   Children 2013 - 021335   2013 $150

Gruelle, Johnny *All About Hansel and Grethel.* New York: Cupples & Leon, 1917. 8 color plates, many black and white illustrations, paper covered boards, very good in like dust jacket, 24mo., previous owner's inscription.   Barnaby Rudge Booksellers   Children 2013 - 021336   2013 $140

Gruelle, Johnny *All About Little Red Riding Hood Retold and Illustrated by...* New York: Cupples & Leon, 1916. 16mo., boards, pictorial paste-on, near fine, 8 wonderful color plates and many black and whites.   Aleph-Bet Books, Inc.   104 - 265   2013 $200

Gruelle, Johnny *Beloved Belindy.* Joliet: Volland, 1926. Twenty first edition, 8vo., pictorial boards, slight rubbing to spine and corners, else very good+, color illustrations.   Aleph-Bet Books, Inc.   105 - 295   2013 $300

Gruelle, Johnny *Friendly Fairies.* Chicago: Volland, 1919. First edition, 8vo., pictorial boards, light wear to spine ends, half title, spotted, very good+ in publisher's box (flaps repaired), uncommon.   Aleph-Bet Books, Inc.   104 - 261   2013 $675

Gruelle, Johnny *Friendly Fairies.* Chicago: Donohue, 1929. 8vo., previous owner's signature on half title, black cloth backed boards, very good, illustrations.   Barnaby Rudge Booksellers   Children 2013 - 020284   2013 $85

Gruelle, Johnny *The Paper Dragon.* Joliet: Volland, 1926. First edition, 2nd issue, 8vo., pictorial boards, wrap around paper spine, as new in fine pictorial box, color illustrations on almost every page as well as full page color illustrations and pictorial endpapers, uncommon, incredible copy.   Aleph-Bet Books, Inc.   104 - 260   2013 $600

Gruelle, Johnny *Raggedy Ann and Andy and the Camel with the Wrinkled Knees.* Joliet: Volland, 1924. First edition, variant, 8vo., cloth backed pictorial boards, minimal wear, near fine in publisher's box (box flap restored), laid-in is printed Volland ad announcing this title as the 'new book' listing Joliet as the city of publication, not Chicago, wonderfully illustrated in color, beautiful copy.   Aleph-Bet Books, Inc.   104 - 258   2013 $500

Gruelle, Johnny *Raggedy Ann at the End of the Rainbow.* Akron: Saalfield, 1947. First and only edition, 8vo., spiral backed boards, corners worn and light cover soil, very good, illustrations in full color and black and white by Ethel Hays, very scarce.   Aleph-Bet Books, Inc.   104 - 259   2013 $250

Gruelle, Johnny *Raggedy Ann in the Deep Deep Woods.* Joliet: P. F. Volland, 1930. First edition, signed and inscribed by Gruelle, very good+ hardback, blue cloth spine with color pictorial paper covered boards, color illustrated endpapers, color illustrations, offsetting from news article, half page gift inscription, soiling to few pages, 8vo., 95 pages.   By the Book, L. C.   36 - 32   2013 $500

Gruelle, Johnny *Raggedy Ann in the Magic Book.* New York: Johnny Gruelle Co., 1939. First edition, 8vo., cloth backed pictorial boards, fine in frayed dust jacket, full color illustrations by Worth Gruelle, nice copy.   Aleph-Bet Books, Inc.   105 - 296   2013 $250

Gruelle, Johnny *Raggedy Ann's Sunny Songs.* New York: Miller, 1930. Folio, pictorial boards, 36 pages, small chip at base of spine, else very good+ in tattered dust jacket, illustrations in color on every page by Gruelle.   Aleph-Bet Books, Inc.   105 - 298   2013 $225

Grunsky, Carl Ewald *Irrigation Near Fresno, California.* Washington: GPO, 1898. First edition, 94 pages, photo plates, numerous text maps, 3 folding maps, text illustrations, extracted, sewn, upper covers slightly jammed, fine.   Argonaut Book Shop   Recent Acquisitions June 2013 - 125   2013 $125

Grunsky, Carl Ewald *Stockton Boyhood. Being the Reminiscences of... Which Cover the Years from 1855 to 1877.* Berkeley: Friends of the Bancroft Library, 1959. First edition, one of 800 copies, 137 pages, printed in red and black, frontispiece, illustrations from detailed drawings, green cloth, gilt lettered spine, very fine.   Argonaut Book Shop   Summer 2013 - 136 2013 $75

Guazzo, Stefano *De Civilii Conversatione Libri Quatuor.* Ambergae: M. Forster, 1598. 24mo., vellum over beveled boards, rules and flora embosses, boards scuffed, free endpapers loose, few wormholes at corners, more evident on pastedowns and endpapers at hinge, but rarely if ever affecting leaves, scattered minor foxing, scattered underlining in red in fine hand with occasional marginalia former owner's name under date on titlepage and on front board though mainly rubbed away, title in like hand to spine also nearly faded, good copy, the copy of Sigmund Maximilian Raid, a 17th century Jena jurist with his name on titlepage and front board.   Kaaterskill Books   16 - 41   2013 $500

Gudde, Erwin G. *California Gold Camps.* Berkeley and Los Angeles: University of California Press, 1975. First edition, x, 467 pages, numerous illustrations and maps, dark gray cloth, very fine, pictorial dust jacket.   Argonaut Book Shop   Recent Acquisitions June 2013 - 126   2013 $150

Guer, Jean Antoine *Moeurs et Usages Des Turcs, Leur Religion, Leur Gouvernement Civil, Militaire et Politique avec un Abrege de l'Histoire Ottomane.* Paris: Chez Merigot & Piget, 1747. Second edition, 2 volumes, 2 engraved titlepages, titles printed in red and black with devices, 28 additional plates, engraved initials, and head and tailpieces, small 4to., contemporary mottled calf, boards ruled in gilt, five raised bands, compartments decorated in gilt, red morocco lettering piece, all edges gilt, wear to extremities with some loss at spine heads, and two small splits at tip of joints on first volume, volume number in one compartment mostly worn away, light scattered foxing and minor offsetting, marginal on plates, one folding panorama with small tear near hinge and upper margin, one with one inch tear to lower section near hinge, otherwise plates quite sharp, overall very good, bookplate of La Verne Baldwin (former consul General at Istanbul), gift to Baldwin from Beth (Bertha) Carp, close friend of Allen Dulles.   Kaaterskill Books   16 - 42   2013 $4000

Guerin, Pierre *Traite sur les Maladies des Yeux, dans Lequel l'Auteur, Apris Avoir Expose les Differentes methodes de Faire l'Operation de la Catarcte, Propose un Instrument Nouveau....* Lyon: Chez V. Requilliat, 1769. First edition, 12mo., headpieces, decorative initials, tailpieces, 1 folding engraved plates, errata, binder's instructions on final page, titlepage torn at gutter, plate foxed and torn at folds (tears closed with japanese tissue), contemporary French tan mottled calf, raised bands, gilt spine, marbled edges, marbled endleaves, rubbed, ms. in notations on half title, bookplate of Jerry F. Donin, very good.   Jeff Weber Rare Books   172 - 117   2013 $350

Guest, Barbara *The Altos.* San Francisco: Hine Editions/Limestone Press, 1991. Limited edition, one of 40 Roman-numeraled copies printed by hand on Somerset paper and signed by author and artist, from a total edition of 120 copies, folio, original full white calf stamped in blind on front cover, as new in original mailing glassine and shipping box.   James S. Jaffe Rare Books   Fall 2013 - 62   2013 $7500

Guevara, Antonio De *The Praise and Happinesse of the Countries-Life.* Newtown: Gregynog Press, 1938. 263/380 copies (of an edition of 400), printed on Arnold handmade paper, 6 head and tailpieces and title vignette by Reynolds Stone, usual light foxing to blank leaves, 16mo., original quarter red morocco, backstrip gilt lettered, mid green boards, printed front cover label, red morocco tipped corners, untrimmed, dust jacket, near fine.   Blackwell's Rare Books   B174 - 346   2013   £300

A Guide to the English Lake District intended Principally for the Use of Pedestrians. London: Simpkin, Marshall & Co. and Windermere: J. Garnett, circa, 1865. Revised edition, original blindstamped cloth, gilt, color frontispiece, 4 folding maps printed in blue, 2 woodcut plates and several tables, signature of James Payn on pastedown.   R. F. G. Hollett & Son   Lake District and Cumbria - 219   2013   £65

A Guide to Pink Elephants: 200 Most requested Mixed Drinks on Alcohol-Resistant Cards. Volume One. New York: Richard Rosen Assoc., 1952. First edition, spiral comb bound illustrated pink wrappers in printed pink box, fine.   Between the Covers Rare Books, Inc.   Cocktails, Etc. - 325196   2013 $85

Guillemeau, Jacques   *Hondert en Dertien Gebreken en Genesinge der Oogen... En nu Vermeerdert door Mr. Johannes Verbrigge...*   Amsterdam: Jan Claesz ten Hoorn, 1678. 12mo., frontispiece (trimmed close at top of fort edge), titlepage vignette, decorative initials, contemporary full calf, raised bands, gilt spine, all edges red, leather scuffed and cracked, outer hinges starting, front free endpaper loose, bookplate of Jerry Donin good.   Jeff Weber Rare Books   172 - 119   2013 $1000

Guillemin, Amedee Victor   *Les Cometes.*   Paris: Librairie Hachette, 1875. First edition, tall 8vo., 78 figures, 11 plates, occasional foxing, early quarter gilt stamped red morocco over blindstamped pebbled red cloth, moire endpapers, 4 raised spines, all edges gilt, corners showing, front hinge strengthened, very good.   Jeff Weber Rare Books   169 - 177   2013 $380

Guinness, Bryan   *A Fugue of Cinderellas.*   London: Heinemann, 1956. First edition, 8vo., original blue cloth, excellent copy in dust jacket, chipped at head of spine, inscribed by author for Cecil Woodham Smith Nov. 1963.   Maggs Bros. Ltd.   1460 - 385   2013   £50

Guinness, Bryan   *Reflexions.*   London: Heinemann, 1947. First edition, 8vo., original yellow cloth, printed paper label on upper cover, excellent copy, inscribed to Cornish poet Ronald Bottrall by author.   Maggs Bros. Ltd.   1460 - 384   2013   £50

Guisnee, Mr.   *Application de l'Algebre a la Geometrie, ou Methode de Demontrer...*   Paris: Jean Boudot and Jacue Quillau, 1705. First edition, woodcut head and tailpieces, 6 folding engraved plates, hint of browning and few scattered spots, 4to., contemporary calf, spine gilt in compartments, red lettering piece, slightly worn, cracks at ends of joints, headcap defective, good.   Blackwell's Rare Books Sciences - 55   2013   £1200

Gundling, Nicolaus Hieronymus   *Gundlingiana. Darinnen Allerhand zur Jurisprudenz.*   Halle in Magdeburgischen: Renger, 1717. 2 volumes of 3 only, i.e. parts 11-30 only of 30 part collection, usually found as 3 volumes, 8vo., blue pencil mark to page 7 volume 1, very occasional marginal notes, contemporary vellum, yapp edges, paper and gilt label to spines, edges sprinkled red, vellum little yellowed and marked, endcaps slightly snagged, illegible ink ownership.   Unsworths Antiquarian Booksellers   28 - 104   2013   £240

Gunn, James   *Deadlier than the Male.*   New York: Duell, Sloan and Pearce, 1942. First edition, advance reading copy, fine in self wrapper with some very faint offsetting on front wrapper, very nice.   Between the Covers Rare Books, Inc.   Mystery & Detective Fiction - 65946   2013 $1250

Gunn, Robert Alexander   *The Truth About Alcohol.*   Chicago and New York: Belford Clarke & Co., 1887. First edition, 24mo., publisher's blue cloth, stamp "From Brewer's Journal" on 3 leaves, small spot on front board, near fine.   Between the Covers Rare Books, Inc.   Cocktails, Etc. - 293919   2013 $65

Gunther, John   *Eden for One: an Amusement.*   New York: Harper & Bros., 1927. First edition, Jazz Age-style bookplate, else fine in near very good dust jacket with offsetting on rear panel, small chips, split along edge of front flap, evidence of old internal repairs and modest stain on front panel, very scarce in jacket.   Between the Covers Rare Books, Inc.   Sci-Fi, Fantasy & Horror - 92228   2013 $400

Guppy, Estella L.   *The Story of the Sequoias. Sequoia Sempervirens (Coast Redwood Tree of California). Sequoia Gigantea or Washingtoniana (Big Tree of the Sierra).*   Pasadena: the author, 1925. First edition, 12mo., 4 tipped in photo illustrations, publisher's stiff brown pictorial wrappers, printed in dark green, very fine.   Argonaut Book Shop Summer 2013 - 137   2013 $60

Gurley, W.   *Manual of Gurley Hydraulic Engineering Instruments.*   Troy: W. & L. E. Gurley, Makers, 1918. First edition, 139, (3) pages, photos, drawings, text maps, charts green cloth gilt, lacking price list in rear pockets, light cover soiling, else fine.   Argonaut Book Shop   Recent Acquisitions June 2013 - 129   2013 $75

Gurney, Ivor   *Severn and Somme.*   London: Sidgwick & Jackson, 1917. First edition, 8vo., original red cloth, printed label on spine, excellent copy, spine faded, inner hinges splitting, ownership signature of W. M. Gurney.   Maggs Bros. Ltd.   1460 - 386   2013   £600

Gutch, John Mathew   *A Lytell Geste of Robin Hode.*   London: Longman, Brown, Green and Longmans, 1847. First edition, 2 volumes, recent simple forest green morocco by a skilled amateur, flat spine with three gilt floral stamps and gilt titling, engraved frontispiece in each volume 140 illustrations in text by F. W. Fairholt, titlepages with ink library stamp mostly effaced; 2 pages with ink pencilled marginalia, isolated minor smudges, printed on inexpensive paper and consequently with overall light browning, otherwise fine, only trivial imperfections internally, bindings as new.   Phillip J. Pirages   63 - 404   2013 $375

Guthrie, A. B. *The Big Sky.* New York: William Sloan, 1947. First edition, signed, limited edition, 1/500 numbered copies signed by author with special printed jacket as well as regular illustrated dust jacket, very good plus to near fine, tiny touch of dampstain to one corner of pages, nearly invisible, special printed jacket is very good plus with some shallow chipping to spine crown and round light stain to front panel, the illustrated jacket near fine with some minor chipping to spine crown.   Ed Smith Books   78 - 24   2013 $500

Guthrie, A. B. *Wild Pitch.*   Boston: Houghton Mifflin, 1973. First edition, fine in dust jacket.   Mordida Books   81 - 22   2013 $65

Guthrie, George James   *On Injuries of the Head Affecting the Brain.*   London: John Churchill, 1842. Tall 4to., recent leather backed cloth boards saving endpapers, faint library stamp on title leaf, light foxing and toning of pages, otherwise very good, rare.   James Tait Goodrich   75 - 109   2013 $2500

Gutierrez Del Cano, Marcelino   *Catalog de Los Manuscritos Existentes en La Bibliothecca Universitaria de Valencia.*   Valencia: Libreria Maraguat, 1913. First edition, no. 119 of 500 copies, 3 volumes, 30 facsimile plates, cloth, spine scuffed and boards rubbed, else very good with scattered foxing.   Kaaterskill Books   16 - 43   2013 $900

Guy, Francis   *Tourists' Handbook to Cork.*   Kilarney: Blackwater, 1882. 8vo., 8, 78 pages, 3 folding maps, 3 plates, disbound, very good.   C. P. Hyland   261 - 463   2013   £70

Guyer, William   *The Merry Mixer or Cocktails and their Ilk: a Booklet on Mixtures and Mulches, Fizzes and Whizzes.*   New York: Geo. T. Stagg Co., 1933. 24mo., 63 pages, vignettes, printed wrappers, name faintly stamped on front wrapper, nice, near fine.   Between the Covers Rare Books, Inc.   Cocktails, Etc. - 321218   2013 $125

H

H., B. *The Twelve Months by B. H.* Zuilichem: Catharijne Press, 1990. Limited to 165 copies, this one of the 150 numbered trade copies, bound by Gus Thurkow and hand coloring by Luc Thurkow, each month with hand colored scene, 4.5 x 6.2cm., paper covered boards with color illustration on front cover, miniature bookplate of Kathryn Rickard, from the collection of Donn W. Sanford.   Oak Knoll Books   303 - 90   2013 $125

H., J. L. *Alphabet. Allegorical & Alliterative & Amusing.* London: Effingham Wilson, 1871. Sole edition, oblong 4to., pages (28), entirely lithographic, title printed in red, few minor marginal tears, lightly spotted or browned in places, original publisher's red half morocco over printed boards, front cover repeating title, extremities worn, name on title. Marlborough Rare Books Ltd.   218 - 88   2013   £250

H., Z. *The Peek-a-Boos Among the Bunnies.* New York: Hodder & Stoughton, n.d circa, 1913. First US edition, square 4to., pictorial boards, pictorial paste-on, some foxing and tips rubbed, else very good, illustrations by Chloe Preston, 8 fine color plates, pictorial endpapers and numerous black and whites by George Howard-Vyse, scarce. Aleph-Bet Books, Inc.   104 - 458   2013 $750

Haab, Otto *An Atlas of Opthalmoscopy.* London: British Optical Association, 1928. New edition, large 8vo., 6 figures, 87 plates, gilt stamped black cloth, front hinge starting, bookplate of St. Bartholomew's Hospital College Library, very good.   Jeff Weber Rare Books   172 - 121   2013 $150

Haagner, Alwin *Sketches of South African Bird-Life.* Cape Town: T. Maskwe Miller, 1914. Second edition, original cloth, gilt, trifle dusty in places, 148 illustrations, pastedowns little spotted.   R. F. G. Hollett & Son   Africana - 83   2013   £140

Haberly, Loyd *Poems.* Long Crendon, Buckinghamshire: Seven Acres Press, 1930. First edition, one of 120 numbered copies, (this neither signed nor numbered), printed on handmade paper, large capital to beginning of many poems printed in green or red, first word to initial poem printed in red with large, beautifully printed initial "T" as the first capital, foolscap 8vo., recent pink boards, printed label, top edge gilt, others untrimmed, fine.   Blackwell's Rare Books B174 - 383   2013   £200

The Habits of Good Society: a Handbook for Ladies and Gentlemen...   New York: Carleton, 1867. First edition, 8vo, pages 430, ads, maroon cloth stamped in blind and gilt, very good.   Second Life Books Inc.   182 - 9   2013 $95

Haddon, A. C. *The Study of Man.* 1898. First edition, Welch photos, original cloth stained, text good, 8vo.   C. P. Hyland   261 - 465   2013   £30

Haddon, Mark *The Curious Incident of the Dog in the Night-Time.* London: Cape, 2003. First edition, original cloth, gilt, dust jacket, pages 272, illustrations, scarcer adult issue.   R. F. G. Hollett & Son   Children's Books - 257   2013   £120

Hader, Berta *Berta and Elmer Hader's Picture Book of Mother Goose.* New York: Coward McCann, 1930. First edition, 4to., pictorial cloth, fine in dust jacket (spine faded, some fraying and small tears), really very good+, decorative border on each page of text, full page color illustrations and black and whites, extremely rare in dust jacket.   Aleph-Bet Books, Inc.   105 - 301   2013 $1500

Hader, Berta *The Cat and the Kitten.* New York: Macmillan, Oct., 1940. First edition, 4to., green pictorial cloth, fine in slightly frayed dust jacket, full page color illustrations, plus many text illustrations, nice, scarce.   Aleph-Bet Books, Inc.   104 - 267   2013 $200

Hadfield, P. Heywood *With a Ocean Liner (Orient Line SS "Otranto") through the Fiords of Norway...*   Stereoscopic & Photographic Co. Ltd. n.d., 1907. Ninth edition, quarto, 70 pages, black and white photos, folding map, original dark green cloth, corners rubbed, inner hinge cracked.   J. & S. L. Bonham Antiquarian Booksellers   Europe - 9869   2013   £75

Hagan, William T. *Quanah Parker, Comanche Chief.* Norman: University of Oklahoma Press, 1993. First edition, 22 vintage photos, 2 maps, maroon cloth, very fine, pictorial dust jacket.   Argonaut Book Shop   Summer 2013 - 139   2013 $50

Hagerty, Donald J. *Leading the West: One Hundred Contemporary Painters and Sculptors.* Flagstaff: Northland, 1997. Limited, first edition, 409 of 500 copies, square folio, frontispiece, illustrations, quarter gilt stamped calf over green cloth, front cover inset color, pictorial, gilt stamped green cloth slipcase, signed by author.   Jeff Weber Rare Books   171 - 154   2013 $200

Haggard, Henry Rider 1856-1925 *Colonel Quaritch, V.C.: a Tale of Country Life.* London: Longman, 1888. First edition, 3 volumes, half titles, original red cloth, front boards and spines lettered in black, spines slightly dulled, small marks on front board volume I and on spine of volume II, nice, crisp copy.   Jarndyce Antiquarian Booksellers   CCV - 120   2013   £450

Haggard, Henry Rider 1856-1925 *Heart of the World.* London: Longmans, 1896. First English edition, frontispiece, illustrations by Amy Sawyer, 24 page catalog Dec. 1895, original dark blue cloth, bevelled boards, spine slightly dulled, very good. Jarndyce Antiquarian Booksellers CCV - 121 2013 £100

Haggard, Henry Rider 1856-1925 *Joan Haste.* London: Longmans, 1895. First edition, 20 illustrations by E. S. Wilson, half title, frontispiece, plates, 24 page catalog July 1895, original dark blue smooth cloth, beveled boards, very slight rubbing to spine, very good. Jarndyce Antiquarian Booksellers CCV - 122 2013 £90

Haggard, Henry Rider 1856-1925 *King Solomon's Mines.* London: Cassell & Co., 1885. First edition, first issue, folding color map inserted as frontispiece, black and white map on page 27, original front cover cloth bound in at back, beautifully bound by Bayntun Riviere in full red morocco, boards ruled in gilt, spine printed and lettered gilt, gilt dentelles, all edges gilt, marbled endpapers, few professional repaired closed tears to folding map, about fine. Heritage Book Shop Holiday Catalogue 2012 - 71 2013 $5000

Haggard, Henry Rider 1856-1925 *King Solomon's Mines.* London: Cassell & Co., 1887. 48th thousand, Half title, folding color frontispiece, 4 pages ads, odd spot, original red cloth, slightly dulled, spine faded, pencil inscription. Jarndyce Antiquarian Booksellers CCV - 123 2013 £125

Hailey, Lord *An African Survey. A Study of Problems Arising in Africa South of the Sahara.* Oxford University Press, 1945. Second edition, thick 8vo., original cloth, gilt, 6 maps, 17 tables. R. F. G. Hollett & Son Africana - 84 2013 £45

Haimo, Oscar *Cocktail and Wine Digest: Encyclopedia & Guide for Home and Bar.* New York: International Cocktail, Wine and Spirit Digest, Inc., 1949. Reprint, possibly third printing, 24mo., printed wrappers, some modest stains to text, small shadow on front wrapper, very good or little better. Between the Covers Rare Books, Inc. Cocktails, Etc. - 321217 2013 $50

Haining, Peter *Movable Books.* London: New English Library, 1979. First edition, folio, black cloth, very good+ in like dust jacket. Barnaby Rudge Booksellers Children 2013 - 021636 2013 $60

Hainsworth, D. R. *The Correspondence of Sir John Lowther of Whitehaven 1693-1698.* British Academy, 1983. First edition, thick 8vo., original cloth, gilt, dust jacket (edges little worn and chipped), 2 plates, 3 maps. R. F. G. Hollett & Son Lake District and Cumbria - 221 2013 £75

Hakluyt, Richard 1552-1616 *The Principal Navigations Voyages & Discoveries of the English Nation Made by Sea or Overland to the Remote & Farthest Distant Quarters of the Earth at Any Time Within the Compasse of These 1600 Yeares.* London: J. M. Dent, 1926. 1936., Small 8vo., green cloth, dust jackets, very good, few volumes have some light soiling to outer edges, jackets worn, slightly soiled and with wear, nicks and some small tears to edges. Schooner Books Ltd. 101 - 143 2013 $75

Haldeman, Joe *The Forever War.* New York: St. Martins, 1974. First edition, fine in fine dust jacket, exceptionally fine in fine dust jacket, exceptionally fresh and crisp copy. Between the Covers Rare Books, Inc. Sci-Fi, Fantasy & Horror - 312885 2013 $1000

Hale, John *The Speech of Lieutenant-General Hale, in Favour of the People, at the Nomination and Election of a Member of Parliament for Yorkshire, in the Room of Sir George Saville.* York: printed by A. Ward, 1785. 8vo., very good in recent marbled boards with red morocco spine label, neat repair to gutter margin of titlepage, very scarce. Ken Spelman Books Ltd. 75 - 41 2013 £295

Hale, Kathleen *Orlando the Marmalade Cat Becomes a Doctor.* London: Country Life, 1944. First edition, folio, pictorial wrappers, some rubbing and marks to covers, very good+, beautiful color lithographs by Hale, this is publisher's proof, clipped inside front cover is typed page with text to be used on dust jacket flap of second edition and a piece of paper marked "PROOF COPY", few handwritten notes with reprint details on copyright page and rear cover text marked for exclusion, quite scarce. Aleph-Bet Books, Inc. 105 - 304 2013 $350

Hale, Kathleen *Orlando's Magic Carpet.* London: John Murray, 1958. First edition, small 4to., pictorial boards, some light cover soil, else very good (no dust jacket), illustrations in color and black and white, scarce. Aleph-Bet Books, Inc. 105 - 305 2013 $300

Hale, Susan *Imitation Nonsense Book a collection of Limericks.* Boston: Marshall Jones, 1919. First edition, oblong 8vo., pictorial boards, slightest of spine wear, very good, printed on one side of paper only, each leaf has humorous limerick with brown line illustration by Hale. Aleph-Bet Books, Inc. 105 - 364 2013 $125

Hales, Stephen *Statical Essays: Containing Vegetable statics.* London: Wilson and Nichol et al, 1769. Fourth and third edition, mixed set, 2 volumes, modern quarter calf with morocco labels. James Tait Goodrich 75 - 110 2013 $595

Hales, William *The Inspector, or Select Literary Intelligence for the Vulgar A.D. 1798 but Correct A.D.1801 to the first Year of the XIXth Century.* printed for J. White and J. Wright, 1799. 8vo., library shelf mark in ink at head of titlepage, some foxing and browning, 19th century purple hard grained cloth, shelfmark in gilt on spine, spine slightly darkened, inscription "to Mrs. James Ivory from Mr. Baron Manres 1799", bookplate of Dundee Free Libraries inside front cover, good. Blackwell's Rare Books B174 - 65 2013 £500

Halevy, Ludovic *The Abbe Constantin.* Philadelphia: Henry T. Coates & Co., circa, 1884. Frontispiece, title in red and green, 11 plates by Madeleine Lemaire, original dark green pictorial cloth,. Jarndyce Antiquarian Booksellers CCV - 124 2013 £45

Haley, Charles Scott *Gold Placers of California.* Sacramento: California State Mining Bureau, 1923. First edition, 167 pages, 36 photo, 7 plates ad maps, folding table, large folding map in rear pocket, brown cloth stamped in black, folding table torn and damaged to one edge, large folding map, few breaks at fold junctions else fine, ink name on end, fine. Argonaut Book Shop Recent Acquisitions June 2013 - 130 2013 $250

Haley, James Evetts *Erle P. Halliburton: Genius with Cement.* Duncan: 1959. Limited to 2000 copies, pictorial cloth, no dust jacket as issued. Dumont Maps & Books of the West 124 - 67 2013 $100

Haley, James Evetts *Fort Concho and the Texas Frontier.* Midland: West Texas Legacy Press, 2006. New edition, illustrations by H. D. Bugbee, maps by Jose Cisneros, brown cloth, very fine, pictorial dust jacket (spine very slightly faded), presentation inscription signed by J. Evetts Haley, Jr. Argonaut Book Shop Summer 2013 - 140 2013 $125

Haley, James Evetts *George W. Littlefield, Texan.* Norman: 1943. First edition, xiv, 287 pages, illustrations by Harold Bugbee, light wedge wear to dust jacket, else near fine. Dumont Maps & Books of the West 122 - 61 2013 $125

Haley, James Evetts *George W. Littlefield, Texan.* Norman: University of Oklahoma Press, 1972. First edition, 2nd printing, tan cloth stamped in dark green, very fine, pictorial dust jacket, presentation inscriptions signed by author. Argonaut Book Shop Summer 2013 - 141 2013 $100

Haley, James Evetts *Jeff Milton: a Good Man with a Gun.* Norman: 1953. Third printing, xiii, 430 pages, illustrations by Harold Bugbee, dust jacket with edge wear and short tears, book clean and very good, inscribed by author to previous owner. Dumont Maps & Books of the West 122 - 62 2013 $75

Haley, James Evetts *On His Native Health...In His Natural Element...* Midland: 1992. (xiii), 287 pages, illustrations, fine in like dust jacket, inscribed by author to previous owner. Dumont Maps & Books of the West 122 - 64 2013 $75

Haley, James Evetts *The XIT Ranch of Texas the Early Days of the Llano Estacado.* Norman: University of Oklahoma Press, 1953. First edition thus, presentation inscription, signed by author, large folding map, single page map, 32 vintage photos, green cloth, fine, lightly used pictorial dust jacket. Argonaut Book Shop Summer 2013 - 142 2013 $325

Haley, Katherine H. *Edward Borein, Artist of the West. From the Katherine H. Haley Collection.* Palm Springs: Palm Springs Desert Museum, 1991. 32 pages, 35 reproductions, 8 smaller photos, stiff brown wrappers with color pastedown on front cover, lettered in gold, fine, presentation inscription signed by Katherine Haley to Glen Dawson. Argonaut Book Shop Recent Acquisitions June 2013 - 33 2013 $60

Halfpenny, Joseph *Fragmenta Vetusta or the Remains of Ancient Buildings in York.* York: J. Halfpenny, 1807. Half title, decorative etched titlepage, dedication leaf, 34 etched plates, very good in contemporary half calf, marbled boards, upper joint little cracked, but very firm, some slight foxing to margins as usual with this work. Ken Spelman Books Ltd. 73 - 12 2013 £260

Halfpenny, Joseph *Gothic Ornaments in the Cathedral Church of York.* York: J. Todd and Sons, 1795-1800. First edition, 4to., engraved titlepage and 105 etched plates, very good 'family' copy bound in contemporary reverse calf with red morocco label, corners slightly bumped and minor wear to foot of spine, tiny worm track to top margin of several plates, Mary and William Halfpenny's copy, signed by Wm. Halfpenny 1798 and with inscription "Mr. Joseph Halfpenny, author of this book died July 11th 1811 aged 62", also signed by Mary Halfpenny. Ken Spelman Books Ltd. 73 - 9 2013 £595

Haliburton, Richard *The Flying Carpet.* Indianapolis: Bobbs Merrill, 1932. Stated first edition, near fine in original black cloth, gilt lettered spine and front cover, page edges, and f.f.e.p. age toned, in very good+ dust jacket with mild edgewear and sun spine, 8vo., 352 pages, rarely found in this condition with dust jacket, signed by author. By the Book, L. C. 36 - 85 2013 $300

Haliburton, Thomas Chandler 1796-1865 *The Bubbles of Canada.* London: Richard Bentley, 1839. First edition, 8vo., original paper covered boards with paper label to spine, outer hinge cracks with piece of top of spine missing, interior very good with only light foxing. Schooner Books Ltd. 101 - 94 2013 $75

Haliday, Charles *The Scandinavian Kingdom of Dublin.* 1884. IUP Facsimile of second edition, 8vo., cloth, very good. C. P. Hyland 261 - 466 2013 £80

Halifax, Nova Scotia and Its Attractions. Halifax: Howard & Kutsche Pub., n.d., 1903. 20.3 x 26.7cm., green cloth, red, white and black design to cover, 208 black and white photo illustrations, previous owner's name, cloth worn at edges, generally very good. Schooner Books Ltd. 104 - 49 2013 $100

Hall, A. Rupert *Henry More Magic: Religion and Experiment.* Cambridge: Basil Blackwell, 1990. 8vo., 304 pages, black cloth, silver stamped spine, dust jacket, inscribed in ink by author to I. Bernard Cohen, Burndy Library bookplate, fine. Jeff Weber Rare Books 169 - 306 2013 $60

Hall, Adam *The Volcanoes of San Domingo.* London: Collins, 1963. First edition, top corners slightly bumped, otherwise fine in dust jacket with small scrape on spine, several short closed tears and chips at corners. Mordida Books 81 - 239 2013 $150

Hall, Anna Maria *Lights and Shadows of Irish Life.* London: Henry Colburn, 1838. First edition, 33 volumes, contemporary half green calf, gilt spines maroon morocco labels, slight rubbing, very good. Jarndyce Antiquarian Booksellers CCV - 125 2013 £280

Hall, Ansel F. *Handbook of Yosemite National Park.* New York: G. P. Putnam's Sons, 1921. First edition, frontispiece, 27 plates, folding map, green pictorial cloth, stamped in white and black on front cover, tiny dents to top and fore-edge of front cover, else very fine. Argonaut Book Shop Summer 2013 - 143 2013 $125

Hall, Brian *Stealing from a Deep Place.* London: Heinemann, 1988. First edition, 8vo., pages 271, map, original green decorative cloth, dust jacket, torn at top of spine. J. & S. L. Bonham Antiquarian Booksellers Europe - 9812 2013 £25

Hall, Donald *Ox-Cart Man.* New York: Viking, 1979. Stated first edition, Oblong 4to., cloth backed pictorial boards, fine in dust jacket (price intact, no award seal, slight wear to base of spine, else near fine), illustrations in color by Barbara Cooney, inscribed by Cooney. Aleph-Bet Books, Inc. 105 - 149 2013 $700

Hall, Florence Howe *Little Lads and Lasses.* Boston: Lothrop, 1898. 4to., cloth backed pictorial boards, edges rubbed an rear cover soil, else very good+, 6 fine full page chromolithographs. Aleph-Bet Books, Inc. 104 - 570 2013 $375

Hall, Frederick Garrison *Book-Plates.* Boston: Troutsdale Press, 1905. 8vo., 24 black and/or red plates, original quarter white paper over gray paper backed boards, front cover tipped in gilt stamped title label, lightly rubbed, spine slightly soiled, bookplate of Jim Lewis, titlepage and first text page library blindstamps and rubber stamps, rear pastedown rubber stamp, very good, scarce. Jeff Weber Rare Books 171 - 156 2013 $75

Hall, G. *Monty the Monkey.* Bombay: Thacker, 1943. 12mo., 61 pages, cloth backed pictorial boards, very good, full page illustrations. Aleph-Bet Books, Inc. 104 - 188 2013 $200

Hall, J. Francis *Sea Breezes: The Hip Lovers' Digest (the Magazine of Ships and the Sea). New Series. Volumes 1-63.* Liverpool: Charles Birchall & sons/Journal of Commerce and Shipping, 1946-1989. First edition, volumes 1-63, color and black and white photos, drawings and plans, 8vo., cloth, lacking only volume 57, 1982; very good to fine, volumes 2-7 rubbed spines, volume 2 with addition photos and articles bound in, volumes 1-46 very good to very good+, volumes 47-63 near fine or fine, 3 volumes in shrink wrap, occasional photocopied index bound in, four earlier volumes with worn dust jackets. Kaaterskill Books 16 - 44 2013 $750

Hall, Jay *Evidently Murdered.* Philadelphia: Dorrance and Co., 1943. First edition, fine in lightly rubbed, very near fine dust jacket, very uncommon, scarce, especially in this condition. Between the Covers Rare Books, Inc. Mystery & Detective Fiction - 87726 2013 $200

Hall, Jeff M. *Linkage of Early-Onset Familial Breast Cancer to Chromosome...* American Assoc. for the Advancement of Science, 1990. Offprint from Science Volume 250 21 Dec. 1990, fine, original printed wrappers. By the Book, L. C. 37 - 38 2013 $300

Hall, Joseph *Mundus alter et Idem sive Terra Australis...* Frankfurt: apud haeredes Ascanii de Rinialme, 1607? 8vo., first state engraved titlepage, 5 folding engraved plates (all first editions) text mixed edition, two gatherings from second printing), somewhat soiled and browned, few outer edges slightly frayed, title slightly abraded, some contemporary manuscript notes, ownership inscriptions to title and flyleaf and Macclesfield embossment to first two leaves, 8vo., original limp vellum, somewhat soiled, ties lost, stitching loosening, Shirburn Castle bookplate, preserved in clamshell morocco. Blackwell's Rare Books B174 - 66 2013 £5500

Hall, Louisa J. *Sophia Morton.* Boston: Bowles and Dearborn, 1827. First edition, fine in original printed card covers, rear wrapper depicting Boston bookshop. Ken Spelman Books Ltd. 75 - 89 2013 £180

Hall, Marshall *The Artists of Cumbria.* Newcastle-upon-Tyne: Marshall Hall Associates, 1979. First edition, 4to., illustrations, original cloth, gilt, dust jacket, variant design with overall illustration of Sam Bough's 'Baggage Wagons', price clipped.   R. F. G. Hollett & Son   Lake District and Cumbria - 222   2013   £30

Hall, Marshall *Lectures on the Nervous System and Its Diseases.* Philadelphia: Carey & Hart, 1836. First American edition, original full brown calf, some wear and rubbing and chipping to leather but binding sound, text with browning and foxing typical for this period.   James Tait Goodrich   S74 - 141   2013 $495

Hall, Marshall *Memoirs on the Nervous System.* London: printed for Sherwood, Gilbert & Piper, 1837. First edition, 3 engraved plates, 4to., modern brown cloth, pages with marginal foxing and some toning, otherwise clean.   James Tait Goodrich   75 - 111   2013 $1500

Hall, Marshall *On the Diseases and Derangements of the Nervous System.* London: H. Bailliere, 1841. 8 plates, original green Victorian cloth, worn and rubbed, ex-library with usual stamps.   James Tait Goodrich   75 - 112   2013 $595

Hall, Oakley *Warlock.* New York: Viking Press, 1958. First edition, very good, cream linen spine, red paper covered boards and red title to spine, few very light spots of foxing to spine and very light edge wear, very good black dust jacket with white title to spine panel, minor wear to edges of jacket, some rubbing to panels, 471 pages.   The Kelmscott Bookshop   7 - 114   2013 $250

Hall, Richard *Stanley. An Adventurer Explored.* Collins, 1974. First edition, original cloth, gilt, dust jacket, 42 illustrations and maps on endpapers.   R. F. G. Hollett & Son   Africana - 85 2013   £35

Hall, Ruth *The Boys of Scrooby.* Boston and New York: Houghton Mifflin and Co., 1899. First edition, frontispiece, original grey pictorial cloth, label removed from leading pastedown, very good.   Jarndyce Antiquarian Booksellers   CCV - 126   2013   £20

Hall, Sidney Prior *Oxford Sketches.* Oxford: J. Ryman, circa, 1868. 170 albumen prints on 154 sheets, mounts affected by damp and stained from glue, prints somewhat yellowed and occasionally faint but generally good, 4to., with 8vo. 'Key', contemporary black pebble grain morocco matching in style although black dye with red undertones on first two volumes and green on third, front boards bordered gilt and lettered "Oxford Sketches/D.C.", glue in volume iii entirely perished and sheets loose, joints rubbed, slight wear to endcaps volumes i and ii, small bookplates recording volumes printed by J. Ryman on front pastedowns, Key in original wrappers, soiled and worn with loss from blank area at foot of gutter, sound.   Blackwell's Rare Books   B174 - 112   2013   £800

Hallday, Brett *Michael Shayne's 50th Case.* New York: Torquil/Dodd, Mead, 1964. First edition, very slightly cocked, else fine in fine, gilt foil dust jacket, inscribed by author to fellow mystery writer John D. MacDonald, outstanding association.   Between the Covers Rare Books, Inc.   Mystery & Detective Fiction - 97549   2013 $1250

Haller, Albrect Von *Deux Memoires sur le Mouvement du Sang...* Paris: chez David, 1756. viii, 343 pages, frontispiece, 8vo., full contemporary polished mottled calf, gilt spine in compartments, head of spine worn, faint dampstaining of lower margins of frontispiece, title and prelims, from the library of Theophile de Bordeu with his armorial bookplate.   James Tait Goodrich   75 - 113   2013 $1295

Halley, Edmund *Astronomical Tables with Precepts both in English and Latin.* London: William Innys, 1752. First edition in English, 4to., engraved frontispiece, lacks half title, offsetting to pastedowns and free endleaves and titlepage opposite frontispiece, some corners browned, else text clean, beautiful gilt stamped double ruled calf, decorative spine, dark red leather spine label, bit rubbed, spine recently replaced to period style and corners renewed, near fine.   Jeff Weber Rare Books   169 - 183   2013 $2750

Halliday Company Limited *Factory Distributors Truro Nova Scotia Head Office Hamilton, Ontario 1921. Catalogue 67.* Hamilton: Halliday Co. Ltd., 1921. Pages 76, quarto, color illustrated paper covers worn with small nicks and tears to edges, pages 36 to 40 have small tear to inner margin.   Schooner Books Ltd.   102 - 66   2013 $75

Halliday, Brett *Die Like a Dog.* New York: Torquil, 1959. First edition, fore edge foxed, else fine in fine, very slightly age toned white dust jacket.   Between the Covers Rare Books, Inc.   Mystery & Detective Fiction - 36611   2013 $50

Halliday, Geoffrey *A Flora of Cumbria.* Lancaster University: Centre for North-West Regional Studies, 1997. First hardback edition, large 4to., original cloth, gilt, dust jacket, 113 color plates, 1190 color maps.   R. F. G. Hollett & Son   Lake District and Cumbria - 226   2013   £75

Halliday, Geoffrey *A Flora of Cumbria...* Lancaster University: Centre for North-West Regional Studies, 1998. First softback reprinted edition, large 4to., original pictorial wrappers, pages 611, with 113 color plates and 1190 colored maps, addenda and corrections on corrigenda slip loosely inserted with the first edition are here corrected.   R. F. G. Hollett & Son   Lake District and Cumbria - 225   2013   £60

Hamady, Walter *Book No. 68.* Mt. Horeb: Perishable Press, 1974. First edition, limited to 34 copies (entire edition), signed by Hamady, irregular 12mo., original wrappers, fine, rare.   James S. Jaffe Rare Books   Fall 2013 - 122   2013 $3500

Hamady, Walter *Closing Flowers.* Mt. Horeb: Perishable Press, 1966. First edition, one of only 30 copies printed on variegated handmade paper, 8vo., unbound signatures as issued, fine, rare. James S. Jaffe Rare Books Fall 2013 - 121 2013 $4500

Hamady, Walter *The Disillusioned Solipsist and Nine Related Poems.* No place: Perishable Press Ltd., 1964. First edition, limited to 60 copies of which this is marked "Artist's proof, Walter Hamady", small 4to., 2 original signed etchings, original photo and 2 drawings by author, original brown paper wrappers, very fine, rare. James S. Jaffe Rare Books Fall 2013 - 120 2013 $9500

Hamady, Walter *For the Hundredth Time, Gabberjab Number Five.* Minor Confluence: Perishable Press, 1981. First edition, one of 200 copies, 12mo., original boards, this copy bears special inscription by printer on back cover, fine, laid in is appealing holograph postcard from Hamady. James S. Jaffe Rare Books Fall 2013 - 124 2013 $1500

Hamady, Walter *Hand Papermaking: Papermaking by Hand.* Minor Confluence: Perishable Press, 1982. First edition, limited to 200 copies printed on various handmade papers, fine, tall 8vo., illustrations by Jim Lee, original cloth, 2 variants of publisher's prospectus laid in. James S. Jaffe Rare Books Fall 2013 - 125 2013 $1750

Hamady, Walter *The Interminable Gabberjabb Volume One (&) Number Four.* Mt. Horeb: Perishable Press, 1975. First edition, one of 60 copies, oblong 12mo., 2 photos by Gregory Conniff, original wrappers, fine. James S. Jaffe Rare Books Fall 2013 - 123 2013 $2500

Hamady, Walter *Neopostmodernism or Gabberjab Number 6.* Mt. Horeb: Perishable Press, 1988. First edition, limited to 125 copies printed on various handmade papers, oblong small 8vo., illustrations, original boards, signed by binder, Marta Gomez, Hamady's assistant, Kent Kasuboske and especially inscribed by Hamady to collector, very fine. James S. Jaffe Rare Books Fall 2013 - 125 2013 $2500

Hamady, Walter *Papermaking by Hand.* Minor Confluence Perry Township: Perishable Press, 1982. One of 200 copies, on a variety of contemporary handmade papers, 13 various Shadwells, Roma and Perusia from Miliani in Fabriano, Canterbury from Barcham Green in Maidstone, Kent (all three retain their watermarks), Barlow from HMP in Woodstock, Conn., Banana-sisal from Carriage House in Brookline, Mass., Yale (in wove and laid surfaces) for Twinrocker in Brookston, Indiana, bound by Bill Anthony & Associates in tan Irish linen over boards, housed in custom made black cloth clamshell box with leather label printed in gold gilt on spine, 56 pages surfaces in 7 signatures, 26 pages of text, 3 illustrations from Diderot and 12 linoleum cuts by Jim Lee, especially for this text, 2 titlepages, one by Hamady and one penned by Hermann Zapf. Priscilla Juvelis - Rare Books 55 - 21 2013 $2500

Hamady, Walter *Papermaking by Hand. A Book of Suspicions.* Minor Confluence, Perry Township: Perishable Press, 1982. One of 200 copies on a variety of contemporary handmade papers, 13 various Shadwells, Roma & Perusia from Miliani in Fabriano, Canterbury from Barcham Green in Maidstone, Kent (all three retain their watermarks), Barlow from HMP in Woodstock, Connecticut, banana sisal from Carriage House in Brookline, Massachsuetts, Yale (in wove and laid surfaces) from Twinrocker in Brookston, Indiana, laid in is original prospectus for book and original invoice from Perishable Press, bound by Bill Anthony & Associates tan Irish linen over boards, pages size 11 x 7 1/2 inches, 56 pages surfaces in 7 signatures, 26 pages of text, page size of prospectus 6 11/16 x 9 11/16 inches, page size of invoice 7 3/16 x 10 7/16 inches, custom made wood veneer clamshell box with brown leather spine banded in vellum, lined in buff felt, fine, 3 illustrations from Diderot and 12 linoleum cuts by Jim Lee especially for this text, there are 2 titlepage - one by Walter Hamady and one penned by Hermann Zapf who also designed typeface, Palatino, used for this text, type was handset and printed by Hamady, 50 of the pages printed in 88 press runs, in 5 basic colors, on 19 different colors of paper, beautiful book. Priscilla Juvelis - Rare Books 56 - 24 2013 $3000

Hambly, Wilfrid D. *Clever Hands of African Negro.* Washington: Associated Publishers, 1945. First edition, owner's note on front fly, else about fine in very good dust jacket with scrape on front panel to lettering (which has been retouched by previous owner), large chip on rear panel, scarce. Between the Covers Rare Books, Inc. 165 - 163 2013 $85

Hamby, Wallace B. *Intracranial Aneurysms.* Springfield: Charles C. Thomas, 1952. First edition, 8vo., 104 figures, maroon cloth, gilt stamped spine title, bookplate removed from front pastedown, presentation signatures of 17 members of the Fellow Society of Montreal Neurological Institute dated 27 Ma7 1955, ownership signature on titlepage, very good. Jeff Weber Rare Books 172 - 122 2013 $325

Hamilton, A. W. *Haji's Book of Malayan Nursery Rhymes.* Sydney: Australasian Pub. Co., 1947. First edition, 4to., cloth, pictorial paste-on, fine in dust jacket torn on rear panel, color and black and whites by Nora Hamerton. Aleph-Bet Books, Inc. 104 - 334 2013 $200

Hamilton, Adrian *The Infamous Essay on Woman or John Wilkes Seated Between Vice and Virtue London.* London: Andre Deutsch, 1972. One of 2000 numbered copies, 4to., 256 pages, set of two copies, one bound in patterned paper with black cloth spine, the other a 'reading' copy, identical but in paper binding, ex-library with labels and bookplates, copiously illustrated, aside from library labels, nice copies in somewhat worn box. Second Life Books Inc. 183 - 153 2013 $85

Hamilton, Anthony 1646-1720 *Memoires de la Vie du Cmte De Grammont...* Cologne: Pierre Marteau, 1713. First edition, 12mo., full calf, raised bands, 6 gilt decorated compartments, marbled endpapers, title in red and black, armorial bookplate of De Constant Rebecque, spine scuffed, else very good with boards rubbed, few tiny worm holes to top edge of rear board, endpapers toned at edges, binding tight, text clean with only some odd foxing. Kaaterskill Books 16 - 45 2013 $500

Hamilton, Anthony 1646-1720 *Memoires du Comte de Grammont.* Paris: de l'Imprimerie de Didot, 1760. 12mo., 2 volumes, some old waterstaining to volume II, slightly dusted, contemporary calf, gilt panelled spines, red and black morocco labels, hinges cracked, head and tail of spines slightly chipped. Jarndyce Antiquarian Booksellers CCIV - 153 2013 £45

Hamilton, Anthony 1646-1720 *Memoirs of Count Grammont.* London and Edinburgh: printed by Jas. Ballantyne & Co. for William Miller and James Carpenter, 1811. 2 volumes, 235 x 146mm., with a total of 143 engraved portrays, including 64 called for, and extra illustrated with 79 additional portraits apparently taken from 1793 edition of the work inserted specially in this copy, large paper copy, splendid crimson straight grain morocco, elegantly and attractively gilt by Zaehnsdorf (stamp signed and dated 1900 on front turn-ins), covers gilt with double ruled border enclosing fleurons and floral sprays, large fleuron cornerpieces accented with circlets and dots, broad raised bands adorned with six gilt rules, spine compartments with filigreen frames echoing the cover decoration, densely gilt filigree turn-ins, marbled endpapers, top edge gilt, other edges untrimmed, noticeable offsetting from portraits whenever there is a facing text page (as opposed to verso of another plate) and rather conspicuous in about half dozen cases, otherwise, extremely fine, text very fresh and clean, beautiful, unworn bindings, extraordinarily bright. Phillip J. Pirages 61 - 131 2013 $1600

Hamilton, Bruce *Too Much of Water.* London: Cresset, 1958. First edition, fine in dust jacket. Mordida Books 81 - 240 2013 $75

Hamilton, Cicely Mary *Marriage as a Trade.* London: Chapman & Hall, 1909. First edition, half title, 8 pages ads, original olive green cloth, slightly dulled and rubbed, evidence of label removed from front board, stamps and label of National Council of Women. Jarndyce Antiquarian Booksellers CCV - 127 2013 £225

Hamilton, Elizabeth *Letters on the Elementary Principles of Education.* Bath: R. CruttwellI, 1801-1802. First edition Volume II, second edition of volume I, 2 volumes, half title to volume II, very good in handsome contemporary half calf, gilt decorated spines, marbled boards and edges, some light foxing, bookplate of Frankland, of Thirkleby, Yorkshire, 8vo. Ken Spelman Books Ltd. 75 - 50 2013 £260

Hamilton, Elizabeth *Memoirs of Modern Philosophers.* Bath: printed by R. Cruttwell and sld by G. & J. Robinson, London, 1804. Fourth edition, 3 volumes, contemporary full speckled calf, gilt borders, spines ruled and with devices in gilt, red morocco labels, small volume number labels in black morocco, contemporary owner's inscription volume I, very good. Jarndyce Antiquarian Booksellers CCV - 128 2013 £380

Hamilton, Owen *Tyrolean Summer.* London: Williams & Norgate, 1934. First edition, 8vo., 319 pages, illustrations, original brown cloth. J. & S. L. Bonham Antiquarian Booksellers Europe - 5320 2013 £30

Hamilton, Virginia *Zeely.* New York: Macmillan, 1967. Stated first printing, review copy with slip laid-in, full page black and whites by Symeon Shimin, very scare, 8vo., cloth, fine in slightly rubbed dust jacket. Aleph-Bet Books, Inc. 104 - 79 2013 $400

Hamilton, William 1704-1754 *Poems on Several Occasions.* Edinburgh: printed for W. Gordon, Bookseller in the Parliament Close, 1760. 8vo., engraved frontispiece, lightly toned and spotted, contemporary cat's paw tan calf, spine gilt in compartments, red morocco label, bit rubbed at extremities, slight wear to headcap and front joint, ink inscription of Wm. Irby August 3rd out of 1769 Mr. Tompsons library at Gottingen" armorial bookplate of William Irby. Unsworths Antiquarian Booksellers 28 - 105 2013 £200

Hamilton, William 1730-1803 *Outlines from the Figures and Compositions Upon the Greek, Roman and Etruscan Vases of the late Sir William Hamilton...* London: published by William Miller, Old Bond Street, Printed by W. Bulmer and Co., Cleveland Row MDCCCIV, 1804. Large paper copy, 4to., 124 plates, being 62 engraved plates, each in two states, colored in red and black and uncolored, contemporary red morocco gilt with crowned cipher of Eugene de Beaucharnais, spine in compartments separated by double raised bands, two lettered gilt possibly by Maurais or Lodigian who provided many bindings for Beaucharnais, watered silk endpapers. Marlborough Rare Books Ltd. 218 - 74 2013 £5000

Hamilton, William Rowan *Researches Respecting Quaternions. in Transactions of Royal Irish Academy Volume XXI Part II.* Dublin: Royal Irish Academy, 1847. Offered are unbound sheets of the Science section, minimal soil, scattered foxing, housed in modern quarter leather marbled board clamshell box with gilt rules, decorations and lettering on spine, printed paper label on front cover. By the Book, L. C. 38 - 51 2013 $3500

Hammer, Victor *Memory and Her Nine Daughters.* New York: printed at the hand press by Carolyn R. Hammer, Victor Hammer has set the pages, 1957. 83/250 copies, printed in Uncial types on handmade paper printed in black save for sub title which is printed in red, one full page diagram, 8vo., original cream boards printed in black overall, backstrip printed in red 'hammer: 4 dialogues", untrimmed, dust jacket, fine, Vivian Ridler's copy with his book ticket, inscribed "in appreciation - C(arolyn) Hammer. Blackwell's Rare Books   B174 - 352   2013   £450

Hammett, Dashiell *The Glass Key.* London: Alfred A. Knopf, 1931. First edition, first issue with Knopf imprint (later issues have Cassell imprint), attractive engraved bookplate on front pastedown, slightly cocked with small, not too obtrusive stain on front board, otherwise near fine, lacking rare dust jacket, very attractive copy. Between the Covers Rare Books, Inc.   Mystery & Detective Fiction - 84799   2013 $4500

Hammett, Dashiell *The Glass Key.* New York: Grosset & Dunlap, 1933. Reprint edition, pages darkened and covers lightly soiled, otherwise near fine in dust jacket with couple of closed tears, small chip a top corner of back panel, nicks at corners.   Mordida Books   81 - 242   2013 $150

Hammett, Dashiell *The Maltese Falcon.* New York: Alfred A. Knopf, 1930. First edition, first printing, octavo, titlepage printed in blue gray and black, decorated light gray cloth, front and spine panels stamped in blue-grey and black running Borzoi stamped in black on rear panel, top edge gilt stained light blue gray, other edges rough trimmed.   L. W. Currey, Inc.   Fall Sampler Sept. 2013 - 144963   2013 $65,000

Hammett, Dashiell *Modern Tales of Horror.* London: Victor Gollancz, 1932. first English edition, page edges slightly darkened, otherwise fine in very good dust jacket with some internal tape reinforcing and repair, strip clipped from internal rear flap, couple of short closed tears. Mordida Books   81 - 241   2013 $450

Hammett, Dashiell *Woman in the Dark.* New York: Lawrence E. Spivak, 1951. First edition, wrappers, digest size paperback original very good+, tiny nick or two and mild wear.   Beasley Books   2013 - 2013 $60

Hammond, Bryan *Josephine Baker.* London: Jonathan Cape, 1988. First edition, quarto, fine in very lightly rubbed, still easily fine dust jacket, heavily illustrated. Between the Covers Rare Books, Inc.   165 - 57   2013 $85

Hammond, Elizabeth *Modern Domestic Cookery and Useful Receipt Book.* printed for Dean & Munday and A. K. Newman, 1824. Fifth edition, additional engraved frontispiece and frontispiece, 4 engraved plates, few spots and stains, especially at beginning, 12mo., contemporary mottled calf, spine with triple gilt rules forming compartments, black lettering piece, cracks in joints and head and tail of spine little worn, good.   Blackwell's Rare Books   Sciences - 34   2013   £700

Hammond, George Peter *New Spain and the Anglo-American West; Historical Contributions Presented to Herbert Eugene Bolton.* Privately printed, 1932. 2 volumes, frontispiece, bright and near fine.   Dumont Maps & Books of the West   122 - 67   2013 $275

Hammond, George Peter *Noticias de California.* San Francisco: Book Club of California, 1958. Limited to 400 copies, quarto, 53 pages, folding frontispiece map, 8 page octavo facsimile and 6 page quarto facsimile with folding map, one illustration, decorated gray boards, black cloth back, gilt, very fine.   Argonaut Book Shop   Recent Acquisitions June 2013 - 131   2013 $90

Hammond, George Peter *The Treaty of Guadalupe Hidalgo Feb. Second 1848.* Berkeley: Friends of the Bancroft Library, 1949. Facsimile edition, one of 500 copies, lacking large folding map in separate folder, original orange and white patterned boards, white linen spine with printed paper label, edges slightly darkened fine, Disturnell map that accompanies text in separate matching folder is lacking.   Argonaut Book Shop   Recent Acquisitions June 2013 - 132   2013 $75

Hammond, William *Experimental Researches Relative to the Nutritive value and Physiological Effects of Albumen, Starch and Gum...* Philadelphia: T. K. and P. G. Collins, 1857. 79 pages, with errata, original ruled printed gray wrappers, light marginal dampstaining and some foxing, quite scarce.   James Tait Goodrich   S74 - 142   2013 $495

Hanapis, Nicolaus De *Exempla Sacre Scripture.* Paris: per Petrum Levet (post), 1494. Portions of titlepage excised (removing ownership inscriptions), remainder mounted, lower margin of final leaf and blank portions of two text leaves, also sometime renewed (one covering small stamp), rubricated throughout, including 6 line initial on first text leaf and recently foliated in pencil, some light browning, old washed ink marks to antepenultimate leaf, 8vo., recased in vellum, preserving an earlier vellum, backstrip lettered in ink, endpapers renewed, sound.   Blackwell's Rare Books   172 - 65   2013   £2500

Handbook of North Carolina. Raleigh: Presses of Edwards & Broughton, 1893. First edition, 8vo., pages 333, printed wrappers, large foldout map in rear, slip tipped to flyleaf "Compliments of/ C.?Root/ Jno Robinson/ Com. of Agriculture" in unknown holograph, very good, photos, scarce.   Second Life Books Inc.   183 - 294   2013 $225

Handcock, William D.   *The History & Antiquities of Tallaght.*   1976.   Tower facsimile of 2nd edition, 8vo., illustrations, cloth, dust jacket, very good.   C. P. Hyland   261 - 468   2013   £60

Handel, George Frideric   *Jephtha. An Oratorio set to Musick by Mr. Handel.*   London: printed for I. Walsh, 1752. First edition, modern half leather, marbled paper boards, raised bands to spine, gilt lettering on maroon spine labels, gilt design to spine, new endpapers, fine navy cloth covered slipcase, title and last page with mild soil, corner chip blank edge, last page not affecting music or text, mild scattered foxing, 4to., 91 pages.   By the Book, L. C.   36 - 3   2013 $1500

Handforth, Thomas   *Mei Li.*   New York: Doubleday Doran, 1938. First edition, folio, orange cloth, some cover soil, very good+ in dust jacket (not price clipped, no medal, slightly frayed at spine ends, few small closed tears), magnificently illustrated in black and white on every page, signed by Handforth.   Aleph-Bet Books, Inc.   104 - 274   2013 $1350

Handley, James E.   *The Irish in Modern Scotland.*   Cork: U.P., 1947. First edition, 8vo., cloth, dust jacket over wrappers, some foxing, else very good.   C. P. Hyland   261 - 469   2013   £40

Handley, John   *Catalogue of Plants Growing in the Sedbergh District...*   Leeds: Richard Jackson, 1898.   First edition, small 8vo., original printed wrappers, foot of backstrip trifle defective and repaired, 48 pages, nice, clean, scarce.   R. F. G. Hollett & Son   Lake District and Cumbria - 228   2013   £40

Hanft, Robert M.   *Pine across the Mountain.*   San Marino: Golden West Books, 1972. First edition, 2nd printing, 224 pages, over 295 photos and illustrations, including maps, wood grain beige cloth, some minor foxing to edges of jacket, but fine with pictorial dust jacket.   Argonaut Book Shop   Recent Acquisitions June 2013 - 133   2013 $75

Hankinson, Alan   *Camera on the Crags.*   London: Heinemann, 1975. 4to., original cloth gilt, dust jacket, 105 pages of plates, ex-libris, scarce.   R. F. G. Hollett & Son   Lake District and Cumbria - 229   2013   £95

Hankinson, Alan   *The Regatta Men.*   Milnthorpe: Cicerone Press, 1988. First edition, oblong large 4to., original pictorial wrappers, pages 27, 10 illustrations and 8 full or double page facsimile maps.   R. F. G. Hollett & Son   Lake District and Cumbria - 230   2013   £25

Hanna, Phil Townsend   *The Dictionary of California Land Names.*   Los Angeles: Automobile Club of Southern California, 1946. First edition, rust cloth, gilt, fine.   Argonaut Book Shop   Recent Acquisitions June 2013 - 134   2013 $75

Hannay, James   *The History of Acadia from Its First Discovery to Its Surrender to England by the Treaty of Paris.*   St. John: printed by J. & A. Macmillan, 1879. Pressed cloth with gilt and black design to front cover, gilt title to spine, 8vo., some very light shelfwear to edges, otherwise very good.   Schooner Books Ltd.   101 - 1   2013 $95

Hannett, John   *An Inquiry into the Nature and Form of the Books of the Ancients...*   London: Richard Groombridge, 1837. First edition, 12mo., iv, 212 pages, frontispiece, 13 plates, woodcuts in text, contemporary cloth.   Marlborough Rare Books Ltd.   218 - 75   2013   £750

Hansberry, Lorraine   *A Raisin in the Sun.*   New York: Random House, 1959. First edition, fine in fine dust jacket, advance review copy with slip laid in.   Between the Covers Rare Books, Inc.   165 - 305   2013 $1000

Hansch, Michael Gottlieb   *Godefridi Guilielmi Leibnitii Principia Philosophiae...*   Frankfurt and Leipzig: Peter Conrad Monath, 1728. First edition, 2 leaves with wormhole in upper margin, contemporary ?Slovak calf, spine gilt in compartment, gilt dull, extremities little worn, spine slightly defective at either end, good.   Blackwell's Rare Books   Sciences - 72   2013   £2000

Hansen, Ron   *Desperadoes.*   New York: Knopf, 1979. First edition, inscribed, fine in dust jacket.   Ed Smith Books   78 - 25   2013 $150

Hanson, Robert   *The Microbibliophile, a Bi-Monthly Review of Literature Concerning Miniature Books.*   Mattituck/Venice: Robert F. Hanson, 1977-2005.   Small 4to. newsletter and small 8vo. magazine, self wrappers and stiff paper wrappers, 10-15 pages each, consecutive run of 162 issues, color photos tipped to cover of each issue in magazine format starting with volume 4, from the collection of Donn W. Sanford.   Oak Knoll Books   303 - 16   2013 $650

Haraszthy, Arpad   *Wine-Making in California.*   San Francisco: Book Club of California, 1978. Limited to 600 copies, 69 pages, illustrations and frontispiece, portraits and facsimiles, maroon cloth, gilt, very fine, pictorial dust jacket.   Argonaut Book Shop   Summer 2013 - 144   2013 $75

Harbou, Thea Von *Metropolis Roman.* Berlin: August Scherl G. m. b. H., 1926. First edition, octavo, original four color pictorial wrappers, all edges untrimmed. L. W. Currey, Inc. Fall Sampler Sept. 2013 - 143430   2013 $7500

Harcourt, Edward Vernon *A Sketch of Madeira...* London: John Murray, 1851. First edition, 8vo., 2 folding maps, 5 illustrations, some occasional light foxing, original brown decorative cloth, spine and corners rubbed.   J. & S. L. Bonham Antiquarian Booksellers   Europe - 8965   2013   £125

Hardy, Charles Frederick *The Hardys of Barbon and some Other Westmorland Statesman; Their Kieth, Kin and Childer.* London: Constable, 1913. First edition, original green cloth, gilt, faint shelf numbers on spine, top edge gilt, map frontispiece and illustrations.   R. F. G. Hollett & Son   Lake District and Cumbria - 232   2013   £60

Hardy, Eric *The Naturalist in Lakeland.* David & Charles, 1973. First edition, original cloth, gilt, dust jacket, 192 pages, illustrations.   R. F. G. Hollett & Son   Lake District and Cumbria - 233   2013   £30

Hardy, Evelyn *Summer in Another World.* 1950. First edition, illustrations, cloth, dust jacket worn, good copy.   C. P. Hyland   261 - 471   2013   £35

Hardy, Florence *The Early Life of Thomas Hardy 1840-1891. (with) The Later Years of Thomas Hardy 1892-1928.* London: Macmillan, 1928-1930. First edition, 2 volumes, 8vo., original light green cloth, gilt lettering, top edge gilt, frontispiece in each volume and 25 plates, cloth slightly worn, fine copies in slightly worn dust jackets, from the Gary Lepper Collection of Thomas Hardy.   The Brick Row Book Shop   Bulletin Nine - 87   2013 $200

Hardy, Florence *The Early Life of Thomas Hardy 1840-1891. (and) The Later Years of Thomas Hardy 1892-1928.* Macmillan, 1928-1933. First editions, 2 volumes, frontispiece portraits, plates and facsimiles, 8vo., original mid green cloth, lettering on backstrips and Hardy medallion on front covers all gilt blocked, faint endpaper foxing, small newspaper clipping pasted to rear free endpaper of volume ii, top edge gilt, dust jackets chipped and with short tears, very good, this was Doctor Vandermin's copy, quite possibly Florence Hardy's doctor with presentation inscription from Florence Hardy Nov. 1928.   Blackwell's Rare Books   172 - 191   2013   £550

Hardy, Florence *Nurse Jane!* London: Castell Bros. n.d. circa, 1910. 12mo., stiff pictorial wrappers, silk ties, some cover soil, else very good+, full page color illustrations, very scarce.   Aleph-Bet Books, Inc.   105 - 308   2013 $225

Hardy, Francis *Memoirs of James Caulfield, Earl of Charlemont.* 1812. Second edition, volume I ex-library, Lord Carbery, Laxton Hall (ownership inscription dated St. Patrick's Day 1875), covers poor, text very good, 8vo., cloth. C. P. Hyland   261 - 177   2013   £95

Hardy, Thomas 1840-1928 *And There Was a Great Calm. 11 November 1918.* London: privately printed for Florence Emily Hardy at the Chiswick press, 1920. First edition, number 3 of 25 numbered copies, initialed by Florence Hardy, 4to., original blue printed wrappers, stitched as issued, edges of wrappers slightly darkened and chipped, fine, from the Gary Lepper Collection of Thomas Hardy. The Brick Row Book Shop   Bulletin Nine - 64   2013 $2500

Hardy, Thomas 1840-1928 *A Call to National Service. An Appeal to America. Cry of the Homeless.* London: privately printed by the Chiswick Press for Florence Hardy, 1917. First edition, one of 25 numbered copies initialed by Florence Hardy on limitation page, inscribed "Corrected by/ Thomas Hardy/May 1917", 4to., original blue wrappers stitched as issued, (8) pages, untrimmed, fine in chemise and quarter morocco slipcase, from the Gary Lepper Collection of Thomas Hardy.   The Brick Row Book Shop   Bulletin Nine - 60   2013 $5000

Hardy, Thomas 1840-1928 *A Catalogue of the Library of Thomas Hardy...* London: Messrs. Hodgson, 1938. First edition, 55 pages, 309 lots, fine, original printed wrappers, 4to., from the Gary Lepper Collection of Thomas Hardy. The Brick Row Book Shop   Bulletin Nine - 94   2013 $250

Hardy, Thomas 1840-1928 *A Changed Man, The Waiting Supper and Other Tales. Concluding with the Romantic Adventures of a Milkmaid.* London: Macmillan, 1913. First edition, colonial issue, 8vo., original decorated pale blue cloth, gilt lettered, frontispiece and double page map, 8 page publisher's catalog, cloth faded, somewhat worn, good copy, from the Gary Lepper Collection of Thomas Hardy. The Brick Row Book Shop   Bulletin Nine - 54   2013 $450

Hardy, Thomas 1840-1928 *A Changed Man, The Waiting Supper and Other Tales. Concluding with the Romantic Adventures of a Milkmaid.* London: Macmillan, 1913. First edition, 8vo., original dark green cloth, gilt lettered, top edge gilt, frontispiece, double page map, 2 pages publisher's terminal ads, edges little worn, very good in like dust jacket (spine darkened, edges worn), from the Gary Lepper Collection of Thomas Hardy.   The Brick Row Book Shop   Bulletin Nine - 52   2013 $400

Hardy, Thomas   1840-1928   *Compassion: an Ode in Celebration of the Royal Society for the Prevention of Cruelty to Animals.*   Dorchester: privately printed,   1924.   First edition, number 8 of 25 numbered copies, initialed by Florence Emily Hardy on colophon page, 4to., original printed wrappers, stitched as issued, 6 pages, fine in chemise and quarter morocco slipcase, from the Gary Lepper Collection of Thomas Hardy.   The Brick Row Book Shop   Bulletin Nine - 69   2013 $3500

Hardy, Thomas   1840-1928   *Desparate Remedies.*   New York: Henry Holt, 1874.   First American edition, 2nd issue binding, 8vo., original decorated mustard yellow cloth, black lettering, endpapers little browned, fine, from the Gary Lepper Collection of Thomas Hardy.   The Brick Row Book Shop   Bulletin Nine - 3   2013 $750

Hardy, Thomas   1840-1928   *The Duke's Reappearance: a Tradition.*   New York: privately printed, 1927.   First separate edition, number 30 of 89 numbered copies, 8vo., original yellow paper boards, printed paper label, boards slightly soiled, fine, from the Gary Lepper Collection of Thomas Hardy.   The Brick Row Book Shop   Bulletin Nine - 78   2013 $250

Hardy, Thomas   1840-1928   *The Dynasts: a Drama of the Napoleonic Wars in Three Parts, Nineteen Acts and One Hundred and Thirty Scenes.*   London: Macmillan, 1903-1908.   First edition, first issue volume one, second issue of volume two with titlepage a cancel, 3 volumes, 8vo., original olive-green cloth, gilt decoration and lettering, bookplate on front pastedown in volume one of Edward Joseph Dent, cloth little worn, hinges in volume one carefully repaired, very good in original printed dust jackets which have had skillful paper restoration to corners and spines, enclosed in chemise and morocco slipcase, from the Gary Lepper Collection of Thomas Hardy.   The Brick Row Book Shop   Bulletin Nine - 46   2013 $4500

Hardy, Thomas   1840-1928   *The Dynasts: a Drama of the Napoleonic Wars, in Three Parts, Nineteen Acts & One Hundred and Thirty Scenes.*   New York and London: Macmillan, 1904-1906.   First American edition of part one and first English edition of Part second, second state as issued, 2 volumes, 8vo., original dark green cloth, gilt decoration and lettering, fine, from the Gary Lepper Collection of Thomas Hardy.   The Brick Row Book Shop   Bulletin Nine - 47   2013 $750

Hardy, Thomas   1840-1928   *The Dynasts: an Epic Poems of the War with Napoleon.*   London: Macmillan, 1910.   First one volume edition, 8vo., original green cloth, gilt lettered, frontispiece, one leaf of publisher's ads, followed by 32 page publisher catalog, fine presentation copy inscribed by author for Miss Alice Balfour, 1912 with her stylized initials, cloth slightly worn, very good, enclosed in morocco clamshell box, from the Gary Lepper Collection of Thomas Hardy.   The Brick Row Book Shop   Bulletin Nine - 50   2013 $6000

Hardy, Thomas   1840-1928   *Earth and Air and Rain: Ten Songs for Baritone and Piano. Words by Thomas Hardy. Music by Gerald Finzi.*   Paris: London: New York: Sydney: Boosey & Hawkes, 1936.   First edition, original orange down printed wrappers slightly worn, 15 pages, fine, from the Gary Lepper Collection of Thomas Hardy.   The Brick Row Book Shop   Bulletin Nine - 93   2013 $125

Hardy, Thomas   1840-1928   *The Famous Tragedy of the Queen of Cornwall at Tintagel in Lyonnesse.*   London: Macmillan, 1923.   First edition, 4to., original decorated green cloth, gilt lettering, frontispiece, one plate, fine in slightly worn and darkened dust jacket, from the Gary Lepper Collection of Thomas Hardy.   The Brick Row Book Shop   Bulletin Nine - 67   2013 $200

Hardy, Thomas   1840-1928   *The Famous Tragedy of the Queen of Cornwall. At Tintagel in Lyonnesse.*   Dorchester: 1923.   First edition, 4to., original blue wrappers, stitched as issued (8) pages, one illustration, 2 news clippings about performance tipped inside front wrappers, little browned at edges and slightly worn, very good, remaining portions of original envelope, from the Gary Lepper Collection of Thomas Hardy.   The Brick Row Book Shop   Bulletin Nine - 71   2013 $400

Hardy, Thomas   1840-1928   *Far from the Madding Crowd.*   New York: Henry Holt, 1874.   First American edition, small 8vo., original decorated white cloth, black lettering, publisher's ads on endpapers dated Nov. 17 1874, cloth somewhat soiled, good copy, from the Gary Lepper Collection of Thomas Hardy.   The Brick Row Book Shop   Bulletin Nine - 4   2013 $100

Hardy, Thomas   1840-1928   *A Group of Noble Dames.*   Melbourne: Sydney and Adelaide: E. A. Petherick; London: James R. Osgood, 1891.   First Australian edition, using sheets of London edition with new titlepage, 8vo., original blue-green cloth, gilt lettered, publisher's ads dated Aug. 1891, cloth little worn, front blank removed, very good, from the Gary Lepper Collection of Thomas Hardy.   The Brick Row Book Shop   Bulletin Nine - 24   2013 $650

Hardy, Thomas   1840-1928   *A Group of Noble Dames.*   New York: Harper and Brothers, 1891.   First American edition, 8vo., 4 pages publisher's terminal ads, original decorated brown cloth, gilt lettered, frontispiece and five plates, printed on thin paper and decorations on spine less elaborate, probably second of two states, edges little rubbed, good, from the Gary Lepper Collection of Thomas Hardy.   The Brick Row Book Shop   Bulletin Nine - 23   2013 $300

Hardy, Thomas 1840-1928 *A Group of Noble Dames.* New York: Harper and Brothers, 1891. First American edition, 8vo., original decorated brown cloth, gilt lettering, frontispiece and five plates, 4 pages of publisher's terminal ads, printed on thick paper and spine decorations more elaborate than subsequent issues, prelims slightly soiled, fine, from the Gary Lepper Collection of Thomas Hardy.   The Brick Row Book Shop   Bulletin Nine - 22   2013 $375

Hardy, Thomas 1840-1928 *A Group of Noble Dames.* London: Osgood, McIlvaine, 1891. First edition, first binding, 8vo., original beige cloth, gilt decorations and brown lettering, bookplate of Newton Hall, Cambridge, fine, from the Gary Lepper Collection of Thomas Hardy.   The Brick Row Book Shop   Bulletin Nine - 21   2013 $275

Hardy, Thomas 1840-1928 *The Hand of Ethelberta: a Comedy in Chapters.* New York: Henry Holt, 1876. First American edition, 8vo., original decorated white cloth, black lettering, publisher's ads on endpapers dated May 9 1876, earliest issue has May 9 1876 date on front free endpaper as here, cloth little soiled, very good, from the Gary Lepper Collection of Thomas Hardy.   The Brick Row Book Shop   Bulletin Nine - 5   2013 $500

Hardy, Thomas 1840-1928 *"How I Built Myself a House." in Chamber's Journal of Popular Literature, Science and Art...* London & Edinburgh: W. & R. Chambers, 18 March, 1865. Third Annual volume, consisting of 24 issues, large 8vo., contemporary brown quarter calf, marbled boards, black leather label, gilt lettering, edges little rubbed, very good, from the Gary Lepper Collection of Thomas Hardy.   The Brick Row Book Shop   Bulletin Nine - 1   2013 $275

Hardy, Thomas 1840-1928 *Human Shows, Far Phantasies, Songs and Trifles.* London: Macmillan, 1925. First edition, 8vo., original olive green cloth, gilt decoration and lettering, slightly soiled, very good, in like dust jacket, from the Gary Lepper Collection of Thomas Hardy.   The Brick Row Book Shop   Bulletin Nine - 72   2013 $125

Hardy, Thomas 1840-1928 *An Indiscretion in the Life of an Heiress.* privately printed for the author's widow, 1934. First edition, 94/100 copies, crown 8vo., original limp cream vellum, yapped fore-edges backstrip gilt lettered, gilt edges, fine.   Blackwell's Rare Books   B174 - 216   2013   £500

Hardy, Thomas 1840-1928 *Jude the Obscure.* London: Osgood, McIlvaine, 1896. First edition, 8vo., original dark green cloth, front blocked in gold with monogram medallion, top edge gilt, gilt lettering, fine, bright copy in original publisher's printed dust jacket (two very small chips at edges), enclosed in chemise and quarter morocco slipcase, from the Gary Lepper Collection of Thomas Hardy.   The Brick Row Book Shop   Bulletin Nine - 35   2013 $30,000

Hardy, Thomas 1840-1928 *Jude the Obscure.* London: Macmillan, 1896. First edition, colonial issue, 8vo., original printed wrappers, (516) pages, map, 7 pages publisher's ads + one leaf of inserted ads, publisher's ads dated March 20 1896, copies were issued in cloth, wrappers little worn and soiled, spine darkened, very good, from the Gary Lepper Collection of Thomas Hardy.   The Brick Row Book Shop   Bulletin Nine - 37   2013 $225

Hardy, Thomas 1840-1928 *Jude the Obscure.* Lakewood: printed for private circulation, 1917. First edition, number 11 of 27 numbered copies, 12mo., original printed gray wrappers, stitched as issued, wrappers slightly browned, fine, the letter was owned by Paul Leperly who privately printed this limited edition, inscribed by Leperly, from the Gary Lepper Collection of Thomas Hardy.   The Brick Row Book Shop   Bulletin Nine - 61   2013 $650

Hardy, Thomas 1840-1928 *Late Lyrics and Earlier with Many Other Verses.* London: Macmillan, 1922. First edition, 8vo., original olive green cloth, gilt decoration and lettering, neat signature on front free endpaper dated June 13 1922, scattered spots of foxing, fine in publisher's dust jacket (just slightly worn), from the Gary Lepper Collection of Thomas Hardy.   The Brick Row Book Shop   Bulletin Nine - 66   2013 $350

Hardy, Thomas 1840-1928 *Life's Little Ironies: a Set of Tales with Some Colloquial Sketches.* London and New York: Macmillan, 1894. First edition, colonial issue, 8vo., original printed wrappers, 301 pages, 7 pages publisher's ads dated July 20 1894, wrappers little soiled and worn, very good, from the Gary Lepper Collection of Thomas Hardy.   The Brick Row Book Shop   Bulletin Nine - 28   2013 $150

Hardy, Thomas 1840-1928 *Maumbury Ring.* Waterville: Colby College Library, 1942. First edition, number 95 of 100 numbered copies, 8vo., original white linen spine, gray boards, red lettering, fine in glassine wrapper, from the Gary Lepper Collection of Thomas Hardy.   The Brick Row Book Shop   Bulletin Nine - 97   2013 $75

Hardy, Thomas 1840-1928 *The Mayor of Casterbridge. The Life and Death of a Man of Character.* London: Smith Elder, 1886. First edition, first binding, 2 volumes, 8vo., original decorated blue cloth, black and gilt lettering, 2 pages of publisher's terminal ads in volume one and four pages in volume two, cloth little worn and soiled, particularly at edges, some light foxing, very good, from the Gary Lepper Collection of Thomas Hardy.   The Brick Row Book Shop   Bulletin Nine - 16   2013 $7500

Hardy, Thomas 1840-1928 *The Greenwood Edition of the Novels and Stories of Thomas Hardy.* London: New York: Macmillan, 1964. Reprint, 18 volumes, 8vo., original blue cloth, gilt lettered, map of Wessex on endpapers, fine in somewhat worn dust jacket, from the Gary Lepper Collection of Thomas Hardy.   The Brick Row Book Shop   Bulletin Nine - 102   2013 $250

Hardy, Thomas 1840-1928 *Old Mrs. Chundle: a Short Story.* New York: Crosby Gaige, 1929. First edition, number 117 of 700 numbered copies, 8vo., original green cloth spine, decorated boards, gilt lettering, untrimmed, vignette title, fine in publisher's glassine, wrapper, from the Gary Lepper Collection of Thomas Hardy.   The Brick Row Book Shop   Bulletin Nine - 90   2013 $75

Hardy, Thomas 1840-1928 *Our Exploits at West Poley by Thomas Hardy.* London: Oxford University Press, 1952. First edition, one of 1000 numbered copies, 8vo., original blue cloth, silver lettering, vignette title and two wood engravings by Lynton Lamb, fine in dust jacket, from the Gary Lepper Collection of Thomas Hardy.   The Brick Row Book Shop   Bulletin Nine - 100   2013 $75

Hardy, Thomas 1840-1928 *The Oxen.* Hove: E. Williams, 1915. First edition, 8vo., original printed wrappers, stitched as issued, 4 pages, fine, from the Gary Lepper Collection of Thomas Hardy.   The Brick Row Book Shop   Bulletin Nine - 57   2013 $100

Hardy, Thomas 1840-1928 *A Pair of Blue Eyes.* Philadelphia: Henry T. Coates, circa, 1897. Later American edition, 8vo., original decorated dark green cloth, gilt lettering, top edge gilt, uncommon, date taken from ink signature on front free endpaper dated Sept. 23 1897, fine, from the Gary Lepper Collection of Thomas Hardy.   The Brick Row Book Shop   Bulletin Nine - 39   2013 $1000

Hardy, Thomas 1840-1928 *Unos Ojos Azules. (A Pair of Blue Eyes).* Barcelona: Gustavo Gili, 1919. First edition in Spanish, 2 volumes, 8vo., original decorated brown pictorial cloth, gilt decorations and lettering, fine, presentation copy inscribed by author to George Douglas, from the Gary Lepper Collection of Thomas Hardy.   The Brick Row Book Shop   Bulletin Nine - 63   2013 $4500

Hardy, Thomas 1840-1928 *The Variorum Edition of the Complete Poems of Thomas Hardy.* London: Macmillan, 1979. First edition, 2nd issue, 4to., original red cloth, gilt lettering, fine in fine dust jacket, signed by editor, John Gibson, from the Gary Lepper Collection of Thomas Hardy.   The Brick Row Book Shop   Bulletin Nine - 104   2013   £100

Hardy, Thomas 1840-1928 *Selected Poems of...* London: Liverpool and Boston: the Medici Society, 1921. First Medici Society edition, number 313 of 1000 numbered copies, signed by Hardy with his holograph note, laid in is note sent Feb. 21 1928 from Florence Hardy to Lucy Chew of Bryn Mawr, PA, 8vo., original tan cloth spine, blue boards and printed paper labels, frontispiece, engraved titlepage, fine in original printed dust jacket, slightly faded and enclosed in chemise and quarter morocco slipcase, from the Gary Lepper Collection of Thomas Hardy.   The Brick Row Book Shop   Bulletin Nine - 67   2013 $3750

Hardy, Thomas 1840-1928 *Selected Poems of Thomas Hardy.* London: Macmillan, 1940. First edition edited by Young, 8vo., original blue cloth, gilt lettering, fine in slightly worn dust jacket, from the Gary Lepper Collection of Thomas Hardy.   The Brick Row Book Shop   Bulletin Nine - 95   2013 $75

Hardy, Thomas 1840-1928 *The Preservation of Ancient Cottages: an Appeal.* London: The Royal Society of Arts, 1927. First edition, 4to., original printed grey wrappers, 16 pages, 8 photographic illustrations, wrappers slightly browned at edges, fine, from the Gary Lepper Collection of Thomas Hardy.   The Brick Row Book Shop   Bulletin Nine - 81   2013 $75

Hardy, Thomas 1840-1928 *The Return of the Native.* London: Smith Elder, 1878. First edition, 3 volumes, 8vo., original decorated brown cloth, gilt lettering, frontispiece, faint evidence of lending library labels on upper boards of each volume, bookplate of American collector Kenyon Starling on front pastedown, below which is the earlier bookplate of illustrator and connoisseur Pickford Waller, designed by Austin Osman Spare circa 1907, cloth little worn and soiled, some light foxing, particularly on prelims, very good, from the Gary Lepper Collection of Thomas Hardy.   The Brick Row Book Shop   Bulletin Nine - 6   2013 $10,000

Hardy, Thomas 1840-1928 *Return of the Native.* New York: London: Harper & Bros., 1929. First edition, number 744 of 1000 numbered copies of American issue, signed by Leighton, 4to., original tan buckram spine, blue paper boards, printed paper label, frontispiece, 11 tipped-on woodcuts and numerous vignettes in text by Clare Leighton, fine in slightly worn dust jacket, from the Gary Lepper Collection of Thomas Hardy.   The Brick Row Book Shop   Bulletin Nine - 89   2013 $350

Hardy, Thomas 1840-1928 *Romantic Adventures of a Milkmaid.* New York: John W. Lovell, 1883. One of several unauthorized American editions, 12mo., original pictorial wrappers, 91 pages, wrappers little stained and soiled, very good, from the Gary Lepper Collection of Thomas Hardy.   The Brick Row Book Shop   Bulletin Nine - 14   2013 $125

Hardy, Thomas   1840-1928   *The Sergeant's Song (1803). Words by Thomas Hardy Music by Gustav Holst.*   London: Edwin Ashdown, 1923.   First edition, 4to., original printed self wrappers, fine, from the Gary Lepper Collection of Thomas Hardy.   The Brick Row Book Shop Bulletin Nine - 68   2013 $350

Hardy, Thomas   1840-1928   *The Short Stories of Thomas Hardy.*   London: Macmillan, 1928. First edition, 8vo., original maroon cloth, gilt lettering, fine in very slightly worn dust jacket, from the Gary Lepper Collection of Thomas Hardy.   The Brick Row Book Shop   Bulletin Nine - 86   2013 $150

Hardy, Thomas   1840-1928   *The Society for the Protection of Ancient Buildings. The General Meeting of the Society: Twenty-Ninth Annual Report of the Committee and Paper Read by Thomas Hardy Esq. June 1906.*   London: 1906.   First edition, 8vo., original printed pale blue wrappers, 98 pages, 2 plates, leaflet about the Society laid in, edges slightly foxed, fine, from the Gary Lepper Collection of Thomas Hardy.   The Brick Row Book Shop   Bulletin Nine - 48   2013 $150

Hardy, Thomas   1840-1928   *Tess of the D'Urbervilles: a Pure Woman Faithfully Presented.*   London: Osgood McIlvaine, 1891.   First edition, 3 volumes, 8vo., sand colored cloth, gilt decorations and lettering after designs by Charles Ricketts, from the British Club Library at Malaga, Spain with their bookplate, from the Gary Lepper Collection of Thomas Hardy, LA Bookseller Maxwell Hunley sold to Estelle Doheny Dec. 3 1932, some foxing, few edges slightly bumped, three hinges skillfully repaired, fine, unusually bright copy, enclosed in chemise and quarter morocco slipcase.   The Brick Row Book Shop   Bulletin Nine - 25   2013 $17,500

Hardy, Thomas   1840-1928   *Tess of the D'Urbervilles: a Pure Woman.*   London: Osgood, McIlvaine, 1892.   First one volume edition, called the "fifth Edition", 8vo., original beige cloth, gilt decorations and brown lettering, frontispiece, later ink signature, cloth slightly soiled, very good, from the Gary Lepper Collection of Thomas Hardy.   The Brick Row Book Shop   Bulletin Nine - 26   2013 $500

Hardy, Thomas   1840-1928   *Tess of the D'Urbervilles. A Pure Woman.*   London: Osgood McIlvaine, 1895.   First Wessex Novels Edition, 8vo., original green cloth, gilt decoration and lettering, top edge gilt, etched frontispiece, one plate, map, from the library of English author A. E. Coppard, paper browning slightly in margins, very good, from the Gary Lepper Collection of Thomas Hardy.   The Brick Row Book Shop   Bulletin Nine - 33   2013 $250

Hardy, Thomas   1840-1928   *Tess of the D'Urbervilles: a Pure Woman.*   London: Macmillan and Co., 1926.   First edition thus, one of 325 large paper copies signed by author, royal 4to., original quarter velum, marbled paper sides, gilt lettering, frontispiece and engravings, fine in nearly fine dust jacket, few mended tears on verso, some slight creases, from the Gary Lepper Collection of Thomas Hardy.   The Brick Row Book Shop   Bulletin Nine - 74   2013 $3500

Hardy, Thomas   1840-1928   *The Thieves Who Couldn't Help Sneezing...*   Waterville: Colby College Library, 1942.   First separate edition, number 78 of 100 numbered copies, 8vo., white linen spine, decorated boards, yellow lettering, from the Gary Lepper Collection of Thomas Hardy.   The Brick Row Book Shop   Bulletin Nine - 96   2013 $75

Hardy, Thomas   1840-1928   *The Three Wayfarers: a Play in One Act.*   Dorchester: printed by Henry Ling (for Florence Emily Hardy), 1935.   First English edition, one of 250 copies, 4to., original printed white wrappers, stitched as issued, wrappers slightly soiled and foxed, very good, from the Gary Lepper Collection of Thomas Hardy.   The Brick Row Book Shop   Bulletin Nine - 92   2013 $125

Hardy, Thomas   1840-1928   *"The Trumpet Major." in Good Words for 1880.*   London: Isbister and Co., 1880.   Thick 8vo., original decorated green cloth, gilt lettering, frontispiece and illustrations. cloth little rubbed at edges, very good, from the Gary Lepper Collection of Thomas Hardy.   The Brick Row Book Shop   Bulletin Nine - 8   2013 $225

Hardy, Thomas   1840-1928   *The Trumpet-Major.*   London: 1880.   First edition in book form, 3 volumes, octavo, volumes I and II without prelim blank, publisher's primary binding of volume I and secondary binding of volumes II and III all of red diagonal fine ribbed cloth, only difference being back covers stamped in blind with double rule (volume 1) or triple rule (volumes 2 and 3) border, front covers decoratively stamped in black with three panel design incorporating two vignettes, on encampment at top, a mill at bottom and lettering in center panel, spines decoratively stamped in gilt and black with standard sword and bugle and lettered in blind and gilt (with imprint at foot of spine, Smith, Elder & Co.), yellow coated endpapers, spines of all volumes bit darkened, cloth of all spines with some wrinkling as well as to cloth of back board of volume one, bit of soiling and rubbing to cloth, some light shelfwear to spines, previous owner's bookplate on front pastedown of each volume, occasional thumb soiling along fore-edges, volumes slightly skewed, overall good set housed in quarter morocco clamshell and chemise.   Heritage Book Shop   Holiday Catalogue 2012 - 72   2013 $7500

Hardy, Thomas 1840-1928 *The Trumpet Major.* London: Smith, Elder & Co., 1880. First edition, without prelim blanks in volumes ii and iii (present in volume i), some finger marking and minor stains, few slightly careless openings, tear in upper margin of one leaf in volume ii, approaching but not touching text, 8vo., original primary binding of red diagonal fine ribbed cloth, blocked in black on front with 3 panel design incorporating 2 vignettes, blocked in blind on back, 2 rule border, spine blocked in gold and black with standard, sword and bugle and lettered in blind and gold, ex-circulating library with evidence of labels removed from top panel of front covers, rebacked, original spines preserved though with minor loss at head and tail and with loss of terminal letter on spine imprint of 2 volumes, spines bit dulled, recased, sound.   Blackwell's Rare Books   172 - 66   2013   £5500

Hardy, Thomas 1840-1928 *The Trumpet Major: a Tale.* London: Smith, Elder, 1880. First edition in book form, 2nd issue binding, 3 volumes, 8vo., original pictorial red cloth, black and gilt lettering, faint evidence of lending library labels on upper boards, edges lightly foxed, minor wear to cloth, very nice in chemises and quarter morocco slipcase, from the Gary Lepper Collection of Thomas Hardy.   The Brick Row Book Shop   Bulletin Nine - 9   2013 $10,000

Hardy, Thomas 1840-1928 *The Trumpet Major. A Tale.* London: Sampson Low Marston, Searle & Rivington, 1881. Cheap edition, first one volume edition, 8vo., original decorated red cloth, gilt lettering, 32 page publisher's catalog dated Jan. 1881, cloth little soiled and worn, very good, morocco clamshell box, inscribed by author for Tindal Atkinson, with holograph note by Hardy on his Max Gate stationery to Atkinson, from the Gary Lepper Collection of Thomas Hardy.   The Brick Row Book Shop   Bulletin Nine - 10   2013 $4500

Hardy, Thomas 1840-1928 *"Two on a Tower". in The Atlantic Monthly May-December 1882.* Boston: Houghton Mifflin, 1882. First appearance in print, 4to., 8 volume, original light brown printed wrappers, wrappers little chipped, worn and soiled, very good, from the Gary Lepper Collection of Thomas Hardy.   The Brick Row Book Shop   Bulletin Nine - 11   2013 $450

Hardy, Thomas 1840-1928 *Two on a Tower.* New York: John W. Lovell, circa, 1882. Pirated American edition, 8vo., original decorated mustard yellow cloth, gilt lettering, 2 pages terminal ads, paper little browned, fine, from the Gary Lepper Collection of Thomas Hardy.   The Brick Row Book Shop   Bulletin Nine - 13   2013 $425

Hardy, Thomas 1840-1928 *Two on a Tower.* New York: Henry Holt, 1882. First American edition, small 8vo., original pictorial mustard yellow cloth, black and gilt lettering, publisher's ads on front and rear endpapers, fine, from the Gary Lepper Collection of Thomas Hardy.   The Brick Row Book Shop   Bulletin Nine - 12   2013 $400

Hardy, Thomas 1840-1928 *The Two Hardys: an Address by Thomas Hardy July 21 1927.* London: printed for private circulation only, 1927. Unauthorized printing, number 49 of 50 numbered copies, single sheet folded to make 4 pages, photo, fine, from the Gary Lepper Collection of Thomas Hardy.   The Brick Row Book Shop   Bulletin Nine - 80   2013 $450

Hardy, Thomas 1840-1928 *Under the Greenwood Tree: a Rural Painting of the Dutch School.* New York: Henry Holt, 1873. First American edition, second issue with the Henry Holt imprint, small 8vo., original decorated yellow cloth, black lettering, cloth little worn, very good, enclosed in clamshell box, from the Gary Lepper Collection of Thomas Hardy.   The Brick Row Book Shop   Bulletin Nine - 2   2013 $600

Hardy, Thomas 1840-1928 *Under the Greenwood Tree: a Rural Painting of the Dutch School.* New York: Hovendon Company, n.d. but circa, 1895. Uncommon later American edition, 8vo., original decorated light green cloth, dark green lettering, cloth slightly worn, fine, from the Gary Lepper Collection of Thomas Hardy.   The Brick Row Book Shop   Bulletin Nine - 34   2013 $175

Hardy, Thomas 1840-1928 *The Well-Beloved: a Sketch of Temperament.* New York: Harper & Brothers, 1897. First American edition, 8vo., original green cloth, gilt decorations and lettering, frontispiece and maps, cloth little spotted, fine in original printed dust jacket which is little browned and slightly stained, overall very good, from the Gary Lepper Collection of Thomas Hardy.   The Brick Row Book Shop   Bulletin Nine - 40   2013 $1000

Hardy, Thomas 1840-1928 *Wessex Poems and other Verses.* Toronto: George N. Morang, 1899. First Canadian edition using sheets of American Harper & Brothers edition of same year, 8vo., original pictorial green cloth, gilt lettering, frontispiece and 29 illustrations, cloth little soiled and worn, very good, from the Gary Lepper Collection of Thomas Hardy.   The Brick Row Book Shop   Bulletin Nine - 41   2013 $350

Hardy, Thomas 1840-1928 *Wessex Tales: Strange, Lively and Commonplace.* London and New York: Macmillan, 1888. First edition, 2 volumes, 8vo., original decorated dark green cloth, gilt lettered, 4 pages publisher's terminal ads in volume one, bookplate of J. Smart, endpapers slightly foxed, edges trifle worn, fine, from the Gary Lepper Collection of Thomas Hardy.   The Brick Row Book Shop   Bulletin Nine - 19   2013 $4500

Hardy, Thomas 1840-1928 *Winter Words in Various Moods and Metres.* New York: Macmillan, 1928. First American edition, advance page proofs, oblong 4to., loose sheets, set up mostly two pages per sheet on rectos only, with few sheets halved, 184 pages, very good, enclosed in chemise and cloth slipcase, from the Gary Lepper Collection of Thomas Hardy.   The Brick Row Book Shop   Bulletin Nine - 83   2013 $1500

Hardy, Thomas 1840-1928 *Winter Words: in Various Moods and Metres.* London: Macmillan, 1928. First edition, 8vo., original light green cloth, gilt decoration and lettering, fine in very good dust jacket, spine somewhat darkened, from the Gary Lepper Collection of Thomas Hardy. The Brick Row Book Shop   Bulletin Nine - 82 2013 $300

Hardy, Thomas 1840-1928 *The Woodlanders.* London and New York: Macmillan, 1887. First edition, first binding, 3 volumes, 8vo., original grey green cloth, gilt lettering, 2 pages publisher's terminal ads in volume one, cloth slightly worn, few hinges starting, very good, from the Gary Lepper Collection of Thomas Hardy.   The Brick Row Book Shop   Bulletin Nine - 17 2013 $5000

Hardy, Thomas 1840-1928 *The Woodlanders.* London and New York: Macmillan, 1887. First edition, 2nd binding, 3 volumes, 8vo., original dark green pebbled cloth, gilt lettering, few hinges repaired, edges lightly rubbed, fine, from the Gary Lepper Collection of Thomas Hardy.   The Brick Row Book Shop   Bulletin Nine - 18 2013 $3500

Hardy, Thomas 1840-1928 *The Woodlanders...* London and New York: Macmillan, 1903. Later printing of 1895 Wessex Novels, 8vo., original blue cloth, gilt decoration and lettering, 10 pages of publisher's terminal ads, cloth slightly worn, very good. from the Gary Lepper Collection of Thomas Hardy.   The Brick Row Book Shop   Bulletin Nine - 45 2013 $3000

Hardy, Thomas 1840-1928 *The Works of Thomas Hardy in Prose and Verse.* London: Macmillan and Co., 1912-1913. 21 volumes, octavo, photogravure frontispieces and double page maps, bound by Zaehnsdorf in 1914, full purple calf, gilt triple border on covers, spines decoratively paneled in gilt, four red morocco floral onlays and purple calf, gilt triple rule, border on covers, spines decoratively paneled in gilt, four red morocco floral onlays and three brown morocco lettering labels, top edge gilt, marbled endpapers, gilt dentelles, bit of rubbing to some board edges and head and tail of few spines, overall near fine, very attractive.   Heritage Book Shop   Holiday Catalogue 2012 - 73 2013 $6000

Hardy, Thomas 1840-1928 *The Works of...* London: Macmillan and Co., 1919-1920. Mellstock edition, limited to 500 copies signed by author, 37 volumes, frontispiece volume 1, few volumes unopened and all uncut in original dark blue cloth, gilt medallion on front boards, elaborate gilt spines, some minor rubbing but attractive example. Jarndyce Antiquarian Booksellers   CCV - 129 2013   £4500

Hardy, Thomas 1840-1928 *The Mellstock Edition of the Works in Thirty-Seven Volumes.* London: Macmillan and Co., 1919-1920. First edition, one of 500 copies signed by author, 37 volumes, 8vo., original blue cloth, gilt decorated and lettered spines, untrimmed, frontispiece, map, fine, from the Gary Lepper Collection of Thomas Hardy.   The Brick Row Book Shop   Bulletin Nine - 62 2013 $12,500

Hardy, Thomas 1840-1928 *Yuletide in a Younger World.* New York: William Edwin Rudge, 1927. First American edition, one of only 27 copies, 12mo., original printed pale yellow wrappers stapled as issued, fine, from the Gary Lepper Collection of Thomas Hardy.   The Brick Row Book Shop   Bulletin Nine - 77 2013 $450

Hare, Davaid *Marcel Duchamp, Andre Breton, Max Ernst et al, VVV Almanac for 1943 Number 2-3.* New York: VVV, 1943. First edition, 144 pages, double issue, about very good copy with small chip to bottom right corner, some other edgewear and creasing, internally nice, scarce in any condition.   Jeff Hirsch Books   Fall 2013 - 129142 2013 $2500

Hargarve, Francis *A Review of the Laws Against the Knowingly Receiving of Stolen Goods and a Proposal for Making a New Law on that Subject.* printed in the year, 1770. 8vo., small circular sticker on titlepage with date in Arabic numerals in pencil, traces of another sticker, in neither case affecting text, outer leaves slightly soiled, disbound, some annotations, good.   Blackwell's Rare Books 172 - 67 2013   £700

Hargrove, E. *Anecdotes of Archery, from the Earliest Ages to the Year 1791...* York: Hargrove's Library, 1845. Good copy, 8vo., color titlepage, 6 plates, original decorative green gilt cloth, spine faded, bookplate, scarce.   Ken Spelman Books Ltd. 75 - 111 2013   £220

Haring, Nikolaus M. *Commentaries on Boethius.* Toronto: Pontifical Institute of Mediaeval Studies, 1971. 8vo., 619 pages, red cloth, gilt stamped spine title, ownership signature, fine.   Jeff Weber Rare Books 169 - 32 2013 $125

Harington, Charles Sumner *Changes Upon Church Bells.* James Nisbet & Co., 1876. New edition, scarce, small 8vo., original blindstamped cloth gilt, spine and edges faded, woodcut frontispiece and text illustrations.   R. F. G. Hollett & Son   Children's Books - 260 2013   £85

Harington, T. *Remarkable Account of the Loss of the Ship Ganges... off the Cape of Good Hope, May 29 1807...* London: printed for Thomas Tegg, 1808. Folding mezzotint frontispiece, frontispiece with little waterstaining, some browning, 8vo., disbound.   Blackwell's Rare Books   B174 - 140   2013   £250

Harlan, George H. *Of Walking Beams and Paddle Wheels. A Chronicle of San Francisco Bay Ferryboats.* San Francisco: Bay Books Ltd., 1951. First edition, signed by George Harlan, frontispiece, photos, map, blue cloth lettered and decorated in silver, minor chip to head of spine, but very fine and bright, pictorial dust jacket.   Argonaut Book Shop   Summer 2013 - 146   2013 $75

Harlan, Robert D. *The Two Hundredth Book: a Bibliography of the Books Published by the Book Club of California 1958-1993.* N.P.: (San Francisco), 1993. 1 of 500 copies following design of the original, this being #200, x, 62 pages, folio, near fine.   Dumont Maps & Books of the West   122 - 45   2013 $100

Harlow, Alvin *Old Waybills: the Romance of the Express Companies.* New York: D. Appleton Century, 1934. First edition, 80 vintage photos, red cloth, very fine with chipped pictorial dust jacket (protected).   Argonaut Book Shop   Summer 2013 - 147   2013 $175

Harlow, Neal *Maps and Surveys of the Pueblo Lands of Los Angeles.* Los Angeles: Dawson's, 1976. First edition, one of 375 copies, 14 plates, two laid into rear pocket, cloth backed decorated boards, gilt lettered spine, small bookplate of noted collector, very fine.   Argonaut Book Shop   Summer 2013 - 148   2013 $350

Harlow, Neal *Maps of the Pueblo Lands of San Diego 1602-1874.* Los Angeles: Dawson's, 1987. First edition, limited to 375 numbered copies, signed by author, small folio, 244 pages, numerous reproductions, tinted or in color, cloth backed decorated boards, small oval bookplate, very fine.   Argonaut Book Shop   Recent Acquisitions June 2013 - 136   2013 $225

Harman, Richard *Country Company.* Blandford Press, 1949. First edition, original cloth, gilt, dust jacket with little edge wear, chip to one corner, 208 pages, 8 color plates.   R. F. G. Hollett & Son   Lake District and Cumbria - 234   2013   £30

Harness, Charles Leonard *Flight into Yesterday.* New York: 1953. First edition, octavo, boards.   L. W. Currey, Inc.   Utopian Literature: Recent Acquisitions (April 2013) - 140063   2013 $250

Harpending, Asbury *The Great Diamond Hoax and Other Stirring Incidents in the Life of...* San Francisco: James H. Barry Co., 1913. First edition, 283 pages, frontispiece, plates, original light blue cloth, light rubbing to extremities, fine.   Argonaut Book Shop   Summer 2013 - 150   2013 $60

Harper, Francis E. W. *Iola Leroy, or Shadows Uplifted.* Philadelphia: Garrigues Brothers, 1892. First edition, dark green cloth gilt, frontispiece lacking (though there is no obvious evidence that this copy ever had one), some slight puckering to cloth on front board from light dampstain and nominal spotting on spine, tight, very good, with gilt bright and mostly unrubbed.   Between the Covers Rare Books, Inc.   165 - 308   2013 $14,000

Harper, Ida Husted *The Life and Work of Susan B. Anthony...* Indianapolis: Bowen-Merril Co. The Hollenbeck Press, 1899. 1898. 1908. First edition, inscribed by Anthony for Miss Florence Holbrook, inscribed by Harper to same, large 8vo., 3 volumes, dark green cloth, gilt stamped medallion portrait of Anthony on each of the front covers, title, author and publisher stamped in gilt on spines, volume III slightly lighter green cloth with gold gilt medallion on front panel, volumes I and II with some rubbing and wear, but generally good sound set, volume III with traces of ex-libris removed from front pastedown and another on front flyleaf, inside hinge split between pages ii-iii, but binding sound, remains of small 3/4 x 1 inch bookseller's ticket on rear pastedown, else very good+ with little rubbing to edges, frontispiece portraits.   Priscilla Juvelis - Rare Books   55 - 2   2013 $5000

Harper, Ida Husted *The Life and Work of Susan B. Anthony.* Indianapolis: Bowen Merrill, 1899. First edition, 2 volumes, large 8vo., illustrations, donor's presentation in both volumes, light blue cloth, cover slightly scuffed and soiled, but very good.   Second Life Books Inc.   182 - 110   2013 $450

Harper, Kenneth *The Story of the Lakeland Diocese 1933-1966.* Carlisle: Charles Thurnam, 1966. First edition, original pictorial wrappers, pages vi, 172.   R. F. G. Hollett & Son   Lake District and Cumbria - 236   2013   £20

Harraden, Richard *Cantabrigia Depicta.* Cambridge: publ by Harraden & Son, Cambridge, R. Cribb and Son, 288 High Holborn, T. Cadell and W. Davies, Strand, London, 1811. One of 100 proof copies on large paper, 4to., engraved titlepage, frontispiece, engraved map and 35 engraved plates, contemporary Russia, spine in compartments and lettered gilt, gilt edges, some abrasions to head of spine and slight cracking to lower joint, fine, bookplate of original subscriber Sir William Brown Ffolkes.   Marlborough Rare Books Ltd.   218 - 76   2013   £450

Harral, Thomas *Anne Boleyn and Caroline of Brunswick Compared...* London: W. Wright, 1820. Portrait, disbound, odd spot, three small holes near inner title margin, from the Renier library. Jarndyce Antiquarian Booksellers CCV - 130 2013 £40

Harrington, Elizabeth Still Stanhope, Countess of *Poems.* London: Henry Sotheran, 1874. Small square 8vo., original blue cloth, covers ruled with double black fillet, spine lettered in gilt, unopened, virtually pristine copy. Marlborough Rare Books Ltd. 218 - 77 2013 £100

Harrington, Elizabeth Still Stanhope, Countess of *The Storks. The False Prince, from the German.* London: Henry Sotheran, 1875. Square 12mo., pages 78, entirely unopened in original blind stamped purple cloth, spine ruled and lettered in gilt, spine discolored due to humidity. Marlborough Rare Books Ltd. 218 - 146 2013 £100

Harris, A. *Cumberland Iron.* Truro: Bradford Barton, 1970. First edition, original cloth, gilt, dust jacket, 12 pages of plates, 4 figures. R. F. G. Hollett & Son Lake District and Cumbria - 237 2013 £35

Harris, Charlaine *Dead Until Dark.* New York: Ace Books, 2001. First edition, small octavo, pictorial wrappers. L. W. Currey, Inc. Fall Sampler Sept. 2013 - 146309 2013 $100

Harris, Clara E. *History of the Woman's Parent Mite Missionary Society of the African Methodist Episcopal Church 1824-1827, 1874-1935.* Baltimore?: Clara E. Harris, 1935. First edition, printed brown stiff wrappers, 176 pages, frontispiece, some smudging to wrappers, small tear at edge of spine, else near fine. Between the Covers Rare Books, Inc. 165 - 306 2013 $650

Harris, Clare Winger *Away from the Here and Now: Stories in Pseudo-Science.* Philadelphia: Dorrance and Co., 1947. First edition, endpapers and fore edge trifle foxed, else fine in near fine dust jacket with small nicks at crown. Between the Covers Rare Books, Inc. Sci-Fi, Fantasy & Horror - 313185 2013 $75

Harris, Frank *The Man Shakespeare and His Tragic Life Story.* London: printed at the Chiswick Press for Frank Palmer, 1909. One of 150 copies of the large paper edition, this copy #34, signed by author, 253 x 156mm., attractive contemporary crimson three quarter morocco over burgundy linen, raised bands, spine gilt in concentric fillet compartments, marbled endpapers, top edge gilt, spine just slightly and uniformly sunned, two faint, small brown spots on dedication page and last page of text, otherwise very fine, text especially clean, fresh and bright, binding virtually unworn. Phillip J. Pirages 63 - 436 2013 $250

Harris, James 1709-1780 *Three Treatises. The First concerning Art. The Second Concerning Music, Painting and Poetry. The Third Concerning Happiness.* London: printing by H. Woodfall for J. Nourse and P. Vaillaint, 1744. First edition, 8vo., toned and lightly spotted, contemporary sprinkled calf, spine gilt in compartments, later orange morocco label, headcap little worn, joints cracking through small old repairs. Unsworths Antiquarian Booksellers 28 - 106 2013 £200

Harris, James 1709-1780 *Three Treatises. The First Concerning Art. The Second Concerning Music, Painting and Poetry. The Third Concerning Happiness.* London: printed for C. Nourse in the Strand, 1783. Fourth edition, frontispiece, 8vo., some offset browning to edges of endpapers, old waterstaining noticeable on edges of a number of leaves, contemporary lattice patterned calf, neatly rebacked with gilt decorated spine and red morocco label, corners and inner hinge expertly, repaired. Jarndyce Antiquarian Booksellers CCIV - 154 2013 £75

Harris, Joel Chandler 1848-1908 *Nights with Uncle Remus.* Boston: James R. Osgood, 1883. First edition, 8vo., brown cloth stamped in gold and black, slight rubbing on endpaper and slightest of wear to spine ends, else near fine, 20 black and white plates, beautiful copy. Aleph-Bet Books, Inc. 105 - 312 2013 $600

Harris, Joel Chandler 1848-1908 *Nights with Uncle Remus.* Boston: Houghton Mifflin Oct., 1917. 4to., cloth, pictorial paste-on, fine, illustrations by Milo Winter with pictorial endpapers, 12 color plates and many black and whites. Aleph-Bet Books, Inc. 105 - 311 2013 $275

Harris, Joel Chandler 1848-1908 *Sister Jane.* Boston: Houghton Mifflin, 1896. First edition, hardcover, very good, spine bit darkened. Beasley Books 2013 - 2013 $65

Harris, Joel Chandler 1848-1908 *Tar Baby and Other Rhymes of Uncle Remus.* New York: D. Appleton, Sept., 1904. 8vo., peach colored cloth (191) pages top edge gilt, slightest of cover soil, else near fine, illustrations by A. B.. Frost and E. W. Kemble, with full page plates and line illustrations, nice. Aleph-Bet Books, Inc. 105 - 313 2013 $450

Harris, Joel Chandler 1848-1908 *Uncle Remus. His Songs and Sayings.* New York: Appleton, 1881. (1880) First edition, first issue with "presumptive" last line, page 9 and first page of ads reading "New Books. A Treatise on the Practice of Medicine...", 12mo., original gilt and black stamped brown cloth (minor rubbing), 8 plates, including frontispiece, endpapers repaired at folds, morocco backed cloth slipcase. Howard S. Mott Inc. 262 - 71 2013 $1500

Harris, Joel Chandler 1848-1908 *Uncle Remus: Hs Songs and Sayings.* New York: D. Appleton, 1906. (1895), 8vo., red cloth stamped in gold and black, 265 pages + ads, some damage to rear cover where cloth is scraped, gilt top dinged in few spots, very good newly illustrated with 112 illustrations by A. B. Frost, this copy inscribed and dated 1906 by Harris, also signed again by Harris on titlepage where he has crossed out his printed name, Harris inscriptions are not common.   Aleph-Bet Books, Inc.   104 - 277   2013 $2500

Harris, Joel Chandler 1848-1908 *Uncle Remus.* London: Raithby, Lawrence, n.d. (originally Nelson 1908), circa, 1915. Folio, cloth, one inconspicuous mend, else very good+, dust jacket with mounted color plate, illustrations by Harry Rowntree with 12 vibrant action packed color plates and by Rene Bull, 84 large pen and inks.   Aleph-Bet Books, Inc.   105 - 314 2013 $900

Harris, Joel Chandler 1848-1908 *Uncle Remus or the Story of Mr. Fox and Brer Rabbit.* Raithby, Lawrence & Co., n.d., 1939. Large 4to., original cloth, 2 small dents to lower board, 12 full page color plates by Harry Rountree and 84 text drawings by Rene Bull, one color plate creased, 2 plates with small edge tears, chip and small scribble, trifle shaken, still very good.   R. F. G. Hollett & Son   Children's Books - 261   2013   £120

Harris, John *Navigantium Atque Itinerantium Bibliotheca...* London: printed for T. Osborne, 1764.   Third and best edition, 2 volumes, folio, with 61 engraved plates, including 15 folding maps, titlepages in red and black, beautifully bound period style, Cambridge paneled speckled calf with blind tooling, spine compartments densely gilt in repeating leaf pattern, red and green morocco gilt lettering labels, marbled endpapers, scattered light foxing, small owner's stamp in purple ink to outer margin of titlepage of volume II, closed tear in center of leaf 5Z2 in volume II has been expertly repaired, overall very good, remarkably clean and bright. Heritage Book Shop   Holiday Catalogue 2012 - 74   2013 $15,000

Harris, Moses *The Aurelian; or Natural History of English Insects.*   for the author, 1766.   and with great additions for J. Robson, 1778, English and French titles, engraved vignette, frontispiece, hand colored engraved diagrammatic key-plate and 44 plates numbered I-XLIV by and after Harris, plate I inscribed by author/artist "Colour'd by me Mr. Harris Sept. 1778" indicating plates were coloured by author throughout, occasional very light spotting and offsetting, several leaves and plates with tears in lower margins, not affecting text or image, folio, 19th century half brown morocco, pinkish pebble grained cloth sides, spine gilt and blind tooled on either side of raised bands, lettered direct, top edge gilt, front inner hinge cracked at top and bottom, extremities rubbed, very slight warping of boards, good. Blackwell's Rare Books   Sciences - 56   2013   £8500

Harris, Walter *De Morbis Acutis Infantum.* Samuel Smith, 1689. First edition, final ad leaf, imprimatur leaf present but cut down, old front endpaper mostly clipped neatly leaving an old purchase note with price, little soiling, especially to final leaf, last 2 leaves with minor tear in gutter, ownership inscription to title margin (trimmed - of John Tolnay? Chirurg. 173-) and to initial blank of Richard Drinkwater, Jr. Surgeon 1753, errata corrected in old hand, 8vo., modern calf boards panelled in blind, backstrip with five raised bands, morocco label in second compartment with remainder with central floral blind tools, new endpapers, good.   Blackwell's Rare Books   Sciences - 57   2013   £2500

Harris, William T. *Hegel's Doctrine of Reflection.* New York: D. Appleton, 1881. First edition, 24cmo., green publishers' cloth, contemporary name stamp of "J.K. Light" on endpapers and some text pages, scattered annotations in pencil, good, moderate rubbing, few spots of faint on board, corners bumped and modest wear at spine ends, scarce. Between the Covers Rare Books, Inc.   Philosophy - 63985 2013 $185

Harris, Wilson *The Eye of the Scarecrow.* London: Faber & Faber, 1965. First edition, fine in fine dust jacket. Beasley Books   2013 - 2013 $60

Harris, Wilson *The Waiting Room.* London: Faber & Faber, 1967. First edition, fine in fine dust jacket. Beasley Books   2013 - 2013 $100

Harris, Wilson *The Whole Armor.* London: Faber & Faber, 1967. First edition, fine in fine dust jacket. Beasley Books   2013 - 2013 $100

Harrison, Ada *Poems.* Hatfield: privately printed for the family of the author at the Stellar Press, 1978.   Number 24 of 50 copies, (49) pages, frontispiece by Robert Austin, fine in original japanese vellum backed patterned boards, 8vo., gilt lettered spine.   Ken Spelman Books Ltd.   75 - 189 2013   £40

Harrison, Edward *An Essay on the Powerful Influence of the Spinal Nerves over the Sexual Organs and through them Upon the General State of the Body...* London: Simpkin and Marshall, 1831. lv, 22 pages, pamphlet which has been disbound from a bound volume, no wrapper. James Tait Goodrich   S74 - 142   2013 $125

Harrison, Harry *Astounding: John W. Campbell Memorial Anthology.* New York: Random House, 1973. First edition, fine in fine dust jacket, beautiful copy.   Between the Covers Rare Books, Inc.   Sci-Fi, Fantasy & Horror - 319032 2013 $100

Harrison, Harry *Captive Universe.* New York: G. P. Putnam's Sons, 1969. First edition, fine in fine, bright and crisp dust jacket with tiny spot of rubbing, superior, unread copy.   Between the Covers Rare Books, Inc.   Sci-Fi, Fantasy & Horror - 316153   2013 $75

Harrison, Harry *The Complete Life of Lena Home.* New York: Pocket Magazines Inc., 1955. First edition, 12mo., stapled photographically illustrated wrappers, faint crease on front wrapper and trifle rubbed, else near fine.   Between the Covers Rare Books, Inc.   Sci-Fi, Fantasy & Horror - 302213   2013 $650

Harrison, Harry *The Complete Life of Lena Home.* New York: Pocket Magazines, 1955. First edition, 12mo., stapled photographically illustrated wrappers, faint crease on front wrapper and trifle rubbed, else near fine.   Between the Covers Rare Books, Inc.   165 - 259   2013 $650

Harrison, Harry *Bill, the Galactic Hero.* Garden City: Doubleday & Co., 1965. First edition, octavo, cloth.   L. W. Currey, Inc.   Utopian Literature: Recent Acquisitions (April 2013) - 141019   2013 $350

Harrison, Jim *Farmer.* New York: Viking, 1976. First edition, signed by author, half title has 3 inch strip where paper has thinned, minor bindery defect, owner's name on f.e.p., otherwise book near fine in very good+ to near fine dust jacket with tiny tear or two.   Beasley Books   2013 - 2013 $100

Harrison, Jim *Legends of the Fall.* New York: Delacorte/Seymour Lawrence, 1979. First edition, signed by author, fine in dust jacket.   Ed Smith Books   75 - 33   2013 $450

Harrison, Joseph *Floricultural Cabinet and Florist's Magazien for 1847.* London: Whittaker and Co., 1847. 8vo., 330 pages, plus 66 pages of ads plus 16 page seed catalog, 11 of 12 hand colored plates, pagination messed up, top edge gilt is in front of ad at rear of book, September is missing, some other pages misplaced.   Barnaby Rudge Booksellers   Natural History 2013 - 017313   2013 $165

Harrison, Michael *The Exploits of Chevalier Dupin.* Sauk City: Mycroft and Moran, 1968. First edition, tiny name stamp on bottom of page edges, small faint date stamped on titlepage, else fine in fine dust jacket.   Between the Covers Rare Books, Inc.   Mystery & Detective Fiction - 89309   2013 $65

Harrison, Sarah *The House-Keeper's Pocketbook, and compleat Family Cook.* printed for R. Ware, 1755. Sixth edition, 2 parts in 1 volume, woodcuts of table settings in text, occasional minor staining, bit of foxing at end, 12mo., contemporary sheep, price 2/6 on title, but not specifying boards or sheep, double gilt fillets on sides, spine gilt ruled in compartments, minor wear, very good.   Blackwell's Rare Books   Sciences - 58   2013   £600

Harrison, Tony *Dramatic Verse 1973-1985.* Newcastle upon Tyne: Bloodaxe Books, 1985. First edition, crown 8vo., original tan boards, backstrip gilt lettered, dust jacket with faded backstrip panel, near fine, signed by author, author's inscription to Rex Collings.   Blackwell's Rare Books   B174 - 217   2013   £100

Harrison, Tony *Newcastle is Peru.* Eagle Press (set up and printed by author and others, 1969. First edition, one of 200 copies (of an edition of 226 copies), with 3 wood engravings, 8vo., original plain white sewn card wrappers, dust jacket, near fine.   Blackwell's Rare Books   B174 - 218   2013   £150

Harris's Cabinet, Numbers One to Four. Griffith & Farran 1883, Square 8vo., original parchment backed boards, spine soiled, edges worn, uncut, facsimiles of original illustrations, endpapers browned.   R. F. G. Hollett & Son   Children's Books - 716   2013   £75

Harrod, Howard L. *Mission Among the Blackfeet.* Norman: University of Oklahoma Press, 1971. First edition, vintage photos, 3 maps, dark green cloth, very fine, slightly rubbed dust jacket.   Argonaut Book Shop   Summer 2013 - 151   2013 $60

Harrower, Molly *I Don't Mix with Fairies.* London: Eyre and Spottiswoode, 1928. First edition, 8vo., blue cloth, owner bookplate, fine in lightly worn pictorial dust jacket, wonderful full page pen and ink illustration by Kathleen Hale, quite scarce.   Aleph-Bet Books, Inc.   105 - 306   2013 $400

Harshaw, Benjamin *American Yiddish Poetry.* Berkeley: University of California, 1986. First printing, large 8vo., gray cloth, small reproductions of woodcuts, cover and edges somewhat spotted, else very good, tight copy in faded dust jacket.   Second Life Books Inc.   183 - 155   2013 $50

Hart, George Edward *The Story of Old Abegweit a Sketch of Prince Edward Island History.* published by author, n.d., 1935. 8vo., card covers stapled at centre, 79 pages, few black and white white photo illustrations, light wear to covers, otherwise good.   Schooner Books Ltd.   104 - 139   2013 $60

Hart, William Lee *History of Base Hospital Number Fifty Three Advance Section, Service of Supply.* Haute Marne: Printed by Base Printing Plant 20th Engineers US Army, 1919. 63, (1) pages, 8 photos, text browned in parts, 3 hole punch to spine, original wrappers with recent rebacking, corner chipping on front wrapper, library stamps. James Tait Goodrich 75 - 18 2013 $395

Harte, Bret 1836-1902 *The Queen of the Pirate Isle.* London: Chatto & Windus, 1886. First edition, binding A, octavo, color frontispiece and 27 text illustrations in color by Kate Greenaway, publisher's original tan cloth, covers pictorially decorated in colors, front cover with illustration on page 13, lower cover with illustrations from page 16, all edges gilt, cloth little bit soiled, lower corner of rear board with small loss of cloth, incredibly rare original gray pictorial dust jacket, printed in brown, jacket has been miraculously and almost invisibly backed by master book restorer, Bruce Levy, spectacular presentation copy, in excessively scarce dust jacket. David Brass Rare Books, Inc. Holiday 2012 Chapter One - DB 01728 2013 $3500

Harte, Walter *Essays on Husbandry.* London: printed for W. Frederick in Bath and sold by J. Hinton..., 1764. First edition, 5 engraved plates, woodcuts in text, 8vo., contemporary calf, double gilt fillets on sides, spine gilt ruled in compartments, red lettering piece (small piece missing, affecting 1 letter), trifle worn, excellent copy. Blackwell's Rare Books Sciences - 59 2013 £700

Hartford, R. R. *Godfrey Day: Missionary, Pastor and Primate.* 1940. First edition, 8vo., illustrations, cloth, dust jacket, very good. C. P. Hyland 261 - 296 2013 £38

Hartley, Gilfird W. *Wild Sports and Some Stories.* Blackwood, 1912. First edition, 2 color plates, 52 black and white illustrations, 8 line drawings, cloth, occasional faint foxing, else very good, scarce. C. P. Hyland 261 - 474 2013 £95

Hartley, Thomas *A Discourse on Mistakes Concerning Religion, Enthusiasm, Experiences &c.* Germantown: reprinted by Christopher Sower, 1759. First American edition, 12mo., 168 pages, disbound. M & S Rare Books, Inc. 95 - 351 2013 $300

Hartmann, Heinz *Essays on Ego Psychology.* New York: IUP, 1964. First edition, owner's name, otherwise fine in near fine dust jacket. Beasley Books 2013 - 2013 $50

Hartnett, Michael *A Farewell to English and Other Poems.* Dublin: Gallery Press, 1975. First edition, 8vo., wrappers, near fine, from the library of Richard Murphy, signed by him. Maggs Bros. Ltd. 1442 - 86 2013 £60

Hartshorne, Charles *Creative Synthesis and the Philosophic Method.* London: SCM Press, 1970. First edition, signed by author, very good++, minimal soil and foxing to edge, cover edge wear in very good+ dust jacket with mild chips, short closed tears, minimal sun spine, 8vo. By the Book, L. C. 38 - 26 2013 $350

Harvard University *Harvard Class of 1908 Thirtieth Anniversary Report June 1938 (Seventh Report).* Norwood: privately printed for the Class by the Plimpton Press, 1938. Red cloth, gilt, fine, poet John Hall Wheelock's copy, signed by him by his statement. Between the Covers Rare Books, Inc. 165 - 202 2013 $200

Harvey, Dan *The Barracks, a History of the Victoria/Collins Barracks.* Cork: Mercier, 1997. First edition, 8vo., 284 pages, illustrations, cloth, dust jacket, fine, signed by both authors. C. P. Hyland 261 - 475 2013 £50

Harvey, John *Dublin: a Study in Environment.* 1949. First edition, color frontispiece and 160 black and white illustrations, 8vo., dust jacket, very good. C. P. Hyland 261 - 476 2013 £30

Harvey, M. *Newfoundland in 1897: Being Queen Victoria's Diamond Jubilee Year and the Four Hundredth Anniversary of the Discovery of the Island of John Cabot.* London: Sampson Low, Marston & Co., 1897. 8vo., blue cloth boards, gilt titles to front and spine, half title, index, 2 frontispiece portraits, 22 illustrations, inner hinge cracks, news articles on Harvey pasted to front endpaper, cloth worn, good only. Schooner Books Ltd. 101 - 33 2013 $55

Harvey, William 1578-1657 *Anatomical Exercitations concerning the Generation of Living Creatures.* London: James Young for Octavian Pulleyn, 1653. Engraved frontispiece, 19th century half morocco, rebacked, cloth folding case, front and back blank leaves lacking. James Tait Goodrich 75 - 115 2013 $4750

Harvey, William 1578-1657 *The Anatomical Exercises of Dr. William Harvey.* London: printed for Richard Lowedes, 1673. Second edition in English, recent full calf, contemporary style, raised bands, gilt label, title leaf bit browned, chipped along top fore edge, some browning, else very good, clean copy, modern slipcase box. James Tait Goodrich 75 - 114 2013 $6500

Harvey, William 1578-1657 *Movement of the Heart and Blood in Animals: an Anatomical Essay.* Oxford: Blackwell Scientific, 1957. 8vo., color frontispiece, illustrations, gilt stamped navy blue cloth, dust jacket worn, Burndy bookplate and ink inscription of I. Bernard Cohen, 1957, near fine in good dust jacket. Jeff Weber Rare Books 172 - 124 2013 $60

Harvey, William Fryer *Midnight House and Other Tales.* London: Dent, 1910. First edition, title printed in red, prelims and final leaves lightly foxed, 16mo., original lime green boards, printed label and darkened backstrip little rubbed, free endpapers browned, untrimmed, good, inscribed with love of Margaret Harvey Xmas 1937. Blackwell's Rare Books B174 - 219 2013 £285

Harwood, Mabel Ada *Little Verses for Little People.* Amonsbury, Bristol: privately published n.d. circa, 1912. Original wrappers trifle marked and creased, 16 pages, few pencilled anntotations, scarce. R. F. G. Hollett & Son Children's Books - 262 2013 £25

Haschid, Democritus *A Mole's-Eye View of New York.* Boston: Charles T. Branford, 1941. First edition, bookplate, light stain on bottom, near fine in attractive, very good dust jacket with couple of moderate tears on rear panel and little age toning, seamier side of city, very scarce in jacket. Between the Covers Rare Books, Inc. New York City - 22048 2013 $225

Haskell, Arnold *Infanatilia. the Archaeology of the Nursery.* Dennis Dobson, 1971. First edition, 4to., original cloth, gilt, dust jacket, illustrations by Stanley Lewis. R. F. G. Hollett & Son Children's Books - 263 2013 £30

Haskell, L., Mrs. *God is Love.* London: Ernest Nister, n.d. circa, 1880. 4to., original cloth backed pictorial boards, edges rubbed, corners little bruised, 24 fine full page color plates. R. F. G. Hollett & Son Children's Books - 351 2013 £75

Hassall, A. G. *Treasures from the Bodleian Library.* New York: Columbia University Press, 1976. Thin 4to., 159 pages, 36 color plates, dark blue cloth, gilt stamped cover and spine titles, housed in gray paper slipcase, institutional ex-library bookplate, fine. Jeff Weber Rare Books 171 - 36 2013 $50

Hassall, Joan *Dearest Sydney. Joan Hassall's Letters to Sydney Cockerell from Italy and France April May 1950.* Wakefield: Fleece Press, 1991. One of 220 copies printed by Simon Lawrence, first line of title and sub title printed in red, frontispiece, 2 other portraits and 2 facsimiles, all lightly tipped in, original quarter orange linen printed label, patterned orange, fawn and light brown boards, rough trimmed, fine. Blackwell's Rare Books 172 - 278 2013 £120

Hastings, Francis, Viscount *The Golden Octopus.* Eveleigh Nash & Grayson, 1928. First edition, one of 750 copies, 12 color printed plates by Blamire Young, each tipped to grey card mount, captioned tissue guards present, 4to., original quarter grey cloth, backstrip gilt lettered, brown decorated batik boards, light free endpaper browning, top edge gilt, others untrimmed good. Blackwell's Rare Books B174 - 220 2013 £120

Hatch, James *Wee Tree's Christmas.* New York: Cromwell Printery, 1956. Large folio, 39 pages, spiral backed thick pictorial board covers bound at top edge, near fine, full page color lithographs, rare. Aleph-Bet Books, Inc. 105 - 136 2013 $275

Hatin, Julius *A Manual of Practical Obstetrics Arranged so as to Afford a Concise and Accurate Description of the Management of Preternatural Labours...* Philadelphia: J. Grigg, 1828. First edition in English, (4), 198 pages plus 2 pages ads, rebound in quarter brown speckled calf and green marbled boards, text foxed and browned. James Tait Goodrich S74 - 144 2013 $895

Hatton, Joseph *Newfoundland: the Oldest British Colony. Its History, Its Present Condition and Its Prospects in the Future.* London: Chapman and Hatton, 1883. 8vo., olive cloth boards, gilt to front and spine, 32 pages of ads dated Nov. 1882, half title, frontispiece and 29 black and white illustrations, cloth very worn with spine missing piece at top, some foxing, interior good. Schooner Books Ltd. 101 - 32 2013 $125

Hauff, Wilhelm *Dwarf Long-Nose.* New York: Random House, 1960. First edition (correct price and ads), 4to., faint marks on back of endpaper, else fine in dust jacket, beautiful copy, scarce, illustrations by Maurice Sendak. Aleph-Bet Books, Inc. 105 - 528 2013 $400

Hauff, Wilhelm *Longnose the Dwarf and Other Fairy Tales.* London: W. Swan Sonnenschein & Allen, 1881. First edition thus, 8vo., blue decorated gilt cloth, all edges gilt, 303 pages, near fine, 14 charming full page illustrations, quite uncommon. Aleph-Bet Books, Inc. 104 - 208 2013 $250

Hauptmann, Gerhart *Fasching.* Berlin: Fischer Verlag, 1925. First Kubin edition, aside from total edition of 450 numbered copies, this is special unnumbered copy, likely publisher's that is signed by Hauptmann, illustrations by Alfred Kubin, with 12 original black and white lithographs, of which 11 are signed in pencil by aritst, 10 of them hors texte, regular edition of 400 with only one plate signed by Kubin, this copy identical to deluxe edition of 50 copies, with 11 plates signed, 33 x 26cm., 40 pages, printed on handmade cream wove paper with deckle edges, half morocco and decorative paper over boards, very clean, almost new. Gemini Fine Books & Arts., Ltd. Art Reference & Illustrated Books - 2013 $1450

Das Hausgesinde. Oldenburg: Stalling, 1925. First edition, 4to., cloth backed pictorial boards, rear cover slightly soiled, light edge rubbing, very good, printed on one side of paper only, each page entirely illustrated in color with 1 line of text below, illustrations, scarce. Aleph-Bet Books, Inc. 104 - 198 2013 $450

Hawes, Hampton *Raise Up Off Me.* New York: Coward, 1974. First edition, near fine but for very slight sunning to spine ends, very good+ dust jacket with little edge toning and tiny tears at folds, nice, 179 pages.   Beasley Books 2013 - 2013 $100

Hawkesbury, Lord *The Heraldry on the Gateway at Kirkham Abbey.* n.p.: 1902. 8vo., good copy, 8vo., contemporary half red calf, spine rubbed, bookplate of Hawkesbury.   Ken Spelman Books Ltd. 73 - 112 2013 £25

Hawking, Stephen *A Brief History of Time.* New York: Bantam Books, 1988. First edition, 8vo., near fine in fine dust jacket, signed by Hawking without personalization.   By the Book, L. C. 38 - 5 2013 $5000

Hawkins, Bisset *Germany: the Spirit of Her History, Literature, Social Condition and National Economy.* London: John W. Parker, 1838. First edition, 8vo., pages xx, 475, contemporary green straight grained morocco, spine faded with small wear to head and tail.   J. & S. L. Bonham Antiquarian Booksellers Europe - 5502 2013 £145

Hawkins, Sheila *Pepito.* London: Hamish, Hamilton, 1938. Large 4to., pictorial cloth, fine in chipped dust jacket, illustrations on every page in color by author.   Aleph-Bet Books, Inc. 105 - 552 2013 $400

Hawtayne, George Hammond *West Indian Yarns.* Demerara: J. Thomson, Georgetown, 1884. Slight spotting, original half glazed, printed drab paper boards, paper label, spine slightly darkened, little rubbed.   Jarndyce Antiquarian Booksellers CCV - 131 2013 £180

Hawthorne, Nathaniel 1804-1864 *Lake Country Notes.* Ambleside: George Middleton, n.d., Tall slim 8vo., original printed wrappers, 16 pages, scarce.   R. F. G. Hollett & Son Lake District and Cumbria - 239 2013 £20

Hawthorne, Nathaniel 1804-1864 *The Marble Faun.* Boston: Ticknor & Fields, 1860. First US edition, 12mo., March 1860 catalog, brown cloth, worn at extremities of spines, rear hinge volume I loose, very good set.   Second Life Books Inc. 183 - 157 2013 $300

Hawthorne, Nathaniel 1804-1864 *Mosses from an Old Manse.* New York: Wiley & Putnam, 1846. First edition, first state, 8vo., original cloth, gilt stamped black leather label, outer hinges cracked, small chip out of label, text foxed, very sound.   M & S Rare Books, Inc. 95 - 143 2013 $850

Hawthorne, Nathaniel 1804-1864 *Passages from the French and Italian Note-Books of Nathaniel Hawthorne.* London: Strahan and Co., 1871. 8vo., 2 volumes, half titles, very good, contemporary half vellum, large red morocco labels and gilt ruled spines, marbled boards, top edges gilt.   Ken Spelman Books Ltd. 75 - 136 2013 £140

Hawthorne, Nathaniel 1804-1864 *Pegasus, the Winged Horse: a Greek Myth Retold by Nathaniel Hawthorne.* New York: Macmillan, 1963. First edition, folio, glossy illustrated boards, fine, beautiful copy.   Between the Covers Rare Books, Inc. Horses, Horsemanship, Horse Racing, Etc. - 279462 2013 $75

Hawthorne, Nathaniel 1804-1864 *The Scarlet Letter.* Boston: Ticknor, Reed and Fields, 1850. First edition, mixed issue with 'reduplicate' for 'repudiate' on page 21, line 20 and contents ending on page 'iv', without publisher's ads inserted, small octavo, titlepage printed in black and red, bound by Atelier Bindery in full blue morocco, boards ruled in gilt with leaf corner devices, front board with scarlet calf letter "A" outlined in gilt, inlaid in center, spine stamped and lettered in gilt, top edge gilt, gilt dentelles, marbled endpapers, original brown cloth bound in at back, slipcase with blue morocco edges, overall very good.   Heritage Book Shop Holiday Catalogue 2012 - 75 2013 $2750

Hawthorne, Nathaniel 1804-1864 *The Scarlet Letter.* Boston: Ticknor, Reed and Fieldsd, 1850. First edition, one of 2500 printed, 12mo., original ribbed blind decorated brown cloth, slight wear at spine tips and corners, 4 pages inserted ads at front dated March 1850, little wear at spine tips and corners, few spots on covers, otherwise very good, better than average, Rampant lion bookplate inside front cover, morocco backed cloth slipcase.   Howard S. Mott Inc. 262 - 72 2013 $4500

Hawthorne, Nathaniel 1804-1864 *Scarlet Letter.* London: Methuen, n.d., 1920. Large thick 4to., blue cloth with extensive gilt decoration, top edge gilt, offsetting on half title, else very fine in publisher's box with color plate over box in very good condition, some scuffing and soil and repairs to flaps, 31 beautiful tipped-in color plates on heavier stock by Hugh Thomson, detailed pen and ink drawings, amazing copy.   Aleph-Bet Books, Inc. 104 - 556 2013 $475

Hawthorne, Nathaniel 1804-1864 *Transformation; or the Romance of Monte Beni.* London: Smith Elder, 1860. First edition, 8vo., half title in volume I, not called for in 2 or 3, later three quarter morocco, very good tight with just minor foxing.   Second Life Books Inc. 183 - 158 2013 $750

Hawthorne, Nathaniel 1804-1864 *Twice Told Tales.* Boston: American Stationers Co., 1837. First edition, 12mo., 4 pages initial ads, 12 page catalog, clean tear to pages 78-79 repaired with archival tape, one gathering misbound, slightly later half dark green calf, gilt compartment, some slight rubbing, but very good. Jarndyce Antiquarian Booksellers CCV - 132 2013 £380

Hawthorne, Nathaniel 1804-1864 *Hawthorne's Wonder Book.* London: Hodder & Stoughton, nd., 1922. First Rackham edition, 4to., red gilt cloth, fine in dust jacket with mounted color plate, dust jacket with margin mends and some soil, but very good+, 24 beautiful color plates, 16 tipped in color plates with printed guards plus 8 color plate drawings, as well as 20 equally as lovely text black and whites and pictorial endpapers. Aleph-Bet Books, Inc. 104 - 470 2013 $900

Hawthorne, Nathaniel 1804-1864 *A Wonder Book.* London: Hodder & Stoughton, 1922. First Rackham edition, 546/600 copies signed by artist, 24 color printed plates of which 16 are lightly tipped to cream card mounts with associated captioned tissue guards, other illustrations in text and endpaper designs all by Arthur Rackham, one hinge strained, large 4to., original white cloth, backstrip and front cover, gilt blocked to a design by Rackham, just little faint edge browning to rear cover, top edge gilt, others untrimmed. Blackwell's Rare Books B174 - 284 2013 £1400

Hay, Daniel *Whitehaven. A Short History.* Whitehaven: Borough Council, 1966. First edition, 152 pages, illustrations, original pictorial boards, protected with self-adhesive film. R. F. G. Hollett & Son Lake District and Cumbria - 240 2013 £35

Hay, Daniel *Whitehaven. A Short History.* Whitehaven: Borough Council, 1968. Pages 152, illustrations, original cloth. R. F. G. Hollett & Son Lake District and Cumbria - 241 2013 £35

Hayden, Arthur *Spode & His Successors. A History of the Pottery Stoke-on-Trent...* London: Cassell, 1925. 8vo., 24 tipped-in color plates, 64 half tone illustrations, original pale blue decorated cloth, spine lettered gilt, original dust jacket slightly toned on spine with some minor chips to head, presentation label tipped in from one of the company directors. Marlborough Rare Books Ltd. 218 - 78 2013 £95

Hayden, Ferdinand Vandiveer 1829-1887 *Geological and Geographical Atlas of Colorado and Portions of Adjacent Territory.* Washington: Jules Bien, 1877. First edition, 20 sheets, elephant folio, original three quarter leather over brown cloth boards, leather label at center of front board, raised bands and title gilt on backstrip, very good, light wear to boards, bookplate on front pastedown. Ken Sanders Rare Books 45 - 36 2013 $3500

Haydock, Roger *A Collection of Christian Writings, Labours, Travels and Sufferings of that Faithful and Approved Minister...* London: by T. Sowle, 1700. First edition, contemporary calf, very worn, spine shabby, part of front free endpaper torn away, light foxing and occasional browning from the library of Sir John Rodes (1670-1743), with his signature. Joseph J. Felcone Inc. Books Printed before 1701 - 49 2013 $300

Haydon, T. *Sporting Reminiscences.* London: Bliss Sands & Co., 1898. First edition, 281 pages (7 pages ads), green cloth with decoration, lettering and top edge gilt, light general wear, very good plus. Between the Covers Rare Books, Inc. Horses, Horsemanship, Horse Racing, Etc. - 65817 2013 $100

Hayek, Friedrich A. *The Road to Serfdom.* Chicago: University of Chicago, 1945. Sixth printing, Signed by author, very good++, ex-library, blindstamp titlepage and numbers on copyright page, label residue r.f.e.p., no other markings, mild sun spine, 8vo. By the Book, L. C. 38 - 17 2013 $750

Hayek, Friedrich A. *Rules, Perception and Intelligibility.* London: Oxford University Press, 1963. Offprint, first separate edition, very good++ in original printed wrappers, mild toning, 8vo., scarce. By the Book, L. C. 38 - 15 2013 $450

Hayek, Friedrich A. *The Sensory Order.* Chicago: University of Chicago, 1952. First edition, 8vo., fine in very good++ dust jacket with mild sun to spine and rear cover, minimal edge wear, scarce. By the Book, L. C. 38 - 16 2013 $400

Hayes, Derek *Historical Atlas of California.* Berkeley: University of California Press, 2007. Folio, 256 pages, vintage photos, prints, maps, very fine with pictorial dust jacket. Argonaut Book Shop Summer 2013 - 153 2013 $75

Hayes, Derek *Historical Atlas of the Pacific Northwest maps of Exploration and Discovery.* Seattle: Sasquatch Books, 2000. Second edition, small folio, 208 pages, profusely illustrated in color, black cloth, very fine, pictorial dust jacket. Argonaut Book Shop Recent Acquisitions June 2013 - 137 2013 $90

Hayes, Maurice *The Flight Path.* Oldcastle: The Gallery Press for The American Ireland Fund, 1996. First edition, one of 500 copies, large 8vo., original quarter burgundy cloth, mock vellum boards, shamrock device blocked in gilt on upper board, fine in matching slipcase, from the library of contributor Richard Murphy. Maggs Bros. Ltd. 1442 - 249 2013 £150

Hayes, Nancy M. *The Plucky Patrol.* London: Cassell, 1924. First edition, original grey cloth with oval pictorial onlay, color frontispiece and 3 plates by John Cameron. R. F. G. Hollett & Son   Children's Books - 271   2013   £25

Hayes, Richard *Interest at one View, Calculated to a Farthing At 2, 3, 4, 5, 6, 7 and 8 per cent....* printed for W. Meadows, 1751. Eighth edition, 16mo., small strip missing form top of first 2 leaves, without loss, little spotted or soiled in places, 19th century hard grained morocco, lettered gilt on spine, patch where author's name should be missing, lacking rear free endpaper, sound.   Blackwell's Rare Books   172 - 69   2013   £250

Hayley, William *The Life and Posthumous Writings of William Cowper...* Chichester: printed by J. Seagrave for J. Johnson, 1803-1806. First edition, 4 volumes including supplementary pages, in three, with 6 plates by William Blake, first impressions of those in volumes i and ii (no second state for those in volume iii) and one plate engraved by Caroline Watson, bound without half titles, little browned in places, some worming in lower margins of volumes i and ii, 4to., contemporary calf, blind roll tooled borders on sides, flat backstrips tooled in blind and lettered gilt direct, gilt inner dentelles, bit rubbed and bumped, spines little darkened, crack at foot on one joint, contemporary ownership of Elizabeth? Cardigan, that of C. Waldegrave dated 1824 in two places and Radstock bookplate in each volume, good.   Blackwell's Rare Books   172 - 70   2013   £450

Hayley, William *The Life, and Posthumous Writings of William Cowper...* Chichester: printed by J. Seagrave for J. Johnson, 1806. New edition, 4 volumes, half titles, frontispiece volume 1, contemporary full diced calf, spines ruled and lettered in gilt, devices in blind, spines and hinges slightly rubbed, armorial bookplates of J. M. Lloyd and later Lloyd family booklabels, nice.   Jarndyce Antiquarian Booksellers   CCIII - 616   2013   £120

Hayley, William *The Triumphs of Temper.* Chichester: printed by J. Seagrave, for T. Cadell and W. Davies, London, 1803. Twelfth edition, 6 plates, few spots, bound without half title, later 'antique' panelled calf by V. A. Brown of Mildenborough, spine gilt in compartments, red and green leather labels, slightly rubbed, all edges gilt, nice, bright copy, signature of Mary Keats on titlepage, pencil notes in prelims by Grant Gration-Maxfield.   Jarndyce Antiquarian Booksellers   CCIII - 7   2013   £650

Haym, Nicola Francesco *Biblioteca Italiana O Sia Ntizia De Libri Rari Nella Lingua Italiana.* Venezia: Presso Angiolo Geremia, 1728. First edition, 4to., first and last leaves little spotted, last with wormtrack to lower margin, few leaves with pale marginal waterstain, 19th century polished calf by Carrs of Glasgow, covers ruled in blind, gilt stamped centerpiece depicting Hunterian Museum, spine rubbed, hinges cracked.   Marlborough Rare Books Ltd.   218 - 79   2013   £345

Haymaker, Webb *The Founders of Neurology.* Springfield: Thomas, 1970. 616 pages, illustrations, original binding, worn dust jacket, copy shows some use, from the library of Hugh Rizzoli, M.D., neurosurgeon.   James Tait Goodrich   S74 - 145   2013 $125

Hayman, Samuel *Guide to St. Mary's Collegiate Church.* 1869. New edition, 35 pages, original front wrapper, some marking of passages, good.   C. P. Hyland   261 - 882   2013   £60

Hayman, Samuel *Hand-Book for Youghal.* Field, 1896. 8vo. 99 pages, wrappers, very good.   C. P. Hyland   261 - 883   2013   £45

Hayman, Samuel *Illustrated Guide to the Blackwater & Ardmore.* W. G. Field, 1898. 44 pages, wrappers, very good.   C. P. Hyland   261 - 883   2013   £35

Hays, Margaret *Wiederseimkiddie-Land.* no publishing information, circa, 1910. 4to., linen like finish, pictorial wrappers, slight cover soil, else near fine, 14 near fine, 14 near full page illustrations by Grace Drayton.   Aleph-Bet Books, Inc.   105 - 202   2013 $275

Hayward, Richard *Where the River Shannon Flows.* 1950. Louis Morrison photos, folding map, 8vo., cloth, very good.   C. P. Hyland   261 - 478   2013   £30

Haywood, Eliza Fowler   1693-1756 *The Fruitless Enquiry.* London: printed for W. Cater, opposite Red Lion Street in Hoborn, 1760. Second edition, 12mo., occasional foxing and light browning, inner boards browned from turn-ins, several blank margins torn without loss of text, endpapers removed, full contemporary calf, raised and gilt banded spine, neatly repaired at foot, some rubbing, corners bumped.   Jarndyce Antiquarian Booksellers   CCIV - 156   2013   £750

Haywood, Helen *The Helen Haywood Christmas Book.* Hutchinson, n.d. mid 1930's, 4to., original cloth backed pictorial boards, pages 120 full color illustrations, lovely fresh copy.   R. F. G. Hollett & Son   Children's Books - 272   2013   £65

Hazard, Willis P. *Comic History of the United States.* New York: Leavitt & Allen, 1861. First edition, Square 8vo., frontispiece and numerous cuts, original blindstamped and gilt decorated cloth, spine mostly shot, numerous cuts and some full page illustrations in text, all colored by contemporary hand, interior bit grubby.   M & S Rare Books, Inc.   95 - 153   2013 $275

Hazlitt, William Carew 1834-1913 *Old Cookery Books and Ancient Cuisine.* London: Elliot Stock, 1886. First edition, 8vo., original quarter gilt stamped copper cloth over brown paper backed boards, corners lightly rubbed, booklabel, very good.   Jeff Weber Rare Books   171 - 158   2013 $140

He is Nothing but a Little Boy.   Skokie: Black Cat Press, 1980. Limited to 240 copies, 2 x 1.8 cm., cloth, title gilt stamped on spine, decoration gilt stamped on front cover, frontispiece, illustrations by Barbara Raheb, from the collection of Donn W. Sanford.   Oak Knoll Books   303 - 55   2013 $225

Head, Henry   *Aphasia and Kindred Disorders of Speech.*   Cambridge: University Press, 1926. First edition, 2 volumes, numerous figures and tables, original blind ruled green cloth, gilt stamped titles, fine copy, like new.   Jeff Weber Rare Books   172 - 126   2013 $600

Head, Henry   *Studies in Neurology.*   Oxford: 1920. First collected edition, 2 volumes, 4to., original cloth, spines bit sunned, otherwise very clean, tight set with no ownership markings.   James Tait Goodrich   S74 - 146   2013 $395

Head, Henry   *Studies in Neurology.*   London: Henry Frowde, Hodder & Stoughton, 1920. 2 volumes, 8vo., 182 figures, original red cloth blindstamped covers, black stamped cover title, gilt stamped spine titles, spines lightly sun faded, ink ownership marks on Edward N. J. Duggan inside front cover, unusually fine set.   Jeff Weber Rare Books   172 - 128   2013 $400

Headlam, Cuthbert   *The Three Northern Counties of England.* Gateshead: Northumberland Press, 1939. Limited edition (500 copies), small 4to., original full dark blue levant morocco gilt, untrimmed, 23 plates, 8 maps and plans, few spots to half title and fore-edges, most attractive, loosely inserted are several letters relating to production of the book between H. L. Honeyman (one of the contributors) and publishers and others, with press cuttings.   R. F. G. Hollett & Son   Lake District and Cumbria - 244   2013   £120

Headlam, Cuthbert   *The Three Northern Counties of England.* Gateshead: Northumberland Press, 1939. First trade edition, small 4to., original cloth, xii, 343 pages, 23 plates and 8 maps and plans, prelims and edges lightly spotted.   R. F. G. Hollett & Son   Lake District and Cumbria - 243   2013   £30

Headlam, Cuthbert   *The Three Northern Counties of England.* Gateshead: Northumberland Press, 1939. First trade edition, small 4to., original cloth, dust jacket spine faded, 23 plates, 8 maps and plans, prelims and edges lightly spotted.   R. F. G. Hollett & Son   Lake District and Cumbria - 242   2013   £50

Headley, J. T. *Grant and Sherman: Their Campaigns and Generals.* New York: E. B. Treat, 1865. First edition, 8vo., original brown cloth with some minor tearing to cloth at top and bottom of spine, 4 pages of ads 608 pages, many illustrations, portraits lacking, very good.   Barnaby Rudge Booksellers   Biography 2013 - 021181   2013 $75

Heaney, Seamus   *After Summer.*   Dublin: Gallery Press, 1978. Limited to 250 copies signed by author, 8vo., original chocolate brown cloth, dust jacket slightly proud at head as usual and therefore slightly creased, fine.   Maggs Bros. Ltd.   1442 - 91   2013   £600

Heaney, Seamus   *Articulations. Poetry, Philosophy and the Shaping of Culture.* Dublin: Royal Irish Academy, 2008. First edition, limited to 450 copies signed by president of RIA, Professor James Sleven, narrow 4to., original decorative wrappers, fine.   Maggs Bros. Ltd.   1442 - 125   2013   £50

Heaney, Seamus   *Ballynahinch Lake. Turning the Millenium.*   Ballynahinch: Co. Galway, private printed for Ballynahinch Castle, 1999.   Limited to 500 numbered copies, this copy inscribed by author "Seamus Heaney, h.c. (hors commerce)", fine, 8vo., single cream card folded.   Maggs Bros. Ltd.   1442 - 113   2013   £275

Heaney, Seamus   *A Boy Driving His Father to Confession.* Farnham, Surrey: Sceptre Press, 1970. First edition, one of 150 numbered copies, small thin 8vo., original white printed wrappers, printed on Glastonbury laid paper, staples beginning to rust as usual, otherwise fine.   James S. Jaffe Rare Books   Fall 2013 - 63   2013 $2000

Heaney, Seamus   *Changes.* N.P.: privately printed for the author by Peter Fallon, 1980. First edition, small 8vo., original green printed wrappers, very fine.   James S. Jaffe Rare Books   Fall 2013 - 67   2013 $1250

Heaney, Seamus   *Death of a Naturalist.*   London: Oxford University Press, 1966. First US edition, one of only 1000 copies, 8vo., original green cloth, fine.   Maggs Bros. Ltd.   1442 - 87   2013   £750

Heaney, Seamus   *Door into the Dark.* New York: Oxford University Press, 1969. One of 1000 copies, first U.S. edition, 8vo., original back cloth, near fine in dust jacket.   Maggs Bros. Ltd.   1442 - 89   2013   £350

Heaney, Seamus   *The Door Stands Open.* Dublin: Irish Writer's Centre, 2005. Limited to 250 copies signed by author, from a total edition of 300, 8vo., original handwove and Zanders Zeta paper bound in stainless steel covers printed in black and folded inside mixed media silkscreen wrapper within black card folding case with author's facsimile signature in silver, fine.   Maggs Bros. Ltd.   1442 - 121   2013   £350

Heaney, Seamus *The Door Stands Open.* Dublin: Irish Writer's Centre, 2005. Limited to 50 copies, signed by author with additional holograph quotation, 8vo., original handwoven and Zanders Zeta paper bound in stainless steel covers printed in black and folded inside mixed-media silk-screen wrap, within frame of twin glass-rods attached to a full mixed metal spine with poet's signature in relief, all housed in slipcase of hand blown clear glass, as new. Maggs Bros. Ltd.   1442 - 122   2013   £850

Heaney, Seamus *Field Work.* London: Faber and Faber, 1979. First edition, 8vo., original brown cloth, dust jacket, slight fading to spine, otherwise fine, inscribed by author May 1981.   Maggs Bros. Ltd.   1442 - 94   2013   £275

Heaney, Seamus *Field Work.* London: Faber, 1979. First edition, crown 8vo., original mid brown boards, backstrip gilt lettered, dust jacket without any fading to backstrip panel, flaps with just little light foxing, near fine. Blackwell's Rare Books   172 - 192   2013   £250

Heaney, Seamus *Haw Lantern.* New York: Farrar Straus Giroux, 1987. First edition, number 129 of 250 copies numbered and signed by author, 8vo., original burgundy linen backed boards, black panel on spine lettered gilt, fine in matching slipcase.   Maggs Bros. Ltd.   1442 - 102   2013   £350

Heaney, Seamus *Human Chain.* London: Faber, 2010. First edition, 175/300 copies (of an edition of 325) signed by author, foolscap 8vo., original brown cloth backed cream boards, printed label, matching boards and cloth slipcase, fine.   Blackwell's Rare Books   172 - 193   2013   £400

Heaney, Seamus *A Keen for the Coins.* Hickory: Lenior Rhyne College, 2002. One of 100 copies, first edition, 12mo., original grey wrappers, printed in black, brown and grey, fine.   Maggs Bros. Ltd.   1442 - 116   2013   £650

Heaney, Seamus *A Keen for the Coins.* Hickory: Lenior-Rhyne College, 2002. First edition, one of 100 copies, though this is an unrecorded variant having reverse of the 1928 Irish coin embossed on both upper and lower covers, 12mo., original grey wrappers printed in black, brown, grey and stitched with mahogany thread, fine.   Maggs Bros. Ltd.   1442 - 117   2013   £750

Heaney, Seamus *The Kilpeck Anthology.* Hereford: Five Seasons Press, 1981. Number 25 of 50 numbered copies, 4to., original quarter brown morocco, canvas boards, lettered gilt, top edge coloured, others uncut, printed letterpress on Barcham Green's handmade Penshurst Light Toned paper with handmade screenprints by Brian Nevitt, with a modicum of wear to head and tail of spine, otherwise fine in matching slipcase.   Maggs Bros. Ltd.   1442 - 98   2013   £200

Heaney, Seamus *Laments.* London: Faber and Faber, 1995. First edition, 8vo., original black cloth, dust jacket, fine in slightly rubbed dust jacket, from the library of Richard Murphy.   Maggs Bros. Ltd.   1442 - 107   2013   £75

Heaney, Seamus *A Lough Neagh Sequence.* Didsbury: Phoenix Pamphlet Poetry Press, 1969. One of 950 copies, from a total edition of 1000, 8vo., original wrappers, fine. Maggs Bros. Ltd.   1442 - 88   2013   £180

Heaney, Seamus *The Midnight Verdict.* Dublin: Gallery Press, 1993. Limited to 925 copies from a total edition of 1000, 8vo., fine, original black cloth, dust jacket.   Maggs Bros. Ltd.   1442 - 106   2013   £150

Heaney, Seamus *North.* London: Faber & Faber, 1975. First edition, 8vo., original cloth, dust jacket, front endsheets darkened as usual, otherwise very fine, virtually as new. James S. Jaffe Rare Books   Fall 2013 - 65   2013 $1000

Heaney, Seamus *North.* New York: Oxford University Press, 1976. First US edition, 8vo., original blue cloth, dust jacket, near fine, from the library of Richard Murphy. Maggs Bros. Ltd.   1442 - 90   2013   £600

Heaney, Seamus *Poems and a Memoir.* New York: Limited Editions Club, 1982. Limited to 2000 copies signed by Heaney, Flanagan and Pearson, 4to., original full brown calf, fine in matching slipcase.   Maggs Bros. Ltd. 1442 - 99   2013   £600

Heaney, Seamus *Preoccupations. Selected Prose 1968-1978.* London: Faber and Faber, 1980. First edition, 8vo., original blue cloth, dust jacket faintly rubbed at head and tail of spine, fine copy.   Maggs Bros. Ltd.   1442 - 96   2013   £250

Heaney, Seamus *Gravities. A Collection of Poems and Drawings.* Newcastle-Upon-Tyne: Charlotte Press, 1979. First edition, oblong 8vo., original black wrappers, near fine. Maggs Bros. Ltd.   1442 - 95   2013   £75

Heaney, Seamus *A Shiver.* Thame: Clutag Press, 2005. First edition, limited to 300 copies, large 8vo., original pale red wrappers, fine in wrappers.   Maggs Bros. Ltd.   1442 - 120   2013   £75

Heaney, Seamus *Sounding Lines: the Art of Translating Poetry.* Berkeley: Doreen B. Townsend Center for the Humanities, 2000. First edition, 32 pages, near fine in wrappers that have some very slight rubbing, seemingly quite uncommon.   Jeff Hirsch Books   Fall 2013 - 129196   2013 $50

Heaney, Seamus *The Sounds of Rain.* Atlanta: Emory University, 1988. Limited to 300 copies, printed at The Shadowy Waters Press, 8vo., original hand stitched pale blue wrappers, white printed label, fine in original printed envelope. Maggs Bros. Ltd. 1442 - 103 2013 £175

Heaney, Seamus *Spelling It Out.* Loughcrew: Gallery Press, 2009. Limited to 400 copies signed by author with only 300 for sale, large 8vo., original green linen, lettered gilt on upper cover printed in black and brown, fine. Maggs Bros. Ltd. 1442 - 127 2013 £150

Heaney, Seamus *The Spirit Label.* London: Faber, 1996. First edition, foolscap 8vo., original mid green boards, backstrip gilt lettered, dust jacket, fine, inscribed by author for Nick Gammage. Blackwell's Rare Books 172 - 194 2013 £300

Heaney, Seamus *Sweeney Praises the Trees.* New York: Kelly/Winterton Press, 1981. First edition, limited to 110 copies, thin 8vo., original wrappers, very fine, rare. James S. Jaffe Rare Books Fall 2013 - 68 2013 $1000

Heaney, Seamus *The Testament of Cresseid.* London: Enitharmon Editions, 2004. Limited edition, signed by author and artist, 4to., original dark green cloth with paper label on spine and color image on upper board, printed on Arches Velin and bound by Fine Bindery, Wellingborough. Maggs Bros. Ltd. 1442 - 119 2013 £300

Heaney, Seamus *A Tribute to Michael McLaverty.* Belfast: Linen Hall Library, 2005. First edition, limited to 250 copies signed by author, narrow 8vo., original marbled paper wrappers, sewn with Barbour thread and hand bound by Sydney Aiken, fine in black four-fold card sleeve. Maggs Bros. Ltd. 1442 - 123 2013 £250

Heaney, Seamus *Ugolino.* Dublin: Andrew Carpenter, 1979. First edition, limited to 125 copies, signed by poet, artist and designer and publisher, Andrew Carpenter, only 30 copies were for sale, 4to., 2 lithographs by Louis Le Brocquy, original limp black goatskin, publisher's slipcase, very fine, rare. James S. Jaffe Rare Books Fall 2013 - 66 2013 $12,500

Heaney, Seamus *Wintering Owl.* New York: Oxford University Press, 1973. First American edition (500 copies), 8vo., original blue cloth bards, very fine in very slightly dust soiled jacket, scarce, poet and critic Ralph Mills Jr's copy with his ownership signature. James S. Jaffe Rare Books Fall 2013 - 64 2013 $1250

Heap, Gwinn Harris *Central Route to the Pacific, from the Valley of the Mississippi to California...* Philadelphia: 1854. 136, 46, pages, 13 plates, without map, included in only a few issues, original cloth covered boards, extremities lightly rubbed, scattered foxing, faint damp mark to few pages, else very good. Dumont Maps & Books of the West 122 - 68 2013 $795

Heard, H. F. *Murder by Reflection.* London: Cassell, 1945. First English edition, tiny light spotting on page edges and name on front endpaper, otherwise near fine in dust jacket with tiny tears at spine ends and wear along folds and edges. Mordida Books 81 - 244 2013 $65

Hearn, Lafcadio 1850-1904 *Buying Christmas Toys and Other Essays.* Tokyo: Hokuseido Press, 1939. First edition, octavo, green cloth, spine panel stamped in gold, publisher's monogram stamped in blind on rear panel, top edge stained black, cream endpapers. L. W. Currey, Inc. Christmas Themed Books - 80585 2013 $200

Hearn, Lafcadio 1850-1904 *Buying Christmas Toys and Other Essays.* Tokyo: Hokuseido Press, 1939. First edition, octavo, green cloth, spine panel stamped in gold, publisher's monogram stamped in blind on rear panel, top edge stained black, cream endpapers. L. W. Currey, Inc. Christmas Themed Books - 80586 2013 $150

Hearn, Lafcadio 1850-1904 *Glimpses of Unfamiliar Japan.* Boston and New York: Houghton Mifflin, 1894. First edition, 8vo., 4 full page illustrations, black cloth stamped in silver, top edge gilt, hinges of volume one starting, nice, clean set, issued in an edition of 1000 copies. Second Life Books Inc. 183 - 161 2013 $275

Hearn, Lafcadio 1850-1904 *Japanese Fairy Tale Series.* 5 volumes, each 5 1/2 x 7 3/4 inches, bound with silk ties and printed on crepe paper, housed in publisher's folding cloth case with pictorial lining and ivory clasps in fine condition, without exception, each book in fine bright condition with delicate silk ties, intact and all have their original rice paper sleeves, each volume hand colored. Aleph-Bet Books, Inc. 105 - 315 2013 $3000

Hearn, Lafcadio 1850-1904 *The Romance of the Milky Way.* Boston and New York: Houghton Mifflin, 1905. First edition, 8vo., very fine, chipped and dust stained dust jacket, lacks 1 inch piece from upper right of front cover from extremities of spine. Second Life Books Inc. 183 - 162 2013 $300

Hearn, Lafcadio 1850-1904 *Shadowings.* Boston: Little Brown, 1900. First edition, 8vo., 268 pages, uncut, five illustrations inserted, blue cloth stamped in different shades of blue and gilt, designed by Bruce Rogers, name on endpaper, untrimmed, top edge gilt, nice, bright copy. Second Life Books Inc. 183 - 163 2013 $350

Hearn, Lafcadio 1850-1904 *Shadowings.* Boston: Little Brown, 1900. First edition, 8vo., 268 pages, top edge gilt, other edges uncut, deep blue cloth stamped in light blue and gilt, rather nice, little nicked dust jacket.   Second Life Books Inc.   183 - 164   2013 $600

Hearn, Lafcadio 1850-1904 *Some Chinese Ghosts.* Boston: Roberts Bros., 1887. First edition, 12mo., original cloth (minor rubbing and slight soiling), pages 185, red morocco backed cloth slipcase.   Howard S. Mott Inc.   262 - 74   2013 $350

Hearne, Thomas *Antiquities of Great Britain.* London: T. Hearne and W. Byrne, 1786. First edition, Volume I only as issued, landscape folio, pages 55 + 52 plates of copper engravings, toned, foxed, particularly around edges of plates, few tissue guards missing and some others creased and with occasional tears, later quarter sheep mottled paper covered boards and endpapers, morocco label to spine, original marbled free endpapers still present, matching marbled edges, upper hinge split releasing spine strip and upper board from text block, lower hinge loosening, spine scraped, joints and edges worn, small loss to bottom corner of f.e.fe.p., small binder's ticket of Carpenter and Co. Old Bond Street.   Unsworths Antiquarian Booksellers   28 - 107   2013   £250

Hearne, Thomas *Reliquiae Harnianae: the Remains of Thomas Hearne, M.A. of Edmund Hall...* Oxford: printed for the editor, 1857. First edition, engraved frontispiece in volume i, prospectus loosely inserted, bit of light dust soiling, 8vo., early 20th century half calf, marbled boards, spines with five raised bands, dark olive morocco lettering pieces, scuffed, touch worn at corners, some scratches and stains, joints just cracking at ends, but strong, bookseller's descriptions pasted to front pastedown, sound.   Blackwell's Rare Books   B174 - 67   2013   £150

Hearne, Vicki *Nervous Horses.* Austin and London: University of Texas Press, 1980. First edition hardcover issue, edges lightly foxed, else fine in slightly spine faded, but near fine dust jacket, Advance Review Copy with publisher's slip laid in, hardcover issue is very uncommon.   Between the Covers Rare Books, Inc.   Horses, Horsemanship, Horse Racing, Etc. - 311147   2013 $275

Heberden, M. V. *That's the Spirit.* Garden City: Doubleday Crime Club, 1950. First edition, pages darkened, otherwise near fine in dust jacket with faint crease on spine.   Mordida Books   81 - 245   2013 $65

Hecht, Anthony *Interior Skies: Late Poems from Liguria.* Camden: Two Ponds Press, 2011. Artist's book, 1 of 75 copies, all on paper made by Velke Losiny in Czech republic, each copy hand numbered, 38 pages, bound by Gray Parrot, his own teal blue pastepaper over boards with coral morocco spine, author and title in gold gilt stamped on spine, handsewn teal headbands housed in matching grey cloth clamshell box with title and author's initials stamped in gold gilt on coral morocco within rules, binder's ticket on lower inside turn-in, 2 engravings by Abigail Rorer printed on Zirkall paper by artist,.   Priscilla Juvelis - Rare Books   55 - 25   2013 $950

Hecht, Anthony *The Seven Deadly Sins.* Northampton: Gehenna Press, 1958. First edition, of 300 copies, this one of just 100 bound in cloth, wood engravings by Leonard Baskin, number 10 signed by author and artist, publisher's cloth backed boards, fine.   Second Life Books Inc.   183 - 165   2013 $1100

Hecker, Justus Friedrich Carl *Der Schwarze tod im Vierzehnten Jahrhundert.* Berlin: Friedrich August Herbig, 1832. First edition, 8vo., pencil underlining and maraginalia, foxed, modern quarter black morocco, German paste paper boards, new endleaves, fine.   Jeff Weber Rare Books   172 - 129   2013 $750

Heckrotte, Warren *California 49. Forty-Nine Maps of California from the Sixteenth Century to the Present.* Quarto, tipped on color frontispiece map, 7 tipped on color plates 38 black and white plates, large color folded leaf in rear pocket, map and name index, half black cloth, pictorial boards, spine label, fine.   Argonaut Book Shop   Recent Acquisitions June 2013 - 138   2013 $125

Hederich, Benjamin *Graecum Lexicon Manuale Primum a Beniamine Hederico Institutum...* Excudit H. Woodfall, 1766. 4to., some light browning, contemporary sprinkled calf, spine with raised bands between double gilt fillets, red morocco lettering piece in second compartment, small gilt crest stamp (a lion) in third, few scratches, very good.   Blackwell's Rare Books   B174 - 68   2013   £300

Hedgecoe, John *Henry Moore. Energy in Space.* Greenwich: New York Graphic Society, 1973. First trade edition, 8vo., 83 pages, signed and inscribed by Henry Moore, near fine hardback, mild soil to edges, near fine dust jacket, price clipped.   By the Book, L. C.   36 - 21   2013 $400

Hedin, Sven *With the German Armies in the West.* London: John Lane, 1915. First edition, 8vo., pages xvi, 402, maps, illustrations, original decorative cloth, half inch nick at top of spine.   J. & S. L. Bonham Antiquarian Booksellers   Europe - 9426   2013   £30

Hedley, William *A Complete System of Practical Arithmetic and Three Forms of Bookeeping...* Newcastle upon Tyne: T. Saint and J. Whitfield & Co., 1779. First and only edition, contemporary speckled sheep, upper joint cracking but firm, early names and scribbles on pastedowns (Richard Lancaster, Kirkby Stephen, Aug. 15th 1791), old inked erasures on title, occasional spots and lightly patched brown patches, rare. R. F. G. Hollett & Son Children's Books - 273 2013 £275

Heedless Harry's Day of Disasters. London: Darton & Clark, n.d., but inscribed 1847, 8vo., wrappers, 23 pages, covers worn and soiled, tight and good, 4 full page and 4 partial page hand colored illustrations. Aleph-Bet Books, Inc. 105 - 222 2013 $450

Hefferman, T. F. *Wood Quay, The Clash over Dublin's Viking Past.* 1988. First edition, 8vo., cloth, dust jacket, fine. C. P. Hyland 261 - 481 2013 £30

Hegel, Georg Wilhelm Friedrich *Gesammelte Werke.* Hamburg: Felix Meiner, 1968-1991. Mixed editions, 14 volumes, incomplete set, 4to., gilt stamped red cloth, blue spine labels, original cardboard slipcases, volume 6 in white dust jacket with gilt stamped blue spine label, volume 9 lacking slipcase, fine. Jeff Weber Rare Books 171 - 159 2013 $1500

Heidenstam, Verner Von *Christmas Eve at Finnstad.* Stockholm: har Haeggstroms Boktryckeri A. B., 1950. First edition of this translation, octavo, original decorated wrappers printed in black, red and yellow, sewn. L. W. Currey, Inc. Christmas Themed Books - 117745 2013 $100

Heinemann, William *The First Step: a Dramatic Moment.* London: John Lane, 1895. 1 of 500 copies, very scarce, original grey green boards with paper title label, label chipped and corners of boards slightly bumped, interior clean, most of the pages unopened, very good, 69 pages + 13 pages of ads. The Kelmscott Bookshop 7 - 115 2013 $200

Heinlein, Robert Anson 1907-1988 *Citizen of the Galaxy.* New York: Charles Scribner's Sons, 1957. First edition, minimal light staining to spine board, else fine in near fine dust jacket with slight wear to top and bottom edges, from the library of Bruce Kakhn. Between the Covers Rare Books, Inc. Sci-Fi, Fantasy & Horror - 304122 2013 $450

Heinlein, Robert Anson 1907-1988 *Citizen of Galaxy.* New York: Charles Scribner's Sons, 1957. First edition, cloth, octavo. L. W. Currey, Inc. Utopian Literature: Recent Acquisitions (April 2013) - 141027 2013 $1500

Heinlein, Robert Anson 1907-1988 *Sixth Column.* New York: Gnome Press, 1949. First edition, octavo, cloth. L. W. Currey, Inc. Utopian Literature: Recent Acquisitions (April 2013) - 141055 2013 $500

Heinlein, Robert Anson 1907-1988 *Starship Troopers.* New York: G. P. Putnam's Sons, 1959. First edition, octavo, cloth. L. W. Currey, Inc. Utopian Literature: Recent Acquisitions (April 2013) - 141058 2013 $2500

Heinsius, Daniel *Poematum.* Lugduni Batavorum: Elzevirum abd J. Maire, 1621. 2 volumes, 8vo., woodcut printer's device to titlepage and some woodcut initials to text, small portrait of Homer page 264, small piece cut form top corner of f.f.e.p., little staining to titlepage 3 leaves with small chips from blank lower margins, one of them just touching text and sometime repaired with few letters supplied in manuscript, contemporary vellum, long sides overlapping, title inked to spine, edges sprinkled red, library code inked to spine, some faint brown stains to upper board, rear endpaper tearing little where turn-in lifting, ownership inscription of O. Preuss. Unsworths Antiquarian Booksellers 28 - 108 2013 £450

Heise, Carl Georg *Genius: Zeitschrift Fur Werdende und Alte Kusnt.* Munchen: Kurt Wolff Verlag, 1919-1921. 6 issues in 3 volumes, 14 x 11 inches, over 1000 pages, hundreds of hand mounted black and white and color plates produced in offset lithography and heliogravure, 16 full page original woodcuts and lithographs, protected with tissue guards, volume 8 in variant publisher's binding but same size as other 2 volumes, volume 1 with bump at spine, some light foxing at some edges of books (not affecting text or images), otherwise remarkably clean and fresh set. Gemini Fine Books & Arts., Ltd. Art Reference & Illustrated Books - 2013 $2500

Heiser, Harvey Michael *Memories of the Fire Service.* Fresno: by the author, 1841. First edition, 179 pages, vintage photos, pictorial gray cloth stamped in red, owner's name erased from top of front cover, small rubber stamped name to top and fore edge of text block, else fine. Argonaut Book Shop Summer 2013 - 155 2013 $150

Heister, Lorenz 1683-1758 *A General System of Surgery in Three Parts.* London: printed for W. Innys and J. Richardson etc., 1757. 4to., 2 volumes in one, 40 folding copper engraved plates, contemporary full calf, gilt ruled edges, early rebacking with spine label laid down, corners repaired, paper repairs, expertly repaired without loss to a6 and plates 16 and 40, occasional minor marginal staining including few plates not affecting image, plate images crisp and sharp, overall very nice. James Tait Goodrich S74 - 147 2013 $1750

Heizer, Robert F. *The California Indians. A Source Book.* Berkeley: University of California Press, 1971. Second edition, photos, maps, text drawings, map endpaper, dark green cloth, very fine, pictorial dust jacket. Argonaut Book Shop Recent Acquisitions June 2013 - 142 2013 $75

Heizer, Robert F. *The Four Ages of Tsurai.* Berkeley: University of California Press, 1952. First edition, 3 figures, 10 illustrations, orange brown cloth, bookplate removed from inner cover with slight remnants, fine in slightly chipped and spine faded dust jacket. Argonaut Book Shop Recent Acquisitions June 2013 - 141 2013 $75

Helen's Babies by Their Latest Victim. Boston: Loring, 1876. First edition mixed state, this copy matches first state with perfect type page 13 and rear over listing 5 titles with this title, last, but has damaged type on page 18, is on wove paper and has ad for 'Pique' inside front cover, very rare in such nice condition, 12mo., wrappers, slightest of edge fraying and soil on fragile paper covers, else fine. Aleph-Bet Books, Inc. 105 - 300 2013 $400

Heller, Joseph *Catch 22.* New York: Simon & Schuster, 1961. First edition, 2nd printing, signed by author, very good, blue cloth boards with white title to spine, slight sunning to spine and edges of boards, light wear to edges and spine ends, dust jacket in first state with original $5.95 price and photo with no blurbs on back panel, jacket has few chips and repaired closed tear top of back panel, few creases and light scuff marks to panel of jacket, front flap present but detached and rear panel neatly detached, 443 pages. The Kelmscott Bookshop 7 - 117 2013 $900

Hellman, Libby Fischer *Chicago Blues.* Madison: Bleak House, n.d., First edition, one of 199 copies signed by 15 contributors, fine in fine dust jacket with DVD. Beasley Books 2013 - 2013 $60

Hellman, Lillian *Candide.* New York: Random House, 1957. First edition, 8vo., fine in little browned dust jacket, inscribed by author. Second Life Books Inc. 183 - 166 2013 $600

Hellman, Lillian *Maybe.* London: Macmillan, 1980. First edition, inscribed by author to V. S. Pritchett and his wife Dorothy, with Pritchett's ownership label, shallow crease to front flyleaf, else fine in near fine, mildly spine faded and dusty dust jacket. Ken Lopez Bookseller 159 - 79 2013 $200

Hellwig, Christoph Von *Nosce te Ipsum vel Anatomicum Vivum Oder Krtz Gefasstes doch Richtig Gestelltes Anatomisches Werck.* Erfurt: George Andreas Muller for Hieronymus Philipp Ritschel, 1716. Engraved portrait on title, 4 engraved plates, small folio, modern quarter calf and marbled boards, text browning in parts. James Tait Goodrich 75 - 116 2013 $1795

Helme, Elizabeth *Saint-Clair des Isles ou les Exiles a l'Isle de Barra...* Paris: H. Nicolle, 1809. 4 volumes, half titles, one with piece torn from outer margin, volume i slightly browned and foxed, others less so, 12mo., contemporary red skiver, roll tooled vine borders on sides, flat spines gilt in compartments, spines and corners slightly darkened where covering and underlying material, good. Blackwell's Rare Books B174 - 69 2013 £450

Helms, Anne Adams *The Descendants of William James Adams and Cassandra Hills Adams.* Salinas: Anne Helms, 1999. First edition, quarto, photos, single page map, stiff red wrappers printed, very fine. Argonaut Book Shop Summer 2013 - 1 2013 $150

Hemans, Felicia *He Giveth His Beloved Sleep.* Boston: Lee and Shepard, 1880. First edition, white cloth backed boards, very good, illustrations by L. B. Humphrey, all edges gilt, color cover illustration by Maud Humphrey, very good. Barnaby Rudge Booksellers Poetry 2013 - 021163 2013 $95

Hemingway, Ernest Millar 1899-1961 *The Dangerous Summer.* New York: Scribners, 1985. First edition, near fine, small corner bump, in like dust jacket. Beasley Books 2013 - 2013 $50

Hemingway, Ernest Millar 1899-1961 *A Farewell to Arms.* New York: Charles Scribner's Sons, 1929. First trade edition, first issue, publisher's seal on copyright page and no legal disclaimer on page (x), octavo, original black cloth with gold paper labels on front cover and spine, lower corners very slightly bumped, faint scratch to spine label, otherwise attractive, original first issue color pictorial dust jacket (flap corners neatly trimmed), housed in quarter morocco clamshell box. David Brass Rare Books, Inc. Holiday 2012 Chapter Five - DB 01410 2013 $5500

Hemingway, Ernest Millar 1899-1961 *For Whom the Bell Tolls.* New York: Scribners', 1940. First edition, solid, clean, very good plus to near fine copy, some offsetting along gutters in clean, near fine, first issue jacket with some expert restoration. Ed Smith Books 78 - 26 2013 $850

Hemingway, Ernest Millar 1899-1961 *For Whom the Bell Tolls.* New York: Scribners, 1940. First edition, solid, clean, very good plus to near fine, some offsetting along gutters in clean, near fine, first issue dust jacket that has some expert restoration. Ed Smith Books 78 - 26 2013 $850

Hemingway, Ernest Millar 1899-1961 *Der Alte Mann und Das Meer. (The Old Man and the Sea).* Hamburg: Johannes Asmus Verlag, 1961. Limited to 500 signed copies, this no. 29, 8vo., loose sheets in plain cream wrappers, spine lettered in grey-green, mild sun spine, soil to covers, minimal bump to lower spine tip, in fine custom made slipcase, typeset in Janson Antiqua on special making of Hahnemuhle-Butten paper. By the Book, L. C. 38 - 86 2013 $500

Hemingway, Ernest Millar 1899-1961 *The Spanish Earth.* Cleveland: J. B. Savage Co., 1938. First edition, first issue with F.A.I. banner on endpapers, #29 of a limited edition of 1000 numbered copies, small 8vo., pages 60, tan cloth printed in orange and black, issued in acetate dust jacket, tan cloth printed in orange and black. Second Life Books Inc. 183 - 167 2013 $3500

Hemingway, Ernest Millar 1899-1961 *To Have and Have Not.* New York: Charles Scribner's Sons, 1937. First edition, publisher's black cloth, spine stamped and lettered green and gilt, front board stamped gilt with Hemingway's signature, dust jacket with $2.50 price, jacket edges with browning, some wear and light creasing, head and tail of jacket spine with few small chips some very light rubbing to cloth and small amount of fraying to head cap, overall near fine, bright unrestored dust jacket. Heritage Book Shop Holiday Catalogue 2012 - 76 2013 $2000

Hemyng, Bracebridge *Money Marks; or the Sailor Highwayman.* London: George Vickers, circa, 1865. Dark brown binder's cloth, illustrations, from the collection of Ronald Rouse, Norwich, very good. Jarndyce Antiquarian Booksellers CCV - 134 2013 £125

Henderson, H. J. *The Cruising Association Library Catalogue.* London: Chiltern Court, 1931-1954. Second edition, third edition, 8vo., 2 frontispiece plates, 98 collotype plates, original plum colored cloth, lettered in gilt, together with third edition of 1954, 16 pages of plates, uniformly bound and supplement of 1965-67 (staple bound pamphlet of 14 pages). Marlborough Rare Books Ltd. 218 - 108 2013 £150

Henderson, James D. *Lilliputian Newspapers.* Worcester: Achille J. St. Onge, 1936. First edition, limited to 1000 copies. tall 12mo., 95 pages, cloth backed boards, leather spine label, top edge gilt, slipcase, number of facsimiles in pocket in back of book, very fine, from the collection of Donn W. Sanford. Oak Knoll Books 303 - 17 2013 $275

Henderson, James D. *Miniature Books.* Leipzig: Tondeur & Sauberlich, 1930. Limited to 260 numbered copies, 16mo., limp leather, covers rubbed, miniature bookplate of Kathryn Rickard, from the collection of Donn W. Sanford. Oak Knoll Books 303 - 18 2013 $300

Henderson, L. R. S., Mrs. *The Magic Aeroplane.* Chicago: Reilly & Britton, 1911. 4to., cloth backed pictorial boards, 96 pages, slight wear to edge of boards, else very good+ in worn and repaired dust jacket, 6 very fine color plates and many full page and smaller black and whites by Emile Nelson, excellent condition. Aleph-Bet Books, Inc. 104 - 211 2013 $600

Henderson, Louis T. *Travel in Stories and Pictures.* Chicago: Donahue, 1939. Folio, cloth backed pictorial boards, tips rubbed, else very good+ in frayed dust jacket, photos. Aleph-Bet Books, Inc. 105 - 455 2013 $200

Henderson, Mary F. *Practical Cooking and Dinner Giving.* New York: Harper, 1876. First edition, covers very dust stained and soiled, one signature loose, fair/good copy. Second Life Books Inc. 182 - 111 2013 $65

Henley, William *Lyra Heroica: A Book of Verse...* London: David Nutt, 1892. First edition, large paper copy, 83 of 100 copies, although not named, this was a presentation copy to one of the contributors, William Johnson Cory, original cream cloth embossed geometric designs, title and editor in red on spine, binding soiled and rubbed, small ink marks at top and bottom of spine, offsetting to first free endpaper affecting inscription but not legibility, otherwise very good, 362 pages. The Kelmscott Bookshop 7 - 116 2013 $475

Henn, T. R. *The Apple & the Spectroscope.* 1951. First edition, 8vo., cloth, dust jacket, near fine. C. P. Hyland 261 - 482 2013 £30

Hennell, Mary *A Outline of the Various Social systems and Communities which Have Been Founded on the principle of Co-operation.* London: Longman, 1844. First edition, author's names added to title in pencil odd pencil annotation, signature of G. J. Holyoake on leading blank, additional later signature of J. J. Deakin, unsympathetic green marbled endpapers, 20th century half green crushed morocco, label on following endpaper of Midlands Workers' Library, very good. Jarndyce Antiquarian Booksellers CCV - 135 2013 £450

Hennepin, Louis *A New Discovery of a Vast Country in America, Extending Above Four Thousand Miles Between New France and New Mexico...* London: for M. Bentley, J. Tonson &c, 1698. First edition in English, Tonson issue, imperfect copy lacking two maps and one plate, engraved fore title, 5 (of 6) folding plates, contemporary calf, early rebacking (hinges and corners worn), text dampstained. Joseph J. Felcone Inc. Books Printed before 1701 - 50 2013 $2200

Hennepin, Louis *A New Discovery of a Vast Country in America.* Chicago: 1903. 2 volumes, plates, folding map, plates, folding map, cloth, light wear externally with light scattered foxing internally, overall very good set. Dumont Maps & Books of the West 125 - 54 2013 $150

Hennessy, John Pope *Sir Walter Raleigh in Ireland.* 1883. First edition, 8vo., vellum binding, top edge gilt, foreedge untrimmed, signed presentation to John Hooper, M.P. Cork, covers dull, text very good.   C. P. Hyland   261 - 740   2013   £150

Hennessy, William M. *The Annals of Loch Ce.*   1939. 2 volumes, frontispiece, original cloth, ex-Prinknash Abbey library, very good.   C. P. Hyland   261 - 483   2013   £225

Henri, Adrian *Lowlands Away. An Oratorio.*   Hinton Charterhouse: Old School Press, 2001. 23/240 copies (of an edition of 280), printed on Rivoli mouldmade paper, 7 full page pastel drawings and a further double page pastel incorporating both frontispiece and titlepage design, all by author, royal 8vo., original yellow cloth backed boards, title gilt lettered longitudinally on front cover, grey-green boards, fine.   Blackwell's Rare Books   B174 - 372   2013   £50

Henry, James *Sketches of Moravian Life and Character.* Philadelphia: J. B. Lippincott, 1859. First edition, 8vo., 317 pages, frontispiece, original purple cloth, faded, lacks free endpaper.   J. & S. L. Bonham Antiquarian Booksellers Europe - 7384   2013   £40

Henry, Marguerite *Wagging Tails.*   Chicago: Rand McNally, 1955. First edition, hardcover, very good with rubbing and no dust jacket, this copy inscribed by author. Beasley Books   2013 - 2013 $100

Henty, George Alfred   1832-1902   *At the Point of the Bayonet.*   Blackie & Son, 1902. First edition, original pictorial dark green cloth, gilt over bevelled boards, neatly recased, 12 illustrations by Wal Paget, nice, bright copy. R. F. G. Hollett & Son   Children's Books - 275   2013   £85

Henty, George Alfred   1832-1902   *By England's Aid; or the Freeing of the Netherlands.*   Blackie, 1891. First edition, frontispiece and 9 other plates by Alfred Pearse, 4 plans in text, crown 8vo., original mid brown bevel edged cloth with soiling overall, backstrip and front cover gilt lettered, designs in black and pink to backstrip and front cover, maroon endpapers, good.   Blackwell's Rare Books   B174 - 221   2013   £100

Henty, George Alfred   1832-1902   *By Pike and Dyke. A Tale of the Rise of the Dutch Republic.*   Blackie, 1890. First edition, frontispiece and 9 other plates by Maynard Brown, double plate map, plate map and 2 other maps on one plate, crown 8vo., original variant light blue bevel edged cloth (Newbolt calls for brown cloth), very light rubbing to corners and head and tail of backstrip, backstrip and front cover pictorially lettered and decorated in gilt and grey and black, maroon endpapers, very good.   Blackwell's Rare Books   B174 - 222   2013   £260

Henty, George Alfred   1832-1902   *By Sheer Pluck.* Blackie & Son, n.d. circa, 1910. Original pictorial red cloth gilt, little edge wear, slight bubbling to cloth on lower board, 8 plates by Gordon Browne, joints cracking, lower flyleaf spotted.   R. F. G. Hollett & Son   Children's Books - 276   2013   £50

Henty, George Alfred   1832-1902   *The Cat of Bubastes.* Blackie, 1889. First edition, frontispiece and 7 other sepia plates, gift inscription reverse of frontispiece, crown 8vo, original light blue cloth, backstrip and front cover gilt lettered, decorated in black, gilt and red, blue endpapers, very good.   Blackwell's Rare Books   B174 - 223   2013   £285

Henty, George Alfred   1832-1902   *The Dash for Khartoum: a Tale of the Nile Expedition.*   Blackie, 1892. First edition, frontispiece and 9 plates, 4 maps on 2 plates, crown 8vo., original brown bevel edged cloth cocked, backstrip and front cover pictorially lettered in gilt and brown and decorated in black, blue and cream, backstrip sunned and rubbed, small scuff mark to front free maroon endpaper. Blackwell's Rare Books   B174 - 224   2013   £100

Henty, George Alfred   1832-1902   *Held Fast for England. A Tale of the Siege of Gibraltar (1779-83).*   Blackie, 1892. First edition, frontispiece, 6 other plates, 2 profile image on further plate, map in text, crown 8vo., original grey-green cloth, backstrip and front cover gilt lettered and with design in various colors on backstrip and front cover, maroon endpapers, fine.   Blackwell's Rare Books   B174 - 225   2013   £400

Henty, George Alfred   1832-1902   *In Greek Waters.* Blackie & Son, 1893. First edition, original pictorial brown cloth, gilt over bevelled boards, 12 plates by W. Stacey and map, front joint just cracking, else most attractive, clean crisp copy.   R. F. G. Hollett & Son   Children's Books - 277   2013   £95

Henty, George Alfred   1832-1902   *In Greek Waters: a Story of the Grecian War of Independence.*   Blackie, 1893. First edition, frontispiece and 11 plates, full page map, crown 8vo., original variant brown bevel edged cloth, backstrip and front cover pictorially blocked and lettered in black and gold, backstrip rubbed at head and tail, rear cover little soiled and spotted, maroon endpapers, burnished olivine edges, good.   Blackwell's Rare Books   B174 - 226   2013   £100

Henty, George Alfred   1832-1902   *The March to Coomassie.*   Tinsley Brothers, 1874. First edition, tall 8vo., original blue cloth blindstamped and gilt, hinges worn and with piece missing, recased with new endpapers, occasional spot and mark, but very good internally, rare.   R. F. G. Hollett & Son   Africana - 86   2013   £850

Henty, George Alfred 1832-1902 *A Roving Commission.* Blackie and Son, 1900. First edition, original pictorial red cloth, gilt over bevelled boards, corners trifle rubbed, spine rather worn and faded, 12 plates by William Rainey.   R. F. G. Hollett & Son   Children's Books - 278 2013   £60

Henty, George Alfred 1832-1902 *St. Bartholomew's Eve.* Blackie & Son, 1894. First edition, original pictorial dark green cloth, gilt over bevelled boards, slight wear to extremities, 12 illustrations, scattered foxing, one section little shaken.   R. F. G. Hollett & Son   Children's Books - 279 2013   £75

Henty, George Alfred 1832-1902 *Through Russian Snows.* Blackie & Son, 1896. First edition, original pictorial blue cloth, gilt, worn and rubbed, corners bumped, 10 plates by W. H. Overed and map, joints badly cracked, foreedge of front flyleaf and frontispiece worn.   R. F. G. Hollett & Son   Children's Books - 280 2013   £45

Henty, George Alfred 1832-1902 *With Buller in Natal.* Blackie & Son, 1901. First edition, original pictorial blue cloth gilt, extremities little worn, 10 illustrations and map, front flyleaf removed two torn pages neatly repaired, few spots.   R. F. G. Hollett & Son   Children's Books - 281 2013   £45

Henty, George Alfred 1832-1902 *With Cochrane the Dauntless.* Blackie & Son, 1897. First edition, original pictorial blue cloth gilt over bevelled boards, slight wear to extremities and few marks to lower board, 12 illustrations by W. H. Margetson, gift inscription dated 1897 on flyleaf.   R. F. G. Hollett & Son   Children's Books - 282 2013   £85

Henty, George Alfred 1832-1902 *With Kitchener in the Soudan.* Blackie & Son, 1903. First edition, early issue with William Rainey, R.I. complete with second full point, original pictorial cloth, gilt, spine little faded, corners slightly worn, 10 plates by William Rainey and 3 maps, trifle shaken.   R. F. G. Hollett & Son   Children's Books - 283 2013   £95

Henty, George Alfred 1832-1902 *With Lee in Virginia.* Blackie, 1890. First edition, frontispiece, 9 other plates by Gordon Browne, double plate map, plate map and 4 other maps, 2 plates, occasional faint foxing, crown 8vo., original bright tan bevel edged cloth, corners just little rubbed, backstrip and front cover pictorially lettered and decorated in gilt and brown and black, maroon endpapers, very good.   Blackwell's Rare Books   B174 - 227 2013   £400

Henty, George Alfred 1832-1902 *With Moore at Corunna.* Blackie & Son, n.d. circa, 1910. Original pictorial blue cloth, upper board little spotted by damp, color frontispiece and 4 plates by Wal Paget, blank label pasted to flyleaf, scattered spotting.   R. F. G. Hollett & Son   Children's Books - 284 2013   £25

Henty, George Alfred 1832-1902 *Young Colonists.* New York: London: Manchester: George Routledge and Sons, n.d., 8vo., rust colored cloth stamped in black, gold and white, near fine, line illustrations.   Aleph-Bet Books, Inc. 105 - 318 2013 $350

Henty, George Alfred 1832-1902 *The Young Carthaginian; or a Struggle for Empire.* Blackie, 1887. First edition, first issue titlepage, frontispiece, 11 other plates, crown 8vo., original bright variant mid brown bevel edged cloth with gilt blocking to upper backstrip and front cover and overall pictorial design to lower backstrip and front cover to design by Staniland, maroon endpapers, school prize bookplate, light erasing of pencilled price to front free endpaper, near fine.   Blackwell's Rare Books B174 - 228 2013   £400

Herb, David   *Ancient and Modern Scottish Songs, Heroic Ballads, etc.* Glasgow: Kerr & Richardson, 1869. 2 volumes, fine large paper set, contemporary half crushed morocco, with most ornate gilt panelled spines, top edge gilt, remainder uncut.   Ken Spelman Books Ltd.   75 - 135 2013   £220

Herball; from The Dialogues of Creatures Moralised. West Burke: Janus Press, 1979. First edition, one of 150 numbered copies printed on Barcham Green deWint paper with hand colored woodcuts and signed by Sigel, mint, scarce, 4to., cloth, printed spine label.   James S. Jaffe Rare Books Fall 2013 - 77 2013 $1000

Herbermann, Charles G.   *The Catholic Encyclopedia.* New York: Encyclopedia Press, 1913. Special edition, 16 volumes, large 8vo., various paginations, frontispieces, illustrations, maps, ribbed green cloth, stamped double ruling and front cover pictorials, gilt stamped spines, spine ends occasionally slightly torn, titlepage ownership signatures, very good.   Jeff Weber Rare Books   171 - 65 2013 $175

Herbert, Frank   *Soul Catcher.* New York: G. P. Putnam's Sons, 1972. First edition, fine in fine dust jacket.   Between the Covers Rare Books, Inc.   Mystery & Detective Fiction - 287152 2013 $65

Herbert, Frank   *Whipping Star.* New York: G. P. Putnam's, 1970. First edition, fine in fine dust jacket, superb, almost as new.   Between the Covers Rare Books, Inc.   Sci-Fi, Fantasy & Horror - 287205 2013 $500

Herbert, George *The Works in Prose and Verse.* London: William Pickering, 1853. 230 x 150mm., 2 volumes, extremely pleasing contemporary Cambridge style calf, handsomely gilt, covers with mitered corner gilt frame formed by plain and decorative rules bounding an inch wide inlay of lighter tan calf, fleuron cornerpieces extending obliquely from frame, raised bands, spines densely gilt in compartments with large central fleuron enclosed in lozenge of small tools and scrolling cornerpieces, each spine with two red morocco labels, densely gilt turn-ins, marbled endpapers, all edges gilt, engraved frontispiece, spines faintly sunned, gilt with slight loss of brightness, extremities bit rubbed (one spine top with small, very shallow loss), mild marginal foxing to plates, other trivial imperfections but still pretty set in excellent condition, text clean and smooth, generous margins, decorative bindings, completely sound with nothing approaching fatal defect.   Phillip J. Pirages   63 - 365   2013 $550

Herbert, Thomas *Some Yeares Travels Into Divers Parts of Asia and Afrique.* London: 1677. Fourth edition, folio, 19th century calf, engraved titlepage, engraved plates (one folding), numerous illustrations and maps.   Maggs Bros. Ltd.   1467 - 52   2013   £4000

Hercules, Frank *I Want a Black Doll.* New York: Simon and Schuster, 1967. First edition, full black morocco gilt, raised bands, just touch of wear, else fine, almost certainly an author's copy.   Between the Covers Rare Books, Inc.   165 - 162   2013 $175

Herd, Richard *Scraps of Poetry.* Sedbergh: Miles Turner, n.d. c., 1900. Sedbergh edition, 12mo., original brown cloth, gilt, lovely copy, scarce.   R. F. G. Hollett & Son   Lake District and Cumbria - 245   2013   £120

Heredia, Jose Maria De *Les Trophees.* Paris: Librairie des Amateurs, 1914. First Rochegrosse edition, number 40 of 75 deluxe copies on Grand Japon paper (total edition 512), initialed in pen by publisher, 33 original etchings, 25 hors texte by Georges Rochegrosse, engraved by Eugene Decisi, each of the etchings in 3 states, 2 of the states with artist's remarques (small proof etching printed on same plate, usually an image different from the larger one), all etchings signed in plate by Rochegrosse and Decisi, total number of etchings is 99, 81 of them hors-texte, in addition, book illustrated with numerous woodcut, over 300 leaves bound in very beautiful signed Master binding by Rene Kieffer, full burgundy backstrip bound in, top edge gilt, matching slipcase, overall size 33 x 24 cm., in excellent condition.   Gemini Fine Books & Arts., Ltd.   Art Reference & Illustrated Books - 2013 $3000

Herivel, John *The Background to Newton's Principia: a Study of Newton's Dynamical Researches in the Years 1664-84.* Oxford: Clarendon Press, 1965. First edition, 8vo., frontispiece, 4 plates, navy blue cloth, gilt stamped spine, dust jacket smudged and with rubbed extremities, very good.   Jeff Weber Rare Books   169 - 321   2013 $185

Herman, Bernhardt *Price List. Herman Bernhardt Formerly Bernhardt Bros. Importer and General Merchant Fine Wines and Liquors.* Buffalo: Herman Bernhardt/The Wenborne-Sumner Co. printers, n.d circa, 1900. 12mo., stapled wrappers embossed in gold, 80 pages, printed in black and red fine.   Between the Covers Rare Books, Inc. Cocktails, Etc. - 275797   2013 $400

Hermes, Gertrude *Wood Engravings.... (with) A Folder of Pulls of the Six Wood Engravings, each numbered XV.* Newtown: Gwasg Gregynog, 1988. xv/xxv copies (of an edition of 240), printed on Zerkall mouldmade paper, with 7 superb full page wood engravings, folio, original full russet straight grain morocco, backstrip gilt lettered, front cover with Hermes design gilt blocked, top edge gilt, others untrimmed, fine, pulls loosely inserted in printed pale pink folder, book and folder in original fawn cloth box, lettered in brown, prospectus loosely inserted.   Blackwell's Rare Books   B174 - 351   2013   £1200

Hermes, Gertrude *Wood Engravings....* Newtown: Gwasg Gregynog, 1988. 193/200 copies, of an edition of 240, printed on Zerkall mouldmade paper, 6 superb full page wood engravings, text printed in black and brown, folio, original quarter fawn cloth, backstrip gilt lettered, patterned brown and white boards, untrimmed, fine, prospects loosely inserted.   Blackwell's Rare Books   B174 - 350   2013   £385

Herndon, William H. *Herndon's Lincoln: The True Story of a Great Life.* Chicago: New York and San Francisco: Belford Clarke & Co., 1889. First edition, 12mo., 3 volumes, 63 plates, original cloth, large library stamp on title of each volume, library bookplates, hinges volume I tender, otherwise very sound and clean set.   M & S Rare Books, Inc.   95 - 200   2013 $600

Herold, J. Christopher *The Age of Napoleon.* New York: American Heritage Pub., 1963. First edition, folio, black cloth, very good+, cover blindstamped "N", very good slipcase with copy picture of Napoleon.   Barnaby Rudge Booksellers   Biography 2013 - 021157   2013 $55

Herrick, Robert 1591-1674 *Hesperides or Works both Hvman and Divine by Robert Herrick. Together with His Noble Nvmbers or His Piouvs Pieces.* London: George Newnes Ltd., New York: Charles Scribner's Sons, 1902. 2 volumes, 165 x 110mm., 26 line drawings in black and white by Reginald Savage, as called for, leaf with printed copy of Robert Bridges poem "In a Volume of Herrick" tipped in at front, verso signed by Bridges and dated June 22, 1905; splendid burgundy morocco, lavishly and intricately gilt in "Scottish Wheel" design by Morrell (stamp-signed), covers with large central wheel of 20 compartments containing slender and elegant floral tools between two lines of dots radiating from central rosette, massed tiny circle tools at head and foot of wheel, triangle formed by small scalloped compartments and multiple tiny flowers above and below the centerpiece, large leaf frond tools at corners and many small tools accenting background, raised bands, interlocking floral garlands forming overall wreath in spine compartments, punctuated on either side by cluster of crescents and other small tools, elegantly and elaborately gilt turn-ins, ivory watered silk endleaves, all edges gilt; top of spine of second volume with barely perceptible loss of leather, silk endleaf in each volume with dampstain (no doubt from removal of bookplate), leaves little browned at edges because of quality of paper, else particularly attractive glittering bindings unusually lustrous. Phillip J. Pirages 61 - 120 2013 $1600

Herrick, Robert 1599-1674 *The Memoirs of an American Citizen.* New York: Macmillan, 1905. First edition, very good, hinges going. Beasley Books 2013 - 2013 $65

Herriot, Edouard *Andre Mare.* Paris: Aux Editions de l'Estampe, 1927. First illustrated edition, from a total edition of 170, this number 86 of 105 copies on Arches wove paper, 40 original black and white lithographs, including 10 hors texte, and extra suite of the 40 lithos, printed in sanguine on Japon, 287 pages, very handsome signed Master binding by Gruel with engraved design of black and gilt geometric decorations on both covers and spine, on rich emerald snakeskin, raised bands, top edge gilt, beautifully designed internal endleaves, wrappers and backstrip well preserved and bound in, overall size 10.5 x 8.75 x 2 inches, spine sunned to nice gold brown, otherwise as new, very handsome binding. Gemini Fine Books & Arts., Ltd. Art Reference & Illustrated Books - 2013 $1300

Herschel, Isabella *The Catalogue of the Herschel Library.* New York: printed for the editor, 2001. 8vo., xii, 578 pages, plates, pictorial boards, fine. Jeff Weber Rare Books 171 - 161 2013 $90

Herschel, John F. W. *Essays from the Edinburgh and Quarterly Reviews, with Addresses and Other Pieces.* London: Longman, Brown, Green, Longmans & Roberts, 1857. First edition of this collection, 8vo., contemporary polished calf, spine gilt, red lettering piece, spine little darkened, crack at head of upper joint, sound. Blackwell's Rare Books 172 - 71 2013 £150

Herschel, William *The Scientific Papers of Sir William Herschel...* London: Royal Society, 1912. First collected edition, 2 volumes, 4to., 5 plates, illustrations, original cloth, rare, near fine set. Jeff Weber Rare Books 169 - 198 2013 $2000

Herskowitz, Mickey *The Golden Age of Pro Football: a Remembrance of Pro Football in the 1950's.* New York: Macmillan, 1974. First edition, quarto, slight spotting to boards, very good in internally repaired about very good dust jacket, signed by several former NFL notables - Paul Hornung, Fuzzy Thurston, Earl Morrall, Joe Perry, Johnny Lattner and Tom Fears. Between the Covers Rare Books, Inc. Football Books - 29280 2013 $400

Hertz, Heinrich Rudolf *Electric Wares: Being Researches on the Propagation of Electic Action with Finite Velocity through Space.* London: Macmillan and Co., 1900. Second edition in English, 8vo., 40 figures, numerous formulae & charts, modern full navy morocco, raised bands, gilt stamped spine title, top edge gilt, fine. Jeff Weber Rare Books 169 - 201 2013 $850

Hervey, Canon G. A. K. *Natural History of the Lake District.* London: Frederick Warne & Co., 1970. First edition, original cloth gilt, dust jacket, 8 colored plates, 24 in black and white and maps on endpapers. R. F. G. Hollett & Son Lake District and Cumbria - 246 2013 £40

Hervey, Harry *School for Eternity.* New York: G. P. Putnam's Sons, 1941. First edition, very near fine in about very good dust jacket with some modest chipping on front panel, this copy with warm, full page inscription by author. Between the Covers Rare Books, Inc. Mystery & Detective Fiction - 98529 2013 $375

Hervey, James *Meditations and Contemplations.* London: printed for John and James Rivington, 1749. Fifth edition, 2 volumes, frontispieces, one full page illustrations, old ink splash page 272 volume i and slight foxing traces of wax seals to inner board and lacking following endpaper volume i, full contemporary calf, gilt ruled borders, raised bands, red morocco labels, spines slightly chipped, leading hinges cracked but firm, inscribed by author to his sister Mary Hervey. Jarndyce Antiquarian Booksellers CCIV - 157 2013 £480

Hervey, John *Racing in America 1922-1936.* New York: Privately printed The Jockey Club, 1937. First edition, folio, quarter cloth and paper covered boards, corners bumped and rubbed, tidemark in upper margins, gradually diminishing away to nothing after the first forty or so pages, dampstain on spine label, good sound copy. Between the Covers Rare Books, Inc. Horses, Horsemanship, Horse Racing, Etc. - 30840 2013 $225

Hessenbruch, Arne *Reader's Guide to the History of Science.* London & Chicago: Fitzroy Dearborn Pub., 2000. Thick 8vo., printed boards, signature of contributor David C. Lindberg, fine.   Jeff Weber Rare Books   169 - 203   2013 $85

Hetherington, William *Branthwaite Hall and Other Poems.* Carlisle: printed for the author by Charles Thurnam, 1837. First edition, modern half polished calf gilt with spine label, complete with half title, original pale green front endpapers preserved, mss. corrections in third line of stanza 6, page 22 and stanza 6 on page 15, maybe in author's hand, scarce.   R. F. G. Hollett & Son   Lake District and Cumbria - 247   2013   £250

Hetherington, William *Branthwaite Hall, Canto III. And Other Poems.* Cockermouth: printed for author by Daniel Fidler, 1850. First edition, original cloth, paper spine label, little darkened, extremities minimally worn, half title, errata slip and blue sugar paper endpapers.   R. F. G. Hollett & Son   Lake District and Cumbria - 248   2013   £140

Heuman, William *Famous Pro Football Stars.* New York: Dodd, Mead, & Co., 1967. First edition, fine in fine, price clipped dust jacket with little wear.   Between the Covers Rare Books, Inc.   Football Books - 82552   2013 $65

Hevelius, Johannes *Selemographia, sive Lunae Descriptio.* New York: Johnson Reprint Corp., 1967. 4to., frontispiece, plates, exquisite gilt stamped red cloth, intricate decorations, publisher's cardboard slipcase (slightly rubbed with ink notation to front panel), mint in very good case.   Jeff Weber Rare Books   169 - 204   2013 $1250

Heward, Constance *Ameliaranne and the Green Umbrella.* Harrap, 1927. Second reprint, original grey boards with pictorial onlay, illustrations in color and black and white by Susan Pearse, occasional slight finger marking, but very good, early issue.   R. F. G. Hollett & Son   Children's Books - 449   2013   £85

Heward, Constance *Ameliaranne Camps Out.* Harrap, 1945. First reprint, original pictorial boards, dust jacket rather worn in places, head of spine defective, illustrations in color and black and white by Susan Pearse.   R. F. G. Hollett & Son   Children's Books - 450   2013   £35

Heward, Constance *Ameliaranne Goes Touring.* Harrap, 1941. First edition, original cloth backed pictorial boards, little worn and faded, illustrations in color and black and white by Susan Pearse, little light creasing and one pencil mark, small inscription, front joint cracking.   R. F. G. Hollett & Son   Children's Books - 451   2013   £25

Heward, Constance *Ameliaranne in Town.* Harrap, 1930. First edition, original grey boards with pictorial onlay (slight scratches), illustrations in color and black and white by Susan Pearse, slight browning to flyleaves.   R. F. G. Hollett & Son   Children's Books - 452   2013   £120

Heward, Constance *The Twins & Tabiffa.* 1933. Original pictorial boards, fragile original glassine dust jacket (edges little chipped), illustrations in color and black and white by Susan Pearse,.   R. F. G. Hollett & Son   Children's Books - 453   2013   £45

Heward, S. L. *Simple Bible Stories for the Little Ones.* Ernest Nister n.d., 1902. Large 4to., original cloth backed pictorial boards, extremities little worn, chromolithographed in color, text and smaller drawings in sepia, occasional brown spot or small patch.   R. F. G. Hollett & Son   Children's Books - 285   2013   £85

Hewitt, John *Hewitt's Tables of Simple Interest, Shewing at one View the Interest of any Sum of Money...*   London: printed for John Clarke and C. Hitch, 1747. Second edition, 12mo., original full calf, gilt stamped double ruling to covers, heavily worn, front cover open tear, lacks original spine, joints reinforced with kozo, internally clean, ownership signature of John Coryton, as is, internally very good, rare.   Jeff Weber Rare Books   171 - 163   2013 $75

Hewitt, John *Out of My Time.* Belfast: Blackstaff Press, 1974. First edition, 8vo., original wrppers, inserted are two ALS's from author to publisher Timothy O'Keefe, letters and book in excellent state.   Maggs Bros. Ltd.   1442 - 359   2013   £350

Hewson, J. B. *A History of the Practice of Navigation.* Glasgow: Brown, Son & Ferguson, 1951. First edition, 8vo., viii, 270 pages, illustrations, dark blue cloth, gilt stamped cover and spine titles, dust jacket worn with pieces missing and tape repair, else very good, Burndy bookplate, rare in jacket, with Charles Singer's bookplate.   Jeff Weber Rare Books   169 - 205   2013 $125

Hewson, John *Beothuk Vocabularies. A Comparative Study.* St. John's: Newfoundland Museum, 1978. Quarto, card covers, illustrations, very good.   Schooner Books Ltd.   101 - 34 2013 $50

Heyer, Georgette *Detection Unlimited.* London: Heinemann, 1953. First edition, fine in price clipped dust jacket.   Mordida Books   81 - 246   2013 $100

Heylyn, Peter 1600-1662 *Theologia Veterum; or the Summe of Christian Theologie.* printed by E. Cotes for Henry Seile, 1654. Folio, some even browning and occasional slight foxing, small early blindstamp at foot of titlepage of Christ's Hospital, gilt stamped on cover board 'Thomas Lee Esq. to Christs Hospitall' contemporary calf, neatly rebacked and corners repaired, some abrasions to boards, with fresh contemporary endpapers and pastedowns. Ken Spelman Books Ltd. 75 - 3 2013 £120

Heyrick, Thomas *Miscellany Poems.* Cambridge: by John Hayes for the author, 1691. Woodcut alma mater device, 4to., late 19th century half morocco, hinges lightly scuffed some foxing and light browning, chiefly on first and last few pages and largely confined to margins, small piece from upper corner of titlepage, short marginal tear on K1, signature of Rd Habgood 1774 on titlepage. Joseph J. Felcone Inc. Books Printed before 1701 - 51 2013 $3000

Hiaasen, Carl *Native Tongue.* New York: Knopf, 1991. First edition, uncorrected proof, fine in wrappers. Between the Covers Rare Books, Inc. Mystery & Detective Fiction - 18474 2013 $60

Hiaasen, Carl *Tourist Season.* New York: Putnam, 1986. First edition, very fine in dust jacket. Mordida Books 81 - 247 2013 $250

Hickey, John J. *Our Police Guardians. History of the Police Department of the City of New York.* New York?: John J. Hickey, 1925. First edition, pictorial cloth, bookplate and stamps of previous owner, else near fine without dust jacket, scarce. Between the Covers Rare Books, Inc. New York City - 292110 2013 $175

Hicks, Frederick Codrington *Forty Years Among the Wild Animals of India from Mysore to the Himalayas.* Allahbad: Pioneer Press, 1910. First edition, profusely illustrated, 25 maps, 103 plates, small 4to., clean and bright, full modern dark green morocco, scarce, signed by Hicks and marked copy 63 of an unspecified number. Maggs Bros. Ltd. 1467 - 53 2013 £1400

Hicks, G. D. *Berkeley.* 1921. First edition, octavo, cloth, ex-library but very good. C. P. Hyland 261 - 36 2013 £27

Hieb, Louis A. *Tony Hillerman: from the Blessing Way to Talking God. A Bibliography.* Tucson: Press of the Gigantic Hound, 1990. First edition, one of 1000 copies, this copy signed by author, (6), 88 pages, 6 photo reproductions, rust cloth, lettered in black, very fine. Argonaut Book Shop Recent Acquisitions June 2013 - 143 2013 $100

Hiemer, Ernst *Der Giftpilz. (The Poisoned Mushroom).* Nurnberg: Sturmer, 1938. 4to., cloth spine and edges, pictorial boards, near fine, illustrations in full color by Fips featuring grossly stereotypical depictions. Aleph-Bet Books, Inc. 104 - 374 2013 $6000

Higgins, Aidan *Balcony of Europe.* London: Calder and Boyars, 1972. First edition, 8vo., original red cloth, dust jacket, from the library of Richard Murphy, signed by him, fine in dust jacket, slightly browned on spine. Maggs Bros. Ltd. 1442 - 129 2013 £50

Higgins, Godfrey *The Celtic Druids.* London: R. Hunter, 1827. First edition, 4to., engraved titlepage on India paper, 9 lithograph plates, 31 other lithograph plates of ancient sites, 7 wood engraved vignettes in text, 7 vignette tailpieces to chapters, 4to., contemporary panelled calf, expertly rebacked, raised bands, blind tooled compartments, inner hinges reinforced with cloth tape, corners rubbed. Jarndyce Antiquarian Booksellers CCIV - 158 2013 £650

High, Philip E. *Come, Hunt an Earthman.* London: Robert Hale and Co., 1973. First edition, little foxing n first couple of leaves and jacket flaps, else fine in lightly rubbed, very near fine dust jacket, very scarce. Between the Covers Rare Books, Inc. Sci-Fi, Fantasy & Horror - 301301 2013 $275

Highsmith, Patricia *The Cry of the Owl.* New York: Harper and Row, 1962. First edition, fine in fine dust jacket, beautiful copy. Between the Covers Rare Books, Inc. Mystery & Detective Fiction - 84676 2013 $400

Highsmith, Patricia *The Talented Mr. Ripley.* New York: Coward McCann, 1955. First edition, fine in fine dust jacket with very tiny nick at edge of crown where it meets front panel and very slight rubbing. Between the Covers Rare Books, Inc. Mystery & Detective Fiction - 74564 2013 $4000

Hijuelos, Oscar *The Mambo Kings Play Songs of Love.* New York: Farrar Straus and Giroux, 1989. First edition, tight, near fine in very near fine dust jacket, signed by author. Jeff Hirsch Books Fall 2013 - 129441 2013 $55

Hijuelos, Oscar *Our House in the Last World.* New York: Persea Books, 1983. First edition, fine, boards slightly splayed in dust jacket. Ed Smith Books 78 - 27 2013 $200

Hildebrand, Wolfgang *Magiae Naturalis.* Leipzig: Henning Grossen des Jungern, 1620. 3 parts in one volume, small 4to., 218 pages of 220?, lacking final 2 pages, 8 woodcuts, 1 map, folding chart with sun at center, astrological chart some leaves slightly trimmed with some loss at bottom margin, browning, disbound, rare. Jeff Weber Rare Books 169 - 206 2013 $1200

Hildebrandt, M. M. *The External School in Carolingian Society.* Leiden: New York and Koln: E. J. Brill, 1992. 8vo., xii, 169 pages, navy cloth gilt stamped cover and spine titles, dust jacket, presentation inscription (non-authorial), fine. Jeff Weber Rare Books 169 - 208 2013 $80

Hildreth, Don *Tiny Tome/Tomo Minisculo.* San Diego: Ash Ranch Press, 1991. Limited to 126 copies, 26 lettered and signed, foldout illustration, 5 x 3.5 cm., leather, title gilt stamped on spine, mounted metal teddy bear on both boards, slipcase, 40 pages, from the collection of Donn W. Sanford. Oak Knoll Books 303 - 38 2013 $200

Hildreth, Richard *The Slave; or Memoir of Archy Moore.* Boston: Whipple and Danrell, 1840. Second edition, 2 volumes, 8vo., original cloth backed boards, front cover nearly detached, binding soiled, light waterstaining. M & S Rare Books, Inc. 95 - 144 2013 $450

Hildreth, Samuel C. *The Spell of the Turf: The Story of American Racing.* Philadelphia: J. B. Lippincott, 1926. First edition, red cloth and gilt lettering and decoration, 286 pages, photos, spine lettering little dull and cloth slightly soiled, very good plus, lacking dust jacket. Between the Covers Rare Books, Inc. Horses, Horsemanship, Horse Racing, Etc. - 67238 2013 $125

Hill, Alan G. *The Letters of William and Dorothy Wordsworth III. The Later Years Part 1 1821-1828.* Oxford University Press, 1978. Second edition, original cloth, gilt, dust jacket, 3 plates, fine. R. F. G. Hollett & Son Lake District and Cumbria - 252 2013 £60

Hill, Allan Massie *Some Chapters of the History of Digby County and Its Early Settlers.* Halifax: McAlpine Pub. Co., 1901. Small 8vo., card covers with title in red on font cover, small 8vo., card covers worn and chipped with small pieces missing from cover edges. Schooner Books Ltd. 105 - 79 2013 $95

Hill, Andrew P. *Save the California Redwoods...* San Francisco: Sempervirens Club of California, Jan., 1901. First edition, square 8vo., (24) pages, including covers, photos, map, pictorial wrappers, each page creased where folded vertically, slight chipping to few extremities, one half inch chip from bottom border of one leaf, very good. Argonaut Book Shop Recent Acquisitions June 2013 - 54 2013 $300

Hill, Daniel G. *Daniel Grafon Hill, R. 1860-1931.* No place: the authors, circa, 1965. First edition, stapled photographic wrappers, (8) pages, illustrations, near fine, very scarce. Between the Covers Rare Books, Inc. 165 - 153 2013 $200

Hill, Forest G. *Roads, Rails & Waterways. The Army Engineers and Early Transportation.* Norman: University of Oklahoma Press, 1957. First edition, 13 illustrations, black cloth, very fine, pictorial dust jacket. Argonaut Book Shop Summer 2013 - 156 2013 $60

Hill, Ira *Antiquities of America Explained.* Hagers-town: William D. Bell, 1831. First edition, 12mo., 131 pages, one text illustration, full contemporary calf, endleaf torn, otherwise very nice. M & S Rare Books, Inc. 95 - 175 2013 $400

Hill, Leslie Pinckney *The Wings of Oppression.* Boston: The Stratford Co., 1921. First edition, front hinge neatly repaired, couple of very modest stains on boards, some wear to corners, near very good lacking rare dust jacket. Between the Covers Rare Books, Inc. 165 - 165 2013 $225

Hill, M. F. *Permanent Way.* Nairobi: East African Railways and Harbours, 1949. First edition, small 4to., library cloth, gilt, edges rather frayed and worn, illustrations, usual library stamps, little underlining in places. R. F. G. Hollett & Son Africana - 88 2013 £30

Hill, Reginald *Ruling Passion.* London: Collins/Crime Club, 1973. First edition, faint offsetting at bottom of front fly, else fine in lightly rubbed dust jacket. Between the Covers Rare Books, Inc. Mystery & Detective Fiction - 68309 2013 $275

Hill, Richard *An Address to Persons of Fashion, Relating to Balls...* Shrewsbury: printed by J. Eddowes, 1771. Sixth edition, 12mo., half title, good clean copy, slight old waterstaining to upper edge of few leaves manuscript footnotes on page 34, blue marginal line marking a paragraph on pages 154-155, recent full calf, raised bands, red morocco label, fresh contemporary endpapers and pastedowns, early signature of Peter Dean. Jarndyce Antiquarian Booksellers CCIV - 160 2013 £200

Hill, Susan *The Woman in Black.* Hamilton, 1983. Uncorrected proof, headpieces and other illustrations by John Lawrence, foolscap 8vo., original pale blue wrappers, front cover printed and illustrated in black and printed "uncorrected book proof", fine, margins trimmed down for uncorrected proof issue to foolscap octavo in size. Blackwell's Rare Books B174 - 229 2013 £100

Hillary, Edmund *No Latitude for Error.* London: Hodder and Stoughton, 1961. First edition, original cloth, gilt, dust jacket, 47 illustrations. R. F. G. Hollett & Son Polar Exploration - 29 2013 £25

Hiller, James K. *The Newfoundland National Convention 1946-1948.* Montreal & Kingston: McGill-Queen's University Press, 1955. Large 8vo., 2 volumes, blue cloth, 2064 pages, photo portraits, fine. Schooner Books Ltd. 101 - 35 2013 $150

Hillerman, Tony *The Blessing Way.* New York: Harper & Row, 1972. Fifth edition, signed by author, fine, price clipped dust jacket with slight spine fading. Mordida Books 81 - 248 2013 $200

Hillerman, Tony *Dance Hall of the Dead.* New York: Harper & Row, 1973. First edition, signed by Hillerman, very fine in dust jacket with tiny scrape on front panel. Mordida Books 81 - 249 2013 $1500

Hillerman, Tony *The Dark Wind.* New York: Harper & Row, 1982. First edition, very fine in dust jacket. Mordida Books 81 - 253 2013 $250

Hillerman, Tony *The Great Taos Bank Robbery.* Albuquerque: University of New Mexico, 1973. First edition, small label removed from front endpaper, otherwise fine in dust jacket with tiny nick at top of spine, first ate with grayish cloth covered boards, single picture of Shiprock on back panel of jacket. Mordida Books 81 - 250 2013 $350

Hillerman, Tony *Listening Woman.* New York: Harper & Row, 1978. First edition, signed by author, pages slightly darkened, otherwise fine in dust jacket. Mordida Books 81 - 251 2013 $650

Hillerman, Tony *People of Darkness.* New York: Harper & Row, 1980. First edition, signed by author, tiny nick on bottom edge of back cover, otherwise fine in dust jacket. Mordida Books 81 - 252 2013 $650

Hillgarth, Alan *The Black Mountain.* New York: Knopf, 1934. First American edition, contemporary gift inscription, top edge of rear board slightly abraded and little light soiling to extremities of binding, still near fine. Between the Covers Rare Books, Inc. Sci-Fi, Fantasy & Horror - 28211 2013 $175

Hillman, Raymond W. *Cities and Towns of San Joaquin County Since 1847.* Fresno: Panorama West Books, 1985. First trade edition, signed by authors, photos, map, beige pictorial cloth, very fine. Argonaut Book Shop Recent Acquisitions June 2013 - 146 2013 $75

Hillman, William *Mr. President.* New York: Farrar, Straus and Young, 1952. First edition, inscribed by President Truman to Jane Lingo, April 10, 1952, laid in is 3 x 5 card is a note in young hand signed by Lingo asking the President to sign the book for her, quarter beige cloth with blue cloth covered boards and gilt title label to spine, toning to edges of boards and small bump along bottom edge of rear board, clean, bright interior with errata slip laid in, blue dust jacket with red title to spine and front panel, large open tear on front of jacket affecting title, few closed tears along edges, very good in good dust jacket, 253 pages. The Kelmscott Bookshop 7 - 133 2013 $1500

Hilton, James *Lost Horizon.* Toronto: Macmillan Company of Canada Limited, 1943. First Canadian edition, very slightly worn and near fine in very good plus dust jacket with very shallow loss at crown and internally repaired split along inside front wrapper, fragile and exceptionally scarce. Between the Covers Rare Books, Inc. Sci-Fi, Fantasy & Horror - 83073 2013 $1500

Hilton, John *Notes on some of the Developmental Functional Relationships Certain Portions of the Cranium.* London: John Churchill, 1855. 93 pages, 9 engraved plates, ad, original cloth, library stamp on title and front board, some wear, author's presentation. James Tait Goodrich 75 - 119 2013 $695

Hilton, Simpson, M. W. *Algiers and Beyond.* Hutchinson & Co., 1906. First edition, original green cloth, gilt over bevelled boards, spine rather browned and trifle nicked at head and foot, 32 illustrations, folding map, flyleaves browned. R. F. G. Hollett & Son Africana - 89 2013 £75

Himes, Chester *A Case of Rape.* New York: Targ Editions, 1980. First American edition, one of 350 copies, signed by author, fine in quarter cloth and paper covered boards in near fine, unprinted glassine dust jacket with small tears at extremities warmly inscribed by publisher to novelist Brad Morrow. Between the Covers Rare Books, Inc. 165 - 169 2013 $250

Himes, Chester *The Heat's On.* New York: Putnam, 1966. First edition, fine in very good plus, price clipped dust jacket with some rubbing. Between the Covers Rare Books, Inc. 165 - 168 2013 $250

Himes, Chester *If He Hollers Let Him Go.* Garden City: Doubleday Doran, 1945. First edition, fine, lacking dust jacket, scarce. Between the Covers Rare Books, Inc. 165 - 167 2013 $300

Himes, Chester *Lonely Crusade.* New York: Alfred A. Knopf, 1947. First edition, slight stain on rear board, else near fine in attractive, very good dust jacket with long tear on front panel small chips on rear panel and some modest stains on rear panel, mostly externally invisible. Between the Covers Rare Books, Inc. 165 - 307 2013 $600

Himes, Chester *The Real Cool Killers.* London: Allison & Busby, 1985.   First hardcover edition, fine in dust jacket.   Mordida Books   81 - 260   2013 $100

Hinchcliffe, Edgar *Appleby Grammar School - from Chantry to Comprehensive.*   Appleby: J. Whitehead & Son, 1974.   First edition, pages 151, 8 plates, original cloth, gilt, dust jacket price clipped, scarce.   R. F. G. Hollett & Son   Lake District and Cumbria - 254   2013   £50

Hinderwell, Thomas *The History and Antiquities of Scarborough and the Vicinity.*   York: printed by Thomas Wilson and Son, 1811.   Supplement Newcastle P Edward Walker, 1831. Second edition, 435, (1) pages, frontispiece, 3 plates, extra illustrated with 6 plates, some laid down and trimmed, rather foxed and browned, folding map worn; with supplement to Mr. Chapman's Report of August 1829 on the Ancient, Intermediate and present state of the Harbour of Scarborough...8vo., the two items in one, later 19th century half calf, gilt label, pebble grain cloth boards.   Ken Spelman Books Ltd.   73 - 150   2013   £95

Hinding, Andrea *Women's History Sources a Guide to Archives and Manuscript Collections in the United States.* New York: Bowker, 1979.   2 volumes, small 4to., rust colored cloth, edges somewhat soiled, corners of covers little bumped, flyleaf missing in volume I, otherwise very good.   Second Life Books Inc.   182 - 113   2013 $125

Hindle, Brian Paul *Roads and Trackways of the Lake District.*   Moorland Pub., 1984.   First edition, original cloth, gilt, dust jacket, 187 pages, illustrations.   R. F. G. Hollett & Son   Lake District and Cumbria - 256   2013   £25

Hinds, James Pitcairn *Bibliotheca Jacksoniana.*   Kendal: Titus Wilson, 1909.   Limited edition, number 76, tall 8vo., original brown cloth, gilt, flyleaves little browned, otherwise fine.   R. F. G. Hollett & Son   Lake District and Cumbria - 257   2013   £85

Hines, Daivd Theo *The Life, Adventures and Opinions of David Theo. Hines of South Carolina, Master of Arts and Sometimes, Doctor of Medicine...*   New York: Bradley Clark, 1840.   First edition, 12mo., 195 pages, original cloth backed boards, printed paper label (rubbed), very nice.   M & S Rare Books, Inc.   95 - 145   2013 $250

Hines, Laurence *Mary, Queen of Scots.*   San Diego: Ash Ranch Press, 1990.   Limited to 33 copies, 26 lettered and 7 state proofs, all signed by author and printer on colophon, this is a lettered copy, frontispieces on both sides, leather, 5.7 x 8cm., brass hinges and studs, purple tinted edges, embossed boards, gilt slipcase with title gilt stamped on signed, included is prospectus limited to 225 copies, illustrations, stiff paper wrappers, front wrapper illustrated with gilt seal of Queen Mary, from the collection of Donn W. Sanford.   Oak Knoll Books   303 - 39   2013 $300

Hinzelin, Emile *Quand Le Grand Napoleon Etait Petit.* Paris: Delagrave, 1932.   Large 4to., cloth backed boards, pictorial paste-on, 44 pages, near fine, illustrations by Job with 8 fine color plates plus 20 line illustrations.   Aleph-Bet Books, Inc.   104 - 301   2013 $500

Hippocrates *De Humoribus Purgandis Liber et de Diaeta Acutorum Libri Tres cum Commentariis Integris Ludovici Dureti...* Leipzig: Breitkopf for Heirs of Lanisch, 1745. First edition of Gunz's recension, title printed in red and black, text in various sizes of Greek and Roman and occasional black letter (German) type, woodcut head and tailpieces, old repair to short tear in lower margin of last (errata) leaf, contemporary half calf, drab paper sides, attractive sponge marbled edges, trifle worn, very good.   Blackwell's Rare Books   Sciences - 60   2013   £450

Hippocrates *Liber se Somniis Cum Iulii Caesaris Scaligeri Commentariis.*   Lugduni: Apud Seb. Gryphium, 1539. First edition of this translation, printer woodcut on title, 2 index leaves misbound at end, small 4to., early full polished calf with gilt paneled spine with raised bands, quite nice, clean crisp copy.   James Tait Goodrich   75 - 117   2013 $1550

Hiram Walker's Cordials: a Rainbow of Flavors.   Peoria: Hiram Walker & Sons Inc. n.d. circa, 1963.   12mo., single leaf folded to make 12 pages, overprinted with name of Maryland liquor store, else fine, drawings.   Between the Covers Rare Books, Inc.   Cocktails, Etc. - 312636   2013 $50

Hirsch, August *Biographisches Lexikon der Hervorragenden Aerzie aller Zeiten und volker. Zweite Auflage.*   Berlin and Vienna: 1929-1935. 1932-1933., 6 volumes with 2 volume supplement and continuation to 1930 by Fischer, 8 volumes in total, large 8vo., original quarter vellum, spine soiled with spine labels, supplemental two volumes bound in half leather, overall good set, tight and unabused.   James Tait Goodrich   75 - 28   2013 $1495

Hirsch, Richard F. *Power Loss: the Origins of Derregulation and Restructuring in the American Electric Utility System.*   Cambridge and London: MIT Press, 1999. First edition, 8vo., x, 406 pages, illustrations, tables, quarter yellow cloth over beige cloth sides, silver stamped spine title, dust jacket, Burndy bookplate, fine.   Jeff Weber Rare Books   169 - 209   2013 $165

Hirst, Damien *I Want to Spend the rest of My Life Everywhere with Everyone, One to One, Always, Forever, Now.*   Booth Clibborn, 1997.   First edition, illustrations, pop-ups, pulls, folding map, moveable wheels, posters, transparencies of cows, large 4to., original red leatherette, gilt and blind blocked dust jacket, original unbroken shrinkwrap enclosure, rare in such state, fine.   Blackwell's Rare Books   172 - 195   2013   £600

Hirt, Michael *Rorschach Science Readings in Theory and Method.* New York: Free Press of Glencoe, 1962. First edition, lightly browned fore edge, else fine in near fine, lightly rubbed dust jacket with some minor edgewear. Between the Covers Rare Books, Inc. Psychology & Psychiatry - 101666 2013 $65

Hirtzler, Victor *The Hotel St. Francis Cook Book.* Chicago: Hotel Monthly Press, 1919. First edition, 432, (10) pages, frontispiece, menu files, classified and general indexes, dark green cloth lettered in gilt on spine and front cover some blotchy type foxing to front ends and title, lower corners lightly jammed else fine. Argonaut Book Shop Recent Acquisitions June 2013 - 147 2013 $250

The Historical, Antiquarian and Picturesque Account of Kirkstall Abbey... London: Longman, 1827. frontispiece, 4 engraved plates, 19th century half morocco, marbled boards, titlepage, joints and corners rubbed, some heavy foxing to frontispiece and titlepage. Ken Spelman Books Ltd. 73 - 116 2013 £95

Historical Description of Westminster Abbey, Its Monuments and Curiosities. London: A. K. Newman & Co., 1830. Original printed paper boards, some slight rubbing, very good, contemporary signature on titlepage. Jarndyce Antiquarian Booksellers CCV - 286 2013 £125

Historicus *The Best Hundred Irish Books.* circa, 1890. Reprinted from Freeman's Journal, 60 pages + 4 pages ads, original cloth on stiff boards, very good. C. P. Hyland 261 - 70 2013 £50

History of Jackey Jingle and Sukey Single. New York: McLoughlin Bros. circa, 1860. 12mo., pictorial wrappers, inconspicuous spine repair, slight soil, near fine, 8 nice half page hand colored illustrations. Aleph-Bet Books, Inc. 104 - 341 2013 $300

The History of Little Goody Twoshoes... Worcester: Printed by Isaiah Thomas, 1787. Second American edition, 32mo. 35 woodcuts, original wrappers blind decorated with grape vines, 3 corners clipped, frontispiece pasted inside front wrapper, nearly fine in morocco backed slipcase. Howard S. Mott Inc. 262 - 81 2013 $3500

The History of Reynard the Fox. Zuilichem: Catharijne Press, 1991. Limited to 190 copies, this one of 175 numbered trade copies, 6.6 x 5.1cm., cloth, paper cover label, wood engraving by Pam Reuter, binding by Luce Thurkow, wood engraved frontispiece signed and numbered in pencil, from the collection of Donn W. Sanford. Oak Knoll Books 303 - 83 2013 $125

The History of Ripon; with Descriptions of Studley-Royal, Fountains' Abbey, Newby, Hackfall &c &c. Ripon: W. Farrer, 1806. Second edition, 314 pages, aquatint frontispiece and woodcuts in text, very good, contemporary half calf, marbled boards, raised gilt bands, blindstamped decoration in each compartment, foolscap 8vo., signature of John Hammond 24th August 1863, later bookplates of Chapman-Purchas and R. J. Rattray. Ken Spelman Books Ltd. 73 - 142 2013 £120

The History of the House that Jack Built. London: Houlston & Son, n.d. circa, 1820. 24mo., pictorial wrappers, fine, woodcuts on each page plus cuts on both covers. Aleph-Bet Books, Inc. 105 - 123 2013 $350

History of the Rebellion in Ireland in the Year 1798, Containing an Impartial Account of the Proceedings of the Irish Revolutionists from the Breaking-out of the Rebellion Till Its Suppression. Workington: printed by W. Borrowdale, 1806. 8vo., woodcut tailpiece ornaments, good, uncut, original drab boards, corners and edges worn, neatly rebacked. Jarndyce Antiquarian Booksellers CCIV - 168 2013 £150

The History of Thirsk; Including an Account of Its Once Celebrated Castle. Thirsk: sold by Robert Peat, 1821. 8vo., frontispiece, 2 woodcut illustrations, half title, uncut, recent half calf, marbled boards, new endpapers, scarce, this copy extra illustrated with two 19th century sepia wash drawings of Byland Abbey. Ken Spelman Books Ltd. 73 - 166 2013 £220

The History of Tommy and Harry. York: Kendrew, n.d. circa, 1820. 16mo., green paper wrappers, (30) pages, fine, 8 nice woodcuts. Aleph-Bet Books, Inc. 105 - 124 2013 $250

History of Trinity Wesleyan Church. Blackburn: no publisher, circa, 1930. Small 8vo., original cloth, gilt, 31 pages, frontispiece. R. F. G. Hollett & Son Wesleyan Methodism - 62 2013 £25

The History of U.S. Army Base Hospital No. 6 and Its Part in the American Expeditionary Forces 1917-1918. Boston: 1924. 161 pages, frontispiece, original cloth, light damp wrinkling of pages, otherwise nice, tight copy with numerous illustrations. James Tait Goodrich S74 - 21 2013 $125

Hitchens, Robert *The Near East: Dalmatia, Greece and Constantinople.* New York: Century Co., 1913. First edition, 8vo., pages x, 268, illustrations, original blue decorative cloth. J. & S. L. Bonham Antiquarian Booksellers Europe - 8706 2013 £65

Hittell, John S. *A History of San Francisco and Incidentally of the State of California.* Berkeley: Berkeley Hills Books, 2000. Frontispiece, reproductions, maps, blue cloth, gilt very fine and bright. Argonaut Book Shop Summer 2013 - 158 2013 $175

Hoare, Edward *Some Account of the Early History & Genealogy of the family of Hore or Hoare.* 1883. First edition, viii, 70 pages, 2 plates, very good, scarce. C. P. Hyland 261 - 394 2013 £120

Hoatson, A. *Merry Words for Merry Children.* London and New York: W. Hagelberg, n.d. circa, 1890. oblong 16mo., stiff pictorial card covers, as new in original pictorial dust jacket, 11 full page chromolithographs and one full page drawing in brown line, remarkable copy, rare in dust jacket. Aleph-Bet Books, Inc. 105 - 572 2013 $450

Hoban, Russell *The Little Brute Family.* New York: Macmillan, 1966. Stated first edition, 12mo, pictorial cloth, fine in lightly soiled, slightly worn dust jacket, illustrations in color by Lillian Hoban. Aleph-Bet Books, Inc. 105 - 319 2013 $450

Hoban, Russell *The Stone Doll of Sister Brute.* New York: Macmillan, 1968. Stated first edition, 12mo., pictorial cloth, fine, rare, illustrations in color by Lillian Russell. Aleph-Bet Books, Inc. 104 - 279 2013 $200

Hobart, Noah *An Attempt to Illustrate and confirm the Ecclesiastical Constitution of the Consociated Churches in the Colony of Connecticut.* New Haven: Mecom, 1765. First edition, 8vo., 44 pages, later plain wrappers, trimmed close all around, affecting first letter and fore edge of several leaves. M & S Rare Books, Inc. 95 - 85 2013 $225

Hobbes, Thomas 1588-1679 *Leviathan or the Matter, Forme and Power of a CommonWealth Ecclesiasticall and Civill.* London: printed for Andrew Crooke, 1651. First edition, first issue with 'head' ornament on titlepage, fine copy, partly effaced ownership signature on title of Edward Waring, possibly the noted English mathematician with some of his ink lines in margins, folio (in 4's), modern full calf antique style, gilt and blind ruled covers, gilt spine, raised bands, leather label, extra engraved title, folding table. Howard S. Mott Inc. 262 - 75 2013 $20,000

Hobbes, Thomas 1588-1679 *Leviathan, or the Matter, Forme & Power of a Common-Wealth Ecclesisticall and Civill.* London: 1651. First edition, first issue with 'head' ornament on titlepage and correct spelling of publisher's name "Crooke", small folio, engraved titlepage and folding table, decorative wood engraved headpiece and initials C.C. in a central oval, with 3 woodcut initials in text, contemporary paneled calf, expertly rebacked, spine lettered gilt, titlepage neatly repaired, engraved title and lower portion of last leaf expertly laid down and mounted, intermittent light browning at beginning and end of text, still, overall an excellent copy. Heritage Book Shop 50th Anniversary Catalogue - 45 2013 $18,500

Hobbs, Anne Stevenson *Beatrix Potter's Art.* London: Warne, 1989. First edition, 4to., original cloth, gilt, dust jacket, pages 192, illustrations in color, related ephemera loosely inserted. R. F. G. Hollett & Son Lake District and Cumbria - 263 2013 £45

Hobbs, William Herbert *Exploring About the North Pole of the Winds.* London: G. P. Putnam's Sons, 1930. First edition, large 8vo., original blue cloth, spine little faded and marked, 26 illustrations, maps on endpapers, decorations by author. R. F. G. Hollett & Son Polar Exploration - 30 2013 £45

Hobhouse, John Cam *Historical Illustrations of the Fourth Canto of Childe Harold...* London: John Murray, 1818. Second edition, contemporary full vellum, spine gilt in compartments, red label slightly marked, small split to leading hinge, ownership inscription "J. Langley 1829", very good. Jarndyce Antiquarian Booksellers CCIII - 150 2013 £110

Hobhouse, John Cam *Imitations and Translations from the Ancient and Modern Classics...* London: Longmans, 1809. First edition, half title, odd spot, handsomely bound in contemporary tree calf, spine gilt and gilt borders, dark green leather label, slightly chipped, at some time expertly repaired, head and tail of spine slightly worn, with one small chip, contemporary signatures, later label and signature of Alex Bridge, scarce. Jarndyce Antiquarian Booksellers CCIII - 391 2013 £750

Hobrecker, Karl *Jahreszeiten Las Frolich Dich Begleiten.* Oldenberg: Stalling, 1927. First edition, 4to., cloth backed pictorial boards, fine in dust jacket frayed but very good, beautiful copy. Aleph-Bet Books, Inc. 104 - 236 2013 $350

Hoch, Edward D. *The Spy Who Read Latin and Other Stories.* Helsinki: Eurographica, 1990. First edition thus, one of 350 numbered copies, boldly signed by author, with date "June 1990", fine copy, perfect bound, original stiff paper wrappers, fine, brown printed dust jacket. Ed Smith Books 78 - 28 2013 $75

Hocking, Anne *Death Disturbs Mr. Jefferson.* Garden City: Doubleday Crime Club, 1950. First edition, pages darkened, otherwise fine in fine, bright dust jacket with faint crease on spine. Mordida Books 81 - 262 2013 $65

Hockney, David *Hockney's Alphabet...* London: Faber for the Aids Crisis Trust, 1991. First edition, intermediate issue signed by Hockey and Stephen Spenser, printed on Exhibition Fine Art Cartridge paper, 27 full page color printed illustrations, large 4to., original bright yellow cloth, backstrip gilt lettered on dark blue ground, cloth slipcase, fine. Blackwell's Rare Books B174 - 230 2013 £250

Hodder, William Reginald *The Vampire.* London: William Rider & Son Ltd., 1913. First edition, octavo, inserted frontispiece with color illustration by E. A. Holloway, titlepage printed in red and black, original blue cloth, front panel stamped in red, black and gold, spine panel stamped in black and gold. L. W. Currey, Inc. Fall Sampler Sept. 2013 - 145580 2013 $2500

Hodeir, Andre *Jazz its Evolution and Essence.* New York: Grove Press, 1956. First American edition, paperback original, near fine, some rubbing, author Ralph Ellison's copy with his ownership signature. Between the Covers Rare Books, Inc. 165 - 170 2013 $250

Hodge, Edmund W. *Enjoying Lakes from Post-Chaise to National Park.* Oliver & Boyd, 1957. First edition, original cloth, dust jacket, 32 illustrations, maps. R. F. G. Hollett & Son Lake District and Cumbria - 264 2013 £25

Hodges, William *The Statute Law Relating to Railways in England and Ireland.* Sweet, 1845. First edition, 8vo., original quarter cloth, very good. C. P. Hyland 261 - 487 2013 £75

Hodgkin, Lucy Violet *Yesterday.* privately printed, 1914. Limited to 150 copies, this an out-of-series copy, original cloth, gilt, spine little worn at head and foot, pages 74, presentation copy inscribed by author to Margie (Margaret Cropper) and dated Oct. 1914. R. F. G. Hollett & Son Lake District and Cumbria - 220 2013 £25

Hodgson, Henry W. *A Bibliography of the History and Topography of Cumberland and Westmorland.* Carlisle: Record Office, 1968. First edition, large 8vo., original cloth, plain dust jacket, pages 301. R. F. G. Hollett & Son Lake District and Cumbria - 265 2013 £50

Hodgson, Herbert *Herbert Hodgson, Printer.* Wakefield: Fleece Press, 1989. One of 340 copies, printed on Hahnemuhle Book Wove, mould made paper, lightly mounted frontispiece, one line of title and both chapter titles printed in red, 8vo., original quarter light brown cloth, printed label, vertically striped multi colored paste paper boards, rough trimmed, fine. Blackwell's Rare Books 172 - 279 2013 £70

Hodgson, John *The Beauties of England and Wales; or Original Delineations, Topographical, Historical and Descriptive...* Harris, Longman, etc., 1814. Modern half blue levant morocco, gilt with double spine labels, spine faded to grey, engraved title, 20 engraved plates, few spots and stains, good copy. R. F. G. Hollett & Son Lake District and Cumbria - 266 2013 £120

Hodgson, John *A Topographical and Historical Description of the County of Westmoreland...* printed for Sherwood, Neely, and Jones and George Cowie and Co., 1820. Old binder's cloth, gilt, untrimmed, 6 engraved plates (bout out of order). R. F. G. Hollett & Son Lake District and Cumbria - 268 2013 £120

Hodgson, John *A Topographical and Historical Description of the County of Westmoreland...* printed for Sherwood, Neely and Jones and George Cowie and Co., 1820. Original publisher's cloth, paper spine label (little rubbed), untrimmed, folding map, engraved title (both little spotted), 6 engraved plates (bound in at end, some upside down), very good. R. F. G. Hollett & Son Lake District and Cumbria - 267 2013 £140

Hodgson, John *A Topographical and Historical Description of the County of Westmoreland...* printed for Sherwood, Neely and Jones, 1820. Old half calf gilt, marbled boards, engraved frontispiece, 7 engraved plates. R. F. G. Hollett & Son Lake District and Cumbria - 269 2013 £145

Hodgson, Ralph *The Skylark and Other Poems.* Fenton: Curwen Press, 1958. 22/50 copies (of an edition of 350, signed by author, (on page 92 as usual) and artist, 5 full page wood engravings and title vignette and tailpiece, all by Reynolds Stone, title printed in black and red, 8vo. original quarter black morocco, backstrip gilt lettered, blue and brown, marbled boards, Stone design of skylark blocked in gilt within blue paper onlay to front cover, top edge gilt, fine. Blackwell's Rare Books B174 - 302 2013 £200

Hodgson, Randolph *On Plain and Peak.* Westminster: Archibald Constable, 1898. First edition, 8vo., pages viii, 254, illustrations, rebound in half green calf. J. & S. L. Bonham Antiquarian Booksellers Europe - 7162 2013 £100

Hodgson, William *Flora of Cumberland.* Carlisle: W. Meals and Co., 1898. First edition, original green cloth gilt, geological map. R. F. G. Hollett & Son Lake District and Cumbria - 271 2013 £85

Hodgson, William Hope *The Ghost Pirates.* Paul, 1909. First edition, frontispiece, library inkstamps erased from titlepage, faint browning to half title and title, foolscap 8vo., original mid green second issue cloth (first issue was red cloth), backstrip gilt lettered and front cover lettered in black, remnants of library label on front cover, tiny nick at head of front cover, short ex-libris note, rough trimmed.   Blackwell's Rare Books   B174 - 231   2013   £1200

Hodgson, William Hope *Men of the Deep Waters.* Eveleigh Nash, 1914. First edition, light foxing to prelims and final few leaves, foolscap 8vo., original maroon cloth, backstrip and front cover gilt lettered that on the lightly faded backstrip tarnished, little damp marking to rear cover, mainly to lower half, rear hinge weak, rubber stamp of "Bristol Ship-Lovers Society", tail edges rough trimmed.   Blackwell's Rare Books   B174 - 232   2013   £800

Hodgson, William Hope *The Voice of the Ocean.* Selwyn & Blount, 1921. First edition, pages 48, 16mo., original blue-green boards, printed label rubbed and little chipped, endpapers browned, edges spotted, good. Blackwell's Rare Books   B174 - 233   2013 $600

Hoexter, Corinne K. *From Canton to California. The Epic of Chinese Immigration.* New York: Four Winds Press, 1976. First edition, photos, red cloth, very fine, pictorial dust jacket.   Argonaut Book Shop   Summer 2013 - 159   2013 $75

Hoffman, Edward *The Drive for Self: Alfred Adler and the Founding of Individual Psychology.* Reading: Addison-Wesley, 1994. First edition, fine in fine dust jacket. Between the Covers Rare Books, Inc.   Psychology & Psychiatry - 92857   2013 $50

Hoffmann-Donner, Heinrich 1809-1894 *The English Struwelpeter or Pretty Stories and Funny Pictures for Little Children.* Frankfurt: Krebs-Schmitt, n.d. circa, 1860. Original printed boards, little stained and sometime rebacked to match, corners worn, pages 24 hand colored throughout, first leaf torn and laid down, few other tears neatly repaired, early hand colored editions are now very scarce.   R. F. G. Hollett & Son   Children's Books - 289   2013   £85

Hoffmann-Donner, Heinrich 1809-1894 *Greedy Peter.* Lowell: J. Merrill, circa, 1870. 4 X 6 inches, yellow pictorial wrappers, some soil, very good, every page illustrated with half page engraving.   Aleph-Bet Books, Inc.   105 - 321   2013 $250

Hoffmann-Donner, Heinrich 1809-1894 *Miss Vanity's Holiday.* New York: McLoughlin Bros., n.d. circa, 1860-1865. 12mo., pictorial wrappers, spot on cover, else fine, color cover plus 8 half page color illustrations.   Aleph-Bet Books, Inc.   104 - 284   2013 $300

Hoffmann-Donner, Heinrich 1809-1894 *Slovenly Betsy.* Philadelphia: Henry Altemus, n.d., 1911. 16mo., cloth backed pictorial boards, pictorial paste-on, 95 pages plus ads, fine, every page with full page color illustration by Walter Hayn, very scarce.   Aleph-Bet Books, Inc.   104 - 282   2013 $450

Hoffmann-Donner, Heinrich 1809-1894 *Petrulus Hirrutus (Slovenly Peter).* Frankfurt: Rutten & Loening, 1956. First Latin edition, 4to., cloth backed pictorial boards, as new in original paper wrapper, printed on rectos only, illustrations in bright color, pamphlet in German in pocket in rear.   Aleph-Bet Books, Inc.   104 - 281   2013 $200

Hoffmann-Donner, Heinrich 1809-1894 *Slovenly Peter's Story Book.* New York: McLoughlin Bros. n.d.,, 12mo. cloth stamped in black and gold, pictorial paste-on, few minor mends, paper worn on one page and finger soil throughout, tight, overall very good, 4 chromolithographs, inscribed 1877.   Aleph-Bet Books, Inc.   104 - 283   2013 $1250

Hoffmann-Donner, Heinrich 1809-1894 *Sruwwelpeter Pictures for Painting.* London: Humphrey Milford/Oxford University Press, n.d. circa, 1930. Large 12mo., pictorial boards, spine paper chipped, some illustrations colored, some soil and wear, really very good, printed in full color on coated paper, facing each colored illustration is same illustration in line meant to be painted by child (6 of 24 neatly painted) very scarce.   Aleph-Bet Books, Inc.   104 - 280   2013 $850

Hoffmann, J. J. *A Japanese Grammar.* Leiden: His Majesty's Minister for Colonial Affairs, 1868. First edition in English, in new wrappers to style with original printed front cover laid down, scattered foxing, few page corners dog eared, soil edges, small 4to, scarce original edition.   By the Book, L. C.   38 - 63   2013   £500

Hofland, Barbara Hoole *The Barbadoes Girl.* London: A. K. Newman & Co., 1825. Fifth edition, 12mo., frontispiece, additional engraved title, slight foxing, following endpaper removed, contemporary quarter rubbed and slightly worn, 'Tremayne' ownership signatures.   Jarndyce Antiquarian Booksellers   CCV - 137   2013   £20

Hofland, Barbara Hoole *Moral Tales for the Young.* New York: C. S. Francis & Co. and Boston: Crosby, Nichols & Co., 1855. Original blue blindstamped cloth, gilt extremities rubbed, backstrip frayed at foot, tissue guarded woodcut frontispiece, woodcut general title and tailpiece.   R. F. G. Hollett & Son   Children's Books - 291   2013   £65

Hofland, Barbara Hoole *Theodore; or the Crusaders.* John Harris and Son circa, 1821. First edition?, small 8vo., original roan backed pictorial boards, little rubbed, head of spine chipped, vignette, 24 woodcut illustrations on 12 plates, little spotting to endpapers, some plates trifle offset, excellent sound copy, scarce. R. F. G. Hollett & Son Children's Books - 292   2013   £175

Hofman, Caroline *Princess Finds a Playmate.* Chicago: Volland, 1918. First edition, 8vo., pictorial boards, fine in publisher's box (flap repaired), Volland flyer laid in, very uncommon, color illustrations by Rachael Elmer. Aleph-Bet Books, Inc.   104 - 573   2013 $250

Hofmann's Confession... Salt Lake City: Utah Lighthouse Ministry, Quarto, wrappers, bound with plastic spines and green translucent covers, very good. Ken Sanders Rare Books   45 - 7   2013 $150

Hogan, Elizabeth *Rivers of the West.* Menlo Park: Lane Pub. Co., 1974. First deluxe edition, quarto, 224 pages, color and black and white photos, maps, half turquoise leather, beige cloth sides, very fine, pictorial slipcase. Argonaut Book Shop   Recent Acquisitions June 2013 - 148   2013 $75

Hogan, James *Letter and Papers Relating to the Irish Rebellion 1642-1646.* 1936. 518 copies printed, 8vo., cloth, very good, ex-libris Seamus Pender. C. P. Hyland   261 - 502   2013   £75

Hogarth, Paul *Paul Hogarth's American Album. Drawings 1962-1965.* 1973. 185 (of approximately 400 copies), numerous full page illustrations, number color printed, title and title to each chapter printed in yellow and orange, folio, original white boards, front cover lettered and with design by Hogarth, dust jacket with short tear, near fine. Blackwell's Rare Books   172 - 300   2013   £50

Hogg, James *The Brownie of Bodsbeck and Other Tales.* Edinburgh: printed for William Blackwood, Prince's Street and John Murray Albemarle St.. London, 1818. First edition, 2 volumes, 12mo., half title leaves present, recently rebound with new endpapers in green leather, front, spine and rear panels stamped in gold and blind, black leather spine labels. L. W. Currey, Inc.   Fall Sampler Sept. 2013 - 145581   2013 $2500

Hogg, Thomas *A Concise and Practical Treatise on the Growth and Culture of the Carnation.* London: G. & W, B. Whittaker, 1822. Boards, 8vo., good+, 6 hand colored flower plates, spine well rubbed. Barnaby Rudge Booksellers   Natural History 2013 - 020229   2013 $125

Holden, Horace *A Narrative of the Shipwreck, Captivity and Sufferings of Horace Holden and Benj. H. Nute...* Boston: Russell, Shattuck and Co., 1836. First edition, 16mo., frontispiece, original cloth, front hinge weak, outer cloth split, very good, with fragile binding not often seen intact. M & S Rare Books, Inc.   95 - 146   2013 $275

Holder, H. W. *The Scarborough Bouquet of Rhymes; Being Recollections of Subjects Amusing and Interesting, brought into Original Verse.* Scarborough: Marshall and Co., circa, 1860. 46 pages, very good, original brick red gilt lettered cloth, scarce. Ken Spelman Books Ltd.   73 - 153   2013   £45

The Holidays at Llandudno. Cassell Petter and Galpin, 1868. First edition, small 8vo., original decorated green cloth gilt, hinges little rubbed, all edges gilt, 4 color plates by Kronheim. R. F. G. Hollett & Son   Children's Books - 16   2013   £50

Holinshed, Raphael *The First (-Laste) Volumes of the Chronicles of England, Scotlande, and Irelande.* London: 1577. First edition, 4 parts in two volumes, folio, woodcut borders, numerous woodcut initials and illustrations, foldout plate of map of Edinburgh (often lacking), 18th century full brown calf, very expertly rebacked preserving original spines, boards ruled in gilt with central gilt device, spines stamped in gilt, red morocco spine labels, lettered gilt, top edge brown, others red, newer endpapers, first titlepage in each volume neatly backed, neat old ink notes on front free endpaper of volume I and small marginal rust hole to pages 107-115 of volume 1, hole has been repaired on pages 111-115 and is barely affecting marginal text notes on pages 111-114, page 469 volume 1 has corner that has been professionally repaired barely affecting text; final four leaves volume I remargined along top edge, barely affecting headline of just one leaf, final leaf of this group has been remargined along fore-edge, not affecting text, volume II with pages 467 889 and 1891 recornered, not affecting text, page 1197 recornered, barely touching text, pages 1005-1010, 1409 and 1423 have been remargined, not affecting text, five inch closed tear to leaf cii of index, partially repaired with no loss of text, occasional browning and light dampstaining, overall excellent and quite large copy. Heritage Book Shop   Holiday Catalogue 2012 - 77   2013 $45,000

Holinshed, Raphael *The First (-Laste) Volumes of the Chronicles of England, Scotlande and Irelande.* London: George Bishop (and) John Hunne, 1577. First edition, 2 volumes, medium folio, numerous woodcut initials of various sizes throughout, may repeated, blank *b*6 lacking in I:2; second leaf of errata lacking from I; several leaves supplied from another genuine copy, map of Edinburgh remargined and with other minor repairs, several paper repairs to titles and text with occasional loss, some printed marginal notes shaved as usual, a made-up copy, this copy with George Bishop title in volume I and remaining titles with John Hunne imprint; early 19th century full tan calf over thick boards, gilt wide fillet bordering on covers, gilt ruled board edges, spines gilt in compartments with six raised bands, yellow endpapers, all edges gilt, little rubbed, few scuffs, hinges and joints just becoming tender, overall very good. Heritage Book Shop   50th Anniversary Catalogue - 46   2013 $25,000

Holland, Elizabeth Gaskell *Poems and Translations.* colophon: Women's Printing Society, Limited, 1891. First edition, titlepage slightly spotted and with minute tear in foremargin, 8vo., contemporary green crushed morocco, single gilt fillet borders on sides, spine lettered direct, spine faded, but not as far as brown, top edge gilt, others uncut, good. Blackwell's Rare Books   B174 - 70   2013   £850

Holland, Eric G. *Coniston Copper. A History.* Milnthorpe: Cicerone Press, 1987. First edition, illustrations, gilt, dust jacket, 104 illustrations, 312 pages.   R. F. G. Hollett & Son   Lake District and Cumbria - 276   2013   £40

Holland, Henry *Travels in the Ionian Seas, Albania, Thessaly, Macedonia, etc. During the Years 1813 and 1814.* London: Longman, Hurst, 1815. First edition, quarto, 12 plates, occasional foxing, contemporary half calf, corners and spine rubbed, split at head of spine.   J. & S. L. Bonham Antiquarian Booksellers   Europe - 8823   2013   £750

Holland, J. J. *The Bannow Farm School 1821-1827.* Dept. of Education, UCD, 1932. 8vo., 36 pages, frontispiece, wrappers, ex-library, very good.   C. P. Hyland   261 - 488   2013   £30

Holliday, J. S. *Rush for Riches, Gold Fever and the Making of California.* Oakland: Museum and University of California Press, 1999. First edition, quarto, profusely illustrated, brown cloth, gilt, very fine with pictorial dust jacket. Argonaut Book Shop   Summer 2013 - 161   2013 $75

Holliday, Robert Cortes *Broome Street Straws.* New York: Doran, 1919. First edition, slight sunning, near fine in very good, white dust jacket with some light foxing, couple of small chips at extremities and couple of faint stains on front panel.   Between the Covers Rare Books, Inc.   New York City - 40239   2013 $85

Holliday, Thomas *A Complete Treatise on Practical Land Surveying.* London: published by Whittaker and Co., 1838. First edition, 229 x 146mm., recent quite pleasing sympathetic quarter calf over contemporaneous paper boards, raised bands, red morocco label, numerous small illustrations and diagrams in text, 20 engraved plates, ownership inscription "Richard A. Knox July 1884", one leaf with few marginal manuscript calculations, isolated underscoring, lower corners bit rubbed, boards with few stains, upper corner of titlepage reinforced with fore edge of one leaf with neat paper repair, occasional minor soiling and isolated foxing, plates lightly offset onto adjacent leaves, otherwise very good internally, text well preserved and with no significant faults, in skillfully restored and attractive binding.   Phillip J. Pirages   63 - 457   2013 $375

Holling, Holling C. *Paddle to the Sea.* Boston: Houghton Mifflin, 1941. First edition, 4to., cloth, tiny edge stain on few pages, else very good in slightly worn dust jacket, illustrations in color.   Aleph-Bet Books, Inc.   105 - 323   2013 $450

Holm, John Cecil *Three Men on a Horse.* New York: Samuel French, 1935. First edition, slight foxing to titlepage, still easily fine in fine dust jacket with some infinitesimal tanning to spine, nice copy.   Between the Covers Rare Books, Inc.   Horses, Horsemanship, Horse Racing, Etc. - 46542   2013 $150

Holme, Constance *He-Who-Came?* London: Chapman & Hall, 1930. First edition, original cloth, gilt, 163 pages, fine, scarce.   R. F. G. Hollett & Son   Lake District and Cumbria - 277   2013   £45

Holmes, Kenneth *Child Art Grows Up.* Studio Publication, 1952. First edition, large 8vo., original red cloth, illustrations.   R. F. G. Hollett & Son   Children's Books - 293   2013   £25

Holmes, Kenneth L. *Covered Wagon Women: Diaries & Letters from the Western Trails.* Glendale: 1983-1993. 11 volumes, totaling 3108 pages, folding maps, fine.   Dumont Maps & Books of the West   124 - 68   2013 $3250

Holmes, Martin *Appleby Castle.* Appleby: Ferguson Industrial Holdings, 1974. Limited edition, number 75 of 250 copies, signed, large 8vo., original parchment backed cloth gilt, pictorial slipcase, illustrations, mostly in color, scarce.   R. F. G. Hollett & Son   Lake District and Cumbria - 278   2013   £120

Holmes, Martin *Proud Northern Lady. Lady Anne Clifford 1590-1676.* Phillimore, 1975. First edition, original cloth, gilt, dust jacket, 12 plates.   R. F. G. Hollett & Son   Lake District and Cumbria - 279   2013   £25

Holmes, Martin *Proud Northern Lady. Lady Anne Clifford 1590-1676.* Phillimore, 1984. Corrected edition, original cloth, gilt, dust jacket, 12 plates.   R. F. G. Hollett & Son   Lake District and Cumbria - 280   2013   £30

Holmes, Mary Jane *Christmas Stories.* New York: G. W. Carleton & Co., Publishers; London: S. Low, Son & Co., 1885. First edition, inserted frontispiece, original decorated brown cloth, front and rear panels stamped in blind, spine panel stamped in gold, buff endpapers.   L. W. Currey, Inc.   Christmas Themed Books - 139668   2013 $75

Holmes, Oliver Wendell 1841-1935 *The Common Law.* Boston: Little Brown and Co., 1881. First edition, octavo, original russet fine cross grain cloth with covers ruled in blind and spine ruled and lettered gilt, extremities lightly worn, spine with slightest bit darkened, bookseller's small stamp on front pastedown and early signature, very good in quarter morocco clamshell.   Heritage Book Shop   Holiday Catalogue 2012 - 78   2013 $1750

Holmes, Oliver Wendell 1841-1935 *The Common Law.* Boston: Little Brown and Co., University Press, John Wilson and Son, Cambridge, 1881. First edition, 8vo., original brick red cloth, slight soiling and very slight wear on lower spine, inner hinge touch tender, penciling in text, mostly at front, otherwise especially nice.   M & S Rare Books, Inc.   95 - 147   2013 $2250

Holmes, Thomas *Cotton Mather: a Bibliography of His Works.* Cambridge: Harvard University Press, 1940. First edition, limited to 500 copies, 3 volumes, 8vo., decorative red title border, illustrations, original quarter dark brown levant over lighter brown cloth, top edge gilt, gilt stamped spine by Harcourt Bindery, Boston, fine, Burndy bookplate, beautiful set, George Sarton's copy (and Harvard University's) bookplate and ownership signature.   Jeff Weber Rare Books   169 - 212   2013 $500

Holt, L. Emmett *The Care and Feeding of Children.* New York: D. Appleton and Co., 1894. First edition, square 16mo., 66 pages, plus ads, original cloth, occasional rubbing, owner's signature dated 1895.   M & S Rare Books, Inc.   95 - 148   2013 $650

The Holtz & Freystedt Co. Importers New York. New York: Holtz & Freystedt, n.d. circa, 1910. First edition, 12mo., wrappers, 80 pages, slight tears to yapped edges, some splitting along edge of spine and sticker shadow on front wrapper, very good.   Between the Covers Rare Books, Inc.   Cocktails, Etc. - 57508   2013 $85

Holtzman, Wayne H. *Holtman Inkblot Technique.* New York: Psychological Corporation, 1958. First edition, fine, colored ink blot cards inside near fine, age toned original publisher's cardstock box.   Between the Covers Rare Books, Inc.   Psychology & Psychiatry - 101553   2013 $250

Holway, John B. *Blackball Stars: Negro league Pioneers.* Westport: Meckler Books, 1988. First edition, boards quite bowed, thus good only, in torn and mildly chipped good plus dust jacket, inscribed by Bill (Ready) Cash for James.   Between the Covers Rare Books, Inc.   165 - 79   2013 $275

Holwell, John Zephaniah *Indian Tracts.* London: printed for T. Becket, 1774. 8vo., full contemporary tree calf, raised gilt banded spine, red morocco label, slight dustiness to outer edge of plate, otherwise very good, clean copy, armorial bookplate of Frankland, Bart, of Thirkleby, North Yorkshire.   Jarndyce Antiquarian Booksellers   CCIV - 161   2013   £380

Holzer, Max *Meditation in Kastilien.* St. Gallen: Erker Presse, 1968. First edition, number 70 of 125 exemplars (total edition of 145) signed by author and artist, 7 original lithographs by Eduardo Chillida, printed on Rives, 32 loose leaves in boards folder and matching slipcase, 4.5 x 39cm., new condition.   Gemini Fine Books & Arts., Ltd.   Art Reference & Illustrated Books - 2013 $3000

Home Book of Natural History. W. Kent & Co. (late D. Bogue), 1859. Small 8vo., original blindstamped cloth, gilt, little marked, spine frayed and chipped at head, 100 wood-cut illustrations.   R. F. G. Hollett & Son   Children's Books - 294   2013   £25

"Home Brewed" Wines and Beers and Bartenders' Guide. Secrets of the Liquor Trace. Racine: published by Johnson Smith & co., n.d. circa, 1930. Edition unknown, illustrated green wrappers, pages browned, pages 31-32 has crease and two short tears, near very good,.   Between the Covers Rare Books, Inc.   Cocktails, Etc. - 284291   2013 $75

Home for Aged Colored Women *Thirty Fourth Annual Report of the Directors of the Home for Aged Colored Women, No. 27 Myrtle Street for the Year 1893.* Boston: Barta Press, 1894. First edition, 12 pages, stapled self wrappers, ink number top of front wrapper, else fine.   Between the Covers Rare Books, Inc.   165 - 156   2013 $375

Home, Francis *Clinical Experiments, Histories and Dissections.* London: J. Murray 1682, i.e., 1782. Second edition, 8vo., toned, rear endleaves waterstained, later full grain calf, gilt stamped black leather spine label, binding worn, outer hinges cracked, white spine library number, mid spine missing small pieces, date incorrectly penned on titlepage as DCLXXXII 37 years before Home was born, inscription from "John Tetsworth(?) to Jonathan (Havesy(?), good. Jeff Weber Rare Books   172 - 141   2013 $650

Homerus *The Crowne of all Homers Workess; Batrachomyomachio; or the Battaile of Frogs and Misc. His Hymn's and Epigrams.* London: John Bill, 1624. First edition of this translation, quarto, engraved titlepage, numerous woodcut headpieces, full 18th century tan calf with gilt borders and corner devices on covers spine bands ruled in gilt, maroon morocco gilt label, gilt board edges and turn-ins, marbled endpapers, titlepage trimmed and mounted, worming to small part of upper rear joint, lower joint and along upper front board, some very light soiling and foxing to few leaves, overall very good. Heritage Book Shop 50th Anniversary Catalogue - 47 2013 $8500

Homerus *Batrachomyomachia Graece and Veterum Exemplarium Fiden Resusa.* London: William Boyer, 1721. 8vo., contemporary full red morocco, small 1 inch splits top of spine, minor wear at corners, gilt decorated borders and centerpieces, gilt decorated spine (bit darkened), leather label, copper engraved folding facsimile, all edges gilt, bookplates of collector Thomas Brooke and Rowland Thomas Baring, 2nd Earl of Cromer. Howard S. Mott Inc. 262 - 76 2013 $850

Homerus *Homeri Ilias (in Greek).* Venice: Aldus Manutius not before 31 October, 1504. First Aldine edition, second edition in Greek, small octavo, bound without final blank, title in Greek and Latin, text in Greek, Greek and Italic types, 30 lines plus headline, capital spaces with guide letters, 19th century vellum over boards, covers bordered with ink rule, smooth spine decoratively tooled in gilt with dark green morocco gilt lettering label turn-ins ruled in gilt, all edges gilt, marbled endpapers, lower blank corner of first leaf of Herodotus's life of Homer renewed, not affecting text, small intermittent dampstain in lower margin, armorial bookplate of George Becher Blomfield on front pastedown, pencilled annotations on verso of front free endpaper, early ink line numbers in outer margin of few leaves. Heritage Book Shop 50th Anniversary Catalogue - 48 2013 $20,000

Homerus *The Iliads of Homer Prince of Poets. (bound with) Homer's Odysses.* London: Nathanielle Butler, 1611. 1615? Rare first complete editions, folio in sixes, engraved titlepages to Iliads with slight early marginal restoration, of the four blank leaves, 2 are lacking, a1 and Ii8, also A2, etched title to Odysses, which was not found in all copies, with the memorial engraving to Prince Henry, without the unsigned sheet (two unsigned leaves inserted before blank Gg8) containing sonnets to Viscounts Cranbourne and Rochester and to Sir Edward Philips, which are usually lacking; contemporary full mottled sheepskin, raised bands, little scuffed and some wear to bottom of spine, still attractive and appropriately bound, scarce in contemporary binding, in Odysses, marginal repairs to first two leaves of dedication (A3 and A4), first leaf of text (B1); tear to Hh2, in Iliads, repair to verso of *3 and *4, repaired tear to H6 and Dd1 with loss of catchword on verso. Heritage Book Shop 50th Anniversary Catalogue - 49 2013 $27,500

Homerus *Homer His Iliads. (with) Homer His Odysses.* London: printed by Thomas Roycroft, 1660. 1665. First illustrated edition and first Ogilby translation of both titles, 2 volumes, folio, Illiad with 53 full page engravings including engraved frontispiece, Odysses with portrait or Ogilby and Ormond, frontispiece and 24 other full page engraved plates, both volumes with engraved head and tailpieces and engraved initials, both titlepages in red and black, both volumes in contemporary paneled, mottled calf, both rebacked with original spines, panels tooled in gilt, Iliad with gilt lettering on spine and gilt medallions in spine compartments, Odysses with gilt spine lettering and tooling, all edges speckled red, bit of rubbing to boards and edges, engraved plate between pages 262-263 with small closed tear bottom left corner of engraving, but with no loss, occasional very light foxing, few minor marginal dampstains, overall very good and internally clean and complete copy. Heritage Book Shop 50th Anniversary Catalogue - 50 2013 $11,000

Homerus *The Iliad of Homer.* London: printed for Henry Lintot, 1743. 6 volumes, engraved portrait bust, folding map, 28 plates, , volume II bound without A2 (blank?), 12mo., contemporary calf, raised and gilt banded spines, heads and tails of 3 volumes little chipped, lacking 4 labels, corners bumped, ownership name on inner front boards of P. Taubman, 1798. Jarndyce Antiquarian Booksellers CCIV - 162 2013 £160

Homerus *The Iliad (and) The Odyssey.* Nonesuch Press, 1931. 1188/1450 copies and 671/1500 copies respectively, on Pannekoek mouldmade paper, printed with J. van Krimpen's Greek Antigone type and monotype Cochin, decorative ornaments, used as headpieces to each section, designed by Rudolph Koch title and section titles printed in red, royal 8vo., original natural niger morocco, backstrips lightly faded, raised bands and gilt lettering in second compartments, double rule gilt border to sides, sides sported, brown marbled endpapers, top edge gilt, others untrimmed, board slipcase to Iliad, good. Blackwell's Rare Books B174 - 367 2013 £900

Homerus *The Odyssey of Homer.* London: printed for T. Osborne (and others), 1763. 3 volumes, 12mo., C2 volume II torn with loss, tear to lower corner of K6 volume III, full contemporary sprinkled calf, raised and gilt banded spines, ownership name of Francisco Chalmer, 19th century armorial bookplate and signature of Robert Chambre Vaughan, Esq. of Burlton Hall Co. Salop. Jarndyce Antiquarian Booksellers CCIV - 163 2013 £200

Homerus *Homeri Odyssea Cum Scholis Veteribus. Accedut Batrachomyomachia, Hymni, Fragmenta.* Oxonii: E Typographeo Clarendoniano, 1827. 228 x 138mm., 2 volumes, very attractive 19th century red pebble grain morocco, covers with multiple frames formed by plain and decorative gilt rules and Greek key roll as well as fleuron cornerpieces, raised bands, spine compartments with similar Greek key and gilt rule borders enclosing fleuron centerpiece, turn-ins gilt, marbled endpaper, all edges gilt, ink ownership inscription "W.M. Thackeray" dated "Arpil 1828", each titlepage with very small oval embossed stamp "W M T" at top, minimal foxing here and there, but especially fine, text very fresh, clean and bright, binding lustrous and virtuallly unworn. Phillip J. Pirages 63 - 464 2013 $3250

Homerus *The Odyssey of Homer.* Cambridge: Houghton Mifflin Co., Riverside Press, 1929. First edition thus, illustrated by N. C. Wyeth, 4to., quarter pigskin, green cloth, gilt stamp on front cover, leather label, 16 tipped in color plates, original tissue guards, uncut, with extra set of plates in original, lightly worn envelope, fine in original box which has been mended at some edges. Howard S. Mott Inc. 262 - 164 2013 $3000

Homerus *Opero (in Greek).* Florence: printer of Virgil C6061, probably Bartolommeo di Libri and Demetrius Damilas...9th December, 1488. but not before Jan. 1488/89 date of dedication. Editio princeps, 2 median folio volumes, unrubricated, early 19th century russia gilt, marbled endpapers and edges, volume II is about 15mm. shorter in its binding, bindings uniform height, inner margin of first leaf strengthened, slight worming at beginning of volume II, some foxing, from the collection of Dr. Charles Burney 1757-1817 whose collection was sold to British Museum (red library stamps), sold as duplicate in 1931 to Alice Millard; to Estelle Doheny. Heritage Book Shop 50th Anniversary Catalogue - 51 2013 $250,000

Homerus *(Opera). Illias cum Brevi Annotatione; Odyssea cum Scholiis Veteribus; Batrachomyomachia; Hymni; Fragmetna.* Oxford: Clarendon Press, 1834. 1827, 4 volumes, text in Greek with footnotes in Latin, occasional trivial spotting, but generally very clean, half vellum, marbled paper boards and endpaper, spines gilt with black and red morocco labels, edges red, slight evidence of removed library stickers to darkened spines, boards rubbed, still very good, armorial bookplate of Aston Walker to each front pastedown, various library tickets and stamps from London Borough of Southwark Metropolitan Special Collection to prelims of each volume, tiny bookseller tickets of W. Winkley, Harrow on the Hill. Unsworths Antiquarian Booksellers 28 - 15 2013 £200

Homes, Geoffrey *And Then There Were Three.* New York: Morrow, 1938. First edition, fine in very good dust jacket with light wear at spine ends, wear along folds and edges. Mordida Books 81 - 263 2013 $185

Homes, Geoffrey *No Hands on the Clock.* New York: Morrow, 1939. First edition, trifle worn, still fine in about near fine dust jacket (scarce) with few tiny chips, mild rubbing and little fading to spine. Between the Covers Rare Books, Inc. Mystery & Detective Fiction - 97537 2013 $1500

Homes, Nathanael *An Essay Concerning the Sabbath.* London: printed for the author, 1673. 12mo., erratic pagination but complete, prelim erratum leaf, tear to G7 without loss, full contemporary sheep, blind ruled borders, spine worn with loss, early signatures of Anne and Jane Watkins, and Katherine. Jarndyce Antiquarian Booksellers CCIV - 15 2013 £85

Hone, William *Conrad the Corsair; or the Pirate's Tale.* London: printed by and for William Hone Reformists' Register Office, 1817. Hone's adaptation, original buff printed wrappers bound into half dark blue crushed morocco, wrappers little dusted, generally well preserved, scarce, 16 pages. Jarndyce Antiquarian Booksellers CCIII - 188 2013 £250

Honorius of Autun *Elucidarius Dvalogicus Theologie Tripertitus: Infinitarum Questionum Resolutiouus.* Landshut: Johann Weyssenburger 20 June, 1514. Scarce edition, title printed in red, and blow in five vignettes, four within circles and altogether surrounded by a square frame, inner margin of first leaf strengthened, few minor spots and stains, 4to. in sixes, early 20th century calf backed buckram, spine faded, blindstamped of C. H. Radford, good. Blackwell's Rare Books 172 - 72 2013 £1500

Hood, Tom *The Knight and the Dragon.* London: Eyre and Spottiswoode, n.d. circa, 1870. 4to., original cloth backed pictorial bevelled boards, corners little worn, illustrations, printed throughout in red and black, new endpapers. R. F. G. Hollett & Son Children's Books - 295 2013 £45

Hooke, Nathaniel *The Roman History....* London: printed by James Bettenham etc., 1738-1771. 4 volumes, engraved frontispiece in each volume, 37 further plates across set (of which 20 are folding), titlepages of volumes i and ii in red and black, some minor spotting volume i bound without ad leaf mentioned i ESTC, 2 leaves in volume ii with closed vertical tears through a few lines of text (no loss), touch of minor worming in gutter of volume ii at end, 2 cancellanda leaves bound before final leaf of volume ii, the cancellans are in their correct place, 4to., contemporary mostly uniform sprinkled calf, spines with five raised bands between double gilt fillets, red morocco lettering pieces, central gilt tools in other compartments, joints cracked but strong, some spine ends worn, few marks to boards, good. Blackwell's Rare Books B174 - 71 2013 £800

Hooper, Robert *The Morbid Anatomy of the Human Brain.* London: printed for the author, 1828. Second edition, 65 pages, 15 hand colored engraved plates, small folio, quarter leather with later morocco rebacking of spine, endpaper renewed, some light toning of paper, else fine.   James Tait Goodrich   S74 - 150   2013 $5900

Hoopes, Penrose R. *Shop Records of Daniel Burna, Clockmaker.* N.P.: Connecticut Historical Society, 1958. Limited to 1000 copies, 265 x 180mm., brown cloth, printed paper cover label and gilt stamped black spine label, cloth very lightly rubbed, previous owner's bookplate and small mailing label, near fine.   Jeff Weber Rare Books   171 - 167   2013 $70

Hooykaas, R. *Fact, Faith and Fiction in the Development of Science: the Gifford Lectures Given in the University of St. Andrews, 1976.* Dordrecht: Boston & London: Kluwer Academic Pub., 1999. 8vo., xvi, 454 pages, navy cloth, gilt stamped spine title, dust jacket, fine.   Jeff Weber Rare Books   169 - 215   2013 $150

Hop O My Thumb. New York: McLoughlin Bros., n.d. circa, 1865. 12mo., pictorial wrappers highlighted in gold, mounted on linen, fine, 8 brightly colored half page illustrations, beautiful copy.   Aleph-Bet Books, Inc.   105 - 245   2013 $300

Hop O' My Thumb. London: Warne, circa, 1910. 4to., stiff pictorial wrappers, fine illustrations by H. M. Brock with 8 color plates printed on glossy paper plus black and whites, beautiful book.   Aleph-Bet Books, Inc.   105 - 92   2013 $325

Hope, Laurence *Five Songs of Laurence Hope.* New York: G. Ricordi & Co., 1915. First edition, quarto, ribbon tied stiff wrappers, faint crease on rear wrapper, else fine.   Between the Covers Rare Books, Inc.   165 - 171   2013 $225

Hope, W. H. St. J. *The Abbey of St. Mary in Furness, Lancashire.* Kendal: T. Wilson, 1902. 2 folding lithographed plans, 20 plates, contemporary half calf gilt, little rubbed, scarce.   R. F. G. Hollett & Son   Lake District and Cumbria - 281   2013   £120

Hopkins, John Henry *Essay on Gothic Architecture, with Various Plans and Drawings for Churches...* Burlington: Smith & Harrington, 1836. First edition, 4to., 13 lithographed plates plus extra lithographed titlepage, original cloth, printed paper label on spine, cloth wrinkled, occasional browning or stains to plates, very good.   M & S Rare Books, Inc.   95 - 11   2013 $1100

Hopkinson, John *Original Papers by the Late John Hopkinson.* Cambridge: Cambridge University Press, 1901. 2 volumes, 8vo., frontispiece, figures, original double ruled maroon cloth, gilt stamped spines, corners and spine ends faintly rubbed, half title, and f.f.e.p. rubber stamps, Dominion Observatory Ottawa Library bookplates very good+.   Jeff Weber Rare Books   169 - 218   2013 $175

Hopwood, John *The Toyland Convention.* Springfield: McLoughlin, 1928. 4to., cloth backed pictorial boards, some edge and tip wear, else very good and clean, full and partial page vibrant color illustrations.   Aleph-Bet Books, Inc.   105 - 238   2013 $225

Horatius Flaccus, Quintus *Carmina Sapphica.* Ashendene Press, 1903. One of 175 copies, printed on Japanese paper, fly-titles and colophons printed in red, large initial letter to each Ode drawn in by Graily Hewitt in blue or red, with large capital "I" to first ode drawn in gold, 16mo., original limp cream vellum, backstrip gilt lettered, rough trimmed, near fine.   Blackwell's Rare Books   B174 - 320   2013   £850

Horatius Flaccus, Quintus *Carmina Sapphica.* Boston: Anne & David Bromer, 1983. Limited to 150 copies, printed by Linnea Gentry using original plates of Ashendene Press edition from 1923, c.5 x 2.6 cm., full morocco with gilt fillets, two raised bands, inserted in tray in larger cloth case with leather spine, which also holds prospectus, in specially made slipcase holding the miniature book, miniature bookplate of Kathryn rickard, binding by David Bourbeau, from the collection of Donn W. Sanford.   Oak Knoll Books   303 - 71   2013 $450

Horatius Flaccus, Quintus *Carminum Libri IV. (The Odes of Horace).* printed at the Curwen Press for Davies, 1926. One of 500 copies, title vignette and numerous color printed vignettes by Vera Willoughby, browning in part to the initial and final pages, crown 8vo., original maroon cloth, backstrip and front cover with overall gilt design and lettering, endpapers foxed, untrimmed and unopened, gold dust jacket, near fine.   Blackwell's Rare Books   B174 - 354   2013   £70

Horatius Flaccus, Quintus *Q. Horatius Flaccus ex Recensione & cum Notis Atque.* Amstelaedami: apud Rd. & Gerh. Wetstenios, 1713. 4to., very good, full contemporary panelled calf, raised bands and remnants of contemporary paper label to spine, small tear without loss to engraved titlepage.   Ken Spelman Books Ltd.   75 - 14   2013   £295

Horatius Flaccus, Quintus *Satires, Epistles and Art of Poetry.* London: printed for Joseph Davidson, 1743. 8vo., lacking imprimatur leaf, titlepage in red and black, small loss to margin of page 347 not affecting text and small tear near gutter of penultimate leaf, servicably recased in modern parchment with part of original label to spine, edges colored red, little grubby, spine slightly darkened, top edge dusty, code in pink pencil to front pastedown, clean internally and still very good. Unsworths Antiquarian Booksellers 28 - 17 2013 £75

Horatius Flaccus, Quintus *Venusini Poetae Lyrici Poemata Omnia Quibus Respondet Index Th. Treteri Nuper Excusus.* Antverpiae: ex officina Christophori Plantini, 1576. Early 19th century gilt ruled calf, gilt banded spine with repeat gilt flower head device, hinges cracked but firm, head of spine slightly chipped, expert repair to lower outer tips of C8 ad n1, some occasional slight foxing, bound without final blank t4 to first part, armorial bookplate of Sir John Trollope. Jarndyce Antiquarian Booksellers CCIV - 16 2013 £280

Horatius Flaccus, Quintus *Opera cum Quilbusdam Annotationibus (of Jacob Locher).* Strassburg: Johann (Reinhard) Gruninger (misspelled Gurninger) 12 March, 1498. First illustrated edition of Horace and first edition printed in Germany, Gothic and Roman types, 3 columns, 74 lines of commentary on either side of text, 168 woodcut illustrations in various combinations, including some repeats, capital spaces with guide letters, initials supplied in red and blue, woodcut printer's device, 18th century paste paper over pasteboard, spine lettered in manuscript, few leaves slightly browned, slight dampstaining in upper corner toward end, some minor marginal loss, short tear to folio LXXXIX, affecting foliation and just entering woodcut on recto and just touching two letters on verso, short marginal tear to folio CLXIX, not affecting text early paper repairs to blank verso of final leaf, occasional early ink marginalia, early ink drawing in margin of folio CXXXI verso, early ink inscription crossed out on folio CXXXII verso, early ink calculations in folio (C)XLIX verso and folio (C)L, early ink ownership inscription at foot of title and ink inscription dated 1498 at head of title, leather bookplate of Eduard J. Bullrich, early ink annotations on front free endpaper, overall excellent copy, housed in black cloth clamshell case. Heritage Book Shop 50th Anniversary Catalogue - 52 2013 $60,000

Horatius Flaccus, Quintus *(Opera) ex recensione & cum Notis Atque Emendationibus Richardi Bentleii.* Cambridge: 1711. First Bentley edition, 4to., engraved half title, engraved frontispiece, one gathering with substantial dampmark in lower corner, and last 50 leaves with marginal dampstain at top, otherwise quite clean, later sprinkled calf, boards bordered with decorative gilt roll, sometime skilfully rebacked preserving original spine, in six compartments with raised bands, red morocco label to second, rest with gilt tooling, boards slightly darkened at fore edges, armorial bookplate and motto "Ducii Amor Patriae". Unsworths Antiquarian Booksellers 28 - 16 2013 £650

Horatius Flaccus, Quintus *Opera.* London: Gulielmus Pickering, 1824. Large paper copy, 32mo., pages 192 + 1 portrait frontispiece, 1 engraved plate, very light occasional foxing, still nice and bright, contemporary red morocco by Joubert, gilt title to spine, gilt dentelles, bright blue morocco doublures, top edge gilt, joints and corners little worn, small split starting at head of lower board, slight discoloration to free endpapers from leather joints, illegible inscription to f.f.e.p. verso, bookseller's pencilled notes to rear. Unsworths Antiquarian Booksellers 28 - 18 2013 £275

Horgan, Paul *Great River: the Rio Grande in North American History.* New York: Rinehart, 1954. First edition, 2 volumes, one of 1000 numbered, specially bound copies signed by author, 2 volumes, 20 reproductions of watercolors by Horgan, rough beige cloth in original publisher's cardboard slipcase with large label, issued without jackets, top edge gilt, near fine. Ed Smith Books 75 - 34 2013 $250

Horgan, Paul *Lamy of Santa Fe. His Life and Times.* New York: Farrar, Straus & Giroux, 1973. First edition, large paper limited edition of 490 copies, signed by author, this number 12, tall 8vo., 20 black and white plates, 12 beautifully colored plates, cloth backed boards, top edge gilt, couple of light age spots on titlepage, otherwise fine in publisher's box, presentation from Hogan for Leon Edel. Second Life Books Inc. 183 - 172 2013 $275

Horizon. A Review of Literature & Art. Volume I No. 1. London: published by the Proprietors, 1940. First edition, 8vo., original brown wrappers, stained on corner of lower cover, otherwise excellent copy in protective folding box, inscribed by Cyril Connolly for Noel Blakiston. Maggs Bros. Ltd. 1460 - 180 2013 £600

Horler, Sydney *The Man Who Walked with Death.* New York: Knopf, 1931. First American edition, endpapers foxed with small spot on bottom edge, else fine in attractive, near fine dust jacket lightly faded on spine with little rubbing. Between the Covers Rare Books, Inc. Mystery & Detective Fiction - 30282 2013 $157

Hornby, Charles Harry St. John *A Descriptive Bibliography of the Books Printed at the Ashendene Press.* Chelsea: Shelley House, 1935. Limited to 390 numbered copies, this #186 printed on special paper made by Joseph Batchelor & sons, 4to., beautiful plates and woodcuts, some initial letters filled by hand by Graily Hewitt, errata slip tipped in, original gilt stamped maroon calf, five raised bands, spine bands, spine professionally rebacked to imitate original corners faintly rubbed, signed by printer Charles Harry St. John Hornby in ink at limitation page, prospectus for later printing laid in, bookplate of Norman J. Sondheim, near fine, gorgeous copy. Jeff Weber Rare Books 171 - 9 2013 $2850

Hornby, Nick *Contemporary American Fiction.* London: New York: Vision Press/St. Martin's Press, 1992. First edition, signed by author, fine in fine dust jacket. Ed Smith Books 78 - 29 2013 $275

Horne, George *A Fair, Candid and Impartial State of the Case Between Sir Isaac Newton and Mr. Hutchinson.* London: G. G. and G. Robinson, F. and C. Rivington and I. Hathard, 1799. Second edition, 8vo., near fine, modern full brown leather with gilt lettering to spine and new endpapers, mild scattered foxing. By the Book, L. C. 38 - 52 2013 $650

Horne, Thomas Hartwell *The Lakes of Lancashire, Westmorland and Cumberland...* London: printed for T. Cadell and W. Davies, 1816. First edition, folio, modern half calf gilt, double page extending map and 43 fine tissue guarded engraved plates, scattered foxing, mainly to plate margins, otherwise very nice, sound and clean. R. F. G. Hollett & Son Lake District and Cumbria - 76 2013 £1250

Hornsby, Henry *The Trey of Sevens.* Dallas: Mathis, Van Nott & Co., 1946. First edition, printed grey cloth, photographs, map endpapers, rubbing and beginning of fraying to edges of boards, corners little bumped, near very good, nicely inscribed by author, rare. Between the Covers Rare Books, Inc. 165 - 292 2013 $600

Hornung, Paul *Football and the Single Man: a Candid Autobiography.* Garden City: Doubleday, 1965. First edition, fine in fine dust jacket, lovely copy. Between the Covers Rare Books, Inc. Football Books - 94581 2013 $100

Horsfall, John *The Wild Geese are Flighting.* Kineton: Roundwood Press, 1976. First edition, tall 8vo., original buckram, gilt, dust jacket, colored extending frontispiece, 12 plates, 3 maps, signed copy. R. F. G. Hollett & Son Africana - 90 2013 £65

Horsley, Victor *The Structure and Function of the Brain and Spinal Cord.* London: 1892. vi, 223 pages, illustrations, original cloth, library spine label and no other markings, otherwise very good, clean, tight copy. James Tait Goodrich S74 - 151 2013 $495

Hort, Richard *The Embroidered Banner and Other Marvels.* London: Johna and Daniel A. Darling, 1850. First edition, color frontispiece and plates by Alfred Ashley, 8 pages catalog on smaller paper, 4 pages ads, original olive green cloth by Josiah Westley, gilt centerpiece "Libertad", spine decorated and lettered in gilt, signed JL (designed by John Leighton) some watermarking on front board. Jarndyce Antiquarian Booksellers CCV - 138 2013 £150

Hosmer, James K. *History of the Expedition of Captains Lewis and Clark 1804-5-6.* Chicago: A. C. McClurg, 1902. Reprint of 1814 edition, 2 volumes, portraits, maps, 8vo., frontispiece, plates, maps, index, some pages unopened, quarter brown cloth over tan cloth sides, gilt stamped spine, top edge gilt, inner hinges neatly reinforced, short tear to joint mend, Burndy bookplates, very good. Jeff Weber Rare Books 169 - 216 2013 $80

Hotaling, Edward *The Great Black Jockeys.* Rocklin: CA Forum/Primo Pub., 1999. First edition, fine in fine dust jacket, 8vo., 380 pages. Beasley Books 2013 - 2013 $100

Houblon, Alice Archer *The Houblon Family, Its Story and Times.* London: Archibald Constable and Co., 1907. 2 volumes, large 8vo, very good in bright original green gilt lettered cloth, very good dust jackets, one just little worn, some foxing to edges of book block. Ken Spelman Books Ltd. 75 - 161 2013 £45

Hough, Charles Henry *A Westmorland Rock Garden.* Ambleside: Frederic Middleton, 1934. Second edition, original cloth backed boards, 40 pages, uncut, 16 plates. R. F. G. Hollett & Son Lake District and Cumbria - 284 2013 £25

Hough, Charles Henry *A Westmorland Rock Garden.* Ambleside: George Middleton, 1929. First edition, original cloth backed boards, 41 pages, uncut, 16 plates. R. F. G. Hollett & Son Lake District and Cumbria - 283 2013 £25

Hough, Franklin B. *The Thousand Islands of the Saint Lawrence.* Syracuse: Davis, Bardeen & Co., 1880. First edition, small octavo, yellow pictorial cloth stamped in black and gilt, LOC duplicate stamp on titlepage, boards little soiled, nice, near fine. Between the Covers Rare Books, Inc. New York City - 284961 2013 $450

Houghton Mifflin & Company *A Catalogue of Authors Whose Works are Published by...* Boston: New York and Chicago: Houghton Mifflin, 1899. First edition, 8vo., 205 pages, cloth backed boards with paper label, illustrations, very good, clean. Second Life Books Inc. 183 - 173 2013 $85

Houghton, Claude *This Was Ivor Trent.* London: Heinemann, 1935. First edition, inscribed by author, fine in very good dust jacket with chips at top of spine and at corners and several short closed tears, Book Society wraparound intact. Mordida Books 81 - 265 2013 $150

Houghton, Claude *Three Fantastic Tales.* London: Frederick C. Joiner, 1934. Limited edition, one of 275 numbered copies signed by author, fine, without dust jacket as issued, frontispiece by John Farleigh. Mordida Books 81 - 254 2013 $125

Houghton, Frederick W. *The Story of the Settle-Carlisle Line.* Bradford: Norman Arch Publications, 1948. First edition, original cloth backed boards, 41 photo illustrations and extending section.   R. F. G. Hollett & Son   Lake District and Cumbria - 285   2013   £65

Houghton, Frederick W. *The Story of the Settle-Carlisle Line.* Huddersfield: Advertiser Press, 1965. Second edition, original cloth, gilt, dust jacket, 40 photographic illustrations and folding section, front flyleaf removed, pastedowns little marked, shelf numbers inked on back of title.   R. F. G. Hollett & Son   Lake District and Cumbria - 287   2013   £40

Houghton, William *British Fresh-Water Fishes.* London: William MacKenzie, 1879. First edition, large 4to., 41 colored full page chromolithographs, 64 engraved vignettes, red and black titlepage, top edge gilt, modern dark brown quarter morocco over original cloth boards, raised bands, gilt stamped spine title, bookplate of James Jones, rare, fine.   Jeff Weber Rare Books   171 - 171   2013 $2200

Houlgate, Deke *The Football Thesaurus: 77 Years on the American Gridiron.* Los Angeles: Nash-U-Nal Pub. Co., 1946. First edition, copy 1858 of unspecified edition, oblong folio, plastic spiral bound boards, very good, extensive annotation in text and on endpapers.   Between the Covers Rare Books, Inc.   Football Books - 76975   2013 $175

House that Jack Built to Which is Added Some Account of Jack Jingle... York: printed by J. Kendrew, circa, 1820. 24mo., pictorial wrappers, 23 pages, fine, woodcuts on each page.   Aleph-Bet Books, Inc.   105 - 327   2013 $275

House, Gordon *London Bridges.* London: Kelpra Studio, 1985. Artist's proofs, number III of V copies, 8 colored etchings from shaped copper plates, contained within blocked portfolio with etched titlepage.   Marlborough Rare Books Ltd.   218 - 82   2013   £1250

Household, Geoffrey *Rogue Male.* Boston: Little Brown and Co., 1939. First American edition, small new bookstore label on front pastedown, else fine in very attractive, near fine, price clipped dust jacket with small nicks at spine ends.   Between the Covers Rare Books, Inc.   Mystery & Detective Fiction - 322145   2013 $1250

Housman, John *A Descriptive Tour and Guide to the Lakes, Caves, Mountains and Other Natural Curiosities...* Carlisle: printed by F. Jollie for C. Law, 1800. First edition, modern quarter calf gilt, marbled boards, frontispiece, large folding map, 2 extending sheets of maps, margins of frontispiece and title foxed, title repaired at fore-edge, faint library stamp to back of one folding map, large map, little weak in folds, otherwise excellent.   R. F. G. Hollett & Son   Lake District and Cumbria - 288   2013   £350

Housman, John *A Descriptive Tour and Guide to the Lakes, Caves, Mountains and Other Natural Curiosities...* Carlisle: F. Jollie, 1812. Fifth edition, original printed boards, little worn and bumped, 4 engraved maps and 6 plates, several folding, large folding hand colored general map, excellent copy.   R. F. G. Hollett & Son   Lake District and Cumbria - 289   2013   £225

Housman, John *A Descriptive Tour and Guide to the Lakes, Caves, Mountains and Other Natural Curiosities...* Carlisle: F. Jollie, 1814. Sixth edition, old full scarlet polished roan, gilt, sometime neatly recased, folding general map, folding plan, 2 folding sheets of plans, 6 folding engraved plates, very nice, uncut.   R. F. G. Hollett & Son   Lake District and Cumbria - 290   2013   £275

Housman, Laurence   1865-1959 *Green Arras.* London: John Lane, 1896. First edition, frontispiece, titlepage illustration and 5 plates by Housman, lovely with Housman's signature gilt Art Nouveau cover design on green cloth, minor creasing to spine ends, otherwise very good, interior pages slightly age toned but clean, 90 pages plus 16 pages ads.   The Kelmscott Bookshop   7 - 75   2013 $200

Housman, Laurence   1865-1959 *Princess Badoura: a Tale from the Arabian Nights.* London: Hodder & Stoughton, n.d., 1913. First edition, 4to., white cloth with elaborate pictorial stamping in blue and gold, slight bit of cover soil, else fine, illustrations by Edmund Dulac with cover design plus 10 magnificent tipped in color plates with pictorial guards.   Aleph-Bet Books, Inc.   105 - 207   2013 $700

Housman, Laurence   1865-1959 *Stories from the Arabian Nights Retold by...* London: Hodder & Stoughton, 1907. First edition, limited to only 350 numbered copies, signed by artist, 50 tipped in color plates by Edmund Dulac, thick 4to., gilt pictorial vellum, top edge gilt, few very small areas of soil, else near fine with new ties and none of the usual warping, nice, very scarce.   Aleph-Bet Books, Inc.   105 - 205   2013 $4250

Houtain, George Julian *Home Brew. Volume I Number 5, June 1922.* Brooklyn: E. D Houtain,, 1922. Small octavo, pictorial wrappers, stapled.   L. W. Currey, Inc.   Fall Sampler Sept. 2013 - 146574   2013 $1650

Houtain, George Julian *Home Brew. Volume I number 3 April 1922.* Brooklyn: E. D. Houtain, April, 1922. Small octavo, single issue, pictorial wrappers, stapled.   L. W. Currey, Inc.   Fall Sampler Sept. 2013 - 146573   2013 $1500

How, William *Phytologia Britannica Natales Exhibens Indigenarum Stirpium Sponte Emergentium.* Richard Cotes for Octavian Pulleyn, 1650. First (only) edition, woodcut device on title, without initial leaf (blank except for signature A on recto), text printed in mixture of Roman, Italic and Black letter, 4 leaves with small holes affecting few letters (apparently not worming), small 8vo., contemporary calf, rebacked, corners worn, crackling of covers, contemporary signature at head of title of Edward Heaston, later indecipherable library stamp in outer margin of title, sound. Blackwell's Rare Books   Sciences - 61   2013   £950

Howard, Alice *Ching-Li and the Dragons.* New York: Macmillan, 1931. First edition, 4to., blue cloth slightly faded, else very good+ in dust jacket with half inch chip off top of spine, full page color lithographs by Lyn Ward. Aleph-Bet Books, Inc.   105 - 584   2013 $225

Howard, Ankaret *The Quarryman.* London: Secker & Warburg, 1936. First edition, original cloth, dust jacket, rather dusty and chipped but neatly repaired on reverse. R. F. G. Hollett & Son   Lake District and Cumbria - 291   2013   £75

Howard, J. H. W. *Bond and Free a True Tale of Slave Times.* Harrisburg: Edwin K. Meyers, 1886. First edition, 12mo., 280 pages, frontispiece, original cloth, some spotting, spine darkened.   M & S Rare Books, Inc.   95 - 151   2013 $950

Howard, O. O. *My Life and Experiences Among Our Hostile Indians.* Hartford: 1907. First edition, 570 pages, 10 chromolithographic plates plus numerous black and white illustrations, original blue cloth, bookplate on front pastedown, extremities lightly rubbed, else remarkably nice, bright, near fine.   Dumont Maps & Books of the West   122 - 69   2013 $250

Howard, Robert Ervin *Skull-Face and Others.* Sauk City: Arkham House, 1946. First edition, large octavo, cloth. L. W. Currey, Inc.   Fall Sampler Sept. 2013 - 144827   2013 $1500

Howard, Robert Ervin *The Sword of Conan.* New York: Gnome Press Inc., 1952. First edition, octavo, cloth.   L. W. Currey, Inc.   Fall Sampler Sept. 2013 - 146546   2013 $850

Howard, Sidney *Yellow Jack, a History by...* New York: Harcourt Brace, 1933. First edition, 8vo., 152 pages, full brown morocco by Brentanos, spine gilt in compartments, initials "G. McC" on first board, little scuffing, near fine, this copy was presented by author to director Guthrie McClintic and bears affectionate presentation for Howard and DeKruif.   Second Life Books Inc.   183 - 174   2013 $375

Howells, John Mead *The Architectural Heritage of the Piscataqua...* N.P.: Architectural Book Pub. Co., 1965. First edition, 4to., 300 illustrations, bookplate, very good, tight copy, dust jacket.   Second Life Books Inc.   183 - 175   2013 $85

Howes, Royce *Death on the Bridge.* Garden City: Doubleday Crime Club, 1935. First edition, scrape on spine, otherwise fine in near fine dust jacket with scrape on front panel and long narrow stain on front panel.   Mordida Books   81 - 266   2013 $250

Howitt, Mary *Hope On, Hope Ever!* London: Simpkin, Marshall, etc. and Sedberg: Jackson & son, 1910. Second edition, original green cloth gilt, uncut, frontispiece, piece cut from flyleaf.   R. F. G. Hollett & Son   Lake District and Cumbria - 293   2013   £45

Howitt, Mary *Hope On, Hope Ever!* Dent: Dales Historical Monographs, 1988. Signed limited edition, no. 2 of 50 copies), half green levant morocco, gilt, 2 illustrations. R. F. G. Hollett & Son   Lake District and Cumbria - 292   2013   £45

Howker, Janni *Martin Farrell.* Julia MacRae Book, 1994. First edition, original boards, gilt, dust jacket, 86 pages, presentation copy inscribed.   R. F. G. Hollett & Son Children's Books - 299   2013   £40

Howson, William *An Illustrated Guide to the Curiosities of Craven.* London: Whittaker & Co., Wildman, Settle, 1850. 134 pages, frontispiece, 4 plates, folding map and woodcuts in text, very good, original blindstamped and gilt lettered cloth, all edges gilt, slight wear to head of spine, scarce. Ken Spelman Books Ltd.   73 - 68   2013   £100

Hoyle, Edmund *The Polite Gamester.* Dublin: printed by James Hoey, 1786. 12mo., slight browning, few corners little creased, full contemporary calf, raised bands, red morocco label of Marquess of Headfort, nice.   Jarndyce Antiquarian Booksellers   CCIV - 164   2013   £320

Hoys, Dudley *English Lake Country.* London: Batsford, 1969. First edition, original cloth, gilt, dust jacket, 224 pages, with 31 plates.   R. F. G. Hollett & Son   Lake District and Cumbria - 295   2013   £25

Hriagain, Mairi Ni *Sean-eion.* Dublin: 1938. First edition, square 8vo., original quarter red cloth, green boards, dust jacket, five tipped in plates in color by Yeats, seven others in black and white, excellent copy in worn dust jacket. Maggs Bros. Ltd.   1442 - 332   2013   £500

Hubbard, Elbert *A Message to Garcia.* East Aurora: 1899. First edition, number 405 of 925 copies signed by author, 8vo., original limp suede, and with titlepage hand illuminated with floral border in blue, green, orange and gold, first page of text with illuminated initial letter, fine in morocco backed cloth slipcase.   Howard S. Mott Inc.   262 - 126   2013 $250

Hubbard, L. Ron *Final Blackout.* Providence: Hadley Pub., 1948. First edition, fine in age toned, else near fine dust jacket with little rubbing, nice.   Between the Covers Rare Books, Inc.   Sci-Fi, Fantasy & Horror - 95070   2013 $400

Hubbard, L. Ron *Slaves of Sleep.* Chicago: 1948. First edition, one of 250 subscriber copies signed by author, signed by author, original grey cloth over boards, spine lettered gilt, original pictorial dust jacket lightly browned along edges and spine, fine, in about fine dust jacket, not price clipped, from the library of collector, Jack Cordes.   Heritage Book Shop   Holiday Catalogue 2012 - 79   2013 $2500

Hubert, Francis *The Life of Edward II. With the Fates of Gavestone and the Spencers.* London: printed for Tho. Harbin, 1721. Engraved frontispiece, titlepage printed in red and black, 12mo., outer leaves little dusted, later marbled paper wrappers, ownership signature of Geoffrey Tillotson, 1942.   Jarndyce Antiquarian Booksellers   CCIV - 165   2013   £120

Hubert, J. *Europe of the Invasions.* New York: Braziller, 1969. First edition, 4to., fine in fine dust jacket.   Beasley Books   2013 - 2013 $50

Huchon, Rene *George Crabbe and His Times 1754-1832.* London: John Murray, 1907. First English edition, half title, frontispiece, facsimiles, occasional notes in text, original brick red cloth, black leather label rubbed to brown, good plus.   Jarndyce Antiquarian Booksellers   CCIII - 627   2013   £25

Huckell, John *Avon, a Poem in three parts.* Birmingham: printed by John Baskerville and sold by R. and J. Dodsley in Pall Mall, 1758. First edition, 78 pages, 4to., leading edge of titlepage rather short perhaps due to wear to inner margin and page inset when rebound, final leaf dusted and marked, repair along leading edge, contemporary marbled boards, simply rebacked, contemporary signature of E. Baker, several contemporary corrections in text.   Jarndyce Antiquarian Booksellers   CCIV - 166   2013   £280

Huddart, Joseph *Memoir of the Late Captain Joseph Huddart, F. R. S. etc.*   printed for private circulation, W. Phillips, 1821. Very scarce, 4to., old half calf gilt, raised bands and Spanish marbled boards, edges little rubbed, spine defective, lithographed portrait (corner waterstained), woodcut vignette on title, extending engraved plates.   R. F. G. Hollett & Son   Lake District and Cumbria - 297   2013   £250

Hudleston, C. Roy *An Armorial for Westmorland and Lonsdale.* Kendal: Titus Wilson, 1975. Signed, limited deluxe edition, no. 30 of 35 copies, original full crimson calf gilt, arms gilt on boards, frontispiece, 4 plates, 5 pages of arms, Whittington Hall copy with bookplate of Brian and Enid Greenwood.   R. F. G. Hollett & Son   Lake District and Cumbria - 301   2013   £150

Hudleston, C. Roy *Cumberland Families and Heraldry with a Supplement to an Armorial for Westmorland and Lonsdale.* Kendal: Titus Wilson, 1978. Limited deluxe edition, no. 13 of 50 copies, original full crimson calf gilt, arms in gilt on boards, frontispiece and 5 pages of illustrations, Whittington Hall copy with bookplate of Brian and Enid Greenwood.   R. F. G. Hollett & Son   Lake District and Cumbria - 300   2013   £150

Hudleston, C. Roy *Howard Family Documents.* Durham: The University, 1968-1970. 3 volumes, folio, unbound, side sewn as issued, pages 219; 216; 125, cyclostyled on each recto.   R. F. G. Hollett & Son   Lake District and Cumbria - 298   2013   £180

Hudleston, C. Roy *Naworth Estate and Household Account 1648-1660.* Durham: Andrews & Co., 1958. Original green cloth, gilt, pages i-vi not present as is correct.   R. F. G. Hollett & Son   Lake District and Cumbria - 302   2013   £65

Hudleston, F. *Penrith Castle.* Kendal: Titus Wilson, 1930. Original wrappers, pages 13-26, 3 plates, 2 plans, presentation copy.   R. F. G. Hollett & Son   Lake District and Cumbria - 303   2013   £35

Hudleston, F. *A Short Description of Hutton John.* 1923. Original ribbed cloth, gilt, plan and photographic illustrations, presentation copy.   R. F. G. Hollett & Son   Lake District and Cumbria - 304   2013   £40

Hudleston, F. *A Short Description of Hutton John.* Kendal: Titus Wilson, 1923. Original wrappers, pages 19, plan and photographic illustrations, signed.   R. F. G. Hollett & Son   Lake District and Cumbria - 305   2013   £30

Hudson's Bay Company *Minutes of the Hudson's Bay Company 1671-1674 and 1679-1684.* London: Hudson's Bay Record Society, 1942. 1945. 1946. First edition, 3 volumes, frontispiece, blue cloth, gilt, slight bumping to corners, fine set, mostly uncut.   Argonaut Book Shop   Summer 2013 - 163   2013 $325

Hudson-Fulton Celebration Commission *The Fourth Annual Report of the Hudson-Fulton Celebration Commission to the Legislature of the State of New York.* Albany: J. B. Lyon Co., 1910. 2 volumes, thick quarto, illustrated green cloth, 1172 pages, hundreds of illustrations, folding ship plans in pocket, 2 bookplates, some rubbing and faint stains along edges of spines, hinges little tender, light dampstain bottom margin of some leaves in volume 2, about very good set. Between the Covers Rare Books, Inc. New York City - 304290 2013 $85

Hudson, Alma *Peter Rabbit and the Fairies.* New York: Cupples & Leon, 1921. First edition, 8 color illustrations and many black and white text illustrations by Richard Hudson, red boards, color illustrated onlay to front cover, light foxing to prelims, very nice, bright copy in original pictorial dust jacket (lightly foxed and soiled). Ian Hodgkins & Co. Ltd. 134 - 49 2013 £65

Hudson, Alma *Peter Rabbit and the Fairies. Peter Rabbit in Mother Goose Land and Peter Rabbit at the Circus.* New York: Cupples & Leon, 1921. First edition, 3 books, illustrations by Richard Hudson, each 48 pages with 8 color illustrations and many black and white text illustrations, light red boards with color illustrated onlay top front covers, together with 6 inch celluloid figure Toy Rattle of Peter Rabbit, backstrip volume 1 little faded with area of surface rubbing to paper on dedication page of same volume, small nick repaired at fore-edge of another volume, thumbing contents, nice set. Ian Hodgkins & Co. Ltd. 134 - 51 2013 £185

Hudson, Alma *Peter Rabbit at the Circus.* New York: Cupples and Leon, 1921. First edition, 8 color illustrations and many black and white text illustrations by Richard Hudson, 48 pages, light red boards with color illustrated onlay to front cover, slight odd mark to contents, very good in slightly soiled dust jacket with few tears. Ian Hodgkins & Co. Ltd. 134 - 50 2013 £65

Hudson, Alma *Peter Rabbit in Mother Goose Land.* New York: Cupples & Leon, 1921. First edition, illustrations by Richard Hudson with 8 color illustrations and many text illustrations, light red boards with color illustrated onlay top front cover, dark red titling to cover and backstrip, very good in slightly soiled dust jacket. Ian Hodgkins & Co. Ltd. 134 - 52 2013 £65

Hudson, Ernest *Barton Records.* Penrith: St. Andrew's Press, 1951. First edition, original cloth, gilt trifle rubbed, 79 pages, illustrations, relevant cuttings on endpapers, presentation copy inscribed by author April 1951 for J. M. Schmidt. R. F. G. Hollett & Son Lake District and Cumbria - 306 2013 £25

Hudson, Gossie Harold *Directory of Black Historians, Ph.D.'s and Others 1975-1976: Essays and Commentaries.* Monticello: Council of Planning Librarians Exchange Bibliographies, 1976. First edition, spiral bound thick quarto, 384 pages, front wrapper lacking, dampstain largely confined to fore edge, some ink notation in text, good only. Between the Covers Rare Books, Inc. 165 - 172 2013 $250

Hudson, John *A Complete Guide to the English Lakes...* London: Longman and Co. and Whittaker and Co. and Kendal: J. Hudson, 1846. Third edition, original blindstamped green cloth, gilt, leather spine label (recased), engraved frontispiece, 4 pages of mountain outlines, 1 plan and diagram, large folding linen backed map, yellow ad sheet tipped to flyleaf. R. F. G. Hollett & Son Lake District and Cumbria - 307 2013 £350

Hudson, John *Sketches of Grange and Neighbourhood.* Kendal: printed by John Hudson, 1850. First edition, small 8vo., original green blindstamped cloth gilt, spine rather faded, 5 tinted lithographic plates, trifle shaken, very scarce. R. F. G. Hollett & Son Lake District and Cumbria - 308 2013 £85

Hudson, Noel *An Early English Version of Hortus Sanitatis, a Recent Bibliographical Discovery.* London: Bernard Quaritch, 1954. limited edition facsimile, one of 550 copies only, 4to, illustrations, gilt stamped cranberry cloth, dust jacket, corners slightly bumped, jacket worn, Burndy bookplate, fine otherwise, rare. Jeff Weber Rare Books 171 - 173 2013 $125

Hudson, Roger *Coleridge Among the Lakes and Mountains.* London: Folio Society, 1991. First edition, original pictorial cloth gilt, 265 pages, numerous color illustrations and 4 maps. R. F. G. Hollett & Son Lake District and Cumbria - 309 2013 £25

Hudson, William *Flora Anglica, Exhibens Platnas per Regnum Angliae Sponte Crescentes, Distributas Secundum Systema Sexuale...* printed for the author and sold by J. Nourse and C. Moran, 1762. First edition, 8vo., contemporary calf, spine gilt with rules on either side of raised bands red lettering piece, little rubbed and scuffed, headcap defective, good. Blackwell's Rare Books 172 - 74 2013 £600

Hudson, William *Flora Anglica...* printed for the author and sold by J. Nourse, 1778. Fragment of fore-edge torn off Aa4 with loss of one letter to a side note, little worming in lower margin volume i, 2 clean tears in Xx1 in volume ii, probably paper flaws, 8vo., contemporary speckled calf, red and green lettering pieces on spines, latter with attractive leaf spray tool, minor wear, good. Blackwell's Rare Books 172 - 75 2013 £400

Hue. Chicago: Johnson Pub. Co., 1957-1958. Volume 5, 12mo., complete run of volume 5 (12 issues. Nov. 1957-Oct. 1958), bound with all wrappers in green buckram ruled in gilt, some light staining to endpapers and boards, very good, internally fine.   Between the Covers Rare Books, Inc.   165 - 189   2013 $300

Hues, Robert   *Tractatus de globus et Eorum Usu. A Treatise Descriptive of the Globes constructed by Emory Molyneux....* London: Hakluyt Society, 1889. 8vo., frontispiece, foldout color map, light blue cloth, gilt stamped cover illustration and spine title, extremities bit stained, spine chipped, inner hinges cracked, pages unopened, Burndy bookplate, good.   Jeff Weber Rare Books   169 - 220   2013 $95

Huggins, Charles   *Endocrine-Induced Regression of Cancer.* Offprint from Science, May 26, 1967. Volume 15, no. 3778, 4to., fine in original printed wrappers.   By the Book, L. C.   38 - 41   2013 $275

Huggins, Nathan Irvin   *Black Odyssey: The Afro-American Ordeal in Slavery.* New York: Pantheon, 1977. First edition, boards little soiled, extensive pencil notes by Samson Raphaelson on endpapers and in text, else very good in very good plus dust jacket with couple of short tears, inscribed by author to Mr. and Mrs. Raphaelson, Christmas 1977.   Between the Covers Rare Books, Inc.   165 - 309   2013 $200

Huggins, William   *On the Photographic Spectra of Stars.* London: Royal Society, 1880. Rare offprint from Philosophical Transactions of the Royal Society Volume 1717, 4to., with cut signature of Huggins above which is printed his address in London, laid-in, near fine in original mildly soiled printed wrappers, with "From the Author" inscribed on front wrapper in unknown hand, offprint and signature are in custom quarter morocco and cloth clamshell box with gilt lettering on spine, black lettering on cover, rare, especially with Huggins' signature.   By the Book, L. C.   38 - 53   2013 $1000

Hughes, Dorothy B.   *Dread Journey.* New York: Duell Sloan and Pearce, 1945. First edition, fine in about very good dust jacket with modest chip at crown and vertical crease to spine.   Between the Covers Rare Books, Inc.   Mystery & Detective Fiction - 60045   2013 $65

Hughes, Edward   *North Country Life in the Eighteenth Century. Volume II: Cumberland and Westmorland 1700-1830.* Oxford University Press, 1965. First edition, original cloth gilt, dust jacket, price clipped, 6 illustrations, map.   R. F. G. Hollett & Son   Lake District and Cumbria - 311   2013   £50

Hughes, Glen   *Four and Twenty Block Prints for Four and Twenty Rhymes.* Seattle: University of Washington Book Store, 1927. Second edition, wrappers, very good, illustrations with blockprints done on different color papers, couple of small tears to top of cover.   Barnaby Rudge Booksellers   Children 2013 - 021650   2013 $75

Hughes, John T.   *Doniphan's Expedition: Containing an Account of the Conquest of New Mexico.* Cincinnati: 1850. 407 pages, illustrations, folding map, original boards, spine faded, rubbing and wear to extremities, some internal foxing, one signature slightly out, binding sound, very good, unsophisticated.   Dumont Maps & Books of the West   125 - 55   2013 $225

Hughes, Langston   *Black Misery.* New York: Eriksson, 1969. First edition, oblong octavo, illustrations by Arouni, about fine in price clipped, near fine dust jacket with tear on rear panel.   Between the Covers Rare Books, Inc.   165 - 109   2013 $100

Hughes, Langston   *The Langston Hughes Reader.* New York: George Braziller, 1958. First edition, endpapers little foxed, small stain on front fly else near fine, in near fine dust jacket with little rubbing and short and unobtrusive tear on front panel.   Between the Covers Rare Books, Inc.   165 - 176   2013 $100

Hughes, Langston   *Shadows in the Sun: Eleven Poems for Voice and Piano.* Hastings-on-Hudson: General Music Pub. Co., 1971. First edition, stapled wrappers, very light wear, near fine, uncommon sheet music, apparently issued in relatively small numbers.   Between the Covers Rare Books, Inc.   165 - 177   2013 $100

Hughes, Langston   *Shakespeare in Harlem.* New York: Alfred A. Knopf, 1945. Second printing, 125 pages, presentation copy signed by author to Gay Dallman, NY July 12, 1947, very good in black cloth with orange cloth spine and purple title to front board and spine, slight fading to spine and bumping to bottom corners, very good dust jacket, price clipped with green spine panel and black title to spine, jacket worn along edges including chip to head of spine and short closed tear, scuffmark to front panel of interior of front flap has light dampstaining, no evidence of dampstaining to boards or exterior of jacket.   The Kelmscott Bookshop   7 - 118   2013 $950

Hughes, Langston   *The Ways of White Folks.* New York: Alfred A. Knopf, 1934. First edition, bookplate on front pastedown with name effaced, small bump on rear board, else clean, near fine, lacking dust jacket.   Between the Covers Rare Books, Inc.   165 - 173   2013 $200

Hughes, Langston *The Weary Blues.* New York: Alfred A. Knopf, 1926. First edition, one of 1500 copies, advance copy with publisher's review slip, giving publication date, laid in, small 8vo., original blue cloth backed decorated boards, pictorial dust jacket, extremely rare in jacket. James S. Jaffe Rare Books Fall 2013 - 69 2013 $25,000

Hughes, Langston *The Weary Blues.* New York: Alfred A. Knopf, 1926. First edition, one of 1500 copies printed, small 8vo., original blue cloth backed decorated boards, presentation copy inscribed by author for George Gershwin, covers lightly rubbed, lacking rare dust jacket, otherwise very good. James S. Jaffe Rare Books Fall 2013 - 70 2013 $45,000

Hughes, Richard *A High Wind in Jamaica.* London: Chatto & Windus, 1929. First Book form edition, crown 8vo., original pale green cloth, foxed backstrip gilt lettered, tail edges rough trimmed, darkened backstrip panel to dust jacket, torn and chipped, wrap around band present, good, from the library of Julian Barnes. Blackwell's Rare Books B174 - 235 2013 £175

Hughes, Robert *The Fatal Shore.* Collins, 1987. 8vo., maps, photos, cloth, dust jacket, very good. C. P. Hyland 261 - 490 2013 £35

Hughes, Rupert *The Fairy Detective.* New York: Harper & Bros., 1919. First edition, drawings by Rhoda Chase, contemporary pencil name on front fly, still easily fine in attractive, fine dust jacket, very scarce in jacket. Between the Covers Rare Books, Inc. Mystery & Detective Fiction - 74191 2013 $400

Hughes, Ted 1930-1998 *Chiasmadon.* Baltimore: Charles Seluzicki, 1977. First edition, #75 of 120 copies for sale, square 8vo., signed by author and artist, Claire Van Vliet, printed wrappers, fine, relief print by Van Vliet. Second Life Books Inc. 183 - 176 2013 $425

Hughes, Ted 1930-1998 *Fangs the Vampire Bat and the Kiss of Truth.* Faber, 1986. First edition, small 4to., original cloth, gilt, dust jacket, pages 96, illustrations by Chris Riddell. R. F. G. Hollett & Son Children's Books - 300 2013 £40

Hughes, Ted 1930-1998 *The Iron Man.* London: Faber, 1968. First edition, 5 full page illustrations by George Adamson, pages 59, 8vo., original pale blue and pink boards, backstrip and front cover lettered in black, blue and white, that on front cover incorporated within design by Adamson, dust jacket repeating design, fine, scarce, particularly in such fine condition, rarely found inscribed, this copy inscribed by author for Nick Gammage. Blackwell's Rare Books 172 - 196 2013 £1500

Hughes, Ted 1930-1998 *Moortown.* London: Faber, 1979. First edition, 3 illustrations by Leonard Baskin, light text browning to poor quality paper as usual, crown 8vo., original scarlet cloth, backstrip gilt lettered, dust jacket, fine. Blackwell's Rare Books 172 - 197 2013 £90

Hughes, Ted 1930-1998 *New Selected Poems.* New York: Harper & Row, 1982. First American edition, 8vo., original black boards, backstrip gilt lettered, very good, inscribed by author. Blackwell's Rare Books B174 - 235 2013 $300

Hughes, Ted 1930-1998 *"Roosting Hawk".* Northampton: Grecourt Review, 1959. First separate edition, offprint, 8vo., original printed wrappers, offsetting from newspaper insert on inside front cover, otherwise fine, presentation copy, inscribed by poet to his mother in law, Aurelia Plath. James S. Jaffe Rare Books Fall 2013 - 71 2013 $8500

Hughes, Ted 1930-1998 *Season Songs.* London: Faber, 1976. First edition, crown 8vo., 80 pages, original light blue boards, backstrip blocked in silver, dust jacket, fine. Blackwell's Rare Books 172 - 198 2013 £60

Hughes, Thomas 1822-1896 *David Livingstone; Charles George Gordon. Englishmen of Action Series.* Macmillan, 1897. Full calf gilt by Bickers, extremities little worn, top of spine frayed, 2 portraits and colored folding map. R. F. G. Hollett & Son Africana - 91 2013 £35

Hughes, Thomas 1822-1896 *Tom Brown's School Days.* London: Macmillan & Co., 1869. First illustrated edition, frontispiece, illustrated title, plates and illustrations, original decorated blue cloth by Burn & Co., bevelled boards, slight repair to upper front corner, otherwise fine, bright copy. Jarndyce Antiquarian Booksellers CCV - 141 2013 £250

Hughs, Mrs. *Emma Mortimer.* Philadelphia: Thomas T. Ash, 1829. First edition, 12mo., 249 pages, leather backed boards, rubbed, some foxed, good copy, all edges gilt. Second Life Books Inc. 183 - 177 2013 $75

Hugill, Robert *Castles and Peles of Cumberland and Westmorland.* Newcastle-upon-Tyne: Frank Graham, 1977. First edition, original cloth, gilt, dust jacket price clipped, illustrations. R. F. G. Hollett & Son Lake District and Cumbria - 319 2013 £50

Hugnet, Georges *La Hampe de l'Imaginaire.* Paris: GLM (Guy Levis Mano), 1936. First edition, from a total edition of 70 impressions, this number 56 signed by Levis-Mano, printed on normandy vellum teinte, full page etching by Oscar Dominguez signed by artist in plate and dated '35', loose as issued, original orange printed wrappers, 25.5 x 19.5cm., specially designed custom box by Ann Repp, overall size 28 x 23 x 4.5cm., excellent condition, quite rare. Gemini Fine Books & Arts., Ltd.   Art Reference & Illustrated Books - 2013 $2700

Hugo, Herman *Pia Desideria....* Antwerp: Lucam de Potter, 1657. 12mo., 45 (of 46) engraved plates, slightly imperfect, having leaf G1 in early pen facsimile and lacking plate facing that leaf, old calf, worn at spine ends and corners, clasps lacking, occasional minor spotting and chips, good, tight copy, bookplate of William S. Heckscher. Joseph J. Felcone Inc.   Books Printed before 1701 - 52   2013 $400

Hugo, Victor   1802-1865 *The Hunchback of Notre Dame.* Philadelphia: Carey, Lea and Blanchard, 1834. First American edition, one of only 1000 copies, 2 volumes, octavo, original quarter blue cloth over drab boards, untrimmed, light toning and foxing throughout as expected, heavy crease to lower corner of front board of volume one, some other minor edgewear, remnants of printed paper labels on untouched cloth spines, original owner's dated (1835) signature on titlepages, very good, rarely found in original binding, chemised and housed within elegantly handsome modern full blue goatskin, gilt decorated, two spine slipcase by Rene Patron. David Brass Rare Books, Inc.   Holiday 2012 Chapter Five - DB 02091   2013 $3850

Hugo, Victor   1802-1865 *Notre Dame de Paris.* Bruxelles: Louis Hauman et Comp., 1834. Second Bruxelles edition, 3 volumes, 12mo., very pretty set, finely bound in near contemporary half calf, marbled boards, spines most ornately covered in geometric gilt lattice tooling with red and black gilt morocco labels, marbled edges and endpapers, armorial bookplate of Stephens Lyne Stephens, scarce.   Ken Spelman Books Ltd.   75 - 96   2013   £295

Hulbert, Hugh *In the Footsteps of William and Dorothy.* Kendal: Titus Wilson, 1950. First edition, original pictorial stiff wrappers, onlay on upper cover and silk tie, little soiled, small ink stain to lower panel.   R. F. G. Hollett & Son   Lake District and Cumbria - 321   2013   £20

Hulke, John Whitaker *A Practical Treatise on the Use of the Ophthalmoscope, Being the Essay for Which the Jacksonian Prize in the Year 1859 was Awarded by the Royal College of Surgeons of England.* London: John Churchill, 1861. First edition, large 8vo., 12 figures, 4 chromolithographic plates, original blind stamped brown cloth gilt spine, rubbed, light corner dampstain to back cover, bookplate of Jerry F. Donin, very good.   Jeff Weber Rare Books   172 - 144   2013 $250

Hull, Clifton E. *Shortline Railroads of Arkansas.* Norman: University of Oklahoma Press, 1969. First edition, 175 photos, 16 maps, red cloth, very fine with pictorial dust jacket.   Argonaut Book Shop   Summer 2013 - 165   2013 $60

Hulsizer, Allan *The Indian Boy's Days.* Smithtown: Exposition Press, 1983. First edition, fine in heavily rubbed, very good dust jacket with tiny corner chips.   Ken Lopez Bookseller   159 - 152   2013 $100

Humber, Robert D. *Heversham. The Story of Westmorland School and Village.* Kendal: Titus Wilson, 1968. First edition, original cloth, gilt, dust jacket, frontispiece.   R. F. G. Hollett & Son   Lake District and Cumbria - 322   2013   £35

Humboldt, Friedrich Heinrich Alexander, Baron Von 1769-1859 *Personal Narrative of Travels to the Equinoctial Regions of America During the Years 1799-1804.* London: George Bell, 1907. Small 8vo., red cloth, spines faded, very good.   Second Life Books Inc.   183 - 179   2013 $85

Hume, David   1711-1776 *An Enquiry Concerning the Principles of Morals.* London: printed for A. Millar, 1751. First edition, first issue with L3 in uncancelled state, 12mo., contemporary brown calf ruled in gilt on covers, gilt stamped on spine with red morocco label, includes half title, errata leaf and final three pages of ads, spine rebacked, half title with previous owner's signature and professional restoration, new endpapers, else fine in custom quarter brown morocco slipcase.   Heritage Book Shop   50th Anniversary Catalogue - 53   2013 $7500

Hume, David   1711-1776 *Essays and Treatises on Several Subjects.* London: printed for A. Millar and A. Kincaid and A. Donaldson, at Edinburgh, 1767. New edition, 2 volumes, modern antique style calf, gilt corners gilt spine, leather labels, raised bands, very good with scattered light foxing.   Howard S. Mott Inc.   262 - 77   2013 $750

Hume, David   1711-1776 *Essays and Treatises on Several Subjects.* Edinburgh: printed by George Caw for Bell and Bradfute, 1800. 2 volumes, some light spotting, 8vo., contemporary sprinkled calf, spines divided by gilt fillets, red and green morocco lettering pieces, rubbed, touch of wear to endcaps and corners, slight cracking to joints, sound.   Blackwell's Rare Books   B174 - 72   2013   £180

Hume, David 1711-1776 *Essays on Suicide and the Immortality of the Soul, Ascribed to the Late David Hume, Esq.* London: printed for M. Smith, 1783. Second edition, despite what titlepage states, small octavo, iv, 107 pages, contemporary full mottled calf, covers ruled in gilt, spine covered in red morocco onlay, decorated with gilt urns and lyres, gilt board edges, marbled endpapers, front blank missing bit from upper corner, superb copy, from the collection of historian Hugh Trevor-Robert (with his bookplate on front pastedown),. Heritage Book Shop 50th Anniversary Catalogue - 55 2013 $15,000

Hume, Fergus *Chronicles of Fairy Land.* Philadelphia: Lippincott, 1911. First edition, 8vo., red gilt cloth, top edge gilt, gilt, 191 pages, covers slightly dull, else very good+, 8 color plates by Maria Kirk and line illustrations in text by M. Dunlop plus pictoral endpapers, scarce. Aleph-Bet Books, Inc. 104 - 306 2013 $225

Humphry, Charlotte Eliza *Manners for Men.* London: James Bowden, 1898. Sixth edition, 4 pages ads, original light brown decorated cloth, slightly marked and dulled, embossed stamp of W. H. Smith. Jarndyce Antiquarian Booksellers CCV - 142 2013 £75

Hungerford, Edward *The Story of the Waldorf Astoria.* New York: G. P. Putnam's Sons, 1925. First edition, publisher's blue cloth gilt, slight foxing to fore edge and endpapers, tight and bright, just about fine. Between the Covers Rare Books, Inc. New York City - 276844 2013 $75

Hungerford, Edward *The Story of the Waldorf Astoria.* New York: G. P. Putnam's and Sons, 1925. First edition, 283 pages, near fine in very good plus dust jacket that has some small edge chips and some chipping and wear to spine, very scarce in dust jacket. Jeff Hirsch Books Fall 2013 - 129448 2013 $250

Hungerford, Edward *The Story of the Baltimore & Ohio Railroad 1827-1927.* New York: and London: G. P. Putnam's Sons, 1928. First edition, 2 volumes, frontispiece, plates, navy cloth, gilt stamped spine title, top edge gilt, dust jackets worn with pieces missing, top spine cloth torn on both volumes (titles affected), bookplates of Burndy Library, good. Jeff Weber Rare Books 169 - 224 2013 $75

Hunt, Frazier *Cap Mossman, Last of the Great Cowman.* New York: Hastings House, 1951. First edition, 16 illustrations by Ross Santee, tan cloth decorated and lettered in dark brown, name erased from endpaper, else very fine, pictorial dust jacket (tiny chip to lower corner of jacket), scarce. Argonaut Book Shop Summer 2013 - 166 2013 $75

Hunt, Gill *Planet X.* London: printed in Great Britain and Published by Curtis Warren Limited, n.d., 1951. First edition, small octavo, pictorial wrappers. L. W. Currey, Inc. Fall Sampler Sept. 2013 - 145376 2013 $75

Hunt, Irvine *Old Lakeland Transport.* Ulverston: Rusland Press, 1978. First edition, oblong 8vo., original pictorial wrappers, illustrations. R. F. G. Hollett & Son Lake District and Cumbria - 325 2013 £25

Hunt, John *Irish Medieval Figure Sculpture.* 1974. First edition, 8vo., cloth, dust jacket, ex-library but very good, 2 volumes,. C. P. Hyland 261 - 491 2013 £105

Hunt, Leigh *A Jar of Honey from Mount Hybla.* London: Smith, Elder, 1848. First edition, 8vo., text illustrations, original blindstamped cloth. J. & S. L. Bonham Antiquarian Booksellers Europe - 7058 2013 £40

Hunt, M. Stuart *Nova Scotia's Part in the Great War.* Halifax: Nova Scotia Veteran Pub. Co., 1920. 8vo., red cloth with NS coat of arms decoration to front, half title, frontispiece, illustrated with half tones, cloth stained and darkened, slight dampstaining to endpapers and paper edges, otherwise very good. Schooner Books Ltd. 104 - 73 2013 $65

Hunt, Marsha *The Way We Wore. Styles of the 1930's and 1940's.* Fallbrook: Fallbrook Pub. Ltd., 1993. Second printing, fine in fine dust jacket, photos, 4to., 438 pages. Beasley Books 2013 - 2013 $60

Hunt, Rachel McMasters Miller *Catalogue of Botanical Books in the Collection of...* Pittsburgh: Hunt Botanical Library, 1958-1961. One of 750 sets, 3 volumes, large 8vo., frontispiece, plates, dark green cloth, gilt stamped cover illustrations and spine titles, Burndy bookplates, fine. Jeff Weber Rare Books 169 - 226 2013 $700

Hunt, Thomas *The Rights of the Bishops to Judge in Capital Cases in Parliament, Cleared.* London: Tho. Braddly for Robert Clavel, 1680. Second edition, folio, (4), 44 pages, later marbled wrappers. Joseph J. Felcone Inc. Books Printed before 1701 - 53 2013 $150

Hunt, Thomas P. *The Cold Water Army.* Boston: Whipple & Damrell, 1840. First edition, 12mo., 36 pages, removed, very good. Second Life Books Inc. 183 - 180 2013 $75

Hunt, Tony *Plant Names of Medieval England.* Cambridge: D. S. Brewer, 1989. First edition, 8vo., green cloth, very slight browning and dustiness to edges of text block, near fine, dust jacket with 4 cm. tear to rear, with other small tears to edges, very good, ownership inscription of Marie Denley. Unsworths Antiquarian Booksellers 28 - 171 2013 £50

Hunter, Andrew *Thornton & Tully's Scientific Books, Libraries and Collectors: a Study of Bibliography and the Book Trade in Relation to the History of Science.* Aldershot, et al: Ashgate, 2000. Fourth edition, 8vo., 8 plates, green cloth, silver stamped spine title, dust jacket, Burndy bookplate, fine.   Jeff Weber Rare Books   169 - 227   2013 $150

Hunter, Dard   1883-1966 *A Papermaking Pilgrimage to Japan, Korea and China.* New York: Pynson Printers, 1936. Limited to 370 signed copies, this #317, signed by Hunter and publisher, Elmer Adler on colophon page, 4to., plates, binding by Gerhard Gerlach, quarter black leather and patterned paper boards with gilt lettering and red design spine, mild foxing to few specimen pages, very good publisher's paper covered printed slipcase with wear and scuffs.   By the Book, L. C.   38 - 64   2013 $3000

Hunter, Dard   1883-1966 *Papermaking by Hand in India.* New York: Pynson printers, 1939. Limited numbered edition of 370 copies signed by author, prospectus loosely inserted, 4to., large full page illustrations, printed wrappers, fine.   Jeff Weber Rare Books   171 - 177   2013 $1300

Hunter, John   1728-1793 *A Treatise on the Blood, Inflammation and Gun-shot Wounds.* London: John Richardson for George Nicol, 1794. First edition, 4to., frontispiece, 9 plates foxed, occasional light scattered foxing throughout text, modern quarter gilt stamped calf over marbled paper backed boards, gilt stamped red leather spine label, corners faintly rubbed, inscribed by David Rice 8/25/1820 for W. Buxton, better than very good.   Jeff Weber Rare Books   172 - 145   2013 $6500

Hunter, John   1728-1793 *A Treatise on the Blood, Inflammation and Gun-Shot Wounds to which is Prefixed a Short Account of the Author's Life.* London: John Richardson for George Nicol, 1794. First edition, 9 engraved plates, lacking frontispiece, 4to., contemporary full sheep, newly rebacked, text foxed in parts, institutional stamps on title and plates.   James Tait Goodrich   75 - 122   2013 $995

Hunter, Stephen *The Day Before Midnight.* New York: Bantam, 1989. First edition, fine in dust jacket.   Mordida Books   81 - 267   2013 $85

Hurlbert, William H. *Ireland Under Coercion. The Diary of an American.* 1888. First edition, 2 volumes, good, cloth, ex-Prinknash Abbey Library.   C. P. Hyland   261 - 492   2013   £75

Hurlbert, William H. *Ireland Under Coercion. The Diary of an American.* 1888. Second edition, 8vo., 3 volumes, cloth, very good.   C. P. Hyland   261 - 493   2013   £95

Hurley, Michael *Irish Anglicanism 1869-1969.* 1970. First edition, 8vo., cloth, dust jacket, near fine.   C. P. Hyland   261 - 494   2013   £50

Hurley, Patrick *Some Account of the Family of O'Hurly.* 1906-1907. 46 pages, 10 photos, pedigrees, stiff printed wrappers, ex-library, some stamps some foxing, good.   C. P. Hyland   261 - 395   2013   £60

Hurlock, Elizabeth B. *The Psychology of Dress.* New York: Ronald Press, 1929. First edition, bookseller label, front pastedown very lightly rubbed, near fine.   Between the Covers Rare Books, Inc. Psychology & Psychiatry - 92953   2013 $100

Hurn, Ethel Alice *Wisconsin Women in the War Between the States.* Wisconsin History Commission, 1911. One of 5000 copies, 8vo., pages xix, 190, illustrations, paper over boards, ex-library with pocket and stamps, front hinge tender, cover little worn at corners and ends of spine, otherwise very good.   Second Life Books Inc.   182 - 115   2013 $65

Hurst, J. L. *Century of Penrith Cricket.* Penrith: 1967. First edition, small 8vo., original cloth, gilt, 91 pages, illustrations, relevant ephemera (Club dinner menu etc.) loosely inserted.   R. F. G. Hollett & Son   Lake District and Cumbria - 326   2013   £25

Hutcheson, Francis *An Essay on the Nature and conduct of the Passions and Affections.* London: printed for A. Ward, 1742. Third edition, 8vo., full contemporary calf, raised bands, red morocco label, slight wear to upper hinge, small scratch to rear board, armorial bookplate of Marquess of Headfort, very good.   Jarndyce Antiquarian Booksellers CCV - 143   2013   £380

Hutchins, Robert Maynard *Great Books of the Western World.* Chicago: Encyclopedia Britannica, 1988. Thirtieth printing, 54 volumes, all near fine or better with only minor wear to corner and edges of spine from normal shelfwear.   Jeff Hirsch Books   Fall 2013 - 129264   2013 $400

Hutchinson, Horace G. *Big Game Shooting.* London: Country Life, 1905. First edition, half dark green roan gilt, top edge gilt, 106 illustrations, very attractive copy.   R. F. G. Hollett & Son   Africana - 93   2013   £120

Hutchinson, Pearse *Barnsley Main Seam.* Oldcastle: Gallery Press, 1995. First edition, 8vo., original black cloth, dust jacket, fine in dust jacket, from the library of Richard Murphy, inscribed for him by author.   Maggs Bros. Ltd.   1442 - 131   2013   £60

Hutchinson, Pearse *Friend Songs.* Dublin: New Writers' Press, 1970. First edition, tall 8vo., original brown stitched wrappers, inscribed by author, number 50 of 100 copies for sale, excellent copy.   Maggs Bros. Ltd.   1442 - 130   2013   £150

Hutchinson, W. H. *The Life and Personal Writings of Eugene Manlove Rhodes. A Bar Cross Man.* Norman: University of Oklahoma Press, 1965. First edition, presentation inscription, signed by author, 18 illustrations, 2 maps, gray-green cloth, very fine, pictorial dust jacket (slightly rough at top edge).   Argonaut Book Shop   Summer 2013 - 167   2013 $90

Hutchinson, William *An Excursion to the Lakes in Westmoreland and Cumberland with a Tour through Part of the Northern Counties in the years 1773 and 1774.* J. Wilkie and W. Charnley, 1776. First edition, near contemporary half calf, marbled boards, neatly rebacked to match, original spine label, relaid, 2 engraved text vignettes, contemporary inscription of James Waring and few pencilled marginalia by later owner, William Ball of Glen Rothay.   R. F. G. Hollett & Son   Lake District and Cumbria - 328   2013   £295

Hutchinson, William *An Excursion to the Lakes in Westmoreland and Cumberland...* J. Wilkie and W. Charnley, 1776. First edition, old speckled calf, little worn, backstrip and hinges cracked but sound, 19 plates, 2 engraved vignettes, few light dampstains to margins, otherwise very good.   R. F. G. Hollett & Son   Lake District and Cumbria - 329   2013   £650

Hutchinson, William *The History of the County of Cumberland...* Carlisle: F. Jollie, 1794. First edition, 2 volumes, large 4to.. contemporary full diced calf gilt, spines with 3 flattened raised bands, gilt panels and rolls at head and foot, hinges trifle rubbed, 2 engraved titles, folding map, 4 folding or double page plans, 50 engraved plates, 4 pages of tables, 1 extending table and over 50 woodcut or engraved illustrations, maps etc. in text, few leaves rather foxed, handsome sound wide margined set, armorial bookplate of Edward Charles Fletcher (of Kenward, Kent) in each volume.   R. F. G. Hollett & Son   Lake District and Cumbria - 332   2013   £495

Hutchinson, William *The History of the County of Cumberland...* Carlisle: F. Jollie, 1794. First edition, 2 volumes, 4to., modern half levant morocco with raised bands and contrasting double spine labels, 2 engraved titles, folding map, 4 folding or double page plans, 50 engraved plates, 4 pages of tables, 1 extending table and over 50 woodcut or engraved illustrations, maps, few neat repairs to folding plates, etc., but handsome, sound set.   R. F. G. Hollett & Son   Lake District and Cumbria - 331   2013   £495

Hutchinson, William *The History of the County of Cumberland...* Carlisle: F. Jollie, 1794. First edition, 4to., 2 volumes, old half calf gilt, boards rubbed, rebacked in pigskin, original lettering pieces and spine panels relaid; 2 engraved titles, 2 folding or double page plans, 50 engraved plates, 4 pages of tables, 1 extending table, over 50 woodcut or engraved illustrations, maps in text, lacks general map and plan of Carlisle, and section on Cumberland animals by Heysham, some browning and foxing in places, good, sound set.   R. F. G. Hollett & Son   Lake District and Cumbria - 330   2013   £350

Hutchison, Isobel Wylie *Stepping Stones from Alaska to Asia.* Blackie, 1937. First edition, original cloth, dust jacket, soiled and defective, pages x, 246 with 20 plates and 2 maps, endpapers little spotted.   R. F. G. Hollett & Son   Polar Exploration - 33   2013   £30

Huth, Hans *Roentgen Furniture. Abraham and David Roentgen: European Cabinet Makers.* London and New York: Sotheby Parke Bernet, 1974. pages viii, 108, highly illustrated with numerous plates, original publisher's cloth, dust jacket with few marginal tears to wrappers.   Marlborough Rare Books Ltd.   218 - 83   2013   £125

Hutin, Jean Mathuria Felix *Anatomie Pathologique des Cicatrices dans les Differents Tissus... (with) Memoire sur la Necessite d'Extraire les Corps Etrangers et les Esquilles, dans le Traitement des Plaies par Armes a feu...* Paris: J. B. Bailliere, 1856. 1851. First separate issues, 2 volumes in 1, 4to., early full black grained morocco, gilt, first title spotted, else near fine, very rare.   Jeff Weber Rare Books   172 - 148   2013 $500

Hutton, Charles *Elements of Conic Sections with Select Exercises in Various Branches of Mathematics and Philosophy.* London: printed by J. Davis, sold by G. G. J. Robinson and J. Robinson, 1787. First (only) edition, diagrams in text, first and last leaves slightly browned (offsetting from acidic flyleaves), 8vo., uncut in early to mid 20th century cloth backed boards, trifle worn, good.   Blackwell's Rare Books   Sciences - 62   2013   £600

Hutton, Charles *The School-Master's Guide; or a Complete System of Practical Arithmetic and Book-Keeping..* Newcastle-upon-Tyne: printed by T. Saint and sold by J. Wilkie, 1771. 12mo., leading edge of B6 dusted, contemporary calf, blind ruled borders to three edges, decorative blindstamped design along left hand borders, raised and gilt banded spine, slightly chipped at head and tail of spine, contemporary note relating to flour weights and pricing at Bradford and Leeds Custom Houses.   Jarndyce Antiquarian Booksellers   CCIV - 167   2013   £250

Hutton, Edward *The Children's Christmas Treasury of Things New and Old.* London: J. M. Dent & Co., 1905. Quarto, 15 full color plates, 15 full page and one text illustration in red and black, 15 drawings in black and white by various artists, original white cloth with full pictorial design by Reginald Knowles dated 1805, near fine, very scarce. David Brass Rare Books, Inc.   Holiday 2012 Chapter One - DB 02161   2013 $1250

Hutton, Samuel King *A Shepherd in the Snow the Life Story of Walter Perrett of Labrador.* London: Hodder and Stoughton, 1936. 8vo., cloth worn and darkened, some offsetting and foxing to endpapers and paper edges. Schooner Books Ltd.   101 - 36   2013 $175

Huxham, John *An Essay on Fevers.* London: printed for J. Hinton, 1757. Third edition, full contemporary calf, raised and gilt banded spine, red morocco label.   Ken Spelman Books Ltd.   75 - 23   2013   £160

Huxley, Aldous Leonard   1894-1963 *Brave new World: a Novel.* London: Chatto & Windus, 1932. First edition, limited issue, number 239 of 325 numbered copies, signed by author, 8vo., original yellow buckram, blue morocco label, gilt lettering, top edge gilt, others untrimmed, bookplate on front pastedown buckram little soiled, spine slightly dull, very good.   The Brick Row Book Shop   Miscellany Fifty-Nine - 28   2013 $4000

Huxley, Aldous Leonard   1894-1963 *The Burning Wheel.* Oxford: Blackwell, 1916. First edition, decorated frontispiece and titlepage, foolscap 8vo., original cream wrappers with light dust soiling, printed labels on front cover and backstrip, rough trimmed, good.   Blackwell's Rare Books   B174 - 236   2013   £285

Huxley, Aldous Leonard   1894-1963 *The Genius and the Goddess.* London: Chatto & Windus, 1935. First edition, small 8vo., near fine, minimal cover edge wear, near fine dust jacket.   By the Book, L. C.   38 - 87   2013 $400

Huxley, Aldous Leonard   1894-1963 *Selected Poems.* Oxford: Blackwell, 1925. First edition, crown 8vo., 64 pages, original orange and tan lettered and patterned boards, corners and backstrip head and tail rubbed, good. Blackwell's Rare Books   B174 - 237   2013   £100

Huxley, Elspeth *The African Poison Murders.* New York: Harper & Bros., 1940. First American edition, fine in near fine dust jacket with short tear on front panel, very fresh copy.   Between the Covers Rare Books, Inc.   Mystery & Detective Fiction - 98109   2013 $275

Huxley, Elspeth *The Flame Trees of Thika.* London: Chatto & Windus, 1959. Original cloth, gilt, 288 pages, frontispiece, dust jacket.   R. F. G. Hollett & Son   Africana - 94   2013   £25

Huxley, Elspeth *Forks and Hope.* London: Chatto & Windus, 1964. First edition, original cloth, gilt, dust jacket, 272 pages, frontispiece.   R. F. G. Hollett & Son   Africana - 95   2013   £25

Huxley, Julian *Africa View.* London: Chatto & Windus, 1931. First edition, large 8vo., original black cloth, gilt, mark to upper board, 50 illustrations and folding map, prelims slightly spotted.   R. F. G. Hollett & Son   Africana - 96   2013   £35

Huxley, Julian *Evolution. The Modern Synthesis.* London: George Allen, 1942. First edition, very good++, owner name, minimal cover edge wear, soil to edges, in very good+ dust jacket with owner ink stamp to front and rear of jacket, mild sun spine and covers, soil, edgewear, 8vo, 645 pages.   By the Book, L. C.   37 - 44   2013 $125

Huxley, Julian *Memories.* London: George Allen & Unwin, 1970. Stated first edition, Francis Crick copy, signed by him, near fine in like dust jacket with minimal chips to spine tips, errata slip laid in, 8vo., 296 pages.   By the Book, L. C.   37 - 45   2013 $400

Huxley, Thomas Henry   1825-1895 *The Crayfish.* London: C. Kegan Paul & Co., 1880. Limited to 250 numbered copies signed by publisher, 8vo., frontispiece, 81 figures, original olive cloth, bevelled boards, gilt stamped spine title, neatly restored spine, fine, quite rare issue.   Jeff Weber Rare Books   169 - 228   2013 $1250

Huxley, Thomas Henry   1825-1895 *On Our Knowledge of the Causes of the Phenomena of Organic Nature.* London: Robert Hardwicke, 1862. First edition, very good++, original blindstamped black binding with gilt lettered spine, binding tight, titlepage with date '1862', owner bookplate, ex-library with stamps on several pages, no other library markings, most listings describe as First editions copies with '1863' on titlepage, clearly such copies are a later printing or edition, quite scarce, 8vo.   By the Book, L. C.   37 - 46   2013 $500

Huygens, Christian *(Cosmotheoros)... sive De Terris Calestibus, Earumque Ornate, Conjecture ad Constantnum Hugenium.* Hagae Comitum: Adrianum Moetjens, 1698. First edition, small 4to., engraved title vignette, engraved headpieces, engraved tailpiece, engraved initials, 5 folding engraved plates, title margin rebuilt, few pages nicked at margin, light foxing, modern full blind tooled antique style dark brown calf, new endpapers, early rubber stamp, very good.   Jeff Weber Rare Books   169 - 229   2013 $4000

Huygens, Christian *Horlogium Oscillatorium; sive de Motu Pendulorum ad Horlogia Aptato Demonstrationes Geometricae.* Bruxelles: Culture et Civilisation, 1966. Facsimile reprint of Paris 1673 edition, 30 cm., illustrations, blue gilt stamped leatherette, bit nicked along bottom edge, fine, otherwise scarce, Burndy bookplate. Jeff Weber Rare Books 171 - 179 2013 $120

Huysmans, J. K. *A Vau-L-Eau.* Paris: Georges Courville, 1933. First edition, limited to 200 numbered copies initialled by publisher, 19 original black and white drypoint etchings by Edgar Chahine, 9 of them hors-texte, 28 x 23cm., 121 pages, handsomely bound three quarter red morocco with 5 raised bands, extensive gilt decoration, signed by Vandyck, exceptionally clean and crisp, from the Jean Jacobs collection with his two small wood engraved bookplates pasted on endleaves. Gemini Fine Books & Arts., Ltd. Art Reference & Illustrated Books - 2013 $1400

Hyde, Evan X. *North Amerikan Blues.* Belize City: the author, 1977. First edition, wrappers, glue has dried up and consequently text block has become detached from wrappers, else very good. Between the Covers Rare Books, Inc. 165 - 178 2013 $65

Hyde, George E. *Indians of the High Plains.* Norman: University of Oklahoma, 1959. First edition, 14 photos, 3 maps, gray-green cloth, bookplate removed from inner rear cover, light scarring, very good, pictorial dust jacket. Argonaut Book Shop Summer 2013 - 168 2013 $50

Hyde, Ralph *The Regents Park Colosseum.* London: Ackermann 3 Old Bond Street, 1982. Limited edition, no. 51 of 200, large 4to., pages 73 (1) colophon, 6 plates, full green morocco gilt, original cloth box. Marlborough Rare Books Ltd. 218 - 84 2013 £450

Hylan, John Francis *Autobiography of John Francis Hylan: Mayor of New York.* New York: Rotary Press, 1922. First edition, Memorial bookplate on front pastedown, gift inscription on front fly, else near fine, front panel of dust jacket reproducing frontispiece laid in, uncommon title. Between the Covers Rare Books, Inc. New York City - 275668 2013 $200

Hyman, Sarah *Patchwork Quill.* N. P.: New York: Gentlemen's Quarterly, n.d. probably, 1958. Folio, 4 loose tall quarto proof sheets printed rectos only, folded once horizontally, with very light wear, near fine. Between the Covers Rare Books, Inc. Sci-Fi, Fantasy & Horror - 845313 2013 $450

I

The I'm Alone Incident Correspondence Between the Governments of Canada and the United States 1929. Ottawa: printed by order of Parliament, 1929. Blue paper wrappers, pages 23, 8vo., very good.   Schooner Books Ltd.   105 - 33   2013 $75

I Wish I Were a Dancer.   Garden City: Garden City Books, 1952.   Oblong 8vo., pictorial boards, folded accordion style, some rubbing, very good, opening to 5 feet, color lithos by Edna Kaula, at end are 2 leaves of die-cut punch-out figures for child to play with.   Aleph-Bet Books, Inc.   105 - 440   2013 $225

Ibsen, Henrik   *A Doll's House.*   London: Fisher Unwin, 1889.   First English edition, limited to 115 copies, this #45, signed by Fisher Unwin, 7 original photos, 8vo., 123 pages, bound in cream vellum boards (little soiled), gilt lettered, untrimmed, top edge gilt.   Second Life Books Inc.   183 - 181   2013 $700

Ibsen, Henrik   *Peer Gynt.*   London: Harrap, 1936. Limited to only 460 copies signed by artist, 4to., full vellum decorated in gold, top edge gilt, some discoloration of vellum, else near fne, pictorial endpapers, 12 color plates plus numerous black and whites by Arthur Rackham, beautiful copy.   Aleph-Bet Books, Inc.   105 - 494   2013 $1850

Ibsen, Henrik   *Peer Gynt: a Dramatic Poems.*   London: George G. Harrap & Co. Ltd., 1936.   First (British) Printing of this edition, 260 x 197mm., original publisher's linen boards, original pictorial dust jacket, 12 color plates, by Arthur Rackham, all protected by tissue guards with descriptive letterpress, dust jacket with thin chip out of bottom edge of back panel and two very minor closed tears at bottom of front panel, little chafing at folds, still, very fine in fine dust jacket.   Phillip J. Pirages   63 - 380   2013 $1950

Ibsen, Henrik   *Peer Gynt, a Dramatic Poem.*   London: Harrap, 1936.   First Rackham edition, 12 color printed plates with captioned tissue guards present, endpaper decorations, decorated half title and titlepage both printed in black and green text illustrations placed as head and tailpieces, all by Arthur Rackham, imperial 8vo., original mid brown cloth, backstrip and front cover lettered and decorated in gilt to a design by Rackham, dust jacket with overall design no present in the book, near fine.   Blackwell's Rare Books   B174 - 285   2013   £500

If Grandma Had the Balls - She'd Be Grandpa. Volume I. San Francisco: Muntjac Press, 1968. First edition, 8vo., original brown wrappers, near fine.   Maggs Bros. Ltd. 1442 - 85   2013   £50

Iguh, Thomas O.   *Tshombe of Katanga. (Drama).* Onitsha: Experience Printing Press, circa, 1960-1965. First edition, stapled photo wrappers, scrape and stain on front wrapper, cheap paper pages browned, about very good, very scarce.   Between the Covers Rare Books, Inc. 165 - 49   2013 $275

Iley, Matthew   *The Life, Writings Opinions and Times of... Lord Byron...*   London: Matthew Iley, 1825.   First edition, 3 volumes, frontispiece volumes I & II, folding frontispiece volume III, frontispieces browned, text slightly spotted, contemporary half calf, gilt spines, dark green and maroon leather labels, slightly rubbed, Renier booklabels, very good. Jarndyce Antiquarian Booksellers   CCIII - 393   2013 £280

Illinois. State Health Commission   *Report of the Health Insurance Commission of the State of Illinois.*   Springfield: Illinois State Journal May 1, 1919.   First edition, 8vo., 647 pages, wrappers, lacks the front, some light marginal stain, consumer advocate Florence Kelley's copy, good.   Second Life Books Inc.   183 - 335   2013 $65

The Illustrated Hand-Book for Harrogate, with Excursions in the Neighbourhood.   Harrogate: Hollins and Moxon, 1883. 2 large folding maps, printed on silk and 7 tinted lithograph plates, small 8vo., good copy, original blind and gilt stamped dark red cloth, all edges gilt, upper board rubbed, spine clean and bright, one page with old sellotape repair along inner margin and some foxing to silk maps, very scarce. Ken Spelman Books Ltd.   73 - 83   2013   £95

Illustrated Historical Atlas of the State of Indiana.   Chicago: Baskin, Forster and Co., 1876.   First edition, 449 x 370mm., 462 pages, publisher's original blindstamped brown boards, upper cover with gilt titling and state seal, corners and spine inexpertly renewed with black leather, hinges reinforced, 58 lithographed portraits, 92 lithographed views, illustrated titlepage and 89 sheets containing 381 maps; joints and extremities somewhat rubbed, four small abrasions to leather on lower cover, boards little faded in patches, last 10 leaves and rear endpaper with two vertical creases, final leaf little soiled, another with short marginal tear, occasional thumbing or corner creases, final leaf little soiled, another with short marginal tear, occasional thumbing or corner creases, other trivial defects, but more than simply a passable copy, binding sturdy and text and illustrations still clean and fresh.   Phillip J. Pirages   63 - 257 2013 $375

Imagination! Los Angeles: Los Angeles Science Fiction Society, 1937-1938. Complete run, 13 monthly issues from Volume 1 No. 1 in October 1937 to Anniversary Issue October 1938, remarkable set, mimeographed productions, in stapled covers, all issues fine, very scarce, the set has folder wrapping the first issue, with ownership name of Roy Squires II.   Ken Lopez Bookseller   159 - 176   2013 $7500

Iman, Yusef   *Something Black!*   No place: Jihad Productions, 1966. First edition, stapled wrappers, little darkened at extremities, else fine.   Between the Covers Rare Books, Inc.   165 - 179   2013 $65

Imbert-De-Lonnes, Ange Bernard   *Progres de la Chirurgie en France ou Phenomenes du Regne Animal, Gueris par des Operations Nouvelle... (with) Operation Courte, Facile et sans Danger, Pour Gueir Surement l'Hydrocele.*   Paris: de l'Imprimerie de la Republique Nivsse, 1799. Avignon: J. J. Niel an XI 1802. First edition, 8vo., 60 pages, frontispiece, 4 plates, original yellow boards, stained, spine chipped and cracked, corners rubbed, very good, choice collector's copy, presentation from author to his father.   Jeff Weber Rare Books   172 - 149   2013 $2750

In Cat Land.   N.P.: USA, circa, 1915. 4to., pictorial wrappers, slight cover soil, very good+, color cover plate plus 4 full page color illustrations and black and whites by Louis Wain.   Aleph-Bet Books, Inc.   105 - 582   2013 $375

In Fair Verona.   privately printed for Hans Schmoller, 1972. One of 100 copies printed on handmade paper, wood engraved vignette and 2 smaller engravings on titlepage, all printed in brown and by Reynolds Stone, folio, original vertically striped brown and cream wrappers over stiff card, backstrip gilt lettered on brown ground, untrimmed, near fine.   Blackwell's Rare Books   B174 - 375   2013   £300

In Praise of the Virtuous Woman.   Zuilichem: Catharijne Press, 1994. Limited to 193 copies, this one of 15 lettered copies, Hebrew characters heightened in gold, 6 x 4cm., white paper covered boards, stamped in gilt, frontispiece, binding by Luce Thurkow, from the collection of Donn W. Sanford.   Oak Knoll Books   303 - 82   2013 $250

Ince, William   *The Universal System of Household Furniture.*   London: sold by Robt. Sayer..., 1762. First edition, first issue, folio, engraved title, additional engraved titlepage in French, printed in sepia, engraved dedication leaf, 101 engraved plates on 95 leaves final 12 leaves with wormholes in upper margins not affecting engravings, text leaves marginally little spotted, overall rather clean and fresh in 20th century full panelled calf with raised bands, contrasting lettering pieces.   Marlborough Rare Books Ltd.   218 - 85   2013   £13,500

Inchbald, Elizabeth   *Nature and Art.*   London: printed for G. G. and J. Robinson, 1796. First edition, half title in volume i, half title probably discarded from volume ii, some soiling and staining, hole in G8 in volume i touching couple of letters on recto, tear in one leaf entering text without loss, 8vo., uncut, contemporary marbled boards, worn at extremities, rebacked, label inside front cover of Rotherham's circulating Library, Coventry, signature of William Thomas in both volumes, one dated, 1857, sound.   Blackwell's Rare Books   B174 - 74   2013   £1200

Inchbald, Elizabeth   *A Simple Story.*   London: printed for G. G. J. and J. Robinson, 1791. Second edition, 4 volumes, half titles discarded, ownership inscription of Jane Panton on titlepages, touch of light soiling and browning, one leaf in volume 1 with small paper flaw to blank margin, one gathering in volume iii, rough at bottom edge (missed by binder's knife), 8vo., late 19th century half calf, sometime rebacked to style, dark brown morocco lettering pieces, marbled boards, edges and endpapers, slightly rubbed, corners bit worn, hinges neatly relined, good.   Blackwell's Rare Books   B174 - 73   2013   £750

Inchbold, Stanley   *Lisbon and Cintra.*   London: Chatto & Windus, 1907. First edition, 8vo., pages xii, 248, illustrations, original red decorative cloth.   J. & S. L. Bonham Antiquarian Booksellers   Europe - 9862   2013   £45

Index Librorum Prohibitorum Pii Sexti Pontificis Maximi Jussu Editus.   Rome: Typographia Camerae Apostolicae, 1786-1817. Small 8vo., additional engraved title, occasional light marginal waterstains, lightly browned in places, otherwise clean in contemporary boards, rubbed, jonts worn.   Marlborough Rare Books Ltd.   218 - 86   2013   £425

Inglis, Henry David   *Spain in 1830.*   Whittaker & Treacher, 1831. First edition, 2 volumes, 8vo., contemporary black half morocco, raised band and gilt, minimal rubbing to spine, handsome set.   J. & S. L. Bonham Antiquarian Booksellers   Europe - 9746   2013   £1250

Ingpen, Roger   *One Thousand Poems for Children.*   Philadelphia: Jacobs, 1923. 4to., green cloth, pictorial paste-on, as new in dust jacket and box (slightly worn), illustrations by Ethel Betts with cover plate, pictorial endpapers plus 8 color plates, incredible copy.   Aleph-Bet Books, Inc.   104 - 71   2013 $500

Ingraham, J. H.   *The South-West.*   New York: Harper & Bros., 1835. First edition, 12mo., original cloth, printed paper labels, spines slightly faded, upper hinges cracking, sound, small piece lacking from one endpaper, foxed.   M & S Rare Books, Inc.   95 - 162   2013 $350

Inman, Henry *The Old Santa Fe Trail: the Story of a Great Highway.* New York: 1897. First edition, xvi, 493 pages, illustrations, folding map, 3 ads, original pictorial boards, top edge gilt, extremities and spines rubbed, light staining or insect nibbling on spine, bookplates on front pastedown, internally very good. Dumont Maps & Books of the West 125 - 56 2013 $100

Innes, Michael *Christmas at Candleshoe.* New York: Dodd, Mead & Co., 1953. First US edition, octavo, boards. L. W. Currey, Inc. Christmas Themed Books - 128803 2013 $300

Innes, Michael *What Happened at Hazelwood.* London: Gollancz, 1946. First edition, slight fading at base of spine, otherwise fine in dust jacket with short closed tear. Mordida Books 81 - 269 2013 $300

An Inquiry into the Causes of the Insurrection of the Negroes in the Island of St. Domingo. London: 1792. First edition, 8vo., fine, stitched and uncut in original printed wrappers. Maggs Bros. Ltd. 1467 - 14 2013 £1250

An Interesting Appendix to Sir William Blackstone's Commentaries on the Laws of England. Philadelphia: Robert Bell, 1773. Second American edition, 8vo., contemporary calf, crudely rebacked, very good, browned, institutional name stamped on free endpaper, name erased from title, bookplate of John C. Williams. M & S Rare Books, Inc. 95 - 31 2013 $3500

International Exhibition, 1862 *A Catalogue of the First (second and last) Portion of... very choice and Valuable Wines Spirits, and Liqueurs... Furniture and fittings Which will be sold by Public Auction by Merrs. Green & Son... in the Exhibition Building on Monday Dec. 8th 1862 and (26) subsequent Days.* London: J. M. Johnson & Son..., 1862-1863. 6 volumes, including especially bound copy in red morocco for Alderman Samuel green, proprietor of Green and Sons, 4 interleaved copies marked-up by auctioneer and his clerk and one further volume interleaved and marked up for the French Wine section sold on the 11th 13th December 1862, bound in flexible roan and lettered gilt on upper covers, unique set of marked up copies. Marlborough Rare Books Ltd. 218 - 87 2013 £2500

International Sporting Club *11th Rallye Automobile. Monte Carlo. Organised by the International Sporting-Club in Conjunction with the Automobile-Club of Monaco... Regulations January 1932.* Monte Carlo: printed by Impremerie Monegasque, 1932. First edition, 27 black and white drawings and sketches, 4 photos, map, stapled paper wrappers, original unused pink detachable entry form and information slips still attached, double page map, numerous ads, photos, scarce, very good, spine worn, wrappers soiled, one leaf torn at lower edge, interior quite bright, few leaves still unopened. Kaaterskill Books 16 - 50 2013 $500

Ireland, John *The Shipwrecked Orphans a True Narrative of the Shipwreck and Sufferings of John Ireland and William Bayley Who Were Wrecked in the Ship Charles Eaton on an Island in the South Seas.* New Haven: S. Babcock, 1845. 12mo., titlepage and 8 plates, original green printed wrappers, spine chipped, some minor dampstaining not affecting text, 64 pages. Maggs Bros. Ltd. 1467 - 80 2013 £1750

Ireland, Joseph N. *Records of the New York Stage from 1750 to 1860.* New York: T. H. Morrell, 1866-1867. First edition, one of 200 octavo copies for subscribers (an additional 60 copies were printed in quarto), octavo, 241 x 159mm., 241 x 159mm., striking 19th century dark brown morocco beautifully gilt by Stikeman (stamp signed), raised bands, spines intricately gilt in double ruled compartments with elaborate inner frame of curls, volutes and fleurons, marbled sides and endpapers, top edge gilt, small oval portraits on titlepages, leaves faintly browned at edges (as no doubt in all copies), boards bit chafed, minor wear to joints and extremities (one corner slightly bumped), still handsomely bound in excellent condition, volumes showing no serious wear, text quite smooth and clean. Phillip J. Pirages 63 - 466 2013 $550

Ireland, Samuel *Picturesque Views on the Thames from Its Source in Gloucestershire ot the Nore with Observations on the Public Buildings and Other Works of Art.* London: Egerton, 1792. First edition, 2 volumes, 8vo., 2 maps, sepia aquatint titlepages, 52 sepia aquatints, some light occasional spotting, mainly in margins, contemporary speckled calf, volume I neatly rebacked using original spine with some small loss at head. J. & S. L. Bonham Antiquarian Booksellers Europe - 9236 2013 £500

Ireland, William Henry 1777-1835 *Memoirs of Jeanne D'Arc Surnamed La Pucelle D'Orleans: with the History of Her Times.* London: Robert Triphook, 1824. 2 volumes bound in 4, 240 x 150mm., pleasing 19th century dark blue three quarter morocco, flat spines decorated in gilt and inlaid with four tan fleurs-de-lys, marbled sides and endpapers, top edge gilt, with 27 plates, and extra illustrated with 22 plates, four of them in color, large paper copy, signature of Charles G. Dill dated 31 May 1909;, joints and extremities with hint of rubbing (but well masked with dye), small chip out of one spine top, backstrips lightly sunned, pretty bindings solid and with no serious condition issues, flyleaves and final leaf in each volume somewhat browned (one opening with small portion of the pages similarly browned from laid-in acidic object), variable offsetting from plates (perhaps a dozen rather noticeably offset), intermittent spotted foxing (isolated leaves more heavily foxed), not without problems internally, text still fresh, without many signs of use and printed within vast margins. Phillip J. Pirages 63 - 267 2013 $850

Ireland, William Henry 1777-1835 *Scribbleomania; or the Printer's Devil's Polichronicon.* London: printed for Sherwood, Neely, & Jones, 1815. First edition, title printed in black and red, 3 pages ads, few internal marks, contemporary half dark green calf, little rubbed, leading hinge splitting and repaired, booklabel of Joan Feisenberger. Jarndyce Antiquarian Booksellers CCIII - 394   2013   £225

The Irish Ancestor. 1969. No. 1 - 1973 No. 1; 1974 No. 1 & 2, 1982, No. 1 - 1985 No. 2 + supplements to 1969, 70 and 71, 21 issues in all, fine in original wrappers. C. P. Hyland   261 - 705   2013   £100

Irish Eloquence. Speeches of the Celebrated Irish Orators, Philips, Curran & Grattan... Philadelphia: Key, Mielke & Biddle, 1832. 8vo., modern cloth, very good.   C. P. Hyland   261 - 497   2013   £50

The Irish Genealogist. Volume 2 No,. 12 July, 1955. through 3/9, 4/1-5/4, 5/6-6/3, 6/5, 7/1-3, /1-12/3, 13/1 & 2, 45 issues in all, original wrappers, very good to fine.   C. P. Hyland   261 - 706   2013   £250

The Irish Genealogist. Volume IV no. 3-6, 1970-1973. No. 3 cover damp damaged, else very good.   C. P. Hyland   261 - 707   2013   £35

The Irish Genealogist. Volume V. No. 1-4, 6, 1974-1977. and 1979, Very good.   C. P. Hyland   261 - 708   2013   £50

The Irish Genealogist. Volume VI no. 1-3, 5, 1980-1982. and 1984, Very good.   C. P. Hyland   261 - 709   2013   £40

The Irish Georgian Society. Volume XII No. 4, Oct., 1970. to XXII No. 2 (June 1980), lacking 2 issues, XVI 3/4 and XVII 1/2, with 1972 prospectus for the Pool & Cash silver plates, 22 items.   C. P. Hyland   261 - 711   2013   £70

The Irish Studies Review. Volume 6 No. 1 April, 1999. - Volume 10 No. 1 April 2002, 13 issues, all in original wrappers, fine.   C. P. Hyland   261 - 712   2013   £80

Irish Sword. Numbers 4, 12--17, 19, 21, 23-28, 43, 54-56, 71-74, 78, 91, 105, all very good in original wrappers, 27 issues.   C. P. Hyland   261 - 713   2013   £200

Irish Theatre Archive *Prompts: Bulletin of Irish Theatre Archive. Nos. 1-4 (of 6).* 1981-1982. 8vo., cloth, very good.   C. P. Hyland   261 - 511   2013   £40

Irvine, W. R. *The Small Back Room.* Belfast: Neatherlea, 2009. First edition, 8vo., original grey suede, lettered in silver, frontispiece.   Maggs Bros. Ltd.   1442 - 126   2013   £350

Irving, Christopher *A Catechism of Jewish Antiquities.* New York: Lockwood, 1824. Second American edition, 18m., 80 pages, frontispiece, original stiff wrappers, rebacked.   M & S Rare Books, Inc.   95 - 177   2013 $425

Irving, John 1942- *The Cider House Rules.* n.p.: Garp Enterprises/Radio Telegraphic Co., 1991. Revised, hand number '42', screenplay dated June 14, 1991, signed by author, 130 pages, stringbound with one remaining brad, foxing to pages, near fine.   Ken Lopez Bookseller   159 - 81   2013 $3500

Irving, John 1942- *The Cider House Rules.* Los Angeles: Film Colony/Miramax, 1995. Screenplay, Revised December 1995 hand numbered '47', with signature of Michael Goldsmith as well as changes and proposed changes to text, apparently in Goldsmith's hand, signed by author, uncommon signed, bradbound in Miramax covers, 139 pages, near fine, working copy, changes and revisions visible.   Ken Lopez Bookseller   159 - 82   2013 $2500

Irving, John 1942- *The Fourth Hand.* Toronto: Knopf Canada, 2001. Uncorrected proof copy of the first Canadian edition, inscribed by author, fine in wrappers with dust jacket art bound in, uncommon proof, especially scarce signed.   Ken Lopez Bookseller   159 - 84   2013 $450

Irving, John 1942- *The Imaginary Girlfriend.* London: Bloomsbury, 1996. Uncorrected proof copy of the first British edition, inscribed by author, fine in near fine proof dust jacket worn, where it overlays proof, with price of £13.99 (later lowered to £9.99), uncommon proof.   Ken Lopez Bookseller   159 - 83   2013 $1000

Irving, John 1942- *In One Person.* New York: Simon & Schuster, 2012. First edition, signed by author, scare thus, one upper corner lightly bumped, else fine in fine dust jacket.   Ken Lopez Bookseller   159 - 86   2013 $500

Irving, John 1942- *A Prayer for Owen Meany.* New York: Morrow, 1989. First edition, number 16 of 250 copies signed by author, cloth in acetate dust jacket and cloth slipcase, new condition.   Gemini Fine Books & Arts., Ltd.   Art Reference & Illustrated Books - 2013 $1250

Irving, John Treat 1812-1906 *Indian Sketches Taken During an Expedition to the Pawnee Tribes (1833).* Norman: University of Oklahoma Press, 1955. First annotated edition, 16 illustrations, double page map, green-gray cloth, very fine, dust jacket.   Argonaut Book Shop   Summer 2013 - 169   2013 $75

Irving, Washington 1783-1859 *The Adventures of Captain Bonneville, USA in the Rocky Mountains and the Far West.* New York and London: G. P. Putnam's Sons, 1898. Pawnee edition, 2 volumes, frontispieces, 26 photogravure plates from prints, drawings and photos, printed tissue guards, large folding map, navy blue decorated cloth, beveled edges, covers stamped with elaborate Indian motif design in gilt by Margaret Armstrong, bookplate on inner covers, beautiful set in very fine. Argonaut Book Shop Summer 2013 - 170   2013 $500

Irving, Washington 1783-1859 *The Alhambra.* London and New York: Macmillan and Co., 1896. One of 500 extra-illustrated copies, 264 x 194mm., xx, 436 pages, numerous illustrations in text and 12 inserted lithographs by Joseph Pennell, magnificent contemporary dark green crushed morocco, extravagantly gilt by Bagguley (signed with firm's ink 'Sutherland' patent stamp on verso of front endleaf), covers with borders of multiple plain and decorative gilt rules, lobed inner frame with fleuron cornerpieces, whole enclosing large and extremely intricate gilt lozenge, raised bands, spine lavishly gilt in double ruled compartments, gilt titling and turn-ins, beautiful vellum doublures elaborately tooled in diapered gilt, red and green Moorish pattern, green watered silk endleaves, top edge gilt, other edges rough trimmed, bookplate of Harold Douthit, boards with slight humpback posture(as often with vellum doublures), otherwise in beautiful condition inside and out, lovely binding with lustrous morocco, vellum and gilt, text virtually pristine. Phillip J. Pirages 61 - 97   2013 $5500

Irving, Washington 1783-1859 *A History of the Life and Voyages of Christopher Columbus and Voyages and Discoveries of the Companions of Columbus.* New York: G. and C. Carvill, 1828. First edition, 4 volumes, uniformly bound in contemporary tan calf, red leather title and volume labels to spines, spine of each book decorated with raised bands and gilt devices, boards ruled gilt and feature blind stamped decorations along edges, few chips to leather on spines of first two volumes and hinges of both cracked although boards remain firmly attached, last two volumes have light rubbing to hinges and spines, all volumes leather cracked on spines and light evidence of dampstaining on boards, endpages marbled and edges speckled in brown, occasional spots of foxing to interiors and top margins, with slight browning, map volume one is present, however, it has two inch closed tear, still attractive set, 399; 367; 420; 350 pages. The Kelmscott Bookshop 7 - 134   2013 $600

Irving, Washington 1783-1859 *A History of the Life and Voyages of Christopher Columbus.* London: John Murray, 1828. First edition, 8vo., 4 volumes, 2 large folding maps, bound into rear of volume IV, all 4 bound with half titles, full calf, stamped in gilt on spine, by Bickers & Son, some rubbed and nicked, very nice, clean set. Second Life Books Inc. 183 - 186   2013 $950

Irving, Washington 1783-1859 *A History of New York...* New York: George P. Putnam, 1850. First edition, illustrations by Felix O. C. Darly, very good, some separation of spine from front board and some offsetting on endpapers. Between the Covers Rare Books, Inc. New York City - 109664   2013 $120

Irving, Washington 1783-1859 *Life of George Washington.* New York: G. P. Putnam, 1860. 235 x 149mm., 5 volumes, pleasant contemporary butterscotch colored half calf, raised bands, spines attractively gilt in compartments with frame composed of entwined scrolls and drawer handle ornaments and a large central fleuron, each spine with one black and one green morocco label, marbled boards, edges and endpapers; 7 engraved portraits, 2 engraved vignettes and 15 maps, 3 of them double page; boards bit chafed, extremities little worn, three not very noticeable short cracks at top of volume V, small abrasions here and there, gilt just slightly dulled, bindings solid, generally well preserved, still attractive, marginal stain of no great consequence on two pages in Table of Contents of volume I, otherwise excellent internally, text quite clean, fresh and smooth. Phillip J. Pirages 63 - 260   2013 $450

Irving, Washington 1783-1859 *Rip Van Winkle.* New York & London: Doubleday Page & William Heinemann, 1905. First US edition, 4to., green gilt cloth, closed split base of spine, articles removed from blank page, slight foxing on text page, really tight and very good+, 51 magnificent mounted color plates plus several black and whites by Arthur Rackham. Aleph-Bet Books, Inc. 104 - 474   2013 $1200

Irving, Washington 1783-1859 *Rip Van Winkle.* London: Heinemann, 1907. Third impression, large 8vo., original pictorial green cloth gilt, short reaired tear to head of upper hinge, 51 tipped in color plates by Arthur Rackham, very good, clean copy. R. F. G. Hollett & Son Children's Books - 492   2013   £300

Irving, Washington 1783-1859 *Rip Van Winkle.* Utrecht: Catharijne Press, 1987. Limited to 165 copies, this one of 150 numbered copies, with 4 tipped in illustrations by Henk van der Haar, 6.5 x 4.5cm, pictorial paper covered boards, miniature bookplate of Kathryn Rickard, from the collection of Donn W. Sanford. Oak Knoll Books 303 - 85   2013 $125

Irving, Washington 1783-1859 *Sketch Book of Geoffrey Crayon, Gent.* New York: printed By C. S. Van Winkel, 1819-1820. First edition, first printings of parts 1-6, second printing of part 7, 2 volumes, 8vo., 20th century crimson straight grained morocco, spine and inner dentelles gilt, all edges gilt, bound without wrappers as usual, 4 ownership signatures of Francis Redding Tillou (1795-1865), very minor occasional browning, fine, beautifully bound. Howard S. Mott Inc. 262 - 79   2013 $5000

Irving, Washington 1783-1859 *Spanish Papers and Other Miscellanies, Hietherto Unpublished or Uncollected by...* New York: Putnam, Hurd and Houghton, 1866. First edition, 8vo., faded purple cloth, stamped on spine, faded, top edge gilt loose in volume one, some offsetting from frontispiece, couple of light stains, good/very good.   Second Life Books Inc.   183 - 187   2013 $125

Irving, Washington 1783-1859 *Tales of a Traveller.* London: John Murray, 1824. First edition, 2 volumes, 231 x 141mm., with five items not included in later First American edition, publisher's blue paper boards, paper labels on spine, edges untrimmed (recently resewn and rebacked, using original backstrips), blue cloth chemise and inside a matching (slightly rubbed and soiled) slipcase, black morocco backed spine designed to appear on shelf as 2 volumes with raised bands and gilt titling, engraved booklabel from which name has been removed; corners worn, boards slightly soiled, original temporary bindings expertly restored now and extremely pleasing, very faint offsetting here and there, just most trivial isolated soiling, otherwise fine internally, leaves especially fresh and clean, margins inordinately ample.   Phillip J. Pirages   63 - 261   2013 $2400

Irving, Washington 1783-1859 *Tales of a Traveller.* New York: Putnam, 1895. First edition, 2 volumes, large 8vo., white cloth with extensive gilt pictorial bindings, signed GWE (George Wharton Edwards), top edge gilt, fine in original printed cloth, dust jackets, 5 illustrations half tone by Arthur Rackham (also illustrated by others), uncommon.   Aleph-Bet Books, Inc.   105 - 497   2013 $450

Isaacs, Alick *Virus Interference I: the Interferon.* London: Royal Society, 1957. 8vo., original printed wrappers, fine.   Jeff Weber Rare Books   172 - 150   2013 $400

Isendoorn, Gisbertus *Cursus Logicus Systematicus & Agonisticus in quo Praeter Theoremata, Quaestiones a Eorum Explicationem Necessariae...* Oxford: by R. Blagrave for W. Hall, 1658. Title within a border of printer's ornaments, defective however, with loss of border at foremargin but without loss of text and mounted, some dampstaining in lower margins and worming, affecting text, 8vo., contemporary calf, double blind ruled borders on sides with an off centre double rule to the left, horizontal blind pairs of rules on spine, spine defective at foot, crude repairs, lower edges worn, sound.   Blackwell's Rare Books   B174 - 76   2013   £750

Isherwood, Christopher *All the Conspirators.* New York: New Directions Book, 1958. First American edition, very good++, 8vo., dust jacket with mild sun to spine.   By the Book, L. C.   38 - 88   2013 $650

Isherwood, Christopher *Lions and Shadows: an Education in the Twenties.* London: Hogarth Press, 1938. First edition, photographic frontispiece portrait, foolscap 8vo., original blue cloth, first issue with backstrip blocked in black, partial browning to free endpapers, dust jacket with design by Robert Medley reproduction on front panel, backstrip panel darkened and trifle frayed at head and tail, few small ink spots to rear panel, good, bookplate of Paul Tabori.   Blackwell's Rare Books   B174 - 238   2013   £250

Isherwood, Christopher *Prater Violet.* London: Methuen, 1946. First edition, foolscap 8vo., original purple cloth, backstrip blocked in green, dust jacket with backstrip panel and fore-edges darkened, small chip in front panel at head and tail, good, bookplate of Paul Tabori.   Blackwell's Rare Books   B174 - 239   2013   £100

Ishiguro, Kazuo *A Pale View of Hills.* London: Faber & Faber, 1982. First edition, fine in very near fine dust jacket with just slight fading to spine, very attractive.   Ken Lopez Bookseller   159 - 88   2013 $1000

Israel, Madeleine *Poemes 1928-1934.* 1938. First edition, 8vo., 126 pages, wrappers, unopened, very good, signed presentation copy to Elizabeth Bowen.   C. P. Hyland   261 - 145   2013   £45

Iverian Society *Report of the Inaugural Meeting of the Ivernian Society.* 1908? 13 pages, original wrappers under modern cloth, very good.   C. P. Hyland   261 - 261   2013   £75

Ives, Joseph C. *Report Upon the Colorado River of the West, Explored in 1857 and 1858...* Washington: GPO, 1861. 1860. First edition, 5 parts in 1, 4to., fine illustrations, numerous steel engravings, minor tears to maps repaired, some browning, spotting and engraving offsetting, page 108 glue spot on plate has pulled some facing text, titlepage with small perforated "LC" and dated 1908, rubber stamp on verso, otherwise clean pages, original pictorial gilt and blind stamped dark brown cloth covers, recent new spine of similarly toned cloth, Library of Congress bookplate, very good, unusually clean and well maintained.   Jeff Weber Rare Books   171 - 197   2013 $1400

Ives, Sarah Noble *The Story of Teddy the Bear.* Springfield: McLoughlin, n.d. circa, 1920. Folio, cloth backed pictorial boards, tips slightly worn, else near fine, 5 full page color plates and many 2 color illustrations, excellent condition.   Aleph-Bet Books, Inc.   104 - 62   2013 $350

Ives, Sidney *The Parkman Dexter Howe Library. Parts I, III & IV.* Gainesville: University of Florida, 1983-1986. 8vo., frontispiece, plates, printed wrappers, near fine.   Jeff Weber Rare Books   171 - 172   2013 $50

J

J. B. Judkins Company *Judkins. Being the Story of a New England Handicraft and Its Honest Expression in Fine Carriages and Motor Car Bodies.* Merrimac: Judkins, circa, 1920's, 8vo., 34 pages, drawings, paper wrappers, rubbing of label on back page, cover soiled, remnants of pencil notation, cover worn at spine, but very good, tight copy. Second Life Books Inc. 183 - 188 2013 $60

J. G., A. *Willie and Lucy at the Sea-Side.* Religious Tract Society, 1868. First edition, square 8vo., original blind-stamped green cloth gilt extra, little worn, all edges gilt, 4 colored plate, 8 text woodcut, little shaken. R. F. G. Hollett & Son Children's Books - 301 2013 £85

Jack & Jill and Old Dame Gill. Banbury: J. G. Rusher, circa, 1820. 16mo., each page but one with woodcut illustration, that on last being full page, slightly foxed, corner torn off lower outer corner of first leaf, 16mo., uncut, self wrappers, sound. Blackwell's Rare Books B174 - 81 2013 £50

Jack the Giant Killer and Other Tales. New York: Blue Ribbon, 1932. Thick 4to., pictorial boards, usual hinge strains, else unusually fine in fine dust jacket, illustrations by Harold Lentz, includng 4 fabulous double page pop-ups. Aleph-Bet Books, Inc. 104 - 434 2013 $900

Jacka, Lois Essary *Enduring Traditions. Art of the Navajo.* Flagstaff: Northland Press, 1994. First edition, tall quarto, color photos by Jerry Jacka, red cloth, very fine. Argonaut Book Shop Recent Acquisitions June 2013 - 150 2013 $60

Jackman, E. R. *The Oregon Desert.* Caldwell: Caxton printers Ltd., 1964. First edition, second printing, photos, endpaper map, grayish blue cloth lettered in black, offsetting to blank flyleaf, fine with slightly chipped pictorial dust jacket. Argonaut Book Shop Summer 2013 - 171 2013 $75

Jackman, Joseph *The Sham-robbery Committed by Elijah Putnam Goodridge on His Own Person, in Newbury...* Concord: printed for the author, 1819. First edition, 12mo., contemporary plain wrappers, text somewhat browned, but nice, crisp copy, very scarce. M & S Rare Books, Inc. 95 - 96 2013 $425

Jackson, Catherine Hannah Charlotte *Lady Jackson's Works.* London: Grolier Society, circa, 1899. One of 150 copies for England and America, "Edition Artistique", 9 x 6 inches, 14 volumes, extremely pleasing crimson crushed three quarter morocco, attractively gilt and inlaid, marbled sides and endpapers, raised bands, spines gilt ruled compartments featuring floral ornaments at corners connected by scalloped stippling along each of four sides and with inlaid olive morocco flower as a centerpiece, top edge gilt, other edges rough trimmed, 10 of the volumes entirely unopened (and two others largely so), with 164 plates, including 82 images, each in two states, usually in black and white on different paper stock, but with 28 of the plates (14 of them frontispieces) in color, lacking two illustrations called for from plate list in "Valois" volume), titles printed partly in yellow and blue-green, one volume with small notch out of bottom of a group of 10 consecutive leaves, but remarkably well preserved copy in quite attractive, very bright bindings, without anything beyond the trivial in terms of wear to leather or signs of use to the (mostly unopened) text. Phillip J. Pirages 63 - 262 2013 $1500

Jackson, Charles James *An Illustrated History of English Plate, Ecclesiastical and Secular.* London: Country Life Limited and B. T. Batsford, 1911. First edition, 2 volumes, 343 x 279mm., original dark green half binding of faux morocco by Western Mail Bindery in Cardiff (with their ticket), cloth sides, spines with raised bands, gilt ruled compartments, gilt titling, top edge gilt, etched frontispiece, 76 photogravure plates and 1500 other illustrations, titles in red and black, text printed on coated stock, plates printed on high quality thick paper, bookplate of Dorothy Riley Brown in each volume, leather somewhat flaked from joints and extremities, few superficial marks to covers, hinges cracked before half title in each volume, bindings otherwise sound and not without appeal. fine set internally, only trivial defects. Phillip J. Pirages 63 - 439 2013 $175

Jackson, Charles Ross *Quintus Oakes.* New York: G. W. Dillington, 1904. First edition, near fine in pictorial brown cloth covers, gold stamped titles on spine. Mordida Books 81 - 270 2013 $150

Jackson, Donald C. *Dams.* Aldershot, et al: Ashgate/ Variorum, 1997. 8vo., photos and illustrations, red cloth, gilt stamped cover and spine titles, fine. Jeff Weber Rare Books 169 - 235 2013 $110

Jackson, G. G. *Trains, Cars and Planes.* Blackie & Son, n.d. 1920's, 8vo., original cloth backed pictorial boards, edges and lower board rather worn and stained, unpaginated, 23 color plates and numerous line drawings. R. F. G. Hollett & Son Children's Books - 302 2013 £25

Jackson, Holbrook *The Anatomy of Bibliomania. (with) The Fear of Books.* London: Soncino Press, 1930. 1931. 1932. First edition, 3 volumes, 8vo., light intermittent spotting to first two volumes, red buckram, spines sunned, boards little marked and rubbed, corners of third volume slightly bumped, top edges gilt as issued, edges dusty with light speckling, endpapers slightly foxed, mostly in volume I, but nice set.   Unsworths Antiquarian Booksellers   28 - 172   2013   £120

Jackson, Holbrook *The Anatomy of Bibliomania.* Soncino Press, 1932. Third edition, xv, 854 pages, octavo, original cloth, some marking, text very good.   C. P. Hyland   261 - 77   2013   £25

Jackson, J. E. *History of St. George's Church, Doncaster Destroyed by Fire, Feb. 28 1853.* for the author, 1855. Folio, frontispiece, 14 lithograph plates, woodcuts in text, very good, contemporary half black calf, marbled boards, joints expertly repaired, some sattered foxing and titlepage little creased, scarce.   Ken Spelman Books Ltd.   73 - 71   2013   £125

Jackson, John Hughlings *Neurological Fragments.* London: 1925. Original cloth, nice, lx, 227 pages.   James Tait Goodrich   S74 - 158   2013 $195

Jackson, John Hughlings *Selected Writings of John Hughlings Jackson.* New York: Basic Books, 1958. 2 volumes, original binding, original dust jackets (bit worn, otherwise nice bright set).   James Tait Goodrich   S74 - 157   2013 $395

Jackson, John N. *The Welland Canals and their Communities...* Toronto: University of Toronto Press, 1997. First edition, 8vo, photos, 13 maps, 11 tables, gray cloth, red stamped spine title, dust jacket, Burndy bookplate, fine.   Jeff Weber Rare Books   169 - 236   2013 $100

Jackson, Jon A. *The Blind Pig.* New York: Random House, 1978. First edition, very fine in dust jacket.   Mordida Books   81 - 271   2013 $200

Jackson, Jon A. *Dead Folk.* Tucson: Dennis McMillan, 1995. First edition, one of 300 numbered copies signed by author, very fine in dust jacket with slipcase.   Mordida Books   81 - 272   2013 $150

Jackson, K. *Farm Stories.* New York: Simon and Schuster, 1946. First edition, one of 650 numbered copies, numbered and signed by three contributors on special plate, 4to., very good+.   Beasley Books   2013 - 2013 $100

Jackson, Kathryn *Nurse Nancy.* New York: S&S, 1952. A., Fine, illustrations in color by Corinne Malerne, beautiful copy, rare.   Aleph-bet Books, Inc.   104 - 241   2013 $400

Jackson, Louise *Beulah. A Biography of the Mineral King Valley of California.* Tucson: Westernlore Press, 1988. First edition, xi, 204 pages, maps, red leatherette, very fine with pictorial dust jacket.   Argonaut Book Shop   Recent Acquisitions June 2013 - 151   2013 $75

Jackson, Mary Ann *The Pictorial Flora; or British Botany Delineated in 1500 Lithographic Drawings...* London: Longman, Orme, Brown, Green and Longmans, 1840. 8vo., 131 lithographed plates, mostly with 12 figures to the page but including appendix including some 300 extra figures (with gap in numbering), foxed, contemporary green vellum, metal catch and clasp, red lettering piece, sound.   Blackwell's Rare Books   172 - 76   2013   £300

Jackson, Mary Catherine *Word-Sketches in the Sweet South.* London: Richard Bentley, 1873. First edition, 8vo., pages 301, frontispiece, late 19th century red full calf, gilt spine, raised bands, school crest on upper cover, fine.   J. & S. L. Bonham Antiquarian Booksellers   Europe - 8978   2013   £350

Jackson, Shirley *The Lottery or the Adventures of James Harris.* London: Victor Gollancz, 1950. First English edition, slightly cocked, else near fine in very good dust jacket with small chips at extremities, inscribed by author to fellow author Paul Radin and Doris.   Between the Covers Rare Books, Inc.   Sci-Fi, Fantasy & Horror - 103778   2013 $2500

Jackson, William *Thirty letters on Various Subjects.* London: T. Cadell and E. Evans in the Strand and B. Thorn and Son in Exeter, 1783. 2 volumes in 1, 12mo., very good, clean copy, recent quarter green gilt morocco, marbled boards, vellum tips.   Ken Spelman Books Ltd.   75 - 38   2013   £280

Jacob, Giles *The Complete Court-Keeper or Land Steward's Assistant.* In the Savoy: London: Henry Lintot for T. Woodward, D. Browne, J. Shcukburgh, T. Osborne...., 1741. Fourth edition, 8vo., 20th century half calf over blue buckram, 5 raised spine bands, gilt stamped red leather spine label, cloth lightly rubbed, titlepage signature upper margin, very good.   Jeff Weber Rare Books   171 - 186   2013 $400

Jacob, Hildebrand *The Fatal Constancy.* London: printed for J. Tonson, 1623. First edition, 8vo., disbound, head of titlepage little close cropped.   Jarndyce Antiquarian Booksellers   CCIV - 169   2013   £45

Jacobs, Joseph *Book of Wonder Voyages.* London: David Nutt, 1896. First edition, 8vo., pictorial cloth, 224 pages, + Nutt catalog, near fine, John Batten plates and illustrations.   Aleph-Bet Books, Inc.   105 - 58   2013 $200

Jacobs, Joseph *More English Fairy Tales.* London: David Nutt, 1894. One of 150 numbered copies for sale, signed by author, 4to., printed on Japan vellum, 8 fine full page illustrations in 2 states by John Batten, many smaller illustrations, flexible cream colored boards, few small spots on cover, else fine and title.   Aleph-Bet Books, Inc.   105 - 244   2013 $850

Jacobs, T. C. H. *Appointment with the Hangman.* New York: Macaulay, 1936. First American edition, foxing to boards, thus very good in very good plus dust jacket, soiling on rear panel.   Between the Covers Rare Books, Inc.   Mystery & Detective Fiction - 97641   2013 $200

Jacobsson, D. *Fifty Golden Years of the Rand 1886-1936.* London: Faber, 1936. Original blue cloth, gilt, extremities rather rubbed, 206 pages, 8 plates, extending plan, scattered spotting.   R. F. G. Hollett & Son   Africana - 98   2013   £25

Jaekel, Blair *The Lands of the Tamed Turk.* Boston: L. C. Page, 1910. First edition, 8vo., 295 pages, map, illustrations, original green decorative cloth, near fine.   J. & S. L. Bonham Antiquarian Booksellers   Europe - 8457   2013   £125

Jahr, G. H. G. *G. H. G. Jahr's Manual of Homoeopathic Medicine.* Allentown: at the Academical Book Store, 1836. First American edition, 588 pages, lacking portion of index, original cloth backed printed boards, covers stained but good, no endpapers, insurance ads (from 1872) pasted on inside of covers.   M & S Rare Books, Inc.   95 - 149   2013 $550

James Watt and the Steam Engine. Religious Tract Society, n.d. circa, 1870. 12mo., original blindstamped cloth gilt, slight mark on lower hinge, all edges gilt.   R. F. G. Hollett & Son   Children's Books - 17   2013   £30

James I, King of Scotland *The Kingis Quair.* Vale Press, 1903. One of 260 copies, (another 10 copies on vellum), 236 x 150mm., lv, (1) pages, printed in red and black, extremely pleasing midnight blue crushed morocco, intricately gilt by Stikeman, stamp signed, covers with gilt frame formed by three rows of tiny gilt circlets enclosing two intertwining veins that combined at 12 intervals to produce a trio of rose blossoms, raised bands, spine gilt in double ruled compartments containing tulip beneath a daisy, flowers surrounded by gilt circlets, inner gilt dentelles, marbled endpapers, top edge gilt, matching morocco backed flat lined solander box, morocco bookplate of Paul Chevalier, inevitable slight offsetting to free endpapers from turn-ins otherwise, most attractive copy in very fine condition, binding lustrous and unworn, text with no signs of use.   Phillip J. Pirages   61 - 125   2013 $3500

James I, King of Scotland *Kingis Quair.* Vale Press, 1903. One of 260 copies (of an edition of 270), printed in black and red on arnold handmade paper, large wood engraved initial letter designed by Charles Ricketts, crown 8vo., original quarter fawn linen, pale blue boards, printed front cover label, faintly brown endpapers as usual, untrimmed and unopened, near fine.   Blackwell's Rare Books   B174 - 395   2013   £250

James II, King of Great Britain *His Majesties Most Gracious Speech to Both Houses of Parliament... 22th of May 1685.* London: by the assigns of John Bill deceas'd and by Henry Hills and Thomas Newcomb, 1685. Folio, 7 pages, modern buckram.   Joseph J. Felcone Inc.   Books Printed before 1701 - 55   2013 $300

James, Cowan, & Co. *Illustrated Catalogue and Net Price List of Carriage and Wagon Hardware Blacksmiths' Supplies No. 10.* London: James Cowan & Co., 1914. 8vo., card covers with tab index in taped spine, pages 350, illustrations with prices, very good.   Schooner Books Ltd.   104 - 156   2013 $95

James, George Payne Rainsford *Philip Augustus or the Brothers in Arms.* London: Smith, Elder and Co., 1845. 241 x 165mm., handsome contemporary brown pebble grain half morocco, marbled sides and endpapers, raised bands, spine heavily and attractively gilt in 6 compartments with repeated motif of center lozenge surrounded by volute border, top edge gilt, engraved frontispiece joints and extremities with minor rubbing, frontispiece somewhat foxed, otherwise excellent, fine internally.   Phillip J. Pirages   63 - 363   2013 $150

James, George Wharton *The 1910 Trip of the H. M. M. B. A. to California and the Pacific Coast.* San Francisco: 1911. 377 pages, ads, illustrations, original cloth, light wear to extremities, even lighter wear internally, overall very good, inscribed by author.   Dumont Maps & Books of the West   122 - 70   2013 $95

James, George Wharton *The Wonders of the Colorado Desert (Southern California) Its Rivers and Its Mountains...* Boston: 1906. First edition, 2 volumes, xliv, 270 pages, illustrations, folding map; xiv, 271-547 pages, illustrations, some external wear and soil, spines faded, hinges starting, overall very good set.   Dumont Maps & Books of the West 124 - 70   2013 $150

James, Henry   1843-1916 *Pardon my Delay. Letters from Henry James to Bruce Richmomd.* Tunbridge Wells: Foundling Press, 1994. First edition, 215/350 copies printed on Zerkall mouldmade paper in black with occasional typographical decorations in red, 2 frontispiece portraits tipped in, crown 8vo., original off-white boards, printed front cover label, untrimmed, fine.   Blackwell's Rare Books B174 - 240   2013   £25

James, Henry   1843-1916 *The Reverberator.* London and New York: Macmillan and Co., 1888. Second edition, American issue, 184 x 127mm., 2 p.l., 229, (1) pages, publisher's original blue cloth with gilt titling and decoration, half title with ink ownership inscription "Kate D. Wilson, Jan. 26th 189(0)", bookplate inscribed "Capt. James Hart, Baltimore 26 Feb. (19)46", spine slightly rolled, tiny snag at top of backstrip and one at bottom, light rubbing to small portions of joints and extremities, still nearly fine, cloth and gilt especially bright, hinges solid, text with virtually no signs of use. Phillip J. Pirages   63 - 263   2013 $250

James, J. T. *Journal of a Tour in Germany, Sweden, Russia, Poland during the Years 1813 and 1814.* London: John Murray, 1816. First edition, quarto, 6 etched plates, 12 sepia aquatint plates, some light browning opposite, vignette on titlepage, plate, 50mm. split at head of spine, good.   J. & S. L. Bonham Antiquarian Booksellers   Europe - 9755   2013   £550

James, P. D. *Death of an Expert Witness.* London: Faber, 1977. First edition, foolscap 8vo., original pink boards, backstrip gilt lettered, dust jacket, fine, signed by author. Blackwell's Rare Books   172 - 200   2013   £120

James, P. D. *Unnatural Causes.* London: Faber & Faber, 1967. First edition, fine in fine, price clipped dust jacket, scarce in this condition.   Between the Covers Rare Books, Inc. Mystery & Detective Fiction - 291791   2013 $3500

James, Robert *The Modern Practice of Physic...* London: printed for J. Hodges, 1746. 2 volumes, blank flyleaf missing in volume I, early contemporary full calf, rubbed, joints cracked and weak, text with foxing and browning, overall good copy.   James Tait Goodrich   S74 - 156   2013 $295

James, Will   1892-1942 *All in the Day's Riding.* New York: Charles Scribner's Sons, 1933. First edition, first issue with date at bottom of titlepage and Scribner's "A" on copyright page, 104 black and white drawings, plus 2 more on jacket, red cloth, very slight rubbing to foot of spine, contemporary owner's name and date on endpaper, very fine, with lightly worn pictorial dust jacket, neat contemporary owner's name and date (1933).   Argonaut Book Shop Recent Acquisitions June 2013 - 152   2013 $900

James, Will   1892-1942 *Flint Spears, Cowboy Rodeo Contestant.* New York: Charles Scribner's, 1938. First edition, without Scribner's 'A' on copyright page with "New York" at bottom of titlepage, neat contemporary owner's name and date (March 1940) at top edge of endpaper, photos, full color frontispiece, 30 black and white drawings by author, 13 pages of 21 photos, orange red cloth stamped in black, fine with pictorial dust jacket (short half inch tear near lower spine, head of spine very slightly chipped).   Argonaut Book Shop   Recent Acquisitions June 2013 - 153   2013 $400

James, Will   1892-1942 *Scorpion. A Good Bad Horse.* New York: Charles Scribner's Sons, 1936. First edition, full color frontispiece, 45 black and white drawings, salmon cloth stamped in black, contemporary owner's inscription, very fine, pictorial dust jacket, very scarce in this condition, neat contemporary owner's five line inscription to upper corner of endpaper, dated Christmas 1936.   Argonaut Book Shop   Recent Acquisitions June 2013 - 154   2013 $450

James, Will   1892-1942 *Smoky.* New York: Charles Scribner's Sons, 1929. 4to., black cloth, pictorial paste-on, mint in publisher's box with mounted color plate on cover, illustrations by James, rare in box, early copy.   Aleph-Bet Books, Inc.   104 - 290   2013 $450

James, William *The Letters of Charlotte, During Her Connexion with Werter.* New York: printed by William A. Davis for Benj. Gomez, 1797. 12mo., 2 volumes in one, half titles and final blank to volume I, some foxing and browning throughout, slight tears to upper corners of G6 and 7 without loss, full contemporary calf, gilt banded spine, red morocco label, rubbed, leading hinge cracked but firm, corners worn.   Jarndyce Antiquarian Booksellers   CCIV - 170 2013   £150

James, William   1842-1910 *Pragmatism: a New Name for Some Old Ways of Thinking.* New York: Longmans, Green and Co., 1919. 22cm., green publisher's cloth with printed paper spine label, label bit worn and little light fraying at spine ends, else near fine, American composer Virgil Thomson's copy with his pencilled ownership signature, March 1920.   Between the Covers Rare Books, Inc. Philosophy - 326790   2013 $400

Jameson, Anna Brownell Murphy 1794-1860 *The Communion of Labour: a Second Lecture on the Social Employments of Women.* London: Longman Brown, Green, Longmans & Roberts, 1856. First edition, small 8vo., small bookplate of Arthur Hoe, flexible cloth, stamped in gilt, cover little soiled, very good, tight copy. Second Life Books Inc. 182 - 123   2013 $225

Jameson, Anna Brownell Murphy 1794-1860 *Diary of an Ennuye.* Boston: Lilly Wait, Colman and Holden, 1833. First American edition, 8vo., pages 268, publisher's linen (lacks front flyleaves), some foxed and toned, very good. Second Life Books Inc.   182 - 122   2013 $125

Jameson, Anna Brownell Murphy 1794-1860 *Memoirs of Early Italian Painters and of the Progress of Painting in Italy.* London: John Murray, 1880. New edition, 187 x 124mm., simple but fine dark brown crushed morocco in Jansenist style for C. E. Lauriat Co. of Boston (stamp-signed), raised bands densely gilt turn-ins, marbled endpapers, all edges gilt, with 58 portraits of Italian artists, isolated faint smudges, otherwise very fine, quite clean, fresh and bright in unworn and remarkably lustrous binding. Phillip J. Pirages   63 - 264   2013 $150

Jameson, James S. *Story of the Rear Column of the Emin Pasha Relief Expedition.* New York: United States Book Co., 1890. First US edition, large thick 8vo., original pictorial cloth, gilt, foot of spine little rubbed, 100 illustrations, 2 folding facsimiles, 2 colored folding maps, scarce, upper joint badly cracked.   R. F. G. Hollett & Son   Africana - 99   2013   £175

Jami *Salaman and Absal: an Allegory.* London: J. W. Parker and Son, 1856. First edition, 213 x 148mm., xvi, 84 pages, frontispiece; lovely early 20th century chestnut brown morocco handsomely gilt by Zaehnsdorf (stamp signed), covers with multiple-rule frame and central panel containing 25 gilt flowers in rows, each flower with long curving leafy stem, background accented with tiny gilt dots and crescents, raised bands, spine gilt in compartments featuring alternating gilt blossom and twining vines, gilt turn-ins, light brown silk endleaves, original blue paper wrappers bound in at rear, slightly rubbed brown morocco felt lined pull-off case with raised bands and gilt title, flyleaf with offset image of leather bookplate of bookplate of Charles Kalbfleisch, bookplate no longer present, trial marginal soiling or dots of foxing on handful of leaves, else especially fine, text fresh and smooth, margins considerably more than ample, glittering decorative binding unworn and especially lustrous. Phillip J. Pirages   61 - 132   2013 $4500

Jamieson, Frances *Ashford Rectory; or the Spoiled Child Reformed...* printed for G. and W. B. Whittaker, 1820. Third edition, frontispiece and one plate, very good in full contemporary dark red calf, 12mo., gilt ruled borders and spine, morocco label.   Ken Spelman Books Ltd.   75 - 80   2013   £60

Jamieson, John *The History of the Royal Belfast Academical Institution 1810-1960.* 1959. First edition, 8vo., illustrations, dust jacket torn, very good.   C. P. Hyland   261 - 513   2013   £50

Jane, Fred T. *Blake of the "Rattlesnake" or the Man who Saved England.* London: Tower Pub. Co., 1895. First edition, 8vo., 269 pages, illustrations, original pictorial cloth, gilt on spine trifle rubbed, very good, presentation inscription signed by author, very rare.   M & S Rare Books, Inc.   95 - 166   2013 $425

Jane, Fred T. *Blake of the "Rattlesnake" or the Man who Saved England.* Tower Publishing Co., 1895. First edition, original pictorial green cloth gilt, neatly recased with new endpapers, 28 illustrations and drawings by author. R. F. G. Hollett & Son   Children's Books - 303   2013   £120

Jane, Fred T. *Blake of the "Rattlesnake" or the Man who Saved England: a Story of Torpedo Warfare in 189-.* London: W. Thacker & Co., 1898. First edition, illustrations by author, corners bit bumped and some rubbing to spinal extremities, handsome, very good or better in pictorial boards, very scarce.   Between the Covers Rare Books, Inc.   Sci-Fi, Fantasy & Horror - 43090   2013 $350

Jankovic, Vladimir *Reading the Skies: a Cultural History of English Weather 1650-1820.* Chicago: University of Chicago Press, 2000. 8vo., frontispiece, illustrations, gilt stamped blue bukram, Burndy bookplate, scarce, fine.   Jeff Weber Rare Books   171 - 188   2013 $60

Janson, Hank *Hotsy, You'll be Chilled.* London: New Fiction Press, 1951. First edition, illustrataed title, original pictorial wrappers, slight spotting, very good.   Jarndyce Antiquarian Booksellers   CCV - 144   2013   £125

Janson, Hank *Ripe for Rapture.* London: Roberts & Vinter, 1960. First edition, half title original pictorial wrappers, very good.   Jarndyce Antiquarian Booksellers   CCV - 145   2013   £40

Janson, Hank *Vengeance.* London: New Fiction Press, 1953. First edition, 2 pages ads, leaves stapled, original wrappers, very good.   Jarndyce Antiquarian Booksellers   CCV - 146   2013   £175

Janson, Hank *Whiplash.* London: New Fiction Press, 1952. First edition, half title, illustrations title, original pictorial wrappers, very good.   Jarndyce Antiquarian Booksellers   CCV - 147   2013   £85

Janvier, Catherine A. *London Mews.* New York & London: Harper & Bros., 1904. First edition, olive cloth backed boards, 4to., very good, corners worn, wonderful hand colored illustrations.   Barnaby Rudge Booksellers   Children 2013 - 020690   2013 $125

Janvier, Thomas *The Mexican Guide.* New York: Scribner's Sons, 1900. This seems to be a reprint of the fourth edition, small 8vo., pages 531, flexible green cloth, stamped in gilt, very good.   Second Life Books Inc.   183 - 191   2013 $85

Japanese Fairy Tales: the Cub's Triumph. Tokyo: Hasegawa, 12mo., crepe paper with silk ties, fine, beautifully illustrated with color woodblocks printed by hand.   Aleph-Bet Books, Inc. 104 - 291   2013 $200

Japanese Fairy Tales: the Mouse's Wedding. Tokyo: Hasegawa, n.d., 12mo., crepe paper with silk ties, fine, color woodblocks printed by hand.   Aleph-Bet Books, Inc. 104 - 292   2013 $200

Japanese Fairy Tales: the Old Man and the Devils. Tokyo: Hasegawa, 8vo., crepe paper with silk ties, fine, color woodblocks printed by hand.   Aleph-Bet Books, Inc.   104 - 293   2013 $200

Japanese Fairy Tales: the Princes Fire-Flash and Fire-Fade. Tokyo: Hasegawa, n.d., 12mo., crepe paper with silk ties, fine, color woodblocks printed by hand.   Aleph-Bet Books, Inc.   104 - 295   2013 $1500

Jarcho, Saul *Human Palaeopathology.* New Haven: Yale University Press, 1966. 29 illustrations, original binding, nice, dust jacket.   James Tait Goodrich   S74 - 159   2013 $125

Jardine, William *The Naturalist's Library. Mammalia. Volume VI. On the Ordinary Cetacea or Whales.* Edinburgh: W. H. Lizars, n.d. circa, 1837. 30 beautiful illustrations, all but one of the plates hand colored, original green cloth, lightly sunned with few small chips on spine, although tightly bound, few gutters exposed due to book having been opened flat, very good, 264 pages.   The Kelmscott Bookshop   7 - 74   2013 $575

Jarrell, Randall *Gingerbread Rabbit.* New York: Macmillan, 1964. Stated first printing, 8vo., pictorial boards, slightest edge rubbing, else very good+ in very good frayed dust jacket with closed tear, price intact, rather uncommon, charming line illustrations by Garth Williams. Aleph-Bet Books, Inc.   105 - 590   2013 $95

Jarry, Hawke *Black Schoolmaster.* New York: Exposition Press, 1970. First edition, fine in near fine dust jacket with tiny puncture in front gutter and price on front flap inked over.   Between the Covers Rare Books, Inc.   165 - 181 2013 $175

Jarvis, Adrian *Port and Harbor Engineering.* Aldershot, et al: Ashgate, 1998. 8vo., photos and illustrations, red cloth, gilt stamped cover and spine titles, Burndy bookplate, fine.   Jeff Weber Rare Books   169 - 238   2013 $175

Jaspers, Karl *Existentialism and Humanism: Three Essays by Karl Jaspers.* New York: Russel F. Moore Co., 1952. First edition, near fine with paper and blue remnants on front and rear pastedowns, lacking dust jacket. Between the Covers Rare Books, Inc.   Philosophy - 103565   2013 $60

Jayne, Caroline Furness *String Figures.* New York: Charles Scribner's Sons, 1906. First edition, small 4to., original blue cloth gilt, neatly recased, 867 figures, few marginal pencil lines to introduction, otherwise excellent copy, inscribed by author to Sir Edward Russell dated 1906.   R. F. G. Hollett & Son   Children's Books - 304   2013   £250

Jeaffreson, John Cordy *The Real Lord Byron.* Leipzig: Bernhard Tauchnitz, 1883. (1896-1905). Copyright edition, 3 volumes, half titles, uncut, original printed cream wrappers, spine torn without loss, volume I little dusted, well preserved copy in clear protective wrappers, Doris Langley Moore's copy.   Jarndyce Antiquarian Booksellers   CCIII - 396   2013   £40

Jeaffreson, John Cordy *The Real Lord Byron: New Views on the Poet's Life.* London: Hurst & Blackett, 1883. First edition, 2 volumes, half titles, 16 pages ads volume II, original brown cloth, spines lettered in gilt, Durdans bookplate of the Earl of Rosebery very good, attractive copy.   Jarndyce Antiquarian Booksellers   CCIII - 395   2013   £75

Jean-Aubry, G. *Twenty Letters to Joseph Conrad.* London: Curwen Press for the First Edition Club, 1926. First edition, 12 separately printed pamphlets, each limited to 220 copies, sewn as issued, double compartment folding case as issued, complete set, uncommon.   Second Life Books Inc.   183 - 192   2013 $350

Jeancon, J. A. *Pathological Anatomy, Pathology and Physical Diagnosis.* Cincinnati: Progress Publishing, 1885. Tall folio, three quarter calf, newly rebacked with cloth spine and original spine laid down, ex-library with stamps, boards rubbed and corners bumped, internally quite clean, lithographed plates are delicately colored.   James Tait Goodrich   75 - 123   2013 $795

Jeanneret-Oehl, Auguste *Souvenirs du Sejour d'un Horloger Neuchatelois en Chine.* Neuchatel: G. Guillaume Fils, 1866. 135 x 205mm., 136 pages, frontispiece, original mustard printed wrappers, few chips, spine paper taped, Sternfeld bookplate, very rare.   Jeff Weber Rare Books 169 - 239   2013 $365

Jeans, Henry William *Hand-Book for the Stars...* London: Robson & Son, 1868. Third edition, frontispiece and illustrations, original green cloth, slightly rubbed, contemporary signature of W. S. Brook on leading pastedown, very good.   Jarndyce Antiquarian Booksellers   CCV - 148 2013   £150

Jefferies, Richard *The Story of a Boy.* London: Jonathan Cape, 1932. First edition, 8vo., cloth, fine in very slightly worn dust jacket, illustrations by E. H. Shepard.   Aleph-Bet Books, Inc.   105 - 546   2013 $100

Jeffers, Robinson 1887-1962 *Granite & Cypress: Rubbings from the Rock...* University of California at Santa Cruz: Lime Kiln Press, 1975. Limited to 100 numbered copies, oblong folio, printed on English Hayle handmade paper, titlepage woodcut by William Prochnow, bound by Schuberth Bookbindery in German linen, open laced deerskin over Monterey Cypress spine, Japanese Uwa endpapers, custom slipcase made of Monterey Cypress inlaid with square 'window' of granite from Jeffers' stoneyard (drawn by the poet from the sea), built to stand erect on felt lined cypress stand, case with hair-line crack, else fine, signed by printer William Everson in ink at limitation page, prospectus signed by Everson and three proof sheets laid in, exceptionally rare.   Jeff Weber Rare Books   171 - 190   2013 $15,000

Jeffers, Robinson 1887-1962 *The Loving Shepherdess.* New York: Random House, 1956. Limited to 155 numbered copies (#64), 4to., quarter gilt stamped black cloth over white paper backed boards, black cloth slipcase by Silverlake Bindery, signed by author and artist, with original etchings by Jean Kellogg, additionally signed and inscribed from Kellogg to Dick McGraw, with prospectus, backing sheet and 3 ALS's laid in, fine.   Jeff Weber Rare Books   171 - 192   2013 $2000

Jeffers, Robinson 1887-1962 *Whom Should I Write For, Dear But For You?* Carmel: Tor House Foundation Jan., 1979. Limited edition of 100 copies, 4to., Douglas Cockerel marbled wrappers with RJ printed label on upper cover.   Jeff Weber Rare Books   171 - 191   2013 $895

Jefferson, T. E. *The Battle Field and The Hermit: Poems.* Sheffield: Robert Leader, 1859. First edition, original red brown cloth wrappers, printed paper label, slightly dulled, 26 pages.   Jarndyce Antiquarian Booksellers   CCV - 149   2013   £50

Jefferson, T. H. *Map of th Emigrant Road from Independence Mo.....* San Francisco: California Historical Society, 1945. One of 300 copies, reprint of extremely rare first edition of 1849, Large folding map (in 4 parts) in rear pocket, original red cloth with printed paper label on front cover, slight offsetting to ends, else fine.   Argonaut Book Shop   Recent Acquisitions June 2013 - 156   2013 $225

Jefferson, Thomas *Report of the Secretary of State on the Subject of Establishing a Uniformity in the Weights, Measures and Coins of the United States.* New York: printed by F. Childs and J. Swaine, 1790. First edition, octavo, blue wrappers, fine in custom quarter red morocco clamshell gilt stamped on spine, very rare.   Heritage Book Shop 50th Anniversary Catalogue - 56   2013 $25,000

Jeffs, Robin *The English Revolution I. Fast Sermons to Parliament.* London: Cornmarket Press, 1970-1971. Facsimile reprints, 34 volumes, 8vo., half brown cloth and half black divided vertically, black printed panel to spine with gilt title, spines little sunned, printed panel rubbed to some volumes, occasional light marks to boards, top edges slightly dusty, some corners bumped, Cornmarket Press compliments slip signed by Ridley Burnett loosely inserted.   Unsworths Antiquarian Booksellers   28 - 159   2013   £1700

Jeffs, Robin *The English Revolution III. Newsbooks 5.* London: Cornmaket Press, 1971-1972. Facsimile reprints, 19 volumes, 8vo., slight vertical crease to final gatherings of volume 13 affecting legibility, green cloth, black printed panel to spine with gilt title, occasional very slight marks to boards, some volumes' endpapers faded a little at edges, very good.   Unsworths Antiquarian Booksellers   28 - 160   2013   £950

Jekels, Ludwig *Selected Papers.* New York: IUP, 1952. First edition, inscribed by author for Melitta Sperling, fine in close to fine dust jacket with light wear at top edge.   Beasley Books   2013 - 2013 $50

Jekyll, Gertrude *Children and Gardens.* London: Country Life, 1908. First edition, 8vo., photos and drawings, green cloth, stamped in gilt, little foxing, owner's name on flyleaf, very small piece missing from corner of one leaf, cover little worn at corners and spine, otherwise very good.   Second Life Books Inc.   183 - 193   2013 $125

Jekyll, Gertrude *Garden Ornament.* London: the Offices of Country Life, 1918. Folio, color frontispiece, titlepage in red and black, photographic illustrations, f.f.e.p. and frontispiece pulling away little bit, tissue guard discolored, slight spotting to titlepage but otherwise excellent internally, blue cloth, gilt title to spine and upper board, all edges gilt, little scuffed, touch of wear, lower joint cracking.   Unsworths Antiquarian Booksellers   28 - 173   2013   £100

Jekyll, Gertrude *Garden Ornament.* London: Country Life, 1927. Second and best edition, Lavishly illustrated with photos, folio, original green cloth, upper cover lettered gilt, block of sculptural sundial, spine lettered gilt, gilt edges, upper cover very slightly and unevenly faded, corners bumped, very good.   Blackwell's Rare Books   172 - 77   2013   £500

Jekyll, Gertrude *Old West Surrey.* London: Longmans, Green, 1904. First edition, 8vo. 330 illustrations from photos by author, green cloth stamped in gilt, cover faded and somewhat faded and somewhat scuffed and bumped, few leaves at beginning of chapter I somewhat soiled and little dented, otherwise, tight.   Second Life Books Inc.   183 - 194   2013 $175

Jelley, S. M. *The Voice of Labor.* Philadelphia: H. J. Smith, 1888. First edition, illustrations, hardcover. Beasley Books   2013 - 2013 $100

Jemison, D. V. *First Annual Message of the Rev. D. Jemison, D.D., LL.D Before the National Baptists Convention USA...* Selma: Pritchett Printing Co., 1941. First edition, stapled printed green wrappers, 19 pages, several very small chips on front wrapper, some age toning, very good, very scarce.   Between the Covers Rare Books, Inc.   165 - 182   2013 $150

Jenkins, John *Education: Its Nature, Import and Necessity.* London: Longman, 1848. 8vo., very good, half title, presentation inscription 'from the writer', original dark green blindstamped and gilt lettered cloth, covers little rubbed.   Ken Spelman Books Ltd.   75 - 116   2013   £65

Jenkins, John H. *I'm Frank Hamer. The Life of a Texas Peace Officer.* Austin: State House Press, 1993. Reprint of 1968 first edition, photos and reproductions, dark blue cloth, very fine, pictorial dust jacket.   Argonaut Book Shop Summer 2013 - 173   2013 $125

Jenkins, Rhys *The Collected Papers of...* Cambridge: Cambridge University Press for the Newcomen Society, 1936. Limited to 300 copies, this #124, signed by author, frontispiece, 7 plates, 26 text figures, 4to., quarter beige cloth over green cloth, gilt stamped spine title (double ruled border), bottom spine end chipped, some light foxing, very good.   Jeff Weber Rare Books 169 - 240   2013 $90

Jenks, Tudor *Romero and Julietta.* Philadelphia: Henry Altemus, 1905. 12mo., pictorial boards, 111 pages, tips rubbed and rear cover soil, else very good+, full page pen and ink drawings, surrounded by red decorative borders and with smaller illustrations in text, by John R. Neill, uncommon Neill title.   Aleph-Bet Books, Inc.   105 - 420   2013 $225

Jenner, Edward *Further Observations on the Varioale Vaccinae or Cow Pox.* London: printed for the author by Sampson Low, 1799. First edition, Half title, title, (6), 64 pages, 4to., uncut, large wide margins, light dampstaining affected outer margins, browned in parts, original blue sugar wrappers, lacking rear one, clamshell protective case, with ALS circa 1800 to Louis Hallady and Rev. W. H. C. Boggs and signed Z. Lewis. Rob. Hart.   James Tait Goodrich   75 - 125   2013 $4500

Jennings, Brendan *Louvain Papers 1606-1827.* 1968. One of only 400 copies, 8vo., original cloth, very good.   C. P. Hyland   261 - 507   2013   £120

Jennings, Linda Deziah *Washington Women's Cook Book...* Seattle: Trade Register Print, 1909. First edition, 8vo., 256 pages, bound in printed boards (little rubbed and soiled), hinges loose, inscription on endpaper, some recipes from "Rhodes Brothers Tea Room" tipped to rear blanks, some wrinkling to fore edge of first titlepage, good, clean copy, rare.   Second Life Books Inc.   182 - 124   2013 $475

Jenson, Nicolas *The Last Will and Testament of the Late Nicolas Jenson.* Chicago: Ludlow Typography Co. Nov., 1928. 299 x 203mm., publisher's original cream colored paper boards, embossed to resemble a 15th century binding, original blue buckram dust jacket, faint spot of foxing to upper board, one leaf with short tear at head edge, otherwise very fine in close to original condition.   Phillip J. Pirages   63 - 265   2013 $125

Jephcott, C. M. *The Postal History of Nova Scotia and New Brunswick 1754-1867.* Toronto: Sissons Pub. Limited, 1964. #378 of 400 copies, 8vo., maroon buckram in dust jacket, half title, index, black and white illustrations, frontispiece, maps, postal markings, very good in torn dust jacket with piece missing from lower front.   Schooner Books Ltd.   104 - 157   2013 $250

Jerome, Jerome K. *John Ingerfield and Other Stories.* London: McClure & Co., 1894. First edition, signed by author, inscribed by author, uncommon thus, bound in original green cloth with faded cover, bumped corners and signs of handling, spine faded, interior pages clean save for occasional foxing, untrimmed edges and darkened, illustrations, nice, very good.   The Kelmscott Bookshop   7 - 119   2013 $250

Jerome, Jerome K. *Told After Supper.* London: Leadenhall Press... Simpkin Marshall, Hamilton, Kent & Co., Ltd., New York: Scribner & Welford, 1891. octavo, 20 full page and many smaller illustrations by Kenneth M. Skeaping, original pictorial red cloth, front and spine panels stamped in black, top edge gilt, other edges untrimmed, variant binding (priority unknown) with '3/6' printed at lower right hand corner of front panel not canceled by over stamping.   L. W. Currey, Inc.   Christmas Themed Books - 138240   2013 $150

Jerrold, Alice *A Cruise in the Acorn.* London: Marcus Ward, 1875. First edition, 8vo., brown gilt and black cloth, pictorial paste-on, fine, 6 unsigned mounted color illustrations, beautiful copy.   Aleph-Bet Books, Inc.   105 - 290   2013 $1500

Jerrold, Blanchard   1826-1884 *A Brage-Beaker with the Swedes; or Notes from the North in 1852.* London: Nathaniel Cooke, 1854. First edition, 8vo., frontispiece, plate, text illustrations, original purple decorative cloth, rebacked in recent cloth.   J. & S. L. Bonham c Booksellers Europe - 8458   2013   £35

Jervis, H. S. *The 2nd Munsters in France.* 1922. First edition, signed presentation from author, 8vo., 2 photos, 13 maps on 9 folding sheets.   C. P. Hyland   261 - 516   2013   £250

Jesse, J. *Black Armed Forces Officers 1736-1971: a Documented Pictorial History. Missing Pages in U.S. History.* Hampton: Hampton Institute, 1971. First edition, quarto, 169 pages, illustrations, fine, almost certainly issued without dust jacket.   Between the Covers Rare Books, Inc.   165 - 215   2013 $150

Jesse, John Heneage *Six Works on English, Including Royal Memoirs.* Boston: printed for Francis A. Niccolls & Co., 1901. First edition, one of 100 copies of the "Edition des Amateurs" (this copy #27), 225 x 149, 22 volumes, rich contemporary red crushed morocco, covers with single blind ruled border, raised bands, gilt titling on spine, turn-ins densely gilt with multiple decorative rolls, brown and gold silk millefleurs endleaves, top edge gilt, other edges rough trimmed, with 336 plates, (the 168 plates, each in two states, the second being printed on Japon), all with captioned tissue guards, large paper copies, ink ownership inscription of Hyman Friedman, spines with faint overall variation in depth of red (three spines with few small areas of uneven darkening), leather with handful of minor nicks, hint of soiling, one plate slightly loose (but still attached), other trivial imperfections, but quite attractive collection, the Jansenist bindings not lavishly adorned, but entirely tight and lustrous and text uniformly fresh, clean and bright, few signs of use.   Phillip J. Pirages   63 - 266   2013 $1250

Jesseph, Douglas M. *Squaring the Circle: the War Between Hobbes and Wallis.* Chicago and London: University of Chicago Press, 1999. First edition, 8vo., figures, black cloth, gilt stamped spine title, Burndy bookplate, fine.   Jeff Weber Rare Books   169 - 241   2013 $95

Jessye, Eva A. *My Spirituals.* New York: Robbins - Engel, 1927. First edition, signed and inscribed by Jessye, very good++, floral and check patterned cloth with printed paper title label spine and front cover, cover edge wear, 4to., 81 pages.   By the Book, L. C.   38 - 35   2013 $550

Jewett, John Howard *Baby Finger Play and Stories.* London & New York: Nister & Dutton, n.d. circa, 1900. 16mo., cloth backed pictorial boards, edges rubbed, else very good, full page chromolithographs.   Aleph-Bet Books, Inc.   104 - 131   2013 $200

Jewett, Sarah Orne   1849-1909 *A Native of Winby and Other Tales.* Boston: Houghton Mifflin, 1893. First edition, 8vo., green cloth, stamped in gilt, spine slightly faded, front hinge little tender, flyleaf starting along hinge, one inch closed tear to lower corner of titlepage, rear hinge little cracked, very good, inscribed by author for LNF.   Second Life Books Inc.   183 - 195   2013 $1250

Jex-Blake, A. J. *Gardening in East Africa.* London: Longman, Green and Co., 1957. Fourth edition, large 8vo., original cloth, gilt, 23 colored plates.   R. F. G. Hollett & Son   Africana - 100   2013   £45

Joan Miro - Derriere le Miroir 57/58/59. Paris: Maeght, 1953. First edition, 12 original color lithographs by Joan Miro, original wrappers, virtually new.   Gemini Fine Books & Arts., Ltd.   Art Reference & Illustrated Books - 2013 $2700

Joan, Natalie *The Joyous Book.* Oxford University Press, n.d., 1923. First edition, original parchment backed boards, trifle worn and darkened, 12 color plates by Millicent Sowerby, front flyleaf removed, odd spot.   R. F. G. Hollett & Son   Children's Books - 560   2013   £85

Jocelyn, Ada Maria *Only a Flirt.* London: George Bell & sons, 1897. Original pink cloth, slightly marked and dulled, nice.   Jarndyce Antiquarian Booksellers   CCV - 150   2013   £35

Joel, A. E. *A History of Engineering and Science in the Bell System.* Bell Laboratories, 1982. First edition, fine in very good dust jacket with few short clean tears.   Beasley Books   2013 - 2013 $60

John Bull. volume IV. No. 44. Nov. 1, 1824. Disbound, slightly marked.   Jarndyce Antiquarian Booksellers   CCIII - 432   2013   £25

John Davies (a memoir). Newtown: Gregynog Press, June, 1938. One of 150 copies,, royal 8vo. original pale blue boards, front cover with design of subject's initials in dark blue, spine faded and very short tear, free endpapers lightly browned, untrimmed, good, with 4 page prospectus for "John Davies Memorial Fund" loosely inserted, page 1 browned.   Blackwell's Rare Books   B174 - 348   2013   £100

John, John St. *To the War with Waugh.* Andoversford: Whittington Press, 1973. 296/600 copies on Saunders' mouldmade paper, signed by author, line drawings by Peter MacKarell, photo portrait tipped in as frontispiece, paste has bled through plate as usual, title printed in green, royal 8vo., original Morris style green willow leaf decorated white cloth printed oval label on front cover, original glassine jacket, near fine.   Blackwell's Rare Books   172 - 312   2013   £75

Johnes, Edward R. *The Johnes Family of Southampton, L.I. 1629-1886.* New York: William Lowey, 1886. First edition, brown cloth stamped in black and gilt, 46 pages, folding charts, cloth eroded near bottom of front joint, good copy, internally fine, scarce.   Between the Covers Rare Books, Inc.   New York City - 292681   2013 $175

Johns, C. A. *Flowers of the Field.* London: SPCK, 1850. 1893. Third edition, 8vo., green cloth, rebacked.   Barnaby Rudge Booksellers   Natural History 2013 - 020479   2013 $65

Johns, Milton V. *California Redwood and Its Distribution.* San Francisco: Redwood Sales Co., 1925. First edition, 12mo., 47 pages, numerous photos, portrait, color samples, map, printed brown wrappers stamped in black and gold, ink number to top edge of front wrapper, else very fine, very scarce.   Argonaut Book Shop   Recent Acquisitions June 2013 - 158   2013 $150

Johns, W. E. *Biggles Sees it Through.* Oxford University Press 1941, but circa, 1942. First edition, later issue, original orange cloth with 'pyramid' design on upper board, dust jacket by Howard Leigh (extremities little rubbed), top edge slightly creased with few short closed tears, color frontispiece and illustrations, very attractive.   R. F. G. Hollett & Son   Children's Books - 305   2013   £450

Johns, W. E. *The Rescue Flight.*   Oxford University Press, 1939. Pyramid edition, original blue pictorial cloth, minimal wear to extremities, color frontispiece and black and white illustrations, some spotting to fore-edge.   R. F. G. Hollett & Son   Children's Books - 306   2013   £150

Johnson & Lund *Catalogue of Dentists' Materials for sale by Johnson & Lund, Manufacturers, Importers, Wholesale and Retail Dealers.*   Philadelphia: July 1, 1871. First edition, illustrations, 8vo., original blue cloth, minor shelf wear.   Howard S. Mott Inc.   262 - 149   2013 $450

Johnson, Alexander Bryan   *A Treatise on Language or the Relation Which Words Bear to Things in Four Parts.*   New York: Harper and Bros., 1836. First edition, 8vo., 32 page catalog, original cloth faded, printed paper label, heavily rubbed, lacking one front endleaf, 2 library stamps on title, foxed.   M & S Rare Books, Inc.   95 - 168   2013 $1500

Johnson, Audrey   *Furnishing Doll's Houses.*   G. Bell & Sons, 1972. First edition, 4to., original cloth, gilt, dust jacket price, pages 284, 19 plates and line drawings, presentation, inscribed by author.   R. F. G. Hollett & Son   Children's Books - 307   2013   £60

Johnson, Charles   *Being and Race: Black Writing Since 1970.*   Bloomington: Indiana University Press, 1988. First edition, fine in very slightly spine sunned dust jacket, warmly inscribed by author to Nicholas Delbanco.   Between the Covers Rare Books, Inc.   165 - 184   2013 $250

Johnson, Charles   *King. The Photobiography of Martin Luther King, Jr.*   New York: Viking, 2000. First edition, this copy signed by Johnson and by Bob Adelman and dated 11/14/00, photos, fine in fine dust jacket.   Ed Smith Books   75 - 37   2013 $100

Johnson, Charles   *The Sorcerer's Apprentice: Tales and Conjurations.*   New York: Atheneum, 1986. First edition, fine in spine sunned dust jacket which is otherwise near fine, nicely inscribed by author for Nick and Elena Delbanco.   Between the Covers Rare Books, Inc.   165 - 183   2013 $200

Johnson, Crockett   *Harold at the North Pole.*   New York: Harper Brothers, 1958. First edition, 16mo., cloth backed pictorial boards, fine in very good+ dust jacket with some wear at spine ends, extremely rare, nice.   Aleph-Bet Books, Inc.   105 - 346   2013 $1500

Johnson, Denis   *The Incognito Lounge.*   New York: Random House, 1982. Uncorrected proof, scarce, couple of tiny spots to covers, near fine in wrappers.   Ken Lopez Bookseller   159 - 90   2013 $350

Johnson, Denis   *The Man Among the Seals.*   Iowa City: Stone Wall Press, 1979. First edition, one of 260 copies, signed by author, label removal abrasions to front endpages and sticker removal mark on front cover, sunning to edges and spine, very good, without dust jacket, as issued, laid in is announcement for a 2008 reading by Johnson and others, scarce.   Ken Lopez Bookseller   159 - 89   2013 $650

Johnson, Edna   *Anthology of Children's Literature.*   Boston: Houghton Mifflin, 1940. First Wyeth edition, 2nd issue without date on titlepage but also without any alter date which appears in later printings, thick small 4to., pictorial cloth, fine in dust jacket frayed on edges and rubbed, 15 magnificent color plates plus glorious pictorial endpapers and illustration on titlepage as well as color pictorial dust jacket, quite rare in this condition.   Aleph-Bet Books, Inc.   104 - 599   2013 $750

Johnson, Edward Austin   *Light Ahead for the Negro.*   New York: Grafton Press, 1904. octavo, original decorated olive green cloth, front and spine panel stamped in black and orange.   L. W. Currey, Inc.   Fall Sampler Sept. 2013 - 153357   2013 $1500

Johnson, Edward Austin   *A School History of the Negro Race in America from 1619 to 1890...*   Chicago: W. B. Conkey, 1893. Revised edition, 200 pages, illustrations, green cloth stamped in black, name stamp and ownership signature, very near fine.   Between the Covers Rare Books, Inc.   165 - 311   2013 $475

Johnson, Henry Lewis   *Gutenberg and the Book of Books.*   New York: William Edwin Rudge, 1932. Limited edition, one of 750 copies, one of 750 copies, folio, 3 color facsimiles, 1 page of color examples, original gilt stamped brown cloth, front upper corner faded, spine ends lightly worn, else near fine, folder with facsimile page from Gutenberg Bible laid in.   Jeff Weber Rare Books   171 - 152   2013 $100

Johnson, Jack *Johnson - In the Ring - and Out.* Chicago: National Sports Pub. Co., 1927. First edition, very near fine, lacking dust jacket, inscribed by Lucius C. Harper, editor of newspaper The Chicago Defender to Bettise Stalling.   Between the Covers Rare Books, Inc.   165 - 17   2013 $850

Johnson, James *Along This Way.* New York: Viking, 1933. First edition, 418 pages, fine in near very good dust jacket, price clipped with some scuffing and repair at spine, suspiciously near where second printing jackets would state that fact, thus offered by us in what we suspect is second printing jacket.   Between the Covers Rare Books, Inc.   165 - 186   2013 $275

Johnson, James Weldon *The Book of American Negro Poetry.* New York: Harcourt Brace and Co., 1922. First edition, 8vo., 48, 217 pages, original cloth backed paper covered boards, paper label, label slightly rubbed, old newsclipping on Negro spirituals pinned to front endpaper, with offsetting.   M & S Rare Books, Inc.   95 - 171   2013 $200

Johnson, James Weldon *God's Trombones.* New York: Viking Press, 1927. First edition, 5th printing, 8vo, 8 full page deco illustrations, original cloth backed printed boards, some light rubbing.   M & S Rare Books, Inc.   95 - 170   2013 $250

Johnson, John *Original Letters Written by the Late Mr. John Johnson of Liverpool. To which is prefixed a Succinct Account of His Writings by the editor (Samuel Fisher, of Norwich).* Norwich: printed and sold by Crouse, Stevenson and Matchett, sold also by W. Robinson, Liverpool, 1798-1800. First edition, 4 volumes, some foxing in both volumes, some worming volume i, confined to upper and lower margins, 8vo., contemporary brown straight grained morocco by S. Curtis with his ticket, triple blind ruled borders on sides, black lettering pieces in 2nd and 4th of 5 compartments on spine, raised bands gilt tooled, hinges rubbed, small knock at foot of spine volume i, some contemporary annotations to first Letter, sound.   Blackwell's Rare Books   172 - 78   2013   £600

Johnson, John H. *Black World Volume XX No. 9.* Chicago: Johnson Pub. July, 1971. First edition, lightly soiled and foxed with few light creases, tiny tear to bottom of spine, some tanning to pages, else very good in wrappers, from the library of poet Gwendolyn Brooks with her address label.   Between the Covers Rare Books, Inc.   165 - 187   2013 $100

Johnson, Leroy *Escape from Death Valley.* Reno: University of Nevada Press, 1987. First edition, quarto, photos, maps, beige cloth, very fine, dust jacket.   Argonaut Book Shop   Recent Acquisitions June 2013 - 160   2013 $90

Johnson, Marjorie R. *Chinatown Stories.* New York: Dodge, 1900. 4to., cloth backed pictorial boards, some cover and finger soil, blank piece of titlepage repaired, very good, illustrations by Amy Johnson, hand colored illustrations, uncommon.   Aleph-Bet Books, Inc.   105 - 126   2013 $225

Johnson, Samuel   1609-1674 *An Essay Concerning Parliaments at a Certainty; or the Kalends of May.* London: for the author to be sold by Richard Baldwin, 1694. 4to., 34, (1) pages, removed.   Joseph J. Felcone Inc.   Books Printed before 1701 - 56   2013 $100

Johnson, Samuel   1709-1784 *The Beauties of Johnson.* London: printed for G. Kearsley at no. 46 in Fleet Street, 1781. First edition, 8vo., bound in fours, marginal tears to Q2-3, some old waterstaining, contemporary sprinkled calf, rebacked rather plainly, but not recently, inner hinge strengthened, new pastedowns, ownership signature of Lt. Colonel Clayton, 1829, later bookplate of Margaret Huntingdon, several 19th century marginal annotations.   Jarndyce Antiquarian Booksellers   CCIV - 171   2013   £125

Johnson, Samuel   1709-1784 *A Dictionary of the English Language.* London: 1755. First edition, 2 large folio volumes, tall paper copies, titlepages printed in red and black, decorative woodcut tailpieces, full brown calf, rebacked to style, spines with original two calf spine labels lettered in gilt, spines ruled gilt in compartments, 6 raised bands, spine label on volume 1, chipped with label professionally repaired, board rubbed and scuffed, titlepage and first page of preface with some professional restoration, not affecting text, previous owner's bookplate, some toning to glue to edges and blanks, overall very nice set.   Heritage Book Shop   Holiday Catalogue 2012 - 81   2013 $20,000

Johnson, Samuel   1709-1784 *A Dictionary of the English Language.* London: J. Johnson and W. J. & J. Richardson, . Baldwin, &c., 1806. Ninth edition, frontispiece volume I, handsomely rebound in half calf, spines gilt, red and green morocco labels, very good, bound without half titles.   Jarndyce Antiquarian Booksellers   CCV - 151   2013   £950

Johnson, Samuel   1709-1784 *A Dictionary of the English Language.* London: for F. and C. Rivington, J. Walker, 1810. Tenth edition, 2 volumes, quarto, engraved frontispiece portrait, contemporary diced calf, ruled in gilt, gilt lettering on spine, marbled endpapers, all edges marbled, 2 former owners bookplates, neatly rebacked to style, very nice, bright.   Heritage Book Shop   Holiday Catalogue 2012 - 80   2013 $2500

Johnson, Samuel   1709-1784   *A Dictionary of the English Language.*   Harlow, Essex: Longman, 1990. 414 x 262mm., 2 volumes, publisher's maroon leatherette, covers with gilt fillet border, raised bands, spine gilt in single ruled compartments with floral cornerpieces, each spine with green morocco label, in slightly scuffed dark red buckram slipcase with paper labels on sides, near mint.   Phillip J. Pirages   63 - 271   2013 $450

Johnson, Samuel   1709-1784   *The History of Rasselas, Prince of Abyssinia.*   London: printed by C. Whittingham for Longman et al, 1806.   163 x 100mm., viii, 1923 pages, very attractive contemporary diced calf, covers framed by three plain and decorative gilt rules, flat spine divided into panels by wide black and thin gilt rules, 3 panels with gilt floral centerpiece, two with gilt titling, marbled endpapers, frontispiece, five engraved plates, armorial bookplate of Sarah Phillott, barely perceptible short crack top of front joint, hint of soil to covers, faint offsetting from plates, other trivial imperfections, quite excellent copy, binding lustrous and scarcely worn and text especially fresh, clean and bright.   Phillip J. Pirages   63 - 268   2013 $250

Johnson, Samuel   1709-1784   *The Idler.*   London: printed for J. Rivington & sons, 1790.   Fifth edition, 2 volumes, half title to volume I, 2 engraved frontispieces, 12mo., good, clean copy internally, contemporary tree calf, hinges cracked, spines rubbed, lacking labels, worn at head and tail and corners.   Jarndyce Antiquarian Booksellers   CCIV - 177   2013   £45

Johnson, Samuel   1709-1784   *A Journey to the Western Islands of Scotland.*   1775.   Second edition, First issue with 6 line errata, contemporary calf, raised bands, red and green morocco labels, expert repairs to head and tail of spine and hinges, case, shelf and division note written in contemporary hand on prelim blank, nice.   Jarndyce Antiquarian Booksellers   CCIV - 173   2013   £380

Johnson, Samuel   1709-1784   *A Journey to the Western Islands of Scotland.*   London: printed for W. Strahan and T. Cadell in the Strand, 1775.   First edition, first issue, with 12 line errata, 8vo., some dusting and browning, lacking following endpaper, slight tear to corner M2, pencil marginalia to page 257, some pencil underlining, contemporary tree calf, neatly rebacked raised bands, retaining original red morocco label, corners bumped, some abrasions to boards, inner hinges repaired.   Jarndyce Antiquarian Booksellers   CCIV - 172   2013   £450

Johnson, Samuel   1709-1784   *The Letters. With Mrs. Thrale's Genuine Letters to Him.*   Oxford: Clarendon Press, 1952.   8vo., 3 volumes, fine, dust jackets.   Ken Spelman Books Ltd. 75 - 180   2013   £90

Johnson, Samuel   1709-1784   *The Letters of Samuel Johnson.*   Oxford: Clarendon Press (first 3 volumes). Princeton: University Press (final two volumes),   1992. 1992. 1992. 1994. 1994, First edition thus, 5 volumes, 8vo., grey cloth, minor signs of use, near fine, dust jackets dusty with light wear and markings, that of volume I with several small tears to edges, still very good, review notes of David Nokes loosely inserted, his pencil underlinings and annotations in text.   Unsworths Antiquarian Booksellers   28 - 175   2013   £150

Johnson, Samuel   1709-1784   *The Letters.*   Oxford: Clarendon Press, 1992.   Hyde edition, 5 volumes, fine hardback set in dust jackets.   Ken Spelman Books Ltd. 75 - 192   2013   £180

Johnson, Samuel   1709-1784   *The Lives of the Most Eminent English Poets...*   London: printed for Bathurst and others, 1783.   New edition, 4 volumes, frontispiece, 375 engraved portrait plates, 8vo., some old not intrusive waterstaining to lower margins, foxing to tissue guards, very handsome set, full contemporary mottled polished calf, gilt borders, ornate gilt decorated spines, red morocco labels, silk markers, all extra plates handwritten initialled on reverse.   Jarndyce Antiquarian Booksellers   CCIV - 174 2013   £1500

Johnson, Samuel   1709-1784   *The Lives of the Most Eminent English Poets.*   Oxford: Clarendon Press, 2006. First edition, boxed set of 4 volumes, no dust jackets issued, light wear and markings to slipcase, from the library of David Nokes with his occasional light pencil underlinings to text and review notes loosely inserted.   Unsworths Antiquarian Booksellers   28 - 176   2013   £300

Johnson, Samuel   1709-1784   *Lives of the Poets.*   New York: Charles Scribner's Sons, 1896.   175 x 114mm., 6 volumes, 24 engraved portraits, tissue guards, pleasing contemporary scarlet three quarter morocco over marbled boards, flat spines adorned with gilt flowering vine, gilt titling, marbled endpapers, top edge gilt, entirely unopened, with 24 engraved portraits, joints and edges with significant rubbing (but no cracks), backstrips sunned toward dark red, one spine with several abrasions and darkened, where these are refurbished, leather little soiled, not as pretty as it once was, but all the volumes entirely sound and text obviously with no signs of use.   Phillip J. Pirages   63 - 269 2013 $175

Johnson, Samuel   1709-1784   *The Prince of Abissinia.* London: printed for R. and J. Dodsley and W. Johnston, 1759.   First edition, first state of volume II with leaf A2, 2 volumes, small 8vo., full contemporary calf, gilt ruled borders, minor wear, usual offsetting to endpapers and titlepages, discrete Blairhame leather book label on front endsheets, otherwise unusually attractive copy in original state with all blanks, preserved in brown half morocco slipcase. James S. Jaffe Rare Books   Fall 2013 - 78   2013 $12,500

Johnson, Samuel 1709-1784 *The Prince of Abissinia. A Tale.* London: printed for R. and J. Dodsley, 1759. Second edition, 12mo., small paper flaw to one leaf of preface volume 1 affecting page numbers, some splash marks to same opening, occasional light browning and slight dusting to text, offset browning affecting endpapers and pastedowns, contemporary mottled calf, expertly rebacked, raised and gilt banded spines, red morocco labels, corners little worn, split to leading edge of rear board volume II, late 19th century ownership name of R. V. Vernon, armorial bookplate "Vernon Semper Viret".   Jarndyce Antiquarian Booksellers   CCIV - 175   2013   £225

Johnson, Samuel 1709-1784 *The Rambler.* London: F. C. and I. Rivington et al, 1820. 2 volumes, 12mo., frontispiece and titlepage to each volume, inscription removed from each half title, few pencil marks to volume I index, publisher's sugar paper covered boards, backed in very faded cloth, paper covering little torn, edges worn and corners fraying, uncut edges, somewhat dusted, ownership inscriptions of M. K. Hislop 1863, bookseller's notes in pencil to front pastedown of volume I.   Unsworths Antiquarian Booksellers   28 - 174   2013   £60

Johnson, Samuel 1709-1784 *The Yale Edition of the Works.* New Haven: Yale University Press, 1958-2005. First edition, 15 volumes, blue cloth, light signs of use to board edges and minor dustiness to text block, volume X lower corner of upper board bumped with small area of damage to cloth, volume XIV crease to joint of upper board, dust jacket for volumes II, XVI, XVII & XVIII with slight creasing to extremities, volume I dust jacket present but with substantial tears, all others lacking dust jackets, David Nokes' intermittent pencil underlinings and annotations to all volumes.   Unsworths Antiquarian Booksellers   28 - 177   2013   £750

Johnson's England. Oxford: Clarendon Press, 1933. First edition, 233 x 152 mm., 2 volumes, pleasing contemporary deep blue crushed three quarter morocco, gilt decorated raised bands flanked by gilt rules, spine panels with central gilt fleuron, marbled endpapers, top edge gilt, other edges rough trimmed, map and 129 monochrome photographic plates, spines lightly sunned to blue-gray, one board with two small white spots to cloth, two corners just slightly bumped, one short closed tear to one leaf, otherwise fine, fresh, clean, bright, internally in unworn attractive bindings.   Phillip J. Pirages   63 - 274   2013 $225

Johnston, Arnid *Animal Families and Where They live.* London: Country Life, 1939. First edition, large 4to., original cloth, dust jacket, 24 pages of color lithograph illustrations, each with page of text and map, little scattered spotting, mainly to fore-edges, but very nice.   R. F. G. Hollett & Son   Children's Books - 308   2013   £45

Johnston, D. C. *The Galaxy of Wit or Laughing Philosopher.* Boston: Stereotyped by J. Reed, 1827. 1826. Second edition of volume 1, 2 volumes in 1, 16mo., 2 engravings signed by Johnston, full contemporary calf, gilt stamped, some wear, 9 wood engravings by Hartwell.   M & S Rare Books, Inc.   95 - 154   2013 $350

Johnston, D. C. *Scraps No. 1 1849.* Boston: Sketched, Etched & published by D. C. Johnston, 1849. First edition, oblong large 4to., 4 leaves with etchings on rectos, tissue guards as issued, original printed and illustrated yellow wrappers, fine.   M & S Rare Books, Inc.   95 - 395   2013 $325

Johnston, Hank *They Felled the Redwoods. A Saga of Flumes and Rails in the High Sierra.* Glendale: Anglo Books, 1983. First edition, 6th printing, 160 pages, 200 photos and 6 maps, orange cloth, very fine with pictorial dust jacket.   Argonaut Book Shop   Recent Acquisitions June 2013 - 161   2013 $60

Johnston, Hank *The Yosemite Grant 1864-1906. A Pictorial History.* Yosemite National Park: Yosemite Association, 1995. First edition, quarto, old photos, prints, facsimiles, pictorial boards, very fine.   Argonaut Book Shop   Recent Acquisitions June 2013 - 163   2013 $60

Johnston, Harry *My Home on the Range: Frontier Ranching in the Badlands.* St. Paul: 1942. xii, 313 pages, illustrations, some edgewear to dust jacket, one corner of text block slightly bumped, else clean and very good.   Dumont Maps & Books of the West   125 - 57   2013 $50

Johnston, Harry *The Uganda Protectorate.* London: Hutchinson, 1902. First edition, 2 volumes, original black pictorial cloth, gilt, recased, new endpapers, 48 color plates 506 illustrations, 9 maps, inscription on each half title, otherwise very good, sound set.   R. F. G. Hollett & Son   Africana - 101   2013   £180

Johnstone, Charles *Chrysal; or the Adventures of a Guinea in America.* London: T. Becket, 1760. First edition, 2 volumes, large 12mo., 19th century antique mottled calf by Riviere, gilt, expertly rebacked, old backs laid down, leather labels, raised bands, inner gilt dentelles, fine, bookplates of John Leveson Douglas Stewart and A. Edward Newton, slipcase.   Howard S. Mott Inc.   262 - 80   2013 $500

Johnstone, Charles *Chrysal; or the Adventures of a Guinea.* London: printed for T. Becket and P. A. De Hondt, 1771. 1768. 1767. 1767. Volume I 7th edition, volume II 6th edition; volumes III-IV, 2nd edition, 4 volumes, 12mo., fine, clean copy, small tear to foot of I5 volume I, full contemporary diced calf, double gilt ruled borders, attractive gilt decorated spines, bookplate of Sarah Phillott.   Jarndyce Antiquarian Booksellers   CCIV - 178   2013   £280

Jolas, Eugene *Transition. No. 22, 23, 25 and 26.* The Hague: Servire Press, 1932-1933. New York: 1936-1937. First editions, 4 separately issued volumes, original pictorial paper wrappers, numerous black and white photos, issue no 22 with original (somewhat chipped, but intact) yellow paper band reading "Revolutionary Romanticism", issue no. 25 with ink inscription "Wallace Liggett/April 18 1946" on rear cover, issue no. 26 with ink stamp of Messageries Dawson, Paris on rear cover, few tiny chips to edge of boards, little light soiling, No. 26 with short scratch and pencilled number on front cover, No. 25 with occasional small, faint stains to fore edge, few inevitable), corner creases, otherwise fine, clean, fresh, bright internally in very well preserved paper wrappers.   Phillip J. Pirages   63 - 289   2013 $1500

Jolly Alphabets and Puzzles.   London: Blackie, n.d. circa, 1930.   4to., cloth backed pictorial boards, edges slightly rubbed, else fine, 2 alphabets with several puzzles at end, charming 3-color cat drawings by A. E. Kennedy, also 2 full color plates by Albert Kayen, 3-color illustrations by C. E. B. Bernard, and 2 color plates by him, puzzles pages have on color plate by Ruth Cobb.   Aleph-Bet Books, Inc.   105 - 11   2013 $275

Jolly Bears ABC.   New York: Charles Graham, n.d. circa, 1907.   Square 4to., flexible card wrappers, slight creasing of corners, very good+, full color illustrations on every page, rare.   Aleph-Bet Books, Inc.   105 - 2   2013 $750

Jones, A. H. M.   *A History of Abyssinia.*   Oxford: Clarendon Press, 1935.   First edition, original cloth, little soiled, single worm track to head of spine, plates and folding map.   R. F. G. Hollett & Son   Africana - 102   2013   £25

Jones, David   *In Parenthesis.*   London: Faber, 1961. 32/70 copies signed by author and T. S. Eliot, 3 plates by Jones, 8vo., original light blue buckram, backstrip lettered in blue on pale grey ground within gilt ruled border, top edge gilt, glassine jacket, fine.   Blackwell's Rare Books   172 - 201   2013   £1600

Jones, Glyn   *The Saga of Llywarch the Old.*   Golden Cockerel Press, 1955.   7/60 special issue copies (of an edition of 200), printed on Green's handmade paper, title vignette and 4 full page brown and green engravings by Dorothea Braby, 8vo., original full tan morocco lettering on sunned backstrip as usual, two designs on covers all gilt blocked, marbled endpapers, top edge gilt, others untrimmed, marbled board slipcase, near fine.   Blackwell's Rare Books   B174 - 340 2013   £220

Jones, Gwyneth   *Band of Gypsys.*   London: Gollancz, 2005.   First edition, octavo, boards.   L. W. Currey, Inc. Utopian Literature: Recent Acquisitions (April 2013) - 140639   2013 $65

Jones, Gwyneth   *Castles Made of Sand.*   London: Gollancz, 2002.   First edition, octavo, boards.   L. W. Currey, Inc.   Utopian Literature: Recent Acquisitions (April 2013) - 140636   2013 $65

Jones, Harold   *Silver Bells and Cockle Shells.*   Oxford University Press, 1979.   First edition, original glazed pictorial boards, illustrations in color.   R. F. G. Hollett & Son   Children's Books - 309   2013   £30

Jones, Harold   *There & Back Again.*   Oxford University Press, 1977.   First edition, original glazed pictorial boards, illustrations in color.   R. F. G. Hollett & Son   Children's Books - 310   2013   £30

Jones, Ifano   *Printing & Printers in Wales & Monmouthshire.*   1925.   First edition, x, 367 pages, publisher's cloth, some wear and tear, ex-public library, text good.   C. P. Hyland   261 - 78   2013   £35

Jones, Jennifer   *Murder al Fresco.*   Garden City: Doubleday Doran/Crime Club, 1939.   First edition, offsetting to endpapers from jacket flaps, near fine in lightly edge-worn, about fine dust jacket with couple of tiny nicks, scarce in jacket.   Between the Covers Rare Books, Inc.   Mystery & Detective Fiction - 85008   2013 $200

Jones, Lloyd   *Co-Operation in Danger.*   London: 1880. First and only edition, 22 pages, moderan wrappers, good. C. P. Hyland   261 - 517   2013   £100

Jones, Mary Joss   *Hump Tree Stories.*   San Francisco: Paul Elder, 1910.   4to., cloth backed pictorial boards, 79 pages, light cover soil, else near fine, printed on heavy brown paper, illustrations by R. L. Hudson with extremely fine and detailed 2-color lithographs.   Aleph-Bet Books, Inc.   105 - 226   2013 $200

Jones, Robert   *Artificial Fireworks, Improved to the Modern Practice from the Minutest to Highest Branches.* Chelmsford: printed and sold by Meggy and Chalk, 1801. 210 x 136mm., very pleasing recent retrospective smooth calf, raised bands, red morocco label, edges entirely untrimmed, 20 copper engraved plates, inscription of Mr. S. Pearson, Steeton in 19th century hand, minor foxing and soiling here and there, generally text in excellent condition, unexpectedly clean and fresh, unworn sympathetic binding. Phillip J. Pirages   63 - 374   2013 $1500

Jones, Robert   *The Muses Garden for Delights or the Fifth Books of Ayres, Onley for the Lute, the Base-vyoll and the Voice.*   Oxford: Daniel Press, 1901.   109/130 copies printed on Van Gelder handmade paper,, full page collotype facsimile of original titlepage, small 4to., original printed mid blue wrappers, projecting edges only trifle frayed, owner's name on front flyleaf, near fine.   Blackwell's Rare Books B174 - 327   2013   £160

Jones, Thomas *The Horrors of War Renewed in Egypt.* London: printed by W. Williams for J. S. Jordan, 1801? Disbound, slight spotting, without half title or initial blank. Jarndyce Antiquarian Booksellers   CCV - 152   2013   £75

Jones, Thomas H. *Experience and Personal Narrative of Uncle Tom Jones.* Boston: sold at Skinner's Rooms, 1855? 8vo., 64 pages, portrait, frontispiece and vignette, original printed and pictorial front wrapper, frayed and stained, some fraying, foxing and browning.   M & S Rare Books, Inc.   95 - 172   2013 $750

Jones, W. Bence *The Life's Work in Ireland of a Landlord Who Tried to Do His Duty.* 1880. First edition, 8vo., original cloth, good, signed "from the author".   C. P. Hyland   261 - 518   2013   £150

Jonson, Ben *The Key Keeper. A Masque for Opening of Britain's Purse April 19 1609.* Tunbridge Wells,: printed... by David Esselmont, Foundling Press, 2002. First edition, 97/300 copies, printed on Zerkall mouldmade paper, 11 line drawings by David Gentlemen, including 5 full page, title printed in red, 8vo., original dark blue cloth, backstrip gilt lettered, tail edges rough trimmed, dust jacket, fine. Blackwell's Rare Books   B174 - 336   2013   £70

Jonson, Ben *The Workes of Benjamin Jonson. (with) The Workes of Benjamin Jonson. The second volume...* London: printed by William Stansby, 1616. 1640-1641. First folio edition, 3 volumes, bound in two, folio, volume II divided into 4 parts, originally issued in two volumes), volume 1 bound with rare initial blank leaf, engraved allegorical title by William Hole, volume 1 full contemporary brown paneled calf expertly rebacked to style, spine with red and green spine labels, lettered gilt, all edges gilt, former owner's signature on top of titlepage not affecting engraving, another signature on front pastedown, volume 2 full brown calf, ruled in blind, expertly rebacked and uniform with volume 1, with red and green spine labels, lettered gilt, previous owner's bookplate, Walter Scott Seton-Karr and John Seton Karr, together a very handsome set.   Heritage Book Shop   Holiday Catalogue 2012 - 82   2013 $35,000

Jonsson-Rose, N. *Lawns and Gardens.* New York: G. P. Putnam's Sons, 1897. 414 pages, 4to., beige cloth, illustrations by author, very good.   Barnaby Rudge Booksellers   Natural History 2013 - 020929   2013 $75

Jordan, David Starr *American Food and Game Fishes.* New York: Doubleday Page & Co., 1902. First edition, scarce thus, quarto, 50 prelim pages plus 573 pages, 111 color plates and halftone illustrations and over 200 text illustrations, dark green cloth lettered gilt on spine, contemporary owner's dated inscription on endpaper, else fine, scarce thus.   Argonaut Book Shop   Recent Acquisitions June 2013 - 166   2013 $300

Jordan, Elizabeth *Red Riding Hood.* New York: Century Co., 1925. First edition, fine in attractive, near fine dust jacket with some edgewear and tiny nicks.   Between the Covers Rare Books, Inc.   Mystery & Detective Fiction - 308382   2013 $200

Jordan, Pat *Black Coach.* New York: Dodd, Mead and Co., 1971. First edition, fore edge foxed, else near fine in lightly rubbed, near fine dust jacket, signed by author. Between the Covers Rare Books, Inc.   Football Books - 84336   2013 $200

Jordan, Pat *Black Coach.* New York: Dodd, Mead & Co., 1971. First edition, fore edge quite foxed, else near fine in lightly rubbed, near fine dust jacket, signed by author. Between the Covers Rare Books, Inc.   165 - 150   2013 $150

Jordanus De Nemore *Opusculum de Ponderosita(te) Nicolai Tartalea(e) Studo Correctum...* Venice: Curzio Troiano, 1565. 4to., woodcut arms on title, woodcut initials and numerous diagrams in text, main text in Latin, corroded ink blot on title resulting in loss of 3 letters, title slightly browned and little browning here and there, 4to., recent limp (old) vellum, good.   Blackwell's Rare Books   Sciences - 64   2013   £2500

Jorgensen, Johannes *Don Bosco.* London: Burns, Oates & Washbourne, 1934. First edition, 8vo., full leather, that on spine scraped, good+.   Barnaby Rudge Booksellers   Biography 2013 - 019843   2013 $50

Josephus, Flavius *Opera quae Exstant...* Geneva: Jacobum Crispinum, 1634. Third Geneva printing, folio, slightly toned, little marginal worming to first few quires, blot from hot wax to page 610 affecting a couple of words and slightly marking the preceding page, small marginal inkstain to several leaves at rear, tan calf, gilt spine and borders, rebacked retaining original spine, boards scratched with a little surface loss suggesting tape removal, few wormholes to upper board, edges and corners worn, upper hinge neatly repaired, ownership inscription of M. D. Macleod, the University Southampton, much older ink inscription to front pastedown.   Unsworths Antiquarian Booksellers   28 - 19   2013   £500

Josephus, Flavius *The Works of Flavius Josephus.* London: printed for R. Sare, 1702. First L'Estrange edition, folio, many errors in pagination but collates complete, at page 196-7 a pin is visible which is holding gathering in place, p. 199 stained at fore-edge, pages 553-88 with little loss to top margin, page 591 remargined, occasional marginal notes, wax spots and short closed tears, tan Cambridge style calf, red morocco and gilt label to spine, edges sprinkled red, spine creased and scratched, loss to endcaps, joints cracked but cords holding, lower board scraped, corners frayed, prelim blanks loose, inscriptions of M. Kenne stating 'the gift of Rnd. Fortiscue' and Albert Victor Murray, Magdalen and Mansfield Colleges Oxford, May 11 1914, pink 'Cancelled' stamp to front pastedown. Unsworths Antiquarian Booksellers 28 - 20 2013 £250

Josephus, Flavius *Opera. quae Reperiri Potuerunt Omnia.* Oxford: Theatro Sheldoniano, 1720. First edition thus, 2 volumes, folio, letter, printer's vignette on titlepage, small tear to lower margin page 942 not affecting text, contemporary dark brown Cambridge style panelled calf, later rebacked and repaired using red morocco, joints worn, upper joint splitting and reback lifting on volume II, some loss of leather at fore-edge, hinges relined with cloth, Gilt Athenaeum Library stamps to both tailcaps and upper board of volume. Unsworths Antiquarian Booksellers 28 - 22 2013 £450

Josephy, Alvin M. *The Nez Perce Indians and the Opening of the Northwest.* New Haven and London: Yale University Press, 1965. First edition, scarce thus, presentation inscription signed by author, pages xx, (4), 703, frontispiece, 11 maps and 24 contemporary photos and sketches, publisher's tan cloth, very fine, pictorial dust jacket. Argonaut Book Shop Recent Acquisitions June 2013 - 167 2013 $225

Joss, Morag *Fearful Symmetry.* London: Hodder & Stoughton, 1999. First edition, fine in dust jacket. Mordida Books 81 - 274 2013 $65

Joss, Morag *Funeral Music.* London: Hodder & Stoughton, 1998. First edition, fine in dust jacket. Mordida Books 81 - 273 2013 $200

Jost, A. C. *Guysborough Sketches and Essays.* Kentville: Kentville Pub. Co., 1950. 8vo., blue cloth, gilt title to front, half title, maps and illustrations, very good. Schooner Books Ltd. 104 - 74 2013 $75

Jouhandeau, Marcel *Le Bal Masque.* Paris: 1967. First edition, one of 71 examples on Arches wove paper signed by Oskar Kokoschka and Marcel Jouhandeau, 7 original color lithographs, each signed with initials in pencil by Kokoschka and separate folder with 66 original photolithographs in colors, signed in plate, all housed in specially designed publisher's box, overall size 60 x 83cm., all leaves and lithos in very good condition, box with minor wear. Gemini Fine Books & Arts., Ltd. Art Reference & Illustrated Books - 2013 $2975

Jourdanet, Denis *Influence de la Pression de l'air sur la Vie de l'Homme Climats d'Altitude et Climats de Montagne.* Paris: G. Masson, 1875. First edition, 2 volumes, large 8vo., 39 engraved plates 3 chromolithographic plates, 8 color maps, figures, numerous tables, foxed and waterstained, text is clean, original reddish brown cloth, gilt stamped cover and spine titles, top edge gilt, extremities stained, ownership ink stamps of Simon D. Woivodich, very good. Jeff Weber Rare Books 172 - 161 2013 $500

Joy, Lynn Sumida *Gassendi the Atomist.* Cambridge et al: Cambridge University Press, 1987. 8vo., green cloth, gilt stamped spine title, dust jacket, ownership signature, near fine. Jeff Weber Rare Books 169 - 156 2013 $60

Joyce, James 1882-1941 *Anna Livia Plurabelle.* New York: Crosby Gaige, 1928. First edition, one of 800 copies signed by author, 180 x 120mm., this copy #195, original publisher's brown cloth stamped in blind and gilt, extremely fine, especially fresh and clean in inside and out and without even trivial imperfection. Phillip J. Pirages 63 - 275 2013 $4250

Joyce, James 1882-1941 *Brideship and Gulls.* New York: Vincent FitzGerald & Co., 1991. One of 25 copies, text on Apta Royale Laid Richard de Bas paper (made in 1938), images on Musee paper, backed on custom made papers by Paul Wong on Dieu Donne papermill, page size 16 x 26 inches, bound by Zahra Partovi in Coptic style mauve grey silk over boards, box by David Bourbeau, Thistle Bindery, fine, 6 original line etchings by Susan Weil hand painted in watercolor and gouache with gold leafing throughout, each mounted on museum board, images surround the 40 page text when sitting in the box and when lifted out become three dimensional paintings; there are also 2 original collages in text and on boards of cover, which is printed in 3 colors, box itself is piece of sculpture. Priscilla Juvelis - Rare Books 55 - 8 2013 $10,000

Joyce, James 1882-1941 *Chamber Music.* London: Elkins Mathews, 1907. First edition (variant C), 164 x 108mm., (20) leaves, original green cloth, gilt tilting on front cover and spine, supplied green linen dust jacket, woodcut border on title, just tiny hint of wear at corners and spine ends, 3 very short fore-edge tears to free endpapers, otherwise extremely fine, entirely clean and bright inside and out. Phillip J. Pirages 63 - 276 2013 $2500

Joyce, James 1882-1941 *Chamber Music.* London: Elkin Mathews, 1907. First edition first issue with horizontal chain lines on endpapers, poems in signature C centered on page, foolscap 8vo., original mid green cloth, backstrip and front cover gilt lettered, backstrip little darkened, endpapers foxed, bookplate, fore-edges rough trimmed, very good.   Blackwell's Rare Books   B174 - 241   2013   £4500

Joyce, James 1882-1941 *Chamber Music.* London: Egoist Press, 1921. First issue of third edition, one of only 107 copies, list of publications of the Egoist Press tipped to rear pastedown, offsetting to endpages, otherwise fine in green cloth, without dust jacket (as issued?).   Ken Lopez Bookseller   159 - 91   2013 $350

Joyce, James 1882-1941 *Collected Poems.* New York: Black Sun Press, 1936. First edition, one of 800 copies (this #166), 170 x 114mm., publisher's cream colored paper boards, covers printed blue with floral frame enclosing central panel of alternating rows of fleurons, blue titling on flat spine, frontispiece by Augustus Johns, printed in dark blue, spine slightly sunned to creamier color, light soiling along bottom inch of back cover, one small faint spot to margin of one page, otherwise very fine, clean and bright inside and out.   Phillip J. Pirages   63 - 277   2013 $1250

Joyce, James 1882-1941 *The Dead.* Pitloochry: Duval and Hamilton, 1982. Number 133 of 150 numbered copies, signed by artist, small folio, original quarter green morocco, spine lettered in gilt, pale yellow Fabriano paper sides, top edge gilt, printed on Magnani handmade paper at Officina Bodoni, fine in matching slipcase.   Maggs Bros. Ltd.   1442 - 140   2013   £750

Joyce, James 1882-1941 *Dubliners.* London: Grant Richards, 1914. First edition, one of 746 copies printed for Richard (504 copies were printed for Huebsch in America, for a total of 1250), 197 x 130mm., 278 pages, original dark red cloth, gilt lettering on spine, and front cover, recent maroon cloth folding box, spine faintly and uniformly darkened (covers with hint of fading at edges), barely perceptible cocking to binding, small dent to fore edge of front board (and one even smaller at bottom edge), perhaps two dozen pages with dot of foxing, excellent copy.   Phillip J. Pirages   63 - 279   2013 $18,000

Joyce, James 1882-1941 *Exiles.* New York: Huebsch, 1918. First American edition, 8vo., 154 pages, cloth backed boards, endpapers foxed, very good tight copy.   Second Life Books Inc.   183 - 199   2013 $325

Joyce, James 1882-1941 *Exiles. A Play in three Acts.* New York: B. W. Huebsch, 1918. First edition, 199 x 128mm., publisher's gray paper boards backed with green buckram, title blindstamped on front cover, gilt titling on spine, original pale yellow dust jacket printed in black, bookplate of John Quinn, photo of Joyce tipped on, 3 short, brown marks to rear cover, otherwise volume very fine in somewhat soiled dust jacket that is slightly torn, chipped and frayed at edges (small hole in middle of spine).   Phillip J. Pirages   63 - 280   2013 $2500

Joyce, James 1882-1941 *Finnegans Wake. (with) A Companion Volume.* Dublin: Houyhnhnm, 2010. One of 150 numbered copies, new edition, 4to., full black calf lettered gilt, printed on 130gsm acid fee paper, 4to., grey boards, printed in black, fine in black cloth slipcase.   Maggs Bros. Ltd.   1442 - 144   2013   £750

Joyce, James 1882-1941 *Finnegans Wake. (together with) A Companion Volume.* Dublin: Houyhnhnm, 2010. New edition, limited to 800 copies, 2 volumes, 4to., original navy blue cloth, lettered gilt, printed on 120gsm acid-free paper, designed by Martino Mardersteig and printed by Stamperia Valdonega, 4to., grey wrappers printed in black.   Maggs Bros. Ltd.   1442 - 143   2013   £250

Joyce, James 1882-1941 *Finnegan's Wake.* London: Faber & Faber and New York: Viking Press, 1939. Number 124 of 425 numbered copies, signed by author, tall 8vo., original red buckram, gilt, top edge gilt, others uncut, near fine, without slipcase.   Maggs Bros. Ltd.   1442 - 136   2013   £6500

Joyce, James 1882-1941 *Finnegan's Wake.* London: Faber & Faber: New York: Viking Press, 1939. First edition, limited to 425 copies signed by author, this copy #206, 260 x 170mm., 4 p.l., (first blank), 628 pages, original brick red buckram, gilt titling on spine, edges untrimmed and mostly unopened, original (very slightly soiled) yellow cloth slipcase and housed in extremely attractive modern dark red morocco backed folding box with raised bands and gilt title, remnants of bookplate, especially fine, binding unworn, virtually pristine internally and even slipcase very well preserved.   Phillip J. Pirages   63 - 281   2013 $22,000

Joyce, James 1882-1941 *Finnegans Wake.* London: Faber and Faber, 1939. First (regular) edition, large octavo, original rough red cloth, spine ruled and lettered in gilt on two panels stamped in blind, top edge stained orange-yellow, others uncut, maroon dust jacket and few minute abrasions to top edge of jacket, almost fine.   Heritage Book Shop   Holiday Catalogue 2012 - 83   2013 $6000

Joyce, James 1882-1941 *Finnegans Wake.* London: Faber and Faber Ltd., 1939. First trade edition, 8vo., original crimson cloth, gilt, from the library of Richard Murphy, signed by him, some spotting to endpapers and dusty at page edges, otherwise excellent.   Maggs Bros. Ltd.   1442 - 136   2013   £500

Joyce, James 1882-1941 *Finnegans Wake.* London: Faber and Faber, 1949. Second printing, with 28 page "Corrections of Misprints" added at end, tall 8vo., original smooth dark red cloth, dust jacket, unusually fine copy in dust jacket.   Maggs Bros. Ltd.   1442 - 138   2013   £450

Joyce, James 1882-1941 *Haveth Childers Everywhere. Fragment from work in Progress.* Paris: Henry Babou and Jack Kahane; New York: The Fountain Press, 1930. First edition, limited issue, one of 100 copies on iridescent handmade Japan, signed by author, this copy #24 (there were an additional 500 on paper and 85 writer's copies), original white paper covers with printed titling on front and spine, leaves untrimmed and unopened in original glassine protective wrapper, whole in original (slightly rubbed), three panel stiff card folder covered with gilt paper (without the original slipcase), title printed in green and black, initials and headlines printed in green, inside front cover of folder with bookplate of John Kobler; corners just slightly bumped, one small faint brown spot to tissue cover, outstanding copy, very fragile and always torn glassine entirely intact and text with no signs of use, most of it never having seen the light of day.   Phillip J. Pirages   63 - 282   2013 $18,000

Joyce, James 1882-1941 *The Mime of Mick Nick and the Maggies. A Fragment from Work in Progress.* The Hague: Servire Press; New York: Gotham Book Mart, 1934. First edition, 242 x 162mm., on Old Antique Dutch, this copy # 631, there were also 29 special signed copies on Japon, plain paper wrappers in white dust jacket, front cover with design by Lucia Joyce, printed in blue and silver, blue titling on front cover and spine, unopened, very rare original dust jacket and housed in slightly worn brown cardboard slipcase, opening initial and tailpiece designed by Lucia Joyce, glassine little wrinkled, one corner just lightly bumped, otherwise pristine.   Phillip J. Pirages   63 - 283   2013 $2000

Joyce, James 1882-1941 *The Mime of Mick, Nick and the Maggies a fragment from work in progress.* The Hague and London: The Servire Press and Faber and Faber Ltd., 1934. First edition, limited to 1000 numbered copies, printed on Antique Dutch paper, this being number 200, octavo, cover illustration, initial letter and tailpiece designed by Lucia Joyce, author's daughter, original unprinted wrappers in original printed dust jacket illustrated in blue, silver and gray, some minor browning to spine and small split at bottom back hinge, fragments of original glassine laid in, else near fine, uncut, mostly unopened, original silver slipcase with pink paper label, lettered in silver, slipcase with bit of wear, still very good.   Heritage Book Shop   Holiday Catalogue 2012 - 84   2013 $1000

Joyce, James 1882-1941 *Pomes Penyeach.* Paris: Shakespeare & Co., 1927. First edition, 16mo., (24) pages, pale green boards (faded to light brown, spine paper chipped and worn), errata slip.   Second Life Books Inc.   183 - 200   2013 $500

Joyce, James 1882-1941 *Poems Penyeach and other Verses.* London: Faber and Faber, 1965. Uncorrected proof copy, new edition, small 8vo. original pink wrappers, Charles Monteith's copy with his book label loosely inserted and his name in non-authorial hand, on cover, near fine.   Maggs Bros. Ltd.   1442 - 139   2013   £200

Joyce, James 1882-1941 *A Portrait of the Artist as a Young Man.* New York: B. W. Huebsch, 1916. First edition, 193 x 125mm, 2 p.l., 299, (1) pages, publisher's blue cloth, blindstamped title on front cover, flat spine with gilt titling, bookplates of John Kobler and of "Porcaro", very slight chafing to joints and extremities, spine ends just little curled, otherwise fine, binding especially clean, spine gilt very bright and text virtually pristine.   Phillip J. Pirages   63 - 284   2013 $9500

Joyce, James 1882-1941 *Stephen Hero, Part of the First Draft of "A Portrait of the Artists as a Young Man".* London: 1944. First edition, 200 x 130mm., 210 pages, publisher's black cloth flat spine with gilt titling, original dust jacket, very nice black clamshell box, bookplate of John Kobler, touch of soil and hint of rumpling to white dust jacket, otherwise fine, volume itself mint.   Phillip J. Pirages   63 - 285   2013 $475

Joyce, James 1882-1941 *Tales Told of Shem and Shaun. Three Fragments from Work in Progress.* Paris: Black Sun Press, 1929. First edition, one of 500 copies on Van Gelder Zonen paper (this copy #249), there were also 50 copies hors commerce and 100 copies on japanese vellum, original white paper wrappers, title printed in black and red on front cover and spine, printer's device on back cover, original glassine dust jacket, slightly worn and expertly repaired, with cardboard slipcase of orange cloth covered with paper and with orange ribbon pull (apparently a variant of publisher's slipcase described by Slocum & Cahoon), frontispiece, original tissue guard, printed in red and black, minuscule chip to glassine at head and tail of spine, otherwise in pristine condition.   Phillip J. Pirages   63 - 286   2013 $2900

Joyce, James 1882-1941 *Two Criterion Miscellany Publications, Offered Together: Anna Livia Plurabelle, Fragment of Work in Progress. (and) Haveth Childers Everywhere, Fragment of Work in Progress.* London: Faber & Faber, 1932. 1931. First work First English edition, fourth impression, Second work, First English edition, 195 x 131mm and 200 x 133mm., first work original stiff card inside publisher's printed paper wrappers (fragmentary) dust jacket, second work: original stiff card, publisher's(?) dust jacket, whole anchored inside a green flexible suede binding with blue cloth label on front cover; back panel of "Anna" dust jacket lacking (front panel with large chip missing at upper inner corner), otherwise fine "Haveth" jacket fold reinforced on verso, front fold of jacket mostly split, rear fold with short tear at head, front panel rather soiled, suede binding bit faded and soiled, text of both items fine.   Phillip J. Pirages   63 - 278   2013 $250

Joyce, James 1882-1941 *Ulysses.* Paris: Shakespeare and Co., 1922. First edition, copy 811 of 750 copies numbered 250 to 1000, 4to., later blue half morocco by Bayntun, blue cloth sides, gilt rules and lettering, top edge gilt, others untrimmed, with half title, bound without printed wrappers, half title slightly smudged, fine.   The Brick Row Book Shop   Miscellany Fifty-Nine - 29   2013 $20,000

Joyce, James 1882-1941 *Ulysses.* London: Egosit Press, by John Rodker, Paris, 1922. One of 200 copies (this #936), 230 x 175mm., 4 leaves of errata tipped on at end, original blue green paper wrappers, white titling on upper cover, edges untrimmed, attractive linen clamshell box backed with blue green morocco, raised bands, gilt titling on spine, wrappers somewhat chipped and flaked at edges and joints (tail of front wrapper with shallow chip two inches wide, front joint torn a third of the way up from bottom), arching eight-inch closed tear to front cover (neatly repaired by backing, the cover with another sheet on verso), binding with condition issues but still solid and fine internally, quite clean, fresh, with trivial defects only.   Phillip J. Pirages   63 - 287   2013 $2400

Joyce, James 1882-1941 *Ulysse.* Paris: La Maison des Amis de Livres, Adrienne Monnier, 1929. First edition, #59 de 100 exemplaires sur papier velin d'arches, limited to 100 copies on velin, this no. 59, fine in original tan wrappers with blue lettering and original mildly worn glassine dust jacket, untrimmed, small 4to.   By the Book, L. C.   38 - 89   2013 $8000

Joyce, James 1882-1941 *Ulysses.* New York: Limited Editions Club, 1935. Limited to 1500 numbered copies, signed by Henri Matisee, the illustrator, quarto, 26 plates by Matisse, original full brown buckram, embossed in gold on front cover and spine from a design by Leroy Appleton, fine copy, housed in publisher's original board slipcase, slightly worn.   Heritage Book Shop   50th Anniversary Catalogue - 57   2013 $3500

Joyce, James 1882-1941 *Ulysses.* London: John Lane, The Bodley Head, 1936. One of 100 copies signed by author, (there were also 900 unsigned copies), 265 x 195mm., 8 p.l., 765, (1) pages, original vellum, gilt titling on spine, large stylized gilt bow on each cover, top edge gilt, other edges untrimmed and mostly unopened, original (slightly worn but very solid), black and white patterned paper slipcase with paper label, housed in fine silk lined gray morocco clamshell box by Sangorski & Sutcliffe, title printed in blue and black, prospectus laid in at front, hint of smudging to vellum (or perhaps just a natural variation in color), but in any case, virtually mint, binding entirely unworn, especially bright and mostly unopened text pristine.   Phillip J. Pirages   63 - 288   2013 $50,000

Joyce, James 1882-1941 *Ulysses.* London: John Lane, the Bodley Head, 1936. First English edition printed in England, one of 900 numbered copies, printed on Japon vellum, out of a total edition of 1000 copies, this being number 748, bound by Zaehnsdorf (stamp signed in gilt on front turn-in) in full green morocco, front cover decoratively stamped in gilt with a Homeric bow (matching original design), spine lettered gilt in compartments, board edges ruled in gilt, turn-ins decoratively tooled in gilt, top edge gilt, others uncut, marbled endpapers, fine.   Heritage Book Shop   Holiday Catalogue 2012 - 85   2013 $4000

Joyce, James 1882-1941 *Ulysses.* London: Bodley Head, 1937. First English trade edition, crown 8vo., original lime green cloth, backstrip gilt lettered, design on Eric Gill's Homeric bow gilt blocked on front cover, tail edges rough trimmed, dust jacket dust soiled and chipped, good.   Blackwell's Rare Books   B174 - 242   2013   £600

Joyce, James 1882-1941 *Ulysses.* San Francisco: Arion Press, 1988. One of 150 numbered copies for sale (this being #96) out of a total edition of 175, signed by artist, thick folio, 40 etchings by Rober Motherwell on 20 folded leaves, of which 20 are in color, printed in Perpetua type on French mouldmade Johannot paper, intaglio printing was done by R. C. Townsend in black and 19 colors on heavier weight Johannot paper; bound with white alum-tawed pigskin on spine and fore-edges of boards which are covered in blue cloth with white flecks, spine lettered blue, fine, original slipcase covered with same fabric and with paper label on spine, with original cardboard shipping carton and publisher's prospectus laid in.   Heritage Book Shop   Holiday Catalogue 2012 - 2   2013 $15,000

Joyce, James 1882-1941 *Ulysses.* Dublin: Lilliput Press, 1997. Limited to 100 numbered copies signed by editor and introducer on limitation leaf, which is printed on Arches mouldmade paper, large 8vo., original full blue Chieftan goatskin, blind embossed and blocked in gold, top edge gilt, fine in matching cloth backed slipcase.   Maggs Bros. Ltd.   1442 - 141   2013   £750

Joyce, Jeremiah *Scientific Dialogues, Intended for the Instruction and Entertainment of Young People...* London: printed for J. Johnson, 1807. 1805, 6 volumes bound in 3, 153 x 88mm., pleasing recent retrospective half calf over marbled boards, raised bands, black morocco label on each spine, 24 plates, leaves of first volume with opening of second with harmless vertical crease down center, splash stain on titlepage of volume II, other occasional minor stains, faint foxing or thuming, but excellent set generally clean, fresh in unworn, sympathetic binding.   Phillip J. Pirages   63 - 425   2013 $400

Joyce, P. W. *Catalogue of the Library of P. W. Joyce.* Hanna & Neale, April, 1914. 36 pages, 8vo., wrappers, very good.   C. P. Hyland   261 - 119   2013   £45

Joyce, P. W. *English as We Speak It in Ireland.* 1910. First edition, xi, 356 pages, 8vo., original gilt decorated cloth, very good.   C. P. Hyland   261 - 523   2013   £35

Joyce, P. W. *On Spenser's Irish Rivers.* 1867. First edition, 13 pages, disbound, 8vo., note "presented to me by author 11th Oct. 1867 Bryan O'Looney".   C. P. Hyland   261 - 790   2013   £45

Judah, Aaron *The Pot of Gold and Two Other Tales.* London: Faber, 1959. First edition, original pictorial red cloth, dust jacket price clipped and overstamped with decimal price, pages 62, illustrations by Mervyn Peake.   R. F. G. Hollett & Son   Children's Books - 445   2013   £60

Judson, A. C. *In Southern Ireland.* Bloomington: Principia Press, 1933. 7 line presentation inscription from author, 8vo., cloth, very good.   C. P. Hyland   261 - 790   2013   £45

Jung, C. G. *Analytsche Psychologie und Erziehung.* Heidelberg: Niels Kampmann Verlag, 1926. First edition, green cloth, gilt, slight wear to corners and little age-toning, else near fine.   Between the Covers Rare Books, Inc.   Psychology & Psychiatry - 296997   2013 $125

Jung, C. G. *Freud and Psychoanalysis. Volume 4 of the Collected Works.* New York: Pantheon Books, 1961. First edition, near fine with owner's bookplate on front pastedown in very good, price clipped dust jacket with some scuffing and scratches.   Between the Covers Rare Books, Inc.   Psychology & Psychiatry - 317236   2013 $75

Jung, C. G. *The Structure and Dynamics of the Psyche. Volume 8 of the Collected Works.* New York: Pantheon Books, 1960. First edition, near fine, owner's bookplate, very good price clipped dust jacket with some scuffing.   Between the Covers Rare Books, Inc.   Psychology & Psychiatry - 317234   2013 $70

Junius, Pseud. *Junius. Stat Nominis Umbra.* London: printed by T. Bensley for Vernor and Hood et al, 1801. 2 volumes, 8vo., engraved titlepage (dated 1797), engraved portrait frontispieces and other engraved plates portrait plates, foxed, contemporary straight grained dark blue morocco, spine gilt in compartments with liberty cap tool, also lettered direct, boards bordered in gilt, bit rubbed at extremities and touched up with blue dye, small printed booklabel 'Gwendolen Branch'.   Unsworths Antiquarian Booksellers   28 - 178   2013   £160

Junker, Wilhelm *Travels in Africa During the Years 1879-1883.* London: Chapman & Hall, 1891. First edition, original pictorial cloth, gilt, head and foot of spine trifle rubbed, illustrations, lacking map.   R. F. G. Hollett & Son   Africana - 103   2013   £150

Junker, Wilhelm *Travels in Africa During the Years 1882-1886.* London: Chapman and Hall, 1892. First edition, original pictorial cloth, gilt, one lower hinge and lower edge to rear board bumped and snagged, illustrations, folding map, occasional light spotting.   R. F. G. Hollett & Son   Africana - 104   2013   £275

Junod, Henri A. *The Life of a South African Tribe.* Neuchatel: Attinger Freres, 1912. First edition, 2 volumes, original pictorial cloth, gilt, spine little rubbed and frayed, few small nicks, numerous illustrations, scattered spotting, front endpapers replaced, but very good set.   R. F. G. Hollett & Son   Africana - 105   2013   £350

Jussieu, Antoine Laurent De *Genera Plantarum Secundum Ordines Natrales Disposita Juxta Methodum in borto Regio Parisieni Exaratam...* Paris: Viduam Herissant et Thephilum Barrois, 1789. First edition, 8vo., headpieces, tailpieces, occasional pencil marginalia, contemporary tree calf, gilt spine, red leather spine label, marbled endleaves rubbed, outer hinges starting at foot of spine, bookplate and blindstamps of Alfred Povah, very good.   Jeff Weber Rare Books   172 - 162   2013 $650

Juster, Norton *The Phantom Tollbooth.* New York: Epstein & Carroll, 1961. First edition, first printing, 4to., blue cloth, fine in dust jacket with some edge rubbing but no tears, illustrations by Jules Feiffer, quite scarce in signed by author, especially in such nice condition.   Aleph-Bet Books, Inc.   105 - 348   2013 $2200

Justin Martyr *Tou Agiou Ioustinou Philosophou Kai Marturos... (bound with) Opera Omnia...* Paris: ex officina Roberti Stephani, 1551. Paris: apud Iacobum Dupuys, 1554. Editio princeps and first edition, first substantial translation respectively, ruled in red throughout, titlepage lightly soiled, tiny dampstain to upper corner at beginning of first work, early French biscuit calf, boards with central decorative oval gilt stamp, name "A. FOURNIER" lettered gilt above, circular gilt stamp in spine compartments, old paper label pasted in second, rebacked preserving original spine (now darkened), new endpapers, boards somewhat scratched and marked, still attractive, silk ties lost, good.   Blackwell's Rare Books   172 - 79   2013   £2200

Juvenalis, Decimus Junius *Satyrae.* Utrecht: Rudolphi a Zyll, 1685. 4to., engraved title, contemporary calf, blind central panel and corner ornaments, very skilfully rebacked retaining original spine, new period style spine label, some dampstaining at beginning and end of text, strip along blank fore-edge of engraved title neatly replaced, else very good.   Joseph J. Felcone Inc.   Books Printed before 1701 - 57   2013 $475

K

Kaberry, C. J. *Our Little Neighbours.* London: Humphrey Milford/Oxford University, n.d., 1921. 4to., cream colored boards, pictorial paste-on, slight soil on corner of rear cover, else fine in pictorial dust jacket (repaired with some pieces off), 11 magnificent mounted color plates by Edmund Detmold, uncommon, rare in dust jacket. Aleph-Bet Books, Inc. 105 - 172   2013 $650

Kafka, Franz 1883-1924 *Der Kubelreiter. The Bucket Rider.* Newark: Janus Press, 1972. First edition, one of 100 copies (entire edition), large 4to., loose sheets in cloth folding box, fine, rare portfolio. James S. Jaffe Rare Books Fall 2013 - 73   2013 $1000

Kahn, Edgar M. *Andrew Smith Hallidie. A Tribute to a Pioneer California Industrialist.* San Francisco: by the author, 1953. First edition, one of 275 copies, presentation inscription signed by author for Ben C. Duniway, title printed in brown and black brown cloth, gilt, very fine, uncut. Argonaut Book Shop   Recent Acquisitions June 2013 - 168   2013 $90

Kahn, Edgar M. *Bret Harte in California. A Character Study.* San Francisco: privately printed and designed for author by Haywood H. Hunt, 1951. First book edition, one of 200 copies, (4), 25 pages plus colophon leaf, frontispiece, tan cloth back, marbled boards, paper cover label, very fine. Argonaut Book Shop   Recent Acquisitions June 2013 - 169   2013 $60

Kahrl, William L. *Water and Power. The Conflict Over Los Angeles' Water Supply in the Owens Valley.* Berkeley: University of California Press, 1982. First edition, numerous portraits and plates form photos, maps, two-tone cloth, very fine with printed dust jacket. Argonaut Book Shop   Recent Acquisitions June 2013 - 171   2013 $75

Kames, Henry Home 1696-1782 *Elements of Criticism.* Edinburgh: printed by Neill and Company for Bell & Bradfute, 1807. 2 volumes, 8vo., faint toning, few spots, contemporary marbled and polished calf, spine divided by gilt rules and decorative pallets, red and black morocco labels, spines lightly sunned, extremities tiny bit rubbed, plain printed booklabel "Fasque", plain printed bookplate "Fasque". Unsworths Antiquarian Booksellers 28 - 169   2013   £150

Kane, Elisha Kent *The Far North: Explorations in the Arctic Regions.* Edinburgh: W. P. Nimmo, 1890. Original pictorial cloth, gilt, 4 woodcut plates. R. F. G. Hollett & Son Polar Exploration - 34   2013   £25

Kane, Thomas Leiper *The Private Papers and Diary of Thomas Leiper Kane, a Friend of the Mormons.* San Francisco: Lilienthal, 1937. First edition, limited to 500 copies, frontispiece, one plate, facsimile letter, title printed in red and black, cloth backed boards, paper spine label, very fine and bright copy. Argonaut Book Shop   Summer 2013 - 174   2013 $125

Kansas State Historical Society *Kansas Forts Series.* Topeka: 1997-2000. First three volumes revised, matching format of others, illustrations, all near fine, softcover, several inscribed by author. Dumont Maps & Books of the West 125 - 58   2013 $75

Kant, Immanuel *The Principles of Critical Philosophy, Selected from the Works of....* London: sold by J. Johnson, W. Richardson; Edinburgh: P. Hill, Manners and Miller; Hamburg: B. G. Hoffmann, 1797. First English edition, 8vo. original quarter paper backed blue drab boards, spine heavily chipped, corners showing, ex-library bookplate, very good, scarce. Jeff Weber Rare Books   171 - 193   2013 $6500

Karaka, D. F. *New York with Its Pants Down.* Bombay: Thacker and Co. Ltd., 1946. First edition, muslin cloth with applied printed paper label, small scrape on front fly, probably from a removed sticker or bookplate, else near fine, lacking dust jacket. Between the Covers Rare Books, Inc. New York City - 107089   2013 $50

Karamanski, Theodore J. *Fur Trade and Exploration. Opening the Far Northwest 1821-1852.* Norman: University of Oklahoma Press, 1983. First edition, 24 illustrations, 8 maps, yellow cloth, very fine, spine faded pictorial dust jacket. Argonaut Book Shop   Summer 2013 - 175   2013 $75

Karamisheff, W. *Mongolia and Western China.* Tientsin: La Librairie Francaise, 1925. First edition, 8vo., 3 foldout maps, very good++ in very good+ dust jacket with chips, mild sun spine, scuffs and minimal foxing, rare. By the Book, L. C. 38 - 65   2013 $1200

Karlsson, Elis *Cruising off Mozambique.* Oxford University Press, 1969. First edition, original two-tone cloth, gilt, dust jacket price clipped, covered in self adhesive plastic film, 8 plates, line drawings by author. R. F. G. Hollett & Son   Africana - 106   2013   £25

Karpinski, Louis C. *Bibliography of Mathematical Works Printed in America through 1850.* Ann Arbor & London: University of Michigan Press & Oxford University Press, 1940. First edition, inscribed by author to Henry P. Kendall, Burndy bookplate, 4to., illustrations, dark blue cloth, blind-stamped cover emblem, gilt stamped spine title, extremities lightly speckled, inner hinge cracked, very good. Jeff Weber Rare Books   169 - 247   2013 $400

Katchmer, George A. *How to Organize and Conduct Football Practice.* Englewood Cliffs: Prentice Hall Inc., 1962. First edition, old and faint price mark on front pastedown and tiny spot on fore edge, still fine in near fine dust jacket with couple of tears, tiny nick, nice, bright copy. Between the Covers Rare Books, Inc.   Football Books - 80527   2013 $65

Kavanagh, Patrick   *Come Dance with Kitty Stobling and Other Poems.*   London: Longmans, 1960. First edition, 8vo, original brown cloth, acetate dust jacket, original price tipped in on corner of front free endpaper, unusual, attractive bookplate, slight fading to spine, otherwise fine. Maggs Bros. Ltd.   1442 - 145   2013   £120

Kavanagh, Patrick   *Lough Derg. A Poem.*   London: Martin Brian & O'Keefe, 1978. First edition, large 8vo., original green cloth, fine in dust jacket.   Maggs Bros. Ltd.   1442 - 150   2013   £125

Kavanagh, Patrick   *Collected Poems.*   London: MacGibbon & Kee, 1964. First edition, number 41 of 110 copies signed by author, tall 8vo., quarter green morocco, paper covered boards, sympathetically rebacked on spine, some offsetting from previous insertion between colophon and half title, otherwise near fine in slipcase.   Maggs Bros. Ltd.   1442 - 146   2013   £1500

Kavanagh, Patrick   *Collected Poems.*   New York: Devin Adair, 1964. First US edition, tall 8vo., original quarter black cloth, burgundy boards, from the library of Richard Murphy, inscribed, nicked at head and tail of spine, otherwise excellent.   Maggs Bros. Ltd.   1442 - 147   2013   £250

Kavanagh, Patrick   *Collected Poems.*   London: MacGibbon & Kee, 1964. First edition, file copy of publisher, stamped "File copy Editorial and inscribed by editorial director Timothy O'Keefe, marked - return to T O K, with his minor marks on 6 pages, 8vo., original fawn cloth, dust jacket, near fine, jacket slightly nicked and worn at extremities.   Maggs Bros. Ltd.   1442 - 360   2013   £650

Kavanagh, Patrick   *The Complete Poems of Patrick Kavanagh.*   New York: Peter Kavanagh Hand Press, 1972. First edition, 8vo., original black cloth, dust jacket, from the library of Richard Murphy, signed by him on front free endpaper, very good in dust jacket, nicked at extremities and browned on spine.   Maggs Bros. Ltd.   1442 - 149   2013   £250

Kavin, Mel   *Catalog of the Thirty-three Miniature Designer Bindings You Can Judge a Book by Its Cover by Bernard C. Middleton.*   Rivera: Kater-Crafts Bookbinders, 1998. Limited to 500 copies, signed by compiler, oblong 4to., cloth, title stamped on spine and cover, color illustrations, from the collection of Donn W. Sanford.   Oak Knoll Books   303 - 19   2013 $180

Keane, John B.   *The Field.*   Cork: Mercier Press, 1966. First Irish edition, small 8vo., original illustrated boards, excellent copy.   Maggs Bros. Ltd.   1442 - 151   2013   £75

Kearton, Richard   *The Adventures of Cock Robin and His Mate.*   London: Cassell & Co., 1904. First edition, original green pictorial cloth, gilt, over 120 illustrations from photos. R. F. G. Hollett & Son   Children's Books - 316   2013   £30

Kearton, Richard   *Wild Bird Adventures.*   London: Cassell & Co., 1923. First edition, original green cloth, spine rather faded, photos by author, scattered spotting.   R. F. G. Hollett & Son   Children's Books - 317   2013   £25

Keary, Eliza   *Pets and Playmates.*   London: Marcus Ward, 1880. First edition, square 8vo., blue cloth backed boards, about good, recased, corners rounded, some pages have tape stains at gutters, wonderful color plates by Edith Scannell.   Barnaby Rudge Booksellers   Children 2013 - 021521   2013 $50

Keating, H. R. F.   *In Kensington Gardens Once...*   Newcastle upon Tyne: Flambard Press, 1997. First edition, original wrappers, illustrations by Gwen Mandley, presentation copy from artist, inscribed.   R. F. G. Hollett & Son   Children's Books - 318   2013   £25

Keating, William H.   *Narrative of a Expedition to the Source of St. Peter's River, Lake Winnepeek, Lake of the Woods...*   Philadelphia: Carey & Lea, 1824. First edition, 8vo., folding map, rebacked and fine, 15 plates, both half titles, new half calf, marbled boards, leather labels, plates foxed, fine set.   M & S Rare Books, Inc.   95 - 185   2013 $1750

Keats, Ezra Jack   *John Henry an American Legend.*   New York: Pantheon, 1965. First edition, pre-publication copy, publisher sheet laid-in, illustrations in color, 4to., cloth, fine in dust jacket.   Aleph-Bet Books, Inc.   104 - 305   2013 $200

Keats, John 1795-1821   *Endymion: a Poetic Romance.*   London: printed for Taylor and Hessye, 1818. First edition, first issue, with one-line erratum on page (xi) and five line errata slip tipped in, watermark on title and sheets '1817', original drab boards, rebacked to style, original printed paper spine label, bit chipped and soiled, uncut, corners lightly bumped and edges flaking bit, little light foxing and browning to edges of leaves, previous owner's bookplate, very good, fragile item, quarter brown calf clamshell case. Heritage Book Shop   Holiday Catalogue 2012 - 86   2013 $8500

Keats, John 1795-1821 *Endymion: a Poetic Romance.* London: printed for Taylor and Hessey, 1818. First edition, 218 x 135mm., 6 p.l., 207 pages, bound without leaf of ads at back; sumptuous chocolate brown crushed morocco, elaborately gilt and inlaid by Zaehnsdorf (signed on front turn-in and with stamped oval, normally marking firm's best work), covers with gilt ruled and inlaid frames of ochre and maroon morocco, central panel intricately diapered with curving ochre acanthus leaves forming original compartments containing maroon fleuron, raised bands, maroon framed compartments with inlaid ochre and maroon centerpiece, brown morocco doublures and endleaves, doublures continuing use of maroon and ochre inlays to form a frame entwined with sinuous leafy vine sprouting berries, all edges gilt, slightly frayed, grey cloth dust jacket with gilt titling, faint foxing on few leaves near back, otherwise only most trivial imperfections, extremely fine, text clean and mostly bright, beautiful binding in perfect condition, bookplate of Francis Kettaneh. Phillip J. Pirages 61 - 133 2013 $9500

Keats, John 1795-1821 *Poems.* Vale Press, 1898. One of 217 copies, 232 x 145nn, 2 volumes, woodcut white-vine initials and intricate full borders on opening leaves by Charles Ricketts, handsome contemporary oxblood crushed morocco (signed "G. P. Putnam's sons" on front turn-ins), covers gilt with graceful leafy frame of twining veins accented with small floral tools and dots as well as intricate floral sprig cornerpieces, raised bands, double ruled spine compartments repeating floral sprig as centerpiece surrounded by small tools and leafy branch cornerpieces, French fillets on turn-ins, Japanese vellum endpapers, top edges gilt, matching felt lined morocco slipcase with slightly soiled paper sides and matching morocco pull-off protective spine cover with gilt tilting, hint of darkening at edges of free endpapers because of turn in glue (as usual), two pages with very minor soling perhaps during printing, but extremely fine set, text and lovely bindings virtually pristine. Phillip J. Pirages 61 - 109 2013 $4500

Keats, John 1795-1821 *The Poetical Works of John Keats.* London: published for the proprietor by William Smith, 1841. First separate British hardcover edition, 12mo., original blindstamped green binding with gilt lettering and decoration to spine, one inch surface split to upper joints, hinges and joints solid, frontispiece portrait foxed with mild offsetting to adjacent titlepage, 12mo., scarce. By the Book, L. C. 38 - 90 2013 $1000

Keats, John 1795-1821 *The Poetical Works and Other Writings.* New York: Charles Scribner's Sons, 1938-1939. Hampstead edition, limited to 1050 numbered copies, this being no. 695, signed by Maurice Buxton Forman and John Masefield, octavo, 8 volumes, photogravure frontispieces with tissue guards and plates, half blue morocco over blue cloth, morocco ruled in gilt, spines stamped and lettered gilt, top edge gilt, others uncut, marbled endpapers, few volumes with small amount of light discoloration to cloth, near fine set. Heritage Book Shop Holiday Catalogue 2012 - 87 2013 $3750

Keats, John 1795-1821 *Collected Sonnets.* Maastricht: Halcyon Press, 1930. 30/325 copies of an edition of 376, printed on Dutch Pannekock laid paper, 11 wood engravings by John Buckland Wright, pages (96), royal 8vo., original mid blue linen lettering on backstrip, hinges cracking very slightly, free endpapers lightly browned, untrimmed, good. Blackwell's Rare Books B174 - 180 2013 £350

Keeler, Harry Stephen *The Case of the Barking Clock.* New York: Phoenix Press, 1947. First edition, spine peaked little and small bookstore label on front pastedown, near fine in like dust jacket with tiny nicks and small tears. Between the Covers Rare Books, Inc. Mystery & Detective Fiction - 322258 2013 $350

Keeler, Harry Stephen *The Case of the Transposed Legs.* New York: Phoenix Press, 1948. First edition, front fly excised and vertical line on pastedowns from old jacket protector, else very good in like dust jacket with modest chips. Between the Covers Rare Books, Inc. Mystery & Detective Fiction - 322259 2013 $275

Keeler, Harry Stephen *The Case of the Two Strange Ladies.* New York: Phoenix Press, 1943. First edition, slightly cocked, else near fine in very good or better dust jacket with light edgewear. Between the Covers Rare Books, Inc. Mystery & Detective Fiction - 286431 2013 $375

Keeler, Harry Stephen *The Man with the Magic Eardrums.* New York: E. P. Dutton, 1933. First edition, front hinge repaired, else fine in very good, price clipped dust jacket with small nicks at spine ends. Between the Covers Rare Books, Inc. Mystery & Detective Fiction - 290365 2013 $350

Keeler, Harry Stephen *The Monocled Monster.* London: Ward Lock and Co., 1947. First English edition, few tiny spots on boards, else near fine in modestly rubbed, very good dust jacket. Between the Covers Rare Books, Inc. Mystery & Detective Fiction - 286428 2013 $400

Keeler, Harry Stephen *The Steeltown Strangler.* London: Ward Lock & Co., 1950. First edition, small bookstore stamp to front pastedown, distributor's stamp on titlepage, else fine in near fine, price clipped dust jacket, signed with greeting by author, scarce. Between the Covers Rare Books, Inc. Mystery & Detective Fiction - 322257 2013 $1250

Keeping, Charles *Charley, Charlotte and Golden Canary.* Oxford University Press, 1967. First edition, 13 color printed illustrations by Keeping, imperial 8vo., original canary yellow cloth backed white boards, illustrated overall to designs by Keeping, front cover printed in black, dust jacket repeats cover images, near fine. Blackwell's Rare Books 172 - 202 2013 £100

Keeping, Charles *Miss Emily and the Bird of Make-Believe.* Hutchinson, 1978. First edition, 30 color printed full page illustrations by Keeping, imperial 8vo., original boards with designs overall by Keeping, backstrip and front cover printed in black, fine.   Blackwell's Rare Books   172 - 203   2013   £100

Keeping, Charles *Wasteground Circus.* Oxford University Press, 1975. First edition, 32 full page color printed illustrations by Keeping, imperial 8vo., original boards illustrated overall to designs by Keeping, backstrip and front cover printed in black, illustrated endpapers, bookplate, dust jacket repeats cover image, fine, signed by Keeping.   Blackwell's Rare Books   172 - 204   2013   £100

Kees, Weldon *The Last Man.* San Francisco: Colt Press, 1943. First edition, 8vo., original cloth backed decorated boards, printed label on spine, signed by Kees, spine label rubbed, otherwise fine.   James S. Jaffe Rare Books   Fall 2013 - 79   2013 $1250

Kees, Weldon *Nonverbal Communication: Notes on the Visual Perception of Human Relations.* Berkeley: and Los Angeles, 1956. First edition, quarto, some modest spotting to boards, else near fine in near very good with few chips.   Between the Covers Rare Books, Inc.   Psychology & Psychiatry - 279943   2013 $100

Kees, Weldon *Poems 1947-1954.* San Francisco: Adrian Wilson, 1954. First edition, tall 8vo., original cloth backed paste paper boards with printed label on spine, printed wraparound band, bit of tape residue from previous dust jacket protector on endsheets, otherwise fine, rarest form of book, with publisher's prospectus laid in.   James S. Jaffe Rare Books   Fall 2013 - 80   2013 $3500

Kees, Weldon *The Collected Poems of Weldon Kees.* Iowa City: Stone Wall Press, 1960. First edition, one of only 20 copies on Rives heavy, French mould made paper, bound in full leather, out of a total edition of 200 copies printed, very fine, rare issue.   James S. Jaffe Rare Books   Fall 2013 - 81   2013 $4500

Keill, James *The Anatomy of the Humane Body Abridg'd or a Short and full View of all the Parts of the Body.* printed for William Keblewite, 1703. Second edition, little bit of light staining in margins, 12mo., contemporary Cambridge style panelled calf, attractive but slightly defective, red lettering piece on spine, extremities worn, joints cracked but cords firm, old pen scribble on titlepage, ownership inscription at top of flyleaf, ex-libris Jacobi Skipper Coll. Cor., i.e. Corpus Christi College 1706 and later armorial bookplate.   Blackwell's Rare Books   Sciences - 66   2013   £250

Keill, John *An Examination of Dr. Burnet's Theory of the Earth.* Oxford: printed at the Theater, 1698. First edition, 8vo., browned old ink strokes in margins, prelim blank leaf torn without loss, some old waterstaining to lower margins, full contemporary unlettered panelled calf, raised bands, armorial bookplate of Rd. Maurice Jones.   Jarndyce Antiquarian Booksellers CCIV - 17   2013   £225

Keith, Alexander *Burns and Folk Song.* Aberdeen: D. Wyllie & Son, 1922. Half title, frontispiece, occasional pencil annotations, untrimmed, original brown cloth, lettered gilt, very good.   Jarndyce Antiquarian Booksellers   CCIII - 60   2013   £20

Keith, L. E. *Female = Filosofy, Fished Out and Fried.* Cleona: Holzapfel, 1894. Volume I, no. 1 of The Coming Kingdom, published quarterly, 8vo., pages 336, illustrations, printed paper wrappers, ex-library, with bookplate and stamps, title little chipped and soiled, edges soiled, cover somewhat worn, especially at spine, otherwise very good.   Second Life Books Inc.   182 - 128   2013 $85

Keith, Thomas *A New Treatise on the Use of Globes.* London: Longmans Brown etc., 1845. New edition, original black fine ribbed cloth, gilt, boards panelled in blind, head of spine frayed, 7 folding copper engraved plates.   R. F. G. Hollett & Son   Children's Books - 319   2013   £60

Keleher, William A. *Maxwell Land Grant.* Santa Fe: Rydal Press, 1942. First edition, one of 750 printed, pages xiii, 168, illustrations, lacking dust jacket, number inked on titlepage, else very good, rare.   Dumont Maps & Books of the West   122 - 72   2013 $95

Kelham, Robert *Domesday Book Illustrated...* London: printed by John Nichols, 1788. 8vo., errata, half title, some occasional foxing, late 19th or early 20th century full pale calf, gilt flower head devices on spine, raised bands, red morocco label, marbled endpapers, carmine red edges.   Jarndyce Antiquarian Booksellers   CCIV - 179   2013   £250

Kellam, Ian *Were the Snow Lay.* Gryffon Publications, 1990. Limited edition, no. 140 of 250 copies, original cloth decorated in green with paper label inlay, pages 128, illustrations by Arthur Keene, music on endpapers, presentation copy inscribed by author.   R. F. G. Hollett & Son   Children's Books - 320   2013   £35

Kelleher, D. L. *The Glamour of Cork.* 1919. First edition, 8vo., quarter cloth, fair.   C. P. Hyland   261 - 526   2013   £20

Kelleher, George D. *Gunpowder to Guided Missles: Ireland's War Industries.* 1993. First edition, private printing, illustrations, xv, 400 pages, 8vo., cloth, dust jacket, near fine.   C. P. Hyland   261 - 527   2013   £40

Keller, David H. *The Homunculus.* Philadelphia: Prime Press, 1949. First edition, one of 112 numbered copies, signed by author, additionally very nicely inscribed by author to collector. Between the Covers Rare Books, Inc. Sci-Fi, Fantasy & Horror - 33945 2013 $245

Kelley, Charles R. *The Ending of Wilhelm Reich's Researches.* Stamford: Interscience Research Institute, 1960. First edition, stapled wrappers, 20 pages, bit sunned, otherwise fine. Beasley Books 2013 - 2013 $65

Kelley, Florence *Wage-Earning Women in War Time: The Textile Industry, with Special Reference in Pennsylvania and New Jersey to Woolen and Worsted Yarn, and in Rhode Island to The Work of Women at Night.* New York: National Consumers' League, 1919. Offprint, 4to. 24 pages, illustrations, self wrappers (cover separate, lacks small piece at lower corner of cover, not affecting any text), author's copy. Second Life Books Inc. 182 - 132 2013 $100

Kelley, Florence *Women in Industry.* New York: National Consumers' League, May, 1916. 8vo., pages 8, printed self wrappers, very good. Second Life Books Inc. 182 - 131 2013 $125

Kelley, Robert *Battling the Inland Sea.* Berkeley: University of California Press, 1989. First edition, numerous photos, green cloth, gilt, very fine, pictorial dust jacket. Argonaut Book Shop Recent Acquisitions June 2013 - 172 2013 $75

Kelley, Robert *Gold vs Grain. The Hydraulic Mining Controversy in California's Sacramento Valley.* Glendale: Arthur H. Clark Co., 1959. First edition, one of 1265 copies, 324 pages, illustrations, brown cloth, gilt, very fine and bright copy. Argonaut Book Shop Recent Acquisitions June 2013 - 173 2013 $150

Kelley, William D. *Speeches, Addresses and Letters on Industrial and Financial Questions to Which is Added an introduction...* Philadelphia: Henry Carey Baird, 1872. First edition, 8vo., green cloth, some external wear, cloth torn along lower hinge, hinges starting, good, presentation from Florence Kelley to her son Nicholas, July 12th 1906. Second Life Books Inc. 182 - 140 2013 $300

Kelley, William D. *Why Colored People in Philadelphia are Excluded from the Street Cars.* Philadelphia: Benj. C. Bacon, 1866. First edition, 8vo., 27 pages, original printed wrappers. M & S Rare Books, Inc. 95 - 186 2013 $1250

Kelley, William Melvin *Dancers on the Shore.* Garden City: Doubleday, 1964. First edition, little foxing to endpapers, near fine in lightly rubbed, frontispiece dust jacket. Between the Covers Rare Books, Inc. 165 - 190 2013 $65

Kelley, William Melvin *Dunfords Travels Everywhere.* Garden City: Doubleday, 1970. First edition, Advance Review copy with slip laid in, fine in very slightly soiled, fine dust jacket. Between the Covers Rare Books, Inc. 165 - 192 2013 $65

Kellogg, Lucy *History of the Town of Bernardston Franklin County, Massachusetts 1736-1900.* Greenfield: E. A. Hall, 1902. First edition, large 8vo., 581 pages, full page portrait, 2 page map, faded cloth, hinges and flyleaf loose, good, clean copy. Second Life Books Inc. 183 - 220 2013 $150

Kellogg, Vernon *Nuova or the New Bee.* Boston: Houghton Mifflin, 1920. 8vo., brown pictorial cloth, fine in dust jacket (with piece off bottom of spine and scrape on front), illustrations by Milo Winter. Aleph-Bet Books, Inc. 105 - 592 2013 $175

Kellsall, Charles *Classical Excursion from Rome to Arpino.* London: Richard Phillips, 1821. First edition, 8vo., pages 107, 2 maps, 3 plates, recent brown quarter calf. J. & S. L. Bonham Antiquarian Booksellers Europe - 6404 2013 £55

Kelly, George *Behold, the Bridegroom.* Boston: Little Brown, 1928. First edition, 8vo. 172 pages, frontispiece, blue cloth with paper label, else near fine in little nicked and soiled, dust jacket, rare in jacket, inscribed by author for Barrett Clark. Second Life Books Inc. 183 - 221 2013 $350

Kelly, Howard A. *Operative Gynecology.* Birmingham: Classics of Medicine, 1992. 2 volumes, 8vo., 24 color plates 592 text figures, full navy leather, gilt stamped covers and spine titles, all edges gilt, fine. Jeff Weber Rare Books 172 - 165 2013 $95

Kelly, J. J. *Irish Varieties.* 1891. First edition, 8vo., 111 pages, original decorated boards (worn), text good. C. P. Hyland 261 - 529 2013 £35

Kelly, Thomas Hughes *Library of the late Thomas Hughes Kelly.* New York: American Art Association, 1934. 8vo., 113 pages, wrappers, very good. C. P. Hyland 261 - 120 2013 £45

Kelman, Janet Havey *The Sea-Shore Shown to the Children.* T. C. & E. C. Jack, n.d, 8vo., original cloth, gilt, pictorial onlay, 48 color plates. R. F. G. Hollett & Son Children's Books - 321 2013 £30

Kelsey, Harry *Juan Rodriguez Cabrillo.* San Marino: Huntington Library, 1986. First edition, numerous illustrations and maps, blue cloth decorated and lettered in silver, very fine with dust jacket. Argonaut Book Shop Recent Acquisitions June 2013 - 174 2013 $60

Keltie, J. Scott *The Partition of Africa.* Edward Stanford, 1895. Second edition, original green ribbed cloth, gilt, 24 tinted folding maps, joints tender, but very good.   R. F. G. Hollett & Son   Africana - 108   2013   £65

Kempe, Martin *Opus Polyhistoricum, Dissertationibus XXV de Osculis.* Frankfurt: Martini Hallervordi Bib. typis Joannis Andreae, 1680. 4to., portrait, titlepage in red and black, contemporary sprinkled calf, extremities very worn and chipped, leather loss at head and foot of spine, hinges cracking, front flyleaves wanting, text with moderate overall foxing and browning, minor marginal worming, good copy.   Joseph J. Felcone Inc.   Books Printed before 1701 - 59   2013 $425

Kendall, George Wilkins *The War Between the United States and Mexico.* New York and Philadelphia: D. & G. S. Appleton, 1851. First edition, large folio, plates in landscape format, iv, 52 pages, plus map and 12 hand finished colored lithographed plates, heightened in gum arabic, all loose as issued, laid into brown cloth portfolio, with gilt cover lettering and black silk ties, titlepage foxed, text with some trace of foxing (as always), plates all very good to fine (very minor foxing in margins, but images clean), especially fine in original format and has not bound up into a book, as it has never been under binder's blade, this is as tall a copy as one can ever hope to find.   Heritage Book Shop 50th Anniversary Catalogue - 60   2013 $35,000

Kendall, Katharine *The Interior Castle.* Worcester: Stanbrook Abbey Press, 1968. One of 310 copies (of an edition of 350 copies), printed in Cancelleresca Bastarda typeface on Hodgkinson white wove handmade paper in black and blue, title printed in maroon, titlepage eagle device printed in gold, with 3 initial letters drawn in by hand in red by Margaret Alexander, errata slip present, original blue silk backed silver fawn Japanese wood veneer boards, front cover gilt lettered, blue dyed Canson Ingres endpapers, top edge gilt, others rough trimmed, original gilt lettered board box split into two parts, fine.   Blackwell's Rare Books   B174 - 387   2013   £85

Kendall, P. F. *Geology of Yorkshire.* for the authors, 1924. First edition, 2 volumes, illustrations, very good in original gilt lettered cloth, some browning to paper as often the case.   Ken Spelman Books Ltd.   73 - 173   2013   £60

Kendall, Phebe M *Maria Mitche. Life, Letters and Journals.* Boston: Lee and Shepard, 1896. First edition, very good, ex-private library with partial sticker on spine and several stamps inside from Headquarters, Professional Woman's League.   Beasley Books   2013 - 2013 $100

Kenealy, Edward *Brallaghan; or the Deipnosophists.* 1845. First edition, original cloth, good.   C. P. Hyland   261 - 531   2013   £55

Kennard, Mary E. *Twilight Tales.* London: F. V. White, 1888. Half title, frontispiece and 5 plates by Edith Ellison, original green cloth, front board blocked and lettered in black, spine blocked and lettered, very slight rubbing, ownership inscription on half title dated 1890, very good.   Jarndyce Antiquarian Booksellers   CCV - 153   2013   £35

Kennedy, Brian P. *Ireland Art into History.* Town House, 1996. First edition, 240 pages, profusely illustrated, cloth, dust jacket, fine.   C. P. Hyland   261 - 530   2013   £40

Kennedy, E. S. *The Astrological History of Masha'allah.* Cambridge: Harvard University Press, 1971. 8vo., orange cloth, white stamped spine title, dust jacket, ownership signature, fine.   Jeff Weber Rare Books   169 - 291   2013 $65

Kennedy, James *Conversations on Religion with Lord Byron and Others, Held in Cephalonia...* London: John Murray, 1830. First edition, half title, folding facsimile plate, 3 pages ads, attractively bound in slightly later half maroon calf by Cox & Ogle of Cambridge gilt spine, black leather label, slight rubbing, F. J. Sebley booklabel, very good.   Jarndyce Antiquarian Booksellers   CCIII - 397   2013   £180

Kennedy, James *Probable Origin of the American Indians, with Particular Reference to that of the Caribs.* London: E. Lumley, 1854. First edition, disbound, spine strengthened with linen backed tape.   Jarndyce Antiquarian Booksellers   CCV - 154   2013   £250

Kennedy, John *Report of the National Convention of Southern Rhodesia.* Salisbury: Amalgamated Pub., 1960. Original wrappers, signed by Kennedy.   R. F. G. Hollett & Son   Africana - 109   2013   £45

Kennedy, John Fitzgerald   1917-1963 *As We Remember Joe.* Cambridge: privately printed, 1945. First edition, first issue, one of about 500 copies distributed to friends and family, with all points as described by Kennedy Library Head, David Powers, titlepage in two colors, with sunken panel on front cover, ivory colored paper and caption on page 64, octavo, 33 black and white photos, including frontispiece, publisher's original full burgundy cloth, front cover stamped in black and gilt on sunken panel, spine lettered in gilt, very small amount of rubbing to spine and back board, otherwise near fine, original glassine, with three ALS's from Powers to Dr. Moury Bromsen.   Heritage Book Shop Holiday Catalogue 2012 - 92   2013 $3750

Kennedy, John Fitzgerald   1917-1963 *Inaugural Address.* Los Angeles: Bela Blau, 1965. Limited to 1000 numbered copies, one of the copies printed on vellum, 4 x 3.5 cm., full vellum stamped in gilt, vellum covered slipcase, handset, printed and bound by Blau, covers show age yellowing of vellum, from the collection of Donn W. Sanford.   Oak Knoll Books   303 - 60   2013 $200

Kennedy, P. J. *The Clonmel Charter School 1747-1886.* Dept. of Education, U. C. D., 1932. First edition, 43 pages, wrappers, ex-library but very good.   C. P. Hyland   261 - 532   2013   £30

Kennedy, Richard *A Boy at the Hogarth Press.* Andoversford: Whittington Press, 1972. First edition, 350/520 copies printed on Wookey Hole mouldmade paper and signed by author, numerous line drawings, title printed in red, folding plan, royal 8vo., original purple lettered cloth, dust jacket, near fine.   Blackwell's Rare Books   B174 - 398   2013   £200

Kennedy, W. R. *Sport, Travel and Adventure in Newfoundland and the West Indies.*   Edinburgh: William Blackwood & Sons, 1885. 8vo., blue cloth with gilt to spine and gilt illustration on front cover, half title, color frontispiece, 1 plate, 16 black and white illustrations in text and color folding map, wear to edges and whiting to outer edge of front and back covers, interior very good.   Schooner Books Ltd.   105 - 35   2013 $175

Kennelly, Brendan *A Time for Voices.* Newcastle upon Tyne: Bloodaxe Books, 1990. First edition, 8vo., wrapper issue, fine, from the library of Richard Murphy, inscribed to him by author.   Maggs Bros. Ltd.   1442 - 153   2013   £50

Kennerly, William Clark *Persimmon Hill. A Narrative of Old St. Louis and the Far West.*   Norman: University of Oklahoma Press, 1948. First edition, 23 illustrations from old prints, views, portraits, green cloth, very fine, pictorial dust jacket, small closed edge tear, quite scarce in this condition.   Argonaut Book Shop   Summer 2013 - 176   2013 $75

Kent, Rockwell *The Bookplates and Marks of Rockwell Kent.*   New York: Random House, 1929. First edition, limited to 1250 copies, this number 196, with proofs of more than 90 bookplates and trademarks printed one side of French folded Japanese paper, prospectus laid in, 12mo., 79 pages, near fine, minimal sun spine and cover edges, in very good++ dust jacket with minimal sun spine, edge wear.   By the Book, L. C.   36 - 66   2013 $600

Kent, Rockwell *Rockwell Kent. The Art of the Bookplate.*   San Francisco: Fair Oaks, 2003. Stated first edition, small 4to., xii, 212 pages. signed and inscribed by author, small 4to., xii, 212 pages, as new in like dust jacket.   By the Book, L. C.   36 - 67   2013 $125

Kenyatta, Charles *Death: "A Rumor in Our Communities" (cover title) Harlem's Free Press: "Revolut! Buy Shotguns! Declare All-Out War!".*   New York: Charles Kenyatta, 1971. Presumed first and probably only edition, quarto, mimeographed and stapled self wrappers (6) pages, fairly sizable but faint stain, about fine.   Between the Covers Rare Books, Inc.   165 - 193   2013 $225

Kernahan, Coulson *Captain Shannon.*   London: Ward Lock, 1897. First edition, name on front endpaper, otherwise near fine in black covered boards.   Mordida Books   81 - 275   2013 $165

Kernahan, Coulson *A World Without a Child: a Story for Women and for Men.*   London: Hodder & Stoughton, 1905. First separate edition, octavo, original blue cloth, front and spine panels stamped in gilt, top edge gilt, fore-edge untrimmed.   L. W. Currey, Inc.   Utopian Literature: Recent Acquisitions (April 2013) - 138731   2013 $200

Kerr, Robert *A General History and Collection of Voyages and Travels, Arranged in Systematic Order. Volume IV (Voyages of Sebastian Cabot and Jacques Cartier to Newfoundland).*   Edinburgh and London: William Blackwood & J. Murray, 1812. Half brown calf, marbled boards, 8vo., extreme wear to edges of binding and outer hinge cracks, foxing to prelim leaves.   Schooner Books Ltd.   104 - 19   2013 $95

Kersowski, Frank *The Outsiders: Ports of Contemporary Ireland.*   Fort Worth: 1975. First edition, wrappers, viii, 201 pages, signed presentation copy, very good.   C. P. Hyland   261 - 533   2013   £29

Kertesz, Andre *Kertesz.*   Hungary: Szentendre, 1987. First edition, 2.5 x 2.5 inches, as new, uncommon, bound in velvet like material with gilt lettering on spine and front panel.   Jeff Hirsch Books   Fall 2013 - 129432   2013 $85

Kesey, Ken *Kesey's Garage Sale.*   New York: Viking, 1973. First edition, scarce hardcover issue, inscribed by author, heavily illustrated with sketches by Kesey, photos, etc., fine in near fine, lightly edgeworn dust jacket.   Ken Lopez Bookseller   159 - 95   2013 $1250

Kesey, Ken *Kesey's Garage Sale.*   New York: Viking, 1973. First edition, quarto, pages 238, very good, scarce cloth edition, dust jacket, illustrations, inscribed by author.   Second Life Books Inc.   183 - 225   2013 $325

Kesey, Ken *One Flew Over the Cuckoo's Nest.*   New York: Viking, 1962. First edition, small crimp to cloth at crown, otherwise fine in very good, modestly spine faded dust jacket with shallow wear to spine extremities and crease to upper front panel, nicer than usual copy, jacket is first jacket with Kerouac blurb.   Ken Lopez Bookseller   159 - 94   2013 $7500

Kesey, Ken *One Flew Over the Cukoo's Nest.*   New York: Viking, 1962. First edition, first issue, 8vo., 311 pages, fine, price clipped dust jacket that is little nicked, one closed tear.   Second Life Books Inc.   183 - 226   2013 $5000

Keynes, John *A Rational, Compendious Way to Convince without any dispute, all Persons Whatsoever, Dissenting from the True Religion.* N.P.: London: printed in the year, 1674. First edition, 12mo., contemporary sheep, nearly fine, with final blank leaf, faint ownership stamp on front endpaper of William J. Onahan (1836-1919).   Howard S. Mott Inc.   262 - 85   2013 $750

Keynes, Richard Darwin *The Beagle Record: Selections from the Original Pictorial Records and Written Accounts of the Voyage of H.M.S. Beagle.*   Cambridge: Cambridge University Press, 1979. First edition, 4to., illustrations, brown cloth, gilt stamped brown cover and spine labels, dust jacket, Burndy, near fine.   Jeff Weber Rare Books   169 - 249   2013 $70

Khazin, E. *Neft. (Oil).* Moscow: Ogiz, 1931. 4to., pictorial wrappers, light cover soil, very good+, illustrations by N. Chifrin.   Aleph-Bet Books, Inc.   104 - 502   2013 $975

Kibre, Pearl *Studies in Medieval Science: Alchemy, Astrology, Mathematics and Medicine.*   London: Hambledon Press, 1984. 8vo., green cloth, gilt stamped cover and spine titles, ownership signature, fine.   Jeff Weber Rare Books   169 - 250   2013 $95

Kidd, Dudley *The Essential Kafir.* A. & C. Black, 1925. Second edition, large 8vo., original decorated cloth, 63 plates, folding map.   R. F. G. Hollett & Son   Africana - 111   2013   £85

Kidder, Daniel P. *The Broken Leg, a Sunday Accident.* New York: Lane & Scott, 1851. First edition, 16mo., 60 pages plus wrappers.   Barnaby Rudge Booksellers   Children 2013 - 021222   2013 $65

Kiell, Norman *Freud Without Hindsight. Review of His Work 1893-1939.*   Madison: IUP, 1988. First edition, stamps on f.e.p., otherwise fine in fine dust jacket.   Beasley Books   2013 - 2013 $50

Kiely, Benedict *All the Way to Bantry Bay and Other Irish Journeys.*   London: Gollancz, 1978. 208 pages, illustrations, dust jacket, near fine, cloth.   C. P. Hyland   261 - 535   2013   £30

Kiely, Benedict *Dogs Enjoy the Morning.* London: Gollancz, 1968. First edition, 8vo., original red cloth, dust jacket, inscribed by author on titlepage, very good in dust jacket, rubbed, overall and nicked at extremities.   Maggs Bros. Ltd.   1442 - 154   2013   £50

Kierkegaard, Soren *Attack upon "Christendom" 1854-1855.* London: Oxford University Press, 1944. First English edition from American sheets, some modest spotting to boards and corners, slightly bumped, very good, without dust jacket.   Between the Covers Rare Books, Inc.   Philosophy - 92923   2013 $150

Kierkegaard, Soren *Christelige Taler. (Christian Discourses).* Copenhagen: C. A. Reitzel, 1848. First edition, presentation state, very good or better in glossy black presentation issue paper covered boards with some surface loss to outer joints and spine, presentation copy inscribed by author for Johan Ludvig Heiberg, the philosopher.   Between the Covers Rare Books, Inc.   Philosophy - 54791   2013 $12,500

Kierkegaard, Soren *Enten - Eller: et Livsfragmet Udgivet af Victor Eremita (Either - Or).* Kjobenhavn: C. A. Reitzel, 1843. First edition, 2 volumes, sympathetically rebound in black morocco, gilt and cloth covered boards, new endpapers and lacking half titles, one of 525 copies, lovely.   Between the Covers Rare Books, Inc.   Philosophy - 78520   2013 $5850

Kierkegaard, Soren *Enten-Eller et Livs Fragment Udgivat of Victor Cremita (pseud.).* Kobenhavn: 1849. Second edition, 8vo., 2 volumes in 1, contemporary half morocco, marbled boards, rubbed along edges, rebacked, original spine laid down, text fine.   M & S Rare Books, Inc.   95 - 299   2013 $1250

Kijewski, Karen *Katapult.* New York: St. Martin's Press, 1990. First edition, fine in fine dust jacket, signed by author, from the library of Bruce Kahn.   Between the Covers Rare Books, Inc.   Mystery & Detective Fiction - 201759   2013 $65

Kilgour, Alexander *Anecdotes of Lord Byron, from Authentic Sources...* London: Knight & Lacey, 1825. First edition, 12mo., half title, frontispiece, with slight dampstain in top outer corner, uncut in original drab boards, paper label, slightly rubbed and odd small mark, but very good, scarce.   Jarndyce Antiquarian Booksellers   CCIII - 398   2013   £450

Killen, John *A History of the Linen Hall Library 1788-1988.* 1990. First edition, 8vo., illustrations, cloth, dust jacket, fine.   C. P. Hyland   261 - 79   2013   £23

Killian, Gustav *The Accessory of the Nose and Their Relations to Neighbouring Parts.* Jena: Gustav Fischer, 1904. First edition, loose folio sheets, 15 colored plates, each with printed glassine overlay, quarter cloth over yellow printed paper with three original black cloth ties, neatly rebacked in black cloth, rare, fine.   Jeff Weber Rare Books   172 - 166   2013 $750

Kilmer, Joyce *Trees and Other Poems.* New York: George H. Doran Co., 1914. First edition, 8vo., original boards, paper labels, fine, 2 small very light spots on front cover, morocco backed cloth folding case. Howard S. Mott Inc. 262 - 86 2013 $250

Kimball, Robert *Reminiscing With Sissle and Blake.* New York: Viking, 1973. First edition, 4to., hardcover, fine in near fine dust jacket with clear tape reinforcement at edges. Beasley Books 2013 - 2013 $50

Kimes, William F. *John Muir: a Reading Bibliography.* Fresno: Panorama West Books, 1986. Second edition, 179 pages, views, portraits, facsimiles, two-tone cloth, 2 corners very slightly jammed, but fine. Argonaut Book Shop Recent Acquisitions June 2013 - 176 2013 $175

Kimo. Joliet: Volland, 1928. First edition, tall 8vo., cloth backed pictorial boards, fine in pictorial publisher's box, illustrations by Lucille Holling, rare in box, beautiful copy. Aleph-Bet Books, Inc. 104 - 285 2013 $375

Kincaid, Jamaica *Among Flowers: a Walk in the Himalaya.* Washington: National Geographic, 2005. First edition, fine in fine dust jacket, inscribed by author for Nicholas Delbanco and his family. Between the Covers Rare Books, Inc. 165 - 197 2013 $200

Kincaid, Jamaica *Annie-John.* New York: Farrar, Straus Giroux, 1985. First edition, fine in spine faded, near fine dust jacket, inscribed by author to daughter of Nicholas Delbanco, Cesca. Between the Covers Rare Books, Inc. 165 - 194 2013 $250

Kincaid, Jamaica *The Autobiography of My Mother.* New York: Farrar Straus Giroux, 1996. First edition, fine in fine dust jacket, inscribed by author for Nicholas and Elena Delbanco. Between the Covers Rare Books, Inc. 165 - 196 2013 $200

Kincaid, Jamaica *A Small Place.* New York: Farrar Straus Giroux, 1988. First edition, fine in fine dust jacket, inscribed by author for Elena, Nick, Cesca and Andrea Delbanco. Between the Covers Rare Books, Inc. 165 - 195 2013 $200

Kindig, Joe *Thoughts on the Kentucky Rifle in Its Golden Age.* New York: Bonanza, n.d., Reprint, fine in very lightly used dust jacket with short tear at rear flap fold, 4to., 561 pages. Beasley Books 2013 - 2013 $60

King-Harman, Robert Douglas *The Kings, Earls of Kingston.* for private circulation, 1959. First edition, xi, 312 pages, illustrations, loose insert "Kingston College, The Prayer", spine faded, else very good. C. P. Hyland 261 - 397 2013 £125

King Winter. Hamburg: Gustav W. Seitz circa, 1860. 12mo., pictorial wrappers, near fine, die cut in shape of Old Man Winter, every page delicately illustrated in color, very scarce. Aleph-Bet Books, Inc. 104 - 528 2013 $850

King, Frank *Operation Honeymoon.* London: Robert Hale, 1950. First edition, near fine with very light wear in very good dust jacket, price clipped with some internally repaired tears and small hole on spine, scarce in jacket. Between the Covers Rare Books, Inc. Mystery & Detective Fiction - 321524 2013 $250

King, Henry Seymour *Visit of Hull Workmen to the Paris Exhibition. Reports on the Visit.* Spottiswoode & Co., 1889. 50 pages, 8vo., original printed wrappers, rather dusty, corners creased, very scarce. Ken Spelman Books Ltd. 73 - 105 2013 £45

King, Jeremiah *Dictionary of Ireland.* 1917-1918. Second edition, parts 1-3, 40, 40, 64 pages, wrappers, very good. C. P. Hyland 261 - 80 2013 £45

King, Joseph L. *History of San Franncisco Stock and Exchange Board.* San Francisco: Jos. I. King, 1910. First edition, 373 pages, facsimile, portraits, illustrations, publisher's gray cloth stamped in dark gray and gold, light rubbing to extremities, small owner's stamp to end, very good. Argonaut Book Shop Summer 2013 - 178 2013 $150

King, Laurie R. *A Grave Talent.* New York: St. Martin's Press, 1993. First edition, 2nd issue, with Hebrew dedication printed correctly, manufacturer's flaw on front pastedown, tear and bump at bottom of board, else fine in fine dust jacket. Between the Covers Rare Books, Inc. Mystery & Detective Fiction - 77667 2013 $275

King, Lester C. *South African Scenery.* Oliver & Boyd, 1951. Second edition, original cloth, gilt, few slight marks, 266 plates, 79 text figures and folding colored map. R. F. G. Hollett & Son Africana - 112 2013 £30

King, Marian *Piccolino.* Chicago: Whitman, 1939. First edition, 4to., cloth, pictorial paste-on, fine in slightly worn dust jacket, rich color lithos by Nell Smock, this copy inscribed by author. Aleph-Bet Books, Inc. 105 - 338 2013 $100

King, Martin Luther *Stride Toward Freedom.* New York: Harper & Bros., 1958. First edition, fine in very good dust jacket with two 1 1/2 inch tears on front panel, inscribed by author to Dr. Charles W. Orr. Between the Covers Rare Books, Inc. 165 - 1 2013 $10,000

King, Philip Parker *Narrative of a Survey of the Intertropical and Western Colonies of Australia. Performed Between the Years 1818 and 1822.* London: 1827. First edition, 2nd issue, 2 volumes, engraved folding chart, 10 uncolored aquatint views, 8 woodcut engravings, plan, contemporary half calf over marbled boards, spines gilt and sound, slightly shelfworn, extremities rubbed, the Sturt family copy with Alington bookplate, lovely association.   Maggs Bros. Ltd.   1467 - 81   2013   £3750

King, Rufus *Design in Evil.* Garden City: Doubleday Crime Club, 1942. First edition, fine in near fine dust jacket with nicks at spine ends and at corners, several short closed tears, light wear along edges.   Mordida Books   81 - 276   2013 $125

King, Stephen   1947- *Black Magic & Music.* Bangor: Bangor Historical Society, 1983. First edition, thin octavo, illustrations, printed wrappers, (8) pages, trifle rubbed, else fine.   Between the Covers Rare Books, Inc.   Sci-Fi, Fantasy & Horror - 315236   2013 $125

King, Stephen   1947- *The Dark Tower III: The Waste Lands.* Hampton Falls: Donald M. Grant, 1991. First trade edition, fine in fine dust jacket with just hit of wear at corners.   Between the Covers Rare Books, Inc.   Sci-Fi, Fantasy & Horror - 309958   2013 $100

King, Stephen   1947- *Fear Itself: the Horror Fiction of Stephen King.* San Francisco: Underwood Miller, 1982. First edition, fine in dust jacket.   Mordida Books   81 - 277   2013 $75

King, Stephen   1947- *Gerald's Game.* New York: Viking, 1992. Uncorrected proof, fine in wrappers.   Between the Covers Rare Books, Inc.   Sci-Fi, Fantasy & Horror - 306621   2013 $85

King, Stephen   1947- *The Regulators.* New York: Dutton, 1996. Advance reading copy, printed wrappers, crease on rear wrapper, thus about very good.   Between the Covers Rare Books, Inc.   Sci-Fi, Fantasy & Horror - 306667   2013 $50

King, Stephen   1947- *Thinner.* New York: NAL Books/ New American Library, 1984. First edition, fine in very near fine dust jacket with just touch of rubbing on front panel.   Between the Covers Rare Books, Inc.   Sci-Fi, Fantasy & Horror - 315960   2013 $100

Kingsborough, Edward King, Viscount *Antiquities of Mexico.* London: Robert Havel, Colnaghi Son and Co., 1831. (for volumes I-VII) and Henry G. Bohn, 1848 (Volumes VI-IX), 9 volumes, large folio, 741 plates, 2 lithographed tables in text volumes with 60 page section for projected volume X bound in at end of volume IX, contemporary green half morocco gilt, spines gilt and gilt lettered in seven compartments, all edges gilt, thin woven paper guards bound into volume three only, some light spotting, scattered, light and mostly marginal foxing or discoloration volume 4 more heavily foxed, especially the chalk lithographs on mounted India paper, 6 plates and paper guards in volume three have smaller repairs, less than 1 inch, on lower corner, not affecting images, fine, colored issue.   Heritage Book Shop   50th Anniversary Catalogue - 61   2013 $135,000

Kingsley, Charles   1819-1875 *Hereward the Wake. "Last of the English".* Macmillan and Co., 1893. 8vo., contemporary olive calf prize binding, spine gilt, red morocco lettering piece, front board with gilt stamp of Oxford High School, marbled edges and endpapers, little rubbed, spine slightly sunned, prize bookplate of R. G. Holliday for Divinity Form VI in the 1896 midsummer examination, very good.   Blackwell's Rare Books   172 - 82   2013   £25

Kingsley, Charles   1819-1875 *His Letters and Memories of His Life.* London: Kegan Paul, 1885. Fifteenth abridged edition, 8vo., very good, handsome contemporary half calf, gilt panelled spines with red and black, morocco labels, marbled boards, endpapers and edges.   Ken Spelman Books Ltd.   75 - 143   2013   £45

Kingsley, Charles   1819-1875 *The Water-Babies.* London & Cambridge: 1863. First edition, first issue, small square octavo, with "L'Evoi" leaf inserted after dedication, inserted frontispiece and full page illustration, original dark green fine-grain cloth, hinges just starting, top of spine with two very small splits, otherwise superlative copy, gilt fresh, very scarce, housed in fleece lined green cloth clamshell case, rare issue.   David Brass Rare Books, Inc.   Holiday 2012 Chapter One - DB 01480   2013 $5500

Kingsley, Charles   1819-1875 *The Water Babies.* London: Macmillan and Co., 1882. New edition, 4 plates, including frontispiece, tan calf school prize binding, red label with gilt title to spine, decorative gilt stamp of St. John's Foundation School to upper board, edges colored red, neatly rebacked, edges little worn, small area of surface loss to lower board, endpapers slightly foxed, still very good, small binder's stamp of Relfe Brothers.   Unsworths Antiquarian Booksellers   28 - 179   2013   £60

Kingsley, Charles   1819-1875 *The Water Babies.* Macmillan, 1891. Full scarlet calf gilt prize binding by Relfe Brothers, few slight scratches, 100 woodcut illustrations by Linley Sambourne.   R. F. G. Hollett & Son   Children's Books - 324   2013   £50

Kingsley, Charles 1819-1875 *Water Babies.* London: Macmillan, 1909. Limited edition, thick quarto, full blue morocco by Sangorski & Sutcliffe, book spine is decorated with gilt and raised bands and covers are heavily decorated with triple gilt rules and floral decorated corners, inside covers there are gilt dentelles and silk doublures (silk lining), book is the magnificent deluxe edition, limited to only 260 copies, printed on handmade paper and illustrated by Warwick Goble with 32 mounted color plates with lettered tissue guards, book housed in velvet lined cradle, on the opposite side of box is a special insert holding original watercolor signed by artist that appears as a full page color plate on page 32 of the book, actual image measures 13 1/2 x 9 1/4 inches, box is 13 1/2 x 17 3/4 inches high with backstrip rounded to simulate spine of a book with extensive gilt decorations and raised bands. Aleph-Bet Books, Inc. 105 - 277 2013 $22,000

Kingsley, Charles 1819-1875 *The Water Babies.* London: T. C. and E. C. Jack, 1910. 12mo., green cloth, 8 color plates by Katharine Cameron , color paste-on illustration on cover, very good. Barnaby Rudge Booksellers Children 2013 - 020260 2013 $50

Kingsley, Charles 1819-1875 *The Water-Babies.* London: Constable, 1915. First edition thus, 8 color plates, numerous black and white full page and line drawings, original pictorial green cloth gilt, spine partially faded, dust jacket with drawings by W. Heath Robinson on upper panel and spine (upper fold and spine torn and frayed at head, but very little loss), inscription, otherwise very nice, clean copy in rare dust jacket. R. F. G. Hollett & Son Children's Books - 518 2013 £450

Kingsley, Charles 1819-1875 *Water Babies.* New York: Nelson, n.d. circa, 1924. 4to., blue cloth, pictorial paste-on, 180 pages, near fine in worn, soiled and chipped dust jacket, illustrations by Anne Anderson with 12 beautiful color plates plus black and whites in text and pictorial endpapers, scarce in dust jacket. Aleph-Bet Books, Inc. 104 - 37 2013 $475

Kingsley, Henry *Ravenshoe.* London: Ward Lock, 1853. New edition, half title, 6 pages ads, 'Yellowback', original printed boards, rubbed and slightly worn, good plus. Jarndyce Antiquarian Booksellers CCV - 155 2013 £55

Kingsley, Henry *Tales of Old Travel.* London: Macmillan and Co., 1869. First edition, half title, frontispiece, 56 page catalog (August 1869), original green decorated cloth by Burn & Co., hinges slightly cracking, W. H. Smith embossed stamp on leading f.e.p. very good, bright. Jarndyce Antiquarian Booksellers CCV - 156 2013 £45

Kingsley, Mary H. *Travels in West Africa.* Macmillan, 1897. Second edition, original maroon ribbed cloth, corners little bumped, 33 plates. R. F. G. Hollett & Son Africana - 113 2013 £95

Kingsley, Sidney *Dead End. A Play in Three Acts.* New York: Random House, 1936. First edition, round robin copy, signed by 26 members of the original cast, including Huntz Hall, Leo Gorcey, Bobby Jordan and Billy Hallop, signature of Dan Duryea also present, near fine, clean in very good plus dust jacket with chipping to spine crown and some darkening to spine. Ed Smith Books 78 - 8 2013 $1250

Kingston, William H. G. *Marmaduke Merry, the Midshipman.* London: Bemrose and Sons, circa, 1882. Fourth edition, 2 p.l., iv, 405 pages, very pleasing contemporary navy blue half morocco over royal blue cloth boards, raised bands, spine attractively gilt in double ruled compartments with scrolling cornerpieces and complex central fleuron, marbled endpapers, all edges gilt, originally highly decorative cloth covers and spine (as well as front free endpaper) bound in, titlepage vignette, charming headpieces, tailpieces, initials and vignettes in text, 7 engraved plates, including frontispiece, armorial bookplate of "Humphries" and gift inscriptions on original flyleaf dated 1882 and 1966; corners rather worn, otherwise fine in attactive binding, with only trivial internal imperfections. Phillip J. Pirages 63 - 297 2013 $150

Kinnaird, Marion *The Story of Happy Holligan.* Springfield: McLoughlin, 1932. Folio, pictorial card covers, some cover soil, very good, illustrations in color on every page by Frederick Opper, quite scarce. Aleph-Bet Books, Inc. 104 - 119 2013 $350

Kinnan, Peter *Order Book Kept by Peter Kinnan July 7-September 4 1776.* Princeton: Privately printed at Princeton University Press, 1931. First edition, black cloth gilt, stamps from library of a newspaper, else near fine. Between the Covers Rare Books, Inc. New York City - 285930 2013 $50

Kinney, Joshua *My Years of Service.* Richmond: privately printed, 1931. First edition, 28 pages, 2 different types of brushed suede with printed paper label, dampstain along bottom marring of pages, near very good, signed by author. Between the Covers Rare Books, Inc. 165 - 198 2013 $65

Kinross, Albert *The Fearsome Island, Being a Modern rendering of the Narrative of One Silas Fordred, Master Mariner of Hythe...* Chicago: Herbert S. Stone, 1896. First American edition, slight rubbing to boards, fine. Between the Covers Rare Books, Inc. Sci-Fi, Fantasy & Horror - 43096 2013 $400

Kinsella, Thomas *Another September.* Dublin: Dolmen Press, 1958. First edition, 8vo., mustard cloth, dust jacket, from the library of Richard Murphy, inscribed by author, near fine, jacket inexorably browned and split on spine. Maggs Bros. Ltd. 1442 - 156 2013 £375

Kinsella, Thomas *Butcher's Dozen.* Dublin: Peppercanister, 1972. First edition, number 107 of 125 numbered copies signed by author, 8vo., original quarter black leather, red boards with coffin device on upper board, fine in acetate dust jacket. Maggs Bros. Ltd. 1442 - 161 2013 £275

Kinsella, Thomas *The Death of a Queen.* Dublin: Dolmen Press, 1956. First edition, tall 8vo., original wrappers, one of 250 copies, fine. Maggs Bros. Ltd. 1442 - 155 2013 £100

Kinsella, Thomas *Downstream.* Dublin: Dolmen Press, 1960. First edition, 8vo., original pale grey cloth, dust jacket, excellent copy, jacket slightly rubbed and nicked at extremities, inscribed by author for Richard Murphy. Maggs Bros. Ltd. 1442 - 158 2013 £250

Kinsella, Thomas *Finistere.* Dublin: Dolmen Press, 1972. First edition, limited to 250 numbered copies, signed by author, square 4to., original blindstamped green cloth, lettered gilt, top edge gilt, fine in acetate dust jacket, from the library of Richard Murphy, loosely inserted receipt for the book to Murphy on Dolmen Press printed invoice sheet. Maggs Bros. Ltd. 1442 - 165I 2013 £350

Kinsella, Thomas *Finistere.* Dublin: Dolmen Press, 1972. First edition, limited to 250 numbered copies signed by author, square 4to., original blindstamped green cloth, lettered gilt, top edge gilt, fine in acetate dust jacket. Maggs Bros. Ltd. 1442 - 166 2013 £250

Kinsella, Thomas *Glenmacnass.* Minnesota: Traffic Street Press, 2003. First edition, limited to 30 numbered copies, from a total of 56, 8vo., original handmade green flax wrappers, fine. Maggs Bros. Ltd. 1442 - 172 2013 £150

Kinsella, Thomas *Glenmacnass.* Minnesota: Traffic Street Press, 2003. Limited to 26 lettered copies from total edition of 56, 8vo., original handmade green flax cloth covered boards, printed letterpress by Paulette Myers-Rich, with slipcase in Japanese silk cloth, fine. Maggs Bros. Ltd. 1442 - 171 2013 £200

Kinsella, Thomas *The Messenger.* Dublin: Peppercanister, 1978. First edition, tall 8vo. limited to 525 copies, original wrappers, near fine, inscribed by author for Richard Murphy. Maggs Bros. Ltd. 1442 - 169 2013 £200

Kinsella, Thomas *Moralities.* Dublin: Dolmen Press, 1960. First edition, one of 500 copies, tall 8vo., original wrappers, from the library of Richard Murphy, inscribed by RM, covers marked and slightly stained, as suggested, otherwise very good. Maggs Bros. Ltd. 1442 - 157 2013 £175

Kinsella, Thomas *Nightwalker.* Dublin: Dolmen Press, 1967. First edition, 8vo., original wrappers, fine, inscribed by author for Richard Murphy. Maggs Bros. Ltd. 1442 - 159 2013 £250

Kinsella, Thomas *Notes from the Land of the Dead.* Dublin: Cuala Press, 1972. First edition, 8vo., original quarter linen, grey boards, fine, from the library of Richard Murphy, inscribed by author for Murphy. Maggs Bros. Ltd. 1442 - 164 2013 £100

Kinsella, Thomas *One Fond Embrace.* Dublin: Peppercanister, 1988. First edition, original wrappers, from the library of Richard Murphy with his signature, inscribed to him by author, limited to 500 copies, near fine. Maggs Bros. Ltd. 1442 - 170 2013 £175

Kinsella, Thomas *Phoenix Park.* Dublin: Irish University Review, 1967. Offprint from Irish University Review, 8vo., original stapled wrappers, inedd. Maggs Bros. Ltd. 1442 - 160 2013 £150

Kinsella, Thomas *The Tain.* 1969. First Dolmen issue, with Le Brocquy illustrations, fine in original box and dust jacket. C. P. Hyland 261 - 537 2013 £750

Kinsella, W. P. *Shoeless Joe.* Boston: Houghton Mifflin, 1982. Uncorrected proof copy, inscribed by author in year of publication, recipient's signature, slight edge sunning and short crease at mid spine, near fine in wrappers. Ken Lopez Bookseller 159 - 97 2013 $1000

Kinsey, W. M. *Portugal Illustrated.* Valpy, 1828. First edition, large 8vo., folding frontispiece, double page map, 16 plates, 10 plates of music (some foxing mainly in margin), 9 colored plates, 19th century half green morocco, spine gilt with raised bands, handsome binding. J. & S. L. Bonham Antiquarian Booksellers Europe - 9513 2013 £650

Kip, Leonard *Hannibal's Man and Other Tales.* Albany: Argus Co., 1878. First edition, 12mo., original decorated bevel edged green cloth, front and rear panels stamped in black, spine panel stamped in gold and black, brown coated endpapers. L. W. Currey, Inc. Christmas Themed Books - 136488 2013 $450

Kipling, Rudyard 1865-1936 *All the Mowgli Stories.* Macmillan, 1933. 4to., original pictorial pale blue cloth, 8 color plates, line drawings. R. F. G. Hollett & Son Children's Books - 325 2013 £45

Kipling, Rudyard 1865-1936 *An Almanac of Twelve Sports by William Nicholson: words by Rudyard Kipling.* London: William Heinemann, 1898. Folio in brown paper boards with hunting illustration to front cover, boards chipped along edges and slightly soiled, linen spine darkened and has tears along front hinge, interior pages very good, usual offsetting of illustrations to text pages and with age toning, illustrations themselves not affected, small book seller sticker, unpaginated.   The Kelmscott Bookshop   7 - 76   2013 $1100

Kipling, Rudyard 1865-1936 *Barrack-Room Ballads and Other Verses.* London: Methuen & Co., 1892. First English edition, one of 30 numbered copies (of which 20 were for sale), printed on Japanese vellum, vellum spine and cloth very slightly soiled, otherwise fine, rare and beautiful issue, in half morocco slipcase.   James S. Jaffe Rare Books   Fall 2013 - 82   2013 $4500

Kipling, Rudyard 1865-1936 *The Jungle Book. (with) The Second Jungle Book.* Macmillan, 1894-1895. First edition and first English edition, foolscap 8vo., occasional faint foxing, illustrations, many full page, frontispiece tissue guard present, original mid blue cloth, lettering and pictorial design on backstrip and further pictorial design on front cover, all gilt blocked, dark blue-green endpapers, rear hinge cracked, gilt edges, very good; foolscap 8vo., illustrations, some leaves lightly foxed, original mid blue cloth, lettering and pictorial design on backstrip and further pictorial design on front cover, all gilt blocked, bookplate of A. E. B. Fair, small paper repair to rear free endpaper, dark blue green endpapers, gilt edges, good, author's signature on slips pasted to reverse of half title of Jungle Book and reverse of titlepage to Second Jungle Book, with Bateman's headed notepaper with typed note "With Mr. Rudyard Kipling's Compliments" tipped to front flyleaf of Second Jungle Book.   Blackwell's Rare Books   172 - 205   2013   £3000

Kipling, Rudyard 1865-1936 *The Jungle Book. (and) The Second Jungle Book.* New York: Century Co., 1903-1909. Later editions, octavo, 2 volumes, numerous illustrations, beautifully bound by Asprey in contemporary full green morocco, elaborately gilt decorated spine and covers, raised bands, brown, gray, burgundy and black morocco animal onlays on each of the four covers, marbled endpapers, all edges gilt, gilt dentelles, previous owner's bookplates on front pastedown of each volume, fine set, custom quarter morocco slipcase, with morocco edges. Heritage Book Shop   Holiday Catalogue 2012 - 93   2013 $3000

Kipling, Rudyard 1865-1936 *Just So Stories for Little Children.* Macmillan, 1902. First edition, large 8vo., original pictorial plum cloth gilt, spine rather rubbed at head and tail, small nick to lower hinge, 249 pages, illustrations by author, endpapers little spotted and lightly browned, otherwise nice, clean copy.   R. F. G. Hollett & Son   Children's Books - 327   2013   £350

Kipling, Rudyard 1865-1936 *Just so Stories for Little Children.* London: Macmillan and Co., 1902. First edition, 4to, red cloth stamped in white and black, one of the earliest copies with covers printed in chalky white ink that had a tendency to fleck off, slight bit of cover fading, else fine, white still bright, in custom clamshell box, illustrations in black and white by author.   Aleph-Bet Books, Inc.   105 - 350   2013 $4000

Kipling, Rudyard 1865-1936 *Just So Stories for Little Children.* London: Folio Society, 1991. First edition, large 8vo., original pictorial cloth gilt, slipcase, illustrations by author.   R. F. G. Hollett & Son   Children's Books - 326   2013   £25

Kipling, Rudyard 1865-1936 *Just So Stories.* Mendocino: Attic Press, 1992. Limited to 75 copies, 3 volumes, 5.3 x 7.3 cm., quarter leather with gilt stamped title set on spine, marbled paper covered boards, paper label on front board, slipcase, from the collection of Donn W. Sanford.   Oak Knoll Books   303 - 43   2013 $225

Kipling, Rudyard 1865-1936 *Land and Sea Tales for Scouts and Guides.* Macmillan, 1923. First edition, large 8vo., original pictorial cloth, dust jacket rather soiled and chipped, backstrip rather browned, bottom section lacking, flyleaves partly browned as usual.   R. F. G. Hollett & Son   Children's Books - 328   2013   £75

Kipling, Rudyard 1865-1936 *Plain Tales from the Hills.* Calcutta: Thacker, Spink & Co., 1888. First edition, half title, 24 page catalog (Dec. 1887), sewing slightly loose, original olive green pictorial cloth, unevenly faded, slight lifting of cloth on back board, hinges slightly cracking, stamp of Thacker & Co. Bombay, along with booklabels of Oliver Corse Hoyt & Christopher Clark Geest, small catalog entry laid down on following pastedown, half red morocco Solander case.   Jarndyce Antiquarian Booksellers   CCV - 157   2013   £420

Kipling, Rudyard 1865-1936 *Poems 1886-1929.* London: Macmillan and Co., 1929. First edition, one of 525 numbered sets, signed by author, this #425, quarto, 3 volumes, engraved portrait, frontispiece with tissue guard, publisher's full red rushed levant morocco, spines lettered gilt, top edge gilt, others uncut, gilt dentelles, bit of light foxing to fore edge and frontispiece, beautiful, about fine copy.   Heritage Book Shop   Holiday Catalogue 2012 - 94   2013 $2000

Kipling, Rudyard 1865-1936 *Poems 1886-1929.* London: Macmillan and Co., 1929. First edition, limited to 525 copies signed by author, octavo, 3 volumes, frontispiece volume 1, original deluxe binding of full crimson polished morocco, original printed dust jackets over glassine wrappers, original box, very fine set, custom made quarter morocco solander case.   David Brass Rare Books, Inc.   Holiday 2012 Chapter Five - DB 01827   2013 $4250

Kipling, Rudyard 1865-1936 *The Works.* New York: Doubleday Page and Co., 1925-1926. Mandalay Edition, 26 volumes bound in 14, 213 x 146mm., recent dark blue highly polished morocco, covers with vaguely Art Deco gilt frame, raised bands decorated with stylized silver Greek key rolls, azure morocco labels, marbled endpapers, top edge gilt, one leaf with two inch tear into text with no loss, isolated mild foxing or other trivial imperfections but in very fine condition, text clean and fresh throughout, bindings as new. Phillip J. Pirages   63 - 298   2013 $2500

Kirby, W. F. *Natural History of the Animal Kingdom...* SPCK, 1889. Folio, original pictorial boards, rather worn and neatly rebacked, 30 fine double page hand colored lithograph plates.   R. F. G. Hollett & Son   Children's Books - 329   2013   £350

Kirchmann, Johann *De Annulis Liber Singularis.* Leiden: Apud Hackios, 1672. 12mo., engraved fore-title, illustrations, early vellum (trifle soiled), light dampstain on upper part of number pages, very good bookplate of Thomas Stewart Traill, M.D.   Joseph J. Felcone Inc.   Books Printed before 1701 - 74   2013 $400

Kirk, Betty *Covering the Mexican Front. The Battle of Europe vs. America.* Norman: University of Oklahoma Press, 1942. First edition, 26 photos, line drawing, red cloth just bit dulled but fine, lightly worn dust jacket, few tape repairs.   Argonaut Book Shop   Summer 2013 - 182   2013 $75

Kirk, E. N. *Sermon, Preached before the American Missionary Association at Its Nineteenth Annual Meeting in Plymouth Church, Brooklyn, New York, October 25, 1865.* New York: American Missionary Association, 1865. First edition, buff printed wrappers, 14 pages, bookplate on inside front wrapper, faint vertical crease and little age toning, else near fine.   Between the Covers Rare Books, Inc.   165 - 199   2013 $125

Kirkland, Caroline Matilda Stansbury 1801-1864 *The Book of Home Beauty.* New York: Putnam, 1852. First edition, 4to., 145 pages, blue cloth stamped in gilt, all edges gilt, ex-library with bookplate and stamps, cover somewhat soiled and scuffed, some wear at edges and ends of spines, little foxing and browning, few leaves loose, rear hinge tender, very good.   Second Life Books Inc.   183 - 228   2013 $100

Kirkland, Caroline Matilda Stansbury 1801-1864 *Our New Home in the West; or Glimpses of Life Among the Early Settlers by Mrs. Mary Calvers.* New York: James Miller, 1874. 8vo., pages 298, very good, tight copy. Second Life Books Inc.   182 - 146   2013 $60

Kirwin, William *Reminiscences of James P. Howley: Selected Years.* Toronto: Champlain Society, 1997. Limited to 925 copies, this unnumbered, red cloth with glt to spine, half title, index, frontispiece and 5 black and white illustrations plus 4 folding maps, 8vo., fine.   Schooner Books Ltd.   105 - 36   2013 $75

Kisch, Bruno *Forgotten Leaders in Modern Medicine.* Philadelphia: June, 1954. Large 4to., original brown printed wrappers, light wear, else very good, numerous illustrations, ex-libris from Sir Geoffrey Jefferson with his bookplate and signature.   James Tait Goodrich   S74 - 165 2013 $145

Kitchener, Henry Thomas *Letters on Marriage on the Causes of Matrimonial Infidelity and on the Reciprocal Relations of the Sexes...* London: C. Chapple, 1812. First edition, 8vo., plain boards, volume 1 with new spine and front cover, volume 2 with new spine, new printed spine labels, little toned, untrimmed, very good or better, scarce. Second Life Books Inc.   182 - 273   2013 $750

Kitchiner, William 1775-1827 *The Art of Invigorating and Prolonging Life, by Food, Clothes, Air, Exercise, Wine, Sleep...* London: printed for Geo. B. Whittaker, 1828. Sixth edition, 168 x 105mm., pleasing contemporary half calf over marbled boards, recently rebacked to style, raised bands, brown morocco label, page 101 with small stamp of "Birmingham Reference Library", two other leaves with library stamps removed (and neatly repaired on verso), paper boards bit chafed and wear at edges, leather corners worn through, two leaves with inch wide black ink blots to text (without loss of legibility), two other leaves with marginal ink stains, additional trivial imperfections but in most ways really excellent copy, internally very clean, fresh and smooth and in solidly restored and generally well preserved binding. Phillip J. Pirages   63 - 299   2013 $300

Kitchiner, William 1775-1827 *The Economy of the Eyes.* London: Hurst, Robinson & Co., 1824. First edition, folding frontispiece, engraved plate, good copy, full contemporary tree calf, double gilt bands to spine, red morocco labels, upper board detached, 19th century booklabel of Mary Addington, scarce.   Ken Spelman Books Ltd.   75 - 86   2013   £125

Klauer-Klattovsky, Wilhelm *A Comprehensive Grammar of the German Language on a New Plan.* Wurtz: Treuttel Jun. and Richter, circa, 1840. 2 folding tables, signed by author to prevent piracy, somewhat browned, dissected and mounted on linen, each folded to 185 x 115mm., marbled paper on front and rear, housed in matching marbled paper slipcase, latter rubbed and worn, each table labelled in contemporary hand, good, rare set.   Blackwell's Rare Books   B174 - 83   2013   £250

Klein, Melanie *Contributions to Psycho-Analysis 1921-1945.* London: Hogarth, 1948. First edition, faint staining to fore edge, thus very good in attractive, price clipped, about very good dust jacket with tanned spine and stain at bottom of spine. Between the Covers Rare Books, Inc. Psychology & Psychiatry - 95824 2013 $50

Klein, Melanie *New Directions in Psycho-analysis: the Significance of Infant Conflict in the Pattern of Adult Behaviour.* New York: Basic Books, 1955. First American edition, fine with publisher's prospectus laid in, very good dust jacket with piece missing at top of rear panel, plus general wear. Between the Covers Rare Books, Inc. Psychology & Psychiatry - 101562 2013 $125

Kleinmichel, Julius *Sugar and Spice and All That's Nice.* London: Strahan & Co., 1882. Square 8vo., original cloth backed glazed pictorial boards, little worn and soiled, 34 pages, illustrations in color, joints cracked. R. F. G. Hollett & Son Children's Books - 314 2013 £45

Klemm, Friederich *A History of Western Technology.* London: Ruskin House, George Allen and Unwin, 1959. English translation of original 154 German edition, 8vo., 59 figures, green cloth, silver stamped spine title, dust jacket, light jacket edgewear, Burndy bookplate, scarce, very good. Jeff Weber Rare Books 169 - 251 2013 $75

Klickman, Flora *The Girl's Own Annual. Volume 49.* Girl's Own Annual n.d., 1928. 4to., original decorated cloth gilt, pictorial onlay, over bevelled boards, colored title and plates, illustrations, endpapers by Maude Angell, very good, clean, sound. R. F. G. Hollett & Son Children's Books - 331 2013 £65

Kline, Otis A. *Call of the Savage.* New York: Clode, 1937. First edition, small spot on fore edge, else fine in very good plus dust jacket, very slightly sunned at spine with several short tears, very scarce in jacket. Between the Covers Rare Books, Inc. Sci-Fi, Fantasy & Horror - 10382 2013 $332

Klingsberg, Harry *Doowinkle, D. A.* New York: Dial, 1940. First edition, pages darkened, otherwise fine in dust jacket with tiny wear at spine ends. Mordida Books 81 - 284 2013 $135

Kluckhohn, Cyde *Beyond the Rainbow.* Boston: Christopher Pub. House, 1933. First edition, 271 pages, octavo, black cloth with title gilt stamped on front board, map endsheets, very good, lettering on backstrip gently faded, name and date small in ink at head of front free endsheet, black and white photos, uncommon. Ken Sanders Rare Books 45 - 37 2013 $1500

Knapp, Moses L. *Address Delivered to the Graduating Class of the Indiana Medical College.* Chicago: 1847. First edition, 8vo., 22, (1) pages, removed. M & S Rare Books, Inc. 95 - 60 2013 $500

Kneeland, Samuel *The Wonders of Yosemite Valley and of California.* Boston: Alexander Moore, 1872. Third edition, 10 mounted albumen photos by Soule, with tissue guards and 3 wood engraved text illustrations, 2 engraved maps, text and photos ruled in red, original publisher's green pebble grain cloth over bevelled boards with front cover and spine decoratively stamped and lettered in gilt and black and rear cover decoratively stamped in blind, all edges gilt, previous owner's small bookplate, over older bookplate that has been partially removed, minimal rubbing to extremities, previous owner's pencil drawings on front and back endpapers dated 1884, pencil lines throughout paper in small area, very clean and bright. Heritage Book Shop Holiday Catalogue 2012 - 95 2013 $1500

Knight, C. *Mind Amongst the Spindles: a Selection from the Lowell Offering...* London: Knight, 1845. First edition, 12mo., rebound in marbled paper with leather spine, some writing inked out at top of title, otherwise nice. Second Life Books Inc. 182 - 148 2013 $300

Knight, Charles *Half Hours of English History from the Roman Period to the Death of Elizabeth.* London: Frederick Warne and Co., 1868. 222 x 146mm., 4 p.l., 687 pages, lavishly gilt contemporary black half calf by Bain (stamp signed on verso front free endpaper), raised bands, decorated with gilt roll, spines in six compartments, two of these with titling labels of red or black, the other four quite intricately gilt with large central filigree ornament framed by scrolling leafy cornerpieces, marbled boards, edges and endpapers, trivial wear to corners and top of spine, nearly fine in attractive binding, leather unusually lustrous and text very clean and fresh. Phillip J. Pirages 63 - 300 2013 $175

Knight, Charles *Half Hours with the Best Authors.* London: Frederick Warne and Co., 1868. 2 volumes, 222 x 143mm., lavishly gilt contemporary black half calf by Bain (stamp signed), raised bands, decorated with gilt roll, spines in six compartments, two of these with titling labels of red or black, other four quite intricately gilt with large central filigree ornament framed by scrolling leafy cornerpieces, marbled board, edges and endpapers, with four plates, each with four engraved portraits, for a total of 16 portraits, boards slightly chafed, hint of wear (only) to joints and extremities, leaves faintly yellow at edges (no doubt as in all copies), excellent set, clean and fresh internally and with solid bindings. Phillip J. Pirages 63 - 301 2013 $300

Knight, Ellis Cornelia 1757-1837 *A Description of Latium; or La Campagna Di Roma.* London: Longman Hurst, 1805. First edition, quarto, 20 tinted sepia etchings, map (lightly foxed), dust jacket brown speckled calf, joints split, covers rubbed, corners worn. J. & S. L. Bonham Antiquarian Booksellers Europe - 9598 2013 £600

Knight, Ellis Cornelia 1757-1837 *Dinarbas: a Tale Being a Continuation of "Rasselas, Prince of Abissinia".* London: printed for Luke Hansard for T. Caldwell, Jun. and W. Davies, 1800. Fourth edition, 178 x 108mm., very attractive contemporary flamed calf, flat spine gilt in panels formed by double rules and decorative rolls and featuring an oval centerpiece encircling a four pointed star with roundel center, crimson morocco label, bookplate of Franz Pollack Parnau, extremities and joints bit flaked, occasional very minor foxing and offsetting, but excellent copy, attractive original binding completely sound with boards lustrous, especially clean, smooth and fresh internally.   Phillip J. Pirages   63 - 272   2013 $175

Knight, Laura   *Oil Paint and Grease Paint. Autobiography of...*   London: Ivor Nicholson & Watso, 1936. Second printing, 8vo., black and white reproductions of artist's work, autographed by Knight to Dorothy M. White, red cloth with paper spine label, ex-library with bookplate and stamps, front hinge tender, edges stained, some foxing, cover scuffed and rubbed, otherwise very good.   Second Life Books Inc.   182 - 149   2013 $85

Knight, Oliver   *Fort Worth Outpost on the Trinity.* Norman: University of Oklahoma Press, 1953. First edition, 18 photo views, portraits, sketch maps, light brown cloth, owner's name and tiny rubber stamp on end, but very fine with slightly chipped pictorial dust jacket.   Argonaut Book Shop   Summer 2013 - 184   2013 $50

Knowles, James S.   *The Dramatic Works.*   1841. 3 volumes, original gilt decorated cloth, very good.   C. P. Hyland   261 - 539   2013   £100

Knowles, Laura   *The Swallow's Tour.*   No publisher, no date, circa, 1870. 4to., original blue cloth gilt, corners rather worn, little marked, neatly recased, unpaginated, all edges gilt, title and monochrome etched plates and decorations in 13 page spreads, little fingering in places, child's address dated 1898, rare.   R. F. G. Hollett & Son Children's Books - 332   2013   £150

Knowlton, Charles   *Fruits of Philosophy...*   London: Freethought Pub. Co. 28 Stonecutter Street, circa, 1877. Original printed wrappers, bit worn, spine chipped, very good plus 8 page 'Catalog of Works sold by the Freethought Publishing Co. 28 Stonecutter Street, E.C." circa 1877.   M & S Rare Books, Inc.   95 - 191   2013 $250

Knox, Rawle   *The Work of E. H. Shepard.*   London: Methuen, 1979. First edition, large 8vo., original cloth, gilt, dust jacket, over 300 illustrations, fine.   R. F. G. Hollett & Son   Children's Books - 333   2013   £50

Knox, Robert   *Ecclesiastical Index, with Rectories...* London: Hodges & Smith, 1839. xii, 180 pages, original cloth, rebacked, some passages pencilled, else very good. C. P. Hyland   261 - 540   2013   £105

Knox, Vicesimus 1752-1821 *Elegant Extracts; or Useful and Entertaining Pieces of Poetry.* (with) *Elegant Extracts; or Useful and Entertaining Passages in Prose.* (with) *Elegant Epistles.*   London: printed for Charles Dilly, 1790. 1789? 1790. Respectively. Second edition of first work, new edition of second work, first work 4 parts in 2 volumes, 2 engraved titlepages, each with vignette, little foxing here and there; second work with engraved titlepage; third work half title discarded; royal 8vo., contemporary tree calf, gilt roll tooled Greek key borders on sides, spines gilt in compartments, red lettering piece and small circular black numbering pieces (on Poetry), slightly worn, head and tail caps of Prose particularly, ownership inscription of Thomas Hewett to blank endpapers, good.   Blackwell's Rare Books   B174 - 84   2013   £1200

Koch, Kenneth   *Ko or a Season on Earth.*   New York: Grove Press, 1959. First edition, limited issue, one of only 4 copies hors commerce and signed by Koch in blank ink on colophon page, present copy, however is numbered '6', suggesting that this issue may have consisted of a few more copies than was originally intended, 8vo., original cloth backed tan paper boards, very fine, rare.   James S. Jaffe Rare Books   Fall 2013 - 84   2013 $1250

Koch, Kenneth   *Poems/Prints.*   New York: Editions of the Tibor de Nagy Gallery, 1953. First edition, 4to., original illustrated card wrappers, stapled, 4 original linoleum cuts by Nell Blaine, one of 300 numbered copies (entire edition), not issued signed by poet or artist, but this copy signed and dated by Blaine on three large mounted prints in bottom margin, very fine, rare in such beautiful condition, with none of the offsetting and staining that so often marks this book. James S. Jaffe Rare Books   Fall 2013 - 83   2013 $4500

Koch, Theodore Wesley   *More Tales for Bibliophiles.* Chicago: Black Cat Press, 1966. First edition, printed in limited number, 5.8 x 4.3cm., full leather, slipcase, 3 volumes, from the collection of Donn W. Sanford.   Oak Knoll Books   303 - 56   2013 $250

Kochno, Boris   *Le Ballet.*   Paris: Arts du Monde/Hachette, 1954. First edition, one of 1000 copies, 12.75 x 9.25 inches, 383 pages, text in French, 415 plates, most printed in heliogravure and about 20 hand mounted photo engravings, frontispiece of book tipped-in original 4-color lithograph by Picasso, signed by artist in plate, red cloth with drawing after Henri Matisse on front cover and publisher's acetate dust jacket, new condition, thus very rare.   Gemini Fine Books & Arts., Ltd.   Art Reference & Illustrated Books - 2013 $1400

Kock, Charles Paul De 1794-1871 *The Works.* London: Boston and Paris: The Frederick J. Quinby Co., 1902-1904. One of 500 copies, the St. Gervaiss Edition, this #180, 229 x 159mm., 25 volumes, extremely pretty contemporary rose colored three quarter morocco, raised bands, spines with large Art Nouveau style Iris in gilt and onlaid mauve morocco, marbled sides and endpapers, top edge gilt, other edges rough trimmed, dozens of plates, some colored, two small marginal tears, exceptionally fine set, clean, fresh text printed on high quality paper within large margins and very lustrous bindings in as close to original condition as one could hope for. Phillip J. Pirages 63 - 302 2013 $3500

Kock, Victor De *Our Three Centuries.* Cape Town: Central Committee for the Van Riebeeck Festival, 1952. 4to., original cloth, gilt, dust jacket very defective, 264 pages, illustrations, partly in color. R. F. G. Hollett & Son Africana - 114 2013 £25

Koebel, W. H. *Portugal: Its Land and People.* London: Archibald Constable, 1909. First edition, 8vo., numerous illustrations, original red decorative cloth, spine slightly faded, Abel Chapman's copy with his signature and bookplate. J. & S. L. Bonham Antiquarian Booksellers Europe - 7971 2013 £80

Koelen, D. *Eduard Chillida: Catalogue Raisonne of the Original Prints.* Munich: Chorus, 1997-1999. First editions, volume 1 is one of 100 deluxe copies with laid-in loose original etching by Chillida, signed and numbered (47/100), large 4to., 3 volumes, 360, 400, 360 pages, with 183, 215, 156 plates in original colors, cloth, dust jackets, new condition, in deluxe cloth-over-boards slipcase. Gemini Fine Books & Arts., Ltd. Art Reference & Illustrated Books - 2013 $3000

Koelliker, Albert Von 1817-1905 *Die Normale Resorption des Knocengewebes ihre Bedeutung fur die Entstehung der Typischen Knochenformen.* Leipzig: F. C. W. Vogel, 1873. 4to., 8 color plates, mustard cloth, black stamped spine title, original printed wrappers bound in at rear, very good. Jeff Weber Rare Books 172 - 171 2013 $600

Koenig, George *Beyond this Place There be Dragons.* Glendale: Arthur H. Clark Co., 1984. First edition, one of 968 copies, 263 pages, photos, drawings, 3 folding maps, red cloth, gilt, very fine in printed dust jacket. Argonaut Book Shop Recent Acquisitions June 2013 - 177 2013 $90

Koenig, George *Death Valley Tailings. Rarely Told Tales of Old Death Valley.* Morongo Valley: Sagebrush Press for the Death Valley '49ers Inc, 1986. First edition, one of 275 copies bound in cloth and issued with dust jackets, there were another 2000 copies in paperback, 125 pages, photos, tan cloth, gilt, very fine, pictorial dust jacket. Argonaut Book Shop Recent Acquisitions June 2013 - 178 2013 $125

Kok, Henri A. R. *The Diary of Anne Frank (1929-1945), a Biography.* Zuilichem: Catharijne Press, 1995. Limited to 190 copies, this one of 15 lettered copies bound thus, 6.5 x 4.2cm., full red leather with 14 ct. gold Star of David mounted on front cover, clamshell box with leather spine and marbled paper covered boards, mounted miniature of Frank as frontispiece, from the collection of Donn W. Sanford. Oak Knoll Books 303 - 84 2013 $275

Kokoschka, Oscar *Oskar Kokoschka: Florentiner Skizzenbuch.* Luzern: Edition Bucher, 1972. First edition, of the total edition of 475 copies, this one of 75 deluxe examples (XVIII/LSSV), with 24 bound in full page color lithographs after Kokoschka's drawings + 2 laid-in loose original lithographs (one in colors) by Kokoschka, numbered and signed by artist in pencil, printed on mould made paper, tan linen, fit in publisher's matching slipcase overall size 48 x 36cm., new condition. Gemini Fine Books & Arts., Ltd. Art Reference & Illustrated Books - 2013 $2600

Kolb, E. L. *Through the Grand Canyon from Wyoming to Mexico.* New York: Macmillan, 1914. First edition, presentation inscription signed by author's brother, Emery Kolb and dated 1916, xx, 344 pages, plus publisher's catalog at end, color frontispiece and 7 plates, 103 photos by author and his brother, decorated dark blue cloth stamped in orange and gilt, color illustration pastedown to front cover, slight rubbing to corners of cover pastedown, but very fine. Argonaut Book Shop Recent Acquisitions June 2013 - 179 2013 $175

Konigsburg, E. L. *View from Saturday.* New York: Atheneum, 1996. Stated first edition, 8vo., as new in new dust jacket (no award seal, not price clipped), inscribed by author, scarce. Aleph-Bet Books, Inc. 104 - 307 2013 $200

Konstam, Gertrude A. *Dreams, Dances and Disappointments.* Thos. de la Rue, n.d. circa, 1890. First edition, large square 8vo., original stiff pictorial wrappers, 12 full page colored plates and other full page and text illustrations. R. F. G. Hollett & Son Children's Books - 334 2013 £40

Konstam, Gertrude A. *The Maypole.* Thos. de la Rue, nd. circa, 1890. First edition, large square 8vo., original stiff pictorial wrappers, pages 26, 8 full page color plates, other full page and text illustrations. R. F. G. Hollett & Son Children's Books - 335 2013 £30

Koontz, Dean R. *The Bad Place.* New York: G. P. Putnam's Sons, 1990. First edition, one of 250 numbered copies, fine in fine slipcase, signed by author, this copy number 248. Between the Covers Rare Books, Inc. Sci-Fi, Fantasy & Horror - 306910 2013 $200

Koontz, Dean R. *Chase.* New York: Random House, 1972. First edition, fine in fine dust jacket, exceptional copy. Between the Covers Rare Books, Inc. Sci-Fi, Fantasy & Horror - 27704 2013 $315

Koontz, Dean R. *Dragonfly.* New York: Random House, 1975. First edition, negligible spine slant still very near fine in fine dust jacket with tiny tear on rear panel. Between the Covers Rare Books, Inc. Sci-Fi, Fantasy & Horror - 10673 2013 $192

Koontz, Dean R. *Hanging On.* London: Barrie & Jenkins, 1974. First English edition, fine in dust jacket with nicks at top of spine and at corners, small chip at bottom edge of back panel. Mordida Books 81 - 285 2013 $250

Koontz, Dean R. *Hideaway.* New York: G. P. Putnam's Sons, 1992. First edition, one of 800 numbered copies, signed by author, fine in fine dust jacket and fine slipcase. Between the Covers Rare Books, Inc. Sci-Fi, Fantasy & Horror - 306549 2013 $150

Koontz, Dean R. *The House of Thunder.* Arlington Heights: Dark Harvest, 1988. First edition thus, one of 550 numbered copies, signed by author and artist, illustrations by Phil Parks, fine in fine dust jacket and fine slipcase. Between the Covers Rare Books, Inc. Sci-Fi, Fantasy & Horror - 306563 2013 $125

Koontz, Dean R. *Lightning.* New York: G. P. Putnam, 1988. Limited to 200 signed copies, this no. 124, 8vo., 351 pages, near fine, half leather and marbled boards, gilt lettered spine. By the Book, L. C. 36 - 51 2013 $450

Koontz, Dean R. *Mr. Murder.* New York: G. P. Putnam's Sons, 1993. First edition, one of 600 numbered copies signed by author, fine in fine dust jacket in fine slipcase. Between the Covers Rare Books, Inc. Sci-Fi, Fantasy & Horror - 306551 2013 $160

Koontz, Dean R. *The Voice of the Night.* Garden City: Doubleday, 1980. First edition, near fine in like dust jacket, excellent copy. Leather Stalking Books October 2013 - 2013 $300

Koran *The Koran, Commonly called the Alcoran of Mohammed.* printed for C. Ackers, 1734. First sale edition, title printed in red and black, 5 engraved plates, including map of Arabia, variable moderate browning, 4to., contemporary panelled calf, blind tooling around central mottled panel, spine gilt in compartments, red lettering piece, gilt Suffield crest in 5th panel, rebacked preserving original spine, but raised bands of lighter new calf, engraved armorial bookplate of Edward Lord Suffield inside front cover, good, well above average copy. Blackwell's Rare Books 172 - 83 2013 £2500

Koran *The Morality of the East; Extracted from the Koran of Mohammed...* Printed for W. Nicoll, 1766. First edition, possibly lacking final blank, small 8vo., contemporary sheep, worn at extremities, spine defective at head, lettering piece missing, good, very scarce. Blackwell's Rare Books B174 - 85 2013 £2000

Kornbluth, Cyril M. *The Mindworm.* London: Michael Joseph, 1955. First edition, octavo, boards. L. W. Currey, Inc. Utopian Literature: Recent Acquisitions (April 2013) - 140168 2013 $100

Kornilov, Boris *Kat Ot Meda U Medvedi a Zuby Nachali Bolet. (The Honey Bear with a Toothache).* Moscow: State Pub., 1935. Large 4to., pictorial wrappers, several edge repairs, very good, chromolithographs on every page. Aleph-Bet Books, Inc. 105 - 517 2013 $500

Kosinski, Jerzy *The Future is Ours, Comrade.* Garden City: Doubleday, 1960. First edition, fine but for owner's name and address (2 lines), lightly used dust jacket with tiny chips. Beasley Books 2013 - 2013 $100

Kossak-Szczucka, Zopfja *The Troubles of a Gnome.* A. & C. Black, 1928. First English edition, 4to., original cloth backed patterned boards, pictorial label, edges little rubbed, 8 fine color plates and 8 line drawings, edges slightly spotted. R. F. G. Hollett & Son Children's Books - 204 2013 £85

Kozisek, Josef *The Magic Flutes.* New York: London & Toronto: Longmans, Green and co., 1929. Oblong large 4to., cloth backed pictorial boards, fine and bright in original slipcase with color plate on cover (box with some chips and slight soil but very good), colorful border on each page of text, in text color illustrations, superb copy. Aleph-Bet Books, Inc. 104 - 336 2013 $600

Krafft, Michael *The American Distiller or the Theory and Practice of Distilling According to the Latest Discoveries and Improvements....* Philadelphia: Thomas Dobson, 1804. First edition, octavo in fours, 22 unnumbered pages between pages 151 and 152 with chapter title "The Manner of Making Malt as described by Sir Robert Murray", 3 figures on 2 folding engraved plates, contemporary tree sheep, rebacked to style, red morocco spine label lettered gilt, spine stamped in gilt, boards with some light wear, corners bit bumped, bit of chipping to spine, pages bit foxed and toned, particularly pages 29-43, first folding chart has minor closed split along margin, not affecting engraving, small hole to first page of ads, marginal paper flaw to page 53, not affecting text, some minor soiling and staining to leaves, final blank and back free endpaper contain old ink notes and recipes for Holland Gin, St. Croix Rum and Jamaica Rum, dated 1834, overall very good, scarce. Heritage Book Shop Holiday Catalogue 2012 - 96 2013 $2750

Krause, Dorothy Simpson *Rivers of Grass: an Homage to Marjory Stoneman Douglas.* Boca Raton: Minerva: the Press at Wimberly, 2012. One of 36 copies on Yu Kou heavy for the images and text and interleaved with Yu Kou light paper, hand numbered and signed by artist on colophon page "D Krause", page size 9 7/8 x 6 7/8 inches, 10 pages, bound loose as issued housed in envelope, 7 x 10 inches, made of terracotta Lokta oil paper fastened with tie (combination of terra cotta and light orange string and tan leather cord) on lozenge shaped seed-pod from mahogany tree serves as the fastener, printed letterpress with small amount of ink, with the words "River of Grass" and "Dorothy Simpson Krause" on lower left of front corner, beautiful book.   Priscilla Juvelis - Rare Books   56 - 15   2013 $875

Krause, Fedor *Die Allgemeine Chirurgie der Gehirnkrankheiten.* Stuttgart: Ferdinand Enke, 1914. First edition, 2 volumes, 255 illustrations partly colored, very good set in original cloth.   James Tait Goodrich   S74 - 167   2013 $495

Krauss, Ruth *Charlotte and the White Horse.* Bodley Head, 1977. First UK edition, small 8vo., original pictorial boards, illustrations in color by Maurice Sendak.   R. F. G. Hollett & Son Children's Books - 542   2013   £60

Krauss, Ruth *A Hole is to Dig.* New York: Harper Bros., 1952. First edition, later printing with 'grrr' present, small 8vo., blue cloth backed pictorial boards, fine in dust jacket frayed at top of spine price intact, illustrations on every page by Sendak, especially nice, inscribed by Kraus.   Aleph-Bet Books, Inc.   104 - 515   2013 $350

Krauss, Ruth *A Hole is to Dig.* Hamish Hamilton, 1963. First UK edition, small square 8vo., original cloth backed pictorial boards, dust jacket little spotted, some repairs to reverse, lettered in brown and illustrated in black and white by Maurice Sendak, booklabel pasted to pictorial flyleaf crinkling the paper.   R. F. G. Hollett & Son   Children's Books - 543   2013   £40

Kren, Claudia *Alchemy in Europe: a Guide to Research.* New York and London: Garland Pub., 1990. 8vo., red cloth, black stamped cover and spine titles, fine.   Jeff Weber Rare Books   169 - 255   2013 $60

Kreymborg, Alfred *Funnybone Alley.* New York: Macauley Co., 1927. First edition, 4to. 7 tipped in color plates by Boris Artzybasheff, with minor creases, signed by author, blue gilt binding, good+.   Barnaby Rudge Booksellers   Children 2013 - 020592   2013 $125

Krimsky, Sheldon *Genetic Alchemy. the Social History of the Recombinant DNA Controversy.* Cambridge: MIT, 1982. First edition, near fine, 8vo., mild soil to covers, very good++ dust jacket with minimal sun spine, cover edge wear.   By the Book, L. C.   37 - 49   2013 $100

Kroeber, A. L. *Handbook of the Indians of California.* Washington: GPO, 1925. First edition, 17 tables, 83 plates and maps, 78 text figures, original gilt lettered olive cloth, spine bit dulled with light rubbing to ends and corners, fine.   Argonaut Book Shop   Recent Acquisitions June 2013 - 180   2013 $250

Kroeber, A. L. *Handbook of the Indians of California.* Berkeley: California Book Co., 1953. Reprint of 1925 first edition, 83 plates and maps, 78 text illustrations, 2 large folding maps in pocket, vertical crease to spine, few spots to ends, very good.   Argonaut Book Shop   Recent Acquisitions June 2013 - 181   2013 $125

Kroeber, A. L. *Handbook of the Indians of California.* Berkeley: California Book Co., 1953. Reprint of 1925 first edition, 83 plates and maps, 78 text illustrations, 2 large folding maps in rear pocket, just hint of fading to extreme top portion of front cover, fine, fresh copy.   Argonaut Book Shop   Summer 2013 - 186   2013 $150

Kroeber, A. L. *Karok Myths.* Berkeley: University of California Press, 1980. First edition, yellow cloth, portraits, maps, very fine, decorated dust jacket.   Argonaut Book Shop   Recent Acquisitions June 2013 - 183   2013 $75

Kroeber, A. L. *Yurok Myths.* Berkeley: University of California Press, 1976. First edition, xl, 488 pages, portraits, maps, yellow cloth, very fine with decorated dust jacket.   Argonaut Book Shop   Recent Acquisitions June 2013 - 182   2013 $125

Kroeber, Theodora *Almost Ancestors.* San Francisco: Sierra Club, 1968. First edition, 4to., 168 pages, photos, very fine with pictorial dust jacket.   Argonaut Book Shop Recent Acquisitions June 2013 - 185   2013 $125

Kroeber, Theodora *The Inland Whale.* Covelo: Yolla Bolly Press, 1987. First edition thus, one of 115 copies on Rives BFK Cream each signed by artist, Karin Wilkstrom and numbered, page size 12 x 14 inches, 94 pages + colophon and sources, bound by Schuberth Bookbindery, tan Belgian linen over flexible boards, laced at spine with linen cord, black and white engraving on front panel, housed in publisher's slipcase of brown roma Fabriano paper, fine, the artist, Karin Wikstrom has hand colored wood engravings, hors texte as well as chapter headings and tailpieces, prints were hand colored in gouache paints applied from her own stencils, lovely book.   Priscilla Juvelis - Rare Books   55 - 27   2013 $600

Kruska, Dennis *Sierra Nevada Big Trees. History of the Exhibitions 1850-1903.* Los Angeles: Dawson's Book Shop, 1985. First edition, one of 500 copies, 63 pages, color frontispiece, drawings, engravings and broadsides, rust cloth, gilt lettered spine, very fine.   Argonaut Book Shop Recent Acquisitions June 2013 - 186   2013 $60

Kruska, Dennis *Twenty-Five Letters from Norman Clyde 1923-1964.* Los Angeles: Dawsons Book Shop, 1998. First edition, one of 500 copies, frontispiece, illustrations, red cloth lettered in black, fine.   Argonaut Book Shop Recent Acquisitions June 2013 - 187   2013 $60

Kucherlapati, Raju *Genetic Recombination.* Washington: American Society for Microbiology, 1988. First edition, mild soil to cover, edges, small 4to., near fine.   By the Book, L. C.   37 - 50   2013 $95

Kuczynski, Jurgen *Labour Conditions in Western Europe 1820 to 1935.* London: Lawrence and Wishart, 1937. First edition, 8vo., black cloth, author's presentation on flyleaf, very good, tight copy in worn dust jacket.   Second Life Books Inc.   183 - 2 30   2013 $75

Kuhn, Carlus Gottlob *Medicorvm Graecorvm Opera Qvae Exstant.* Lipsiae: 1821-1833. 20 volumes, 19th century buckram, ex-library with stamp on title, bindings worn in parts, couple of volumes have front joint split, overall clean, tight set.   James Tait Goodrich   75 - 127   2013 $4500

Kumm, H. Karl W. *From Hausaland to Egypt, through the Sudan.* London: Constable, 1910. First edition, large 8vo., original pictorial cloth, gilt over bevelled boards, extremities trifle rubbed, 6 color plates, over 70 illustrations, portrait, folding map, upper joint cracked, otherwise very nice.   R. F. G. Hollett & Son   Africana - 115   2013   £180

Kunhardt, Dorothy *Tiny Nonsense Stories.* New York: Simon & Schuster, 1949. Wonderful set of 12 miniature books, 2 x 3 1/16 inch, each bound in thick pictorial boards, housed in color pictorial slipcase that simulates room of a house, case has removable sliding cover, box shows slight wear, else books and box in very good condition, lithographs by Garth Williams.   Aleph-Bet Books, Inc.   104 - 588   2013 $350

Kussmaul, Adolf *Die Storungen der Spraceh.* Leipzig: Verlag von G. C. W. Yogel, 1877. x, 299 pages, early patterned boards, with new black linen spine, endpapers renewed, nice tight copy.   James Tait Goodrich   S74 - 168   2013 $750

Kuttner, Henry *Fury.* New York: Grosset & Dunlap, 1950. First edition, octavo, boards.   L. W. Currey, Inc. Fall Sampler Sept. 2013 - 145677   2013 $75

Kuznetzov, V. *Vazar.* Ogiz: 1938. 8vo., pictorial wrappers, slight edge wear, else fine, beautiful chromolithographs by Korodova.   Aleph-Bet Books, Inc.   105 - 515   2013 $350

Kyne, Peter B. *They Also Serve.* New York: Cosmopolitan Book Corp., 1927. First edition, illustrations by C. Leroy Baldridge, decorations by Paul Brown, fine in near fine dust jacket with several modest tears.   Between the Covers Rare Books, Inc.   Horses, Horsemanship, Horse Racing, Etc. - 97657   2013 $125

L

L'Empereur Constant *The Tale of the Emperor Coustans and of Over Sea.* Kelmscott Press, 1894. One of 545 copies (20 of which were on vellum), 142 x 106mm., 2 p.l., 130 pages, elegant crimson crushed morocco, handsomely gilt by Doves Bindery (stamp-signed and dated 1901 on rear turn-in), covers tooled gilt with French fillet frame punctuated with dots and with rose leaf cornerpieces, raised bands, spine beautifully gilt in compartments with Tudor rose centerpiece and rose leaves at corners, gold tooled turn-ins featuring multiple fillets and leaf clusters at corners, all edges gilt with typical simple stippling, with white-vine borders of twining grape clusters and leaves on each of the two full page woodcuts as well as on first page of text of both stories, three line foliated woodcut initials, shoulder notes (in red) on every page, breath of rubbing to extremities, one very faint marginal smudge, outstanding copy, simply sparkling inside and out. Phillip J. Pirages 61 - 102 2013 $4500

L'Engle, Madeleine *Dare to Be Creative!* Washington: Library of Congress, 1984. 30 pages, stapled wrappers, fine. Ken Lopez Bookseller 159 - 119 2013 $75

L'Engle, Madeleine *Separation from the Stars The Fifth Archibald Yell Smith IV Lecture and The Rewards of Failure...* Chattanooga: The Baylor School, 1986. First edition, stapled printed wrappers, 24 pages, slight paperclip indentation and touch of age toning, both on front wrapper, else fine, very scarce. Between the Covers Rare Books, Inc. Sci-Fi, Fantasy & Horror - 96847 2013 $200

L'Engle, Madeleine *Small Rain.* New York: Vanguard, 1945. First edition, 8vo., cloth, 371 pages, very good+ in dust jacket (very worn along front fold, slightly chipped at base of spine with triangular piece off top of spine), signed by author. Aleph-Bet Books, Inc. 105 - 366 2013 $800

L'Estrange, A. G. *Conna and Desmond.* Bristol: 1902. 8vo., illustrations, viii, 178 pages, autograph pasted in, very good. C. P. Hyland 261 - 552 2013 £100

La Calprenede, Gaultier De Cost, Seigneur De *Hymen's Praeludia; or Love's Master-Piece.* printed for Ralph Smith, 1698. Title with double rules, occasional paper flaw, rust or other small holes with loss of odd letter, minor ink, wax of other stains, few leaves foxed, slightly browned in places, final ad leaf discarded, folio in 4's, near contemporary mottled calf rebacked, corners worn, inscription on flyleaf recording purchase of it on 3 Oct. 1699 for 18/6, few emendations to text in same early hand, 19th century bookplate of Marquess of Headfort, good. Blackwell's Rare Books B174 - 86 2013 £2000

La Fontaine, Jean De 1621-1695 *Contes et Nouvelles en Vers. Tome Premier (-Second).* Londres: (Paris Cazin), 1780. 2 volumes, engraved frontispiece, 24 engraved plates, little foxing and few plates slightly browned, 12mo., contemporary mottled calf, gilt ruled borders on sides, gilt in compartments, citron lettering piece, gilt edges, little worn, head caps defective, 1951 inscription, good. Blackwell's Rare Books B174 - 87 2013 £1200

La Fontaine, Jean De 1621-1695 *Contes et Nouvelles en Vers.* Paris: De l'Imprimerie de P. Didot l'Aine, 1795. First printing of the Fragonard edition, 2 volumes, very fine honey brown crushed morocco, handsomely gilt by Noulhac (stamp-signed and dated 1902 on front turn-ins), covers with French fillet border and sawtooth edging with very elegant large floral ornaments in corners, raised bands, spines very attractively gilt in compartments formed by triple rules and featuring poppy centerpiece framed by leafy sprays wide and lovely turn-ins with gilt flowers linked by sprays and ribbons, marbled endpapers, all edges gilt, 3 full page portraits, one smaller portrait, one vignette, 20 very fine plates 'Before Letters" from the original edition, (16 of them after Fragonard), in addition 57 etchings "Before Letters) published in 1880 by Rouquette Based on Fragonard's 57 planned illustrations for the 1795 edition, along with 16 original sepia wash drawings done in 1869, slightest hint of foxing internally (perhaps half dozen leaves more foxed, but worst being just about negligible), perhaps 10 leaves expertly repaired short marginal tears (typically less than an inch and never anywhere near text), very special copy in beautiful condition, finely executed lovely bindings lustrous and virtually without wear, margins nothing short of vast, text and plates and inserted material all extraordinarily fresh and clean. Phillip J. Pirages 61 - 115 2013 $17,500

La Fontaine, Jean De   1621-1695   *Fables.*   Boston: published by Elizur Wright Jr. and Tappan and Dennet, 1841. First American printing, 235 x 149mm., 2 volumes, 240 charming illustrations by J. J. Granville, facing texts in French and English, pleasing contemporary red morocco, covers with multiple gilt rule border and leafy blindstamped frame, inner frame of dotted gilt rule with scrolling cornerpieces, gilt decorated with raised bands, gilt titling, all edges gilt, front hinge of each volume tightened, remnants of removed bookplate on front pastedown, joints bit worn with just hint of cracking, corners little bumped, light soiling to covers, back board of volume II with two small abrasions, mild to moderate (but never offensive) foxing throughout because of paper stock used, very slight smudging here and there, very good, without any serious problems, text still fresh and pleasing, contemporary bindings sturdy and lustrous.   Phillip J. Pirages   63 - 304   2013 $600

La Fontaine, Jean De   1621-1695   *Fables De La Fontaine.*   Paris: Garnier, 1868. 4to., 2 volumes in 1, leather spine with gilt decoration in compartments, red cloth, all edges gilt, slight foxing on first pages, else near fine, profusion of exquisitely detailed engravings by J. J. Grandville. Aleph-Bet Books, Inc.   104 - 249   2013 $600

La Fontaine, Jean De   1621-1695   *Fables of La Fontaine.* London: Society for Promoting Christian Knowledge, n.d. circa, 1880. 4to., cloth backed pictorial boards, light edgewear and few minor mends at tabs, else very good+, 6 moveable plates in full color, very scarce, excellent condition.   Aleph-Bet Books, Inc.   104 - 364   2013 $875

La Fontaine, Jean De   1621-1695   *Fables De La Fontaine presentees par Jean de la Varende.* Paris: Marcus, 1949. Large 4to., cloth backed pictorial boards fine in dust jacket, illustrations by Felix Lorioux in gold, full color on every page. Aleph-Bet Books, Inc.   104 - 329   2013 $500

La Fontaine, Jean De   1621-1695   *Fables.*   Boston: Alphabet Press, 1981. Folio, cloth, fine in dust jacket and slipcase, magnificent color illustrations by Marie Angel, with separate pamphlet that translates fables into English. Aleph-Bet Books, Inc.   105 - 41   2013 $85

La Morliere, Charles Jacques Louis Auguste Rochette   *Angola Histoire Indiene.*   A Agra (i.e. Paris): Avec Privilege du Grand Mogol, 1748. 2 volumes in 1, 12mo., contemporary leather backed marbled boards, spine title partly effaced, each volume with copper engraved titlepage with vignette, engraved by P. F. Tardieu de la Montagne, nearly fine.   Howard S. Mott Inc.   262 - 89   2013 $350

La Motte Fouque, Friedrich Heinrich Karl, Freiherr De 1777-1843   *Undine.*   London: New York: William Heinemann/Doubleday,, Page & Co., 1909. First UK trade edition, tall octavo, 15 full page color mounted illustrations, 30 black and white text illustrations by Arthur Rackham, publisher's blue cloth, original light brown dust jacket, with Heinemann post card, in mint condition, laid in, light foxing and offsets to endpapers, near fine in very scarce, near fine dust jacket.   David Brass Rare Books, Inc.   Holiday 2012 Chapter One - DB 01886   2013 $780

La Motte Fouque, Friedrich Heinrich Karl, Freiherr De 1777-1843   *Undine.*   London: New York: William Heinemann/Doubleday Page & Co., 1909. Edition deluxe, limited to 100 large paper copies, signed by artist, quarto, 15 color plates, original full vellum, original ribbon ties, bookplate, minimal dusting to boards, otherwise fine and bright. David Brass Rare Books, Inc.   Holiday 2012 Chapter One - DB 01983   2013 $2500

La Motte Fouque, Friedrich Heinrich Karl, Freiherr De 1777-1843   *Undine.*   London & New York: Heinemann & Doubleday, 1909. First American edition, 14 beautiful tipped in color plates mounted on heavy paper, pictorial endpapers, lovely line illustrations in text, cloth backed pictorial boards, edges slightly rubbed, else near fine in slightly worn dust jacket.   Aleph-Bet Books, Inc.   104 - 478   2013 $600

La Motte, Guillaume Mauquet de   *Traite Complet des Accouchemens Naturels, Non Naturels et Contre Nature.* Paris: Chez Laurent d'Houry, 1721. Tall 4to., contemporary full mottled calf, gilt paneled spine, pages cracked, corners and edges rubbed, contemporary signature on title date 1753.   James Tait Goodrich   75 - 131   2013 $995

La Perouse, M. De   *A Voyage Round the World Performed in the Years 1785, 1786, 1787, 1788...* Boston: Joseph Bumstead, 1801. First American edition, scarce, 8vo., contemporary calf, spine gilt, extremities slightly rubbed, slightly browned as usual, some dampstaining to titlepage, very good.   Maggs Bros. Ltd.   1467 - 82   2013   £2250

La Place, Pierre Simon   *Elementary Illustrations of the Celestial Mechanics of LaPlace.*   London: John Murray, 1832. First edition, 8vo., very good++ in modern quarter leather and marbled boards, new endpapers, printed paper spine label, mild scuffs to covers, minimal cover edge wear. By the Book, L. C.   38 - 54   2013 $500

La Place, Pierre Simon   *Mecanique Celeste.*   Boston: 1829-1839. First edition, large and thick quarto, 4 volumes, library buckram, entirely untrimmed, unusual thus, ex-library with small library stamps and ink markings, but very nice. M & S Rare Books, Inc.   95 - 34   2013 $3500

La Place, Pierre Simon *Oeuvres de Laplace.* Paris: Imprimerie Royale, 1843-1847. First collected edition, 7 volumes bound in 4, 4to., contemporary calf, two lettering pieces on each spine, covers ruled in gilt, marbled endpapers, bright yellow edges, joints repaired, rear joint of first and second volume starting, extremities rubbed, good. Blackwell's Rare Books   Sciences - 67   2013   £1800

La Rochefoucauld, Francois, Duc De   1613-1680 *Maxims and Moral Reflections by....*   London: printed for Lockyer Davis, printer to the Royal Society, 1775. First of five printings, 12mo., full contemporary calf, gilt spine, red morocco label, boards with some old scratches, worn at head and tail, hinges cracked.   Jarndyce Antiquarian Booksellers   CCIV - 180   2013   £85

La Rochefoucauld, Francois, Duc De   1613-1680 *Maxims and Moral Reflections...* 1781. 12mo., late 19th or early 20th century ink annotations to text, contemporary quarter calf, marbled boards, vellum tips, gilt ruled spine, black morocco label, boards rubbed, ownership name of A. R. Winnington-Ingram, name erased from front endpaper. Jarndyce Antiquarian Booksellers   CCIV - 181   2013   £85

La Rochefoucauld, Francois, Duc De   1613-1680 *Moral Reflections, Sentences and Maxims.* New York: William Gowans, 1851. First edition, octavo, steel engraved frontispiece, device in gilt on front cover, owner's name in neat ink on front pastedown, very good in brown publisher's cloth with some light staining and fading, corners bumped, text pages clean and tight.   Between the Covers Rare Books, Inc.   Philosophy - 134819   2013 $70

La Valliere, Louise Francoise De La Baume Le Blanc, Duchess De   *Lettres De Madame La Duchesse De La Valliere, Morte Religieuse Carmelite...*   Paris: Antoine Boudet, 1767. 12mo., brown speckled boards, leather label, bookplate and signature of Horace White, Paris 1875. Second Life Books Inc.   182 - 151   2013 $225

Laban, Samuel   *Cherokee Outlet Cowboy. Recollections of Laban Samuel Records.*   Norman: University of Oklahoma Press, 1995. First edition, scarce in this condition, vintage photo portraits and views, maps, charts, reproductions, beige cloth, very fine, pictorial dust jacket.   Argonaut Book Shop   Summer 2013 - 289   2013 $60

Labarraque, Antoine Germain   *De l'Emploi de Chlorures d'Oxide de Sodium et de Chaux.*   Paris: Madame Huzard, 1825. First edition, 8vo., 48 pages, tears at page 47 repaired with only minor loss of text, some staining and spotting on various leaves, modern marbled wrappers, housed in cloth clam shell box, red gilt stamped leather label on spine of box, bookplate of Haskell Norman, inscribed by author for Pierre Adolph Piorry, very good, scarce.   Jeff Weber Rare Books   172 - 177   2013 $1450

Labillardiere, Jacques Julien Houton De   *Relation du Voyage a la Recherche de La Perouse, Fait par Ordre de l'Assemblee Constituante, Pendant les annes 1791, 1792...*   Paris: Chez H. J. Jansen, An VIII de la Republique Francoise, 1799-1800. First edition, quarto issue, 2 volumes, quarto, atlas with engraved title, double page route map, 43 plates engraved by Copia after drawings by Piron, and botanical plates by Redoute, contemporary French mottled calf by Courteval, covers with borders of rope and disc design enclosed between gilt rules, smooth spines divided into sections using wide gilt bands stripped vertically, sections with large gilt designs, black morocco gilt lettering labels, gilt board edges turn-ins decorated gilt in gilt greek-key pattern, marbled endpapers, edges speckled yellow, atlas corners and caps expertly strengthened, old and scattered oxidation stains to pages 148-149 in volume II (text), plate 10 with old, opaque stain to lower corner (into plate margin but not affecting image), four other plates with browning to spots to lower blank margin, truly exceptional set, beautifully bound, very tall and very clean.   Heritage Book Shop   Holiday Catalogue 2012 - 97   2013 $15,000

Labillardiere, Jacques Julien Houton De   *Voyage in Search of La Perouse Performed by Order of the Constituent Assembly During the Years 1791, 172, 1793 and 1794.*   London: Stockdale, 1800. 8vo., 2 volumes, 45 engraved plates with large folding map, contemporary tree calf, superb copy from Berkeley Castle, having had only very minor restoration to headcap of first volume.   Maggs Bros. Ltd.   1467 - 83   2013   £2750

Lachendes Leben: Fibel Fur Berliner Kinder.   Berlin: Oehmigke mit Union Dt. Verlagsges, 1936. First edition, 4to., clothbacked pictorial boards, 112 pages, faint corner stain on first few leaves, else very good+, color illustrations. Aleph-Bet Books, Inc.   105 - 417   2013 $975

Lacroix, Paul   *Ma Republique.*   Paris: Librairie L. Conquet, 1902. One of 40 special copies with two extra states of the plates and inscribed by publisher to Monsieur L. Rattier, limited edition of 100 copies on Japan vellum (out of a total edition of 400 copies), 7 etchings, each in three states (for a total of 21 plates) by Edmond Adolphe Rudaux; very fine crimson morocco gilt and inlaid by Chambolle-Duru (stamp signed), covers with broad border comprised of seven gilt fillets, raised bands, spine compartments outlined with five concentric gilt rules, doublures of brown crushed morocco featuring stylized flowers of inlaid olive brown morocco, elegant arching gilt stems, cloth endleaves, marbled flyleaves, all edges gilt, original printed wrappers bound in, virtually mint.   Phillip J. Pirages   61 - 114   2013 $3250

Ladd-Franklin, Christine   *Colour and Colour Theories.*   New York: Harcourt, 1929. First edition, few private library stamps and homemade pocket, some erased pencilling in introduction (only), otherwise very good+, color plates. Beasley Books   2013 - 2013 $100

Lafargue, Paul *The Sale of an Appetite.* Chicago: Charles H. Kerr & Co., 1904. First edition in English, 3 inserted plates, original grey cloth, front cover stamped in black, pictorial paper onlay affixed to front cover, all edges untrimmed.   L. W. Currey, Inc.   Utopian Literature: Recent Acquisitions (April 2013) - 137399   2013 $100

Lafferty, Raphael Aloysius *Nine Hundred Grandmother.* London: Dennis Dobson, 1975. First British and first hardcover edition, octavo, boards.   L. W. Currey, Inc.   Utopian Literature: Recent Acquisitions (April 2013) - 140090   2013 $350

Laforgue, Jules *L'Imitation de Notre Dame La Lune.* Paris: Les Cent Une, 1974. First Jansem edition, number LXXIX (79) of 122 exemplars on velin d'Arches (total edition 122), signed by Jansem, Club's President and VP on justification page, 4 original hors texte etchings by Jean Jansem in multiple tones of black and grey, about 110 pages, loose leaves in publisher's wrappers, boards chemise and slipcase, this exemplar with 2 extra suites of 4 loose original hors texte etchings, each of the 8 etchings signed and numbered in pencil by Jansem, overall size 30 x 24cm., new condition.   Gemini Fine Books & Arts., Ltd.   Art Reference & Illustrated Books - 2013 $1400

Lait, Jack *All the Funny Folks.* New York: The World Today, 1926. Large 4to., cloth, pictorial paste-on, 112 pages, 2 tiny margin mends, else near fine, illustrations in full bold color on every page, rare in this condition.   Aleph-Bet Books, Inc.   104 - 118   2013 $500

Laking, Guy Francis *The Furniture of Windsor Castle.* London: Bradbury Agnew & Co., 1905. First edition, 47 black and white plates, 4to. quarter tan calf over linen boards with embossed red and gilt monogram of Edward VII, silk bookmark sewn in, very good boards rubbed with some darkening, mostly to rear cover, offsetting on tissue guards, plates quite fine and bright, binding tight.   Kaaterskill Books   16 - 51   2013 $500

Laking, Guy Francis *Sevres Porcelain of Buckingham Palace and Windsor Castle.* London: Bradbury, Agnew & Co., 1907. First edition, 4to., 63 color plates, quarter tan calf over cream muslin boards, gilt title, silk bookmark sewn in, very good, spine rubbed, light soiling on boards, text and plates sharp, binding tight.   Kaaterskill Books   16 - 52   2013 $750

Lalley, Des *Captivating Brightness, Ballynahinch.* Ballynahinch: Ballynahinch Castle Hotel, 2008. Limited to 250 numbered copies in hardback, signed by artist below tipped in plate, of which 150 only are for sale, large 8vo., original grey cloth, lettered in silver, color frontispiece by Cecil Maguire.   Maggs Bros. Ltd.   1442 - 124   2013   £175

Lamartine, Alphonse *Memoirs of Celebrated Characters.* London: Richard Bentley, 1858. Third edition, 187 x 12mm., most appealing 19th century light tan highly polished half calf, raised bands decorated with gilt floral roll, spines richly gilt in double ruled compartments with volute cornerpieces and central pomegranate surrounded by small tools, marbled sides and endpapers, bookplate of John Francis Harris in each volume, small handful of leaves lightly toned, corners just little rubbed, quite pretty set in nearly fine condition, text clean and fresh, attractive decorative binding scarce worn and especially lustrous.   Phillip J. Pirages   63 - 305   2013 $450

Lamb, Caroline *Glenarvon.* London: Henry Colburn, 1816. First edition, 3 volumes, bound without half titles, contemporary half calf, spines gilt in compartments with crest at tails, dark green leather labels, bookplate of Corinna Cochrane volume I.   Jarndyce Antiquarian Booksellers   CCIII - 402   2013   £1200

Lamb, Charles 1775-1834 *The Life, Letters and Writings.* London: Gibbings & Co., 1897. Temple edition, 6 volumes, 179 x 114mm., pictorial titlepage, 17 portraits, pleasant enough contemporary burgundy half morocco over marbled boards, raised bands, spine panels with gilt acorn ornament, marbled endpapers, top edge gilt, other edges rough trimmed, 2 volumes unopened, armorial bookplate of William R. Cabrera, hint of rubbing to joints and extremities, 3 leaves with two inch tears into text (no loss), other small marginal tears here and there from rough opening, additional trivial imperfections, perfectly satisfactory copy, text fresh and clean (though not printed on bright stock) and entirely sound, bindings without any serious wear.   Phillip J. Pirages   63 - 306   2013 $95

Lamb, Charles 1775-1834 *A Masque of Days.* London: Cassell & Co., 1901. First edition, 4to., original cloth backed pictorial boards, edges rubbed and corners little rounded, plates 40, illustrations, nice bright copy.   R. F. G. Hollett & Son   Children's Books - 147   2013   £150

Lamb, Charles 1775-1834 *Mrs. Leicester's School.* London: J. M. Dent, 1899. First edition, square 8vo., color plates, very good, rebacked with original spine laid down, grey decorated cloth.   Barnaby Rudge Booksellers   Children 2013 - 017490   2013 $75

Lamb, Charles 1775-1834 *Poetry for Children.* London: The Leadenhall Press, 1892. One of 112 copies, signed by press founder, Andrew White Tuer (this copy #2), 157 x 99mm., 2 volumes, charming contemporary batik textured calf by Zaehnsdorf (stamp-signed in gilt on front turn-in), covers gilt with fillets and dogtooth roll border, upper cover with thick festooned garland of fruit and leaves, flat spines divided into panels by plain and decorative rules, densely gilt turn-ins, marbled endpapers, top edge gilt, each volume with engraved frontispiece, engraved bookplate of A. Edward Newton of Oak Knoll with (loose) bookplate of H. Marion Soliday, minor offsetting from frontispieces, just vaguest hint of rubbing to extremities, but very fine, bindings bright and scarcely worn, text with virtually no signs of use. Phillip J. Pirages   63 - 67   2013 $1500

Lamb, Charles 1775-1834 *Tales from Shakespeare.* London: printed for Thomas Hodgkins at the Juvenile Library, 1807, actually, 1806. First edition, first impression, with imprint of printer T. Davison verso of page 235 volume I and Hanway Street address at top of first page of ads in volume II, 2 volumes, full blue crushed levant morocco by Wood, gilt decorated corners, elaborately gilt spine, raised bands, dentelles with gilt decorated corners, top edge gilt, others untrimmed, etchings, bookplate in each volume "E. R. Mc. C", morocco backed slipcase.   Howard S. Mott Inc. 262 - 88   2013 $3000

Lamb, Charles 1775-1834 *Tales from Shakespeare.* New York: Trulove Hanson & Comb, n.d., 1899. First edition, thick 8vo., 372 pages, red gilt pictorial cloth, top edge gilt, very good+, 10 full page woodcuts by Robert Anning Bell.   Aleph-Bet Books, Inc.   104 - 40   2013 $225

Lamb, Charles 1775-1834 *Tales from Shakespeare.* London: Ernest Nister, circa, 1905. Original pictorial blue cloth gilt over bevelled boards, extremities little worn, all edges gilt, 6 color plates and 70 half tone illustrations by W. Paget, neat inscription on flyleaf, scattered foxing, very good, sound copy.   R. F. G. Hollett & Son   Children's Books - 337   2013   £45

Lamb, Charles 1775-1834 *(The Works).* London: Macmillan and Co., 1891-1898. 178 x 121mm., 7 volumes, fine honey brown crushed morocco handsomely gilt by Doves Bindery (stamp signed with bindery name and '18 C-S 98" on rear turn-in of each volume), raised bands, spines in extremely attractive gilt compartments featuring dense gouge work in the shape of stemmed hearts, along with open circles and circlets, turn-ins ruled in gilt with cornerpieces incorporating heart and tulip tools, all edges gilt, (stippled gauffering), frontispiece in volume V, joints of first volume little worn at juncture of raised bands, extremely slight wear to joints and extremities of other volumes, spines uniformly sunned to very pleasing lighter brown (minor irregular fading to small areas on covers), still most attractive set, beautifully designed bindings solid and with no significant wear, pristine internally.   Phillip J. Pirages   61 - 103   2013 $8500

Lamb, Frank *Indian Baskets of North America.* Riverside: Rubidoux Pub. Co, 1972. First edition, signed by author, quarto, (6), 155 pages, color frontispiece plate, photos, maps, endpaper maps, cloth, very fine, pictorial dust jacket. Argonaut Book Shop   Recent Acquisitions June 2013 - 188   2013 $75

Lamb, J. Parker *Perfecting the American Steam Locomotive.* Bloomington & Indianapolis: Indiana University Press, 2003. First edition, tall 8vo., xi, 197 pages, photos and illustrations, tables, quarter tan cloth with brown paper boards, brown stamped spine title, dust jacket, fine, Burndy bookplate.   Jeff Weber Rare Books   169 - 258   2013 $65

Lamb, Martha, J. *History of the City of New York: Its Origin, Rise and Progress.* New York: and Chicago: A. S. Barnes and Co., 1877. First edition, 2 volumes, small quarto, publisher's half morocco and marbled paper covered boards, bookplate fine ach volume, bit of rubbing at extremities, slight nicks at corners, handsome, else near fine. Between the Covers Rare Books, Inc.   New York City - 299526   2013 $400

Lamb, Patrick *Royal Cookery; or the Compleat Court-Cook.* London: printed for J. Nutt and A. Roper, 1716. Second edition, 8vo. 40 engraved plates, some occasional browning, leading edge of three plates, little dusted and creased, endpapers and pastedowns dusted and browned, full contemporary panelled calf, raised bands, red morocco label, head of spine chipped and darkened.   Jarndyce Antiquarian Booksellers   CCIV - 182   2013   £1800

Lamb, Ursula *Cosmographers and Pilots of the Spanish Maritime Empire.* Aldershot and Brookfield: Variorum, 1995. 8vo., illustrations, gilt stamped blue cloth, fine, Burndy bookplate.   Jeff Weber Rare Books   169 - 259   2013 $120

Lambe, John Lawrence *To Theodore Watts-Dunton: Sonnets 1912-1914.* Tiptree: privately printed for Anchor Press, 1915. First edition, about very good, some minor wear to edges of boards, moderate foxing and with some rough openings to some of the pages with author and critic Clement K. Shorter's attractive bookplate, signed by author, uncommon thus.   Jeff Hirsch Books   Fall 2013 - 129356   2013 $60

Lambert, A. J. *The Chapel on the Hill.* Bristol: St. Stephen's Press, circa, 1930. Limited to 200 copies, original pictorial boards, illustrations.   R. F. G. Hollett & Son   Wesleyan Methodism - 15   2013   £25

Lambert, Edward *The Art of Confectionary.* London: printed for T. Taylor by the Meuse-gate in Castle-Street, 1750? 8vo., tear without loss to top inner corner of C3, and to head of F1 just affecting page numbers, final two leaves, slightly browned, rear blank dusted and marked, disbound. Jarndyce Antiquarian Booksellers   CCIV - 183   2013   £500

Lamont, J. D. *Historiette of Methodism in Cork Wesley Chapel Centenary 1805-1905.* 1905. First edition, 1905 pages 64 pages, 8vo., photos, very good, owner inscribed by a member of the Centenary Committee.   C. P. Hyland   261 - 541   2013   £45

Lamothe-Langdon, Etienne Leon Baron De *Private Memoirs of the Court of Louis XVIII.* London: Henry Colburn and Richard Bentley, 1830. First edition in English, 2 volumes, 225 x 143mm., very pleasing 19th century green half morocco over marbled boards and endpapers, raised bands, spine panels with flower cluster centerpiece, top edge gilt, spines faded evenly to a shade darker than leather on covers, really excellent, bindings showing virtually no wear, fine internally with only trivial defects.   Phillip J. Pirages   63 - 324   2013 $350

Lancaster, Albert Edmund *"All's Dross but Love" a Strange Record of Two Reincarnated Souls...* New York: John W. Lowell Co., 1889. First edition, flyleaves at front and rear, original brown cloth, front panel stamped in black.   L. W. Currey, Inc.   Christmas Themed Books - 117541   2013 $150

Lancaster, Clay *Prospect Park Handbook.* New York: Walton H. Rawls, 1967. First edition, fine in fine original glassine dust jacket, signed by Lancaster and by Marianne Moore, provided foreword, beautiful copy.   Between the Covers Rare Books, Inc.   New York City - 99835   2013 $150

Lancisi, Giovanni Maria *Dissertatio de Nativis Deque Adventitiis Romani coeli Qualitatibus...* Rome: Francisco Gonzaga, 1711. First edition, 4to., engraved allegorical titlepage vignette, engraved historiated initials, headpieces, tailpieces, errata foxed, contemporary full vellum, ms.. spine title, small chip in fore edge of top cover, paper label at foot of spine, titlepage with perforated library ownership mark, very good.   Jeff Weber Rare Books   172 - 178   2013 $1600

Lander, Eric *Calculating the Secrets of Life.* Washington: National Academy Press, 1995. First edition, 8vo., as new hardback, signed 3 times by Eric S. Lander as editor and on both of his contributions.   By the Book, L. C.   37 - 51   2013 $175

Landor, Walter Savage 1775-1864 *Poems from the Arabic and Persian.* Warwick: printed by H. Sharpe and sold by Mesrrs. Rivigntons, London, 1800. First edition, 4to., half title, old horizontal fold, sewn as issued, very nice, rare.   Jarndyce Antiquarian Booksellers   CCV - 158   2013   £780

Landseer, Thomas *Twenty Engravings of Lions, Tigers, Panthers & Leopards.* London: I. & H. L. Hunt and J. Landseer, 1823. First edition, landscape 4to., frontispiece, engraved title, plates, edges of frontispiece slightly spotted with damp mark to upper margin of first 4 plates, contemporary half black calf, gilt spine, little rubbed, 35 pages.   Jarndyce Antiquarian Booksellers   CCV - 159   2013   £385

Lane, Charles *Lane's Telescopic View of the Interior of the Exhibition.* London: published by C. Lane, June 3rd, 1851. 8 hand colored lithographic panels and back science panel, front panel with hand colored title vignette, with peep-hole, without the mica lens which is usually missing, measuring 175 x 160mm., extending with paper bellows to c. 900mm., front panel bit soiled.   Marlborough Rare Books Ltd.   218 - 65   2013   £1250

Lane, Horace *Five Years in State's Prison...* New York: printed for author by Luther Pratt & son, 1835. Fifth edition, 8vo., 24 pages, sewn as issued, stitching coming loose, title quite foxed, some foxing in text, else very good, fore and bottom margins untrimmed.   M & S Rare Books, Inc.   95 - 294   2013 $500

Lane, Margaret *A Calabash of Diamonds.* London: Heinemann, 1961. First edition, original cloth, few marks, dust jacket, frontispiece, 12 plates and maps on endpapers.   R. F. G. Hollett & Son   Africana - 116   2013   £30

Lane, Withrop *Uncle Same Jailer.* Chicago: Industrial Workers of the World, n.d., First edition, first printing, wrappers, very good with wrinkling, 12mo., 40 pages.   Beasley Books   2013 - 2013 $50

Lanes, Selma G. *The Art of Maurice Sendak.* New York: Harry Abrams, 1980. First edition, oblong large 4to., original pictorial boards, printed glassine dust jacket, 261 illustrations, 94 color plates, 3 folding plates, mint in publisher's original mailing box.   R. F. G. Hollett & Son   Children's Books - 338   2013   £150

Lanfranco, of Milan *Wundartznel Des Hocherfarnen unnd Weitberumpten H. D. Lanfranci Verteuscht.* Frankfort: 1566. Small 8vo., well margined, rebound in 19th century three quarter burgundy and marbled boards, light foxing and browning of text and one page repaired in blank margin.   James Tait Goodrich   75 - 130   2013 $6500

Lang, Jeanie *Stories from the Iliad...* London: T. C. & E. J. Jack, n.d., 1907? First edition, small 8vo., original limp blue cloth, edges trifle frayed, 8 color plates by W. Heath Robinson, very scarce.   R. F. G. Hollett & Son   Children's Books - 519   2013   £50

Lang, Andrew *The All Sorts of Stories Book.* London: Longmans, Green and Co., 1911. First edition, original purple cloth gilt, spine rather faded, 5 color plates by H. J. Ford, few spots to endpapers.   R. F. G. Hollett & Son   Children's Books - 343   2013   £65

Lang, Andrew *The Animal Story Book.* Longman, Green and Co., 1914. New impression, original blue cloth gilt, spine little dulled, illustrations by H. J. Ford.   R. F. G. Hollett & Son   Children's Books - 344   2013   £25

Lang, Andrew *The Blue Fairy Book.* London: Longmans, Green and Co., 1889. First edition, 8vo., original gilt decorated blue cloth, frontispiece, 8 plates, many in text illustrations, all edges gilt, fine.   Howard S. Mott Inc.   262 - 90   2013 $5000

Lang, Andrew *The Book of Romance.* London: Longmans, Green and Co., 1902. First edition, original blue pictorial cloth gilt, extremities worn, spine rather creased and chipped at head, numerous illustrations, slight adhesion damage to first plate and its tissue, rear joint cracked.   R. F. G. Hollett & Son   Children's Books - 339   2013   £65

Lang, Andrew *Book of Romance.* London: Longmans, Green, 1902. First edition, first printing, 8vo., blue gilt pictorial cloth, all edges gilt, fine and bright, 8 color plates, 35 beautiful black and white plates, smaller black and whites in text, pictorial endpapers, great copy.   Aleph-Bet Books, Inc.   104 - 308   2013 $425

Lang, Andrew *The Book of Romance.* London: Longmans, Green and Co., 1903. New impression, original decorated blue cloth, gilt extra, trifle worn, lower board rather marked, all edges gilt, 8 color and 35 black and white plates, 8 text illustrations by H. J. Ford.   R. F. G. Hollett & Son   Children's Books - 345   2013   £120

Lang, Andrew *The Book of Saints and Heroes.* London: Longmans Green, 1912. 8vo., blue pictorial cloth, top edge gilt, toning on endpaper from dust jacket, else fine in dust jacket, illustrations by H. J. Ford, great copy, rare in jacket.   Aleph-Bet Books, Inc.   104 - 309   2013 $300

Lang, Andrew *The Brown Fairy Book.* London: Longmans, Green and Co., 1904. First edition, original brown pictorial cloth, gilt, fore-edges of boards rather damped, all edges gilt, 8 color plates and numerous other illustrations by H. J. Ford, upper joint cracking, otherwise nice, clean copy.   R. F. G. Hollett & Son   Children's Books - 346   2013   £180

Lang, Andrew *The Crimson Fairy Book.* London: Longmans, Green and Co., 1903. First edition, original crimson pictorial cloth gilt, spine rather faded, trifling wear to extremities, all edges gilt, 8 color plates, numerous illustrations by H. J. Ford, tissue go frontispiece little creased and browned, faintly offset on to title, but very good with series prospectus loosely inserted.   R. F. G. Hollett & Son   Children's Books - 347   2013   £250

Lang, Andrew *The Gold of Faimilee.* Bristol London: Arrowsmith & Simpkin, Marshall, n.d. circa, 1880. Number 41 of an unstated limitation (150?), large paper copy, 4to., half parchment paper, brown gilt cloth, top edge gilt, general cover soil and offsetting on blank endpaper, else tight and internally fine, 15 beautiful chromolithographs by E. A. Lemann, frontispiece by T. Scott, printed on handmade paper.   Aleph-Bet Books, Inc.   104 - 310   2013 $600

Lang, Andrew *The Gold of Faimilee.* Bristol & London: Arrowsmith, & Simpkin, Marshall, n.d. circa, 1880. First edition, 4to., green cloth, slight cover soil, else very good+, 15 chromolithographs, printed on handmade paper.   Aleph-Bet Books, Inc.   105 - 352   2013 $400

Lang, Andrew *The Green Fairy Book.* London: Longmans, Green, 1892. First edition, first printing, 8vo., green gilt pictorial cloth, all edges gilt, rear hinge bit rubbed but not weak, scattered foxing, bright and very good+, illustrations by H. J. Ford, with 101 beautiful black and whites.   Aleph-Bet Books, Inc.   104 - 311   2013 $800

Lang, Andrew *The Green Fairy Book.* London: Longmans, Green and Co., 1920. Fourteenth impression, original blindstamped pictorial green cloth, gilt, little rubbed, illustrations by H. J. Ford, card prize label laid on to flyleaf.   R. F. G. Hollett & Son   Children's Books - 348   2013   £30

Lang, Andrew *Homer and the Epic.* London: and New York: Longmans, Green, 1893. First edition, one of only 107 large paper copies, uncut, partially unopened, bound in little warped and soiled parchment backed boards, library bookplates and name stamp, library numeral on spine which is worn and chipped, nice, clean copy.   Second Life Books Inc.   183 - 234   2013 $450

Lang, Andrew *Johnny Nut and the Golden Goose.* London: Longmans, Green and Co., 1887. Large tall 8vo., original decorated cloth gilt over bevelled boards, extremities trifle worn, pages 45, top edges gilt, printed on one side of each leaf, illustrations and decorations by A. M. Lynen, little light foxing in places, very nice tight copy.   R. F. G. Hollett & Son   Children's Books - 340   2013   £175

Lang, Andrew *The Princess Nobody.* London: Longman, Green and Co. n.d., 1884. First edition, large 8vo., original cloth backed pictorial boards, corners little rounded, neatly recased, pages 56, with 26 color printed and 26 sepia illustrations, pictorial endpapers printed in white on green, fore edge of first flyleaf neatly strengthened, one short tear repaired, otherwise really nice. R. F. G. Hollett & Son Children's Books - 341   2013   £395

Lang, Andrew *Prince Ricardo of Pantouflia: Being the Further Adventures of Prince Prigio's Son.* Bristol: Arrowsmith, n.d., 1893. First edition, 4to., vellum and brown cloth, 204 pages, vellum slightly age toned, else fine, large paper presentation copy (so stamped), rare in this edition, illustrations by Gordon Browne, with 12 plates plus 12 illustrations in text. Aleph-Bet Books, Inc.   105 - 353   2013 $500

Lang, Andrew *The Red Book of Animal Stories.* London: Longmans Green & Co., 1899. First edition, original red pictorial cloth gilt extra, spine little faded and slightly worn at head, all edges gilt, 32 plates by H. J. Ford. R. F. G. Hollett & Son   Children's Books - 349   2013   £75

Lang, Andrew *The Red Book of Heroes.* London: Longmans, Green and Co., 1909. First edition, original pictorial cloth, gilt extra, spine lightly faded, all edges gilt, 8 colored plate, few spots to prelims, lower joint cracked, very good, bright. R. F. G. Hollett & Son   Children's Books - 342   2013   £75

Lang, Andrew *The Red Book of Heroes.* London: Longmans, Green, 1909. First edition, first printing, 8vo., red gilt cloth, all edges gilt, spine very slightly dull else fine with beautiful and elaborate gilt cover design, 8 lovely color plates, 17 black and white plates, 23 black and whites in text, pictorial endpapers. Aleph-Bet Books, Inc.   105 - 354   2013 $300

Lang, Andrew *The Red Romance Book.* London: Longmans, Green, 1905. First edition, first printing, 8vo., red gilt cloth, all edges gilt spine slightly faded, else near fine with beautiful and elaborate gilt over design, 8 color plates and 28 beautiful black and white plates, smaller black and whites in text, pictorial endpapers. Aleph-Bet Books, Inc.   104 - 312   2013 $300

Lang, Blanche Leonora *The Book of Princes and Princesses.* London: Longmans, 1908. First edition, 8vo., 361 pages + ads, blue cloth, extensive gilt pictorial binding, all edges gilt, few spots on endpaper, else mint in dust jacket (only slightly worn on edges), 8 color plates and full page black and whites by H. J. Ford and lovely text illustrations, amazing copy, rare. Aleph-Bet Books, Inc.   105 - 351   2013 $1350

Lang, Blanche Leonora *The Strange Story Book.* London: Longmans, Green, 1913. First edition, First printing, 8vo., pink cloth stamped in gold, top edge gilt, 312 pages, fine, 12 color plates and 18 black and white plates, frontispiece is photogravure.   Aleph-Bet Books, Inc.   104 - 313   2013 $325

Lang, Johannes *Clinical Anatomy of the Head. Neurocranium, Orbit, Craniocervical.* Berlin: Heidelberg; New York: Springer Verlag, 1983. 4to., 189 diagrams, 99 tables, black cloth, white and red stamped cover and spine titles, dust jacket, original paper slipcase with label, ownership signature inside front covers, fine, rare.   Jeff Weber Rare Books   172 - 179   2013 $450

Langdon, Arthur G. *Old Cornish Crosses...* Truro: Joseph Pollard, 1896. First edition, large paper limited edition, number 37 of 54 copies, signed by Langdon, Folio, black and white plates, diagrams, 1 folding map, frontispiece, folio, quarterbound brown morocco over blue cloth boards, gilt titles and devices to spine and front board, top edge gilt, fore and bottom edges deckled, scarce in this edition, boards and spine rubbed, gilt bright, front free endpaper offset, small tears to front joint but binding still firm, rear endpapers bit darkened, leaves clean and crisp, very good or better.   Kaaterskill Books   16 - 54   2013 $600

Langtry, J. *History of the Church In Eastern Canada and Newfoundland with Map.* London: Society for Promoting Christian Knowledge, 1892. Red cloth, gilt to spine and front cover as well as black decorative design to front cover, half title, color folding map as frontispiece, small 8vo., slight wear to cloth, Sunday school library bookplate inside front cover partially torn off generally very good.   Schooner Books Ltd.   102 - 134   2013 $60

Lansdale, Joe R. *Act of Love.* New York: Kensington/Zebra, 1981. Paperback original, signed by author, dated 11/1/86, stamp of recipient Stanley Wiater, spine creased, very good in wrappers, laid in is folded autograph note signed by author to Wiater.   Ken Lopez Bookseller   159 - 98   2013 $150

Lansdale, Joe R. *By Bizarre Hands.* Shingletown: Mark V. Ziesing, 1989. First edition, one of 500 numbered copies signed by Lansdale, Potter and Nelson, very fine in dust jacket with slipcase.   Mordida Books   81 - 287   2013 $75

Lansdale, Joe R. *Cold in July.* New York: Bantam, 1989. Publisher's copy, (indicated "P/C" on colophon) of limited edition, which was issued with numbered limitation of 100 copies, signed by author, colophon laid in, having detached as glue which is tipped in has dried, glue stains at hinge and light spine crease, ownership stamp of Stanley Wiater, very good in wrappers, uncommon issue of this paperback original.   Ken Lopez Bookseller   159 - 101   2013 $100

Lansdale, Joe R. *Dead in the West.* New York: Space and Time, 1986. First edition, review copy, only issued in softcover, inscribed by author for Stanley Wiater, with his bookplate, near fine in wrappers, publisher's promotional material laid in.   Ken Lopez Bookseller   159 - 99   2013 $125

Lansdale, Joe R. *The Drive-in 2.* New York: Bantam, 1989. Uncorrected proof, inscribed by author to Stanley Wiater, with his bookplate, edge sunned with small crown bump, near fine in wrappers.   Ken Lopez Bookseller   159 - 102   2013 $75

Lansdale, Joe R. *Freezer Burn.* Holyoke: Crossroads Press, 1999. Uncorrected proof of this limited edition, signed by author, comb-bound with both printed and acetate covers, stamp of Stanley Wiater, near fine in wrappers.   Ken Lopez Bookseller   159 - 105   2013 $150

Lansdale, Joe R. *Mucho Mojo.* Baltimore: CD Publications, 1994. Limited edition, one of 400 numbered copies signed by author and artist, Mark Nelson.   Mordida Books   81 - 291   2013 $85

Lansdale, Joe R. *My Dead Dog, Bobby.* Sacramento: Cobblestone Books, 1995. One of 750 numbered copies, signed by author, Norman Partridge (introduction) and Joe Virgil (artist), illustrations, bookplate of Stanley Wiater, fine in stapled wrappers.   Ken Lopez Bookseller   159 - 104   2013 $75

Lansdale, Joe R. *The Nightrunners.* Arlington Heights: Dark Harvest, 1987. Publisher's copy (indicated "P/C" on colophon), deluxe edition, issued in numbered limitation of 300 copies, signed by Lansdale, also signed by Dean Koontz and by Gregory Manchess, who provided introduction and illustrations respectively, slightly musty, else fine in near fine dust jacket and very good, edge stained slipcase.   Ken Lopez Bookseller   159 - 100   2013 $150

Lansdale, Joe R. *Tarzan: The Last Adventure...adapted by Lonsdale.* Milwaukee: Dark Horse, 1995. First edition, very fine in soft covers.   Mordida Books   81 - 292   2013 $100

Lansdowne, J. E. *Birds of the Eastern Forest 1 and 2.* Boston: Houghton Mifflin, 1968-1970. First edition, folio, 2 volumes, very good+ in like dust jackets.   Beasley Books 2013 - 2013 $100

The Laundry Manual... Chicago: National Laundry Journal, 1898. First edition, 8vo., 370 pages, illustrations, original cloth, rear hinge tender, some soiling to cover, very good.   Second Life Books Inc.   183 - 238   2013 $65

Lapham, L. A. *Report of the Disastrous Effects of the Destruction of Forest Trees, Now Going on so Rapidly in... Wisconsin.* Madison: 1867. First edition, 104 pages, contemporary boards, leather spine, front cover detached.   M & S Rare Books, Inc.   95 - 393   2013 $375

Lardner, Dionysius *Hand-Book of Natural Philosophy: Hydrostatics, Pneumatics and Heat.* London: Walton and Maberly, 1855. First edition, 181 x 114mm., appealing contemporary published calf presentation binding, covers with double gilt rule border with floral cornerpieces and inner frame of blind dotted rule, upper cover with gilt insignia of school of the City of London, raised bands, spine densely gilt in compartments with large and intricate central fleuron and curling cornerpieces maroon morocco label, marbled edges and endpapers, frontispiece and 292 illustrations; ink inscription "2nd Prize for proficiency in Writing awarded to John Debney, Thos. Hall BA Master of the First Class July 1858", joints and extremities slightly rubbed, hinge open at titlepage (but no structural fragility), other trivial imperfections internally, but excellent copy, text clean, fresh and smooth, decorative binding sturdy and not without charm.   Phillip J. Pirages   63 - 307   2013 $125

Larkey, Joann Leach *Davisville '68. The History and Heritage of the City of Davis, Yolo County, California.* Davis: Davis Historical and Landmarks Commission, 1969. First edition, illustrations by Jeanette Nunn Copley, brown cloth, gilt, very fine.   Argonaut Book Shop   Summer 2013 - 188   2013 $50

Larkin, George *The Visions of John Bunyan; Being His Last Remains...* London: printed for A. Millar, W. Law and R. Cater and for Wilson, Spence and Mawman, York, 1793. 12mo., some browning and staining, contemporary half calf over marbled boards, large vellum cornerpieces, themselves marbled, rebacked, a series of 3 early 19th century inscriptions inside front cover and on flyleaves passing book on, sound.   Blackwell's Rare Books   172 - 85   2013   £250

Larkin, Philip   1922-1985 *The Fantasy Poets. Number Twenty One.* Swinford: Fantasy Press, 1954. First edition, entire issue devoted to Larkin, approximately 300 copies printed, signed by Larkin on front cover, very fine, preserved in half morocco slipcase.   James S. Jaffe Rare Books   Fall 2013 - 86   2013 $4500

Larkin, Philip   1922-1985 *The Less Deceived. Poems.* Hessle: Marvell Press, 1955. First edition, first issue, first binding, one of 120 copies of the first impression with list of subscribers bound in at back, out of total first printing of 300 copies, bound with strip of stiffening mull in spine, with all textual points noted by Bloomfield as present in first edition, signed by Larkin on titlepage, bottom edge of boards and base of spine little dampstained, otherwise fine in jacket with minute nick at base of spine and short closed tear at top right hand corner of jacket at front fold.   James S. Jaffe Rare Books   Fall 2013 - 87   2013 $5000

Larkin, Philip 1922-1985 *XX Poems.* N.P.: privately printed, 1951. First edition printed in an edition of 100 copies, 8vo., original printed white wrappers, presentation copy inscribed to his editor at Faber, Charles Monteith, beautiful copy, none of the discoloration typical of paper used to bind this publication, cloth folding box.   James S. Jaffe Rare Books   Fall 2013 - 85   2013 $15,000

Larkin, Philip 1922-1985 *The Whitsun Weddings. Poems.* London: Faber & Faber, 1964. First edition, one of 3910 copies, Harry Chambers' copy with his ownership signature and inscription "Harry Chambers February 10th 1964 (Publication date Feb. 28th)," signed and dated by Larkin on front free endpaper, Chambers' light pencil marks in text, otherwise fine.   James S. Jaffe Rare Books   Fall 2013 - 88   2013 $4500

Larkin, Thomas Oliver *California in 1846.* San Francisco: Grabhorn Press, 1934. One of 550 copies, frontispiece, four facsimile color lithographs, 5 facsimile documents, handset style, black cloth spine, gilt stamped blue boards, paper spine label, very fine and bright.   Argonaut Book Shop   Summer 2013 - 189   2013 $150

Larrey, Dominique Jean *Memoires de Chirurgie Militaire et Campagnes.... (with) Relation Medicale de Campagnes et voyages de 1815 a 1840...* Paris: J. Smith, 1812-1817. Paris: J. B. Bailliere, 1841. First edition, first work in 4 volumes, 8vo., 6 plates, occasional light scattered foxing, especially to plates, volume I minor waterstain to top and right margins throughout and volume II waterstain to lower and right margins, not affecting text, modern half navy blue cloth over turquoise marbled paper backed boards, gilt stamped green leather spine labels, half title, titlepage and p. 1 rubber stamped in all volumes and no pages preceding plates in volumes I and III, volume I half title with early ink gift inscription donating set to Bibliotheque Hosptial Mre. d'Inston de Strasbourg, additional ink inscription May 11 1948 from Dr. Alfred Haas to Prof. H. K. (Hanson Kelly) Corning, Basel, with his rubber stamp in all 4 volumes, very good, scarce; second work 8vo., 2 folding plates, all edges marbled light occasional foxing scattered throughout, later quarter calf over contemporary marbled paper backed boards, gilt stamped and leather spine label, covers creased and scuffed, edges rubbed, bookseller ticket of Paul Hober NY, very good, this set belonged to Dr. Eugene Courtiss (1930-200), plastic surgeon.   Jeff Weber Rare Books   172 - 180   2013 $175

Laskey, John K. *Alethes, or, The Roman Exile: a Tale.* St. John: printed for the author by Robert Shives, Market Square, 1840. Small 8vo., original floral designed cloth with printed paper label to spine, wear to edges of covers and foxing to interior.   Schooner Books Ltd.   101 - 15   2013 $475

Laszlo *Our Block.* Crown, 1951. 4to., pictorial boards, light spine wear, very good+, with punch-out die cut people and objects, unread and really great.   Aleph-Bet Books, Inc.   105 - 431   2013 $200

Latassa Y Ortin, Felix De *Bibliotecas Antigua y Nueva de Escritores Aragoneses de Latassa Amuentadas y Refundidas en Forma de Diccionario Bibliografico-Biografico.* Zaragoza: Imprenta de Calisto Arino, 1884. 1885. 1886. First edition, 3 volumes, small 4to., cloth, near fine, foxing on top edges, leaves slightly browned, occasional soiling, else clean.   Kaaterskill Books   16 - 55   2013 $500

Latchford, Benjamin *The Loriner.* London: printed by Herbert Fitch, 1883. 4to., 14 double page plates with 138 illustrations, 10 pages, contemporary half black roan, very good.   Jarndyce Antiquarian Booksellers   CCV - 160   2013   £280

Latest Information from the Settlement of New Plymouth on the Coast of Taranake, New Zealand. London: Smith, Elder & Co., 1842. First edition, woodcut frontispiece and woodcut vignette, 12mo., fine copy, original printed wrappers, crisp copy.   Maggs Bros. Ltd.   1467 - 86   2013   £450

Lathan, T. D. *An Address, Advice, Hints &c to the Roman Catholics.* Cork: Bolster, 1826. 8vo., viii, 196 pages, disbound, clean.   C. P. Hyland   261 - 542   2013   £60

Lathbury, Mary *Fleda and the Voice.* New York: Nelson Phillips, 1876. 4to., gilt pictorial cloth, beveled edges, few small spots on cover, else near fine, engravings by author, elaborate cover design, attractive.   Aleph-Bet Books, Inc. 105 - 236   2013 $200

Latimer, Hugh, Bp. of Worcester *The Sermons of... Many of Which were Preached Before King Edward VI... on the Religious.* printed for J. Scott, 1758. First collected edition, engraved frontispiece in each volume and 1 engraved plate, one gathering in volume i foxed, 8vo., contemporary polished calf, panelled gilt, spines gilt in compartments with dolphin within crowed circle, red lettering pieces, numbered gilt direct, 3 later inkstamps on flyleaves, very good, attractive copy, fairly scarce.   Blackwell's Rare Books   172 - 86   2013   £800

Latimer, Jonathan *Solomon's Vineyard.* Santa Barbara: Neville, 1982. First American edition, one of 26 lettered copies bound in full leather and signed by author, very fine without dust jacket.   Mordida Books   81 - 296   2013 $300

Latta, Frank F. *California Indian Folklore as told to F. F. Latta.* Shafter: 1936. First edition, octavo, 209 pages, photos, brown cloth lettered in black, small spot to front cover, covers slightly dulled, very good, very scarce.   Argonaut Book Shop   Recent Acquisitions June 2013 - 191   2013 $200

Latta, Frank F. *Handbook of Yokuts Indians.* Santa Cruz: Bear State Books, 1977. Second edition, first issue, one of 5000 copies, xxxi, 765 pages, photos, map endpapers, original gilt pictorial green cloth, very fine.   Argonaut Book Shop   Recent Acquisitions June 2013 - 189   2013 $100

Latta, Frank F. *Tailholt Tales.* Santa Cruz: Bear State Books, 1976. First edition, frontispiece, photos, light green cloth, pictorially stamped in black, very fine.   Argonaut Book Shop   Recent Acquisitions June 2013 - 190   2013 $75

Laud, William *A Relation of the Conference Between William Laud... and Mr. Fisher the Jesuit...* London: by Ralph Holt for Thomas Bassett, Thomas Dring and John Leigh, 1686. Folio, title in red and black, nearly sprinkled calf, gilt arms on covers, spine with gilt ornaments, heavy noticeable dampstain at bottom of first and last several leaves, upper hinges splitting at bottom, but very good, sound.   Joseph J. Felcone Inc.   Books Printed before 1701 - 60   2013 $400

Lauder, Thomas Dick *Lochandhu, Histoire du XVIIIe Siecle...* Paris: Charles Gosselin...and Mame et Delaunay-Vallee, 1828. First edition in French, 4 volumes, some foxing at beginning of volume i and in volumes iii, and iv, 12mo., contemporary? Austrian half calf, 4 raised bands on spines with blue skiver lettering pieces in second and fourth compartments, remainder gilt, blue and pink strip of paper pasted on towards foot, spines trifle faded, Brunsee libary label inside front cover, very good, rare.   Blackwell's Rare Books   B174 - 89   2013   £300

Laughlin, James *New Directions in Poetry and Prose.* Norfolk: New Directions, 1936. First edition, printed boards, some soiled, signed by author and inscribed to Aquinto Jack from E. B. D.   Second Life Books Inc.   183 - 235   2013 $300

Laughlin, James *New Directions in Poetry and Prose.* Norfolk: New Directions, 1941. First edition, tan cloth little soiled, dust jacket nicked and some worn and missing some pieces, very good, this copy signed by Delmore Schwartz and John Berryman.   Second Life Books Inc. 183 - 237   2013 $250

Laughlin, James *This Is My Blood.* Covelo: Yolla Bolly Press, 1989. First edition, one of 55 copies signed by author and hand numbered from a total issue of 255 (200 not signed and bound in paper wrappers), 100 pages, tan cloth with tan paper label, printed in slightly deeper tan with title on front panel, matching publisher's slipcase with title printed on spine fine.   Priscilla Juvelis - Rare Books   55 - 28   2013 $150

The Laundry Manual... Chicago: National Laundry Journal, 1898. First edition, 8vo., 370 pages, illustrations, original cloth, rear hinge tender, some soiling to cover, very good.   Second Life Books Inc.   182 - 153   2013 $65

Laurence, Edward *The Duty of a Steward to His Lord...* London: Shuckburgh at the Sun, 1727. First edition, 4to., 212 pages, charts, folding plates, fine, crisp copy in contemporary calf, front cover almost separate.   Second Life Books Inc.   183 - 239   2013 $650

Laurents, Arthur *The Way We Were.* New York: Harper & Row, 1972. First edition, inscribed by author for Pierre Sicari, fine dust jacket, price clipped, would be fine but for blue line from old style glassine jacket protector.   Ed Smith Books   78 - 30   2013 $125

Laval, Jerome D *As "Pop" Saw It. The Great Centra Velly of California...* Fresno: Graphic Technology Co., 1975-1976. First edition, 2 volumes, quarto, photos, pictorial cloth, owner's small and neat inscription in each volume, fine set with pictorial dust jacket (chip to head of jacket spine on volume I).   Argonaut Book Shop   Recent Acquisitions June 2013 - 192   2013 $100

Lavender, David *Bent's Fort.* Garden City: 1954. First edition, 450 pages, map endpapers, dust jacket price clipped and worn with short tears, but complete, book very good, signed by author.   Dumont Maps & Books of the West   125 - 60   2013 $50

Lavender, David *Land of Giants. The Drive to the Pacific Northwest 1750-1950.* Garden City: Doubleday & Co., 1958. First edition, 4 maps, green cloth, gilt, owner's name on end, very fine, pictorial dust jacket, presentation inscription signed by author.   Argonaut Book Shop   Summer 2013 - 191   2013 $90

Lavin, Mary *The Great Wave and Other Stories.* London: Macmillan, 1961. First edition, 8vo., original green cloth, presentation from author to Tom Kinsella and his wife Eleanor, with stamp of Lavin's literary agents A. D. Peters below the inscription and bookmark from New Yorker magazine, early gatherings loose and boards close to asunder at spine, good copy only.   Maggs Bros. Ltd.   1442 - 174   2013   £125

Lavin, Mary *The Patriot Son and other Stories.* London: Michael Joseph, 1956. First edition, 8vo. original black cloth, dust jacket, excellent copy, jacket rubbed and marked, most notably at spine, inscribed by author for Richard Murphy.   Maggs Bros. Ltd.   1442 - 175   2013   £175

Law, William *An Extract from a Treatise by William Law, M.A. called The Spirit of Prayer...* Philadelphia: B. Franklin and D. Hall, 1760. First edition, 12mo., 19th century half morocco gilt, 48 pages, crisp copy.   Maggs Bros. Ltd.   1467 - 121   2013   £1000

Lawick, Hugo Van *Among Predators and Prey.* Elm Tree Books, 1986. First edition, small folio, original cloth, dust jacket, 224 pages, illustrations in color.   R. F. G. Hollett & Son   Africana - 117   2013   £40

Lawley, Robert Nevill *The Battle of Marston-Moor. A Lecture Delivered in the School-Room at Marston.* New York: John Sampson, Coney Street, 1865. 8vo., 56 pages, half title, very good, disbound.   Ken Spelman Books Ltd.   73 - 125   2013   £45

Lawlor, C. F. *The Mixicologist or How to Fix All Kinds of Fancy Drinks.* Cincinnati: Lawlor & Co./The Robert Clarke Company, Hawleys..., 1895. stated "Revised edition" but OCLOC record no earlier copies, printed wrappers soiled and small tape repairs at spine ends, internally near fine, sound copy, very uncommon.   Between the Covers Rare Books, Inc.   Cocktails, Etc. - 318066   2013 $385

Lawlor, Hugh J. *The Fasti of St. Patrick's Dublin.* 1930. First edition, 8vo., cloth, cover faded and some wear, text good.   C. P. Hyland   261 - 544   2013   £56

Lawrence, David Herbert 1885-1930 *Birds, Beasts and Flowers, Poems.* London: Secker, 1923. First English edition, 208 pages, 8vo. original quarter black cloth, printed label, bright yellow boards, light free endpaper browning, untrimmed, fragile dust jacket faded with tears to backstrip panel, good.   Blackwell's Rare Books   B174 - 244   2013   £80

Lawrence, David Herbert 1885-1930 *Etruscan Places.* Secker, 1932. First edition, 20 plates, pages 200, 8vo., original pale blue bevel edged cloth, backstrip gilt lettered, blindstamped etruscan design on front cover, untrimmed and partly unopened, dust jacket little frayed and with 2 short tears to slightly darkened backstrip panel, very good.   Blackwell's Rare Books   B174 - 245   2013   £150

Lawrence, David Herbert 1885-1930 *Lady Chatterley's Lover.* Florence: printed by the Tipografia Giuntina, 1928. First edition, one of 1000 copies signed by author, 232 x 168mm., original mulberry colored paper boards, edges untrimmed and unopened, original plain cream colored jacket, 2 pages with breath of foxing, narrow band inside front flap of jacket bit spotted, just the slightest fraying and wrinkling on jacket spine ends, but extraordinarily fine, volume virtually pristine and jacket in marvelous condition.   Phillip J. Pirages   63 - 308   2013 $21,000

Lawrence, David Herbert 1885-1930 *Lady Chatterley's Lover.* Secker, 1932. First English edition and first authorised expurgated edition, 328 pages, foolscap 8vo., original brown cloth, backstrip gilt lettered, bookplate, tail edges rough trimmed, dust jacket frayed, backstrip panel browned and defective for the top 3 cms., very good.   Blackwell's Rare Books   B174 - 246   2013   £350

Lawrence, David Herbert 1885-1930 *Lady Chatterley's Lover.* Penguin, 1960. First English unexpurgated edition, poor quality paper browned, 16mo., 320 pages, original printed cream and orange wrappers, very good.   Blackwell's Rare Books   B174 - 247   2013   £100

Lawrence, David Herbert 1885-1930 *Lady Chatterley's Lover.* Penguin, 2006. One of 100 numbered copies, printed in purple, 8vo., original purple cloth, white cotton dust jacket with overall sewn design of flowers and lettering by Paul Smith, clear perspex slipcase with limitation label, plastic cellophane seal broken, original white card protective box with limitation label, fine.   Blackwell's Rare Books   B174 - 248   2013   £600

Lawrence, David Herbert 1885-1930 *Love Among the Haystacks and Other Pieces.* Nonesuch Press, 1930. First edition, 555/1600 copies, printed on Auvergne handmade paper, 8vo., original fawn canvas, black leather label, canary yellow buckram sides, browned endpapers, untrimmed, two tiny spots on backstrip panel, dust jacket, near fine.   Blackwell's Rare Books   B174 - 368   2013   £100

Lawrence, David Herbert 1885-1930 *The Lovely Lady.* London: Secker, 1932. First edition, 248 pages, foolscap 8vo., original mid brown cloth, backstrip gilt lettered, dust jacket with backstrip panel chipped and little darkened, good.   Blackwell's Rare Books   B174 - 249   2013   £250

Lawrence, David Herbert 1885-1930 *A Modern Lover.* London: Secker, 1934. First edition, light foxing to prelims and fore-edges, 312 pages, foolscap 8vo. original mid brown cloth, backstrip gilt lettered, dust jacket trifle frayed, backstrip panel browned, good.   Blackwell's Rare Books   B174 - 250   2013   £85

Lawrence, David Herbert 1885-1930 *Psychoanalysis and the Unconscious.* Secker, 1923. First English edition, foolscap 8vo. pages 128, original maroon cloth, printed label, prelims and final few leaves lightly foxed, dust jacket with backstrip panel trifle darkened, very good.   Blackwell's Rare Books   B174 - 251   2013   £100

Lawrence, David Herbert 1885-1930 *St. Mawr Together with the Princess.* Secker, 1925. First edition, variant 1 with text block 7/8 inch across, prelims trifle foxed, pages 240, foolscap 8vo., original chocolate brown cloth, gilt lettering on lightly faded backstrip tarnished, rough trimmed, very good.   Blackwell's Rare Books   B174 - 252   2013   £50

Lawrence, Josephine *Man in the Moon Stories told Over the Radio Phone.* New York: Cupples and Leon, 1922. 4to., blue cloth, pictorial paste-on, some shelfwear and rubbing very good, illustrations by Johnny Gruelle, cover plate, double page pictorial endpapers, 8 color plates plus black and whites in text.   Aleph-Bet Books, Inc.   104 - 264   2013 $500

Lawrence, Robert Means *The Descendants of Major Samuel Lawrence of Groton, Massachusetts with Some Mention of allied Families.* Cambridge: printed at the Riverside Press, 1904. First edition, 241 x 15mm., extremely attractive contemporary crimson half morocco, marbled sides and endpaper, raised bands, spine gilt in double ruled compartments with tulip cornerpieces, top edge gilt, photogravure frontispiece, inscribed by author for Miss Jessie Degen Boston, March 30th 1915, back cover with small areas of soiling, corners just slightly rubbed, still fine, binding lustrous, internally pristine. Phillip J. Pirages 63 - 309 2013 $250

Lawrence, Thomas Edward 1888-1935 *Crusader Castles.* Golden Cockerel Press, 1936. First edition, 2 volumes, 6/ 1000 sets printed on Portals and mouldmade paper, 106 reproductions of photos, diagrams and drawings, titles printed in red, 2 maps present in fine state and inserted in their foxed envelope, 4to., original half russet red morocco, backstrips gilt lettered between raised bands, cream linen sides with light foxing, top edge gilt, others untrimmed, near fine. Blackwell's Rare Books 172 - 291 2013 £1600

Lawrence, Thomas Edward 1888-1935 *Men in Print. Essays in Literary Criticism.* Golden Cockerel Press, 1940. First edition, 68/470 copies (of an edition fo 500 copies), printed on Arnold's mouldmade paper, 4to., original quarter mid blue crushed morocco, lightly faded backstrip gilt lettered between raised bands, cream cloth sides, top edge gilt, others untrimmed, card slipcase, near fine. Blackwell's Rare Books 172 - 292 2013 £450

Lawrence, William *Lectures on Physiology, Zoology and Natural History of Man Delivered at the Royal College of Surgeons.* printed for J. Callow, 1819. Suppressed first edition, 12 engraved plates little foxed, 8vo., 19th century half calf for Vet Med Association, spine with intricate blind tooling and gilt roll tooling on raised bands, red lettering piece, good. Blackwell's Rare Books Sciences - 68 2013 £650

Lawrence, William *Two Lectures on Political Economy.* New York: G. & C. & H. Carvill, 1832. First edition, removed. M & S Rare Books, Inc. 95 - 198 2013 $325

Laws Concerning Property in Literary Production, in Engravings, Designings and Etchings... London: printed for Jordan No. 166 Fleet Street, 1795? 8vo., uncut, titlepage slightly dusted, disbound. Jarndyce Antiquarian Booksellers CCIV - 44 2013 £1500

The Laws Concerning the Election of Members of Parliament; with Determinations of the House of Commons Thereon and all Their Incidents... London: printed for W. Owen, 1768. First edition, 8vo., some light browning, foxing to endpapers and pastedowns, contemporary calf, blind-stamped inner borders, expertly rebacked, raised bands, gilt device, red morocco label, armorial bookplate of Sir Edward Blackett, Bart. Jarndyce Antiquarian Booksellers CCIV - 45 2013 £350

Lawson, J. Murray *Record of the Shipping of Yarmouth, N.S..... (with) Appendix.... from 1876 to 1884.* St. John: J. & A. McMillan, Yarmouth, 1876. Appendix - Yarmouth: printed at the Herald Office, 1884, 8vo., half title has been torn out, pressed brown cloth with gilt to spine and front board, some foxing, cloth very speckled and faded, interior generally good, errata tipped to page 258, appendix very good with only minor wear to cloth edges. Schooner Books Ltd. 101 - 105 2013 $225

Lawson, J. Murray *Yarmouth Past and Present. A Book of Reminiscences.* Yarmouth: Yarmouth Herald Office, 1902. Light green cloth with gold titles, index, 3 large folding photo illustrations backed on linen and 64 photos and engravings, large 8vo., cloth worn and stained, interior very good, views very good, errata slip inserted at front. Schooner Books Ltd. 102 - 72 2013 $125

Lawson, Mary Jane Katzmann *History of Townships of Dartmouth, Preston and Lawrencetown, Halifax County, N.S.* Halifax: Morton and Co., Provincial Book Store, 1893. 8vo., rebound in blue library cloth, frontispiece, original title label pasted to inside front cover, previous owner's names, news clipped taped to front endpaper, binding slightly cocked, generally good. Schooner Books Ltd. 104 - 77 2013 $150

Lawson, Robert *Country Colic.* Boston: Little Brown, March, 1944. First edition, 8vo. tan cloth, fine in dust jacket frayed at spine ends, black and white illustrations. Aleph-Bet Books, Inc. 104 - 315 2013 $100

Lawson, Robert *Rabbit Hill.* New York: Viking, Sept., 1944. First edition, tall 8vo., fine in dust jacket with few very small chips, illustrations, with price intact and without medal. Aleph-Bet Books, Inc. 104 - 316 2013 $275

Lawson, Robert *Smeller Martin.* New York: Viking, 1950. First edition, 4to., green cloth, 157 pages, fine in very slightly frayed dust jacket, illustrations by author. Aleph-Bet Books, Inc. 104 - 317 2013 $150

Layden, Elmer *It Was a Different Game: The Elmer Layden Story.* Englewood Cliffs: Prentice Hall, 1969. First edition, fine in fine dust jacket with short tear on rear panel signed by author. Between the Covers Rare Books, Inc. Football Books - 80532 2013 $400

Layne, J. Gregg *Annals of Los Angeles from the Arrival of the First White Man to the Civil War 1769-1861.* San Francisco: California Historical Society, 1935. First book edition, 3 color reproductions, green cloth lettered in black on spine, printed pictorial label on front cover, very fine, bright, very scarce. Argonaut Book Shop Summer 2013 - 212 2013 $200

Lazer, Hank *On Equal Terms. Poems by Charles Bernstein, David Ignatow, Denise Levertov, Louis Simpson, Gerald Stern.* Tuscaloosa: Symposium Press, 1984. First edition, limited to 275 copies, although not called for, this copy signed by all contributors, one of the few copies we've seen signed by any of the poets, 4to., original green wrappers, as new. James S. Jaffe Rare Books Fall 2013 - 5 2013 $450

Le Baron, Gaye *Santa Rosa. A Nineteenth Century Town.* N.P.: Historia Ltd., 1985. First limited edition, one of 5000 numbered copies with printed signatures of all 4 contributors, additionally this copy signed by LeBaron, Dee Blackman and Joann Mitchell, old photos, brochures, maroon cloth, gilt, very fine in very good dust jacket. Argonaut Book Shop Summer 2013 - 192 2013 $75

Le Breton, J. G. *Kenya Sketches.* London: Allen & Unwin, 1935. First edition, small 8vo., original decorated brown cloth, dust jacket rather worn and chipped and repaired with tape on reverse, edges rather spotted. R. F. G. Hollett & Son Africana - 119 2013 £25

Le Carre, John 1931- *Absolute Friends.* London: Hodder and Stoughton, 2003. First edition, signed by author, very fine in dust jacket. Mordida Books 81 - 308 2013 $125

Le Carre, John 1931- *Call for the Dead.* London: Hodder & Stoughton, 1992. 8vo., pages 144, original black boards, backstrip gilt lettered, dust jacket, fine, inscribed by author for his secretary, Fritz Rummler. Blackwell's Rare Books 172 - 206 2013 £235

Le Carre, John 1931- *The Honourable Schoolboy.* London: Hodder & Stoughton, 1990. Lamplighter edition, 8vo., original black boards, backstrip gilt lettered, endpapers, final leaf of text and edges foxed, waterstaining faintly to tail of covers and interior of dust jacket, good, inscribed by author for his secretary Fritz Rummler. Blackwell's Rare Books 172 - 207 2013 £200

Le Carre, John 1931- *A Murder of Quality.* New York: Walker, 1963. First American edition, fine in dust jacket with slightly faded spine, exceptional copy. Mordida Books 81 - 302 2013 $2300

Le Carre, John 1931- *A Murder of Quality.* London: Hodder & Stoughton, 1990. Lamplighter edition, 8vo., 144 pages, original black boards, backstrip gilt lettered, prelims and edges foxed, dust jacket, titlepage inscribed to his secretary, Fritz Rummler. Blackwell's Rare Books 172 - 208 2013 £200

Le Carre, John 1931- *The Night Manager.* London: Hodder & Stoughton, 1993. First edition, signed by author, very fine in dust jacket. Mordida Books 81 - 304 2013 $175

Le Carre, John 1931- *Our Game.* New York: Knopf, 1995. First American edition, 8vo., original black cloth, tail of rear cover affected by damp, damp also intruding onto tail of rear endpaper and associated area of dust jacket, backstrip gilt lettered, endpaper maps, fore edge rough trimmed, dust jacket, good, inscribed by author for his secretary. Blackwell's Rare Books 172 - 209 2013 £350

Le Carre, John 1931- *Our Game.* London: Hodder & Stoughton, 1995. First English edition, very fine in dust jacket. Mordida Books 81 - 305 2013 $300

Le Carre, John 1931- *A Perfect Spy.* New York: Alfred A. Knopf, 1986. First American edition, signed by author, very fine in dust jacket. Mordida Books 81 - 303 2013 $150

Le Carre, John 1931- *A Small Town in Germany.* London: Hodder & Stoughton, 1991. Lamplighter edition, 8vo., original black boards, backstrip gilt lettered, foxing to edges, dust jacket, very good, inscribed by author for his secretary Fritz Rummler. Blackwell's Rare Books 172 - 210 2013 £200

Le Carre, John 1931- *Single & Single.* London: Hodder & Stoughton, 1999. Uncorrected proof, fine in wrappers. Mordida Books 81 - 307 2013 $100

Le Carre, John 1931- *The Tailor of Panama.* London: Hodder & Stoughton, 1996. First edition, signed by author, very fine in dust jacket. Mordida Books 81 - 306 2013 $100

Le Clerc, Daniel *Bibliotheca Anatomica; sive Recens in Anatomia Inventorum Thesaurus...* Geneva: Jean Antoine Chouet & David Ritter, 1699. Second edition, 2 large folio volumes, lacks allegorical title in volume one and half title leaf in volume two, with 123 (of 124?) plates, nice contemporary blindstamped vellum with arabesque pattern, boards somewhat warped, light wrinkling of text, some plates browned, overall a tall quite handsomely bound set. James Tait Goodrich 75 - 134 2013 $1750

Le Clerc, Daniel *A Natural and Medicinal History of Worms Bred in the Bodies of Men and Other Animals.* London: J. Wilcox, 1721. 3 folding plates, recent quarter calf and marbled boards, raised bands, endpapers renewed, text foxed in parts, margins of title bit brittle with light loss of blank margin, text underlining and annotations in early hand. James Tait Goodrich   S74 - 170   2013 $895

Le Clezio, J. M. G. *The Book of Flights.* New York: Atheneum, 1972. First American edition, inscribed by author, recipient's signature and date (173), fine in very near fine price clipped dust jacket with one short tear, closed edge tear, very nice, uncommon.   Ken Lopez Bookseller 159 - 111   2013 $450

Le Clezio, J. M. G. *Desert.* St. Amand: Folio, 1991. French language paperback reissue, inscribed by author, recipient's signature, fine in wrappers.   Ken Lopez Bookseller   159 - 116   2013 $200

Le Clezio, J. M. G. *Diego & Frida.* Paris: Stock, 1993. First edition (French), warmly inscribed by author, recipient's signature, fine in wrappers.   Ken Lopez Bookseller   159 - 117   2013 $450

Le Clezio, J. M. G. *Fever.* London: Hamish Hamilton, 1966. First English language edition, inscribed by author, uncommon, scarce signed, inscribed by author, recipient's name, fine in very good dust jacket with several edge tears and small sticker removal shadow to front panel.   Ken Lopez Bookseller   159 - 107   2013 $850

Le Clezio, J. M. G. *Fever.* New York: Atheneum, 1966. First edition, inscribed by author. recipient's signature, small spot to top stain, light sunning to board edges, near fine in very good, rubbed and price clipped dust jacket with moderate edgewear and mild fading to red block on spine.   Ken Lopez Bookseller   159 - 108   2013 $750

Le Clezio, J. M. G. *The Flood.* New York: Atheneum, 1968. First American edition, review copy, inscribed by author, recipient's signature, trace sunning to board edges, else fine in very good, lightly rubbed dust jacket with mild edgewear, scarce,.   Ken Lopez Bookseller   159 - 109 2013 $950

Le Clezio, J. M. G. *The Giants.* New York: Atheneum, 1975. First American edition, inscribed by author, recipient's signature, fine in near fine dust jacket, with small abrasion to lower rear spine fold.   Ken Lopez Bookseller   159 - 114   2013 $375

Le Clezio, J. M. G. *Terra Amata.* New York: Atheneum, 1969. First American edition, inscribed by author, recipient's signature, fine in very good, spine sunned dust jacket, scarce.   Ken Lopez Bookseller   159 - 110   2013 $500

Le Clezio, J. M. G. *War.* London: Jonathan Cape, 1973. First English language edition, hardcover issue, inscribed by author, recipient's signature, some fading to top stain, else fine in very good price clipped dust jacket with small mended chip at upper rear panel.   Ken Lopez Bookseller   159 - 112   2013 $500

Le Clezio, J. M. G. *War.* London: Wildwood House, 1973. Simultaneous softcover issue of first English language edition, inscribed by author, recipient's signature, near fine in wrappers.   Ken Lopez Bookseller   159 - 113 2013 $375

Le Conte, Joseph N. *A Yosemite Camping Trip 1889.* Berkeley: University of California, 1990. First edition, scarce, 13 photo reproductions, dark grey-green wrappers printed in black on light green background, very fine. Argonaut Book Shop   Summer 2013 - 195   2013 $90

Le Corbeau, Adrien *The Forest Giant.* Cape, 1935. First illustrated edition, frontispiece and 8 other full page wood engravings by Agnes Miller-Parker, prelims and edges foxed, pages 160, foolscap 8vo., original lime green cloth, backstrip gilt lettered, two bookplates, untrimmed, internal tape reinforcing to dust jacket chipped and darkened on backstrip panel, good.   Blackwell's Rare Books   B174 - 253   2013   £60

Le Cron, Helen Cowles *Animal Etiquette Book.* New York: Frederick Stokes, 1926. First edition, 8vo., cloth, pictorial paste-on, 95 pages, title and frontispiece foxed, else very good, illustrations by Maurice Day with full color frontispiece and 24 full page black and white line illustrations. Aleph-Bet Books, Inc.   105 - 231   2013 $150

Le Fanu, Joseph Sheridan 1814-1873 *Carmilla.* New York: Alsparck, 1983. First Fini edition, number 70 of 267 copies on Arches wove paper with deckle edges (total edition 297), signed in pencil by the artist, Leonor Fini on justification page, about 110 pages, 23 prints in color, 15 original lithographs in-texte and 8 original silkscreens hors texte, each of the 23 prints numbered and signed by Fini loose leaves in very handsome publisher's box with display window on front cover, overall size 60 x 50 x 6 cm. excellent condition.   Gemini Fine Books & Arts., Ltd.   Art Reference & Illustrated Books - 2013 $3000

Le Fanu, Joseph Sheridan 1814-1873 *In a Glass Darkly.* London: Peter Davies, 1929. Half title, frontispiece, illustrations by Edward Ardizzone, contemporary half dark green crushed morocco, spine faded to brown, slight nick to tail of spine.   Jarndyce Antiquarian Booksellers CCV - 161   2013   £150

Le Gallienne, Richard   1866-1947   *Robert Louis Stevenson: an Elegy and Other Poems Mainly Personal.*   London: John Lane, 1887.   First edition, half title, title portrait vignette, uncut, 16 page catalog (1895), pencil doodles on following f.e.p., original blue cloth, front board slightly marked, very good.   Jarndyce Antiquarian Booksellers   CCV - 254   2013   £50

Le Gallienne, Richard   1866-1947   *The Romance of Zion Chapel.*   London: John Lane, The Bodley Head, 1898.   Half title, partly uncut in original blue cloth, spine lettered in gilt, library label at foot of spine, slightly rubbed, library stamps of staffs T.C. and M.C.   Jarndyce Antiquarian Booksellers   CCV - 162   2013   £35

Le Guin, Ursula K.   *The Dispossessed.*   New York: Evanston: San Francisco: London: Harper & Row, 1974.   First edition, octavo, cloth backed boards.   L. W. Currey, Inc.   Utopian Literature: Recent Acquisitions (April 2013) - 140069   2013 $450

Le Mettrie, Julien Offray De   *Abrege de la Theorie Chymique.*   Paris: Lambert & Durand, 1741.   First edition, woodcut ornament on title, headpiece and initials, divisional title to traite du Vertige (but pagination continuous), little staining here and there, 12mo., contemporary speckled calf, gilt scallop shell at each corner on both covers, spine gilt in compartments, red lettering piece, little worn, joints cracked but cords holding, the copy deposited in the library of the chancelier Henri Francois d'Aguesseau by terms of the Privilege, with neat accession numbers on rear flyleaf, bibliographical notes at front, red ink stamp of P. E. Cathelineau of Paris and Vaas on page 111 (19th century), 20th century notes in French in blue ink to first part, good.   Blackwell's Rare Books   172 - 84   2013   £2200

Le Perouse, Jean Francois De Galaup, Comte De   *A Voyage Round the World Which was Performed (sic) in the Years 1785 ...*   Edinburgh: printed by J. Moir for T. Brown..., 1798.   folding engraved map, 3 engraved plates, bound without half title, map and plates and some pages bit browned, small 8vo., contemporary tree calf, spine gilt in compartments with ship in each, green lettering piece, black lettering piece in top compartment with crest and initials RT, slightly rubbed, head of spine chipped, Headfort armorial bookplate inside front cover, good.   Blackwell's Rare Books   B174 - 88   2013   £1500

Le Prince, Nicolas Theodore   *Essai Historique Sur la Bibliotheque Du Roi...*   Paris: Chez Belin, 1782.   First edition, 12mo., corner of Q4 torn away, contemporary mottled calf, spine gilt, red morocco label, head and foot of spine lightly chipped.   Marlborough Rare Books Ltd.   218 - 92   2013   £550

Le Queux, William   *The Eye of Ishtar.*   New York: Stokes, 1897.   First American edition, illustrations by Alfred Pearse, endpapers little foxed, spine slightly rubbed, at least very good copy.   Between the Covers Rare Books, Inc.   Sci-Fi, Fantasy & Horror - 45396   2013 $250

Le Sage, Alain Rene   1668-1747   *The History and Adventures of Gil Blas de Santillane.*   Edinburgh: printed for J. Massey and W. Sprout, 1775?   4 volumes, half titles, engraved frontispiece to each volume, 12mo., small tear to blank top corner volume I F9-11, slight browning, contemporary sheep, red and dark green morocco labels, some loss to lower edge of two boards where they meet spine, insect damage on one rear board, spines rather rubbed, one with vertical crack.   Jarndyce Antiquarian Booksellers   CCIV - 184   2013   £150

Le Sage, Alain Rene   1668-1747   *The Adventures of Gil Blas of Santillane.*   London: T. M'Lean, 1819.   3 volumes, hand colored frontispiece and plates, bound without half titles in 20th century full dark red morocco, lined and decorated in gilt, raised bands, compartments gilt and with gilt dentelles, all edges gilt, fine set.   Jarndyce Antiquarian Booksellers   CCV - 163   2013   £850

Le Sage, Alain Rene   1668-1747   *The Adventures of Gil Blas of Santillane.*   London: J. C. Nimmo and Bain, 1881.   3 volumes, 190 x 120mm., reddish brown crushed morocco gilt by Bayntun (stamp signed), covers with gilt French fillet border and circlet cornerpieces, raised bands, spine compartments similarly decorated, gilt ruled turn-ins, marbled endpapers, all edges gilt, 12 original etchings by de Los Rios, as called for, extra illustrated with 95 hand colored plates by Warner, Tomlinson and others, one board detached, other joints rather worn, couple with older cracks repaired by glue, spines bit scuffed, other general wear, couple of tiny fore edge tears to one plate, otherwise text and inserted plates in especially fine condition.   Phillip J. Pirages   63 - 317   2013 $850

Le Sage, Alain Rene   1668-1747   *The Adventures of Gil Blas of Santillana.*   Edinburgh: William Paterson, 1886.   3 volumes, 248 x 165mm., quite pleasing three quarter vellum over sturdy textured cloth boards by Tout (stamp signed), flat spines heavily gilt in compartments in antique style featuring large and intricate central fleuron, three brown morocco labels on each spine, marbled endpapers, gilt tops, title vignettes and 21 fine etched plates, including frontispiece by Adolphe Lalauze, large attractive bookplate of Hilda Leyel signed "A M H 1940" in each volume, top corners of volume 1 slightly bumped, turn-ins little spotted (trivial spots and superficial marks elsewhere to covers and spines, particularly to labels, otherwise excellent set, no significant wear, gilt still bright and attractive, slight offsetting from plates but very fine internally.   Phillip J. Pirages   63 - 319   2013 $550

Lea, Tom *The King Ranch.* Boston: Little Brown & Co., 1957. First edition, first issue, 4to., 2 volumes, signed by Tom Leaf in volume I, fine set in publisher's binding, housed in original publisher's decorated slipcase, which shows some wear. Ed Smith Books 75 - 38 2013 $450

Leach, Morgan Lewis *A History of Grand Traverse Region.* Traverse City: Grand Traverse Herald, 1883. First edition, 59 pages, quarto, original tan printed wrappers, near fine, minor foxing to wrappers, few small chip at extremities of rear panel, uncommon. Ken Sanders Rare Books 45 - 23 2013 $2500

Leadman, Alex D. H. *Battles Fought in Yorkshire: Treated Historically and Topographically.* printed for the author, 1891. First edition, 8vo., frontispiece, folding plan, 2 plates, text plates, good copy in original red cloth, gilt spine little dull, small mark to upper board, ownership name of H. A. Andrews at head of preface page, scarce. Ken Spelman Books Ltd. 73 - 171 2013 £35

Leaf, Munro *The Story of Ferdinand.* New York: Viking, Sept., 1936. First edition, first printing, 8vo., cloth backed pictorial boards, few spots on endpapers, else near fine in dust jacket (very nice, some spine sunning, few small chips on corners and slight fraying at spine ends), illustrations by Robert Lawson, inscribed and signed and dated by Leaf, exceedingly scarce, signed and in such nice condition. Aleph-Bet Books, Inc. 105 - 362 2013 $15,000

Leaf, Munro *Wee Gillis.* New York: Viking, 1938. First edition, limited to 525 copies signed by Robert Lawson and Munro Leaf, this copy also inscribed by Leaf, 4to., burlap covered boards, spine darkened, else fine in slipcase. some wear to case, full page illustrations by Lawson, nice. Aleph-Bet Books, Inc. 105 - 360 2013 $600

Leakey, L. S. B. *White African.* London: Hodder and Stoughton, 1937. First edition, original black cloth lettered in white, 24 plates, scattered spots, very good. R. F. G. Hollett & Son Africana - 120 2013 £75

Lear, Edward 1812-1888 *The Book of Nonsense.* London: F. Warne and Co., n.d., Twenty fifth edition, oblong 4to., original cloth, gilt over bevelled boards, trifle worn, 100 illustrations, front hinge cracking, few spots, inscription dated 1888. R. F. G. Hollett & Son Children's Books - 357 2013 £120

Lear, Edward 1812-1888 *A Book of Nonsense.* London: Routledge, Warne and Rougledge, preface dated, 1863. Tenth edition, oblong small 4to, older leather backed marbled boards, (112) pages, very good+, wood engraved text, pictures and verses, very scarce. Aleph-Bet Books, Inc. 105 - 363 2013 $975

Lear, Edward 1812-1888 *More Nonsense.* London: Frederick Warne & co., 1888. Oblong 4to., original cloth, gilt over bevelled board, corners little worn, neatly recased, printed on rectos only, mss. limerick (very bad one) written in ink, with drawing on verso of page 29, slight fingering to one or two leaves, but nice. R. F. G. Hollett & Son Children's Books - 358 2013 £150

Lear, Edward 1812-1888 *The New Vestments.* N.P.: Chamberlain Press, 1978. Limited to 100 numbered copies signed by Sarah Chamberlain, printed on very fine Kitakata paper, illustrations by Sarah Chamberlain with 2 wonderful wood engravings, 8vo., wrappers, fine. Aleph-Bet Books, Inc. 104 - 319 2013 $250

Lear, Edward 1812-1888 *Nonsense Songs and Stories.* London: Frederick Warne and Co., 1901. Ninth edition, large 8vo., original two-tone pictorial cloth gilt, trifle rubbed, illustrations by Lear. R. F. G. Hollett & Son Children's Books - 359 2013 £65

Lear, Edward 1812-1888 *The Pelican Chorus and Other Nonsense Verses.* London: F. Warne & co., n.d. 1950's, Square 8vo., original cloth, dust jacket rather torn and chipped, price of 9/- on flap, 7 full page color plates, numerous line drawings and endpapers by L. Leslie Brooke. R. F. G. Hollett & Son Children's Books - 360 2013 £25

Lear, Edward 1812-1888 *The Pelican Chorus and Other Nonsense Verses.* London: and New York: Frederick Warne, 1931. Square 8vo., 6 color plates plus numerous black and whites by L. Leslie Brooke, white cloth backed boards, previous owner's inscription dated 1931. Barnaby Rudge Booksellers Children 2013 - 020693 2013 $55

Lear, Edward 1812-1888 *Teapots and Quails and Other New Nonsenses.* London: John Murray, 1953. First edition, original pictorial boards, dust jacket trifle browned and spotted, 64 page, illustrations by Lear. R. F. G. Hollett & Son Children's Books - 361 2013 £40

Leatham, Diana *Celtic Sunrise: an Outling of Celtic Christianity.* 1951. First edition, maps, illustrations, 8vo., cloth, dust jacket, very good. C. P. Hyland 261 - 546 2013 £35

Leaves from a Life: Being the Reminiscences of Montagu Williams, Q. C. Macmillan, First edition, 2 volumes, portrait, good, cloth. C. P. Hyland 261 - 872 2013 £30

Leavitt, Nancy Ruth *Floating through the Desert.* Stillwater: 1988. Artist's book copy number one of a series of 7, hand painted and hand lettered in watercolor and gouache on Rives BFK paper by artist/author and signed by her, 7 x 10 inches, 14 leaves, bound loose as issued in handmade case of green cotton fabric with purple and darker green exposed threads, lined with acrylic pastepaper with malachite clasp, hand lettered and painted in watercolor and gouache,.   Priscilla Juvelis - Rare Books   56 - 16   2013 $2000

Leblanc, Maurice *Arsene Lupin Versus Herlock Sholmes.* New York: Ogilvie, 1910. First American edition?, soft covers, very good in soiled pictorial wrappers with some chipping to page edges and scrape on front cover.   Mordida Books   81 - 298   2013 $100

Leblanc, Maurice *The Confessions of Arsene Lupin.* Garden City: Doubleday Page, 1913. First American edition, corners rubbed, otherwise near fine, without dust jacket.   Mordida Books   81 - 299   2013 $125

Leblanc, Maurice *The Golden Triangle.* New York: Macaulay, 1917. First American edition, name on front endpaper, otherwise very good without dust jacket.   Mordida Books   81 - 300   2013 $85

Lecciones de Fortificacion de Campana, Sacadas de la Obras Modernas que Tratan del Arte Militar, y Particularmente de la Obra Clasica Francesa Titulada Diaro del Oficial de Ingenieros.   Paris: Libreria Americana, 1830. First edition, 114 pages, 24mo., period quarter calf over marbled boards, gilt decorations on spine, boards rubbed, signature on titlepage, faint dampstain to early leaves, later foxing and spotting, still about very good.   Kaaterskill Books   16 - 33   2013 $500

Leckie, William H. *The Military Conquest of the Southern Plains.* Norman: University of Oklahoma Press, 1963. First edition, numerous black and white photos and maps, gray cloth, very fine, pictorial dust jacket.   Argonaut Book Shop   Summer 2013 - 193   2013 $75

Lecky, E. *Letter from Old Father Christmas.* London: Raphael Tuck, n.d. circa, 1890. 4to., cloth backed pictorial card covers die-cut in shape of Santa, one small corner repaired, else near fine, beautiful chromolithographs by Emily Harding, very fine, rare.   Aleph-Bet Books, Inc.   104 - 122   2013 $650

Lecompte, Janet *Pueblo, Hardscrabble Greenhorn: The Upper Arkansas 1832-1856.* Norman: University of Oklahoma Press, 1978. First edition, portraits, photos, prints, maps, light blue cloth, very fine, pictorial dust jacket.   Argonaut Book Shop   Summer 2013 - 194   2013 $60

Leconte de Lisle, C. R. M. *Les Erinnyes Tragedie Antique.* Paris: A. Romagnol Editeur, 1908. First edition, number 184 of 190 copies on Arches paper (total edition 301), 25 original etchings + 12 original woodcut decorations and wood engraved color frames on each page by Frank Kupka, 11.25 x 8 inches, 89 pages, very handsome lightly brown morocco, signed by by Lemardeley, front cover with inlaid original copper plate for one of the etchings, spine with 5 raised bands, gilt lettering, all edges gilt, beautifully designed dentelles, nicely designed double endleaves and edges of covers, housed in matching slipcase, very handsome in as new condition. Gemini Fine Books & Arts., Ltd. Art Reference & Illustrated Books - 2013 $2500

Ledwidge, Francis *Selected Poems.* Dublin: New Island Books, 1992. First edition, 8vo., wrapper issue, near fine, from the library of Richard Murphy, inscribed for him by Seamus Heaney (provides introduction).   Maggs Bros. Ltd.   1442 - 105   2013   £200

Lee, Craig L. *Breaking through the Past to Modernity: The Art of Xgu.* Presumed first edition, numerous illustrations, very near fine, some very slight wear, beautiful copy, scarce.   Jeff Hirsch Books   Fall 2013 - 129219   2013 $200

Lee, Fred J. *Casey Jones.* Kingsport: Southern Pub., 1939. First edition, hardcover, very good, photos.   Beasley Books   2013 - 2013 $50

Lee, G. Herbert *An Historical Sketch of the First Fifty years of the Church of England in the Province of New Brunswick (1783-1833).* St. John: New Brunswick Historical Society, 1880. 12mo., purple pressed cloth boards, gilt titles and blindstamped to rear, covers worn and stained, sunned to spine, previous owner's name on inside front pastedown, author's presentation copy.   Schooner Books Ltd.   105 - 16   2013 $75

Lee, Harper *To Kill a Mockingbird.* Philadelphia: Lippincott, 1960. First issue of advance reading copy, slight spine lean, mild spine creasing, one small red spot and some edge sunning to off white wrappers, near fine.   Ken Lopez Bookseller   159 - 118   2013 $7500

Lee, Harper *To Kill a Mockingbird.* London: Heinemann, 1960. First English edition, crown 8vo., 296 pages, original maroon boards backstrip lettered silver, faint endpaper browning, edges faintly spotted, dust jacket head edge little frayed, one very short tear, very good.   Blackwell's Rare Books   B174 - 254   2013   £700

Lee, Harriet *Canterbury Tales.* London: G. G. and J. Robinson, 1797-1805. First edition, 5 volumes, 8vo., half titles in volumes 2, 3, 5 as issued not called for in others, lacks errata in volume 4, modern quarter calf, spine gilt with red morocco lettering pieces, scattered minor foxing and stains, very good, tight, clean set.   Second Life Books Inc.   183 - 240   2013 $1500

Lee, Katie *The Ballad of Gutless Ditch.* Jerome: Katydid Books & Music, 2012. 1/500 copies, 84 pages, quarto, brown cloth, fine, signed by Lee and illustrator, Robin John Anderson. Ken Sanders Rare Books 45 - 45 2013 $75

Lee, Laurie *Cider with Rosie.* London: Hogarth Press, 1959. First edition, first issue, line drawings by John Ward, prelims and edges lightly foxed, crown 8vo., original mid green boards, backstrip gilt lettered, owner's name on front free endpaper, bright, clean dust jacket with two very short tears, very good. Blackwell's Rare Books B174 - 255 2013 £185

Lee, Laurie *I Can't Stay Long.* Deutsch, 1975. First edition, frontispiece, line drawing by William Thomson, crown 8vo., original pale green boards, backstrip gilt lettered and decorated, dust jacket chipped at head, very good, inscribed by author. Blackwell's Rare Books 172 - 211 2013 £80

Lee, Laurie *We Made a Film in Cyprus.* London: Longmans Green, 1947. First edition, 8vo., illustrations, original buff cloth, small stain to base, dust jacket with small tear. J. & S. L. Bonham Antiquarian Booksellers Europe - 9770 2013 £45

Lee, Samuel *The Travels of Ibn Batuta.* London: 1829. First edition, extra title in red, black and blue with covering letter, 4to., original wrappers, some light wear to edges, colored title in red, black and blue identifying this as the copy printed for "His Grace the Duke of Leeds, a Subscriber to the Oriental Translation Fund". Maggs Bros. Ltd. 1467 - 54 2013 £1500

Lee, Sidney *A Life of William Shakespeare.* London: Smith, Elder & Co., 1898. Second edition, octavo, 2 photogravure plates, and four additional plates, bound by Riviere & son (stamp signed gilt on front turn-in), full brown crushed levant morocco expertly and almost invisibly rebacked, original spine laid down, front cover set with large oval miniature scene on ivory under glass by Miss C.B. Currie (stamped in gilt on front doublure:"Miniatures by C. B. Currie") within elaborate gilt frame incorporating onlaid red morocco gilt roses, spine in 6 compartments with five raised bands, gilt lettered in two compartments, with gilt date at foot, remaining four compartments decoratively tooled in gilt in similar design with onlaid red morocco gilt roses, board edges ruled in gilt, turn-ins ruled in gilt with gilt floral ornaments with onlaid red morocco gilt roses, green watered silk doublures and liners, top edge gilt, signed in gilt on fore-edges of front and rear boards "Cosway Binding" and "Invented by J. H. Stonehouse", superb example, inserted certificate leaf signed by Stonehouse and Currie and numbered in ink identifies this as being copy "No. 804 of the Cosway Bindings invented by J. H. Stonehouse, with Miniatures on Ivory by Miss Currie". Heritage Book Shop Holiday Catalogue 2012 - 32 2013 $13,500

Lee, Sophia *The Recess.* Dublin: G. Burnet et al, 1791. Third Irish edition, 2 volumes, 12mo., pages 236, 219, contemporary calf with leather label, light brown stains on some early leaves, some foxing and browning, horizontal tear in front endpaper of volume I. Second Life Books Inc. 183 - 241 2013 £350

Leet, Frank *Polka-Dot Cat.* Akron: Saalfield, 1930. Oblong 4to., diecut in shape of toy gingham cat on wheels, fine and unread, front and back covers illustrate front and back of a toy cat sitting on wheeled base, illustrations by Fern Bisel Peat, rare. Aleph-Bet Books, Inc. 104 - 413 2013 $375

Lefevre D'Etaples, Jacques *Musica Libris Quator Demonstrata.* Paris: Guillaume Cavellat, 1551. First separate edition, 4to., 44 leaves, Cavellat's large woodcut, printer's device on title, text diagrams, tables, woodcut initials, early 19th century calf, gilt, neatly rebacked retaining original spine, title very slightly soiled, faint marginal foxing, modern booklabel. Joseph J. Felcone Inc. Books Printed before 1701 - 62 2013 $4800

Lefevre, Raoul *Le Recueil des Histoires de Troyes.* Bruges: William Caxton, 1473. First edition in French, small folio, Lettre batarde, lacking 32 printed leaves and two blanks, early 19th century brown straight grain morocco by Charles Lewis, gilt and blind ruled in geometric patterns, gilt inner dentelles, gilt edges, fine, unrestored, the missing leaves are internal and first and last printed leaves are present from the collection of the Duke of Roxburghe (sale 1812) of the third Earl Spencer (sale 1823), John Dent, with his notes (sale 1827), P. A. Hanrott (sale 1834) the Earl of Ashburnham (sale 1897); Richard Bennett with his bookplate and John Pierpont Morgan with his bookplate and shelfmark. Heritage Book Shop 50th Anniversary Catalogue - 62 2013 $950,000

Lefevre, Raoul *Le Recueil des Hystoires Troyennes, ou est Comte nuc la Genealogie de Satume (&) de Juipter...* Lyons: Jacques Sacon, 1510. Extremely rare, small folio, lacks final blank, Gothic type, 98 woodcuts, 6 full page cuts, large device of Saccon on titlepage, on reverse is full page cut of the Siege, divided horizontally into two compartments, this also on n6; on I3 is the full page "Troye la Grande" repeated on I6, another full page cut on I6 and The Stratagem of the Horse on F6, in text are 92 cuts with only few repeated, 19th century crimson morocco gilt extra, by A. Motte, gilt dentelles, morocco doublures, gilt interlacements, gilt edges and clean and fresh, nicely margined copy in fine binding, from the renowned Fairfax Murray collection of French Books. Heritage Book Shop 50th Anniversary Catalogue - 63 2013 $85,000

The Legend of Saint Robert, the Hermit of Knaresborough. Knaresborough: Hargrove & Sons, 1818. 8 pages, small 8vo., uncut stitched as issued, disbound, old paste marks down the 'binding' edge, scarce. Ken Spelman Books Ltd. 73 - 118 2013 £50

Legendre, Adrien Marie *Essai sue la Theorie des Nombres.* Paris: Duprat, An VI, 1798. First edition, occasional slight browning or spotting, 4to., 19th century calf backed boards, vellum tips to corners, rebacked, preserving original spine, good.   Blackwell's Rare Books   Sciences - 69   2013   £2750

Legendre, Adrien Marie *Essai sue la Theorie des Nombres.* Paris: Courcier, 1808-1825. Second edition, with the two supplements, 3 parts in 1 volume, folding engraved plate to first supplement, occasional spotting, 1 gathering browned in first part, 4to., contemporary green speckled calf, gilt tooled borders on sides, stamp of College Royal de St. Louis, Universite de France, wreathed and crowned at centre of upper cover, flat spine gilt with twin red lettering pieces, marbled edges, matching pastedowns and front free endpapers, by Rivage with his ticket, spine and lower cover unevenly faded, head of spine little worn, good.   Blackwell's Rare Books Sciences - 70   2013   £500

Legge, Alfred O. *Sunny Manitoba: Its Peoples and Its Industries.* London: 1893. 297 pages, plates, colored folding map, original printed boards, recased, new endpapers, discrete library blindstamped on titlepage, no other markings.   Dumont Maps & Books of the West   124 - 73   2013 $100

Legh, Thomas *Narrative of a Journey in Egypt and the Country Beyond the Cataracts.* London: John Murray, 1817. Second edition, old full blind ruled calf, rather rubbed and stained, corners worn, rebacked in morocco, all edges gilt, frontispiece, folding map, 9 further plates.   R. F. G. Hollett & Son   Africana - 121   2013   £350

Lehane, Dennis *Mystic River.* New York: William Morrow, 2001. First edition, inscribed by author, very fine in dust jacket.   Mordida Books   81 - 311   2013 $65

Lehane, Dennis *Prayers for Rain.* New York: Morrow, 1999. First edition, uncorrected proof, signed by author, very fine in slick pictorial wrappers.   Mordida Books   81 - 310   2013 $60

Lehane, Dennis *Sacred.* New York: Morrow, 1997. First edition, advance reading copy signed by author, very fine in pictorial wrappers.   Mordida Books   81 - 309   2013 $60

Lehman, Agnes C. *The Flahertys of Aran.* Harrap, 1940. First edition, original cloth, dust jacket, slight chipping to head of spine, price clipped, illustrations by author.   R. F. G. Hollett & Son   Children's Books - 362   2013   £25

Lehmann, Rudolph Chambers *The Adventures of Picklock Holes Together with Perversion and a Burlesque.* London: 1901. First edition, 8vo., original green cloth, spine browned, 11 plates, front hinge cracked with some glue residue in gutter, endpapers browned, some light scattered foxing, still good copy.   Howard S. Mott Inc.   262 - 45   2013 $200

Leiber, Fritz *(Fafhrd and the Gray Mouser Saga): Swords and Deviltry; Swords Against Death; Swords in the Mist; Swords Against Wizardry; The Swords of Lankhmar; and Swords and Ice Magic.* Boston: Gregg Press, 1977. First U.S. hardcover edition, octavo, volumes, cloth.   L. W. Currey, Inc.   Fall Sampler Sept. 2013 - 144547   2013 $450

Leiber, Fritz *The Green Millennium.* New York: Lion Books (Lion Library), 1954. First paperback edition, light rubbing at extremities, pretty much fine, very scarce.   Between the Covers Rare Books, Inc.   Sci-Fi, Fantasy & Horror - 57054   2013 $600

Leiber, Fritz *The Secret Songs.* London: Rupert Hart Davis, 1968. First edition, octavo, boards.   L. W. Currey, Inc.   Utopian Literature: Recent Acquisitions (April 2013) - 140073   2013 $350

Leibniz, Gottfried Wilhelm *"Nouvelle Arithmetique Binaire. (with) explication de l'Arithmetique Binaire quie se Sert des Seuls Caracteres 0 & 1." in Historie (et Memoires) de l'Academie Royale des Sciences Annee MDCCIII.* Paris: Hocherau, 1720. 4to., complete volume, 12 engraved plates, some folding, original speckled calf, spine gilt in compartments, rebacked, preserving original spine, spine slightly worn, good.   Blackwell's Rare Books Sciences - 71   2013   £950

Leigh Fermor, Patrick *Three Letters from the Andes.* London: Murray, 1991. First edition, full page map, title vignette, 2 full page illustrations and jacket design by John Craxton, crown 8vo., original mid blue boards, backstrip gilt lettered, dust jacket, fine, signed by author.   Blackwell's Rare Books   172 - 212   2013   £200

Leigh, Edward *Select and Choice Observations Concerning All the Roman and Greek Emperors.* London: printed for J. Williams and are to be sold by Amos Curteyne Bookseller in Oxford, 1670. Third edition, woodcut portraits, 8vo., very good, clean, contemporary unlettered calf, raised bands, leading hinge cracked at head but firm, slight wear to board edges, armorial bookplate of Marquess of Headfort & 19th century bookseller's label of W. A. Masson.   Jarndyce Antiquarian Booksellers   CCIV - 18   2013   £380

Leigh, Elizabeth Medora *Medora Leigh: a History and Autobiography.* London: Richard Bentley, 1869. Half title, original orange cloth, some marks, spine faded, otherwise very good.   Jarndyce Antiquarian Booksellers   CCIII - 404   2013   £85

Leigh, Percival *The Comic English Grammar...* London: Richard Bentley, 1840. First edition, frontispiece plate, tailpiece and 48 illustrations after drawings by John Leech, very attractive polished calf, handsomely gilt by Riviere & Son (signed), covers bordered with gilt French fillet and small roundel cornerpieces, raised bands, spine gilt in compartments featuring elegant floral cornerpieces, sidepieces and centerpiece with surrounding small dots and stars, decorative bands at head and foot, red morocco label, gilt inner dentelles, marbled endpapers, top edge gilt, front joint very expertly repaired, original cloth bound in at end, morocco bookplate of Alexander McGrigor, very fine in especially pretty binding.   Phillip J. Pirages   63 - 312   2013 $350

Leigh, Percival *The Comic Latin Grammar.* London: Charles Tilt, 1840. First edition, 197 x 127mm., very attractive polished calf, handsomely gilt by Riviere & Son (signed on verso of front endpaper), covers bordered with French fillet and small roundel cornerpieces, raised bands, spine gilt in compartments, featuring elegant floral cornerpieces, sidepieces, and centerpiece with surrounding small dots and stars, decorative bands at head and foot, red morocco label, gilt inner dentelles, marbled endpapers, top edge gilt, 54 illustrations in text and 8 engraved plates after drawings by John Leech, joints slightly flaked (front joint just beginning to crack at head and foot), one inch tear in fore edge of one leaf (well away from text), excellent copy in very pretty binding, covers quite lustrous and text smooth, fresh and clean, bookplate of Alexander McGrigor.   Phillip J. Pirages   63 - 313   2013 $350

Leighton, John M. *Select Views of Glasgow and Its Environs.* Glasgow: Published by Joseph Swan, 1828. First edition, 276 x 216mm., handsome 19th century polished calf, covers with elaborate ruled and floral roll frame in gilt and blind, raised bands decorated with four gilt rules terminating in an arabesque at either end, gilt compartments formed by thick, thin and dotted rules, tan morocco title label, turn-ins tooled in blind, all edges gilt; with 33 engraved scenic plates printed on India paper and mounted, engravings done by Joseph Swan after drawings by J. Feming and J. Knox, original tissue guards (one missing), very thin crack along top three inches of front joint, joints otherwise not seriously worn, one large and two small abrasions to lower cover, original decorative binding solid, especially lustrous and altogether pleasing, hint of foxing (only) to some plates (two plates bit more foxed), endpapers and first few leaves at front and back with faint discoloration at corners, apparently from blue, otherwise fine internally, fresh and bright, clean throughout, first rate impressions of engravings.   Phillip J. Pirages   63 - 314   2013 $1250

Leikin, Nikolai Aleksandrovich *Where the Oranges Grow.* London: Greening and Co., 1901. First English edition, half title with ad on verso, title in black and red, original green pictorial cloth, slightly dulled but good plus copy.   Jarndyce Antiquarian Booksellers   CCV - 165   2013   £65

Leinster, Murray *Three Stories.* Garden City: Doubleday, 1967. First edition, fine in fine dust jacket, with tiny tear at foot, especially crisp and bright.   Between the Covers Rare Books, Inc.   Sci-Fi, Fantasy & Horror - 319790   2013 $50

Leland, John *The Itinerary of John Leland the Antiquary in Nine Volumes.* Oxford: printed at the Theatre, 1745. 1744. 1742. Second edition, 9 volumes, 8vo., some illustrations in text, light toning, occasional brown leaves particularly to volumes III and V, some slight marginal staining, contemporary light brown calf, gilt spines with red morocco labels, gilt borders, edges sprinkled red, scratched and rubbed, spines chipped with some small losses to endcap, pages worn, many cracking, upper board of volume VIII nearly loose, armorial bookplate to front pastedown and second armorial bookplate of John Gage, Lincoln's Inn.   Unsworths Antiquarian Booksellers   28 - 110   2013   £600

Lematire, Jules *ABC par Jules Lemaitre.* Tours: Mame, 1919. First edition, 4to., cloth backed pictorial boards, tips lightly rubbed, else near fine, illustrations by Job with full and partial page color illustrations.   Aleph-Bet Books, Inc.   104 - 8   2013 $475

Lemon, Mark *A Christmas Hamper.* London: George Routledge and Sons, 1875. 8 pages initials ads, frontispiece, 4 pages ads, 'Yellowback', original pictorial yellow boards, little rubbed and soiled, good plus.   Jarndyce Antiquarian Booksellers   CCV - 166   2013   £120

Leng, Charles W. *Staten Island and Its People: A History.* New York: Lewis Historical Publishing Co., 1930. First edition, 5 volumes, quarto, half buckram and cloth, 2 bookplates, small gouge in spine of volume five, else near fine or better, very uncommon.   Between the Covers Rare Books, Inc.   New York City - 291528   2013 $1250

Lenglet Dufresnoy, Nicolas *Geographia Antiqua et Nova; or a System of Antient and Modern Geography...* London: printed for John and Paul Knapton, 1742. 33 double page maps on guards, old waterstaining to first few leaves, rather faint, full contemporary calf, slight cracks to upper inch of both joints, but very firm, some worming to upper margin towards end, just touching ruled border of final two maps.   Ken Spelman Books Ltd.   75 - 19   2013   £395

Lenglet Dufresnoy, Nicolas *Geography for Children; or a Short and Easy method of Teaching and Learning Geography...* Shrewsbury: printed by Sandford and Maddocks, 1800. Folding double hemisphere world map as frontispiece, 3 engraved plates, 12mo., original sheep, roll tooled borders on sides, joints split, ends of spine worn, owners name in ink on upper cover, good, rare.   Blackwell's Rare Books   172 - 90   2013   £450

Lenier, Jules *A Midget Book of Mighty Mental Magic.* Fullerton: Baffles Press, 1994. Limited to 50 numbered copies, signed by author, 6.5 x 7.8 cm., cloth, slipcase with labels, from the collection of Donn W. Sanford.   Oak Knoll Books   303 - 44   2013 $350

Lennox, Sarah *The Life and Letters of Lady Sarah Lennox... also a Short Political Sketch of the Years 1760 to 1763 by Henry Fox, 1st Lord Holland.* London: John Murray, 1901. First edition, third printing, 2 volumes, especially attractive contemporary moss green three quarter morocco over lighter green linen by Wood of London (stamp signed), raised bands, spines handsomely gilt in compartments with large central fleuron within a lozenge of small tools and scrolling cornerpieces accented with gilt dots, marbled endpapers, top edge gilt, 30 photogravures of portraits, many by Sir Joshua Reynolds, engraved bookplate of F. Ambrose Clark, leather of spine and edges of boards darkened (as nearly always with green morocco) to olive-brown, offsetting to endpapers from bookplate and turn-in, fine set, the stiffly opening volumes with virtually no signs of use and handsome bindings lustrous and unworn.   Phillip J. Pirages   63 - 317   2013 $375

Lennox, Sarah *The Life and Letters of Lady Sarah Lennox 1745-1826.* London: John Murray, 1901. Third printing, 8vo., 30 plates, fine, specially bound in full contemporary dark red crushed morocco, raised ands and gilt ruled spine, gilt title to each upper board, set within gilt wreath, all edges gilt, gilt dentelles, silk markers, inscribed by John Murray and Evelyn Murray April 1902 for Miss Evelyn Moreton, some scattered foxing.   Ken Spelman Books Ltd. 75 - 154   2013   £220

Lenski, Lois *San Francisco Boy.* Philadelphia: J. B. Lippincott, 1955. First edition, 8vo., 176 pages, signed by Lenski, fine in very good++ dust jacket with minimal sun spine, soil, edgewear.   By the Book, L. C.   36 - 33   2013 $200

Lenski, Lois *Strawberry Girl.* Philadelphia: Lippincott, 1945. Stated first edition, 8vo., green cloth, fine in lightly soiled dust jacket, small piece off lower corner, irregular chip across top of spine, overall very good, 84 black and whites by Lenski, rare dust jacket, with handwritten letter from Lenski on her personal stationery laid in.   Aleph-Bet Books, Inc.   104 - 320   2013 $1200

Lenski, Lois *We Live in the Country.* Philadelphia: Lippincott, 1960. First edition, 8vo., 127 pages, fine in rubbed dust jacket.   Aleph-Bet Books, Inc.   104 - 321   2013 $100

Lentz, Harold *The Pop-Up Mother Goose.* New York: Blue Ribbon, 1934. Square 4to., pictorial boards, fine, illustrations by Harold Lentz with 3 great double page color pop-ups plus many black and whites.   Aleph-Bet Books, Inc.   105 - 467   2013 $350

Leonard, Elmore *Bandits.* New York: Mysterious Press, 1987. First edition, one of 26 specially bound lettered copies signed by author, very fine in slipcase without dust jacket, as issued.   Mordida Books   81 - 316   2013 $125

Leonard, Elmore *Bandits.* New York: Arbor House, 1987. First edition, inscribed by author, recipient's signature, fine in fine, price clipped dust jacket.   Ken Lopez Bookseller   159 - 120   2013 $150

Leonard, Elmore *La Brava.* New York: Arbor House, 1983. First edition, uncorrected proof copy, very fine in printed wrappers.   Mordida Books   81 - 315   2013 $85

Leonard, Elmore *City Primeval.* New York: Arbor House, 1980. First edition, very fine in dust jacket.   Mordida Books   81 - 314   2013 $90

Leonard, Elmore *Get Shorty.* New York: Delacorte Press, 1990. First edition, signed by author in blue ink, octavo, original quarter white linen over black boards, front cover stamped in blind with palm tree, spine lettered green, fine, original color pictorial dust jacket.   David Brass Rare Books, Inc.   Holiday 2012 Chapter Five - DB 00354   2013 $100

Leonard, Elmore *Gold Coast.* Allen, 1982. First hardback edition, usual marginal browning to text leaves, foolscap 8vo., original light blue boards, backstrip gilt lettered, dust jacket trifle creased at head of rear panel, light foxing to flaps, very good.   Blackwell's Rare Books   B174 - 256   2013   £500

Leonard, Elmore *Killshot.* New York: Arbor House/ Morrow, 1989. First edition, inscribed by author in year of publication, recipient's signature, fine in very near fine dust jacket with little lamination lift to top edge of front panel and small sticker (Macmillan of Canada) over price on front flap.   Ken Lopez Bookseller   159 - 121   2013 $150

Leonard, Elmore *The Switch.* London: Secker & Warburg, 1979. First hardcover edition, fine in price clipped dust jacket with small tar at lower corner of rear flap.   Mordida Books   81 - 313   2013 $300

Leonard, Hugh *Stephen D. A Play in Two Acts.* London: Evans Brothers, 1964. First edition, 8vo., original white cloth, lettered in black, dust jacket, uncommon, excellent copy, jacket slightly rubbed at extremities.   Maggs Bros. Ltd.   1442 - 176   2013   £50

Leonard, John William *History of the City of New York 1609-1909...* New York: Journal of Commerce and Commercial Bulletin, 1910. First edition, very good with rubbing to edges, head and tail of spine, bumps to corners and some scattered soiling to boards. Between the Covers Rare Books, Inc. New York City - 306764 2013 $200

Leonard, Zenas *Adventures of Zenas Leonard, Fur Trader.* Norman: University of Oklahoma Press, 1959. First edition thus, plates, maps, black cloth, very fine with pictorial dust jacket. Argonaut Book Shop Summer 2013 - 196 2013 $90

Leonardo Da Vinci 1452-1519 *Atlas der Anatomischen Studies in der Sammlung Ihrer Majestat Windsor Castel.* Johnson Reprint Co., 1980. Copy 198 of 300, 3 volumes, large folio, 2 volumes of text and one volume of plates, 400 facsimile plates, Nigerian royal blue goatskin quarter leather and linen boards with facsimiles placed in clamshell box, leather spine. James Tait Goodrich 75 - 135 2013 $4500

Leonardo Da Vinci 1452-1519 *Leonardo Da Vinci on the Human Body. The Anatomical, Physiological and Embryological Drawings of Leonardo Da Vinci.* New York: Schuman, 1952. Large 4to., pictorial boards, 506 pages, no dust jacket, nice, tight copy, nicely illustrated. James Tait Goodrich S74 - 173 2013 $125

Leonardo, Richard A. *History of Gynecology.* New York: Froben Press, 1944. Frontispiece, 25 illustrated plates, very good in original blue cloth, clean and tight. James Tait Goodrich S74 - 197 2013 $125

Leopardi *The Poems.* Cambridge: 1923. Large 8vo., 544 pages, very good, original cloth. Ken Spelman Books Ltd. 75 - 169 2013 £40

Lepecq De La Cloture, Louis *Observations sur les Maladies Epidemiques (Annee) (with) Collection d'Oservations sur les Maladies et Constitutions Epidemiques.* Paris: Rouen: De l'impr. de Vincent/Chez Didot et Mequignon; A Rouen: De l'imprimerie privilegiee, 1776-1778. First editions, 4to., full continental cat's paw calf, spine with five raised bands, two morocco lettering pieces, red on two volumes, brown and tan on the other, four compartments decorated with gilt florals, board edges ruled in gilt, marbled endpapers, all edges gilt, spines rubbed, one volume with shallow chip at head of spine and small chip at lower edge, few scuff marks to boards, otherwise bindings solid, leaves clean, very good set. Kaaterskill Books 16 - 56 2013 $2500

Lepper, John Heron *History of the Grand Lodge of Free and Accepted Masons of Ireland.* London: 1925. 1957. First edition, 2 volumes, illustrations, lower fore corner of volume 1 damaged, signed presentation copy from Crossle to a fellow mason, otherwise very good set. C. P. Hyland 261 - 548 2013 £500

Lerner, Howard D. *Primitive Mental States and the Rorschach.* Madison: International Universities Press, 1988. First edition, minor bumping to extremities else fine in very good dust jacket with tidemark at foot, tears to extremities and soiling to underside. Between the Covers Rare Books, Inc. Psychology & Psychiatry - 101508 2013 $55

Leroux, Gaston *The Phantom of the Opera.* New York: Bobbs Merrill, 1911. First American edition, color frontispiece and 4 striking two page color illustrations by Andre Castaigne as issued, contemporary owner name on front fly, bottom corners trifle bumped, near fine in very good example of the exceptionally rare dust jacket (some professional internal repair and some modest chipping at spine ends that continues a bit onto rear panel near crown, some modest flaws), true rarity. Between the Covers Rare Books, Inc. Sci-Fi, Fantasy & Horror - 85405 2013 $55,000

Leroux, Gaston *The Phantom of the Opera.* New York: Indianapolis: The Bobbs Merrill Co., 1911. First edition in English, octavo, one single page and four double page inserted plates with color illustrations by Andre Castaigne, original pictorial brown cloth, front and spine panels stamped in white and blind. L. W. Currey, Inc. Fall Sampler Sept. 2013 - 146513 2013 $1850

Leroux, Gaston *The Phantom of the Opera.* New York: Grosset & Dunlap 1911, really, 1925. Photoplay edition, page edges little soiled, else about fine in striking, very good dust jacket with some tears and small chips, attractive copy. Between the Covers Rare Books, Inc. Sci-Fi, Fantasy & Horror - 78336 2013 $850

Leskell, Lars *Stereotaxis and Radiosurgery. An Operative System.* Springfield: Charles C. Thomas, 1971. First edition, 8vo., 51 figures, gilt stamped black cloth, dust jacket, rubber stamps of Bland Wilson Cannon, M.D., scarce with jacket, very good. Jeff Weber Rare Books 172 - 183 2013 $450

Leslie, Frank, Mrs. *California. A Pleasure Trip from Gotham to the Golden Gate (April, May, June 1877).* New York: G. W. Carleton & Co., 1877. First edition, 24 woodcut plates, text illustrations, grayish brown cloth stamped in black and gold, light rubbing to spine ends, covers slightly stained, contemporary owner's inscription in pencil on end, very good, internally fine and clean. Argonaut Book Shop Summer 2013 - 197 2013 $175

Leslie, Joan *Two Faced Murder.*   Garden City: Doubleday Crime Club, 1946.   First edition, some faint spotting on endpapers, else fine in fine, bright dust jacket with faint crease on spine.   Mordida Books   81 - 321   2013 $65

Leslie, Shane   *The Cuckoo Clock and Other Poems.* Tilley Printing, Ledbury: under the Direction of the Stanbrook Abbey Press... for Iris C. Leslie, Worcester, 1987.   One of 30 copies (of an edition of 200), printed in black on cream wove handmade paper by Tilley printing, with illustrations, a number hand tinted by Margaret Adams, four color offset lithographic reproductions of 2 paintings by Irish Leslie, small folio, original tan cloth, backstrip printed in brown, cuckoo clock device and reproduction of author's signature blocked in brown on front cover, rough trimmed, fine. Blackwell's Rare Books   B174 - 388   2013   £250

Lessing, Doris   *The Habit of Loving.*   New York: Crowell, 1957.   First American edition, inscribed by author, recipient's signature, faint age toning to some pages, very near fine in very good, rubbed dust jacket with fading to red spine lettering.   Ken Lopez Bookseller   159 - 122   2013 $350

Lessons of Louisville: A White Community Response to Black Rebellion.   Louisville: SCEF Press/Southern Conference Educational Fund Press, 1970.   First edition, quarto, stapled wrappers, 24 pages, illustrations, some wrinkles on rear wrapper caused by production flaw, near fine. Between the Covers Rare Books, Inc.   165 - 81   2013 $175

Letchworth, Thomas   *Twelve Discourses, Delivered Chiefly at the Meeting-House of the People Called Quakers in the Park, Southwark.*   London: printed by J. W. Galabin, 1787.   First edition, 8vo., endpapers and blanks rather foxed, titlepage little browned, early 19th century half calf, marbled boards, leading hinge cracked, spine rubbed and slightly worn at head.   Jarndyce Antiquarian Booksellers CCIV - 185   2013   £85

Lethem, Jonathan   *Travelers.*   New York: Aperture, 2008. First edition, photos, inscribed by Lethem, tear to lower margin of first page of his story, else fine in illustrated boards, uncommon signed.   Ken Lopez Bookseller   159 - 123   2013 $125

A Letter to a Person of Quality, Occasion'd by the News of the Ensuing Parliament.   London: 1688?   4to., 8 pages, caption title, removed.   Joseph J. Felcone Inc.   Books Printed before 1701 - 75   2013 $90

A Letter to the author of the Vindication of the Ecclesiastical Commissioners Concerning the Legality of that Court. Oxford: 1688.   4to., 8 pages, caption title, removed. Joseph J. Felcone Inc.   Books Printed before 1701 - 63 2013 $100

Letters from the Front. Being a Record of the Part Played by Officers of the Bank in the Great War 1914-1919.   Toronto and Montreal: Canadian Bank of Commerce, Printed by Southern Press Limited, 1921.   Large 8vo., 2 volumes, red cloth with gilt to spine and gilt emblem of the bank on front cover, half title, 145 plates and folding map, cloth worn, generally good.   Schooner Books Ltd.   105 - 125   2013 $75

Lettre a Mon Peintre: Raoul Dufy.   Paris: Librairie Academique Perrin, 1965.   First edition, number 590 of 6200 numbered copies on velin de rives with extra suite of 27 lithographs, 27 lithographs, 18 by Dufy, very good plus in white paper wrappers with few light smudge marks to panels and interior, the book and extra lithographs housed in grey chemise with white leather spine that is soiled along hinges, light foxing to folder holding extra lithographs, not affecting them, slightly worn slipcase, 193 pages.   The Kelmscott Bookshop   7 - 73   2013 $1750

Levaillant, F.   *Second Voyage Dans L'Interieure de 'Afrique...*   Paris: chez J. Jansen et Compe, l'an 3 de La Republique, 1795.   First edition, 3 volumes, early 20th century half crimson morocco gilt by Christian of Eastbourne, small label removed from foot of each spine, top edge gilt, uncut, 3 half titles, 22 engraved plates, labels removed from endpapers, small stamps of Bibliotheca Oatesiana and an earlier German library, otherwise excellent, clean, sound set. R. F. G. Hollett & Son   Africana - 122   2013   £850

Leveling, Henrich Palmaz   *Anatomische Erklarung der Original Figuern von Andreas Vessa...*   Anton Attenhoeur, 1783.   Second issue of Leveling's edition, 2 folding plates, woodcut frontispiece, 22 full page woodcuts and numerous woodcuts in text, all printed from original woodblocks, folio, early 19th century quarter vellum boards, signature on title, inner edge of frontispiece remargined but not affecting image, tall well margined uncut copy, plates sharply impressed.   James Tait Goodrich   75 - 211   2013 $12,000

Levens, Peter   *A Right Profitable Booke for All Disease called the Pathway to Health.*   London: John Bale for Robert Bird, 1632.   Fifth edition, Text in black letter, paper toned in parts, paper erosion along edges, marginal fraying of pages and some text loss of last several leaves, title soiled and frayed and mounted, clean tear across H4, 4to., full modern mottled calf done in period style with morocco lettering label, nice, rare.   James Tait Goodrich   75 - 136 2013 $1500

Lever, Charles   1806-1872   *Confessions of Con. Cregan: the Irish Gil Blas.*   London: Wm. S. Orr, 1849-1850.   First edition, 14 monthly parts in 13 (as issued), original illustrated blue wrappers, 28 plates and numerous vignettes by Phiz, some wear to wrappers, small neat repairs to front wrappers of four issues, front wrapper to final part supplied from earlier issue, very good set, enclosed in two chemises and cloth slipcases.   The Brick Row Book Shop Miscellany Fifty-Nine - 31   2013 $800

Lever, Charles   1806-1872   *Roland Cashel.*   London: Chapman and Hall, 1850. First Book edition, 8vo., marbled paper over boards, three quarter leather, cover little worn at edges, otherwise very good, tight copy.   Second Life Books Inc.   183 - 242   2013 $150

Lever, Darcy   *The Young Sea Officer's Sheet Anchor; or a Key to the Leading and Rigging and to Practical Seamanship.*   London: sold by John Richardson, 1819. Second edition, 4to., engraved titlepage, 57 plates, uncut in original printed boards, expertly rebacked, later blue cloth, dust jacket, attractive copy.   Jarndyce Antiquarian Booksellers   CCV - 167   2013   £420

Levere, Trevor H.   *Chemists and Chemistry in Nature and Society 1770-1878.*   Aldershot and Brookfield: Variorum, 1994. 8vo. blue cloth, gilt stamped cover and spine titles, illustrations, bookplate of Burndy Library, fine.   Jeff Weber Rare Books   169 - 269   2013 $75

Levertov, Denise   *Embroideries.*   Los Angeles: Black Sparrow, 1969. First edition, a total of 700 copies, this one of 250 copies, sewn in wrappers (little soiled), signed by author Oct. 16th 1984, very good.   Second Life Books Inc.   183 - 243   2013 $50

Levine, Bernard R.   *Knifemakers of Old San Francisco.*   San Francisco: Badger Books, 1978. First edition, 4to., drawings, photos, gray cloth lettered in black, small rubber stamp to upper corner of front end, fine, pictorial dust jacket.   Argonaut Book Shop   Summer 2013 - 198   2013 $90

Levinson, Andre   *The Designs of Leon Bakst for the Sleeping Princess.*   London: Benn Brothers Ltd., 1923. 1/1000 copies, first edition, folio, vellum backed cloth top edge gilt, 54 mounted color plates with printed tissue guards and 2 other mounted decorations by Leon Bakst, full page portrait of Bakst after drawing by Pablo Picasso, endpapers slightly spotted, covers lightly soiled, spine darkened and rubbed, extremities slightly bumped, overall very good.   Gemini Fine Books & Arts., Ltd.   Art Reference & Illustrated Books - 2013 $3000

Levinson, C.   *"If There is a Why, You Can Live by Any How".*   Berkeley: Huey Newton Defense Committee, 1969? Mimeographed sheets, four pages printed rectos only, stapled in upper left hand corner, illustrated with 2 images of Newton, little age toning to extremities, two light horizontal folds, tiny tears, else about fine, scarce.   Between the Covers Rare Books, Inc.   165 - 230   2013 $150

Levis, Larry   *Elegy with a Thimbleful of Water in the Cage.*   Richmond: Laurel Press, 1994. First edition, one of 40 copies printed by hand on Lana gravure paper and signed by author and artist, large 4to., 2 original etchings by David Freed, original Echizen Washi over boards sewn Japanese style, very fine, beautiful book.   James S. Jaffe Rare Books   Fall 2013 - 92   2013 $850

Levy, Julien   *Surrealism.*   New York: Black Sun Press, 1936. First edition, one of 1500 copies on various color papers, 65 black and white images, cover design and jacket illustrated with collage by Joseph Cornell, clean, near fine, with some very slight bumping to top corner and vintage bookstore sticker to base of the rear pastedown in very good plus dust jacket with some minor edge wear and minuscule piece missing on front panel, scarce in any jacket.   Jeff Hirsch Books   Fall 2013 - 129107   2013 $750

Lewelyn, William   *An Exposition of the Beginning of Genesis.*   Leominster: printed by F. Harris (volume V: Glocester, printed by R. Raikes), 1790-1792. 5 volumes, 8vo., rare set, touch of marginal worming in 2 volumes, some dust soiling and browning, contemporary tree calf, spines divided by double gilt fillets, red morocco lettering pieces and small green oval labels (lost or defective on several volumes), old paper labels at foot of spines, very rubbed and scratches, some wear to endcaps and joint ends, sound.   Blackwell's Rare Books   172 - 91   2013   £900

Lewes, George Henry   *The Life and Works of Goethe.*   Boston: Ticknor and Fields, 1856. First American edition, 8vo., blindstamped brown cloth, some staining inside, but very good.   Second Life Books Inc.   183 - 244   2013 $150

Lewis, Angelo John   1839-1919   *More Magic.*   London: George Routledge and Sons, 1890. 8vo., titlepage vignette many illustrations in text, titlepage and index foxed and quite marked, pencil notes on magic to titlepage verso, occasional further foxing, brown pictorial cloth, gilt, all edges gilt, endcaps and corners lightly worn, pages rubbed, bit dusty, still good.   Unsworths Antiquarian Booksellers   28 - 180   2013   £60

Lewis, Clive Staples   1898-1963   *The Last Battle.*   London: Bodley Head, 1956. First edition, line drawings, some full page by Pauline Baynes, pages 184, crown 8vo., original pale blue boards, backstrip lettered in silver, little faint edge spotting, dust jacket trifle rubbed at head and tail of backstrip panel, foxed on rear panel as is usually the case, very good.   Blackwell's Rare Books   B174 - 257   2013   £900

Lewis, Clive Staples   1898-1963   *The Last Battle.*   London: Bodley Head, 1956. First edition, fine in dust jacket slightly frayed at top of spine, else nice and free of tears, illustrations by Pauline Baynes, nice.   Aleph-Bet Books, Inc.   104 - 322   2013 $2400

Lewis, Clive Staples   1898-1963   *The Last Battle.* London: Bodley Head, 1956. First edition, line drawings, by Pauline Baynes, crown 8vo., original pale blue boards, backstrip lettered in silver, little faint edge spotting, dust jacket trifle rubbed at head and tail of backstrip panel, with small delta shaped chip 1 x 1 cm. to rear panel adjacent to backstrip and tiny chip .5 x 1.1.cm and short tear to adjacent area of front panel, very good.   Blackwell's Rare Books   172 - 214   2013   £4000

Lewis, Clive Staples   1898-1963   *Perelandra.* London: John Lane, Bodley Head, 1943. First edition, original cloth, gilt, spine partially faded, dust jacket little worn and chipped, lower third of spine, lacking lower third of spine, fine and clean internally.   R. F. G. Hollett & Son   Children's Books - 364   2013   £180

Lewis, Clive Staples   1898-1963   *Prince Caspian: the Return to Narnia.* London: Geoffrey Bles, 1951. First edition, first printing, 8vo., blue cloth, 195 pages, slight lean a few faint spots, very slight rubbing, else very good+ in near very good dust jacket with some fraying and few small closed tears, illustrations by Pauline Baynes, this copy signed by author, rare thus.   Aleph-Bet Books, Inc.   105 - 368   2013 $7500

Lewis, Clive Staples   1898-1963   *The Silver Chair.* London: Geoffrey Bles, 1953. First edition, first printing, 8vo., navy blue cloth, 217 pages, fine in nice dust jacket with price intact, dust jacket has few soil marks on front panel, frayed at corners and spine ends, few small closed tears, illustrations by Pauline Byanes with black and white frontispiece, pictorial endpapers and black and white throughout text.   Aleph-Bet Books, Inc.   104 - 323   2013 $3850

Lewis, Clive Staples   1898-1963   *Vivisection.* London: National Anti-Vivisection Society, 1948. Frontispiece portrait, original blue wrappers, stapled as issued, slight marked, spine slightly faded, 12 pages.   Jarndyce Antiquarian Booksellers   CCV - 168   2013   £120

Lewis, Clive Staples   1898-1963   *The Voyage of the Dawn Treader.* Bles, 1952. First edition, line drawings throughout, some full page by Pauline Baynes, pages 224, crown 8vo., original pale blue boards lightly stained, backstrip lettered in silver, front endpaper maps, dust jacket just little frayed, mainly to head and tail of backstrip panel which is unfaded, faint browning to white area on backstrip panel and rear panel little soiled, overall in much better state than usual, very good.   Blackwell's Rare Books   B174 - 258   2013   £2000

Lewis, Ernest A.   *The Fremont, Cannon, High Up and Far Back.* Glendale: Arthur H. Clark, 1981. First edition, 17 illustrations, blue cloth, gilt, very fine.   Argonaut Book Shop   Summer 2013 - 116   2013 $125

Lewis, Janet   *The Wife of Martin Guerre.* San Francisco: Colt Press, 1941. First edition, large 8vo., decorations by Valenti Angelo, this one of 300 copies, hand colored by artist and signed by him, fine in slightly nicked dust jacket.   Second Life Books Inc.   183 - 245   2013 $100

Lewis, Meriwether   1774-1809   *Travels to the Source of the Missouri River and across the American Continent to the Pacific Ocean.* London: Longman, Hurst, Rees, Orme and Brown, 1814. First British edition, quarto, one large folding engraved map, 5 engraved plans on 3 plates, one page publisher's ads, bound with half title, original boards, spine professionally reinforced, original printed paper label, uncut, board edges and corners bumped and worn, paper label, bit chipped, barely affecting print, some minor professional repairs to back of map, in folds, few pages with some minor tears, not affecting text, final leaf with reinforcement along bottom edges, small old library stamp 2 previous owner's bookplates, very good.   Heritage Book Shop   Holiday Catalogue 2012 - 98   2013 $30,000

Lewis, Norman   *Naples '44.* London: Collins, 1978. First edition, 8vo., 206 pages, original red cloth, dust jacket, near fine.   J. & S. L. Bonham Antiquarian Booksellers   Europe - 9810   2013   £45

Lewis, Norman   *Voices of the Sea.* London: Hamish Hamilton, 1984. First edition, 8vo., 202 pages, original blue cloth, dust jacket.   J. & S. L. Bonham Antiquarian Booksellers   Europe - 9781   2013   £35

Lewis, Oscar   *The Big Four. The Story of Huntington, Stanford, Hopkins and Corcker and of the Building of the Central Pacific.* New York: Knopf, 1938. First edition, numerous illustrations, dark blue cloth, decorated and lettered gilt, very fine and bright.   Argonaut Book Shop   Summer 2013 - 201   2013 $90

Lewis, Oscar   *The First 75 Years. The Story of The Book Club of California.* San Francisco: Book Club of California, 1987. First edition, one of 1200 copies, 54 pages, title within decorative color border, numerous illustrations, color photos, cloth backed boards, decorated and lettered in gold very fine.   Argonaut Book Shop   Summer 2013 - 27   2013 $60

Lewis, Oscar   *Sea Routes to the Gold fields. The Migration by Water to California in 1849-1852.* New York: Alfred A. Knopf, 1949. First edition, illustrations, folding map, blue cloth, gilt, very fine, pictorial dust jacket (lightly worn at extremities), presentation inscription signed by author.   Argonaut Book Shop   Summer 2013 - 202   2013 $75

Lewis, Oscar   *Silver Kings: The Lives and Times of Mackay, Fair, Flood and O'Brien, Lord of the Nevada Comstock Lode.* New York: Knopf, 1947. First edition, signed by author, 306 pages, portraits, plates, fine with dust jacket, slightest of chipping to spine ends.   Argonaut Book Shop   Summer 2013 - 203   2013 $60

Lewis, Sinclair 1885-1951 *Main Street.* New York: Harcourt Brace and Howe, 1920. First edition, first issue (mixed issue?), with folio 54 unbattered but the 'y' in 'may' on page 387 imperfect, inscribed by author to Hugh Palmer, Aug. 20 1947, on front pastedown facing inscription is ownership inscription of Von Jagermann 1920, original dark blue cloth stamped in orange on front cover and spine, spine lightly sunned and edges of spine with small amount of wear, bit of light foxing to prelims, overall very good. Heritage Book Shop   Holiday Catalogue 2012 - 88   2013 $2000

Lewis, T. Percy *The Book of Cakes.* London: MacLaren & Sons, 1903. Large 4to., half title, rubricated text, color plates, original olive green cloth, slightly rubbed and dulled, hinges little weak. Jarndyce Antiquarian Booksellers   CCV - 169   2013   £450

Lewis, William *The Philosophical Commerce of Arts...* printed for the author, 1765. First edition, 4to., contemporary calf, red lettering piece, some worming at foot of spine and slight wear to extremities, Christie's Matthew Boulton label inside front cover, good. Blackwell's Rare Books   172 - 92   2013   £650

Lewis, Wyndham 1862-1957 *America and Cosmic Man.* London: Nicholson & Watson, 1948. Fine in blue cloth, nearly fine dust jacket with tiny scrape on spine, 8vo., 231 pages. Beasley Books   2013 - 2013 $60

Lewis, Wyndham 1862-1957 *The Art of Being Ruled.* Santa Rosa: Black Sparrow Press, 1989. New edition, one of 26 lettered copies, fine in fine dust jacket, 8vo., 460 pages. Beasley Books   2013 - 2013 $100

Lewis, Wyndham 1862-1957 *The Complete Wild Body.* Santa Barbara: Black Sparrow Press, 1982. Number 177 of 276 numbered copies signed by editor, Bernard Lafourcade on tipped in leaf, fine in fine, acetate dust jacket, large 8vo., 414 pages, illustrations by Lewis. Beasley Books   2013 - 2013 $60

Lewis, Wyndham 1862-1957 *Journey into Barbary. Morocco Writings and Drawings.* Santa Barbara: Black Sparrow Press, 1983. New edition, first printing, one of 26 lettered copies, signed by editor on tipped in leaf, fine in fine dust jacket, 15 drawings by Lewis, 8vo., 234 pages. Beasley Books   2013 - 2013 $100

Lewis, Wyndham 1862-1957 *Left Wings Over Europe; or How to Make a War About Nothing.* London: Cape, 1936. First edition, prelims and final few leaves lightly foxed, pages 336, crown 8vo., original scarlet cloth, backstrip and front cover blocked in black, tail edges rough trimmed, dust jacket soiled and chipped, good. Blackwell's Rare Books   B174 - 259   2013   £100

Lewitt, Alina *Blue Peter.* London: Faber & Faber, 1943. First edition, 4to., cloth backed pictorial board covers, fine in slightly worn dust jacket, illustrations by Lewitt and Him, rare. Aleph-Bet Books, Inc.   104 - 325   2013 $475

Lhote, Henri *The Search for the Tassili Frescoes.* RU, 1960. Original cloth, dust jacket price clipped, 237 pages, 4 maps, 101 illustrations, including extending centre-folding plate. R. F. G. Hollett & Son   Africana - 124   2013   £25

Lhuilier, Simon *Elemens Raisonnes d'Algebre.* Geneva: J. J. Paschoud, 1804. First edition, one folding engraved plate, few leaves slightly browned, 8vo., contemporary half sheep, very good. Blackwell's Rare Books   Sciences - 73   2013   £450

Lichtenberger, Henri *The Gospel of Superman: the Philosophy of Friedrich Nietzsche.* Edinburgh: T. N. Foulis, 1910. First edition, no. 1594 of 2000 copies, 20.5 cm., near fine in publisher's blue cloth with light fading to spine and age toning to endpapers. Between the Covers Rare Books, Inc.   Philosophy - 328155   2013 $60

Lichtenberger, James P. *Women in Public Life in The Annals, Volume LVI, November 1914.* Philadelphia: American Academy of Political and Social Science, 1914. First edition, 8vo., pages v, 194, index, maroon cloth, spine stamped in gilt, blindstamped on front with seal of Academy, front hinge tender, otherwise very good. Second Life Books Inc.   182 - 155   2013 $225

Lida *Coucou.* Paris: Flammarion, 1939. Oblong 4to., stiff pictorial wrappers, fine, beautifully illustrated with color and black and white lithographs by Feodor Rojankovsky. Aleph-Bet Books, Inc.   105 - 507   2013 $250

Lida *Quipic.* Paris: Flammarion, 1937. 4to. pictorial wrappers, near fine, brightly colored full page and in text lithos by Rojankovsky. Aleph-Bet Books, Inc.   104 - 497   2013 $250

Lida *Scaf La Foca. (The Seal).* Milano: Bompiani, n.d. circa, 1936. 4to., stiff pictorial wrappers, some cover soil, else fine, beautiful color lithographs by Feodor Rojankovsky, scarce. Aleph-Bet Books, Inc.   105 - 506   2013 $225

Liddell Hart, Basil Henry *Lawrence of Arabia.* N.P.: Corvinus Press, 1936. First edition, number 69 of 128 numbered copies, signed by both authors, fine in publisher's slipcase (somewhat worn), 4to., original tan cloth spine, decorated paper boards, gilt lettering. The Brick Row Book Shop   Miscellany Fifty-Nine - 30   2013 $325

Liddy, James *Moon and Star Moments.* New York: At Swin Press, 1982. First edition, 16mo., original blue wrappers, limited to 300 copies, fine, from the library of Richard Murphy. Maggs Bros. Ltd.   1442 - 177   2013   £100

Liebermeister, Carl Von *Handbuch der Pathologie und Therapie des Fiebers.* Leipzig: Verlag von F. C. W. Vogel, Contemporary half red morocco with raised bands, tooled spine, black cloth boards, light foxing and toning of paper, else very good.   James Tait Goodrich   S74 - 174   2013 $595

Liebig, Justus *Researches on the Chemistry of Food.* printed for Taylor and Walton, 1847. First edition, slightly foxed at either end, 8vo., original cloth with elaborate blind-stamped panel on sides, spine lettered gilt by Remnant and Edmonds, slightly worn at extremities, signature of Rev. Chas. Popham Miles, Glasgow 1848, inside front cover very good.   Blackwell's Rare Books   Sciences - 74   2013   £200

Liebman, Ellen *California Farmland. A History of Large Agricultural Landholdings.* Totowa: Rowman and Allanheld, 1983. First edition, text maps, green cloth, very fine, scarce. Argonaut Book Shop   Summer 2013 - 207   2013 $75

Liebreich, Richard *Atlas der Ophthalmmoscopie Darstellung des Augengrundes im Gesunden und Krankhaften Zustande.* Berlin: August Hirschwald; Paris: Germer Bailliere, 1863. First edition, folio, 12 chromolithographic plates, foxed, paper brittle (edges chipped), original printed wrappers mounted on modern case, new endleaves, quarter dark green cloth, cloth corners, original wrappers heavily rubbed, bottom edge of front cover re-enforced with dark beige paper, bookplate of Jerry F. Donin.   Jeff Weber Rare Books   172 - 185   2013 $1500

Liechtenstein, Marie Henriette Norberte, Prinzessin Von *Holland House...* London: Macmillan and Co., 1874. Large paper copy, photos, 2 volumes, 4to., 38 photos mounted on thick paper, numerous other text and full page plates, some foxing as usual, original blue morocco backed decorative cloth blocked in gold and black, top edges gilt, spines slightly sunned and cloth rubbed on corners, some slight damp marks to lower corner volume II, bookplates of Philip Currie, 1st Baron Currie (1834-1906).   Marlborough Rare Books Ltd.   218 - 93   2013   £385

Lieutaud, Joseph *Essais Anatomiques Contenant l'Histoire exacte de Toutes les Parties qui Composent le Corps de l'Homme...* Paris: Chez D'Houry, Guillyn, P. F. didot, 1766. New edition, 8vo., titlepage vignette, headpieces, decorative initials, tailpieces, 6 engraved folding plates, full contemporary mottled calf, raised bands, red leather spine label, gilt spine, all edges marbled, marbled endleaves, leather on top cover scuffed, very good.   Jeff Weber Rare Books   172 - 186   2013 $500

The Life and Confession of Peregrine Hutton, Who, with His Companion, Morris N. B. Hull, Was Executed in Baltimore July 14 1820 for Robbing the Mail and Murdering the Driver.... Baltimore: Benjamin Edes, 1820. 8vo., 29 pages, disbound, browned and foxed, edges chipped.   M & S Rare Books, Inc.   95 - 242   2013 $500

The Life and Death of Jenny Wren. York: Kendrew, n.d. circa, 1820. 16mo., yellow pictorial wrappers, 16 pages, fine, 16 nice woodcuts.   Aleph-Bet Books, Inc.   104 - 195   2013 $150

The Life and Memoirs of Mr. Ephraim Tristram Bates Commonly Called Corporal Bates, a Broken-Hearted Soldier... London: printed by Malachi *** for Edith Bates, relict of the aforesaid Mr. Bates and sold by W. Owen, 1756. First edition, 12mo., some offset browning to titlepage edges and final leaf, light browning to text, recent full calf, double gilt bands, gilt label. Jarndyce Antiquarian Booksellers   CCIV - 46   2013   £680

The Life Of Man Symbolised by the Months of the Year in a Series of Illustrations. London: Longmans, Green Reader and Dyer, 1866. First edition, 291 x 225mm., engraved title and allegorical frontispiece, numerous illustrations in text, 24 full page engravings by John Leighton, once splendid and still presentable contemporary pebbled grain green morocco, covers with elaborate gilt frames formed by plain rules and floral rolls, raised bands, spine gilt in compartments with corner volutes and intricate central fleuron, turn-ins gilt with cresting floral roll, marbled endpapers, all edges gilt, engraved title and allegorical frontispiece, numerous illustrations, 24 full page engravings by John Leighton, joints rather rubbed and flaked (with tiny cracks beginning), leather dulled in spots from preservative and little faded, small areas of gilt lost, other minor defects, binding still quite sound, front free endpaper with tiny tears and chips at fore edges, isolated minor marginal smudges, otherwise fine internally.   Phillip J. Pirages   63 - 316   2013 $125

Lightfoot, John *Flora Scotica; or a Systematic Arrangement, in the Linnaean Method of the Native Plants of Scotland and the Hebrides.* printed for B. White, 1777. First edition, 2 volumes, additional engraved titles, including illustration and 35 engraved plates, some folding, small hole in one leaf touching 2 letters on verso, short tear in lower margin of one leaf, occasional mild foxing, letterpress impression faint in few places, 8vo., contemporary sprinkled calf, gilt rules on either side of raised bands on spine, green lettering pieces, numbered direct, slight wear ad cracking of joints but good and solid, ownership inscription on flyleaves of both volumes of Wm. Burton Lightfoot dated 1817 and of C. A. Pitowsky dated 1872, good.   Blackwell's Rare Books   Sciences - 75   2013   £900

Lighton, William Beebey *Narrative of the Life and Sufferings of a Young British Captive.* Concord: Pub. by the author, Allison and Forst, Printers, 1836. First edition, 12mo., 9 plates, contemporary paper covered boards with leather spine, worn, upper hinge cracking, title and text stained, spotty foxing, one leaf with clean tear, fair only, lacks frontispiece. M & S Rare Books, Inc. 95 - 50 2013 $200

Lima, Antonieetta Iolanda *Soleri, Architecture as Human Ecology.* N. P.: Cosenti/Jaca Book, n.d., Special print for the Cosanti Foundation, fine in near fine dust jacket, laid in is Soleri's Bubble Diagram printed on special card, 4to., 407 pages. Beasley Books 2013 - 2013 $65

Linche, Richard *Diella: Certaine Sonnets.* Edinburgh: E. & G. Goldsmid, 1887. One of two copies (this copy unnumbered), there were also 97 copies on paper, 197 x 130mm., pleasing modern black half morocco over marbled boards, flat spine with vertical gilt titling, marbled endpapers, top edge gilt, titlepage printed in red and black, one gathering with mild (naturally occurring) discoloration to vellum, otherwise pristine in unworn binding. Phillip J. Pirages 63 - 478 2013 $1250

Lincoln, Abraham 1809-1865 *Political Debates Between Hon. Abraham Lincoln and Hon. Stephen A. Douglas in the Celebrated Campaign of 1858 in Illinois...* Columbus: Follett, Foster and Co., 1860. First edition, later issue with numeral '2' at bottom of page 13, royal octavo, original brown textured cloth with blindstamped borders tied by floral devices in corners and with blindstamped central device, spine lettered gilt, gilt slightly faded, head and tail with some light shelfwear, edges lightly rubbed, foxing throughout as usual, quite light, previous owner's bookplate, overall beautiful copy. Heritage Book Shop Holiday Catalogue 2012 - 100 2013 $1000

Lindbergh, Anne Morrow *North to the Orient.* New York: Harcourt Brace & Co., 1935. Fourth printing, 255 pages, original cloth, silvered, frontispiece and maps by Charles Lindbergh, few spots. R. F. G. Hollett & Son Polar Exploration - 35 2013 £25

Lindeberg, David C. *Studies in the History of Medieval Optics.* London: Variorum Reprints, 1983. 8vo., teal cloth, gilt stamped cover and spine titles, fine, rare. Jeff Weber Rare Books 169 - 272 2013 $140

Linder, Robert *Explorations in Psychoanalysis: a Tribute to the Work of Theodor Reik.* New York: Julian Press, 1953. First edition, very good with light wear to spine ends, good only dust jacket with extensive wear to spine and along top edge, significant use of clear tape on spine, signed by Reik on frontispiece. Between the Covers Rare Books, Inc. Psychology & Psychiatry - 283263 2013 $200

Linderman, Frank Bird *Recollections of Charley Russell.* Norman: University of Oklahoma Press, 1963. First edition, review copy with slip laid in portraits, reproductions, drawings by Russell, aqua cloth, very fine, pictorial dust jacket. Argonaut Book Shop Summer 2013 - 210 2013 $90

Lindgren, Astrid *Pippi in the South Seas.* New York: Viking, 1959. First edition, 8vo., cloth, 126 pages, fine in slightly worn dust jacket, color dust jacket and full and partial page pen and inks by Louis Glanzman. Aleph-Bet Books, Inc. 105 - 369 2013 $200

Lindman, Maj *Dear Little Dear.* Chicago: Whitman, 1953. 4to., cloth, pictorial paste-on, fine in dust jacket with chip and closed tear, color lithos by Lindman. Aleph-Bet Books, Inc. 105 - 370 2013 $225

Lindman, Maj *Flicka, Ricka, Dicka Bake a Cake.* Chicago: Whitman, 1955. First edition, first printing, 4to., cloth pictorial paste-on, fine in fine+ dust jacket, many lovely full page lithos by author, scarce in such nice condition. Aleph-Bet Books, Inc. 104 - 326 2013 $225

Lindsay, J. *History of the Muskerry Foxhounds 1742-1914.* 1914. First edition, 11 pages, wrappers, erratum slip, very good. C. P. Hyland 261 - 553 2013 £45

Lindsay, Lady *About Robins.* London: Frederick Warne, n.d. circa, 1890. 4to., original cloth backed pictorial boards, trifle marked, pages 155, 7 pages in color and numerous drawings, scattered spotting. R. F. G. Hollett & Son Children's Books - 368 2013 £75

Lindsay, Lady *About Robins. Songs, Facts and Legends Collected and Illustrated by...* London: Routledge, circa, 1890. 4to., black paper over boards stamped in faded gilt, ex-library with private bookplate, donor's presentation on blank, stickers on cover, cover worn at edges, hinges tender, rear flyleaf creased, otherwise very good, 7 color plates. Second Life Books Inc. 183 - 247 2013 $100

Lindsay, Norman *The Magic Pudding: Adventures of Bunyip Bluegum and His friends Bill Barncle & Sam Sawnoff.* Sydney: L. Angus & Robertson, 1918. First edition, first issue with patterned endpapers and spine stamped in gold, 4to., cloth backed pictorial boards, slight bit of toning to edge of covers, else fine condition in dust jacket with mounted color plate, dust jacket is very good+ with old repairs on verso at folds, color plate title plus full and partial page black and whites by author. Aleph-Bet Books, Inc. 105 - 371 2013 $6250

Lindsay, Norman *The Magic Pudding.* Sydney: Angus & Robertson, 1954. Original blue cloth, little marked, pages 171, illustrations. R. F. G. Hollett & Son Children's Books - 369 2013 £25

Lindt, J. W. *Picturesque New Guinea with an Historical Introduction and Supplementary Chapters on the Manners and Customs of the Papuans.* London: 1887. First edition, 50 full page autotype plates, original green cloth, gilt, little rubbed, inscribed by author for Revd. J. Dawson 1919. Maggs Bros. Ltd.   1467 - 84   2013   £1500

Linen Hall Library *Catalogue of the Books in the Irish Section.* 1917. First edition, 8vo., cloth, very good.   C. P. Hyland   261 - 85   2013   £75

Ling, Roth H. *Great Benin.* London: Routledge & Kegan Paul, 1968. Reissued edition, small 4to., original cloth gilt, dust jacket little worn and creased, 275 illustrations, scarce. R. F. G. Hollett & Son   Africana - 125   2013   £180

Lingenfelter, Richard E. *Death Valley and the Amargosa. A Land of Illusion.* Berkeley: University of California Press, 1986. First edition, viii, 664 pages, photos, facsimiles and maps, gilt lettered brown cloth, very fine with pictorial dust jacket.   Argonaut Book Shop   Recent Acquisitions June 2013 - 193   2013 $60

Linne, Carl Von   1707-1778   *A Dissertation of the Sexes of Plants.* London: printed for the author and sold by George Nicol, 1786. 8vo., half title, final ad leaf, uncut, partially unopened, disbound.   Jarndyce Antiquarian Booksellers   CCIV - 187   2013   £220

Lionni, Leo *Fish is Fish.* Pantheon Books, 1970. First edition, folio, lime green cloth, book very good+ in like dust jacket, one quarter inch mark on dust jacket cover, some light foxing to bottom edge of boards.   Barnaby Rudge Booksellers   Children 2013 - 021333   2013 $90

Lionni, Leo *The Greentail Mouse.* Pantheon Books, 1973. First edition, blue cloth, very good+ in like dust jacket, folio, $4.50 price on dust jacket with 10/73 at bottom of flap.   Barnaby Rudge Booksellers   Children 2013 - 021332   2013 $150

Lipman, Peter W. *The 1980 Eruptions of Mount St. Helens, Washington.* Washington: GPO, 1981. First edition, thick quarto, photos, graphs, charts, maps, pictorial cloth, covers lightly rubbed, fine.   Argonaut Book Shop   Recent Acquisitions June 2013 - 194   2013 $175

Lippincott, Sara Jane *New Life in New Lands: Notes of Travel...* New York: J. B. Ford, 1873. First edition, 8vo., 413 pages, 8 pages ads, pictorial cloth, nice, bright copy. Second Life Books Inc.   182 - 156   2013 $150

Lipschutz, Peggy *The World of Peggy Lipschutz. A Portfolio of Her Graphic Work.* Chicago: Comm. to Salute PL, probably 1970's, First edition, portfolio signed by Lipschutz, loose sheets in portfolio, 9 x 12 inches, this set with extra suite of prints, fine.   Beasley Books   2013 - 2013 $50

Lissauer, Frank *A Visit to Ireland.* Leicester/ Wymondham: Cog Press/Brewhouse Press, 1975. Number 78 of 120 hand numbered copies, large 8vo., original green cloth, decorated in gilt, fine.   Maggs Bros. Ltd.   1442 - 84   2013   £50

Lister, Joseph   1827-1912   *The Collected Papers of Joseph Baron Lister.* Oxford: Clarendon Press, 1909. First collected edition, thick 4to., 2 volumes, frontispiece photos, 14 plates, tables, full gilt stamped black cloth (blue cloth volume 2), hinges starting, head and base of spine chipped, extremities bit rubbed (volume I), early ownership signatures of Robert Broh-Khan, very good.   Jeff Weber Rare Books   172 - 188   2013 $350

Lister, Martin *Conchyliorum Bivalvium Utriusque Aquae Exercitatio Anatomica Tertia. Huic Accedit Dissertatio Medicinalis de Calculo Humano.* London: Sumptiubs authoris impressa, 1696. First edition, 4to., 10 engraved plates, terminal blank Z4 in first work, the Dissertatio with its own titlepage and pagination, contemporary sprinkled calf, very skillfully rebacked period style, small early shelf mark in red ink on endpaper and on title, minor paper flaw in S2 just grazing catchword, very faint foxing in fore-edge, very lovely copy, text and plates clean and fresh, armorial bookplate of A. Gifford, DD of the Museum, presentation copy inscribed by author for Mr. Dalone.   Joseph J. Felcone Inc.   Books Printed before 1701 - 64   2013 $10,000

Lister, R. P. *Allotments.* Andoversford: Whittington Press, 1985. 237/300 copies (of an edition of 335), printed on Zerkall mouldmade paper and signed by author and artist, 41 delightful wood engravings by Miriam Macgregor, text printed in black and green, oblong 8vo., original quarter brown cloth, printed label, cream boards with repeated pale and dark green engravings overall, untrimmed, board slipcase with printed label, fine.   Blackwell's Rare Books 172 - 313   2013   £200

Lister, Raymond *The Emblems of Theodosius of the Unity of Endymion.* Cambridge: Golden Head Press, 1969. 43/50 copies (of an edition of 59), 9 plate, 4to., original bright blue wrappers, good.   Blackwell's Rare Books B174 - 344   2013   £50

Literary and Political Examiner Feb. - May 1818. Cork: Bolster, 1818. 4 issues, 251 pages, modern boards with leather label, very good.   C. P. Hyland   261 - 554   2013   £500

Little Ah Sid. London: Raphael Tuck, n.d. circa, 1890. 8vo., pictorial wrappers, all edges gilt, near fine, illustrations by Willie Ostrander and T. R. Kennedy, magnificent wrap-around pictorial covers with heavy gilt highlights with chromos on every page of text, excellent condition.   Aleph-Bet Books, Inc.   105 - 127   2013 $300

A Little Black Book. Marcham: The Alembic Press, 1995. Limited to 100 numbered copies, 7.2 x 6 cm., sewn in 8 sections with a Coptic binding in heavy textured black boards, 63 pages, printed in black and red, from the collection of Donn W. Sanford.   Oak Knoll Books   303 - 30   2013 $125

Little Boy Blue. Bobbs Merrill, 1917. Large 4to., pictorial boards, fine in dust jacket (dusty), illustrations by Fanny Cory with 6 color plates and in 2 color one very page of text.   Aleph-Bet Books, Inc.   105 - 150   2013 $325

Little Boy Blue and Other Nursery Rhymes. Blackie and Son, n.d. 1930's, Large 8vo., original card wrappers, glazed pictorial upper board by artist, John Hassall, drawings by Hassall, some brown stains to lower margins in places, otherwise very good, scarce.   R. F. G. Hollett & Son   Children's Books - 266   2013   £85

Little Folks: a Magazine for the Young. London: Cassell, 1887-1894. Parts 1 and 2, 13 bi-annual volumes, large 8vo., contemporary half red roan gilt, original owner's name (Emily Barratt) in gilt on each upper board, some rubbing to extremities, few surface defects to leather in places, each volume with 2 chromolithographs and numerous full page and text illustrations, some tinted, attractive collection.   R. F. G. Hollett & Son   Children's Books - 133   2013   £450

The Little Gleaner. London: Houlston & Wright, 1960-1961. Volumes VII and VIII, thick 12mo., original half roan gilt, 1 pictorial titles and 2 frontispieces.   R. F. G. Hollett & Son   Children's Books - 370   2013   £30

Little Marian. Philadelphia: American Sunday School Union, n.d. circa, 1860. 8vo., pictorial wrappers, neat spine mends, tight and very good+, diecut in shape of little girl, delicately illustrated with color lithographs by F. Moras, quite rare.   Aleph-Bet Books, Inc.   105 - 542   2013 $1200

Little Miss Muffet. New York: McLoughlin, 1902. Small 8vo., wrappers, 8 pages, including covers, very good.   Barnaby Rudge Booksellers   Children 2013 - 021497   2013 $55

Little Old Woman. New York: McLoughlin Bros., n.d. circa, 1865. 12mo., pictorial wrappers highlighted in gold, mounted on linen, fine, 8 brightly colored three quarter page illustrations that are well printed, full page color pictorial title, nice copy, beautiful copy.   Aleph-Bet Books, Inc.   104 - 342   2013 $300

The Little Ones' Sunday Picture Book. London: Ernest Nister, n.d. circa, 1900. 4to., original cloth backed pictorial boards, lower boards little bruised, tinted illustrations.   R. F. G. Hollett & Son   Children's Books - 416   2013   £75

Little Red Riding Hood. London: Dean and Son, 1894. First edition, tall 8vo., glazed card covers shaped at top, 4 chromolithographs plus cover, spine repaired with archival repair tape, very good.   Barnaby Rudge Booksellers   Children 2013 - 021320   2013 $85

Little Red Riding Hood. New York: Blue Ribbon, 1935. 8vo., pictorial boards, some cover soil, else very good, illustrations by Harold Lentz with pictorial endpapers, full page and in text black and whites plus one wonderful double page pop-up in vibrant color.   Aleph-Bet Books, Inc.   105 - 466   2013 $150

Little Red Riding Hood Cutouts. Racine: Whitman, 1939. Oblong 4to. stiff card wrappers, name on cover and slightly dusty, else fine and unused, 6 pages of die-cut cardboard cut-outs in color.   Aleph-Bet Books, Inc.   104 - 206   2013 $250

Little Will. Oakland: California Pacific Press, inscribed 1886, 3 x 4.5 inches, 16 pages, wrappers, some cover rubbing, very good.   Aleph-Bet Books, Inc.   105 - 211   2013 $200

The Little Would-Nots. New York: Samuel Gabriel Sons & Co., 1922-1925. 4to., cloth with pictorial paste-on, corner of one page repaired, else fine in dust jacket with mounted color plate, illustrations by Mary La Fetra Russell, beautiful copy, scarce.   Aleph-Bet Books, Inc.   104 - 423   2013 $750

Little, Constance   *The Black Piano.* Garden City: Doubleday Crime Club, 1948. First edition, pages darkened, otherwise very good in price clipped dust jacket with couple of closed tears and tiny wear at top of spine.   Mordida Books   81 - 322   2013 $100

Lively, Penelope   *Moon Tiger.* London: Andre Deutsch, 1987. First edition, fine, crisp copy, dust jacket price clipped.   Ed Smith Books   78 - 31   2013 $100

Livermore, Mary A. *My Story of the War...* Hartford: Worthington, 1889. 8vo., 700 pages, illustrations, front hinge tender, edges little soiled, red cloth blindstamped and printed in gilt, ex-library with bookplate and stamps, very good.   Second Life Books Inc.   182 - 157   2013 $60

The Lives of Illustrious and Eminent Persons of Great Britain. London: printed for Longman, Hurst, Rees, Orme and Brown, 1820. First edition, 63 engraved portraits; quite pretty brown morocco gilt and inlaid in most animated design by Andrew Grieve of Edinburgh (stamp-signed), covers bordered by multiple plain and decorative gilt rules enclosing unusual gilt frame of baroque style flowers, leaves, volutes, swirls and quatrefoils, cornerpieces of inlaid red morocco quatrefoils outlined in gilt, central panel dominated by red morocco oval medallion adorned with gilt laurel wreath, oval with four red morocco petals from which spring gilt fronds and quatrefoils, these terminating at top and bottom of panel with ochre morocco outlined mandorlas containing gilt floral sprig, background of panel exuberantly decorated with many small gilt flowers, inlaid green morocco dots, ochre morocco half moons and assorted small tools, raised bands, spine elegantly gilt in compartments with central red morocco oval framed in gilt with oval branch cornerpieces, turn-ins with gilt frames formed by multiple decorative rules, marbled endpapers, all edges gilt, intermittent minor foxing, more prominent on first few leaves, one page with small inkspot obscuring a couple of letters, otherwise fine, text clean and fresh, binding lustrous and virtually unworn.   Phillip J. Pirages   61 - 111   2013 $1500

Lives of the Fathers. Oxford: John Henry Parker, 1840-1856. 15 titles bound in 14 volumes, original gilt lettered dark blue cloth, volume 6 chipped on spine, otherwise good sound set.   Ken Spelman Books Ltd.   75 - 107   2013   £100

Living Picture Book with the Wonder of Spectacles. London: W. Walker, n.d. circa, 1930. Oblong 4to.., pictorial boards, fine, 15 pages of photos can only be seen by using the 3-d glases provided in front pocket, illustrations in blue on bottom of each page.   Aleph-Bet Books, Inc.   104 - 420   2013 $225

Livingstone, David   1813-1873   *The Last Journals of David Livingstone, in Central Africa, from 1875 to His Death.* London: John Murray, 1874. First edition, 2 volumes, original pictorial plum cloth gilt, spines faded and little rucked and repaired at head and foot, 21 full page illustrations, 24 text woodcuts and 2 colored folding maps, one in rear pocket to volume 1 (little browned on reverse) scattered spotting, but very good, sound set, pictorial bookplate of F. Ransom.   R. F. G. Hollett & Son   Africana - 131   2013   £395

Livingstone, David   1813-1873   *Missionary Travels and Researches in South Africa.* London: John Murray, 1857. First edition, original brown embossed cloth gilt, neatly recased with much of backstrip relaid, extending wood engraved frontispiece by J. W. Whymper, engraved portrait, 2 folding maps (1 in rear pocket), 22 full page woodcut plates, folding plan, text woodcuts, very nice, armorial bookplate of Tindall Lucas, later issue with woodcuts replacing tinted lithographs of first issue.   R. F. G. Hollett & Son   Africana - 127   2013   £275

Livingstone, David   1813-1873   *A Popular Account of Dr. Livingstone's Expedition to the Zambesi and Its Tributaries....* London: John Murray, 1875. Original green cloth, gilt over bevelled boards, folding map, 34 woodcut illustrations, flyleaves foxed, prize label on pastedown, joints just cracking, otherwise very nice.   R. F. G. Hollett & Son   Africana - 128   2013   £85

Livingstone, David   1813-1873   *A Popular Account of Missionary Travels and Researches in South Africa.* London: John Murray, 1861. First edition, original plum pebble grain cloth, gilt, extremities trifle bumped or frayed, 34 woodcut illustrations, including folding frontispiece, and folding map.   R. F. G. Hollett & Son   Africana - 129   2013   £120

Livingstone, David N.   *Geography and Enlightenment.* Chicago and London: University of Chicago Press, 1999. First edition, 8vo., illustrations, figures, navy cloth, gilt stamped spine title, Burndy bookplate, fine.   Jeff Weber Rare Books   169 - 276   2013 $85

Livius, Titus   *Titi Livii Patavini Historiarum Libri Qui Extant.* Paris: apud Fredericum Leonard, 1679. 5 volumes bound as 6, 4to., engraved half title and 2 engraved maps, folding engraved plate and 1 other engraved plate, light toning and some spotting, contemporary Cambridge style panelled calf, spines darkened with stain and paneled gilt, red morocco labels, rubbed at joints and corners, joints cracked, endcaps worn, some labels lost, contemporary armorial bookplate of "Sr Robert Clayton of the City of London/Knight Alderman & Mayor thereof Ano. 1679", covered up by later plain endpapers (volume 4 excavated locally to reveal identity), early 19th century armorial bookplate of Stephen Lowdell.   Unsworths Antiquarian Booksellers   28 - 24   2013   £450

The Livre Rouge; or the Red Book... Dublin: Byrne, 1790. First Irish edition, 8vo., 160 pages, front hinge loose, bound in leather backed paper boards, rubbed, somewhat worn, paper lacking from front cover, some library stamps inside, good copy, entirely printed in red.   Second Life Books Inc.   183 - 8   2013 $1100

Lizars, John   *Observations on Extractions of Diseased Ovaria.* Edinburgh: Danie Lizars, 1825. Folio in original publisher boards with alter renewed cloth spine, light toning and foxing, five hand colored plates.   James Tait Goodrich   75 - 137   2013 $3750

Llewellyn, L. L. Jones   *Fiberositis (Gouty, Infective, Traumatic): So Called Chronic Rheumatism Including Villous Synopsis of Knee and Hip and Sacro-Iliac Relaxation.* London: William Heinemann, 1915. Thick 8vo., color plates, photos, figures, errata slip inserted on page 1, blue cloth, gilt stamped spine title, extremities worn and with some staining, inner hinges cracked, good, scarce.   Jeff Weber Rare Books   172 - 192   2013 $100

Llewellyn, Richard *How Green Was My Valley.* New York: Macmillan, 1941. (1940). Later printing, round-robin, signed in fountain pen on location during making of the film on July 19 1941, gift copy from Freda Knill (niece of cast member Thomas A. Hughes) to her daughter, with autographs and inscriptions of Roddy McDowall, Maureen O'Hara, Walter Pidgeon, Donald Crisp, Barry Fitzgerald, Sara Allgood, Anna Lee, T. Arthur Hughes, Richard Fraser and Evan H. Evans; fair to good only, binding intact, shaken and with fraying to edges of cloth, in very good supplied dust jacket with some rubbing and light wear at extremities. Ed Smith Books   75 - 39   2013 $1750

Lloyd, Elizabeth Maria *Exercises in the Gospel Narrative of the Life of Our Lord...* London: Sampson Low, 1833. Second edition, 4 pages ad, original green limp cloth, all edges gilt, with 4 folding plates backed on linen with 50 numbered plates, original green limp cloth, in original green paper box, paper label, remarkably well preserved, very good.   Jarndyce Antiquarian Booksellers   CCV - 171   2013   £250

Lloyd, H. E. *The German Tourist.* London: D. Nutt, 1837. First edition, 8vo., 200 pages, 17 steel engravings, contemporary purple blindstamped morocco bound boards, all edges gilt, joints little rubbed, plates foxed or browned, original blindstamped morocco, all edges gilt, spine rubbed.   J. & S. L. Bonham Antiquarian Booksellers   Europe - 3960   2013   £160

Lloyd, Nathaniel *A History of the English Country House from Primitive Times to the Victorian Period.* London: Architectural Press, 1951. Third impression, folio, numerous half tone plates and illustrations, original green cloth, upper cover and spine lettered gilt, original printed dust jacket, frayed at edges.   Marlborough Rare Books Ltd.   218 - 94   2013   £65

Lloyd, Richard *The Prayer and the Address to the Volunteer Association of the Bank of England Upon the Consecration of Its Colours on September 2 1799...* printed by John March, 1799. Printed on thick paper, flyleaves foxed, 24 pages, small 4to., contemporary navy blue straight grained morocco, gilt ruled borders on sides, upper cover gilt lettered with salient part of the title, gilt edges, minor wear, front inner hinge broken but stitching holding, very good.   Blackwell's Rare Books   B174 - 6   2013   £800

Llwyd, Richard *The Poetical Works of...* Whittaker and Co., 1837. First collected edition, portrait and frontispiece plate, very good in original blindstamped and gilt lettered cloth, some wear to head and tail of spine.   Ken Spelman Books Ltd.   75 - 102   2013   £50

Llywelyn, Robin *Portmeirion. Images by Leslie Gerry.* Andoversford: Whittington Press, 2008. 161/225 copies (of an edition of 350), printed in concertina form on sturdy cream Zerkall mouldmade paper and signed by author and artist with 7 superb double page illustrations drawn on an electronic tablet and digitally colored by Leslie Gerry and a further 3 decorations in same form, text imposed on intermediate double page openings with further double page text opening at beginning of text, titlepage printed in black and orange, small folio, original unlettered boards, illustrated overall, reproducing one of Gerry's illustrations, board slipcase, new.   Blackwell's Rare Books   172 - 314   2013   £145

Lobagola, Bata Kindai Amgoza ibn *An African Savage's Own Story.* Alfred A. Knopf, 1930. First edition, original cloth, 6 illustrations.   R. F. G. Hollett & Son   Africana - 132   2013   £35

Lobstein, J. F. Daniel *A Treatise Upon the Semeiology of the Eye for the Use of Physicians and of the Countenance for Criminal Jurisprudence.* New York: C. S. Francis, 1830. First edition, 8vo., original cloth backed boards, printed paper label, minor wear and waterstaining, quite good.   M & S Rare Books, Inc.   95 - 204   2013 $300

Locke, John   1632-1704 *An Abridgement of Mr. Locke's Essay Concerning Humane Understanding.* Dublin: printed by and for J. Hyde and E. Dobson, 1728. Fourth edition, small chip from blank margin of first text leaf (clear of text), 12m., contemporary sprinkled calf, slightly later hand lettered paper label to spine (chipped at edges), bit of wear to fore corners, small waxmark to front board, very good, scarce.   Blackwell's Rare Books   B174 - 92   2013   £550

Locke, John   1632-1704 *An Essay Concerning Humane Understanding.* London: 1690. First edition, first issue, with the "Eliz. Holt" imprint, the "SS" of "Essay" correctly printed and typographical ornament aligned, this copy contains two ms. corrections in prelims found in most copies of first issue and 52 additional errata neatly listed in three columns under printed errata on a2 verso, folio, one of 10 copies specially bound by John Graves for presentation in full dark red morocco, covers with double gilt fillet enclosing a central gilt panel of the same fillet with stylized floral devices at each corner, spine in seven compartments with six raised bands, elaborately framed gilt device in each compartment, gilt board edges, all edges gilt, few tiny wormholes to front cover, some light marginal dampstaining, overall excellent copy, housed in quarter red morocco clamshell case. Heritage Book Shop   50th Anniversary Catalogue - 64   2013 $85,000

Locke, John   1632-1704 *Letters Concerning Toleration.* London: printed for A. Millar, 1765. First collected edition, quarto, frontispiece, full contemporary calf, rebacked preserving original spine, decorated in gilt, previous owner's bookplate and signature, handsome copy.   Heritage Book Shop   50th Anniversary Catalogue - 65   2013 $10,000

Locke, John 1632-1704 *Some Thoughts Concerning Education.* London: printed for A. and J. Churchill at the Black Swan in Pater Noster Row, 1693. First edition, octavo, contemporary calf, expertly rebacked at early date preserving original spine, covers bordered on three sides with double blind rule and with floriated blind border at joints, spine in six compartments with five raised bands, sprinkled edges, holograph ink title on front board "Education of Young Persons", early holograph notes on pastedown endpapers, signatures D-F with small wormtracks affecting approximately 12 leaves, manuscript ex-libris of Philip Webber on titlepage dated 1745 with another ink signature on verso of title, minor soiling in few places, very good. Heritage Book Shop   50th Anniversary Catalogue - 66   2013 $9000

Locke, John 1632-1704 *Some Thoughts Concerning Education.* Dublin: printed by Will. Forrest, 1728. Ninth edition, 12mo., frontispiece, full contemporary panelled calf, central panel with small tulip cornerpiece decorations, raised bands, red morocco label, armorial bookplate of the Marquess of Headfort.   Jarndyce Antiquarian Booksellers   CCV - 172   2013   £480

Locker-Lampson, Hannah Jane *What the Blackbird Said.* London: George Routledge, 1881. First edition, small 4to., original decorated cloth, excellent copy, cloth little soiled, extremities worn, inscribed by author for Kate Greenaway, excellent copy, cloth little soiled, extremities worn.   Maggs Bros. Ltd.   1460 - 368   2013   £450

Lockhart, J. G. *Rhodes. A New Biography Based, for the first time, On Unrestricted Use of the Rhodes Papers.* London: Hodder and Stoughton, 1963. Original cloth, gilt dust jacket, 18 plates and maps on endpapers.   R. F. G. Hollett & Son   Africana - 133   2013   £25

Lockhart, John Gibson 1794-1854 *John Bull's Letter to Lord Byron.* Norman: University of Oklahoma Press, 1947. Half title, plates, original maroon cloth, booklabel of Alex Bridge, very good in slightly worn price clipped dust jacket. Jarndyce Antiquarian Booksellers   CCIII - 406   2013   £35

Lockhart, John Gibson 1794-1854 *Letter to the Right Hon. Lord Byron for John Bull.* London: printed by and for William Wright, 1821. First edition, disbound, top edge slightly damp affected, booklabel of Alex Bridge.   Jarndyce Antiquarian Booksellers   CCIII - 405   2013   £450

Lockhart, John Gibson 1794-1854 *The Life of Robert Burns.* Edinburgh: Constable & Co., 1828. First edition, portrait, contemporary half calf, spine with raised bands and devices in gilt, dark green leather label, hinges little rubbed, armorial stamp "DTM" contemporary ownership inscription of D. Mackay.   Jarndyce Antiquarian Booksellers   CCIII - 61   2013   £125

Lockhart, John Gibson 1794-1854 *The Life of Sir Walter Scott.* Edinburgh: Adam and Charles Black, 1853. 8vo., full leather, 11 engravings, gilt decorated spine, all edges gilt, joints repaired.   Barnaby Rudge Booksellers   Biography 2013 - 020942   2013 $75

Lockhart, John Gibson 1794-1854 *Memoirs of the Life of Sir Walter Scott.* Boston and New York: Houghton Mifflin and Co., 1902. Cambridge edition, 213 x 149mm, 5 volumes, lovely contemporary red half morocco, beautifully gilt in style of Doves Bindery, raised bands, spines in fine gilt compartments featuring sprays of tulips, marbled boards and endpapers, top edge gilt, other edges untrimmed and (except for the prefatory material in the first volume), entirely unopened, frontispiece portraits, small portions of two spine bands, corners and just few joints with insignificant wear (the rubbing carefully refurbished), one leaf with jagged fore edge from rough opening, but lovely set in nearly fine condition, bindings unusually lustrous and text virtually pristine, because obviously unread.   Phillip J. Pirages   63 - 431   2013 $2400

Lockman, John *The Entertaining Instructor; in French and English.* London: printed for A. Millar, 1765. First edition, complete with half title, one or two spots here and there, 12mo., original speckled sheep, black lettering piece on spine, joints cracked and corners worn, armorial bookplate inside front cover of Smithe of Exeter, good.   Blackwell's Rare Books   B174 - 93   2013   £350

Lockman, John *The History of Greece.* London: printed for C. Hitch and L. Hawes and others, 1761. 12mo., some light foxing and browning, contemporary mottled calf, raised bands, spine rubbed, slightly worn at head, label chipped with loss.   Jarndyce Antiquarian Booksellers   CCIV - 188   2013   £45

Loeb, Harold A. *Doodah.* New York: Boni & Liveright, 1925. First edition, foxing to endpages and edges of text block, near fine, very good dust jacket with some blended staining and tanning, minor edge chipping and narrow, closed tear at mid spine.   Ken Lopez Bookseller   159 - 124   2013 $600

Loederer, Richard *A Voodoo Fire in Haiti.* London: Jarrolds, 1935. First edition, hardcover.   Beasley Books   2013 - 2013 $50

Lofting, Hugh *Doctor Dolittle's Caravan.* New York: Frederick Stokes, Oct., 1926. Stated first edition, illustrations by Lofting with beautiful color frontispiece, color pictorial endpapers, plus a profusion of black and whites in text. Aleph-Bet Books, Inc.   104 - 328   2013 $225

Lofting, Hugh *Doctor Dolittle's Circus.* New York: Stokes, 1924. First edition, 8vo., yellow pictorail cloth, pictorial paste-on, some cover soil and rubbing, very good, illustrations by Lofting, scarce.   Aleph-Bet Books, Inc.   105 - 373   2013 $300

Lofting, Hugh *The Story of Doctor Dolittle.* New York: Stokes, 1920. First edition, 8vo., orange cloth, color plate on cover, 180 pages, pictorial endpapers, color frontispiece, black and white plates plus many full page line illustrations, scarce. Aleph-Bet Books, Inc. 104 - 328 2013 $1000

Logan, John Daniel *The New Apocalypse and Other Poems of Days and Deeds in France.* Halifax: T. C. Allen & Co., 1919. 8vo., pages 39, frontispiece, illustrated card covers, slightly frayed at edges, otherwise very good. Schooner Books Ltd. 101 - 103 2013 $50

Lomas, John *In Spain.* London: A. & C. Black, 1908. First edition, 8vo. folding map, illustrations, original red decorative cloth. J. & S. L. Bonham Antiquarian Booksellers Europe - 8982 2013 £30

London Almanack for the Year of Christ 1792. London: printed for the Company of Stationers, 1792. (24) pages, engraved view of Guild Hall folded into binding forming 4 pages, 64mo., slight dusting, tax stamp on first opening, original marbled paper covers. Jarndyce Antiquarian Booksellers CCIV - 38 2013 £125

London, Jack 1876-1916 *Before Adam.* New York: Macmillan Co., 1907. First edition, painted spine lettering rubbed but easily readable, small spot on front board, slight foxing on titlepage, otherwise tight, near fine, lacking rare dust jacket. Between the Covers Rare Books, Inc. Sci-Fi, Fantasy & Horror - 94487 2013 $300

London, Jack 1876-1916 *The Call of the Wild.* New York: Macmillan Co., 1903. First edition, octavo, frontispiece, 10 color plates included in pagination, text illustrations, some printed in blue and some in color, titlepage printed in blue and black, original vertically ribbed green cloth, front cover and spine decoratively stamped in white, red, black, and gilt, top edge gilt, others uncut, pictorial endpapers, printed in blue with dog-team and mountain scene, original dark grey printed dust jacket, jacket with restoration along folds, bit of dampstaining to top edge of front panel, closed tear along spine of jacket, cloth extremities slightly worn and bumped, occasional finger soiling to few margins of text, binding slightly skewed, very good, scarce edition. Heritage Book Shop Holiday Catalogue 2012 - 101 2013 $5000

London, Jack 1876-1916 *Jack London at Yale.* Westwood: Connecticut State Committee/Ariel Press, wrappers, good, both front and rear wrapper detached, as is frontispiece, but all present with small chip to corner of front wrapper, uncommon as first edition, 8vo. Beasley Books 2013 - 2013 $65

London, Jack 1876-1916 *The Turtles of Tasman.* New York: Macmillan, 1916. First edition, 8vo., 268 pages + ad, mauve cloth stamped in yellow, orange and blue, little light soiling on cover and nick at extremities of spine, otherwise near fine. Second Life Books Inc. 183 - 250 2013 $300

London, Jack 1876-1916 *White Fang.* New York: Macmillan, 1906. First edition, second printing with titlepage tipped in, 8vo., original slate blue vertically ribbed cloth (little faded), stamped in white, gold and blue black, very good in morocco backed cloth slipcase. Howard S. Mott Inc. 262 - 92 2013 $275

London, Jack 1876-1916 *The Works.* New York: The Review of Reviews Company, 1917. 192 x 132mm., 12 volumes, publisher's blue buckram, spines with black and gilt pictorial titling, top edge gilt, 32 black and white plates, including frontispiece in each volume, one double page map and numerous illustrations in text, one board with small indentation, hint of rubbing to extremities, isolated short marginal tears, other trivial imperfections, otherwise very fine set, clean, bright and unworn. Phillip J. Pirages 63 - 321 2013 $175

The Long Vacation. London: H. Hills, 1708. Second edition, a Hills piracy, 12mo., modern cloth, 16 pages. Howard S. Mott Inc. 262 - 93 2013 $175

Long, A. A. *The Hellenistic Philosophers, volume 2: Greek and Latin Texts.* Cambridge, et al: Cambridge University Press, 1988. 8vo., x, 512 pages, red cloth, gilt stamped cover and spine titles, ownership signature, fine, rare in cloth. Jeff Weber Rare Books 169 - 277 2013 $60

Long, Frank Belknap *John Carstairs Space Detective.* London: Fantasy Books, n.d., 1951. First British edition, octavo, pictorial wrappers. L. W. Currey, Inc. Fall Sampler Sept. 2013 - 145361 2013 $125

Long, Haniel *Malinche (Dona Marina).* Santa Fe: 1939. First edition, dust jacket with horizontal crease, book near fine. Dumont Maps & Books of the West 124 - 74 2013 $75

Long, James *The Book of the Pig. Its Selection, Breeding, Feeling and Management.* London: Upcott Gill, 1886. First edition, 8vo., 36 wood engraved plates, frontispiece slightly foxed, occasional light fingermarks to margins, original decorative boards in green cloth and gilt with embossed illustrations and faux pigskin grain, little cocked, very proficiently rebacked with original spine retained, almost intact, corners and lower hinge repaired, very good, three inkstamps of Chas. and Thos. Harris & Co. Ltd. to prelims, 1904 leaflet from Board of Agr. & Fisheries on Pig Breeding and Feeding loosely inserted. Unsworths Antiquarian Booksellers 28 - 181 2013 £400

Long, John *Voyages and Travels of an Indian Interpreter and Trader.* London: printed for the author, 1791. First edition, folding engraved map, 4to., contemporary calf, gilt spine rubbed, some offsetting to map, lovely copy.   Maggs Bros. Ltd.   1467 - 122   2013   £2750

Long, Manning *Vicious Circle.* New York: Duell, Sloan & Pearce, 1942. First edition, very good in good+ dust jacket, scarce, tape ghosts to endpapers and pastedowns, some paper loss to rear pastedown where dust jacket has been taped and was removed, Kraft paper glued to verso of dust jacket, presumably the remains of old style jacket protector, dust jacket trimmed approximately 1/4 inch at lower edge with some loss of lettering, despite flaws, scarce jacket remains intact without fading.   Leather Stalking Books October 2013 - 2013 $50

Long, Stephen H. *Voyage in a Six-Oared Skiff to the Falls of Saint Anthony in 1817.* Philadelphia: 1860. First edition, 88 pages, map, original printed wrappers, binding reinforced, wrappers soiled with minor chip to back wrapper, else clean and very good.   Dumont Maps & Books of the West   124 - 75   2013 $125

Longard, John R. *Knots, Volts and Decibels, an Informal History of the Naval Research Establishment 1940-1967.* (with) *Seas, Ships and Sensors, an Informal History of the Defence Research Establishment Atlantic 1968-1995.* Dartmouth: Defence Research Establishment Atlantic, 1993. 2003., Quarto, half title, maps, diagrams, numerous black and white illustrations, both in very good condition, previous owner's address label to half title.   Schooner Books Ltd.   104 - 160   2013 $75

Longfellow, Henry Wadsworth   1807-1882 *Courtship of Miles Standish.* Boston: Houghton Mifflin, 1920. First Wyeth edition, 4to., green gilt cloth, pictorial paste-on, very fine in original dust jacket (spine darkened, else near fine), illustrations by N. C. Wyeth, rare in such nice jacket. Aleph-Bet Books, Inc.   104 - 593   2013 $850

Longfellow, Henry Wadsworth   1807-1882 *The Courtship of Miles Standish.* Boston and New York: Houghton Mifflin Co., 1920. Tercentenary Edition, 241 x 178mm., 8 color plates by N. C. Wyeth, original publisher's cloth with full color illustration by Wyeth mounted on front cover, illustrated endpaper, original dust jacket repeating cover illustration, verso of dust jacket reinforced with seven short pieces of transparent tape, several very minor closed tears at jacket edges, white portions of wrapper somewhat soiled, but illustrated panel bright and pleasing and jacket as a whole still very good, volume itself with very narrow band of faint discoloration along back of cover, otherwise extremely fine.   Phillip J. Pirages   63 - 505   2013 $450

Longfellow, Henry Wadsworth   1807-1882 *Evangeline.* London: George Routledge & Co., 1856. New edition, 31 engravings, original dark blue gilt decorated cloth, some slight rubbing, new front endpaper.   Ken Spelman Books Ltd.   75 - 119   2013   £35

Longfellow, Henry Wadsworth   1807-1882 *Golden Legend.* Hodder & Stoughton, 1910. 4to., gilt pictorial cloth, fine in publisher's box, illustrations by Sidney Meteyard, with magnificent tipped in color plates.   Aleph-Bet Books, Inc.   104 - 73   2013 $850

Longfellow, Henry Wadsworth   1807-1882 *Hyperion a Romance.* New York: Samuel Colman, 1839. First edition, Volumes I-II, 12mo., original tan boards, brown endpapers, printed paper labels slightly rubbed, minimal wear and chipping to these fragile boards, very superior, most unusual in fine condition.   M & S Rare Books, Inc.   95 - 205   2013 $375

Longfellow, Henry Wadsworth   1807-1882 *The Poetical Works.* London: Routledge, 1861. New edition, frontispiece and wood engraved illustrations, original blue morocco grained cloth, bevelled boards, ornate gilt blocked covers with title set within gilt roundel, spine gilt decorated, corners and head and tail of spine little rubbed, early inscription on front endpaper.   Ken Spelman Books Ltd.   75 - 127   2013   £40

Longfellow, Henry Wadsworth   1807-1882 *Tales of a Wayside Inn.* Boston: Ticknor & Fields, 1863. First American edition, first printing state of ads dated "November 1863", 12mo., original brown cloth (lower 2 inch front hinge repaired, little faded), extra engraved title, couple of leaves have small pieces of corners off, excellent copy in folding case, Christmas 1863 gift inscription in pencil.   Howard S. Mott Inc.   262 - 94   2013 $200

Longfellow, Henry Wadsworth   1807-1882 *The Works.* Boston and New York: Houghton Mifflin Co. circa, 1904. Riverside edition, 200 x 130mm., not unpleasant contemporary dark brown half calf by Ernst Hertzberg & sons (signed on rear turn-in), raised bands, spines with elongated compartment decorated with drawer handle cornerpieces, red morocco label on each spine, marbled endpapers, top edge gilt, other edges rough trimmed, frontispiece, spines faded to olive green and bit marked and abraded, handful of joints with wear, one volume with occasional minor foxing in margins, additional minor problems, otherwise excellent, binding sturdy and not without appeal, text showing almost no signs of use.   Phillip J. Pirages   63 - 323 2013 $95

Longinus, Dionysius *On the Sublime.* London: E. Johnson, successor to Mr. B. Dod, 1770. Fourth edition, 8vo., engraved frontispiece, internally bright, publisher's ads at end, few pencil marks to margins plus pencilled notes to r.f.e.p., versos and rear pastedown, contemporary tan calf, red morocco label to spine, gilt title and borders, spine very lightly scuffed, upper joint little creased but overall very good.   Unsworths Antiquarian Booksellers   28 - 25   2013   £175

Longley, Michael *A Jovial Hullabaloo.* London: Enitharmon Press, 2008.   Number 9 of 50 copies signed by author, tall 8vo., original quarter burgundy cloth, marbled paper boards, printed paper label in black and red, printed letterpress by Sebastian Carter on Somerset Laid paper.   Maggs Bros. Ltd.   1442 - 187   2013   £200

Longley, Michael *Lares.* London: Poet and Printer, 1972.   First edition, small 8vo., original grey wrappers, fine.   Maggs Bros. Ltd.   1442 - 180   2013   £60

Longley, Michael *Selected Poems.* London: Jonathan Cape, 1988.   First edition, original red cloth, touch foxed on top edge, otherwise fine, dust jacket, inscribed by author for Richard Murphy.   Maggs Bros. Ltd.   1442 - 181   2013   £120

Longley, Michael *Secret Marriages.* Didsbury: Phoenix Pamphlet Poets Press, 1968.   Number 33 of 50 numbered copies, signed by author and additionally inscribed by him for friend Solly Lipsitz, near fine, small 8vo., original red cloth, dust jacket with minor loss at head of lower wrapper.   Maggs Bros. Ltd.   1442 - 168   2013   £600

Longley, Michael *Snow Water.* London: Jonathan Cape, 2004.   First edition, original wrappers, 8vo., fine, inscribed by author for Richard Murphy.   Maggs Bros. Ltd.   1442 - 183   2013   £100

Longley, Michael *Ten Poems.* Belfast: Festival Publications, Queen's University, 1965.   First edition, 8vo., original wrappers, slightly marked, otherwise excellent copy, ownership copy of Henry Kelly with his inscription.   Maggs Bros. Ltd.   1442 - 178   2013   £350

Longley, Michael *Wavelengths, Various Translations.* London: Enitharmon Press, 2009.   Limited to 175 copies signed by author, large 8vo., original marbled wrappers, printed paper label on upper cover, printed letterpress on 125gsm Caneletto paper, fine.   Maggs Bros. Ltd.   1442 - 188   2013   £55

Longstaff, John *Frog Went a-Courtin'.* New York: Harcourt Brace, 1955.   Stated first edition, 4to., boards, fine in very good+ dust jacket with few tiny closed edge tears with price intact, illustrations by Feodor Rojankovsky, with fabulous lithographs.   Aleph-Bet Books, Inc.   105 - 505   2013 $1500

Longstreth, T. Morris *Murder at Belly Butte.* New York: Century, 1931.   First edition, fine in dust jacket with nicks at base of spine, couple of short closed tears and light wear along folds.   Mordida Books   81 - 323   2013 $125

Longus *Dapnhis et Chloe.* Paris: H. Piazza, 1926.   First edition thus, number VI of 111 copies on Rives BFK with 24 original wood engravings in colors by Carlos Schwabe, including 12 hors texte + beautiful titlepage engraved in colors, 12 full page prints, each signed in plate and come with tissue guards, contemporary full buckram, very clean, almost new, no foxing, overall size about 12 by 9.25 inches.   Gemini Fine Books & Arts., Ltd.   Art Reference & Illustrated Books - 2013 $1500

Longus *Les Amours Pastorale de Daphnis et Chloe.* Ashendene Press, 1933.   One of 290 copies (of an edition of 310), printed in black and red on Batchelor handmade paper, 4 full page and 24 smaller wood engravings by Gwendolen Raverat, large initial letters and paragraph marks hand drawn in blue by Graily Hewitt and his assistants, imperial 8vo., original quarter white vellum, lettering within panels on backstrip and front cover device all gilt blocked, lime green boards, vellum tipped corners, bookplate, untrimmed, board slipcase, near fine.   Blackwell's Rare Books   172 - 263   2013   £1700

Longworth, Thomas *Longworth's American Almanac, New York Register and City Directory for the Forty Fourth Year of American Independence.* New York: Published for Jona. Olmstead... Joseph Desnoues, printer, 1819.   Rebound in later blue buckram with leather spine label, few pages of ads with some old repair to edges, small stains and pencil notes in text, about very good.   Between the Covers Rare Books, Inc.   New York City - 288059   2013 $550

Longworth's American Almanac, for the Fifty-Second Year of American Independence. New York: published by Thomas Longworth, 1827.   557 pages, rebound in later red buckram, evidence of former library ownership, bookplate removed, call letters on spine, stain bottom of pages, few tears, one half of one page torn away, good copy.   Between the Covers Rare Books, Inc.   New York City - 313834   2013 $300

Lonsdale, Earl of *Lowther Castle. the Major Part of the Earl of Lonsdale's Collection Fifty Series - Tues. 20th May and two following days.* Maple & Co. and Thomas Wyatt, 1947.   4to., original wrappers, pages 49, some lots priced in pencil.   R. F. G. Hollett & Son   Lake District & Cumbria - 51   2013   £30

Lope De Vega Y Carpio, Felix Arturo *Arauco Domado por el Excelentisimo Senor Don Garcia Hurtado de Mendoza.* Santiago: Sociedad de Bibliofilos Chilenos, 1963. First edition, number 90 of 100 copies for Society members (of a total run of 300), 234 pages, 4 black and white plates and 3 drawings, folio, loose in stiff paper portfolio slipcase, each plate other than frontispiece signed by artist, very good, unopened (uncut), spine tanned, 2 inch tear at head, light soiling on wrappers, few small tears, contents near fine, very good marbled slipcase. Kaaterskill Books 16 - 58 2013 $500

Lopez, Barry *Arctic Dreams.* New York: Charles Scribner's Sons, 1986. First edition, inscribed by author to major book collector, Carter Burden, 464 pages with index, fine in dust jacket. Ed Smith Books 78 - 34 2013 $200

Lopez, Barry *Children in the Woods.* Eugene: Lone Goose Press, 1992. first edition thus, 4to., one of 75 copies signed by author and artist, both text, handset in Perpetua and relief images printed on Vandercook 219 proofing press, text and cover papers made by Margaret Prentice from the plant fiber abaca with patterns created in papers body by colored pulp, housed in original publisher's cloth clamshell box, spine label, fine. Ed Smith Books 78 - 35 2013 $500

Lopez, Barry *Giving Birth to Thunder, Sleeping with His Daughter: Coyote Build North America.* Kansas City: Andrews & McMeel, 1977. First edition, fine, tight copy in near fine dust jacket with minor rubbing at edges, one small tear to bottom of rear panel. Ed Smith Books 78 - 32 2013 $175

Lopez, Barry *The Mappist.* San Francisco: Pacific Editions, 2005. First edition thus, one of 48 copies, all on BFK Rives paper, signed by author and artist, Charles Hobson, in pencil and numbered by Hobson, page size 11 x 12 inches, original USGS maps for the concertina binding, which when opened creates its own vista of mountain and valleys representing the maps that figure prominently in the Lopez story, covers made of paper over boards, paper reproducing a 1911 map of Bogota, publisher's slipcase of wood grained paper over boards, with brass toned metal label holder attached to spine of box holding white paper label with title and author in black, all suggesting a map cabinet, further housed in tan corrugated paper board slipcase, slipcase and board covers made by John De Merrit with assitance of Kris Langan, new. Priscilla Juvelis - Rare Books 56 - 23 2013 $2100

Lopez, Barry *River Notes. The Dance of Herons.* Kansas City: Andrews and McNeel, 1979. First edition, fine in near fine dust jacket with some rubbing to extremities. Ed Smith Books 78 - 33 2013 $125

Lorac, E. C. R. *A Screen for Murder.* Garden City: Doubleday Crime Club, 1948. First American edition, light offsetting to endpapers, else near fine in very good dust jacket with modest scrape on spine. Between the Covers Rare Books, Inc. Mystery & Detective Fiction - 318105 2013 $60

Lorand, Sandor *Technique of Psychoanalytic Therapy.* New York: IUP, 1952. First edition, third printing, inscribed by author, fine in near fine dust jacket. Beasley Books 2013 - 2013 $50

Lord, Eliot *Comstock Mining and Miners.* Berkeley: Howell-North, 1959. Facsimile reprint of 1883 edition, x, 451 pages, 117 illustrations, 2 maps, folding map in rear pocket, grey cloth, fine in pictorial dust jacket. Argonaut Book Shop Recent Acquisitions June 2013 - 195 2013 $60

Lord, Kenneth *Certain Members of the Lord Family Who Settled in New York City...* privately printed, 1945. First edition, limited edition, number 317, 4to., fine, white backstrip over gray boards. Beasley Books 2013 - 2013 $100

Lord, Tom *Clarence Williams.* Chigwell: Storyville, 1976. First edition, blue cloth, slight wear to spine, else near fine, issued without dust jacket. Beasley Books 2013 - 2013 $100

Loreau, Max *Cerceaux 'Sorcellent.* Paris: 1967. First edition, one of 750 numbered copies, 11 x 8.75 inches, 56 silkscreened pages with 21 original color silkscreens by Jean Dubuffet, signed and inscribed by author and artist for Mr. and Mrs. Ralph Colin, as new in sitff wrappers and slipcase. Gemini Fine Books & Arts., Ltd. Art Reference & Illustrated Books - 2013 $1200

Lorenzini, Carlo 1829-1890 *Story of a Puppet or the Adventures of Pinocchio.* London: T. Fisher Unwin, 1892. First edition in English, 12mo., decorative cloth with design repeated on edges, 232 pages, cloth lightly faded and spine age toned, else very good+, illustrations by C. Mazzanti. Aleph-Bet Books, Inc. 105 - 144 2013 $8000

Lorenzini, Carlo 1829-1890 *Pinocchio's Adventures in Wonderland.* Boston: Jordan Marsh, 1898. First edition printed in America, 12mo., half blue pictorial cloth, edges and corners rubbed, else very good+,clean and tight, 212 pages, very scarce, black and white chapter head and tailpieces. Aleph-Bet Books, Inc. 104 - 128 2013 $900

Lorenzini, Carlo 1829-1890 *Le Avventure di Pinocchio.* Firenze: Societa Editrice toscana, n.d. circa, 1923. 4to., cloth, pictorial paste-on, 191 pages, paper aging on edges, 2 leaves creased, good to very good, illustrations by C. Toppi with 7 color plates, 7 half tone plates and many line illustrations by C. Sarri.   Aleph-Bet Books, Inc.   104 - 127   2013 $450

Lorenzini, Carlo 1829-1890 *Pinocchio.* New York: Sears, 1926. 4to., cloth, pictorial paste on, 236 pages, fine in frayed dust jacket, illustrations by Christopher Rule, with color frontispiece, pictorial endpapers plus wide pictorial borders in orange to every page.   Aleph-Bet Books, Inc.   105 - 147   2013 $225

Lorenzini, Carlo 1829-1890 *Les Aventures de Pinocchio.* Lausanne: Librarie Payot, 1945. First of this new edition, 12mo., pictorial boards, 171 pages, fine in slightly worn dust jacket, 8 full page color illustrations and many black and whites by J. J. Mennet.   Aleph-Bet Books, Inc.   105 - 146   2013 $225

Loti, Pierre *La Troisieme Jeunesse de Madame Prune.* Paris: Les Editions d'Art Devambez, 1926. Number 190 of 325 exemplars, on velin Arches with publisher's watermark (total edition of 458), 17 original color etchings by Foujita, 11 are hors texte and 6 in-texte, Monod erroneously sites 13 hors-texte and 4 in-texte), 27 x 22cm., 175 pages, original wrappers, rare publisher's slipcase, minor offsetting from original tissue guards, otherwise very good.   Gemini Fine Books & Arts., Ltd.   Art Reference & Illustrated Books - 2013 $1400

Louisa's Fairy Legends. New York: McLoughlin Bros., n.d. circa, 1875. 4to., brown cloth stamped in black and gold, pictorial paste-on slight rubbing, else near fine.   Aleph-Bet Books, Inc.   105 - 247   2013 $600

Louisiana Territory *The Laws of the Territory of Louisiana Comprising All Those Which are Now Actually in Force with the Same.* St. Louis: printed by Joseph Charles, printer to the Territory, 1808. First edition, 8vo., full new morocco leather label, early leaves with some thumbing and browning in outer margin, slightly frayed, two old tape stains on edges, two old signatures on title, near fine.   M & S Rare Books, Inc.   95 - 196   2013 $45,000

Lounsbury, Ralph Greenlee *The British Fishery at Newfoundland 1634-1763.* New Haven: Yale University Press, 1934. First edition, red cloth with gilt to spine in dust jacket, half title, folding color map in rear and 1 black and white single page map, 8vo., very good, dust jacket very good.   Schooner Books Ltd.   101 - 41   2013 $100

Loutherbourg, Phillippe Jacques De *The Romantic and Picturesque Scenery of England and Wales...* London: T. Bensley for R. Bowyer, 1805. First edition, first issue, folio, watermarked J. Whatman 1801/1805, 18 hand colored aquatint plates, modern black half morocco, spine lettered gilt.   Marlborough Rare Books Ltd.   218 - 98   2013   £3500

Louys, Pierre *Aphrodite.* Paris: Librarie L. Borel, 1900. 8vo. plates, many illustrations in text, contemporary quarter red morocco binding with marbled paper boards, spine gilt, top edge gilt, other edges uncut and little discolored, joints and edges rubbed.   Unsworths Antiquarian Booksellers   28 - 182   2013   £30

Louys, Pierre *Mimes des Courtisanes de Lucien.* Paris: Ambrose Vollard, 1935. Limited to one of 325 copies, on Rives paper, this being number 138, illustrations by Edgar Degas, 83 pages of text, 12 intertextual woodcuts in brown and 22 loose etchings by Maurice Potin after Degas, of the 22 etchings, four are in color, original stiff printed wrappers and original glassine, wrappers and titlepage printed in black and red, leaves uncut and unbound, loose etchings housed in separate folder, fine.   Heritage Book Shop   Holiday Catalogue 2012 - 37   2013 $3500

Love, Mary *A Peep at the Equimaux; or Scene on the Ice to Which is Annexed a Polar Pastoral.* London: 1828. Second edition, 40 hand colored plates, 12mo., original dark red backed marbled boards, very good.   Maggs Bros. Ltd.   1467 - 137   2013   £3000

Lovechild, Thomas *Sketches of Little Girls.* New York: McLoughlin Bros., n.d. circa, 1863-1870. 12mo., cloth backed pictorial boards (64) pages, edges rubbed, some soil, very good, illustrations bny J. H. Howard with 8 full page colored illustrations, including color pictorial titlepage.   Aleph-Bet Books, Inc.   105 - 322   2013 $750

Lovecraft, H. P. *Collected Poems.* Sauk City: Arkham House, 1963. First edition, illustrations by Frank Utpatel, tiny name stamp on bottom page edge, small faint, date stamp on titlepage, else fine in fine, fresh and bright dust jacket, nicely inscribed by artist, beautiful copy.   Between the Covers Rare Books, Inc.   Sci-Fi, Fantasy & Horror - 89257   2013 $400

Lovecraft, H. P. *The Conservative July 1923 (Whole number 13).* Providence: H. P. Lovecraft, July, 1923. Small octavo, printed wrappers, stapled.   L. W. Currey, Inc.   Fall Sampler Sept. 2013 - 146509   2013 $1250

Lovecraft, H. P. *The Dream Quest of Unknown Kadath.* Buffalo: Shroud Pub., 1955. First edition, Currey's issue D (2) in second state of jacket, stated one of 1500 copies this number 491, black cloth stamped in gilt on spine, fine in very good or better yellow dust jacket with few small nicks and tears, little age toning,.   Between the Covers Rare Books, Inc.   Sci-Fi, Fantasy & Horror - 89343   2013 $850

Lovecraft, H. P. *Fungi From Yuggoth.* Salem: Bill Evans, June, 1943. First edition, large octavo, mimeographed from typewritten copy self wrappers, stapled. L. W. Currey, Inc. Fall Sampler Sept. 2013 - 146510   2013 $1850

Lovecraft, H. P. *H. P. Lovecraft: Letters to Robert Bloch and Supplement.* West Warwick: Necronomicon Press, 1993. First edition, 2 pamphlets, first is 91 pages, supplement is 18, both fine in wrappers. Between the Covers Rare Books, Inc. Sci-Fi, Fantasy & Horror - 286581 2013 $250

Lovecraft, H. P. *Selected Letters.* Sauk City: Arkham House, 1965-1976. First editions, 5 volumes complete, tiny name stamp on bottom page edge of 3 volumes, small date stamp on titlepage of some volumes, else fine in fine dust jackets with odd tiny tear. Between the Covers Rare Books, Inc. Sci-Fi, Fantasy & Horror - 89280   2013 $500

Lovejoy, Joseph Cammett *The Law and the Offence.* Boston: Moody, 1852. First edition, 8vo., 16 pages, sewn self wrappers, little foxed and soiled, very good. Second Life Books Inc. 183 - 252   2013 $75

Lovelace, Ralph Milbanke, Earl of *Astarte; a Fragment of Truth Concerning George Gordon Byron...* London: printed at the Chiswick Press, 1905. First edition, half title, frontispiece slightly spotted, plates facsimiles, original blue boards, brown cloth spine, paper label slightly chipped, little dulled, Lord Rosebery's copy with letter from Lord Lovelace tipped in, Doris Langley Moore's copy with few pencil notes. Jarndyce Antiquarian Booksellers   CCIII - 108   2013   £85

Lovell, Ernest James *Captain Medwin: Friend of Byron and Shelley.* Austin: University of Texas Press, 1962. First edition, half title, original blue cloth, very good in slightly worn dust jacket, Doris Langley Moore's copy, few pencil notes by her. Jarndyce Antiquarian Booksellers CCIII - 420 2013 £25

Lovell, Mansfield *Correspondence Between the War Department and General Lovell, Relating to the Defences of New Orleans.* Richmond: R. M. Smith, Public printer, 1863. First edition, 8vo., original self wrappers, stitched as issued, front and rear wrappers little soiled, very good. The Brick Row Book Shop Miscellany Fifty-Nine - 10 2013 $500

Lover, Samuel *Legends and Stories of Ireland.* Dublin: W. F. Wakeman, 1831. Etchings by author, contemporary full tan calf by C. Lewis, gilt ownership stamp lettered "Vigilantibus" on boards, the stamp is that of Archibald Acheson, 3rd Earl of Gosford 1806-1864 gilt spine, green morocco label, some marking, but very good. Jarndyce Antiquarian Booksellers   CCV - 180   2013   £180

Lovesey, Peter *A Case of Spirits.* London: Macmillan, 1975. First edition, pages bit browned, else fine in fine dust jacket, signed by author. Between the Covers Rare Books, Inc. Mystery & Detective Fiction - 61205 2013 $65

Low, A. P. *Report on the Dominion Government Expedition to Hudson Bay and the Arctic Island on Board the D. G. S. Neptune.* Ottawa: Government Printing Bureau, 1906. Original green pictorial cloth, gilt fore edge of upper board little stained, lower board damped and marked, well illustrated with large folding map in rear pocket, little dampstaining to fore-edges at beginning and end, but very good. R. F. G. Hollett & Son Polar Exploration - 36   2013   £75

Lowe, Constance *Hide and Seek Pictures.* London: Ernest Nister, n.d., 1913. Folio, original cloth backed glazed pictorial boards, trifle marked and edges slightly rubbed, 10 leaves illustrated, 6 of which bear two chromo-lithographed roundels with silk pull, each to transform the page, set under central bar with verse and behind a decorated oval border, border defective on first sheet and tear to backing sheet, both pulls missing on second and sixth, one full missing on fifth, front joint strained, little shaken, very acceptable copy, scare moveable. R. F. G. Hollett & Son Children's Books - 371   2013   £350

Lowe, Peter *A Discovrse of the Whole Art of Chyrvrgerie.* London: printed by Thomas Purfoot, 1636. 4to., recent full English paneled calf, raised bands, gilt spine, burgundy label, endpapers renewed, title with toning, text with toning and browning and areas of foxing, page 147 lacking part of lower blank margin, page 203 lacking part of lower blank margin just catching one letter of text, overall most pleasing copy of a book that was obviously well appreciated and used by a former owner, throughout are contemporary inked line outs and corrections. James Tait Goodrich 75 - 138 2013 $3950

Lowell, James Russell 1819-1891 *The Writings.* London: Macmillan and Co., 1890. Riverside edition, 10 volumes, 194 x 130mm., 3 of the volumes with portrait frontispiece, beautiful early 20th century olive green textured calf handsomely gilt by Sangorski & Sutcliffe (stamp signed), covers with double ruled gilt border and blindstamped in basket weave pattern, raised bands, spines lavishly gilt in compartments with central cruciform ornament framed by wide densely gilt cornerpieces filled with leaves, flowers and small tools, each spine with two maroon morocco labels, turn-ins gilt in lacy filigree, marbled endpapers, top edge gilt, other edges rough trimmed, light rubbing and flaking to one joint (only), spines uniformly sunned to a mellow olive brown, one leaf with triangular tear at upper right just into text (no loss), isolated very minor stains or foxing, otherwise beautiful set in fine condition, handsome bindings very lustrous and with no significant wear, text fresh, clean and bright. Phillip J. Pirages 61 - 145 2013 $1750

Lowell, James Russell 1819-1891 *The Complete Writings.* Cambridge: Riverside Press, 1904. One of 1000 copies, 222 x 146mm, 16 volumes, Edition de luxe, 80 mounted photogravure illustrations on India paper, original tissue guards, very handsome dark green morocco, extravagantly gilt, covers with wavy gilt border and charming floral ornaments at corners, central panel (with square notched corners) formed by six parallel gilt lines, raised bands, spine compartments attractively gilt with scrolling flowers and foliate enclosing a floral fleuron centerpiece, wide turn-ins with elaborate gilt decoration featuring many large and small roses and leaves on stylized lattice work, turn-ins enclosing scarlet colored polished morocco doublures crimson watered silk free endleaves, top edge gilt, other edges rough trimmed, mostly unopened (six of the volumes entirely unopened, and all but one of the others largely so), front joint of first volume bit worn (wear joint little flaked), half dozen other joints with hint of rubbing, spines evenly sunned to attractive olive brown, one small cover scuff, two leaves roughly opened (no serious consequences), other isolated trivial imperfections, nearly fine, attractive binding, leather lustrous, (mostly unopened), text essentially undisturbed. Phillip J. Pirages 61 - 127 2013 $3000

Lowell, Josephine Shaw *Industrial Arbitration and Conciliation.* New York: Putnam's, 1894. First edition, 8vo., red cloth stamped in black, from the library of reformer Florence Kelley (1859-1932). Second Life Books Inc. 182 - 160 2013 $75

Lowell, Percival *Mars and Its Canals.* New York: Macmillan, 1911. Reprint, 8vo., frontispiece, 70 illustrations, gilt stamped green cloth, inside front hinge, blindstamp of Lowell Observatory Library, better than very good. Jeff Weber Rare Books 169 - 279 2013 $150

Lower, Mark, A. *English Surnames.* London: 1875. Fourth edition, 2 volumes, original cloth, some damp marking, text fine. C. P. Hyland 261 - 398 2013 £35

Lowry, Alexander *Big Basin.* Los Altos: Sempervirens Fund, 1973. First edition, one of 500 hardbound copies, this being #99, quarto, black and white photos, some vintage photos by A. P. Hill, map, light brown cloth lettered in dark brown with photographic pastedown on front cover, very fine. Argonaut Book Shop Recent Acquisitions June 2013 - 196 2013 $75

Loy, Mina *Lunar Baedeker & Time-Tables. Selected Poems.* Highlands: Jonathan Williams, 1958. First edition, one of only 50 hardbound copies of an Author's Edition, numbered and signed by Loy, tall 8vo., titlepage illustration by Emerson Woelffer, original cloth, printed paper spine label, presentation copy inscribed by book's publisher, Jonathan Williams to Denise Levertov, who contributed one of the introductions, extremities lightly rubbed, few small faint spots near bottom edge of front cover, some barely perceptible offset from binding adhesive along endpaper gutters, otherwise near fine. James S. Jaffe Rare Books Fall 2013 - 93 2013 $2500

Lucanus, Marcus Annaeus *Pharsalia.* Leiden: Samuel Luchtmans, 1728. 4to., frontispiece and foldout map, diagrams in text, part of one leaf pages 549-50, torn away with loss of text, some corners creased, contemporary Dutch vellum prize binding with handwritten title to spine, blind embossed boards, edges sprinkled, vellum darkened and rather grubby, some staining at edges, but strong and still very good, library ticket holder and armorial bookplate of Pierce Butler with motto 'Soyez Ferme' to front pastedowns, inkstamp of Metropolitan Special Collections, Southwark to both sides of f.f.e.p., titlepage and to all rear endpapers. Unsworths Antiquarian Booksellers 28 - 26 2013 £95

Lucas, E. V. *The Book of Shops.* London: Grant Richards, 1899. Oblong folio, 24 full page color printed illustrations on right hand pages, slight stain to upper margin of endpapers, original printed boards, brown cloth spine, gilt lettered, edges and corners bit rubbed. Jarndyce Antiquarian Booksellers CCV - 181 2013 £650

Lucas, E. V. *Book of Shops.* London: Grant Richards n.d. circa, 1900. Probable first edition, large oblong 4to., cloth backed pictorial boards, some soil, two small margin mends, very good+, 24 full page color illustrations plus 3 additional color illustrations (by F. Bedford) for half title, title and contents pages, extremely scarce. Aleph-Bet Books, Inc. 104 - 65 2013 $1200

Lucas, E. V. *Four and Twenty Toilers.* London: Grant Richards, n.d., Oblong 4to., original cloth backed pictorial boards, corners little worn, light surface defect to bottom of lower boards, 24 colored plates, text illustrations, joints strengthened, very nice and clean and bright copy. R. F. G. Hollett & Son Children's Books - 53 2013 £220

Lucas, E. V. *Four and Twenty Toilers.* London: Grant Richards, n.d., 1900. Large oblong, 103 pages, cloth backed pictorial boards, cover scratched, some with edge and corner wear, else tight, clean and very good, 24 full page color illustrations by F. D. Bedford. Aleph-Bet Books, Inc. 104 - 66 2013 $850

Lucas, E. V. *Playtime and Company.* London: Methuen, 1925. First edition, large 8vo., original cloth backed pictorial boards, extremities little worn, illustrations, nice, clean copy. R. F. G. Hollett & Son Children's Books - 554 2013 £45

Lucas, George *Star Wars: from the Adventures of Luke Skywalker.* New York: Ballantine Books, 1976. True first edition, paperback original, fine with light rubbing to rear wrapper, from the library of Bruce Kahn. Between the Covers Rare Books, Inc. Sci-Fi, Fantasy & Horror - 310997 2013 $225

Lucas, Mr. *The Strolling Player; or Life and Adventures.* London: printed by B. McMillan, 1802. 3 volumes, 8vo., uncut, text browned and foxed, tears without loss to volume II, F8 and M7, rebound in quarter calf, marbled boards, gilt banded spines, red morocco labels.   Jarndyce Antiquarian Booksellers   CCIV - 189   2013   £950

Lucas, Richard *Enquiry After Happiness.* London: printed for R. Gosling; printed for W. Innys and R. Manby, 1734-1735. Parts I-II sixth edition Part III Fifth edition, 2 volumes, contemporary sprinkled calf, spines divided by gilt rules, red morocco labels, boards bordered with gilt rule, touch rubbed at extremities, few corners lightly worn, contemporary ink ownership inscription "Thomas Price 1740". Unsworths Antiquarian Booksellers   28 - 111   2013   £350

Lucia, Ellis *Mr. Football: Amos Alonzo Stagg.* South Brunswick & New York: A. S. Barnes, 1970. First edition, staining to upper edge of both boards, thus very good in like dust jacket, rubbed.   Between the Covers Rare Books, Inc.   Football Books - 71463   2013 $60

Lucian *Dialogi Morales.* Neapoli: typis Onuphrii Zambraja, 1794. First edition thus, octavo, 20cm., owner's signature in neat ink, very good, full contemporary vellum, red morocco spine label, with moderate foxing to endpapers and scattered light foxing to text pages, scarce.   Between the Covers Rare Books, Inc.   Philosophy - 338033   2013 $350

Lucian *Opera Omnia.* Paris: Julien Bertault, 1615. First edition by Jean Bourdelot, folio, lacking 2 leaves from prelims, dedicatory poems and a life of Lucian, usually found between preface and index, titlepage in red and black, little dusty, small hole to last page of prelims and substantial marginal paper flaw to page 505, neither affecting text, contemporary dark brown calf, gilt border, rebacked in olive green with dark green morocco spine label, corners crudely repaired in sheep, now rubbed, some stains to spine, boards crackled, little worming to upper edges and corners worn, bookplate of William Orme Foster.   Unsworths Antiquarian Booksellers   28 - 27   2013   £350

Luckombe, P. *The History and Art of Printing.* London: printed by W. Adlard and J. Browne, 1771. Reissue, 8vo. frontispiece, woodcut illustrations, each page framed within decorative typographic border, some browning to frontispiece, titlepage and final leaf, recent sprinkled calf, raised bands, rather bright red morocco label.   Jarndyce Antiquarian Booksellers   CCIV - 191   2013   £380

Lucretius Carus, Titus *De Rerum Natura Libri Sex.* Glasguae: in Aedibus Academicis Excudebant Robertus et Andreas Foulis, 1759. 8vo., some browning to pastedowns and endpapers, full contemporary calf, raised and gilt banded spine, red morocco label, covers rubbed, head of spine slightly worn, ownership name dated 1939 at head of front endpaper.   Jarndyce Antiquarian Booksellers   CCIV - 192   2013   £40

Lucretius Carus, Titus *De Rerum Natura Libri Sex.* London: in aedibus Ricardi Taylor et socii, 1824. 4to., printer's vignette to titlepage and at colophon, light foxing in places, contemporary tan calf, rebacked with old spine relaid, boards ruled in blind and gilt, slightly scratched, patches of surface-loss near bottom edge of lower board, corners worn, marbled edges and endpapers, prelims (only) creased and starting to loosen at gutter, gift inscription of Dr. Keate.   Unsworths Antiquarian Booksellers   28 - 28   2013   £150

Ludlam, Rose *Under the Moon.* Leicester: Edgar Backus, 1943. 12mo., pictorial boards, near fine, full page color illustrations by Anthony Rado.   Aleph-Bet Books, Inc.   105 - 385   2013 $200

Ludolf, H. *A New History of Ethiopia.* London: for Samuel Smith, 1682. First edition in English, folio, 8 engraved plates, engraved plate of Ethiopic alphabet, folding table, contemporary or early 18th century calf, front hinge cracked but held by cords, corners worn, some light browning, but very good, signatures of Edmund and Rufus Marsden, latter dated 1762, Herz booklabel.   Joseph J. Felcone Inc.   Books Printed before 1701 - 65   2013 $2200

Ludwig, Arnold M. *The Price of Greatness: Resolving the Creativity and Madness Controversy.* New York: Guilford Press, 1995. First edition, fine in fine dust jacket.   Between the Covers Rare Books, Inc.   Psychology & Psychiatry - 101030   2013 $95

Ludwig, Emil *Doctor Freud: an Analysis and a Warning.* New York: Hellman Williams & Co., 1947. First American edition, near fine in very good dust jacket.   Between the Covers Rare Books, Inc.   Psychology & Psychiatry - 289894   2013 $50

Lumb, Norman *Gonococcal Infection in the Male for Students and Practitioners.* London: John Bale Sons & Danielson Ltd., 1920. 8vo., 13 tissue guarded color plates, 165 figures in text and photo plates, original red cloth, gilt stamped cover and spine titles, water damage to covers, corners bumped, ex-library bookplate and ink stamp, bookplate and inkstamps of Andrew Davidson, very good, rare.   Jeff Weber Rare Books   172 - 194   2013 $75

Lummis, Charles F. *The Man Who Married the Moon.* New York: Century Co., 1894. First edition, spine darkened, with cloth showing modest overall handling, very good, without dust jacket.   Ken Lopez Bookseller   159 - 154   2013 $200

Lund, John *The Newcastle Rider, or, Ducks and Pease...* York: printed by J. Kendrew, c., 1800. 2 woodcuts tailpieces and one illustration in text, bit browned, outer pages soiled and rubbed, 12mo., self wrappers, overstitched, sound.   Blackwell's Rare Books   B174 - 95   2013   £450

Lunn, Arnold *John Wesley.* London: Cassell, 1929. First edition, original cloth, boards little marked, spine slightly creased, 382 pages, frontispiece, presentation copy, inscribed by author and dated March 1929.   R. F. G. Hollett & Son   Wesleyan Methodism - 16   2013   £25

Lupi, Antonio Maria *Dissertatio et Animadversiones ad Nuper Inventum Severae Martyris Epitaphium.*   Palermo: ex typographia Stephani Amato, 1734.   First edition, small folio, 15 leaves of plates, additional woodcut illustrations, edges speckled red, occasional light soiling, small closed tear to blank margin of one folding plate, contemporary vellum boards, gilt to spine, soiled, touch of wear to tail of spine, 3 small spots of worming to pastedowns, ownership inscription of Geo. Errington and bookplate of library of Prinknash Abbey, few early marginal pen notes.   Unsworths Antiquarian Booksellers   28 - 29   2013   £800

Lupoff, Richard A.   *Stroka Prospekt.*   West Branch: Toothpaste Press, 1982.   First edition, one of 100 numbered copies, specially bound and signed by author and artist, illustrations by Ann Mikolowski, quarter cloth and decorated paper over boards, fine.   Between the Covers Rare Books, Inc.   Sci-Fi, Fantasy & Horror - 312225   2013 $125

Luprian, Hildegard   *Ducky Drake.*   Springfield: McLoughlin, 1932.   4to., thick pictorial card covers, fine in box, bold art deco color and black and whites by author, box cover has window through which a duck's head bobs back and forth when moved.   Aleph-Bet Books, Inc. 105 - 408   2013 $250

Lupton, Daniel   *The Glory of their Times, or the Lives of Ye Primitive Fathers....* London: I. Oakes, 1640.   First edition, small 4to., contemporary calf, binding worn and tender, endpapers gone, armorial bookplate, some marginal staining, whole printed inside of ruled borders, 43 engraved portraits.   Second Life Books Inc.   183 - 253   2013 $700

Luther, Martin   1483-1546   *A Commentarie Upon the Fifteen Psalmes, Called Psalmi Graduum... (bound with) A Commentarie of M. Doctor Martin Luther upon the Epistle of S. Paul to the Galathians.*   London: by Richard Field, 1615-1616.   4to., black letter, 2 works bound together in 18th century calf, very neatly rebacked retaining original spine label, titlepage of first work soiled, minor dampstains on first few leaves, else very good, armorial bookplate of John Brogden.   Joseph J. Felcone Inc.   Books Printed before 1701 - 66   2013 $2800

Luther, Martin   1483-1546   *A Commentary on the Galatians.*   Chester: printed and sold by Jones and Crane, 1796.   8vo., rare printing, titlepage soiled, light browning and soiling, pencil inscription, contemporary sheep, rebacked and repaired, green morocco lettering piece, old leather darkened around edges, boards bowing outward slightly, sound.   Blackwell's Rare Books   172 - 93   2013   £800

Luther, Martin   1483-1546   *An Den Christlichen Adel Teutscher Nation, con des Christlichen Standes Besserung.*   Wittenberg: Melchior Lotter, 1520.   First edition, small quarto, 6 line decorative woodcut initial, modern limp vellum, edges sprinkled red, title and final leaf very slightly browned, small portion of lower corner of title renewed, first and last gatherings strengthened at inner margin, some light dampstaining, ink notation at foot of title, few additional ink notations in text, overall excellent copy, housed in quarter red morocco clamshell, gilt stamped on spine.   Heritage Book Shop   50th Anniversary Catalogue - 68   2013 $18,500

Luys, Georges   *A Text-Book of Gonorrhea and Its Complications.*   London: Bailliere Tindall and Cox, 1913.   8vo., 3 chromolithographic plates, titlepage lightly foxed, black stamped gray cloth, rubbed, edges foxed, ownership signature title, very good, scarce.   Jeff Weber Rare Books   172 - 193   2013 $65

Lycophron   *Alexandra, sive Cassandro.*   Basel: Ex officina Joannis Oporini, 1546.   First separate edition, 2 parts in one folio, title and text in Greek and Latin, contemporary half blindstamped pigskin over wooden boards, 2 clasps, spine lettered in manuscript with four raised bands, from the library of Joseph von Lassberg, 2 additional early ink inscriptions, very minor worming in lower margin of last five leaves and to rear endpapers, small margin stain to Pp2 and Pp3, housed in custom quarter brown morocco clamshell, gilt stamped.   Heritage Book Shop   50th Anniversary Catalogue - 69   2013 $25,000

Lycophron   *Alexandra (...) Accedunt Versiones, Variantes Lectiones, Emendationes, Annotationes, & Indices Necessarii.*   Oxford: E Theatro Sheldoniano, 1697.   2 parts in 1 volume, folio, Greek and Latin text, full page engraved frontispiece, titlepage with engraved vignette, tiny burn hole to frontispiece, unobtrusive embossed Athenaeum Library stamp to titlepage, small tear to lower margin page 7 not affecting text, contemporary speckled calf, rebacked in sheep gilt Athenaeum Library stamps to spine not affecting text, contemporary speckled calf, rebacked in sheep, gilt Athenaeum Library stamps to spine and upper board, edges and pages worn, corners fraying, hinges repaired with cloth, armorial bookplate of Jeremiah Miles to front pastedown.   Unsworths Antiquarian Booksellers   28 - 30   2013   £350

Lyda, John W.   *The Negro in the History of Indiana.*   Terra Haute: John W. Lyda, 1953.   First edition, wire stitched into stiff blue wrappers printed in black, 136 pages, bookplate on inside front wrapper, couple of tiny and unnecessary Japanese paper repairs to first couple of leaves, else nice, near fine, author's name stamp on rear fly, warmly inscribed by author to former student.   Between the Covers Rare Books, Inc.   165 - 312   2013 $350

Lydgate, John *Table Manners for Children.* Salisbury: Perdix Press, 1989. First edition thus, 8vo., red buckram boards, Caxton's colophon blindstamped to upper board, fore and bottom edges uncut, fine, dust jacket with deckle to bottom edge, fine, printer's compliments card with inscription loosely inserted, limited edition of 265 copies, this one unnumbered, with facsimile reprint of Caxton's 1476 Black letter printing to rectos and modern rendering to facing pages.   Unsworths Antiquarian Booksellers   28 - 183   2013   £30

Lyman, Nanci *Print America's Graphic Design Magazine XIII: 6 November/December 1959.* New York: Kaye-Cadel Pub., 1959. First edition, near fine, little bit of creasing to top edge of spine, light edge wear and slight soiling of covers.   Jeff Hirsch Books   Fall 2013 - 129531   2013 $50

Lynam, E. W. *The Irish Character in Print 1571-1923.* 1924. Offprint, (47) pages, octavo, cloth, mint.   C. P. Hyland   261 - 45   2013   £40

Lynd, Robert *Rambles in Ireland.* Boston: Dana Estes and Co., 1912. First US edition, large 8vo., original green cloth lettered in gilt, top edge gilt, neat bookplate on front pastedown and some pages slightly foxed, otherwise excellent.   Maggs Bros. Ltd.   1442 - 330   2013   £220

Lyons, Arthur *The Dead are Discreet.* New York: Mason & Lipscomb, 1974. First edition, fine in rubbed dust jacket. Mordida Books   81 - 324   2013 $200

Lyons, Cicely *Salmon: Our Heritage. The Story of a Province and an Industry.* Vancouver: British Columbia Packers Ltd., 1969. First edition, signed by author, color frontispiece, numerous photos, portraits, maps, errata slip tipped in, dark blue cloth, gilt, very fine with dust jacket. Argonaut Book Shop   Summer 2013 - 215   2013 $90

Lyons, F. S. L. *Charles Stewart Parnell.* 1977. First edition, 704 pages, cloth, dust jacket, fine.   C. P. Hyland   261 - 681   2013   £38

Lysaght, A. M. *Joseph Banks in Newfoundland & Labrador, 1766.* London: Faber, 1971. First edition, large 4to., original cloth, gilt, dust jacket price clipped, 12 color plates, 91 monochrome plates, 6 text figures and 9 facsimiles.   R. F. G. Hollett & Son   Polar Exploration - 37   2013   £75

Lysaght, E. E. *Irish Eclogues.* Maunsel, 1915. First edition, quarter parchment, very good.   C. P. Hyland   261 - 579   2013   £32

Lysaght, E. E. *Self-Government & Business Interests.* Dublin: Maunsel, 1918. First edition, 33 pages, original printed wrappers, very good.   C. P. Hyland   261 - 562   2013   £30

Lysaght, Elizabeth Jane *Sealed Orders.* London: Richard Bentley & Son, 1886. First edition, 3 volumes, 8vo., original black cloth, gilt lettered, on upper board of each volume is white envelope with red seal, embossed in cloth, cloth worn, endpapers little stained, very good.   The Brick Row Book Shop   Miscellany Fifty-Nine - 18   2013 $500

Lysons, Daniel *Magna Britannia...* London: printed for T. Cadell and W. Davies, 1806-1822. Large paper copy, 6 volumes bound in 10, 346 x 260mm., pleasing contemporary red hard-grain half morocco over marbled boards by J. Mackenzie & Son (stamp-signed), raised bands, spines attractively gilt in compartments with very large and complex central fleuron surrounded by small tools and volute cornerpieces, gilt titling, marbled endpapers, all edges gilt, 398 plates of maps, plans, views and architecture, 264 as called for and extra illustrated with 134, the total, including 72 double page, 7 folding and 13 in color; armorial bookplate of Arthur G. Soames, signed and dated by plate by C. Helard (18)99, paper boards somewhat chafed, extremities (especially bottom edges of boards) rather rubbed, spines slightly (but uniformly) darkened, few of the leather corners abraded, small portions of morocco dulled from preservatives, but bindings completely solid - with no cracking to joints - and still impressive on shelf, handsomely decorated spines unmarked, majority of plates with variable foxing (usually minimal but perhaps two dozen noticeably foxed), number of engravings with small faint dampstains at very edge of top margin, but text itself in very fine condition, looking remarkably clean, fresh and smooth within its vast margins. Phillip J. Pirages   63 - 325   2013 $6500

Lyttelton, George Lyttelton, 1st Baron   1709-1773 *The Poetical Works...* London: For Cadell and Davies, 1801. 12mo., titlepage vignette and 5 engraved plates, contemporary dark green half straight grain morocco, marbled boards, gilt decorated spine.   Ken Spelman Books Ltd.   75 - 53   2013   £45

Lytton, Edward George Earle Lytton Bulwer-Lytton, 1st Baron   1803-1873 *The Pilgrims of the Rhine.* London: Saunders & Otley, 1834. First edition, 8vo., plates, vignettes, contemporary brown calf spine rubbed and worn, corners rubbed.   J. & S. L. Bonham Antiquarian Booksellers   Europe - 6258   2013   £65

M

M'Clintock, Captain *The Voyage of the Fox in the Arctic Seas.* London: John Murray, 1859. First edition, original pictorial blue cloth gilt, neatly recased, 18 illustrations and sketch maps, few spots to title, lacking folding map.   R. F. G. Hollett & Son   Polar Exploration - 38   2013   £95

M'Collum, William *California as I Saw It.* Los Gatos: Talisman Press, 1960. Reprint of the extremely rare first edition, 219 pages, titlepage vignette, 1 illustration, map endpapers, cloth backed pictorial boards, paper spine label, very fine and bright, with dust jacket.   Argonaut Book Shop Summer 2013 - 216   2013 $90

M'Kim, J. M. *A Sketch of the Slave Trade in the District of Columbia, Contained in Two Letters.* Pittsburgh: republished by the Pittsburgh and Allegheny Anti-Slavery Society, 1838. First edition, 12mo., 15 pages, sewn, browned and waterstained, sound and decent, very rare.   M & S Rare Books, Inc.   95 - 25   2013 $425

M'Leod, Alexander *Trial of Alexander M'Leod for the Murder of Amos Durfee; and as an Accomplice in the Burning of the Steamer Caroline, in the Niagara River During the Canadian Rebellion in 1837-38.* New York: printed at the Sun Office, 1841. First edition, 8vo., 32 pages, sewn as issued, unopened, foxed.   M & S Rare Books, Inc.   95 - 52   2013 $750

M., J. *The True Story of Lord and Lady Byron as told by Lord Macaulay, Thomas Moore, Leigh Hunt, Thomas Campbell, the Countess of Blessington, Lord Lindsay, The Countess Guiccioli by Layd Byron...* London: John Camden Hotten, 1869. First edition, frontispiece, slight spotting, contemporary half calf, brown leather label, little rubbed, Doris Langley Moore's copy.   Jarndyce Antiquarian Booksellers   CCIII - 384   2013   £150

M., J. *The True Story of Lord and Lady Byron as told by Lord Macaulay, Thomas Moore, Leigh Hunt, Thomas Campbell, the Countess of Blessington, Lord Lindsay, The Countess Guiccioli by Lady Byron...* London: John Camden Hotten, 1869. First edition, frontispiece, 16 page catalog (1869), slightly spotted, original blue cloth, lettered in silver, slightly marked, spine slightly darkened, nice, bright copy.   Jarndyce Antiquarian Booksellers   CCIII - 353   2013   £200

Maberly, Catherine Charlotte *The Love Match.* London: David Bryce, 1856. New edition, contemporary half maroon calf, spine decorated n gilt, black leather label, spine and corners little rubbed, from the Headfort library, signed 'Bective 1854', good plus.   Jarndyce Antiquarian Booksellers   CCV - 182   2013   £45

Maberly, Samuel Edward *The Pictorial Humpty Dumpty Sketches and Etched by...* London: Tilt & Bogue, 1843. Narrow 4to., slight cover soil and rubbing, else near fine, hand colored etched plates, excellent copy, rarely found so clean.   Aleph-Bet Books, Inc.   105 - 437   2013 $4250

Mac-Orlan, Pierre *Nuits aux Bouges. Eaux-Fortes de Dignimont.* Paris: Ernest Flammarion, 1929. Limited edition, 83 of 50 special copies on Holland Van Gelder Zonen paper (of a total 890), 4to., 69 pages, 5 etched plates after illustrations by Dignimont, original printed wrappers, illustrated cover plate, later cloth backed, slipcase with patterned paper backed boards designed by Vance Gerry, with Gerry bookplate, fine.   Jeff Weber Rare Books   171 - 103   2013 $300

Mac Flogg'em, Peter, Pseud. *Aesculapian Secrets Revealed; or Friendly Hints and Admonitions Addressed to gentlemen of the Medical Profession...* printed (by W. Flint) for C. Chapple, 1813. First edition, fine hand colored folding aquatint frontispiece, signed, little spotting her and there, 12mo., uncut in original blue paper wrappers, contemporary ownership inscription of G. D. P. Thomas, very good.   Blackwell's Rare Books   Sciences - 76   2013   £1200

MacAlister, John MacNeill *Leabhar Gabhala: The Book of Conquests of Ireland Book I (all published).* circa, 1915. Lacks, titlepage and wrapper, 285 pages, text good.   C. P. Hyland   261 - 564   2013   £30

MacArthur, Wilson *The Desert Watches.* Rupert Hart-Davis, 1954. First edition, original cloth, gilt, dust jacket, little worn and price clipped, 15 plates.   R. F. G. Hollett & Son   Africana - 135   2013   £30

MacAskill, Wallace R. *Out of Halifax: a Collection of Sea Pictures.* New York: Derrydale Press, 1937. Limited to 950 copies, this #663, quarto, blue cloth spine and light blue cloth boards, gilt titles to front and spine, half title, frontispiece, 99 plates, all edges of covers have wear and some light browning.   Schooner Books Ltd.   105 - 86   2013 $175

Macaulay, Thomas Babington Macaulay, 1st Baron 1800-1859 *Critical and Historical Essays, contributed to the Edinburgh Review.* London: Longman, Brown, Green, Longmans & Roberts, 1858. Ninth edition, 3 volumes, 229 x 152mm., extra illustrated with 122 engraved plates, primarily portraits, lovely contemporary honey brown crushed morocco, elegantly gilt, by Morrell (signed on front turn-in), covers with double gilt rule frame, raised bands, spine gilt in charming Arts and Crafts design of interlocking flowers and leaves gilt titling, turn-ins with gilt floral roll, top edges gilt, other edges rough trimmed, upper cover of third volume in one inch and two-three inch scratches (all shallow and well masked with dye), thin band of offsetting to free endpapers from gilt turn-ins (as usual), some plates with minor foxing and bit offset onto facing pages, otherwise quite handsome set in fine condition, text fresh and clean, bindings very lustrous and virtually no wear to joints or extremities. Phillip J. Pirages 61 - 121 2013 $850

MacBeth, George *The Screens.* London: Turret Books, 1967. First edition, copy 58 of only 200 copies, a collection of 6 loose folded sheets with each having illustration and poem, loose sheets in fine condition and housed in close to near fine folded portfolio that has some tanning to edges, signed by Macbeth. Jeff Hirsch Books Fall 2013 - 129310 2013 $50

MacBride, Alexander *The Rev. Mr. Elder and the Supporters of the Gladstone Irish Policy.* Printed by John Chalmers, Rothesay, circa, 1870. 7 pages, modern wrappers, very good. C. P. Hyland 261 - 565 2013 £90

MacBride, MacKenzie *Wild Lakeland.* London: A. & C. Black, 1922. First edition, original blue blindstamped cloth gilt, extremities little rubbed, 32 colored plates by A. Heaton Cooper and maps. R. F. G. Hollett & Son Lake District & Cumbria - 309 2013 £40

MacCarthy, C. J. F. *Regional Defence, a Nation in Arms.* Cork: Forum Press, 1944. 139 pages, ads, wrappers, 8vo., signed, good. C. P. Hyland 261 - 567 2013 £45

Macclesfield, George Parker, Earl of *Remarks upon the Solar and Lunar Years, The Cycle of 19 Years, Commonly called the Golden Number...* printed for Charles Davis, 1750. First separate edition, folding table at ed, 4to., later (not recent) marbled boards, very good. Blackwell's Rare Books Sciences - 92 2013 £550

MacCreagh, Gordon *The Last of Free Africa.* Century Co., 1928. First edition, original brown cloth gilt, well illustrated. R. F. G. Hollett & Son Africana - 136 2013 £35

MacCulloch, John 1773-1835 *A Geological Classification of Rocks...* published by Longman, Hurst, Rees, Orme and Brown, 1821. First edition, large 8vo., uncut in original boards, rebacked in nearly matching paper, slightly damaged label preserved, corners bumped, pencil ownership inscription inside front cover of James Edmonstone FGS dated 8173, neat drawing by him and hammer opposite and pencil note inside back cover, indexing reference to Corstorphine Hill, small oval Edmondstone stamp on title, very good. Blackwell's Rare Books Sciences - 77 2013 £750

MacCurdy, Rahno Mabel *The History of the California Fruit Growers Exchange.* Los Angeles: printed by G. Rice and Sons, 1925. First edition, 4 photo plates, one full page engraving, gilt lettered green wrappers, fine. Argonaut Book Shop Recent Acquisitions June 2013 - 197 2013 $125

MacDermot, H. E. *Sir Thomas Roddick His Work in Medicine and Public Life.* Toronto: MacMillan Co., 1938. 8vo., cloth, dust jacket is very good, signed by author, erratum tipped in, illustrations. Schooner Books Ltd. 101 - 42 2013 $65

MacDonagh, Donagh *Veterans and other Poems.* Dublin: Cuala Press, 1941. Number 183 of 270 numbered copies, 8vo., original linen backed blue paper boards, title printed in black on upper panel and printed paper label on spine, uncut, dust jacket, fine in original numbered tissue dust jacket. Maggs Bros. Ltd. 1442 - 53 2013 £150

MacDonagh, Micahel *The Life of William O'Brien.* 1928. First edition, portrait, illustrations, 8vo., cloth, very good. C. P. Hyland 261 - 623 2013 £40

MacDonald, George 1824-1905 *At the Back of the North Wind.* New York: George Routledge & Sons, 1871. First American edition printed from British sheets with the same dates on both titlepages, this one of a few copies sent to US to secure copyright, 8vo., blue cloth stamped in gold and black, all edges gilt, 378 pages, chip at head of spine, binding lightly rubbed, really nice, bright copy, very good+, illustrations by Arthur Hughes, quite scarce. Aleph-Bet Books, Inc. 104 - 331 2013 $2100

MacDonald, James S. *Annals North British Society of Halifax Nova Scotia with Portraits and Biographical Notes 1768-1903.* Halifax: McAlpine Pub., 1905. Third edition, blue cloth with gilt spine and front cover, tartan endpapers, portraits and illustrations, 8vo., binding starting to loosen with inner hinge crack, interior very good. Schooner Books Ltd. 101 - 113 2013 $60

MacDonald, John D. *The Deep Blue Good-Bye.* Philadelphia and New York: Lippincott, 1975. First American hardback edition, very good, clean copy, would be near fine except for few pinholes to front endpaper, also top edge remainder mark in near fine or better dust jacket with 6.95 flap price and minor wear to extremities.   Ed Smith Books   78 - 36   2013 $150

MacDonald, John D. *Dress Her in Indigo.* London: Hale, 1971. First English edition, fine in dust jacket with short closed tear and crease on front and rear flap.   Mordida Books   81 - 331   2013 $300

MacDonald, John D. *The Girl in the Plain Brown Wrapper.* Philadelphia and New York: Lippincott, 1973. First American hardcover edition, near fine in brown boards with few spots to bottom edge, neat bookplate, very good plus jacket with few short vertical rubs on back panel, date code of 373 and flap price of $5.95.   Ed Smith Books   78 - 39   2013 $175

MacDonald, John D. *No Deadly Drug.* Garden City: Doubleday, 1968. First edition, fine in near fine dust jacket, signed and inscribed by author, scarce thus.   Leather Stalking Books   October 2013 - 2013 $450

MacDonald, John D. *One Fearful Yellow Eye.* Philadelphia and New York: Lippincott, 1977. First American hardbound edition, near fine, foxing to edges, near fine, clean dust jacket, slightly shorter than book.   Ed Smith Books   78 - 38   2013 $175

MacDonald, John D. *The Quick Red Fox.* Philadelphia and New York: Lippincott, 1964. First American hardcover edition, fine, faint offsetting to pastedowns from flaps, in fine dust jacket which is slightly shorter than the book, 1/16 of an inch.   Ed Smith Books   78 - 37   2013 $450

MacDonald, John D. *The Scarlet Ruse.* New York: Lippincott & Crowell, 1973. First American hardcover edition, fine in near fine dust jacket with tiny tears to spine folds.   Ed Smith Books   78 - 40   2013 $200

MacDonald, John D. *S*E*V*E*N.* London: Robert Hale, 1974. First hardcover edition, fine in dust jacket with some slight spine fading.   Mordida Books   81 - 333   2013 $75

MacDonald, John D. *A Tan and Sandy Silence.* Philadelphia: J. B. Lippincott, 1971. First American hardcover edition, fine in fine dust jacket with none of the usual spine fading and just touch of rubbing, very nice.   Between the Covers Rare Books, Inc.   Mystery & Detective Fiction - 291537   2013 $400

MacDonald, John D. *A Tan and Sandy Silence.* London: Hale, 1973. First hardcover edition, fine in dust jacket.   Mordida Books   81 - 332   2013 $300

MacDonald, John D. *Three for McGee - Nightmare in Pink. A Purple Place for Dying. The Deep Blue Good-by.* Garden City: Doubleday, 1967. Omnibus, fine in dust jacket, nicks at spine ends and at corners.   Mordida Books   81 - 329   2013 $200

MacDonald, John D. *The Turquoise Lament.* Philadelphia: J. B. Lippincott, 1973. First edition, 8vo., foxing, very good++, in very good+ dust jacket with chips, short closed tears, minimal sun spine, dust jacket price clipped as is common with this title, '1073' code intact on flap.   By the Book, L. C.   38 - 91   2013 $1000

MacDonald, Philip *Forbidden Planet.* New York: Farrar, Straus and Cudahy, 1956. First edition, fine in price clipped, very good plus dust jacket that has one small nick at top of front panel and some light rubbing at extremities, very nice, very scarce thus.   Between the Covers Rare Books, Inc.   Sci-Fi, Fantasy & Horror - 56131   2013 $2000

MacDonald, Philip *Warrant for X.* Garden City: Doubleday Crime Club, 1938. First American edition, fine in near fine dust jacket with lightly frayed spine ends, wear along front panel fold and some light stains on back panel.   Mordida Books   81 - 334   2013 $350

MacDonald, Ross *Archer in Hollywood.* New York: Knopf, 1967. First omnibus edition, fine in price clipped dust jacket.   Mordida Books   81 - 339   2013 $100

MacDonald, Ross *Archer in Hollywood.* New York: Alfred A. Knopf, 1967. First edition, near fine in very good++ dust jacket with mild soil, minimal sun spine and edge wear, 8vo., ix, 528 pages, signed, inscribed and dated by author.   By the Book, L. C.   36 - 52   2013 $750

MacDonald, Ross *Archer in Jeopardy.* New York: Knopf, 1979. Omnibus edition, fine in dust jacket with slight spine fading.   Mordida Books   81 - 345   2013 $75

MacDonald, Ross *The Barbarous Coast.* New York: Knopf, 1956. First edition, some discoloring along top of page edges, otherwise fine in dust jacket with couple of short closed tears, light wear at corners and faint stain on back panel.   Mordida Books   81 - 337   2013 $300

MacDonald, Ross *The Chill.* New York: Knopf, 1964. First edition, fine in dust jacket with tiny wear at spine ends and lightly soiled back panel.   Mordida Books   81 - 338   2013 $200

MacDonald, Ross *A Collection of Reviews.* Northridge: Lord John, 1979. First edition, unbound uncorrected flat page proof with two pages to a sheet, very fine.   Mordida Books   81 - 344   2013 $250

MacDonald, Ross *The Drowning Pool.* New York: Knopf, 1950. First edition, cover edges slightly darkened, otherwise very good in dust jacket with internal tape mends along flap-fold, tears along folds, wear along spine folds and at corners.   Mordida Books   81 - 335   2013 $375

MacDonald, Ross *Find a Victim.* New York: Knopf, 1954. First edition, fine in lightly soiled dust jacket with several short closed tears.   Mordida Books   81 - 336   2013 $500

MacDonald, Ross *The Goodbye Look.* London: Collins Crime Club, 1969. First English edition, fine in dust jacket, tiny wear at corners and tiny tear.   Mordida Books   81 - 340   2013 $65

MacDonald, Ross *The Instant Enemy.* London: Collins Crime Club, 1969. First English edition, fine in price clipped dust jacket.   Mordida Books   81 - 341   2013 $85

MacDonnell, Eneas *Plain Facts, Demonstrating the Injustice and Inconsistency of Anti-Catholic Hostility.* Cork: Connor, circa, 1815. 39 pages, disbound, foxed but good.   C. P. Hyland   261 - 574   2013   £75

MacDougall, J. L. *History of Inverness County, Nova Scotia.* Belleville: Mika Pub,, 1972. Facsimile edition of original 1922 edition, 8vo., half title, frontispiece, portrait, tables, green cloth with gilt to spine and front cover, very good.   Schooner Books Ltd.   101 - 104   2013 $75

Macedo, Antonio *Breve Memoria.* Ponta Delagada: n.p., 1853. First edition, 8vo., 35 pages, original yellow wrappers, worn.   J. & S. L. Bonham Antiquarian Booksellers   Europe - 8953   2013   £30

MacEoin, Uinseann *Survivors: the Story of Ireland's Struggle.* 1980. First edition, Colman Doyle photos, 8vo., cloth, dust jacket, very good.   C. P. Hyland   261 - 575   2013   £90

MacGregor, Barrington *King Longbeard or Annals of the Golden Dreamland. A Book of Fairy Tales.* London and New York: John Lane and the Bodley Head, 1898. 262 pages plus 1 ad, initials, vignettes and full page plates by Charles Robinson, blue cloth boards, charming gilt illustrations, gift inscription and few pencil markings to front endpages and embossed ownership stamp in rear endpage, browning to all endpapers, otherwise interior is clean, very good.   The Kelmscott Bookshop   7 - 67   2013 $300

Machen, Arthur 1863-1947 *The Cosy Room and Other Stories.* London: Rich and Cowan Ltd., 1936. First edition, octavo, original pink brown cloth, spine panel lettered in green, top edge stained green.   L. W. Currey, Inc.   Fall Sampler Sept. 2013 - 146173   2013 $1500

Machen, Arthur 1863-1947 *The Green Round.* Sauk City: Arkham House, 1968. First American edition, fine in fine dust jacket, very bright, as new.   Between the Covers Rare Books, Inc.   Sci-Fi, Fantasy & Horror - 317379   2013 $120

Machen, Arthur 1863-1947 *The Terror.* London: Duckworth, 1917. First edition, pages browned as always, tiny chips from bottom corner of several pages and small spot on front board, still attractive, very good plus lacking dust jacket, label laid in indicating that this volume was from the library of Donald Wandrei.   Between the Covers Rare Books, Inc.   Sci-Fi, Fantasy & Horror - 43094   2013 $200

Machiavelli, Niccollo 1469-1527 *The Works of the Famous Nicholas Machiavel, Citizen and Secretary of Florence.* London: printed for T(homas) W(ood) for A. Churchill (and 10 others), 1720. Third edition, folio, some very slight worming to extreme outer edge of leading margin, otherwise fine, clean copy, full contemporary calf, double gilt ruled borders, raised and gilt banded spine with small repair 'flower head' motif, red and black gilt labels.   Jarndyce Antiquarian Booksellers   CCV - 185   2013   £850

MacInnes, Colin *City of Spades.* New York: Macmillan, 1958. First American edition, tiny ink date on front fly, else fine in near fine dust jacket with touch of rubbing and couple of tiny nicks, very attractive.   Between the Covers Rare Books, Inc.   165 - 204   2013 $250

MacIntyre, Heather *Country Roads I and II. History of Mira (Cape Breton).* N.P.: n.p. 1960's and, 1984. 2 volumes, illustrated card covers, stapled, quarto, 44 and 66 pages, numerous maps and black and white illustrations, quarto, volume I has previous owner's stamp to prelim leaves and light soiling to covers and outer edges, volume II has previous owner's stamp to front cover and first flyleaf, otherwise very good.   Schooner Books Ltd.   102 - 78   2013 $75

MacIsaac, Fred *The Mental Marvel.* Chicago: A. C. McClurg, 1930. First edition, fine in internally repaired, good only dust jacket with scrape on front panel, much of spine lettering faded, some modest overall wear.   Between the Covers Rare Books, Inc.   Sci-Fi, Fantasy & Horror - 178062   2013 $200

Mack, Lizzie *A Christmas Tree Fairy.* Griffin Farran, Okeden & Welsh, n.d., 1887. First edition, original cloth backed glazed pictorial boards, corners trifle bruised, neatly recased, unpaginated, 10 color plates and tinted text vignettes, occasional very slight fingering and few faint spots, but very good, scarce.   R. F. G. Hollett & Son   Children's Books - 375   2013   £225

Mack, Robert Ellice *Nister's Holiday Annual 1890.* Ernest Nister, 1890. Small 4to., original cloth backed glazed, pictorial boards, rather worn, corners bruised and rounded, 6 fine chromolithograph plates and numerous full page and text woodcuts, including full page drawing by Louis Wain, rather shaken and loose. R. F. G. Hollett & Son   Children's Books - 376   2013   £75

MacKay-Smith, Alexander *American Foxhunting Stories.* Millwood: Millwood House, 1996. Expanded edition, illustrations, 4to., signed on special autographed leaf, fine. Beasley Books   2013 - 2013 $100

MacKenzie, Alexandre *Tableau Historique et Politique Du Commerce Des Pelleteries Dans Le Canada Depuis 1608.* Paris: 1807. 8vo., original paper wrappers with printed paper title label to spine, half title, frontispiece, paper wrappers very worn with paper repairs to edges of covers. Schooner Books Ltd.   105 - 159   2013 $1200

MacKenzie, Alister *The Spirit of St. Andrews.* Chelsea: Sleeping Bear Press, 1995. First edition, copy 688 from an edition of 1500, 324 pages, numerous illustrations, fine, green leather, fine slipcase, without dust jacket as issued. Jeff Hirsch Books   Fall 2013 - 129300   2013 $150

MacKenzie, Eneas *A Descriptive and Historical Account of the Town and Country of Newcastle Upon Tyne...* Newcastle upon Tyne: printed and published by Mackenzie and Dent, 1827. 2 volumes bound as 1, 4to., frontispiece and other engraved plates, foxed in places, modern half calf by John Henderson 1976, armorial bookplate of Archibald Dawnay.   Unsworths Antiquarian Booksellers   28 - 184   2013   £250

MacKenzie, Eneas *An Historical, Topographical and Descriptive View of the County Palatine of Durham.* Newcastle upon Tyne: 1834. 2 volumes, 4to., folding engraved map frontispieces and other engraved plates, plates foxed, frontispiece offset onto title, contemporary half tan calf, marbled boards, spines divided by false raised bands, compartments infilled with blind tools, brown morocco labels.   Unsworths Antiquarian Booksellers   28 - 185   2013   £250

MacKenzie, Henry *The Man of Feeling.* London: printed by W. M'Dowal, Pemberton Row, for Harrison and Co., 1803. 12mo., signed in fours, 7 engraved plates, 3 parts bound in 1, but with continuation pagination for parts two and three, occasional slight browning, full contemporary mottled calf, gilt spine, black morocco label, 1956 ownership inscription.   Jarndyce Antiquarian Booksellers   CCIV - 193   2013   £65

MacKenzie, Therese *Dromana: The Memoirs of an Irish Family.* 1907. Deluxe edition first edition, vellum bound, ms. notes by member of the Villiers Stuart family.   C. P. Hyland   261 - 413   2013   £350

MacKnight, Thomas *History of the Life and Times of Edmund Burke.* London: Chapman and Hall, 1858. First edition, 3 volumes, handsome set, full contemporary calf, gilt ruled borders, gilt panelled spines with original red and green morocco labels, marbled edges and endpapers, inscription dated 1866, some foxing to endpapers.   Ken Spelman Books Ltd.   75 - 124   2013   £160

Mackworth-Praed, Cyril Winthrop *Birds of Eastern and North Eastern Africa.* London: Longmans, Green and Co., 1957-1960. Second edition, 2 volumes, thick 8vo., original cloth, gilt, dust jackets, 1000 color illustrations, 20 plates and numerous marginal drawings and maps, endpaper maps little browned, otherwise excellent sound set.   R. F. G. Hollett & Son   Africana - 138   2013   £180

Mackworth, John *The Raid of the Terribore: a Modern Adventure Story.* Philadelphia: London: J. B. Lippincott Co., 1937. First US edition, octavo, inserted frontispiece with color illustration by Reginald Mills, black and white illustrations in text, some full page by Thomas Somerfield, original pictorial blue cloth, front panel stamped in black and white, spine panel stamped in black, top edge stained black. L. W. Currey, Inc.   Fall Sampler Sept. 2013 - 146522   2013 $150

MacLean, Alistair *The Last Frontier.* London: Collins, 1959. First edition, bookplate, fine in dust jacket.   Mordida Books   81 - 347   2013 $100

MacLeish, Archibald *Einstein.* Paris: Black Sun Press, 1929. First edition, one of 100 numbered copies (of 150 copies), printed in black & red on Van Gelder handmade paper, this unnumbered being stamped H(ors) Commerce) and reserved for presentation purposes, frontispiece of MacLeish by Paul Emile Becat, tissue guard present, 4to., printed cream wrappers, untrimmed, tissue jacket, somewhat defective, fine, half title inscribed by author for Bob and Odile Lovett 12th Jan. 1930.   Blackwell's Rare Books   172 - 269   2013   £500

MacLeish, Archibald *The Pot of Earth.* Boston and New York: Houghton Mifflin, 1925. First edition, 1/100 copies, 12mo., pages 45, cloth backed printed boards, some dust worn, very nice, untrimmed.   Second Life Books Inc.   183 - 255   2013 $100

MacLeod, Charles Stuart *Peter Rabbit and the Big Brown Bear.* Philadelphia: Henry Altemus, 1924. First edition, frontispiece and 13 color illustrations by Bess Goe Willis, red cloth backed purple boards, color illustration pasted front cover, edges covers with very slight fading, some marking to margins page 6/7, occasional thumbing and other odd mark contents, very good in soiled and slightly worn dust jacket. Ian Hodgkins & Co. Ltd.   134 - 9   2013   £60

MacLiammoir, Michael *The Importance of Being Oscar.* London: Heinemann, 1968. Uncorrected proof, 8vo., original wrappers, excellent copy.   Maggs Bros. Ltd.   1442 - 205   2013   £75

MacLiammoir, Michael *Oidhcheanna Sidhe: Fairy Nights.* Talbot Press, 1922. First edition, color stiff wrappers, 93 pages, color frontispiece, black and white text illustrations, cover dull, text very good, very rare, 8vo., cloth.   C. P. Hyland   261 - 578   2013   £350

Maclure, William *Opinions on Various Subjects.* Harmony: printed at the School Press, 1831-1838. First complete edition, 8vo., dust jacket three quarter black calf, marbled sides, marbling on volume III differs slightly but all 3 volumes contain old library labels of Marietta Public Library & binder's ticket of Peterson of Philadelphia pages 475-6 (one leaf) in volume I lack the bottom five lines of text, same volume was cracked down spine and repaired at front cover is nearly detached, text browned, volumes II-III are very nice, intact, clean and unfoxed.   M & S Rare Books, Inc.   95 - 208   2013 $2750

MacNeice, Louis *Collected Poems 1925-1948.* London: Faber and Faber, 1954. First edition, 8vo., original blue cloth, dust jacket, near fine, jacket slightly browned. Maggs Bros. Ltd.   1442 - 2076   2013   £50

MacNeill, Marie *The Festival of Lughnasa.* London: Oxford University Press, 1962. First edition, 8vo., original green cloth, near fine in slightly chipped and rubbed dust jacket, from the library of Richard Murphy, inscribed by author for Murphy.   Maggs Bros. Ltd.   1442 - 208   2013   £250

Macray, William Dunn *A Manual of British Historians to A.D. 1600.* London: William Pickering, 1845. 8vo., half title, decorative initial letters, good, contemporary blind panelled dark calf with new red morocco label, ownership names struck through on endpapers.   Ken Spelman Books Ltd.   75 - 110   2013   £85

MacSweeney, Patrick M. *A Group of Nation Builders.* 1913. First edition, portraits, 8vo., cloth, very good.   C. P. Hyland   261 - 586   2013   £55

MacVicar, Agnus *The Canisbay Conspiracy.* London: Long, 1956. First edition, inscribed by author, fine in dust jacket with slight spine fading and short closed tear.   Mordida Books   81 - 354   2013 $85

Madan, Martin *The Elyphthora; or a Treatise on Female Ruin...* London: Dodsley, 1781. Second edition of volumes 1 and 2, first edition of volume 3, 8vo., top edge gilt, later three quarter calf, stamped in gilt, first signature loose in volume 3, otherwise very good.   Second Life Books Inc.   182 - 274   2013 $1250

Madden, R. R. *Catalogue of the Library of Dr. R. R. Madden.* Bennett & Son, 1886. 114 pages, wrappers, good.   C. P. Hyland   261 - 122   2013   £50

Madeira. Funchal: n.p., n.d., 1910. First edition, small oblong folio, 12 color plates, original grey decorative wrappers.   J. & S. L. Bonham Antiquarian Booksellers   Europe - 8972   2013   £30

Madison, Lucy Foster *Washington.* Philadelphia: Penn, 1925. First edition, thick 4to., blue gilt cloth, pictorial paste-on, 399 pages, mint in publisher's box with color plate on cover, illustrations by Brandywine school artist Frank Schoonover, rare in box.   Aleph-Bet Books, Inc.   104 - 511   2013 $500

Madurell Marimon, Jose Maria *Documentos para la Historia de la Imprenta y Libreria en Barcelona 1474-1553.* Barcelona: Gremios de Editores de Libreros y de Maestros Impresores, 1955. First edition, gift copy, from the library of Alberto Parreno (bookplate), small 4to., loose gatherings in printed wrapper and slipcase, unopened copy (uncut), small stain to margin of one leaf, else fine in worn wrapper and lightly soiled slipcase.   Kaaterskill Books   16 - 59   2013 $500

Maeterlinck, Maurice *Tyltyl.* New York: Dodd Mead, 1920. First edition, 4to., blue cloth, pictorial paste-on, 159 pages, nearly as new in publisher's pictorial box (some soil and flap repair but very good+ box), illustrations by Herbert Paus with 8 very lovely tipped in color plates with guards, pictorial endpapers, amazing copy.   Aleph-Bet Books, Inc.   105 - 374   2013 $325

Maeterlinck, Maurice *La Vie des Abeilles. La Vie des Fourmis. La Vie des Termites.* Paris: Artisan du Livre, 1930. First edition, 3 volumes, of the total edition of 780 copies, this deluxe example is one of 20 de tete, printed on Japon imperial paper, none of which were for sale, about 750 pages, 32 original black and white etchings, with additional suite of 32 etchings, all hors texte, all full page etchings signed in plate, 3 volumes in publisher's wrappers, original chemise and slipcase, 8 x 6 inches, excellent copy, most pages unopened, very rare with 37 hors text etchings verus 5 in regular issue.   Gemini Fine Books & Arts., Ltd.   Art Reference & Illustrated Books - 2013 $1500

Magalaner, Marvin *A James Joyce Miscellany: Second Series.* Carbondale: 1959. First edition, 8vo., cloth, dust jacket, very good, scarce.   C. P. Hyland   261 - 520   2013   £40

Magee, David *The Hundredth Book; A Bibliography of the Publications of the Book Club of California.* n.p.: San Francisco, 1958. 1 of 400 copies, xxiii, 80 pages, illustrations, folio, some age toning, else near fine, tan linen spine, paper label and decorated boards.   Dumont Maps & Books of the West   122 - 44   2013 $225

Mager, Gus *Hawkshaw the Detective.* Akron: Saalfield Pub. Co., 1917. First edition, oblong quarto, illustrated wrappers, cheap paper browned with few very small chips in margins, some soiling and faint creases to wrappers, but solid, good or better copy.   Between the Covers Rare Books, Inc.   Mystery & Detective Fiction - 283466   2013 $200

Maggi, Girolamo *De Tintinnabulis Liber Postumus. (with, as issued) De Equleo Liber Postumus...* Amsterdam: Sumptibus Andreae Frisii, 1664. Enlarged edition, engraved half title and 5 engraved plates, numerous full page engravings within pagination, 12mo., 19th century biscuit calf, spine lettered in gilt, marbled edges and endpapers, bit rubbed and marked, bookplate of Rev. George Innes of the College, Warwick, good.   Blackwell's Rare Books   172 - 95   2013   £600

Maggs Bros. Ltd. *Food and Drink through the Ages 2500 BC to 1937 A.D: a Catalogue of Antiquities, Manuscripts, Books...* London: Maggs Bros. Ltd., 1937. First edition, wrappers slightly soiled, very near fine, ex-James Gabler.   Between the Covers Rare Books, Inc.   Cocktails, Etc. - 83257   2013 $125

The Magic Lantern; or Green Bag Plot Laid Open: a Poem. London: S. W. Fores, 1820. (44) pages, illustrations, disbound.   Jarndyce Antiquarian Booksellers   CCV - 47   2013   £40

Magloire-Saint-Aude, Clement *Veillee.* Port-au-Prince: Imprimerie Renelle, 1956. First edition, signed by author with full page inscription to poet Barbara Howes, stitching absent, staining to covers, good in wrappers, with wraparound band addressed to Howes in author's hand, excellent association.   Ken Lopez Bookseller   159 - 125   2013 $750

Magnus, Olaus *Historia de Gentibus Septentrionalibus.* Antwerp: Jean Bellere, 1562. 8vo., woodcut printer's device on title and innumerable woodcuts in text, final leaf with corroded ink blot with loss of text to last 5 lines, rust spot in outer margin of another leaf touching initial letter of a side-note, contemporary calf, 3 panels blind ruled on covers with connecting diagonals, central panels with gilt a snowflake at each corner and a prancing reindeer at centre, 17th century paper manuscript lettering piece on spine, in superior compartment a similar shelf number, traces of later label at foot of spine, headcaps defective, old repair to that at head, few abrasions to lower cover, corners little worn, one early 17th century and one later ownership inscription of Jesuit College of Cordoba, with ink stamp of same provenance, unsuccessful attempt having been made to bleach out part of inscriptions, one or two early marginal annotations, printer's waste endpapers, two bifolia from 1548 Lyons printing of works of Horace, good, attractive copy.   Blackwell's Rare Books   172 - 96   2013   £1600

Maguire, J. F. *Home Government for Ireland, Being a Series of Articles from the Cork Examiner.* Dublin: Falconer, 1872. 8vo., 48 pages, disbound, very good.   C. P. Hyland   261 - 590   2013   £35

Mahabharata. Bhagavadgita *Song Celestial, or the Bhagavad Gita.* Philadelphia: David McKay, 1934. 4to., black cloth, stamped in silver, pictorial paste-on, mint in publisher's box, 18 gravure plates by Willy Pogany.   Aleph-Bet Books, Inc.   105 - 462   2013 $300

Mahan, A. T. *Some Neglected Aspects of War.* Boston: Little Brown, 1970. First edition, very good, darkened spine.   Beasley Books   2013 - 2013 $50

Mahan, D. H. *An Elementary Course of Civil Engineering for the Use of Cadets of the United States' Military Academy.* New York: Wiley and Putnam, 1837. First edition, large 8vo., 14 large folding plates, original cloth back hinge cracked, but sound, light foxed.   M & S Rare Books, Inc.   95 - 209   2013 $275

Mahon, Derek *Antarctica.* Dublin: Gallery Press, 1985. First edition, 8vo., original black cloth, dust jacket, signed by author on titlepage, fine in dust jacket.   Maggs Bros. Ltd.   1442 - 196   2013   £150

Mahon, Derek *Art Notes.* Oldcastle: Gallery Press, 2006. First edition, limited to 175 copies, signed by author and artist, (150 for sale), 8vo., original blue handsewn wrappers, fine in dust jacket.   Maggs Bros. Ltd.   1442 - 199   2013   £60

Mahon, Derek *High Time, After Moliere.* Dublin: Gallery Press, 1985. First edition, 8vo., original black cloth, fine in dust jacket.   Maggs Bros. Ltd.   1442 - 195   2013   £75

Mahon, Derek *High Water.* Oldcastle: Gallery Press, 2000. First edition, limited to 175 copies, 8vo., single card folded once, fine.   Maggs Bros. Ltd.   1442 - 197   2013   £75

Mahon, Derek *Homage to Gaia.* Loughcrew: Gallery Press, 2008. First edition, limited to 175 copies signed by author and artist (150 for sale), fine in dust jacket, 8vo., original yellow wrappers printed in black and hand sewn with black thread.   Maggs Bros. Ltd.   1442 - 201   2013   £75

Mahon, Derek *A Kensington Notebook.* London: Anvil Press Poetry, 1984. First edition, number 142 of 250 numbered copies, signed by author, from a total edition of 500, small 8vo., original red wrappers, sky blue marbled paper wrappers, fine.   Maggs Bros. Ltd.   1442 - 194   2013   £50

Mahon, Derek *Lives.* London: Oxford University Press, 1972. First edition, 8vo., original wrappers, near fine. Maggs Bros. Ltd. 1442 - 190 2013 £75

Mahon, Derek *Poems 1962-1978.* Oxford: Oxford University Press, 1979. First edition, 8vo., signed by author, original brown cloth, fine in dust jacket. Maggs Bros. Ltd. 1442 - 193 2013 £120

Mahon, Derek *Resistance Days.* Oldcastle: Gallery Press, 2001. First edition, limited to 150 copies, signed by author and artist, from a total edition of 175, 8vo., original grey wrappers, hand-sewn with black thread, fine, drawings by Michael Kane. Maggs Bros. Ltd. 1442 - 198 2013 £75

Mahon, Derek *The Sea in Winter.* Dublin: Gallery Press, 1979. First edition, limited to 300 copies signed by author, 8vo., original black cloth, dust jacket, fine. Maggs Bros. Ltd. 1442 - 192 2013 £150

Mahon, Derek *Sextus and Cynthia.* Dublin: Gallery Press, 2009. Number 143 of 175 copies signed by author (150 for sale), drawings by Hammnd Journeaux, 8vo., original lilac wrappers, hand sewn with black thread, fine. Maggs Bros. Ltd. 1442 - 202 2013 £55

Mahon, Derek *Twelve Poems.* Belfast: Festival Publications, Queen's University of Belfast, 1965. First edition, 8vo., original white wrappers, purple sun device on upper cover, slight production crease at corners of couple of leaves, otherwise fine. Maggs Bros. Ltd. 1442 - 189 2013 £450

Mahony, Francis S. *The Reliques of Father Prout.* 1860. Revised edition, 8vo., cloth, illustrations, good. C. P. Hyland 261 - 592 2013 £25

Maidment, James *A Book of Scottish Pasquils 1568-1715.* Edinburgh: William Paterson, 1868. One of 3 copies on vellum, (there were a limited but unspecified, number of copies, also printed on paper), 206 x 128mm., handsome contemporary crimson morocco, attractively gilt by Andrew Grieve (stamp signed), covers gilt with multiple plain and decorative rules enclosing a delicate dentelle frame, large intricate fleuron at center of each cover, spine gilt in double ruled compartments with complex fleuron centerpiece and scrolling floral cornerpieces, turn-ins decorated with plain and decorative gilt rules, patterned burgundy and gold silk endleaves, top edge gilt, slightly worn matching morocco lipped slipcase; woodcut titlepage illustration, numerous decorative tailpieces and occasional woodcut vignettes in text; armorial bookplate of H. D. Colvill-Scott, armorial bookplate of Clarence S. Bemens; tiny dark spot on spine, corners with just hint of rubbing, couple of leaves with slightly rumpled fore edge, still fine, text clean, smooth and bright, binding unusually lustrous and with virtually no wear. Phillip J. Pirages 63 - 479 2013 $4800

Main, Neville *The Bookworms.* Brockhampton Press, n.d. circa, 1960. Oblong 12mo., original cloth backed pictorial wrappers, rebacked and rather creased, 2 illustrations per page, printed in red and black. R. F. G. Hollett & Son Children's Books - 377 2013 £25

Maitland, Barry *The Marx Sisters.* London: Hamilton, 1994. First edition, fine in price clipped dust jacket with crease on inner rear flap. Mordida Books 81 - 355 2013 $500

Major, Clarence *Swallow the Lake.* Middletown: Wesleyan University Press, 1970. First edition, hardcover issue, top corners very slightly bumped, else fine in dust jacket. Between the Covers Rare Books, Inc. 165 - 205 2013 $100

Major's Alphabet. New York: McLoughlin Bros. n.d. circa, 1870. 8vo., pictorial wrappers, slight bit of margin soil on rear cover, else fine+ condition, beautiful copy, featuring 3 pictures per page. Aleph-Bet Books, Inc. 104 - 12 2013 $425

Makkreel, Rudolf A. *Imagination and Interpretation in Kant: the Hermeneutical Import of the Critique of Judgment.* Chicago: University of Chicago Press, 1990. First edition, fine in fine dust jacket. Between the Covers Rare Books, Inc. Philosophy - 100497 2013 $65

Malanga, Gerard *Screen Tests: A Diary.* New York: Kulchur Press, 1967. First edition, from an edition of less than 500, octavo, 54 black and white screen text portraits, by Andy Warhol, each portrait printed on vellum translucent paper and accompanied by a poem by Malanga on facing page, in original full color photographic wrappers, title, authors and $2 printed in white on front wrapper, spine lettered in red and blue, some light creasing to front and back wrapper, spine chipped and repaired, few small pieces missing from spine, most letters intact, slight wrinkle to photograph number 43, final 3 portraits, very good, scarce. Heritage Book Shop Holiday Catalogue 2012 - 155 2013 $2750

Malapert, Charles *Poemata.* Dilingen: Ulrich Rem, 1622. 12mo., woodcut Jesuit device on title, gap in margin between first leaf and next (turn-in from binding around first leaf having drawn it apart), minor staining here and there. Blackwell's Rare Books B174 - 96 2013 £250

Malcolm, Elizabeth *Ireland Sober, Ireland Free.* 1986. First edition, 8vo., review copy, cloth, dust jacket, fine. C. P. Hyland 261 - 593 2013 £40

Malcolmson, Anne *The Song of Robin Hood.* Boston: Houghton Mifflin, 1947. First edition, large 4to., pictorial cloth, near fine in very good dust jacket with chips off spine ends, slight fraying on edges, illustrations by Virginia Burton with black and whites on every page, this copy signed by Burton. Aleph-Bet Books, Inc.   105 - 108   2013 $850

Malinowski, Bronislaw *The Sexual Life of Savages.* New York: Eugenics Pub. Co., 1929. Later printing, very good with light wear to spine ends, pages darkened uniformly, without dust jacket as issued.   Between the Covers Rare Books, Inc.   Psychology & Psychiatry - 100726   2013 $50

Maloney, Ralph *The 24 Hour Drink Book: a Guide to Executive Survival.* New York: Ivan Obolensky Inc./Productions 14, 1962. First edition, illustrations by Leo Summers, fine in attractive, very near fine dust jacket with just touch of age toning and small finger puncture on front gutter, very scarce.   Between the Covers Rare Books, Inc.   Cocktails, Etc. - 279992   2013 $250

Malory, Thomas *The Noble and Joyous Book Entytled Le Morte Darthur...* Chelsea: At the Ashendene Press, 1913. One of 147 copies on paper (not 145 as stated in colophon), out of a total edition of 155, folio, printed in red and black in Subiaco type, chapter headings and shoulder notes in red, initial letters designed by Graily Hewitt and printed in alternating red and blue, 2 full page woodcuts, one at beginning and one at end of book, 27 smaller woodcuts, original full brown calf, gilt lettered spine with raised bands, board edges and turn-ins ruled in blind, corners very slightly bumped with lower back corner slightly rubbed through, few minor surface closed cracks to edges of spine top corner of front free endpaper with small professional repair, some light browning and foxing, mainly to preliminary and final blanks, near fine.   Heritage Book Shop   Holiday Catalogue 2012 - 5   2013 $10,000

Malory, Thomas *Le Morte D'Arthur.* London: Dent, 1927. 1/600 copies, 4to., lvi, 538 pages, plates and numerous illustrations by Aubrey Beardsley in text, 10 extra illustrations not included in first two printings, 22 full page and double page illustrations by Beardsley, including fine frontispiece, black cloth stamped in gilt, cloth and paper of rear hinge splitting, little bumped at corner, untrimmed, very good.   Second Life Books Inc.   183 - 257   2013 $2000

Malory, Thomas *The Most Ancient and Famous History of the Renowned Prince Arthur King of Britainne.* London: printed by William Stansby for Jacob Bloome, 1634. Sixth edition, small quarto, 3 parts in 1 volume with separate titlepages each with facing woodcut of King Arthur and the Knights of the Round Table, black letter text, Roman and italic prelims, headlines, rubrics and proper names, first title skilfully repaired in inner and lower margins, frontispieces to parts I and II skilfully renewed in outer margins, that of 11 also restored at inner corner, with few letters supplied in facsimile, and just shaved at foot, E3 Part 1 mounted on guard, one catchword and headline at beginning of part II shaved, tiny rust hole in PP1 of Part II affecting one letter of headline, natural paper flaw affecting few letters in part III; bound by Bedford in 19th century brown morocco, ruled gilt on covers, decorated gilt on spine, all edges gilt, housed in custom brown cloth clamshell, very good, extremely rare.   Heritage Book Shop   50th Anniversary Catalogue - 70   2013 $40,000

Malouf, David *Johnno.* Queensland: University of Queensland Press, 1975. Correct first Australian edition, signed by author, bit of shelfwear to lower board edges, else fine in very near fine dust jacket with mild fading to spine, scarce, especially in such condition and signed.   Ken Lopez Bookseller   159 - 126   2013 $750

Malpighi, Marcello *Tetra Anatomicarum Epistolarum de Lingua et Cerebro Quibus Anonymi Accessit Exercitatio de Ormento... (bound with) De Externo Tactus Organ Anatomica Observatio.* Bologna: Vittorio Benacci, 1665. Naples: Aegidius Longus, 1665. First issue of first work and first edition, 2nd complete issue of second work, 3 folding engraved plates, 12mo., 18th century full calf, spine in gilt panels, vellum label applied to upper spine, one plate has tear repaired, light wear, else very good, tight copy, rare. James Tait Goodrich   75 - 139   2013 $12,500

Malpighi, Marcello *Opera Posthuma.* London: Impensis A. & J. Churchill, 1697. Portrait, 19 engraved plates, engraved allegorical frontispiece plus engraved portrait, title in red and black, folio, rebound in handsome quarter leather and marbled boards, text browning, occasionally heavy in spots, tear in frontispiece skillfully repaired, staining affecting lower blank margins of final leaves.   James Tait Goodrich   75 - 140   2013 $1750

Malthus, Thomas Robert 1766-1834 *Additions of the Fourth and Former Editions of an Essay on the Principle of Population.* London: John Murray, 1817. First edition, 229 x 152mm., original blue paper boards, rebacked in buff paper, original printed paper spine label, untrimmed edges, 19th century bookplate, spine label chipped and rubbed, significant loss of legibility, little soil and wear to original sides (as expected), but boards surprisingly well preserved, well restored binding absolutely tight, first few leaves and last three gatherings freckled with foxing, minor foxing elsewhere, few trivial spots, excellent internally, still rather fresh and not at all darkened or browned.   Phillip J. Pirages   63 - 326   2013 $950

Malthus, Thomas Robert 1766-1834 *An Essay on the Principle of Population or a View of Its Past and Present Effects on Human Happiness...* London: J. Johnson, 1806. Third edition, 2 volumes, traces of library blindstamps on titles, ink pressmarks, handsomely rebound in half calf, red labels.   Jarndyce Antiquarian Booksellers   CCV - 186   2013   £450

Malthus, Thomas Robert 1766-1834 *Principles of Political Economy Considered with a View to Their Practical Application.* London: William Pickering, 1836. Second edition, very good, original cloth with remnant of paper title label to spine, 8vo., hinges archivally and subtly strengthened, cover edge wear, sunning to spine and covers, owner name, dampstain to lower edge, pastedowns and endpapers, minimal scattered foxing.   By the Book, L. C.   38 - 18   2013 $900

Malton, Thomas *Views of Oxford.* London: White & Co.; Oxford: R. Smith, 1810. First complete edition, 411 x 315mm., appealing 19th century circa 1860s?), dark green half morocco over lighter green textured cloth by T. Aitken (stamp signed), upper cover with gilt titling, raised bands, spine gilt incompartments with elongated fleuron centerpiece and scrolling cornerpieces, gilt titling, marbled endpapers, all edges gilt (small, very expert repairs to upper outer corners and perhaps top of joints), mezzotint frontispiece after Gilbert Stuart, engraved title, 30 fine plates, 24 of then aquatints and 6 of them etched, armorial bookplates of Sir Mayson M. Beeton and Sir Richard Farrant, ink presentation inscription "Sir Charles Locock, Bart./ with Captn. Malton's kindest regards/Nov. 1860", subscription proposal for the work printed by T. Bensley and dated "London, May 30, 1301" (i.e. "1801"), laid in at front, couple of small smudges to boards, portrait faintly foxed and browned, isolated small stains (not affecting images), still fine, plates especially clean, fresh and smooth and pleasing binding with virtually no wear.   Phillip J. Pirages   63 - 327   2013 $9500

Mamet, David *The Frog Prince: a Play.* New York: Vincent FitzGerald & Co., 1984. One of 130 copies on rives paper, printed at Wild Carrot Letterpress by Karen with one original etching, signed and numbered in pencil by artist and 4 plates after drawing by Edward Koren. etching was pulled by Lynn Rogan of Printmaking Workshop, 4 additional illustrations printed on Misu paper at the Meriden Gravure Co., titlepage calligraphy by Jerry Kelly, all copies signed by Mamet and Korne, bound in orange cloth stamped in frog-green handmade endpapers by Gerard Charriere.   Priscilla Juvelis - Rare Books   56 - 8   2013 $700

Man, George Flagg *The Geranium Leaf.* Boston: Marsh, Capen, Lyon & Webb, 1840. First edition, fine, signed binding, 12mo., original gilt lettered and decorated green ribbon embossed cloth, blindstamped on both covers "Copeland Binder", signed by Robert McCleary Copeland, with 20th century gift inscription.   Howard S. Mott Inc.   262 - 95   2013 $200

Manchester, Henry Montagu, 1st Earl of *Manchester al Mondo.* London: printed by Iohn Haviland for Francis Constable, 1635. Title printed within double rules, twin line of printer's ornaments towards foot of page, text within single rules with empty column on outside, headpiece of triple row of printer's ornaments, sections with single row of ornaments at head, some soiling, paper flaws and few tears, but without loss, plentiful early annotations and later notes by Bernard G. Hall, 12mo., original calf double blind ruled borders on sides, corners worn, rebacked, sound.   Blackwell's Rare Books   B174 - 104   2013   £600

Mandeville, Bernard *The Fable of the Bees.* Oxford: 1957. 2 volumes, very good, 8vo., original gilt lettered dark blue cloth, dust jackets.   Ken Spelman Books Ltd.   75 - 182   2013   £80

Manget, Jean Jacques *Theatrum Anatomicum...* Geneva: Cramer & Perachon, 1717. First edition, frontispiece, 136 engraved plates, large folio, contemporary calf, rich gilt spine with compartments done in ornaments and filigrees, binding worn and rubbed, joints splitting, text foxing and light browning in text, overall pleasing, tight set.   James Tait Goodrich   75 - 141   2013 $3795

Maning, Hugo *Dead Seasons' Heritage.* Buenos Aires: Francisco Columbo, 1942. First edition, 93 pages, text in English, about very good in blue printed wrappers, somewhat soiled, some minor staining to rear panel, some creasing and bumping to corners, signed and inscribed by Manning, very uncommon thus.   Jeff Hirsch Books   Fall 2013 - 129287   2013 $150

Mankell, Henning *Pyramiden.* Stockholm: Ordfront Forlag, 1999. First Swedish edition, inscribed by author in year of publication, fine in fine dust jacket.   Ken Lopez Bookseller   159 - 127   2013 $250

Mankiewicz, Don M. *See How They Run.* New York: Alfred A. Knopf, 1951. First edition, fine in fine dust jacket, single short tear, very attractive copy, inscribed by author's mother with card laid in from his mother to recipient.   Between the Covers Rare Books, Inc.   Horses, Horsemanship, Horse Racing, Etc. - 283973   2013 $150

Mankowitz, Wolf *The Day of the Woman and the Night of the Men.* Ahakista: Ahaksita Press, 2000. Limited to 25 numbered copies, signed by author, although this copy neither numbered nor signed as author died before publication, 8vo., original brown cloth, lettered gilt, near fine in matching slipcase.   Maggs Bros. Ltd.   1442 - 209   2013   £60

Mankowitz, Wolf *XII Poems.* Ahakista: Ahaksita Pess, 1972. Limited to 250 numbered copies signed by author though this copy is neither numbered nor signed, original linen, lettered in gilt, fine in acetate dust jacket.   Maggs Bros. Ltd.   1442 - 67   2013   £50

Manly, William Lewis *Death Valley in '49.* San Jose: Pacific Tree and Vine Co., 1894. First edition, 498 pages, 4 halftone plates, illustrated chapter tailpieces, flora endpapers, publisher's decorated mustard cloth stamped in black on front cover stamped in blind on rear cover, spine lettered in gilt, tiny nick to head of spine (hardly noticeable), superior copy, very fine, clean and tight, housed in custom half leather clamshell box. Argonaut Book Shop Recent Acquisitions June 2013 - 200 2013 $1500

Manly, William Lewis *Death Valley in '49.* Los Angeles: Borden Pub. Co., 1949. Centennial edition, 524 pages, 31 full page photos, large folding map, tan cloth stamped in dark brown, very fine, pictorial dust jacket. Argonaut Book Shop Recent Acquisitions June 2013 - 201 2013 $75

Manly, William Lewis *The Jayhawkers' Oath and Other Sketches.* Los Angeles: Warren F. Lewis, 1949. First edition in book form, signed by editor, 168 pages, numerous illustrations, portraits, large folding map, tan cloth decorated in brown, very fine with pictorial dust jacket. Argonaut Book Shop Recent Acquisitions June 2013 - 202 2013 $90

Mann, J. H. *History of Gibraltar and Its Sieges.* London: Provost, 1873. Second edition, 8vo., map, 16 photos, some foxing but mainly in margins, plate frayed on fore-edge not affecting image, all photos clean, original red decorative cloth, rebacking using original spine. J. & S. L. Bonham Antiquarian Booksellers Europe - 9420 2013 £750

Mann, James *Time-Limited Psychotherapy.* Cambridge: Harvard University Press, 1973. First edition, small dampspot on front board, thus near fine in near fine dust jacket with smaller corresponding stain that is barely visible. Between the Covers Rare Books, Inc. Psychology & Psychiatry - 99281 2013 $50

Mann, Leonard *Murder in Sydney.* London: Cape, 1937. First edition, page edges spotted, otherwise very good in dust jacket with frayed spine ends, soiled back panel, wear along folds, couple of short closed tears. Mordida Books 81 - 356 2013 $100

Mann, Thomas *Schopenhauer.* Stockholm: Bermann-Fischer, 1938. First edition, printed self wrappers, spine little age toned, else near fine. Between the Covers Rare Books, Inc. Philosophy - 296899 2013 $50

The Manners of Polite Society; or Etiquette for Ladies and Gentlemen. London: Ward, Lock & Tyler, 1875. Half title preceding title, illustrations, 16 page catalog, original green cloth, bevelled boards, decorated in gilt and black, hinges little weak, spine slightly rubbed at head and tail, attractive copy. Jarndyce Antiquarian Booksellers CCV - 7 2013 £65

Manners, Janetta *Encouraging Experiences of Reading and Recreation Rooms; Aims of Gilds; Nottingham Social Gild...* Edinburgh: William Blackwood & Sons, 1886. Half titles, original pink paper wrappers, spine cracked with some slight loss, little dulled, presentation inscription from author for Mr. Humphreys. Jarndyce Antiquarian Booksellers CCV - 188 2013 £120

Manning, Frederick Edward *Old New Zealand; a Tale of the Good Old Times.* Auckland: Robert J. Creighton & Alfred Scales, 1863. Second edition, half title, occasional spotting, original green publisher's cloth, neatly recased maintaining original spine, good plus. Jarndyce Antiquarian Booksellers CCV - 187 2013 £180

Manning, Hugo *The Secret Sea.* London: Trigram Press, 1968. First edition, copy 57 from an edition of 100 specially bound and printed on T. Edmonds Mould-Made Blue Laid paper, 63 pages, fine in fine dust jacket, signed by Manning. Jeff Hirsch Books Fall 2013 - 129242 2013 $50

Manning, P. L. *The Destroyers.* London: John Spencer & Co. Ltd. n.d., 1958. First edition, small octavo, pictorial wrappers. L. W. Currey, Inc. Fall Sampler Sept. 2013 - 144015 2013 $100

Manning, R. *Trout Fishing.* Cork: Shandon Printing Works, 1915. First (and) only edition, 32 pages, portrait, 5 photos, original cloth with gilt titling, good. C. P. Hyland 261 - 595 2013 £150

Mansfield, Joseph K. F. *Mansfield on the condition of the Western Forts 1853-1854.* Norman: University of Oklahoma Press, 1963. First edition, 29 facsimiles, green cloth, very fine, dust jacket. Argonaut Book Shop Summer 2013 - 223 2013 $60

Mansfield, Katherine 1888-1923 *The Garden Party and Other Stories.* London: Verona, 1939. Limited to 1200 copies, this no. 170, small 4to., minimal cover edgewear, near fine dust jacket with mild sun to spine, original slipcase with mild wear, near fine copy, colored lithographs by Marie Laurencin. By the Book, L. C. 38 - 93 2013 $1300

Mansfield, Katherine 1888-1923 *In a German Pension.* New York: Knopf, 1926. First American edition, pages 200, foolscap 8vo., original medium green cloth, printed label, rough trimmed, dust jacket with faint backstrip panel fading, near fine. Blackwell's Rare Books B174 - 260 2013 £100

Manson, T. *Zig-Zag: Rambles of a Naturalist.* Darlington: Wm. Dresser, 1898. Second edition, 8vo., illustrations, original blue decorative cloth. J. & S. L. Bonham Antiquarian Booksellers Europe - 9310 2013 £35

Manwaring, Edward *Institutes of Learning: Taken from Aristotle, Plutarch, Longinus... and Many Other Writers Ancient and Modern.*   W. Innys and R. Manby, 1737.   8vo., very good, disbound.   Ken Spelman Books Ltd.   75 - 18   2013   £50

Maran, Rene *Batouala.*   New York: Thomas Seltzer, 1922.   First edition, 2 inch tear in rear joint, very good.   Beasley Books   2013 - 2013 $65

Maran, Rene *Batouala.*   New York: Limited Editions Club, 1932.   First edition thus, illustrations by Miguel Covarrubias, spine bit rubbed, else near fine in full pigskin in worn cardboard slipcase, lacking couple of pieces, signed by artist.   Between the Covers Rare Books, Inc.   165 - 313   2013 $225

Marcel-Turenne Des Pres, Francois *Children of Yayoute: Folk Tales of Haiti.*   Port-au-Prince: Editions Henri Deschamps, 1949.   First edition, illustrated paper wrappers, spine cocked, some foxing on wrappers, very good.   Between the Covers Rare Books, Inc.   165 - 206 2013 $85

Marcet, Jane Haldimand *Conversations of Political Economy; in which the Elements of that Science are Familiarly Explained.*   London: Longman, Hurst, Rees, Orme and Brown, 1821.   Fourth edition, 12mo., initial 12 page catalog (July 1884), half title, uncut in original grey boards, paper label, spine slightly rubbed and marked, very good.   Jarndyce Antiquarian Booksellers   CCV - 189   2013   £150

Marcosson, Isaac F. *An African Adventure.*   New York: John Lane, 1921.   First edition, original cloth, gilt, little bumped and marked, label removed from upper board, 48 plates.   R. F. G. Hollett & Son   Africana - 139   2013   £25

Marcy, Randolph Barnes   1812-1887 *Border Reminiscences.*   New York: 1872.   Original stamped boards, slight wear to extremities, dusty on top edge, previous owner's bookplate, else clean and very good.   Dumont Maps & Books of the West   124 - 76   2013 $150

Marge *Little Lulu and Her Magic Tricks.*   New York: S&S, 1954.   A, fine, illustrations by Marge, with the package of Klennex tissue on cover to be used to make the magic tricks, rare.   Aleph-Bet Books, Inc.   104 - 240   2013 $275

Margoliouth, Moses *Curates of Riversdale: Recollections in the Life of a Clergyman.*   London: Hurst and Blackett, 1860.   First edition, 3 volumes, half dark blue calf, marbled boards, expertly and handsomely rebacked, inscription to leading f.e.p. volume from author for Mrs. Buckley, later signature of M. Jane Hole.   Jarndyce Antiquarian Booksellers   CCV - 190   2013   £750

Maricain, Raissa *Chagall ou l'Orage Enchante.*   Geneve/Paris: Editions des Trois Collines, 1948.   Small quarto, half title, original color drawing and inscription by Marc Chagall for Samuel and Helen Slosberg, 8 full color plates tipped in with descriptions under the flaps, numerous black and white photographic plates and illustrations, many of which are full page, publisher's full green illustrated dust jacket wrapper, jacket illustrated and lettered in black ink, uncut and partially unopened, jacket with very slight amount of sunning to spine and minimal rubbing to spine extremities and edges, overall very good with beautiful original drawing.   Heritage Book Shop   Holiday Catalogue 2012 - 28   2013 $12,500

The Mariner's Concert, Being a New Collection of the Most Favorite Sea Songs...   printed by J. Evans, 1797.   4to., large woodcut vignette on title, poorly printed on cheap paper with bit of consequent browning, pages 8, early 20th century navy blue buckram lettered on upper cover, slightly worn, pencil note inside front cover, good, from the library of Lovat Fraser.   Blackwell's Rare Books   B174 - 132   2013   £375

Marino, Giambattista *L'Adone, Poems.*   Amsterdam: 1651.   2 volumes, 12mo. bound in sixes, small marginal tear to V1 volume II, some light browning, few ink splashes but very good, most handsome early 19th century dark blue straight grain morocco, gilt ruled borders, attractive gilt panelled spines decorated with flower head, open circles and small gilt dots, pink endpapers and pastedowns, armorial bookplate of John Barron, early inscription of J. Stirling, alter 19th century bookplate of Alfred Coco of Middle Temple, ownership name of J. Stroud Read, London Nov. 1928, earlier hand notes "Will. Roscoe's Library", all edges gilt.   Jarndyce Antiquarian Booksellers   CCV - 191   2013   £620

Maritain, Jacques *The Responsibility of the Artist.*   New York: Charles Scribner's Sons, 1960.   First edition, endpapers little darkened, else fine in very slightly spine faded , very near fine dust jacket, complimentary slip from author laid in, very nice.   Between the Covers Rare Books, Inc.   Philosophy - 91554   2013 $85

Maritain, Raissa *Patriarch Tree. thirty Poems.*   Worcester: Stanbrook Abbey Press, 1965.   390/500 copies (of an edition of 550), printed in black and red, on Barcham Green handmade paper, reproduction of photographic portrait tipped in, 4 large initial letters printed in green, imperial 8vo., original quarter black morocco, backstrip gilt lettered, patterned black boards, top edge gilt, tail edges untrimmed, board slipcase, fine.   Blackwell's Rare Books   B174 - 389   2013   £175

Marjoribanks, Alexander *Tour to the Loire and La Vendee in 1835...* London: Effingham Wilson, 1836. Second edition, frontispiece, original pink paper boards, green glazed cloth spine, paper label, spine slightly faded, signature of J. Menzies and library stamp of St. Mary's College, Blairs on leading pastedown, 'Eastern Division' stamp on title, very good.   Jarndyce Antiquarian Booksellers   CCV - 192   2013   £280

Markham, Clements Robert   1830-1916 *The Gaunches of Tenerife, the Holy Image of Our Lady of the Candelaria and the Spanish Conquest and Settlement.* London: Hakluyt, 1907. First edition, 8vo., illustrations, original green half calf, spine and edges worn, library label on upper endpaper.   J. & S. L. Bonham Antiquarian Booksellers   Europe - 6350   2013   £60

Markham, Clements Robert   1830-1916 *A Life of John Davis, the Navigator 1550-1605, Discoverer of Davis Straits.* London: 1889. vi, 301 pages, ads, illustrations, maps, slight shelfwear, bit cocked, bookplate on front pastedown, else clean and very good.   Dumont Maps & Books of the West   122 - 73   2013 $65

Markino, Yoshio *The Japanese Dumpy Book.* London: Grant Richards, 1902. First edition, 24mo., 96 pages, top edge gilt and list of dumpy books in facsimile, green cloth, good+.   Barnaby Rudge Booksellers   Children 2013 - 020273   2013 $60

Markovskaia, V. *Chto Takoye Khorosho Chto Takoye Plokho. (What Is Good and What is Bad?).* State publisher, 1930. 12mo. pictorial wrappers, light spine wear, corner creased, very good, illustrations by A. Lapmeva, with color lithographs.   Aleph-Bet Books, Inc.   105 - 514   2013 $600

Marlantes, Karl *Some Desperate Glory.* Berkeley: New York: El Leon/Grove Atlantic, 2010. Advance copy, early state reading copy labeled "Unedited Bound manuscript" with title Some Desperate Glory, signed by author, scarce early issue, stray ink mark on lower edge of block, else fine in wrappers.   Ken Lopez Bookseller   159 - 205   2013 $500

Marlow, Joyce *Captain Boycott and the Irish.* 1973. First edition, cloth, very good, octavo.   C. P. Hyland   261 - 147   2013   £32

Marmaduke, Mary Ellen Dandy *Walter Dandy: the Personal Side of a Premier Neurosurgery.* Philadelphia: 2002. 182 pages, numerous photos and illustrations, printed in small print run, scare.   James Tait Goodrich   S74 - 72   2013 $125

Marmion, Anthony *Ancient and Modern History of the Maritime Ports of Ireland.* 1860. Fourth edition, ex-library, but except for the presence of library stamps on each chapter head, very good.   C. P. Hyland   261 - 596   2013   £150

Marmontel, Jean Fracois   1723-1799 *Belisarius.* London: printed for and sold by P. Vaillant, 1767. First English edition, 12mo., some offsetting from turn-ins on to endpapers, full contemporary sprinkled calf, double gilt ruled borders, raised and gilt banded spine, red morocco label, hinges slightly cracked, head and tail of spine slightly chipped, corners little worn.   Jarndyce Antiquarian Booksellers   CCIV - 202   2013   £110

Marquand, John P. *The Late George Apley.* Boston: Little Brown, 1937. First edition, 8vo., near fine in very good dust jacket (small chips at spine and board corners and with one inch abrasion to front panel, not affecting either picture or text, probably from sticker removal).   Ed Smith Books   75 - 40   2013 $950

Marquardt, H. Michael *Early and Later Patriarchal Blessings of the Church of Jesus Christ of Latter-day Saints.* Salt Lake City: Smith Pettit Foundation, 2007-2012. First edition, 2 volumes, 447, 648 pages, quarto, maroon cloth boards with stamped gilt titles on covers and spines, both volumes new in publisher's shrink-wrap.   Ken Sanders Rare Books   45 - 24   2013 $350

Marriage of Cock Robin & Jenny Wren. London: Warne, circa, 1870. 4to., stiff pictorial wrappers mounted on linen, some wear to paper on rear cover and spine, very good, 8 very fine full page chromolithographs.   Aleph-Bet Books, Inc.   105 - 142   2013 $275

Marriott, Crittenden *The Isle of Dead Ships.* Philadelphia: Lippincott, 1909. First edition, color frontispiece and additional illustrations by Frank McKernan, slight wear to spine extremities, else fine in pictorial boards, very scarce.   Between the Covers Rare Books, Inc.   Sci-Fi, Fantasy & Horror - 45423   2013 $450

Marryat, Frederick   1792-1848 *Peter Simple.* London: Saunders & Otley, 1834. Third edition, 3 volumes, bound for the library of Nun-Appleton Hall in contemporary half green calf, gilt spines with family crest of a winged horse at head, maroon morocco labels, slight rubbing, but very good, attractive set, bookplate of Sir William Mordaunt Sturt Milner, 4th Baronet, Nun Appelton.   Jarndyce Antiquarian Booksellers   CCV - 193   2013   £150

Marryat, Frederick   1792-1848 *Poor Jack.* London: Longman, 1840. First edition, 38 plates and tailpieces, very good in contemporary dark green half morocco, gilt banded spine, marbled edges and endpapers, old stain to head of first few leaves and some slight foxing to plates.   Ken Spelman Books Ltd.   75 - 106   2013   £60

Marsden, Richard *Cotton Waving: Its Development, principles and Practice.* Chiswick Press for George Bell and Sons, and Manchester: Marsden, 1895. First edition, oval inkstamp of G. Peltzer - Teacher - Manchester on title, 8vo., original cloth, good.   Blackwell's Rare Books   Sciences - 119   2013   £60

Marsh, A. E. W. *Sketches and Adventures in Madeira, Portugal and the Andalusias of Spain.* New York: Harper Bros., 1856. First edition, 8vo., 445 pages, frontispiece, illustrations, original blue decorative cloth, small wear to head and tail of spine, very good.   J. & S. L. Bonham Antiquarian Booksellers   Europe - 8937   2013   £200

Marsh, J. B. T. *The Story of the Jubilee Singers, with Their Songs.* Boston: Houghton Mifflin Co., 1880? Revised edition, seventy-fifth thousand, frontispiece, wear to spine ends and corners, label on front fly, good or better copy. Between the Covers Rare Books, Inc.   165 - 242   2013 $100

Marsh, Ngaio *Final Curtain.* London: Collins Crime Club, 1947. First edition, page edges lightly soiled, otherwise fine in near fine dust jacket with slightly faded spine, wear along spine-fold and nicks at base of spine.   Mordida Books   81 - 360   2013 $185

Marsh, Ngaio *The Nursing Home Murder.* New York: Sheridan House, 1941. First American edition, some wear along cover edges, otherwise near fine in very good dust jacket with internal tape mends, external tape mend at base of spine chipping at base of spine, chipped lower corner of front panel, wear aong folds.   Mordida Books   81 - 362   2013 $250

Marsh, Ngaio *Overture to Death.* New York: Furman, 1939. First American edition, advance review copy with slip tipped in on front endpaper, some slight darkening on pastedowns, otherwise fine in dust jacket with light soiling on spine and nicks at top of spine.   Mordida Books   81 - 358   2013 $600

Marsh, Ngaio *Singing in the Shrouds.* London: Collins Crime Club, 1959. First English edition, some tiny spotting and darkening on page edges, otherwise fine in dust jacket with some spotting on back panel and tiny wear at corners.   Mordida Books   81 - 361   2013 $90

Marsh, Ngaio *Surfeit of Lampreys.* London: Collins Crime Club, 1941. First edition, some staining on spine and spine slightly faded otherwise very good in dust jacket with staining at base of spine, wear at corners and along spine ends, couple of short closed tears.   Mordida Books   81 - 359   2013 $650

Marsh, Ngaio *Vintage Murder.* London: Bles, 1937. Later edition, signed by Marsh, name and address on half titlepage and some scattered spotting on page edges, otherwise fine in red cloth covered black titles.   Mordida Books   81 - 357   2013 $200

Marshak, S. *Detke V Kletke. (Animal Babies in a Cage - Zoo Babies).* Leningrad: Ogiz, 1935. first edition with Charushin's illustrations, color lithographs, 4to., cloth backed pictorial boards, edges rubbed and cover toned, else very good.   Aleph-Bet Books, Inc.   104 - 501   2013 $800

Marshak, S. *Doska Sorevnovaniya. (Board of Soviet Competition).* Moscow: Maladaya Guardiya, 1931. First and only edition, small 4to., pictorial wrappers, very good to fine, illustrations in black and white by V. Lebedev.   Aleph-Bet Books, Inc.   104 - 505   2013 $2000

Marshak, S. *Bikvy (Living Letters).* Moscow: Goznak, 1947. 4to., pictorial wrappers, near fine, illustrations by Vladimir Lebedev, black and white lithographs.   Aleph-Bet Books, Inc.   105 - 365   2013 $2750

Marshak, S. *Posha.* Detizdat: n.d., circa, 1930. 4to., rich color illustrations on every page by N. Bondarenko, pictorial wrappers, near fine.   Aleph-Bet Books, Inc.   105 - 513   2013 $800

Marshal, Andrew *The Morbid Anatomy of the Brain, in Mania and Hydrophobia with the Pathology of These Two Diseases as Collected from the Papers of Andrew Marshal M.D...* London: Longman et al, 1815. 295 pages, silhouette frontispiece, offsetting of silhouette onto title, 295 pages, recent quarter calf and marbled boards, light browning of paper, else near fine, newly rebound, rare.   James Tait Goodrich   75 - 143   2013 $1250

Marshal, William *The Rural Economy of the Midland Counties....* Dublin: J. Moore, 1793. First Irish edition, some light spotting, 8vo., contemporary marbled calf, spine divided by double gilt fillets, red and green morocco lettering pieces, tiny chip to head of spine of volume i, old paper label to foot, bookplates of Essex Agricultural Society Lending Library and Essex Institute , very good.   Blackwell's Rare Books   B174 - 98   2013   £300

Marshall, Alfred *Principles of Economics Volume I (all published).* London: Macmillan and Co., 1890. First edition, scarce, original dark green diaper grain cloth, covers ruled in blind and spine ruled and lettered gilt, dark green coated endpapers, previous owner's signature, corners lightly bumped with some minor repairs to top and bottom of spine, light foxing to half title, otherwise very good. Heritage Book Shop   Holiday Catalogue 2012 - 102   2013 $7500

Marshall, John *The Life of George Washington.* London: printed for Richard Phillips by T. Gillt, 1804-1807. First English edition, 280 x 216mm., 5 volumes, large paper quarto edition, 16 engravings, as called for, including 12 folding maps, portrait and 3 views; publisher's quarter red roan over green paper boards, raised bands, spines attractively rebacked to style in modern times in panels with blind tooling and foliate gilt centerpiece, apparently original endpapers (hinges expertly reinforced, with matching paper); paper boards bit soiled and chafed, extremities little rubbed, by sympathetically rebacked bindings sturdy and attractive on shelf, one leaf with 3 inch tear into text (minimal loss), another with light brown stain touching but not obscuring text, one gathering somewhat foxed, occasional mild offsetting, otherwise clean and fresh internally with wide margins an few signs of use. Phillip J. Pirages 63 - 488 2013 $7500

Marshall, Joseph A. *Stonewall: a Biography of a Firefighter.* Philadelphia: Judson Press, circa, 1975. First edition, illustrated stapled wrappers, 19, (1) pages, frontispiece, fine, promotional flyer for book laid in, very scarce. Between the Covers Rare Books, Inc. 165 - 207 2013 $300

Martel, Yann *Life of Pi.* Canongate, 2002. First English edition, crown 8vo., original dark blue boards, backstrip blocked in silver, illustrated endpapers, rare first issue dust jacket with folds incorrectly aligned causing misalignment of backstrip panel, fine, titlepage inscribed by author to a member of Canongate's Export sales staff, Aline Hill. Blackwell's Rare Books 172 - 217 2013 £300

Martell, Dominic *Gitana.* London: Orion, 2001. First edition, very fine in dust jacket. Mordida Books 81 - 363 2013 $85

Martial, Marcus Valerius *Epigrammaton Libros Omnes, Plenis Commentariis, Novo Studio Confectis, Explicatos Emendatos.* Ingolstadt: Adam Sartorius, 1611. Second edition, 2 plates, titlepage in red and black with engraved vignette, very occasional light dampstaining to fore-edge, marginal tear to bottom of page 469, not affecting text, dark brown contemporary calf, neatly rebacked, gilt spine and borders, little cocked, few wormholes to upper board, some crackling to leather with sporadic areas of surface loss sympathetically painted in, bookplate of B(althazar) H(enri) de Fourcy to front pastedown, also more recent bookplate of "C.F." numbered 262 below it. Unsworths Antiquarian Booksellers 28 - 31 2013 £800

Martial, Marcus Valerius *Epigrammata Demptis Obscenis.* Paris: Apud Viduam Simonis Benard, 1693. 12mo., armorial binding, contemporary brown morocco, covers with gilt fleur de lys and interlaced crescents at alternate corners, large ornate gilt arms of town of Bordeaux, edges gilt, very pretty, bookplates (two) of Camille Aboussouan. Joseph J. Felcone Inc. Books Printed before 1701 - 11 2013 $600

Martial, Marcus Valerius *The Epigrams of M. Val. Martial in Twelve Books.* London: printed by Baker and Galabin, 1782. First edition of Elphinston's complete translations, 4to., engraved frontispiece, some foxing and browning in places, final ad leaf discarded, contemporary diced Russia, spine divided by raised bands between gilt rules, black morocco label, marbled endpapers, edges yellow, joints and endcaps rubbed, Ingleby family heraldic crest and monogram gilt stamped in compartments 1 and 6 respectively. Unsworths Antiquarian Booksellers 28 - 32 2013 £350

Martin, Annie *Home Life of an Ostrich Farm.* George Philip & Son, 1890. First edition, original cloth gilt, applied decorated paper panels, that on spine little chipped, 10 illustrations, lower hinge tender. R. F. G. Hollett & Son Africana - 140 2013 £60

Martin, Annie *Home Life on an Ostrich Farm.* New York: Appleton, 1891. First American edition, 8vo., orange cloth stamped in black and gilt, very good, tight copy. Second Life Books Inc. 183 - 260 2013 $100

Martin, Benjamin *A Course of Lectures in Natural and Experimental Philosophy, Geography and Astronomy...* Reading: printed and sold by J. Newberry and C. Micklewright (and others in London and the provinces), 1743. First edition, 8 folding engraved plates, some browning and spotting, 4to., recent half calf by Bernard Middleton, early 20th century ownership inscription, sound. Blackwell's Rare Books Sciences - 80 2013 £1500

Martin, Benjamin *Micrographia Nova; or a New Treatise n the Microscope and Microscopic Objects.* Reading: printed and sold by J. Newberry and C. Micklewright (and others in London),, 1742. First edition, 2 large folding engraved plates, both plates with long tears across middle repaired, some foxing, 4to., recent half calf by Bernard Middleton, sound. Blackwell's Rare Books Sciences - 79 2013 £1800

Martin, Benjamin *The Philosophical Grammar...* London: J. Noon, J. Rivington, G. Keith, et al, 1762. 8vo., 26 folding engraved plates, 2 folding tables, tears to plates, original full brown calf, raised bands, gilt stamped black leather spine label, rebacked to period style, corners bumped and showing, very good. Jeff Weber Rare Books 169 - 288 2013 $350

Martin, C. F. J. *Robert Grosseteste on the Six Days of Creation.* Oxford: Oxford University Press, 1996. 8vo., ix, 373 pages, navy cloth, gilt stamped spine title, dust jacket, ownership signature, fine, scarce. Jeff Weber Rare Books 169 - 174 2013 $100

Martin, Edward Winslow *The Secrets of the Great City: a Work Descriptive of the Virtues and Vices, the Mysteries, Miseries and Crimes of New York City.* Philadelphia: National Publishing Co., 1868. Large 8vo., original cloth. M & S Rare Books, Inc. 95 - 253 2013 $125

Martin, Ernest *Histoire des Monsires Depuis l'antiquite Jusqua Nos Jours.* Paris: C. Reinwald, 1880. Half title, uncut, early vellum backed marbled boards, light marginal dampstaining, else fine.   James Tait Goodrich   75 - 144   2013 $495

Martin, Frederick *The Life of John Clare.* London and Cambridge: Macmillan & Co., 1865. First edition, half title, vignette title, original green cloth, borders blocked in blind, spine lettered gilt, slightly rubbed, presentation "from the publisher", very good, bright.   Jarndyce Antiquarian Booksellers   CCIII - 489   2013   £110

Martin, J. Wallis *A Likeness in Stone.* London: Hodder & Stoughton, 1997. First edition, fine in dust jacket.   Mordida Books   81 - 364   2013 $250

Martin, Liam C. *Dublin Sketchbook.* Special edition for the Irish Georgian Society, Dolmen Press, 1962. Original cartridge paper wrappers with a 30th sketch 37 x 25 cm., 20 pages, very good.   C. P. Hyland   261 - 597   2013   £60

Martineau, Robert A. S. *Rhodesian Wild Flowers.* Longman, Green and Co. for the Trustees of the national Museums of Southern Rhodesia, 1953. First edition, small 4to., original cloth, gilt, dust jacket, edges little rubbed in places, price clipped, 34 colored plates, flyleaves lightly browned.   R. F. G. Hollett & Son   Africana - 141   2013   £30

Martyn, Thomas *Thirty-Eight Plates, with Explanations: Intended to Illustrate Linnaeus's System of Vegetables...* London: printed for B. White and Son, 1788. First edition, 8vo., modern antique calf, gilt leather labels, raised bands, black and white plates, blank corner of one leaf, otherwise fine.   Howard S. Mott Inc.   262 - 97   2013 $300

Martyn, Thomas *Thirty-Eight Plates, with Explanations: Intended to Illustrate Linnaeus's System of Vegetables...* London: printed for J. White, 1799. Third edition, hand colored edition, 8vo., modern antique calf, leather labels, raised bands, 38 engraved colored plates, without publisher's 2 pages ads, fine.   Howard S. Mott Inc.   262 - 98   2013 $450

Marx, Karl 1818-1883 *Kapital.* St. Petersburg: Izd N.P. Poliakova, 1872. First edition in Russian, 8vo., half contemporary Russian roan over black cloth, four raised bands, two compartments with Cyrillic lettering in gilt, boards rubbed and stained, front endpapers soiled, most of rear and paper removed, faint dampstain to lower portion of leaves, overall still very good.   Kaaterskill Books   16 - 60   2013 $10,000

Mary Mary Quite Contrary and Other Rhymes. New York: McLoughlin Bros., 1897. Tall 8vo., 3 chromolithographs inside and one on each of the covers, wrappers, very good.   Barnaby Rudge Booksellers   Children 2013 - 021331   2013 $60

Mascarenhas, Jose Freire de Monterroyo *Relacam dos Progressos das Armas Portuguezas no Estado da India...* Lisbon: Pascoal de Sylva, 1715-1716. First edition, 4 parts in one volume, 4to., 20th century polished blue morocco by Emile Rouselle, gilt dentelles and spine, some very light staining to titlepage of second part, otherwise very clean, attractive volume.   Maggs Bros. Ltd.   1467 - 55   2013   £3500

Masefield, John 1878-1967 *The Tragedy of Nan and Other Plays.* London: Grant Richards, 1909. First English edition, one of 500 copies, 8vo., original cloth, presentation copy from author to John Galsworthy, inscribed and dated Sept. 13th 1909, with Galsworthy's bookplate, covers faded, head of spine rubbed, evidently well read, presumably by recipient.   James S. Jaffe Rare Books   Fall 2013 - 95   2013 $1250

Masel, Arlene *Funny Little Woman.* New York: Dutton, 1972. Stated first edition, oblong 4to., cloth, fine in soiled dust jacket with seal, illustrations by Blair Lent.   Aleph-Bet Books, Inc.   105 - 367   2013 $200

Masich, Andrew E. *The Civil War in Arizona. the Story of the California Volunteers 1861-1865.* Norman: University of Oklahoma Press, 2006. First edition, photos, prints, reproductions, maps, cloth backed boards, very fine, pictorial dust jacket.   Argonaut Book Shop Summer 2013 - 226   2013 $75

Maskelyne, Nevil *Astronomical Observations Made at the Royal Observatory at Greenwich from the year MDCCLXV to the Year MDCCLXXIV.* printed by William Richarson and sold by J. Nourse, 1776. First edition, occasional foxing or browning, folio ?original boards, marbled edges (French style), sometime rebacked with paper, front pastedown formed of strips of large type French ads for epicierie, good.   Blackwell's Rare Books   Sciences - 81   2013   £500

Mason, A. E. W. *The Three Gentlemen.* Garden City: Doubleday Doran, 1932. First American edition, fine in price clipped dust jacket with tiny wear along edges.   Mordida Books   81 - 365   2013 $125

Mason, Edward T. *Songs of Fairyland.* New York: G. P. Putnam, 1889. First edition, 252 pages, illustrations by Maud Humphrey, blue gilt decorated binding, 252 pages plus ads.   Barnaby Rudge Booksellers   Poetry 2013 - 021327   2013 $75

Mason, George Henry *The Costume of China.* London: printed for W. Miller, Old Bond Street by S. Gosnell, Little Queen Street, Holborn, 1800, but, 1822. Folio, English and French letterpress, pages (16), (120), 60 hand colored stipple engraved costume plates from original drawings, watermarked 1823, contemporary blue panelled morocco with decorative borders in blind and gilt, spine in compartments, two lettered tilt, gilt edges.   Marlborough Rare Books Ltd.   218 - 101   2013   £4000

Mason, James *Cornelia and Alcestis: Two Operas.* London: printed for T. Payne, 1810. First edition, 195 x 125mm., harmless contemporary purple straight grain morocco, covers with gilt fillet border, raised bands flanked by plain gilt rules, gilt titling, all edges gilt, with excellent later fore-edge painting of Acropolis, joints bit rubbed and flaked, boards little stained and rather faded, rear board with two small abraded patches, otherwise excellent copy, clean and fresh internally in solid, inoffensive binding, with vividly colored painting in fine condition.   Phillip J. Pirages   63 - 188   2013 $1100

Mason, W. M. *History and Antiquities of the... Church of St. Patrick.* for the author, 1819. Lacks second page contents, with frontispiece and 5 plates, curious copy, parchment covered boards, subscriber's copy no. 63 and 3 pages ads tipped in at front, original binding.   C. P. Hyland   261 - 599   2013   £250

Mason, William *Poems.* York: printed by A. Ward, 1779. Fifth edition, 8vo., lightly toned and spotted, original quarter calf with marbled boards, spine gilt in compartments with raised bands, red morocco label, boards scuffed and edges worn, front joint and headcap neatly renewed, contemporary ink ownership inscription "T. James, "Isabella Octavia James", later heraldic bookplate Percy S. Godman.   Unsworths Antiquarian Booksellers   28 - 112   2013   £125

Mass, Nuri *Magic Australia.* Sydney: Angus & Robertson, 1943. First edition, 4to., cloth, 164 pages, fine in slightly worn dust jacket, illustrations by Celeste Mass with 4 color plates, 4 full page black and whites plus text illustrations.   Aleph-Bet Books, Inc.   105 - 48   2013 $300

Massachusetts Medical Society *Address to the Community of the Necessity of Legalizing the Study of Anatomy by Order of the Massachusetts Medical Society.* Boston: Perkins & Marvin, 1829. 27 page pamphlet bound in modern quarter cloth, penned note at top of title slightly cropped, from the collection of Willard Parker.   James Tait Goodrich   75 - 6   2013 $750

Massey, Gerald *Robert Burns: a Centenary Song and Other Lyrics.* London: W. Kent & Co. (late D. Bogue), 1859. First edition, 2 pages ads, contemporary full purple morocco blocked and lettered gilt, spine and edges rubbed and worn, initial blank signed Emma Sanderson June 1859, good, sound copy.   Jarndyce Antiquarian Booksellers   CCIII - 63   2013   £65

Masson, David *Chatterton: a Story of the Year 1770.* London: Macmillan, 1874. First separate edition, Half title 4 pages ads + 32 page catalog (Sept. 1874), original brown cloth, little dulled and rubbed, leading inner hinge with slight splitting, W. H. Smith, Dublin & Belfast library label.   Jarndyce Antiquarian Booksellers   CCIII - 659   2013   £35

Master Chubb and His Dog. no publication information, circa, 1880. Housed in color pictorial wrappers, on 8 panel panorama that unfolds vertically, each panel has charming chromolithographed illustrations.   Aleph-Bet Books, Inc.   105 - 188   2013 $350

Mastin, John *Through the Sun in an Airship.* London: Charles Griffin, 1909. First edition, 2nd issue, slight spotting to front board modest scattered foxing, very good plus in near fine dust jacket, with couple of small nicks at crown.   Between the Covers Rare Books, Inc.   Sci-Fi, Fantasy & Horror - 45397   2013 $650

Mathers, Edward Powys *Red Wise.* Waltham St. Lawrence: Golden Cockerel Press, 1926. Limited to 500 copies, quarter buckram, red boards, 8vo., very good.   C. P. Hyland   261 - 445   2013   £150

Mathes, W. Michael *Missions.* San Francisco and Los Angeles: California Historical Society, 1980. First edition, number 543 of 950 copies, signed by photographer Stanley Truman, signed by Mathes, quarto, 96 pages, cloth backed decorated boards, photos, cloth backed boards, very fine.   Argonaut Book Shop   Recent Acquisitions June 2013 - 204   2013 $75

Matheson, G. F. G. *Journal of a Tour in Ireland During the Months of October and November 1835.* for private circulation, 1836. 8vo., original boards (worn), some staining in text but generally good.   C. P. Hyland   261 - 600   2013   £550

Matheson, Richard *I Am Legend.* Springfield: Gauntlet Publications, 1995. First edition thus, special edition limited to 500 numbered copies signed by author, Dan Simmons (introduction), George Clayton Johnson (introduction) and Dennis Etchison (afterword), full red leather with gilt lettering housed in publisher's leather covered black slipcase, fine.   Ed Smith Books   75 - 41   2013 $300

Matheson, Richard *Collected Stories.* Los Angeles: Dream/Press, 1989. Limited to 100 leather bound copies, this no. 49, full black leather, gilt lettering and illustrations to spine, all edges gilt, marbled endpapers, original near fine quarter red cloth clamshell box, small 4to.   By the Book, L. C.   38 - 94   2013 $365

Matheson, Robert E. *Varieties & Synonymes of Surnames & Christian Names in Ireland.* London: HMSO, 1901. First edition, 8vo., 94 pages, disbound, very good.   C. P. Hyland   261 - 401   2013   £50

Mathews, Charles *Memoirs of the Youthful Days of Mr. Mathews..* London: J. Limbird, 1825. Color frontispiece, disbound. Jarndyce Antiquarian Booksellers CCV - 194 2013 £140

Mathews, Charles *Mr. Mathews at Home! In His Youthful Days. Part I... Part II.* London: printed and published by M. Merford, 1822? 26 pages including plate, stabbed as issued, slightly dusted and creased at corners. Jarndyce Antiquarian Booksellers CCV - 195 2013 £220

Mathews, Charles *Mr. Mathews' Memorandum-Book of Peculiarities, Character and Manners, Collected by Him on His Various Trips.* Duncombe, 1826. Second edition, folding color frontispiece, disbound, 24 pages. Jarndyce Antiquarian Booksellers CCV - 196 2013 £160

Mathews, Cornelius *Indian Fairy Book from the Original Legends.* New York: Mason Brothers, 1856. (1855), 8vo., blue gilt cloth, extensive gilt decorations, all edges gilt, 338 pages + ads, some foxing, very good-fine, tight, 4 fine engravings by John McLenan, rare. Aleph-Bet Books, Inc. 105 - 334 2013 $750

Mathews, Harry *Singular Pleasures.* New York: Grenfell Press, 1988. First edition, one of 324 numbered copies, signed by author and artist, illustrations by Francesco Clemente, 8vo., illustrations, original black cloth, printed paper spine, as new. James S. Jaffe Rare Books Fall 2013 - 97 2013 $450

Mathews, Harry *Singular Pleasures.* New York: Grenfell Press, 1988. First edition, one of 26 deluxe copies printed on Japanese papers, 8vo., lithographs by Francesco Clemente, specially bound in original full black morocco, ruled in blind, with red morocco lettering strip by Claudia Cohen, in publisher's red morocco and paper over boards slipcase, specially bound with original signed watercolor by Clemente, signed by author and artist out of a total edition of 350, this copy unlettered and out-of-series, very fine. James S. Jaffe Rare Books Fall 2013 - 96 2013 $2750

Mathews, Joanna *Benny, The Boy Who Was Always Right and Mother's Honest Little Boy.* New York: American Tract Society, 1848. First edition, 12mo., inscription, frontispiece, red cloth, very good. Barnaby Rudge Booksellers Children 2013 - 021556 2013 $55

Mathews, Mitford M. *A Dictionary of Americanisms on Historical Principles.* Chicago: University of Chicago, 1956. Third printing, 1 volume edition, 1946 pages, very good in like dust jacket. Beasley Books 2013 - 2013 $65

Mathias, Thomas James *The Pursuit of Literature. (bound with) A Translation of the Passages from Greek, Latin, Italian and French Writers...* London: printed for T. Becket, 1799. 1798. Third edition, 2 volumes in 1, 8vo., lightly spotted, contemporary diced and polished tan calf spine divided by Greek key rolls and lettered gilt direct, other compartments with gilt centerpieces, marbled edges and endpapers, rubbed at extremities, spine sunned, armorial bookplate of Richard Hopton, signed binding by T. B. Watkins/Hereford with his ticket. Unsworths Antiquarian Booksellers 28 - 113 2013 £150

Matrix 6. Andoversford: Whittington Press, 1986. 237//800 copies (of an edition of 900 copies), printed in black and green on Sommerville and Zerkall mouldmade papers, text illustrations, including wood engravings, several plates of photos, imperial 8vo., original stiff mid green wrappers over dark green card, backstrip faded, printed in black and dark green, untrimmed, near fine. Blackwell's Rare Books 172 - 315 2013 £140

Matrix 7. Andoversford: Whittington Press, 1987. One of 850 copies (of an edition of 960), printed in black on Sommerville and Zerkall Mouldmade papers, numerous inserts, including reproductions of photos, examples of printing and illustrations, including folding plates, imperial 8vo., original stiff yellow wrappers over orange patterned white boards, backstrip panel faded, untrimmed, near fine. Blackwell's Rare Books 172 - 316 2013 £110

Matrix 30. Andoversford: Whittington Press, 2011. One of 655 copies (of an edition of 725), printed on mouldmade papers, numerous tipped in plates, including 4 folding plates, small folio, original unlettered mauve boards, front cover design blocked in black, untrimmed, dust jacket, fine. Blackwell's Rare Books B174 - 399 2013 £135

Matson, Norman *Bats in the Belfry.* Garden City: Doubleday Doran, 1943. First edition, fine in nice, near fine dust jacket, but for small chip on rear panel, very attractive. Between the Covers Rare Books, Inc. Sci-Fi, Fantasy & Horror - 85489 2013 $225

Matta, Roberto Sebastian *Le Coeur Est un Oeil.* Paris: J. H. Bernard, 1981. First edition, one of 125 copies on velin d'Arches, with Matta's 'visual and tactile poem translated in braille' and etched in colors, 3 excellent color etchings, each signed and numbered by artist, 20 pages, loose sheets, as issued, pink cloth covered clamshell box with plexiglass window in shape of a heart, displaying enclosed cover design, excellent copy. Gemini Fine Books & Arts., Ltd. Art Reference & Illustrated Books - 2013 $1400

Matthews, Charles G. *Manual of Alcoholic Fermentation and the Allied Industries.* London: Edward Arnold, 1902. First edition, octavo, 295, 8 pages ads, original blue cloth gilt, owner name front fly, corners bit bumped, sound, very good copy, exceptionally uncommon, ex-James Gabler. Between the Covers Rare Books, Inc.   Cocktails, Etc. - 83341   2013 $200

Matthiae, Christian, Pseud. *Theatrum Historicum Theoretico-Praticum.* Amsterdam: Ludovicum and Danielem Elzevirios, 1656. Second edition, 4to. little occasional very light dampstaining near fore edge, marginal note to page 854, small ink spill to last few pages of index, mostly top margin only but affecting few letters, contemporary vellum, handwritten ink title to spine, long sides overlapping, edges sprinkled blue, vellum soiled including ring stain to upper board, spine darkened, endcaps nicked, some wear to edge and corners, small excision from top of f.f.e.p. perhaps to remove ownership inscription, illegible ink inscription.   Unsworths Antiquarian Booksellers   28 - 134   2013   £300

Matthiessen, Peter *Partisans.* New York: Viking, 1955. First edition, near fine but for previous owner signature and date on pastedown, nearly hidden by dust jacket flap, in like dust jacket (some minute rubbing at extremities, just hint of sunning to spine and one tiny chip in lower edge of rear panel, superior copy.   Leather Stalking Books   October 2013 - 2013 $325

Matthiessen, Peter *Seal Pool.* New York: Doubleday, 1972. First edition, 8vo., pictorial cloth, fine in slightly soiled and price clipped dust jacket, illustrations in color by William Pene Du Bois.   Aleph-Bet Books, Inc.   104 - 337   2013 $375

Maudslay, Alfred P. *Biologia Centrali Americani... Archaeology.... (with) A Note on the Position and Extent of the Great Temple Enclosure of Tenochititlan and the Position, Structure and Orientation of Teocalli of Huitzlopochtli.* London: 1889-1912. First edition, 18 volumes (2 text and 16 atlas), 404 plates, most autotypes, some tinted and some colored lithographs, large oblong folio, lightly rubbed, text in modern cloth, atlases in original printed boards, rebacked, some marginal annotations in red pencil, most folding plates repaired at fold, some small marginal tear not affecting images.   Maggs Bros. Ltd.   1467 - 113   2013   £25,000

Maugham, William Somerset   1874-1965 *Ashenden or the British Agent.* Garden City: Doubleday Doran and Co., 1928. First American edition, fine in attractive very good plus dust jacket with two small chips at crown and some slight age toning, pretty copy.   Between the Covers Rare Books, Inc.   Mystery & Detective Fiction - 291777   2013 $2500

Maugham, William Somerset   1874-1965 *Lady Frederick. A Comedy in Three Acts.* London: Heinemann, 1912. First edition, 16mo., original champagne wrappers, printed overall in brown, backstrip little darkened, overall near fine.   Blackwell's Rare Books   B174 - 262   2013   £200

Maunder, Samuel *The Biographical Treasury.* London: Longmans, Brown, Green, Longmans, 1847. Sixth edition, 8vo., 913 pages plus engraved frontispiece and extra engraved titlepage, gilt decorations and red morocco label on spine, well rubbed, rebacked with original spine laid down.   Barnaby Rudge Booksellers   Biography 2013 - 020253   2013 $65

Maunsell, Robert George *History of Maunsell or Mansel.* Cork: 1903. First edition, 28 plates, this copy contains many blank leaves inserted for notes, much neat pencil annotations with a great deal of added information, cloth, very good useful copy.   C. P. Hyland   261 - 402   2013   £150

Maupassant, Guy Du   1850-1893 *Oeuvres Completes Illustrees.* Paris: Societe d'Editions Litteraires et Artistiques, circa, 1920. 29 volumes, very good in later gilt lettered red cloth with original decorative front wrappers mounted on each front board.   Ken Spelman Books Ltd.   75 - 166   2013   £150

Maurer, David W. *The Big Con: the Story of the Confidence Man and the Confidence Game.* Indianapolis/New York: Bobbs Merrill, 1940. First edition, endpapers negligibly foxed, still easily fine in bright, attractive near fine dust jacket with moderate sized accordion tear (which as been flattened) on rear panel.   Between the Covers Rare Books, Inc.   Mystery & Detective Fiction - 71195   2013 $5000

Maurice, C. Edmund *Life of Octavia Hill, as told in Her Letters.* London: Macmillan, 1913. First edition, 8vo., 591 pages, portraits, untrimmed and partially unopened, very good, tight, clean copy, this the copy of Jane Addams (Hull House), with her ownership signature, from the library of reformer Florence Kelley (1859-1932).   Second Life Books Inc.   182 - 165   2013 $250

Mauriceau, A. M. *The Married Woman's Private Medical Companion.* New York: 1854. 16mo., original cloth, very nice.   M & S Rare Books, Inc.   95 - 23   2013 $200

Maurois, Andre *Byron.* Paris: Bernard Grasset, 1930. 2 volumes, half titles, volume II slightly browned, original grey wrappers, blocked in green, spines faded and with some old neat repairs, signed presentation from author.   Jarndyce Antiquarian Booksellers   CCIII - 410   2013   £30

Maury, M. F. *The Physical Geography of the Sea.* New York: 1855. First edition, 8vo., original cloth, rebacked, portion of spine laid down, endpapers stained, but nice. M & S Rare Books, Inc. 95 - 228 2013 $275

Mavor, William Fordyce *Mavor's Spelling-Book Arranged for Use of Preparatory Schools.* London: Somers & Isaacs, 1800. 16mo., 10 pages, including wrappers, very good. Barnaby Rudge Booksellers Children 2013 - 021640 2013 $95

Mawe, Thomas *Every Man His Own Gardener.* London: printed for William Griffin, 1773. Sixth edition, 8vo., 4 engraved frontispieces, couple of leaves with small tears to blank margins, bit of light spotting in places, contemporary sheep, rubbed, joints and edges worn, spine cracking but sound, several deaths and baptisms in Smith family recorded in old hand on endpapers and blank recto of frontispiece. Unsworths Antiquarian Booksellers 28 - 114 2013 £95

Maxton, Hugh *The Enlightened Cave.* Washington: 1983, 1983. First edition, printed in an edition of 75, Single long sheet of paper folded 10 times to create 12 pages, very near fine, signed by Maxton, scarce. Jeff Hirsch Books Fall 2013 - 129490 2013 $125

Maxwell, Colonel Montgomery *My Adventures.* London: Henry Colburn, 1845. First edition, 2 volumes, 200 x 126mm., special very attractive presentation binding of contemporary Oxblood pebble grain morocco, elaborately gilt, covers with blind ruled borders and complex gilt frame featuring shell head and tailpieces, scrolling corners and sides, many floral tools, raised bands, spine compartments gilt with flower basket centerpiece and leaf frond corners, blind tooled turn-ins, all edges gilt, frontispiece portraits, ink presentation inscription for Reginald Porter from friend, James Nelson Palmer on his leaving Eton Xmas 3rd 1846, spines slightly and uniformly sunned, gilt still bright, one board with little dulling because of leather preservative, otherwise very fine, clean, fresh, smooth internally in handsome binding with virtually no wear. Phillip J. Pirages 63 - 332 2013 $600

Maxwell, John *True Reform; or Character a Qualification for the Franchise.* Edinburgh: Thomas Constable & Co., 1860. Half green calf, red label, slightly faded, presentation from the author with later signature and bookplate of David Murray, very good, 50 pages. Jarndyce Antiquarian Booksellers CCV - 197 2013 £50

Maxwell, Marcus *Big Game Photographs from the Times Taken in Kenya and Tanganyika.* The Times, n.d., Oblong 4to., original blue cloth, gilt, extremities little rubbed, unpaginated, 27 full page sepia plates, leaf of text, few spots. R. F. G. Hollett & Son Africana - 142 2013 £30

Maxwell, Marius *Stalking Big Game with Camera in Equatorial Africa.* London: Heinemann, 1925. First trade edition, large 4to., original cloth, gilt, little faded, top edge gilt, 113 plates after photos by author, double page frontispiece, extending plate and map. R. F. G. Hollett & Son Africana - 143 2013 £50

Maxwell, William H. *Wild Sports of the West.* London: 1973. Facsimile of 1850 edition, 8vo. cloth, near fine, dust jacket. C. P. Hyland 261 - 602 2013 £35

Maydon, H. C. *Big Game Shooting in Africa.* London: Seeley Service and Co., 1932. First edition, original two tone brown buckram gilt, dust jacket (rather rubbed and chipped, spine darkened), 150 illustrations. R. F. G. Hollett & Son Africana - 144 2013 £85

Mayer, Henry *A Trip to Toyland.* London: Grant Richards, 1900. First edition, oblong folio, cloth backed pictorial boards, tips slightly rubbed and very slight cover soil, very good-fine, full page color illustrations printed on one side of the page, rare. Aleph-Bet Books, Inc. 104 - 426 2013 $1200

Mayer, Luigi *Views in Egypt, Palestine and Other Parts of the Ottoman Empire.* London: Thomas Bensley for R. Bowyer, 1801-1804. First editions in book form, 482 x 335mm., 3 separately published works bound in 1 volume, very fine contemporary russia, elaborately gilt by Staggemeier & Welcher (their ticket), covers gilt with frame of Greek-key rolls on either side of cresting roll, this frame enclosing another role of linked palmettes, raised bands, spine expertly rebacked retaining original backstrip, its compartments with unusual Egyptian hieroglyphic designs, turn-ins with gilt chain roll, marbled endpapers, all edges gilt; with engraved frontispiece and 96 fine hand colored aquatint views of near east; bookplate of Dayton Art Institute (but sold with their authorization at auction), corners slightly bumped, few small portions of the spine with vague crackles, occasional minor offsetting from plates, isolated faint marginal foxing, thumbing or rust spots, but still fine, especially clean and fresh internally, generous margins and richly colored plates, solidly restored, lustrous binding that retains virtually all of its original considerable appeal. Phillip J. Pirages 63 - 333 2013 $18,500

Mayfield, J. W. *History of Springhead Waterworks and How the Pearson Park was Obtained for the People.* Hull: A. Brown & Sons, 1909. 8vo., original printed wrappers, very scarce. Ken Spelman Books Ltd. 73 - 106 2013 £40

Mayhew, Augustus *Paved with Gold; or the Romance and Reality of the London Streets.* London: Chapman & Hall, 1858. First edition, illustrations by Phiz, frontispiece, added engraved title and plates, uncut in original dark green cloth by Bone & Son, bookseller's ticket of J. Philipson, North Shields on leading pastedown, very good, bright copy. Jarndyce Antiquarian Booksellers CCV - 198 2013 £150

Mayhew, Henry *London Labour and the London Poor; the Condition an Earnings of Those that Will Work, Cannot Work and Will Not Work. (with) the Extra Volume: Those that Will Not Work.* London: Charles Griffin, 1864. 1862, 4 volumes, frontispieces in volumes 3 and 4, plates, illustrations, maps, tar with loss to following f.e.p. volume II, original maroon cloth by Deighton, volume I slightly damp marked, little rubbed, contemporary signature on title volume I. Jarndyce Antiquarian Booksellers CCV - 199 2013 £850

Mayhew, The Brothers *Acting Charades or Deeds not Words.* D. Bogue, 1850. First edition, small square 8vo., original red cloth gilt by Bone and Son, stamped in blind and gilt, extremities trifle rubbed, all edges gilt, hand colored frontispiece, title and silhouette illustrations in text by H. G. Hine. R. F. G. Hollett & Son Children's Books - 381 2013 £120

Mayne, Ethel Colburn *Byron.* London: Methuen & Co., 1912. 2 volumes, half titles, frontispiece portraits, plates, 31 page catalog in both volumes, original dark blue/green cloth, lettered gilt and blind, tiny nick in spine cloth volume II, otherwise very good, Doris Langley Moore's copy with occasional notes by her in text. Jarndyce Antiquarian Booksellers CCIII - 413 2013 £35

Mazzei, Filippo *Recherches Historiques et Politiques sur les Etats-Unis de l'Amerique Septentrionale.* Paris: 1788. First edition, 12mo., 4 volumes, half titles in each volume, full gilt stamped speckled calf, leather labels, minor rubbing, fine set. M & S Rare Books, Inc. 95 - 230 2013 $925

McAlmon, Robert *Contact Collection of Contemporary Writers.* Paris: Contact Editions/Three Mountains Press, 1925. First edition, one of 300 copies, 8vo., original printed wrappers, very fine, bright copy tiny nick at head of spine, touch of soiling at base of spine, usually found in poor condition, this is as fine a copy as we have seen. James S. Jaffe Rare Books Fall 2013 - 3 2013 $3500

McAlmon, Robert *A Hasty Bunch.* Dijon: Contact Editions, 1922. First edition, 8vo., original printed wrappers, with scarce broadside "From an h'English to an English publisher" laid in, unopened and as new. James S. Jaffe Rare Books Fall 2013 - 04 2013 $1250

McAlpine's Halifax City Directory for 1895-1896. Halifax and St. John: McAlpine Directory Co., 1895. 8vo., printed paper covered boards, green calf spine, gilt title and ad, 645 pages, index, illustrated ads, covers worn, front and rear hinge cracks, some foxing and browning to edges. Schooner Books Ltd. 104 - 97 2013 $200

McAlpine's Maritime and Newfoundland Gazetteer for Nova Scotia, New Brunswick and Prince Edward Island and the Island of Newfoundland. Saint John: McAlpine Directory Co., 1898. 8 x 6 inches, red cloth, gilt to spine, 8vo, cloth worn and top and bottom of spine frayed, interior hinge starting to crack, interior generally very good with stain to outer edges of last 400 pages. Schooner Books Ltd. 102 - 118 2013 $125

McAuley, James J. *A New Address.* Dublin: Dolmen Press, 1965. Uncorrected proof, small 8vo., original pale grey wrappers printed in black, fine. Maggs Bros. Ltd. 1442 - 64 2013 £175

McBain, Ed *The 87th Precinct.* New York: Simon & Schuster, 1959. First combined and first hardcover edition, octavo, boards. L. W. Currey, Inc. Fall Sampler Sept. 2013 - 146533 2013 $150

McBain, Ed *The Heckler.* New York: Simon & Schuster, 1960. First edition, pages slightly darkened, otherwise fine in dust jacket with small chip at top of spine and couple of closed tears along folds. Mordida Books 81 - 326 2013 $150

McBain, Ed *I Saw Mommy Killing Santa Claus.* Los Angeles: Mysterious Bookshop, 1999. First edition, octaov, pictorial wrappers. L. W. Currey, Inc. Christmas Themed Books - 126803 2013 $75

McBain, Ed *The Interview and Other Stories.* Helsinki: Eurographica, 1986. First edition thus, one of 350 numbered copies boldly signed by author adding '1986', fine, perfect bound in original wrappers, fine brown printed dust jacket. Ed Smith Books 78 - 42 2013 $75

McBain, Ed *See Them Die.* New York: Simon and Schuster, 1960. First edition, pages slightly darkened, otherwise fine in dust jacket. Mordida Books 81 - 325 2013 $300

McBain, Ed *See Them Die.* New York: Simon and Schuster, 1960. First edition, octavo, boards. L. W. Currey, Inc. Fall Sampler Sept. 2013 - 146535 2013 $250

McBain, Ed *Ten Plus One.* New York: Simon and Schuster, 1963. First edition, fine in dust jacket. Mordida Books 81 - 327 2013 $300

McCabe, Eugene *The Love of Sisters.* Dublin: Tusker Rock Press, 2009. First edition, number X of 25 roman numeralled copies signed by author, small 8vo., original black leather lettered gilt on spine, fine in charcoal grey cloth backed slipcase.   Maggs Bros. Ltd. 1442 - 211 2013 £100

McCabe, Pat *Carn.* Nuffield: Aidan Ellis, 1989. First edition, 8vo., original black cloth, dust jacket, fine.   Maggs Bros. Ltd. 1442 - 212 2013 £65

McCaffrey, Anne *Habit is an Old Horse.* Bellevue: Dryad Press, 1986. First edition, one of 342 copies published in wrappers, fine, printed wrappers.   Between the Covers Rare Books, Inc. Sci-Fi, Fantasy & Horror - 287058 2013 $250

McCaffrey, Anne *A Time When.* Nefsa Press, 1975. First edition, with TLS by author explaining circumstances of publication, "Author's Copy" written on top and fore edges, several holograph corrections to text in same hand, small 8vo., clear plastic dust jacket, near fine.   By the Book, L. C. 38 - 95 2013 $750

McCammon, Robert R. *Mystery Walk.* New York: Holt Rinehart and Winston, 1983. First edition, fine in fine dust jacket.   Between the Covers Rare Books, Inc. Sci-Fi, Fantasy & Horror - 319506 2013 $55

McCance, S. *History of the Royal Munster Fusiliers 1652-1922.* London: 1927. First edition, 2 volumes, 5 color plates, 31 photos on 12 plates, 20 maps, 3 color plates, 58 photos on 37 plates, 21 maps, good, cloth.   C. P. Hyland 261 - 566 2013 £600

McCarthy, Cormac *All the Pretty Horses.* New York: Knopf, 1992. Advance reading copy, issued in wrappers and publisher's folding box, signed by author, uncommon thus.   Ken Lopez Bookseller 159 - 130 2013 $750

McCarthy, Cormac *All the Pretty Horses.* New York: Esquire, 1992. Offprint, quarto, fine in stapled wrappers.   Between the Covers Rare Books, Inc. Horses, Horsemanship, Horse Racing, Etc. - 315728 2013 $200

McCarthy, Cormac *All the Pretty Horses.* New York: Alfred A. Knopf, 1992. Uncorrected proof, third state, in gray wrappers.   Between the Covers Rare Books, Inc. Horses, Horsemanship, Horse Racing, Etc. - 307450 2013 $300

McCarthy, Cormac *All the Pretty Horses.* London: Picador, 1993. First English edition, fine in fine dust jacket.   Between the Covers Rare Books, Inc. Horses, Horsemanship, Horse Racing, Etc. - 282886 2013 $100

McCarthy, Cormac *The Border Trilogy. All the Pretty Hoses. The Crossing. Cities of the Plain.* New York: Alfred A. Knopf, 1992. 1994. 1998. First editions, 3 volumes, 301, 425, 291 pages, octavo, quarter black cloth over matching boards, all volumes near fine, all volumes signed.   Ken Sanders Rare Books 45 - 48 2013 $4500

McCarthy, Cormac *Child of God.* New York: Random House, 1973. First edition, very near fine in very good dust jacket with small chip to upper rear panel, bit of fading to red spine title, attractive copy, overall, without remainder stamp.   Ken Lopez Bookseller 159 - 129 2013 $750

McCarthy, Cormac *No Country for Old Men.* New Orleans: B. E. Trice, 2005. Limited to 325 numbered copies, this copy 134, signed by author, quarto, 309 pages, half brown calf over marbled boards, title gilt stamped on backstrip, publisher's slipcase, both book and slipcase fine.   Ken Sanders Rare Books 45 - 46 2013 $1500

McCarthy, Cormac *No Country for Old Men.* New York: Alfred A. Knopf, 2005. First edition, first issue, signed by author on tipped in leaf as usual for this title, octavo, publisher's pictorial dust jacket, not price clipped, original black boards, spine lettered gilt, fore edge uncut, fine, unread.   Heritage Book Shop Holiday Catalogue 2012 - 104 2013 $850

McCarthy, Cormac *Outer Dark.* New York: Random House, 1968. First edition, modest edge sunning to boards, very near fine in like dust jacket with minor wear at spine extremities, one short edge tear, hint of sunning to spine title, nice.   Ken Lopez Bookseller 159 - 128 2013 $1750

McCarthy, Cormac *Suttree.* New York: Random House, 1979. First edition, no remainder mark, nor price clip, fine, tight, nearly fine dust jacket with light sunning to title on spine.   Ed Smith Books 75 - 43 2013 $2500

McCarthy, F. M. *Handbook for Youghal.* 1849. Errata slip, folding frontispiece, folding map, 12mo., original quarter cloth, some staining on wrappers & text, very scarce.   C. P. Hyland 261 - 887 2013 £250

McCarthy, J. G. *The History of Cork: a Lecture.* Guy, 1869. 70 pages, 4 maps, cloth, good,.   C. P. Hyland 261 - 568 2013 £65

McCarthy, Justin *Four Works: History of Our Own Times. The Four Georges & William IV. The French Revolution. The Regin of Queen Anne.* London: Chatto & Windus, 1884-1901. First editions of the last three works, 222 x 144mm., 15 volumes, pleasing contemporary dark blue three quarter morocco by Bickers & son (stamp signed), raised bands, spine gilt in single ruled compartments, marbled endpapers, top edges gilt, tiny chip to top of one spine, three joints with short cracks at head, minor dulling from leather preservative, first volume with hinge open at rear (but volume quite sound), one leaf with older tissue paper repair to head-edge tear into text, but legibility not lost), other trivial defects, but still quite attractive set in excellent condition, clean and fresh internally, bright, solid bindings showing little wear. Phillip J. Pirages 63 - 334 2013 $650

McCarthy, Justin *Irish Recollections.* 1911. First edition, 12 mounted plates, good, 8vo., cloth. C. P. Hyland 261 - 571 2013 £30

McCarthy, Justin *The Story of an Irishman.* 1904. First edition, Chatto & Windus catalog for June 1904, some pencil notes, 8vo., cloth, good. C. P. Hyland 261 - 570 2013 £30

McCarthy, Mary *Emily.* Boston: 2011. Artist's book, one of 20 copies from a total edition of 30, all on Lanaquarell 90lb hot pressed paper, each signed and numbered by artists, Mary McCarthy and Shirley Veenema, page size 5 x 7 inches, 56 pages, bound by McCarthy, white weave Asahi cloth on spine and Nasumi white Japanese paper over boards, title stamped in gold gilt on front panel, handmade pale green Thai Mango paper endpapers, custom made green suede open front box with button and silk tie close, box opens to book laid in on left side and an original collage used as the art which was scanned and bound with poems, text printed in 12 point imprint MT Shadow with Epson Stylus Pro 3800 printer, original images of mixed media and paper added to a single piece of Stonehenge paper were crafted by both artists responding to one another's work and to the verse, there are 25 images reproduced in with 12 of the 12 poems, bound book is laid in on one side of box and an original collage is laid in on the other side. Priscilla Juvelis - Rare Books 56 - 20 2013 $975

McCarthy, Mary *Fighting Fitzgerald & Other Papers.* 1930. First edition, 8vo., cloth, illustrations, very good. C. P. Hyland 261 - 427 2013 £30

McCarthy, S. T. *Three Kerry Families (Mahony, Conway, Spotswood).* Folkstone, 1923. first issue, 72 pages, pedigrees, quarter leather, very good, scarce, autographed "With the Author's compliments". C. P. Hyland 261 - 400 2013 £95

McClintock, F. R. *Holiday in Spain: Being Some Account of Two Tours in that Country in the Autumns of 1880 and 1881.* London: Ed Stanford, 1882. First edition, 8vo., frontispiece, 3 plates, original red decorative cloth, waterstain on spine, small area excised from front endpaper, good copy. J. & S. L. Bonham Antiquarian Booksellers Europe - 8427 2013 £150

McCloskey, Robert *Make Way for Ducklings.* New York: Viking, 1941. First edition, 4to., cloth, fine in very good++ dust jacket (spine slightly faded, some fraying to spine ends, no tears), great copy of 20th century rarity. Aleph-Bet Books, Inc. 104 - 338 2013 $18,500

McCloskey, Robert *Make Way for Ducklings.* New York: Viking, 1941. (First Published Aug. 1941). First edition, first printing, 4to., cloth, fine in very good+ dust jacket (no medal, with small narrow 1 x 1/4 inch chip off top of rear panel and faded on spine and small part of covers, few tiny closed tears). Aleph-Bet Books, Inc. 105 - 375 2013 $16,5000

McCloskey, Robert *One Morning in Maine.* New York: Viking Press, 1952. First edition, fine in very good dust jacket with 2 inch piece missing lower spine tip affecting name of author and publisher, short closed tears and chips, 4to., 64 pages. By the Book, L. C. 36 - 34 2013 $400

McCloskey, Robert *One Morning in Maine.* New York: Viking, 1952. First edition, folio, pictorial cloth, 64 pages, fine in very good dust jacket with few mends on verso, chips on spine ends, illustrations on every page. Aleph-Bet Books, Inc. 104 - 339 2013 $850

McConkey, Phil *Simms to McConkey: Blood, Sweat and Gatorade.* New York: Crown, 1987. First edition, fine in dust jacket, signed by Simms, McConkey and Schaap, scarce thus. Between the Covers Rare Books, Inc. Football Books - 29211 2013 $475

McConnor, Vincent *The French Doll.* New York: Hill & Wang, 1965. First edition, small stain on front fly and fore edge, else near fine in very good plus dust jacket with few short tears. Between the Covers Rare Books, Inc. Mystery & Detective Fiction - 41712 2013 $65

McCord, David *Stow Wengenroth's New England.* Barre: Barre Pub., 1969. First edition, limited to 350 copies, with original pencil signed lithograph, 8.5 x 11 inches, 108 pages printed on Rives heavyweight paper, red cloth spine and handmade Crepe Kaji made in Japan, gilt lettering spine, near fine slipcase with printed paper title label. By the Book, L. C. 36 - 13 2013 $140

McCord, Margaret *Abbeys and Churches.* Belfast: Crannog Press, 1971. Limited to 100 numbered copies, printed in black and colors, small 4to., original pale red and dark navy lettering in gilt on spine, near fine.   Maggs Bros. Ltd.   1442 - Crannog   2013   £150

McCorkle, George Washington *Part One Poems of Perpetual Memory (revised) and Part Two Rhymes from the Delta. (Cover title).*   High Point: George Washington McCorkle, circa, 1945. First edition, 119 pages, frontispiece, photos, printed brown wrappers, splitting at spine folds, small chips at wrappers, essentially good copy.   Between the Covers Rare Books, Inc.   165 - 209   2013 $200

McCormick, Richard C. *The Duty of the Hour. An Oration Delivered at Jamaica Long Island, July 4th 1863.* New York: Geoge A. Whitehorne, Steam Printer, 1863. First edition, sewn buff wrappers, 36 pages, owner's name, offsetting and spotting on wrappers, else very good.   Between the Covers Rare Books, Inc.   New York City - 285584   2013 $300

McCoy, Horace *Scalpel.* New York: Appleton, 1952. First edition, fine in dust jacket with tiny wear at corners.   Mordida Books   81 - 328   2013 $135

McCoy, Horace *Scalpel.* New York: Appleton Century Crofts, 1952. First edition, fine in near fine dust jacket with slight sunning at spine.   Between the Covers Rare Books, Inc.   Mystery & Detective Fiction - 291540   2013 $275

McCracken, Eileen *The Irish Woods Since Tudor Times; Distribution and Exploitation.* 1971. First edition, 8vo., cloth, dust jacket, signed by author, near fine.   C. P. Hyland   261 - 573   2013   £50

McCullough, John *Our House.* New York: William Scott, 1943. First edition, 4to., pictorial boards, fine in dust jacket with few small closed tears, black and white illustrations by Roger Duvoisin.   Aleph-Bet Books, Inc.   105 - 210   2013 $325

McCullough, Niall *Dublin. An Urban History. The Plan of the City.* Dublin: Associated Editions, 2007. First edition, number 55 of 755 copies signed by author, this copy signed by designer Anne Brady, oblong 4to., original full black cloth blindstamped with plan of Dublin, spine lettered silver, fine in silver slipcase.   Maggs Bros. Ltd.   1442 - 213   2013   £250

McDarrah, Fred W. *New York, N. Y.* New York: Corinth, 1964. First edition, hardcover issue, fine in lightly rubbed just about fine dust jacket, hardcover issue is uncommon especially in this condition.   Between the Covers Rare Books, Inc.   New York City - 291572   2013 $125

McDermott, John Francis *George Caleb Bingham, Rivert Portraitist.* Norman: University of Oklahoma Press, 1959. First edition, quarto, 112 reproductions, drawings, brown cloth, very fine, lightly rubbed pictorial dust jacket, slight chipping to head of jacket spine.   Argonaut Book Shop   Summer 2013 - 217   2013 $125

McElroy, Joseph *A Smuggler's Bible.* New York: Harcourt Brace, 1966. First edition, near fine in very good+ engraved plates with sunned spine and tiny chip on rear panel.   Beasley Books   2013 - 2013 $100

McEvoy, Arthur F. *The Fisherman's Problem. Ecology and Law in California Fisheries 1850-1980.* Cambridge: Cambridge University Press, 1986. First edition, photos, blue cloth, gilt, very fine with pictorial dust jacket.   Argonaut Book Shop   Recent Acquisitions June 2013 - 198   2013 $90

McEwan, Ian *Atonement.* London: Cape, 2001. First edition, original black boards, backstrip lettered silver, dust jacket fine, signed by author.   Blackwell's Rare Books   172 - 215   2013   £125

McFarland, J. Randall *Water for a Thirsty Land.* Selma: Consolidated Irrigation District, 1996. First edition, quarto, 176 page, photos, maps, reproductions, pictorial boards, very fine.   Argonaut Book Shop   Recent Acquisitions June 2013 - 199   2013 $60

McFarling, Lloyd *Exploring the Northern Plains.* Caldwell: Caxton Printers, 1955. First edition, from the library of John M. Carroll with his signed bookplate, numerous maps, brown cloth, bookplate, very fine with lightly rubbed pictorial dust jacket.   Argonaut Book Shop   Summer 2013 - 218   2013 $75

McGahern, John *Amongst Women.* London: Faber, 1990. First edition, 8vo., original orange boards, backstrip lettered in black, dust jacket, fine.   Blackwell's Rare Books   B174 - 260   2013   £100

McGahern, John *The Barracks.* London: Faber and Faber, 1963. First edition, 8vo., original red cloth, very good, dust jacket torn at head and tail of spine with small loss here and there and nicked extremities, from the library of Richard Murphy, signed by him.   Maggs Bros. Ltd.   1442 - 214   2013   £600

McGahern, John *The Collected Stories.* London: Faber & Faber, 1990. First edition, 8vo., burgundy cloth, fine in slightly rubbed dust jacket, inscribed by author for Richard Murphy.   Maggs Bros. Ltd.   1442 - 217   2013   £450

McGahern, John *Memoir.* London: Faber and Faber, 2005. First edition, number 54 of 250 numbered copies signed by author, 8vo., original quarter burgundy cloth, spine stamped gilt on black panel, fine in matching slipcase. Maggs Bros. Ltd. 1442 - 218 2013 £350

McGahern, John *Memoir.* London: Faber and Faber, 2005. First edition, 8vo., original black cloth, dust jacket, signed by author, fine in dust jacket. Maggs Bros. Ltd. 1442 - 219 2013 £120

McGahern, John *Nightlines.* London: Faber, 1970. First edition, crown 8vo., original mid-blue cloth lightly dampspotted, gilt lettered partly on black ground, endpapers browned, ownership signature of publisher Harry Chambers, dust jacket with some browning, good. Blackwell's Rare Books 172 - 216 2013 £100

McGahern, John *The Pornographer.* London: Faber and Faber, 1979. First edition, 8vo., original brown cloth, dust jacket, fine. Maggs Bros. Ltd. 1442 - 216 2013 £60

McGinnies, William G. *Deserts of the World. An Appraisal of Research into Their Physcial and Biological Environments.* Tucson: University of Arizona Press, 1968. First edition, quarto, maps, peach cloth, lettered in black. Argonaut Book Shop Summer 2013 - 219 2013 $50

McGivern, William *Blondes Die Young.* New York: Dodd Mead and Co., 1952. First edition, octavo, boards. L. W. Currey, Inc. Fall Sampler Sept. 2013 - 146530 2013 $250

McGovern, Melvin *Specimen Pages of Korean Movable Types.* Los Angeles: Dawson's Book Shop, 1966. Limited edition of 300 copies, 95 of which are Primary edition and 205 the regular edition, this copy #187; with 2 original tipped-in specimens printed from moveable type dated from 1795 and 1815 with 20 facsimile specimen pages of movable type which date from 1420 to 1858, fine, vibrant patterned yellow covered paper made by Kim Dong-Khyu, original near fine plain yellow dust jacket and slipcase. By the Book, L. C. 36 - 68 2013 $3750

McGowan, Edward *Narrative...Including a Full Account of the Author's Adventures and Perils While Persecuted by the San Francisco Vigilance Committee of 1856.* San Francisco: Published by author, 1857. First edition, 12mo., 248 pages, illustrations, new half calf and marbled board, corners of text worn and turned, one leaf with marginal replacement. M & S Rare Books, Inc. 95 - 231 2013 $750

McGraw, DeLoss *Hard Traveling.* San Diego: Brighton Press, 1985. Limited edition of 100 numbered copies, signed by artist, 350 x 287mm., folio, contents loose as issued in clamshell box with original painted binding by McGraw on front cover, 10 full color hand painted etchings and woodcuts, 4 additional three dimensional cut-out images in plastic sleeves, hand painted folding case with tie and button, like new. Jeff Weber Rare Books 171 - 50 2013 $4000

McGuff, Joe *Winning It All: The Chiefs of the AFL.* Garden City: Doubleday, 1970. First edition, fine save for loss of cloth over foot of spine, near fine dust jacket with chipping in same area. Between the Covers Rare Books, Inc. Football Books - 73550 2013 $65

McGuffey's Newly Revised Eclectic Primer. New York: American Book Co., 1867. 16mo., 34 pages, pictorial wrappers, illustrated with cuts. Aleph-Bet Books, Inc. 104 - 9 2013 $125

McGuinness, Brian *Wittgenstein, a Life: Young Ludwig 1889-1921.* Berkeley: The University of California Press, 1988. First edition, fine in fine, lightly rubbed dust jacket. Between the Covers Rare Books, Inc. Philosophy - 105304 2013 $70

McGuinness, Frank *Booterstown.* Loughcrew: Gallery Press, 1994. First edition, 8vo., original black cloth, dust jacket, fine, signed by author. Maggs Bros. Ltd. 1442 - 223 2013 £50

McGuinness, Frank *Observe the Sons of Ulster Marching Towards the Somme.* London: Faber and Faber, 1986. First edition, 8vo., original wrappers, signed by author on half title, near fine. Maggs Bros. Ltd. 1442 - 221 2013 £60

McGuinness, Frank *The Sea with No Ships.* Loughcrew: Gallery Press, 1999. First edition, signed by author, 8vo., original black cloth, dust jacket, fine. Maggs Bros. Ltd. 1442 - 222 2013 £50

McHarg, William *Let's Pretend.* Chicago: Volland, 1914. Stated first edition, 8vo., pictorial boards, slightest of cover soil, else fine, rare, illustrations by Bonnibe Butler. Aleph-Bet Books, Inc. 105 - 576 2013 $300

McKenney, Thomas Lorraine *History of the Indian Tribes of North America, with Biographical Sketches and Anecdotes of the Principal Chiefs.* Kent: Published by Volair Limited, 1978. 265 x 170mm., 2 volumes, full brown leatherette, elaborately gilt, edges gilt, watered silk endpapers, volumes housed in very sturdy (just slightly smudged cloth slipcase, 123 full page color plates plus 2 black and white maps and portrait of McKenney. Phillip J. Pirages 63 - 336 2013 $375

McKim, Alicia *Greetings from California.* Denver: 2009. Artist's book, one of 50 copies, each containing five dioramas of three separate layers each of vintage postcards, printed on inkjet printer with pigmented ink on neutral pb paper, each copy numbered by author, page size 5 1/2 x 6 1/2 inches, carousel book, bound by the artist, paper over boards, blue cloth spine and blue ribbon ties, housed in publisher's stiff white board folding box.   Priscilla Juvelis - Rare Books   56 - 21   2013 $500

McKinley, Robin *Blue Sword.* New York: Greenwillow, 1982. Stated first edition, first printing with correct number code, 8vo., cloth, fine in dust jacket slightly rubbed, else fine, no award seal.   Aleph-Bet Books, Inc.   105 - 377   2013 $325

McMasters, Susanne *The Gallant Heart: the Story of a Race Horse.* Garden City: Doubleday, 1954. First edition, illustrations by Paul Brown, bookplate on front pastedown, else fine in very good or better dust jacket with very slight loss at crown and few very small nicks and tears, scarce.   Between the Covers Rare Books, Inc.   Horses, Horsemanship, Horse Racing, Etc. - 56364   2013 $225

McMillian, Terry *Mama.* Boston: Houghton Mifflin and Co., 1987. First edition, first printing, near fine in very good dust jacket with some soiling and minor wear.   Jeff Hirsch Books   Fall 2013 - 129194   2013 $75

McMurtry, Larry *In a Narrow Grave.* Austin: Encino, 1968. First printing, with "skycrapers" for skyscrapers" on page 105, although not called for, this copy signed by author, fine in fine dust jacket, flawless copy, from the Bruce Kahn collection.   Ken Lopez Bookseller   159 - 132   2013 $12,500

McMurtry, Larry *The Last Picture.* New York: Dial, 1966. First edition, fine in near fine dust jacket with very shallow wear to top edge and short tear at upper rear spine fold, agency copy with label of Ziegler-Ross Agency of LA.   Ken Lopez Bookseller   159 - 131   2013 $1000

McMurtry, Larry *Terms of Endearment.* New York: Simon and Schuster, 1975. First edition, inscribed by author, 8vo., brown cloth backstrip over beige paper boards, spine lettered gilt, dust jacket, text browned as usual, else near fine.   Heritage Book Shop   Holiday Catalogue 2012 - 105   2013 $600

McNally, Robert *Old Ireland.* 1965. First edition, 8vo., cloth, dust jacket, near fine.   C. P. Hyland   261 - 582   2013   £45

McNeil, Marion *Jingleman Jack Circus Man.* Akron: Saalfield, 1930. 8vo., pictorial boards, fine in box (scuffed and slightly worn), illustrations by Corinne Bailey with full page color and black and whites.   Aleph-Bet Books, Inc.   105 - 138   2013 $200

McNeil, Marion *Little Green Cart.* Akron: Saalfield, 1931. 4to., pictorial boards, very good+, illustrations by Francoise, scarce.   Aleph-Bet Books, Inc.   104 - 220   2013 $300

McQuade, Ruth *Badge of the Baronets of Nova Scotia.* Ottawa: Author, 1976. Quarto, card covers with plastic binding at spine, frontispiece, other illustrations.   Schooner Books Ltd.   105 - 88   2013 $60

McTernan, John *Here's to Their Memory.* Mercier, 1977. First edition, 427 pages, photos, cloth, very good, dust jacket.   C. P. Hyland   261 - 587   2013   £35

McWatters, George S. *Knots Untied: or, Ways and By-Ways in the Hidden Life of American Detectives.* Hartford: J. B. Burr and Hyde, 1872. First edition, publisher's purple cloth gilt, contemporary owner's name, later bookplate, spine bit faded, tight, near very good copy.   Between the Covers Rare Books, Inc.   New York City - 293171   2013 $50

McWilliams, Jay *Passing the Three Gates: Interviews with Charles Johnson.* Seattle: University of Washington, 2004. First edition, fine in fine dust jacket, warmly inscribed by author to Nicholas Delbanco.   Between the Covers Rare Books, Inc.   165 - 310   2013 $200

Mead, James R. *Hunting and Trading on the Great Plains 1859-1875.* Norman: University of Oklahoma Press, 1986. First edition, vintage photos, maps, blue cloth, very fine with pictorial dust jacket, quite scarce in this condition.   Argonaut Book Shop   Summer 2013 - 227   2013 $125

Mead, Margaret 1901-1978 *The Mountain Arapesh. V. The Record of Unabelin with Rorschach Analyses.* New York: American Museum of Natural History, 1949. First edition, paperback, wrappers, near fine with few chips.   Beasley Books   2013 - 2013 $65

Meade, J. A. *The Meades of Inishannon.* Victoria: 1955. No. 1- (of?), signed presentation copy from author, to noted Cork historian, John T. Collins, 14 plates, 59 pages, very good.   C. P. Hyland   261 - 403   2013   £125

Meader, Stephen W. *Cedar's Boys.* New York: Harcourt Brace and Co. 1949, but probably, 1957. Reprint ("C" - probably third printing), illustrations by Lee Towsend fine in price clipped, about fine dust jacket with very slight wear, bright copy.   Between the Covers Rare Books, Inc.   Horses, Horsemanship, Horse Racing, Etc. - 89631   2013 $125

Meader, Stephen W. *Red Horse Hill.* New York: Harcourt Brace and Co., 1930, but really, 1957. Seventh printing ("G"), illustrations by Lee Townsend, fine in modestly rubbed, very good dust jacket, price clipped with some tears. Between the Covers Rare Books, Inc. Horses, Horsemanship, Horse Racing, Etc. - 89638 2013 $85

Meader, Stephen W. *Wild Pony Island.* New York: Harcourt Brace and Co., 1959. First edition, illustrations by Charles Beck, fine in near fine dust jacket with bit of darkening and little rubbing, mostly at spine. Between the Covers Rare Books, Inc. Horses, Horsemanship, Horse Racing, Etc. - 89761 2013 $225

Meadowcourt, Richard *A Critical Dissertation with Notes on Milton's Paradise Regain'd.* London: printed for A. Millar, 1748. Second edition, 8vo., some marking to titlepage, occasional foxing, original stab holes, disbound. Jarndyce Antiquarian Booksellers CCIV - 203 2013 £125

Means, James *The Aeronautical Annual Nos. 1-(2, 3).* Boston: W. B. Clarke, 1895. 1896. 1897. 1910. First editions, 8vo., 69 plates, original printed and pictorial wrappers, fine, nearly original condition. M & S Rare Books, Inc. 95 - 4 2013 $2750

Means, James *Manflight.* Boston: James Means, 1891. First edition, 8vo., 29 pages, original printed wrappers, fine, fresh copy. M & S Rare Books, Inc. 95 - 5 2013 $250

Mecanno Magazine. Volume XXVI Jan.- Dec. 1941. Liverpool: Meccano Magazine, 1941. 4to., binder's red cloth, gilt, 396 pages, illustrations. R. F. G. Hollett & Son Children's Books - 383 2013 £50

Mechain, Pierre Francois Andre *Base du Systeme Metrique Decimal, ou Mesure d l'arc du Meridien Compris entre les Paralleles de Dunkerque...* Paris: Boudoin, 1806-1810. First edition, rare, 3 volumes, quarto, 28 folding engraved plates by C. Collin, numerous tables in text, contemporary French tree calf with gilt borders, smooth spines stamped and lettered gilt, red morocco spine labels, all edges marbled, marbled endpapers, lacking endpapers in volume 1, some insignificant pale marginal dampstaining, few small splits to joints, corners and boards bit rubbed, some staining to boards volumes I and III, bookplate of Frank Streeter, overall very nice. Heritage Book Shop Holiday Catalogue 2012 - 106 2013 $35,000

Mechel, Christian Von *Catalogue des Tableaux de la Galerie Imperiale et Royale De Vienne.* Basle: J. Thourneisen, for the author, 1784. 8vo., pages xxx, (2), 384, engraved and woodcut vignettes, head and tailpieces in text, four large folding engraved plates, French 19th century cloth stamped in blind, title in gilt on spine, little sunned. Marlborough Rare Books Ltd. 218 - 103 2013 £450

The Medical Classics, or a General and complete Library of Physicians, Surgeons, Anatomists, Chymists, Apothecaries &c. and sold by M. Lister, 1788. First edition, engraved allegorical frontispiece, second general title, 4 parts in one volume, each with titlepage, engraved portrait of Huxham, 14 engraved plates in the Sharpe, main texts, internal tear in one leaf in Sharpe with loss of couple of letters, but these adhering to a spot of glue on succeeding page having caused the tear, ink spots on one page of Monro, obscuring a few letters, contemporary half calf, red lettering piece on spine, gilt numeral in one compartment, joints cracked cords holding, corners worn, good, very rare. Blackwell's Rare Books Sciences - 82 2013 £1250

Medicina Flagellata; or the Doctor Scarificed. printed for J. Bateman and J. Nicks, 1721. First edition, additional letterpress title with engraved vignette, 8vo., contemporary tree calf, flat spine gilt in compartments, red lettering piece, minor wear, top of upper joint snagged foot of spine chipped, contemporary signature at head of title of W. Beeson, engraved bookplate of Sir Thomas Hesketh, and Easton Neston Library shelf label, very good. Blackwell's Rare Books Sciences - 101 2013 £750

Medwin, Thomas 1788-1869 *Journal of the Conversations of Lord Byron Noted During Residence with His Lordship at Pisa in the Years 1821 and 1822.* Paris: L. Gaudry, 1824. 2 volumes, half titles, frontispiece volume I, prelims slightly dampmarked, some spotting to text, 2 volumes in 1, contemporary quarter dark brown morocco, slightly rubbed. Jarndyce Antiquarian Booksellers CCIII - 417 2013 £125

Medwin, Thomas 1788-1869 *Conversations of Lord Byron with Thomas Medwin.* London: Henry Colburn & Richard Bentley, 1832. 2 volumes in 1, frontispiece little spotted, folding facsimile letter, 2 volumes in 1 as issued, original purple cloth, blocked in blind, slightly rubbed, spine faded to brown, booklabel of James Robert Brown. Jarndyce Antiquarian Booksellers CCIII - 419 2013 £50

Medwin, Thomas 1788-1869 *Journal of the Conversations of Lord Byron, Noted During a Residence with His Lordship at Pisa in the Years 1821 and 1822.* London: Henry Colburn, 1824. First edition, 4to., half title, frontispiece facsimile with slight offsetting on title, 2 pages ads (Oct. 1824), contemporary half calf, black label, little rubbed, armorial booklabel of Joseph Bainbridge. Jarndyce Antiquarian Booksellers CCIII - 415 2013 £250

Medwin, Thomas 1788-1869 *Conversations of Lord Byron Noted During Residence with His Lordship at Pisa in the Years 1821 and 1822.* London: Henry Colburn, 1824. Second edition, half title, folding facsimile frontispiece, slightly damp affected, slightly later half dark brown morocco, maroon leather labels, slightly chipped, little rubbed. Jarndyce Antiquarian Booksellers CCIII - 416 2013 £150

Medwin, Thomas 1788-1869 *Conversations of Lord Byron Noted During Residence with His Lordship at Pisa in the Years 1821 and 1822.* London: Henry Colburn, 1825. New edition, 2 volumes, half titles, frontispiece portrait volume I, folding facsimile volume II, slightly spotted, contemporary half calf, spines and corners little worn.   Jarndyce Antiquarian Booksellers   CCIII - 418   2013   £65

Mee, John *The Three Little Frogs.* Chicago: Volland, 1924. First edition, 8vo., no additional printings, pictorial boards, very good+ in pictorial box, illustrations by John Rae.   Aleph-Bet Books, Inc.   104 - 576   2013 $325

Meehan, Paula *The Sea.* Minnesota: Traffic Street Press, 2007. Limited to 26 lettered copies, signed by author, from a total edition of 56, first edition, oblong 8vo., original Canapetta linen on boards, printed letterpress by Paulette Myers-Rich on Johannot paper, photos printed in ultrachrome inks on vellum, fine in matching slipcase.   Maggs Bros. Ltd.   1442 - 224   2013   £175

Meighan, Clement W. *Prehistoric Trails of Atacama: Archaeology of Northern Chile.* Los Angeles: Institute of Archaeology, University of California, 1980. First edition, quarto, 61 photo plates, numerous text illustrations, maps, leatherette spine, cloth sides, very fine with pictorial dust jacket.   Argonaut Book Shop   Recent Acquisitions June 2013 - 206   2013 $125

Melanchthon, Philipp 1779-1848 *Moralis Philosophiae Epitome.* Lyon: Sebastien Gryphius, 1542. Small 8vo., woodcut printer's device on titlepage, woodcut of a Griffin on verso of last leaf, 3 woodcut initials, few minor stains, modern calf backed boards, portions of dedication ruled through in pencil (as if censored, but if so inefectually), good.   Blackwell's Rare Books   B174 - 100   2013   £450

Melvile, James *The Memoirs of Sir James Melvil of Halhil.* Glasgow: printed for Robert Urie, 1751. Third edition, 12mo., lightly age toned few spots, contemporary sheep, rebacked and rcornered by Chris Weston, old leather bit rubbed at edges, early MS ink annotations cropped by binder, occasional ink annotations in foremargins and occasional manicules, 19th century ink ownership of Thos. Barclay.   Unsworths Antiquarian Booksellers   28 - 115   2013   £150

Melville, Herman 1819-1891 *Moby-Dick; or the Whale.* New York: Harper & Bros., 1851. First American edition, 12mo., BAL first binding of publisher's red "A" cloth, original brown-orange coated endpapers, double flyleaves at front and back, headcap and small areas of front and rear joint expertly and almost invisibly restored by master restorer Bruce Levy, inner hinges untouched, spectacular copy in rarest original binding.   David Brass Rare Books, Inc.   Holiday 2012 Chapter Five - DB 02001   2013 $45,000

Melville, Herman 1819-1891 *The Works of Herman Melville.* London: Bombay: Sydney: Constable and Co. Ltd., 1922-1924. Standard edition, limited to 750 sets,, 16 volumes, tall 8vo., original cloth, top edge gilt, seven of the volumes with original dust jackets, which are extremely rare and fragile, having been printed on heavy, acidic paper, remnants of other dust jackets, chiefly inside flaps included in a few of the other volumes, the set is exceptionally fine, all hinges firm and tight, with no fading to spines.   James S. Jaffe Rare Books   Fall 2013 - 98   2013 $20,000

Memorial of a Delegation from the Cherokee Indians. Washington: 1931. First edition, 8vo., 8 pages, unbound, untrimmed and unopened, single sheet folded to from four leaves, edges little browned with couple of tears in fore-edge, nice.   M & S Rare Books, Inc.   95 - 160   2013 $100

Mencken, H. L. *The Gist of Nietzsche.* Boston: John W. Luce and Co., 1910. First edition, cloth and paper labels, fine, lacking unprinted glassine dust jacket.   Between the Covers Rare Books, Inc.   Philosophy - 108821   2013 $200

Mencken, H. L. *The Philosophy of Friedrich Nietzsche.* Boston: Luce and C., 1908. First edition, frontispiece, 21.5 cm., in dark red publisher's cloth, small name in ink of noted collector, modest wear at spinal extremities and light rubbing to lettering at base of spine, very good, without dust jacket, scarce.   Between the Covers Rare Books, Inc.   Philosophy - 47437   2013 $245

Mendelssohn, Felix *Letters.... 1833-1847.* London: Longmans, 1864. 8vo., half title, frontispiece, near fine, original cloth.   Ken Spelman Books Ltd.   75 - 129   2013   £50

Mendoza, George *The Inspector.* Garden City: Doubleday and Co., 1970. First edition, illustrations by Peter Parnall, very near fine, illustrated boards, in very good plus dust jacket with tear to top of spine that has been repaired on verso with tape, another small tear at base of front panel and some very slight wear, still very nice, uncommon.   Jeff Hirsch Books   Fall 2013 - 129438   2013 $125

Mengs, Anthony Raphael *The Works.* R. Faulder, 1796. First English edition, 3 volumes in 1, engraved titlepages to volumes I and II and printed sectional title to volume III, some foxing and browning, mid 19th century half calf, marbled boards, morocco label, small tear to foot of first titlepage and leather rather rubbed.   Ken Spelman Books Ltd.   75 - 47   2013   £95

Mercer, A. S. *The Bandit of the Plains; or the Cattlemen's Invasion of Wyoming in 1892.* San Francisco: George Fields, 1935. Limited to 1000 copies, titlepage vignette and 17 headpieces in brown by Arvilla Parker, cloth backed boards, paper spine label, minor offsetting to ends, but very fine and bright, publisher's plain dust jacket. Argonaut Book Shop   Summer 2013 - 229   2013 $150

Mercier, Vivian *The Irish Comic Tradition.* 1962. First edition, 8vo., cloth, dust jacket, some marks, owner inscribed by J. M. Kerrigan (actor), very good.   C. P. Hyland   261 - 603   2013   £50

Merck's Index an Encyclopedia for the Chemist, Pharmacist and Physician. Merck & Co., 1930. 1940. 1952., 3 editions included, 4th, 5th and 6th edition, 2nd printing, original cloth.   James Tait Goodrich   S74 - 183   2013 $95

Merington, Marguerite *The Custer Story. The Life and Letters of General George A. Custer and His Wife Elizabeth.* New York: Devin-Adair Co., 1950. First edition, frontispiece, photos, map, dark blue cloth, gilt, very fine, pictorial dust jacket, minor chipping to spine ends.   Argonaut Book Shop   Summer 2013 - 230   2013 $150

Meriton, George *The Touchestone of Wills, Testaments and Administrations.* Printed for W. Leak, A. Roper, F. Tyton, T. Dring, J. Place, W. Place, J. Starkey, T. Basset, R. Pawlet & S. Herrick, 1668. First edition, slightly browned and spotted, small 8vo., contemporary calf, very worn, upper joint half split, piece missing from upper cover, upper outer corner, page of contemporary notes on flyleaf and annotations in text, sound.   Blackwell's Rare Books   B174 - 90   2013   £550

Meriwether, David *My Life in the Mountains and on the Plains.* Norman: University of Oklahoma Press, 1965. First edition, photos and drawings, brown cloth, gilt lettered spine, very fine with slightly rubbed pictorial dust jacket. Argonaut Book Shop   Summer 2013 - 231   2013 $60

Meriwether, Susan *Playbook of Robin Hood.* New York: Harper and Bros., 1927. First edition, folio, stiff pictorial card covers, corner of one flap frayed a bit, else fine an unused, bold color illustrations, unusually fine, rare in unused condition.   Aleph-Bet Books, Inc.   104 - 488   2013 $500

Merriam, Charles C. *Report of the City Council Committee on Crime of the City of Chicago.* Chicago: H. G. Adair March 22, 1915. First edition, 8vo., pages 916, foldout-charts, printed wrappers (cover nearly separate, lacks rear), from the library of reformer Florence Kelley (1859-1932). Second Life Books Inc.   182 - 39   2013 $150

Merrill, Marion *The Animated Peter Rabbit.* New York: Cima Pub. Co., 1945. First edition, 3 tab operated moveable pages + other color illustrations, pages 22, spiral bound color pictorial boards, edges of pages lightly browned, very nice in partly worn dust jacket, scarce.   Ian Hodgkins & Co. Ltd.   134 - 44   2013   £190

Merritt, A. *Burn Witch Burn!* New York: Liveright, 1933. First edition, 8vo., bookplate of previous owner, fine, except for dime sized chip at top corner of spine, would be near fine dust jacket.   Ed Smith Books   75 - 44   2013 $1250

Merritt, A. *Dwellers in the Miracle.* Providence: The Grandon Co., 1932. First edition thus, nearly fine, bright copy in near fine dust jacket with one missing chip to spine crown.   Ed Smith Books   75 - 46   2013 $125

Merritt, A. *Dwellers in the Mirage.* New York: Liveright, 1932. First edition, owner's neat name front fly, spine gilt dull but readable, very good, without dust jacket.   Between the Covers Rare Books, Inc.   Sci-Fi, Fantasy & Horror - 319917   2013 $65

Merritt, A. *The Face in the Abyss.* West Kingston: Donald Grant, 1991. First edition thus, with these illustrations, one of 375 copies signed by artist, Ned Dameron, fine in fine dust jacket and fine slipcase.   Between the Covers Rare Books, Inc.   Sci-Fi, Fantasy & Horror - 306568   2013 $50

Merritt, A. *Seven Footprints to Satan.* New York: Boni & Liveright, 1928. First edition, very good, solid copy, publisher's decorated binding, lacking rare dust jacket, couple of bumps to board edges, bookplate to front endpaper.   Ed Smith Books   75 - 45   2013 $125

Merritt, A. *The Ship of Ishtar.* New York: Putnams, 1926. First edition, 8vo., dark reddish brown weave cloth with tan lettering and no top staining (one of several bindings - priority unknown), pictorial bookplate of Henry Eichner, tape ghosts to front and back free endpapers (probably from jacket protector), else bright and fresh in very good pictorial dust jacket (internal tape at foot of spine), some wear at corners and edges and somewhat darkened spine, scarce, especially in dust jacket.   Ed Smith Books   75 - 47   2013 $850

Merritt, A. *The Ship of Ishtar.* Los Angeles: Borden Pub. Co., 1949. Memorial edition, illustrations by Virgil Finlay, fine in fine dust jacket.   Between the Covers Rare Books, Inc.   Sci-Fi, Fantasy & Horror - 320946   2013 $70

The Merry Mixer from the House of Schenley. New York: Schenley Products, 1938. 24mo., (24) pages, vignettes, stapled illustrated wrappers, just about fine.   Between the Covers Rare Books, Inc.   Cocktails, Etc. - 321220   2013 $100

Merryman, Bryan *Cuirt an Mheadhon Oidhche.* 1912. First edition, 8vo., cloth, some light shading on boards, else very good.   C. P. Hyland   261 - 604   2013   £100

Mersereau, John *The Corpse Comes Ashore.* Philadelphia: J. B. Lippincott, 1941. First edition, publisher's file copy, so stamped on front fly, else fine in near fine, price clipped dust jacket with some rubbing and couple of short tears, very scarce in dust jacket.   Between the Covers Rare Books, Inc.   Mystery & Detective Fiction - 86707   2013 $285

Mertens, Charles De *An Account of the Plague which Raged at Moscow in 1771.* London: printed for F. and C. Rivington, 1799. First English edition, 8vo., modern green quarter calf, marbled paper sides, gilt lettering, lacking front and rear blanks, very good.   The Brick Row Book Shop   Miscellany Fifty-Nine - 34   2013 $500

Merton, Thomas   1915-1968 *The Pasternak Affair in Perspective.* New York: Thought, 1960. First separate edition, offprint, tall 8vo., original printed wrappers, presentation from author for Mark (Van Doren), wrappers partially faded at margins, front outer corners bumped, otherwise very good, rare.   James S. Jaffe Rare Books   Fall 2013 - 102   2013 $3500

Merton, Thomas   1915-1968 *Prometheus/A Meditation. Pro Manuscripto.* Lexington: Margaret I King Library Press, University of Kentucky, Spring, 1958. First edition, limited to 150 copies, 8vo., original boards, printed label on spine, presentation from author for Mark and Dorothy Van Doren 1958, with drawing, fine, rare.   James S. Jaffe Rare Books   Fall 2013 - 101   2013 $7500

Merton, Thomas   1915-1968 *The Solitary Life.* Lexington: Stamperia del Santuccio, 1960. First edition, one of 60 copies, hand printed by Victor Hammer at Stamperia del Santuccio and signed by Merton, fine in dust jacket which is sunned near spine and back panel, rare, 8vo., original brown boards, printed label, dust jacket.   James S. Jaffe Rare Books   Fall 2013 - 103   2013 $2500

Merton, Thomas   1915-1968 *Thirty Poems.* Norfolk: New Directions/Poets of the Year, 1944. First edition, scarce hardbound issue, signed by author, laid in is TLS 1 page April 5 , 1945 to E. R. Underwood from the Abbot of Our Lady Gethsemani Monastery, spine ends trifle bumped, small bookseller's label on front pastedown, otherwise very fine and bright copy.   James S. Jaffe Rare Books   Fall 2013 - 99   2013 $3500

Merton, Thomas   1915-1968 *The Tower of Babel.* Norfolk: New Directions, 1957. First edition, one of 250 numbered copies printed by hand press of Richard Von Sichowsky in Hambuurg and signed by Merton and Marcks, noted Bauhaus artist, folio, original boards, fine in slipcase which is starting to split at ends of spine.   James S. Jaffe Rare Books   Fall 2013 - 100   2013 $1500

Merzbach, Uta C. *Carl Friedrich Guass: a Bibliography.* Wilmington: Scholarly Resources, 1984. 4to., dark blue green cloth, gilt stamped spine, bookplate of Burndy Library, fine.   Jeff Weber Rare Books   169 - 158   2013 $95

Messinger, W. C. *W. C. Messinger's Illustrated Catalogue of Dental Furniture, Instruments and Materials.* Pittsburgh: 1897. First edition, 8vo., original printed cloth, tipped in errata, nearly fine.   Howard S. Mott Inc.   262 - 150   2013 $500

Methodist Episcopal Church in America *Minutes Taken at the Several Conferences of the Methodist Episcopal Church, in America, for the Year 1789.* New York: printed by Wm. Ross in Broad Street, 1789. Slightly browned around edges, cut close at fore-edge, just touching one letter on title, pages 14, 12mo., disbound and loose, very rare. Blackwell's Rare Books   172 - 98   2013   £550

The Methodist Magazine for the Year 1814. Thomas Cordeaux, 1814. Volume XXXVII, old full polished tree calf gilt with leather spine label, 12 steel engraved portraits.   R. F. G. Hollett & Son   Wesleyan Methodism - 46   2013   £75

Mettler, Cecilia C. *History of Medicine.* Philadelphia: Blakiston, 1947. 16 plates, good copy, original cloth, some sun fading to upper front board.   James Tait Goodrich   75 - 145   2013 $135

Metz, Leon Claire *The Shooters.* El Paso: 1976. Silver Bullet Edition, one of 300 bound thus, quarter rawhide leather and red cloth with bullet inlaid in front board, signed and numbered, this number 000, 300 pages, illustrations, spine little faded, else near fine in like slipcase, issued without dust jacket.   Dumont Maps & Books of the West   125 - 61   2013 $375

Mewshaw, Michael *Man in Motion.* New York: Random House, 1970. One of the dedication copies, inscribed to Dr. Herbert Schaumann, one of the three dedicatees, one section marked in text, fading to cloth edges and two tiny spots on prelims, near fine in like dust jacket with slight corner chipping and small ink number on rear panel.   Ken Lopez Bookseller   159 - 134   2013 $450

Meyer, Carl *Nach dem Sacramento. Resiebilder Eines Heimgekehrten von Carl Meyer.* Aarau: Druck und Verlag von H. R. Sauerlander, 1855. First edition, quite rare, especially in this condition, small octavo, publisher's yellow pictorial wrappers, printed in black, just a hint of occasional foxing, slight soiling to wrappers, very fine, uncut, unread. Argonaut Book Shop   Summer 2013 - 232   2013 $1500

Meyer, Franz *Marc Chagall.* New York: Harry N. Abrams, 1963. First edition, over 1250 illustrations, includes 53 tipped in color plates, tight, near fine copy in very good dust jacket with tear and some minor wear to top of spine.   Jeff Hirsch Books   Fall 2013 - 129146   2013 $75

Meyer, Michael C. *Water in the Hispanic Southwest.* Tucson: University of Arizona Press, 1984. First edition, photographs, facsimiles, maps, grey cloth, very fine, pictorial dust jacket. Argonaut Book Shop Recent Acquisitions June 2013 - 207 2013 $60

Meyerowitz, Joel *A Summer's Day.* New York: Times Books, 1985. First edition, 65 color photos, very near fine in like dust jacket. Jeff Hirsch Books Fall 2013 - 129489 2013 $55

Meynell, Laurence W. *The Door in the Wall.* New York: Harper & Bros., 1937. First American edition, fine in lovely, very near fine dust jacket with slight rubbing on spine, very nice, scarce. Between the Covers Rare Books, Inc. Mystery & Detective Fiction - 54285 2013 $400

Miall, A. Bernard *Nocturnes and Pastorals: a Book of Verse.* London: Leonard Smithers, 1896. First edition, rare first book, original dark blue cloth, chipping to spine ends and bumping to corners, otherwise very nice, offsetting to free endpapers and slight browning to page edges, but clean and tight, bookplates of W. MacDonald MacKay, Charles Hiatt (writer on art) and Barry Humphries (actor), illegible signature in ink, 109 pages. The Kelmscott Bookshop 7 - 121 2013 $450

Michael, A. C. *An Artist in Spain.* London: Hodder & Stoughton, 1920. First edition, quarto, pages 205, 26 colored illustrations original red decorative cloth. J. & S. L. Bonham Antiquarian Booksellers Europe - 8401 2013 £60

Michell, Thomas *History of the Scottish Expedition to Norway i 1612.* London: T. Nelson & Sons, 1886. First edition, 8vo., 189 page, map, illustrations, original brown decorative cloth, spine faded, small wear to upper fore edge. J. & S. L. Bonham Antiquarian Booksellers Europe - 8980 2013 £90

Middlesex Mechanic Association *A Catalogue of the Library of the Middlesex Mechanic Association at Lowell, Mass. with the Act of Incorporation and the Constitution and By-laws....* Lowell: S. J. Varney, 1853. First edition, 8vo., 165, (1), removed. M & S Rare Books, Inc. 95 - 33 2013 $175

Middleton, Charles *A New and Complete System of Geography.* London: 1777-1779. 2 volumes, folio, maps, plates, rebound in full leather, contents browned with some marginal staining, one map with some loss to neat line. Dumont Maps & Books of the West 125 - 62 2013 $3750

Middleton, W. N. *The China Punch.* Hong Kong: China Mail Office dated between May 28 1867 - May 28,1868. November 5, 1872 - November 22nd, 1876, First and only edition, 3 volumes bound in one, Volume I No. 1-24, Volume 2 No. 1-19, Volume 3 No. 1-7, 28 color lithograph plates, numerous woodcut illustrations, folio, volume 1 bound in contemporary half calf, minor restoration, volumes 2 and 3 bound in contemporary red half morocco, some very minor worming and edge wear, overall very good, very rare. Maggs Bros. Ltd. 1467 - 57 2013 £26,000

Mikelsen, Ajnar *Lost in the Arctic.* London: Heinemann, 1913. First edition, large 8vo., original blue cloth, silvered, neatly recased, pages xviii, 400, numerous illustrations, large folding map, endpapers little dusty, otherwise very good. R. F. G. Hollett & Son Polar Exploration - 39 2013 £195

Mikovaro, E. *Book of Pirates.* Racine: Whitman, 1932. Large 4to., cloth backed pictorial boards, 95 pages, nearly as new in fine pictorial dust jacket, 16 full page and 1 double page color plates by G. R. Taylor, remarkable copy. Aleph-Bet Books, Inc. 105 - 458 2013 $225

Miles, Henry A *Lowell, As It Was and As It Is.* Lowell: Powers and Bagley, 1845. First edition, 12mo., 234 pages, foldout map, one foldout engraving, brown cloth, stamped on spine in gilt, owner's name on flyleaf, front cover nearly detached, spine and corners lacking some of the cloth, just good. Second Life Books Inc. 182 - 171 2013 $65

The Militant. October 31 1969-February 6, 1970, Broken run, issues between 33:43 and 34:4, 11 issues, near fine. Beasley Books 2013 - 2013 $100

Milizia, Francesco *Del Teatro.* Venezia: Giambatista Pasquali, 1773. First edition with these plates, 4to., engraved titlepage and 6 folding engraved plates, modern cloth backed boards, printed spine label, some minor foxing, soiling, light dampstain, very good, tight copy. Second Life Books Inc. 183 - 172 2013 $1700

Mill, John Stuart 1806-1873 *Autobiography.* London: Longmans, Green Reader & Dyer, 1874. Third edition, 23cm., green publisher's cloth, very good with light rubbing and modest wear to spine ends, else near fine, clean and tight. Between the Covers Rare Books, Inc. Philosophy - 62546 2013 $75

Mill, John Stuart 1806-1873 *Principles of Political Economy with Some of their Applications to Social Philosophy.* New York: D. Appleton and Co., 1868. From the fifth London edition, 2 volumes, 616, 603 pages, 23cm, in brown publishers' cloth, two small owner's bookplates on front pastedowns and free endpapers respectively, both volumes very good, moderate rubbing to boards and darkening to spines, else near fine set with text pages clean, tight and unopened. Between the Covers Rare Books, Inc. Philosophy - 62510 2013 $85

Mill, John Stuart 1806-1873 *The Subjection of Women.* Philadelphia: Lippincott, 1869.   First American edition, 8vo., 174 pages, brown cloth, owner's name and date on blank, cover faded and little spotted, worn at corners and ends of spine, otherwise very good, tight copy.   Second Life Books Inc.   182 - 172   2013 $350

Mill, John Stuart 1806-1873 *The Subjection of Women.* London: 1869.   First edition, octavo, original mustard sand grain cloth with covers decoratively stamped in blind, spine ruled and ruled and lettered in gilt, original brown coated endpapers, binder's ticket on rear pastedown, slight extremity wear and spine darkening, owner's signature, very good.   Heritage Book Shop   50th Anniversary Catalogue - 71   2013 $4500

Millais, John Guille *A Breath from the Veldt.* London: Henry Sotheran, 1895.   Large paper signed limited edition, number 31 of 60 copies, folio, original half crimson morocco gilt by Sotheran with cream boards, upper board with vignettes of sable and kudu antelope, extremities little rubbed and boards trifle soiled in places, short soiled tear to cloth of upper panel, top edge gilt, untrimmed, etched frontispiece, 12 further full page electro etched plates, 12 full page plates and numerous text illustrations, little scattered foxing to plates, small Oatesiana roundel stamp to title, most handsome copy, armorial bookplates of William Edward Oates and Robert Washington Oates, presentation label of latter and printed label of Newton Library.   R. F. G. Hollett & Son   Africana - 145   2013   £1950

Miller, Alfred Jacob *The West of Alfred Jacob Miller (1837) from the Notes and Water Colors in the Walters Art Gallery...* Norman: University of Oklahoma Press, 1951.   First edition, 4to., color frontispiece and 200 black and white plates, tan cloth, spine lettered in dark green with gilt, very fine, lightly worn pictorial dust jacket.   Argonaut Book Shop   Summer 2013 - 234   2013 $150

Miller, Arthur *Death of a Salesman.* New York: Limited Editions Club, 1984.   First edition, 1/500 copies, signed by author and artist, 4to., full brown morocco by Gray Parrot, fine in original slipcase, little worn, five etchings by Leonard Baskin.   Second Life Books Inc.   183 - 275   2013 $750

Miller, David L. *The Philosophy of George V. Gentry.* Austin: Minneapolis: Burgess Pub. Co., 1938.   First edition, mimeographed sheets bound in printed stiff card covers, 203 pages, stain on titlepage, card covers cracked, sound, good plus, apparently issued in small numbers, scarce.   Between the Covers Rare Books, Inc.   Philosophy - 62212   2013 $300

Miller, Henry 1891-1980 *Maurizius Forever.* San Francisco: Colt Press, 1946.   First edition, one of 500 copies, 8vo., pages 78, teal cloth in plain brown dust jacket (toning to pastedown from dust jacket), illustrations from original drawings and water colors by Miller.   Second Life Books Inc.   183 - 276   2013 $200

Miller, Henry 1891-1980 *To Paint is to Love Again.* New York: Grossman, 1968.   First edition, tan cloth with white lettering to front cover and white and orange lettering to spine, very good++ dust jacket, price clipped with minimal soil and faint blue offsetting from previous dust jacket cover, 4to., color frontispiece and 19 color plates.   By the Book, L. C.   38 - 96   2013 $265

Miller, Hugh, Mrs. *Stories of the Cat and Her Cousins the Lion, the Tiger ad the Leopard.* T. Nelson & Sons, 1880.   Small 8vo., original brown pictorial cloth, gilt over bevelled boards, little soiled and rubbed, chromolithograph frontispiece and 29 woodcuts, frontispiece and title heavily dampstained, endpapers spotted or scribbled upon, joints cracked, few spots or finger marks in text, one leaf, badly defective, rare.   R. F. G. Hollett & Son   Children's Books - 385   2013   £120

Miller, Kelly *The Disgrace of Democracy: Open Letter to President Woodrow Wilson.* Washington: Kelly Miller, 1917.   Stapled gray printed wrappers, small stain on edges of pages, near fine.   Between the Covers Rare Books, Inc.   165 - 318   2013 $475

Miller, Kelly *Eugenics of the Negro Race.* New York?: Science Press, 1917.   Offprint, stapled, printed self wrappers, tiny tear and little spotting on front wrapper, good or better.   Between the Covers Rare Books, Inc.   165 - 218   2013 $350

Miller, Kelly *The Howard Spirit.* Washington: Howard University, n.d.,   First edition, printed self wrappers, single folded leaf, (4) pages, punch holes on left hand margin, front leaf soiled and with small tears, good.   Between the Covers Rare Books, Inc.   165 - 316   2013 $400

Miller, Kelly *Is Race Prejudice Innate or Acquired?* No place: no publisher, n.d.,   First edition, stapled printed self wrappers trifle soiled, near fine.   Between the Covers Rare Books, Inc.   165 - 315   2013 $500

Miller, Kelly *Is the American Negro to Remain Black or Become Bleached.* Durham: Reprinted from the South Atlantic Quarterly/Duke University Press, 1926.   Offprint, stapled printed self wrappers, scraping and an old tissue repair to unprinted rear wrapper where it seems to have been affixed to another page, scrape on front wrapper, fair.   Between the Covers Rare Books, Inc.   165 - 219   2013 $300

Miller, Kelly *The Negro Sanhedrin: a Call to Conference.* Washington: Howard University, 1923.   First edition, printed brown wrappers, staples oxidized and small stains on rear wrapper, probably where pamphlet was removed from a scrapbook leaf, else nice, near fine.   Between the Covers Rare Books, Inc.   165 - 319   2013 $950

Miller, Kelly *The Political Capacity of the Negro.* Washington: Murray Bros. Press, 1910. Offprint, stapled printed self wrappers, stab holes near spine and wrappers and pages stained, small chips on front wrapper. Between the Covers Rare Books, Inc. 165 - 317 2013 $400

Miller, Kelly *Roosevelt and the Negro.* Washington: Kelly Miller/Haworth Pub. House, 1907. First edition, stapled printed wrappers, 23 pages, two stab holes near spine, very faint stain on first leaf, else near fine. Between the Covers Rare Books, Inc. 165 - 217 2013 $350

Miller, Kelly *"Social Equality.".* Washington: Kelly Miller, 1905? Offprint, stapled printed self wrappers, staples lacking, thus disbound, trifle foxed, else very good. Between the Covers Rare Books, Inc. 165 - 216 2013 $250

Miller, M. Catherine *Flooding the Courtrooms Law and Water in the Far West.* Lincoln: University of Nebraska, 1993. First edition, 4 maps, green cloth lettered in silver, very fine. Argonaut Book Shop Recent Acquisitions June 2013 - 208 2013 $75

Miller, Maria Morris *Wild Flowers of Nova Scotia and New Brunswick.* Halifax: published by M. L. Katzman and John Snow, Paternoster Row, London,, 1866. Part V - third series, 3 full color plates, with original printed titlepage, text plate and tissue guards, plates in very good condition, covers split down spine/fold and have some soiling to front. Schooner Books Ltd. 102 - 102 2013 $2500

Miller, Olive Beaupre *My Book House.* Chicago: Book House for Children, 1925. 6 volumes, 8vo., illustrations, green cloth, very good, clean set with minor scratches to cover pictures, top edge gilt. Barnaby Rudge Booksellers Children 2013 - 020581 2013 $210

Miller, Olive Beaupre *My Book House.* Chicago: Book House for Children, 1937. 8vo., 13 volumes, including guide book, blue cloth, good, volume 1 has scratches to front picture and childs drawings on blank front endpapers, other volumes nice and clean. Barnaby Rudge Booksellers Children 2013 - 020708 2013 $75

Miller, Paul Eduard *Esquire's Jazz Book.* Chicago: Esquire, 1943-1944. First edition, paperback illustrations, wrappers, folio, very good. Beasley Books 2013 - 2013 $50

Miller, Philip *The Abridgement of the Gardeners Dictionary.* London: printed for the author and sold by John Rivington (and others), 1763. 4to., engraved frontispiece and 12 folding plates, clean tear without loss of Xx4, contemporary calf, double gilt ruled borders, expertly rebacked, raised and gilt banded spine, morocco label, corners very neatly repaired, early signature of Robert Chapman verso of frontispiece. Jarndyce Antiquarian Booksellers CCIV - 204 2013 £750

Miller, Philip *The Practical Gardener Containing Plain and Familiar Instructions for Propagating and Improving the Different Kinds of Fruit Trees, Plants and Flowers...* printed by W. Day & Co. for M. Jones, 1805. First edition, 9 engraved plates, 2 folding, others turned in, 1 frayed and dust soiled at fore-edge, not affecting engraved surface, 8vo., contemporary tree calf, backed marbled boards, ownership inscription of Thomas Sneyd dated 1807 and his armorial bookplate as Thomas Sneyd Kynnersley (of Loxley Park, Staffs, added Kynnersley to his name in 1815), very good. Blackwell's Rare Books Sciences - 83 2013 £120

Miller, Robert Ryall *For Science and National Glory. The Spanish Scientific Expedition to America 1862-1866.* Norman: University of Oklahoma Press, 1968. First edition, title color illustrations, 48 illustrations from photos, yellow cloth, very fine with dust jacket. Argonaut Book Shop Summer 2013 - 235 2013 $60

Miller, Robert Ryall *Shamrock and Sword. The Saint Patrick's Battalion in the U.S. Mexican War.* Norman: University of Oklahoma Press, 1989. First edition, photos, reproductions, views, maps, green cloth, very fine, pictorial dust jacket. Argonaut Book Shop Summer 2013 - 237 2013 $75

Miller, Thomas *Picture Sketches of London Past and Present.* London: National Illustrated Library, n.d., 1854. First edition, 8vo., 306 pages, illustrations, original blue blindstamped cloth. J. & S. L. Bonham Antiquarian Booksellers Europe - 8340 2013 £50

Miller, Wade *Pop Goes the Queen.* New York: Farrar Straus, 1947. First edition, some light spotting on covers, otherwise near fine in dust jacket with small chips and nicks at spine ends and couple of tears. Mordida Books 81 - 366 2013 $65

Miller, Walter M. *Conditionally Human.* London: Victor Gollancz, 1963. First edition, owner's name on front fly, spine lightly faded, corners modestly bumped, else very good, lacking dust jacket. Between the Covers Rare Books, Inc. Sci-Fi, Fantasy & Horror - 138767 2013 $300

Millett, Benignus *The Irish Franciscans 1651-1665.* Rome: Gregorian U. P., 1964. 8vo., wrappers, near mint. C. P. Hyland 261 - 605 2013 £60

Million, A. *Pere Marquette Power.* Alderman: C. & O. Historical Society, 1984. First edition, 4to., wrappers, fine. Beasley Books 2013 - 2013 $60

Mills, George H. *Mohammed, the Arabian Prophet.* Boston: Philips, Sampson & Co., 1850. First edition, 12mo., original cloth, bottom of spine chipped, inscribed by George H. Mills to Ellen M. Clopper, Feb. 28 1851.   M & S Rare Books, Inc.   95 - 235   2013 $125

Mills, John *An Essay on the Weather, with Remarks on the Shepherd of Banbury's Rules for Judging of it's Changes and Directions for Preserving Lives and Buildings from the Fatal Effects of Lightening.* printed for S. Hoper, 1770. First edition, one or two spots, 8vo., calf backed boards, rebacked notes on front flyleaf, slightly affected by one time too generous application of glue, good.   Blackwell's Rare Books   172 - 99   2013   £1200

Mills, John *The Life of a Racehorse.* The Office of "the Field", 1854. First bookform edition, frontispiece, title vignette and vignette at end, frontispiece, small 8vo., contemporary green calf, single gilt fillet on sides, spine gilt in compartments, red lettering piece, few slight marks, good, attractive copy, scarce.   Blackwell's Rare Books   B174 - 102   2013   £200

Mills, W. H. *Evolution of Society, from Primitive Savagery to the Industrial Republic.* New York: New York Labor News, 1927. First edition, one of 100 numbered and signed copies on tinted paper, very good+, publisher's address change stamp on titlepage, promo brochure for book laid in, lightly chipped plain brown dust jacket, Louis Fisher's copy with his embossed stamp.   Beasley Books   2013 - 2013 $65

Milman, Henry Hart *The Fall of Jerusalem: a Dramatic Poem.* London: John Murray, 1820. New edition, 222 x 140mm., attractive contemporary crimson straight grain morocco, gilt covers with wide gilt dentelles comprising closely spaced palmettes, flat spine in gilt compartments formed by three thin rules and decorated in roman style, scrolling foliate cornerpieces and charming floral centerpiece incorporating morocco onlaid circle, turn-ins with gilt decoration echoing outer dentelles, all edges gilt, with very fine fore-edge painting of Monk Soham in Suffolk, titlepage with signature of E. A. Majendie, dated May 1839. corners quite worn, spine ends very slightly chipped, joints rather flaked, spine somewhat darkened, few marks on front board, binding still quite solid with bright covers, narrow faint dampstain along fore edge throughout (probably related to the process of painting), first half of text with variable foxing, but no major problems internally, leaves still fresh with ample margins.   Phillip J. Pirages   63 - 189   2013 $1250

Milman, Henry Hart *The Fall of Jerusalem.* London: John Murray, 1820. New edition, 8vo., toned and foxed, corner damp marked, contemporary half calf, marbled boards, spine divided by flat raised bands, gilt lettered direct, compartments tooled in blind, marbled edges and endpapers, little rubbed, headcap chipped, boards scuffed, contemporary ink ownership inscription "Anne Creyke" at upper fore corner of titlepage, signed binding by "W/ Forth/ book-binder.   Unsworths Antiquarian Booksellers   28 - 186   2013   £75

Milne, Alan Alexander   1882-1956   *An April Folly in Three Acts.* London: Small French, 1922. First edition French's Acting edition, 8vo., 57 pages, wrappers, fine, 2 photos of sets, signed by author.   Aleph-Bet Books, Inc.   105 - 389   2013 $250

Milne, Alan Alexander   1882-1956   *Christopher Robin Birthday Book.* London: Methuen, 1930. First edition, 12mo., cloth, 215 pages, fine, unused in nice dust jacket (backstrip toned, slight wear to head of backstrip), illustrations by E. H Shepard, quite uncommon, great copy.   Aleph-Bet Books, Inc.   104 - 355   2013 $1200

Milne, Alan Alexander   1882-1956   *A Gallery of Children.* Stanley Paul and Co., 1925. Second edition, large 4to., original blue cloth gilt, pictorial onlay, trifle marked, extremities little rubbed, 12 fine color plates, piece torn from lower corner of one text leaf, otherwise very nice, clean copy.   R. F. G. Hollett & Son   Children's Books - 353   2013   £120

Milne, Alan Alexander   1882-1956   *House at Pooh Corner.* London: Methuen, 1928. First edition, deluxe edition, 8vo., full calf with gilt vignettes and floral decoration, all edges gilt, 103 pages, fine in original publisher's box with printed label, box rubbed with light soil, illustrations by E. H. Shephard, scarce in this binding, beautiful copy.   Aleph-Bet Books, Inc.   104 - 353   2013 $2700

Milne, Alan Alexander   1882-1956   *The House at Pooh Corner.* London: Methuen, 1928. First edition, original cloth gilt, head of spine trifle faded, dust jacket (spine little darkened, trifling edgewear to head and foot of backstrip, short closed tear to top of lower panel), titlepage, decorations by E. H. Shepard, narrow faintly browned strip on each flyleaf, else fine.   R. F. G. Hollett & Son   Children's Books - 389   2013   £1250

Milne, Alan Alexander   1882-1956   *The House at Pooh Corner.* London: Metheun, 1928. First edition, original cloth, gilt, head of spine trifle faded, dust jacket extremities creased and worn, backstrip worn and darkened, pieces missing from head and foot, top edge gilt gilt, decorations by Ernest H. Shepard, narrow lightly browned strip on each fly-leaf.   R. F. G. Hollett & Son   Children's Books - 386   2013   £400

Milne, Alan Alexander 1882-1956 *The House at Pooh Corner.* London: Methuen, 1928. First edition, deluxe issue, original limp red calf gilt, spine and upper board gilt decorated, spine trifle rubbed and canted, all edges gilt, decorations and pink endpapers by E. H. Shepard, very nice, clean.   R. F. G. Hollett & Son   Children's Books - 387   2013   £450

Milne, Alan Alexander 1882-1956 *The House at Pooh Corner.* London: Methuen, 1928. Second edition, original cloth gilt, spine trifle faded, top edge gilt, decorations by E. H. Shepard, very nice, bright, clean copy.   R. F. G. Hollett & Son   Children's Books - 388   2013   £85

Milne, Alan Alexander 1882-1956 *More Very Young Songs from When We Were Very Young and Now We Are Six.* London: Methuen, 1928. First edition, 32/100 copies, printed on Japanese paper and signed by Milne, Fraser-Simson and E. H. Shepard, decorations by Shepard, large 4to., original quarter dark blue cloth, pale grey boards, front cover label, untrimmed and unopened, near fine.   Blackwell's Rare Books   B174 - 263   2013   £800

Milne, Alan Alexander 1882-1956 *More Very Young Songs.* London: Methuen, 1928. First edition, cloth backed boards, folio, fine in dust jacket (just slight soil and wear, else very good+), illustrations by Ernest Shepard, great copy.   Aleph-Bet Books, Inc.   104 - 354   2013 $300

Milne, Alan Alexander 1882-1956 *Now We Are Six.* New York: E. P. Dutton and Co., 1927. First American edition, large paper edition, one of 200 copies, signed by author and artist, this being #8, small quarto, printed on Japon vellum, with signed limitation leaf, text illustrations by E. H. Shepard, original half pink cloth over light blue illustrated paper boards, printed paper spine label, blue laid endpapers, publisher's light blue printed jacket and illustrated box, top edge cut, others untrimmed, mostly unopened, jacket spine lightly sunned, box slightly browned, some chips and repairs, box missing left side handsome, fine.   Heritage Book Shop   Holiday Catalogue 2012 - 107   2013 $3000

Milne, Alan Alexander 1882-1956 *Now We Are Six.* London: Methuen, 1927. First edition, original cloth, gilt, dust jacket spine little darkened, some loss to head and little wear to foot, short closed tear to lower edge and wear to hinges of flaps, decorations by E. H. Shepard, slight browning to inner third of half title and final leaf, otherwise contents fine.   R. F. G. Hollett & Son   Children's Books - 392   2013   £500

Milne, Alan Alexander 1882-1956 *Now We Are Six.* London: Methuen, 1927. First edition, original cloth, gilt dust jacket (spine and folds browned and rubbed, little loss to head and foot of spine and folds, light fingering in places), top edge gilt, decorations by E. H. Shepard, slight browning to inner third of half title and final leaf, pencilled inscription on flyleaf dated Christmas 1927, otherwise contents fine.   R. F. G. Hollett & Son   Children's Books - 394   2013   £450

Milne, Alan Alexander 1882-1956 *Now We Are Six.* London: Methuen, 1927. First edition, deluxe issue, original full limp blue leather gilt, spine little faded, decorations by E. H. Shepard, contents fine.   R. F. G. Hollett & Son   Children's Books - 393   2013   £650

Milne, Alan Alexander 1882-1956 *Now We Are Six.* London: Methuen, 1927. First edition, deluxe issue, drawings and endpaper designs by E. H. Shepard, browning (faint) to initial and final page as usual, foolscap 8vo., original mid blue calf (copies were also issued in green or maroon calf), gilt lettered and decorated backstrip lightly faded, front cover with gilt double fillet border and a Shepard vignette, owner's name on front free endpaper of decorated endpapers, gilt edges, very good.   Blackwell's Rare Books   B174 - 264   2013   £650

Milne, Alan Alexander 1882-1956 *Now We Are Six.* London: Methuen, 1927. Second edition, original cloth, gilt, spine rather faded, top edge gilt, decorations by E. H. Shepard, half title browned, flyleaves lightly spotted.   R. F. G. Hollett & Son   Children's Books - 390   2013   £85

Milne, Alan Alexander 1882-1956 *Now We Are Six.* London: Methuen, 1927. Third edition, original cloth, gilt, spine rather darkened, dust jacket (spine rubbed and browned, few small edge chips), top edge gilt, decorations by E. H. Shepard, neat name on half title.   R. F. G. Hollett & Son   Children's Books - 391   2013   £180

Milne, Alan Alexander 1882-1956 *Once on a Time.* London: Hodder & Stoughton, n.d., 1925. First edition with these illustrations, 8vo., blue gilt pictorial cloth, gilt decorative spine, 269 pages, illustrations by Charles Robinson.   Aleph-Bet Books, Inc.   105 - 390   2013 $500

Milne, Alan Alexander 1882-1956 *Other People's Lives.* London: Samuel French, 1935. First edition, 8vo., 79 pages, wrappers, fine, 2 scene plans, this copy signed by author.   Aleph-Bet Books, Inc.   105 - 388   2013 $250

Milne, Alan Alexander 1882-1956 *When We Were Very Young.* London: Methuen, 1924. 7th printing, first deluxe leather printing, 8vo., full blue leather deluxe binding, spine ends rubbed and spine slightly faded, owner name verso of free endpaper, very good, rare.   Aleph-Bet Books, Inc.   104 - 352   2013 $1850

Milne, Alan Alexander 1882-1956 *When We Were Very Young.* London: Methuen, 1924. #36 of only 100 numbered copies signed by author and artist, first edition, 4to., cloth backed boards, except for few faint oxidation marks, very fine in very good+ dust jacket (spine sunned and with two small chips off top of spine), custom quarter leather box, rare, beautiful copy.　Aleph-Bet Books, Inc.　104 - 351　2013　$24,000

Milne, Alan Alexander 1882-1956 *When We Were Very Young.* London: Methuen, 1924. Second edition, original blue cloth, gilt, top edge gilt, decorations by E. H. Shepard, few faint spots to flyleaves, but very nice, clean bright copy.　R. F. G. Hollett & Son　Children's Books - 396　2013　£150

Milne, Alan Alexander 1882-1956 *When We Were Very Young.* London: Methuen, 1924. Fourth edition, original blue cloth gilt, dust jacket (most of backstrip lacking, rather soiled, edges worn), top edge gilt, decorations by E. H. Shepard, inscription, else very good.　R. F. G. Hollett & Son　Children's Books - 395　2013　£150

Milne, Alan Alexander 1882-1956 *When I Was Very Young.* New York: Fountain Press, 1930. Limited to 603 copies for America, signed by author, 842 copies in all, 4to., pictorial cloth, fine in slightly worn slipcase, printed on handmade paper, beautiful illustrations by Ernest Shepard on fine paper.　Aleph-Bet Books, Inc.　104 - 356　2013　$750

Milne, Alan Alexander 1882-1956 *When We Were Very Young.* London: Methuen Children's Books, 1974. One of 300 copies, signed by Christopher Milne, this #157, 193 x 120mm., xii, 100 pages, publisher's sky blue crushed morocco, upper cover with gilt figure of Little Bo Peep, flat spine adorned with twining floral vine around which cherubic children frolic, all edges gilt, illustrations by E. H. Shepard, spine and edges of covers very slightly sunned, otherwise pristine.　Phillip J. Pirages　63 - 337　2013　$950

Milne, Alan Alexander 1882-1956 *Winnie-the-Pooh.* London: Methuen, 1926. First edition, deluxe issue, drawings and endpaper designs by E. H. Shepard, foolscap 8vo., original apple-green calf (copies were also issued in blue or red calf), gilt lettered and decorated backstrip darkened to brown and rubbed at head, tail and a little on rear joint, front cover with gilt double fillet border and Shepard vignette, endpaper maps, green silk marker detached, gilt edges, good.　Blackwell's Rare Books　B174 - 265　2013　£1000

Milne, Alan Alexander 1882-1956 *Winnie-the-Pooh.* London: Methuen, 1926. First edition, original green cloth gilt, trifle rubbed at extremities, small patch of cockling to lower board, top edge gilt, decorations by E. H. Shepard, excellent, sound copy.　R. F. G. Hollett & Son　Children's Books - 398　2013　£450

Milne, Alan Alexander 1882-1956 *Winnie-the-Pooh.* London: Methuen, 1926. First edition, drawings and endpaper designs by E. H. Shepard, foolscap 8vo., original dark green cloth, backstrip lettering and Shepard designs of Pooh and Christopher Robon on front cover all gilt blocked, endpaper maps by E. H. Shepard, partial browning to free endpapers as usual, top edge gilt, others rough trimmed, dust jacket with backstrip panel little darkened, but otherwise in fine bright condition, near fine.　Blackwell's Rare Books　B174 - 266　2013　£1900

Milne, Alan Alexander 1882-1956 *Winnie the Pooh.* London: Methuen, 1926. First edition, drawings and endpaper maps by E. H. Shepard, gift inscription, crown 8vo., original dark green cloth, backstrip lettering and Shepard designs on front cover, all gilt blocked, faint offsetting to endpaper maps as usual, top edge gilt, others rough trimmed, very good.　Blackwell's Rare Books　172 - 219　2013　£800

Milne, Alan Alexander 1882-1956 *Winnie the Pooh.* London: Methuen, 1926. First edition, deluxe edition, 8vo., full green publisher's morocco, gilt pictorial cover with extensive gilt pictorial spine, all edges gilt, fine, illustrations by E. H. Shepard.　Aleph-Bet Books, Inc.　104 - 350　2013　$4500

Milne, Alan Alexander 1882-1956 *Winnie-the-Pooh...* London: Methuen & Co., 1926. First edition, half title, illustrations, original green cloth blocked in gilt, minor mark to spine, some slight rubbing, but very good, bright copy.　Jarndyce Antiquarian Booksellers　CCV - 200　2013　£750

Milne, Alan Alexander 1882-1956 *Winnie-the-Pooh.* London: Methuen, 1927. Fourth edition, original green cloth gilt, extremities little worn, dust jacket (soiled and chipped, loss to head of backstrip, pencil scribbles to lower panel), top edge gilt, decorations by E. H. Shepard, trifle shaken, contents nice and clean.　R. F. G. Hollett & Son　Children's Books - 397　2013　£120

Milne, Alan Alexander 1882-1956 *Winnie-the-Pooh.* London: Methuen, 1928. Sixth edition, original green cloth gilt, xi, 160 pages, top edge gilt, decorations by E. H. Shepard, lovely clean and bright copy with no inscriptions or marking of any kind.　R. F. G. Hollett & Son　Children's Books - 399　2013　£150

Milner, Joe *California Joe, Noted Scout and Indian Fighter.* Caldwel: Caxton Printers, 1935. First edition, 27 vintage photos, gilt stamped dark green cloth, light offsetting to endpapers but very fine and bright, quite scarce in this condition.　Argonaut Book Shop　Summer 2013 - 238　2013　$350

Milner, John *A Practical Grammar of the Latin Tongue.* London: printed for John Noon, 1742. Second edition, 8vo., lightly toned, fore-edge sometimes cut little close, contemporary polished sheep, plain spine, paper label lettered in ink, edges speckled, joints cracking but strong, corners and endcaps worn, later ink ownership inscription 'W. Carr/1794". Unsworths Antiquarian Booksellers 28 - 33 2013 £95

Milnor, William *An Authentic Historical Memoir of the Schuylkill Fishing Company of the State in Schuylkill. (with) Memoirs of the Gloucester for Hunting Club, near Philadelphia.* Philadelphia: Judah Dobson, 1930. Frontispiece and 2 portraits, 127 pages; second work with frontispiece and plate, 56 pages, errata leaf, spotting throughout, occasionally heavy; uncut, original pink cloth boards, paper label on front board, spine slightly faded, slight mark to tail, very good in original binding, half red morocco slipcase. Jarndyce Antiquarian Booksellers CCV - 201 2013 £650

Milosz, Czeslaw *The Captive Mind.* New York: Alfred A. Knopf, 1953. First US edition, signed by author on bookplate tipped in on titlepage, very good in blue cloth boards with gilt title to spine, gentle wear to edges of boards and foxing/toning to endpapers, otherwise clean bright copy, dust jacket with few chips to edges, few creases and some marks to front panel, jacket very good, 151 pages. The Kelmscott Bookshop 7 - 122 2013 $350

Milton, John 1608-1674 *Literae Pseudo-Senatus Anglicani, Cromwellii Reliquorumque Perduellium Nomine ac Jussu Conscriptae a Joanne Miltono.* Amsterdam: Impressae by Peiter and Willem Blaeur for Moses Pitt, London?, 1676. 12mo, woodcut device to titlepage, complete with final 3 blank leaves, full contemporary calf, upper board loose but attached, some browning to endpapers and pastedowns. Ken Spelman Books Ltd. 75 - 8 2013 £220

Milton, John 1608-1674 *Literae Pseudo-Sentaus Anglicani, Cromwellii....* Brussels?: Impressae anno, 1676. First edition, 12mo., woodcut fruit on title, modern full calf, very skilfully executed in period style, original pastedowns retained, fine, lovely copy. Joseph J. Felcone Inc. Books Printed before 1701 - 69 2013 $900

Milton, John 1608-1674 *Paradise Lost.* London: printed for Jacob Tonson, 1707. Eighth edition, engraved frontispiece dated 1670, 12 engraved plates, some browning and waterstaining, clean tears without loss to one plate and Gg3, small pencil dots in margin mark certain passages, full contemporary calf, ruled borders, small thistle device in each corner, gilt panelled spine, red morocco label, expert repairs to hinges & head and tail of spine, early ownership signature of Martha Drew, 1748 and 19th century bookplate of Mary Wood, handsome copy. Jarndyce Antiquarian Booksellers CCV - 203 2013 £350

Milton, John 1608-1674 *The Paradise Lost of Milton.* London: 1827. First (Imperial Quarto) edition, one of only 50 copies with smaller set of engravings, 2 volumes bound in 1, 24 mezzotint plates in smaller format, with tissue guards, contemporary burgundy pebble grain morocco, covers decoratively paneled gilt, spines paneled and lettered in gilt compartments, gilt spine bands, gilt board edges, wide gilt tooled dentelles, marbled endpapers and doublures, all edges gilt, some light foxing, mainly to plate margins and prelims, excellent copy, scarce. Heritage Book Shop Holiday Catalogue 2012 - 108 2013 $9500

Milton, John 1608-1674 *Le Paradis Reconquis.* Paris: chez Cailleau, Place du Pont Saint Michel du cote du Quai des Augustins..., 1730. 8vo., old rather faint waterstain to lower corners of preface, full contemporary calf, gilt panelled spine, red morocco label, marbled endpapers, carmine edges, silk marker, slight insect damage to surface leather on upper board, nice, bookplate of Jacqueline Hilpert. Jarndyce Antiquarian Booksellers CCV - 202 2013 £320

Milton, John 1608-1674 *The Poetical Works...* London: printed under the direction of J. Bell British Library, Strand, 1788. 4 volumes in 2, frontispiece, engraved titlepage to each part, fine contemporary tree calf, greek key gilt borders, gilt spines, decorative bands and flowerhead motifs, red and black morocco labels, early name of Maria Hole on endpapers, another early signature struck through at head of each titlepage, name also neatly clipped from top corner of front endpapers. Jarndyce Antiquarian Booksellers CCIV - 205 2013 £95

Milton, John 1608-1674 *The Poetical Works of John Milton.* printed for C. Cooke, 1796. 2 volumes, 12mo., engraved frontispiece and additional titlepage in each volume, plus 7 engraved plates (all lightly foxed), most with tissue guards, contemporary quarter sprinkled calf with marbled boards, corners tipped in vellum, spines divided by gilt fillet, red morocco lettering pieces, ownership inscription of W. E. Goodchild to initial blank, slightly rubbed, touch of wear to few corners, good. Blackwell's Rare Books B174 - 103 2013 £150

Milton, John 1608-1674 *The Poetical Works of...* Boston: Hilliard, Gray and Co., 1839. New edition, 251 x 152mm., 2 volumes, publisher's purple-brown pebble grain buckram, gilt titling and anchor device on flat spines, recent brown cardboard slipcase, frontispiece by O. Pelton, miniature of the same size by Faithorne, original tissue guard, large paper copy, ad leaf for 1839 issues of North American Review (published by Hilliard) laid in at rear volume I; spines sunned to light brown, one spine with thin four inch vertical line of soil, mild rubbing to extremities, minor browning to head and tail portions of frontispiece not protected by tissue guard, other trivial imperfections, particularly fine, text clean, fresh and bright, margins especially spacious, bindings with no significant wear. Phillip J. Pirages 63 - 338 2013 $475

Milton, John   1608-1674   ... *Pro Populo Anglicano defensio, contras Claudii Anonymi Alias.*   London: i.e Gouda?: Typis du Gardianis, 1652.   False imprint, probably from Gouda, 12mo., 192 pages, woodcut arms on title, modern calf, antique, one inch piece torn from titlepage margin, not affecting type and neatly repaired, else very good, Eric Quayle's copy with his bookplate.   Joseph J. Felcone Inc. Books Printed before 1701 - 70   2013 $750

Milton, William Fitzwilliam, Viscount   1839-1877   *The North-West Passage by Land: Being the Narrative of an Expedition from the Atlantic to the Pacific.*   London: 1875. Eighth edition, xviii, 396 pages, illustrations, folding map, ads, original printed boards, extremities rubbed, hinges just starting, gift inscription.   Dumont Maps & Books of the West   124 - 77   2013 $95

Minarik, Else Homelund   *A Kiss for Little Bear.*   New York: Harper Row, 1968.   8vo., pictorial boards, fine in frayed dust jacket, scarce in such nice condition, wonderful color illustrations by Maurice Sendak.   Aleph-Bet Books, Inc.   105 - 527   2013 $350

The Miners' Own Book...   San Francisco: Book Club of California, 1949.   One of 500 copies, xi, 35 pages, numerous illustrations, pictorial cloth backed boards, paper label, fine.   Argonaut Book Shop   Recent Acquisitions June 2013 - 209   2013 $75

Miniature Book News.   St. Louis: n.p., 1965-2001.   Small 8vo., nos. 1-108, complete run, self paper wrappers, variously paginated, illustrations, from the collection of Donn W. Sanford.   Oak Knoll Books   303 - 20   2013 $450

Miniature Book Society   *Catalogue of the Miniature Book Competitions and Exhibitions.*   N.P.: Miniature Book Society, 1988-2002.   14 volumes, excluding 1994, miniature books, various sizes, stiff paper wrappers, from the collection of Donn W. Sanford.   Oak Knoll Books   303 - 13   2013 $350

Minshull, John   *A Comic Opera.*   New York: printed for the author, 1801.   First edition, 8vo., removed, evidently lacking frontispiece, title leaf detached, some soiling.   M & S Rare Books, Inc.   95 - 106   2013 $250

Mirabeau, Honore Gabriel de Riquetti, Comte De   1749-1791   *Errotika Biblion.*   Rome: de l'Imprimerie du Vatican MDCCLXXXIII (i.e. Germany circa, 1860.   12mo., 263 pages, some light spotting, 20th century half blue morocco over marbled boards, marbled endpapers, top edge gilt, one corner lightly bumped, Purchase inscription to titlepage with initials (blocked out) and place and date (1869). Unsworths Antiquarian Booksellers   28 - 187   2013   £125

Miro, G.   *Jan Gabriel Daragnes. Semaine Sainte.*   Lyon: Societe les XXX, 1931.   First edition, number 3 of 30 'exemplaires nominatifs', with 19 hand colored engravings, of which 7 are hors texte and an additional suite of 18 hand colored engravings, all hors texte by Daragnes, printed on velin d'Arches filigrane paper, circa 13 x 1 inches, page size 360 x 270mm., 61 pages, signed binding by Manuel Gerard, blue snakeskin with inlaid large geometric wood panels, plain spine with gilt lettering, dark blue painted endleaves, top edge gilt, original wrappers bound in, morocco trimmed matching slipcase, few faint fox marks, otherwise fine, rare.   Gemini Fine Books & Arts., Ltd.   Art Reference & Illustrated Books - 2013 $1450

The Mirror No. 423.   April 10, 1830.   Disbound, slightly marked.   Jarndyce Antiquarian Booksellers   CCIII - 434   2013   £30

Mises, Ludwig Von   *A Critique of Interventionism.*   New Rochelle: Arlington House, 1977.   First edition in English, 8vo., scarce edition, near fine, age darkening to endpapers, very good+++ dust jacket with mild edgewear.   By the Book, L. C.   38 - 20   2013 $200

Mises, Ludwig Von   *The Free and Prosperous Commonwealth (Liberalism).*   New York: Van Nostrand, 1962.   First English language edition, 8vo., scarce, near fine with minimal sun spine, in very good+ price clipped dust jacket with minimal soil and stains, edgewear and sun spine. By the Book, L. C.   38 - 21   2013 $225

Mises, Ludwig Von   *The Ultimate Foundation of Economic Science.*   Princeton: D. Van Nostrand, 1962.   First edition, 8vo., fine in very good++ dust jacket with sun spine, minimal soil and scuffs.   By the Book, L. C.   38 - 19   2013 $300

Mistral, Gabriela   *Selected Poems of Gabriela Mistral.* Bloomington: Indiana University Press, 1957.   First edition, text in Spanish and English, bookplate, owner's name and offsetting from a clipping on the front fly, else near fine in very good dust jacket with tear and very shallow loss at spine ends.   Between the Covers Rare Books, Inc.   165 - 220   2013 $100

Mitchell, Abe   *Down to Scratch.*   London: Methuen, 1933. First edition, 8vo., xi, 145 pages, mild scuffs to spine and rear cover, owner name to front pastedown, minimal soil, very good++ in very good+ dust jacket with edge wear and soil.   By the Book, L. C.   36 - 71   2013 $300

Mitchell, Annie R.   *The Way It Was. The Colorful History of Tuylare County.*   Fresno: Panorama West Pub., 1987. Second printing, 4to., photos and portraits, map, brown cloth, very fine, pictorial dust jacket.   Argonaut Book Shop Recent Acquisitions June 2013 - 210   2013 $75

Mitchell, David *Black Swan Green.* Sceptre, 2006. First edition, 8vo., original dark green boards, backstrip blocked in silver, dust jacket, fine, inscribed by author. Blackwell's Rare Books   B174 - 267   2013   £100

Mitchell, Edmund *Chickabiddy Stories.* Wells Gardner, Darton and Co., n.d. circa, 1922. Second edition, Large 8vo., original pictorial green cloth, 4 color plates tipped on to brown card and 26 line drawings by Norman Hardy, contemporary inscription, else very nice, scarce.   R. F. G. Hollett & Son   Children's Books - 402   2013   £120

Mitchell, J. Leslie *Three Go Back.* Indianapolis: Bobbs Merrill, 1932. First American edition, boards little soiled, top edge little darkened, very good or better in very good plus dust jacket with two scratches on spine and few tiny nicks and tears, laid in is ALS from author's widow (R. Mitchell) telling her correspondent that her husband died in 1932, letter has old, light glue stain on verso where it was presumably affixed in an album, else near fine.   Between the Covers Rare Books, Inc.   Sci-Fi, Fantasy & Horror - 84977   2013 $450

Mitchell, James *A Tour through Belgium, Holland, Along the Rhine and through the North of France in the Summer of 1816.* London: printed for Longman, Hurst (and others), 1816. xii, 390 pages, folding frontispiece, 8vo., slight foxing, map offset on to titlepage, contemporary polished calf, gilt ruled borders, gilt panelled spine, black morocco label, hinges cracked, chip to foot of spine, William Beckford's copy with 2 pages of his pencil notes written on prelim blank.   Jarndyce Antiquarian Booksellers   CCIV - 206   2013   £1500

Mitchell, Margaret *Gone with the Wind.* New York: Macmillan, 1936. First edition, first printing with "Published May 1936" on copyright page, in second issue dust jacket, 8vo., original gray cloth, little drab, couple of minor splits at top of spine, jacket very good with few blank pieces missing from top and bottom of spine, some short tears.   Howard S. Mott Inc.   262 - 102   2013 $950

Mitchell, Margaret *Gone with the Wind.* New York: Macmillan Co., 1936. First edition, first issue (with "published May, 1936" on copyright page and no note of further printing), signed by author, 222 x 152mm., 4 p.l., 1037 pages, very pleasing gray crushed morocco by Sangorski & Sutcliffe (stamp signed on front turn-in), covers with single gilt rule border, raised bands, decorated with stippled rule and flanked by gilt rules, panels with intricate gilt fleuron centerpiece and gilt tilting, gilt ruled turn-ins, marbled endpapers, top edge gilt, upper right corner of back cover slightly soiled (with a series of short, thin, faint parallel lines about two of three inches in length descending from top edge), spine slightly and evenly sunned to pleasant light brownish gray, trivial internal imperfections, otherwise very fine. Phillip J. Pirages   63 - 342   2013 $7500

Mitchell, Samuel Latham   1764-1831 *The Picture of New York or the Traveller's Guide, through the Commercial Metropolis of the United States.* New York: I. Riley and Co., 1807. First edition, 16mo.. contemporary quarter leather and paper covered boards, contents pages (217)-223 are inserted before text, ex-library with stamp on copyright page, withdrawn stamp on front fly, name struck through on titlepage, fair only, lacking folding map, spine partially perished and replaced with older book cloth repair, itself worn and wear to boards.   Between the Covers Rare Books, Inc. New York City - 301352   2013 $500

Mitchell, Silas Weir   1829-1914 *The Tendon-Jerk and Muscle-Jerk in Disease and Especially in Posterior Sclerosis.* Offprint from American Journal of Medical Science, Oct., 1886. 10 pages, original publisher's printed green wrappers, nice copy.   James Tait Goodrich   S74 - 186   2013 $150

Mitchnik, Helen *Egyptian & Sudanese Folk-Tales Retold.* Oxford University Press, 1978. First edition, original cloth, gilt, dust jacket, illustrations by Eric Fraser.   R. F. G. Hollett & Son Africana - 146   2013   £25

Mitford, Mary Russell   1787-1855 *Our Village.* London: Macmillan, 1910. First color plate edition, 4to., green gilt cloth bubbled in few places, else fine in dust jacket (frayed), illustrations by Hugh Thomson with 100 black and white drawings and by Alfred Rawlings with 16 beautiful tipped in color plates, nice, scarce in dust jacket.   Aleph-Bet Books, Inc.   104 - 555   2013 $400

Miura, Kerstin Tini *My World of Bibliophile Binding.* Berkeley: University of California Press, 1984. First edition, 343 x 268mm., original blindstamped lilac colored cloth, flat spine with vertical titling, matching slipcase with printed paper label on cover, 152 pages of color photos, including double folding plate, bookplate of Terese Blanding, as new. Phillip J. Pirages   63 - 70   2013 $225

Mivart, George *Man and Apes, an Exposition of Structural Resemblances and Differences Bearing Upon Questions of Affinity and Origin.* London: Robert Hardwicke, 1873. First edition, very good, purple cloth with gilt lettered spine, sun spine, scuffs and wear to spine, gift inscription, scattered foxing, rear hinge archivally repaired, 8vo.   By the Book, L. C.   37 - 57   2013 $200

Mockler-Ferryman, A. F. *In The Northman's Land...* London: Sampson Low, Marston, 1896. First edition, 8vo., half title, map, 16 photogravures, 2 illustrations in text, original maroon cloth, gilt vignette on upper cover, crease on lower cover.   J. & S. L. Bonham Antiquarian Booksellers   Europe - 8984   2013   £35

Moctezuma, Eduardo Matos *Teotihuacan. The City of the Gods.* New York: Rizzoli, 1990. First English language edition, quarto, 239 pages, color and black and white photos, black boards, very fine with pictorial dust jacket. Argonaut Book Shop   Recent Acquisitions June 2013 - 211   2013 $75

Model Menagerie with Natural History Stories... London: Nister, n.d. circa, 1895.   Large oblong 4to. cloth backed pictorial boards, lacks rear blank endpaper and front endpaper chipped, else very good+, beautiful book with 6 full page chromolithographed pages of animals in cages that emerge when page is turned, quite often found with bars of cage detached or missing, this copy nice.   Aleph-Bet Books, Inc.   104 - 444   2013 $900

The Modern Couple; or the History of Mr. and Mrs. Davers. Dublin: printed by and for J. A. Husband, 1776.   12mo., some browning and foxing, some pages dusted, slight adhesion from wax on page 83, full contemporary calf, double gilt banded spine, dark green morocco label, expert repairs to hinges, head and tail of spine and corners.   Jarndyce Antiquarian Booksellers   CCIV - 48   2013   £2800

A Modern Delineation of the Town and Port of Kingston Upon Hull... Hull: printed by and for W. Turner, 1805. 8vo., half title, very good, recent calf backed cloth, some light browning to paper, scarce.   Ken Spelman Books Ltd.   73 - 97   2013   £120

Moerenhout, Jacques Antoine *The Inside Story of the Gold Rush.* San Francisco: California Historical Society, 1935. First book edition, 7 plates, map, large folding map, yellow cloth with paper spine label and color pictorial pastedown, very fine, bright, quite scarce.   Argonaut Book Shop   Summer 2013 - 240   2013 $250

Mogridge, George *Sergeant Bell and His Raree-Show.* printed for Thomas Tegg, 1839.   First edition, original red blindstamped cloth, gilt, rather

soiled and darkened, neatly recased, new endpapers, all edges gilt, title vignette and numerous woodcuts, lacks frontispiece and leaf FF1, few light spots and finger marks, foredge of one leaf rather dusty, titlepage vignette and some other illustrations by Cruikshank.   R. F. G. Hollett & Son Children's Books - 403   2013   £175

Mohr, Richard *The Platonic Cosmology.* Leiden: E. J. Brill, 1985.   8vo., printed wrappers, ownership signature, fine, rare.   Jeff Weber Rare Books   169 - 302   2013 $75

Moir, Robert Gordon *Dunning, Dundee and Dartmouth. A Moir Story. Parts 1 and 2.* Dartmouth: privately printed, 1995.   2006., Card covers, 87 and 24 pages, photo illustrations, family trees, quarto, both very good.   Schooner Books Ltd.   104 - 104   2013 $55

Molesworth, Mary Louisa Stewart   1839-1921 *The February Boys.* W. & R. Chambers, 1909.   Original pink pictorial boards, gilt, 266 pages, 8 charming color plates, scarce.   R. F. G. Hollett & Son   Children's Books - 37 2013   £85

Molesworth, Robert *An Account of Denmark as it was in the year 1692.* London: n.p., 1694. First edition, 8vo., 271 pages, recent red quarter morocco, clean, crisp copy.   J. & S. L. Bonham Antiquarian Booksellers   Europe - 9277 2013   £175

Molina, Alfonso De *Vocabulario en Lenguo Castellana y Mexicana...* Mexico: En Casa de Antonio de Spinosa, 1571.   Second (first complete) edition, 2 parts in one folio volume, first title supplied in early facsimile, decorative woodcut initials, contemporary limp vellum, title in manuscript on spine, some worming heavier in first part, occasionally affecting few letters wormholes repaired on title of second part, Part 1 with early paper repair to lower margin of leaf *2, just touching few letters on recto, paper flaw in lower margin of g2, just touching a few letters, short marginal tear to leaf f1, not affecting text, part II with short marginal tears to A5 A6 and N4, early paper repairs in lower margin of C4 just touching few letters in lower margin of C5, G8, M7 and R8 and in upper margin of V8, not affecting text, final leaf strengthened in margins on verso, few small stains, early ink library stamp of Dr. Manuel A. R. de Arellano, Mexico in several places, few early ink annotations, overall excellent copy, extremely rare.   Heritage Book Shop   50th Anniversary Catalogue - 72   2013 $30,000

Molineux, T. *An Introduction to Byrom's Universal English Short-Hand.* Macclesfield: printed for the author by E. S. Bayley, 1823.   Sixth edition, modern calf backed marbled boards, gilt, original engraved label relaid on upper board, frontispiece, 6 plates, faint marginal blindstamped on title and final leaf.   R. F. G. Hollett & Son   Children's Books - 404   2013   £85

Mollien, G. *Travels in Africa, to the Sources of the Sengal and Gambia in 1818.* printed for Sir Richard Phillips, 1825. Second UK edition, old half morocco gilt, recased with new spine label, corners little bruised, 4 steel engraved plates and folding map (little spotted).   R. F. G. Hollett & Son Africana - 148   2013   £180

Molnar, E. F. *The Slave of Ea: a Sumerian Legend.* Philadelphia: Dorrance and Co., 1934.   First edition, fine in fine dust jacket with very slight wear, lovely copy.   Between the Covers Rare Books, Inc.   Sci-Fi, Fantasy & Horror - 73798   2013 $350

Moloney, Colette *The Irish Music Manuscripts of Edward Bunting (1773-1843).* Dublin: 2000.   4to., fine hardback copy.   Ken Spelman Books Ltd.   75 - 193   2013   £45

Momigliano, Arnaldo *Claudius: the Emperor and His Achievement.* Oxford: Clarendon Press, 1934. First edition in English, 8vo., original red cloth, excellent copy, slightly foxed, slight wear to head and tail of spine, inscribed by Robert Graves for Mrs. Thomas Ashby (May Ashby). Maggs Bros. Ltd. 1460 - 361 2013 £425

Monakow, Constantin Von *Gehimpathologies.* Wien: Alfred Holder, 1905. Second edition, 1316 pages, 357 text engravings and illustration, later plain red buckram, internally good. James Tait Goodrich S74 - 187 2013 $750

Monfort, Eugene *La Belle-Enfant ou l'Amour a Quarante Ans.* Paris: Ambroise Vollard Editeur, 1930. First Dufy edition, one of 245 numbered copies (total edition 390) on Arches paper, 250 pages, 110 original etchings by Dufy, 94 of which are half or full page plates, 41 of these hors texte, each with tissue guard, all leaves loose in wrappers, chemise and slipcase, overall size 13.5 x 11 x 2.25 inches, generally lean and crisp. Gemini Fine Books & Arts., Ltd. Art Reference & Illustrated Books - 2013 $2950

Monier, Pierre *The History of Painting, Sculpture, Architecture, Graving and of Those Who Have Excell'd in Them.* London: T. Bennet and others, 1699. First English edition, 8vo., little browned, frontispiece, small hole at inner margin, contemporary panelled calf, rebacked with black morocco lettering piece. Marlborough Rare Books Ltd. 218 - 105 2013 £575

Monkey Tricks. New York: McLoughlin Bros., 1894. 6 x 9 1/2 inch die-cut in shape of a monkey, inconspicuous mend on one page, minimal soil, very good+, 6 chromolithographed pages and other pages, illustrations in brown line to accompany poems about monkeys, cats and other animals, scarce title. Aleph-Bet Books, Inc. 104 - 530 2013 $275

Monkhouse, W. *The Churches of York.* London: J. G. and F. Rivington, 1843. First edition, hand colored lithograph titlepage, lithograph dedication leaf, (i) subscribers list noting only 68 names + viii + (48) pages, 23 fine tinted lithograph plates and 3 ground plans, original blind and gilt stamped cloth, with later gilt lettered morocco spine, some foxing to dedication leaf, few other leaves but generally clean, old waterstain to lower inner blank corner, but not intrusive apart from dedication leaf leading edge of titlepage slightly torn and with several faint color splashes, with signature and note of John Bevan dated 1904 "This book was given my by my father in 1903 - the illustrations were drawn on stone by my grandfather William Bevan of York about 1863...". Ken Spelman Books Ltd. 73 - 24 2013 £380

Monod, Jacques *Selected Papers in Molecular Biology.* New York: Academic, 1978. 8vo., near fine, remainder mark to lower edge, 8vo. By the Book, L. C. 37 - 48 2013 $200

Monro, Alexander *Observations on Hydrocephalus Chronicus.* Edinburgh: printed by A. Neill and Co., 1803. First edition, 8vo., 32 pages, folding plate, some discoloration with text lightly spotted, recently rebound in modern quarter calf and marbled boards, author's presentation copy, for Mr. Considen, rare. James Tait Goodrich 75 - 150 2013 $3500

Monro, Alexander *Observations on the Structure and Functions of the Nervous System.* Edinburgh: W. Creech, 1783. First edition, 50 engraved plates, atlas folio in original blue sugar bards, original vellum corners, newly rebacked in calf, raised bands, burgundy calf label with gilt ruling in contemporary style tall, uncut unsophisticated copy internally quite pristine with only minimal foxing, near fine copy. James Tait Goodrich 75 - 148 2013 $7500

Monro, Alexander *Three Treatises. On the Brain, the Eye and the Ear.* Edinburgh & London: Bell & Bradfute, 1797. First edition, 24 engraved plates, 4to., contemporary tree calf, newly rebacked in calf, offsetting from plates, some foxing, else very good, tall crisp well margined copy. James Tait Goodrich 75 - 149 2013 $2250

Monro, Alexander *The Works of Alexander Monro, M.D. Fellow of the Royal Society, Fellow of the Royal College of Physicians and Late Professor of Medicine and Anatomy in the University of Edinburgh.* Edinburgh: Macfarquhar and Elliot for Charles Elliot, 1781. First collected edition, frontispiece, 7 folding plates, thick 4to., contemporary full calf, newly rebacked in calf, offsetting from plates and portrait, lacks half title. James Tait Goodrich 75 - 147 2013 $1295

Monroe, Forest *Maid of Montauk.* New York: William R. Jenkins, 1902. First edition, very faint stain of edge of spine, else nice, near fine. Between the Covers Rare Books, Inc. New York City - 286972 2013 $100

Montagu, M. F. Ashley *Edward Tyson, M.D., F.R.S. (1650-1708) and the Rise of Human and Comparative Anatomy in England: a Study in the History of Science.* Philadelphia: American Philosophical Society, 1943. First edition, 8vo., frontispiece, illustrations, red cloth, gilt stamped cover and spine titles, corners slightly bumped, else fine, Burndy bookplate. Jeff Weber Rare Books 169 - 305 2013 $65

Montagu, Mary Pierrepone Wortley 1689-1762 *Select Passages from Her Letters.* London: Seeley and Co. Ltd., 1892. First edition, 206 x 140mm. 4 p.l., 308 pages, very attractive contemporary dark blue three quarter morocco by Tout (stamp signed), raised bands, spine lavishly gilt in compartments with central oval medallion containing a floral spray, medallion within a frame of entwined volutes, floral tools and stippling, marbled boards and endpapers, top edge gilt, fine, binding very bright, virtually unworn, and obviously unread text especially clean and fresh; 9 engraved portraits after Sir Godfrey Kneller and other artist, bookplate of William Eyres Sloan.   Phillip J. Pirages   63 - 343   2013 $450

Montague, John *The Bread God.* Dublin: Dolmen Press, 1968. Limited to 250 copies, signed by author, 4to., original wrappers, near fine.   Maggs Bros. Ltd.   1442 - 228   2013   £125

Montague, John *Drunken Sailor.* Oldcastle: Gallery Press, 1995. First edition, 8vo., original black cloth, dust jacket, bumped at head, otherwise near fine, inscribed by author for Richard Murphy.   Maggs Bros. Ltd.   1442 - 230   2013   £175

Montague, John *Home Again.* Belfast: Festival Publications, Queen's University of Belfast, 1966. First edition, 8vo., original green wrappers lettered in black, fine, from the library of Richard Murphy, signed by him.   Maggs Bros. Ltd.   1442 - 226   2013   £75

Montague, John *Hymn to the New Omagh Road.* Dublin: Dolmen Press, 1968. First edition, limited to 175 copies, large 8vo., original wrappers, hand stitched with red cotton, rear cover and facing page marked with damp, else good, from the library of Timothy O'Keefe and inscribed by author.   Maggs Bros. Ltd.   1442 - 362   2013   £125

Montague, John *Hymn to the New Omagh Road.* Dublin: Dolmen Press, 1968. First edition, limited to 175 copies signed by author, large 8vo., original tan wrappers, hand stitched with red cotton, some uneven fading on covers, otherwise near fine, from the library of Richard Murphy.   Maggs Bros. Ltd.   1442 - 227   2013   £225

Montague, John *O'Riada's Farewell.* Cork: Golden Stone, 1974. First edition, 8vo., original wrappers, excellent, inscribed by author for Richard Murphy.   Maggs Bros. Ltd.   1442 - 229   2013   £175

Montague, John *Poisoned Lands.* London: MacGibbon & Kee, 1961. First edition, 8vo., original mottled grey cloth, dust jacket, book slightly dampstained at rear, else excellent copy in dust jacket, loosely inserted c. 90 word autographed postcard from author's Dublin address to publisher Timothy O'Keefe dated 2nd Jan. 1961 in English with some Gaelic, card in excellent state.   Maggs Bros. Ltd.   1442 - 361   2013   £175

Montaigne, Michel De 1533-1592 *Les Essais...* Paris: chez Michel Sonnius, 1595. Folio, errata, modern maroon morocco, morocco label, raised bands, old gilt edges, contents skillfully washed and sized, few marginal tears not affecting text, some scattered pencil marginalia, very good.   Heritage Book Shop   50th Anniversary Catalogue - 73   2013 $25,000

Montaigne, Michel De 1533-1592 *The Essayes or Morall, Politike, and Militarie Discourses.* printed by M. Flesher for Rich. Royston, 1632. Third edition, additional engraved architectural titlepage by Martin Droeshout, leaf A6, bound at front as usual, engraved title little proud and slightly rumpled at fore-edge, some browning and occasional spotting, few rust stains, in one instance with loss of a letter on either side of the leaf, one rust hole in blank margin, another margin with a scorched hole, two leaves with marginal tears (or paper flaws) in upper fore-margins, in second case touching a sidenote, small hole (paper flaw) in one leaf with loss of 3 letters on verso, folio in 6's, contemporary calf, double blind ruled borders on sides rebacked preserving most of the original spine, lettered (later) in gilt, recornered, some scuffing to covers, red edges, early lettering to fore-edge and similarly early manuscript title label loosely inserted, good.   Blackwell's Rare Books   B174 - 105   2013   £2500

Montaigne, Michel De 1533-1592 *Essais.* Paris: chez Jean Serviere, Jean Francois Bastien, 1793. 3 volumes, 8vo., half titles, frontispiece, 8vo., some very slight foxing, otherwise fine, clean copy, one gathering in volume III printed on different stock of slightly tinted paper, lower corner of L4 volume I torn with loss not affecting text, slight tear to margin B2 volume II, full contemporary tree calf, gilt borders, gilt panelled spine, red morocco labels, armorial bookplate of C. B. Caldwell, handsome set.   Jarndyce Antiquarian Booksellers   CCIV - 207   2013   £780

Montaigne, Michel De 1533-1592 *The Complete Works of...* London: John Templeman, 1842. First edition, 2 volumes, large 8vo., engraved portrait, engraved titlepage in volume one, presentation by Ralph Waldo Emerson for George Phillips, July 1848, three quarter black morocco, raised bands, some rubbed and scuffed, very good set, some holograph notes on rear blank, probably by Phillips.   Second Life Books Inc.   183 - 279   2013 $3500

Montefiore, Arthur *David Livingstone: His Labours and His Legacy.* S. W. Partridge, n.d. circa, 1890. Twentieth-Eighth thousand, original pictorial cloth gilt, little sued, spine darkened, woodcut illustrations, poor quality paper rather browned at edges.   R. F. G. Hollett & Son   Africana - 149   2013   £30

Montefiore, Leonard A. *Essays and Letters.* London: privately printed, 1881. 8vo., full leather, very good+, 345 pages, full green leather with gilt title to spine, all edges gilt, bookplate of AGM Dagart.   Barnaby Rudge Booksellers   Biography 2013 - 021273   2013 $85

Montesquieu, Charles Louis de Secondat, Baron De La Brede *Oeuvres. Tome Premier - Tome Cinquieme.* Paris: Plassan, Regent Bernard et Gregoire, 1796. 5 volumes, 4to., frontispiece and 2 folding maps to volume I and 13 further engraved copper plates, second map little foxed, some very occasional light underlining, small closed tears to only a few margins, contemporary tan marbled calf, dark green and brown morocco labels and gilt to spines, gilt borders and dentelles, all edges gilt, pink marbled endpapers, boards scratched with areas of surface loss repaired or colored to blend in, endcaps worn, joints worn with volume I upper starting to split a little, ownership inscriptions of Dr. Guerreiro to initial blanks or half titles. Unsworths Antiquarian Booksellers 28 - 116 2013 £2000

Montgomery, James *Poems on the Abolition of the Slave Trade.* London: printed for R. Bowyer, the Proprietor, 1809. First edition, large quarto, sympathetically rebound in later quarter morocco and marbled paper covered boards, dark red spine label, engraved title and 12 plates, some staining and foxing to title and plates, smudging to front fly, else handsome, very good. Between the Covers Rare Books, Inc. 165 - 314 2013 $2250

Montgomery, L. M. *Anne of Avonlea.* Boston: L. C. Page and Co., 1909. Stated first impression, color frontispiece by George Gibbs, 8vo., tan cloth, pictorial paste-on, extremely scarce, beautiful copy. Aleph-Bet Books, Inc. 104 - 357 2013 $1500

Montgomery, L. M. *Anne's House of Dreams.* Toronto: McClelland & Stewart, 1922. Later edition, 8vo., blue cloth boards with dark blue lettering to spine and front cover in dust jacket, some light wear to edges, dust jacket baldy torn with pieces missing and taped, signed by author, inscription "Ann Cleveland August 28th 1941". Schooner Books Ltd. 104 - 141 2013 $375

Montgomery, L. M. *Emily of New Moon.* New York: Frederick Stokes, 1923. First edition, 8vo., blue cloth, pictorial paste-on, fine in dust jacket (heavily worn with old tape repairs), illustrations by Maria Kirk with color. Aleph-Bet Books, Inc. 104 - 358 2013 $850

Montgomery, L. M. *Jane of Lantern Hill.* New York: Frederick A. Stokes, 1937. First edition, 8vo., green cloth stamped in gold, fine in dust jacket slightly chipped at head of spine, uncommon, color frontispiece, very scarce. Aleph-Bet Books, Inc. 104 - 359 2013 $850

Montgomery, L. M. *Rainbow Valley.* New York: Frederick Stokes, 1919. First edition, 8vo., green cloth, pictorial paste-on, near fine in dust jacket with old restoration on top edge, illustrations by Maria Kirk with tissue guarded frontispiece, quite scarce. Aleph-Bet Books, Inc. 104 - 360 2013 $750

Montgomery, L. M. *The Story Girl.* Boston: L. C. Page and Co., May, 1911. First edition, first impression, 8vo., light green cloth with color pictorial panel on front cover and gilt titles to spine and front cover, color frontispiece with tissue guard, wear to pictorial panel and covers, front inner hinge cracks and very small brown spot to pages 1 to 4, previous owner's gift inscription. Schooner Books Ltd. 105 - 120 2013 $95

Montorgueil, Georges *La Cantiniere: France son Historie.* Paris: Felix Juven, n.d. circa, 1899. Folio, color pictorial cover, slightest of rubbing, else fine, magnificent full page and partial page color illustrations by Job. Aleph-Bet Books, Inc. 105 - 344 2013 $500

Montorguiel, G. *Jouons a L'Histoire.* Paris: Boivin, 1908. First edition, 4to., cloth backed pictorial boards, near fine, full page color illustrations by Job (pages hinged individually into book). Aleph-Bet Books, Inc. 104 - 300 2013 $800

Moodie, Susanna *Roughing It in the Bush; or Forest Life in Canada.* Toronto: Maclear & Co., 1871. First Canadian edition, 8vo., original dark grey cloth, gilt title to spine and title and men in woods design in gilt to front cover, half title, black and white frontispiece, 6 black and white plates. Schooner Books Ltd. 102 - 137 2013 $125

Moody, Anne *Mr. Death: Four Stories.* New York: Harper & Row, 1975. First edition, fine in near fine dust jacket with touch of foxing, poet Gwendolyn Brook's copy with letter laid in from publisher presenting the book. Between the Covers Rare Books, Inc. 165 - 110 2013 $85

Moon, Bucklin *The Darker Brother.* Garden City: Doubleday, 1943. First edition, fine in very good with proof dust jacket included. Beasley Books 2013 - 2013 $50

Moon, Henry *An Account of the Wreck of H. M. Sloop "Osprey" with the Encampment of Her Crew and Their March Across the Island of New Zealand...* Arnett & Robinson, 1858. First edition, 12mo., original cloth, spine very lightly sunned, lovely copy, rare. Maggs Bros. Ltd. 1467 - 85 2013 £2500

Moor, J. H. *Notices of the Indian Archipelago and Adjacent Countries.* Singapore: Mission Press, 1837. First edition, 6 folding lithograph maps, charts and town plans, 5 colored in outline with usual bleed through, one repaired, 4to., contemporary half calf, some foxing, very rare. Maggs Bros. Ltd. 1467 - 58 2013 £12,000

Moorat, Joseph *Thirty Old-Time Nursery Songs.* T. C. and E. C. Jack, n.d., 4to., original cloth backed pictorial boards, little spotted and marked, corners worn, pAges 34, illustrations in color, front joint strengthened, little light fingering here and there, but very good. R. F. G. Hollett & Son Children's Books - 727 2013 £75

Moorcock, Michael *Warrior of Mars.* London: New English Library/Times Mirror, 1981. First hardcover edition, cover corners lightly bumped, else fine in fine dust jacket with fine printed wraparound band, especially rare with wraparound band.   Between the Covers Rare Books, Inc.   Sci-Fi, Fantasy & Horror - 314703   2013 $500

Moore, Brian *The Feast of Lupercal.* London: Andre Deutsch, 1958. First UK edition, original red cloth, near fine, signed by author.   Maggs Bros. Ltd.   1442 - 232   2013   £300

Moore, Charles Herbert *Development and Character of Gothic Architecture.* New York: Macmillan, 1899. Second edition, 8vo., 10 plates in photogravure and 242 illustrations in text, bound in black cloth stamped in gilt, little scratched, bookplate, very good, tight clean copy.   Second Life Books Inc.   183 - 280   2013 $50

Moore, Clement Clarke   1779-1863 *Night Before Christmas.* Philadelphia: Willis P. Hazard, 1858. this edition marks first use of this title as opposed to A Visit from St. Nicholas, Large 8vo., pictorial wrappers, (16) pages, including covers, lacks outer wrapper, last leaf has 2 triangular pieces off inner edges (no loss of text), spine worn, corners rounded, some soil and chipping, good to very good 3 full page wood engravings plus large engraving on cover, 2 full page engravings, 1 large engraving, rare.   Aleph-Bet Books, Inc.   105 - 131   2013 $2750

Moore, Clement Clarke   1779-1863 *A Visit from Santa Claus.* Publisher's imprint on front outer wrapper of either Boston or Philadelphia, circa, 1866. 4to., pictorial wrappers, 8 pages, not including cover, lacks decorative front outer wrapper, else very good laid into contemporary paper folder titled Christmas Roses, full page engravings, rare.   Aleph-Bet Books, Inc.   105 - 132   2013 $1850

Moore, Clement Clarke   1779-1863 *A Visit of St. Nicholas.* New York: McLoughlin Bros. n.d. circa, 1875. printed on one side of paper, 4to., yellow pictorial wrappers, binding inconspicuously strengthened, some cover soil and small corner stain on few pages, really nice, very good, 6 fabulous full page chromolithographs and wonderfully detailed black and white drawings on text pages by Thomas Nash, extremely scarce.   Aleph-Bet Books, Inc.   105 - 133   2013 $850

Moore, Clement Clarke   1779-1863 *The Night Before Christmas.* Philadelphia: John C. Winston (Porter & Coates), 1883. 8vo., cloth backed pictorial white boards, fine in publisher's box (soiled), illustrations in black and white, great copy.   Aleph-Bet Books, Inc.   105 - 130   2013 $700

Moore, Clement Clarke   1779-1863 *The Night Before Christmas or a Visit of St. Nicholas.* New York: McLoughlin Bros., 1888. Folio, pictorial wrappers, cover crease, corner and spine repairs, some margin repairs, overall tight and good condition, 12 full page, one double page and two half page fabulous chromolithographs plus great color covers and color illustrations in text, quite scarce.   Aleph-Bet Books, Inc.   105 - 129   2013 $650

Moore, Clement Clarke   1779-1863 *Denslow's Night Before Christmas.* New York: G. W. Dillingham Co., 1902. First edition, 2nd issue with cloth binding, quarto, 64 pages, publisher's dust jacket, full olive/tan cloth, front board and spine lettered in brown, illustrated plate affixed to front board, pictorial endpapers, inner hinges starting, previous owner's inscription dated 1911, few instances of marginal closed tears and finger smudges, not affecting illustrations, jacket faded, soiled, dampstained and quite chipped along edges, still intact, overall very good.   Heritage Book Shop Holiday Catalogue 2012 - 38   2013 $2500

Moore, Clement Clarke   1779-1863 *The Night Before Christmas.* London: George Harrap, n.d., 1932. Limited to 275 copies for England and 275 copies for the US numbered and signed by artist, 8vo., full limp vellum, top edge gilt, fine, no slipcase, illustrations by Arthur Rackham with pictorial endpapers, 4 color plates, charming black and whites in text.   Aleph-Bet Books, Inc.   105 - 493   2013 $2200

Moore, Courtney *Con Hegarty: a Story of Irish Life.* Cofl Pub., 1897. First edition, 142 pages, top fore-corner of first 3 leaves damaged, else very good, cloth.   C. P. Hyland   261 - 607   2013   £35

Moore, Francis *Vox Stellarum; or a Royal Almanack for the Year of Human Redemption 1799.* London: the Company of Stationers, 1799. 12mo., pages 48 + occasional blank leaves, semi-limp brown morocco with marbled paper lined flap to upper board, flap partially torn and a rudimentary repair made with linen thread, holes to spines, all edges worn, text block coming loose in blind, blue wax seal affixed to front pastedown, note of money received from Mr. Carr dated Aug. 1799.   Unsworths Antiquarian Booksellers   28 - 117   2013   £35

Moore, Frank *Women of the War: Their Heroism and Self Sacrifice.* Hartford: Scranton, 1866. First edition, 8vo., pages 596, green cloth stamped in gilt, cover worn at ends of spine and corners, some foxing throughout, hinges beginning tender, otherwise very good.   Second Life Books Inc.   182 - 174   2013 $50

Moore, George *The Brook Kerith: a Syrian Story.* New York: Macmillan, 1929. Limited to 500 numbered copies for America signed by author and artist,, 4to.. vellum backed cloth, fine in slipcase lacking top flap, 9 full page and 3 partial page engravings by Gooden, beautiful and richly detailed.   Aleph-Bet Books, Inc.   105 - 281   2013 $200

Moore, George *Celibate Lives.* London: William Heinemann, 1927. First edition, large 8vo., original quarter brown cloth, printed paper label on spine, excellent copy, light shelfwear to upper cover, inscribed by Arnold and Dorothy Bennett to the future Lady Rothschild, Barbara Hutchinson. Maggs Bros. Ltd. 1460 - 84 2013 £250

Moore, George H. *Historical Notes on the Employment of Negroes in the American Army of the Revolution.* New York: 1862. First edition, 8vo., 24 pages, original printed wrappers. M & S Rare Books, Inc. 95 - 238 2013 $200

Moore, John 1729-1802 *Mordaunt.* London: printed for G. G. and J. Robinson, 1800. First edition, 216 x 130mm., 3 volumes, fine contemporary full tree calf, flat spines divided into panels by multiple plain and decorative rules, each panel with central floral medallion, 2 green morocco labels on each spine, booklabel of "Fasque", spines just slightly dry, one cover with minor insect damage, one signature with touch of soil, other trivial imperfections, but quite excellent set, text especially clean, fresh and bright, attractive bindings lustrous, no significant wear. Phillip J. Pirages 63 - 344 2013 $650

Moore, John 1729-1802 *A View of Society and Manners in Italy.* Dublin: printed for H. Chamberlaine, 1786. Third edition, 3 volumes, half titles in volumes I and II, prelim blank volume III, 12mo., very good, attractive set in full contemporary calf, gilt banded spines, red and olive green morocco labels, form the library of John Musgrave, with armorial bookplates and contemporary signatures of Frances Musgrave. Jarndyce Antiquarian Booksellers CCIV - 208 2013 £480

Moore, John 1729-1802 *A View of Society and Manners in France, Switzerland and Germany.* London: A. Strahan & T. Cadell, 1786. Sixth edition, 2 volumes, 8vo., contemporary brown full calf, upper cover volume 1 detached, joints and corners rubbed, labels chipped, internally clean. J. & S. L. Bonham Antiquarian Booksellers Europe - 9180 2013 £130

Moore, John Hamilton *The New Practical Navigator.* London: printed for F. C. and J. Rivington et al, 1814. Nineteenth edition, 1817 ownership signature, 8vo., contemporary calf, rebacked, new leather label, tables, engraved plates. Howard S. Mott Inc. 262 - 104 2013 $200

Moore, Joseph *Outlying Europe and the Nearer Orient...* Philadelphia: J. B. Lippincott, 1880. First edition, 8vo., 554 pages, original blue blindstamped cloth, presentation copy to Katherine Baker. J. & S. L. Bonham Antiquarian Booksellers Europe - 8339 2013 £140

Moore, Marianne 1887-1972 *Observations.* New York: Dial Press, 1924. First edition, 8vo., original black three quarter cloth and boards, gold dust jacket, rare jacket lightly worn at extremities, otherwise very good, S. Foster Damon's copy with his ownership signature and his pencil annotations. James S. Jaffe Rare Books Fall 2013 - 105 2013 $1500

Moore, Marianne 1887-1972 *The Pangolin and Other Verse.* London: Brendin Pub. Co., 1936. First edition, limited to 120 copies, 8vo., illustrations by George Plank, original decorated paper boards with printed label on front cover, presentation copy inscribed by author for Laurence Scott, extremely rare signed or inscribed, very fine. James S. Jaffe Rare Books Fall 2013 - 106 2013 $3500

Moore, Marianne 1887-1972 *Poems.* London: Egoist Press, 1921. First edition, 8vo., original decorated wrappers, presentation copy inscribed by author for owner of Grolier Bookshop, Gordon Cairnie, very fine, virtually as new, none of the foxing usually found in this book in half morocco slipcase, rarely found signed or inscribed. James S. Jaffe Rare Books Fall 2013 - 104 2013 $4500

Moore, Maude *Fairy Helpers.* Boston: D. C. Heath, 1927. 8vo., pictorial cloth, 155 pages, near fine, illustrations by Dorothy Rittenhouse Morgan in color on nearly every page. Aleph-Bet Books, Inc. 105 - 235 2013 $200

Moore, Michael *Stupid White Men.* New York: Regan Books, 2001. First edition, fine in fine dust jacket, scarce printing, sharp copy. Leather Stalking Books October 2013 - 2013 $125

Moore, Thomas *British Wild Flowers Familiarly described in The Four Seasons.* London: Reeve and Co., 1867. New edition, 24 hand colored plates, very good, 8vo., green cloth. Barnaby Rudge Booksellers Natural History 2013 - 020464 2013 $95

Moore, Thomas *Lalla Rookh, an Oriental Romance.* London: Longman, Hurst, Rees, Orme, Brown and Green, 1824. 218 x 136mm., 2 pl., 397, (1) pages, very pleasing contemporary midnight blue crushed morocco attractively gilt, covers with fillet borders and delicate inner frame, wide raised bands decorated with horizontal gilt fillets and floral tool terminations, spine gilt in compartments featuring unusual obliquely oriented quatrefoil ornament, gilt titling and turn-ins, all edges gilt, with fine later(?) fore-edge painting of an animated London street scene, bookplate of Oscar Ehrhardt Lancaster, touch of rubbing to joints and extremities (but this successfully masked with dye), chalky endpapers a bit blotchy from chemical reaction, slight separation and discoloration at hinge before title leaf, very few trivial marginal spots, still excellent copy, leaves quite clean, fresh and smooth, original decorative binding bright and without any significant wear and painting very well preserved. Phillip J. Pirages 61 - 53 2013 $1250

Moore, Thomas *Lalla Rookh, an Oriental Romance.* London: Longman, Rees Orme, Brown & Green, 1828. 165 x 99mm., 2 p.l., 376 pages, extra engraved titlepage with vignette and 3 engraved plates after designs by Richard Westall; quite attractive contemporary dark green straight grain morocco, ornately gilt covers with 13 gilt or blind (mostly gilt) rules and frames (including elegant palmette frame), tulip cornerpieces at board edges and scrolling foliate cornerpieces closer in, central panel with large and elaborate lyre, raised bands, spine gilt in compartments with foliate cornerpieces and central lyre surrounded by small tools, densely gilt turn-ins, all edges gilt, gauffered in diapered pattern; with fine fore-edge painting of an oriental landscape, very surprisingly hidden beneath guaffered edge; spine evenly sunned to softer green, just hint of wear to joints and extremities, minor offsetting from mild foxing to plates, otherwise fine, binding sound and pleasing, text quite clean, fresh and bright and fore-edge painting well preserved.   Phillip J. Pirages   61 - 57   2013 $1750

Moore, Thomas *Lalla Rookh.* New York: Leavitt & Allen, 1870. Small 4to., full leather, blind tooled covers with gilt title, joints repaired, very good.   Barnaby Rudge Booksellers   Poetry 2013 - 020888   2013 $55

Moore, Thomas *The Life of Lord Byron and His Letters and Journals.* London: John Murray, 1847. New edition, frontispiece, engraved title printed title, index unopened, uncut in original purple cloth, lettered and blocked with armorial monogram in gilt, slight faded, but very good. Jarndyce Antiquarian Booksellers   CCIII - 325   2013   £75

Moore, Thomas *Loves of the Angels.* 1823. First edition, 213 X 135mm., once handsome and still appealing elaborately decorated blue-green calf, covers with gilt floral border enclosing a frame of a dozen blind rules with central panel blindstamped in basket weave design, upper cover with "Newby Hall" home of Thomas Philip Weddell, Baron Grantham & 2nd Earl de Grey (1781-1859) stamped in gilt between joint and gilt frame, gilt decorated raised bands, red morocco backstrip label, gilt spine compartments formed by half a dozen rules featuring tulip cornerpieces and flanked by blindstamped diapering, marbled endpapers and edges; engraved bookplate of Earl de Grey, with coronet and cypher, small gouge to lower cover, half dozen scratches to upper cover, leather bit faded, spotted and soiled, hint of wear to joints and extremities, otherwise fine, text especially clean and fresh, original decorative binding, completely sound and retaining much of its original appeal.   Phillip J. Pirages   63 - 345   2013 $500

Moorehead, Warren K. *The Stone Age in North America...* London: Constable, 1911. First English edition, large 8vo., colored frontispiece and 15 colored plates, black and white illustrations, green cloth worn and stained, hinges loose, clean inside worn binding.   Second Life Books Inc.   183 - 282   2013 $250

Moorhead, Ethel *The Quarter.* Paris: the editors, 1925. Volume I, no. 1, plates, original wrappers, neat repair to hinges, few small marginal tears but nice, foldover box. Jarndyce Antiquarian Booksellers   CCV - 204   2013   £420

Moorman, Madison Berryman *The Journal of.... 1850-1851.* San Francisco: California Historical Society, 1948. First edition, frontispiece, folding map, gilt lettered dark green cloth, spine and edges faded as usual, offsetting to front ends from news clipping, very good, presentation inscription signed by editor, Irene Paden.   Argonaut Book Shop   Summer 2013 - 243   2013 $75

Morand, Paul *Closed All Night.* London: Guy Chapman, 1924. First edition, #151 o4 275 signed, fine in dust jacket with chip to head of spine and label wear.   Beasley Books 2013 - 2013 $65

Morden, William *Our African Adventure.* London: Seeley Service, 1954. First edition, 2ith 2 ANS' by author and APS signed by Morden laid in, near fine in very good+ dust jacket with edge chips, mild scuffs, mild sun spine.   By the Book, L. C.   36 - 86   2013 $325

More, Hannah 1745-1833 *The Works of.* New York: Harper, 1836. First complete American edition, 2 volumes, large 8vo., frontispiece in volume 1, embossed brown cloth, faded to tan, owners' bookplate, name on flyleaves, light foxing, covers somewhat worn at corners and spines, otherwise very good.   Second Life Books Inc.   183 - 283   2013 $75

More, Thomas 1478-1535 *The Debellacyon of Salem and Bizance.* London: printed by W. Rastell, 1533. First edition, 2 parts in one small octavo volume, bound without final blank leaf, this copy has leaf C8 in probable facsimile and lacks rare bifolium, Black Letter, title within woodcut border, woodcut historiated initials, early 20th century brown crushed levant morocco by Riviere and Son, covers ruled in gilt and blind with gilt corner ornaments, spine ruled in gilt and blind decoratively tooled and lettered gilt in compartments, board edges ruled in gilt, turn-ins ruled in gilt and blind, all edges gilt, marbled endpapers, washed prelims and few other leaves with slight discoloration at upper corners, leaf a4 with crease marks to covers and short tear at upper margin, final leaves slightly discolored, excellent copy of this extremely rare work, from the library of William Foyle with his bookplate, quarter brown morocco clamshell. Heritage Book Shop   50th Anniversary Catalogue - 74   2013 $12,500

More, Thomas 1478-1535 *A Frutefull Pleasaunt & Wittie Worke...called Utopia.* London: Abraham Vele, 1556. Second edition in English second state with colophon on (S8), 12mo., 144 leaves, many misnumbered, full red morocco by Riviere and Sons, covers ruled in gilt, spine lettered gilt in compartments, cream endpapers, all edges gilt, former signature and bookplate of W. A. Foyle, title with some soiling, overall beautiful copy, elegantly bound, housed in custom black morocco clamshell, gilt stamped. Heritage Book Shop   50th Anniversary Catalogue - 75 2013 $45,000

More, Thomas 1478-1535 *Utopia.* London: Sold by Reeves & Turner, 1893. One of 300 copies on paper, out of a total edition of 308, octavo, printed in red and black in Chaucer and Troy types, decorative woodcut borders and initials, original full limp vellum with yapp edges, spine lettered gilt, all edges uncut, back bottom tie renewed, previous owner's bookplate, about fine.   Heritage Book Shop   Holiday Catalogue 2012 - 90   2013 $6500

Moreau, Francois Joseph *A Practical Treatise on Midwifery, Exhibiting the Present Advanced State of the Science.* Philadelphia: Carey & Hart, 1844. Folio, 80 color plates, foxing, few plates stained, original brown blind-stamped cloth, gilt stamped cover and spine titles, neatly rebacked, fine, hand colored lithographs.   Jeff Weber Rare Books   172 - 195   2013 $1500

Moreau, Jacob Nicholas *Nouveau Memoire pour Server a l'Histoire des Cacauacs.* Amsterdam: i.e. Paris, 1757. First edition, 8vo., original floral wrappers, soiled, spine perished, lower cover separated but present, uncut, very good in original condition, few soiled edges and minor scattered foxing.   Howard S. Mott Inc.   262 - 105   2013 $600

Morgagni, Giovanni Battista 1682-1771 *De Sedibus e Causis Morborum per Anatomen Indagatis.* Venice: Remondin, 1761. First edition, 2 volumes bound as one, first title printed in red and black, both titles with same engraved vignette, with engraved frontispiece, scattered foxing and browning, mainly mild, Birmingham Central Hospital Library stamp in numerous places but not overwhelming, some 150 pages manuscript at end, folio, 20th century calf, red lettering piece on spine "Birmingham medical Institute" in small gilt letters at foot of spine, crack at head of upper joint, Johnstone family bookplate inside front cover and a portion of the original front pastedown or flyleaf, recording book as being James Johnstone's and a further inscription by his grandson John dated 1834, good.   Blackwell's Rare Books   Sciences - 84   2013   £11,000

Morgagni, Giovanni Battista 1682-1771 *De Sedibus et Causis Morborum per Anatomen Indagatis.* Patavii: Sumptibus Remondianais, 1765. Second edition, engraved full page portrait, 2 volumes bound in one, folio in contemporary full vellum gilt binding with gold scrolling and filigrees around fore-edges, spine bit worn and soiled with contents clean and bright, title in red and black, some light wear, otherwise very nice tight copy.   James Tait Goodrich   75 - 151   2013 $3500

Morgan, Dale L. *Bibliography of the Church Of Jesus Christ.* (28) pages, octavo, blue publisher's buckram, gilt stamped title on front board, tipped in frontispiece of facsimile titlepage of "The Ensign" by William Bickerton, fine, ex-libris Albert Zobell Jr. with his signature.   Ken Sanders Rare Books   45 - 26   2013 $200

Morgan, Dale L. *Jedediah Smith and the Opening of the West.* New York: Bobbs Merrill, 1953. First edition, 458 pages, numerous illustrations, endpaper maps, slight remnants from removed bookplate on blank flyleaf, else fine with dust jacket, long presentation inscription, signed and dated by author to well-known collector Ralph Velich. Argonaut Book Shop   Summer 2013 - 244   2013 $175

Morgan, John *A Discourse Upon the Institution of Medical Schools in America.* Philadelphia: William Bradford, 1765. 19th century full blond paneled calf, endpapers renewed, top edge gilt remargined along inner edge, text foxed, dampstaining affecting outer upper blank corner of pages, presentation copy to John Shaw Billings, from John Stockton, quite rare.   James Tait Goodrich   75 - 153   2013 $8995

Morgan, Lewis H. *The American Beaver and His Works.* Philadelphia: 1868. 330 pages, illustrations, folding map, inscribed by author, original cloth, spine cloth, spine faded with minor loss at top and bottom, internally clean and very good.   Dumont Maps & Books of the West   125 - 64   2013 $200

Morgan, Ruth Stemm *My Whirligig Fair Book.* Minneapolis: Gordon Volland Buzza, 1929. Folio, cloth backed pictorial boards, slight bit of cover soil, else fine, each page completely and brightly illustrated in typical Volland colors, 8 moveable pages operated with notched wheels with gear mechanisms so that turning one wheel causes another wheel to turn and 2 pieces move, rare. Aleph-Bet Books, Inc.   104 - 368   2013 $1250

Morgan, Thomas Hunt *Experimental Zoology.* New York: Macmillan, 1907. First edition, 8vo., very good+, minimal cover edge and spine wear, owner name, age darkening to page edges, rare.   By the Book, L. C.   37 - 59   2013 $300

Morley, Christopher 1890-1957 *Where the Blue Begins.* London and New York: Heinemann & Doubleday Page, 1922. First US edition, 4to., blue gilt cloth, top edge gilt, fine in chipped and worn dust jacket, 4 beautiful and unusual color plates plus black and whites in text, pictorial endpapers by Arthur Rackham.   Aleph-Bet Books, Inc.   105 - 499   2013 $600

Morley, Henry *English Writers Volume I, Part I, Celts and Anglo-Saxons.* 1867. First edition, 8vo., original cloth, hinges worn, text good.   C. P. Hyland   261 - 88   2013   £60

Morley, Henry *Jerome Cardan. The Life of Girolamo Cardano.* London: Chapman an Hall, 1854. First edition, woodcut medallion of Cardano, bust portrait of Tartaglia, one or two scattered spots, 8vo., contemporary half burgundy morocco, spines gilt, some corners, bit worn, good. Blackwell's Rare Books   172 - 100   2013   £200

The Morning Chronicle, No. 13, 994. Feb. 21, 1814. Disbound, few small holes in text, little fragile.   Jarndyce Antiquarian Booksellers   CCIII - 431   2013   £25

Morreale, Marie T. *Fiesta Ware.* Kansas City: Andrews McNeel Publishing, 2001. First edition, 48mo., 80 pages, fine in fine dust jacket, color chart, color photos.   Beasley Books   2013 - 2013 $100

Morrell, L. A. *The American Shepherd: being a History of the Sheep, with their Breeds, Management and Diseases.* New York: Harper and Bros., 1850. 8vo., illustrations, original cloth, minor chipping to ends of spine, foxed, this copy was awarded to Ransom Harmon for best black lambs by B. P. Janson, Rochester, NY 1857.   M & S Rare Books, Inc.   95 - 340   2013 $100

Morris, Cora *The Gypsy Story Teller.* New York: Macmillan, 1931. First edition, 4to., cloth, fine in chipped dust jacket, color frontispiece and many striking full page black and whites by Frank Dobias.   Aleph-Bet Books, Inc.   104 - 169   2013 $150

Morris, Ethelberta *Ameliaranne Bridesmaid.* Harrap, 1946. First edition, original pictorial boards, dust jacket, extremities little chipped and worn, illustrations in color and black and white by Susan Pearse.   R. F. G. Hollett & Son Children's Books - 454   2013   £50

Morris, Francis Orpen 1810-1893 *A Natural History of the Nests and Eggs of British Birds.* London: John C. Nimmo, 1896. 3 volumes, large 8vo., 248 plates, chiefly colored by hand, occasional light foxing to pastedowns and free endpapers or text block edges, not affecting text or plates, ruled gilt stamped olive green morocco, gilt stamped front cover and blindstamped rear cover nest pictorials, extremities lightly worn, fine plates in very good binding. Jeff Weber Rare Books   169 - 310   2013 $450

Morris, Francis Orpen 1810-1893 *A Series of Picturesque Views of Seats of the Noblemen and Gentlemn of Great Britain and Ireland.* London: William Mackenzie, circa, 1880. First edition in book form, 7 volumes, 4to., additional color printed titles and 234 plates printed in colors from wood engravings by Fawcett, original cloth, spines and upper covers elaborately gilt blocked, gilt edges, some spotting to contents as usual, otherwise fine and tight. Marlborough Rare Books Ltd.   218 - 106   2013   £400

Morris, Henry *No. V-109, the Biography of a Printing Press.* N.P.: Anne and David Bromer, 1978. First edition, limited to 150 numbered copies, printed by hand by Henry Morris, very scarce, 6.1 x 4.7 cm., quarter leather over pastepaper covered boards, from the collection of Donn W. Sanford.   Oak Knoll Books   303 - 72   2013 $525

Morris, Henry *Roller-Printed Paste Papers for Bookbinding.* North Hills: Bird and Bull Press, 1975. First edition, limited to 215 copies, this no. 49, text set in Centaur and Codex types and printed on Hodgkinson handmade paper, fine, all of the paste paper made at the press and binding done by Edward G. Parrot II, bound in quarter vellum with gilt lettered spine and blue patterned paper covers, 6 x 9.5 inches, 42 pages + samples.   By the Book, L. C.   36 - 69   2013 $275

Morris, James *Venice.* London: Faber, 1960. First edition, 8vo., 337 pages, maps, illustrations, original brown cloth, dust jacket.   J. & S. L. Bonham Antiquarian Booksellers   Europe - 9795   2013   £35

Morris, Jan *The Vennetian Empire.* London: Faber, 1980. First edition, 8vo., 192 pages, illustrations, original black cloth, dust jacket.   J. & S. L. Bonham Antiquarian Booksellers   Europe - 9776   2013   £30

Morris, Kenneth *Book of the Three Dragons.* New York: Junior Literary Guild, 1930. First edition thus, near fine, lacking scarce dust jacket, very attractive copy in yellow cloth with three green dragons on cover.   Leather Stalking Books   October 2013 - 2013 $100

Morris, William 1834-1896 *A Dream of John Ball and a King's Lesson.* Kelmscott Press, 1892. (One of 300 copies) of an edition of 311, printed in Golden types on handmade paper, in black with shoulder notes and 2 small areas of text printed in red, wood engraved frontispiece by Edward Burne-Jones, wood engraved leaf border and wood engraved vine border to adjacent page of text designed by Morris, large and small wood engraved initial letters throughout, crown 8vo., original limp cream vellum, backstrip gilt lettered, front free endpaper, little darkened, green silk ties, untrimmed and unopened, recent maroon cloth, solander case with gilt lettered black leather labels, near fine, inscribed by Morris to friend Theodore Watts-Dunton. Blackwell's Rare Books   B174 - 356   2013   £4000

Morris, William 1834-1896 *The Earthly Paradise, a Poem.* London: F. S. Ellis, 1870. (for volumes I, II Fifth edition). Boston: Roberts Brothers 1870-1871 (volumes III, IV Fourth impression. Mixed early editions,, deep burgundy half morocco over wine colored textured buckram, mixed bands flanked by black and gilt rules, spine panels with central gilt fleuron, top edge gilt, with Burne-Jones' woodcut of the Three Graces on titlepages and in colophons; spine faded to hazel brown, joints and extremities somewhat worn (tiny chip out of top of one spine), leaves with overall slight browning because of quality of paper, but perfectly usable copy with some shelf appeal, original morocco bindings mellowed but solid and without any fatal flaw and text with almost no signs of use. Phillip J. Pirages 63 - 346 2013 $250

Morris, William 1834-1896 *The Earthly Paradise.* London: Reeves and Turner, 1890. Revised edition, octavo. titlepage vignette after design by Burne-Jones, bound by Riviere & Son in full green morocco with gilt central floral design and single gilt fillet border on covers, gilt title and floral design on spine, gilt fillet on turn-ins, top edges gilt, marbled endpapers rubbing to front joint, spine little toned, else near fine. Between the Covers Rare Books, Inc. Philosophy - 337508 2013 $350

Morris, William 1834-1896 *Love is Enough, or the Freeing of Pharamond: a Morality.* Hammersmith: sold by the Trustees of the Late William Morris at the Kelmscott Press, 1897. One of 300 paper copies, out of a total edition of 308, large quarto, 2 full page illustrations designed by Sir Edward Burne-Jones, decorative woodcut borders and initials, printed in black, red and blue in Troy and Chaucer types, original full limp vellum with green silk ties, spine lettered in gilt, bookplate of Estelle Doheny, overall excellent copy. Heritage Book Shop Holiday Catalogue 2012 - 89 2013 $6000

Morris, William 1834-1896 *News from Nowhere; or an Epoch of Rest, Being Some Chapters from a Utopian Romance.* Boston: Roberts, 1890. First edition, issued in an edition of 1500 copies, 8vo., frontispiece by Walter Crane, maroon cloth with floral endpapers, name on flyleaf, very good, quite scarce. Second Life Books Inc. 183 - 284 2013 $350

Morris, William 1834-1896 *The Story of Sigurd the Volsung and the Fall of the Niblungs.* Kelmscott Press, 1898. Limited to 160 copies on paper out of an edition of 166, small folio, 2 wood engraved illustrations, section titles and shoulder titles printed in red, original limp vellum, yapp edges, silk ties, previous owner's bookplates, aside from bit of typical foxing on sheet edges, as usual truly remarkable copy, housed in custom green cloth open ended slipcase. Heritage Book Shop 50th Anniversary Catalogue - 58 2013 $12,500

Morrison, Toni *The Bluest Eye.* London: Chatto & Windus, 1979. First British edition, inscribed by author, recipient's signature, fine in fine dust jacket. Ken Lopez Bookseller 159 - 138 2013 $750

Morrison, Toni *Jazz.* New York: Alfred A. Knopf, 1992. Uncorrected proof, fine in wrappers. Between the Covers Rare Books, Inc. 165 - 223 2013 $75

Morrison, Toni *Lecture and Speech of Acceptance Upon the Ward of the Nobel Prize for Literature...* New York: Alfred A. Knopf, 1994. Stated first edition, signed by author, small 8vo., 37 pages, red cloth over boards with gilt lettered spine, gilt square with black paper title label within it to front cover. By the Book, L. C. 36 - 53 2013 $350

Morrison, Toni *The Tortoise or the Hare.* New York: Simon & Schuster, 2010. Advance copy in the form of unbound signatures, laid into dust jacket, fine, uncommon. Ken Lopez Bookseller 159 - 140 2013 $100

Morrison, Toni *The Tortoise or the Hare.* New York: Simon & Schuster, 2010. First edition, signed by author on bookplate, illustrations by Joe Cepeda, fine in fine dust jacket. Ken Lopez Bookseller 159 - 139 2013 $125

Morse, John F. *Illustrated Historical Sketches of California with a Minute History of Sacramento Valley Together with an Appendix of General Views.* Sacramento: John Hand, March, 1854. Number 1 (all published), frontispiece, 8vo., original printed pictorial wrappers, lovely copy, rare. Maggs Bros. Ltd. 1467 - 123 2013 £2000

Morse, William *Catalogue of the William Inglis Morse Collection of Books, Pictures, Maps, Manuscripts, Etc. at Dalhousie University Library Halifax, Nova Scotia.* Plaistow: Curwen Press, 1938. Limited edition, this 244 of 250, blue cloth boards, gilt to front and spine, half title, frontispiece, 6 illustrations, quarto, very good. Schooner Books Ltd. 101 - 109 2013 $75

Morse, William Inglis *Acadiensia Nova.* London: Bernard Quaritch, Curwen Press, Plaistow, 1935. Limited to 375 copies (no limitation o this copy), 8vo., half title, maps, charts and illustrations, green buckram, gilt titles to spines, dust jackets, both volumes very good as are jackets with only very light soiling. Schooner Books Ltd. 101 - 3 2013 $200

Morten, Baker E. *No More Nigger Thinking.* New York: Vantage, 1972. First edition, fine in lightly worn, about fine dust jacket, warmly inscribed by author, very uncommon. Between the Covers Rare Books, Inc. 165 - 224 2013 $85

Mortenson, Greg *Three Cups of Tea.* New York: Viking, 2006. First printing, uncommon, signed by author, ticket and program for Mortenson reading (of Stones into Schools) at which this copy was signed is laid in, fine in fine dust jacket in custom clamshell case. Ken Lopez Bookseller   159 - 141   2013 $500

Mortenson, Greg *Three Cups of Tea.* New York: Viking, 2006. Advance reading copy, signed by author and by David Relin, fine in wrappers and custom clamshell case, scarce.   Ken Lopez Bookseller   159 - 142   2013 $750

Mortimer, Alfred *S(t.) Mark's Church Philadelphia and its Lady Chapel with an Account of Its History and Treasures.* New York: privately printed by the De Vinne Press, 1909. One of 400 copies, 300 x 235mm., 71 pages, 127 photo plates, 20 of these in color, all with captioned tissues, remarkably animated gothic style black morocco, very elaborately decorated gilt and blind by Zaehnsdorf (stamp signed on front turn-in), covers with ornate frames comprised of 16 compartments, 8 of these intricately gilt featuring repeating Maltese crosses, rose windows and flame design, other 8 with blindstamp of one of the four evangelists (at corners), or else the Salvator, frame enclosing large central panel stamp within gilt frame enclosing large central panel stamp within gilt frame, that on upper cover depicting St. Mark with his lion and that on lower cover showing Virgin Mary holding lily, raised bands, spine compartments with central blindstamped fleuron flanked by gilt rules and several small gilt stamps, turn-ins repeating gilt elements in cover frames, cream color watered silk endleaves, all edges gilt, just hint of rubbing to corners, otherwise choice copy. Phillip J. Pirages   63 - 68   2013 $1900

Mortimer, Favell Lee *Far Off.* Hatchards, 1890. New edition, fifty-fourth thousand, small 8vo., original pictorial blue cloth, gilt, trifle rubbed, 28 illustrations and folding colored map.   R. F. G. Hollett & Son   Children's Books - 406   2013   £45

Mortimer, Favell Lee *The Peep of Day.* Religious Tract Society, n.d. circa, 1920. Original blue cloth, gilt, pictorial onlay, all edges gilt in rough, 8 striking color plates, scarce. R. F. G. Hollett & Son   Children's Books - 405   2013   £35

Mosch, Lucas *Arithmeticus Practicus Utilitati Publicae Oblatus per Patrem Lucam a S. Edmundo e Clericis Pauperibus Matris Dei Scholarum Piarum.* Tyrnaviae: Typis Academicis per Joannem Andream Hormann, 1697. First edition, 8vo. worming to lower blank margin and inner rear board, not affecting text, full contemporary unlettered calf, very slightly worming to tools of spine.   Jarndyce Antiquarian Booksellers   CCIV - 24   2013   £480

Mosdell, H. M. *Newfoundland Its Manifold Attractions for the Capitalist, the Settler and the Tourist.* St. John's: Executive government of Newfoundland, 1920. Paper wrappers, numerous black and white illustrations, 8vo., covers stained and worn, bottom corner torn off, previous owner's notations to pages 2, 4 and 5, plus first flyleaf, some foxing to outer margins and pencil underlining to first 10 pages.   Schooner Books Ltd.   102 - 33   2013 $65

Moses, Kingsley *New Shoes: a Hockey Story. in Sport Story Magazine February 8 1925.* New York: Street and Smith, 1925. Tiny chips to wrappers, some tears to extremities of yapped edges, pages browned as usual, some light but fairly pervasive dampstaining, mostly on front wrapper, else about very good.   Between the Covers Rare Books, Inc.   Horses, Horsemanship, Horse Racing, Etc. - 73088   2013 $75

Mosley, Walter *Devil in a Blue Dress.* New York: Norton, 1990. First edition, signed by Mosley, very fine in dust jacket, correct first state dust jacket with price of $18.95. Mordida Books   81 - 371   2013 $150

Mosley, Walter *Devil in a Blue Dress.* New York: W. W. Norton and Co., 1990. First edition, fine in fine dust jacket, signed by author.   Between the Covers Rare Books, Inc. Mystery & Detective Fiction - 306951   2013 $200

Mosley, Walter *White Butterfly.* New York: Norton, 1992. First edition, signed and dated by author 7/30/92, very fine in dust jacket.   Mordida Books   81 - 372   2013 $150

Mother Goose *The Comic Adventures of Old Mother Hubbard and Her Dog.* York: Kendrew, n.d. circa, 1820. 16mo., yellow wrappers, 16 pages, fine, 15 fine and well printed half page woodcuts.   Aleph-Bet Books, Inc.   104 - 361   2013 $300

Mother Goose *Favorite Jingles from Mother Goose.* New York: McLoughlin Bros., 1870. First edition, 8vo., 12 pages, including wrappers, excellent condition inside and out.   Barnaby Rudge Booksellers   Children 2013 - 021663   2013 $75

Mother Goose *The Jessie Wilcox Smith Mother Goose.* New York: Dodd, Mead & Co., 1914. First edition, 2nd issue, large oblong quarto, 17 full pages plates, 12 of which are in color, including frontispiece, many illustrations in text, titlepage in black and blue, publisher's full black cloth, color pictorial label on front cover, spine lettered in white, pictorial label with few very small spots of rubbing, previous owner's inscription, few instances of finger soiling, overall near fine, housed in rare publisher's pictorial box, box bit tattered and missing one flap end.   Heritage Book Shop   Holiday Catalogue 2012 - 142   2013 $1250

Mother Goose *Mother Goose Chimes.* New York: McLoughlin Bros., 1898. Folio, pictorial wrappers, near fine, 4 fine full page chromolithographed pages and 10 page illustrated in 2-colors plus pictorial cover. Aleph-Bet Books, Inc. 105 - 401 2013 $475

Mother Goose *Mother Goose Gift Box.* New York: Upples & Leon, 1916. 3 books, except for slight soil, near fine, box has pictorial label and measures 4 1/2 x 6 inches, books in pictorial boards with color labels, fine, color plates by Johnny Gruelle. Aleph-Bet Books, Inc. 104 - 263 2013 $500

Mother Goose *Mother Goose... Her Alphabet.* Akron: Saalfield, 1946. Oblong 4to., spiral backed boards, fine in dust jacket with few pieces off back panel and with repairs on verso, full color illustrations by Jane Francis. Aleph-Bet Books, Inc. 104 - 15 2013 $225

Mother Goose *Mother Goose Melodies.* New York: McLoughlin Bros., 30 Beekman St., n.d. circa, 1865. 6 1/2 inches high, die-cut in shape of Mother Goose, one illustration rubbed, else near fine, busily illustrated in bright colors on salmon colored background. Aleph-Bet Books, Inc. 105 - 543 2013 $950

Mother Goose *Mother Goose Melodies.* New York: McLoughlin Bros., 1894. folio, pictorial wrappers, near fine, 12 fine full page chromolithographed pages and pictorial covers. Aleph-Bet Books, Inc. 105 - 400 2013 $475

Mother Goose *Mother Goose: the Old Nursery Rhymes.* London: Heinemann, 1913. First edition, limited to 1130 numbered copies signed by artist, large 4to., original white gilt pictorial cloth, top edge gilt, owner bookplate, light finger soil and spine slightly toned as common, else very good-fine, tight and clean with not one bit of spotting, 13 fabulous tipped in color plates mounted on heavy paper plus a profusion of beautiful black and whites, text with reproductions far superior to those in trade edition, illustrations by Arthur Rackham. Aleph-Bet Books, Inc. 104 - 472 2013 $2950

Mother Goose *Mother Goose.* Racine: Whitman, 1939. Oblong 4to., stiff card wrappers, slightly dusty, else fine and unused, 6 pages of brightly colored die-cut cardboard cut-outs in color. Aleph-Bet Books, Inc. 105 - 403 2013 $250

Mother Goose *Mother Goose Nursery Tales.* Philadelphia: Altemus, n.d. circa, 1924. 16mo., cloth backed pictorial boards, pictorial paste-on fine, 45 color and black and white illustrations by John Neill, scarce. Aleph-Bet Books, Inc. 104 - 378 2013 $225

Motley, John Lothrop 1766-1851 *Correspondence.* New York: Harper & Bros., 1889. First edition, 2 volumes, 251 x 175mm., attractive contemporary dark green half morocco over marbled boards by Stikeman (stamp signed). raised bands, spines gilt in compartments with tulip centerpiece and scrolling cornerpieces, gilt titling, marbled endpapers, top edge gilt, frontispiece in volume I, bookplate of W. M. Burden; little wear to joints and extremities (five corner tips worn through), spines uniformly darkened toward brown, otherwise fine, clean and fresh internally, in solid pleasing bindings. Phillip J. Pirages 63 - 350 2013 $150

Motley, John Lothrop 1766-1851 *History of the United Netherlands: from the Death of William the Silent to the Twelve Years' Truce.* New York: Harper & Bros., 1874. 4 volumes, very pretty decorative contemporary half calf, raised bands, spines handsomely gilt in double ruled compartments with scrolling cornerpieces and intricate central lozenge, one red and one green morocco label on each spine, marbled boards, edges and endpapers, frontispiece and one folding map, very small area of slight discoloration at head of one spine, vague hint of chafing to paper sides, otherwise really excellent set with only very minor imperfections, decorative bindings showing little wear, text remarkably smooth, fresh and clean. Phillip J. Pirages 63 - 348 2013 $450

Motley, John Lothrop 1766-1851 *The Rise of the Dutch Republic, a History.* New York: Harper and Brothers, 1870. 235 x 152mm., 3 volumes, very pretty decorative contemprary half calf, raised bands spines handsomely gilt in double ruled compartments with bands of tangent concentric circles at top and bottom, delicate inner frame with curling and dotted borders, looping cornerpieces the whole enclosing a central wheel design formed by fleur-de-lys, marbled boards, edges and endpapers, frontispiece portraits; boards little chafed, neat repair to fore edge of one leaf, occasional minor foxing, excellent set, clean, fresh text, scarcely worn bindings, very pleasing on shelf. Phillip J. Pirages 63 - 349 2013 $450

Motley, Willard *Llamad A Cualquier Perta. (Knock on Any Door).* Mexico: Compania Editorial Continental S. A., 1955. First Mexican edition, pages bit browned, else fine in fine self wrappers. Between the Covers Rare Books, Inc. 165 - 226 2013 $85

Motley, Willard *We Fished All Night.* New York: Appleton Century Crofts, 1951. First edition, corners bit bumped, otherwise fine in slightly rubbed, near fine dust jacket with tiny tears. Between the Covers Rare Books, Inc. 165 - 225 2013 $150

Mott, Ed *The Black Homer of Jimtown.* New York: Grosset and Dunlap, 1900. First edition, 8vo. 286 pages, original cloth, photogravure, fine in original printed pictorial dust jacket (frayed, with some splitting but complete). M & S Rare Books, Inc. 95 - 240 2013 $250

The Mottoes of the Spectators, Tatlers and Guardians. London: printed for Richard Wellington, 1737. 12mo., paper toned and bit spotted, contemporary sprinkled calf, spine ruled in gilt, red morocco label, edges sprinkled red, rubbed around edges, joints cracking at head, contemporary ink ownership inscription 'Ann Tonnereau hr Book 17:46:7". Unsworths Antiquarian Booksellers 28 - 64 2013 £95

Moulton, Gary F. *Atlas of the Lewis and Clark Expedition.* Lincoln and London: University of Nebraska Press, 1983. First edition, 126 facsimile maps, dark blue cloth decorated in light blue and lettered in gilt on spine and front cover, very fine, as new in original shipping box. Argonaut Book Shop Summer 2013 - 204 2013 $2250

Moulton, Gary F. *The Journals of the Lewis and Clark Expedition. volume 4 only.* Lincoln and London: University of Nebraska Press, 1987. First edition, blue cloth, very fine with dust jacket. Argonaut Book Shop Summer 2013 - 205 2013 $100

Mowat, Farley *People of the Deer.* Boston: Little Brown and Co., 1954. Original cloth, gilt, dust jacket rather worn. R. F. G. Hollett & Son Polar Exploration - 42 2013 £30

Moyer, Kenneth E. *Attention Spans of Children for Experimentally Designed Toys.* No Place: The Journal of Genetic Psychology, 1955. Offprint, stapled self wrappers, tiny stain front wrapper, else fine. Between the Covers Rare Books, Inc. Psychology & Psychiatry - 92904 2013 $50

Mozart, Wolfgang Amadeus *Cosi I'am Tutte.* New York: Limited Editions Club, 2001. First edition, one of 300 copies signed by Balthus, this being number 249, folio, numerous color woodcuts by Balthus, publisher's full peacock green silk, front board with black leather label on lettered gilt, fine, housed in publisher's matching suede lined silk clamshell with black leather label, lettered gilt on spine, with Limited Editions Club newsletter laid in. Heritage Book Shop Holiday Catalogue 2012 - 110 2013 $2500

Mozart, Wolfgang Amadeus *Figaro's Hochzeit: Oper von W. A. Mozart.* Berlin: F. Weidle, n.d. circa, 1840. Beautiful copy, engraved titlepage, rebound in quarter dark red leather with five raised bands and gilt title to spine, boards marbled, interior pages browned, otherwise clean, very good, 231 pages. The Kelmscott Bookshop 7 - 135 2013 $300

Mrabet, Mohammed *The Lemon.* New York: McGraw Hill, 1972. First American edition, inscribed by author for Mary Robbins, Tangier 14/IV/90, fine in very near fine dust jacket with slight rubbing to spine colors. Ken Lopez Bookseller 159 - 23 2013 $300

Mrs. Lovechild's Golden Present for all Good Little Boys and Girls. York: Kendrew, circa, 1820. 2 1/2 x 4 inches, printed wrappers, 31 pages, fine, 26 charming woodcuts, full page woodcut frontispiece and 6 other woodcuts in text. Aleph-Bet Books, Inc. 105 - 7 2013 $325

Muir, Agustus *The Shadow on the Left.* Indianapolis: Bobbs Merrill, 1928. First American edition, fine in near fine dust jacket with slightly faded spine, nicks on spine, some small faint lettering along top edge of dust jacket. Mordida Books 81 - 378 2013 $85

Muir, Edwin *We Moderns: Enigmas and Guesses.* London: George Allen & Unwin Ltd., 1918. First edition, one of 1030 copies printed, of which 190 unbound copies were destroyed in the Blitz, dedication copy inscribed by author for A. R. Orage, small 8vo., original pebble grained blue cloth with printed paper label on spine, extremities of spine lightly rubbed, one short quarter inch tear at top, spine label worn, but very good. James S. Jaffe Rare Books Fall 2013 - 107 2013 $3000

Muir, John 1838-1914 *My First Summer in the Sierra.* Covelo: Yolla Bolly Press, 1988. First edition thus, limited edition, one of 125 bound in linen from a total edition of 150 copies, all on Incisioni cream, mould made paper at Magnani paper mill at Pescia, Italy, all signed by artist, Michael McCurdy, 162 pages, bound by Schuberth Bookbindery in tan linen handwoven at Myung Jin Fabricus with endsheets of handmade bark paper, housed in blue-grey publisher's slipcase with tan paper label with brown border printed with author and title in black, fine, 12 wood engravings by McCurdy, type is Jan Van Krimpen's Van Dijck and Caslon, was handset at Press and by Monotype at MacKenzie-Harris Corporation. Priscilla Juvelis - Rare Books 55 - 29 2013 $900

Muldoon, Paul *Feet of Clay.* Oxford: Candles Press, 2011. First edition, 84/100 copies (of an edition of 112), printed on Magnani paper and signed by author, with large 3 color titlepage engraving by Neil Bousfield, 8vo., original plain white sewn card untrimmed, dust jacket, new. Blackwell's Rare Books B174 - 269 2013 £75

Muldoon, Paul *Kerry Slides.* Loughcrew: Gallery Press, 1996. First edition, 4to., original black cloth, dust jacket, signed by author, fine. Maggs Bros. Ltd. 1442 - 236 2013 £125

Muldoon, Paul *Medley for Morin Khur.* London: Enitharmon Press, 2005. First edition, xxiv of xxv lettered copies, signed by author, from a total edition of 200, 8vo., original green marbled wrappers, printed paper label, fine. Maggs Bros. Ltd. 1442 - 241 2013 £150

Muldoon, Paul *Mules.* London: Faber and Faber, 1977. First edition, 8vo., original wrappers, brown fading to green spine as usual, otherwise near fine, inscribed by author for Richard Murphy.   Maggs Bros. Ltd.   1442 - 234   2013   £275

Muldoon, Paul *Prince of the Quotidian.* Loughcrew: Gallery Press, 1994. First edition, 8vo., original black cloth, dust jacket, exceedingly uncommon hardback edition, fine in fine dust jacket, lightly faded on spine.   Maggs Bros. Ltd.   1442 - 235   2013   £175

Muldoon, Paul *Unapproved Road.* Hopewell: Pied Oxen Printers, 2002. First edition thus, one of 125 copies, 100 of which are for sale, all on somerset Textured Soft White paper each signed by the poet, the printer, David Sellers and the artist, Diarmuid Delargy on each of his two intaglio prints, print size 10 x 13 inches, 26 pages, , designed and printed by Sellers, hand set in Palatino with title in Sistina, both designed by Hermann Zapf and cat by Stempel AG and printed on Vandercook Universal I proof press, intaglio prints involve both etching and aquatint and printed by artist from steel faced copper plates at Beflast Print Workshop.   Priscilla Juvelis - Rare Books   56 - 26   2013 $1250

Muldoon, Paul *Wayside Shrines.* Loughcrew: Gallery Press, 2009. First edition, number 160 of 400 copies signed by author, 350 for sale, large 8vo., paintings and drawings by Keith Wilson, original burgundy linen with title blindstamped on upper cover, printed in color on Rives artist paper, dust jacket, fine.   Maggs Bros. Ltd.   1442 - 242   2013   £120

Mulford, Anna *A Sketch of Dr. John Smith Sage, of Sag Harbor, NY with an Appendix.* Sag Harbor: John B. Hunt, 1897. First edition, printed textured wrappers, approximately 2 inch tear on front fly, else very near fine.   Between the Covers Rare Books, Inc. New York City - 286591   2013 $150

Muller, Hermann Joseph *The Mechanism of Crossing-Over.* New York: American Naturalist, 1916. Offprint from American Naturalist, 1916, very good++, original printed wrappers, small chip archivally repaired to rear cover, small piece missing lower spine tip, short closed tear front cover, cover edge wear.   By the Book, L. C.   37 - 62   2013 $500

Muller, Hermann Joseph *The Production of Mutations.* Washington: American Genetic Assoc., 1947. First separate edition, offprint from Journal of Heredity, volume 38 No. 9 September 1947, Near fine, original printed wrappers, owner name to front wrapper, 8vo.   By the Book, L. C.   37 - 61   2013 $400

Muller, Herta *The Land of Green Plums.* New York: Metropolitan/Holt, 1996. First American edition, awarded IMPAC prize, inscribed by author to Greg Gatenby, one of IMPAC judges, Muller has also drawn a caricature of Gatenby, as well as adding her address, phone and fax, also inscribed by translator, Michael Hofmann, stamp of the award on front flyleaf, hint of crown bump, fine in very near fine dust jacket with shallow vertical crease to spine, remarkable copy.   Ken Lopez Bookseller   159 - 143   2013 $1000

Muller, Johann *Uber die Phantastischen Gesichtsercheinungen.* Coblenz: Jacob Holscher, 1826. x, 117 pages, original plain wrappers, front wrapper detached, uncut with large margins, text foxed.   James Tait Goodrich   S74 - 190   2013 $1495

Muller, Johann *Versuch Eienr Asthetik der toilette oder Winke fur Damen sich nach den Grundregeln der Malerei Geschmackvoll zu Kleiden...* Leipzig: im Industrie-Comptoir, circa, 1805. First edition, 8 leaves of plates, 8 colored, one bound as frontispiece, contemporary green boards imitating morocco, edged and tooled in gilt, spine ruled and lettered gilt, some loss to paper on spine, boards and spine generally worn, stamp at foot of title, initials PvH surmounted by a crown, sound, very rare.   Blackwell's Rare Books   172 - 101   2013   £3500

Mumey, Nolie *The Art and Activities of John Dare (Jack) Howland.* Boulder: 1973. Limited to 350 numbered and signed copies, xix, 237 pages, illustrations, tiny chip from corner of title block on spine, else near fine in slipcase.   Dumont Maps & Books of the West   122 - 74   2013 $125

Munby, A. N. L. *Book Collecting in Britain in the 1930's.* Nevada City: 1973. 403/675 copies printed in black and red on Curtis Tweedweave paper, 24 pages, 16mo., original cinnamon sewn card wrappers, front cover printed in black and red.   Blackwell's Rare Books   B174 - 353   2013   £40

Munro-Fraser, J. P. *History of Marin County, California: Including Its Geography, Geology, Topography and Climatology.* Petaluma: Charmaine Burdell Veronda, 1972. Reprint of rare 1880 edition, 36 lithographed portrait plates, map, maroon leatherette, very fine.   Argonaut Book Shop Summer 2013 - 224   2013 $150

Munro, H. H. *The Novels and Plays of Saki.* New York: Viking Press, 1933. Stated "Second Omnibus" volume, rebound in blue half morocco gilt and paper covered boards, probably soon after publication, spine expertly preserved, otherwise nice, near fine, with two identical examples of the armorial bookplate of Thomas Ruggles Pynchon, presumably the bookplate of author's (Thomas Pynchon) father, also named Thomas Ruggles Pynchon.   Between the Covers Rare Books, Inc. Sci-Fi, Fantasy & Horror - 86650   2013 $950

Munro, Leaf *Wee Gillis.* New York: Viking, 1938. First edition, inscribed by Leaf with two sketches, illustrations in black and white by Robert Lawson, green endpapers, special copy.   Aleph-Bet Books, Inc.   104 - 319   2013 $425

Murakami, Haruki *1Q84. Books 1 & 2 Together with Book 3.* London: Harvill Secker, 2011. First edition, Red Edge Limited edition, with both books being limited to 1500 copies with all edges stained red, fine in fine dust jacket.   Ed Smith Books   75 - 49   2013 $300

Murakami, Huraki *After the Quake.* New York: Knopf, 2002. First American edition, signed by author and stamped on half titlepage, fine in fine dust jacket, somewhat uncommon collection, scarce signed.   Ken Lopez Bookseller   159 - 144   2013 $850

Muratori, Ludovico Antonio *Raccolta delle Opere Minor di Ludovico Antonio Muratori.* Napoli: A Spese di G. Ponzelli volume 2-3, Nella STamperia di G. Ponzelli, volume 4-21, Nella Stamepria di Tommaso Alfano volume 22, Nella stamperia degli eredi di Tommaso Alfano, 1757-1764. First edition, 2 engraved portraits, 1 folding map, numerous title vignettes, head and tailpieces and initials, 4to., full vellum, gilt embossed titles and borders, sewn in silk bookmarks, vellum bright but with scattered soiling, spine ends rubbed, little bumped, one volume with vellum split at top edge near spine and one volume with vellum split and damaged at head of spine down through label, both due to dampness, foxing, occasionally heavy though mainly on front and rear signatures, occasional staining at top margins, but text almost crisp, leaves otherwise clean, bindings tight and sound, seminary library bookplate, small bookseller's ticket to front pastedowns, 2 volumes, about good, remaining 20 are very good.   Kaaterskill Books   16 - 61   2013 $2450

Murdoch, Beamish *A History of Nova Scotia or Arcadie.* Halifax: James Barnes, 1865-1867. 3 volumes, 8vo., rebound in half leather and blue buckram, new endpapers, leather slightly scuffed at edges, titlepages slightly foxed, previous owner's name inside front cover volume I.   Schooner Books Ltd.   105 - 89   2013 $250

Murdoch, Iris *Nuns and Soldiers.* New York: Viking Press, 1981. First American edition, 8vo., original quarter mid brown cloth, backstrip gilt lettered, fawn boards, dust jacket trifle rubbed, near fine.   Blackwell's Rare Books   172 - 221   2013   £100

Murdoch, Iris *Sartre, Romantic Rationalist.* Cambridge: Bowes and Bowes, 1953. First edition, near fine, lacking dust jacket.   Between the Covers Rare Books, Inc.   Philosophy - 104308   2013 $100

Murphy, Dervla *Cameroon with Egbert.* London: John Murray, 1989. First edition, original cloth, gilt, dust jacket, 14 illustrations and map.   R. F. G. Hollett & Son   Africana - 150   2013   £25

Murphy, Dervla *Muddling through in Madagascar.* London: John Murray, 1985. First edition, original cloth, gilt, dust jacket, 21 illustrations and map.   R. F. G. Hollett & Son   Africana - 151   2013   £25

Murphy, Dominick *Sketches of Irish Nunneries. 1st Series.* 1865. First edition, iv, 18 pages, cloth, good.   C. P. Hyland   261 - 609   2013   £100

Murphy, John N. *Terra Incognita: The Convents of the United Kingdom.* 1873. First edition, signed presentation copy, xi, 753 pages, with 24 page publisher's catalog, original cloth, recased, good.   C. P. Hyland   261 - 610   2013   £50

Murphy, Lois Barclay *Personality in Young Children.* New York: Basic Books, 1956. fourth printings, 2 volumes, hardcover, fine in near fine dust jackets with rubbed rear pane on volume 2.   Beasley Books   2013 - 2013 $50

Murphy, Patricia *Nonplus.* Dublin: Nonplus, 1959-1960. Numbers 1-4 all published, 8vo., original wrappers, near fine, from the library of Richard Murphy.   Maggs Bros. Ltd.   1442 - 61   2013   £250

Murphy, Richard *The Archaeology of Love.* Dublin: Dolmen Press, 1955. First edition, 8vo., original quarter sand buckram, grey boards, fine in original acetate jacket (only slightly worn), author's copy.   Maggs Bros. Ltd.   1442 - 244   2013   £275

Murphy, Richard *Beehive Sell.* Winston Salem: printed at the Shadowy Waters Press for Distribution to Participants in the XXIII Annual Meeting of the American Committee for Irish Studies, 1985. First edition, limited to 150 copies printed on mould made paper, fine, 16mo., original stitched mid blue wrappers, signed by author, fine.   Maggs Bros. Ltd.   1442 - 247   2013   £125

Murphy, Richard *Care.* Amsterdam: Cornamona Press, 1983. One of 125 copies in wrapeprs, from a total edition of 200, 4to., original marbled paper wrappers, printed on Ossekop paper, fine in yellow slipcase.   Maggs Bros. Ltd.   1442 - 246   2013   £175

Murphy, Richard *The Kick.* London: Granta, 2002. First edition, 8vo., original black cloth, dust jacket, near fine, inscribed by author for Beatrice Roethke Lushington, the dedicatee was wife of poet Theodore Roethke.   Maggs Bros. Ltd.   1442 - 250   2013   £50

Murphy, Richard *The Mirror Wall.* Newcastle-upon-Tyne: Dublin: Bloodaxe Books/Wolfhound Press, 1985. First edition, number 81 of 100 copies signed by author, each with original holograph manuscript poem by author, 8vo., original full brown leather, marbled endpapers, near fine, matching slipcase.   Maggs Bros. Ltd.   1442 - 248   2013   £250

Murphy, Richard *The Woman of the House.* Dublin: Dolmen Press, 1959. First edition, limited to 250 copies, 8vo., original wrappers, covers unevenly browned, otherwise excellent, author's copy signed by him.   Maggs Bros. Ltd.   1442 - 245   2013   £250

Murphy, Robert *Murder in Waiting.* New York: Scribners, 1938. First edition, fine in dust jacket with some slight fading on spine.   Mordida Books   81 - 379   2013 $100

Murphy, Robert Cushman *Oceanic Birds of South America.* New York: Macmillan Co. and the American Museum of Natural History, 1936. First edition, small quarto, 16 color plates, 72 black and white photos, text maps, dark green cloth, slight etching to front hinge volume II, fine set.   Argonaut Book Shop   Recent Acquisitions June 2013 - 214   2013 $275

Murphy, Thomas *The Morning After Optimism.* Dublin and Cork: Mercier Press, 1973. First edition, small 8vo., signed by author, original wrappers, near fine.   Maggs Bros. Ltd.   1442 - 251   2013   £60

Murphy, Tom *On the Outside/On the Inside.* Dublin: Gallery Press, 1976. First edition, one of an unstated number of hardbound copies signed by author, 8vo., original black cloth, fine in dust jacket.   Maggs Bros. Ltd.   1442 - 252   2013   £75

Murray, Albert *The Hero and Blues.* Columbia: University of Missouri Press, 1973. First edition, 107 pages, fine in fine dust jacket with tiny nick on rear panel, scarce.   Between the Covers Rare Books, Inc.   165 - 320   2013 $200

Murray, Alexander *An Easy English Grammar for the Use of Schools.* Newcastle upon Tyne: T. Angus for the author, 1784. First edition, 8vo., contemporary calf, blindstamped border, ms. ownership inscription "Jno K. Murray" to title and ms. annotations to front pastedown and free endpapers, slightly browned with some pale dampstaining, rare.   Maggs Bros. Ltd.   1467 - 124   2013   £2750

Murray, David Christie *First Person Singular, a Novel.* London: Chatto & Windus, 1887. New edition, half title, initial ad leaf, 32 page catalog, July 1887, slightly dusted, 'yellowback', original printed boards, slightly rubbed, very good.   Jarndyce Antiquarian Booksellers   CCV - 206   2013   £90

Murray, David Christie *In His Grip.* London: Long, 1907. First edition, name on copyright page and page edges soiled and lightly foxed, otherwise fine in pictorial blue cloth covered boards with gold stamped titles on spine.   Mordida Books   81 - 380   2013 $200

Murray, Florence *The Negro Handbook 1942.* New York: Wendell Malliet & Co., 1942. First edition, first issue, 269 pages, fine in very good plus dust jacket with several very small nicks and tears, some modest overall age toning, handsome copy, scarce in dust jacket.   Between the Covers Rare Books, Inc.   165 - 228   2013 $150

Murray, Johann Andreas *Spina Bifidae ex Malaossivm Conformatione Initia.* Gottingae: Litteris Joannis Christian Dietrich, 1779. Only edition, 26 pages, 4to., later mottled wrappers.   James Tait Goodrich   75 - 154   2013 $495

Murray, John *John Murray 50 Albermarle St. 1768-1930.* London: Artist Illustrators, n.d., 1930. First edition, 8vo., pages 13, illustrations, original brown wrappers.   J. & S. L. Bonham Antiquarian Booksellers   Europe - 9232   2013   £50

Murray, John *The Letters of John Murray to Lord Byron.* Liverpool University Press, 2007. First edition, half title, original dark blue cloth, mint in dust jacket.   Jarndyce Antiquarian Booksellers   CCIII - 421   2013   £45

Murray, Judith Sargent *The Life of Rev. John Murray Preacher of Universal Salvation.* Boston: Universalist Pub. House, 1882. New edition, 8vo., 408 pages, brown cloth, stamped gilt on spine, private bookplate on endpaper, poem tipped to free endpaper, some pencil scribbling on a rear blank.   Second Life Books Inc.   182 - 177   2013 $125

Murray, Lindley *A Compendium of Religious Faith and Practice. (with) The Duty and Benefit of a Daily Perusal of the Holy Scriptures...* York: printed for W. Alexander, printed by Thomas Wilson and Sons, 1815. 1817. First editions, small 8vo., contemporary half calf gilt, label at base of spine, little spotting.   R. F. G. Hollett & Son   Children's Books - 408   2013   £85

Murray, Lindley *English Exercises, Adapted to Murray's English Grammar...* York: printed by Thomas Wilson & Sons, etc., 1813. Eighteenth edition, original speckled sheep gilt, hinges little cracked at head and foot, one gathering springing, much contemporary scribbling on endpapers.   R. F. G. Hollett & Son   Children's Books - 409   2013   £75

Murray, Lindley *English Exercises.* York: Thomas Wilson and Sons, 1816. Twenty-second edition, some light foxing and few ink splashes, with name Edward Rawlinson 1819 on front endpaper, contemporary calf, expert repairs to joints, some ink splashes to boards, 12mo.   Ken Spelman Books Ltd.   75 - 76   2013   £65

Murray, Lindley *An English Grammar...* York: Thomas Wilson and Son, 1809. Second edition, very good, handsome contemporary half calf with broad gilt bands, blind and gilt decorated spines 8vo., marbled boards and edges, some foxing, quite heavy in places.   Ken Spelman Books Ltd.   75 - 63   2013   £140

Murray, Richard *Alethia; or a General System of Moral Truths and Natural Religion...* printed for T. Osborne, 1747. First edition, bit of light browning, small early inscription erased from titlepage, 8vo., contemporary calf, borders bordered with double gilt fillet, spines with five raised bands between double gilt fillets, lettering pieces lost, rubbed and scratched, slight loss form headcaps, sound, scarce.   Blackwell's Rare Books   B174 - 106   2013   £800

Murtagh, Harman *Irishmen in War 1800-200: Essays from the Irish Sword. Volume II.* IAP, 2006. xiii, 306 pages, 8vo., cloth, dust jacket, fine.   C. P. Hyland   261 - 611   2013   £50

Musae Seatonianae. A Complete Collection of the Cambridge Prize Poems from the First Institution of that Premium by the Rev. Mr. Tho. Seaton in 1750 to 1770. London: printed. sold by Deighton, 1787. 8vo., contemporary half calf, marbled boards, leading hinge cracked but firm, head of spine slightly chipped, armorial bookplate of Peter Acklom Reaston.   Jarndyce Antiquarian Booksellers   CCIV - 81   2013   £85

Musae Seatonianae. A Complete Collection of the Cambridge Prize Poems from the First Institution of that Premium by the Rev. Mr. Tho. Seaton in 1750 to 1806. Cambridge: printed by F. Hodson for J. Deighton, 1808. 8vo. slight paper flaw volume I, not affecting text, full contemporary calf, double gilt ruled and blind borders, raised gilt bands, twin black gilt labels, small gilt spine devices, marbled edges, contemporary inscription "Thomas Waddington the gift of his brother, W. P. Waddington", nice copy.   Jarndyce Antiquarian Booksellers   CCIV - 82   2013   £150

Museum of the Yorkshire Philosophical Society *A Descriptive Account of the Antiquities in the Grounds and in the Museum of the Yorkshire Philosophical Society.* York: H. Sotheran, 1852. Original linen backed boards rather dusty and corner of one leaf torn without loss, presentation copy from author, inscribed, bookplate of Thos. Brayshaw of Settle.   Ken Spelman Books Ltd.   73 - 29   2013   £45

Musgrave, Richard *Memoirs of the Different Rebellions in Ireland.* 1802. Third edition, 2 volumes, 8vo., 10 folding plates, half calf worn, binding tight, text very good.   C. P. Hyland   261 - 612   2013   £250k

Musil, Robert *The Man Without Qualities.* London: Secker & Warburg, 1953. 1954. 1960. First English edition, 3 volumes, first 2 exhibit bit of loss to spine stamping and first volume has slight fore edge foxing, books otherwise fine in near fine, spine tanned dust jackets, the first two of which are price clipped.   Ken Lopez Bookseller   159 - 145   2013 $1000

Musseau, J. C. L. *Manuel Des Amateurs D'Estampes.* Paris: chez J. L. F. Foucault, Libraire, rue des Noyers No. 37, 1821. Small 8vo., pages 242, (2), contemporary half calf, rubbed, upper board detached.   Marlborough Rare Books Ltd.   218 - 107   2013   £165

Muybridge, Eadweard *Descriptive Zoopraxography or the Science of Animal Locomotion.* Philadelphia: University of Pennsylvania, 1893. First edition, hinges professionally and seamlessly reinforced and tips of cloth spine ends restored, nice, very good plus, this copy inscribed by author to noted publisher of photographic stereocard "George Ennis with compliments of the author. University of Pennsylvania 9 June 1894", rare thus.   Between the Covers Rare Books, Inc.   Horses, Horsemanship, Horse Racing, Etc. - 45757   2013 $4500

My ABC Book. London: Frederick Warne, n.d. circa, 1910. Folio, cloth backed decorative boards, color pictorial paste-on, name inked out inside cover, else very good+, every page mounted on linen, printed on rectos only, 2 letters per page, each printed in color, charming chromo illustrations.   Aleph-Bet Books, Inc.   104 - 21   2013 $250

My Book of Alphabet Rhymes and Jingles. Boston: De Wolfe Fisk, circa, 1880. 4to., cloth backed pictorial boards, light shelf wear, very good+, 4 charming full page chromolithographs and photogravures.   Aleph-Bet Books, Inc.   105 - 17   2013 $300

My Book of Noble Deeds. Blackie & Son, n.d circa, 1907. Large 8vo., original cloth backed glazed pictorial boards, little soiled, 4 color plates, other plates and illustrations, inscribed by Joan Ruskin for John Hext.   R. F. G. Hollett & Son   Children's Books - 71   2013   £75

My First Jig-Puzbook. John Leng & Co. n.d circa, 1930. Small 4to., original cloth backed pictorial boards, few scrapes and scratches, corners worn, 4 heavy card leaves and 5 colored jigsaws built in with opposing text, one small piece missing few small flaws and some scattered fingering.   R. F. G. Hollett & Son   Children's Books - 363   2013   £75

My Guinea Pig. Akron: Saalfield, 1912. First edition, 8vo., wrappers, 8 page storybook cut in shape of guinea pig, bound by ribbon.   Barnaby Rudge Booksellers   Children 2013 - 021659   2013 $75

My Honey ABC. London: Tuck, n.d. circa, 1900. Oblong 8vo., printed cloth, some soil and fraying and staining, overall very good, printed in full color on cloth, rare. Aleph-Bet Books, Inc. 104 - 2 2013 $1850

My Life Story by P. Uppy. New York: Sam'l. Gabriel, n.d. circa, 1920. 4to., cloth backed pictorial boards, nearly as new in original publisher's box (slightly worn, but very good+), 4 charming full page color illustrations and pen and inks on text pages. Aleph-Bet Books, Inc. 105 - 189 2013 $400

Myers, Colin *The Book Decorations of Thomas Lowinsky.* Oldham: Incline Press, 2001. Limited edition of 250 copies, 4to., 120 pages, sepia frontispiece, 86 illustrations, half brown cloth over green patterned paper boards, gilt stamped spine title, Mylar wrappers, housed in blue cloth slipcase, printed paper spine label, as new, fine. Jeff Weber Rare Books 171 - 194 2013 $350

Myers, Dwight *In Celebration of the Book: Literary New Mexico.* Albuquerque: 1982. 1 of 500 signed by all involved, xxv, 222 pages, fine in fine slipcase. Dumont Maps & Books of the West 122 - 75 2013 $75

Myers, James P. *Elizabethan Ireland: a Selection of Writings.* 1983. First edition, x, 261 pages, 8vo., 2 maps, cloth, near fine. C. P. Hyland 261 - 613 2013 £35

Myers, Peter Hamilton *The Young Patroon or Christmas in 1690.* New York: George P. Putnam; London: Putnam's American Agency, removed from Paternoster Row to J. Chapman, 1849. First edition, 12mo., original decorated purple cloth stamped in gold and blind. L. W. Currey, Inc. Christmas Themed Books - 133146 2013 $100

Mylar, Isaac L. *Early Days at the Mission San Juan Bautista.* San Juan: Bautista Historical Society, 1970. Facsimile reprint of 1929 edition, 204 pages, vintage photos, gilt lettered maroon cloth, light foxing to extreme fore-edge of text block, else very fine with pictorial dust jacket. Argonaut Book Shop Summer 2013 - 247 2013 $60

Myres, J. N. L. *A Corpus of Anglo-Saxon Pottery of the Pagan Period.* Cambridge: University Press, 1977. 2 volumes, folio, cloth, minimal shelfwear to dust jackets, with 4mm. closed tear to upper inner corner of volume 2, otherwise very good. Unsworths Antiquarian Booksellers 28 - 188 2013 £60

Myrick, David F. *Rails Around the Bohemian Grave.* San Francisco: Bohemian Club, 1973. First edition, 39 pages, plates, maps, pictorial green boards, spine lightly faded, fine and clean, illustrations. Argonaut Book Shop Summer 2013 - 248 2013 $50

The Mystery Magazine. March 1933 (volume 7 number 3). Dunellen: Tower Magazines, Inc. March, 1933. Large octavo, pictorial wrappers. L. W. Currey, Inc. Fall Sampler Sept. 2013 - 146580 2013 $450

The Mystery Magazine June 1934. (volume 9 number 6). Dunellen: Tower Magazines Inc. June, 1934. Large octavo, pictorial wrappers. L. W. Currey, Inc. Fall Sampler Sept. 2013 - 146581 2013 $350

The Mystery Magazine. October 1934 (volume 10 number 4). Dunellen: Tower Magazines Inc., Large octavo, pictorial wrappers. L. W. Currey, Inc. Fall Sampler Sept. 2013 - 146582 2013 $400

N

Nais, R. De *A Bibliography of Limerick History.* Limerick: 1965. 61 pages, 8vo., wrappers, very good.   C. P. Hyland   261 - 54   2013   £30

The Nameless Crime: a Mystery Shown in Two Tableau Vivants. London: printed by Whipwell & Co., Bottom Lane, circa, 1889. One of 250 copies printed but not numbered, beautifully printed in pink and black on handmade paper, uncut in contemporary vellum, lettered gilt, extra buckle on spine, slightly dulled, 46 pages.   Jarndyce Antiquarian Booksellers   CCV - 8   2013   £380

Nannini, Remigio *Civill Considerations Upon Many and Sundrie Histories as well Ancient as Moderne...* London: by F(elix) K(ingston) for Matthew Lowndes, 1601. Folio, woodcut device on titlepage, woodcut head and tailpieces and initials with cancel bifolium C1.2, contemporary calf with 1603 Towneley arms of Richard Towneley of Towneley stamped (in blind?) on both covers, remains of green cloth ties, front blank A1 and rear blank 2A6 present and seemingly correct, binding very heavily worn and scuffed, early reinforcing to inner hinges, blank lower corner of G5 and O3 torn away, dampstain in upper left margin of first several leaves and reappearing toward rear of text, occasional spotting and soiling and browning but very nice internally, Richard Towneley's copy with armorial bookplate dated 1702, signature of Cha.. Towneley, probably Richard's father.   Joseph J. Felcone Inc.   Books Printed before 1701 - 71   2013 $3500

Nansen, Fridtjof   1861-1930   *'Farthest North'.* London: George Newnes, 1898. 2 volumes, original pictorial cloth, gilt and silvered over bevelled boards, extremities faintly rubbed, complete with colored plate, 120 plates and maps, one joint trifle tender, few spots, but very nice.   R. F. G. Hollett & Son   Polar Exploration - 44   2013   £140

Nansen, Fridtjof   1861-1930   *'Farthest North'.* George Newnes, 1898. 2 volumes, original pictorial cloth, gilt and silvered over bevelled boards, heads of spines, rather chipped and frayed, colored plate, 120 plates and maps, some flyleaves spotted.   R. F. G. Hollett & Son   Polar Exploration - 43   2013   £120

Nansen, Fridtjof   1861-1930   *Sporting Days in Wild Norway.* London: Thornton Butterworth, 1925. First edition, 8vo., 270 pages, illustrations, original purple cloth, spine faded.   J. & S. L. Bonham Antiquarian Booksellers   Europe - 8803   2013   £48

Narrative and Confessions of Lucretia P. Cannon, Who was tried, Convicted and Sentenced to be Hung at Georgetown, Delaware... New York: printed for the publishers, 1841. First edition, 8vo., 23 (of 24) pages, frontispiece and illustrations, title leaf, old plain blue wrappers, backed with tape, browned with some bad lower cover stains.   M & S Rare Books, Inc.   95 - 244   2013 $275

Nash, John *Wood-Engravings: a Catalogue of the Wood-Engravings, Early Lithographs, Etchings and Engravings on Metal.* Liverpool: Wood Lea Press, 1987. One of 750 copies (of an edition of 1811 copies), frontispiece, reproductions, lithography and etchings and engravings on metal, few of the wood engravings reproduced in colored form, folio, original quarter mid green cloth, backstrip gilt lettered, cream boards with repeated Nash design printed in brown overall, remains of bookplate pasted to front pastedown, matching cloth slipcase, very good.   Blackwell's Rare Books   B174 - 270   2013   £100

Nash, Paul *A Catalogue of the Wood Engravings, Pattern Papers, Etchings and an Engraving on Copper.* Woodbridge, Suffolk: Wood Lea Press, 1997. 34/60 copies (of an edition of 550), several tipped-in color printed plates and numerous reproductions of engravings, pages 144, small folio, original quarter mid grey morocco, backstrip gilt lettered, black, white and yellow Curwen patterned boards, matching cloth slipcase, fine, with single proof pull, also present with this issue of the edition, loosely inserted in box.   Blackwell's Rare Books   B174 - 363   2013   £350

Natalibus, Petrus De *Catalogu Sanctorum et Gestorum Eorum ex Diversis Volminibus Collectus.* Vicenza: Henricus de Sancto Ursio 12 Dec., 1493. First edition, folio 331 (of 332) leaves, lacks final blank, Roman type, title in red and black, woodcut initials throughout, 19th century Italian vellum, gilt, rather unattractive brown dampstaining confined largely to gutters through most of volume but occasionally extending as much as 3 inches into top and bottom blank margins, scattered early marginalia occasional cropped.   Joseph J. Felcone Inc.   Books Printed before 1701 - 72   2013 $4500

National American Woman Suffrage Association *Forty-Fifth Annual Convention New Masonic Temple...* Washington: November 29 to December 5, 1913. Pages 14, little soiled printed wrappers, laid in is the "Constitution of the National American Woman Suffrage Association" and a proposed "Constitution for the NAWSA", scarce.   Second Life Books Inc.   182 - 179   2013 $225

National Park Service *A Survey of the Recreational Resources of the Colorado River Basin.* Washington: 1950. xxiv, 242 pages, illustrations, 15 maps in rear pocket, printed wrappers, some soil to wrappers, else clean and very good.   Dumont Maps & Books of the West   124 - 79   2013 $60

Neale, Hannah *Amusement Hall: or an Easy Introduction to the Attainment of Useful Knowledge.* T. Gardiner, 1806. Third edition, contemporary full roan, front hinge cracked but cords folding, half title and steel engraved frontispiece. R. F. G. Hollett & Son   Children's Books - 410   2013   £45

Neale, John Preston *Views of the Seats of Noblemen and Gentlemen in England, Wales, Scotland and Ireland.* London: Sherwood, Neely ad Jones, 1820-1829. Large paper copy, 11 volumes, 4to., 11 engraved titles and 721 plates, all on india paper and marked 'proof, mounted, 7 wood engraved text vignettes, late 19th century purple half morocco by Sotheran & Co.   Marlborough Rare Books Ltd.   218 - 109   2013   £3000

Neale, Thomas *An Abstract of the Sea-Laws, as Established in Most Kingdoms of Europe, But More Particularly in England and Scotland.* London: printed for Isaac Cleave next Serjeants Inn in Chancery Lane, 1704. 8vo., tear to titlepage neatly repaired not affecting text, part of ruled border made good in pen and ink, old waterstaining to lower margins, some worming to leading edge, repaired on final three leaves touching a few leaves in marginal notes and ad, lower margin of ad leaf neatly repaired, full contemporary calf, blind ruled and decorated borders, raised bands, some wear to foot of spine, lower sections of hinges cracked.   Jarndyce Antiquarian Booksellers   CCIV - 213   2013   £420

Nearing, Scott *Social Adjustment.* New York: Macmillan, 1911. First edition, very good, 376 pages, hardcover. Beasley Books   2013 - 2013 $65

Neasham, V. Aubrey *The City of the Plain. Sacramento in the Nineteenth Century.* Sacramento: Sacramento Pioneer Foundation, 1969. First edition, quarto, 230 pages, color frontispiece, drawings, paintings, vintage photos, gold yellow cloth, gilt, three tiny stamps on ends, fine, uncut.   Argonaut Book Shop   Summer 2013 - 250   2013 $75

The Negro Review. Atlanta: American Enterprises Sept., 1953. Volume I ,number 1, 12mo., fine, first issue. Between the Covers Rare Books, Inc.   165 - 188   2013 $125

Neil, James *Rays from the Realm of Nature; or Parables of Plant Life.* Cassell, Petter, Galpin & Co., n.d. circa, 1890. Fifth edition, original pictorial green cloth, gilt, color lithograph frontispiece and numerous text woodcuts, front flyleaf removed, little pencilled marginal lining. R. F. G. Hollett & Son   Children's Books - 411   2013   £30

Nelson, Byron *Shape Your Swing the Modern Way.* Norwalk: Golf Digest, 1976. First edition, small 8vo., 127 pages, fine, minimal cover edgewear in very good++ dust jacket with minimal edgewear, short closed tears, scuffs, signed and inscribed by author.   By the Book, L. C.   36 - 72   2013 $200

Nelson, Hugh Lawrence *Kill with Care.* New York: Rinehart, 1953. First edition, fine in near fine dust jacket with few small faint stains on rear panel.   Between the Covers Rare Books, Inc.   Mystery & Detective Fiction - 39301   2013 $65

Nelson, June Kompass *Harry Bertoia Sculptor.* Detroit: Wayne State University Press, 1970. First edition, hardcover, 137 pages, numerous black and white illustrations, clean, close to near fine copy but for some paperclip impressions to top of a number of pages in close to near fine dust jacket with price sticker shadow to front flap, signed and warmly inscribed by Bertoia to his agents.   Jeff Hirsch Books   Fall 2013 - 129108   2013 $750

Nequam, Alexander *The Schools and the Cloister: the Life and Writings of Alexander Nequam (1157-1217).* Oxford: Clarendon Press, 1984. 8vo., xiii, 165 pages, navy cloth, gilt stamped spine title, dust jacket, ownership signature, fine, rare.   Jeff Weber Rare Books   169 - 314   2013 $60

Nesbit, Edith *Book of Dogs.* London: J. M. Dent, 1898. First edition, first printing, oblong 4to., pictorial cloth, near fine, illustrations by Winifred Austin with gravure portrait frontispiece and with black and whites in text, uncommon, beautiful copy.   Aleph-Bet Books, Inc.   105 - 424   2013 $125

Nesbit, Edith *The Five Children.* New York: Junior Literary Guild, 1930. Profusely illustrated, including color frontispiece, near fine in very good+ dust jacket, spine of dust jacket modestly sunned, light general wear and soiling, very scarce in dust jacket.   Leather Stalking Books   October 2013 - 2013 $100

Nesbit, Edith *Five of Us and Madeline.* London: T. Fisher Unwin, 1925. 8vo., red cloth, 310 pages, neat owner inscription, slight foxing, else near fine, illustrations by Nora Unwin with color frontispiece and black and white plates. Aleph-Bet Books, Inc.   104 - 381   2013 $400

Nesbit, Edith *Harding's Luck.* London: Hodder & Stoughton, 1909. First edition, 8vo., red gilt cloth, top edge gilt, 281 pages, slight darkening on bottom edge of front cover and very occasional foxing, tight, near fine, illustrations by H. R. Millar with 16 plates and pen and ink drawings, rare.   Aleph-Bet Books, Inc.   104 - 382   2013 $750

Nesbit, Edith *In Homespun.* London: John Lane; Boston: Roberts Brothers, 1896. First edition, 8vo., pictorial cloth, 189 pages + publisher's catalogues, fine, beautiful copy, pictorial titlepage.   Aleph-Bet Books, Inc.   104 - 383   2013 $325

Nesbit, Edith *The New Treasure Seekers.* London: Fisher Unwin, 1904. First edition, original red pictorial cloth gilt, lower board rather marked, spine faded, neatly recased, top edge gilt, 33 illustrations by Gordon Browne and Lewis Baumer, little fingering in places. R. F. G. Hollett & Son Children's Books - 413 2013 £75

Nesbit, Edith *Oswald Bastable and Others.* London: Wells Gardner Darton, 1905. First edition, first issue, with page 96 mistakenly printed on page 69, 8vo., maroon cloth, top edge gilt, small blemish on cover and fore edge soil, illustrations by C. E. Brock and H. R. Millar with 22 black and white plates plus pictorial titlepage. Aleph-Bet Books, Inc. 104 - 384 2013 $400

Nesbit, Edith *The Rainbow and the Rose.* London: Longmans, Green & Co., 1905. First edition, rare presentation copy from author to Olindo Malagodi, July 1905, original green cloth with lovely floral and fleur-de-lis design in gilt on front cover along with author and title, light bumping and small light stain to top of rear cover, otherwise beautiful, front and rear endpapers foxed but interior pages bright and clean, each section preceded by blank page with flower illustration, each illustration is different color, 143 pages, 4 pages ads. The Kelmscott Bookshop 7 - 123 2013 $2000

Nesbit, Edith *Rosy Cheeks and Golden Ringlets.* London: Raphael Tuck, n.d. circa, 1900. Slim 8vo., cloth backed pictorial boards, corners rubbed, some finger soil, very good+, 4 lovely chromolithographed plates and 4 illustrations in brown line, scarce. Aleph-Bet Books, Inc. 105 - 425 2013 $200

Nesbit, Edith *Royal Children of English History.* London: Raphael Tuck, n.d. circa, 1896. 4to., blue cloth stamped in gold, all edges gilt, 94 pages, slight edgewear and toning to some pages, near fine, illustrations by Francis Brundage with 10 fine chromolithograph plates and many black and white drawings and half tones by M. Bowley, rare in such nice condition. Aleph-Bet Books, Inc. 104 - 385 2013 $200

Nesbit, Edith *The Story of the Five Rebellious Dolls.* London: Nister, 1904. Oblong folio, cloth backed pictorial boards, covers very lightly rubbed and 2 mends else, beautiful, very good+ copy, 8 fabulous and detailed color plates plus other illustrations in brown line and pictorial endpapers by E. Stuart Hardy. Aleph-Bet Books, Inc. 105 - 197 2013 $750

Nesbit, Edith *Winter Songs and Sketches.* Griffith, Farran and Co., n.d., 1886. Square 8vo., original chromolithographed pictorial card wrappers, spine chipped, illustrations in grey and sepia. R. F. G. Hollett & Son Children's Books - 415 2013 £30

Nesbit, Edith *The Wouldbegoods.* Harper and Brothers, 1901. First US edition, 16 plates by Reginald Birch, nice, clean copy, original brown pictorial cloth gilt. R. F. G. Hollett & Son Children's Books - 414 2013 £95

Netterville, Luke *The Queen of the World or Under the Tyranny.* London: Lawrence and Bullen Ltd., 1900. octavo, original red cloth, front and spine panels stamped in gold, edges untrimmed. L. W. Currey, Inc. Utopian Literature: Recent Acquisitions (April 2013) - 139159 2013 $850

Neuhaus, Eugen *The Art of the Exposition Personal Impressions of the Architecture, Sculpture, Mural, Decorations, Color Scheme and Other Aesthetic Aspects of the Panama-Pacific International Exposition.* San Francisco: Paul Elder, 1915. First edition, 8vo., pages 94, illustrations, untrimmed, dust jacket with pieces missing to fore edge, part of lower corner of front board nicked and about 1 inch of paper missing, good copy, from the library of reformer Florence Kelley (1859-1932), with presentation to her from Katherine Philips Edson May 29th 1915. Second Life Books Inc. 182 - 180 2013 $95

Neuhaus, Eugen *The Art of Treasure Island.* Berkeley: University of California Press, 1939. First edition, 51 photo plates, double page ground plan, blue cloth, slight rubbing to spine ends, fine. Argonaut Book Shop Summer 2013 - 251 2013 $50

Nevill, E. Mildred *Interest Ah Fu: A Chinese River Boy.* New York: Friendship Press, n.d. circa, 1928. 16mo., pictorial cloth, fine in slightly worn dust jacket, full page color illustrations by Elsie Anna Wood. Aleph-Bet Books, Inc. 105 - 125 2013 $200

Nevins, Allan *Fremont, Pathmaker of the West.* New York: D. Appelton Century Co., 1939. First edition, 16 illustrations, 9 maps, blue cloth lettered gilt, light offsetting to front ends, very fine, lightly worn dust jacket. Argonaut Book Shop Summer 2013 - 117 2013 $125

New Brunswick Museum *Museum Memoir Volume I Number 1 March 1969 - Volume 7 Number 2 June 1975.* St. John's: New Brunswick Museum, 1975. 8vo., rebound in red buckram, black and white photo illustrations, previous owner's name to front pastedown, remnants of paper pocket to front pastedown, name blocked out to free endpaper, otherwise very good. Schooner Books Ltd. 105 - 19 2013 $55

New Brunswick. Board of Agriculture *The Seventh Annual Report of the Board of Agriculture of th Province of New Brunswick.* Fredericton: G. E. Fenety, 1867. 8vo., paper wrappers, 97 pages, illustrations, very good. Schooner Books Ltd. 105 - 6 2013 $75

New Brunswick. Chief Superintendent of Schools *Annual Report of the Chief Superintendent of Schools for New Brunswick.* Fredericton: J. Simpson, 1859. 8vo., paper wrappers creased and stained, corners torn, interior good. Schooner Books Ltd. 105 - 7 2013 $75

New Brunswick. General Assembly *Acts of the General Assembly of Her Majesty's Province of New Brunswick, Passed in July 1856 and March and July 1857.* Fredericton: J. Simpson, 1857. 8vo. paper wrappers, 8vo., slight water damage to bottom creased covers, interior good. Schooner Books Ltd. 105 - 18 2013 $50

The New England Journal of Medicine and Surgery and the Collateral Branches of Science. Boston: published by Bradford and Read, 1816-1817. Volume V and VI, early quarter calf and marbled boards, binding worn and rubbed, joints cracked, text with some foxing, portion of title torn off affecting word 'Journal' in first volume, 2 volumes bound in 1. James Tait Goodrich S74 - 192 2013 $250

New Mexico The Last Great West. Chicago: 1917. Pages 177, illustrations, maps, some wear, boards soiled, generally good. Dumont Maps & Books of the West 124 - 80 2013 $95

New York City Guide. New York: Random House, 1939. First edition, 2nd printing without the supplementary chapter on the World's Fair, gray cloth in blue jacket fine in very good dust jacket with few small chips at extremities, map of New York in pocket in rare as issued, very nice copy of the WPA guide, John Cheever was an editorial assistant this copy signed by Cheever. Between the Covers Rare Books, Inc. New York City - 318527 2013 $750

New York Produce Exchange *Report of the New York Produce Exchange with Charter, By-laws and the Several Trace Rules Adopted by the Exchange and a List of Its Members from July 1 1912 to July 1 1913.* New York: New York Produce Exchange, 1913. Brick red cloth stamped in black and gilt, bookplate, small smudge to front board, else fine. Between the Covers Rare Books, Inc. New York City - 285548 2013 $85

New York State Communist Party *Negro History Week 1952.* NYSCP Education Dept., 1952. First edition, wrappers, double issue, 8 x 11, 72 pages, fine. Beasley Books 2013 - 2013 $50

New York State Communist Party *Party Voice 3-6, 8.* New York: State Communist Party, 1956. 5 issues, wrappers, about 32 pages, very good. Beasley Books 2013 - 2013 $50

New York. (City) *Manual of the Corporation of the City of New York for 1850.* New York: Mcspedon & Baker, 1850. First edition, publisher's pale green cloth stamped in blind and gilt, 552 pages, duotones, color plates and engravings, many foldout maps and facsimiles, one map detached but present, couple of small repairs to folding plates, light stain on rear board, else nice, very good or better two bookplates one with "Bequeathed to Robert Sterling Clark by his father Alfred Corning Clark 1896". Between the Covers Rare Books, Inc. New York City - 299892 2013 $500

New York. (City) *Manual of the Corporation of the City of New York for 1854.* New York: D. T. Valentine, 1854. First edition, 560 pages, duotones, color plates and engravings, many foldout maps and illustrations, 2 bookplate, one from a library with minimal marking, front fly lacking, corners bumped, small tears at spine ends, about very good. Between the Covers Rare Books, Inc. New York City - 299896 2013 $300

New York. (City) *Manual of the Corporation of the City of New York for 1856.* New York: D. T. Valentine, 1856. Publisher's brown cloth stamped in blind and gilt, duotones, color plates and engravings, many foldout maps and facsimiles, small tears to one or two of the foldouts and few small tears to cloth, else fresh and near fine, bookplate of Lewis E. Waterman. Between the Covers Rare Books, Inc. New York City - 291609 2013 $750

New York. (City) *Manual of the Corporation of the City of New York for 1861.* New York: D. T. Valentine, 1861. 700 pages, duotones, color plates, engravings, many foldout maps and illustrations, original purple cloth decorated in blind and gilt, 3 bookplates, one of Samuel W. Galpin, another from a library (with minimal marking), spine little sunned, else very good plus, inscribed by Galpin to Maine Congressman Daniel Somes. Between the Covers Rare Books, Inc. New York City - 299888 2013 $450

Newbald Benefit Society *Rules and Orders for the Regulation of the Newbald Benefit Society, Instituted at Newbald April 11th 1850 for the Mutual Relief and Maintenance of Its Dependent Members...* Beverley: John Kemp, 1850. 8vo., 15, (1) pages, very good, disbound, recent marbled wrappers, rare. Ken Spelman Books Ltd. 73 - 129 2013 £95

Newbald Benefit Society *Rules and Orders for the Regulation of the Newbald Benefit Society, Instituted at Newbald April 11th 1850...* Beverley: John Kemp Market Place, 1850. 8vo., very good, recent marbled wrappers, rare. Ken Spelman Books Ltd. 75 - 117 2013 £55

Newbery, John *The Newtonian System of Philosophy.* Philadelphia: Johnson & Warner, Lydia R. Railey, 1808. 16m. 140 pages, 5 full page plates, numerous text woodcuts, contemporary calf, leather label, very good. M & S Rare Books, Inc. 95 - 183 2013 $350

Newbigging, Thomas *Sketches and Tales.* London: Sampson Low, Marston and Co., 1883. First edition, half title, original green cloth, very good, bright.   Jarndyce Antiquarian Booksellers   CCV - 208   2013   £50

Newbigin, Alice M. S. *A Wayfarer in Spain.* London: Methuen, 1926. First edition, 8vo., map on endpaper, illustrations, original brown cloth, small stain where label removed, small nick at head of spine.   J. & S. L. Bonham Antiquarian Booksellers   Europe - 6377   2013   £30

Newcastle, Thomas Pelham Hollis, 1st Duke of *A Tale of Two Tubs; or the B---rs in Querpo.* London: printed or A. Price, 1749. First edition, 8vo., early quarter calf, marbled boards, half title, title, pages 55 + folding engraved plate. Howard S. Mott Inc.   262 - 107   2013 $700

Newell, Peter *Jungle-Jangle.* New York: Peter Newell, copyright applied for, 1909. 4to., pictorial wrappers, neat spine and page strengthening, slight cover soil, very good+, printed on one side of paper only, first 3 leaves have holes cut out in strategic places so that eyes and mouths appear in different places in each succeeding illustration; illustrations in color, rare.   Aleph-Bet Books, Inc.   105 - 426   2013 $1850

Newell, Peter *The Rocket Book.* New York: Harper & Bros. Oct., 1912. First edition, 8vo., cloth, pictorial paste-on, very fine in dust jacket with some old tape mends on verso, else very good, full page illustrations, rare in dust jacket.   Aleph-Bet Books, Inc.   104 - 387   2013 $3000

Newfoundland Conference of the Methodist Church *Minutes of the Proceedings of the Twelfth Session of the Newfoundland Conference of the Methodist Church June 25th 1895.* St. John's: G. S. Milligan, 1895-1903. 8vo., green cloth with gilt title to spine, 5 black and white illustrations in 1899 session and numerous tables, 8vo.. binding worn and quite sunned, generally very good interior with the exception of the 1900 session which has hole to inner margin of titlepage, not into text.   Schooner Books Ltd.   105 - 38   2013 $225

The Newgate Calendar; Comprising Interesting Memoirs of the Most Notorious Characters Who Have Been Convicted of Outrages on the Laws of England... London: J. Robins and Co., 1824-1828. 4 volumes, frontispiece and illustrations, odd spot, slightly later half crimson calf, very good.   Jarndyce Antiquarian Booksellers   CCV - 209   2013   £550

Newstead Abbey. Lord Byron. Colonel Wildman. A Reminiscence. Leeds: Fenteman & Sons, 1856. Some internal marks, uncut in original printed wrappers, dusted, chipped and worn, spine defective, small news clipping pasted on to preface, booklabel of Alex Bridge & ownership inscription.   Jarndyce Antiquarian Booksellers   CCIII - 339   2013   £180

Newte, Thomas *Prospectus and Observations; on a Tour in England and Scotland...* London: printed for G. G. J. and J. Robinson, 1792. First edition, 4to., plates slightly foxed, occasional spotting, uncut in original blue paper boards, cream paper spine, 'Newt's Tour' in contemporary ink on spine, some slight rubbing, excellent copy in original boards.   Jarndyce Antiquarian Booksellers   CCV - 212   2013   £750

Newton, Catherine *The Trial of the Hon. Mrs. Catherine Newton, Wife of John Newton, Esq. and Daughter of the Right Honourable and Reverend Lord Francis Seymour, at the Consistory Court of Doctors Commons...* London: printed for G. Lister No. 46 Old Bailey, 1782. 8vo., etched frontispiece, uncut, titlepage slightly dusted, slight foxing, later boards, plain cloth spine slightly worn, bookplate of Coningsby Disraeli, Hughenden, Manor House.   Jarndyce Antiquarian Booksellers   CCIV - 215   2013   £350

Newton, Isaac 1642-1727 *The Mathematical Principles of Natural Philosophy.* London: printed for Benjamin Motte at the Middle-Temple Gate in Fleetstreet, 1729. First edition, 2 volumes, with hgh quality facsimiles for the frontispieces and titlepages of both volumes and plate XXV in volume I is facsimile, all else original, 25 folding plates in volume I and 22 folding plates in volume II, as called for, modern matching brown speckled leather with spine in five compartments, gilt lettering to spine label, gilt decorations to spine, original endpapers preserved, owner name to front pastedown volume I, edges volume I yellow tint, volume II green tint, scattered foxing initial pages but overall clean set with wide margins, 8vo., plates, tables.   By the Book, L. C.   38 - 7   2013 $12,500

Newton, Isaac 1642-1727 *Mathematical Principles of Natural Philosophy. Book the First (all published).* London: printed by A. Strahan for T. Cadell Jun. and W. Davies, 1802. 22 folding engraved plates, some dampstaining, mainly marginal throughout, usually pale but little more pronounced in places 4to., 19th century half calf and marbled boards, flat spine gilt tooled on either side of raised bands, skilfully rebacked and recornered, new labels stamp of Melchet Court, Romsey, with initial A circled by crown, few mathematical notes in margins.   Blackwell's Rare Books   Sciences - 89   2013   £3000

Newton, Isaac 1642-1727 *Opticks; or a Treatise of the Reflections, Refractions, Inflections and Colours of Light.* London: printed for William and John Innys, 1721. Third edition, 12 folding engraved plates, trifle browed in places, 1 plate bit dust soiled on verso, contemporary panelled calf, rebacked, few old scratches on covers, ownership at head of title "George Palmes 1796" (of Naburn in Yorkshire) and his armorial bookplate inside front cover.   Blackwell's Rare Books   Sciences - 86   2013   £3500

Newton, Isaac 1642-1727 *Opuscula Mathematica, Philosophica et Philologia.* Lausanne & Geneva: Marc-Michel Bousquet, 1744. First collected edition, titlepages printed in red and black with engraved title vignettes of two putti surrounding a medallion portrait of Newton, 64 engraved plates, 2 folding tables, tables in text, decorative head and tailpieces, 4to., near contemporary marbled boards, backstrips ruled in gilt with red labels and gilt lettering, slightly rubbed, corner bumped, good.   Blackwell's Rare Books   Sciences - 87   2013   £2500

Newton, Isaac 1642-1727 *Philosophiae Naturalis Principia Mathematica.* London: Joseph Streater for the Royal Society, 1687. One of 1000 copies, large 8vo., rust cloth, gilt stamped spine, spine head slightly torn, ownership signature of I. Bernard Cohen with his scattered notes and underlining, booklabel of Burndy Library with bookplate, very good.   Jeff Weber Rare Books   169 - 317   2013 $300

Newton, Isaac 1642-1727 *Philosophiae Nautralis Principia Mathematica.* Amsterdam: Sumptibus Societatis, 1714. First Amsterdam edition, contemporary full leather, spine in six compartments, gilt decorations and titling to spine, covers with mild wear, joints strengthened, bookplate of renowned French Blouet de Camilly family, endpapers with mild soil scattered foxing, titlepage printed in black and red, engraved vignette, folding plate of comet orbits, 4to., attractive copy.   By the Book, L. C.   38 - 6   2013 $15,000

Newton, Isaac 1642-1727 *Unpublished Scientific Papers of Isaac Newton.* Cambridge: University Press, 1962. First edition, 8vo., 5 plates, red cloth, gilt stamped spine title, dust jacket, Burndy bookplate, very good.   Jeff Weber Rare Books   169 - 318   2013 $125

Newton, Isaac 1642-1727 *Opera Qua Extant Omnia.* printed by John Nichols, 1779-1785. First edition, diagrams in text, 33 engraved plates, some folding, half title to volume iv slightly soiled, very occasional spotting and little dampstaining in lower margin of volume v, contemporary mottled calf, all volumes sturdily rebacked preserving most all of the original spines, which are gilt in compartments, red lettering piece, numbering pieces absent, Snelston Hall bookplate in each volume, ink signature of ?George Legge erased in each volume, good.   Blackwell's Rare Books   Sciences - 88   2013   £6500

Newton, John *Trigonometria Britanica; or the Doctrine of Triangles, in Two Books.* printed by R. and W. Leybourn and are to be sold by George Hurlock, Joshuah Kirton, Thomas Pierrepont and William Fisher, 1658. First edition, 4 parts in one volume, sectional titles to last 3 parts, woodcut diagrams in text in first part, woodcut initials and headpieces, browned in places, titlepage ill attached to a later (rather stiff) flyleaf, last leaf folding with errata pasted to verso of flap, folio in 4s, contemporary panelled mottled calf, rebacked, preserving most of original spine, edges parti-colored, the 2 canones logarithmorum red, remainder marbled, the Macclesfield copy with blindstamps and bookplate, few annotations in the hand of John Collins, sound.   Blackwell's Rare Books   Sciences - 85   2013   £2000

Newton, William *The History and Antiquities of Maidstone, the Country-Town of Kent.* London: printed for the author and sold by J. and P.. Knapton, 1741. 8vo., uncut, slight foxing and little browning, nineteenth century half calf, expertly rebacked, raised gilt bands, top edge gilt, armorial bookplate of noted collector, Frances Mary Richardson Currer.   Jarndyce Antiquarian Booksellers   CCIV - 217   2013   £250

Nexo, Martin Andersen *Pelle the Conqueror.* New York: Holt, 1917. 2 volumes, 8vo., red cloth stamped in black, from the library of consumer advocate Florence Kelley with her ownership signature, covers scuffed, spotted and faded, volume I has front hinge tender, volume II has small tear top side of spine and rear hinge tender, very good.   Second Life Books Inc.   183 - 290   2013 $65

The Niagara Book, a Complete Souvenir of Niagara Falls Containing Sketches. Buffalo: Underhill and Nicholas, 1893. First edition, 2nd/3rd printing (copyright notice in 3 lines and 4 pages of ads in rear), 8vo., pages 225+ ads, frontispiece, headpieces, half tone reproductions from sketches by Harry Fenn, 6 views, original pictorial green cloth, some dust soiled, wrinkle and nicks to fore-edge of flyleaf, some light waterstain to top margin of text, in all, very good, rare.   Second Life Books Inc.   183 - 78   2013 $350

Nichols, Robert *Wings Over Europe: a Dramatic Extravaganza on a Pressing Theme.* London: Chatto and Windus, 1932. First English edition, with two page author's note that appears here for the first time, bookplate of Mary Landon Baker, stain at bottom rear board and bottom page edge, just touch the body of a few pages, else near fine, lacking dust jacket, inscribed by author for Baker, Venice Oct. 15 1937.   Between the Covers Rare Books, Inc.   Sci-Fi, Fantasy & Horror - 98482   2013 $300

Nichols, Thomas *A Handbook for Readers at the British Museum.* London: Longmans, 1866. First edition, 8vo., very good in original cloth.   Ken Spelman Books Ltd.   75 - 134   2013   £45

Nichols, Walter *Essays and Miscellaneous Writings of Walter Nichols, A. B. of Hempstead, Long Island.* New York: printed by Charles N. Baldwin, 1826. First edition, original paper covered boards with red morocco spine label gilt, some spotting to boards and pastedowns, nicks at corners of gutters, but nice, very good or better copy. Between the Covers Rare Books, Inc.   New York City - 291733   2013 $225

Nicholson, Ben *Ben Nicholson: Drawings, Paintings and Reliefs 1911-1968.* New York: Harry N Abrams, 1969. First edition, 298 illustrations, 78 tipped in color plates, near fine and tight copy in close to near fine dust jacket with tear to top of front panel and to top of spine, tanning to spine and front panel.   Jeff Hirsch Books   Fall 2013 - 129126   2013 $200

Nicholson, Francis *Six Views of Scarborough and Its Vicinity Drawn from Nature and on Stone.* Scarborough: Pub. by W. Wilson, 1822. 6 lithograph plates, plates generally clean with just some slight foxing, original printed sugar paper wrappers rather worn at edges, lower left hand corner of each page has some wear, well clear of image. Ken Spelman Books Ltd.   73 - 146   2013   £220

Nicholson, G. W. L. *The Fighting Newfoundlander. (with) More Fighting Newfoundlanders. A History of Newfoundland's Fighting Forces.* St. John's: Government of Newfoundland & Labrador, 1964. 1969, 2 volumes, white decorative paper covered boards, map endpapers, dust jackets, color frontispiece, 15 maps, full page portrait, numerous black and white illustrations, 8vo., both volumes and jackets very good.   Schooner Books Ltd.   101 - 48   2013 $150

Nicholson, James B. *Manual of the Art of Bookbinding....* Philadelphia: Henry Carey Baird, 1856. First edition, 8vo., pages 318, (20 ads), 12 lithograph plates, 7 samples of marbled papers and numerous wood engraved text figures, publisher's brown vertical grained cloth, blocked in blind and spine lettered gilt head and foot of spine defective, corners slightly worn.   Marlborough Rare Books Ltd.   218 - 110   2013   £950

Nicholson, Norman *Wednesday Early Closing.* London: Faber, 1975. First edition, 8vo., original tan cloth, fore edges trifle faded, backstrip gilt lettered, endpapers and dust jacket lightly foxed, very good.   Blackwell's Rare Books   172 - 223   2013   £40

Nicholson, Peter *The Carpenter and Joiner's Assistant...* printed for I. and J. Taylor at the Architectural Library, 1979. First edition, 79 engraved plates, first few leaves little frayed at fore-edge, 4 page catalog dated Jan. 2 1802, 4to., modern calf backed boards, good.   Blackwell's Rare Books   Sciences - 90   2013   £850

Nicholson, Peter *The New Practical Builder and Workman's Companion.* London: Thomas Kelly, 1823. 1825. First edition, 4to., half title, frontispiece, plates, slightly foxed, full contemporary mottled calf, raised bands, gilt band, red and black morocco labels, expert repairs to hinges, boards slightly rubbed and marked, ownership label W. Smith 1829.   Jarndyce Antiquarian Booksellers   CCV - 213   2013   £520

Nicholson, William *An Introduction to Natural History.* Philadelphia: T. Dobson, 1795. 25 folding illustrated plates, recent quarter calf and marbled boards, some light marginal worming, text browned and foxed in parts, plates better condition, clean tear in plate xxii, overall nice set. James Tait Goodrich   S74 - 193   2013 $750

Nicholson, William *The Pirate Twins.* London: Faber & Faber, 1929. Special edition, limited to 60 numbered copies signed by Nicholson, color lithographs, oblong 8vo., pictorial boards, magnificent copy, very rare.   Aleph-Bet Books, Inc.   104 - 388   2013 $6500

Nicholson, William *The Square Book of Animals.* London: Heinemann, 1900. First edition, 4to., cloth backed boards, covers somewhat darkened and tips rubbed, else fine, 12 magnificent full page color woodblock illustrations. Aleph-Bet Books, Inc.   105 - 427   2013 $2000

Nickel, George Wilmarth *Following the Cattle King.* Berkeley: Bancroft Library Regional Oral History Office, 2002. First edition, quarto, mounted frontispiece in color, numerous black and white and color photos, reproductions, blue cloth, gilt, very fine.   Argonaut Book Shop   Recent Acquisitions June 2013 - 218   2013 $125

Nicklaus, Jack *My Golden Lessons 100-Plus Ways to Improve Your Shots...* New York: Simon & Schuster, 2002. First edition, signed and dated by author, 8vo., 176 pages, fine in fine dust jacket.   By the Book, L. C.   36 - 73   2013 $250

Nicklin, Susan *Address to a Young Lady on Her Entrance into the World.* London: printed for Hookham and Carpter, 1796. 1 volumes, 8vo., slight tears to inner edge of titlepage volume I small hole at foot of A1 affecting signature letter (probably printing fault), slight damp marks to fore edge final three leaves, old rather faint waterstaining towards end of volume II, full contemporary tree calf, gilt spines decorated with sunburst and floral devices, black morocco labels, spines rubbed, slight abrasions to boards, corners bumped, scarce.   Jarndyce Antiquarian Booksellers   CCIV - 218   2013   £580

Nidever, George *Life and Adventures of George Nidever (1802-1883).* Berkeley: University of California Press, 1937. First edition, 3 plates, facsimile, dark peach cloth lettered in gilt and dark green, very fine, with printed dust jacket (fading to spine and top edge of jacket).   Argonaut Book Shop   Summer 2013 - 254   2013 $90

Niedecker, Lorine *My Friend Tree. Poems.* Edinburgh: Wild Hawthorn Press, 1961. First edition, oblong 8vo., original wrappers, dust jacket, extremely rare, fine association copy, inscribed by author for her publisher Jonathan Williams.   James S. Jaffe Rare Books   Fall 2013 - 108   2013 $7500

Nietzsche, Friedrich *The Birth of Tragedy or Hellenism and Pessimism.* Edinburgh: T. N. Foulis, 1910. Volume One of the complete works, 2nd edition, no. 2876 of 3000 copies, 20cm., near fine in publishers' blue cloth with some light rubbing to boards, age toning to endpapers.   Between the Covers Rare Books, Inc.   Philosophy - 339939   2013 $75

Nietzsche, Friedrich *The Case of Wagner.* Edinburgh: T. N. Foulis, 1911. Volume 8 of the complete works, first edition, no. 1194 of 1500 copies, 20cm., very good in publisher's blue cloth with rubbing to boards and light soiling to endpapers, owner's signature, W. J. Kingsland Jr.   Between the Covers Rare Books, Inc.   Philosophy - 339996   2013 $125

Nietzsche, Friedrich *The Dawn of Day.* Edinburgh: T. N. Foulis, 1911. Volume 9 of the Complete Works, no. 1158 of 1500 copies, 20cm., very good in publisher's blue cloth with rubbing to boards, age toning to endpapers.   Between the Covers Rare Books, Inc.   Philosophy - 34000   2013 $125

Nietzsche, Friedrich *Early Greek Philosophy and Other Essays.* London & Edinburgh: T. N. Foulis, 1911. Number 1271 of 1500 copies, 20 cm., very good in publisher's green cloth with light scuffng to front board and bottom edge and age toning to endpapers, else near fine.   Between the Covers Rare Books, Inc.   Philosophy - 339938   2013 $270

Nietzsche, Friedrich *The Joyful Wisdom.* London: T. N. Foulis, n.d., Second edition (no. 450 of 1250 copies), 20 cm., very good in publisher's blue cloth with rubbing to boards, age toning to endpapers, light staining and chipping to bottom edges.   Between the Covers Rare Books, Inc.   Philosophy - 240002   2013 $100

Nietzsche, Friedrich *On the Future of Our Educational Institutions, Homer and Classical Philology.* Edinburgh: T. N. Foulis, 1910. Volume 3 of complete works, second edition, number 1498 of 3000 copies, very good in publisher's blue cloth with light rubbing to boards and age toning to endpapers, else near fine.   Between the Covers Rare Books, Inc.   Philosophy - 339939   2013 $75

Nietzsche, Friedrich *Thus Spake Zarathustra.* Edinburgh: T. N. Foulis, 1914. Volume 11 of the complete works, third edition, no. 887 of 2000 copies, 20 cm., very good in publisher's blue cloth with rubbing to boards, thin white stain along fore edge of front board and light age toning to endpapers, owner's signature in neat ink on front endpaper.   Between the Covers Rare Books, Inc.   Philosophy - 340005   2013 $65

Nietzsche, Friedrich *The Twilight of the Idols: The Antichrist.* Edinburgh: T. N. Foulis, 1912. Volume 16 of the collected works part 1 is third edition (no. 189 of 1000), part 2 is third edition (no. 2025 of 3000 copies), 20cm., 2 volumes, near fine in publisher's blue cloth, light rubbing to boards and age toning to endpapers.   Between the Covers Rare Books, Inc.   Philosophy - 339940   2013 $225

Night Visions 4. Arlington Heights: Dark Harvest, 1988. First edition, one of 500 numbered copies, signed by all contributors, fine in fine dust jacket and fine slipcase, illustrations by Kevin Davies.   Between the Covers Rare Books, Inc.   Sci-Fi, Fantasy & Horror - 306903   2013 $100

Night Visions 6. Arlington Heights: Dark Harvest, 1988. First edition, one of 600 numbered copies, signed by all contributors and illustrator, Phil Parks, fine in fine dust jacket and fine slipcase.   Between the Covers Rare Books, Inc.   Sci-Fi, Fantasy & Horror - 312712   2013 $65

Nightingale, B. *Lancashire Nonconformity... Volume II.* Manchester: John Heywood, 1891. First edition, original cloth gilt, extremities trifle frayed, 32 illustrations, flyleaves rather browned.   R. F. G. Hollett & Son   Wesleyan Methodism - 20   2013   £65

Nightingale, B. *Lancashire Nonconformity; or Sketches, Historical and Descriptive of the Congregational and Old Presbyterian Churches in the County. Volume III: the Churches of Manchester, Oldham, Ashton &c.* Manchester: John Heywood, 1893. First edition, large paper copy, thick 4to., original cloth, gilt , head of spine worn away, foot little nicked, 45 illustrations.   R. F. G. Hollett & Son   Wesleyan Methodism - 19   2013   £180

Nightingale, Florence 1820-1910 *Notes on Nursing; What It Is and What It Is Not.* New York: D. Appleton, 1860. First American edition, 12mo., 140 pages, original cloth, portion of front endleaf lacking.   M & S Rare Books, Inc.   95 - 266   2013 $550

Nihon Fuzouku (Japanese Customs). Osaka: printed by Oshima Yosuke for Tsujiko Kumataro 2550, 1890. 2 volumes, 16mo., 26, 27 pages, frenchfold color pictorial paper with sewn bindings, housed in original pictorial envelope holder, this set in fine condition, fine illustrations.   Aleph-Bet Books, Inc.   104 - 297   2013 $1250

Nims, John Frederick *The Six Cornered Snowflake.* New York: Sea Cliff Press, 1991. First edition, one of only 60 copies numbered and signed by Nims and Dean Bornstein, this copy no.5, an author's copy, lovely accordion folded paper bound in paper covered boards, printed sleeve, fine.   Beasley Books   2013 - 2013 $100

Nin, Anais *D. H. Lawrence: an Unprofessional Study.* Paris: Edward W. Titus, 1932. First edition, one of 550 copies, of which 500 were numbered 1 to 500 for subscribers, this copy #425; 203 x 133mm., publisher's black buckram, gilt titling on upper cover and spine, in original green dust jacket, 2 facsimile ms. pages from "Lady Chatterley's Lover", jacket with little fading, couple of tiny chips to head edge of jacket, little fading, couple of tiny chips to head edge of jacket, spine very slightly cocked, but really excellent copy, bright and clean in well preserved jacket.   Phillip J. Pirages   63 - 356   2013 $600

Nin, Anais *House of Incest.* Paris: Siana Editions, 1936. First edition, one of 249 copies, 4to. pages 89, stain to endpapers and blanks opposite frontispiece by Ian Hugo and in rear, printed wrappers, some shelfwear and browning, front hinge strengthened, nice, untrimmed copy in cloth slipcase.   Second Life Books Inc.   183 - 292   2013 $1250

Nininger, Harvey H. *Find a Falling Star.* New York: Paul S. Erikkson, 1972. First edition, 8vo., x, 254 pages, near fine, owner name, age darkening to page edges, inscribed, signed and dated by author.   By the Book, L. C.   36 - 99   2013 $175

Nitsch, Friedrich August *A General and Introductory View of Professor Kant's Principles Concerning Man, The World and the Deity...* London: J. Downes, 1796. First edition, 8vo., very good++, modern quarter leather with gilt lettering on morocco spine label, owner name to titlepage, minimal cover edge wear, marginal note in ink, scarce.   By the Book, L. C.   38 - 27   2013 $1200

Nixon, Richard Milhous *The Inaugural Address of Richard Milhous Nixon, President of the United States.* Worcester: Achille J. St. Onge, n.d. circa, 1969. Limited to 1500 copies, 6.6 x 4.6cm., full leather, all edges gilt, tipped in frontispiece portrait, printed in Holland by Enschede on handmade Hayle paper made at the Hayle mill in England, this copy signed by Nixon beneath frontispiece portrait, from the collection of Donn W. Sanford.   Oak Knoll Books   303 - 27   2013 $750

Noah's Ark Primer. Syracuse: Handford Manufacturing, 1912. 5 x 7 inches, pictorial wrappers, some edge fraying, else very good, illustrations on every page in full color.   Aleph-Bet Books, Inc.   104 - 19   2013 $225

Noble, Joseph A. *From Cab to Caboose. Fifty Years of Railroading.* Norman: University of Oklahoma Press, 1964. First edition, photos, map, black cloth, very fine, pictorial dust jacket.   Argonaut Book Shop   Summer 2013 - 255   2013 $50

Noel, Augusta *Effie's Friends; or Chronicles of the Woods and Shore.* London: James Nisbet, 1865. Second edition, original blue cloth, gilt over bevelled boards, extremities little worn, decorated title and chapter head and tails, joints cracking and rather shaken in places.   R. F. G. Hollett & Son   Children's Books - 418   2013   £65

Noel, R. R. *Grundzuge der Phenolgie oder Anleitung zum Studium Dieser Wissenschaft...* Leipzig: Arnold, 1842. Frontispiece, 6 engraved plates, 19th century quarter brown linen spine with green patterned boards, some wear to bindings, ownership markings on title, otherwise very good. James Tait Goodrich   S74 - 2-9   2013 $495

Nolhac, Pierre De *The Trianon of Marie Antoinette.* London: T. Fisher Unwin Ltd., 1925. First edition in English, 222 x 146mm., 234 pages (2) leaves (ads), quite pretty contemporary dark blue three quarter morocco, raised bands, spine gilt in panels containing three closely spaced intricately gilt harp ornaments (with cresting rolls above and below), marbled sides and endpapers, top edge gilt, other edges rough trimmed, frontispiece, 4 photos; spine slightly sunned toward a pleasing dark blue green, one leaf with three inch tear from fore edge into text due to rough opening, otherwise fine with only trivial imperfections, bright, attractive binding unworn.   Phillip J. Pirages   63 - 328   2013 $275

Norden, Hermann *White and Black in East Africa...* Boston: Small Maynard and Co., 1924. First American edition, 304 pages, fine in good or better dust jacket with several chips, illustrations.   Between the Covers Rare Books, Inc.   165 - 321a   2013 $275

Norden, John *A Mirror for the Multitude, or Glasse, Wherein Maie be Seene the Violence, the Error, the Weakness and Rash Content of the Multitude and the Dangerous Resolution of Such as Without Regard of the Truth...* London: printed by John Windet, 1586. First edition, 8vo., ornate border to titlepage, headpieces and some woodcut initials, printer's waste used as r.f.e.p., small marginal hole to titlepage, little dampstaining to bottom margin page 49 onwards, few spots and smudges, 17th century brown calf, small paper label to spine, blind tooled triple fillet to spine and borders, single gilt fillet to edges 'Edward Gwynn' in gilt to upper board and initials E.G. to lower board, joints little creased, upper inner hinge splitting a little but binding strong, endpapers soiled, small label pasted to bottom of titlepage reading "Ex Bibliotheca . Cl. Eusebii Renaudot quam Monasterio sancti Germani a Pratis legacvit anno Domini 1720", also to titlepage in ink, E. 1714 and old MS note opposite.   Unsworths Antiquarian Booksellers   28 - 118   2013   £3000

Nordenskiold, Gustaf *Ruiner af Klippbonigar I Mesa Verde's Canons. (The Cliff Dwellers of the Mesa Verde).* Stockholm: P. A. Norstedt & Soners Florlag, 1893. First edition, 193 pages, folio, original maroon cloth with decorative blindstamped borders to front and backstrip, title gilt stamped on backstrip, near fine, minor rubbing to corners of boards, subtle fading to backstrip, text in Swedish.   Ken Sanders Rare Books   45 - 38   2013 $1250

Norman, Howard *The Bird Artist.* New York: Farrar, 1994. First edition, fine in fine dust jacket with bookstore's original price sticker still in place on rear panel.   Beasley Books   2013 - 2013 $50

Norman, W. H. *Journals of the Voyage and Proceedings of HMCS "Victoria" in search of Shipwrecked People at the Auckland and Other Islands.* Melbourne: John Ferres, 1865? 8vo., recent half calf.   Maggs Bros. Ltd.   1467 - 87   2013   £950

Norris, Frank 1870-1902 *Complete Works of Frank Norris.* New York: Doubleday Page, 1903. First collected edition, number 98 of 100 numbered copies, 7 volumes, large 8vo., tan buckram spines, blue paper boards, blue paper labels, gilt lettering, untrimmed, frontispiece and 3 plates in volume 6, frontispiece in volume 7 as called for, cloth and boards somewhat stained and worn, very good set.   The Brick Row Book Shop   Miscellany Fifty-Nine - 32   2013 $850

Norris, John *A Collection of Miscellanies; Consisting of Poems, Essays, Discourses and Letters, Occasionally Written. (bound with) The Theory and Regulation of Love.* Oxford: printed at the Theatre for John Crosley, 1687. Oxford: printed at the Theatre for Hen. Clements, 1688. First edition, engraved vignette on title, slightly browned and one or two spots; second work large or thick paper copy, 8vo., bound together in contemporary calf, blind ruled borders ons ides, roll tooled border at inner edge repeated an inch out, spine gilt in compartments, red lettering piece, rebacked, preserving original spine, covers rubbed and with some craquelure, contemporary ownership inscription at head of dedication "S. Pendarves 89", few notes in his hand to text of Miscellanies, 18th century inscription of Eliz. Kekenick, Norris's Postscript, retracting the Considerations upon the nature of Sin, copied out apparently in her hand on verso of its sectional title, good.   Blackwell's Rare Books   B174 - 109   2013   £750

North, J. D. *Stars, Minds and Fate: Essays in Ancient and Medieval Cosmology.* London and Ronceverte: Hambledon Press, 1989. 8vo., green cloth, gilt stamped cover and spine titles, ownership signature, fine, rare.   Jeff Weber Rare Books   169 - 325   2013 $75

North, Mary Remsen *Down the Colorado by a Lone Girl.* New York: 1930. First edition, xiii, 164 pages, ads, illustrations, clean, very good, no dust jacket.   Dumont Maps & Books of the West   125 - 66   2013 $75

North, Robert Carver *Bob North with Dog Team and Indians.* G. P. Putnam's Sons, 1929. First edition, original cloth, gilt, 24 illustrations and pictorial endpapers.   R. F. G. Hollett & Son   Polar Exploration - 45   2013   £30

North, Thomas *A Chronicle of the Church of S. Martin In Leicester During the Reigns of Henry VIII Edward VI Mary and Elizabeth with some Account of its Minor Altars and Ancient Guilds. (with) The Accounts of the Churchwardens of S. Martin's, Leicester 1489-1844.* London: Bell and Daldy, Leicester: Crossley and Clarke, Leicester: Samuel Clarke, 1866. 1884, 2 volumes, 8vo., very slightly browned to edges, some spotting, not affecting text or illustrations, some staining to rear pastedown to volume I, bound uniformly in brown cloth, gilt lettering to spine, blindstamp decorations to both volumes, little bumped and worn to extremities in both volumes, but binding sound, volume I, author's inscription and ALS tipped to front pastedown, ownership signatures one of P. A. Slack, bookplate of antiquary John Edwin Cussans.   Unsworths Antiquarian Booksellers   28 - 189   2013   £80

Northbrook, Thomas George Baring, Earl of *The Northbrook Gallery.* London: S. Low Martson, Searle and Rivington, 1885. 36 black and white plates with letterpress tissue guards, folio, full pebble tan calf, gilt rules and fillets to boards, raised bands, six compartments with gilt titles, and rules, elaborate inner gilt dentelles, top edge gilt, marbled endpapers, very good, extremities rubbed wear to upper fore corner, binding tight, leaves crisp, handsome copy.   Kaaterskill Books   16 - 64   2013 $500

Northcote, William *The Anatomy of the Human Body.* 8vo., full modern brown calf with raised bands and gilt leather spine label in red, endpapers renewed, titlepage repaired with top and bottom margins repaired which has resulted in eliminating the first line "The" from title, text has some soiling and foxing of paper, nice, rebound in fine modern calf.   James Tait Goodrich   S74 - 194   2013 $850

Northleigh, John *Topographical Descriptions with Historico-Political Observations...* London: Tooke, 1702. First edition, 2 parts in 1 volume, 8vo., 2 leaves of catalog creased and lightly soiled, contemporary brown panelled calf, scuff mark on upper cover, good copy.   J. & S. L. Bonham Antiquarian Booksellers   Europe - 8398   2013   £350

Norton, Andre *The Beast Master.* New York: Harcourt Brace and Co., 1959. First edition, foxing confined to endpapers (and jacket flaps), else fine in very near fine dust jacket, signed by author, scarce in nice condition, uncommon signed.   Between the Covers Rare Books, Inc.   Sci-Fi, Fantasy & Horror - 91271   2013 $1250

Norton, Mary *Are All the Giants Dead?* London: Dent, 1975. First edition, 8vo., faint stain on last leaf of text, very good in dust jacket with one closed tear and faint stain on rear edge, illustrations by Brian Froud with color dust jacket (front and back) in black and white, tipped in bookplate reproducing illustration on back of book, signed by Norton. Aleph-Bet Books, Inc.   105 - 430   2013 $200

Norton, Mary *The Borrowers Afield.* New York: Harcourt Brace and Co., 1955. First US edition, octavo, illustrations by Beth and Joe Krush, cloth.   L. W. Currey, Inc.   Fall Sampler Sept. 2013 - 146481   2013 $100

Norton, Mary Beth *Guide to Historical Literature.* New York: Oxford, 1995. Third edition, 2 volumes, small 4to., red cloth, edges slightly soiled, else nice set.   Second Life Books Inc.   183 - 295   2013 $75

Norwood, R. W. *Driftwood.* North Sydney: W. Lane, Dec., 1898. 12mo., green card covers, printed on heavy bound paper, cover has few small waterstains and edges worn. Schooner Books Ltd.   101 - 112   2013 $55

Nostradamus *The True Prophecies or Prognostications of Michael Nostradamus.* London: Thomas Radcliffe and Nathaniel Thompson, 1672. First English edition, small folio, engraved frontispiece, decorated woodcut initials and headpieces, titlepage printed in red and black, contemporary mottled calf, neatly rebacked, retaining original red morocco lettering label spine with five raised bands, gilt board edges, marbled edges, 18th century armorial bookplate of Sir George Cooke of Westminster, slightly browned, otherwise very good.   Heritage Book Shop   50th Anniversary Catalogue - 77   2013 $11,000

Nostradamus, Michael *The Complete Fortune-Teller Being the Magic Mirror of....* London: Lawrence and Bullen Ltd., 1899. First edition, elaborately illustrated yellow boards with front board die-cut and revolving disk inset on verso of front board, owner's pencil name, boards little soiled, small stain, little fraying top one corner, else very good, exceptionally uncommon.   Between the Covers Rare Books, Inc.   Sci-Fi, Fantasy & Horror - 299310   2013 $800

Notes Respecting the Church of St. Peter, Ballyodan and County of Cork. London: printed by the Boys of the Door-Step Brigade, 1874. 54 pages, 4to., all edges gilt, half leather, rubbed, very good.   C. P. Hyland   261 - 16   2013   £120

Nott, J. C. *Indigenous Races of the Earth, or New Chapters of Ethnological Enquiry.* Philadelphia & London: 1857. First edition, 4to., 656 pages, lacking original wrappers and most of spine, folding table, litho frontispiece and 8 plates, fore and bottom edges uncut, some soiling to frontispiece, internally fine.   M & S Rare Books, Inc.   95 - 269   2013 $450

Nott, Stanley Charles *Voices from the Flowery Kingdom.* New York: Chinese Culture Study of America, 1947. First edition, limited to 500 signed copies, this number 172, very good+, mild sun spine, foxing, mild soil to edges, in good+ dust jacket with 2 inch piece missing, dust jacket spine tip affecting title, 2 inch piece missing from jacket lower spine tip affecting publisher, chips and soil, 4to., scarce.   By the Book, L. C.   38 - 67   2013 $500

Nourse, Alan Edward *Trouble on Titan.* Philadelphia: Toronto: John C. Winston Co., 1954. First edition, octavo, cloth.   L. W. Currey, Inc.   Fall Sampler Sept. 2013 - 146544   2013 $350

Nouvelle Ecole Publique des Finances ou l'Art de Voler sans Ailes par Toutes les Regions du Monde. Paris: Chez Robert le Turc, rue d'enfer a la Hache d'Or, 1707. First edition, title printed in red and black, woodcut device, 12mo., contemporary speckled calf, rubbed, joints cracked but cords holding, armorial bookplate of Sir John Eden, Bart, good.   Blackwell's Rare Books   172 - 17   2013   £950

Nova Scotia Furnishing Co, *Catalogue No. 6 "The Complete Home Furnisher".* Halifax: Nova Scotia Furnishing Co., 1900's, 9.25 x 7.25 inches, decorative card covers in black and red, black and white illustrations, some have red 'cancelled' stamp, covers badly worn and front cover detached, spine torn, titlepage detached, few small tears to edges.   Schooner Books Ltd.   101 - 115   2013 $125

Nova Scotia Historical Society *Collections of the Nova Scotia Historical Society for the Year 1892. Volume VIII.* Halifax: Nova Scotia Historical Society, 1895. 8vo., paper covered boards, covers slightly worn, interior good. Schooner Books Ltd.   105 - 90   2013 $75

Novik, Naomi *Temeraire, Throne of Jake, Black Powder War and Empire of Ivory.* London: Harper Voyager, 2006-2007. First British and first hardbound editions, small 4to. and 8vo., 4 volumes, one of 100 copies numbered and signed by author on titlepage, fine in fine dust jackets.   Ed Smith Books   75 - 50   2013 $2250

Nunez, Antonio *Distribucion de Las Obras Ordinarias y Extraordinarias del dia, Para Hazerlas Perfectamente...* En Mexico: por la Viuda de Miguel de Ribera Calderon, 1712. First and only edition, 16 pages, titlepage set within typographic border, and one woodcut in text, very good in full contemporary limp vellum with original ties, some very slight foxing and vellum now mellowed in color.   Ken Spelman Books Ltd.   75 - 13   2013   £495

Nunn, D. Merlin *Spiraling Out of Control Lessons Learned from a Boy in Trouble December 2006.* Halifax: 2006. Quarto, pages xvi, 381, card covers, very good.   Schooner Books Ltd.   105 - 92   2013 $55

Nunn, Kem *Tapping the Source.* New York: Delacorte Press, 1984. First edition, fine in fine dust jacket, signed by author, from the library of Bruce Kahn. Between the Covers Rare Books, Inc. Mystery & Detective Fiction - 302254 2013 $350

Nunn, Kem *Tijuana Straits.* New York: Scribner, 2004. First edition, fine in fine dust jacket, signed by author, from the library of Bruce Kahn. Between the Covers Rare Books, Inc. Mystery & Detective Fiction - 392223 2013 $65

Nura *All Aboard We Are Off.* New York: The Studio Publications and Junior Literary Guild, 1944. 4to., cloth, fine in dust jacket (very good+, rubbed at folds and frayed st spine ends), beautiful color and black and white at deco style color lithographs. Aleph-Bet Books, Inc. 105 - 434 2013 $200

Nursery ABC. Akron: Saalfield, 1906. Some soil, fraying and creasing, good+, on printed cloth, illustrations in bright colors. Aleph-Bet Books, Inc. 104 - 17 2013 $125

Nursery ABC and Simple Speller. New York: McLoughlin Bros., n.d., circa, 1870. 8vo., pictorial wrappers (12) pages including covers, slight cover wear, else near fine. Aleph-Bet Books, Inc. 104 - 13 2013 $350

Nursery Colored Picture Book. New York: McLoughlin Bros. circa, 1870. 4to., cloth, pictorial paste-on, edges rubbed, very good+, 16 full page chromolithographs, uncommon. Aleph-Bet Books, Inc. 104 - 343 2013 $400

Nursery Rhyme Rag Book. London: Dean, n.d. circa, 1910. 4to., pictorial cloth, some wear and soil very good, full page color illustrations by Drayton, printed on cloth, rare. Aleph-Bet Books, Inc. 105 - 203 2013 $450

Nusbaumer, Louis *Valley of Salt, Memories of Wine. A Journal of Death Valley 1849.* Berkeley: Friends of the Bancroft Library, 1967. First edition, 67 pages, portrait, facsimile, illustrations, from photos by Ansel Adams, folding map by Robert Becker, light green cloth, fine. Argonaut Book Shop Recent Acquisitions June 2013 - 215 2013 $60

Nuttall, Thomas *Journal of Travels into the Arkansa (sic) territory During the Year 1819.* Philadelphia: printed and published by Thos. H. Palmer, 1821. First edition, five aquatint plates, folding map, one plate in facsimile but an original of the same image, from another copy, laid in (blank borders bit trimmed), outer hinges cracked but cords strong, paper spine fragile with some fading, some spotting or light foxing within, but fine, untrimmed, housed in sumptuous half morocco custom slipcase, bookplate of collector Herbert McLean Evans, excessively rare. Argonaut Book Shop Summer 2013 - 257 2013 $6000

Nuttall, Thomas *A Journal of Travels into the Arkansas Territory During the Year 1819.* Norman: University of Oklahoma Press, 1980. First edition thus, frontispiece, reproductions, plates, maps, gray cloth lettered in silver, very fine with pictorial dust jacket. Argonaut Book Shop Summer 2013 - 258 2013 $75

Nuttall, Thomas *Manual of the Ornithology of the United States and Canada and the Water Birds.* Boston: Hilliard Gray and Co., 1834. First edition, good+, brown cloth, 8vo., 627 pages, foxing mainly to endpapers, very top of spine torn. Barnaby Rudge Booksellers Natural History 2013 - 021249 2013 $150

O

O'Bannon, Romonia Gray *Zora's House.* New York: Vantage Press, 1995. First edition, illustrations by Jane Kucharnik, fine in fine dust jacket with couple of tiny marks on front panel, scarce. Between the Covers Rare Books, Inc. 165 - 111 2013 $175

O'Brian, Patrick *The Road to Samarcand.* Rupert Hart Davis, 1954. First edition, original cloth, gilt, dust jacket, edges little worn and spine slightly dulled, label removed, leaving few slight paste stains. R. F. G. Hollett & Son Children's Books - 420 2013 £350

O'Brian, Patrick *The Unknown Shore.* London: Rupert Hart-Davis, 1959. First edition, original cloth, gilt, dust jacket trifle worn, spine faded, scarce. R. F. G. Hollett & Son Children's Books - 421 2013 £350

O'Brian, Patrick *The Yellow Admiral.* New York: W. W. Norton, 1996. First edition, signed by author, 8vo., fine in fine dust jacket. By the Book, L. C. 38 - 97 2013 $400

O'Brien, Darcy *A Way of Life, Like Any Other.* London: Martin Britain & O'Keefe, 1977. Proof copy, 8vo., original yellow wrappers, author's pencilled corrections sprinkled throughout, inscribed by publisher Timothy O'Keefe, excellent copy. Maggs Bros. Ltd. 1442 - 363 2013 £175

O'Brien, Edward *The Lawyer, His Character and Rule of Holy Life.* London: William Pickering, 1842. First edition, 167 x 105mm., pleasing contemporary rose colored pebble grain morocco by Birdsall & Son (stamp signed), covers with multiple blind rule frame, raised bands, spine compartments ruled in blind, gilt tooling, gilt ruled turn-ins, marbled endpapers, all edges gilt, decorative frame on titlepage, headpieces and tailpieces, spine somewhat faded, joints and extremities little rubbed, one opening with offsetting from old laid-in clipping, excellent copy, clean and fresh internally, sound, well executed binding. Phillip J. Pirages 63 - 310 2013 $175

O'Brien, Flann *The Third Policeman.* MacGibbon & Kee, 1967. First edition, pages 200, 8vo. original dark brown boards, backstrip gilt lettered, dust jacket, very good. Blackwell's Rare Books 172 - 223 2013 £450

O'Brien, George *Dancehall Days.* Leamington Spa: Sixth Chamber Press, 1988. First edition, number XXI of 25 roman numeral copies, signed by author, 8vo., original quarter green leather, marbled paper boards, fine in matching green cloth slipcase (slightly rubbed). Maggs Bros. Ltd. 1442 - 253 2013 £125

O'Brien, Henry *The Round Towers of Ireland; or the Mysteries of Freemasonry of Sabaism and of Budhism for the First Time Unveiled.* 1834. First edition, half calf, 4 plates, many text illustrations, quarter leather, not a pretty copy but it has owner inscription of the doyen of Cork antiquaries, John Windele, pasted to front loose leaf an appreciation of O'Brien from "A Gallery of Literary Characters No. LXIII" and on rear free endpaper some correspondence by Windele and another from the Southern Reporter. C. P. Hyland 261 - 620 2013 £250

O'Brien, R. Barry *A Hundred Years of Irish History.* Pitman, 1911. Second edition, 184 pages + 24 page publisher's catalog, very good, owner inscribed by Frederick MacNeice. C. P. Hyland 261 - 621 2013 £30

O'Brien, Sophie *Golden Memories. The Love Letters and Prison Letters of William O'Brien.* 1929. First edition of volume I, 2nd impression of volume 2, 2 volumes, 8vo., cloth, good, dust jacket, signed presentation copy. C. P. Hyland 261 - 624 2013 £50

O'Brien, Tim *Northern Lights.* New York: Delacorte/Seymour Lawrence, 1975. First edition, bookplate signed by author laid in, poorly made book is actually perfect bound hardback with pages glued into boards, as issued, nearly fine, some light fading to boards, as usual, but in fine dust jacket. Ed Smith Books 75 - 52 2013 $950

O'Brien, Tim *Speaking of Courage.* Santa Barbara: Neville, 1980. First edition, presentation copy inscribed to Mary Dumont Nov. 7 1980, from author, bound in same green cloth as the 300 numbered copies, with spine and cover labels, there was also a deluxe edition of 26 lettered copies (bound in leather), this one marked "Presentation Copy", original glassine (one chip), issued without printed dust jacket, near fine. Ed Smith Books 75 - 51 2013 $300

O'Bryen, Christopher *Naval Evolutions; or a System of Sea-Discipline, Extracted from the Celebrated Treatise of P. L'Hoste, Professor of Mathematics...* London: printed for W. Johnston, 1762. 4to., large uncut copy, expertly bound in recent quarter calf, marbled boards, vellum tips, gilt spine, red morocco label. Jarndyce Antiquarian Booksellers CCIV - 219 2013 £1800

O'Callaghan, E. B. *Laws and Ordinances of New Netherland 1638-1674.* Albany: Weed, Parsons and Co., 1868. First edition, contemporary half morocco and marbled paper covered boards with wax seal of State of New York on spine, xxxii, 602 pages, bookplate, light wear to extremities, handsome near fine.   Between the Covers Rare Books, Inc.   New York City - 291414   2013 $750

O'Callaghan, Jeremiah *Atheism of Brownson's Review. Unity & Trinity of God...* Burlington: 1852. First edition, 308 pages, faint staining to early leaves, 8vo., original cloth (some wear), good, sound copy.   C. P. Hyland   261 - 628   2013   £60

O'Callaghan, Jeremiah *Usury, Funds and Banks...* London: printed for the author, 1834. 380 pages, 8vo., cloth, very good.   C. P. Hyland   261 - 627   2013   £250

O'Callaghan, Jeremiah *Usury or Interest Proved to be Repugnant in Divine and Ecclesiastical Laws and Descriptive to Civil Society.* London: C. Clements, 1825. First London edition, 8vo., boards with paper spine, very good.   C. P. Hyland   261 - 625   2013   £350

O'Callaghan, Jeremiah *Usury or Interest Proved to be Repugnant in Divine and Ecclesiastical Laws and Descriptive to Civil Society.* London: Cobbett, 1828. Second edition, 8vo., original quarter cloth with original spine label (small tear on spine cloth), text spotless.   C. P. Hyland   261 - 626   2013   £375

O'Callaghan, John *History of the Irish Brigades in the Service of France.* 1854. First edition, viii 451 pages, 8 pages ads, 8vo., original cloth, hinges broken, text very good.   C. P. Hyland   261 - 629   2013   £90

O'Connell, Carol *Mallory's Oracle.* New York: G. P. Putnams Sons, 1994. First edition, fine in fine dust jacket, signed by author, from the library of Bruce Kahn.   Between the Covers Rare Books, Inc.   Mystery & Detective Fiction - 301912   2013 $65

O'Connell, Daniel *The Correspondence of Daniel O'Connell. Volume II. 1814-1823.* IUP for IMC, 1972. 543 pages, 8vo., cloth, dust jacket, very good.   C. P. Hyland   261 - 632   2013   £50

O'Connell, Daniel *The Correspondence of Daniel O'Connell. Volume III 1824-1828.* IUP for IMC, 1974. 8vo., 441 pages, cloth, dust jacket, very good.   C. P. Hyland   261 - 633   2013   £50

O'Connell, Daniel *The Correspondence of Daniel O'Connell. Volume IV 1829-1832.* IUP for IMC, 1977. 494 pages, 8vo., cloth, dust jacket, very good.   C. P. Hyland   261 - 634   2013   £50

O'Connell, M. J., Mrs. *The Last Colonel of the Irish Brigade.* 1977. Tower reprint, 2 volumes in 1, 8vo., cloth, dust jacket, fine.   C. P. Hyland   261 - 635   2013   £60

O'Connell's Cork Almanack 1894. 16 + 116 pages, 8vo., original wrappers (light stain on lower fore corner), good.   C. P. Hyland   261 - 209   2013   £25

O'Connor, Flannery 1925-1964 *Everything that Rises Must Converge.* New York: Farrar, 1965. First edition, near fine with trace of sunning to top edge, fine dust jacket, 269 pages.   Beasley Books   2013 - 2013 $100

O'Connor, Frank 1903-1966 *Bones of Contention.* London: Macmillan, 1936. First edition, 8vo., original red cloth, near fine, dusty on top and slightly darkened on spine,.   Maggs Bros. Ltd.   1442 - 255   2013   £150

O'Connor, Frank 1903-1966 *The Saint and Mary Kate.* London: Macmillan, 1932. First edition, 8vo., original green cloth, near fine, dust jacket lightly nicked at head of spine and faintly rubbed at corners.   Maggs Bros. Ltd.   1442 - 254   2013   £175

O'Connor, G. B. *Elizabethan Ireland, Native and English.* n.d. circa, 1903. 8vo., folding maps, cloth, good.   C. P. Hyland   261 - 637   2013   £100

O'Connor, G. B. *Stuart Ireland, Catholic & Protestant.* 1910. First edition, xv, 236 pages, cloth, some light staining on publisher's cloth, else very good.   C. P. Hyland   261 - 638   2013   £55

O'Connor, Joseph *Ghost Light.* London: Harvill Secker, 2010. First edition, number 19 of 75 specially bound copies, signed by author, 8vo., original full green leather lettered gilt, cream scroll design on upper cover, decorated paper endpapers, fine in matching slipcase.   Maggs Bros. Ltd.   1442 - 257   2013   £175

O'Connor, Joseph *True Believers.* London: Sinclair Stevenson, 1991. First edition, large 8vo., original black cloth, fine in dust jacket, inscribed by author for Ian.   Maggs Bros. Ltd.   1442 - 256   2013   £50

O'Conor, Matthew *The Irish Brigades; or Memoirs of the Most Eminent Irish Military Commanders Who Distinguished Themselves in the Elizabethan and Wiliamite Wars in their Own Country...* Dublin: 1855. First edition, 8vo., original cloth, subjected to amatuerish repairs, ex-library C. P. Curran (Francis Henry bookplate).   C. P. Hyland   261 - 639   2013   £160

O'Croly, David *A Farewell Address to the Roman Catholics of the Diocese of Cork.* Dublin: Milliken, 1836. 35 pages, printed wrappers, very good.   C. P. Hyland   261 - 641   2013   £45

O'Daly, Aenghus *The Tribes of Ireland: a Satire.* 1852. First edition, 112 pages, original wrappers, damage to both fore-corners from page 55 (no text affected), else good.   C. P. Hyland   261 - 642   2013   £95

O'Dea, Agnes *Bibliography of Newfoundland.* Toronto: University of Toronto and Memorial University, 1986.   8vo., 2 volumes, illustrated brown cloth boards, half title, 8vo., fine.   Schooner Books Ltd.   101 - 49   2013 $100

O'Dell, Scott *The King's Fifth.* Boston: Houghton Mifflin, 1966.   Stated first edition, illustrations by Samuel Bryant, 8vo., cloth, neat owner inscription on endpaper, else fine in very nice contemporary, no award and seal, price clipped, illustrations by Samuel Bryant.   Aleph-Bet Books, Inc.   104 - 397   2013 $275

O'Donoghue, Bernard *Poaching Rights.* Dublin: Gallery Press, 1986.   First edition, 8vo., original black cloth, dust jacket, inscribed by author for Richard Murphy, fine in slightly rubbed dust jacket, uncommon.   Maggs Bros. Ltd.   1442 - 258   2013   £125

O'Donoghue, D. J. *The Poets of Ireland.* 1901. 1905. Revised edition, Parts I and II (of projected V), 128 pages, octavo, wrappers.   C. P. Hyland   261 - 92   2013   £45

O'Donovan, John *The Antiquities of County Clare.* Clasp, 1997.   First edition, limited to 1000 copies, 8vo., color and black and white illustrations, cloth, dust jacket, very good.   C. P. Hyland   261 - 644   2013   £50

O'Driscoll, Dennis *All the Living.* Minnesota: Traffic Street Press, 2008.   Number 10 of 23 numbered copies (from total edition of 49) initialled by printer and signed by author, large 8vo., original blue decorative Japanese paper wrappers with printed paper label on upper cover, printed letterpress and bound by Paulette Myers-Rich, with etching by Nial Naessens, fine.   Maggs Bros. Ltd.   1442 - 260   2013   £200

O'Driscoll, Dennis *All the Living.* Minnesota: Traffic Street Press, 2008.   First edition, Letter H of 26 lettered copies (from a total edition of 49), initalled by printer and signed by author, large 8vo., original navy blue cloth, printed paper label on upper cover, printed letterpress and bound by Paulette Myers-Rich, etching by Niall Naessens inkjet printed in ultrachrome inks, fine in mustard and blue slipcase, printed paper label on spine.   Maggs Bros. Ltd.   1442 - 259   2013   £250

O'Driscoll, Dennis *Kist.* Mountrath: Dolmen Press, 1982.   First edition, 8vo., original grey wrappers printed in blue, near fine.   Maggs Bros. Ltd.   1442 - 26   2013   £35

O'Faolain, Julia *We Might See Sights and Other Stories.* London: Faber and Faber, 1968.   First edition, original red cloth dust jacket, fine in dust jacket.   Maggs Bros. Ltd. 1442 - 263   2013   £75

O'Faolain, Sean *Midsummer Night Madness.* London: Jonathan Cape, 1932.   First edition, 8vo. original light green cloth, dust jacket, near fine, jacket price clipped and slightly rubbed at extremities of spine.   Maggs Bros. Ltd. 1442 - 264   2013   £225

O'Flaherty, Liam   1897-1984   *The Fairy Goose and Two Other Stories.*   New York: Faber and Gwynn/Crosby Gaige, 1927.   First edition, 16mo., original quarter buckram, shamrock patterned boards, paper label, slight nicking to spine label, else fine, inscribed by author for Percy Muir.   Maggs Bros. Ltd.   1442 - 267   2013   £150

O'Flaherty, Liam   1897-1984   *The Informer.*   1930.   First edition, 8vo., original green cloth, excellent copy, dust jacket lightly nicked at edges.   Maggs Bros. Ltd.   1442 - 266 2013   £1500

O'Flaherty, Liam   1897-1984   *The Martyr.*   London: Victor Gollancz, 1933.   First edition, 8vo., original black cloth, spine lettered green, fine in dust jacket slightly rubbed dust jacket.   Maggs Bros. Ltd.   1442 - 265   2013   £150

O'Flaherty, Liam   1897-1984   *Shame the Devil.*   London: Grayson and Grayson, 1934.   First edition, number 89 of 105 numbered copies, signed by author, 8vo., original red cloth, dust jacket, top edge gilt, others uncut, loosely inserted is page from typescript, with 3 inked corrections in author's hand and half a dozen or so typed emendations, also inserted newspaper cuttings from Sunday Times (April 8 1934) and Daily Telegraph, containing reviews of the book, near fine, dust jacket slightly sunned on spine and nicked at extremities, typescript page twice folded and housed in envelope.   Maggs Bros. Ltd.   1442 - 268   2013   £675

O'Flaherty, Roderic *A Chorographical Description of West Or H-iar Connaught.* Dublin: for the Irish Archaeological Society, 1846.   First edition, small square 4to., recent blue cloth, lettered gilt, excellent copy, from the library of Richard Murphy with his inscription, illustrations by James Hardiman. Maggs Bros. Ltd.   1442 - 269   2013   £175

O'Flanagan, James Roderick *The Blackwater in Munster.* 1844.   First edition, map, 3 plates, original cloth, some foxing, all edges gilt, 8vo.   C. P. Hyland   261 - 650   2013 £200

O'Flanagan, James Roderick *The Blackwater in Munster.* Tower Books, 1975.   8vo., map, 3 plates, cloth, dust jacket, very good.   C. P. Hyland   261 - 651   2013   £120

O'Flanagan, James Roderick *Impressions at Home and Abroad; or a Year of Real Life.* London: Smith, Elder, 1837. First edition, 2 volumes original quarter cloth, worn, labels still on spine but dull, volume I lacks front flyleaf. C. P. Hyland   261 - 649   2013   £200

O'Flanagan, James Roderick *The Munster Circuit.* 1880. First edition, Later publisher's catalog April 1880, 8vo., damage to front hinge, else good, cloth. C. P. Hyland   261 - 652   2013   £30

O'Grady, Desmond *The Gododdin. Ink Paintings by Louis Brocquy.* Dublin: Dolmen Press, 1977. First edition, 4to., original black cloth, dust jacket, limited to 650 copies, fine, dust jacket slightly rubbed. Maggs Bros. Ltd.   1442 - 271   2013   £175

O'Grady, Desmond *Reilly. Roma MCMLXI.* London: Phoenix Press, 1961. First edition, 4to., original black cloth, dust jacket stained and nicked, excellent copy, inscribed, but not signed, by author for Richard Murphy. Maggs Bros. Ltd.   1442 - 270   2013   £150

O'Grady, Standish *Finn and His Companions.* London: T. Fisher Unwin, 1892. First edition, small 8vo., original white cloth, lettered and decorated all over in blue, all edges printed with same pattern in blue, spine browned and covers slightly marked, else excellent. Maggs Bros. Ltd.   1442 - 327   2013   £150

O'Hagan, Andrew *Be Near Me.* Dublin: Tuskar Rock Press, 2006. First edition, numbet IX of 15 roman numeral copies in morocco (only 12 for sale), from a total edition of 75, fine in mid blue slipcase, as issued, 8vo., original full red morocco lettered gilt on spine, with red and yellow head and tail bands, bound by The Fine Bindery. Maggs Bros. Ltd.   1442 - 272   2013   £225

O'Hanlon, John *Life and Scenery in Missouri: Reminiscences of a Missionary Priest.* Dublin: James Duffy & Co. Ltd., 1890. 153 x 99mm., xii, 292 pages, (2) leaves (ads), publisher's green buckram, upper cover with gilt Irish harp wreathed by shamrocks, flat spine with gilt titling, volume tightened, with new endpapers, hint of wear to spine, joints and extremities, other trivial imperfections, but excellent copy, clean and fresh, binding with no significant defects. Phillip J. Pirages   63 - 341   2013 $200

O'Hanlon, Redmond *Joseph Conrad and Charles Darwin.* Edinburgh: Salamander Press, 1984. First edition, inscribed by author, recipient's name, fine in near fine dust jacket with wear at spine extremities, uncommon first book. Ken Lopez Bookseller   159 - 162   2013 $450

O'Hara, Frank *A City Winter and Other Poems.* New York: Tibor De Nagy Gallery, 1951, but, 1952. First edition, one of 20 numbered copies printed by hand in Bodoni types on Japanese Kochi paper by Ruthven Todd, tall 8vo., specially bound with original frontispiece drawing by Larry Rivers and reproductions of 2 drawings by Rivers, original cloth backed decorated boards, the drawing signed by Rivers, edges bit rubbed, spine lightly faded, but very good, rare issue, preserved in scarlet half morocco slipcase. James S. Jaffe Rare Books   Fall 2013 - 109   2013 $15,000

O'Hara, Frank *A City Winter and Other Poems.* New York: Tibor De Nagy Gallery, 1951, i.e., 1952. First edition, deluxe issue, one of 20 numbered copies, specially bound with original frontispiece drawing by Larry Rivers, this copy number 13, tall 8vo., original signed frontispiece drawing and reproductions of 2 drawings by Larry Rivers, original cloth backed decorated boards, the Thomas B. Hess - Elaine de Kooning copy, specially signed by O'Hara, also signed by Hess, with de Kooning's ownership stamp, covers lightly worn, along bottom edge and lower fore-corners, small stain to cloth near top of front panel, one page shows some faint indentations, otherwise very good. James S. Jaffe Rare Books   Fall 2013 - 110   2013 $45,000

O'Hara, Frank *Love Poems.* New York: Tibor de Nagy Gallery, 1965. Limited to 500 copies, this no. 17 of only 20 numbered and signed copies, signed and dated by author, near fine, original printed wrappers with minimal soil, spotting, offsetting from cover design to titlepage, rare, 8vo., 30 pages. By the Book, L. C.   36 - 5   2013 $3000

O'Hara, Frank *Love Poems.* New York: Tibor De Nagy Editions, 1965. First edition, limited to 500 copies, square 8vo., original wrappers, presentation copy inscribed by author for Ted (Berrigan), marvelous association, covers lightly soiled, but very good, enclosed in half leather and marbled board clamshell box. James S. Jaffe Rare Books   Fall 2013 - 116   2013 $5000

O'Hara, Frank *Love Poems (Tentative Title).* New York: Tibor De Nagy Editions, 1965. First edition, one of only 20 copies numbered and signed by author, out of a total edition of 500 copies, square 8vo., original striped wrappers, usual offsetting to titlepage from striped wrappers, otherwise very fine. James S. Jaffe Rare Books   Fall 2013 - 117   2013 $4500

O'Hara, Frank *Lunch Poems.* San Francisco: City Lights Books, 1964. First edition, one of 1500 copies, small 8vo., original printed wrappers, very fine, virtually as new, extremely rare. James S. Jaffe Rare Books   Fall 2013 - 114   2013 $1000

O'Hara, Frank *Meditations in an Emergency.* New York: Grove Press, 1957. First edition, 8vo. this copy numbered "10" and signed by author, original green cloth, publisher's slipcase, some light foxing to endpapers, bit of foxing to cloth, otherwise fine.   James S. Jaffe Rare Books   Fall 2013 - 112   2013 $2500

O'Hara, Frank *Meditations in an Emergency.* New York: Grove Press, 1957. First edition, one of an unknown number of unnumbered (out of series) hardbound copies, small 8vo., original green cloth, glassine dust jacket, presentation copy inscribed by author for poet James Schuyler, very fine, lacking slipcase.   James S. Jaffe Rare Books   Fall 2013 - 113   2013 $7500

O'Hara, Frank *Meditations in an Emergency.* New York: Grove Press, 1957. First edition, 8vo., wrapper issue, review copy with publisher's printed slip laid in, original printed wrappers, very fine, rare in this condition.   James S. Jaffe Rare Books   Fall 2013 - 111   2013 $750

O'Hara, John *Appointment in Samarra.* New York: Harcourt Brace, 1934. First edition, fine in fine, first issue dust jacket, errata slip present, from the Bruce Kahn collection.   Ken Lopez Bookseller   159 - 163   2013 $15,000

O'Hara, Mary *My Friend Flicka.* Philadelphia: J. B. Lippincott, 1941. First edition, faint pencil name on front fly, fine in attractive, very good dust jacket with small nicks and tears at extremities, very slight loss at crown, exceptionally uncommon in dust jacket.   Between the Covers Rare Books, Inc.   Horses, Horsemanship, Horse Racing, Etc. - 97185   2013 $3500

O'Kelly, Eoin *Old Private Banks & Bankers of Munster.* Cambridge University Press, 1959. First edition, xiv 173 pages, original cloth, dust jacket over damp marked publisher's cloth, very good.   C. P. Hyland   261 - 656   2013   £40

O'Laidhin, T. *Sidney State Papers 1565-1570.* IMC, 1962. 8vo., cloth, dust jacket, near fine.   C. P. Hyland   261 - 503   2013   £60

O'Leary, Con *Wayfarer in Ireland.* 1935. First edition, map endpapers, and another, folding in end pocket, frontispiece, 26 photos on 15 plates, 8vo., cover faded, else good.   C. P. Hyland   261 - 660   2013   £30

O'Leary, John *Recollections of Fenians and Fenianism.* IUP, First issue, 2 volumes in 1, 8vo., cloth, very good.   C. P. Hyland   261 - 663   2013   £40

O'Longain, Pol *Gairdin an Anma.* 1844. 13 x 8 cm., 113 pages, errata page, presentation to James O'Connor from C. M. O'Connell, subsequent presentation inscription, rear (blue) wrapper under calf, badly repaired, not very good.   C. P. Hyland   261 - 666   2013   £105

O'Mahony, Colman *The Maritime Gateway to Cork.* Tower, 1986. First edition, 8vo., cloth, dust jacket, very good, signed presentation copy.   C. P. Hyland   261 - 668   2013   £125

O'Mara, Michael *Private Interlude.* San Diego: Brighton Press, n.d., Numbered edition, signed by author, this being number 16, etchings from copperplates, one etching loosely inserted in pocket on back pastedown, which is signed, 7.5 x 6.7cm., cloth, unpaginated, accordion folded, from the collection of Donn W. Sanford.   Oak Knoll Books   303 - 66   2013 $450

O'Meara, Dominic J. *Pythagoras Revived: Mathematics and Philosophy in Late Antiquity.* Oxford: Clarendon Press, 1989. 8vo., navy cloth, gilt stamped spine title, dust jacket, ownership signature, fine, rare in cloth.   Jeff Weber Rare Books   169 - 361   2013 $75

O'Murchadha, Ciaran *Sable Wings Over the Land: Ennis and His Wider Community during the Great Famine.* Clasp, 1998. First edition, 8vo., color and black and white illustrations, cloth, dust jacket, very good.   C. P. Hyland   261 - 670   2013   £50

O'Neill, Eugene Gladstone   1888-1953 *Anna Christie.* New York: Liveright, 1930. First edition, limited to 775 large paper copies signed by author, 8vo., pages 161, uncut, unopened, fine in dust jacket.   Second Life Books Inc.   183 - 297   2013 $400

O'Neill, Eugene Gladstone   1888-1953 *Before Breakfast.* New York: Frank Shay, 1916. First edition, 12mo., wrappers binding A, about fine.   Second Life Books Inc.   183 - 298   2013 $300

O'Neill, Eugene Gladstone   1888-1953 *Dynamo.* New York: Liveright, 1929. First edition, one of 775 copies signed by author, large paper limited edition, 8vo., 150 pages, fine, untrimmed, blue flexible boards, spine faded, little rubbed publisher's box, printed in Calson in two colors.   Second Life Books Inc.   183 - 299   2013 $400

O'Neill, Eugene Gladstone   1888-1953 *The Iceman Cometh.* New York: Limited Editions Club, 1982. First edition, one of 2000 copies, all signed by artist, this copy with lithograph signed, small 4to., drawings and lithograph by Leonard Baskin, original slipcase, as new, little bumped at top of spine.   Second Life Books Inc.   183 - 301   2013 $300

O'Neill, Eugene Gladstone 1888-1953 *Lazarus Laughed.* New York: Boni & Liveright, 1927. First limited edition, number 503 of 775 numbered copies, signed by author, 179 pages, publisher's batik paper cover boards, parchment paper spine with printed spine label, untrimmed edges, spine slightly darkened, else fine, uncut, worn slipcase.   Argonaut Book Shop   Recent Acquisitions June 2013 - 219   2013 $350

O'Neill, Eugene Gladstone 1888-1953 *Eugene O'Neill: Complete Plays 1913-1920. Eugene O'Neill: Complete Plays 1920-1931. Eugene O'Neill: Complete Plays 1932-1943.* New York: Library of America, 1988. First edition thus, fine in near fine dust jacket, 3 volumes, boxed set, first volume has bump on rear board, otherwise fine, dust jacket near fine, last volumes fine in near fine dust jackets, box has bump to rear top panel, otherwise close to fine, small 8vo., 1004, 1092, 1007 pages.   Beasley Books   2013 - 2013 $60

O'Neill, Eugene Gladstone 1888-1953 *Thirst and Other One-Act Pays.* Boston: Gorham Press, 1914. First edition, small 8vo., 168 pages, very good, clean, tight copy.   Second Life Books Inc.   183 - 304   2013 $250

O'Neill, F. Gordon *Ernest Reuben Lilienthal and His Family.* Palo Alto: Stanford University Press, 1949. First edition, small quarto, frontispiece, photos, dark blue cloth, gilt, bookplate, very fine, presentation inscription signed to William Gilman with his bookplate.   Argonaut Book Shop Summer 2013 - 208   2013 $125

O'Neill, Rose *The Kewpies their Book Written and Illustrated by...* New York: Frederick Stokes Nov., 1913. 4to., boards, pictorial paste-on, slightest bit of rubbing, else near fine, pictorial endpapers, cover plate, plus numerous 2 color illustrations on every page, sold with book is boxed set of 3 kewpie handkerchiefs, rare.   Aleph-Bet Books, Inc. 104 - 398   2013 $2200

O'Nolan, Brian *The Hard Life.* London: MacGbbon & Kee, 1961. First edition, 8vo., original black flecked red cloth, fine in slightly rubbed dust jacket.   Maggs Bros. Ltd. 1442 - 273   2013   £250

O'Nolan, Brian *Myles. Portraits of Brian O'Nolan.* London: Martin Brian & O'Keefe, 1973. First edition, one of 100 specially bound copies, from total edition of 110, 8vo., original pale burgundy cloth lettered gilt, near fine in acetate dust jacket and matching slipcase.   Maggs Bros. Ltd. 1442 - 274   2013   £150

O'Nolan, Brian *Myles Away from Dublin.* London: Granada, 1985. First edition, 8vo., original orange cloth, dust jacket, from the library of Richard Murphy and inscribed to him by selector, Martin Green, fine in dust jacket.   Maggs Bros. Ltd.   1442 - 275   2013   £125

O'Nuallain, Brian *The Best of Myles.* 1968. First edition, 400 pages, cloth, dust jacket worn, text very good.   C. P. Hyland   261 - 671   2013   £35

O'Shea, J. J. *Subject and Name Index of Entries in the Council Book 1710 to 1841.* 1891. Photocopy of typescript, 635 leaves, bound in 3 volumes, cloth, very good.   C. P. Hyland   261 - 674   2013   £500

O'Shiel, Kevin R. *Handbook fo the Ulster Question.* London: Stationary Office, 1923. First edition, 8vo., 5 large folding maps, quarter cloth, very good.   C. P. Hyland   261 - 675   2013   £75

O'Siochfradha, Padraig *An Seanshaidhe Muimhneach.* 1832. First edition, 8vo., cloth, dust jacket, very good.   C. P. Hyland   261 - 676   2013   £50

O'Sullivan, Vincent *The Green Window.* London: Leonard Smithers & Co., 1899. First edition, second issue (issued by Grant Richards with his name at foot of spine), scarce, original brown cloth with title and author in gilt to spine, some chipping and bumping to spine ends and corners, otherwise very good, typical offsetting to free endpapers and one or two gatherings slightly pulled away, still very good, undated ownership signature of Mary O'Sullivan, 113 pages.   The Kelmscott Bookshop   7 - 124   2013 $300

O'Sullivan, William *The Economic History of Cork City from the Earliest Times.* Cork University Press, 1937. First edition, maps, diagrams, cloth, very good.   C. P. Hyland   261 - 678   2013   £90

O'Sullivan, William *The Economic History of Cork City from the Earliest Times.* 1937. First edition, 8vo., maps, diagrams, cloth, linen lined dust jacket (frayed), signed presentation copy, very good.   C. P. Hyland   261 - 679   2013   £125

Oakley, Francis *Natural Law, Conciliarism and Consent in the Late Middle Ages: Studies in Ecclesiastical and Intellectual History.* London: Variorum Reprints, 1984. Teal cloth, gilt stamped cover and spine titles, ownership signature, fine, rare.   Jeff Weber Rare Books   169 - 329   2013 $75

Oakley, Violet *Cathedral of Compassion.* Philadelphia: Women's International League, 1955. Limited edition, 8vo. pages 104, uncut, ivory cloth, stamped in red, signed by author, owner's name and address on verso of flyleaf, ex-library with stamps, cover somewhat soiled, little worn at corners and ends of spine, otherwise very good.   Second Life Books Inc.   183 - 305   2013 $65

Oakley, Violet *The Law Triumphant.* Published by Oakley, 1932. Limited to 300 numbered copies signed by Violet Oakley, large folio, full leather, embossed and gilt stamped, metallic endpapers, closed with 2 brass clasp, leather very slightly spotted in places, fine, original plain box, printed on high quality San Marco paper, illustrations - 71 tipped in plates in color and black and white, rare. Aleph-Bet Books, Inc.   104 - 395   2013 $2250

Oates, Frank *Matabele Land and the Victoria Falls.* C. Kegan Paul Co., 1881. First edition, large 8vo, original pictorial cloth, gilt over bevelled boards, trifling rubbing to head of backstrip, unopened, frontispiece, title vignette, 6 tissue guarded chromolithographs, 10 hand colored plates, few spots to prelims and large map, neat repair to stub of large map, otherwise splendid, unused copy, with delightful later presentation inscription.   R. F. G. Hollett & Son Africana - 152   2013   £1200

Ober, Frederick A. *Camps in the Caribbees. the Adventures of a Naturalist in the Lesser Antilles.* Boston: Lee and Shepard, 1899. Reprint, 8vo., frontispiece and illustrations, very good, original printed dust jacket, tight copy.   Second Life Books Inc.   183 - 306   2013 $150

Occum, Samson *A Sermon Preached at the Execution of Moses Paul, an Indian, Who was Executed at New Haven on the 2nd of September 1772 for the Murder of Mr. Moses Cook...* New London: T. Green, 1772. First edition, scarce, 8vo., original printed wrappers, small tear to rear wrapper, affecting five lines of text, faint contemporary ownership inscription to front wrapper.   Maggs Bros. Ltd. 1467 - 126   2013   £3000

Ocellus, Lucanus *De Universi Natura.* Bologna: e Typographia Ferroniana, 1646. 5o., intermittent marginal dampstaining, few gatherings browned, one leaf with repaired marginal tear, 18th century vellum boards, spine divided by blind rules, one compartment dyed yellow and lettered gilt, another lettered direct, somewhat soiled and stained, gilt stamp of Birmingham Medical Inst. to spine and their small stamp to title.   Unsworths Antiquarian Booksellers   28 - 34   2013   £800

Ochsner and Percy New Manual of Surgery Civil and Military. Chicago: Cleveland Press, 1917. Fifth edition, 817 pages, text illustrations, original printed tan wrappers, some wear and discoloration, overall good, tight copy. James Tait Goodrich   S74 - 185   2013 $75

Octavio Paz: A Celebration. New York: Academy of American Poets and the Mexican Cultural Institute, 1994. First edition, 8vo., original wrappers, although not called for, this copy signed by Paz, Mark Strand, John Ashbery, Bei Dao and Charles Tomlinson.   James S. Jaffe Rare Books Fall 2013 - 6   2013 $750

Odlum, Jerome *Nine Lives Are Not Enough.* New York: Sheridan House, 1940. First edition, fine in dust jacket with tiny wear at spine ends and at corners.   Mordida Books   81 - 381   2013 $500

Odum, Howard W. *Cold Blue Moon: Black Ulysses Afar Off.* Indianapolis: Bobbs Merrill, 1931. First edition, fine in near fine, price clipped dust jacket with very slight spine fading, scarce.   Between the Covers Rare Books, Inc. 165 - 231   2013 $125

Odum, Howard W. *The Negro and His Songs.* Chapel Hill: University of NC, 1925. First edition, f.e.p. excised, otherwise fine and bright in variant binding of black cloth but not embossed stamping on front board and no gold rules on spine.   Beasley Books   2013 - 2013 $100

Odum, Howard W. *Race and Rumors of Face: Challenge to American Crisis.* Chapel Hill: University of North Carolina Press, 1943. First edition, mild edgewear, near fine, without dust jacket, signed by author Thanksgiving 1943.   Between the Covers Rare Books, Inc.   165 - 232   2013 $85

Of, By & About Henry Miller. Yonkers: Oscar Baradinsky/ Alicat Bookshop, 1947. One of 1000 copies, of which 750 were for sale, near fine in oversize stapled wrappers.   Ken Lopez Bookseller   159 - 135   2013 $175

Official Automobile Blue Book 1925 Standard Touring Guide of America Volume Four. New York: Automobile Blue Book Pub. Co., 1925. 706 pages, octavo, black cloth, covered flexible wrappers, very good with minor wear and marginalia, large folding map present in attached map holder with some chipping at edges and minor splitting at folds, text block just barely beginning to crack at page 547, pages mildly age toned.   Ken Sanders Rare Books   45 - 39 2013 $300

Official Handbook of the Panama Canal 1915. Washington: GPO, 1915. First edition, 58 pages, photos, folding map, pale green pictorial wrappers, printed in black and red, fine. Argonaut Book Shop   Recent Acquisitions June 2013 - 226 2013 $90

The Official History of the California Midwinter International Exposition. San Francisco: H. S. Crocker Co., 1894. First edition, hundreds of photographic illustrations map, original three quarter red leather, black pebble cloth sides, title in gilt on spine, corners show light wear one leaf with 2 inch stain at lower edge from tape, owner's name stamped on one page (John J. Deane), very good.   Argonaut Book Shop Summer 2013 - 233   2013 $1500

Ogden, Peter Skene *Traits of American Indian Life and Character.* San Francisco: Grabhorn Press, 1933. Limited to 500 copies, 6 full page illustrations, printed in red and black, cloth backed boards, paper labels on spine and front cover, very fine and bright. Argonaut Book Shop Summer 2013 - 261 2013 $150

Ogilby, John *Britannia Depicta; or Ogilby Improv'd.* London: printed and sold by Tho. Bowles, 1753. Fourth edition, engraved titlepage set within elaborate border, engraved maps, fine, clean copy, contemporary sprinkled calf, hinges cracked, head and tail of spine and corners worn. Jarndyce Antiquarian Booksellers CCIV - 220 2013 £580

Ogilby, John *Ogilby's Road Maps of England and Wales from Ogilby's Britannia 1675.* Reading: Osprey Pub. Ltd., 1971. Folio, pages (14), 100 double page maps, original red cloth, spine with black label lettered gilt, upper cover lettered gilt. Marlborough Rare Books Ltd. 218 - 113 2013 £75

Ogle, Nathaniel *The Colony of Western Australian: a Manual for Emigrants to that Settlement or Its Dependencies...* London: James Fraser, 1839. First edition, very good, first issue complete with folding map, 4 engraved plates, 8vo., original green cloth. Maggs Bros. Ltd. 1467 - 88 2013 £3000

Ohnet, Georges *The Marl-Pit Mystery.* London: Vizetelly & Co., 1890. Third edition, half title, original glazed maroon boards, blocked and lettered in blue and black, spine little sunned, some slight rubbing, good plus in unusual fragile binding. Jarndyce Antiquarian Booksellers CCV - 214 2013 £65

Ol' King Coal. Kenosha: Samuel Lowe, circa, 1950. 8 x 6 inches, pictorial boards die-cut in shape of coal truck, fine, illustrations in color. Aleph-Bet Books, Inc. 104 - 531 2013 $150

Olby, Robert *Origins of Mendelism.* London: Constable, 1966. First edition, signed by Olby, very good+, foxing to edges, endpapers, scuff to f.f.e.p., in very good dust jacket with mild chips, mild soil, mild foxing, 8vo., 204 pages, scarce signed volume. By the Book, L. C. 37 - 65 2013 $150

Olby, Robert *The Path to the Double Helix.* Seattle: University of Washington Press, 1974. First edition, 8vo., inscribed to a professor of Biology with notes and minimal underlining in his hand, very good++ with minimal sun spine and cover edges, owner inscription, very good+ dust jacket with internal tape reinforcement, minimal edge wear. By the Book, L. C. 37 - 66 2013 $250

Olcott, Frances Jenkins *Stories from the Arabian Nights.* Harrap, 1913. First edition, original ribbed blue cloth gilt, spine and top edges faded, small bump and frayed patch to edges, top edge gilt, 15 color plates by Monro Orr. R. F. G. Hollett & Son Children's Books - 424 2013 £30

The Old Ballad of Dick Whittington. London: Warne, n.d. circa, 1870. 4to., wrappers, slight offsetting on text pages, else near fine, each page mounted on linen, 6 very fine full page chromolithographs. Aleph-Bet Books, Inc. 105 - 242 2013 $300

The Old Crow Mixing Guide and Almanac. Frankfort: The Old Crow Distillery Co., n.d. circa, 1963. 12mo., 28 pages, illustrations from drawings and photos, fine. Between the Covers Rare Books, Inc. Cocktails, Etc. - 312640 2013 $50

Old Mother Hubbard. New York: McLoughlin Bros, n.d. circa, 1869. 8vo., stiff decorative card covers, erroneously bound upside down in covers, else fine, 6 fine full page color illustrations. Aleph-Bet Books, Inc. 105 - 380 2013 $400

Old Mother Hubbard and Her Dog. Banbury: J. G. Rusher, circa, 1814. Each page illustrated with one or two Bewickesque woodcuts, that on last being full page, little frayed, 16mo., uncut, self wrappers, good. Blackwell's Rare Books B174 - 80 2013 £65

Old Time Fairy Tales and Nursery Rhymes. Raphael Tuck & Sons, n.d., 1931. Original red cloth gilt over bevelled boards with pictorial and lettered paper onlay to upper board, spine faded, 6 dramatic color plates and numerous black and white illustrations, scattered spotting. R. F. G. Hollett & Son Children's Books - 259 2013 £95

The Old Woman and Her Silver Penny. London: Dean & son 11 Ludgate Hill 1858 code on rear cover, 4to, cloth backed pictorial boards, slight bit of edge rubbing, else really near fine, 8 fine hand colored moveable plates operated by tabs with several pieces moving simultaneously, beautiful copy. Aleph-Bet Books, Inc. 104 - 363 2013 $3250

The Old Woman who Lived in a Shoe. Racine: Whitman, 1931. 4to., stiff pictorial wrappers, fine, die-cut in shape of large shoe-house with moveable roof, internally, pages are also die-cut in varying widths and heights to that there is a three dimensional effect, illustrations by Ethel Bonney Taylor. Aleph-Bet Books, Inc. 104 - 532 2013 $200

Oldenburg, Jastro *Cornhill Epitomes of Three Sciences. Comparative Philology, Psychology ...* Chicago: Open Court, 1890. First edition, hardcover, fine. Beasley Books 2013 - 2013 $50

Olds, Sharon *The Sign of Saturn. Poems 1980-1987.* London: Secker & Warburg, 1991. First edition, faint marginal browning, pages x, 94, 16mo., original printed white wrappers, near fine.   Blackwell's Rare Books   B174 - 271   2013   £150

Oliphant, Margaret Oliphant Wilson   1828-1897 *Jerusalem: Its History and Hope.* London: Macmillan, 1891. First edition, half title, frontispiece, illustrations some light foxing, uncut in original green cloth, bevelled boards, spine lettered in gilt, front board with shield blocked in gilt and silver, armorial bookplate of William Blackwood, top edge gilt, very good, bright copy, loosely inserted printed slip "From the author".   Jarndyce Antiquarian Booksellers   CCV - 215   2013   £120

Oliphant, Margaret Oliphant Wilson   1828-1897 *The Literary History of England in the End of the Eighteenth and Beginning of the Nineteenth Century.* Macmillan and Co., 1882. First edition, Volumes I-III, extra illustrated by insertion of 112 portraits and views, some illustrations foxed, some of these offsetting into text, 8vo., mid 20th century dark brown morocco by Bayntun, French fillets on sides with arabesque corner ornaments, spines gilt, gilt edges, lower joint volume ii tender, spines slightly faded, one or two minor knocks, good.   Blackwell's Rare Books   B174 - 110   2013   £450

Oliphant, Margaret Oliphant Wilson   1828-1897 *Makers of Modern Rome.* London and New York: Macmillan and Co., 1895. 222 x 154mm., handsome contemporary red crushed morocco gilt by Howell of Liverpool (stamp signed), covers with gilt fillet border and triple fillet framed central panel with ornate fleur-de-lys cornerpieces, raised bands, spine attractively gilt in compartments with fleur-de-lys centerpiece within lozenge of small tools and with scrolling cornerpieces, densely gilt turn-ins, all edges gilt, pleasing later fore-edge painting of the eternal city, signed with cypher formed by initials "A" and "V", with 25 full page illustrations and numerous illustrations in text, slight rubbing to joints, lower inner corner with faint arching dampstain extending into part of bottom four lines of text, very few tiny dots of foxing, otherwise fine, attractive decorative binding bright, text fresh and clean, painting very well preserved.   Phillip J. Pirages   63 - 190   2013 $650

Oliver, Amanda S. *Revelations.* Strasburg: Shenandoah Publishing House, 1932. First edition, tall 8vo., pages 173, textured light blue cloth with pictorial stamping in gilt, titlepage trifle loose, but very good tight copy.   Second Life Books Inc.   182 - 182   2013 $125

Oliver, George *The Monumental Antiquities of Great Grimsby.* Hull: printed by Isaac Wilson, Lowgate, 1825. double page plan, 2 plates, 8vo., some foxing to plates but not plan and to several pages, uncut in original boards, paper spine label, bookplates, joints cracked but firm, corners bumped, scarce.   Ken Spelman Books Ltd.   73 - 81   2013   £120

Oliver, J. R. *The Olivers of Cloghanodfoy and their Descendants.* 1897. Second edition, 43 pages, printed wrappers (repaired), text very good.   C. P. Hyland   261 - 405   2013   £35

Olivers, Thomas *Thomas Olivers of Tregynon. The Life of an Early Methodist Preacher, Written by Himself.* Newtown: Gregynog Press, 1979. Limited edition, no. 272 of 375 copies, original cloth, paper spine label, frontispiece, spare label tipped in.   R. F. G. Hollett & Son   Wesleyan Methodism - 21   2013   £30

Olsen, Jack *Last Man standing: the Tragedy and Triumph of Geronimo Pratt.* New York: Doubleday, 2000. First edition, fine in very good dust jacket with couple of small tears, some soiling on rear panel and little overall wear, signed by author, Geronimo Pratt, Johnny Cochrane and one other signature that we can't confidently decipher.   Between the Covers Rare Books, Inc.   165 - 326   2013 $450

Olson, Charles *Causal Mythology.* San Francisco: Four Seasons, 1969. First edition, near fine in wrappers, inscribed by author to fellow poet and his wife Vince (Ferrini) and Mary (Shore), near fine in wrappers.   Ken Lopez Bookseller   159 - 165   2013 $450

Olson, Charles *Projective Verse.* New York: Totem, 1959. First separate edition, near fine in stapled wrappers, one spot to front cover, warmly inscribed by author to poet Vince Ferrini and his wife, Mary Shore.   Ken Lopez Bookseller   159 - 164   2013 $750

Omar Khayyam *The Rubaiyat of Omar Khayyam.* London: Hodder and Stoughton, n.d., 1909. First trade edition, large quarto, 20 color plates mounted on buff vellum-like paper with gilt over tan decorative borders, with descriptive tissue guards, text printed on rectos only within brown decorative border, bound in full red calf by Bayntun-Riviere, gorgeous copy, housed in red cloth slipcase.   David Brass Rare Books, Inc.   Holiday 2012 Chapter One - DB 01778   2013 $1100

Omar Khayyam *Rubaiyat of Omar Khayyam.* London: Harrap, 1909. First edition, 4to., full limp brown suede binding stamped in gold, top edge gilt, except for few scattered oxidation spots on first few pages, this is very fine in original pictorial box, flaps repaired, pictorial endpapers, 24 tipped in color plates and decorative text pages with calligraphy by Willy Pogany, magnificent copy.   Aleph-Bet Books, Inc.   104 - 431   2013 $1200

Omar Khayyam *The Rubaiyat of Omar Khayyam.* London: Hodder & Stoughton, n.d. circa, 1915. 4to., illustrations by Edmund Dulac, maroon cloth, elaborate gilt pictorial decoration, plain endpapers, spot on half title else fine in publisher's box with double elephant design in green (box flaps repaired, some soil and rubbing), 20 beautiful tipped in color plates with lettered tissue guards (guards have elephant design), mounted on heavier cream stock surrounded by decorative borders in dull gilt over green, green decorative border on text pages.   Aleph-Bet Books, Inc.   104 - 185   2013 $750

Omar Khayyam *Rubaiyat of Omar Khayyam.* New York: Dodd Mead and Co., 1920. First American edition, large 8vo., pages 193, uncut, frontispiece, 38 full page tipped in black and white and color illustrations by Ronald Balfour, tan paper with text and line drawings, green cloth stamped in gilt, little rubbed at tips and tear to cloth at bottom of spine, very good, tight.   Second Life Books Inc.   183 - 227   2013 $300

Omar Khayyam *Rubaiyat.* 1973. 2/25 copies actually bound by Susan Allix (of an edition of 75 copies), signed and numbered by her, French folded, with 30 copper etchings in various colors by Susan Allix, titlepage printed in brown, 4to., original dark pink morocco, backstrip longitudinally gilt lettered, front cover with gilt lattice work design overall, interspersed with 3 lines of small stars, untrimmed, cloth slipcase, fine.   Blackwell's Rare Books   B174 - 392   2013   £3000

Onderdonk, Henry *Documents and Letters Intended to Illustrate the Revolutionary Incident of Queens County, NY...* Hempstead: Lott Van De Water, 1884. First edition, unprinted blue green wrappers, modest chips to front wrapper, some erosion on spine, nice, sound, very good copy, tipped into pamphlet is presentation slip, inscribed and initialled by Onderdonk.   Between the Covers Rare Books, Inc.   New York City - 285273   2013 $225

100 Soldiers on Parade. Springfield: Milton Bradley Co. n.d. circa, 1910. Housed in original pictorial box is a complete set of 100 toy soldiers on heavy card with wooden bases, box measures 22" wide x 11 3/4" with great chromolithographed cover, flaps have been neatly strengthened and box is solid and in very good condition, each of the soldiers is 6 inches tall, all with bright chromolithographed uniforms and except for few minor creases they are all in fine condition, instructions for play inside box lid, unusual survival.   Aleph-Bet Books, Inc.   105 - 384   2013 $975

125th Anniversary 1871-1996 Mt. Zion Baptist Church of Germantown. Philadelphia: Mt. Zion Baptist Church of Germantown, 1996. First edition, quarto, black cloth gilt, 208 pages, illustrations, small gift inscription, still fine, issued without dust jacket, uncommon.   Between the Covers Rare Books, Inc.   165 - 252   2013 $125

Onetti, Juan Carlos *The Shipyard.* New York: Charles Scribner's Sons, 1968. First American edition, fine in dust jacket with minor wear to extremities.   Ed Smith Books   78 - 43   2013 $150

Onyeama, Dillibe *Nigger at Eton.* London: Leslie Frewin, 1972. First edition, fine but for '2F' inked on f.e.p. (smallish), lightly edgeworn dust jacket, uncommon.   Beasley Books   2013 - 2013 $100

Opie, Amelia Alderson *Illustrations of Lying In all Its Branches.* London: Longman, 1825. Second edition, 2 volumes, slight spotting, contemporary half maroon roan, slight rubbing, armorial bookplate of Frederick Greenwood, attractive copy.   Jarndyce Antiquarian Booksellers CCV - 216   2013   £100

Opie, Iona *The Lore and Language of Schoolchildren.* Oxford: Clarendon Press, 1959. First edition, large 8vo., original cloth, gilt, dust jacket price clipped, 11 distribution maps.   R. F. G. Hollett & Son   Children's Books - 430   2013   £50

Opie, Iona *A Nursery Companion.* Oxford University Press, 1980. First edition, 4to., original cloth, gilt, dust jacket, price clipped, pages 128, illustrations in color.   R. F. G. Hollett & Son   Children's Books - 426   2013   £40

Opie, Iona *The Oxford Dictionary of Nursery Rhymes.* Oxford: Clarendon Press, 1952. Original cloth gilt, dust jacket (front edge and inner flap rather defective), 24 plates, 13 pages of text illustrations.   R. F. G. Hollett & Son   Children's Books - 427   2013   £50

Opie, Iona *The Oxford Nursery Rhyme Book.* Oxford: Clarendon Press, 1957. First edition, large 4to., original cloth, gilt, dust jacket, illustrations in color.   R. F. G. Hollett & Son   Children's Books - 429   2013   £35

Opie, Iona *Tail Feathers from Mother Goose.* Walker Books, 1988. First UK edition, large square 8vo., original pink boards with pictorial onlay, large square 8vo., original pink boards with pictorial onlay, dust jacket, pages 125, illustrations in color.   R. F. G. Hollett & Son   Children's Books - 425   2013   £30

Oppenheim, E. Phillips *The Double Traitor.* New York: A. L. Burt, n.d., Reprint, name and address on front endpaper, else fine in dust jacket.   Mordida Books   81 - 382   2013 $75

Oppenheim, E. Phillips *The Evil Shepherd.* Boston: Little Brown, 1922. First edition, spine slightly darkened, otherwise near fine in fine Burt reprint dust jacket with short crease tear on spine.   Mordida Books   81 - 385   2013 $85

Oppenheim, E. Phillips *General Besserley's Puzzle Box.* London: Hodder & Stoughton, 1935. First edition, 8vo., original light blue cloth. Howard S. Mott Inc. 262 - 108 2013 $65

Oppenheim, E. Phillips *The Great Prince Shan.* Boston: Little Brown, 1922. First American edition, spine slightly darkened, otherwise near fine in Burt reprint dust jacket with long rubbed streak on spine. Mordida Books 81 - 388 2013 $75

Oppenheim, E. Phillips *The Kingdom of the Blind.* Boston: Little Brown, 1916. First edition, pages lightly spotted and slightly darkened, otherwise fine in fine A. L. Burt reprint dust jacket. Mordida Books 81 - 383 2013 $85

Oppenheim, E. Phillips *Matroini's Vineyard.* Boston: Little Brown, 1928. First American edition, name-stamp on front endpaper, otherwise very good in very good dust jacket with crease on back panel. Mordida Books 81 - 388 2013 $100

Oppenheim, E. Phillips *The Mystery Road.* Boston: Little Brown, 1923. First edition, spine slightly darkened otherwise fine in Burt reprint dust jacket. Mordida Books 81 - 387 2013 $85

Oppenheim, E. Phillips *The Pawns Court.* Boston: Little Brown, 1918. First American edition, name and date on front endpaper, otherwise near fine in fine Burt reprint dust jacket. Mordida Books 81 - 374 2013 $85

Orczy, Emmuska, Baroness *Eldorado; a Story of the Scarlet Pimpernel.* Leipzig: Bernahrd Tauchnitz, 1913. Copyright edition, 2 volumes, half titles, uncut in contemporary half red calf, spine elaborately blocked in gilt, dark green morocco labels, top edge gilt, very good. Jarndyce Antiquarian Booksellers CCV - 217 2013 £75

Orczy, Emmuska, Baroness *The Laughing Cavalier.* London: Hodder and Stoughton, 1914. First edition, 8vo., original red cloth, color pictorial label on front cover, 406 pages, nearly fine. Howard S. Mott Inc. 262 - 109 2013 $95

Orleans, Charles Duc D' *Poemes de Charles d'Orleans.* Paris: Teriade Editeur, 1950. One of 1200 numbered copies, out of a total edition of 1230, signed by artist on limitation leaf, this being number 789, large folio, 54 full page color lithographed illustrations by Henri Matisse, lithographed text in artist's hand printed in black within lithographed borders in color, loose as issued in original color lithographed wrappers, endleaves present, lower corners very slightly bumped, near fine in original glassine, housed in newer cloth slipcase. Heritage Book Shop Holiday Catalogue 2012 - 103 2013 $7500

Ormsby, Frank *A Northern Spring.* Dublin/London: Gallery Press/Secker & Warburg, 1986. First edition, 8vo., original black cloth, fine in dust jacket, slightly discolored, from the library of Richard Muphy, inscribed by author for Murphy. Maggs Bros. Ltd. 1442 - 276 2013 £40

Orwell, George 1903-1950 *Animal Farm: a Fairy Story.* London: Secker & Warburg, 1945. First edition, octavo, original green cloth spine panel stamped in white. L. W. Currey, Inc. Fall Sampler Sept. 2013 - 146553 2013 $15,000

Orwell, George 1903-1950 *Burmese Days.* New York: Harper, 1934. Stated first edition, very good++, 8vo., mild spotting at spine, mild stain to front cover. By the Book, L. C. 38 - 99 2013 $1000

Orwell, George 1903-1950 *Burmese Days.* New York: Harper and Brothers, 1934. First edition, 8vo., original orange cloth, lettered in black, binding and titling slightly stained, otherwise excellent, inscribed by author as Eric Blair, with undated TNS by Adrian Fierz, describing the provenance of the book. Maggs Bros. Ltd. 1460 - 109 2013 £18,500

Orwell, George 1903-1950 *The Road to Wigan Pier.* London: Victor Gollancz, 1937. First edition, Left Book Club Edition, 216 x 140mm., pleasing modern red three quarter morocco, raised bands, spine panels with gilt fleurons or gilt titling, marbled endpapers, top edge gilt, original orange cloth spine and covers bound in at rear, with 32 black and white photos; couple of leaves with trivial marginal foxing, but very fine, text especially clean and fresh, binding unworn. Phillip J. Pirages 63 - 357 2013 $400

Orwell, George 1903-1950 *The Road to Wigan Pier.* London: Victor Gollancz, 1937. First edition, 8vo., original limp orange cloth lettered in black, signed by author, slightly nicked on lower spine and a name partially erased from front blank, otherwise excellent copy in protective folding box. Maggs Bros. Ltd. 1460 - 110 2013 £7500

Osborn, Sherard *Japanese Fragments.* London: Bradbury & Evans, 1861. First edition, very good hardback, original brown cloth, gilt lettered spine, gilt lettered illustration to front cover, all edges gilt, cover edge wear, discoloration to rear cover, minimal foxing to endpapers and pastedowns, 6 hand colored illustrations, 8vo., 139 pages. By the Book, L. C. 36 - 91 2013 $475

Osborne, Edward B. *Letters from the Woods.* Poughkeepsie: The Author, 1893. First edition, lacks free front endpaper, else near fine, scarce. Between the Covers Rare Books, Inc. New York City - 286806 2013 $250

Osier, Donald V. *A Century of Serial Publications in Psychology 1850-1950.* Millwood: Kraus, 1984. First edition, fine, hardcover, issued without dust jacket. Beasley Books 2013 - 2013 $60

Osler, William 1849-1919 *Bibliotheca Osleriana. A Catalogue of Books Illustrating the History of Medicine...* Oxford: 1929. First edition, Thick 4to., original blue cloth, some wear, overall nice copy, now scarce, bookplate "The first hundred copies of this Catalogue, in accordance with the late Lady Osler's Instructions, are sent to those friends and libraries whose names she herself indicated. W. W. Francis, Librarian Osler Library McGill University, Montreal.", on front pastedown is engraved invitation to dedication of Osler Library. James Tait Goodrich 75 - 158 2013 $995

Osler, William 1849-1919 *"Christmas and the Microscope." in Hardwicke's Science Gossip, Feb. 1 1869.* London: 1870. Volume 5, royal 8vo., 19th century plain cloth, spine sunned, rubbing to cloth, internally very good, quite scarce. James Tait Goodrich S74 - 202 2013 $495

Osler, William 1849-1919 *The Principles and Practice of Medicine.* New York: D. Appleton and Co., 1892. First edition, first state, large 8vo., original green cloth, some rubbed and bumped, rebacked with original spine laid down, first state with misspelling 'Georgias' for Gorgias' facing contents page and second set of ads dated Nov. 1891, holograph presentation by Dr. George B. Shattuck, Jan. 2 1897 with ownership signature of Edward N. Libby, small date stamp on top of titlepage, very good, clean, tight copy. Second Life Books Inc. 183 - 308 2013 $7500

Osler, William 1849-1919 *The Principles and Practice of Medicine Designed for the Use of Practitioners and Students of Medicine.* New York: D. Appleton, 1897. Second edition, thick 8vo., original calf backed cloth, some scuffing and slight chipping, very sound. M & S Rare Books, Inc. 95 - 277 2013 $250

Ossoli, Sarah Margaret Fuller, Marchesa D' 1801-1850 *Memoirs of Margaret Fuller Ossoli.* Boston: Roberts, 1852. First edition, first issue, binding 1, 2 volumes, 8vo., 351, 352 pages + ads, wear to extremities of spine, little foxed, but good tight set. Second Life Books Inc. 182 - 70 2013 $250

Ossoli, Sarah Margaret Fuller, Marchesa D' 1801-1850 *Woman in the Nineteenth Century, and Kindred Papers Relating to the Sphere...* Boston: Roberts Bros., 1875. New edition, 8th printing, 8vo., pages 420, ownership bookplate, brown cloth, spine faded, hinge starting in front, good, tight, clean copy. Second Life Books Inc. 182 - 183 2013 $100

Our Exagmination Round His Factification for Incamination of Work in Progress. Paris: Shakespeare and Co., 1929. First printing, one of 96 special copies in the limited edition (there was also a trade edition of 200 copies, original printed paper wrappers designed by Sylvia Beach, front flyleaf with ink ownership inscription of Arthur W. Poulin/November 1944/San Francisco", one inch tears at top of front and bottom of rear joint, spine little scuffed, covers with faint soiling, two small chips to fore edge of front cover, otherwise fragile wrappers in excellent condition, except for slight browning at edges because of paper stock, fine internally. Phillip J. Pirages 63 - 293 2013 $5000

Our Children: Sketched from Nature in Pencil and Verse. Dean & son, n.d circa., 1867. Small 4to., original green blindstamped cloth gilt, neatly recased, pages (56), lithographed throughout with pencil drawings, little light spotting to first few leaves, inscription dated July 6th 1867. R. F. G. Hollett & Son Children's Books - 18 2013 £75

Oursler, Will *Folio on Florence White.* New York: Simon and Schuster, 1942. First edition, fine in dust jacket. Mordida Books 81 - 389 2013 $65

Outcault, R. F. *Buster Brow Goes Fishing.* Akron: Saalfield, 1905. 12mo., cloth, some cover and margin soil, very good, printed in colors on cloth. Aleph-Bet Books, Inc. 105 - 435 2013 $300

Outcault, R. F. *Pore Lil Mose. His Letters to His Mammy.* Brooklyn: Grand Union Tea Co./NY Herald, 1902. Oblong folio, cloth backed pictorial card covers, corners worn and slight cover soil, else near fine, printed on rectos only, each leaf gloriously illustrated in color, very rare. Aleph-Bet Books, Inc. 104 - 80 2013 $4000

Outland, Charles F. *Man-Made Disaster: the Story of the St. Francis Dam...* Glendale: Arthur H. Clark Co., 1963. First edition, 249 pages, illustrations, maps, portraits, brown cloth, bookplate, very fine, pictorial dust jacket, presentation inscription signed by author for friend Harvey Starr, extremely scarce. Argonaut Book Shop Recent Acquisitions June 2013 - 220 2013 $500

Outland, Charles F. *Man-Made Disaster: the Story of the St. Francis Dam...* Glendale: Arthur H. Clark Co., 1963. First edition, one of 2059 copies, extremely scarce, 249 pages, illustrations, maps, portraits, brown cloth, lacking dust jacket, owner's neat signature, very fine. Argonaut Book Shop Recent Acquisitions June 2013 - 221 2013 $250

Outland, Charles F. *Man-Made Disaster: the Story of the St. Francis Dam...* Glendale: Arthur H. Clark Co., 1977. Revised edition, one of 1517 copies, 275 pages, illustrations, maps, portraits, pictorial "Lexotone" fabric over boards, fine with pictorial dust jacket. Argonaut Book Shop Recent Acquisitions June 2013 - 222 2013 $125

Outland, Charles F. *Stagecoaching on el Camino Real.* Glendale: Arthur H. Clark Co., 1973. First edition, 339 pages, numerous photos, 2 maps, red cloth, very fine, printed dust jacket. Argonaut Book Shop Recent Acquisitions June 2013 - 223 2013 $225

The Outsider: a complete set of #1-#5. New Orleans/Tucson: Loujon Press, 1961-1969. First edition, First three issues in pictorial wrappers with issue 4/5 hardcover with glassine dust jacket, scarce complete run, near fine. Charles Agvent Charles Bukowski - 65 2013 $600

Ovidius Naso, Publius *The Heroycall Epistles of the Learned Poet Publius Ovidius Naso.* London: Cresset Press, 1928. Limited edition, one of the special issues on better paper limited to 30 copies, this number V of XXX copies on handmade paper, of a total 380 copies, 4to., 10 illustrations by Hester Sainsbury, top edge gilt, green tinted vellum over boards, gilt stamped black leather spine label, slightly rubbed, front pastedown offsetting (bookplate removed), interior fine. Jeff Weber Rare Books 171 - 84 2013 $625

Ovidius Naso, Publius *Metamorphoses.* London: Folio Society, 2008. First edition, large hardcover, #1137 from an edition of 2750, printed on Vizile Ivoire Laid paper, very fine in full Nigerian goatskin with design by Simon Brett, fine clamshell box, beautiful production. Jeff Hirsch Books Fall 2013 - 129478 2013 $400

Ovidius Naso, Publius *Ovid's Epistles with His Amours.* London: printed for J. & R. Tonson, and S. Draper, 1748. 12mo. 2 engraved frontispieces, some light browning and occasional foxing, bound in later half calf, marbled boards, attractive blind tooled spine, raised bands, brown morocco label, 19th century ownership of George Proctor. Jarndyce Antiquarian Booksellers CCIV - 221 2013 £85

Owen, David Dale 1807-1860 *Report of a Geological Reconnoissance of the Chippewa Land District of Wisconsin and Incidentally of a Portion of the Kickapoo Country and of a Part of Iowa and the Minnesota Territory.* Washington: 1848. 134 pages, 23 plates, 14 folding section, large folding map, rebound in quarter cloth and patterned paper over board, scattered foxing, else very good. Dumont Maps & Books of the West 125 - 67 2013 $350

Owen, Gordon R. *The Two Alberts: Fountain ad Fall.* Las Cruces: Yucca Tree Press, 1996. First edition, signed by author, brick cloth, very fine with pictorial dust jacket. Argonaut Book Shop Summer 2013 - 264 2013 $60

Owen, H. *The History of Shrewsbury. Parts V and VI.* London: printed for Harding, Mavor and Lepard, 1823. 1824, Folio, 5 plates, small repair to page 325, half green cloth with marbled paper boards, original paper wrappers with publisher's ads to rear retained inside binding, spine faded, board edges and corners worn, edges uncut and little discolored, some unopened, very good, ownership inscription of P. A. Slack April 1976 and initials BRH. Unsworths Antiquarian Booksellers 28 - 190 2013 £90

Owen, Mary Alicia *Old Rabbit the Voodoo and Other Sorcerers...* London: T. Fisher Unwin, 1893. First edition, octavo, inserted frontispiece and numerous illustrations, original light blue cloth, front panel stamped in black, tan and brown, spine panel stamped in gold and black, publisher's monogram stamped in black on rear panel, edges untrimmed. L. W. Currey, Inc. Fall Sampler Sept. 2013 - 146511 2013 $225

Owston, Lucy M. *Hunmanby East Yorkshire.* Scarborough: G. A. Pindar & Son, 1948. (4), 75 pages, frontispiece and 7 plates, good in original blue cloth, scarce. Ken Spelman Books Ltd. 73 - 108 2013 £25

Ox-Tales (Elements): Original Stories from Remarkable Writers: Earth, Air, Fire, Water. Green Profile, 2009. First edition, 36/150 sets signed by contributors, a total of 38 signatures, 4 volumes, 16mo., original green, white, orange or blue cloths, front covers titled in white, cotton markers, books enclosed in drop-down back box, fine. Blackwell's Rare Books B174 - 272 2013 £495

Oxenbury, Helen *Pig Tale.* London: Heinemann, 1973. First edition, numerous color printed illustrations by author, imperial 8vo., original white boards and illustrated overall, illustrated endpapers, dust jacket fine, inscribed by Oxenbury. Blackwell's Rare Books 172 - 225 2013 £120

Oxenham, Elsie Jeanette *Mistress Nanciebel.* Oxford University Press, n.d., 1930. Original red blindstamped cloth, gilt, dust jacket (bottom third of spine and back panel missing, chips to other corners), color frontispiece, pictorial endpapers, fore edge little spotted. R. F. G. Hollett & Son Children's Books - 432 2013 £85

Oxtravels. Meetings of Remarkable Travel Writers. Profile Books, 2011. 49/100 copies (of an edition of 250) signed by each of the contributors on specially printed stamps pasted as the titlepage to their particular contribution, with a reproduction of their photographic portrait on the reverse, pages 432, 16mo., original dark blue cloth, backstrip and front cover lettered in white, yellow cotton marker, cloth, slipcase, fine. Blackwell's Rare Books B174 - 273 2013 £385

Ozanam, Jacques *Recreations Mathematical and Physical...* printed for R. Bonwick, W. Freeman, Tim Goodwin (and 7 others), 1708. First edition in English, 26 engraved plates, numerous woodcut diagrams and illustrations in text, some dampstaining and browning throughout and few leaves dust soiled, couple of glue spots on one plate have lifted a small amount of letterpress on opposite page (present on plate, whose engraved area is not affected), 8vo., late 18th century tree calf, flat spine gilt in compartments, black lettering piece, crack in upper joint, headcap defective, armorial bookplate inside front cover of Sir Richard Bempde Johnstone, sound. Blackwell's Rare Books Sciences - 91 2013 £700

Ozick, Cynthia *Trust.* New York: New American Library, 1966. First edition, signed by author, publisher's review slip laid in, scarce especially signed, fine in very good dust jacket. Ed Smith Books 75 - 54 2013 $750

P

P., M. *The Child's Introduction to Thorough Bass, In Conversations of a Fortnight, Between a Mother and Her Daughter of Ten Years Old.* London: for Baldwin, Cradock and Joy, 1819. 3 engraved plates, musical notation set within text, very good in contemporary half roan, marbled boards, large printed paper label on upper cover, some slight foxing, scarce. Ken Spelman Books Ltd. 75 - 79 2013 £320

Pacchioni, Antonio *Opera.* Romae: Apud Thomam & Nicolulaum Pagliarinos, 1741. 8 engraved plates on 6 sheets, 1 with discoloration to fore-margin, engraving on titlepage, 2 large decorative engraved headpieces, 5 tail-pieces, 3 historiated initials, small faint stamp on title little scattered foxing and few minor stains, but generally crisp copy printed on heavy stock paper, 4to., recent half calf, extremely uncommon, very rare. James Tait Goodrich 75 - 162 2013 $3500

Pace, William B. *Rifle and Light Infantry Tactics...* Salt Lake City: Deseret News Print, 1865. First edition, 192 page, 24mo., half black calf over back grained cloth, title bands gilt stamped on backstrip, near fine, gentle rubbing to corners, inscribed to Lester J. Herrick, 23 plans. Ken Sanders Rare Books 45 - 9 2013 $5000

Packe, Edmund *An Historical Record of the Royal Regiment of Horse Guards or Oxford Blues.* London: printed and sold by William Clowes, 1834. First edition, 229 x 146mm., frontispiece and engraved title, illustrations by G. E. Manderley, publisher's original blue cloth decorated and titled gilt and blind, engraved frontispiece, one other black and white engraving, hand colored vignette on engraved title, 6 hand colored plates as issued, original watercolor dated 1842, laid in at front, illustrations, engraved armorial bookplate of Herbert John Buckmaster, laid in watercolor equestrian portrait showing new silver helmets instead of bearskin, top and bottom edge of front board with small nick near middle, isolated minor foxing and corner creases, otherwise extremely fine, insubstantial binding, sound, clean and pleasing, text nearly pristine, richly colored plates very well preserved. Phillip J. Pirages 63 - 411 2013 $450

Page, David *The Mutual Duties of Parents and Teachers, a Lecture Delivered before the American Institute of Instruction at the Ninth Annual Anniversary at Lowell, Mass.* Boston: William D. Ticknor, 1838. First separate edition, 8vo., sewn as issued, outside leaves little browned and very lightly soiled, some spotty foxing throughout, very good, wide margined copy. M & S Rare Books, Inc. 95 - 112 2013 $150

Page, William *The Victoria History of the County of Nottingham.* London: Archibald Constable and Co., 1906. Volumes I and II (all published), very good in original red gilt cloth, folio. Ken Spelman Books Ltd. 75 - 160 2013 £95

Pagel, Walter *From Paracelsus to Van Helmont.* London: Variorum Reprints, 1986. Teal cloth, gilt stamped cover and spine titles, ownership signature, fine, rare. Jeff Weber Rare Books 169 - 335 2013 $75

Pagel, Walter *Paracelsus: an Introduction to Philosophical Medicine in the Era of the Renaissance.* Basel & New York: S. Karger, 1958. First edition, 8vo., xii, 368 pages, illustrations, blue cloth, gilt stamped cover and spine titles, dust jacket worn with pieces missing, else very good, Burndy bookplate. Jeff Weber Rare Books 169 - 336 2013 $175

Pagel, Walter *William Harvey's Biological Ideas: Selected Aspects and Historical Background.* New York: S. Karger, 1967. 8vo., 394 pages, illustrations, light pencil marginalia, gilt stamped blue cloth, sunned, Burndy bookplate, formerly belonging to Robert M. McKeon, very good. Jeff Weber Rare Books 172 - 125 2013 $120

Paget, J. Otho *Beagles and Beagling.* London: Hutchnson & Co., 1923. First edition, 8vo., 34 plates, original gilt lettered dark blue cloth with wear to head of spine and some foxing. Ken Spelman Books Ltd. 75 - 167 2013 £45

Paget, Violet 1856-1935 *Althea: a Second Book of Dialogues on Aspirations and Duties.* London: Osgood, McIlvaine & Co., 1894. First edition, inscribed by author, original green cloth with gilt title and author to spine, very good with very light bumping to corners, interior pages have browning to margins but otherwise very good, scarce. The Kelmscott Bookshop 7 - 129 2013 $350

Paine, Albert Bigelow *The Arkansaw Bear.* Harrap & Co., 1919. Large 8vo., original pictorial boards, hinges little chipped, pages 123, 8 color plates by Harry Rountree. R. F. G. Hollett & Son Children's Books - 434 2013 £30

Paine, Robert Treat *The Ruling Passion: an Occasional Poem... Spoken... in the Chapel of the University, Cambridge July 20th 1797.* Boston: Manning & Loring for the author, 1797. First edition, 32 pages, later wrappers, half morocco slipcase. Joseph J. Felcone Inc. English and American Literature to 1800 - 19 2013 $200

Paine, Thomas 1737-1809 *Agrarian Justice Opposed to Agrarian Law and to Agrarian Monopoly Being a Plan for Meliorating the Condition of Man.* Philadelphia: Printed by R. Fowell for Benjamin Franklin Bache, 1797. First American edition, 8vo., 32 pages, later boards, couple of closed tear to top of titlepage, front hinge glued down, some staining to inner margins and toning to some leaves, good. Second Life Books Inc.   183 - 445   2013 $950

Paine, Thomas 1737-1809 *Letters from... to the Citizens of America, After an Absence of Fifteen Years in Europe.* London: printed by and for T. C. Rickman, 1804. First edition, 8vo., titlepage browning at head and with two largish brown spots, disbound, inscribed "From the Editor to Mr. Gurney", good.   Blackwell's Rare Books   172 - 106   2013   £1100

Paine, Thomas 1737-1809 *Mr. Paine's Letter to Mr. Secretary Dundas.* London: printed and distributed gratis by the Society for Constitutional Information, 1792. 8vo., 16 pages, uncut as issued with stab holes, some browning.   Jarndyce Antiquarian Booksellers   CCIV - 222   2013   £125

Paine, Thomas 1737-1809 *Rights of Man Being an Answer to Mr. Burke's Attack on the French Revolution.* London-Derry: printed at the desire of a Society of Gentlemen, 1791. First Londonderry edition, 8vo., disbound, removed from a larger volume, leaves toned, dampstain to first few and last few leaves, titlepage split along spine, lacking wrappers, few upper fore-corners bent or chipped with loss to few words on two lines on one leaf, overall still good, rare.   Kaaterskill Books   16 - 66   2013 $750

Paine, Thomas 1737-1809 *Rights of Man.* London: J. S. Jordon, 1791. First edition, 2nd issue, octavo in fours, bound without half title, previously stab-stitched copy in old linen over boards, slightly browned, former owners ink signatures on front endpapers, modern bookplate, apart from light foxing very good copy, housed in custom quarter green morocco slipcase over green cloth, gilt stamped on spine. Heritage Book Shop   50th Anniversary Catalogue - 78   2013 $5000

Paine, Thomas 1737-1809 *Rights of Man: Being an Answer to Mr. Burke's Attack on the French Revolution.* London: printed for J. S. Jordon, 1791. Second edition, with "Jordan" imprint and added preface, octavo in fours, half title present, scarce original plain blue wrappers, string tied to binding, all edges uncut, title and date hand-written in pencil on front wrapper, wrappers with bit of creasing and edgewear, few small tears to middle of wrapper spine, internally quite clean, overall very good, housed in quarter green straight grain morocco slipcase. Heritage Book Shop Holiday Catalogue 2012 - 111   2013 $2500

Paine, Thomas 1737-1809 *Rights of Man: Being an Answer to Mr. Burke's Attack on the French Revolution.* London: printed for J. S. Jordan, 1791. Sixth edition, half title, 8vo., later plain boards, hand lettered on spine. Jarndyce Antiquarian Booksellers   CCIV - 223   2013   £180

Pajot, Charles *Dictionarum Novum Latino-Gallico-Graecum, cum ad Versionem Authorum Latinae Locutionis in Gallicam Linguam...* Rouen: apud Richardum Lallemant, 1700. 4to., lightly foxed in places, paper slightly age softened, old ownership inscriptions on title and front pastedown, 4to., contemporary vellum, spine bit darkened, boards marked, slightly ruckled, good, scarce.   Blackwell's Rare Books   172 - 107   2013   £350

Palaephatus *De Incredibilibus.* Amsterdam: Ludovicum Elzevirium, 1649. 12mo., titlepage in red and black, round inkstamp, single pen trial and smudge of wax to titlepage, small holes to leaf **4 affecting few letters, contemporary vellum, ink title to spine, Yapp edges, edges green, small patch repair, joints little cracked and alum thongs missing from upper board, illegible ink ownership inscription, ink library code opposite titlepage.   Unsworths Antiquarian Booksellers 28 - 35   2013   £300

Palahniuk, Chuck *Fugitives and Refugees: a Walk in Portland, Oregon.* New York: Crown Journeys/Crown Publishers, 2003. First edition, fine in fine dust jacket, signed by author, from the library of Bruce Kahn. Between the Covers Rare Books, Inc.   Mystery & Detective Fiction - 304849   2013 $200

Paley, William 1743-1805 *The Principles of Moral and Political Philosophy.* London: F. C. & J. Rivington, 1822. 3 volumes, engraved frontispieces and titlepages, full contemporary straight grain morocco with gilt decorated borders and spines, dark green morocco labels, some slight even fading to leather.   Ken Spelman Books Ltd.   75 - 82   2013   £60

Palfyn, Jean *Description Anatomique des Parties de la Femme qui Fervent a la Generation Avec un traite des Monstres, De Leur Causes, De Leur Natur, Se de Leue Differences et une Description Anatomique.* Leide: Chez Bastiaan Schouten, 1708. Engraved allegorical frontispiece, title in red and black, 72 pages, folding engraved plates, 19th century green polished calf, gilt paneled spine with raised bands, marbled paper boards, some foxing and toning of pages, overall very good, tight copy, rare.   James Tait Goodrich   75 - 163   2013 $4500

Palgrave, Francis Turner 1824-1897 *The Children's Treasury of Lyrical Poetry.* Macmillan and Co., 1922. Small 8vo., full brown morocco, gilt prize binding, title vignette, prize label of Sedbergh Preparatory School.   R. F. G. Hollett & Son   Children's Books - 435   2013   £25

Palladio, Andrea *The Four Books of Andrea Palladio's Architecture.* London: published by Isaac Ware, 1755. Folio, 205 plates, contemporary calf, rebacked to style, spine in compartments, profusely decorated in gilt, brown label lettered in gilt, inscribed "G. Morrison given the Earl of Burlington 1746", armorial bookplate of G. Morrison. Marlborough Rare Books Ltd.   218 - 115   2013   £1250

Palladio, Andrea *The Architecture of A. Palladio: in Four Books.* London: printed by John Darby for the author and all the plates by John Vantack, 1721.   Second Leoni edition, folio, frontispiece and 203 engraved plates and 12 text illustrations, lacking engraved portrait of George II, contemporary calf, rebacked to style, spine in compartments profusely decorated in gilt, brown label lettered in gilt. Marlborough Rare Books Ltd.   218 - 114   2013   £1250

The Palladium of Conscience; or the Foundation of Religious Liberty Displayed, Asserted and Established... Philadelphia: printed for the Subs: by Robert Bell, 1773. Second American edition or printing, 8vo., contemporary calf, 5 raised bands, red leather label, some browning and moderate staining, but very nice.   M & S Rare Books, Inc.   95 - 32   2013 $7500

Palliser, Fanny Marryat   1805-1878 *History of Lace.* London: Sampson Low, Son & Marston, 1865. First edition, 209 x 140mm., iv, 460 pages, very attractive blue-gray crushed morocco by Riviere & Son (stamp signed), covers with blind and gilt rules enclosing wide gilt filigree frame, raised bands, spine panels gilt in similar intricate pattern, gilt inner dentelles, marbled endpapers, all edges gilt, original purple and gilt cloth bound in at rear, engraved frontispiece, more than 150 illustrations in text and 26 plates of lace patterns, small portions of joints and extremities very slightly rubbed (and carefully refurbished), spine sunned to a hazel brown (hint of fading to portions of boards as well), once very handsome binding, still quite impressive and almost none of the original appeal diminished, beautiful internally, text and illustrations especially clean, fresh and smooth. Phillip J. Pirages   63 - 303   2013 $375

Palmer, David *New Brunswick and ther Poems.* Saint John: McMillan, 1869.   Maroon cloth, gold titles, half title, small 8vo., slightly sunned along spine and slight staining to cloth, lower edges have some waterstaining not affecting text.   Schooner Books Ltd.   101 - 16   2013 $75

Palmer, E. Clephan *The Young Blackbird.* Allan Wingate, 1953.   First edition, original cloth, dust jacket, trifle dusty. R. F. G. Hollett & Son   Children's Books - 446   2013   £65

Palmer, Frederick *The Last Shot.* New York: Charles Scribner's Sons, 1914.   First edition, owner name on front fly, few small and unobtrusive spots on boards, very good in rubbed and faded, good plus dust jacket with several internally repaired small chips and tears.   Between the Covers Rare Books, Inc.   Sci-Fi, Fantasy & Horror - 82706   2013 $300

Palmer, Raymond A. *Strange Offspring.* London: Utopian Pub. Limited, n.d., 1946.   First edition, small octavo, original pictorial self wrappers, stapled.   L. W. Currey, Inc.   Fall Sampler Sept. 2013 - 146555   2013 $350

Palmer, Samuel *Moral Essays on Some of the Most Curious and Significant English, Scotch and Foreign Proverbs.* printed by Tho. Hodgkin for R. Bonwicke etc., 1710.   First edition, contemporary blind panelled calf with spine label, little bumped and scratched, few slight defects, lacks front flyleaf, index leaves little damaged by damp and worm at bottom margins, nowhere affecting text, otherwise very good, scarce.   R. F. G. Hollett & Son   Wesleyan Methodism - 64   2013   £250

Palmer, Stuart *Rook Takes Knight.* New York: Random House, 1968.   First edition, fine in fine, price clipped dust jacket.   Between the Covers Rare Books, Inc.   Mystery & Detective Fiction - 105402   2013 $65

Palmer, T. S. *Chronology of the Death Valley Region in California 1849-1949.* Washington: printed by Byron S. Adam, 1952.   First edition, presentation copy signed by author, beige stiff wrappers printed in black on front cover, fine.   Argonaut Book Shop   Recent Acquisitions June 2013 - 224   2013 $100

Palmer, W. T. *The English Lakes.* A. & C. Black, 1908. Second edition, large 8vo., original decorative cloth gilt, top edge gilt, 75 colored plates by A. Heaton Cooper, rear endpapers lightly spotted, otherwise very good, fresh copy.   R. F. G. Hollett & Son   Lake District & Cumbria - 310   2013 £75

Palmer, W. T. *The English Lakes.* A. & C. Black, 1908. Second edition, large 8vo., original decorative cloth gilt, top edge gilt, 75 colored plates by A. Heaton Cooper, tape stains to corners of flyleaves, edges lightly spotted, otherwise very attractive copy, in scarce dust jacket.   R. F. G. Hollett & Son   Lake District & Cumbria - 311   2013   £140

Palmquist, Peter E. *Redwood and Lumbering in California Forests: a Reconstruction of the Original Edgar Cherry Edition.* San Francisco: Book Club of California, 1983. First edition thus, limited to 600 copies, frontispiece, numerous photo plates, full linen stamped in brown on spine, pictorial pastedown to front cover, very fine.   Argonaut Book Shop   Recent Acquisitions June 2013 - 225   2013 $150

Palou, Francisco *The Expedition into California of the Venerable Padre Fray Junipero Serra and His Companions in the Year 1769...* San Francisco: Nueva California Press, 1934.   First edition, first issue, quarto, 124 pages, frontispiece, 4 facsimiles, folding map, vellum backed golden boards, lettered in red on front cover and spine, vellum backed golden boards, lettered in red on front cover and spine, very fine and bright copy, uncut with printed dust jacket, news article removed from front flap of jacket.   Argonaut Book Shop   Summer 2013 - 266   2013 $225

Palou, Francisco *Historical Memoirs of New California.* Berkeley: University of California Press, 1926. First edition in English, 4 volumes, approximately 400 pages per volume, frontispiece, 25 plates, 3 folding maps, navy blue cloth, gilt, slightest of rubbing to few spine ends and corners, fine set. Argonaut Book Shop   Recent Acquisitions June 2013 - 29   2013 $600

Paltock, Robert *The Life and Adventures of Peter Wilkins, a Cornish Man.* Berwick: printed for W. Phorson and B. Law, 1784. 12mo., signed in sixes, half dark green crushed morocco by Sangorski & Sutcliffe, top edge gilt, very good, clean copy.   Jarndyce Antiquarian Booksellers CCIV - 224   2013   £500

Pangborn, Edgar *The Judgment of Eve.* New York: Simon & Schuster, 1966. First edition, fine in fine dust jacket with small ink price on front flap, lovely, unrubbed and unread.   Between the Covers Rare Books, Inc.   Sci-Fi, Fantasy & Horror - 318819   2013 $75

Pankhurst, Christabel *Seeing the Future.* New York: Harper, 1929. Fourth printing, 8vo., 328 pages, author's 4 line presentation, clear tape over signature, brown cloth, news clippings on front pastedown, very good, tight copy. Second Life Books Inc.   183 - 310   2013 $85

Pankhurst, E. Sylvia *The Suffragette Movement, an Intimate Account of Persons and Ideals with Illustrations.* London: Longmans Green, 1931. First edition, 8vo., frontispiece, 631 pages, bookplate, small name sticker on endpaper, another removed from front blank otherwise fine, without dust jacket, scarce, from the library of reformer Florence Kelley (1859-1932).   Second Life Books Inc. 182 - 186   2013 $175

Panorama of Monks. No publication information, Italian, circa, 1850. very good in plain slipcase, chipped, 2 3.4 x 4 inches, boards, spine repaired, else very good, 36 very fine hand colored illustrations, opening accordion style.   Aleph-Bet Books, Inc.   104 - 402   2013 $700

Papanicolaou, George N. *Diagnosis of Uterine Cancer by Vaginal Smear.* New York: Commonwealth Fund, 1943. First edition, signed and inscribed by author, very good++, 4to., color plates A-K with facing legend pages minimal spotting and edge wear to cover, very good dust jacket with 1 inch chip upper left corner front panel of dust jacket, other small chips, age darkening, spotting to dust jacket.   By the Book, L. C.   38 - 42   2013 $2500

Papworth, John Buonarotti   1775-1847 *Rural Residences....* London: R. Ackermann, 1818. First edition, large 8vo., 27 hand colored aquatint plates, some minor spotting, modern marbled paper boards, spine with label lettered in gilt.   Marlborough Rare Books Ltd.   218 - 116 2013   £985

Papworth, John Buonarotti   1775-1847 *Rural Residences...* London: R. Ackerman, 1818. First edition, imperial 8vo., pages (109), 27 color aquatint plates, contemporary diced calf, later leather back, rubbed, inner joints strengthened, some foxing and minor soiling, clean fresh sheets and bright plates, bookplates on front pastedown, another removed from front free endpaper.   Second Life Books Inc.   183 - 437   2013 $3750

Papworth, John Buonarotti   1775-1847 *Rural Residences.* London: printed for R. Ackermann..., 1832. Second edition, large 8vo., 27 hand colored aquatint plates, original green cloth, upper and lower covers with dolphin and fountain design, sympathetically rebacked, inscribed by Samuel Clegg Jun 1840.   Marlborough Rare Books Ltd. 218 - 117   2013   £1400

Pardies, Ignace Gaston *Dell'Anima delle Bestie e sue Funzioni.* Venice: Per Andrea Poletti, 1696. Contemporary ownership inscription, slightly browned edges untrimmed, 16mo., original carta rustica, spine lettered in ink soiled, spine darkened, very good.   Blackwell's Rare Books 172 - 108   2013   £650

Pardoe, Julia *The Beauties of the Bosophorus...* London: published for the proprietors by George Virtue, 1838. First edition, small 4to., 81 steel engravings, frontispiece, titlepage vignette, 78 view plates, 1 map, three quarter dark green morocco over marbled boards, boards ruled in gilt, five raised bands ruled in gilt, 4 compartments with floral gilt decorations, two with gilt titles, marbled endpapers, all edges gilt, very good, boards and extremities rubbed, owner's bookplate to free front endpaper, small faint semi circular stain to fore edge of first two prelim leaves, tissue guard and engraved title foxed and offset, faint dampstain to lower inner corner, marginal only, scattered foxing to plates, nearly all marginal or blank backs, otherwise plates crisp, text clean, binding solid, very handsome.   Kaaterskill Books 16 - 67   2013 $1200

Pare, Ambrose *The Works of that Famous Chirurgion Ambrose Pare.* London: printed by Th. Cotes and R. Young, 1634. First edition in English, tall folio, contemporary full polished calf, raised bands, red leather spine label, front joint just beginning to split along top 4 inches, text with some browning and staining, some marginal fraying of couple of leaves, overall generally clean copy, lacks "To the reader" and the "dedication leaf".   James Tait Goodrich 75 - 165   2013 $10.500

Paretsky, Sara *Bitter Medicine.* New York: Morrow, 1987. First edition, signed by author, very fine in dust jacket.   Mordida Books   81 - 391   2013 $100

Paris, J. A. *Philosophy in sport Made Science in Earnest.* London: John Murray, 1861. Ninth edition, original green cloth, gilt, woodcut frontispiece and numerous text illustrations, prelims rather foxed, shaped armorial bookplate of Woodthorpe Brandon.   R. F. G. Hollett & Son   Children's Books - 436   2013   £85

Paris, Matthew   1200-1259   *Flores Historiarum pr Matthaeum Westmonasteriensem Collecti, Praecipue de Rebus Britannicis ab Exordio Mundi Usque ad Annum Domini 1307.*   Ex officina Thomae Marshii, 1570.   Second printed edition, Folio, titlepage trimmed close to woodcut border, final blank leaf discarded, index bound at front of text, one leaf with original paper flaw affecting a few characters, first leaf of index with bottom margin folded over to preserve early ms. note, verso of title also filled with text in early ms. (trimmed at bottom), few short notes or marks later on, last dozen leaves showing faint but substantial dampmark, some soiling/minor staining elsewhere, touch of worming to blank fore-edge margin, two leaves remargined, gathering Ttt in earlier(?) state without (and not calling for) the additional unsigned singleton leaf, 18th century mottled calf, spine with five raised bands, red morocco lettering pieces in second and third compartment, rubbed, front joint cracking (but strong), little peeling to leather, light wear to endcaps, marbled endpapers, bookplates of Robert Surtees (1779-1834) and his Mainsforth Library, sound.   Blackwell's Rare Books   172 - 109   2013   £1600

Parish, Peggy   *Amelia Bedelia.*   New York et al: Harper and Row, 1972.   Stated first edition, illustrations in color by Wallace Tripp, 8vo., glazed pictorial boards, fine in slightly worn dust jacket, scarce.   Aleph-Bet Books, Inc.   105 - 85   2013 $200

Park, Katharine   *The Cambridge History of Science. Volume 3. Early Modern Science.*   Cambridge: Cambridge University Press, 2006.   thick 8vo., green cloth, gilt stamped cover and spine titles, dust jacket, fine.   Jeff Weber Rare Books   169 - 337   2013 $140

Park, Mungo   *The Life and Travels of Mungo Park.* Edinburgh: William P. Nimmo, 1881.   Modern half blue levant morocco, full page woodcut illustrations, scattered spotting, few slight edge repairs, very attractive copy.   R. F. G. Hollett & Son   Africana - 153   2013   £85

Parker, Al   *Baseball Giant Killers: The Spudders of the 20's.*   Quanah: 1976.   illustrations, dust jacket with slight wear, two abrasions, front endpaper stained from old newspaper clipping, else about very good, inscribed by author, quite scarce.   Dumont Maps & Books of the West   125 - 68   2013 $55

Parker, B.   *Arctic Orphans.*   London & Edinburgh: W. & R. Chambers, n.d. circa, 1920.   Oblong folio, pictorial boards, slight tip rubbing, else fine in dust jacket (chipped with few mends), illustrations by N. Parker with 13 incredible full page color illustrations plus illustrations in text, pictorial endpapers and striking color covers, rare.   Aleph-Bet Books, Inc.   105 - 441   2013 $2000

Parker, B.   *Book of Baby Birds.*   New York: Frederick Stokes, 1905.   Large 4to, pictorial boards, 54 pages, covers and edges worn, else tight, clean and very good, 12 fine full page illustrations and line illustrations by N. Parker, scarce.   Aleph-Bet Books, Inc.   104 - 406   2013 $600

Parker, B.   *Larder Lodge.*   London: Chambers circa, 1910.   Large oblong 4to., pictorial boards, some chipping to spine paper, slight edge rubbing tight and very good+, 14 fine full page color illustrations.   Aleph-Bet Books, Inc. 104 - 407   2013 $1200

Parker, E. H.   *John Chinaman and a Few Others.*   New York: E. P. Dutton, 1902.   First edition, 8vo., very good+, owner bookplate, minimal sun spine, mild soil and foxing. By the Book, L. C.   38 - 70   2013 $225

Parker, George   *Studley Royal, Fountains Abbey, Past and Present, etc.*   Ripon: George Parker, Kirkgate House, circa, 1905.   Frontispiece, titlepage vignette folding plan and text engravings, small 8vo., some browning to leading edge of several pages and tear to blank edge of one leaf, original wrappers with later paper backstrip.   Ken Spelman Books Ltd.   73 - 76   2013   £25

Parker, H.   *Mail and Passenger Steamships of the Nineteenth Century.*   London: Sampson Low, 1928.   4to., color and black and white plates, good in original cloth, spine little rubbed.   Ken Spelman Books Ltd.   75 - 173 2013   £50

Parker, Robert Andrew   *Ein Deutsches Worterbuch.* Cornwall: March, 2011.   Only edition, 12mo., 28 hand colored flexible card leaves, each 7 1/2 x 5 inches, uncut, laid into cloth backed hand painted cardboard and wooden box fabricated by artist, fine.   Howard S. Mott Inc.   262 - 110 2013 $1500

Parker, Robert Andrew   *Travels with Bob: Words and Pictures.*   New York: Ink, Inc., 2009.   First edition, one of 100 copies printed and signed by author/artist, this one designated 'h/c' or 'hors commerce' and unnumbered, prospectus containing 2 signed letterpress relief prints, hand colored by artist, labeled, "A/P" or "artists proof", over 300 reproductions, all in full color, fine.   Howard S. Mott Inc.   262 - 111 2013 $750

Parker, Robert B. *Pale Kings and Princes.* New York: Delacorte, 1987. First edition, uncorrected proof copy, one of 500 numbered copies signed by Parker on publisher's bookplate, very fine in printed wrappers. Mordida Books 81 - 400 2013 $65

Parker, Robert B. *Poodle Springs.* New York: Putnam, 1989. First edition, advance reading copy, signed by author, very fine in pictorial wrappers. Mordida Books 81 - 402 2013 $75

Parker, Robert B. *The Private Eye in Hammett and Chandler.* Northridge: Lord John, 1984. First edition, one of 300 numbered copies signed by Parker, very fine without dust jacket as issued. Mordida Books 81 - 394 2013 $150

Parker, Robert B. *Valediction.* New York: Delacorte/ Seymour Lawrence, 1984. First edition, uncorrected proof, fine in printed wrappers. Mordida Books 81 - 395 2013 $65

Parker, Robert B. *The Widening Gyre.* New York: Delacorte/Seymour Lawrence, 1983. First edition, signed by author, very fine in dust jacket. Mordida Books 81 - 392 2013 $65

Parker, Theodore *The Critical and Miscellaneous Writings of...* Boston: Munroe, 1843. First edition, 8vo., pages 360 plus ads, black cloth, partially unopened, from the library of consumer advocate Florence Kelley, front hinge tender, cover somewhat faded and little worn at corners and ends of spine, else very good, ownership signatures of Judge, abolitionist and Congressman, William D. Kelley. Second Life Books Inc. 183 - 311 2013 $85

Parker, Thomas N. *An Essay on the Construction, Hanging and Fastening of Gates...* Printed by C. Whittingham, 1804. Second edition, narrow 4to., contemporary half calf, drab paper boards, green morocco label, hinges and head and tail of spine very neatly repaired. Jarndyce Antiquarian Booksellers CCIV - 225 2013 £380

Parkes, Samuel *A Chemical Catechism with Copious Notes, a Vocabulary of Chemical terms...* printed for the author by Richard Taylor, 1807. Second edition, engraved frontispiece, frontispiece foxed, little bit of foxing and mild browning elsewhere, 8vo., uncut, original boards, hand lettered title on spine, trifle worn and one or two spots, good. Blackwell's Rare Books Sciences - 93 2013 £475

Parkin, Louise *Voice from the Mountains: Life and Works of Joe Hills Johnson.* Mesa: Joel Hills Johnson Arizona Committee, 1982. First edition, 329 pages, octavo, brown grained buckram with gilt title on front board and backstrip, map on front endsheet and pastedown, very good, light rubbing to corners of boards. Ken Sanders Rare Books 45 - 10 2013 $125

Parkinson, John *Theatrum Botanicum...* London: Tho. Cotes, 1640. First edition, Folio, added engraved titlepage with inset portrait of author by W. Marshall, headpieces, tailpieces, decorative initials, more than 2700 woodcut illustrations, engraved title remargined with few small holes or tears closed, last leaf remargined with minor loss to index and page number, margins brittle and occasionally waterstained or with small tears, with pencil marginalia and underlining, corners torn at pages 611-612 and 1687-1688 without loss, full modern dark brown calf, blind ruled covers and spine, raised bands/brown leather spine label, gilt spine, fine. Jeff Weber Rare Books 169 - 338 2013 $8000

Parkinson, Sydney *A Journal of a Voyage to The South Seas in His Majesty's Ship The Endeavour.* London: 1773. First edition, 4to., map, portrait, 26 engraved plates, tall copy, early plain calf, rebacked, original back laid down, original red morocco label. Maggs Bros. Ltd. 1467 - 89 2013 £11,000

Parkman, Francis 1823-1893 *The California and Oregon Trail.* New York: George P. Putnam, 1849. First edition, one of 500 copies of the second printing April 7 1849, good copy, morocco backed cloth slipcase, 8vo., original blue-gray cloth, general overall shelfwear, inner hinge strengthened, frontispiece and extra lithographed title. Howard S. Mott Inc. 262 - 112 2013 $2500

Parkman, Francis 1823-1893 *The Oregon Trail.* Boston: Little Brown, 1925. Limited to 950 numbered copies for sale, 6 1/2 x 9 1/4 inches, illustrations by N. C. Wyeth and Frederick Remington, cloth backed boards with cloth tips top edge gilt, fine in dust jacket and slipcase with limitation number on printed label (dust jacket with repair and piece off back panel), case very good, strengthened along joints, rare with jacket and slipcase. Aleph-Bet Books, Inc. 105 - 597 2013 $1250

Parkman, Francis 1823-1893 *The Works.* Boston: Little Brown and Co., 1897. 12 volumes, 203 x 137mm., 12 volumes, pleasant contemporary polished half calf, raised bands, spines gilt in compartments with central floral sprig and scrolling cornerpieces, each spine with one red and one green morocco label, marbled boards and endpapers, top edge gilt, 3 frontispiece portraits, 25 plates of plans and maps, five of them folding, bookplates of Irwin Library, Butler University (underneath bookplate noting that the book is 'the gift of Spaan memorial", stamp of Butler University Library in each volume, spines little dried and marked, hint of wear to joints, about half the volumes with rubbing at top of spine, but bindings tight and still attractive with no cracking to joints, fine internally, text very fresh, clean and smooth. Phillip J. Pirages   63 - 359   2013 $250

Parks, Gordon *Camera Portraits: The Techniques and Principles of Documentary Portraits.* New York: Franklin Watts, 1948. First edition, quarto, 94 pages, boards quite soiled and small stain at top of first several pages, else very good in good dust jacket with a number of modest chips and tears, reasonable copy, uncommon.   Between the Covers Rare Books, Inc.   165 - 239 2013 $275

Parnell, Henry *A Treatise on Roads.* London: printed for Longman, Orme, Brown Green and Longmans, 1838. Second edition, 229 x 152mm., appealing recent sympathetic half calf over marbled paper boards, raised bands, black morocco label, few gatherings at rear unopened, 9 folding engraved plates, isolated light marginal soiling, few pencilled markers and diagrams in margins, plates slightly foxed, otherwise internally in excellent condition, binding as new. Phillip J. Pirages   63 - 400   2013 $550

Parr, Harriet 1828-1900 *Tuflongob's Journey in Search of Ogres; with Some Accounts of His Early Life and How His Shoes Got Worn Out.* London: Smith, Elder and Co., 1862. First edition, half title, hand colored frontispiece and 5 plates, uncut in original green pebble grained pictorial cloth, owner's inscription on leading f.e.p., dated 1864, good plus, scarce.   Jarndyce Antiquarian Booksellers   CCV - 164   2013   £85

Parrot, Louis *Paul Eluard.* Paris: Pierre Sechers Editeur, 1951. New edition, 12mo., original wrappers, folding box, good copy, slightly soiled, spine worn with some loss at head, inscribed by Paul Eluard for Douglas Glass.   Maggs Bros. Ltd.   1460 - 278   2013   £150

Parry, William *The Last Days of Lord Byron, with His Lordship's Opinions on Various Subjects.* London: printed for Knight & Lacey, 1825. First edition, frontispiece, 3 color aquatint plates, one or two gatherings slightly proud, contemporary half calf, gilt spine, maroon leather label, little dulled and rubbed, Marquess of Headfort's armorial bookplate.   Jarndyce Antiquarian Booksellers   CCIII - 428   2013   £320

Parry, William Edward 1790-1855 *Journal of a Second Voyage for the Discovery of a North-West Passage from the Atlantic to the Pacific Performed n the Years 1821, 1822 and 1823 in His Majesty's Ships Fury and Hecla.* London: 1824. First edition, 40 engraved maps, charts, views, 4to, contemporary calf, expertly rebacked with contemporary style endpapers, inscribed by author for Thomas Martyn.   Maggs Bros. Ltd.   1467 - 138   2013   £3250

Parry, William Edward 1790-1855 *Journal of a Second Voyage for the Discovery of a North-West Passage from the Atlantic to the Pacific Performed in the Years 1821-22-23...* London: John Murray, 1824. First edition, large 4to., modern full tan calf gilt, spine with four flattened raised bands and contrasting spine label, engraved frontispiece, 30 aquatint and engraved tissue guarded plates, 4 folding charts, 4 folding plates, 121 text illustrations, excellent large, untrimmed copy.   R. F. G. Hollett & Son   Polar Exploration - 46   2013   £1250

Parsons, George F. *The Life and Adventures of James W. Marshall.* San Francisco: George Fields, 1935. Reprint of 1870 first edition, small 8vo., folding color plates, folding tinted plate, folding color map, original early ephemera tipped or laid-in, green boards, printed paper label on spine, printed pictorial pastedown on front cover, folding map, split to portion of one fold, repaired, else very fine.   Argonaut Book Shop   Summer 2013 - 269   2013 $300

Parsons, Usher *Sailor's Physician...* Providence: printed by Barnum Field & Co., 1824. Second edition, 12mo., original light green boards, paper label, 203 pages, uncut, inscribed "A present by Dr. Parsons Mach 30th 1825, Natha(nia)l Bachelder", with Bachelder's ownership signature.   Howard S. Mott Inc.   262 - 113   2013 $450

Parsons, William Barclay *Robert Fulton and the Submarine.* New York: Columbia University Press, 1922. First edition, 8vo., xiii, 154 pages, frontispiece, plates, burgundy cloth, gilt stamped cover emblem and spine title, dust jacket chipped with pieces missing, else very good, Burndy bookplate, rare in original edition with jacket.   Jeff Weber Rare Books   169 - 339   2013 $75

Partington, J. R. *A History of Greek Fire and Gunpowder.* Cambridge: W. Heffer, 1960. First edition, tall 8vo., 3 plates, including frontispiece, illustrations, red cloth, gilt stamped spine title, dust jacket rubbed with some edgewear and manuscript paper spine label, very good, Burndy bookplate.   Jeff Weber Rare Books   169 - 340   2013 $65

Parton, Mary Field *Autobiography of Mother Jones.* Chicago: Charles H. Kerr, 1925. First edition, 8vo., 242 pages, 4 photos, blue cloth, owner's name on flyleaf, cover little faded and slightly worn at corners and ends of spine, else very good, tight copy.   Second Life Books Inc.   183 - 312   2013 $150

Party Wine Punches and Wine Cocktails. San Francisco: Italian Swiss Colony, n.d. circa, 1963. 24mo., single leaf folded to make 12 pages, illustrations from photos, few light pencil notations on last panel (apparently calculations on the expense of making wine punch), else fine. Between the Covers Rare Books, Inc. Cocktails, Etc. - 312644 2013 $50

Pascal, Blaise *Monsieur Pascall's Thoughts, Meditations and Prayers...* London: printed for Jacob Tonson, 1688. First English edition, without A1, prelim blank leaf, with small piece out of blank corner of A7, superior copy, 12mo., contemporary paneled calf, raised bands, rebacked, old back laid down. Howard S. Mott Inc. 262 - 114 2013 $2850

Pascal, Blaise *Penses de M. Pascal sur la Religion et sur Quelques Autres Sujets qui Ont este... (bound with) Discours sur les Pensees de M. Pascal...* Amsterdam: chez Abraham Wolganck..., 1672-1673. 2 volumes bound in 1, full contemporary vellum, paper spine label, covers little rubbed, armorial bookplate. Ken Spelman Books Ltd. 75 - 5 2013 £380

Passer, Harold C. *The Electrical Manufacturers 1875-1900...* Cambridge: Harvard University Press, 1953. First edition, 8vo., illustrations, tables, diagrams, light gray cloth, black stamped spine title, dust jacket heavily chipped with pieces missing, Burndy bookplate, very good. Jeff Weber Rare Books 169 - 341 2013 $65

Passeron, Roger *Andre Masson: Graphik.* Fribourg: Office d Livre, 1973. First edition in German, one of 50 deluxe copies from a total edition of 700, numbered "D50" and signed by Masson with pencil, 2 volumes, volume i is bound book in publisher's dust jacket and cloth slipcase, 180 pages of text, 51 handsome photolithographic plates, most in colors, bound in are 3 hors-texe original color lithographs printed by Gernand Mourlot; volume ii publisher's deluxe portfolio case with extra suite of 1 drypoint etching and 4 color lithographs, each of the 5 original prints signed and numbered "50/50" by Masson, 14.25 x 11.75 inches, excellent condition. Gemini Fine Books & Arts., Ltd. Art Reference & Illustrated Books - 2013 $3000

Passport to Trader Vic's Exotic Cocktails. San Francisco: Trader Vic's, n.d. circa, 1960. 12mo., stapled illustrated wrappers (20) pages, illustrations in color from drawings, fine. Between the Covers Rare Books, Inc. Cocktails, Etc. - 312616 2013 $50

Pasteur, Louis *Studies on Fermentation, the Diseases of Beer, Their Causes and the Means of Presenting Them.* London: Macmillan, 1879. First edition in English, 8vo., 12 plates, original black stamped dark grey-green cloth, gilt stamped spine, neatly repaired hinges, bookplate of H.D. (Humphrey Desmond) Murray, rubber stamps of Murray, Bull & Spencer, limited, canceled titlepage ownership signature "Union Brewery 1889". Jeff Weber Rare Books 169 - 342 2013 $375

Pastimes of James Joyce. New York: Joyce Memorial Fund, 1941. First edition, one of 100 copies signed by editors and artists, this #37, there were also 700 unsigned copies, 305 x 230mm., original blue-gray paper boards, facsimile of Joyce's signature on upper cover, flat spine, frontispiece by Jo Davidson, with 3 pages of facsimile manuscript, laid in at rear, article from 28 September 1916 edition of "The Listener" entitled "James Joyce: A First Impression" by James Stern, half the length of each joint with thin crack, faint offsetting (from news article?) to titlepage and frontispiece, otherwise especially clean and fresh inside and out. Phillip J. Pirages 63 - 292 2013 $950

Pater, Walter 1839-1894 *Marius the Epicurean: His Sensations and Ideas.* London: Macmillan and Co., 1892. Sixth thousand, inscribed by author to Lady Brooke, Ranee of Sarawak, original dark blue cloth with gilt title and author to spine, some bumping and rubbing but in very good condition, hinges volume I tender and discoloration to endpapers, otherwise very good, booklabel of Arnold Muirhead affixed to front pastedown of each volume, 2 volumes, 165; 246 pages. The Kelmscott Bookshop 7 - 126 2013 $875

Pater, Walter 1839-1894 *Marius the Epicurean.* London: Macmillan and Co., 1910. 224 x 140mm, 2 volumes, titlepage printed in red and black, excellent contemporary russet morocco, gracefully tooled in gilt and inlaid in Arts and Crafts style, covers delicately framed in gilt with cornerpieces of inlaid ivory flowers and gilt leaves, front covers with large central medallion composed of thin, linked gilt ovals accented with gilt dots and enclosing lozenge of inlaid ivory flowers and green leaves with green daisy at center (total of 90 floral or foliate inlays in all), raised bands, spine compartments with finely tooled flower centerpieces and gilt dots at corners, turn-ins with multiple gilt rules, all edges gilt, titlepage printed in red and black, very slight variations in color of leather (some of this due to fading?), one corner little bruised, leaves bit browned at edges because of paper stock quality (no doubt same as in all copies), first volume with occasional minor spotting, otherwise very appealing set, fresh internally and generally very well preserved with nothing approaching significant condition problem. Phillip J. Pirages 61 - 98 2013 $1250

Pater, Walter 1839-1894 *The Marriage of Cupid and Psyche.* New York: Limited Editions Club, 1951. Limited to 1500 numbered copies, signed by artist, Edmund Dulac with 6 color plates, beautiful copy, 4to., full vellum stamped in gold, fine in fine slipcase. Aleph-Bet Books, Inc. 104 - 187 2013 $750

Paterson, Katherine Jacob *Have I Loved.* New York: Crowell, 1980. Stated first edition, 8vo., quarter cloth, fine in fine dust jacket (not price clipped, no award medal). Aleph-Bet Books, Inc. 105 - 444 2013 $200

Patmore, Coventry *The Children's Garland from the Best Poets.* Macmillan, 1862. First edition, original cloth, gilt, little worn and neatly recased, new endpapers, half title and vignette on title.   R. F. G. Hollett & Son   Children's Books - 437   2013   £130

Paton, Alan *Cry, The Beloved Country.*   New York: Charles Scribner's Sons, 1948. First US edition, original decorated grey cloth, spine trifle darkened, slightly stained booklabel.   R. F. G. Hollett & Son   Africana - 155   2013   £30

Paton, Maggie Whitecross *Letters and Sketches for the New Hebrides.* London: Hodder and Stoughton, 1894. Second edition, original green cloth gilt, frontispiece, map and 23 illustrations.   R. F. G. Hollett & Son   Polar Exploration - 47   2013   £75

Paton, Maggie Whitecross *Letters and Sketches from the New Hebrides.* London: Hodder and Stoughton, 1894. Second edition, original green cloth, gilt, slightly used, labels removed from spine, frontispiece, map and 23 illustrations, front joint cracking, few spots, library label of front pastedown.   R. F. G. Hollett & Son   Polar Exploration - 48   2013   £50

Patoun, Archibald *A Compleat Treatise of Practical Navigation, Demonstrated from Its First Principles...*   printed for R. Willock, 1730. First edition, folding engraved plate, diagrams in text, tear in plate which is frayed at fore-edge, without loss, bit of foxing at either end and occasionally elsewhere, 8vo., original calf, double gilt fillets on sides, spine gilt ruled in compartments, paper lettering piece without flyleaves, rubbed and worn, headcap lacking, sound.   Blackwell's Rare Books   Sciences - 94   2013   £850

Patrick, Chann *The House of Retrogression.*   New York: Jacobsen, 1932. First edition, fine in dust jacket.   Mordida Books   81 - 404   2013 $300

Patron, Susan *Higher Power of Lucky.*   New York: Atheneum, 2006. Stated first edition, first printing with correct number code, 8vo., boards, 134 pages, as new in as new dust jacket, illustrations by Matt Phelan.   Aleph-Bet Books, Inc.   105 - 445   2013 $150

Pattee, William S. *A History of Old Braintree and Quincy...*   Quincy: Green and Prescott, 1878. First edition, 8vo., pages 660, three quarter calf and gilt stamped cloth, hinges neatly reinforced with tape, very good, tight, clean copy, name on endpaper, 14 engraved illustrations.   Second Life Books Inc.   183 - 313   2013 $95

Patterson, George *Missionary Life among the Cannibals Being the Life of Rev. John Geddie...* Toronto: James Campbell & Son, 1882. 8vo., green cloth boards, gilt titles to front and spine, frontispiece & black and white illustrations, edges worn, front hinge crack and some foxing.   Schooner Books Ltd.   105 - 95   2013 $65

Patterson, James *Cat and Mouse.*   Boston: Little Brown, 1997. First edition, hardcover, inscribed by author, fine in fine dust jacket.   Beasley Books   2013 - 2013 $50

Patterson, Terry Ezekiel *Narrative of the Adventures and Sufferings of Samuel Patterson, Experienced in the Pacific Ocean and Many Other Parts of the World....*   Palmer: May 1, 1817. First edition, second issue?, 16mo., 144 pages, contemporary calf, leather label, binding worn but sound.   M & S Rare Books, Inc.   95 - 281   2013 $950

Pattison, Mark *Isaac Casaubon 1559-1614.*   London: Longmans, 1875. First edition, good in original dark green gilt lettered cloth, some minor rubbing and slight mark to foot of titlepage.   Ken Spelman Books Ltd.   75 - 139   2013   £70

Patton, Annaleone D. *California Mormons by Sail and Trail.*   Salt Lake City: Deseret Book Company, 1961. First edition, inscribed and signed by author, illustrated from old prints and photos, turquoise cloth, gilt, light offsetting to front ends from news clipping, else fine, very slightly chipped pictorial dust jacket, inscribed and signed by author.   Argonaut Book Shop   Summer 2013 - 271   2013 $75

Paul, Doris A. *The Navajo Code Talkers.*   Pittsburgh: Dorrance Pub., 1990. Seventh printing, 8vo., signed by fourteen Navajo code talkers, including Albert Smith (President 4th Mar. Div. 4th Sig. Co.), Paul Blatchford, Bill Toledo, Harold Foster, George Smith, Harold Evan and others, fine in near fine dust jacket.   By the Book, L. C.   38 - 38   2013 $900

Paul, Elliot *Hugger-Mugger in the Louvre.*   New York: Random House, 1940. First edition, some darkening on pastedowns, otherwise fine in dust jacket.   Mordida Books   81 - 405   2013 $200

Paul, Elliot *Intoxication Made Easy.*   New York: Modern Age, 1941. of 100 numbered copies, copy number 103, cloth, paper covered boards, slipcase, little darkening to paper spine label, else fine in very good or better, edgeworn slipcase, signed by uthor and artist.   Between the Covers Rare Books, Inc.   Cocktails, Etc. - 304992   2013 $175

Paul, Rodman W. *The California Gold Discovery Sources, Documents, Accounts and Memoirs Relating to the Discovery of Gold at Sutter's Mill.* Georgetown: Talisman Press, 1966. First edition, scarce thus, 237 pages, portraits, maps, illustrations, dark red cloth spine, printed yellow boards, very fine in pictorial dust jacket. Argonaut Book Shop   Recent Acquisitions June 2013 - 229   2013 $125

Paulhan, Jean *Les Paroles Transparentes.* Paris: Les Bibliophiles de l'Union Francaise, 1955. First edition, one of the total issue of 132 exemplars produced for members of the club (no copies were for sale), signed in pencil by Braque, Paulhan and Leon Leal, club's President, 14 original lithographs in tones of blue, four of these hors-texte, printed on handmade Auvergne du Moulin Richard de Bas paper, 84 loose leaves in wrappers, boards chemise and slipcase, overall size 18 x 14, slipcase with minor imperfections, otherwise excellent. Gemini Fine Books & Arts., Ltd.   Art Reference & Illustrated Books - 2013 $2500

Pauli, Wolfgang *Writings on Physics and Philosophy.* Berlin: Springer-Verlag, 1994. First edition, without dust jacket as issued, slight bump to middle of front cover and price sticker on rear cover, else fine. Between the Covers Rare Books, Inc.   Philosophy - 101222   2013 $70

Paulin, Tom *Selected Poems. 1972-1990.* London: Faber and Faber, 1993. Uncorrected unbound page proofs, 4to., original white wrappers, stapled on upper corner, upper page slightly rubbed and creased, rear leaf detached from staple, otherwise excellent. Maggs Bros. Ltd.   1442 - 277   2013   £75

Paulsen, Martha *Toyland.* Akron: 1944. Oblong 4to., spiral backed boards, slight wear to spine else very good-fine, 4 great moveable plates and many color black and whites by Julian Wehr. Aleph-Bet Books, Inc.   105 - 414   2013 $200

Paulus Aegineta *Medicinae totius Enchiridion, Septem Libris Universam Recte Mendendi Rationem Complectens, Nuncque Denueo Multo Quam Antea & Emendatius & Forma Artis Huius Studiosis Commodiore i Lucem Editum.* Basel: 1551. 8vo., small marginal tear in title repaired with sellotape, few small old marginal marks, some light toning and dustiness, contemporary vellum boards, long sides overlapping, spine labelled in ink, few small marks and faint dust soiling to vellum, vellum covering detached from front hinge (but joint and endpaper both holding strong), gilt stamp of Birmingham Medical Inst. to spine, and small stamp to title. Unsworths Antiquarian Booksellers   28 - 36   2013   £600

Paulus Aegineta *Pavli Aeginetae Medici Insignis Opus Divinum Qvc vtr Le Vastissimvm Totivs Artis Oceaniun, Laconica Breuitate Sensibus Argutis Areris Aphorismmis in Epitomen Redegit... (bound with) Pro Conservanda Sanitate Tuendaque Prospera Valetudine...* Basel: Andreas Cratander & Johann Bebel, 1532. Mainz: 1531. First edition, folio, recent full English paneled calf, raised bands and nicely blind tooled spine, panels on front and back in lighter tone, elegant binding, title soiled and creased and has been mounted, some light marginal dampstaining and foxing. James Tait Goodrich   75 - 166   2013 $2475

Payne, Bucker H. *The Negro: What Is His Ethnological Status?* Cincinnati: published for the proprietor, 1867. Second edition, 12mo., 48 pages, original printed wrappers, slightly dusty, faint tide marks in text, very good.   M & S Rare Books, Inc.   95 - 282   2013 $225

Payton, Charles *Days of a Knight.* Hutchinson, 1924. Original cloth, spine rather faded, 16 plates.   R. F. G. Hollett & Son   Africana - 156   2013   £45

Payton, Lew *Did Adam Sin and Other Stories of Negro Life in Comedy, Drama and Sketches.* Los Angeles: the author, 1937. 132 pages, illustrated stiff wrappers, fine. Between the Covers Rare Books, Inc.   165 - 146   2013 $100

Payton, Lew *Did Adam Sin? Also Stories of Negro Life.* Los Angeles: the author, 1937. First edition, stiff wrappers, quite fine.   Beasley Books   2013 - 2013 $50

Paz, Octavio *Sight and Touch.* New York: Limited Editions Club, 1994. Limited to 300 copies, signed by author and artist on limitation page, this being number 249, large folio, 3 full-color woodcuts by Balthus, publisher's quarter tan morocco over tan cloth, front cover with printed paper label, lettered in brown, housed in publisher's tan, felt lined cloth clamshell, clamshell with tan morocco lettering label on front, publisher's newsletter laid in, fine. Heritage Book Shop   Holiday Catalogue 2012 - 113   2013 $1750

Peacham, Henry *The Period of Mourning.* London: printed by T. S. for John Helme, 1613. Reprint, 8vo., 4 woodcut vignettes, uncut, some dusting to titlepage and fore-edges, final page lists errata and (like all copies) has manuscript correction relating to page 32 and corresponding manuscript correction to that page, 19th century quarter calf, marbled boards, little rubbed, corners bumped. Jarndyce Antiquarian Booksellers   CCIV - 226   2013   £260

Peacock, George *A Treatise of Algebra. Volume I. Volume II.* Cambridge: printed at the University Press, 1842-1845. 8vo., contemporary or slightly later tan calf, double gilt fillets on sides, arms of Jesus College, Oxford blocked in gilt at centre of covers, spines gilt in compartments, contrasting lettering pieces, marbled edges matching endleaves, spine slightly faded and with some loss of gilt, covers little spotted, flyleaves foxed, good.   Blackwell's Rare Books   Sciences - 95   2013   £350

Peake, Mervyn   1911-1968 *Boy in Darkness.* Wheaton, 1976. Original pictorial stiff wrappers, 5 illustrations.   R. F. G. Hollett & Son   Children's Books - 440   2013   £35

Peake, Mervyn   1911-1968 *Boy in Darkness.* Hodder Children's Books, 1996. First edition, original cloth, gilt, dust jacket, light crease to lower panel, illustrations.   R. F. G. Hollett & Son   Children's Books - 439   2013   £25

Peake, Mervyn   1911-1968 *Captain Slaughterboard Drops Anchor.* Macmillan, circa, 1987. First US edition, small 4to., original glazed pictorial boards, matching dust jacket (closed tear and slight surface defect to upper panel), illustrations in yellow and black.   R. F. G. Hollett & Son   Children's Books - 441   2013   £85

Peake, Mervyn   1911-1968 *Letters from a Lost Uncle.* London: Eyre and Spottiswoode, 1948. First edition, 2nd issue with original price of 7s.6d overprinted and 3s6d printed below, small 8vo., original pictorial yellow cloth, dust jacket spine chipped, worn and darkened, chip to upper edge of lower panel, unpaginated, illustrations.   R. F. G. Hollett & Son   Children's Books - 442   2013   £225

Pears, Iain *The Last Judgment.* London: Victor Gollancz, 1993. First edition, fine in fine dust jacket, signed by author.   Between the Covers Rare Books, Inc.   Mystery & Detective Fiction - 313179   2013 $60

Pearsall, Doris *The Story of the Four Little Sabots.* London: Frederick Warne, 1906. First edition, 4 x 6 inches, printed boards, pictorial paste-on, 86 pages, near fine, full page color illustrations.   Aleph-Bet Books, Inc.   105 - 446   2013 $250

Pearse, G. E. *The Cape of Good Hope 1652-1833.* Pretoria: J. L. van Schaik, 1956. First edition, 4to., original cloth, gilt, dust jacket rather worn and torn, loss and repair, 180 illustrations and map, label removed from pastedown.   R. F. G. Hollett & Son   Africana - 157   2013   £45

Pearson, Jim Berry *The Maxwell Land Grant.* Norman: University of Oklahoma Press, 1961. First edition, 16 photos, 3 maps, light brown cloth, owner's light inscription, else very fine, lightly rubbed dust jacket, scarce.   Argonaut Book Shop   Summer 2013 - 273   2013 $90

Pearson, John *Critici Sacri, sive, Annotata Doctissimorum Virorum in Vetus ac Novum Testamentum...* Amstelaedami: excudunt Henricus et Vidua Theodori Boom, Joannes & Aegidius Janssonii a Waesberge..., 1698. Editio nova, 13 engraved plates, 34 woodcuts, 2 engravings, numerous decorated initial letters and tailpieces, 2 titlepages in red and black with large engraved vignettes, folio, later vellum over marbled paper covered boards, morocco spine labels lettered in gilt, vellum soiled, boards rubbed, few tears and splits to vellum, small shallow chip to head of spine on oe volume, shadows of spine labels, some edge wear, small institutional bookplate to front pastedowns, leaves with some scattered staining and soiling, often at rear of volumes, one volume with minor marginal worming, partially repaired, 2 leaves at rear of one volume reattached, occasional repair, one leaf with marginal tear, leaves mostly clean, folding maps without tears but with some minor soiling or staining, one plate creased, one with extra fold, few with dampstain to edges, one scuffed at top and repaired on verso, overall very good.   Kaaterskill Books   16 - 5   2013 $9500

Pearson, Ridley *The Seizing of Yankee Green Mall.* New York: St. Martins, 1987. First edition, fine in fine dust jacket.   Between the Covers Rare Books, Inc.   Mystery & Detective Fiction - 67785   2013 $65

Pease, Theodore Calvin *The Story of Illinois.* Chicago: A. C. McClurg, 1925. First edition, first printing, very good+ to near fine with tiny rub to one joint, in rarely seen dust jacket, very good with small tears and chips, 8vo., maps.   Beasley Books   2013 - 2013 $50

Peche Francaise de la Baleine dans le Mers du Sud en 1829. Harve: Hue, 1829. Offprint from Le Navigateur, frontispiece and folding lithograph plate, 8vo., fine in quarter calf over marbled boards, spine gilt, crisp, clean copy, rare.   Maggs Bros. Ltd.   1467 - 130   2013   £3750

Peck, George Washington *Aurifodina; or Adventures in the Gold Region.* New York: Baker and Scribner, 1849. First edition, 12mo., 103 pages, original boards, front cover highly decorated and attractively so, although whether by publisher seems dubious.   M & S Rare Books, Inc.   95 - 283   2013 $100

Peck, George Washington *Peck's Bad Boy and His Pa.* Chicago: Belford Clarke & Co., 1883. First edition, first issue, first state with rules above and below copyright notice, and with no text, save ads, after page 916, 12mo., original pictorial cloth, moderate rubbing at edges, 19 plates, including frontispiece, very good in morocco backed cloth slipcase.   Howard S. Mott Inc.   262 - 115   2013 $1500

Peck, Samuel *Fair Women of To-Day.* New York: Stokes, 1895. 4to., three quarter blue cloth, fine, full page chromolithographs by Caroline Lovell, remarkable copy.   Aleph-Bet Books, Inc.   104 - 218   2013 $600

Pedley, Charles *The History of Newfoundland From the Earliest Times to the Year 1860.* London: Longman, Green, Longman, Roberts and Green, Spottiswoods and Co., 1863. Brown cloth, half title, large map in pocket, 8vo., expertly rebacked in original cloth, very good association with bookplate of Gardiner Green Hubbard inside front cover, with GBF initials in ink on front endpaper. Schooner Books Ltd. 104 - 23 2013 $450

Peepshow Pictures. London: Nister, n.d. circa, 1890. Small 4to., cloth backed pictorial boards, some normal edge rubbing, else very good+, with 4 magnificent chromolithographed pop-out scenes, brown illustrations on every page. Aleph-Bet Books, Inc. 104 - 445 2013 $1350

Peet, Creighton *Mike the Cat.* New York: Henry Holt, 1939. First Holt edition, oblong 4to., cloth, fine in dust jacket (slightly frayed), artful black and white photos. Aleph-Bet Books, Inc. 105 - 454 2013 $85

Pegge, Samuel *Anecdotes of the English Language...* London: J. Nichols, Son & Bentley, 1814. Second edition, occasional light foxing, original drab boards, green cloth spine, paper label, some slight wear to fore-edges, corners little bumped, nice in original boards. Jarndyce Antiquarian Booksellers CCV - 219 2013 £200

Pegge, Samuel *Curialia; or an Historical Account of Some Branches of the Royal Household, &c.* printed by J. Nichols, 1791. 3 parts in one volume, errata leaf bound at end, light browning, few marginal paper flaws repaired, 4to., 20th century half calf, brick red pebbled cloth sides, spine with five raised bands, red morocco lettering piece, scratched and marked, good. Blackwell's Rare Books B174 - 114 2013 £150

Peirce, Cyrus *Crime: its Cause and Cure. An Essay.* Boston: Crosby Nichols and Co., 1854. First edition, 12mo., 63 pages, original flexible cloth, bit spotted and unevenly faded, text damp wrinkled, good, pencilled inscription. M & S Rare Books, Inc. 95 - 95 2013 $150

Peirce, Melusina Fay *New York: a Sympyhonic Study in three Parts.* New York: Neale Pub. Co., 1918. First edition, red publisher's cloth gilt, fine, very scarce. Between the Covers Rare Books, Inc. New York City - 286283 2013 $225

Peirce, Norman A. *The White Man Cometh!* Red Cloud: Self published, late 1950's, First edition, signed by author, mild sunning, near fine in wrappers. Ken Lopez Bookseller 159 - 156 2013 $125

Pelecanos, George P. *The Big Blowdown.* New York: St. Martin's, 1996. First edition, very fine in dust jacket. Mordida Books 81 - 409 2013 $75

Pelecanos, George P. *A Firing Offense.* New York: St. Martin's, 1992. First edition, signed by Pelecanos, very fine in dust jacket with tiny tear. Mordida Books 81 - 406 2013 $275

Pelecanos, George P. *A Firing Offense.* New York: St. Martin's Press, 1992. First edition, inscribed by author '1/28/93', fine in near fine dust jacket with few tiny impressions. Ed Smith Books 78 - 44 2013 $100

Pelecanos, George P. *Hard Revolution.* Tucson: Dennis McMillan, 2004. First edition, one of 300 numbered copies, signed by author, very fine in dust jacket with slipcase. Mordida Books 81 - 412 2013 $150

Pelecanos, George P. *Hell to Pay.* Tucson: Dennis McMillan, 2002. First edition, one of 350 numbered copies signed by author, very fine in dust jacket with slipcase. Mordida Books 81 - 411 2013 $150

Pelecanos, George P. *King Suckerman.* Boston: Little Brown, 1997. First edition, minor spotting to lower board edge, near fine in fine dust jacket, inscribed by author for Kent Anderson. Ken Lopez Bookseller 159 - 166 2013 $250

Pelecanos, George P. *Nick's Trip.* New York: St. Martins, 1993. First edition, very fine in dust jacket with tiny nick at top of spine. Mordida Books 81 - 407 2013 $500

Pelecanos, George P. *Shoedog.* New York: St. Martin's, 1994. First edition, signed by author, very fine dust jacket. Mordida Books 81 - 408 2013 $500

Pellegrino, Camillo *Historia Principum Langobardorum: Quae continet Antiqua Aliquot Opuscula de Rebus Langobardorum Beneventana Olim Provinciae...(bound with) Dell' Origine del' Antica Famiglia Detta di Colimenta. (bound with) Due Discorsi di Camillo Pellegrino...* Neapoli: ex typographica Francisci Sauii..., 1643. 4to., folding map, 2 folding tables, tear to blank lower corner B4 in first work, part II appears to have been bound with final 16 pages noted in Copac, and 3 further folding tables misbound into following work, slight marginal worming to final 2 leaves of last work, bound together in contemporary vellum, hand lettered spine, some light browning, vellum darkened on spine, slight wear to head of spine, Italian ownership name dated 1728 on front endpaper, with another by English owner in 1933. Jarndyce Antiquarian Booksellers CCIV - 25 2013 £750

Pellew, Claughton *Five Wood Engravings Printed from Original Wood Blocks with a Biographical Note by Anne Stevens.* Wakefield: Fleece Press, 1987. One of 150 sets printed on Zerkall mouldmade paper, folio, original plain white sewn wrappers, untrimmed, dust jacket with wood engraving by Pellew reproduced in line block on label on front cover, fine, with five wood engravings, each printed on a separate sheet and loosely enclosed in pale or mid blue card folder with printed title, book and prints enclosed in grey buckram, card lined, fold down back box with same design of label as that used for the book on its front, fine. Blackwell's Rare Books   172 - 280   2013   £350

Pemberton, Henry *Observations on Poetry, Especially the Epic, Occasioned by the Late Poem Upon Leonidas.* London: printed by H. Woodfall, 1738. 8vo., little light spotting, contemporary sprinkled tan calf, spine panelled in gilt with raised bands, orange morocco label, boards bordered with gilt rules, spine sometime regilded in coppery color and then glazed, slight wear to headcap. Unsworths Antiquarian Booksellers   28 - 120   2013   £125

Penada, Jacopo *Saggio D'Osservazioni E Memorie Medico-Anatomiche...* Padova: per Biovanbattista Penada e figli, 1793-1804. First edition, 3 volumes, 4to., original limp interim bookseller's pattern papers, fine well margined copy, some wear to spines and joints, internally beautiful clean, crisp copy, folding engraved plates quite pristine, very rare set.   James Tait Goodrich   75 - 167   2013 $9950

Pendexter, Hugh *Tiberius Smith.* New York: Harper and Brothers, 1907. First edition, green cloth, applied illustration and painted lettering, fine, without dust jacket, lovely copy.   Between the Covers Rare Books, Inc.   Mystery & Detective Fiction - 85033   2013 $200

Penn, John *A Timely Appeal to the Common Sense of the People of Great Britain in General...* London: printed for J. Hatchard (second work) by W. Bulmer, 1798-1800. 2 works in 1 volume, first bound without half title or final ad leaf, the whole interleaved, titlepage of second slightly soiled and with reddish stain in fore-margin which persists for a few leaves, 8vo. (text) and 4to. (interleaves), contemporary calf, rebacked, corners worn, pencil notes on interleaves, some quite extensive, to first 42 pages, bookplate of Peter Isaacs, good.   Blackwell's Rare Books   B174 - 115   2013   £1200

Penn, William *No Cross, No Crown. A Discourse Shewing the Nature and Discipline of the Holy Cross of Christ.* Boston: Rogers and Fowle, 1747. Seventh edition, 5 3/4 x 4 inches, contemporary American brown calf panelled in blind, small abrasion n title affecting one word, small tear with small loss to text on E1 (with words affected noted in ink).   M & S Rare Books, Inc.   95 - 284   2013 $850

Penn, William *The Sandy Foundation Shaken; or Those so Generally Believe and Applauded Doctrines of One God, Subsisting in Three Distinct and Separate Persons...* printed in the year, 1668. First edition, short wormtrail in lower margin, often just touching a character but with no loss of sense, reinforced on first 8 leaves with clear tape, light browning and few fox spots, 4to., extracted from a volume and preserved in folding case, sound.   Blackwell's Rare Books   172 - 112   2013   £5000

Pennant, Thomas   1726-1798 *A Tour from Downing to Alston Moor.* London: Oriental Press, 1801. First edition, quarto, 27 plates, light occasional light foxing, recent brown half calf.   J. & S. L. Bonham Antiquarian Booksellers Europe - 9113   2013   £250

Pennell, Cholmondeley *The Family Fairy Tales.* London: John Camden Hotten, 1865. Second edition, original blue ribbed cloth gilt, rather rubbed, extremities little frayed, 6 hand colored plates by M. Ellen Edwards, little fingered and marked and slightly shaken, scarce.   R. F. G. Hollett & Son Children's Books - 455   2013   £150

The Penny Mechanic. A Magazine of the Arts and Sciences. Published by D. A. Doudney, at the Holloway Press and G. Berger, 1836-1843. 9 annual volumes of weekly issues (bound as 5), each number with wood engraving on front and occasional illustrations and diagrams in text, prefaces and annual titlepages to most years, additional engraved frontispieces to three annual volumes, frontispiece on yellow paper facing an ad, 8vo., contemporary purple roan backed drab boards, neatly rebacked, very good, rare.   Blackwell's Rare Books   172 - 113   2013   £1500

Pennyroyal Press *Flyer for Alice's Adventures in Wonderland.* Northampton: Pennyroyal, Folio, folded cover and one leaf, 2 lithographs by Barry Moser, little soiled, yellowed and chipped, very good, full page of Madhatter signed by Moser.   Second Life Books Inc.   183 - 314   2013 $150

Penton, Stephen *The Guardian's Instruction of the Gentleman's Romance...* London: printed for the author and sold by Simon Miller near the West-end of St. Paul's, 1688. One of 3 variants of first edition, this with colon at end of fifth line on titlepage, 12mo., prelim imprimatur leaf and final contents leaf, full contemporary sprinkled calf, double blind ruled borders, unlettered, double ruled spine, slight cracking at head and tail of spine, some offset browning on endpapers, near contemporary hand has identified author at head of front endpaper. Jarndyce Antiquarian Booksellers CCIV - 26   2013   £580

Pepler, Hilary Douglas Clark *The Devil's Devices or Control Versus Service.* Hampshire House Workshops: St. Dominic's Press, 1915. First edition, 11 wood engravings by Eric Gill, foolscap 8vo., original quarter black cloth, scarlet boards, Gill engraving and lettering on front cover, all printed in black, covers rubbed, more so on rear cover, untrimmed, good, Eric Gill's bookplate.   Blackwell's Rare Books   B174 - 382   2013   £250

Pepler, Hilary Douglas Clark *In Petra. Being a Sequel to 'Nisi Dominus', together with a Preface and Notes by Eric GIll ad Hilary Pepler.*   Ditchling, Sussex: Saint Dominic's Press, 1923.   First edition, printed on handmade paper, 3 wood engravings by David Jones and 6 by Eric Gill, including a title engraving (and colophon) both printed in red, 16mo., original light blue canvas, backstrip faded, front cover label including printed price '51', untrimmed, good.   Blackwell's Rare Books   B174 - 382   2013   £250

Pepoon, H. S. *An Annotated Flora.*   Chicago: Chicago Academy of Sciences, 1927.   First edition, 554 pages, black and white photographic reproductions, tight close to near fine copy in green cloth boards with couple of small spots to front panel and tiny bit of other wear, very nice and clean.   Jeff Hirsch Books   Fall 2013 - 129167   2013 $50

Pepys, Samuel   1633-1703   *The Diary.*   London: G. Bell and Sons Ltd., 1924.   8 volumes bound in 3, frontispiece, fine in contemporary terra cotta crushed morocco by Sangorski & Sutcliffe (signed on front turn-in), double gilt fillet border on covers, upper covers with gilt insignia incorporating initials "S P" crossed anchors and looping ropes with Pepys' (misspelled) motto in Latin on ribbon above it, raised bands, spines gilt in double ruled compartments with central ornament of either a crown, a sailor's knot, an anchor or crossed quills, turn-ins ruled in gilt, marbled endpapers, all edges gilt, spines lightly and uniformly sunned toward pink, otherwise extremely pleasing set in beautiful condition inside and out.   Phillip J. Pirages   61 - 146   2013 $1250

Pepys, Samuel   1633-1703   *Everybody's Pepys: The Diary...*   London: G. Bell & Sons, 1926.   195 x 133mm., attractive contemporary tree calf, gilt by Riviere & Son (stamp signed), covers with decorative gilt rule border, raised bands, spine gilt in compartments with intricate scrolling cornerpieces and side fleurons, two with anchor centerpiece, two with lyre, two tan morocco labels, densely gilt turn-ins, marbled endpapers (showing maps) bound in at rear, with 60 plates by E. H. Shepard; presentation inscription from Christmas in year of publication; lower cover with faint circular mark, very light wear to joints and extremities, but binding still solid and appealing, fine internally, text especially fresh and clean.   Phillip J. Pirages   63 - 362   2013 $125

Pepys, Samuel   1633-1703   *Memoires Relating to the State of the Royal Navy of England.*   London: printed Anno, 1690.   First edition, issue for private distribution without commercial imprint on titlepage, 8vo., contemporary panelled calf, red morocco label, gilt decorations and lettering, frontispiece and folding table, early ink signature of "Northesk", which is probably that of John Carnegie, 7th Earl of Northesk, edges little rubbed, upper joints starting, but sound, fine.   The Brick Row Book Shop   Miscellany Fifty-Nine - 33   2013 $4500

Pepys, Samuel   1633-1703   *Memoirs of Samuel Pepys.*   London: Henry Colburn, 1825.   First edition, quarto, 2 volumes, with half titles in each volume, frontispiece in each volume, 11 engraved plates and embellished with 2 engraved illustrations in text, uncut in contemporary half brown morocco over marbled boards, spines with gilt bands, gilt panelled compartments and gilt lettering, marbled endpapers, top edge gilt, armorial bookplate, small divet from 3k in first volume, one marginal tear in second volume, some general rubbing and fading to boards, overall very clean and excellent copy.   Heritage Book Shop   Holiday Catalogue 2012 - 115   2013 $4500

Pepys, Samuel Ananias   *A True Narrative of a Visit to Liddesdayle.*   Edinburgh: by H. & J. Pillans & Wilson, n.d. but c., 1918.   4to., ff., (iii), 33, Bartholomew color printed map tipped in as frontispiece and 20 photos, mounted on 19 sewn-in leaves, little spotting to some plate mounts, contemporary russet goarskin, plain spine, "Liddesdayle" gilt at upper fore corner of front board, marbled endpapers, top edge gilt, others uncut, rubbed at extremities, few tiny marks, 2 initial blank leaves with lengthy MS inscriptions from author and photographer to "Cozen Tomm" who features heavily in text.   Unsworths Antiquarian Booksellers   28 - 191   2013   £200

Percyvall, Richard   *A Dictionarie in Spanish and English.... (bound with) A Spanish Grammar...*   imprinted by Edm. Bollifant, 1599.   First edition by Minsheu, 2 works (the second in 2 parts) in one volume, woodcut printer's device on both titles and part title, the Dictionarie printed in 3 columns within rules, the Grammar mainly in black letter, Dialogues with parallel texts in double columns, first few leaves browned at top edge, title little stained, few spots and stains here and there, occasional minor browning, some waterstaining at very end, little worming in lower margins, folio in '6s, modern calf, contrasting lettering pieces on spine by Period Binders, annotated throughout in mid to late 17th century English hand (more profusely in first quarter but nonetheless throughout) and with various ownership inscriptions, good.   Blackwell's Rare Books   B174 - 116   2013   £2750

The Perfectionist.   Putney: 1843-1845.   Volume III-IV, lacking volume V for completeness.   M & S Rare Books, Inc.   95 - 275   2013 $750

Peret, Benjamin *Air Mexicain.* Paris: Librairie Arcanes, 1952. One of 24+ copies with extra suite from a total issue of 274, 1 on Van Gelder, 24 on Renage with an extra suite numbered; 229 on BFK de Rives, 20 H.C., this copy on B.F.K. Rives but contains extra suite of lithographs on Renage, laid in is ALS signed by Peret, concerning physical makeup of this book and another single sheet that is the copy for the colophon, with holograph envelope, fine, page size 7 1/2 x 9 1/2 inches, bound loose in original wrappers printed in red and black, housed in publisher's pink slipcase, fine, with 4 splendid color lithographs by Rufino Tamayo, text printed over outline lithographs, text handset and printed by M. Arrault et Cie, lithographs editioned at the studios of M. Desjobert, fine.   Priscilla Juvelis - Rare Books   56 - 33   2013 $6000

Perkins, Eleanor Ellis *News from Notown.* Boston: Houghton Mifflin, 1919. First edition, 4to., pictorial cloth, (108) pages, fine in worn dust jacket missing most of back panel, many fine full page illustrations by Lucy Fitch Perkins. Aleph-Bet Books, Inc.   104 - 416   2013 $200

Perkins, John *A Profitable Book of Mr. Iohn Perkins, Sometimes Fellow of the Inner Temple.* London: for Matthew Walbanck, 1657. (30), 333 pages, early 19th century calf, neatly rebacked in period style, heavily browned and bit brittle, cropped with occasional running head shaved.   Joseph J. Felcone Inc.   Books Printed before 1701 - 61   2013 $300

Perkins, Kenneth *Voodoo'd.* New York: Harper and Brothers, 1931. First edition, old bookstore stamp on rear pastedown, slight soiling to boards, else about fine in attractive, fine dust jacket with small stains on rear panel and front flap fold and couple of tiny tears.   Between the Covers Rare Books, Inc.   Mystery & Detective Fiction - 64289   2013 $375

Perkins, William *Three Years in California...* Berkeley: University of Oklahoma Press, 1964. First English language edition, photo illustrations, rust cloth, very fine with pictorial dust jacket.   Argonaut Book Shop   Summer 2013 - 276   2013 $75

Perkins, William *Two Treatises. I. Of the Nature and Practise of Repentance. II. Of the Combat of the Flesh and Spirit.* printed by Iohn Legate, 1597. 4to., somewhat browned (and sometimes touched by damp) around the edges, few leaves with more substantial light marks, modern quarter calf, marbled boards, good.   Blackwell's Rare Books   B174 - 117   2013   £750

Perrault, Charles 1628-1703 *Cinderella or the Little Glass Slipper.* New York: published by D. Longworth at the Dramatic Repository, Shakespeare Gallery, 1807. First American edition, 12mo., disbound, 12 pages, small spot on title, else fine.   Howard S. Mott Inc.   262 - 117   2013 $500

Perrault, Charles 1628-1703 *Contes de Perrault.* Paris: Theofore Lefevre circa, 1910. 4to., red cloth with elaborate gold and black decorative binding, all edges gilt, 217 pages, near fine, engravings by LeFrancq after Desandre and wood engravings, beautiful edition.   Aleph-Bet Books, Inc.   104 - 417   2013 $175

Perrault, Charles 1628-1703 *The Histories of Passed Times, or the Tales of Mother Goose. With Morals.* London: printed and sold at Brussels: B. Le Francq, 1785. New edition, 2 volumes, 12mo., 10 engraved plates including frontispiece, text parallel in French and English, titlepages to both volumes, printed in red and black in both French and English, contemporary full sheep, spines stamped in gilt, green morocco spine labels, lettered gilt, board edges stamped in gilt, previous owner's old ink signature dated 1794 on English titlepage of each volume, boards bit scuffed, some wear to head and tail of spines and corners, board joints, cracked but firm, overall very good, scarce, housed in full morocco clamshell.   Heritage Book Shop Holiday Catalogue 2012 - 116   2013 $12,500

Perrault, Charles 1628-1703 *Little Red Riding Hood.* London and New York: John Lane The Bodley Head, 1898. 4to., pictorial wrappers, (12) pages, including covers and endpapers, fine, magnificent full page color signed by author by Walter Crane.   Aleph-Bet Books, Inc.   104 - 135   2013 $275

Perrault, Charles 1628-1703 *Sleeping Beauty.* Philadelphia and London: Lippincott & Heinemann, 1920. First edition, 4to., cloth backed pictorial boards, fine in slightly frayed dust jacket, pictorial endpapers, tipped in color frontispiece, many full page and in text beautiful silhouettes and drawings by Arthur Rackham, nice.   Aleph-Bet Books, Inc.   105 - 496   2013 $750

Perret, Jacques *Les Sept Peches Capitaux.* Nice: La Belle Page, 1967. First Lenor Fini edition, number 69 of 149 exemplars on gand velin d'Arches, signed by Fini (total edition 201), 8 original color lithographs by Fini, each signed by artist, 116 pages, loose sheets in publisher's thick paper folder and solander box, overall size 44 x 36cm., fine.   Gemini Fine Books & Arts., Ltd.   Art Reference & Illustrated Books - 2013 $2500

Perry, Anne *Resurrection Row.* New York: St. Martin's, 1981. First edition, very fine in dust jacket.   Mordida Books   81 - 415   2013 $250

Perry, John *The State of Russia Under the Present Czar.* London: Benjamin Tooke, 1716. First edition, 8vo., fine folding map, contemporary full panelled calf, rebacked sensitively using the original spine, new black morocco label.   J. & S. L. Bonham Antiquarian Booksellers   Europe - 8661   2013   £750

Perry, William *The Royal Standard English Dictionary.* Boston: Thomas & Andrews, 1810? Square 12mo., 491 pages, full contemporary calf, leather label, text foxed, very sound.   M & S Rare Books, Inc.   95 - 101   2013 $150

Pervigilium Veneris.   Doves Press, 1910.   One of 150 copies (of an edition of 162), printed in black on handmade paper with title, initials and refrain at end of each verse, printed in red, 8vo., original russet morocco, backstrip gilt panelled between seven raised bands, second and third gilt lettered and with date 1910 at tail, single gilt rule border to sides, green leather booklabels of Willis Vickery and Cortland Bishop, with some offsetting to front free endpaper, gilt edges, by Doves Bindery, fine.   Blackwell's Rare Books   172 - 272   2013   £1500

Pervomai.   Detizdat: 1938.   Large 4to., pictorial wrappers, light cover sol, very good+, illustrations in color on every page by V. Konashevich, nice, very scarce.   Aleph-Bet Books, Inc.   104 - 503   2013 $1200

Pesotta, Rose   *Bread upon the Waters.*   New York: Dodd, Mead, 1944.   First edition, 8vo., red cloth stamped in black, author's presentation on flyleaf, cover little faded and scuffed at edges, interior slightly rippled on first few leaves, otherwise very good.   Second Life Books Inc.   183 - 317   2013 $75

Petavius, Dionysius   *Rationarium Temporum: in Quo Aetatum Omnium Sacra Profanaque Historia Chronolgoicis Probationibus Munita Summatim Traditur.*   Leiden: Apud Theodorum Haak, 1724.   8vo., 3 parts in 1 volume, frontispiece, additional engraved titlepage and 6 plates, lightly toned, some minor spotting, contemporary vellum boards, spine lettered in ink, small gilt decoration to centre of boards, soiled and small tear to head of spine, ownership inscription of Mitford dated 1803 with a later paragraph long biographical note, from the collection (but without any signs of ownership) of Ferdinand Tonnies (1855-1936). Unsworths Antiquarian Booksellers   28 - 121   2013   £200

Peter Pan's ABC.   New York: Hodder & Stoughton, 1913. First US edition, 4to., cloth backed pictorial boards, near fine, illustrations by Flora White with 26 especially lovely color plates.   Aleph-Bet Books, Inc.   105 - 16   2013 $800

Peter Parley's Annual. A Christmas and New Year's Present. Darton & Co., 1849.   Small square 8vo., original blind-stamped cloth gilt, extremities trifle worn, all edges gilt, color printed frontispiece and title and numerous woodcut illustrations.   R. F. G. Hollett & Son   Children's Books - 460 2013   £45

Peter Parley's Annual 40th Year 1881.   Ben George, 1881. Original decorated red cloth, gilt over bevelled boards, spine rather rubbed, all edges gilt, chromolithographs, few edges little chipped and soiled.   R. F. G. Hollett & Son   Children's Books - 458   2013   £40

Peter Parley's Annual 43rd Year 1884.   Ben George, 1884. original decorated red cloth gilt over bevelled boards, rather damped, spine label lacking, all edges gilt, 9 chromolithograph and 12 monochrome illustrations, rather shaken.   R. F. G. Hollett & Son   Children's Books - 459   2013   £35

Peter Parley's Annual 44th Year 1885.   Ben George, 1885. Original decorated red cloth gilt over bevelled board, little rubbed, part of spine label lacking, all edges gilt, 9 chromolithographs and 11 monochrome illustrations, upper joint cracked, ownership stamp on back of frontispiece. R. F. G. Hollett & Son   Children's Books - 457   2013   £40

Peter Parley's Annual 45th Year 1886.   Ben George, 1886. Original decorated red cloth gilt over bevelled boards, trifle rubbed, all edges gilt, 16 chromolithographs, back of frontispiece rather spotted, lower joint tender.   R. F. G. Hollett & Son   Children's Books - 456   2013   £45

Peter Rabbit. Tracing and Drawing Book.   M A. Donohue, n.d., Later issue, illustrated dust jacket and 19 half page black and white illustrations for tracing, 16 pages, card covers with color illustrations and titling repeated to both covers, 15 x 9 3/4 inches, covers very slightly used, 2 outlines have been traced and couple of pictures have been colored, very good.   Ian Hodgkins & Co. Ltd.   134 - 57   2013 £38

Peter Rabbit and Other Stories.   Castle, 1977.   11 x 8 1/4 inches, illustrations in color, 94 pages, color pictorial laminated boards and color illustrated character endpapers,. Ian Hodgkins & Co. Ltd.   134 - 41   2013   £22

Peter Rabbit, Little Red Hen & Owl and Pussy Cat. Charles E. Graham, n.d.,   First edition thus, 16 full page color plates and other illustrations in black and white or black and orange, pages 40, cloth backed brown paper covered boards, square color pictorial onlay centre front cover with black titling, black and white character decorated endpapers, 12 x 10 inches, corners with some rubbing and wear along very edges of boards, very slight wear to edge of titlepage and one page with small margin tear, little thumbing, very nice, scarce.   Ian Hodgkins & Co. Ltd.   134 - 76 2013   £175

Peter Rabbit: Painting Book.   New York: Charles E. Graham and Co., n.d.,   Title printed in red and green, 33 pages of black and white illustrations for painting, some colored examples for children to copy, some places left totally blank for own picture drawing + line text each page, blue cloth backed thick card covers, corner cut from top front, some rubbing and little wear along edges of boards, some light creasing, small repaired tear fore edge and last page with small piece torn from fore edge margin, very good, unused copy.   Ian Hodgkins & Co. Ltd.   134 - 78   2013   £130

Peter Rabbit: Painting Book. New York: Charles E. Graham And Co. copyright, 1913. Title printed in red and green, 33 pages of black and white illustrations for painting, some colored examples for children to copy, some places left totally blank for own picture drawing + line text each page telling the story, maroon cloth backed thick card covers, color illustrations with boards shaped around edges, very nice.   Ian Hodgkins & Co. Ltd.   134 - 77   2013   £125

The Peter Rabbit Playtime Story Book. Henry Altemus, 1931. Frontispiece and 116 color illustrations by Bess Goe Willis, red cloth, backstrip faded and slightly worn top/bottom, name dated 1932 front pastedown, slight thumbing to contents, very good, uncommon.   Ian Hodgkins & Co. Ltd.   134 - 17   2013   £65

The Peter Rabbit Story Book for Little Boys & Girls. Henry Altemus, n.d., 1924. First edition thus, frontispiece and 13 color plates, blue cloth with large color pictorial label pasted front cover, fine in partly worn dust jacket.   Ian Hodgkins & Co. Ltd.   134 - 18   2013   £140

Peters, Ellis   *Dean Man's Ransom.* London: Macmillan, 1984. First edition, pages slightly darkened, otherwise fine in dust jacket.   Mordida Books   81 - 426   2013 $200

Peters, Ellis   *Death Mask.* London: Collins Crime Club, 1959. First edition, near fine in dust jacket with light wear and tiny tears at spine ends.   Mordida Books   81 - 416   2013 $175

Peters, Ellis   *Death to the Landlords!* London: Macmillan, 1972. First edition, very fine in dust jacket.   Mordida Books   81 - 417   2013 $350

Peters, Ellis   *The Devil's Novice.* London: Macmillan, 1983. First edition, signed by authorv ery fine in dust jacket.   Mordida Books   81 - 425   2013 $375

Peters, Ellis   *The Devil's Novice.* London: Macmillan, 1983. First edition, fine in nearly fine, crisp dust jacket.   Ed Smith Books   78 - 48   2013 $150

Peters, Ellis   *An Excellent Mystery.* London: Macmillan, 1985. First edition, pages slightly darkened, otherwise fine in dust jacket.   Mordida Books   81 - 428   2013 $200

Peters, Ellis   *The Heretic's Apprentice.* London: Headline, 1989. First edition, pages slightly darkened, otherwise fine in dust jacket.   Mordida Books   81 - 431   2013 $85

Peters, Ellis   *The Hermit of Eyton Forest.* London: Headline, 1987. First edition, pages slightly darkened, otherwise fine in dust jacket.   Mordida Books   81 - 430   2013 $85

Peters, Ellis   *The Leper of Saint Giels.* London: Macmillan, 1981. First edition, page edges lightly darkened, otherwise fine in price clipped dust jacket.   Mordida Books   81 - 422   2013 $350

Peters, Ellis   *The Marriage of Meggotta.* London: Macmillan, 1979. First edition, some light spotting on page edges, else fine in dust jacket.   Mordida Books   81 - 419   2013 $75

Peters, Ellis   *Monk's Hood.* London: Macmillan, 1980. First edition, near fine with few tiny spots to yellow cloth (tiny corner nudges) in nearly fine dust jacket.   Ed Smith Books   78 - 45   2013 $350

Peters, Ellis   *Monk's Hood.* London: Macmillan, 1980. First edition, very fine in dust jacket.   Mordida Books   81 - 420   2013 $500

Peters, Ellis   *One Corpse Too Many.* London: Macmillan, 1979. First edition, fine in dust jacket.   Mordida Books   81 - 417   2013 $650

Peters, Ellis   *The Pilgrim of Hate.* London: Macmillan, 1984. First edition, fine in fine dust jacket.   Ed Smith Books   78 - 49   2013 $150

Peters, Ellis   *The Pilgrim of Hate.* London: Macmillan, 1984. First edition, fine in dust jacket.   Mordida Books   81 - 427   2013 $200

Peters, Ellis   *The Raven in the Foregate.* London: Macmillan, 1986. First edition, fine in black cloth with gilt spine lettering in fine dust jacket.   Ed Smith Books   78 - 50   2013 $150

Peters, Ellis   *The Rose Rent.* London: Macmillan, 1986. First edition, pages slightly darkened, else fine in dust jacket.   Mordida Books   81 - 429   2013 $85

Peters, Ellis   *The Rose Rent.* London: Macmillan, 1986. First edition, fine in fine dust jacket.   Ed Smith Books   78 - 51   2013 $150

Peters, Ellis   *Saint Peter's Fair.* London: Macmillan, 1981. First edition, fine in dust jacket.   Mordida Books   81 - 421   2013 $400

Peters, Ellis   *Saint Peter's Fair.* London: Macmillan, 1981. First edition, fine in fine dust jacket (with price clip).   Ed Smith Books   78 - 47   2013 $150

Peters, Ellis   *The Sanctuary Sparrow.* London: Macmillan, 1983. First edition, pages slightly darkened, else fine in dust jacket.   Mordida Books   81 - 424   2013 $250

Peters, Ellis *The Summer of the Danes.* London: Headline, 1991. First edition, pages slightly darkened, else fine in dust jacket. Mordida Books 81 - 432 2013 $85

Peters, Ellis *The Virgin in the Ice.* London: Macmillan, 1982. First edition, pages slightly darkened, otherwise fine in dust jacket. Mordida Books 81 - 423 2013 $300

Peters, Harry T. *California on Stone.* New York: Doubleday, 1935. First edition, number 37 of 501 numbered copies, 112 plates on 99 leaves, 12 in color, glazed linen stamped on front cover and spine in black and gold, beveled edges, tipped in bookplate, very fine and bright with printed dust jacket and slipcase, jacket spine faded with quarter inch tear to head. Argonaut Book Shop Summer 2013 - 277 2013 $500

Peters, John P. *Labor and Capital.* New York: Putnam's, 1902. First edition, 8vo., red cloth, edges little spotted, owner's name on blank, otherwise very good, tight copy. Second Life Books Inc. 183 - 318 2013 $165

Petersham, Maud *An American ABC.* New York: MacMillan, Sept., 1941. First edition, 4to., cloth, fine in dust jacket, color lithographs, this copy signed by Maud and Miska Petersham. Aleph-Bet Books, Inc. 104 - 418 2013 $450

Petersham, Maud *Get-a-Way and Hary Janos.* New York: Viking, 1933. First edition, 4to., cloth backed pictorial boards, fine in dust jacket with some chips and mends, illustrations by Maud and Miska Petersham. Aleph-Bet Books, Inc. 104 - 419 2013 $375

Peterson, Arthur Everett *New York as Eighteenth Century Municipality.* New York: Longmans, Green and Co., 1917. First edition, news article affixed to front fly, else fine and bright. Between the Covers Rare Books, Inc. New York City - 286254 2013 $75

Peterson, Frederick *A Text-Book of Legal Medicine and Toxicology.* Philadelphia: and London: W. B. Saunders & Co., 1903-1904. First edition, 2 volumes, 8vo., 23 plates, 1975 text figures, original olive cloth, gilt stamped spine titles, neatly rebacked preserving original spines, new endpapers, ink signature of Roger G. Perkins, 1904, Cleveland, fine, rare. Jeff Weber Rare Books 172 - 197 2013 $450

Petko, Edward *Fine Printing and the '80's.* Los Angeles: Columbian 415 Chappel, 1980. Limited to 100 numbered copies, this copy with presentation by author to Roger Levenson, 7.3 x 5.9cm., marbled cloth, label with title on spine, top edge cut, other edges uncut, from the collection of Donn W. Sanford. Oak Knoll Books 303 - 99 2013 $150

Petrakis, Harry Mark *Chapter Seven from the Hour of the Bell, a Novel Concerning the Greek War of Independence.* Mt. Horeb: Perishable Press, 1976. One of 150 copies, all on Frankfurt and Frankfurt Cream paper signed by author, laid in is broadside prospectus for book printed Frankfurt Cream paper with titlepage illustration by Warrington Colescott reproduced in a reduced size, book page size 9 3/4 x 7 1/4 inches, 44 pages, 22 of which are printed, broadside size 16 3/4 x 11 1/2 inches, bound by Bill Anthony, hand marbled paper by Norma Rubovits over boards, each book with different patterned marbled paper, black blind-stamped oasis spine, fine in acetate jacket, reset monotype Jan Van Krimpen Spectrum (1955), titlepage illustration by Warrington Colescott which the printer calls his best to date'. Priscilla Juvelis - Rare Books 56 - 25 2013 $275

Petry, Ann *Tituba of Salem Village.* New York: Crowell, 1964. First edition, very faint stain on front board, barely worthy of mention, else fine in very near fine dust jacket with very small stain and slight toning to white spine, scarce especially in nice condition. Between the Covers Rare Books, Inc. 165 - 325 2013 $200

Petry, Ann *Harriet Tubman: Conductor on the Underground Railroad.* New York: Thomas Y. Crowell, 1955. First edition, very near fine in about very good dust jacket with couple of holes in spine and small nicks and tears, very uncommon. Between the Covers Rare Books, Inc. 165 - 112 2013 $100

Pets and Playfellows. Dean & Sons, n.d. circa, 1890. 4to., original printed wrappers, top and fore edge shaped, few tears to edges, 5 fine chromolithographs, including 1 double page spread of rabbits and guinea pigs. R. F. G. Hollett & Son Children's Books - 19 2013 £25

Pettee, Florence *The Who Bird and other Whimsies.* Chicago: Whitman, 1920. Small 4to., cloth backed pictorial boards, fine in pictorial box (shows wear with flap repairs), illustrations by author in color on every page. Aleph-Bet Books, Inc. 104 - 204 2013 $200

Pettigrew & Oulton *The Dublin Almanac & General Register of Ireland 1837.* viii 360 pages, bookseller's ticket of Osborne Savage & Son, 112 Patrick Street, Cork and bookplate of Horace Townsend, text good, original cloth with damaged label. C. P. Hyland 261 - 724 2013 £175

Pettit, S. F. *This City of Cork 1700-1900.* 1977. 303 pages, photos, cloth, dust jacket, very good. C. P. Hyland 261 - 725 2013 £45

Petty, John *The History of the Primitive Methodist Connexion from Its Origin to the Conference of 1860...* John Dickenson, 1880. Revised edition, full black calf gilt extra over heavy bevelled boards, neatly recased, spine little scraped and dulled, all edges gilt, frontispiece, flyleaves foxed, gold printed presentation slip to the Duke of Devonshire.   R. F. G. Hollett & Son   Wesleyan Methodism - 23   2013   £95

Petty, William *The Political Anatomy of Ireland.* IUP Facsimile reprint of 1691 edition, 1970. 8vo., cloth, near fine.   C. P. Hyland   261 - 727   2013   £50

Petvin, John *Letters Concerning Mind.* printed for John and James Rivington, 1750. First edition, title reinforced at inner margin, occasional light spotting, modern half calf, sound.   Blackwell's Rare Books   172 - 114   2013   £400

Phalaris *Epistolae. Ex Mss. Recensuit, Versione, Annotationibus & Vita Insuper Authoris Donavit Car. Boyle ex Aede Christi.* Oxford: e typographeo Clarendoniano, 1718. Second impression, 8vo., engraved frontispiece, Greek and Latin text, little soiling at beginning and end, contemporary Cambridge style panelled calf, rebacked and repolished preserving original red morocco label, hinges relined, bookplate of Cheshunt College Library with 'Withdrawn" stamps.   Unsworths Antiquarian Booksellers   28 - 38   2013   £475

Phelps, Elizabeth Stuart 1815-1852 *Sealed Orders.* Boston: Houghton Osgood and Co., 1879. First edition, boards and end of spine lightly worn, else near fine.   Between the Covers Rare Books, Inc.   Sci-Fi, Fantasy & Horror - 53284   2013 $250

Phelps, William Dane *Fremont's Private Navy. The 1846 Journal of Captain William Dane Phelps.* Glendale: Arthur H. Clark Co., 1987. First edition, one of 500 numbered copies, signed by editor, Briton Cooper Busch, green cloth, gilt, very fine.   Argonaut Book Shop   Summer 2013 - 118   2013 $125

Philip or the Autobiography of a Dope Fiend. N.P.: Demarest Book Concern, n.d., wrappers, very scarce, 16mo., 16 pages.   Beasley Books   2013 - 2013 $100

Philipon, Charles *Album Pour Rire.* Paris: chez Ostervald, n.d. circa, 1828-1829. First issue, oblong folio, 12 hand colored lithographs, 10 numbered, 2 unnumbered, one suite (unidentified), contemporary full dark green morocco, gilt ruled borders, gilt panel, gilt lettering and ornaments to spine, some foxing to margins not affecting text, otherwise attractive copy, scarce.   David Brass Rare Books, Inc.   Holiday 2012 Chapter Two - DB 01881   2013 $3250

Philips, Francis Charles *As In a Looking Glass.* London: Ward & Downey, 1889. Large 8vo., half title, frontispiece, plates, small tear to lower edge of leading f.e.p., uncut in original brown cloth, blocked in gilt, little rubbed, slightly knocked, variant binding with brown and gold endpapers.   Jarndyce Antiquarian Booksellers   CCV - 220   2013   £75

Phillimore, W. P. *An Index to Changes of Name 1760-1901.* 1905. First edition, 8vo., ex-Doneraile Court Library, cloth, very good.   C. P. Hyland   261 - 408   2013   £75

Phillips, Allan *The Birds of Arizona.* Tucson: University of Arizona Press, 1964. First edition, 4to., fine in near fine dust jacket with few short tears and some tape staining on rear panel (may be offsetting from another book).   Beasley Books   2013 - 2013 $50

Phillips, Caryl A. *Cambridge.* New York: Alfred A. Knopf, 1992. First American edition, fine in fine dust jacket, inscribed by author for Nicholas Delbanco.   Between the Covers Rare Books, Inc.   165 - 235   2013 $125

Phillips, Caryl A. *Crossing the River.* Toronto: Alfred A. Knopf, 1994. First Canadian edition, fine in dust jacket, inscribed by author to Nicholas Delbanco.   Between the Covers Rare Books, Inc.   165 - 236   2013 $125

Phillips, Caryl A. *State of Independence.* New York: Farrar, Straus & Giroux, 1986. First American edition, fine in fine dust jacket, inscribed by author to Nicholas Delbanco.   Between the Covers Rare Books, Inc.   165 - 234   2013 $125

Phillips, Catherine Coffin *Jessie Benton Fremont: a Woman Who Made History.* San Francisco: printed by John Henry Nash, 1935. first edition, one of 1000 copies, frontispiece, portraits, plates and illustrations, lovely floral headbands and chapter initials, linen backed boards, paper spine label, bookplate on inner cover, very fine with printed dust jacket (spine slightly faded).   Argonaut Book Shop   Summer 2013 - 109   2013 $175

Phillips, Catherine Coffin *Portsmouth Plaza: The Cradle of San Francisco.* San Francisco: Nash, 1932. First edition, one of 1000 copies, 464 pages, 18 portrait headbands, 88 text illustrations, vellum backed marbled boards, spine gilt lettered and decorated, bookplate on inner cover, 2 minor rubbed spots at spine ends but very fine, publisher's slipcase (paper label on spine).   Argonaut Book Shop   Summer 2013 - 279   2013 $250

Phillips, Edward *Theatrum Poetarum Anglicanorum: Containing the Names and Characters of All the English Poets.* London: Canterbury, 1800. first printing of this enlarged updated edition, 203 x 120mm., appealing recent brown quarter morocco over linen boards, raised bands, red morocco label, front flyleaf with inscription "G. D./ Canonbury" (George Daniel), titlepage with small embossed stamp of "Mark Pattison, Lincoln College, Oxon", exceptionally fine.   Phillip J. Pirages   63 - 320   2013 $750

Phillips, Jayne Anne *How Mickey Made It.*   St. Paul: Bookslinger, 1981.   First edition, one of 150 specially bound copies, numbered and signed by author, fine. Beasley Books   2013 - 2013 $50

Phillips, Maud Gillette *Law Unwrit.*   New York: Frederick H. Hitchcock, 1925.   First edition, fine in very nearly fine dust jacket but for very small chip at bottom front flap fold. Between the Covers Rare Books, Inc.   Sci-Fi, Fantasy & Horror - 43882   2013 $200

Phillips, Samuel *Essays from the London Times. Second Series.*   New York: D. Appleton, 1852.   First edition, 12mo., original printed red cloth, minor foxing, mostly to endpapers, otherwise excellent.   Howard S. Mott Inc.   262 - 118   2013 $125

Phillips, Samuel *Guide to the Crystal Palace and Park.* London: Bradbury and Evans, 1856.   First edition, 8vo., 193 pages, ads, 1 folding map, 2 folding plates, contemporary black half morocco, joints and corners rubbed.   J. & S. L. Bonham Antiquarian Booksellers   Europe - 8366   2013   £195

Philo of Alexandria *Opera Quae Reperiri Potuerunt Omnia.*   London: G. Bowyer, 1742.   2 volumes, folio, some light intermittent staining, very occasional pencil notes to volume I, one or two minor marginal tears, contemporary brown Cambridge style calf, gilt spines, upper boards detached, lower pages splitting, rather worn, labels largely lost, bookplate of Cheshunt College Library, with pink 'Cancelled" stamp to each front pastedown, embossed stamp of same to each titlepage.   Unsworths Antiquarian Booksellers   28 - 39   2013   £450

Philostratus *(Opera) quae supersunt omnia. Vita Apolloni Libris VIII, Vitae Sophistorum Libris II, Heroica, Imagines, Priores atque Posteriores et Epistolae...*   Leipzig: Apud Thomam Fritsch, 1709.   First edition thus, folio, titlepage in red and black, printer's vignette, occasional small engravings in text, ink smudge to volume II page 379 not affecting text, toned throughout with occasional darker browning, early 20th century half dark brown sheep, textured dark brown cloth boards, gilt spines with Athenaeum gilt stamp to tail, extremities worn, spine scuffed, ink split to top edge continuing down fore-edge and pooling slightly at bottom fore-edge corner, only intruding occasionally onto margins, some illegible notes pencilled on prelim blank in volume I. Unsworths Antiquarian Booksellers   28 - 40   2013   £500

Picard, Raymond *Les Prestiges.*   1947.   First edition, 8vo., wrappers, very good, signed presentation copy for Elizabeth Bowen.   C. P. Hyland   261 - 143   2013   £40

Pichette, Henri *Dents de Lait, Dents de Loup (Milk Teeth, Teeth of Wolf).*   Paris: Pierre de Tartas, 1959.   First edition, number 94 of 135 copies (total edition 211), signed in pencil by Pierre de Tartas, Jacques Villon and Henri Pichette, 13 etchings, 7 in-texte and 6 hors-texte), 75 loose leaves printed on rives wove paper with text and 12 etchings in wrapper folder, 13th etching is front cover, this copy with extra publisher's exhibition folder, containing text extract, 3 original etchings and original photo of Villon and de Tartas at work, all housed in publishers folding cloth box, overall size 16 x 12, excellent condition.   Gemini Fine Books & Arts., Ltd.   Art Reference & Illustrated Books - 2013 $1400

Pichon, Thomas *Genuine Letters and Memoirs Relating to the Natural, Civil and Commercial History of the Islands of Cape Breton and Saint John...*   J. Nourse, 1760.   First English edition, very good, contemporary mottled calf, expertly rebacked, raised and gilt banded spine with red morocco label, some light browning, scarce.   Ken Spelman Books Ltd.   75 - 24   2013   £850

Pick, William *Pedigrees and Performances of the Most Celebrated Racehorses, that have Appeared Upon the English Turf, Since the Time of Basto, Flying Childers &c.*   By W. Pick of York, 1785.   8vo., 132 pages, very good, full contemporary calf, expert repairs to joints and corners, contemporary inscription "Thomas B. Beale from his friend" and armorial bookplate with ornate monogram GR.   Ken Spelman Books Ltd.   73 - 8   2013   £295

Pickens, William *Bursting Bonds.*   Boston: Jordan and More Press, 1923.   Second edition, 8vo., 222 pages, boards, paper label (lacking some paper on spine, some staining to cover), nice and clean inside, from the library of reformer Florence Kelley (1859-1932), inscribed by author for Kelley June 11 1924.   Second Life Books Inc.   182 - 191   2013 $325

Pickering, Leslie P. *Lord Byron, Leigh Hunt and the "Liberal".*   London: Drane's Ltd., 1925.   Half title, frontispiece, original red cloth, bevelled boards, lettered gilt, spine little faded, small split at head, Doris Langley Moore's copy. Jarndyce Antiquarian Booksellers   CCIII - 309   2013   £30

Picott, J. Rupert *A Quarter Century of the Black Experience in Elementary and Secondary Education 1950-1975.*   No place: J. Rupert Piccot, 1976.   First edition, black cloth lettered in silver, 94 pages, photos, trifle rubbed at extremities, else very near fine, without dust jacket, possibly as issued.   Between the Covers Rare Books, Inc.   165 - 243   2013 $125

Pictet, Benedict *An Antidote Againtt a Careless Indifferency in Matters of Religion, Being a Treatise in Opposition to Those that Believe that all Religions are Indifferent and...* North Allerton: printed by L. Langdale, 1802. Third edition, 12mo., tan sheep with simple blind tooled border, edges colored yellow, spine sunned and bit worn, slightly scuffed, still very good. Unsworths Antiquarian Booksellers   28 - 192   2013   £30

Picton, J. Allanson *The Conflict of Oligarchy and Democracy.* London: Alexander & Shepheard, 1885. 4 pages, original green cloth, very good. Jarndyce Antiquarian Booksellers CCV - 221   2013   £20

Pictures of English History. George Routledge & Co., n.d., 1869. 4to., original green cloth gilt, little worn, full page frontispiece, 24 plates, 4 illustrations, all printed in colors, joints tightened, little fingering in places, but very good.   R. F. G. Hollett & Son   Children's Books - 336   2013   £65

Picturesque America. London: Paris: and Melbourne: Cassell & Co. Ltd., 1894-1897. First English edition, 4 volumes, 320 x 240mm., original publisher's blue grey cloth, upper covers with gilt title and eagle insignia within arched frame of red and gold, flat spines with gilt decoration and titling, all edges gilt, with 48 full page steel engravings as called for, more than 800 wood engravings, 2 faint creases in an endpaper, hint of rubbing to extremities and trivial soiling to cloth, but very fine, especially clean and fresh internally and in remarkably well preserved original publisher's bindings.   Phillip J. Pirages   63 - 366   2013 $1400

Picturesque Detroit and Environs. Northampton: Picturesque Pub., 1893. First edition, 4to., 151 pages, frontispiece, some soiling, green cloth, very good, tight.   Second Life Books Inc.   183 - 320   2013 $150

Picturesque Guide to the English Lakes. Adam and Charles Black, 1850. Fourth edition, original blindstamped green cloth gilt, rather faded and marked, folding map frontispiece, 3 woodcut vignette plates, 6 outlines of mountains and 4 maps.   R. F. G. Hollett & Son   Lake District & Cumbria - 124   2013   £75

Picturesque Guide to the English Lakes. Adam and Charles Black, 1870. Original pictorial green limp boards, hinges cracked, lower board creased, double page map frontispiece, 1 full page woodcut, 9 text maps.   R. F. G. Hollett & Son   Lake District & Cumbria - 123   2013   £45

Pienkowski, Jan *Haunted House.* London: Heinemann, 1982. Large 8vo., original glazed pictorial boards, illustrations in color, 6 elaborate pop-ups with tabs, overlays, etc.   R. F. G. Hollett & Son   Children's Books - 461   2013   £40

Pierce, Michael D. *The Most Promising Young Officer.* Norman: University of Oklahoma Press, 1993. First edition, 14 illustrations and portraits, from early photos, 6 maps, dark blue cloth, very fine, pictorial dust jacket.   Argonaut Book Shop   Summer 2013 - 280   2013 $60

Piers, Harry *The Evolution of the Halifax Fortress 1749-1928.* Halifax: Public Archives Nova Scotia, 1947. Green card covers, tables, folding map to rear, 8vo., covers worn and sunned, interior good.   Schooner Books Ltd.   101 - 114   2013 $55

Piers, Harry *Master Goldsmiths and Silversmiths of Nova Scotia and Their Marks.* Halifax: Antiquarian Club, 1948. 8vo., blue cloth boards, gilt decoration and title to front cover, half title, frontispiece and 60 plates, cloth worn and scuffed, signed by Una Thomson, artist.   Schooner Books Ltd.   101 - 116   2013 $175

Pigott, Richard *Personal Recollections of an Irish National Journalist.* 1970. Facsimile reproduction of first edition, xii, 447 pages, cloth, dust jacket.   C. P. Hyland   261 - 728   2013   £80

Pike, Mary Hayden Green *Ida May: A Story of Things Actual and Possible by Mary Mangon.* Boston: Phillips, Sampson, 1857. 52nd thousand, 8vo., publisher's cloth stamped in blind and gilt, very good, tight copy, contemporary ownership of Miss Elizabeth Dickinson.   Second Life Books Inc.   183 - 121   2013 $65

Pike, Zebulon Montgomery 1779-1839 *Exploratory Travels through the Western Territories of North America.* Denver: W. H. Lawrence and Co., 1889. Reissue of very rare London 1811 edition, 394 pages, frontispiece, 4 maps, tastefully rebound in full French beige cloth, black leather spine label, fine.   Argonaut Book Shop   Recent Acquisitions June 2013 - 231   2013 $500

Piles, Roger D. *Nouveau Tratie d'Anatomie Accomodee aux Arts & Peinture et de Sculpture part Tortebat.* Paris: Chez Jean, 1799. 5 text leaves on green tinted paper margined and tipped in, 10 engraved plates, tall folio, contemporary calf backed boards, engraved titlepage with armorial crests in elaborate facade, tall quite crisp copy.   James Tait Goodrich   S74 - 209   2013 $1895

Pillsbury, Parker *Acts of the Anti Slavery Apostles.* Concord: Clague, Wegman, Schlicht & Co., 1883. First edition, green cloth gilt, contemporary name stamp on endpapers and half title, corners very slightly rubbed through, still nice, near fine copy, much nicer than usually found.   Between the Covers Rare Books, Inc.   165 - 244   2013 $300

Pinchard, Elizabeth Sibthorpe *The Two Cousins, a Moral Story...* London: printed for E. Newbery, 1798. 12mo., full contemporary tree calf, double gilt banded spine, hinges cracked but very firm. Jarndyce Antiquarian Booksellers CCIV - 229 2013 £225

Pinchbeck, Ivy *Children in English Society. Volume I: from Tudor times to the Eighteenth Century.* London: Routledge & Kegan Paul, 1869. First edition, original cloth, gilt, dust jacket with very slight wear to fold, 18 plates. R. F. G. Hollett & Son Children's Books - 463 2013 £25

Pindarus *Pindari Carmnia Juxta Exemplar Heynianum.* London: T. Cadell and W. Davies, 1814. 2 volumes 8vo., Text in Greek with Latin paraphrase and notes in Latin, interleaved with plain notepaper, most of which unused but with sporadic pencil notes and also marginalia, contemporary tan calf, black label and gilt to spine, gilt border, neatly rebacked with original spine relaid, corners repaired but little worn, endpapers foxed hinges reinforced with heavy paper. Unsworths Antiquarian Booksellers 28 - 41 2013 £120

Pinel, Philippe *Tratado Medico Filosofico de la Enangenacion del Alma o Mania Escrito e Frences por Felipe Pinel.* Madrid: en la Imprenta Real, 1804. First edition in Spanish, 2 engraved plates, folding table, little browned or foxed in places, small 8vo., original tree sheep, flat spine gilt ruled in compartments, red lettering piece, red edges, very minor wear, very good. Blackwell's Rare Books Sciences - 96 2013 £1500

Pingret, Edouard *Voyage de S. M. Louis-Philippe Ier, Roi de Francais Au Chateau de Windsor Dedie ASM.* Paris: Ed. Pingret, London: Ackermann and Co., 1846. Elephant folio, 25 lithographed plates, some tinted, pages 13 and 14 misnumbered, text in French, titlepages printed partly in gilt, second with ornate colored border, tissue interleaving discolored, some torn or creased, occasionally missing, some foxing, particularly near fore edge, later quarter blue morocco with blue marbled boards, gilt title to spine, little scuffed, endcaps fraying, slight wear, marbled endpapers beginning to crack a little at hinges, bookplate of Bibliotheque de M. Laplalgne Barris. Unsworths Antiquarian Booksellers 28 - 193 2013 £850

Pinnock, W. *The Golden Treasury; Being a Guide to Youth in their Social, Moral and Religious Duties...* Shepherd and Sutton, 1843. New edition, original blindstamped red cloth gilt upper hinge splitting at head, backstrip little frayed at head and foot, engraved frontispiece portrait, 1 woodcut plate and 18 plates each with four panels, one section shaken, scarce. R. F. G. Hollett & Son Children's Books - 464 2013 £85

Pinnock, W. *Whittaker's Improved Editions of Pinnock's Catechisms.* Whittaker & Co. 1820's, 8vo., original red cloth gilt, spine mellowed, 11 separate titles from a series, bound together, each with frontispiece, engraved title and woodcuts, most titles have 72 pages and there are 6 pages ads at end. R. F. G. Hollett & Son Children's Books - 465 2013 £275

Pinter, Harold *The Caretaker.* Encore Pub., 1960. First edition, true first, foolscap 8vo., original black and white stapled card wrappers, near fine. Blackwell's Rare Books 172 - 226 2013 £250

Piozzi, Hester Lynch Salusbury Thrale *Mrs. Thrale, afterwards Mrs. Piozzi, a Sketch of Her Life and Passages from Her Diaries, Letters & Other Writings.* London: Seeley and Co., 1891. 206 x 140mm., very attractive contemporary dark blue three quarter morocco by Tout (stamp signed), raised bands, spine lavishly gilt in compartments with central oval medallion containing a flora spray, medallion within a frame of entwined volutes, floral tools and stippling, marbled boards and endpapers, top edge gilt, frontispiece, 8 portraits, bookplate of William Eyres Sloan, very fine in especially pretty binding, only most trivial imperfections. Phillip J. Pirages 63 - 367 2013 $450

Piper, Watty *The Bumper Book.* New York: Platt & Munk, 1946. Folio, cloth, pictorial paste-on, some cover soil and rubbing to cover plate, else very good+, illustrations in color by Eulalie. Aleph-Bet Books, Inc. 105 - 240 2013 $250

Pisan, Christine De *Poemes et Ballades du Temps Passe.* Paris: Imprime pour Charles Meunier "Maison du Livre", 1902. One of 115 copies, 100 of which were for sale (this #53), 320 x 233mm., with additional state of illustrated wrapper, woodcut tailpieces by Pierre Gusman and 50 large etchings by Albert Robida beginning each of the poems and ballads, and (bound in at back), extra suite of tailpieces on China paper as well as extra suite of etchings in two states (black and bistre) on China paper, (and tipped in at front), fine full page original signed pen and wash painting in sepia tones by Robida, text printed in red and black; remarkably attractive and animated 'Cuir-Cisele' binding of mahogany morocco over heavy bevelled boards by Charles Meunier (signed, with tiny inscription in leather at bottom of front cover, as well as stamp-signed gilt and dated 1904 on front turn-in), both covers with elaborately detailed sculpted scenes filling large brown calf panel, upper cover featuring golden sword hilt at top middle and skull at foot with swirling acanthus leaves emanating from each and framing head and foot of panel, large lyre at center acting as scabbard for sword and incorporating cartouche bearing title, and beneath that shield and troubadour's hat over crossed rifles and swords, all highlighted with silver or gold paint, this intricate frame laid down as whole on ground of sharkskin stippled in blind, lower cover with similar elements but very differently designed, featuring 'cuir-cisele' acanthus leaf cornerpieces and larger centerpiece medallion on much later ground of stippled sharkskin, centerpiece with shield over two crossed swords and lance, lute and horn hanging from latter these elements highlighted with silver or gold paint and encircled by laurel branch, raised bands, center spine panel with gilt titling, panels above and below it with simple gilt floral medallion, turn-ins consisting of light brown morocco punctuated with inlaid mahogany morocco overall, gold watered silk endleaves, marbled flyleaves, all edges gilt, original pictorial paper wrappers bound in, few trivial smudges, but very fine, impressive binding unusually lustrous and virtually unworn, text with almost no signs of use. Phillip J. Pirages 61 - 116 2013 $6500

Pisani, Donald J. *From the Family Farm to the Agribusiness. The Irrigation Crusade in California and the West 1850-1931.* Berkeley: University of California Press, 1984. First edition, portraits, text maps, brown cloth, very fine with dust jacket. Argonaut Book Shop Recent Acquisitions June 2013 - 232 2013 $75

Pitman, Isaac *Manuscript Writing & Lettering.* 1921. Second edition, 8 plate, quarter cloth, some staining on boards, text very good, inscribed "Edith Somerville from BTS July 1926" in her own hand. C. P. Hyland 261 - 786 2013 £35

Pitt, Robert *The Craft and Frauds of Physick Expos'd.* printed for Tim Childe, 1702. First edition, little bit browned and soiled, 8vo., contemporary gilt panelled calf, rebacked, corners worn, contemporary signature of J. Collinson and his book label inside front cover giving his place of residence as Lancaster, sound. Blackwell's Rare Books Sciences - 97 2013 £750

Pittman, Philip *The Present State of the European Settlements on the Mississippi.* Cleveland: 1908. One of 549 numbered copies, 165 pages, 8 maps on 7 folding sheets (x ads), cloth, no dust jacket, spine faded, minor repairs to top and bottom of spine and rear board, interior and maps very good. Dumont Maps & Books of the West 122 - 76 2013 $125

Placido, Titi *Primum Mobile with Theses to the Theory and Canons for Practice.* London: Davis and Dickson, n.d., circa, 1814. First edition translated into English, quarto, tables, diagrams and one engraved plate, 22cm., printed on wove paper with 1812 watermark plate, owner's signature in neat ink, with extensive manuscript annotations and marginalia by Thomas Henry Huxley, contemporary brown half morocco and marbled paper boards, morocco spine label, gilt title, raised bands, marbled endpapers, boards scuffed and detached, else very good with light age toning and scattered foxing to text pages, housed in professionally made clamshell box, dark brown quarter morocco on rounded spine, raised bands, gilt spine title and tooling, interior lined in black felt, signed "T. Huxley, Leamington, Warwickshire Sept. 14 1842", scarce. Between the Covers Rare Books, Inc. Philosophy - 332721 2013 $3000

The Plan of Campaign Illustrated. ILPU, 1888. 24 pages, disbound, good. C. P. Hyland 261 - 733 2013 £50

Planche, J. R. *Descent of the Danube; from Ratisbon to Vienna during the Autumn of 1827.* London: James Dunkan, 1828. First edition, 8vo., 320 pages, map, frontispiece, vignette on titlepage, light foxing to map and margins of frontispiece, contemporary black polished calf with gilt spine and raised bands, handsome. J. & S. L. Bonham Antiquarian Booksellers Europe - 9110 2013 £200

Planck, Max *Where is Science Going?* New York: W. W. Norton, 1932. Stated first edition, 8vo., 221 pages, very good++ with minimal cover edge wear and foxing to edges in very good+ dust jacket with sun spine, small pieces missing spine tips and chips, rare in dust jacket. By the Book, L. C. 36 - 100 2013 $500

Plant, C. P. *Handbook for the Guidance of Shipmaster on the Ichang-Chunking Section of the Yangtze River.* Shanghai: Statistical Department of the Inspectorate General of Customs, 1920. First edition, small 4to., vi, 91 pages, 5 foldout plates, 28 additional plates, very good+ in original yellow paper covered boards and red cloth spine with mild soil, edge wear, owner's signature on front cover and f.f.e.p., few pencilled notes inside. By the Book, L. C. 36 - 92 2013 $650

Plater, F. *Praxeos seu de Cognoscendis, Praedicensis Praecavendis...* Basel: C. Waldkich, 1608-1609. 3 volumes, contemporary vellum with hand lettered spines, some soiling and discoloration to vellum, rubbed, inner hinges weak, text foxed and strained in parts, early ownership stamps on title. James Tait Goodrich S74 - 210 2013 $695

Plath, Sylvia 1932-1963 *Ariel.* London: Faber, 1965. First edition, crown 8vo., original pink cloth, backstrip gilt lettered, dust jacket with light sunning to backstrip panel, very good. Blackwell's Rare Books 172 - 229 2013 £700

Plath, Sylvia 1932-1963 *"Dialogue en Route." in Smith Review Exam Blues Issues Jan. 1955.* Northampton: Smith Review, 1955. First appearance of this poem, 8vo., original blue printed wrappers, fine. James S. Jaffe Rare Books Fall 2013 - 129 2013 $1500

Plath, Sylvia 1932-1963 *"Sculptor. To Leonard Baskin".* N.P: Grencourt Review, n.d. but circa, 1959-1960. First separate edition, probably no more than 25 copies were produced, 8vo., original printed wrappers, very fine. James S. Jaffe Rare Books Fall 2013 - 128 2013 $2500

Plath, Sylvia 1932-1963 *Uncollected Poems.* Turret Books 1965, but published, 1966. First edition, one of 165 copies, double plate facsimile printed on pink paper, pages 20, foolscap 8vo., original plain white stapled card wrappers, stiff card dust jacket faded at spine and little soiled, good, superb association inscribed by Ted Hughes to fellow poet Richard Murphy. Blackwell's Rare Books B174 - 276 2013 £850

Plato *Dialoghi di Platone Intitolati l'Eutifrone Ouero Della Santita, l'Apologiae di Socrate, il Critone o Di quel che s'ha affare, il Fedone o Della Immortalita....* Venice: presso Giovanni Varisco e Comapgni, 1574. First Italian edition of three dialogues, some light foxing and browning, small rusthole in final leaf affecting three characters, 8vo., contemporary limp vellum, spine lettered vertically in ink, yapp edges, bit ruckled, slightly marked, ties removed and front flyleaf lost, good. Blackwell's Rare Books 172 - 115 2013 £1500

Plato *Dialogues of Plato.* London: printed for W. Sandby, 1767. 1773. First collected edition, 8 (of 13) parts, in 2 volumes, quarto, engraved folding plate in volume II, each part containing special titlepage, contemporary full tan calf, rebacked to style, gilt single rule border on covers, gilt board edges, marbled endpapers, brown calf spine labels, lettered gilt, corners worn and boards slightly scuffed, occasional light foxing, previous owner's armorial bookplate, very good, crisp. Heritage Book Shop Holiday Catalogue 2012 - 118 2013 $4000

Platts, John *The Literary and Scientific Class-Book...* Whittaker, Treacher and Co., 1830. Second edition, original black roan gilt, rather rubbed and scratched, spine defective at head and foot, engraved frontispiece, 2 engraved plates and numerous text woodcuts, some pencilled crosses in text and little fingering in places in first half of work, rather shaken, scarce. R. F. G. Hollett & Son Children's Books - 466 2013 £75

Plautus, Marcus Accius *Comoediae Interpretation et Notis Illustravit Jacobus Operarius... i Usum Serenissimi Delphini.* Paris: Apud Fredericum Leonard Regis, Srenissimi Delphini & Cleri Gallicani Typograhum via Jacobea, 1679. 2 volumes, 4to., engraved half title, browned and spotted, bit of marginal dampstaining, contemporary Dutch blind panelled vellum, red morocco labels, ink date in fifth compartments, edges red, vellum soiled, front pages just cracking, parts of volume I spine defective. Unsworths Antiquarian Booksellers 28 - 42 2013 £250

Playfair, John 1745-1820 *Outlines of Natural Philosophy, Being Heads of Lectures Delivered in the University of Edinburgh.* Edinburgh: printed for Archibald Constable and Co., 1819. Volume 1 3rd edition, volume 2 second edition, 7 engraved plates, 8vo., bound without half titles, full contemporary calf, gilt ruled borders, attractive gilt panelled spines, light brown morocco labels, library stamp in gilt at head of each spine, hinges slightly cracked but very firm, small oval stamp of United Presbyterian Library verso of titlepages. Jarndyce Antiquarian Booksellers CCIV - 231 2013 £170

The Playground. New York: 1909-1914. 26 issues, approximately 24 pages each, wrappers, photo illustrations, very good. Beasley Books 2013 - 2013 $100

The Playmate Book. Santa Monica: General Pub., 1996. First edition, this copy signed by Hugh Hefner, Gretchen Edgren and at least 7 of the playmates, fine in fine dust jacket. Ed Smith Books 75 - 58 2013 $300

Pleasant Surprises. Boston: Lothrop Pub. Co. n.d. circa, 1870. 4to., cloth backed pictorial boards, no titlepage as issued, covers soiled, else very good, 6 fine chromolithographed pages folded accordion style, when pulled open a surprise picture is revealed, also illustrated in brown line. Aleph-Bet Books, Inc. 105 - 406 2013 $600

Pleynet, Marclein *Robert Motherwell.* Paris: Edition Daniel Papierski, 1989. First edition, Copy 2832 from an edition of 7000, Motherwell paintings along with original lithograph bound in as frontispiece, fine in fine dust jacket and very near fine slipcase, very attractive book. Jeff Hirsch Books Fall 2013 - 129135 2013 $250

Plimpton, George *Writers at Work: the Paris Review Interviews. Second Seris.* New York: Viking Press, 1963. First edition, 8vo., fine in fine, bright dust jacket (top corner of front flap clipped, but price remains). Ed Smith Books 75 - 56 2013 $75

Plimpton, Sarah *Storms.* New York: 2011. Artist's book, one of 15 copies only, all on Somerset black paper, each signed and numbered by author/artist, Plimpton, loose as issued in tan cloth over card stock envelope printed with author and title in black on front panel, the nine pages are all original woodcuts as well as text printed letterpress in Caslon, this is a 'jigsaw' book, i.e. three 'jigsaw' woodcuts printed in white on black paper, carved block is cut by jigsaw and then reassembled on letterpress bed and printed with white ink on black paper. Priscilla Juvelis - Rare Books 55 - 23 2013 $950

Plinius Secundus, C. *Historia Mundi.* Basel: Froben Press, 1525. Lacking leaf Y1 (pages 529/530), numerous woodcut initial letters, marginalia throughout in early hand, early ownership signatures on title, early 17th century vellum soiled and worn still tight, some foxing and some marginal worming in lower inside corner involving approximately 20 leaves, this copy lacks one leaf and it appears that it likely was never bound in, otherwise very good. James Tait Goodrich S74 - 212 2013 $2950

Plinius Secundus, C. *The Historie of the World commonly called the Natural Historie.* London: Adam Islip, 1634. Second Holland edition, 2nd edition in English, Thick folio, lacks initial and final blanks, 2 volumes bound in 1, full contemporary calf, rebacked, endpapers renewed, marginal dampstaining, title in volume I trimmed and mounted, first 3 prelims rather primitively. James Tait Goodrich 75 - 170 2013 $1995

Plowden, Francis *The History of Ireland from Its Union and Great Britain in January 1801 to October 1811.* Dublin: Boyce, 1811. Volume 1 (of 3), full contemporary calf (worn), binding tight, text good. C. P. Hyland 261 - 729 2013 £35

Plumb, Joseph Hudson *Trading West: a Novel.* Boston: Bruce Humphries, 1940. First edition, fine in very near fine dust jacket with touch of rubbing. Between the Covers Rare Books, Inc. 165 - 245 2013 $100

Plummer, T. Arthur *The Bonfire Murder.* New York: Macaulay Co., 1937. First American edition, top corners slightly bumped, else fine in fine dust jacket, beautiful copy, scarce thus. Between the Covers Rare Books, Inc. Mystery & Detective Fiction - 89167 2013 $200

Plumptre, Anne *Narrative of a Residence in Ireland During the Summer of 1814 (and 1815).* London: Coburn, 1817. First edition, portrait, 9 (of 11) plates, modern half calf, very good, scarce. C. P. Hyland 261 - 730 2013 £550

Plunkett, James *Strumpet City.* London: Hutchinson, 1959. First edition, original black cloth, dust jacket, fine, inoffensively price clipped dust jacket, inscribed by author. Maggs Bros. Ltd. 1442 - 365 2013 £175

Plunkett, James *The Trusting and Maimed.* New York: Devon Adair Co., 1955. First edition, 8vo., original quarter blue cloth, dust jacket, inscribed by author, with name and address, from the library of publisher Timothy O'Keefe, bumped at extremities, otherwise very good, nicked and torn dust jacket. Maggs Bros. Ltd. 1442 - 364 2013 £200

La Plus Vielle Histoire Du Monde. Paris: Jardin des Modes, n.d., 1931. Oblong 4to., printed on cloth, slightest of cover soil, near fine, quite scarce, nice copy, full color illustrations on every page by Francoise, one of the first Batik printed books (using vegetable dyes). Aleph-Bet Books, Inc. 104 - 219 2013 $1200

Plutarchus *Plutarchi Chaeronensis.* London: ex Officina Jacobi Tonson & Johannis Watts, 1723-1729. First edition thus, 5 volumes, 4to., frontispiece in volume 1, engraved portrait headpieces, numerous woodcut head and tailpieces, titlepage volume I in red and black, volumes 2-5 titles in Greek, half brown morocco over marbled boards, heads, tails and raised bands, decorated in gilt, gilt volume numbers and titles to two compartments, blind tooled, decorations to three compartments, all edges marbled, marbled endpapers, spines scuffed, extremities rubbed, sort splits to joints near heads on 2 volumes, tears to head of spines, some minor loss on 3 volumes, top edge trimmed, occasional browning or toning, still overall very good. Kaaterskill Books 16 - 68 2013 $1850

Plutarchus *Plutarch's Lives (with) a Life of Plutarch.* London: printed by C. Baldwin for J. Mawman et al, 1819. Third printing of this edition, 6 volumes, pleasing contemporary diced russia skillfully rebacked to style (in early 20th century?), flat spines divided into panels by blind tooling and gilt rules, square panels at head and tail with gilt central floral arabesque and blindstamped flower cornerpieces, elongated central panel with gilt floral spray centerpiece inside blind tooled floral frame, each spine with one black and one reddish brown morocco label, marbled endpapers; frontispiece in volume I; bookplate of George and Nora Ranney, extremities somewhat rubbed, half corners worn through, boards little soiled and stained, two gatherings in volume V noticeably foxed, faint offsetting it text, still excellent set, clean and fresh internally, solidly restored bindings that look good on the shelf. Phillip J. Pirages 63 - 368 2013 $650

Plutarchus *Plutarch's Lives...* London: W. Robinson and Sons, R. Jennings, 1823. 6 volumes, frontispiece volume 1, partially unopened in original green cloth boards, paper label, boards slightly bumped, otherwise exceptional copy in original binding. Jarndyce Antiquarian Booksellers CCV - 222 2013 £350

Plutarchus *Les Ouvvres Morales & Meslees du Plutarque.* Paris: De l'Impriemrie de Michel de Vascosan, 1572. First edition, title creased and slightly frayed at edges, short closed tear reinforced with tissue, some light spotting elsewhere, few sections toned, folio 18th century calf, scraped and worn at edges, rebacked, black morocco lettering piece, hinges relined, bookplate of drama critic Joseph Knight (1829-1907), sound.   Blackwell's Rare Books   172 - 116   2013   £3500

Pocock, Doris A. *Self or School?* Cassell, 1926. First edition, original grey cloth, oval pictorial onlay, color frontispiece and 3 plates by Stanley Lloyd.   R. F. G. Hollett & Son   Children's Books - 467   2013   £25

Poe, Edgar Allan   1809-1849 *The Bells and Other Poems.* London: Hodder and Stoughton, n.d., 1912. Edition deluxe, limited to 750 copies, numbered and signed by artist, large quarto, 28 mounted color plates, 10 black ink headpieces and portrait by Edmund Dulac, one of a very few copies bound for special customers in publisher's dark green morocco, near fine.   David Brass Rare Books, Inc.   Holiday 2012 Chapter One - DB 02158   2013 $3000

Poe, Edgar Allan   1809-1849 *The Conchologist's First Book.* Philadelphia: Pub. for the author by Haswell, Barrington and Haswell, 1840. Second edition, 12 lithographic plates, original green printed leather backed boards, worn at extremities of spine, covers rubbed and some worn, occasional light foxing, but very good, fragile.   Second Life Books Inc.   183 - 322   2013 $950

Poe, Edgar Allan   1809-1849 *"The Purloined Letter." in The Gift: A Christmas, New Year and Birthday Present.* Philadelphia: Carey & Hart, 1845. First appearance of Poe's story, octavo, 8 engraved plates, including frontispiece and engraved titlepage, plates with tissue guards, full maroon morocco publisher's special gift binding, elaborate gilt stamping on boards ad spine, spine lettered gilt, all edges gilt, corners with some rubbing, some scattered foxing, very nice in beautiful binding.   Heritage Book Shop Holiday Catalogue 2012 - 119   2013 $2000

Poe, Edgar Allan   1809-1849 *The Raven.* New York: Harper Bros., 1884. First edition thus, illustrations by Gustave Dore, with wood engraved plates with guards, 2 other text engravings, folio, grey gilt pictorial cloth, all edges gilt, except for slight foxing to endpapers and half title, fine in publisher's box (some soil and repair to box), rarely found in such fine condition with box.   Aleph-Bet Books, Inc.   105 - 198   2013 $4000

Poe, Edgar Allan   1809-1849 *Tales.* New York: Wiley and Putnam, 1845. First edition, third printing, octavo, half title, bound by Curtis Walters c. 1910-20 in full brown morocco, original green cloth preserved at rear, joints expert and almost invisible repair, near fine, internally fresh and clean, original chamois-lined leather edged slipcase.   David Brass Rare Books, Inc.   Holiday 2012 Chapter Five - DB 02101   2013 $9500

Poe, Edgar Allan   1809-1849 *Tales of Mystery and Imagination.* New York: Brentano's, n.d. circa, 1923. Color plate edition, large thick 4to., black cloth, pictorial paste-on, top edge tinted black, others trimmed, no decoration on spine, 412 numbered pages, black endpapers, slightest bit of fading, near fine in dust jacket (frayed), illustrations by Harry Clarke with 24 detailed black and white plates and 26 other vignettes.   Aleph-Bet Books, Inc.   104 - 125   2013 $950

Poe, Edgar Allan   1809-1849 *Tales of Mystery and Imagination.* Philadelphia: J. B. Lippincott Co., 1935. First American trade edition, large octavo, 12 color plates with descriptive tissue guards, 17 full page black and white illustrations by Arthur Rackham, publisher's red linen, lettered and pictorially stamped in gilt, pictorial endpapers, excellent copy in fine dust jacket.   David Brass Rare Books, Inc.   Holiday 2012 Chapter One - DB 01891   2013 $480

Poe, Edgar Allan   1809-1849 *Tales of Mystery and Imagination.* Philadelphia: Lippincott, 1935. First American Rackham illustrated edition, 4to., old paper clip mark on end of endpaper, else fine in dust jacket, red pictorial cloth, dust jacket very good with 'v' shaped piece off top of spine, frayed at base of spine, 12 fine color plates by Arthur Rackham, tissue guards, plus many black and whites.   Aleph-Bet Books, Inc.   104 - 477   2013 $875

Poe, Edgar Allan   1809-1849 *Tales of Mystery and Imagination.* London: Harrap, 1935. Limited to 460 numbered copies, signed by artist, thick 4to., full gilt decorated vellum, small bruise to vellum on edge of spine, else fine in original publisher's slipcase (taped on edges), 12 mounted color plates with lettered tissue guards plus a profusion of text drawings by Arthur Rackham, nice.   Aleph-Bet Books, Inc.   104 - 476   2013 $3300

Poe, Edgar Allan   1809-1849 *Tales of Mystery and Imagination.* Philadelphia: Lippincott, 1935. First American edition, frontispiece, 11 other illustrations in color, 17 line drawings, bound in red cloth, covers little bowed, stain to top of leaves near spine, spine cloth rubbed and worn, clean inside.   Second Life Books Inc.   183 - 444   2013 $200

Poe, Edgar Allan 1809-1849 *Two Poems.* Utrecht: Catharijne Press, 1984. Limited to 100 numbered copies, each with signed and numbered photogravure by Johan de Zoete, 4 x 6.5cm., full leather, vellum cover label on set, bound by Luce Thurkow, from the collection of Donn W. Sanford.   Oak Knoll Books   303 - 87   2013 $200

Poe, Edgar Allan 1809-1849 *The Works. (with) The Literati. (with) The Works of the Late Edgar Allan Poe.* New York: Redfield, 1850. 1850. 1856. First collected edition, first issue, 2nd issue of volume I and II first issue of volume III, first and only printing of volume IV, together 4 volumes, 12mo., frontispiece in volume 1, volumes I and II original light purple cloth, covers blindstamped with double rule frame, cornerpieces and ornate centerpiece, spines blindstamped with simple rules, lettered gilt and with gilt stamped rule between volume number and volume title, cloth bit rubbed on these 2 volumes and uniformly sunned, small amount of shelfwear, tiny hole to spine hinge volume II, Volume III in blue cloth with matching blindstamped and gilt as previous 2 volumes, bit of edge and shelfwear, spine sunned, volume IV in original purple cloth, covers blindstamped with five rule frame, spine lettered gilt and stamped gilt with bust of Athene and raven, pale yellow endpapers, spine sunned, volumes I-III with previous owner's inscription, volume IV with previous owner's old ownership stamp on titlepage, bit of light foxing, overall very good each book chemised and housed in quarter morocco slipcase, bit of soiling to slipcase.   Heritage Book Shop   Holiday Catalogue 2012 - 120   2013 $5000

Poehlmann, Jo Anna *Escargot Under Glass. A Day in the Life of a Forest Snail.* Milwaukee: 2011. Artist's book, one of 35 copies on white stock, hand numbered by artist on verso of titlepage, page size 1 7/16 inches in diameter, 34 pages, bound by artist accordion fold with card stock as titlepage and endpage, housed in small metal circular box with glass lid showing cover of book, hand painted and lettered by Jo Anna Poehlmann, then copied and then hand colored by her, charming homage.   Priscilla Juvelis - Rare Books   56 - 29   2013 $140

Poems by Dobson, Locker and Praed. New York: Stokes, 1892. 4to., two tone cloth stamped in gold pictorial paste-on, top edge gilt, slight cover soil, very good+, illustrations by Maud Humphrey with 6 beautiful color plates and in black and white by other artists, rare.   Aleph-Bet Books, Inc.   104 - 288   2013 $950

Poems for Alan Hancox. Andoversford: Whittington Press, 1993. Sole edition, 56/300 copies (of an edition of 350), printed on Zerkall mouldmade paper, 2 wood engravings by Miriam Macgregor on titlepage printed in cinnamon, imperial 8vo., original quarter mid brown linen, backstrip gilt lettered, pink boards with overall design of vertical decorative lines, top edge gilt, others untrimmed, fine.   Blackwell's Rare Books   172 - 307   2013   £50

Poetry of the Anti-Jacobin. London: printed for J. Wright, 1799. First edition, contemporary full dark blue morocco by Dillon of Chelsea, spine lettered and ruled gilt, slightly rubbed, all edges gilt, very good.   Jarndyce Antiquarian Booksellers   CCIII - 629   2013   £65

Pogany, Nander *Hungarian Fairy Book.* New York: Frederick Stokes, n.d. circa, 1913. 8vo., blue pictorial cloth, 287 pages, slightest bit of soil, else near fine, color frontispiece and a profusion of full and partial page black and whites by Willy Pogany, very scarce.   Aleph-Bet Books, Inc.   104 - 429   2013 $500

Pogany, Willy *Willy Pogany's Mother Goose.* Thomas Nelson & Sons, 1928. Perhaps a later printing with 'lalch' corrected to latch' in Crosspatch rhyme, Large 8vo., original blue decorated cloth gilt, upper board, trifle marked, unpaginated, superbly illustrated in color and black and white in art deco style, couple of small smudges, endpapers lightly browned, bookplate on flyleaf slightly offset onto half title with little adhesion damage, small edge tear, but excellent copy.   R. F. G. Hollett & Son   Children's Books - 468   2013   £250

Pogany, Willy *Willy Pogany's Mother Goose.* New York: Nelson, 1928. First edition, first issue (with mis-spelling of 'lalch' for 'latch' in 'Crosspatch' verse),, many full page color illustrations, also black and whites, blue cloth, elaborate gilt pictorial cover and spine, top edge gilt, fine in original color pictorial wrapper (very good+, very slightly frayed).   Aleph-Bet Books, Inc.   105 - 459   2013 $975

Pohl, Frederik *The Reefs of Space.* London: Dennis Dobson, 1965. First British (and first hardcover edition, octavo, boards.   L. W. Currey, Inc.   Utopian Literature: Recent Acquisitions (April 2013) - 138543   2013 $100

Pohl, Frederik *Slave Ship.* New York: Ballantine Books, 1957. First edition, boards and endpapers foxed, thus very good in very good plus dust jacket with modest soiling and tiny tears, very scarce.   Between the Covers Rare Books, Inc.   Sci-Fi, Fantasy & Horror - 84945   2013 $650

Pohl, Frederik *Starchild.* London: Dennis Dobson, 1966. First British and first hardcover edition, octavo, boards.   L. W. Currey, Inc.   Utopian Literature: Recent Acquisitions (April 2013) - 138544   2013 $100

Poilroux, Jacques Barthelemy *Traite de Medecine Legale Criminelle.* Paris: Levrault, 1834. First edition, last leaf slightly stained, small circular library stamp on verso of title, 8vo., uncut in original yellow paper wrappers, paper label on spine, lettered in ink, small label inside front cover partly excised, minor defects to spine, very good.   Blackwell's Rare Books   Sciences - 98 2013   £850

Polidori, John William 1795-1821 *The Vampyre: a Tale.* Paris: Galignani, 1819. Second edition, half title, contemporary half maroon calf, gilt spine, little rubbed, very slightly worn, damage to leather of following board, good plus, scarce item.   Jarndyce Antiquarian Booksellers   CCIII - 436   2013   £600

Polignac, Melchior De *Anti-Lucretius, siue, de Deo et Natura, Libri Novem... Opus Posthumum...* Amsterdam: Marc-Michel Rey, 1748. Small 8vo., titlepages printed in red and black, half title frayed at edges, minor dampstain in lower margins at start, small 8vo., contemporary calf, roll tooled border towards spine on upper cover, rebacked, corners worn, sound.   Blackwell's Rare Books   172 - 117   2013   £120

The Polite Jester; or, Theatre for Wit. printed by and for J. Drew, 1796. First edition, engraved frontispiece, frontispiece trimmed at fore margin with slight loss of image and 3 letters of the legend (sense recoverable), 12mo., early pink card wrappers, paper spine, cracks on spine, with ownership inscription "Elizabeth Savil(le) May 1st 1809, a quatrain in pencil in early hand on verso of flyleaf in German and another, in English on recto of frontispiece, good.   Blackwell's Rare Books   B174 - 78   2013   £700

Politi, Leo *A Boat for Peppe.* New York: Charles Scribner's Sons, 1950. First edition, 4to., cloth, fine in dust jacket (slightly frayed at spine ends), beautiful color illustrations, inscribed by Politi with lovely watercolor embellishments on entire endpaper.   Aleph-Bet Books, Inc.   105 - 463   2013 $375

Politi, Leo *Little Leo.* New York: Charles Scribner's Sons, 1951. First edition, 4to., cloth, fine in slightly worn dust jacket, illustrations by Politi, inscribed by Politi with watercolor embellishments.   Aleph-Bet Books, Inc.   105 - 464   2013 $400

Politics; or the History of Will and Jane: a Tale for the Times. Printed by A. Paris, 1796. Half title, 4to., final leaf foxed, otherwise very clean, expertly bound in recent quarter calf, marbled boards, vellum tips, gilt banded spine, red morocco label.   Jarndyce Antiquarian Booksellers   CCIV - 49   2013   £380

Pollux, Julius *Onomaticum Graece & Latine.* Amstelaedami: ex Officina Wetsteniana, 1706. 2 volumes, folio, double page plate to volume II, additional engraved titlepage, engraved frontispiece, titlepage in red and black, Gathering 8N in volume I bound out of sequence, small hole to page 373 affecting a few letters, repair to corner of rear endpaper in volume I, tan Cambridge style calf with catspaw staining to frame, neatly rebacked with red morocco gilt spine labels, edges sprinkled red, boards scratched, some small areas of surface loss, corners worn, hinges relined, to each volume bookplate of Robert Edward Way, bookplate of William Sedgwick, Queens College Cambridge and inscription of Caroli Beaumont, another inscription beneath oval inkstamp of Queens College Library.   Unsworths Antiquarian Booksellers   28 - 43   2013   £750

Ponting, Herbert G. *The Great White South or with Scott in the Antarctic.* London: Duckworth, 1923. Fifth impression, 164 illustrations, map, 2 drawings, modern half blue levant morocco, gilt.   R. F. G. Hollett & Son   Polar Exploration - 50   2013   £120

Poole, Robert *Time's Alteration: Calendar Reform in Early Modern England.* London and Bristol: UCL Press, 1998. 8vo., xix, 243 pages, figures, tables, black cloth, gilt stamped spine title, dust jacket, rare, fine, Burndy Library bookplate.   Jeff Weber Rare Books   169 - 352   2013 $170

Poor Cock Robin. New York: McLoughlin Brothers, n.d circa, 1870. 8vo., pictorial wrappers, cover rubbed, inconspicuous margin mend, very good, 6 fine full page chromolithographs and with small black and white.   Aleph-Bet Books, Inc.   105 - 143   2013 $200

Pope, Alexander 1688-1744 *The Dunciad Variorum. (bound with) Supremacy and Infallibility Examin'd...* London: A. Dod/J. Roberts, 1729. 1729. First edition of Dunciad, 2 works bound in one, contemporary board binding with vellum spine in five compartments, spine lettering in pen, very good, covers with mild edge wear, soil, bookplate, foxing, small 4to., rare.   By the Book, L. C.   38 - 8   2013 $2500

Pope, Alexander 1688-1744 *The Dunciad.* London: printed for Lawton Gilliver at Homer's Head against St. Dunstan's Church, Fleetstreet, 1729. 8vo., bound without final ad leaves, titlepage in red and black, the "Ass" frontispiece, titlepage and frontispiece little dusted, some light browning, front endpaper, chipped with crude repair to top corner, contemporary panelled calf, rebacked with unsympathetic label, corners worn, inner hinges repaired, signatures dated 1758 and 1924.   Jarndyce Antiquarian Booksellers   CCIV - 233   2013   £120

Pope, Alexander 1688-1744 *An Essay on Man...* 1748. Engraved frontispiece, titlepage printed in red and black, with small portrait vignette, 8vo., some dusting and occasional marks, following endpaper creased, contemporary panelled calf, raised bands, slight wear.   Jarndyce Antiquarian Booksellers   CCIV - 235   2013   £40

Pope, Alexander 1688-1744 *The Rape of the Lock.* London: printed by T. Bensley for F. J. Du Roveray, 1798. 8vo., bound without half title, some foxing to plates, slight dusting, contemporary half calf, marbled boards, spines and corners rubbed, head and tail chipped.   Jarndyce Antiquarian Booksellers   CCIV - 236   2013   £75

Pope, Alexander 1688-1744 *The Rape of the Lock.* London: printed by W. Bulmer and Co. for F. J. Du Roveray, 1801. Re-issue of 1798 edition, half title, frontispiece, 5 engraved plates, 8vo., some foxing to plates, full contemporary calf, double gilt ruled borders, blind tooled spine, double gilt rule dividers, very good.   Jarndyce Antiquarian Booksellers   CCIV - 237   2013   £95

Pope, Alexander 1688-1744 *Selecta Poemata Italorum qui Latine Scripsersunt.* Londini: Impensis J. & P. Knapton, 1740. 2 volumes, 8vo., touch of foxing to titlepages, contemporary sprinkled calf, spines in six compartments with raised bands and morocco labels, numbered in gilt, rest with gilt decoration (much rubbed), joints and corners repaired spines bit darkened, ownership inscriptions to front endpaper of Geoffrey Woledge, Birmingham 1937 and A. Montague Summers (1899).   Unsworths Antiquarian Booksellers   28 - 122   2013   £300

Pope, Alexander 1688-1744 *The Works. Volume IV. Part I.* London: printed for T. Cooper, 1742. 3 parts in 1, 8vo., some occasional browning and foxing, inner board and first seven leaves wormed with slight loss of some letters, contemporary sprinkled calf, double gilt ruled borders, raised gilt bands, later red morocco label, leading hinge slightly cracked at foot, 18th century armorial bookplate of Jeremiah Curteis, 19th century bookplate of Wm. Fred D'arley.   Jarndyce Antiquarian Booksellers   CCIV - 232   2013   £50

Pope, Alexander 1688-1744 *The Works of.* Edinburgh: printed for J. Balfour, 1764. Volumes I-VI, engraved frontispiece in volume i, one titlepage bit browned, 12mo., contemporary speckled calf, single gilt fillets, spines with double gilt rules, either side of raised bands, tan lettering pieces, minor wear at extremities, very good.   Blackwell's Rare Books   B174 - 120   2013   £1400

Pope, Jessie *Adventures of Silversuit.* New York: Dodge, circa, 1910. Small 4to., cloth backed boards, pictorial paste-on small chip of paper in corner and edges rubbed, else tight, clean and very good, full page color illustrations by Augustine MacGregor.   Aleph-Bet Books, Inc.   104 - 422   2013 $325

Pope, Thomas *A Treatise on Bridge Architecture in which the Superior Advantages of the Flying Pedent Lever Bridge are Fully Proved.* New York: printed for the author by Alexander Niven, 1811. First edition, 15 engraved plates and 2 vignettes, recent cloth and label, light to moderate waterstaining.   M & S Rare Books, Inc.   95 - 301   2013 $1250

Popham, Hugh *To the Unborn - Greetings. Three Cantos.* Dropmore Press, 1946. 30/75 copies (of an edition of 81 copies), printed on Barcham Green handmade paper and signed by author, crown 8vo., original cream vellum, backstrip gilt lettered, light grey cloth sides, front cover lettered ad with press device all blocked in red, untrimmed, fine.   Blackwell's Rare Books   B174 - 330   2013   £85

Popper, Karl R. *Conjectural Knowledge: My Solution of the Problem of Induction.* Brussels: Revue Inernationale de Philosophie, 1971. First separate edition, offprint, original printed wrappers, signed and inscribed by author to Mario Bunge and his wife, fine.   By the Book, L. C.   38 - 28   2013 $500

Portal, Antoine *Observations sur La Nature et sur Le Traitement du Rachitisme ou des Courbures De La Colonne Vertebrale...* Paris: chez Merlin, 1797. 8vo., 19th century quarter brown calf and marbled boards, light rubbing, some foxing, marginal dampstaining affecting first 30 leaves, overall nice, tight copy.   James Tait Goodrich   75 - 171   2013 $595

Portal, Gerald *The British Mission to Uganda.* Edward Arnold, 1894. First edition, original pictorial cloth gilt, rather worn, little marked, etched portrait, 38 illustrations, frontispiece, folding colored map, very good.   R. F. G. Hollett & Son   Africana - 159   2013   £120

Porter Dean A. *Taos Artists and Their Patrons 1898-1950.* Notre Dame: 1999. First (only) edition, 400 pages, illustrations, dust jacket very lightly rubbed, else bright, near fine.   Dumont Maps & Books of the West   124 - 81   2013 $275

Porter, Clyde *Matt Field on the Santa Fe Trail.* Norman: University of Oklahoma Press, 1960. First edition, color frontispiece, illustrations from portraits and drawings, green cloth, very fine, pictorial dust jacket.   Argonaut Book Shop Summer 2013 - 282   2013 $60

Porter, Edward J. D. *The Pictorial History of New Mexico Military Institute 1891-1983.* N.P.: 1983. 207 pages, illustrations, map endpaper, issued without dust jacket, near fine, signed by author.   Dumont Maps & Books of the West   125 - 69   2013 $50

Porter, Eliot *Eliot Porter.* New York: New York Graphic Society, 1987. First edition, 4to., 130 photos, gray cloth, donor's presentation, remainder mark on top edge, otherwise nice in very slightly soiled and nicked dust jacket. Second Life Books Inc. 183 - 323 2013 $150

Porter, Eliot *The Place No One Knew: Glen Canyon on the Colorado.* San Francisco: Sierra Club, 1966. First edition, folio 186 pages, 80 color photos, cloth very fine, pictorial dust jacket. Argonaut Book Shop Recent Acquisitions June 2013 - 234 2013 $175

Porter, Eliot *Portfolio Two: Iceland.* San Francisco: Sierra Club, 1866. First edition, signed by artist, limited to 110 copies of which 100 were for sale, 11 (of 12) 8 x 10 1/2 inch dye transfer color prints mounted on 20 x 15 inch heavy backing, tissue guards, stamped on verso of each mount "Portfolio II, (Iceland), Eliot Porter, printer number and portfolio number and Printed by the artist, Santa Fe, New Mexico 1975", light line of toning across titlepage, photos and mounts about fine, housed in blue cloth string-tied folding case, case with bit of light scuffing. Heritage Book Shop Holiday Catalogue 2012 - 122 2013 $4500

Porter, Eugene O. *San Elizario a History.* Austin: 1973. 1 of 50 copies, pages (14), 86, illustrations by Jose Cisneros, quarter leather and vellum, boards slightly bowed and discolored, else near fine in slipcase. Dumont Maps & Books of the West 124 - 82 2013 $250

Porter, Jane *The Scottish Chiefs.* London: Hodder & Stoughton, 1921. First edition, small 4to., original red pictorial cloth, spine trifle faded, crease to lower board, 14 color plates and endpapers by N. C. Wyeth. R. F. G. Hollett & Son Children's Books - 728 2013 £65

Porter, Whitworth *History of the Knights of Malta; on the Order of the Hospital of St. John of Jerusalem.* London: Longman Brown, 1858. First edition, 2 volumes, 8vo., frontispieces, map, 2 plates, original purple decorative cloth, slightly faded, but near fine, unopened copy. J. & S. L. Bonham Antiquarian Booksellers Europe - 9649 2013 £300

Porter, William Sydney 1862-1910 *An O. Henry Gift from Henry, The Gift of the Magi.* North Hills: Bird & Bull Press, 1979. Limited to 250 copies, 2.125 x 50 inches (scroll), housed in protective "plastic pill box", this copy does not have a mailing label attached so it was probably one of those produced for booksellers, from the collection of Donn W. Sanford. Oak Knoll Books 303 - 48 2013 $100

Porter, William Sydney 1862-1910 *The Complete Writings of O. Henry.* Garden City: Doubleday Page and Co., 1917. One of 1075 copies, Memorial Edition and Edition deluxe, 229 x 152mm., 14 volumes, 90 plates (45 images, each in two states), including color frontispiece in each volume, one in volume 1 signed by artist), as well as engraved half title with vignette, signed by publishers, original tissue guards, prelim page of first volume with folding leaf of manuscript, apparently in Porter's hand, tipped in, titlepages and half titles in blue and black lovely dark blue crushed lavishly gilt by Stikeman, covers with very broad and animated gilt borders of swirling foliage, flowers and butterflies in style of Derome, raised bands, spine compartments attractively gilt with antique tools red morocco doublures, multiple rules and other gilt elaboration, watered silk free endleaves, top edge gilt, others untrimmed, entirely unopened, spines evenly sunned, one leaf with marginal tear at fore edge, otherwise extraordinarily beautiful set in virtually faultless condition. Phillip J. Pirages 61 - 124 2013 $11,500

Portinaro, Pierluigi *The Cartography of North America 1500-1800.* New York: Crescent Books, 1987. First American edition, folio, 319 pages, profusely illustrated with reproductions of maps and portraits, dark blue boards, very fine in dust jacket. Argonaut Book Shop Recent Acquisitions June 2013 - 235 2013 $100

Portugal, Franklin H. *A Century of DNA, a History of the Discovery of the Structure and Function of the Genetic Substance.* Cambridge: MIT Press, 1977. First edition, near fine in very good dust jacket with chips, small pieces missing rear of dust jacket, scuffs, minimal sun spine, 8vo., signed and inscribed and dated by author. By the Book, L. C. 37 - 67 2013 $250

Posey, Alexander *The Poems of Alexander Lawrence Posey.* Topeka: Crane & Co., 1910. First edition, bit of wear to edges of cloth, spine gilt intact, near fine, photos. Ken Lopez Bookseller 159 - 157 2013 $350

Poska, Valentine J. *Microbibliotrivia, a Curious Adventure in Miniature Books.* San Antonio: privately printed, 1984-1989. Issues 1-5, 4to., stiff paper wrappers, plastic comb binding, not paginated, miniature bookplate of Kathryn Rickard, 5th in the series signed by author, from the collection of Donn W. Sanford. Oak Knoll Books 303 - 22 2013 $250

Post, Emily *Etiquette in Society, in Business, in Politics and at Home.* New York: Funk and Wagnalls, 1922. First edition, very good++, mild edge wear, small owner blindstamp, 8vo., custom cloth clamshell box with images of cover and spine of book tipped on clamshell. By the Book, L. C. 38 - 9 2013 $2000

Post, Melville Davisson *The Silent Witness.* New York: Farrar & Reinhart, 1929. First edition, slight offsetting to endpapers, else fine in attractive dust jacket with several internal repairs.   Between the Covers Rare Books, Inc.   Mystery & Detective Fiction - 47309   2013 $280

Pote, Joseph *The Foreigner's Guide; or a Necessary and Instructive Companion...* London: printed and sold by K. Kent, E. Comyns and Jo. Jollifee, 1752. Third edition, 12mo., contemporary sheep, 213 pages + 3 pages of publisher's terminal ads, ownership signature of Ellis Iles dated 1760 on front free endpaper, with price paid of 2/6, front hinge nearly detached, edges little rubbed, small tear in one leaf with minor loss, but not to sense, very good.   The Brick Row Book Shop   Miscellany Fifty-Nine - 46   2013 $1200

Potter, Beatrix   1866-1943 *All About Peter Rabbit.* New York: Cupples & Leon, 1914. 5 1/4 x 4 inches, frontispiece and 7 color plates and black and white line drawings, red paper covered boards with oblong color pasted label top front cover, very nice in lightly soiled and slightly worn dust jacket.   Ian Hodgkins & Co. Ltd.   134 - 47   2013   £55

Potter, Beatrix   1866-1943 *The Fairy Caravan.* Philadelphia: David McKay, 1929. First US edition, 8vo., 225 pages, green cloth, pictorial -paste-on, as new in dust jacket with most minor edge wear, else fine, 6 color plates and 20 full page and 42 smaller black and white drawings, magnificent copy.   Aleph-Bet Books, Inc.   104 - 453   2013 $2000

Potter, Beatrix   1866-1943 *Ginger & Pickles.* London: Frederick Warne and Co., 1909. First edition, small quarto, color frontispiece and 9 full page color illustrations, original greenish tan boards, color pictorial endpapers, previous owner's ink presentation, near fine, original slightly later (circa 1911) glazed paper glassine, dust jacket with small closed tear to front panel and another closed tear to back panel, not affecting text.   David Brass Rare Books, Inc.   Holiday 2012 Chapter One - DB 00685   2013 $3800

Potter, Beatrix   1866-1943 *The Kitten Who Bumped It's Head.* Charles E. Graham, n.d., 6 color illustrations, pages 12 within pictorial color borders color illustrated boards, slight wear to backstrip and boards, slightly dust soiled, very good, scarce.   Ian Hodgkins & Co. Ltd.   134 - 73   2013   £95

Potter, Beatrix   1866-1943 *Peter Rabbit Story Book.* Philadelphia: Altemus, various dates, 1924. Thick 4to., cloth, pictorial paste-on, 256 pages, fine in slightly worn dust jacket, pictorial endpapers, plus 14 large color plates by Margaret Campbell Hoopes.   Aleph-Bet Books, Inc.   105 - 480   2013 $275

Potter, Beatrix   1866-1943 *Peter Rabbit with Great big cut-outs.* Akron: Saalfield, 1936. Folio, stiff pictorial wrappers small ink check on cover, else near fine and unused, 6 large die-cut pages of cut out Potter figures, rare.   Aleph-Bet Books, Inc.   105 - 478   2013 $800

Potter, Beatrix   1866-1943 *The Pie and the Patty-Pan.* Warne, 1905. Early edition, pages 52, 10 color plates and line text illustrations, square 8vo., original light maroon boards with roundel onlay to upper board, trifle faded and rebacked in matching cloth, lettered in white, slight stain to lower corner of pastedowns and last few leaves, otherwise very nice.   R. F. G. Hollett & Son   Children's Books - 474   2013   £225

Potter, Beatrix   1866-1943 *The Roly-Poly Pudding.* London: Warne & Co., 1908. Square 8vo., original cloth backed pictorial boards, spine and edges little worn and faded, 18 color plates and other illustrations, edges of title little creased and worn, some fingering and light creases, small piece torn from lower margin of 1 leaf, not affecting text, 2 inch tear to another text leaf, early issue.   R. F. G. Hollett & Son   Children's Books - 475   2013   £120

Potter, Beatrix   1866-1943 *The Roly-Poly Pudding.* New York: Warne, 1908. First edition, 3rd printing, 8vo., red cloth stamped in green and gold, beveled edges, as new, 18 wonderful color plates including title and 38 black and white drawings by Potter, extraordinary copy.   Aleph-Bet Books, Inc.   104 - 454   2013 $750

Potter, Beatrix   1866-1943 *The Story of Miss Moppet and Other Stories.* Charles E. Graham, n.d.,   9 x 6 1/2 inches, frontispiece and black and white illustrated titlepage + 9 black and white illustrations, cloth backed blue boards with color illustrations and titling to front cover, slight discoloration to hinge edge front cover, extremities very slightly worn, free endpapers broken at hinge, very good.   Ian Hodgkins & Co. Ltd.   134 - 80   2013   £85

Potter, Beatrix   1866-1943 *The Story of Miss Moppet.* Charles E. Graham, n.d., 6 color text illustrations, 4 in black and white, 3 illustrations verso last page, 12 pages (unpaginated), each with decorative ruled border color pictorial paper covered boards with color illustration inset on front, light rubbing to backstrip, few areas of surface rub rear cover and few faint marks top covers, very good.   Ian Hodgkins & Co. Ltd.   134 - 81   2013   £80

Potter, Beatrix   1866-1943 *The Story of Miss Moppet.* London: Frederick Warne and Co., n.d. after, 1913. First edition in book form, 12mo., color frontispiece and 14 color plates, original grey boards, color pictorial endpapers, very slight foxing to prelims, otherwise very fine, original glazed paper glassine dust jacket, housed in full dark green morocco gilt clamshell case, extremely scarce in jacket.   David Brass Rare Books, Inc.   Holiday 2012 Chapter One - DB 00675   2013 $7800

Potter, Beatrix   1866-1943   *The Tailor of Gloucester.*   F. Warne & Co., 1903.   First edition, 2nd printing, 12mo., original dark green boards with shaped pictorial inlay, rebacked in matching levant morocco lettered in white, 86 pages, illustrations in color, very attractive.   R. F. G. Hollett & Son   Children's Books - 476   2013   £350

Potter, Beatrix   1866-1943   *The Tale of Benjamin Bunny.*   London: Frederick Warne and Co., 1904.   First edition, 12mo., color frontispiece and 26 color plates, black and white vignette on titlepage, original deluxe binding of tan fine diagonally ribbed cloth, front cover decoratively stamped and lettered gilt, spine lettered gilt, all edges gilt, color pictorial endpapers, bare minimum of rubbing to corners and spine extremities, otherwise superb, near fine.   David Brass Rare Books, Inc.   Holiday 2012 Chapter One - DB 0733   2013 $9500

Potter, Beatrix   1866-1943   *The Tale of Johnny Town-Mouse.*   Frederick Warne & Co., 1918.   Second printing with N restored to London on imprint, 12mo., original grey pictorial boards lettered in white, shaped onlay, pages 86, illustrations in color, pictorial endpapers, lovely, fresh copy.   R. F. G. Hollett & Son   Children's Books - 477   2013   £450

Potter, Beatrix   1866-1943   *Tale of Johnny Town-Mouse.*   London: Frederick Warne Ltd. n.d., 1918.   First edition, slightly later printing with correct endpapers and with quote marks before first line of page 39, with the 'n' in London on title and 'Ltd' in imprint, 12mo., brown boards, pictorial paste-on, (85) pages, fine, charming color illustrations, beautiful copy.   Aleph-Bet Books, Inc.   105 - 475   2013 $1250

Potter, Beatrix   1866-1943   *The Tale of Little Pig Robinson.*   Frederick Warne & Co., 1930.   First reprint, large 8vo., original cloth gilt, spine and edges rather rubbed, pages 96, 6 colored plates and 22 drawings.   R. F. G. Hollett & Son   Children's Books - 478   2013   £65

Potter, Beatrix   1866-1943   *Tale of Mr. Jeremy Fisher.*   London & New York: Warne, 1906.   First edition, 12mo., lavender cloth, gilt lettering and decorations, pictorial paste-on, all edges gilt, paste-on scraped, some rear cover soil, hinge rubbing, deluxe binding, 26 color illustrations, rare in this binding.   Aleph-Bet Books, Inc.   104 - 450   2013 $3500

Potter, Beatrix   1866-1943   *The Tale of Mr. Jeremy Fisher.*   London: Frederick Warne and Co., 1906.   First edition, 12mo., original green boards with oval pictorial onlay to the upper board, rebacked in paper relettered to match, pages 86, gift inscription to back of frontispiece, few old tape marks to front endpapers and odd finger mark, tape marks to front endpapers and odd finger mark.   R. F. G. Hollett & Son   Children's Books - 479   2013   £450

Potter, Beatrix   1866-1943   *The Tale of Mrs. Tittlemouse.*   London: Frederick Warne and Co., 1910.   First edition, 12mo., pictorial label, frontispiece, 26 illustrations in color, original blue boards, printed in white, color pictorial paper label on front cover, pictorial endpapers, top of spine little bumped, spine lightly sunned, small bookseller stamp blank verso of front free endpaper, overall very good to fine.   Heritage Book Shop   Holiday Catalogue 2012 - 123   2013 $750

Potter, Beatrix   1866-1943   *The Tale of Mrs. Tittlemouse.*   London: Warne, 1910.   First edition, 12mo., blue boards, pictorial paste-on, rub marks on corner of half title, else near fine.   Aleph-Bet Books, Inc.   104 - 451   2013 $1000

Potter, Beatrix   1866-1943   *The Tale of Peter Rabbit.*   Buffalo: Berger Pub. Co.,   Color frontispiece and 5 color illustrations and pictorial titlepage and 21 black and white text illustrations, 24 pages (unpaginated), grey paper covered boards with color square, set diagonally within which is illustration of Peter, blue and gold lettering to front cover, backstrip rubbed with much paper loss towards bottom, corners little worn and slight rubbing to extremities, name to rear pastedown, thumbing to contents, still good copy, scarce.   Ian Hodgkins & Co. Ltd.   134 - 38   2013   £48

Potter, Beatrix   1866-1943   *The Tale of Peter Rabbit.*   Chicago: M. A. Donohue, n.d.,   57 pages, unpaginated, red cloth with large color pictorial label pasted to front cover, few areas of fading to cloth and few tiny holes on backstrip, short tear to fore-edge of one page and slight thumbing, very good copy in worn and creased dust jacket.   Ian Hodgkins & Co. Ltd.   134 - 60   2013   £68

Potter, Beatrix   1866-1943   *The Tale of Peter Rabbit.*   New York: Sam L. Gabriel, n.d.,   12 large color illustrations and 2 black and white line drawings, pages 14 including inside covers, printed on linenette, red cloth backed glossy color illustrated card covers with titling in several colors on front, covers with light soiling and slight marks, name dated 1943 to top edge of last page, very good.   Ian Hodgkins & Co. Ltd.   134 - 69   2013   £40

Potter, Beatrix   1866-1943   *Tale of Peter Rabbit.*   Charles E. Graham, n.d.,   2 full page color plates, 2 black and white illustrations, on linen, color pictorial linen covers, crease and rubbing across center where folded, some creasing and little wear, very good.   Ian Hodgkins & Co. Ltd.   134 - 75   2013   £55

Potter, Beatrix   1866-1943   *Peter Rabbit.*   The Goldsmith Pub. Co. n.d.,   Pages 16, illustrated titlepage in black and red, 7 illustrations in red and black and 8 in black and white, color pictorial die-cut card covers, tiny puncture hole near fore edge cover and pages, covers slightly rubbed at extremities, very good, scarce.   Ian Hodgkins & Co. Ltd.   134 - 72   2013   £75

Potter, Beatrix   1866-1943   *The Tale of Peter Rabbit.* Chicago: M. A. Donohue, n.d., Pages 57 (unpaginated), 28 black and white illustrations, pale green and white lined cloth with color pictorial label to front cover, slight rubbing to extremities, pages browned as usual, pencil inscription dated 1926, very good.   Ian Hodgkins & Co. Ltd.   134 - 59   2013   £55

Potter, Beatrix   1866-1943   *Peter Rabbit.*   Ohio: The Goldsmith Pub. co. n.d., 7 black and red text illustrations and 6 illustrations in black and white, pages (unpaginated), color pictorial card covers, stapled, first and last page lightly browned, fine.   Ian Hodgkins & Co. Ltd.   134 - 71   2013   £30

Potter, Beatrix   1866-1943   *The Tale of Peter Rabbit.* Chicago: M. A. Donohue, n.d., 54 pages (unpaginated), 26 full page color illustrations, red cloth with small black vignette of Peter on front above a black checked line, black titling to front cover red and white checked endpapers, very nice in worn dust jacket (some loss).   Ian Hodgkins & Co. Ltd.   134 - 56   2013   £40

Potter, Beatrix   1866-1943   *The Tale of Peter Rabbit.* Chicago: M. A. Donohue, n.d., 63 pages, 28 illustrations in color, red cloth with large color pictorial onlay to front cover, covers with some soiling and small area surface rubbing to onlay near top front cover, pencil inscription dated 1916, thumbing to pages, very good.   Ian Hodgkins & Co. Ltd.   134 - 58   2013   £48

Potter, Beatrix   1866-1943   *The Tale of Peter Rabbit.* London: F. Warne & Co.,, 1902. First edition, first issue with 'wet big tears' on page 51, 12mo., original brown boards with pictorial onlay, little rubbed and neatly rebacked in maroon levant morocco lettered in white, illustrations in color, leaf patterned endpapers, flyleaves laid down, title creased, corner of one page torn away and replaced (not affecting text), few light stains here and there, little edge wear in places, very acceptable, nicely restored copy of author's first book.   R. F. G. Hollett & Son   Children's Books - 485   2013   £1800

Potter, Beatrix   1866-1943   *The Tale of Peter Rabbit.* Philadelphia: Henry Altemus Co., 1904. 5 3/8 x 4 inches, frontispiece and 30 color illustrations, 127 pages, grey cloth with three quarter color patterned paper only front cover, with oval color illustration printed thereon, some fading and rubbing to cloth and covering with gilt dull edges rubbed and little worn, rear endpapers repaired at hinge, thin mark down fore-edge page 123 and other odd scattered mark and thumbing to contents, very good.   Ian Hodgkins & Co. Ltd.   134 - 23   2013   £125

Potter, Beatrix   1866-1943   *The Tale of Peter Rabbit.* Philadelphia: Henry Altemus, 1904. 5 3/8 x 4 inches, frontispiece and 30 color illustrations, grey/green cloth, color illustrated front cover, some fading to covers with spotting to edges, contents slightly shaken, very good.   Ian Hodgkins & Co. Ltd.   134 - 25   2013   £140

Potter, Beatrix   1866-1943   *The Tale of Peter Rabbit.* Philadelphia: Henry Altemus, 1904. 5 3/8 x 4 inches, frontispiece and 31 color illustrations, pages 63, red cloth backed purple boards, color illustration pasted front cover, cloth slightly faded and boards with some fading at edges, slight wear to corners, slight thumbing and light crease on one page, very good.   Ian Hodgkins & Co. Ltd.   134 - 26   2013   £60

Potter, Beatrix   1866-1943   *The Tale of Peter Rabbit.* Philadelphia: Henry Altemus, 1904. 5 3/8 x 4 inches, frontispiece and 30 color illustrations, smooth green cloth, color illustrated front cover, tips of backstrip with very slight wear, odd slight thumb mark, very nice.   Ian Hodgkins & Co. Ltd.   134 - 24   2013   £130

Potter, Beatrix   1866-1943   *Peter Rabbit.*   New York: Hurst and Co., 1906. Copyright by Selden Anderson 4to., printed on cloth, some creasing and light soil, very good+, illustrations in full color.   Aleph-Bet Books, Inc.   105 - 477   2013 $400

Potter, Beatrix   1866-1943   *The Tale of Peter Rabbit.* Philadelphia: Henry Altemus, 1907. 8 1/8 x 6 inches, 31 color illustrations, 63 pages, (unpaginated), maroon cloth backed brown boards, color pictorial onlay, name to free endpaper, slight paper remains on rear pastedown, very nice.   Ian Hodgkins & Co. Ltd.   134 - 27   2013   £75

Potter, Beatrix   1866-1943   *The Tale of Peter Rabbit.* Philadelphia: Henry Altemus, 1907. 31 color illustrations, red cloth with blue and green printed illustration, backstrip lightly marked and little faded, covers lightly dust soiled and slight mark top corner, short ink note, mild crease to top corner 16 pages and few spots same area on page 33, very good.   Ian Hodgkins & Co. Ltd.   134 - 29   2013   £90

Potter, Beatrix   1866-1943   *The Tale of Peter Rabbit.* Philadelphia: Henry Altemus, 1907. 8 1/8 x 6 inches, 31 color illustrations, blue cloth color pictorial onlay, very nice copy in torn and slightly worn dust jacket.   Ian Hodgkins & Co. Ltd.   134 - 28   2013   £78

Potter, Beatrix   1866-1943   *Tale Of Peter Rabbit.* Philadelphia: Henry Altemus, 1907. 8vo., grey pictorial cloth, 70 pages, very good+, full color frontispiece plus 30 full page black and whites, each illustration has another illustration embedded in it that is obscured or hidden and the child has to try to find, uncommon.   Aleph-Bet Books, Inc.   105 - 475   2013 $300

Potter, Beatrix 1866-1943 *The Tale of Peter Rabbit.* Philadelphia: Henry Altemus, 1907. First edition, color frontispiece and 30 full page black and white illustrations, grey cloth with color pictorial front cover, couple tiny holes in cloth on outer hinge, some offset of dust jacket on endpapers, slight thumbing and odd mark, very nice in remains of dust jacket.   Ian Hodgkins & Co. Ltd.   134 - 30   2013   £78

Potter, Beatrix 1866-1943 *Peter Rabbit.* Donohue & Co., 1913. Pages 12, color pictorial card covers, very nice, number 795 stamped in ink on bottom front cover.   Ian Hodgkins & Co. Ltd.   134 - 55   2013   £65

Potter, Beatrix 1866-1943 *Tale of Peter Rabbit.* Charles E. Graham, 1917. 4 full page color plates, 2 black and white illustrations, pages 10, including inside covers, color pictorial gloss card covers, ink name top front cover, some dust soiling, top corner little worn and corners little creased, contents very good.   Ian Hodgkins & Co. Ltd.   134 - 74   2013   £68

Potter, Beatrix 1866-1943 *The Tale of Peter Rabbit.* New York: Sam L. Gabriel, 1920. 12 large color illustrations and 2 black and white line drawings, pages 14 (including inside covers) printed on 'linenette', glossy color illustrated card covers, some wear along backstrip, covers lightly soiled and little marked, very good.   Ian Hodgkins & Co. Ltd.   134 - 67   2013   £38

Potter, Beatrix 1866-1943 *The Tale of Peter Rabbit.* New York: Platt & Munk, n.d. circa, 1930. Original pictorial wrappers, with 8 line poem on back panel, illustrations in color and line, no publisher's imprint inside front panel.   R. F. G. Hollett & Son   Children's Books - 484   2013   £40

Potter, Beatrix 1866-1943 *Peter Rabbit.* The Federal Rubber Co., 1931. Title and facing illustration in red and black, 7 full page color illustrations + text illustrations, wrappers, federal patterned endpapers, slight browning to wrappers and little wear to lower edges, small crease top corner, very good, scarce.   Ian Hodgkins & Co. Ltd.   134 - 62   2013   £50

Potter, Beatrix 1866-1943 *The Tale of Peter Rabbit.* New York: Platt & Munk, 1932. Original pictorial wrappers, illustrations in color and line.   R. F. G. Hollett & Son   Children's Books - 483   2013   £35

Potter, Beatrix 1866-1943 *Peter Rabbit.* New York: Sam L. Gabriel Sons, 1939. Pages 10, each with color illustration, printed on Linenette, wrappers with color illustrations and titling to front cover, stapled, slightly used and little soiled, very good.   Ian Hodgkins & Co. Ltd.   134 - 66   2013   £28

Potter, Beatrix 1866-1943 *The Tale of Peter Rabbit.* New York: Grosset & Dunlap, 1942. Large square 8vo., original pictorial boards, spine little bruised at head and foot, illustrations, color pictorial endpaper 2 booklabels on front pastedown.   R. F. G. Hollett & Son   Children's Books - 480   2013   £35

Potter, Beatrix 1866-1943 *The Tale of Peter Rabbit.* Chicago: Merrill Pub. Co., 1943. Large 4to., original pictorial wrappers, printed on linen-effect paper and illustrations in color, corners and lower wrappers, trifle creased, otherwise very nice fresh copy.   R. F. G. Hollett & Son   Children's Books - 482   2013   £25

Potter, Beatrix 1866-1943 *The Tale of Peter Rabbit.* Ohio: American Crayon Co., 1943. Large 4to., original pictorial wrapper, 6 color plate and line drawings by Fern Bisel Peat, very nice, fresh, uncreased and clean copy.   R. F. G. Hollett & Son   Children's Books - 481   2013   £45

Potter, Beatrix 1866-1943 *The Tale of Peter Rabbit. Retold for little Children.* Sandusky: American Crayon Co., 1943. 13 x 9 1/2 inches, 6 full page color plates and several black and white text illustrations by Fern Bisel Peat, pages 14 (unpaginated), yellow boards with color illustrations and titling on front, fine in slightly torn dust jacket. Ian Hodgkins & Co. Ltd.   134 - 33   2013   £48

Potter, Beatrix 1866-1943 *The Tale of Peter Rabbit.* Michigan: Fideler Co., 1946. First edition thus, illustrations in color by Dirk, 26 pages, color pictorial boards, top/bottom backstrip worn and little wear to front hinge, faint inscription to free endpaper and light soiling around hinge area, bright copy in very slightly worn dust jacket.   Ian Hodgkins & Co. Ltd.   134 - 64   2013   £50

Potter, Beatrix 1866-1943 *Peter Rabbit.* Chicago: Children's Press, 1947. Pictured by Phoebe Erickson, illustrations in color and black and white, 36 pages, light tan linson, dark brown titling and illustrated front cover, titled backstrip, yellow and white star patterned endpapers, very nice, review copy, label pasted to free endpaper.   Ian Hodgkins & Co. Ltd.   134 - 43   2013   £28

Potter, Beatrix 1866-1943 *The Tale of Peter Rabbit.* New York: Sam L. Gabriel, 1948. 12 large color illustrations and 2 black and white line drawings, pages 14, including inside covers, printed on Linenette, glossy color illustrated card covers, titling in several colors on front, 12 9 3/4 inches, some light dust soiling and small bump to corner, very good.   Ian Hodgkins & Co. Ltd.   134 - 68   2013   £45

Potter, Beatrix 1866-1943 *The Tale of Peter Rabbit.* New York: Golden Press, 1958. First edition, Little Golden Book series, color pictorial title, color illustrations by Adriana Mazza Saviozzi, 24 pages (unpaginated), silver & brown patterned paper backed thick card covers, tiny nick bottom edge rear cover, very good.   Ian Hodgkins & Co. Ltd.   134 - 70   2013   £22

Potter, Beatrix 1866-1943 *The Story of Peter Rabbit.* printed in Japan for Child Guidance Products of New York, n.d. pre, 1963.   5 pages text + 5 full page color illustrations, covered with clear plastic, which 'move' as the book opens, the whole printed on thick card sheets, green laminated boards with color illustrations and titling on front, titling to backstrip and ad for series on rear, 7 1/2 x 10, very nice. Ian Hodgkins & Co. Ltd.   134 - 42   2013   £60

Potter, Beatrix 1866-1943 *The Tale of the Faithful Dove.* London: Frederick Warne, 1955. Limited to only 100 numbered copies, 12mo., green cloth stamped in gold, as new in as new dust jacket, magnificent copy, of utmost rarity. Aleph-Bet Books, Inc.   105 - 474   2013 $2000

Potter, Beatrix 1866-1943 *The Tale of the Faithful Dove.* London: Frederick Warne, 1971. First edition thus, 12mo., original pictorial boards, dust jacket, pages 48 with 22 color plates.   R. F. G. Hollett & Son   Children's Books - 486   2013   £50

Potter, Beatrix 1866-1943 *Tale of Timmy Tiptoes.* London: Warne, 1911. 12mo., dark green boards, pictorial paste-on, small owner inscription, else fine in original printed glassine wrapper (with half inch chip top of spine, base of spine has '1-net' price, few smaller chips elsewhere, but overall very good), color frontispiece, 26 color plates, pictorial endpapers, exceptional copy, rare in wrapper.   Aleph-Bet Books, Inc.   104 - 452   2013 $3250

Potter, Beatrix 1866-1943 *Tonton-le-Voltigeur. (Translated from the Tale of Timmy Tiptoes").*   London: F. Warne and Co., 1978. First edition, 12mo., original light brown boards with pictorial onlay, dust jacket, illustrations in color.   R. F. G. Hollett & Son   Children's Books - 488   2013   £25

Potter, Beatrix 1866-1943 *The Tale of Tom Kitten.* London: F. Warne and Co., 1907. First edition, 12mo., original blue/green boards lettered in white, pictorial onlay, few surface mark, rebacked in matching levant morocco lettered in white, illustrations in color, top edge gilt of front flyleaves little dusty, neat name on flyleaf.   R. F. G. Hollett & Son   Children's Books - 487   2013   £250

Potter, Beatrix 1866-1943 *Toto Le Minet. (The Tale of Tom Kitten).* London: F. Warne and Co., 1973. First edition, 12mo., original corn yellow boards with pictorial onlay, dust jacket, pages 59, illustrations in color.   R. F. G. Hollett & Son   Children's Books - 489   2013   £25

Potter, Beatrix 1866-1943 *The Tale of Two Bad Mice.* London: Frederick Warne and Co., 1904. First edition, 12mo., color frontispiece and 26 color plates, black and white vignette on titlepage (expertly hand colored in this copy), original deluxe binding of maroon cloth, color pictorial label on front cover, color pictorial endpapers, all edges gilt, minimal rubbing to spine extremities and corners, very small watercolor stain in margin of titlepage and in lower margin of frontispiece, inscription "Little Jackie/Feb. 21st 1906/ Johannesburg", otherwise excellent copy, original plain glazed paper glassine dust jacket.   David Brass Rare Books, Inc.   Holiday 2012 Chapter One - DB 00668   2013 $5800

Potter, Beatrix 1866-1943 *Wag by Wall.* Boston: Horn Book, 1944. First edition, 12mo., buckram, pictorial paste-on, fine in dust jacket, lovely woodcuts by J. J. Lankes. Aleph-Bet Books, Inc.   104 - 455   2013 $475

Potter, Dennis *The Singing Detective.*   London: Faber & Faber, 1986. First edition, usual age toning to pages, else fine in fine dust jacket, errata slip laid in, very scarce. Between the Covers Rare Books, Inc.   Mystery & Detective Fiction - 291643   2013 $450

Potter, John *Archaeologia Graeca, sive Veterum Graecoru Praecipue Vero Atheniensium, Ritus Civiles, Reliugiosi, Militares et Domestici, Fusius...*   Venetiis: Typis Johan Mariae Lazzaroni, 1734. First edition, 2 volumes, quarto, 9 folding engraved plates, titlepage in volume one printed in red and black, bound with half title in volume I, contemporary vellum, one hinge starting little bit, otherwise very nice, clean crisp.   Second Life Books Inc.   183 - 325   2013 $450

Potter, Miriam Clark *The Gigglequicks.* Chicago: Volland, 1918. First edition, 8vo., pictorial boards, as new in original dust jacket (slight wear to box), very hard to find in any condition, rare in box.   Aleph-Bet Books, Inc.   105 - 520   2013 $650

Potts, Thomas *An Inquiry into the Moral and Political of the Religion Called Roman Catholic.* London: printed for G. G. J. and J. Robinson, 1790. First edition, 8vo., full contemporary sprinkled calf, gilt floral spine, hinges cracked but firm, lacking label, ownership inscription "Eliza Giffard - Nequis, Flintshire, 1807".   Jarndyce Antiquarian Booksellers   CCIV - 238   2013   £75

Poulson, George *The History and Antiquities of the Seigniory of Holderness.* Hull: Robert Brown, 1840. 2 volumes, 4to., 41 plates and maps as required, numerous woodcuts in text, one extra plate inserted, 8vo., very good, 19th century full calf, gilt ruled borders, gilt bands and red and black morocco labels.   Ken Spelman Books Ltd.   73 - 87   2013   £320

Pound, Ezra Loomis 1885-1972 *Cathay.* London: Elkin Mathews, 1915. First edition, limited to 1000 copies, small thin 8vo., original printed wrappers (somewhat dust soiled and rubbed, few faint stains on covers, otherwise very good), enclosed in half morocco slipcase, inscribed by author in month before publication for Harriet Monroe. James S. Jaffe Rare Books Fall 2013 - 131 2013 $17,5000

Pound, Ezra Loomis 1885-1972 *Quia Pauper Amavi.* London: Egoist Ltd., 1919. First edition, number 30 of 100 copies signed by author, with ink correction by Pound of the misprint on line 24 of page 34, correcting "Wherefore" to "Wherefrom" (some copies were not corrected), printed on handmade paper, one short tear margin of page 21, five pages have very minor fox marks, back endpapers with very minor waterstain at lower margin, binding with very slight discoloration, overall very crisp, very good, from the Quentin Keynes collection. Gemini Fine Books & Arts., Ltd. Art Reference & Illustrated Books - 2013 $2400

Poussin, Nicolas *Vita della Gran Madre di Dio Incise in XXII. Rami de Felice Polanzani sy li Desegni Originali del Celebre Pittoree Nicolo Pussino.* Rome: Venanzio Monaldini, 1783. Second edition, folio, mid 19th century Italian gilt lettered and decorated full vellum, inner gilt dentelles, marbled endpapers, 22 engraved plates measuring 320 x 223cm., inside plate marks, all edges gilt, negligible binding wear, internally fine. Howard S. Mott Inc. 262 - 140 2013 $3000

Powell, Anthony *Agents and Patients.* London: Duckworth, 1936. First edition, faint foxing to prelims and final few leaves little to edges, foolscap 8vo., original pink cloth cocked, faded backstrip gilt lettered and with chafing to its head and tail, good, with friendly 2 page ALS from author loosely tucked into book, dated 29 Dec. 1945 and addressed to Gerald Reitlinger. Blackwell's Rare Books 172 - 231 2013 £1000

Powell, Anthony *Talk About Byzantium Anthony Powell & the BBC.* Charingworth: Evergreen, 2006. First edition, one of 200 numbered copies, 8vo., stitched paper wrappers, handset and printed by John Grice in Centaur type on Zerkall mould made paper, laid in is original letter from Powell to William Claire with ink corrections and additions. Second Life Books Inc. 183 - 326 2013 $1500

Powell, Anthony *Hearing Secret Harmonies.* London: Heinemann, 1975. First edition, foolscap 8vo., original red cloth, backstrip gilt lettered on black ground, faint foxing to pastedowns, dust jacket, near fine. Blackwell's Rare Books B174 - 281 2013 £50

Powell, H. M. C. *The Santa Fe Trail to California 1849-1852.* San Francisco: Book Club of California, 1931. One of 300 copies, folio, 272 pages, 16 plates, 2 folding maps, on handmade paper by Van Gelder Zonen of Holland, publisher's prospectus laid in, quarter orange niger over tan linen boards, spine stamped in blind with four raised bands, fore edge and bottom edge uncut, spine slightly sunned, overall near fine. Heritage Book Shop Holiday Catalogue 2012 - 69 2013 $1500

Powell, John Wesley 1834-1902 *The Colorado River Region and John Wesley Powell.* Washington: Geological Survey Professional Paper, 1969. First edition, quarto, xi, 145 pages, photos and maps, pictorial cloth, fine. Argonaut Book Shop Recent Acquisitions June 2013 - 238 2013 $65

Powell, John Wesley 1834-1902 *Report on the Lands of the Arid Region of the United States.* Cambridge: Belknap Press of Harvard University Press, 1962. Maps, 2 large folding maps in rear pocket, rust cloth lettered in gilt, fine with dust jacket. Argonaut Book Shop Recent Acquisitions June 2013 - 237 2013 $125

Powell, Lawrence Clark *Bookshops.* Los Angeles: 1965. No limitation given, but obviously very small, bound by Bela Blau, 6 x 4.3 cm., leather, presentation "W.T.'s. book from L.P.' 65", from the collection of Donn W. Sanford. Oak Knoll Books 303 - 65 2013 $250

Power, P. *Ardmore - Deaglain. A Popular Guide to the Holy City.* Waterford: Catholic Record Office, 1919. First edition, Frontispiece, 35 pages, 13 x 9 6 cm., very good. C. P. Hyland 261 - 736 2013 £30

Power, Patrick *A Bishop of the Penal Times: Being Letters and Reports of John Brenan (Waterford & Cashel 1671-93).* Cambridge University Press, 1932. 8vo., wrappers, mint. C. P. Hyland 261 - 151 2013 £35

Powers, Alan *A Book of Jugs.* Andoversford: Whittington Press, 1990. One of 950 copies, titlepage printed in black and blue, 10 full page illustrations in black and blue and cover designs by Alan Powers, oblong 16mo., original printed sewn wrappers, untrimmed, fine. Blackwell's Rare Books 172 - 317 2013 £30

Powers, Alan *The Story of High Street.* Sparham, Norwich: Mainstone Press, 2008. One of 750 copies, numerous illustrations, majority in color, reproductions of sketches, letters and photos, imperial 8vo., original slate grey cloth, backstrip lettered in silver, printed label inlaid to front cover, illustrated endpapers, board slipcase, new. Blackwell's Rare Books B174 - 289 2013 £485

Powers, Richard *The Echo Maker.* New York: Farrar, Straus & Giroux, 2006. First edition, later printing, signed by author on bookplate, near fine in grey cloth boards with silver title to spine, slight bumping to corners and edge of rear board, very small spot bottom of rear board, else fine, white dust jacket with red title to spine and front panels, 451 pages.   The Kelmscott Bookshop   7 - 127   2013 $500

Powers, Richard *Three Farmers on their Way to a Dance.* New York: William Morrow, 1985. First edition, fine, minor foxing to edges, in fine dust jacket with trace of wear to extremities.   Ed Smith Books   78 - 54   2013 $250

Powers, Richard *Three Farmers on their Way to a Dance.* New York: William Morrow, 1985. First edition, uncorrected bound galleys, photographic postcard laid in, as issued, near fine, solid, rare, corner crease to laid in photo postcard.   Ed Smith Books   78 - 53   2013 $750

Powers, Shirley Dare *The Ugly-Girl Papers or Hints for the Toilet.* New York: Harper and Brothers, 1875. Second edition, 8vo., brown cloth stamped in black and gilt, little offsetting to a couple of pages from a now removed clipping, very good, tight copy, scarce.   Second Life Books Inc.   182 - 194   2013 $150

Powers, Stephen *Tribes of California.* Berkeley: University of California Press, 1976. Reprint, 480 pages, maps and engravings, brown cloth, very fine, pictorial dust jacket.   Argonaut Book Shop   Recent Acquisitions June 2013 - 239   2013 $75

Praeger, Robert Lloyd *Tourist's Flora of the West of Ireland.* Dublin: Hodges, Figgis & Co., 1909. First edition, 8vo., 5 colored maps, 27 plates, original grey decorated cloth.   Maggs Bros. Ltd.   1442 - 278   2013   £150

Pratchett, Terry *The Colour of Magic.* Smythe, Gerrards Cross, 1983. First edition, pages 208 crown 8vo., original mid green boards with faint rubbing to backstrip head and tail, backstrip gilt lettered, dust jacket with publisher's overlay on front flap carrying the revised text, near fine.   Blackwell's Rare Books   B174 - 282   2013   £8000

Pratchett, Terry *Sourcery.* London: Gollancz, 1988. First edition, 8vo., original bright yellow boards, backstrip gilt lettered, dust jacket, near fine, inscribed by author to Peter More.   Blackwell's Rare Books   172 - 232   2013   £200

Prather, Maria *Willem De Kooning: Paintings.* Washington: & New Haven: National Gallery of Art/Yale University Press, 1994. First edition, hardcover, 231 pages, numerous black and white illustrations, 84 color plates, light, very near fine in very near fine black cloth slipcase with color plate affixed to front panel.   Jeff Hirsch Books   Fall 2013 - 129469   2013 $150

Pratt, Anne *The Field, The Garden and the Woodland or Interesting Facts Respecting Flowers and Plants in General.* London: Charles Knight, 1838. First edition, 12mo., all edges gilt, illustrations, frontispiece colored by hand, drab cloth stamped in gilt, very good, clean copy.   Second Life Books Inc.   183 - 328   2013 $150

Pratt, Anne *Flowers and Their Associations.* London: Charles Knight, 1840. First edition, 12mo., 4 hand colored plates, names on endpapers, red cloth stamped in gilt, marginal waterstaining on rear endpaper and along top edge of last few pages, very good, clean copy.   Second Life Books Inc.   183 - 329   2013 $225

Pratt, Anne *Haunts of the Wild Flowers.* London: George Routledge, 1866. First edition, 12mo., 8 color plates, green gilt binding, good.   Barnaby Rudge Booksellers   Natural History 2013 - 020484   2013 $55

Pratt, George B. *Salt Lake City: Picturesque and Descriptive.* Neenah: Art Publishing Co., 1889. 9 parts, (58) pages, quarto, tan wrappers with printed titles on front panel, all volumes very good, crease to rear panel of part one, part five shows some minor bumping to fore edge and subtle discoloring to front panel, minor discoloration to front panel of part 8, part 9 has small hole in rear panel.   Ken Sanders Rare Books   45 - 11   2013 $1250

Pratt, John *Pratt Family Records.* for private circulation, 1931. 8vo., signed presentation to H. P. Gordon, added pencil notes from Horace E. Jones, very good.   C. P. Hyland   261 - 409   2013   £250

Pratt, Lucy *Ezekiel.* Boston and New York: Houghton Mifflin, 1914. First Houghton Mifflin edition, illustrations by Frederic Dorr Steele, owner's signature on front fly, fine in near fine dust jacket with slight nicks and tears, very scarce in jacket.   Between the Covers Rare Books, Inc.   165 - 246   2013 $200

Pratt, Parley Parker 1807-1857 *Proclamation of the Twelve Apostles of the Church of Jesus Christ Latter-Day Saints...* Liverpool: Published by Wilford Woodruff, 1845. First UK printing, 16 pages, octavo, wrappers, previously bound in with other works with stab holes near spine, first leaf detached but present, short closed tear to front panel.   Ken Sanders Rare Books   45 - 27   2013 $1250

Pratt, Samuel Jackson *Pity's Gift - a Collection of Interesting Tales to Excite the Compassion of Youth for the Animal Creation.* London: printed for T. N. Longman, 1798. 12mo. 15 woodcut headpiece vignettes in text, uncut, expertly rebacked, original boards.   Jarndyce Antiquarian Booksellers   CCIV - 240   2013   £150

Prendergast, J. P. *Ireland from the Restoration to the Revolution 1660-1690.* 1887. First edition, 8vo., xix, 206 pages, original cloth stained, text very good, signed presentation to Col. Sir William Butler.   C. P. Hyland   261 - 737   2013   £225

Preoprashensky, N. *Pesni Truda I Revolutsii Dlya Detei. (Songs of Labor & Revolution for Children).* Moscow: State Pub., 1924. 4to., pictorial wrappers, 46 pages light wear, very good+, rare.   Aleph-Bet Books, Inc.   105 - 510   2013 $400

Prescott, Harriet B. *Catalogue of the Avery Architectural Library. A Memorial of Library of Architecture, Archaeology and Decorative Art.* New York: Library of Columbia College, 1895. Limited to 1000 copies, large 8vo., frontispiece, illustrations, half calf, marbled paper sides and raised spinal bands, gilt stamped spine title, top edge gilt, extremities worn, small marginal hole punched through page 1107 to rear endpapers, text unaffected, bookplate, ex-library with painted spine call number and front pocket, good.   Jeff Weber Rare Books   171 - 11   2013 $350

Prescott, William Hickling   1796-1859 *History of the Conquest of Mexico.* London: Swan Sonnenschein & Co., 1906. 8vo., 2 maps, one handwriting facsimile plate, 8vo., contemporary tree calf, boards with gilt roll border, spine in five compartments with raised bands, green morocco lettering piece, compartments with gilt floral centrepieces and corner vine sprays, marbled edges and endpapers, gilt prize stamp Cambridge Local Examinations Southport Centre, at front board and prize bookplate, inside binder's ticket of Edward Howell, Liverpool, spine gently sunned, near fine, awarded to W. T. Waterhouse for First Class Honors in History and Geography.   Blackwell's Rare Books   172 - 119   2013   £95

Prescott, William Hickling   1796-1859 *History of the Conquest of Peru.* London: Swan Sonnenschein & Co., 1907. 8vo., contemporary tree calf boards with gilt roll border, spine in five compartments with raised bands, green morocco lettering piece, compartments with gilt floral centrepieces and corner vine sprays, marbled edges and endpapers, gilt prize stamp (Cambridge Local Examinations, Southport Centre) to front board and prize bookplate inside, binder's ticket of Edward Howell, Liverpool, spine gently sunned, awarded to W. T. Waterhouse for First Class Honours in English 1908.   Blackwell's Rare Books   172 - 120   2013   £95

Preston, Chloe *The Peek-a-Boos and Mr. Plopper.* London: Henry Frowde, Hodder & Stoughton, n.d. inscribed 1915, 4to., boards, pictorial paste-on, slight soil and rubbing, very good+, 8 color plates, many line illustrations and pictorial endpapers.   Aleph-Bet Books, Inc.   104 - 457   2013 $650

Preston, Jack *The Desert Battalion.* Hollywood: Murray & Gee, 1944. First edition, wrappers, very good, laid in are signatures of Trixie Robinson and several others.   Beasley Books   2013 - 2013 $100

Preston, William L. *Vanishing Landscapes. Land and Life in the Tulare Lake Basin.* Berkeley and Los Angeles: University of California Press, 1981. First edition, x, 278 pages, well illustrated with maps and charts, graphs, photos, brown cloth, very fine with pictorial dust jacket.   Argonaut Book Shop   Recent Acquisitions June 2013 - 240   2013 $90

Prevert, Jacques *Les Chiens ont Soif.* Paris: Au Pont des Arts, 1964. First edition, one of 250 exemplars (total edition 320), complete book with text and 2 hors-texte original color etchings, each signed by Max Ernst in pencil, 26 lithographs after drawings by Ernst, printed by Mourlot on Arches, 43 x 31cm., 63 pages of text, loose leaves in lithographed paper folder, housed in publisher's linen box, excellent copy.   Gemini Fine Books & Arts., Ltd.   Art Reference & Illustrated Books - 2013 $2975

Prevert, Jacques *To Paint the Portrait of a Bird.* East Sussex: Graphic Ideas, 1994. First edition, 1/1000, fine, hardcover.   Beasley Books   2013 - 2013 $100

Price-Mars, Jean *Ainsi Parla L'Oncle.... Essais D'Ethnographie.* Haiti: Imprimerie De Compiegne, 1928. First edition, large octavo, printed wrappers, little soiling and light wear, very good, errata slip laid in on cheap paper, browned, inscribed by author.   Between the Covers Rare Books, Inc.   165 - 328   2013 $3500

Price, Anthony *The Labyrinth Makers.* London: Gollancz, 1970. First edition, some tiny staining on fore-edge, otherwise fine in very soiled dust jacket with scraping at lower part of spine, chipping at base of spine and at corners, some staining on front panel.   Mordida Books   81 - 433   2013 $200

Price, Edward *Norway: Views of Wild Scenery and Journal.* Hamilton Adams, 1834. First edition, quarto, 21 aquatint plates, contemporary plum half morocco, joints and corners rubbed, very good, clean.   J. & S. L. Bonham Antiquarian Booksellers   Europe - 9731   2013   £550

Price, G. Ward *In Morocco with Legion.* Beacon Library, 1937. Original cloth, edges little worn in places, small nick to spine, 288 pages, frontispiece.   R. F. G. Hollett & Son   Africana - 160   2013   £25

Price, Mary *A Treasury of Great Recipes.* N.P.: Ampersand Press Inc., 1965. First edition, hardcover, clean and tight very near fine in near fine glassine, much nicer than usual.   Jeff Hirsch Books   Fall 2013 - 129426   2013 $75

Price, Reynolds *Permanent Errors.* New York: Atheneum, 1970. First edition, fine in dust jacket, sharp, apparently unread copy. Leather Stalking Books   October 2013 - 2013 $75

Prideaux, John *An Easy and Compendious Introduction for Reading All Sorts of Histories.* Oxford: by Leon Lichfield, 1672. 4to., very good in near contemporary panelled calf with expert repairs to joints and head and tail of spine, some offset browning from turn-ins onto endpapers and margins of titlepage. Ken Spelman Books Ltd.   75 - 6   2013   £260

Prideaux, Sarah Treverbian *Bookbinders and their Craft.* London: printed by the Gilliss Press for Zaehnsdorf Cambridge Works, 1903. One of 500 numbered copies, this #122, numerous black and white photos of bindings in text, beautiful contemporary midnight blue crushed morocco, very handsomely gilt and inlaid by De Sauty, cornerpieces adorned with floral sprays of inlaid ivory morocco four petaled blossoms on background of tiny dots, large central medallion formed by inlaid ivory flowers on leafy gilt stems radiating from a central circle of gilt hearts, gilt titling in panels above and below centerpiece, raised bands, spine very handsomely gilt in compartments with similar gilt and inlaid decoration, binding with 79 floral inlays in all, edges gilt, minor wear to front joint, otherwise especially fine, striking binding extremely lustrous and internally pristine. Phillip J. Pirages   61 - 118   2013 $2900

Pridham, Caroline *Domestic Pets; Their Habits and Treatment, Anecdotal and Descriptive.* S. W. Partridge & Co., 1893. First edition, 4to., 112 pages, frontispiece and numerous full page and vignette text illustrations, fine in original decorative cloth. Ken Spelman Books Ltd.   75 - 147   2013   £95

Priestley, Joseph *A Familiar Introduction to the Study of Electricity.* London: Dodsley, 1768. First edition, 4 fine full page engraved plates, modern half calf, marbled boards, front joint just starting, slight foxing and browning, otherwise very good. James Tait Goodrich   75 - 172   2013 $1395

Priestley, Joseph *A Free Discussion of the Doctrines of Materialism and Philosophical Necessity, in a Correspondence between Dr. Price and Dr. Priestley.* printed for J. Johnson, 1778. First edition, lightly toned and dust soiled, few fox marks and marginal pencil marks, 8vo., contemporary sprinkled calf, smartly rebacked with backstrip with five raised bands between double gilt fillets, red morocco label in second compartment, rest plain, later marbled endpapers, light dampmark to lower board, corners renewed, good. Blackwell's Rare Books   172 - 121   2013   £500

Priestley, Joseph *The Important and Extent of Free Inquiry in Matters of Religion: a Sermon preached Before the Congregations of the Old and New Meeting of Protestant Dissenters at Birmingham, Nov. 5 1785.* Birmingham: printed by M. Swinney, 1785. 8vo., lower corner of titlepage torn away, first two leaves rather dusted and marked, disbound. Jarndyce Antiquarian Booksellers   CCIV - 242   2013   £80

Priestley, Joseph *A Letter to the Reverend John Blair Lin, A. M. Pastor...* Northumberland: printed by Andrew Kennedy for P. Byrne, Philadelphia, 1803. First edition, 8vo., old waterstaining to text, marginal worming to leading edges, not affecting text, recent half calf, marbled boards. Jarndyce Antiquarian Booksellers   CCIV - 243   2013   £95

Prieto, Guillermo *San Francisco in the Seventies. The City as Viewed by a Mexican Political Exile.* San Francisco: printed by John Henry Nash, 1938. First English translation, 90 pages, portrait, plates, blue cloth backed marbled boards, paper spine label, very fine and bright with printed dust jacket. Argonaut Book Shop   Summer 2013 - 284   2013 $90

Prime, William C. *Boat Life In Egypt and Nubia.* New York: Harper Brothers, 1860. Original blue grained cloth gilt, spine flaking and rather defective at head, but stabilised, text woodcuts. R. F. G. Hollett & Son   Africana - 161   2013   £35

The Primitive Methodist Magazine for the Year of Our Lord 1852. Volume X of the Third Series. Thomas Holliday, 1852. Original blindstamped cloth, gilt, rather worn and chipped, 13 steel engraved portraits (some dampstained). R. F. G. Hollett & Son   Wesleyan Methodism - 47   2013   £45

The Primitive Methodist Magazine for the Year of Our Lord 1859. Richard Davies, 1859. Volume XVI, Old half calf, rubbed and worn but sound, 12 steel engraved portraits. R. F. G. Hollett & Son   Wesleyan Methodism - 48   2013   £85

Prince, David *Illustrations of Deformities and Their Treatment.* Jacksonville: printed at the Jacksonville Journal Office, 1866. First edition, 8vo., 32 pages, contents comprising 61 text figures, original printed wrappers, chipped with some loss, signature torn from one margin, some spotty foxing and faint stains internally, not quite very good, with second contemporary signature of Dr. Snyder. M & S Rare Books, Inc.   95 - 232   2013 $750

Prince, Richard *Richard Prince.* New York: Barbara Gladstone, 1988. First edition, softcover, clean, very near fine copy, paperclip impression to front cover and first few pages from gallerys complementary card that is still present. Jeff Hirsch Books   Fall 2013 - 129105   2013 $1000

Prince, Thomas *The Vade Mecum for America: or a Companion for Traders and Travelers...* Boston: S. Kneeland and T. Green for D. Henchman and T. Hancock, 1732. Second edition, narrow 12mo., contemporary calf, chipped, hinges cracked, very good. M & S Rare Books, Inc. 95 - 302 2013 $2250

Princeton University *A Catalogue of the Cotsen Children's Library Volumes I and II.* Princeton: Princeton University Press, 2000-2003. 2 volumes, large folio, handsome color reproductions, decorative endpapers, gilt stamped pictorial green Japanese cloth, gilt stamped black leather spine label, fine, signed presentation inscription by collector Lloyd Cotsen to Jeff Weber in volume I. Jeff Weber Rare Books 171 - 79 2013 $400

The Principal Contents of Corby Castle Cumbria. Edinburgh: Phillips, 1994. Large 8vo., original stiff pictorial wrappers, trifle creased, pages 70, illustrations in color, 585 lots, most lots priced n ink, with some annotations. R. F. G. Hollett & Son Lake District & Cumbria - 50 2013 £30

The Principles and Practice of Gynaecology. Philadelphia: Henry C. Lea, 1880. 875 pages, 32 pages publisher's ads, 133 illustrations, original dark brown binding, rubbed and worn, text toned in parts. James Tait Goodrich S74 - 198 2013 $95

Pringle, Roger *A Garland for the Laureate. Poems Presented to Sir John Betjeman on His 75th Birthday.* Stratford-upon-Avon: The Celandine Press, 1981. First edition, number 307 of 350 numbered copies, folio, fine in original marbled wrappers, printed paper label to upper cover, fore and bottom edges uncut, fine. Maggs Bros. Ltd. 1460 - 103 2013 £75

Pringle, Roger *Poems for Shakespeare 6.* London: Globe Playhouse Trust Publications, 1977. Number 4 of 120 copies signed by contributors, 8vo., original blue cloth, lettered gilt on spine with gilt title on upper board, all edges gilt, fine in matching slipcase. Maggs Bros. Ltd. 1442 - 152 2013 £200

Prior, Matthew 1664-1721 *Selected Poems of Matthew Prior.* London: Kegan Paul, Trench & Co., 1889. 12mo., frontispiece, original burgundy cloth, very good, spine faded, some slight wear to head and tail of spine, inscribed by Austin Dobson to French scholar and wine writer George Saintsbury. Maggs Bros. Ltd. 1460 - 230 2013 £150

Proceedings of the Grand Council of Alabama at the Annual Convocation Held In the City of Montgomery, commencing Dec. 6th 1865. Montgomery: 1866. First edition, 8vo., 39 pages, original printed wrappers. M & S Rare Books, Inc. 95 - 216 2013 $125

Procter, Bryan Waller *Bryan Waller Procter (Barry Cornwall). An Autobiographical Fragment and Biographical Notes...* London: George Bell and Sons, 1877. First edition, half title, frontispiece, original purple/brown cloth, spine little darkened and with slight wear at head and tail, slightly marked, ex-library, shadow of library label on front board and fragment of library label on half title. Jarndyce Antiquarian Booksellers CCIII - 610 2013 £50

Procter, Bryan Waller *Dramatic Scenes.* Boston: Ticknor & Fields, 1857. Frontispiece, original brown cloth, blocked in blind, very good, bright copy. Jarndyce Antiquarian Booksellers CCIII - 602 2013 £40

Procter, Bryan Waller *Dramatic Scenes.* New York: D. Appleton & Co., 1857. Slightly spotted, illustrations, contemporary quarter black sheep, pink glazed boards, rubbed, some loss of glazed paper on following board, corners worn, Renier booklabel, good, sound copy. Jarndyce Antiquarian Booksellers CCIII - 601 2013 £30

Procter, Bryan Waller *Dramatic Scenes.* London: Chapman & Hall, 1857. Half title, illustrations, slightly spotted, original dark green cloth, tiny nick in tail of following hinge, spine cloth slightly lifting. Jarndyce Antiquarian Booksellers CCIII - 600 2013 £40

Procter, Bryan Waller *English Songs, and Other Small Poems.* London: Edward Moxon, 1846. 12mo., contemporary marbled boards, maroon cloth spine faded to brown, very slightly rubbed. Jarndyce Antiquarian Booksellers CCIII - 608 2013 £35

Procter, Bryan Waller *English Songs.* London: G. Bell and Sons, 1880. Original royal blue cloth, spine lettered in gilt, fine, bright copy. Jarndyce Antiquarian Booksellers CCIII - 609 2013 £30

Procter, Bryan Waller *The Flood of Thessaly, The Girl of Provence and Other Poems.* London: Henry Colburn, 1823. First edition, half title, uncut in original drab boards, paper label, front board marked, head of spine slightly rubbed, bumped corners carefully strengthened, signed "Charles Milner", good plus. Jarndyce Antiquarian Booksellers CCIII - 607 2013 £85

Procter, Bryan Waller *Marcian Colonna: an Italian Tale with Three Dramatic Scenes and Other Poems.* London: John Warren & C. & J. Ollier, 1820. First edition, half title, final ad leaf, occasional spotting, uncut in original drab boards, expertly rebacked, name torn from corner of leading f.e.p., inscribed by author for his mother. Jarndyce Antiquarian Booksellers CCIII - 604 2013 £150

Procter, Bryan Waller *Mirandola; a Tragedy.* London: John Warren, 1821. First edition, half title, disbound, very good. Jarndyce Antiquarian Booksellers CCIII - 606 2013 £35

Procter, Bryan Waller *Mirandola; a Tragedy.* London: John Warren, 1821. First edition, half title, expertly rebound in sympathetic half calf, very good.   Jarndyce Antiquarian Booksellers   CCIII - 605   2013   £150

Procter, Bryan Waller *The Poetical Works.* London: Henry Colburn & Co., 1822. First edition, second edition and first edition, 3 volumes, occasional dampstaining and spotting, contemporary full dark blue morocco, gilt spines, borders & dentelles, maroon silk endpapers, slight rubbing to spines and corners, attractive set, all edges gilt, armorial bookplate of Edward Butler in volumes I and III, removed from volume II.   Jarndyce Antiquarian Booksellers   CCIII - 598   2013   £150

Procter, Bryan Waller *A Sicilian Story with Diego de Montilla and Other Poems.* (bound with) *Dramatic Scenes and Other Poems.* C. & J. Ollier, 1820. First edition, 2nd edition, 2 works bound in 1 volume, contemporary full calf, spine gilt in compartments, olive green leather label, hinges slightly rubbed and beginning to split at head, ownership details, 1821, partially erased from title, attractive.   Jarndyce Antiquarian Booksellers   CCIII - 603   2013   £50

Procter, E. H. *The Rabbits Day in Town.* London: Blackie, n.d. circa, 1905. 4to., cloth backed pictorial boards, light rubbing, very good+, illustrations in bold colors by Walton Corbould.   Aleph-Bet Books, Inc.   104 - 425   2013 $400

Professional Mixing Guide: the Accredited List of Recognized and Accepted Standard Formulas for Mixed Drinks. New York: Angostura-Wuppermann Corporation, 1945. Second edition, stapled stiff printed wrappers, 32mo., 95, (1) pages, some rubbing and slight crease on front wrapper, nice, sound, very good.   Between the Covers Rare Books, Inc.   Cocktails, Etc. - 96457   2013 $125

Proudfoot, Merrill *Diary of a Sit-In.* Chapel Hill: University Of North Carolina Press, 1962. First edition, fine in price clipped and lightly worn, very good plus dust jacket, advance review copy with slip laid in, author and organizer Herbert Aptheker's copy with his ownership signature.   Between the Covers Rare Books, Inc.   165 - 248   2013 $75

Proulx, Annie *Close Range: Wyoming Stories.* New York: Scribner, 1999. First edition, fine in fine dust jacket, illustrations by William Matthews, with 6 watercolors.   Leather Stalking Books   October 2013 - 2013 $150

Prout, Samuel *Sketches in France, Switzerland & Italy.* London: Hodgson and Graves, 1839. First printing, 560 x 380mm., publisher's blue moire cloth boards, upper cover with original gilt titling, later (flat) spine of blue morocco with titling in gilt, 26 pleasing hand colored lithographic plates, bookplate of Giannalisa Feltrinelli; corners little bumped, upper board with small (but noticeable) white (paint?) stain and darkened three inch wide horizontal strip, open plate with very small brown marginal spot, still an extremely desirable copy, because remarkably fine internally, beautifully colored plates, especially clean, fresh and bright, in solid binding retaining much of its original materials.   Phillip J. Pirages   63 - 371   2013 $9500

Provensen, Alice *Glorious Flight.* New York: Viking, 1983. First edition, review copy with slip laid in, oblong 4to., pictorial boards, as new in dust jacket, color illustrations.   Aleph-Bet Books, Inc.   104 - 460   2013 $200

Prowse, D. W. *A History of Newfoundland from the English, Colonial and Foreign Records.* Belleville: Mika Studio, 1972. Facsimile edition, half title, numerous maps and illustrations, plus folding map to rear, 8vo., blue cloth boards, gilt to front and spine, very good.   Schooner Books Ltd.   101 - 59   2013 $65

Prowse, D. W. *The Newfoundland Guide Book 1905...* London: Bradbury, Agnew & Co. Ltd., 1905. 8vo., beige cloth, frontispiece, folding map, numerous black and white photos, sketches, line drawings, interior very good, author's presentation to Theodore Roberts dated Jan. 1906.   Schooner Books Ltd.   101 - 60   2013 $175

Ptolemaeus, Claudius *(Almagest) Composition Mathematique de Claude Ptolemee...* Paris: J. M. Ebehart, chez Henri Grand, 1813-1816. First edition of this translation, engraved frontispiece in volume i, engraved vignette on both title, engraved portrait in volume ii, engraving and diagrams, and tables in text in both volumes, parallel Greek and French text, some foxing and marginal dampstaining (more pronounced in volume i) and little marginal worming at beginning of volume i, 4to., recased in contemporary vellum backed boards, sound.   Blackwell's Rare Books   Sciences - 99   2013   £1200

Ptolemaeus, Claudius *(Greek) Klaudiou Ptolemaiou Hypotheseis kai Planomenon Archai Kai Proklou Diadochous Hypotyposeis.* Paris: Merlin, 1820. First edition of this translation, engraved vignette on title, engraved portrait, engravings in text, 3 engraved plates, 2 folding tables, Greek and French, some localised foxing and browning, 4to., contemporary vellum backed marbled boards, slightly worn, good.   Blackwell's Rare Books   Sciences - 100   2013   £750

Ptolemaeus, Claudius *Omnia Quae Extant Opera.* Basel: 1541. First collected edition, folio, 2 large double page woodcut (one dated 1532), 2 leaves of woodcut diagrams at beginning and numerous woodcut diagrams, including some instruments in text, printer's device on last leaf, contemporary vellum with yapp edges, brown morocco gilt spine label, upper spine with short repaired tear, some contemporary marginalia (few retained in rebinding and folded back), few leaves browned, light scattered foxing, planispheres with old repairs down center fold lines (loss of couple of letters in sub-heading), titlepage with initials "EJS" written in pen, tips bit bumped, overall very good.   Heritage Book Shop   50th Anniversary Catalogue - 79   2013 $15,000

Puckett, Newbell Niels *Folk Beliefs of the Southern Negro.* Chapel Hill: The University of North Carolina Press, 1926. First edition, publisher's cloth, tears to cloth at crown and along joints, good copy without dust jacket, complimentary copy with handwritten presentation to Leonard Outhwaite with compliments of University of North Carolina Pres.   Between the Covers Rare Books, Inc.   165 - 248   2013 $85

Pugin, Augustus Charles   1762-1832 *Gothic Furniture.* London: M. A. Nattali... circa, 1845. 4to., pages iv, 27, 27 hand colored aquatint plates, including additional aquatint pictorial titlepage and 26 plates, titlepage somewhat browned, later brown half morocco.   Marlborough Rare Books Ltd.   218 - 120   2013   £1800

Pugin, Augustus Welby Northmore   1812-1852 *Designs for Iron and Brass Work in the Style of the XV and XVI Centuries.* London: Ackermann & Co., 1836. 4to., engraved titlepage and 26 plates, some slight foxing but internally very good, original grey brown embossed patterned cloth, large engraved paper label in black and red, expertly recased maintaining original spine strip, slightly rubbed, signature of John Shelly(?), pencil drawing of a building and its gardens on partly torn single sheet loosely inserted.   Jarndyce Antiquarian Booksellers   CCV - 223   2013   £280

Puissant, Louis *Traite de Topographie, d'Arpentage et de Nivellement.* Paris: Mme. Ve. Courcier, 1820. Second edition, 4to., 9 engraved plates, 42 pages of tables, original quarter brown calf over marbled boards, gilt stamped spine bands, gilt stamped red calf spine title label light wear to covers, corners bumped, minor pencil signature and ink stamp on titlepage, very good.   Jeff Weber Rare Books   169 - 359   2013 $800

Pullen, H. F. *The Pullen Expedition in Search of Sir John Franklin.* Toronto: Arctic History Press, 1979. Copy #272 of limited edition of 1000 copies, blue leather with gilt titles to spine and front cover, pages 230, half title, index, 4 folding maps and 7 plates, 8vo., author's name worn off spine, otherwise very good, lacks slipcase, 2 page handwritten letter from Pullen describing the expedition.   Schooner Books Ltd.   105 - 99   2013 $150

Pullman, Philip *The Golden Compass.* New York: Alfred A. Knopf, 1995. (1-10 code). First US edition, 8vo., cloth backed boards, as new in as new dust jacket, this copy signed by Pullman, great copy.   Aleph-Bet Books, Inc.   104 - 461   2013 $750

Pumphrey, Bevan *Through the Years a Miscellany of Memoirs.* London: Intype, 1994. Limited edition of 100 copies, 8vo., pages 178, frontispiece, color illustrations, frontispiece, buckram, fine, presentation copy with hand written letter from author, offering this book as a gift.   Schooner Books Ltd.   101 - 61   2013 $75

The Punishments of China.. London: printed for William Miller by W. Bulmer and Co., 1801. First edition, 357 x 267mm., (27) leaves, 22 hand colored stippled engravings, contemporary marbled boards and endpapers, rebacked and recornered to style, flat spine in panels with central gilt star tool, gilt titling; armorial bookplate of Thomas Tyndall Jr., paper boards bit chafed and darkened by glue near spine and corners, bit rubbed along top and bottom edges of boards, occasional thumbing or minor stains to very generous margins, otherwise excellent, binding scarcely worn and internally clean, fresh and bright, without any of the usual offsetting from text to plates.   Phillip J. Pirages   63 - 331   2013 $2500

Purcell, Henry *Orpheus Britannicus.* London: printed by William Pearson and sold by John Cullen, 1706. 1711. Second edition, first issue, 2 volumes, folio, contemporary full paneled calf, rebacked with original spine, red morocco spine labels, lettered in gilt, boards and spines ruled and stamped in gilt, marbled endpapers, all edges speckled red, board edges tooled gilt, front inner hinge cracked, firm in volume II, page 169, volume I with closed tear to lower margin, barely affecting text, contents very clean.   Heritage Book Shop   Holiday Catalogue 2012 - 124   2013 $3500

Purcell, Mac Fisher *History of Contra Costa County.* Berkeley: Gillick Press, 1940. First edition, tan cloth, gilt, bookplate tipped in, light rubbing to extremities, but fine, scarce.   Argonaut Book Shop   Summer 2013 - 57   2013 $250

Purdy, Helen Throop *San Francisco: As It Was - As It Is - and How to See It.* San Francisco: Paul Elder, 1912. First edition, profusely illustrated with light brown decorated boards, pictorial paper pastedown on front cover, one lower corner just showing, very fine with very elusive dust jacket (slight chipping), scarce in this condition.   Argonaut Book Shop   Summer 2013 - 285   2013 $175

Purdy, Richard L. *Thomas Hardy 1840-1928: Catalogue of a Memorial Exhibition of First Editions, Autograph Letters and Manuscripts.* New Haven: Yale University Library, 1928. First edition, one of 25 copies on rag paper, designed by Carl Purington, 8vo. original tan linen spine, blue boards, black lettering, untrimmed, presentation copy from Purdy to American Literature scholar and curator, Gilbert Troxell, with note and Hardy keepsake, also produced by Purdy laid in, fine, from the Gary Lepper Collection of Thomas Hardy. The Brick Row Book Shop Bulletin Nine - 85 2013 $300

Purmannus, Mattheus Gothofredus *Chirurgia Curiosa or the Newest and most curious Observations and Operations in the Whole Art of Chirurgery.* London: printed for D.. Browned, 1706. Small folio, contemporary 18th century paneled calf, spine repaired with early spine laid down, original endleaves and pastedowns saved as part of binding. James Tait Goodrich 75 - 173 2013 $3500

Purvis, Robert *A Tribute to the Memory of Thomas Shipley, the Philanthropist.* Philadelphia: 1836. First edition, 8vo., 20 pages, original printed wrappers, embossed library stamp on title, some soiling to wrappers, but very good. M & S Rare Books, Inc. 95 - 305 2013 $1250

Pushkin, Aleksandr Sergeevich 1799-1837 *Arion.* San Francisco: Arion Press, 2002. First edition translated by Seamus Heaney, 8vo., published in edition of 400 copies, original blue wrappers printed in black, fine. Maggs Bros. Ltd. 1442 - 115 2013 £300

Pushkin, Aleksandr Sergeevich 1799-1837 *Il Cavaliere di Bronzo.* Verona: Officina Bodoni, 1968. 47/165 copies, printed on Magnani handmade paper in parallel texts of Cyrillic and Italian and signed by both type designers, Mardersteig and Lazursky with heliogravure title vignette, small folio, original quarter cream vellum, backstrip gilt lettered, patterned boards of thin vertical stripes of pink, grey and white, top edge gilt, others untrimmed, board slipcase, fine. Blackwell's Rare Books B174 - 371 2013 £680

Pushkin, Aleksandr Sergeevich 1799-1837 *The Golden Cockerel.* New York: Thomas Nelson and sons, 1938. 4to., original cloth, gilt, rather soiled and stained, unpaginated, 12 pages in full color and numerous black and white illustrations by Willy Pogany, littler fingering in places, inscriptions on front free endpaper. R. F. G. Hollett & Son Children's Books - 471 2013 £95

Pushkin, Aleksandr Sergeevich 1799-1837 *The Golden Cockerel.* New York: Limited Editions Club, n.d., 1950. Limited to 1500 numbered copies signed by artist, 4to., cloth with gold plated brass figure on cover, fine in glassine, pictorial chemise and card slipcase (slightly faded), illustrations by Edmund Dulac, LEC Monthly Letter laid in. Aleph-Bet Books, Inc. 104 - 186 2013 $400

Puss in Boots. London: Fold Books, 1951. First edition, 8vo., cloth backed pictorial boards, light edgewear, very good, wonderful peepshow book, illustrations in color, with 6 3 dimensional color scenes that form a pentagonal shaped Pop-up display when opened. Aleph-Bet Books, Inc. 104 - 272 2013 $350

Puss in Boots. London: Bancroft, 1961. Oblong 4to., cloth backed pictorial boards, light wear, very good+, illustrations by Kubasta with 8 fine pop-up scenes, several of which have moveable tabs as well. Aleph-Bet Books, Inc. 104 - 442 2013 $225

Putnam, Frank *City Govemment in Europe.* Houston: 1913. 137 pages, illustrations, original cloth, cover little faded, else very good. Dumont Maps & Books of the West 125 - 70 2013 $100

Putnam, Nina Wilcox *Sunny Bunny.* Chicago: Volland, 1918. 8vo., pictorial boards, fine in box (slight wear), grat copy, illustrations by Gruelle. Aleph-Bet Books, Inc. 105 - 299 2013 $450

Putnam, Nina Wilcox *Twinkle and Lollypop.* Joliet: Volland, 1918. Fifteenth edition, 8vo., pictorial board, slightest cover soil, else near fine in original box (flaps repaired), beautiful color illustrations by Katherine Sturges Dodge, lovely, uncommon, in excellent condition. Aleph-Bet Books, Inc. 105 - 580 2013 $350

Putsche, Carl Wilhelm Ernst *Versuch Einer Monographie Der Kartoffeln.* Weimer: im Verlage des Gr. H. S. priv Landes-Industrie-Comptoir, 1819. First edition, 260 x 216mm., plates, very pleasing contemporary half calf over marbled paper boards, flat spine divided into six panels by gilt pentaglyph and metope roll, four panels with central gilt calligraphic flourish, fifth panel with gilt initials "AV" inside laurel wreath, tan morocco label, blue patterned endpapers, four uncolored plates of equipment, 9 extremely attractive hand colored plates of potato plants and tubers, front pastedown with evidence of bookplate removal, titlepage with remnants of round ownership ?, tail of spine with small remnant of paper shelf label, corners somewhat bumped, paper boards bit chafed, isolated spots of foxing, exceptionally fine, binding scarcely worn, leaves entirely clean and unusually fresh, charming plates richly colored. Phillip J. Pirages 63 - 370 2013 $4800

Pychon, Thomas *Against the Day.* New York: Penguin Press, 2006. Advance reading copy, issued in limited quantities to sales reps and reviewers, sales rep's name on titlepage, some copies misprinted pages, this copy appears not to, this copy was given by sales rep to reviewer Steven Moore with note signed by Moore to that effect laid in, Moore has made several small pencilled check marks in margins (and noted few typos), bulky book, slightly cocked, near fine, with Moore's handwritten notes for review (4 pages), his typed review (2 pages) and copy of Washington Post Book World Nov. 19 2006 with his review.   Ken Lopez Bookseller   159 - 168   2013 $3500

Pycraft, W. P. *The Sea-Shore.* London: SPCK, 1920. Original decorated cloth, color frontispiece, numerous illustrations and 2 maps.   R. F. G. Hollett & Son   Children's Books - 490   2013   £25

Pyle, Howard *Yankee Doodle: an Old Friend in a New Dress.* New York: Dodd Mead, 1881. First edition, square 4to., pictorial boards, tips and edges worn as is common, else tight, clean and unusually nice, 8 full page color illustrations, plus extensive blue illustrations. very scarce.   Aleph-Bet Books, Inc.   105 - 488   2013 $1500

Pynchon, Thomas *Inherent Vice.* New York: Penguin Press, 2009. Advance reading copy, issued in very limited quantities to sales reps and reviewers sales rep's name on titlepage, bump to upper rear spine corner, thus near fine in wrappers, extremely scarce.   Ken Lopez Bookseller 159 - 169   2013 $3000

Pynchon, Thomas *V.* Philadelphia: Lippincott, 1963. First edition, small lower corner bump, else fine with rich top stain, near fine dust jacket with some light rubbing but no fading to fold on lower spine, as frequently the case, very nice.   Ken Lopez Bookseller   159 - 167   2013 $3500

Pyne, Stephen J. *The Ice. A Journey to Antarctica.* Arlington Books, 1987. First English edition, original cloth, gilt, dust jacket, 16 pages of plates.   R. F. G. Hollett & Son Polar Exploration - 52   2013   £25

Pyne, William Henry   1769-1843 *The History of the Royal Residences of Windsor Castle, St. James's Palace, Carlton House, Kensington Palace, Hampton Court....* London: printed for A. Dry...., 1819. First edition, large paper copy, 3 volumes, 100 hand colored aquatint plates, plate of Frogmore Exterior supplied from smaller copy, full green morocco by Charles E. Lauriat Boston, USA, covers with ruled borders enclosing spandrels of leafy sprigs and flower beads, spines in six compartments, four similarly decorated and lettered gilt, dates at foot, silk endpapers, bookplate of Thomas W. Lawson.   Marlborough Rare Books Ltd.   218 - 121   2013 £7500

Q

Quarles, Francis *Enchiridion Miscellaneum.* reprinted for Charles Baldwyn, 1822. 12th impression, 2 volumes, frontispiece, contemporary full vellum, gilt borders, red leather labels, slightly marked, volume II little discolored, booklabels of John Porter, top edge gilt, very good, with unsigned inscription by Henry Nelson Coleridge, signed by Sara and Edith Coleridge.   Jarndyce Antiquarian Booksellers   CCIII - 597   2013   £350

Queen Summer of the Journey of the Lily and the Rose. London: Paris: Melbourne: Cassell, 1891. 4to., cloth backed pictorial boards, 40 pages, slightest bit of tip wear, else near fine, printed on one side of paper only, each page with beautifully intricate color illustration by Walter Crane. Aleph-Bet Books, Inc.   105 - 157   2013 $600

Queen, Ellery, Pseud. *The Dragon's Teeth.* New York: Stokes, 1939. First edition, staining on covers, otherwise very good in dust jacket with internal tape mends, external tape mend at lower corner of front panel, several closed tears and nicks at base of spine.   Mordida Books   81 - 434   2013 $200

Queen, Ellery, Pseud. *The Female of the Species: The Great Women Detectives and Criminals.* Boston: Little Brown, 1943. First edition, bookplate on front endpaper, fine in dust jacket with slightly faded spine and several short closed tears.   Mordida Books   81 - 435   2013 $85

Queen, Ellery, Pseud. *The King is Dead.* Boston: Little Brown, 1952. First edition, fine in price clipped dust jacket with internal tape mends and couple of crease tears on front panel.   Mordida Books   81 - 436   2013 $85

Queen, Ellery, Pseud. *Queen's Quorum: a History of the Detective Crime Short Story as Revealed in the 106 Most Important Books Published in this Field Since 1845. Supplements through 1967.* New York: Biblio & Tannen, 1969. Revised edition, fine in very near fine dust jacket with tiny smudge on front panel.   Between the Covers Rare Books, Inc.   Mystery & Detective Fiction - 92638   2013 $60

Queen, Ellery, Pseud. *The Roman Hat Mystery.* New York: Frederick A. Stokes, 1929. Fifth printing, very good, original endpapers missing, and one internal page is torn, however this is an interesting copy in that according to a "Property of" sticker, this book was donated to Beverly Library in 1933 by H. C. Lodge, Jr., U.S. Senator.   Leather Stalking Books   October 2013 - 2013 $100

Quick, Michael *George Inness: a Catalogue Raisonne (Volume One 1841-1879. Volume Two 1880-1894.* New Brunswick and London: Rutgers University Press, 2007. First edition, 2 volumes, frontispiece to both volumes, 234 color plates, numerous black and white reproductions, brown cloth, gilt stamped black spine labels, dust jacket, housed in large cloth slipcase, fine.   Jeff Weber Rare Books   171 - 183   2013 $375

Quigley, John Grodon *A Century of Rifles 1860-1960. The Halifax Rifles.* Halifax: McNab & Son Ltd., 1960. 6 x 9 inches, card covers, double frontispiece, 24 photo illustrations.   Schooner Books Ltd.   105 - 132   2013 $55

Quiller-Couch, Arthur Thomas   1863-1944 *In Powder and Crinoline.* London: Hodder & Stoughton, n.d., 1913. First trade edition, second state bound all in cloth instead fo cloth backed boards, 4to., lavender pictorial cloth, as new in plain paper wrapper in beautiful original publisher's pictorial box with mounted color plate, illustrations by Kay Nielsen, with 24 tipped in color plates and pictorial tissue guards, pictorial endpapers plus text decorations, rarely found in original box.   Aleph-Bet Books, Inc.   104 - 391   2013 $2500

Quiller-Couch, Arthur Thomas   1863-1944 *Shakespeare's Christmas and Other Stories.* London: Smith, Elder & Co., 1905. First edition, octavo, 8 inserted plates, original red cloth, front and spine panels stamped in black.   L. W. Currey, Inc.   Christmas Themed Books - 138257   2013 $85

Quiller-Couch, Arthur Thomas   1863-1944 *The Sleeping Beauty.* London: Hodder and Stoughton, n.d., 1910. 4to., publisher's red imitation morocco with extensive gilt decorated cover, 129 pages, light foxing on margins of text pages, else very good+, 30 very beautiful color plates with decorative borders (and tissue guards) by Edmund Dulac, nice copy.   Aleph-Bet Books, Inc.   105 - 206   2013 $875

Quiller-Couch, Mabel *The Treasure Book of Children's Verse.* New York: Hodder & Stoughton, n.d. circa, 1910. Very thick 4to., 335 pages, blue cloth with elaborate gilt pictorial design, top edge gilt, fine, 20 mounted color plates, excellent condition.   Aleph-Bet Books, Inc.   104 - 250   2013 $350

Quillinan, Edward *Journal of a Few Months' Residence in Portugal and Glimpses of the South of Spain.* London: Ed Moxon, 1847. First edition, 2 volumes, 8vo., original green blindstamped cloth, spines worn, with small loss, internally clean, inscribed copy to Anna Maria Briggs from author.   J. & S. L. Bonham Antiquarian Booksellers   Europe - 8979   2013   £180

Quincy, John *Pharmacopoeia Officinalis & Extemporanea.* London: R. Bell, Fifth edition, final leaves of index remendiorum lacking, old calf boards nicely rebacked in calf, new spine label, early notes on pastedowns, endleaves with early notes, annotations, text foxed and browned.   James Tait Goodrich   S74 - 214   2013 $450

Quine, Willard Van Orman *Selected Logic Papers.* New York: Random House, 1966.   Stated first edition, 8vo., fine, in very good++ dust jacket with mild scuffs, edgewear, minimal sun to spine.   By the Book, L. C.   38 - 30   2013 $1250

Quine, Willard Van Orman *Set Theory and Its Logic.* Cambridge: Belknap Press, Harvard University, 1963.   First edition, inscribed by author, near fine, mild edge soil, minimal cover edge wear, near fine dust jacket, price clipped.   By the Book, L. C.   38 - 31   2013 $1250

Quine, Willard Van Orman *The Time of My Life. An Autobiography.* Cambridge: MIT Press, 1985.   First edition, 8vo., fine in very good++ dust jacket with minimal sun to spine and edge wear.   By the Book, L. C.   38 - 29   2013 $850

Quinn, Elisabeth V. *The Kewpie Primer.*   George G. Harrap & Co., n.d., 1916.   First UK edition, original brown pictorial boards, little faded, spine rubbed and defective at head, orange and black illustrations, flyleaves lightly browned, short closed edge tear to half title, small piece torn from corner of contents leaf, faint fingering to first few leaves, else very nice, clean and sound.   R. F. G. Hollett & Son   Children's Books - 423   2013   £95

Quinn, Seabury *The Complete Adventures of Jules De Grandin.*   Shelburne: Ontario: and Sauk City: Battered Silicon Dispatch Box/George A. Vanderburgh, 2001.   First edition, hardbound issue, 3 volumes, quarto, fine in very slightly rubbed, still easily fine dust jacket, somewhat amateurishly produced (the elaborate color Xeroxed dust jackets have been pieced together with tape as issued), very uncommon.   Between the Covers Rare Books, Inc.   Sci-Fi, Fantasy & Horror - 315979   2013 $750

Quinnell, A. J. *The Mahdi.*   London: Macmillan, 1981.   First edition, fine in dust jacket.   Mordida Books   81 - 438   2013 $65

Qurra, Thabit B. *The Astronomical Works of Thabit B. Qurra.*   Berkeley & Los Angeles: University of California Press, 1960.   8vo., 262 pages, printed wrappers, ownership signature, fine.   Jeff Weber Rare Books   169 - 364   2013 $100

R

Raban, Jonathan *Coasting.* Collins Harvill, 1986. First edition, 8vo., 301 pages, original black cloth, dust jacket, near fine.   J. & S. L. Bonham Antiquarian Booksellers   Europe - 9797   2013   £28

Rabelais, Francois *The Works.* London: Gibbings and Co. Ltd., 1901. 175 x 110 mm., 5 volumes, appealing contemporary scarlet three quarter calf by Bayntun (stamp signed), raised bands, spine panels with central gilt anthemion, gilt titling, marbled boards and endpapers, top edge gilt, volumes II and IV with 2 engraved plates, each as called for, but volume I bound without 7 plates called for and volume V without its frontispiece, 2 volumes with light soiling to leather on front covers, just breath of rubbing to extremities, bit of offsetting to endleaves from turn-ins, 2 small closed foreedge tears from rough opening, other trivial imperfections, still excellent set, text clean and fresh, pretty bindings with almost no wear.   Phillip J. Pirages   63 - 375   2013 $125

Racinet, Auguste *Le Costume Historique.* Paris: Librairie Firmin-Didot, 1876-1888. First edition, Deluxe Grad Quarto Large Paper Versions, 420 x 300mm., 6 volumes, serviceable modern maroon library buckram, flat spine, gilt titling, reinforced hinges, 486 often very pleasing chromolithographic and lithographic plates (on 480 leaves), small dark mark to one spine, half dozen leaves with repaired tears into text, another half dozen with short closed marginal tears, occasional minor smudges or stains, otherwise generally excellent set, clean and fresh internally and sturdy bindings, with no signs of wear.   Phillip J. Pirages   63 - 376   2013 $1250

Rack, Henry D. *Reasonable Enthusiast. John Wesley and the Rise of Methodism.* Epworth Press, 1989. First edition, original cloth, gilt, dust jacket.   R. F. G. Hollett & Son   Wesleyan Methodism - 24   2013   £25

Rackham, Arthur *The Allies' Fairy Book.* London: William Heinemann, n.d., 1916. Limited to 525 numbered copies signed by Rackham, this copy 369, quarto, 12 color plates mounted on heavy brown paper, descriptive tissue guards, 24 drawings in black and white, original blue buckram front cover, decoratively stamped and lettered gilt, spine stamped and lettered gilt, top edge gilt, others uncut, illustrated endpapers, fine.   Heritage Book Shop   Holiday Catalogue 2012 - 125   2013 $2000

Rackham, Arthur *The Allies' Fairy Book.* London: Heinemann, n.d., 1916. Limited to 525 numbered copies, signed by Rackham, 4to., blue gilt cloth, top edge gilt, slightest bit of cover darkening usual offsetting on endpaper, else fine in custom slipcase, 12 magnificent tipped in color plates, profusion of line illustrations.   Aleph-Bet Books, Inc.   104 - 465   2013 $2500

Rackham, Arthur *The Arthur Rackham Fairy Book.* London: George G. Harrap & Co. Ltd., 1933. First trade edition, octavo, 8 full page color plates and 60 drawings in black and white, pictorial endpapers printed in green, publisher's original brick red cloth pictorially stamped, original color pictorial dust jacket (little chipped at spine extremities but with no lettering loss), bright, fine, excellent dust jacket.   David Brass Rare Books, Inc.   Holiday 2012 Chapter One - DB 01806   2013 $750

Rackham, Arthur *Arthur Rackham's Book of Pictures.* London: William Heinemann, 1913. Limited to 1030 numbered copies signed by Rackham, large 4to., white gilt decorated cloth, top edge gilt, spine slightly toned and light soil on edge of cover, else very good-fine, clean and tight with no spotting or foxing, 44 beautiful mounted color plates, lettered guards and several charming black and whites, nice, very scarce.   Aleph-Bet Books, Inc.   104 - 466   2013 $2750

Radcliffe, Ann Ward   1764-1823 *The Mysteries of Udolpho.* London: printed for G. G. and J. Robinson, 1794. First edition, 4 volumes, 12mo., bound without half titles, extra-illustrated with 12 small engravings as headpieces, 4 leaves in volume I with small hole at inner margin, touching two letters, three leaves in volume II short in upper and outer margins (2 contiguous), one or two corners torn in lower margin without loss of text, contemporary dark purple half calf gilt ruled spines, decorated in blind, some slight rubbing, ownership inscription of C. Ellis.   Jarndyce Antiquarian Booksellers   CCIV - 246   2013   £3200

Radcliffe, Ann Ward   1764-1823 *The Mysteries of Udolpho.* Philadelphia: J. B. Lippincott & Co., 1864. 8vo., 534 pages, frontispiece, very good in original blindstamped and gilt lettered cloth, very slight wear to head and tail of spine.   Ken Spelman Books Ltd.   75 - 130   2013   £25

Radcliffe, Charles Bland *The Diseases of the Spine and the Nerves.* Philadelphia: Henry C. Lea, 1871. Contemporary linen backed marbled boards, text foxed and browned, worst being the flyleaf and title, rest of the book quite good, uncommon.   James Tait Goodrich   S74 - 215   2013 $395

Radcliffe, Garnett *The Return of Ceteosaurus and Other Tales.* London: Drane's Limited n.d., 1926. First edition, lightly rubbed and soiled, still near fine, without dust jacket, very scarce.   Between the Covers Rare Books, Inc.   Sci-Fi, Fantasy & Horror - 84981   2013 $500

Radcliffe, John *Pharmacopoeia Radcliffeana; or Dr. Radcliff's Prescriptions Faithfully Gather'd...* London: printed for Charles Rivington, 1716. Second edition, frontispiece, 12mo., some browning to endpapers and pastedowns, contemporary sprinkled sheep, expertly rebacked retaining original red morocco label, signature of R. Cawley, 1759, with 19th century name H. Gordon Burning. Jarndyce Antiquarian Booksellers   CCIV - 248   2013   £480

Raddall, Thomas H. *Saga of the Rover.* Liverpool: Mersey Paper Co., 1931. First edition, 2nd issue, without ad for paper company in front, limited to 250, small 8vo., decorated vellum boards and map endpapers, frontispiece plus 9 other plates, piece of vellum missing from top of spine and inner and outer hinge cracks and two small brown spots to front cover, obituary of Thomas W. Hayhurst attached to Raddall & Jones on back of titlepage. Schooner Books Ltd.   104 - 103   2013 $200

Radko, Christopher *Christopher Radko. The First Decade 1986-1995.* Dobbs Ferry: the author, 1996. First edition, fine in fine dust jacket.   Beasley Books   2013 - 2013 $100

Rae, Wynedd *Mostly Mary.* London: Routledge, 1941. Original pale blue boards, spine little faded and rucked at head and foot, short indented mark to upper board, pages 95, illustrations by Irene Williamson, flyleaves lightly spotted. R. F. G. Hollett & Son   Children's Books - 493   2013   £25

Raffald, Elizabeth *The Experienced English Housekeeper for the Use and Ease of Ladies, Housekeepers, Cooks, etc.* London: printed for R. Baldwin, 1786. Tenth edition, frontispiece, 3 folding plates, final ad leaf, frontispiece and ad leaf laid down on endpapers, contemporary vellum, soiled, strangely attractive.   Jarndyce Antiquarian Booksellers   CCV - 224   2013   £280

Raffalovich, George *On the Loose.* London: publishing Office of the Equinox, n.d. circa, 1910. Reprint, cloth, gilt, bookplate, little edgewear to spine, near fine, probably issued without dust jacket.   Between the Covers Rare Books, Inc.   Sci-Fi, Fantasy & Horror - 87925   2013 $250

Raffles, Thomas *Memoirs of the Life and Ministry of the Late Reverend Thomas Spencer of Liverpool.* Liverpool: Reston & Taylor, 1817. Fourth edition, frontispiece, contemporary half calf, marbled boards, gilt banded and gilt lettered spine, frontispiece little dusty and with slight waterstain at foot, Providincial bookseller's label for W. Turner, Market Place, Driffield.   Ken Spelman Books Ltd.   75 - 77   2013   £30

Rahmas, Sigrid *A Day in Fairy Land.* Helsingborg: Helsingbors Litografiska AB, n.d. circa, 1945. Folio, original cloth backed pictorial boards, very slight wear to edges, small hole in upper hinge, full color illustrations, excellent, clean and sound.   R. F. G. Hollett & Son   Children's Books - 528   2013   £180

Raine, James *Saint Cuthbert; with an Account of the state in Which His Remains Were Found Upon the Opening of His Tomb in Durham Cathedral in the Year MDCCCCXXVII.* Durham: Geo. Andrews and J. B. Nichols, London, 1828. 4to., half title, title in red and black, plates and illustrations, uncut in original drab boards, brown moire cloth spine, rubbed, paper label, spine little rubbed, corners bumped, bookseller's ticket of R. D. Steedman, Newcastle. Jarndyce Antiquarian Booksellers   CCV - 225   2013   £150

Rainey, George *The Cherokee Strip.* Guthrie: Co-Opoerative Publishing Co., 1933. First enlarged edition, over 100 vintage photo portraits and views, red cloth, gilt, spine faded, small spot on top edge of front cover, near fine, tight copy, internally fine and clean, presentation inscription signed by author for friend Martha Garber Earles. Argonaut Book Shop   Summer 2013 - 286   2013 $225

Rainolds, John *De Romanae Ecclesiae Idololatria (sic) in Cultu Sanctoru, Reliquiarum, Imaginum, Aquae Salis Olei Aliarumque Rerum Consecratum & Sacramenti Eucharistiae, Operis Inchoati Libri Duo...* Oxford: Joseph Barnes, 1596. Lacking initial blank, faint browning around edges of last few leaves at either end, square 8vo., recent half calf, original red stain to edges, good.   Blackwell's Rare Books   B174 - 122   2013   £850

Rakow, Edwin *Inside My Skin.* La Porte: The Dierkes Press, 1946. First edition, 4to pages, near fine in very good plus dust jacket that is somewhat soiled and with tear at top of spine, signed and with full page inscription, scarce. Jeff Hirsch Books   Fall 2013 - 129458   2013 $50

Ralli, Constantine *Vanessa.* London: Paris: New York: Melbourne: Cassell & Co., 1904. First edition, octavo, original blue cloth, spine panel stamped in gold marbled endpapers.   L. W. Currey, Inc.   Utopian Literature: Recent Acquisitions (April 2013) - 141161   2013 $300

Ralph, Benjamin *The School of Raphael; or the Student's Guide to Expression in Historical Painting.* London: printed for John Boydell, 1782. Second edition, folio, 102 plates numbered I-XII, 1-45 with additional 45 unnumbered plates made up of the 'celebrated heads' in outline only, largely inoffensive damp mark to lower margin of most plates, affecting image of plates II, VI and VII, 19th century half dark blue calf, slight rubbing.   Jarndyce Antiquarian Booksellers   CCV - 226   2013   £2500

Ralph, James *The Fashionable Lady; or Harlequin's Opera.* London: printed for J. Watts, 1730. First edition, 8vo., later grey paper boards, printed paper label on upper board, one leaf of publisher's terminal ads, musical scores, text lightly foxed, some minor paper flaws and worming in margins, insignificant loss, very good.   The Brick Row Book Shop   Miscellany Fifty-Nine - 35   2013 $2500

Ralston, W. *Tippoo: a Tale of a Tiger.* London: George Routledge and Sons, n.d. circa, 1905. Oblong large 8vo., original pictorial wrappers, one short edge tear and chip, pages 28, illustrations.   R. F. G. Hollett & Son   Children's Books - 497   2013   £85

Ramazzini, Bernardini *Opera Omnia medica et Physiologica i Duos Tomos Distributa.* Neapoli: Veneunt Venetiis Apud Andream Poletti, 1750. 4to., 5 engraved plates, early limp boards, text foxing, uncut.   James Tait Goodrich   75 - 176   2013 $1250

Ramey, Earl *The Beginnings of Marysville.* San Francisco: California Historical Society, 1936. First book edition, very scarce, frontispiece, titlepage map in color, 4 plates, 2 full page facsimiles, large folding map, rust cloth backed tan boards, printed paper labels on spine and front cover, small oval bookplate, very fine, mostly uncut.   Argonaut Book Shop   Summer 2013 - 225   2013 $350

Ramierez, Carolyn *Small as a Raisin Big as the World.* Irvington-on-Hudson: Harvey Books, 1961. First edition, tall hardcover, illustrations by Carl Ramirez, very near fine in like dust jacket, scarce thus.   Jeff Hirsch Books   Fall 2013 - 129361   2013 $75

Ramsay, Alexander *Anatomy of the Heart, Cranium and Brain.* Edinburgh: printed by George Ramsay and Co. for Archibald Constable and Co. and London Longman, Hurst, Rees, Orme and Brown, 1813. Second edition, 15 hand colored aquatint plates, recent quarter calf and marbled boards, text with foxing and some toning, light marginal chipping to blank borders of plates, signature C (text) foxed, some light scattered spotting and very small marginal chips to blank borders of plates, attractive modern half calf with marbled sides.   James Tait Goodrich   75 - 175   2013 $4500

Ramsay, Allan *The Ever Green.* Edinburgh: printed for Alexander Donaldson, 1761. 12mo., 2 volumes, frontispiece, contents leaf to volume II misbound at end of volume I, some slight dusting and foxing, generally very clean, rather tightly, in 19th century dark green cloth, gilt bands & lettering to spines, 19th century armorial bookplate of Julius Charles Hare 1795-1855, ownership label of Maurice Powell.   Jarndyce Antiquarian Booksellers   CCIV - 249   2013   £85

Ramsaye, Terry *A Million and One Nights.* New York: Simon and Schuster, 1926. First edition, limited to 327 copies signed by author and Thomas Edison, quarto, frontispiece, black and white photo reproductions, publisher's blue buckram, bordered with single blind rule on front cover and with center device stamped in gilt, spines lettered gilt, bit of gilt lettering slightly rubbed from spines, light staining to endpapers due to glue used on pastedown endpapers, else very handsome, near fine.   Heritage Book Shop   Holiday Catalogue 2012 - 53   2013 $4500

Ramsden, Charles *Bookbinders of the United Kingdom (Outside London) 1780-1840.* privately printed, 1954. One of 500 copies, octavo, xv, 250 pages, cloth, fine.   C. P. Hyland   261 - 98   2013   £40

Ramsden, Charles *French Bookbinders 1789-1848.* 1950. First edition, prospectus loosely enclosed indicates this publication was limited to 950 copies, 8vo., cloth, fine, signed presentation copy.   C. P. Hyland   261 - 97   2013   £60

Ramsden, Charles *London Bookbinders 1780-1840.* London: Batsford, 1956. 8vo., xiv, 155 pages, cloth, very good.   C. P. Hyland   261 - 99   2013   £40

Rand, Ann *Sparkle and Spin: a Book About Words.* New York: Harcourt Brace and World, 1957. Stated first edition, 4to., pictorial boards, fine in dust jacket with few mends on verso, quite scarce in jacket, illustrations by Paul Rand.   Aleph-Bet Books, Inc.   104 - 483   2013 $500

Rankin, D. J. *A History of the County of Antigonish, Nova Scotia.* Toronto: Macmillan Co., 1929. First edition, large 8vo., blue cloth, gilt title to spine, first flyleaf missing and some light wear to edges, very good condition.   Schooner Books Ltd.   102 - 85   2013 $100

Ransome, Arthur *Aladdin and His Wonderful Lamp.* London: Nisbet, n.d., 1919. Limited to only 250 numbered copies signed by artist, large 4to., white cloth with elaborate gilt pictorial cover, top edge gilt, other edges uncut, slightest of fading to spine, else fine, 12 magnificent tipped in color plates with tissue guards, decorative initials and text borders, a profusion of black and whites on every page by Thomas MacKenzie, rare limited format.   Aleph-Bet Books, Inc.   104 - 332   2013 $6250

Ransome, Arthur *The Big Six.* London: Cape, 1940. First edition, original cloth, gilt, later dust jacket, 23 illustrations and 2 maps and 2 color maps on endpapers.   R. F. G. Hollett & Son   Children's Books - 498   2013   £85

Ransome, Arthur *Coot Club.* London: Cape, 1934. First edition, original cloth gilt, trifle rubbed, 22 illustrations and 2 colored maps on endpapers, joints cracked, few spots to flyleaves.   R. F. G. Hollett & Son   Children's Books - 499   2013   £65

Ransome, Arthur *Great Northern?* London: Cape, 1947. First edition, original cloth gilt, 23 illustrations and maps on endpapers.   R. F. G. Hollett & Son   Children's Books - 500   2013   £65

Ransome, Arthur *Missee Lee.* London: Cape, 1941. First edition, original cloth, gilt, 26 illustrations and colored maps on endpapers.   R. F. G. Hollett & Son   Children's Books - 501   2013   £45

Ransome, Arthur *The Picts and the Martyrs: or Not Welcome at All.* London: Cape, 1943. First edition, original cloth, gilt, 20 illustrations and 2 color maps on endpapers.   R. F. G. Hollett & Son   Children's Books - 502   2013   £30

Ransome, Arthur *The Picts and the Martyrs: or not Welcome At All.* London: Cape, 1943. First edition, original cloth, gilt, faint creasing to upper board, dust jacket extremities trifle rubbed 20 illustrations and 2 color maps on endpapers.   R. F. G. Hollett & Son   Children's Books - 503   2013   £325

Ransome, Arthur *Pigeon Post.* London: Cape, 1936. First edition, original cloth, gilt, pages 384, 23 illustrations and colored maps on endpapers, rear joint cracked, inscription.   R. F. G. Hollett & Son   Children's Books - 504   2013   £65

Ransome, Arthur *Secret Water.* London: Cape, 1939. First edition, original cloth, gilt, 41 illustrations and colored maps on endpapers.   R. F. G. Hollett & Son   Children's Books - 505   2013   £45

Ransome, Arthur *Secret Water.* London: Cape, 1939. First edition, frontispiece, title vignette, numerous line drawings in text, some full page and color printed map endpapers, all by author, crown 8vo., original mid green cloth backstrip gilt lettered, front cover titled in blind, dust jacket, faint browning to backstrip panel and just trifle rubbed, overall delightful copy, very good.   Blackwell's Rare Books   B174 - 288   2013   £1000

Ransome, Arthur *Swallowdale.* London: Cape, 1941. Original green cloth gilt, spine trifle faded, pages 453, numerous illustrations and colored maps on endpapers.   R. F. G. Hollett & Son   Children's Books - 506   2013   £25

Ransome, Arthur *We Didn't Mean to Go to Sea.* London: Cape, 1937. First edition, original cloth, gilt, 34 illustrations and maps on endpapers, few light spots to flyleaves and fore-edge.   R. F. G. Hollett & Son   Children's Books - 507   2013   £120

Rapelje, George *A Narrative of Excursions, Voyages and Travels, Performed at Different Periods in America, Europe, Asia and Africa.* New York: printed for the author by West & Trow, 1834. First edition, 8vo., 416 pages, frontispiece, original cloth, edges worn.   M & S Rare Books, Inc.   95 - 309   2013 $375

Rashad, Johari *(R)evolutions.* Washington: The author, 1982. Advance review copy, stapled wrappers, fine, signed by author requesting a review.   Between the Covers Rare Books, Inc.   165 - 250   2013 $275

Raskin, Ellen *The Westing Game.* New York: Dutton, 1978. Review copy with slip laid in, 8vo., quarter cloth and boards, fine in near fine dust jacket (no award seal, not price clipped), review copy with slip laid in.   Aleph-Bet Books, Inc.   104 - 484   2013 $400

Rasmussen, Louis J. *San Francisco Ship Passenger Lists Volume I.* Colma: San Francisco Historic Record & Genealogy Bulletin, 1965. First edition, 3 plates from old photos, frontispiece, black cloth, lower corners lightly worn, else fine.   Argonaut Book Shop   Summer 2013 - 287   2013 $90

Ratcliffe, Dorothy Una *Island of the Little Years.* Frederick Muller, 1947. First edition, large 8vo., original patterned cloth, dust jacket little worn and chipped, price clipped, illustrations by Franc Martin, including tipped in color frontispiece.   R. F. G. Hollett & Son   Children's Books - 509   2013   £30

Rattigan, Terence *The Winslow Boy.* London: Hamish Hamilton, 1946. First edition, 8vo. 109 pages, very good, signed by 10 f the 11 cast members of the first London production, including Kathleen Harrison, Emelyn Williams, Michael Newell, etc.   Second Life Books Inc.   183 - 330   2013 $350

Rauschenberg, Robert *Rauschenberg Photographs.* New York: Pantheon, 1981. First American edition, signed by Rauschenberg, fine in near fine dust jacket, 122 black and white photos, 4to.   By the Book, L. C.   36 - 14   2013 $900

Rauwolf, Leonard *Aigentliche Beschreibung der Rais...* I. Reinmichel, 1582. First edition, small 4to., modern calf, gilt title to spine, (16), 488 pages.   Maggs Bros. Ltd.   1467 - 30   2013   £2500

Ravaton, Hughes *Chirurgie d'Armee ou traite des Plaies d'Armes a Feu, et d'Armes Blanxes avec Des Observations sur ces Maladies...* Paris: Chez P. Fr. Didot le Jeune, 1768. 7 engraved plates, contemporary full mottled calf, gilt compartments on spine, light wear and head and tail of spine, all edges in red, text very clean and crisp with marginal worming only rarely affecting text, overall near fine, tight, crisp copy. James Tait Goodrich 75 - 177 2013 $995

Raven, J. E. *Pythagoreans and Eleatics: an Account of the Interaction Between the two Opposed Schools During the Fifth and Early Fourth Centuries.* Cambridge: Cambridge University Press, 1948. Small 8vo., blue cloth, gilt stamped spine title, ownership signatures, very good, rare. Jeff Weber Rare Books 169 - 370 2013 $75

Ravilious, Eric *For Shop Use Only: Curwen and Dent Stock Blocks and Devices with Contributions by John Lewis, Enid Marx and Robert Harling.* Devizes: Garton, 1933. Limited to 75 copies in edition "A", this no. 42, 8vo, 47 pages, original wood engravings by Ravilious tipped in and 20 wood engravings loose in card mounts, blue cloth spine and white paper with red patterned boards, red lettering on white paper label spine, book and engravings housed in matching blue cloth covered clamshell box. By the Book, L. C. 36 - 15 2013 $600

Ravizzotti, Gaetano *Viridarium Latinum; ou Recueil des Pensees et Bons-mots le Plus Remarquables...* De l'Imprimerie de W. et C. Spilsbury, Snowhill, 1801. First edition, titlepage (cancel) signed by author to prevent piracy, poor quality paper browned and foxed, 8vo. contemporary brown cloth, black lettering piece to spine, cloth slightly bubbled, touch of wear to extremities, scarce. Blackwell's Rare Books B174 - 123 2013 £400

Rawlings, Marjorie Kinan *The Yearling.* New York: Charles Scribner's Sons, 1939. A. Limited to 750 copies for sale, signed by author and artist, 4to., bluish green cloth, top edge gilt, fine in matching chemise with leather label and publisher's blue slipcase (slightly rubbed on edges, else sound and very good+), new signature with correction was inserted but not before some sheets were distributed, this copy has the corrected pages, illustrations by N. C. Wyeth, very scarce. Aleph-Bet Books, Inc. 105 - 599 2013 $4250

Rawlings, Marjorie Kinnan *Yearling.* New York: Scribner, 1940. (1939, 1938) First Scribner Classic edition, 4to., black cloth, color plate on cover, fine, publisher's box with color plate on cover, box flap replaced, illustrations by N. C. Wyeth, scarce in box. Aleph-Bet Books, Inc. 104 - 597 2013 $950

Rawls, James J. *Dan DeQuille of the Big Bonanza.* San Francisco: Book Club of California, 1980. First edition, limited to 650 copies printed, 128 pages, frontispiece, plates, cloth backed patterned boards, gilt lettered spine, very fine. Argonaut Book Shop   Recent Acquisitions June 2013 - 241 2013 $75

Ray, John *The Wisdom of God Manifested in the Works of the Creation.* Glasgow: printed by J. Bryce and D. Paterson, 1756. Thirteenth edition, 324 pages, 12mo., very good in full contemporary sprinkled calf, raised and gilt banded spine with red morocco label, some slight rubbing to spine and board edges, tiny amount of worming to front endpaper and foot of title, armorial bookplate of John Headlam, early signature of W. Milner. Ken Spelman Books Ltd. 75 - 21 2013 £120

Raymond, Dora Neill *The Political Career of Lord Byron.* London: George Allen & Unwin, 1925. First English edition, original red cloth, slightly marked, spine slightly faded, booklabel of David A.. Lyttleton, from the library of Doris Langley Moore. Jarndyce Antiquarian Booksellers CCIII - 438 2013 £30

Raymond, Margaret *Roberta Goes Adventuring.* Chicago: Volland, 1931. First edition, small 4to., cloth backed pictorial boards, slightest of cover soil, else near fine, very rare, illustrations in bold colors by Eleanor Campbell. Aleph-Bet Books, Inc. 105 - 577 2013 $275

Read Me a Story Books. Joliet: Volland, 1928. 5 Volland picture books, all in fine condition in dust jackets, illustrated in bold colors art deco style, housed in publisher's box with color plate on cover, super, ultra rare. Aleph-Bet Books, Inc. 104 - 577 2013 $1500

Reasons Assigned by the Church in North Wrentham for Withdrawing from Their Masonic Brethren and others and Being Formed into a Distinct and Separate Church. Boston: 1830. First edition, 8vo., 32 pages, original printed wrappers, uncut. M & S Rare Books, Inc. 95 - 214 2013 $125

Reay, Henry Utrick *A Short Treatise on the Useful Invention Called the Sportsman's Friend; or, the Farmer's Footman.* Newcastle: printed by Edward Walker; London: Sold by R. Faulder..., 1801. First (only) edition, copper engraved frontispiece and two fine full page wood engravings by Thomas Bewick, uncut and partly unopened, 8vo., original blue paper wrappers, split at foot of upper joint, author's own copy, engraved bookplate of author on inside front cover, preserved in fleece lined morocco backed folding box, very good. Blackwell's Rare Books B174 - 7 2013 £1200

Recreations in Natural History, or Popular Sketches of British Quadrupeds. London: William Clarke Etc., 1815. First edition, three quarter leather, 8vo., 24 full page engravings, some foxing, very good. Barnaby Rudge Booksellers Natural History 2013 - 016074   2013 $95

Recupero, Giuseppe *Storia Naturale e Generale Dell'Etna.* Catania: Dalla Stamperia della Regia Universita Degli Studj, 1815. First edition, 2 volumes, 298 x 215mm., volume II with pages 22 and 23 blank (text accidentally omitted during printing) and with pages 173-76 supplied in excellent bound-in facsimile; 6 folding wood engravings, frontispiece, a large map of Mount Etna, a topographical map and 3 views, verso of titlepage with British Museum's 'Duplicate' stamp; pleasing recent half calf over marbled boards, raised bands, each spine with red morocco label, edges untrimmed (slightly soiled publisher's blue paper wrappers bound in; occasional minor foxing or dust soiling to margins, one opening with printing smudges to margins and footnotes (obscuring one word), two gatherings in volume II little browned, one with half inch worm trail touching eight letters, other trivial imperfects (short closed marginal tears, isolated rust spots, corner creases), generally excellent, fresh with good margins and in unworn bindings. Phillip J. Pirages 63 - 483   2013 $2500

Red Riding Hood. New York: McLoughlin Bros. n.d. circa, 1880. 4to., pictorial wrappers, (16) pages, including covers, faint crease on rear cover, few small margin mends, very good, 8 large and very fine chromolithographs. Aleph-Bet Books, Inc.   104 - 207   2013 $250

Redding, Cyrus *Every Man His Own Butler.* London: Whitaker and Co., 1839. First edition, engraved title, small tear to upper corner of leading f.e.p., original ribbed purple cloth, illustrations in gilt with decanter & two wine glasses on a tray, neat repair to tear in spine with no loss, leading hinge slightly cracked at tail, later ink inscription. Jarndyce Antiquarian Booksellers   CCV - 227   2013   £520

Redding, Cyrus *A History and Description of Modern Wines.* London: Whittaker, Treacher and Arnot, 1833. First edition, original green publisher's cloth, old rebacking, original spine laid down, some wear, old signature on half title. James Tait Goodrich   75 - 178   2013 $575

Redding, Cyrus *Literary Reminiscences and Memoirs of Thomas Campbell.* London: Charles J. Keet, 1860. First edition, 2 volumes, frontispiece volume i, slightly dampstained in inner margin, original black cloth, patterned with cream dots, spines little dulled, inner hinges slightly cracking, booklabels of Samuel Allen, good plus. Jarndyce Antiquarian Booksellers   CCIII - 476   2013   £110

Redi, Francesco *Experimenta circa Generationem Insectorum.* Amsterdam: Andreas Frisius, 1761. Additional engraved title, engraved vignette on title, 2 engravings in text, 38 engraved plates, very slightly browned in places, 12mo., original vellum, yapp edges, soiled (as one would expect), very good, contemporary ownership inscription of Jo. Ballard, repeated at end with cost code. Blackwell's Rare Books   Sciences - 103   2013   £750

Redinger, David H. *The Story of Big Creek.* Glendale: Trans-Anglo Books, 1987. Revised edition, quarto, vintage photos, gilt lettered blue cloth, very fine, slightly chipped pictorial dust jacket. Argonaut Book Shop   Recent Acquisitions June 2013 - 242   2013 $75

Redmond, Patrick *The Wishing Game.* London: Hodder & Stoughton, 1999. First edition, very fine in dust jacket. Mordida Books   81 - 441   2013 $85

Redpath, James *The Public Life of Capt. John Brown.* Boston: Thayer and Eldridge, 1860. First edition, 8vo., 407 pages, frontispiece, publisher's brown cloth stamped in blind and titled in gilt, some little external wear, rear hinge repaired, ownership signature of Edward B. Tinsley on endpaper, very good, tight. Second Life Books Inc.   183 - 332   2013 $150

Reed, Ishmael *Mumbo Jumbo.* Garden City: Doubleday, 1972. First edition, fine in lightly rubbed, otherwise fine dust jacket, inscribed by author to Nick Delbanco. Between the Covers Rare Books, Inc.   165 - 251   2013 $275

Reed, John *Daughter of the Revolution and Other Stories.* New York: Vanguard, 1927. First edition, 12mo., 164 pages, yellow cloth, near fine. Second Life Books Inc. 183 - 333   2013 $85

Reed, John *Sangar to Lincoln Steffens.* Riverside: Hillacre, 1913. First edition, one of only 500 copies, tall 8vo., 6 pages, frontispiece with tissue guard, printed boards, little foxed, nice clean, untrimmed, scarce. Second Life Books Inc.   183 - 333a   2013 $300

Reed, Joseph *Tom Jones, a comic Opera As it is Performed at the Theatre Royal in Covent Garden.* London: Becket and De Hondt and Richardson and Urquhart, 1769. First edition, 8vo., later wrappers, 62 pages, without half title, very good. The Brick Row Book Shop   Miscellany Fifty-Nine - 24   2013 $225

Reed, William *Improved Tables of Gain and Discount; Shewing Real Profits from 2 per Cent to 50 per Cent on the Prime Cost of Goods at any Price from One Penny to £2000...* printed for the author by Henry Kent-Cuaston, 1806. First edition, signed by author, bit browned in places, titlepage fragile at edges, 8vo. in fours, modern half calf, good. Blackwell's Rare Books B174 - 124   2013   £400

Rees, Ennis *Lions and Lobsters and Foxes and Frogs.* Reading: Young Scott Book, 1971. First edition, oblong 4to., pictorial boards, fine in like dust jacket, illustrations in color on every page, nice. Aleph-Bet Books, Inc. 104 - 243 2013 $100

Rees, Fred *On Peak, Pyramid and Prairie.* Arthur H. Stockwell, n.d., 1910. First edition, small 8vo., original green cloth, gilt, pages 95, portrait, 7 pages of illustrations, scattered foxing, some pencilled annotations, uncommon. R. F. G. Hollett & Son Africana - 162 2013 £45

Rees, W. D. Wood *A History of Barmby Moore from Pre-Historic Times.* Pocklington: W. & C. Forth, 1911. Portrait and illustrations, good copy, original gilt lettered cloth, carce. Ken Spelman Books Ltd. 73 - 60 2013 £25

Reeve, Arthur B. *Craig Kennedy Listens in.* New York: Harper, 1923. First edition, page edges and endpapers darkened, otherwise very good in dust jacket with small chips at spine ends and at corners. Mordida Books 81 - 442 2013 $100

Reformiana; or Tit-for-Tat. Carlisle: Henry Lowes, 1841. 36 pages, sewn as issued in original buff printed wrappers, very good. Jarndyce Antiquarian Booksellers CCIII - 338 2013 £500

The Register of Prohibited Publications to 1961. Dublin: GPO, 1961. 432 pages, wrappers, card glued inside "Catahl O Dubb (Charles Duff?), good. C. P. Hyland 261 - 95 2013 £70

Regnier, Henri De *Les Rencontres de Mr. de Breot.* Paris: chez Sylvain Sauvage, 1927. First Sauvage edition, number 15 of 25 copies on Japon Imperial, from a total edition of 177; 46 original pochoir enhanced color woodcuts printed by Pierre Bouchet, 248 pages, superb Art Deco signed master binding by Henri Creuzevault, front panel with mosaic of stylized guitar with onlaid multi color leathers, spine with 4 raised bands, top edge gilt, doublures with fillets of gilt and morocco, framing moire fabric, fit in slipcase, overall size 11.5 x 10 inches, in excellent condition. Gemini Fine Books & Arts., Ltd. Art Reference & Illustrated Books - 2013 $2700

Reid, Forrest *Illustrations of the Sixties.* Faber & Gwyer, 1928. First edition, illustrations, 8vo., original green cloth, gilt titling, some light fading, else very good. C. P. Hyland 261 - 741 2013 £75

Reid, Hugo, Mrs. *Woman, Her Education and Influence.* New York: Fowler and Wells, 1848. Stereotype edition, 8vo., numerous illustrations, rebound in yellow cloth, small leather spine label, bookplate, little foxing, few light marks in margins, nice, tight copy. Second Life Books Inc. 182 - 197 2013 $125

Reid, Mayne 1818-1883 *The Young Yagers; or a Narrative of Hunting.* London: David Bogue, 1857. First edition, half title with ads on verso, frontispiece and plates, 4 pages ads, original purple brown morocco grained cloth, some slight rubbing, boards unevenly faded, long inscription on leading f.e.p. to 12 year old James Hibbert from his father Oct. 14 1857. Jarndyce Antiquarian Booksellers CCV - 228 2013 £150

Reid, Sam. C. *International Law: the Case of the Private Armed Brig of War Gen. Armstrong.* New York: Banks Gould & Co., 1857. First edition, 8vo., contemporary sheep, front cover detached. M & S Rare Books, Inc. 95 - 197 2013 $225

Reid, Thomas 1710-1796 *Essays on the Intellectual Powers of Man. (with) Essays on the Active Powers of Man.* Edinburgh: printed for John Bell, G. G. J. & J. Robinson, London, 1785-1788. First editions, 2 volumes, half titles and ads in both volumes, few leaves slightly browned, one or two minor spots or stains, tear in fore-margin of one leaf in Intellectual Powers (not affecting text), 4to., uniform tree calf, gilt lines on either side of raised bands on spine, red lettering pieces, yellow edges, first page of text of first volume signed in pencil G. E., more or less contemporary, excellent. Blackwell's Rare Books 172 - 122 2013 £5000

Reik, Theodor *Fragment of a Great Confession: a Psychoanalytic Autobiography.* New York: Farrar Straus and Co., 1949. First edition, near fine in nice, near fine dust jacket, inscribed by author to another psychiatrist. Between the Covers Rare Books, Inc. Psychology & Psychiatry - 2842662 2013 $275

Reik, Theodor *Haunting Melody: Psychoanalytic Experiences in Life and Music.* New York: Farrar, Straus and Young, 1953. First edition, offsetting from clipping on front fly, thus very good in slightly spine tanned, else near fine dust jacket, clipping partially offset onto inscription. Between the Covers Rare Books, Inc. Psychology & Psychiatry - 97042 2013 $200

Reilly, Philip R. *Abraham Lincoln's DNA and other Adventures in Genetics.* Cold Spring Harbor: Cold Spring Harbor Lab. Press, 2000. Fourth printing, 8vo. mild stain to fore edge, near fine in fine dust jacket. By the Book, L. C. 37 - 1 2013 $75

Reinhardt, Karl Heinrich Leopold *Lettres sur Dresde A Madame Contenant une Esquisse...* Berlin: H. Frolich, 1800. Small 8vo., pages xxiv, 262, 19th century half morocco, engraved armorial bookplate of Duff-Gordon, Aberdeen bookseller's ticket inside front cover. Marlborough Rare Books Ltd. 218 - 122 2013 £575

Reisner, Mary *Shadows on the Wall.* New York: Dodd Mead and Co., 1943. First edition, trifle worn at foot of spine, still about fine in very good dust jacket with tiny nick at crown, some modest rubbing at spine ends, inscribed by author for Judge and Mrs. Crabites. Between the Covers Rare Books, Inc. Mystery & Detective Fiction - 57180 2013 $275

Reiter, H. W. *The Merry Gentlemen of Japan.* New York: Bass, 1935. First edition, 4to., cloth, pictorial paste-on, very good+. Aleph-Bet Books, Inc. 105 - 275 2013 $150

A Relation of the Defeating Card. Mazarine and Oliv. Cromwel's Designs to Have Taken Ostend by Treachery in the Year 1658. printed for Hen. Herrington, 1666. 12mo., washed and pressd, headline in sig. B cropped and preliminary leaves cut close, 20th century panelled calf, gilt, spine gilt, red lettering piece, rebacked preserving original spine, sound. Blackwell's Rare Books B174 - 41 2013 £500

Religious Experience and Death of Eliza Van Wyck. New York: American Tract Society, 1833. First edition, 24mo., 32 pages plus wrappers, 7 woodcuts, previous owner inscription, good. Barnaby Rudge Booksellers Children 2013 - 021317 2013 $65

Remarques Historique sur la Bastille, sa Demolition & Revolutions de Paris en Juillet 1789. Londres: 1789. Folding plan, without half title, 8vo., marginal paper flaw to d2 of second part, some old waterstaining towards end, titlepage foxed, 19th century half dark green calf by R. Jenkins with his ticket, marbled boards, hinges and corners rubbed, few marks to spine. Jarndyce Antiquarian Booksellers CCIV - 57 2013 £180

Reminiscences of Charles Butler, Esq. 1822. First edition, half calf, 8vo. good. C. P. Hyland 261 - 919 2013 £38

Renard, Maurice *New Bodies for Old or The Strange Experiments of Dr. Lerne.* New York: Macaulay, 1923. First American edition, and first edition in English, very slight scuff to fore edge, else fine in fine dust jacket, superb, as new copy. Between the Covers Rare Books, Inc. Sci-Fi, Fantasy & Horror - 15302 2013 $750

Rendell, Ruth *A Guilty Thing Surprised.* Garden City: Doubleday Crime Club, 1970. First US edition, fine in near fine dust jacket with one clean tear at head of front panel. Beasley Books 2013 - 2013 $100

Rennell, James *The Geographical System of Herodotus.* London: printed by W. Bulmer and Co., 1800. First edition, frontispiece (foxed) and 11 engraved maps (all but one folding, all lightly foxed), paper evenly toned throughout, touch of spotting and offsetting from plates in places, 4to., contemporary dark blue straight grained morocco, boards bordered with triple gilt fillet, spine with five raised bands, compartments bordered with triple gilt fillet, second compartment gilt lettered direct, decorative gilt rolls at head and foot, and on bands, marbled edges and endpapers, small gilt armorial stamp (Earls of Camden) on boards, little rubbed at extremities, spine lightly faded, good. Blackwell's Rare Books 172 - 123 2013 £850

Renouard, Antoine Augustin *Catalogue d'une Precieuse Collection De Livres...* Paris: Firmin Didot for Poitier and Jules Renouard in Paris and Barthez and Lowel in London, 1854-1855. 8vo., portrait etched by G. Staal on India, evenly lightly browned, portrait little foxed, later red morocco backed marbled boards, spine with raised bands and lettered in gilt, upper edge gilt, price list with original printed wrappers bound in, bookplate of R. Chevanne inside front cover. Marlborough Rare Books Ltd. 218 - 123 2013 £500

Rentoul, A. I. *Mollie's Staircase.* Melbourne: M. L. Hutchinson, 1906. First edition, oblong 4to., string bound printed wrappers, (52) pages, titlepage foxed, scattered foxing, string bound printed wrappers, titlepage foxed, scattered foxing and faint crease on other pages, otherwise remarkably intact and very good+, 12 full page black and whites, printed on one side of paper plus several smaller illustrations in text. Aleph-Bet Books, Inc. 104 - 401 2013 $2500

Rentoul, Annie R. *Fairyland.* New York: Frederick A. Stokes, 1929. First American edition, folio, red gilt cloth, pictorial paste-on, as new in fine pictorial dust jacket with large color illustration housed in original publisher box (flaps repaired), with large color plate mounted on cover, pictorial endpapers, 19 magnificent large color plates, 32 large and incredibly detailed black and white plates plus drawings in text, magnificent, rare with jacket and box. Aleph-Bet Books, Inc. 104 - 400 2013 $6000

Renwick, George *Romantic Corsica; Wanderings in Napoleon's Isle with a Chapter on Climbing...* London: Fisher Unwin, 1909. First edition, 8vo., 333 pages, folding color map, frontispiece, illustrations, original blue cloth, gilt vignette. J. & S. L. Bonham Antiquarian Booksellers Europe - 6409 2013 £30

The Repentence and Happy Death of the Celebrated Earl of Rochester. Nottingham: printed by Sutton and Son, 1814. 8vo., titlepage woodcut and tailpiece, uncut folded sheet in fine state, containing two unseparated copies of the work. Ken Spelman Books Ltd. 75 - 70 2013 £80

Report of the Trials of the Insurgent Negroes Before a General Court Martial Held at Georgetown, Demarara on the 25th August 1823 and Continued by Adjournement Until the 11th of October Following. Demerara: A. Stephenson at the Guiana Chronicle Office, Georgetown, 1824. First edition, 8vo., contemporary half calf, slightly shelfworn, rare, this copy belonged to William Bruce Ferguson.   Maggs Bros. Ltd.   1467 - 4   2013   £3000

Reports Respecting Distilleries in Scotland, by Committees of the Honourable the House of Commons, Appointed in 1798 and 1799... London: printed (by S. Gosnell) for J. Wright, 1799. 8vo., date Oct. 5th neatly added to imprint in contemporary hand, uncut and partially unopened, disbound.   Jarndyce Antiquarian Booksellers   CCIV - 264   2013   £580

Repton, Humphrey   1752-1818   *The Red Books.* London: Basilisk Press, 1976. Limited edition, number 111 of an edition of 525 copies, 4 volumes, various sizes facsimiles, half red morocco in fitted brown cloth case, fine reprints.   Marlborough Rare Books Ltd.   218 - 124   2013   £1750

Repton, Humphrey   1752-1818   *Sketches and Hints on Landscape Gardening...* London: W. Bulmer & Co. for J. & J. Boydell and G. Nicol, 1794. First edition, landscape folio, half title, pages xvi, 83, (4), 10 hand colored aquatint engravings, each with one or more over-slips and 6 aquatint plates printed in black with single tint added, 2 wood engraved illustrations, 1 wood engraved tailpiece, contemporary green morocco backed cloth boards, spine lettered gilt, raised bands, very good.   Marlborough Rare Books Ltd.   218 - 125   2013   £12,500

Reresby, John   *The Memoirs of Sir John Reresby of Thrybergh, Bart, M.P. for York &c. 1634-1689.* London: Longmans,, 1875. xiv, 466 pages, original gilt lettered cloth, spine faded with some wear.   Ken Spelman Books Ltd.   73 - 40   2013   £40

Restoration Love Songs. Preston, Hitchin: printed at the Oxford University Press, 1950. 145/660 copies, printed in Fell types on Arnold mouldmade paper, 6 collotype plates, 2 color printed folding frontispieces all by Rex Whistler, crown 8vo., original quarter pale blue buckram, grey leather label, blue, brown and white marbled boards, corners trifle bumped, top edge gilt, others untrimmed, glassine jacket, near fine.   Blackwell's Rare Books   B174 - 326   2013   £120

Retz, Jean Francois Paul De Gondi, Cardinal De   *Memoirs of the Cardinal de Retz...*   London: printed for Jacob Tonson, 1723. 4 volumes, 12mo., worming to lower inner margin volume I, disappearing to single hole by B4 of main text and also to outer blank margin of final five leaves of volume III, full contemporary panelled calf, raised bands, red morocco labels, little rubbed and worn, armorial bookplate of Marquess of Headfort, signature of Thomas Taylor dated 1756.   Jarndyce Antiquarian Booksellers   CCIV - 250   2013   £185

Rey, C. F.   *The Romance of the Portuguese in Abyssinia.* London: H. F. and G. Witherby, 1929. First edition, 8vo. 16 plates and two foldout maps as called for, some marginal foxing, small tear to second map but still very good, green cloth, gilt title to spine, dust jacket, endcaps little creased, edges foxed but very good, dust jacket edges bit worn with some small tears, spine little darkened, somewhat marked, still very good.   Unsworths Antiquarian Booksellers   28 - 194   2013   £175

Reynard the Fox in South Africa: or Hottentot Fables and Tales. London: Trubner, 1864. First edition, 8vo., green cloth, excellent condition.   Aleph-Bet Books, Inc.   105 - 81   2013 $275

Reynard, Adeline   *Histoires Pour Ride.*   no imprint, circa, 1905. Folio, cloth backed pictorial boards, tiny mends to paper next to tabs, else fine, 6 moveable plates operated by pull tabs, , 7 large drawings in text.   Aleph-Bet Books, Inc.   104 - 345   2013 $3500

Reynolds, Alastir   *The Perfect.* London: Gollancz, 2007. First edition,   L. W. Currey, Inc.   Utopian Literature: Recent Acquisitions (April 2013) - 141361   2013 $75

Reynolds, James   *Equality: a History of Lithconia.* Philadelphia: published by the Liberal Union, 1837. First edition, small octavo, original green boards rebacked with facsimile brown cloth shelf back closely resembling original, facsimile paper spine label.   L. W. Currey, Inc.   Utopian Literature: Recent Acquisitions (April 2013) - 140667   2013 $8500

Reynolds, John   *A Discourse Upon Prodigious Abstinence, Occasioned by the Twelve Moneths Fasting of Martha Taylor, the Famed Derbyshire Damosell..*   London: printed by R(obert W(hite) for Nevill Simmons, 1669. 4to., rather browned and foxed, imprimatur and final leaf expertly repaired along inner margin, expertly bound in full sprinkled calf triple blind ruled borders, raised bands, fresh endpapers and pastedowns.   Jarndyce Antiquarian Booksellers   CCIV - 27   2013   £2250

Reynolds, John *The Triumphs of Gods Revenge Against the Crying and Exercable Sin of Wilful and Premeditated Murther...* London: Griffin, 1704. Seventh edition, folio, pages 481, engraved titlepage and 30 text engravings, contemporary calf, rubbed, rebacked with binder's tape on hinges, later bookplate, some intermittent worming, many of the leaves foxed and toned but not obscuring text, titlepage in red and black, all editions are rare. Second Life Books Inc. 183 - 439 2013 $500

Reynolds, John Hamilton *The Fancy.* London: Elkin Mathews, 1905. 13 illustrations by Jack B. Yeats, small 8vo., original grey wrappers lettered in black, edges untrimmed, small leather booklabel, attractive bookplate on front free endpaper and some browning to spine, otherwise excellent, delicate binding. Maggs Bros. Ltd. 1442 - 328 2013 £250

Reynolds, Tim *The Women Poem.* New York: Phoenix Book Shop, 1973. First edition, one of 100 hardbound copies, 8vo., quite fine. Beasley Books 2013 - 2013 $50

Rhazes, Abu Bakr Muhammad Ben Zakariya Al-Razi *Divisiones Rasis Filli Zachariae Viaticum Co(n)stanini Monachi.* Lyon: G. de Villiers impensis V. de Portonariis, 1510. First edition, 2 volumes, bound in 1, 17th century vellum with yapped edges, repaired defect in rear board, light browning of text otherwise, very nice tight copy, some early annotations in text, woodcut initials. James Tait Goodrich 75 - 1179 2013 $6000

Rhijne, Willem Ten *Meditationes.* Leiden: Johannes vvan Schuylenburgh, 1672. First edition, engraved frontispiece, folding engraved plate both designed by author, little dampstaining in upper margin, 12mo., original vellum over boards, lettered in ink on spine, minor staining, contemporary ownership inscription of Venetian Jesuit, very good. Blackwell's Rare Books Sciences - 104 2013 £2000

Rhode, John *Death at Breakfast.* New York: Dodd Mead, 1936. First American edition, covers and page pages spotted, otherwise very good in dust jacket with internal and external tape mends, large chips at spine ends and along edges and heavy wear along folds. Mordida Books 81 - 457 2013 $65

Rhode, John *Open Verdict.* London: Geoffrey Bles, 1956. First edition, page endges darkened and lightly spotted, otherwise very good in dust jacket with nicks at spine ends, small chip at lower corner front panel and some faint stains on inner flaps. Mordida Books 81 - 460 2013 $175

Rhode, John *The Robthorne Mystery.* Toronto: Dodd Mead, 1934. First Canadian edition, name stamp on front endpaper, otherwise fine in very good dust jacket with chipped and frayed spine ends, chips at corners and wear along edges. Mordida Books 81 - 455 2013 $75

Rhode, John *The Venner Crime.* London: Odhams, 1933. First edition, front cover mottled otherwise fine in dust jacket with small chip at top corner of spine and at top corner of front panel. Mordida Books 81 - 455 2013 $75

Rhodes, Henry T. *The Craft of Forgery.* London: John Murray, 1934. First edition, very good in fine dust jacket, price clipped. Mordida Books 81 - 461 2013 $150

Ricardo, David *On the Principles of Political Economy and Taxation.* London: John Murray, 1817. First edition, octavo, index, some very slight foxing to prelim and final leaves, few underlinings and marginal annotations in ink and pencil, contemporary calf neatly rebacked to style, bound without two pages of publisher's ads as usual, very good, extremely scarce. Heritage Book Shop 50th Anniversary Catalogue - 80 2013 $22,500

Riccoboni, Marie Jeanne *Historie de Miss Jenny...* Paris: chez Brocas & Humblot, 1764. Reissue of 1764 4 volume first edition, 2 volumes, 12mo., frontispieces, 2 engraved plates, small tear to leading edge of volume II F1, some light browning and foxing, pretty copy in full contemporary mottled calf, ornate gilt floral spines, red and green morocco labels, slight wear to foot of volume II, small handwritten contemporary paper label on inner front boards "Bibl. Stadel". Jarndyce Antiquarian Booksellers CCIV - 251 2013 £180

Riccoboni, Marie Jeanne *Letters from Juliet Lady Catesby to her friend Lady Henrietta Campley.* London: J. Dodsley, 1780. Sixth edition, half title, good copy, full contemporary calf, double gilt ruled borders, raised and gilt banded spine with red morocco label, clean tear to one leaf without loss, contemporary ownership name of Maria Therese De Limvilan (?) on half title, later signature on inner front board recording the purchase of this volume in Dijon in 1926. Ken Spelman Books Ltd. 75 - 37 2013 £95

Rice, Anne *The Feast of All Saints.* New York: Simon and Schuster, 1979. First edition, fine in fine dust jacket. Between the Covers Rare Books, Inc. Sci-Fi, Fantasy & Horror - 306546 2013 $65

Rice, Canon *The Catholic Religion and Irish Politics.* 1890. First edition, 28 pages, printed wrappers, initialed presentation copy. C. P. Hyland 261 - 743 2013 £60

Rice, Craig *The Big Midget Murders.* New York: Simon and Schuster, 1942. First edition, pages edges slightly darkened, otherwise near fine in dust jacket with nicks at top of spine, crease tear and split with attendant one inch narrow piece missing along spine front panel fold. Mordida Books 81 - 462 2013 $200

Rice, Craig *The Sunday Pigeon Murders.* New York: Simon and Schuster, 1942. First edition, fine in dust jacket with tiny wear at spine ends and at corner, small slightly faded area at lower corner of front panel and closed tear. Mordida Books   81 - 463   2013 $200

Rice, William B. *The Los Angeles Star 1851-1864.* Berkeley: University of California Press, 1947. First edition, green cloth, very fine in slightly worn dust jacket. Argonaut Book Shop   Summer 2013 - 291   2013 $60

Rich, Adrienne *Letters Censored, Shredded, Returned to Sender or Judged Unfit to Send.* Hopewell: Pied Oxen Printers, 2009. First edition thus, one of 100 copies, 85 of which are for sale, all on Somerset Book wove paper, each signed by poet, by artist, Nancy Grossman on each of her two prints and by printer/designer, David Sellers, who has also hand numbered each copy on colophon page, page size 16 5/8 x 12 7/8 inches, 22 pages, bound by David Sellers hand sewn in tan Belgian linen over boards, headbands, author and title printed in black on pastepaper with black rule inset on front panel, title printed on marbled paper on spine, fine, designed band bound by Sellers, printed by Sellers and his son Jonathan, book set in ATF Garamond 459 and 460 and printed on 1848 Hopkinson & Cope Albion Press, 2 intaglio prints drawn on copper plates by the artist, Nancy Grossman and etched, steel faced and printed by Marjorie Van Dye at Van Deb Editions. Priscilla Juvelis - Rare Books   56 - 27   2013 $3500

Rich, Benjamin Erastus *"Truths" from Latter Day Prophets.* Chattanooga: Ben E. Rich, circa, 1908. First edition, 52 leaves, oblong octavo, string bound green cloth with title gilt stamped on front board, floral pastedown, very good, light rubbing to corners and minor spotting to front board, short inscription from previous owner to front pastedown, presentation from Rich. Ken Sanders Rare Books   45 - 28   2013 $500

Richards, George *The Aboriginal Britons a Prize Poem.* Oxford: sold by D. Prince and J. Cooke, 1791. Second edition, 24 pages, foxed, disbound. Jarndyce Antiquarian Booksellers   CCIV - 252   2013   £45

Richards, George *Modern France: a Poem.* Oxford: sold by J. Cooke, 1793. First edition, 4to., occasional foxing, expertly bound in recent quarter calf, marbled boards, vellum tips, red morocco label. Jarndyce Antiquarian Booksellers   CCIV - 253   2013   £280

Richards, Robert J. *Darwin and the Emergence of Evolutionary Theories of Mind and Behavior.* Chicago: University of Chicago, 1987. Second printing, 8vo., near fine in like dust jacket. By the Book, L. C.   37 - 68   2013 $150

Richardson, Albert D. *Beyond the Mississippi from the Great River to the Great Ocean.* Hartford: American Pub. Co., 1867. First edition, 8vo., 572 pages, illustrated titlepage, illustrations, double page map, publisher's stamped cloth, hinges tender. Second Life Books Inc.   183 - 336   2013 $135

Richardson, Charles Leland *Selected Shore Plants of Southern California.* Pasadena: Weather Bird Press, 1992. Limited edition, one of 20 copies, rare deluxe edition, tall 8vo., 86 pages, 16 signed color pochoir prints, bound loose in separate case, original full cloth by Allwyn O'Mara printed paper spine labels, matching folding print case, housed within matching drop back box, fine, with the separate set of color plates, individually signed and numbered by Gerry, along with the original drawing of 'Sea Rocket', signed by author and Gerry. Jeff Weber Rare Books   171 - 134   2013 $2000

Richardson, John *The Polar Regions.* Edinburgh: Adam and Charles Black, 1861. First edition, original blindstamped cloth, rebacked in matching maroon levant morocco, gilt, extending map (rather foxed), rather large near contemporary name on titlepage. R. F. G. Hollett & Son   Polar Exploration - 54   2013   £150

Richardson, John *Wacousta; or the Prophecy.* Philadelphia: Waldie's Select Circulating Library, April 16, 1833. to May 7th 1833. First American edition, Volume I No. 14 to Volume I. No. 17, half brown calf with marbled boards, quarto, extreme wear to edges of covers and front board almost detached, foxing to interior, especially first 20 pages. Schooner Books Ltd.   101 - 145   2013 $375

Richardson, Jonathan 1665-1745   *An Essay on the Theory of Painting.* London: printed by W. Bowyer, 1715. First edition, 8vo., little browned in places, contemporary panelled sheep, worn, especially upper corners splits at extremities of joints, early signature at head of title, Eliz Creyke, good. Blackwell's Rare Books   172 - 124   2013   £350

Richardson, Samuel 1689-1761   *Clarissa; or The History of a Young Lady...* London: printed for J. Rivington (and others), 1768-1769. Sixth edition, 8 volumes, frontispiece in all volumes, folding leaf of engraved music in volume II, 12mo., some occasional slight foxing and browning, attractive full contemporary sprinkled calf, raised bands, gilt compartments with floral motif, red and olive green gilt sprinkled calf, raised bands, gilt compartments with floral motif red and olive green gilt morocco labels, following hinge volume III little cracked at foot, slightly chipped. Jarndyce Antiquarian Booksellers   CCIV - 254   2013   £680

Richardson, Samuel 1689-1761 *The History of Sir Charles Grandison.* London: printed for S. Richardson, 1754. (1753-1754). Second edition, 6 volumes, 8vo., some occasional foxing and browning, minor marginal tears without loss, blank corner of Q8 Volume III and S5 Volume VI torn with no loss of text, B7 Volume IV torn without loss of text, full contemporary calf, gilt panelled spines, red and black morocco labels, slight chipping to head of two spines, armorial bookplate of Patrick Craufurd, Esq., contemporary ownership name of Sarah James , Stratford.   Jarndyce Antiquarian Booksellers   CCV - 229   2013   £450

Richardson, Samuel 1689-1761 *The Works.* London: printed for William Miller and James Carpenter, 1811. 187 x 127mm., 19 volumes, very pleasing contemporary polished calf, handsomely gilt flat spines with panels formed by bands of multiple fillets, each spine with panel at top featuring lozenge centerpiece and three other panels diapered with azured and solid diagonals as well as with one red and two dark blue morocco labels (four spines with small repairs to paste down loose pieces of leather), engraved frontispiece in first volume, 19th century booklabel in each volume of Josiah Wedgwood; some joints bit flaked, extremities little rubbed, isolated abrasions on covers, other minor defects but very decorative original bindings without any major problems and generally very pleasing, unambitious worming in first few leaves of one volume two minor tears into text without loss, other trivial imperfections excellent copy internally, text uniformly clean and smooth.   Phillip J. Pirages   63 - 398   2013 $1800

Richmond, Legh *The Young Cottager.* Religious Tract Society, n.d., circa, 1839. 12mo., original cloth, gilt, little rubbed, 13 woodcuts, some fingering in places, front pastedown removed.   R. F. G. Hollett & Son   Children's Books - 511   2013   £35

Richter, Carl *Biological Clocks in Medicine and Psychiatry.* Springfield: Charles C. Thomas, 1965. First edition, boards fine, library stamps and pocket removal traces internally, white dot on very good+ dust jacket spine.   Beasley Books 2013 - 2013 $50

Richter, Henry James *Day-Light: a Recent Discovery in the Art of Painting...* London: R. Ackermann, 1817. First and only edition, 8vo., pages ix, 67, hand colored woodcut illustrations, occasionally little spotted, uncut in original publisher's boards with printed label on upper cover, rebacked, little spotted and worn.   Marlborough Rare Books Ltd. 218 - 126   2013   £1250

Rickard, V., Mrs. *The Story of the Munsters at Etreux...* 1918. First edition, 11 photos, 2 sketch maps, 8vo., original quarter cloth, labels, very good.   C. P. Hyland 261 - 744 2013   £75

Ricketts, Charles 1866-1931 *Pages on Art.* London: Constable, 1913. First edition, frontispiece tissue guarad present, 8vo., original blue green cloth, backstrip blocked in green and front cover in blind, untrimmed, dust jacket frayed at head and with chip to head of backstrip panel, very good.   Blackwell's Rare Books   B174 - 290   2013   £150

Rickman, John *Journal of Captain Cook's Last Voyage to the Pacific Ocean on Discovery, Performed in the Years 1776, 1777, 1778, 1777 and 1780.* London: E. Newbery, 1785. Second edition, folding map repaired without loss and 10 engraved plates (one folding), 8vo., contemporary calf, rebacked.   Maggs Bros. Ltd.   1467 - 90   2013 £4250

Riddle, Kenyon *Records and Maps of the Old Santa Fe Trail.* West Palm Beach: John K. Riddle, 1963. First edition, 147 pages, 8 separate folded maps, photos, original blue cloth lettered gilt on front board and spine, very fine-. Argonaut Book Shop   Recent Acquisitions June 2013 - 243 2013 $125

The Ride on the Sled; or the Punishment of Disobedience. Boston: New England Sabbath School Union, 1839. 12mo., original blindstamped cloth gilt, covers little damped, neatly recased, new endpaper, 64 pages, woodcut frontispiece and tailpiece.   R. F. G. Hollett & Son   Children's Books - 20   2013   £85

Rideing, William H. *Boys Coastwise or All Along the Shore.* New York: Appleton, 1884. First edition?, 8vo., pictorial covers, black and white illustrations, very good, tight copy.   Second Life Books Inc.   183 - 377   2013 $50

Ridge, John R. *Joaquin Murieta: The Brigand Chief of California.* San Francisco: Grabhorn Press, 1932. Reprint of 1859 edition, 8 color reproductions from drawings by Charles Nahl, silhouettes by Valenti Angelo, folding facsimile broadside, cloth backed boards, light offsetting to endpapers, but very fine with plain yellow dust jacket.   Argonaut Book Shop   Summer 2013 - 293   2013 $150

Riding, Laura *Description of Life.* New York: Targ Editions, 1980. First edition, one of 350 numbered copies, signed by author, fine in lightly used glassine dust jacket, 8vo., 75 pages.   Beasley Books   2013 - 2013 $100

Ridler, Anne *The Jesse Tree.* Oxford: printed at the University Press for The Lyrebird Press and Editions Poetry London, 1972. First edition, 6/100 copies on wove handmade paper signed by author and artist, colored frontispiece and 9 illustrations, in text, all by John Piper, royal 4to., original quarter dark blue-green buckram with faintly faded gilt lettered backstrip, canary yellow boards with a Piper sketch repeated in maroon on front cover, untrimmed, board slipcase trifle split, very good.   Blackwell's Rare Books   172 - 227 2013   £175

Ridley, Humphrey *The Anatomy of the Brain.* London: Sam Smith and Benjamin Walford, 1695. 5 folding engraved plates, imprimatur leaf present before title, contemporary full calf, rebacked, pages somewhat toned in parts, some shaving of headline of dedication leaf.   James Tait Goodrich   75 - 180   2013 $13,500

Ridley, Matt *Francis Crick. Discoverer of the Genetic Code.* New York: Atlas Books/Harper Collins, 2006. Stated first edition, signed and inscribed by Ridley, fine in fine dust jacket, small 8vo.   By the Book, L. C.   37 - 31   2013 $200

Rieman, Margo *Twelve Company Dinners or the Well-Fed Guest Made Easy.* New York: Simon and Schuster, 1957. First edition, 242 pages, very good with some splitting to top of front hinge internally in clean very near fine dust jacket, signed by Rieman on half titlepage and with wraparound band from Kroch's & Brentanos, scarce signed.   Jeff Hirsch Books   Fall 2013 - 129306   2013 $50

Riesenberg, Felix *Portrait of New York.* New York: Macmillan Co., 1939. First printing, near fine, touch of browning to spine.   Between the Covers Rare Books, Inc. New York City - 293720   2013 $50

The Rightful Power of Congress to Confiscate and Emancipate. Boston: 1862. First edition, 8vo., 24 pages, original printed wrappers.   M & S Rare Books, Inc.   95 - 118   2013 $125

Riley, Athelston *Athos; or the Mountain of the Monks.* London: Longmans, Green, 1887. First edition, 8vo. map, 8 plates, text illustrations, original red cloth, very clean, scarce.   J. & S. L. Bonham Antiquarian Booksellers Europe - 9617   2013   £750

Riley, Frederic *Rhymes and Recitations for the Children. Book 2.* Settle: printed by J. W. Lambert, 1917. Original wrappers, edges little browned, illustrations by author, very scarce.   R. F. G. Hollett & Son   Children's Books - 512   2013   £30

Riley, Harvey *The Mule.* New York: Dick & Fitzgerald, 1867. First edition, 12mo., 107 pages, 14 plates, original pictorial cloth, some stains, tear in one leaf and last leaf loose, good.   M & S Rare Books, Inc.   95 - 12   2013 $135

Riley, James A. *The All-Time All-Stars of Black Baseball.* Cocoa: TK Pub., 1983. First edition, 306 pages, photos, fine in fine dust jacket with just touch of toning, inscribed by author for Cliff Kachline, scarce.   Between the Covers Rare Books, Inc.   165 - 17   2013 $850

Riley, James A. *Dandy, Day and the Devil.* Cocoa: TK Pub., 1987. First edition, illustrated wrappers, 153 pages, photos, trifle rubbed, still fine in wrappers, uncommon, signed by player Ray Dandridge on page 5 by his picture.   Between the Covers Rare Books, Inc.   165 - 74   2013 $250

Riley, James Whitcomb   1849-1916 *The Poems and Prose Sketches.* New York: Charles Scribner's Sons, 1908-1914. Homestead edition, 197 x 133mm., 16 volumes, pleasing contemporary dark brown half morocco, raised bands, spine panels with gilt ear of corn ornament, gilt millefleur patterned boards and endpapers, top edge gilt, other edges untrimmed, mostly unopened, frontispiece, each volume stamped "Private Library of Barnum B. Wixom", backstrips just a touch less dark than leather on sides (one spot just percepitbly lighter than the others), one leaf with marginal tears from rough opening (no loss), but very fine set, clean and fresh internally and in virtually unworn binding.   Phillip J. Pirages   63 - 399   2013 $1500

Riley, James Whitcomb   1849-1916 *The Raggedy Man.* Indianapolis: Bobbs Merrill, 1907. First edition, large 4to., green cloth, pictorial paste-on, fine, printed on coated paper, illustrations by Ethel Betts with 8 magnificent rich color plates and decorative border, line illustrations on each page, nice, beautiful book.   Aleph-Bet Books, Inc.   104 - 72   2013 $400

Riley, James Whitcomb   1849-1916 *While the Heart Beats Young.* Indianapolis: Bobbs Merrill, 1906. First edition, first issue with misnumbered table of contents, green cloth, very good+, 16 color plates plus color paste on picture on cover all in beautiful condition, by Ethel Franklin Betts, slight bumping to cover edge, gilt titles on spine bright.   Barnaby Rudge Booksellers   Children 2013 - 021174   2013 $95

Riley, James Whitcomb   1849-1916 *While the Heart Beats Young.* Indianapolis: Bobbs Merrill, 1906. First edition, small 4to., 16 color plates plus color paste on picture on cover, all in beautiful condition, slight bumping to cover edge, gilt titles on spine bright, first issue with misnumbered table of contents, very good+.   Barnaby Rudge Booksellers Poetry 2013 - 021174   2013 $95

Rilke, Rainer Maria   1875-1926 *For the Sake of a Single Verse.* New York: Atelier Mourlot, 1968. First edition, one of 200 copies signed by artist, out of a total edition of 950, this being number 18, with 24 lithographs by Ben Shahn on Richard de Bas handmade paper, each signed by artist, large folio, lithographs loose as issued, housed in half vellum over cloth clamshell, clamshell embossed on front with image of hand with a pen, spine of clamshell lettered gilt, fine.   Heritage Book Shop   Holiday Catalogue 2012 - 133   2013 $13,500

Ring, John *Reflections on the Surgeon's Bill: in Answer to Three Pamphlets.* printed for Hookham and Carpenter and J. Johnson, 1798. First edition, first few gatherings somewhat foxed, little browning and just staining elsewhere, 8vo., uncut in original boards, rebacked, inscribed on title "Dr. Granville with the author's best respects" and with Granville's stamp, inscribed "Dr. (John Coakley) Lettsom from the author" with Lettsom's booklabel inside front cover, sound, scarce.   Blackwell's Rare Books   Sciences - 105   2013   £1200

Ringgold, Cadwalader *A Series of Charts, with Sailing Directions, Embracing Surveys of the Farallones...* Washington: printed by Jno. T. Towers, 1852. Fourth edition, very good+, original green cloth with gilt lettering and decorated upper cover, cover edge wear, soil and sunned, spine archivally repaired to style, scattered foxing, engraved plates, 12 images and 6 folding maps in nice condition.   By the Book, L. C.   38 - 37   2013 $3000

Rink, Evald *Technical Americana: a Checklist of Technical Publications Printed before 1831.* Millwood: Kraus International Pub., 1981. First printing, large 8vo., small title vignette, index, some yellow highlighting dark mustard cloth, gilt stamped black cover an spine labels, Burndy bookplate, ownership signature, very good.   Jeff Weber Rare Books   169 - 377   2013 $200

Riordon, William L. *Plunkitt of Tammany Hall...* New York: McClure Philips and Co., 1905. First edition, red cloth with white lettering, lettering dull but readable on spine, else near fine, inscribed by subject of the book G. W. Plunkitt for Senator A P. Gorman.   Between the Covers Rare Books, Inc.   New York City - 302462   2013 $1250

The Riot at New Haven Between the Students and the Town Boys on the Night of March 17, 1854. New Haven: Richardson's Book Magazine and Newspaper Depot, 1854. First edition, 12mo., 47 pages, original printed and pictorial wrappers, removed, worn along spine and gutter, short tear without loss in fore-edge of front wrapper and first leaf, two short side lines in ink, small shelf label on first leaf, withal very good, signature "E. Tracy".   M & S Rare Books, Inc.   95 - 109   2013 $225

Riska, Augustim *Wittgenstein, the Vienna Circle and Critical Rationalism: Proceedings of the 3rd International Wittgenstein Symposium 13th to 19th Aug. 1978.* N.P.: n.p., 1978. Offprint, near fine with crease down middle, inscribed by author.   Between the Covers Rare Books, Inc.   Philosophy - 105284   2013 $50

Riss, Jacob A. *Theodore Roosevelt, The Citizen.* New York: Outlook, 1904. First edition, Beasley Books   2013 - 2013 $65

Ritchie, Anne Isabella Thackeray   1837-1919 *To Esther and Other Sketches.* London: Smith, Elder, 1869. First edition, vo., pages (viii), 394, bound with half title in later three quarter calf, spine gilt, rubbed along hinges, very good, tight, clean copy.   Second Life Books Inc.   182 - 244   2013 $150

Ritchie, Anne Isabella Thackeray   1837-1919 *Toilers and Spinsters and Other Essays.* London: Smith, Elder, 1874. First edition, 8vo., bound with half title in later three quarter calf, spine gilt, rubbed along hinges, very good, tight, clean copy.   Second Life Books Inc.   182 - 245   2013 $135

Ritson, John *Remarks, Critical and Illustrative on the Text and Notes of the Last Edition.* London: J. Johnson, 1783. 8vo., large uncut copy, attractively bound in recent marbled paper boards, paper spine label, author's name added on titlepage with date 1783 at foot.   Jarndyce Antiquarian Booksellers   CCIV - 267   2013   £350

Ritson, Joseph *An Essay on Abstinence from Animal Food, as a Moral Duty.* London: printed for Richard Phillips No. 71, St. Paul's Church Yard, 1802. First edition, 8vo., little light foxing, contemporary quarter calf, marbled boards with vellum cornerpieces, gilt banded spine with ducal gilt crest and letter 'N' at foot, red gilt morocco label, very good.   Jarndyce Antiquarian Booksellers   CCV - 230   2013   £580

Ritson, Joseph *A Select Collection of English Songs, with their Original Airs and a Historical Essay.* London: printed for F.. C. and Rivington &, 1813. Second edition, 3 volumes, slight spotting, later (1931) half dark brown calf.   Jarndyce Antiquarian Booksellers   CCV - 231   2013   £320

Rittenhouse, Jack *Disturnell's Treaty Map: The Map that was Part of the Guadalupe Hidalgo Treaty on Southwestern Boundaries, 1848.* Santa Fe: 1965. 20 pages, large folding map, gilt spine title slightly faded, else near fine, issued without a dust jacket inscribed by author to previous owner,.   Dumont Maps & Books of the West   122 - 77   2013 $125

Rittenhouse, Jack *The Man Who Owned Too Much: Maxwell's Land Grant.* Houston: 1958. Limited to 450 copies, viii, 52 pages, illustrations, boards, slipcase faded and rubbed, glassine wrapper chipped, book very good.   Dumont Maps & Books of the West   124 - 84   2013 $75

Ritzenthaler, Pat *The Fon of Bafut.* London: Cassell, 1967. First UK edition, original boards, dust jacket, 32 pages of plates, near fine.   R. F. G. Hollett & Son   Africana - 163   2013   £25

Rivard, Gilles *Competition in Transportation Policy and Legislation in Review.* Ottawa: Transportation Act Review Commission, 1993. 8vo., both volumes in blue leather with silver, leather covered slipcase, 8vo., Commissioner's copy with his name (John Gratwick) embossed on front cover both volumes, inscribed to him by Rivard, very good. Schooner Books Ltd. 105 - 160 2013 $95

Rivers, Elizabeth *Out of Bedlam.* Glenageary: Dolmen Press, 1956. First edition, 120/225 copies signed by artist, printed on Irish paper, 27 superb wood engravings by Rivers, 8vo., original stiff grey plain wrappers, backstrip gilt lettered, wood engraving blocked in red at centre of front cover, dust jacket little browned in part, very good. Blackwell's Rare Books B174 - 328 2013 £400

Rivers, John *Greuze and His Models.* London: Hutchinson & Co., 1912. First edition, 225 x 171mm., 9 p.l., including frontispiece, 282 pages, fine contemporary emerald green crushed morocco for Hatchards (done according to pencilled note at front, by Zaehnsdorf), covers gilt in Arts and Crafts design of interlocking plain rule frames with floral stamps at corners and gilt titling flanked by leaves and berries, raised bands, spine gilt in double ruled compartments with central floral sprig and three circles in each corner, gilt ruled turn-ins, gray endpapers, all edges gilt, extra engraved titlepage and 44 plates, 40 with tissue guards, spine faintly sunned to pleasing slightly darker green front free endpaper with two small very faint vestiges of tape, quite fine, handsomely bound in unworn, clean and fresh, bright inside and out. Phillip J. Pirages 63 - 69 2013 $400

Riviere, Lazare 1589-1655 *The Practice of Physick, in Seventeen Several Books...* London: printed by J. Streater and sold by G. Sawbridge, 1672. Small folio, pagination erratic, frontispiece, small marginal repairs to few leaves, few scattered spots, overall very good in 18th century full calf with red leather spine label. James Tait Goodrich 75 - 182 2013 $1795

Rivolier, Jean *Emperor Penguins.* Blek, 1956. First English edition, original cloth, gilt, dust jacket rather worn and price clipped, 22 illustrations, scarce. R. F. G. Hollett & Son Polar Exploration - 55 2013 £50

Robarts, Edith *Robinson Crusoe Retold for Little Folk.* Blackie & Son, n.d. circa, 1910. 4to., original cloth backed pictorial boards, edges and corners worn and rounded, little scratched, 6 full page color plates and fine color centrefold by John Hassall, top quarter of flyleaf cut off. R. F. G. Hollett & Son Children's Books - 270 2013 £35

Robbins, Tom *Even Cowgirls Get the Blues.* Boston: Houghton Mifflin, 1976. First edition, signed by author, fine in fine dust jacket with closed tear at top of front panel. Ed Smith Books 75 - 62 2013 $1250

Roberson, Francena *Echoes from the Ghetto.* Boston: the author, 1979. First edition, stapled gold wrappers, slightly smudged, just about fine, scarce. Between the Covers Rare Books, Inc. 165 - 253 2013 $225

Robert *Cocktails: How to Mix Them.* London: Herbert Jenkins, n.d. circa, 1930. Sixth printing, 12mo., original decorated cloth, soiling and some small stains on front board, small liquor stains on first two leaves, about very good. Between the Covers Rare Books, Inc. Cocktails, Etc. - 296779 2013 $125

Robert *Cocktails" How to Mix Them.* London: Herbert Jenkins, n.d. circa, 1935. Sixteenth edition, 12mo., green decorated cloth, tiny owner's name, else near fine, in very good example of the uncommon dust jacket with few stains. Between the Covers Rare Books, Inc. Cocktails, Etc. - 324593 2013 $175

Roberts, Austin *Birds of South Africa.* South African Bird Book Fund, 1961. Fourth edition, original cloth, gilt, dust jacket little cut down, 56 colored plates and 8 black and white plates. R. F. G. Hollett & Son Africana - 164 2013 £35

Roberts, Austin *The Mammals of South Africa.* South Africa: Trustees of "The Mammals of South Africa" Book Fund, First edition, 4to., original cloth, gilt, 24 colored plates, 54 photo plates. R. F. G. Hollett & Son Africana - 165 2013 £140

Roberts, Austin *The Mammals of South Africa.* South Africa: Trustees of The Mammals of South Africa Book Fund, 1951. First edition, 4to., modern half green levant morocco gilt with raised bands and spine label, 24 colored plates, 54 photo plates, handsome copy. R. F. G. Hollett & Son Africana - 166 2013 £250

Roberts, Brigham Henry *Life of John Taylor; third President of the Church of Jesus Christ of Latter-Day Saints.* Salt Lake City: George Q. Cannon & Sons, 1892. First edition, 468 pages, octavo, full leather, gilt stamped title on front board and backstrip, all edges gilt, 1 plates, fine, ex-libris Frederick A. Mitchell with his name in ink on front free endsheet. Ken Sanders Rare Books 45 - 39 2013 $1000

Roberts, Brigham Henry *Seventy's Course in Theology.* Salt Lake City: Deseret Book Co., Skelton Pub., Caxton Press, Deseret News, 1907-1912. 5 volumes bund in 2 books, octavo, three quarter dark reddish brown leather with black cloth covered boards and gilt stamped titles on spines, very good, books show some wear, some marginalia, books sturdy. Ken Sanders Rare Books 45 - 29 2013 $250

Roberts, Charles *Poems of Wild Life.* London: Walter Scott, 1888. 12mo., dark gray cloth with printed paper label to spine, extreme wear to top and bottom of spine and corners, light waterstains to front cover, signed by Roberts for Miss Jessie Blanchard. Schooner Books Ltd. 105 - 21 2013 $75

Roberts, Howard *The Story of Pro Football.* New York: Rand McNally, 1953. First edition, fine in very good or better dust jacket with short edge tears and spine bit tanned. Between the Covers Rare Books, Inc. Football Books - 73548 2013 $75

Roberts, Jack *Celeste L'Hippotoame Rose.* Paris: Tolmer, 1926. 8vo., color lithographed cover and text mounted on slightly larger decorative board, fine, pink and black lithographs printed on thick grey paper. Aleph-Bet Books, Inc. 104 - 486 2013 $1500

Roberts, James *Introductory Lessons, with Familiar Examples in Landscape, for the use of Those who are Desirous of Gaining some Knowledge of the Pleasing Art of Painting in Water Colours.* London: printed by W. Bulmer and Co. for the author and sold by G. and W, Nicol, 1800. 8 engraved plates, of which 5 are hand colored, pages browned, large but faint dampmark throughout (not visibly affecting the coloring on the plates), darker stain in top margin, first and last leaves just slightly rubbed at fore edge, leaf D1 bound following E1, 4to., modern half black calf, marbled boards, red morocco lettering piece, sound, scarce. Blackwell's Rare Books B174 - 125 2013 £1500

Roberts, John B. *Surgery of Deformities of the Face Including Cleft Palate.* New York: William Wood, 1912. Original green cloth, some rubbing and wear, internally very good, 273 figures and engravings. James Tait Goodrich 75 - 183 2013 $595

Roberts, John S. *Africa and African Travel Including the Life and Travels of Dr. Livingstone, Stanley, Cameron and the Ancient and Modern Explorers.* W. P. Bennett & Co., n.d. circa, 1875. First one volume edition, 3 volumes in 1, large thick 4to., modern quarter calf gilt, spine rather faded and spotted, all edges gilt, tinted litho title, titlepage for volume 1 only (as issued), double page colored map, 30 full page plates, numerous text woodcuts, couple of short edge tears, otherwise very good. R. F. G. Hollett & Son Africana - 167 2013 £175

Roberts, Keith *The Chalk Giants.* London: Hutchinson, 1974. First edition, fine in fine dust jacket, especially crisp copy. Between the Covers Rare Books, Inc. Sci-Fi, Fantasy & Horror - 319787 2013 $125

Roberts, Kenneth *Northwest Passage.* Collins, 1938. Original cloth, gilt, lettering trifle dulled, maps on endpapers, edges little spotted. R. F. G. Hollett & Son Polar Exploration - 56 2013 £20

Roberts, Kenneth *Trending Into Maine.* Boston: Little Brown, May, 1938. First Wyeth edition, limited to 1075 numbered copies signed by author and artist, 4to., white cloth spine, blue cloth, fine in original plain paper wrapper and slipcase, paper label (case toned on backs trip, few spots, else tight and very good+), 15 beautiful color plates and endpapers by N. C. Wyeth, with extra suite of plates in original envelope, scarce thus. Aleph-Bet Books, Inc. 104 - 595 2013 $2500

Roberts, Verne L. *Bibliotheca Mechanica.* New York: Jonathan Hill, 1991. One of 1100 copies, 4to., frontispiece, 49 illustrations, quarter gilt stamped beige cloth over illustrated paper backed boards, fine. Jeff Weber Rare Books 169 - 379 2013 $150

Roberts, W. Adolphe *The Haunting Hand.* New York: Macauley, 1926. First edition, ex-library copy from private lending library, library marks on endpapers, extremities of boards rubbed and worn, fair only, lacking dust jacket. Between the Covers Rare Books, Inc. 165 - 254 2013 $250

Robertson, David *Reports of the Trials of Colonel Aaron Burr... for Treason, and for a Misdemeanor in Preparing the Means of a Military Expedition Against Mexico...* Philadelphia: Hopkins and Earle, 1808. Second edition, 8vo., 2 volumes, original two-toned boards, uncut, sound, boards nearly loose, spines rubbed, remnants of labels only. M & S Rare Books, Inc. 95 - 43 2013 $375

Robertson, H. R. *Plants We Play With.* Wells Gardner, Darton & Co., n.d., Original pictorial cloth, spine faded and little rubbed, 40 plates. R. F. G. Hollett & Son Children's Books - 513 2013 £25

Robertson, J. E. *The Life of David Livingstone, the Great Missionary Explorer.* London: Walter Scott, 1882. 6 tinted plates, original tan cloth gilt, boards little speckled by damp, all edges gilt, tinted lithograph title, 6 tinted plates. R. F. G. Hollett & Son Africana - 168 2013 £35

Robertson, James A. *Gaelic Topography of Scotland and What It Proves.* Edinburgh: William P. Nimmo, 1869. First edition, 8vo., large foldout map in color, repaired in places, but with several further tears and protruding little from textblock at lower edge, titlepage in red and black, later blue half calf, blue cloth boards, gilt title to spine, top edge gilt, spine faded, some marks and scratches, still good, inkstamp of Wm. Jackson Bookbinders, Aberdeen, embossed stamp of Glenrinnes, Dufftown, Banfshire. Unsworths Antiquarian Booksellers 28 - 195 2013 £50

Robertson, Joseph Clinton *London, or Interesting Memorials of Its Rise, Progress and Present State.* London: printed for T. Boys, 1823. First edition, 157 x 93mm., 3 volumes, recent attractive retrospective three quarter calf over marbled boards, raised bands, each spine with red morocco label, edges untrimmed, 7 woodcut head and tailpieces, five engraved plates, large folding map of London, expertly backed with heavy stock, map little soiled and tiny spot of loss near fold, prelim leaves in first volume perhaps washed, fore margin of 3 dozen leaves in first volume with small brown spots, other minor browning and foxing here and there, still excellent set, text generally clean and fresh, unworn sympathetic bindings. Phillip J. Pirages 63 - 322 2013 $450

Robertson, William 1721-1793 *An Historical Disquisition Concerning the Knowledge Which the Ancients Had of India...* London: printed for Cadell and Davies et al, 1812. Sixth edition, 222 x 140mm., without half title, handsome contemporary sprinkled calf, flat spine attractively gilt in panels divided by multiple decorative gilt rules, panels with large central fleuron, spine with one red and one green morocco label, 2 large engraved foldout maps, Danish library stamp of Bibliotheket paa Glorup; joints with short thin cracks at head, corners little bumped, two inch tear edge of one map (no loss), occasional minor foxing, smudges or offsetting, really excellent copy, binding solid, lustrous and with only minor wear, text especially clean, bright and fresh. Phillip J. Pirages 63 - 401 2013 $450

Robertson, William 1721-1793 *History of America.* London: printed by A. Strahan for A. Strahan, T. Cadell and W. Daivesn, 1800. Ninth edition, 218 x 130mm., pleasing contemporary tree calf, expertly and attractively rebacked with complementary modern calf, raised bands flanked by double gilt rules, red and black morocco labels, marbled endpapers, four large engraved folding maps and one folding plate, bookplate of Fred(eric)k L. Hutchins and engraved armorial bookplate of Frederick Edwin Eyre; corners very worn, boards with several small abrasions and patches of lost patina, opening and closing leaves bit foxed, faint offsetting in text, one map rather wrinkled and two small tears along folds, still appealing copy, text fresh and clean, well restored bindings quite solid and very attractive on shelf. Phillip J. Pirages 63 - 402 2013 $400

Robertson, William 1721-1793 *History of the Reign of Charles the Fifth.* London: Routledge & Co., 1857. First edition, BAL first issue with titlepage of volume 1 with period present after the word 'street' in imprint and comma present on titlepage of volume 2 after the word 'abdication', 8vo., name on top of each titlepage, full calf, raised bands, gilt on spine, rubbed, marbled endpapers, very good set. Second Life Books Inc. 183 - 338 2013 $150

Robertson, William 1721-1793 *The Works.* London: printed for T. Cadell et al, 1821. 10 volume, 214 x 135mm., once very handsome and still quite appealing contemporary black polished calf, covers with simple rule border, raised bands, spines attractively gilt in compartments with Romantic-style frames formed by volutes, fleurons and small tools, two burgundy morocco labels, top edge gilt, frontispiece portraits, 6 folding maps and one folding illustrated plate, front pastedowns with bookplate of Butler University Library, joints and extremities little rubbed (though well masked with dye), two spine ends very slightly damaged, one leaf with tear length of page neatly repaired without loss, engraved matter somewhat foxed and with variable offsetting, other minor foxing here and there, still quite pleasing set, text fresh and clean, bindings entirely solid especially lustrous and with no serious wear. Phillip J. Pirages 63 - 403 2013 $275

Robin Hood *Robin Hood.* New York: McLoughlin Bros., 1895. Large 4to., stiff pictorial wrappers, die-cut in shape of Robin Hood, very good+, 4 full page and one double page chromolithographs and with great color cover. Aleph-Bet Books, Inc. 105 - 502 2013 $200

Robinson, Emily Parker *Blacks in the Deep South.* New York: Vantage Press, 1974. First edition, owner name written on top and bottom of page edges, else fine in rubbed, very good plus dust jacket with tiny nick and tear, nicely inscribed by author, very scarce. Between the Covers Rare Books, Inc. 165 - 255 2013 $175

Robinson, Helen *Sally Dick and Jane.* Chicago: Scott Foresman and Co., 1962. oblong small 4to., pictorial wrappers, slightest bit of cover soil and crease on rear cover else fine, illustrations in color by Bob Childress. Aleph-Bet Books, Inc. 105 - 179 2013 $275

Robinson, Hugh *Shcolae Wintoniensis Phrases Latinae.* London: printed for A. M. to be sold by R. Boulter, 1670. Seventh edition, 8vo., titlepage laid down and page 347 repaired, small loss to bottom corner of page 201 affecting a few letters, occasional Ms notes and ink blots, possibly some blanks bottom corner of page 201, affecting a few letters, occasional MS notes and ink blots, possibly some blanks excised to rear with notes covering the remaining stubs, otherwise having survived schoolboy usage relatively unscathed, recent dark brown slightly scuffed morocco, blind tooled, red label with gilt title to spine, marbled endpapers, ownership inscription (P?) Johannes Higgins (Rev.?) Waterford 1724. Unsworths Antiquarian Booksellers 28 - 44 2013 £400

Robinson, John *An Account of Sueden, together with an Extract of the History of that Kingdom.*   London: printed for Tim Goodwin at the Queen's Head, 1694. First edition, first leaf bars half title on recto and an ad on verso, 8vo., lower outer corner of F4 torn with slight loss not affecting text, 18th century marbled boards, vellum spine, some rubbing to boards, slight wear at foot of spine, withdrawn stamp of Worcester College at head of titlepage and on inner front board, early ownership name of W. Gower.   Jarndyce Antiquarian Booksellers   CCIV - 28   2013   £220

Robinson, John *An Account of Sueden; Together with an Extract of the History of that Kingdom.*   London: Tim Goodwin, 1717. Third edition, 12mo., contemporary brown speckled calf, spine rubbed.   J. & S. L. Bonham Antiquarian Booksellers   Europe - 8421   2013   £200

Robinson, Lennox *Pictures in a Theatre.*   Dublin: Abbey Theatre, 1947. First edition, 8vo., original wrappers, inscribed by author on front cover "Lennox Robinson August 1947" and further inscription from Eileen Crowe.   Maggs Bros. Ltd.   1442 - 281   2013   £75

Robinson, Lewis *Every Patient His Own Doctor; or the Sick Man's Triumph Over Death and the Grave.*   London: printed for J. Cooke, 1779? 8vo., slightly dusted, clean tear without loss to leading edge of one leaf, original wrappers, rubbed and worn, inscribed on inside rear wrapper "Thomas Beedon Junior, His Book March the 14th 779".   Jarndyce Antiquarian Booksellers   CCIV - 255   2013   £225

Robinson, Nicholas *A New System of the Spleen, Vapours and Hypochondriack Melancholy...*   London: printed for A. Bettesworth, W. Innys and C. Rivington, 1729. Full contemporary English paneled and polished calf, front joint cracked and starting to split, part of spine label lacking, spine gilt.   James Tait Goodrich   75 - 181   2013 $1500

Robinson, Stanford F. H. *Celtic Illuminative Art in the Gospel Books of Durrow, Lindisfarne and Kells.*   Dublin: 1908. First edition, ex-library in library cloth, frontispiece, 51 plates, cloth, very good.   C. P. Hyland   261 - 747   2013   £190

Robinson, W. W. *The Indians of Los Angeles. Story of the Liquidation of a People.*   Los Angeles: Glen Dawson, 1952. First edition, one of 200 copies, 12mo., 42 pages, gray cloth, printed paper cover label, slight darkening to foot of spine, fine copy.   Argonaut Book Shop   Recent Acquisitions June 2013 - 244   2013 $125

Robinson, W. W. *Maps of Los Angeles from Ord's Survey of 1849 to the End of the Book of the Eighties.*   Los Angeles: Dawson's Bookshop, 1966. First edition, number 160 fo 380 copies, signed by Robinson, quarto, 90 pages, 27 reproductions of maps (some tipped-in, many folding, one in rear pocket), decorated gray cloth, gilt lettered red leather label, small oval bookplate, very fine.   Argonaut Book Shop   Summer 2013 - 295   2013 $350

Robinson, Walter *The Landlord's Pocket Lawyer or the Complete Landlord and Tenant...*   printed for S. Bladon, 1780. First edition, 8vo., little light browning and spotting, contemporary half calf, boards rather rubbed and corners worn, spine sometime polished and just slightly chipped at ends, good, very scarce.   Blackwell's Rare Books   172 - 125   2013   £450

Robinson, William Heath *The Adventures of Uncle Lubin.*   New York: Brentanos, 1902. First US edition, 8vo., pictorial cloth stamped in blue, green and white, expertly recased, else clean and very good+, color frontispiece, 55 full page black and whites and 72 vignettes plus pictorial endpapers, rare.   Aleph-Bet Books, Inc.   104 - 490   2013 $3000

Robinson, William Heath *The Child's Arabian Nights.*   London: Grant Richards, 1903. 1 page initial ads, half title, color frontispiece, full page color illustrations, vignettes in text, binding cracked but firm at page 46-47, original pictorial paper boards, red cloth spine, boards little marked and dulled, slightly rubbed at extremities, faded inscription on leading f.e.p., good, scarce.   Jarndyce Antiquarian Booksellers   CCV - 232   2013   £350

Robinson, William Heath *Heath Robinson On Leather.*   London: Connolly Bros. n.d., Folio, grey simulated leather wrappers, pictorial covers, 48 pages, some cover soil and wear, very good, drawings by Robinson, uncommon.   Aleph-Bet Books, Inc.   105 - 504   2013 $700

Robinson, William Heath *My Line of Life.*   London: Blackie & son, 1938. First edition, 4to., pictorial cloth, 198 pages, slightest bit of soil to spine ends, else fine in dust jacket (frayed at spine ends, else very good), 16 half tone plates, 11 full page line illustrations.   Aleph-Bet Books, Inc.   104 - 491   2013 $400

Robson, W. J. *Silsden Primitive Methodism.*   Silsden: Briggs Bros., 1910. First edition, original ribbed green cloth, profusely illustrated, flyleaves little spotted and browned, scarce.   R. F. G. Hollett & Son   Wesleyan Methodism - 25   2013   £85

Roche-Mazon, J. *Le Mariage De La Tour Eiffel.*   Paris: Boivin, 1931. Tall 4to., cloth backed metallic silver pictorial boards, very good+, color illustrations by V. Le Campion.   Aleph-Bet Books, Inc.   105 - 43   2013 $600

Roche, Paul *Enigma Variations And.* Gloucester: Thornhill Press, 1974. First edition, 8vo., original blue cloth, dust jacket, signed by Duncan Grant who designed the cover and by author, near fine in price clipped dust jacket.   Maggs Bros. Ltd.   1460 - 357   2013   £350

Rochfort, John A. *Business and General Directory of Newfoundland 1877...* Montreal: Lovell Printing and Publishing, 1877. 8vo., light blue paper covered boards with leather spine, 18 pages ads, spine very worn and chipped, boards have some foxing, interior very good.   Schooner Books Ltd.   101 - 63   2013 $225

Rock, J. F. *The Indigenous Tree of the Hawaiian Islands.* Rutland: Charles E. Tuttle and Co. and Lawai, Kaui, Hawaii: Pacific Tropical Botanical Garden, 1974. New edition, profusely illustrated with photographic plates, gilt lettered dark green cloth, owner's name on end, very fine, pictorial dust jacket and printed slipcase.   Argonaut Book Shop   Summer 2013 - 296   2013 $300

Rockwell, Donald S. *Women of Achievement.* New York: House of Field, 1940. First edition, Press numbered edition, number 206, 4to., 213 pages, white cloth, heavily embossed, stamped in gilt, cover worn at corners and ends of spine, spine split along part of its length, one hinge tender, some marginal chips to leaves, otherwise very good, signed by Rockwell and photographer, G. Maillard Kesslere.   Second Life Books Inc.   182 - 201   2013 $75

Rockwell, John *Sinatra, an American Classic.* New York: Rolling Stone/Random House, 1984. First edition, 4to., fine in fine dust jacket but for short tear at flap fold.   Beasley Books   2013 - 2013 $65

Rocque, John *An Exact Survey of the City's of London, Westminster... and the Country 10 Miles Round London (and) A Plan of the Cities of London...* Lymphe Castle: H. Margary, 1971. Large folio, double page title, double page explanation, 16 double page map sheets, 1 double page map, double page sheets A1-H3, the whole contents stub mounted, original red cloth with paper label on upper cover.   Marlborough Rare Books Ltd.   218 - 127   2013   £250

Roddenberry, Gene *The Making of Star Trek.* New York: Ballantine, 1970. Sixth printing, paperback original, owner label of Fred Durant III with small bookstore stamp, near fine with light wear, nicely inscribed by author for Durant, marvelous association.   Between the Covers Rare Books, Inc.   Sci-Fi, Fantasy & Horror - 43900   2013 $500

Rodell, Marie *Mystery Fiction: Theory and Technique.* New York: Duell, Sloan & Pearce, 1843. First edition, fine in dust jacket.   Mordida Books   81 - 449   2013 $75

Rodriguez De Castro, Jose *Biblioteca Espanola.* Madrid: En la Imprenta Real de la Gazeta, 1781-1786. First edition, half titles, final errata leaf in volume 2, folio, 18th century mottled sheep, decorated gilt with morocco lettering pieces, edges stained red, sizes not uniform, some dampstaining, mainly to edges of first and last two dozen leaves in volume 1 and top edge in volume 2, minor worming in blank margins, 19th century institutional stamp on first text page in each volume, unidentified branded ownership mark on top edges, otherwise leaves quite bright.   Kaaterskill Books   16 - 69   2013 $5000

Roederer, Joannis Georgii *Elementa Artist Obstetriciae in Usum Auditorum Denuo Edidit.* Gottingen: Apvd Vidvan Abrami Vandenhoeckii, 1766. Third Latin edition, Engraved title, folio, early quarter calf and patterned boards, rubbed, corners bumped, some light foxing to text.   James Tait Goodrich   S74 - 198   2013 $595

Roethel, H. *Wassily Kandinsky: Das Graphische Werk.* Koln: DuMont, 1970. First edition, one of a total edition of 1500 numbered copies on Phonix Kunstdruck and Zerkal-Butten paper, text in German, large stout 4to., 504 pages, hundreds of plates, blue cloth, gilt stamping, dust jacket and red boards slipcase, overall almost as new.   Gemini Fine Books & Arts., Ltd.   Art Reference & Illustrated Books - 2013 $1500

Roethke, Theodore *Party at the Zoo.* New York: Crowell Collier, 1963. First edition, 4to., pictorial cloth, slight edge rubbing, very good+, illustrations in color by Al Swiller.   Aleph-Bet Books, Inc.   104 - 493   2013 $225

Roethke, Theodore *Sequence Sometimes Metaphysical. Poems.* Iowa City: Stone Wall Press, 1963. First edition, one of 60 specially bound copies, signed by author and artist, small 4to., original quarter leather and pictorial boards, publisher's slipcase, very fine, illustrations by John Roy.   James S. Jaffe Rare Books   Fall 2013 - 132   2013 $3500

Roger, Noelle *He Who Sees.* London: George G. Harrap & Co., 1935. First English edition, boards slightly bowed some very light scattered foxing, else about fine in very attractive near fine dust jacket with rubbed tear at crown, rare in jacket.   Between the Covers Rare Books, Inc.   Sci-Fi, Fantasy & Horror - 50066   2013 $1000

Rogers, Bruce   1870-1957 *Venetian Printers: a Conversation on the Fourth Day of the Bibliographical Decameron of Thomas Frognall Dibdin with Annotation.* Mt. Vernon: Press of William Edwin Rudge, 1924. Limited to 223 copies, original printed wrappers, cover edges bit bumped and worn, else very good.   Jeff Weber Rare Books   171 - 102   2013 $85

Rogers, Fred B. *Bear Flag Lieutenant. The Life Story of Henry L. Ford (182-1860) Together with some Reproductions of Related and Contemporary Paintings by Alexander Edouart.* San Francisco: California Historical Society, 1951. First edition in book form, one of 250 numbered copies, 87 pages, printed in red and black, frontispiece portrait, 5 plates, tan cloth lettered in red, tippped in bookplate, very fine. Argonaut Book Shop Summer 2013 - 297 2013 $100

Rogers, James Edwin Thorold 1823-1890 *Speeches on Questions of Public Policy by John Bright, M.P.* 1868. First edition, 2 volumes, portrait, 8vo., cloth, good, sound. C. P. Hyland 261 - 154 2013 £70

Rogers, Julia *Little Red Riding Hood.* Rochester: Stecher, 1929. Large square 4to., pictorial wrappers, (16) pages, including covers, light wear, very good+, full page color lithographs by Frances Brundage. Aleph-Bet Books, Inc. 105 - 102 2013 $200

Rogers, Samuel *Italy, a Poem. (and) Poems.* London: T. Cadell, 1830. 1834., 197 x 140mm. 2 separately published volumes (though often sold together), quite appealing light tan polished calf by Tout & Sons (stamp signed on verso of front free endpaper), covers with plain gilt rule frame, raised bands, spines richly gilt in compartments filled with fleurons and curls, each backstrip and two red morocco labels (title in second compartment and thin strip with publication information at bottom), gilt turn-ins, marbled endpapers, all edges gilt, 54 fine engraved vignettes, joints and extremities little rubbed, intermittent minor foxing to head margin, otherwise fine, especially clean, fresh and bright, solid, lustrous and attractive bindings. Phillip J. Pirages 63 - 405 2013 $200

Rogers, Samuel *Italy, a Poem.* London: Edward Moxon, 1838. 297 x 213mm., 114 fine engraved plates, 54 of these with additional state, being proof 'before letters' along with one proof plate of engraved tailpiece and four proofs on India paper, large paper copy; very striking dark green morocco with extraordinarily elaborate gilt and inlaid decoration, for the Guild of Women Binders (stamp-signed), covers with exceptionally animated and complex design featuring central stippled cruciform radiating a controlled riot of gilt tooling and more than 600 inlays of red, moss green, gray and ochre morocco forming flowering vines and geometrical shapes, raised bands, spine panels each decorated with six inlaid flowers and multiple teardrop tools, second panel with gilt tooling, azure morocco doublures with attractive Art Nouveau frame featuring delicate gilt tooling and inlaid dark green sidepieces, orange dot accents, vellum endleaves with tiny gilt heart at each corner, all edges gilt, very fine velvet lined modern dark green morocco folding box, occasional faint foxing to margins and to about one-third of the plates, one plate with old repaired two inch tear to tail edge, in amazing condition, text fresh and bright, margins immense, plates richly impressed, unusually exuberant binding, especially lustrous and entirely unworn. Phillip J. Pirages 61 - 107 2013 $24,000

Rogers, Samuel *The Pleasures of Memory, with other Poems.* London: printed by Thomas Bentley... for T. Cadell, 1801. 12mo., very clean crisp copy in fine contemporary full sprinkled calf with gilt borders, multiple gilt bands to spine decorated with gilt lyre motifs, black morocco label, marbled endpapers and pastedowns, neat contemporary inscription. Ken Spelman Books Ltd. 75 - 54 2013 £75

Rogers, Samuel *Poems.* London: t. Cadell, 1834. First edition thus, engravings by Turner and Sothard, later 19th century dark blue morocco, gilt crests to head and tail of spine and both boards, all edges gilt, some slight foxing, recent bookplate. Ken Spelman Books Ltd. 75 - 97 2013 $95

Rogerson, Ian *Barnett Freedman, the Graphic Art.* Upper Denby: Fleece Press, 2006. One of 500 copies on Monadnock Dulcet mouldmade paper, numerous color printed reproductions of artist's work throughout, including tipped in double page plates, pages 256, small folio, original pink cloth, printed label, pocket on rear pastedown with DVD of documentary "The King's Stamp", fine. Blackwell's Rare Books 172 - 277 2013 £225

Rohde, Eleanour Sinclair *The Old English Gardening Books.* London: Martin Hopkinson, 1924. First edition, 8vo. illustrations, uncut, gray paper over boards, cloth spine, top edge little spotted, some foxing, very good in tight copy, somewhat worn, neatly mended dust jacket. Second Life Books Inc. 183 - 339 2013 $175

The Rohrschach Evalograph. Beverly Hills: Western Psychological Services, 1954. 28 pages, stapled self wrappers printed in black and red, slight toning, probably from over roiled printing Press, else fine. Between the Covers Rare Books, Inc. Psychology & Psychiatry - 300140 2013 $250

Roland, Philip *1957 Foto Features.* St. Louis: The School Press, 1957. First edition, thick 12mo., stapled orange printed wrappers, 179 pages, small spots on front wrapper, very good. Between the Covers Rare Books, Inc. 165 - 28 2013 $500

Rolewinck, Werner *Fasciculus Temporum.* Venice: Erhard Ratdolt 28 May, 1484. Third Ratdolt edition, first issue, folio, Gothic letter, numerous woodcuts (some repeated) and diagrams in text, two large woodcut white-vine initials (one thirteen line and one ten-line), early 20th century Continental full red calf richly gilt with multi colored calf onlays, gilt board edges, turn-ins ruled in gilt with two narrow bands on onlaid black morocco, all edges gilt marbled, endpaper, first leaf with repaired tear on recto, not affecting text on verso, small marginal wormhole repaired on first 15 leaves, not affecting text, another small wormhole repaired on first 39 leaves, just touching few letters, first and last leaves browned, overall excellent copy. Heritage Book Shop 50th Anniversary Catalogue - 81 2013 $13,500

Rolf, Gero *Teatro Comico di Burattini.* Pub. by Arnoldo Mondadori, 1949. First edition, oblong folio, 45 ff., pictorial wrappers, fine and unused in dust jacket that when removed unfolds into a giant poster (repaired at folds), bold primary color illustrations, the book includes pages to create 27 puppets operated by hand as well as 7 plays and accessories needed to create a puppet threatre.   Aleph-Bet Books, Inc.   105 - 483   2013 $875

Rolle, Andrew F. *The Lost Cause. The Confederate Exodus to Mexico.* Norman: University of Oklahoma Press, 1965. First edition, 8 photographic portraits and views, map, black cloth, very fine, pictorial dust jacket.   Argonaut Book Shop   Summer 2013 - 298   2013 $60

Rollin, Charles *The Ancient History of the Egyptians, Carthaginians, Assyrians, Babylonians, Medes and Persians, Macedonians and Grecians.* London: John & Paul Knapton, 1749. Third edition, 12 volumes, 12mo., frontispiece, final ad leaf, volume VIIII; slight loss to margin of lower corner of titlepage, volume IV; contemporary mottled calf, raised bands, compartments ruled in gilt, red morocco labels, small wormhole to foot of spine, volume XI, corners slightly bumped with some slight rubbing, very attractive, original Scottish binding from the Invercauld Library.   Jarndyce Antiquarian Booksellers   CCV - 233   2013   £750

Rollin, Charles *The Ancient History of Egyptians, Carthaginians, Assyrians, Babylonians...* Boston: printed & published by Samuel Walker, 1823. 2 volumes, contemporary tree calf, corners little rubbed, spine stamped in blind and gold, black morocco lettering pieces, 2 engraved titles, yellow mottled edges + 16 engraved plates, 7 engraved maps, with 1 1/2 worm track on one cover of each binding, unusually fine, text free of foxing, only one plate little browned.   Howard S. Mott Inc.   262 - 123   2013 $350

Rollins, William *Notes on X-Light.* Boston: pub. by the author, 1904. First edition, very good++, original dark grey cloth, 8vo., gilt lettered front board, spine, with owner bookplate, offsetting to endpapers, minimal cover edge wear.   By the Book, L. C.   38 - 43   2013 $500

A Roman Story. London: printed in the Year, 1711. First edition, 8vo., later marbled boards, brown leather label, gilt lettering, some light foxing, very good.   The Brick Row Book Shop   Miscellany Fifty-Nine - 17   2013 $475

Romen, Jean Joseph Therese *L'Inoculation Poeme en Quatre Chants.* Amsterdam & Paris: Chez Lacomee, 1773. First edition, Engraved frontispiece, 8vo. original full tan mottled calf, gilt paneled spine, all edges marbled, light rubbing to binding, internally fine, from the library of Dr. Blanchard with his bookplate, tipped post card from Paris (1891) with note by A. Corlieu in regards to this book.   James Tait Goodrich   S74 - 217   2013 $495

Ron, Moshe *Catalog of the Sidney M. Edelstein Collection of the History of Chemistry, Dyeing and Technology.* Jerusalem: Jewish National and University Library Press, 1981. 4to., 182 pages, frontispiece, illustrations, beige cloth, gilt stamped cover and spine titles, Burndy bookplate, fine.   Jeff Weber Rare Books   169 - 383   2013 $145

Ronayne, C. O'L. *History of the Earls of Desmond and Earl of Cork & Sir Walter Raleigh in Munster.* 1929. First edition, 8vo., cloth, very good, Eoin 'The Pope' O'Mahony's copy with his bookplate, very good.   C. P. Hyland   261 - 410   2013   £150

Ronayne, J. P. *How "Liberal" England Governs Catholic Ireland as Exemplified in the County of Cork.* 1873. 8vo., 42 pages, large folding chart, disbound but good.   C. P. Hyland   261 - 750   2013   £75

Rondelet, Guillaume *Liber de Piscibus marinis...* Lugduni: apud Matthiam Bonbomme, 1554-1555. many illustrations, 2 volumes bound together in 17th century full vellum, spine hand lettered with floral drawing on lower spine, later endpapers, lower front joint just starting to split, early marginalia in brown ink, title missing in upper right with partial loss (top 4mm) of two letters of title lower outer portion of title has paper defect in blank margin, similar in next leaf, text toned throughout, 217-242 pages and index leaves have brown stain in outer blank margin.   James Tait Goodrich   75 - 184   2013 $6500

Rooke, Octavius *The Channel Islands: Pictorial Legendary and Descriptive.* London: L. Booth, 1856. First edition, 8vo., text illustrations, contemporary green morocco, gilt, handsome copy.   J. & S. L. Bonham Antiquarian Booksellers   Europe - 8349   2013   £350

Roosevelt, Theodore   1858-1919   *African Game Trails.* New York: Scribner's, 1910. One of 500 large paper copies, signed by author, printed on Ruisdael paper, 2 volumes, 8vo., original half pigskin, minor rubbing at corners, uncut, few blank corners of text leaves offset from pigskin corners and some fading of blindstamped title on spine volume I, otherwise fine.   Howard S. Mott Inc.   262 - 124   2013 $7500

Root, Sidney *Primary Bible Questions for Young Children.* Atlanta: Franklin Steam Publishing House, 1864. Third edition, 16mo., 80 pages, original printed wrappers, spine and one corner chipped, very brown, but quite good.   M & S Rare Books, Inc.   95 - 78   2013 $250

Roscoe, H. E. *A Treatise on Chemistry.* New York: D. Appleton, 1878-1889. 8 volumes, frontispiece, illustrations, frontispiece and title detached from volume I, some inner hinges cracked, brown cloth, gilt stamped spine titles, extremities worn, including fraying of corners and spine ends, ex-library copies with usual markings and defects, previous owner's signatures, fair, rare.   Jeff Weber Rare Books   169 - 381   2013 $250

Roscoe, Thomas *The Landscape Annual for 1836. The Tourist in Spain, Andalusia.* London: Robert Jennings, 1836. First edition, seventh volume of the annual, 21 engraved plates and 10 wood engravings, small 8vo., green morocco stamps in blind, gilt titles on spine, all edges gilt, very good, joints rubbed, head of spine worn, light scattered foxing, small booksellers ticket, owner's stamp on free endpaper, contents crisp.   Kaaterskill Books   16 - 70   2013 $400

Roscoe, Thomas *The Landscape Annual for 1838. The Tourist in Spain and Morocco.* London: Robert Jennings, 1838. First edition, 9th volume of the Annual, 21 engraved plates, small 8vo., green morocco stamped in bind, gilt titles on spine, all edges gilt, small chip at head of spine, else very good, joints rubbed, light scattered foxing, owner's stamp on free endpaper, plates crisp.   Kaaterskill Books   16 - 71   2013 $400

Roscoe, William *Butterfly's ball and Grasshopper's feast.* Boston: Anne & David Bromer, 1977. Limited to 150 copies, this one of 25 deluxe copies, bound in full leather by Gray Parrot and containing a pocket in back with extra prints of woodcut illustrations, printed letterpress by Sarah Chamberlain at her press, she has signed and lettered this copy, 6 x 5 cm., full green leather stamped in gilt, (24) pages, from the collection of Donn W. Sanford.   Oak Knoll Books   303 - 73   2013 $850

Roscoe, William *The Butterfly's Ball and the Grasshopper's Feast.* London: printed for J. Harris, Jan. 1st, 1807. First edition, first issue with (18)06 watermark on final leaf, fine, hand colored illustrations after drawings by W. Mulready, morocco backed cloth slipcase, later marbled wrappers, frontispiece, title and 13 unnumbered leaves, printed on one side only.   Howard S. Mott Inc.   262 - 125   2013 $500

Roscoe, William *The Nurse, a Poem.* Liverpool: McCreery for Cadell and Davies, London, 1800. Second edition, 8vo., little worn, contemporary calf, rebacked, 3 small engravings.   Second Life Books Inc.   183 - 341   2013 $325

Roscoe, William *Strictures on Mr. Burke's Two Letters Addressed to a Member of the Present Parliament.* London: printed for G. G. J. and J. Robinson, 1796. First edition, outer leaves trifle soiled, pages 79, 8vo., disbound, good, rare.   Blackwell's Rare Books   172 - 126   2013   £575

The Rose-Poseie Book. Thomas Nelson, 1920. 12 full page color plates and 12 monochrome by Anne Anderson, decorated pages of text, printed on opposing pages, versos blank, original cream boards with pictorial onlay, little marked, corners trifle bruised.   R. F. G. Hollett & Son   Children's Books - 11   2013   £85

Rose, Barbara *Claes Oldenburg.* New York: Museum of Modern Art, 1970. First edition, oblong padded vinyl binding, checklist laid in, about very good with some offsetting to front panel and other slight wear, internally clean, signed and dated by Oldenburg in 1973 and additionally inscribed by Rose on titlepage.   Jeff Hirsch Books   Fall 2013 - 129137   2013 $500

Rose, Billy *Wine, Women and Words.* New York: Simon and Schuster, 1948. First edition, limited to unspecified number of copies signed by author, this number 1451, octavo, illustrations by Salvador Dali, inscription from Henry Miller for Pierre Sicari, quarter gold cloth over pictorial boards, spine printed in black, top edge black, red endpapers, red silk placemarker, boards bit rubbed, edges with some light wear and corners bumped, small stain top of fore-edge, very good.   Heritage Book Shop   Holiday Catalogue 2012 - 34   2013 $1500

Rose, Gene *Yosemite's Tioga Country. A History and Appreciation.* Yosemite National Park: Yosemite Association, 2006. First edition, quarto, profusely illustrated with vintage photos, maps, brown cloth, gilt, very fine in pictorial dust jacket.   Argonaut Book Shop   Recent Acquisitions June 2013 - 247   2013 $60

Rose, Paul *The Manchester Martyrs; the Story of a Fenian Tragedy.* Lawrence & Wishart, 1970. First edition, 8vo., cloth, illustrations, dust jacket, very good.   C. P. Hyland   261 - 751   2013   £30

Rose, Susan *Medieval Naval Warfare 1000-1500.* London and New York: Routledge, 2002. First edition, xvi, 155 pages, 5 plates, 3 maps, black cloth, gilt stamped cover and spine titles, Burndy bookplate, fine.   Jeff Weber Rare Books   169 - 385   2013 $75

Rosen, George *Journal of the History of Medicine and Allied Sciences.* New York: Henry Schuman, 1947-1972. 20 volumes, tall 8vo. various paginations, illustrations, navy buckram, gilt spines, bookplate of Elmer Belt, very good.   Jeff Weber Rare Books   172 - 138   2013 $750

Rosenberg, Isaac *Poems.* London: William Heinemann, 1922. First edition, 8vo., original black cloth, lower and fore edges uncut, one long crease to front cover, otherwise excellent copy, inscribed by T. S. Eliot for Ottoline Morrell.   Maggs Bros. Ltd.   1460 - 262   2013   £2500

Rosenberg, Isaac *Poems.* London: Heinemann, 1922. First edition, 500 copies printed, frontispiece, foolscap 8vo., original black cloth, printed label, tail edges rough trimmed, dust jacket with backstrip panel darkened, head and tail rubbed and with internal professional restoration to split along front fold of backstrip panel, very good.   Blackwell's Rare Books   B174 - 291   2013   £485

Rosenberg, Jakob *Rembrandt.* Cambridge: Harvard University Press, 1948. First edition, 2 volumes, attractive rose colored half morocco for Lauriat's of Boston (stamp signed), raised bands, spines gilt in compartments with central fleuron, top edge gilt, color frontispiece, 281 black and white plates by Rembrandt, spine slightly and uniformly darkened, mild soiling to cloth on one board, one corner little rubbed, otherwise fine set, signs of use to text or bindings. Phillip J. Pirages   63 - 397   2013 $150

Rosenblatt, Julia Carlson *Dining with Sherlock Holmes.* Indianapolis: Bobbs Merrill, 1976. First edition, fine in dust jacket.   Mordida Books   81 - 153   2013 $100

Rosenthal, Franz *Science and Medicine in Islam: A Collection of Essays.* Aldershot: Variorum, 1990. 8vo., blue cloth, gilt stamped cover and spine titles, fine, ownership signature.   Jeff Weber Rare Books   169 - 387   2013 $125

Rosenthal, Leonard *The Kingdom of the Pearl.* London: Nisbet, 1920. Limited to 675 numbered copies, 4to., quarter white cloth, grey pictorial boards, top edge gilt, slight wear to tip, near fine, illustrations by Edmund Dulac with cover design, decorative endpapers plus 10 very beautiful tipped in color plates with tissue guards, very lovely. Aleph-Bet Books, Inc.   105 - 208   2013 $1000

Rosenthal, Mark *Jasper Johns Work Since 1974. Exhibition at the Philadelphia Museum of Art Oct 23 1988 - January 8 1989.* Philadelphia: Thames and Hudson in association with Philadelphia Museum of Art, 1988. First edition, signed by Johns, fine, in fine dust jacket, 75 illustrations, 36 in color, and one foldout triptych, 4to., 112 pages, scarce signed.   By the Book, L. C.   36 - 11   2013 $1000

Ross, Albert *A Black Adonis.* New York: G. W. Dilingham, 1895. First edition, contemporary quarter black cloth and paper covered boards, possibly rebound from wrappered issue, hinge little tender, private lending library stamp on titlepage, nice, very good or better.   Between the Covers Rare Books, Inc.   165 - 329   2013 $300

Ross, D. K. *The Pioneers and Churches, the Pioneers and Families of Big Brook and West Branch.* New Glasgow: Hector Pub. Co., n.d., 8vo., card cover with taped spine, photo illustrations, covers slightly darkened, otherwise very good.   Schooner Books Ltd.   102 - 87   2013 $75

Ross, Frederick *Contributions towards a History of Driffield and the Surrounding Wolds District in the East Riding of the County of York.* Driffield: 1898. First edition, very good, original decorative cloth, some rubbing to edges and head and tail of spine, scarce.   Ken Spelman Books Ltd.   73 - 72   2013   £50

Ross, James *They Don't Dance Much.* Boston: Houghton Mifflin Co., 1940. First edition, contemporary owner name, cloth on spine, bit foxed and soiled, very good in edgeworn, very good dust jacket with modest chip at foot and some nicks and short tears at extremities, signed by author, extremely uncommon thus.   Between the Covers Rare Books, Inc.   Mystery & Detective Fiction - 81720   2013 $3000

Ross, John *Narrative of a Second Voyage in Search of a North-West Passage and of a Residence in the Arctic Regions During the Years 1829-1833.* A. W. Webster, 1835. First edition, large paper issue, large 4to., modern half blue levant morocco gilt with raised bands and double contrasting spine labels, 30 engraved plates, maps and charts (of which 8 are hand colored and final chart is large folding map), one plate cut down to plate-mark and re-laid, little faint dampstaining to some top margins, few neat repairs, little loss to corner of folding map, but handsome large copy.   R. F. G. Hollett & Son   Polar Exploration - 57   2013   £950

Ross, Patricia *The Magic Forest.* New York: Knopf, 1948. Stated first edition, 8vo., 128 pages, cloth backed pictorial boards, fine in dust jacket, illustrated in full colors by Carlos Merida.   Aleph-Bet Books, Inc.   104 - 346   2013 $275

Ross, Sam *The Sidewalks are Free.* New York: Farrar, Straus & Cudahy, 1956. First edition, boards slightly soiled, else fine in attractive, near fine dust jacket with rubbing and tiny nicks near crown.   Between the Covers Rare Books, Inc.   Mystery & Detective Fiction - 83293 2013 $65

Ross, Sam *The Tight Corner.* New York: Farrar, Straus and Cudahy, 1956. First edition, about fine in very good dust jacket with chipping at spine ends, nicely inscribed by author to Max Lamb.   Between the Covers Rare Books, Inc.   Mystery & Detective Fiction - 71263   2013 $275

Rossetti, Christina 1830-1894 *Goblin Market.* London: George G. Harrap & Co., 1933. One of 410 copies (400 for sale), signed by artist, 241 x 165mm., illustrated endpapers, half title and titlepage, text illustrations and 4 color plates all by Arthur Rackham, titlepage partly printed in green, original publisher's limp vellum, original (?) tissue dust jacket, original slipcase with printed paper label on top, slight fraying and tiny chips missing along top of front panel of dust jacket, otherwise almost amazing copy, even slipcase being unusually clean and volume itself virtually pristine.   Phillip J. Pirages   63 - 381   2013 $2250

Rossetti, Christina 1830-1894 *Poems by Christina Rossetti.* London: Blackie & Son, n.d., 1910. Thick 4to., white cloth with extensive gilt decoration, top edge gilt, very fine in original pictorial dust jacket, illustrations by Florence Harrison with 36 magnificent mounted color plates (on heavy stock) 34 full page black and white illustrations plus many black and whites in text, magnificent copy, rare in dust jacket. Aleph-Bet Books, Inc. 104 - 278 2013 $1800

Rossetti, Christina 1830-1894 *The Prince's Progress and Other Poems.* London: Macmillan, 1866. First edition, half title, frontispiece, vignette title, additional printed title, untrimmed in original green glazed cloth by Burn & Kirby's decorated and lettered in gilt, John Sparrow's small booklabel, very good, bright copy. Jarndyce Antiquarian Booksellers CCV - 234 2013 £850

Rossetti, Dante Gabriel 1828-1882 *Ballads and Narrative Poems.* London: published by Ellis & Elvey, 1893. One of 310 paper copies, out of a total edition of 316 copies, octavo, printed in red and black in Golden type, decorative woodcut borders and initials, printed by William Morris, original full limp, yapp edges, original silk ties, spine lettered gilt, slightest crease to vellum on spine, previous owner Brion Stilwell bookplate on front pastedown, small purple ownership stamp of Helen Ladd Corbett also on front pastedown, housed in custom black slipcase, near fine. Heritage Book Shop   Holiday Catalogue 2012 - 88 2013 $300

Rostand, Edmond *Cyrano De Bergerac. A Play in Five acts.* Mount Vernon: Peter Pauper Press, 1941. Small 4to., fully bound n red leather, gilt stamping, very good. Beasley Books 2013 - 2013 $100

Roth, Philip *Portnoy's Complaint.* New York: Random House, 1969. First trade edition, fine, minor spot to front endpaper, near fine dust jacket with standard price clip (price present) and touch of sunning to spine. Ed Smith Books 78 - 55 2013 $125

Rothenstein, William *Men and Memories.* New York: Coward McCann Inc., 1931-1932. First editions, 2 volumes, 244 x 159mml., striking black three quarter morocco by Whitman Bennett for Stewart Kidd (stamp signed), raised bands, spines gilt in compartments with centerpiece of artist's palette and brushes, geometrically patterned paper boards and endpapers, top edge gilt, other edges rough trimmed (second volume largely unopened), 96 collotype plates, just touch of wear to joints and extremities, paper boards, lightly chafed, paper clip impression to front free endpaper of volume I (also affecting pastedown and flyleaf), otherwise quite appealing set in fine condition, bindings especially lustrous and with only minor rubbing, text quite clean and fresh. Phillip J. Pirages 63 - 408 2013 $225

Rothmann, Johann *Keipomantia; or the Art of Divinity by the Lines and Signatures Engraven in the Hand of Man, by the Hand of Nature...* London: printed by J. G. for Nathaniel Brooke, at the Angell in Corne Hill, 1652. First edition, frontispiece, illustrations, small internal hole affecting 2 leaves (pages 107-110) and 4 words, contemporary sheep double ruled blind tooling, corners bumped, hinges slightly rubbed, faint sign of later label removed from spine, armorial bookplate of Mark Dineley, good in original binding. Jarndyce Antiquarian Booksellers CCV - 235 2013 £2250

Rotsler, William *Zandra.* Garden City: Doubleday and Co., 1978. First edition, fine in fine dust jacket, as new. Between the Covers Rare Books, Inc. Sci-Fi, Fantasy & Horror - 320015 2013 $65

Rottenberg, Dan *Fight On, Pennsylvania: a Century of Red and Blue Football.* Philadelphia: University of Pennsylvania, 1985. First edition, quarto, fine in very near fine dust jacket with little rubbing and few very tiny tears, moderately uncommon. Between the Covers Rare Books, Inc. Football Books - 71433 2013 $60

Roucher-Deratte, Claude *Lecon Physiologico-Meteorologique sur les Constitutions des Saisons, Relativement a l'Economie Animale et Vegetale.* Montpellier: Auguste Ricard L 11 floreal an XII, 1804. First edition, some light dampstaining in gutters of few gatherings, last two leaves repaired in inner margin, 8vo., largely unopened, contemporary pink wrappers handwritten paper label on spine, spine bit frayed, very good, rare. Blackwell's Rare Books Sciences - 107 2013 £700

Rourke, L. *Men Only in the Air.* London: C. Arthur Pearson, 1941. First reprint, original blue stiff wrappers, pages 96, frontispiece, line drawing, tailpieces, scattered foxing, mainly to half title and final leaf, very scarce. R. F. G. Hollett & Son Children's Books - 523 2013 £45

Rourke, Thomas *The Scarlet Flower.* London: Ivor Nicholson & Watson, 1934. First English edition, fine in dust jacket. Mordida Books 81 - 464 2013 $375

Rousseau, Jean Jacques 1712-1778 *Les Confessions de J. J. Rousseau suivi des Reveries du Promeneur Solitaire Tome Premier (-Second).* Geneva: 1782. First edition of the first six books of the Confessions and the Reveries of a Solitary Walker, 2 volumes, octavo, woodcut headpieces and vignette and arabesque tailpiece, typographic ornaments, contemporary full polished mottled calf, spines decorated in gilt red and green morocco spine labels, French curl pattern endpapers, green silk markers, edges stained red, small paper flaws to volume I f. I7-8; marginal tear to volume II f. 2D1 (not affecting text), scattered foxing, heavier on two or three gatherings in each volume, some minor scuffing to binding, near fine overall early letterpress bookplates in each volume of M. Gautherin.   Heritage Book Shop   50th Anniversary Catalogue - 82   2013 $7500

Rousseau, Jean Jacques 1712-1778 *The Confessions.* Philadelphia: Gebbie and Co., 1902. One of 53 copies for sale (of a total of 56) of the Astral Edition, this #9, 12 parts in 6 volumes, 310 x 230mm., vignette on limitation page, title vignettes and vignette headpieces and tailpieces as well as 48 fine plates by Maurice Leloir, printed on fine Japon vellum, titles in red and black, striking reddish brown inlaid and gilt Spanish calf, covers with ornately framed gilt panel featuring prominent gray morocco inlaid fleur-de-lys in center and smaller inlays at corners, spines in compartments featuring inlaid fleur-de-lys of white and green morocco (four per spine), beautiful green morocco doublures panelled in gilt and featuring quite large and very striking spray of lilies in gilt and 7 inlays of red or white, ivory watered silk endleaves, top edges gilt, other edges untrimmed, this set especially designed and bound for Alfred Raymond, very fine, exceptionally attractive.   Phillip J. Pirages   61 - 117   2013 $7500

Rousseau, Jean Jacques 1712-1778 *The Cunning-Man.* London: printed for T. Becket and P. A. de Hondt, 1766. First edition in English, earliest issue with misprint 'published' in publisher's ads, 8vo., modern brown quarter morocco, gray-green boards, gilt lettering, half title and leaf of publisher's ads for other works by Rousseau, half title and final blank little soiled, very good.   The Brick Row Book Shop   Miscellany Fifty-Nine - 36   2013 $650

Rousseau, Jean Jacques 1712-1778 *Emilius; or a Treatise of Education.* Edinburgh: printed by A. Donaldson, 1763. 3 volumes, some browning to paper, very slight chips to edges of titlepages of two volumes, bound in rather plain recent full calf, raised and gilt banded spines, red labels.   Ken Spelman Books Ltd.   75 - 25   2013   £195

Rousseau, Jean Jacques 1712-1778 *Emilius and Sophia; or a New System of Education.* London: printed by H. Baldwin, 1783. 12mo., 4 volumes, engraved frontispieces, 2 engraved plates, bound without half titles, paper flaw to foot of volume III, B2 with loss to a catchword, one corner not trimmed and neatly folded back, contemporary tree calf gilt banded spines, red morocco labels, hinges cracked, spines rubbed and slightly chipped at head and tail.   Jarndyce Antiquarian Booksellers   CCIV - 256   2013   £380

Rousseau, Jean Jacques 1712-1778 *Letters on the Elements of Botany Addressed to a Lady.* B. & J. White, 1794. Fourth edition, 8vo., hardcover, very good. Barnaby Rudge Booksellers Natural History 2013 - 019961   2013 $125

Routledge's Japanese Almanac. Boston: W. B. Clark & Carruth, 1886. Printed in New York, copyright by Joseph Blamire, 24mo., cloth backed pictorial boards, fine, 8 beautiful full page chromolithographs and with smaller chromos on every text page, all in Japanese style, very lovely.   Aleph-Bet Books, Inc.   105 - 340   2013 $325

Rowan, A. B. *The Old Countess of Desmond...* University Press, 1860. First edition, one of 100 copies, 50 pages, photo frontispiece, very good.   C. P. Hyland   261 - 752   2013   £240

Rowan, Richard Wilmer *Spy and Counter Spy: The Development of Modern Espionage.* New York: Viking, 1928. First edition, spine and page edges darkened, otherwise very good in fine contemporary.   Mordida Books   81 - 465   2013 $135

Rowe, C. Francis *The Currency and Medals of Newfoundland.* Toronto: J. Douglas Ferguson Historical Research Foundation, 1983. Quarto, cloth, illustrations, very good in like dust jacket.   Schooner Books Ltd.   101 - 65   2013 $95

Rowe, Nicholas *The Dramatick Works of Nicholas Rowe, Esq.* printed and sold by T. Jauncy, 1720. First collected edition, Volume 1 and 2, 3 engraved plates in each volume, 12mo., contemporary calf, boards ruled in gilt, rebacked in slightly different shade, red morocco lettering pieces, new endpapers, slightly rubbed, good.   Blackwell's Rare Books B174 - 126   2013   £200

Rowe, Nicholas *The Works...* London: W. Lowndes et al, 1792. 12mo., portrait frontispiece, 11 plates (1 folding creased at gutter margin), all offset, some light spotting, early 19th century straight grain dark green roan, backstrips with raised bands, red morocco lettering pieces in second compartments, volume numbers lettered direct in third, remainder gilt panelled with convolvulus corner ornaments and central flower spray, triple gilt gillet border on sides, gilt roll on board edges and turn-ins, marbled endpapers, all edges gilt, minor rubbing to joints, very good. Blackwell's Rare Books 172 - 127 2013 £250

Rowling, J. K. *Harry Potter and the Chamber of Secrets.* New York: Scholastic, 1999. First American edition, fine, crisp copy in fine dust jacket. Ed Smith Books 78 - 56 2013 $500

Rowling, J. K. *Harry Potter and the Philosopher's Stone and the Chamber of Secrets and the Prisoner of Azkaban and the Goblet of Fire, and the Order of the Phoenix and The Half Blood Prince and the Deathy Hallows. With the Beedle in the Bard.* London: Bloomsbury, 1999-2007. First printings, deluxe editions, clothbound with pictorial onlays, all edges gilt, fine without dust jackets as issued, with a collector's edition of The tales of Beedle the Bard (London: Children's High Level Group, 208), leatherbound Beedle is in drawstring bag, which, with 10 illustrations by Rowling, are housed together in large box made to look like a textbook, which is contained in publisher's sleeve. Ken Lopez Bookseller 159 - 171 2013 $3800

Rowling, J. K. *Harry Potter and the Prisoner of Azkaban.* Bloomsbury, 1999. Uncorrected proof, owner's signature, foolscap 8vo., original green and white wrappers, covers printed in black, cover printed "Uncorrected Proof Copy", publication data printed on rear cover, corners little creased, very good. Blackwell's Rare Books B174 - 292 2013 £1200

Rowntree, B. Seebohm *Poverty and Progress. A Second Social Survey of York.* London: Longmans, 1941. First edition, very good, original gilt lettered dark blue cloth, dust jacket little worn, inscribed 'a gift from Arnold Rowntree, Ernest Taylor, John Harvey, Oct. 1941'. Ken Spelman Books Ltd. 73 - 54 2013 £35

Rowson, Susanna *Charlotte Temple. A Tale of Truth.* Concord: New Hampshire, 1815. 2 volumes in one, 132 pages, some browning to paper, contemporary calf backed boards, gilt banded and lettered spine has some insect damage at foot, corners bumped. Ken Spelman Books Ltd. 75 - 74 2013 £95

Roy, Bernard *Le Buffon des Enfants: Les Oiseaux Exotiques.* Paris: Marcus, 1948. First edition, Square 4to., pictorial boards, near fine, stunning full page color illustrations by Felix Lorioux. Aleph-Bet Books, Inc. 104 - 330 2013 $400

Roy, J. *History of Canada for the Use of Schools and Families.* Montreal: H. Ramsay, 1856. Original blind-stamped cloth, rebacked in matching cloth, new endpapers, titlepage rather browned, few scattered spots, but very good, sound copy. R. F. G. Hollett & Son Children's Books - 524 2013 £65

Roy, Jessie Hailstalk *Pioneers of Long Ago.* Washington: Associated Publishers, 1951. First edition, illustrations by Lois Mailou Jones, fine, lacking dust jacket. Between the Covers Rare Books, Inc. 165 - 257 2013 $100

Roy, William *The Military Antiquities of the Romans in the North of Britain and Particularly, Their Ancient System of Castramentation...* London: pub. by order and expense of the Society of Antiquaries, 1793. Elephant folio, 51 plates of maps and plans, some double page or folding as called for, internally bright, only occasional very light spotting limited to text rather than plates, few finger smudges to title and half title, contemporary half dark brown morocco with marbled boards, gilt and blind tooling to spine, more recent red morocco label, somewhat worn, boards rubbed, endpapers flat with signs of previous creases, ownership inscription of R. Morison? Unsworths Antiquarian Booksellers 28 - 125 2013 £750

Royal Folly; or the Danger of Being Tempted by Harlots. printed for Thomas Robins, 1740. Half title, little minor marginal worming, pages 23, 8vo, disbound, loose. Blackwell's Rare Books 172 - 68 2013 £300

The Royal Illuminated Book of Legends. Edinburgh: William P. Nimmo, n.d. circa., 1870. Oblong large 8vo., original cloth backed pictorial boards, edges and corners little worn, 18 colored plates, accompanying text, piece torn from lower margin of one text leaf, lower edge of one leaf rather worn, new endpapers. R. F. G. Hollett & Son Children's Books - 702 2013 £150

Royal Munster Fusiliers Association *Journal.* No. 12, 13, 15-22(?), Spring, 1998. - Autumn 2003, Lacking spring 1999. TLS from Hon. Sec. 1998 acknowledging photos, 10 issues with annual reports, etc., fine. C. P. Hyland 261 - 719 2013 £35

Royal Society *Medical Essay and Observations Relating to the Practice of Phsyic and Surgery abridg'd from the Philosophical Transactions.* London: printed by J. Newbery, 1745. 4 folding engraved plates, 5 folding engraved plates, 2 volumes, recently bound in quarter calf and marbled boards, very pleasing binding. James Tait Goodrich 75 - 168 2013 $1295

Roy's Revenge and Friends and Friendship. New York: T. Nelson, 1880. 24mo., frontispiece, brown cloth, stamp from L. E. Kinsey Druggist and Bookseller. Barnaby Rudge Booksellers Children 2013 - 021391 2013 $60

Rubens, Alfred *A History of Jewish Costume.* London: Peter Owen Ltd., 1981. Revised edition, 4to., pages xvi, 221, (1), profusely illustrated, original cloth, dust jacket, some shelfwear.   Marlborough Rare Books Ltd.   218 - 131   2013   £75

Rubin, Gerald M. *Genetic Transformation of Drosophila with Transposable Element Vectors.* American Assoc. for the Advancement of Science, 1982.   Offprint from Science Volume 281, 4to., fine in self wrappers.   By the Book, L. C.   37 - 69   2013 $100

Rubin, Gerry R. *Durban 1942: a British Troopship Revolt.* Hambledon Press, 1992. First edition, original cloth, gilt, dust jacket.   R. F. G. Hollett & Son   Africana - 172   2013   £30

Rudavsky, Tamar *Divine Omniscience and Omnipotence in Medieval Philosophy: Islamic, Jewish and Christian Perspectives.* Dordrecht, Boston & Lancaster: D. Reidel, 1985. Blue cloth, gilt stamped spine title, dust jacket chipped, ownership signature, very good, scarce in jacket.   Jeff Weber Rare Books   169 - 392   2013 $100

Ruddock, Red *Arch Bridges and their Builders 1735-1835.* Cambridge: Cambridge University Press, 1979. First edition, 4to., half tone frontispiece, 203 illustrations, figures, brown cloth, gilt stamped red spine label, dust jacket, bookplate of Burndy Library, fine.   Jeff Weber Rare Books   169 - 393   2013 $275

Rudolphi, Carolo Asmund *De Ventriculis Cerebri Gryphiae Typis I.* H. Eckhardt, 1795. 4to., later marbled boards, leather label, uncut, well margined, some light foxing, very uncommon.   James Tait Goodrich   75 - 185   2013 $595

Rudwin, Maximilian Joseph *Devil Stories: an Anthology.* New York: Alfred A. Knopf, 1921. First edition, variant (probably later) binding, octavo, original decorated light reddish brown cloth, front and spine panels stamped in black, running Borzoi stamped in black on rear panel, all edges trimmed.   L. W. Currey, Inc. Fall Sampler Sept. 2013 - 144478   2013 $2500

Ruess, Everett *On Desert Trails with Everett Ruess.* El Centro: Desert Magazine Press, 1950. Second edition, 80 pages, quarto, tan cloth with title gilt stamped on front board, very good/near fine, few small nicks at corners of jacket, small piece of jacket chipped at foot of rear panel, scotch tape on reverse of jacket at head and foot and near folds, overall clean jacket.   Ken Sanders Rare Books   45 - 48   2013 $400

Ruess, Everett *On Desert Trails with Everett Ruess.* El Centro: Desert Magazine Press, 1950. Second edition, Advance Readers copy? 80 pages, quarto, tan publisher's wrappers with title printed on front panel, very good, minor discoloring to spine and surrounding area of panel, prints and photos, warmly inscribed by author's brother, Waldo Ruess for Jim and Stephanie Ure.   Ken Sanders Rare Books   45 - 49   2013 $300

Ruffin, Edmund *Anticipations of the Future, to Serve as Lessons for the Present Time.* Richmond: J. W. Randolph, 1860. First edition, 12mo., original cloth, library bookplate and slip on front endpapers, but very nice, rare.   M & S Rare Books, Inc.   95 - 333   2013 $1250

Ruffman, Allan *Ground Zero. A Reassessment of the 1917 Explosion in Halifax Harbour.* Halifax: Nimbus Pub. Ltd. & The Gorsebrook Research Inst., 1994. 9.5 x 6.5 inches, 8vo. binding slightly brittle due to illness.   Schooner Books Ltd.   104 - 113   2013 $75

Ruiz, Ramon *Facsimile Edition of California's First Book; Reglamento Provicional Printed at Monterey in 1834...* San Francisco: Designed and printed by Lawton Kennedy for the Book Club of California, 1954. Limited to 400 copies, printed in red, blue and black, 16 page facsimile in rear pocket, spine faded, else very fine.   Argonaut Book Shop Recent Acquisitions June 2013 - 248   2013 $75

Rules and Orders to be Observed and Kept by the Members of the Friendly Society, Established on the 7th Day of January 1828... Hull: printed by T. Topping 51 Lowgate, 1829. 12 pages, some old and rather faint waterstaining, recent marbled wrappers, rare.   Ken Spelman Books Ltd.   75 - 91   2013   £120

Rumford, Benjamin Thompson, Count *Proposals for Forming by Subscription in the Metropolis of the British Empire, a Public Institution for diffusing the Knowledge and Facilitating the General Mechanical Inventions and Improvements and for Teaching, by Courses of Philosophical Lectures and Experiments, The Application of Science to the Common Purposes of Life.* London: n.p., 1799. uncut, unopened, disbound, 8vo., printed on wove paper.   Jarndyce Antiquarian Booksellers   CCIV - 257   2013   £350

Rumi, Jalaluddin Mohammad *Divan e Shams.* New York: Vincent FitzGerald & Co., 1996. Signed limited edition, one of 50 copies, all on handmade papers by Dieu Donne and BFK Rives, bound by Craig Jensen at BookLab in ivory linen in coptic style binding with brown and gray endpapers that are etchings of various leaves, housed in silver silk over boards custom made clamshell box, title in palladium on spine and engraved ornament on front panel of box, fine, extremely beautiful, with graphic works and one sculpture (glass laid in to back of custom made clamshell box) by 15 artists, some mounted, some on multiple or folded leaves, some on colored or translucent paper, most signed in pencil by respective artist. Priscilla Juvelis - Rare Books 55 - 9 2013 $15,000

Rumi, Jalaluddin Mohammad *Letters.* New York: Vincent FitzGerald, 1987. One of 75 copies, each signed by artist, Agnes Murray and translator, Zahra Partovi, 3 colored lithographs each containing 12 plates, bound by Partovi accordion style, turquoise Japanese paper over boards with label on front panel on buff handmade paper with title printed in gold gilt, housed in salmon colored paper envelope with black silk tie and silver sealing wax, fine, calligraphy is by Jerry Kelly and printed by John Hutcheson, lithographs by Murray and editioned by Murray and Partovi at Bob Blackburn's Printmaking Workshop, page size is 9 1/3 x 6 1/2 inches, beautiful book. Priscilla Juvelis - Rare Books 56 - 9 2013 $700

Rumi, Jalaluddin Mohammad *The Reed.* New York: Vincent FitzGerald & Co., 1989. One of 50 copies only on handmade J. B. Green paper, each signed by artist and translator, illustrations by Susan Weil with 18 original hand colored line etchings, mirrored on verso in colored mezzotints by Shigemitsu Tsukaguchi, text hand printed by Dan Keleher at Wild Carrot Letterpress in Diotima type by Gudrun Zapf-von Hesse with calligraphy by Jerry Kelly and Zahra Partovi, 9 1/2 x 6 1/2 inches, bound gray Dieu-Donne handmade paper over boards in Japanese style binding, title in silver gilt on lighter gray paper label bordered in green paper on front cover, housed in matching gray Dieu-Donne paper folding box with ebony and silk ribbon closure, English text printed in slate grey over delicate grey-green lines of the etch on gray paper, Persian text with its calligraphy printed on gray paper, etchings by Susan Weil. Priscilla Juvelis - Rare Books 56 - 10 2013 $3500

Rundell, Maria *Flora and Thalia: or Gems of Flowers and Poetry.* London: Henry Washbourne, 1835. First edition, 12mo., 26 hand colored plates, green cloth, lower cover little loose, extremities worn. Barnaby Rudge Booksellers Poetry 2013 - 020230 2013 $125

Ruppli, Michel *The Savoy Label. A Discography.* Westport: Greenwood Press, 1980. First edition, fine, issued without dust jacket. Beasley Books 2013 - 2013 $100

Rusch, Kristine Kathryn *Pulphouse: the Hardback Magazine. Issue Two.* Eugene: Pulphouse Pub., 1988. First edition, one of 25 publisher's copy (appropriately marked "PC"), full leather gilt, fine in fine slipcase, full leather, signed by all contributors. Between the Covers Rare Books, Inc. Sci-Fi, Fantasy & Horror - 297823 2013 $300

Rush, Benjamin 1745-1813 *An Enquiry into the Effects of Public Punishments Upon Criminals and Upon Society.* Philadelphia: printed: London: reprinted for C. Dilly, 1787. 8vo., some spotting, modern boards, good. Blackwell's Rare Books B174 - 128 2013 £1250

Rush, Benjamin 1745-1813 *An Oration, Delivered Before the American Philosophical Society Held in Philadelphia on the 27th of Feb. 1786...* Philadelphia: printed: London: reprinted for C. Dilly, 1786. Second edition, few spots here and there, 8vo., modern boards, good. Blackwell's Rare Books B174 - 127 2013 £750

Rushdie, Salman *Shame.* London: Jonathan Cape, 1983. First edition, signed by author, fine, crisp copy in fine. Ed Smith Books 78 - 57 2013 $300

Ruskin, John 1819-1900 *Dame Wiggins of Lee and Her Seven Wonderful Cats: A Humorous Tale...* Sunnyside, Orpington: George Allen, 1885. First edition, small 8vo., original illustrated green cloth, endpapers split, long tear in back free endpaper, some wear to extremities and one gathering little loose, pencilled address in child's hand to rear endpaper, otherwise good, illustrations by Kate Greenaway, inscribed by Greenaway dated 1886. Maggs Bros. Ltd. 1460 - 369 2013 £300

Ruskin, John 1819-1900 *Dame Wiggins of Lee and Her Seven Wonderful Cats.* Sunnyside Orpington, Kent: George Allen, 1885. First edition with Kate Greenaway illustrations, large paper copy limited to 400 copies issued on fine Whatman paper, charming woodcuts including 4 illustrations by Kate Greenaway, 4to. brown gilt pictorial cloth, 20 pages, fine. Aleph-Bet Books, Inc. 105 - 291 2013 $750

Ruskin, John 1819-1900 *Deucalion Collected Studies of the Lapse of Waves and Life of Stones.* Orpington, Kent: George Allen, 1879-1880. 8 parts in 2 volumes, 212 x 141mm., 11 plates in form of drawings by Ruskin, two of them in several colors and two in blue; lovely chestnut brown morocco, handsomely gilt by Doves Bindery (turn-ins at back signed and dated '19 C-S 09'), covers with French fillet border enclosing two rectangular strapwork frames with semicircular interlacing at top and bottom, inner frame interlaced further with two strapwork triangles that form a six-sided star at center, each point of star surmounted with small open circles (and top and bottom point with additional three petalled floral design), star surrounding a garland composed of two leafy sprays, raised bands, spines gilt in compartments featuring concentric square frames enclosing prominent daisy within lozenge, turn-ins with rules and petalled floral cornerpieces, all edges gilt and with stippled gauffering, original front wrappers as well as extra titlepages, bound in at back of each volume, very dark blue full morocco pull-off suede-lined cases in the shape of a book (just slightly rubbed) with raised bands and gilt titling; pastedown of first volume with bookplate of Dr. Samuel L. Siegler, pastedown of second volume with bookplate of "E. R. McC." (Edith Rockefeller McCormick) and with vestige of removed Siegler bookplate, beautifully bound set in pristine condition, even original wrappers in perfect shape.   Phillip J. Pirages   61 - 104   2013 $10,000

Ruskin, John 1819-1900 *The Ethics of the Dust.* New York: John Wiley & Son, 1866. First edition, from the library of the first woman physician, Elizabeth Blackwell, octavo, Blackwell's signature and date of 1866, bookplate, publisher's full purple cloth, decoratively ruled in blind, spine lettered gilt, dampstaining and wrinkling to cloth, spine sunned and soiled, head and tail of spine chipped some foxing to blanks, otherwise very clean, Blackwell's inscription, custom half morocco clamshell, very good.   Heritage Book Shop   Holiday Catalogue 2012 - 15   2013 $3500

Ruskin, John 1819-1900 *King of the Golden River.* London: George Harrap, 1932. Limited to 550 numbered copies for sale, signed by artist, slim 8vo., full limp vellum, fine, publisher's slipcase (soiled, lacking 1 inch piece off edge), pictorial endpapers 4 fine color plates, beautiful red and black textual illustrations. printed on high quality paper.   Aleph-Bet Books, Inc.   105 - 492   2013 $1250

Ruskin, John 1819-1900 *The Queen's Gardens.* Manchester: printed in Aid of the St. Andrews Schools Fund, 1864. First printing, 221 x 144mm., 19, (1) pages, very fine dark blue morocco by Doves Bindery (signed and dated 1911), covers with gilt fillet border and central oval wreath of tudor roses and rose leaves, raised bands, spine with gilt fillet compartments containing vertical titling, gilt ruled turn-ins, all edges gilt, slightly scuffed felt lined tan morocco pull-off box by Riviere & Son, bookplate of Edith Rockefeller McCormick, usual minor offsetting to free endpapers from turn-ins, otherwise sparkling copy.   Phillip J. Pirages   61 - 105   2013 $2500

Ruskin, John 1819-1900 *Unto this Last.* Edinburgh: printed at the Ballantyne Press and published by George Allen, 1902. One of 400 copies (of an edition of 411), printed in black with shoulder titles, ornate wood engraved initial letters and large initial letters, all printed in red, large floral wood engraved border to five pages, crown 8vo., original limp clean cream vellum with yapped edges, backstrip gilt lettered, gilt design to front cover, faint endpaper foxing, gift inscription, pink silk ties, untrimmed, very good.   Blackwell's Rare Books   B174 - 321   2013   £200

Russ, Joanna *And Chaos Died.* Boston: Gregg Press, 1978. First hardcover edition, octavo, cloth.   L. W. Currey, Inc.   Utopian Literature: Recent Acquisitions (April 2013) - 140096   2013 $650

Russell, Bertrand 1872-1970 *The Australasian Journal of Psychology and Philosophy: Volume I Number 2 June 1923.* Sydney: Australasian Association of Psychology and Philosophy, 1923. First edition, very good in somewhat soiled wrappers, few tiny tears around extremities.   Between the Covers Rare Books, Inc.   Philosophy - 108420   2013 $50

Russell, Bertrand 1872-1970 *Mysticism and Logic.* New York: W. W. Norton, 1929. first Norton Printing, signed by author, very good++ with mild cover edge wear, soil to edges, in very good+ dust jacket with chips, sun spine, small piece missing from dust jacket spine affecting word "Logic" in title, 8vo., 234 pages.   By the Book, L. C.   38 - 32   2013 $900

Russell, Charles Edward *Railroad Melons Rates and Wages.* Chicago: Kerr, n.d., First edition, blue cloth, fine in fine dust jacket.   Beasley Books   2013 - 2013 $65

Russell, Charles M. *Good Medicine...* Garden City: Doubleday, Doran & Co., 1930. First trade edition, large quarto, color illustrations, facsimiles, pictorial endpapers, hand set type, illustrations from lithographed plates, tan buckram, gilt small ink price to upper corner of free endpaper, tear to front tissue protector, fine.   Argonaut Book Shop   Recent Acquisitions June 2013 - 249   2013 $500

Russell, Colin A. *Edward Frankland: Chemistry, Controversy and Conspiracy in Victorian England.* Cambridge: Cambridge University Press, 1996. First edition, tall 8vo., illustrations, tables, burgundy cloth, gilt stamped spine title, dust jacket, fine.   Jeff Weber Rare Books   169 - 396   2013 $90

Russell, Eric Frank *Sinister Barrier.* London: Fantasy Books, n.d., 1952. First British paperback edition, octavo, pictorial wrappers.   L. W. Currey, Inc.   Fall Sampler Sept. 2013 - 145367   2013 $55

Russell, Fred *Big Bowl Football: the Great Postseasons Classics.* New York: Ronald Press, 1963. First edition, fine in lightly rubbed, else fine dust jacket. Between the Covers Rare Books, Inc. Football Books - 73943 2013 $85

Russell, George William 1867-1935 *The Candle of Vision.* London: Macmillan, 1918. First edition, 8vo., original blue cloth, excellent copy in scarce dust jacket, creased and torn at head of spine. Maggs Bros. Ltd. 1442 - 282 2013 £220

Russell, Hugh *A Journey from Time to Eternity; Seriously Recommended to all Who Call Themselves Christians...* Nottingham: printed by C. Sutton for the Flying Stationers, c., 1815. 8 pages, titlepage woodcut, 8vo., uncut folded sheet in fine state. Ken Spelman Books Ltd. 75 - 73 2013 £40

Russell, John *Francis Bacon.* London: Thames and Hudson, 1971. First edition, 4to., original brown cloth, inscribed by Francis Bacon for Muriel Belcher, near fine in slightly rubbed dust jacket, signed by Belcher. Maggs Bros. Ltd. 1442 - 1 2013 £2500

Russell, Rachel Wriothesley Vaughan 1636-1732 *Letters of Lady Rachel Russell.* London: printed for Edward and Charles Dilly, 1773. Second edition, half title, 4to., single wormhole to lower margins, lower corner F1 torn, possibly an original paper flaw, some browning to inner margins of final two leaves, uncut and unpressed in recent drab boards, paper spine label. Jarndyce Antiquarian Booksellers CCIV - 258 2013 £120

Russell, William *Extraordinary Women; their Girlhood and Early Life.* London: Routledge, 1857. Frontispiece, plates, original green cloth, blocked in blind, spine elaborately blocked and lettered in gilt, slightly dulled, bookseller's stamp and later signature on leading f.e.p., very good. Jarndyce Antiquarian Booksellers CCV - 236 2013 £45

Rust, Brian *Jazz Records 1897 to 1931.* Hatch end: the author, 1962. First edition, very good- shaken with loosening pastedown, rear hinge going. Beasley Books 2013 - 2013 $100

Rust, Graham *The Painted House.* New York: Knopf, 1988. First edition, oblong 4to., fine in close to fine dust jacket with short tear on rear panel. Beasley Books 2013 - 2013 $100

Ruthenberg, C. E. *A Communist Trial.* New York: National Defense Committee, 1920. First edition, wrappers, good to very good-, 80 pages, SWP (Boston) stamps, some corner chipping, spine wear. Beasley Books 2013 - 2013 $100

Ryan, Desmond *The Fenian Chief. A Biography of James Stephens.* Gill, 1967. First edition, very good. C. P. Hyland 261 - 799 2013 £45

Ryan, Desmond *The Phoenix Flame: a Study of Fenianism & John Devoy.* Barker, 1937. First edition, 8vo., cloth, very good. C. P. Hyland 261 - 762 2013 £45

Ryan, Richard *Biographia Hibernica. A Biographical Dictionary of the Worthies of Ireland.* 1821. First edition, 2 volumes, portrait, 8vo., cloth, full diced calf (worn), reback, ex- Institutional Library, good,. C. P. Hyland 261 - 764 2013 £500

Ryan, W. F. *Pseudo-Aristotle: The Secret of Secrets.* London: Warburg Institute, University of London, 1982. 8vo., 148 pages, printed wrappers, ownership signature on half title, fine, rare. Jeff Weber Rare Books 169 - 397 2013 $75

Ryff, Walter Hermenius *Des Aller Furtrefflichesten, Hochsten unnd Adelichsten Gachopffs aller Creaturen, von Got dem Herren, Schopffer aller Ding auff Erden...* Strassburg: Balthassar Beck, 1541. Small folio, 17th century full vellum, hand lettered spine label, light foxing, some brown staining in parts overall most pleasing tight copy, plates. James Tait Goodrich 75 - 186 2013 $25,000

Ryle, Gilbert *Plato's Progress.* Cambridge: Cambridge University Press, 1966. First edition, 8vo., signed and inscribed "with the author's compliments" and dated by Ryle, 2 TLS's by Ryle laid in, fine in near fine dust jacket. By the Book, L. C. 38 - 33 2013 $700

Ryser, Fred A. *Birds of the Great Basin. A Natural History.* Reno: University of Nevada Press, 1985. First edition, drawings by Jennifer Dewey, 60 color photos, dark blue cloth, gilt, very fine, pictorial dust jacket. Argonaut Book Shop Recent Acquisitions June 2013 - 251 2013 $75

S

S. T. E. Lawrence Boxwood Blockmaker. Wood Engravings Collected in Honour of His Eightieth Birthday. printed at the Whittington Press for Simon Lawrence, Wakefield, 1980. 18/250 copies on Zerkall mouldmade paper, wood engraved frontispiece by Leo Wyatt printed in brown and 37 other wood engravings by leading engravers of the period, each printed on separate leaf with engraved name printed in brown beneath, titlepage printed in black and brown, small folio, original quarter mid brown cloth, backstrip gilt lettered, orange and brown marbled boards, top edge gilt, others untrimmed, board slipcase, fine.   Blackwell's Rare Books   B174 - 400   2013   £385

Sabartes, J. *Toreros (A Los Toros).* Monte Carlo: A. Sauret, 1961. First German edition, 10 x 13 inches, 154 pages, numerous plates, including 4 original lithos, fine in slipcase, lithographs in excellent condition.   Gemini Fine Books & Arts., Ltd.   Art Reference & Illustrated Books - 2013 $2750

Sabin, Elijah R. *The Life and Reflections of Charles Observator...* Boston: Rowe & Hooper, 1816. First edition, 12mo, 271 pages, contemporary calf, slightly warped, but very good, text foxed, early owner's small bookplate.   M & S Rare Books, Inc.   95 - 338   2013 $250

Sackett, Susan *Letters to Star Trek.* New York: Ballantine, 1977. First edition, paperback original, small scrape to top of front panel, near fine in wrappers, inscribed by author to noted scientist Fred Durant, splendid association.   Between the Covers Rare Books, Inc.   Sci-Fi, Fantasy & Horror - 43908   2013 $275

Sackville-West, Edward *The Rescue.* London: Secker and Warburg, 1945. First edition, 185/850 copies, 8 color printed plates by Henry Moore, 96 pages, 8vo., original light blue cloth, backstrip gilt lettered, front cover very faintly damp spotted, two small bleach stains to front free endpaper, top edge gilt, others untrimmed, dust jacket with few short tears and two internal tape repairs, good.   Blackwell's Rare Books   B174 - 268   2013   £50

Sackville-West, Victoria Mary 1892-1962 *Aphra Behn, the Incomparable Astrea.* Howe, 1927. First edition, frontispiece, foolscap 8vo., original dark blue cloth, backstrip gilt blocked, front cover with design blocked in blind, endpapers, lightly foxed, fore-edges rough trimmed, chipped dust jacket detached at front backstrip panel fold, very good.   Blackwell's Rare Books   172 - 234   2013   £50

Sackville, George Germain, Viscount *The Proceedings of a General Court Martial Held at the Horse-Guards on Friday the 7th and Continued by Several Adjournments to Monday the 24th of March 1760 and of a General court Martial held at the Horse Guards on Tuesday the 25th of March and continued by Several Adjournments to Saturday the 5th of April 1760 Upon the Trial of lord GeorgeSackville.* London: printed for A. Millar, 1760. 8vo., 224 pages, first few and final leaves little browned and dusted, D4 torn and neatly repaired, contemporary quarter calf, marbled boards, corners worn, hinges cracked but firm, spine worn at head and tail, label chipped with loss.   Jarndyce Antiquarian Booksellers   CCIV - 261   2013   £180

Sade, Jacques Francois Paul Aldonce De *The Life of Petrarch.* London: printed by T. Bensley for the Associated Booksellers, 1797. 2 volumes, 8vo., some old waterstaining to plates offset on to facing page, early 19th century dark green half calf, marbled boards, ornate gilt decorated spines, hinges and corners rubbed, some insect damage to marbled paper, old stain at foot of rear board volume II.   Jarndyce Antiquarian Booksellers   CCIV - 262   2013   £85

Sadger, J. *Sleep Walking and Moon Walking. A Medico-Literary Study.* New York: Washington: NMD Pub., 1909. First edition, wrappers, fine.   Beasley Books   2013 - 2013 $50

Sadler, Marie *Mamma's Angel Child in Toyland.* Chicago: Rand McNally, 1915. First edition, 8vo., boards, pictorial paste-on, 115 pages, cover slightly rubbed, else very good+, illustrations by M. T. Ross, with 24 fabulous full page color illustrations plus numerous smaller color illustrations, and detailed black and whites, very scarce.   Aleph-Bet Books, Inc.   104 - 498   2013 $350

Sag-Harbor Tippicanoe Club *By-laws of the Sag-Harbor Tippicanoe Club: Adopted July 2 1840.* Sag Harbor: printed at the Corrector Office, 1840. First edition, 24mo., 7 pages, stitched, unprinted blue wrappers, vertical crease, slight stain on front wrapper, near fine, scarce.   Between the Covers Rare Books, Inc.   New York City - 314254   2013 $450

Sage, Betty *Rhymes of Real Children.* New York: Fox Duffield, Oct., 1903. First edition, Large square 4to. cloth backed pictorial boards, tips and edges lightly rubbed, else fine, illustrations by Jessie Willcox Smith, mounted on front endpaper is charming 2 page typed poem signed by William Lloyd Garrison Jr. dedicating the book and poem to recipient Garrison Hadley, great copy.   Aleph-Bet Books, Inc.   104 - 541   2013 $675

Sage, Bryan *Alaska and its Wildlife.* Hamlyn, 1973. First edition, 4to., original cloth, gilt, dust jacket, illustrations, partly in color.   R. F. G. Hollett & Son   Polar Exploration - 58   2013   £20

Saint George and the Dragon. London: Virtue and Co., circa, 1868? 4to., frontispiece, plates and illustrations, contemporary hand painted full vellum, signed "H.W." and dated 1905, all edges gilt, 31 pages.   Jarndyce Antiquarian Booksellers   CCV - 237   2013   £650

Saint John, Judith   *The Osborne Collection of Early Children's Books 1566-1910.* Toronto: Toronto Public Library, 1966. Volume I, large 8vo., original pictorial boards, numerous plates and illustrations.   R. F. G. Hollett & Son   Children's Books - 569   2013   £65

Saint Pierre, Jacques Henri Bernardin De   1737-1814   *Paul and Virginia.* London: for G. G. and J. Robinson, 1795. Probable first edition in English, 12mo., xii, 212 pages, contemporary paper covered boards, undecorated paper spine, occasional very light foxing, boards soiled and rubbed with half inch piece missing at bottom of spine.   Joseph J. Felcone Inc.   English and American Literature to 1800 - 3   2013 $300

Saint Pierre, Jacques Henri Bernardin De   1737-1814   *The Studies of Nature to which are added the Indian Cottage and Paul and Virginia.* published by W. Emans, printed by J. Briscoe, 1836. 3 volumes, 6 superior engravings on steel, engraved frontispiece, occasional light foxing, 8vo., original cloth blacked drab boards, printed paper labels, corners bumped, spine touch faded and with few marks, labels, corners bumped, spine touch faded and with few mark, labels darkened, small pieces missing, good.   Blackwell's Rare Books   Sciences - 108   2013   £750

Saint Real, Caesar Vischard De   *The Memoirs of the Dutchess Mazarine (Hortense Mancini).* London: William Cademan, 1676. First edition, 8vo., errata, license leaf, modern full calf, rust hole in blank margin of B6, some minor staining and browning, very good.   Second Life Books Inc.   183 - 342   2013 $500

Sainte-Maure, Charles De   *A New Journey through Greece, Aegypt, Palestine, Italy, Swissenland, Alstatia and the Netherlands.* London: J. Battey, 1735. Second edition, 8vo., contemporary full speckled calf, joints cracked, covers worn, clean and crisp.   J. & S. L. Bonham Antiquarian Booksellers   Europe - 8974   2013   £280

Sainthill, Richard   *The Old Countess of Desmond: an Inquiry.* Private printing, 1861-1863. 2 volumes, 76 + 105 pages, 2 plates, 3 pedigrees, very good, 2 ALS's from Caulfield, 1 from Sainthill, many cuttings.   C. P. Hyland   261 - 766   2013   £350

Sakel, Manfred   *Schizopherenia.* New York: Philosophical Library, 1958. First edition, fine in lightly used dust jacket with short tears.   Beasley Books   2013 - 2013 $65

Salaman, M. C.   *Modern Book Illustrators and their Work.* London: The Studio, 1914. First edition, owner inscription Mary Hutton, very good, 8vo., cloth.   C. P. Hyland   261 - 767   2013   £85

Saldern, Friedrich Christoph Von   *Elements of Tacticks and Introduction to Military Evolutions for the Infantry by a Celebrated Prussian General with Plates.* printed for the author, sold by P. Elmsley and J. Egerton, 1787. First edition in English, 18 folding engraved plates, slightly browned in places, few spots, 8vo., contemporary mottled calf, rebacked, corners worn, good.   Blackwell's Rare Books   B174 - 101   2013   £1200

Salinger, Jerome David   *The Catcher in the Rye.* Boston: Little Brown, 1951. First edition, 8vo., 277 pages, near fine un unrestored, unclipped dust jacket (showing some nicking at top of spine, little wear at tips, letter marred on rear jacket flap because of old removal of tape), name erased from endpaper, first issue jacket with Saligner's photo portrait, "Book of the Month Club" notation at bottom of rear flap.   Second Life Books Inc.   183 - 343   2013 $11,500

Salinger, Jerome David   *Catcher in the Rye.* Boston: Little Brown, 1951. Stated first edition, black cloth, bookplate removed from endpaper, else fine in dust jacket with some expert restoration at base of spine and at folds, nice in first issue dust jacket.   Aleph-Bet Books, Inc.   105 - 518   2013 $6500

Salinger, Jerome David   *Raise High the Roof Beam, Carpenters and Seymour an Introduction.* New York: Little Brown, 1963. First edition, first issue, exceptionally scarce issue, fine in very near fine dust jacket with tiny closed catch to spine, from the Bruce Kahn collection.   Ken Lopez Bookseller   159 - 172   2013 $5000

Salisbury, Robert Cecil   *The Copies of a Letter to the Right Honourable, the Earl of Leycester, Lieutenant General of all Her Majesties Forces in the United Provinces of the Low Countreys...* London: Christopher Barker, 1586. 4to., without final blank leaf, woodcut arms on A, verso, facing titlepage, large woodcut initials, this copy is variant A, recto starting "Albeit with earnest...", bound by Pratt in 19th century brown crushed morocco with gilt arms on both covers, all edges gilt, bookplate of Fairfax of Cameron, fine copy.   Second Life Books Inc.   182 - 207   2013 $4000

Sallustius Crispus, C. *La Conjuracion de Catilina y la Guerro de Juguria.* Madrid: Per Joachim Ibarra, 1772. First Ibarra edition, folio, engraved title with border, and engraved medallion portrait by C. Montfort, engraved map 8 engraved plates, numerous engraved illustrations, head and tailpieces, initials, bound without half title, contemporary Spanish red morocco, covers decoratively bordered gilt, gilt spine, tooled in compartments with black morocco label, gilt board edges and inner dentelles, all edges gilt, blue moire silk endpapers, small library stamp on lower edge of title and on fore edge, modern bookplate on front pastedown, very light marginal foxing on few leaves, generally fine, crisp.   Heritage Book Shop   50th Anniversary Catalogue - 85   2013 $15,000

Salmon, Thomas *A Complete Collection of State-Trials and Proceedings for High Treason and Other Crimes and Misdemeanours...* London: printed for J. Walthoe, R. Vincent J. and J. Knapton, R. Knaplock, J. Roberts (and 33 others in London), 1730. Second edition, 6 volumes, numerous errors in paging throughout, titlepages in red and black, engraved head and tailpieces, folio, contemporary brown calf, rebacked in tan, calf boards decoratively paneled in blind with floral designs at corners, spine with five raised bands, dark brown morocco label lettered gilt, very good, boards worn, occasional soiling, minor tear to one titlepage, few leaves with worn holes in one volume, just nicking a few letters, faint dampstain to lower edge of few gatherings in another volume, overall contents clean.   Kaaterskill Books   16 - 72   2013 $1200

Salmon, William *The Country Builder's Estimator, or the Architect's Companion.* printed for James Hodges at the Looking Glass on London Bridge, 1737. Second edition, few diagrams and illustrations in text, washed and repaired, 12mo., fairly modern (1954) tan Niger goatskin by Anthony Gardner, OBE, blind tooled borders on sides, lettered direct in gilt on spine, binder' Apologia penned inside front cover in sepia ink in accomplished calligraphic italic script, his detailed invoice-cum-letter to the then owner loosely inserted, very good.   Blackwell's Rare Books   Sciences - 109   2013   £1250

Saloman, Charlotte *Life or Theatre?* London: Allen Lane, Gary Swartz, 1971. Large 4to., pages xvi, 784, original cloth, pictorial dust jacket.   Marlborough Rare Books Ltd.   218 - 133   2013   £55

Salsman, Lillian V. *Homeland: Country Harbour, Nova Scotia 1783-1983. Volume I. (with) Homeland Country Harbour, Nova Scotia 1783-1983 Genealogies. , Volume II: Homeland a Girl from the County Harbour, Nova Scotia, her Autobiography Volume III.* Hantsport & Marblehead: Lancelot Press (volume 1) Davis Associates (volumes 2 & 3), 1984. 9 x 6 inches, card covers, volumes I and II worn, previous owner's annotations in rear, volume III very good.   Schooner Books Ltd.   104 - 117   2013 $75

Salve Regina! Or, a Lay of Sympathy and Loyal Homage to a Persecuted Woman and a Legitimate Queen Caroline of England. London: printed and published by John Fairburn, 1820. Half title, 15 pages, disbound.   Jarndyce Antiquarian Booksellers   CCV - 48   2013   £80

Salzman, Michael *New Water for a Thirsty World.* Los Angeles: Science Foundation Press, 1960. First edition, brown cloth, lettered green, corners slightly jammed, else fine with dust jacket.   Argonaut Book Shop   Recent Acquisitions June 2013 - 252   2013 $75

Sampaio, Manuel De Castro *Os Chins de Macau. (The Chinese Macao).* Hong Kong: Noroha & Filhos, 1867. First edition, one folding map, folded albumen map, frontispiece, 8vo., contemporary half calf.   Maggs Bros. Ltd.   1467 - 62   2013   £2750

Sample, Ann Aliza *Fluffy Cat's Tail.* Chicago: Whitman, 1931. First edition, oblong small 4to., cloth, pictorial paste-on, slight soil very good+, full page silhouette scissor cuts. Aleph-Bet Books, Inc.   104 - 120   2013 $125

Sampson, John *XXI Welsh Gypsy Folk Tales.* Newtown, Powys: Gregynog Press, 1933. 216/235 copies (of an edition of 250), printed on Portal handmade paper, title vignette and 7 other exquisite wood engravings by Agnes Miller Parker, imperial 8vo., original mustard yellow bevel edged sheepskin, backstrip rubbed, more so at head and tail, edges and corners also with some fairly light rubbing, design of horizontal lines on front cover incorporating the title lettering and lettering on backstrip, all gilt blocked, usual offsetting fro turn-ins and faint tape stains to free endpapers, bookplates of M. Weiss and Norman J. Sondheim, untrimmed, good.   Blackwell's Rare Books   172 - 293   2013   £1250

San Lazarro et Ses Amis: Hommage au Fondateur de la Revue XXe Siecle. Paris: 1975. First edition, one of 575 copies, 25 lithographs, 145 pages on velin d'Arches paper, loose sheets in publisher's wrapper folder and clamshell linen box, photo of San Lazarro by Pierre Volboudt glued to inside of front cover, of the 25 full page lithos, 15 are original lithographs by Max Bill, Alexander Calder (signed and dated in Plate, March Chagall, Max Ernst (signed in plate), Hans Hartung, Joan Miro, Henry Moore, Graham Sutherland ad Zao Wou-Ki, 10 full page lithos are from the 2nd edition by Georges Braque, Lucio Fontana, Alberto Magnelli (signed and dated in plate), Rene Magritte (titled and signed in plate), Picasso (signed in plate) and Serge Poliakoff. Gemini Fine Books & Arts., Ltd.   Art Reference & Illustrated Books - 2013 $3000

San Lazzaro, G. Di *Homage to Matisse.*   New York: Tudor Pub. Co., 1970. First edition, 126 pages, numerous color and black and white illustrations, linocut executed by Mastisse in 1938 for XXe Siecle, near fine in about very good dust jacket with tear to top of front panel which also has tiny nick at base and with chip and tear to top of rear panel as well, still nice copy.   Jeff Hirsch Books   Fall 2013 - 129109   2013 $55

Sanchez, Gonzalo *The Edwin Smith Papyrus.*   Atlanta: Lockwood Press, 2012. Colored frontispiece, colored plates, tall 4to., color pictorial boards, numerous illustrations in text.   James Tait Goodrich   S74 - 99   2013 $250

Sandeman, Christopher *Thyme and Bergamot.*   Dropmore Press, 1947. 137/525 copies of an edition of 550, printed on Hodgkinson handmade paper, 3 quarter wood engraved border to titlepage and 8 other delightful wood engravings all by John O'Connor, imperial 8vo., original light blue linen cloth, gilt lettering on backstrip and gilt press device to front cover, untrimmed, dust jacket, fine.   Blackwell's Rare Books   B174 - 331   2013   £80

Sandes, Elise *Enlisted; or My Story, Incidents of Life & Work, Among Soldiers.*   Cork: 1897. 224 pages, 8vo., frontispiece, wood engravings in text, card covers (worn), text good.   C. P. Hyland   261 - 768   2013   £50

Sandes, Elise *Enlisted; or My Story: Incidents of Life and Work Among Soldiers.*   Curragh: 1915. Fourth edition, 277 + (6) pages, 11 photos, illustrations, 8vo., card covers, very good.   C. P. Hyland   261 - 769   2013   £45

Sandler, Martin W. *American Image Photographing One Hundred Fifty Years in the Life of a Nation.*   Chicago: Contemporary Books, 1989. First edition, 4to., 266 pages, black cloth, nice, little scuffed and slightly soiled dust jacket.   Second Life Books Inc.   183 - 346   2013 $50

Sands, Benjamin *Metamorphosis or a Transformation of Pictures with Poetical Explanations for the Amusement of Young Persons.*   New York: Samuel Wood and Sons, 1814. One sheet folded to 8 pages, breaks in some threads, becoming disbound, one half inch sliver missing on one plate.   M & S Rare Books, Inc.   95 - 184   2013 $2250

Sandwith, Humphry *The Hekin Bashi; or the Adventures of Giuseppe Antonelli, a Doctor in the Turkish Service.*   London: Smith, Elder and Co., 1864. First edition, 2 volumes, half titles, some occasional pencil underlining, 2 volumes in 1, original olive green remainder cloth, blocked in blind, slightly rubbed and marbled.   Jarndyce Antiquarian Booksellers   CCV - 238   2013   £350

Sanfilippo, Luigi *General Catalog of Duke Ellington's Recorded Music.*   Palermo: Centro Studi di Musica, 1966. Second edition, wrappers, 109 pages, printed rectos only, pages darkened, few loosened, thus very good+.   Beasley Books   2013 - 2013 $50

Sanger, Margaret *Woman and the New Race.*   New York: Brentano's, 1923. Sixth printing, 8vo., author's presentation on half title under scotch tape, red cloth stamped in black, ex-lbrary with bookplate and stamps, rear hinge near tender, otherwise very good.   Second Life Books Inc.   182 - 210   2013 $50

Sanginaticus, Georgius *Introductio Anatomica.*   Leiden: Phillipp Bonk, 1744. First illustrated edition, engraved title vignette, 3 full page engravings on 2 leaves, nice in contemporary vellum, light warping of boards, very good.   James Tait Goodrich   75 - 187   2013 $1795

Sanial, Lucien *General Bankruptcy or Socialism?*   New York: Co-operative Press, 1913. First edition, 20 pages, wrappers, folding chart at rear, near fine.   Beasley Books   2013 - 2013 $50

Sansay, Leonora Hassall *Secret History; or the Horrors of St. Domingo...*   Philadelphia: Bradford & Inskeep, R. Carr, 1808. Only edition, 12mo., contemporary tree calf, corners rubbed, hinges starting, leather label, lacks free half of front endpaper and has 1 inch wide strip clipped off at top of titlepage, undoubtedly excising an ownership signature, some foxing and staining, still very good, scarce.   Howard S. Mott Inc.   262 - 128   2013 $1250

Santa Claus Book.   Newark: Charles Graham, circa, 1915. Small 8vo., pictorial wrappers, fine, die cut in shape of Santa, illustrations.   Aleph-Bet Books, Inc.   105 - 135   2013 $150

Santa Gertrudes Magna, Francisco De Paula *Encomio Poetico ao Illustrissimo e Excellentissimo Senhor D. Marcos de Noronha...*   Rio de Janeiro: Na Impressao Regia..., 1812. First edition, 8vo., very good.   Howard S. Mott Inc.   262 - 129   2013 $1250

Santorio, Santorio 1561-1636 *Medicina Statica.*   London: W. & J. Newton, 1720. Second edition, Engraved frontispiece, folding chart, elegant gilt polish speckle calf by Riviere, gilt panel spine, gilt ruled edges and inner dentelles, all edges gilt, lower outer board with small gash in letter, otherwise fine binding, near fine copy.   James Tait Goodrich   S74 - 220   2013 $495

Santos, Francisco De Los *The Escurial; or a Description of that Wonder of the World for Architecture and Magnificence of Structure.* London: printed for T. Collins and J. Ford, 1671. First edition in English, small 4to., 19th century polished calf by Ramage, gilt decorations and lettering, all edges gilt, from the library of Hispanophile Richard Ford (1796-1858) with his bookplate and signature dated 1836, later small bookplate of Henry Huth with clipped description of this book from Sotheby's Huth Sale catalog laid in, some light foxing, margins trimmed little close in places, very good.   The Brick Row Book Shop   Miscellany Fifty-Nine - 37   2013 $3000

Sapori, Armando *I Libri Di Comemrcio Dei Peruzzi.* Milano: Fratelli Treves, 1934. First edition, folio, blue cloth, leather spine label, near fine, label creased but extra label loose within.   Kaaterskill Books   16 - 63   2013 $600

Saposs, David J. *The Labor Movement in Post-War France.* New York: Columbia University Press, 1931. First edition, hardcover, very good with spine wear.   Beasley Books   2013 - 2013 $50

Sappho *The Songs of Sappho...* New York: Frank Maurice, 1925. One of 750 numbered copies, large 8vo., pages xiv, 435, 10 plates, green paper over boards, owner's bookplate on pastedown, name on title, frontispiece detached, some pencil marking throughout, notes on rear blank, very good.   Second Life Books Inc.   182 - 212   2013 $75

Sarawak *Evidence Given before the Commission of Enquiry into the Charges Against Sir James Brooke, K.C.B.* Singapore: at the Free Press, 1854. First edition, foling map, original printed orange paper wrappers, upper wrapper torn with some loss, text in double column.   Maggs Bros. Ltd.   1467 - 63   2013   £12,500

Sargent, Pamela *Venus of Dreams.* Norwalk: Easton Press, 1990. First hardcover edition, octavo, illustrations by Ron Miller, full decorated leather.   L. W. Currey, Inc.   Utopian Literature: Recent Acquisitions (April 2013) - 139955   2013 $100

Sarjeant, Thomas *Elementary Principles of Arithmetic... (with) An Introduction to the Counting House...* Philadelphia: printed by Thomas Dobson..., 1788, i.e., 1789. First edition, 8vo., original tree calf, front hinge starting, leading edges gilt rolled, half title, rare, fine save for cracked front hinge, 4 ownership signatures of Jeremiah Lott.   Howard S. Mott Inc.   262 - 130   2013 $3500

Saroyan, William *Don't Go Away Mad and Two Other Plays.* New York: Harcourt Brace, 1949. First edition, 8vo., 238 pages full page inscription, nice, dust jacket.   Second Life Books Inc.   183 - 349   2013 $375

Saroyan, William *Harlem as Seen by Hirschfeld.* New York: Hyperion Press, 1941. First edition, limited to 1000 numbered copies, this being #511, large folio, 6 pages text by Saroyan, 24 original lithographic captioned plates by Albert Hirschfeld, printed on handmade Canson paper, original cream cloth, lettered on front cover and spine, illustration from book reproduced and colored by hand on front cover, spine bit bumped and rubbed, some minor spotting and soiling to cloth as often seen, else very good, handsome copy, 24 wonderful illustrations, plates clean and bright.   Heritage Book Shop   Holiday Catalogue 2012 - 128   2013 $3000

Sarsfield-Hall, E. G. *From Cork to Khartoum, Memoirs 1886-1936.* Private printing, 1975. First edition, 123, vii pages, photos, maps, cloth, dust jacket, very good.   C. P. Hyland   261 - 770   2013   £40

Sassoon, Siegfried Lorraine   1886-1967 *The Daffodil Murderer.* Richmond, 1913. First edition, just few fox spots on half title, crown 8vo., original bright yellow wrappers printed in red, covers just trifle dust soiled, very good.   Blackwell's Rare Books   B174 - 293   2013   £285

Sassoon, Siegfried Lorraine   1886-1967 *Memoirs of a Fox Hunting Man. Memoirs of an Infantry Officer. Sherston's Progress.* London: Faber, 1928. 126/260 copies; 275/750 copies/ 15/300 copies respectively, all printed on handmade paper, each signed by author, 8vo., original light blue buckram, light bumping to front head corner of Infantry Officer, backstrips gilt lettered, backstrip to "Sherston's Progress" unfaded, other two only very slightly faded, faint free endpaper browning, that to Fox Hunting more so, top edge gilt, others untrimmed, overall much better set than usually met with, very good.   Blackwell's Rare Books   B174 - 294   2013   £1650

Sassoon, Siegfried Lorraine   1886-1967 *Memoirs of an Infantry Officer.* London: Faber, 1931. First illustrated edition, 150/320 copies, printed on handmade paper and signed by author and artist, 15 plates and numerous other head and tailpieces by Barnett Freedman, 8vo., original parchment with color printed design overall by Barnett Freedman, pictorial endpapers, top edge gilt, others untrimmed and partly unopened, illustrated dust jacket, fine.   Blackwell's Rare Books   B174 - 295   2013   £1800

Sassoon, Siegfried Lorraine   1886-1967 *The Old Huntsman and Other Poems.* London: Heinemann, 1917. First edition, pages x, 110, crown 8vo., original grey boards, printed label chipped, joints flaking, rough trimmed, good.   Blackwell's Rare Books   B174 - 296   2013   £335

Sassoon, Siegfried Lorraine   1886-1967 *Satirical Poems.* London: William Heinemann, 1926. First edition, publisher's dark blue cloth, gilt titled on cover and spine, original dust jacket, jacket spine lightly and evenly sunned, else fine in like jacket.   Phillip J. Pirages   63 - 420   2013 $150

Sassoon, Siegfried Lorraine 1886-1967 *Siegfried's Journey 1916-1920.* London: Faber and Faber Ltd., 1945. First edition, 224 pages, near fine in about good dust jacket with a number of tears, small chips and larger chip to top of rear panel, scarce in jacket.   Jeff Hirsch Books   Fall 2013 - 129496   2013 $50

Satge Saint Jean, Caroline De, Viscountess *The Cave of the Hugenots; a Tale of the XVIIth Century and Other Poems.* Bath: Binns & Goodwin, 1852? Engraved frontispiece, list of subscribers with 6 names added in ms. to 'Additional Subscribers' list, 3 engraved plates, 10 page catalog, plates foxed at margins, original dark green diagonal grained cloth, coloured to give uniform pale green vertical stripes, elaborately blocked in gilt, owner's inscription, August 1866, all edges gilt, exceptional copy in attractive presentation binding.   Jarndyce Antiquarian Booksellers   CCV - 240   2013   £150

Saunders, Edward Manning *History of the Baptists of the Maritime Provinces.* Halifax: Press of John Burgoyne, 1902. Brown cloth, gilt to spine and front cover, 136 portraits, frontispiece, 2 illustrations of hand writing, 8vo., cloth scuffed to front, inner hinges cracked, front endpaper missing, binding shaky with some pages loose but all there.   Schooner Books Ltd.   105 - 162   2013 $55

Saunders, J. B. *Andreas Vesalius Bruxellensis: the Bloodletting Letter of 1539.* New York: Schuman, 1948. 95 pages, original binding.   James Tait Goodrich   S74 - 232   2013 $125

Saunders, Louise *Knave of Hearts.* New York: Scribner, 1925. First edition, Folio, black cloth, pictorial paste-on, fine in original box (restored as usual), beautiful copy, pictorial endpapers and magnificent full page color illustrations by Maxfield Parrish.   Aleph-Bet Books, Inc.   104 - 408   2013 $4000

Sauvan, Jean Baptiste Balthazar *Picturesque Tour of the Seine, from Paris to the Sea with Particulars Historical and Descriptive.* London: R. Ackermann, 1821. 345 x 275mm., publisher's red buckram, covers with blindstamped frame, upper cover with gilt titling, flat spine stamped with gilt strapwork panels and with gilt titling, all edges gilt, engraved color vignette on titlepage, unsigned aquatint vignette at foot of last page, engraved color map, 24 fine hand colored aquatint plates by Augustus Pugin and John Gendall; presentation bookplate to Master E. Cockayne as reward of merit by Mr. Bowling/Milk Street Academy, Sheffield June 23rd 1848; binding little soiled, joints and extremities bit worn, just slightest offsetting from some plates onto text, one plate with offsetting from text ad half dozen others with just hint of same, other trivial imperfections, very desirable copy.   Phillip J. Pirages   63 - 422   2013 $6000

Savile, Henry *Rerum Anglicarum Scriptores post Bedam Praecipui ex Vertustissimis Codicibus Manuscriptis Nunc Primum in Lucem Editi.* Execudebant G. Bishop, R. Nuberie and R. Barker, 1596. First edition, publisher's device on titlepage, four divisional titlepages with wood engraved architectural borders, small patches on ff. 190v and 191r with loss of text to six lines due to mutual adhesion, another pair similarly affected but rather less so, but with separate small hole in one of them with loss of couple of letters on either side, some browning, first divisional titlepage with small flaw to blank lower corner, folio in 4s, late 19th century mid brown calf, boards with elaborate central panel blocked in blind, surrounded by gilt fillets and blind frame, brown morocco lettering piece to spine, edges gilt, rebacked preserving original backstrip, new endpapers touch worn at extremities, good.   Blackwell's Rare Books   B174 - 129   2013   £950

Saville, Jenny *Closed Contact.* New York: Gagosian Gallery, 2002. First edition, 48 pages, small folio, very good in boards with some minor soiling and fading along top edge of boards.   Jeff Hirsch Books   Fall 2013 - 129132   2013 $250

Saville, Malcolm *Lone Pine London.* Aylesbury: John Goodchild, 1986. Revised edition, Original cloth gilt, dust jacket, pages 202, 2 maps, ex-library, labels and stamps on flyleaf and stamp on back of title.   R. F. G. Hollett & Son   Children's Books - 526   2013   £25

Sawyer, John *Automatic Arithmetic: a New System for Multiplication and Division without Mental Labour and Without the Use of Logarithms.* London: William Clowes and Sons for George Bell and Sons, 1878. First edition, presentation copy, inscribed to good friend Frederick Brown, oblong 8vo., pages 17, 3, final linen covered and blank, 10 tables printed in red and black, 9 of which cut into horizontal strips of increasing length, original plum pebble grained cloth, covers ruled in blind, gilt stamped lettering on front cover, light wear to extremities, front inner hinges strengthened with cloth strips at early date.   Marlborough Rare Books Ltd.   218 - 136   2013   £750

Sawyer, Ruth *Roller Skates.* New York: Viking Press, Oct., 1936. First edition, 8vo., pictorial cloth, fine in slightly worn dust jacket with few small chips, illustrations by Valenti Angelo.   Aleph-Bet Books, Inc.   104 - 39   2013 $200

Saxo Grammaticus *Danorum Regum Heroumque Historiae...* Paris: Jodocus Badius Ascensius, 1514. Rare first edition, folio, bound without final blank leaf, title printed in red within architectural woodcut border enclosing a woodcut of the Danish king at head of his army, fine woodcut crible initials, including several specially designed for the book incorporating a portrait of the King of Demark and the royal arms; early 18th century limp vellum with leather ties, spine lettered gilt on rose wash panel, edges stained blue, title border shaved at head, some minor mostly marginal worming, few marginal stains, early ink inscription of Christianus Torndallius, Helsing; Danorum (Elsinore) and another early ink inscription, bookplate of Hjalmar Hartmann, some scattered early ink marginalia and underlining, overall excellent copy. Heritage Book Shop 50th Anniversary Catalogue - 86 2013 $20,000

Sayers, Dorothy L. *Even the Parrot.* London: Methuen, 1944. First edition, small 8vo., original cloth, gilt, dust jacket, spine little rubbed and faded, chipped at head and foot, endpapers little browned in gutters. R. F. G. Hollett & Son Children's Books - 527 2013 £75

Sayers, Dorothy L. *The Just Vengeance. The Lichfield Festival Play for 1946.* London: Gollancz, 1946. First edition, pages 80, foolscap 8vo., original black cloth, backstrip gilt lettered, dust jacket with chipped and sunned backstrip panel, very good, inscribed by author for Charles Richardson, further inscribed to him by artist and theatre designer Norah Lambourne, inscribed by the play's producer, Frank Napier and by composer Anthony Hopkins. Blackwell's Rare Books 172 - 235 2013 £300

Sayili, Aydin *The Observatory in Islam and Its Place in the General History of the Observatory.* Ankara: Turk Tarih Kurumu Basimevi, 1960. First printing, 8vo., 7 plates, orange cloth, black stamped cover and spine titles, ownership signatures, fine, rare. Jeff Weber Rare Books 169 - 401 2013 $160

Scaligero, Giulio Cesare *Ivlii Caesaris Scaligeri Exotericarvm Exercitationvm Liber XV. De Subtilitate ad Hieronymvm Cardanvm.* Francofurti: Apud Haeredes Andr. Wechelus, 1582. 8vo., titlepage vignette, few diagrams, figures in text, index, printer's device on final leaf, minor waterstaining and also some minor worming affecting upper margin of Epistola and final four leaves (no loss), original full dark calf with blind embossed devices on either board, some worming to spine, bottom head cap loosening, light wear to covers which are generally very good, signature of early owner, very good. Jeff Weber Rare Books 171 - 63 2013 $1250

Scarron, Paul *Scarron's Comical Romance; or a Facetious History of a Company of Strowling Stage-Players Interwoven with Divers Choice Novels...* London: by J(ames) C(ottrell) for William Crooke, 1676. Second edition in English, folio, lacks frontispiece, contemporary calf, rebacked and recornered with later endpapers, scattered foxing and browning throughout. Joseph J. Felcone Inc. Books Printed before 1701 - 76 2013 $650

The Sceptic. London: John Russell Smith, printed in Crewkerne, 1850. 12mo., half title, original blue cloth, blocked in blind, spine lettered gilt, at some time excellently rebacked retaining original spine strip, very good. Jarndyce Antiquarian Booksellers CCV - 10 2013 £525

Sceve, Maurice *Visages Pour Delie.* Geneve: Ethis, 1974. First edition, one of LXXV deluxe exemplars on Japon (total edition of 320), 12 color lithographs, each signed and numbered by the artist, Leonor Fini, loose leaves in publisher's folding box, overall size 69 x 53cm., 4 lithos with insignificant spots in lower right corners/margins, otherwise very good, possibly lacking justification page, with 2 additional signed lithographs. Gemini Fine Books & Arts., Ltd. Art Reference & Illustrated Books - 2013 $1500

Schaaf, Gregory *American Indian Jewelry III: M-Z 2,100 Artist Biographies.* Santa Fe: 2013. First edition, 415 pages, illustrations, new. Dumont Maps & Books of the West 125 - 73 2013 $70

Schaarschmidt, Samuel *Semiotic, oder Lehre von den Kennzeichen des Innerlichen Zustandes des Menschlichen Korpers.* Berlin: Gottlieb August Lange, 1756. First edition, lightly browned throughout (due to paperstock), 8vo., contemporary mottled boards, spine with label titled in ink, some light rubbing, very good. Blackwell's Rare Books Sciences - 110 2013 £1250

Scharff, Robert *Standard Handbook of Salt Water Fishing.* New York: Thomas Y. Crowell, 1959. First printing, 2 owner's names, including that of Ralph Ellison, else fine in presentable about very good dust jacket with small nicks and tears. Between the Covers Rare Books, Inc. 165 - 148 2013 $275

Schedel, Hartmann *Liber Chronicarum.* Nuremberg: Anton Koberger for Sebald Schreyer and Sebastian Kammermeister 12 July, 1493. First edition, large folio, 325 leaves, woodcut title and 1809 woodcut illustrations, one large (fourteen-line) initial in blue, red and brown, other large (four-six, seven and eight line) initials in red and blue, this copy with 3 numbered leaves blank except for headlines and five additional (unnumbered) leaves containing De Sarmacia regione and the poem on Maximilian and subsequent blank, portrait of Pope Joan usually missing, present and unmutilated, double page map free from restoration, with full margins visible, 16th century calf over wooden boards, neatly rebacked retaining original spine, few marginal restorations and minor repairs, several leaves reinforced at inner margin, few leaves slightly smaller and probably supplied, few early ink marginalia, overall very good, unusually clean, extremely tall, housed in custom clamshell, gilt stamped. Heritage Book Shop 50th Anniversary Catalogue - 87 2013 $150,000

Schele, Linda *A Forest of Kings. The Untold Story of the Ancient Maya.* New York: William Morrow and Co. Inc., 1990. First edition, 542 pages, cover 250 text drawings and photos, maps, cloth backed boards, very fine with pictorial dust jacket. Argonaut Book Shop Recent Acquisitions June 2013 - 253 2013 $75

Scheme for Crash Evacuation of Certain of the Homeless after a "blitz" Air-Raid. Kingston upon Hull: Jan., 1941. 76 pages, with additional specimen evacuation slips at end, fine in original card covers, punch holes and original string ties, scarce. Ken Spelman Books Ltd. 73 - 107 2013 £40

Schiff, Stuart David *Whispers Volume 6 Nos. 1-2. Whole Number 21-22.* Binghampton: Stuart David Schiff, 1984. First edition, hardcover issue, one of 350 numbered copies signed by several contributors, octavo, blue cloth, gilt. Between the Covers Rare Books, Inc. Sci-Fi, Fantasy & Horror - 317020 2013 $100

Schiller, Johann Christoph Friedrich Von 1759-1805 *The Death of Wallenstein.* London: T. N. Longman and O. Rees, 1809. First English edition, translated by S. T. Coleridge, Disbound, very good. Jarndyce Antiquarian Booksellers CCIII - 509 2013 £150

Schiller, Johann Christoph Friedrich Von 1759-1805 *The Piccolomini or the First Part of Wallenstein. (with) The Death of Wallenstein.* London: T. N. Longman & O. Rees, 1800. First edition translated by Samuel T. Coleridge, handsomely bound in full green morocco by Brian Frost and Co., gilt borders and dentelles, spine fading to brown, all edges gilt, very good. Jarndyce Antiquarian Booksellers CCIII - 507 2013 £650

Schiller, Johann Christoph Friedrich Von 1759-1805 *Wallenstein. (with) The Death of Wallenstein.* London: T. N. Longman & O. Rees, 1800. First editions translated by S. T. Coleridge, frontispiece slightly spotted, 3 pages ads part II, little browned, contemporary full calf, gilt borders, black label, lower corners slightly chipped, spine sympathetically rebacked. Jarndyce Antiquarian Booksellers CCIII - 508 2013 £500

Schiller, Johann Christoph Friedrich Von 1759-1805 *The Works.* Philadelphia: George Barrie, 1883. 300 x 222mm., 4 volumes, publisher's appealing black half morocco over textured black cloth boards, front covers with gilt titling, raised bands, spine compartments heavily gilt with interlacing leafy cornerpieces and differing centerpieces, textured ivory endpapers, all edges gilt, headpieces, tailpieces, engraved titlepages, more than 400 woodcut illustrations, 150 full page plates, titlepages in red and black, spines little chafed, in all other ways, outstanding copy, virtually without any signs that volumes have been used. Phillip J. Pirages 63 - 423 2013 $650

Schillings, C. G. *With Flashlight and Rifle.* London: Hutchinson & Co., 1906. First London edition, 302 photos, 2 volumes, 4to., very good in original dark green decorative cloth, bookplate. Ken Spelman Books Ltd. 75 - 159 2013 £120

Schlein, Miriam *Fast Is Not a Ladybug.* New York: William R. Scott, 1953. First edition, 4to., pictorial boards, fine in chipped dust jacket, illustrations by Leonard Kessler with great 3 color illustrations on every page. Aleph-Bet Books, Inc. 105 - 523 2013 $200

Schlesigner, Leon *Porky Pig's Duck Hunt.* Akron: Saalfield, 1938. Folio, stiff pictorial linen like wrappers, fine, color illustrations. Aleph-Bet Books, Inc. 105 - 122 2013 $250

Schmid, J. *Speculum Chirurgicum oder Spiegel der Wund-Artzney...* Augsburg & Frankfurt: Hermsdorff, 1675. Later edition, Thick 4to., engraved title, early vellum which is worn and rubbed, front joint starting. James Tait Goodrich S74 - 223 2013 $1395

Schmidt, Erich F. *Flights Over Ancient Cities of Iran.* Chicago: University of Chicago Press, 1940. Folio, 119 large photographic plates, map endleaves, pictorial cloth, joints rubbed, very good, scarce. Jeff Weber Rare Books 171 - 184 2013 $1500

Schmoller, Hans *Mr. Gladstone's Washi.* Newtown: Bird & Bull Press, 1984. 110/500 copies, printed on Hahnemuhle mouldmade paper, with Japanese characters printed in brown, woodcut facsimiles, printed on 16 leaves of handmade Japanese Torinoko Gampi and lithographic reproductions (totalling 19 in color) on Mohawk vellum, also with 3 folding facsimiles of contemporary engraved illustrations, complete with additional suite of 19 color printed plates all loosely inserted in pale grey printed card folder, imperial 8vo., original quarter maroon crushed morocco, black leather label, red, blue and grey decorated boards, reproduced from paper sample in Parkes collection, untrimmed, board slipcase, fine.   Blackwell's Rare Books   172 - 267   2013   £225

Schneider, Herman *Let's Find Out.* New York: William Scott, 1946. 4to., pictorial boards, very good in chipped dust jacket with piece out of spine, illustrations by Jeanne Bendick, quite scarce.   Aleph-Bet Books, Inc.   104 - 512   2013 $150

Schnick Schnack: Trifles for the Little Ones. London: Routledge, 1867. 8vo. green cloth with extensive gilt pictorial cover, near fine, 32 fine full color plates.   Aleph-Bet Books, Inc.   105 - 573   2013 $250

Schofield, Lily *Billy Ruddylox an Ancient British Boy.* London: Swan Sonnenschein & Co., 1904. Brown cloth, 16mo., 89 pages with 21 color plates, very good.   Barnaby Rudge Booksellers   Children 2013 - 020249   2013 $75

Scholder, Fritz *Fritz Scholder. Painting and Monotypes.* Altadena: Twin Palms Pub., 1988. First edition, limited to 5000 casebound copies, 4to., signed and dated by Scholder, fine in very good++ dust jacket with chips, minimal sun spine and covers, "Autographed Copy" sticker front of dust jacket, typeface Goudy, plates printed four-color process on matte finished paper stock and text signatures are uncoated Japanese paper stock printed and bound in Singapore through Palace Press, San Francisco.   By the Book, L. C.   36 - 20   2013 $100

The School for Satire or a Collection of Modern Satirical Poems Written During the Present Reign. London: printed and sold by Jacques and Co., 1801. First edition, 8vo., bound without half title, contemporary half sheep, slightly scuffed.   Marlborough Rare Books Ltd.   218 - 135   2013   £225

The School of Wisdom; or Repository of the Most Valuable Curiosities of Art & Nature. Gainsbroguh (sic): printed by John Mozley and sold by J. F. and C. Rivington, London, 1776. First edition, unevenly browned, lower margins trimmed close, touching text in couple of instances, poor impression of type in few places, 8vo., recent half diced calf gilt, floral printed boards, sound.   Blackwell's Rare Books   172 - 60   2013   £550

Schools of Illumination: Reproductions from Manuscripts in the British Museum. London: printed by Order of the Trustees of the British Museum, 1914-1922. 4 volumes, 398 x 283mm., loose as issued in green linen ties, 61 plates on thick paper, 8 in color with gold, booklabel of Bernard M. Rosenthal, spine bit faded, faint soiling to boards, fine set, few signs of use.   Phillip J. Pirages   63 - 394   2013 $250

Schoonmaker, Nancy M. *The Actual Government of Connecticut.* New York: National Woman Suffrage Pub. Co., 1919. First edition, 8vo., tan cloth, ex-library with stamps and bookplate, edges of cover little bumped and scuffed, otherwise very good, tight copy.   Second Life Books Inc.   182 - 214   2013 $65

Schreiner, Olive 1855-1920 *The Story of an African Farm.* New York: printed for the Members...at the Westerham Press, 1961. One of 1500 numbered copies, (this unnumbered, but initialled "P.H." beneath Paul Hogarth's signature, full page color printed illustrations and endpapers and line drawings in text by Hogarth, small folio, original russet bark cloth, red leather label, board slipcase with printed label, fine.   Blackwell's Rare Books   172 - 298   2013   £50

Schreiner, Olive 1855-1920 *Woman and Labor.* New York: Stokes, 1911. First edition, near fine, owner's name and few mild spots to spine.   Beasley Books   2013 - 2013 $65

Schrodinger, Erwin *What is Life? The Physical Aspect of the Living Cell.* Cambridge: at the University Press, 1945. First reprint, 8vo., original green cloth, inscribed by Samuel Beckett for nephew Gerald Beckett, near fine copy.   Maggs Bros. Ltd.   1460 - 57   2013   £1250

Schroeder, Frederick A. *Report of the Celebration of the 100th Anniversary of American Independence in Brooklyn, NY July 3-4 1876 under the Auspices of the Municipality...* Brooklyn: Daily Times Print, 1876. First edition, pale grey wrappers printed in blue, 32 pages, tiny chip, else near fine.   Between the Covers Rare Books, Inc.   New York City - 283515   2013 $225

Schuchat, Simon *Caveman.* New York: January, 1978. First edition, unnumbered issue, large narrow 4to., original stapled printed self wrappers, annotated throughout with Ted Berrigan's holograph notes identifying the author of many of the Pseudonymous contributions, very light overall use and dust soiling (bit heavier on back wrapper), otherwise near fine.   James S. Jaffe Rare Books   Fall 2013 - 22   2013 $2500

Schultz, Leon *L'Univers des Enfats.* Paris: Larousse, n.d., 1934. Spiral backed pictorial boards, fine, illustrations by Leon Schultz.   Aleph-Bet Books, Inc.   105 - 407   2013 $675

Schuyler, James *The Fireproof Floors of Witley Court, English Songs and Dances...* West Burke: Janus Press, 1976. First edition, limited to 150 numbered copies, torn, cut and bound by Claire Van Vliet, although not issued signed, this copy signed by Schuyler, 8vo., architectural cut-out endpapers fashioned after topiary gardens at Levens Hall, Westmorland, original orange decorated wrappers, narrow three quarter inch strip of light fading along top of front cover, otherwise fine. James S. Jaffe Rare Books Fall 2013 - 135 2013 $2500

Schwann, Theodor *Mikroskopische Untersuchungen uber Die...* Berlin: G. E. Reimer, 1839. First edition, octavo, all four folding plates at rear, strictly contemporary German speckled boards with red paper gilt lettering label, light blue endpapers, edges stained red, ownership inscription, cloth clamshell case, some minor rubbing to front outer joint, minor foxing to pastedowns, overall very clean and bright, appropriate binding. Heritage Book Shop Holiday Catalogue 2012 - 129 2013 $25,000

Schwerd, Friedrich Magnus *Die Beugungserscheinungen aus den Fundamentalgesetzen der Undulationstheorie.* Manheim: Schwan and Goetz, 1835. First edition, 18 large folding lithographed plates, 2 hand colored, contents bound out of order before introduction, 4to., contemporary half cloth, very good, very scarce. Blackwell's Rare Books Sciences - 111 2013 £950

Schwing, Ned *The Browning Superposed, John M. Browning's Last Legacy.* Iola: Krause Pub., 1996. First edition, very rare, quarto, 496 pages, profusely illustrated with black and white and color photos, facsimiles, charts, reproductions, black boards, gilt, very fine with pictorial dust jacket. Argonaut Book Shop Recent Acquisitions June 2013 - 255 2013 $450

The Science Fiction Syndicate. Austin: pub. by the Science Fiction Syndicate, 1935. First edition, octavo, printed self wrappers, stapled. L. W. Currey, Inc. Fall Sampler Sept. 2013 - 146568 2013 $150

Scoresby, William *Journal of a Voyage to the Northern Whale Fishery...* Edinburgh: 1823. First edition, one large and one other folding map, 6 engraved plates, further illustrations in text, 8vo. contemporary half calf marbled boards, upper joint repaired, occasional very light browning as usual, with distinctive library stamp of Rudmose-Brown. Maggs Bros. Ltd. 1467 - 139 2013 £850

Scotland's Opposition to the Popish Bill. Edinburgh: printed by David Paterson, 1780. 8vo., some browning in places, contemporary sprinkled sheep, flat spine divided by triple gilt fillet, red morocco lettering piece, some old scratches to boards, armorial bookplate of Brown of Waterhaughs and ownership inscription of David Murray, Glasgow, with few of his notes on endpapers, very good. Blackwell's Rare Books 172 - 118 2013 £425

Scott, C. Rochefort *Excursions in the Mountains of Ronda and Granada.* London: Henry Colburn, 1838. First edition, 2 volumes, 8vo., frontispieces (light foxing in margins), original purple blindstamped cloth, very small ownership stamp at base of titlepages, very good set. J. & S. L. Bonham Antiquarian Booksellers Europe - 9734 2013 £1750

Scott, H. Percy *Seeing Canada and the South.* Toronto: William Briggs, 1911. Small 8vo. red cloth boards, gilt titles to front and spine, waterstain to bottom edge of back cover, dust jacket worn with small nicks and tears to edges. Schooner Books Ltd. 101 - 122 2013 $55

Scott, J. M. *Icebound. Journey to the Northwest Sea.* Gordon & Cremonisi, 1977. First edition, tall 8vo., original cloth, gilt, dust jacket price clipped, 16 pages of illustrations and drawings in text. R. F. G. Hollett & Son Polar Exploration - 60 2013 £30

Scott, J. M. *The Polar Regions.* London: Chatto & Windus, circa, 1935. First edition, large 8vo., original cloth, gilt, spine trifle rubbed and faded 100 photos. R. F. G. Hollett & Son Polar Exploration - 62 2013 £25

Scott, Jonathan *Tales, Anecdotes and Letters.* Shrewsbury: printed by J. and W. Eddowes, 1800. 8vo., large clean, uncut copy, unpressed, original sugar paper bands, expertly rebacked, front inner hinge neatly repaired. Jarndyce Antiquarian Booksellers CCV - 242 2013 £220

Scott, Peter *Wild Geese and Eskimos.* London: Country Life, 1951. First edition, original cloth, gilt, faded, colored frontispiece, 36 illustrations and 2 maps, front joints strengthened with linen tape. R. F. G. Hollett & Son Polar Exploration - 63 2013 £30

Scott, Robert Falcon 1868-1912 *The Voyage of the Discovery.* London: Smith, Elder & Co., 1905. Second impression, 2 volumes, very good set in bright original blue gilt cloth some slight foxing. Ken Spelman Books Ltd. 75 - 158 2013 £380

Scott, Walter 1771-1832 *The Field of Waterloo: a Poem.* Edinburgh: printed by James Ballantyne & Co., 1815. First edition, half title, old brown mark to one leaf, some slight foxing, late 19th century half calf, gilt label, upper joint worn and covers unevenly faded. Ken Spelman Books Ltd. 75 - 75 2013 £40

Scott, Walter   1771-1832   *Halidon Hill; A Dramatic Sketch from Scottish History.*   Edinburgh: printed for Archibald Constable and Co., 1822.   First edition, first impression, original publisher's drab paper wrappers, titling printed on cover, untrimmed edges, bookplate of Graham W. Murdoch, tiny losses to backstrip, covers very slightly soiled, leaves faintly browned at edges with occasional minor foxing, excellent copy, fragile original wrappers, still entirely sound, text clean and fresh.   Phillip J. Pirages   63 - 426   2013 $275

Scott, Walter   1771-1832   *Harold the Dauntless: a poem in six cantos.*   Edinburgh: printed by James Ballantyne and Co. for Longman et al, 1817.   First edition, 175 x 108mm., pleasing mid 19th century brown three quarter morocco over green marbled boards by Root and Son (stamp signed), raised bands, spine gilt in compartments with curling frame and large lozenge containing thistle centerpiece, gilt titling, marbled endpapers, top edge gilt, 2 engraved plates, engraved bookplate of John Waugh dated 1896; bit of carefully refurbished rubbing to corners and spine bands, about two thirds of leaves with thin brown stains, sustained before binding?, right at fore and tail edge and well away from text, additional trivial defects, otherwise excellent copy, text fresh and clean, ample margins and in binding solid and appealing.   Phillip J. Pirages 63 - 427   2013 $200

Scott, Walter   1771-1832   *The Lady of the Lake.*   Edinburgh: John Ballantyne and Co., 1810.   Third edition, half title, contemporary tree calf, attractive gilt decorated spine with large circular ornaments, one set against a red morocco onlay, green morocco title label and author's name in green morocco at foot of spine, joints cracked but firm, some slight rubbing, few leaves little creased at top corner.   Ken Spelman Books Ltd.   75 - 65   2013   £85

Scott, Walter   1771-1832   *The Lady in the Lake.*   Edinburgh: printed for Arch. Constable and Co., 1822.   2 volumes (volumes IV and V of the Poetical Works of Sir Watler Scott), each volume with fore-edge painting, volume IV with fore-edge painting of Craigmiller Castle, and volume V with fore-edge painting of Loch Leven Castle; full navy blue straight grain morocco, boards stamped with vignette in gilt of a countryside scene and paneled in blind, spine stamped and lettered gilt, all edges gilt, blue drab endpapers bit of foxing and dampstaining, mainly to blank preims and not affecting fore-edge, overall very good.   Heritage Book Shop   Holiday Catalogue 2012 - 64   2013 $1000

Scott, Walter   1771-1832   *The Life of Napoleon Buonaparte, Emperor of the French...*   Edinburgh: printed by Ballantyne and Co. for Longman, Rees, Orme, Brown & Green, 1827.   First edition, first issue (half titles in each volume), 220 x 130mm., collation irregular in last gathering of volume I, but complete, with half titles in all volumes, errata in first seven, 9 volumes, not unpleasant contemporary black half calf, flat spines heavily gilt in one elongated compartment filled with repeating pattern of flowers and twining leaves, newer black morocco label on each spine, marbled boards, endpapers and top edges, other edges untrimmed; bookplate of Martin Holdich Green, Trinity College, Oxford; half joints bit rubbed and flaked (but not cracking) paper sides rather chafed, couple of spines slightly abraded with minor loss of gilt, leaves with frequent minor foxing and faint offsetting (never serious but intermittently present throughout), not without condition problems, still pleasing set, volumes quite sound, text with no fatal defects.   Phillip J. Pirages   63 - 352   2013 $750

Scott, Walter   1771-1832   *Marmion: a Tale of Flodden Field.*   Edinburgh: Archibald Constable and Co., 1808.   First edition first impression, 287 x 221mm., contemporary burgundy half morocco, two raised bands setting off elongated central spine panel, backstrip with gilt rules, botanical head and tailpiece and gilt titling, marbled boards, edges and endpapers, extra illustrated with engraved titlepage and 6 engraved plates by Richard Westall from 1809, large engraved bookplate and armorial bookplate with ink ownership inscriptions of Charles Leeson Prince, engraved bookplate of Edward S. Marsh dated 1909, flyleaf with armorial bookplate of Johnson Phillott, front joint and hinge cracked with slight bit of give to board, paper sides noticeably chafed, extremities and bands rather rubbed, significant offsetting from plates, half dozen leaves at front and back somewhat foxed, other minor imperfections with condition issues, still intact and internally fresh and clean as well as desirable for its added illustrations and special provenance.   Phillip J. Pirages   63 - 428   2013 $250

Scott, Walter   1771-1832   *Minstrelsy of the Scottish Border.*   Edinburgh: printed by J. Ballantyne and Co., 1810.   Fourth edition, second (Large Paper) impression, 240 x 145mm., pleasing contemporary black straight grain morocco, covers with gilt floral frame enclosing central panel with blindstamped thistle cornerpieces, raised bands, spines heavily gilt in compartments with much swirling foliate, gilt turn-ins, marbled endpapers, all edges gilt, volume I with attractive fore-edge painting of the Mercat Cross in Melrose, Roxburghshire; pastedown volumes II and III with engraved bookplate of W. J. Denison, volume I with evidence of bookplate removal, copy of engraving of Boston Church, Lancashire laid in at rear volume II, joints and extremities somewhat rubbed, boards bit marked and abraded, minor foxing here and there in text, 9 gatherings with faint overall browning due to poor quality paper, still excellent set, leaves clean, once quite dazzling bindings still sound and pleasing, fore edge painting well preserved.   Phillip J. Pirages   63 - 191   2013 $1250

Scott, Walter 1771-1832 *Miscellaneous Poems.* Edinburgh: printed for Archibald Constable and Co., 1820. First edition, 2nd issue, 235 x 143mm., original publisher's drab paper boards with paper title label on spine, fore and tail edges untrimmed in (rather soiled, scuffed and faded), green linen covered slipcase with red morocco spine label, pencilled ownership inscription of E. B. Rose 62 Burton Crescent", front board detached parts of backstrip missing, spine label rather abraded (with considerable loss of letterpress), isolated spots of light foxing, otherwise fine internally text quite clean fresh and bright.   Phillip J. Pirages   63 - 429   2013 $75

Scott, Walter 1771-1832 *Nigels Afventyr.* Stockholm: 1827. 3 volumes, 8vo., contemporary Swedish (?) half calf, gilt spines, volumes look well on shelf, but marbled paper boards have severe insect damage and text is rather heavily foxed, scarce.   Ken Spelman Books Ltd.   75 - 90   2013   £50

Scott, Walter 1771-1832 *Redgauntlet.* Edinburgh: printed for Archibald Constable and Co., 1824. First edition, first state with 1823 watermark and comma following title on titlepage of volumes I and II, 3 volumes, 203 x 129mm., without 2 leaves of ads at end of volume 3, pleasing 19th century brown quarter morocco over marbled boards by Rene Asper of Geneva (stamp signed), raised bands, gilt titling, edges untrimmed, hint of rubbing to joints, trivial scratch to one board, occasional minor foxing, other insignificant defects, still excellent set, text fresh and and clean, bindings showing little wear.   Phillip J. Pirages   63 - 430   2013 $200

Scott, Walter 1771-1832 *Rokeby.* Edinburgh: printed for John Ballentyne and Co. by James Ballantyne and Co., 1813. First edition, 4to., toned and somewhat spotted, early 20th century dark blue Niger morocco, spine divided by four broad flat raised bands, tooled in gilt, lettered gilt direct, top edge gilt with others uncut, scratched, front joint and ends of rear joint renewed, ink ownership inscription "C & Q A Head, from original endpaper archivally pasted at upper forecorner of pastedown, ex-libris heraldic bookplate of Vincent Henry Stanton, signed binding "Bound by Stoakley Late Hawes".   Unsworths Antiquarian Booksellers   28 - 197   2013   £50

Scott, Walter 1771-1832 *Works.* Edinburgh: printed for Robert Cadell and Whittaker and Co., London, 1830-1834. 62 volumes, foolscap 8vo., engraved titles and frontispieces in every volume, contemporary half green morocco over marbled boards, matching marbled edges, spines gilt, minor wear, very good.   Blackwell's Rare Books   B174 - 131   2013   £1000

Scoville, Wilbur L. *The Art of Compounding.* Philadelphia: Blakiston, 1895. Original green cloth, wear and rubbing to cloth.   James Tait Goodrich   S74 - 207   2013 $65

Scowrers and Molly Maguires of San Francisco *West by One and by One.* San Francisco: privately pub., 1965. First edition, fine in dust jacket, laid in is program for the 20th Anniversary Dinner for The Scowers & Molly Maguires at the Lepard Cafe in San Francisco May 1964.   Mordida Books   81 - 156   2013 $200

Scribonius Largus *Compositiones Medicae.* Padua: typis Pauli Frambotti, 1655. 4to, 2 plates, 2 leave, large dark stains, causing paper damage to blank area of sectional title, sometime repaired, no loss, small repair to margin of following leaf, few minor spots elsewhere, gathering O bound out of order, contemporary vellum boards, long sides overlapping, slightly soiled, endpapers renewed, new leather label to spine, small stamp to title and gilt stamp to spine of Birmingham Medical Institute, red stamp of the Libraria Colona to title, endpaper and several leaves of plates.   Unsworths Antiquarian Booksellers   28 - 45   2013   £950

Scudder, Horace Elisha *The Game of Croquet.* New York: Abercrombie & Fitch, 1968. First edition, fine in very good dust jacket with nicks at spine ends, several closed tears and light wear along folds and at corners.   Mordida Books   81 - 494   2013 $125

Scultetus, Johann *...Cheiroplotheke Armamentarium Chirurgicum...* The Hague: ex officina Adriani Vlacq 1656, i.e., 1657. First octavo edition, contemporary calf, newly rebacked in calf, endpapers renewed, signed inscription of Sir Charles Sherrington.   James Tait Goodrich   75 - 188   2013 $2500

Searle, Mark *Turnpikes and Toll-Bars.* London: Hutchinson & Co., 1930. Limited edition, numbered 411 of 500 copies, 2 volumes, 4to., numerous illustrations, half red rexine, original dust jackets.   Marlborough Rare Books Ltd.   218 - 138   2013   £500

Seaver, George *Edward Wilson: Nature-Lover.* London: John Murray, 1937. First edition, original cloth, gilt, spine label, few marks, 14 color plates, numerous other plates and illustrations.   R. F. G. Hollett & Son   Polar Exploration - 64   2013   £35

Sebald, W. G. *Austrlitz.* Hamilton: 2001. Uncorrected proof copy, 53/100 copies signed by author, illustrations, foolscap 8vo., original cream boards printed in black, white and yellow, illustrated overall on front cover, very light bumping to backstrip tail, near fine.   Blackwell's Rare Books   B174 - 297   2013   £700

Sebald, W. G. *"Unerzahlt. 33 Miniaturen.* Munchen: Carl Hanser Verlag, 2002. First edition, one of only 33 numbered copies signed by Hans Magnus Enzensberger who contributes prefatory poem, small 4to., original half morocco and gray cloth, silk ribbon marker, matching original cloth and cardstock slipcase, 33 original signed prints by Tripp, signed frontispiece etching by Tripp, as new, acid free box and publisher's shipping carton.   James S. Jaffe Rare Books   Fall 2013 - 136   2013 $7500

Seccombe, Joseph *Some Occasional Thoughts on the Influence of the Spirit.* Boston: S. Kneeland and T. Green, 1742. First edition, 8vo., modern plain wrappers, lacks half title, foxed.   M & S Rare Books, Inc.   95 - 338   2013 $300

Seccombe, T. S. *Comic Sketches from English History for Children of all Ages.* London: W. H. Allen & Co. n.d. circa, 1885. Oblong large 8vo., original cloth backed pictorial boards, worn and soiled, pages 55, 12 full page color plates, numerous text illustrations, scattered light foxing.   R. F. G. Hollett & Son   Children's Books - 529   2013   £30

Seccombe, Thomas *The Bookman Illustrated History of English Language.* London: Hodder & Stoughton, 1907. 290 x 210m, 2 volumes bound in 1, with 51 "Rembrandt" photogravures of author portraits and scenes from literary works; striking contemporary Arts and Crafts style dark brown crushed morocco elaborately gilt and inlaid, covers with borders containing quotes from Emerson and Pope as well as inlaid green quatrefoil cornerpieces, central panel framed by intricately entwined flowering vine (the vine on the front cover with dozens of inlaid green leaves and ivory blossoms), very large window-like central panel divided into 24 'panes' of various sizes by linking and parallel gilt lines, 14 of the intersections of these lines on each cover with variably intricate stylized floral and leafy decoration (upper board with these decorations incorporating inlaid ivory, ochre and green morocco dots), large square centerpiece with similar intricate tooling, multiple inlays and gilt dots (centerpiece on lower cover with gilt only), raised bands, spine compartments with looping gilt tooled decoration accented by inlaid and gilt dots, foot of spine with initials "A.F.W." and date "1909", 2 braided leather and brass fore-edge clasps, rich green morocco doublures framed in brown with borders of multiple plain and dotted gilt rules, vellum endleaves, all edges gilt, leather little dulled in spots (apparently by preservative), just hint of rubbing to extremities, first and last gatherings in second part rather browned, occasional minor foxing, particularly to opening and closing leaves, but impressive with no significant internal condition problems, extremely handsome and animated binding showing virtually no wear.   Phillip J. Pirages   61 - 100   2013 $2800

Sedaris, David *Barrel Fever.* Boston: Little Brown and Co., 1994. First edition, 196 pages, clean, very near fine in very near fine dust jacket with very slight crease to front flap, very nice.   Jeff Hirsch Books   Fall 2013 - 129217   2013 $75

Sedgwick, Adam *Adam Sedgwick's Dent.* Sedbergh: R. F. G. Hollett & Son, 1985. First edition, attractively bound in green leather cloth, paper spine label to match original editions, 2 plates, inex.   R. F. G. Hollett & Son   Lake District & Cumbria - 147   2013   £25

Sedgwick, Anne Douglas *Christmas Roses and Other Stories.* Boston and New York: Houghton Mifflin, 1920. First edition, octavo, original decorated green cloth.   L. W. Currey, Inc.   Christmas Themed Books - 113128   2013 $75

Seeds of Change. Boulder: Boulder Public Library, 1993. Brochure, symposium program and activities, fine in hand lettered "Teacher's Packet" folder.   Ken Lopez Bookseller   159 - 158   2013 $75

Seegmiller, Wilhelmina *Other Rhymes for Little Readers.* Chicago: Rand McNally, 1911. Folio, pictorial cloth, pictorial paste on, (72) pages, fine, every page with beautiful sepia illustrations by Ruth Hallock plus color plate on cover, printed on heavy coated paper.   Aleph-Bet Books, Inc.   104 - 273   2013 $250

Segal, Hyman R. *They Called Him Champ.* New York: Citadel Press, 1959. First edition, near fine in very good dust jacket, signed and inscribed by Harry Champ Segal, uncommon.   Leather Stalking Books   October 2013 - 2013 $125

Seidenberg, Caryl *Insomnia.* Winnetka: The Vixen Press, 2008. One of 12 copies, each signed and numbered by artist/author/printer, all on Somerset cover stock, page size 5 3/4 x 7 inches, 20 pages, bound by artist, black cover stock, exposed spine with three white ribbons printed by author woven behind wires that are affixed to each page with tape, ribbons extend on to front and back panels, front label with hand printed relief print in black that resembles a bid or open curtains (with eyes peering out), and a sleeping pill and the title "In somnia", text handset in Eusebius and printed on a number 4 Vandercook, images are hand painted relief prints as well as drawings translated to polymer plates, beautiful book.   Priscilla Juvelis - Rare Books   56 - 36   2013 $1200

Seidenberg, Caryl *Operation Rescue.* Winnetka: Vixen Press, 1980. Artist's book, one of 35 copies only, all on Arches paper, each signed and numbered by artist/author/printer/binder, Caryl Seidenberg, page size 6 x 8 1/8 inches, 16 pages, bound by artist, sewn, brown paper over boards, tan cloth spine, brown Fabriano endsheets, label printed in brown with title and artist on front panel, poem printed letterpress on Number 4 Vandercook in 18 pt. Caslon Openface, 12 pt. Bauer Bodoni Italic, 12 pt. Bodoni Book and 10 p.t Bauer Bodoni.   Priscilla Juvelis - Rare Books   56 - 37   2013 $500

Selbourne, Joanna *Gwen Raverat, Wood Engraver.* Denby Dale: Fleece Press, 1996. One of 260 copies (of an edition of 300), printed on Zerkall mouldmade paper, printed in black, title and chapter headings printed in brown, numerous reproductions of wood engravings by Raverat, small number tipped in with tipped in color printed self portrait of artist, small folio, original quarter mustard cloth, printed label, marbled brown and yellow boards, rough trimmed, few small stains on cloth and board slipcase, fine. Blackwell's Rare Books 172 - 281 2013 £350

Selby, Thomas G. *As the Chinese See Us.* London: T. Fisher Unwin, 1901. First edition, 8vo., few pages unopened, very good+, inscribed "R. Regs. Esq. with author's compliments". By the Book, L. C. 38 - 71 2013 $200

Selden, John *An Historicall Discourse of the Uniformity of the Government of England.* London: for Mathew Walbancke, 1647. First edition, 4to., engraved fore-title, contemporary calf, faint dampstain bottom margin, extremities of engraved fore-title discolored from leather turn-ins, front hinge scuffed and cracking at top, very nice, as issued. Joseph J. Felcone Inc. Books Printed before 1701 - 77 2013 $750

Selden, John *An Historical Discourse of the Uniformity of the Government of England.* (with) *The Continuation of an Historicall Discourse of the Government of England...* London: printed for Matthew Walbancke, 1647-1651. (i.e. 1672), 2 volumes bound as one, 4to., browned and spotted, intermittent underlining and some marginal notes in red pencil, pencilled index to final blank, fore margin of that leaf, also repaired somewhat crudely, modern half calf in antique style, spine lettered and decorated in blind, bit rubbed. Unsworths Antiquarian Booksellers 28 - 126 2013 £500

Semonides *De Mulieribus. Recensuit Atque Animadversionibus Illustratvit Georgius David Koeler.* Gottingen: Sumtibus viduae Vandenhoeck, 1781. First separate edition, titlepage little dusty, edges entirely untrimmed and bumped as result, 8vo., stitched (top stitch loose), original blue paper wrappers, bit soiled, few small tears at edges, sometime backed with matching paper, this lettered longitudinally in ink, good. Blackwell's Rare Books 172 - 129 2013 £225

Sen, Amartya *On Economic Inequality.* New York: W. W. Norton, 1973. First American edition, signed and dated by author, near fine, 8vo., very good++ dust jacket with minimal scuffs and edgewear. By the Book, L. C. 38 - 22 2013 $650

Sendak, Jack *Happy Rain.* New York: Harper Bros., 1956. 4to., blue cloth stamped in yellow, some fading in areas of covers, else fine in dust jacket with price intact and with some soil and small chip on rear edge, color dust jacket and full page and smaller black and whites by Maurice Sendak, rare. Aleph-Bet Books, Inc. 105 - 526 2013 $850

Sendak, Maurice *Nutshell Library. Alligators All Around; Chicken Soup with Rice. One was Johnny. Pierre.* Harper & Row, 1962. First edition, 4 volumes, 12mo., original pink cloth, dust jackets (extremities little worn and chipped in places), pictorial slipcase, latter rather worn, taped repair, price sticker torn off damaging the surface of one panel, each volume illustrated in color. R. F. G. Hollett & Son Children's Books - 535 2013 £75

Sendak, Maurice *Caldecott & Co.* Reinhardt Books and Viking, 1989. First edition, original cloth, gilt, dust jacket, 216 pages, fine. R. F. G. Hollett & Son Children's Books - 531 2013 £40

Sendak, Maurice *Collection of Books, Posters and Original Drawings.* New York: Justin G. Schiller Ltd., 1984. Square 4to., original pictorial wrappers, 77 illustrations. R. F. G. Hollett & Son Children's Books - 532 2013 £35

Sendak, Maurice *Hector Protector and As I Went Over the Water.* New York: Harper and Row, 1965. First edition, oblong 8vo., original cloth backed pictorial boards, dust jacket price clipped, unpaginated, illustrations in color. R. F. G. Hollett & Son Children's Books - 533 2013 £75

Sendak, Maurice *In the Night Kitchen.* Harper & Row, 1970. First US edition, original cloth with pictorial roundel, dust jacket, illustrations in color, fine copy of later impression with unpriced wrapper (rear flap printed same as first edition). R. F. G. Hollett & Son Children's Books - 534 2013 £180

Sendak, Maurice *Seven Little Monsters.* London: The Bodley Head, 1977. First UK edition, long oblong 8vo., original pictorial boards, no dust jacket issued, illustrations in color, 6 panel foldout 'leporello' at end. R. F. G. Hollett & Son Children's Books - 537 2013 £75

Sendak, Maurice *Seven Little Monsters.* Harper Collins, 1977. Long oblong 8vo., original plain boards, dust jacket, illustrations in color. R. F. G. Hollett & Son Children's Books - 536 2013 £50

Sendak, Maurice *Stories & Pictures.* Harper Collins, circa, 1991. First edition, small square 8vo., original pictorial wrappers, concertina of 16 panels, printed in color on stiff coated paper, unfolding to a length of 250mm, top edges die cut to shape of illustrations. R. F. G. Hollett & Son Children's Books - 538 2013 £60

Sendak, Maurice *We Are All in the Dumps with Jack and Guy.* Harper Collins, 1993. First edition, oblong large 8vo., original fawn boards, dust jacket, unpaginated, illustrations in color, fine.   R. F. G. Hollett & Son   Children's Books - 539   2013   £60

Sendak, Maurice *Where the Wild Things Are.*   New York: Harper & Row, 1963. Oblong 4to., cloth backed pictorial boards, fine in dust jacket with $4.95 price, inscribed by Sendak with wonderful pen drawing dated 1975.   Aleph-Bet Books, Inc.   104 - 513   2013 $1750

Sendak, Philip *In Grandpa's House.*   Harper & Row, 1985. First edition, original cloth, gilt, dust jacket price clipped, illustrations by Maurice Sendak.   R. F. G. Hollett & Son   Children's Books - 546   2013   £45

Seneca, Lucius Annaeus *Tragoediae.* Florence: studio et impensa Philippi di Giunta, 1506. 8vo., final blank discarded, rather foxed in places, some soiling, intermittent stain in gutter, few early ink marks, early ownership inscription to second leaf, 8vo., later vellum, spine with four raised bands lettered in ink somewhat soiled and splayed, bookplates of Bibloteca Senequiana and the Prince of Liechtenstein, sound.   Blackwell's Rare Books   B174 - 133   2013   £950

Senff, Carolus Fridericus *Nonnulis de Incremento Ossium Embryonum in Primus Graviditatis Menisbus.* Haiae: Typis Baltheanis, n.d. crica, 1870. 84 pages, one folding table, one folding anatomical plate, 4to., later plain wrappers with engraved fetal skull on titlepage, text foxed and browned, very few copies.   James Tait Goodrich   75 - 189   2013 $395

Senior, Nassau William   1790-1864 *A Journey Kept in Turkey and Greece, in the Autumn of 1857 and the Beginning of 1858.*   London: Longman, Brown, Green, 1859. First edition, 8vo., half title, 2 double page maps colored in outline, 2 colored lithographs, original green blindstamped cloth, corners rubbed, small evidence of rubbing on upper cover, very good.   J. & S. L. Bonham Antiquarian Booksellers   Europe - 9174   2013   £600

Sennart, Daniel *Institutionum Medicinae Libri V.* Wittenberg: Zachariam Schuurerum, 1620. Second edition, Engraved allegorical title, portrait of author and folding plate (repaired at folds), thick large 4to., newly rebound in quarter calf and marbled boards, raised bands, early underlining and marginalia, text toned and foxed, scattered page and paper repairs, inner edge of title has been reinforced. James Tait Goodrich   S74 - 224   2013 $1495

Sequeira, Louis De *Breve Relacion sobre la Persecuion de Nuestra Santa Fe en la Provincia de Kiamnan y Otras....* Manila: en la Imprenta de la Compania de Iesus por D. Nicolas de la Cruz Bagay, 1751. First edition, small 4to., rebound in early 20th century speckled calf, title with minor marginal repairs, overall fine.   Maggs Bros. Ltd.   1467 - 64   2013 $26,000

Serrano Y Morales, Jose Enrique *Resena Historica en Forma de Diccionario de la Imprentas que han Existido en Valencia desde la Introduccion del Arte Tipografico en Espana Hasta el Ano 1868.*   Valencia: Impr. de F. Domenech, 1898-1899. First edition, number 45 of 100 copies, inscribed by author, 4to., black and white reproductions full autumn leaf calf, raised bands, compartments decorated in gilt, sides decorated in gilt, marbled endpapers, original wrappers bound in, very good or better, extremities rubbed, rear board with few scuffs.   Kaaterskill Books   16 - 74   2013 $500

Serviss, Garrett P. *The Columbus of Space.*   New York and London: D. Appleton and Co., 1911. First edition, pictorial cloth, both hinges neatly repaired, few light stains in text, else very good.   Between the Covers Rare Books, Inc.   Sci-Fi, Fantasy & Horror - 292479   2013 $200

Seth, Vikram *A Suitable Boy.*   London: Sixth Chamber Books, 1993. First edition, letter Q from an edition of only 26 copies, fine in full leather, signed with 6 line holograph quotation from the book.   Jeff Hirsch Books   Fall 2013 - 129213   2013 $950

Seth, Vikram *A Suitable Boy.*   Sixth Chamber Press, 1993. First edition, 61/100 copies (of an editio of 126 copies), signed by author 8vo., original quarter tan morocco, backstrip gilt lettered, dark brown boards, fine.   Blackwell's Rare Books   B174 - 298   2013   £250

Seton, Ernest Thompson   1860-1946 *Bannertail.* London: Hodder and Stoughton, 1922. First US edition, original green cloth with pictorial onlay, 8 plates, 100 drawings by author.   R. F. G. Hollett & Son   Children's Books - 547   2013   £35

Seton, Ernest Thompson   1860-1946 *Rolf in the Woods.* London: Constable, 1911. First edition, original blindstamped green cloth gilt, partially faded, untrimmed, over 200 illustrations. R. F. G. Hollett & Son   Children's Books - 551   2013   £30

Seton, Ernest Thompson   1860-1946 *Wild Animals I Have Known and 200 Drawings.*   New York: Charles Scribner's, 1898. First edition, first state, with page 265, last paragraph, omitting line "The Angel whispered don't go", one of 1640 copies printed for this country, of an edition of 2000, 8vo., original pictorial green cloth, some fading, little wear at spine tips, 29 plates, top edge gilt, top and bottom edges uncut.   Howard S. Mott Inc.   262 - 131   2013 $400

Severn, David *Burglars and Bandicoots.* New York: Macmillan Co., 1952. First American edition (from English sheets), illustrations by J. Kiddell-Monroe, fine in fine dust jacket with tiny tear, beautiful copy. Between the Covers Rare Books, Inc. Mystery & Detective Fiction - 98350 2013 $65

Severus, Sulpicius *Opera Omnia.* Leiden & Rotterdam: Apud Elzevirios, apud Hackios, 1665. Editio tertia, 8vo., some browning and spotting, contemporary vellum, yapped edges, spine lettered ink, spine soiled, boards bowed and stained, large line engraving pasted to front pastedown, sound. Blackwell's Rare Books 172 - 130 2013 £95

Sevigne, Marie De Rabutin-Chantal, Marquise De 1626-1696 *Lettres Choisies De Mme. De Sevinge...* Paris: Chez Bossange, 1817. 12mo., 3 volumes in French, 2 frontispiece portraits, half leather, very good. Barnaby Rudge Booksellers Biography 2013 - 016107 2013 $90

Sewall, May Wright *The World's Congress of Representative Women a Historical Resume...* Chicago: Rand McNally, 1894. 2 volumes, large 8vo., portraits, blue cloth, stamped in gilt, ex-library with bookplate and stamps, cover scuffed at edges, corners little bumped, otherwise very good, tight set. Second Life Books Inc. 182 - 216 2013 $225

Seward, Anna *Memoirs of the Life of Dr. Darwin, Chiefly During His Residence at Lichfield,...* London: Printed for J. Johnson by T. Bensley, 1804. First edition, occasional light foxing, 8vo., 19th century half calf by E. Clulow of Derby, slightly worn, neatly recased, titlepage inscribed "From the author", recipient's name erased, with number of pencil notes to text, good. Blackwell's Rare Books Sciences - 112 2013 £650

Seward, Anna *Monody on Major Andre.* Lichfield: printed and sold by J. Jackson for the author, sold also...London, Oxford, Cambridge & Bath, 1781. First edition, 4to., contemporary half calf, marbled boards, leather label, first couple of leaves foxed, otherwise fine, signed by author on page 28, as usual to protect from piracy. Howard S. Mott Inc. 262 - 132 2013 $1350

Seward, William W. *The Hibernian Gazetteer...* Dublin: Alex Stuart, 1789. 8vo., contemporary calf (worn), text age browned, worm-traces pages liii-lxviii, lower margin, text not affected, fairly good. C. P. Hyland 261 - 772 2013 £300

Seward, William W. *Topographia Hibernica; or the Topography of Ireland.* Dublin: Alex Stewart, 1795. 4to., (366) pages, folding map, chart, contemporary mottled calf, front hinge broken, text very good. C. P. Hyland 261 - 773 2013 £375

Sewell, Anna *Black Beauty; the Autobiography of a Horse.* London: Jarrold and Sons, 1878. Fourth edition, frontispiece and name cut from upper margin with slight loss of image, carefully replaced with smaller paper, 8 pages ads, brown endpapers, original dark blue diagonal fine ribbed cloth, blocked ad lettered in black and gilt, lettering reversed out of gilt, little rubbed and dulled, but nice. Jarndyce Antiquarian Booksellers CCV - 243 2013 £420

Sewell, Anna *Black Beauty.* London: J. M. Dent, 1915. Limited edition, signed, number 20 of 600 copies, large 4to., original green cloth gilt, large gilt embossed roundel of horses' heads on upper board, trifling wear to extreme corners, top edge gilt, uncut, 30 colored plates tipped on to fawn mounts, few scattered spots but lovely copy, inscribed "T. M. Walker, to myself Christmas 1915". R. F. G. Hollett & Son Children's Books - 322 2013 £795

Sewell, Anna *Black Beauty.* Jarrolds for Boot's the Chemist, n.d. circa, 1930. First edition thus, Large 8vo., original pictorial blue cloth gilt, extremities little worn, 18 color plates by Cecil Aldin tipped in with tissue guards. R. F. G. Hollett & Son Children's Books - 9 2013 £120

Sewell, William Grant *Ordeal of Free Labor in the British West Indies.* New York: Harper and Bros., 1862. Second edition, some slight spotting, original purple cloth, little rubbed and dulled, nice. Jarndyce Antiquarian Booksellers CCV - 244 2013 £120

Sexton, Anne *Love Poems.* Boston: Houghton Mifflin, 1969. First edition, very good with several dog eared pages, very good dust jacket with small chip at head of front spine fold. Beasley Books 2013 - 2013 $100

Seymann, Jerrold *Colonial Charters Patents and Grants to the Communities Comprising the City of New York.* New York: Board of Statutory Consolidation of the City of New York, 1939. First edition, one of 500 copies, blue buckram, 612 pages, folding plates, fine. Between the Covers Rare Books, Inc. New York City - 286985 2013 $150

Seymour, Mary F. *Report of the International Council of Women, Assembled by the National Woman Suffrage Association, Washington DC... March 25 to April 1 1888.* Washington: Darby, 1888. First edition, large 8vo., rust cloth, stamped in gilt, frontispiece portrait, ex-library with bookplate and edges stamps, hinges tender, owner's name, cover scuffed at edges and spine, otherwise very good. Second Life Books Inc. 182 - 218 2013 $750

Seymour, W. D. *Journal of a Voyage Round the World.* Cork: Guy, 1877. First edition, vii, 169 pages, mounted portrait photo, very good. C. P. Hyland 261 - 774 2013 £750

Shackelford, Jane Dabney *The Child's Story of the Negro.* Washington: Associated Pub., 1938. First edition, 219 pages, illustrations by Lois Milou Jones, some soiling to boards and fraying at base of spine, about very good in very good plus dust jacket, slightly frayed at spine, signed by artist, Lois Mailou Jones.   Between the Covers Rare Books, Inc.   165 - 24   2013 $1000

The Shade of Byron: a Mock Heroic Poem... London: James Burns, 1871.   Double frontispiece, some light foxing, occasional annotations and underlinings in red ink, original blue cloth, blocked in blind and gilt, pine lettered gilt, slightly rubbed, spine darkened, following hinge beginning to slit.   Jarndyce Antiquarian Booksellers   CCIII - 341   2013   £165

Shahn, Ben *The Alphabet of Creation: an Ancient Legend from Zohar.* New York: Spiral Press for Pantheon, 1954. First edition, one of 50 copies printed on Umbria handmade paper, signed by artist with original drawing by him, this copy being number five, tall octavo, (44) pages, including colophon and numerous Shahn illustrations plus frontispiece of original Shahn watercolor, signed by him, publisher's natural linen cloth with black morocco, gilt spine label, cover label, publisher's cardboard slipcase with small split at bottom, overall fine.   Heritage Book Shop   Holiday Catalogue 2012 - 132   2013 $1850

Shakespeare, William   1564-1616 *The Beauties of Shakespeare...* for J. Walker, 1818.   12mo., engraved title, half title, very good in contemporary half calf, gilt banded spine with red morocco label, marbled edges.   Ken Spelman Books Ltd.   75 - 78   2013   £40

Shakespeare, William   1564-1616 *The Comedies of William Shakespeare.*   New York: Harper and Bros., 1895. First edition, one of 750 copies, this copy #560, 4 volumes, 264 x 186mm., pleasant contemporary blue-gray half morocco, raised bands, spines in unusual wavy ruled and lobed gilt compartments, with clusters of small dots as corner and side pieces and jester's head or theatrical masks as centerpiece, marbled boards and endpapers, top edge gilt, other edges untrimmed, 131 photogravure plates by Edwin Abbey, as called for, all with lettered tissue guards; spines very faintly and uniformly faded, but bindings in fine condition, without any of the expected rubbing to joins or chafing to paper sides, hint of edge browning a few leaves roughly opened, ample four inch stain at bottom of one page, other trivial imperfections, but generally quite fine internally, text and plates very fresh and clean, margins especially ample.   Phillip J. Pirages   63 - 434   2013 $500

Shakespeare, William   1564-1616 *The Comedy of Errors. (with) Much Ado About Nothing.*   London: printed for H. Herringman, E. Brewster and R. Bentley, 1685. Extracted from Fourth folio, folio, attractively bound in half orange morocco over marbled boards, spine lettered gilt, front board with orange morocco label, lettered and ruled gilt, edges speckled red, some minor marginal dampstaining, overall very good.   Heritage Book Shop   Holiday Catalogue 2012 - 138   2013 $4500

Shakespeare, William   1564-1616 *The Tragedie of Cymbeline.*   printed at the Shakespeare Head press for Benn, 1923.   374/500 copies (from a total of 6066 copies), 5 color printed plates and 29 decorations in text, all by Ablert Rutherson, titlepage, printed in red and black, large 4to., original quarter grey linen, backstrip lettered in black, pale grey boards, small neat gift inscription, faint free endpaper foxing, untrimmed, very good.   Blackwell's Rare Books   B174 - 385   2013   £50

Shakespeare, William   1564-1616 *Dramatic Works of Shakespeare.*   Edinburgh: William Paterson, 1883.   8 volumes, octavo, etchings, three quarter red morocco over red linen boards, spines stamped and lettered gilt, marbled endpapers, top edge gilt, others uncut, some hinges with bit of very light rubbing, overall very good, handsome set.   Heritage Book Shop   Holiday Catalogue 2012 - 134   2013 $1500

Shakespeare, William   1564-1616 *Merry Wives of Windsor.*   New York: Frederick Stokes, 1910.   First US edition, thick 4to., green gilt pictorial cloth, fine, 40 beautiful tipped-in color plates (with guards), uncommon title, great copy, illustrations by Hugh Thomson.   Aleph-Bet Books, Inc.   105 - 560   2013 $300

Shakespeare, William   1564-1616 *A Midsummer Nights Dream.*   London and New York: Heinemann & Doubleday, 1908.   First edition, 4to., tan cloth, stamped in gold, fine, 40 magnificent tipped in color plates by Arthur Rackham, with lettered guards, many lovely black and whites in text.   Aleph-Bet Books, Inc.   104 - 471   2013 $1200

Shakespeare, William   1564-1616 *The Late and Much Admired Play, Called Pericles, Prince of Tyre.*   London: Thomas Coles, 1635.   Sixth edition, octavo in fours, printer's device on titlepage, full 20th century red morocco, boards double ruled gilt spine lettered gilt, gilt dentelles, edges speckled red from earlier binding, spine slightly sunned and worn at edges, old ink signature of William Glegh.   Heritage Book Shop   Holiday Catalogue 2012 - 135   2013 $60,000

Shakespeare, William   1564-1616   *The Plays and Poems of William Shakespeare...*   London: printed for F. C. and J. Rivington et al, 1821.   21 volumes, six engraved plates, one folding plate and 5 folding letterpress tables, plates spotted, occasional spotting elsewhere, 8vo., later tan calf, spines gilt in compartments with two red morocco labels (nine replaced, a number of others chipped or partly defective), marbled edges and endpapers, rubbed, touch of wear to some extremities, good.   Blackwell's Rare Books   B174 - 135   2013   £900

Shakespeare, William   1564-1616   *Poems on Several Occasions.*   London: sold by A. Murden &c, circa, 1775? vi, 250 pages, engraved frontispiece, 12mo., small hole to A11 affecting few letters, some foxing and light browning, expertly bound in recent quarter sprinkled calf, marbled boards, vellum tips, raised and gilt banded spine, red morocco label.   Jarndyce Antiquarian Booksellers   CCIV - 266   2013   £380

Shakespeare, William   1564-1616   *The Tempest.*   London: Hodder & Stoughton, 1908.   Limited to 500 numbered copies signed by artist, large 4to., full gilt vellum, silk ties renewed, top edge gilt, near fine, 40 beautiful tipped in color plates by Edmund Dulac, on heavy stock, magnificent copy.   Aleph-Bet Books, Inc.   104 - 182   2013 $2500

Shakespeare, William   1564-1616   *The Tempest.*   London: William Heinemann Ltd. and New York: Doubleday, Page & Co., 1926.   First trade edition, quarto, 20 mounted color plates and 25 drawings in black and white by Arthur Rackham, original black cloth over boards, minimal spotting in text, otherwise exceptionally fine, original cream colored pictorial dust jacket printed in red and listing 16 other books illustrated by Rackham, neat ink name and date Dec. 24th 1926.   David Brass Rare Books, Inc.   Holiday 2012 Chapter One - DB 01619   2013 $1500

Shakespeare, William   1564-1616   *The Tempest.*   London: Heinemann, 1926.   First Rackham edition, 20 color printed plates, 25 illustrations in text all by Arthur Rackham, imperial 8vo., original dark grey cloth, few minor smudges to front cover and tiny bump to head of rear cover adjacent to backstrip, gilt blocked lettering and designs to backstrip and front cover by Rackham, tail edges rough trimmed, very good.   Blackwell's Rare Books   B174 - 286   2013 £500

Shakespeare, William   1564-1616   *The Tempest. (with) The Two Gentlemen of Verona.*   London: printed for H. Herringman, C. Brewster and R. Bentley, 1685.   Extracted from the fourth folio, folio, attractively bound in half orange morocco over marbled boards, spine lettered gilt, front board with orange morocco label, lettered and ruled gilt, edges speckled red, some minor marginal dampstaining, pages 23-26 with some soiling and approximately one half inch trimmed from bottom margin, not affecting text, 7 inch closed tear, overall very good.   Heritage Book Shop Holiday Catalogue 2012 - 137   2013 $3500

Shakespeare, William   1564-1616   *The Works of William Shakespear, (with) The Works of Mr. William Shakespear. Volume the seventh.*   London: printed for Jacob Tonson, 1709.   London: printed for C. Curll, 1710, First illustrated edition, 7 octavo volumes, engraved plates, frontispiece in each volume and 43 additional plates, volume VII has the plate, often missing, before Venus and Adonis, contemporary calf, panels stamped in blind on covers, gilt spines decoratively tooled in compartments, gilt board edges, edges sprinkled red, volume VIII, published one year later, bound in contemporary calf not matching the preceding six, as seems usual with this set, all in fine contemporary condition, joints repaired, previous owner's bookplate.   Heritage Book Shop   50th Anniversary Catalogue - 89   2013 $25,000

Shakespeare, William   1564-1616   *The Works of...*   Edinburgh: printed for Bell and Bradfute et al, 1795.   8 volumes, some light browning, occasional foxing and few small marginal paper flaws, contemporary tree calf, spines divided by gilt fillet, red morocco lettering pieces and small circular green morocco numbering pieces, the latter lost on volume iii, spines rubbed, few headcaps chipped, ownership inscriptions of George Buchanan of Ladrishmore, good. Blackwell's Rare Books   B174 - 134   2013   £800

Shakespeare, William   1564-1616   *The Pictorial Edition of the Works of Shak(e)speare.*   London: Charles Knight and Co., 1839-1843.   254 x 171mm., 8 volumes, attractive contemporary rose colored pebble grain morocco, covers with blind ruled border and central gilt armorial crest featuring three stages of an azured escutcheon, whole surrounded by plumes, ribbons, and foliage, raised bands flanked by blind rules, elaborate gilt floral gilt turn-ins, marbled endpapers, all edges gilt, approximately 900 steel engravings and woodcuts, many full page, light soiling to bindings joints and extremities slightly rubbed (one joint with short crack just beginning), occasional minor foxing another trivial imperfections, but excellent set, clean, fresh text in solid and appeal offprint, near fine with crease down middle, inscribed by authoring binding, showing little wear.   Phillip J. Pirages 63 - 432   2013 $2400

Shakespeare, William   1564-1616   *The Works.*   London: Edward Moxon, 1857.   First printing of this edition, 222 x 140mm., one gathering in third volume with leaves bound out of order, but complete, 6 volumes, frontispiece and one title leaf bit foxed, beautiful contemporary tree calf by Andrew Grieve of Edinburgh for William Paterson, Edinburgh bookseller (stamp-signed with both names on verso front free endpaper of each volume), covers with gilt double fillets and twining leaf border, raised bands, spines very attractively gilt in compartments with graceful floral cornerpieces and elaborate fleuron centerpiece, red and dark green morocco title labels, gilt rolled turn-ins, marbled endpapers and edges, isolated very minor foxing elsewhere, couple of very faint scratches to covers, exceptionally fine, lovely bindings lustrous and virtually unworn, text showing no signs of use.   Phillip J. Pirages   61 - 112   2013 $4800

Shakespeare, William 1564-1616 *The Works of William Shakespeare.* London: Bickers and Son, 1864. 4to., half title, engraved frontispiece, fine, superbly bound in full contemporary straight grain red morocco, wide gilt decorated borders, ornate gilt panelled spine decorated with thistles and floral motifs, all edges gilt, gilt dentelles, armorial bookplate of William Preston of Ellel Grange. Ken Spelman Books Ltd.   75 - 132   2013   £320

Shakespeare, William 1564-1616 *The Works.* New York: Sheldon & Co., 1869. Large 8vo., 979 pages, frontispiece, plates, full brown pebbled cloth, stamped in black and gilt, stamped dentelles, all edges gilt, some very minor scuffing, very good, clean, tight copy.   Second Life Books Inc.   183 - 353   2013 $150

Shakespeare, William 1564-1616 *The Works of...* New York: Virtue & Yorston, 1873-1876. Imperial edition, 3 volumes, large heavy folio, all edges gilt, profusely illustrated with full page steel engravings, vignette half title and frontispiece, black three quarter morocco, spine stamped in gilt, very nice clean set.   Second Life Books Inc.   183 - 354   2013 $2500

Shakespeare, William 1564-1616 *The Works.* London: George Routledge & Sons, circa, 1875. 2 volumes, 262 x 179mm., extremely pleasing contemporary light tan three quarter calf, raised bands, spines elegantly gilt in compartments with lily cornerpieces sporting graceful curling foliage and large central lozenge formed by botanical stamps, whole accented by other small tools, two crimson morocco labels on each spine, marbled boards, edges and endpapers, with 340 text illustrations by Sir John Gilbert, small external defects (edges bit rubbed, few tiny abrasions, one small dampstain) but handsome binding very lustrous and with no significant wear, 2 leaves with minor marginal ink stains, otherwise very fine internally, text quite fresh, clean and smooth.   Phillip J. Pirages   63 - 433   2013 $400

Shakespeare, William 1564-1616 *The Works.* London: Macmillan And Co., 1902-1905. Cambridge Edition, 235 x 159mm., 9 volumes, very appealing olive brown half morocco over green linen by Zaehnsdorf (stamp-signed on verso of front free endpaper), raised bands, spines gilt in double ruled compartments with dotted inner frame and floral cornerpieces as well as large central ornament formed by crossed swords, a crown and a garland, marbled endpapers, top edges gilt, other rough trimmed, spines uniformly sunned to a pleasing honey brown, first volume with shallow chip at top of spine with one band little abraded, otherwise only trivial defects, bindings in all other ways showing only very minor signs of use and text quite clan and fresh.   Phillip J. Pirages   63 - 435   2013 $2500

Shakespeare, William 1564-1616 *Works. The Text of the First Folio with Quarto Variants and a Selection of Modern Readings.* Nonesuch Press, 1929-1933. 579/1600 sets, printed on Pannekoek mouldmade paper using Fournier type with recut capitals, 8vo., original tan niger morocco, gilt lettered backstrips trifle faded, raised bands ruled in blind, double gilt rule borders to sides and single gilt rule to inner borders, few faint scratches to rear cover of one volume, bookplates, top edge gilt, on the rough, others untrimmed, very good.   Blackwell's Rare Books   172 - 303   2013   £2250

Shakespeare, William 1564-1616 *Complete Works.* London: Oxford University Press, 1969. 8vo., 1166 pages, publisher's cloth, very good, tight copy, bookseller Larry McMurtry's copy with his 1969 ownership inscription and "Booked Up" card with 7 lines of holograph laid in, second slip of paper with 6 lines of holograph in laid in as well.   Second Life Books Inc.   183 - 352   2013 $50

The Shamrock. Jan., 1900-. May 1901, 55 issues (ex 73), lacks March, May & July 1900 and March 1901, bound in one volume, cloth, hinges broken, text goodish.   C. P. Hyland   261 - 720   2013   £35

Shange, Ntozake *Sassafras, Cypress & Indigo.* New York: St. Martin's, 1982. Uncorrected proof, faint stain on front wrapper, else fine in wrappers.   Between the Covers Rare Books, Inc. 165 - 260   2013 $100

Shanks, Edward *Images from the Progress of Seasons.* Dropmore Press, 1947. First edition, 17/50 copies (of an edition of 450) printed in black and red on handmade paper, signed by author and artist, 10 engravings on grey or pink tinted backgrounds by Charles Berry, crown 8vo., original full bottle green morocco, backstrip longitudinally gilt lettered between gilt ruled raised bands, untrimmed and partly unopened, fine.   Blackwell's Rare Books   B174 - 333   2013   £85

Sharp, Granville 1734-1813 *The System of Colonial Law Compared with the Eternal Laws of God...* London: Richard Edwards, 1807. Only edition, 8vo., fine, contemporary wrappers, paper label.   Maggs Bros. Ltd.   1467 - 12   2013   £950

Sharp, William *Practical Observations on Injuries of the Head.* London: John Churchill, 1841. Half title, x - 108 pages + ads, original red publisher's linen cloth, spine and front board sunned, clean tight binding and internally fine, very uncommon.   James Tait Goodrich   75 - 190 2013 $795

Shavykin, A. *Nashi Vorogy. (Our Enemies).* Kiev: Molodyi Bolshavyk , n..d., circa, 1930. 4to., pictorial wrappers, cover soiled, else very good+, rare, illustrations by J. Nizhnyka.   Aleph-Bet Books, Inc.   105 - 509   2013 $3500

Shaw, Alexander *An Account of Sir Charles Bell's Classification of the Nervous System.* London: printed by Moyes and Barclay, 1841. 30 pages, stamp on title, old pamphlet boards, author's presentation to Sir Benjamin Brodie.   James Tait Goodrich   75 - 23   2013 $950

Shaw, Bishop Alexander P. *What Must the Negro Do to Be Saved.* Baltimore: Bishop Alexander P. Shaw/Clarke Press, circa, 1935. First edition, 24mo., stapled printed gray wrappers, 31 pages.   Between the Covers Rare Books, Inc.   165 - 330   2013 $475

Shaw, Bob *One Million Tomorrows.* New York: Ace Books, 1970. First edition, folio, loose sheets, printed rectos only.   L. W. Currey, Inc.   Utopian Literature: Recent Acquisitions (April 2013) - 140299   2013 $250

Shaw, George Bernard   1856-1950 *The Adventures of the Black Girl in Her Search for God.* 1932. First edition, 208 x 135mm., original black pictorial boards and endpapers, designed and engraved by John Farleigh, in custom made gilt titled black cloth folding box (slightly soiled), illustrated titlepage and 18 woodcut engravings by John Farleigh, with proofs of the cover, endpapers and 19 engravings (one a trial version of a scene), all signed in pencil by Fairleigh and numbered "3/9" the cover with Farleigh's inscription "This set was Specially printed for William Maxwell" (proofs contained in portfolio inside folding box), front flyleaf with inscription by Shaw for Maxwell, hint of rubbing to edges, couple of faint spots of foxing, proof copy of cover slightly wrinkled at edges, otherwise fine copy, fresh, bright and unworn.   Phillip J. Pirages   63 - 437   2013 $2500

Shaw, George Bernard   1856-1950 *Cashel Byron's Profession.* London: Modern Press, 1886. First edition, smaller issue, tall 8vo., original blue wrappers, smaller variant, measuring c. 23.3 x 14.8 cm., with prelim blank leaf bound in at end, some discoloration to wrappers, otherwise very good in blue cloth slipcase.   Maggs Bros. Ltd.   1442 - 285   2013   £350

Shaw, George Bernard   1856-1950 *Fabian Essays in Socialism.* London: Walter Scott, 1890. Reprint of 1889 edition, 8vo., modern handling wear, very good.   Second Life Books Inc.   183 - 357   2013 $50

Shaw, George Bernard   1856-1950 *Man and Superman.* New York: Dodd, Mead, 1947. First edition, 8vo., 743 pages, very good in little worn dust jacket, signed by Malcolm Keen, Chester Stratton, Victor Sutherland, Carmen Mathews, Jack Manning, Phoebe Mackay and Tony Bickley.   Second Life Books Inc.   183 - 356   2013 $450

Shaw, George Bernard   1856-1950 *The Quintessence of Ibsenism.* London: Constable, 1929. First edition thus, 12mo., very nice, clean copy, light green cloth, scarce.   Second Life Books Inc.   183 - 354   2013 $2500

Shaw, George Bernard   1856-1950 *Saint Joan: a Chronicle Play in Six Scenes and an Epilogue.* London: Constable and Co., 1924. Limited to 750 copies, large paper format, folio, cloth backed pictorial boards, fine in original pictorial dust jacket, illustrations by Charles Ricketts with 16 art deco tipped in plates in color and black and white, outstanding copy, rarely found with dust jacket which has really protected beautiful pictorial cover.   Aleph-Bet Books, Inc.   105 - 501   2013 $1350

Shaw, J. Beverly F. *The Negro in the History of Methodism.* Nashville: Parthenon Press, 1954. First edition, small owner stamp bottom textblock and on copyright page, bookplate of author Ralph Lord Roy, else near fine in very good dust jacket with small chips at spine ends, scarce in this condition.   Between the Covers Rare Books, Inc.   165 - 261   2013 $200

Shaw, John *How to Order Any Land, So as It May Reteyne All the Moysture that Falleth Thereon...* N.P.: n.p., n.d. London: Bernard Alsop, 1637. First edition, 4to., pages (8), little browned, uncut with backstrip hinged into modern wrappers, few passages underlined in ink in contemporary hand.   Marlborough Rare Books Ltd.   218 - 139   2013   £1250

Shaw, Joseph T. *Blood on the Curb.* New York: Dodge Pub. Co., 1936. First edition, pastedown little browned from binder's glue, else fine in fine and bright contemporary with tiny nicks at crown, inscribed by author to noted mystery writer George Harmon Coxe.   Between the Covers Rare Books, Inc.   Mystery & Detective Fiction - 94557   2013 $3000

Shaw, Simeon *History of the Staffordshire Potteries and the Rise and Progress of the Manufacture of Pottery and Porcelain with References to Genuine Specimens and Notices of Eminent Potters.* Hanley: for the author, 1829. First edition, 12mo., pages viii, 244, original boards, rebacked with cloth, printed lettering piece.   Marlborough Rare Books Ltd.   218 - 140   2013   £700

Sheahan, Thomas *Articles of Irish Manufacture or Portions of Cork History.* 1833. First edition, modern cloth, very good, very scarce.   C. P. Hyland   261 - 777   2013   £250

Shearing, Joseph *The Spider in the Cup.* New York: Smith and Haas, 1934. First American edition, delicate green dyes in boards moderately faded else fine in fine dust jacket with very minor rubbing, lovely copy.   Between the Covers Rare Books, Inc.   Mystery & Detective Fiction - 46574   2013 $315

Sheehy, Shawn *A Pop-Up Field Guide to North American Wildflowers with a Language of Flowers for the 21st Century.* Chicago: 2011. Artist's book, one of 30 copies, all on commercial cover paper in various weights from various manufacturers, each copy signed and numbered by artist, page size 6 1/2 x 4 1/2 x 1 1/4 inches, 30 pages, including 12 double page spread pop-up wildflowers, bound in drab boards with green paper spine, small collaged floral decoration on front panel, housed in custom made box, brightly colored papers as base for wildflowers printed letterpress in Italian by Sarah Vogel, 12 brightly colored wildflowers concevied, engineered and designed by Shawn Sheey, assembled by both contributors.   Priscilla Juvelis - Rare Books   56 - 31   2013 $1750

Sheehy, Shawn *A Pop-Up Field Guide to North American Wildflowers with a Language of Flowers for the 21st Century.* Chicago: 2011. Artist's book, one of 30 copies, all on commercial cover paper in various weights from various manufacturers, each copy signed and numbered by Sheehy, 30 pages, including 12 double page spread pop-up wildflowers, bound in drab boards with green paper spine, small collaged floral decoration on front panel, housed in custom made box, brightly colored papers at base for wildflowers printed letterpress in Italian by Sarah Vogel with common name as well as botanical name of each flower, 12 colored wildflowers conceived, engineered and designed by Sheey, assembly is by both contributors.   Priscilla Juvelis - Rare Books   55 - 24   2013 $1500

Sheldon, Edward *"The Nigger:" An American Play in Three Acts.* New York: Macmillan Co., 1910. First edition, publisher's blue cloth gilt, contemporary owner name on front fly, light crease on front board, else near fine, scarce.   Between the Covers Rare Books, Inc.   165 - 262   2013 $250

Shelley, Jane Gibson *Shelley Memorials from Authentic Sources. Edited by Lady Shelley.* London: Edward Moxon, 1862. Second edition, errata slip, fine in contemporary half red morocco, ornate gilt spine, marbled boards and edges, some slight foxing.   Ken Spelman Books Ltd.   75 - 121   2013   £120

Shelley, Percy Bysshe   1792-1822 *Lines and Fragments.* Belfast: Crannog Press, 1977. One of 100 numbered copies, 7 illustrations by artist, small 8vo., original dark blue cloth, gold patterned endpapers, printed paper label, fine.   Maggs Bros. Ltd.   1442 - Crannog   2013   £100

Shelley, Percy Bysshe   1792-1822 *Poems of Shelley.* London: Caxton Pub. Co., 1907. 12mo., brown cloth decorated in orange and gilt, top edge gilt, 246 pages, fine in beautiful, near fine pictorial dust jacket, frontispiece and title page vignette by A. S. Hartrick and with 8 beautiful color plates by Jessie King, rare in jacket.   Aleph-Bet Books, Inc.   105 - 349   2013 $650

Shelley, Percy Bysshe   1792-1822 *The Poetical Works.* London: Edward Moxon, 1857. 3 volumes, 8vo., fine set, contemporary half red morocco, ornate gilt spines, marbled boards and edges, gilt bookplate.   Ken Spelman Books Ltd.   75 - 120   2013   £250

Shelley, Percy Bysshe   1792-1822 *Queen Mab, a Philosophical Poem with Notes.* London: printed by P. B. Shelley, 1813. First edition, 8vo., full green morocco by Bedford, gilt rules and lettering, gilt inner dentelles, top edge gilt, others untrimmed, edges slightly rubbed, fine.   The Brick Row Book Shop   Miscellany Fifty-Nine - 39   2013 $18,000

Shelley, Percy Bysshe   1792-1822 *The Revolt of Islam.* printed for John Brooks, 1829. First edition, first state sheets, remainder issue, lightly browned and spotted, errata corrected in early hand, 8vo., untrimmed in original boards, rubbed and bit soiled, rebacked in calf with green morocco lettering piece, hinges relined, good.   Blackwell's Rare Books   B174 - 136   2013   £950

Shelley, Percy Bysshe   1792-1822 *The Works.* printed and published by John Ascham..., 1834. 2 volumes, 12mo., frontispiece in volume i, portrait offset onto title, half title volume i discarded, few minor spots or stains, contemporary burgundy hard grained morocco, elaborate gilt and blind tooled panels on sides, flat spines gilt, pink silk doublures and endleaves, gilt edges, short crack at foot of upper joint on volume i, extremities slightly worn, good.   Blackwell's Rare Books   B174 - 137   2013   £500

Shelley, Percy Bysshe   1792-1822 *The Complete Works.* London and Boston: Virtue and Co., 1904-1906. One of 1000 copies of the Laurel edition, this set #221, 235 x 160mm., 8 volumes, unusual (amateur?) contemporary honey-brown half morocco, raised bands, spine panels decorated with graceful Art Nouveau style flowers and leaves, partly gilt and partly handpainted in red and green, marbled boards and endpapers, top edges gilt, other edges untrimmed, 3 volumes, unopened, others partially so, with 40 plates, including hand colored portrait, all with lettered tissue guards, spines lightly sunned, extremities bit rubbed, 3 volumes with slight chipping at head of spine, leather with small minor stains and abrasions, three inch dampstain to one front board, older repair to head of one joint, bindings quite solid and still pleasing, fine internally, text clean, bright and with fresh with few signs of use.   Phillip J. Pirages   63 - 438   2013 $350

Shelvocke, George *A Voyage Round the World by Way of the Great South Sea Performed in the Years 1719, 20, 21, 22...* London: printed for J. Senex, W. and J. Innys and J. Osborn & T. Longman, 1726. First edition, 8vo., frontispiece, very good+, contemporary paneled calf with modern rebacking, spine in five compartments with gilt rules, leather spine label gilt lettered, folding frontispiece map, scattered foxing.   By the Book, L. C.   38 - 11   2013 $6000

Shepard, Lucius *The Jaguar Hunter.* Sauk City: Arkham House, 1987. First edition, review copy, inscribed by author to Stanley Wiater, one of 3194 copies, illustrations by J. K. Potter, with Wiater's Gahan Wilson designed bookplate, near fine in like dust jacket with review slip laid in. Ken Lopez Bookseller 159 - 177 2013 $350

Shepard, Sam *Hawk Moon. Short Stories, Poems & Monologues.* Los Angeles: Black Sparrow Press, 1973. First edition, one of 200 numbered copies signed by author, small 4to., fine in original acetate dust jacket, as issued. Ed Smith Books 75 - 64 2013 $200

Shepard, Thomas *The Parable of the Ten Virgins Opened & Applied: Being the Substance of Divers Sermons on Matth. 25, 1, -13...* London: re-printed and carefully corrected in the year, 1695. Small folio, modern full calf, very skillfully executed in period style, title bit soiled and with early stamp on verso, small burn hole in F3 costing a few letters, corner of K4 torn way affecting type rule, minor soiling and spotting but very good in handsome period style binding. Joseph J. Felcone Inc. Books Printed before 1701 - 79 2013 $1000

Sherard, Robert Harborough *Oscar Wilde: the Story of an Unhappy Friendship.* London: privately printed at the Hermes Press, 1902. First edition, 254 x 198mm., 277, (1) pages, handsome contemporary olive green morocco lavishly gilt in Art Nouveau style by Stikeman (stamp-signed on rear turn-in), covers with multiple plain and decorative gilt rules enclosing large quatrefoil with very prominent floral cornerpieces and floral tool accents, central panel of that on upper cover containing coronet imposed upon crossed writing tools, raised bands, spine attractively gilt in compartments with large central lily framed by drawer hand tools, intricate gilt floral turn-ins, marbled endpapers, top edge gilt, original paper and cloth bound in, frontispiece photo of Wilde, five other portraits and two facsimiles of letters as called for, large paper copy, morocco bookplates of Helen Janssen Wetzel and Mary Pinkerton Carlisle, spine sunned to rich brown, just touch of rubbing to joints, usual offsetting to free endpapers from turn-ins, titlepage little browned from acidic(!) tissue guard (now removed), last page with faint darkening from bound-in cloth cover, handful of leaves with small, light brown stains along gutter (from binder's glue), other trivial imperfections but still excellent copy, leaves fresh, clean and bright, margins enormous and animated, glittering binding scarcely worn. Phillip J. Pirages 61 - 126 2013 $1250

Sheraton, Thomas *The Cabinet Dictionary...* London: printed by W. Smith and sold by W. Row, J. Mathews...., 1803. First edition, 8vo., 87 engraved plates, several are folding, minimally spotted in places only, original reversed calf, covers and spine ruled gilt, gilt stamped red morocco lettering piece on spine, extremities worn, with repairs, front inner hinge with repair. Marlborough Rare Books Ltd. 218 - 141 2013 £950

Sheraton, Thomas *The Cabinet Dictionary....* London: printed by W. Smith and sold by W. Row, Matthews, Vernon and Hood and M. Jones, 1803. First edition, 89 engraved plates, several folding, plates irregularly numbered and sometimes misbound, with a plate 81 not called for, last few leaves at either end stained from binding turn-ins, occasional browning or foxing, waterstain to front flyleaves, 8vo., contemporary mottled calf, skillfully rebacked, original green lettering piece, signature at head of introduction of Edward Jones, sound. Blackwell's Rare Books B174 - 138 2013 £750

Sheridan, Richard Brinsley Butler 1751-1816 *The School for Scandal.* London, et al: Hodder & Stoughton, n.d., 1911. 4to., pictorial cloth stamped in gold on spine and in red and blue on cover, nearly as new in publisher's pictorial box (flap repairs, 25 beautiful tipped in color plates as well as numerous other line illustrations and pictorial endpapers by Hugh Thomson), outstanding copy very beautiful. Aleph-Bet Books, Inc. 105 - 561 2013 $475

Sheridan, Thomas *The Life of the Rev. Swift, Dean of St. Patrick's, Dublin.* London: printed for C. Bathurst et al, 1784. First edition, 8vo, 2 engraved portrait plates, discoloration on page 24-5 (transfer from inserted envelope), speckled tan calf, rebacked, red and green morocco labels and gilt to spine, little worn, top edge dusty, bookplate of University of London Library, library ticket of same, small inkstamp to verso of titlepage and final page, letter from Prof. H. T. Mason to Dr. D. Nokes dated 3rd Oct. 1983 loosely inserted. Unsworths Antiquarian Booksellers 28 - 128 2013 £200

Sherlock, William *A Practical Discourse Concerning Death.* London: printed for R. Baldwin, 1751. 8vo., full contemporary calf, raised and gilt bands, hinges cracked but firm, head of spine chipped, corners bumped, old stain to upper board. Jarndyce Antiquarian Booksellers CCIV - 269 2013 £50

Sherman, Murray H. *Psychoanalysis in America: Historical Perspectives.* Springfield: Charles C. Thomas, 1966. First edition, 518 pages, fine in fine dust jacket. Beasley Books 2013 - 2013 $50

Sherman, Thomas *Divine Breathings.* Philadelphia: printed by William Gibbons, 1792. First American edition, small inscription excised from head of titlepage, toned, few leaves stained, 12mo., original marbled boards, rebacked with smooth dark calf, lettered gilt, boards rubbed, booklabel of Aimwll School Library, sound. Blackwell's Rare Books 172 - 131 2013 £450

Sherry, Sylvia *Girl in a Blue Shawl.* London: Hamish Hamilton, 1982. First edition, 8vo., original brown cloth, near fine in dust jacket with wraparound band and 'puff' from Grahame Greene, inscribed by author for Vivien Greene. Maggs Bros. Ltd. 1460 - 378 2013 £125

Sherwood, E. Hugh *Bobbie Bubbles.* Chicago: Rand McNally, 1916. Later edition, 8vo., pictorial boards, 64 pages, slight rubbing, very good+, illustrations by E. Hugh Sherwood with 14 full page color illustrations, 5 full page black and whites and partial page black and whites. Aleph-Bet Books, Inc.   105 - 253   2013 $100

Sherwood, Mary Martha Butt   1775-1851 *The History of the Fairchild Family or the Child's Manual.* London: printed for J. Hatchard, 1818. First edition, 8vo., frontispiece, very bright with only occasional slight creases to some page corners, publisher's list at rear, light brown calf, blind tooled spine, gilt borders, upper joint split, edges and top part of upper board worn, some scratches, f.f.e.p. removed, inscription to prelim blank "Frances Katharine Sarah Knight gift of her friend Mrs. Wright, Bosgrove, Oct. 3 1854".   Unsworths Antiquarian Booksellers   28 - 198 2013   £150

Shiel, M. P. *The Last Miracle.* London: Victor Gollancz, 1929. Reissue of 1906 title, modest edgewear, nice, very good, without dust jacket inscribed to head of his American publisher Vanguard, James Henle.   Between the Covers Rare Books, Inc.   Sci-Fi, Fantasy & Horror - 27817   2013 $850

Shiel, M. P. *Prince Zaleski.* Leyburn: Tartarus Press, 2002. First printing of this expanded edition, octavo, drawings by Robert Arrington and a facsimile reproduction of original titlepage from John Lane first edition of 1895, original decorated navy blue cloth, front and spine panels stamped in silver, all edges gilt, marbled endpapers.   L. W. Currey, Inc.   Fall Sampler Sept. 2013 - 146174   2013 $100

Shiel, M. P. *The Yellow Danger or What Might Happen if the Division of the Chinese Empire Should Estrange all European Countries.* New York: R. F. Fenno & Co., 1899. First American edition, boards little soiled, nice, very good. Between the Covers Rare Books, Inc.   Sci-Fi, Fantasy & Horror - 286818   2013 $275

Shields, Carol *Others.* Ottawa: Borealis, 1972. inscribed by author to Canadian poet and novelist Rosemary Aubert, spine faded, little tear to spine base, near fine in wrappers.   Ken Lopez Bookseller   159 - 178   2013 $750

Shields, Carol *Small Ceremonies.* Toronto: McGraw-Hill Ryerson Ltd., 1976. First edition, fine in dust jacket with minor rubbing to extremities.   Ed Smith Books   78 - 59   2013 $250

Shillibeer, J. *A Narrative of Briton's Voyage to Pitcairn's Island...* Taunton: printed for the author, 1817. First edition, 16 engraved plates, one in bisque, several folding, fine in later polished calf, spine elaborately gilt with black morocco labels, fine copy of rare first edition.   Maggs Bros. Ltd.   1467 - 91   2013   £3500

Shipley, Jonathan *A Sermon Preached Before the Incorporated Society for the Propagation of the Gospel in Foreign Parts... on Friday Feb. 19, 1773.* London: printed, Boston: reprinted, sold by Thomas and John Fleet, 1773. First American edition, 8vo., 17 pages, stitched, uncut as issuued, some staining and browning, nearly fine.   Howard S. Mott Inc.   262 - 135   2013 $350

Shirley Smith, Richard *Bookplates.* Upper Denby: Fleece Press, 2005, i.e., 2006. One of 235 copies (of an edition of 275), printed on Saunders paper, 65 illustrations by Richard Shirley Smith , photographic reproduction of Shirley Smith also tipped in, title printed in brown, crown 8vo., original quarter lime-green linen, printed label, matching stained wood veneer boards, untrimmed, green linen slipcase with printed label, fine.   Blackwell's Rare Books   B174 - 334   2013   £140

Shirley Smith, Richard *The Paintings & Collages 1957 to 2000.* Murray: Studio House, 2002. 130/140 copies (of an edition of 150), signed by Shirley Smith and printed on glossy art paper with substantial number of color printed reproductions of artist's work, a number full page, small number of wood engravings in black and white, color photo portrait of artist, title printed in black, cream and red, 4to., original quarter grey cloth, backstrip gilt lettered, lime green boards, cloth slipcase, fine with 2 engraving pulls signed by artist and loosely inserted in pocket on rear pastedown. Blackwell's Rare Books   172 - 236   2013   £175

Shiverick, Nathan C. *Joram's Feast.* Boston: Atlantic Monthly Press/Little Brown and Co., 1964. First edition, illustrations by Esther Constable, very near fine in like dust jacket with clip to bottom corner of front flap but price still present on top corner, clean copy.   Jeff Hirsch Books   Fall 2013 - 129358   2013 $85

Shoberl, Frederic   1775-1853 *Forget me Not: a Christmas New Year's and Birthday Present for MDCCCXXXVI.* London: published by Ackerman and Co., 1835. First edition, 12mo., 11 inserted plates, including presentation plate and frontispiece, original decorated full brown leather, all panels elaborately tooled in gold and blind, all edges gilt, yellow coated endpapers.   L. W. Currey, Inc.   Christmas Themed Books - 136004   2013 $100

Shore, Evelyn Berglund *Born on Snowshoes.* Robert Hale, 1955. First UK edition, original cloth, gilt, dust jacket chipped and torn, spine defective, price clipped, 16 plates, double page map.   R. F. G. Hollett & Son   Polar Exploration - 67   2013   £25

Shore, Joseph *In Old St. James (Jamaica): a Book of Parish Chronicles containing the Story of the Jamaica Ancestry of Mrs. Barrett Browning: the True Tale of Rose Hall; What an Estate Slave-Book tells, etc.* Kingston: Aston W. Gardner & Co., 1911. First edition, illustrations, stiff printed cardboard covers, 160 pages, scarce. Between the Covers Rare Books, Inc. 165 - 180 2013 $250

Shorthouse, Joseph Henry *John Inglesant; a Romance.* Birmingham: Cornish Brothers, 1880. Only 100 copies printed, half title, original parchment by Burn and Co., lettered in red on front and spine, slightly rubbed and marked, minor repairs, leading inner hinge cracking, bookplate of Alex Bridge on front pastedown, overall very good, handsome custom made maroon cloth slipcase, black leather spine label, scarce. Jarndyce Antiquarian Booksellers CCV - 247 2013 £650

Shout, 60, 61, 62, 63. November, 1970-. February 1971, Wrappers, fine copies, photos. Beasley Books 2013 - 2013 $50

Shouvuos Tie. Cincinnati: Union Amer. Hebrew Congregations, 1947. 4to., spiral backed wrappers, fine, illustrations in color. Aleph-Bet Books, Inc. 104 - 299 2013 $100

The Showa Anthology 2. Modern Japanese Short Stories 1961-1984. New York: Kodansha, 1985. Fine in fine dust jacket, Kenzaburo Oe's copy which he used as a reading copy at Toronto's Harbourfront International Festival of Authors in 1985, inscribed by Oe to Greg Gatenby, director of the festival, with Gatenby's signature. Ken Lopez Bookseller 159 - 161 2013 $1000

Shuffrey, W. A. *The Churches of the Deanery of North Craven.* Leeds: J. Whitehead and Sons, 1914. Large 8vo., 28 illustrations, very good, original gilt lettered dark blue cloth, scarce. Ken Spelman Books Ltd. 73 - 70 2013 £50

Shuldham, E. *Pictures from Birdland.* London & New York: J. M. Dent & E. P. Dutton, 1899. First edition, 4to., pictorial boards, fine but for small amount of edge and corner rubbing, fine except for small amount of edge and corner rubbing, 24 magnificent color plates by Maurice and Edward Detmold. Aleph-Bet Books, Inc. 105 - 169 2013 $2350

Shuman, E. L. *Rainy Day Scrap Book.* Chicago: Reilly & Britton, 1910. Narrow 4to., pictorial cloth, near fine in chipped dust jacket, in envelope in front of book are half tone illustrations, the child is to cut out photo illustrations and paste them with their proper description (some already done). Aleph-Bet Books, Inc. 104 - 421 2013 $200

Sibson, Francis *Medical Anatomy or Illustrations of the Relative Position and Movements of the Internal Orangs.* London: John Churchill, 1869. 21 superb partially hand colored plates, engraved illustrations, large elephant folio, skillfully rebacked original blue cloth, some wear at corners, oval library stamp on some leaves and verso of plates, some scattered foxing. James Tait Goodrich 75 - 195 2013 $2995

Sicard, J. A. *Le Liquide Cephalo Rachidien.* Paris: Masson, 1902. 192 pages, original printed green wrappers, uncut, unopened, text pages bit toned, otherwise nice, tight copy. James Tait Goodrich 75 - 192 2013 $495

Siddons, George A. *The Cabinet Maker's Guide; or Rules and Instructions in the Art of Varnishing, Dying, Staining, Japanning, Polishing, Lackering....* London/Dublin: printed for Knight and Lacey, Paternoster Row and Westley and Tyrrell, 1825. New edition, 16mo., printed paper covered boards, spine repaired with binder's tape boards rubbed with few chips at edges, few scuff marks, one affecting the word 'wood' on front board and one affecting a few letters of ads on rear board, front endpapers soiled, flyleaf torn and split from gutter, small chips to top edge of a1 and a2 probably from opening roughly, some staining to last page of of index and blank, occasional finger soiling, overall remarkably roughly, some staining to last page of index and blank, occasional finger soiling, overall remarkably clean, crisp and tight and evern scarcer thus. Kaaterskill Books 16 - 20 2013 $2500

Sidgwick, Cecily *Children's Book of Gardening.* London: Adam & Charles Black, 1909. First edition, half title, color frontispiece and plates, original dark green cloth, pictorial onlay, gift inscription with 8 lines of verse on leading f.e.p., very good. Jarndyce Antiquarian Booksellers CCV - 247 2013 £45

Sidney, Algernon *The Very Copy of a Paper Delivered to the Sheriffs Upon the Scaffold on Tower Hill... Decemb. 7 1683.* London: for R. H. J. B. ad J. R. and are to be sold by Walter Davis, 1683. Folio, (3) pages, caption title, fair copy, cropped at bottom with loss of one or two lines of text on pages 1-2, edges chipped and slightly brittle. Joseph J. Felcone Inc. Books Printed before 1701 - 80 2013 $300

Sidney, Margaret *Five Little Peppers Abroad.* Boston: Lathrop Pub. Co. May, 1902. First edition, 8vo., green pictorial cloth with gilt lettering, 449 pages, great copy, rarely found so bright, fine. Aleph-Bet Books, Inc. 104 - 536 2013 $275

Sidney, Margaret *Five Little Peppers and Their Friends.* Boston: Lothrop Pub. Co. May, 1902. First edition, 8vo., green pictorial cloth with gilt lettering, 449 pages, fine, great copy, rarely found so bright. Aleph-Bet Books, Inc. 104 - 537 2013 $275

Sidney, Margaret *Lullabies and Jingles.* Boston: D. Lothrop, 1893. First edition, small 4to., 5 full page chromolithographs plus color paste on picture, illustrated boards, good+, paper on very top of front cover torn showing some of the cloth backing the spine, corners well worn, inside clean.   Barnaby Rudge Booksellers   Children 2013 - 020796   2013 $55

Sidney, Margaret *Phronsie Pepper.* Boston: Lothrop Pub. Co., 1897. First edition, 8vo., green cloth, ornate pictorial cover and spine in red, brow and gold, 437 pages, fine, binding stunning and rarely found so bright, illustrations in black and white by Jessie McDermott.   Aleph-Bet Books, Inc.   105 - 548   2013 $300

Sigerson, George *The Poets and Poetry of Munster.* Dublin: O'Daly, 1860. First edition, original blind embossed green cloth, worn and dull, titlepage defaced, text good, rare.   C. P. Hyland   261 - 782   2013   £75

Sigsby, William *Life and Adventures of Timothy Murphy, the Benefactor of Scholarie.* Scholarie: W. H. Gallup Jan, 1839. First edition, 8vo., 32 pages, sewn and uncut as issued, tall copy, very rare, slight staining, slight pinkish hue to outer leaves.   M & S Rare Books, Inc.   95 - 341   2013 $950

Sillitoe, Alan *The Loneliness of the Long-Distance Runner.* Allen, 1959. First edition, pages 176, foolscap 8vo., original grey green cloth, backstrip gilt lettered, free endpapers partly lightly browned as usual, dust jacket little frayed at head, very good, inscribed by author for film critic Clive Hirschhorn.   Blackwell's Rare Books   B174 - 299   2013   £525

Sillitoe, Alan *Saturday Night and Sunday Morning.* Allen, 1958. First edition, 216 pages, foolscap 8vo., original red boards, backstrip gilt lettered, faint staining to free endpaper edges, bookplate, dust jacket, faintly waterstained, good, inscribed by author to film critic Clive Hirschhorn.   Blackwell's Rare Books   B174 - 300   2013   £600

Sillman, Leonard *Here Lies Leonard Sillman.* New York: Citadel, 1959. First edition, inscribed by author, fine in bit dusty, but near fine dust jacket.   Beasley Books   2013 - 2013 $50

Silver, Arthur P. *Farm-Cottage, Camp and Canoe in Maritime Canada; or the Call of Nova Scotia to the Emigrant and Sportsman.* London: 1907. xviii, 249 pages, illustrations, original board, extremities slightly rubbed, internally clean, very good and largely unopened, many illustrations from photos.   Dumont Maps & Books of the West   124 - 85   2013 $95

Silverberg, Robert *To Open the Sky.* New York: Ballantine Books, 1967. Unpaged long galleys of the first edition, tall octavo, original unprinted cream wrappers, sheets secured in wrappers by metal clasp at top, publisher's printed paper affixed to front wrapper.   L. W. Currey, Inc.   Utopian Literature: Recent Acquisitions (April 2013) - 140302   2013 $200

Silverberg, Robert *To Open the Sky.* Boston: Gregg Press, 1977. First hardcover edition, octavo, cloth.   L. W. Currey, Inc.   Utopian Literature: Recent Acquisitions (April 2013) - 141797   2013 $150

Silvers, Willys K. *The Coat Colors of Mice.* New York: Springer, 1979. Stated first edition, 8vo., 66 illustrations and 3 color plates, minimal cover edge wear.   By the Book, L. C.   37 - 62 2013 $125

Silverstein, Shel *The Missing Piece.* New York: Harper & Row, 1976. Stated first edition, 4to., cloth, fine in dust jacket, black and white drawings by author, signed by author with drawing.   Aleph-Bet Books, Inc.   104 - 538   2013 $1200

Simak, Clifford D. *Cemetery World.* New York: G. P. Putnam's Sons, 1973. First edition, fine in fine dust jacket, beautiful, unread copy.   Between the Covers Rare Books, Inc.   Sci-Fi, Fantasy & Horror - 316298   2013 $100

Simenon, Georges *Inspector Maigret and the Killers.* Garden City: Doubleday/Crime Club, 1954. First American edition, fine in lightly rubbed, very good or better dust jacket with closed tear to top of back panel, nice copy of cheaply made volume.   Between the Covers Rare Books, Inc.   Mystery & Detective Fiction - 51905   2013 $60

Simenon, Georges *Maigret Takes a Room.* London: Hamish Hamilton, 1960. First English edition, tiny bookseller to label, fine in fine dust jacket, beautiful, unread copy, very scarce thus.   Between the Covers Rare Books, Inc.   Mystery & Detective Fiction - 316762   2013 $250

Simenon, Georges *Maigret Travels South.* New York: Harcourt Brace, 1940. First American edition, bookplate, some scattered tiny spotting on fore-edge, otherwise fine in dust jacket with nicks at spine ends and couple of tiny tears.   Mordida Books   81 - 468   2013 $350

Simenon, Georges *The Shadow Falls.* New York: Harcourt Brace & Co., 1945. First American edition, fine in fine dust jacket, spectacular copy.   Between the Covers Rare Books, Inc.   Mystery & Detective Fiction - 10159   2013 $280

Simington, Robert C. *The Civil Survey AD 1654-6. County of Tipperary.* 1931. Volume I of 2, map, 8vo., cloth, very good, ex-libris Seamus Pender. C. P. Hyland 261 - 504   2013   £90

Simington, Robert C. *The Civil Survey AD 1654-6. County of Waterford.* 1942. 500 copies printed, 2 maps, 8vo., cloth, very good. C. P. Hyland 261 - 505   2013   £110

Simington, Robert C. *The Civil Survey AD 1654-6. Volume X Miscellanies.* 1962. large folding map in end-pocket, 8vo., cloth, very good, ex-libris Seamus Pender. C. P. Hyland 261 - 506   2013   £90

Simmons, Dan *Children of the Night.* New York: G. P. Putnam's Sons, 1992. First edition, fine in fine dust jacket, signed by author. Between the Covers Rare Books, Inc. Sci-Fi, Fantasy & Horror - 308787   2013 $60

Simmons, Dan *The Hollow Man.* New York: Bantam Books, 1992. First edition, tiny bump to top front corners, else fine in fine dust jacket, signed and dated by author. Between the Covers Rare Books, Inc. Sci-Fi, Fantasy & Horror - 308783   2013 $50

Simmons, Dan *Phases of Gravity.* London: Headline, 1989. First edition, just bit of age toning to pages, else fine in dust jacket, signed by author. Between the Covers Rare Books, Inc. Sci-Fi, Fantasy & Horror - 308791   2013 $60

Simmons, Dan *Prayers to Broken Stones.* Arlington Heights: Dark Harvest, 1990. First edition, fine in fine dust jacket, signed by author, illustrations. Between the Covers Rare Books, Inc. Sci-Fi, Fantasy & Horror - 313553   2013 $55

Simmons, Dan *Summer Sketches.* Northridge: Lord John Press, 1992. First edition, fine in fine dust jacket, signed by author. Between the Covers Rare Books, Inc. Sci-Fi, Fantasy & Horror - 313551   2013 $50

Simmons, Dan *Summer of Night.* New York: G. P. Putnam's Sons, 1991. Uncorrected proof, fine in wrappers, signed by author. Between the Covers Rare Books, Inc. Sci-Fi, Fantasy & Horror - 313547   2013 $50

Simmons, Dan *Worlds Enough and Time.* Burton: Subterranean Press, 2002. First edition, one of 26 lettered copies, signed by author, fine in fine dust jacket and fine gilt cloth clamshell slipcase; from the library of Bruce Kahn. Between the Covers Rare Books, Inc. Sci-Fi, Fantasy & Horror - 311781   2013 $600

Simmons, James *Ballad of a Marriage.* Belfast: Festival Publications, 1965. First edition, small 8vo., original white wrappers, printed in black with sun device in purple, near fine. Maggs Bros. Ltd. 1442 - 286   2013   £200

Simmons, James *Constantly Singing.* Belfast: Blackstaff Press, 1980. First edition, 8vo., original wrappers, near fine, from the library of Richard Murphy, inscribed for him by author. Maggs Bros. Ltd. 1442 - 288   2013   £65

Simmons, James *No Land is Waste, Dr. Eliot.* Richmond: Keepsake Press, 1972. First edition, number 28 of 30 hardbound copies, numbered and signed by author, 8vo., original green buckram, fine. Maggs Bros. Ltd. 1442 - 287   2013   £225

Simmons, Marc *Albuquerque, a Narrative History.* Albuquerque: 1982. xvi, 443 pages, illustrations, near fine in like dust jacket, scarce. Dumont Maps & Books of the West   124 - 86   2013 $65

Simmons, Owen *The Book of Bread.* London: Maclaren & Sons, 1903. First edition, large 4to., half title, rubricated text, 8 photographic plates tipped on to black paper, 2 silver gelatin photo plates tipped on to green paper, 12 color plates, 4 additional illustrations, original olive green cloth, dulled and little marked. Jarndyce Antiquarian Booksellers CCV - 248   2013   £650

Simon, George T. *The Best of the Music Makers.* Garden City: Doubleday, 1979. First edition, inscribed by author, advance review copy with promo laid in, fine in near fine dust jacket. Beasley Books   2013 - 2013 $65

Simon, George T. *Glenn Miller and His Orchestra.* New York: Thomas Crowell, 1974. First edition, fine in fine dust jacket. Beasley Books   2013 - 2013 $65

Simonde De Sismondi, Jean Charles Leonard   1773-1842 *De La Richesse Commerciale, ou Principes d'Econmie Politique, Appliques a la Legislation du Commerce.* Geneva: Chez J. J. Puschoud An XI, 1893. Scarce first edition, original blue paper wrappers with printed paper spine labels (labels defective), library shelf label at foot of spine, joints split but firm, very clean and fresh uncut and largely unopened, housed in red cloth clamshell case. Heritage Book Shop 50th Anniversary Catalogue - 90   2013 $8000

Simonds, John *The Story of Manual Labor.* Chicago: R. S. Peale, 1887. First edition, hardcover, very good with f.e.p. detached (but present). Beasley Books   2013 - 2013 $65

Simons, Lao Genevra *Bibliography of Early American Textbooks on Algebrae...* Yeshiva College, 1936. 68 pages, 8vo., navy cloth, gilt stamped cover and spine titles, Burndy library bookplate, near fine. Jeff Weber Rare Books 169 - 413 2013 $65

Simple Samuel and Other Stories. Charles E. Graham, n.d., One color plate, 8 black and white illustrations, green cloth with color illustration onlay front cover, little rubbing backstrip, light browning pages and some thumbing to contents, very good, scarce. Ian Hodgkins & Co. Ltd. 134 - 79 2013 £68

Simple Simon and His friends. Greening and Co. n.d., 1906. Oblong folio, original cloth backed boards, unpaginated 12 superb full page color plates, half page plate illustrating 2 page ad for Brown & Polson's Paisley Flour, presentation copy inscribed for Bruce Low from Brown and Polson, staples little rusted, otherwise lovely, clean, fresh and tight copy. R. F. G. Hollett & Son Children's Books - 148 2013 £375

Simpson, Anna Pratt *Problems Women Solved.* San Francisco: Woman's Board, 1915., i.e., 1916. First edition, Thick octavo, tipped-on photographic portraits, views, publisher's brown paper covered boards, linen spine, printed paper label, one lower corner just showing, fine, uncut, very nice and tight copy. Argonaut Book Shop Summer 2013 - 267 2013 $200

Simpson, Dorothy *Six Feet Under.* London: Michael Joseph, 1982. First English edition, near fine with faint offsetting to endpapers and pastedown, 2 tiny holes to tail of lower board, owner inscription, fine dust jacket with light soiling and little wear. Between the Covers Rare Books, Inc. Mystery & Detective Fiction - 51675 2013 $275

Simpson, James Young *History of Modern Anaesthetics.* Edinburgh: Edmonston and Douglas, 1870. 8vo., original purple paper wrappers, some wear, else good. James Tait Goodrich 75 - 193 2013 $595

Simson, John *A Summary View of Professor Simon's Errors; Prov'd Against Him in the Double Process Before the General Assembly; with Some Thoughts Upon the Whole.* Edinburgh: 1729. Bit browned, minor staining to title, pages 16, 8vo., modern marbled wrappers, sound. Blackwell's Rare Books B174 - 142 2013 £300

Sinclair, John *The Code of Agriculture; Including Observations on Gardens, Orchards, Woods, and Plantations.* Hartford: 1818. First American edition, 8vo., 8 plates, full contemporary tree calf, leather label. M & S Rare Books, Inc. 95 - 344 2013 $325

Singer, Charles *A History of Technology.* London: Oxford University Press, 1954-1958. 4 volumes, reprints, large 8vo., thin paper issue, tables, illustrations, color frontispieces, plates, navy blue cloth, gilt stamped spines, dust jackets slightly torn especially at spine ends, spines faded, bookplates, ownership signatures of David C. Lindberg, near fine very good jackets. Jeff Weber Rare Books 169 - 415 2013 $75

Singer, Charles *A History of Technology.* Oxford: Clarendon Press, 1958. 5 volumes, preferred issue (thicker paper stock), thick 8vo., maps, tables, illustrations, color frontispieces, pastedowns and free endpapers foxed, else text and plates clean, navy blue cloth, gilt stamped spines, dust jackets torn and foxed, volume V with slip reading "Spare copy returned by Lord McGowan. with Compliments of Imperial Chemical Industries Limited" laid in, very good in good jackets. Jeff Weber Rare Books 169 - 414 2013 $185

Singer, Charles *Studies in the History and Method of Science.* Oxford: at the Clarendon Press, 1917-1921. Colored frontispiece, 40 plates, colored frontispiece, royal 8vo., original cloth, volume 1 has sunned spine, signed by author April 1932, from the library of Meyer Friedman, with his bookplates. James Tait Goodrich 75 - 194 2013 $595

Singer, Isaac Bashavis *Zlateh the Goat.* New York: Harper & Row, 1966. First edition, 8vo., gilt cloth, dust jacket, 17 magnificent full page illustrations by Maurice Sendak, review copy with slip laid-in. Aleph-Bet Books, Inc. 105 - 530 2013 $325

Singer, Isaac Bashevis *Satan in Goray.* New York: Sweetwater Editions, 1981. Sweetwater editions, limited to 50 copies signed by author and artist, out of a total edition of 475, this being number 20, 10 original signed copperplate etchings and forty drawings, by Ira Moskowitz, tissue guards, with additional clamshell portfolio with set of 10 signed copperplate etchings, original signed drawing from book, quarto, original full burgundy morocco, front board and spine stamped and lettered gilt, housed in cloth slipcase along with additional portfolio, about fine. Heritage Book Shop Holiday Catalogue 2012 - 140 2013 $1500

Singer, Isaac Bashevis *Old Love.* New York: Farrar, Straus & Giroux, 1979. First US edition, very near fine in like dust jacket, signed by author. Jeff Hirsch Books Fall 2013 - 129414 2013 $50

Singer, Isaac Bashevis *A Young Man In Search of Love.* New York: Doubleday, 1978. Limited to 300 numbered copies, signed by author with extra color print signed by artist, 8vo., fine, illustrations by Raphael Soyer, 8vo., cloth, fine in slipcase. Aleph-Bet Books, Inc. 104 - 539 2013 $400

Sinyavsky, Andrei *A Voice from the Chorus.* London: Collins, 1976. First English edition, 8vo., original green cloth, dust jacket slightly rubbed, near fine, with Graham Greene's ownership inscription and some manuscript notes in his hand and further marginal stress marks spread sparsely throughout. Maggs Bros. Ltd. 1460 - 377 2013 £350

Siodmak, Curt *Hauser's Memory.* New York: Putnams, 1968. First edition, fine in bright, near fine dust jacket with two barely noticeable tears, nicely inscribed, attractive. Between the Covers Rare Books, Inc. Sci-Fi, Fantasy & Horror - 36502 2013 $175

Siskind, Aaron *Photographs/Poems.* Rochester: Visual Studies Workshop, 1976. First edition, one of 600 copies, with black and white photos by Aaron Siskind, 34 pages, fine in very near fine dust jacket. Jeff Hirsch Books Fall 2013 - 129512 2013 $50

Sitwell, George *On the Making of Gardens.* Dropmore Press, 1949. First edition, 499/900 copies (of an edition of 1000), printed on Hodgkinson handmade paper and signed by Osbert Sitwell and John Piper, 6 2-color plates, 8vo., original apple green buckram, fading to extreme edges of gilt lettered backstrip with Piper design gilt blocked to front cover, untrimmed, foxed dust jacket with sunned backstrip panel, very good. Blackwell's Rare Books B174 - 274 2013 £150

Six Lectures... before the Cork Young Men's Association... During ... 1851-2. Cork: Religious Tract & Book Society, 1852. 6mo., vii, 219 pages, original red cloth, hinges worn, gilt titling, inscribed by J. N. Lombard to his son, very good. C. P. Hyland 261 - 253 2013 £75

Six-Line Wood Letter Alphabets. Marcham: Alembic Press, 1995-1997. Limited to 100 numbered copies, 6 miniature books, 7 x 5 cm., sewn, stiff paper wrappers, paper covered slipcase, from the collection of Donn W. Sanford. Oak Knoll Books 303 - 31 2013 $125

Skeffington, F. Sheehy *Michael Davitt: Revolutionary, Agitator and Labour Leader.* Four Courts, 2007. First edition, 314 pages, photos, cloth, dust jacket, near fine. C. P. Hyland 261 - 295 2013 £30

Skelton, Robin *An Irish Album.* Dublin: Dolmen Press, 1969. Proof copy, 8vo., original pale grey wrappers, bound with cream binder's tape and printed on rudimentary paper on rectos only, excellent copy. Maggs Bros. Ltd. 1442 - 65 2013 £175

Skelton, Robin *A Valedictory Poem.* Victoria: privately circulated, 1963. First edition, limited to 100 copies, 8vo., original wrappers, fine, inscribed by author for Beatrice Roethke. Maggs Bros. Ltd. 1442 - 289 2013 £50

Sketch of a Railway Judiciously Constructed Between Desirable Points (in Pennsylvania). New York: Egbert Hedge, Railroad Journal Office, 1841. First edition, 8vo., 125 pages, 2 folding maps, contemporary finely ribbed cloth, title stamped in gilt on upper cover, edges and corners worn, spine effectively if artlessly backed with leather, library book plate and stamp on front pastedown with pocket in rear, shelf number neatly inked on margin of first page of text and stamp on blank verso of last page of text, boldly inscribed by Samuel Lyman for Archibald Maclay. M & S Rare Books, Inc. 95 - 308 2013 $375

A Sketch of the Blackwater from Youghal to Fermoy. 1860. First edition, 14 pages, frontispiece, octavo, original wrappers, very good. C. P. Hyland 261 - 128 2013 £80

Sketlon, John *The Poetical Works.* London: Thomas Rodd, 1843. 2 volumes, attractive contemporary polished calf, covers with double gilt fillet border, raised bands, spines gilt in compartments with quatrefoil centerpiece enclosed by rosettes and small tools as well as paisley cornerpieces, each spine with one black and one red label, marbled endpapers and edges, armorial bookplate of Edmund Philips, very slight rubbing to spines, joints and extremities, two covers with (naturally occurring?) tiny dark spots, second volume with handful of gatherings variably foxed, never serious, other trivial imperfections but excellent set, decorative bindings sound and still lustrous, text clean and fresh. Phillip J. Pirages 63 - 441 2013 $375

Skey, William *The Heraldic Calendar: a List of the Nobility and Gentry Whose Arms are Registered & Pedigrees Recorded in the Herald's Office in Ireland.* Dublin: 1846. 62 pages, 8vo., some foxing, original red cloth, spine worn, gilt titling, very good. C. P. Hyland 261 - 411 2013 £120

Skinner, B. F. *Walden Two.* London: Macmillan, 1969. Revised edition, signed and inscribed by author, 8vo., fine in fine dust jacket. By the Book, L. C. 38 - 100 2013 $800

Skinner, E. L. *Merry Tales.* Cincinnati & Chicago: American Book Co., 1915. 8vo., pictorial cloth, 232 pages, very good-fine, 12 lovely color plates plus dozens of delicate pen and inks by Maginel Wright Enright. Aleph-Bet Books, Inc. 105 - 228 2013 $200

Skinner, Fanny J. *John Trevenen Penrose: a Memoir.* 1921. First edition, 6 photos, original boards, light staining, text very good. C. P. Hyland 261 - 684 2013 £30

Skjoldebrand, Anders Fredrik *A Picturesque Journey to the North Cape.* London: J. M. Richardson, 1813. First English edition, 8vo., 2 hand tinted plates, some occasional light foxing, recent brown half calf. J. & S. L. Bonham Antiquarian Booksellers Europe - 9662 2013 £550

Slade, Dorothea *Gutter-Babies.* London: Heinemann, 1912. First edition, original blue cloth, gilt, pictorial onlay to upper board, spine rather faded, 12 color plates by Lady Stanley, titlepage stamped 'presentation copy'.   R. F. G. Hollett & Son   Children's Books - 555   2013   £35

Sladen, Douglas Brooke Wheelton *In Cornwall and Across the Sea...* London: Griffith, Farran, Okeden & Welsh, 1885. Half title, 32 page catalog (1/85), partly unopened in original cream decorated cloth, dulled, slight cracking to front board leading to lifting of cloth, presentation inscription, Teddie Fiske from Douglas Sladen.   Jarndyce Antiquarian Booksellers CCV - 249   2013   £35

Slate Pictures Drawing for Beginners. Boston: L. Prang & Co., 1863. First edition, 12mo., 16 pages of drawings in white on black paper in very good condition, this # 5 in the series of 6, repair to one leaf.   Barnaby Rudge Booksellers Children 2013 - 021312   2013 $75

Sleeping Beauty. New York: McLoughlin Bros. n.d. circa, 1865. 12mo, pictorial wrappers highlighted in gold, mounted on linen, fine, 8 brightly colored half page illustrations, beautiful copy.   Aleph-Bet Books, Inc.   104 - 209   2013 $300

Sleeping Beauty. New York: Thomas Nelson and Sons, 1928. Small 8vo., 35 pages, pictorial boards, 40 pages, slight wear, very good, 4 full page color plates, 29 large partial page color illustrations with large partial page line illustrations by Anne Anderson, printed on coated paper, scarce.   Aleph-Bet Books, Inc.   105 - 40   2013 $250

Sleeping Beauty. Bancroft, 1961. 8 superb color double page concertina pop-ups printed on thick card paper, 2 incorporating movable elements, illustrations by Kubasta, including endpapers, oblong 8vo., original quarter lime green unlettered cloth, color printed boards illustrated overall, front cover also with one movable tab, fine.   Blackwell's Rare Books   B174 - 277   2013   £130

Slidell-Mackenzie, Alexander *A Year in Spain.* London: John Murray, 1831. First edition, 2 volumes, 8vo., recent brown half calf, clean, crisp copy.   J. & S. L. Bonham Antiquarian Booksellers   Europe - 8408   2013   £190

Sloan, Edward L. *Utah Gazetteer and Directory of Logan, Ogden, Provo and Salt Lake Cities for 1884.* Salt Lake City: printed for Sloan and Dunbar by Herald Printing and Pub. Co., 1884. Original edition, 634 pages, octavo, black cloth with title (faint) on backstrip, boards faded and rubbed, name and ink stamp with small ink on second free endsheet, otherwise very good, large foldout map present at front.   Ken Sanders Rare Books   45 - 12   2013 $650

Slobodkina, Esphyr *The Clock.* New York: Abelard Schuman, 1956. First edition, 4to., pictorial boards, fine in slightly worn, very good+ dust jacket,.   Aleph-Bet Books, Inc.   105 - 549   2013 $400

Slocum, Joshua *Sailing Alone Around the World.* New York: 1901. Second edition, numerous illustrations, 8vo., modern full green morocco, gilt and blindstamped, custom cloth dropback box, duplicating design of original cover, inscription from author Feb. 18 1902 for C. E. Borgshgrevink, Commander of the British Antarctic Expedition.   Maggs Bros. Ltd.   1467 - 144   2013   £2750

Sloss, Frank H. *Only on Monday. Papers Delivered Before the Chit-Chat Club.* San Francisco: Designed and printed by Lawton R. Kennedy for the author, 1978. First edition, one folding plate, rus cloth, very fine, presentation from author for Ben Duniway.   Argonaut Book Shop   Recent Acquisitions June 2013 - 258   2013 $60

A Small Book of Fists. Oxford: Alembic Press, 1990. Limited to 100 numbered copies, 4 volume set, 4.3 x 6.2 cm., quarter cloth, marbled paper covered boards, marbled slipcase, 2 volumes with title gilt stamped on spine, two with label, from the collection of Donn W. Sanford.   Oak Knoll Books   303 - 32   2013 $250

Smallwood, Joseph R. *Encyclopedia of Newfoundland and Labrador.* St. John's: Smallwood Heritage Foundation, 1981-1993. Volume 1-5, all blue cloth, illustrated color endpapers, gilt title to front and spine, frontispiece and black and white illustrations, maps, quarto, all very light wear to covers, otherwise very good.   Schooner Books Ltd.   101 - 74   2013 $450

Smart, Christopher *Musae Seatonianae.* printed by T. Wright for G. Pearch, 1772. First edition, touch of minor browning, ownership inscription of Nicolson Calvert (1816), 8vo., contemporary sprinkled calf, spine divided by gilt milled rolls, black lettering piece in second compartment, rest with central octagonal tools containing sunbursts, rubbed, front joint splitting, ownership inscription of Henry Waldron Bradley, sound.   Blackwell's Rare Books   B174 - 143 2013   £300

Smeaton, John *An Experimental Enquiry Concerning the Natural Powers of Water and Wind to Turn Mills and Other Machines, Depending on a Circular Motion.* London: 1760. First edition, small 4to, 20th century calf backed marbled boards, 3 folding plates, fine.   Howard S. Mott Inc.   262 - 137   2013 $850

Smedley, R. C. *History of the Underground Railroad in Chester and the Neighbouring Counties of Pennsylvania.* Lancaster: printed at the Office of the Journal, 1883. First edition, original cloth titled gilt, 407 pages, small pencil name, 2 church library stamps on titlepage and frontispiece, markings removed from endpapers, some slight spotting to boards, else tight and sound, very good.   Between the Covers Rare Books, Inc.   165 - 263   2013 $300

Smellie, William *The Philosophy of Natural History.* Philadelphia: printed for Robert Cambell, bookseller, North East Corner of second and Chesnut Street, 1791. First American edition, 8vo. browned, few page edges chipped, blank corner of title excised, contemporary sprinkled sheep, red morocco label, little rubbed, head and tail of spine renewed, few old scrapes to boards.   Unsworths Antiquarian Booksellers   28 - 129   2013   £175

Smiddy, Richard *An Essay on the Druids, the Ancient Churches & Round Towers of Ireland.* 1871. First edition, 8vo., cloth, cover dull, text very good, "With the author's respects".   C. P. Hyland   261 - 783   2013   £95

Smiley, Jane *Barn Blind.* New York: Harper & Row, 1980. First edition, signed by author, near fine, light foxing to top edge, fine dust jacket.   Ed Smith Books   78 - 60   2013 $650

Smith, Adam   1723-1790 *An Enquiry into the Nature and Causes of the Wealth of Nations.* Dublin: printed by William Porter, 1793. Fifth edition, 2 volumes, 8vo., little minor spotting and soiling, one leaf with portion of blank corner torn away, contemporary Irish sprinkled calf, spines divided by double gilt fillets, red and green morocco lettering pieces, small patches of shallow insect nibbling to extremities volume i, touch of rubbing elsewhere, all edges citron, very good.   Blackwell's Rare Books   172 - 132   2013   £1800

Smith, Adam   1723-1790 *Essays on Philosophical Subjects to Which is Prefixed an Account of the Life and Writings of the Author by Dugald Stewart.* London: printed for T. Cadell Jun and W. Davies etc., 1795. First edition, quarto, contemporary boards, rebacked, small library stamp on title and verso and on last page, small ink smudge on title, previous owner's bookplate, overall very good, large paper copy, totally uncut.   Heritage Book Shop 50th Anniversary Catalogue - 91   2013 $10,000

Smith, Adam   1723-1790 *An Inquiry into the Nature and Causes of the Wealth of Nations.* London: printed for W. Strahan and T. Cadell, 1776. First edition, 2 volumes, large quarto, half title in volume II, none called for in volume I, final blank leaf end volume 1, contemporary mottled calf, boards tooled with border and gilt floral devices, spines densely stamped in gilt in compartments, blue and green morocco gilt lettering labels, gilt dentelles, edges speckled blue, marbled endpapers, outer hinges bit cracked but holding very firm, bit of chipping to head and tail of spines, some minor flaking of leather along outer hinges, slight crease down center of spine of volume II, in volume II pages 563-566 have been bond out of order, between pages 554 and 555, which is not entirely uncommon, small closed marginal tear with no restoration to leaf 4A2 not affecting text, overall very clean, near fine, housed in full tree calf clamshell, elaborately embellished in gilt.   Heritage Book Shop Holiday Catalogue 2012 - 141   2013 $185,000

Smith, Adam   1723-1790 *An Inquiry into the Nature and Causes of the Wealth of Nations.* London: A. Strahan and T. Cadell, 1796. Eighth edition, 3 volumes, 8vo., pencil note to margin of pages 340 volume II and one front endpaper, full contemporary mottled calf, gilt banded spines, black morocco labels, expert repairs to hinges and head and tail of spines, little rubbed, early 19th century endpapers and pastedowns.   Jarndyce Antiquarian Booksellers   CCIV - 271   2013   £1500

Smith, Adam   1723-1790 *The Theory of Moral Sentiments.* London: printed for A. Strahan and T. Cadell, 1790. Volume 1 (of two) only, presentation copy, inscribed by author for Professor Millar, octavo, half title, contemporary tree calf, neatly rebacked and recornered to style, covers decoratively bordered gilt, board edges tooled in blind, edges sprinkled blue, marbled endpapers, early ink signature of "J. Millar, Millheugh" and Milheugh bookplate, excellent copy, housed in custom green cloth slipcase.   Heritage Book Shop   50th Anniversary Catalogue - 92   2013 $37,500

Smith, Agnes *Glimpses of Greek Life and Scenery.* London: Hurst & Blackett, 1884. First edition, 8vo.., vignette on titlepage, color folding map, frontispiece, 3 plates, original brown decorative cloth, vignette on front cover, spine faded, inner hinges cracked.   J. & S. L. Bonham Antiquarian Booksellers   Europe - 6013   2013   £250

Smith, Albert *The Pottleton Legacy, a Story of Town and Country Life.* London: D. Bogue, 1849. First edition, 8vo., pages viii, 472, 20 engraved plates by Phiz, half calf, gilt tooled spine, labels, marbled boards, matching edges and endpapers.   Marlborough Rare Books Ltd.   218 - 143   2013   £90

Smith, Arthur H. *China in Convulsion.* New York: Fleming H. Revell Co., 1901. First edition, 2 volumes, 8vo., xvi, 364, (viii); 365-770, five maps, owner inscription, age darkening and foxing to endpapers, mild stains to page edges, near fine, volume I dust jacket very good++ with mild edge wear, volume II dust jacket very good+ with stain on front flap fold, rear flap fold has chips, rare in dust jackets which have protected covers wonderfully. By the Book, L. C. 36 - 93 2013 $800

Smith, Charles *The Ancient and Present State of the County & City of Waterford.* 1774. Second edition, Only 2 plates present, pages 23-26 excised, replaced on loose leaf mss., working copy only, in contemporary calf. C. P. Hyland 261 - 784 2013 £60

Smith, Charles H. *Alfred Russel Wallace: an Anthology of His Shorter Writings.* Oxford: Oxford University Press, 1991. First edition, 8vo., very good++, mild soil to edges, in very good++ dust jacket with short closed tears and cover edgewear. By the Book, L. C. 37 - 2 2013 $150

Smith, Charles Hamilton *The Ancient Costume of Great Britain and Ireland from the Seventh to the Sixteenth Century.* London: Henry G. Bohn, 1848. Improved edition, folio, 61 color plates, text only titlepage foxed, but only very slight marginal toning and occasional finger marks elsewhere, near contemporary dark red half morocco with marbled paper boards, skilfully rebacked retaining original gilt spine, all edges gilt, boards scuffed, corners little worn, two gift inscriptions to f.f.e.p., both to "Barbara from Auntie E" one dated 14th June 1935 and one dated Xmas 1944, clippings from auction catalogs loosely inserted. Unsworths Antiquarian Booksellers 28 - 199 2013 £750

Smith, Charlotte Curtis *The Old Cobblestone House: a Ghost Story.* Rochester: Craftsman Press, 1917. First edition, endpapers slightly foxed, still fine in very good dust jacket with few modest chips, small triangular chip at bottom of front panel and slight loss at crown, exceptionally scarce in jacket. Between the Covers Rare Books, Inc. Sci-Fi, Fantasy & Horror - 56678 2013 $450

Smith, Dodie *The Hundred and One Dalmations.* London: Heinemann, 1956. First edition, 8vo., cloth, fine in slightly frayed, very good+ dust jacket, illustrations by Janet and Anne Grahame-Johnstone with color dust jacket, pictorial endpapers plus 58 other black and white's scarce. Aleph-Bet Books, Inc. 104 - 539 2013 $400

Smith, E. Boyd *Fun in the Radio World.* New York: Frederick Stokes, 1923. First edition, 12 color plates plus pictorial endpapers and pen and ink drawings in text, rare in dust jacket. Aleph-Bet Books, Inc. 105 - 550 2013 $575

Smith, E. J. *Jo, a Telegraphic Tale.* Fort Worth: 1885. 211 pages, frontispiece, original half leather, extremities rubbed, some internal staining, hinges reinforced, final two leaves have loss of paper, repaired with loss of text. Dumont Maps & Books of the West 122 - 78 2013 $150

Smith, Edward E. *The Skylark of Space: the Tale of the First Inter-Stellar Cruise.* Cranston: Buffalo Book Co., 1946. First edition, little modest edgewear, very good, without dust jacket. Between the Covers Rare Books, Inc. Sci-Fi, Fantasy & Horror - 286937 2013 $200

Smith, Emmitt *The Emmitt Zone.* New York: Crown Pub., 1994. First edition, fine in fine dust jacket, signed by Smith. Between the Covers Rare Books, Inc. Football Books - 290430 2013 $225

Smith, Ernest Bramah *English Farming and Why I Turned It Up.* Leadenhall Press, 1894. First edition, faint marginal browning to poor quality paper, foolscap 8vo., original stiff pale grey morocco grained cloth, covers lettered an decorated in dark blue and front cover further lettered gilt, backstrip with faint fading, very good. Blackwell's Rare Books B174 - 15 2013 £120

Smith, F. Nicoll *English and American System of Handicapping Running Races: a Complete Treatise Explaining Scientific Handicapping.* New York: F. Nicoll Smith, n.d. circa, 1890. Probable first edition, 16mo., full leather, 30 pages, considerable staining to endpapers, encroaching somewhat on interior gutters, couple of pencil notes, still sound and presentable good copy, laid in are some slips with betting notes and couple of small clippings, exceptionally scarce. Between the Covers Rare Books, Inc. Horses, Horsemanship, Horse Racing, Etc. - 96571 2013 $450

Smith, Fay Jackson *Father Kino in Arizona.* Phoenix: 1966. Limited edition, #188 of 200 copies, signed, xvi, 142 pages, illustrations, folding map, maps, fine hardcover, quarter leather, very good. Dumont Maps & Books of the West 124 - 87 2013 $100

Smith, Fay Jackson *Father Kino in Arizona.* Phoenix: Arizona Historical Foundation, 1966. First edition, 142 pages, quarto, folding map, illustrations, facsimiles, single page map, half black leatherette, gilt decorated blue cloth, very fine. Argonaut Book Shop Summer 2013 - 181 2013 $90

Smith, Gregory Ian *Willie Whiskers.* Blackie & Son, 1950. First edition, square 8vo., original cloth backed pictorial boards, edges little worn, corners bumped, child's drawing on blank lower board, illustrations in color, few short tears to lower gutter. R. F. G. Hollett & Son Children's Books - 556 2013 £30

Smith, Horace 1779-1849 *Brambletye House; or Cavaliers and Roundheads.* London: Henry Collins, 1826. Third edition, 3 volumes, 191 x 12mm., lavishly gilt contemporary olive green straight grain morocco, covers divided into three square panels at top and bottom of an elongated panel at right and left, these panels densely gilt with repeated versions of a large stamp formed by a floral cross radiating oak leaves, central panel with gilt rule frame featuring spiral cornerpieces decorated with acanthus leaves and flowers, raised bands, spine compartments heavily gilt repeating fleuron stamps used on covers, gilt turn-ins, marble endpapers, all edges gilt; each volume with handsome fore-edge painting of a picturesque location important to plot of the novel; engraved bookplate of Emily Lynch Lowe (NY artist), extremities and joints slightly rubbed (but well masked with dye), occasional minor foxing or stains, really excellent set, remarkably decorative bindings lustrous and most appealing, text clean and fresh, expert fore-edge paintings in fine condition. Phillip J. Pirages 61 - 55 2013 $3500

Smith, Horace 1779-1849 *Rejected Addresses; or the New Theatrum Poetarum.* London: John Miller, 1812. First edition, half title, final ad leaf, some spotting, uncut in original drab boards, covered with marbled paper and respined, chipped and slightly defective, booklabel of Lord Elton of Headington, Oxon. Jarndyce Antiquarian Booksellers CCIII - 152 2013 £85

Smith, Horace 1779-1849 *Rejected Addresses; or the New Theatrum Poetarum.* London: John Miller, 1812. Third edition, 12mo, occasional internal marks and pencil notes, slightly later half vellum, slightly marked, spine little dulled, edges trimmed, some loss of owner signature and date on title. Jarndyce Antiquarian Booksellers CCIII - 153 2013 £25

Smith, Horace 1779-1849 *Rejected Addresses; or the New Theatrum Poetarum. (with) Horace in London.* London: John Miller, 1813. 11th edition and 2nd edition respectively, 2 volumes in 1, 12mo., contemporary half calf, lacking label, slightly rubbed, very good. Jarndyce Antiquarian Booksellers CCIII - 155 2013 £35

Smith, Horace 1779-1849 *(Rejected Addresses). A Sequel to the "Rejected Addresses"; or the Theatrum Poetarum Minorum.* London: Sherwood, Neely & Jones, 1813. First edition, uncut in original drab boards, spine slightly chipped, paper label defective, Renier booklabel. Jarndyce Antiquarian Booksellers CCIII - 157 2013 £75

Smith, Jedediah Strong 1779-1831 *The Southwest Expedition of Jedediah S. Smith.* Glendale: Arthur H. Clark Co., 1977. First edition, 2nd printing, one of 513 copies, 259 pages, 3 maps, red cloth, fine, becoming quite scarce. Argonaut Book Shop Recent Acquisitions June 2013 - 259 2013 $90

Smith, Jessie Willcox *The Jessie Willcox Smith Mother Goose.* New York: Dodd Mead, 1914. First edition, third issue, Large oblong 4to., black cloth, pictorial paste-on, margin of frontispiece slightly frayed, else fine, cover plate, pictorial title page, 12 color plates, 5 black and white plates, plus many illustrations. Aleph-Bet Books, Inc. 105 - 551 2013 $875

Smith, John *The Late Reverend Richard Smith. An Appreciation.* New York: 1911. 8vo., card covers with string binding at spine, rear end flap, 34 pages, frontispiece, missing front endflap, covers very slightly scuffed, interior good. Schooner Books Ltd. 102 - 49 2013 $75

Smith, John *A Letter to J. K(elly) M.D. with an account of the Case of Mr. T----n of the City of Oxford.* Oxford: printed for D. Prince, 1765. 4to., 5 line initial in red at beginning, smaller initials in red rubricated, first page slightly soiled and initial a little rubbed, very minor browning in few margins, few early notes, early to mid-19th century pebble grained brown cloth, very good, rare. Blackwell's Rare Books 172 - 133 2013 £350

Smith, John *The Principles and Practice of Vegetarian Cookery, Founded on Chemical Analysis and Embracing the Most Approved Methods of the Art.* London: Simpkin Marshall and Co., 1860. First edition, half title, odd spot, original green cloth, slightly rubbed, very good. Jarndyce Antiquarian Booksellers CCV - 250 2013 £180

Smith, Lucy Mack *Biographical Sketches of Joseph Smith the Prophet and His Progenitors for Many Generations.* Liverpool: Published for Orson Pratt by S. W. Richard, 1853. First edition, duodecimo, full dark brown morocco with decorative flora gilt stamping to boards and backstrip, title gilt stamped on backstrip, gilt dentelles, decorative green and gold pastedowns and endsheets, near fine, matching leather clamshell. Ken Sanders Rare Books 45 - 32 2013 $7500

Smith, Lucy Toulmin *York Plays. The Plays Performed by the Crafts or Mysteries of York on the Day of Corpus Christi in the 14th, 15th and 16th Centuries.* Oxford: at the Clarendon Press, 1885. First edition, 3 folding plates, very good in original red gilt cloth, few marginal pencil notes, scarce. Ken Spelman Books Ltd. 73 - 45 2013 £45

Smith, Mary *Eskimo Stories.* Chicago: Rand McNally, 1902. First edition, 4to., cloth pictorial paste-on, 175 pages, endpaper creased, else fine in dust jacket (chipped), printed on coated paper, illustrations by Howard V. Brown, with color frontispiece, 17 black and white plates, many black and whites in text, uncommon. Aleph-Bet Books, Inc. 104 - 201 2013 $200

Smith, Nora Arch *Boys and Girls of Bookland.* Philadelphia: McKay, Cosmopolitan, 1923. Large 4to., brown cloth, pictorial paste-on, paper with slight aging, else fine in dust jacket chipped and lightly soiled, illustrations by Jessie Willcox Smith with cover plate plus 11 large color plates.   Aleph-Bet Books, Inc.   104 - 542   2013 $200

Smith, Patti *Just Kids.* New York: Ecco Press, 2010. Signed limited edition, 1/1000 copies, original publisher's box, unopened.   Ed Smith Books   75 - 67   2013 $300

Smith, Patti *Just Kids.* New York: Ecco Press, 2010. First edition, signed by author, with sticker to front dust jacket "Signed @ Book Soup" and flyer for the signing laid in, fine in dust jacket.   Ed Smith Books   75 - 66   2013 $150

Smith, S. Percy *The Eruption of Tarawera; a Report of the Surveyor General.* Wellington: 1886. First edition, 8vo., 7 original photos laid down, lithographs and maps, contemporary cloth.   Maggs Bros. Ltd.   1467 - 92   2013   £750

Smith, Stevie *The Holiday.* London: Chapman and Hall, 1949. First edition, foolscap 8vo., original pale grey cloth, backstrip lettered in silver on pink ground, few small chips to dust jacket with design by author, very good.   Blackwell's Rare Books   B174 - 301   2013   £100

Smith, Tom Robb *Child 44.* New York: Grand Central Pub., 2008. First edition, advance reading copy, signed by author, slight spine roll, else fine in wrappers, laid in is printed flyer entitled "How Do You Solve an Impossible Crime?"   Ken Lopez Bookseller   159 - 179   2013 $150

Smith, Truman *Speech of Mr. Smith, of Conn. on the Bill "To Admit California into the Union to Establish Territorial Governments for Utah and New Mexico...* Washington: Gideon & Co., 1850. First edition, 8vo., 32 pages, unbound, uncut and partly unopened, minor browning.   Howard S. Mott Inc.   262 - 138   2013 $200

Smith, W. Eugene *Minamata.* New York: Holt, Rinehart & Winston, 1975. First edition, 4to., 192 pages, near fine, original printed wrappers, signed by Eugene and Aileen Smith.   By the Book, L. C.   36 - 25   2013 $350

Smith, Walker C. *The Everett Massacre a History of the Class Struggle in the Lumber Industry.* Chicago: I. W. W. Pub. Bureau, 1917? First edition, 8vo., photos, publisher's cloth stamped in gilt, hinges tender, good, former owner's signature on copyright page.   Second Life Books Inc.   183 - 359   2013 $125

Smith, Wallace *Garden of the Sun.* Fresno: Fresno State College, 1960. Eighth edition, (14) 568 pages, frontispiece, photos, drawings, text maps, beige cloth stamped in copper, green and red, very fine.   Argonaut Book Shop Recent Acquisitions June 2013 - 260   2013 $60

Smith, Wallace *Prodigal Sons. the Adventures of Christopher Evans and John Sontag.* California History Books, 1973. Reprint of rare first edition, 434 pages frontispiece, plates, portraits, red cloth, small oval bookplate, fine with slightly chipped dust jacket.   Argonaut Book Shop Recent Acquisitions June 2013 - 2611   2013 $75

Smith, William   1728-1793 *History of New York from the First Discovery to the Year MDCCXXXII.* Albany: printed by Ryer Schermerhorn, 1814. Second American edition, 512 pages, original paper covered boards, title printed on spine, large dampstain throughout text, paper over boards, spine largely eroded, but sound, good.   Between the Covers Rare Books, Inc.   New York City - 205893   2013 $225

Smith, William   1728-1793 *The History of the Province of New York from the First Discovery to the Year MDCCXXXII.* London: Thomas Wilcox, 1757. First edition, folding frontispiece, 4to., later red morocco, spine gilt.   Maggs Bros. Ltd.   1467 - 127   2013   £4250

Smith, William   1813-1893 *Dictionary of Greek and Roman Biography and Mythology. (and) Dictionary of Greek and Roman Geography. (and) Dictionary of Greek and Roman Antiquities.* Boston: Charles C. Little and James Brown; Boston: Little Brown and Co., 1849-1859. Apparently first edition of the first two works, second edition of Antiquities, 230 x 149mm., 3 works in 6 volumes, pleasing half calf in tan, olive or black over buckram or marbled paper, raised bands flanked by thick and thin gilt rules, morocco labels, numerous woodcuts in text, titlepages with contemporary ink inscription "Ex Libris J. Kelly", joints and extremities with bit of rubbing, boards lightly chafed, but fine, fresh little used copies with only most trivial internal imperfections and in solid bindings that make attractive appearance on the shelf.   Phillip J. Pirages   63 - 442   2013 $2000

Smith, William Gardner *South Street.* New York: Farrar, Straus and Young, 1954. First edition, spine ends and corners lightly bumped, else near fine in very good dust jacket with short nicks to spine ends and small pen scribble on verso, signed by author, scarce in this condition.   Between the Covers Rare Books, Inc.   165 - 332   2013 $700

Smithson, J. S. *A Useful Book for Farmers.* Carlisle: 1877. 72 pages, 8vo., wrappers (worn), text good.   C. P. Hyland   261 - 454   2013   £30

Smollett, Tobias George   1721-1771   *The Adventures of Covnt Fathom.*   London: Navarre Society Ltd. circa, 1902. One of 2000 copies, 181 114mm., 2 volumes, very fine burgundy morocco, handsome gilt and onlaid, by Harcourt Bindery of Boston (stamp-signed on front flyleaf), boards with triple fillet border, each cover with elaborate heraldic frame of gilt and onlaid green morocco around an empty oval, raised bands, very pretty gilt spine compartments, featuring looping tendril frame enclosed a charming flower centerpiece densely gilt turn-ins, marbled endpapers, top edge gilt, 2 frontispieces by G. Cruikshank, very fine, bindings especially bright, text with virtually no signs of use.   Phillip J. Pirages   63 - 443   2013 $400

Smollett, Tobias George   1721-1771   *The Adventures of Peregrine Pickle.*   London: Navarre Society Ltd. circa., 1902.   One of 2000 copies, 4 volumes, 181 x 114mm., very fine burgundy morocco, handsomely gilt and onlaid by Harcourt Bindery of Boston (stamp signed), boards with triple fillet border, each cover with elaborate heraldic frame of gilt and onlaid green morocco around an empty oval, raised bands, very pretty gilt spine compartments featuring looping tendril frame enclosing a charming flower centerpiece, densely gilt turn-ins, marbled endpapers, titlepage, 4 frontispiece drawings by George Cruikshank, very fine, bindings bright, text with virtually no signs of use.   Phillip J. Pirages 63 - 444   2013 $600

Smollett, Tobias George   1721-1771   *The Adventures of Roderick Random.*   Gotha: printed for Steudel and Keil, 1805.   12mo., some unintrusive foxing, F8 volume III torn with slight loss, contemporary green glazed boards, later grain cloth, spine and corners, booklabel of F. Stahlschmidt. Jarndyce Antiquarian Booksellers   CCIV - 272   2013 £225

Smollett, Tobias George   1721-1771   *The Adventures of Roderick Random.*   London: Navarre Society Ltd. circa, 1902.   One of 2000 copies, 3 volumes, 181 x 114mm., very fine burgundy morocco, handsomely gilt onlaid by Harcourt Bindery of Boston (stamp signed), boards with triple fillet border, each cover with elaborate heraldic frame of gilt and onlaid green morocco around an empty oval, raised bands, very pretty gilt spine compartments featuring looping tendril frame enclosing a charming flower centerpiece, densely gilt turn-ins, marbled endpapers, top edge gilt, three frontispiece drawings by George Cruikshank, very fine, bindings especially bright and text virtually unused.   Phillip J. Pirages 63 - 445   2013 $550

Smollett, Tobias George   1721-1771   *The Expedition of Humphry Clinker.*   London: printed for W. Johnston, 1771. First edition, Rothschild variant A4, 3 volumes, half titles but bound without final blanks volumes I and II, leading edge of titlepage volume II trimmed, occasional foxing and light browning, fresh contemporary endpapers to two volumes, contemporary calf neatly rebacked, gilt bands to morocco labels, corners worn, inner hinges neatly repaired. Jarndyce Antiquarian Booksellers   CCIV - 273   2013 £580

Smollett, Tobias George   1721-1771   *The Expedition of Humphry Clinker.*   London: W. Johnston and B. Collins in Salisbury, 1671, i.e., 1771.   First edition, 3 volumes, 12mo., contemporary calf (front hinge volume 1 cracked and slightly chipped at head of spine), leather titlepieces, raised bands, excellent copy, with all half titles, early ownership signature "Arch. Wilson/Dedham", old stamp of "W. C. Day" and bookplate of Chicago book collector Harold Greenhill (1893-1968) in each volume, morocco backed cloth folding case.   Howard S. Mott Inc.   262 - 139   2013 $1350

Smollett, Tobias George   1721-1771   *The Expedition of Humphry Clinker.*   C. Cooke, 1794.   2 volumes, 12mo, superb engravings, frontispieces and 3 plates, faces on two of the plates have been blacked over by contemporary hand, rebound, not recently, in full polished calf, raised bands, black gilt labels, some scattered foxing.   Ken Spelman Books Ltd.   75 - 45   2013   £95

Smollett, Tobias George   1721-1771   *Travels through France and Italy...*   London: printed for R. Baldwin, 1766. Second edition, 2 volumes, 8vo., some slight foxing, endpapers replaced with laid paper, full contemporary sprinkled calf, raised and gilt banded spines, red morocco labels, corners little worn, contemporary signature of John How on half title and head of first page of text.   Jarndyce Antiquarian Booksellers   CCIV - 274   2013   £380

Smollett, Tobias George   1721-1771   *The Works.* London: Bickers and Son and H. Sotheran and Co., 1872. 221 x 144mm., 8 volumes, appealing contemporary sprinkled half calf, raised bands, spines in double gilt ruled compartments, black and burgundy morocco labels, marbled boards and endpapers, frontispiece portrait and engraved plate in volume 1, touch of wear to joints and extremities, one leaf with one inch fore-edge chip, other trivial imperfections but quite excellent set, clean, fresh text and in sound, pleasing bindings with no serious condition problems. Phillip J. Pirages   63 - 446   2013 $400

Smollett, Tobias George   1721-1771   *The Works.*   New York: Jenson Society, 1911.   One of 1000 sets, 236 x 146mm., 12 volumes, this copy #317, very pleasing contemporary rose colored three quarter calf spines with slightly raised bands, unusual gilt decoration in compartments, two with gilt roses flanking a central helix and two with central rose in lozenge and with trefoil cornerpieces, marbled boards and endpapers, top edge gilt, other edges untrimmed, 6 frontispieces in color and 6 additional plates as called for all by John Ward Dunsmore, lettered tissue guards, spines sunned to a softer pink, very small portions of extremities with hint of rubbing, one rear board with small scratch to leather, trivial internal imperfections, but excellent set, text clean, fresh and bright and pleasant bindings with no significant wear.   Phillip J. Pirages   63 - 447   2013 $450

Smooth, Joseph *Ye Second Book of Nursery Rhymes Set to Music.* London: George Allen, 1896. First edition, green cloth, album 4to., illustrations, joints repaired, good. Barnaby Rudge Booksellers   Children 2013 - 021524   2013 $75

Smyth, Henry De Wolf *A General Account of the Development of Methods of Using Atomic Energy for Military Purposes Under the Auspices of the United States Government 1940-1945.* Washington: GPO, 1945. First Government Printing Office Edition, octavo, few black and white charts within text, printed beige cardboard wrappers, with staples, back wrapper bit sunned, wrappers with few light creases, otherwise about fine.   Heritage Book Shop Holiday Catalogue 2012 - 143   2013 $500

Snead, Sam *The Education of a Golfer.* New York: Simon & Schuster, 1962. First edition, 8vo., vii, 248 pages, near fine, minimal cover edge wear in very good+ dust jacket with chips and short closed tears, signed and inscribed by author.   By the Book, L. C.   36 - 74   2013 $250

Snell, Edmund *The Z Ray.* Philadelphia: Lippincott, 1932. First edition, fine in very attractive, near fine dust jacket with slight tanning and small nick, both at spine. Between the Covers Rare Books, Inc.   Sci-Fi, Fantasy & Horror - 87164   2013 $250

Snell, George D. *Search for Rational Ethics.* New York: Springer, 1988. Stated first edition, fine, 8vo., fine dust jacket, inscribed and signed by author.   By the Book, L. C.   37 - 73   2013 $325

Snell, Hannah *The Female Soldier.* London: R. Walker, 1750. First edition, frontispiece, 3 plates, 8vo., contemporary half calf, border slightly trimmed on one plate, very rare. Maggs Bros. Ltd.   1467 - 45   2013   £6500

Snell, Willebrord *Tiphys Batavus, sive Histioromice de Navium Cusribus et re Navali.* Leiden: Elzevier, 1624. First edition, woodcut printer's device on title, diagrams in text, 3 engraved plates, chart just shaved at for margin, trifle browned in plates minor dampstaining, 4to., contemporary deerskin, gilt and blind ruled borders on sides, spine gilt in compartments, lettered in gilt direct, in top compartment, blue edges, spine faded and defective at top and tail, ownership inscriptions and notes in French and Dutch on flyleaves, the Macclesfield copy with blindstamp and bookplate.   Blackwell's Rare Books   Sciences - 113   2013   £1500

Snicket, Lemony *A Series of Unfortunate Events.* Egmont, 2001-2006. First UK edition, 13 volumes, small 8vo., original pictorial matt glazed boards, illustrations by Brett Helquist, 3 volumes with child's name on printed ex-libris on flyleaf, else fine unmarked, complete set.   R. F. G. Hollett & Son   Children's Books - 557   2013   £250

Snider, Denton J. *Psychology and the Psychosis Intellect.* St. Louis: Sigma Co., 1896. First edition, very good, library marks on endpapers, penciling at early pages.   Beasley Books   2013 - 2013 $65

Snow White. Duenewald: 1950. 4to., pictorial wrappers, small neat reinforcement on inside, else near fine, text printed on rear panel, inside are 2 full page color lithographed pages by Julian Wehr, one has tab operated moveable, and other has 2 color illustrated hankies tucked into slots in illustrations, rare.   Aleph-Bet Books, Inc.   105 - 413   2013 $400

Snyder, Dee *The ABC's of Baker Street: a Guide to the Holmesian Habitat.* Skokie: Black Cat Press, 1983. Limited to 249 copies, 7.3 x 5.2 cm., cloth, title gilt stamped on spine and front cover, marbled endpapers, 97, (5) pages, illustrations, bound by Bela Blau, from the collection of Donn W. Sanford.   Oak Knoll Books   303 - 58   2013 $100

Snyder, Fairmont *The Lovely Garden.* Chicago: Volland, 1919. First edition, illustrations, very good+ with child's name pencilled inside, in damaged illustrated box, missing several blank side pieces, unusually well preserved. Beasley Books   2013 - 2013 $100

Snyder, Gary *Sixteen T'ang Poems.* Hopewell: Pied Oxen Printers, 1993. First edition, one of 126, 100 of which were for sale all on Rives paper, each signed by poet and translator, Gary Snyder on author's Notes pages, and hand numbered on colophon, frontispiece Hanga woodcut by Bill Paden, on kizuki-kozo, sarashi paper made by Kazuo Yamaguchi is also signed and numbered, page size 8 1/4 x 11 1/2 inches, 26 pages, bound by printer/designer, David Sellers, handsewn in handmade paper from India over boards, stamped with Chinese characters in black on front panel, title in back type in contrasting red label on spine, fine.   Priscilla Juvelis - Rare Books   56 - 28   2013 $950

Social Harmony, or the Feast of Apollo, a collection of the Most Esteemed, Scarce and Celebrated Glees, Catches, Madrigals, Canzonets, Rounds and Cannons. Jones & Co., 1825. Royal 8vo., engraved throughout, apart from letterpress index at end, titlepage with vignette, some thumbing and soiling, occasional slight browning, poor impression at foot of contents and occasionally elsewhere near plate mark, modern tan calf, red lettering piece on spine, good. Blackwell's Rare Books   B174 - 107   2013   £450

Societe Astronomique de France *Bulletin de la Societe Astronomique de France et Revue Mensuelle d'Astronomie de Meterologie et de Physique de Globe.* Paris: Au Siege de la Societe, Hotel des Societes Savantes, 1899-1931. 1933-1934, 35 volumes, 8vo., various paginations, illustrations and figures, beautiful later half red morocco over marbled paper backed boards, gilt stamped spines, Carnegie Inst. of Washington, Solar Observatory, blindstamps, near fine, handsome set.   Jeff Weber Rare Books   169 - 21   2013 $1500

Society of Antiquaries *List of Printed Books in the Library of the Society of Antiquaries of London.* London: Pickton for The Society, 1861. First edition, 8vo., light marginal offsetting from binder's glue to title and blank, otherwise clean in original publisher's cloth, front cover lettered in gilt, hinges with short slits at head and tail, little spotted. Marlborough Rare Books Ltd. 218 - 144 2013 £75

Society of Antiquaries *Vetusta Monumenta...* London: various printers, 1747-. 1789-1796-1810-1815, First editions, 4 volumes in two, large folio, engraved plates, 5 engravings in text, occasionally little foxed, early 19th century calf, spines and covers ornamented in gilt, gilt stamped red morocco lettering pieces, hinges and corners restored. Marlborough Rare Books Ltd. 218 - 145 2013 £2500

Soemmerring, Samuel Thomas Von *De Basi Encephali et Orginibus Nervorum Cranio Egredientium. (bound with) Dispvtationem Inavgvrale de Base Encephall et Originibvs Nervorvm...* Gottingen: Prostat apud Abr. Vadenhoeck Viduam, 1778. Gottingae:... Ion. christ Dieterich, 4to., early parchment boards, light wear, printed on thicker and heavy stock of paper than what is usually seen, library stamps on title but no external markings, rare work. James Tait Goodrich 75 - 196 2013 $5500

Soldier ABC. New York: McLoughlin Bros. circa, 1900. Folio, pictorial wrappers, few margin mends, spine mend, very good+ brightly illustrated with 2 full page chromolithographs and 6 full page brown and whites. Aleph-Bet Books, Inc. 104 - 14 2013 $400

Solis Y Ribadeneyra, Antonio De 1610-1686 *The History of the Conquest Mexico by the Spaniards.* London: printed for T. Woodward... J. Hooke... and J. Peele, 1724. First English edition, five parts in one volume, folio, 2 engraved maps, 6 engraved plates, bound without engraved frontispiece portrait, engraved head and tailpieces, ornamental initials, contemporary full tree calf, rebacked, boards tooled in gilt floral motif, original red morocco spine label lettered gilt, marbled endpapers, corners bit bumped, boards with few minor scuffs and scrapes, titlepage has been trimmed and is laid down, closed tear professionally repaired and fold reinforced to folding plate between pages 68/69 of book III, small old ink binding instructions also written on plate, top margin of plate reinforced, four inch closed tear to page 243, some foxing and toning, overall very good. Heritage Book Shop   Holiday Catalogue 2012 - 144 2013 $2000

Solleysel, Jacques De *The Compleat Horseman: or Perfect Farrier.* London: printed for R. Bonwicke, W. Freeman, Tim Goodwin (and others), 1711. Second edition, octavo, 376, (16) pages, 7 plates, including folding frontispiece and five other folding plates, rebacked with new endpapers and some erosion to edges of original or contemporary boards later gift inscription, faint, pretty much unreadable library stamp (with tiny 'cancelled' stamp), scattered foxing, some modest dampstains on some of the folding plates, sound, very good. Between the Covers Rare Books, Inc. Horses, Horsemanship, Horse Racing, Etc. - 304404 2013 $1200

Solzhenitsyn, Alexander *August 1914.* New York: Farrar Straus Giroux, 1971. First American edition, near fine, minimal soil, foxing to edges, 8vo., 622 pages, in very good++ dust jacket with short closed tear, tape, minimal foxing. By the Book, L. C. 36 - 55 2013 $1000

Some British Ballads. London: Constable & Co., 1919. One of 575 copies signed by artist, this #379, 286 x 229mm., very attractive red engraved plates morocco (stamp signed "Putnams"), raised bands, spine handsomely gilt in compartments formed by plain and decorative rules, quatrefoil centerpiece, surrounded by densely scrolling cornerpieces, sides and endleaves of rose colored linen, top edge gilt, with titlepage, vignette, black and white illustrations in text and 17 color plates by Arthur Rackham, all tipped on and with letterpress guards, morocco bookplate of W. A. M. Burden; only most trivial signs of use externally, exceptionally fine inside and out, especially lustrous handsome gilt binding. Phillip J. Pirages 63 - 382 2013 $1500

Some "Kernel" Arguments Opposed to Woman's Suffrage: Suffrage Not a matter of "Right" Creature o Government for Government. Ohio?: 1912. 16mo., self wrappers, front cover browned, lacks lower corner of cover not affecting text, very good. Second Life Books Inc. 183 - 10 2013 $75

Some Papers Given in by the Commissioners of the Parliament of Scotland, to the... Parliament of England... Concerning the Disposing of His Majesties Person. Edinburgh: by Evan Tyler, 1646. 4to., (2), 30 pages, modern cloth, text bit browned. Joseph J. Felcone Inc. Books Printed before 1701 - 81 2013 $325

Some Who Do... and One Who Doesn't. Exton, Devon: Bishops Books, printed by the Whittington Press, 1998. One of 150 numbered copies printed on Zerkall mouldmade paper, this unnumbered, but listed 'out of series', titlepage printed in black and green, royal 8vo., original plain cream sewn card, untrimmed, dust jacket, fine. Blackwell's Rare Books 172 - 318 2013 £45

Somers, Ray *History of Logan.* Logan: Somers Historic Press, 1993. Oblong quarto, black cloth spines with illustrated wrappers, very good, covers gently discolored. Ken Sanders Rare Books 45 - 13 2013 $200

Somervell, Arthur *Singing Time.* Elkin & Co., n.d. circa, 1900. 4to., original cloth backed pictorial board, black and white illustrations, joints cracking, little loose. R. F. G. Hollett & Son Children's Books - 89 2013 £45

A Song in Favour of Bundling. Orpheus Press for the Twelve by Eight, 1961. 188/200 copies, 4to., 22 pages, full page illustrations by Rigby Graham, very good in original vellum backed marbled boards. Ken Spelman Books Ltd. 75 - 183 2013 £65

Songs and Lyrics from the Dramatists 1533-1777. London: George Newnes; New York: Charles Scribner's Sons, 1905. 164 x 88mm., xiv, 242, (1) pages, 81 illustrations, decorative titlepage and head and tailpieces; excellent olive brown morocco by Morrell, heavily and flamboyantly decorated gilt in "Scottish Wheel" design, each cover with large central wheel of 20 compartments containing slender and elegant floral tools between two lines of dots radiating from central rosette, all contained within two scalloped concentric rings filled with dense and very regular stippling, wheel with tangent massed gilt circlets at top and bottom and then complex fleurons farther above and below featuring a very charming cherub, corners with triangular floral ornaments, other small tools surrounding central wheel, raised bands, spine compartments attractively gilt in playful scrolling manner with interwoven design including two shell ornaments, very wide turn-ins with intricate and complementary gilt decoration, pastedowns and free endpapers of bright crimson watered silk, all edges gilt, minor fading to leather, still lavish binding in very fine condition, internally with virtually no signs of use. Phillip J. Pirages 61 - 119 2013 $750

Sons of the Copper Beeches *Leaves from the Copper Beeches.* Philadelphia: Baker Street Irregulars, 1959. First edition, short tear along bottom edge of back cover, otherwise fine without dust jacket as issued. Mordida Books 81 - 155 2013 $125

Soos, Troy *Murder at Fenway Park.* New York: Kensington, 1994. First edition, very fine in dust jacket. Mordida Books 81 - 25 2013 $135

Sophocles *Quae Exstant Omnia cum Veterum Grammaticorum Scholiis.* Strasbourg: Apud Joannem Georgium Treuttel, 1786. First Brunck edition, 2 volumes, bound without final leaf in volume ii (blank except for colophon on verso, often missing), few minor spots, small early manuscript date to volume i title, 4to., contemporary russia, boards bordered with gilt roll with torch tools at corners, spines divided by double gilt fillet, second and fourth compartments gilt lettered direct, rest with central gilt tool of mask and instruments, all edges gilt, marbled endpapers, front board of volume i with prize inscription lettered direct in gilt and enclosed on top and sides by gilt flower and pearl tools, old repair to spine ends in slightly different colour, some cracking to front of volume i, few old scratches and marks, bookplate of author Nevil Shute and lending label of the Sandford Press to front endpapers, good. Blackwell's Rare Books B174 - 144 2013 £900

Sophocles *Sophoclis Tragoediae...* Argentorati: Treuttel et Wurtz, 1788. One of only 250 copies, 8vo., three quarter maroon morocco over marbled boards, ruled gilt, four raised bands, compartments paneled gilt, gilt titles, all edges gilt, marbled endpapers, very good set, boards rubbed, spines lightly sunned, boards on final volume with repaired paper splits. Kaaterskill Books 16 - 75 2013 $1250

Sorenstam, Annika *Golf Annika's Way.* New York: Gotham, 2004. Stated first edition, 8vo., 271 pages, fine in near fine dust jacket with minimal edgewear. By the Book, L. C. 36 - 76 2013 $120

Soth, Alec *Dog Days Bogota.* Germany: Steidl Publishers, 2007. First edition, very fine in like dust jacket, signed by Soth. Jeff Hirsch Books Fall 2013 - 129131 2013 $150

Soth, Alec *Sleeping By the Mississippi.* Gottingen: Steidl Publishers, 2004. First edition, color photos, fine copy in boards, issued without dust jacket, signed and inscribed by Soth. Jeff Hirsch Books Fall 2013 - 129115 2013 $1500

South, Robert *Ecclesiastical Policy the Best Policy; or Religion the Best Reason of State in a Sermon Delivered before the Honourable Society of Lincolnes Inn.* Oxford: printed by A. L. for Tho. Robinson, 1660. 4to. disbound, contemporary marginal note to one page. Jarndyce Antiquarian Booksellers CCIV - 30 2013 £20

Southall, Rita *The Black Letters: Love Letters from a Black Soldier in Viet Nam.* Washington: Nuclassics and Science Pub. co., 1972. First edition, small owner name, small owner name, a mark (possibly a remainder mark) on both top and bottom page edges some scuffing and rubbing to boards, very good, lacking dust jacket, very scarce. Between the Covers Rare Books, Inc. 165 - 264 2013 $85

Southcott, Joanna *Answer to five charges in the Leeds Mercury, Four of Which are Absolutely false...*   London: Seale, 1805. First edition, 8vo., 24, removed from bound volume, fine.   Second Life Books Inc.   182 - 226   2013 $500

Southcott, Joanna *Answer to Five Charges in the Leeds Mercury, Four of Which are Absolutely False.*   London: Seale, 1805. First edition, 8vo., removed from bound volume.   Second Life Books Inc.   183 - 360   2013 $500

Souvenir: Irish National Teachers Congress.   Cork: 1931. Special binding of ITA, 86 pages, 8vo., photos, decorative boards, very good.   C. P. Hyland   261 - 245   2013   £45

Souvenir of Madeira.   Funchal: Perestrelos, n.d., 1910. First edition, small oblong folio, 12 colored plates, original brick red decorative wrappers.   J. & S. L. Bonham Antiquarian Booksellers   Europe - 8970   2013   £30

Souvenir of the Canal and Republic of Panama.   Panamas: I. L. Maduro, n.d. circa, 1912. First edition, oblong 8vo., 79 photographic illustrations, original color pictorial stiff wrappers, minor chipping to hinge and corners of front wrapper, near fine, internally fine.   Argonaut Book Shop   Recent Acquisitions June 2013 - 227   2013 $75

Sowerby, G. B. *Grasses of Great Britain.*   London: 1861. 8vo., blue cloth, 84 color plates, titlepage and a number of pages lacking, fair condition.   Barnaby Rudge Booksellers   Natural History 2013 - 020995   2013 $89

Sowerby, Githa *The Bright Book.*   London: Henry Frowde, Hodder & Stougton, n.d., 1916. Original embossed pictorial boards, little marked, spine slightly worn, 12 full page color plates, illustrations by Millicent Sowerby.   R. F. G. Hollett & Son   Children's Books - 562   2013   £75

Sowerby, Githa *Childhood.*   New York: and London: Duffield & Chatto and Windus, 1907. 4to., cloth, pictorial paste-on, 46 pages, very good, line illustrations by Millicent Sowerby.   Aleph-Bet Books, Inc.   104 - 543   2013 $250

Sowerby, Githa *The Dainty Book.*   London: Henry Frowde, Hodder & Stoughton, n.d., 1915. First edition, original embossed pictorial boards, little soiled and rubbed, 12 full page color plates, decorations by Millicent Sowerby, scarce.   R. F. G. Hollett & Son   Children's Books - 563   2013   £75

Sowerby, Githa *The Gay Book.*   London: Henry Frowde, Hodder & Stoughton, n.d., 1915. First edition, original embossed pictorial boards, little marked in places, 12 full page color plates by Millicent Sowerby, scarce.   R. F. G. Hollett & Son   Children's Books - 564   2013   £95

Sowerby, Githa *The Pretty Book.*   London: Henry Frowde, Hodder & Stoughton, n.d., 1915. First edition, original embossed pictorial boards, little marked in places, 12 full page color plates and decorations in green by Millicent Sowerby, scarce.   R. F. G. Hollett & Son   Children's Books - 565   2013   £95

Sowerby, J. G. *Afternoon Tea.*   London: Frederick Warne & Co., n.d., 1880. 4to., original pictorial glazed boards, edges little worn, corners rounded, pages 64, color illustrations, floral patterned endpapers, half title and final leaf lightly browned,.   R. F. G. Hollett & Son   Children's Books - 558   2013   £95

Spaeth, Sigmund *Maxims to Music.*   New York: McBride, 1939. Stated first edition, 4to., fine in slightly worn dust jacket, very scarce, illustrations in color by Tony Sarg, laid in is card from publisher.   Aleph-Bet Books, Inc.   104 - 510   2013 $300

Spafford, Horatio Gates *Gazetteer of the State of New York...*   Albany: B. D. Packard, 1824. First edition, full calf with black morocco spine label, spine titled and decorated in gilt, 620 pages, folding map, some wear to top of the joints, slight nicking at spine ends, nice, very good.   Between the Covers Rare Books, Inc.   New York City - 200902   2013 $550

Spaher, Micahel *A Survey of the Microcosme or the Anatomy of the Bodies of Man and Woman.*   London: printed for Dan. Midwinter and Tho. Leigh, 1702. Second edition, titlepage and 4 manikin plates with text legends, plates and leaves appear complete except for the first manakin leaf where the 'chastity' leaf might be missing, recently bound in simple quarter calf and linen boards, marginal dampstaining along outer fore edge, with two extra Vesalian plates (18th century?) pasted on pastedown leaves, very rare.   James Tait Goodrich   75 - 198   2013   £3950

Spallanzani, Lazzaro *Dissertazioni Due dell' Abate Spallanzani...*   Modena: ededi di Bartolomeo Soliani, 1765. Very good in contemporary limp boards, covered in speckled patterned paper with scattered edge wear, scuffs to binding, contemporary scuffed spine label, light dampstaining to first pages and scattered foxing, 2 engraved foldout plates, custom modern quarter leather clamshell box.   By the Book, L. C.   38 - 12   2013 $3000

Sparkes, Boyden *The Witch of Wall Street: Hetty Green.*   Garden City: Doubleday Doran & Co., 1935. Reprint, bookplate and some sunning to green cloth, very good in good or better price clipped dust jacket with some chips on front panel and soiling to spine.   Between the Covers Rare Books, Inc.   New York City - 288313   2013 $85

Sparrow, Anthony *A Rationale Upon the Book of Common Prayer of the Church of England...* London: printed for Robert Pawlet, 1672. Sixth edition, 12mo., frontispiece, 2 engraved titles, 3 engraved portrait plate, edges of frontispiece and first engraved title repaired, little spotting elsewhere, contemporary speckled calf, resewn and rebacked by Chris Weston, old leather touch rubbed and chipped, contemporary ink inscription 'Lv Dl' on printed titlepage. Unsworths Antiquarian Booksellers 28 - 130 2013 £250

Speare, Elizabeth George *Bronze Bow.* Boston: Houghton Mifflin, 1961. First edition, 8vo., cloth, 255 pages, owner name on endpaper, fine in fine dust jacket (price clipped), nice. Aleph-Bet Books, Inc. 104 - 544 2013 $250

Speare, Elizabeth George *Witch of Blackbird Pond.* Boston: Houghton Mifflin, 1958. First edition, 8vo., cloth, near fine in very good dust jacket, price clipped, no award seal, some closed tears, very scarce. Aleph-Bet Books, Inc. 104 - 545 2013 $375

Spears, John R. *Illustrated Sketches of Death Valley and Other Borax Deserts of the Pacific Coast.* New York: Rand McNally and Co., 1892. First edition, 56 photo plates, 1 map, publisher's blue cloth, gilt lettering on spine and front cover, bookplate tipped on, slightest of rubbing to spine ends and corners, but very fine and bright, very rare. Argonaut Book Shop Recent Acquisitions June 2013 - 262 2013 $900

Specimens of the Yorkshire Dialect, in Various Dialogue, Tales and Songs. Otley: William Walker, circa, 1840. 8vo., 34 pages, folding woodcut frontispiece, titlepage vignette, fine in original lemon yellow decorative printed wrappers, scarce. Ken Spelman Books Ltd. 73 - 136 2013 £75

Spedon, Andrew Learmont *Rambles Among the Blue Noses; or, Reminiscences of a Tour through New Brunswick and Nova Scotia, During the Summer of 1862.* Montreal: John Lovell, 1863. Original green pressed cloth, gilt to front cover, small 8vo., very good. Schooner Books Ltd. 104 - 121 2013 $225

Speight, Harry *Kirkby Overblow and District.* London: Elliot Stock, 1903. Large paper copy, 4to., 169, (3) pages, frontispiece, map and illustrations, very good, recent half morocco, marbled boards, gilt lettered spine. Ken Spelman Books Ltd. 73 - 110 2013 £40

Speight, Harry *Nidderdale from Nun Munkton to Whernside.* Elliott Stock, 1906. First edition, 571 pages, folding map, folding table, illustrations, inner hinges worn, otherwise very good in original decorative gilt lettered cloth. Ken Spelman Books Ltd. 73 - 130 2013 £25

Spence, Catherine Helen *A Week in the Future.* Sydney: Hale & Iremonger, 1987. First edition, large octavo, drawings and vignettes, boards. L. W. Currey, Inc. Utopian Literature: Recent Acquisitions (April 2013) - 139860 2013 $100

Spence, Joseph 1699-1766 *An Essay on Mr. Pope's Odyssey.* London: printed for S. Wilmot, Bookseller in Oxford, 1737. Second edition, 12mo., engraved frontispiece, toned and little bit spotted, contemporary sheep, later olive morocco label, joints cracking but strong, boards marked, little rubbed at extremities, ink ownership inscription " J. Filmer 1774" at upper forecorner of f.f.e.p. printed booklabel of John Sparrow. Unsworths Antiquarian Booksellers 28 - 131 2013 £175

Spence, Joseph 1699-1766 *Polymetis; or an Enquiry concerning the Agreement Between the Works of the Roman Poets and the Remains of the Antient Artists.* London: printed for R. and J. Dodsley, 1755. Second edition, engraved frontispiece and 41 other engraved plates, some minor spotting, plates offset onto facing pages, folio, contemporary calf, neatly rebacked preserving original gilt spine, gilt now somewhat worn, new green morocco lettering piece to style, boards with elaborate stencilled frame dyed a lighter brown, marbled endpapers, some tidy repairs to corners, rubbed, bookplates of Strathallen and Southouse, good. Blackwell's Rare Books B174 - 145 2013 £650

Spence, William *The Radical Cause of the Present Distresses of the West-India Planters Pointed Out...* London: 1807. First edition, 8vo., lacks half title, removed. M & S Rare Books, Inc. 95 - 351 2013 $300

Spencer, Edmund *Sketches of Germany and the Germans...* Whittaker & Co., 1836. Second edition, 2 volumes, hand colored frontispieces (light foxing), large folding map, original green blind stamped cloth, spines faded, joints worn, neat library stamps on endpapers. J. & S. L. Bonham Antiquarian Booksellers Europe - 9615 2013 £300

Spencer, Edmund *Travel in Circassia, Krim Tartary &c.* London: 1837. First edition, 2 volumes, 2 folding maps, 2 color lithograph frontispiece and 2 further lithograph plates, 8vo., contemporary calf, spines gilt. Maggs Bros. Ltd. 1467 - 46 2013 £1500

Spender, Harold *At the Sign of the Guillotine.* London: Fisher Unwin, 1895. Half title, uncut, original red pictorial cloth, spine slightly fade, bookseller's stamp of Dalton, Scarborough, on leading f.e.p., very good. Jarndyce Antiquarian Booksellers CCV - 251 2013 £120

Spender, Stephen *The Still Centre.* London: Faber, 1939. First edition, crown 8vo., original pink cloth, backstrip gilt lettered, untrimmed, partly unopened, dust jacket chipped at backstrip panel head, very good. Blackwell's Rare Books 172 - 237 2013 £60

Spenser, Edmund   1552-1599   *The Faerie Queene Disposed into XII Bookes.*   London: printed by H(umphrey) L(ownes) for Mathew Lownes, 1609.   First folio and first complete edition, small folio in sixes, bound without final blank, as usual, woodcut printer's device, colophon and numerous head and tailpieces and initials, bound by Riviere & Son in antique style full sprinkled calf, covers bordered gilt, spine decoratively tooled in gilt in compartments, lettered gilt on brown morocco labels, marbled endpapers, all edges gilt, gilt turn-ins and gilt board edges, Lytton Strachey's copy with his bookplate, and that of Roger Senhouse, hinges slightly tender, minimal wear to spine, superb copy, fresh and clean, lovely copy.   Heritage Book Shop   50th Anniversary Catalogue - 83   2013 $10,000

Spenser, Edmund   1552-1599   *The Faerie Queene.*   London: printed by William Faden, 1758.   4 volumes, 8vo. some slight browning, contemporary sprinkled calf, gilt banded spines, morocco labels, one label chipped, hinges cracked, head and tail of spines little worn, overall good plus.   Jarndyce Antiquarian Booksellers   CCIV - 275   2013   £150

Spenser, Edmund   1552-1599   *The Loves of Bregog and Mulla.*   Dublin: Dolmen Press, 1956.   One of 250 copies, tall 8vo., original wrappers, fine, hand colored monotypes by Leslie MacWeeney.   Maggs Bros. Ltd.   1442 - 60   2013   £85

Spenser, Edmund   1552-1599   *The Loves of Bregog and Mulla.*   Dublin: Dolmen Press, 1956.   First edition, one of 250 copies, tall 8vo., original wrappers, fine, hand colored monotypes by Leslie MacWeeney.   Maggs Bros. Ltd.   1442 - 290   2013   £60

Spenser, Edmund   1552-1599   *Minor Poems, Containing The Shepheardes Calender, Complaints, Daphnaida, Colin Clovts Come Home again, Amoretti, Hymnes, Epithalamion, Prothalamion, Sonnets and Svndrie other Verses.*   Ashendene Press, 1925.   One of 200 copies printed in black, blue and red on Batchelor handmade paper, folio, original quarter dark brown cowhide, backstrip lettered in gilt with raised bands, joints rubbed, four inches of rear joint just cracking at head, natural vellum sides, untrimmed, god.   Blackwell's Rare Books   172 - 264   2013   £1700

Spenser, Edmund   1552-1599   *Poems of Spenser. Selected with Introduction by W. B. Yeats.*   Edinburgh: T. C. and E. C. Jack, 1906.   8vo., illustrations by Jessie M. King, frontispiece, vignette title, further color illustrations by King, 8vo., deep purple cloth, gilt design on cover and spine, top edge gilt, other edges trimmed, excellent copy.   Maggs Bros. Ltd.   1442 - 339   2013   £200

Spenser, Edmund   1552-1599   *The Poetical Works of...*   Boston: Little Brown, 1848.   First American edition, small 8vo., purple cloth stamped in blind, spines uniformly faded, stamped gilt, very nice, clean set.   Second Life Books Inc.   183 - 361   2013 $600

Spenser, Edmund   1552-1599   *Prothalamion & Epithalamion.*   Boston and New York: Houghton Mifflin, 1902.   First edition, with illustrations and decorations in old red on India paper, excellent copy, small folio, original yellow boards, little browned and dusty, uncut.   Howard S. Mott Inc.   262 - 121   2013 $85

Spenser, Edmund   1552-1599   *A View of the State of Ireland.*   1970.   New edition, 8vo., illustrations, cloth, dust jacket, very good.   C. P. Hyland   261 - 788   2013   £40

Spenser, Edmund   1552-1599   *The Works.*   London: Bell and Daldy, 1862.   First edition, five volumes, octavo, frontispiece in volume 1, titlepages printed in red and black, decorative woodcut head and tailpieces and initials, 20th century three quarter red morocco over red buckram boards, spines decoratively tooled and lettered gilt in compartments, top edge gilt, marbled endpapers, fine set.   Heritage Book Shop   Holiday Catalogue 2012 - 145   2013 $1000

Spicer, Jack   *After Lorca.*   San Francisco: White Rabbit Press, 1957.   First edition, one of 26 lettered copies signed by Spicer with drawing by poet, out of a total edition of 500, 8vo., original pictorial wrappers with cover drawing by Jess, covers somewhat foxed, spine portion rubbed, otherwise very good, rare.   James S. Jaffe Rare Books   Fall 2013 - 137   2013 $6500

Spiegel, F.   *Ha Pininah Ha Anakeet. (The Gigantic Pearl).*   Tel Aviv: Pressa, n.d., circa, 1947.   Printed in Palestine, 4to., pictorial wrappers, archival spine strengthening, very good+, woodblock illustrations by Elizabeth Hermann.   Aleph-Bet Books, Inc.   105 - 84   2013 $350

Spielmann, M. H.   *The Iconography of Andreas Vesalius.*   London: John Bale, Sons & Danielson Ltd., 1925.   4to., original blue cloth, titlepage plate printed from original woodblock, nice.   James Tait Goodrich   S74 - 233   2013 $495

Spielmann, M. H.   *Kate Greenaway.*   London: A. & C. Black, 1905.   Thick 8vo., original decorated cloth gilt, spine trifle faded, top edge gilt, 52 color plates, color endpapers, 3 monochrome plates, 90 text illustrations, slight creasing to corner of flyleaf, bookplate of G. F. Reiss.   R. F. G. Hollett & Son   Children's Books - 567   2013   £150

Spielmann, M. H.   *Kate Greenaway.*   London: A. & C. Black, 1905.   Limited to 500 numbered copies, signed by John Greenaway and with original pencil sketch done by Kate Greenaway, which is matted and bound in with John Greenaway's signature of authenticity, more than 50 color plates plus many black and whites, rarely found with white binding so clean, large thick 4to., white cloth, top edge gilt, near fine.   Aleph-Bet Books, Inc.   104 - 251   2013 $2000

Spielmann, M. H. *The Rainbow Book.* London: Chatto & Windus, 1909. First edition later issue without top edge gilt, 8vo., pink cloth blindstamped, gilt lettering, gilt on spine faded, normal shelfwear, very good, 7 full page black and whites, frontispiece, several in text black and whites. Aleph-Bet Books, Inc. 104 - 482 2013 $200

Spielmann, Percy Edwin *Catalogue of the Library of Miniature Books Collected by...* London: Edward Arnold, 1961. Limited to 500 numbered copies, 8vo., cloth backed patterned paper covered boards, dust jacket, chip out of dust jacket at top of spine, scarce, from the collection of Donn W. Sanford. Oak Knoll Books 303 - 10 2013 $300

Spiers, James *Travellers' Tales.* Seeley, Jackson & Halliday, 1875. First edition, original pictorial blue cloth gilt, spine and corners rather worn, 45 woodcut illustrations, inscription dated Xmas 1874. R. F. G. Hollett & Son Children's Books - 566 2013 £25

Spillane, Mickey *The Big Kill.* New York: Dutton, 1951. First edition, some light spotting on endpapers and small stain on back cover, otherwise fine in dust jacket with couple of closed tears and tiny wear at spine ends. Mordida Books 81 - 469 2013 $2000

Spillane, Mickey *Kiss Me, Deadly.* New York: Dutton, 1952. First edition, bookplate, fine in dust jacket with tiny wear at spine ends. Mordida Books 81 - 471 2013 $1250

Spillane, Mickey *My Gun is Quick.* New York: Dutton, 1950. First edition, some light spotting on endpapers and small stain on back cover, else fine in dust jacket with couple of closed tears and tiny wear at spine ends. Mordida Books 81 - 469 2013 $2000

Spinckes, Nathaniel *The Sick Man Visited...* London: C. Rivington, 1731. Fourth edition, engraved frontispiece, 8vo., worming to lower gutter on pages 13-35 not affecting text, small marginal tear to O1, full contemporary calf, gilt ruled borders, raised and gilt banded spine, hinges slightly cracked, corners bumped, some rubbing to boards. Jarndyce Antiquarian Booksellers CCIV - 276 2013 £75

Spinden, Herbert J. *A Study of Maya Art: Its Subject Matter and Historical Development.* Cambridge: 1913. Folio, xxiii, 285 pages, 29 plates, folding map, handsomely rebound in quarter leather and marbled boards (original wrappers not present), small chip from few prelim pages, else clean and very good. Dumont Maps & Books of the West 122 - 79 2013 $295

Spinoza, Benedict De *Tractatus Theologico-Politicus.* Amsterdam: printed by Christoffel Conrad for Jan Rieuwertsz, circa, 1672. or later. First edition, although not the virtually unobtainable first issue, small quarto, contemporary gilt decorated red paper boards, somewhat worn and soiled, spine chipped, joints and rear hinge cracked, front hinge reinforced, early ink inscriptions and notes on front endpapers, and titlepage, some leaves lightly browned or foxed, though generally very fresh and bright, overall very good, unsophisticated copy, scarce in such fragile and lovely contemporary binding, housed in custom quarter black morocco clamshell, gilt stamped on spine. Heritage Book Shop 50th Anniversary Catalogue - 95 2013 $12,500

Spinoza, Benedict De *Opera Posthuma.* Amsterdam: J. Rieuwertsz, 1677. First edition, quarto, lacking portrait, as usual, woodcut vignette on title, woodcut illustrations, diagrams and initials in text, contemporary mottled calf, expertly rebacked to style, covers decoratively bordered in blind, spine tooled and lettered gilt from the library of Herbert McLean Evans, with his bookplate, some marginal browning, lightly dampstained, mostly marginal, overall very good. Heritage Book Shop 50th Anniversary Catalogue - 94 2013 $11,000

Spinrad, Norman *Bug Jack Barron.* New York: Walker and Co., 1969. First edition, octavo, boards. L. W. Currey, Inc. Utopian Literature: Recent Acquisitions (April 2013) - 139612 2013 $150

Spolasco, Baron *Narrative of the Wreck of the Killarney Steamer.* Cork: 1838. First edition, 72 pages, portrait and plate, 20th century cloth, very good, very scarce. C. P. Hyland 261 - 794 2013 £150

Spon, Isaac *The History of the City and State of Geneva...* London: Bernard White, 1687. First edition, folio, 5 plates, contemporary brown full polished calf, joints cracked, corners rubbed, internally clean and crisp. J. & S. L. Bonham Antiquarian Booksellers Europe - 8716 2013 £650

Sport in Frogland. London: Sandle Bros. printed in Holland, n.d. circa, 1930. Oblong small 4to., pictorial wrappers, slight soil, very good+, illustrations. Aleph-Bet Books, Inc. 104 - 225 2013 $125

A Sporting Garland. London: Sands, n.d. circa, 1900. Oblong folio, cloth backed pictorial boards, covers lightly rubbed and tips worn, else fine, pictorial half titles, frontispieces, full page color illustrations by Cecil Aldin, printed on heavy coated paper. Aleph-Bet Books, Inc. 105 - 30 2013 $1750

Sprague, Henry H. *Women Under the Law of Massachusetts, Their Rights, Privileges and Disabilities.* Boston: Clarke & Carruth, 1884. First edition, 8vo., 70 pages, news clipping pinned to rear endpaper, near fine. Second Life Books Inc. 182 - 228 2013 $225

Springenschmid, Karl *Eine Wahre Geschichte Worte und bilder von Zwei Deutschen nus dem Auslande.* Stuttgart: Frankh'sche Verlagshandlung, 1936. First edition, 4to., cloth backed pictorial boards, occasional mark, else near fine, illustrations in color on evey page by Poldi Muhlmann, rare.   Aleph-Bet Books, Inc.   105 - 416   2013 $3500

Spyri, Johanna *Heidi.* New York: Golden Press, 1962. Pictorial box 9 1/2 x 16 x 4 inches, cover opens like a book, inside front cover is affixed a copy of the Little Golden Book Version of Heidi, illustrated in color by Corinne Malverne, opposite book in deep portion of box is an original Jolly Doll dressed as Heidi appears in the book, book and doll fine, doll still in original plastic covering, box scuffed but very good, rare.   Aleph-Bet Books, Inc.   104 - 239   2013 $575

Squirrell, Robert *The Maxims of Health; or, An Essay on Indigestion...* printed by J. Hawe, and sold by Highley... Callow... and by the author, 1817. Supposed 10th edition, minor foxing at either end and trifle browned in places, 12mo., contemporary dark blue straight grained morocco, wide gilt and blind tooled borders on sides, flat spine gilt in compartments, gilt and blind tooled doublures, pale blue silk paste downs and endleaves, gilt edges, very good.   Blackwell's Rare Books   Sciences - 114   2013   £350

St. Clair, Henry *The United States Criminal Calendar or Awful Warning to the Youth of America...* Charles Gaylor: 1835. First edition, 8vo., 356 pages, illustrations, original cloth backed printed and pictorial boards, printed paper label on spine, printed paper on covers damaged, especially on back cover, hinges cracked but sound, foxed, one leaf of text torn, without loss.   M & S Rare Books, Inc.   95 - 97   2013 $175

Staal, Marguerite Jeanne Baronne De *Memoirs of Madame de Staal de Launay.* London: Richard Bentley & Son, 1877. 8vo., 16 plates, cloth, extra illustrated edition, scattered foxing, mainly to prelims and edges of added plates, else fine, slipcase lightly worn at extremities, bookplate of Jay B. Lippincott.   Kaaterskill Books   16 - 80   2013 $300

Stael-Holstein, Anne Lousie Germaine Necker, Baronne De 1766-1817 *De L'Allemagne.* Stuttgart: Charles Hoffmann, 1830. New edition, 3 volumes, 12mo., leather backed paper boards, rubbed, lacking front flyleaf in volumes 1-2, good set, contemporary owner has written table of contents on rear flyleaf.   Second Life Books Inc.   183 - 103   2013 $125

Stael-Holstein, Anne Lousie Germaine Necker, Baronne De 1766-1817 *Corina o Italia.* Paris: Pillet Aine, 1839. Revised edition, 2 volumes in one, 12mo., 2 illustrations, black paper over boards, leather spine, cover little worn at edges and spine, rear upper corner cracked, still very tight.   Second Life Books Inc.   183 - 101   2013   £75

Stagg, Tom *New Orleans, the Revival.* Dublin: Bashall Eaves, 1973. First edition, near fine, owner's small booklabel, plastic dust jacket, mispaginated, but complete, 8vo., 307 pages.   Beasley Books   2013 - 2013 $60

Stahl, William Harris *Martianus Capella and the Seven Liberal Arts.* New York: Columbia University Press, 1971-1977. 2 volumes, olive cloth, gilt stamped spine titles, fine.   Jeff Weber Rare Books   169 - 424   2013 $75

Stamp, Tom *Greenland Voyager.* Whitby: Caedmon, 1983. First edition, original cloth, gilt, dust jacket, illustrations.   R. F. G. Hollett & Son   Polar Exploration - 69   2013   £30

Stanger, Frank M. *Sawmills in the Redwoods. Logging on the San Francisco Peninsula 1849-1967.* San Mateo: San Mateo County Historical Association, 1967. First edition, frontispiece, illustrations from photos, text maps, folding map in rear, green cloth, fine.   Argonaut Book Shop   Recent Acquisitions June 2013 - 265   2013 $75

Stanger, Frank M. *Who Discovered the Golden Gate?* San Mateo: San Mateo County Historical Association, 1969. First edition, one of 1500 copies, scarce, 4to., drawings, maps, map endpapers, dark blue cloth, fine.   Argonaut Book Shop   Recent Acquisitions June 2013 - 267   2013 $90

Stanley, Thomas *The History of Philosophy.* London: printed for Thomas Bassett at the George in Fleet Street, Dorman Newman at Kings Arms and Thomas Cockerill, at the Three Leggs in the Poultry, 1687. Second edition, engraved frontispiece, 26 further engraved portraits, plus few in text charts, diagrams and figures, folio, cloth, titlepage printed in red and black, very good copy, few scattered marginal notations and sketches in ink and pencil, thin stain at vvv2-xxx3, tear at F2 and small chip at G4, all within lower margins.   Kaaterskill Books   16 - 81   2013 $2000

Stanley, William *Rejected Addresses; or the Triumph of the Ale-King: a Farce.* London: John Cawthorn, 1813. First edition, half title, disbound, scarce.   Jarndyce Antiquarian Booksellers   CCIII - 158   2013   £150

Stansberry, Domenic *The Spoiler.* New York: Atlantic Monthly, 1987. First edition, signed by author, very fine in dust jacket.   Mordida Books   81 - 28   2013 $80

Stanton, Carey *An Island Memoir.* Los Angeles: Zamorano Club, 1984. First edition, one of 350 copies, 38 pages, frontispiece, 29 illustrations from photos, map endpapers, brown/gray cloth, gilt lettered spine, very fine.   Argonaut Book Shop   Recent Acquisitions June 2013 - 268   2013 $60

Stanton, Elizabeth Cady *History of Woman Sufferage.* New York: Fowler & Wells, 1881. First edition, volume I only, 1848-1861, 8vo., 878 pages, steel engravings, maroon cloth, cover quite scuffed, somewhat worn at spine and corners, little foxing, otherwise very good, with presentation by editor Matilda Joslyn Gage.　Second Life Books Inc.　182 - 230　2013　$350

Stanton, Elizabeth Cady *History of Woman Sufferage.* New York: Susan B. Anthony, 1887. First edition, Volume III only, 1876-1885, 8vo., steel engravings, maroon cloth, cover quite scuffed and spotted, slightly worn at spine and corners, little foxing, front hinge tender and blank leaf partly detached, otherwise very good.　Second Life Books Inc.　182 - 231　2013　$300

Stark, Richard *The Blackbird.* New York: Macmillan, 1969. First edition, fine in fine dust jacket, fresh jacket, lovely as new copy, especially uncommon.　Between the Covers Rare Books, Inc.　Mystery & Detective Fiction - 316556　2013　$250

Stark, Richard *The Score.* London: Allison & Busby, 1985. First hardcover edition, fine in dust jacket.　Mordida Books　81 - 474　2013　$65

Stark, Richard *The Sour Lemon Score.* London: Allison & Busby, 1986. First English edition, fine in fine dust jacket, lovely, unread copy.　Between the Covers Rare Books, Inc.　Mystery & Detective Fiction - 316555　2013　$200

Starrett, Vincent *Murder in Peking.* New York: Lantern Press, 1946. First edition, endpapers and top edge foxed, else fine in near fine dust jacket with little light edgewear.　Between the Covers Rare Books, Inc.　Mystery & Detective Fiction - 33274　2013　$192

Starrett, Vincent *Oriental Encounters.* Chicago: Normandie House, 1938. First edition, one of 249 numbered copies, fine in acetate dust jacket.　Mordida Books　81 - 476　2013　$150

Starrett, Vincent *Persons from Porlock.* Chicago: Bookfellows, 1923. First separate edition, signed by author, back page darkened, otherwise fine in string tied printed wrappers.　Mordida Books　81 - 475　2013　$85

Starrett, Vincent *The Private Life of Sherlock Holmes.* New York: Macmillan, 1933. First edition, inscription, otherwise near fine in very good, price clipped dust jacket with dampstaining on back panel and at base of spine, spine darkened, wear along edges and corners.　Mordida Books　81 - 156　2013　$150

A Statistical Inquiry into the Condition of the People of Colour of the City and Districts of Philadelphia. Philadelphia: 1849. First edition, 8vo., 44 pages, original printed wrappers.　M & S Rare Books, Inc.　95 - 349　2013　$1250

Statius, Publius Papinius *Sylvarum Libri V. Thebaidos Libro XII. Achilleidos Libri II.* (bound with) *Orthographia ex Flexus Dictrionum Graecarum Omnium apud Statius cum Accentib. et Generib. ex varaiis utriusque linguae authoribus.* Paris: Apud Simonem Colinaeum, 1530. 8vo., some light staining, old and slightly discolored repairs to blank areas of first and last leaf, few small marginal tears, frequent later annotations in pencil and ink, late 19th century olive calf, largely faded to brown, boards with blind frame with gilt cornerpieces, spine to compartments with central gilt stamps, second compartment gilt lettered direct, all edges gilt, rubbed, small chip from head of spine, short crack to front joint, ownership inscription of Raymond Breckpol (contemporary with binding?) to head of titlepage, date of publication and an old cypher stamp both in violet ink to f.f.e.p., same repeated on rear pastedown (though cypher here handwritten), along with inscription of Chad Carbacusend(?) 1913 and small colored pictorial label.　Unsworths Antiquarian Booksellers　28 - 47　2013　£650

Statius, Publius Papinius *Sylvarum Libri V. Thebaidos Lib. XII Achilleidos Lib II.* Lyon: apud Haered Seb. Gryphii, 1559. 16mo., printer's device on title hand colored, somewhat crudely, one leaf (p1) with small paper flaw affecting two words, bit of light dampmarking and soiling, old ownership inscription (M. Flinck(?) and shelf number on title, contemporary vellum dyed brown, boards with central oval decorative gilt stamp bordered gilt and blind with gilt cornerpieces, these repeated above and below central oval, spine with five raised bands, small gilt floral stamp in each compartment, gilt darkened and rubbed in places, particularly lower board, edges gilt and gauffered, bit rubbed at extremities, front flyleaf loosening, armorial bookplate, good. Blackwell's Rare Books　B174 - 147　2013　£750

Statius, Publius Papinius *The Thebaid.* London: T. Becket, 1773. Second edition of this William Lillington Lewis translation, 2 volumes, 8vo., internally very clean and tidy, some minor flaws to margins but none interfering with text, later half red morocco with red faux morocco boards, five raised bands to spine, gilt with Athenaeum emblem and date, pages and corners scraped, white library codes to upper boards, top edges dusty, upper hinge cracked in volume I with f.f.e.p. beginning to come away, armorial bookplate of John Proctor Anderdon, "Athenaeum Library. Cancelled" ink stamps.　Unsworths Antiquarian Booksellers　28 - 49　2013　£80

Statius, Publius Papinius *Opera, ex recensione et cum notis I Frederici Gronovii.* Venice: Apud Nicolaum Pezzana, 1712. Scarce edition, 12mo., little light spotting, large but faint dampstain to final leaves, titlepage laid down, contemporary vellum boards, brass clasps mounted on vellum tabs, edges sprinkled red and blue, lightly soiled, old ownership inscription, partly rubbed out.   Unsworths Antiquarian Booksellers   28 - 48   2013   £80

Stauffacher, Jack Werner *The Continuity of Horace.* San Francisco: Greenwood Press, 1992. 305 x 190mm., 32 pages, 38 figures, 2 additional text illustrations, printed wrappers, fine.   Jeff Weber Rare Books   171 - 169   2013 $150

Stawell, George D. *A Quantock Family: the Stawells of Somerton & Devonshire and the County Cork.* 1910. First edition, 53 plates, text illustrations, 14 folding pedigrees, very good, very scarce, signed presentation copy to Mary Longfield.   C. P. Hyland   261 - 412   2013   £400

Stead, W. T. *Books for the Bairns.* Review of Reviews, Mowbray House, n.d. circa, 1895-1903. Small thick 8vo., original binder's cloth gilt, 11 titles bound together, illustrations.   R. F. G. Hollett & Son   Children's Books - 571   2013   £65

Stead, W. T. *The First Birdie Book.* Review of Reviews Office, n.d. circa, 1900. Small 8vo., original pictorial wrappers, 48 wood engravings.   R. F. G. Hollett & Son   Children's Books - 570   2013   £30

Stead, W. T. *Real Ghost Stories: a Record of Authentic Apparitions.* London: Publishing Office of the Review of Reviews, n.d., 1891-1892. First editions, Large octavo, 2 volumes, illustrations, the two parts bound together in original publisher's blue green cloth printed in black.   L. W. Currey, Inc.   Wandering Ghosts & Itinerant Souls (10/12) - 101359   2013 $350

Stearns, Harold E. *The Street I Know.* New York: Lee Furman, 1935. First edition, near fine in modestly worn, very good, advance review copy with slip tipped in.   Between the Covers Rare Books, Inc.   New York City - 279235   2013 $275

Stearns, Samuel *The American Herbal or Materia Medica.* Walpole: David Carlise for Thomas & Thomas and the author, 1801. 12mo., 360 pages, full modern calf, gilt spine rules, red gilt stamp spine label, 19th century style, some browning as might be expected, small stamp on title verso, early ownership signatures of A. E. Bigelow MD (1893), J. Henry Jackson (1870) and Fred K. Jackson (1903), very good, rare.   Jeff Weber Rare Books   169 - 426   2013 $3500

Stearns, Samuel *The Mystery of Animal Magnetism Revealed to the World.* London: sold by Mr. Parsons No. 21 Pater Noster Row, 1791. 8vo., 2 leaves of 'Proposals for printing by subscription, the American oracle' and final ad leaf, 8vo., marginal tear to B4 margins, slightly dusted, uncut and partially unopened, disbound.   Jarndyce Antiquarian Booksellers   CCIV - 277   2013   £580

Stebbing, Henry *A Short and True Account of a Confernece Held at a Quakers Meeting House in Suffolk with Joseph Middleton of Hempton-Abbey in Norfolk, Spaker...* London: John Pemberton, William and John Innys, 1714. 1715. 1716. 1725., 4 works bound in 1, 8vo., lightly toned with some spotting tail edges of f.f.e.p. and titlepage fragile and frayed, not affecting any text, some dampstaining to lower margins, associated occasional mould-spotting, contemporary vellum, soiled and darkened, loss of approximately 10mm across headcap including loss of headband, corners worn, endpapers somewhat crumpled with odd notes and small areas of loss, MS. note to front pastedown stating that the Stebbing volumes came from the library of Anthony Collins and that handwritten index opposite was added by him.   Unsworths Antiquarian Booksellers   28 - 132   2013   £250

Steel, Kurt *Madman's Buff.* Boston: Little Brown, 1941. First edition, fine in dust jacket.   Mordida Books   81 - 478   2013 $165

Steele, Richard *The Conscious Lovers.* London: printed for J. Tonson, 1723. 8vo., some old waterstaining to inner margins at top of pages, later 18th century note on final page, disbound.   Jarndyce Antiquarian Booksellers   CCIV - 278   2013   £60

Stegmaier, Mark J. *James F. Milligan: His Journal of Fremont's Fifth Expedition 1853-1854. His Adventurous Life on Land and Sea.* Glendale: Arthur H. Clark Co., 1988. First edition, collector's edition, one of 64 special copies bound in 'lexohyde', numbered and signed by Steigmaier, 30 pages, illustrations, maps, portraits, publisher's brown leather, very fine.   Argonaut Book Shop   Summer 2013 - 119   2013 $150

Stegner, Wallace *Clarence Edward Dutton: an Appraisal.* Salt Lake City: University of Utah Press, 1935. First edition, 23 pages, octavo, gray printed wrappers, near fine faint age toning near spine, otherwise bright and clean.   Ken Sanders Rare Books   45 - 50   2013 $10,000

Stegner, Wallace *Conversations with Wallace Stegner on Western History and Literature.* Salt Lake City: University of Utah Press, 1983. First edition, 207 pages, fine in very near fine dust jacket, signed by Stegner and Etulain, very nice.   Jeff Hirsch Books   Fall 2013 - 129189   2013 $300

Stegner, Wallace *Crossing to Safety.* New York: Random House, 1987. First edition, inscribed by author, fine in dust jacket. Ed Smith Books 78 - 62 2013 $175

Stegner, Wallace *Fire and Ice.* New York: Duell Sloan and Pearce, 1941. First edition, 214 pages, blue cloth, octavo, near fine in like dust jacket, minor age toning to jacket rear, and spine subtly faded, few small nicks at corners, internally clean and nice, signed by author. Ken Sanders Rare Books 45 - 51 2013 $3000

Stegner, Wallace *Mormon Country.* New York: Duell, Sloan & Pierce, 1942. First edition, near fine, bright copy in very good plus to near fine dust jacket, inscribed by Edward Hyde Cox (1914-1998). Ed Smith Books 78 - 61 2013 $850

Stegner, Wallace *The Potter's House.* Muscatine: Prairie Press, 1938. First edition, 1/490 copies, 75 pages, octavo, gray cloth gilt stamped title on backstrip, very good, minor age toning to spine and extremities of boards, very faint foxing to endsheets and pastedowns, uncommon. Ken Sanders Rare Books 45 - 53 2013 $2000

Stegner, Wallace *Shooting Star.* New York: Viking Press, 1961. Advance edition/first edition, 433 pages, octavo, red boards with title gilt stamped on backstrip and "Advance Edition" gilt stamped at foot of front board, near fine in fine dust jacket. Ken Sanders Rare Books 45 - 54 2013 $500

Stegner, Wallace *Wolf Willow: A History, A Story and a Memory of the Last Plains Frontier.* New York: Viking Press, 1962. First edition, octavo, 306 pages, brown cloth, near fine, signed by author. Ken Sanders Rare Books 45 - 55 2013 $500

Stegner, Wallace *The Women on the Wall.* Boston: Houghton Mifflin Co., 1950. First edition, signed by author, 277 pages, octavo, light blue cloth, very good, in like dust jacket, light nicking to corners, price clipped with faint creasing to head of front panel, light rubbing to corners of boards. Ken Sanders Rare Books 45 - 56 2013 $750

Steichen, Edward *The Family of Man.* New York: Museum of Modern Art/Maco, 1955. First edition, special deluxe edition with pictorial endpapers and the special portfolio by Stoller, signed by Steichen, near fine, original black cloth backed light blue paper boards with spotting to top edge, spine lettering is silver, designs on front cover bronze, silver and black, custom cloth backed clamshell box, spine and cover of clamshell have reproductions of spine and cover of book itself, scarce, signed work. By the Book, L. C. 38 - 13 2013 $2250

Steig, William *Sylvester and the Magic Pebble.* New York: Simon and Schuster/Windmill, 1969. Stated first edition, large 4to., green cloth, edges faded, else fine in dust jacket (not price clipped, no award medal, light stain on upper corner), illustrations by William Stieg in color on every page, quite hard to find in first edition. Aleph-Bet Books, Inc. 104 - 546 2013 $1500

Stein, Gertrude 1874-1946 *Portrait of Mabel Dodge at the Villa Curonia.* Florence: privately printed, 1912. First edition, one of 300 copies, 8vo., original floral Florentine wallpaper wrappers with printed label on front cover, fine, rare, presentation copy inscribed by author for Natalie Clifford Barney. James S. Jaffe Rare Books Fall 2013 - 138 2013 $25,000

Stein, Gertrude 1874-1946 *What are Masterpieces?* Los Angeles: Conference Press, 1940. First edition, fine in lightly used dust jacket with internal mend on rear panel. Beasley Books 2013 - 2013 $100

Steinbeck, John Ernst 1902-1968 *Flight. A Story by John Steinbeck.* Covelo: Carolyn and James Robertson/ Yolla Bolly Press, 1984. Limited to 250 signed and numbered copies, this number 91, signed by Wallace Stegner (provided afterword) and by (artist) Karin Wilkstrom, 4to., 52 pages, card from publisher laid-in, typeface is Goudy Modern, fine in pattered cloth with paper covered slipcase, slipcase fine, illustrations printed direct from artist's blocks over lithographed color lithographs tipped-in. By the Book, L. C. 36 - 56 2013 $290

Steinbeck, John Ernst 1902-1968 *In Dubious Battle.* New York: Covici Friede, 1936. First edition, tiny bookstore stamp lower rear pastedown, fine in fine dust jacket, custom clamshell box, from the Bruce Kahn collection, beautiful copy. Ken Lopez Bookseller 159 - 181 2013 $8500

Steinbeck, John Ernst 1902-1968 *Once There Was a War.* London: Heinemann, 1959. First UK edition, proof copy, green printed wrappers, solid, very good in very good to near fine dust jacket. Ed Smith Books 78 - 63 2013 $150

Steinbeck, John Ernst 1902-1968 *The Red Pony.* New York: Viking, 1945. First illustrated edition, possibly a variant thereof, fine in beige cloth, in very good, slightly soiled slipcase, illustrations in color by Wesley Dennis, this issue printed by Rogers Kellogg Stilson. Between the Covers Rare Books, Inc. Horses, Horsemanship, Horse Racing, Etc. - 67852 2013 $275

Steinbeck, John Ernst   1902-1968   *The Red Pony.*   New York: Viking, 1945.   First illustrated edition, fine in worn, good plus slipcase, variant issue, fine beige glazed cloth with "Printed by Zeese-Wilkinson Co.", but with tan paper board slipcase, not blue-gray slipcase usually seen.   Between the Covers Rare Books, Inc.   Horses, Horsemanship, Horse Racing, Etc. - 57149   2013 $125

Steinbeck, John Ernst   1902-1968   *The Winter of Our Discontent.*   New York: Viking Press, 1961.   First edition, very good with owner signature and address to front free endpaper in an about very good price clipped dust jacket that has chipping to top of spine and to top edge and corners and some other very slight wear, still presentable copy.   Jeff Hirsch Books   Fall 2013 - 129433   2013 $50

Steiner, Charlotte   *Annie's ABC Kitten.*   New York: Alfred Knopf, 1965.   4to., cloth, fine in dust jacket, illustrations on every page by Steiner, with wonderful color lithographs, scarce.   Aleph-Bet Books, Inc.   105 - 553   2013 $375

Steiner, Stan   *The Last Horse.*   New York: Macmillan, 1961.   First edition, 71 pages, illustrations by Beatien Yazz, fine in fine, price clipped dust jacket with very light wear.   Between the Covers Rare Books, Inc.   Horses, Horsemanship, Horse Racing, Etc. - 49354   2013 $65

Stellwagen, Charlotte Fisher   *Mrs. Andrew Johnson Jones' Handmaid.*   Washington: W. F. Roberts Co., 1912.   First edition, illustrations by Clifford Berryman, bookplate on front pastedown, corners slightly bumped, very near fine, nicely inscribed by author.   Between the Covers Rare Books, Inc.   165 - 265   2013 $200

Stenhouse, T. B. H., Mrs.   *"Tell It All" The Story of a Life's Experience in Mormonism.*   Hartford: Worthington, 1875.   8vo., 28 full page illustrations, and steel plate portrait, green cloth, decorative stamping in gilt, frontispiece detached, ex--library with stamps and bookplate, cover scuffed at edges, otherwise very good.   Second Life Books Inc.   182 - 235   2013 $125

Step, Edward   *Wayside and Woodland Blossoms.*   London & Frederick Warne: 1895.   First edition, red cloth, good+, 12mo., 156 color plates, previous owner's inscription dated 1895.   Barnaby Rudge Booksellers   Natural History 2013 - 020460   2013 $75

Stephens, Ian   *The Engraver's Cut.*   printed at the Rampant Lions Press for Primrose Academy, Stratton Audley, 2001.   8/135 copies signed by artist and printed on Zerkall mouldmade paper, 30 wood engravings on rectos of 25 leaves and with a further 3 engravings printed in blue, all by Stephens, royal 8vo., original light blue cloth backed light blue boards, backstrip gilt lettered, overall repeat pattern of an engraving of a bee, board slipcase, fine.   Blackwell's Rare Books   B174 - 391   2013   £135

Stephensky, V.   *Sakhalin Calendar.*   Sakhalin: printed in the typography on the Sakhalin Island, 1899.   First edition, 4 lithographed plates, 8vo., period style red half morocco with raised bands, gilt tooled spine, six leaves, margins neatly strengthened, overall very good.   Maggs Bros. Ltd.   1467 - 44   2013   £2000

Steptoe, John   *Stevie.*   New York: Harper & Row, 1969.   First edition, fine in fine dust jacket.   Between the Covers Rare Books, Inc.   165 - 113   2013 $100

Stereographic Library Animals.   Keystone View Co., 1920.   First edition, 8vo., volumes 1 and 2 in original case that looks like 2 books, 100 stereo views like new, black cloth, very good.   Barnaby Rudge Booksellers   Natural History 2013 - 021688   2013 $175

Sterling, George   *The Caged Eagle and Other Poems.*   San Francisco: A. M. Robertson, 1916.   First edition, first issue with the two errors called for by Johnson on pages 34 and 162, olive green cloth, gilt lettered spine and front cover, inner front hinge with short crack, spine gilt slightly dulled, else fine, presentation inscription signed by author, for George Sterling, with corrections in Sterling's hand for the issue point errors (pages 34, 162) as well as corrections in his hand on page 161 for errors not noted by bibliographers.   Argonaut Book Shop   Recent Acquisitions June 2013 - 271   2013 $350

Sterling, George   *The House of Orchids.*   San Francisco: A. M. Robertson, 1911.   First edition, first issue with two errors called for by Johnson on pages 31 and 48, one of the errors corrected in hand of Sterling, presentation inscription signed by author for Cushing (Ben Cushing Duniway), 140 pages, purple pictorial cloth with gilt decoration on front cover, free endpaper darkened from publisher's glue (as usual), spine slightly faded, fine.   Argonaut Book Shop   Recent Acquisitions June 2013 - 272   2013 $450

Sterling, George   *Sails and Mirage and Other Poems.*   San Francisco: A. M. Robertson, 1921. First edition, 119 pages, green cloth, gilt lettered spine and front cover, spine gilt slightly dulled, else fine, presentation copy inscribed by author for Cushing (Ben Cushing Duniway).   Argonaut Book Shop   Recent Acquisitions June 2013 - 263   2013 $225

Sterling, George   *The Testimony of Suns and Other Poems.*   San Francisco: A. M. Robertson, 1907.   Third edition, 142 pages, blue cloth, decorated and lettered in silver, spine lightly faded with some spotting, else fine, presentation inscription from author for Cushing (Ben Cushing Duniway).   Argonaut Book Shop   Recent Acquisitions June 2013 - 274   2013 $200

Sterling, George *A Wine of Wizardry and Other Poems.* San Francisco: A. M. Robertson, 1909. First edition, variant (without the front cover ornament), 137 pages, burgundy cloth, gilt lettered spine and front cover, free endpapers darkened from publisher's glue (as usual), spine slightly dulled, else fine, presentation inscription from author for Cushing (Ben Cushing Duniway). Argonaut Book Shop Recent Acquisitions June 2013 - 275   2013 $350

Stern, Philip Van Doren *The Midnight Reader: Great Stories of Haunting and Horror.* New York: Henry Holt and Co., 1942. First edition, octavo, original black cloth, front and spine panels stamped in white. L. W. Currey, Inc. Fall Sampler Sept. 2013 - 146496   2013 $125

Sterne, Laurence   1713-1768 *The Life and Opinions of Tristram Shandy, Gentleman.* Vienna: printed for R. Sammer, Bookseller, 1798. 9 volumes bound in 4, 4 engraved frontispieces, marbled paper pasted on to page 119-20 of volume II, 12mo., some occasional foxing but very good set in early 19th century boards, paper spine labels reading 'Sterne Select Works', some slight rubbing and darkening to spines, minor cracks to leading hinges. Jarndyce Antiquarian Booksellers   CCIV - 280   2013   £160

Sterne, Laurence   1713-1768 *Voyage Sentimental en France.* Dijon: De l'Imprimerie de L. N. Frantin, 1797. First Dijon edition, 2 volumes in 1, very good, wide margined copy, 19th century marbled paper wrappers, hand written spine label. Ken Spelman Books Ltd.   75 - 48   2013   £120

Sterne, Laurence   1713-1768 *A Sentimental Journey through France and Italy.* Dublin: printed for G. Faulkner, 1768. 2 volumes in 1, 12mo., half titles, very good, full contemporary calf, slight chip to head of spine and upper joint cracked but firm, old waterstain to corner of front endpaper and prelim blank, very slight tear to lower corner of 1, B1, not affecting text, in quarter bound solander box in red morocco with dark red cloth, gilt lettering, bookplate of Donald S. Tuttle. Ken Spelman Books Ltd.   75 - 27   2013   £250

Sterne, Laurence   1713-1768 *A Sentimental Journey through France and Italy.* London: for T. Becket and P. A. De Hondt, 1768. First edition, text variant 2 in volume 1 and text variant 1 in volume 2, as usual, 2 volumes, 8vo., engraved coat of arms, with half titles and list of subscribers' names, but, as usual, without rare inserted ad leaf, full sprinkled calf, fully gilt by Riviere, spines bit dry, hinges worn, small chip at crown of volume 2, Hobart F. Cole bookplate. Joseph J. Felcone Inc.   English and American Literature to 1800 - 21   2013 $900

Sterne, Laurence   1713-1768 *A Sentimental Journey through France and Italy.* London: for T. Becket and P. A. De Hondt, 1768. Second edition, 2 volumes, very good, contemporary calf, expertly rebacked, raised and gilt banded spines with red morocco labels, some darkening to edges of boards, corners neatly repaired, 12mo. Ken Spelman Books Ltd.   75 - 26   2013   £395

Sterne, Laurence   1713-1768 *A Sentimental Journey through France and Italy.* Dublin: printed for G. Faulkner, 1769. Third edition, full contemporary calf with distinctive patterning to boards, joints cracked but firm, lacking label, corners worn and some browning and light foxing to paper, armorial bookplate, shelfmark 172/H on front endpaper, which is rather loose. Ken Spelman Books Ltd.   75 - 29   2013   £120

Sterne, Laurence   1713-1768 *A Sentimental Journey through France and Italy. (with) Yorick's Sentimental Journey...* London: T. Becket and P. A. De Hondt, 1770. New edition and second edition respectively, 12mo., 4 volumes, very good full contemporary calf, double gilt fillet borders, raised and gilt banded spines with simple volume numbers tooled directly onto spines, some slight chipping to head and tail of spines, strictly unsophisticated state, bookplate "C. T. C. Luxmoore", signature "Cha. Luxmore" in all volumes, pencilled note 'obit 1863' in volumes 3-4 'St John's Col. Camb'. Ken Spelman Books Ltd.   75 - 32   2013   £395

Sterne, Laurence   1713-1768 *Voyage Sentimental.* Amsterdam: chez Changuion; Paris: chez Le Jay, 1774. Nouvelle edition, 2 volumes, very good in original blue paper boards, contemporary hand written paper spine labels (volume number label missing from volume 1), some rubbing to head and tail of spines and to joints, volume 1 closed tear H4 slightly affecting text, minor loss of M1, not affecting text, slightly greater loss at top of n3 again not affecting text. Ken Spelman Books Ltd.   75 - 36   2013   £295

Sterne, Laurence   1713-1768 *A Sentimental Journey through France and Italy.* P. Miller and J. White, 1774. Probably printed edition, 328 pages, five volumes in one, each with separate titlepage but continuous pagination, 328 pages, very good, 8vo., 19th century half calf, gilt panelled spine, signature of Agnes Wagstaffe 1777 on first titlepage. Ken Spelman Books Ltd.   75 - 35   2013   £120

Sterne, Laurence   1713-1768 *A Sentimental Journey through France and Italy.* London: printed for W. Strahan, 1780. 12mo., some offset browning from pastedowns to endpapers and prelim and final blanks, full contemporary calf, gilt panelled spine, red morocco label, little rubbed, hinges cracked but firm, 19th century bookplate of Walter de Laci Devereux. Jarndyce Antiquarian Booksellers   CCIV - 281   2013   £85

Sterne, Laurence   1713-1768   *A Sentimental Journey through France and Italy.*   for T. Osborne, in St. Paul's Church-Yard and J. Mozley, in Gainsborough,   1784.   12mo., 4 volumes complete in one, frontispiece, very good in full contemporary calf, raised and gilt banded spine with original ted gilt morocco label, head and tail of spine slightly chipped, early booklabel of "J. L. Haddon" and signature of same on titlepage.   Ken Spelman Books Ltd.   75 - 40   2013   £200

Sterne, Laurence   1713-1768   *Voyage Sentimental en France.*   Paris: Duchene, 1788.   2 volumes, 12mo., very good, original marbled paper boards with contemporary manuscript labels on pink paper, joints cracked but very firm, some loss to marbled paper at foot of spines, learned annotation in ink dealing with Bevoriskius in lower margins of volume 2 pages 10-11.   Ken Spelman Books Ltd.   75 - 43   2013   £280

Sterne, Laurence   1713-1768   *A Sentimental Journey through France and Italy.*   Aix: printed by Antony Henricy, 1796.   New edition, 2 volumes, 12mo., some light browning and foxing, full contemporary mottled calf, gilt spines, black morocco labels, spines rubbed, corners slightly worn.   Jarndyce Antiquarian Booksellers   CCIV - 282   2013   £200

Sterne, Laurence   1713-1768   *A Sentimental Journey through France and Italy.*   Vienna: printed for R. Sammer, Bookseller, 1798.   Second edition, engraved plates, 12mo., small marginal tear to I2 volume 1, some occasional foxing and light browning, 4 volumes in 2, contemporary dark green roan backed marbled boards, ornate gilt decorated spines, gilt initials DM at foot of spines, attractive.   Jarndyce Antiquarian Booksellers   CCIV - 283   2013   £200

Sterne, Laurence   1713-1768   *A Sentimental Journey through France and Italy.*   London: Navarre Society, circa, 1926.   One of 2000 copies, 181 x 114mm., frontispiece, very fine burgundy morocco, handsomely gilt and onlaid by Harcourt Bindery of Boston (stamp signed), boards with triple fillet border, reach cover with elaborate heraldic frame of gilt and onlaid green morocco around an empty oval, raised bands, very pretty gilt spine compartments, featuring looping tendril frame enclosing a charming flower centerpiece, densely gilt turn-ins, marbled endpapers, top edge gilt, very fine, bindings especially bright, text with virtually no signs of use.   Phillip J. Pirages   63 - 450   2013 $375

Sterne, Laurence   1713-1768   *The Works.*   London: printed for W. Strahan, J. Rivington and Sons, J. Dodsley, 1780.   10 volumes, octavo, frontispiece, other engraved plates, contemporary full tree calf, spines stamped gilt, each volume with red and green morocco spine labels, green labels with small red morocco oval inlay with volume number stamped in gilt, board edges stamped gilt, bit of scattered light foxing, generally very clean, about fine.   Heritage Book Shop Holiday Catalogue 2012 - 146   2013 $3000

Sterne, Laurence   1713-1768   *The Works of Laurence Sterne.*   London: W. Strahan, 1783.   10 volumes, very good, early 20th century crushed red morocco with spines gilt in six compartments containing gilt floral and leaf motifs, gilt labels, top edge gilt, some slight darkening to spines, handsome set, large 12mo.   Ken Spelman Books Ltd.   75 - 39   2013   £350

Sterne, Laurence   1713-1768   *Yoricks Empfindsame Reise durch Frankreich und Italien, aus dem Englischen Ubersetzt. Erster (Zweyter) Band. Dritte Auflage.*   Hamburg und Bremen: Johann Henrich Cramer, 1770.   4 volumes bound in one, contemporary marbled paper boards with later printed paper spine label, some small paper flaws to rather cheap quality paper it was printed on, 12mo.   Ken Spelman Books Ltd.   75 - 31   2013   £295

Steuart, James   *An Inquiry into the Principles of Political Economy.*   London: printed of A. Millar and T. Cadell,   1767.   First edition, 2 volumes, quarto, bound without prelim blank in volume I, as is often the case, 2 folding tables, contemporary mottled calf, expertly and almost invisibly rebacked to style, original contrasting morocco labels laid down, spines decoratively gilt tooled in compartments, contemporary booklabel written in manuscript of Lieut. Colonel Fane in each volume and a modern bookplate, slight marginal offsetting to first few leaves of each volume and occasional light foxing, overall very good in attractive contemporary binding.   Heritage Book Shop   50th Anniversary Catalogue - 96   2013 $11,000

Stevens, Doris   *Jailed for Freedom.*   New York: Liveright, 1920.   First edition, 8vo., 388 pages, illustrations, purple cloth, cover little scuffed and stained at edges, front hinge repaired, some light waterstain at top of prelim matter, otherwise very good in worn dust jacket, from the library of reformer Florence Kelley (1859-1932) with her ownership signature.   Second Life Books Inc.   182 - 236   2013 $250

Stevens, Frank Walker   *The Beginnings of the New York Central Railroad: a History.*   New York: G. P. Putnam's Sons, 1926.   First edition, foldout map laid in, blue cloth, gilt letters on front board and spine, top edge gilt, owner's inscription on prelim page, page fine edges lightly foxed, small stain on rear board, thus very good, lacking dust jacket.   Between the Covers Rare Books, Inc.   New York City - 316725   2013 $75

Stevens, John   *The History of Portugal...*   London: W. Rogers, 1698.   First edition, 8vo., table, contemporary brown speckled calf, covers scuffed, good copy, library label of Baron Rolle.   J. & S. L. Bonham Antiquarian Booksellers   Europe - 8419   2013   £500

Stevens, Thomas   *Scouting for Stanley in East Africa.*   New York: 1890.   First edition, frontispiece, 15 further plates, 8vo., fine, original pictorial cloth, gilt.   Maggs Bros. Ltd.   1467 - 24   2013   £2250

Stevens, Wallace 1879-1955 *Esthetique du Mal.* Cummington: Cummington Press, 1945. First edition, 8vo., original quarter black morocco and rose Natsume paper covered boards, glassine dust jacket, one of only a few copies bound thus, out of an edition of 300 copies printed on Pace paper, very fine, preserved in cloth folding box, pen and ink drawings by Wightman Williams.   James S. Jaffe Rare Books   Fall 2013 - 139   2013 $7500

Stevens, Wallace 1879-1955 *Harmonium.* New York: Alfred A. Knopf, 1923. First edition, 3rd printing, 8vo., 140 pages, original blue cloth, printed paper label, soiling of edges of binding and marginal chipping of title label, fellow poet, Kenneth Rexroth's copy with partially faint penciled signature.   M & S Rare Books, Inc.   95 - 354   2013 $1250

Stevens, Wallace 1879-1955 *Three Academic Pieces. The Realm of Resemblance, Someone Puts a Pineapple Together, Of Ideal Time and Choice.* Cummington: Cummington Press, 1947. First edition, one of 102 copies printed on Worthy Dacian paper and bound thus by Arno Werner out of a total edition of 246 copies, small 8vo., original bright green paper covered hand decorated boards, plain unprinted dust jacket, fine, bright copy in rare dust jacket.   James S. Jaffe Rare Books   Fall 2013 - 140   2013 $2250

Stevenson, D. Alan *The World's Lighthouses Before 1820.* London: New York and Toronto: Oxford University Press, 1959. First edition, large 8vo., illustrations, green cloth, gilt stamped cover emblem and spine title, dust jacket, inner hinges beginning to crack, Burndy bookplate, very good.   Jeff Weber Rare Books   169 - 429   2013 $65

Stevenson, John *Yoshitoshi's Thirty-Six Ghosts.* New York: Weatherhill/Blue Tiger, 1983. First edition, folio, spine tail lightly bumped, else fine in fine dust jacket.   Between the Covers Rare Books, Inc.   Sci-Fi, Fantasy & Horror - 291632   2013 $300

Stevenson, John Hall *Makarony Fables; with the New Fable of the Bees.* London: printed for J. Almon, 1768. Second edition, 4to., half title, final ad leaf, slightly sunned, sewn as issued.   Jarndyce Antiquarian Booksellers   CCV - 252   2013   £180

Stevenson, Robert Louis Balfour 1850-1894 *The Black Arrow.* New York: Charles Scribners Sons, 1936. Large 8vo., original black cloth gilt, pictorial onlay, spine lettering dulled, 9 color plates and color endpapers by N. C. Wyeth.   R. F. G. Hollett & Son   Children's Books - 572   2013   £30

Stevenson, Robert Louis Balfour 1850-1894 *A Child's Garden of Verses.* London: John Lane and The Bodley Head, 1896. First edition thus, small 8vo., original decorated green cloth gilt, corner third of lower board rather badly damped, all edges gilt, illustrations by Charles Robinson, several name stamps on front pastedown.   R. F. G. Hollett & Son   Children's Books - 514   2013   £45

Stevenson, Robert Louis Balfour 1850-1894 *A Child's Garden of Verses.* London: John Lane, The Bodley Head, 1896. One of 150 large paper copies, printed on Japon vellum paper, octavo, over 150 line drawings by Charles Robinson, original dark red cloth as issued with green cloth covers of trade edition as doublures, with ALS Oct. 8 1896 from London bookseller P. Appleby Robson of Robson & Co., very fine.   David Brass Rare Books, Inc.   Holiday 2012 Chapter One - DB 01507   2013 $1850

Stevenson, Robert Louis Balfour 1850-1894 *A Child's Garden of Verses.* London: Longmans, Green & Co., 1885. First edition, first printing, printing of 1000 copies with apostrophe on spine shaped like the number 7, the word "OF" in smaller type on spine with no mention of "Two Series" in the list of other works by author; small 8vo. blue cloth stamped in gold, top edge gilt, x, 101 pages, except for usual offsetting on endpaper, clean, bright and fine, housed in beautiful custom half leather box, especialy fine.   Aleph-Bet Books, Inc.   104 - 547   2013 $6000

Stevenson, Robert Louis Balfour 1850-1894 *A Child's Garden of Verses.* London: Longmans, Green and Co., 1885. First edition, first printing, one of 1000 copies, 12mo., original dark blue cloth, minor soiling, pages x, 101, top edge gilt, fore and bottom edges uncut, usual browning of endpapers, little rubbing to extremities, else fine in morocco backed cloth slipcase.   Howard S. Mott Inc.   262 - 141   2013 $2950

Stevenson, Robert Louis Balfour 1850-1894 *A Child's Garden of Verses.* New York: Scribners, 1905. First edition, 4to., illustrations by Jessie Willcox Smith, few scratches on cover, bookplate inside front cover, 1905 date on both titlepage and copyright page, 11 of 12 plates, plate opposite page 10 has rough edges and no tissue guard, black cloth, very good.   Barnaby Rudge Booksellers   Children 2013 - 021617   2013 $65

Stevenson, Robert Louis Balfour 1850-1894 *A Child's Garden of Verses.* London: John Lane the Bodley Head, 1913. Original decorated red cloth gilt, spine trifle faded, top edge gilt, illustrations by Charles Robinson, flyleaves partly browned.   R. F. G. Hollett & Son   Children's Books - 515   2013   £30

Stevenson, Robert Louis Balfour 1850-1894 *A Child's Garden of Verses.* London: Collins, n.d. circa, 1925. 4to., full leather with found gilt pictorial vignette on cover, top edge gilt, (192) pages, fine in publisher's box with color plate on cover, some fading to box, illustrations by Kate Elizabeth Oliver with color pictorial endpapers, 4 color plates plus numerous full and partial page black and whites, very scarce edition, rare in box. Aleph-Bet Books, Inc. 104 - 548 2013 $675

Stevenson, Robert Louis Balfour 1850-1894 *A Child's Garden of Verses.* London: Harrap, 1931. First edition thus, oblong small 4to., original cloth backed pictorial boards, trifle marked and bubbled in places, 12 color plate, top edge of title little dusty, otherwise nice, clean copy. R. F. G. Hollett & Son Children's Books - 356 2013 £180

Stevenson, Robert Louis Balfour 1850-1894 *The Merry Men and Other Tales and Fables.* London: Chatto & Windus, 1887. First edition, half title, 32 pages catalog (Sep. 1886), original blue cloth, front board and spine decorated in black and silver, spine lettered gilt, slight mark to lower board, very good. Jarndyce Antiquarian Booksellers CCV - 253 2013 £120

Stevenson, Robert Louis Balfour 1850-1894 *Napa Wine.* San Francisco: Westwind Books, 1974. First edition thus, one of 950 copies, small octavo, (6), 38 pages, frontispiece, titlepage printed in green, red and black, beige cloth spine, decorative boards printed in white, red and green, title printed in black on spine, very fine, original semi-transparent dust jacket. Argonaut Book Shop Recent Acquisitions June 2013 - 276 2013 $90

Stevenson, Robert Louis Balfour 1850-1894 *Poems.* Florence Press, 1913. Number 276 of 500 copies on handmade paper, fine in full vellum, 400 pages, large 8vo. Ken Spelman Books Ltd. 75 - 165 2013 £95

Stevenson, Robert Louis Balfour 1850-1894 *Songs with Music. From "A Child's Garden of Verses".* T. C. and E. C. Jack, n.d., 1915. First edition, small 4to, original cloth backed pictorial boards, rather worn and soiled, color frontispiece, title and headings throughout, occasional faint fingering. R. F. G. Hollett & Son Children's Books - 584 2013 £25

Stevenson, Robert Louis Balfour 1850-1894 *Strange Case of Dr. Jekyll and Mr. Hyde.* London: Longmans, Green and Co., 1886. First British edition, octavo, original decorated buff wrappers printed in blue and red. L. W. Currey, Inc. Wandering Ghosts & Itinerant Souls (10/12) - 130677 2013 $6500

Stevenson, Robert Louis Balfour 1850-1894 *Strange Case of Dr. Jekyll and Mr. Hyde.* London: Longmans Green and Co., 1886. First English edition, wrapper issue, nicely rebound in half red morocco gilt, wrappers bound in at rear, housed in red quarter morocco slipcase, pleasing copy. Between the Covers Rare Books, Inc. Sci-Fi, Fantasy & Horror - 291851 2013 $5500

Stevenson, Robert Louis Balfour 1850-1894 *Treasure Island.* London: Cassell & Co., 1883. First edition, first issue, octavo, original olive green diagonal fine ribbed cloth, exceptionally fine, gilt on spine bright and fresh, the Bradley Martin copy with bookplate of Mildred Greenhill on front pastedown, chemised in quarter green morocco slipcase. David Brass Rare Books, Inc. Holiday 2012 Chapter Five - DB 00036 2013 $32,500

Stevenson, Robert Louis Balfour 1850-1894 *Treasure Island.* London: Cassell, 1883. First edition, frontispiece map, initial letter of 'vain' broken on page 40, 'a' not present in line 6 on page 63, the 8 to be found in pagination on page 83 and 7 is present on page 127, the full stop missing following word 'opportunity' on page 178 and word 'worse' in uncorrected form on page 197, foolscap 8vo., original lime green cloth, small mark to rear cover and faintly to backstrip, backstrip gilt lettered, pencilled gift inscription dated Jan 1 86 on grey-black endpapers, front hinge professionally restored, faint shadow of removed bookplate, rear hinge just beginning to crack at tail, still unusually nice. Blackwell's Rare Books B174 - 148 2013 £7000

Stevenson, Robert Louis Balfour 1850-1894 *Virginbus Puerisque an Essay in Four Parts.* East Aurora: Roycrofters, 1903. First edition, 8vo., suede, very good, some light stains on back cover. Barnaby Rudge Booksellers Poetry 2013 - 020639 2013 $75

Stevenson, Sarah Hackett *Boys and Girls in Biology: Simple Studies of the Lower Forms of Life...* New York: Appleton, 1894. Second edition, 8vo., 2 early library bookplates, maroon cloth, stamped in black and gilt, covers darkened, rubbed along edges, very good. Second Life Books Inc. 182 - 237 2013 $150

Stewart, George R. *John Phoenix, Esq. The Veritable Squibob.* New York: Henry Holt and Co., 1937. First edition, xiv, 252 pages, frontispiece, 19 plates and illustrations, maroon cloth gilt, ends bit darkened at gutter, else very fine, pictorial dust jacket. Argonaut Book Shop Recent Acquisitions June 2013 - 89 2013 $75

Stewart, Mary *Ludo and the Star Horse.* Brockhampton Press, 1974. First edition, original cloth, gilt, dust jacket price clipped, illustrations by Gino D'Achille. R. F. G. Hollett & Son Children's Books - 573 2013 £25

Stewart, Mary *Wildfire at Midnight.* London: Hodder & Stoughton, 1956. First reprint, original cloth, dust jacket rather worn, plan. R. F. G. Hollett & Son Children's Books - 574 2013 £45

Stiles, H. R. *A History of the Medical Profession of the County of Kings and the City of Brooklyn NY....* Brooklyn: Reprinted from The Illustrated History of Kings County, 1884. Offprint, quarto, printed wrappers, 69 pages, inserted portrait plates, paper spine perished, soiling and small nicks and tears to wrappers, threatening to disbind, but currently holding together, good copy, fragile and very uncommon offprint. Between the Covers Rare Books, Inc. New York City - 317348 2013 $300

Still, George Frederic *The History of Pediatrics.* London: Oxford University Press, 1931. First edition, very good++ in original green cloth, 8vo., gilt lettering to spine, mild scuffs to covers, cover edge wear, minimal spotting to endpapers. By the Book, L. C. 38 - 44 2013 $500

Stillingfleet, Edward *The Unreasonableness of Separation; or an Impartial Account of the... Present Separation from the Communion of the Church of England.* London: T. N. for Henry Mortlock, 1681. First edition, 4to., some spotting and toning, first few leaves soiled, title a touch worn at fore edge, contemporary calf, marbled edges, rebacked and recornered by Chris Weston, old leather scratched and crackled early ink inscription Christopher Metcalfe, also printed booklabel Rev. Richard Gibbons Binnali, M.A. Unsworths Antiquarian Booksellers 28 - 133 2013 £275

Stinson, Alvah *Woman Under the Law.* Boston: Hudson, 1914. First edition, 8vo., frontispiece, author's presentation on blank, blue cloth stamped in gilt, very good. Second Life Books Inc. 182 - 238 2013 $150

Stith, William *A History of the First Discovery and Settlement of Virginia.* Williamsburg: printed by William Parks, 1747. First edition, third issue possibly printed in 1753, 8vo., polished crimson morocco (finely rebacked, old back laid down), gilt ruled covers, spine elaborately gilt, wide inner gilt crimson borders, marbled endpapers, signed "Toof & Co./Zahn", fine copy in fine signed binding by Otto Zahn (1857-1928), signature on endpaper of Massachusetts politician Gaspar G. Bacon (1886-1947). Howard S. Mott Inc. 262 - 142 2013 $8500

Stock, Joseph *A Narrative of What Passed at Killalla, in the County of Mayo and the Parts Adjacent During the French Invasion in the Summer of 1798.* Dublin: printed by and for R. E. Mercier and Co., 1800. 8vo., bound with 2 final ad leaves, titlepage lightly foxed, some browning, small hole at blank head of H8, contemporary half red morocco, marbled boards, spine rubbed and dull, corners bumped, some abrasions to boards, presentation form author "F. H. Lewis given by the Bishop of Killala 1806", 19th century armorial bookplate of H. M. Williamson and pencil signature of Michael Foot. Jarndyce Antiquarian Booksellers CCIV - 284 2013 £480

Stock, Sarah Geraldina *Missionary Heroes of Africa.* London: London Missionary Society, 1897. Large 8vo., original pictorial green cloth, trifle worn, 75 woodcuts and map, joints cracking, some fingering. R. F. G. Hollett & Son Children's Books - 575 2013 £25

Stockley, W. F. P. *Essays in Irish Biography.* CUP, 1933. First edition, 8vo., 191 pages, dust jacket, cloth, very good, signed presentation copy. C. P. Hyland 261 - 800 2013 £40

Stockton, Frank *John Gayther's Garden and the Stories Told Therein.* New York: Charles Scribner's Sons, 1902. First edition, pictorial green cloth, very near fine. Between the Covers Rare Books, Inc. Sci-Fi, Fantasy & Horror - 317904 2013 $75

Stockton, Frank *Ting a Ling.* New York: Hurd and Houghton, 1870. First edition, 8vo., original gold stamped green cloth, 187 pages, all edges gilt, very nice with minor rubbing to corners and spine extremities, lower 2 inches of front inner hinge cracked, internally fine, with 1875 gift inscription. Howard S. Mott Inc. 262 - 145 2013 $500

Stockton, Frank *Ting-a-Ling.* New York: Hurd & Houghton, 1870. First edition, 8vo., green cloth stamped in black and gold, very faint small corner stain, else near fine, engravings by E. B. Bensell. Aleph-Bet Books, Inc. 105 - 555 2013 $650

Stoddard, Charles Augustus *Across Russia; from the Baltic to the Danube.* London: Chapman & Hall, 1892. First UK edition, 8vo., 12 illustrations, original black and yellow decorative cloth. J. & S. L. Bonham Antiquarian Booksellers Europe - 8775 2013 £65

Stoddard, Charles Warren *Summer Cruising in the South Seas...* London: Chatto & Windus, 1874. First English edition, 8vo., original pictorial green cloth, gilt lettering, frontispiece and 21 plates, 48 page publisher's terminal catalog, uncommon, little shaken and worn, inner hinges starting, very good. The Brick Row Book Shop Miscellany Fifty-Nine - 43 2013 $325

Stoker, Bram 1847-1912 *Dracula.* Westminster: Archibald Constable and Co. June, 1897. First edition, later issue, original yellow cloth bordered and lettered in red on boards and spine, boards lightly soiled, red stamping faded, spine darkened and soiled, head and tail of spine chipped and frayed, inner hinge starting, some toning and foxing, primarily to endpapers and prelims, marginal tear to page 53, not affecting text, previous owner's old ink signature dated 1898, previous owner's bookplate, some pages of ads unopened, some pages of ads opened roughly, still very good housed in quarter black morocco clamshell case. Heritage Book Shop   Holiday Catalogue 2012 - 147   2013 $7500

Stoker, Bram 1847-1912 *The Jewel of Seven Stars.* New York: Harpers, 1904. First American edition, very good in later (1920's) dust jacket with internal tape mends and wear along folds.   Mordida Books   81 - 479   2013 $350

Stokes, Vernon *Mountaineers.* Collins, 1941. First edition, large 4to., original blue cloth, dust jacket, some edge chips and tears, lower part of backstrip missing, illustrations.   R. F. G. Hollett & Son   Children's Books - 576   2013   £50

Stone, Irving *Men to Match My Mountains. The Opening of the Far West 1840-1900.* New York: Doubleday & Co. Inc., 1956. First trade edition, green cloth, very fine in pictorial dust jacket (chip to head of jacket spine), very scarce thus.   Argonaut Book Shop   Recent Acquisitions June 2013 - 277   2013 $75

Stone, John A. *Put's Original California Songster, Giving in a Few Words what Would Occupy Volumes, Detailing the Hopes, Trials and Joys of Miner's Life.* San Francisco: D. E. Appleton, 1868. Fifth edition, 12mo., 64 pages, original illustrated wrappers, top covers loose and chipped at extremities, scarce, very good.   Jeff Weber Rare Books   171 - 58   2013 $250

Stone, Mary *Children's Stories that Never grow Old.* Chicago: Reilly & Britton, 1908. First edition, 8vo., yellow pictorial cloth, 312 pages + ads, near fine, illustrations by John R. Neill with over 70 full page color illustrations and several black and whites.   Aleph-Bet Books, Inc.   104 - 376   2013 $750

Stone, Wilbur Macey *The Thumb Bible of John Taylor.* Brookline: The LXIVMOS, 1928. Limited to 100 copies, this one of 10 large paper copies with "One of ten large paper copies specially bound. To my good friends Mr. & Mrs. William Hand with all good wishes, Wilbur Macey Stone, March 1928", 12mo., decorated paper covered boards, paper label on front cover, slightly rubbed at extremities, loosely inserted is typed errata slip pointing out an error and a handwritten note from Stone to Jane Hand meant to accompany this gift copy, miniature bookplate of Jane Beulah Hand, spine slightly age darkened, very scarce, from the collection of Donn W. Sanford.   Oak Knoll Books   303 - 23   2013 $450

Stone, Wilbur Macey *The Thumb Bible of John Taylor.* Brookline: the LXIVMOS, 1928. Limited to 100 copies, 12mo., cloth backed boards, paper label, illustrations, rubbed along edges, miniature bookplate of Kathryn Rickard with acquisition date of 1990 added in ink beneath bookplate, pages 65-68 (one sheet) loose from not being sewn in, from the collection of Donn W. Sanford.   Oak Knoll Books   303 - 24   2013 $200

Stoney, Samuel Gaillard *Black Genesis.* New York: Macmillan Co., 1930. First edition, illustrations by Martha Bensley Bruere, decorated green cloth, little light staining on rear board, else near fine in near very good dust jacket price clipped with several small chips and tears, publisher's bookmark listing this title laid in, handsome copy, very scarce.   Between the Covers Rare Books, Inc.   165 - 331   2013 $350

Stong, Phil *Cowhand Goes to Town.* New York: Dodd Mead, 1939. Stated first edition, 4to., cloth backed pictorial boards, fine in chipped dust jacket, color lithographs by Kurt Wiese.   Aleph-Bet Books, Inc.   105 - 587   2013 $150

Stong, Phil *The Other Worlds.* New York: Wilfred Funk Inc., 1941. First edition, octavo, original light gray cloth, spine panel stamped in green.   L. W. Currey, Inc.   Fall Sampler Sept. 2013 - 146498   2013 $125

Stonier, George Walter *The Memoirs of a Ghost.* London: Grey Walls Press, 1947. First edition, octavo, cloth.   L. W. Currey, Inc.   Wandering Ghosts & Itinerant Souls (10/12) - 63749   2013 $100

Stoppard, Tom *Jumpers.* London: Faber & Faber, 1972. First edition, signed by author, fine in nearly fine, crisp dust jacket with minor soiling to back panel.   Ed Smith Books   78 - 64 2013 $500

Stoppard, Tom *Night and Day.* London: Faber & Faber, 1978. First edition, uncorrected proof in original perfect bound printed wrappers, very good plus with some light sunning to spine.   Ed Smith Books   78 - 67   2013 $300

Stoppard, Tom *The Real Thing.* London: Fraser & Dunlap Scripts Ltd. Feb., 1982. First edition, early pre-publication version from playwright's literary agent, xeroxed leaves (8.5 x 11), brad bound in paper covers with cut-out title window, very good plus to near fine. Ed Smith Books 78 - 68 2013 $350

Stoppard, Tom *Travesties.* London: Faber & Faber, 1975. First edition, softcover issue, signed by author, 2 newspaper reviews tipped to rear, with 16 page program for this play at the Albery Theatre, London in June of 1974, staple bound, very good to near fine. Ed Smith Books 78 - 66 2013 $100

Stories by a Mother for the Use of Her Own Children. London: Harvey and Darton, 1820. 16mo., 96 pages, roan backed marbled boards, spine extremes chipped, else very good, 6 fine engraved plates. Aleph-Bet Books, Inc. 105 - 221 2013 $350

Story Magazine. Volume XXIV #106. New York: Story Magazine March-April, 1944. First edition, printed wrappers, near fine, contains Charles Bukowski's first appearance in print, near fine, tight, clean copy. Charles Agvent Charles Bukowski - 70 2013 $2000

The Story of Old Mother Hubbard and Her Dog. Blackie & Son, n.d. circa, 1930. Large 4to, original cloth backed boards with pictorial onlay, little surface abrasion to corners and edges, pages (32), 12 full page color illustrations, numerous black and white drawings and 2 color pictorial endpapers, very nice. R. F. G. Hollett & Son Children's Books - 2 2013 £65

Story of the Apostles. New York: McLoughlin Bros. n.d. circa, 1865. 12mo., 32 pages, pictorial wrappers, fine, illustrations by W. H. Herrick with 13 fine half page copper engravings, decorative initials and with color pictorial cover. Aleph-Bet Books, Inc. 105 - 381 2013 $250

The Story of the Charmed Fawn. New York: Elton & Co., 1858. on titlepage and front and rear cover read New York: John McLoughlin, n.d. circa, 12m., pictorial wrappers, nearly as new, illustrations by Harrison Wier with 6 full page hand colored wood engravings, rarely found in this condition. Aleph-Bet Books, Inc. 104 - 344 2013 $800

Story, Jack Trevor *Mix Me a Person.* New York: Macmillan, 1960. First American edition, pages little darkened, else fine in fine dust jacket with spine unfaded, especially nice. Between the Covers Rare Books, Inc. Mystery & Detective Fiction - 76657 2013 $65

Story, Robert *Love and Literature; Being the Reminiscences Literary Opinions and Fugitive Pieces of a Poet in Humble Life.* for Longman Brown, 1842. First edition, errata and ad, half title good copy in original blind-stamped and gilt lettered cloth, head of spine neatly repaired and little faded, scarce. Ken Spelman Books Ltd. 73 - 79 2013 £75

Stothard, Charles Alfred *The Monumental Effigies of Great Britain.* London: printed by J. M'Creery for the author, 1817-1832. Large paper edition, richly colored and gilt frontispiece, 1 portrait, second frontispiece and 144 numbered color and duo tone plates plus 9 vignettes, folio, contemporary three quarter red morocco over marbled boards, five raised bands, gilt title, top edge gilt, marbled endpapers, very good with wear at spine ends, boards scuffed with wear along edges, occasional foxing or soiling, colors brilliant, binding tight. Kaaterskill Books 16 - 82 2013 $1500

Stourbridge Glazed Brick and Fireclay Co. Ltd. *A Small Brick but It is a Product of the Stourbridge Glazed Brick and Fireclay Co. Ltd.* Blowers Green Dudley Birmingham: Drew & Hopwood Ltd., 1935. 4to., pages (2), 15, half tone and one color illustration, original decorated wrappers, cord ties. Marlborough Rare Books Ltd. 218 - 64 2013 £95

Stout, Rex *Before Midnight.* New York: Viking, 1955. First edition, bookplate, fine in dust jacket with nicks and tiny wear top of spine. Mordida Books 81 - 491 2013 $250

Stout, Rex *Before Midnight.* New York: Viking, 1955. First edition, octavo, cloth. L. W. Currey, Inc. Fall Sampler Sept. 2013 - 146494 2013 $350

Stout, Rex *Death of a Doxy.* New York: Viking, 1966. First edition, fine in dust jacket. Mordida Books 81 - 493 2013 $150

Stout, Rex *Fer-De-Lance.* New York: Farrar & Rinehart, 1934. First edition, spine lettering faded, otherwise very good, without dust jacket. Mordida Books 81 - 480 2013 $400

Stout, Rex *Fer-De-Lance.* New York: Otto Penzler, 1996. Exact facsimile of 1934 edition, very fine in dust jacket. Mordida Books 81 - 481 2013 $200

Stout, Rex *Homicide Trinity.* New York: Viking, 1962. First edition, bookplate, fine in dust jacket, with crease tear at lower edge of front panel and tiny wear at spine ends. Mordida Books 81 - 492 2013 $200

Stout, Rex *The League of Frightened Men.* New York: Farrar & Rinehart, 1935. First edition, spine lettering slightly faded, otherwise fine without dust jacket. Mordida Books 81 - 482 2013 $500

Stout, Rex *Murder by the Book.* New York: Viking, 1951. First edition, fine in dust jacket with very slightly faded spine, bookplate. Mordida Books 81 - 490 2013 $200

Stout, Rex *Not Quite Dead Enough.* New York: Farrar & Rinehart, 1944. First edition, fine in dust jacket with some tiny nicks at spine ends, several short closed tears and crease along spine. Mordida Books 81 - 485 2013 $850

Stout, Rex *The Red Box.* New York: Farrar & Rinehart, 1937. First edition, darkening along internal hinges and faint stains on fore edge, otherwise very good, without dust jacket. Mordida Books 81 - 483 2013 $250

Stout, Rex *The Second Confession.* New York: Viking, 1949. First edition, very good in dust jacket with few nicks along edges, couple of short closed tears and some slight spine fading. Mordida Books 81 - 487 2013 $90

Stout, Rex *The Second Confession.* New York: Viking, 1949. First edition, 8vo., 245 pages, with TLS by Stout, mild cover edge wear in very good+ dust jacket with chips, minimal sun spine, scuffs. By the Book, L. C. 36 - 57 2013 $500

Stout, Rex *The Silent Speaker.* New York: Viking, 1946. First edition, very good in dust jacket with label removed from base of spine, chipping at top of spine, darkened spine, wear along front flap fold. Mordida Books 81 - 486 2013 $200

Stout, Rex *Some Buried Caesar.* New York: Farrar & Rinehart, 1939. First edition, staining along front cover hinge and along internal hinges, spine slightly darkened, stamp on front endpaper, otherwise very good, without dust jacket. Mordida Books 81 - 484 2013 $150

Stout, Rex *Three Doors to Death.* New York: Viking, 1950. First edition, very good in dust jacket with internal tape mends, chips at base of spine and at corners, several closed tears, wear along folds and along edges. Mordida Books 81 - 489 2013 $80

Stout, Rex *Trouble in Triplicate.* New York: Viking, 1949. First edition, fine in very good dust jacket with few nicks along edges, couple of short closed tears, some slight spine fading. Mordida Books 81 - 488 2013 $150

Stow, John *The Annales of England.* London: by Peter Short, Felix Kingston and George Eld for George Bishop and Thomas Adams, 1605. Early edition, quarto in 8's, collages complete and same as British Library, elaborate woodcut titlepage and numerous woodcut initials, black letter, beautifully bound in full panelled calf, elaborately stamped in blind, spine stamped in blind and lettered in gilt, board edges and dentelles tooled in blind, all edges gilt, marbled endpapers, top outer corner of mostly first half with light dampstaining, occasional old ink marginalia, front and back boards, professionally repaired at outer hinges, final two leaves with some professional paper repairs, not affecting text, previous owner's bookplate, overall very nice. Heritage Book Shop 50th Anniversary Catalogue - 97 2013 $3000

Stow, John *A Survey of the Cities of London.* London: W. Innys et al, 1754-1755. Sixth and best edition, 2 volumes, folio, titles printed in red and black, 132 engraved plates, neat early 20th century brown morocco, spines in seven compartments with raised bands, lettered and dated gilt, inner gilt dentelles, gilt edges by Riviere. Marlborough Rare Books Ltd. 218 - 147 2013 £16,500

Stowe, Harriet Elizabeth Beecher 1811-1896 *The Edmondson Family and the Capture of the Schooner Pearl.* Cincinnati: American Reform Tract and Book Society, circa, 1856. Early edition, original figured green cloth gilt contemporary pencil gift inscription, foxing and some creases at corners of few pages, else nice, very good. Between the Covers Rare Books, Inc. 165 - 266 2013 $300

Stowe, Harriet Elizabeth Beecher 1811-1896 *Lady Byron Vindicated: a History of the Byron Controversy...* Boston: Fields, Osgood & Co., 1870. First edition, initial ad leaf, prelims slightly marked, original dark green cloth, spine little darkened and slightly worn at head and tail, booklabel and stamp of J. J. Worley Memorial Library. Jarndyce Antiquarian Booksellers CCIII - 356 2013 £40

Stowe, Harriet Elizabeth Beecher 1811-1896 *Novels and Stories.* New York: Sully and Kleinteich, 1899. University edition, 213 x 148mm., 9 volumes, publisher's brown buckram, flat spines with gilt titling, mostly unopened, each volume with frontispiece, tiny tears to head of three spines, just hint of rubbing to extremities, text with touch of browning to edges isolated short closed tears to margins, other trivial imperfections, still quite fine set, clean, smooth and fresh, few signs of use inside and out. Phillip J. Pirages 63 - 452 2013 $275

Stowe, Harriet Elizabeth Beecher 1811-1896 *Sam Lawson's Oldtown Fireside Stories.* Boston: Houghton Mifflin and Co., 1881. First printing of the expanded edition, 12mo., 13 full page illustrations by F. O. C. Darley, Augustus Hoppin and John J. Harley, plus chapter vignettes and tailpieces, original bevel edged decorated green cloth, front and spine panels stamped in gold, brown coated endpapers. L. W. Currey, Inc. Wandering Ghosts & Itinerant Souls (10/12) - 134557 2013 $250

Stowe, Harriet Elizabeth Beecher 1811-1896 *Woman Sacred in History.* New York: J. B. Ford and Co. 1873 i.e., 1874? First complete edition, thick 4to., publisher's full brown Turkey morocco, title stamped in blind, gold border, inner gilt dentelles, coated moire silk doublures, 400 pages + frontispiece and 24 inserted plates, each with printed tissue, all edges gilt, nearly fine, all printed tissue guards present, although four have tear holes in blank areas, with no loss of print, spine title printed in gold with name "E. D. Waterman" stamped in gold at bottom, minor browning to top of some leaves,.   Howard S. Mott Inc.   262 - 144   2013 $450

Stowe, Marietta Lois Beers *Probate Confiscation, Unjust Laws Which Govern Women.* Boston: by the author, 1879. Fourth edition, rust cloth, stamped in gilt, ex-library with bookplate, cover scuffed and slightly worn at edges, hinges tender, flyleaf, frontispiece and title loose, otherwise very good.   Second Life Books Inc.   182 - 240   2013 $75

Strachey, Alix *The Unconscious Motives of War.* New York: IUP, n.d., First edition, from UK plates, fine in near fine dust jacket.   Beasley Books   2013 - 2013 $50

Strange, John Stephen *For the Hangman.* Garden City: Crime Club, 1934. First edition, spotting to boards, very good in good plus dust jacket and rubbing to spine. Between the Covers Rare Books, Inc.   Mystery & Detective Fiction - 40865   2013 $65

Stratton, Clarence *Swords and Statues.* Philadelphia: John C. Winston, 1937. First edition, First 8vo., blue cloth stamped in gold, 254 pages, offsetting on title, else fine in slightly worn dust jacket. color wrapper, color frontispiece, several full and partial page black and whites by Robert Lawson.   Aleph-Bet Books, Inc.   105 - 360   2013 $600

Straub, Julia *Julia.* New York: Coward, McCann & Geoghegan, 1975. Advance copy, uncorrected proof of first edition, octavo, printed orange wrappers.   L. W. Currey, Inc.   Wandering Ghosts & Itinerant Souls (10/12) - 107150   2013 $350

Straub, Peter *Floating Dragon.* San Francisco: Underwood Miller, 1982. First edition, fine in fine dust jacket, one of 500 numbered copies, signed by Straub and jacket artists Leo and Diane Dillon, this copy number 5. Between the Covers Rare Books, Inc.   Sci-Fi, Fantasy & Horror - 309570   2013 $125

Straub, Peter *Ghost Story.* New York: Coward McCann & Geohegan, 1979. First edition, octavo, cloth backed boards.   L. W. Currey, Inc.   Wandering Ghosts & Itinerant Souls (10/12) - 139023   2013 $100

Straub, Peter *Mrs. God.* Hampton Falls: Donald Grant, 1990. First separate edition, one of 600 numbered copies, signed by author and artist, Rick Berry, quarter morocco and cloth with applied illustration in slipcase, fine.   Between the Covers Rare Books, Inc.   Sci-Fi, Fantasy & Horror - 306898   2013 $75

Straub, Peter *The Throat.* Baltimore: Borderlands Press, 1993. First edition, one of 350 numbered copies, signed by author fine in fine dust jacket and fine slipcase.   Between the Covers Rare Books, Inc.   Sci-Fi, Fantasy & Horror - 306906   2013 $60

Streamlined Trains. Findon Publications, n.d., 1945. Oblong 8vo., original pictorial colored card wrappers, pages (14), illustrations in color, fine, scarce.   R. F. G. Hollett & Son   Children's Books - 712   2013   £35

Streatfieild, Noel *Skating Shoes.* New York: Random House, 1951. Stated first edition, 8vo., pictorial cloth, 245 pages, fine in chipped and frayed dust jacket, black and white illustrations by Richard Floethe, scarce in jacket. Aleph-Bet Books, Inc.   104 - 549   2013 $275

Strickland, Agnes *Fisher's Juvenile Scrap-book.* Fisher, Son & Co., 1839. Original heavily blind embossed cloth gilt, spine and edges rather faded, all edges gilt, steel engraved title and 15 engraved plates, some little foxed. R. F. G. Hollett & Son   Children's Books - 580   2013   £65

String-Field, John K. *Souvenir Catalogue of the Thoroughbreds (Stallions and Mares) Belonging to the Melbourne Stud. The Property of William S. Barnes. Lexington, Fayette County Kentucky.* Cincinnati: John K. Stringfield, 1901. First edition, green cloth, decorated and titled in silver, 252 pages, illustrations, small tears to edges of front fly and titlepage, dampstaining to bottom of pages, presentable copy, good only, stamped in gilt "Complimentary to Sporting Editor New York World", scarce.   Between the Covers Rare Books, Inc.   Horses, Horsemanship, Horse Racing, Etc. - 295106   2013 $275

Strong, Leonard Alfred George *The Hansom Cab and Pigeons Being Random Reflections Upon the Silver Jubilee of King Georg V.* Golden Cockerel Press, 1935. First edition, 18/212 special issue copies (of an edition of 1212), printed on Arnold handmade paper and signed by author, wood engraved frontispiece and 16 other engravings in text by Eric Ravilious, 8vo., 52 pages, original quarter royal blue crushed morocco, faded silver gilt lettered backstrip, boards marbled in various shades of blue on cream ground, top edge silver, others untrimmed, very good.   Blackwell's Rare Books   B174 - 341   2013   £300

Struther, Jan *Sycamore Square.* London: Methuen, 1932. 8vo., cloth, 63 pages, fine in slightly browned dust jacket, 12 plates and 40 text illustrations, uncommon. Aleph-Bet Books, Inc.   105 - 547   2013 $225

Strutt, Jacob George *Sylva Britannica; or Portraits of Forest Trees...* London: published for the author, n.d., 1831-1836. Royal 8vo., pages viii, 151, additional etched vignette title and 49 plates, all on india paper, title and front flyleaf with repaired holes to lower inner margins, corner of one plate with repair, only occasional light foxing, contemporary green pebble grain cloth, black paper label on spine, rebacked relaying original backstrip. Marlborough Rare Books Ltd. 218 - 150 2013 £1250

Stuart, Francis *Arrow of Anguish.* Dublin: Raven Arts Press, 1995. First edition, 8vo., original wrappers, limited to 400 copies, fine, signed by author. Maggs Bros. Ltd. 1442 - 295 2013 £60

Stuart, Francis *Black List, Section H.* London: Martin Brian & O'Keefe, 1975. First UK edition, 8vo., original black cloth, dust jacket, near fine. Maggs Bros. Ltd. 1442 - 293 2013 £40

Stuart, Francis *Faillandia.* Dublin: Raven Arts Press, 1985. First edition, 8vo., original wrappers, signed by author on titlepage, near fine. Maggs Bros. Ltd. 1442 - 292 2013 £100

Stuart, Francis *States of Mind. Selected Short Prose 1936-1983.* Dublin/London: Raven Arts Press/Martin Brian & O'Keefe, 1984. First edition, limited to 400 copies, original blue cloth, slightly bumped on lower spine, otherwise fine in dust jacket, scarce. Maggs Bros. Ltd. 1442 - 294 2013 £50

Stuart, Francis *We Have Kept the Faith.* Dublin: Raven Arts Press, 1985. First edition, 8vo., original green cloth, inscribed by author to his UK publisher Timothy O'Keefe, page slightly browning, otherwise excellent copy in dust jacket, incised at bottom of upper wrapper. Maggs Bros. Ltd. 1442 - 366 2013 £350

Stuart, Ruth McEnery *Carlotta's Intended and Other Tales.* New York: Harper and Bros., 1894. First edition, octavo, original decorated red cloth, front and spine panels stamped in black and gold. L. W. Currey, Inc. Christmas Themed Books - 113181 2013 $100

Stuart, Ruth McEnry *Daddy Do-Funny's Wisdom Jingles.* New York: Century, 1913. First edition, 8vo., cloth, 95 pages, edges of covers soiled, else very good, illustrations on every page by G. H. Clements, very scarce. Aleph-Bet Books, Inc. 104 - 82 2013 $225

Stuart, Villers H. *Adventures Amidst the Equatorial Forests and Rivers of South America...* London: John Murray, 1891. First edition, 268 pages, 21 illustrations and two folded maps, about good in illustrated blue cloth boards with loss to spine ends, near to corners and some foxing to pages as well as vintage bookstore sticker, small vintage price sticker, very serviceable copy of somewhat uncommon book in original edition. Jeff Hirsch Books Fall 2013 - 129431 2013 $175

Stuckey, Ronald *The Lithographs of Stow Wengenroth 1931-1972.* Boston: Boston Public Library/Barre Pub., 1974. Limited to 100 copies with pencil, signed lithograph, this is no. 17, with signed original lithograph pulled form stone at workshop of George C. Miller and Son of NY City, 4to., 295 pages, quarter black leather with gilt lettering spine, marbled paper covered boards, illustrated endpapers, original soiled paper covered slipcase with paste-on, printed title label. By the Book, L. C. 36 - 12 2013 $500

Stucki, John Stettler *Family History Journal of John S. Stuckii: Handcart Pioneer of 1860.* Salt Lake City: Pyramid Press, 1931. First edition, 164 pages, 20cm., red marbled yapp wrappers with title and illustration on front panel, very good, extremities rubbed, more so at corners, faded notation on rear panel in ink, inscribed by author, ex-libris Dale Morgan, with his name in pencil. Ken Sanders Rare Books 45 - 14 2013 $600

Studer, Jacob H. *The Birds of North America.* New York: Natural Science Assoc. of America, 1888. 391 x 300mm., , publisher's original turkey half morocco and buckram, upper cover with gilt decorative titling, joints and tips renewed with calf, original backstrip preserved, spine panels with blind-stamped fleuron, floral patterned endpapers, all edges gilt, frontispiece, 119 chromolithographs of North American Birds after crayon drawings by Theodore Jasper, all with tissue guards, some rubbing and scuffing to spine joints, and extremities (noticeable without being severe), small white stain to upper cover, frontispiece rather foxed, isolated minor smudges or thumbing, otherwise very good, text and plates clean and fresh and binding completely sound. Phillip J. Pirages 63 - 453 2013 $750

Sturgeon, Theodore *More than Human.* New York: Farrar Straus Young, 1953. Stated first edition, 8vo., signed and inscribed by author, very good+, owner name and scuff to front pastedown, minimal cover edge wear in contemporary+ dust jacket with short closed tears, minimal sun spine, soil, scuffs and edge wear, 8vo., scarce. By the Book, L. C. 38 - 101 2013 $500

Sturgis, Edith *My Busy Days.* New York: D. Appleton, Oct., 1908. First edition, folio, cloth backed pictorial boards, some edge wear and cover rubbing, else very good+, illustrations by Margaretta Hinchman. Aleph-Bet Books, Inc. 104 - 424 2013 $1350

Sturt, Charles *Two Expeditions into the Interior of Southern Australia During the Years 1828, 1829, 1830 and 1831....* London: Smith, Elder & Co., 1833. First edition, 2 volumes, large folding engraved map, chart and 5 lithograph views, further 4 hand colored lithographs of birds and 4 lithographic illustrations of geological specimens, 8vo., very good original purple cloth, backs fade as usual, one or town tiny nicks here and there, entirely unrestored. Maggs Bros. Ltd. 1467 - 94   2013   £5000

Sturtevant, A. H. *Essays on Evolution.* Quarterly Review of Biology Volume 12 No. 4 Dec., 1937. Offprint, near fine, owner stamp and mild scuffs to front cover, 8vo., original printed wrappers.   By the Book, L. C.   37 - 76   2013 $150

Sturtevant, A. H. *Preferential Segregation in Triplo-iv Females of Drosophila Melanogaster.* Genetics, 1936. Offprint from Genetics 21, July 1936, author's name underlined, owner stamp to front cover, 8vo., good++ in original printed wrappers.   By the Book, L. C.   37 - 77   2013 $95

Sturtevant, A. H. *The Relations of Inversions in the X chromosome of Drosophila Melanogaster to Crossing Over and Disjunction.* Genetics, 1936. Offprint from Genetics 21 Sept. 1936, 8vo., very good+, original printed wrappers, author's names underlined, soil to front cover.   By the Book, L. C.   37 - 81   2013 $250

Sturtevant, A. H. *Sequence of Correspondence Third-Chromosome genes in Drosophila Melano-Gaster and D. Simulans.* Biological Bulletin Volume I, No. 1 Jan., 1926. Offprint, near fine 8vo., original printed wrappers, owner stamp to front cover, mild toning and wear to cover edges. By the Book, L. C.   37 - 80   2013 $100

Sturtevant, A. H. *The Spatial Relations of Genes.* National Academy of Sciences, 1919. Offprint from Proceedings of Nat. Academy of Sciences Volume 5, May 1919, 8vo., very good+ in plain wrappers, author's names underlined, owner stamp toning and edge wear.   By the Book, L. C.   37 - 83   2013 $90

Sturtevant, A. H. *The Use of Mosaics in the Study of the Developmental Effect of Genes.* Sixth International Congress of Genetics, Volume I, 1932. Offprint, near fine in original printed wrappers, faint red underlining and owner stamp to front cover, 8vo.   By the Book, L. C.   37 - 79   2013 $150

Suarez, Raoul Quintana *Libertad O' Meurte! Episodios de la Revolution.* Habana: Dibjuos Pub. Luque circa, 1960. 4to., pictorial wrappers, 40 pages, some cover soil, very good+ and complete, 325 numbered picture cards, each card mounted in numbered space with printed caption, very rare.   Aleph-Bet Books, Inc.   105 - 482   2013 $4500

The Substance of Three Sermons, Preached at Edinburgh, the 8th, 9th, and 10th Days of July 1787 by Moses the Jew Who Was Lately Converted to the Christian Religion. Nottingham: Charles Sutton, reprinted, 1812. 8vo., 8 pages, uncut sheet as issued.   Ken Spelman Books Ltd.   75 - 68   2013   £50

Suckling, John *Fragmenta Aurea.* London: for Humphrey Moseley, 1646. First edition, first state with "FRAGMENTA AVREA" in upper case, a period after Churchyard in imprint and rule under the date; A3v:16 reads "allowed", second state of frontispiece re-incised with heavier lines around leaves of the garland and the bulge in the left sleeve, according the Beaurline and Clayton, the plate was most certainly re-incised in course of printing and is fairly evenly distributed with the various states of title; engraved portrait, contemporary calf, gilt fillet and cornerpieces, red morocco spine label, portrait and 2 first 2 leaves with two very tiny holes at gutter, worm trail in lower margin of first three gatherings, else very nice in lovely contemporary binding; bookplate of C. Pearl Chamberlain and booklabel of Abel Berland, fine red morocco pull-off case; with ALS of John Suckling (1569-1627) father of the poet.   Joseph J. Felcone Inc.   Books Printed before 1701 - 83   2013 $6000

Suckling, John *Fragmenta Aurea.* London: for Humphrey Moseley, 1646. First edition, first state, engraved portrait, contemporary calf, gilt fillet and cornerpieces, red morocco spine label, portrait and first two leaves with two very tiny holes at gutter, worm trail in lower margin of first three gatherings, else very nice in lovely dust jacket binding, bookplate of C. Pearl Chamberlain and book label of Abel Berland, fine red morocco pull-off case, with ALS from John Suckling (1569-1627), father of poet to unnamed recipient.   Joseph J. Felcone Inc.   English and American Literature to 1800 - 22   2013 $6000

Sudek, Josef *Sudek.* New York: Clarkson N. Potter, n.d., First edition, 4to., very good in near fine dust jacket. Beasley Books   2013 - 2013 $65

Sue, Eugene 1804-1857 *The Works.* Boston: Dana Estes & Co. circa, 1899-1900. Illustrated Cabinet condition, 11 works in 20 volumes, 197 x 140mm., attractive contemporary oxblood half morocco over textured green cloth, raised bands, spines gilt in compartments with inlaid green morocco quatrefoil centerpiece and lacy cornerpieces, marbled endpapers, top edges gilt, entirely unopened, 86 engraved plates, cloth little faded at head edge and with minor discoloration on sides (from binder's glue?), couple of tiny scuff marks, otherwise especially fine set, bindings unworn, quite pleasing on shelf unread interiors immaculate. Phillip J. Pirages   63 - 454   2013 $800

Suetonius Tranquillus, Gaius *Caesarum XII Libri a Mendis ad Interpretum Sententiam & Vetustorum Exemplarium fidem Repeurgati...* Basel: per Henricum Petrum, 1537. First Gallus edition, touch of soiling to titlepage, institutional stamp and small paper shelfmark label at foot, earlier inscription at head, contemporary wooden boards backed in blindstamped pigskin, spine dyed black and with three raised bands, later paper labels in second and fourth compartments, two clasps (both lost), little bit rubbed, old inscriptions to front endpapers (one the purchase note of Jonas Christian Weber), very good. Blackwell's Rare Books 172 - 136 2013 £1400

Suetonius Tranquillus, Gaius *Duodecim Caesares et de Illustrbus Grammataicis & Claris Rhetribus, Libelli Duo.* Leiden: ex officina Plantiniana Apud Franciscum Raphelengium, 1596. 8vo., browned and dampstained in places, some soiling and underlining, small area excised from margin of titlepage and another blank area patched, as well as inscription rubbed and causing small damage to paper, contemporary vellum, boards ruled in blind, long sides overlapping, rear board rather stained and somewhat rumpled, corner of f.f.e.p. repaired, old ownership inscriptions to titlepage, mostly rubbed out our excised but dated 1693 and 1761 and initials J. B. A. C. still visible. Unsworths Antiquarian Booksellers 28 - 50 2013 £300

Suetonius Tranquillus, Gaius *The Lives of the Twelve Caesars.* Chicago: Argus Book Shop, 1930. One of 2000 numbered copies, of which 1500 are for America and 500 for England (this copy #a9), 270 x 186mm., frontispiece, striking orange morocco by Bennett of NY (stamp signed), covers with gilt panelled frame containing 8 large gilt rosettes (at corners and middle of each side), rosettes radiating black dotted lines or fleurons, raised bands, spine compartments with similar design, deep blue morocco doublures framed by decorative gilt rolls, leather hinges, indigo watered silk endleaves, top edge gilt, other edges rough trimmed, with illustrated title, 23 figures in text, 16 full page illustrations, all with patterned tissue guards, binding lightly soiled, joints and extremities bit rubbed, otherwise excellent, unusual binding solid and without serious condition problems, immaculate internally. Phillip J. Pirages 63 - 455 2013 $175

Suffer Little Children. London: Ernest Nister, n.d. circa, 1897. 4to., original cloth backed pictorial boards, edges worn, some dampstaining, 14 chromolithographed plates and sepia illustrations, rather shaken and loose in places, little fingering. R. F. G. Hollett & Son Children's Books - 417 2013 £45

Sullivan Bros. *The Clans of Ireland, Their Battles, Chiefs & Princes with Territorial Map.* n.d., 8vo., cloth, almost fine. C. P. Hyland 261 - 804 2013 £80

Sullivan, Maurice S. *Jedediah Smith, Trader and Trail-Breaker.* New York: Press of the Pioneers, 1936. First edition, 227 pages, 7 illustrations, red cloth, barely noticeable tiny embossed name at top of half title, spine slightly dulled, else fine. Argonaut Book Shop Recent Acquisitions June 2013 - 279 2013 $125

Sullivan, Timothy Daniel *Speeches from the Dock or Protests of Irish Patriotism.* Dublin: Gill & Son, circa, 1910? 8vo., 160 pages, illustrations, puckered publisher's cloth, spine faded, signed on endpaper by F. M. Sullivan, very good. Second Life Books Inc. 183 - 366 2013 $75

Summers, Montague *Victorian Ghost Stories.* London: Fortune Press, n.d., 1933. First edition, octavo, original black cloth, spine panel stamped in gold. L. W. Currey, Inc. Wandering Ghosts & Itinerant Souls (10/12) - 136687 2013 $450

Summersett, Henry *The Fate of Sedley: a Novel.* London: printed for William Lane, Minerva Press, Leadenhall Street, 1795. 12mo., some occasional foxing, but generally in good, clean condition, contemporary quarter calf, marbled boards, vellum tips, gilt banded spines, red morocco labels, spines chipped at head and little rubbed, library shelf number '85' blindstamped at head of spines, contemporary ownership name of Mary Lyon. Jarndyce Antiquarian Booksellers CCIV - 285 2013 £1500

Sumner, E. V. *Tactics for Gatling Gun Cal. 45 Proposed by Captain E. V. Sumner, 1st Cavalry.* San Francisco: Adjutant General's Office, Headquarters Dept. of California, Feb. 14, 1876. First edition, 12mo., 4 pages, original printed wrappers, one vertical crease, very rare. M & S Rare Books, Inc. 95 - 236 2013 $375

The Sunday Scholars' Magazine and Juvenile Miscellany for 1847 and 1848. J. Bakewell, Methodist New Commission Book Room, 1847-1848. Volumes XXIV and XXV, 12mo., original half green sheep gilt by Mason of Thorne with his ticket, little rubbed, numerous woodcuts, scattered spotting, scarce. R. F. G. Hollett & Son Wesleyan Methodism - 51 2013 £65

The Sunday-School Boy. Philadelphia: American Sunday School Union, 1849. 16mo., wrappers, woodcuts, 8 pages, very good. Barnaby Rudge Booksellers Children 2013 - 019749 2013 $50

Sunshine for Little Children. Philadelphia: A. T. Zeising & Co., 1883. First edition, folio, illustrations, color frontispiece, wood engravings, green cloth backed boards, good. Barnaby Rudge Booksellers Children 2013 - 021522 2013 $75

Surtees, Robert Smith 1803-1884 *Hunting with Mr. Jorrocks, from Handley Cross.* Oxford: Oxford University Press, 1956. First Ardizzone edition, 8 color printed plates by Edward Ardizzone, 8vo., original pale grey cloth, lightly faded backstrip gilt lettered on red ground, endpapers foxed, dust jacket, good.   Blackwell's Rare Books   172 - 159   2013   £40

Surtees, Robert Smith 1803-1884 *Jorrocks's Jaunts and Jollities.* London: Rudolph Ackermann Eclipse Sporting Gallery, 1843. Second edition, octavo, hand colored engraved vignette title and 14 hand colored aquatint plates, plates watermarked 1832, handsomely bound by Wood of London circa 1920, full red crushed levant morocco, contemporary covers and spine bound in at end, housed in red cloth slipcase.   David Brass Rare Books, Inc.   Holiday 2012 Chapter Two - DB 02169   2013 $1500

Surtees, Robert Smith 1803-1884 *Mr. Facey Romford's Hounds.* London: Bradbury and Evans, 1865. First edition, frontispiece and 23 hand colored plates by John Leech, very good in contemporary half calf, marbled boards, gilt banded spine with green morocco label, some rubbing to marbled paper and slight foxing.   Ken Spelman Books Ltd.   75 - 133   2013   £75

Surtees, Robert Smith 1803-1884 *Soapey Sponge's Sporting Tour.* London: George Routledge, 1893. Half title, 6 page ads, 'yellowback', original printed boards, slightly dulled and worn, some damp marking, good, sound copy.   Jarndyce Antiquarian Booksellers   CCV - 255   2013   £60

Survey of London, Volume XVII. The Strand (St. Martin-in-the Fields Part II). London: published for the Greater London Council, 1937. Limited edition, no. 421 of 700 copies, 4to., pages xxii, (2), 163, (2), colored frontispiece, 111 photo plates, several text illustrations, original blue cloth, original printed dust jacket.   Marlborough Rare Books Ltd.   218 - 97   2013   £50

Sutherland, Captain *A Tour Up the Straits from Gibraltar to Constantinople...* London: J. Johnson, 1790. First edition, 8vo., contemporary brown half calf, small crack at base of spine, corners rubbed, library label on front endpaper, but no stamps in text, good.   J. & S. L. Bonham Antiquarian Booksellers   Europe - 8380   2013   £400

Sutter, John A. *New Helvetia Diary. A Record of Events... from September 9 1845 to May 25, 1848.* San Francisco: Society of California Pioneers, 1939. First edition, one of 950 copies, color frontispiece, 2 plates, map, cloth backed decorated boards, paper spine label, very fine.   Argonaut Book Shop   Recent Acquisitions June 2013 - 280   2013 $225

Svevo, Italo *James Joyce: a Lecture Delivered in Milan 1927.* Milan: Officine Grafiche 'Esperia', 1950. One of 1600 copies, this #837, 102 x 77mm., (34) leaves, original paper wrappers in original dust jacket showing a photo of Joyce by Man Ray on front cover and a photo of Svevo on rear, tiny dent to jacket at head of spine, otherwise extremely fine, very fragile item, quite clean and bright inside and out, few signs of use.   Phillip J. Pirages   63 - 294 2013 $200

Swain, Edmund Gill *The Stoneground Ghost Tales Compiled from the Recollections of the Reverend Roland Batchel, Vicar of the Parish.* Cambridge: W. Heffer & Sons Ltd., 1912. First edition, octavo, original pictorial blue cloth, front and spine panels stamped in black.   L. W. Currey, Inc.   Wandering Ghosts & Itinerant Souls (10/12) - 102703   2013 $1250

Swain, Edmund Gill *The Stoneground Ghost Tales.* Cambridge: Heffer, 1912. First edition, prelims and final few leaves lightly foxed, foolscap 8vo., original bright light blue cloth, lettering on backstrip and front cover and overall design on front cover, all blocked in dark blue and white, small faint stain to front cover.   Blackwell's Rare Books   172 - 238   2013   £450

Swammerdam, Jan *Histoire Generale des Insectes...* Utrecht: Jean Ribbius, 1685. Second edition in French, 4to., 13 engraved plates, folding table, later half calf antique, extremities of spine bit rubbed, else very good.   Joseph J. Felcone Inc.   Books Printed before 1701 - 84   2013 $1200

Swan, James G. *The Northwest Coast; or Three Years' Residence in Washignton Territory.* New York: Harper & Bros., 1857. First edition, 195 x 125mm., publisher's brown buckram, flat spine with gilt titling, 28 illustrations by author, folding map, inscribed by author to Mrs. C. W. Philbrick, Port Townsend Oct. 13th 1876, with signature of Ellen Philbrick, and bookplate of Frederick V. Holman; spine sunned, extremities slightly worn, small patches of water(?) stains to boards, other trivial imperfections, but really excellent copy, fresh and clean internally, original fragile binding still solid and generally well preserved.   Phillip J. Pirages   63 - 358   2013 $1250

Swan, Joseph *Illustrations of the Comparative Anatomy of the Nervous System.* London: 1835. 35 engraved plates, 4to., contemporary quarter calf with morocco label, institutional stamps on title and verso of plates, moderate foxing of plates, binding showing bit of wear with spine ends and raised bands bit worn.   James Tait Goodrich   75 - 197   2013 $1595

Swan, Kay *Tick-Tock Clock Book.* New York: Stoll & Edwards, 1929. Large 4to., pictorial boards, fine in original pictorial box, slight repair to box, cover has cloth with moveable hands, illustrated in bold colors.   Aleph-Bet Books, Inc.   104 - 197   2013 $300

Swan, Oliver *Deep Water Days.* Philadelphia: Macrae Smith, 1929. Stated first edition, 4to., green pictorial cloth, top edge blue, mint in original pictorial box (slightly rubbed but very good+), illustrations by N. C. Wyeth, Frank Schoonover and Stanley Arthurs, etc., rare in this condition. Aleph-Bet Books, Inc.   104 - 594   2013 $600

Swannell, Mildred *Paper Silhouettes.* George Philip & Son, 1929. Small 4to., original boards, little rubbed, lower board spotted, color frontispiece and 150 diagrams in black and white.   R. F. G. Hollett & Son   Children's Books - 581   2013   £35

Swanwick, Michael *The Nature of Mirrors.* Philadelphia: Dragonstairs Press, 2011. First edition, small octavo, pictorial wrappers, sewn.   L. W. Currey, Inc.   Utopian Literature: Recent Acquisitions (April 2013) - 140673   2013 $100

Swanzy, H. B. *The Family of Green of Youghal.* for private circulation, 1902. 105 pages, cloth over original wrappers, presentation ALS from Swanzy to Philip Crossle tipped in at rear, presentation copy later presented to Horace E. Jones, Ms. additions and death notices tipped in throughout, Jones's bookplate, very good+.   C. P. Hyland   261 - 391   2013   £300

Swedenborg, Emanuel *On the Worship and Love of Gold. (bound with) A Treatise on the Nature of Influxe or of the Intercourse Between the Soul and Body...* printed at the Aurora Press by J. Hodson, 1801. Second work printed and sold by R. Hindmarsh, 1788, Third edition of second work, 12mo; first work toned and dust soiled, some corners creased, second work browned and dust soiled, short wormtrail deep in gutter, 12mo., modern quarter calf, marbled boards, green morocco lettering piece, sound.   Blackwell's Rare Books   172 - 138   2013   £600

Swedenborg, Emanuel *A Treatise Concnering Heaven and Hell and of the Wonderful Things Therein as Heard and Seen.* Chester: printed by C. W. Leadbeater, 1800. Fourth edition, printed on poor quality greyish paper, slightly browned with occasional light spotting, slight damage to titlepage in 3 places, slight loss from one character of author's name, 8vo., later half calf, marbled boards rubbed, neatly rebacked preserving old black lettering piece, red edges, old ownership inscription of Hugh Thornton of Bunbury, Cheshire, to initial binder's blank and beginnings of manuscript index in ink and pencil at end, sound, rare. Blackwell's Rare Books   172 - 137   2013   £400

Sweeney, Matthew *Broken Flowers.* Banholt: Bonnefant Press, 2007. Limited to 99 copies, printed on Zerkall mouldmade paper, tall 8vo., original pink wrappers, fine. Maggs Bros. Ltd.   1442 - 296   2013   £75

Swendsen, Haagen *The Tryals of Haagen Swendsen, Sarah Baynton, John Hartwell and John Spurt.* London: printed for Isaac Cleave, 1703. Folio, stain on first 8 leaves, diminishing in size, sewn as issued, stamp of Gloucestershire County Library on title verso.   Jarndyce Antiquarian Booksellers   CCV - 256   2013   £125

Swieten, Gerard Van *The Commentaries Upon the Aphorisms of Dr. Herman Boerhaave.* London: John and Paul Knapton and Robert Horsfield & Thomas Longman, 1744-1765. 10 of 18 volumes, lacking volumes 3, 11, 13-18, small 8vo., frontispiece in volume 12, folding plates in volume 4, occasional worm tracks slightly affecting text, original brown calf, gilt ruled covers, raised bands, gilt stamped red leather spine labels, few hinges weak or starting, ownership signature William Clapham and few volumes signed M. A. Halloway.   Jeff Weber Rare Books   172 - 34   2013 $1700

Swift, Jonathan 1667-1845 *A Complete Collection of Genteel and Ingenious Conversation, According to the Most Polite Mode and Method Now Used at Court...* London: printed for B. Motte and C. Bathurst, 1738. 8vo., prelim ad leaf, endpapers and pastedowns browned and dusted, contemporary calf, double gilt ruled borders, hinges cracked but firm, spine worn at head and tail, corners bumped and worn. Jarndyce Antiquarian Booksellers   CCIV - 289   2013   £750

Swift, Jonathan 1667-1845 *The Correspondence of Jonathan Swift.* Oxford: Clarendon Press, 1963. 1965. First edition, five volumes, 8vo., red cloth, light wear to extremities, slight dusting and browning to edges, very good, jackets with light wear with creasing and small tears to some edges, very good, handwritten notes loosely inserted in volume I.   Unsworths Antiquarian Booksellers   28 - 200   2013   £225

Swift, Jonathan 1667-1845 *Directions to Servants in General and in Particular to the Butler, Cook, Footman, Coachman, Groom, House, Steward and Land-Steward, Porter, Dairy-Maid.* London: printed for R. Dodsley, 1745. 8vo., some slightly foxing and browning, final contents leaf dusted, stab holes visible in gutter of final leaves, titlepage trimmed and laid into contemporary paper, 19th century half calf, marbled boards, gilt banded spine, spine slightly worn at head.   Jarndyce Antiquarian Booksellers   CCV - 257   2013   £1250

Swift, Jonathan 1667-1845 *Gulliver's Travels.* Paris: 1826. New edition, 9 plates, 2 volumes bound in one, quarter leather, scuffed and worn, 15 x 10 cm., much foxing. C. P. Hyland   261 - 807   2013   £75

Swift, Jonathan   1667-1845 *Gulliver's Travels into Several Remote Nations of the World.*   New York: E. P. Dutton and Co., 1909.   First American trade edition, octavo, 12 full color plates, including frontispiece, 2 black and white full page illustrations, tailpieces, by Arthur Rackham, publisher's maroon cloth pictorially gilt stamped, original light gray dust jacket pictorially decorated and lettered in black on front cover and spine, bright, fine copy in near fine, price clipped dust jacket.   David Brass Rare Books, Inc.   Holiday 2012 Chapter One - DB 01889   2013 $550

Swift, Jonathan   1667-1845 *Gulliver's Travels, a Voyag to Lilliput.*   Zuilichem: Catharijne Press, 1995.   Limited to 190 copies, this one of 15 lettered copies, bound thus and with extra suite of the illustrations, hand colored, under passe-partout and placed in a second volume, bound by Luce Thurkow, 6.7 x 4.2cm., paper covered boards, slipcase, from the collection of Donn W. Sanford.   Oak Knoll Books   303 - 89   2013 $275

Swift, Jonathan   1667-1845 *Miscellanies.*   London: printed in the year, 1722.   Fourth edition, 12mo., frontispiece, some light browning, faint old waterstaining to first 20 leaves, contemporary sprinkled calf, gilt panelled spine, red morocco label, slight damp marks to boards causing slight bowing and cracking to upper inch of both hinges.   Jarndyce Antiquarian Booksellers   CCIV - 290   2013   £150

Swift, Jonathan   1667-1845 *A Modest Proposal for Preventing the Children of Poor People from Being a Burthen to their Parents of the Country and for Making Them Beneficial to the Publick.*   Dublin: printed and reprinted at London for Weaver Bickerton, 1730.   Third edition, 8vo., half title, some light offsetting from turn-ins to prelim and final blank leaves, original stab stitch holes visible, 19th century half red morocco, gilt lettered spine.   Jarndyce Antiquarian Booksellers   CCIV - 291   2013   £8500

Swift, Jonathan   1667-1845 *The Poetical Works...*   Edinburgh: 1736.   Frontispiece, woodcut device to titlepage, 12mo., titlepage torn without loss, neatly repaired, expertly bound in recent sprinkled half calf, retaining neat contemporary marbled boards, gilt banded spine, dark green morocco label, bookplate removed from inner pastedown.   Jarndyce Antiquarian Booksellers   CCIV - 287   2013   £250

Swift, Jonathan   1667-1845 *The Poetical Works...*   Edinburgh: at the Apollo Press by the Martins, 1772.   4 volumes in 2, frontispiece, additional engraved titlepage to each volume, general and divisional printed titlepages to each volume, 8mo., slight full contemporary tree calf, gilt decorated spines, twin red morocco labels, armorial bookplate of William Waddington.   Jarndyce Antiquarian Booksellers   CCIV - 288   2013   £150

Swift, Jonathan   1667-1845 *Reason Against Coition: a Discourse...*   London: H. Hook, 1732.   64 pages, modern quarter calf good copy.   C. P. Hyland   261 - 806   2013   £750

Swift, Jonathan   1667-1845 *Remarks on the Life and Writings of Dr. John Swift...*   London: printed for A. Millar, 1752.   Second edition, frontispiece, 8vo., slight browning and occasional foxing, contemporary calf, double gilt fillet border, plainly rebacked, raised bands, unsympathetic red label, some cracking to surface leather on boards, corners worn, inner hinges repaired, early signature of Samuel Cam.   Jarndyce Antiquarian Booksellers   CCIV - 293   2013   £65

Swift, Jonathan   1667-1845 *A Tale of a Tub.*   London: printed for John Nutt, 1704.   First edition, second state with page 320, with blank space on line 10 after 'furor' (but with 'uterinus' not inked in), octavo, lacking rear flyleaf, excellent, fresh and crisp copy in contemporary panelled calf, tooled in blind, skillfully rebacked with original spine laid down, edges sprinkled red, contemporary signature on titlepage, former owner's signature on front free endpaper dated 13 June 1704, very clean except for last few pages with bit of foxing and few prelim leaves with light waterstaining, overall, very good.   Heritage Book Shop   50th Anniversary Catalogue - 98   2013 $5000

Swift, Jonathan   1667-1845 *Travels into Several Remote Nations of the World.*   London: printed for Benj. Motte, 1726.   Teerink's "B" edition, one of three 8vo. editions printed the same year the first "A" published, 2 volumes, 8vo., 19th century speckled calf by Robson & Kerslak (hinges repaired), leather labels, raised bands, inner gilt dentelles, marbled endpapers, frontispiece, 3 maps, 1 diagram, minor scattered foxing.   Howard S. Mott Inc.   262 - 146   2013 $3500

Swift, Jonathan   1667-1845 *Travels in to Several Remote Nations of the World.*   London: printed for Benj. Motte, 1726.   First edition, Teerink's state A with 4 necessary points, frontispiece in second state, 4 maps, 2 plans, decorative woodcut and typographic head and tailpieces and initials, contemporary panelled calf, spines with raised bands, brown morocco gilt lettering labels, board edges decoratively tooled gilt, edges sprinkled red, joints just starting portion of rear free endpaper volume II torn away, short tear to lower gutter margin of c2, not affecting text, small waterstain to outer margin of 17-k4 in part II, few additional minor stains or soil marks, armorial bookplate of Rt. Hon. Lord Viscount Lymington in each volume, sensational copy, totally unsophisticated, chemised in quarter red morocco pull off case.   Heritage Book Shop   Holiday Catalogue 2012 - 148   2013 $125,000

Swift, Jonathan 1667-1845 *Travels into Several Remote Nations of the World.* London: printed for Benj. Motte..., 1726. First edition, Teerink's state A, 4 parts in 2 volumes, octavo, frontispiece in second state, 4 maps, 2 plans, modern antique style mottled calf, gilt double rule border on covers, gilt spines with red and green morocco labels, gilt board edges, edges sprinkled red, marbled endpapers, small inkstain on frontispiece, short tear to upper margin of B7 in part 1, some inoffensive washing at beginning of volume II, little light foxing and soiling, early ink signatures on recto of frontispiece and on titlepage volume I, otherwise excellent set. Heritage Book Shop 50th Anniversary Catalogue - 99 2013 $45,000

Swift, Jonathan 1667-1845 *Travels into Several Remote Nations of the World.* London: printed for Benj. Motte at the Middle Temple Gate in Fleet-street, 1727. Second edition, frontispiece, 5 engraved maps, engraved plate, 8vo. tear with loss of text to A3 (contents leaf) volume II from wax adhesion with verso of plate III, undamaged though wax visible through plate, some browning and foxing, first titlepage and frontispiece dusted, old waterstain at head from attempt to remove later 18th century signature, later endpapers and pastedowns, contemporary calf, recased not recently, retaining original backstrips, later morocco labels, corners neatly repaired, some abrasions to boards, inner leading hinges cracked but firm, signatures of Samuel Coote Martin 1787 on titlepages, overall very good. Jarndyce Antiquarian Booksellers CCIV - 292 2013 £1650

Swift, Jonathan 1667-1845 *The Works.* Dublin: printed by George Faulkner in Essex Street, 1738. Volume II dated 1737, 5 engraved maps and 1 plan in volume III, frontispiece portraits in volumes I-IV, possibly lacking a final blank leaf in volume II, 8vo., some occasional foxing and several gatherings rather browned, one leaf torn with slight loss to leading edge not affecting text, contemporary marbled boards, leading edges tipped with vellum, recent calf spines, raised bands, gilt labels, near contemporary signature of George Ledwith. Jarndyce Antiquarian Booksellers CCIV - 286 2013 £750

Swift, Jonathan 1667-1845 *The Posthumous Works.* Edinburgh: printed for John Balfour, 1766. 3 volumes, 12mo., contemporary Scottish speckled calf, gilt ruled compartments on spines, tan morocco lettering pieces numbered "1"-"3" direct in gilt, little rubbed and worn, contemporary signature "Leven" at heads of titles of volumes i-ii, later booklabel of one Douglas Grant with separately printed shelfmark label, good. Blackwell's Rare Books B174 - 149 2013 £750

Swift, Roger *The Irish in Victorian Britain.* Four Courts, 1999. 320 pages, wrappers, 8vo., fine. C. P. Hyland 261 - 813 2013 £20

Swinburne, Algernon Charles 1837-1909 *Poems and Ballads.* London: John Camden Hotten, 1866. Second edition, 12mo., pages viii, 344 pages, green cloth, owner's name and address on pastedown, hinges tender, cover little scuffed and worn at edges, otherwise very good. Second Life Books Inc. 183 - 368 2013 $200

Swinburne, Algernon Charles 1837-1909 *The Springtide of Life.* London: William Heinemann, 1918. One of 765 copies signed by artist, this #369, 286 x 232mm., very attractive red three quarter morocco, raised bands, spine handsomely gilt in compartments, formed by plain and decorative rules, quatrefoil centerpiece surrounded by densely scrolling cornerpieces, sides and endleaves of rose colored linen, top edge gilt, numerous black and white illustrations, fine color plates as called for, by Arthur Rackham, all tipped onto brown paper and with letterpress guards; morocco bookplate of W. A. M. Burden; hint of offsetting from brown mounting paper, otherwise very fine, bright, fresh and clean inside and out, only most trivial of imperfections. Phillip J. Pirages 63 - 383 2013 $1600

Swinburne, Algernon Charles 1837-1909 *Springtide of Life: Poems of Childhood.* London: Heinemann, 1918. Limited to only 765 numbered copies (100 for US), signed by artist, large 4to., vellum backed pictorial boards, tips rubbed, covers toned on edges, else very good+, 8 beautiful color plates and 52 black and whites by Arthur Rackham, very uncommon. Aleph-Bet Books, Inc. 104 - 475 2013 $1450

Swinburne, Henry *Travel through Spain in the Years 1775 and 1776.* London: P. Elmsley, 1787. Second edition, 2 volumes, 8vo., frontispiece, 10 plates, 2 maps, contemporary brown polished calf, rebacked using original gilt decorated spines. J. & S. L. Bonham Antiquarian Booksellers Europe - 8448 2013 £550

Swinton, John *Striking for Life. Labor's Side of the Labor Question.* American Manufacturing & Pub., 1894. First edition, very good, spine wear and f.e.p. excised, 500 pages, many illustrations, portraits. Beasley Books 2013 - 2013 $65

Swinton, John *Striking for Life, Labor's Side of the Labor Question...* New York: American Manufacturing and Publishing, 1894. First edition?, 8vo., 498 pages, maroon cloth, pictorial stamping on front in black and gilt, cover somewhat scuffed and soiled, rear hinge just beginning tender, otherwise very good, tight copy. Second Life Books Inc. 183 - 369 2013 $75

"Sydney's" Letter to the King; and Other Correspondence, Connected with the Exclusion of Lord Byron's Monument from Westminster Abbey. London: James Cawthorne, 1828. First edition, half title, original drab boards, spine slightly worn and repaired in places, Renier booklabel. Jarndyce Antiquarian Booksellers CCIII - 337 2013 £180

Sykes, D. F. E. *Huddersfield and Its Vicinity.* Huddersfield: Advertiser Press, 1898. First edition, half title, errata leaf, plates, good in original green gilt cloth, binding little rubbed.   Ken Spelman Books Ltd.   73 - 90   2013   £28

Sykes, Godfrey   *The Colorado Delta.*   Washington: 1937. vii, 193 pages, folding map, cloth, shelf wear, else near fine.   Dumont Maps & Books of the West   122 - 80   2013 $85

Sylla, Edith   *Texts and Contexts in Ancient and Medieval Science: Studies on the Occasion of John E. Murdoch's Seventieth Birthday.*   Leiden: New York & Koln: Brill, 1997. 8vo., maroon cloth, gilt stamped cover and spine title, ownership signature, fine.   Jeff Weber Rare Books   169 - 312   2013 $80

Sylvius   *Opera Medic Tam Hactenus Inedita quam Variis Locis & Formis Edita...*   Paris: Apud Frederick Leonard, 1679. First edition, title printed in red and black, inserted large folding engraved portrait, 4to., modern brown calf, gilt spine with raised bands, black leather gilt label, some early ink inscriptions, title with marginal loss and two repairs to verso, final index leaf with hole and loss of text, very pale, mostly marginal dampstaining at beginning and end, very good Paris bookseller's label pasted over imprint.   James Tait Goodrich   S74 - 226   2013 $950

Syme, James   *The Principles of Surgery.*   Philadelphia: Carey & Lea, 1832. First American edition, 220 x 135mm, attractive recent retrospective three quarter calf over marbled boards, raised bands, brown morocco label, frontispiece, leaves little browned, title and frontispiece with dozen or so short, thin brown stains, one opening heavily splattered with dark brown (almost certainly blood) stains also affecting adjacent leaves, otherwise excellent copy in attractive, unworn binding.   Phillip J. Pirages   63 - 456   2013 $225

Symonds, John   *The Isle of Cats.*   London: Werner Laurie, 1955. First edition, original cloth, top inner corners of boards rather faded, dust jacket trifle soiled, price clipped, 6 color plates and numerous drawings.   R. F. G. Hollett & Son   Children's Books - 290   2013   £65

Symonds, John Addington   1807-1871   *A Problem in Modern Etchics.*   London: John Addington Symonds, 1896. First edition, one of 100 copies, few small bumps on rear board, else very good.   Between the Covers Rare Books, Inc.   Philosophy - 41278   2013 $100

Synge, John Millington   1871-1909   *John M. Synge: a Few Personal Recollections.*   Dublin: Cuala Press, 1910. Number 235 of 350 copies, 8vo., original quarter linen over blue boards, printed paper label, slightly marked on lower cover, otherwise near fine.   Maggs Bros. Ltd.   1442 - 55   2013   £175

Synge, John Millington   1871-1909   *The Well of the Saints.*   Dublin/London: A. H. Bullen, the Abbey Theatre, 1905. First edition, small 8vo., original wrappers, slightly nicked on spine, otherwise excellent, scarce.   Maggs Bros. Ltd.   1442 - 297   2013   £375

Synge, John Millington   1871-1909   *Collected Works.*   Oxford University Press, 1962-1968. 8vo., frontispiece and illustrations to each volume, cloth, very good to near fine.   C. P. Hyland   261 - 815   2013   £165

T

Tacitus, Cornelius *The Works of...* London: printed for G. G. J. and J. Robinson, 1793. 4 volumes, 4to., folding engraved maps, plates somewhat foxed, contemporary speckled calf, spines gilt in compartments, red and black morocco labels, rubbed, corners and endcaps worn, joints cracking, label from first two and partly lost from third volumes, stipple engraved booklabel of Theo. Leigh/Toft, ink ownership inscription 'Theodosia Leigh'. Unsworths Antiquarian Booksellers 28 - 51 2013 £300

Taekel, Blair *The Lands of the Tamed Turk.* Boston: L. C. Page, 1910. First edition, 8vo., pages 295, illustrations, folding map, original green decorative cloth, near fine. J. & S. L. Bonham Antiquarian Booksellers Europe - 8324 2013 £125

Tahsin al-Din *The Loves of Camarupa and Camelata, an Ancient Indian Tale.* London: printed for T. Cadell, 1793. First edition of this translation, staining from turn-in affecting borders of few leaves at either end, cancelled library stamp on half title, 8vo., contemporary sheep, gilt rules on flat spine forming compartments, red lettering piece, upper hinge repaired, spine darkened and with vertical crack ascending little over half of the height, contemporary armorial bookplate (Ferdinand) Graf on Wintzingerode, sound. Blackwell's Rare Books B174 - 150 2013 £750

Taine, John *The Gold Tooth.* New York: E. P. Dutton and Co., 1927. First edition, fine in age toned, very good or better dust jacket with couple of shallow chips on rear panel, nice, scarce. Between the Covers Rare Books, Inc. Sci-Fi, Fantasy & Horror - 290450 2013 $500

Tait, John *The Cave of Morar, the Man of Sorrows.* Bookseller to the Royal Academy and sold by J. Bew and J. Balfour, at Edinburgh, 1774. First edition, lacking half title, 4to., disbound, last leaf working loose. Blackwell's Rare Books B174 - 151 2013 £250

Talbot, J. H. *A Biographical History of Medicine.* New York: 1970. 1211 pages, many portraits and illustrations, nice just light wear, original binding. James Tait Goodrich S74 - 227 2013 $175

Talcott, Dudley Vaill *North of North Cape.* London: John Lane, Bodley Head, 1936. First English edition, original cloth, gilt, faint signs of numbers having been removed from spine, illustrations by author, with maps, drawings and photos, piece cut out of title. R. F. G. Hollett & Son Polar Exploration - 71 2013 £40

Tale of Patchy Pig. Volland, 1927. Squarish 8vo., cloth, some cover rubbing, very good, illustrations. Aleph-Bet Books, Inc. 104 - 579 2013 $200

The Tale of Tsarevich Ivan. The Fire Bird and Grey Wolf. Moscow: 1901. Folio, pictorial wrappers, near fine, illustrations by Ivan Bilibin, with 3 full page and 5 smaller magnificent chromolithographs. Aleph-Bet Books, Inc. 105 - 80 2013 $1200

Tales from Fairyland with Cut-Out and Stand-Up Pictures. Akron: Saalfield, n.d. circa, 1905. 4to., pictorial wrappers, light cover rubbing, else near fine, unused, full page die-cut chromolithographs, child is meant to remove characters from each die-cut and stand them up for play using die-cut stands provided, colors rich, illustrations lovely, rarely found intact. Aleph-Bet Books, Inc. 104 - 447 2013 $1250

Talfourd, Thomas Noon *Literary Sketches and Letter: Being the Final Memorials of Charles Lamb...* New York and Philadelphia: Appleton, 1849. Second edition, 8vo., black blindstamped cloth, spine stamped in gilt "I. Metcalf, Providence 1852" on flyleaf, very good, tight copy. Second Life Books Inc. 183 - 371 2013 $65

Talfourd, Thomas Noon *A Speech in the House of Commons 18th May 1837.* 1837. First edition, 8vo., 16 pages, disbound, very good. C. P. Hyland 261 - 104 2013 £75

Talirunili, Joe *Portfolio of Prints.* Quebec: La Federation de Cooperatives du Noveau Quebec, 1974. Oblong folio, original pictorial wrappers, 12 leaves of prints of hunting scenes, printed in black and white. R. F. G. Hollett & Son Polar Exploration - 72 2013 £75

Tallack, William *Malta; Under the Phoenicians, Knights and English.* London: A. W. Bennett, 1861. First edition, 8vo., pages vii, 322, ads, 2 tinted lithographs, 2 illustrations, original brown blindstamped cloth, slight rubbing to head and tail of spine. J. & S. L. Bonham Antiquarian Booksellers Europe - 9434 2013 £220

Tambimuttu *Festschrift for Marianne Moore's Seventy Seventh Birthday by Various Hands...* New York: Tambimuttu & Mass, 1964. First edition, 8vo. 137 pages, fine in printed dust jacket by Leonard Baskin, little soiled, fine, spine stamp blacked out and new title stamped as seen on most copies. Second Life Books Inc. 183 - 281 2013 $100

Tapply, William *Dead Meat.* New York: Scribners, 1987. First edition, inscribed by author, very fine in dust jacket. Mordida Books 81 - 498 2013 $65

Tapply, William *Death at Charity's Point.* New York: Scribners, 1984. First edition, signed by author, very fine in dust jacket. Mordida Books 81 - 485 2013 $200

Tapply, William *Follow the Sharks.* New York: Scribners, 1985. First edition, signed by author, very fine in dust jacket. Mordida Books 81 - 496 2013 $65

Tapply, William *The Marine Corpse.* New York: Scribners, 1986. First edition, signed by author, very fine in dust jacket. Mordida Books 81 - 497 2013 $65

Tarbell, Ida M. *A Reporter for Lincoln: The Story of Henry E. Wing.* New York: Macmillan Co., 1927. First edition, very good plus, spine lettering dulled and some lettering on front panel flaked off in about very good dust jacket with some chipping to spine ends and some soiling as well as internal strengthening to corners and joints, signed and dated by Tarbell. Jeff Hirsch Books Fall 2013 - 129502 2013 $100

Targ, William *The Making of the Bruce Rogers World Bible.* Cleveland: World Pub. Co., cop., 1949. First edition, signed by Rogers and A. Colish copy number 10, fine, without slipcase, 4to., illustrations, original red cloth. Howard S. Mott Inc. 262 - 122 2013 $100

Tarkington, Booth 1869-1946 *The Works of Booth Tarkington.* Garden City: Doubleday Page and Co., 1918-1922. One of 565 copies of the "Autograph Edition", signed by author, this #539, 217 x 140mm., 16 volumes (of 27) (The works in 12 volumes, Volumes XIII ad XIV in our set have a publication date of 1919 and volumes XV and XVI were published in 1922, apparently Doubleday produced 11 additional volumes in this series), very attractive contemporary olive green crushed three quarter morocco over light green linen raised bands, spine gilt in four compartments, one at head and one large compartment with stylized Art Nouveau floral centerpieces and scrolling cornerpieces (the other two with titling), textured green endpapers, top edges gilt, other edges untrimmed, 11 volumes, mostly or entirely unopened, each volume with frontispiece in two states, one in color, all with lettered tissue guards, volume V with 11 full page illustrations and volume XIV with four full page illustrations, both as called for, light marks to couple of boards and other trivial imperfections, otherwise handsomely bound set in fine condition, few signs of use inside or out. Phillip J. Pirages 63 - 461 2013 $950

Tarrant, Margaret *The Children's Year.* Modern Art Society, England, n.d., Small 8vo., original blue boards, pictorial onlay by artist on upper board, unpaginated, double page title and line drawing in blue, full page color illustrations. R. F. G. Hollett & Son Children's Books - 585 2013 £75

Tarrant, Margaret *Fairy Tales.* Ward, Lock & co. n.d. circa, 1920. Original cloth, oval pictorial onlay, dust jacket edges trifle chipped, 44 color plates, color pictorial endpapers by Margaret Tarrant, very nice. R. F. G. Hollett & Son Children's Books - 583 2013 £150

Tarry, Ellen *The Third Door.* New York: McKay, 1955. First edition, 8vo., pages ix, 304, aqua cloth, author's presentation, top edge gilt slightly soiled, otherwise very good, tight copy in scuffed and little chipped and soiled dust jacket. Second Life Books Inc. 182 - 242 2013 $150

Tart, Charles T. *On Being Stoned. A Psychological Study of Marihuana Intoxication.* Palo Alto: Science and Behavior Books, 1971. First edition, near fine in very good+ dust jacket with short tears at edges, 8vo. Beasley Books 2013 - 2013 $50

Tartaglia, Niccolo *La Nova Scientia...* colophon: Venice: n.p. (C. Troiano di i Navo), 1558. Third edition, elaborate woodcut on titlepage, woodcut illustrations and diagrams in text, titlepage little browned and with repairs to edges, especially lower but just without loss, verso of #2 with very faint impression of last three lines, partially supplied in manuscript, but last line an half scarcely discernable, small 4to., later limp yellowish vellum, ink stamp on title of Biblioteca Aprosiana obscuring the last name of a contemporary ownership inscription (first name Giorgio), good. Blackwell's Rare Books 172 - 139 2013 £2200

Tate, Allen *The Hovering Fly and Other Essays.* Cummington: Cummington Press, 1949. First edition, one of only 12 copies on Van Gelder paper with original drawing and woodcuts hand colored, this copy specially bound and signed by author and artist, out of a total edition of 245 copies, 8vo., woodcuts by Wightman Williams, full russet morocco with inlaid hand colored panel on front cover by Arno Werner, this the binder's copy, signed by Werner "Arno Werner Bookbinder 1949", very fine, half morocco, folding box with Werners booklabel. James S. Jaffe Rare Books Fall 2013 - 36 2013 $15,000

Tate, James *If It Would All Please Harry. A Poem.* Amherst: Shanchie Press, 1980. First edition, one of only 10 lettered copies reserved for author and artist (this being copy "J") out of total edition of 35 copies produced, of which 25 roman numeraled copies were for sale, all copies signed by poet and artist, with each of the original prints also numbered and signed in margin by artist, folio, 10 original etchings and engravings by Stephen Riley, on Arches over White paper, loose sheets in folding box, presentation copy inscribed by Tate and Riley to Stanley Wiater, portfolio lightly soiled, otherwise very fine, rare. James S. Jaffe Rare Books Fall 2013 - 141 2013 $5000

Tate, William *Chemistry: Relating ot Mine Ventilation.* Leeds: A. Megson, 1882. Some soiling of leaves through use, particularly at beginning, 8vo., original dark green pebble grained cloth, blindstamped borders on sides, lettered gilt on upper cover slightly worn, front inner hinge strained, good.   Blackwell's Rare Books   Sciences - 115   2013   £350

Tatham, Herbert Francis William *The Footprints in the Snow and Other Tales.* London: Macmillan and Co., Limited, 1910. First edition, octavo, inserted frontispiece, original blue cloth, front and rear panels stamped in blind, spine panel stamped in gold, all edges untrimmed.   L. W. Currey, Inc.   Wandering Ghosts & Itinerant Souls (10/12) - 114143   2013 $350

The Tatler, (and The Guardian). Stereotyped, printed and sold by A. Wilson, 1814. Engraved titlepage and 7 engraved plates, contemporary dark blue half calf, gilt panelled spine with red morocco label, marbled boards, binder's ticket of F. Brown, Durham, some foxing to plates.   Ken Spelman Books Ltd.   75 - 71   2013   £60

Taylor, Alison G. *Simeon's Bride.* London: Hale, 1995. First edition, fine in price clipped dust jacket.   Mordida Books   81 - 501   2013 $250

Taylor, Ann *The Family Mansion.* printed (by T. Miller) for Taylor and Hessy, 1819. First edition, with engraved frontispiece foxed and offset in either direction, 12mo., original plum polished calf, double gilt fillets on sides, spine richly gilt in compartments, marbled endleaves and matching the marbled edges, spine trifle faded, minor wear to corners, very good.   Blackwell's Rare Books   B174 - 152   2013   £1200

Taylor, Ann *My Mother.* New York: McLoughlin, 1867. First edition, 12mo., 10 pages plus wrappers, 7 1/2 page color illustrations, some light writing outside frame on cover, spine reinforced with archival tape.   Barnaby Rudge Booksellers   Children 2013 - 021635   2013 $75

Taylor, Arthur Adelbert *California Redwood Park, Sometimes Called Sempervirens Park. An Appreciation.* Sacramento: William Richardson, 1912. First edition, 14 photos, brown cloth lettered in dark brown, endpaper bit darkened, fine, scarce.   Argonaut Book Shop   Recent Acquisitions June 2013 - 281   2013 $90

Taylor, Bayard   1825-1878 *Eldorado or Adventures in the path of Empire...* New York: 1850. Second edition, 2 volumes, 8 full page tinted lithographs, original blindstamped cloth, spines faded, slight loss of cloth at top of spine of volume I, extremities rubbed, previous owner's name and name stamp, overall very good, unsophisticated set.   Dumont Maps & Books of the West   125 - 75   2013 $450

Taylor, Bayard, Mrs. *On Two Continents: memories of Half a Century.* London: Smith Elder, 1905. First edition, 8vo., pages 309, frontispiece, tissue guard, illustrations, original red cloth, spine slightly rubbed.   J. & S. L. Bonham Antiquarian Booksellers   Europe - 4364   2013   £30

Taylor, Charles Edwin *An Island in the Sea.* St. Thomas: 1895. First edition, frontispiece and 10 plates, 8vo., very good in original plum pictorial cloth, gilt, all edges gilt, extremities slightly rubbed,.   Maggs Bros. Ltd.   1467 - 114   2013   £750

Taylor, Deems *The Nutcracker Suite.* Collins, n.d. early 1940's, First English edition, large square 8vo., original cloth backed decorated boards, edges little worn, one corner slightly creased, unpaginated, illustrations in color and monochrome, scarce.   R. F. G. Hollett & Son   Children's Books - 587   2013   £65

Taylor, Deems *Walt Disney's Fantasia.* New York: Simon and Schuster, 1940. First edition, folio, profusely illustrated in color and black and white, including 16 tipped in color illustrations, titlepage printed in red, black and blue, bound by Zaehnsdorf, circa 1977 for E. Joseph, full brown crushed levant morocco, front cover and smooth spine lettered in gilt after original binding lettering, board edges ruled gilt, turn-ins decoratively tooled in gilt, pale gray watered silk doublures and liners, all edges gilt, very fine.   David Brass Rare Books, Inc.   Holiday 2012 Chapter One - DV00420   2013 $1800

Taylor, Emily *Purples and Blues.* Groombridge & Sons, n.d. circa, 1860. 12mo., original blue wrappers trifle worn, woodcut illustrations.   R. F. G. Hollett & Son   Children's Books - 588   2013   £25

Taylor, George H. *An Exposition of the Swedish Movement Cure Embracing the History and Philosophy of the System of Medical Treatment...* New York: Fowler and Wells, 1860. Text illustrations, original green blindstamped cloth, cloth bit faded, otherwise very good.   James Tait Goodrich   S74 - 228   2013 $175

Taylor, Jane   1783-1824 *City Scenes or a Peep into London.* London: Harvey and Darton, 1828. Fourth edition, original blind panelled cloth gilt, rebacking in cloth, copper engraved title and 875 copper engraved illustrations on 29 leaves.   R. F. G. Hollett & Son   Children's Books - 590   2013   £450

Taylor, Jane   1783-1824 *Hymns for Infant Minds.* Jackson and Walford, 1840. Thirty-second edition, 12mo., original roan backed marbled boards, gilt, edges and corner little rubbed or worn, woodcut vignette frontispiece, some early leaves little fingered with some contemporary annotations, very scarce, this copy inscribed "Master W. B. Willyams Oct. 1841".   R. F. G. Hollett & Son   Children's Books - 591   2013   £45

Taylor, Jane   1783-1824   *Little Ann and Other Poems.*   London: George Routledge & Sons, n.d., 1883.   Tall 8vo., original cloth backed pictorial boards, scratched and soiled, pages 64, with 39 color illustrations and numerous endpieces, all by Greenaway, front flyleaf little creased and slightly marked, otherwise contents fine and clean.   R. F. G. Hollett & Son   Children's Books - 253   2013   £140

Taylor, Jane   1783-1824   *Meddlesome Matty and Other Poems for Infant Minds.*   London: John Lane Bodley Head, 1925.   First edition, original cloth backed pictorial boards, color illustrations, flyleaves lightly spotted, prize label on front pastedown.   R. F. G. Hollett & Son   Children's Books - 589   2013   £45

Taylor, Jane   1783-1824   *Original Poems for Infant Minds.*   London: Harvey & Darton, 1836.   New edition, 2 volumes, 12mo., original red blind stamped cloth, gilt both volumes neatly recased, nice, clean set, 2 engraved frontispieces.   R. F. G. Hollett & Son   Children's Books - 520   2013   £120

Taylor, John   *Reminiscences of Isaac Marsden, of Doncaster.*   Charles H. Kelly, 1902.   Ninth thousand, original blue cloth, gilt, portrait.   R. F. G. Hollett & Son   Wesleyan Methodism - 27   2013   £35

Taylor, Peter   *The Widows of Thornton.*   New York: Harcourt Brace, 1954.   First edition, inscribed by author in 1968, trace wear to board edge, else fine in rubbed, thus very good, dust jacket.   Ken Lopez Bookseller   159 - 182   2013 $850

Taylor, Philip Meadows   *Seeta.*   London: Henry S. King & Co., 1872.   First, second and second edition, 3 volumes, 32 page catalog volume I, final ad leaf volume III, original green cloth, decorated in black, unusual blocking of edition statement on spines of volumes II and III, near fine.   Jarndyce Antiquarian Booksellers   CCV - 258   2013   £750

Taylor, R. H., Mrs.   *The Airedale Fairy Stories.*   Keighley: Keighley printers, 1926.   First edition, original pictorial boards, illustrations and decorations by B. M. Cass, scarce.   R. F. G. Hollett & Son   Children's Books - 593   2013   £50

Taylor, Samuel   *Sistema Universale e Completo di Stenografia o sia Maniera di Scrivere in Compendio Applicabile a tutti gli'idiomi...*   Paris: for Emilio Amanti, 1809.   Engraved frontispiece and titlepage, 8 engraved plates, imprint cropped at foot of title, trifle spotted at end, 8vo., contemporary calf backed boards, faded, gilt lettering and tooling on spine, signed by author for authenticity, good.   Blackwell's Rare Books   B174 - 141   2013   £250

Taylor, Thomas   *The Life of William Cowper.*   London: Smith, Elder & Co., 1833.   Second edition, frontispiece, 16 page catalog, original dark green cloth, very slightly marked, very good.   Jarndyce Antiquarian Booksellers   CCIII - 617   2013   £60

Taylor, W. C.   *The Natural History of Society in the Barbarous and Civilized State.*   1840.   First edition, 2 volumes in 1, 8vo., front hinge broken, else good, cloth.   C. P. Hyland   261 - 817   2013   £120

Teffi, N. A.   *Baba Yaga.*   Paris: YMCA Press, 1932.   First edition, folio, pictorial wrappers, slightest of cover soil, else near fine, color lithographs by Nathalie Parain.   Aleph-Bet Books, Inc.   104 - 403   2013 $650

Tegg, Thomas   *Remarks on the Speech of Sergeant Talfourd.*   1837.   First edition, 23 pages, 8vo., disbound, very good.   C. P. Hyland   261 - 105   2013   £45

Temple, Bert   *A.O.F.B.: Do You Gollop Beer with Zest? If So! You are Unanimously Elected as a Member of Ye Ancient Order of Froth Blowers.*   London: Bert Temple, 1927.   Third edition, 24mo., stapled white cloth boards, owner name in provided place, boards little soiled and cocked, date stamped "Sept 14 1927" on front board, near very good, scarce.   Between the Covers Rare Books, Inc.   Cocktails, Etc. - 83944   2013 $200

Temple, J. H.   *History of the Town of Palmer, Massachusetts, Early Known as the Elbow Tracts...*   Palmer: published by the town, 1889.   First edition, 8vo., illustrations, 4 maps, publishers' cloth, hinges loose, good copy.   Second Life Books Inc.   183 - 375   2013 $200

Temple, John   *The Irish Rebellion; or an History of the Beginnings and First Progresse of the General Rebellion.. 1641.*   London: 1646.   First London edition, full calf, few brown spots on text, small corner torn from lower fore edge pages 89/90 with loss of few letters from marginal summary, else textually very good.   C. P. Hyland   261 - 818   2013   £1200

Temple, William   *Miscellanea, containing a Survey of the Constitutions and Interests of the Empire, Sweden, Denmark, Spain and Holland, France and Flanders.*   London: Jacob Tonson, 1697.   Fifth edition, 2 volumes in 1, 8vo., contemporary brown panelled calf, spine worn at head, internally clean and crisp.   J. & S. L. Bonham Antiquarian Booksellers   Europe - 8719   2013   £220

Temple, William   *Observations Upon the United Provinces of the Netherlands.*   London: for Jacob Tonson and Awnsham Churchill, 1693.   Sixth edition, contemporary black morocco, covers gilt in panel design, spine gilt in compartments, edges gilt, marbled endpapers, extremities rubbed, but nice, tight copy.   Joseph J. Felcone Inc.   Books Printed before 1701 - 85   2013 $300

Ten Little Niggers. London: Dean circa, 1904. 8vo., printed on cloth, some creasing, soil and discoloration, illustrations by R. James Williams, with color illustrations on every page, very scare. Aleph-Bet Books, Inc. 104 - 83 2013 $650

(Ten Little Niggers) Sma Negerpojkar. Stockholm: Ringens Florlag, 1932. Pictorial wrappers, light cover soil, very good+, color illustrations by Einar Nerman, scarce. Aleph-Bet Books, Inc. 104 - 84 2013 $850

Ten Little Pickaninnies. Kansas City: Faultless Starch circa, 1910. 16mo., pictorial wrappers, 15 pages, illustrations in blue on every page. Aleph-Bet Books, Inc. 105 - 87 2013 $225

Tench, Watkin *Letters Written in France to a Friend in London Between the Month of November 1794 and the Month of May 1795.* London: J. Johnson, 1796. First edition, 8vo., fine in period style full crimson morocco, spine gilt. Maggs Bros. Ltd. 1467 - 98 2013 £3750

Tench, Watkin *A Narrative of the Expedition to Botany Bay...* London: 1789. First edition, 8vo., later full red morocco, gilt, lacking half title. Maggs Bros. Ltd. 1467 - 96 2013 £12,000

Tench, Watkin *Voyage a la Baie Botanique...* Paris: Letellier, 1789. First French edition, folding map, 8vo., original paste paper wrappers, uncut, slightly worn, inner joints mended with plain paper some time ago, and ms. label added to spine, old signature and stamp of Albert Spitaels (probably the Dutch banker), housed in black cloth box, with rare map "Carte de le Baye Botanique et Harvres Adjacens...". Maggs Bros. Ltd. 1467 - 97 2013 £5000

Tenfold. Poems for Frances Horowitz. Knotting: Martin Booth, 1983. First edition, number 22 of 50 numbered copies signed by contributors, from total edition of 500, tall 8vo., original blue wrappers printed in deep red, fine. Maggs Bros. Ltd. 1442 - 100 2013 £450

Tenn, William *The Human Angle.* New York: Ballantine Books, 1956. First edition, small octavo, cloth. L. W. Currey, Inc. Utopian Literature: Recent Acquisitions (April 2013) - 140588 2013 $450

Tenn, William *The Human Angle.* New York: Ballantine Books, 1956. First edition, small octavo, cloth. L. W. Currey, Inc. Utopian Literature: Recent Acquisitions (April 2013) - 140052 2013 $1000

Tennyson, Alfred Tennyson, 1st Baron 1809-1892
Ballads and Other Poems. London: C. Kegan Paul and Co., 1880. First edition, with 3 pages ads at back, 8vo., original green cloth panelled in blind, presentation copy, inscribed by author for F. T. Palgrave, spine panel slightly rubbed, few soft creases in front free endpaper, otherwise very good, preserved in cloth clamshell box. James S. Jaffe Rare Books Fall 2013 - 143 2013 $2500

Tennyson, Alfred Tennyson, 1st Baron 1809-1892
Come Into the Garden. Boston: Lee and Shepard, 1880. First edition, small 4to., brown cloth backed boards, very good, truly scarce, black and white illustrations by Edmund Garrett, all edges gilt, color cover illustration by Maud Humphrey. Barnaby Rudge Booksellers Poetry 2013 - 021159 2013 $125

Tennyson, Alfred Tennyson, 1st Baron 1809-1892
Guinevere. New York: George Routledge, 1868. Large folio, green gilt decorated cloth, all edges gilt, slight wear to tips and spine ends, hinges neatly strengthened, very good+, 9 exquisitely detailed engraved plates by Dore, rare, excellent copy. Aleph-Bet Books, Inc. 105 - 199 2013 $800

Tennyson, Alfred Tennyson, 1st Baron 1809-1892 *The Holy Grail and Other Poems.* London: Strahan and Co., 1870. First edition, 2 pages ads at back, 8vo., original green cloth panelled in blind, presentation copy inscribed by author for Charles Ellis (1824-1908), booklabel of William Harrison Arnold, small newsprint clipping affixed verso of half titlepage, another to verso of first section-title, otherwise fine, full morocco slipcase. James S. Jaffe Rare Books Fall 2013 - 142 2013 $1750

Tennyson, Alfred Tennyson, 1st Baron 1809-1892
Poems. London: Routledge, Warne & Routledge, 1864. New edition, half title, frontispiece, illustrations, some occasional minor spotting, handsomely bound in contemporary full crushed green morocco over heavy boards, elaborate gilt borders and dentelles with red floral cornerpieces, raised bands, spine blocked in red and gilt, spine very slightly faded, contemporary inscription on leading blank, all edges gilt, very good. Jarndyce Antiquarian Booksellers CCV - 259 2013 £280

Tennyson, Alfred Tennyson, 1st Baron 1809-1892
Poems. printed... at the University Printing House Cambridge, 1974. 144/2000 copies, signed by artist, numerous wood engraved vignettes by Reynolds Stone, small folio original quarter maroon morocco, black leather label, orange cloth sides, black oval relief bust of author on front cover, board slipcase with printed label, fine. Blackwell's Rare Books 172 - 299 2013 £50

Tennyson, Alfred Tennyson, 1st Baron 1809-1892 *The Princess: a Medley.* London: Edward Moxon and Co., 1860. 218 x 147mm., 3 p.l., 188 pages, 26 illustrations engraved on wood by Dalziel, Green, Thomas and E. Williams from drawings by Daniel Maclise, R.A., sumptuous dark green morocco, very densely gilt intricately inlaid and adorned with jewels by Sangorski & Sutcliffe (stamp-signed), covers with diapered central panel enclosed by wide and ornate frame of inlaid brown and green strapwork on heavily stippled gilt ground accented with leafy fronds of gold, inner edge of frame punctuated at corners and on sides by dozen lotus blossoms of purple and green morocco, upper cover with large central medallion framed by green blue and brown strapwork with knots at head and foot, with a total of 6 cabochon sapphires and the frame inset set with 10 cabochon emeralds, medallion filled with swirling gilt vines, tiny red morocco berries and flowers on very densely stippled ground, whole with dramatically superimposed "A T" monogram of inlaid green morocco at center, lower cover with similar central medallion in which red dots of inlaid morocco take place of gemstones and centerpiece is gilt quatrefoil with inlaid circles of green morocco, raised bands, spine richly gilt in compartments with inlaid brown strapwork, gilt leaves, red morocco berries, much gilt stippling, chestnut brown morocco doublures inside wide green morocco frame decorated with plain dotted gilt rules and floral spray cornerpieces of inlaid lavender flowers, red hearts and gilt rose leaves, panel of front doublure with sunken scalloped oval medallion containing a portrait of poet on ivory under glass, this encircled by wide, thickly gilt collar with 10 cabochon turquoises, near doublure with similar sunken panel featuring a large floral spray of roses and tulips in gilt and inlaid morocco within inlaid strapwork frame, whole surrounded by wide band of heavy gilt, brown watered silk endleaves, edges gilt, gauffered and painted, in delicate diapered floral pattern, in matching straight grain morocco solander box lined with felt (slightly scuffed, with front joint expertly renewed), occasional mild foxing but dazzling copy in exceptionally fine condition. Phillip J. Pirages 61 - 144 2013 $35,000

Tennyson, the Brothers *Poems by Two Brothers.* London: printed by R. and R. Clark; Edinburgh for Macmillan and Co., 1893. Large paper limited edition, 10 pages of facsimiles at end, royal 8vo., contemporary red morocco by Zaehnsdorf with their exhibition stamp, single gilt fillet borders on sides enclosing an inner border of leafy tendrils, interstices filled with gilt dots, area widening at foot and incorporating 3 onlaid flower heads in darker red, both covers lettered gilt in fancy 'Japanese' style, spine similarly decorated but conventionally lettered, gilt inner dentelles, top edge gilt, others uncut, short cracked at head of upper joint, very good. Blackwell's Rare Books B174 - 13   2013   £1500

Terentius Afer, Publius *Comoediae ad Optimorum Exemplarium Fidem Recensitae.* Cambridge: Typis Academicis, impensis Jacobi Tonson, 1701. 4to., frontispiece, some light spotting and toning, bookplate removed from title verso with corresponding dampmark visbile on recto, blank corner of one leaf torn, modern quarter calf, marbled boards, spine lettered gilt. Unsworths Antiquarian Booksellers 28 - 53   2013   £275

Terentius Afer, Publius *The Comedies of Terence.* London: printed for T. Becket and P. A. De Hodnt, 1765. First edition of this translation, 4to., engraved frontispiece and additional 8 engraved plates, toned and lightly spotted, contemporary mottled and polished calf, spine divided by raised bands, orange morocco label, edges speckled red, rubbed and scratched, corners worn, joints just cracking. Unsworths Antiquarian Booksellers 28 - 54   2013   £300

Terentius Afer, Publius *Terence in English.* Cantabrigiae: ex officina Iohannis legat, 1607. Second edition of Richard Bernard's translation, 4to., first and last leaf mounted, small marginal wormhole to last half, large dampmark to first few leaves, occasional other marks, later speckled calf, rubbed, spine gilt but now rubbed and darkened, some wear to endcaps, spine label defective, joints cracking, Latin quotation to front endpaper, ownership inscription of S. Bateman and Jacob Bishop. Unsworths Antiquarian Booksellers 28 - 52   2013   £950

Terrell, Mary Church *The Progress of Colored Women.* New York: Congregational Rooms, 1898. First edition, small 12mo., self wrappers, stapled, sheets tanned, small tear to upper corner of last leaf. M & S Rare Books, Inc. 95 - 27   2013 $650

The Terrific Register; or Record of Crimes, Judgments, Providences and Calamaties. London: Sherwood and Co., printed by T. Richardson, 1825. First edition, 2 volumes, general woodcut titles, handsomely rebound in half calf, blank labels. Jarndyce Antiquarian Booksellers CCV - 260   2013   £750

The Testament of Charlotte B. Marlborough: Libanus Press, 1988. XXXII/L copies (of an edition of 220), printed on Amtruda handmade paper and signed by editor, 7 superb wood engravings by Richard Shirley Smith, all printed in mauve, crown 8vo., original quarter mauve morocco, backstrip printed in silver, pale grey boards, covers printed in black with overall design by Shirley Smith, also printed in mauve, white silk marker, top edge gilt, tail edge untrimmed, pale grey linen box, backstrip blocked in silver, fine. Blackwell's Rare Books 172 - 297   2013   £150

Tetlow, Richard John *An Historical Account of the Borough of Pontrefact in the County of York and the Definition of a Borough in General...* Leeds: printed by G. Wright, 1769. 8vo., disbound, hole to inner blank margin of titlepage. Jarndyce Antiquarian Booksellers CCIV - 294   2013   £150

Tevis, Walter *The Man Who Fell to Earth.* Greenwich: Gold Medal Books, 1963. First edition, paperback original, small ink stroke to top edge, else fine, unread, scarce thus. Between the Covers Rare Books, Inc. Sci-Fi, Fantasy & Horror - 78408 2013 $100

Thacher, James 1754-1844 *A Military Journal During the American Revolutionary War...* Boston: 1823. First edition, 8vo., 603 pages, contemporary three quarter calf, neatly rebacked, title browned, but very nice. M & S Rare Books, Inc. 95 - 363 2013 $525

Thacher, James 1754-1844 *Observations on Hydrophobia.* Plymouth: published by Joseph Avery, 1812. 302 pages, one hand colored plate, original blue sugar boards with tan paper spine, spine shows wear about head and tail, text browned, uncut, nice protective linen case, black morocco spine label. James Tait Goodrich 75 - 199 2013 $495

Thackeray, William Makepeace 1811-1863 *The History of Pendennis.* printed by W. S. Cowell, 1961. 1411/1500 sets, 32 full page color printed illustrations by Charles Stewart, titlepage printed in black and blue, 8vo., original light yellow cloth, backstrips gilt lettered on blue grey ground, covers including backstrips, decorative design blocked in blind overall, tissue jackets, board slipcase, fine. Blackwell's Rare Books B174 - 362 2013 £60

Thackeray, William Makepeace 1811-1863 *The Virginians.* London: Bradbury and Evans, 1857-1859. First edition, (with 'actresses' instead of 'ancestresses' on page 207), 222 x 142mm., original printed yellow paper wrappers, housed in red linen chemises inside two very fine red crushed morocco pull-off cases, numerous illustrations in text and 48 plates by Thackeray, as called for, chemise flaps with bookplate of John (i.e. James) A. Spoor, signed "Emery Walker" in the plate and dated 1921, mild soiling to wrappers (only No. 1 significantly affected), two covers neatly reattached, another with renewed fore edge of 8 plates little browned around edges, occasional minor foxing or short marginal tears, other trivial defects, still excellent set, fresh and generally well preserved, without any of the usual wretchedness afflicting this item, having been well protected at least during the last 90 years by the attractive morocco boxes. Phillip J. Pirages 63 - 472 2013 $1250

Thackeray, William Makepeace 1811-1863 *The Works.* London: Smith, Elder & Co., 1869-1886. First collected edition, 222 x 146mm., 24 volumes, 436 plates, extremely pleasing three quarter morocco handsomely gilt by Root & Son (stamp signed), raised bands, spines craefully gilt in compartments with central floral spray inside a lozenge of small tools, whole framed by scrolling cornerpieces and fleuron side ornaments, marbled boards and newer(?) marbled endpapers, top edge gilt, half the volumes unopened, leather vaguely soiled, few small marginal tears from rough opening, other trivial defects, quite pretty set in early fine condition, lustrous bindings with only very slightest wear and text with just minor signs of use. Phillip J. Pirages 63 - 463 2013 $1800

Thackwray, Jerome *The History of Jerome Thackwray, the Ivy House Poet.* Bradford: E. Smith, 1861. 24 pages, 12mo., original printed wrappers, slight edge browning, but very good, scarce. Ken Spelman Books Ltd. 73 - 62 2013 £30

Thaxter, Celia *An Island Garden.* Boston and New York: Houghton Mifflin, 1895. Color frontispiece, plates and illustrations, original light green cloth, decorated with 5 tall gilt flowers on front and back boards, very good. Jarndyce Antiquarian Booksellers CCV - 262 2013 £350

Thelma Gooch ABC. New York: Grosset & Dunlap, 1941. Folio, cloth backed stiff pictorial wrappers, fine, charming color lithographs, scarce. Aleph-Bet Books, Inc. 105 - 12 2013 $200

Theophrastus *(in Greek) Theophrastu Peri Pyros.* Paris: Adrien Turnebe, 1552. Editio princeps, titlepage, little soiled, trifle browned, pages 24, 4to., 20th century marbled boards, good. Blackwell's Rare Books Sciences - 120 2013 £1100

Thicknesse, Philip *A Year's Journey through France and Part of Spain.* N. Brown, 1778. Second edition, 2 volumes in one, 8vo., 10 plates, 3 music sheets, 3 pages with marginal tears, contemporary brown speckled calf, joint cracked, spine worn and rubbed. J. & S. L. Bonham Antiquarian Booksellers Europe - 9636 2013 £200

Thirty Prints of Places Mentioned in the Holy Scriptures Illustrative of the Fulfilment of Prophecy. London: Society for Promoting Christian Knowledge, printed by R. Clay, n.d. circa, 1860. First edition, First edition in large format, folio, title leaf and 30 hand colored copper plate line engravings, publisher's original cloth, superior issue with plates colored and imprint on each plate "Price 3/4dd. Plain; 2d Coloured". David Brass Rare Books, Inc. Holiday 2012 Chapter Two - DB 02078 2013 $1250

This is the House that Jack Built. London: Marcus Ward & Co., 1890. First edition, 8vo., wrappers, good+, 12 page booklet. Barnaby Rudge Booksellers Children 2013 - 021661 2013 $95

This Little Pig. London: Marcus Ward, n.d. circa, 1890. Stiff pictorial wrappers, die-cut in shape of a hand, faint stain inside cover, else very good+, charming chromolithographs on every page by E. Caldwell, rare.   Aleph-Bet Books, Inc.   105 - 544   2013 $350

Thom, Robert   *Wang Keaou Lwan Pih Neen Chang Han; or the Lasting Resentment of Miss Keaou Lwan Wang. A Chinese Tale.*   Canton: Canton Press Office, 1839.   First edition, one lithograph plate, small 4to., modern half calf, original front wrapper (worn and repaired) preserved and bound in, some wear throughout, margin of title stained and frayed, lower corner repaired, library stamp, title with presentation inscription from author's brothers "To the Manchester New College for D. Thom 1842".   Maggs Bros. Ltd.   1467 - 65   2013   £4200

Thomas A'Kempis   1380-1471   *The Christian's Pattern.*   J. Mason, 1842.   24mo., original straight grained morocco gilt, little rubbed, front flyleaf removed, pastedowns little damped.   R. F. G. Hollett & Son   Wesleyan Methodism - 63   2013   £25

Thomas A'Kempis   1380-1471   *Imitatio Christi.*   Augsburg: Gunther Zuiner before 5 June, 1473.   First edition, folio, two to six line Lombard initials (some pearled) supplied in red, few in brown ink, 19th century (circa 1840) dark blue morocco by J. Clarke (stamp signed), covers decoratively paneled in blind, spine decoratively tooled in blind and lettered in gilt in compartments, board edges and turn-ins ruled in gilt, all edges gilt, marbled endpapers, tiny portion of upper blank corner of fol. 8 renewed, upper blank corner of fol. 22 renewed, small portion of lower blank corner of folio 49 renewed, few additional minor marginal repairs, few marginal wormholes or wormtracks, those in lower gutter throughout, and in upper margin of first twenty-nine leaves neatly filled, few leaves with faint marginal dampstaining, overall, wonderful copy.   Heritage Book Shop   50th Anniversary Catalogue - 100   2013 $200,000

Thomas Aquinas, Saint   *Selections from His Works.*   New York: printed by W. and J. Mackay for the Limited Editions Club, 1969.   89/1500 copies, signed by artist, 19 wood engraved medallions and lettering blocks by Reynolds Stone, all printed in grey, 4to., original light grey cloth, overall blindstamped Crusader cross pattern to covers, backstrip gilt lettered, board slipcase with black cotton pull, fine.   Blackwell's Rare Books   B174 - 359   2013   £50

Thomas Aquinas, Saint   *Opus Aureum Sancti Tome de Aquino sup Quator Euangelia Nuperrime Reuisuz...*   Venice: Octavianus Scotus, 1521.   4to., woodcut at head of titlepage, some partially removed MS below, some woodcut initials and device at end, wax blot to ff. 185-6 also visible on adjacent pages but not obscuring text, slight marginal worming from f 269 onwards, intermittent dampstaining to lower corner of margins, occasional spotting, ff. 45-6 with small losses to lower margin not affecting text, small very neat paper repairs to first and last few leaves, neatly rebound in vellum with earlier vellum laid down, retaining spine with large ink title, few wormholes and several sums in old hand to lower board, endpapers replaced, scarce.   Unsworths Antiquarian Booksellers   28 - 65   2013   £950

Thomas, David Hurst   *Columbian Consequences. Archaeological and Historical Perspectives on the Spanish Borderlands.*   Washington: Smithsonian Institution Press, 1989.   1990. 1991. Second printing of volume 1, first printings of volumes 2 and 3, 3 volumes, photos, text drawings, maps, publisher's cloth, very fine, pictorial dust jackets.   Argonaut Book Shop   Recent Acquisitions June 2013 - 282   2013 $250

Thomas, Dylan Marlais   1914-1953   *A Child's Christmas in Wales.*   New York: New Directions, 1969.   Limited to only 100 numbered copies printed at Thistle Press, signed by artist, 2 volumes, text in leather backed buckram, plates in folio cloth portfolio, 5 full page wood engravings by Fritz Echenberg, portfolio contains separate suite of plates in larger format, signed by artist, rare special edition.   Aleph-Bet Books, Inc.   105 - 557   2013 $2500

Thomas, Dylan Marlais   1914-1953   *Deaths and Entrances. Poems.*   London: J. M. Dent & Sons Ltd., 1946.   First edition, one of 3000 copies, 12mo., original orange cloth, dust jacket, very fine.   James S. Jaffe Rare Books   Fall 2013 - 144   2013 $1500

Thomas, Dylan Marlais   1914-1953   *18 Poems.*   Fortune Press, circa, 1942.   32 pages, 8vo., original brown morocco grain boards, backstrip gilt lettered, untrimmed, dust jacket faded in part, very good.   Blackwell's Rare Books   B174 - 303   2013   £100

Thomas, Dylan Marlais   1914-1953   *Letters to Vernon Watkins.*   Dent: Faber, 1957.   Proof copy, pencilled note "Proof only Publication 14 Nov 57", crown 8vo., original tan wrappers, front cover printed in black and with "Proof Copy" also printed across cover, dust jacket which stand little proud of proof and is little frayed, very good.   Blackwell's Rare Books   B174 - 395   2013   £65

Thomas, Dylan Marlais   1914-1953   *Collected Poems 1934-1952.*   London: Dent, 1952.   First edition, frontispiece, 8vo., original mid blue cloth, gilt lettered backstrip, price clipped dust jacket, trifle chipped and wine stained on rear panel, short tear to front fold, very good, inscribed by author to his American agent John Malcolm Brinnin.   Blackwell's Rare Books   B174 - 304   2013   £2500

Thomas, Dylan Marlais   1914-1953   *Quite Early One Morning.*   Dent, 1954.   First edition, frontispiece, foolscap 8vo., original light blue cloth, backstrip gilt lettered, dust jacket with just touch of rubbing and one short tear, very good.   Blackwell's Rare Books   B174 - 306   2013   £60

Thomas, Dylan Marlais   1914-1953   *Twenty-Six-Poems.*   Printed at the Officina Bodoni for James Laughlin and J. M. Dent, 1949.   First English edition, 37/60 copies (of an edition of 150) signed by author, printed in black on Fabriano handmade paper with press mark printed in red, small folio, original quarter cream canvas, printed label on backstrip which is just at touch browned, white boards closely patterned overall in black and green, untrimmed, some wear to board slipcase, near fine.   Blackwell's Rare Books   172 - 304   2013   £3000

Thomas, Edward   *The Pocket Book of Poems and Songs for the Open Air.*   London: E. Grant Richards, 1907.   First edition, small 8vo., original blue decorated cloth, Rupert Brooke's copy, signed in pencil by him, there is also a pencilled correction to index, changing Ramal to De La Mare and this is almost certainly in Brooke's hand, covers slightly worn, otherwise very good.   Maggs Bros. Ltd.   1460 - 143   2013   £950

Thomas, Frederick   *Humorous and Other Poetic Pictures, Legends and Stories of Devon.*   London: W. Kent & Co., 1883.   First edition, Original red decorated cloth, slightly dulled and marked, inscription "May B. Wood - from Mother Ot. 1891".   Jarndyce Antiquarian Booksellers   CCV - 263   2013   £30

Thomas, Jerry   *The Bon Vivant's Companion or How to Mix Drinks.*   New York: Alfred A. Knopf, 1928.   First edition thus, one of 160 numbered copies, signed by editor, Herbert Asbury, cloth, gilt decorated pastepaper boards, fine in lightly worn, near fine slipcase with paper spine label, beautiful copy, exceptionally uncommon.   Between the Covers Rare Books, Inc.   Cocktails, Etc. - 98301   2013 $2000

Thomas, Louis   *Nos Elegances & la Mode Masculine.*   Paris: Societe Generale d'Impression, August 1, 1911, December 1, 1911.   Five issues, probably all published, small folio, each with 32 pages profusely illustrated in half tone, lithographic wrappers printed in two colors, clean and fresh, rare.   Marlborough Rare Books Ltd.   218 - 104   2013   £1750

Thomas, Lowell   *Doolittle: a Biography.*   Garden City: Doubleday, 1976.   8vo., 67 illustrations, quarter gilt stamped black cloth over maroon cloth, dust jacket rear slightly soiled, signed and inscribed from Doolittle to Larry Seyferth in ink, very good.   Jeff Weber Rare Books   171 - 108   2013 $200

Thomas, Myfanwy   *Letters from Myfanwy.*   printed privately (at the Whittington Press), 2009.   One of 50 copies (of an edition of 100), printed on Kozo handmade paper in black with acknowledgement at end printed in green, signed by Masatsuga Ohtake in Japanese calligraphy and stamped with his seal, 20 small wood engraved designs by Hellmuth Weissenborn printed in green or yellow, 8vo., original cinnamon morocco, backstrip gilt lettered, marbled endpapers by Christopher Rowlatt, untrimmed, fine; with a Portfolio of 20 proof pulls of the engravings, all loosely inserted in grey paper portfolio, book and portfolio within board slipcase, fine.   Blackwell's Rare Books   172 - 319   2013   £335

Thomas, R. S.   *The Mountains.*   New York: printed at the Rampant Lions Press for Chilmark editions, 1968.   First edition, 14/240 copies on Wookey Hole mouldmade paper, each of the 10 wood engravings placed on separate page, titlepage printed in cinnamon and black, small folio, original dark green linen backed pale green boards with overall illustration blocked in dark green, backstrip gilt lettered, untrimmed, board slipcase, fine.   Blackwell's Rare Books   172 - 239   2013   £800

Thomas, Robert   *The Modern Practice of Physic, Exhibiting the Character, Causes, Symptoms, Prognostics, Morbid Appearances...*   New York: Collins and Co., 1817.   Thick 8vo., back cover detached, front cover lacking, some staining to latter sheets, notes laid in.   M & S Rare Books, Inc.   95 - 365   2013 $450

Thomas, Ross   *The Backup Men.*   New York: Morrow, 1971.   First edition, signed by author, fine in dust jacket with tiny closed tear at top of spine.   Mordida Books   81 - 597   2013 $200

Thomas, Ross   *The Brass Go-Between.*   London: Hodder & Stoughton, 1970.   First English edition, signed by author, fine in dust jacket with nicks at spine ends and along lower edge of front panel.   Mordida Books   81 - 505   2013 $150

Thomas, Ross   *Briarpatch.*   New York: Simon and Schuster, 1984.   First edition, fine in dust jacket.   Mordida Books   81 - 515   2013 $65

Thomas, Ross   *Cast a Yellow Shadow.*   New York: Morrow, 1967.   First edition, signed by author, fine in dust jacket.   Mordida Books   81 - 503   2013 $250

Thomas, Ross *The Fools in Town are on Our Side.*   New York: Morrow, 1971.   First American edition, fine in dust jacket.   Mordida Books   81 - 508   2013 $200

Thomas, Ross *The Highbinders.*   New York: Morrow, 1973.   First edition, uncorrected proof, small dampspot on front wrapper, owner stamp, very good in wrappers, signed by author, scarce format.   Between the Covers Rare Books, Inc.   Mystery & Detective Fiction - 2609   2013 $210

Thomas, Ross *The Highbinders.*   New York: Morrow, 1974.   First edition, inscribed by author, fine in dust jacket.   Mordida Books   81 - 511   2013 $175

Thomas, Ross *If You Can't Be Good.*   New York: Morrow, 1973.   First edition, fine in dust jacket.   Mordida Books   81 - 510   2013 $150

Thomas, Ross *The Money Harvest.*   New York: Morrow, 1975.   First edition, small spot on bottom of page edges, otherwise fine in dust jacket with short closed tear.   Mordida Books   81 - 512   2013 $90

Thomas, Ross *No Questions Asked.*   New York: Morrow, 1976.   First edition, signed by author Oct. 7 1987, fine in lightly soiled dust jacket with tiny staining at top of spine.   Mordida Books   81 - 513   2013 $150

Thomas, Ross *The Procane Chronicle.*   New York: Morrow, 1972.   First edition, signed by author, very good in dust jacket with considerable internal dampstaining, some staining and wrinkling on back panel, chipped spine ends, some short closed tears, wear at corners.   Mordida Books   81 - 509   2013 $85

Thomas, Ross *Protocol for a Kidnapping.*   New York: Morrow, 1971.   First edition, signed by author, very fine in dust jacket.   Mordida Books   81 - 506   2013 $400

Thomas, Ross *The Seersucker Whipsaw.*   New York: Morrow, 1967.   First edition, name on front endpaper and small label removed from same, otherwise fine in dust jacket.   Mordida Books   81 - 502   2013 $400

Thomas, Ross *The Singapore Wink.*   New York: Morrow, 1969.   First edition, signed by author, fine in dust jacket with crease on front and rear flap.   Mordida Books   81 - 504   2013 $300

Thomas, Ross *Twilight at Mac's Place.*   New York: Mysterious Press, 1990.   First edition, one of 26 lettered specially bound copies signed by author, very fine in slipcase, without dust jacket as issued.   Mordida Books   81 - 516   2013 $100

Thomas, Ross *Yellow-Dog Contract.*   New York: Morrow, 1977.   First edition, signed by author, fine in dust jacket.   Mordida Books   81 - 514   2013 $150

Thompson, Edward Maunde *An Introduction to Greek and Latin Palaeography.*   Oxford: 1912.   First edition, deluxe binding,, plates, very good in contemporary morocco backed, decorative cloth boards, gilt lettered spine, slight rubbing, top edge gilt.   Ken Spelman Books Ltd.   75 - 164   2013   £100

Thompson, Francis *Shelley.*   London: Burns & Oates, 1911.   Twelfth thousand, 8vo., original brown buckram, marked and spine darkened, but very good, inscribed by Dora Carrington.   Maggs Bros. Ltd.   1460 - 160   2013   £500

Thompson, Francis *Works.*   London: Burns & Oates, 1913.   First edition, 211 x 143mm., 3 volumes, attractive contemporary olive brown crushed three quarter morocco over green cloth boards, raised bands, spines gilt in compartments formed by plain and dotted rules and trefoil cornerpieces, gilt titling, top edge gilt, other edges rough trimmed, each volume with different frontispiece, spines uniformly sunned to rich brown, occasional minor marginal foxing, otherwise fine set, clean and fresh internally and in appealing bindings with few signs of wear.   Phillip J. Pirages   63 - 467   2013 $275

Thompson, George *Christianity Versus Slavery, or a Report, Published in the 'Glasgow Angus' Newspaper November 8 1841, a Lecture Delivered at an Anti-Slavery Meeting in the City...*   Dublin: printed by W. Powell for the benefit of the Sisters of Charity, 1841.   Unopened in original cream wrappers, sewn as issued, fine.   Jarndyce Antiquarian Booksellers   CCV - 264   2013   £220

Thompson, George *A Sentimental Tour, Collected from a Variety of Occurrences from Newbiggin, near Penrith...*   Penrith: printed by Anthony Soulby for the author, 1798.   12mo., old splash mark to H12, ink note at foot of p. 234, uncut, recent boards, paper spine label, contemporary ownership name of Thos. Scott at head of titlepage and under author's name is presentation inscription, presumably from author to J. H. Allinson from his preceptor.   Jarndyce Antiquarian Booksellers   CCIV - 295   2013   £380

Thompson, Hunter S. *The Curse of Lono.*   New York: Bantam, 1983.   First edition, illustrations by Ralph Steadman, signed by artist with original full page caricature by him of Thompson, only issued in wrappers, near fine.   Ken Lopez Bookseller   159 - 183   2013 $350

Thompson, Hunter S. *Fear and Loathing in Las Vegas.*   New York: Random House, 1971.   First edition, signed by author, signed by Ralph Steadman with Steadman drawing and dated 3 May '95, about fine with minimal sunning to top of boards in near fine dust jacket with few creases to flaps.   Ed Smith Books   75 - 72   2013 $2750

Thompson, Hunter S. *Fire in the Nuts.* Woody Creek: Gonzo International/Steam Press, 2004. First edition, illustrations by Ralph Steadman, one of 150 numbered copies signed in full by author and artist (of a total edition of 176), quarter bound in black Asahi cloth with color illustrations to boards and black leather spine label stamped in gold, very fine.   Ed Smith Books   75 - 78   2013 $1500

Thompson, Hunter S. *The Great Shark Hunt. Gonzo Papers. Volume 1. Strange Tales from a Strange Time.* New York: Summit Books, 1979. First edition, signed by author in red, dated underneath 10/12/79, 602 pages, light foxing to all edges, otherwise very good, in very good plus dust jacket with few creases to front flap.   Ed Smith Books   75 - 75   2013 $850

Thompson, Hunter S. *Hell's Angels.* New York: Random House, 1967. First edition, laid in (loose) is bookplate signed by author, fine in near fine dust jacket with few minor edge tears (small piece of tape on verso).   Ed Smith Books   75 - 71   2013 $2250

Thompson, Hunter S. *Kingdom of Fear.* New York: Simon & Schuster, 2003. First edition, signed by author, as new in dust jacket, 8vo., xx, 354 pages.   By the Book, L. C.   36 - 58   2013 $600

Thompson, Hunter S. *Mistah Leary - He Dead.* San Francisco/New Orleans: X-Ray Book Co/Perdido Press, 1996. First edition, deluxe issue, being one of 26 lettered copies (of total edition of 326), front and rear grey wrappers foldout, on rear foldout is attached a scored simulated sheet of blotter acid printed in magneta on white sheet, fine.   Ed Smith Books   75 - 73   2013 $1250

Thompson, Hunter S. *"The Nonstudent Left." in The Nation September 27 1965.* New York: The Nation Co., 1965. Signed by author on front cover, mild age toning, else fine in stapled wrappers.   Ken Lopez Bookseller   159 - 184   2013 $450

Thompson, Hunter S. *Screwjack.* Santa Barbara: Neville, 1991. First edition, one of only 26 lettered copies, deluxe issue signed in full by author on colophon page, small book, 38 pages, brown leather with gilt decoration, issued without dust jacket, fine.   Ed Smith Books   75 - 74   2013 $3000

Thompson, J. Harry *Report of Columbia Hospital for Women and Lying-in Asylum.* Washington: GPO, 1873. 19 plates, tables, occasional light foxing, modern maroon cloth, gilt spine, new endleaves, very good.   Jeff Weber Rare Books   172 - 56   2013 $350

Thompson, Jim *A Hell of a Woman.* New York: Lion, 1954. First edition, paperback edition, unread copy, fine in crisp wrappers with just touch of rubbing at extremities.   Between the Covers Rare Books, Inc.   Mystery & Detective Fiction - 24228   2013 $315

Thompson, Jim *King Blood.* New York: Armchair Detective, 1993. First hardcover edition, one of 26 lettered copies signed by Ellroy, very fine in slipcase without dust jacket.   Mordida Books   81 - 517   2013 $100

Thompson, Jim *Ni Mas Ni Menos Que un Asesinato. (Nothing More than Murder).* Mexico City: Editorial Novaro-Mexico, 1958. First Mexican edition, probably first Spanish language edition, pages bit browned, spine slightly sunned, spine edges little rubbed, still handsome, very good plus in wrappers as issued.   Between the Covers Rare Books, Inc.   Mystery & Detective Fiction - 64287   2013 $275

Thompson, Jim *Roughneck.* New York: Lion Book, 1954. First edition, paperback original, little edgewear along edges of front wrapper, still especially fresh, near fine.   Between the Covers Rare Books, Inc.   Mystery & Detective Fiction - 314626   2013 $250

Thompson, John *The Tule Breakers.* Stockton: Stockton Corral of Westerners and the University of the Pacific, 1983. First trade edition, one of 2450 copies, signed by Ed Dutra, photos, maps, plans, dark brown leatherette, very fine, pictorial dust jacket.   Argonaut Book Shop   Recent Acquisitions June 2013 - 283   2013 $90

Thompson, Mildred *The Gilly Willies.* Hamburg: Mildred Thompson/Franz Berg, 1960. First edition, cloth and illustrated paper covered boards, little wear to paper covering the bottom of boards, near fine in very good plus dust jacket with bit of tanning and few faint stains on spine, inscribed by author.   Between the Covers Rare Books, Inc.   165 - 25   2013 $4500

Thompson, R. A. *The Russian Settlement in California, Fort Ross....* Oakland: Biobooks, 1951. First edition, limited to 700 copies, two-tone black and red cloth, fine.   Argonaut Book Shop   Recent Acquisitions June 2013 - 284   2013 $75

Thompson, Ruth Plumly *The Cowardly Lion of Oz.* Chicago: Reilly & Lee, 1945. 8vo., brown cloth, vey nice later printing with no color plates, very good.   Barnaby Rudge Booksellers   Children 2013 - 021169   2013 $65

Thompson, Ruth Plumly *Grampa in Oz.* Chicago: Reilly & Lee, 1924. First edition, first state with perfect type on page 171 numeral, 189 last worn penultimate line (H-G XVIII), 8vo., brick red cloth, pictorial paste-on, occasional finger soil hinges discreetly strengthened, very good+, illustrations by J. R. Neill with 12 color plates.   Aleph-Bet Books, Inc.   104 - 55   2013 $600

Thompson, Ruth Plumly *The Perhappsy Chaps.* Chicago: Volland, 1918. First edition, 8vo., pictorial boards, few tiny pinholes on rear outer joints, else very good-fine, illustrations by Arthur Henderson with beautiful pictorial covers, pictorial endpapers plus many lovely full and partial page color illustrations, rare.   Aleph-Bet Books, Inc.   105 - 558   2013 $975

Thompson, Ruth Plumly *Purple Prince of Oz.* Chicago: Reilly & Lee, 1932. First edition, first state, 4to., deep purple cloth, pictorial paste-on, tiny rub area on rear corner, else fine in very good+ dust jacket slightly frayed ($1.75 price and ads on title), illustrations by J. R. Neill, beautiful copy.   Aleph-Bet Books, Inc.   104 - 53   2013 $2000

Thompson, Ruth Plumly *Tommy Frog and the Pirate and Tommy Frog Goes Fishing.* N.P.: Donohue, n.d. circa, 1920. 4to., pictorial wrappers, slightest of soil, near fine, illustrations by Charles Coll, 6 full color illustrations, sever page half tones and color covers, very scarce.   Aleph-Bet Books, Inc.   105 - 559   2013 $350

Thompson, Ruth Plumly *The Wishing Horse of Oz.* Chicago: Reilly & Lee, 1935. First edition (H-G XXIX), 4to., green cloth, pictorial paste-on, corner of cover plate rubbed, else fine in very good+ dust jacket (correct price and ads through this title, frayed at head of spine), cover plate, 12 beautiful color plates, black and whites in text by J. R. Neill, beautiful copy.   Aleph-Bet Books, Inc.   104 - 54   2013 $1750

Thomsen, Vilhelm *The Relations Between Ancient Russia and Scandinavia and the Origin of the Russian State.* Oxford: James Parker, 1877. First edition, 8vo., original brown blindstamped cloth, blindstamped on titlepage, very good, unopened.   J. & S. L. Bonham Antiquarian Booksellers   Europe - 8822   2013   £100

Thomson, Alexander *The Choice.* Edinburgh: printed for William Creech, 1788. 4to., small hole to D1 shaving one letter, final page dusted, some ocasional foxing, expertly bound in recent quarter calf, marbled boards, vellum tips, gilt banded spine, red morocco label.   Jarndyce Antiquarian Booksellers   CCIV - 296   2013   £380

Thomson, Charles *An Enquiry into the Causes of the Alienation of the Delaware and Shawanee Indians from the British Interest and into the Measures Taken for Recovering the Friendship.* London: J. Wilkie, 1759. First edition, folding engraved map, 8vo., uncut, modern half morocco, chemise and half morocco slipcase.   Maggs Bros. Ltd.   1467 - 129   2013   £8500

Thomson, Christine Campbell *Not at Night.* London: Selwyn & Blount, n.d., 1925. First edition, octavo, original red boards, front and spine panels stamped in black.   L. W. Currey, Inc.   Fall Sampler Sept. 2013 - 146514   2013 $2250

Thomson, David F. E. *Interim General Report of Preliminary Expedition to Arnhem Land, Northern Territory of Australia 1935-1936.* Canberra: Dept. of the Interior, 1936. Folio, 2 colored maps, grey paper wrappers, some staining to front and back resulting from rusted hinges, slightly bumped, contents, 49 pages.   Maggs Bros. Ltd.   1467 - 99   2013   £1250

Thomson, James 1700-1748 *Coriolanus.* London: for A. Millar, 1749. First edition, half title present, contemporary calf, neatly rebacked, paper flaw on B6 extending one inch into text, else fine, clean copy, booklabel of T. R. Francis.   Joseph J. Felcone Inc.   English and American Literature to 1800 - 23   2013 $150

Thomson, James 1700-1748 *Edward and Eleonora.* London: printed for the author and sold by A. Millar, 1739. First edition, marked up with cuts, substitutions and additions, in contemporary hand, bit of thumbing, soiling and occasional foxing, 8vo., later blue paper wrappers (frayed) formerly disbound (traces of calf on spine) some fore-edges uncut, others with manuscript notes very slightly cropped, good.   Blackwell's Rare Books   B174 - 153   2013   £2000

Thomson, James 1700-1748 *Liberty, a Poem.* London: for A. Millar, 1735-1736. First editions of all five parts, 4to., lacks final ad leaf in part 1 and half titles in parts 2-5, later half calf, first title leaf dust soiled, final three leaves with repairs in lower corner affecting few letters, booklabel of T. R. Francis, lacking one ad leaf and four half titles.   Joseph J. Felcone Inc.   English and American Literature to 1800 - 24   2013 $750

Thomson, James 1700-1748 *The Poetical Works.* London: printed for L. J. Higham, 1803. 12mo., some slight foxing, very good, contemporary quarter calf, marbled boards, vellum tips.   Ken Spelman Books Ltd.   75 - 56   2013   £75

Thomson, James 1700-1748 *The Seasons.* London: printed for A. Millar, 1752. 4 engraved plates, titlepage vignette, some light browning, contemporary mottled calf, raised and gilt banded spine, red morocco label, hinges cracked but firm, head of spine worn, corners little bumped.   Jarndyce Antiquarian Booksellers   CCIV - 297   2013   £65

Thomson, James 1700-1748 *The Seasons, with His Life and a Complete Index and Glossary.* London: printed by and for J. Chapman, 1795. 8vo., 5 plates, further illustrations in text, bound without final ad leaf found in some copies, dark brown calf, gilt spine and borders, marbled endpapers, neatly rebacked, corners worn, front hinge repaired with marbled paper though just starting to crack, gift inscription to Henrietta Marshall from Evelyn Marshall Aug. 6 '07 to prelim blank.   Unsworths Antiquarian Booksellers   28 - 135   2013   £80

Thomson, James 1700-1748 *The Seasons.* London: P. W. Tomkins, 1797. Magnificent edition, imperial folio, frontispiece and dedication leaf, five full page engravings, 10 head and tailpieces and five vignettes, extra illustrated with four later engraved full page plates, each with vignette, beautifully bound by Riviere in full dark red levant morocco, boards ruled in gilt tooling, spine elaborately stamped and lettered in gilt, gilt dentelles, all edges gilt, marbled endpapers, previous owner's bookplate, some restoration to outer hinges, overall beautiful copy. Heritage Book Shop Holiday Catalogue 2012 - 150 2013 $3500

Thomson, Joseph John *Conduction of Electricity through Gases.* Cambridge: at the University Press, 1903. First edition, trifle browned, emanating from the pastedowns and flyleaves 8vo., uncut in original green cloth, gilt lettered on upper cover and spine, trifling signs of wear, very good. Blackwell's Rare Books Sciences - 121 2013 £275

Thomson, June *Holmes and Watson.* London: Constable, 1995. First edition, fine in dust jacket. Mordida Books 81 - 157 2013 $90

Thomson, William *The Land and the Book or Biblical Illustrations Drawn from the Manners and Customs...* New York: Harper, 1880. Reprint, thick 8vo., green cloth stamped in gilt, black, red, front hinge little tender but very good, clean copy. Second Life Books Inc. 183 - 379 2013 $145

Thorburn, Grant *Forty Years' Residence in America...* Boston: Russell, Odiorne & Metcalf, 1834. First edition, publisher's green pebble grain cloth, leather spine label, 264 pages, ownership signature of author Susan Anne Livingston Ridley Sedgwick, light scattered foxing, near fine,. Between the Covers Rare Books, Inc. New York City - 292192 2013 $400

Thorburn, William *A Contribution to the Surgery of the Spinal Cord.* London: Charles Griffin, 1889. Original red cloth, light wear with some soiling and marking of covers. James Tait Goodrich 75 - 200 2013 $695

Thoreau, Henry David 1817-1862 *Walden; or Life in the Woods.* Boston: Ticknor & Fields, 1854. First edition, 2000 copies published July 12 1854, covers lightly spotted, book recased some time ago by binder who could have done a better job putting the book back together, signatures in middle sprung, 1855 pencil signature of H. W. Stinson from Cypress Hills, Long Island, i.e. Brooklyn, morocco backed slipcase, 12mo., original lined decorated brown cloth, rebacked and recased, old back laid down, minor rubbing at corners. Howard S. Mott Inc. 262 - 147 2013 $3000

Thoreau, Henry David 1817-1862 *Wild Apples.* Worcester: Achille J. St. Onge, 1956. Limited to 950 copies, 7.5 x 5.1 cm., full leather, gilt lettering on spine and both covers, designed by Bruce Rogers, from the collection of Donn W. Sanford. Oak Knoll Books 303 - 28 2013 $200

Thoreau, Henry David 1817-1862 *The Writings.* Boston and New York: Houghton Mifflin Co., 1906. One of 700 copies, 20 volumes, 104 black and white and 20 colored plates, mostly photogravures, with a portion of manuscript in Thoreau's hand, as called for in this edition; fine dark green three quarter morocco, marbled sides and endpapers, spines very handsomely gilt in animated compartments filed with floral stamps and stars, top edge gilt, other edges rough trimmed, most volumes unopened; spines faded uniformly and very slightly to a pleasing brown (just hint of fading to perimeter of covers), a total of four leaves with expertly repaired tears (one tear of four inches entering the text, the others smaller and marginal, and no loss in any case), otherwise very fine, bindings quite bright and virtually unworn and leaves without any significant signs of use, majority of text obviously never having been read. Phillip J. Pirages 63 - 468 2013 $18,000

Thorn, Ismay *Captain Geoff.* Wells, Gardner, Darton & Co. circa, 1894. 8vo., half title, frontispiece and plates, fine in most attractive contemporary gilt binding, floral decoration to boards and spines, all edges gilt. Ken Spelman Books Ltd. 75 - 148 2013 £120

Thorne, Kip S. *Black Holes and Time Warps.* New York: W. W. Martin, 1994. First edition, 8vo., 619 pages, near fine in like dust jacket. By the Book, L. C. 36 - 102 2013 $125

Thorne, Robert *Structural Iron and Steel 1850-1900.* Aldershot, et al: Ashgate/Variorum, 2000. 8vo., photos, illustrations, red cloth, gilt stamped cover and spine titles, Burndy bookplate, fine. Jeff Weber Rare Books 169 - 447 2013 $190

Thornhill, Bonnie *The Road to St. Ann's...* Sydney: St. Ann's Baddeck Waipu Twinning Society, 2007. Quarto, card covers black and white photo illustrations, fine, signed by editor. Schooner Books Ltd. 104 - 123 2013 $75

Three Famous New Songs Called Effect of Whisky, The Valley Below, Larry O'Gaff. Paisley: printed by and for G. Caldwell, circa, 1825. 8 pages, small 8vo., woodcut, very good, disbound. Ken Spelman Books Ltd. 75 - 85 2013 £30

Three Little Kittens. New York: Simon & Schuster, 1942. First edition, cloth backed pictorial boards, name in ownership box and faint erased name on edge of title, else fine, illustrations in color by Masha, scarce. Aleph-Bet Books, Inc. 105 - 279 2013 $300

Three Remarkable and Scarce Trials. viz. 1. The Trial Between Theophilus Cibber... and William Sloper... II. The Trial of Richard Lyddel, Es. for Criminal Conversation with Lady Abergavenny. III. The Trial of Col. Chartres for a Rape, Committed on the Body of Anne Bond, His Servant. London: printed by and for Isaac Holyroyd, 1764. 32 pages, 8vo., text with typographic head and tailpiece decoration for each trial, disbound.   Jarndyce Antiquarian Booksellers   CCIV - 299   2013   £650

Three Young Rats and Other Rhymes. New York: Museum of Modern Art, 1944. 1946. Limited to 3000 copies, large 4to., red cloth, fine in worn dust jacket, illustrations by Alexander Calder, numerous black and whites.   Aleph-Bet Books, Inc.   104 - 112   2013 $200

Thubron, Colin *Among the Russians.* London: William Heinemann, 1983. First edition, 8vo., ix, 212, original grey cloth, dust jacket, signed.   J. & S. L. Bonham Antiquarian Booksellers   Europe - 9806   2013   £45

Thubron, Colin *Journey into Cyprus.* London: Heinemann, 1975. First edition, 8vo., pages xi, 256, map, illustrations, original green cloth, dust jacket, very good.   J. & S. L. Bonham Antiquarian Booksellers   Europe - 9804   2013   £50

Thucydides *De Bello Peloponnesiaco Libri Octo.* Geneva: Excudebat Henricus Stephanus, 1564. First Estienne edition, folio, titlepage in red and black, dampstain to top margin (reaching down to 4th line of text), lower inner corner, some other light browning and spotting, few pencil marginal notes, library stamp of a school at Douai to title, old vellum, spine with six raised bands, red morocco lettering piece, possibly preserved from earlier binding in second compartment, rest with central gilt decorative lozenge, boards ruled with double gilt fillet, somewhat stained and since polished, joints just cracking, plain vellum patch, sometime applied over lower spine compartment, old note in Greek to flyleaf, sound.   Blackwell's Rare Books   172 - 140   2013   £1500

Thucydides *History of the Peloponnesian War.* Chelsea: printed at the Ashendene Press, 1930. One of 260 copies on paper (240 for sale), out of a total edition of 280 (257 for sale), folio, printed in black in Ptolemy type with 3 line initials at beginning of each chapter and larger initials and opening line of each of the 8 books designed by Graily Hewitt and printed in red, marginal chapter summaries also in red in Blado italic type, printer's mark D printed in black, publisher's white pigskin by W. H. Smith & Son Ltd., spine lettered gilt, raised bands, all edges gilt, spine very slightly darkened, overall very good.   Heritage Book Shop Holiday Catalogue 2012 - 4   2013 $4000

Thurman, Wallace *Fire!! Quarterly Devoted to the Younger Negro Artists Volume One Number One November 1926.* Metuchen: The Fire!! Press, 1982. Facsimile reprint, one of 1400 copies, fine in stapled pictorial wrappers in original mailing envelope.   Between the Covers Rare Books, Inc.   165 - 268   2013 $175

Thurston, Clara Bell *The Jingle of a Jap.* Boston: Caldwell, 1906. Small 4to., elaborately illustrated pictorial cloth with oriental design, fine in original box (soiled but sound and very good+), complete with original real Japanese doll in cloth dress that ties to cover of the book (doll has her feet repaired), illustrations by author, very rare with doll and box.   Aleph-Bet Books, Inc.   104 - 296   2013 $975

Thurston, Joseph *The Toilette.* printed for Benj. Motte, 1730. Second edition, 47 (1) pages, engraved frontispiece, titlepage printed in red and black and with typographic ornament, 19th century linen backed wrappers, little dusted.   Ken Spelman Books Ltd.   75 - 16   2013   £120

Thygesen, Helge *Black Swan. The Record Label of the Harlem Renaissance.* Nottingham: VJM Publications, 1996. First edition, illustrations, wrappers, fine.   Beasley Books   2013 - 2013 $100

Tickell, John *Church-Rules to the Church in Abingdon and Approved by Them.* Oxford: printed by L. Lichfield, 1656. First edition, browned and brittle at fore-edge, last leaf little waterstained, 4to., disbound, sound.   Blackwell's Rare Books   172 - 1   2013   £400

Tickell, Richard *Anticipation: containing the Substance of His M-----y's most Gracious Speech to both H-----e of C-----S on the Motion for the Address, and the Amendment.* London: printed for T. Becket, 1778. Without half title, ad leaf, 8vo., upper corner of final page stained, some tears to upper margins without loss, disbound.   Jarndyce Antiquarian Booksellers   CCIV - 298   2013   £45

Tidyman, Ernest *The Last Shaft.* London: Weidenfeld and Nicholson, 1975. First edition, dedication copy, signed by author 3 Feb. 1975 beneath printed dedication for Judith Loth, recipient was Judy Oppenheimer Loth, uncommon.   Between the Covers Rare Books, Inc.   Mystery & Detective Fiction - 98993   2013 $1000

Tidyman, Ernest *Shaft.* New York: Macmillan, 1970. First edition, tiny dot at top edge, else fine in fine dust jacket, scarce in this condition.   Between the Covers Rare Books, Inc.   Mystery & Detective Fiction - 102112   2013 $200

Tifft, Wilton *Ellis Island.*   New York: W. W. Norton and Co., 1971.   First edition, oblong small quarto, fine in near fine dust jacket with short tear on rear panel.   Between the Covers Rare Books, Inc.   New York City - 293957   2013 $75

Tilman, H. W. *Mischief Among the Penguins.*   Rupert Hart Davis, 1961.   First edition, original cloth, gilt, dust jacket (small chip and repair to reverse), pages 192, 20 plates and 4 maps and diagrams.   R. F. G. Hollett & Son   Polar Exploration - 74   2013   £85

Tilman, H. W. *Mischief Goes South.*   Hollis & Carter, 1968.   First edition, original cloth, gilt, dust jacket little worn and chipped, 190 pages, 18 plates, 3 maps and diagrams.   R. F. G. Hollett & Son   Polar Exploration - 75   2013   £85

Tilman, H. W. *Mischief in Patagonia.*   Travel Book Club, 1957.   Original cloth, dust jacket little chipped and soiled, 2 maps.   R. F. G. Hollett & Son   Polar Exploration - 76   2013   £30

Tilman, H. W. *Triumph and Tribulation.*   Lymington: Nautical Pub. Co., 1977.   First edition, original cloth, gilt, dust jacket, map and illustrations.   R. F. G. Hollett & Son   Polar Exploration - 77   2013   £35

Tilney, Frederick *The Brain from Ape to Man.*   New York: Paul B. Hoeber, 1928.   First edition, 2 volumes, 4to., original black cloth, gilt lettered spine, scattered foxing, soil and stains to edges minimal cover edge wear, illustrations, many in color, very good+.   By the Book, L. C. 37 - 84   2013 $175

Timbs, John *The History of Wonderful Inventions.*   New York: Harper & Bros., 1849.   First US edition, 12mo., 2 parts, numerous engravings on wood, original decorated dark blue cloth, stamped on front and rear cover in blind, stamped in spine panel in gold and blind.   L. W. Currey, Inc.   Fall Sampler Sept. 2013 - 145407   2013 $125

Timperley, Charles Henry *Encyclopaedia of Literary and Topographical Anecdotes...*   London: Henry G. Hohn, 1842.   Second edition, small folio, plates illustrations, slight damp mark to leading endpapers and first 4 leaves, original brown cloth, blocked in blind, spine decorated in gilt, ownership signatures on leading f.e.p., ticket of Fletcher, Forbes and Co., modern booklabel tipped onto leading pastedown, remarkably well preserved and attractive copy.   Jarndyce Antiquarian Booksellers   CCV - 265   2013   £350

Tiny Tots' ABC.   London: Children's Press, n.d. circa, 1945.   Oblong 4to., pictorial wrappers, fine, bright illustrated with color lithographs by G. I. Smith, printed on blue backgrounds.   Aleph-Bet Books, Inc.   104 - 22   2013 $200

Titus, Sara Alice Smith *This is a Fine Day: The Letters of Benjamin Wilson Marsh 1874-1875.*   Long Beach: 1959.   Limited edition of 100 copies, numbered and signed.   Dumont Maps & Books of the West   124 - 88   2013 $75

Tocqueville, Alexis Charles Henri Maurice Clerel De 1805-1859 *De La Democratie en Amerique.*   Paris: Librairie de Charles Gosselin, 1835-1840.   First edition, 4 volumes, small octavo, hand colored folding lithograph map in volume 1, uniformly bound by De Vauchelle in modern antique-style quarter black calf over marbled boards, smooth spines ruled and decoratively tooled in gilt in compartments, red and olive green calf gilt lettering labels marbled endpapers, sprinkled edges, expertly clean, wonderful copy.   Heritage Book Shop   50th Anniversary Catalogue - 191   2013 $40,000

Toda Y Guell, Eduardo *Bibliografia Espanola de Cerdena.*   Madrid: Tipografia de los Huerfanos, 1890.   First edition, small 4to., full marbled calf, red morocco lettering piece, five raised bands ruled in gilt, marbled endpapers, very good, spine rubbed, small paper slip on front pastedown, institutional stamp opposite titlepage.   Kaaterskill Books   16 - 85   2013 $350

Todd, Marilyn *I, Claudia.*   London: Macmillan, 1995.   First edition, very fine in dust jacket.   Mordida Books   81 - 518   2013 $65

Toibin, Colm *Brooklyn.*   Dublin: Tuskar Rock Press, 2009.   First edition, number VII of 25 roman numeral copies in morocco from total edition of 100, 8vo., original full yellow morocco lettered gilt on spine, red and yellow head and tail bands, cream laid paper endpapers, bound by Fine Bindery, fine in matching yellow slipcase.   Maggs Bros. Ltd.   1442 - 300   2013   £450

Toibin, Colm *Brooklyn.*   Dublin: Tuskar Rock Press, 2009.   First edition, number 46 of 75 numbered copies in cloth, form total edition of 110, 8vo., original yellow cloth, lettered gilt on spine, red and yellow head and tail bands, cream laid paper endpapers, bound by Fine Bindery, fine in matching yellow slipcase.   Maggs Bros. Ltd.   1442 - 301   2013   £175

Toibin, Colm *Dubliners.*   London: MacDonald, 1990.   First edition, photos by Tony O'Shea, signed by author, original black cloth, oblong 4to., fine in dust jacket.   Maggs Bros. Ltd.   1442 - 299   2013   £75

Tolkien, John Robert Reuel 1892-1973 *Some Contributions to Middle English Lexicography.*   London: Sidgwick & Jackson, 1925.   First edition, 8 pages, crown 8vo., original tan sewn wrappers printed in black, fine, from the library of J. R. R. Tolkien, with his pencilled note.   Blackwell's Rare Books   172 - 240   2013   £2000

Tolstoi, Lev Nikolaevich   1828-1910 *Anna Karenina.* New York: Thomas Y. Crowell & Co., 1886. 8vo., 773 pages, original cloth.   M & S Rare Books, Inc.   95 - 367   2013 $650

Tolstoi, Lev Nikolaevich   1828-1910 *The Novels and other Works.* New York: Charles Scribner's Sons, 1907. 24 volumes, 217 x 148mm., pleasing publisher's royal blue gilt decorated cloth, flat spines, top edge gilt, other edges untrimmed, each volume with engraved frontispiece and letterpress tissue guard, one in-text map, printed on specially made paper watermarked with Tolstoy's monogram, titlepages printed in red and black; few boards with faint white or scuff marks, some volumes with pages roughly opened so that edges are rather uneven (never threatening any text), spines slightly and evenly sunned to a pleasing light blue, but quite attractive overall, especially for a cloth set, generally very clean, fresh and bright inside and out with scarcely any wear to bindings.   Phillip J. Pirages   63 - 469   2013 $650

Tolstoi, Lev Nikolaevich   1828-1910 *Work While Ye Have the Light.* London: William Heinemann, 1890. First English edition, Half title, 6 pages ads, 16 page catalog (Octo 1890), original pink cloth, spine and front board lettered in black, cloth little darkened.   Jarndyce Antiquarian Booksellers   CCV - 277   2013   £45

Tombleson's Views of the Rhine from Cologne to Mayence. London: Tombleson, 1852. First edition, 8vo., folding map frontispiece, vignette on titlepage, 67 steel engravings, all edges gilt, contemporary half black morocco, purple pebbled boards, joints rubbed, few plates affected by marginal foxing, otherwise very good.   J. & S. L. Bonham Antiquarian Booksellers   Europe - 4398   2013   £295

Tomlin, Henry *Courtship and Marriage of Henry Tomlin.* Dallas: n.d., circa, 1908. 22 pages, original printed wrappers, covers worn and faded, red color bleeding onto edges of first and last few pages, short tear to several pages, else clean, very rare.   Dumont Maps & Books of the West   125 - 37   2013 $125

To-Night! or the Total Eclipse. London: J. J. Stockdale, 1818. Fifteenth edition, half title, 6 color plates by C. William bound together following title, uncut in original pink boards, marked, spine reinforced with later cream paper, ink title, bookplates of R. D. G. Jones and Renier.   Jarndyce Antiquarian Booksellers   CCIII - 630   2013   £60

Tony and the Circus Boy. London: Bancroft, 1960. Folio, cloth backed pictorial boards, covers very slightly wavy, else very good+, huge double page color pop-up by Kubasta. Aleph-Bet Books, Inc.   104 - 443   2013 $300

Tony and the Circus Boy. Bancoft, circa, 1960. Text on 8 pages, illustration in color on rear endpaper which when lifted reveals double page pop-up of a circus ring including performing animals, covers and endpapers by Kubasta, illustration and pop-up, small folio, original pink cloth backed card wrappers illustrated overall, rusting to staples with resultant corrosion to cloth, good.   Blackwell's Rare Books   B174 - 278   2013   £150

Toomer, Jean *Essentials.* Chicago: Private Edition, 1931. First edition, one of 1000 copies, this #400, fine, lacking dust jacket.   Between the Covers Rare Books, Inc.   165 - 269   2013 $350

Torrey, Jesse *A Portraiture of Domestic Slavery, in the United States: Proposing National Measures for the Education, and Gradual Emancipation of the Slaves, Without Impairing the Legal Privileges of the Possessor...* Balston Spa: The author, 1818. Second edition, original quarter calf and paper covered boards, very faint tidemark to edges of first few pages, some modest rubbing and light wear, sound, very good or better, bookplate of Ransom Cook which covers Cook's easily readable signature.   Between the Covers Rare Books, Inc.   165 - 270   2013 $1250

Tory, James Cranswick *Addresses Delivered by Hn. James Cranswick Tory, LL.D.* Ottawa: Mortimer Co., 1932. Half dark blue calf, gilt to spine and blue cloth boards, 8vo., wear to edges, otherwise very good.   Schooner Books Ltd.   105 - 108   2013 $55

Tothill, William *Transactions of the High Court of Chancery, Both by Practice and President.* London: R. Best and J. Place, 1671. 8vo., original mottled calf, rebacked with lighter calf and gilt stamped red leather spine label, bookplate of Algernon Capell, Earl of Essex, Viscount Maldon & Baron Capell of Hadham 1701 (partially affected by burn), good.   Jeff Weber Rare Books   171 - 116   2013 $200

Toudouze, Gustave *Le Roy Soleil.* Paris: Boivin, 1917. Folio, pictorial cloth, all edges gilt, near fine, printed on heavy paper with each page individually hinged into book, full page color illustrations.   Aleph-Bet Books, Inc.   104 - 224   2013 $350

The Tourist's Illustrated Handbook for Ireland.. London: John Cassell, 1853. Deluxe edition, gilt decorated calf with silk endpapers, all edges gilt, ex-Malahide Castle, text interleaved throughout with rice paper guards, sadly foldover of Plan of the Building has been torn-off from the crease.   C. P. Hyland   261 - 822   2013   £200

Tourtel, Mary *The Little Bear and the Ogres.* Thomas Nelson and Sons, n.d., 1922. First edition, small square 8vo., original pictorial boards, upper board trifle creased, patch of surface abrasion at foot, corners rounded and backstrip lacking, illustrations in orange and black, few spots and marks, little light fingering to some lower margins, otherwise very good. R. F. G. Hollett & Son Children's Books - 603 2013 £350

Tourtel, Mary *Margot the Midget and Little Bear's Christmas.* Thomas Nelson and Sons, n.d., 1922. First edition, small squre 8vo., original pictorial boards, trifle soiled, corners rounded and backstrip lacking, illustrations in orange and black, final 4 pages rather stained with brown patches, otherwise very good. R. F. G. Hollett & Son Children's Books - 604 2013 £295

Tourtel, Mary *The Monster Rupert.* Sampson Low, Marston & Co., 1948. 4to., original cloth backed pictorial boards, edges little worn, illustrations, first illustrations neatly colored in with crayon, ownership box on pastedown filled in. R. F. G. Hollett & Son Children's Books - 605 2013 £50

The Tower of Babel. West Burke: Janus Press, 1975. First edition, limited to 100 copies signed by artist, Claire Van Vliet, small folio, loose signatures in wrapper and folding linen box, fine. James S. Jaffe Rare Books Fall 2013 - 75 2013 $1000

Towgood, Micaiah *A Calm and Plain Answer to the Enquiry.* Tamworth: printed by J. Hilditch and sold by Longman & Co., 1808. 8vo., pages 66, bit of light spotting, modern blue sugar paper wrappers, good. Blackwell's Rare Books 172 - 142 2013 £60

Towle, Tony *Poems.* N.P.: printed at the A.I.G.A. workshop of James Hendrickson, 1966. First edition, one of 80 numbered copies signed by Towle (entire edition), 4to., original printed wrappers, very fine, rare. James S. Jaffe Rare Books Fall 2013 - 145 2013 $1250

The Town and Country Almanack for the Year MDCCLXXXVIII. Edinburgh: printed for T. Ruddiman and Co., 1788. 12mo., 168 pages, some occasional browning and foxing, original wallet style calf binding, blind ruled borders, part of original ties attached to flap, gilt stamped T on spine, official tax stamp dated 1788 on titlepage, rear board worn from where original ties were knotted and rubbed through surface leather, marbled paper lining to flap worn, scarce. Jarndyce Antiquarian Booksellers CCIV - 39 2013 £180

Townes, Charles H. *How the Laser Happened.* New York: Oxford University Press, 1999. First edition, 8vo., 200 pages, fine in like dust jacket, signed by author. By the Book, L. C. 36 - 103 2013 $650

Townsend, Joseph *Elements of Therapeutics or a Guide to Health...* Boston: Thomas & Andrew et al, 1802. 612 pages, full contemporary calf, very rubbed, worn, boards present but off, text foxed and browned in parts. James Tait Goodrich S74 - 229 2013 $295

Townsend, R. W. *Report on Railway Communication Between Cork and Skibbereen & Bantry.* 1845. 12 pages, folding map, very good, rare, cloth. C. P. Hyland 261 - 824 2013 £150

Townsend, R. W. *Report on the Proposed Cork, Passage & Kinsale Railway.* Purcell, 1845. 8vo, (10) pages, map, plan/section, disbound, very good, rare. C. P. Hyland 261 - 825 2013 £150

Townsend, Reginald T. *Mother of Clubs: Being the History of the First Hundred Years of the Union Club of City of New York 1836-1936.* New York: Union Club, 1936. First edition, number 1186 of 1500 copies, very good without dust jacket. Between the Covers Rare Books, Inc. New York City - 274254 2013 $125

Townsend, W. J. *A New History of Methodism.* London: Hodder and Stoughton, 1909. First edition, 2 volumes, large 8vo., original blue cloth, slight wear to extremities, 2 color frontispiece and 64 plates, half titles browned as usual, very good set. R. F. G. Hollett & Son Wesleyan Methodism - 29 2013 £75

Townsend, William R. *Letters on Furze, Prickley, Comfrey, Proper Payment of Labour & Little Things.* Cork: Landon Bros., 1862. 8vo., 92 pages, peculiar binding, original appears to have been paper back but was stitched into green leather diary(?) cover. C. P. Hyland 261 - 827 2013 £75

Townshend, Horace *Stories and Songs: a Venture in Verse.* Lloyd, 1904. First edition, 8vo., 77 pages, cloth, good. C. P. Hyland 261 - 826 2013 £45

Toy Animals and Tinkle the Tired Fairy. Chicago: Volland, 1922. Oblong folio, limp pictorial cloth, some soil, very good+, illustrations by John Rae, rare. Aleph-Bet Books, Inc. 104 - 580 2013 $400

Tracy, George *A History of the Typographical Union.* International Typographical Union, 1913. First edition, 1164 pages, stout 8vo., green cloth, ex-library with call numbers on spine, half of f.e.p. clipped and stamps on edges. Beasley Books 2013 - 2013 $50

Traill, Catherine Parr Strickland *Canada and Oregon. (with) The Oregon Territory...* London: M. A. Nattali, 1846. Frontispieces, illustrations, stamp of the Union Club Manchester on title, rebound in half maroon calf, very good. Jarndyce Antiquarian Booksellers   CCV - 267   2013   £280

Train, Arthur *Mr. Tutt Finds a Way.* New York: Scribner's, 1945. First edition, fine in dust jacket.   Mordida Books   81 - 521   2013 $75

Train, Arthur *Tut, Tut! Mr. Tutt.* New York: Scribner's, 1923. First edition, inscribed and dated Nov. 8, 1923 by Train, near fine in very good, heavily chipped and internally mended dust jacket with 2 inch piece missing at base of spine.   Mordida Books   81 - 520   2013 $175

Train, Arthur Cheney *The Man Who Rocked the Earth.* Garden City: Doubleday Page and Co., 1915. First edition, octavo, inserted frontispiece with color illustrations by Walter L. Green, original pictorial dark blue cloth, front panel stamped in lavender, black and gold, spine panel stamped in gold, pictorial endpapers.   L. W. Currey, Inc.   Fall Sampler Sept. 2013 - 143135   2013 $850

Transtromer, Tomas *Baltics.* Berkeley: Oyez, 1975. First edition in English, one of 125 numbered copies signed by Transtromer and translator, Samuel Charters, 8vo., grey-green cloth spine, pictorial boards and printed paper label, slight spotting on printed label, fine.   The Brick Row Book Shop   Miscellany Fifty-Nine - 44   2013 $250

Transylvania University *A Catalaogue of the Officers and Students of Transylvania University.* Lexington: printed by Herndon & Savary, 1831. First edition, 8vo., 16mo., removed, foxed.   M & S Rare Books, Inc.   95 - 369   2013 $225

Trant, Dominick *Considerations on the Present Disturbances in.. Munster.* Dublin: 1787.   (iv), 90 pages, disbound, dusty.   C. P. Hyland   261 - 828   2013   £50

Traubel, Hoarce L. *In Re Walt Whitman.* Philadelphia: David McKay, 1893. First edition, 1 of 1000 copies, 8vo., recent half leather, marbled boards, inscribed by author Sept. 12 1893 for Robert G. Ingersoll.   M & S Rare Books, Inc.   95 - 370   2013 $950

Travers, P. L. *Mary Poppins.* New York: Reynal & Hitchcock, 1934. First American edition, 8vo., blue cloth, 206 pages, very fine+ in beautiful dust jacket with few tiny closed edge tears, illustrations by Mary Shepard with pictorial endpapers plus many charming full page and smaller black and whites, excellent copy.   Aleph-Bet Books, Inc.   104 - 558   2013 $1200

Travers, P. L. *Mary Poppins in the Park.* New York: Harcourt Brace and Company, 1952. Stated first American edition, 8vo., blue cloth, 206 pages, fine in dust jacket (near fine), illustrations by Mary Shepard with pictorial endpapers plus many charming full page and smaller black and whites, great copy.   Aleph-Bet Books, Inc.   105 - 563   2013 $275

Treadwell, Edward F. *The Cattle King.* frontispiece, portraits, map endpapers, tan cloth lettered in blue, light rubbing to spine ends, owner's name, spine faded, upper corners slightly jammed very good, presentation for Ben C. Duniway.   Argonaut Book Shop   Recent Acquisitions June 2013 - 285   2013 $90

Treat, Roger *The Official National Football League Football Encyclopedia.* New York: A. S. Barnes, 1952. First edition, very good with spine and board edges sunned, few small worn spots in cloth, lacking dust jacket.   Between the Covers Rare Books, Inc.   Football Books - 71426   2013 $85

Trelawny, Edward John *Adventures of a Younger Son.* London: Richard Bentley, Engraved frontispiece and title, small hole in engraved title slightly affecting text, original plum cloth (Sadleir binding style A), one label slightly chipped and another missing, otherwise good plus. Jarndyce Antiquarian Booksellers   CCIII - 443   2013   £50

Trelawny, Edward John *Memoires d'un Cadet de Familie...(Adventures of a Younger Son).* Bruxelles: J. P. Meline, 1833.   3 volumes, uncut, half titles, original grey printed wrappers, slight browning and staining, bookseller's stamp on titlepages, well preserved.   Jarndyce Antiquarian Booksellers   CCIII - 442   2013   £120

Trelawny, Edward John *Adventures of a Younger Son.* London: T. Fisher Unwin, 1890. New edition, half title, frontispiece, plates, original red cloth, dulled, minor damp marks, slight worming inner margin of upper board through half title, bookplates of E. G. Thomson.   Jarndyce Antiquarian Booksellers   CCIII - 444   2013   £30

Trelawny, Edward John *Records of Shelley, Byron and the author.* London: Pickering & Chatto, 1887. New edition, half title, frontispiece, original dark blue cloth, paper label slightly rubbed, following board slightly marked, booklabel of Alex Bridge, very good.   Jarndyce Antiquarian Booksellers   CCIII - 445   2013   £65

Tremaudan, A. H. De *The Hudson Bay Road.* London: 1915. xvi, 264 pages, illustrations, folding map, dust jacket lightly soiled with foxed spine and couple of spots of loss, book with dusty top edge and foxed edges, but clean and bright internally.   Dumont Maps & Books of the West   124 - 89   2013 $100

Tremaux, Pierre *Voyages au Soudan Orientale et dans l'Afrique Septentrionale.* Paris: Borani, 1852-1858. First edition, 9 original photos, 4 maps, 50 lithograph plates, oblong folio, modern half straight grain morocco marbled boards, spine gilt, red morocco label, printed on recto only. Maggs Bros. Ltd. 1467 - 25 2013 £33.000

Tresslet, Alvin *White Snow Bright Snow.* New York: Lothrop Lee Shepard, 1947. First edition, first printing, 4to., pictorial boards, slight rubbing to spine ends, else fine in dust jacket (very good+, slightly frayed at spine ends, not price clipped and no award seal), color illustrations, excellent copy. Aleph-Bet Books, Inc. 104 - 191 2013 $950

Trevathan, Charles E. *The American Thoroughbred.* New York: Macmillan Co., 1905. First edition, 493 pages, ads, frontispiece, illustrations, lovely fine copy. Between the Covers Rare Books, Inc. Horses, Horsemanship, Horse Racing, Etc. - 66707 2013 $250

Trevigar, Luke *Sectionum Conicarum Elementa Methodo Facillima (sic) Demonstrata.* Cambridge: University Press, 1731. First edition, 11 folding engraved plates, little browned in places, 4to., contemporary plain calf, red lettering piee, worn, contemporary ownership inscription on title of Tho. Johnson, Magd(alene College), sound. Blackwell's Rare Books Sciences - 122 2013 £350

Trevor, William 1928- *Angels at the Ritz and Other Stories.* London: Bodley Head, 1975. First edition, 256 pages, 8vo., original navy blue boards, gilt lettered and blocked backstrip, endpapers and dust jacket flaps lightly foxed, very good. Blackwell's Rare Books 172 - 241 2013 £90

Trevor, William 1928- *A Bit on the Side.* London: Viking, 2004. First edition, 8vo., original black cloth, signed by author on dust jacket, fine in dust jacket. Maggs Bros. Ltd. 1442 - 304 2013 £75

Trevor, William 1928- *The Boarding House.* London: Bodley Head, 1965. First edition, 8vo., original brown cloth, near fine in lightly rubbed, browned and price clipped dust jacket. Maggs Bros. Ltd. 1442 - 303 2013 £150

Trevor, William 1928- *The Children of Dynmouth.* London: Bodley Head, 1976. First edition, pages 222, foolscap 8vo., original light green boards backstrip gilt lettered, faint front endpaper and edge browning, dust jacket, near fine. Blackwell's Rare Books B174 - 307 2013 £50

Trevor, William 1928- *Fools of Fortune.* London: Galway: Jonathan Cape/Kenny's of Galway, 1983. First edition, number 47 of 50 copies, signed by author, 8vo., original quarter brown leather, marbled paper boards, neat booklabel on front pastedown, otherwise fine, matching slipcase. Maggs Bros. Ltd. 1442 - 308 2013 £450

Trevor, William 1928- *Men of Ireland.* Oundle: Oundle Festival of Literature, 2008. Number 18 of 120 copies signed by author, small 8vo., original patterned paper boards, printed on Somerset Laid mould-made paper and bound by Fine Book Bindery, Wellingborough. Maggs Bros. Ltd. 1442 - 306 2013 £175

Trevor, William 1928- *Mrs. Eckdorf in O'Neill's Hotel.* New York: Viking, 1970. First American edition, signed by author, owner name front flyleaf, near fine in very good dust jacket faded at spine and flap folds. Ken Lopez Bookseller 159 - 190 2013 $250

Trevor, William 1928- *Nights at the Alexandra.* Hutchinson, 1987. First edition, 8vo., original quarter black cloth backstrip and front cover blocked in gilt, pink boards, dust jacket, fine, signed by author. Blackwell's Rare Books B174 - 308 2013 £100

A Tribute to Henry W. Sage from the Women Graduates of Cornell University. Ithaca: 1895. Large 8vo., 3 small wood engravings by Annie Comstock, white cloth, stamped in gilt, cover spotted, little worn at edges, but very good, tight. Second Life Books Inc. 182 - 13 2013 $75

Tributes ot Sir Robert Mayer on His Ninetieth Birthday 5 June 1969. London: privately printed, 1969. First edition, large 8vo., original green cloth, lettered gilt on upper cover, fine. Maggs Bros. Ltd. 1442 - 66 2013 £150

Tricks of Naughty Boys. London: H. Grevel, n.d., 1899. First English edition with new illustrations by Lothar Meggendorfer, folio, cloth backed pictorial boards, slight cover soil, slight wear to paper near tabs else fine, 6 slatted transformation plates, also illustrated in line on text pages. Aleph-Bet Books, Inc. 105 - 383 2013 $3500

Trimmer, Sarah *Fabulous Histories.* London: Grant & Griffith, circa, 1860. Frontispiece, vignette title, final ad leaf, original glazed yellow boards, printed in green and black, expertly rebacked with new spine strip, very good. Jarndyce Antiquarian Booksellers CCV - 268 2013 £50

Trioen, Cornelii *Observationum Medico Chirurgicarum Fasiculus.* Lugduni Batavorum: Apud Petrum Vander Eye Jacobum van der Kluis, 1743. 4to., title in black and red, 13 engraved plates, text dusty and old smoke stain in parts, uncut and partially unopened, 4to., new quarter linen and marbled boards, small library stamps on title on plates. James Tait Goodrich 75 - 303 2013 $595

Troil, Uno Von, Abp. of Upsala 1746-1803 *Letters on Iceland, Containing Observations on the Civil, Literary, Ecclesiastical and Natural History.* London: J. Robson, 1780. First London edition, 8vo., pages xxiv, 400, frontispiece (marginal foxing and browning), folding map (small tear repaired), contemporary marbled boards, later reback in brown half calf, titlepage thumbed in lower corner, lacks endpapers, uncut. J. & S. L. Bonham Antiquarian Booksellers Europe - 9729 2013 £380

Troil, Uno Von, Abp. of Upsala 1746-1803 *Letters on Iceland: Containing Observations on the Civil, Literary, Ecclesiastical and Natural History...* London: J. Robson, W. Richardson, N. Conant, 1780. Second edition, 8vo. engraved frontispiece and foldout map, lacking half title, small handling tear to map at mount, 2 small repairs to page margins, otherwise internally good and clean, contemporary tree calf, efficiently rebacked and recornered, booklabel of W. R. Stuart Majendie and pen inscription of G. Selby, pen inscription of Levin Munksgaard. Unsworths Antiquarian Booksellers 28 - 136 2013 £450

Trollope, Anthony 1815-1882 *The American Senator.* London: Chapman and Hall, 1877. First edition in book form, half titles, 3 volumes, 184 x 127mm., fine contemporary dark olive morocco bound for the Earl of Carysfort (with his arms in gilt on center of front covers and monogram at foot of spines), backstrips titled in gilt raised bands flanked by multiple gilt rules, marbled endpapers, all edges gilt, Carysfort bookplate; front joint of 2 volumes with hint of wear, one leaf with two tiny tears at top, but fine, attractive set, text immaculate, and in a lustrous elegant binding. Phillip J. Pirages 63 - 471 2013 $2250

Trollope, Anthony 1815-1882 *Australia and New Zealand.* Melbourne: George Robertson, 1873. Second (First Australian) edition, 8vo., contemporary full polished calf by George Mercer, Geelong, Victoria, gilt arms of Geelong Anglican school within circle with motto, spine elaborately gilt, leather label, inner gilt dentelles, binder's ticket inside front cover. Howard S. Mott Inc. 262 - 152 2013 $275

Trollope, Anthony 1815-1882 *Castle Richmond.* Leipzig: 1860. 2 volumes bound in 1, cloth, very good. C. P. Hyland 261 - 830 2013 £95

Trollope, Anthony 1815-1882 *Castle Richmond, a Novel.* 1860. First edition, 3 volumes, modern cloth, may be in the process of this rebind, corners of the fore-edge were shaved (to prevent dog ears), otherwise good, scarce. C. P. Hyland 261 - 829 2013 £300

Trollope, Anthony 1815-1882 *Orley Farm.* London: Chapman and Hall, 1862. First edition, 2 volumes, 40 plates with some foxing, original purple brown wavy grained cloth, boards blocked in blind, spines decorated and lettered in gilt, small repairs to heads and tails of spines, endpapers little marked, booklabels partly removed, signatures of R. Hesketh 1883. Jarndyce Antiquarian Booksellers CCV - 269 2013 £400

Trollope, Frances *Hargrave; or the Adventures of a Man of Fashion.* London: Henry Colburn, 1843. First edition, 3 volumes, contemporary half red calf, gilt spines, dark green morocco labels, spines little dulled, volume II signed Mrs. Alcock on titlepage in contemporary hand, attractive set. Jarndyce Antiquarian Booksellers CCV - 270 2013 £850

Trollope, Frances *The Mother's Manual; or Illustrations of Matrimonial Economy.* London: Treuttel & Wurtz & Richter, 1833. First edition, frontispiece, vignette title and 18 plates, all attractively hand colored, slightly later full scarlet morocco by Bayntun of Bath, gilt spine borders an dentelles, all edges gilt, very good in custom made fold over box, scarce. Jarndyce Antiquarian Booksellers CCV - 271 2013 £2250

Trotskii, Lev 1879-1940 *Problems of the Chinese Revolution.* New York: Pioneer Pub., 1932. First edition, hardcover, little spine war, f.e.p. excised, otherwise near fine. Beasley Books 2013 - 2013 $50

Trotter, Thomas *A Treatise on Geology: in Which the Discoveries of that Science are Reconciled with the Scriptures and the Ancient Revolutions of the Earth are Shown to be Sources of Benefit to Man.* Pictou: Geldert & Patterson, Eastern Chronicle Office, 1845. Original light brown cloth, paper label to spine, 8vo., some wear to edges and spotting to outer edges, else very good. Schooner Books Ltd. 104 - 124 2013 $275

True Stories of the Olden Days. Blackie & son, n.d. circa, 1907. Large 8vo., original cloth backed glazed pictorial boards, upper board little soiled, especially at one corner, 4 color plates, other plates and illustrations, inscribed by Joan Ruskin Severn for John Hext. R. F. G. Hollett & Son Children's Books - 72 2013 £65

True Strange Stories November 1929. Volume 1 number 8. Dunellen: True Strange Stories Pub. Co. Nov., 1929. Volume I, number 8, large octavo, pictorial wrappers. L. W. Currey, Inc. Fall Sampler Sept. 2013 - 146578 2013 $450

True, Louise *Number Men.* Chicago: Children's Press, 1948. Oblong 4to., pictorial boards, slightest of cover soil, else near fine in dust jacket, illustrations by Lillian Owens. Aleph-Bet Books, Inc. 105 - 151 2013 $200

Trumbull, H. Clay *Child Life in Many Lands.* New York: Fleming H. Revell, 1903. First edition, 8vo., very good, tight, clean copy with no real faults, 215 pages plus 6 pages of ads and 8 photos. Barnaby Rudge Booksellers Children 2013 - 021318   2013 $85

Trumbull, M. M. *The Free Trade Struggle in England.* Chicago: Open Court, 1892. Second edition, near fine. Beasley Books   2013 - 2013 $65

Truro, Nova Scotia. The Hub of the Province. Truro: and Grand Rapids, n.d., 1900. 7 x 9 inches, decorative card covers, 76 black and white photo illustrations by Lewis Rice, very good. Schooner Books Ltd.   105 - 109   2013 $125

Tschiffely, A. F. *The Tale of Two Horses.* New York: Junior Literary Guild and Simon and Schuster, 1935. First American edition, illustrations by Kurt Wiese, tiny ink owner name and light pencil inscription, else fine in very good or better, price clipped dust jacket with small chip on rear panel an some modest rubbing.   Between the Covers Rare Books, Inc.   Horses, Horsemanship, Horse Racing, Etc. - 63110   2013 $175

Tubb, Edwin Charles *City of No Return.* London: Scion Limited, 1954. First edition, pictorial wrappers, octavo. L. W. Currey, Inc.   Fall Sampler Sept. 2013 - 143749   2013 $150

Tubb, Edwin Charles *The Stellar Legion.* London: Scion Distributors Ltd., 1954. First edition, octavo, pictorial wrappers. L. W. Currey, Inc.   Fall Sampler Sept. 2013 - 143802   2013 $125

Tuck, Raphael *Our Railway ABC.* Raphael Tuck & Sons, n.d. circa, 1930. Oblong large 8vo., original glazed colored pictorial stiff wrappers, one lower corner little chipped, illustrations in red and black, 4 fine color plates, scarce. R. F. G. Hollett & Son   Children's Books - 606   2013   £75

Tucker, Abraham *Vocal Sounds by Edward Search, Esq.* London: printed by T. Jones and sold by T. Payne, 1773. First edition, small 8vo., 19th century half maroon morocco by E. Riley & Son, very good.   Blackwell's Rare Books 172 - 143   2013   £1500

Tucker, Benjamin R. *Instead of a Book by a Man Too Busy to Write One.* New York: Benj. R. Tucker, 1897. Second edition, 8vo., frontispiece, original printed wrappers, for a book with such poor paper this copy amazing fine and sound, very rare.   M & S Rare Books, Inc.   95 - 371   2013 $300

Tucker, Charlotte M. *Idols in the Hart: a Tale.* T. Nelson and Sons, 1863. Small 8vo., original blindstamped cloth gilt extra, little rubbed, 302 pages, joints cracking, little skewed. R. F. G. Hollett & Son   Children's Books - 608   2013   £25

Tucker, Charlotte M. *The Mine; or Darkness and Light.* T. Nelson and sons, 1888. Original pictorial blue cloth gilt, hinges and edges rubbed in places, pages 175, all edges gilt, 7 woodcut plates, front flyleaf removed, half title browned. R. F. G. Hollett & Son   Children's Books - 609   2013   £25

Tucker, Elizabeth *Baby Folk.* New York: Frederick Stokes, 1898. 4to. cloth backed pictorial boards, edges rubbed, margin of one plate strengthened, else tight and very good+, pictorial borders, 6 magnificent full page chromolithograph illustrations by Maud Humphrey.   Aleph-Bet Books, Inc.   105 - 330   2013 $950

Tucker, Elizabeth *Little Rosebuds.* New York: Stokes, 1898. 4to., cloth backed pictorial boards, edges slightly rubbed, else tight, very good-fine, 6 magnificent full page chromolithograph illustrations by Maud Humphrey, very scarce.   Aleph-Bet Books, Inc.   104 - 287   2013 $850

Tuckey, C. Lloyd *Psycho-Therapeutics; or Treatment by Hypnotism and Suggestion.* London: Bailliere, Tindall & Cox, 1891. Third edition, very good, owner's name on title, small tear at head of front joint, mend to f.e.p.   Beasley Books   2013 - 2013 $100

Tuckey, Francis H. *The County and City of Cork Remembrancer; or Annals of the County and City.* Tower Press, 1980. Facsimile of 1837 first edition, 8vo. cloth, dust jacket, fine. C. P. Hyland   261 - 831   2013   £100

Tudor, Tasha *Amanda and the Bear.* New York: Oxford University Press, 1951. First edition, first printing, 8vo., blue boards, fine in very good+ fine dust jacket, full page color illustrations, nice copy.   Aleph-Bet Books, Inc.   105 - 567   2013 $950

Tudor, Tasha *First Prayers.* New York: Oxford University Press, 1952. First edition, 16mo., blue cloth, pictorial paste-on, fine in very slightly worn dust jacket, nice, beautiful color illustrations by Tudor.   Aleph-Bet Books, Inc.   105 - 566   2013 $300

Tudor, Tasha *Linsey Woolsey.* New York: Oxford University Press, 1946. First edition, 16mo., yellow polka dotted cloth, fine in slightly soiled, very good+ dust jacket, rare, illustrations by Tudor.   Aleph-Bet Books, Inc.   104 - 560   2013 $650

Tudor, Tasha *Pumpkin Moonshine.* New York: Oxford University Press, 1938. First edition, first printing, 16mo., polka-dot patterned boards, cloth very slightly faded on edges and occasional finger soil, else near fine in dust jacket (with old tape mark on verso and small chip at spine end), scarce.   Aleph-Bet Books, Inc.   105 - 565   2013 $2750

Tudor, Tasha *A Tale for Easter.* London: Oxford University Press, 1941. First edition, first state, near fine in very good++ price clipped dust jacket with mild soil and chips, 16mo., signed and inscribed by author.   By the Book, L. C.   36 - 36   2013 $500

Tudor, Tasha *A Tale for Easter.* New York: Oxford University Press, 1941. First edition, 8vo., cloth, near fine in very lightly soiled dust jacket, color illustrations by Tudor.   Aleph-Bet Books, Inc.   104 - 561   2013 $500

Tudor, Tasha *White Goose.* New York: Oxford University Press, 1943. First edition, grey cloth, near fine in slightly worn dust jacket, beautiful full page illustrations, opposite each page of text, nice.   Aleph-Bet Books, Inc.   104 - 562   2013 $500

Tuer, Andrew White   1838-1900 *The History of the Horn-Book.* London: Leadenhall Press, 1897.   4to. 3 examples of Horn Books in pocket at rear, 231 text illustrations, good copy in original cloth, lettered in gilt and black, some rubbing to covers but clean copy internally, signature dated 1897 on front endpaper and later bookplate.   Ken Spelman Books Ltd.   75 - 151   2013   £220

Tuer, Andrew White   1838-1900 *Stories from Old Fashioned Children's Book.* Leadenhall Press, 1899-1900. First edition, original blue cloth gilt extra, little worn and marked, top edge gilt, untrimmed, 250 illustrations, new endpapers.   R. F. G. Hollett & Son   Children's Books - 610   2013   £50

Tuke, Daniel Hack *Illustrations of the Influence of the Mind Upon the Body.* Philadelphia: Henry C. Lea, 1873. Second US edition, faint call numbers on spine, boards sunned, quarter inch chip to finish at head of spine, thus very good.   Beasley Books   2013 - 2013 $100

Tuke, Samuel *Account of the Rise and Progress of the Asylum, Proposed to be Established Near Philadelphia, for the Relief of Persons Deprived of their Reason.* New Jersey: circa, 1970. Facsimile of 1814 edition, 72 pages, 12mo., illustrations, very good, printed paper wrappers, slight chip at head of front cover.   Ken Spelman Books Ltd. 73 - 16   2013   £20

Tuke, Samuel *Description of the Retreat, an Institution near York, for Insane Persons of the Society of Friends.* York: W. Alexander, 1813. First and only edition, large paper, frontispiece view foxed, 2 plans 4to., very good, contemporary mid brown calf with gilt hatched raised bands between double gilt rules, gilt morocco label, marbled boards and edges, drab endpapers, bookplate of Frances Mary Richardson Currer and later owner's small book ticket.   Ken Spelman Books Ltd.   73 - 15   2013   £1250

Tull, Jethro *Horse-Hoeing Husbandry or an Essay on the Principles of Vegetation and Tillage.* printed for A. Millar, 1762. 7 folding engraved plates, small stain on title, occasional minor spotting, 8vo., original speckled calf, red lettering piece, lower corners bumped, spine minimally defective at foot, excellent.   Blackwell's Rare Books   Sciences - 123   2013   £400

Tupper, Martin Farquhar *Geraldine, a sequel to Coleridge's Christabel.* Boston: Saxton & Kelt, 1846. First American edition, half title, endpapers little browned, original purple cloth, blocked in blind, spine lettered gilt, slight wear to head and tail of spine, some uneven fading, early bookplate of CLF, good plus.   Jarndyce Antiquarian Booksellers   CCIII - 532   2013   £75

Turenne, Raymond *The Last of the Mammoths.* London: Chatto & Windus, 1907. First edition, corners bit bumped and some uniform and modest overall soiling, very good or better, very scarce.   Between the Covers Rare Books, Inc.   Sci-Fi, Fantasy & Horror - 54810   2013 $250

Turgenev, Ivan Sergeevich   1818-1883 *Fathers and Sons.* London: Ward, Lock and Co., 1983. First English edition, Contemporary blue pebble grained binder's cloth, very good.   Jarndyce Antiquarian Booksellers   CCV - 272   2013   £250

Turgenev, Ivan Sergeevich   1818-1883 *The Jew and Other Stories.* New York: Charles Scribner's Sons, 1904. 213 x 146mm., frontispiece lovely contemporary dark rose colored morocco, ornately gilt by Sickles (stamp signed), covers with border of double gilt rules enclosing an Art Nouveau style frame of wavy rules connecting large cornerpieces, these with small oval medallion onlaid black morocco enclosed by gilt drawer handle tools and leafy sprays, upper cover with circular stylized monogram "C E B" at center, raised bands, spines gilt in double ruled compartments decorated with drawer handles and circlets, wide turn-ins with gilt frame featuring pretty fleuron cornerpieces, ivory watered silk pastedowns and free endleaves, top edge gilt, spine evenly faded to soft rose, three leaves with uneven fore edges from rough opening, half a dozen leaves with corner creases, other trivial imperfections, but fine, text clean, fresh and bright and handsome binding, lustrous and virtually unworn.   Phillip J. Pirages   63 - 472   2013 $375

Turgenev, Ivan Sergeevich 1818-1883 *A Month in the Country.* London: Heinemann, 1943. First English edition, 8vo., 94 pages, very good in dust jacket, bookplate of Hugh Beaumont on front endpaper, inscribed by Emlyn Williams for Beaumont, signed by 13 members of the opening night cast including Michael Redgrave, David Baxter, Winifred Hindle, etc.   Second Life Books Inc.   183 - 383   2013 $400

Turgenev, Ivan Sergeevich 1818-1883 *Phantoms and Other Stories.* New York: Charles Scribner's Sons, 1904. 213 x 146mm., frontispiece, lovely contemporary dark rose colored morocco, ornately gilt by Sickles (stamp signed), covers with border of double gilt rules enclosing an Art Nouveau style frame of wavy rules connecting large cornerpieces, these with small oval medallion onlaid black morocco enclosed by gilt drawer handle tools and leafy sprays, upper cover with circular stylized monogram "C E B" at center, raised bands, spines gilt in double ruled compartments decorated with drawer handles and circlets, wide turn-ins with gilt frame featuring pretty fleuron cornerpieces, ivory watered silk pastedowns and free endleaves, top edge gilt, except for even fading of spine, very fine and very pretty copy.   Phillip J. Pirages   63 - 473   2013 $350

Turgenev, Ivan Sergeevich 1818-1883 *A Reckless Character, and Other Studies.* New York: Charles Scribner's Sons, 1904. 213 x 146mm., frontispiece, lovely contemporary dark rose colored morocco, ornately gilt by Sickles (stamp signed), covers with border of double gilt rules enclosing an Art Nouveau style frame of wavy rules connecting large cornerpieces, these with small oval medallion onlaid black morocco enclosed by gilt drawer handle tools and leafy sprays, upper cover with circular stylized monogram "C E B" at center, raised bands, spines gilt in double ruled compartments decorated with drawer handles and circlets, wide turn-ins with gilt frame featuring pretty fleuron cornerpieces, ivory watered silk pastedowns and free endleaves, top edge gilt, spine evenly faded very small dark spot on upper cover, otherwise very attractive decorative binding in fine condition, first half of book with very faint dampstain in upper quarter of page (front endleaves with slightly larger and darker dampstain), four leaves with cellotape mends to short marginal tears (none touching text), one page with 3 marginal inkspots, otherwise excellent internally.   Phillip J. Pirages   63 - 474   2013 $125

Turgenev, Ivan Sergeevich 1818-1883 *Collected Works.* Moscow: 1953. 12 volumes, Russian text, 8vo., very good set in green gilt cloth.   Ken Spelman Books Ltd.   75 - 181   2013   £40

Turgot, Anne Robert Jacques *Reflexions sur La Formation et la Distribution des Richesses.* N.P.: 1788. First edition in book form, octavo, half title, mid 19th century brown diced morocco, triple gilt fillet border on covers, additional vertical lines stamped in gilt and decorative blind tooling extending from spine, spine decoratively gilt tooled in compartments, maroon morocco lettering label, gilt board edges and turn-ins, marbled endpapers, all edges gilt, spine ends and corners slightly rubbed, armorial bookplate of Scottish Judge Thomas Maitland, Lord Dundrennan (1792-1851), occasional very light foxing, otherwise exceptionally good, clean and sound, exceedingly scarce, housed in custom full brown morocco clamshell, gilt stamped.   Heritage Book Shop   50th Anniversary Catalogue - 102   2013 $17,500

Turley, Charles *The Voyages of Captain Scott.* London: Smith, Elder & Co., 1914. Original pictorial cloth, gilt, hinges trifle rubbed, 38 plates, folding map little torn and repaired.   R. F. G. Hollett & Son   Polar Exploration - 78   2013   £30

Turner, Daniel *A Discourse Concerning Fevers in Two Letters to a Young Physician.* London: J. Clark, 1727. Complete with printer's pagination error, later red cloth, ex-library with faint stamp on title, gilt stamp bottom of spine, overall very good, tight copy.   James Tait Goodrich   75 - 205   2013 $1250

Turner, Don *A Plea for Heroes: T. R. and Rough Riders.* Amarillo: 1971. Number 12 of 300, hand printed and signed, frontispiece, 40 pages, 12mo., boards, issued without dust jacket, little rubbed, title on front board faded, else very good.   Dumont Maps & Books of the West   125 - 76   2013 $50

Turner, Frederick J. *The Character and Influence of the Indian Trade in Wisconsin.* Baltimore: John Hopkins Press Nov. and Dec., 1891. First edition, 8vo., 94 pages plus ads and half title, original printed wrappers, chipped and detached, text fine.   M & S Rare Books, Inc.   95 - 372   2013 $250

Turner, J. B. *Mormonism in All Ages; or the Rise, Progress and Causes of Mormonism...* New York: Platt and Peters, 1842. First edition, 12mo., original cloth, rubbed, foxed, some staining to front cover.   M & S Rare Books, Inc.   95 - 239   2013 $550

Turner, Judith *The Parthenon Pediments.* New York: Vincent FitzGerald & Co., 1993. One of 25 copies, each signed and numbered by Turner, portfolio of etchings, all on BFK Rives paper and paper from Paul Wong, Dieu Donne Papermill, page size 30 x 15, 6 leaves, loose in green paper portfolio with title in silver gilt on front panel by BookLab, 24 photographic images by Turner, laid out in horizontally on five rectangular sheets of paper.   Priscilla Juvelis - Rare Books   55 - 10   2013 $7500

Turner, R. *An Easy Introduction to the Arts and Sciences...* London: F. C. and J. Rivington, 1814. Sixteenth edition, 12mo., original calf, very worn, 3 plates and numerous text woodcuts, considerable soiling and fingering in places, lacks final leaf of text. R. F. G. Hollett & Son Children's Books - 617 2013 £25

Turner, R. *The Fashionable Letter-Writer, or Art of Polite Correspondence in Original Letters.* Dean and Son, circa, 1874. engraved frontispiece and printed and engraved titlepages, very good, clean in decorative blue gilt cloth, gilt rather dulled. Ken Spelman Books Ltd. 75 - 138 2013 £45

Turner, R. L. *A Comparative Dictionary of the Indo-Aryan Languages. (with) Addenda and Corrigenda.* London: Oxford University Press, 1989. 1985. Third impression of 1966 first edition, addenda first edition, 2 volumes, 4to., green cloth, dust jacket little faded, creases and some small nicks to spine at head and tail, price label to lower board, still very good, volume 2 wrappers very slightly dusty and shelfworn, near fine. Unsworths Antiquarian Booksellers 28 - 201 2013 £150

Turpin, Richard *The Trial of the Notorious Highwayman Richard Turpin at York Assizes on the 22d Day of March 1793 Before the Hon. Sir William Chapple Knt. Judge of Assize and one of His Majesty's Justices of the Court of King's Bench...* York: printed by Ward and Chandler, 1739. 8vo. little light browning, original stab holes visible, early 20th century half calf, marbled boards, armorial bookplate of Moncure Biddle. Jarndyce Antiquarian Booksellers CCIV - 300 2013 £3800

Tuskegee Institute *The 1939 Tuskeana of Tuskegee Institute.* Tuskegee: Senior Class, 1939. Quarto, padded leatherette, several student inscriptions, some slight wear to spinal extremities, near fine, with author Albert Murray's inscription beneath his senior picture. Between the Covers Rare Books, Inc. 165 - 227 2013 $750

Tusser, Thomas *Five Hundred Points of Husbandry...* London: printed for M. Cooper, 1744. 8vo., clean tears without loss to F1, M1, blank lower corners torn on O1-2, paper flaws to X1 and 3 with slight loss, upper margins slightly close cropped affecting some running heads, handsome near contemporary tree calf, gilt borders, attractive gilt decorated spine, red morocco label and onlay at tree calf, gilt borders, attractive gilt decorated spine, red morocco label and onlay at foot of spine, early signature of Edwd. Cooper, slightly later inscription "The Revd George Ashby's gift to The Revd Jonathan Carter". Jarndyce Antiquarian Booksellers CCV - 273 2013 £420

Tustin, Fances *Autistic States in Children.* London: Routledge and Kegan Paul, 1981. First British edition, near fine with light foxing at top edge in near fine dust jacket with tiny hole on front panel and bumping to extremities of book and jacket. Between the Covers Rare Books, Inc. Psychology & Psychiatry - 101501 2013 $65

Tuthill, Franklin *The History of California.* San Francisco: H. H. Bancroft, 1866. First edition, publisher's brown cloth, gilt spine lettering, spine faded and worn at spine ends, some spotting to covers, minimal foxing to extreme fore-edge of text block, overall very good, internally clean and generally without any foxing. Argonaut Book Shop Recent Acquisitions June 2013 - 287 2013 $275

Tuttle, Lisa *Gabriel.* London: Severn House, 1987. First edition, octavo, cloth. L. W. Currey, Inc. Wandering Ghosts & Itinerant Souls (10/12) - 106495 2013 $85

Tuttle, Richard *Richard Tuttle.* Amsterdam: The Hague: Institute of Contemporary Art/Sdu Publishers, 1991. First edition, 203 pages, numerous color and black and white illustrations, very good, some bumping to spine ends and corners and in very good plus dust jacket with two sticker shadows to top of front panel and some other slight wear. Jeff Hirsch Books Fall 2013 - 129202 2013 $60

Tweedie, Ethel Brilliana *Women the World Over; a Sketch Both Light and Gay, Perchance Both Dull and Stupid.* London: Hutchinson, 1914. First edition, half title, frontispiece and plates and illustrations, 4 pages ads, original red cloth, lettered in gilt, front board blocked in white with image of Venus de Milo; very slightly faded, Park Close bookplate, top edge gilt, very good. Jarndyce Antiquarian Booksellers CCV - 274 2013 £30

Tweedsmuir, Lord *Hudson's Bay Trader.* Clerke & Cockeran, 1951. First edition, original cloth, gilt, head and tail of spine little faded, dust jacket little worn and torn, more than 80 illustrations, small stamp at base of titlepage. R. F. G. Hollett & Son Polar Exploration - 79 2013 £25

Tweedsmuir, Susan Charlotte Buchan *John Buchan by His Wife and Friends.* London: Hodder and Stoughton Ltd., 1947. First edition, large 8vo., original black cloth, inscribed by Buchan's widow Susan Tweedsmuir to Sam Morison, below which is a pencilled note by recipient, inscribed photo of Lady Tweedsmuir, inscribed postcard and ALS from John Buchan to recipient, excellent copy with Morison's bookplate, now loose. Maggs Bros. Ltd. 1460 - 149 2013 £175

XXIII Psalm: a Psalm of David. Canberra: Bookarts, 2001. Limited to 15 presentation copies and 150 numbered copies, this copy numbered and signed by publishers, John and Joy Tonkin, 7 x 4. cm., leather, brass clasp, 4 raised bands on spine, excess leather tied in topknot, marbled endpapers, in leather pouch unpaginated, from the collection of Donn W. Sanford. Oak Knoll Books 303 - 64 2013 $200

The Twigs or Christmas at Ruddock Hall. printed in Bavaria for Castell Brothers, n.d. circa, 1890. Oblong small 8vo., original stiff card pictorial wrappers, tasselled silk cord ties, 8 chromolithographs and other illustrations, scattered foxing, but very good, sound, rare title. R. F. G. Hollett & Son Children's Books - 175   2013   £95

The Twins. New York: & London: Hodder & Stoughton, n.d., 1910. First American edition, large 4to., cloth backed boards, pictorial paste-on, tips and edges rubbed, respined, tight, clean and very good++, illustrations by Cecil Aldin with 24 fabulous color plates plus pictorial endpapers and titlepage, nice. Aleph-Bet Books, Inc.   105 - 33   2013 $500

Twisleton, Tom *Poems in the Craven Dialect.* Settle: Edmondson and Wilson, 1907. Sixth edition, 166 pages, frontispiece, signed by author, very good in original brown and black gilt lettered cloth. Ken Spelman Books Ltd.   73 - 69   2013   £30

Twitchell, Ralph E. *Leading Fact of New Mexico History.* Santa Fe: 2007. 2 volumes, illustrations, hardcover. Dumont Maps & Books of the West   125 - 77   2013 $130

Two Hundreth Anniversary of the First Reformed Protestant Dutch Church of Schenectady. Schenectady: Daily and Weekly Union Steam Printing House, 1880. First edition, green cloth, gilt, contemporary owner's name, corners little bumped, small faint stain on one leaf, nice, very good or better copy. Between the Covers Rare Books, Inc.   New York City - 28749   2013 $225

Two Jolly Mariners. London: Blackie, n.d. circa, 1918. Oblong 4to., cloth backed pictorial boards, slightly edgewear, very good+, 24 full page color illustrations by Stewart Orr. Aleph-Bet Books, Inc.   104 - 399   2013 $225

Two Worlds. New York: Two Worlds Pub., September, 1925. September 1926, First editions, each one of 500 copies, issues 1-5, original printed paper wrappers, first four issues in original (somewhat worn) black cardboard slipcases, issue 5 with 8 full page illustrations and numerous illustrations in text, issue No. 3 with ink owner inscription of Harry Marshall, No. 4 with same signature inside front wrapper, paper wrapper of first issue coming loose from spine, wrappers bit darkened, spines slightly wrinkled, two spines with minor chips, isolated faint smudges, other trivial imperfections, otherwise in excellent condition, generally clean, fresh and bright. Phillip J. Pirages   63 - 290   2013 $500

Two Worlds Monthly. New York: July, 1926. September 1927, First 11 issues, original printed paper wrappers, isolated pencilled marginalia, five spines with minor chip at tail, short splits to head of six joints, covers of last issue detached and chipped around edges, covers little soiled, couple of short fore-edge tears, occasional corner creases or short marginal tears, leaves clean and fresh, fragile volumes, otherwise well preserved. Phillip J. Pirages   63 - 291   2013 $4000

Tyerman, L. *The Life and Times of the Rev. John Wesley, M.A., Founder of the Methodists.* London: Hodder and Stoughton, 1871. Second edition, 3 volumes, old half calf, gilt, rather rubbed and scraped in places but sound, 3 tissue guarded portraits, excellent set. R. F. G. Hollett & Son Wesleyan Methodism - 30   2013   £85

Tyerman, L. *The Oxford Methodists: Memoirs of the Rev. Messrs. Clayton, Ingham, Gambold, Hervey and Broughton...* New York: Harper and Brothers, 1873. First US edition, original brown cloth, gilt, paneled in black, over bevelled boards, engraved composite portrait frontispiece. R. F. G. Hollett & Son   Wesleyan Methodism - 31   2013   £95

Tyler, Anne 1941- *Breathing Lessons.* Franklin Center: Franklin Library, 1988. First edition, true first, signed by author, gilt stamped blue leather, all edges gilt, ribbon marker. Beasley Books   2013 - 2013 $100

Tymme, Thomas *A Silver Watch Bell, the Sound Whereof is Able (by the Grace of God) to Win the Most Prophane Worldling and Careless Liver...* London: printed by John Haviland for Thomas Alchorn, 1638. Small octavo, lacking A2 (titlepage) and I2 (pages 115-116), text within double ruled border, with headline, page numbers and marginal glosses inside outer border, 16 headpieces, 14 ornamental initials and 2 tailpieces, contemporary marbled boards, rebacked (possibly in 1915, according to pencil note on front pastedown), with speckled calf, modern red and white paper spine label lettered in ink, plain endpapers, all edges speckled red, some trimmed close to headlines and in a few cases to marginal inscriptions, boards worn, hinges cracked, tiny rust or ink hole to top of front free endpaper, tiny wormhole to outer margin of beginning leaves, affecting a letter or two of marginal glosses, over opened at a few places, still very good, from the library of John Locke with ink inscriptions, signatures and marginal notations in at least five different hands, (John Locke, Ri. Yolland, Emmanual Bayhind, William Yoo and Riettell). Heritage Book Shop 50th Anniversary Catalogue - 67   2013 $35,000

Tynan, Katharine 1861-1931 *The Holy War.* London: Sidgwick and Jackson, 1916. First edition, small 8vo., original blue cloth, paper label to spine, inscribed by author for Ettie Grenfell, with library label of Taplow Court, spine label slightly nicked, otherwise excellent. Maggs Bros. Ltd. 1442 - 309   2013   £125

Tynan, Katherine   **1861-1931**   *A Little Book for John O'Mahony's Friends.*   Mosher, 1909.   8vo., cloth, dust jacket, slipcase, very good, signed presentation from author to Mary Hutton.   C. P. Hyland   261 - 669   2013   £70

Tynan, Kenneth   *Persona Grata.*   London: Allan Wingate, 1954.   First reprint, 4to. original blue cloth, excellent copy in slightly rubbed and nicked dust jacket, inscribed by Cecil Beaton to Maurice Chevalier, photos by Beaton, excellent copy, in slightly rubbed and nicked dust jacket.   Maggs Bros. Ltd.   1460 - 55   2013   £300

Tyndale-Biscoe, E. D.   *Fifty Years Against the Stream.*   Mysore: Wesleyan Mission Press, 1930.   First edition, small 4to., original red pictorial cloth, spine little faded, 54 illustrations, errata slip tipped in.   R. F. G. Hollett & Son   Wesleyan Methodism - 65   2013   £50

Tyndale, William   *The Whole Workes of W. Tyndall, John Frith and Doct. Barnes, three worthy Martyrs...*   London: printed by John Daye, 1573.   First edition, 3 parts in one, folio, black letter and roman letter, woodcut border, half page woodcut illustrations on A4, woodcut historiated and foliate initials, typographical ornaments, 18th century calf, neatly rebacked to style, covers decoratively bordered in blind, board edges tooled gilt marbled edges, early paper repair to outer margin of D4 in first part, not affecting text, lower blank corner of Xs3 (pages 405/406) renewed, not affecting text, repaired tear to lower margin of DD1 (pages 461/462), just touching a few letters, but with no loss, paper repair to lower corner of Mmm5 (pages 321/322) in third part, not affecting text, few minor marginal paper flaws not affecting text, small dampstain in lower corner of end of second part and throughout third part, date '1572' on general title has been altered ink to '1573' as in several copies noted in STC.   Heritage Book Shop   50th Anniversary Catalogue - 103   2013 $35,000

A Typesticker's Tract on Typefaces What They Are & What He Thinks they Ought Not to Be; with a Review of the Opinions of Others on This.   Los Angeles: W. M. Cheney, 1949.   Labeled 'reading copy' on front board, 10.3 x 7.3 cm., paper covered boards, label on front, from the collection of Donn W. Sanford.   Oak Knoll Books   303 - 95   2013 $125

Tytler, Sarah   *Childhood a Hundred Years Ago.*   Marcus Ward & Co. n.d., 1877.   Original decorated cloth gilt over bevelled boards, extremities trifle worn, 6 chromolithographs after Reynolds laid in, prize label on pastedown, very nice.   R. F. G. Hollett & Son   Children's Books - 618   2013   £40

U

Unaipon, David *Native Legends.* Adelaide: Hankin, Ellis & King, 1929. First edition, stapled wrappers, small faint stain to front photo wrapper, else fine, rare. Between the Covers Rare Books, Inc. 165 - 11 2013 $1500

Underwood, Thomas Richard *A Narrative of Memorable Events in Paris... in the Year 1814... Also Anecdotes of Buonaparte's Journey to Elba.* London: printed for the editor, 1828. First edition, publisher's pinkish brown muslin, flat spine with original printed paper label, edges untrimmed, slight fading to spine and around board edges, extremities bit bumped and wrinkled (as expected), front cover with couple of small stains, one opening with faint shadow of laid-in object (a ribbon?), other trivial imperfections, but quite excellent, original insubstantial binding entirely solid, leaves remarkably clean and fresh. Phillip J. Pirages 63 - 353 2013 $600

United Mine Workers of America *United Mine Workers of America Journal Volume XXXI Nos. 7, 9, 20 and 24.* Indianapolis: United Mine Workers, 1920. 4 issues, 4to., newsprint, little chipped at edges and slightly browned, but very good. Second Life Books Inc. 183 - 385 2013 $65

United States. Department of Agriculture - 1900 *Report on the Big Trees of California. Prepared in the Division of Forestry, US Dept. of Agriculture.* Washington: GPO, 1900. First edition, 30 pages, 19 photo illustrations on 15 plates, 2 large folding maps, publisher's blind and gilt stamped cloth, spotting and slight rubbing to spine, ink number on spine, slight damage to outer blank margin of last few text leaves, else nice, maps are fine. Argonaut Book Shop Recent Acquisitions June 2013 - 24 2013 $250

United States. Library of Congress - 1910 *Preliminary Catalogue: American & English Genealogies in the Library of Congress.* Washington: 1910. First issue, 805 pages, original cloth, some damp marking, text very good. C. P. Hyland 261 - 51 2013 £65

United States. Navy Department - 1959 *Dictionary of American Naval Fighting Ships.* Washington: Navy Department, 1959-1981. 8 volumes, large 8vo., photos, maroon cloth, gilt stamped cover and spine titles, Burndy bookplates, near fine. Jeff Weber Rare Books 169 - 452 2013 $350

United States. Supreme Court - 1857 *The Case of Dred Scott in the United States Supreme Court.* New York: Greeley & McElrath, 1857. First New York edition, 104 pages, sewn self wrappers, old owner's stamp effaced, else nice, near fine. Between the Covers Rare Books, Inc. 165 - 30 2013 $400

United States. War Department - 1917 *War Surgery of the Nervous System.* Washington: GPO, 1917. 360 pages, original leather boards, newly rebacked, fore edges chipped and worn, lower corner lacking outer leather about 1 inch, internally very good. James Tait Goodrich 75 - 67 2013 $495

An Universal History from the Earliest Account of Time. London: printed for T. Osborne, A. Millar & J. Osborne, 1747-1748. 20 volumes, plates, uniformly bound in contemporary Scottish full calf, raised bands, gilt compartments, red morocco label, some occasional slight rubbing, slight nick to head of volume I, fine in original binding. Jarndyce Antiquarian Booksellers CCV - 275 2013 £2500

Unsworth, Barry *Mooncranker's Gift.* Boston: Houghton Mifflin, 1974. First American edition, inscribed by author in Toronto in 1993, owner name, fine in near fine, very slightly spine tanned dust jacket with one small spot to rear panel and 3 small edge tears. Ken Lopez Bookseller 159 - 191 2013 $200

Updike, John 1932- *Bech: a Book.* New York: Knopf, 1970. First edition, inscribed by author for Cyril and Sylvia Wismar, foxing to top edge of text block, else fine in near fine dust jacket foxed on verso and with couple of small edge chips. Ken Lopez Bookseller 159 - 192 2013 $650

Updike, John 1932- *Buchanan Dying.* New York: Knopf, 1974. First edition, inscribed by author for Cyril Wismar, half dozen instances of underlining in as many pages, presumably by Wismar, foxing to fore edge, thus near fine in like dust jacket, price clipped. Ken Lopez Bookseller 159 - 193 2013 $750

Updike, John 1932- *The Centaur.* New York: Alfred A. Knopf, 1963. First edition, clean and tight near fine copy in about very good dust jacket, small chips from spine ends and decent amount of scratching to front panel. Jeff Hirsch Books Fall 2013 - 128427 2013 $65

Updike, John 1932- *Due Considerations.* New York: Knopf, 2007. Uncorrected proof copy, bulky text, nearly 700 pages with shallow corner creasing to covers, near fine in yellow wrapper with cover art bound in. Ken Lopez Bookseller 159 - 201 2013 $125

Updike, John 1932- *The Early Stories 1953-1975.* New York: Knopf, First edition, fine in near fine dust jacket, signed and inscribed by author to Harvard classmate. Leather Stalking Books   October 2013 - 2013 $300

Updike, John 1932- *Five Poems.* Cleveland: Bits Press, 1980. Of a total edition of 185, this one of 135 numbered copies, signed by author, this #184, additionally inscribed by author for Sylvia and Cyril Wismar, some staining to fore edge of cover, bit of foxing to fore edge of text block, fine in saddle stitched wrappers.   Ken Lopez Bookseller   159 - 195   2013 $375

Updike, John 1932- *Hawthorne's Creed.* New York: Targ, 1981. One of 250 signed by author, inscribed by author for Sylvia & Cyril Wismar, together with a deck of Pinochle playing cards inscribed on case "From John & Martha Updike" in unknown hand, cards and case near fine, book fine in near fine, unprinted dust jacket (mildly sunned).   Ken Lopez Bookseller   159 - 196   2013 $550

Updike, John 1932- *Hugging the Shore.* New York: Knopf, 1983. First edition, inscribed by author for Robert Starer, book appears read, with some sagging to bulky text block and modest fading to covers, in very good to near fine dust jacket.   Ken Lopez Bookseller   159 - 197   2013 $350

Updike, John 1932- *Jester's Dozen.* Northridge: Lord John Press, 1984. First edition, limited to 50 numbered copies, specially bound, this no. 13, 8vo., signed by author, fine, paper is Frankfurt White, the Spectrum type as handset by Denise Grimsman, binding by Campbell-Logan in quarter black cloth and patterned paper covered boards, printed paper spine label.   By the Book, L. C.   38 - 103   2013 $400

Updike, John 1932- *My Father's Tears and Other Stories.* New York: Knopf, 2009. Uncorrected proof copy, few light spots to covers, near fine in wrappers.   Ken Lopez Bookseller   159 - 202   2013 $125

Updike, John 1932- *Problems and Other Stories.* New York: Knopf, 1979. First edition, inscribed by author for Sylvia and Cyril Wismar, trace of fore edge foxing, else fine in very near fine dust jacket.   Ken Lopez Bookseller   159 - 194   2013 $750

Updike, John 1932- *Bessere Verbaltnisse. (Rabbit is Rich).* Berlin: Verlag Volt und Welt, 1986. German language edition, inscribed by author for Cyril Wismar, mild age toning to acidic paper and foxing to top edge of text block, near fine in fine dust jacket.   Ken Lopez Bookseller   159 - 198   2013 $250

Updike, John 1932- *S.* Deutsch, 1988. First English edition, 17/175 copies (of an edition of 97), signed by author, 8vo., original quarter green morocco, slightly faded, backstrip gilt lettered and banded, board slipcase, near fine.   Blackwell's Rare Books   B174 - 309   2013   £250

Updike, John 1932- *The Same Door.* New York: Alfred A. Knopf, 1959. First edition in book form, 210 x 133mm., original blue quarter cloth over paper boards, original dust jacket frayed and with small chips at head of spine (without loss of lettering), slight fraying at corners, short tear at head of rear board, front panel with very minor abrasions, but bright and attractive nevertheless (volume itself in fine condition), quite pleasing copy, rarely seen in truely fine jacket.   Phillip J. Pirages   63 - 475   2013 $450

Updike, John 1932- *A Soft Spring Night in Shillington.* Northbridge: Lord John Press, 1986. First edition, limitd to 50 deluxe, specially bound signed copies, this no. 2, 8vo., 43 pages, fine, brown leather spine and tan cloth covered boards, gilt lettered spine and patterned endpapers by Marianna Blau, fine in original cloth covered slipcase, paper is Simpson Coronado Opaque and type is Schneidler.   By the Book, L. C.   36 - 59   2013 $400

Updike, John 1932- *Thanatopses.* Cleveland: Bits Press, 1991. One of 237 copies, this copy inscribed by author for Cyril Wismar, fine in saddle stitched self wrappers.   Ken Lopez Bookseller   159 - 199   2013 $250

Updike, John 1932- *Toward the End of Time.* New York: Knopf, 1997. First edition, fine in fine dust jacket, inscribed by author for Cyril Wismar.   Ken Lopez Bookseller   159 - 200   2013 $250

Upfield, Arthur W. *The Bachelors of Broken Hill.* Garden City: Doubleday Crime Club, 1950. First edition, fine in dust jacket with tiny wear at spine ends at corners and along folds.   Mordida Books   81 - 532   2013 $400

Upfield, Arthur W. *The Battling Prophet.* London: Heinemann, 1956. First edition, fine in price clipped dust jacket with short closed tear.   Mordida Books   81 - 533   2013 $150

Upfield, Arthur W. *The Bone is Pointed.* Garden City: Doubleday Crime Club, 1947. First American edition, very good in dust jacket with internal tape mends, numerous short closed tears, chipping at spine ends and at corners.   Mordida Books   81 - 531   2013 $100

Upfield, Arthur W. *Bony and the Black Virgin.* London: Heinemann, 1959. First edition, name on front endpaper, top of page edges slightly spotted, otherwise fine in dust jacket with lightly soiled back panel and couple of short closed tears.   Mordida Books   81 - 534   2013 $100

Upfield, Arthur W. *Death of a Swagman.* Garden City: Doubleday Crime Club, 1945. First edition, fine in near fine dust jacket with internal tape reinforcing, minor color restoration at base of spine, several short closed tears, crease on back panel, attractive unfaded copy. Mordida Books 81 - 530 2013 $350

Upfield, Arthur W. *Gripped by Drought.* Missoula: Dennis McMillan, 1990. First American edition, one of 450 copies, fine in fine dust jacket, scarce. Between the Covers Rare Books, Inc. Mystery & Detective Fiction - 316971 2013 $350

Upfield, Arthur W. *Murder Down Under.* Garden City: Doubleday Crime Club, 1943. First American edition, fine in dust jacket with some very slight spine fading, some short closed tears and wear at top corners. Mordida Books 81 - 527 2013 $500

Upfield, Arthur W. *The Mystery of Swordfish Reef.* Garden City: Doubleday Crime Club, 1943. First American edition, very good in dust jacket with half inch piece missing top of spine, chipping at base of spine, corners and along edges, internal tape mends, numerous closed tears, wear along folds. Mordida Books 81 - 529 2013 $80

Upfield, Arthur W. *Wings Above the Claypan.* Garden City: Doubleday Crime Club, 1943. First American edition, page edges slightly darkened, else fine in very good dust jacket with internal tape, slightly faded spine, chipping at top of spine and at top edge of front panel, several short closed tears. Mordida Books 81 - 528 2013 $250

Upham, Charles W. *Life, Explorations and Public Service of John Charles Fremont.* Boston: Ticknor and Fields, 1856. First edition, small octavo, portrait, 13 engraved plates, blind embossed and gilt stamped blue cloth, slightest of foxing to frontispiece, light rubbing to spine ends, very fine. Argonaut Book Shop Summer 2013 - 120 2013 $250

Upton, Bertha *Golliwogg in the African Jungle.* Longman Green and Co., 1909. First edition, oblong small 4to., original cloth backed pictorial boards, boards rubbed, corners rather worn, pages 64, illustrations in color, contents very clean, free of any tears or markings, nice, scarce. R. F. G. Hollett & Son Children's Books - 619 2013 £450

Upton, Bertha *The Golliwogg's Air-Ship.* London: Longmans, Green and Co., n.d., First edition, oblong small 4to., original cloth backed pictorial boards, little rubbed and soiled, edges and corners worn and repaired, nicely rebacked to match, illustrations in color, contents clean and untorn. R. F. G. Hollett & Son Children's Books - 620 2013 £450

Upton, Bertha *Golliwogg's Air-ship.* London: Longmans, 1902. First edition, oblong 4to., cloth backed pictorial boards, corners slightly rubbed, slight cover soil and few inconspicuous archival margin mends, else clean, tight, very good+, full page color illustrations by Florence Upton are superb. Aleph-Bet Books, Inc. 104 - 563 2013 $900

Upton, Bertha *The Golliwogg's "Auto-Go-Cart".* London: Longman, Green and Co., 1901. First edition, oblong small 4to., original cloth backed pictorial boards, little soiled, edges and corners worn, illustrations in color, joints cracked, few short edge tears, spots and marks, very good. R. F. G. Hollett & Son Children's Books - 621 2013 £350

Upton, Bertha *The Golliwogg's Bicycle Club.* London: Longmans, Green and Co., 1903. New edition, oblong small 4to., original cloth backed pictorial boards, little soiled, corners rather worn, illustrations in color, little spotting and small pencilled name to title, else contents very clean and free of any tears or markings. R. F. G. Hollett & Son Children's Books - 622 2013 £350

Upton, Bertha *Little Hearts.* London: George Routledge, 1897. First edition, 4to., cloth backed pictorial boards, some edge wear and slight bit of cover soil, very good+, illustrations in color by Florence Upton, rare. Aleph-Bet Books, Inc. 104 - 564 2013 $1500

Uris, Leon *Trinity.* Deutsch, 1976. First edition, 8vo., cloth, dust jacket, very good. C. P. Hyland 261 - 840 2013 £30

Usher, James *An Answer to a Challenge Made by a Jesuit in Ireland.* London: printed for Benjamin Tooke, 1686. 4to., very good, 18th century half calf, gilt banded spine, red morocco label, marbled boards, top corner of final leaf torn, not affecting text, some light browning to endpapers and titlepage. Ken Spelman Books Ltd. 75 - 9 2013 £420

Ussher, Arland *The Mines of Siberiay.* Dublin: Dolmen Press, 1956. First edition, one of 250 copies, tall 8vo., original wrappers, fine. Maggs Bros. Ltd. 1442 - 310 2013 £60

Utah Brand Book 1922. Salt Lake City: Utah State Board of Agriculture, circa, 1922. 231 pages, octavo, flexible red cloth wrappers, gilt stamped title on front wrapper, good, extremities gently rubbed, front cover has some very light staining and rear cover has numerous small stains. Ken Sanders Rare Books 45 - 15 2013 $295

Utah. Constitution *Constitution of the State of Utah. Adopted by the Convention April 27 1882. Ratified by the People May 22 1882.* Salt Lake City: 1882. Original printed wrappers, pages browned, some soil to wrappers, else very good. Dumont Maps & Books of the West 125 - 38 2013 $150

Utley, Robert M. *Billy the Kid: a Short and Violent Life.* Lincoln: 1989. xii, 302 pages, illustrations, near fine in like dust jacket, inscribed by author to previous owners. Dumont Maps & Books of the West   125 - 78   2013 $50

Uyeda, Makoto *GA Houses 5.* Japan: A. D. A. Edita, 1978. First edition, numerous color and black and white illustrations, near fine copy, little wear to edges and very slight soiling to covers.   Jeff Hirsch Books   Fall 2013 - 129274   2013 $50

Uzanne, Octave *Son Altesse, La Femme.* Paris: A. Quantin, 1885. First edition, one of 100 special large paper copies on Japon, 292 x 216mm, vignette on title, small illustrations or vignettes on 50 text pages, 11 vignette borders or headpieces (3 of them in color, 10 of them in one or two extra states) and 10 color plates, each in two states (before and after letters), beautifully and elaborately gilt contemporary blue-gray crushed morocco by Zaehnsdorf (signed on front turn-in), covers framed with single rule around very broad and intricate floral border of many leaves, blossoms and tendrils enclosing central field of rows of alternating flower and small stars, raised bands, spine compartments similarly decorated, very handsome densely gilt inner dentelles, marbled endpapers, top edge gilt, other edges untrimmed, original paper and silk materials bound in; armorial bookplate of Sir David Salomons, spine slightly and uniformly faded, one inch cut in lower margin of one leaf, else extremely fine and beautifully bound set.   Phillip J. Pirages   61 - 135   2013 $2500

V

Vachell, Horace Annesley *Quinney's Adventures.* New York: Doran, 1924. First American edition, little darkening to gutters, else fine in very good plus dust jacket rubbed on front panel, very faint stain on spine and couple of tiny nicks at crown.   Between the Covers Rare Books, Inc.   Sci-Fi, Fantasy & Horror - 43250   2013 $250

Vachss, Andrew *Flood.* New York: Fine, 1985. First edition, signed by author, very fine in dust jacket.   Mordida Books   81 - 535   2013 $125

Vachss, Andrew *Strega.* New York: Knopf, 1987. First edition, inscribed by author, very fine in dust jacket.   Mordida Books   81 - 536   2013 $90

Valentiner, Karl Wilhelm *Handworterbuch der Astronomie Unter Mitwirkung.* Wroclaw: Eduard Trewendt, 1897-1902. 4 volumes in 5 book, numerous illustrations, 11 plates, endleaves occasionally faintly foxed, beautiful modern half gilt stamped black morocco over blue pebbled cloth, few corners gently rubbed, volume IV front cover slightly smudged, near fine, spectacular set.   Jeff Weber Rare Books   169 - 458   2013 $1500

Valin, Jonathan *Dead Letter.* New York: Dodd Mead, 1981. First edition, signed by author, fine in dust jacket with tiny rubbing on spine.   Mordida Books   81 - 543   2013 $75

Valin, Jonathan *Final Notice.* New York: Dodd, Mead, 1980. First edition, very fine in dust jacket.   Mordida Books   81 - 542   2013 $125

Vallee, Louis Leger *Traite de la Geometrie Descriptive. (with) Planches Gravees par Ambroise Tardieu.* Paris: widow Courcier, 1819. First edition, 2 volumes in 1, lithographed frontispiece, engraved titlepage to atlas, comprising 60 engraved plates, 3 double page, minor dampstain in upper outer corner towards end, little offsetting of plates, 4to., contemporary half calf, corners worn, good.   Blackwell's Rare Books   Sciences - 124   2013   £1000

Vallee, Rudy *Vagabond Dreams Come True.* New York: Dutton, First edition, 8vo., 262 pages, photos, very good, inscribed by author for Harry Chaffin.   Second Life Books Inc.   183 - 386   2013 $100

Valpy, Richard *Elements of Greek Grammar.* London: printed by A. J. Valpy, 1830. New edition, 8vo., 2 fold-out plates, very occasional pencil annotations, little soiled, particularly near front, tan half calf with brown label to spine and marbled boards, upper joint splitting, edges bit worn, boards rubbed, ownership inscription of William Melland.   Unsworths Antiquarian Booksellers   28 - 55   2013   £30

Van *Fun with Faces.* Garden City: Garden City Books, 1950. 4to., spiral backed boards, tiny bit of rubbing, else near fine, bright color illustrations by Julain Wehr, 6 comical color plates operated with tabs letting reader made comical faces, rare.   Aleph-Bet Books, Inc.   104 - 369   2013 $450

Van Allsburg, Chris *Garden of Abdul Gasazi.* Boston: Houghton Mifflin, 1979. First edition, large oblong 4to., cloth, fine in dust jacket with long closed tear on front panel, full page illustrations, very scarce.   Aleph-Bet Books, Inc.   105 - 570   2013 $750

Van Allsburg, Chris *Jumanji.* Boston: Houghton Mifflin Co., 1981. First edition, oblong quarto, original green linen grain cloth over boards with copper gold lettering on front cover and spine, tan endpapers, fine in original green printed dust jacket, this copy with gold Caldecott Medal affixed to front panel.   David Brass Rare Books, Inc.   Holiday 2012 Chapter One - DB 00808   2013 $550

Van Der Elst, Violet *Deaths of the Vampire Baroness and Other Thrilling Stories.* London: published by Modern Fiction, n.d., 1945. First edition, octavo, pictorial wrappers, side stamped.   L. W. Currey, Inc.   Fall Sampler Sept. 2013 - 146554   2013 $150

Van Der Post, Laurens *Journey into Russia.* London: Hogarth Press, 1964. Third impression, 8vo., folding map, original blue cloth, inscribed copy from author to Field Marshal Lord Montgomery.   J. & S. L. Bonham Antiquarian Booksellers   Europe - 9805   2013   £45

Van Derzee, James *James Van Derzee, Photographer.* New York: James van DerZee Inst./Beefeater Foundatiaon, 1972. First edition, small quarto, stapled wrappers, fine in original glassine sleeve, although not called for this copy signed by Van Derzee.   Between the Covers Rare Books, Inc.   165 - 527   2013 $850

Van Derzee, James *The World of James Van Derzee: a Visual Record of Black Americans.* New York: Grove Press, 1969. First edition, quarto, near fine dust jacket with couple of very short tears.   Between the Covers Rare Books, Inc.   165 - 240   2013 $125

Van Evrie, John H. *Subgenation; the Theory of the Normal Relation of the Races an Answer to "Miscegnation".* New York: 1864. First edition, 12mo., 72 pages, original printed wrappers.   M & S Rare Books, Inc.   95 - 375   2013 $375

Van Gulik, Robert *The Chinese Bell Murders.* London: Michael Joseph, 1958. First English edition, some darkening on endpapers, otherwise fine in dust jacket with nicks at corners and tiny wear at top of spine.   Mordida Books   81 - 553   2013 $300

Van Gulik, Robert *The Chinese Gold Murders.* London: Michael Joseph, 1959. First English edition, darkening on endpapers, small scrape on front endpaper, otherwise very good in dust jacket with soiled back panel, wear at corners and nicks at spine ends.   Mordida Books   81 - 554   2013 $150

Van Gulik, Robert *The Chinese Lake Murders.* London: Michael Joseph, 1960. First English edition, fine in dust jacket with several closed tears, one of which on back panel is about an inch and a half in length.   Mordida Books   81 - 555   2013 $200

Van Gulik, Robert *Vier Vingers. (Four Fingers).* Amsterdam: Netherlands Society, 1964. First edition, fine in soft covers with short crease at corner and tiny wear at corners.   Mordida Books   81 - 557   2013 $100

Van Gulik, Robert *Judge Dee at Work.* London: Heinemann, 1967. First English edition, fine in dust jacket with light wear at corners and couple of tiny closed tears.   Mordida Books   81 - 559   2013 $175

Van Gulik, Robert *The Lacquer Screen.* London: Heinemann, 1964. First English edition, small stain on top of page edges, otherwise fine in dust jacket with very slightly faded spine.   Mordida Books   81 - 556   2013 $200

Van Gulik, Robert *The Monkey and the Tiger.* London: Heinemann, 1965. First English edition, name and address stamped on front endpaper, otherwise near fine in dust jacket with some tiny tears and wear.   Mordida Books   81 - 558   2013 $90

Van Loan, Charles E. *Old Man Curry; Race Track Stories.* New York: George H. Doran, 1917. First edition, slight wear to boards, still easily near fine in lightly soiled, fine dust jacket.   Between the Covers Rare Books, Inc.   Horses, Horsemanship, Horse Racing, Etc. - 72547   2013 $85

Van Vechten, Carl 1880-1964 *Les Paradis des Negres. (Nigger Heaven).* Paris: Simon Kra, 1927. First French edition, one of 200 numbered copies on velin, orange printed wrappers, some erosion to paper on spine, front wrappers loose, sound, fair copy, uncommon.   Between the Covers Rare Books, Inc.   165 - 272   2013 $275

Van Vechten, Carl 1880-1964 *Le Paradis des Negres. (Nigger Heaven).* New York: Alfred A. Knopf, 1927. Eleventh printing, little light foxing in text, else near fine, without dust jacket, inscribed by author for M. P. Shiel, July 4 1927.   Between the Covers Rare Books, Inc.   Sci-Fi, Fantasy & Horror - 273811   2013 $850

Van Vechten, Carl 1880-1964 *Nigger Heaven.* New York: Alfred A. Knopf, 1927. Eleventh printing, little light foxing in text, else near fine, without dust jacket, bookplate of "Realm of Redonda" and its monarchs M. P. Shiel and John Gawsworth, inscribed by author for Shiel.   Between the Covers Rare Books, Inc.   165 - 271   2013 $850

Van Vliet, Claire *Sky and Earth; Variable Landscape.* Newark: Janus Press, 1976. First limited edition, one of 100 unnumbered, unsigned copies (entire edition), 4to., original cloth, paper onlay to front cover, printed paper spine label with 39 pieces of die-cut acetate and Navaho colored paper landscape elements in triangular pocket, very fine, rare.   James S. Jaffe Rare Books   Fall 2013 - 74   2013 $1250

Van Vogt, A. E. *Null A3.* Berkshire/Beverly Hills: Morrison, Raven-Hill Co., 1984. Limited to 750 signed copies with page section from original manuscript tipped in, 8vo., 213 pages, signed and inscribed by Lydia and A. E. Van Vogt, fine dust jacket, fine original slipcase, quite scarce, fine copy.   By the Book, L. C.   36 - 60   2013 $1250

Vance, Jack *Emphryio.* Garden City: Doubleday and Co., 1969. First edition, fine in fine dust jacket, exceptional, nearly as new.   Between the Covers Rare Books, Inc.   Sci-Fi, Fantasy & Horror - 287138   2013 $850

Vance, Jack *Maske: Thaery. Fantastic Adventure of the Far Future.* New York: Berkeley/Putnam, 1976. First edition, signed by author on titlepage.   Ed Smith Books   78 - 69   2013 $150

Vance, John Holbrook *Emphyrio.* Garden City: Doubleday & Co., 1969. First edition, octavo, cloth.   L. W. Currey, Inc.   Utopian Literature: Recent Acquisitions (April 2013) - 141496   2013 $750

Vance, John Holbrook *The Fox Valley Murders.* Indianapolis: Bobbs Merrill Co., 1966. First edition, fine in fine dust jacket with slightest of rubbing, beautiful copy.   Between the Covers Rare Books, Inc.   Mystery & Detective Fiction - 286698   2013 $200

Vance, John Holbrook *The Fox Valley Murders.* Indianapolis: Bobbs Merrill, 1967. First English edition, fine in dust jacket with light wear at corners and couple of tiny closed tears.   Mordida Books   81 - 560   2013 $150

Vance, John Holbrook *The View from Chickweed's Window.* San Francisco: Underwood/Miller, 1979. First edition, limited to 750 copies, though not called for, this copy signed, 8vo., 194 pages, fine in fine dust jacket.   By the Book, L. C.   36 - 50   2013 $200

Vane, C. W. *A Steam Voyage to Constantinople.* London: Henry Colburn, 1842. First edition, 2 volumes, 8vo., frontispieces, plate, contemporary green half calf, small loss of leather on spine, internally clean and crisp.   J. & S. L. Bonham Antiquarian Booksellers   Europe - 9695   2013   £1100

Vane, Roland *Sin Stained.* Stoke-on-Trent: The Archer Press, 1950. Leaves stapled, original pictorial wrappers. Jarndyce Antiquarian Booksellers   CCV - 276   2013   £75

Varcaresco, Helene *The Bard of the Dimbovitza: Romanian Folk-Songs Second Series Collected from the Peasants.* London: Osgood, McIlvaine, 1896. First edition, presentation copy from principal translator, Carmen Sylva (Pseud. of Elizabeth, Queen of Romania) to Benjamin Duryea Woodward, original brown cloth, gilt front cover and spine by Charles Ricketts, binding very good with some rubbing and fading, some foxing to endpapers but interior pages clean with edges untrimmed, 130 pages.   The Kelmscott Bookshop   7 - 128   2013 $500

Vardon, Thomas *Index to Local and Personal Acts 1798-1839.* Luke, 1840. First edition, 485 pages, octavo, original cloth, worn, text good, office stamp of Mallow Co., Cork, solicitors.   C. P. Hyland   261 - 107   2013   £60

Vassalli, Mikiel Anton *Grammatica della Lingua Maltese.* Malta: Stampata per l'Autore, 1827. 8vo., original cloth backed plain grey wrappers, folding table, uncut, inscribed "A Maltese Grammar presented by the Committee of the Church Missionary Society for the Library March 3rd 1828, fine, ex-British & Foreign Bible Society Library and later ex-Cambridge University Library with stamp.   Howard S. Mott Inc.   262 - 154   2013 $850

Vaughan, Henry *The Works.* Oxford: Clarendon Press, 1914. 228 x 142mm., 2 volumes, appealing contemporary hunter green half calf, raised bands, spines attractively gilt in compartments with large central fleuron and volute cornerpieces, one red and one black morocco label, marbled endpapers, top edges gilt, other edges unopened, spines uniformly sunned to soft brown, minor rubbing to extremities, but bindings quite sound, generally pleasant and immaculate copy internally, obviously unread text very clean, fresh and bright with generous margins.   Phillip J. Pirages   63 - 276   2013 $350

Veblen, Thorstein *Absentee Ownership and Business Enterprise in Recent Times. The Case of America.* New York: B. W. Huebsch, 1923. 8vo., very good++ in original green cloth, gilt lettering, minimal cover wear and stain to edges, signed and inscribed by author in year of publication.   By the Book, L. C.   38 - 23   2013 $1750

Veblen, Thorstein *The Theory of the Leisure Class.* New York: Macmillan and Co., 1899. First edition, 190 x 131mm., original dark green cloth, spine lettered and ruled in gilt, front board ruled in blind, top edge gilt, others uncut, bit of soiling to cloth of front cover, spine very slightly darkened, overall very good, housed in full green morocco clamshell.   Heritage Book Shop   Holiday Catalogue 2012 - 152   2013 $5000

Veer, Gerrit De *Tre Navigationi Fatte Dagli Olandesi, e Zelandesi Al Settentrione Nela Norvegia Moscovia, e Tartaria Verso il Catai e Regno de Sini, Doue Scopersero di Mare di Veygatz...* Venice: Jeronimo Porro, 1599. First Italian edition, engraved vignette on titlepage, engraved full page compass rose and 31 half page plates, 4to., old calf, rubbed.   Maggs Bros. Ltd.   1467 - 145   2013   £6000

Venn, H. *The Complete Duty of Man; or a System of Doctrinal & Practical Christianity.* Religious Tract Society, circa, 1847. New edition, very good, 8vo., full contemporary plum pebble grain morocco, ornate gilt panels and spine, all edges gilt, tear to lower outer corner of titlepage and foxing to frontispiece, inscription dated 1847 on endpaper, little rubbing, pretty contemporary binding.   Ken Spelman Books Ltd.   75 - 113   2013   £60

Venn, John *Annals of a Clerical Family.* London: Macmillan and Co., 1904. 8vo., folding map, plates, recent half blue morocco, gilt lettered spine, uncut edges, some slight foxing.   Ken Spelman Books Ltd.   75 - 167   2013   £40

Veresaev, Vikentii Vikent'Evich *In the War. Memoirs of V. Veresaev.* New York: Mitchell Kennerley, 1917. First edition, small 8vo., cloth with gilt titles, very scarce in printed dust jacket, bright, near fine, unopened, uncut, near fine in lightly rubbed dust jacket.   Kaaterskill Books   16 - 86   2013 $150

Verey, David *A Shell Guide to Mid Wales. The Counties of Brecon, Radnor and Montgomery.* London: Faber, 1960. First edition, numerous reproductions of photos, color printed title vignette, pages 88, 8vo., original tan cloth, backstrip blocked in green, dust jacket rubbed and with small piece torn from head of front panel of the John Piper designed dust jacket, good.   Blackwell's Rare Books   172 - 228   2013   £50

Vergilius Maro, Publius *The Nyne Fyrst Bookes of the Eneidos of Virgil Converted Into Englishe Verse by Thomas Phaer.* London: by Rouland Hall for Nicholas England, 1562. Rare early edition, 4to., (220) pages, woodcut on title, text in black letter, 19th century morocco, ruled in gilt, edges gilt, extremities lightly worn, minor scuffing, first quire washed and neatly extended at top edge, possibly supplied from another copy, few internal repairs, else very good, with excellent full margins, Rubislaw House bookplate of John Morgan.   Joseph J. Felcone Inc. Books Printed before 1701 - 86   2013 $11,000

Vergilius Maro, Publius *The Aeneid of Virgil.* London: printed for R. Dodsley, 1740. First complete edition, 2 volumes, 4to., contemporary paneled calf, rebacked with sheep at early date, corners worn, early leather labels, 1918 bookplate of John W. Thomson whose parents bought Fanny Kemble's Lenox Mass. residence, gift inscription from Charles L. Hibbard, prominent Pittsfield Mass. judge.   Howard S. Mott Inc.   262 - 119   2013 $1250

Vergilius Maro, Publius *The Aeneids.* London: Ellis and White, 1876. Second, i.e. first edition, 2nd issue), 186 x 143mm., appealing contemporary navy blue morocco by Bickers & Son (stamp signed on verso of front free endpaper), covers with gilt French fillet border, raised bands flanked by plain gilt rules, spine panels with daisy centerpieces and gilt titling, turn-ins densely gilt, marbled endpapers, all edges gilt, booklabel of Abel Berland, spine uniformly sunned toward blue-green, bottom.   Phillip J. Pirages   63 - 347   2013 $275

Vergilius Maro, Publius *Aeneid.* London: Folio Society, 2010. Copy 846 of an edition of 1750, 448 pages, numerous color illustrations, very fine in decorated full leather binding done in Wassa goatskin in very near fine clamshell box, beautiful production.   Jeff Hirsch Books   Fall 2013 - 129476   2013 $400

Vergilius Maro, Publius *Bucolicorum Eclogae Decem. The Bucolicks of Virgil with an English Translation.* London: printed by R. Reily for T. Osborne, 1749. Second edition of John Martyn's translation, 8vo., frontispiece, one folding map and 3 other plates, final 2 leaves of ads present, titlepage printed in red and black, tiny bit of spotting but generally quite clean, map with small handling tear at mount, contemporary calf, spine in six compartments with low raised bands, red morocco label in second compartment, joints repaired but headcap chipped, boards with double gilt rule border, corners worn, old leather little scratched and rubbed at extremities, ownership inscription of George Hales, Christ. Coll. Cam. 1846 and different hand a monogram (EJA) vignette of a stork and crown.   Unsworths Antiquarian Booksellers   28 - 59   2013   £250

Vergilius Maro, Publius *Bucolica, Georgica, et Aeneis.* Glasguae: in aedibus Academicus Excudebat Andreas Foulis, 1778. First Foulis folio, 2 volumes bound in 1, folio, bound without list of subscribers, very occasional slight toning to some gatherings, contemporary crimson morocco boards, rebacked with some attempt made to match original color, gilt title and border, gilt Athenaeum Library stamp to spine and upper board, joints worn, boards scuffed and little chipped, some patch repairs, new endpapers pasted over old marbled boards.   Unsworths Antiquarian Booksellers   28 - 60   2013   £600

Vergilius Maro, Publius *Les Bucoliques de Virgile.* Paris: Scripta & Picta, 1953. First Villon edition, one of 245 copies (total edition), 45 (44 in color) original lithographs by Jacques Villon, hors and in texte, printed on Arches wove paper by F. Mourlot, xxx, 136 loose leaves in publisher's paper folder, boards chemise and slipcase.   Gemini Fine Books & Arts., Ltd.   Art Reference & Illustrated Books - 2013 $2750

Vergilius Maro, Publius *Georgica Publii Virgilii Maronis Hexaglotta.* E Typographeo Gulielmi Nicol, 1827. presentation copy from English translator and printer, half title inscribed "For the library of the Royal Institution from William Sotheby 12 Grosvenor Street Feby 19 1833", letter front printer presenting the volume tipped in, some light dust soiling, imperial 4to., contemporary half purple roan over marbled boards, edges untrimmed, spine divided by triple gilt filets, second compartment gilt lettered direct, rubbed at extremities, worn, front hinge cracking after title, rear flyleaf removed 'withdrawn' stamp to front pastedown, good.   Blackwell's Rare Books   172 - 147   2013   £1400

Vergilius Maro, Publius *Opera quae quidem Exstant Omnia.* Basilae: Sebastianum Henriepetri, 1613. Folio, little worming to fore-edge margins around columns 180 and 279, toning at very edge of margins to varying degrees, occasional discoloration around text esecially to volumes 1079-1802 and 1901-1904, contemporary speckled tan calf, neatly rebacked and corners repaired, red morocco gilt spine label, boards heavily scratched, few dents, edges worn, armorial bookplate of Sir William Molesworth with ink inscription of Kenneth J. Cox, Dalton Hall Victoria Park, Manchester 14 added, old ink ownership inscription of Johannis Glover on titlepage, small contemporary (?) list of Latin names for various vegetables and herbs loosely inserted.   Unsworths Antiquarian Booksellers   28 - 57   2013   £500

Vergilius Maro, Publius *Opera, Emembranis Compluribus lisque Antiquissimis recensuit.* Amsterdam: Elzevir, 1676. 12mo., foldout map, engraved titlepage trimmed down and mounted, gilt border and decoration added, 18th century red straight grain morocco, gilt spine and borders, marbled endpapers, all edges gilt, spine little scuffed, upper joint expertly repaired, hinge split, upper board very slightly marked.   Unsworths Antiquarian Booksellers   28 - 58   2013   £300

Vergilius Maro, Publius *The Works of Virgil...* London: printed for Jacob Tonson, 1697. First edition, first issue of Dryden's translation, large paper copy, 416 x 265mm., engraved frontispiece and 102 engraved plates, light dampmark to fore-edge throughout with some resultant purple spotting to lower corner, frontispiece and couple of other plates with short tears and old repairs to that corner, one plate just shaved at fore-edge, some spotting and soiling, folio, 18th century reversed calf, red morocco lettering piece, rubbed, worn at extremities, front joint cracked, gutter cracking in few places, sound.   Blackwell's Rare Books   B174 - 155   2013   £2000

Vergilius Maro, Publius *(Works). P. Virgilius Maro: in Usum Scholarum/ Ad Novissimam Heynii Editionem Exactus.* Londini: Imprensis J. Johnson et al, 1809. 250 x 147mm., 2 p.l., 700 pages, handsome contemporary navy blue straight grain morocco, densely gilt, covers with thick and thin gilt rule border and large central laurel wreath, that on front with Latin motto "Honoris Causa", that on rear with name Thomas T. Churton and date 1817, raised bands, spine lavishly gilt in compartments filled with foliage and small tools emanating from a central fleuron gilt titling and turn-ins, all edges gilt, with splendid later painting of Mount Etna on the Fore Edge, recent plush lined folding cloth box with gilt spine titling, ink stamp of Bolton Public Library on verso of title and first page of text, corners slightly bumped, boards little faded, first two gatherings mildly foxed, isolated dust spots or faint freckled foxing, still especially attractive copy, handsome binding virtually unworn, text clean and smooth and unusual fore-edge painting, very well preserved.   Phillip J. Pirages   63 - 192   2013 $2900

Vergilius Maro, Publius *Pvblivs Virgilivs Maro Varietate Lectionis et Perpetva Adnotatione. (Opera).* Lipsiae: Sumtibus Librariae Hahnianae; Londini: Apud Black, Young & Young, 1830-1841. Fourth edition, 223 x 14mm., 5 volumes bound in 9, engraved allegorical frontispiece, 6 title vignettes, 120 headpieces, 80 tailpieces and 2 plates; fine contemporary red morocco, gilt, covers with gilt double ruled frames and quatrefoil cornerpieces, raised bands, spines in gilt double ruled compartments with intricate fleuron centerpiece, gilt titling and turn-ins, marbled endpapers, all edges gilt, armorial bookplate of John Clerk Brodie, one tiny nick to upper cover of last volume, isolated faint offsetting, three gatherings in volume III, part 1, very lightly browned, isolated mild foxing to last volume, but extraordinarily fine, text especially clean, fresh and bright on thick luxurious paper and handsome bindings, quite lustrous with virtually no wear, opening only reluctantly as an indication of very little use.   Phillip J. Pirages   63 - 482   2013 $3200

Vergilius, Polydorus *De Gli Invenotri Delle Cose.* Florence: Per Filippo e Iacopo Giunti e Fratelli, 1587. First edition of this translation, light foxing, little toning, additional colophon leaf at end of text, cancelled with ink stroke but not removed, correct colophon leaf also present after index, old vellum boards, backstrip with dyed label lettered in gilt, edges mottled red and blue, scattering of wormholes to backstrip (none through to paper), hinges cracking but strong, few light marks, very good.   Blackwell's Rare Books   172 - 146   2013   £750

Vergilius, Polydorus *Proverbiorum Libellus.* Colophon: Venice: per Ioannem de Cereto de Tridino alias Tacuinum, 1503. Rare early edition, 4to., roughly half the gatherings browned, some light spotting, frequent marginal notes and underlining in early hand, some shaved, recto of final leaf dusty, modern boards covered with incunable leaf, lightly soiled and spotted, good.   Blackwell's Rare Books   172 - 145   2013   £2500

Verheyen, Philip *Corporis Humani Anatomiae liver Primus in quo Tam Veteru...* Brussels: Apd Fratres Serstevens, 1710. 2 volumes in one, 46 engraved folding plates, small 4to., contemporary full calf, gilt spine with raised bands, joints just starting, light browning to text, some fraying to plate edges, otherwise very clean, tight copy.   James Tait Goodrich   75 - 208   2013 $1795

Verlaine, Paul 1844-1896 *Parallelement.* Paris: Pierre de Tartas, 1969. First Leonor Fini edition, one of 60 dexlue exemplars (total edition 311), signed by Fini and Tartas, 13 original color lithographs by Fini, 12 of them hors texte + extra deluxe suite of 6 double page + one duplicate + one refusee color lithographs, of the 22 lithographs in total, 18 are individually signed by Leonor Fini in pencil, book printed on grand velin d'Arches paper, all plates with tissue guards (one missing), publisher's 3 paper folders inside original box, overall size 39 x 29 x 8 cm., excellent condition.   Gemini Fine Books & Arts., Ltd.   Art Reference & Illustrated Books - 2013 $3000

The Vermin Killer; Being a complete and Necessary Family Book... printed for John Thompson...and sold by T. Lochead, Glasgow: W. Chambers, Leith and every Bookseller and Dealer in books in the United Kingdom, circa, 1820. Page references in pencil to vermin, little staining and spotting, pages 40, 12mo., original printed blue paper wrappers, contemporary stitched into calf backed boards, inside front of these with ownership inscription "Charles L. Phillips, Dunds Vale 1820" and inside back cover, Table of Contents in ink, good, rare.   Blackwell's Rare Books   Sciences - 125   2013   £425

Verne, H. G. *(The) Spelling (Rebus:) Bee.* J. T. Wood & Co., circa, 1876. Title with very large woodcut of a magnified bee, printed on very thin paper, songs printed in minuscule type in 7 columns, very fragile, small piece missing from top of first two leaves, removing "The" of title and few lines from songs, some fraying and small tears, unbound, folio.   Blackwell's Rare Books   172 - 147   2013   £275

Verne, Jules 1828-1905 *Michael Strogoff the Counter of the Czar.* London: Sampson, Low, Marston, Searle & Rivington, 1877. First English edition, Original red brown pictorial cloth, bevelled boards, leading f.e.p. removed, all edges gilt, foldout map, 88 full page engravings, 24 page catalog (Oct. 1876), original red brown pictorial cloth, bevelled boards, leading f.e.p. removed, all edges gilt. Jarndyce Antiquarian Booksellers CCV - 277 2013 £280

Verne, Jules 1828-1905 *Michael Strogoff.* New York: Charles Scribner's, 1927. First edition, 4to., black cloth, pictorial paste-on, fine in dust jacket with mounted color plate, dust jacket very slightly worn, else near fine, illustrations by N. C. Wyeth, incredible copy. Aleph-Bet Books, Inc. 105 - 596 2013 $1500

Verne, Jules 1828-1905 *De La Terre a La Lune: Trajet Direct en 97 Heures.* Paris: Bibliotheque d'Education et de Recreation, J. Hetzel, 18 rue Jacob, 1865. First edition, octavo, original buff wrappers printed in black, all edges untrimmed. L. W. Currey, Inc. Fall Sampler Sept. 2013 - 144948 2013 $10,000

Verne, Jules 1828-1905 *Twenty Thousand Leagues Under the Sea.* London: Ward, Lock & Tyler, 1876. 2 volumes in 1, 4 color plates, 6 page catalog, clean tear to pages 43/44, original light brown pictorial cloth, all edges gilt, embossed stamp of W. H. Stamp of W. H. Smith on leading f.e.p., exceptionally bright copy. Jarndyce Antiquarian Booksellers CCV - 278 2013 £350

Verne, Jules 1828-1905 *The Vanished Diamond: a Tale of South Africa.* London: Sampson Low, Marston & Co., 1896. New edition, half title, frontispiece and plates, original olive green pictorial cloth, slightly dulled, very good plus. Jarndyce Antiquarian Booksellers CCV - 279 2013 £85

Verne, Jules 1828-1905 *The Wreck of the Chancellor.* Boston: James R. Osgood, 1875. First American edition, 12mo., 285 pages, green cloth stamped in gilt, all edges stained red, some rubbing at extremities of spine, very nice, tight copy. Second Life Books Inc. 183 - 387 2013 $300

Verney, Frances Parthenope *Memoirs of the Verney Family.* London: Longmans Green and Co., 1892. 1894. 1899. First edition, royal 8vo., 69 engravings, drawings and woodcuts, 2 foldouts, pebbled brown cloth, red and gilt edge bands, gilt titles and coat of arms, top edge gilt, inscribed by Margaret Verney, author of volume III, very good or better set with wear to extremities. Kaaterskill Books 16 - 87 2013 $350

Verney, Frances Parthenope *Memoirs of the Verney Family Volumes I-IV.* London: Longmans, Green and Co., 1892. 1892. 1894. 1899. First editions, 4 volumes, 8vo., 50 plates as called for, further woodcuts and illustrations to text, protective tissue removed from volume I frontispiece, brown cloth, gilt spine and armorial centerpiece, top edge gilt, fore-edges uncut, endcaps creased, pages and edges little worn, boards faded, minor dent to upper board volume I, upper hinge of volume II cracking but bindings sound, very good internally, armorial bookplate of Frances Fortescue Urquhart of Balliol College 1909 to each front pastedown and his ownership inscription, bookplate of R. C. Mowat, pencilled ownership of P. A. Slack. Unsworths Antiquarian Booksellers 28 - 202 2013 £120

Verney, Frances Parthenope *Memoirs of the Verney-Family During the Seventeenth Century.* London: Longmans Green and Co., 1907. Second edition, 203 x 143mm., 2 volumes, appealing contemporary chestnut brown three quarter morocco, raised bands decorated with a row of five gilt dots, spine compartments framed with gilt rules, gilt titling, marbled endpapers, top edges gilt, other edges rough trimmed, folding genealogical chart and 26 black and white photo plates as called for, leather with only vaguest evidence of use, spines just slightly sunned, but fine quite clean, fresh internally, pleasant bindings lustrous and virtually unworn. Phillip J. Pirages 63 - 480 2013 $200

Versteeg, Dingman *Manhattan in 1628 as described in the Recently Discovered Autograph letter of Jonas Michaelius...* New York: Dodd, Mead and Co., 1904. First edition, one of 175 numbered copies on Holland handmade paper (of a total of 225), signed by printer, Frank C. Hopkin, small quarto, 18 collotype illustrations using Bierstadt process, cloth and paper covered boards and spine, bookplate, slight nicking to paper on spine, else near fine. Between the Covers Rare Books, Inc. New York City - 291430 2013 $250

Vertot, Rene Aubert De *The History of the Knights Hospitallers of St. John of Jerusalem...* Edinburgh: printed for Alexander Donaldson, 1770. 12mo., some foxing and browning, mainly affecting titlepages and final leaves, 19th century half calf, marbled boards, raised and gilt banded spines, later morocco labels, hinges and corners rubbed. Jarndyce Antiquarian Booksellers CCV - 280 2013 £450

Vertot, Rene Aubert De *Revolutions de Portugal.* Paris: Chez les Libraires Associes, 1773. Small 8vo., frontispiece, folding genealogical plate, small 8vo., blank lower corner Ci torn, paper flaw to leading edge R1, otherwise fresh, clean copy, full contemporary mottled calf, triple gilt ruled borders, gilt spine, brown morocco label, little rubbed, all edges gilt, armorial bookplate of Marquess of Headfort. Jarndyce Antiquarian Booksellers CCIV - 301 2013 £150

Vertrees, John J. *An Address to the Men of Tennessee on Female Suffrage.* Nashville: 1916. Square 8vo., pages 20, self wrappers, first leaf separate, last loose, with stab holes, scarce. Second Life Books Inc. 182 - 252 2013 $135

Vesalius, Andreas *De Humani Corporis Fabrica.* Basel: Oporinus, 1555. Second folio edition, folio, engraved frontispiece/title, early 17th century full speckled calf with gilt paneled spine, light wear to fore edges, joints just starting but firm, some peeling to leather on front board, very good showing some light wear, printing impressions of plates excellent, light staining and foxing, 2 inscriptions skilfully removed from title, rear flyleaf with rubber stamp of Arnold Kelbs, M.D. James Tait Goodrich 75 - 210 2013 $79,500

Vesalius, Andreas *Tabulae Anatomicae Sex.* London: privately printed for Sir William Maxwell, 1874. 6 engraved plates, 14 leaves, elephant portfolio, original leather backed marbled boards, some light wear to spine. James Tait Goodrich 75 - 209 2013 $12,500

Vesling, Johannes *Syntagma Anatomicvm Locis Plurimis Auctum, Emendatum.* Patavii: Typis Pauli Framboitti Bibliopale, 1647. First illustrated edition, frontispiece, 24 full page engraved plates, 4 to., full modern calf with gilt spine done in panels, boards have gilt ruling and fleur de les engravings, some occasional mild dampstaining, first illustrated edition. James Tait Goodrich 75 - 215 2013 $2495

Vesling, Johannes *Syntagma Anatomicvm Locis Plurimis Auctum Amendatum.* Patavii: Typis Pauli Frambotti Bibliopolae, 1647. 4to., old plain boards, title and final plate remargined along inner border, some soiling and foxing of pages, final leaf shaved at bottom affecting one line of text, engraved frontispiece, engraved portrait, 24 engraved plates, 24 leaves of handwritten figure elgends done in cursive brown ink. James Tait Goodrich 75 - 214 2013 $3500

Vian, Louis Rene *Arts Decoratifs a Bord des Paquebots Francais 1880/1960.* Paris: Fonmare, 1992. First edition, 319 pages, color and black and white photos, drawings and plans, 4to., full grey decorated cloth, gray deco endpapers, hard to fine in such pristine condition, fine in lightly rubbed dust jacket, small transparent bookseller's label on lower edge of front pastedown. Kaaterskill Books 16 - 23 2013 $900

Vicq D'Azyr, Felix *Traite d'Anatomie et de Physiologie.* Paris Didot l'aine: 1786. 69 plates with separate black and white outline plates and one black and white plate, lacking frontispiece and accompanying text leaf, otherwise complete with all plates, some light foxing and text browning, plates with bright coloring, full contemporary calf, newly backed with corners repaired, small library stamp verso of title. James Tait Goodrich 75 - 216 2013 $25,000

The Victoria Jubilee in Twelve Reliefs. London, et al: Raphael Tuck, n.d., 1887. Pictorial wrappers, covers have neat spine strengthening, else very good+, 12 panel panorama of die-cut chromolithographs opening to 57 inches (reinforced at folds on blank verso, few minor creases, else very good), illustrations in color by Arthur and Harry Payne, quite remarkable survival in such nice condition. Aleph-Bet Books, Inc. 105 - 438 2013 $975

Vidocq, Eugene Francois *Histoire de Vidocq, Chef De La Brigade De La Surete.* Paris: Chez Delarue, 1830. Second edition, 2 volumes bound in one, half titles, probably contemporary black pebble grain morocco, covers ruled in blind, spine with raised bands and gilt lettering, marbled endpapers, folding frontispiece, text lightly foxed and softened because of poor quality paper stock, otherwise excellent, binding with only trivial wear. Phillip J. Pirages 63 - 481 2013 $350

La Vieille Garde Imperiale. Tours: Alfred Mame et Fils, 1902. Thick 4to., contemporary newer cloth matching original with original silk pictorial cover laid down, near fine, 19 fine full page color engraved plates and 38 detailed half page engravings, fine quality paper. Aleph-Bet Books, Inc. 105 - 345 2013 $1200

Vieilles Chansons et Rondes. Paris: Plon Nourrit, n.d., Oblong 4to., decorative grey cloth, as new in original dust jacket slightly soiled, color illustrations, rarely found in dust jacket. Aleph-Bet Books, Inc. 104 - 86 2013 $375

Viereck, Peter *The First Morning.* New York: Scribner's Sons, 1952. First edition, 8vo., 120 pages, very good in nicked and torn dust jacket, inscribed by his infamous father. Second Life Books Inc. 183 - 388 2013 $150

Viereck, Peter *Terror and Decorum Poems 1940-1948.* New York: Charles Scribner's Sons, 1948. First edition, 8vo., 120 pages, very good in nicked dust jacket, inscribed to his infamous father. Second Life Books Inc. 183 - 389 2013 $250

A View of London and Westminster, or the Town Spy. (bound with) A Second part of a View of London and Westminster. London: sold by T. Warner and by the booksellers, 1728. London; sold by J. Isted... and by all booksellers, 1725. Fourth edition? and first edition, 2 parts in one volume, 8vo., pages (iv), 59, (1) blank; half title, folding engraved plate, (ii), 62, titlepage with repaired tear, no loss of surface and text unaffected, 19th century calf gilt by W. Pratt, spine sometime neatly repaired, very good. Marlborough Rare Books Ltd. 218 - 95 2013 £3850

Views of the Halifax Catastrophe Showing Effects of Explosion December Sixth 1917. Halifax: Royal Print & Litho Ltd., 1917. 6 x 9 inches, 40 black and white photo illustrations, (32) pages, covers slightly worn, interior good. Schooner Books Ltd. 105 - 77 2013 $75

Views of the Parish Churches in York; with a Short Account of Each. York: A. Barclay, 1831. 23 mounted india paper lithograph plates, some foxing, rather heavy in places, little chipping to fore-edges of some leaves, recent wrappers with original printed front wrapper bound in, scarce. Ken Spelman Books Ltd.   73 - 19   2013   £120

Viger, Denis B.   *The Year of the Maple.*   N.P.: Margaret Challenger, 2000. Limited to 20 numbered copies, 7 x 5.8 cm., printed paper covered boards in maple leaf design, slipcase with paper cover label, bound accordion style, (14) leaves, with 2 Canadian 6 cent stamps and two Canadia 7 cent stamps tipped in, from the collection of Donn W. Sanford.   Oak Knoll Books   303 - 93   2013 $145

Vigo, Johannes De   *Practica Copiosa in Arte Chirugica* (sic).   Venice: heirs of Octavianus Scotus, 1520.   First Venice edition, Folio, 2 parts in one volume, part 1 with final blank, woodcut initials, text dampstained with some worming which is mostly in margins but also affecting some text especially in gatherings M-N, paper repairs in last two leaves, part 2 lacking final blank, modern vellum by Omega Bindery, spine lettered in manuscript.   James Tait Goodrich   75 - 217   2013 $5750

Villiers De L'Isle-Adam, Auguste   *Olympe and Henriette.*   No location given: Joseph D'Ambrosio, 1992. Limited edition of 75 numbered copies, this one of 10 artist proofs, 8vo., 24 pages, printed letterpress on misty-rose paper with folds and two-level pages backed with fabric, hand-sewn in 'book-in-a-box' modular type binding with decorative fabric and Roma paper backed boards, original prospectus laid in, signed by author, fine.   Jeff Weber Rare Books   171 - 95   2013 $500

Villon, Francois   *Les Neiges D'Antan. Poems.*   Belfast: Crannog Press, 1973. One of 85 numbered copies, so bound, from total edition of 100 copies, 6 single page and one double page linocut illustrations by artist, large 8vo., original dark blue cloth, printed paper label.   Maggs Bros. Ltd.   1442 - Crannog   2013   £120

A Vindication of Lady Byron.   London: Richard Bentley & son, 1871. First edition, original brick brown cloth, inner hinges slightly cracking, slightly rubbed, spine little worn at head and tail, T. J. Wise's copy.   Jarndyce Antiquarian Booksellers   CCIII - 350   2013   £180

Vinge, Joan D.   *Dune Storybook.*   New York: Putnam, 1984. First edition, 4to., signed by Vinge and Frank Herbert, with ALS signed and dated Oct. 10, 1972 by Herbert, book near fine in original color pictorial binding with mild wear to cover, no dust jacket issued, ALS fine.   By the Book, L. C.   36 - 48   2013 $650

Vinycomb, John   *Fictitious & Symbolic Creatures in Art...*   1906. First edition, 8vo., profusely illustrated, very good.   C. P. Hyland   261 - 109   2013   £80

Vinycomb, John   *On the Processes for... Production of Ex Libris (Bookplates).*   1894. First edition, color frontispiece (offset on titlepage) and many black and white and monochrome illustrations, very good, very scarce, cloth.   C. P. Hyland   261 - 108   2013   £100

Viollet-le-Duc, Eugene   *The Habitations of Man in all Ages.*   London: Sampson Low, Marston, Searle and Rivington, 1876. First English edition, 8vo, color frontispiece and 8 further plates, illustrations in text, decorative green cloth embossed in gilt and black, endcaps worn and little torn, boards lightly scuffed, upper hinge splitting but very good, bookplate of Lieut. General Fox Pitt-Rivers, pencilled inscription.   Unsworths Antiquarian Booksellers   28 - 203   2013   £50

Virchow, Rudolf   *Die Cellularpathogie in Ihrer Begrilundung and Physiologie und Pathologische Gewebelehre, Vierte neu Bearbeitete und Stark Vermehrte Auflage.*   Berlin: Hirschwald, 1871. 582 pages, 157 illustrations, half contemporary leather worn, ex-library usual markings, internally clean.   James Tait Goodrich   75 - 218   2013 $595

Virgin, Christoph Adolph   *Kongliga Svenska Fregatten Eugenies Resa Omkring Jorden under befal of C. A. Virgin Aren 1851-1853.*   Uppsala & Stockholm: Almqvist & Wiksells Boktryckeri, 1857-1910. First edition in Swedish, 3 volumes in five parts, 54 lithographic plates and 1 shaded folding map, 4to., original paper wrappers, very good or better mostly unopened, uncut and untrimmed copies, minor edge wear, scattered foxing, mainly marginal, including a few plates, mostly in insect volume, else plates and maps about fine.   Kaaterskill Books   16 - 88   2013 $600

A Visit to Aunt Agnes.   London: Religious Tract Society, n.d circa, 1868.   Square small 8vo., original blindstamped cloth, gilt extra, spine and edges faded, pages 80, all edges gilt, text woodcuts and 4 Kronheim color plates, pencilled signature dated 1868 on flyleaf.   R. F. G. Hollett & Son Children's Books - 21   2013   £85

A Visit to the Tower.   Religious Tract Society, n.d., circa, 1890.   large 8vo., original pictorial wrappers, little soiled, pages 6, plus 6 colored plates, all linen backed, edges little frayed, little fingered in places.   R. F. G. Hollett & Son Children's Books - 22   2013   £45

Vizcaino, Sebastian   *The Voyage of Sebastian Vizcaino.*   San Francisco: Book Club of California, 1933. First edition, one of 240 copies, large folding map, cloth backed boards, paper spine label, beautiful, very fine copy with plain blue dust jacket (spine faded), quite scarce in this condition.   Argonaut Book Shop   Recent Acquisitions June 2013 - 291   2013 $350

Vladimirov, V. *Miteshniki.* Moscow: Ravotnik Prosveschehenye (Worker Education), 1929. 8vo., 60 pages, pictorial wrappers, light cover soil, unopened with few pages with tiny repairs where opened roughly, very good+, color cover plus full page and smaller black and whites by M. Shervinski.   Aleph-Bet Books, Inc.   105 - 516   2013 $400

Vlaminck, Maurice De *En Noir et en Couleurs. Lithographs by Maurice de Vlaminck.* Paris: Aux Depens d'un Amateur, 1962. First edition, one of 75 deluxe examples (total edition of 298), printed on grand velin d'Arches, 33 original lithographs of which 5 are in colors + one hors texte in bistre (front cover) + 10 large black and white lithos with text, 1 full page original lithographs as frontispiece + 19 smaller woodcuts in texte, in addition this copy contains 1) extra suite of 11 hors-texte lithos; 2) an extra suite of the 5 hors-texte color lithos (not called for in the colophon); 3) an extra suite of 8 color proofs; 40 x 30cm., 100 pages in French, loose leaves, as issued, publisher's wrapper folder, boards chemise and linen over boards folding box, excellent condition, no foxing or other defects.   Gemini Fine Books & Arts., Ltd.   Art Reference & Illustrated Books - 2013 $2800

Volland *Volland Book Catalogue: Books Good for Children.* n.d. circa, 1929. 3.5 x 6 inches, pictorial wrappers, 35 pages, fine, illustrations in black and white with great color covers by Ellery Friend, rare.   Aleph-Bet Books, Inc.   105 - 575   2013 $400

Vollmann, William T. *The Grave of Lost Stories.* Sacramento: CoTangent Press, 1993. Artist's book, one of 15 deluxe copies only, 13 of which are for sale, all on Johannot paper, each signed and numbered by artist/author and binder, from an edition of 200, 185 regular edition, bound by Ben Pax, steel and grey marble box (tomb) fitted to custom steel hinge by means of a copper sheet riveted to the steel and then crimped upward to form a pan, hinge is powder-coated black as is the interior, front cover incised with title, author's initials and Poe's dates, copy number appears in roman numeral on back cover, along fore-edge of box (tomb) 13 cow's teeth have been set in handmade silver bezels, inside covers each have four brass and copper rods (oxidized green), book itself is bound in boards with linen spine which are "leafed, and variegated and painted in metallic fungoid patterns over which the author has painted a female figure to represent one of the stories", gessoed boards are copper colored and female is in blue with onlays of four small white bones outlining skeleton, book lays into marble box (tomb), the four illustrations are hand colored by author who has also made a number of small revisions in text, titlepage printed in three colors, guards of black and gold gilt Japanese paper.   Priscilla Juvelis - Rare Books 55 - 26   2013 $5000

Volney, Constantin Francois *Les Ruines, ou Meditation sur les Revolutons des Empires.* Paris: Chez Desenne Volland, Plassan, 1791. First edition, 3 leaves of plates, 8vo., titlepage little dusted, occasional minor foxing, blank upper corner of aii torn, late 19th century half vellum, marbled boards, ruled spine, slightly rubbed black morocco label, signature of Michael Foot.   Jarndyce Antiquarian Booksellers   CCIV - 302   2013   £380

Volney, Constantin Francois *The Ruins; or a Survey of the Revolutions of Empires.* London: J. Johnson, 1795. Second English edition, 8vo., frontispiece, 2 folding plates (1 waterstained and partially backed with paper), contemporary brown half calf, joints rubbed, small split at base of spine.   J. & S. L. Bonham Antiquarian Booksellers   Europe - 8327   2013   £150

Voltaire, Francois Marie Arouet De   1694-1778 *Candide. (bound with) Seconde Partie.* London?: John Nourse, 1759. and n.p., 1761, 12mo., woodcut fleuron of interlocking Es on title, repeated on page 34 and 279, woodcut vignette of Adam Digging on title of 'second part', first title trifle browned and creased, second part slightly browned, modern red morocco, top edges gilt, 1884 presentation inscription in Latin, with quatrain from Rubaiyat of Omar Khayyam, good.   Blackwell's Rare Books   172 - 149   2013   £2000

Volusenus, Florentius *De Animi Tranquilitate Dialogus.* Lyons: Sebastian Gryphius, 1543. First edition, woodcut printer's device on title, 2 large woodcut initials, top outer corner of title renewed and first two leaves guarded, some waterstaining in lower margins, browned in few places, contemporary? French calf with three concentric frames stamped in blind with fleurons at innermost corners and in centre, rebacked and re-edged preserving most of original covers and about half of the spine, red edges, contemporary lettering on lower edges, inscription at end dated 1596, 18th century inscription on title partly erased, sound.   Blackwell's Rare Books   172 - 150   2013   £900

Von Harbou, Theo *Metropolis.* Berlin: August Scherl, 1926. First paperback photoplay edition, octavo, 8 photogravure illustrations from the Fritz Lang film on 4 inserted pages, original pictorial printed color wrappers printed in red, blue and black, title printed in red, spine printed in black, spine and back wrapper, some very light smudging, top of spine with smallest amount of chipping, small crease to lower right corner of titlepage, still near fine, extremely rare, fragile.   Heritage Book Shop   Holiday Catalogue 2012 - 153   2013 $2500

Von Leskoschek, Axel *Der Blitz Fft-Pfs-Ft.* Nurnberg: Stalling, 1926. 16mo., pictorial boards, slight edge wear, very good-fine, pictorial covers, wonderful 24 panel panorama, scarce. Aleph-Bet Books, Inc. 104 - 234 2013 $600

Von Neumann, John *Mathematische Grundlagen der Quantenmechanik.* Berlin: Julius Springer, 1932. First edition, 4 diagrams in text, single fox mark on 4 early leaves, 8vo., contemporary black cloth, spine and corners fine grained, boards pebble grained, very good. Blackwell's Rare Books   Sciences - 126   2013   £500

Von Neumann, John *Theory of Games and Economic Behavior.* Princeton: University Press, 1944. First edition, first printing, errata leaf tipped onto front free endpaper, 8vo., original publisher's cloth, spine ruled and lettered gilt, little rubbed, spine faded, top corner of front board bumped, former owner's bookplate, sound.   Blackwell's Rare Books   Sciences - 127   2013   £1500

Von Nostrand, Jeanne *The First Hundred Years of Painting in California 1775-1875.* San Francisco: John Howell Books, 1980. First edition, limited to 2500 copies, quarto, 135 pages, 40 full page plates, gilt lettered blue cloth, fine with light blue dust jacket.   Argonaut Book Shop   Recent Acquisitions June 2013 - 289   2013 $75

Von Puckler-Muskau, Prince *A Tour in England, Ireland and France in the Years 1828/1829.* 1832. 2 volumes, 8vo., rebacked, quarter cloth, original boards, feint foxing, untrimmed, very good.   C. P. Hyland   261 - 841   2013   £175

Von Puttkamer, Jesco *Star Trek: The New Voyages 2.* New York: Bantam, 1978. First edition, paperback original, near fine with just few reading creases, inscribed by author to Fred Durant, with longer typed note from author to same.   Between the Covers Rare Books, Inc.   Sci-Fi, Fantasy & Horror - 43910   2013 $275

Von Taube, Max *Der Bunte Hans.* Leipzig: Carl Reissner, n.d. circa, 1880. Large 4to., cloth backed boards, some cover soil and mild internal wear, very good, printed on heavy boards, each page individually hinged onto book and printed on one side only, each page printed in different color, illustrations by Adolf Reinheimer, rare.   Aleph-Bet Books, Inc.   105 - 270   2013 $1200

Von Wright, G. H. *A Portrait of Wittgenstein as a Young Man: from the Diary of David Hume Pinsent 1912-1914.* Oxford: Basil Blackwell Ltd., 1990. First edition, fine in near fine dust jacket with tiny tear at crown.   Between the Covers Rare Books, Inc.   Philosophy - 105301   2013 $125

Vonnegut, Kurt *Bogombo Snuff Box: Uncollected Short Fiction.* New York: Putnams, 1999. First trade edition, signed by author, fine in dust jacket.   Ed Smith Books   75 - 79   2013 $150

Vonnegut, Kurt *Cat's Cradle.* London: Gollancz, 1963. First English edition, crown 8vo., original orange boards, backstrip gilt lettered, dust jacket, rear panel creased at head, dust jacket, wraparound band little foxed in part, very good.   Blackwell's Rare Books   172 - 242   2013   £600

Vonnegut, Kurt *A Man Without a Country.* New York/ London: Seven Stories Press/Bloomsbury, 2005-2006. First American edition and a copy of the First British edition, American edition signed by author with self caricature and dated 4/4/06 and British edition signed by author with self caricature and dated 7/12/06 each fine in fine dust jacket and two are housed together in custom clamshell case.   Ken Lopez Bookseller   159 - 207   2013 $2000

Vonnegut, Kurt *The Sirens of Titan.* Boston: Houghton Mifflin, 1961. First hardcover edition, only 2500 copies printed, signed by author with self caricature in 2006, near fine in very good dust jacket with two small gutter nicks and sunning to spine lettering and on rear panel where (presumably) a smaller book stood next to it on a bookshelf, in custom clamshell case.   Ken Lopez Bookseller   159 - 206   2013 $8500

Vossius, Gerardus Joannes   *...De Theologia Gentili et Physiologia Christiana, sive de Origine ac Progressu Idololatriae.* Amsterdam: Joannes Blaeu, 1668. Folio, 2 volumes in 1, possibly lacking portrait, contemporary vellum, old seminary label on pastedown, else very good, clean and tight.   Joseph J. Felcone Inc.   Books Printed before 1701 - 87   2013 $900

The Voyage of Marco Polo. London: Bancroft, 1962. First edition, 4to., pop-up book, near fine.   Beasley Books   2013 - 2013 $100

Vrchlicky, Jaroslav *Jaroslav Vrchlicky Mertev!* Praha: 1912. 8 pages, 6 black and white photos, folio, 6 loose red leaves with mounted photos laid into folded, printed sheet within a tan printed portfolio (soiled, otherwise very good).   Kaaterskill Books   16 - 89   2013 $250

Vredenburg, Edric *My Book of Mother Goose Nursery Rhymes.* Philadelphia: Tuck & McKay, n.d. circa, 1925. 4to., cloth, pictorial paste-on, near fine, illustrations by Jennie Harbour with 12 stunning color plates and a profusion of full and partial page blank and whites in typical 20's Art Deco style, really nice one, quite scarce.   Aleph-Bet Books, Inc.   104 - 276   2013 $675

W

Wa-Sha-Quoin-Asin, Grey Owl *Pilgrims of the Wild.* Toronto: Macmillan Co., 1934. First edition, 281 pages, illustrations, tight, very near fine cloth in black cloth boards.   Jeff Hirsch Books   Fall 2013 - 129462   2013 $50

Wadd, William *Cases in Surgery.* London: Printed for J. Callow, 1815-1819. 3 volumes bound in one, tall 4to., later 19th century plain burgundy cloth, library stamps (faint) on title and plates, some toning and foxing of the pages and plates.   James Tait Goodrich   75 - 220   2013 $1095

Wade, William Richard *A Journey in the Northern Island of New Zealand, Interspersed with Various Information.* Hobart Town: George Rolwegan, 1842. First edition, 8vo., original cloth backed patterned boards, some light staining, extremities rubbed with little loss of paper, rebacked with original spine laid down.   Maggs Bros. Ltd.   1467 - 100   2013   £950

Wadia, A. R. *The Ethics of Feminism. A Study of the Revolt of Woman.* New York: Doran, 1923. First American edition, 8vo., 256 pages, blue cloth, paper spine label, ex-library with stamps, cover little worn at corners and ends of spine, otherwise very good.   Second Life Books Inc.   182 - 254   2013 $60

Wadsworth, Edward *The Graphic Work.* Woodbridge: Wood Lea Press, 2002. One of 450 copies (of 500), with over 100 color reproductions of Wadsworth's work, folio, original white boards with overall design in black, board slipcase, fine.   Blackwell's Rare Books   B174 - 396   2013   £80

Wadsworth, L. A. *Mystery at the Black Cat.* New York: Farrar & Rinehart, 1941. First edition, illustrations by George Porter Jr., fine in price clipped, else near fine dust jacket with couple of tiny nicks at extremities, scarce.   Between the Covers Rare Books, Inc.   Mystery & Detective Fiction - 57188   2013 $275

Wagner, Bruce *Force Majeure.* New York: Random House, 1991. First edition, inscribed by author to Michael Millikan, fine in fine dust jacket.   Ken Lopez Bookseller   159 - 209   2013 $150

Wagner, Henry Raup   1862-1957 *The Cartography of the Northwest Coast of America to the Year 1800.* Mansfield Center: Maurizio Martino, 1999. Second reprint edition, quarto, 2 volume in one, 40 maps, tan cloth, very fine.   Argonaut Book Shop   Recent Acquisitions June 2013 - 282   2013 $125

Wagner, Henry Raup   1862-1957 *Juan Rodriguez Cabrillo, Discoverer of the Coast of California.* San Francisco: California Historical Society, 1941. First edition, one of 750 copies, 94 pages, decorations by Robert Windrem, initials by Fred Glauser, chapter notes, printed in red and black, cloth backed decorated boards, paper spine label, very fine.   Argonaut Book Shop   Recent Acquisitions June 2013 - 294   2013 $125

Wagner, Henry Raup   1862-1957 *The Plains and the Rockies: a Critical Bibliography of Exploration, Adventure and Travel in the American West 1800-1865.* San Francisco: John Howell Books, 1982. Fourth edition, 745 pages, frontispiece, plus several illustrations, very fine.   Argonaut Book Shop   Recent Acquisitions June 2013 - 298   2013 $150

Wagner, Henry Raup   1862-1957 *Sir Francis Drake's Voyage Around the World: its Aims and Achievements.* San Francisco: John Howell Books, 1926. First edition, although not indicated, limited to 1100 copies, quarto, maps, photos, facsimiles, maroon cloth, gilt lettered spine, spine slightly faded, else very fine.   Argonaut Book Shop   Recent Acquisitions June 2013 - 295   2013 $450

Wagner, Henry Raup   1862-1957 *The Spanish Southwest 1542-1794. An Annotated Bibliography.* Albuquerque: The Wuivira Society, 1937. Second edition, 2 volumes, frontispiece, 113 facsimiles, folding map, white cloth spines, tan boards, gilt, four minor spots to inner cover of each volume, from removed bookplate, fine and clean set.   Argonaut Book Shop   Recent Acquisitions June 2013 - 296   2013 $675

Wagner, Henry Raup   1862-1957 *The Spanish Voyages to the Northwest Coast of America in the Sixteenth Century.* Amsterdam: Nico Israel, 1966. Reprint, quarto, text maps and plans, 16 map plates, facsimiles, gilt lettered blue cloth, fine.   Argonaut Book Shop   Recent Acquisitions June 2013 - 297   2013 $225

Wagner, Richard   1813-1883 *Parsifal.* London: Harrap, 1912. 4to., grey pictorial and gilt cloth, except for slight lean, fine and bright, illustrations by Willy Pogany with 16 tipped in color plates plus numerous full page color illustrations, full page black and whites, pictorial borders on text pages, pictorial endpaper and calligraphic text, printed on heavy grey stock, beautiful copy, scarce.   Aleph-Bet Books, Inc.   105 - 461   2013 $900

Wagner, Richard 1813-1883 *Rhinegold & The Valkyrie.* London and New York: Heinemann and Doubleday, 1910. Limited to 1150 numbered copies (105 for US) signed by artist, 34 magnificent tipped in color plates and 14 black and whites by Arthur Rackham. large 4to., full vellum, some rubbing, spine and cover, endpapers slightly foxed, else beautiful copy, silk ties renewed.   Aleph-Bet Books, Inc.   105 - 495   2013 $1800

Wagner, Richard 1813-1883 *The Rhinegold and the Valkyrie. Siegfried and the Twilight of the Gods.* London: Heinemann, 1911-1912. First Rackham edition, 2 volumes, numerous color printed plates and line drawings in text by Arthur Rackham, 4to., original tan buckram, gilt lettering and decoration to backstrips and front covers, rear cover to Rhinegold just little waterstained, backstrips faded, good.   Blackwell's Rare Books   B174 - 287   2013   £600

Wahl, Jan *Pleasant Fieldmouse.* New York: Harper Row, 1964. Probable first edition but need price for definitive determination, 4to., pictorial boards, fine in price clipped, dust jacket, lovely color pictorial cover and intricate black and whites on every page by Maurice Sendak, nice, very scarce.   Aleph-Bet Books, Inc.   104 - 516   2013 $200

Wain, Louis *Daddy Cat.* New York: Dodge, 1925. 8vo., cloth backed boards, pictorial paste-on, slight edge wear, else fine, 32 rich full page color illustrations plus few illustrations in line and pictorial endpapers, beautiful copy, scarce.   Aleph-Bet Books, Inc.   105 - 581   2013 $2000

Wain, Louis *Merry Times with Louis Wain.* London: Raphael Tuck & Sons Ltd., n.d. circa, 1939. Unrecorded second edition, quarto, full color frontispiece, black and white and two-color text illustrations, titlepage illustration, quarter red cloth over pictorial boards, rear board illustrated in full color, neat gift and ownership signature dated 1939, mild edgewear and some minor soiling, internally crisp and clean, wonderful copy, scarce.   David Brass Rare Books, Inc. Holiday 2012 Chapter One - DB 01788   2013 $750

Wait, Benjamin *Letters from Van Dieman's Land.* Buffalo: A. G. Wilgus, 1843. First edition, 12mo., 356 pages, frontispiece and folding map, contemporary calf backed cloth, spine quite worn, folding portion of map lacking, although essentially complete, text foxed.   M & S Rare Books, Inc.   95 - 51   2013 $550

Waiting at Table: a Practical Guide. London: Frederick Warne, 1894. Half title, 4 pages ads, original blue grey cloth, front board slightly marked.   Jarndyce Antiquarian Booksellers   CCV - 11   2013   £125

Wake, C. Staniland *Serpent-Worship and Other Essays with a Chapter on Totemism.* George Redway, 1888. 8vo. good in original gilt lettered dark green cloth, some slight rubbing to extremities of covers.   Ken Spelman Books Ltd.   75 - 146   2013   £75

Wake, William *The Missionarie's Arts Discovered; or an Account of their Ways of Insinuation, their Articles and Several Methods of Which They Serve themselves in Making Converts.* London: by Randal Taylor, 1688. First edition, 4to., imprimatur and errata leaf, modern wrappers, minor paper flaw in margin G4, without loss, else near fine.   Joseph J. Felcone Inc.   Books Printed before 1701 - 2   2013 $500

Wakefield, Herbert Russell *They Return at Evening: A Book of Ghost Stories.* New York: D. Appleton and Co., 1928. First US edition, first printing with "(1)" at base of text on page (266), octavo, original black cloth, front and spine panels stamped in gold.   L. W. Currey, Inc.   Wandering Ghosts & Itinerant Souls (10/12) - 75878   2013 $350

Wakefield, P. *Mental Improvement or the Beauties and Wonders of Nature and Art.* Dublin: printed by T. Burnside for P. Wogan, H. Colbert and J. Gough, 1799. Rare first Dublin edition, 12mo., contemporary tree sheep, gilt ruled, compartments on spine, red lettering piece, crack at head of upper joints, ownership inscription "Edward Johnsons Book, Carrickfergus, July 20th 1811", good.   Blackwell's Rare Books   Sciences - 128   2013   £600

Walcott, Derek *The Fortunate Traveller.* New York: Farrar Straus Giroux, 1981. First edition, fine in near fine dust jacket with some small stains on back panel, signed by author on half title.   Between the Covers Rare Books, Inc.   165 - 274   2013 $100

Walcott, Derek *The Star-Apple Kingdom.* New York: Farrar Straus and Giroux, 1979. Uncorrected proof, fine in wrappers and fine proof dust jacket, signed by author.   Between the Covers Rare Books, Inc.   165 - 273   2013 $200

Walcott, MacKenzie *The Minsters & Abbey Ruins of the UK.* 1860. First edition, 8vo., x, 265 pages plus 16 pages ads, good, cloth.   C. P. Hyland   261 - 842   2013   £40

Waldberg, Patrick *Aux Petits Agneaux.* Paris: Au Pont des Arts (Galerie Lucie Weill), 1971. First edition, one of 52 collaborators' exemplars published without the additional suite (there were also 122 copies with a suite), 19 original color lithographs by Max Ernst, signed by artist and author, 84 pages, 330 x 257mm., printed on Velin d'Arches, loose in lithographed wrapper chemise ad cloth clamshell box, box with very minor corner bump and bit of fading, else good in excellent condition.   Gemini Fine Books & Arts., Ltd.   Art Reference & Illustrated Books - 2013 $2600

Waldie, Jane *Narrative of a Residence in Belgium During the Campaign of 1815 and of a Visit to the Field of Waterloo.* London: John Murray, 1817. First edition, 8vo., pages vii, 351, contemporary brown diced calf, expertly rebacked, some occasional light foxing.   J. & S. L. Bonham Antiquarian Booksellers   Europe - 8722   2013   £290

Wales, Hubert *The Brocklebank Riddle.* New York: Century Co., 1914. First edition, octavo, original pictorial blue grey cloth, front and spine panels stamped in black and gold. L. W. Currey, Inc. Wandering Ghosts & Itinerant Souls (10/12) - 109329 2013 $85

Walford, Edward *The County Families of the U.K.* 1860. First edition, original cloth, showing signs of its age, needs recasing, text clean. C. P. Hyland 261 - 414 2013 £100

Walford, Edward *The County Families of the U.K.* 1904. Original cloth (worn), text good. C. P. Hyland 261 - 415 2013 £40

Walford, Edward *Tales of Our Great Families.* 1877. First edition, 2 volumes, 8vo., original red cloth, very good. C. P. Hyland 261 - 416 2013 £55

Walker, A. Earl *A History of Neurological Surgery.* Baltimore: William & Wilkins, 1951. First edition, signed, dated and inscribed, near fine, in very good dust jacket with mild soil, sun spine, edge wear, 1 inch chip front dust jacket panel, 8vo. By the Book, L. C. 38 - 45 2013 $500

Walker, A. Earl *A History of Neurological Surgery.* Baltimore: Williams & Wilkins, 1951. 583 pages, original cloth, no dust jacket. James Tait Goodrich S74 - 235 2013 $150

Walker, Alice 1944- *The Color Purple.* New York: Harcourt Brace Jovanovich, 1982. First edition, near fine, clean copy in near fine, first issue dust jacket. Ed Smith Books 78 - 70 2013 $500

Walker, Alice 1944- *Good Night, Willie Lee, I'll See You in the Morning.* New York: Dial Press, 1979. First edition, uncorrected proof, black canvas spine and yellow wrappers, fine, scarce. Between the Covers Rare Books, Inc. 165 - 277 2013 $850

Walker, Alice 1944- *Her Blue Body Everything We Know: Earthling Poems 9165-1990 Complete.* San Diego: Harcourt Brace Jovanovich, 1990. First edition, fine in fine slipcase, one of 111 numbered copies, signed by author. Between the Covers Rare Books, Inc. 165 - 280 2013 $350

Walker, Alice 1944- *In Love & Trouble: Stories of Black Women.* New York: Harcourt Brace Jovanovich, 1973. First edition, fine in fine dust jacket, very slightly rubbed, inscribed by author to Howard Zinn and his wife. Between the Covers Rare Books, Inc. 165 - 276 2013 $950

Walker, Alice 1944- *In Search of Our Mothers' Gardens: Womanist Prose.* New York: Harcourt Brace Jovanovich, 1983. Uncorrected proof, fine in wrappers. Between the Covers Rare Books, Inc. 165 - 279 2013 $75

Walker, Alice 1944- *Revolutionary Petunias and Other Poems.* New York: Harcourt Brace Jovanovich, 1973. First edition, trifle rubbed at base of spine, else fine in near fine dust jacket with minimal soiling, warmly inscribed by author to Howard Zinn and wife Roz, very scarce thus. Between the Covers Rare Books, Inc. 165 - 335 2013 $600

Walker, Alice 1944- *You Can't Keep a Good Woman Down.* New York: Harcourt Brace Jovanovich, 1981. First edition, trifle foxed on top edge, still fine in fine dust jacket, inscribed by author to her editor, John Ferrone. Between the Covers Rare Books, Inc. 165 - 278 2013 $850

Walker, Dorothy *Modern Art in Ireland.* Dublin: Lilliput Press, 1997. Number 89 of 100 specially bound, numbered copies, signed by author and Seamus Heaney, provided introduction, 4to., original red cloth, lettered gilt on spine over black, fine in black slipcase. Maggs Bros. Ltd. 1442 - 110 2013 £1200

Walker, J. Crampton *Irish Life and Landscape.* circa, 1926. 8vo., 32 color and 35 black and white reproductions, stiff card wrappers ex-Prinknash Abbey Library, near fine. C. P. Hyland 261 - 743 2013 £75

Walker, J. U. *History of Wesleyan Methodism in Halifax and Its Vicinity, from its Commencement to the Present Period.* Halifax: Hartley and Walker, 1836. First edition, original watered cloth, paper spine label rather rubbed, head of spine little chipped, scarce. R. F. G. Hollett & Son Wesleyan Methodism - 32 2013 £140

Walker, James *A Sermon Preached in Brooklyn, Connecticut at the Installation of Rev. Samuel Joseph May, Nov. 5 1823.* Boston: 1824. First edition, 8vo., 40 pages, sewn and uncut as issued, inscribed in ink on titlepage by May. M & S Rare Books, Inc. 95 - 229 2013 $150

Walker, James J. *Mayor James J. Walker's Answer to Governor Franklin D. Roosevelt Together with the Decision of the Governor and Editorial Comment.* New York: Office of the Mayor, 1931. First edition, stapled printed wrappers, 60 pages, little age toning to wrappers and foxing to first leaf, else near fine. Between the Covers Rare Books, Inc. New York City - 291297 2013 $175

Walker, Josiah *An Account of the Life and Character of Robert Burns.* Edinburgh: printed by John Moir, 1811. Few internal marks, contemporary full mottled calf, olive green leather label, leading hinge weakening, presentation inscription from author to Mrs. Thomson. Jarndyce Antiquarian Booksellers CCIII - 68 2013 £85

Walker, Margaret *For My People.* New Haven: Yale University Press, 1942. First edition, very slight soiling to boards, about fine, lacking dust jacket.   Between the Covers Rare Books, Inc.   165 - 281   2013 $85

Walker, Margaret *For My People.* New York: Limited Editions Club, 1992. First edition, one of 400 numbered copies, signed by author and artist, 6 bound-in unsigned hors texte original color lithographs by Elizabeth Catlett, housed in handsome folding cloth box, overall size 22.5 18.5 inches, new condition.   Gemini Fine Books & Arts., Ltd.   Art Reference & Illustrated Books - 2013 $1250

Walker, Robert *The City of Cork.* Guy & Co., 1883. First edition, 20 pages, 3 folding plates, 2 illustrations lacking, original wrappers under functional half cloth, author's own copy, with pencil inscription on front wrapper, scarce.   C. P. Hyland   261 - 845   2013   £150

Walker, Robert *Plebeian Politics; or The Principles and Practices of Certain Mole-Eyed Maniacs Vulgarly Called Warrites...* Salford: printed by Cowdroy & Slack, 1801. 8vo., frontispiece, vignette titlepage, 6 engraved plates, rather browned and foxed, some old waterstaining, one page torn without loss, recent plain half calf, dark green cloth boards, gilt lettered spine.   Jarndyce Antiquarian Booksellers   CCIV - 303   2013   £160

Walker, Rowland *Dastral of the Flying Corps.* S. W. Partridge, n.d., 1918. Original pictorial cloth, gilt, 4 plates.   R. F. G. Hollett & Son   Children's Books - 626   2013   £25

Walker's Hiberian Magazine or Compendium of Entertaining Knowledge. Jan.-June, 1811. 336 pages, color frontispiece, 6 copper plates, 3 needle work patterns, half calf worn, text good.   C. P. Hyland   261 - 846   2013   £120

Walkingame, Francis *The Tutor's Assistant...* Gainsborough: Henry Mozley, 1801. New edition, 5 parts, contemporary full blindstamped calf, little worn and hinges cracking, folding table, frontispiece (edges rather worn), joints cracked.   R. F. G. Hollett & Son   Children's Books - 627   2013   £45

Wall, Alexander J. *A List of New York Almanacs 1694-1850.* New York: New York Public Library, 1921. First edition, cloth bound with wrappers bound in, slight foxing in text, else fine, ownership signature of Wilberforce Eames, inscribed by Wall for Eames, Eames has corrected a few entries in list and laid in are few pages of additional notes in his hand.   Between the Covers Rare Books, Inc.   New York City - 317972   2013 $275

Wallace, Alfred Russel   1823-1913 *Contributions to the Theory of natural Selection.* New York: Macmillan, 1871. Second American edition, 8vo., very good+, brown cloth with gilt lettered spine, mild cover edge wear, paper label to spine base, soil and spotting to edges, owner name, owner ink stamp.   By the Book, L. C.   37 - 86   2013 $175

Wallace, Alfred Russel   1823-1913 *The Malay Archipelago: the Land of the Orang-Utan and the Bird of Paradise.* London: Macmillan and Co., 1869. First edition, 2 volumes, 2 frontispieces, 9 maps, 6 plates, numerous illustrations, 8vo., original green cloth, hinges repaired, extremities slightly rubbed.   Maggs Bros. Ltd.   1467 - 67   2013   £4000

Wallace, Alfred Russel   1823-1913 *My Life: a Record of Events and Opinions.* New York: Dodd, Mead, 1906. 2 volumes, 8vo., frontispiece, plates, maroon cloth, gilt stamped cover and spine titles, , extremity edges worn, inner hinges cracked, Burndy Library bookplate, bookplate of Seafarer's Education Service, very good.   Jeff Weber Rare Books   169 - 467   2013 $175

Wallace, Dillon *Left on the Labrador: a Tale of Adventure Down North.* Toronto: McClelland & Stewart, 1927. 8vo., pictorial blue grey cloth with black titles to front and spine, illustrations, including frontispiece, cloth slightly worn at edges, otherwise very good.   Schooner Books Ltd.   101 - 78   2013 $75

Wallace, Dillon *The Long Labrador Trail Illustrated.* New York: Outing Pub. Co., 1907. First edition, dark blue cloth with white and black design and gilt to front cover and spine, gilt titles to spine and front cover, half title, color frontispiece and 29 black and white photo illustrations and folding map, 8vo., cloth slightly worn, generally very good.   Schooner Books Ltd.   104 - 30   2013 $65

Wallace, Edgar *Cirumstantial Evidence.* London: Newes, 1929. First edition, original paprback, 8vo., original colored pictorial wrappers (little worn), 128 pages, exceedingly scarce, printed on cheap paper which has browned.   Howard S. Mott Inc.   262 - 155   2013 $200

Wallace, Edgar *Fighting Snub Reilly.* London: Newnes, 1929. First edition of original paperback, 8vo., original garish pictorial wrappers, 2 corners off, pages 127, printed on cheap paper which is browned, exceedingly scarce.   Howard S. Mott Inc.   262 - 156   2013 $150

Wallace, Frederick William *Record of Canadian Shipping.* Toronto: Musson Book Co. Ltd., 1929. Limited to 1000, this #147 signed by author, 8vo., black cloth, gilt to cover and spine, map endpapers, half title, 102 black and white illustrations, some light foxing to front pastedown and first flyleaf, otherwise very good, with typed list of ships built at River John, Pictou County, plus few loose notes.   Schooner Books Ltd.   105 - 164   2013 $100

Wallace, Frederick William *The Shack Locker: Yarns of the Deep Sea Fishing Fleets.* Toronto and Montreal: Industrial and Educational Press Ltd., 1916. First edition, 8vo., decorated card covers, some wear to edges of spine, otherwise very good, author's presentation copy dated Feb. 1951. Schooner Books Ltd. 101 - 126 2013 $95

Wallace, John William *An Address Delivered at the Celebration by the New York Historical Society May 20 1863 of the Two Hundredth Birthday of Mr. William Bradford.* Albany: J. Munsell, 1863. First edition, 114 pages, 3 folding plates, half calf and marbled paper covered boards, black morocco spine label, elaborate gilt decorations on spine, slight rubbing at corners and spine ends, else near fine, tipped to front fly is 2 page ALS from author. Between the Covers Rare Books, Inc. New York City - 291883 2013 $225

Wallace, Robert B. *The Georgia Tech Yellow Jackets 1966.* Atlanta: Georgie Inst. of Technology/Sports Publications, 1966. First edition, quarto, probably issued without dust jacket, illustrations, uncommon. Between the Covers Rare Books, Inc. Football Books - 71434 2013 $150

Wallace, William A. *Galileo, the Jesuits and the Medieval Aristotle.* London: Variorum, 1991. 8vo., teal cloth, gilt stamped cover and spine titles, ownership signature, fine. Jeff Weber Rare Books 169 - 468 2013 $75

Waller, Augustus *Nouvelle Methode Anatomique pour l'Investigation Du Systeme Nerveauz Premiere Patie Etant une Letter Evoyee a L'Academie Des Sciences De Paris Le 23 Novembre 1851.* Bon: Charles Georgi, 1852. 28 pages, 2 plates, large 4to., new marbled wrappers, text with some foxing, otherwise tall, uncut copy, wide margins, rare. James Tait Goodrich 75 - 221 2013 $1495

Waller, Henry D. *History of the Town of Flushing, Long Island, New York.* Flushing: J. H. Ridenour, 1899. First edition, fair with torque in spine, boards and spine cover detached but present, text block split in several places, few pages loose, ink notation on half titlepage. Between the Covers Rare Books, Inc. New York City - 288613 2013 $50

Wallin, Georg *Forsta Res Fran Cairo till Arabiska Oknen 1 April 1845.* Helsingfors: Simelius, 1853. First edition, map, 8vo., viii, 126 pages. Maggs Bros. Ltd. 1467 - 31 2013 £1100

Walling, William English *Russia's Message. The True World Import of the Revolution.* New York: Doubleday Page, 1908. First American edition, 8vo., photos, from the library of consumer advocate Florence Kelley, with her ownership signature, green cloth, stamped in gilt on spine, top edge gilt, owner's name on flyleaf, cover bumped at corners and scuffed at corners and ends of spine, else very good. Second Life Books Inc. 183 - 391 2013 $85

Wallingford, Richard *Richard Wallingford. An Edition of His Writings and Introductions.* Oxford: Clarendon Press, 1976. 3 volume, 8vo., plates, navy cloth, gilt stamped spine titles, dust jackets, fine. Jeff Weber Rare Books 169 - 458 2013 $375

Walpole, Horace *Catalogue of the Classic Contents of Strawberry Hill, Collected by Horace Walpole.* London: George Robins, 1842. 4to., title, pages xxiv, 250, lithographic portrait frontispiece on India paper, wood engraved title and text vignettes, some foxing to frontispiece, occasionally little spotted, modern calf backed green cloth, spine with red label lettered in gilt. Marlborough Rare Books Ltd. 218 - 149 2013 £150

Walpole, Horace *Historic Doubts on the Life and Reign of King Richard the Third.* London: J. Dodsley, 1768. First edition, one of 1250 copies, 4to., 2 engraved plates, expertly bound in recent half calf, retaining original marbled boards, raised and gilt banded spine and red morocco label, inscribed by author for friend Thomas Astle " A Present from the author. Thos. Astle", very faint stamp "disposed of by the Royal Institution". Ken Spelman Books Ltd. 75 - 28 2013 £1250

Walpole, Horace *Horace Walpole and His Words: Select Passages from His Letters.* London: Seeley and Co. Ltd., 1892. Fourth edition, 206 x 140mm., frontispiece and 7 portraits, very attractive contemporary dark blue three quarter morocco by Tout (stamp signed), raised bands, spine lavishly gilt in compartments with central oval medallion containing a floral spray, medallion within frame of entwined volutes, floral tools and stippling, marbled boards and endpapers, top edge gilt, other edges rough trimmed; spine slightly and evenly sunned to pleasing dark blue green, otherwise very fine, no signs of use inside or out; bookplate of William Eyres Sloan. Phillip J. Pirages 63 - 485 2013 $375

Walpole, Horace *The Letters.* London: Richard Bentley and Son, 1891. 9 volumes, 230 x 149mm., 43 engraved plates, protected by tissue guards; extremely pleasing polished calf for Hatchards (stamp signed), blind ruled triple frame on covers, raised bands, spine compartments of thick and thin gilt rules enclosing decorative frames with dotted sides and volute cornerpieces, each spine, two morocco labels, top edges gilt; one joint mostly and two joints partly, cracked (but nothing loose), faint hairline scratches on few covers, couple of volumes with slightest hint of wear to extremities, otherwise fine, attractive binding, looking handsome on the shelf, text entirely fresh and clean. Phillip J. Pirages 63 - 484 2013 $950

Walpole, Hugh *All Souls' Night: a Book of Stories.* London: Macmillan and Co. Ltd., 1933. First edition, octavo, titlepage printed in red and black, original decorated green cloth, front panel stamped in blind, spine panel stamped in gold and blind. L. W. Currey, Inc. Wandering Ghosts & Itinerant Souls (10/12) - 130580 2013 $350

Walsdorf, John J. *Printers on Morris.* Beaverton: Beaverdam Press, 1981. Limited to 326 copies, this is one of 300 bound thus, 7.6 x 5.6 cm., leather spine, floral paper covered boards, (36) pages, frontispiece by Barry Moser, 4 page prospectus loosely inserted, from the collection of Donn W. Sanford.   Oak Knoll Books   303 - 47   2013 $125

Walsh, Basil   *A Unique Victorian Composer.* IAP, 2008. First edition, xxiii, 296 pages, illustrations, cloth, dust jacket, fine.   C. P. Hyland   261 - 15   2013   £30

Walsh, Christy   *College Football and All America Review.* Hollywood: House Warven Pub., 1951. First edition, remainder sheets of the first edition issued in 1949 with cancel titlepage, pages bit browned, fine save for small scrape to spine, very good, yellowed dust jacket with matching scrape, reverse side of jacket folds out to double size poster featuring 25th year All America Football Team players. Between the Covers Rare Books, Inc.   Football Books - 74700   2013 $175

Walsh, Christy   *Intercollegiate Football: a Complete Pictorial and Statistical Review from 1869 to 1934.* New York and St. Paul: Doubleday, Doran for Intercollegiate Football, 1934. First edition, drawings by Homer Peace, very good plus in pictorial leatherette with spine lettering dimmed, lacking dust jacket.   Between the Covers Rare Books, Inc.   Football Books - 71447   2013 $125

Walsh, James Morgan   *Vanguard to Neptune.* London: Fantasy Books, n.d., 1952? octavo, pictorial wrappers.   L. W. Currey, Inc.   Fall Sampler Sept. 2013 - 145369   2013 $125

Walsh, Robert   *Constantinople and the Scenery of the Seven Churches of Asia Minor. First Series.* London: Fisher, Son and Co. circa, 1838. First series only, 4to., 47 engraved plates, dampstaining towards front and rear, plates little foxed with some discoloration to top edge, black half calf, marbled paper boards, gilt spine, marbled paper rubbed, substantial surface loss to lower board, joints scuffed and corners fraying, small label of Pickering Booksellers, West Street, Fareham.   Unsworths Antiquarian Booksellers   28 - 144   2013   £200

Walsh, William   *Story of Santa Klaus.* New York: Moffat Yard, 1909. First edition, 8vo., pictorial cloth, 222 pages, plus illustrations, near fine.   Aleph-Bet Books, Inc.   105 - 134   2013 $200

Walter, J. G.   *Observationes Anatomicae. Historia Monstri Bicorporis, Duobus, Capitibus, Tribus Pedibus, Pectore Pelvique Concreti.* Berolini: Apud Gottlieb Augustum Lange, 1775. Folio, engraved title vignette, 13 engraved copper plates, 2 are folding plates, tall, uncut, some foxing and text browning, old worn wrappers, binding loose and shaken, front wrapper off.   James Tait Goodrich   S74 - 236   2013 $3500

Walter, William   *A Discourse Delivered Before the Humane Society of Massachusetts Twelfth of June1798.* Boston: printed by John and Thomas Fleet at the Bible and Heart, Cornhill, 1798. First edition, small 4to., contemporary marbled paper wrappers, endpapers little stained, some light soiling, small stamp of later owner on inside front wrapper, attractive copy, with half title, with "Hon. Elbridge Gerry ESq." on front flyleaf.   M & S Rare Books, Inc.   95 - 224   2013 $275

Walters, Minette   *The Scold's Bridle.* Bristol: Scorpion, 1994. First edition, one of 75 specially bound numbered copies signed by author, very fine.   Mordida Books   81 - 564   2013 $200

Walton, Izaak   1593-1683   *The Complete Angler...* London: printed for F. and C. Rivington, 1792. Fifth edition, frontispiece, 9 plates, 2 engraved leaves of music, woodcuts, 8vo., slight browning and occasional foxing to plates, expertly bound in recent full sprinkled calf, raised and gilt bands, gilt device to spine, red morocco label, handsome.   Jarndyce Antiquarian Booksellers   CCIV - 304   2013   £480

Walton, Izaak   1593-1683   *The Complete Angler.* Chiswick: printed by C. Whittingham sold by Thomas Tegg, etc., 1824. First Tegg edition, 2 volumes, 16mo., original printed boards, frontispieces, uncut, partly unopened, fine, rare in this condition, morocco backed cloth folding case. Howard S. Mott Inc.   262 - 157   2013 $750

Walton, Izaak   1593-1683   *The Complete Angler.* London: D. Bogue, 1844. Sixth (titled fourth) John Major edition, 12 steel engravings, 74 woodcuts, early 20th century binding by Riviere & Son in full forest green levant morocco, fine, unique copy with four signed watercolors by John Absolon, from the renowned collection of John T. Spaulding. David Brass Rare Books, Inc.   Holiday 2012 Chapter Five - DB 01876   2013 $3850

Walton, Izaak   1593-1683   *The Compleat Angler or the Contemplative Man's Recreation.* London: George G. Harrap, 1931. One of 775 copies signed by artist, 270 x 203mm., original vellum covered boards, gilt titling and decoration on front cover and spine, top edge gilt, other edges untrimmed and unopened, titlepage and endpapers, 24 illustrations in text and 12 color plates by Arthur Rackham, 3 minuscule dots near top of spine, else virtually faultless and rare thus.   Phillip J. Pirages   63 - 384   2013 $2100

Walton, Izaak 1593-1683 *The Compleat Angler or the Contemplative Man's Recreation.* London: Harrap, 1931. First Rackham edition, one of 775 numbered copies, this unnumbered, but inscribed by Arthur Rackham above his signature on limitation page 'Special Copy' and printed on Millbourn, handmade paper, 12 color printed plates, each with captioned tissue guard, 25 drawings and pictorial endpapers, all by Rackham, titlepage printed in black and green, 4to., original white buckram, backstrip and front cover gilt lettered and decorations and triple line border in gilt to a design by Rackham, top edge gilt, others untrimmed and partly unopened, near fine. Blackwell's Rare Books 172 - 233 2013 £875

Walton, Izaak 1593-1683 *The Lives of John Donne, Sir Henry Wotton, Mr. Richard Hooker, Mr. George Herbert and Dr. Robert Sanderson.* New York: privately printed (at the Chiswick Press) for the Scott-Thaw Co., 1904. One of 200 copies for sale, signed by publisher, this copy #88, 362 x 22mm., engraved titlepage and historiated initials by Dion Clayton Calthrop, printer's device in colophon and 6 engraved portraits, original tissue guards, printed in black and red on thick textured paper; simply decorated but quite elegant modern retrospective olive brown crushed morocco by Grace-Bindings (stamp signed), cover with slender chain gilt roll border, raised bands, spine panels with gilt titling and central 8 point sunburst lozenge, marbled endpapers, untrimmed, bottom edges, other edges rough trimmed, original paper spine label from publisher's cloth binding tipped in a rear of volume), four (of the 9) blank flyleaves vaguely browned, isolated trivial foxing, but very fine, excellent edition, binding unworn, text especially bright, fresh and clean. Phillip J. Pirages 63 - 486 2013 $950

Walton, Todd *Forgotten Impulses.* New York: Simon & Schuster, 1980. First edition, with ALS signed by author, with envelope, book near fine in fine dust jacket. Ken Lopez Bookseller 159 - 211 2013 $150

Walton, Todd *Inside Moves.* Garden City: Doubleday, 1978. First edition, signed by author in 1981, to noted film critic Pauline Kael, with long letter included here in photocopy, asking Kael why she did not review the film made from the book, fine in near fine dust jacket. Ken Lopez Bookseller 159 - 210 2013 $100

Walton, William *A Memoir Addressed to Proprietors of Mountain and Other Waste Lands and Agriculturists of the United Kingdom on the Naturalization of the Alpaca.* printed by C. Reynell, London for the Natural History Society of Liverpool, 1841. First edition, wood engraved frontispiece, little foxing, mostly on endpapers which are also dust soiled, minor dampstaining at lower inner corners, 8vo., original ripple grain cloth, single gilt fillet around sides, 'Alpaca' stamped gilt in centre of upper cover, unevenly faded and worn at extremities, inscription beneath author's name on gilt, giving author's address and stating that it has been sent at request of William Danson of Liverpool, sound. Blackwell's Rare Books Sciences - 129 2013 £400

Wandrei, Donald *The Eye and the Finger.* Sauk City: Arkham House, 1944. First edition, name stamp, small, faint date stamp on titlepage, else fine in very lightly worn, fine dust jacket with small nicks and tears, very nice. Between the Covers Rare Books, Inc. Sci-Fi, Fantasy & Horror - 89278 2013 $450

Ward, Edward *A Compleat and Humorous Account of all the Remarkable Clubs and Societies in the Cities of London and Westminster...* London: printed for J. Wren at the Bible and Crown, 1756. Seventh edition, 12mo., few pages slightly foxed, contemporary mottled calf, gilt ruled borders, raised bands, spines gilt in compartments, olive green morocco label, spine and corners little rubbed, slight wear to corners. Jarndyce Antiquarian Booksellers CCIV - 305 2013 £580

Ward, Edward *Hudibras Redivivus; or a Burlesque Poem on the Times Part the First (-Twelfth).* London: printed and sold by B. Bragge, 1705-1707. First editions, 4to., rather browned, some pages heavily foxed, later endpapers, contemporary calf, double blind ruled borders, rebacked, not recently, red morocco label, hinges cracked but firm, spine rubbed. Jarndyce Antiquarian Booksellers CCIV - 306 2013 £750

Ward, John *Skipton Castle: Including Sketches of Its Noble Owners and Its Historical Associations.* Skipton: James Tasker, 1866. 9, (1) pages, frontispiece, very good in original blindstamped and gilt lettered cloth, evidence of removal of bookplate from inner front board, scarce. Ken Spelman Books Ltd. 73 - 163 2013 £45

Ward, Lock *A Guide to Cork, Queenstown, Glengariff Killarney the South West of Ireland.* 1950. Tenth edition, 5 maps, 20 photos, cloth, very good. C. P. Hyland 261 - 860 2013 £30

Ward, Lock *Illustrated Guide to and Popular History of Dublin and Its Neighbourhood.* circa, 1889. 118 pages (102+ pages ads), 2 maps, chromolithographs, many black and white illustrations, original green boards worn, lacks map of Killarney, good. C. P. Hyland 261 - 851 2013 £55

Ward, Lock *A Pictorial & Descriptive Guide to Cork, Queenstown, Glengariff, Killarney and the South West of Ireland.* 1912. Sixth edition, 8vo., 2 maps, 60 photos, cloth, good. C. P. Hyland 261 - 852 2013 £30

Ward, Lock *A Pictorial & Descriptive Guide to Cork, Queenstown, Glengariff, Killarney and the South West of Ireland.* 1926. Seventh edition, 8vo., 5 maps, 39 photos, cloth, very good. C. P. Hyland 261 - 854 2013 £32

Ward, Lock *A Pictorial & Descriptive Guide to Cork, Queenstown, Glengariff, Killarney and the South West of Ireland.* 1931. Eighth edition, 8vo., 5 maps, 39 photos, cloth, very good.   C. P. Hyland   261 - 855   2013   £32

Ward, Lock *A Pictorial & Descriptive Guide to Cork, Queenstown, Glengariff, Killarney and the South West of Ireland.* 1938. Ninth edition, 5 maps, 39 photos, cloth, very good.   C. P. Hyland   261 - 858   2013   £30

Ward, Lock *Pictorial and Historical Guide to Killarney... With Excursions to Cork...* circa, 1887. 3 folding maps (2 torn but complete), 118 pages (84 + pages ads), 11 chromolithographs, many black and white illustrations, original boards worn, lacks maps of Killarney & Cork city, good.   C. P. Hyland   261 - 850   2013   £55

Ward, Lock *Pictorial and Historical Guide to Killarney... With Excursions to Cork...* 1886. 1 folding map (torn but complete), 118 pages, many pages of ads, 11 chromolithographs, many black and white illustrations, original boards worn, lacks maps of Killarney & Cork City, good.   C. P. Hyland   261 - 849   2013   £45

Ward, Mary Augusta Arnold   1851-1920 *The History of David Grieve.* London: Smith, Elder, 1892. First edition, 3 volumes, 8vo., original blindstamped purple cloth, gilt lettering, spines rebacked with original preserved, edges little browned, very good, inscribed on half title to her brother, W. T. Arnold and Henrietta Arnold.   The Brick Row Book Shop   Miscellany Fifty-Nine - 47   2013 $1750

Ward, R., Mrs. *The Child's Guide to Knowledge...* London: Simpkin Marshall & Co., 1907. Sixty second edition, 12mo., original roan backed marbled boards, edges worn, upper board scraped, 480 pages.   R. F. G. Hollett & Son   Children's Books - 704   2013   £30

Ward, Samuel *A Modern System of Natural History.* London: printed for F. Newbery, 1775-1776. 12 volumes, 12mo. 117 of 118 plates, volume 3 lacks plate xxvii, occasional slight browning, but very good and bright internally, publisher's ad included in several volumes and 4 page recommended reading list to volume VIII, volume I has inkstain to margin of page 146; volume III titlepage affected by short tear to fore-edge and small hole, volume V titlepage title discolored at edges, slight marginal worming around page 100 for volume VI, contemporary tan sheep, gilt volume numbers to spines, rather worn, most joints splitting by all boards attached (with repairs to volumes I and IV).   Unsworths Antiquarian Booksellers   28 - 137   2013   £900

Warden, Florence *Miss Ferriby's Clients.* London: Laurie, 1910. First edition, page edges darkened and spotted, otherwise near fine in green pictorial cloth covered boards.   Mordida Books   81 - 565   2013 $150

Warhol, Julia *Holy Cats by Andy Warhol's Mother.* New York: privately printed, 1957. First edition, 20 leaves, each leaf printed recto with photolithographic image of cat and corresponding calligraphic text, leaves in a variety of different colored papers, front blank with unsigned inscription by Julia Warhol, very good, original buff pictorial paper over boards, spine brittle and chipped, missing one inch portion from bottom of spine, edges of boards bit toned, overall very good, custom cloth clamshell with two red morocco spine labels.   Heritage Book Shop   Holiday Catalogue 2012 - 154   2013 $6000

Waring, George *The Squirrels and Other Animals.* Harvey and Darton, n.d. circa, 1840. Square 12mo., original cloth, gilt, spine trifle rubbed and faded, neatly recased, frontispiece (top margin repaired), title vignette and 6 full page woodcut vignettes (little spotting).   R. F. G. Hollett & Son   Children's Books - 705   2013   £65

Warner, Charles Dudley *In the Levant.* Boston & New York: Houghton Mifflin, 1893. Reprint, 8vo., 2 volumes, 215 photogravures, tissue guards, one loose, quarter bound in red and green cloth sides, with gilt decoration, covers little soiled, staining to fore edges of prelim matter, good set.   Second Life Books Inc.   183 - 393   2013 $100

Warner, F. *The History of the Rebellion and Civil War in Ireland.* Dublin: James Williams, 1768. First edition, volume 2 of 2, 332 pages, contemporary calf (worn), binding tight, text good.   C. P. Hyland   261 - 862   2013   £40

Warner, Rex *The Wild Goose Chase.* London: Boriswood, 1937. First edition, near fine in attractive, very good dust jacket with dampstains on edges of flaps and rear panel.   Between the Covers Rare Books, Inc.   Sci-Fi, Fantasy & Horror - 306823   2013 $75

Warner, Richard *Excursions from Bath.* Bath: printed by R. Cruttwell, 1801. First edition, 8vo., titlepage vignette, 4 maps set within text, slight foxing and light browning, small tear to head of A3, pencil notes in margins of four pages, 19th century half calf, marbled boards, gilt lozenges & bands to spine, gilt label, modern booklabel for Castle Hacket on inner front board, attractive copy.   Jarndyce Antiquarian Booksellers   CCIV - 307   2013   £225

Warner, Samuel *Authentic and Impartial Narrative of the Tragical Scene Which was Witnessed in Southampton County (Virginia) on Monday 22nd of August Last,...* New York: printed for Warner & West, 1831. First edition, 8vo., 38 pages, contemporary plain wrappers, uncut, lacks pages 35-38 and folding frontispiece, all supplied in facsimile.   M & S Rare Books, Inc.   95 - 373   2013 $1250

Warren, Constance Whitney *Constance Whitney Warren 1888-1948: Memorial Exhibition Feb. 2-15, 1953.* New York: Fearagil Galleries, 1953. First edition, quarto, self wrappers, just touch of wear, very near fine, 19 full page plates, scarce.   Between the Covers Rare Books, Inc.   Horses, Horsemanship, Horse Racing, Etc. - 81940   2013 $85

Warren, Edward *Some Account of the Letheon; or Who is the Discoverer?* Boston: Dutton and Wentworth, 1847. Third edition, first issue, 88 pages, original printed publisher's wrappers, author's presentation to Dr. J. Ware.   James Tait Goodrich   S74 - 15   2013 $1750

Warren, J. Russell *Murder in the Blackout.* New York: Sheridan House, 1940. First American edition, very good or little better with edgeworn, very good dust jacket with several small internal repairs, very scarce.   Between the Covers Rare Books, Inc.   Mystery & Detective Fiction - 85027   2013 $200

Warren, John Collins *The Great Tree on Boston Common.* Boston: John Wilson, 1955. First edition, large 8vo., 20 pages, inscribed by author to John Wells, wood engraved frontispiece with tissue guard, double page map.   Second Life Books Inc.   183 - 395   2013 $250

Warren, John E. *Etherization: with Surgical Remarks.* Boston: Ticknor, 1848. Original pressed Victorian brown cloth, some light toning to paper, binding showing some light wear, overall very good.   James Tait Goodrich   75 - 7   2013 $1295

Warren, Joseph *Revenge.* New York: Grosset & Dunlap, 1928. First edition, endpapers slightly darkened, otherwise fine in dust jacket with nicks and small chips at spine ends, couple of closed tears and wear at corners.   Mordida Books   81 - 566   2013 $150

Warren, Robert Penn 1905-1989 *Night Rider.* Boston: Houghton Mifflin, 1939. First edition, 8vo., near fine, clean copy in very good plus to near fine bright jacket with shallow chipping at spine crown (tad browned at spine).   Ed Smith Books   75 - 80   2013 $400

Warren, Robert Penn 1905-1989 *Selected Poems New and Old.* New York: Random House, 1966. First edition, 8vo., #235 of 250 large paper copies, printed on special paper and specially bound, signed by author, small stain to fore-edge, otherwise fine in dust jacket and publisher's box.   Second Life Books Inc.   183 - 396   2013 $225

Warton, Thomas *The Lives of those Eminent Antiquaries John Leland, Thomas Hearne and Anthony a Wood...* Oxford: printed at the Clarendon Press, 1772. First edition, 2 frontispieces, 9 engraved plates, 8vo., some offset browning on endpapers, occasional minor foxing and light browning, 19th century calf, gilt crest to each board, competently rebacked with rather unsympathetic red morocco labels, extremities rubbed, corners repaired.   Jarndyce Antiquarian Booksellers   CCIV - 308   2013   £180

Warton, Thomas *The Union or Select Scots and English Poems.* London: printed for R. Baldwin, 1759. Second edition, small 8vo., browned and dusted throughout tear to B1 without loss, old wax seals on inner boards, contemporary calf, raised bands, red morocco label, boards rubbed, corners worn, early names of J. Heap, Brasenose Coll. and William Hutchinson on endpaper.   Jarndyce Antiquarian Booksellers   CCIV - 309   2013   £150

Warwick, Arthur *Spare Minutes; or resolved Meditations and Premeditated Resolutions.* London: printed by G. M. for Walter Hammond, 1822. Sixth edition, small 4to., half title, frontispiece, plate, contemporary full vellum, gilt borders, blue leather label slightly faded, slightly marked, top edge gilt, very good, inscribed by Henry Nelson Coleridge for his wife Sara and signed by him with initials, later signature of their daughter Edith Coleridge.   Jarndyce Antiquarian Booksellers   CCIII - 596   2013   £250

Wasatch Front Volume 58 Number 1. Salt Lake City: University of Utah, 1971. 52 pages, octavo, stapled gray and white illustrated wrappers, near fine.   Ken Sanders Rare Books   45 - 44   2013 $300

Wascher-James, Sande *Just a Woman.* Whidbey Island: 2012. Artist's book, one of 12 copies only, each signed and numbered by artist, all on 1 ply museum board (triple layered), the figure of Marian Anderson made from 100 per cent black cotton rag, a series of double sided paper dolls with faces of women on photo paper and their costumes of Liberty Lawn fabrics, the figures are the pages so there are 24, each about 10 inches tall, those with hats about 12 inches, housed in black cloth over boards box fastened with black gros-grain ribbon with Velcro, figures of the 12 women are placed within board guides.   Priscilla Juvelis - Rare Books   55 - 32   2013 $2500

Washburn, A. L. *Recent Polar Publications. Supplement to No. 10 of "The Polar Times".* New York: American Polar Society, 1940. 4to., cloth binder, label removed from upper board, 41 pages, duplicated.   R. F. G. Hollett & Son   Polar Exploration - 80   2013   £35

Washburn, Robert Collyer *The Jury of Death.* Garden City: Doubleday Crime Club, 1930. First edition, name and address on front endpaper and top corner slightly bumped, otherwise fine in very fine, as new dust jacket.   Mordida Books   81 - 567   2013 $200

Washington, Booker T. *The Future of the American Negro.* Boston: Small Maynard, 1899. First edition, 244 pages, frontispiece, maroon cloth, publisher's promotional pamphlet laid in, spine slightly faded, else fine, tight, gilt on spine and front board intact and easily readable, increasingly scarce in nice condition.   Between the Covers Rare Books, Inc.   165 - 282   2013 $600

Washington, Doris V. *Yulan.* New York: Carlton Press, 1964. First edition, fine in near fine dust jacket.   Between the Covers Rare Books, Inc.   165 - 283   2013 $150

Washington, George *Official Letters to the Honorable American Congress, written during the War Between the United Colonies and Great Britain.* London: printed for Cadell Junior and Davies, 1795. 2 volumes, one leaf of preface bound out of order, 8vo., contemporary tree calf, gilt banded spine, black morocco labels, expert repairs to hinges and head and tail of spines, later bookplate in both volumes.   Jarndyce Antiquarian Booksellers   CCIV - 310   2013   £450

Washington, Walter E. *H: the Student's Handbook Howard University 1937-1938.* Washington: Howard University, 1937. Second edition, 24mo., flexible blue cloth decorated in white, 178 pages, ads, only modest wear at extremities, nice, very good or better, laid in is a ticket for Student Council Opening reception.   Between the Covers Rare Books, Inc.   165 - 284   2013 $150

Watanabe, Sadao *Biblical Prints.* Tokyo: Shinkyo Shuppansha; Boston: Biblical Research, 1986. First edition, folio, fine, mustard colored cloth boards, brown lettered spine and front cover, fine original orange cloth covered tri-fold folder with title printed in Japanese on paste-on paper label.   By the Book, L. C.   38 - 73   2013 $600

Waterland, Daniel *Scripture Vindicated; In Answer to Book Intituled Christianity as Old as the Creation. Part I-(II).* London: printed for W. Innys, Cambridge: printed for Cornelius Crownfield and John Crownfield, 1730. 2 parts bound as 1, with collective half title, 8vo., few minor spots, lower corner of first leaf worn, plain calf by Chris Weston.   Unsworths Antiquarian Booksellers   28 - 138   2013   £150

Waterloo, Stanley *The Story of Ab: a Tale of the time of the Cave Man.* Chicago: Way and Williams, 1897. First edition, first issue, neat contemporary pencil owner name on titlepage, especially fine and bright.   Between the Covers Rare Books, Inc.   Sci-Fi, Fantasy & Horror - 88335   2013 $500

The Waters of the Earth. Religious Tract Society, circa, 1840. First edition, 12mo., original blindstamped cloth gilt, pages iv, 160, all edges gilt, woodcut title and numerous full page and vignette woodcuts, fine.   R. F. G. Hollett & Son   Children's Books - 23   2013   £65

Waters, D. W *The Rutters of the Sea: The Sailing Directions of Pierre Garcie. A Study of the First English and French Printed Sailing Directions...* New Haven: Yale University Press, 1967. First edition, large 4to., frontispiece, 14 illustrations, 3 tables, dark blue cloth, blind-stamped cover illustration, gilt stamped blue spine label, dust jacket worn, very good, Burndy bookplate.   Jeff Weber Rare Books   169 - 470   2013 $83

Waters, Frank *Flight from Fiesta.* Santa Fe: 1986. Limited edition, one of 200 numbered and signed copies, (iv), 140 pages, prospectus laid in, as new in slipcase, paper covered boards.   Dumont Maps & Books of the West   124 - 93   2013 $95

Waters, John *Long Black Coat.* Dublin: New Island Books, 1995. First edition, limited to 150 copies, signed by author for customers of Kenny's Bookshop in Galway, 8vo., original grey cloth, fine in dust jacket, loosely inserted is card reproducing a black and white drawing by author entitled "Eh Sam", signed.   Maggs Bros. Ltd.   1442 - 311   2013   £75

Waters, Thomas *The Reflections of a Policeman.* Boston: Wentworth, 1856. First authorized American edition, contemporary owner name, bottom of boards worn through in some places, as well as some lesser wear to corners and at spinal extremities, else nice, very good copy with spine lettering fresh and readable.   Between the Covers Rare Books, Inc.   Mystery & Detective Fiction - 11043   2013 $315

Waterton, Charles *Wanderings in South America, the North-West of the United States and the Antilles in the Years 1812, 1820, 1824.* London: F. Fellowes, 1828. Second edition, engraved plate, early green cloth, light wear and foxing, else clean, tight copy.   James Tait Goodrich   75 - 9   2013 $695

Wathen, James *Journal of a Voyage in 1811 and 1812 to Madras & China Returning by the Cape of Good Hope and St. Helena in the H.C.S. The Hope, Capt. James Pendergrass.* London: 1814. First edition, 24 hand colored aquatint views, some very slight offsetting from text to plate on few plates, 4to., modern quarter morocco.   Maggs Bros. Ltd.   1467 - 68   2013   £5000

Watkins-Pitchford, D. J. *Meeting Hill.* Hollis & Carter, 1948. First edition, 4to., original cloth, head of spine little faded, dust jacket price clipped, extremities chipped, 15 color plates, few spots to flyleaves, but very nice.   R. F. G. Hollett & Son   Children's Books - 707   2013   £250

Watkins-Pitchford, D. J. *Wandering Wind.* Hamish Hamilton, 1959. Second impression, original yellow cloth, dust jacket rather worn and little soiled, some loss to head of spine, illustrations by author, pencil scribbles on flyleaf and fore-edge, scarce.   R. F. G. Hollett & Son Children's Books - 708   2013   £175

Watkins, T. H. *Gold Rush Country.* San Francisco: California Historical Society, 1981. First edition, large quarto, 96 pages, 63 high gloss black and white photos, map, photo endpapers, brown cloth spine, gilt over dark green pictorial boards stamped in brown, slight fading to spine, else very fine. Argonaut Book Shop Recent Acquisitions June 2013 - 302 2013 $60

Watson, Andrew G. *A Descriptive Catalogue of the Medieval Manuscripts of Exeter College, Oxford.* Oxford: Oxford University Press, 2000. First edition, 4to., color frontispiece, 4 color plates, 4 black and white plates, navy cloth, gilt stamped spine title, dust jacket, Burndy bookplate, fine. Jeff Weber Rare Books 169 - 471 2013 $215

Watson, James D. *Genes, Girls and Gamow.* New York: Alfred A. Knopf, 2002. First American edition, signed by Watson, Cecilia Gilbert and Walter Gilbert, fine in fine dust jacket, 8vo. By the Book, L. C. 37 - 88 2013 $300

Watson, James D. *The Genetical Implications fo the Structure of Deoxyribonucleic Acid. in Nature Sat. May 30, 1953 No. 4361 volume 171.* London: Nature, 1953. Entire issue offered, very good++ original wrappers in modern blue wrappers with printed label on front cover, issue has been slightly trimmed without any loss of text or images, dampstain to first page. By the Book, L. C. 37 - 87 2013 $500

Watson, James D. *Molecular Biology of the Gene.* Menlo Park: Benjamin Cummings, 1977. Third edition, 2nd printing, 4to., signed and dated by Marshall Nirenberg, few pages dog eared, original color illustrated cloth, scarce association. By the Book, L. C. 37 - 89 2013 $200

Watson, James D. *A Passion for DNA. Genes, Genomes and Society.* Cold Springs Harbor: Cold Springs Harbor Lab. Press, 2000. First edition, 8vo., signed by Watson, as new in like dust jacket. By the Book, L. C. 37 - 90 2013 $400

Watson, John F. *Historic Tales of Olden Time...* New York: Collins and Hannay, 1832. First edition, small octavo, 214 pages, contemporary quarter cloth, paper over boards with printed spine label, small chips on spine, small dampstain on blank leaf, very good, no restoration. Between the Covers Rare Books, Inc. New York City - 316236 2013 $200

Watson, John F. *Historic Tales of Olden Time...* New York: Collins and Hannay, 1832. First edition, rebound in sturdy red buckram, spotting to boards, small repair to frontispiece, moderate foxing and spotting throughout, sound but good only. Between the Covers Rare Books, Inc. New York City - 292639 2013 $65

Watson, Joseph *Autumn Leaves.* London?: printed for private circulation, 1859. Half title, photo frontispiece and title vignette, original brown cloth by Westleys and Co., bevelled boards, borders and title in gilt, little rubbed with slight loss to head and tail of spine, all edges gilt, bookplate of Joshua Watson, presentation inscription for Watson from his niece Mary Spence Watson with uncle Fossy's best wishes, recent blue ink notes on leading f.e.p.'s. Jarndyce Antiquarian Booksellers CCV - 282 2013 £450

Watson, Lucy *Coleridge at Highgate.* London: Longmans, 1925. Half title, frontispiece, plates, few pencil notes, lacking leading f.e.p., original maroon cloth, spine faded with repair at tail. Jarndyce Antiquarian Booksellers CCIII - 589 2013 £30

Watson, Richard *Anecdotes of the Life of Richard Watson, Bishop of Landaff.* London: printed for T. Cadell and W. Davies, 1818. 2 volumes, 8vo., stipple engraved portrait frontispiece, titlepages foxed, light foxing elsewhere, contemporary half dark blue polished calf with marbled boards, spines gilt in six compartments, lettered direct in gilt and numbered within a geometrical gilt frame, edges sprinkled red boards little scuffed, touch of rubbing to spine ends. Unsworths Antiquarian Booksellers 28 - 204 2013 £120

Watteson, Henry *History of the Manhattan club of New York: a Narrative of the Activities of Half a Century.* New York: The Manhattan Club/the De Vinne Press, 1915. First edition, one of 650 copies, this copy for Franklin Bein, rebound in red buckram gilt, else fine, gravure portraits. Between the Covers Rare Books, Inc. New York City - 292253 2013 $150

Watts, Alaric *Lyrics of the Heart: with Other Poems.* London: Longman, Brown, Green and Longmans, 1851. First edition, 211 x 132mm., superb late 19th century olive brown crushed morocco gilt and inlaid by Fazakerley (stamp signed on front turn-in), covers with frames of gilt rules, dots and inlaid tan morocco, central panel of upper cover with inlaid red morocco rectangle emblazoned with title gilt at head, below it a large topiary-shaped, symmetrical design in inlaid morocco and gilt tooling, incorporating 34 heart shaped green leaves on curling hairline stems as well as five lotus blossoms with lavender petals and inverted red heart centers (lower cover with smaller version of same inlaid elements inside plain ruled panel), raised bands, gilt spine compartments continuing same design (each with four inlaid leaf cornerpieces and central lotus flower), turn-ins with gilt and dot frames and lotus and leaf cornerpieces, ivory silk endleaves, marbled flyleaves, edges gilt and elaborately gauffered with deep gouging (in similar floral pattern), fore edge with three exquisitely painted scenes, within pointed frames, these vignettes taken from illustrations appearing within book, felt lined slipcase; with 41 engraved headpieces, as called for, engraved bookplate of Rodman Wanamaker, spine and front board sunned to pleasing uniform tan (as almost always with this color of morocco), occasional minor foxing, more prominent on first and last gatherings), still extremely fine, lovely, morocco lustrous and without perceptible wear, edges with particularly brilliant gilding, 3 painted fore-edge vignettes in perfect condition. Phillip J. Pirages   61 - 79   2013 $12,500

Watts, Edith Ballad *Jesse's Book of Creole and Deep South Recipes.* New York: Viking Press, 1954. First edition, fine in attractive, very good or better dust jacket, slightly spine faded, scarce in this condition.   Between the Covers Rare Books, Inc.   165 - 124   2013 $100

Watts, Isaac *Divine and Moral Songs for Children.* R. Miller, 1816. New edition, beautiful vignettes, 12mo, modern full calf gilt, engraved title with vignette and 40 leaves on thin card, all copper engraved with poem, each with engraved vignette at head, 2 ad leaves at end rather browned and stained, but very good, rare.   R. F. G. Hollett & Son   Children's Books - 709   2013   £450

Watts, Isaac *Logic; or the right Use of Reason in the Enquiry after Truth...* printed for Thomas Tegg, 1811. 12mo., original sheep, gilt, rubbed, frontispiece rather stained, some pencil scribbles to flyleaves.   R. F. G. Hollett & Son   Children's Books - 710   2013   £35

Watts, Louisa *Pretty Little Poems for Pretty Little People...* Halifax: William Milner, 1846. 12mo., original blindstamped cloth, gilt, all edges gilt, woodcut frontispiece (rather foxed). R. F. G. Hollett & Son   Children's Books - 711   2013   £65

Watts, Richard *ABC's of Forest Fire Prevention.* Ottawa: Cloutier, 1950. 8vo., pictorial wrappers, near fine, illustrations in color on every page.   Aleph-Bet Books, Inc.   104 - 6   2013 $200

Waugh, Ida *Ideal Heads.* Philadelphia: Sunshine Pub. Co., 1890. Folio, gold cloth stamped in gold and colors, all edges gilt, (92) pages, light cover soil, several insignificant archival margin mends, else very good, printed on heavy paper and illustrated by Waugh with 20 magnificent color lithographs also illustrated with numerous full and partial page black and whites by Jessie Willcox Smith.   Aleph-Bet Books, Inc.   104 - 584   2013 $1200

Wauthier, J. M. *The Geographical Institutions; or a Set of Classical and Analytical Tables Forming a complete Course of Gradual Lessons in Ancient and Modern Geography. First Part (second part).* printed by Schulze and Dean... for Longman, Hurst, Rees, Orme and Brown... and J. M. Wauthier... sold also by Messrs. Bossange and Masson, 1816-1815. First edition of both parts, 2 parts in 1 volume, 3 folding engraved hand colored maps, slight foxing at either end, folding table, 4to., original calf backed boards, rebacked and recornered, original large printed label on upper cover, good, very rare.   Blackwell's Rare Books 172 - 152   2013   £900

Wayland, John W. *The Pathfinder of the Seas: the Lifie of Matthew Fontaine Maury.* Richmond: Garrett & Massie, 1930. First edition, 8vo., frontispiece, decorative blue title border, plates, green cloth, black stamped cover and spine titles, Burndy bookplate, inscribed by author, very good. Jeff Weber Rare Books   169 - 472   2013 $75

Wead, Frank *Gales, Ice and Men.* London: Methuen, 1938. First edition, original cloth, spine littl faded, 20 illustrations, including color frontispiece, maps on endpapers. R. F. G. Hollett & Son   Polar Exploration - 81   2013   £25

Weatherby, James *The General Stud-Book: containing (with few exceptions, the pedigree of every horse, mare &c. of note that has appeared on the turf for the last fifty years...).* London: printed by H. Reynell, 1793. 8vo. slight marking to few pages, full contemporary tree calf, expertly rebacked, gilt spine, red morocco label, two slight scratches to front board.   Jarndyce Antiquarian Booksellers   CCIV - 311   2013   £425

Weatherley, Fred E. *Color Plate Sunbeams.* London & New York: Hildesheimer & Faulkner and Whitney, circa, 1885. 4to., cloth backed pictorial boards, corners worn, else very good+, full page chromolithographs by E. K. Johnson.   Aleph-Bet Books, Inc.   105 - 574   2013 $175

Weatherley, Fred E. *Our Darlings' Surprise Pictures.* London: Ernest Nister, n.d circa, 1895. 8 color transformation pictures, black and white illustrations, small folio, original color glazed pictorial boards, very fine.   David Brass Rare Books, Inc.   Holiday 2012 Chapter One - DB01761 2013 $1850

Weatherley, Fred E. *Pleasant Pastime Pictures.* London: Nister, 1894. 8vo., cloth backed pictorial boards, slightest bit of rubbing, else fine, 6 very charming slatted moveable chromolithographed plates that reveal new pictures when tabs are pulled, illustrations in black and white on text pages. Aleph-Bet Books, Inc. 105 - 411 2013 $950

Weatherley, Fred E. *Told in the Twilight.* New York: E. P. Dutton & Co. n.d. circa, 1884. Original cloth backed pictorial boards, corners little worn, 64 pages, illustrations in color and tints. R. F. G. Hollett & Son Children's Books - 713 2013 £65

Weatherley, Fred E. *Touch and Go.* London: Ernest Nister/New York: E. P. Dutton, n.d. circa, 1890. Small folio, 8 chromolithographed transformation pictures, original color glazed pictorial boards some light soiling to covers, bit of light edgewear, hinges expertly strengthened, otherwise excellent copy, with each moveable plate in original working order and scarce thus. David Brass Rare Books, Inc. Holiday 2012 Chapter One - DB 02097 2013 $1850

Web, Dan *Sounds Pretty.* New York: Harper and Brothers, First edition, fine, very clean copy, scarce. Jeff Hirsch Books Fall 2013 - 129420 2013 $50

Webb, Frank J. *The Garies and Their Friends.* London: G. Routledge and Co., 1857. First edition, one gathering slightly proud, slightly later half navy blue calf, raised bands, gilt compartments, spine slightly faded, very slightly rubbed, very good, scarce. Jarndyce Antiquarian Booksellers CCV - 283 2013 £5800

Webb, Marion St. John *The Littlest One.* George G. Harrap, 1928. First reprint, 4to., original cloth backed pictorial boards, upper board little marked, signs of label removed, 4 color plates by Margaret Tarrant. R. F. G. Hollett & Son Children's Books - 586 2013 £65

Webb, T. T. *From Spears to Spades.* Melbourne: Book Depot, 1944. Second printing, stapled wrappers, 12mo., 80 page, photo, owner name, small stain on fore edge and tiny crease on front wrapper, very good or better. Between the Covers Rare Books, Inc. 165 - 56 2013 $60

Weber, Carl J. *Hardy Music at Colby. A Check-List Compiled with an Introduction.* Waterville: Colby College Library, 1945. First edition, one of 200 copies, fine, 8vo. original salmon paper boards, printed paper label, from the Gary Lepper Collection of Thomas Hardy. The Brick Row Book Shop Bulletin Nine - 99 2013 $85

Weber, Francis J. *Smallpaxweber.* San Diego: Ash Ranch Press, 1989. Limited to 128 copies, 100 numbered, deluxe edition lettered A-Z and 2 state deluxe proofs, this is lettered copy, signed by author and publisher, Don Hildreth, Artwork by Isabel Piczek and Leo Politi, photo by Alphonse Antczak, color frontispiece, 4.6 x 6.1cm., quarter leather with raised bands, title gilt stamped on spine, decorated cloth boards, clamshell box with inset color illustration, 23, (3) pages, from the collection of Donn W. Sanford, miniature bookplate of Kathryn Rickard. Oak Knoll Books 303 - 41 2013 $200

Weber, Francis J. *What Happened to Junipero Serra?* Los Angeles: Bela Blau, 1969. Limited to 1000 numbered copies, handset, printed and bound by Bela Blau, 3.5 x 5.2 cm., dark green leather stamped in gilt, patterned paper endpapers, from the collection of Donn W. Sanford. Oak Knoll Books 303 - 62 2013 $150

Weber, Franics J. *Bela Blau Bookbinder 1914-1993.* Los Angeles: Privately printed for Mariana Blau, 1993. Limited to 150 copies, one of the numbered deluxe copies bound thus, bound and signed by Mariana Blau, 5.2 x 4 cm., full dark brown leather with inset full color photo of Bela Blau on front cover, slipcase, each contributor has signed their contribution, from the collection of Donn W. Sanford. Oak Knoll Books 303 - 61 2013 $225

Weber, Jeff *An Annotated Dictionary of Fore-edge Painting Artists and Binders.* Los Angeles: Weber Rare Books, 2010. Limited to 980 copies, 10 x 7 inches, approximately 432 pages, illustrations, cloth, dust jacket, signed by author, new. Jeff Weber Rare Books 171 - 195 2013 $400

Weber, Jeff *Portfolio of 25 Fore-Edge Paintings.* Los Angeles: Jeff Weber Rare Books, 2012. One of 50 copies, oblong 4to., color illustrations, black cloth, pictorial dust jacket, new. Jeff Weber Rare Books 171 - 196 2013 $75

Weber, Richard *O'Reilly.* Dublin: Dolmen Press, 1957. First edition, one of 250 copies, tall 8vo., original wrappers, some creasing, otherwise excellent. Maggs Bros. Ltd. 1442 - 312 2013 £50

Webster, C. A. *St. Patrick's Lodge, No. 8 1808-1908.* Offprint JCHAS, 1909. 39 pages, many portraits, cloth, presentation copy from Hedley Webster. C. P. Hyland 261 - 863 2013 £35

Webster, Daniel *On the Powers of Government Assigned to It by the Constitution from His Address in the United States Senate May 7, 1834.* Worcester: New Hampshire Historical Society, 1952. Limited to 100 copies, 8 x 5.5 cm., red cloth stamped in gilt, from the collection of Donn W. Sanford. Oak Knoll Books 303 - 29 2013 $175

Webster, Daniel 1782-1852 *Speech.. in Rely (sic) to Mr. Hayne of South Carolina, The Resolution Offered by Mr. Foot, Relative to the Public Lands, Being Under Consideration. Delivered in the Senate Jan. 26 1830.* Washington: Gales & Seaton, 1830. First edition, 2nd issue, 12mo., 76 pages, removed, title foxed and slightly chipped, contemporary ms. note "From the Hon. D. Webster" in secretarial hand.   M & S Rare Books, Inc.   95 - 383   2013 $200

Webster, George *Rip Van Winkle.* New York: McLoughlin Bros. n.d. circa, 1875. 4to., pictorial wrappers, (16) pages, including covers, old marks from stitching, pages foxed with light spine wear, very good, illustrations by Thomas Nast, 6 wonderful full page chromolithographs printed on one side of paper, 9 very detailed illustrations.   Aleph-Bet Books, Inc.   105 - 415   2013 $450

Webster, George *The Story of Rip Van Winkle.* New York: McLoughlin Bros., 1889. Retold by Webster, 4to., pictorial wrappers, 4 fine full page and 1 double page chromolithographs.   Aleph-Bet Books, Inc.   105 - 336   2013 $250

Webster, John Clarence 1863-1950 *The Forts of Chignecto. A Study of the Eighteenth Century Conflict Between France and Great Britain in Acadia.* Shediac: pub. by the author, 1930. Number 60 of a limited edition of 400 copies, card covers, color frontispiece, folding map, other maps, sketches, plans and portraits, large 8vo., covers slightly faded, generally very good, previous owner's bookplate and inscription.   Schooner Books Ltd.   104 - 127   2013 $200

Webster, Noah 1758-1843 *An American Dictionary of the English Language.* New York: published by S. Converse, printed by Hezekiah Howe, 1828. First edition, 2 volumes, large quarto, frontispiece, with final leaf "Additions" and "Corrections" at end volume ii, often lacking, contemporary tree calf, outer hinges restored, spines ruled gilt in compartments with red and black morocco lettering labels, occasional light foxing and offsetting to first and last few pages, binding extremities lightly rubbed, previous owner's bookplate and library bookplate, no library markings, overall excellent.   Heritage Book Shop   Holiday Catalogue 2012 - 156   2013 $27,500

Webster, Noah 1758-1843 *An American Dictionary of the English Language.* New York: published by S. Converse printed by Hezekiah Howe, New Haven, 1828. First edition, 290 x 227 mm., 2 volumes, including terminal leaf (not infrequently missing) of 'Additions' in second volume, engraved frontispiece in volume 1, contemporary marbled boards expertly convincingly rebacked and recornered by Courtland Benson using diced Russia of the period, spines divided into panels by double gilt rules, gilt titling, paper boards bit chafed, two inch abrasion to leather on lower board of volume i, but artfully and cleverly restored retrospective bindings showing no important wear at same time that they retain their period feel, 2 gatherings (only) with significant foxing (frontispiece title and few leaves here and there with quite minor foxing), other trivial imperfections but altogether pleasing internally, text remarkably fresh and clean, especially fine, looks very attractive on shelf.   Phillip J. Pirages   63 - 489   2013 $22,500

Webster, Noah 1758-1843 *A Plain and Comprehensive Grammar of the English Language...* Philadelphia: printed for W. Young, 1789. First edition with this title, 12mo., contemporary calf, rebacked, old back laid down, leading edge of rear cover signed, minor pitting, corners rubbed, despite binding wear, very good, especially internally, with mild occasional browning.   Howard S. Mott Inc.   262 - 159   2013 $500

Wechsberg, Joseph *Dining at the Pavilion.* Boston: Little Brown and Co., 1962. First edition, 227 pages, fine in near fine dust jacket with tiny tear and crease to top of front panel and couple of other miniscule tears, fresh copy otherwise.   Jeff Hirsch Books   Fall 2013 - 129301   2013 $75

Wedl, Carolus *Dissertatio Inauguralis Medica De Influuxu Anatomiae Patholgicae in Medicinam...* Vidobonae: typis Caroli Ueberreuter, 1839. 8vo., original green silk pattern cloth, later rebacking, edges of boards and paper edges all ruled in gilt, author's presentation copy with penned not to family member on front flyleaf.   James Tait Goodrich   S74 - 237   2013 $495

Weedon, Lucy L. *Fine Fun for Everyone.* London: Ernest Nister, n.d., 1898. First edition, small folio, original cloth backed glazed pictorial boards, cracked and scratched in places, edges rather worn, unpaginated, illustrations in color and line.   R. F. G. Hollett & Son   Children's Books - 715   2013   £120

The Weekly Magazine of Original Essays, Fugitive Pieces and Interesting Intelligence. Philadelphia: James Watters and Co. Volume I nos. 1-13, Feb. 3 through April 28, 1798. 2 engraved plates, contemporary half sheep, worn and scuffed but sound, usual foxing, occasional spotting.   Joseph J. Felcone Inc.   English and American Literature to 1800 - 25   2013 $500

Weems, Mason Locke 1759-1825 *God's Revenge Against Adultery, Awfully Exemplified....* Philadelphia: printed for the author, 1818. Third edition, 8vo., 48 pages, frontispiece trimmed close at top, removed. M & S Rare Books, Inc. 95 - 385 2013 $200

Weems, Mason Locke 1759-1825 *The Philanthropist; or a Good Twenty-five Cents Worth of Political Love Powder for Honest Adamites and Jeffersonians.* Dumfries: 1799. First edition, 8vo., 30 pages, sewn and uncut as issued. M & S Rare Books, Inc. 95 - 386 2013 $750

Wegelin, Oscar *Jupiter Hammon, American Negro Poet: Selections from His Writings and a Bibliography.* New York: Chas. Fred. Heartman, 1915. First edition, full morocco gilt, joints visibly repaired, very good, of a total of 99 copies, this one of 8 numbered copies on Japan vellum, this copy unnumbered, rare. Between the Covers Rare Books, Inc. 165 - 304 2013 $2000

Weir, Robert Fulton *Contribution to the Diagnosis and Surgical Treatment of Tumors of the Derebrum.* Reprinted from American Journal of Medical Sciences, 1888. Author's offprint, 8vo., 48 pages, text illustrations, paper spine as issued. James Tait Goodrich 75 - 222 2013 $495

Weisheipl, James A. *Nature and Motion in the Middle Ages.* Washington: Catholic University of America Press, 1985. 8vo., xii, 292 pages, green cloth, silver stamped spine title, dust jacket, ownership signature, fine, rare. Jeff Weber Rare Books 169 - 475 2013 $95

Weisman, Nochem *Dos Meidele Mitn Rotten Kleidele.* Brooklyn: Osborn, 1940. 4to., cloth, near fine, illustrations by Weisy with full page blue and white illustrations. Aleph-Bet Books, Inc. 104 - 298 2013 $125

Weiss, Edoardo *Sigmund Freud as a Consultant.* New York: Intercontinental Med. Book, 1970. First edition, fine, hardcover, issued without dust jacket. Beasley Books 2013 - 2013 $50

Weiss, Ruth *A New View of Matter/Novy Pohled Na Vec.* Prague: Mata, 1999. First edition, bi-lingual Czech-English, with photo section at rear, fine in fine dust jacket, inscribed by author, signed by photographer, Paul Blake. Beasley Books 2013 - 2013 $100

Weiss, Sara *Decimon Huydas: a Romance of Mars.* Rochester: Austin Pub. Co., 1906. First edition, octavo, flyleaves at front and rear, inserted frontispiece, 6 inserted plates, titlepage printed in orange and black, original green cloth, front panel stamped in red and black, spine panel stamped in black. L. W. Currey, Inc. Wandering Ghosts & Itinerant Souls (10/12) - 89991 2013 $65

Weissenborn, Hellmuth *Engraver.* Andoversford: Whittington Press, Acorn Press, 1983. 29/40 copies (of an edition of 260), printed on fawn and white Zerkall mould-made papers, reproduction of photographic frontispiece, 2 further photographic portraits in introduction, 448 perspex, vinyl or wood engravings by Weissenborn printed in a variety of colours, folio, original cream canvas, printed label on backstrip and label carrying a wood engravings on front cover, untrimmed, board slipcase with cloth head and tail, fine. Blackwell's Rare Books 172 - 320 2013 £200

Weissenborn, Hellmuth *Fantasy.* Acorn Press, 1978. One of 100 numbered copies signed by artist (this copy neither numbered nor signed), printed on Wookey Hole handmade paper, with 21 linocuts by Weissenborn, printed in blue or brown and finished with hand coloring, each with printed title, large 4to., original mid green boards with faded backstrip, printed front cover label, untrimmed, matching board slipcase with printed label, near fine. Blackwell's Rare Books B174 - 319 2013 £50

Welcome, S. Byron *From Earth's Center: a Polar Gateway Message.* Chicago: Charles H. Kerr, 1894. First edition, original pictorial white wrappers printed in black. L. W. Currey, Inc. Utopian Literature: Recent Acquisitions (April 2013) - 139599 2013 $750

Wellbeloved, Charles *A Sermon Preached on Wednesday October 19 1803 at Day of National Humiliation, to a Congregation of Protestant Dissenters in St. Saviourgate, York...* York: T. Wilson and R. Spence, 1803. 8vo., disbound, titlepage dusty, another York sermon, lacking title, bound in at end. Ken Spelman Books Ltd. 73 - 11 2013 £30

Welles, Gideon *Regulations for the Uniform of the United States Navy.* Washington: GPO, 1864. First edition, 8vo., self wrappers, sewn, fine. M & S Rare Books, Inc. 95 - 69 2013 $100

Wellman, Manly Wade *The Beasts from Beyond.* Manchester: published by World Distributors, 1950. First edition, octavo, pictorial wrappers. L. W. Currey, Inc. Fall Sampler Sept. 2013 - 144002 2013 $250

Wells, Carveth *Jungle Man and His Animals.* New York: Duffield, 1928. Stated second edition, large 4to., cloth backed pictorial boards, 68 pages, corners worn, light cover soil with 2 dents on rear cover, else very good, 13 color plates by Tony Sarg, two plates frayed with small edge tears, plus a profusion of black and whites, this copy signed by Sarg with drawing of an elephant, this is a special copy of a rare Sarg title. Aleph-Bet Books, Inc. 105 - 521 2013 $450

Wells, Herb *Comrades in Arms a History of Newfoundlanders in Action.* St. John's: 1987-1988. 2 volumes, cloth, dust jackets, illustrations, quarto, very good in like jackets, both volumes signed by author.   Schooner Books Ltd.   101 - 80   2013 $150

Wells, Herbert George   1866-1946 *The Adventures of Tommy.* London: Amalgamated, 1928. #544 of a limited numbered edition deluxe, published for private circulation only, wrappers, cover reinforced, good.   Barnaby Rudge Booksellers   Children 2013 - 015790   2013 $75

Wells, Herbert George   1866-1946 *The Country of the Blind and Other Stories.* Nelson, 1911. First edition, color frontispiece by Dudley Tennant, crown 8vo., original royal blue cloth, faintly sunned backstrip gilt lettered and just touch rubbed at head and tail, backstrip and front cover decoratively blocked in blind, very good.   Blackwell's Rare Books   172 - 243   2013   £160

Wells, Herbert George   1866-1946 *The Food of the Gods and How It Came to Earth.* London: Macmillan and Co., 1904. First edition, octavo, 16 page publisher catalog dated 20.7.04 inserted at rear, first binding in original decorated green cloth, front panel stamped in gold and blind, spine panel stamped in gold, top edge gilt.   L. W. Currey, Inc. Utopian Literature: Recent Acquisitions (April 2013) - 139598   2013 $300

Wells, Herbert George   1866-1946 *Men Like Gods.* London: Cassell, 1923. First edition, foolscap 8vo., original sage green cloth, backstrip gilt lettered, decoration to backstrip and front cover lettering and decoration all blocked in blind, publishers name correctly spelt 'Cassell' at foot of backstrip, light endpaper browning, gift inscription dated 1923 on front free endpaper, tail edges rough trimmed, dust jacket with browning to backstrip panel short tear to tail of front flap fold, very good.   Blackwell's Rare Books   B174 - 310   2013   £275

Wells, Herbert George   1866-1946 *Russia in the Shadows.* London: Hodder and Stoughton, 1920. First edition, Frontispiece and 10 other plates, foolscap 8vo., original pink cloth, lightly faded backstrip and front cover lettered and bordered in black, scarce dust jacket in nice condition save for short tears, near fine.   Blackwell's Rare Books   172 - 244   2013   £350

Wells, Herbert George   1866-1946 *Tono-Bungay.* New York: Harcourt Brace Jovanovich, 1982. First edition, near fine, clean in near fine, first issue dust jacket.   Ed Smith Books   78 - 70   2013 $500

Wells, Herbert George   1866-1946 *What is Coming?* London: Cassell, 1916. First edition, wartime issue paper browned at margins as usual, original dark green cloth, rubbing to head and tail of gilt blocked backstrip, front cover blocked in blind, ownership signature dated 1916. Blackwell's Rare Books   B174 - 311   2013   £55

Wells, Herbert George   1866-1946 *The Works of H. G. Wells.* New York: Charles Scribner's Sons, 1924-1927. One of 1670 (of which 1050 for America - 1000 for sale), signed by author, this copy #982; 235 x 159mm., 28 volumes, original publisher's linen backed green paper boards, paper title labels on flat spines, edges rough trimmed, half the volumes unopened and all encased in original slightly worn slipcases (one slipcase a modern replica); photographic frontispiece in each volume, titlepages printed in red and black, printed on high quality rag paper; most volumes with extra paper labels, spines slightly darkened, rough edges bit yellowed, three leaves with open marginal tears well away from text (no doubt from rough opening), other trivial imperfections, nearly fine, many of the volumes near pristine, much of text never having been read.   Phillip J. Pirages   63 - 490   2013 $3500

Wells, James L.   *The Bronx and Its People A History 1609-1927.* New York: Lewis Historical Pub. Co., 1927. First edition, 3 volumes, publisher's cloth gilt, bookplate in each volume, moderately rubbed, else near fine set.   Between the Covers Rare Books, Inc.   New York City - 292281   2013 $350

Wells, Junius   *The Contributor, Representing the Young Men's and Young Ladies' Mutual Improvement Associations of the Latter Day Saints.* Salt Lake City: Deseret News Co., 1896. 17 volume set, octavo, issued in binding, except volumes 3 and 17 have been rebound (both in blue cloth, but differing shades), volumes 1, 2, 4, 5, 6, 7, 8. 9 and 14 bound in three quarter over black boards with gilt bands and title on backstrip, front board of volume 14 detached but present, volumes 10, 11, 12, 13, 15 and 16 bound in black cloth with gilt gilt stamped on backstrip and blindstamped on front board, most volumes are very good or better, the last issue (October 1896) of volume 17 is missing.   Ken Sanders Rare Books   45 - 21   2013 $1000

Wells, Margaret *Moths.* Wellington: Harry Tombs, n.d., 4to., boards, pictorial paste-on, very good+, illustrations by Edna Kuala with 1 color plate, 4 black and white plates plus numerous black and whites in text.   Aleph-Bet Books, Inc.   105 - 237   2013 $275

Wells, Margaret *A Selection of Wood Engravings.* Woolley, Wakefield: Fleece Press, 1985. One of 170 copies of an edition of 200, printed on Arches paper, with 15 wood engravings and vignette by Margaret Wells in text, titlepage printed in black and blue, imperial 8vo., original canary yellow cloth, printed backstrip label and with Wells' engraving onlaid to front cover, untrimmed, fine. Blackwell's Rare Books   172 - 282   2013   £70

Wells, Nathaniel Armstrong *The Picturesque Antiquities of Spain...* London: Richard Bentley, 1846. First edition, 8vo., 10 plates, illustrations, original brown decorative cloth, inner hinges cracked, good.   J. & S. L. Bonham Antiquarian Booksellers   Europe - 9487   2013   £150

Wells, Roger *Insurrection, the British Experience 1795-1803.* Sutton, 1983. 8vo., cloth, dust jacket, near fine. C. P. Hyland   261 - 866   2013   £35

Welsh, Doris Varner *A Bibliography of Miniature Books (1470-1965).* New York: Kathryn I. Rickard, 1989. First edition, limited to 500 copies, 4to., cloth, dust jacket, signed by author, with presentation from publisher on facing page "Dear Mr. Sanford, Welcome to a new World. Kathryn V. Rickard 8.30.90", corner bumped, from the collection of Donn W. Sanford.   Oak Knoll Books   303 - 25   2013 $200

Welsh, Irvine *Trainspotting.* London: Secker & Warburg, 1993. First edition, inscribed by author in 2002, owner name to first blank, fine in self wrappers.   Ken Lopez Bookseller   159 - 213   2013 $500

Welsh, Irvine *Trainspotting.* London: Secker & Warburg, 1993. Simultaneous softcover issue, signed by author, owner name on first blank, some age toning apparent to fore edge, very near fine in self wrappers.   Ken Lopez Bookseller   159 - 212   2013 $500

Welsh, Richard *Kiddie-Kar Book.* Philadelphia: Lippincott, 1920. First and probably only edition, large oblong 4to., cloth backed boards, pictorial paste-on, corner of free endpaper repaired else fine in frayed and soiled dust jacket, detailed pictorial borders and 9 fine color plates plus pictorial endpapers and other smaller line illustrations, rare. Aleph-Bet Books, Inc.   105 - 554   2013 $750

Welty, Eudora *Losing Battles.* New York: Random House, 1970. First trade edition, inscribed by author, fine in fine dust jacket.   Ed Smith Books   75 - 81   2013 $250

Wentworth, Lady *Drift of the Storm.* Oxford: George Donald, 1951. First edition, 8vo., original light blue cloth, the spine little faded with odd small nick to edge of dust jacket and jacket spine slightly browned, inscribed by Lord Dunsany to Walter de la Mare, loosely inserted ALS from Dunsay to a Mrs. Mathews with signed photo.   Maggs Bros. Ltd.   1460 - 260   2013 £350

Werdenhagen, Johannes *Introductio Vniversalis in Omnes Respublicas, sive Politica Generalis.* Amsterdam: Apud Guilielum Blaeu, 1632. Later edition, 16mo., contemporary vellum, remains of old typewritten label on spine. Joseph J. Felcone Inc.   Books Printed before 1701 - 89   2013 $125

Werner, Charles J. *Historical Miscellanies Relating to Long Island.* Huntington: Privately printed, 1917. First edition, one of 100 copies, this copy unnumbered, blue cloth gilt, two tiny stains on rear board, else fine.   Between the Covers Rare Books, Inc.   New York City - 286966 2013 $125

Wescott, Glenway *The Babe's Bed.* Harrison of Paris, 1930. First edition, no. 87 of 375 copies printed on Pannekoek paper, numbered and signed by author, fine but for tiny tears at top edge of rear pastedown, next to what looks like remains of price sticker, 8vo., 45 pages.   Beasley Books   2013 - 2013 $100

Wesley, J. *Life of the Rev. J. W. Fletcher, Vicar of Madeley.* London: Religious Tract Society, n.d., 12mo., old roan gilt, rather rubbed, endpapers rather soiled, some browning or fingering in places.   R. F. G. Hollett & Son   Wesleyan Methodism - 33   2013   £35

Wesley, John   1703-1791 *A Collection of Hymns, for the Use of People called Methodists.* London: printed and sold at the New Chapel, City Road, 1788. Sixth edition, 12mo., one page slightly proud in binding, full contemporary sprinkled calf, gilt bands, small diamond motifs, red morocco label, near contemporary ownership name of James Williams.   Jarndyce Antiquarian Booksellers   CCIV - 312   2013   £280

Wesley, John   1703-1791 *A Collection of Hymns for the Use of the People Called Methodists.* Wesleyan Conference Office, 1877. Full black divinity calf gilt, extremities rather rubbed, all edges gilt, endpapers little marked, very good, sound.   R. F. G. Hollett & Son   Wesleyan Methodism - 60   2013   £45

Wesley, John   1703-1791 *A Compendium of Natural Philosophy...* London: Thomas Tegg and Son, 1835-1838. 3 volumes, small 8vo., original printed cloth, spines little darkened, few small snags and chips, 3 engraved frontispieces, very good, sound set.   R. F. G. Hollett & Son   Wesleyan Methodism - 34   2013   £275

Wesley, John   1703-1791 *The Desideratum; or Electricity Made Plain and Useful.* London: Bailliere, Tindall and Cox, 1871. Second edition, original brown decorated cloth, gilt corners and edges trifle marked, first 10 or so leaves more or less stained from early greasy insertion, scarce.   R. F. G. Hollett & Son   Wesleyan Methodism - 38   2013   £95

Wesley, John   1703-1791 *Explanatory Notes Upon the New Testament.* London: printed by William Bowyer, 1755. First edition, 4to., contemporary full straight grained calf, gilt, boards little rubbed, corners worn, hinges cracked and repaired, front flyleaf removed, lacks portrait as so often, near contemporary mss. transcription of epitaph on Wesley's tombstone on pastedown, very scarce.   R. F. G. Hollett & Son   Wesleyan Methodism - 35   2013   £450

Wesley, John   1703-1791 *The Journal.* London: J. M. Dent & Sons, 1938. 4 volumes, small 8vo., original cloth, gilt, dust jackets (edges and spines little darkened), excellent set.   R. F. G. Hollett & Son   Wesleyan Methodism - 36   2013   £95

Wesley, John   1703-1791 *Primitive Physic: or an Easy and Natural Method of Curing Most Diseases.* published for the booksellers, 1848-1850. 12mo., original blindstamped cloth, gilt, frontispiece, 2 titlepages and few woodcut illustrations, ex-libris.   R. F. G. Hollett & Son   Wesleyan Methodism - 40   2013   £175

Wesley, John   1703-1791 *Sermons on Several Occasions.* London: John Mason, 1838. 3 volumes, old half calf, gilt, marbled boards, spines rubbed and lettering faded, frontispiece, flyleaves rather spotted, very good set.   R. F. G. Hollett & Son   Wesleyan Methodism - 37   2013   £120

Wesley, John   1703-1791 *Sermons on Several Occasions. First Series.* Wesleyan Methodist Book Room, n.d. circa, 1889. Original blindstamped maroon cloth, gilt, fore-edge lightly spotted.   R. F. G. Hollett & Son   Wesleyan Methodism - 39   2013   £25

The Wesleyan-Methodist Magazine for the Year 1823. J. Kershaw, 1823. Volume II of the third series, old half calf, gilt, boards rubbed and scraped, 12 steel engraved portraits, some fingering and creasing label of T. Sewell, stationer and bookbinder.   R. F. G. Hollett & Son   Wesleyan Methodism - 50   2013   £45

Wesleyan Methodist Church. Conference *Minutes of Some Late Conversations Between the Rev. Mr. Wesley and Others.* Leeds: 1789. First edition, 12mo., printer's woodcut ornament on title, little browned around edges, 12mo., disbound and more or less loose.   Blackwell's Rare Books   172 - 153   2013   £300

The Wesleyan Sunday-School Magazine and Educational Journal for the Year 1866. New Series. Volume I. Wesleyan Conference Office, 1866. Old half black roan gilt, extremities rubbed, lower hinge cracked and repaired.   R. F. G. Hollett & Son   Wesleyan Methodism - 49   2013   £35

West, Mrs. *Letters Addressed to a Young Man on his First Entering Into Life...* London: Longman, 1809. Fifth edition, 12mo., full contemporary tree calf, gilt banded spines, black title labels, one joint cracked lacks small oval volume labels, name on bookplate rubbed through.   Ken Spelman Books Ltd.   75 - 61   2013   £95

West, Nathanael *The Day of the Locust.* New York: Random House, 1939. First edition, octavo, publisher's full red cloth, orange paper label on spine, printed in black, top edge black, bright publisher's dust jacket with $2.00 price, jacket with some minor wear along edges and some light rubbing, small circle stain to back panel of jacket and back board of book, outer joints of book just slightly darkened, still near fine.   Heritage Book Shop   Holiday Catalogue 2012 - 157   2013 $4500

West, Nathanael *The Dream Life of Balso Snell.* Paris: Contact Editions, 1931. First edition, limited to 500 copies, this no. 197, 8vo., very good, original printed wrappers, mild soil and foxing to covers, age darkening to spine and cover edges, cover edge wear, owner name, reference note inside front cover, small pieces of glassine glued to inside covers, mild foxing to edges.   By the Book, L. C.   38 - 106   2013 $650

West, Will *A Directory and Picture of Cork and Its Environs.* 1810. 8vo., 142 pages, folding frontispiece, original wrappers, good.   C. P. Hyland   261 - 212   2013   £500

West, William *Symbolaeography, Which May Be Termed the Art, Description or Image of Instruments, Extra Iudicial...* imprinted... by Richard Tottle, 1592. 8vo., printer's ornaments at head of title, woodcut initials, partly printed in black Letter, little worming in front flyleaves reduced to just couple of small holes in margin of titlepage, minor soiling to titlepage, contemporary calf, blind ruled borders on sides, blindstamped medallions in centre of covers, vestiges of ties, worn at extremities, split at foot of upper joint, manuscript notes on flyleaf including note of purchase cost in 1642 'five shillings', good.   Blackwell's Rare Books   B174 - 91   2013   £3000

Westall, William *Picturesque Tour of the Thames.* London: R. Ackermann, 1828. First edition, first issue plates, large paper copy, with two spots of discoloration in sky on Twickenham plate, folio, 24 hand colored aquatint plates, 2 aquatint vignettes and double page engraved map laid down on linen, elegantly bound by Zaehnsdorf in full crimson crushed morocco, internally pristine, very scarce in large paper format.   David Brass Rare Books, Inc.   Holiday 2012 Chapter Two - DB 02070   2013 $12,500

Westell, W. Percival *Fifty-Two Nature Rambles.* Religious Tract Society, 1917. Fifth impression, full black calf gilt prize binding, 5 colored plates, 160 illustrations, scattered spotting.   R. F. G. Hollett & Son   Children's Books - 717   2013   £35

Westlake, Donald E. *Horse Laugh and Other Stories.* Helsinki: Eurographica, 1990. First edition thus, one of 350 numbered copies boldly signed by Westlake on titlepage, he has added "12 July 1990", fine copy, perfect bound in original wrappers, fine brown printed dust jacket with flaps, as issued.   Ed Smith Books   78 - 72   2013 $75

Weston, Brett *Brett Weston: Photographs from Five Decades.* New York: Aperture Monograph, 1980. First edition, limited to 400 copies signed by artist, being number 241, original silverprint photo signed by author, original photo "Reeds, Oregon, 1975", numerous black and white photos, original full oatmeal linen cloth, spine lettered gilt, housed in matching slipcase (in opened original plastic wrap), original signed silverprint housed separately in portfolio made from oatmeal colored boards, portfolio lettered in gilt, fine, book and portfolio housed in publisher's original cardboard shipping box.   Heritage Book Shop   Holiday Catalogue 2012 - 158   2013 $5000

Westropp, M. S. D. *Irish Glass.* Allen Figgis, 1978. Revised edition, illustrations, 248 pages, cloth, dust jacket, very good.   C. P. Hyland   261 - 867   2013   £60

Westrup, E. Kate *Hunting Alphabet.* Blackie and Son, n.d. circa, 1906. Oblong 8vo., original cloth backed pictorial boards, edges rather worn and bumped, unpaginated and french-folded, 24 colored plates, few Victorian scraps pasted to flyleaves and one to upper board, joints cracked, very good, rare.   R. F. G. Hollett & Son   Children's Books - 718   2013   £375

Wetherbee, F. I. *Teddy Bears Painting and Drawing Book.* New York: H. B. Claflin, 1907. First edition, oblong 4to., cloth backed pictorial boards, edges rubbed and some normal shelfwear, some blank pages artfully colored, very good, rare.   Aleph-Bet Books, Inc.   104 - 63   2013 $500

Wexberg, Erwin *Individual Psychology.* New York: Cosmopolitan Book Co., 1929. First edition, fine in lightly sued dust jacket.   Beasley Books   2013 - 2013 $50

Wexley, John *They Shall Not Die.* New York: Alfred A. Knopf, 1934. First edition, fine in fine dust jacket with very short rubbed tear on rear panel, warmly inscribed by author to journalist John Spivak.   Between the Covers Rare Books, Inc.   165 - 337   2013 $475

Weyman, Stanley *Sophia.* New York: Longmans, Green and Co., 1900. First American edition, contemporary owner's name front fly, little rubbing on spine, else near fine, publisher's pamphlet for Weyman's books laid in.   Between the Covers Rare Books, Inc.   Sci-Fi, Fantasy & Horror - 319846   2013 $100

Whalen, Philip *Self-Portrait, from another Direction.* San Francisco: Auerhahn Press, 1959. First edition, single folded sheet tipped into stiff wrappers, very good plus in wrappers with some creasing to corners, signed and warmly inscribed by Whalen to another poet in year of publication, nice.   Jeff Hirsch Books   Fall 2013 - 129224   2013 $100

Whalley, Peter *An Enquiry into the Learning of Shakespeare with Remarks on Several Passages of His Plays.* London: printed for T. Waller, 1748. 8vo., titlepage dusted and neatly repaired along gutter, evidence of original stab holes, later but not recent half calf, marbled boards, raised and gilt banded spine, red morocco label.   Jarndyce Antiquarian Booksellers   CCIV - 268   2013   £180

Wharton, Edith   1862-1937 *The Decoration of Houses.* New York: Charles Scribner's Sons, 1897. First edition, 8vo., original marbled paper boards and printed paper label, 57 plates, from the library of poetry editor, Susan Hayes Ward, with her signature, boards somewhat rubbed, rear hinge repaired, tissue guard little foxed, very good.   The Brick Row Book Shop   Miscellany Fifty-Nine - 48   2013 $450

Wharton, Edith   1862-1937 *The Glimpses of the Moon.* New York: D. Appleton, 1922. First edition, 8vo., very nice, little soiled cloth.   Second Life Books Inc.   183 - 398   2013 $50

Wharton, Edith   1862-1937 *Here and Beyond.* New York: London: D. Appleton & Co., 1926. First edition, octavo, original dark blue moire patterned cloth, front and spine panels stamped in gold, pictorial endpapers, fore and bottom edges, rough trimmed, first printing with "(1)" below last line of text on page (325).   L. W. Currey, Inc.   Wandering Ghosts & Itinerant Souls (10/12) - 137056   2013 $850

Wharton, Edith   1862-1937 *Italian Villas and their Gardens.* New York: Century, 1910. (1904), 4to., green gilt pictorial cloth, top edge gilt, some wear to spine ends, else very good+, illustrations by Maxfield Parrish.   Aleph-Bet Books, Inc.   104 - 409   2013 $1200

Wharton, Edith   1862-1937 *The Mother's Recompense.* New York: D. Appleton, 1925. First edition, 8vo., very nice, little soiled cloth.   Second Life Books Inc.   183 - 399   2013 $50

Wharton, Edith   1862-1937 *Tales of Men and Ghosts.* New York: Charles Scribner's Sons, 1910. First edition, first printing with Scribner device and "Published October 1910" on copyright page, titlepage printed in orange and black, original red cloth, front panel stamped in gold and ruled in blind, spine panel stamped in gold, top edge gilt, other edges untrimmed.   L. W. Currey, Inc.   Wandering Ghosts & Itinerant Souls (10/12) - 136052   2013 $250

Wharton, Edith 1862-1937 *Twelve Poems.* Riccardi Press for the Medici Society, 1926. First edition, 128/130 copies, facsimile signature of Wharton as usual, 8vo., original quarter light blue cloth faded, worn at head and rubbed at tail, light blue boards with gilt lettered author and title details on front cover boards faded light tape stains at tail where tape was at one time wrapped around cloth backstrip, ex-libris rubber stamp to lightly browned free endpaper, few remains of brown card to rear free endpaper, top edge gilt, others untrimmed, rare. Blackwell's Rare Books   172 - 245   2013   £2000

Wharton, Edith 1862-1937 *Xingu and Other Stories.* New York: Charles Scribner's, 1916. First edition, first printing, with "Published October 1916" and Scribner device on copyright page, octavo, titlepage printed in red and black, original reddish brown cloth, front panel stamped in gold and ruled in blind, spine panel stamped in gold, fore-edge untrimmed. L. W. Currey, Inc.   Wandering Ghosts & Itinerant Souls (10/12) - 109095   2013 $750

Wharton, Henry *The History of the Troubles and Tryal of... William Laud, Lord Arch-Bishop of Canterbury.* London: printed for Ri. Chiswell, 1695. Folio, engraved portrait frontispiece, title bit dusty, few minor splits elsewhere, contemporary speckled calf, spine ruled in blind, red morocco label, boards bordered in blind, touch rubbed, joints cracking, front joint bit defective at head, some scratches to boards, ink inscription "W. Danby", armorial 18th century bookplate "William Danby". Unsworths Antiquarian Booksellers   28 - 139   2013   £350

What is This? What is That? London: Dean's Rag Book Co. Ltd., n.d. circa, 1915. Oblong 8vo., pictorial cloth, 10 pages, as new, illustrations by Edith Sarah Berkeley. Aleph-Bet Books, Inc.   105 - 141   2013 $200

Whatman, Susanna *Her Housekeeping Book.* Cambridge: printed for Presentation, 1952. One of 250 copies, printed on Whatman handmade paper, collotype frontispiece, 14 etched illustrations, titlepage engraved by H. K. Wolfenden, tipped in tissue guards, 8vo., original pale flecked dark grey cloth, faded backstrip with gilt blocked monogram, large gilt lettered pink cloth label on front cover, good. Blackwell's Rare Books   B174 - 323   2013   £150

Wheat, Carl Irving *Books of the California Gold Rush, a Centennial Selection.* San Francisco: Colt Press, 1949. first edition, one of 500 copies, title in red and black, one reproduction of a photo and five facsimiles, some on colored paper, red cloth spine, decorated boards in yellow, red and gold, printed paper spine label, offsetting to ends, else very fine. Argonaut Book Shop   Recent Acquisitions June 2013 - 305   2013 $350

Wheat, Carl Irving *Mapping the American West.* N.P.: Bibliographical Society of America, 1956. First separate edition, 16 page, original printed tan wrappers, fine. Argonaut Book Shop   Recent Acquisitions June 2013 - 308   2013 $90

Wheat, Carl Irving *The Maps of the California Gold Region 1848-1857...* Storrs-Mansfield: Maurzio Martino, 1995. Reprinted from rare first edition, small folio, 27 facsimile maps, original tan cloth printed in red on white background on spine, very fine. Argonaut Book Shop Recent Acquisitions June 2013 - 309   2013 $150

Wheat, Carl Irving *Pioneers. The Engaging Tale of Three Early California Printing Presses and Their Strange Adventures.* privately printed in the "Pueblo of Los Angeles": printed for private distribution by Elmer R. King, Mike Ferry and Carl I. Whet, 1934. First separate edition, one of 250 copies, (2), 29 pages, tipped-on frontispiece plate, beige wrappers printed in dark brown, fine. Argonaut Book Shop   Recent Acquisitions June 2013 - 311   2013 $75

Wheat, Carl Irving *The Pioneer Press of California.* Oakland: Grabhorn Press for Biobooks, 1948. First edition, one of 450 copies, quarto, (4), 33 pages, woodcuts by Mallette Dean, 3 facsimiles, red cloth back, marbled boards, paper spine label, offsetting from facsimiles, else very fine. Argonaut Book Shop   Recent Acquisitions June 2013 - 310   2013 $150

Wheat, Carl Irving *A Sketch of the Life of Theodore D. Judah.* San Francisco: Southern Pacific Co., 1925. First separate edition, (2), 53 pages, 5 photo plates, including maps and portraits, original gray wrappers printed in black, fine. Argonaut Book Shop   Recent Acquisitions June 2013 - 313   2013 $125

Wheat, Carl Irving *Trailing the Forty-Niners through Death Valley.* San Francisco: printed by Taylor & Taylor for the author, 1939. First separate edition, 37 pages, 6 photo plates, folding map at rear printed wrappers. Argonaut Book Shop   Recent Acquisitions June 2013 - 314   2013 $60

Wheeler, John Archibald *At Home in the Universe.* Woodbury: AIP American Institute of Physics, 1994. First edition, 8vo., 371 pages, fine in near fine dust jacket, inscribed and dated by author. By the Book, L. C.   36 - 104   2013 $250

Wheelock, Sean D. *Buck O'Neil: a Baseball Legend.* Mattituck: Amereon House, 1994. First edition, simultaneous paperbound issue, lightly rubbed, still easily fine in wrappers, scarce. Between the Covers Rare Books, Inc.   165 - 77   2013 $65

Wheelock, Sean D. *Buck O'Neil: a Baseball Legend.* Mattituck: American House, 1994. First edition, hardcover issue fine in boards, without dust jacket as issued, inscribed by Buck O'Neil, very uncommon.   Between the Covers Rare Books, Inc.   165 - 76   2013 $250

Wheelwright, C. A. *Poems, Original and Translated...*   A. J. Valpy, 1810. 8vo., uncut, original boards, worn, covers detached, Earl of Hardwicke's copy, later in the library of John Sparrow, with tipped-in printed slip requesting subscribers to pay for their copies on delivery.   Ken Spelman Books Ltd.   75 - 66   2013   £35

Whishaw, Francis *The Railways of Great Britain and Ireland.* London: Simpkin, Marshall and Co., 1840. First edition, 290 x 215mm., recent very appealing retrospective full calf, raised bands, maroon morocco label, illustrations, 12 folding tables, occasional pencilled marginalia, minor foxing to opening leaves and plates, one folding plate and neat early repairs on blank verso, other trivial imperfections, but excellent, leaves clean and fresh, attractive sympathetic binding unworn.   Phillip J. Pirages   63 - 386   2013 $900

Whishaw, Fred *The Diamond of Evil.* London: Long, 1902. First edition, endpapers darkened and page edges spotted, otherwise fine in red pictorial cloth covered boards with gold stamped titles on spine.   Mordida Books   81 - 571   2013 $175

Whitaker, Thomas Dunham *The History and Antiquities of the Deanery of Craven in the County or York.* Leeds: Joseph Dodgson, 1878. Third edition, portrait, 59 plates (many tinted), 29 genealogical tables, numerous text illustrations, very good in contemporary half morocco with handsome blind tooled spine and green gilt label, thick 4to.   Ken Spelman Books Ltd.   73 - 67   2013   £295

Whitaker, Thomas Dunham *The History and Antiquities of the Deanery of Craven in the County of York.* London: J. Nichols and Son, 1812. Second edition, engraved plates, tables, numerous text illustrations, very good, clean in contemporary calf, most handsomely rebacked with ornate gilt panelled spine and red morocco label, all plates complete, lacks portrait frontispiece.   Ken Spelman Books Ltd.   73 - 66   2013   £195

White, Adam *The Instructive Picture Book, or a few Attractive Lessons from the Natural History of Animals.* Edinburgh: Edmonston & Douglas, n.d. circa, 1875. Ninth edition, folio, old full black roan gilt, surface rather worm eaten in places, head and foot of spine defective, pages 36, hand colored title and 27 fine double page hand colored plates.   R. F. G. Hollett & Son   Children's Books - 719   2013   £350

White, Charles *A Treatise on the Management of Pregnant and Lying-in Women and the Means of Curing, and More Especially of Preventing the Principal Disorders to which they are liable.*   printed for Edward and Charles Dilly, 1773. First edition, 2 engraved plates, slight dampstaining around edges of titlepage, uniformly very lightly browned, 8vo., contemporary calf, red lettering piece on spine, slightly worn, ownership inscription "Rich. Penfold", good.   Blackwell's Rare Books   Sciences - 130   2013   £850

White, Charles W. *The Hidden and the Forgotten: Buckingham Blacks.* Marceline: The Author, 1990. Fourth printing, green glazed paper covered boards lettered and decorated in white, fine, inscribed by author.   Between the Covers Rare Books, Inc.   165 - 285   2013 $125

White, E. V. *Senegambian Sizzles: Negro Stories.* Dallas: Banks Upshaw and Co., 1945. First edition, illustrations by Leta Mae Calhoun, near fine, about very good dust jacket with tanning to spine, modest chip at crown, scarce in jacket.   Between the Covers Rare Books, Inc.   165 - 286   2013 $150

White, Edward Lucas *Narrative Lyrics.* New York: G. P. Putnam's Sons, 1908. First edition, fine in edge chipped, otherwise very good dust jacket, signed by White, with many corrections in his hand on 14 different pages, rare in jacket.   Between the Covers Rare Books, Inc.   Sci-Fi, Fantasy & Horror - 85483   2013 $500

White, Gilbert   1720-1793 *The Journals.* Century, 1986. 3 volumes, 8vo., fine set in dust jackets.   Ken Spelman Books Ltd.   75 - 192   2013   £75

White, Gilbert   1720-1793 *The Natural History and Antiquities of Selborne and a Garden Kalendar.* S. T. Freemantle, 1900. Number 135 of 160 copies signed by editor and artists, 4to., numerous full page and vignette illustrations, very good in original full vellum, colored gilt crest to each upper board, spines lettered in red with gilt crest, some slight mellowing to vellum as usual and some occasional foxing to tissue guards.   Ken Spelman Books Ltd.   75 - 153   2013   £320

White, Gilbert   1720-1793 *Writings.* Nonesuch Press, 1938. 44/850 sets, 2 volumes, wood engraved titlepages and numerous head and tailpieces by Ravilious, collotye map, folding line block map, imperial 8vo., original grey buckram, gilt blocked lettering and decoration on faded backstrips and on front covers, all designed by Ravilious, faint endpaper foxing, top edge gilt on the rough, untrimmed, near fine.   Blackwell's Rare Books   B174 - 369   2013   £900

White, Gilbert 1720-1793 *The Writings of Gilbert White of Selborne.* London: Nonesuch Press, 1938. Number 418 of 850 copies, 2 volumes, folding map, fine wood engraved titlepages and engraved head and tailpieces, fine set in original gilt decorated cloth, with flower, animal and insect motifs to each spine, top edge gilt, remainder uncut, spines completely unfaded.   Ken Spelman Books Ltd.   75 - 176   2013   £595

White, Henry Kirke *The Poetical Works of Henry Kirke White.* London: Charles Whittingham for William Pickering, 1853. 168 x 105mm., lviii, 252 pages, elegant contemporary dark green morocco inlaid, embossed and elaborately gilt, each cover with broad inlaid ochre morocco frame intricately gilt, large central mandorla of heavily embossed and gilt morocco of same color (both frame and centerpiece highlighted with red painted rules, raised bands, spine gilt in compartments framed by plain and decorative gilt rules, floral centerpiece and lancet cornerpieces richly gilt turn-ins, cream colored watered silk endleaves, all edges gilt, pleasing fore-edge painting of Nottingham Castle; engraved portrait and printer's anchor device on titlepage, pencilled inscription to Bessie Carey from Walter Shipper dated 13 October 1868, pastedown with morocco bookplate of Estelle Doheny, bookplate of Edward Laurence Doheny, bookplate of Carrie Estelle Doheny, bookplate of Dorothy Jayne Pedrini Shea; hint of wear to joints and corners, red paint bit rubbed with minor loss, minor foxing to portrait and titlepage, other trivial imperfections, but excellent copy, handsome binding solid and lustrous, text clean and fresh, fore-edge painting very well preserved.   Phillip J. Pirages   63 - 193   2013 $1100

White, J. Grove *Record of the Doneraile Rangers.* Offprint of JHAS, 1893.   14 pages, 8vo., cloth, very good.   C. P. Hyland   261 - 868   2013   £30

White, James *The Watch Below.* London: Ronald Whiting & Wheaton, 1966.   First British and first hardcover edition, octavo, boards.   L. W. Currey, Inc.   Utopian Literature: Recent Acquisitions (April 2013) - 141859   2013 $100

White, James W.   *Dental Materia Medica.*   Philadelphia: Samuel S. White, 1868.   First edition, 12mo., original brown cloth, nearly fine.   Howard S. Mott Inc.   262 - 162   2013 $650

White, Joshua   *Memoirs of the Professional Life of the Right Honourable Horatio Lord Viscount Nelson...* London: Albion Press printed: published by James Cundee, 1806. 2 parts in 1, continuous pagination, frontispiece, plates little dusted, slight browning, full contemporary straight grained morocco, gilt borders, gilt spine with small flower head motif, marbled editions.   Jarndyce Antiquarian Booksellers   CCIV - 214   2013   £125

White, Michael G.   *Brother's Blood.*   New York: Harper Collins, 1996.   First edition, very fine in dust jacket.   Mordida Books   81 - 572   2013 $85

White, Newport *Extent of Irish Monastic Possessions 1540-1541.* 1943. First edition, 8vo., cloth, very good, ex-libris Seamus Pender.   C. P. Hyland   261 - 508   2013   £45

White, Newport *Irish Monastic & Episcopal Deeds 1200-1600.* 1936. 512 copies printed, 8vo, cloth, very good, ex-libris Seamus Pender.   C. P. Hyland   261 - 509   2013   £100

White, Newport *A Short Catalogue of the English Books in Archbishop Marsh's Library, Dublin, Printed Before MDCXLI.* 1905.   viii, 90 pages, original wrappers (front loose), very good.   C. P. Hyland   261 - 110   2013   £56

White, Patrick   *Happy Valley.* London: Harrap, 1939. Advance proof copy and so printed on front cover, foolscap 8vo, 328 pages, original printed tan wrappers, small chip to tail of backstrip and tear to bottom half of rear joint, good.   Blackwell's Rare Books   B174 - 312   2013   £2500

White, Petrus De   *Wederlegginge der Socinaensche Dwaligen, Uty-Gegeven, Visitatie en Approbatie des E. Classis.* Amstelaedami: Baltes Boeckholt en Arent van den Heuvel..., 1662. Third edition, 3 volumes in one, 8vo., contemporary vellum, embossed in blind, ribbon ties, good copy, split at top half of front joint, boards soiled, engraved title with small repair affecting image and one letter on verso, first few leaves bit ragged at edges, small chips to corners, light dampstain mainly to fore edge or corner of leaves.   Kaaterskill Books   16 - 91   2013 $950

White, Randy Wayne   *Captiva.* New York: Putnam, 1996. First edition, uncorrected proof, fine in slick pictorial wrappers.   Mordida Books   81 - 573   2013 $65

White, Randy Wayne   *North of Havana.* New York: Putnam, 1997.   First edition, signed by White, very fine in dust jacket.   Mordida Books   81 - 574   2013 $75

White, Robert W.   *A History of the Cadiz Short Line Railroad.* Chicago: Black Cat Press, 1966.   Limited to 200 copies, 5.5 x 7.8 cm., black and white illustrations, leather, miniature bookplate of Kathryn Rickard, from the collection of Donn W. Sanford.   Oak Knoll Books   303 - 59   2013 $200

White, Samuel S.   *Catalogue of Dental Materials, Furniture, Instruments, etc. for Sale by Samuel S. White, Manufacturer, Importer and Wholesale Dealer...* Philadelphia: 1876.   First edition, 8vo., original green cloth, tipped in erratum, excellent copy.   Howard S. Mott Inc.   262 - 151   2013 $750

Whitehead, William *The Historian's Pocket Companion; or Memory's Assistant.* Newcastle: printed by T. Angus..., 1777. 12mo., little soiled, foxed and browned, recent calf backed boards with original marbled paper covers laid down, ownership inscriptions on engraved title of John Hudson and Ruth Borrowman, sound, rare. Blackwell's Rare Books 172 - 103 2013 £450

Whitehorn, Mary *The Skoojee Book or the Enchanted Hit and Miss Hooked Rug.* Norwood: Whitehorn, 1927. First and probably only edition, 4to., pictorial card covers, string tied, some edge chipping, few tiny pinholes on last leaf, else very good+, illustrations by Edna May Whitehorn with 12 hand colored full page color woodblock prints, rare. Aleph-Bet Books, Inc. 105 - 251 2013 $1200

Whiteing, Richard *All Moonshine.* London: Hurst and Blackett Limited, 1907. First edition, octavo, original decorated red cloth, front panel stamped in white, spine panel stamped in gold, fore and bottom edges, rough trimmed. L. W. Currey, Inc. Wandering Ghosts & Itinerant Souls (10/12) - 63850 2013 $65

Whitelaw, Marjory *The Dalhousie Journals.* Oberon: 1978. 8vo., 3 volumes, cloth with dust jackets, slight foxing to paper edges volume 2, generally all volumes very good, dust jacket volume 1 is torn and crease, other jackets very good. Schooner Books Ltd. 104 - 132 2013 $100

Whitelock, Bulstrode *Memorials of the English Affairs; or an Historical Account of what Passed from the Beginning of the Reign of King Charles the First to King Charles the Second his Happy Restauration.* London: printed for Nathaniel Ponder, 1682. Folio, lightly browned edges occasionally bit frayed with one or two marginal tears, 20th century red buckram, spine sunned, bit scratched and marked, slight wear to extremities. Unsworths Antiquarian Booksellers 28 - 140 2013 £250

Whitfield, Christopher *Lady from Yesterday.* Waltham St. Lawrence: Golden Cockerel Press, 1939. First edition, unlimited issue, title vignette and 5 full page wood engravings, 72 page, crown 8vo., original pale blue wrappers, good. Blackwell's Rare Books B174 - 343 2013 £40

Whitfield, Raoul *Silver Wings.* New York: Knopf, 1930. First edition, illustrations by Frank Dobias, 2 blanks excised (but not the patterned art deco-design endpapers), else near fine, lacking very scarce dust jacket, inscribed by author. Between the Covers Rare Books, Inc. Mystery & Detective Fiction - 46201 2013 $3500

Whitlock, Abel *Co-Operation. the Sure Way to Wealth by Labor in Business Co-operation.* Port Chester: 1881? First edition, 8vo., 64 pages, sewn, removed, printed wrappers chipped along spine and edges, signatures becoming loose, poorly printed on cheap paper otherwise internaly very good. M & S Rare Books, Inc. 95 - 348 2013 $175

Whitman, Walt 1819-1892 *Calamus. A Series of Letters Written During the Years 1868-1880.* Boston: published by Laurens Maynard at 287 Congress Street, 1897. First (trade) edition, first issue following limited edition of 35 large paper copies signed by Dr. Bucke, of which 25 were for sale, small 8vo., frontispiece and facsimile, original yellow green cloth with blindstamped covers, presentation copy inscribed for Patrick Doughery with regards of Pete Doyle, very fine, without printed jacket as issued, half morocco folding box. James S. Jaffe Rare Books Fall 2013 - 151 2013 $12,500

Whitman, Walt 1819-1892 *Leaves of Grass.* Philadelphia: McKay, 1891-1892. Deathbed edition, ninth separate edition, 8vo., portrait inserted, original heavy grey wrappers, printed yellow spine label, inscribed to Whitman's nurse Warren Fritzinger, Jan. 7 1892, extremely rare issue, front lower wrapper split approximately 2 1/2 inches at joint, otherwise fine, unopened copy in half morocco slipcase. James S. Jaffe Rare Books Fall 2013 - 147 2013 $35,000

Whitman, Walt 1819-1892 *Two Rivulets.* Camden: 1876. First edition, first printing of only 100 copies, 8vo., signed and dated by author on frontispiece (albumen photo of author), near fine, in fine Sangorski & Sutcliffe/Zaehnsdorf green full morocco leather with gilt lettering and rules on spine which is in 6 compartments, custom marbled paper covered, lined slipcase. By the Book, L. C. 36 - 61 2013 $6500

Whitney, Adeline Dutton Train *Mother Goose for Grown Folks.* New York: Rudd & Carleton, 1860. First edition, inserted frontispiece wood engraving, original green pebbled cloth, front panel stamped in gold and blind, rear panel stamped in blind, rose coated endpapers. L. W. Currey, Inc. Christmas Themed Books - 111379 2013 $65

Whitney, Elspeth *Paradise Restored: The Mechanical Arts from Antiquity through the Thirteenth Century.* Philadelphia: American Philosophical Society, 1990. Volume 80, Part 1, 8vo., 169 pages, printed wrappers, ownership signature, fine, scarce. Jeff Weber Rare Books 169 - 478 2013 $65

Whitten, Leslie H. *Moon of the Wolf.* Garden City: Doubleday Crime Club, 1967. First edition, name on front endpaper, otherwise fine in dust jacket with slightly darkened back panel. Mordida Books 81 - 575 2013 $85

Whittier, John Greenleaf 1807-1892 *The Literary Remains of John G(ardiner) C(alkis) Brainard with a Sketch of His Life.* Hartford: P. B. Goodsell, 1832. First edition, 8vo., later full calf, little rubbed along for edge and along hinges, top edge gilt, with gilt dentelles by Stikeman, bookplate of Charles B. Foote.   Second Life Books Inc.   183 - 400   2013 $300

Whittier, John Greenleaf 1807-1892 *Moll Pitcher, a Poem.* Boston: Carter and Hendee, 1832. First edition, 8vo., original printed blue wrappers, uncut, slight chipping of spine, Mass. library stamp at top of verso of titlepage, great rarity in wrappers.   M & S Rare Books, Inc.   95 - 388   2013 $15,000

Whittier, John Greenleaf 1807-1892 *Snow-Bound.* Chicago: Reilly & Britton, 1909. 8vo., cloth, pictorial paste-on, top edge gilt, 123 pages, very fine in original pictorial box ad plain paper wrapper (neat flap mend on box), illustrations by John Neil, excellent condition.   Aleph-Bet Books, Inc.   104 - 379   2013 $350

Whittingham, Bernard *Notes on the Late Expedition Against the Russian Settlements in Easter Siberia...* London: Longman, 1856. First edition, folding map, 8vo., contemporary half morocco, trifle stained here and there, scarce.   Maggs Bros. Ltd.   1467 - 47   2013   £1750

Whittington Press *A Miscellany of Type.* Andoversford: Whittington Press, 1990. 113/460 copies (of an edition of 530), printed on Zerkall mouldmade paper throughout in black and a variety of autumn colors through the browns to orange, all heightened with a selections of illustrations from earlier Whittington books and inserted type facsimiles, folio, original quarter orange buckram, backstrip gilt lettered, cream boards patterned in green and orange, untrimmed, matching board slipcase, fine.   Blackwell's Rare Books   172 - 309   2013   £250

Whittington, Harry *Strangers on Friday.* London: and New York, 1959. First edition, slightly cocked, else fine in very good with couple of tears on front panel, rubbing and some smudges on rear panel.   Between the Covers Rare Books, Inc.   Mystery & Detective Fiction - 73277   2013 $275

Whittle, Glenn *1935 Supplement to the Intercollegiate Football 1869-1934.* St. Paul: Intercollegiate Football Association, 1935. Thin quarto, wrappers, slight wear and short tear top of spine, else very good, ownership stamp, facsimile of his signature of Elmer Layden on titlepage.   Between the Covers Rare Books, Inc.   Football Books - 83773   2013 $125

Why I Am an Agnostic (Why I am a Jew, Catholic, Protestant). Chicago: Popular Interest Series, 1932. First edition, 64 pages, wrappers, very good.   Beasley Books   2013 - 2013 $50

Whymper, F. *The Sea: Its Stirring Story of Adventure, Peril and Heroism.* Cassell, Petter & Galpin, n.d. circa, 1877-1880. 4 volumes in 2, contemporary half calf gilt with raised bands and spine labels, slight wear to short length of one fore-edge, color plate of flags and 400 full page and text woodcut illustrations, excellent set.   R. F. G. Hollett & Son   Children's Books - 720   2013   £180

Whyte-Melville, George John *Songs and Verses.* London: Ward, Lock, circa, 1890. New edition, initial ad leaf, 'yellow' back, original printed boards, near fine.   Jarndyce Antiquarian Booksellers   CCV - 288   2013   £110

Whyte, James Christie *History of the British Turf, from the Earliest Period to the Present Day.* London: Henry Colburn, 1840. First edition, 2 volumes, half title, volume i, frontispiece, illustrations, original dark green moire cloth, little rubbed, odd mark, but very good, bright copy, partly torn bookseller's receipt, completed in manuscript tipped in on recto of frontispiece, volume i.   Jarndyce Antiquarian Booksellers   CCV - 287   2013   £420

Whytt, Robert *Observations on Nature, Causes and Cure of Those Diseases Which Have Been Commonly called Nervous Hypochondriac or Hysteric.* Edinburgh: T. Beckett and P. du Hondt, 1765. New full calf, stamp on title, text foxed in parts, author's presentation copy for Jo. Gregory 1765.   James Tait Goodrich   75 - 224   2013 $2795

Wicks, Mark *To Mars via The Moon: an Astronomical Story.* Philadelphia: J. B. Lippincott, 1911. First American edition, scattered foxing, elaborate spine gilt bright and unrubbed, very near fine.   Between the Covers Rare Books, Inc.   Sci-Fi, Fantasy & Horror - 292863   2013 $450

Wied-Neuwied, Maximillian Alexander Philipp, Prinz Von 1782-1867 *The Children of the Sun: Myths of the Mandan and Minnetaree.* Salt Lake City: Red Butte Press, 1985. 1/50 copies, (16) pages, quarto, string bound gray wrappers with embossed sun on front panel, near fine, this copy #23.   Ken Sanders Rare Books   45 - 57   2013 $700

Wied-Neuwied, Maximillian Alexander Philipp, Prinz Von 1782-1867 *Reise nach Brasilien in den Jahren bis 1817.* Frankfurt: H. L. Broenner & Wein: Carl Gerold, 1820-1821. Second edition, 2 volumes plus 3 atlases, 2 folding maps and 16 engraved plates, 8vo. and 4to., fine set in original wrappers.   Maggs Bros. Ltd.   1467 - 107   2013   £1950

Wiggershaus, Rolf *The Frankfurt School: its History, Theories and Political Significance.* Frankfurt: Cambridge: MIT Press, 1994. First American edition, hardcover issue, fine in fine dust jacket, beautiful copy.   Between the Covers Rare Books, Inc.   Philosophy - 93353   2013 $85

Wiggin, Kate Douglas *The Writings.* Boston and New York: Houghton Mifflin, 1907-1917. Quillcote Edition, 197 x 130mm., 10 volumes, appealing contemporary black half morocco, raised bands flanked by plain gilt rules, spine panels adorned with delicate gilt weather vane marbled boards and endpapers, top edge gilt, 112 plates, 22 of them in color, one spine with small portion of upper corner of top panel missing, gilt ornament just slightly grazed, little wear at tops of other spines, about a fourth of the joints and corners with slight rubbing, bindings solid and not displeasing despite faults, very fine, internally leaves and plates surprisingly clean, fresh and bright especially for books intended for juvenile use.   Phillip J. Pirages   63 - 493   2013 $450

Wilanski-Stekelis, Miriam *Dudaim.* Tel Aviv: Penina, 1947. Oblong 4to., cloth backed stiff pictorial wrappers, near fine, wonderful silhouette by Meir Gur-Arie.   Aleph-Bet Books, Inc.   105 - 342   2013 $375

Wilberforce, Edward *The Idler, Magazine of Fiction, Belles Lettres, News and Comedy. No. 1-6 (all published).* London: Robert Hardwicke & Houston and Stoneman, 1856. First edition, later issue, 6 serial parts, 8vo., original printed yellow wrappers, some minor wear at edges, in fine condition, in chemise and quarter morocco slipcase,.   The Brick Row Book Shop   Miscellany Fifty-Nine - 19   2013 $800

Wilberforce, William *A Practical View of the Prevailing Religious System of Professed Christians, in the Higher Middle Classes in this Country, Contrasted with Real Christianity.* London: T. Cadell and W. Davies, 1805. Eighth edition, 8vo., few leaves foxed, some light browning, full contemporary tree calf, gilt ruled spine, red morocco label, leading hinge cracked but firm, slight wear, early ownership name of Wm. Hamilton (Clerk of Hoole, Cheshire), nice copy.   Jarndyce Antiquarian Booksellers   CCIV - 313   2013   £85

Wilbrandt, Conrad *Des Herrn Friedrich Ost Erlebnisse in Der Welt Bellamy's Mitteilungen aus den Jahren 2001 und 2002.* Wismar: Instorffsche Hofbuchhandlung Verlagsconto, 1891. First edition, Small octavo, original three quarter blue grey cloth and decorated boards, spine panel stamped in gold.   L. W. Currey, Inc.   Fall Sampler Sept. 2013 - 144005   2013 $1250

Wild, Charles *Twelve Perspective Views of the Exterior and Interior Parts of the Metropolitical Church of York...* London: W. Bulmer & Co., 1809. Folio, 14 plates, including 12 fine aquatints, very good, large uncut copy in original sugar paper boards, printed label on upper cover, neatly rebacked, corners and board edges rubbed, slightly worn, fresh contemporary front endpaper, inscribed John Lewis Wolfe, Oct. 1813 from Mr. Namien, scarce.   Ken Spelman Books Ltd.   73 - 13   2013   £650

Wilde, Oscar   1854-1900 *After Reading. Letters of Oscar Wilde to Robert Ross.* London: Beaumont Press, 1921. One of 400 copies on handmade paper, color woodcuts by Ethelbert White, large 8vo., patterned boards, cloth back, one of 400 copies on handmade paper, near fine.   Maggs Bros. Ltd.   1442 - 323   2013   £50

Wilde, Oscar   1854-1900 *C.3.3. The Ballad of Reading Gaol.* London: Leonard Smithers, 1898. First edition, limited to 800 copies, 8vo., linen backed mustard boards, uncut, neat bookplate, spine browning, otherwise excellent copy.   Maggs Bros. Ltd.   1442 - 321   2013   £600

Wilde, Oscar   1854-1900 *Essays, Criticisms and Reviews.* London: privately printed, 1901. First edition, one of 300 copies (ths #250), 258 x 188mm., unusual red and crimson morocco by May Rosina Prat (stamp signed in blind "M R I" and dated "1903" on rear doublure), covers tooled in black with three vertical rows of stylized tulips, each row within a panel formed by plain rules, these floral rows set against red morocco, but with undecorated vertically oriented panels of crimson in between red, raised bands, spine titling in black, red morocco doublures with black ruled frame and tulip cornerpieces, in a lightly worn matching morocco trimmed slipcase (almost certainly by the binder), first few and last few leaves with vague rumpling, otherwise especially fine, text quite clean and fresh, binding unworn.   Phillip J. Pirages   63 - 494   2013 $750

Wilde, Oscar   1854-1900 *Essays, Criticisms and Reviews.* London: privately printed, 1901. First edition, number 27 of 300 copies, large 8vo., original card wrappers printed in black, small tear at tail of spine, otherwise excellent copy.   Maggs Bros. Ltd.   1442 - 322   2013   £100

Wilde, Oscar   1854-1900 *The Happy Prince and Other Tales.* London: David Nutt, 1888. First edition, 4to., illustrations by Crane and Hood, original cream paper boards printed in red and black, one of 1 thousand copies printed, spine browned and chipped at head, corners bumped, bookplate of William Forbes Morgan, otherwise very good.   Maggs Bros. Ltd.   1442 - 317   2013   £600

Wilde, Oscar   1854-1900 *The Happy Prince.* London: Duckworth, 1913. First edition with these illustrations, 4to., gilt pictorial purple cloth, top edge gilt, offsetting on endpaper, else near fine, illustrations by Charles Robinson with 12 magnificent tipped in color plates with lettered tissue guards plus numerous text drawings as well as pictorial endpapers and titlepage, nice.   Aleph-Bet Books, Inc.   105 - 503   2013 $1250

Wilde, Oscar   1854-1900   *A House of Pomegranates.* London: James R. Osgood, McIlvaine & Co., 1891.   First edition, 4to., titlepage and text design, ornament, decorations and decorated endpapers by Charles Ricketts, 4 plates by C. H. Shannon, original cream linen boards, moss green cloth spine, upper cover decorated overall and lettered in pale red and with gilt design of peacock, running fountain and basket of split pomegranates, the 4 plates faint as usual, small bookplate to top left corner of front pastedown, short repair to cloth at foot, otherwise excellent and bright. Maggs Bros. Ltd.   1442 - 316   2013   £500

Wilde, Oscar   1854-1900   *The House of Judgement.* Utrecht: Catharijne Press, 1986.   Limited to 165 copies, this one of 150 numbered copies, 5 x 6.7cm., brown cloth with paper cover label, printed in four colors by Hans Hartzheim with calligraphed original by J. H. Moesman, colophon separately printed on four pages and loosely inserted in pocket in back, miniature bookplate of Kathryn Rickard, from the collection of Donn W. Sanford.   Oak Knoll Books   303 - 91   2013 $150

Wilde, Oscar   1854-1900   *An Ideal Husband.*   London: Leonard Smithers and Co., 1899.   One of 1000 copies, 8vo., original lilac cloth, decorated gilt, slightly bruised at head and tail of spine and some foxing to endpapers, otherwise excellent.   Maggs Bros. Ltd.   1442 - 314   2013   £850

Wilde, Oscar   1854-1900   *An Ideal Husband.*   London: Leonard Smithers and Co., 1899.   First edition, one of 1000 copies, small quarto, original mauve cloth decoratively stamped in gilt on covers and spine, designs by Charles Shannon, spine lettered gilt, some minor foxing, spine sunned, bit of wrinkling to cloth, head of spine with some minor wear, overall very good.   Heritage Book Shop Holiday Catalogue 2012 - 160   2013 $2000

Wilde, Oscar   1854-1900   *Lady Windermeres.*   London: Elkin Mathews and John Lane, 1893.   One of 500 copies, 16 pages ads dated Sept. 1893, small 4to., original red-brown cloth, gilt designs by Charles Shannon, spine lettered and ornamented gilt, fore and bottom edges untrimmed, covers slightly worn, otherwise excellent.   Maggs Bros. Ltd.   1442 - 319   2013   £600

Wilde, Oscar   1854-1900   *A Letter from Oscar Wilde.* Edinburgh: Tragara Press, 1954.   First edition, number 33 of 40 copies, 8vo., original white wrappers, dust jacket in patterned green and red with printed paper label, rare, fine copy.   Maggs Bros. Ltd.   1442 - 326   2013   £250

Wilde, Oscar   1854-1900   *Letters to the Sphinx from Oscar Wild with Reminiscences of the author by Ada Leverson.*   London: Duckworth, 1930.   First edition, large 8vo., original blue cloth, lettered gilt on spine, number 64 of 275 copies signed by author, bookplate of John Sparrow, near fine.   Maggs Bros. Ltd.   1442 - 325   2013   £275

Wilde, Oscar   1854-1900   *Lord Arthur Savile's Crime.* London: Osgood McIlvaine, 1891.   First edition, 8vo., original buff paper over boards, printed and decorated in brown, vertical crease along length of spine, hinges very weak, label removed from upper cover, much used copy.   Maggs Bros. Ltd.   1442 - 318   2013   £250

Wilde, Oscar   1854-1900   *The Picture of Dorian Gray.* London: Petersburg Press, 1968.   Limited edition signed and numbered by artist, Jim Dine, this number 29 of 200 in edition A, folio, complete set of 12 lithographs in color, with set of additional 6 loose lithographs issued in portrait, each annotated "Edition A' on reverse and numbered 29/200 and signed by artist, original full fuchsia (red) velvet boards, front board lettered silver, additional black cloth portfolio, fine. Heritage Book Shop   Holiday Catalogue 2012 - 161   2013 $4500

Wilde, Oscar   1854-1900   *Ravenna.*   Oxford: Thos. Shrimpton & Son, 1878.   First edition, 8vo., slightly later half green morocco over marbled boards, ownership signature of Ada Leverson.   Maggs Bros. Ltd.   1442 - 313   2013   £3500

Wilde, Oscar   1854-1900   *Salome.*   1912.   First edition thus, 8vo., original cloth, 16 drawings by Aubrey Beardsley, very good, clean.   Ken Spelman Books Ltd.   75 - 162   2013   £95

Wilde, Oscar   1854-1900   *The Sphinx.*   London: privately printed, 1901.   Number 34 of 50 copies on Japanese vellum from a total edition of 300, 4to., original cream boards, slightly rubbed overall, bumped at corners, otherwise excellent copy.   Maggs Bros. Ltd.   1442 - 315   2013   £500

Wilde, Oscar   1854-1900   *The Sphinx.*   London: John Lane, Bodley Head, 1920.   First edition, 1 of 1000 copies, 36 pages, 9 full page illustrations with captioned tissue guards and two extra illustrations in front and back, by Alastair, bound in off-white linen with elaborate gilt design with turquoise moon crescent on front board, said to be by Charles Ricketts, minor browning to spine, few light spots of soiling to boards, light foxing and browning to interior, bookplate, very good.   The Kelmscott Bookshop   7 - 77   2013 $1000

Wilde, Oscar   1854-1900   *A Woman of No Importance.* London: John Lane, 1894.   One of 500 copies, first edition, small 4to. original red brown cloth, gilt designs by Charles Shannon, spine lettered and ornamented in gilt, excellent. Maggs Bros. Ltd.   1442 - 320   2013   £600

Wilde, Oscar 1854-1900 *The Young King and Other Tales.* London: Ashendene Press, 1924. First edition, 8vo., original full brown morocco and printed on vellum, bound by W. H. Smith with his monogram under the direction of Douglas Cockerell, spine in six panels with raised bands, each panel with gilt border and dots at each corner, gilt lettering, double gilt borders on turn-ins pencilled ownership inscription of R. Antony Hornby, fine.   Maggs Bros. Ltd.   1442 - 324   2013   £16,500

Wilde, William R. *The Beauties of the Boyne & Its Tributary, The Blackwater.* 1845. Tower Books facsimile of 1850 edition, 8vo., map, illustrations, cloth, dust jacket, very good.   C. P. Hyland   261 - 869   2013   £75

Wilde, William R. *The Closing Years of Dean Swift's Life...* 1849. Frontispiece, text illustrations, portrait dampstained, cloth, spine frayed, else very good, inscription indicates it was Prize for Arithmetic in 1854 at Ouse Gate School, Selby.   C. P. Hyland   261 - 811   2013   £150

Wildenstein, A. *Odilon Redon: Catalogue Raisonne de l'Oeuvre Peint et Dessine.* Paris: Wildenstein Institute/La Bibliotheque de Arts, 1992-1998. First edition, folios, each volume with 30 pages, and about 900 black and white and color plates and illustrations, cloth, dust jackets and slipcases, new condition.   Gemini Fine Books & Arts., Ltd.   Art Reference & Illustrated Books - 2013 $1500

Wilder, Laura Ingalls *By the Shores of Silver Lake.* New York: Harper & Bros., 1939. Stated first edition, 8vo., pictorial cloth, fine in very slightly worn dust jacket, color dust jacket and frontispiece by Helen Sewell and in line by Mildred Boyle, this was Boyle's own copy inscribed by her for her niece.   Aleph-Bet Books, Inc.   105 - 588   2013 $3500

Wilder, Laura Ingalls *Farmer Boy.* New York: Harper Bros., 1933. Not first edition, 8vo., pictorial cloth, fine with front flap and part of front panel of dust jacket, illustrations by Helen Sewell, this copy signed by author, rare thus.   Aleph-Bet Books, Inc.   104 - 585   2013 $4000

Wilder, Laura Ingalls *Little Town on the Prairie.* New York: Harper Bros., 1941. Not first edition, 8vo., pictorial cloth, near fine in dust jacket with old tape mends and 3 pieces out of backstrip, signed by author, rare thus.   Aleph-Bet Books, Inc.   104 - 586   2013 $4000

Wildman, Thomas *A Treatise on the Management of Bees...* London: printed for W. Strahan and T. Cadell, 1770. Second edition, 3 folding engraved plates, 8vo. tears to blank leading edge of N, two following leaves, narrower with minor tears, offset browning to endpapers and pastedowns, otherwise very clean, contemporary calf, gilt borders expertly rebacked in matching style, raised gilt bands, red morocco label.   Jarndyce Antiquarian Booksellers   CCIV - 314   2013   £450

Wildsmith, Brian *The Little Wood Duck.* Oxford University Press, 1972. First edition, color printed illustrations by author 4to., original white boards, illustrated overall, dust jacket, fine.   Blackwell's Rare Books   172 - 246   2013   £30

Wildsmith, Brian *The Tunnel: Le Tunnel.* Oxford University Press, 1933. First edition, color printed illustrations by author, moveable wheel, 4to., original boards illustrated overall, fine.   Blackwell's Rare Books   172 - 247   2013   £30

Wilkes, Charles 1798-1877 *Narrative of the United States Exploring Expedition During the Years 1838, 1839, 1840, 1841, 1842.* Philadelphia: Lea and Blanchard, 1845. First trade edition, 5 volumes plus atlas, 9 double page maps, 64 engraved plates and 5 large folding maps in atlas, numerous illustrations in text, tall 8vo., original pictorial cloth, gilt still bright, one or two minor repairs.   Maggs Bros. Ltd.   1467 - 146   2013   £6750

Wilkes, John *The Life of John Wilkes Patriot.* Lion and Unicorn Press, 1955. 62/200 copies printed on Chariot Cartridge paper, 14 full page illustrations by Donald Higgins, each printed in black and one other color, small folio, original tan boards, backstrip gilt lettered, front cover with gilt blocked design, fine.   Blackwell's Rare Books   172 - 301   2013   £60

Wilkie's Family Almanack & Cork Annual for 1881. Original quarter cloth, 8vo., very good.   C. P. Hyland   261 - 213   2013   £30

Wilkie's Family Almanack & Cork Annual for 1883. 8vo., original wrappers, good.   C. P. Hyland   261 - 214   2013   £30

Wilkins, John *Of the Principles and Duties of Natural Religion.* London: printed for R. Chiswell, W. Battersby and C. Brome, 1699. Fourth edition, 8vo., engraved frontispiece, browned and spotted, intermittent oil stain to lower corner, contemporary speckled calf, rebacked to style with original label relaid and corners repaired by Chris Weston, contemporary ink inscription.   Unsworths Antiquarian Booksellers   28 - 141   2013   £200

Wilkins, Thurman *Clarence King.* Albuquerque: University of New Mexico Press, 1988. Revised edition, 32 plates, very fine, pictorial dust jacket.   Argonaut Book Shop   Recent Acquisitions June 2013 - 316   2013 $60

Wilkinson, George *Practical Geology and Ancient Architecture of Ireland.* 1845. First edition, 17 plates, 72 woodcuts, 8vo., original cloth (faded), rebacked, text very good.   C. P. Hyland   261 - 879   2013   £250

Wilkinson, John Gardner *Manners and Customs of the Ancient Eygptians, Including their Private Life, Government, Laws, Arts, Manufactures, Religion, Agriculture and Early History.* London: John Murray, 1847. Third edition, 5 volumes, 94 lithographed plates, some color, double page and or folding and over 500 woodcuts, 8vo., contemporary tree calf, rebacked, raised bands, red morocco title label, black morocco volume label, both in gilt, boards ruled and bordered gilt, edges ad turn-ins decorated with gilt dentelles, marbled endpapers, very good, extremities rubbed, one volume with top fore-corners bumped and worn, minor loss, labels with some chipped edges, owner's bookplate on front pastedowns, binding solid, contents fine, beautiful set, bookplates of Edward Huth.   Kaaterskill Books   16 - 90   2013 $950

Wilkinson, Spencer *Hannibal's March through the Alps.* Oxford: Clarendon Press, 1911. 8vo., 48 pages, 2 plates, grey paper covered boards, deteriorating spine, corners bumped, somewhat discolored, titlepage browned, author's gift inscription.   Unsworths Antiquarian Booksellers   28 - 205   2013   £45

Wilkinson, Tate *Memoirs of His Own Life.* York: printed for author by Wilson, Spence and Mawman, 1790. 4 volumes, all with half titles, errata leaf at end volume IV and list of subscribers volume I, 12mo., uncut, some light foxing, offsetting from loosely inserted news cutting on to following endpaper; contemporary calf, marbled boards, gilt band spines, red morocco labels, spines rubbed, some loss of surface leather, slight insect damage in two places, neat corrections to text in contemporary hand from errata list. Jarndyce Antiquarian Booksellers   CCIV - 315   2013   £380

Willeford, Charles *The Burnt Orange Heresy.* New York: Crown, 1971. First edition, fine in dust jacket with some darkening along top edges.   Mordida Books   81 - 579   2013 $250

Willeford, Charles *Cockfighter Journal.* Santa Barbara: Neville, 1989. First edition, one of 300 numbered copies (of a total edition of 326), signed by Burke, fine, cloth. Between the Covers Rare Books, Inc.   Mystery & Detective Fiction - 15914   2013 $300

Willeford, Charles *The Difference.* Tucson: Dennis McMillan, 1999. First edition, very fine in dust jacket. Mordida Books   81 - 585   2013 $65

Willeford, Charles *Everybody's Metamorphosis.* Missoula: Dennis McMillan, 1988. First edition, one of 400 copies signed by author, very fine in dust jacket.   Mordida Books   81 - 583   2013 $300

Willeford, Charles *A Guide for the Undehemorrhoided.* Boynton Beach: Star Pub., 1977. First edition, uncommon, light foxing to endpages, else fine in fine, but slightly dust jacket.   Ken Lopez Bookseller   159 - 214   2013 $200

Willeford, Charles *High Priest of California & Wild Wives.* New York: Beacon, 1956. First edition, paperback original, fine, unread copy in wrappers, Willeford misspelled 'Williford" on cover.   Mordida Books   81 - 578   2013 $400

Willeford, Charles *Miami Blues.* New York: St. Martin's, 1984. First edition, fine in dust jacket with crease on inner front flap and some tiny rubbing on back panel.   Mordida Books   81 - 580   2013 $275

Willeford, Charles *New Hope for the Dead.* New York: St. Martin's, 1985. First edition, fine in dust jacket with slightly faded spine.   Mordida Books   81 - 581   2013 $150

Willeford, Charles *Poontang and Other Poems.* Crescent City: privately printed/New Atheneum Press, 1967. First edition, stapled wrappers, seemingly scarcer variant in grey wrappers, no prioity, signed by author, rare thus.   Between the Covers Rare Books, Inc.   Mystery & Detective Fiction - 45959   2013 $3500

Willeford, Charles *Proletarian Laughter.* Yonkers: Alicat Bookshop, 1948. First edition, published in an edition of 1000 copies, fine in stapled soft covers,.   Mordida Books   81 - 577   2013 $250

Willeford, Charles *Something About a Soldier.* New York: Random House, 1986. First edition, very fine in dust jacket.   Mordida Books   81 - 582   2013 $65

Willeford, Charles *The Whip Hand.* Greenwich: Gold Medal, 1961. First edition, paperback original, touch of browning to page edges and tiny bump to one corner, else fine, fresh, scarce.   Between the Covers Rare Books, Inc. Mystery & Detective Fiction - 31599   2013 $280

William Morris, Wallpapers. Zuilichem: Catharijne Press, 1997. Limited to 190 copies, of which this is one of the 15 lettered copies bound thus, and with a separate "wallpaper book" containing an extra suite of the plates in larger format, bound by Luce Thurkow, 11 specimens of wallpaper, 6.6 x 4.3cm., paper covered boards, paper cover label (1st volume); cloth ties (2nd volume), clam shell box covered with reproduction of Morris wallpaper, paper cover label, from the collection of Donn W. Sanford.   Oak Knoll Books   303 - 92 2013 $325

William III, King of Great Britain *The Prince of Orange his Declaration: Shewing the Reasons why He Invades England.* London: by Randal Taylor, 1688. 4to., 32 pages, modern calf backed marbled boards.   Joseph J. Felcone Inc.   Books Printed before 1701 - 90   2013 $325

Williams, Aaron *The Harmony Society at Economy, Penn'a. Founded by George Rapp A.D., 1805.* Pittsburgh: W. S. Haven, 1866. First edition, 16mo., 182 pages, original cloth, very bright, very fine.   M & S Rare Books, Inc.   95 - 390   2013 $1000

Williams, Charles *Aground.* New York: Viking, 1960. First edition, fine in very good dust jacket with internal staining, several short closed tears and wear at spine and end, at corners and along folds.   Mordida Books   81 - 588   2013 $100

Williams, Charles *All Hallows Eve.* London: Faber & Faber, 1945. First edition, edges of boards very slightly soiled, else fine in very good plus dust jacket with very shallow loss at crown and small stain on rear panel, very nice, author's fragile and uncommon final novel.   Between the Covers Rare Books, Inc.   Sci-Fi, Fantasy & Horror - 73791   2013 $875

Williams, Charles *Man on a Leash.* New York: Putnam, 1973. First edition, fine in fine dust jacket.   Between the Covers Rare Books, Inc.   Mystery & Detective Fiction - 12572   2013 $60

Williams, Charles *Silvershell; or the Adventures of an Oyster.* Judd & Glass, 1857. Second edition, original green blindstamped cloth, gilt, spine and edges mellowed to brown, frontispiece, 18 text woodcuts, scarce.   R. F. G. Hollett & Son   Children's Books - 722   2013   £160

Williams, Desmond *The Irish Struggle 1916-1926.* Routledge K. P., 1968. First edition, 8vo., cloth, dust jacket, ex-library, very good.   C. P. Hyland   261 - 871   2013   £30

Williams, Garth *The Rabbits' Wedding.* New York: Harper and Brothers, 1958. Large 4to., illustrations, cloth backed pictorial boards, fine in dust jacket with price intact, jacket very good+ (lightly worn on spine ends with few small closed tears).   Aleph-Bet Books, Inc.   104 - 587   2013 $600

Williams, Gordon *Ravens & Crows.* Los Angeles: William Cheney, 1966. 2.4 x 1.7cm., paper covered boards, miniature bookplate of Kathryn Rickard, from the collection of Donn W. Sanford.   Oak Knoll Books   303 - 96   2013 $100

Williams, Harcourt *Tales from Ebony.* Nattali & Maurice, 1947. New edition, original cloth gilt, dust jacket, some edge tears and pieces lost from extremities, price clipped, 33 fine color plates and black and white head and tailpieces, name on flyleaf, scarce.   R. F. G. Hollett & Son   Children's Books - 616   2013   £75

Williams, Harold *The Motte Edition of Gulliver's Travels.* Oxford University Press, 1925. Motte edition, (35) pages, 3 photos, wrappers, very good.   C. P. Hyland   261 - 812   2013   £30

Williams, Helen Maria *Poems; Moral, Elegant and Pathetic....* London: printed for J. Harris, 1803. 12mo., plates slightly waterstained, one of which is detached, full contemporary tree calf, gilt borders, gilt banded spine, rubbed, some insect damage at foot of spine, lacking, label, inscription dated 1946.   Jarndyce Antiquarian Booksellers   CCIV - 316   2013   £125

Williams, James R. *Annual Address Delivered by James R. Williams M.W. Grand Master, State of Pennsylvania at the 11th Annual Session of the Most Worshipful Grand Lodge...* Philadelphia: James, printer, 1927. First edition, stapled wrappers, 20 pages, photograph frontispiece, small, very faint stain top of pages and on rear wrapper, very good plus, scarce.   Between the Covers Rare Books, Inc.   165 - 152   2013 $150

Williams, John *The Holy Table, Name and Thing, More Anciently, Properly and Literally Used Under the New Testament...* London: printed for the Diocese of Lincoln, 1637. 4t., later ink markings around edges of page 198 intruding into spaces in text, final leaf of main text cropped along upper edge affecting page numbers, tear without loss to lower margin, titlepage dusted and little marked, expertly bound in recent quarter calf, marbled boards, vellum tips, raised and gilt banded spine, red morocco label.   Jarndyce Antiquarian Booksellers   CCIV - 31 2013   £280

Williams, John A. *Sissie.* New York: Farrar, Straus and Cudahy, 1963. First edition, pages age toned, else fine in lightly rubbed, near fine dust jacket, uncommon in nice condition.   Between the Covers Rare Books, Inc.   165 - 287   2013 $150

Williams, John A. *Sons of Darkness, Sons of Light: a Novel of Some Probability.* Boston: Little Brown, 1969. First edition, fine in near fine dust jacket, fresh, bright copy, minuscule rubbing to extremities of dust jacket.   Leather Stalking Books   October 2013 - 2013 $75

Williams, Jonathan *Affilati Attrezzi Per I Giardini Di Catullo.* Milano: Lerici Editori, 1966. First edition, 8vo., 121 pages, paper wrappers, English and Italian on facing pages, inscribed by author for Metcalf, very good, little soiled.   Second Life Books Inc.   183 - 403   2013 $50

Williams, Jonathan *A Celestial Centennial Reverie for Mr. Charles Ives.* Highlands: Jonathan Williams Feb. 20-27, 1975. Produced on Xerox 4000, in an edition of 100 for friends, 4to., 24 pages, self wrappers, plastic binder, inscribed by author for Paul and Nancy Metcalf.   Second Life Books Inc.   183 - 407   2013 $150

Williams, Jonathan *Elite/Elate Poems. Selected Poems 1971-1975.* Jargon Society, 1979. First edition, #36 of 150 copies, portfolio of photos by Guy Mendes, 4to., 220 pages, little streak on cloth, otherwise fine in dust jacket, little worn, inscribed by author to Paul and Nancy Metcalf.   Second Life Books Inc.   183 - 410   2013 $200

Williams, Jonathan *The Empire Finals at Verona.* Jargon, 1958. First edition, 4to., paper wrappers, unnumbered, very good.   Second Life Books Inc.   183 - 411   2013 $65

Williams, Jonathan *Glees Swarthy Monotonies Rince Cochon & Chozzerai for Simon.* Roswell: DBA Editions, 1980. First edition, 1/128 copies distributed for friends, not for sale, 4to., 94 pages, very good, inscribed by author for friend Paul Metcalf, #74 for Paul from the Colonel Highlands 1980", in addition author has circled in pen the statement on titlepage "May contain language that is offensive to children".   Second Life Books Inc.   183 - 412   2013 $100

Williams, Jonathan *Homage, Umbrage Quibble & Chicane.* Roswell: DBA Editions, 1981. First edition, one of 120 copies , this #68, inscribed by author for Paul and Nancy Metcalf, 4to., 72 pages.   Second Life Books Inc.   183 - 413   2013 $125

Williams, Jonathan *In England's Green and A Garland and a Clyster.* San Francisco: Auerhahn Press, 1962. First edition, 8vo., printed wrappers, very nice, one of 750 copies, hand bound in Rhododendron cover paper, handset in Palatino roman and italic types and printed on curtis rag paper by Dave Haselwood and Andrew Hoyem.   Second Life Books Inc.   183 - 414   2013 $75

Williams, Jonathan *The Lucidities, Sixteen in Visionary Company.* London: Turret Books, 1967. First edition, 18 pages, bound in cloth with illustrations by John Furnival on foil, fine, of a total edition of 280 this is one of 250 for sale, inscribed by author for poet Paul Metcalf and his wife Nancy.   Second Life Books Inc.   183 - 416   2013 $125

Williams, Jonathan *Lullabies Twisters Gibbers Drags.* Highlands: Nantahala Foundation, 1963. Oblong wrappers, very good, inscribed by author for Paul Metcalf.   Second Life Books Inc.   183 - 417   2013 $75

Williams, Jonathan *Madeira & Toasts for Basil Buntings 75th Birthday.* Highlands: Jargon, 1977. 1/1250 copies, 8vo., pages not numbered, paper wrappers, very good.   Second Life Books Inc.   183 - 424   2013 $50

Williams, Jonathan *Portrait Photographs.* Frankfort: Gnomon, 1979. One of 1800 copies, square 8vo., not numbered, 30 color portraits, paper wrappers, nice, slightly soiled tissue dust jacket and paper slipcase.   Second Life Books Inc.   183 - 420   2013 $75

Williams, Jonathan *62 Climerikews to Amuse Mr. Lear.* Roswell/Denver: DBA/JCA Editions Christmas, 1983. #62 of 200 numbered copies, this signed for Paul and Nancy (Metcalf), 4to., printed wrappers, nice.   Second Life Books Inc.   183 - 402   2013 $150

Williams, Jonathan *Untinears & Antennae for Maurice Ravel.* St. Paul: Truck Books, 1977. First edition, printed wrappers, very nice, inscribed by author for Paul and Nancy Metcalf.   Second Life Books Inc.   183 - 422   2013 $50

Williams, Martin *The Art of Jazz.* New York: Oxford, 1959. First edition, fine in very good, price clipped dust jacket.   Beasley Books   2013 - 2013 $65

Williams, Martin *Jazz Panorama.* New York: Crowell-Collier, 1962. First edition, fine but for owner's inscription, rubbed dust jacket.   Beasley Books   2013 - 2013 $50

Williams, Steven J. *The Secret of Secrets.* Ann Arbor: University of Michigan Press, 2003. 8vo., navy cloth, silver stamped spine title, ownership signature, fine, scarce.   Jeff Weber Rare Books   169 - 481   2013 $65

Williams, T. *Every Man His Own Lawyer; or Complete Law Library...* London: printed for Sherwood, Neely and Jones, 1812. 8vo., very good, full contemporary diced calf, gilt borders, attractively gilt panelled spine red morocco label, crack to upper two inches of leading hinge.   Jarndyce Antiquarian Booksellers   CCIV - 317   2013   £120

Williams, Tennessee 1911-1983 *Androgyne, Mon Amour.* New York: New Directions, 1977. Uncorrected galley proofs, narrow unbound folio sheets, folded once and stapled at corner, publisher's review slip added to galleys giving publication date and pricing of different editions, also including is 6 1/4 x 9 1/2 inch photo of mock-up for dust jacket cover, long galley proofs like these are earliest typeset form of text and seldom survive, some chipping along fold and at bottom corner of first sheet, very good, rare galleys, housed in elegant red cloth chemise and slipcase of same cloth, but gilt stamped red morocco spine with raised bands.   Ed Smith Books   75 - 83   2013 $750

Williams, Tennessee 1911-1983 *(contributor) Five Young American Poets. Third Series.* Norfolk: New Directions, 1944. First edition, 215 pages, very good plus in yellow and blue decorated cloth, very good plus dust jacket.   Ed Smith Books   78 - 73   2013 $150

Williams, Tennessee 1911-1983 *I Rise in Flame, Cried the Phoenix.* Norfolk: New Directions, 1951. First edition, one of 310 copies signed by Williams, this #243, 4to., very good original publisher's slipcase with label, near fine, bookplate of Robert W. Woodruff Library, Emory University stamped "withdrawn", bookplate of Merle Armitage, signed by him.   Ed Smith Books   78 - 77   2013 $300

Williams, Tennessee 1911-1983 *Pieces of White Shell. A Journey to Navajoland.* New York: Scribner's, 1984. First edition, illustrations by Clifford Byrcelea, signed by author, fine in near fine dust jacket. Ed Smith Books 78 - 81 2013 $175

Williams, Tennessee 1911-1983 *The Kingdom of Earth with Hard Candy: A Book of Stories.* New York: New Directions, 1954. One of 100 copies signed by author (this is copy #15), 248 x 152mm., cancel titlepage tipped in, as on all copies, publisher's linen backed patterned paper boards, flat spine, author's name in gilt, original blue cardboard slipcase with paper title label to front cover, one small, only vaguely visible discolored spot at head of spine, otherwise mint, leaves that open only reluctantly. Phillip J. Pirages 63 - 495 2013 $1900

Williams, Tennessee 1911-1983 *One Arm and Other Stories.* New York: New Directions, 1954. First trade edition, signed by author, near fine in very good with chip to top of rear panel (price clipped), evidence of small bookplate removed from front pastedown, clean copy signed by author. Ed Smith Books 75 - 82 2013 $350

Williams, Tennessee 1911-1983 *The Roman Spring of Mrs. Stone.* London: John Lehmann, 1950. First British edition, very good+ to near fine in very good plus dust jacket with few tiny chips to spine foot, presentation copy inscribed by author to Paul Bigelow. Ed Smith Books 78 - 76 2013 $850

Williams, Tennessee 1911-1983 *Summer and Smoke.* London: John Lehmann, 1952. First UK edition, briefly inscribed by author, very good plus to near fine in orange cloth with sunning to extremities in very good, clean dust jacket with sunning to spine and two tiny chips to spine crown. Ed Smith Books 78 - 78 2013 $450

Williams, Tennessee 1911-1983 *Summer and Smoke.* London: John Lehmann, 1952. First British edition, uncommon proof copy with titlepage printed in black and red, brown paper wrappers with hand printed title and author, very good copy. Ed Smith Books 78 - 79 2013 $450

Williams, Tennessee 1911-1983 *Tennessee Williams' Letters to Donald Windham 1940-1965.* Verona: Sandy Campbell, 1976. First edition, one of 500 numbered copies, #187, small 4to., 333 pages with index, publisher's original slipcase, fine copy, perfect bound in original wrappers with glassine dust jacket. Ed Smith Books 78 - 80 2013 $175

Williams, Tennessee 1911-1983 *You Touched Me!* New York: Samuel French, 1947. First edition, one of only 506 copies, small 8vo., 4 photo plates inserted, fine in dark green cloth with front cover and spine lettered in gilt, only mild rubbing to cloth, near fine dust jacket (bit rubbed, toned and foxed), this copy inscribed by Williams, Key West 1971. Ed Smith Books 78 - 75 2013 $2000

Williams, Tennessee 1911-1983 *You Touched Me!* New York: Samuel French, 1947. First edition, one of 506 copies, small 8vo., 4 photo plates inserted, fine in dark green cloth with front cover and spine lettered in gilt, only mild rubbing to cloth in nearly fine dust jacket, rare. Ed Smith Books 78 - 74 2013 $750

Williams, Terry Tempest *The Illuminated Desert.* Moab: Canyonlands Natural History Association/Back of Beyond Books, 2008. First edition, "X" of 26 copies, folio, (42) pages, half brown calf over blue boards, title gilt stamped on backstrip, matching slipcase, decorative color title label attached to front board, signed by author. Ken Sanders Rare Books 45 - 58 2013 $800

Williams, Urusula Moray *The Nine Lives of Island MacKenzie.* London: Chatto and Windus, 1959. First edition, 24 illustrations by Edward Ardizzone, 8vo., 128 pages, occasional light foxing, original mid green boards, backstrip gilt lettered, color printed endpaper, substantial remains of dust jacket loosely inserted, good, inscribed by author Christmas 1960. Blackwell's Rare Books B174 - 162 2013 £60

Williams, Valentine *The Knife Behind the Curtain.* Boston: Houghton Mifflin, `930. First American edition, spine lightly soiled, otherwise very good in very fine, as new dust jacket. Mordida Books 81 - 589 2013 $100

Williamson, Hamilton *Lion Club.* New York: Doubleday Doran, 1931. First edition, small 4to., pictorial boards, near fine in slightly chipped dust jacket, illustrations in color and black and white by Berta & Elmer Hader. Aleph-Bet Books, Inc. 104 - 268 2013 $200

Williamson, Passmore *Case of Passmore Williamson. Report of the Proceedings on the Writ of Habeas Corpus, Issued by the Hon. John K. Kane, Judge of the District Court of the U.S. for the Eastern District of Pennsylvania, in the Case of the U.S. of America ex Rel. John H. Wheeler vs. Passmore Williamson...* Philadelphia: Uriah Hunt & Son, 1856. First edition, original cloth, bookplate of defunct library on front pastedown, pocket removed from rear pastedown and call letters on spine, cloth worn down at spine ends, still bright, very good, inscribed by subject of the case, Williamson for H. G. Jones, most certainly Horatio Gates Jones, historian. Between the Covers Rare Books, Inc. 165 - 288 2013 $1850

Willis, Browne *A Survey of the Cathedral Church of St. David's and the Edifices Belonging To It as they Stood in the year 1715.* printed for R. Gosling, 1717. 8vo., 2 folding engraved plates and 2 plates of armorials, prelim ad leaf and final errata, very good, clean, bound in later 18th century calf, gilt banded spine rubbed.   Ken Spelman Books Ltd.   75 - 15   2013   £95

Willis, James *The Irish Nation, Its History & Biography.* Fullarton, 1875. 4 volumes, 8vo., original cloth (worn), text good.   C. P. Hyland   261 - 111   2013   £150

Willis, James *Lives of Illustrious & Distinguished Irishmen from the Earliest Times to the Present Period.* 1847. 9 parts bound in 3 volumes, half calf, needs attention, text very good.   C. P. Hyland   261 - 112   2013   £75

Willis, Nathaniel Parker   1806-1867 *American Scenery; or Land, Lakes and River Illustrations of Transatlantic Nature. (with) Canadian Scenery. (First Quarterly Part (-Concluding Part).* London: publ. for the Proprietors by G. Virtue, 27 Ivy Lane, 1840-1842. First edition, 4to., engraved plates including 4 additional titles with vignettes, one portrait, original roan back printed and illustrated green boards, some foxing to text and plates, but very sound, some rubbing to roan and bumping of corners, but very nice, large vignette on front cover of all volumes.   M & S Rare Books, Inc.   95 - 15   2013 $4250

Willis, Nathaniel Parker   1806-1867 *The Scenery and Antiquities of Ireland.* n.d., 2 volumes, bound in 1, full red morocco by Guy Brothers, Academy St. Cork, gilt and blind impresses, some rubbing at edges, 118 plates, 2 vignette titlepages, map, all plates protected by rice paper tissue guards, marginal foxing to greater or less extent - on almost all plates.   C. P. Hyland   261 - 26   2013   £300

Willis, Thomas *The Anatomy of the Brain and Nerves.* Montreal: McGill University Press, 1965. Limited to 2000 sets, 2 small folio volumes, slipcase, light soiling to box and spines, internally fine, very special edition, photogravure plates.   James Tait Goodrich   75 - 226   2013 $395

Willis, Thomas *De Anima Brutorum Quae Hominis Vitalis ac Sensitiva est Exercitationes Duae, Prior Physiologica Ejusdem Naturam Partes Potentias...* London: Typis E. F. Impensis Ri. Davis, 1672. First octavo edition, 8 engraved plates, recently rebound in full contemporary style, English panel calf, handsome binding, very nice, clean, tight copy.   James Tait Goodrich   75 - 225   2013 $3995

Willis, Thomas *Cerebri Anatome cui accessit Nervorum Descriptio et Usus Studio Thomae Willis, ex Aede Christi Oxon, M.d....* Londini: typis J. Flesher, 1664. First edition, 15 engraved plates, 4to., initial imprimatur leaf dated 1663, prelim leaves little dusted, slight marginal browning, tiny wormholes to extreme leading edge of four leaves, minor tear without loss to one plate, expertly bound in recent panelled calf, raised bands, blind tooled decoration, dark green morocco label.   Jarndyce Antiquarian Booksellers   CCIV - 32   2013   £8500

Willis, Thomas *Dr. Willis's Practice of Physick.* London: printed for T. Dring, C. Harper and J. Leigh, 1684. Small folio, newly rebound in full English panel calf, raised bands with tooled compartments, text with light browning and foxing, very mild worming in margins and some of the marginal notes have been slightly shaved.   James Tait Goodrich   75 - 229   2013 $8500

Willis, Thomas *Pathologie Cerebri et Nervosi Generis Specimen....* London: Jacobum Allestry, 1668. Second edition, portrait, 12mo., full early polished calf, likely early 18th century, ruled spine, very nice, tight copy, just light foxing.   James Tait Goodrich   75 - 227   2013 $2995

Willis, Thomas *Opera Omnia Nitidius Quam Anquam Hacienus Edita...* Amsterdam: Apud Henricum Wetstenium, 1682. Engraved allegorical titlepage, plus 36 (of 37) engraved plates, lacks plate 8, large 4to., in quarter 19th century calf and marbled boards, newly rebacked, calf spine, some light text browning, otherwise very good.   James Tait Goodrich   75 - 228   2013 $895

Willis, Walter H. *The Anglo-African Who's Who and Biographical Sketch Book 1907.* London: L. Upcott Gill, 1907. 4to., half title, original red cloth, dulled and little marked.   Jarndyce Antiquarian Booksellers   CCV - 291   2013   £150

Willison, Paul H. *Past, Present & Future of Fresno Irrigation District.* Fresno: Prepared and Submitted by Paul H. Willison August 1, 1980. First edition, quarto photos, graphs and maps, folding facsimiles, stiff yellow pictorial wrappers printed in black, black tape spine over stapled sheets, fine.   Argonaut Book Shop   Recent Acquisitions June 2013 - 317   2013 $150

Willson, Beckles *The Life and Letters of James Wolfe.* London: William Heinemann, 1909. 8vo., blue cloth with gilt titles to spine and top edge gilt, half title, black and white frontispiece with tissue guard, text in black and red on titlepage, numerous black and white illustrations and 6 plans, 8vo., some wear to edges and corners bumped, otherwise very good.   Schooner Books Ltd.   105 - 155   2013 $55

Wilson, Adrian *A Medieval Mirror: Speculum Humanae Salvationis 1324-1500.* Berkeley: Los Angeles and London: The University of California Press, 1984. First edition, 349 x 248mm., original cloth, dust jacket, 8 color plates, many illustrations in text, nearly mint.   Phillip J. Pirages   63 - 396   2013 $95

Wilson, Andrew *Naval History of the United Kingdom...* Cork: John Conner, 1807. Volume * (of 3), stitched in uncovered boards, unopened.   C. P. Hyland   261 - 876   2013   £65

Wilson, August *The Piano Lesson.* New York: Dutton, 1990. First edition, fine in fine dust jacket.   Between the Covers Rare Books, Inc.   165 - 289   2013 $275

Wilson, Bill *My Name is Bill.* New York: Simon & Schuster, 2004. Stated first edition, signed and inscribed by Susan Cheever, 8vo., 306 pages, fine in fine dust jacket. By the Book, L. C.   36 - 80   2013 $150

Wilson, Daniel *Chatterton. A Biographical Study.* London: Macmillan, 1869. First edition, 8vo., original burgundy cloth, faded on spine and lower cover, otherwise excellent copy, inscribed by Thomas Carlyle for Miss Olivia Sinclair (The Henk, Lockaby), Jan. 7 1870, further inscription author author's compliments presumably to Carlyle.   Maggs Bros. Ltd.   1460 - 161   2013   £500

Wilson, Edward *Diary of the Discovery Expedition to the Antarctic Regions 1901-1904.* Blandford Press, 1966. First edition, 4to., original cloth, gilt, dust jacket, edges chipped, lower edges damped, 48 color plates, numerous monochrome illustrations, 6 text maps, folding map.   R. F. G. Hollett & Son   Polar Exploration - 83   2013   £75

Wilson, James P. *An Easy Introduction to the Knowledge of the Hebrew Language without Points.* Philadelphia: 1812. First edition, old calf, one hinge crudely rebacked. M & S Rare Books, Inc.   95 - 391   2013 $750

Wilson, John Leighton *A Grammar of the Mpongwe Language with Vocabularies.* New York: Snowden & Prall, 1847. First edition, 2 folding tables on very thin paper, 8vo., publisher's marbled boards with original paper label rebacked, ex-library with stamps, old shelving label clumsily removed from front free endpaper, 94 pages.   Maggs Bros. Ltd.   1467 - 26   2013   £600

Wilson, Neill C. *Silver Stampede. The Career of Death Valley's Hell-Camp, Old Panamint.* New York: Macmillan Co., 1937. First edition, signed by author and by painter, E. A. Burbank, map endpapers, photos and drawings, light blue cloth, extremities well rubbed, very good.   Argonaut Book Shop   Recent Acquisitions June 2013 - 317   2013 $125

Wilson, Thomas 1703-1784 *Distilled Spirituous Liquors the Bane of the Nation...* London: printed for J. Roberts, 1736. Second edition, removed or disbound, 60 xxii pages, few small stains on titlepage, else near fine.   Between the Covers Rare Books, Inc.   Cocktails, Etc. - 299699   2013 $400

Wilson, Thomas, Bp. of Sodor & Man 1663-1755 *The Knowledge and Practice of Christianity Made Easy to the Meanest Capacotoes...* London: Osborne, 1743. Fourth edition, title in red and black, 19th century three quarter morocco, ex-library, some foxing and soiling, very good, bound with ad leaf in front.   Second Life Books Inc.   183 - 425   2013 $400

Wilson, William *Newfoundland and Its Missionaries.* Cambridge: Printed by Dakin & Metcalf..., 1866. First edition, 8vo., original black cloth, blindstamp design to front and rear boards, gilt title to spine, covers worn and top and bottom of spine frayed, first blank flyleaf missing. Schooner Books Ltd.   104 - 33   2013 $350

Wilson's Almanacks 1872-1885. 1887-1910. 1872-1910. 2 volumes, binder's cloth gilt, unpaginated, monthly household almanack.   R. F. G. Hollett & Son   Lake District & Cumbria - 22   2013   £85

Wind, Herbert Warren *The Story of American Golf.* New York: Simon & Schuster, 1956. Second edition, first printing, small 4to., 563 pages, minimal foxing in near fine dust jacket, signed and inscribed by author.   By the Book, L. C.   36 - 77   2013 $1250

Windle, B. C. A. *A Genealogical Note on the Family of Cramer or Coghill.* JCHAS bound offprint, 1910. 8vo., cloth, very good, ownership and bookplate of Windle plus typescript pedigree of a branch of the family.   C. P. Hyland   261 - 877   2013   £60

Wingfield, R. D. *Winter Frost.* London: Constable, 1999. First edition, very fine in dust jacket.   Mordida Books   81 - 590   2013 $100

Winslow, Anna Green *Diary of Anna Green Winslow. A Boston Girl of 1771.* Cambridge: Boston and New York: Houghton Mifflin Co., Riverside Press, 1894. First edition, 8vo., canvas covered boards with ties in blue, red, green and black on front cover, half title, black and white frontispiece, facsimile and 5 black and white illustrations, spine darkened and inscription on first flyleaf "Mrs. Mills with compliments Nellie F. Booth 1895".   Schooner Books Ltd.   101 - 128   2013 $55

Winslow, Charles *A Cool Breeze on the Underground.* New York: St. Martin's Press, 1991. First edition, fine in fine dust jacket, signed by author.   Between the Covers Rare Books, Inc.   Mystery & Detective Fiction - 306967   2013 $250

Winslow, Don *The Trail to Buddha's Mirror.* New York: St. Martins, 1992. First edition, signed by author, fine in dust jacket. Mordida Books 81 - 591 2013 $200

Winslow, Don *Way Down on the High Lonely.* New York: St. Martin's Press, 1993. First edition, fine in fine dust jacket, signed by author. Between the Covers Rare Books, Inc. Mystery & Detective Fiction - 314299 2013 $60

Winslow, Forbes E. *The Children's Fairy History of England.* David Stott, 1889. Large 8vo., original pictorial green cloth gilt, few stains to lower boards, 200 woodcut illustrations. R. F. G. Hollett & Son Children's Books - 723 2013 £50

Winthrop, John *Two Lectures on Comets... also, an Essay on Comets....* Boston: W. Wells and T. B. Wait and Co., 1811. First edition, 12mo., recent calf backed marbled boards, uncut, some chipping of edges. M & S Rare Books, Inc. 95 - 392 2013 $375

Wintle, William James *Ghost Gleams: Tales of the Uncanny.* London: Heath Cranston, Ltd. n.d., 1921. First edition, octavo, original charcoal gray cloth, front and spine panels lettered in orange. L. W. Currey, Inc. Wandering Ghosts & Itinerant Souls (10/12) - 107061 2013 $1250

Winward, Walter *Rough Deal.* London: Weidenfeld & Nicolson, 1977. First edition, fine in dust jacket with tiny wear at corners. Mordida Books 81 - 592 2013 $75

Wisdom, John Oulton *The Unconscious Origin of Berkeley's Philosophy.* London: Hogarth Press, 1953. First edition, frontispiece, green publisher's cloth, near fine in very good, lightly soiled dust jacket with tanning to spine and some small chips and tears to extremities. Between the Covers Rare Books, Inc. Philosophy - 101932 2013 $85

Wise, Henry A. *Los Gringos; or an Inside view of Mexico and California with Wanderings in Peru, Chili and Polynesia.* New York: 1850. Second edition, xvi, 453 pages, original stamped boards, foxing, slightly cocked, contemporary owner's name, still tight, very good. Dumont Maps & Books of the West 125 - 80 2013 $100

Wise, Larry *Playette Phone Book.* New York: Playette Corp., 1945. 4to., spiral backed pictorial boards, as new in original pictorial box (flaps repaired), illustrations. Aleph-Bet Books, Inc. 104 - 393 2013 $275

Wiseman, Richard *Eight Chirurgical Treatises on the Following Heads...* London: Benjamin Tooke and Luke Meredith, 1696. Small folio, few short tears, faint dampstaining in few gatherings, wormtrack bottom margin of few gatherings touching a few letters, contemporary paneled calf with blind rulings, skillfully rebacked saving endpapers, raised bands, green gilt label bookplate of John Kirkup, Thomas Marsh, William Viger (ownership signature dated 1751), light marginalia. James Tait Goodrich S74 - 239 2013 $975

Wiseman, Richard *Eight Chirurgical Treaties on these Following Heads Viz. 1. cf. Tumours. II. Cf. Ulcers. III. Cf. Diseases of the Anus. IV. Cf. the King's Evil. V. Cf. wounds. VI. Cf. Gun-Shot Wounds. VII. Cf. Fractures and Luxations. VIII Cf. the Lues Venerea.* London: for B. T. & L. M. and sold by W. Keblewhite and J. Jones, 1697. Third edition, folio, including half title A1, 18th century paneled calf, very skilfully rebacked retaining original gilt spine, period style label, tiny (half inch) repaired tear in lower margin of third leaf, else remarkably fine, fresh copy, contemporary ownership signature of Stewart Sparkes. Joseph J. Felcone Inc. Books Printed before 1701 - 68 2013 $3200

Wiseman, Richard *Eight Chirurgical Treatises on These Following Heads...* London: B. Tooke et al, 1719. 2 volumes, contemporary English panel calf, newly rebacked text with some browning, occasional light dampstaining, otherwise nice, clean tight copy. James Tait Goodrich 75 - 230 2013 $695

Wiseman, Richard *Several Chirurgicall Treatises.* London: E. Flesher and J. Macock for R. Royston, 1676. Half title, small folio, contemporary English panel calf with blind ruling on boards, which have been skilfully rebacked with minor repairs to corners, endpapers saved, small marginal loss in E2, occasional light soiling, staining and short tears in margins, final leaf with large loss in blank margin, touching two letters and laid down, early ownership signatures of William Taylor, from the library of John R. Kirkup with his bookplate. James Tait Goodrich S74 - 238 2013 $2500

Wister, Owen 1860-1938 *Owen Wister's Medicine Bow.* Salisbury: Lime Rock Press, 1981. First edition, deluxe edition, #6/100 copies, signed by photographer on limitation leaf, also signed on frontispiece photograph, with 4 additional 4to. original photos signed on verso and each housed in separate presentation mat, photos by Tryntje Van Ness Seymour, in a separate cloth and board folder with ties is a 'scrapbook' of various items about Wister, his book, The Virginian and Medicine Bow, Wyoming (21 items in all), entirely housed in brown cloth solander box with title stamped to top, fine. Ed Smith Books 78 - 82 2013 $350

The Witches or a Trip to Naples. London: G. Martin 6 Great St. Thomas Apostle, n.d., 1817-1835. based on publisher's address, 4 panels 3 x 7 1/2 inches when folded, fine in original wrapper with printed label housed in custom morocco backed folding box, 4 large sections, each folded over at top and bottom, divided in middle, each section has 4 fine hand colored engraved illustrations and by lifting the flaps the reader reveals the continuation of the story and a new illustration below.   Aleph-Bet Books, Inc.   105 - 310   2013 $15,500

Wither, George   *Extracts from Juvenilia or Poems.* London: printed by George Bigg, 1785. 12mo., final leaf foxed, titlepage dusted and foxed, note 'by Alexander Dalrymple Esq', written under author's name, this appears to have been a stitched pamphlet which in the early 19th century as cased in linen backed drab paper boards, it is loosely attached by thread at rear, pasted to inner edge of final page. covers now worn with some old waterstaining.   Jarndyce Antiquarian Booksellers   CCIV - 318   2013   £150

Withering, William   *An Account of the Foxglove and Some Medical Uses.* London: Broomsleigh Press, Facsimile limited edition of 1785 edition, #240/250 copies, half title and hand colored frontispiece, quarter morocco and linen boards, printed on fine heavy rag paper, uncut and unopened, full folding colored frontispiece.   James Tait Goodrich   75 - 231   2013 $495

Withering, William   *An Account of the Foxglove and Some of Its Medical Uses.* London: M. Sinney for G. G. and J. Robinson, 1785. First edition, Half title and hand colored frontispiece present but detached, original paper backed blue sugar boards, front board off, title handwritten on spine, uncut spine quite worn, paper spine missing from top and bottom compartments, boards spotted and rubbed, folding plate has three short tears not affecting image, some browning and spotting of plate and text, placed in quarter morocco slipcase, rare.   James Tait Goodrich   75 - 232   2013 $12,500

Withering, William   *An Account of the Foxglove and Some of Its Medical Uses.* Birmingham: printed by M. Swinney for G. G. J. and J. Robinson, London, 1785. First edition, large folding hand colored engraved plate, first state with large leaf pointing to right and without signature of artist Sowerby (usually bound as frontispiece, but here, appropriately enough, opposite page with "Of the Plate"), plate with several repairs to a tear from inside margin almost but not quite reaching engraved surface, lower horizontal fold reinforced, some splitting to remaining folds and upper outer portion (a blank area) split along its fold, some foxing, no persistent or heavy, initial leaf blank except for signature a, discarded, but half title present, 8vo., modern brown crushed morocco, single blind rule along outer edges, flat spine, black lettering piece, preserved in cloth folding box, box little worn, sound.   Blackwell's Rare Books   172 - 155   2013   £5500

Witherspoon, John   *A Serious Inquiry into the Nature and Effects of the Stage.* New York: by Whiting & Watson, 1812. First American edition, 171 x 108mm., extremely attractive contemporary flamed sheep, flat spine with simple gilt rules and black morocco label, modern booklabel of Amos Tuck French; minor offsetting throughout text, one gathering rather foxed and browned, isolated stains of no great consequence, internally with some problems caused by inferior paper stock, but most of the text still surprisingly fresh, inexpensive binding in superb condition, unworn and very bright.   Phillip J. Pirages   63 - 497   2013 $700

The Writs Magazine and Attic Miscellany. London: Thomas Tegg, 1818. First and only edition, 20 original parts in 2 volumes, 2 volumes, small octavo, 40 hand colored etchings, 16 by George Cruikshank and 24 by Thomas Rowlandson, elegantly bound circa 1900 by Riviere & Son, full blue crushed levant morocco, upper joint of volume one very slightly cracked but still sound, exceptionally fine, clean.   David Brass Rare Books, Inc.   Holiday 2012 Chapter Two - DB 02094   2013 $11,500

Witte, B.   *Walter Benjamin: an Intellectual Biography.* Detroit: Wayne State University Press, 1991. First edition, previous owner's pencil notations on front fly, else fine in fine dust jacket with price sticker on rear panel.   Between the Covers Rare Books, Inc.   Philosophy - 101957   2013 $75

Witte, Henning   *Memoriae Medicorum Nostri Seculi Clarissimorum Renovatate decas Prima.* Frankfurt am Main: Joannes Andreae for Martin Hallerword, 1676. First edition, frontispiece, eary 19th century boards, some foxing in text, front joint showing wear.   James Tait Goodrich   75 - 236   2013 $495

Wittgenstein, Ludwig   *Remarks on Colour.* Berkeley: University of California Press, 1977. First edition, fine in fine dust jacket with light bumping to extremities.   Between the Covers Rare Books, Inc.   Philosophy - 105279   2013 $50

Wittie, Robert   *Scarbrough-Spaw; or a Description of the nature and Vertues of the Spaw at Scarbrough in Yorkshire.* Charles Tyus at the three Bibles on London Bridge and by Richard Lambert in York..., 1660. First edition, leading edge of titlepage worn and lower corner of some leaves chipped, lacking pages 107-8, 121-122, 125-136, recent full sheep, gilt lettered spine, small 8vo.   Ken Spelman Books Ltd.   73 - 145   2013   £95

Wm. Lloyd Garrison to Chas. Sumner. Review of the Senator's Career. Greeleyism Exposed! Boston: 1872. First edition, tall 8vo. leaflet, 8 pages, single sheet folded to form four leaves, unopened, untrimmed, fine.   M & S Rare Books, Inc.   95 - 312   2013 $300

Wofsey, Tammy *The Pest.* New York: Plotzing Press at Bob Blackburn's Printmaking Workshop, 1998. Artist's book, one of 10 copies, all on Rives BFK paper, each signed and numbered by artist, page size 6 1/2 x 7 x 6.6 inches, 280 pages, 140 double page black and white linoleum cuts, bound by artist accordion fold with pages hinged with Gampi paper with two original linoleum cuts from book inset into green cloth over boards as the ends, housed in custom made black cloth over boards clamshell box (also made by artist), with title in small white paper square lettered in black in center of front panel, clamshell 8 x 8 x 8 inches; there are 10 pages of text printed letterpress starting with five pages at front, including titlepage "The Pest" set in 10 pt. Times New Roman with succeeding pages repeating the title in every increasing point size.   Priscilla Juvelis - Rare Books   56 - 39   2013 $4000

Wolcot, John   1738-1819 *The Convention Bill, an Ode.* London: printed for J. Walker, 1795. 4to., without final ad leaf, disbound, some tears to inner margins rather foxed. Jarndyce Antiquarian Booksellers   CCIV - 319   2013   £35

Wolcot, John   1738-1819 *Hair Powder: a Plaintive Epistle to Mr. Pitt by Peter Pindar, Esq.* London: printed for J. Walker, 1795. First edition, 4to., lacking half title, final leaf foxed an soiled on blank verso, some other occasional foxing, disbound.   Jarndyce Antiquarian Booksellers   CCIV - 320   2013   £35

Wolcot, John   1738-1819 *An Ode to the Livery of London on their Petition to His Majesty for Kicking Out his Worthy Ministers.* London: printed for John Walker, 1797. 4to., disbound.   Jarndyce Antiquarian Booksellers   CCIV - 321   2013   £45

Wolcot, John   1738-1819 *One Thousand Seven Hundred and Ninety-Six.* London: printed for John Walker, 1797. 48 pages 4to., engraved portrait plate mounted on front endpaper and Wolcot's signature, note on titlepage verso states "distinguish the genuine edition from any pirated one that may appear...", lacking final unpaged leaf, disbound, some dusting and light browning to titlepage.   Jarndyce Antiquarian Booksellers   CCIV - 322   2013   £35

Wolcot, John   1738-1819 *The Works of Peter Pindar.* London: Printed for John Walker, 1794-1796. 4 volumes, engraved titlepages, engraved frontispiece, bit foxed in places, extremities touch rubbed, contemporary marbled and polished tree calf, spines gilt in compartments, red and green morocco labels, boards bordered with Greek key roll, marbled endpapers, extremities touch rubbed.   Unsworths Antiquarian Booksellers   28 - 142   2013   £100

Wolcot, John   1738-1819 *The Works of Peter Pindar, Esq.* London: printed for John Walker, 1794-1801. 3 volumes (extended to five), contemporary half calf, labels, attractive set.   Jarndyce Antiquarian Booksellers   CCIV - 323   2013   £150

Wolf, Hieronymus *Demosthenis et Aeschinis Principum Graeciae Oratorum Opera...* Francofurti: Apud Cladium Marnium & Haeredes Iohannis Aubrii, 1604. Second edition, folio, 3 engraved, head and tailpieces, initials, quarter bound alter morocco over marbled paper covered boards, Greek and Latin in parallel columns, scarce, 17 x 11cm. section of titlepage, which includes printer's device, has been excised, leaf neatly repaired, top edge lightly trimmed, boards and spine rubbed, scuffing to top edge, otherwise very clean with occasional cross references pencilled in margins, binding tight, very nice, institutional bookplate noting the book was a gift of Michael J. O'Farrell, first Bishop of the Diocese of Trenton.   Kaaterskill Books   16 - 24   2013 $1000

Wolff, Christian *A Treatise of Algebra, with the Application of It to a Variety of Problems in Arithmetic, to Geometry, Trigonometry and Conic Sections.*   printed for A. Bettersworth and C. Hitch, 1739. First edition in English, 8 folding engraved plates, one or two spots or stains, but crisp copy, 8vo. , contemporary unlettered polished calf, double gilt ruled borders on sides, gilt rules on either side of raised bands on backstrip, trifle worn, short crack at top of upper joint, two signatures inside front cover, earlier being that of Chas. Berkeley the other of Saml. Rippiner, Builder, Oundle May 1850, very good.   Blackwell's Rare Books   Sciences - 131   2013   £750

Wolff, Jens *Sketches and Observations Taken on a Tour Through a Part of the South of Europe.* W. Wilson, 1801. First English edition, quarto, contemporary brown half cloth, vignette on titlepage and in text, very light foxing on titlepage, upper cover detached, clean.   J. & S. L. Bonham Antiquarian Booksellers   Europe - 9870   2013   £190

Wolley, Hannah *The Queen-Like Closet or Rich Cabinet...* London: printed for Richard Lowndes at the White Lion in Duck Lane near West Smithfield, 1672. Second edition, 12mo., prelim license leaf, engraved frontispiece, 12mo., unusually good, clean copy, very slight browning, two tiny ink splashes to book block edge, not intruding onto page surface, expertly bound in sprinkled calf, blind ruled borders, decorative raised bands, contemporary endpapers. Jarndyce Antiquarian Booksellers   CCIV - 33   2013 £4200

Wollstonecraft, Mary   1759-1797 *A Vindication of the Rights of Woman: with Strictures on Political and Moral Subjects.* London: printed for J. Johnson, 1792. Second edition, contemporary mottled calf, gilt bands, slightly chipped red morocco label, spine little rubbed, corners slightly bumped, good plus.   Jarndyce Antiquarian Booksellers   CCV - 292   2013   £1500

Wollstonecraft, Mary   1759-1797 *A Vindication of the Rights of Woman...* London: Unwin, 1891. New edition, 8vo., blue cloth stamped in gilt, cover scuffed and slightly worn at edges and spine, hinges tender, front flyleaf loose, else very good.   Second Life Books Inc.   182 - 261   2013 $65

Womack, Jack *Heathern.* New York: Tor, 1990. First US edition, octavo, boards.   L. W. Currey, Inc.   Utopian Literature: Recent Acquisitions (April 2013) - 139257   2013 $100

Womack, Laurence *Sober Sadness; or Historicall Observations upon the Proceedings, Pretences and Designes of a Prevailing Party in both Houses of Parliament...* London: for W. Webb, 1643. 4to, 19th century sheep backed boards (shabby and broken), internally very good, Buxton Forman's copy with his bookplate.   Joseph J. Felcone Inc.   Books Printed before 1701 - 91   2013 $350

Woman's Christian Temperance Union   *Report of the Convention of the...*   WCTU, 1891-1992. 8vo., 27 volumes, most good or very good condition, most at leas 100 pages, printed wrappers, broken run.   Second Life Books Inc.   183 - 427   2013 $500

Women of all Nations. A Record of Their Characteristics, Habits, Manners, Customs and Influence.   London and elsewhere: Cassell and Co. Ltd., 1908. First edition, 287 x 200mm., 2 volumes, 26 color plates, 54 full page black and white photos and hundreds of other black and white photos in text, pleasing burgundy half morocco, raised bands, spine gilt in double ruled compartments with scrolling cornerpieces, gilt titling, marbled endpapers, top edge gilt, spines just little darkened and faintly dulled, hint of rubbing to extremities, otherwise fine, text clean, fresh and bright and bindings with negligible wear; bookplates of Henry Bartholomay.   Phillip J. Pirages   63 - 498   2013 $450

Women's Democratic Campaign Manual 1924.   Washington: Democratic National Committee, 1924. Small 8vo., 152 pages, ex-library with stamps, paper wrappers, small cartoons at chapter heads, cover little worn especially at spine, some leaves dog-eared, edges soiled, otherwise very good.   Second Life Books Inc.   182 - 15   2013 $65

Wonder ABC Book: Three Jolly Alphabets.   London: Collins circa, 1930. 4to., cloth backed pictorial boards, some rubbing, very good+ illustrations in bright colors by Cecily Stead and EWB.   Aleph-Bet Books, Inc.   104 - 23   2013 $175

Wonderful Doings of Fairy Blackshine and Fairy Whiteshine.   London: Reckitt & Sons, circa, 1915. 16mo., pictorial wrappers, slight rubbing, very good, 4 full page, 1 double page, color illustrated color covers and black and whites by H. M. Brock, rare.   Aleph-Bet Books, Inc.   105 - 93   2013 $225

Wonderful Rum Drinks.   New York: Rums of Puerto Rico, n.d. circa, 1963. 12mo., 16 pages, photos, fine.   Between the Covers Rare Books, Inc.   Cocktails, Etc. - 312648   2013 $50

The Wonders of Nature and Art.   Halifax: Milner and Sowerby, 1862. First edition, 12mo., original blindstamped cloth, gilt, little worn, frontispiece and title, lower joint cracked.   R. F. G. Hollett & Son   Children's Books - 400   2013   £45

Wonders of the Waters.   Religious Tract Society, n.d., Small 8vo., original blue decorated cloth, gilt upper hinge trifle rubbed, woodcut illustrations, hinges tender.   R. F. G. Hollett & Son   Children's Books - 724   2013   £25

Wondriska, William   *A Long Piece of String.*   New York: Holt, Rinehart and Winston, 1963. First edition, small oblong hardcover, fine in very near fine dust jacket with tiny tear to bottom of front panel, very fresh copy, scarce.   Jeff Hirsch Books   Fall 2013 - 19279   2013 $175

Wood, Charles W.   *Glories of Spain.*   London: Macmillan, 1901. First edition, 8vo., illustrations, original green decorative cloth.   J. & S. L. Bonham Antiquarian Booksellers   Europe - 7347   2013   £65

Wood, Clement   *The Greenwich Village Blues.*   New York: Henry Harrison, 1926. First edition, little wear at extremities, front fly lightly offset, very good or better, without dust jacket.   Between the Covers Rare Books, Inc.   New York City - 317107   2013 $65

Wood, Ellen 1814-1887   *East Lynne.*   London: Richard Bentley & son, 1879. 96th thousand, half title, frontispiece, original dark green cloth, blocked in blind, lettered in gilt, signed "Ellen Simons" in contemporary hand, very good, bright.   Jarndyce Antiquarian Booksellers   CCV - 293   2013   £45

Wood, Ellen 1814-1887   *Oswald Cray.*   Edinburgh: Adam and Charles Black, 1864. First edition, 3 volumes, half titles, original dark green morocco grained cloth boards, attractively blocked in blind, gilt spines, very good, presentation inscription from the author "For Harry, from Momma".   Jarndyce Antiquarian Booksellers   CCV - 294   2013   £1200

Wood, John George *Our Living World: an Artistic Edition of the Rev. J. G. Wood's Natural History of Animate Creation.* New York: Selmar Hess circa, 1898. 332 x 249mm., 3 volumes, publisher's black half roan over burgundy buckram, gilt pictorial upper covers with ornate titling, raised bands, spine panels with gilt arabesque centerpiece, textured endpapers, all edges gilt, illustrated titlepage, numerous woodcuts, 84 full page woodcuts and 42 chromolithographic plates, original tissue guards, front flyleaf with penciled ownership inscription of Rebecca and Louise Popper; joints and extremities somewhat rubbed, three inch crack in one joint, front board of volume I nearly detached, three boards with scattering of small white spots, occasional mild foxing or marginal stains, other minor imperfections, bindings obviously with condition issues, but internally excellent copy, richly colored plates and few signs of use. Phillip J. Pirages   63 - 499   2013 $450

Wood, Lawson *The Lawson Wood Nursery Rhyme Book.* Thomas Nelson, n.d. circa, 1930. First edition, small 4to., original cloth backed glazed pictorial boards, little scratched, edges slightly worn, 7 thick board leaves with rounded corners, 16 color plates.   R. F. G. Hollett & Son   Children's Books - 725   2013   £75

Wood, Nicholas *A Practical Treatise on Rail-Roads...* London: printed for Longman, Rees, Orme, Brown and Green, 1832. Second edition, 235 x 146mm., attractive recent retrospective half calf over marbled boards, raised bands, spine with red morocco title label, edges untrimmed, 11 plates, 8 of them folding, folding table, small paper repair to titlepage, 3 one inch tears to folds of table, 2 leaves with minor tears to fore edge, errata leaf missing tip of lower corner, otherwise fine, clean and fresh internally and in unworn, sympathetic binding.   Phillip J. Pirages   63 - 387   2013 $500

Wood, Thomas *The Mosaic Creation.* W. Baynes, 1811. 8vo., some light foxing but good, contemporary half calf, marbled boards, gilt label, spine and corners rather rubbed. Ken Spelman Books Ltd.   75 - 67   2013   £85

Woodall, John *The Surgeons Mate or Military and Domestique Surgery...* London: Robert Young (J. Legate? and E. Purslowe) for Nicholas Bourne, 1639. Modern calf by Period bookbinders, blind tooling on boards, done in contemporary style, early signature of John Spence, some marginalia, Bath Medical Library with few marginal stamps. James Tait Goodrich   S74 - 240   2013 $3750

Woodhull, Victoria *The Human Body The Temple of God; or The Philosophy of Sociology....* London: 1890. First edition, 8vo., 618 pages, maroon cloth, stamped in gilt, 2 frontispiece portraits, several engravings, hinges tender, half title and flyleaf loose, cover little worn at edges and ends of spine, otherwise very good, very scarce.   Second Life Books Inc.   182 - 267   2013 $1200

Woodhull, Victoria *The Human Body the Temple of God...* London: 1890. First edition, 8vo., 618 pages, maroon cloth, stamped in gilt, 2 frontispiece portraits, several engravings, hinges tender, half title and flyleaf loose, cover little worn at edges and ends of spine, otherwise very good, very scarce. Second Life Books Inc.   183 - 428   2013 $1200

Woodhull, Victoria *The Origin, Tendencies and Principles of Government; or a Review of the Rise and Fall of Nations...* New York: Woodhull, Claflin, 1871. First edition, 8vo., 247 pages, rust cloth stamped in gilt, frontispiece, cover scuffed and little worn at corners and ends of spine, otherwise very good, very scarce.   Second Life Books Inc. 182 - 268   2013 $750

Woodiwiss, John Cecil *Some New Ghost Stories.* London: Simpkin Marshall, 1931. First edition, octavo, original pictorial gray boards, front and spine panels printed in black.   L. W. Currey, Inc.   Wandering Ghosts & Itinerant Souls (10/12) - 119092   2013 $450

Woodleigh House or the Happy Holidays.   T. Nelson and Sons, 1852. 12mo., original blindstamped crimson cloth gilt, hinges trifle rubbed, engraved title, 6 engraved vignette plates (rather foxed).   R. F. G. Hollett & Son   Children's Books - 24   2013   £35

Woodrell, Daniel *Woe to Live On.* New York: Henry Holt Co., 1987. First edition, fine in fine dust jacket, signed by author, beautiful copy.   Between the Covers Rare Books, Inc.   Mystery & Detective Fiction - 306964   2013 $375

Woodroffe, Patrick *A Closer Look at the Art and Techniques of Patrick Woodroffe.* Limpsfield: Dragon's World, 1986. First softback edition, 4to., original pictorial stiff wrappers, illustrations in color.   R. F. G. Hollett & Son   Children's Books - 726   2013   £25

Woodruff, Elizabeth *Dickey Byrd.* Springfield: Milton Bradley, 1928. First edition, folio, black imitation leather stamped in yellow, very good+, scarce, 6 large and magnificent tipped in color plates, plus many charming full page and in text illustrations by Tenggren and Wehde.   Aleph-Bet Books, Inc.   104 - 551   2013 $875

Woods, Daniel B. *Sixteen Months at the Gold Diggings.* New York: Harper & Brothers, 1851. First edition, 12mo., original cloth, ends of spine chipped, some severe browning, particularly to lower corners, sound if not especially attractive copy.   M & S Rare Books, Inc.   95 - 49   2013 $225

Woods, Margaret Louisa *The Invader.* New York and London: Harper & Bros., 1907. First US edition, titlepage printed in orange and black, original pictorial light orange cloth, front cover stamped in gray, white and black, spine panel stamped in white and black.   L. W. Currey, Inc. Wandering Ghosts & Itinerant Souls (10/12) - 111342   2013 $150

Woodson, Carter Godwin *The Negro in Our History.* Washington: Associated Publishers, 1962. Tenth edition, extensively illustrated, facing pages roughly opened resulting in tiny chips, else near fine, spine faded, very good dust jacket, with internal repairs to flap folds.   Between the Covers Rare Books, Inc.   165 - 291   2013 $375

Woodward, Daniel *The Key to the Goodman Encyclopedia of the California Gold Rush Fleet.* Los Angeles: Fleeting Gold Press for the Zamorano Club, 1996. One of 275 (of total 375) copies, large 8vo., (7)ff., 17 folded charts, loose, housed in original folding pictorial wrappers within gilt stamped blue cloth case front cover inset ship pictorial, mint.   Jeff Weber Rare Books   171 - 57   2013 $90

Woodward, J. J. *The Medical and Surgical History of the War of the Rebellion 1861-1865.* Washington: 1870-1888. Mixed set with some second issue volumes, 6 volumes, in large 4to., binding states mixed with some being ex-library, several volumes recased, one volume rebound in new green cloth, matching original style.   James Tait Goodrich   75 - 47   2013 $1500

Woodward, J. J. *The Medical and Surgical History of the War of the Rebellion 1861-1865. Volume II Part III Surgical History.* Washington: 1883. Second issue, large 4to., original green cloth, binding showing shelfwear, internally very good.   James Tait Goodrich   75 - 46   2013 $700

Woodward, John *The State of Physick and of Diseases with an Inquiry into the Causes of the late Increase of them, but More Particularly of the Small-Pox.* London: printed for T. Horne, 1718. First edition, full contemporary calf gilt panelled spine, head of spine neatly repaired, author's presentation for Thomas Hearne.   James Tait Goodrich   75 - 237   2013 $1500

Woodward, Llewellyn *British Foreign Policy in the Second World War.* London: HMSO, 1970-1976. First edition, 5 volumes, 4to., brown cloth, minor dustiness to edges of text block, brown cloth, minor dustiness to edges of text block, very good, dust jackets in protective plastic, few signs of use, very good, dust jacket of volume IV with tape to spine, folds adhered to pastedowns with tape, ownership inscription of John Charmley, volume IV ex-libris copy with associated plates and stamps.   Unsworths Antiquarian Booksellers   28 - 206   2013   £200

Woodward, W. E. *Bread and Circuses.* New York: Harper, 1925. First edition, fine in lightly used dust jacket.   Beasley Books   2013 - 2013 $50

Woodward, Woody *Jazz Americana.* Los Angeles: Trend Books, 1956. First edition, illustrations, wrappers, 128 pages, close to fine.   Beasley Books   2013 - 2013 $50

Wool, Christopher *Psychopts.* New York: J Mc & GHB, 2008. Copy 37 from an edition of only 50 in this format, fine in fine dust jacket and fine slipcase, signed by Wood and Richard Hell.   Jeff Hirsch Books   Fall 2013 - 129136   2013 $350

Woolf, Virginia   1882-1941 *Granite and Rainbow.* London: Hogarth Press, 1958. First edition, 222 x 140mm., publisher's blue cloth with gilt titling on flat spine, original dust jacket designed by Vanessa Bell, spine of jacket just beginning to turn a creamier color than side panels, two extremely faint indications of creasing at top of back cover of jacket, otherwise nearly mint, very fine jacket, especially clean and bright.   Phillip J. Pirages   63 - 500   2013 $450

Woolf, Virginia   1882-1941 *The Moment and Other Essays.* London: Hogarth Press, 1947. First edition, crown 8vo., 192 pages, original maroon cloth, backstrip gilt blocked, tail of front pastedown just little wrinkled, tail edges rough trimmed, dust jacket, sunned, trifle chipped as usual, very good.   Blackwell's Rare Books   B174 - 313   2013   £150

Woolf, Virginia   1882-1941 *A Room of One's Own.* London: published by Leonard and Virginia Woolf at Hogarth Press, 1929. First edition, small octavo, original cinnamon cloth lettered gilt on spine, original pale pink dust jacket designed by Vanessa Bell, jacket spine very lightly sunned, minor offsetting to front free endpaper, some light foxing to edges of text block, near fine.   Heritage Book Shop Holiday Catalogue 2012 - 162   2013 $6500

Woolf, Virginia   1882-1941 *Three Guineas.* New York: Harcourt Brace and Co., 1938. First American edition issued in same year as London printing, 208 x 138mm., publisher's pink cloth, original dust jacket designed by Vanessa Bell, five black and white photo plates, jacket with scarcely noticeable tiny pinholes (apparently from thumb tacks?) but very fine in otherwise fine dust jacket with just hint of darkening to spine.   Phillip J. Pirages   63 - 501   2013 $400

Woolf, Virginia   1882-1941 *To the Lighthouse.* Hogarth Press, 1927. First edition, prelims just little foxed, crown 8vo., pages 320, original light blue cloth, backstrip gilt lettered, light partial browning to free endpapers, with expert cleaning and restoration of the dust jacket mainly to backstrip panel, where tears have been repaired in folds and to its head and tail, near fine.   Blackwell's Rare Books   B174 - 314   2013   £6850

Woolf, Virginia   1882-1941 *The Years.* London: published by Leonard and Virginia Woolf at the Hogarth Press, 1937. First edition, 191 x 127mm., publisher's light green cloth, printed dust jacket, very faint uniform darkening to jacket spine, otherwise especially fine in very fine dust jacket, virtually faultless inside and out.   Phillip J. Pirages   63 - 502   2013 $5500

Woolf, Virginia 1882-1941 *The Years.* London: Hogarth Press, 1937. First edition, half title little browned in part, foolscap 8vo., original sea green cloth, front endpapers foxed, dust jacket little foxed backstrip panel lightly browned and very small stain to head of front fold, good. Blackwell's Rare Books   B174 - 315   2013   £800

Woolf, Virginia 1882-1941 *The Years.* Hogarth Press, 1937. First edition, foolscap 8vo., original sea green cloth, backstrip gilt lettered, Vanessa Bell designed dust jacket with backstrip panel lightly browned, little chipped at head and tail, tiny hole, panels trifle dust soiled.   Blackwell's Rare Books   172 - 248   2013   £900

Woolman, John *A Journal of the Life, Gospel Labours and Christian Experiences of that Faithful Minister of Jesus Christ, John Woolman...* Dublin: printed b R. Jackson at the Globe, 1776. First Irish edition, 8vo., some occasional browning mainly offsetting from turn-ins, full contemporary calf raised bands, hinges racked but firm, spine rubbed and worn at head and tail, lacking label, corners bumped. Jarndyce Antiquarian Booksellers   CCIV - 324   2013   £150

Woolnough, C. W. *A Pretty Mysterious Art. A Lecture.* Denby Dale: Fleece Press, 1996. One of 270 copies (of an edition of 300), printed on grey Cross Pointe paper in black with title, list of samples and fly-title in red, 10 samples of marbled papers tipped in, 16mo., original quarter yellow cloth, printed label, marbled boards, untrimmed, terracotta linen fold down back box with printed label, fine. Blackwell's Rare Books   172 - 284   2013   £80

Woolrich, Cornell *Angels of Darkness.* New York: Mysterious Press, 1978. First edition, one of 250 numbered copies signed by author of introduction, Harlan Ellison, very fine in dust jacket and slipcase.   Mordida Books   81 - 600   2013 $150

Woolrich, Cornell *The Best of William Irish.* Philadelphia: Lippincott, 1944. First edition, fine in lightly rubbed, very good plus dust jacket with bit of rubbing and two parallel but unobtrusive tears, scarce.   Between the Covers Rare Books, Inc. Mystery & Detective Fiction - 24064   2013 $157

Woolrich, Cornell *"Black Cargo." in Argosy Weekly July 1937.* New York: Frank A. Munsey, 1937. Small chip at base of spine, else very good.   Mordida Books   81 - 593   2013 $75

Woolrich, Cornell *Darkness at Dawn.* Carbondale: Southern Illinois University Press, 1985. First edition, lovely copy, fine in fine dust jacket.   Between the Covers Rare Books, Inc. Mystery & Detective Fiction - 287149   2013 $65

Woolrich, Cornell *The Doom Stone.* New York: Avon, 1960. First edition, paperback original Avon No. T408, very fine unread copy in wrappers.   Mordida Books   81 - 597   2013 $100

Woolrich, Cornell *First You Dream Then You Die.* New York: Mysterious Press, 1988. First edition, very fine in dust jacket.   Mordida Books   81 - 601   2013 $65

Woolrich, Cornell *Hotel Room.* New York: Random House, 1958. First edition, fine in price clipped dust jacket with closed tear.   Mordida Books   81 - 596   2013 $150

Woolrich, Cornell *"Men Must Die." in Black Mask Augsut 1939.* London: Atlas, 1939. Stamp on front cover, else near fine.   Mordida Books   81 - 594   2013 $85

Woolrich, Cornell *Nightwebs.* New York: Harper, 1971. First edition, fine in dust jacket.   Mordida Books   81 - 599   2013 $100

Woolrich, Cornell *Strangler's Serenade.* New York: Rinehart, 1951. First edition, some faint darkening on endpapers, otherwise fine in very good dust jacket with tape mark on front and rear flaps and three quarter inch strip missing at top of inner front flap.   Mordida Books   81 - 595   2013 $150

Woolrich, Cornell *The Ten Faces of Cornell Woolrich.* New York: Simon and Schuster, 1965. First edition, fine in dust jacket with couple of tiny tears.   Mordida Books   81 - 598   2013 $200

Woolrich, Cornell *A Young Man's Heart.* New York: Mason Pub. Co., 1930. First edition, trifle sunned at crown, still easily fine in very attractive, very good dust jacket with chip at crown which affects the "A" of title, very scarce in jacket.   Between the Covers Rare Books, Inc. Mystery & Detective Fiction - 33846   2013 $1750

Woolsey, Edward John *Specimens of Fancy Turning Executed on the Head or Foot Lathe...* Philadelphia: Henry Carey Baird, 1869. First edition, 4to., 30 plates with photographic copies of various sizes laid down, a number of plates little creased, original green cloth, slightly dulled, very good.   Jarndyce Antiquarian Booksellers   CCV - 295   2013   £950

Worcester, G. R. G. *The Junks and Sampans of the Yangtze.* Shanghai: Statistical Department of the Inspectorate General of Customs, 1947. 2 volumes, 4to., xxviii, 245 pages; xv, 247-506 pages, rare, in particularly nice condition, near fine in original green cloth with gilt lettered spine ad front covers, minimal cover edgewear toning to endpapers and page edges.   By the Book, L. C.   36 - 94   2013 $1250

Worcester, G. R. G. *The Junks and Sampans of the Yangtze. A Study in Chinese Nautical Research. China. the Maritime Customs III. Miscellaneous Series. No. 53 and 54.* Shanghai: Statistical Dept. of the Inspectorate General of Customs, 1947. First edition thus, 4to., original green cloth with gilt lettered spine and front covers, minimal cover edge wear, toning to endpapers and page edges, rare set, particularly in such nice condition. By the Book, L. C. 38 - 74 2013 $1250

A Word of Advice to Honest Country People. sold by G. and W. Nicol, Messrs. Rivington and Darton and Harvey, printed by W. Bulmer, 1800. Titlepage browned, 12mo., disbound, good. Blackwell's Rare Books 172 - 44 2013 £450

Wordsworth, Christopher *Athens & Attica: a Journal of a Resistance There.* London: John Murray, 1836. First edition, 8vo., frontispiece, map, 2 lithographic plates, folding table, inscriptions to some foxing to the frontispiece and plates, otherwise fine, Marquis of Camden's copy. J. & S. L. Bonham Antiquarian Booksellers Europe - 9215 2013 £400

Wordsworth, William 1770-1850 *Lyrical Ballads with Other Poems.* London: T. N. Longman and O. Rees, 1800. Second edition, first edition, 2 volumes, volume I titlepage torn and carefully repaired, fly title to The Idiot Boy (pages 105/106) in facsimile, small hole in final leaf of text (page 215) affecting the word 'everywhere' in line 1, volume II titlepage torn in upper right corner and carefully repaired, final leaf of text (pages 227/228) torn with loss along lower margin not affecting text, well bound in 20th century full pigskin over rather thick boards, spines with raised bands, lettered and devices in gilt, good plus, scarce. Jarndyce Antiquarian Booksellers CCIII - 511 2013 £1500

Wordsworth, William 1770-1850 *Lyrical Ballads.* London: Duckworth & Co., 1898. Half title, frontispiece, plate, 4 pages ads (June 1898), original light brown cloth, spine lettered in gilt, slightly dulled. Jarndyce Antiquarian Booksellers CCIII - 512 2013 £25

Wordsworth, William 1770-1850 *Memorials of a Tour on the Continent, 1820.* London: Longman, Hurst, Rees, Orme and Brown, 1822. First edition, tall 8vo., 4 pages ads dated March 1822, untrimmed and bound with half title, contemporary boards, rebacked with later cloth and leather label, contemporary ownership signature of Hannah Hoare. Second Life Books Inc. 183 - 431 2013 $1250

Wordsworth, William 1770-1850 *Poems, in Two Volumes.* London: printed for Longman Hurst Rees & Orme, 1807. First edition, 2 volumes, 8vo., original drab boards with pink paper covered spines as issued, one of 500 copies printed, with cancels D11-12 in volume I and B2 in volume II, Volume I has half title and erratum leaf H8, Volume II has half title, sectional half title B1 and first sheet F9 (i) volume 2, contemporary ownership inscription to Anne Watson in volume I with her pencil ownership signature on titlepage, bookplates of Simon Nowell-Smith and his wife, light foxing, covers slightly chipped and worn, but very good. James S. Jaffe Rare Books Fall 2013 - 152 2013 $27,500

Wordsworth, William 1770-1850 *The Complete Poetical Works.* Boston and New York: Houghton Mifflin, 1910-1911. Large paper edition, one of 500 copies, 10 volumes, 279 x 159mm., lovely dark olive brown three quarter crushed morocco, handsomely gilt, marbled sides and endpapers, raised bands, spine compartments, densely gilt with floral and foliate tools emanating from a large central rose, top edge gilt, other edges untrimmed, entirely unopened, vignette titlepage, map, 75 photogravure plates with letterpress tissue guards, including one hand colored plate at beginning with duplicates a black and white plate elsewhere in the volume, titlepage in red and black, each volume with tipped in bookplate of Fannie May Howard; in remarkably fine condition, essentially without any wear, virtually pristine internally and obviously used so little that volumes open unwillingly. Phillip J. Pirages 63 - 503 2013 $3500

Wordsworth, William 1770-1850 *The Prelude or Growth of a Poet's Mind.* London: Edward Moxon, 1850. First edition, 8vo., original brown cloth, blocked in blind, preserved in folding box, inscribed by Cyril Connolly for Noel Blakiston Jan 17.27, very good, lower joint splitting, extremities worn, plain and large earlier bookplate, issue without publisher's ads. Maggs Bros. Ltd. 1460 - 177 2013 £650

Wordsworth, William 1770-1850 *Yarrow Revisited and Other Poems.* London: Longman, Rees, Orme, Brown, Green and Longman, 1835. First edition, presentation copy, inscribed by author to Eliza M. Hamilton as a token of affectionate esteem from W. M. Wordsworth on a slip of paper pasted to verso of title and with "From the Author" written on half title by publisher's clerk, erratum slip tipped in, ads discarded, 12mo., slightly later 19th century olive pebble grain morocco by Tuckett ('binder to the Queen'), backstrip panelled and ruled in gilt and infilled with volutes and other tools, lettered in gilt in second compartment, sides with triple gilt fillet borders, inner panel with cornerpieces and central panels of curving lines, all edges gilt, marbled endpapers, booklabel of J. O. Edwards, small scrape to upper board, extremities slightly rubbed, good. Blackwell's Rare Books B174 - 159 2013 £3500

World's Columbian Exposition Chicago 1893. 4to., cloth spine, slight edge wear, else fine, chromolithographed covers open to reveal multi-dimensional pop-ups. Aleph-Bet Books, Inc. 104 - 448 2013 $675

World Federation of Trade Union *IInd World Trade Union Congress 28 June; 9 July 1949. Report of Proceedings.* Paris: World Federation of Trade Union, 1949. First edition, wrappers, 760 pages, good+ with chipping and front wrapper missing. Beasley Books 2013 - 2013 $50

Wormald, B. H. G. *Clarendon: Politics Historiography and.* Cambridge University Press, 1989. New edition, 8vo., cloth, dust jacket, near fine, initialled presentation from author. C. P. Hyland 261 - 189 2013 £50

Worsley, Henry *Juvenile Depravity.* London: Charles Gilpin, 1849. First edition, 210 x 133mm., pleasing recent half calf over marbled paper boards, raised bands, original cloth spine label pasted in second spine panel, one leaf creased in corner, occasional very minor marginal soiling, fine, internally very clean and well preserved, retrospective binding unworn. Phillip J. Pirages 63 - 295 2013 $350

Wotton, Henry *Reliquiae Wottonianae; or a Collection of Lives, Letters, Poems.* London: by T. Roycroft for R. Marriott, 1672. Third edition, 8vo., portraits, 19th century red morocco, early signatures of J. Grien? 1725, Thomas Price and John Francis Cole, 1828, bookplates of J. J. Chapman and Molly Flagg Gibb, very good. Joseph J. Felcone Inc. English and American Literature to 1800 - 26 2013 $900

Wotton, Henry *Reliquiae Wottonianae. Or a Collection of Lives, Letters, Poems...* by T. Rycroft for R. Marriott, 1672. Third edition, 8vo., some light browning and very faint old waterstaining to few leaves, bound in handsome recent full panelled calf, raised and gilt banded spine with morocco label, several leaves of preface misbound, original error, noted by 17th century manuscript footnote. Ken Spelman Books Ltd. 75 - 7 2013 £195

Wraxall, Nathaniel William 1751-1831 *The Historical and the Posthumous Memoirs.* London: Bickers and Son, 1884. 5 volumes, 221 x 149mm., pleasing contemporary dark plum half morocco over marbled boards by Riviere & Son (stamp signed on verso of front free endpaper), raised bands, spines gilt in compartments with delicate fleuron centerpiece, gilt titling, marbled endpapers, top edge gilt, 14 engraved portraits, front pastedown with faint discoloration, apparently from bookplate removal, 2 joints with bit of rubbing, paper boards little chafed and with some light soiling, leaves faintly browned at right edges (because of quality of paper stock), otherwise quite excellent set, text fresh and clean with few signs of use, attractive bindings with no significant wear. Phillip J. Pirages 63 - 504 2013 $375

Wraxall, Nathaniel William 1751-1831 *Memoirs of the Courts of Berlin, Dresden, Warsaw and Vienna in the Years 1777, 1778 and 1779.* London: T. Cadell, 1806. Third edition, 2 volumes, 8vo., contemporary tan decorative full calf, joints rubbed. J. & S. L. Bonham Antiquarian Booksellers Europe - 8950 2013 £75

Wray, J. Jackson *Nestleton Magna: a Story of Yorkshire Methodism.* London: Cassell Petter & Galpin, n.d. 1880's, Original blue pictorial cloth gilt, extremities trifle rubbed, ex-library with usual labels removed and few stamps. R. F. G. Hollett & Son Wesleyan Methodism - 52 2013 £25

Wren, Percival Christopher *Mysterious Ways.* New York: Frederick Stokes, 1930. First American edition, fine in dust jacket with short closed tear. Mordida Books 81 - 602 2013 $200

Wrench, Richard *Eminent Divines. Biographical and Critical Sketches of Richard Watson and Robert Hall.* Selby: Brown and Frobisher, 1861. 80 pages, good, 8vo., disbound. Ken Spelman Books Ltd. 73 - 156 2013 £25

Wright, Allen Kendrick *To the Poles by Airship or Around the World Endways.* Los Angeles: Ca. Baumgardt Pub. Co., 1909. First edition, octavo, frontispiece, one illustration in text, original green cloth, front panel stamped in white. L. W. Currey, Inc. Utopian Literature: Recent Acquisitions (April 2013) - 137411 2013 $750

Wright, Barton *Hallmarks of the Southwest.* West Chester: Schiffer Pub., 1989. First edition, red cloth, very fine with color pictorial dust jacket, presentation copy signed by author. Argonaut Book Shop Recent Acquisitions June 2013 - 319 2013 $125

Wright, Barton *Kachinas of the Zuni.* Flagstaff: Northland Press and the Southwest Museum, 1985. First edition, oblong 4to., xiv, 151 pages, original paintings by Duane Dishta, black cloth, very fine, pictorial dust jacket. Argonaut Book Shop Recent Acquisitions June 2013 - 320 2013 $200

Wright, Barton *The Unchanging Hopi.* Flagstaff: Northland Press, 1975. First edition, limited to 100 copies with original signed scratch board drawing by Barton Wright, this no. 60, quarter black cloth and tan marbled paper covers, silver lettering spine, set in Linotype Granjon and Garamond display, bound at Roswell Bookbinding, fine original matching paper covered slipcase, small 4to., 109 pages, with ANS by Wright laid in, fine copy. By the Book, L. C. 36 - 27 2013 $200

Wright, Barton *The Unchanging Hopi.* Flagstaff: Northland Press, 1975. First edition, quarto, x, 109 page, illustrations, black cloth, very fine with pictorial dust jacket. Argonaut Book Shop Recent Acquisitions June 2013 - 321 2013 $75

Wright, Charles *Yard Journal. Poem.* Richmond: Laurel Press, 1986. First edition, one of 30 copies (entire edition) printed on Rives and signed by Wright and Freed, as new, 4to., 7 colored intaglio etchings by David Freed, original quarter leather and boards, publisher's slipcase. James S. Jaffe Rare Books   Fall 2013 - 154   2013 $1500

Wright, Dare *Edith and Little Bear Ned a Hand.* New York: Random House, 1972. First edition, folio, pictorial boards, near fine in slightly worn dust jacket, illustrations by author.   Aleph-Bet Books, Inc.   105 - 593   2013 $300

Wright, Dare *Holiday for Edith and the Bears.* New York: Doubleday, 1958. Stated first edition, folio, cloth backed photographic boards, slight edgewear, else very good+ in slightly worn dust jacket, photos by author.   Aleph-Bet Books, Inc.   104 - 591   2013 $300

Wright, Dare *Lona: a Fairy Tale.* London: Oldbourne, 1964. First UK edition, folio pictorial boards, fine in slightly frayed dust jacket, illustrations by author with photos. Aleph-Bet Books, Inc.   104 - 175   2013 $250

Wright, E. H. *Andre Besnard: A tale of Old Cork.* Cork: Mahony, 1889. First edition, 8vo., 3 plates absent, original wrappers under 20th century cloth.   C. P. Hyland   261 - 879   2013   £150

Wright, Esther Clark *Planters and Pioneers: Nova Scotia 1749-1775.* Wolfville: Printed in Hantsport, N.S., by Lancelot Press Limited, 1982. Second printing, 8vo., green card covers, very good.   Schooner Books Ltd.   102 - 100   2013 $75

Wright, Frances   1795-1852 *Course of Popular Lectures as Delivered by Frances Wright, in New York, Philadelphia, Baltimore, Boston, Cincinnati....* New York: printed at the office of the Free Enquirer, Hall of Science, 1831. Fourth edition, 12mo., original drab paper over boards, pink linen spine and printed spine label, bit soiled, browning on pastedowns, generally very good, tight copy, scarce.   Second Life Books Inc.   182 - 270   2013 $1250

Wright, Frances   1795-1852 *Introductory Address Delivered by Frances Wright at the Opening of the Hall of Science, New York on Sunday April 26, 1829.* New York: George H. Evans, 1829. First edition, 8vo., pages 18, sewn but removed from a nonce volume, lightly browned, very good, clean copy, scarce.   Second Life Books Inc.   183 - 434   2013 $450

Wright, Frances   1795-1852 *Parting Address as Delivered in the Bowery Theatre to the People of New York in June 1830.* New York: printed at the office of the Free Enquirer, Hall of Science, 1830. First edition, 8vo., 22 pages, sewn self wrappers, fine, scarce.   Second Life Books Inc.   182 - 271   2013 $450

Wright, Frances   1795-1852 *Views of Society and Manners in America.* New York: Bliss and White, 1821. First American edition, 8vo. original burled calf, maroon spine title band, some foxing, cover and spine edges rubbed, hinges tender, otherwise very good.   Second Life Books Inc.   183 - 95   2013 $450

Wright, Frances   1795-1852 *Views of Society and Manners in America...* London: Longman, 1822. Second edition, 8vo., modern full cloth, name stamp on endpaper, former owner's name on 'James Bowley', very good, tight copy.   Second Life Books Inc.   183 - 432   2013 $225

Wright, George R. *The Last Day at Leeds!* printed for private circulation only, 1863. 8vo., original wrappers, covers dusty and little chipped, scarce.   Ken Spelman Books Ltd.   73 - 77   2013   £25

Wright, J. S. *The Prairie Farmer...* Chicago: J. S. Wright, 1846. Volume #1-12 Jan. -Dec. 1846, 12 issues, rare, tall 8vo., 384 pages, illustrations, contemporary three quarter calf and cloth, ex-Newbery Library with bookplate and release stamp.   M & S Rare Books, Inc.   95 - 61   2013 $1350

Wright, James *Two Citizens.* New York: Farrar, Straus and Giroux, 1973. First edition, uncorrected proof, near fine in wrappers, with publisher information sheets affixed to front panel.   Jeff Hirsch Books   Fall 2013 - 129510   2013 $65

Wright, Jay *The Homecoming Singer.* New York: Corinth, 1971. First edition, fine in somewhat rubbed, near fine dust jacket, scarce hardcover.   Between the Covers Rare Books, Inc.   165 - 293   2013 $150

Wright, L. R. *The Suspect.* Toronto: Doubleday, 1985. First Canadian edition, name stamped on front endpaper, else fine in dust jacket.   Mordida Books   81 - 603   2013 $150

Wright, Lyle H. *American Fiction 1774-1900.* San Marino: Huntington Library 1969, 1965. 1966. Second edition of volume 1, first editions of volumes 2 and 3, 3 volumes, grey, red and blue cloth respectively, top corner of few leaves crunched, else very fine set with spine faded printed dust jackets.   Argonaut Book Shop   Recent Acquisitions June 2013 - 322   2013 $225

Wright, Richard   1908-1960 *Black Boy.* New York: Harper & Brothers, 1947. First edition, tiny ink price on front fly, gilt on spine little rubbed, very good, in nice, very good dust jacket with few small chips and internally repaired tear.   Between the Covers Rare Books, Inc.   165 - 338   2013 $750

Wright, Richard 1908-1960 *The Outsider.* London: Sydney: Angus and Robertson, 1954. First Australian edition, stains on fore edge, else near fine in price clipped, good dust jacket with some shallow chipping at extremities. Between the Covers Rare Books, Inc. 165 - 294 2013 $75

Wright, Thomas 1859-1936 *The Life of William Blake.* Olney, Bucks: Thomas Wright, 1929. First edition, 2 volumes, 4to., half titles, frontispieces and plates, original dark green cloth, lettered gilt, occasional small mark, otherwise near fine. Jarndyce Antiquarian Booksellers CCIII - 11 2013 £85

Wright, Willard Huntington 1888-1939 *The Garden Murder Case.* New York: Scribners, 1935. First edition, bottom corners slightly bumped, still fine in rubbed, very good dust jacket with some modest nicking at extremities, Advance Review copy with slip laid in, mystery writer Henry C. Beck's copy with his ownership signature. Between the Covers Rare Books, Inc. Mystery & Detective Fiction - 39296 2013 $400

Wright, Willard Huntington 1888-1939 *The Winter Murder Case.* New York: Charles Scribner's Sons, 1936. First edition, bookplate and some marks on pastedown from old jacket protector, else near fine in about very good dust jacket with shallow loss to crown and some shallow chips on front panel and rear flap. Between the Covers Rare Books, Inc. Mystery & Detective Fiction - 291100 2013 $200

Wright, William *A History of the Comstock Silver Lode & Mines.* Virginia, Nevada: Boegle, 1889. First edition, 12mo., 158 pages, original grey wrappers printed in black, foot of spine with small chip to fore-edge of front wrapper slightly rough, wrappers bit darkened, overall fine copy of this fragile book. Argonaut Book Shop Recent Acquisitions June 2013 - 216 2013 $425

Wright, William *Washoe Rambles.* Los Angeles: Westernlore Press, 1963. First book edition, one of 100 copies, 169 pages, 9 illustrations, map endpapers, brown cloth, very fine with pictorial dust jacket. Argonaut Book Shop Recent Acquisitions June 2013 - 217 2013 $50

Wrisberg, Henry *Observationes Anatomicae de Qvinto Pare Nervorvm Encephali et de Nervis qvi Eodem Dvram Matrem Ingredi Falso Dicvntve.* Goettingae: apud Joann Christian Dietriech, 1777. 28 pages plus folding anatomical plate, 4to., uncut in recent marbled wrappers, rare. James Tait Goodrich 75 - 235 2013 $495

Wrisberg, Henry *Vena Azyga Dyplici Allisquve Hvivs Venae Varietatibvs.* Gottingae: apud Joann Christian Dieterich, 1778. 22 pages, folding anatomical plate, tall 4to., uncut, beautifully detailed engravings, some light foxing, else fine in recent marbled wrappers, extremely uncommon. James Tait Goodrich 75 - 234 2013 $395

Wunderlich, Paul *Paul Wunderlich.* Offenbach am Main: Edtion Voker Huber, 1981-1983. 4 complete cloth portfolio cases, each with loose title, justification page in German, 3 original lithographs, each numbered as one of 1000 and signed in pencil by Wunderlich, total number of lithographs is 12, 11 of which are in colors, all printed on Rives wove paper, each litho size 60 x 48cm., in excellent condition. Gemini Fine Books & Arts., Ltd. Art Reference & Illustrated Books - 2013 $3000

Wyeth, Betsy James *The Stray.* New York: Farrar Straus, Giroux, 1979. First edition, signed with original drawing on titlepage by Jamie Wyeth, octavo, color pictorial dust jacket, black and white illustrations, publisher's full orange cloth, spine lettered gilt, blue endpapers, book about fine, dust jacket with some minor toning, otherwise about fine. Heritage Book Shop Holiday Catalogue 2012 - 153 2013 $500

Wyeth, John *Wyeth's Repository of Sacred Music. Part Second.* Harrisburg: John Wyeth, 1813. First edition, oblong 8vo., 133 pages, contemporary calf backed boards, very worn, front cover becoming loose and cracked, corners of text bent and browned with some light staining, limp, complete and unsophisticated and very rare. M & S Rare Books, Inc. 95 - 246 2013 $2000

Wyler, Michael *A Glimpse at the Past.* UK: Jazz Publications, 1957. First edition, number 270 of a limited edition, paperback, illustrations, wrappers, 32 pages, printed on rectos only, fine. Beasley Books 2013 - 2013 $50

Wylie, Elinor 1885-1928 *Nets to Catch the Wind.* New York: Harcourt Brace and Co., 1921. First edition, 12mo., 47 pages, original two toned brown cloth, offsetting from paper on title, otherwise fine. M & S Rare Books, Inc. 95 - 400 2013 $1000

Wylie, Philip *Corpses at Indian Stones.* New York: Farrar and Rinehart, 1943. First edition, little offsetting from flaps to endpapers, else near fine in moderately. Between the Covers Rare Books, Inc. Mystery & Detective Fiction - 75938 2013 $200

Wyman, W. E. A. *The Clinical Diagnosis of Lameness in the Horse.* New York: William R. Jenkins Co., 1898. First American edition, bookplate and owner's name, corners little bumped, very good or better. Between the Covers Rare Books, Inc. Horses, Horsemanship, Horse Racing, Etc. - 287313 2013 $100

Wyndham, John *The Midwich Cuckoos.* Joseph, 1957. First edition, 240 pages, foolscap 8vo., original black boards backstrip gilt lettered, dust jacket, front panel with short snag and resultant tiny hole, good. Blackwell's Rare Books B174 - 316 2013 £235

Wyndham, John *The Outward Urge.* London: Joseph, 1959. First edition, pages 192, foolscap 8vo., original black boards, backstrip blocked in white, dust jacket with rear panel foxed, very good. Blackwell's Rare Books B174 - 317 2013 £70

Wynn, Marcia Rittenhouse *Desert Bonanza: the Story of Early Randsburg, Mojave Desert Mining Camp.* Glendale: Arthur H. Clark Co., 1963. Second edition, one of 2112 copies, 275 pages, illustrations, folding map, brown cloth, very fine, spine darkened dust jacket. Argonaut Book Shop Recent Acquisitions June 2013 - 323 2013 $75

Wynne, Maud *An Irishman and His Family: Lord Morris and Killanin.* 1937. First edition, illustrations, cloth, dust jacket, ex-Prinknash Abbey Library, very good. C. P. Hyland 261 - 396 2013 £35

Wynne, May *Peter Rabbit & The Big Black Crows.* Philadelphia: Henry Altemus, 1931. First edition, frontispiece and color illustrations by Bess Goe Willis, orange cloth backed purple boards, this copy in variant orange cloth backstrip, color illustration pasted front cover, very nice, small sticker pastedown and name free endpaper, rarest title in the Altemus series of Peter Rabbit books. Ian Hodgkins & Co. Ltd. 134 - 8 2013 £68

X-Ray Magazine. 1-10. San Francisco: Ventura: Pasadena: X-Ray Co., 1993-2004. First edition, complete run, issue 1, 62/100 in original mailing envelope with TLS from publisher laid in, issue 2, 61/200 in original mailing envelope with ALS from publisher, issue 3, 71/200; issue 4, (first of lettered issue) Copy B of 26, signed by Hunter Thompson (one of only 11 thus), issue 5, copy # of 26, signed by Allen Ginsberg, Jaime Hernandez and others; issue 6, 13/200; issue 7, copy Z of 26; issue 8, 57/100 (first issued in box); issue #9, 1/100; issue #10, 1/100, all in fine condition. Ed Smith Books 75 - 84 2013 $6500

X-Ray Magazine No. 7. San Francisco: X-Ray Book Co. Fall, 1998. First edition, #129 of 200 numbered copies of a total edition of 226, 7 x 8 1/2 inches, card covers with mylar overlays and Surebind (plastic post) binding, 7 x 8 1/2 inches, various items laid in or tipped in, fine, with broadside poem by Charles Bukowski and color photo of poet by Michael Montford. Charles Agvent Charles Bukowski - 43 2013 $100

X Y Z

Xenophon *The Banquet of Xenophon.* Glasgow: printed by Robert Urie, 1750. 8vo., some dust soiling and light browning, old vellum tipped boards recently recovered in antique style marbled paper and backed in brown morocco, preserving original endpapers, spine with raised bands and red morocco lettering piece, good.   Blackwell's Rare Books   B174 - 160   2013   £250

Yahsiro, Yukio *Sandro Botticelli.* London: Medici Society, 1925.   First edition, number 182 of 630 copies, frontispieces, plates with tissue guards, folio, natural linen with brown morocco lettering pieces in gilt, bevel edges, top edge gilt, fore and bottom edges deckled, ex-libris Giovanni Corradini, linen soiled as common, labels chipped, leaves unopened (uncut), scattered foxing, overall still very good+, magnificent set.   Kaaterskill Books   16 - 93   2013 $450

Yancey, Bessie Woodson *Echoes from the Hills.* Washington: Associated Pub. Inc., 1939.   First edition, small owner's stamp on front fly and tiny tear at crown, else near fine, lacking rare dust jacket.   Between the Covers Rare Books, Inc.   165 - 339   2013 $450

Yankee Doodle's Cousins. Boston: Houghton Mifflin, 1941. First edition, 4to., red cloth, fine in nice dust jacket with 1 inch piece off spine, illustrations by Robert McCloskey with pictorial endpapers and a profusion of full page and smaller illustrations throughout text.   Aleph-Bet Books, Inc.   104 - 340   2013 $425

Yarrow & Company *Steam Launches and Torpedo Baots.* London: Poplar, circa, 1885.   Oblong large 8vo., title printed in mauve on card, 94 photos (103 x 152mm), each mounted on card with printed numbers and ornamental framework, cards bit browned, few photos spotted, original tan morocco ruled in black and gilt, remnants of brass clasp, front cover titled in gilt "Little Screws", inner dentelles gilt, all edges gilt, somewhat rubbed, front cover with small portion worm damaged.   Marlborough Rare Books Ltd.   218 - 142   2013   £2750

Yasuda, Yuri *Story of Shitakiri-Suzume the Tongue-Cut Sparrow.* printed in Japan, 1946.   12mo., pictorial boards, very good+, many full page color illustrations by Yoshinobu Sakakura, this copy inscribed by author.   Aleph-Bet Books, Inc.   105 - 341   2013 $200

Yates, Frederick Henry *Mr. Yates' New Entertainment.* London: Duncombe, Son, 1827.   Folding color frontispiece, spotted with some offsetting, last leaf creased and torn, without loss, stabbed as issued, 26 pages.   Jarndyce Antiquarian Booksellers   CCV - 296   2013   £120

Yeats, Grant David *A Statement of the Early Symptoms Which Lead to the Disease.* London: printed for J. Callow, 1815.   Half title, 16 page catalog and ad leaf at end, modern quarter calf and marbled boards.   James Tait Goodrich   75 - 238   2013 $2500

Yeats, Jack Butler 1871-1957 *Broadside Characters: Drawings.* Dublin: Cuala Press, 1971.   Number 268 of 300 copies, hand colored engravings, 11 leaves, unopened, original blue buckram with color onlay.   Jarndyce Antiquarian Booksellers   CCV - 297   2013   £380

Yeats, Jack Butler 1871-1957 *Life in the West of Ireland.* Dublin: Maunsel and Co., 1912.   First edition, 4to., color frontispiece, 7 color plates, 15 black and white plates and 32 black and white drawings by Jack Yeats, original blue cloth, gilt, cloth slightly rubbed and worn, otherwise excellent, inscribed by James Stephens for Bethel Solomons, Xmas 1912, with his attractive bookplate.   Maggs Bros. Ltd.   1442 - 329   2013   £2000

Yeats, Jack Butler 1871-1957 *Sligo.* London: Wishart & Co., 1930.   First edition, 8vo., pale olive green cloth, stamped gilt on spine, bottom edge untrimmed, neat name on front free endpaper, else fine in dust jacket.   Maggs Bros. Ltd.   1442 - 331   2013   £250

Yeats, John Butler 1839-1922 *Passages from the Letters of John Butler Yeats...* Dundrum: Cuala Press, 1917.   Limited to 400 copies, 8vo., first edition, original quarter linen, blue boards, printed paper label on spine, neat bookplate on front pastedown, otherwise excellent.   Maggs Bros. Ltd.   1442 - 52   2013   £150

Yeats, William Butler 1865-1939 *The Arrow Volume One Number One.* Dublin: Abbey Theatre Oct. 20, 1906.   First edition, small 4to., original grey illustrated paper wrappers, stapled as issued, excellent copy.   Maggs Bros. Ltd.   1442 - 340   2013   £275

Yeats, William Butler 1865-1939 *The Arrow. Volume One Number Two.* Dublin: Abbey Theatre Nov. 24, 1906. First edition, small 4to., original grey illustrated paper wrappers stapled as issued, excellent copy.   Maggs Bros. Ltd. 1442 - 341   2013   £275

Yeats, William Butler 1865-1939 *Autobiographies: Reveries Over Childhood and Youth and The Trembling of the Veil.* Macmillan, 1926. First edition, portrait frontispiece, 4 other plates, tissue guards, prelims and final few leaves foxed, crown 8vo., original apple green cloth, backstrip gilt blocked, faded backstrip and front cover blindstamped to a design by Charles Ricketts, untrimmed, good. Blackwell's Rare Books   172 - 249   2013   £75

Yeats, William Butler 1865-1939 *The Celtic Twilight. Men, Women, Dhouls and Faeries.* London: Lawrence & Bullen, 1893. First edition, first issue, frontispiece, 12mo., original green cloth, fore and bottom edges uncut, spine slightly faded, small nick on lower spine, otherwise very good.   Maggs Bros. Ltd.   1442 - 336   2013   £350

Yeats, William Butler 1865-1939 *The Celtic Twilight. Men and Women, Dhouls and Faeries.* London: Lawrence & Bullen, 1893. Uncommon first issue, with publisher's name in uppercase on spine, 12mo., original green cloth, fore and bottom edge, uncut, neat contemporary inscription on front free endpaper, otherwise excellent.   Maggs Bros. Ltd.   1442 - 335   2013   £450

Yeats, William Butler 1865-1939 *The Cutting of an Agate.* London: Macmillan and Co., 1919. First edition, 8vo., original blue buckram, lettered gilt on spine and upper cover, signed by author, excellent copy.   Maggs Bros. Ltd. 1442 - 344   2013   £950

Yeats, William Butler 1865-1939 *Dramatis Personae 1896-1902.* London: Macmillan, 1936. First edition, 8vo., original cloth backed Curwen paper boards, dust jacket, near fine, jacket slightly nicked at head and tail of spine and with small stain on upper cover.   Maggs Bros. Ltd.   1442 - 352   2013   £120

Yeats, William Butler 1865-1939 *Early Poems and Stories.* London: Macmillan, 1925. First edition, 8vo., original pale green cloth decorated in blind, dust jacket worn at head and tail of spine, excellent copy.   Maggs Bros. Ltd. 1442 - 346   2013   £225

Yeats, William Butler 1865-1939 *Easter 1916.* No place: privately printed by Clement Shorter, 1917. First edition, one of 25 copies, on colophon this copy numbered 10 and signed by publisher, 4to., original bright green printed wrappers, extremely rare, fine, bright copy, preserved in green half morocco slipcase.   James S. Jaffe Rare Books   Fall 2013 - 155   2013 $45,000

Yeats, William Butler 1865-1939 *Essays.* London: Macmillan, 1924. First edition, crown 8vo., original apple green cloth, backstrip gilt blocked, faded backstrip and front cover blindstamped to design by Charles Ricketts, untrimmed, very good.   Blackwell's Rare Books   172 - 251   2013   £60

Yeats, William Butler 1865-1939 *Fairy and Folk Tales of the Irish Peasantry.* London: Walter Scott, 1888. First edition, first issue, 6 pages of ads and errata slip, 8vo., original blue cloth, edges untrimmed, slight browning to spine, otherwise excellent copy.   Maggs Bros. Ltd.   1442 - 333 2013   £350

Yeats, William Butler 1865-1939 *A Full Moon in March.* London: Macmillan, 1935. First edition, one of 2000 copies pub. Nov. 22nd 1935, 8vo., original green cloth, spine lettered gilt, dust jacket, very good in slight nicked and marked dust jacket, browned on spine and stained on rear panel, from the library of Richard Murphy, signed by him. Maggs Bros. Ltd.   1442 - 350   2013   £150

Yeats, William Butler 1865-1939 *The Golden Helmet.* New York: 1908. First edition, 25/50 copies, light waterstaining to bottom third of text, 16mo., original grey boards, rebacked to match, printed label on front cover, grey endpapers, untrimmed, protective dark blue cloth box with printed label, good, inscribed by author to friend Frederick James Gregg, schoolmate of Yeats.   Blackwell's Rare Books   172 - 252   2013   £3000

Yeats, William Butler 1865-1939 *The Green Helmet and Other Poems.* Churchtown, Dundrum: Cuala Press, 1910. First edition, one of 400 copies, colophon printed in red, erratum slip loosely inserted, printed label tipped to front pastedown "this book is now published by Mitchell Kennerley", crown 8vo., original quarter cream linen, printed label on darkened backstrip, grey boards also trifle darkened, untrimmed, very good.   Blackwell's Rare Books   B174 - 325   2013   £700

Yeats, William Butler 1865-1939 *Irish Fairy Tales.* Fourth impression, 2 illustrations by Jack B. Yeats, original cloth, front cover decorated with painting (believed to be by George Russell), in specially made baize-lined box.   C. P. Hyland   261 - 881   2013   £750

Yeats, William Butler 1865-1939 *Irish Fairy Tales.* London: T. Fisher Unwin, 1892. First edition, 8vo., pinafore cloth with pattern repeated on edges, lettered in blue on spine and upper cover, binding titled and covers slightly soiled, otherwise very good, browned on spine, otherwise excellent copy.   Maggs Bros. Ltd.   1442 - 334   2013 £200

Yeats, William Butler 1865-1939 *Is the Order of R. R. & A. C. to Remain a Magical Order?* April, 1901. First edition, 8vo., original brown printed paper wrappers, excellent copy, overlapping edges of wrappers little crumpled, loosely inserted is note (on his personal card) by Colin Smythe asserting that this copy belonged to Yeats.   Maggs Bros. Ltd.   1442 - 337   2013   £4000

Yeats, William Butler   1865-1939   *The King of the Great Clock Tower, Commentaries and Poems.*   Dublin: Cuala Press, 1934.   Limited to 400 copies, 8vo., original quarter linen, grey boards, printed paper label on spine, boards slightly rubbed and marked, label browned otherwise very good.   Maggs Bros. Ltd.   1442 - 51   2013   £175

Yeats, William Butler   1865-1939   *The King's Threshold.*   New York: printed for Private Circulation, 1904.   First edition, number 24 of 100 copies, this copy signed by author, large 8vo., original grey boards, lettered in gilt on spine, top edge gilt, others uncut, printed on Italian handmade paper, near fine.   Maggs Bros. Ltd.   1442 - 338   2013   £2250

Yeats, William Butler   1865-1939   *Last Poems and Plays.*   London: MacMillan & Co., 1940.   First edition, 8vo., original green cloth blocked in blind after design by Sturge Moore, neat name on front free endpaper, otherwise excellent copy, scarce dust jacket only lightly spotted and rubbed.   Maggs Bros. Ltd.   1442 - 353   2013   £400

Yeats, William Butler   1865-1939   *Later Poems.*   Macmillan, 1922.   First edition, crown 8vo., original apple green cloth, backstrip gilt lettered, faded backstrip and front cover blindstamped to design by Charles Ricketts, front hinge just little wear at head, untrimmed, dust jacket little frayed, very good.   Blackwell's Rare Books   B174 - 318   2013   £400

Yeats, William Butler   1865-1939   *Plays in Prose and Verse.*   Macmillan, 1922.   First edition, brown 8vo., original apple green cloth, backstrip faded and front cover blindstamped to design by Charles Ricketts untrimmed, scarce in dust jacket, frayed at head, very good.   Blackwell's Rare Books   172 - 254   2013   £300

Yeats, William Butler   1865-1939   *Plays in Prose and Verse.*   New York: Macmillan, 1924.   First American edition, crown 8vo., original apple green cloth, backstrip gilt lettered, front cover with overall blindstamped design by Sturge Moore, dust jacket with faded backstrip panel, very good.   Blackwell's Rare Books   172 - 255   2013   £200

Yeats, William Butler   1865-1939   *Plays and Controversies.*   London: Macmillan, 1923.   First edition, frontispiece, 7 other plates, titlepage tissue guard present, crown 8vo., original apple green cloth, backstrip gilt blocked, faded backstrip and front cover blindstamped to design by Charles Ricketts, untrimmed, very good, with "Presentation Copy" embossed stamp on titlepage.   Blackwell's Rare Books   172 - 253   2013   £50

Yeats, William Butler   1865-1939   *Plays and Controversies 1924. Plays in Prose and Verse, 1924. Later Poems 1924. Essays 1924. Early Poems and Stories 1925. Autobiographies 1927.*   New York: Macmillan, 1924-1927.   First US editions, each volume limited to 250 copies signed by author, 6 volumes, 8vo., original blue-grey cloth, brown paper boards, printed paper label on spine and upper board, spine labels browning as usual, else near fine, each volume housed in folding grey card cases, whole within presentation slipcase.   Maggs Bros. Ltd.   1442 - 355   2013   £8500

Yeats, William Butler   1865-1939   *Selected Poems. Lyrical and Narrative.*   London: Macmillan, 1929.   First edition, small 8vo., titlepage heliotype portrait by John Singer Sargent, original embossed blue cloth dust jacket, presentation copy inscribed by author for Edith Ellen "Nelly" Tucker, very fine in fine dust jacket, uncommon.   James S. Jaffe Rare Books   Fall 2013 - 159   2013 $17,500

Yeats, William Butler   1865-1939   *Collected Poems.*   Macmillan, 1933.   First English edition, frontispiece, crown 8vo., original purple cloth, backstrip blocked in blind and gilt, partial free endpaper browning, top edge gilt, price clipped dust jacket, near fine.   Blackwell's Rare Books   172 - 250   2013   £300

Yeats, William Butler   1865-1939   *Poems.*   Dublin: Cuala Press, 1935.   First edition, small 8vo., frontispiece, hand colored and heightened with gold, illustrated with hand-drawn ornaments by Elizabeth Corbet Yeats, original light blue paper wrappers, some very minor spotting, gatherings slightly pulled at gutter, otherwise fine, rare, navy blue half morocco slipcase.   James S. Jaffe Rare Books   Fall 2013 - 160   2013 $17,500

Yeats, William Butler   1865-1939   *The Poems of W. B. Yeats.*   London: Macmillan, 1949.   First 'definitive' edition, number 357 from a total edition of 375, signed by author, specimen pages laid in, 2 volumes, 8vo, olive green buckram with beveled boards, printed on Glastonbury Ivory Toned antique laid paper, monogram of author's initials inside circle stamped in gilt on upper cover, top edge gilt, others untrimmed, near fine in matching green slipcase.   Maggs Bros. Ltd.   1442 - 354   2013   £2500

Yeats, William Butler   1865-1939   *Poems.*   Macmillan, 1949.   364/350 sets (of a total 375 sets), signed by author and printed on Glastonbury Ivory Toned Antique Laid paper, frontispiece, 8vo., original olive green bevel edged buckram, backstrips gilt lettered, front covers gilt blocked with author's initials inside gilt circle, top edge gilt, faint endpaper foxing, board slipcase, near fine, with 4 page prospectus for this work loosley inserted, sheets for this edition were signed by Yeats.   Blackwell's Rare Books   172 - 257   2013   £3000

Yeats, William Butler 1865-1939 *The Variorum Edition of the Poems of W. B. Yeats.* New York: Macmillan, 1957. First edition, limited to 825 copies, signed by Yeats, thick 8vo., two-toned cloth, glassine dust jacket, slipcase, very fine, rare glassine, none of the usual discoloration of spine or slipcase.   James S. Jaffe Rare Books   Fall 2013 - 161   2013 $3500

Yeats, William Butler 1865-1939 *Responsibilities and Other Poems.* Macmillan, 1916. First edition, usual offsetting to initial and final pages, crown 8vo., original mid blue cloth, faded backstrip and front cover gilt blocked overall to design by Sturge Moore, backstrip rubbed at head and tail, rough trimmed, good.   Blackwell's Rare Books   172 - 258   2013   £225

Yeats, William Butler 1865-1939 *Shadowy Waters.* London: Hodder and Stoughton, 1900. First edition, 8vo., original dark blue cloth, backstrip and front cover gilt blocked, gilt lettered quarter dark blue morocco and cloth, book-form box fine, inscribed by author, this was originally Oliver St. John Gogarty's copy with his bookplate, subsequently, in ownership of Sean O'Faolain and inscribed by him, photo of Yeats tipped to front free endpaper.   Blackwell's Rare Books   172 - 259   2013   £3250

Yeats, William Butler 1865-1939 *The Speckled Bird.* Dublin: Cuala Press, 1974. First editions, number 94 of 500 copies, 2 volumes, 8vo., natural linen with blue-grey paper covered boards, lettered black on spine, printed label on spine, near fine, original white opaque paper dust jackets, matching grey slipcase, printed paper label.   Maggs Bros. Ltd.   1442 - 356   2013   £175

Yeats, William Butler 1865-1939 *Stories of Michael Robartes and His Friends: an Extract from a Record Made by His Pupils.* Dublin: Cuala Press, 1931. One of 450 copies, 8vo., original quarter linen over blue boards, printed paper label, unusually fine.   Maggs Bros. Ltd.   1442 - 54   2013   £180

Yeats, William Butler 1865-1939 *The Tables of the Law and Adoration of the Magi.* Stratford upon Avon: Shakespeare Head Press, 1914. Second published edition, 108 of 510 numbered copies, small 8vo., original mottled cloth, lettered on upper cloth, ownership copy of poet Robin Wilson, excellent copy.   Maggs Bros. Ltd.   1442 - 343   2013   £125

Yeats, William Butler 1865-1939 *The Tower.* London: Macmillan, 1928. First edition, small 8vo., original gilt decorated cloth by T. Sturge Moore, dust jacket with very slight wear at extremities, fine, bright copy, increasingly scarce thus.   James S. Jaffe Rare Books   Fall 2013 - 157   2013 $4000

Yeats, William Butler 1865-1939 *The Trembling of the Veil.* London: T. Werner Laurie, 1922. First edition, number 600 of 1000 copies signed by author, large 8vo., quarter parchment over blue boards, printed paper label, excellent copy, without dust jacket.   Maggs Bros. Ltd.   1442 - 345   2013   £500

Yeats, William Butler 1865-1939 *Wheels and Butterflies.* London: Macmillan, 1934. First edition, one of 3000 copies, 8vo., original green cloth, endpapers spotted, browned on spine, otherwise excellent copy in price clipped dust jacket, slightly nicked at head and tail of spine.   Maggs Bros. Ltd.   1442 - 349   2013   £175

Yeats, William Butler 1865-1939 *Wheels and Butterflies.* London: Macmillan and Co., 1934. First edition, one of 3000 copies, original green cloth, fine in dust jacket, slightly creased at head and tail of spine.   Maggs Bros. Ltd.   1442 - 348   2013   £220

Yeats, William Butler 1865-1939 *Wheels and Butterflies.* Macmillan, 1934. First edition, title vignette by Edmund Dulac repeated in gilt on front cover, flyleaves darkened in part, foolscap 8vo., original lime green cloth, backstrip lettering and front cover design all gilt blocked, faint free endpaper and edge foxing, rough trimmed, dust jacket chipped at head of darkened backstrip panel, very good, at one time Anne Ridler's copy with her address embossed on front free endpaper.   Blackwell's Rare Books   172 - 260   2013   £150

Yeats, William Butler 1865-1939 *The Wild Swans at Coole.* London: Macmillan & Co., 1919. First edition, one of 1500 copies printed, 8vo., original blue cloth, dust jacket, fine, in rare dust jacket, which is faded at spine and lightly soiled and worn at extremities.   James S. Jaffe Rare Books   Fall 2013 - 156   2013 $3500

Yeats, William Butler 1865-1939 *The Wild Swans at Coole.* Macmillan, 1919. First Trade edition, foolscap 8vo., original dark blue cloth, backstrip and front cover gilt blocked with design by Sturge Moore, backstrip dull, untrimmed, good.   Blackwell's Rare Books   172 - 261   2013   £200

Yeats, William Butler 1865-1939 *The Wind Among the Reeds.* London: Elkin Mathews, 1907. Fifth edition, 8vo., original quarter linen, grey paper boards, printed paper label on spine, excellent copy.   Maggs Bros. Ltd.   1442 - 342   2013   £50

Yeats, William Butler 1865-1939 *The Winding Stair and Other Poems.* London: Macmillan and Co., 1933. First edition, only 2000 copies printed on Sept. 19th 1933, 8vo., original olive green cloth, spine decorated and lettered gilt, fore and bottom edges uncut, near fine in dust jacket, lightly nicked at head and tail of spine.   Maggs Bros. Ltd.   1442 - 347   2013   £950

Yeats, William Butler 1865-1939 *The Winding Stair and Other Poems.* London: Macmillan, 1933. First edition, one of 2000 copies, 8vo., original pictorial olive green cloth, pictorial dust jacket, very fine, virtually as new.   James S. Jaffe Rare Books   Fall 2013 - 158   2013 $3500

Yeats, William Butler 1865-1939 *The Collected Works in Prose and Verse.* Stratford-on-Avon: imprinted at the Shakespeare Head Press, 1908. First edition, 8 volumes, publisher's brown buckram lettered gilt, top edge gilt, others uncut, frontispieces to four volumes, some light rubbing to boards, spine ends and corners lightly bumped, otherwise fine, clean sharp set.   Ed Smith Books   75 - 85   2013 $1350

Yee, Chiang *Chin-Pao and the Giant Pandas.* London: Country Life, 1939. First edition, original cloth, gilt, dust jacket little torn and soiled, pages 84, color frontispiece and text illustrations, endpapers lightly spotted.   R. F. G. Hollett & Son   Children's Books - 729   2013   £30

Yee, Chiang *Chinpao at the Zoo.* London: Methuen, 1941. First edition, original cloth, gilt, dust jacket few short closed edge tears, spine little darkened, colored frontispiece and text illustrations by author, presentation copy inscribed, scarce.   R. F. G. Hollett & Son   Children's Books - 730   2013   £45

Yee, Chiang *Dabbitse.* Transatlantic Arts, 1945. Second edition, large 8vo., original cloth, gilt, dust jacket, 4 colored plates and numerous illustrations, scarce.   R. F. G. Hollett & Son   Children's Books - 731   2013   £40

Yee, Chiang *Lo Cheng.* Penguin Books, n.d. circa, 1942. Oblong 8vo., original pictorial wrappers, little dusty, lower panel chipped and rather torn, illustrations in color and black and white, scarce.   R. F. G. Hollett & Son   Children's Books - 732   2013   £25

Yeo, William *The Method of Ullaging and Inching all sorts of Casks and Utensils Used by Common Brewers...* London: printed for the author by E. Owen, 1749. First and only edition, 8vo., little abrasion to titlepage with few letters renewed, recent library stamp to titlepage verso, contemporary tan mottled calf, red label with gilt title to spine, headcap chipped and spine and corners little worn, mark to upper board possibly from tape removal, small area of surface loss to lower board, endpapers sympathetically replaced with remains of old bookplate just visible behind front pastedowns, ownership inscription Owen Jones June 23 1753 to titlepage, inscription of Edward Evans specifying "Not His Book", clipping from bookseller catalog tipped onto front pastedown.   Unsworths Antiquarian Booksellers   28 - 143   2013   £500

Yictove, D. J. *Soliloquy.* Newark: Thrown Stone Press, 1988. First edition, small ink stain on front wrapper, else about fine in wrappers, very scarce.   Between the Covers Rare Books, Inc.   165 - 295   2013 $150

Yonge, Charlotte Mary 1823-1901 *Aunt Charlotte's Stories of German History for the Little Ones.* Marcus Ward and Co., 1878. Original decorated cloth gilt, neatly creased, all edges gilt, chromolithographed frontispiece and title and woodcut illustrations.   R. F. G. Hollett & Son   Children's Books - 734   2013   £65

Yonge, Charlotte Mary 1823-1901 *The History of Sir Thomas Thumb.* Hamilton, Adams and Co. and Edinburgh: Thomas Constable and Co., 1855. First edition, original cloth, little rubbed and marked, all edges gilt, little rubbed and marked, all edges gilt, full page and other drawings by J. Blackburn, occasional finger mark, very good.   R. F. G. Hollett & Son   Children's Books - 733   2013   £160

Yonge, Charlotte Mary 1823-1901 *The Instructive Picture Book; or Lessons from the Vegetable World.* Edinburgh: Edmonston & Douglas, 1858. Tall 4to., modern quarter morocco gilt with raised bands and green cloth boards, 31 hand colored double page plates, all linen backed bound without text.   R. F. G. Hollett & Son   Children's Books - 735   2013   £650

Yorinks, Arthur *Hey Al.* New York: Farrar Straus Giruoux, 1986. Stated first edition, 4to., cloth, fine in dust jacket slightly frayed at spine ends with few margin mends, great illustrations by Richard Egielski, this copy sold with review proof copy with review slip laid in, proof is loose in dust jacket as sent for review.   Aleph-Bet Books, Inc.   105 - 600   2013 $300

York *City of York Year Books 1886-1915.* York: Dailey Herald Office, 1886-1915. 27 volumes, lacking 1887, 1900 & 1914, each c. 180 pages, very good in original full limp red gilt morocco, all edges gilt.   Ken Spelman Books Ltd.   73 - 46   2013   £120

York Historian. Yorkshire Architectural & York Archaeological Society, 1976-2001. 4to., very good in original wrappers, from the library of the Borthwick Institute, with bookplate and small stamps.   Ken Spelman Books Ltd.   73 - 56   2013   £40

Yorkminster Historical Tracts. York: 1927. 1-, 9, 11-22, 24-29, each 16 pages, very good in original printed wrappers, upper wrapper on part one is worn at corners and leading edge.   Ken Spelman Books Ltd.   73 - 53   2013   £40

Yosemite Tourist. Yosemite National Park: Yosemite Falls Studio, 1926. First edition, think quarto, 8 pages, stapled within printed brown wrappers, wrappers somewhat darkened.   Argonaut Book Shop   Recent Acquisitions June 2013 - 324   2013 $90

The Young Man's Own Book. A Manual of Politeness, Intellectual Improvement and Moral Deportment. for Thomas Tegg and Son, Cheapside, 1834. Second edition, some slight foxing, but good copy in contemporary half calf, marbled boards, gilt spine with red morocco label, slight crack to joint at foot of spine, contemporary bookplate and note 'lent to Master Ed. Cole for two months, March 1, 1836', scarce.   Ken Spelman Books Ltd.   75 - 95   2013   £120

Young, Al   *Dancing.*   New York: Corinth Books, 1969. First edition, one of 3000 copies, bit soiled, else near fine, inscribed by author for poet Nicholas Dellbanco.   Between the Covers Rare Books, Inc.   165 - 296   2013 $65

Young, Al   *Geography of the Near Past.*   New York: Holt, Rinehart & Winston, 1976. First edition, fine in spine sunned, otherwise near fine dust jacket, warmly inscribed by author to fellow author Nicholas Delbanco.   Between the Covers Rare Books, Inc.   165 - 298a   2013 $85

Young, Al   *Sitting Pretty.*   New York: Holt, Rinehart & Winston, 1976. First edition, fine in slightly sunned, near fine dust jacket, warmly inscribed by author to fellow author Nicholas Delbanco.   Between the Covers Rare Books, Inc.   165 - 299   2013 $100

Young, Al   *Snakes.*   New York: Holt Rinehart & Winston, 1970. First edition, bookplate of Earl David McDaniel, fine in fine dust jacket, signed by author, inscribed by author and additionally inscribed by him for David E. McDaniel.   Between the Covers Rare Books, Inc.   165 - 297   2013 $100

Young, Arminius   *One Hundred Years of Mission Work in the Wilds of Labrador.*   London: Arthur H. Stockwell, n.d., 1931. Pencil inscription to first flyleaf dated Sept. 20th 1931, blue cloth, small 8vo., very good.   Schooner Books Ltd.   105 - 49   2013 $95

Young, David   *The Discovery of Evolution.*   Cambridge: Cambridge University Press, 1992. First edition, tall 8vo., 2556 pages, frontispiece, photos and illustrations, blue cloth, gilt stamped spine title, dust jacket, Burndy Library bookplate, scarce cloth issue.   Jeff Weber Rare Books   169 - 486   2013 $100

Young, Edward   1683-1765   *Busiris, King of Egypt.*   London: printed for J. Tonson, 1719. 8vo., without half title, final page dusted and torn without loss, some creasing at corners, top edge close cropped affecting some running heads, disbound.   Jarndyce Antiquarian Booksellers CCIV - 330   2013   £30

Young, Edward   1683-1765   *The Complaint; or Night Thoughts.*   Newburyport: John Mycall, 1790. Early American printing, 408 pages, full leather, good+, pages browned as usual, some stains, primarily in index.   Barnaby Rudge Booksellers   Poetry 2013 - 020528   2013 $7

Young, Edward   1683-1765   *The Complaint and the Consolation; or Night Thoughts.*   London: 1797. First edition, 43 copperplate engravings by William Blake, with the "Explanation of the Engravings" leaf at end, often lacking, full tree calf with old rebacking, to style, boards triple ruled in gilt, spine stamped and lettered gilt, red and black morocco spine label, lettered in gilt, all edges speckled red, marbled endpapers, some wear to board edges and to extremities, previous owner's armorial bookplate and small bookseller label on front pastedown, occasional very minor offsetting or light foxing to leaves, generally not affecting engravings, exceptionally nice.   Heritage Book Shop Holiday Catalogue 2012 - 16   2013 $12,500

Young, Edward   1683-1765   *Night Thoughts on Life, Death and Immortality.*   London: J. Walker, 1807. 140 x 75mm, very pretty contemporary red straight grain morocco, covers with gilt fillet border and blind tooled floral frame, upper cover with central medallion containing crest of Hope family surrounded by motto "At Spes Non Facta" and a wreath, raised bands, spine panels with cruciform centerpiece tooled in gilt and blind, gilt titling and turn-ins, all edges gilt, engraved frontispiece and pictorial title, front pastedown with booklabel of Abel Berland, spine bit darkened, joints just slightly rubbed, mild foxing to opening leaves, otherwise fine, clean and fresh internally and in solid, pleasing binding with little wear.   Phillip J. Pirages   63 - 506   2013 $150

Young, J. T.   *Faith, Medical Alchemy and Natural Philosophy: Johann Moriaen, Reformed Intelligencer and the Hartlib Circle.*   Aldershot: Ashgate, 1998. First edition, black cloth, gilt stamped spine title, dust jacket, Burndy bookplate.   Jeff Weber Rare Books   169 - 487   2013 $75

Young, John   *The Letters of Agricola on the Principles of Vegetation and Tillage....*   Halifax: Holland and Co., 1822. 8vo., original paper covered boards, printed label to spine, diagrams and tables, covers worn and rubbed, some light staining, inkstain bottom edge page 400 to 450 not into text, some foxing, good, handwritten letter tipped in at front dated Sept. 23 1870.   Schooner Books Ltd.   101 - 129   2013 $175

Young, John P.   *Journalism in California. (and) Pacific Coast and Exposition Biographies.*   San Francisco: Chronicle Pub. Co., 1915. First edition, x, 362 pages, photos, portraits, gray cloth, gilt, fine.   Argonaut Book Shop Recent Acquisitions June 2013 - 325   2013 $75

Young, Thomas *"The Bakerian Lecture, on the Theory of Light and Colours." in Philosophical Transactions of the Royal Society of London.* London: printed by W. Bulmer and Co. and sold by G. and W. Nicol, 1802. First edition, quarto, engraved folding plate, extracted from the Transactions and bound in full burgundy morocco with gilt spine lettering, clean and fine.   Heritage Book Shop   Holiday Catalogue 2012 - 164   2013 $2000

Young, William *Portugal in 1828 Comprising Sketches of the State of Private Society and of Religion in that Kingdom Under Don Miguel...* London: Henry Colburn, 1828. First edition, 8vo., contemporary brown half calf, gilt stamp of the Signet Library on covers, no stamps in text.   J. & S. L. Bonham Antiquarian Booksellers   Europe - 8452   2013   £250

Young, Witney M. *To Be Equal.* New York: McGraw Hill, 1964. First edition, bookplate, else fine in lightly rubbed, very good plus dust jacket, inscribed by author.   Between the Covers Rare Books, Inc.   165 - 300   2013 $125

Your Carstairs Authentic Blueprint and Plans for Making a Corner Shelf and Recipes to Drink. Baltimore: Carstairs Distilling Co., n.d. circa, 1963. 24mo. single leaf folded to make 6 pages, small stain, else near fine, drawings.   Between the Covers Rare Books, Inc.   Cocktails, Etc. - 312630   2013 $50

Youthful Recreations. Philadelphia: J. Johnson, n.d. circa, 1805. 3 pages have margins trimmed close to text or picture, else fine, 15 fine full page engravings, illustrations, very sharp reproductions, rare, 2 1/2 x 3 3/4 inches, flexible boards.   Aleph-Bet Books, Inc.   104 - 193   2013 $1850

Zafran, Eric M. *Calder in Connecticut.* Hartford and New York: Wadsworth Atheneum Museum of Art in Association with Rizzoli International Publications, 2000. First edition, numerous color and black and white illustrations, very near fine in near fine dust jacket.   Jeff Hirsch Books   Fall 2013 - 121982   2013 $75

Zaitlin, Joyce *Gilbert Stanley Underwood. His Rustic, Art Deco and Federal Architecture.* Malibu: Pangloss Press, 1989. First edition, photos, plans, drawings, beige cloth lettered in white, very fine with pictorial dust jacket.   Argonaut Book Shop   Recent Acquisitions June 2013 - 326   2013 $125

Zamenhof, Stephen *The Chemistry of Heredity.* Springfield: Charles C. Thomas, 1959. First edition, 8vo., fine in very good+ dust jacket with mild chips, soil and stains.   By the Book, L. C.   37 - 94   2013 $100

Zamorano Club *The Zamorano 80.* Los Angeles: Zamorano Club, 1945. First edition, limited to 500 copies, this is no. 383, 8vo., 66 pages, foldout frontispiece, owner bookplate, minimal cover edge wear, soil to edges, very good+ dust jacket with soil, mild sun to spine, small piece missing.   By the Book, L. C.   36 - 63   2013 $400

Zeichen-Mahler und Stickerbuch zur Selbstebelhrung fur Damen. Leipzig: Voss Und Compagnie, 1795. First edition, oblong folio, 17 x 10 1/2 inches, contemporary half calf, part of original blue wrapper on edge of title, tiny hole in last few leaves, fine unused.   Aleph-Bet Books, Inc.   104 - 194   2013 $22,500

Zeitlin, Ida *Tales and Legends of Old Russia.* New York: Doran, 1926. 4to., blue gilt cloth, top edge gilt, 335 pages, fine, illustrations by Theodore Nadejen with pictorial endpapers plus 24 magnificent and striking tipped-in color plates plus black and whites in text.   Aleph-Bet Books, Inc.   104 - 509   2013 $125

Zelazny, Roger *Damnation Alley.* New York: G. P. Putnam's Sons, 1969. First edition, fine in fine dust jacket, bright, as new, very uncommon thus.   Between the Covers Rare Books, Inc.   Sci-Fi, Fantasy & Horror - 287201   2013 $1250

Zelazny, Roger *Doorways in the Sand.* New York: Harper & Row, 1976. First edition, stated as such with the number line to one, slightest bit cocked, else fine in fine dust jacket with tiny tear fresh, scarce.   Between the Covers Rare Books, Inc.   Sci-Fi, Fantasy & Horror - 313904   2013 $750

Zelazny, Roger *The Dream Master.* London: Rupert Hart Davies, 1968. First English and first hardcover edition, slight bump to foot, still easily fine in fine dust jacket, exceptional copy.   Between the Covers Rare Books, Inc.   Sci-Fi, Fantasy & Horror - 287137   2013 $850

Zelazny, Roger *Eye of the Cat.* San Francisco: and Columbia: Underwood-Miller, 1982. First edition, #4 of 333 numbered copies, signed by author, fine in pictorial cloth boards.   Between the Covers Rare Books, Inc.   Sci-Fi, Fantasy & Horror - 313337   2013 $175

Zelazny, Roger *Here There Be Dragons. (and) Way Up High.* Hampton Falls: Donald M. Grant, 1992. First edition, #24 of 1000 numbered copies, signed by author, 2 volumes, illustrations by Vaughn Bode, fine in fine dust jackets and fine slipcase.   Between the Covers Rare Books, Inc.   Sci-Fi, Fantasy & Horror - 313342   2013 $125

Zelazny, Roger *Lord of Light.* Garden City: Doubleday & Co. Inc., 1967. First edition, octavo, cloth.   L. W. Currey, Inc.   Utopian Literature: Recent Acquisitions (April 2013) - 138555   2013 $3500

Zelazny, Roger *Madwand.* Huntington Woods: Phantasia Press, 1981. First edition, trade edition, one of 750 numbered copies, signed by author, fine in fine dust jacket and fine slipcase. Between the Covers Rare Books, Inc. Sci-Fi, Fantasy & Horror - 313341 2013 $50

Zelazny, Roger *Trumps of Doom.* San Francisco and Columbia: Underwood-Miller, 1985. First edition, #16 of 500 numbered copies, signed by author fine in fine dust jacket, fine suede covered slipcase. Between the Covers Rare Books, Inc. Sci-Fi, Fantasy & Horror - 313340 2013 $85

Zemach, Harve *Duffy and the Devil.* New York: Farrar Straus Giroux, 1973. Stated first edition, very good++, mild sun spine and covers, scattered foxing, in very good+ dust jacket with faint ink writing to front of jacket, chips, small pieces missing spine tips affecting "D" in "Duffy", no medal on dust jacket or mention of Caldecott Award, small 4to, illustrations by Margot Zemach. By the Book, L. C. 36 - 38 2013 $175

Zimara, Marco Antonio *Questio de Primo Cognito.* Lyon: Venundantur apud Scipionem de Gabiano (colophon) Impressum per Jacobi Myt, 1530. Scarce separate printing, title printed in red and black within woodcut border, first leaf little frayed at edges, bit browned in first half, 8vo., 19th century German sheep backed boards, newer endleaves, good. Blackwell's Rare Books 172 - 156 2013 £1500

Zimmerman, Heinrich *Dernier Voyage du Captain Cook Autour du Monde, ou se Trouvent Les Circomstances de Sa Mort.* Berne: 1783. Second French language edition, 8vo., sewn as originally issued, large margins, drop-back box, black morocco label to spine. Maggs Bros. Ltd. 1467 - 101 2013 £6250

Zion, Gene *Hide and Seek Day.* New York: Harper Bros., 1954. First edition, 4to., cloth backed boards, slight soil, else near fine in dust jacket with few chips illustrations by Margaret Bloy Graham, scarce. Aleph-Bet Books, Inc. 104 - 600 2013 $250

Zola, Emile *His Excellency Eugene Rougon.* London: Vizetelly & Co., 1887. First English edition, Half title, original publisher's slip inserted before title, original dark blue cloth, spine slightly darkened, good plus. Jarndyce Antiquarian Booksellers CCV - 298 2013 £200

Zola, Emile *His Masterpiece.* London: Vizetelly & Co., 1886. First English edition, Portrait of author, half title with ad on verso, frontispiece, 24 page catalog (Apr. 1886), original green pictorial cloth spine lettered faded, good, sound copy. Jarndyce Antiquarian Booksellers CCV - 299 2013 £150

Zschokke, Johann Heinrich Daniel *The History of the Invasion of Switzerland by the French...* London: J. Taylor for T. N. Longman & O. Rees, 1803. First English edition, frontispiece map, 3 pages ads, contemporary half calf, handsomely rebacked, very good. Jarndyce Antiquarian Booksellers CCV - 300 2013 £280

Association Copies

Association – Aboussouan, Camille

Martial, Marcus Valerius *Epigrammata Demptis Obscenis.* Paris: Apud Viduam Simonis Benard, 1693. 12mo., armorial binding, contemporary brown morocco, covers with gilt fleur de lys and interlaced crescents at alternate corners, large ornate gilt arms of town of Bordeaux, edges gilt, very pretty, bookplates (two) of Camille Aboussouan. Joseph J. Felcone Inc. Books Printed before 1701 - 11 2013 $600

Association – Adams, C. E.

Betham, Matilda *Elegies and Other Small Poems.* Ipswich: printed by W. Burrell, 1797. Half title discarded, lightly spotted, few leaves with small chips from blank margins, 2 early inscriptions (A. H. Cole - cropped) and (cropped 'to C. E. Adams 1810'), 12mo., slightly later half sprinkled calf, marbled boards, spine divided by sextuple gilt fillets, red morocco lettering piece, other compartments infilled with wave pallets or with central decorative gilt stamp, somewhat rubbed, good. Blackwell's Rare Books 172 - 22 2013 £700

Association – Adams, Rosamund

Adams, Richard *Watership Down.* London: Penguin Books, 1976. First illustrated edition, large 8vo., original cloth backed boards, dust jacket, slipcase, inscribed by author to his editor, John Guest, further signed on dedication page by dedicatee, the author's daughter, Rosamund Adams, near fine in dust jacket, edges lightly browned. Maggs Bros. Ltd. 1460 - 8 2013 £675

Association – Addington, Mary

Kitchiner, William 1775 - 1827 *The Economy of the Eyes.* London: Hurst, Robinson & Co., 1824. First edition, folding frontispiece, engraved plate, good copy, full contemporary tree calf, double gilt bands to spine, red morocco labels, upper board detached, 19th century booklabel of Mary Addington, scarce. Ken Spelman Books Ltd. 75 - 86 2013 £125

Association – Adelman, Bob

Johnson, Charles *King. The Photobiography of Martin Luther King, Jr.* New York: Viking, 2000. First edition, this copy signed by Johnson and by Bob Adelman and dated 11/14/00, photos, fine in fine dust jacket. Ed Smith Books 75 - 37 2013 $100

Association – Agate, James

Baring, Maurice *Tinker's Leave.* London: Heinemann, 1927. First edition, large 8vo., original brown cloth dust jacket, very good, jacket spine browned and chipped at head and tail, inscribed by author for James Agate 1948 August 19. Maggs Bros. Ltd. 1460 - 34 2013 £175

Association – Alcock, Mrs.

Trollope, Frances *Hargrave; or the Adventures of a Man of Fashion.* London: Henry Colburn, 1843. First edition, 3 volumes, contemporary half red calf, gilt spines, dark green morocco labels, spines little dulled, volume II signed Mrs. Alcock on titlepage in contemporary hand, attractive set. Jarndyce Antiquarian Booksellers CCV - 270 2013 £850

Association – Alexander, H. E.

Bailey, Hamilton *Demonstrations of Physical Signs in Clinical Surgery.* Bristol: John Wright and Sons, 1933. Fourth edition, 8vo., 335 illustrations, original gilt stamped black cloth, extremities worn, especially at spine ends, signed and inscribed by author for H. E. Alexander in ink at half title, very good. Jeff Weber Rare Books 172 - 9 2013 $75

Association – Ali, Tariq

Brenton, Howard *Diving for Pearls.* London: Nick Hern Books, 1989. First edition, 8vo., original black cloth, fine in dust jacket, inscribed by author for Tariq Ali. Maggs Bros. Ltd. 1460 - 135 2013 £175

Association – Alington

King, Philip Parker *Narrative of a Survey of the Intertropical and Western Colonies of Australia. Performed Between the Years 1818 and 1822.* London: 1827. First edition, 2nd issue, 2 volumes, engraved folding chart, 10 uncolored aquatint views, 8 woodcut engravings, plan, contemporary half calf over marbled boards, spines gilt and sound, slightly shelfworn, extremities rubbed, the Sturt family copy with Alington bookplate, lovely association. Maggs Bros. Ltd. 1467 - 81 2013 £3750

Association – Allanson, Thomas

Fisher, George *The Instructor or Young Man's Best Companion..* printed for A. Millar, W. Cadell and W. Cater, 1794. Engraved frontispiece, one folding engraved plate, inscription "Thomas Allanson's Book, Hutton, 1804", woodcut illustrations in text, bit of spotting, staining and thumbing, 12mo., original calf in contemporary covering of fine suede, curiously sewn together over inside front covers, good. Blackwell's Rare Books 172 - 57 2013 £400

Association – Allen, Samuel

Redding, Cyrus *Literary Reminiscences and Memoirs of Thomas Campbell.* London: Charles J. Keet, 1860. First edition, 2 volumes, frontispiece volume i, slightly damp-stained in inner margin, original black cloth, patterned with cream dots, spines little dulled, inner hinges slightly cracking, booklabels of Samuel Allen, good plus. Jarndyce Antiquarian Booksellers CCIII - 476 2013 £110

Association – Allingham, William

Browning, Elizabeth Barrett 1806-1861 *Aurora Leigh.* London: Chapman and Hall, 1859. Fourth edition, presentation copy from author to William Allingham, dated Paris October 1858 on slip of paper glued to verso of titlepage, Allingham's pencil notes on about 15 pages, mostly detailing differences between text and that of 1857 first edition, original green cloth with blindstamp design to covers and gilt title and author to spine, spine ends and corners bumped and spine faded, otherwise very good, interior pages clean except for some foxing and offsetting to front endpaper, very good, 403 pages. The Kelmscott Bookshop 7 - 88 2013 $3850

Association – Allinson, J. H.

Thompson, George *A Sentimental Tour, Collected from a Variety of Occurrences from Newbiggin, near Penrith...* Penrith: printed by Anthony Soulby for the author, 1798. 12mo., old splash mark to H12, ink note at foot of p. 234, uncut, recent boards, paper spine label, contemporary ownership name of Thos. Scott at head of titlepage and under author's name is presentation inscription, presumably from author to J. H. Allinson from his preceptor. Jarndyce Antiquarian Booksellers CCIV - 295 2013 £380

Association – Alvarez De Toledo, Pedro De Alcantara

Anquetil, Louis Pierre *Compendio de la Historia de Espana.* Madrid: Imprenta real, 1806. Corrected edition, 8vo., 54 engravings, three quarter polished calf over marbled boards, five raised bands, 4 compartments decorated gilt, brown morocco labels, 3 of four boards detached, edges worn, rear board volume I worn through, otherwise contents quite clean, images sharp, gift from Pedro de Alcantara Alvarez de Toledo and Salm-Salm, to Sr Charles Richard Vaughan, with ALS from Alvarez de Toledo to Vaughan. Kaaterskill Books 16 - 77 2013 $500

Association – Alvin, A. P.

Cicero, Marcus Tullius (Opera). *Orationes, Epistolarum ad Atticum, Philosophicorum.* Strasbourg: Impensis Iosiae Rihelii & Iacobi Dupuys, 1581. 5 volumes only (form a 9 volume set of the works), 8vo., toned and sometimes spotted, fifth volume with staining to first half, third volume with occasional early ink notes, uniformly bound in contemporary pigskin dyed yellow, boards with blind rolled borders and central portrait stamp, all edges red and gauffered, intials 'APA' stamped in black to front board, ownership inscription of A. P. Alvin (1801) and Andreae Petri Aubogiensis (i. e. Andreas Petrus of Arboga in Sweden) dated 1591. Unsworths Antiquarian Booksellers 28 - 8 2013 £625

Association – Amery, L. S.

Gregory, Isabella Augusta Perse 1859-1932 *Hugh Lane's Life and Achievement.* London: John Murray, 1921. First edition, 8vo., original dark grey cloth, printed paper label, inscribed by author March 21 '26 for Rt. Hon. L. S. Amery, spine label browned, otherwise excellent. Maggs Bros. Ltd. 1460 - 381 2013 £300

Association – Amis, Kingsley

Aldiss, Brian W. *Intangibles Inc. & Other Stories.* London: Faber and Faber, 1969. First edition, 8vo., original red cloth, dust jacket, near fine in dust jacket, inscribed by author for Kingsley Amis. Maggs Bros. Ltd. 1460 - 11 2013 £175

Association – Amson, John

Cotton, Charles *Poems on Several Occasions.* printed for Tho. Basset, Will. Hensmann and Tho. fox, 1689. First edition, little browned and stained in places, one leaf dust stained in fore-margin and frail at foot, rust hole in one leaf in blank area, 8vo., contemporary panelled calf, rebacked preserving most of the original spine, gilt almost entirely faded away, red lettering piece, contemporary initials EJL on flyleaf, inscription of John Amson dated 1722 on title and also on flyleaf, later armorial bookplate of E. and F. Bolton, good. Blackwell's Rare Books B174 - 39 2013 £650

Association – Anderdon, John Proctor

Statius, Publius Papinius *The Thebaid.* London: T. Becket, 1773. Second edition of this William Lillington Lewis translation, 2 volumes, 8vo., internally very clean and tidy, some minor flaws to margins but none interfering with text, later half red morocco with red faux morocco boards, five raised bands to spine, gilt with Athenaeum emblem and date, pages and corners scraped, white library codes to upper boards, top edges dusty, upper hinge cracked in volume I with f.f.e.p. beginning to come away, armorial bookplate of John Proctor Anderdon, "Athenaeum Library. Cancelled" ink stamps. Unsworths Antiquarian Booksellers 28 - 49 2013 £80

Association – Anderson, David

Ferrier, Susan *Destiny; or the Chief's Daughter.* Edinburgh: printed for Robert Cadell, 1831. First edition, 3 volumes, 8vo., lightly foxed and spotted, contemporary polished half calf with marbled boards, rebacked to style by Chris Weston, boards scuffed, contemporary ink ownership inscription of David Anderson of St. Germains.   Unsworths Antiquarian Booksellers 28 - 162   2013   £180

Association – Anderson, Gwyneth

Anderson, John Redwood *White the Fates Allow.* Beckenham: The Bee & Blackthorn Press, 1962. First edition, number 1 of 10 special copies, 8vo., original white cloth, dust jacket, inscribed by author for his wife Gwyneth, near fine, jacket spine little faded.   Maggs Bros. Ltd. 1460 - 13   2013   £150

Association – Anderson, J. Redwood

Gibson, Wilfrid *Islands. Poems, 1930-1932.* London: Macmillan and Co., 1932. First edition, 8vo., original green cloth, darkened at spine and edges, dust jacket in two pieces, having split at lower hinge, little chipped at edges, very good, inscribed by author for J. Redwood Anderson. Maggs Bros. Ltd.   1460 - 336   2013   £100

Association – Anderson, Kent

Pelecanos, George P. *King Suckerman.* Boston: Little Brown, 1997. First edition, minor spotting to lower board edge, near fine in fine dust jacket, inscribed by author for Kent Anderson.   Ken Lopez Bookseller   159 - 166   2013 $250

Association – Anderton, Anne

Austen, Jane 1775-1817 *Emma: a Novel.* London: John Murray, 1816. First edition, 3 volumes, 12mo., nick to upper margin of title, volume I, bound without half titles, contemporary half brown calf, gilt bands, compartments in blind, light brown morocco labels, some slight rubbing to extremities, but very nice, inscription "Elizabeth Anne Sandford with affectionate love from her Aunt, Anne Anderton, Wake Green Dec. 29, 1869".   Jarndyce Antiquarian Booksellers   CCV - 12   2013   £15,000

Association – Andrew, W. P.

Chesney, Francis Rawdon *Reports on the Navigation of the Euphrates.* London: 1833. First edition, folding map and folding diagram, folio, contemporary calf, gilt, worn, original upper wrapper bound in, presentation "W. P. Andrew Esq. from the author", rare.   Maggs Bros. Ltd.   1467 - 29   2013   £3000

Association – Andrews, H. A.

Leadman, Alex D. H. *Battles Fought in Yorkshire: Treated Historically and Topographically.* printed for the author, 1891. First edition, 8vo., frontispiece, folding plan, 2 plates, text plates, good copy in original red cloth, gilt spine little dull, small mark to upper board, ownership name of H. A. Andrews at head of preface page, scarce.   Ken Spelman Books Ltd.   73 - 171   2013   £35

Association – Ansted, Clara

Ansted, Daivd Thomas *The Gold-Seeker's Manual.* London: John Van Voort, 1849. Second edition, 8vo., original cloth, paper labels to spine and upper board, some minor staining, library stamp to title, near fine, inscribed by author for Clara Ansted.   Maggs Bros. Ltd.   1467 - 117   2013   £1250

Association – Antonini, A. G.

Breton, Andre *Poemes.* Paris: Gallilmard, 1948. First edition, 8vo. , original wrappers preserved in folding box, near fine, inscribed by author for A. G. Antonini.   Maggs Bros. Ltd.   1460 - 136   2013   £350

Association – Aparici, Francisco

Directori de la Vistita del General del Principat de Catalunya y Comptats de Rossello y Cerdanya... Barcelona: en casa de Rafel (sic) Figuero, 1698. Woodcut arms on title, tear in last leaf passing through one letter on recto (verso blank) without loss, lacking initial blank, square 8vo., contemporary limp vellum, remains of ties little soiled, rear endleaf partially torn away, contemporary ownership inscription "Del Fran(cis)co Aparici", very good.   Blackwell's Rare Books B174 - 26   2013   £1500

Association – Aptheker, Herbert

Proudfoot, Merrill *Diary of a Sit-In.* Chapel Hill: University Of North Carolina Press, 1962. First edition, fine in price clipped and lightly worn, very good plus dust jacket, advance review copy with slip laid in, author and organizer Herbert Aptheker's copy with his ownership signature. Between the Covers Rare Books, Inc.   165 - 248   2013 $75

Association – Arbor, Newell

Green, J. F. N. *The Age of the Chief Intrusions of the Lake District.* Geologists' Association, 1917. Original wrappers, pages 30, 2 extending color lithograph maps, presentation copy inscribed Dr. Newell Arbor, with author's compliments. R. F. G. Hollett & Son   Lake District and Cumbria - 196 2013   £30

Green, J. F. N. *The Structure of the Eastern Part of the Lake District.* Geologists' Association, 1915. Reprinted from Proceedings of Geological Association volume XXVI, 4 illustrations, large edition, color lithograph of sections, large folding colored , presentation copy from author for Dr. Newell Arbor, lithograph map of the area loosely inserted, original wrappers. R. F. G. Hollett & Son Lake District and Cumbria - 200 2013 £30

Association – Ardizzone, Philip

Freedman, Barnett *Real Farmhouse Cheese.* Milk Marketing Board, 1949. First edition, 8 lithographs by Freedman, printed in black and green or yellow, pages 16, folio, original sewn linen wrappers over card with design, overall in grey, green and yellow by Freedman, trifle rubbed at heads and tails of fold, near fine, scarce, Philip Ardizzone's copy (son of Edward) with his signature. Blackwell's Rare Books B174 - 209 2013 £450

Association – Arlott, John

Gerhardi, William *Resurrection.* London: Cassell, 1934. First edition, original green cloth, front endpapers and first gathering lightly foxed, excellent copy, inscribed by author for John Arlott. Maggs Bros. Ltd. 1460 - 332 2013 £150

Association – Armitage, Merle

Williams, Tennessee 1911-1983 *I Rise in Flame, Cried the Phoenix.* Norfolk: New Directions, 1951. First edition, one of 310 copies signed by Williams, this #243, 4to., very good original publisher's slipcase with label, near fine, bookplate of Robert W. Woodruff Library, Emory University stamped "withdrawn", bookplate of Merle Armitage, signed by him. Ed Smith Books 78 - 77 2013 $300

Association – Armstrong, Elizabeth

Anacreon *Teij Odae. Ab Henrico Stephano Luce & Latinate...* Paris: Apud Henricum Stephanum, 1554. Editio princeps, browned in places, Henri Estienne's name censored n title with early ink, 8vo., modern quarter vellum, pasteboard boards, backstrip plain, small booklabel of Elizabeth Armstrong, good. Blackwell's Rare Books 172 - 8 2013 £1600

Association – Armstrong, George Francis

Armstrong, Edmund John *Essays and Sketches.* London: Longmans, 1877. First edition, half title with small tear in upper margin due to careless opening, 2 pages ads, original dark green cloth, bevelled boards, little rubbed, very good, signed presentation from editor, George Francis Armstrong to his cousins. Jarndyce Antiquarian Booksellers CCIII - 634 2013 £45

Association – Arnold, Henrietta

Ward, Mary Augusta Arnold 1851-1920 *The History of David Grieve.* London: Smith, Elder, 1892. First edition, 3 volumes, 8vo., original blindstamped purple cloth, gilt lettering, spines rebacked with original preserved, edges little browned, very good, inscribed on half title to her brother, W. T. Arnold and Henrietta Arnold. The Brick Row Book Shop Miscellany Fifty-Nine - 47 2013 $1750

Association – Arnold, W. T.

Ward, Mary Augusta Arnold 1851-1920 *The History of David Grieve.* London: Smith, Elder, 1892. First edition, 3 volumes, 8vo., original blindstamped purple cloth, gilt lettering, spines rebacked with original preserved, edges little browned, very good, inscribed on half title to her brother, W. T. Arnold and Henrietta Arnold. The Brick Row Book Shop Miscellany Fifty-Nine - 47 2013 $1750

Association – Arnold, William Harrison

Tennyson, Alfred Tennyson, 1st Baron 1809-1892 *The Holy Grail and Other Poems.* London: Strahan and Co., 1870. First edition, 2 pages ads at back, 8vo., original green cloth panelled in blind, presentation copy inscribed by author for Charles Ellis (1824-1908), booklabel of William Harrison Arnold, small newsprint clipping affixed verso of half titlepage, another to verso of first section-title, otherwise fine, full morocco slipcase. James S. Jaffe Rare Books Fall 2013 - 142 2013 $1750

Association – Arnold-Forster, F. G.

Blake, William 1757-1827 *Songs of Innocence and Experience.* London: Pickering, 1866. Vellum, gilt decorated, all edges gilt, monogram on front cover FAF, inscribed Eleanor Alicia O'Brien with Anne Martineau's afft. love Nov. 1866 and F. G. Arnold-Forster from R. V. O'Brien Aug. 1891, New Hall, and Flora Vere O'Brien Sept. 19, 1921, very good. C. P. Hyland 261 - 187 2013 £105

Association – Ashbee, C. R.

Emerson, Ralph Waldo 1803-1882 *An April Day. A Poem Recited at Concord at the Celebration of the One Hundred and twenty-Fifth Anniversary of Concord Fight April 19th 1900.* Cambridge: Riverside Press, 1900. First edition, 8vo., contemporary cloth backed boards, original wrappers bound in, excellent copy, inscribed by author to C. R. Ashbee. Maggs Bros. Ltd. 1460 - 279 2013 £375

Association – Ashbery, John

Octavio Paz: A Celebration. New York: Academy of American Poets and the Mexican Cultural Institute, 1994. First edition, 8vo., original wrappers, although not called for, this copy signed by Paz, Mark Strand, John Ashbery, Bei Dao and Charles Tomlinson. James S. Jaffe Rare Books Fall 2013 - 6   2013 $750

Association – Ashburnham, Earl of

Lefevre, Raoul *Le Recueil des Histoires de Troyes.* Bruges: William Caxton, 1473. First edition in French, small folio, Lettre batarde, lacking 32 printed leaves and two blanks, early 19th century brown straight grain morocco by Charles Lewis, gilt and blind ruled in geometric patterns, gilt inner dentelles, gilt edges, fine, unrestored, the missing leaves are internal and first and last printed leaves are present from the collection of the Duke of Roxburghe (sale 1812) of the third Earl Spencer (sale 1823), John Dent, with his notes (sale 1827), P. A. Hanrott (sale 1834) the Earl of Ashburnham (sale 1897); Richard Bennett with his bookplate and John Pierpont Morgan with his bookplate and shelfmark. Heritage Book Shop 50th Anniversary Catalogue - 62   2013 $950,000

Association – Ashby, May

Momigliano, Arnaldo *Claudius: the Emperor and His Achievement.* Oxford: Clarendon Press, 1934. First edition in English, 8vo., original red cloth, excellent copy, slightly foxed, slight wear to head and tail of spine, inscribed by Robert Graves for Mrs. Thomas Ashby (May Ashby). Maggs Bros. Ltd.   1460 - 361   2013   £425

Association – Ashmore, Ann

Birdwood, James *Heart's Ease in Heart Trouble: or A Sovereign Remedy Against All Trouble of Heart that Christ's Disciples are Subject to...* London: printed for W. Johnston at the Golden Ball in Ludgate Street, 1762. 12mo., frontispiece, original hessian cloth, very good, signature of Ann Ashmore Mr. 14 1836.   Jarndyce Antiquarian Booksellers CCV - 25   2013   £200

Association – Ashton, Winifred

Beaton, Cecil *My Royal Past.* London: B. T. Batsford, 1939. First edition, 4to., original orange brown cloth, dust jacket, excellent copy in dust jacket, chipped at extremities and browned on spine inscribed by author for Winifred Ashton.   Maggs Bros. Ltd.   1460 - 51   2013   £250

Association – Astle, Thomas

Walpole, Horace *Historic Doubts on the Life and Reign of King Richard the Third.* London: J. Dodsley, 1768. First edition, one of 1250 copies, 4to., 2 engraved plates, expertly bound in recent half calf, retaining original marbled boards, raised and gilt banded spine and red morocco label, inscribed by author for friend Thomas Astle " A Present from the author. Thos. Astle", very faint stamp "disposed of by the Royal Institution".   Ken Spelman Books Ltd.   75 - 28   2013   £1250

Association – Atherton, A.

Coleridge, Samuel Taylor 1772-1834 *Specimens of the Table Talk.* London: John Murray, 1836. Second edition, frontispiece, slightly damp marked in lower margin, original dark pink cloth, spine fading to brown and little ink spotted, good plus, signature of A. Atherton.   Jarndyce Antiquarian Booksellers CCIII - 556   2013   £40

Association – Atherton, Charles Gordon

Fremont, John Charles 1813-1890 *Report of the Exploring Expedition to the Rocky Mountains in the Year 1842 and to Oregon and North California in the Years 1843-'44.* Washington: Gales and Seaton, 1845. First edition, 693 pages, 4 maps, 22 lithographed plates, large Preuss map not present, blindstamped brown cloth, gilt, expertly recased, preserving original cloth, new endpapers, occasional light foxing, few minor exceptions, plates bright and clean, beautifully preserved in original cloth, collated complete, with short contemporary presentation signed by Hon. C(harles) G(ordon) Atherton (1804-1853).   Argonaut Book Shop   Recent Acquisitions June 2013 - 115   2013 $2500

Association – Atkinson, Tindall

Hardy, Thomas 1840-1928 *The Trumpet Major. A Tale.* London: Sampson Low Marston, Searle & Rivington, 1881. Cheap edition, first one volume edition, 8vo., original decorated red cloth, gilt lettering, 32 page publisher's catalog dated Jan. 1881, cloth little soiled and worn, very good, morocco clamshell box, inscribed by author for Tindal Atkinson, with holograph note by Hardy on his Max Gate stationery to Atkinson, from the Gary Lepper Collection of Thomas Hardy.   The Brick Row Book Shop   Bulletin Nine - 10   2013 $4500

Association – Auchincruive

Campbell, Thomas 1777-1844 *Gertrude of Wyoming: a Pennsylvanian Tale and Other Poems.* London: T. Bensley published for the author by Longman, Hurst, Rees and Orme, 1809. First edition, 4to., lacks ads and errata slip, half gilt stamped green calf, extremities worn, bookplate of Auchincruive, very good.   Jeff Weber Rare Books   171 - 60   2013 $125

Association – Auden, Wystan Hugh

Betjeman, John 1906-1984 *Murray's Buckinghamshire Guide.* London: John Murray, 1948. First edition, 4to., original red cloth, dust jacket, inscribed by author for W. H. Auden, excellent copy in rubbed price clipped dust jacket, chipped at extremities. Maggs Bros. Ltd. 1460 - 91 2013 £1250

Association – Austin, Samuel

Edwards, Jonathan *Dissertation Concerning Liberty and Necessity.* Worcester: 1797. First edition, 8vo., 23 pages plus errata leaf, rubbed contemporary calf, chipped at extremities of spine, endpapers soiled, text block little browned, very good, inscribed by Rev. Sam'l Austin of Worcester, Oct. 15 1806 for Joseph Goffes. Second Life Books Inc. 183 - 123 2013 $300

Association – Avedon, Richard

Arbus, Doon *The Sixties.* New York: Random House, 1999. First edition, photos by Richard Avedon, fine in very good dust jacket with few edge tears, signed and inscribed by Avedon and additionally signed by Arbus, uncommon signed by both. Jeff Hirsch Books Fall 2013 - 129140 2013 $500

Association – Aydelott, A. L.

Blaine, Nell *Nell Blaine Sketchbook.* New York: The Arts Publisher, 1986. First edition, one of 100 copies, original tipped in frontispiece etching "Flowers" numbered and signed by Blaine, out of a total edition of 726 copies numbered and signed by artist, this copy additionally inscribed by Blaine to "A.L.", 4to., illustrations in color and black and white, original two-toned cloth, matching publisher's slipcase, printed at Mardersteig's Stamperia Valdonega, Verona, on Tintoretto paper, etching was printed at the Center Street Studio, Gloucester, laid in are invitation to publication party at Metropolitan Museum of Art on April 9, 1986, similar card noting where the book was printed, and a color reproduction of Blaine's painting "Summer Interior with Open Book 1986" from the "Collection of Mr. and Mrs. A. L. Aydelott", presumably the person to whom this copy is inscribed, slipcase lightly soiled, otherwise fine, far scarcer than limitation would suggest. James S. Jaffe Rare Books Fall 2013 - 11 2013 $1500

Association – Bachelder, Nathanial

Parsons, Usher *Sailor's Physician...* Providence: printed by Barnum Field & Co., 1824. Second edition, 12mo., original light green boards, paper label, 203 pages, uncut, inscribed "A present by Dr. Parsons Mach 30th 1825, Natha(nia)l Bachelder", with Bachelder's ownership signature. Howard S. Mott Inc. 262 - 113 2013 $450

Association – Bachrach, Alexandre

Gide, Andre 1869-1951 *Journal des Faux-Monnayeurs.* Paris: Gallimard, 1938. Twenty-fifth edition, 8vo., original wrappers, acetate dust jacket, preserved in folding box, good copy, wrappers little worn at extremities, dust jacket chipped and worn, inscribed by author for Alexandre Bachrach. Maggs Bros. Ltd. 1460 - 339 2013 £500

Association – Bacon, Francis

Russell, John *Francis Bacon.* London: Thames and Hudson, 1971. First edition, 4to., original brown cloth, inscribed by Francis Bacon for Muriel Belcher, near fine in slightly rubbed dust jacket, signed by Belcher. Maggs Bros. Ltd. 1442 - 1 2013 £2500

Association – Bacon, Gaspar

Stith, William *A History of the First Discovery and Settlement of Virginia.* Williamsburg: printed by William Parks, 1747. First edition, third issue possibly printed in 1753, 8vo., polished crimson morocco (finely rebacked, old back laid down), gilt ruled covers, spine elaborately gilt, wide inner gilt crimson borders, marbled endpapers, signed "Toof & Co./Zahn", fine copy in fine signed binding by Otto Zahn (1857-1928), signature on endpaper of Massachusetts politician Gaspar G. Bacon (1886-1947). Howard S. Mott Inc. 262 - 142 2013 $8500

Association – Bainbridge, Beryl

Barnes, Julian *The Lemon Table.* London: Jonathan Cape, 2004. First edition, 8vo., original brown cloth, dust jacket, inscribed by author for Beryl Bainbridge, fine in dust jacket. Maggs Bros. Ltd. 1460 - 39 2013 £150

Association – Bainbridge, Joseph

Medwin, Thomas 1788-1869 *Journal of the Conversations of Lord Byron, Noted During a Residence with His Lordship at Pisa in the Years 1821 and 1822.* London: Henry Colburn, 1824. First edition, 4to., half title, frontispiece facsimile with slight offsetting on title, 2 pages ads (Oct. 1824), contemporary half calf, black label, little rubbed, armorial booklabel of Joseph Bainbridge. Jarndyce Antiquarian Booksellers CCIII - 415 2013 £250

Association – Baker A.

Eldridge, Elleanor *Memoirs of...* Providence: Albro, 1828. First edition, 12mo., 128 pages, cloth backed boards, some foxed and soiled, portrait, some stained and foxed, very good, very scarce, notes in pencil "Mrs. E. Choate/from her affectionate/ aunt A. Baker/ New Bedford/ Jan 22nd/ 1939/ I purchased this book/ of Eleanor herself". Second Life Books Inc. 183 - 442 2013 $600

Association – Baker, E.

Huckell, John *Avon, a Poem in three parts.* Birmingham: printed by John Baskerville and sold by R. and J. Dodsley in Pall Mall, 1758. First edition, 78 pages, 4to., leading edge of titlepage rather short perhaps due to wear to inner margin and page inset when rebound, final leaf dusted and marked, repair along leading edge, contemporary marbled boards, simply rebacked, contemporary signature of E. Baker, several contemporary corrections in text. Jarndyce Antiquarian Booksellers   CCIV - 166   2013   £280

Association – Baker, John

Crabbe, George   1754-1832 *Poems.* London: printed for J. Hatchard, 1810. Fifth edition, 2 volumes, half titles, contemporary full vellum, gilt spines, borders and dentelles, red leather labels, little dulled, inscription of Octavia Cholmely 1854, later booklabel of John Baker in volume II, all edges gilt.   Jarndyce Antiquarian Booksellers   CCIII - 622   2013   £65

Association – Baker, Katherine

Moore, Joseph *Outlying Europe and the Nearer Orient...* Philadelphia: J. B. Lippincott, 1880. First edition, 8vo., 554 pages, original blue blindstamped cloth, presentation copy to Katherine Baker.   J. & S. L. Bonham Antiquarian Booksellers   Europe - 8339   2013   £140

Association – Baldwin, La Verne

Guer, Jean Antoine *Moeurs et Usages Des Turcs, Leur Religion, Leur Gouvernement Civil, Militaire et Politique avec un Abrege de l'Histoire Ottomane.* Paris: Chez Merigot & Piget, 1747. Second edition, 2 volumes, 2 engraved titlepages, titles printed in red and black with devices, 28 additional plates, engraved initials, and head and tailpieces, small 4to., contemporary mottled calf, boards ruled in gilt, five raised bands, compartments decorated in gilt, red morocco lettering piece, all edges gilt, wear to extremities with some loss at spine heads, and two small splits at tip of joints on first volume, volume number in one compartment mostly worn away, light scattered foxing and minor offsetting, marginal on plates, one folding panorama with small tear near hinge and upper margin, one with one inch tear to lower section near hinge, otherwise plates quite sharp, overall very good, bookplate of La Verne Baldwin (former consul General at Istanbul), gift to Baldwin from Beth (Bertha) Carp, close friend of Allen Dulles.   Kaaterskill Books   16 - 42   2013 $4000

Association – Balfour, Alice

Hardy, Thomas   1840-1928 *The Dynasts: an Epic Poems of the War with Napoleon.* London: Macmillan, 1910. First one volume edition, 8vo., original green cloth, gilt lettered, frontispiece, one leaf of publisher's ads, followed by 32 page publisher catalog, fine presentation copy inscribed by author for Miss Alice Balfour, 1912 with her stylized initials, cloth slightly worn, very good, enclosed in morocco clamshell box, from the Gary Lepper Collection of Thomas Hardy.   The Brick Row Book Shop   Bulletin Nine - 50   2013 $6000

Association – Balfour, Charlotte

Belloc, Hilaire   1870-1953 *Essays of a Catholic Layman in England.* London: Sheed & Ward, 1931. First edition, 8vo., original blue cloth, excellent copy, spine faded, closed tear to head of cloth of spine, inscribed by author for Charlotte Balfour.   Maggs Bros. Ltd.   1460 - 77   2013   £200

Belloc, Hilaire   1870-1953 *Europe and the Faith.* London: Constable, 1920. First edition, large 8vo., original blue cloth, inscribed by author 8th Sept. 1920 for Charlotte Balfour, excellent copy, spine faded.   Maggs Bros. Ltd.   1460 - 76   2013   £350

Association – Ballard, J.

Redi, Francesco *Experimenta circa Generationem Insectorum.* Amsterdam: Andreas Frisius, 1761. Additional engraved title, engraved vignette on title, 2 engravings in text, 38 engraved plates, very slightly browned in places, 12mo., original vellum, yapp edges, soiled (as one would expect), very good, contemporary ownership inscription of Jo. Ballard, repeated at end with cost code.   Blackwell's Rare Books   Sciences - 103   2013   £750

Association – Ballard, Thomas

Butler, Samuel   1835-1902 *Ex Voto.* London: Trubner & Co., 1888. First edition, inscribed by author to T(homas) Ballard, close friend of author, very good, bumping and small chips to cloth on corners, interior clean and tight, several illustrations from photos, 277 pages, 3 pages ads, very nice.   The Kelmscott Bookshop   7 - 130   2013 $450

Association – Bardon, T.

Beddoes, Thomas 1760-1808 *Hygeia or Essays Moral and Medical on the Causes Affecting the Personal State of Our Middling and Affluent Classes.* Bristol: J. Mills for R. Phillips, 1802-1803. First edition, 8vo., new buff flyleaves, some light waterstaining to margin of last few leaves of volume II, modern half tan calf, over marbled boards, gilt stamped spines with raised bands and black leather, gilt stamped labels, ink stamp at top and bottom of volume II titlepage ink stamp of T. Bardon, rare. Jeff Weber Rare Books 172 - 13 2013 $1350

Association – Baringer, J. Richard

Cushing, Harvey Williams 1869-1939 *Papers Relating to the Pituitary Body, Hypothalamus and Parasympathetic Nervous System.* Springfield & Baltimore: Charles C. Thomas, 1932. 8vo., 99 figures, 2 color plates, 2 charts, 4 tables, green blind and gilt stamped cloth, rubbed, corners showing, ink ownership signature of J. Richard Baringer, Oct. 1961, very good. Jeff Weber Rare Books 172 - 64 2013 $300

Association – Barker, M. R.

Euripides *Opera Omnia.* London: Richard Priestley, 1821. 9 volumes, 8vo., text in Greek with Latin footnotes, printer's list in volume vi, triangular closed tear to page ix in volume vii (no loss of text) sporadic foxing, occasional light pencil annotations, half vellum, marbled paper boards and endpapers, black morocco label to spine, edges red, boards rubbed, edges worn with occasional small bumps but still very good, armorial bookplate of Aston Walker to each front pastedown, various library tickets and inkstamps from London Borough of Southwark Special Collection to prelims, pencilled ownership inscription of M. R. Barker to half title. Unsworths Antiquarian Booksellers 28 - 13 2013 £300

Association – Barnes, Henry Hickman

Bloomfield, Robert *Rural Tales, Ballads and Songs.* (bound with) *Wild Flowers; of Pastoral and Local Poetry.* (bound with) *The Farmer's Boy: a Rural Poem.* London: Vernor, Hood and Sharpe, Poultry, 1811. London: Longman etc., 1816. London: Longman &c. 1837. Seventh and fifteenth edition, 3 volumes in 1, contemporary half green calf, spine gilt in compartments, maroon leather label, armorial bookplate of Henry Hickman Barnes, with his name crossed through and that of Arthur Swinbourne added, Barnes' name has been struck through where present, very good. Jarndyce Antiquarian Booksellers CCIII - 14 2013 £75

Association – Barnes, Julian

Hughes, Richard *A High Wind in Jamaica.* London: Chatto & Windus, 1929. First Book form edition, crown 8vo., original pale green cloth, foxed backstrip gilt lettered, tail edges rough trimmed, darkened backstrip panel to dust jacket, torn and chipped, wrap around band present, good, from the library of Julian Barnes. Blackwell's Rare Books B174 - 235 2013 £175

Association – Barney, Natalie Clifford

Stein, Gertrude 1874-1946 *Portrait of Mabel Dodge at the Villa Curonia.* Florence: privately printed, 1912. First edition, one of 300 copies, 8vo., original floral Florentine wallpaper wrappers with printed label on front cover, fine, rare, presentation copy inscribed by author for Natalie Clifford Barney. James S. Jaffe Rare Books Fall 2013 - 138 2013 $25,000

Association – Barrachina y Almeda, Jaime

Blanco, Francisco Manuel *Flora de Filipinas.* Manila: Impr. de St. Thomas, 1837. First edition, 4to., lacking final leaf of errata (should be 2ff. last a blank), waterstains first and last leaves torn and repaired, last leaves loose (also with some loss), original gilt stamped brown tree calf with red and black calf spine labels, rubbed, good, rare on market, bookplate of Howard Sprague Reed and ownership inscription Jaime Barrachina y Almeda, Madrid 1929. Jeff Weber Rare Books 172 - 33 2013 $1600

Association – Barratt, Emily

Little Folks: a Magazine for the Young. London: Cassell, 1887-1894. Parts 1 and 2, 13 bi-annual volumes, large 8vo., contemporary half red roan gilt, original owner's name (Emily Barratt) in gilt on each upper board, some rubbing to extremities, few surface defects to leather in places, each volume with 2 chromolithographs and numerous full page and text illustrations, some tinted, attractive collection. R. F. G. Hollett & Son Children's Books - 133 2013 £450

Association – Barron, John

Marino, Giambattista *L'Adone, Poems.* Amsterdam: 1651. 2 volumes, 12mo. bound in sixes, small marginal tear to V1 volume II, some light browning, few ink splashes but very good, most handsome early 19th century dark blue straight grain morocco, gilt ruled borders, attractive gilt panelled spines decorated with flower head, open circles and small gilt dots, pink endpapers and pastedowns, armorial bookplate of John Barron, early inscription of J. Stirling, alter 19th century bookplate of Alfred Coco of Middle Temple, ownership name of J. Stroud Read, London Nov. 1928, earlier hand notes "Will. Roscoe's Library", all edges gilt. Jarndyce Antiquarian Booksellers CCV - 191 2013 £620

Association – Barrymore, Baron

Greater Cork International Exhibition 1903 *Official Catalogue.* 132 pages, map, silk bound, ex-library Baron Barrymore (one of the Vice Presidents), spine faded, else very good.   C. P. Hyland   261 - 221   2013   £95

Association – Bartholomay, Henry

Women of all Nations. A Record of Their Characteristics, Habits, Manners, Customs and Influence. London and elsewhere: Cassell and Co. Ltd., 1908. First edition, 287 x 200mm., 2 volumes, 26 color plates, 54 full page black and white photos and hundreds of other black and white photos in text, pleasing burgundy half morocco, raised bands, spine gilt in double ruled compartments with scrolling cornerpieces, gilt titling, marbled endpapers, top edge gilt, spines just little darkened and faintly dulled, hint of rubbing to extremities, otherwise fine, text clean, fresh and bright and bindings with negligible wear; bookplates of Henry Bartholomay.   Phillip J. Pirages   63 - 498   2013 $450

Association – Bartley, P.

Dodd, James Solas *An Essay Towards a Natural History of the Herring.* London: printed for T. Vincent, 1752. First edition, 8vo., contemporary calf, double gilt fillet borders on sides, spine gilt ruled in compartments later green paper label, lettering in ink faded, slightly worn, contemporary ownership inscription of P. Bartley with note of the price (5s), armorial bookplate of Alexander David Seton of Mounie Castle, with pencil Mounie shelfmark inside front cover, good.   Blackwell's Rare Books   Sciences - 44   2013   £400

Association – Batchford, Paul

Paul, Doris A. *The Navajo Code Talkers.* Pittsburgh: Dorrance Pub., 1990. Seventh printing, 8vo., signed by fourteen Navajo code talkers, including Albert Smith (President 4th Mar. Div. 4th Sig. Co.), Paul Blatchford, Bill Toledo, Harold Foster, George Smith, Harold Evan and others, fine in near fine dust jacket.   By the Book, L. C.   38 - 38   2013 $900

Association – Baxter, David

Turgenev, Ivan Sergeevich   1818-1883   *A Month in the Country.* London: Heinemann, 1943. First English edition, 8vo., 94 pages, very good in dust jacket, bookplate of Hugh Beaumont on front endpaper, inscribed by Emlyn Williams for Beaumont, signed by 13 members of the opening night cast including Michael Redgrave, David Baxter, Winifred Hindle, etc.   Second Life Books Inc.   183 - 383   2013 $400

Association – Bayhind, Emmanual

Tymme, Thomas   *A Silver Watch Bell, the Sound Whereof is Able (by the Grace of God) to Win the Most Prophane Worldling and Careless Liver...*   London: printed by John Haviland for Thomas Alchorn, 1638. Small octavo, lacking A2 (titlepage) and I2 (pages 115-116), text within double ruled border, with headline, page numbers and marginal glosses inside outer border, 16 headpieces, 14 ornamental initials and 2 tailpieces, contemporary marbled boards, rebacked (possibly in 1915, according to pencil note on front pastedown), with speckled calf, modern red and white paper spine label lettered in ink, plain endpapers, all edges speckled red, some trimmed close to headlines and in a few cases to marginal inscriptions, boards worn, hinges cracked, tiny rust or ink hole to top of front free endpaper, tiny wormhole to outer margin of beginning leaves, affecting a letter or two of marginal glosses, over opened at a few places, still very good, from the library of John Locke with ink inscriptions, signatures and marginal notations in at least five different hands, (John Locke, Ri. Yolland, Emmanual Bayhind, William Yoo and Riettell).   Heritage Book Shop   50th Anniversary Catalogue - 67   2013 $35,000

Association – Beale, Thomas

Pick, William   *Pedigrees and Performances of the Most Celebrated Racehorses, that have Appeared Upon the English Turf, Since the Time of Basto, Flying Childers &c.* By W. Pick of York, 1785. 8vo., 132 pages, very good, full contemporary calf, expert repairs to joints and corners, contemporary inscription "Thomas B. Beale from his friend" and armorial bookplate with ornate monogram GR.   Ken Spelman Books Ltd.   73 - 8   2013   £295

Association – Beaton, Cecil

Auden, Wystan Hugh   1907-1973   *The Poet's Tongue. An Anthology.* London: G. Bell, 1935. First edition, 8vo., original blue cloth, dust jacket, inscribed by author for Cecil Beaton, excellent copy in slightly rubbed dust jacket.   Maggs Bros. Ltd.   1460 - 25   2013   £675

Colette, Sidonie Gabrielle   1873-1954   *Claudine's en va.* Monte Carlo: Editions Du Livre, 1946. Later edition, one of 3000 copies, this copy unnumbered, 8vo., original wrappers, acetate dust jacket preserved in folding box, near fine, dust jacket just little chipped at head and tail of spine, inscribed by the artist, Christian Berard for Cecil Beaton.   Maggs Bros. Ltd.   1460 - 53   2013   £175

Tynan, Kenneth   *Persona Grata.* London: Allan Wingate, 1954. First reprint, 4to. original blue cloth, excellent copy in slightly rubbed and nicked dust jacket, inscribed by Cecil Beaton to Maurice Chevalier, photos by Beaton, excellent copy, in slightly rubbed and nicked dust jacket.   Maggs Bros. Ltd.   1460 - 55   2013   £300

Association – Beaucharnais, Eugene De

Hamilton, William 1730-1803 *Outlines from the Figures and Compositions Upon the Greek, Roman and Etruscan Vases of the late Sir William Hamilton...* London: published by William Miller, Old Bond Street, Printed by W. Bulmer and Co., Cleveland Row MDCCCIV, 1804. Large paper copy, 4to., 124 plates, being 62 engraved plates, each in two states, colored in red and black and uncolored, contemporary red morocco gilt with crowned cipher of Eugene de Beaucharnais, spine in compartments separated by double raised bands, two lettered gilt possibly by Maurais or Lodigian who provided many bindings for Beaucharnais, watered silk endpapers. Marlborough Rare Books Ltd. 218 - 74 2013 £5000

Association – Beaufort, Duke of

Davenant, William 1606-1668 *The Works of Sr. William Davenant Kt...* London: by T. N. for Henry Herringman, 1673. First collected edition, folio, portrait, turn of the century red levant morocco, gilt arabesque centerpiece on covers, all edges gilt, by Riviere, very skillfully rebacked, though the new leather at joints and on cords has uniformly faded, unusually fine, fresh, wide margined copy with fine impression of the portrait, leather tipped fleece lined slipcase, edges rubbed, bookplates of Duke of Beaufort, E. F. Leo, A. E. Newton. Joseph J. Felcone Inc. English and American Literature to 1800 - 12 2013 $2200

Association – Beaumont, Hugh

Turgenev, Ivan Sergeevich 1818-1883 *A Month in the Country.* London: Heinemann, 1943. First English edition, 8vo., 94 pages, very good in dust jacket, bookplate of Hugh Beaumont on front endpaper, inscribed by Emlyn Williams for Beaumont, signed by 13 members of the opening night cast including Michael Redgrave, David Baxter, Winifred Hindle, etc. Second Life Books Inc. 183 - 383 2013 $400

Association – Beauvoir, Simone De

Algren, Nelson *The Man With the Golden Arm.* Garden City: Doubleday & Co., 1949. First edition, 8vo., original pale brown cloth, inscribed by author for Simone de Beauvoir, excellent copy, very slightly rubbed at extremities. Maggs Bros. Ltd. 1460 - 12 2013 £650

Association – Beck, Henry

Wright, Willard Huntington 1888-1939 *The Garden Murder Case.* New York: Scribners, 1935. First edition, bottom corners slightly bumped, still fine in rubbed, very good dust jacket with some modest nicking at extremities, Advance Review copy with slip laid in, mystery writer Henry C. Beck's copy with his ownership signature. Between the Covers Rare Books, Inc. Mystery & Detective Fiction - 39296 2013 $400

Association – Beckett, Gerald

Schrodinger, Erwin *What is Life? The Physical Aspect of the Living Cell.* Cambridge: at the University Press, 1945. First reprint, 8vo., original green cloth, inscribed by Samuel Beckett for nephew Gerald Beckett, near fine copy. Maggs Bros. Ltd. 1460 - 57 2013 £1250

Association – Beckett, John

Beckett, Samuel 1906-1989 *All that Fall.* London: Faber and Faber, 1957. First edition, 8vo., original pictorial wrappers, chipped at head and tail of spine, otherwise very good, inscribed by author to cousin, John. Maggs Bros. Ltd. 1460 - 62 2013 £1200

Beckett, Samuel 1906-1989 *En Attendant Godot.* Paris: Les Editions de Minuit, 1952. First edition, 8vo., original white wrappers printed in black and blue, very good with inch or so lost from tail of spine, wrappers touch rubbed at extremities, inscribed by author to his cousin John Beckett and wife Vera. Maggs Bros. Ltd. 1460 - 58 2013 £5000

Beckett, Samuel 1906-1989 *Comedie et Actes Divers.* Paris: Les Editions de Minuit, 1966. First edition, 8vo., original white wrappers lettered in black and blue, covers slightly rubbed, otherwise excellent copy in protective folding box, inscribed by author for cousin John Beckett and wife Vera. Maggs Bros. Ltd. 1460 - 65 2013 £1200

Beckett, Samuel 1906-1989 *First Love.* London: Calder and Boyars, 1973. First edition, 8vo., original pink cloth, dust jacket with fading to spine, fine, inscribed by author for John Beckett and Ruth David. Maggs Bros. Ltd. 1460 - 66 2013 £1200

Beckett, Samuel 1906-1989 *How It Is.* London: John Calder, 1964. First edition, 8vo., original grey cloth, dust jacket, excellent copy, inscribed by author to cousin John Beckett and wife Vera, with John's ownership signature. Maggs Bros. Ltd. 1460 - 63 2013 £1200

Beckett, Samuel 1906-1989 *Ill Seen Ill Said.* New York: Grove Press, 1981. First edition, 8vo., original quarter cream cloth, near fine, inscribed by author for John Beckett and Ruth David. Maggs Bros. Ltd. 1460 - 67 2013 £1000

Beckett, Samuel 1906-1989 *Nouvelles et Textes pour Rien.* Paris: Les Editions de Minuit, 1955. First edition, number 46 of 50 numbered hors commerce on Velin from total edition of 1185, 8vo., original white wrappers, lettered in black and blue, chipped at heel of spine and rubbed overall, otherwise very good in protective folding box, inscribed by author to cousin John Becket and wife Vera. Maggs Bros. Ltd.   1460 - 60   2013   £1500

Beckett, Samuel 1906-1989 *Worstward Ho.* London: Calder and Boyars, 1983. First edition, 8vo., original green cloth, fine in dust jacket with fading to spine, inscribed by author for John Beckett and Ruth David.   Maggs Bros. Ltd.   1460 - 67   2013   £1000

Association – Beckett, Samuel

Schrodinger, Erwin *What is Life? The Physical Aspect of the Living Cell.* Cambridge: at the University Press, 1945. First reprint, 8vo., original green cloth, inscribed by Samuel Beckett for nephew Gerald Beckett, near fine copy.   Maggs Bros. Ltd.   1460 - 57   2013   £1250

Association – Beckett, Vera

Beckett, Samuel 1906-1989 *En Attendant Godot.* Paris: Les Editions de Minuit, 1952. First edition, 8vo., original white wrappers printed in black and blue, very good with inch or so lost from tail of spine, wrappers touch rubbed at extremities, inscribed by author to his cousin John Beckett and wife Vera.   Maggs Bros. Ltd.   1460 - 58   2013   £5000

Beckett, Samuel 1906-1989 *Comedie et Actes Divers.* Paris: Les Editions de Minuit, 1966. First edition, 8vo., original white wrappers lettered in black and blue, covers slightly rubbed, otherwise excellent copy in protective folding box, inscribed by author for cousin John Beckett and wife Vera. Maggs Bros. Ltd.   1460 - 65   2013   £1200

Beckett, Samuel 1906-1989 *How It Is.* London: John Calder, 1964. First edition, 8vo., original grey cloth, dust jacket, excellent copy, inscribed by author to cousin John Beckett and wife Vera, with John's ownership signature. Maggs Bros. Ltd.   1460 - 63   2013   £1200

Beckett, Samuel 1906-1989 *Nouvelles et Textes pour Rien.* Paris: Les Editions de Minuit, 1955. First edition, number 46 of 50 numbered hors commerce on Velin from total edition of 1185, 8vo., original white wrappers, lettered in black and blue, chipped at heel of spine and rubbed overall, otherwise very good in protective folding box, inscribed by author to cousin John Becket and wife Vera. Maggs Bros. Ltd.   1460 - 60   2013   £1500

Association – Beckford, William

Mitchell, James *A Tour through Belgium, Holland, Along the Rhine and through the North of France in the Summer of 1816.* London: printed for Longman, Hurst (and others), 1816. xii, 390 pages, folding frontispiece, 8vo., slight foxing, map offset on to titlepage, contemporary polished calf, gilt ruled borders, gilt panelled spine, black morocco label, hinges cracked, chip to foot of spine, William Beckford's copy with 2 pages of his pencil notes written on prelim blank. Jarndyce Antiquarian Booksellers   CCIV - 206   2013   £1500

Association – Bective

Maberly, Catherine Charlotte *The Love Match.* London: David Bryce, 1856. New edition, contemporary half maroon calf, spine decorated n gilt, black leather label, spine and corners little rubbed, from the Headfort library, signed 'Bective 1854', good plus.   Jarndyce Antiquarian Booksellers   CCV - 182   2013   £45

Association – Bedford, Francis, Duke of

Bolingbroke, Henry St. John, 1st Viscount 1678-1751 *Letters on the Study and Use of History.* London: printed for T. Cadell, 1779. New edition, 8vo., some occasional foxing, several marginal notes in contemporary hand, full contemporary calf, gilt banded spine, head and tail slightly chipped, armorial bookplate of Francis, Duke of Bedford, Oakley House, recent bookplate of Thomas Duffy. Jarndyce Antiquarian Booksellers   CCIV - 65   2013   £40

Association – Bedford, William, Duke of

Galt, John 1779-1839 *Sir Andrew Wylie, of that Ilk.* Edinburgh: printed for William Blackwood, 1822. 3 volumes, 8vo., lightly browned, contemporary straight grained half green morocco with marbled boards, spine in compartments with central gilt tools, lettered and numbered in gilt direct, edges marbled, spines gently sunned, armorial bookplate of William, Duke of Bedford, Edinburgh, signed binding by Feaston, with his circular red ticket on front pastedown. Unsworths Antiquarian Booksellers   28 - 165   2013   £180

Association – Beedon, Thomas

Robinson, Lewis *Every Patient His Own Doctor; or the Sick Man's Triumph Over Death and the Grave.* London: printed for J. Cooke, 1779? 8vo., slightly dusted, clean tear without loss to leading edge of one leaf, original wrappers, rubbed and worn, inscribed on inside rear wrapper "Thomas Beedon Junior, His Book March the 14th 779". Jarndyce Antiquarian Booksellers   CCIV - 255   2013   £225

Association – Beeson, W.

Medicina Flagellata; or the Doctor Scarificed. printed for J. Bateman and J. Nicks, 1721. First edition, additional letterpress title with engraved vignette, 8vo., contemporary tree calf, flat spine gilt in compartments, red lettering piece, minor wear, top of upper joint snagged foot of spine chipped, contemporary signature at head of title of W. Beeson, engraved bookplate of Sir Thomas Hesketh, and Easton Neston Library shelf label, very good.   Blackwell's Rare Books   Sciences - 101   2013   £750

Association – Beeton, Mayson

Malton, Thomas *Views of Oxford.* London: White & Co.; Oxford: R. Smith, 1810. First complete edition, 411 x 315mm., appealing 19th century circa 1860s?), dark green half morocco over lighter green textured cloth by T. Aitken (stamp signed), upper cover with gilt titling, raised bands, spine gilt in compartments with elongated fleuron centerpiece and scrolling cornerpieces, gilt titling, marbled endpapers, all edges gilt (small, very expert repairs to upper outer corners and perhaps top of joints), mezzotint frontispiece after Gilbert Stuart, engraved title, 30 fine plates, 24 of then aquatints and 6 of them etched, armorial bookplates of Sir Mayson M. Beeton and Sir Richard Farrant, ink presentation inscription "Sir Charles Locock, Bart./ with Captn. Malton's kindest regards/Nov. 1860", subscription proposal for the work printed by T. Bensley and dated "London, May 30, 1301" (i.e. "1801"), laid in at front, couple of small smudges to boards, portrait faintly foxed and browned, isolated small stains (not affecting images), still fine, plates especially clean, fresh and smooth and pleasing binding with virtually no wear.   Phillip J. Pirages   63 - 327   2013 $9500

Association – Belcher, Muriel

Russell, John *Francis Bacon.* London: Thames and Hudson, 1971. First edition, 4to., original brown cloth, inscribed by Francis Bacon for Muriel Belcher, near fine in slightly rubbed dust jacket, signed by Belcher.   Maggs Bros. Ltd.   1442 - 1   2013   £2500

Association – Bellairs, Mrs.

Clare, John   1754-1832 *The Shepherd's Calendar; with Village Stories, and Other Poems.* London: published for John Taylor, Waterloo Place by James Duncan, Paternoster Row and sold by J. A. Hessey 93 Fleet Street, 1827. First edition, 2 pages publisher's ads at back, presentation copy inscribed by author to Mrs. Bellairs, April 30 1827, spine perished, boards somewhat soiled, gatherings bit loose, otherwise good copy with rare inscription, Bradley Martin copy preserved in folding cloth box.   James S. Jaffe Rare Books Fall 2013 - 32   2013 $8500

Association – Bellamy, Emma

Bellamy, Edward *Looking Backward 2000-1887.* Boston: Houghton Mifflin, 1926. Riverside Library, 8vo., pages 337, very good in publisher's cloth, stain on hinge of rear endpaper, inscribed by author's wife, Emma for Walter James Henry, also inscribed by his daughter Marian Bellamy Ernshaw Oct. 24 1935, laid in is 9 x 6 inch handbill advertising talk given by Marion and Emma Bellamy at the Seattle Civic Auditorium, scarce.   Second Life Books Inc.   183 - 21   2013 $300

Association – Bellis

Bell, Charles   1774-1842 *The Hand: Its Mechanism and Vital Endowments as Evincing Design.* London: William Pickering, 1833. Second edition, 8vo., illustrations, lacks half title, modern blue cloth, red leather spine label, head of spine expertly repaired, spine faded, label rubbed, ownership signature of Charles A. Carton, ownership rubber stamp of Bellis on title, fine.   Jeff Weber Rare Books   172 - 19   2013 $750

Association – Belt, Elmer

Rosen, George *Journal of the History of Medicine and Allied Sciences.* New York: Henry Schuman, 1947-1972. 20 volumes, tall 8vo. various paginations, illustrations, navy buckram, gilt spines, bookplate of Elmer Belt, very good.   Jeff Weber Rare Books   172 - 138   2013 $750

Association – Beltrand, Jacques

Dorgeles, Roland *Vacances Forcees.* Paris: Editions Vialetay, 1956. First edition, one of several deluxe copies "nominatif" (Marcelle Blanchet), produced for collaborators on book, from total edition of 233, printed on Rives wove paper, signed in ink by Dorgeles, Jacques Beltrand and the publisher, on justification page, 24 original color woodcuts, including 23 in texte, engraved by Beltrand after original watercolors by Raoul Dufy + a suite of 23 hors texte woodcuts on thin Japon paper in separate folder, woodcuts are color decompositions of one plate + a suite of 22 hors texte color decomposition woodcuts on Rives wove paper + one 'etat incomplet' woodcut, also in separate folder, also included is publisher's ad brochure, this exemplar inscribed to Marcelle Blanchet and signed by Beltrand, book's designer, page size 13 x 10 inches, overall size 14 x 1.5 x 3 inches, 224 pages, all sheets loose, as issued in wrapper portfolio, all housed in boards chemise and slipcase, unusually fine.   Gemini Fine Books & Arts., Ltd.   Art Reference & Illustrated Books - 2013 $3000

Association – Bemens, Clarence

Maidment, James *A Book of Scottish Pasquils 1568-1715.* Edinburgh: William Paterson, 1868. One of 3 copies on vellum, (there were a limited but unspecified, number of copies, also printed on paper), 206 x 128mm., handsome contemporary crimson morocco, attractively gilt by Andrew Grieve (stamp signed), covers gilt with multiple plain and decorative rules enclosing a delicate dentelle frame, large intricate fleuron at center of each cover, spine gilt in double ruled compartments with complex fleuron centerpiece and scrolling floral cornerpieces, turn-ins decorated with plain and decorative gilt rules, patterned burgundy and gold silk endleaves, top edge gilt, slightly worn matching morocco lipped slipcase; woodcut titlepage illustration, numerous decorative tailpieces and occasional woodcut vignettes in text; armorial bookplate of H. D. Colvill-Scott, armorial bookplate of Clarence S. Bemens; tiny dark spot on spine, corners with just hint of rubbing, couple of leaves with slightly rumpled fore edge, still fine, text clean, smooth and bright, binding unusually lustrous and with virtually no wear. Phillip J. Pirages 63 - 479 2013 $4800

Association – Bennett, Arnold

Gide, Andre 1869-1951 *Le Retour de L'Enfant Prodique.* Paris: Nouvelle Revue Francaise, 1912. First edition, 8vo., original wrappers bound in to half red leather, slight fading to spine, otherwise near fine, inscribed by author for Arnold Bennett. Maggs Bros. Ltd. 1460 - 338 2013 £3000

Moore, George *Celibate Lives.* London: William Heinemann, 1927. First edition, large 8vo., original quarter brown cloth, printed paper label on spine, excellent copy, light shelfwear to upper cover, inscribed by Arnold and Dorothy Bennett to the future Lady Rothschild, Barbara Hutchinson. Maggs Bros. Ltd. 1460 - 84 2013 £250

Association – Bennett, Dorothy

Moore, George *Celibate Lives.* London: William Heinemann, 1927. First edition, large 8vo., original quarter brown cloth, printed paper label on spine, excellent copy, light shelfwear to upper cover, inscribed by Arnold and Dorothy Bennett to the future Lady Rothschild, Barbara Hutchinson. Maggs Bros. Ltd. 1460 - 84 2013 £250

Association – Bennett, Richard

Lefevre, Raoul *Le Recueil des Histoires de Troyes.* Bruges: William Caxton, 1473. First edition in French, small folio, Lettre batarde, lacking 32 printed leaves and two blanks, early 19th century brown straight grain morocco by Charles Lewis, gilt and blind ruled in geometric patterns, gilt inner dentelles, gilt edges, fine, unrestored, the missing leaves are internal and first and last printed leaves are present from the collection of the Duke of Roxburghe (sale 1812) of the third Earl Spencer (sale 1823), John Dent, with his notes (sale 1827), P. A. Hanrott (sale 1834) the Earl of Ashburnham (sale 1897); Richard Bennett with his bookplate and John Pierpont Morgan with his bookplate and shelfmark. Heritage Book Shop 50th Anniversary Catalogue - 62 2013 $950,000

Association – Benson, Frances

Brydges, Samuel Egerton *Sonnets and Other Poems.* London: B. & J. White, 1795. New edition, contemporary full tree calf, spine with bands and devices in gilt, dark green leather label, gilt wearing from spine, corners and hinges little rubbed, ownership inscription of Lady Frances Benson, gift inscription of Miss Louisa Brown, Nov. 1836. Jarndyce Antiquarian Booksellers CCIII - 40 2013 £125

Association – Berard, Christian

Colette, Sidonie Gabrielle 1873-1954 *Claudine's en va.* Monte Carlo: Editions Du Livre, 1946. Later edition, one of 3000 copies, this copy unnumbered, 8vo., original wrappers, acetate dust jacket preserved in folding box, near fine, dust jacket just little chipped at head and tail of spine, inscribed by the artist, Christian Berard for Cecil Beaton. Maggs Bros. Ltd. 1460 - 53 2013 £175

Association – Berger, Anna

Brecht, Bertolt *Poems on the Theatre.* Northwood: Scorpion Press, 1961. First edition, 8vo., original wrappers, inscribed by John and Anna Berger for Basil (probably Basil Bunting), near fine. Maggs Bros. Ltd. 1460 - 86 2013 £200

Association – Berger, John

Brecht, Bertolt *Poems on the Theatre.* Northwood: Scorpion Press, 1961. First edition, 8vo., original wrappers, inscribed by John and Anna Berger for Basil (probably Basil Bunting), near fine. Maggs Bros. Ltd. 1460 - 86 2013 £200

Association – Bergner, Elisabeth

Baring, Maurice *Selected Poems.* London: Heinemann, 1930. First edition, 8vo., excellent copy, original green cloth, inscribed by author for Elisabeth Bergner. Maggs Bros. Ltd. 1460 - 35 2013 £125

Association – Berkeley Castle

Labillardiere, Jacques Julien Houton De *Voyage in Search of La Perouse Performed by Order of the Constituent Assembly During the Years 1791, 172, 1793 and 1794.* London: Stockdale, 1800. 8vo., 2 volumes, 45 engraved plates with large folding map, contemporary tree calf, superb copy from Berkeley Castle, having had only very minor restoration to headcap of first volume. Maggs Bros. Ltd. 1467 - 83 2013 £2750

Association – Berkeley, Charles

Wolff, Christian *A Treatise of Algebra, with the Application of It to a Variety of Problems in Arithmetic, to Geometry, Trigonometry and Conic Sections.* printed for A. Bettersworth and C. Hitch, 1739. First edition in English, 8 folding engraved plates, one or two spots or stains, but crisp copy, 8vo. , contemporary unlettered polished calf, double gilt ruled borders on sides, gilt rules on either side of raised bands on backstrip, trifle worn, short crack at top of upper joint, two signatures inside front cover, earlier being that of Chas. Berkeley the other of Saml. Rippiner, Builder, Oundle May 1850, very good. Blackwell's Rare Books Sciences - 131 2013 £750

Association – Berland, Abel

Fraunce, Abraham *The Lawiers Logike...* London: by William How for Thomas Gubbin and T. Newman, 1588. First edition, 4to., folding table, title within type ornament border, woodcut initials, mixed black letter and roman, full red gilt panelled morocco, edges gilt by Bedford, first two leaves lightly washed, short closed tear on table, blank corner of 2K4 replaced, else fine clean copy, armorial bookplate of Sir Edwin Priaulx and booklabel of Abel E. Berland. Joseph J. Felcone Inc. Books Printed before 1701 - 40 2013 $8000

Suckling, John *Fragmenta Aurea.* London: for Humphrey Moseley, 1646. First edition, first state with "FRAGMENTA AVREA" in upper case, a period after Churchyard in imprint and rule under the date; A3v:16 reads "allowred", second state of frontispiece re-incised with heavier lines around leaves of the garland and the bulge in the left sleeve, according the Beaurline and Clayton, the plate was most certainly re-incised in course of printing and is fairly evenly distributed with the various states of title; engraved portrait, contemporary calf, gilt fillet and cornerpieces, red morocco spine label, portrait and 2 first 2 leaves with two very tiny holes at gutter, worm trail in lower margin of first three gatherings, else very nice in lovely contemporary binding; bookplate of C. Pearl Chamberlain and booklabel of Abel Berland, fine red morocco pull-off case; with ALS of John Suckling (1569-1627) father of the poet. Joseph J. Felcone Inc. Books Printed before 1701 - 83 2013 $6000

Suckling, John *Fragmenta Aurea.* London: for Humphrey Moseley, 1646. First edition, first state, engraved portrait, contemporary calf, gilt fillet and cornerpieces, red morocco spine label, portrait and first two leaves with two very tiny holes at gutter, worm trail in lower margin of first three gatherings, else very nice in lovely dust jacket binding, bookplate of C. Pearl Chamberlain and book label of Abel Berland, fine red morocco pull-off case, with ALS from John Suckling (1569-1627), father of poet to unnamed recipient. Joseph J. Felcone Inc. English and American Literature to 1800 - 22 2013 $6000

Young, Edward 1683-1765 *Night Thoughts on Life, Death and Immortality.* London: J. Walker, 1807. 140 x 75mm, very pretty contemporary red straight grain morocco, covers with gilt fillet border and blind tooled floral frame, upper cover with central medallion containing crest of Hope family surrounded by motto "At Spes Non Facta" and a wreath, raised bands, spine panels with cruciform centerpiece tooled in gilt and blind, gilt titling and turn-ins, all edges gilt, engraved frontispiece and pictorial title, front pastedown with booklabel of Abel Berland, spine bit darkened, joints just slightly rubbed, mild foxing to opening leaves, otherwise fine, clean and fresh internally and in solid, pleasing binding with little wear. Phillip J. Pirages 63 - 506 2013 $150

Association – Bernhardt, Sarah

Cocteau, Jean *Portraits - Souvenir 1900-1914.* Paris: Editions Bernard Grasset, 1935. Reprint, 8vo. original wrappers, near fine in protective folding box, lettered, inscribed by author for Sarah Bernhardt. Maggs Bros. Ltd. 1460 - 172 2013 £500

Association – Bernheimer, Earle

Frost, Robert Lee 1874-1963 *North of Boston.* London: David Nutt, 1914. First edition, one of 350 copies bound in coarse green linen out of a total edition of 1000, fine, preserved in black cloth slipcase and chemise, presentation copy inscribed by author for Earle Bernheimer.   James S. Jaffe Rare Books   Fall 2013 - 51   2013 $15,000

Association – Bernstein, Charles

Lazer, Hank *On Equal Terms. Poems by Charles Bernstein, David Ignatow, Denise Levertov, Louis Simpson, Gerald Stern.* Tuscaloosa: Symposium Press, 1984. First edition, limited to 275 copies, although not called for, this copy signed by all contributors, one of the few copies we've seen signed by any of the poets, 4to., original green wrappers, as new.   James S. Jaffe Rare Books   Fall 2013 - 5   2013 $450

Association – Berrigan, Ted

O'Hara, Frank *Love Poems.* New York: Tibor De Nagy Editions, 1965. First edition, limited to 500 copies, square 8vo., original wrappers, presentation copy inscribed by author for Ted (Berrigan), marvelous association, covers lightly soiled, but very good, enclosed in half leather and marbled board clamshell box.   James S. Jaffe Rare Books   Fall 2013 - 116   2013 $5000

Schuchat, Simon *Caveman.* New York: January, 1978. First edition, unnumbered issue, large narrow 4to., original stapled printed self wrappers, annotated throughout with Ted Berrigan's holograph notes identifying the author of many of the Pseudonymous contributions, very light overall use and dust soiling (bit heavier on back wrapper), otherwise near fine.   James S. Jaffe Rare Books   Fall 2013 - 22   2013 $2500

Association – Betjeman, John

Clark, Kenneth *The Nude. A Study of Ideal Art.* London: John Murray, 1956. First edition, small 4to., original red cloth, excellent copy, inscribed by John Betjeman to his wife Penelope Chetwoad.   Maggs Bros. Ltd.   1460 - 95   2013   £500

Association – Bevan, John

Monkhouse, W. *The Churches of York.* London: J. G. and F. Rivington, 1843. First edition, hand colored lithograph titlepage, lithograph dedication leaf, (i) subscribers list noting only 68 names + viii + (48) pages, 23 fine tinted lithograph plates and 3 ground plans, original blind and gilt stamped cloth, with later gilt lettered morocco spine, some foxing to dedication leaf, few other leaves but generally clean, old waterstain to lower inner blank corner, but not intrusive apart from dedication leaf leading edge of titlepage slightly torn and with several faint color splashes, with signature and note of John Bevan dated 1904 "This book was given my by my father in 1903 - the illustrations were drawn on stone by my grandfather William Bevan of York about 1863...".   Ken Spelman Books Ltd.   73 - 24   2013   £380

Association – Biddle, Moncure

Turpin, Richard *The Trial of the Notorious Highwayman Richard Turpin at York Assizes on the 22d Day of March 1793 Before the Hon. Sir William Chapple Knt. Judge of Assize and one of His Majesty's Justices of the Court of King;s Bench...* York: printed by Ward and Chandler, 1739. 8vo. little light browning, original stab holes visible, early 20th century half calf, marbled boards, armorial bookplate of Moncure Biddle.   Jarndyce Antiquarian Booksellers   CCIV - 300   2013   £3800

Association – Bigelow, A. E.

Stearns, Samuel *The American Herbal or Materia Medica.* Walpole: David Carlise for Thomas & Thomas and the author, 1801. 12mo., 360 pages, full modern calf, gilt spine rules, red gilt stamp spine label, 19th century style, some browning as might be expected, small stamp on title verso, early ownership signatures of A. E. Bigelow MD (1893), J. Henry Jackson (1870) and Fred K. Jackson (1903), very good, rare.   Jeff Weber Rare Books   169 - 426   2013 $3500

Association – Bigelow, Paul

Williams, Tennessee 1911-1983 *The Roman Spring of Mrs. Stone.* London: John Lehmann, 1950. First British edition, very good+ to near fine in very good plus dust jacket with few tiny chips to spine foot, presentation copy inscribed by author to Paul Bigelow.   Ed Smith Books   78 - 76   2013 $850

Association – Bignold, C. Robert

Byron, George Gordon Noel, 6th Baron   1788-1824
Don Juan. (Cantos I to V).   London: printed by G. Smeeton, 1821?   Color frontispiece bound in at page 207, engraved title, printed title, 5 other hand colored plates by I. R. Cruikshank, small tear in outer margin page 101/102 not affecting text, few internal marks, later full tree calf, gilt spine and borders, black leather label, marbled endpapers, slightly rubbed, lacking title label, armorial bookplate of C. Robert Bignold, very good, scarce.   Jarndyce Antiquarian Booksellers   CCIII - 265   2013   £280

Association – Billings, John Shaw

Morgan, John   *A Discourse Upon the Institution of Medical Schools in America.*   Philadelphia: William Bradford, 1765. 19th century full blond paneled calf, endpapers renewed, top edge gilt remargined along inner edge, text foxed, dampstaining affecting outer upper blank corner of pages, presentation copy fto John Shaw Billings, from John Stockton, quite rare.   James Tait Goodrich   75 - 153   2013 $8995

Association – Binnali, Richard Gibbons

Stillingfleet, Edward   *The Unreasonableness of Separation; or an Impartial Account of the... Present Separation from the Communion of the Church of England.* London: T. N. for Henry Mortlock, 1681.   First edition, 4to., some spotting and toning, first few leaves soiled, title a touch worn at fore edge, contemporary calf, marbled edges, rebacked and recornered by Chris Weston, old leather scratched and crackled early ink inscription Christopher Metcalfe, also printed booklabel Rev. Richard Gibbons Binnali, M.A.   Unsworths Antiquarian Booksellers   28 - 133   2013   £275

Association – Birch, A. F.

Campbell, Thomas   1777-1844   *The Poetical Works.* London: Edward Moxon, 1854.   Half title, frontispiece, illustrations, contemporary full green morocco, gilt spine borders and dentelles, slightly rubbed, spine little darkened, armorial booklabel of Viscount Newry and neat gift inscription "Newry from A. F. Birch. Eton Election 1858", all edges gilt, attractive copy.   Jarndyce Antiquarian Booksellers   CCIII - 454   2013   £45

Association – Bishop, C.

Burke, Edmund   1729-1797   *A Philosophical Enquiry into the Origin of Our Ideas of the Sublime and Beautiful.* London: printed for J. Dodsley, 1767.   8vo., some occasional foxing and light browning, full contemporary calf, gilt panelled spine, red morocco label, leading hinge cracked but firm, slight insect damage, spine chipped at head, 18th century armorial bookplate of Rev. Chas. Bishop, with name A. R. Winnington-Ingram 1880 who has underlined many sections of text in pencil and added several marginal notes to his reading.   Jarndyce Antiquarian Booksellers   CCIV - 78   2013   £125

Association – Bishop, Cortland

Pervigilium Veneris.   Doves Press, 1910.   One of 150 copies (of an edition of 162), printed in black on handmade paper with title, initials and refrain at end of each verse, printed in red, 8vo., original russet morocco, backstrip gilt panelled between seven raised bands, second and third gilt lettered and with date 1910 at tail, single gilt rule border to sides, green leather booklabels of Willis Vickery and Cortland Bishop, with some offsetting to front free endpaper, gilt edges, by Doves Bindery, fine.   Blackwell's Rare Books   172 - 272   2013   £1500

Association – Blackwell, Elizabeth

Ruskin, John   1819-1900   *The Ethics of the Dust.*   New York: John Wiley & Son, 1866.   First edition, from the library of the first woman physician, Elizabeth Blackwell, octavo, Blackwell's signature and date of 1866, bookplate, publisher's full purple cloth, decoratively ruled in blind, spine lettered gilt, dampstaining and wrinkling to cloth, spine sunned and soiled, head and tail of spine chipped some foxing to blanks, otherwise very clean, Blackwell's inscription, custom half morocco clamshell, very good.   Heritage Book Shop   Holiday Catalogue 2012 - 15   2013 $3500

Association – Blackwell, Miss

Boreman, Thomas   *The Gigantick History of the Two Famous Giants and Other Curiosities in Guildhall, London.* London: printed for Tho. Boreman, 1740.   Second edition, 64mo., woodcut frontispiece, full page woodcut illustrations, decorative tailpieces, gathered in eights, some slight browning but very good, contemporary quarter calf, embossed floral boards, lacking hinge cracked but firm, corners little rounded, early name of Miss Blackwell on inner front board. Jarndyce Antiquarian Booksellers   CCIV - 68   2013   £1500

Association – Blackwood, William

Oliphant, Margaret Oliphant Wilson 1828-1897
Jerusalem: Its History and Hope. London: Macmillan, 1891. First edition, half title, frontispiece, illustrations some light foxing, uncut in original green cloth, bevelled boards, spine lettered in gilt, front board with shield blocked in gilt and silver, armorial bookplate of William Blackwood, top edge gilt, very good, bright copy, loosely inserted printed slip "From the author".   Jarndyce Antiquarian Booksellers CCV - 215   2013   £120

Association – Blaine, Nell

Ashbery, John *Locus Solus.* France: Locus Solus, 1960-1962. First edition, regular issue being the second (trimmed state of the first volume), 4 volumes, 8vo. original printed wrappers, fine set, artist Nell Blaine's set with her ownership signature.   James S. Jaffe Rare Books   Fall 2013 - 12   2013 $1250

Ashbery, John *The Tennis Court Oath. A Book of Poems.* Middletown: Wesleyan University Press, 1962. First edition, one of only 750 copies, 8vo., original cloth, dust jacket, fine in fine dust jacket, presentation copy inscribed by author for artist Nell Blaine.   James S. Jaffe Rare Books Fall 2013 - 10   2013 $2500

Koch, Kenneth *Poems/Prints.* New York: Editions of the Tibor de Nagy Gallery, 1953. First edition, 4to., original illustrated card wrappers, stapled, 4 original linoleum cuts by Nell Blaine, one of 300 numbered copies (entire edition), not issued signed by poet or artist, but this copy signed and dated by Blaine on three large mounted prints in bottom margin, very fine, rare in such beautiful condition, with none of the offsetting and staining that so often marks this book. James S. Jaffe Rare Books   Fall 2013 - 83   2013 $4500

Association – Blair-Bell, W.

Byron, George Gordon Noel, 6th Baron 1788-1824
Sardanapalus. London: John Murray, 1823. First separate edition, uncut in original blue boards, drab spine and paper label slightly chipped, hinges slightly cracked, armorial bookplate of Prof. W. Blair-Bell, Renier booklabel. Jarndyce Antiquarian Booksellers CCIII - 301   2013   £35

Association – Blairhame

Johnson, Samuel 1709-1784 *The Prince of Abissinia.* London: printed for R. and J. Dodsley and W. Johnston, 1759. First edition, first state of volume II with leaf A2, 2 volumes, small 8vo., full contemporary calf, gilt ruled borders, minor wear, usual offsetting to endpapers and titlepages, discrete Blairhame leather book label on front endsheets, otherwise unusually attractive copy in original state with all blanks, preserved in brown half morocco slipcase. James S. Jaffe Rare Books   Fall 2013 - 78   2013 $12,500

Association – Blake, Paul

Weiss, Ruth *A New View of Matter/Novy Pohled Na Vec.* Prague: Mata, 1999. First edition, bi-lingual Czech-English, with photo section at rear, fine in fine dust jacket, inscribed by author, signed by photographer, Paul Blake. Beasley Books   2013 - 2013 $100

Association – Blakiston, Noel

Acton, Harold *The Bourbons of Naples. (and) The Last Bourbons of Naples.* London: Methuen, 1956-1961. First editions, 2 volumes, 8vo., original blue cloth, dust jackets excellent copies, jackets slightly rubbed, inscribed by author to Noel Blakiston.   Maggs Bros. Ltd.   1460 - 5   2013 £650

Connolly, Cyril 1903-1974 *The Condemned Playground. Essays 1927-1944.* London: Routledge, 1945. First edition, 8vo., frontispiece by Augustus John, original black cloth, dust jacket nicked at extremities, near fine, inscribed by author for Noel Blakiston.   Maggs Bros. Ltd.   1460 - 185   2013   £750

Connolly, Cyril 1903-1974 *Enemies of Promise.* London: George Routledge, 1938. First edition, large 8vo., original blue cloth, dust jacket browned and slightly creased and nicked at edges, excellent copy, inscribed by author to Noel Blakiston.   Maggs Bros. Ltd.   1460 - 178   2013   £1250

Connolly, Cyril 1903-1974 *The Unquiet Grave.* London: Horizon, 1944. First edition, 8vo., original wrappers, inscribed by author for Noel Blakiston, with further 45 word note beneath, slightly chipped, otherwise near fine in protective box.   Maggs Bros. Ltd.   1460 - 182 2013   £750

Horizon. A Review of Literature & Art. Volume I No. 1. London: published by the Proprietors, 1940. First edition, 8vo., original brown wrappers, stained on corner of lower cover, otherwise excellent copy in protective folding box, inscribed by Cyril Connolly for Noel Blakiston.   Maggs Bros. Ltd.   1460 - 180   2013   £600

Wordsworth, William 1770-1850 *The Prelude or Growth of a Poet's Mind.* London: Edward Moxon, 1850. First edition, 8vo., original brown cloth, blocked in blind, preserved in folding box, inscribed by Cyril Connolly for Noel Blakiston Jan 17.27, very good, lower joint splitting, extremities worn, plain and large earlier bookplate, issue without publisher's ads.   Maggs Bros. Ltd.   1460 - 177   2013   £650

Association – Blanchard, Dr.

Romen, Jean Joseph Therese *L'Inoculation Poeme en Quatre Chants.* Amsterdam & Paris: Chez Lacomee, 1773. First edition, Engraved frontispiece, 8vo. original full tan mottled calf, gilt paneled spine, all edges marbled, light rubbing to binding, internally fine, from the library of Dr. Blanchard with his bookplate, tipped post card from Paris (1891) with note by A. Corlieu in regards to this book.   James Tait Goodrich   S74 - 217   2013 $495

Association – Blanchard, Jessie

Roberts, Charles *Poems of Wild Life.* London: Walter Scott, 1888. 12mo., dark gray cloth with printed paper label to spine, extreme wear to top and bottom of spine and corners, light waterstains to front cover, signed by Roberts for Miss Jessie Blanchard.   Schooner Books Ltd.   105 - 21   2013 $75

Association – Blanchet, Marcelle

Dorgeles, Roland *Vacances Forcees.* Paris: Editions Vialetay, 1956. First edition, one of several deluxe copies "nominatif" (Marcelle Blanchet), produced for collaborators on book, from total edition of 233, printed on Rives wove paper, signed in ink by Dorgeles, Jacques Beltrand and the publisher, on justification page, 24 original color woodcuts, including 23 in texte, engraved by Beltrand after original watercolors by Raoul Dufy + a suite of 23 hors texte woodcuts on thin Japon paper in separate folder, woodcuts are color decompositions of one plate + a suite of 22 hors texte color decomposition woodcuts on Rives wove paper + one 'etat incomplet' woodcut, also in separate folder, also included is publisher's ad brochure, this exemplar inscribed to Marcelle Blanchet and signed by Beltrand, book's designer, page size 13 x 10 inches, overall size 14 x 1.5 x 3 inches, 224 pages, all sheets loose, as issued in wrapper portfolio, all housed in boards chemise and slipcase, unusually fine.   Gemini Fine Books & Arts., Ltd.   Art Reference & Illustrated Books - 2013 $3000

Association – Blanding, Terese

Miura, Kerstin Tini *My World of Bibliophile Binding.* Berkeley: University of California Press, 1984. First edition, 343 x 268mm., original blindstamped lilac colored cloth, flat spine with vertical titling, matching slipcase with printed paper label on cover, 152 pages of color photos, including double folding plate, bookplate of Terese Blanding, as new.   Phillip J. Pirages   63 - 70   2013 $225

Association – Blaq, R.

Church of England. Book of Common Prayer *The Booke of Common Prayer and Administration of the Sacraments and Other Rites and Ceremonies of the Church of England.* London: by Robert Barker, printer to the Kings most excellent Majesty, 1634. 4to., very good, 19th century quarter calf, pebble grain cloth boards, armorial bookplate of A. C. Gloucester, with near contemporary name Rog. Blaq in blank space at foot of titlepage border with few manuscript emendations to text, verse numbers noted at head of titlepage.   Ken Spelman Books Ltd.   75 - 2   2013   £350

Association – Blencowe, William

Bion *(Bion and Moschus) Opera.* Londini: T. Bensley, 1795. Large paper copy, 8vo., occasional spotting, little toning to edges of front and rear blanks, tan sheep very slightly diced, spine gilt, gilt dentelles, marbled edges and endpapers upper joint cracked but board still firmly attached, lower joint starting, loss to endcaps, spine and edges rubbed, corner tips worn, name Gulielmus (William) M. Blencowe in gilt to upper board and 'Honoris Causu" similarly gilt to lower board.   Unsworths Antiquarian Booksellers   28 - 5   2013   £125

Association – Blomfield, George Becher

Homerus *Homeri Ilias (in Greek).* Venice: Aldus Manutius not before 31 October, 1504. First Aldine edition, second edition in Greek, small octavo, bound without final blank, title in Greek and Latin, text in Greek, Greek and Italic types, 30 lines plus headline, capital spaces with guide letters, 19th century vellum over boards, covers bordered with ink rule, smooth spine decoratively tooled in gilt with dark green morocco gilt lettering label turn-ins ruled in gilt, all edges gilt, marbled endpapers, lower blank corner of first leaf of Herodotus's life of Homer renewed, not affecting text, small intermittent dampstain in lower margin, armorial bookplate of George Becher Blomfield on front pastedown, pencilled annotations on verso of front free endpaper, early ink line numbers in outer margin of few leaves.   Heritage Book Shop   50th Anniversary Catalogue - 48   2013 $20,000

Association – Blouet de Camilly

Newton, Isaac 1642-1727 *Philosophiae Nautralis Principia Mathematica.* Amsterdam: Sumptibus Societatis, 1714. First Amsterdam edition, contemporary full leather, spine in six compartments, gilt decorations and titling to spine, covers with mild wear, joints strengthened, bookplate of renowned French Blouet de Camilly family, endpapers with mild soil scattered foxing, titlepage printed in black and red, engraved vignette, folding plate of comet orbits, 4to., attractive copy. By the Book, L. C. 38 - 6 2013 $15,000

Association – Blumenbach, Joseph Friedrich

Du Verney, Joseph Guichard *Tractatus de Organo Auditus, Continens Structuarm Usum et Morbos Omnium auris Partium.* Nuremberg: Johann Zieger, 1684. First edition in Latin, 4to., (12), 48 pages, with 16 engraved folding plates, 19th century paper wrappers, plate 16 neatly backed, title very lightly soiled, else very good, Joseph Friedrich Blumenbach's copy with his signature, fine morocco backed clamshell box. Joseph J. Felcone Inc. Books Printed before 1701 - 67 2013 $4800

Association – Blunt, Scawen

Boyer, Abel *Boyer's Royal Dictionary Abridged.* London: printed for Messrs, Bathurst, Pote, Rivingtons, Owen, Buckland, Longman (and 23 others), 1786. Sixteenth edition, one folding table, some light spotting, 8vo., contemporary sheep rebacked preserving original morocco lettering piece, corners repaired, hinges neatly relined, old leather marked, bookplate of Scawen Blunt (probably Francis, father of poet Wilfrid), good. Blackwell's Rare Books B174 - 14 2013 £300

Association – Boette, Michael

Boerhaave, Hermann *Praelectiones Academicae in Proprias Institutiones rei medicae...* Naples: Sumptibus Dom,inci Terres ex typographia Josephi Raymundi, 1754-1755. 7 volumes, title of volume i printed in red and black, each titlepage with woodcut vignette, two small burn holes in B2 of volume vi with loss of few letters, some very minor marginal dampstaining and occasional light foxing, 4to., original carta rustica, front inner hinge volume i little weak, slight soiling, contemporary signature on each title of Michael Boette, very good. Blackwell's Rare Books 172 - 30 2013 £1500

Association – Boggs, W. H. C.

Jenner, Edward *Further Observations on the Varioale Vaccinae or Cow Pox.* London: printed for the author by Sampson Low, 1799. First edition, Half title, title, (6), 64 pages, 4to., uncut, large wide margins, light dampstaining affected outer margins, browned in parts, original blue sugar wrappers, lacking rear one, clamshell protective case, with ALS circa 1800 to Louis Hallady and Rev. W. H. C. Boggs and signed Z. Lewis. Rob. Hart. James Tait Goodrich 75 - 125 2013 $4500

Association – Bok, Mary Louise Curtis

English Lyrics. London: printed at the Chiswick Press for Kegan Paul, Trench & Co., 1883. First edition, one of 50 large paper copies, this #32, 206 x 130mm., fine turn-of-the-century Hazel brown crushed morocco, very elaborately gilt by Zaehnsdorf (stamp signed on front turn-in, oval blind-stamp on rear pastedown), covers richly gilt with very wide floral border featuring many tendrils and small tools, border enclosing panel filled with alternating rows of floral sprigs and leaves (tiny stars in between), raised bands, spine compartments gilt with either floral bouquet or rows of leaves and flowers, densely gilt turn-ins, gray silk endleaves, top edge gilt, other edges untrimmed, armorial bookplate of Mary Louise Curtis Bok, half title with pencilled note "Wedding present to M.L.C./from Charles Scribner October 1896", (spine just slightly sunned toward a darker brown, front joint and very top and bottom of back joint little worn, with flaking and thin cracks, but no looseness), corners slightly rubbed, still especially attractive with lovely binding with glistening covers and beautifully printed text pristine. Phillip J. Pirages 63 - 65 2013 $1250

Association – Bolton, E.

Cotton, Charles *Poems on Several Occasions.* printed for Tho. Basset, Will. Hensmann and Tho. fox, 1689. First edition, little browned and stained in places, one leaf dust stained in fore-margin and frail at foot, rust hole in one leaf in blank area, 8vo., contemporary panelled calf, rebacked preserving most of the original spine, gilt almost entirely faded away, red lettering piece, contemporary initials EJL on flyleaf, inscription of John Amson dated 1722 on title and also on flyleaf, later armorial bookplate of E. and F. Bolton, good. Blackwell's Rare Books B174 - 39 2013 £650

Association – Bolton, F.

Cotton, Charles *Poems on Several Occasions.* printed for Tho. Basset, Will. Hensmann and Tho. fox, 1689. First edition, little browned and stained in places, one leaf dust stained in fore-margin and frail at foot, rust hole in one leaf in blank area, 8vo., contemporary panelled calf, rebacked preserving most of the original spine, gilt almost entirely faded away, red lettering piece, contemporary initials EJL on flyleaf, inscription of John Amson dated 1722 on title and also on flyleaf, later armorial bookplate of E. and F. Bolton, good.   Blackwell's Rare Books   B174 - 39   2013   £650

Association – Bone, Gertrude

Bone, Gavin *Anglo-Saxon Poetry.* Oxford: Clarendon Press, 1944. First reprint, 8vo., original cream cloth, excellent copy, inscribed by Muirhead and Gertrude Bone to A. S. F. Gow.   Maggs Bros. Ltd.   1460 - 125   2013   £50

Association – Bone, Muirhead

Bone, Gavin *Anglo-Saxon Poetry.* Oxford: Clarendon Press, 1944. First reprint, 8vo., original cream cloth, excellent copy, inscribed by Muirhead and Gertrude Bone to A. S. F. Gow.   Maggs Bros. Ltd.   1460 - 125   2013   £50

Association – Bonhoff, Friedrich Karl Paul

Dieffenbach, Johann Friedrich *Ueber die Durchschneidung der Sebnen und Muskeln.* Berlin: Albert Forstner, 1841. First edition, 8vo., 20 lithographed plates, occasional foxing, original brown cloth backed boards, printed paper spine label, extremities worn, bookplate of Dr. Fr. Bonhoff, rare.   Jeff Weber Rare Books   172 - 78   2013 $1250

Association – Booth, Nellie

Winslow, Anna Green *Diary of Anna Green Winslow. A Boston Girl of 1771.* Cambridge: Boston and New York: Houghton Mifflin Co., Riverside Press, 1894. First edition, 8vo., canvas covered boards with ties in blue, red, green and black on front cover, half title, black and white frontispiece, facsimile and 5 black and white illustrations, spine darkened and inscription on first flyleaf "Mrs. Mills with compliments Nellie F. Booth 1895".   Schooner Books Ltd.   101 - 128   2013 $55

Association – Booth, S. M.

Bowles, William Lisle *Sonnets with other Poems.* Bath: printed by R. Cruttwell and sold by C. Dilly, Poultry, London, 1794. Third edition, half title, contemporary full calf, gilt spine, border and dentelles, dark green leather label, bit rubbed, hinges little worn, one or two small splits, possibly author's copy with armorial bookplate "Revd. Mr. Bowles", also small booklabel of Charles Wells and gift inscription "Anna Maria Pinney 1835. From S. M. Booth", blindstamped and labels of Birkbeck College Library.   Jarndyce Antiquarian Booksellers   CCIII - 33   2013   £150

Association – Borrowman, Ruth

Whitehead, William *The Historian's Pocket Companion; or Memory's Assistant.* Newcastle: printed by T. Angus..., 1777. 12mo., little soiled, foxed and browned, recent calf backed boards with original marbled paper covers laid down, ownership inscriptions on engraved title of John Hudson and Ruth Borrowman, sound, rare.   Blackwell's Rare Books   172 - 103   2013   £450

Association – Borthwick, John

Cowley, Abraham   1618-1667 *The Works of Mr. Abraham.* London: printed for J. Tonson, Charles Harper, 1710-1711. Ninth edition, 3 volumes, 8vo., frontispiece, 17 engraved plates, frontispiece, 9 engraved plates, frontispiece and 4 engraved plates, lightly browned, little minor spotting, contemporary calf, plain spine with red morocco labels, boards bordered in blind, edges sprinkled red, rubbed at extremities, neatly conserved by Chris Weston replacing original labels, f.f.e.p. removed from first volume, early ink ownership inscription "Anne Pitt and large armorial bookplate John Borthwick/Crookston".   Unsworths Antiquarian Booksellers   28 - 87   2013   £225

Association – Bosanquet, George Jacob

Escobar, Juan De *Romancero a Historia del Muy Valeroso Cavallero El cid Ruy Diaz en Lenguge Antiguo.* Cadiz: Pedro Ortiz, 1702. Second Cadiz edition, woodcut printer's device on title, top of gutter of one opening torn by intrusive sewing, entering text but without loss paper flaw in one leaf affecting 3 or 4 letters on either side, slight ocasional browning or soiling, fairly tightly sewn, long 12mo., recased in original vellum, lettered ink on spine, marbled edges, armorial bookplate, inside front cover of George Jacob Bosanquet, good.   Blackwell's Rare Books   172 - 53   2013   £650

Association – Bottrall, Ronald

Guinness, Bryan *Reflexions.* London: Heinemann, 1947. First edition, 8vo., original yellow cloth, printed paper label on upper cover, excellent copy, inscribed to Cornish poet Ronald Bottrall by author.   Maggs Bros. Ltd.   1460 - 384   2013   £50

Association – Boulton, Matthew

Lewis, William *The Philosophical Commerce of Arts...* printed for the author, 1765. First edition, 4to., contemporary calf, red lettering piece, some worming at foot of spine and slight wear to extremities, Christie's Matthew Boulton label inside front cover, good. Blackwell's Rare Books 172 - 92   2013   £650

Association – Bowen, Elizabeth

Bowes Lyon, Lilian *Collected Poems.* London: Jonathan Cape, 1948. First edition, 8vo., original blue cloth, excellent copy, spine slightly faded, inscribed by author for Elizabeth Bowen. Maggs Bros. Ltd.   1460 - 128   2013   £125

Israel, Madeleine *Poemes 1928-1934.* 1938. First edition, 8vo., 126 pages, wrappers, unopened, very good, signed presentation copy to Elizabeth Bowen. C. P. Hyland   261 - 145   2013   £45

Picard, Raymond *Les Prestiges.* 1947. First edition, 8vo., wrappers, very good, signed presentation copy for Elizabeth Bowen. C. P. Hyland   261 - 143   2013   £40

Association – Bowlby, Henry

Dacier, Andre *The Life of Pythagoras with his Symbols and Golden Verses. Together with the Life of Hierocles...* London: printed for Jacob Tonson within Grays-Inn Lane, 1707. First English translation, 8vo., some browning to titlepage, early name written down leading margin, expertly bound in recent quarter sprinkled calf, marbled boards, vellum tips, raised and gilt banded spine, red morocco label, bookplate of Henry Bowlby. Jarndyce Antiquarian Booksellers   CCIV - 103   2013   £280

Association – Bowles, George

Bowles, John *The Retrospect; or a Collection of Tracts, Published at Various Periods of the War...* London: printed for T. N. Longman, 1798. 19th century half morocco, spine neatly repaired at head and tail, family copy, signature of George Bowles Junr., Jan. 1852 on titlepage. Ken Spelman Books Ltd.   75 - 49   2013   £120

Bowles, William Lisle *The Missionary: a Poems.* London: John Murray, 1813. Second edition, full contemporary dark blue morocco, gilt and blind spine and borders, gilt dentelles, spine slightly rubbed, slight wear to head small booklabel of John Sparrow, all edges gilt, inscribed "from the author..." Latin ownership and note, armorial bookplate of George Downing Bowles, of Fawley, Southampton. Jarndyce Antiquarian Booksellers   CCIII - 34   2013   £150

Association – Bowling, Mr.

Sauvan, Jean Baptiste Balthazar *Picturesque Tour of the Seine, from Paris to the Sea with Particulars Historical and Descriptive.* London: R. Ackermann, 1821. 345 x 275mm., publisher's red buckram, covers with blindstamped frame, upper cover with gilt titling, flat spine stamped with gilt strapwork panels and with gilt titling, all edges gilt, engraved color vignette on titlepage, unsigned aquatint vignette at foot of last page, engraved color map, 24 fine hand colored aquatint plates by Augustus Pugin and John Gendall; presentation bookplate to Master E. Cockayne as reward of merit by Mr. Bowling/Milk Street Academy, Sheffield June 23rd 1848; binding little soiled, joints and extremities bit worn, just slightest offsetting from some plates onto text, one plate with offsetting from text ad half dozen others with just hint of same, other trivial imperfections, very desirable copy. Phillip J. Pirages   63 - 422   2013 $6000

Association – Boyle, Kay

Beckett, Samuel   1906-1989 *Compagnie.* Paris: Editions de Minuit, 1980. First edition, foolscap 8vo., original printed white wrappers, fine, Kay Boyle's copy with her signature, inscribed for her by author, parcel address label written by Beckett, loosely inserted in book. Blackwell's Rare Books   172 - 161   2013   £750

Beckett, Samuel   1906-1989 *That Time.* London: Faber, 1976. First edition, 16mo., original printed wrappers, front cover with image of Beckett, near fine, inscribed by author for Kay Boyle. Blackwell's Rare Books   172 - 165   2013   £650

Association – Boyle, Mildred

Wilder, Laura Ingalls *By the Shores of Silver Lake.* New York: Harper & Bros., 1939. Stated first edition, 8vo., pictorial cloth, fine in very slightly worn dust jacket, color dust jacket and frontispiece by Helen Sewell and in line by Mildred Boyle, this was Boyle's own copy inscribed by her for her niece. Aleph-Bet Books, Inc.   105 - 588   2013 $3500

Association – Bradley, Henry Waldron

Smart, Christopher *Musae Seatonianae.* printed by T. Wright for G. Pearch, 1772. First edition, touch of minor browning, ownership inscription of Nicolson Calvert (1816), 8vo., contemporary sprinkled calf, spine divided by gilt milled rolls, black lettering piece in second compartment, rest with central octagonal tools containing sunbursts, rubbed, front joint splitting, ownership inscription of Henry Waldron Bradley, sound. Blackwell's Rare Books   B174 - 143   2013   £300

Association – Brady, Anne

McCullough, Niall *Dublin. An Urban History. The Plan of the City.* Dublin: Associated Editions, 2007. First edition, number 55 of 755 copies signed by author, this copy signed by designer Anne Brady, oblong 4to., original full black cloth blindstamped with plan of Dublin, spine lettered silver, fine in silver slipcase.   Maggs Bros. Ltd.   1442 - 213   2013   £250

Association – Brailsford, John William

Donne, John   1571-1631 *Poems, &c. With Elegies on the Author's Death.* London: printed by T. N. for Henry Herringman, 1669. Fifth edition, complete with initial and terminal blanks, some dampstaining in later half of volume, contemporary calf, double blind ruled borders on sides, ornamental corner pieces, binder's flyleaf at end of early 16th century text printed in red and black, bearing contemporary (1669), signature of William Stanell, rebacked, cover crackled, bookplate of archaeologist John William Brailsford.   Blackwell's Rare Books   B174 - 50   2013   £3250

Association – Braithwaite, D. B.

Braithwaite, J. Bevan *J. Bevan Braithwaite.* London: Hodder & Stoughton, 1909. First edition, original blue cloth, gilt, untrimmed, 19 illustrations, scattered spotting, inscribed by D. B. Braithwaite for Alexander Dunlop.   R. F. G. Hollett & Son   Lake District & Cumbria - 166   2013   £40

Association – Branch, Gwendolen

Junius, Pseud. *Junius. Stat Nominis Umbra.* London: printed by T. Bensley for Vernor and Hood et al, 1801. 2 volumes, 8vo., engraved titlepage (dated 1797), engraved portrait frontispieces and other engraved plates portrait plates, foxed, contemporary straight grained dark blue morocco, spine gilt in compartments with liberty cap tool, also lettered direct, boards bordered in gilt, bit rubbed at extremities and touched up with blue dye, small printed booklabel 'Gwendolen Branch'.   Unsworths Antiquarian Booksellers   28 - 178   2013   £160

Association – Brandom, I. M.

Bell, Charles   1774-1842 *Institutes of Surgery; Arranged in the Order of the Lectures Delivered in the University of Edinburgh.* Edinburgh: Adam and Charles Black; London: Longman, Orme, Brown, Green & Longmans, 1838. First edition, 2 volumes, 12mo., original green cloth, printed paper spine labels, rubbed, volume II faded, ownership signatures of I. M. Brandon 1839, very good.   Jeff Weber Rare Books   172 - 18   2013 $375

Association – Brandon, Woodthorpe

Paris, J. A. *Philosophy in sport Made Science in Earnest.* London: John Murray, 1861. Ninth edition, original green cloth, gilt, woodcut frontispiece and numerous text illustrations, prelims rather foxed, shaped armorial bookplate of Woodthorpe Brandon.   R. F. G. Hollett & Son   Children's Books - 436   2013   £85

Association – Brayshaw, Thomas

Museum of the Yorkshire Philosophical Society *A Descriptive Account of the Antiquities in the Grounds and in the Museum of the Yorkshire Philosophical Society.* York: H. Sotheran, 1852. Original linen backed boards rather dusty and corner of one leaf torn without loss, presentation copy from author, inscribed, bookplate of Thos. Brayshaw of Settle.   Ken Spelman Books Ltd.   73 - 29   2013   £45

Association – Breckpol, Raymond

Statius, Publius Papinius *Sylvarum Libri V. Thebaidos Libro XII. Achilleidos Libri II. (bound with) Orthographia ex Flexus Dictrionum Graecarum Omnium apud Statius cum Accentib. et Generib. ex varaiis utriusque linguae authoribus.* Paris: Apud Simonem Colinaeum, 1530. 8vo., some light staining, old and slightly discolored repairs to blank areas of first and last leaf, few small marginal tears, frequent later annotations in pencil and ink, late 19th century olive calf, largely faded to brown, boards with blind frame with gilt cornerpieces, spine to compartments with central gilt stamps, second compartment gilt lettered direct, all edges gilt, rubbed, small chip from head of spine, short crack to front joint, ownership inscription of Raymond Breckpol (contemporary with binding?) to head of titlepage, date of publication and an old cypher stamp both in violet ink to f.f.e.p., same repeated on rear pastedown (though cypher here handwritten), along with inscription of Chad Carbacusend(?) 1913 and small colored pictorial label.   Unsworths Antiquarian Booksellers   28 - 47   2013   £650

Association – Bridge, Alex

Bailey, Thomas *Hand-book to Newstead Abbey.* London: Simpkin, Marshall & Co., 1855. 2 plates, frontispiece, 9 pages ads, original printed yellow wrappers, printed in black, elaborate embossed floral borders, small scratch on front wrapper, slightly dusted, booklabel of Alex Bridge, very good.   Jarndyce Antiquarian Booksellers   CCIII - 343   2013   £125

Byron, George Gordon Noel, 6th Baron   1788-1824 *The Corsair, a Tale.* London: John Murray, 1814. Fourth edition, first issue, half title, 8 page catalog, later drab wrappers, spine with two small repaired tears, ink title, booklabel of Alex Bridge and ownership inscription of Charles Strachey, very good.   Jarndyce Antiquarian Booksellers   CCIII - 184   2013   £30

Byron, George Gordon Noel, 6th Baron   1788-1824 *The Deformed Transformed. (bound with) The Island, or Christian and His Comrades.*   London: printed for J. & H. L. Hunt, 1824. London: John Hunt, 1823. Second edition and third edition, 2 volumes in 1, half titles, contemporary half calf, gilt spine, rubbed, corners and spine little worn, booklabel ad signature of Alex Bridge, library label of Harry Matthews.   Jarndyce Antiquarian Booksellers   CCIII - 319   2013   £180

Byron, George Gordon Noel, 6th Baron   1788-1824 *Don Juan. (Cantos I to V).*   Benbow, printer and publisher 1822, 1824. 12mo., frontispiece and title (122), printed title (1824) with Sudbury imprint), slight browning, uncut in original drab boards, paper label, rubbed, spine cracked and little darkened, booklabel and signature of Alex Bridge.   Jarndyce Antiquarian Booksellers   CCIII - 266   2013   £90

Byron, George Gordon Noel, 6th Baron   1788-1824 *English Bards and Scotch Reviewers.*   London: James Cawthorn, 1812. Third edition, half title, 3 pages ads, interleaved with blanks, edges slightly affected by damp, maroon floral cloth circa 1830, spine lettered in gilt, faded to brown, booklabel of Alex Bridge.   Jarndyce Antiquarian Booksellers   CCIII - 121   2013   £60

Byron, George Gordon Noel, 6th Baron   1788-1824 *English Bards and Scotch Reviewers.*   London: James Cawthorn, 1817. Mixture of fourth and fifth third edition, half title, 3 pages ads, unopened, uncut in contemporary drab boards, pale green paper spine, head and tail of spine slightly chipped, booklabel of Alex Bridge, good plus.   Jarndyce Antiquarian Booksellers   CCIII - 123   2013   £65

Byron, George Gordon Noel, 6th Baron   1788-1824 *English Bards and Scotch Reviewers.*   London: James Cawthorn, 1818. Third edition, uncut in original pale blue boards, faded purple spine strip, paper label, small ink stain on front board, very good, bookplate of Alex Bridge.   Jarndyce Antiquarian Booksellers   CCIII - 127   2013   £75

Byron, George Gordon Noel, 6th Baron   1788-1824 *English Bards and Scotch Reviewers.*   London: James Cawthorn, 1818. Eighth spurious third edition, without half title, contemporary half black calf, gilt spine, bit rubbed, booklabel of Alex Bridge.   Jarndyce Antiquarian Booksellers   CCIII - 126   2013   £60

Byron, George Gordon Noel, 6th Baron   1788-1824 *English Bards and Scotch Reviewers.*   London: James Cawthorn, 1818. Sixth spurious third edition, half title, 1 page following ad contemporary full tan calf gilt spine, hinges weak, lacking spine label, booklabel of Alex Bridge, offsetting to leading f.e.p. from previous owner's bookplate.   Jarndyce Antiquarian Booksellers   CCIII - 124   2013   £45

Byron, George Gordon Noel, 6th Baron   1788-1824 *English Bards and Scotch Reviewers.*   London: James Cawthorn, 1809. Second edition, half title, final ad leaf, contemporary full tan calf by F. Bedford, gilt spine, borders and dentelles, green leather label, spine slightly rubbed, leading hinge repaired, armorial bookplate of Laurence Currie and Alex Bridge booklabel, all edges gilt, good plus.   Jarndyce Antiquarian Booksellers   CCIII - 118   2013   £220

Byron, George Gordon Noel, 6th Baron   1788-1824 *Fugitive Pieces.*   New York: Columbia University Press, 1933. Half title, original brown cloth, very good, signature and booklabel of Alex Bridge.   Jarndyce Antiquarian Booksellers   CCIII - 108   2013   £60

Byron, George Gordon Noel, 6th Baron   1788-1824 *(Hebrew Melodies) Fugitive Pieces and Reminiscences.*   London: Whittaker, Treacher and Co., 1829. 12 page catalog, odd spot, uncut in original drab boards, green cloth spine, paper label, slightly chipped, hinges splitting in places, boards with some surface wear, booklabel of Alex Bridge.   Jarndyce Antiquarian Booksellers   CCIII - 206   2013   £480

Byron, George Gordon Noel, 6th Baron   1788-1824 *The Giaour, a Fragment of a Turkish Tale.*   London: printed by T. Davison for John Murray, 1813. Eighth edition, half title, slightly spotted, later marbled wrappers, spine slightly dulled and with small chip at tail, ownership inscription of Mrs. Crampton on half title, booklabel of Alex Bridge.   Jarndyce Antiquarian Booksellers   CCIII - 166   2013   £30

Byron, George Gordon Noel, 6th Baron   1788-1824 *Lara, a Tale.*   London: John Murray, 1815. Fifth edition, half title, slight browning sympathetic later drab boards, booklabel and signature of Alex Bridge, very good.   Jarndyce Antiquarian Booksellers   CCIII - 201   2013   £35

Byron, George Gordon Noel, 6th Baron   1788-1824 *Lord Byron's Historical Tragedy of Sardanapalus.*   Manchester: John Heywood, 1877? 5 pages ads, original buff wrappers, printed in red and black, slightly marked, spine chipped, booklabel and signature of Alex Bridge.   Jarndyce Antiquarian Booksellers   CCIII - 302   2013   £120

Byron, George Gordon Noel, 6th Baron   1788-1824 *Marino Faliero, Doge of Venice. The Prophecy of Dante, a Poem.*   London: John Murray, 1821. First edition,, first issue, half title, uncut in original pale blue boards, drab spine, paper label, small nick in front board, hinge little worn, armorial bookplate of J.G.B., booklabel of Alex Bridge, good plus.   Jarndyce Antiquarian Booksellers   CCIII - 288   2013   £150

Byron, George Gordon Noel, 6th Baron 1788-1824
Marino Faliero, Doge of Venice. The Prophecy of Dante, a Poem. London: John Murray, 1821. First edition, 2nd issue, half title, final ad leaf, uncut in original drab boards, paper label, hinges and head and tail of spine little worn, one corner slightly creased, booklabel and signature of Alex Bridge, nice copy.   Jarndyce Antiquarian Booksellers   CCIII - 290   2013   £250

Byron, George Gordon Noel, 6th Baron 1788-1824
Marino Faliero, Doge of Venice. The Prophecy of Dante, a Poem. London: John Murray, 1823. Third edition, half title, uncut in original pink boards, paper label, spine little worn and chipped at ends, label partially removed from tail of spine, booklabel and signature of Alex Bridge.   Jarndyce Antiquarian Booksellers   CCIII - 294   2013   £85

Byron, George Gordon Noel, 6th Baron 1788-1824
Mazeppa, a Poem. London: John Murray, 1819. First edition, 2nd issue, half title, final ad leaf and 8 page catalog & July 1819, spotted, uncut in original drab wrappers, spine little chipped, contemporary ownership inscription, booklabel and signature of Alex Bridge.   Jarndyce Antiquarian Booksellers   CCIII - 246   2013   £350

Byron, George Gordon Noel, 6th Baron 1788-1824 *The Miscellaneous Works.* London: Hunt & Clarke, 1830. 2 volumes in one as issued, uncut and partially unopened in original brown boards, green cloth spine, paper label chipped, slightly marked, spine dulled but very good as originally issued, booklabel of Alex Bridge.   Jarndyce Antiquarian Booksellers   CCIII - 97   2013   £125

Byron, George Gordon Noel, 6th Baron 1788-1824
Monody on the Death of the Right Honourable R. B. Sheridan... London: John Murray, 1817. New edition, half title, later drab boards, booklabel and signature of Alex Bridge, very good.   Jarndyce Antiquarian Booksellers   CCIII - 233   2013   £25

Byron, George Gordon Noel, 6th Baron 1788-1824
Ode to Napoleon Bonaparte. London: John Murray, 1814. Fourth edition, half title, disbound, booklabel & signature of Alex Bridge.   Jarndyce Antiquarian Booksellers   CCIII - 191   2013   £30

Byron, George Gordon Noel, 6th Baron 1788-1824
Ode to Napoleon Bonaparte. London: John Murray, 1815. Eleventh edition, half title, final ad leaf, slightly browned, disbound, booklabel of Alex Bridge.   Jarndyce Antiquarian Booksellers   CCIII - 193   2013   £25

Byron, George Gordon Noel, 6th Baron 1788-1824
Poems on His Domestic Circumstances. &c &c. With the Star of the Legion of Honour and Four Other Poems. London: printed for W. Hone, 1816. Second edition, title slightly browned, later drab wrappers, booklabel and signature of Alex Bridge.   Jarndyce Antiquarian Booksellers   CCIII - 217   2013   £65

Byron, George Gordon Noel, 6th Baron 1788-1824
Poems On His Domestic Circumstances &c &c. With His Memoirs and Portrait. London: W. Hone &c., 1816. Ninth edition, frontispiece, some light spotting, slight offsetting, disbound, booklabel and signature of Alex Bridge.   Jarndyce Antiquarian Booksellers   CCIII - 220   2013   £40

Byron, George Gordon Noel, 6th Baron 1788-1824
Poems Original and Translated. Newark: printed and sold by S. & J Ridge, 1808. (1811 or 1812). Second edition, issued without half title, frontispiece, contemporary half calf, at some time rebacked with brown morocco, corners rubbed and worn, booklabel and signature of Alex Bridge.   Jarndyce Antiquarian Booksellers   CCIII - 113   2013   £150

Byron, George Gordon Noel, 6th Baron 1788-1824
Poems Original and Translated. Newark: printed and sold by S. and J. Ridge, 1808. Second edition, half title, frontispiece, few minor internal marks, full brown morocco by Bayntun, gilt spine, borders and dentelles, bookplate and signature of Alex Bridge, top edge gilt, very good, attractive.   Jarndyce Antiquarian Booksellers   CCIII - 112   2013   £500

Byron, George Gordon Noel, 6th Baron 1788-1824 *The Rare Quarto Edition of Lord Byron's "Fugitive Pieces" (1806).* Nottingham: printed for private circulation, Derry & sons, 1919. Frontispiece, plates, uncut in original white boards, white cloth spine, lettered in black, little dusted, bookplate and signature of Alex Bridge, good plus.   Jarndyce Antiquarian Booksellers   CCIII - 107   2013   £60

Dallas, Robert Charles   *Recollections of the Life of Lord Byron, from the Year 1808 to the end of 1814...* London: printed for Charles Knight, 1824. First edition, half title, frontispiece, facsimile letter, few internal spots, uncut in original drab boards, paper label, spine little chipped at head, booklabels of Alastair Forbes & Alex Bridge.   Jarndyce Antiquarian Booksellers   CCIII - 369   2013   £280

Don Juan: with a Biographical Account of Lord Byron and His Family; Anecdotes of His Lordship's Travels and Residence in Greece, at Genev &c. London: William Wright, 1819. First edition, half title, 3 pages ads, lacking frontispiece and with mention of it inked out on titlepage, some internal marks and slight dampstaining to last few pages, uncut in original boards, early spine replacement with appropriate pink paper, rubbed and marked, booklabel and signature of Alex Bridge.   Jarndyce Antiquarian Booksellers   CCIII - 272   2013   £250

Hobhouse, John Cam *Imitations and Translations from the Ancient and Modern Classics...* London: Longmans, 1809. First edition, half title, odd spot, handsomely bound in contemporary tree calf, spine gilt and gilt borders, dark green leather label, slightly chipped, at some time expertly repaired, head and tail of spine slightly worn, with one small chip, contemporary signatures, later label and signature of Alex Bridge, scarce.   Jarndyce Antiquarian Booksellers   CCIII - 391   2013   £750

Lockhart, John Gibson   1794-1854   *John Bull's Letter to Lord Byron.*   Norman: University of Oklahoma Press, 1947. Half title, plates, original maroon cloth, booklabel of Alex Bridge, very good in slightly worn price clipped dust jacket.   Jarndyce Antiquarian Booksellers   CCIII - 406   2013   £35

Lockhart, John Gibson   1794-1854   *Letter to the Right Hon. Lord Byron for John Bull.*   London: printed by and for William Wright, 1821. First edition, disbound, top edge slightly damp affected, booklabel of Alex Bridge.   Jarndyce Antiquarian Booksellers   CCIII - 405   2013   £450

Shorthouse, Joseph Henry   *John Inglesant; a Romance.* Birmingham: Cornish Brothers, 1880. Only 100 copies printed, half title, original parchment by Burn and Co., lettered in red on front and spine, slightly rubbed and marked, minor repairs, leading inner hinge cracking, bookplate of Alex Bridge on front pastedown, overall very good, handsome custom made maroon cloth slipcase, black leather spine label, scarce.   Jarndyce Antiquarian Booksellers   CCV - 247   2013   £650

Trelawny, Edward John   *Records of Shelley, Byron and the author.*   London: Pickering & Chatto, 1887. New edition, half title, frontispiece, original dark blue cloth, paper label slightly rubbed, following board slightly marked, booklabel of Alex Bridge, very good.   Jarndyce Antiquarian Booksellers   CCIII - 445   2013   £65

Association – Bridges, Robert

Herrick, Robert   1591-1674   *Hesperides or Works both Hvman and Divine by Robert Herrick. Together with His Noble Nvmbers or His Piouvs Pieces.*   London: George Newnes Ltd., New York: Charles Scribner's Sons, 1902. 2 volumes, 165 x 110mm., 26 line drawings in black and white by Reginald Savage, as called for, leaf with printed copy of Robert Bridges poem "In a Volume of Herrick" tipped in at front, verso signed by Bridges and dated June 22, 1905; splendid burgundy morocco, lavishly and intricately gilt in "Scottish Wheel" design by Morrell (stamp-signed), covers with large central wheel of 20 compartments containing slender and elegant floral tools between two lines of dots radiating from central rosette, massed tiny circle tools at head and foot of wheel, triangle formed by small scalloped compartments and multiple tiny flowers above and below the centerpiece, large leaf frond tools at corners and many small tools accenting background, raised bands, interlocking floral garlands forming overall wreath in spine compartments, punctuated on either side by cluster of crescents and other small tools, elegantly and elaborately gilt turn-ins, ivory watered silk endleaves, all edges gilt; top of spine of second volume with barely perceptible loss of leather, silk endleaf in each volume with dampstain (no doubt from removal of bookplate), leaves little browned at edges because of quality of paper, else particularly attractive glittering bindings unusually lustrous.   Phillip J. Pirages   61 - 120   2013 $1600

Association – Brigg, J. J.

Bronte, Charlotte   1816-1855   *Villette.*   London: Smith, Elder and Co., 1853. First edition, 3 volumes, 12 page catalog (Jan. 1853) volume I, colophon leaf volume III, pale yellow endpapers, small marginal tear to pages 209.210 volume 1, and pages 79/80 and 196 volume II, original dark brown cloth by Westley's and Co., boards blocked in blind, spines blocked in blind and lettered in gilt, some small expert repairs to hinges and tail of volume 1, small pencil inscription of J. J. Brigg, very good.   Jarndyce Antiquarian Booksellers   CCV - 34   2013   £380

Association – Briggs, Anna Maria

Quillinan, Edward   *Journal of a Few Months' Residence in Portugal and Glimpses of the South of Spain.*   London: Ed Moxon, 1847. First edition, 2 volumes, 8vo., original green blindstamped cloth, spines worn, with small loss, internally clean, inscribed copy to Anna Maria Briggs from author.   J. & S. L. Bonham Antiquarian Booksellers   Europe - 8979   2013   £180

Association – Briggs, John

Adams, Charlotte *Boys at Home.* London: Routledge, 1857. New edition, original red blindstamped cloth gilt extra, pages 414, 8 full page tissue guarded woodcuts by John Gilbert, nice, bright copy, contemporary school prize inscription Wesleyan School, Ulverston presented to John Briggs, Christmas 1857. R. F. G. Hollett & Son Children's Books - 1 2013 £45

Association – Bright, Addison

Barrie, James Matthew 1860-1937 *The Little White Bird.* London: Hodder and Stoughton, 1902. First edition, 8vo., original black cloth, excellent copy, some foxing to page edges and endpapers, spine lightly faded, inscribed by author for Addison Bright. Maggs Bros. Ltd. 1460 - 41 2013 £450

Barrie, James Matthew 1860-1937 *Tommy and Grizel.* London: Cassell, 1900. First edition, 8vo., original blue cloth, inscribed by author for Addison Bright Nov. 1 1900, excellent copy, some light foxing, spine lightly faded. Maggs Bros. Ltd. 1460 - 40 2013 £450

Association – Brink, Andre

Coetzee, J. M. *A Land Apart. A South African Reader.* London: Faber and Faber, 1986. Uncorrected proof copy, signed by Coetzee and co-editor Andre Brink, owner signature, near fine in wrappers, uncommon proof, rare. Ken Lopez Bookseller 159 - 48 2013 $500

Association – Brinnin, John Malcolm

Thomas, Dylan Marlais 1914-1953 *Collected Poems 1934-1952.* London: Dent, 1952. First edition, frontispiece, 8vo., original mid blue cloth, gilt lettered backstrip, price clipped dust jacket, trfile chipped and wine stained on rear panel, short tear to front fold, very good, inscribed by author to his American agent John Malcolm Brinnin. Blackwell's Rare Books B174 - 304 2013 £2500

Association – Brockett, William Henry

Forster, Westgarth *A Treatise on a Section of the Strata, from Newcastle-upon-Tyne, to the Mountains of Cross Fell, in Cumberland.* Alston: printed for the author at the Geological Press and sold by John Pattinson, etc., 1821. 12mo., original boards, corners worn, attractively rebacked in pigskin with green lettering piece, uncut, 12 plates, mostly folding or extending and including 3 colored plates of sections, large folding table of superposition of strata, 12 hand colored pages of sections of strata and 8 further hand colored woodcuts, little scattered browning, excellent wide margined copy, rare, with 12mo. ad leaf, tipped in before title, text woodcuts are not usually found colored, armorial bookplates of William Henry Brockett and Edward Joicey of Whinney House. R. F. G. Hollett & Son Lake District and Cumbria - 136 2013 £650

Association – Brodie, John Clerk

Vergilius Maro, Publius *Pvblivs Virgilivs Maro Varietate Lectionis et Perpetva Adnotatione. (Opera).* Lipsiae: Sumtibus Librariae Hahnianae; Londini: Apud Black, Young & Young, 1830-1841. Fourth edition, 223 x 14mm., 5 volumes bound in 9, engraved allegorical frontispiece, 6 title vignettes, 120 headpieces, 80 tailpieces and 2 plates; fine contemporary red morocco, gilt, covers with gilt double ruled frames and quatrefoil cornerpieces, raised bands, spines in gilt double ruled compartments with intricate fleuron centerpiece, gilt titling and turn-ins, marbled endpapers, all edges gilt, armorial bookplate of John Clerk Brodie, one tiny nick to upper cover of last volume, isolated faint offsetting, three gatherings in volume III, part 1, very lightly browned, isolated mild foxing to last volume, but extraordinarily fine, text especially clean, fresh and bright on thick luxurious paper and handsome bindings, quite lustrous with virtually no wear, opening only reluctantly as an indication of very little use. Phillip J. Pirages 63 - 482 2013 $3200

Association – Brogden, John

Luther, Martin 1483-1546 *A Commentarie Upon the Fifteen Psalmes, Called Psalmi Graduum... (bound with) A Commentarie of M. Doctor Martin Luther upon the Epistle of S. Paul to the Galathians.* London: by Richard Field, 1615-1616. 4to., black letter, 2 works bound together in 18th century calf, very neatly rebacked retaining original spine label, titlepage of first work soiled, minor dampstains on first few leaves, else very good, armorial bookplate of John Brogden. Joseph J. Felcone Inc. Books Printed before 1701 - 66 2013 $2800

Association – Broh-Khan, Robert

Lister, Joseph 1827-1912 *The Collected Papers of Joseph Baron Lister.* Oxford: Clarendon Press, 1909. First collected edition, thick 4to., 2 volumes, frontispiece photos, 14 plates, tables, full gilt stamped black cloth (blue cloth volume 2), hinges starting, head and base of spine chipped, extremities bit rubbed (volume I), early ownership signatures of Robert Broh-Khan, very good.   Jeff Weber Rare Books   172 - 188   2013 $350

Association – Bromsen, Moury

Kennedy, John Fitzgerald 1917-1963 *As We Remember Joe.* Cambridge: privately printed, 1945. First edition, first issue, one of about 500 copies distributed to friends and family, with all points as described by Kennedy Library Head, David Powers, titlepage in two colors, with sunken panel on front cover, ivory colored paper and caption on page 64, octavo, 33 black and white photos, including frontispiece, publisher's original full burgundy cloth, front cover stamped in black and gilt on sunken panel, spine lettered in gilt, very small amount of rubbing to spine and back board, otherwise near fine, original glassine, with three ALS's from Powers to Dr. Moury Bromsen.   Heritage Book Shop Holiday Catalogue 2012 - 92   2013 $3750

Association – Brook, W. S.

Jeans, Henry William *Hand-Book for the Stars...* London: Robson & Son, 1868. Third edition, frontispiece and illustrations, original green cloth, slightly rubbed, contemporary signature of W. S. Brook on leading pastedown, very good.   Jarndyce Antiquarian Booksellers   CCV - 148   2013   £150

Association – Brooke, J.

Davis, William *A Complete Treatise of Land Surveying by the Chain, Cross and Offset Staffs Only.* London: printed for the author, 1798. 8vo., 6 folding plates, numerous diagrams in text, slight foxing, mainly to leading edges and plates, contemporary half calf marbled boards, gilt morocco label, expert repairs to hinges and corners, spine repaired, contemporary signature of J. Brooke and of William Wilson, Tilsey.   Jarndyce Antiquarian Booksellers   CCIV - 105   2013   £320

Association – Brooke, Lady

Pater, Walter 1839-1894 *Marius the Epicurean: His Sensations and Ideas.* London: Macmillan and Co., 1892. Sixth thousand, inscribed by author to Lady Brooke, Ranee of Sarawak, original dark blue cloth with gilt title and author to spine, some bumping and rubbing but in very good condition, hinges volume I tender and discoloration to endpapers, otherwise very good, booklabel of Arnold Muirhead affixed to front pastedown of each volume, 2 volumes, 165; 246 pages.   The Kelmscott Bookshop   7 - 126   2013 $875

Association – Brooke, Rupert

Thomas, Edward *The Pocket Book of Poems and Songs for the Open Air.* London: E. Grant Richards, 1907. First edition, small 8vo., original blue decorated cloth, Rupert Brooke's copy, signed in pencil by him, there is also a pencilled correction to index, changing Ramal to De La Mare and this is almost certainly in Brooke's hand, covers slightly worn, otherwise very good.   Maggs Bros. Ltd.   1460 - 143   2013   £950

Association – Brooke, Thomas

Homerus *Batrachomyomachia Graece and Veterum Exemplarium Fiden Resusa.* London: William Boyer, 1721. 8vo., contemporary full red morocco, small 1 inch splits top of spine, minor wear at corners, gilt decorated borders and centerpieces, gilt decorated spine (bit darkened), leather label, copper engraved folding facsimile, all edges gilt, bookplates of collector Thomas Brooke and Rowland Thomas Baring, 2nd Earl of Cromer.   Howard S. Mott Inc.   262 - 76   2013 $850

Association – Brooks, Gwendolyn

Fine Arts Festival, Talladega College, Talladega Alabama. Kent: Institute for African American Affairs, Kent State University, 1975. Stapled decorated wrappers, (20) pages, modest horizontal crease on front wrapper, else very good plus, although not otherwise indicated, from the library of Gwendolyn Brooks.   Between the Covers Rare Books, Inc.   165 - 92   2013 $75

Ford, Edsel *Love is the House It Lives In.* Fort Smith: Homestead House, 1965. First edition, stapled stiff unprinted card wrappers, fine in fine dust jacket, inscribed by author to poet Gwendolyn Brooks, laid in is printed slip for ordering additional copies on verso of which Ford has penned a brief note, signed to Brooks.   Between the Covers Rare Books, Inc.   165 - 151   2013 $175

Johnson, John H. *Black World Volume XX No. 9.* Chicago: Johnson Pub. July, 1971. First edition, lightly soiled and foxed with few light creases, tiny tear to bottom of spine, some tanning to pages, else very good in wrappers, from the library of poet Gwendolyn Brooks with her address label.   Between the Covers Rare Books, Inc.   165 - 187   2013 $100

Moody, Anne *Mr. Death: Four Stories.* New York: Harper & Row, 1975. First edition, fine in near fine dust jacket with touch of foxing, poet Gwendolyn Brook's copy with letter laid in from publisher presenting the book.   Between the Covers Rare Books, Inc.   165 - 110   2013 $85

Association – Brophy, Brigid

Greene, Graham 1904-1981 *Travels with my Aunt.* London: Bodley Head, 1969. First edition, 8vo., original dark green cloth, excellent copy, dust jacket unevenly browned along top and on spine, original dark green cloth, dust jacket, inscribed by author for Brigid Brophy.   Maggs Bros. Ltd.   1460 - 375   2013   £750

Association – Brown

Scotland's Opposition to the Popish Bill. Edinburgh: printed by David Paterson, 1780. 8vo., some browning in places, contemporary sprinkled sheep, flat spine divided by triple gilt fillet, red morocco lettering piece, some old scratches to boards, armorial bookplate of Brown of Waterhaughs and ownership inscription of David Murray, Glasgow, with few of his notes on endpapers, very good.   Blackwell's Rare Books   172 - 118   2013   £425

Association – Brown, Bridget

Brown, Christy *My Left Foot.* London: Secker & Warburg, 1954. First edition, 8vo., original maroon cloth, dust jacket, excellent copy in dust jacket, little chipped at head and tail of spine, inscribed by author for Ismay Philips 30/5/56 and inscribed below this by his mother Bridget Brown, half title and rear endpaper contain 31 signatures of unknown personages.   Maggs Bros. Ltd.   1460 - 144   2013   £275

Association – Brown, Dorothy Riley

Jackson, Charles James *An Illustrated History of English Plate, Ecclesiastical and Secular.* London: Country Life Limited and B. T. Batsford, 1911. First edition, 2 volumes, 343 x 279mm., original dark green half binding of faux morocco by Western Mail Bindery in Cardiff (with their ticket), cloth sides, spines with raised bands, gilt ruled compartments, gilt titling, top edge gilt, etched frontispiece, 76 photogravure plates and 1500 other illustrations, titles in red and black, text printed on coated stock, plates printed on high quality thick paper, bookplate of Dorothy Riley Brown in each volume, leather somewhat flaked from joints and extremities, few superficial marks to covers, hinges cracked before half title in each volume, bindings otherwise sound and not without appeal, fine set internally, only trivial defects.   Phillip J. Pirages   63 - 439   2013 $175

Association – Brown, Frederick

Sawyer, John *Automatic Arithmetic: a New System for Multiplication and Division without Mental Labour and Without the Use of Logarithms.*   London: William Clowes and Sons for George Bell and Sons, 1878. First edition, presentation copy, inscribed to good friend Frederick Brown, oblong 8vo., pages 17, 3, final linen covered and blank, 10 tables printed in red and black, 9 of which cut into horizontal strips of increasing length, original plum pebble grained cloth, covers ruled in blind, gilt stamped lettering on front cover, light wear to extremities, front inner hinges strengthened with cloth strips at early date.   Marlborough Rare Books Ltd.   218 - 136   2013   £750

Association – Brown, Ivor

Drinkwater, John 1882-1937 *Shakespeare.* London: Duckworth, 1933. Second impression, 12mo., original red cloth, excellent copy, spine little darkened, some rubbing to edges of spine, inscribed by author for Ivor Brown.   Maggs Bros. Ltd.   1460 - 252   2013   £50

Association – Brown, James Robert

Medwin, Thomas 1788-1869 *Conversations of Lord Byron with Thomas Medwin.* London: Henry Colburn & Richard Bentley, 1832. 2 volumes in 1, frontispiece little spotted, folding facsimile letter, 2 volumes in 1 as issued, original purple cloth, blocked in blind, slightly rubbed, spine faded to brown, booklabel of James Robert Brown. Jarndyce Antiquarian Booksellers   CCIII - 419   2013   £50

Association – Brown, Louisa

Brydges, Samuel Egerton *Sonnets and Other Poems.* London: B. & J. White, 1795. New edition, contemporary full tree calf, spine with bands and devices in gilt, dark green leather label, gilt wearing from spine, corners and hinges little rubbed, ownership inscription of Lady Frances Benson, gift inscription of Miss Louisa Brown, Nov. 1836.   Jarndyce Antiquarian Booksellers   CCIII - 40   2013   £125

Association – Brown, Marcia

Cinderella *Cinderella.* New York: Scribner, 1954. A. First edition, first printing, 4to., cloth, corner slightly worn, else fine in very good dust jacket (not price clipped, no award seal, small chips off spine ends), illustrations in color by Marcia Brown, this copy signed by Brown.   Aleph-Bet Books, Inc.   104 - 91   2013 $1500

Dick Whittington and His Cat. New York: Scribner, 1950. A. First edition, 4to., pictorial cloth, fine in nice dust jacket with few small edge chips, wonderful linoleum cuts by Marcia Brown, this copy inscribed by Brown.   Aleph-Bet Books, Inc.   105 - 94   2013 $600

Association – Browne, John

Dickens, Charles 1812-1870 *Christmas Books.* London: Chapman and Hall, 1852. First English collected edition, frontispiece final ad leaf, ads on endpapers, original olive green cloth, blocked in blind, spine blocked and lettered in gilt, armorial bookplate of John Browne, small bookseller's ticket, G. Mann, very good, close to fine copy. Jarndyce Antiquarian Booksellers   CCV - 83   2013   £400

Association – Brunnich, Morten Thrane

Gronovius, Johann Friederich *Bibliotheca Regni Animalis Atique Lapidei seu Recensio Auctorum et Librorum qui de Regno Animali et Lapideo.* Leiden: for the author, 1760. First edition, some foxing, dampstaining towards end, chiefly in lower margins, few ink smudges, 4to., contemporary or slightly later half calf, rebacked, corners worn, presentation copy with numerous manuscript notes (few slightly trimmed), inscribed by author for Mortren Thrane Brunnich 1737-1827, Danish zoologist, good.   Blackwell's Rare Books   172 - 64   2013   £1750

Association – Buchan, John

Tweedsmuir, Susan Charlotte Buchan *John Buchan by His Wife and Friends.* London: Hodder and Stoughton Ltd., 1947. First edition, large 8vo., original black cloth, inscribed by Buchan's widow Susan Tweedsmuir to Sam Morison, below which is a pencilled note by recipient, inscribed photo of Lady Tweedsmuir, inscribed postcard and ALS from John Buchan to recipient, excellent copy with Morison's bookplate, now loose.   Maggs Bros. Ltd.   1460 - 149   2013   £175

Association – Buchanan, George

Shakespeare, William 1564-1616 *The Works of...* Edinburgh: printed for Bell and Bradfute et al, 1795. 8 volumes, some light browning, occasional foxing and few small marginal paper flaws, contemporary tree calf, spines divided by gilt fillet, red morocco lettering pieces and small circular green morocco numbering pieces, the latter lost on volume iii, spines rubbed, few headcaps chipped, ownership inscriptions of George Buchanan of Ladrishmore, good. Blackwell's Rare Books   B174 - 134   2013   £800

Association – Buckley, Mrs.

Margoliouth, Moses *Curates of Riversdale: Recollections in the Life of a Clergyman.* London: Hurst and Blackett, 1860. First edition, 3 volumes, half dark blue calf, marbled boards, expertly and handsomely rebacked, inscription to leading f.e.p. volume from author for Mrs. Buckley, later signature of M. Jane Hole.   Jarndyce Antiquarian Booksellers   CCV - 190   2013   £750

Association – Bull, Charlotte

Churchill, Winston 1620-1688 *Divi Britannici being a Remark Upon the Lives of all the Kings of This Isle...* London: printed by Tho. Roycroft, 1675. Folio, small wormhole in text from page 77 onwards, often touching a letter never affecting sense, gatherings e and d bound in reverse order, lightly browned, occasional spotting, watermark traced in pencil on verso of titlepage, contemporary speckled calf, crackled and rubbed, now rebacked and recornered with reverse calf, printed paper label to spine, new f.f.e.p., ownership inscriptions of Charlotte Bull (19th century) and John Woodford of Pembroke College, Oxford (18th century) to titlepage.   Unsworths Antiquarian Booksellers   28 - 83   2013   £750

Association – Bullock, Adrian

Grimeston, Edward *A Generall Historie of the Netherlands...* London: A. Islip and G. Eld., 1609. First edition, 2nd issue, folio, engraved titlepage with historiated border, many near full page illustrations in text, paper flaw resulting in small hole to first leaf, little marginal worming to first few leaves, tiny burn holes to pages 111, 117 and 597 affecting a few letters, occasional light ink smudges to margins, few slight creases, contemporary dark brown calf, gilt border and centerpiece, symapthetically rebacked with parts of original spine retained and some gilt reapplied to style, evidence of clasps though none remain, bookplate of Adrian Bullock, Sherringham, Norfolk 1988, recently handwritten list of illustrations.   Unsworths Antiquarian Booksellers   28 - 101   2013   £1250

Association – Bullrich, Eduard J.

Horatius Flaccus, Quintus *Opera cum Quilbusdam Annotationibus (of Jacob Locher).* Strassburg: Johann (Reinhard) Gruninger (misspelled Gurninger) 12 March, 1498. First illustrated edition of Horace and first edition printed in Germany, Gothic and Roman types, 3 columns, 74 lines of commentary on either side of text, 168 woodcut illustrations in various combinations, including some repeats, capital spaces with guide letters, initials supplied in red and blue, woodcut printer's device, 18th century paste paper over pasteboard, spine lettered in manuscript, few leaves slightly browned, slight dampstaining in upper corner toward end, some minor marginal loss, short tear to folio LXXXIX, affecting foliation and just entering woodcut on recto and just touching two letters on verso, short marginal tear to folio CLXIX, not affecting text early paper repairs to blank verso of final leaf, occasional early ink marginalia, early ink drawing in margin of folio CXXXI verso, early ink inscription crossed out on folio CXXXII verso, early ink calculations in folio (C)XLIX verso and folio (C)L, early ink ownership inscription at foot of title and ink inscription dated 1498 at head of title, leather bookplate of Eduard J. Bullrich, early ink annotations on front free endpaper, overall excellent copy, housed in black cloth clamshell case.   Heritage Book Shop   50th Anniversary Catalogue - 52   2013 $60,000

Association – Bunge, Mario

Popper, Karl R. *Conjectural Knowledge: My Solution of the Problem of Induction.* Brussels: Revue Inernationale de Philosophie, 1971. First separate edition, offprint, original printed wrappers, signed and inscribed by author to Mario Bunge and his wife, fine. By the Book, L. C.   38 - 28   2013 $500

Association – Burbank, E. A.

Wilson, Neill C. *Silver Stampede. The Career of Death Valley's Hell-Camp, Old Panamint.* New York: Macmillan Co., 1937. First edition, signed by author and by painter, E. A. Burbank, map endpapers, photos and drawings, light blue cloth, extremities well rubbed, very good. Argonaut Book Shop   Recent Acquisitions June 2013 - 317   2013 $125

Association – Burden, Carter

Lopez, Barry *Arctic Dreams.* New York: Charles Scribner's Sons, 1986. First edition, inscribed by author to major book collector, Carter Burden, 464 pages with index, fine in dust jacket.   Ed Smith Books   78 - 34   2013 $200

Association – Burden, W. A. M.

Motley, John Lothrop 1766-1851 *Correspondence.* New York: Harper & Bros., 1889. First edition, 2 volumes, 251 x 175mm., attractive contemporary dark green half morocco over marbled boards by Stikeman (stamp signed). raised bands, spines gilt in compartments with tulip centerpiece and scrolling cornerpieces, gilt titling, marbled endpapers, top edge gilt, frontispiece in volume I, bookplate of W. M. Burden; little wear to joints and extremities (five corner tips worn through), spines uniformly darkened toward brown, otherwise fine, clean and fresh internally, in solid pleasing bindings.   Phillip J. Pirages   63 - 350   2013 $150

Some British Ballads. London: Constable & Co., 1919. One of 575 copies signed by artist, this #379, 286 x 229mm., very attractive red engraved plates morocco (stamp signed Putnams"), raised bands, spine handsomely gilt in compartments formed by plain and decorative rules, quatrefoil centerpiece, surrounded by densely scrolling cornerpieces, sides and endleaves of rose colored linen, top edge gilt, with titlepage, vignette, black and white illustrations in text and 17 color plates by Arthur Rackham, all tipped on and with letterpress guards, morocco bookplate of W. A. M. Burden; only most trivial signs of use externally, exceptionally fine inside and out, especially lustrous handsome gilt binding.   Phillip J. Pirages   63 - 382   2013 $1500

Swinburne, Algernon Charles 1837-1909 *The Springtide of Life.* London: William Heinemann, 1918. One of 765 copies signed by artist, this #369, 286 x 232mm., very attractive red three quarter morocco, raised bands, spine handsomely gilt in compartments, formed by plain and decorative rules, quatrefoil centerpiece surrounded by densely scrolling cornerpieces, sides and endleaves of rose colored linen, top edge gilt, numerous black and white illustrations, fine color plates as called for, by Arthur Rackham, all tipped onto brown paper and with letterpress guards; morocco bookplate of W. A. M. Burden; hint of off-setting from brown mounting paper, otherwise very fine, bright, fresh and clean inside and out, only most trivial of imperfections.   Phillip J. Pirages   63 - 383   2013 $1600

Association – Burlington, Earl of

Palladio, Andrea *The Four Books of Andrea Palladio's Architecture.* London: published by Isaac Ware, 1755. Folio, 205 plates, contemporary calf, rebacked to style, spine in compartments, profusely decorated in gilt, brown label lettered in gilt, inscribed "G. Morrison given the Earl of Burlington 1746", armorial bookplate of G. Morrison. Marlborough Rare Books Ltd.   218 - 115   2013   £1250

Association – Burndy Library

Allibone, S. Austin *A Critical Dictionary of English Literature and British and American Authors.... (with) A Supplement to Albion's Critical Dictionary...* Philadelphia: J. B. Lippincott, 1886-1898. 5 volumes, large 8vo., green cloth, gilt stamped spines, extremities rubbed, some volumes waterstained, some hinges cracked but still strong, bookplates of Burndy Library.   Jeff Weber Rare Books   169 - 4   2013 $275

Brock, Alan St. H. *A History of Fireworks.* London, et al: George G. Harrap, 1949. First edition, 8vo., 280 pages, 40 plates, including frontispiece, text illustrations, dark blue cloth, gilt stamped spine, dust jacket worn, Burndy bookplate, very good, signed by Cyril Stanley Smith.   Jeff Weber Rare Books   169 - 44   2013 $125

Brockett, Paul *Bibliography of Aeronautics.* Washington: Smithsonian Institution, 1910. First edition, 8vo., xiv, 940 pages, printed wrappers, worn, small front cover library blindstamp, very good, Burndy bookplate.   Jeff Weber Rare Books   169 - 45   2013 $75

Camper, Petrus *Optical Dissertation on Vision 1746.* Nieuwkoop: B. de Graaf, 1962. 8vo., 31 pages, frontispiece, illustrations, cream marbled gilt stamped paper backed boards, folding archival case, Burndy Library bookplate, fine.   Jeff Weber Rare Books   172 - 47   2013 $75

Cartwright, David Edgar *Tides: a Scientific History.* Cambridge: Cambridge University Press, 1999. First edition, tall 8vo., xii, 292 pages, frontispiece, illustrations, figures, black cloth, silver stamped spine, dust jacket, Burndy bookplate, fine, rare in cloth with jacket. Jeff Weber Rare Books   169 - 56   2013 $100

Chrimes, Mike *The Civil Engineering of Canals and Railways Before 1850.* Aldershot, et al: Ashgate, 1997. Volume 7, 8vo., illustrations, tables, red cloth, gilt stamped cover and spine titles, Burndy bookplate, fine. Jeff Weber Rare Books   169 - 65   2013 $100

Cox, Edward Godfrey *A Reference Guide to the Literature.* Seattle: University of Washington, 1935-1949. First printing, 3 volumes, large 8vo., printed wrappers, wrappers and spine worn (with pieces missing on volumes I and II), volume I front cover detached, volume II rear cover missing, Burndy bookplates rubber stamps and markings of MIT libraries. Jeff Weber Rare Books   169 - 80   2013 $100

Davis, Audrey *Bloodletting Instruments in the National Museum of History and Technology.* Washington: Smithsonian Institution Press, 1979. First edition, tall 8vo., v, 103 pages, illustrations, printed wrappers, lightly rubbed, spine sunned, else near fine, Burndy bookplate. Jeff Weber Rare Books   169 - 90   2013 $220

Davis, Tenney L. *Chymia: Annual Studies in the History of Chemistry. Nos. 1-12.* Philadelphia: University of Pennsylvania Press, 1948-1967. 8vo., frontispieces, illustrations, blue cloth (nos. 1-4), green cloth (no. 7), red cloth (nos. 8 & 12), black cloth (no. 9), grey cloth (no. 10), yellow cloth (no. 11), gilt stamped spines, dust jackets, nos. 1-4 lacking jackets, rubber stamps, near fine, Burndy Library bookplates. Jeff Weber Rare Books   169 - 91   2013 $850

Dawson, Andrew *Lives of Philadelphia Engineers: Capital Class and Resolution 1830-1890.* Aldershot: Ashgate, 2004. 8vo., 5 tables, 2 charts, 20 figures, pictorial backed boards, Burndy library bookplate, fine. Jeff Weber Rare Books   169 - 92   2013 $75

Deacon, Margaret *Scientists and the Sea 1650-1900: a Study of Marine Science.* Aldershot: and Brookfield: Ashgate, 1997. Second edition, 8vo., xl, 459 pages, illustrations, aqua cloth, silver stamped spine, dust jacket, fine, Burndy bookplate. Jeff Weber Rare Books   169 - 94   2013 $90

Edwards, Llewellyn Nathaniel *A Record of History and Evolution of Early American Bridges.* Orono: University Press, 1959. 8vo., frontispiece, 54 illustrations on 36 pages of plates, gilt stamped textured navy cloth, rubbed, Burndy bookplate, pencil and ink note with signature, very good. Jeff Weber Rare Books   171 - 112   2013 $85

Ferchl, Fritz *A Pictorial History of Chemistry.* London: William Heinemann, 1939. First edition in English, 8vo., viii, 214 pages, illustrations, navy cloth, gilt stamped spine title, near fine, Burndy bookplate. Jeff Weber Rare Books   169 - 138   2013 $95

Frith, Francis *Francis Frith in Egypt and Palestine: A Victorian Photographer Abroad.* Princeton and Oxford: Princeton University Press, 2004. First printing, 4to., 239 pages, frontispiece, 75 duotone plates, 10 black and white plates, quarter brown cloth over pictorial paper backed boards gilt stamped spine, dust jacket, bookplate of Burndy library, fine. Jeff Weber Rare Books   169 - 144   2013 $75

Gardiner, Robert *Frigates of the Napoleonic Wars.* Annapolis: Naval Institute Press, 2000. First edition, 4to., 208 pages, frontispiece, illustrations, tables, navy paper boards, gilt stamped spine, dust jacket bookplate of Burndy library, fine. Jeff Weber Rare Books   169 - 154   2013 $85

Gellibrand, Henry *A Discourse Mathematical on the Variation of the Magnetical Needle.* Berlin: A. Asher, 1897. Facsimile reprint of 1635 London edition, 8vo., diagrams and charts, half green cloth over green paper backed boards, gilt stamped spine, bookplate of Burndy Library and previous owner, near fine. Jeff Weber Rare Books   169 - 160   2013 $50

Goldberg, Benjamin *The Mirror and Man.* Charlottesville: University Press of Virginia, 1985. First edition, 8vo., xii 260 pages, 38 illustrations, grey cloth with white paper boards, silver stamped spine title, dust jacket, Burndy bookplate. Jeff Weber Rare Books   169 - 167   2013 $115

Grafton, Anthony *Commerce with the Classics: Ancient Books & Renaissance Readers.* Ann Arbor: University of Michigan Press, 2000. 8vo., plates, gilt stamped black cloth, dust jacket, fine, Burndy bookplate. Jeff Weber Rare Books   171 - 145   2013 $50

Hall, A. Rupert *Henry More Magic: Religion and Experiment.* Cambridge: Basil Blackwell, 1990. 8vo., 304 pages, black cloth, silver stamped spine, dust jacket, inscribed in ink by author to I. Bernard Cohen, Burndy Library bookplate, fine. Jeff Weber Rare Books   169 - 306   2013 $60

Hewson, J. B. *A History of the Practice of Navigation.* Glasgow: Brown, Son & Ferguson, 1951. First edition, 8vo., viii, 270 pages, illustrations, dark blue cloth, gilt stamped cover and spine titles, dust jacket worn with pieces missing and tape repair, else very good, Burndy bookplate, rare in jacket, with Charles Singer's bookplate. Jeff Weber Rare Books 169 - 205 2013 $125

Hirsch, Richard F. *Power Loss: the Origins of Derregulation and Restructuring in the American Electric Utility System.* Cambridge and London: MIT Press, 1999. First edition, 8vo., x, 406 pages, illustrations, tables, quarter yellow cloth over beige cloth sides, silver stamped spine title, dust jacket, Burndy bookplate, fine. Jeff Weber Rare Books 169 - 209 2013 $165

Holmes, Thomas *Cotton Mather: a Bibliography of His Works.* Cambridge: Harvard University Press, 1940. First edition, limited to 500 copies, 3 volumes, 8vo., decorative red title border, illustrations, original quarter dark brown levant over lighter brown cloth, top edge gilt, gilt stamped spine by Harcourt Bindery, Boston, fine, Burndy bookplate, beautiful set, George Sarton's copy (and Harvard University's) bookplate and ownership signature. Jeff Weber Rare Books 169 - 212 2013 $500

Hosmer, James K. *History of the Expedition of Captains Lewis and Clark 1804-5-6.* Chicago: A. C. McClurg, 1902. Reprint of 1814 edition, 2 volumes, portraits, maps, 8vo., frontispiece, plates, maps, index, some pages unopened, quarter brown cloth over tan cloth sides, gilt stamped spine, top edge gilt, inner hinges neatly reinforced, short tear to joint mend, Burndy bookplates, very good. Jeff Weber Rare Books 169 - 216 2013 $80

Hues, Robert *Tractatus de globus et Eorum Usu. A Treatise Descriptive of the Globes constructed by Emory Molyneux....* London: Hakluyt Society, 1889. 8vo., frontispiece, foldout color map, light blue cloth, gilt stamped cover illustration and spine title, extremities bit stained, spine chipped, inner hinges cracked, pages unopened, Burndy bookplate, good. Jeff Weber Rare Books 169 - 220 2013 $95

Hungerford, Edward *The Story of the Baltimore & Ohio Railroad 1827-1927.* New York: and London: G. P. Putnam's Sons, 1928. First edition, 2 volumes, frontispiece, plates, navy cloth, gilt stamped spine title, top edge gilt, dust jackets worn with pieces missing, top spine cloth torn on both volumes (titles affected), bookplates of Burndy Library, good. Jeff Weber Rare Books 169 - 224 2013 $75

Hunt, Rachel McMasters Miller *Catalogue of Botanical Books in the Collection of...* Pittsburgh: Hunt Botanical Library, 1958-1961. One of 750 sets, 3 volumes, large 8vo., frontispiece, plates, dark green cloth, gilt stamped cover illustrations and spine titles, Burndy bookplates, fine. Jeff Weber Rare Books 169 - 226 2013 $700

Hunter, Andrew *Thornton & Tully's Scientific Books, Libraries and Collectors: a Study of Bibliography and the Book Trade in Relation to the History of Science.* Aldershot, et al: Ashgate, 2000. Fourth edition, 8vo., 8 plates, green cloth, silver stamped spine title, dust jacket, Burndy bookplate, fine. Jeff Weber Rare Books 169 - 227 2013 $150

Huygens, Christian *Horlogium Oscillatorium; sive de Motu Pendulorum ad Horlogia Aptato Demonstrationes Geometricae.* Bruxelles: Culture et Civilisation, 1966. Facsimile reprint of Paris 1673 edition, 30 cm., illustrations, blue gilt stamped leatherette, bit nicked along bottom edge, fine, otherwise scarce, Burndy bookplate. Jeff Weber Rare Books 171 - 179 2013 $120

Jackson, John N. *The Welland Canals and their Communities...* Toronto: University of Toronto Press, 1997. First edition, 8vo, photos, 13 maps, 11 tables, gray cloth, red stamped spine title, dust jacket, Burndy bookplate, fine. Jeff Weber Rare Books 169 - 236 2013 $100

Jarvis, Adrian *Port and Harbor Engineering.* Aldershot, et al: Ashgate, 1998. 8vo., photos and illustrations, red cloth, gilt stamped cover and spine titles, Burndy bookplate, fine. Jeff Weber Rare Books 169 - 238 2013 $175

Jesseph, Douglas M. *Squaring the Circle: the War Between Hobbes and Wallis.* Chicago and London: Universty of Chicago Press, 1999. First edition, 8vo., figures, black cloth, gilt stamped spine title, Burndy bookplate, fine. Jeff Weber Rare Books 169 - 241 2013 $95

Karpinski, Louis C. *Bibliography of Mathematical Works Printed in America through 1850.* Ann Arbor & London: University of Michigan Press & Oxford University Press, 1940. First edition, inscribed by author to Henry P. Kendall, Burndy bookplate, 4to., illustrations, dark blue cloth, blind-stamped cover emblem, gilt stamped spine title, extremities lightly speckled, inner hinge cracked, very good. Jeff Weber Rare Books 169 - 247 2013 $400

Keynes, Richard Darwin *The Beagle Record: Selections from the Original Pictorial Records and Written Accounts of the Voyage of H.M.S. Beagle.* Cambridge: Cambridge University Press, 1979. First edition, 4to., illustrations, brown cloth, gilt stamped brown cover and spine labels, dust jacket, Burndy, near fine. Jeff Weber Rare Books 169 - 249 2013 $70

Klemm, Friedrich *A History of Western Technology.* London: Ruskin House, George Allen and Unwin, 1959. English translation of original 154 German edition, 8vo., 59 figures, green cloth, silver stamped spine title, dust jacket, light jacket edgewear, Burndy bookplate, scarce, very good. Jeff Weber Rare Books 169 - 251 2013 $75

Lamb, J. Parker *Perfecting the American Steam Locomotive.* Bloomington & Indianapolis: Indiana University Press, 2003. First edition, tall 8vo., xi, 197 pages, photos and illustrations, tables, quarter tan cloth with brown paper boards, brown stamped spine title, dust jacket, fine, Burndy bookplate. Jeff Weber Rare Books 169 - 258 2013 $65

Lamb, Ursula *Cosmographers and Pilots of the Spanish Maritime Empire.* Aldershot and Brookfield: Variorum, 1995. 8vo., illustrations, gilt stamped blue cloth, fine, Burndy bookplate. Jeff Weber Rare Books 169 - 259 2013 $120

Levere, Trevor H. *Chemists and Chemistry in Nature and Society 1770-1878.* Aldershot and Brookfield: Variorum, 1994. 8vo. blue cloth, gilt stamped cover and spine titles, illustrations, bookplate of Burndy Library, fine. Jeff Weber Rare Books 169 - 269 2013 $75

Livingstone, David N. *Geography and Enlightenment.* Chicago and London: University of Chicago Press, 1999. First edition, 8vo., illustrations, figures, navy cloth, gilt stamped spine title, Burndy bookplate, fine. Jeff Weber Rare Books 169 - 276 2013 $85

Merzbach, Uta C. *Carl Friedrich Guass: a Bibliography.* Wilmington: Scholarly Resources, 1984. 4to., dark blue green cloth, gilt stamped spine, bookplate of Burndy Library, fine. Jeff Weber Rare Books 169 - 158 2013 $95

Montagu, M. F. Ashley *Edward Tyson, M.D., F.R.S. (1650-1708) and the Rise of Human and Comparative Anatomy in England: a Study in the History of Science.* Philadelphia: American Philosophical Society, 1943. First edition, 8vo., frontispiece, illustrations, red cloth, gilt stamped cover and spine titles, corners slightly bumped, else fine, Burndy bookplate. Jeff Weber Rare Books 169 - 305 2013 $65

Newton, Isaac 1642-1727 *Philosophiae Naturalis Principia Mathematica.* London: Joseph Streater for the Royal Society, 1687. One of 1000 copies, large 8vo., rust cloth, gilt stamped spine, spine head slightly torn, ownership signature of I. Bernard Cohen with his scattered notes and underlining, booklabel of Burndy Library with bookplate, very good. Jeff Weber Rare Books 169 - 317 2013 $300

Pagel, Walter *Paracelsus: an Introduction to Philosophical Medicine in the Era of the Renaissance.* Basel & New York: S. Karger, 1958. First edition, 8vo., xii, 368 pages, illustrations, blue cloth, gilt stamped cover and spine titles, dust jacket worn with pieces missing, else very good, Burndy bookplate. Jeff Weber Rare Books 169 - 336 2013 $175

Pagel, Walter *William Harvey's Biological Ideas: Selected Aspects and Historical Background.* New York: S. Karger, 1967. 8vo., 394 pages, illustrations, light pencil marginalia, gilt stamped blue cloth, sunned, Burndy bookplate, formerly belonging to Robert M. McKeon, very good. Jeff Weber Rare Books 172 - 125 2013 $120

Parsons, William Barclay *Robert Fulton and the Submarine.* New York: Columbia University Press, 1922. First edition, 8vo., xiii, 154 pages, frontispiece, plates, burgundy cloth, gilt stamped cover emblem and spine title, dust jacket chipped with pieces missing, else very good, Burndy bookplate, rare in original edition with jacket. Jeff Weber Rare Books 169 - 339 2013 $75

Partington, J. R. *A History of Greek Fire and Gunpowder.* Cambridge: W. Heffer, 1960. First edition, tall 8vo., 3 plates, including frontispiece, illustrations, red cloth, gilt stamped spine title, dust jacket rubbed with some edgewear and manuscript paper spine label, very good, Burndy bookplate. Jeff Weber Rare Books 169 - 340 2013 $65

Passer, Harold C. *The Electrical Manufacturers 1875-1900...* Cambridge: Harvard University Press, 1953. First edition, 8vo., illustrations, tables, diagrams, light gray cloth, black stamped spine title, dust jacket heavily chipped with pieces missing, Burndy bookplate, very good. Jeff Weber Rare Books 169 - 341 2013 $65

Poole, Robert *Time's Alteration: Calendar Reform in Early Modern England.* London and Bristol: UCL Press, 1998. 8vo., xix, 243 pages, figures, tables, black cloth, gilt stamped spine title, dust jacket, rare, fine, Burndy Library bookplate. Jeff Weber Rare Books 169 - 352 2013 $170

Rink, Evald *Technical Americana: a Checklist of Technical Publications Printed before 1831.* Millwood: Kraus International Pub., 1981. First printing, large 8vo., small title vignette, index, some yellow highlighting dark mustard cloth, gilt stamped black cover an spine labels, Burndy bookplate, ownership signature, very good. Jeff Weber Rare Books 169 - 377 2013 $200

Ron, Moshe *Catalog of the Sidney M. Edelstein Collection of the History of Chemistry, Dyeing and Technology.* Jerusalem: Jewish National and University Library Press, 1981. 4to., 182 pages, frontispiece, illustrations, beige cloth, gilt stamped cover and spine titles, Burndy bookplate, fine. Jeff Weber Rare Books 169 - 383 2013 $145

Rose, Susan *Medieval Naval Warfare 1000-1500.* London and New York: Routledge, 2002. First edition, xvi, 155 pages, 5 plates, 3 maps, black cloth, gilt stamped cover and spine titles, Burndy bookplate, fine. Jeff Weber Rare Books 169 - 385 2013 $75

Ruddock, Red *Arch Bridges and their Builders 1735-1835.* Cambridge: Cambridge University Press, 1979. First edition, 4to., half tone frontispiece, 203 illustrations, figures, brown cloth, gilt stamped red spine label, dust jacket, bookplate of Burndy Library, fine. Jeff Weber Rare Books 169 - 393 2013 $275

Simons, Lao Genevra *Bibliography of Early American Textbooks on Algebrae...* Yeshiva College, 1936. 68 pages, 8vo., navy cloth, gilt stamped cover and spine titles, Burndy library bookplate, near fine. Jeff Weber Rare Books 169 - 413 2013 $65

Stevenson, D. Alan *The World's Lighthouses Before 1820.* London: New York and Toronto: Oxford University Press, 1959. First edition, large 8vo., illustrations, green cloth, gilt stamped cover emblem and spine title, dust jacket, inner hinges beginning to crack, Burndy bookplate, very good. Jeff Weber Rare Books 169 - 429 2013 $65

Thorne, Robert *Structural Iron and Steel 1850-1900.* Aldershot, et al: Ashgate/Variorum, 2000. 8vo., photos, illustrations, red cloth, gilt stamped cover and spine titles, Burndy bookplate, fine. Jeff Weber Rare Books 169 - 447 2013 $190

United States. Navy Department - 1959 *Dictionary of American Naval Fighting Ships.* Washington: Navy Department, 1959-1981. 8 volumes, large 8vo., photos, maroon cloth, gilt stamped cover and spine titles, Burndy bookplates, near fine. Jeff Weber Rare Books 169 - 452 2013 $350

Wallace, Alfred Russel 1823-1913 *My Life: a Record of Events and Opinions.* New York: Dodd, Mead, 1906. 2 volumes, 8vo., frontispiece, plates, maroon cloth, gilt stamped cover and spine titles, , extremity edges worn, inner hinges cracked, Burndy Library bookplate, bookplate of Seafarer's Education Service, very good. Jeff Weber Rare Books 169 - 467 2013 $175

Waters, D. W *The Rutters of the Sea: The Sailing Directions of Pierre Garcie. A Study of the First English and French Printed Sailing Directions...* New Haven: Yale University Press, 1967. First edition, large 4to., frontispiece, 14 illustrations, 3 tables, dark blue cloth, blind-stamped cover illustration, gilt stamped blue spine label, dust jacket worn, very good, Burndy bookplate. Jeff Weber Rare Books 169 - 470 2013 $83

Watson, Andrew G. *A Descriptive Catalogue of the Medieval Manuscripts of Exter College, Oxford.* Oxford: Oxford University Press, 2000. First edition, 4to., color frontispiece, 4 color plates, 4 black and white plates, navy cloth, gilt stamped spine title, dust jacket, Burndy bookplate, fine. Jeff Weber Rare Books 169 - 471 2013 $215

Wayland, John W. *The Pathfinder of the Seas: the Lifie of Matthew Fontaine Maury.* Richmond: Garrett & Massie, 1930. First edition, 8vo., frontispiece, decorative blue title border, plates, green cloth, black stamped cover and spine titles, Burndy bookplate, inscribed by author, very good. Jeff Weber Rare Books 169 - 472 2013 $75

Young, David *The Discovery of Evolution.* Cambridge: Cambridge University Press, 1992. First edition, tall 8vo., 2556 pages, frontispiece, photos and illustrations, blue cloth, gilt stamped spine title, dust jacket, Burndy Library bookplate, scarce cloth issue. Jeff Weber Rare Books 169 - 486 2013 $100

Association – Burnett, Ridley

Jeffs, Robin *The English Revolution I. Fast Sermons to Parliament.* London: Cornmarket Press, 1970-1971. Facsimile reprints, 34 volumes, 8vo., half brown cloth and half black divided vertically, black printed panel to spine with gilt title, spines little sunned, printed panel rubbed to some volumes, occasional light marks to boards, top edges slightly dusty, some corners bumped, Cornmarket Press compliments slip signed by Ridley Burnett loosely inserted. Unsworths Antiquarian Booksellers 28 - 159 2013 £1700

Association – Burney, Charles

Homerus *Opero (in Greek).* Florence: printer of Virgil C6061, probably Bartolommeo di Libri and Demetrius Damilas...9th December, 1488. but not before Jan. 1488/89 date of dedication. Editio princeps, 2 median folio volumes, unrubricated, early 19th century russia gilt, marbled endpapers and edges, volume II is about 15mm. shorter in its binding, bindings uniform height, inner margin of first leaf strengthened, slight worming at beginning of volume II, some foxing, from the collection of Dr. Charles Burney 1757-1817 whose collection was sold to British Museum (red library stamps), sold as duplicate in 1931 to Alice Millard; to Estelle Doheny. Heritage Book Shop 50th Anniversary Catalogue - 51 2013 $250,000

Association – Burning, H. Gordon

Radcliffe, John *Pharmacopoeia Radcliffeana; or Dr. Radcliff's Prescriptions Faithfully Gather'd...* London: printed for Charles Rivington, 1716. Second edition, frontispiece, 12mo., some browning to endpapers and pastedowns, contemporary sprinkled sheep, expertly rebacked retaining original red morocco label, signature of R. Cawley, 1759, with 19th century name H. Gordon Burning. Jarndyce Antiquarian Booksellers   CCIV - 248   2013   £480

Association – Burns, William

Dunbar, Paul Laurence *When Malindy Sings.* New York: Dodd Mead & Co., 1903. First edition, frontispiece and photo illustrations, professionally recased, two moderate stains on rear board, else very good in very good plus, supplied example of the rare dust jacket with couple of very small chips and in internally repaired text, housed in custom half leather and marbled paper clamshell case, inscribed by author for Dr. William "Buf" Burns, physician from Dayton. Between the Covers Rare Books, Inc.   165 - 37   2013 $4500

Association – Burr, Hervey

Adams, Andy *The Log of a Cowboy.* Boston and New York: Houghton Mifflin & Co., 1903. First edition, first state without a map and without mention of map in list of illustrations, beautiful copy, 12mo., original pictorial cloth, pages 387, some offset from jacket flaps which have become separated in interim, this copy otherwise fine, quarter blue morocco slipcase, 1903 bookplate of Hervey E. Burr, future Conn. banker.   Howard S. Mott Inc.   262 - 2   2013 $1000

Association – Burton, Dame Nellie

Behrman, S. N. *Brief Moment.* New York: Farrar & Rinehart Inc., 1931. First edition, inscribed by Behrman to Dame Nellie Burton, Berhman's landlady when he stayed in London, red cloth with title and author in black on front cover and spine, interior bright and clean, some light spotting to fore edge, jacket has small tears to top and bottom of spine, near fine, very good dust jacket.   The Kelmscott Bookshop   7 - 85   2013 $300

Association – Burton, Mabel

Dodgson, Charles Lutwidge   1832-1898 *Eight or Nine Wise Words about Letter-Writing. (with) The Wonderland Postage Stamp Case.* Oxford: Emberlin and Son, 1890. First edition, presentation copies "Wise Words" inscribed on first page to Mabel Burton 'from the author, July 10, 1890', stamp case inscribed inside "M.B. from C.L.D. ap. 4 1890", 24mo., "Wise Words" stitched as issued, lightly spotted and with slight wear to spine ends, stamp case lightly foxed and with outer color printed cotton lined paper sleeve, very good. Blackwell's Rare Books   172 - 41   2013   £4000

Association – Burton, Virginia

Malcolmson, Anne *The Song of Robin Hood.* Boston: Houghton Mifflin, 1947. First edition, large 4to., pictorial cloth, near fine in very good dust jacket with chips off spine ends, slight fraying on edges, illustrations by Virginia Burton with black and whites on every page, this copy signed by Burton.   Aleph-Bet Books, Inc.   105 - 108   2013 $850

Association – Bury, Edward

The British Florist; or Lady's Journal of Horticulture. London: Henry G. Bohn, 1846. First edition, 8vo., 14 hand colored plates, rebound in modern green cloth, volume 4 only, of 6, very good, bookplate of Edward Bury.   Barnaby Rudge Booksellers   Natural History 2013 - 020458   2013 $110

Association – Buspell, M. M.

Aringhi, Paolo *Triumphus Poenitentiae sive Selectae Poenitentim Mortes ex Variis Probatisque Historiarum Monumentis...* Romae: typis Philippi Mariae Mancini, 1670. 4to., original full vellum, some minor worming at gutter, generally fine, rubber ownership stamp of St. Joseph's Retreat, Highgate Hill, London, signature of M. Math. Buspell?, rare.   Jeff Weber Rare Books   171 - 5   2013 $750

Association – Butcher, Matilda

Byron, George Gordon Noel, 6th Baron   1788-1824 *The Works.* London: John Murray, 1833. 17 volumes, engraved frontispieces and vignette titles, printed titles, slightly later full dark green morocco, spines lettered in gilt, some spines very slightly faded, each volume with dust jacket gift inscription to Matilda Butcher from her sister, all edges gilt, very good, bright.   Jarndyce Antiquarian Booksellers   CCIII - 77   2013   £620

Association – Bute

Archimedes *De Iis quae Vehuntur in Aqua Libri Duo. (bound with) Commandino (Federico) Liber de centro Gravitatis Solidorum.* Bologna: Alexander Benacius, 1565. First edition, 2 works in one volume, fine large historiated woodcut initials, numerous geometrical diagrams in text, contemporary limp vellum, later black morocco spine label, Bute bookplate, very good, scarce in contemporary binding. Blackwell's Rare Books   Sciences - 8   2013   £5850

Association – Butler, Andrew Pickens

The Bank Case. A Report in the Cases of the Bank of South Carolina and the Bank of Charleston Upon Scire Facias to Vacate with the Final Argument and Determination Thereof in the Court for the Correction and Errors of South Carolina, in the Years 1842 and 1843. Charleston: W. Riley, Nov., 1844. First edition, large 8vo., full contemporary sheep, leather label on spine, light foxing, very good, inscribed in ink "Hon. A. P. Butler//with respects of the Atty. Genl./Jan. 1845", beneath that signed in ink "M. C. Butler 1857".   M & S Rare Books, Inc.   95 - 350   2013 $1500

Association – Butler, Edward

Procter, Bryan Waller *The Poetical Works.* London: Henry Colburn & Co., 1822. First edition, second edition and first edition, 3 volumes, occasional dampstaining and spotting, contemporary full dark blue morocco, gilt spines, borders & dentelles, maroon silk endpapers, slight rubbing to spines and corners, attractive set, all edges gilt, armorial bookplate of Edward Butler in volumes I and III, removed from volume II.   Jarndyce Antiquarian Booksellers   CCIII - 598   2013   £150

Association – Butler, Matthew C.

The Bank Case. A Report in the Cases of the Bank of South Carolina and the Bank of Charleston Upon Scire Facias to Vacate with the Final Argument and Determination Thereof in the Court for the Correction and Errors of South Carolina, in the Years 1842 and 1843. Charleston: W. Riley, Nov., 1844. First edition, large 8vo., full contemporary sheep, leather label on spine, light foxing, very good, inscribed in ink "Hon. A. P. Butler//with respects of the Atty. Genl./Jan. 1845", beneath that signed in ink "M. C. Butler 1857".   M & S Rare Books, Inc.   95 - 350   2013 $1500

Association – Butler, Pierece

Lucanus, Marcus Annaeus *Pharsalia.* Leiden: Samuel Luchtmans, 1728. 4to., frontispiece and foldout map, diagrams in text, part of one leaf pages 549-50, torn away with loss of text, some corners creased, contemporary Dutch vellum prize binding with handwritten title to spine, blind embossed boards, edges sprinkled, vellum darkened and rather grubby, some staining at edges, but strong and still very good, library ticket holder and armorial bookplate of Pierce Butler with motto 'Soyez Ferme' to front pastedowns, inkstamp of Metropolitan Special Collections, Southwark to both sides of f.f.e.p., titlepage and to all rear endpapers.   Unsworths Antiquarian Booksellers   28 - 26   2013   £95

Association – Butler, Richard

Bond, Edward *Saved.* London: Methuen, 1966. First edition, original wrappers, near fine, inscribed by author for actor Richard Butler, loosely inserted is Christmas card, also inscribed by author.   Maggs Bros. Ltd.   1460 - 123   2013   £175

Association – Buxton, W.

Hunter, John   1728-1793 *A Treatise on the Blood, Inflammation and Gun-shot Wounds.* London: John Richardson for George Nicol, 1794. First edition, 4to., frontispiece, 9 plates foxed, occasional light scattered foxing throughout text, modern quarter gilt stamped calf over marbled paper backed boards, gilt stamped red leather spine label, corners faintly rubbed, inscribed by David Rice 8/25/1820 for W. Buxton, better than very good.   Jeff Weber Rare Books   172 - 145   2013 $6500

Association – Cabral De Melo Neto, Joao

Bishop, Elizabeth *Poems: North & South - a Cold Spring.* Boston: Houghton Mifflin, 1955. First edition, one of 2000 copies printed, 8vo., original blue cloth, dust jacket, presentation copy inscribed by author for Brazilian poet Joao Cabral de Melo Neto, Dec. 18th 1955, pencil annotations to poems on table of contents page, representing a numerical tally of the number of words and lines, head of spine bit frayed, otherwise very good in dust jacket with some shallow chipping and light foxing to spine, extremely rare.   James S. Jaffe Rare Books   Fall 2013 - 24   2013 $4500

Association – Cabrera, William

Lamb, Charles 1775-1834 *The Life, Letters and Writings.* London: Gibbings & Co., 1897. Temple edition, 6 volumes, 179 x 114mm., pictorial titlepage, 17 portraits, pleasant enough contemporary burgundy half morocco over marbled boards, raised bands, spine panels with gilt acorn ornament, marbled endpapers, top edge gilt, other edges rough trimmed, 2 volumes unopened, armorial bookplate of William R. Cabrera, hint of rubbing to joints and extremities, 3 leaves with two inch tears into text (no loss), other small marginal tears here and there from rough opening, additional trivial imperfections, perfectly satisfactory copy, text fresh and clean (though not printed on bright stock) and entirely sound, bindings without any serious wear. Phillip J. Pirages 63 - 306 2013 $95

Association – Caher, Baron

Cooper, Ambrose *The Complete Distiller.* printed for P. Vaillant, 1757. First edition, folding engraved plate, slight offsetting on plate, tendency to browning, 8vo., contemporary calf, rebacked preserving original spine, corners worn, ownership inscription on title of Joseph Leay, Feb. 26th 1822 on title, pencil scribblings on verso of half title in same hand, armorial bookplate of one of the Barons Caher, good. Blackwell's Rare Books Sciences - 36 2013 £950

Association – Cairnie, Gordon

Moore, Marianne 1887-1972 *Poems.* London: Egoist Press, 1921. First edition, 8vo., original decorated wrappers, presentation copy inscribed by author for owner of Grolier Bookshop, Gordon Cairnie, very fine, virtually as new, none of the foxing usually found in this book in half morocco slipcase, rarely found signed or inscribed. James S. Jaffe Rare Books Fall 2013 - 104 2013 $4500

Association – Caldwell, C. B.

Montaigne, Michel De 1533-1592 *Essais.* Paris: chez Jean Serviere, Jean Francois Bastien, 1793. 3 volumes, 8vo., half titles, frontispiece, 8vo., some very slight foxing, otherwise fine, clean copy, one gathering in volume III printed on different stock of slightly tinted paper, lower corner of L4 volume I torn with loss not affecting text, slight tear to margin B2 volume II, full contemporary calf, gilt borders, gilt panelled spine, red morocco labels, armorial bookplate of C. B. Caldwell, handsome set. Jarndyce Antiquarian Booksellers CCIV - 207 2013 £780

Association – Cam, Samuel

Swift, Jonathan 1667-1845 *Remarks on the Life and Writings of Dr. John Swift...* London: printed for A. Millar, 1752. Second edition, frontispiece, 8vo., slight browning and occasional foxing, contemporary calf, double gilt fillet border, plainly rebacked, raised bands, unsympathetic red label, some cracking to surface leather on boards, corners worn, inner hinges repaired, early signature of Samuel Cam. Jarndyce Antiquarian Booksellers CCIV - 293 2013 £65

Association – Camden, Marquis of

Wordsworth, Christopher *Athens & Attica: a Journal of a Resistance There.* London: John Murray, 1836. First edition, 8vo., frontispiece, map, 2 lithographic plates, folding table, inscriptions to some foxing to the frontispiece and plates, otherwise fine, Marquis of Camden's copy. J. & S. L. Bonham Antiquarian Booksellers Europe - 9215 2013 £400

Association – Cammaerts, Emile

De La Mare, Walter 1873-1956 *On the Edge.* London: Faber and Faber, 1930. First edition, 8vo., original blue cloth, gilt, endpapers foxed, spine faded, cloth little scuffed and marked, otherwise very good, wood engravings by Elizabeth Rivers, inscribed by author for poet Emile Cammaerts. Maggs Bros. Ltd. 1460 - 214 2013 £100

Association – Campbell, G. J.

Colvil, Samuel *The Whigs Supplication or the Scotch-Hudibras.* Glasgow: printed by Robert Urie, 1751. 8vo., pages 164, lightly spotted and browned, recent dark brown half calf, marbled boards, spine with two raised bands, middle compartment lettered vertically in gilt, 18th century armorial bookplate of "Geo. Jas. Campbell Esqr./of Treesbank, relaid on front pastedown, above in the paper ex-libris of J. L. Weir. Unsworths Antiquarian Booksellers 28 - 84 2013 £125

Association – Campbell, Grace

Charteris, Leslie *The Saint on the Spanish Main.* Garden City: Doubleday Crime Club, 1955. First edition, some darkening on endpapers and small light stain top of spine, otherwise near fine in very good dust jacket with closed three inch tear on front panel that has had internal tape repair removed but has bled through, couple of other internal tape repairs with tape removed, some wear along folds, inscribed by author for Grace Campbell. Mordida Books 81 - 76 2013 $350

Association – Campbell, John

D'Obsonville, Foucher *Philosophic Essays on the Manners of Various Foreign Animals: With Observations on the Laws and Customs of Several Eastern Nations.* printed for John Johnson, 1784. First edition, little browned or foxed in places, 8vo. near contemporary flyleaves watermarked 1797, tree calf, separate contrasting lettering pieces on spine few abrasions, cracks (or worming) at head of spine, armorial bookplate inside front cover of John Campbell of Orange Bay, Jamaica, very good. Blackwell's Rare Books 172 - 45 2013 £750

Association – Cannon, Bland Wilson

Dandy, Walter *Intracranial Arterial Aneurysms.* Ithaca: Comstock, 1947. Third printing, 8vo., 6 folding charts, blue cloth, gilt stamped spine, extremities rubbed, ownership rubberstamps and signature of Bland Wilson Cannon, M.D., with related original signature, scarce, very good. Jeff Weber Rare Books 172 - 69 2013 $125

Leskell, Lars *Stereotaxis and Radiosurgery. An Operative System.* Springfield: Charles C. Thomas, 1971. First edition, 8vo., 51 figures, gilt stamped black cloth, dust jacket, rubber stamps of Bland Wilson Cannon, M.D., scarce with jacket, very good. Jeff Weber Rare Books 172 - 183 2013 $450

Association – Capel, Bob

Bret, Antoine *Ninon De Lenclos.* London: Arthur L. Humphreys, 1904. 214 x 154mm., attractive contemporary russet morocco in Arts and Crafts style, covers with frame of plain gilt rules and oak leaves and dots at intersections of lines, gilt titling on upper cover, raised bands, spine gilt in double ruled compartments with three large gilt dots at each corner connected by lines of tiny dots, gilt ruled turn-ins, all edges gilt, engraved bookplate of Victoria Sackville West, with best wishes from Bob Capel Xmas 1904, black and white photo portrait of Ninon de Lenclos tipped onto verso of half title, with identifying inscription in Victoria Sackville-West's hand, spine bit sunned, little mild soiling at boards, extremities lightly rubbed, hint of moisture here and there to tail edge margin, otherwise excellent, binding sound, text unusually bright clean and fresh. Phillip J. Pirages 63 - 417 2013 $250

Association – Carbacusend, Chad

Statius, Publius Papinius *Sylvarum Libri V. Thebaidos Libro XII. Achilleidos Libri II.* (bound with) *Orthographia ex Flexus Dictrionum Graecarum Omnium apud Statius cum Accentib. et Generib. ex varaiis utriusque linguae authoribus.* Paris: Apud Simonem Colinaeum, 1530. 8vo., some light staining, old and slightly discolored repairs to blank areas of first and last leaf, few small marginal tears, frequent later annotations in pencil and ink, late 19th century olive calf, largely faded to brown, boards with blind frame with gilt cornerpieces, spine to compartments with central gilt stamps, second compartment gilt lettered direct, all edges gilt, rubbed, small chip from head of spine, short crack to front joint, ownership inscription of Raymond Breckpol (contemporary with binding?) to head of titlepage, date of publication and an old cypher stamp both in violet ink to f.f.e.p., same repeated on rear pastedown (though cypher here handwritten), along with inscription of Chad Carbacusend(?) 1913 and small colored pictorial label. Unsworths Antiquarian Booksellers 28 - 47 2013 £650

Association – Carbery, Lord

Hardy, Francis *Memoirs of James Caulfield, Earl of Charlemont.* 1812. Second edition, volume I ex-library, Lord Carbery, Laxton Hall (ownership inscription dated St. Patrick's Day 1875), covers poor, text very good, 8vo., cloth. C. P. Hyland 261 - 177 2013 £95

Association – Cardiff Castle

Byron, George Gordon Noel, 6th Baron 1788-1824 *Hours of Idleness: a Series of Poems.* Newark: S. & J. Ridge, 1807. First edition, first issue, half title, uncut in full calf by F. Bedford, expertly rebacked retaining gilt spine and dentelles, dark green morocco label, armorial booklabel of Cardiff Castle, top edge gilt, very good, handsome. Jarndyce Antiquarian Booksellers CCIII - 109 2013 £1850

Association – Cardigan, Elizabeth

Hayley, William *The Life and Posthumous Writings of William Cowper...* Chichester: printed by J. Seagrave for J. Johnson, 1803-1806. First edition, 4 volumes including supplementary pages, in three, with 6 plates by William Blake, first impressions of those in volumes i and ii (no second state for those in volume iii) and one plate engraved by Caroline Watson, bound without half titles, little browned in places, some worming in lower margins of volumes i and ii, 4to., contemporary calf, blind roll tooled borders on sides, flat backstrips tooled in blind and lettered gilt direct, gilt inner dentelles, bit rubbed and bumped, spines little darkened, crack at foot on one joint, contemporary ownership of Elizabeth? Cardigan, that of C. Waldegrave dated 1824 in two places and Radstock bookplate in each volume, good. Blackwell's Rare Books 172 - 70 2013 £450

Association – Carey, Bessie

White, Henry Kirke *The Poetical Works of Henry Kirke White.* London: Charles Whittingham for William Pickering, 1853. 168 x 105mm., lviii, 252 pages, elegant contemporary dark green morocco inlaid, embossed and elaborately gilt, each cover with broad inlaid ochre morocco frame intricately gilt, large central mandorla of heavily embossed and gilt morocco of same color (both frame and centerpiece highlighted with red painted rules, raised bands, spine gilt in compartments framed by plain and decorative gilt rules, floral centerpiece and lancet cornerpieces richly gilt turn-ins, cream colored watered silk endleaves, all edges gilt, pleasing fore-edge painting of Nottingham Castle; engraved portrait and printer's anchor device on titlepage, pencilled inscription to Bessie Carey from Walter Shipper dated 13 October 1868, pastedown with morocco bookplate of Estelle Doheny, bookplate of Edward Laurence Doheny, bookplate of Carrie Estelle Doheny, bookplate of Dorothy Jayne Pedrini Shea; hint of wear to joints and corners, red paint bit rubbed with minor loss, minor foxing to portrait and titlepage, other trivial imperfections, but excellent copy, handsome binding solid and lustrous, text clean and fresh, fore-edge painting very well preserved.   Phillip J. Pirages   63 - 193   2013 $1100

Association – Carleton, Lorna

Christian, Anne Hait *The Search for Holmes, Robson, Hind, Steele and Graham Families of Cumberland and Northumberland, England.* California: La Jolla, 1984. Privately printed limited edition no. 53 of 1033 copies, small 4to., original blue cloth gilt, 75 illustrations, chart, presentation copy inscribed by author for Lorna Carleton.   R. F. G. Hollett & Son   Lake District & Cumbria - 268   2013   £65

Association – Carlingford, Chichester Fortescue

Coleridge, Samuel Taylor   1772-1834 *On the Constitution of Church and State...* London: William Pickering, 1839. Second edition, half title, some browning in prelims, contemporary full calf, spine gilt in compartments, dark brown leather label, little rubbed, Carlingford armorial bookplate with his signature as Chichester Fortescue, Oxford 1849.   Jarndyce Antiquarian Booksellers   CCIII - 554   2013   £60

Association – Carlingford, Lord

Byron, George Gordon Noel, 6th Baron   1788-1824 *Byroniana. The Opinions of Lord Byron on Men, Manners and Things...* London: Hamilton, Adams & Co., 1834. 16mo., engraved frontispiece, slightly later purple binder's cloth, spine little faded, armorial bookplate and signature of Lord Carlingford, 1875.   Jarndyce Antiquarian Booksellers   CCIII - 99   2013   £200

Association – Carlisle, Mary Pinkerton

Sherard, Robert Harborough *Oscar Wilde: the Story of an Unhappy Friendship.* London: privately printed at the Hermes Press, 1902. First edition, 254 x 198mm., 277, (1) pages, handsome contemporary olive green morocco lavishly gilt in Art Nouveau style by Stikeman (stamp-signed on rear turn-in), covers with multiple plain and decorative gilt rules enclosing large quatrefoil with very prominent floral cornerpieces and floral tool accents, central panel of that on upper cover containing coronet imposed upon crossed writing tools, raised bands, spine attractively gilt in compartments with large central lily framed by drawer hand tools, intricate gilt floral turn-ins, marbled endpapers, top edge gilt, original paper and cloth bound in, frontispiece photo of Wilde, five other portraits and two facsimiles of letters as called for, large paper copy, morocco bookplates of Helen Janssen Wetzel and Mary Pinkerton Carlisle, spine sunned to rich brown, just touch of rubbing to joints, usual offsetting to free endpapers from turn-ins, titlepage little browned from acidic(!) tissue guard (now removed), last page with faint darkening from bound-in cloth cover, handful of leaves with small, light brown stains along gutter (from binder's glue), other trivial imperfections but still excellent copy, leaves fresh, clean and bright, margins enormous and animated, glittering binding scarcely worn.   Phillip J. Pirages   61 - 126   2013 $1250

Association – Carlyle, Ellen

Campbell, Thomas   1777-1844 *The Pleasures of Hope, with Other Poems.* Edinburgh: printed for Mundell, Doig & Stevenson &c, 1810. Plates dated 1808, contemporary full mottled calf, gilt spine, borders and dentelles, black label, bit rubbed, hinges slightly worn but holding, inscription to Ellen Carlyle the gift of her Aunt Bowers Augs. 2nd 1813.   Jarndyce Antiquarian Booksellers   CCIII - 462   2013   £25

Association – Carlyle, Thomas

Wilson, Daniel *Chatterton. A Biographical Study.* London: Macmillan, 1869. First edition, 8vo., original burgundy cloth, faded on spine and lower cover, otherwise excellent copy, inscribed by Thomas Carlyle for Miss Olivia Sinclair (The Henk, Lockaby), Jan. 7 1870, further inscription author author's compliments presumably to Carlyle.   Maggs Bros. Ltd.   1460 - 161   2013   £500

Association – Carlyon, Horatio

Bacon, Francis Viscount St. Albans 1561-1626 *The Twoo Bookes of Francis Bacon, of the Proficience and Advancement of Learning, Divine and Humane.* London: for Henri Thomes, 1605. First edition, 4to., lacks final blank 3H2 and, as always, the rare two leaves of errata at end, late 18th century half calf and marbled boards, (extremities of boards worn), very skilfully and imperceptively rebacked retaining entire original spine, small worm trail in bottom margin of quires 2D-2F, occasional minor marginalia in early hand, else lovely copy, early signature of Row'd Weatherald and signature of Horatio Carlyon, 1861, Sachs bookplate and modern leather book label, calf backed clamshell box.   Joseph J. Felcone Inc.   Books Printed before 1701 - 5   2013 $7500

Association – Carmichael, Michael

Goring, C. R. *Micrographia: Containing Practical Essays on Reflecting, Solar, Oxy Hydrogen Gas Microscopies, Micrometers; Eye-pieces &c.*   Whittaker and Co., 1837. First edition, folding engraved frontispiece, 2 engraved plates and one full page illustration, 8vo., original boards, surface cracks at joints, contemporary signature of Michael Carmichael at head of title and his arms stencilled inside front cover, bookplate of D. J. Schuitema Meier, very good.   Blackwell's Rare Books   Sciences - 52   2013   £400

Association – Carp, Bertha

Guer, Jean Antoine *Moeurs et Usages Des Turcs, Leur Religion, Leur Gouvernement Civil, Militaire et Politique avec un Abrege de l'Histoire Ottomane.*   Paris: Chez Merigot & Piget, 1747. Second edition, 2 volumes, 2 engraved titlepages, titles printed in red and black with devices, 28 additional plates, engraved initials, and head and tailpieces, small 4to., contemporary mottled calf, boards ruled in gilt, five raised bands, compartments decorated in gilt, red morocco lettering piece, all edges gilt, wear to extremities with some loss at spine heads, and two small splits at tip of joints on first volume, volume number in one compartment mostly worn away, light scattered foxing and minor offsetting, marginal on plates, one folding panorama with small tear near hinge and upper margin, one with one inch tear to lower section near hinge, otherwise plates quite sharp, overall very good, bookplate of La Verne Baldwin (former consul General at Istanbul), gift to Baldwin from Beth (Bertha) Carp, close friend of Allen Dulles.   Kaaterskill Books   16 - 42   2013 $4000

Association – Carr, W.

Milner, John *A Practical Grammar of the Latin Tongue.* London: printed for John Noon, 1742. Second edition, 8vo., lightly toned, fore-edge sometimes cut little close, contemporary polished sheep, plain spine, paper label lettered in ink, edges speckled, joints cracking but strong, corners and endcaps worn, later ink ownership inscription 'W. Carr/1794".   Unsworths Antiquarian Booksellers 28 - 33   2013   £95

Association – Carrington, Dora

Thompson, Francis *Shelley.* London: Burns & Oates, 1911. Twelfth thousand, 8vo., original brown buckram, marked and spine darkened, but very good, inscribed by Dora Carrington.   Maggs Bros. Ltd.   1460 - 160   2013 £500

Association – Carroll, John

McFarling, Lloyd *Exploring the Northern Plains.* Caldwell: Caxton Printers, 1955. First edition, from the library of John M. Carroll with his signed bookplate, numerous maps, brown cloth, bookplate, very fine with lightly rubbed pictorial dust jacket.   Argonaut Book Shop Summer 2013 - 218   2013 $75

Association – Carter, Lillie Bland

Carter, Leon J. *Black Windsongs.* London: Mitre Press, 1973. First edition, fine in lightly worn, near fine dust jacket, inscribed by author's mother, Lillie Bland Carter. Between the Covers Rare Books, Inc.   165 - 99   2013 $225

Association – Carton, Charles

Bell, Charles 1774-1842 *The Hand: Its Mechanism and Vital Endowments as Evincing Design.* London: William Pickering, 1833. Second edition, 8vo., illustrations, lacks half title, modern blue cloth, red leather spine label, head of spine expertly repaired, spine faded, label rubbed, ownership signature of Charles A. Carton, ownership rubber stamp of Bellis on title, fine.   Jeff Weber Rare Books   172 - 19 2013 $750

Bell, Charles 1774-1842 *Observations on Injuries of the Spine and of the Thigh Bone in Two Lectures Delivered in the School of Great Windmill Street.* London: printed for Thomas Tegg, 1824. First edition, 4to., 9 engraved plates, with plate 9 bound in as frontispiece, light offsetting associated with plates marginal waterstains, quarter red buckram, boards, gilt spine, cover soil, blindstamp of Presbyterian Hospital, Ludlow Library, Philadelphia, ownership signature of Charles A. Carton, very good, unopened, rare.   Jeff Weber Rare Books   172 - 21   2013 $1200

Association – Carver, Raymond

Doctorow, E. L. *Drinks Before Dinner.* New York: Random House, 1979. First edition, fine in fine dust jacket, inscribed by author for Ray Carver.   Ken Lopez Bookseller   159 - 55   2013 $350

Burke, Bill *Portraits by Bill Burke.* New York: Ecco Press, 1987. First edition, signed in full by Raymond Carver and inscribed by him for James and Norma Ray, June 1988, fine in near fine dust jacket.   Ed Smith Books   75 - 14   2013 $750

Association – Carysfort, Earl of

Trollope, Anthony   1815-1882   *The American Senator.* London: Chapman and Hall, 1877. First edition in book form, half titles, 3 volumes, 184 x 127mm., fine contemporary dark olive morocco bound for the Earl of Carysfort (with his arms in gilt on center of front covers and monogram at foot of spines), backstrips titled in gilt raised bands flanked by multiple gilt rules, marbled endpapers, all edges gilt, Carysfort bookplate; front joint of 2 volumes with hint of wear, one leaf with two tiny tears at top, but fine, attractive set, text immaculate, and in a lustrous elegant binding.   Phillip J. Pirages   63 - 471   2013 $2250

Association – Cash, Bill

Holway, John B.   *Blackball Stars: Negro league Pioneers.* Westport: Meckler Books, 1988. First edition, boards quite bowed, thus good only, in torn and mildly chipped good plus dust jacket, inscribed by Bill (Ready) Cash for James.   Between the Covers Rare Books, Inc.   165 - 79   2013 $275

Association – Casson, Hugh

Betjeman, John   1906-1984   *The Illustrated Summoned by Bells.* London: John Murray, 1989. First edition, 4to., original green cloth, near fine in price clipped dust jacket, with original watercolor by artist and inscribed by him "Hugh Casson Nov. 1991".   Maggs Bros. Ltd.   1460 - 104   2013   £750

Association – Castle Archdale

Babbage, Charles   1792-1871   *On the Economy of Machinery and Manufactures.* London: Charles Knight, 1832. (1833). Third edition, titlepage, vignette slightly spotted, original purple wavy grained cloth, spine lettered gilt with gilt border, boards slightly marked, spine faded to brown, embossed stamp of Castle Archdale, Irvinestown, very good.   Jarndyce Antiquarian Booksellers   CCV - 14   2013   £450

Association – Castle Hacket

Warner, Richard   *Excursions from Bath.* Bath: printed by R. Cruttwell, 1801. First edition, 8vo., titlepage vignette, 4 maps set within text, slight foxing and light browning, small tear to head of A3, pencil notes in margins of four pages, 19th century half calf, marbled boards, gilt lozenges & bands to spine, gilt label, modern booklabel for Castle Hacket on inner front board, attractive copy.   Jarndyce Antiquarian Booksellers   CCIV - 307   2013   £225

Association – Castlestewart, Arthur, Earl of

Dickens, Charles   1812-1870   *David Copperfield.* London: Bradbury & Evans, 1850. First edition, half title, frontispiece, vignette title, plates by Phiz, some plates browned, generally quite clean, contemporary half dark green calf, spine decorated in gilt, black leather label, bit rubbed, signed F. E. Stevens in contemporary hand on printed title, loose armorial bookplate of Arthur Earl of Castlestewart.   Jarndyce Antiquarian Booksellers   CCV - 85   2013   £450

Association – Cathelineau, P. E.

Le Mettrie, Julien Offray De   *Abrege de la Theorie Chymique.* Paris: Lambert & Durand, 1741. First edition, woodcut ornament on title, headpiece and initials, divisional title to traite du Vertige (but pagination continuous), little staining here and there, 12mo., contemporary speckled calf, gilt scallop shell at each corner on both covers, spine gilt in compartments, red lettering piece, little worn, joints cracked but cords holding, the copy deposited in the library of the Chancelier Henri Francois d'Aguesseau by terms of the Privilege, with neat accession numbers on rear flyleaf, bibliographical notes at front, red ink stamp of P. E. Cathelineau of Paris and Vaas on page 111 (19th century), 20th century notes in French in blue ink to first part, good.   Blackwell's Rare Books   172 - 84   2013   £2200

Association – Caulfield

Sainthill, Richard   *The Old Countess of Desmond: an Inquiry.* Private printing, 1861-1863. 2 volumes, 76 + 105 pages, 2 plates, 3 pedigrees, very good, 2 ALS's from Caulfield, 1 from Sainthill, many cuttings.   C. P. Hyland   261 - 766   2013   £350

Association – Cawley, R.

Radcliffe, John   *Pharmacopoeia Radcliffeana; or Dr. Radcliff's Prescriptions Faithfully Gather'd...* London: printed for Charles Rivington, 1716. Second edition, frontispiece, 12mo., some browning to endpapers and pastedowns, contemporary sprinkled sheep, expertly rebacked retaining original red morocco label, signature of R. Cawley, 1759, with 19th century name H. Gordon Burning.   Jarndyce Antiquarian Booksellers   CCIV - 248   2013   £480

Association – Chadwick, Owen

Canney, Margaret *University of London Library. Catalogue of the Goldsmiths' Library of Economic Literature.* Cambridge: Cambridge University Press, 1970. First edition, oversize 8vo., frontispiece, dark green cloth, gilt stamped cover emblem and spine title, ownership signature of Owen Chadwick, fine.   Jeff Weber Rare Books   171 - 61   2013   £135

Association – Chadwyck-Healey

Byron, George Gordon Noel, 6th Baron   1788-1824 *Childe Harold's Pilgrimage. Canto the Fourth.* London: John Murray, 1818. First edition, 4th issue, 12 page catalog preceding title, final ad leaf, uncut in original pale blue boards, paper label, small ink stain on front board, spine and hinges little worn, armorial bookplate of Chadwyck-Healey, good copy, custom made blue morocco and cloth slipcase by Riviere & son.   Jarndyce Antiquarian Booksellers   CCIII - 148   2013   £300

Byron, George Gordon Noel, 6th Baron   1788-1824 *Childe Harold's Pilgrimage. Canto the Third.* London: John Murray, 1816. First edition, 2nd issue, 2nd variant, half title, 4 pages ads (Dec. 1816), uncut in original drab wrappers, spine slightly chipped at tail, leading hinge splitting, good plus as originally issued in later blue cloth folder, armorial bookplate of Chadwyck-Healey, loosely inserted is letter dated 1930 in original envelope from T. J. Wise to Oliver Nowell Chadwyck-Healey.   Jarndyce Antiquarian Booksellers   CCIII - 144   2013   £350

Byron, George Gordon Noel, 6th Baron   1788-1824 *Ode to Napoleon Bonaparte.* London: printed for John Murray by W. Bulmer and Co., 1814. First edition, retains often missing half title, final ad leaf, slight spotting to prelims, handsomely bound in full royal blue crushed morocco by Riviere & Son, gilt spine, borders and dentelles, armorial bookplate of Chadwyck-Healey, very good, attractive copy.   Jarndyce Antiquarian Booksellers   CCIII - 189   2013   £850

Association – Chaffin, Harry

Vallee, Rudy *Vagabond Dreams Come True.* New York: Dutton, First edition, 8vo., 262 pages, photos, very good, inscribed by author for Harry Chaffin.   Second Life Books Inc.   183 - 386   2013 $100

Association – Chagall, Marc

Maricain, Raissa *Chagall ou l'Orage Enchante.* Geneve/Paris: Editions des Trois Collines, 1948. Small quarto, half title, original color drawing and inscription by Marc Chagall for Samuel and Helen Slosberg, 8 full color plates tipped in with descriptions under the flaps, numerous black and white photographic plates and illustrations, many of which are full page, publisher's full green illustrated dust jacket wrapper, jacket illustrated and lettered in black ink, uncut and partially unopened, jacket with very slight amount of sunning to spine and minimal rubbing to spine extremities and edges, overall very good with beautiful original drawing.   Heritage Book Shop   Holiday Catalogue 2012 - 28   2013 $12,500

Association – Chalmer, Francisco

Homerus *The Odyssey of Homer.* London: printed for T. Osborne (and others), 1763. 3 volumes, 12mo., C2 volume II torn with loss, tear to lower corner of K6 volume III, full contemporary sprinkled calf, raised and gilt banded spines, ownership name of Francisco Chalmer, 19th century armorial bookplate and signature of Robert Chambre Vaughan, Esq. of Burlton Hall Co. Salop.   Jarndyce Antiquarian Booksellers   CCIV - 163   2013   £200

Association – Chamberlain, C. Pearl

Suckling, John *Fragmenta Aurea.* London: for Humphrey Moseley, 1646. First edition, first state with "FRAGMENTA AVREA" in upper case, a period after Churchyard in imprint and rule under the date; A3v:16 reads "allowred", second state of frontispiece re-incised with heavier lines around leaves of the garland and the bulge in the left sleeve, according the Beaurline and Clayton, the plate was most certainly re-incised in course of printing and is fairly evenly distributed with the various states of title; engraved portrait, contemporary calf, gilt fillet and cornerpieces, red morocco spine label, portrait and 2 first 2 leaves with two very tiny holes at gutter, worm trail in lower margin of first three gatherings, else very nice in lovely contemporary binding; bookplate of C. Pearl Chamberlain and booklabel of Abel Berland, fine red morocco pull-off case; with ALS of John Suckling (1569-1627) father of the poet.   Joseph J. Felcone Inc.   Books Printed before 1701 - 83   2013 $6000

Suckling, John *Fragmenta Aurea.* London: for Humphrey Moseley, 1646. First edition, first state, engraved portrait, contemporary calf, gilt fillet and cornerpieces, red morocco spine label, portrait and first two leaves with two very tiny holes at gutter, worm trail in lower margin of first three gatherings, else very nice in lovely dust jacket binding, bookplate of C. Pearl Chamberlain and book label of Abel Berland, fine red morocco pull-off case, with ALS from John Suckling (1569-1627), father of poet to unnamed recipient.   Joseph J. Felcone Inc.   English and American Literature to 1800 - 22   2013 $6000

Association – Chambers, Harry

Larkin, Philip 1922-1985 *The Whitsun Weddings. Poems.* London: Faber & Faber, 1964. First edition, one of 3910 copies, Harry Chambers' copy with his ownership signature and inscription "Harry Chambers February 10th 1964 (Publication date Feb. 28th)," signed and dated by Larkin on front free endpaper, Chambers' light pencil marks in text, otherwise fine.   James S. Jaffe Rare Books   Fall 2013 - 88   2013 $4500

McGahern, John *Nightlines.* London: Faber, 1970. First edition, crown 8vo., original mid-blue cloth lightly dampspotted, gilt lettered partly on black ground, endpapers browned, ownership signature of publisher Harry Chambers, dust jacket with some browning, good.   Blackwell's Rare Books   172 - 216   2013   £100

Association – Chapin, Susan Revere

Fulton, John Farquhar *Grace Revere Osler. Her Influence on Men of Medicine.* Offprint from Bulletin of the History of Medicine, 1949. Original printed wrappers, penned presentation note from Lady Osler's sister, Susan Revere Chapin.   James Tait Goodrich   S74 - 122   2013 $225

Association – Chaplin, Kate

Fraser, James George *The Golden Bough.* London: Macmillan and Co., 1923. Abridged edition, frontispiece, 8vo., original blue cloth, decorated in gilt, inscribed by author for Kate and Mabel Chaplin, excellent copy, spine very slightly faded, extremities lightly rubbed.   Maggs Bros. Ltd.   1460 - 299   2013   £250

Association – Chaplin, Mabel

Fraser, James George *The Golden Bough.* London: Macmillan and Co., 1923. Abridged edition, frontispiece, 8vo., original blue cloth, decorated in gilt, inscribed by author for Kate and Mabel Chaplin, excellent copy, spine very slightly faded, extremities lightly rubbed.   Maggs Bros. Ltd.   1460 - 299   2013   £250

Association – Chapman, Abel

Koebel, W. H. *Portugal: Its Land and People.* London: Archibald Constable, 1909. First edition, 8vo., numerous illustrations, original red decorative cloth, spine slightly faded, Abel Chapman's copy with his signature and bookplate.   J. & S. L. Bonham Antiquarian Booksellers   Europe - 7971   2013   £80

Association – Chapman, Harriet Ann

A Glance at New York: Embracing the City Government, Theaters, Hotels, Churches...   New York: A. Greene, 1837. First edition, 12mo., contemporary quarter morocco gilt, unprinted paper covered boards, later bookplate and two earlier names, including that of Harriet Ann Chapman, joints rubbed and worn, front hinge little tender, still reasonably tight, just about very good.   Between the Covers Rare Books, Inc.   New York City - 300867   2013 $350

Association – Chapman, J. J.

Wotton, Henry *Reliquiae Wottonianae; or a Collection of Lives, Letters, Poems.* London: by T. Roycroft for R. Marriott, 1672. Third edition, 8vo., portraits, 19th century red morocco, early signatures of J. Grien? 1725, Thomas Price and John Francis Cole, 1828, bookplates of J. J. Chapman and Molly Flagg Gibb, very good.   Joseph J. Felcone Inc.   English and American Literature to 1800 - 26   2013 $900

Association – Chapman, Robert

Miller, Philip *The Abridgement of the Gardeners Dictionary.* London: printed for the author and sold by John Rivington (and others), 1763. 4to., engraved frontispiece and 12 folding plates, clean tear without loss of Xx4, contemporary calf, double gilt ruled borders, expertly rebacked, raised and gilt banded spine, morocco label, corners very neatly repaired, early signature of Robert Chapman verso of frontispiece.   Jarndyce Antiquarian Booksellers   CCIV - 204   2013   £750

Association – Chapman-Purchas

The History of Ripon; with Descriptions of Studley-Royal, Fountains' Abbey, Newby, Hackfall &c &c. Ripon: W. Farrer, 1806. Second edition, 314 pages, aquatint frontispiece and woodcuts in text, very good, contemporary half calf, marbled boards, raised gilt bands, blindstamped decoration in each compartment, foolscap 8vo., signature of John Hammond 24th August 1863, later bookplates of Chapman-Purchas and R. J. Rattray.   Ken Spelman Books Ltd.   73 - 142   2013   £120

Association – Charles, Hilary

Arlen, Michael *Men Dislike Women. A Romance.* New York: Doubleday Doran and Co., 1931. First edition, 8vo., original cloth, very good, cloth little soiled, lettering to spine faded, inscribed by author for Hilary Charles.   Maggs Bros. Ltd.   1460 - 17   2013   £50

Association – Charlton, William Henry

Byron, George Gordon Noel, 6th Baron   1788-1824   *The Works... with His Letters and Journals and His Life.* London: John Murray, 1832-1833.   17 volumes, half titles (not in volumes I, IX), frontispieces and titles, illustrations, small repair to half title volume III, original dark green moire cloth, green paper label volume I, gilt, little rubbed and bumped, slightly marked armorial bookplates of William Henry Charlton.   Jarndyce Antiquarian Booksellers   CCIII - 76   2013   £480

Association – Charmley, John

Woodward, Llewellyn   *British Foreign Policy in the Second World War.*   London: HMSO, 1970-1976.   First edition, 5 volumes, 4to., brown cloth, minor dustiness to edges of text block, brown cloth, minor dustiness to edges of text block, very good, dust jackets in protective plastic, few signs of use, very good, dust jacket of volume IV with tape to spine, folds adhered to pastedowns with tape, ownership inscription of John Charmley, volume IV ex-libris copy with associated plates and stamps.   Unsworths Antiquarian Booksellers   28 - 206   2013   £200

Association – Charrington, John

Chaucer, Geoffrey   1340-1400   *The Works of...* Hammersmith: Kelmscott Press, 1896.   One of 425 copies on paper, out of a total edition of 438, folio, 87 woodcut illustrations after Sir Edward Burne-Jones, woodcut titlepage, 14 variously repeated woodcut borders, 18 variously repeated woodcut frames around illustrations, 26 nine-line woodcut initial words, numerous three, six and ten line woodcut initial letters and woodcut printer's device, printed in black and red in Chaucer type, original holland backed blue paper boards, printed paper label on spine, spine and label very lightly browned, with little chipping to label, occasional light foxing or spotting on fore-edge, otherwise fine, bookplate of John Charrington, full brown morocco slipcase.   Heritage Book Shop   Holiday Catalogue 2012 - 91   2013 $85,000

Association – Chase, Robert

Bell, Charles   1774-1842   *Letters Concerning the Diseases of the Urethra.*   Boston: W. Wells & T. B. Wait; Philadelphia: Edward Earle, 1811.   First American edition, small 4to., 6 engraved plates, untrimmed, last 2 plates moderately foxed, original printed boards, extremities and spine chipped, bookplate of Robert A. Chase, very good, very rare in original printed boards, laid in new blue cloth drop back box, black calf spine label.   Jeff Weber Rare Books   172 - 20   2013 $600

Association – Chase, Samuel

Duche, Jacob   *Observations on a Variety of Subjects, Literary, Moral and Religious in a Series of Original Letters.*   Philadelphia: John Dunlap, 1774.   First edition, 12mo., contemporary calf, rebacked corners rubbed, new leather label, errata, this copy belonged to Samuel Chase, signer from Maryland, of the Declaration of Independence, later Supreme Court justice, occasional staining.   Howard S. Mott Inc.   262 - 46   2013 $2750

Association – Cheever, Susan

Wilson, Bill   *My Name is Bill.*   New York: Simon & Schuster, 2004.   Stated first edition, signed and inscribed by Susan Cheever, 8vo., 306 pages, fine in fine dust jacket.   By the Book, L. C.   36 - 80   2013 $150

Association – Chetwoad, Penelope

Clark, Kenneth   *The Nude. A Study of Ideal Art.*   London: John Murray, 1956.   First edition, small 4to., original red cloth, excellent copy, inscribed by John Betjeman to his wife Penelope Chetwoad.   Maggs Bros. Ltd.   1460 - 95   2013   £500

Association – Chetwynd, George, 3rd Baronet

Chesterfield, Philip Dormer Stanhope, 4th Earl of   1694-1773   *Letters Written... to His Son, Philip Stanhope Esq...*   London: printed for J. Dodsley, 1774.   First edition, first state (erratum on page 55 of volume i uncorrected), 2 volumes, frontispiece volume i, bound without errata leaf in volume ii (but with blank leaf of matching paper in its place) some light foxing, embossment of Grendon Hall 1850 (the belonging to Sir George Chetwynd, 3rd Baronet), 4to., modern biscuit calf, spines gilt with red morocco lettering pieces, circular red morocco numbering pieces on green morocco grounds, new endpapers, preserving old bookplates of William Frederick, 2nd Duke of Gloucester and Edinburgh, manuscript letter loosely inserted, very good.   Blackwell's Rare Books   B174 - 146   2013   £900

Association – Chevalier, Maurice

Tynan, Kenneth   *Persona Grata.*   London: Allan Wingate, 1954.   First reprint, 4to. original blue cloth, excellent copy in slightly rubbed and nicked dust jacket, inscribed by Cecil Beaton to Maurice Chevalier, photos by Beaton, excellent copy, in slightly rubbed and nicked dust jacket.   Maggs Bros. Ltd.   1460 - 55   2013   £300

Association – Chevalier, Paul

James I, King of Scotland *The Kingis Quair.* Vale Press, 1903. One of 260 copies, (another 10 copies on vellum), 236 x 150mm., lv, (1) pages, printed in red and black, extremely pleasing midnight blue crushed morocco, intricately gilt by Stikeman, stamp signed, covers with gilt frame formed by three rows of tiny gilt circlets enclosing two intertwining veins that combined at 12 intervals to produce a trio of rose blossoms, raised bands, spine gilt in double ruled compartments containing tulip beneath a daisy, flowers surrounded by gilt circlets, inner gilt dentelles, marbled endpapers, top edge gilt, matching morocco backed flat lined solander box, morocco bookplate of Paul Chevalier, inevitable slight offsetting to free endpapers from turn-ins otherwise, most attractive copy in very fine condition, binding lustrous and unworn, text with no signs of use. Phillip J. Pirages   61 - 125   2013 $3500

Association – Chevanne, R.

Renouard, Antoine Augustin *Catalogue d'une Precieuse Collection De Livres...* Paris: Firmin Didot for Poitier and Jules Renouard in Paris and Barthez and Lowel in London, 1854-1855. 8vo., portrait etched by G. Staal on India, evenly lightly browned, portrait little foxed, later red morocco backed marbled boards, spine with raised bands and lettered in gilt, upper edge gilt, price list with original printed wrappers bound in, bookplate of R. Chevanne inside front cover.   Marlborough Rare Books Ltd.   218 - 123   2013   £500

Association – Chew, Lucy

Hardy, Thomas   1840-1928   *Selected Poems of...* London: Liverpool and Boston: the Medici Society, 1921. First Medici Society edition, number 313 of 1000 numbered copies, signed by Hardy with his holograph note, laid in is note sent Feb. 21 1928 from Florence Hardy to Lucy Chew of Bryn Mawr, PA, 8vo., original tan cloth spine, blue boards and printed paper labels, frontispiece, engraved titlepage, fine in original printed dust jacket, slightly faded and enclosed in chemise and quarter morocco slipcase, from the Gary Lepper Collection of Thomas Hardy.   The Brick Row Book Shop   Bulletin Nine - 67   2013 $3750

Association – Chilcot, Gilbert

Coleridge, Samuel Taylor   1772-1834   *Hints Towards the Formation of a More Comprehensive Theory of Life.* London: John Churchill, 1848. First edition, half title, postscript leaf, original vertical grained purple cloth, blocked in blind, fading to brown and slightly rubbed, signature of Gilbert Chilcot on title, very good, scarce.   Jarndyce Antiquarian Booksellers   CCIII - 566   2013   £180

Association – Child, Paul

Child, Julia   *Julia Child.* New York: Alfred A. Knopf, 1978. First edition, clean very near fine in close to near fine, price clipped dust jacket with few small edge tears and some very slight wear, signed by Julia and Paul Child, very nice.   Jeff Hirsch Books   Fall 2013 - 129480   2013 $400

Association – Choate, E., Mrs.

Eldridge, Elleanor   *Memoirs of...*   Providence: Albro, 1828. First edition, 12mo., 128 pages, cloth backed boards, some foxed and soiled, portrait, some stained and foxed, very good, very scarce, notes in pencil "Mrs. E. Choate/from her affectionate/ aunt A. Baker/ New Bedford/ Jan 22nd/ 1939/ I purchased this book/ of Eleanor herself".   Second Life Books Inc.   183 - 442   2013 $600

Association – Cholmely, Octavia

Crabbe, George   1754-1832   *Poems.*   London: printed for J. Hatchard, 1810. Fifth edition, 2 volumes, half titles, contemporary full vellum, gilt spines, borders and dentelles, red leather labels, little dulled, inscription of Octavia Cholmely 1854, later booklabel of John Baker in volume II, all edges gilt.   Jarndyce Antiquarian Booksellers   CCIII - 622   2013   £65

Association – Churton, Thomas

Vergilius Maro, Publius   (Works). *P. Virgilius Maro: in Usum Scholarum/ Ad Novissimam Heynii Editionem Exactus.*   Londini: Imprensis J. Johnson et al, 1809. 250 x 147mm., 2 p.l., 700 pages, handsome contemporary navy blue straight grain morocco, densely gilt, covers with thick and thin gilt rule border and large central laurel wreath, that on front with Latin motto "Honoris Causa", that on rear with name Thomas T. Churton and date 1817, raised bands, spine lavishly gilt in compartments filled with foliage and small tools emanating from a central fleuron gilt titling and turn-ins, all edges gilt, with splendid later painting of Mount Etna on the Fore Edge, recent plush lined folding cloth box with gilt spine titling, ink stamp of Bolton Public Library on verso of title and first page of text, corners slightly bumped, boards little faded, first two gatherings mildly foxed, isolated dust spots or faint freckled foxing, still especially attractive copy, handsome binding virtually unworn, text clean and smooth and unusual fore-edge painting, very well preserved. Phillip J. Pirages   63 - 192   2013 $2900

Association – Claire, William

Powell, Anthony   *Talk About Byzantium Anthony Powell & the BBC.*   Charingworth: Evergreen, 2006. First edition, one of 200 numbered copies, 8vo., stitched paper wrappers, handset and printed by John Grice in Centaur type on Zerkall mould made paper, laid in is original letter from Powell to William Claire with ink corrections and additions. Second Life Books Inc.   183 - 326   2013 $1500

Association – Clapham, William

Swieten, Gerard Van *The Commentaries Upon the Aphorisms of Dr. Herman Boerhaave.* London: John and Paul Knapton and Robert Horsfield & Thomas Longman, 1744-1765. 10 of 18 volumes, lacking volumes 3, 11, 13-18, small 8vo., frontispiece in volume 12, folding plates in volume 4, occasional worm tracks slightly affecting text, original brown calf, gilt ruled covers, raised bands, gilt stamped red leather spine labels, few hinges weak or starting, ownership signature William Clapham and few volumes signed M. A. Halloway.   Jeff Weber Rare Books   172 - 34   2013 $1700

Association – Clapp, Cornelia

Eastman, Sophie E. *In Old South Hadley.* Chicago: Blakely Pub. Co., 1912. First edition, 8vo., illustrations, spine little wrinkled but very good, clean, ownership signature of professor Cornelia M. Clapp.   Second Life Books Inc.   183 - 119   2013 $75

Association – Clark, Alfred Corning

New York. (City) *Manual of the Corporation of the City of New York for 1850.* New York: Mcspedon & Baker, 1850. First edition, publisher's pale green cloth stamped in blind and gilt, 552 pages, duotones, color plates and engravings, many foldout maps and facsimiles, one map detached but present, couple of small repairs to folding plates, light stain on rear board, else nice, very good or better two bookplates one with "Bequeathed to Robert Sterling Clark by his father Alfred Corning Clark 1896".   Between the Covers Rare Books, Inc.   New York City - 299892   2013 $500

Association – Clark, Barrett

Kelly, George *Behold, the Bridegroom.* Boston: Little Brown, 1928. First edition, 8vo. 172 pages, frontispiece, blue cloth with paper label, else near fine in little nicked and soiled, dust jacket, rare in jacket, inscribed by author for Barrett Clark.   Second Life Books Inc.   183 - 221   2013 $350

Association – Clark, F. Ambrose

Lennox, Sarah *The Life and Letters of Lady Sarah Lennox... also a Short Political Sketch of the Years 1760 to 1763 by Henry Fox, 1st Lord Holland.* London: John Murray, 1901. First edition, third printing, 2 volumes, especially attractive contemporary moss green three quarter morocco over lighter green linen by Wood of London (stamp signed), raised bands, spines handsomely gilt in compartments with large central fleuron within a lozenge of small tools and scrolling cornerpieces accented with gilt dots, marbled endpapers, top edge gilt, 30 photogravures of portraits, many by Sir Joshua Reynolds, engraved bookplate of F. Ambrose Clark, leather of spine and edges of boards darkened (as nearly always with green morocco) to olive-brown, offsetting to endpapers from bookplate and turn-in, fine set, the stiffly opening volumes with virtually no signs of use and handsome bindings lustrous and unworn.   Phillip J. Pirages   63 - 317   2013 $375

Association – Clark, Jane Heaton Cunyngham

Dodgson, Charles Lutwidge   1832-1898 *The Hunting of the Snark.* London: Macmillan, 1876. First edition, small 8vo., original red cloth, gilt decoration, all edges gilt, slightly bumped at head and tail of spine, otherwise excellent, this is the special presentation binding, 100 were bound thus, inscribed on dary of publication Mar 29 1876 for Jane Heaton Cunyngham Clark.   Maggs Bros. Ltd.   1460 - 231   2013   £3500

Association – Clark, Robert Sterling

New York. (City) *Manual of the Corporation of the City of New York for 1850.* New York: Mcspedon & Baker, 1850. First edition, publisher's pale green cloth stamped in blind and gilt, 552 pages, duotones, color plates and engravings, many foldout maps and facsimiles, one map detached but present, couple of small repairs to folding plates, light stain on rear board, else nice, very good or better two bookplates one with "Bequeathed to Robert Sterling Clark by his father Alfred Corning Clark 1896".   Between the Covers Rare Books, Inc.   New York City - 299892   2013 $500

Association – Clarke, H. N.

Cumbria Parish Registers *Ulverston: The Registers of Ulverston Parish Church.* Ulverston: James Atkinson, 1886. First (only) edition, very thick large 8vo., publisher's half black morocco gilt, raised bands, all edges and endpapers marbled, armorial bookplate of H. N. Clarke, handsome copy, extremely scarce.   R. F. G. Hollett & Son   Lake District & Cumbria - 364   2013   £850

Association – Clarkson, John

Du Moulin, Pierre *The Antibarbarian; or a Treatise Concerning an Unknowne Tongue.* printed by George Miller for George Edwards, 1630. Lacking initial and two terminal blanks though the ante-penultimate present, titlepage little soiled and fragment of doeskin cord adhering and partially obscuring one letter, small 8vo., textblock sometime rather ruthlessly over stitched and all but loose in its original limp vellum, contemporary ownership inscription "John Clarkson His Book", soiled.   Blackwell's Rare Books   B174 - 52   2013   £900

Association – Clayton, Lt. Colonel

Johnson, Samuel   1709-1784   *The Beauties of Johnson.* London: printed for G. Kearsley at no. 46 in Fleet Street, 1781.   First edition, 8vo., bound in fours, marginal tears to Q2-3, some old waterstaining, contemporary sprinkled calf, rebacked rather plainly, but not recently, inner hinge strengthened, new pastedowns, ownership signature of Lt. Colonel Clayton, 1829, later bookplate of Margaret Huntingdon, several 19th century marginal annotations.   Jarndyce Antiquarian Booksellers   CCIV - 171   2013   £125

Association – Clayton, Robert

Livius, Titus   *Titi Livii Patavini Historiarum Libri Qui Extant.* Paris: apud Fredericum Leonard, 1679. 5 volumes bound as 6, 4to., engraved half title and 2 engraved maps, folding engraved plate and 1 other engraved plate, light toning and some spotting, contemporary Cambridge style panelled calf, spines darkened with stain and paneled gilt, red morocco labels, rubbed at joints and corners, joints cracked, endcaps worn, some labels lost, contemporary armorial bookplate of "Sr Robert Clayton of the City of London/Knight Alderman & Mayor thereof Ano. 1679", covered up by later plain endpapers (volume 4 excavated locally to reveal identity), early 19th century armorial bookplate of Stephen Lowdell.   Unsworths Antiquarian Booksellers   28 - 24   2013   £450

Association – Clegg, Samuel

Papworth, John Buonarotti   1775-1847   *Rural Residences.*   London: printed for R. Ackermann..., 1832. Second edition, large 8vo., 27 hand colored aquatint plates, original green cloth, upper and lower covers with dolphin and fountain design, sympathetically rebacked, inscribed by Samuel Clegg Jun 1840.   Marlborough Rare Books Ltd.   218 - 117   2013   £1400

Association – Clements, Henry

Addison, Joseph   1672-1719   *The Works of.* Birmingham: printed by John Baskerville, 1761. 4 volumes, without the very scarce "Directions to the Binder" leaf in volume i (which carried instruction that it be cut out) but with 7 plates in volume ii (probably not printed by Baskerville, and sometimes missing), frontispiece and titlepage of volume I browned, little browning elsewhere, occasional foxing, mostly sparse but heavier on few gatherings, 4to., contemporary red morocco, single gilt fillet borders on sides, upper covers with arms of Joshua Hutchinson blocked in gilt at centre, gilt rules around raised bands on spines, gilt edges, lower edges of boards with waterstain of varying height (not affecting textblock), not exceeding 1 inch, engraved Hutchinson bookplate inside front cover, later bookplate opposite Henry J. B. Clements, good.   Blackwell's Rare Books   B174 - 2   2013   £1200

Association – Clerk, John

Darwin, Charles Robert   1809-1882   *On the Origin of Species by means of Natural Selection or the Preservation of Favoured Races in the Struggle for Life.*   London: John Murray, 1859.   First edition, first issue, octavo, one folding diagram, original green cloth decoratively stamped in blind on covers, hinges expertly repaired, spine decorated and lettered in gilt (Freeman variant 'a'), extremities and corners slightly rubbed, binder's ticket of Edmonds & Remnants of London on back pastedown, contemporary bookplate of John Clerk with his signature dated "Jun 1859" and Roberto Salinas Price bookplate, overall very good, housed in full green morocco clamshell case.   Heritage Book Shop   50th Anniversary Catalogue - 28   2013 $160,000

Association – Cleveland, Ann

Montgomery, L. M.   *Anne's House of Dreams.*   Toronto: McClelland & Stewart, 1922.   Later edition, 8vo., blue cloth boards with dark blue lettering to spine and front cover in dust jacket, some light wear to edges, dust jacket baldy torn with pieces missing and taped, signed by author, inscription "Ann Cleveland August 28th 1941".   Schooner Books Ltd.   104 - 141   2013 $375

Association – Cloetta, Yvonne

Connell, Mary   *Help is on the Way (Poems).*   Reinhardt, 1986.   First edition, line drawings by author, crown 8vo., original light blue card wrappers printed in black, red and white, fine, inscribed by Grahame Greene for Yvonne Cloetta.   Blackwell's Rare Books   172 - 190   2013   £1500

Association – Clopper, Ellen

Mills, George H. *Mohammed, the Arabian Prophet.* Boston: Philips, Sampson & Co., 1850. First edition, 12mo., original cloth, bottom of spine chipped, inscribed by George H. Mills to Ellen M. Clopper, Feb. 28 1851. M & S Rare Books, Inc. 95 - 235 2013 $125

Association – Coburn, Kathleen

Coleridge, Samuel Taylor 1772-1834 *Omniana; or Horae Otiosiores.* London: Longman &c., 1812. First edition, 2 volumes, odd spot, small tear from corner of leading f.e.p., contemporary full diced calf, excellent rebacked, slightly rubbed, booklabels of Kathleen Coburn, neat signatures of M. E. Hawkins. Jarndyce Antiquarian Booksellers CCIII - 524 2013 £200

Association – Cockayne, E.

Sauvan, Jean Baptiste Balthazar *Picturesque Tour of the Seine, from Paris to the Sea with Particulars Historical and Descriptive.* London: R. Ackermann, 1821. 345 x 275mm., publisher's red buckram, covers with blindstamped frame, upper cover with gilt titling, flat spine stamped with gilt strapwork panels and with gilt titling, all edges gilt, engraved color vignette on titlepage, unsigned aquatint vignette at foot of last page, engraved color map, 24 fine hand colored aquatint plates by Augustus Pugin and John Gendall; presentation bookplate to Master E. Cockayne as reward of merit by Mr. Bowling/Milk Street Academy, Sheffield June 23rd 1848; binding little soiled, joints and extremities bit worn, just slightest offsetting from some plates onto text, one plate with offsetting from text ad half dozen others with just hint of same, other trivial imperfections, very desirable copy. Phillip J. Pirages 63 - 422 2013 $6000

Association – Coco, Alfred

Marino, Giambattista *L'Adone, Poems.* Amsterdam: 1651. 2 volumes, 12mo. bound in sixes, small marginal tear to V1 volume II, some light browning, few ink splashes but very good, most handsome early 19th century dark blue straight grain morocco, gilt ruled borders, attractive gilt panelled spines decorated with flower head, open circles and small gilt dots, pink endpapers and pastedowns, armorial bookplate of John Barron, early inscription of J. Stirling, after 19th century bookplate of Alfred Coco of Middle Temple, ownership name of J. Stroud Read, London Nov. 1928, earlier hand notes "Will. Roscoe's Library", all edges gilt. Jarndyce Antiquarian Booksellers CCV - 191 2013 £620

Association – Cohen, I. Bernard

Hall, A. Rupert *Henry More Magic: Religion and Experiment.* Cambridge: Basil Blackwell, 1990. 8vo., 304 pages, black cloth, silver stamped spine, dust jacket, inscribed in ink by author to I. Bernard Cohen, Burndy Library bookplate, fine. Jeff Weber Rare Books 169 - 306 2013 $60

Newton, Isaac 1642-1727 *Philosophiae Naturalis Principia Mathematica.* London: Joseph Streater for the Royal Society, 1687. One of 1000 copies, large 8vo., rust cloth, gilt stamped spine, spine head slightly torn, ownership signature of I. Bernard Cohen with his scattered notes and underlining, booklabel of Burndy Library with bookplate, very good. Jeff Weber Rare Books 169 - 317 2013 $300

Association – Cole, A. H.

Betham, Matilda *Elegies and Other Small Poems.* Ipswich: printed by W. Burrell, 1797. Half title discarded, lightly spotted, few leaves with small chips from blank margins, 2 early inscriptions (A. H. Cole - cropped) and (cropped 'to C. E. Adams 1810'), 12mo., slightly later half sprinkled calf, marbled boards, spine divided by sextuple gilt fillets, red morocco lettering piece, other compartments infilled with wave pallets or with central decorative gilt stamp, somewhat rubbed, good. Blackwell's Rare Books 172 - 22 2013 £700

Association – Cole, Hobart

Sterne, Laurence 1713-1768 *A Sentimental Journey through France and Italy.* London: for T. Becket and P. A. De Hondt, 1768. First edition, text variant 2 in volume 1 and text variant 1 in volume 2, as usual, 2 volumes, 8vo., engraved coat of arms, with half titles and list of subscribers' names, but, as usual, without rare inserted ad leaf, full sprinkled calf, fully gilt by Riviere, spines bit dry, hinges worn, small chip at crown of volume 2, Hobart F. Cole bookplate. Joseph J. Felcone Inc. English and American Literature to 1800 - 21 2013 $900

Association – Cole, John Francis

Wotton, Henry *Reliquiae Wottonianae; or a Collection of Lives, Letters, Poems.* London: by T. Roycroft for R. Marriott, 1672. Third edition, 8vo., portraits, 19th century red morocco, early signatures of J. Grien? 1725, Thomas Price and John Francis Cole, 1828, bookplates of J. J. Chapman and Molly Flagg Gibb, very good. Joseph J. Felcone Inc. English and American Literature to 1800 - 26 2013 $900

Association – Coleridge, Edith

Quarles, Francis *Enchiridion Miscellaneum.* reprinted for Charles Baldwyn, 1822. 12th impression, 2 volumes, frontispiece, contemporary full vellum, gilt borders, red leather labels, slightly marked, volume II little discolored, booklabels of John Porter, top edge gilt, very good, with unsigned inscription by Henry Nelson Coleridge, signed by Sara and Edith Coleridge.   Jarndyce Antiquarian Booksellers   CCIII - 597   2013   £350

Warwick, Arthur *Spare Minutes; or resolved Meditations and Premeditated Resolutions.* London: printed by G. M. for Walter Hammond, 1822. Sixth edition, small 4to., half title, frontispiece, plate, contemporary full vellum, gilt borders, blue leather label slightly faded, slightly marked, top edge gilt, very good, inscribed by Henry Nelson Coleridge for his wife Sara and signed by him with initials, later signature of their daughter Edith Coleridge.   Jarndyce Antiquarian Booksellers   CCIII - 596   2013   £250

Association – Coleridge, G. H. B.

Allsop, Thomas *Letters Conversations and Recollections of S. T. Coleridge.* London: Edward Moxon, 1836. First edition, 2 volumes, half titles, pencil notes in text volume I, original dark green cloth, paper label volume I chipped and missing entirely volume II, spines faded and slightly worn at heads and tails, inscribed to G. H. B. Coleridge by W. King. Mar 14 1944.   Jarndyce Antiquarian Booksellers   CCIII - 557   2013   £85

Association – Coleridge, Henry Nelson

Quarles, Francis *Enchiridion Miscellaneum.* reprinted for Charles Baldwyn, 1822. 12th impression, 2 volumes, frontispiece, contemporary full vellum, gilt borders, red leather labels, slightly marked, volume II little discolored, booklabels of John Porter, top edge gilt, very good, with unsigned inscription by Henry Nelson Coleridge, signed by Sara and Edith Coleridge.   Jarndyce Antiquarian Booksellers   CCIII - 597   2013   £350

Warwick, Arthur *Spare Minutes; or resolved Meditations and Premeditated Resolutions.* London: printed by G. M. for Walter Hammond, 1822. Sixth edition, small 4to., half title, frontispiece, plate, contemporary full vellum, gilt borders, blue leather label slightly faded, slightly marked, top edge gilt, very good, inscribed by Henry Nelson Coleridge for his wife Sara and signed by him with initials, later signature of their daughter Edith Coleridge.   Jarndyce Antiquarian Booksellers   CCIII - 596   2013   £250

Association – Coleridge, Sara

Quarles, Francis *Enchiridion Miscellaneum.* reprinted for Charles Baldwyn, 1822. 12th impression, 2 volumes, frontispiece, contemporary full vellum, gilt borders, red leather labels, slightly marked, volume II little discolored, booklabels of John Porter, top edge gilt, very good, with unsigned inscription by Henry Nelson Coleridge, signed by Sara and Edith Coleridge.   Jarndyce Antiquarian Booksellers   CCIII - 597   2013   £350

Warwick, Arthur *Spare Minutes; or resolved Meditations and Premeditated Resolutions.* London: printed by G. M. for Walter Hammond, 1822. Sixth edition, small 4to., half title, frontispiece, plate, contemporary full vellum, gilt borders, blue leather label slightly faded, slightly marked, top edge gilt, very good, inscribed by Henry Nelson Coleridge for his wife Sara and signed by him with initials, later signature of their daughter Edith Coleridge.   Jarndyce Antiquarian Booksellers   CCIII - 596   2013   £250

Association – Colin, Ralph

Loreau, Max *Cerceaux 'Sorcellent.* Paris: 1967. First edition, one of 750 numbered copies, 11 x 8.75 inches, 56 silkscreened pages with 21 original color silkscreens by Jean Dubuffet, signed and inscribed by author and artist for Mr. and Mrs. Ralph Colin, as new in stiff wrappers and slipcase.   Gemini Fine Books & Arts., Ltd.   Art Reference & Illustrated Books - 2013 $1200

Association – Colish, A.

Targ, William *The Making of the Bruce Rogers World Bible.* Cleveland: World Pub. Co., cop., 1949. First edition, signed by Rogers and A. Colish copy number 10, fine, without slipcase, 4to., illustrations, original red cloth.   Howard S. Mott Inc.   262 - 122   2013 $100

Association – Collet, Clara

Gissing, George *Sleeping Fires.* London: T. Fisher Unwin, 1895. First edition, tall 12mo., recently bound in pale brown calf, burgundy label lettered gilt on spine, terminal 10 pages of ads, inscribed by author for Miss Clara Collet Dec. 1895, and signed in full on titlepage, excellent copy.   Maggs Bros. Ltd.   1460 - 343   2013   £1250

Association – Collins, John

Euclides *Geometricorum Elementorum Libri XV.* Paris: Henri Estienne, 7 January, 1516-1517. Sixth edition, Roman types with numerous woodcut geometrical diagrams in margins, fine crible initials in a variety of styles and sizes, titlepage soiled and cut down and mounted on old paper, one diagram just cropped at its extreme outer corner, folio, 19th century half brown calf by Hatton of Manchester, marbled edges, original order for the binder loosely inserted (in fact calling for half Russia), the Macclesfield copy with bookplate but no blindstamps and annotated by John Collins, preserved in cloth folding box, good.   Blackwell's Rare Books   Sciences - 48   2013   £15,000

Meade, J. A. *The Meades of Inishannon.*   Victoria: 1955. No. 1- (of?), signed presentation copy from author, to noted Cork historian, John T. Collins, 14 plates, 59 pages, very good.   C. P. Hyland   261 - 403   2013   £125

Newton, John *Trigonometria Britanica; or the Doctrine of Triangles, in Two Books.*   printed by R. and W. Leybourn and are to be sold by George Hurlock, Joshuah Kirton, Thomas Pierrepont and William Fisher, 1658.   First edition, 4 parts in one volume, sectional titles to last 3 parts, woodcut diagrams in text in first part, woodcut initials and headpieces, browned in places, titlepage ill attached to a later (rather stiff) flyleaf, last leaf folding with errata pasted to verso of flap, folio in 4s, contemporary panelled mottled calf, rebacked, preserving most of original spine, edges parti-colored, the 2 canones logarithmorum red, remainder marbled, the Macclesfield copy with blindstamps and bookplate, few annotations in the hand of John Collins, sound.
Blackwell's Rare Books   Sciences - 85   2013   £2000

Association – Collins, William

Blunden, Edmund *Undertones of War.*   London: Richard Cobden Sanderson, 1929.   Seventh impression, 8vo., original black cloth, author has inscribed the poem How Sleep the Brave on front free endpaper and written beneath "William Collins was the Expeditionary Force in Flanders 1745-1746 with Edmund Blunden's best wishes to all those who came from Ireland into Flanders in 1914-1918 May 15 1930", excellent copy.   Maggs Bros. Ltd.   1460 - 113   2013   £500

Association – Collinson, J.

Pitt, Robert   *The Craft and Frauds of Physick Expos'd.*   printed for Tim Childe, 1702.   First edition, little bit browned and soiled, 8vo., contemporary gilt panelled calf, rebacked, corners worn, contemporary signature of J. Collinson and his book label inside front cover giving his place of residence as Lancaster, sound.   Blackwell's Rare Books   Sciences - 97   2013   £750

Association – Colvill-Scott, H. D.

Maidment, James   *A Book of Scottish Pasquils 1568-1715.*   Edinburgh: William Paterson, 1868.   One of 3 copies on vellum, (there were a limited but unspecified, number of copies, also printed on paper), 206 x 128mm., handsome contemporary crimson morocco, attractively gilt by Andrew Grieve (stamp signed), covers gilt with multiple plain and decorative rules enclosing a delicate dentelle frame, large intricate fleuron at center of each cover, spine gilt in double ruled compartments with complex fleuron centerpiece and scrolling floral cornerpieces, turn-ins decorated with plain and decorative gilt rules, patterned burgundy and gold silk endleaves, top edge gilt, slightly worn matching morocco lipped slipcase; woodcut titlepage illustration, numerous decorative tailpieces and occasional woodcut vignettes in text; armorial bookplate of H. D. Colvill-Scott, armorial bookplate of Clarence S. Bemens; tiny dark spot on spine, corners with just hint of rubbing, couple of leaves with slightly rumpled fore edge, still fine, text clean, smooth and bright, binding unusually lustrous and with virtually no wear.
Phillip J. Pirages   63 - 479   2013 $4800

Association – Comerford, James

A Description of Stonehenge, Abiry &c. in Wiltshire. Salisbury: printed and sold by Collins and Johnson, sold also by J. Wilkie, London, 1776.   First edition, 6 woodcut plates on leaves which form part of gatherings, but not included in pagination, 12mo., original mottled sheep, double gilt fillet borders on sides, rebacked preserving most of original lettering piece lettered ('STONE/HINGE'), armorial bookplate inside front cover of James Comerford, placed over another good.   Blackwell's Rare Books   172 - 135   2013   £750

Association – Connolly, Cyril

Graves, Robert   1895-1985   *Treasure Box.*   London: Chiswick Press, 1919.   First edition, 8vo., original blue unprinted wrappers, excellent copy in protective over sized folding box, leather label, lettered in gilt, inscribed by author and Nancy Nicholson for Robert Graves, inherited by his son Alec Waugh who gave it to Cyril Connolly at Christmas 1967.   Maggs Bros. Ltd.   1460 - 359   2013   £1750

Horizon. A Review of Literature & Art. Volume I No. 1. London: published by the Proprietors, 1940.   First edition, 8vo., original brown wrappers, stained on corner of lower cover, otherwise excellent copy in portective folding box, inscribed by Cyril Connolly for Noel Blakiston.   Maggs Bros. Ltd.   1460 - 180   2013   £600

Wordsworth, William 1770-1850 *The Prelude or Growth of a Poet's Mind.* London: Edward Moxon, 1850. First edition, 8vo., original brown cloth, blocked in blind, preserved in folding box, inscribed by Cyril Connolly for Noel Blakiston Jan 17.27, very good, lower joint splitting, extremities worn, plain and large earlier bookplate, issue without publisher's ads. Maggs Bros. Ltd. 1460 - 177 2013 £650

Association – Conrad, Jessie

Conrad, Joseph 1857-1924 *Laughing Anne. One Day More. Two Plays.* New York: Doubleday Pag and Co., 1925. first US edition, 8vo., original dark blue cloth, spine and upper cover lettered gilt, inscribed by author's widow Jessie for R. B. Cunninghame Graham, excellent copy. Maggs Bros. Ltd. 1460 - 192 2013 £450

Association – Conroy, Donald

Conroy, Pat *The Great Santini.* Boston: Houghton Mifflin, 1976. First edition, 8vo., original red cloth, dust jacket, signed by author and by his father Donald Conroy, near fine in dust jacket. Maggs Bros. Ltd. 1460 - 194 2013 £350

Association – Conroy, Jack

Bontemps, Arna *Anyplace but Here.* New York: Hill and Wang, 1966. First edition, small stain on rear board, else fine in slightly spine faded, very good dust jacket, full page inscription from Jack Conroy. Between the Covers Rare Books, Inc. 165 - 84 2013 $150

Association – Constable

Cook, Eliza *Diamond Dust.* London: F. Putman, 1865. First edition, half title, 8 pages ads, original sand grained green cloth, bevelled boards, blocked and lettered gilt, inscription from author for Misses Constable. Jarndyce Antiquarian Booksellers CCV - 75 2013 £85

Association – Constable, D.

Dodsley, Robert 1703-1764 *The Economy of Human Life.* London: printed for William Lane at the Minerva Press, 1799. 24mo., frontispiece, some minor browning to endpapers, slight offsetting from frontispiece, contemporary sheep expertly rebacked, gilt banded spine, corners little worn, contemporary ownership name of D. Constable. Jarndyce Antiquarian Booksellers CCIV - 115 2013 £125

Association – Cook, Minnie

Blake, William 1757-1827 *The Poetical Sketches.* Basil Montagu Pickering, 1868. Uncut in original brown cloth boards damp affected, spine little worn at head and tail, paper label slightly chipped, good, sound copy, signed Minnie Cook 3873. Jarndyce Antiquarian Booksellers CCIII - 2 2013 £90

Association – Cook, Ransom

Torrey, Jesse *A Portraiture of Domestic Slavery, in the United States: Proposing National Measures for the Education, and Gradual Emancipation of the Slaves, Without Impairing the Legal Privileges of the Possessor...* Balston Spa: The author, 1818. Second edition, original quarter calf and paper covered boards, very faint tidemark to edges of first few pages, some modest rubbing and light wear, sound, very good or better, bookplate of Ransom Cook which covers Cook's easily readable signature. Between the Covers Rare Books, Inc. 165 - 270 2013 $1250

Association – Cooke, George

Nostradamus *The True Prophecies or Prognostications of Michael Nostradamus.* London: Thomas Radcliffe and Nathaniel Thompson, 1672. First English edition, small folio, engraved frontispiece, decorated woodcut initials and headpieces, titlepage printed in red and black, contemporary mottled calf, neatly rebacked, retaining original red morocco lettering label spine with five raised bands, gilt board edges, marbled edges, 18th century armorial bookplate of Sir George Cooke of Westminster, slightly browned, otherwise very good. Heritage Book Shop 50th Anniversary Catalogue - 77 2013 $11,000

Association – Coppard, A. E.

Hardy, Thomas 1840-1928 *Tess of the D'Urbervilles. A Pure Woman.* London: Osgood McIlvaine, 1895. First Wessex Novels Edition, 8vo., original green cloth, gilt decoration and lettering, top edge gilt, etched frontispiece, one plate, map, from the library of English author A. E. Coppard, paper browning slightly in margins, very good, from the Gary Lepper Collection of Thomas Hardy. The Brick Row Book Shop Bulletin Nine - 33 2013 $250

Association – Coppinger, W. A.

Genealogical Notes of the O'Briens of Kilcor. privately printed, 1887. 14 pages, very good, 8vo., 4 ALS's to W. A. Coppinger. C. P. Hyland 261 - 404 2013 £100

Association – Corlieu, A.

Romen, Jean Joseph Therese *L'Inoculation Poeme en Quatre Chants.* Amsterdam & Paris: Chez Lacomee, 1773. First edition, Engraved frontispiece, 8vo. original full tan mottled calf, gilt paneled spine, all edges marbled, light rubbing to binding, internally fine, from the library of Dr. Blanchard with his bookplate, tipped post card from Paris (1891) with note by A. Corlieu in regards to this book. James Tait Goodrich   S74 - 217   2013 $495

Association – Cornford, Frances

Aragon, Louis *La Diane Francaise.* Paris: Editions Pierre Seghers, 1945. First trade edition, 8vo., later blue cloth, excellent copy, spine slightly faded and marked, inscribed by author to poet Frances Cornford.   Maggs Bros. Ltd.   1460 - 16   2013   £750

Association – Corradini, Giovanni

Yahsiro, Yukio *Sandro Botticelli.* London: Medici Society, 1925. First edition, number 182 of 630 copies, frontispieces, plates with tissue guards, folio, natural linen with brown morocco lettering pieces in gilt, bevel edges, top edge gilt, fore and bottom edges deckled, ex-libris Giovanni Corradini, linen soiled as common, labels chipped, leaves unopened (uncut), scattered foxing, overall still very good+, magnificent set.   Kaaterskill Books   16 - 93   2013 $450

Association – Coryton, John

Hewitt, John *Hewitt's Tables of Simple Interest, Shewing at one View the Interest of any Sum of Money...* London: printed for John Clarke and C. Hitch, 1747. Second edition, 12mo., original full calf, gilt stamped double ruling to covers, heavily worn, front cover open tear, lacks original spine, joints reinforced with kozo, internally clean, ownership signature of John Coryton, as is, internally very good, rare. Jeff Weber Rare Books   171 - 163   2013 $75

Association – Cotsen, Lloyd

Princeton University *A Catalogue of the Cotsen Children's Library Volumes I and II.* Princeton: Princeton University Press, 2000-2003. 2 volumes, large folio, handsome color reproductions, decorative endpapers, gilt stamped pictorial green Japanese cloth, gilt stamped black leather spine label, fine, signed presentation inscription by collector Lloyd Cotsen to Jeff Weber in volume I.   Jeff Weber Rare Books   171 - 79   2013 $400

Association – Cottrell, Leonard

Bruce, J. Collingwood *Handbook to the Roman Wall.* Newcastle upon Tyne: Andrew Reid & Co., 1957. Eleventh edition, original cloth, dust jacket, numerous illustrations and 12 maps, ex-libris of Leonard Cottrell on flyleaf.   R. F. G. Hollett & Son   Lake District & Cumbria - 196   2013   £25

Divine, David *The North-West Frontier of Rome.* MacDonald, 1969. Original cloth, gilt, dust jacket, 16 plates, 5 diagrams and map, ex-libris of Leonard Cottrell. R. F. G. Hollett & Son   Lake District and Cumbria - 39 2013   £25

Association – Coulet, Francois

Gary, Romain *The Colours of the Day.* London: Michael Joseph, 1953. First edition, 8vo., original black cloth, dust jacket, near fine, jacket just little worn at head and tail of spine, inscribed by author to fellow diplomat, Mons. et Madam Francois Coulet.   Maggs Bros. Ltd.   1460 - 325 2013   £175

Association – Cowen, Antonia Joyce

Cowen, William Joyce *They Gave Him a Gun.* New York: Harrison Smith and Robert Haas, 1936. First edition, fine in attractive, very good plus dust jacket with small nicks at corners, nicely inscribed by author to his daughter Antonia Joyce Cowen, Jan. 27 1936.   Between the Covers Rare Books, Inc.   Mystery & Detective Fiction - 97568 2013 $1500

Association – Cowley, Wilfrid

Day Lewis, Cecil *Country Comets.* London: Martin Hopkinson, 1928. First edition, small 8vo., rebound in pale green boards, printed paper label, excellent copy, pages lightly browned and foxed, inscribed by author for friend Wilfrid Cowley.   Maggs Bros. Ltd.   1460 - 206   2013 £125

Association – Cox, E. M.

Flatman, Thomas *Poems and Songs.* London: printed for Benjamin Tooke at the Ship in St. Paul's church-yard, 1682. 8vo., frontispiece, small mark to foot of frontispiece, minor tear to foot of titlepage, slight browning, bound without prelim blank but with two final errata and ad leaves, manuscript correction from errata on page 101, bound by Riviere and son in full dark red crushed morocco gilt, ruled border, elaborate gilt decorated spine, inner gilt cornerpiece decoration, marbled endpapers, slight rubbing to board edges, corners little bruised, contemporary signature at head of titlepage, bookplates of E. M. Cox and John Drinkwater, latter adding bibliographical pencil note to leading endpaper, all edges gilt, variant with M74 and the ad, in a different setting, beginning on verso.   Jarndyce Antiquarian Booksellers   CCV - 102   2013   £620

Association – Cox, Edward Hyde

Stegner, Wallace *Mormon Country.* New York: Duell, Sloan & Pierce, 1942. First edition, near fine, bright copy in very good plus to near fine dust jacket, inscribed by Edward Hyde Cox (1914-1998).   Ed Smith Books   78 - 61   2013 $850

Association – Cox, Hyde

Frost, Robert Lee   1874-1963 *You Came Too.* New York: Henry Holt, 1959. First edition, 8vo., original cloth, fine in very good dust jacket, signed by author and by editor, Hyde Cox.   Howard S. Mott Inc.   262 - 53   2013 $850

Association – Cox, Kenneth J.

Vergilius Maro, Publius *Opera quae quidem Exstant Omnia.* Basilae: Sebastianum Henriepetri, 1613. Folio, little worming to fore-edge margins around columns 180 and 279, toning at very edge of margins to varying degrees, occasional discoloration around text especially to volumes 1079-1802 and 1901-1904, contemporary speckled tan calf, neatly rebacked and corners repaired, red morocco gilt spine label, boards heavily scratched, few dents, edges worn, armorial bookplate of Sir William Molesworth with ink inscription of Kenneth J. Cox, Dalton Hall Victoria Park, Manchester 14 added, old ink ownership inscription of Johannis Glover on titlepage, small contemporary (?) list of Latin names for various vegetables and herbs loosely inserted.   Unsworths Antiquarian Booksellers   28 - 57   2013   £500

Association – Cox, Richard

Collins, William   1721-1759 *The Poetical Works of Mr. William Collins.* London: for T. Becket and P. A. DeHondt, 1765. First collected edition, final blank M6, contemporary calf, spine gilt in compartments, covers sprinkled with stencil in interlacing bordered pattern within a gilt fillet, edges sprinkled blue green, marbled endpapers, extremities worn, crown of spine chipped away, respectable copy, fine internally, armorial bookplate of Richard. Cox.   Joseph J. Felcone Inc.   English and American Literature to 1800 - 10   2013 $1000

Association – Coxe, George Harmon

Shaw, Joseph T. *Blood on the Curb.* New York: Dodge Pub. Co., 1936. First edition, pastedown little browned from binder's glue, else fine in fine and bright contemporary with tiny nicks at crown, inscribed by author to noted mystery writer George Harmon Coxe.   Between the Covers Rare Books, Inc.   Mystery & Detective Fiction - 94557   2013 $3000

Association – Crabites, Judge

Reisner, Mary *Shadows on the Wall.* New York: Dodd Mead and Co., 1943. First edition, trifle worn at foot of spine, still about fine in very good dust jacket with tiny nick at crown, some modest rubbing at spine ends, inscribed by author for Judge and Mrs. Crabites.   Between the Covers Rare Books, Inc.   Mystery & Detective Fiction - 57180   2013 $275

Association – Crahan, Marcus

Bigmore, E. C. *A Bibliography of Printing with Notes and Illustrations.* London: Bernard Quaritch, 1880-1886. small 4to., 3 volumes in 1, two color title (printed in red and black), illustrations, original brown leather (signed by Bennett, NY), professionally rebacked by Bruce Levy, gilt stamped spine title with raised spine bands, top edge gilt, some marginal checkmarks, bookplates of Marcus Crahan and the Zamorano Club (gift of Crahan), signature P. R. Lee Jr. (1939), near fine, choice copy.   Jeff Weber Rare Books   171 - 31   2013 $750

Association – Crampton, Mrs.

Byron, George Gordon Noel, 6th Baron   1788-1824 *The Giaour, a Fragment of a Turkish Tale.* London: printed by T. Davison for John Murray, 1813. Eighth edition, half title, slightly spotted, later marbled wrappers, spine slightly dulled and with small chip at tail, ownership inscription of Mrs. Crampton on half title, booklabel of Alex Bridge.   Jarndyce Antiquarian Booksellers   CCIII - 166   2013   £30

Association – Crensman, John

Graves, Robert 1895-1985 *More Poems 1961.* London: Cassell, 1961. First edition, 8vo., original maroon cloth, near fine, dust jacket torn at head and tail of spine, inscribed by author for John Crensman May 26 1961.   Maggs Bros. Ltd.   1460 - 364   2013   £150

Association – Crewe, Marquis of

Cogniard, Hippolyte *Byron a l'Ecole d'Harrow, Episode Mele de Couplets...* Paris: J. Breaute, 1834. 24mo., contemporary full green marbled morocco, wheat sheaf device of Lord Houghton in gilt on upper board, armorial booklabel of Marquis of Crewe, all edges gilt, very good, attractive copy.   Jarndyce Antiquarian Booksellers   CCIII - 364   2013   £450

Association – Crews, Donald

Crews, Donald *Freight Train.* New York: Greenwillow, 1978. First edition, first printing with number code 1-10, oblong 4to., pictorial cloth, fine in dust jacket with award seal, illustrations in color by Donald Crews, this copy inscribed and dated 1979 by Crews who has also added some smoke coming from the picture of the train on endpaper, first printings are scarce, signed copies even more so.   Aleph-Bet Books, Inc.   105 - 82   2013 $325

Association – Creyke, Anne

Milman, Henry Hart *The Fall of Jerusalem.* London: John Murray, 1820. New edition, 8vo., toned and foxed, corner damp marked, contemporary half calf, marbled boards, spine divided by flat raised bands, gilt lettered direct, compartments tooled in blind, marbled edges and endpapers, little rubbed, headcap chipped, boards scuffed, contemporary ink ownership inscription "Anne Creyke" at upper fore corner of titlepage, signed binding by "W/ Forth/ book-binder.   Unsworths Antiquarian Booksellers   28 - 186   2013   £75

Association – Creyke, E.

Richardson, Jonathan 1665-1745 *An Essay on the Theory of Painting.* London: printed by W. Bowyer, 1715. First edition, 8vo., little browned in places, contemporary panelled sheep, worn, especially upper corners splits at extremities of joints, early signature at head of title, Eliz Creyke, good.   Blackwell's Rare Books   172 - 124   2013   £350

Association – Crichton, A.

Deeping, Warwick *Sorrell and Son.* London: Cassell & Co., 1925. First edition, 8vo., original red cloth, spine slightly faded, excellent copy, inscribed by author for A Crichton.   Maggs Bros. Ltd.   1460 - 223   2013   £75

Association – Crisp, Charles Birch

Coleridge, Hartley *Biographia Borealis; or Lives of Distinguished Northerns.* London: Whitaker, Treacher & Co., 1833. First edition, frontispiece, plates, contemporary half maroon morocco, spine slightly faded, little rubbed, bookplate of Charles Birch Crisp, good plus.   Jarndyce Antiquarian Booksellers   CCIII - 591   2013   £90

Association – Cromer, Rowland Thomas Baring, 2nd Earl of

Homerus *Batrachomyomachia Graece and Veterum Exemplarium Fiden Resusa.* London: William Boyer, 1721. 8vo., contemporary full red morocco, small 1 inch splits top of spine, minor wear at corners, gilt decorated borders and centerpieces, gilt decorated spine (bit darkened), leather label, copper engraved folding facsimile, all edges gilt, bookplates of collector Thomas Brooke and Rowland Thomas Baring, 2nd Earl of Cromer.   Howard S. Mott Inc.   262 - 76   2013 $850

Association – Cronyn, Hume

Albee, Edward *A Delicate Balance.* New York: Atheneum, 1966. First edition, signed by author as well as six members of the original cast, Jessica Tandy, Hume Cronyn, Rosemary Murphy, Carmen Matthews, Henderson Forsythe and Marian Seldes, fine in nearly fine dust jacket.   Ed Smith Books   78 - 3   2013 $750

Association – Cropper, Margaret

Hodgkin, Lucy Violet *Yesterday.* privately printed, 1914. Limited to 150 copies, this an out-of-series copy, original cloth, gilt, spine little worn at head and foot, pages 74, presentation copy inscribed by author to Margie (Margaret Cropper) and dated Oct. 1914.   R. F. G. Hollett & Son Lake District and Cumbria - 220   2013   £25

Association – Crosby, Caresse

Connolly, Cyril 1903-1974 *The Unquiet Grave.* London: Horizon, 1944. First edition, one of 1000 copies, 8vo., original wrappers bound in full Oxford blue calf, lettered gilt within compartments, slightly rubbed, otherwise near fine, inscribed by author for Caresse Crosby, presentation binding.   Maggs Bros. Ltd.   1460 - 181   2013   £750

Association – Cross, John Nevill

Dickens, Charles 1812-1870 *Nicholas Nickleby.* London: Chapman & Hall, 1839. First edition, half title, frontispiece, 39 plates by Phiz, uncut in later full olive green crushed morocco by Riviere & Son, gilt spine, borders and dentelles, front wrapper to part XIV bound in at end, armorial bookplate of John Nevill Cross, top edge gilt, very good, handsome copy. Jarndyce Antiquarian Booksellers CCV - 88   2013   £850

Association – Crossle

Lepper, John Heron *History of the Grand Lodge of Free and Accepted Masons of Ireland.* London: 1925. 1957. First edition, 2 volumes, illustrations, lower fore corner of volume 1 damaged, signed presentation copy from Crossle to a fellow mason, otherwise very good set.   C. P. Hyland   261 - 548   2013   £500

Association – Crouch, Walter

Derham, William 1657-1735 *Astro-Theology.* London: Printed for J. Richardson, 1758. Ninth edition, 8vo., 3 folding copper engraved plates, offset browning on endpapers and titlepage, one plate rather foxed, contemporary sprinkled calf, double gilt ruled borders, expertly rebacked, raised and gilt banded spine, red morocco labels, corners neatly repaired, early signature of Wm. J. Staines, ownership name of Walter Crouch, Wanstead.   Jarndyce Antiquarian Booksellers CCIV - 112   2013   £250

Association – Crowe, Eileen

Robinson, Lennox *Pictures in a Theatre.* Dublin: Abbey Theatre, 1947. First edition, 8vo., original wrappers, inscribed by author on front cover "Lennox Robinson August 1947" and further inscription from Eileen Crowe.   Maggs Bros. Ltd. 1442 - 281 2013   £75

Association – Cunard, Nancy

Douglas, Norman 1868-1952 *Paneros. Some Words on Aphrodisiacs and the Like.* privately printed for subscribers by G. Orioli, Lungarno, Dec., 1930. First edition, out of series copy of the stated 250 numbered and signed copies, 8vo., original decorated and 'vermiculated' gold cloth boards, black leather spine label, inscribed by publisher Pino Orioli for Nancy Cunard, then passed on to her principal assistant Winifred Henderson by author, with Henderson's bookplate, extremities slightly rubbed, otherwise excellent. Maggs Bros. Ltd.   1460 - 242   2013 £750

Association – Cunninghame Graham, Robert B.

Conrad, Joseph 1857-1924 *Tales of Hearsay.* London: T. Fisher Unwin, 1925. First edition, 8vo., original dark green cloth, spine and upper cover lettered in gilt, excellent copy, spine dulled, inscribed from R. B. Cunninghame Graham (provided preface).   Maggs Bros. Ltd. 1460 - 193 2013   £250

Conrad, Joseph 1857-1924 *Laughing Anne. One Day More. Two Plays.* New York: Doubleday Pag and Co., 1925. first US edition, 8vo., original dark blue cloth, spine and upper cover lettered gilt, inscribed by author's widow Jessie for R. B. Cunninghame Graham, excellent copy. Maggs Bros. Ltd.   1460 - 192   2013   £450

Conrad, Joseph 1857-1924 *The Rescue.* London: J. M. Dent & Sons Ltd., 1920. First edition, 8vo., original green cloth inscribed by author for Robert Cunninghame Graham, excellent copy.   Maggs Bros. Ltd. 1460 - 190 2013 £6500

Association – Curran, C. P.

Goddard, H. Orpen *The Orpen Family...* for private circulation, 1930. 8vo., cloth, very good, photo of Monksgrange & specimen leaves, interesting copy with 2 ALS's to C. P. Curran.   C. P. Hyland 261 - 406   2013   £450

O'Conor, Matthew *The Irish Brigades; or Memoirs of the Most Eminent Irish Military Commanders Who Distinguished Themselves in the Elizabethan and Williamite Wars in their Own Country...* Dublin: 1855. First edition, 8vo., original cloth, subjected to amateurish repairs, ex-library C. P. Curran (Francis Henry bookplate).   C. P. Hyland   261 - 639   2013   £160

Association – Currer, Frances Mary Richardson

Tuke, Samuel *Description of the Retreat, an Institution near York, for Insane Persons of the Society of Friends.* York: W. Alexander, 1813. First and only edition, large paper, frontispiece view foxed, 2 plans 4to., very good, contemporary mid brown calf with gilt hatched raised bands between double gilt rules, gilt morocco label, marbled boards and edges, drab endpapers, bookplate of Frances Mary Richardson Currer and later owner's small book ticket. Ken Spelman Books Ltd.   73 - 15   2013   £1250

Association – Currie, Laurence

Byron, George Gordon Noel, 6th Baron   1788-1824
English Bards and Scotch Reviewers.   London: James Cawthorn, 1809.   Second edition, half title, final ad leaf, contemporary full tan calf by F. Bedford, gilt spine, borders and dentelles, green leather label, spine slightly rubbed, leading hinge repaired, armorial bookplate of Laurence Currie and Alex Bridge booklabel, all edges gilt, good plus.   Jarndyce Antiquarian Booksellers   CCIII - 118   2013   £220

Association – Currie, Philip

De La Ramee, Louise   1839-1908   *Two Offenders.* London: Chatto & Windus, 1893.   First edition, presentation copy in author's presentation binding, to Sir Philip and Lady Currie, cream cloth with gilt ruling and design to front cover, boards smudged and show other signs of handling, small red spot on front board that may be ink, spine browned and slightly chipped, interior has light foxing to some pages and slight loosening of few signatures, although text block tight, all edges gilt, very good, 254 pages.   The Kelmscott Bookshop   7 - 125   2013 $750

Liechtenstein, Marie Henriette Norberte, Prinzessin Von
Holland House...   London: Macmillan and Co., 1874. Large paper copy, photos, 2 volumes, 4to., 38 photos mounted on thick paper, numerous other text and full page plates, some foxing as usual, original blue morocco backed decorative cloth blocked in gold and black, top edges gilt, spines slightly sunned and cloth rubbed on corners, some slight damp marks to lower corner volume II, bookplates of Philip Currie, 1st Baron Currie (1834-1906).   Marlborough Rare Books Ltd.   218 - 93   2013   £385

Association – Curry, Julian

Beckett, Samuel   1906-1989   *Waiting for Godot.*   London: Faber and Faber, 1956.   First edition in English, 8vo., original fawn cloth, lettered in red, dust jacket, first issue with jacket price of '9s 6d' and publisher's ads for their James Joyce titles, publisher's note tipped in, ownership of actor Julian Curry with his signature, usual offsetting to endpapers, otherwise excellent copy in dust jacket, slightly creased and rubbed at extremities.   Maggs Bros. Ltd.   1442 - 14   2013   £300

Association – Curteis, Jeremiah

Pope, Alexander   1688-1744   *The Works. Volume IV. Part I.*   London: printed for T. Cooper, 1742.   3 parts in 1, 8vo., some occasional browning and foxing, inner board and first seven leaves wormed with slight loss of some letters, contemporary sprinkled calf, double gilt ruled borders, raised gilt bands, later red morocco label, leading hinge slightly cracked at foot, 18th century armorial bookplate of Jeremiah Curteis, 19th century bookplate of Wm. Fred D'arley.   Jarndyce Antiquarian Booksellers   CCIV - 232   2013   £50

Association – Cushing, Katherine Crowell

Fulton, John Farquhar   *Harvey Cushing: A Biography.* Springfield: Charles C. Thomas, 1946.   8vo., frontispiece, figures, blue cloth, gilt stamped spine, spine faded, extremities worn, especially at spine ends, signed and inscribed by Cushing's wife, Katherine Crowell Cushing to Dr. Frank Glenn, her signature seldom seen, good.   Jeff Weber Rare Books   172 - 68   2013 $450

Association – Cussans, John Edwin

North, Thomas   *A Chronicle of the Church of S. Martin In Leicester During the Reigns of Henry VIII Edward VI Mary and Elizabeth with some Account of its Minor Altars and Ancient Guilds. (with) The Accounts of the Churchwardens of S. Martin's, Leicester 1489-1844.*   London: Bell and Daldy, Leicester: Crossley and Clarke, Leicester: Samuel Clarke, 1866.   1884, 2 volumes, 8vo., very slightly browned to edges, some spotting, not affecting text or illustrations, some staining to rear pastedown to volume I, bound uniformly in brown cloth, gilt lettering to spine, blind-stamp decorations to both volumes, little bumped and worn to extremities in both volumes, but binding sound, volume I, author's inscription and ALS tipped to front pastedown, ownership signatures one of P. A. Slack, bookplate of antiquary John Edwin Cussans.   Unsworths Antiquarian Booksellers   28 - 189   2013   £80

Association – Custer, Elizabeth Bacon

Bruce, Robert   *Custer's Last Battle.*   New York: 1927.   40 pages, maps and illustrations, original printed wrappers, large magazine format, slight wear and soil to wrappers, else fine, signature of Elizabeth Bacon Custer.   Dumont Maps & Books of the West   124 - 50   2013 $125

Association – D'Aguesseau, Henri Francois

Le Mettrie, Julien Offray De   *Abrege de la Theorie Chymique.*   Paris: Lambert & Durand, 1741.   First edition, woodcut ornament on title, headpiece and initials, divisional title to traite du Vertige (but pagination continuous), little staining here and there, 12mo., contemporary speckled calf, gilt scallop shell at each corner on both covers, spine gilt in compartments, red lettering piece, little worn, joints cracked but cords holding, the copy deposited in the library of the chancelier Henri Francois d'Aguesseau by terms of the Privilege, with neat accession numbers on rear flyleaf, bibliographical notes at front, red ink stamp of P. E. Cathelineau of Paris and Vaas on page 111 (19th century), 20th century notes in French in blue ink to first part, good.   Blackwell's Rare Books   172 - 84   2013   £2200

Association – D'Arcy, M. C.

Eliot, Thomas Stearns 1888-1965 *The Cocktail Party.* London: Faber and Faber, 1950. First edition, 8vo., original green cloth, excellent copy in slightly nicked dust jacket, browned on spine, presentation copy inscribed by author for M. C. D'Arcy 6.iii.50.   Maggs Bros. Ltd.   1460 - 272   2013 £2000

Association – D'Arley, W. F.

Pope, Alexander 1688-1744 *The Works. Volume IV. Part I.* London: printed for T. Cooper, 1742. 3 parts in 1, 8vo., some occasional browning and foxing, inner board and first seven leaves wormed with slight loss of some letters, contemporary sprinkled calf, double gilt ruled borders, raised gilt bands, later red morocco label, leading hinge slightly cracked at foot, 18th century armorial bookplate of Jeremiah Curteis, 19th century bookplate of Wm. Fred D'Arley.   Jarndyce Antiquarian Booksellers   CCIV - 232   2013   £50

Association – Dallman, Gay

Hughes, Langston *Shakespeare in Harlem.* New York: Alfred A. Knopf, 1945. Second printing, 125 pages, presentation copy signed by author to Gay Dallman, NY July 12, 1947, very good in black cloth with orange cloth spine and purple title to front board and spine, slight fading to spine and bumping to bottom corners, very good dust jacket, price clipped with green spine panel and black title to spine, jacket worn along edges including chip to head of spine and short closed tear, scuffmark to front panel of interior of front flap has light dampstaining, no evidence of dampstaining to boards or exterior of jacket.   The Kelmscott Bookshop   7 - 118   2013 $950

Association – Damon, S. Foster

Moore, Marianne 1887-1972 *Observations.* New York: Dial Press, 1924. First edition, 8vo., original black three quarter cloth and boards, gold dust jacket, rare jacket lightly worn at extremities, otherwise very good, S. Foster Damon's copy with his ownership signature and his pencil annotations.   James S. Jaffe Rare Books   Fall 2013 - 105   2013 $1500

Association – Danbey, Frances

Arblay, Frances Burney D' 1752-1840 *Evelina; or a Young Lady's Entrance into the World.* London: printed by S. Wright Gracechurch Street for and sold by the Booksellers, circa, 1820. New edition, 12mo., signature of Frances Danbey 1820, full contemporary tree calf, neatly rebacked retaining original gilt decorated spines, corners repaired.   Jarndyce Antiquarian Booksellers   CCIV - 80   2013   £65

Association – Danby, William

Wharton, Henry *The History of the Troubles and Tryal of... William Laud, Lord Arch-Bishop of Canterbury.* London: printed for Ri. Chiswell, 1695. Folio, engraved portrait frontispiece, title bit dusty, few minor splits elsewhere, contemporary speckled calf, spine ruled in blind, red morocco label, boards bordered in blind, touch rubbed, joints cracking, front joint bit defective at head, some scratches to boards, ink inscription "W. Danby", armorial 18th century bookplate "William Danby".   Unsworths Antiquarian Booksellers   28 - 139   2013   £350

Association – Dandridge, Ray

Riley, James A. *Dandy, Day and the Devil.* Cocoa: TK Pub., 1987. First edition, illustrated wrappers, 153 pages, photos, trifle rubbed, still fine in wrappers, uncommon, signed by player Ray Dandridge on page 5 by his picture.   Between the Covers Rare Books, Inc.   165 - 74   2013 $250

Association – Daniel, George

Phillips, Edward *Theatrum Poetarum Anglicanorum: Containing the Names and Characters of All the English Poets.* London: Canterbury, 1800. first printing of this enlarged updated edition, 203 x 120mm., appealing recent brown quarter morocco over linen boards, raised bands, red morocco label, front flyleaf with inscription "G. D./ Canonbury" (George Daniel), titlepage with small embossed stamp of "Mark Pattison, Lincoln College, Oxon", exceptionally fine.   Phillip J. Pirages   63 - 320   2013 $750

Association – Dannay, Fred

Cohen, Octavius Roy *Jim Hanvey Detective.* New York: Dodd, Mead and Co., 1923. First edition, 12mo., original green cloth, slightly cocked and little rubbed, 283 pages, mildly browned, inscribed in pencil "For Dannay 10/1/42 sorry it is read out of shape. J.S" in Fred Dannay's hand.   Howard S. Mott Inc.   262 - 33   2013 $150

Association – Danson, John Raymond

Gronow, Rees Howell *The Reminiscences and Recollections of Captain Gronow...* London: printed by Ballantyne and Co. for C. Nimmo, 1889. One of 870 copies printed for England and America with 25 plates in two states (this copy #22), 268 x 169mm., 2 volumes, 50 plates (comprising 25 images, each in two states; one proofs before letters done on plate paper, the other on Whatman paper titled and hand colored), as called for, a large paper copy; extremely handsome red crushed morocco, ornately gilt by Zaehnsdorf (stamp-signed on front turn-ins and with special oval gilt stamp on rear pastedowns), cover with wide filigree frame with massed densely scrolling fleurons, raised bands, unevenly spaced in the continental style, forming five compartments, second and two small bottom compartments with titling, top and elongated middle compartment decorated with intricate gilt in same way as boards, broad inner gilt dentelles, marbled endpapers (with thickly gilt lining between dentelles and pastedowns), top edge gilt, other edges untrimmed, engraved bookplate of John Raymond Danson, couple of very faint scratches on back cover volume II, just hint of rubbing at top and bottom of lower joint of same volume, especially fine in gloriously decorated morocco, text virtually pristine and bindings extremely lustrous and scarce worn. Phillip J. Pirages 63 - 66 2013 $1900

Association – Danson, William

Walton, William *A Memoir Addressed to Proprietors of Mountain and Other Waste Lands and Agriculturists of the United Kingdom on the Naturalization of the Alpaca.* printed by C. Reynell, London for the Natural History Society of Liverpool, 1841. First edition, wood engraved frontispiece, little foxing, mostly on endpapers which are also dust soiled, minor dampstaining at lower inner corners, 8vo., original ripple grain cloth, single gilt fillet around sides, 'Alpaca' stamped gilt in centre of upper cover, unevenly faded and worn at extremities, inscription beneath author's name on gilt, giving author's address and stating that it has been sent at request of William Danson of Liverpool, sound. Blackwell's Rare Books Sciences - 129 2013 £400

Association – Dao, Bei

Octavio Paz: A Celebration. New York: Academy of American Poets and the Mexican Cultural Institute, 1994. First edition, 8vo., original wrappers, although not called for, this copy signed by Paz, Mark Strand, John Ashbery, Bei Dao and Charles Tomlinson. James S. Jaffe Rare Books Fall 2013 - 6 2013 $750

Association – David, Ruth

Beckett, Samuel 1906-1989 *First Love.* London: Calder and Boyars, 1973. First edition, 8vo., original pink cloth, dust jacket with fading to spine, fine, inscribed by author for John Beckett and Ruth David. Maggs Bros. Ltd. 1460 - 66 2013 £1200

Beckett, Samuel 1906-1989 *Ill Seen Ill Said.* New York: Grove Press, 1981. First edition, 8vo., original quarter cream cloth, near fine, inscribed by author for John Beckett and Ruth David. Maggs Bros. Ltd. 1460 - 67 2013 £1000

Beckett, Samuel 1906-1989 *Worstward Ho.* London: Calder and Boyars, 1983. First edition, 8vo., original green cloth, fine in dust jacket with fading to spine, inscribed by author for John Beckett and Ruth David. Maggs Bros. Ltd. 1460 - 67 2013 £1000

Association – Davidson, Andrew

Lumb, Norman *Gonococcal Infection in the Male for Students and Practitioners.* London: John Bale Sons & Danielson Ltd., 1920. 8vo., 13 tissue guarded color plates, 165 figures in text and photo plates, original red cloth, gilt stamped cover and spine titles, water damage to covers, corners bumped, ex-library bookplate and ink stamp, bookplate and inkstamps of Andrew Davidson, very good, rare. Jeff Weber Rare Books 172 - 194 2013 $75

Association – Davies, Daniel

Byron, George Gordon Noel, 6th Baron 1788-1824 *Don Juan. (Cantos III, IV & V).* London: printed for Sherwin & Co., 1821. Pirated edition, uncut in original brown wrappers, very neatly rebacked, contemporary ownership inscription of Daniel Davies, very good in later brown cloth slipcase. Jarndyce Antiquarian Booksellers CCIII - 259 2013 £120

Association – Davis, H. W. C.

Blunt, Wilfrid Scawen *A New Pilgrimage and Other Poems.* 1889. First edition, 8vo., cloth, very good, ownership inscription by Historian H. W. C. Davis, top edge gilt. C. P. Hyland 261 - 130 2013 £75

Association – Dawes, Rose Marie

D'Ambrosio, Joseph J. *Birds in Paradise.* Los Angeles: Woman's Graphic Center & Joseph D'Ambrosio, 1984. Limited to 50 numbered copies, 10 artist proofs, this copy an artist proof, 8vo., black and gold trimmed leather frame style binding with original illustrations beneath glass at front and rear, black felt lined slipcase, slipcase pivotal hinge, no longer functional (separated), else fine, signed by author, ALS from D'Ambrosio to Wally and Rose Marie Dawes laid in, rare. Jeff Weber Rare Books 171 - 91 2013 $1500

D'Ambrosio, Joseph J. *Nineteen Years and Counting: a Retrospective Bibliography 1969 to 1988.* Arizona: Joseph J. D'Ambrosio, 1989. Limited to 75 numbered copies and 10 artist proofs, 8vo., 129 pages, decorative title and preface, 60 photographic tipped in plates, gray leather backed metal hinged boards, polished copper overlay in gray cloth chemise (signed) edged in marbled paper backed boards, signed and inscribed from author to Rose Marie and Wally Dawes, titlepage signed and with holograph "A.P." (for Artist Proof), fine.   Jeff Weber Rare Books   171 - 92   2013 $500

Association – Dawes, Wally

D'Ambrosio, Joseph J. *Birds in Paradise.* Los Angeles: Woman's Graphic Center & Joseph D'Ambrosio, 1984. Limited to 50 numbered copies, 10 artist proofs, this copy an artist proof, 8vo., black and gold trimmed leather frame style binding with original illustrations beneath glass at front and rear, black felt lined slipcase, slipcase pivotal hinge, no longer functional (separated), else fine, signed by author, ALS from D'Ambrosio to Wally and Rose Marie Dawes laid in, rare.   Jeff Weber Rare Books   171 - 91   2013 $1500

D'Ambrosio, Joseph J. *Nineteen Years and Counting: a Retrospective Bibliography 1969 to 1988.* Arizona: Joseph J. D'Ambrosio, 1989. Limited to 75 numbered copies and 10 artist proofs, 8vo., 129 pages, decorative title and preface, 60 photographic tipped in plates, gray leather backed metal hinged boards, polished copper overlay in gray cloth chemise (signed) edged in marbled paper backed boards, signed and inscribed from author to Rose Marie and Wally Dawes, titlepage signed and with holograph "A.P." (for Artist Proof), fine.   Jeff Weber Rare Books   171 - 92   2013 $500

D'Ambrosio, Joseph J. *You Dress "Funny": an Experience.* No location given: Joseph D'Ambrosio, 1970. Limited to 100 copies, this is an artist's proof, 8vo., 44ff., printed using a variety of papers and textures, including tracing paper, newsprint, silver foil, gold foil, machine copy paper, black construction paper and clear acetate with serigraphic graphics, quarter brown cloth over silver cloth, screwed holed binder, brown cloth gently rubbed, author later had many copies rebound in silver cloth over boards, this this copy in earlier format, signed by author, from the collection of Wally Dawes.   Jeff Weber Rare Books   171 - 93   2013 $500

Association – Dawson, J.

Lindt, J. W. *Picturesque New Guinea with an Historical Introduction and Supplementary Chapters on the Manners and Customs of the Papuans.* London: 1887. First edition, 50 full page autotype plates, original green cloth, gilt, little rubbed, inscribed by author for Revd. J. Dawson 1919.   Maggs Bros. Ltd.   1467 - 84   2013   £1500

Association – Dawson, John

Barnard, George *The Theory and Practice of of Landscape Painting in Water Colours.* London: William S. Orr, 1855. Large 8vo., 26 plates, 43 woodcuts, index, occasional light foxing, especially verso plates, decorative blindstamped brown cloth, gilt stamped front cover and spine extremities lightly worn, rare hinge cracked, bookplate of Agnes A. Parkin, titlepage signature of John Dawson, very good.   Jeff Weber Rare Books   171 - 12   2013 $200

Association – Day, W. C.

Smollett, Tobias George   1721-1771 *The Expedition of Humphrey Clinker.* London: W. Johnston and B. Collins in Salisbury, 1671, i.e., 1771. First edition, 3 volumes, 12mo., contemporary calf (front hinge volume 1 cracked and slightly chipped at head of spine), leather titlepieces, raised bands, excellent copy, with all half titles, early ownership signature "Arch. Wilson/Dedham", old stamp of "W. C. Day" and bookplate of Chicago book collector Harold Greenhill (1893-1968) in each volume, morocco backed cloth folding case.   Howard S. Mott Inc.   262 - 139   2013 $1350

Association – De Bathe, W. P.

Byron, George Gordon Noel, 6th Baron   1788-1824 *The Island, or Christian and His Comrades.* London: printed for John Hunt, 1823. Second edition, occasional unobtrusive pencil annotations in contemporary hand, contemporary half calf carefully rebacked, corners slightly rubbed, ownership inscription W. P. de Bathe 1824, nice, scarce.   Jarndyce Antiquarian Booksellers   CCIII - 313   2013   £150

Association – De Champ-Repus, Marigues

Estienne, Henri   1528-1598 *Traicte de la Conformite du Langage Francois avec le Grec, Divise en Trio Liures dont les Deux Premiers Traictent des Manieres de Parler Conformes le Troisieme...* Paris: Robert Estienne, 1569. First Paris edition, small 8vo., all edges gilt, Zaehnsdorf style full brown morocco, blind ruled covers and spine, gilt stamped ornaments, raised bands, gilt stamped title, gilt stamped turn-ins, 19th century leather armorial bookplate of Marigues de Champ-Repus, fine.   Jeff Weber Rare Books   171 - 118   2013 $2500

Association – De Kruif, Paul

Howard, Sidney *Yellow Jack, a History by...* New York: Harcourt Brace, 1933. First edition, 8vo., 152 pages, full brown morocco by Brentanos, spine gilt in compartments, initials "G. McC" on first board, little scuffing, near fine, this copy was presented by author to director Guthrie McClintic and bears affectionate presentation for Howard and DeKruif.   Second Life Books Inc.   183 - 174   2013 $375

Association – De La Mare, Walter

Wentworth, Lady *Drift of the Storm.* Oxford: George Donald, 1951. First edition, 8vo., original light blue cloth, the spine little faded with odd small nick to edge of dust jacket and jacket spine slightly browned, inscribed by Lord Dunsany to Walter de la Mare, loosely inserted ALS from Dunsany to a Mrs. Mathews with signed photo. Maggs Bros. Ltd. 1460 - 260 2013 £350

Association – De Limvilan, Therese

Riccoboni, Marie Jeanne *Letters from Juliet Lady Catesby to her friend Lady Henreitta Campley.* London: J. Dodsley, 1780. Sixth edition, half title, good copy, full contemporary calf, double gilt ruled borders, raised and gilt banded spine with red morocco label, clean tear to one leaf without loss, contemporary ownership name of Maria Therese De Limvilan (?) on half title, later signature on inner front board recording the purchase of this volume in Dijon in 1926. Ken Spelman Books Ltd. 75 - 37 2013 £95

Association – De Quincey, Thomas

Giles, Henry *Illustrations of Genius in Some Relation to Culture and Society.* Boston: Ticknor and Fields, 1854. First edition, 8vo., original brown embossed cloth, lettered in gilt, excellent copy inscribed by publisher for Thomas De Quincey. Maggs Bros. Ltd. 1460 - 222 2013 £325

Association – De Selincourt, Hugh

Ellis, Henry Havelock 1859-1939 *My Confessional.* London: John Lane, The Bodley Head, 1934. First edition, 8vo., original green cloth, spine little faded, otherwise excellent copy, inscribed by author for Hugh de Selincourt. Maggs Bros. Ltd. 1460 - 276 2013 £250

Association – Deakin, J. J.

Hennell, Mary *A Outline of the Various Social systems and Communities which Have Been Founded on the principle of Co-operation.* London: Longman, 1844. First edition, author's names added to title in pencil odd pencil annotation, signature of G. J. Holyoake on leading blank, additional later signature of J. J. Deakin, unsympathetic green marbled endpapers, 20th century half green crushed morocco, label on following endpaper of Midlands Workers' Library, very good. Jarndyce Antiquarian Booksellers CCV - 135 2013 £450

Association – Deal, Dennis

Adams, Ansel *My Camera in Yosemite Valley.* Boston: Virginia Adams, Yosemite National Park and Houghton Mifflin, 1949. 70 pages, inscribed by Adams for Dennis Deal, Carmel 4-18-84, 24 full page photos, soft covers bound with white spiral comb which is broken in several places, front cover present but detached, edges of both covers worn, minor staining to rear cover, light rubbing to covers, interior clean and bright on glossy paper. The Kelmscott Bookshop 7 - 91 2013 $450

Association – Deane, John

The Official History of the California Midwinter International Exposition. San Francisco: H. S. Crocker Co., 1894. First edition, hundreds of photographic illustrations map, original three quarter red leather, black pebble cloth sides, title in gilt on spine, corners show light wear one leaf with 2 inch stain at lower edge from tape, owner's name stamped on one page (John J. Deane), very good. Argonaut Book Shop Summer 2013 - 233 2013 $1500

Association – Debney, John

Lardner, Dionysius *Hand-Book of Natural Philosophy: Hydrostatics, Pneumatics and Heat.* London: Walton and Maberly, 1855. First edition, 181 x 114 mm., appealing contemporary published calf presentation binding, covers with double gilt rule border with floral cornerpieces and inner frame of blind dotted rule, upper cover with gilt insignia of school of the City of London, raised bands, spine densely gilt in compartments with large and intricate central fleuron and curling cornerpieces maroon morocco label, marbled edges and endpapers, frontispiece and 292 illustrations; ink inscription "2nd Prize for proficiency in Writing awarded to John Debney, Thos. Hall BA Master of the First Class July 1858", joints and extremities slightly rubbed, hinge open at titlepage (but no structural fragility), other trivial imperfections internally, but excellent copy, text clean, fresh and smooth, decorative binding sturdy and not without charm. Phillip J. Pirages 63 - 307 2013 $125

Association – Deffoux, Leon

Colette, Sidonie Gabrielle 1873-1954 *Cheri. Roman.* Paris: Artheme Fayard, 1920. First edition, 8vo., original yellow wrappers, acetate dust jacket, near fine, slight wear to foot of spine, one short closed tear at top edge of upper cover, inscribed by author for Leon Deffoux. Maggs Bros. Ltd. 1460 - 176 2013 £500

Association – Degen, Jessie

Lawrence, Robert Means *The Descendants of Major Samuel Lawrence of Groton, Massachusetts with Some Mention of allied Families.* Cambridge: printed at the Riverside Press, 1904. First edition, 241 x 15 mm., extremely attractive contemporary crimson half morocco, marbled sides and endpaper, raised bands, spine gilt in double ruled compartments with tulip cornerpieces, top edge gilt, photogravure frontispiece, inscribed by author for Miss Jessie Degen Boston, March 30th 1915, back cover with small areas of soiling, corners just slightly rubbed, still fine, binding lustrous, internally pristine. Phillip J. Pirages 63 - 309 2013 $250

Association – Delbanco, Andrea

Kincaid, Jamaica *A Small Place.* New York: Farrar Straus Giroux, 1988. First edition, fine in fine dust jacket, inscribed by author for Elena, Nick, Cesca and Andrea Delbanco. Between the Covers Rare Books, Inc. 165 - 195 2013 $200

Association – Delbanco, Cesca

Kincaid, Jamaica *Annie-John.* New York: Farrar, Straus Giroux, 1985. First edition, fine in spine faded, near fine dust jacket, inscribed by author to daughter of Nicholas Delbanco, Cesca. Between the Covers Rare Books, Inc. 165 - 194 2013 $250

Kincaid, Jamaica *A Small Place.* New York: Farrar Straus Giroux, 1988. First edition, fine in fine dust jacket, inscribed by author for Elena, Nick, Cesca and Andrea Delbanco. Between the Covers Rare Books, Inc. 165 - 195 2013 $200

Association – Delbanco, Elena

Kincaid, Jamaica *The Autobiography of My Mother.* New York: Farrar Straus Giroux, 1996. First edition, fine in fine dust jacket, inscribed by author for Nicholas and Elena Delbanco. Between the Covers Rare Books, Inc. 165 - 196 2013 $200

Kincaid, Jamaica *A Small Place.* New York: Farrar Straus Giroux, 1988. First edition, fine in fine dust jacket, inscribed by author for Elena, Nick, Cesca and Andrea Delbanco. Between the Covers Rare Books, Inc. 165 - 195 2013 $200

Johnson, Charles *The Sorcerer's Apprentice: Tales and Conjurations.* New York: Atheneum, 1986. First edition, fine in spine sunned dust jacket which is otherwise near fine, nicely inscribed by author for Nick and Elena Delbanco. Between the Covers Rare Books, Inc. 165 - 183 2013 $200

Association – Delbanco, Nicholas

Dove, Rita *Through the Ivory Gate.* New York: Vintage Books, 1993. First Vintage Books, wrappers, warmly inscribed by Dove to fellow author, Nicholas Delbanco. Between the Covers Rare Books, Inc. 165 - 133 2013 $75

Everett, Percival *Aulus.* Sag Harbor: The Permanent Press, 1990. First edition, fine in fine dust jacket but for crease on front flap, nicely inscribed by author for Nicholas Delbanco. Between the Covers Rare Books, Inc. 165 - 143 2013 $75

Gaines, Ernest J. *A Lesson Before Dying.* New York: Alfred A. Knopf, 1993. First edition, fine in very lightly worn, but still fine dust jacket, ownership signature of author Nicholas Delbanco. Between the Covers Rare Books, Inc. 165 - 154 2013 $85

Johnson, Charles *Being and Race: Black Writing Since 1970.* Bloomington: Indiana University Press, 1988. First edition, fine in very slightly spine sunned dust jacket, warmly inscribed by author to Nicholas Delbanco. Between the Covers Rare Books, Inc. 165 - 184 2013 $250

Johnson, Charles *The Sorcerer's Apprentice: Tales and Conjurations.* New York: Atheneum, 1986. First edition, fine in spine sunned dust jacket which is otherwise near fine, nicely inscribed by author for Nick and Elena Delbanco. Between the Covers Rare Books, Inc. 165 - 183 2013 $200

Kincaid, Jamaica *Among Flowers: a Walk in the Himalaya.* Washington: National Geographic, 2005. First edition, fine in fine dust jacket, inscribed by author for Nicholas Delbanco and his family. Between the Covers Rare Books, Inc. 165 - 197 2013 $200

Kincaid, Jamaica *The Autobiography of My Mother.* New York: Farrar Straus Giroux, 1996. First edition, fine in fine dust jacket, inscribed by author for Nicholas and Elena Delbanco. Between the Covers Rare Books, Inc. 165 - 196 2013 $200

Kincaid, Jamaica *A Small Place.* New York: Farrar Straus Giroux, 1988. First edition, fine in fine dust jacket, inscribed by author for Elena, Nick, Cesca and Andrea Delbanco. Between the Covers Rare Books, Inc. 165 - 195 2013 $200

McWilliams, Jay *Passing the Three Gates: Interviews with Charles Johnson.* Seattle: University of Washington, 2004. First edition, fine in fine dust jacket, warmly inscribed by author to Nicholas Delbanco. Between the Covers Rare Books, Inc. 165 - 310   2013 $200

Phillips, Caryl A. *Cambridge.* New York: Alfred A. Knopf, 1992. First American edition, fine in fine dust jacket, inscribed by author for Nicholas Delbanco. Between the Covers Rare Books, Inc. 165 - 235   2013 $125

Young, Al *Dancing.* New York: Corinth Books, 1969. First edition, one of 3000 copies, bit soiled, else near fine, inscribed by author for poet Nicholas Dellbanco. Between the Covers Rare Books, Inc. 165 - 296   2013 $65

Young, Al *Geography of the Near Past.* New York: Holt, Rinehart & Winston, 1976. First edition, fine in spine sunned, otherwise near fine dust jacket, warmly inscribed by author to fellow author Nicholas Delbanco. Between the Covers Rare Books, Inc. 165 - 298a   2013 $85

Young, Al *Sitting Pretty.* New York: Holt, Rinehart & Winston, 1976. First edition, fine in slightly sunned, near fine dust jacket, warmly inscribed by author to fellow author Nicholas Delbanco. Between the Covers Rare Books, Inc. 165 - 299   2013 $100

Association – Deloria, Vine

Burke, James Lee *Sunset Limited.* New York: Doubleday, 1998. First edition, inscribed by author for author Vine Deloria, Jr., minor bowning to boards, else fine in fine dust jacket. Ken Lopez Bookseller 159 - 28   2013 $250

Association – Denison, W. J.

Scott, Walter 1771-1832 *Minstrelsy of the Scottish Border.* Edinburgh: printed by J. Ballantyne and Co., 1810. Fourth edition, second (Large Paper) impression, 240 x 145mm., pleasing contemporary black straight grain morocco, covers with gilt floral frame enclosing central panel with blindstamped thistle cornerpieces, raised bands, spines heavily gilt in compartments with much swirling foliate, gilt turn-ins, marbled endpapers, all edges gilt, volume I with attractive fore-edge painting of the Mercat Cross in Melrose, Roxburghshire; pastedown volumes II and III with engraved bookplate of W. J. Denison, volume I with evidence of bookplate removal, copy of engraving of Boston Church, Lancashire laid in at rear volume II, joints and extremities somewhat rubbed, boards bit marked and abraded, minor foxing here and there in text, 9 gatherings with faint overall browning due to poor quality paper, still excellent set, leaves clean, once quite dazzling bindings still sound and pleasing, fore edge painting well preserved. Phillip J. Pirages 63 - 191   2013 $1250

Association – Dent, Edward Joseph

Hardy, Thomas 1840-1928 *The Dynasts: a Drama of the Napoleonic Wars in Three Parts, Nineteen Acts and One Hundred and Thirty Scenes.* London: Macmillan, 1903-1908. First edition, first issue volume one, second issue of volume two with titlepage a cancel, 3 volumes, 8vo., original olive-green cloth, gilt decoration and lettering, bookplate on front pastedown in volume one of Edward Joseph Dent, cloth little worn, hinges in volume one carefully repaired, very good in original printed dust jackets which have had skillful paper restoration to corners and spines, enclosed in chemise and morocco slipcase, from the Gary Lepper Collection of Thomas Hardy. The Brick Row Book Shop Bulletin Nine - 46   2013 $4500

Association – Dent, Elizabeth

Binns, Joseph *Exercises, Instructive and Entertaining in false English...* Leeds: printed by Edward Baines, for T. Binns and sold by J. Johnson, D. Ogilvy and Crosby and Co. and Vernot and Hood, London, 1803. 12mo., pages viii, 111, original sheep, little worn, contemporary ownership inscription of Elizabeth Dent dated 1805, good. Blackwell's Rare Books 172 - 29   2013   £350

Association – Dent, John

Lefevre, Raoul *Le Recueil des Histoires de Troyes.* Bruges: William Caxton, 1473. First edition in French, small folio, Lettre batarde, lacking 32 printed leaves and two blanks, early 19th century brown straight grain morocco by Charles Lewis, gilt and blind ruled in geometric patterns, gilt inner dentelles, gilt edges, fine, unrestored, the missing leaves are internal and first and last printed leaves are present from the collection of the Duke of Roxburghe (sale 1812) of the third Earl Spencer (sale 1823), John Dent, with his notes (sale 1827), P. A. Hanrott (sale 1834) the Earl of Ashburnham (sale 1897); Richard Bennett with his bookplate and John Pierpont Morgan with his bookplate and shelfmark. Heritage Book Shop 50th Anniversary Catalogue - 62   2013 $950,000

Association – Desalus, B. A.

Brooke, Frances *Histoire de Julie Maneville; ou Lettres...* Paris: Chez Duchesne, 1764. 2 volumes, half titles, 12mo., slight paper flaw to leading blank edge of two leaves volume I, uncut and unpressed in original marbled paper wrappers, handwritten title and shelf labels on each spine, chipped at head and tail, contemporary signature B. A. Desalus and later stamps on titlepages. Jarndyce Antiquarian Booksellers CCIV - 75   2013   £250

Association – Devereux, Walter De Laci

Sterne, Laurence 1713-1768 *A Sentimental Journey through France and Italy.* London: printed for W. Strahan, 1780. 12mo., some offset browning from pastedowns to endpapers and prelim and final blanks, full contemporary calf, gilt panelled spine, red morocco label, little rubbed, hinges cracked but firm, 19th century bookplate of Walter de Laci Devereux. Jarndyce Antiquarian Booksellers CCIV - 281 2013 £85

Association – Devonshire, Duke of

Petty, John *The History of the Primitive Methodist Connexion from Its Origin to the Conference of 1860...* John Dickenson, 1880. Revised edition, full black calf gilt extra over heavy bevelled boards, neatly recased, spine little scraped and dulled, all edges gilt, frontispiece, flyleaves foxed, gold printed presentation slip to the Duke of Devonshire. R. F. G. Hollett & Son Wesleyan Methodism - 23 2013 £95

Association – Dewhurst, Kenneth

Clarke, Edwin *An Illustrated History of Brain Function.* UC Press, 1972. 154 pages, numerous illustrations, 4to. in dust jacket with some light wear, signed by Kenneth Dewhurst. James Tait Goodrich 75 - 48 2013 $225

Association – Dickinson, Elizabeth

Pike, Mary Hayden Green *Ida May: A Story of Things Actual and Possible by Mary Mangon.* Boston: Phillips, Sampson, 1857. 52nd thousand, 8vo., publisher's cloth stamped in blind and gilt, very good, tight copy, contemporary ownership of Miss Elizabeth Dickinson. Second Life Books Inc. 183 - 121 2013 $65

Association – Digby, John

Burke, Edmund 1729-1797 *A Philosophical Enquiry into the Origin of Our Ideas of the Sublime and Beautiful.* London: printed for R. and J. Dodsley, 1757. First edition, limited to 500 copies, octavo, bound without half title, contemporary calf, early ink inscription of John Digby Jr. and armorial bookplate of John Hamilton Siree, very good. Heritage Book Shop 50th Anniversary Catalogue - 17 2013 $3500;

Association – Digby, Kenelm

Baldelli, Francesco *Di Polidoro Virgilio Da Vrbino de Gli Invetori Delle Cose, Libri Otto.* In Florenza: per Filippo Givnti, 1692. 4to., rebound by Bernard Middleton in contemporary style full panel English calf, endpapers renewed, first 8 leaves washed, title browned, text foxed in parts, overall very good, clean, crisp copy, Sir Kenelm Digby's copy with his gold signature and signature of John Shipton. James Tait Goodrich 75 - 17 2013 $1495

Association – Dill, Charles

Ireland, William Henry 1777-1835 *Memoirs of Jeanne D'Arc Surnamed La Pucelle D'Orleans: with the History of Her Times.* London: Robert Triphook, 1824. 2 volumes bound in 4, 240 x 150mm., pleasing 19th century dark blue three quarter morocco, flat spines decorated in gilt and inlaid with four tan fleurs-de-lys, marbled sides and endpapers, top edge gilt, with 27 plates, and extra illustrated with 22 plates, four of them in color, large paper copy, signature of Charles G. Dill dated 31 May 1909;, joints and extremities with hint of rubbing (but well masked with dye), small chip out of one spine top, backstrips lightly sunned, pretty bindings solid and with no serious condition issues, flyleaves and final leaf in each volume somewhat browned (one opening with small portion of the pages similarly browned from laid-in acidic object), variable offsetting from plates (perhaps a dozen rather noticeably offset), intermittent spotted foxing (isolated leaves more heavily foxed), not without problems internally, text still fresh, without many signs of use and printed within vast margins. Phillip J. Pirages 63 - 267 2013 $850

Association – Dillon, Diane

Aardema, Verna *Why Mosquitoes Buzz in People's Ears.* New York: Dial Press, 1975. Stated first printing, square 4to., pictorial cloth with touch of fading on edge, else fine in near fine dust jacket (no award medal, not price clipped), illustrations by Leo and Diane Dillon, this copy signed by the Dillons. Aleph-Bet Books, Inc. 105 - 83 2013 $875

Association – Dillon, C. W.

Equiano, Olaudah *The Interesting Narrative of the Life of Olaudah Equiano or Gustavus Vassa, the African.* Dublin: printed for and sold by the author, 1791. Fourth edition, frontispiece, 8vo., some foxing and browning to a number of gatherings, old marginal waterstain to frontispiece, inksplash to tissue guard, full contemporary calf, gilt banded spine, red morocco label, rather rubbed, spine little chipped at tail, wear to lower following hinge, with slightly later name of C. W. Dillon on inner board, possibly a relation of Irish subscriber Richard Dillon. Jarndyce Antiquarian Booksellers CCIV - 123 2013 £480

Association – Dillon, Leo

Aardema, Verna *Why Mosquitoes Buzz in People's Ears.* New York: Dial Press, 1975. Stated first printing, square 4to., pictorial cloth with touch of fading on edge, else fine in near fine dust jacket (no award medal, not price clipped), illustrations by Leo and Diane Dillon, this copy signed by the Dillons. Aleph-Bet Books, Inc. 105 - 83 2013 $875

Association – Dillon, Richard

Equiano, Olaudah *The Interesting Narrative of the Life of Olaudah Equiano or Gustavus Vassa, the African.* Dublin: printed for and sold by the author, 1791. Fourth edition, frontispiece, 8vo., some foxing and browning to a number of gatherings, old marginal waterstain to frontispiece, inksplash to tissue guard, full contemporary calf, gilt banded spine, red morocco label, rather rubbed, spine little chipped at tail, wear to lower following hinge, with slightly later name of C. W. Dillon on inner board, possibly a relation of Irish subscriber Richard Dillon. Jarndyce Antiquarian Booksellers CCIV - 123 2013 £480

Association – Dineley, Mark

Rothmann, Johann *Keipomantia; or the Art of Divinity by the Lines and Signatures Engraven in the Hand of Man, by the Hand of Nature...* London: printed by J. G. for Nathaniel Brooke, at the Angell in Corne Hill, 1652. First edition, frontispiece, illustrations, small internal hole affecting 2 leaves (pages 107-110) and 4 words, contemporary sheep double ruled blind tooling, corners bumped, hinges slightly rubbed, faint sign of later label removed from spine, armorial bookplate of Mark Dineley, good in original binding. Jarndyce Antiquarian Booksellers CCV - 235 2013 £2250

Association – Disraeli, Coningsby

Newton, Catherine *The Trial of the Hon. Mrs. Catherine Newton, Wife of John Newton, Esq. and Daughter of the Right Honourable and Reverend Lord Francis Seymour, at the Consistory Court of Doctors Commons...* London: printed for G. Lister No. 46 Old Bailey, 1782. 8vo., etched frontispiece, uncut, titlepage slightly dusted, slight foxing, later boards, plain cloth spine slightly worn, bookplate of Coningsby Disraeli, Hughenden, Manor House. Jarndyce Antiquarian Booksellers CCIV - 215 2013 £350

Association – Dobson, Austin

Prior, Matthew 1664-1721 *Selected Poems of Matthew Prior.* London: Kegan Paul, Trench & Co., 1889. 12mo., frontispiece, original burgundy cloth, very good, spine faded, some slight wear to head and tail of spine, inscribed by Austin Dobson to French scholar and wine writer George Saintsbury. Maggs Bros. Ltd. 1460 - 230 2013 £150

Association – Doheny, Edward Laurence

White, Henry Kirke *The Poetical Works of Henry Kirke White.* London: Charles Whittingham for William Pickering, 1853. 168 x 105mm., lviii, 252 pages, elegant contemporary dark green morocco inlaid, embossed and elaborately gilt, each cover with broad inlaid ochre morocco frame intricately gilt, large central mandorla of heavily embossed and gilt morocco of same color (both frame and centerpiece highlighted with red painted rules, raised bands, spine gilt in compartments framed by plain and decorative gilt rules, floral centerpiece and lancet cornerpieces richly gilt turn-ins, cream colored watered silk endleaves, all edges gilt, pleasing fore-edge painting of Nottingham Castle; engraved portrait and printer's anchor device on titlepage, pencilled inscription to Bessie Carey from Walter Shipper dated 13 October 1868, pastedown with morocco bookplate of Estelle Doheny, bookplate of Edward Laurence Doheny, bookplate of Carrie Estelle Doheny, bookplate of Dorothy Jayne Pedrini Shea; hint of wear to joints and corners, red paint bit rubbed with minor loss, minor foxing to portrait and titlepage, other trivial imperfections, but excellent copy, handsome binding solid and lustrous, text clean and fresh, fore-edge painting very well preserved. Phillip J. Pirages 63 - 193 2013 $1100

Association – Doheny, Estelle

Burgess, Gelett 1866-1951 *The Lark. Book the First Nos. 1 to 12. May 1895 to April 1896. Book the Second Nos. 13 to 24 May 1896 to April 1897.* San Francisco: William Doxey, 1896-1897. First edition, 2nd issue with Doxey imprint, 2 volumes, original colored pictorial cloth, uncut, excellent copy, ex-libris of Estelle Doheny in each volume. Howard S. Mott Inc. 262 - 26 2013 $400

Greenaway, Kate 1846-1901 *Marigold Garden.* London: George Routledge and Sons, n.d., 1885. First edition, first issue, quarto, over 50 colored illustrations, many full page, original green glazed pictorial boards, brown cloth backstrip, corners very slightly rubbed, otherwise fine, Estelle Doheny copy, original woodblock for on page 54, both items housed together in custom quarter tan calf over marbled boards clamshell case. David Brass Rare Books, Inc. Holiday 2012 Chapter One - DB 02024 2013 $3250

Hardy, Thomas 1840-1928 *Tess of the D'Urbervilles: a Pure Woman Faithfully Presented.* London: Osgood McIlvaine, 1891. First edition, 3 volumes, 8vo., sand colored cloth, gilt decorations and lettering after designs by Charles Ricketts, from the British Club Library at Malaga, Spain with their bookplate, from the Gary Lepper Collection of Thomas Hardy, LA Bookseller Maxwell Hunley sold to Estelle Doheny Dec. 3 1932, some foxing, few edges slightly bumped, three hinges skillfully repaired, fine, unusually bright copy, enclosed in chemise and quarter morocco slipcase. The Brick Row Book Shop Bulletin Nine - 25 2013 $17,500

Homerus *Opero (in Greek).* Florence: printer of Virgil C6061, probably Bartolommeo di Libri and Demetrius Damilas...9th December, 1488. but not before Jan. 1488/89 date of dedication. Editio princeps, 2 median folio volumes, unrubricated, early 19th century russia gilt, marbled endpapers and edges, volume II is about 15mm. shorter in its binding, bindings uniform height, inner margin of first leaf strengthened, slight worming at beginning of volume II, some foxing, from the collection of Dr. Charles Burney 1757-1817 whose collection was sold to British Museum (red library stamps), sold as duplicate in 1931 to Alice Millard; to Estelle Doheny. Heritage Book Shop 50th Anniversary Catalogue - 51 2013 $250,000

Morris, William 1834-1896 *Love is Enough, or the Freeing of Phramond: a Morality.* Hammersmith: sold by the Trustees of the Late William Morris at the Kelmscott Press, 1897. One of 300 paper copies, out of a total edition of 308, large quarto, 2 full page illustrations designed by Sir Edward Burne-Jones, decorative woodcut borders and initials, printed in black, red and blue in Troy and Chaucer types, original full limp vellum with green silk ties, spine lettered in gilt, bookplate of Estelle Doheny, overall excellent copy. Heritage Book Shop Holiday Catalogue 2012 - 89 2013 $6000

White, Henry Kirke *The Poetical Works of Henry Kirke White.* London: Charles Whittingham for William Pickering, 1853. 168 x 105mm., lviii, 252 pages, elegant contemporary dark green morocco inlaid, embossed and elaborately gilt, each cover with broad inlaid ochre morocco frame intricately gilt, large central mandorla of heavily embossed and gilt morocco of same color (both frame and centerpiece highlighted with red painted rules, raised bands, spine gilt in compartments framed by plain and decorative gilt rules, floral centerpiece and lancet cornerpieces richly gilt turn-ins, cream colored watered silk endleaves, all edges gilt, pleasing fore-edge painting of Nottingham Castle; engraved portrait and printer's anchor device on titlepage, pencilled inscription to Bessie Carey from Walter Shipper dated 13 October 1868, pastedown with morocco bookplate of Estelle Doheny, bookplate of Edward Laurence Doheny, bookplate of Carrie Estelle Doheny, bookplate of Dorothy Jayne Pedrini Shea; hint of wear to joints and corners, red paint bit rubbed with minor loss, minor foxing to portrait and titlepage, other trivial imperfections, but excellent copy, handsome binding solid and lustrous, text clean and fresh, fore-edge painting very well preserved. Phillip J. Pirages 63 - 193 2013 $1100

Association – Donaghy, Lyle

Gregory, Isabella Augusta Perse 1859-1932 *The Kiltartan History Book.* London: T. Fisher Unwin, 1926. First UK edition, small 8vo., original red cloth, lettered gilt, near fine, inscribed by author for Lyle Donaghy. Maggs Bros. Ltd. 1460 - 382 2013 £500

Association – Donald, Alex

Bennet, William *Songs of Solitude.* Glasgow: W. R. M'Phun, 1831. First edition, contemporary half black calf, spine with raised gilt bands and blind devices, black leather label little rubbed, ownership inscription of Alex Donald. Jarndyce Antiquarian Booksellers CCIII - 643 2013 £75

Association – Donin, Jerry

Anagnostakis, Andreas *Essai sur l'Exploration de la Retine et des Milieux de l'Oeil sur le Vivant...* Paris: Rignoux, 1854. First edition, 8vo., 2 folding wood engraved plates, modern quarter maroon morocco, marbled boards, gilt ruled covers, brown leather spine label, gilt spine, library rubber stamp on verso of plate I, fine, bookplate of Jerry F. Donin, rare. Jeff Weber Rare Books 172 - 6 2013 $2000

Fontana, Felice *Dei Moti Dell'Iride.* Lucca: Jacopo Giusti, 1765. First edition, 8vo., signature D browned, original boards, ms. spine title, stained, spine with minor damage, top rear corner chipped, bookplate of Jerry Donin, housed in modern brown cloth drop-back box, brown leather spine label, gilt spine, very good. Jeff Weber Rare Books 172 - 94 2013 $575

Gorter, Johannes De *Cirugia Expurgada.* Madrid: Pedro Marin, 1780. First Spanish edition, 8vo., errata, headpieces, decorative initials, tailpieces, indexes, materia medica, 3 engraved folding plates, top and fore edges of prelims and titlepage waterstained, first 100 pages of text waterstained (gradually lessens), occasional light foxing, modern full Spanish tree calf, raised bands, maroon leather spine label, gilt spine, all edges red, new endleaves, ms. notation on title, ownership mark, very good, bookplate of Jerry F. Donin. Jeff Weber Rare Books 172 - 108 2013 $900

Graefe, Friedrich Wilhelm Ernst Albrect Von *Symptomenlehre der Augenmuskellabmungen.* Berlin: Hermann Peters, 1867. First edition, 8vo., modern quarter dark red morocco, marbled boards, black leather spine label, gilt spine, new endleaves, bookplate of Jerry Donin, fine. Jeff Weber Rare Books 172 - 112 2013 $800

Guerin, Pierre *Traite sur les Maladies des Yeux, dans Lequel l'Auteur, Apris Avoir Expose les Differentes methodes de Faire l'Operation de la Catarcte, Propose un Instrument Nouveau....* Lyon: Chez V. Requilliat, 1769. First edition, 12mo., headpieces, decorative initials, tailpieces, 1 folding engraved plates, errata, binder's instructions on final page, titlepage torn at gutter, plate foxed and torn at folds (tears closed with japanese tissue), contemporary French tan mottled calf, raised bands, gilt spine, marbled edges, marbled endleaves, rubbed, ms. in notations on half title, bookplate of Jerry F. Donin, very good. Jeff Weber Rare Books 172 - 117 2013 $350

Guillemeau, Jacques *Hondert en Dertien Gebreken en Genesinge der Oogen... En nu Vermeerdert door Mr. Johannes Verbrigge...* Amsterdam: Jan Claesz ten Hoorn, 1678. 12mo., frontispiece (trimmed close at top of fort edge), titlepage vignette, decorative initials, contemporary full calf, raised bands, gilt spine, all edges red, leather scuffed and cracked, outer hinges starting, front free endpaper loose, bookplate of Jerry Donin good.   Jeff Weber Rare Books   172 - 119   2013 $1000

Hulke, John Whitaker *A Practical Treatise on the Use of the Ophthalmoscope, Being the Essay for Which the Jacksonian Prize in the Year 1859 was Awarded by the Royal College of Surgeons of England.* London: John Churchill, 1861. First edition, large 8vo., 12 figures, 4 chromolithographic plates, original blind stamped brown cloth gilt spine, rubbed, light corner dampstain to back cover, bookplate of Jerry F. Donin, very good.   Jeff Weber Rare Books   172 - 144   2013 $250

Liebreich, Richard *Atlas der Ophthalmmoscopie Darstellung des Augengrundes im Gesunden und Krankhaften Zustande.* Berlin: August Hirschwald; Paris: Germer Bailliere, 1863. First edition, folio, 12 chromolithographic plates, foxed, paper brittle (edges chipped), original printed wrappers mounted on modern case, new endleaves, quarter dark green cloth, cloth corners, original wrappers heavily rubbed, bottom edge of front cover re-enforced with dark beige paper, bookplate of Jerry F. Donin.   Jeff Weber Rare Books   172 - 185   2013 $1500

Association – Donovan, Terence

Bradbury, Malcolm *The History of Man.* Boston: Houghton Mifflin, 1976. First US edition, 8vo., original black cloth, near fine in dust jacket lightly faded on spine, inscribed by author to photographer Terence Donovan.   Maggs Bros. Ltd.   1460 - 130   2013   £250

Association – Doolittle, James

Glines, Carroll V. *Doolitte's Tokyo Raiders.* New York: Arno Press, 1980. Reprint, 8vo., illustrations, gilt stamped blue cloth, signed and inscribed by James Doolittle to Larry Seyferth in ink, near fine.   Jeff Weber Rare Books   171 - 107   2013 $75

Thomas, Lowell *Doolittle: a Biography.* Garden City: Doubleday, 1976. 8vo., 67 illustrations, quarter gilt stamped black cloth over maroon cloth, dust jacket rear slightly soiled, signed and inscribed from Doolittle to Larry Seyferth in ink, very good.   Jeff Weber Rare Books   171 - 108   2013 $200

Association – Douglas, George

Hardy, Thomas 1840-1928 *Unos Ojos Azules. (A Pair of Blue Eyes).* Barcelona: Gustavo Gili, 1919. First edition in Spanish, 2 volumes, 8vo., original decorated brown pictorial cloth, gilt decorations and lettering, fine, presentation copy inscribed by author to George Douglas, from the Gary Lepper Collection of Thomas Hardy.   The Brick Row Book Shop   Bulletin Nine - 63   2013 $4500

Association – Douglas, John Scott

Concanen, Matthew *The Flower-Piece.* London: printed for J. Walthoe, 1731. First edition, little browned in places, 2 leaves crinkled, 12mo., contemporary speckled calf, double gilt fillet borders on sides, spine gilt in compartments, red lettering piece spine worn at head and tail, slightly darkened, upper joint cracked but cords firm, 18th century armorial bookplate of Sir Atwill Lake, with that of Sr John J. Scott Douglas (engraved by Lizars) superimposed, good.   Blackwell's Rare Books   B174 - 38   2013   £350

Association – Douthit, Harold

Irving, Washington 1783-1859 *The Alhambra.* London and New York: Macmillan and Co., 1896. One of 500 extra-illustrated copies, 264 x 194mm., xx, 436 pages, numerous illustrations in text and 12 inserted lithographs by Joseph Pennell, magnificent contemporary dark green crushed morocco, extravagantly gilt by Bagguley (signed with firm's ink 'Sutherland' patent stamp on verso of front endleaf), covers with borders of multiple plain and decorative gilt rules, lobed inner frame with fleuron cornerpieces, whole enclosing large and extremely intricate gilt lozenge, raised bands, spine lavishly gilt in double ruled compartments, gilt titling and turn-ins, beautiful vellum doublures elaborately tooled in diapered gilt, red and green Moorish pattern, green watered silk endleaves, top edge gilt, other edges rough trimmed, bookplate of Harold Douthit, boards with slight humpback posture(as often with vellum doublures), otherwise in beautiful condition inside and out, lovely binding with lustrous morocco, vellum and gilt, text virtually pristine.   Phillip J. Pirages   61 - 97   2013 $5500

Association – Downshire

Buxton, Thomas Fowell *The African Slave Trade and Its Remedy.* London: John Murray, 1840. 14 page prospectus, folding map, original brown publisher's cloth, blocked in blind, spine lettered gilt, armorial Downshire bookplate, very good.   Jarndyce Antiquarian Booksellers   CCV - 42   2013   £450

Association – Dowson, Maisie

De Morgan, William *Alice-for-Short. A Dichronism.* London: William Heinemann, 1907. First edition, 8vo., original green cloth very slightly soiled and spine faded, otherwise very good, inscribed by author to Maisie Dowson. Maggs Bros. Ltd.   1460 - 220   2013   £150

Association – Doyle, Peter

Whitman, Walt   1819-1892   *Calamus. A Series of Letters Written During the Years 1868-1880.* Boston: published by Laurens Maynard at 287 Congress Street, 1897. First (trade) edition, first issue following limited edition of 35 large paper copies signed by Dr. Bucke, of which 25 were for sale, small 8vo., frontispiece and facsimile, original yellow green cloth with blindstamped covers, presentation copy inscribed for Patrick Doughery with regards of Pete Doyle, very fine, without printed jacket as issued, half morocco folding box.   James S. Jaffe Rare Books   Fall 2013 - 151   2013 $12,500

Association – Drew, Henry

Drew, Frederic   *The Jummoo and Kashmir Territories.* London: 1875. First edition, large folding map (in front pocket), 6 further folding maps (on 5 sheets), 7 folding profiles (on 2 sheets), frontispiece and 4 Woodbury type photographic plates, further illustrations, large 8vo., original cloth, rebacked, old spine laid down, small stamp on margin of title, 1 map with tear at fold, xv, 568 pages, presentation inscription from author for his brother Henry Drew.   Maggs Bros. Ltd.   1467 - 50   2013   £900

Association – Drew, Martha

Milton, John   1608-1674   *Paradise Lost.* London: printed for Jacob Tonson, 1707. Eighth edition, engraved frontispiece dated 1670, 12 engraved plates, some browning and waterstaining, clean tears without loss to one plate and Gg3, small pencil dots in margin mark certain passages, full contemporary calf, ruled borders, small thistle device in each corner, gilt panelled spine, red morocco label, expert repairs to hinges & head and tail of spine, early ownership signature of Martha Drew, 1748 and 19th century bookplate of Mary Wood, handsome copy.   Jarndyce Antiquarian Booksellers   CCV - 203   2013   £350

Association – Drinkwater, John

Flatman, Thomas   *Poems and Songs.* London: printed for Benjamin Tooke at the Ship in St. Paul's church-yard, 1682. 8vo., frontispiece, small mark to foot of frontispiece, minor tear to foot of titlepage, slight browning, bound without prelim blank but with two final errata and ad leaves, manuscript correction from errata on page 101, bound by Riviere and son in full dark red crushed morocco gilt, ruled border, elaborate gilt decorated spine, inner gilt cornerpiece decoration, marbled endpapers, slight rubbing to board edges, corners little bruised, contemporary signature at head of titlepage, bookplates of E. M. Cox and John Drinkwater, latter adding bibliographical pencil note to leading endpaper, all edges gilt, variant with M74 and the ad, in a different setting, beginning on verso.   Jarndyce Antiquarian Booksellers   CCV - 102   2013   £620

Bennett, Arnold   1867-1931   *The Truth About an Author.* New York: George H. Doran, 1911. New edition, 8vo., original cream cloth, printed paper label on spine, inscribed by author for Duff (Alistair Tayler - sic), excellent copy, loosely inserted is ALS to Duff from John Drinkwater. Maggs Bros. Ltd.   1460 - 80   2013   £350

Association – Drinkwater, Richard

Harris, Walter   *De Morbis Acutis Infantum.* Samuel Smith, 1689. First edition, final ad leaf, imprimatur leaf present but cut down, old front endpaper mostly clipped neatly leaving an old purchase note with price, little soiling, especially to final leaf, last 2 leaves with minor tear in gutter, ownership inscription to title margin (trimmed - of John Tolnay? Chirurg. 173-) and to initial blank of Richard Drinkwater, Jr. Surgeon 1753, errata corrected in old hand, 8vo., modern calf boards panelled in blind, backstrip with five raised bands, morocco label in second compartment with remainder with central floral blind tools, new endpapers, good.   Blackwell's Rare Books   Sciences - 57   2013   £2500

Association – Dubuffet, Jean

Loreau, Max   *Cerceaux 'Sorcellent.* Paris: 1967. First edition, one of 750 numbered copies, 11 x 8.75 inches, 56 silkscreened pages with 21 original color silkscreens by Jean Dubuffet, signed and inscribed by author and artist for Mr. and Mrs. Ralph Colin, as new in stiff wrappers and slipcase.   Gemini Fine Books & Arts., Ltd.   Art Reference & Illustrated Books - 2013 $1200

Association – Duff, Admiral

Dodsley, Robert 1703-1764 *A Collection of Poems in Six Volumes.* London: for R. and J. Dodsley, 1763. 6 volume, 2 engraved plates, engraved title vignettes and headpieces, half titles present, contemporary mottled calf, spines gilt, red and black spine labels, bindings moderately rubbed at extremities, few hinges cracking but secure, very attractive set, armorial bookplates of James Perrot and Admiral Duff, latter dated 1858.   Joseph J. Felcone Inc.   English and American Literature to 1800 - 8   2013 $500

Association – Duff-Gordon

Reinhardt, Karl Heinrich Leopold *Lettres sur Dresde A Madame Contenant une Esquisse...* Berlin: H. Frolich, 1800. Small 8vo., pages xxiv, 262, 19th century half morocco, engraved armorial bookplate of Duff-Gordon, Aberdeen bookseller's ticket inside front cover. Marlborough Rare Books Ltd.   218 - 122   2013   £575

Association – Duffy, Thomas

Bolingbroke, Henry St. John, 1st Viscount 1678-1751 *Letters on the Study and Use of History.* London: printed for T. Cadell, 1779. New edition, 8vo., some occasional foxing, several marginal notes in contemporary hand, full contemporary calf, gilt banded spine, head and tail slightly chipped, armorial bookplate of Francis, Duke of Bedford, Oakley House, recent bookplate of Thomas Duffy. Jarndyce Antiquarian Booksellers   CCIV - 65   2013   £40

Association – Duggan, Edward N.

Head, Henry *Studies in Neurology.* London: Henry Frowde, Hodder & Stoughton, 1920. 2 volumes, 8vo., 182 figures, original red cloth blindstamped covers, black stamped cover title, gilt stamped spine titles, spines lightly sun faded, ink ownership marks on Edward N. J. Duggan inside front cover, unusually fine set.   Jeff Weber Rare Books   172 - 128   2013 $400

Association – Dugmore, J.

Ferguson, James 1710-1776 *Lectures on Select Subjects in Mechanics, Hydrostatics, Hydraulics, Pneumatics and Optics.* London: printed for W. Strahan, 1776. Fifth edition, 13 folding engraved plates, 8vo., bound without half title, leading edge of one plate, little browned and chipped, expertly bound in recent quarter sprinkled calf, marbled boards, vellum tips, raised and gilt banded spine, red morocco label, signature on title of J. Dugmore. Jarndyce Antiquarian Booksellers   CCIV - 129   2013   £350

Association – Dumont, Mary

O'Brien, Tim *Speaking of Courage.* Santa Barbara: Neville, 1980. First edition, presentation copy inscribed to Mary Dumont Nov. 7 1980, from author, bound in same green cloth as the 300 numbered copies, with spine and cover labels, there was also a deluxe edition of 26 lettered copies (bound in leather), this one marked "Presentation Copy", original glassine (one chip), issued without printed dust jacket, near fine.   Ed Smith Books   75 - 51   2013 $300

Association – Duniway, Ben Cushing

Kahn, Edgar M. *Andrew Smith Hallidie. A Tribute to a Pioneer California Industrialist.* San Francisco: by the author, 1953. First edition, one of 275 copies, presentation inscription signed by author for Ben C. Duniway, title printed in brown and black brown cloth, gilt, very fine, uncut. Argonaut Book Shop   Recent Acquisitions June 2013 - 168   2013 $90

Sterling, George *The House of Orchids.* San Francisco: A. M. Robertson, 1911. First edition, first issue with two errors called for by Johnson on pages 31 and 48, one of the errors corrected in hand of Sterling, presentation inscription signed by author for Cushing (Ben Cushing Duniway), 140 pages, purple pictorial cloth with gilt decoration on front cover, free endpaper darkened from publisher's glue (as usual), spine slightly faded, fine.   Argonaut Book Shop Recent Acquisitions June 2013 - 272   2013 $450

Sterling, George *Sails and Mirage and Other Poems.* San Francisco: A. M. Robertson, 1921. First edition, 119 pages, green cloth, gilt lettered spine and front cover, spine gilt slightly dulled, else fine, presentation copy inscribed by author for Cushing (Ben Cushing Duniway).   Argonaut Book Shop   Recent Acquisitions June 2013 - 263   2013 $225

Sterling, George *The Testimony of Suns and Other Poems.* San Francisco: A. M. Robertson, 1907. Third edition, 142 pages, blue cloth, decorated and lettered in silver, spine lightly faded with some spotting, else fine, presentation inscription from author for Cushing (Ben Cushing Duniway).   Argonaut Book Shop   Recent Acquisitions June 2013 - 274   2013 $200

Sterling, George *A Wine of Wizardry and Other Poems.* San Francisco: A. M. Robertson, 1909. First edition, variant (without the front cover ornament), 137 pages, burgundy cloth, gilt lettered spine and front cover, free endpapers darkened from publisher's glue (as usual), spine slightly dulled, else fine, presentation inscription from author for Cushing (Ben Cushing Duniway).   Argonaut Book Shop Recent Acquisitions June 2013 - 275   2013 $350

Treadwell, Edward F. *The Cattle King.* frontispiece, portraits, map endpapers, tan cloth lettered in blue, light rubbing to spine ends, owner's name, spine faded, upper corners slightly jammed very good, presentation for Ben C. Duniway.   Argonaut Book Shop   Recent Acquisitions June 2013 - 285   2013 $90

Association – Dunlop, Alexander

Braithwaite, J. Bevan *J. Bevan Braithwaite.* London: Hodder & Stoughton, 1909.   First edition, original blue cloth, gilt, untrimmed, 19 illustrations, scattered spotting, inscribed by D. B. Braithwaite for Alexander Dunlop.   R. F. G. Hollett & Son   Lake District & Cumbria - 166 2013 £40

Association – Dunsany, Edward John Moreton Drax Plunkett

Wentworth, Lady *Drift of the Storm.* Oxford: George Donald, 1951.   First edition, 8vo., original light blue cloth, the spine little faded with odd small nick to edge of dust jacket and jacket spine slightly browned, inscribed by Lord Dunsany to Walter de la Mare, loosely inserted ALS from Dunsay to a Mrs. Mathews with signed photo.   Maggs Bros. Ltd.   1460 - 260   2013 £350

Association – Dunsmore, John Ward

Smollett, Tobias George   1721-1771 *The Works.* New York: Jenson Society, 1911.   One of 1000 sets, 236 x 146mm., 12 volumes, this copy #317, very pleasing contemporary rose colored three quarter calf spines with slightly raised bands, unusual gilt decoration in compartments, two with gilt roses flanking a central helix and two with central rose in lozenge and with trefoil cornerpieces, marbled boards and endpapers, top edge gilt, other edges untrimmed, 6 frontispieces in color and 6 additional plates as called for all by John Ward Dunsmore, lettered tissue guards, spines sunned to a softer pink, very small portions of extremities with hint of rubbing, one rear board with small scratch to leather, trivial internal imperfections, but excellent set, text clean, fresh and bright and pleasant bindings with no significant wear.   Phillip J. Pirages 63 - 447   2013 $450

Association – Durant, Fred

Roddenberry, Gene *The Making of Star Trek.* New York: Ballantine, 1970.   Sixth printing, paperback original, owner label of Fred Durant III with small bookstore stamp, near fine with light wear, nicely inscribed by author for Durant, marvelous association.   Between the Covers Rare Books, Inc.   Sci-Fi, Fantasy & Horror - 43900   2013 $500

Sackett, Susan *Letters to Star Trek.* New York: Ballantine, 1977.   First edition, paperback original, small scrape to top of front panel, near fine in wrappers, inscribed by author to noted scientist Fred Durant, splendid association.   Between the Covers Rare Books, Inc.   Sci-Fi, Fantasy & Horror - 43908   2013 $275

Von Puttkamer, Jesco *Star Trek: The New Voyages 2.* New York: Bantam, 1978.   First edition, paperback original, near fine with just few reading creases, inscribed by author to Fred Durant, with longer typed note from author to same. Between the Covers Rare Books, Inc.   Sci-Fi, Fantasy & Horror - 43910   2013 $275

Association – Dusenburg, W. A.

Chamberlain, George Agnew *The Silver Cord.* New York: G. P. Putnam's Sons, 1927.   First edition, small, nearly invisible dampstain on edge of couple of leaves, else fine in very near fine dust jacket, nicely inscribed by author for W. A. Dusenburg, scarce.   Between the Covers Rare Books, Inc. Mystery & Detective Fiction - 295502 2013 $450

Association – Duxbury, Arthur

Behrend, Arthur *Unlucky for Some.* London: Eyre & Spottiswoode, 1955.   First edition, original cloth, gilt, dust jacket, pages 190, presentation copy from author for A(rthur) Duxbury June 1958, with APC from author loosely inserted. R. F. G. Hollett & Son   Lake District & Cumbria - 96   2013 £30

Association – Eagen, George

Bell, John   1763-1820 *The Anatomy and Physiology of the Human Body.* New York: Collins, 1817-1822.   Complete set, mixed set, volumes I and II third American edition, volume III fourth American edition, 3 volumes, small 4to., 35 engraved plates, foxed, browned, volume III heavily, occasional ink marginalia, volumes I and II, offsetting from plates and figures, occasional marginal waterstaining, original tree calf, gilt spine, brown leather spine labels, rebacked, preserving original spines, rubbed, ownership signatures of George Eagen, Cranford, Montgomery, New York, N.D. 1837 and William H. Mann, John Mann and Arthur H. Mann Jr., Baltimore, very good.   Jeff Weber Rare Books   172 - 23 2013 $750

Association – Easton Neston Library

Medicina Flagellata; or the Doctor Scarificed. printed for J. Bateman and J. Nicks, 1721. First edition, additional letterpress title with engraved vignette, 8vo., contemporary tree calf, flat spine gilt in compartments, red lettering piece, minor wear, top of upper joint snagged foot of spine chipped, contemporary signature at head of title of W. Beeson, engraved bookplate of Sir Thomas Hesketh, and Easton Neston Library shelf label, very good.   Blackwell's Rare Books   Sciences - 101   2013   £750

Association – Eden, John

Nouvelle Ecole Publique des Finances ou l'Art de Voler sans Ailes par Toutes les Regions du Monde. Paris: Chez Robert le Turc, rue d'enfer a la Hache d'Or, 1707. First edition, title printed in red and black, woodcut device, 12mo., contemporary speckled calf, rubbed, joints cracked but cords holding, armorial bookplate of Sir John Eden, Bart, good.   Blackwell's Rare Books   172 - 17   2013   £950

Association – Edgecumbe, Richard

Chatterton, Thomas 1752-1770 *Poems, Supposed to Have Been Written at Bristol, by Thomas Rowley and Others in the Fifteenth Century.* London: for T. Payne and Son, 1777. First edition, 2nd state, with leaf c4 a cancel, plate of purported Rowley manuscript facsimile, contemporary calf, rebacked in morocco, tiny hole in blank margin of G3, corners very worn with board exposed, armorial bookplate of Richard Edgcumbe.   Joseph J. Felcone Inc.   English and American Literature to 1800 - 5   2013 $750

Association – Edgren, Gretchen

The Playmate Book. Santa Monica: General Pub., 1996. First edition, this copy signed by Hugh Hefner, Gretchen Edgren and at least 7 of the playmates, fine in fine dust jacket.   Ed Smith Books   75 - 58   2013 $300

Association – Edmonstone, James

MacCulloch, John 1773-1835 *A Geological Classification of Rocks...* published by Longman, Hurst, Rees, Orme and Brown, 1821. First edition, large 8vo., uncut in original boards, rebacked in nearly matching paper, slightly damaged label preserved, corners bumped, pencil ownership inscription inside front cover of James Edmonstone FGS dated 8173, neat drawing by him and hammer opposite and pencil note inside back cover, indexing reference to Corstorphine Hill, small oval Edmondstone stamp on title, very good.   Blackwell's Rare Books   Sciences - 77   2013   £750

Association – Edwards, F. L.

Cowper, William 1731-1800 *Poems.* London: printed for J. Johnson, 1793. Fifth edition, 2 volumes, contemporary tree calf, spines ruled gilt, later red morocco labels, numbered direct, unobtrusive repairs to hinges, leading f.e.p. volume I inscribed "Richard Forster French 1739 the gift of Mrs. Nicholas", later bookplate of F. L. Edwards, nice copy.   Jarndyce Antiquarian Booksellers   CCIII - 611   2013   £150

Association – Edwards, Florence

Blackwood, Algernon *A Prisoner in Fairyland.* London: Macmillan, 1925. Reprint, 8vo., original green cloth, excellent copy, inscribed by author to Florence Edwards.   Maggs Bros. Ltd.   1460 - 107   2013   £75

Association – Edwards, J. O.

De La Mare, Walter 1873-1956 *Songs of Childhood.* London: Longmans, Green and Co., 1902. First edition, 8vo., frontispiece after Richard Doyle, original half parchment and pale blue linen over boards, top edge gilt, dust jacket, author's own copy, signed by poet and inscribed below to his nurse and companion of many years, Sister Nathalie Saxton, backstrip lightly rubbed along joints, otherwise fine in dust jacket with very small chip out of bottom spine panel and offsetting from two small old cello-tape repairs at bottom spine and bottom front flap fold, preserved in half morocco slipcase, booklabel of J. O. Edwards, beautiful and distinguished association copy, in extremely rare jacket.   James S. Jaffe Rare Books   Fall 2013 - 37   2013 $12,500

Wordsworth, William 1770-1850 *Yarrow Revisited and Other Poems.* London: Longman, Rees, Orme, Brown, Green and Longman, 1835. First edition, presentation copy, inscribed by author to Eliza M. Hamilton as a token of affectionate esteem from W. M. Wordsworth on a slip of paper pasted to verso of title and with "From the Author" written on half title by publisher's clerk, erratum slip tipped in, ads discarded, 12mo., slightly later 19th century olive pebble grain morocco by Tuckett ('binder to the Queen'), backstrip panelled and ruled in gilt and infilled with volutes and other tools, lettered in gilt in second compartment, sides with triple gilt fillet borders, inner panel with cornerpieces and central panels of curving lines, all edges gilt, marbled endpapers, booklabel of J. O. Edwards, small scrape to upper board, extremities slightly rubbed, good.   Blackwell's Rare Books   B174 - 159   2013   £3500

Association – Egerton, Helen

Dodgson, Charles Lutwidge 1832-1898 *The Game of Logic.* London: Macmillan and Co., 1887. Second edition, one of only 500 copies, 8vo., original scarlet cloth, gilt frontispiece, plans, envelope containing printed plan and full complement of nine counters, four red and five gray, slightly faded on spine and rubbed at head and tail of spine, front endpapers cracked at hinge, otherwise excellent copy, envelope slightly foxed, inscribed by author Feb. 19th 1894 for Helen M. Egerton. Maggs Bros. Ltd. 1460 - 233 2013 £950

Association – Eichner, Henry

Merritt, A. *The Ship of Ishtar.* New York: Putnams, 1926. First edition, 8vo., dark reddish brown weave cloth with tan lettering and no top staining (one of several bindings - priority unknown), pictorial bookplate of Henry Eichner, tape ghosts to front and back free endpapers (probably from jacket protector), else bright and fresh in very good pictorial dust jacket (internal tape at foot of spine), some wear at corners and edges and somewhat darkened spine, scarce, especially in dust jacket. Ed Smith Books 75 - 47 2013 $850

Association – Eldon, John Scott, 1st Earl of

Bowles, William Lisle *The Plain Bible and the Protestant Church in England, with reflections on Some Important Subjects of existing Religious Controversy.* Bath: Richard Cruttwell, 1818. First edition, large 8vo., uncut in contemporary blue boards, drab spine, paper label, corners slightly knocked, very good, as issued, presentation from author, signature and small armorial roundel of John Scott, first Earl of Eldon. Jarndyce Antiquarian Booksellers CCIII - 35 2013 £150

Association – Eliot, Thomas Stearns

Auden, Wystan Hugh 1907-1973 *New Year Letter.* London: Faber and Faber, 1941. First edition, 8vo., original cream cloth, one of 2000 copies, very good, cloth stained on back cover and tail of spine, inscribed by T. S. Eliot for Michael Tipett. Maggs Bros. Ltd. 1460 - 269 2013 £750

Rosenberg, Isaac *Poems.* London: William Heinemann, 1922. First edition, 8vo., original black cloth, lower and fore edges uncut, one long crease to front cover, otherwise excellent copy, inscribed by T. S. Eliot for Ottoline Morrell. Maggs Bros. Ltd. 1460 - 262 2013 £2500

Association – Elizabeth, Queen of Romania

Varcaresco, Helene *The Bard of the Dimbovitza: Romanian Folk-Songs Second Series Collected from the Peasants.* London: Osgood, McIlvaine, 1896. First edition, presentation copy from principal translator, Carmen Sylva (Pseud. of Elizabeth, Queen of Romania) to Benjamin Duryea Woodward, original brown cloth, gilt front cover and spine by Charles Ricketts, binding very good with some rubbing and fading, some foxing to endpapers but interior pages clean with edges untrimmed, 130 pages. The Kelmscott Bookshop 7 - 128 2013 $500

Association – Ellidge, Mary

Graves, Robert 1895-1985 *Impenetrability or the Proper Habit of English.* London: published by Leoanrd & Virginia Woolf at Hogarth Press, 1926. First edition, small 8vo., original pale blue-green boards lettered in black, inscribed by author for Mary with pencilled ownership inscription of Mary Ellidge, browned at edges as ever, otherwise excellent. Maggs Bros. Ltd. 1460 - 360 2013 £1500

Association – Elliot, Gilbert Compton

Byron, George Gordon Noel, 6th Baron 1788-1824 *(Hebrew Melodies) Fugitive Pieces and Reminiscences.* London: Whittaker, Treacher & Son, 1829. Half title, 12 page catalog, handsomely bound in later half tan calf by G. H. May of London, spine with raised bands and devices gilt, armorial bookplate of Gilbert Compton Elliot, top edge gilt, very good, handsome. Jarndyce Antiquarian Booksellers CCIII - 207 2013 £480

Byron, George Gordon Noel, 6th Baron 1788-1824 *Marino Faliero, Doge of Venice. The Prophecy of Dante, a Poem.* London: John Murray, 1821. First edition first issue, half title, final ad leaf, uncut in slightly later tan calf by G. H. May of London, spine with raised bands and gilt devices, armorial bookplate of Gilbert Compton Elliot, top edge gilt, very handsome, neatly tipped into prelims are 3 printed playbills, in excellent condition. Jarndyce Antiquarian Booksellers CCIII - 286 2013 £1800

Byron, George Gordon Noel, 6th Baron 1788-1824 *The Prisoner of Chillon.* London: John Murray, 1816. First edition, first issue, half title with watermark, final ad leaf and 4 pages ads, uncut in original drab wrappers, bound into later half tan calf, armorial bookplate of Gilbert Compton Elliot, very good. Jarndyce Antiquarian Booksellers CCIII - 226 2013 £350

Association – Ellis, Charles

Tennyson, Alfred Tennyson, 1st Baron 1809-1892 *The Holy Grail and Other Poems.* London: Strahan and Co., 1870. First edition, 2 pages ads at back, 8vo., original green cloth panelled in blind, presentation copy inscribed by author for Charles Ellis (1824-1908), booklabel of William Harrison Arnold, small newsprint clipping affixed verso of half titlepage, another to verso of first section-title, otherwise fine, full morocco slipcase.   James S. Jaffe Rare Books Fall 2013 - 142   2013 $1750

Association – Ellis, Dick

Golding, Louis *Sicilian Noon.* London: Chatto and Windus, 1925. First edition, 8vo., original black cloth, excellent copy, inscribed by author for Dick Ellis.   Maggs Bros. Ltd. 1460 - 346   2013   £120

Association – Ellis, John Henry

Crabbe, George 1754-1832 *Poems. Containing The Library, The Village, The Newspaper, The Parish Register, The Borough.* London: John James Chidley, 1846. New edition, frontispiece and engraved title, printed title, contemporary dark blue morocco, decorated in gilt, leading hinges slightly rubbed, beginning to split at tail, armorial bookplate of Rev. John Henry Ellis & Ellis family inscription, all edges gilt, attractive copy.   Jarndyce Antiquarian Booksellers CCIII - 623   2013   £40

Association – Ellison, Ralph

Barrett, Marvin *The Jazz Age.* New York: G. P. Putnam's Sons, 1959. First edition, quarto, picture edition, boards bit soiled, good or better, without dust jacket, Ralph Ellison's copy with his ownership signature.   Between the Covers Rare Books, Inc. 165 - 322   2013 $500

Bates, Joseph D. *Spinning for Salt Water Game Fish.* Boston: Little Brown and Co., 1957. First edition, fine in very good dust jacket with crease on spine and short tears, author Ralph Ellison's copy with his ownership signature. Between the Covers Rare Books, Inc. 165 - 19 2013 $350

Ferris, William *Local Color: a Sense of Place in Folk Art.* New York: McGraw Hill, 1982. First edition, paperback issue, very near fine in wrappers, inscribed by author for Ralph Ellison.   Between the Covers Rare Books, Inc. 165 - 149   2013 $200

Hodeir, Andre *Jazz its Evolution and Essence.* New York: Grove Press, 1956. First American edition, paperback original, near fine, some rubbing, author Ralph Ellison's copy with his ownership signature.   Between the Covers Rare Books, Inc. 165 - 170   2013 $250

Scharff, Robert *Standard Handbook of Salt Water Fishing.* New York: Thomas Y. Crowell, 1959. First printing, 2 owner's names, including that of Ralph Ellison, else fine in presentable about very good dust jacket with small nicks and tears.   Between the Covers Rare Books, Inc. 165 - 148 2013 $275

Association – Elton, Lord

Smith, Horace 1779-1849 *Rejected Addresses; or the New Theatrum Poetarum.* London: John Miller, 1812. First edition, half title, final ad leaf, some spotting, uncut in original drab boards, covered with marbled paper and respined, chipped and slightly defective, booklabel of Lord Elton of Headington, Oxon.   Jarndyce Antiquarian Booksellers   CCIII - 152   2013   £85

Association – Emerson, Ralph Waldo

Montaigne, Michel De 1533-1592 *The Complete Works of...* London: John Templeman, 1842. First edition, 2 volumes, large 8vo., engraved portrait, engraved titlepage in volume one, presentation by Ralph Waldo Emerson for George Phillips, July 1848, three quarter black morocco, raised bands, some rubbed and scuffed, very good set, some holograph notes on rear blank, probably by Phillips. Second Life Books Inc. 183 - 279   2013 $3500

Association – Enders, David

Crisp, Quentin *The Naked Civil Servant.* London: Jonathan Cape, 1968. First edition, 8vo., cloth, dust jacket lightly browned, fine, inscribed by author to David Enders. Maggs Bros. Ltd. 1460 - 201   2013   £250

Association – English, Mrs.

Doyle, Arthur Conan 1859-1930 *The Poems of Arthur Conan Doyle.* London: John Murray, 1922. Collected edition, 8vo., original blue cloth, very good, lettering to spine faded and some evidence of paper having been stuck onto back pastedown and removed, inscribed by author Xmas 1922 to Mrs. English.   Maggs Bros. Ltd. 1460 - 248 2013   £500

Association – Ennis, George

Muybridge, Eadweard *Descriptive Zoopraxography or the Science of Animal Locomotion.* Philadelphia: University of Pennsylvania, 1893. First edition, hinges professionally and seamlessly reinforced and tips of cloth spine ends restored, nice, very good plus, this copy inscribed by author to noted publisher of photographic stereocard "George Ennis with compliments of the author. University of Pennsylvania 9 June 1894", rare thus.   Between the Covers Rare Books, Inc.   Horses, Horsemanship, Horse Racing, Etc. - 45757   2013 $4500

Association – Enniskillen

Byron, George Gordon Noel, 6th Baron   1788-1824 *The Bride of Abydos.* London: John Murray, 1813. Fifth edition, slightly spotted, disbound, ownership inscription Enniskillen, all edges gilt.   Jarndyce Antiquarian Booksellers   CCIII - 173   2013   £25

Association – Ernshaw, Marian Bellamy

Bellamy, Edward *Looking Backward 2000-1887.* Boston: Houghton Mifflin, 1926. Riverside Library, 8vo., pages 337, very good in publisher's cloth, stain on hinge of rear endpaper, inscribed by author's wife, Emma for Walter James Henry, also inscribed by his daughter Marian Bellamy Ernshaw Oct. 24 1935, laid in is 9 x 6 inch handbill advertising talk given by Marion and Emma Bellamy at the Seattle Civic Auditorium, scarce.   Second Life Books Inc.   183 - 21   2013 $300

Association – Errington, George

Lupi, Antonio Maria *Dissertatio et Animadversiones ad Nuper Inventum Severae Martyris Epitaphium.* Palermo: ex typographia Stephani Amato, 1734. First edition, small folio, 15 leaves of plates, additional woodcut illustrations, edges speckled red, occasional light soiling, small closed tear to blank margin of one folding plate, contemporary vellum boards, gilt to spine, soiled, touch of wear to tail of spine, 3 small spots of worming to pastedowns, ownership inscription of Geo. Errington and bookplate of library of Prinknash Abbey, few early marginal pen notes.   Unsworths Antiquarian Booksellers   28 - 29   2013   £800

Association – Esher, Lord

Cobbett, William *Cobbett's Oppression!!* London: printed and published by T. Gillet & sold by Sherwood, Neely & Jones, 1809. 8vo., evidence of original stab holes, some browning, early 20th century cloth, armorial bookplate of Lord Esher and later signature of Michael Foot.   Jarndyce Antiquarian Booksellers   CCIV - 96   2013   £225

Cobbett, William *A New Year's Gift to the Democrats; or Observations on a Pamphlet, entitled "A Vindication of Mr. Randolph's Resignation".* Philadelphia: published by Thomas Bradford, 1796. Second edition, some tanning and foxing, early 20th century linen backed boards, armorial bookplate of Lord Esher & later signature of Michael Foot.   Jarndyce Antiquarian Booksellers   CCIV - 98   2013   £280

Association – Esher, Oliver Brett, Viscount

Graves, Robert   1895-1985 *Poems 1929.* Seizin Press, 1929. First edition, 76/225 copies, printed on Batchelor handmade paper and signed by author foolscap 8vo., original apple green buckram, faded backstrip gilt lettered, faint band of fading also to head of rear cover, browned free endpapers, booklabel of Simon Nowell-Smith and bookplate of Oliver Brett, First Viscount Esher, very good.   Blackwell's Rare Books   B174 - 214   2013   £300

Association – Essex, Algernon Capell, Earl of

Tothill, William *Transactions of the High Court of Chancery, Both by Practice and President.* London: R. Best and J. Place, 1671. 8vo., original mottled calf, rebacked with lighter calf and gilt stamped red leather spine label, bookplate of Algernon Capell, Earl of Essex, Viscount Maldon & Baron Capell of Hadham 1701 (partially affected by burn), good.   Jeff Weber Rare Books   171 - 116   2013 $200

Association – Evan, Harold

Paul, Doris A. *The Navajo Code Talkers.* Pittsburgh: Dorrance Pub., 1990. Seventh printing, 8vo., signed by fourteen Navajo code talkers, including Albert Smith (President 4th Mar. Div. 4th Sig. Co.), Paul Blatchford, Bill Toledo, Harold Foster, George Smith, Harold Evan and others, fine in near fine dust jacket.   By the Book, L. C.   38 - 38   2013 $900

Association – Evans, Evan H.

Llewellyn, Richard *How Green Was My Valley.* New York: Macmillan, 1941. (1940). Later printing, round-robin, signed in fountain pen on location during making of the film on July 19 1941, gift copy from Freda Knill (niece of cast member Thomas A. Hughes) to her daughter, with autographs and inscriptions of Roddy McDowall, Maureen O'Hara, Walter Pidgeon, Donald Crisp, Barry Fitzgerald, Sara Allgood, Anna Lee, T. Arthur Hughes, Richard Fraser and Evan H. Evans; fair to good only, binding intact, shaken and with fraying to edges of cloth, in very good supplied dust jacket with some rubbing and light wear at extremities.   Ed Smith Books   75 - 39   2013 $1750

Association – Evans, Herbert McLean

Fremont, John Charles 1813-1890 *Memoirs of My Life...* Chicago and New York: Belford, Clarke & Co., 1887. First edition, thick quarto, frontispiece, 80 plates, wood engravings, photogravures, etc., 1 chromolithograph and 7 maps, publisher's pictorial cloth stamped in various colors, small bookplate on inner cover, just hint of rubbing to spine ends, front and rear inner hinges expertly and beautifully reinforced, very fine, from the library of Herbert McLean Evans with his small oval bookplate, quite scarce in this condition. Argonaut Book Shop   Recent Acquisitions June 2013 - 114   2013 $1250

Nuttall, Thomas *Journal of Travels into the Arkansa (sic) territory During the Year 1819.* Philadelphia: printed and published by Thos. H. Palmer, 1821. First edition, five aquatint plates, folding map, one plate in facsimile but an original of the same image, from another copy, laid in (blank borders bit trimmed), outer hinges cracked but cords strong, paper spine fragile with some fading, some spotting or light foxing within, but fine, untrimmed, housed in sumptuous half morocco custom slipcase, bookplate of collector Herbert McLean Evans, excessively rare.   Argonaut Book Shop Summer 2013 - 257   2013 $6000

Spinoza, Benedict De *Opera Posthuma.* Amsterdam: J. Rieuwertsz, 1677. First edition, quarto, lacking portrait, as usual, woodcut vignette on title, woodcut illustrations, diagrams and initials in text, contemporary mottled calf, expertly rebacked to style, covers decoratively bordered in blind, spine tooled and lettered gilt from the library of Herbert McLean Evans, with his bookplate, some marginal browning, lightly dampstained, mostly marginal, overall very good. Heritage Book Shop   50th Anniversary Catalogue - 94   2013 $11,000

Association – Eyre, Frederick Edwin

Robertson, William 1721-1793 *History of America.* London: printed by A. Strahan for A. Strahan, T. Cadell and W. Davies, 1800. Ninth edition, 218 x 130mm., pleasing contemporary tree calf, expertly and attractively rebacked with complementary modern calf, raised bands flanked by double gilt rules, red and black morocco labels, marbled endpapers, four large engraved folding maps and one folding plate, bookplate of Fred(eric)k L. Hutchins and engraved armorial bookplate of Frederick Edwin Eyre; corners very worn, boards with several small abrasions and patches of lost patina, opening and closing leaves bit foxed, faint offsetting in text, one map rather wrinkled and two small tears along folds, still appealing copy, text fresh and clean, well restored bindings quite solid and very attractive on shelf. Phillip J. Pirages   63 - 402   2013 $400

Association – Facloner, A. R.

Bible. English - 1910 *The New Testament of Our Lord and Saviour Jesus Christ.* London: Oxford University Press, circa, 1910. 8vo., limp black morocco, 'Antarctic Expedition Terra Nova 1910' gilt to upper cover, inscribed by A. R. Falconer, Sailor's Missionary Dunedin, for Captain Robert Falcon Scott.   Maggs Bros. Ltd.   1467 - 141   2013   £6000

Association – Fair, A. E. B.

Kipling, Rudyard 1865-1936 *The Jungle Book. (with) The Second Jungle Book.* Macmillan, 1894-1895. First edition and first English edition, foolscap 8vo., occasional faint foxing, illustrations, many full page, frontispiece tissue guard present, original mid blue cloth, lettering and pictorial design on backstrip and further pictorial design on front cover, all gilt blocked, dark blue-green endpapers, rear hinge cracked, gilt edges, very good; foolscap 8vo., illustrations, some leaves lightly foxed, original mid blue cloth, lettering and pictorial design on backstrip and further pictorial design on front cover, all gilt blocked, bookplate of A. E. B. Fair, small paper repair to rear free endpaper, dark blue green endpapers, gilt edges, good, author's signature on slips pasted to reverse of half title of Jungle Book and reverse of titlepage to Second Jungle Book, with Bateman's headed notepaper with typed note "With Mr. Rudyard Kipling's Compliments" tipped to front flyleaf of Second Jungle Book.   Blackwell's Rare Books   172 - 205   2013   £3000

Association – Fairfax

Salisbury, Robert Cecil *The Copies of a Letter to the Right Honourable, the Earl of Leycester, Lieutenant General of all Her Majesties Forces in the United Provinces of the Low Countreys...* London: Christopher Barker, 1586. 4to., without final blank leaf, woodcut arms on A, verso, facing titlepage, large woodcut initials, this copy is variant A, recto starting "Albeit with earnest...", bound by Pratt in 19th century brown crushed morocco with gilt arms on both covers, all edges gilt, bookplate of Fairfax of Cameron, fine copy. Second Life Books Inc.   182 - 207   2013 $4000

Association – Fairleigh, John

Shaw, George Bernard 1856-1950 *The Adventures of the Black Girl in Her Search for God.* 1932. First edition, 208 x 135mm., original black pictorial boards and endpapers, designed and engraved by John Farleigh, in custom made gilt titled black cloth folding box (slightly soiled), illustrated titlepage and 18 woodcut engravings by John Farleigh, with proofs of the cover, endpapers and 19 engravings (one a trial version of a scene), all signed in pencil by Fairleigh and numbered "3/9" the cover with Farleigh's inscription "This set was Specially printed for William Maxwell" (proofs contained in portfolio inside folding box), front flyleaf with inscription by Shaw for Maxwell, hint of rubbing to edges, couple of faint spots of foxing, proof copy of cover slightly wrinkled at edges, otherwise fine copy, fresh, bright and unworn. Phillip J. Pirages 63 - 437 2013 $2500

Association – Fairweather, Jack

Bird, Will R. *The Two Jacks: the Amazing Adventures of Major Jack M. Veness and Major Jack L. Fairweather.* Toronto: Ryerson Press, 1954. First edition, green cloth with gilt to spine in dust jacket, half title, 22 black and white photo illustrations, 8vo., previous owner's bookplate on front endpaper, otherwise very good, dust jacket chipped and worn with small pieces missing form lower spine, signed by author and Jack Veness and Jack Fairweather. Schooner Books Ltd. 105 - 56 2013 $75

Association – Fane, Lieut. Colonel

Steuart, James *An Inquiry into the Principles of Political Economy.* London: printed of A. Millar and T. Cadell, 1767. First edition, 2 volumes, quarto, bound without prelim blank in volume I, as is often the case, 2 folding tables, contemporary mottled calf, expertly and almost invisibly rebacked to style, original contrasting morocco labels laid down, spines decoratively gilt tooled in compartments, contemporary booklabel written in manuscript of Lieut. Colonel Fane in each volume and a modern bookplate, slight marginal offsetting to first few leaves of each volume and occasional light foxing, overall very good in attractive contemporary binding. Heritage Book Shop 50th Anniversary Catalogue - 96 2013 $11,000

Association – Farjeon, Francis

Bartlett, Vernon *No Man's Land.* London: George Allen and Unwin, 1930. First edition, 8vo., original black cloth, dust jacket, inscribed by author for Francis and Joe Farjeon, excellent copy, jacket faded on spine and creased and worn at head. Maggs Bros. Ltd. 1460 - 44 2013 £50

Association – Farjeon, Joe

Bartlett, Vernon *No Man's Land.* London: George Allen and Unwin, 1930. First edition, 8vo., original black cloth, dust jacket, inscribed by author for Francis and Joe Farjeon, excellent copy, jacket faded on spine and creased and worn at head. Maggs Bros. Ltd. 1460 - 44 2013 £50

Association – Farra, Aubrey

Graves, Robert 1895-1985 *Over the Brazier.* London: Poetry Bookshop, 1916. Second edition, 8vo., original wrappers worn and slightly nicked, otherwise very good, protected within folding slipcase, author's copy with his armorial bookplate which bears the gift inscription from him to Aubrey Farra, there are substantial manuscript revisions by Graves to two of the poems. Maggs Bros. Ltd. 1460 - 358 2013 £1500

Association – Farrant, Richard

Malton, Thomas *Views of Oxford.* London: White & Co.; Oxford: R. Smith, 1810. First complete edition, 411 x 315mm., appealing 19th century circa 1860s?), dark green half morocco over lighter green textured cloth by T. Aitken (stamp signed), upper cover with gilt titling, raised bands, spine gilt in compartments with elongated fleuron centerpiece and scrolling cornerpieces, gilt titling, marbled endpapers, all edges gilt (small, very expert repairs to upper outer corners and perhaps top of joints), mezzotint frontispiece after Gilbert Stuart, engraved title, 30 fine plates, 24 of then aquatints and 6 of them etched, armorial bookplates of Sir Mayson M. Beeton and Sir Richard Farrant, ink presentation inscription "Sir Charles Locock, Bart./ with Captn. Malton's kindest regards/Nov. 1860", subscription proposal for the work printed by T. Bensley and dated "London, May 30, 1301" (i.e. "1801"), laid in at front, couple of small smudges to boards, portrait faintly foxed and browned, isolated small stains (not affecting images), still fine, plates especially clean, fresh and smooth and pleasing binding with virtually no wear. Phillip J. Pirages 63 - 327 2013 $9500

Association – Fasque

Beattie, James 1735-1803 *An Essay on the Nature and Immutability of Truth, in Opposition to Sophistry and Sceptisim.* London: printed for J. Mawman, 1807. Seventh edition, 8vo, some light spotting in places, contemporary straight grain dark blue morocco, spine divided by gilt rules, small central tools in compartments, boards bordered with greek key roll, marbled endpapers, all edges gilt, corners and pages bit rubbed, boards unevenly sunned, contemporary ownership inscription "Ann Gladstone/ Liverpool/1808" at head of titlepage, plain printed booklabel "Fasque" on front pastedown. Unsworths Antiquarian Booksellers 28 - 146 2013 £125

Association – Feisenberg, Joan

Ireland, William Henry 1777-1835 *Scribbleomania; or the Printer's Devil's Polichronicon.* London: printed for Sherwood, Neely, & Jones, 1815. First edition, title printed in black and red, 3 pages ads, few internal marks, contemporary half dark green calf, little rubbed, leading hinge splitting and repaired, booklabel of Joan Feisenberger. Jarndyce Antiquarian Booksellers CCIII - 394 2013 £225

Association – Feltrinelli, Giannalisa

Prout, Samuel *Sketches in France, Switzerland & Italy.* London: Hodgson and Graves, 1839. First printing, 560 x 380mm., publisher's blue moire cloth boards, upper cover with original gilt titling, later (flat) spine of blue morocco with titling in gilt, 26 pleasing hand colored lithographic plates, bookplate of Giannalisa Feltrinelli; corners little bumped, upper board with small (but noticeable) white (paint?) stain and darkened three inch wide horizontal strip, open plate with very small brown marginal spot, still an extremely desirable copy, because remarkably fine internally, beautifully colored plates, especially clean, fresh and bright, in solid binding retaining much of its original materials. Phillip J. Pirages 63 - 371 2013 $9500

Association – Fernandez, Ramon

Eliot, Thomas Stearns 1888-1965 *Triumphal March.* London: Faber and Faber, 1931. First edition, 8vo., original grey wrappers, fine, inscribed by author for Ramon Fernandez. Maggs Bros. Ltd. 1460 - 267 2013 £650

Association – Ferrini, Vince

Olson, Charles *Projective Verse.* New York: Totem, 1959. First separate edition, near fine in stapled wrappers, one spot to front cover, warmly inscribed by author to poet Vince Ferrini and his wife, Mary Shore. Ken Lopez Bookseller 159 - 164 2013 $750

Association – Ffennell, William

Clinton, George *Memoirs of the Life and Writings of Lord Byron.* London: James Robins & Co., 1826. Frontispiece, plates, few internal spots, contemporary half dark green morocco, spine gilt in compartments, leading hinge weak and repaired with archival tape, little rubbed, armorial bookplate of William E. Ffennell. Jarndyce Antiquarian Booksellers CCIII - 361 2013 £120

Association – Ffolkes, William Brown

Harraden, Richard *Cantabrigia Depicta.* Cambridge: publ by Harraden & Son, Cambridge, R. Cribb and Son, 288 High Holborn, T. Cadell and W. Davies, Strand, London, 1811. One of 100 proof copies on large paper, 4to., engraved titlepage, frontispiece, engraved map and 35 engraved plates, contemporary Russia, spine in compartments and lettered gilt, gilt edges, some abrasions to head of spine and slight cracking to lower joint, fine, bookplate of original subscriber Sir William Brown Ffolkes. Marlborough Rare Books Ltd. 218 - 76 2013 £450

Association – Fielding, Daphne

Boulle, Pierre *The Bridge on the River Kwai.* London: Secker and Warburg, 1954. First edition, 8vo., original black cloth, excellent copy in slightly rubbed and chipped dust jacket, inscribed by translator, Xan Fielding for his wife Daphne. Maggs Bros. Ltd. 1460 - 283 2013 £375

Association – Fielding, Xan

Boulle, Pierre *The Bridge on the River Kwai.* London: Secker and Warburg, 1954. First edition, 8vo., original black cloth, excellent copy in slightly rubbed and chipped dust jacket, inscribed by translator, Xan Fielding for his wife Daphne. Maggs Bros. Ltd. 1460 - 283 2013 £375

Association – Fierz, Adrian

Orwell, George 1903-1950 *Burmese Days.* New York: Harper and Brothers, 1934. First edition, 8vo., original orange cloth, lettered in black, binding and titling slightly stained, otherwise excellent, inscribed by author as Eric Blair, with undated TNS by Adrian Fierz, describing the provenance of the book. Maggs Bros. Ltd. 1460 - 109 2013 £18,500

Association – Filmer, J.

Spence, Joseph 1699-1766 *An Essay on Mr. Pope's Odyssey.* London: printed for S. Wilmot, Bookseller in Oxford, 1737. Second edition, 12mo., engraved frontispiece, toned and little bit spotted, contemporary sheep, later olive morocco label, joints cracking but strong, boards marked, little rubbed at extremities, ink ownership inscription " J. Filmer 1774" at upper forecorner of f.f.e.p. printed booklabel of John Sparrow. Unsworths Antiquarian Booksellers 28 - 131 2013 £175

Association – Firebrace, Cordell William

Byron, George Gordon Noel, 6th Baron   1788-1824
Poetical Works. London: Henry Frowde, Oxford University Press, 1910. Oxford edition, half title, frontispiece, contemporary half tan crushed morocco by Bickers & Son, ruled in gilt, armorial bookplate of Cordell William Firebrace, top edge gilt, very good in fine binding.   Jarndyce Antiquarian Booksellers   CCIII - 84   2013   £120

Association – Fiske, Teddie

Sladen, Douglas Brooke Wheelton *In Cornwall and Across the Sea...* London: Griffith, Farran, Okeden & Welsh, 1885. Half title, 32 page catalog (1/85), partly unopened in original cream decorated cloth, dulled, slight cracking to front board leading to lifting of cloth, presentation inscription, Teddie Fiske from Douglas Sladen.   Jarndyce Antiquarian Booksellers CCV - 249   2013   £35

Association – Fisketion, Gary

Ford, Richard *Women with Men.* New Orleans: B. E. Trice, 1997. Limited edition, true first edition, this copy has printed on colophon "Gary Fisketion's Copy" and shares its design with lettered issue, quarterbound in leather, signed by Ford, fine in fine slipcase, presentation issue.   Ken Lopez Bookseller   159 - 65   2013 $750

Association – Fitzpatrick

Byron, George Gordon Noel, 6th Baron   1788-1824
Choice Works of Lord Byron. The Giaour, Bride of Abydos, The Corsair, Lara, Childe Harold (Canto I and II) with Miscellaneous Poems and Life of the Author. London: Thomas Allman, 1844. 32mo., frontispiece, engraved title, original dark green cloth, slightly rubbed, slight wear to head of spine, armorial bookplate of Fitzpatrick of Grantstown Manor.   Jarndyce Antiquarian Booksellers   CCIII - 102   2013   £35

Association – Fletcher, Commander

Borden, Mary *The Forbidden Zone.* London: Heinemann, 1929. First edition, 8vo., original black cloth, dust jacket, excellent copy, jacket slightly rubbed and browned at spine, inscribed by author to Commander Fletcher.   Maggs Bros. Ltd.   1460 - 126   2013   £125

Association – Fletcher, Edward Charles

Hutchinson, William *The History of the County of Cumberland...* Carlisle: F. Jollie, 1794. First edition, 2 volumes, large 4to.. contemporary full diced calf gilt, spines with 3 flattened raised bands, gilt panels and rolls at head and foot, hinges trifle rubbed, 2 engraved titles, folding map, 4 folding or double page plans, 50 engraved plates, 4 pages of tables, 1 extending table and over 50 woodcut or engraved illustrations, maps etc. in text, few leaves rather foxed, handsome sound wide margined set, armorial bookplate of Edward Charles Fletcher (of Kenward, Kent) in each volume.   R. F. G. Hollett & Son   Lake District and Cumbria - 332   2013   £495

Association – Fletcher, John Gould

Eliot, Thomas Stearns   1888-1965 *A Song for Simeon.* London: Faber and Gwyer, 1928. First edition, 8vo., original pale blue wrappers, wrappers split at spine, now loose, otherwise excellent, inscribed by author for John Gould Fletcher.   Maggs Bros. Ltd.   1460 - 264   2013   £900

Association – Flinck, M.

Statius, Publius Papinius *Sylvarum Libri V. Thebaidos Lib. XII Achilleidos Lib II.* Lyon: apud Haered Seb. Gryphii, 1559. 16mo., printer's device on title hand colored, somewhat crudely, one leaf (p1) with small paper flaw affecting two words, bit of light dampmarking and soiling, old ownership inscription (M. Flinck(?) and shelf number on title, contemporary vellum dyed brown, boards with central oval decorative gilt stamp bordered gilt and blind with gilt cornerpieces, these repeated above and below central oval, spine with five raised bands, small gilt floral stamp in each compartment, gilt darkened and rubbed in places, particularly lower board, edges gilt and gauffered, bit rubbed at extremities, front flyleaf loosening, armorial bookplate, good.
Blackwell's Rare Books   B174 - 147   2013   £750

Association – Flint, Austin

Channing, Walter *A Treatise on Etherization in Childbirth.* Boston: 1848. First edition, 400 pages, original cloth with horizontal cracks across backstrip, boards partly detached, contemporary morocco bookplate of Austin Flint, M.D., library notes this copy was donated by Flint.   James Tait Goodrich   75 - 42   2013 $995

Association – Flower, John Wickham

Godwin, William 1756-1836 *Life of Geoffrey Chaucer the Early English Poet...* London: printed by T. Davison for Richard Phillips, 1804. Second edition, 4 volumes, 8vo., frontispieces, lightly browned and foxed, titles bit dusty, contemporary plum half calf with marbled boards, edges sprinkled brown, marbled endpapers, rebacked to style by Chris Weston, boards scuffed, armorial bookplate of John Wickham Flower/Park III/Croydon. Unsworths Antiquarian Booksellers 28 - 166 2013 £400

Association – Flugel, J. C.

Freud, Sigmund 1856-1939 *Die Traumdeutung. (The Interpretation of Dreams).* Leipzig: Franz Deuticke, 1909. Second edition, good with soiling and wear along edges, without dust jacket as issued, ownership signature of J. C. Flugel. Between the Covers Rare Books, Inc. Psychology & Psychiatry - 274302 2013 $500

Association – Foley, Sam

Donne, John 1571-1631 *Pseudo-Martyr: Wherein Out of Certain Propositions and Gradations...* London: printed by W. Stansby for Walter Burre,, 1610. 392 pages, 4to., 18th century half calf and marbled boards, black leather label, gilt rules and lettering, 2 often missing leaves following Table of the Chapters, containing ad to reader and errata; ink signature "Sam Foley/1689" in upper margin of titlepage, below is earlier signature that has been marked through, apparently by Foley, and is not decipherable by ordinary means, minor wear to binding including some rubbing to joints, few minor waterstains and occasional foxing, some line borders trimmed by binder in upper margin, as usual with this book, still unusually large, fresh and attractive copy. The Brick Row Book Shop Miscellany Fifty-Nine - 15 2013 $27,500

Association – Fontann, Lynn

Coward, Noel 1899-1973 *Quadrille.* London: Heinemann, 1952. First edition, 8vo., 116 pages, signed by 17 members of the English cast and producer Jack Wilson and by Lynn Fontann and Alfred Lunt, inscribed by author to Dorothy Sands (Octavia in NY production). Second Life Books Inc. 183 - 83 2013 $500

Association – Fonteyn, Margot

Bombal, Susana *Green Wings.* Buenos Aires: Ediciones Losange, 1959. First edition, 8vo., original green wrappers, inscribed by author to Margot Fonteyn, near fine, just slightly rubbed at extremities. Maggs Bros. Ltd. 1460 - 122 2013 £100

Association – Foorthe, Albinia

Allestree, Richard *The Art of Contentment.* Oxford: at the Theatre, 1675. First edition, 8vo., original speckled calf, spine elaborately gilt, gilt lettered, raised bands, front hinge starting at top, very small chip out of top of spine, original owner's signature Albinia Foorthe 1675. Howard S. Mott Inc. 262 - 6 2013 $500

Association – Foot, Isaac

Buchan, John 1875-1940 *John Macnab.* London: Hodder & Stoughton, 1925. First edition, half title, frontispiece, original light blue cloth, rubbed and worn, signed presentation from author for Isaac Foot. Jarndyce Antiquarian Booksellers CCV - 38 2013 £150

Association – Foot, Michael

Cobbett, William *A New Year's Gift to the Democrats; or Observations on a Pamphlet, entitled "A Vindication of Mr. Randolph's Resignation".* Philadelphia: published by Thomas Bradford, 1796. Second edition, some tanning and foxing, early 20th century linen backed boards, armorial bookplate of Lord Esher & later signature of Michael Foot. Jarndyce Antiquarian Booksellers CCIV - 98 2013 £280

Cobbett, William *Cobbett's Oppression!!* London: printed and published by T. Gillet & sold by Sherwood, Neely & Jones, 1809. 8vo., evidence of original stab holes, some browning, early 20th century cloth, armorial bookplate of Lord Esher and later signature of Michael Foot. Jarndyce Antiquarian Booksellers CCIV - 96 2013 £225

Stock, Joseph *A Narrative of What Passed at Killalla, in the County of Mayo and the Parts Adjacent During the French Invasion in the Summer of 1798.* Dublin: printed by and for R. E. Mercier and Co., 1800. 8vo., bound with 2 final ad leaves, titlepage lightly foxed, some browning, small hole at blank head of H8, contemporary half red morocco, marbled boards, spine rubbed and dull, corners bumped, some abrasions to boards, presentation form author "F. H. Lewis given by the Bishop of Killala 1806", 19th century armorial bookplate of H. M. Williamson and pencil signature of Michael Foot. Jarndyce Antiquarian Booksellers CCIV - 284 2013 £480

Volney, Constantin Francois *Les Ruines, ou Meditation sur les Revolutons des Empires.* Paris: Chez Desenne Volland, Plassan, 1791. First edition, 3 leaves of plates, 8vo., titlepage little dusted, occasional minor foxing, blank upper corner of aii torn, late 19th century half vellum, marbled boards, ruled spine, slightly rubbed black morocco label, signature of Michael Foot. Jarndyce Antiquarian Booksellers CCIV - 302 2013 £380

Association – Foote, Charles

Whittier, John Greenleaf 1807-1892 *The Literary Remains of John G(ardiner) C(alkis) Brainard with a Sketch of His Life.* Hartford: P. B. Goodsell, 1832. First edition, 8vo., later full calf, little rubbed along for edge and along hinges, top edge gilt, with gilt dentelles by Stikeman, bookplate of Charles B. Foote.   Second Life Books Inc.   183 - 400   2013 $300

Association – Forbes, Alastair

Dallas, Robert Charles *Recollections of the Life of Lord Byron, from the Year 1808 to the end of 1814...* London: printed for Charles Knight, 1824. First edition, half title, frontispiece, facsimile letter, few internal spots, uncut in original drab boards, paper label, spine little chipped at head, booklabels of Alastair Forbes & Alex Bridge.   Jarndyce Antiquarian Booksellers   CCIII - 369   2013   £280

Association – Forbes, Bryan

Dahl, Roald *Switch Bitch.* London: Michael Joseph, 1974. First edition, 8vo., original blue cloth, fine in price clipped dust jacket, inscribed by author to Bryan Forbes.   Maggs Bros. Ltd.   1460 - 204   2013   £375

Association – Ford, Marianne

Byron, George Gordon Noel, 6th Baron 1788-1824 *Lara, a Tale. Jacqueline, a Tale.* London: printed for J. Murray by T. Davison, 1814. First edition, first variant, original half dark green sheep, spine chipped at head and tail, hinges and corners rubbed and worn, Renier booklabel, contemporary booklabel and signature of Marianne Ford, good, s
ound copy.   Jarndyce Antiquarian Booksellers   CCIII - 195   2013   £65

Association – Forget, P.

Fodere, Francois Emmanuel *Traite de Medecine Legale et d'Hygene Publique ou de Police de Sante...* Paris: Mame, 1813. Second edition, 6 volumes, frontispiece, 2 folding tables, foxed, early quarter red morocco, morocco corners, gilt spine, rubbed, ownership signature of P. Forget, bookseller's ticket, very good, beautifully bound set.   Jeff Weber Rare Books   172 - 92   2013 $1500

Association – Forman, Buxton

Womack, Laurence *Sober Sadness; or Historicall Observations upon the Proceedings, Pretences and Designes of a Prevailing Party in both Houses of Parliament...* London: for W. Webb, 1643. 4to, 19th century sheep backed boards (shabby and broken), internally very good, Buxton Forman's copy with his bookplate.   Joseph J. Felcone Inc.   Books Printed before 1701 - 91   2013 $350

Association – Forsythe, Henderson

Albee, Edward *A Delicate Balance.* New York: Atheneum, 1966. First edition, signed by author as well as six members of the original cast, Jessica Tandy, Hume Cronyn, Rosemary Murphy, Carmen Matthews, Henderson Forsythe and Marian Seldes, fine in nearly fine dust jacket.   Ed Smith Books   78 - 3   2013 $750

Association – Fortiscue, R.

Josephus, Flavius *The Works of Flavius Josephus.* London: printed for R. Sare, 1702. First L'Estrange edition, folio, many errors in pagination but collates complete, at page 196-7 a pin is visible which is holding gathering in place, p. 199 stained at fore-edge, pages 553-88 with little loss to top margin, page 591 remargined, occasional marginal notes, wax spots and short closed tears, tan Cambridge style calf, red morocco and gilt label to spine, edges sprinkled red, spine creased and scratched, loss to endcaps, joints cracked but cords holding, lower board scraped, corners frayed, prelim blanks loose, inscriptions of M. Kenne stating 'the gift of Rnd. Fortiscue' and Albert Victor Murray, Magdalen and Mansfield Colleges Oxford, May 11 1914, pink 'Cancelled' stamp to front pastedown.   Unsworths Antiquarian Booksellers   28 - 20   2013   £250

Association – Foster, Aida

De Selincourt, E. *The Letters of William and Dorothy Wordsworth.* Oxford University Press, 1935-1939. 6 volumes, original cloth, gilt, spines trifle faded, 2 facsimiles and map in first volume, excellent sound, clean set, all but one volume with bookplate of Aida Foster, who ran stage and drama school and agency in London.   R. F. G. Hollett & Son   Lake District and Cumbria - 21   2013   £275

Association – Foster, Harold

Paul, Doris A. *The Navajo Code Talkers.* Pittsburgh: Dorrance Pub., 1990. Seventh printing, 8vo., signed by fourteen Navajo code talkers, including Albert Smith (President 4th Mar. Div. 4th Sig. Co.), Paul Blatchford, Bill Toledo, Harold Foster, George Smith, Harold Evan and others, fine in near fine dust jacket.   By the Book, L. C.   38 - 38   2013 $900

Association – Fountain, Dorrit W.

Dickens, Charles 1812-1870 *Little Dorrit.* London: Bradbury and Evans, 1857. First bookform edition, frontispiece and title and 38 etched plates by Phiz, plates generally somewhat spotted, as usual with dampstains in lower outer corners (plates only, not text), 8vo., contemporary half green calf, spine richly gilt, red lettering piece, minor shelfwear, contemporary ownership inscription of C. J. Hallam, early 20th century M. A. Hallam below this and below this inscription of Dorrit W. Fountain, Christmas 1922, good. Blackwell's Rare Books   B174 - 46   2013   £300

Association – Fournier, A.

Justin Martyr *Tou Agiou Ioustinou Philosophou Kai Marturos... (bound with) Opera Omnia...* Paris: ex officina Roberti Stephani, 1551. Paris: apud Iacobum Dupuys, 1554. Editio princeps and first edition, first substantial translation respectively, ruled in red throughout, titlepage lightly soiled, tiny dampstain to upper corner at beginning of first work, early French biscuit calf, boards with central decorative oval gilt stamp, name "A. FOURNIER" lettered gilt above, circular gilt stamp in spine compartments, old paper label pasted in second, rebacked preserving original spine (now darkened), new endpapers, boards somewhat scratched and marked, still attractive, silk ties lost, good. Blackwell's Rare Books   172 - 79   2013   £2200

Association – Foyle, William

Eden, Frederick Morton *The State of the Poor; or an History of the Labouring Classes in England, from the Conquest to the Present Period...* London: printed by I. J. Davis, for B. & J. White..., 1797. First edition, 3 volumes, quarto, bound without half titles, but with "Directions to Binder" leaf at end of volume III, which is often lacking, errata leaf to volume 1 bound before the preface, folding table facing page viii of appendix (in volume III), contemporary calf, neatly rebacked to style, covers with decorative gilt border, spines decoratively tooled in gilt in compartments, with red and green morocco gilt lettering labels, board edges and turn-ins decoratively tooled in gilt, some light foxing and minor soiling, 1.5 inch crack to bottom of outer front hinge volume I, corners bit bumped, short tear to outer margin f 3U3 in volume 1, not affecting text, from the library of William A. Foyle, with his red morocco bookplate, excellent copy. Heritage Book Shop   Holiday Catalogue 2012 - 52   2013 $13,500

More, Thomas 1478-1535 *The Debellacyon of Salem and Bizance.* London: printed by W. Rastell, 1533. First edition, 2 parts in one small octavo volume, bound without final blank leaf, this copy has leaf C8 in probable facsimile and lacks rare bifolium, Black Letter, title within woodcut border, woodcut historiated initials, early 20th century brown crushed levant morocco by Riviere and Son, covers ruled in gilt and blind with gilt corner ornaments, spine ruled in gilt and blind decoratively tooled and lettered gilt in compartments, board edges ruled in gilt, turn-ins ruled in gilt and blind, all edges gilt, marbled endpapers, washed prelims and few other leaves with slight discoloration at upper corners, leaf a4 with crease marks to covers and short tear at upper margin, final leaves slightly discolored, excellent copy of this extremely rare work, from the library of William Foyle with his bookplate, quarter brown morocco clamshell. Heritage Book Shop   50th Anniversary Catalogue - 74   2013 $12,500

Association – Fraget, A.

Byron, George Gordon Noel, 6th Baron 1788-1824 *Childe Harold's Pilgrimage. Canto the Fourth.* London: John Murray, 1818. First edition, 2nd issue, disbound, some light foxing, ownership inscription of A. Fraget (?) Dartmouth.   Jarndyce Antiquarian Booksellers   CCIII - 147   2013   £50

Association – Franchetti, Luigino

Gerhardi, William *Pretty Creatures.* London: Ernest Best, 1927. First edition, 8vo., original black cloth little soiled, spine faded, otherwise very good, inscribed by author for Yvonne and Luigino Franchetti. Maggs Bros. Ltd.   1460 - 330   2013   £250

Association – Franchetti, Yvonne

Gerhardi, William *Pretty Creatures.* London: Ernest Best, 1927. First edition, 8vo., original black cloth little soiled, spine faded, otherwise very good, inscribed by author for Yvonne and Luigino Franchetti. Maggs Bros. Ltd.   1460 - 330   2013   £250

Association – Francis, T. R.

Thomson, James 1700-1748 *Coriolanus.* London: for A. Millar, 1749. First edition, half title present, contemporary calf, neatly rebacked, paper flaw on B6 extending one inch into text, else fine, clean copy, booklabel of T. R. Francis.   Joseph J. Felcone Inc.   English and American Literature to 1800 - 23   2013 $150

Thomson, James 1700-1748 *Liberty, a Poem.* London: for A. Millar, 1735-1736. First editions of all five parts, 4to., lacks final ad leaf in part 1 and half titles in parts 2-5, later half calf, first title leaf dust soiled, final three leaves with repairs in lower corner affecting few letters, booklabel of T. R. Francis, lacking one ad leaf and four half titles. Joseph J. Felcone Inc. English and American Literature to 1800 - 24 2013 $750

Association – Frankland

Hamilton, Elizabeth *Letters on the Elementary Principles of Education.* Bath: R. Cruttwelll, 1801-1802. First edition Volume II, second edition of volume I, 2 volumes, half title to volume II, very good in handsome contemporary half calf, gilt decorated spines, marbled boards and edges, some light foxing, bookplate of Frankland, of Thirkleby, Yorkshire, 8vo. Ken Spelman Books Ltd. 75 - 50 2013 £260

Holwell, John Zephaniah *Indian Tracts.* London: printed for T. Becket, 1774. 8vo., full contemporary tree calf, raised gilt banded spine, red morocco label, slight dustiness to ouer edge of plate, otherwise very good, clean copy, armorial bookplate of Frankland, Bart, of Thirkleby, North Yorkshire. Jarndyce Antiquarian Booksellers CCIV - 161 2013 £380

Association – Franklin, Alfred

Browne, Thomas 1605-1682 *Pseudodoxia Epidemica...* London: Miller, 1650. Second edition, small folio in fours, contemporary English paneled calf, later rebacking in calf with renewed endpapers, top front corner repaired, title laid down and rather marked, last blank with some contemporary calculations in brown ink, errata correct in early hand, occasional foxing and marginal marking, page numbers of page 266 and page 271 transposed which is typical, leaves Qq2 and Qq3 transposed, good overall, from the library of Alfred W. Franklin, co-founder of Osler Club. James Tait Goodrich S74 - 36 2013 $1295

Cushing, Harvey Williams 1869-1939 *The Life of Sir William Osler.* Oxford University Press, 1925. First impression, nice in blue cloth, some light wear to cloth, near fine internally, ownership inscription of Alfred Franklin on front flyleaf, with rare "Corrigenda and Addenda to the Life of Sir William Osler" issued by Cushing August 1936, penned in brown ink at top "Alfred Franklin with regards HC", with TLS from Cushing to Alfred Franklin May 20 1937. James Tait Goodrich 75 - 161 2013 $2995

Association – Fraser, Richard

Llewellyn, Richard *How Green Was My Valley.* New York: Macmillan, 1941. (1940). Later printing, round-robin, signed in fountain pen on location during making of the film on July 19 1941, gift copy from Freda Knill (niece of cast member Thomas A. Hughes) to her daughter, with autographs and inscriptions of Roddy McDowall, Maureen O'Hara, Walter Pidgeon, Donald Crisp, Barry Fitzgerald, Sara Allgood, Anna Lee, T. Arthur Hughes, Richard Fraser and Evan H. Evans; fair to good only, binding intact, shaken and with fraying to edges of cloth, in very good supplied dust jacket with some rubbing and light wear at extremities. Ed Smith Books 75 - 39 2013 $1750

Association – French, Amos Tuck

Witherspoon, John *A Serious Inquiry into the Nature and Effects of the Stage.* New York: by Whiting & Watson, 1812. First American edition, 171 x 108mm., extremely attractive contemporary flamed sheep, flat spine with simple gilt rules and black morocco label, modern booklabel of Amos Tuck French; minor offsetting throughout text, one gathering rather foxed and browned, isolated stains of no great consequence, internally with some problems caused by inferior paper stock, but most of the text still surprisingly fresh, inexpensive binding in superb condition, unworn and very bright. Phillip J. Pirages 63 - 497 2013 $700

Association – French, Richard Forster

Cowper, William 1731-1800 *Poems.* London: printed for J. Johnson, 1793. Fifth edition, 2 volumes, contemporary tree calf, spines ruled gilt, later red morocco labels, numbered direct, unobtrusive repairs to hinges, leading f.e.p. volume I inscribed "Richard Forster French 1739 the gift of Mrs. Nicholas", later bookplate of F. L. Edwards, nice copy. Jarndyce Antiquarian Booksellers CCIII - 611 2013 £150

Association – Frere, Henry Bartle

Frere, John Hookham *The Monks and the Giants.* London: John Murray, 1821. Fourth edition, half title, uncut, original blue boards, drab spine, paper label and spine chipped, inscribed to revd. Thomas Price by Henry Bartle Frere, brother of author. Jarndyce Antiquarian Booksellers CCIII - 382 2013 £65

Association – Friedman, Harry

Cushing, Harvey Williams 1869-1939 *Meningiomas: Their Classification, Regional Behavior, Life History and Surgical End Results.* Springfield: Charles C. Thomas, 1938. First edition, 8vo., frontispiece, illustrations, original navy blue cloth, gilt stamped spine, dust jacket, spine faded, jacket spine ends chipped, ownership signature of Dr. Murl E. Kinal, bookplate of Harry B. Friedman, very good in like dust jacket.   Jeff Weber Rare Books   172 - 67   2013 $1500

Cushing, Harvey Williams 1869-1939 *Tumors of the Nervus Acusticus and the Syndrome of the Cerebellopontile Angle.* Philadelphia: W. B. Saunders, 1917. First edition, 8vo., 262 figures, original double ruled green cloth, gilt stamped spine, extremities lightly rubbed, bookplate of Harry B. Friedman, rare, very good.   Jeff Weber Rare Books   172 - 66   2013   £800

Association – Friedman, Meyer

Singer, Charles *Studies in the History and Method of Science.* Oxford: at the Clarendon Press, 1917-1921. Colored frontispiece, 40 plates, colored frontispiece, royal 8vo., original cloth, volume 1 has sunned spine, signed by author April 1932, from the library of Meyer Friedman, with his bookplates.   James Tait Goodrich   75 - 194   2013 $595

Association – Friel, Helen Otillie

Browning, Robert 1812-1889 *Some Poems by Robert Browning.* Ergany Press, 1904. One of 215 copies on paper (an additional 11 copies printed on vellum), 210 x 134mm., 64 pages, (3) leaves, lovey wood engraved color frontispiece, large decorative initials and device at end, all by Lucien and Esther Pissarro, very fine handsomely gilt and inlaid cordovan crushed morocco by Zaehnsdorf (signed on front turn-in), covers ruled in gilt, inlaid olive green morocco frame decorated with gilt scrolling foliation and inlaid pink morocco roses, raised bands, spine compartments similarly decorated with gilt and inlays, turn-ins gilt with inner toothed roll, ruled borders and foliation, top edge gilt, original paper covers bound in rear, bookplate of John Whiting Friel and Helen Otillie Friel, area under frontispiece with ink inscription dated 1905, now very faded (presumably after an attempt to wash it out?), printed in black and red, very few leaves with quite minor foxing but (setting aside inscription on frontispiece), very fine in splendid binding, especially fresh, bright inside and out.   Phillip J. Pirages   61 - 130   2013 $3500

Association – Friel, John Whiting

Browning, Robert 1812-1889 *Some Poems by Robert Browning.* Ergany Press, 1904. One of 215 copies on paper (an additional 11 copies printed on vellum), 210 x 134mm., 64 pages, (3) leaves, lovey wood engraved color frontispiece, large decorative initials and device at end, all by Lucien and Esther Pissarro, very fine handsomely gilt and inlaid cordovan crushed morocco by Zaehnsdorf (signed on front turn-in), covers ruled in gilt, inlaid olive green morocco frame decorated with gilt scrolling foliation and inlaid pink morocco roses, raised bands, spine compartments similarly decorated with gilt and inlays, turn-ins gilt with inner toothed roll, ruled borders and foliation, top edge gilt, original paper covers bound in rear, bookplate of John Whiting Friel and Helen Otillie Friel, area under frontispiece with ink inscription dated 1905, now very faded (presumably after an attempt to wash it out?), printed in black and red, very few leaves with quite minor foxing but (setting aside inscription on frontispiece), very fine in splendid binding, especially fresh, bright inside and out.   Phillip J. Pirages   61 - 130   2013 $3500

Association – Fritzinger, Warren

Whitman, Walt 1819-1892 *Leaves of Grass.* Philadelphia: McKay, 1891-1892. Deathbed edition, ninth separate edition, 8vo., portrait inserted, original heavy grey wrappers, printed yellow spine label, inscribed to Whitman's nurse Warren Fritzinger, Jan. 7 1892, extremely rare issue, front lower wrapper split approximately 2 1/2 inches at joint, otherwise fine, unopened copy in half morocco slipcase.   James S. Jaffe Rare Books   Fall 2013 - 147   2013 $35,000

Association – Fuller, Roy

Abse, Dannie *Way Out in the Centre.* London: Hutchinson, 1981. First edition, 8vo., original black cloth, dust jacket, inscribed by author for Roy Fuller, near fine.   Maggs Bros. Ltd.   1460 - 3   2013   £75

Association – Furness, R. A.

Dickinson, Goldsworthy Lowes *Poems.* N.P.: privately Printed at Chiswick Press, 1896. First edition, 8vo., original printed blue-gray wrappers (68) pages, untrimmed, pictorial title, inscribed "R.A. Furness from the author June 20", wrappers worn and somewhat chipped around top edges, very good, uncommon.   The Brick Row Book Shop   Miscellany Fifty-Nine - 14   2013 $150

Association – Gabler, James

Matthews, Charles G. *Manual of Alcoholic Fermentation and the Allied Industries.* London: Edward Arnold, 1902. First edition, octavo, 295, 8 pages ads, original blue cloth gilt, owner name front fly, corners bit bumped, sound, very good copy, exceptionally uncommon, ex-James Gabler. Between the Covers Rare Books, Inc.   Cocktails, Etc. - 83341   2013 $200

Association – Gage, Matilda Joslyn

Stanton, Elizabeth Cady   *History of Woman Sufferage.* New York: Fowler & Wells, 1881. First edition, volume I only, 1848-1861, 8vo., 878 pages, steel engravings, maroon cloth, cover quite scuffed, somewhat worn at spine and corners, little foxing, otherwise very good, with presentation by editor Matilda Joslyn Gage.   Second Life Books Inc.   182 - 230   2013 $350

Association – Gajani, Guglielmo

Emerson, Ralph Waldo   1803-1882   *Representative Men: Seven Lectures.* Boston: Phillips, Sampson and Co., 1850. First edition, 8vo., original brown cloth, gilt, preserved in folding box, inscribed by author for Professor Guglielmo Gajani, excellent copy, endpapers lightly browned and foxed, cloth worn at head and tail of spine.   Maggs Bros. Ltd.   1460 - 280   2013   £3500

Association – Galpin, Samuel

New York. (City) *Manual of the Corporation of the City of New York for 1861.*   New York: D. T. Valentine, 1861.   700 pages, duotones, color plates, engravings, many foldout maps and illustrations, original purple cloth decorated in blind and gilt, 3 bookplates, one of Samuel W. Galpin, another from a library (with minimal marking), spine little sunned, else very good plus, inscribed by Galpin to Maine Congressman Daniel Somes.   Between the Covers Rare Books, Inc.   New York City - 299888   2013 $450

Association – Galsworthy, John

Masefield, John   1878-1967   *The Tragedy of Nan and Other Plays.* London: Grant Richards, 1909.   First English edition, one of 500 copies, 8vo., original cloth, presentation copy from author to John Galsworthy, inscribed and dated Sept. 13th 1909, with Galsworthy's bookplate, covers faded, head of spine rubbed, evidently well read, presumably by recipient.   James S. Jaffe Rare Books   Fall 2013 - 95   2013 $1250

Association – Gammage, Nick

Heaney, Seamus   *The Spirit Label.* London: Faber, 1996. First edition, foolscap 8vo., original mid green boards, backstrip gilt lettered, dust jacket, fine, inscribed by author for Nick Gammage.   Blackwell's Rare Books   172 - 194   2013   £300

Hughes, Ted   1930-1998   *The Iron Man.* London: Faber, 1968.   First edition, 5 full page illustrations by George Adamson, pages 59, 8vo., original pale blue and pink boards, backstrip and front cover lettered in black, blue and white, that on front cover incorporated within design by Adamson, dust jacket repeating design, fine, scarce, particularly in such fine condition, rarely found inscribed, this copy inscribed by author for Nick Gammage.   Blackwell's Rare Books   172 - 196   2013   £1500

Association – Gandarillas, Carmen

Eluard, Paul   *Au Rendez-vous Allemand.* Paris: Les Editions de Minuit, 1945.   Nouvelle edition, 8vo., later red morocco, original wrappers bound in, morocco slightly discolored with few marks, inscribed by author for Carmen Gandarillas.   Maggs Bros. Ltd.   1460 - 277   2013   £450

Association – Gaskell, B

Amory, Thomas   *The Life of John Bucle, Esq.* London: printed for T. Becket and P. A. Dehondt and T. Cadell, 1770. New edition, 4 volumes, 12mo., few minor spots, late 19th/ early 20th century sprinkled and polished tan calf by Riviere, rebacked to style by Chris Weston, board edges slightly rubbed, ink ownership inscription 'B. Gaskell' with 'Thomas House' added in volume 4, armorial bookplate of Charles George Milnes Gaskell.   Unsworths Antiquarian Booksellers   28 - 62   2013   £300

Association – Gaskell, Charles George Milnes

Amory, Thomas   *The Life of John Bucle, Esq.* London: printed for T. Becket and P. A. Dehondt and T. Cadell, 1770. New edition, 4 volumes, 12mo., few minor spots, late 19th/ early 20th century sprinkled and polished tan calf by Riviere, rebacked to style by Chris Weston, board edges slightly rubbed, ink ownership inscription 'B. Gaskell' with 'Thomas House' added in volume 4, armorial bookplate of Charles George Milnes Gaskell.   Unsworths Antiquarian Booksellers   28 - 62   2013   £300

Flaubert, Gustave 1821-1880 *Madame Bovary, Moeurs de Province.* Paris: Michel Levy Freres, Libraires Editeurs, 1857. First edition, 2 volumes, dedication leaf, volume I, half titles, with original wrappers cut down and laid on to green paper, bound before half titles, near contemporary quarter blue cloth, light brown morocco labels, marbled boards, leading inner hinge slightly cracking, with unidentified armorial bookplate on leading pastedowns and armorial bookplate of Charles George Milnes Gaskell, very good. Jarndyce Antiquarian Booksellers   CCV - 103   2013   £2800

Association – Gatenby, Greg

Acker, Kathy *Pussy, King of the Pirates.* New York: Grove, 1996. First edition, review copy, full page inscription by author to Greg Gatenby, founding Artistic Director of Toronto's International Festival of Authors, Gatenby's signature on half title, fine in fine dust jacket with publisher's press release laid in.   Ken Lopez Bookseller   159 - 3   2013 $350

Alexie, Sherman *Indian Killer.* New York: Atlantic Monthly Press, 1996. First edition, inscribed by author to Greg Gatenby, with Gatenby's signature, fine in fine dust jacket. Ken Lopez Bookseller   159 - 146   2013 $250

Muller, Herta *The Land of Green Plums.* New York: Metropolitan/Holt, 1996. First American edition, awarded IMPAC prize, inscribed by author to Greg Gatenby, one of IMPAC judges, Muller has also drawn a caricature of Gatenby, as well as adding her address, phone and fax, also inscribed by translator, Michael Hofmann, stamp of the award on front flyleaf, hint of crown bump, fine in very near fine dust jacket with shallow vertical crease to spine, remarkable copy.   Ken Lopez Bookseller   159 - 143   2013 $1000

The Showa Anthology 2. Modern Japanese Short Stories 1961-1984. New York: Kodansha, 1985. Fine in fine dust jacket, Kenzaburo Oe's copy whih he used as a reading copy at Toronto's Harbourfront International Festival of Authors in 1985, inscribed by Oe to Greg Gatenby, director of the festival, with Gatenby's signature.   Ken Lopez Bookseller   159 - 161   2013 $1000

Association – Gautier, Judith

Dodgson, Charles Lutwidge 1832-1898 *Adventures D'Alice Au Pays Des Merveilles. (Alice's Adventures in Wonderland).* Paris: Hachette, 1907. One of only 20 copies printed on vellum, large 4to., full vellum discolored on corners of both covers, else fine, 13 large, fabulous tipped in color plates by Arthur Rackham with guards, numerous full page and in-text illustrations in line and pictorial endpapers, rare and special copy, this copy has an extra printed presentation page reading "Exemplaire Reserve Pour Madame Judith Gautier" (daughter of Theophile).   Aleph-Bet Books, Inc.   105 - 490   2013 $7500

Association – Geddes, G. D.

Anacreon *Teiou Mele: Praefixo Commentario quo Poetae Genus...* Parma: Bodoni, 1791. One of 150 copies, 16mo. in 4's, 2 engraved portraits, text i Greek, commentaries in Latin, very occasional marginal foxing, small marginal tear to page 91, contemporary vellum, spine gilt with black morocco labels, all edges gilt, upper joint split but neatly repaired with vellum, lower joint starting, binding little soiled, particularly at spine, labels slightly chipped, armorial bookplate of John Wells Esq. to front pastedown, with small Greek inscription, armorial bookplate of Gul. D. Geddes. Unsworths Antiquarian Booksellers   28 - 1   2013   £600

Association – Gedeon, Andras

Benard, Claude *Lecons des Anesthesiques et sur l'Asphysie.* Paris: J. B. Bailliere et fils, 1875. First edition, 8vo., 7 text figures, modern quarter black morocco over marbled boards, raised bands, gilt stamped spine title, original paper wrappers bound in, bookplate of Andras Gedeon, fine.   Jeff Weber Rare Books   172 - 24   2013 $700

Cesalpino, Andrea *Quaestionum Peripateticarum Lib. V. Daemonum Investigatio Peripatetica. Quaestionum Medicorum Libri II.* Venetiis: Giunta, 1593. Second edition, 8vo., woodcut printer's device on title, several woodcut figures, contemporary ink notations on front endpaper, contemporary full vellum, manuscript spine title, spine lightly chipped, early ink stamp on titlepage and final leaf, bookplate of Andras Gedeon, very good, quite scarce.   Jeff Weber Rare Books   172 - 57   2013 $9500

Association – Gent, Thomas

Aristophanes *The Comedies of Aristophanes.* London: R. Clavel, 1695. 8vo., some dustiness, volume rebound in unsympathetic quarter morocco, marbled boards, poor gilt label, Thomas Gent's copy, he bought a defective copy, lacking the first gathering, and has made his own pen and ink titlepage to which he signs his name dated 1770.   Ken Spelman Books Ltd.   73 - 6   2013   £495

Association – Gere, John, A. G.

Clare, John 1754-1832 *The Village Minstrel and Other Poems.* (with) *Poems Descriptive of Rural Life and Scenery.* London: Taylor & Hessey, 1821. Stamford: E. Drury, 1821. First edition and fourth edition, uniformly bound as "Clare's Poems" in contemporary full purple panelled calf, gilt spines, small chip at head of leading hinge volume 1, hinges and edges little worn, fading to brown in places, contemporary ownership inscription of W. Dawson Kent and armorial bookplates of John A. G. Gere.   Jarndyce Antiquarian Booksellers   CCIII - 480   2013   £850

Association – Gerry, Elbridge

Walter, William *A Discourse Delivered Before the Humane Society of Massachusetts Twelfth of June 1798.* Boston: printed by John and Thomas Fleet at the Bible and Heart, Cornhill, 1798. First edition, small 4to., contemporary marbled paper wrappers, endpapers little stained, some light soiling, small stamp of later owner on inside front wrapper, attractive copy, with half title, with "Hon. Elbridge Gerry ESq." on front flyleaf.   M & S Rare Books, Inc.   95 - 224   2013 $275

Association – Gerry, Vince

Mac-Orlan, Pierre *Nuits aux Bouges. Eaux-Fortes de Dignimont.* Paris: Ernest Flammarion, 1929. Limited edition, 83 of 50 special copies on Holland Van Gelder Zonen paper (of a total 890), 4to., 69 pages, 5 etched plates after illustrations by Dignimont, original printed wrappers, illustrated cover plate, later cloth backed, slipcase with patterned paper backed boards designed by Vance Gerry, with Gerry bookplate, fine.   Jeff Weber Rare Books   171 - 103   2013 $300

Association – Gershwin, George

Hughes, Langston *The Weary Blues.* New York: Alfred A. Knopf, 1926. First edition, one of 1500 copies printed, small 8vo., original blue cloth backed decorated boards, presentation copy inscribed by author for George Gershwin, covers lightly rubbed, lacking rare dust jacket, otherwise very good.   James S. Jaffe Rare Books   Fall 2013 - 70   2013 $45,000

Association – Gibb, Molly Flagg

Wotton, Henry *Reliquiae Wottonianae; or a Collection of Lives, Letters, Poems.* London: by T. Roycroft for R. Marriott, 1672. Third edition, 8vo., portraits, 19th century red morocco, early signatures of J. Grien? 1725, Thomas Price and John Francis Cole, 1828, bookplates of J. J. Chapman and Molly Flagg Gibb, very good.   Joseph J. Felcone Inc.   English and American Literature to 1800 - 26   2013 $900

Association – Gibbon, Charles

Byron, George Gordon Noel, 6th Baron 1788-1824 *Childe Harold's Pilgrimage.* London: John Murray, 1816. First edition, 2nd issue, half title 8 pages ads (No. 1816), edges little dusted, uncut in original drab wrappers, spine weakening and slightly chipped, small label and ink spot on front wrapper, ownership inscription of Charles Gibbon on initial blank and title, good plus.   Jarndyce Antiquarian Booksellers   CCIII - 142   2013   £150

Association – Gibson, David

Abse, Dannie *O. Jones, O. Jones.* London: Hutchinson, 1970. First edition, 8vo., original grey cloth, dust jacket, inscribed by author for David Gibson, near fine.   Maggs Bros. Ltd.   1460 - 1   2013   £50

Association – Gibson, Dorinda

Gibson, C. B. *The History of the County and City of Cork.* 1861. First edition, 2 volumes, map, signed presentation copy to his daughter, Dorinda, in Guy's special red morocco binding, gilt embossed, all edges gilt, lacks signature 31 (pages 72-89) of volume 2, else very good.   C. P. Hyland   261 - 447   2013   £750

Association – Gibson, John

Hardy, Thomas 1840-1928 *The Variorum Edition of the Complete Poems of Thomas Hardy.* London: Macmillan, 1979. First edition, 2nd issue, 4to., original red cloth, gilt lettering, fine in fine dust jacket, signed by editor, John Gibson, from the Gary Lepper Collection of Thomas Hardy.   The Brick Row Book Shop   Bulletin Nine - 104   2013   £100

Association – Gide, Andre

Bennett, Arnold 1867-1931 *Riceyman Steps.* London: Cassell, 1923. First edition, 8vo., original pale green cloth, excellent copy, dust jacket rubbed and nicked dust jacket, long closed tear at outer edge, inscribed by author to Andre Gide.   Maggs Bros. Ltd.   1460 - 83   2013   £1850

Association – Giffard, Eliza

Brooke, Henry *The Fool of Quality; or the History of Henry Earl of Moreland.* London: printed for Edward Johnston, 1777. 12mo., some offset browning on endpapers and pastedowns, paper flaw to leading edge of D1 volume IV, gatherings D & E in volume IV rather heavily foxed, contemporary full sprinkled calf, hinges cracked, slight wear to head and tail of spines, lacks all labels and volume numbers, ownership inscription of Eliza Giffard, Nerquis, Flintshire 1807.   Jarndyce Antiquarian Booksellers   CCIV - 76   2013   £125

Potts, Thomas *An Inquiry into the Moral and Political of the Religion Called Roman Catholic.* London: printed for G. G. J. and J. Robinson, 1790. First edition, 8vo., full contemporary sprinkled calf, gilt floral spine, hinges cracked but firm, lacking label, ownership inscription "Eliza Giffard - Nequis, Flintshire, 1807". Jarndyce Antiquarian Booksellers   CCIV - 238   2013   £75

Association – Gilbert, Cecilia

Watson, James D. *Genes, Girls and Gamow.* New York: Alfred A. Knopf, 2002. First American edition, signed by Watson, Cecilia Gilbert and Walter Gilbert, fine in fine dust jacket, 8vo.   By the Book, L. C.   37 - 88   2013 $300

Association – Gilbert, Edward

Burroughs, Edgar Rice   1875-1950 *Tarzan and the Jewels of Opar.* Chicago: A. C. McClurg, 1918. First edition, 8vo., original blue cloth, spine faded, otherwise excellent copy, inscribed by author to his brother-in-law Edward Gilbert.   Maggs Bros. Ltd.   1460 - 151   2013   £350

Association – Gilbert, Walter

Watson, James D. *Genes, Girls and Gamow.* New York: Alfred A. Knopf, 2002. First American edition, signed by Watson, Cecilia Gilbert and Walter Gilbert, fine in fine dust jacket, 8vo.   By the Book, L. C.   37 - 88   2013 $300

Association – Gill, Eric

Pepler, Hilary Douglas Clark *The Devil's Devices or Control Versus Service.* Hampshire House Workshops: St. Dominic's Press, 1915. First edition, 11 wood engravings by Eric Gill, foolscap 8vo., original quarter black cloth, scarlet boards, Gill engraving and lettering on front cover, all printed in black, covers rubbed, more so on rear cover, untrimmed, good, Eric Gill's bookplate.   Blackwell's Rare Books   B174 - 382   2013   £250

Association – Gill, Evan

Gill, Eric   1882-1940 *Songs without Clothes, being a Dissertation on the Song of Solomon and Such-Like Songs...* Ditchling, Sussex: Saint Dominic's Press, 1921. First edition, one of 240 copies, printed on Batchelor handmade paper, the 'c' in McNabb on titlepage not 'skied', 16mo., original quarter white linen, plain grey brown boards, light browning to free endpapers, trimmed plain (original?) dust jacket, Evan Gill's copy with his letterpress bookplate. Blackwell's Rare Books   B174 - 380   2013   £250

Association – Gillman, Alexander

Coleridge, Samuel Taylor   1772-1834 *Confessions of an Inquiring Spirit.* London: William Pickering, 1840. First edition, half title, contemporary half black morocco by Hayday, slightly rubbed, top edge gilt, signature and bookplate of Alexander W. Gillman and of Peter Mann 1951. Jarndyce Antiquarian Booksellers   CCIII - 562   2013   £180

Association – Gilman, William

Dressler, Albert *California's Pioneer Artist, Ernest Narjoi, a Brief Resume of the Career of a Versatile Genius.* San Francisco: Albert Dressler, 1936. First edition, of a total of 150 copies, this number 15 of 15 reserved for private distribution, presentation inscription from author for Bill Gilman, 2 tipped in reproductions, printed gold wrappers, fine. Argonaut Book Shop   Summer 2013 - 249   2013 $90

O'Neill, F. Gordon *Ernest Reuben Lilienthal and His Family.* Palo Alto: Stanford University Press, 1949. First edition, small quarto, frontispiece, photos, dark blue cloth, gilt, bookplate, very fine, presentation inscription signed to William Gilman with his bookplate.   Argonaut Book Shop Summer 2013 - 208   2013 $125

Association – Gladstone, Ann

Beattie, James   1735-1803 *An Essay on the Nature and Immutability of Truth, in Opposition to Sophistry and Sceptisim.* London: printed for J. Mawman, 1807. Seventh edition, 8vo, some light spotting in places, contemporary straight grain dark blue morocco, spine divided by gilt rules, small central tools in compartments, boards bordered with greek key roll, marbled endpapers, all edges gilt, corners and pages bit rubbed, boards unevenly sunned, contemporary ownership inscription "Ann Gladstone/ Liverpool/1808" at head of titlepage, plain printed booklabel "Fasque" on front pastedown.   Unsworths Antiquarian Booksellers   28 - 146   2013   £125

Association – Glass, Douglas

Bates, Herbert Ernest   1905-1974 *Edward Garnett.* London: Max Parrish, 1950. First edition, small 8vo., original brown cloth, dust jacket, offset foxing to endpapers, else excellent copy in worn, creased and lightly soiled and nicked dust jacket, inscribed by author to photographer Douglas Glass, 1/58.   Maggs Bros. Ltd.   1460 - 49   2013   £100

Beaton, Cecil *Cecil Beaton's Diaries 1948-1955. The Strenuous Years.* London: Weidenfeld and Nicolson, 1973. First edition, 8vo., original red cloth, dust jacket, excellent copy, jacket spine faded, worn at extremities, inscribed by author for Douglas Glass, loosely inserted is short ALS from Beaton to Glass.   Maggs Bros. Ltd.   1460 - 56   2013   £200

Beaton, Cecil *Photobiography.* London: Odhams Press, 1951. First edition, 4to., original cream cloth, covers rubbed and stained, otherwise very good, detached dust jacket loosely inserted at rear, inscribed by Beaton for Douglas Glass 1952.   Maggs Bros. Ltd.   1460 - 54   2013   £200

Frost, Robert Lee   1874-1963 *Complete Poems of Robert Frost.* New York: Henry Holt and Co., 1949. First US edition, 8vo., original green cloth, rubbed and soiled but very good, inscribed by author for Douglas Glass, Oct. 1953, with few manuscript poem in Glass's hand on back endpapers.   Maggs Bros. Ltd.   1460 - 313   2013   £1500

Frost, Robert Lee   1874-1963 *Selected Poems.* London: Penguin Books, 1955. First edition thus, 8vo., original wrappers, preserved in folding box, pages browned, wrappers torn and worn, good copy, inscribed by author of Douglas Glass May 1957.   Maggs Bros. Ltd.   1460 - 314   2013   £450

Gorer, Geoffrey *The Revolutionary Ideas of the Marquis de Sade.* London: Wishart and Co., 1934. First edition, 8vo., original cream cloth worn at extremities and little soiled, but very good, inscribed by author for Frances, tipped in ALS from author to photographer Douglas Glass. Maggs Bros. Ltd.   1460 - 354   2013   £75

Association – Glegh, William

Shakespeare, William   1564-1616 *The Late and Much Admired Play, Called Pericles, Prince of Tyre.* London: Thomas Coles, 1635. Sixth edition, octavo in fours, printer's device on titlepage, full 20th century red morocco, boards double ruled gilt spine lettered gilt, gilt dentelles, edges speckled red from earlier binding, spine slightly sunned and worn at edges, old ink signature of William Glegh.   Heritage Book Shop   Holiday Catalogue 2012 - 135   2013 $60,000

Association – Glenn, Frank

Fulton, John Farquhar *Harvey Cushing: A Biography.* Springfield: Charles C. Thomas, 1946. 8vo., frontispiece, figures, blue cloth, gilt stamped spine, spine faded, extremities worn, especially at spine ends, signed and inscribed by Cushing's wife, Katherine Crowell Cushing to Dr. Frank Glenn, her signature seldom seen, good.   Jeff Weber Rare Books   172 - 68   2013 $450

Association – Glenrinnes

Robertson, James A. *Gaelic Topography of Scotland and What It Proves.* Edinburgh: William P. Nimmo, 1869. First edition, 8vo., large foldout map in color, repaired in places, but with several further tears and protruding little from textblock at lower edge, titlepage in red and black, later blue half calf, blue cloth boards, gilt title to spine, top edge gilt, spine faded, some marks and scratches, still good, inkstamp of Wm. Jackson Bookbinders, Aberdeen, embossed stamp of Glenrinnes, Dufftown, Banfshire.   Unsworths Antiquarian Booksellers   28 - 195   2013   £50

Association – Gloucester, A. C.

Church of England.   Book of Common Prayer *The Booke of Common Prayer and Administration of the Sacraments and Other Rites and Ceremonies of the Church of England.* London: by Robert Barker, printer to the Kings most excellent Majesty, 1634. 4to., very good, 19th century quarter calf, pebble grain cloth boards, armorial bookplate of A. C. Gloucester, with near contemporary name Rog. Blaq in blank space at foot of titlepage border with few manuscript emendations to text, verse numbers noted at head of titlepage.   Ken Spelman Books Ltd.   75 - 2   2013   £350

Association – Gloucester & Edinburgh, William Frederick, 2nd Duke of

Chesterfield, Philip Dormer Stanhope, 4th Earl of   1694-1773 *Letters Written... to His Son, Philip Stanhope Esq...* London: printed for J. Dodsley, 1774. First edition, first state (erratum on page 55 of volume i uncorrected), 2 volumes, frontispiece volume i, bound without errata leaf in volume ii (but with blank leaf of matching paper in its place) some light foxing, embossment of Grendon Hall 1850 (the belonging to Sir George Chetwynd, 3rd Baronet), 4to., modern biscuit calf, spines gilt with red morocco lettering pieces, circular red morocco numbering pieces on green morocco grounds, new endpapers, preserving old bookplates of William Frederick, 2nd Duke of Gloucester and Edinburgh, manuscript letter loosely inserted, very good.   Blackwell's Rare Books   B174 - 146   2013   £900

Association – Glover, Johannis

Vergilius Maro, Publius *Opera quae quidem Exstant Omnia.* Basilae: Sebastianum Henriepetri, 1613. Folio, little worming to fore-edge margins around columns 180 and 279, toning at very edge of margins to varying degrees, occasional discoloration around text especially to volumes 1079-1802 and 1901-1904, contemporary speckled tan calf, neatly rebacked and corners repaired, red morocco gilt spine label, boards heavily scratched, few dents, edges worn, armorial bookplate of Sir William Molesworth with ink inscription of Kenneth J. Cox, Dalton Hall Victoria Park, Manchester 14 added, old ink ownership inscription of Johannis Glover on titlepage, small contemporary (?) list of Latin names for various vegetables and herbs loosely inserted. Unsworths Antiquarian Booksellers 28 - 57 2013 £500

Association – Goffes, Joseph

Edwards, Jonathan *Dissertation Concerning Liberty and Necessity.* Worcester: 1797. First edition, 8vo., 23 pages plus errata leaf, rubbed contemporary calf, chipped at extremities of spine, endpapers soiled, text block little browned, very good, inscribed by Rev. Sam'l Austin of Worcester, Oct. 15 1806 for Joseph Goffes. Second Life Books Inc. 183 - 123 2013 $300

Association – Gogarty, Oliver St. John

Yeats, William Butler 1865-1939 *Shadowy Waters.* London: Hodder and Stoughton, 1900. First edition, 8vo., original dark blue cloth, backstrip and front cover gilt blocked, gilt lettered quarter dark blue morocco and cloth, book-form box fine, inscribed by author, this was originally Oliver St. John Gogarty's copy with his bookplate, subsequently, in ownership of Sean O'Faolain and inscribed by him, photo of Yeats tipped to front free endpaper. Blackwell's Rare Books 172 - 259 2013 £3250

Association – Goldsmith, Michael

Irving, John 1942- *The Cider House Rules.* Los Angeles: Film Colony/Miramax, 1995. Screenplay, Revised December 1995 hand numbered '47', with signature of Michael Goldsmith as well as changes and proposed changes to text, apparently in Goldsmith's hand, signed by author, uncommon signed, bradbound in Miramax covers, 139 pages, near fine, working copy, changes and revisions visible. Ken Lopez Bookseller 159 - 82 2013 $2500

Association – Gomez, Marta

Hamady, Walter *Neopostmodernism or Gabberjab Number 6.* Mt. Horeb: Perishable Press, 1988. First edition, limited to 125 copies printed on various handmade papers, oblong small 8vo., illustrations, original boards, signed by binder, Marta Gomez, Hamady's assistant, Kent Kasuboske and especially inscribed by Hamady to collector, very fine. James S. Jaffe Rare Books Fall 2013 - 125 2013 $2500

Association – Goodall, Edyth

Ashford, Daisy *The Young Visiters, or Mr. Salteena's Plan.* London: Chatto & Windus, 1919. Reprint, 8vo., frontispiece and one facsimile, original marbled boards, black cloth, printed paper label, signed by author and inscribed by actress Edyth Goodall and one Agnes Strang, worn along edges of boards and lettering piece, otherwise very good. Maggs Bros. Ltd. 1460 - 23 2013 £75

Association – Goodchild, W. E.

Milton, John 1608-1674 *The Poetical Works of John Milton.* printed for C. Cooke, 1796. 2 volumes, 12mo., engraved frontispiece and additional titlepage in each volume, plus 7 engraved plates (all lightly foxed), most with tissue guards, contemporary quarter sprinkled calf with marbled boards, corners tipped in vellum, spines divided by gilt fillet, red morocco lettering pieces, ownership inscription of W. E. Goodchild to initial blank, slightly rubbed, touch of wear to few corners, good. Blackwell's Rare Books B174 - 103 2013 £150

Association – Gordon, H. P.

Pratt, John *Pratt Family Records.* for private circulation, 1931. 8vo., signed presentation to H. P. Gordon, added pencil notes from Horace E. Jones, very good. C. P. Hyland 261 - 409 2013 £250

Association – Gordon, Lindsay

Gordon, Adam Lindsay *Bush Ballads and Galloping Rhymes.* Melbourne: Clarson, Massina and Co., 1870. First edition, 8vo., original burgundy cloth, lettered gilt, inscribed by author for Lindsay Gordon, wear to head and tail of spine, otherwise very good. Maggs Bros. Ltd. 1460 - 353 2013 £375

Association – Gould, Jay

Ferrier, Auger *A Learned Astronomical Discourse of the Iudgement of Natiuiies.* printed at the widdow Charlewoods House, for Edwarde White, 1593. First edition in English, title within elaborate woodcut border, without final blank, title bit browned and stained, weak area causing short vertical split with loss of couple of letter, hole in inside border with slight less of engraved surface, text slightly browned, dampstain at head, headline of table shaved, last couple of leaves frayed in fore margin, ink trials on verso of last leaf seeping through three small holes, two of which touch letters, small 4to, later sheep rebacked, fore edges worn, early ownership inscription, later bookplate of Jay Gould (railway magnate) and at end that of his daughter, sound. Blackwell's Rare Books Sciences - 49 2013 £4000

Association – Gow, A. S. F.

Bone, Gavin *Anglo-Saxon Poetry.* Oxford: Clarendon Press, 1944. First reprint, 8vo., original cream cloth, excellent copy, inscribed by Muirhead and Gertrude Bone to A. S. F. Gow. Maggs Bros. Ltd. 1460 - 125 2013 £50

Association – Gower, W.

Robinson, John *An Account of Sweden, together with an Extract of the History of that Kingdom.* London: printed for Tim Goodwin at the Queen's Head, 1694. First edition, first leaf bars half title on recto and an ad on verso, 8vo., lower outer corner of F4 torn with slight loss not affecting text, 18th century marbled boards, vellum spine, some rubbing to boards, slight wear at foot of spine, withdrawn stamp of Worcester College at head of titlepage and on inner front board, early ownership name of W. Gower. Jarndyce Antiquarian Booksellers CCIV - 28 2013 £220

Association – Grant, Douglas

Burke, Edmund 1729-1797 *Reflections on the Revolution in France and on the Proceedings in Certain Societies in London Relative to that Event.* London: printed for J. Dodsley, 1790. Seventh edition, uncut in original pale blue boards, drab swine, spine little darkened and slightly chipped, corners slightly knocked, following board bit marked, small label and signature of Douglas Grant, good plus, internally clean. Jarndyce Antiquarian Booksellers CCIII - 651 2013 £250

Association – Grant, Duncan

Roche, Paul *Enigma Variations And.* Gloucester: Thornhill Press, 1974. First edition, 8vo., original blue cloth, dust jacket, signed by Duncan Grant who designed the cover and by author, near fine in price clipped dust jacket. Maggs Bros. Ltd. 1460 - 357 2013 £350

Association – Granville, Dr.

Ring, John *Reflections on the Surgeon's Bill: in Answer to Three Pamphlets.* printed for Hookham and Carpenter and J. Johnson, 1798. First edition, first few gatherings somewhat foxed, little browning and just staining elsewhere, 8vo., uncut in original boards, rebacked, inscribed on title "Dr. Granville with the author's best respects" and with Granville's stamp, inscribed "Dr. (John Coakley) Lettsom from the author" with Lettsom's booklabel inside front cover, sound, scarce. Blackwell's Rare Books Sciences - 105 2013 £1200

Association – Gration-Maxfield, Grant

Hayley, William *The Triumphs of Temper.* Chichester: printed by J. Seagrave, for T. Cadell and W. Davies, London, 1803. Twelfth edition, 6 plates, few spots, bound without half title, later 'antique' panelled calf by V. A. Brown of Mildenborough, spine gilt in compartments, red and green leather labels, slightly rubbed, all edges gilt, nice, bright copy, signature of Mary Keats on titlepage, pencil notes in prelims by Grant Gration-Maxfield. Jarndyce Antiquarian Booksellers CCIII - 7 2013 £650

Association – Gratwick, John

Rivard, Gilles *Competition in Transportation Policy and Legislation in Review.* Ottawa: Transportation Act Review Commission, 1993. 8vo., both volumes in blue leather with silver, leather covered slipcase, 8vo., Commissioner's copy with his name (John Gratwick) embossed on front cover both volumes, inscribed to him by Rivard, very good. Schooner Books Ltd. 105 - 160 2013 $95

Association – Graves, R. P.

Clough, Arthur Hugh *Poems.* Cambridge: Macmillan, 1862. First collected edition, 8vo., original green honeycomb cloth, gilt, minor wear to extremities, good, inscribed by author for Rev'd. R. P. Graves. Blackwell's Rare Books B174 - 34 2013 £450

Association – Graves, Robert

Momigliano, Arnaldo *Claudius: the Emperor and His Achievement.* Oxford: Clarendon Press, 1934. First edition in English, 8vo., original red cloth, excellent copy, slightly foxed, slight wear to head and tail of spine, inscribed by Robert Graves for Mrs. Thomas Ashby (May Ashby). Maggs Bros. Ltd. 1460 - 361 2013 £425

Association – Gray, Ian

Bennett, Alan *Habeas Corpus.* London: Faber and Faber, 1973. First edition, 8vo., original grey cloth, inscribed by author for Ian Gray, excellent copy in dust jacket, rubbed at edges with 2cm. chunk missing from lower spine. Maggs Bros. Ltd. 1460 - 79 2013 £350

Association – Grayson, William

Green, William *The Tourist's New Guide Containing a Description of the Lakes, Mountains, and Scenery, in Cumberland, Westmorland and Lancashire.* Kendal: R. Lough and Co., etc., 1819. First edition, 2 volumes in 1, old half red morocco gilt, little worn, with second half title, only 4 engraved plates, one section bound out of order, mss. copy of inscription n Green's tombstone in Grasmere churchyard on final blank; from the library of William Grayson of Simonswood (Liverpool). R. F. G. Hollett & Son Lake District and Cumbria - 203 2013 £350

Association – Green, Martin

O'Nolan, Brian *Myles Away from Dublin.* London: Granada, 1985. First edition, 8vo., original orange cloth, dust jacket, from the library of Richard Murphy and inscribed to him by selector, Martin Green, fine in dust jacket. Maggs Bros. Ltd. 1442 - 275 2013 £125

Scott, Walter 1771-1832 *The Life of Napoleon Buonaparte, Emperor of the French...* Edinburgh: printed by Ballantyne and Co. for Longman, Rees, Orme, Brown & Green, 1827. First edition, first issue (half titles in each volume), 220 x 130mm., collation irregular in last gathering of volume I, but complete, with half titles in all volumes, errata in first seven, 9 volumes, not unpleasant contemporary black half calf, flat spines heavily gilt in one elongated compartment filled with repeating pattern of flowers and twining leaves, newer black morocco label on each spine, marbled boards, endpapers and top edges, other edges untrimmed; bookplate of Martin Holdich Green, Trinity College, Oxford; half joints bit rubbed and flaked (but not cracking) paper sides rather chafed, couple of spines slightly abraded with minor loss of gilt, leaves with frequent minor foxing and faint offsetting (never serious but intermittently present throughout), not without condition problems, still pleasing set, volumes quite sound, text with no fatal defects. Phillip J. Pirages 63 - 352 2013 $750

Association – Greenaway, Kate

Locker-Lampson, Hannah Jane *What the Blackbird Said.* London: George Routledge, 1881. First edition, small 4to., original decorated cloth, excellent copy, cloth little soiled, extremities worn, inscribed by author for Kate Greenaway, excellent copy, cloth little soiled, extremities worn. Maggs Bros. Ltd. 1460 - 368 2013 £450

Association – Greene, Graham

Gough, J. W. *John Locke's Political Philosophy: Eight Studies.* Oxford: Clarendon Press, 1950. First edition, small label from London bookseller Blackwell's near fine, without dust jacket, Graham Greene's ownership signature, which has been lightly struck through with another name beneath it. Between the Covers Rare Books, Inc. Philosophy - 328306 2013 $350

Sinyavsky, Andrei *A Voice from the Chorus.* London: Collins, 1976. First English edition, 8vo., original green cloth, dust jacket slightly rubbed, near fine, with Graham Greene's ownership inscription and some manuscript notes in his hand and further marginal stress marks spread sparsely throughout. Maggs Bros. Ltd. 1460 - 377 2013 £350

Association – Greene, Vivien

Bayley, Nicola *One Old Oxford Ox.* London: Cape, 1977. First edition thus, large 8vo., pages not numbered, illustrations in color, pictorial paper over boards, cover slightly faded at spine, otherwise nice, Vivien Green's book from the estate of Graham Greene. Second Life Books Inc. 183 - 19 2013 $75

Greene, Graham 1904-1981 *Lord Rochester's Monkey, Being the Life of John Wilmot, Second Earl of Rochester.* London: Bodley Head, 1974. First edition, 4to., original brown cloth, dust jacket, near fine, jacket little worn at head and tail of spine, inscribed by author to his wife Vivien. Maggs Bros. Ltd. 1460 - 376 2013 £2250

Sherry, Sylvia *Girl in a Blue Shawl.* London: Hamish Hamilton, 1982. First edition, 8vo., original brown cloth, near fine in dust jacket with wraparound band and 'puff' from Grahame Greene, inscribed by author for Vivien Greene. Maggs Bros. Ltd. 1460 - 378 2013 £125

Association – Greenhill, Harold

Smollett, Tobias George 1721-1771 *The Expedition of Humphrey Clinker.* London: W. Johnston and B. Collins in Salisbury, 1671, i.e., 1771. First edition, 3 volumes, 12mo., contemporary calf (front hinge volume 1 cracked and slightly chipped at head of spine), leather titlepieces, raised bands, excellent copy, with all half titles, early ownership signature "Arch. Wilson/Dedham", old stamp of "W. C. Day" and bookplate of Chicago book collector Harold Greenhill (1893-1968) in each volume, morocco backed cloth folding case. Howard S. Mott Inc. 262 - 139 2013 $1350

Association – Greenhill, Mildred

Burgess, Gelett 1866-1951 *Goops and How to Be Them.* New York: Frederick A. Stokes, 1900. First edition, 4to., original pictorial red cloth, excellent, Mildred Greenhill/H. Bradley Martin copy.   Howard S. Mott Inc.   262 - 24   2013 $300

Stevenson, Robert Louis Balfour 1850-1894 *Treasure Island.* London: Cassell & Co., 1883. First edition, first issue, octavo, original olive green diagonal fine ribbed cloth, exceptionally fine, gilt on spine bright and fresh, the Bradley Martin copy with bookplate of Mildred Greenhill on front pastedown, chemised in quarter green morocco slipcase.   David Brass Rare Books, Inc.   Holiday 2012 Chapter Five - DB 00036   2013 $32,500

Association – Greenshields, J. Blackwood

Cervantes Saavedra, Miguel De 1547-1616 *The Life and Exploits of the Ingenious Gentleman Don Quixote de la Mancha.* London: printed for J. and R. Tonson, 1749. Second edition, 2 volumes, engraved frontispiece, 23 engraved plates, 8vo., some light browning, expertly rebacked in matching style, raised and gilt banded spines, red morocco labels, armorial bookplate of John Hallifax, Esq., Kenilworth on inner front boards, 19th century bookplate of J. Blackwood Greenshields.   Jarndyce Antiquarian Booksellers   CCIV - 86   2013   £1500

Association – Greenwood, Brian

Boumphrey, R. S. *An Armorial for Westmorland and Lonsdale.* Kendal: Titus Wilson, 1975. Limited deluxe edition, no. 30 of 35 copies, signed, original full crimson calf gilt, arms in gilt on boards, frontispiece, 4 plates and 5 pages arms, Whittingon Hall copy with bookplate of Brian dated Enid Greenwood.   R. F. G. Hollett & Son   Lake District & Cumbria - 150   2013   £150

Hudleston, C. Roy *An Armorial for Westmorland and Lonsdale.* Kendal: Titus Wilson, 1975. Signed, limited deluxe edition, no. 30 of 35 copies, original full crimson calf gilt, arms gilt on boards, frontispiece, 4 plates, 5 pages of arms, Whittington Hall copy with bookplate of Brian and Enid Greenwood.   R. F. G. Hollett & Son   Lake District and Cumbria - 301   2013   £150

Association – Greenwood, Enid

Boumphrey, R. S. *An Armorial for Westmorland and Lonsdale.* Kendal: Titus Wilson, 1975. Limited de luxe edition, no. 30 of 35 copies, signed, original full crimson calf gilt, arms in gilt on boards, frontispiece, 4 plates and 5 pages arms, Whittingon Hall copy with bookplate of Brian dated Enid Greenwood.   R. F. G. Hollett & Son   Lake District & Cumbria - 150   2013   £150

Hudleston, C. Roy *An Armorial for Westmorland and Lonsdale.* Kendal: Titus Wilson, 1975. Signed, limited deluxe edition, no. 30 of 35 copies, original full crimson calf gilt, arms gilt on boards, frontispiece, 4 plates, 5 pages of arms, Whittington Hall copy with bookplate of Brian and Enid Greenwood.   R. F. G. Hollett & Son   Lake District and Cumbria - 301   2013   £150

Association – Greenwood, Frederick

Opie, Amelia Alderson *Illustrations of Lying In all Its Branches.* London: Longman, 1825. Second edition, 2 volumes, slight spotting, contemporary half maron roan, slight rubbing, armorial bookplate of Frederick Greenwood, attractive copy.   Jarndyce Antiquarian Booksellers CCV - 216   2013   £100

Association – Gregg, Frederick James

Yeats, William Butler 1865-1939 *The Golden Helmet.* New York: 1908. First edition, 25/50 copies, light waterstaining to bottom third of text, 16mo., original grey boards, rebacked to match, printed label on front cover, grey endpapers, untrimmed, protective dark blue cloth box with printed label, good, inscribed by author to friend Frederick James Gregg, schoolmate of Yeats.   Blackwell's Rare Books   172 - 252   2013   £3000

Association – Gregory, Augusta

Gaskell, Elizabeth Cleghorn 1810-1865 *Cranford.* London: Macmillan, 1891. First reprint, 8vo., original green cloth, excellent copy, cloth just little marked and scuffed, inscribed by Lady Augusta Gregory for Arabella Waithman, Dec. 25 1981.   Maggs Bros. Ltd.   1460 - 379   2013   £250

Association – Gregory, J.

Whytt, Robert *Observations on Nature, Causes and Cure of Those Diseases Which Have Been Commonly called Nervous Hypochondriac or Hysteric.* Edinburgh: T. Beckett and P. du Hondt, 1765. New full calf, stamp on title, text foxed in parts, author's presentation copy for Jo. Gregory 1765.   James Tait Goodrich   75 - 224   2013 $2795

Association – Grenfell, Ettie

Tynan, Katharine 1861-1931 *The Holy War.* London: Sidgwick and Jackson, 1916. First edition, small 8vo., original blue cloth, paper label to spine, inscribed by author for Ettie Grenfell, with library label of Taplow Court, spine label slightly nicked, otherwise excellent.   Maggs Bros. Ltd.   1442 - 309   2013   £125

Association – Grey, Ida

Grey, Zane 1872-1939 *The Vanishing American.* New York: Harper, 1925. First edition, 8vo., very good++ with mild cover edge wear, offsetting to endpapers, very good+ price clipped dust jacket with edgewear, mild soil, small corner chips, signed, inscribed and dated by author to his sister, Ida.   By the Book, L. C.   38 - 34   2013 $1750

Association – Grien, J.

Wotton, Henry *Reliquiae Wottonianae; or a Collection of Lives, Letters, Poems.* London: by T. Roycroft for R. Marriott, 1672. Third edition, 8vo., portraits, 19th century red morocco, early signatures of J. Grien? 1725, Thomas Price and John Francis Cole, 1828, bookplates of J. J. Chapman and Molly Flagg Gibb, very good.   Joseph J. Felcone Inc.   English and American Literature to 1800 - 26   2013 $900

Association – Guerreiro, Dr.

Montesquieu, Charles Louis de Secondat, Baron De La Brede *Oeuvres. Tome Premier - Tome Cinquieme.* Paris: Plassan, Regent Bernard et Gregoire, 1796. 5 volumes, 4to., frontispiece and 2 folding maps to volume I and 13 further engraved copper plates, second map little foxed, some very occasional light underlining, small closed tears to only a few margins, contemporary tan marbled calf, dark green and brown morocco labels and gilt to spines, gilt borders and dentelles, all edges gilt, pink marbled endpapers, boards scratched with areas of surface loss repaired or colored to blend in, endcaps worn, joints worn with volume I upper starting to split a little, ownership inscriptions of Dr. Guerreiro to initial blanks or half titles.   Unsworths Antiquarian Booksellers   28 - 116   2013   £2000

Association – Guest, John

Adams, Richard *Watership Down.* London: Penguin Books, 1976. First illustrated edition, large 8vo., original cloth backed boards, dust jacket, slipcase, inscribed by author to his editor, John Guest, further signed on dedication page by dedicatee, the author's daughter, Rosamund Adams, near fine in dust jacket, edges lightly browned.   Maggs Bros. Ltd.   1460 - 8   2013   £675

Association – Gurney, J. H.

Andersson, Charles John *Notes on the Birds of Damara Land and the Adjacent Countries of South-West Africe.* John van Voorst, 1872. First edition, original green blind panelled cloth, gilt, spine slightly worn and scraped at head ad foot, frontispiece map, 4 lithographed plates, presentation from editor, J. H. Gurney to his friend Jules Verraux (1807-1873), engraved bookplates on endpapers of David Simson of Ickleford.   R. F. G. Hollett & Son   Africana - 2   2013   £450

Association – Gurney, Mr.

Paine, Thomas 1737-1809 *Letters from... to the Citizens of America, After an Absence of Fifteen Years in Europe.* London: printed by and for T. C. Rickman, 1804. First edition, 8vo., titlepage browning at head and with two largish brown spots, disbound, inscribed "From the Editor to Mr. Gurney", good.   Blackwell's Rare Books   172 - 106   2013   £1100

Association – Gurney, W. M.

Gurney, Ivor *Severn and Somme.* London: Sidgwick & Jackson, 1917. First edition, 8vo., original red cloth, printed label on spine, excellent copy, spine faded, inner hinges splitting, ownership signature of W. M. Gurney.   Maggs Bros. Ltd.   1460 - 386   2013   £600

Association – Guyt, Corrie

Cox, Morris *From a London Suburb.* London: Gogmagog Press, 1975. Copy number 2 of 24 copies, numbered and signed by author on colophon, double page spread titlepage reverse offset print from lace and four reverse/direct offset prints on colored papers, Corrie Guyt's copy printed on Japanese handmade Yamato-Chiri and Mingei papers, bound in green silk boards with acetate dust jacket, laid in is long TLS 1 page 4to. 28 Nov. 1975 from author to Guyt, very fine.   James S. Jaffe Rare Books   Fall 2013 - 60   2013 $1250

Association – Gwynn, Edward

Norden, John *A Mirror for the Multitude, or Glasse, Wherein Maie be Seene the Violence, the Error, the Weakness and Rash Content of the Multitude and the Dangerous Resolution of Such as Without Regard of the Truth...* London: printed by John Windet, 1586. First edition, 8vo., ornate border to titlepage, headpieces and some woodcut initials, printer's waste used as r.f.e.p., small marginal hole to titlepage, little dampstaining to bottom margin page 49 onwards, few spots and smudges, 17th century brown calf, small paper label to spine, blind tooled triple fillet to spine and borders, single gilt fillet to edges 'Edward Gwynn' in gilt to upper board and initials E.G. to lower board, joints little creased, upper inner hinge splitting a little but binding strong, endpapers soiled, small label pasted to bottom of titlepage reading "Ex Bibliotheca . Cl. Eusebii Renaudot quam Monasterio sancti Germani a Pratis legacvit anno Domini 1720", also to titlepage in ink, E. 1714 and old MS note opposite.   Unsworths Antiquarian Booksellers   28 - 118   2013   £3000

Association – Gwynn, Stephen

Gibson, Wilfrid *Challenge.* London: Oxford University Press, 1942. First edition, 8vo., original red wrappers, near fine, protective folding box, inscribe by author to Stephen Gwynn. Maggs Bros. Ltd. 1460 - 337 2013 £125

Association – Habgood, R.

Heyrick, Thomas *Miscellany Poems.* Cambridge: by John Hayes for the author, 1691. Woodcut alma mater device, 4to., late 19th century half morocco, hinges lightly scuffed some foxing and light browning, chiefly on first and last few pages and largely confined to margins, small piece from upper corner of titlepage, short marginal tear on K1, signature of Rd Habgood 1774 on titlepage. Joseph J. Felcone Inc. Books Printed before 1701 - 51 2013 $3000

Association – Haddon, J. L.

Sterne, Laurence 1713-1768 *A Sentimental Journey through France and Italy.* for T. Osborne, in St. Paul's Church-Yard and J. Mozley, in Gainsborough, 1784. 12mo., 4 volumes complete in one, frontispiece, very good in full contemporary calf, raised and gilt banded spine with original ted gilt morocco label, head and tail of spine slightly chipped, early booklabel of "J. L. Haddon" and signature of same on titlepage. Ken Spelman Books Ltd. 75 - 40 2013 £200

Association – Hadley, Garrison

Sage, Betty *Rhymes of Real Children.* New York: Fox Duffield, Oct., 1903. First edition, Large square 4to. cloth backed pictorial boards, tips and edges lightly rubbed, else fine, illustrations by Jessie Willcox Smith, mounted on front endpaper is charming 2 page typed poem signed by William Lloyd Garrison Jr. dedicating the book and poem to recipient Garrison Hadley, great copy. Aleph-Bet Books, Inc. 104 - 541 2013 $675

Association – Hague, Michael

Baum, Lyman Frank *The Wizard of Oz.* New York: Holt, 1982. 4to., pictorial boards mint in dust jacket, illustrations by Michael Hague, with color illustrations, signed by Hague with wonderful drawing of an Oz character. Aleph-Bet Books, Inc. 105 - 64 2013 $325

Association – Hailstone, Edward

Baines, Edward *A Companion to the Lakes of Cumberland, Westmoreland and Lancashire...* London: Hurst, Chance and Co., 1829. First edition, original cloth, paper spine label, boards rather marked, spine faded and joints cracked but firm, lacks folding map, errata slip tipped in, Edward Hailstone's copy with his label, very scare. R. F. G. Hollett & Son Lake District & Cumbria - 60 2013 £150

Association – Haining, Peter

Doherty, Hugh *The Discovery; or the Mysterious Separation of Hugh Doherty, Esq. and Ann His Wife.* London: sold at no. 12, Temple Place &c, 1807. Third edition, 12mo., illustrations, slight spotting and occasional small marginal tears, contemporary marbled boards, later tan calf spine, gilt ands and compartments, maroon morocco label, signature of author Hugh Doherty on title, very slightly trimmed through, additional signature of J. Wolus, Rysbrooke, 1878, recent bookplate of Peter Haining. Jarndyce Antiquarian Booksellers CCV - 93 2013 £580

Association – Hall, Cayton

Boumphrey, R. S. *Armorial for Westmorland and Lonsdale.* Lake District Museum Trust and CWAAS, 1975. Original crimson rexine gilt, frontispiece and 5 pages illustrations, inscribed by Roy Hudleston for his cousin Cayton Hall and dated Ambleside 1 Sept. 1976. R. F. G. Hollett & Son Lake District & Cumbria - 149 2013 £65

Association – Hall, Thomas

Lardner, Dionysius *Hand-Book of Natural Philosophy: Hydrostatics, Pneumatics and Heat.* London: Walton and Maberly, 1855. First edition, 181 x 114mm., appealing contemporary published calf presentation binding, covers with double gilt rule border with floral cornerpieces and inner frame of blind dotted rule, upper cover with gilt insignia of school of the City of London, raised bands, spine densely gilt in compartments with large and intricate central fleuron and curling cornerpieces maroon morocco label, marbled edges and endpapers, frontispiece and 292 illustrations; ink inscription "2nd Prize for proficiency in Writing awarded to John Debney, Thos. Hall BA Master of the First Class July 1858", joints and extremities slightly rubbed, hinge open at titlepage (but no structural fragility), other trivial imperfections internally, but excellent copy, text clean, fresh and smooth, decorative binding sturdy and not without charm. Phillip J. Pirages 63 - 307 2013 $125

Association – Hallady, Louis

Jenner, Edward *Further Observations on the Varioale Vaccinae or Cow Pox.* London: printed for the author by Sampson Low, 1799. First edition, Half title, title, (6), 64 pages, 4to., uncut, large wide margins, light dampstaining affected outer margins, browned in parts, original blue sugar wrappers, lacking rear one, clamshell protective case, with ALS circa 1800 to Louis Hallady and Rev. W. H. C. Boggs and signed Z. Lewis. Rob. Hart.   James Tait Goodrich   75 - 125   2013 $4500

Association – Hallam, C. J.

Dickens, Charles   1812-1870 *Little Dorrit.* London: Bradbury and Evans, 1857. First bookform edition, frontispiece and title and 38 etched plates by Phiz, plates generally somewhat spotted, as usual with dampstains in lower outer corners (plates only, not text), 8vo., contemporary half green calf, spine richly gilt, red lettering piece, minor shelfwear, contemporary ownership inscription of C. J. Hallam, early 20th century M. A. Hallam below this and below this inscription of Dorrit W. Fountain, Christmas 1922, good.   Blackwell's Rare Books   B174 - 46   2013   £300

Association – Hallam, M. A.

Dickens, Charles   1812-1870 *Little Dorrit.* London: Bradbury and Evans, 1857. First bookform edition, frontispiece and title and 38 etched plates by Phiz, plates generally somewhat spotted, as usual with dampstains in lower outer corners (plates only, not text), 8vo., contemporary half green calf, spine richly gilt, red lettering piece, minor shelfwear, contemporary ownership inscription of C. J. Hallam, early 20th century M. A. Hallam below this and below this inscription of Dorrit W. Fountain, Christmas 1922, good.   Blackwell's Rare Books   B174 - 46   2013   £300

Association – Hallifax, John

Cervantes Saavedra, Miguel De   1547-1616 *The Life and Exploits of the Ingenious Gentleman Don Quixote de la Mancha.* London: printed for J. and R. Tonson, 1749. Second edition, 2 volumes, engraved frontispiece, 23 engraved plates, 8vo., some light browning, expertly rebacked in matching style, raised and gilt banded spines, red morocco labels, armorial bookplate of John Hallifax, Esq., Kenilworth on inner front boards, 19th century bookplate of J. Blackwood Greenshields.   Jarndyce Antiquarian Booksellers   CCIV - 86   2013   £1500

Association – Halloway, M. A.

Swieten, Gerard Van *The Commentaries Upon the Aphorisms of Dr. Herman Boerhaave.* London: John and Paul Knapton and Robert Horsfield & Thomas Longman, 1744-1765. 10 of 18 volumes, lacking volumes 3, 11, 13-18, small 8vo., frontispiece in volume 12, folding plates in volume 4, occasional worm tracks slightly affecting text, original brown calf, gilt ruled covers, raised bands, gilt stamped red leather spine labels, few hinges weak or starting, ownership signature William Clapham and few volumes signed M. A. Halloway.   Jeff Weber Rare Books   172 - 34   2013 $1700

Association – Hamady, Walter

Duncan, Robert *Six Prose Pieces.* Rochester: Perishable Press Ltd., 1966. First edition, special issue, one of only 15 copies printed on handmade paper made by Walter Hamady, the printer/publisher, signed by Duncan, out of a total edition of 70 copies, illustrations by author, unbound folded & gathered signatures, natural linen cloth chemise, facsimile signature printed in red, matching slipcase, presentation copy from author inscribed and signed in full by Duncan for Hamady, slipcase very slightly soiled otherwise fine, scarce.   James S. Jaffe Rare Books   Fall 2013 - 44   2013 $6000

Association – Hamblen, William Henry Smith, Viscount

Defoe, Daniel *The Dyet of Poland, a Satyr.* printed at Dantzick, 1705. 4to. some light spotting and browning, few small expert paper repairs, bound by Riviere in full crushed red morocco, elaborate gilt borders and dentelles, raised bands, gilt compartments, armorial bookplate of William Henry Smith, Viscount Hambleden, all edges gilt, very good, handsome.   Jarndyce Antiquarian Booksellers   CCIV - 107   2013   £850

Association – Hamilton, E.

Wordsworth, William   1770-1850 *Yarrow Revisited and Other Poems.* London: Longman, Rees, Orme, Brown, Green and Longman, 1835. First edition, presentation copy, inscribed by author to Eliza M. Hamilton as a token of affectionate esteem from W. M. Wordsworth on a slip of paper pasted to verso of title and with "From the Author" written on half title by publisher's clerk, erratum slip tipped in, ads discarded, 12mo., slightly later 19th century olive pebble grain morocco by Tuckett ('binder to the Queen'), backstrip panelled and ruled in gilt and infilled with volutes and other tools, lettered in gilt in second compartment, sides with triple gilt fillet borders, inner panel with cornerpieces and central panels of curving lines, all edges gilt, marbled endpapers, booklabel of J. O. Edwards, small scrape to upper board, extremities slightly rubbed, good.   Blackwell's Rare Books   B174 - 159   2013   £3500

Association – Hamilton, G.

Coleridge, Samuel Taylor 1772-1834 *The Poetical Works.* London: William Pickering, Reprint of 1834 edition, 3 volumes, 16 page catalog in volume 1, original dark blue cloth, paper labels, spine little faded and slightly marked, G. Hamilton booklabels, nice. Jarndyce Antiquarian Booksellers CCIII - 492 2013 £90

Association – Hamilton, William

Wilberforce, William *A Practical View of the Prevailing Religious System of Professed Christians, in the Higher Middle Classes in this Country, Contrasted with Real Christianity.* London: T. Cadell and W. Davies, 1805. Eighth edition, 8vo., few leaves foxed, some light browning, full contemporary tree calf, gilt ruled spine, red morocco label, leading hinge cracked but firm, slight wear, early ownership name of Wm. Hamilton (Clerk of Hoole, Cheshire), nice copy. Jarndyce Antiquarian Booksellers CCIV - 313 2013 £85

Association – Hamilton, Yvonne

Auden, Wystan Hugh 1907-1973 *Collected Shorter Poems 1930-1944.* London: Faber & Faber, 1950. First edition, 8vo., original blue cloth, spine very slightly faded, as is top inch of lower cover, inscribed by author for Yvonne Hamilton. Maggs Bros. Ltd. 1460 - 26 2013 £300

Capote, Truman 1924-1985 *The Grass Harp.* London: Heinemann, 1952. First UK edition, 8vo., original brown cloth, inscribed by author for Yvonne Hamilton, with her ownership signature, excellent copy. Maggs Bros. Ltd. 1460 - 157 2013 £2500

Capote, Truman 1924-1985 *Other Voices Other Rooms.* London: Heinemann, 1948. First UK edition, 8vo., original brown cloth, excellent copy, inscribed by author for Yvonne Hamilton, with her ownership signature. Maggs Bros. Ltd. 1460 - 156 2013 £2000

Connolly, Cyril 1903-1974 *Previous Convictions.* London: Hamish Hamilton, 1963. First edition, large 8vo., original blue cloth, near fine in dust jacket slightly browned on spine, inscribed by author for Yvonne Hamilton. Maggs Bros. Ltd. 1460 - 188 2013 £450

Association – Hammond, John

The History of Ripon; with Descriptions of Studley-Royal, Fountains' Abbey, Newby, Hackfall &c &c. Ripon: W. Farrer, 1806. Second edition, 314 pages, aquatint frontispiece and woodcuts in text, very good, contemporary half calf, marbled boards, raised gilt bands, blindstamped decoration in each compartment, foolscap 8vo., signature of John Hammond 24th August 1863, later bookplates of Chapman-Purchas and R. J. Rattray. Ken Spelman Books Ltd. 73 - 142 2013 £120

Association – Hammond, William

Blackwell, Thomas *An Enquiry into the Life and Writings of Homer.* London: printed for J. Oswald in the year, 1736. Second edition, 8vo., engraved frontispiece, folding engraved map, lightly spotted in places, corner of one leaf torn just touching page number, contemporary sprinkled and polished calf, spine divided by gilt rules, edges sprinkled red, lightly rubbed, slightly worn at endcaps and corners, few small scrapes to boards, armorial bookplate of William Hammond Esqr. of East Kent, contemporary inscription "Will= Hammond" at upper forecorner of titlepage. Unsworths Antiquarian Booksellers 28 - 6 2013 £125

Association – Handerson, H. E.

Baas, J. H. *Outlines of the History of Medicine and the Medical Profession.* New York: Vail, 1889. First English edition, 1173 pages, original cloth, inner hinges just starting to split, light rubbing, otherwise good, tight copy, translator's presentation from H. E. Handerson to Dr. G. H. Monks. James Tait Goodrich 75 - 14 2013 $495

Association – Hanna, Justice

Gogarty, Oliver St. John 1878-1957 *As I Was Going Down Sackville Street.* London: Rich & Cowan, 1937. First reprint, 8vo., original green cloth, this book was the subject of famous Dublin legal suit taken against the author by the brothers William and Harry Sinclair who felt that they had been libelled in the book, ownership copy of the presiding judge in the case, Mr. Justice Hanna with his inked signature and clipping tipped-in to rear with account of opening of the trial from The Irish Times June 8 1937. Maggs Bros. Ltd. 1460 - 345 2013 £450

Association – Hanrott, P. A.

Lefevre, Raoul *Le Recueil des Histoires de Troyes.* Bruges: William Caxton, 1473. First edition in French, small folio, Lettre batarde, lacking 32 printed leaves and two blanks, early 19th century brown straight grain morocco by Charles Lewis, gilt and blind ruled in geometric patterns, gilt inner dentelles, gilt edges, fine, unrestored, the missing leaves are internal and first and last printed leaves are present from the collection of the Duke of Roxburghe (sale 1812) of the third Earl Spencer (sale 1823), John Dent, with his notes (sale 1827), P. A. Hanrott (sale 1834) the Earl of Ashburnham (sale 1897); Richard Bennett with his bookplate and John Pierpont Morgan with his bookplate and shelfmark. Heritage Book Shop 50th Anniversary Catalogue - 62 2013 $950,000

Association – Harbin

Bailey, Nathan *Dictionarium Rusticum, Urbanicum & Botanicum; or a Dictionary of Husbandry...* London: printed for James and John Knapton, 1726. 2 engraved plates, repair and little worn along leading edge, numerous woodcuts in text, 8vo., contemporary panelled calf, raised bands, hinges slightly cracked but very firm, some wear, contemporary name Harbin on each front endpaper. Jarndyce Antiquarian Booksellers CCIV - 54 2013 £580

Association – Hardwicke, Earl of

Wheelwright, C. A. *Poems, Original and Translated...* A. J. Valpy, 1810. 8vo., uncut, original boards, worn, covers detached, Earl of Hardwicke's copy, later in the library of John Sparrow, with tipped-in printed slip requesting subscribers to pay for their copies on delivery. Ken Spelman Books Ltd. 75 - 66 2013 £35

Association – Hardy, Florence

Hardy, Thomas 1840-1928 *Selected Poems of...* London: Liverpool and Boston: the Medici Society, 1921. First Medici Society edition, number 313 of 1000 numbered copies, signed by Hardy with his holograph note, laid in is note sent Feb. 21 1928 from Florence Hardy to Lucy Chew of Bryn Mawr, PA, 8vo., original tan cloth spine, blue boards and printed paper labels, frontispiece, engraved titlepage, fine in original printed dust jacket, slightly faded and enclosed in chemise and quarter morocco slipcase, from the Gary Lepper Collection of Thomas Hardy. The Brick Row Book Shop Bulletin Nine - 67 2013 $3750

Association – Hardy, Thomas

Griersn, Francis *Modern Mysticism and Other Essays.* London: George Allen, 1899. First edition, 12mo., original green cloth, gilt lettering, cloth waterstained, very good, from Thomas Hardy's library with his posthumous Max Gate bookplate and his signature, tipped to front free endpaper is printed presentation slip from publisher, George Allen, from the Gary Lepper Collection of Thomas Hardy. The Brick Row Book Shop Bulletin Nine - 43 2013 $750

Association – Hare, H. P. C.

Conrad, Joseph 1857-1924 *The Rover.* London: T. Fisher & Unwin, 1924. Fourth impression, 8vo., original green vertically ribbed cloth, spine and upper cover lettered in gilt, good copy, little waterstaining at foot of front cover, inscribed by author for H. P. C. Hare. Maggs Bros. Ltd. 1460 - 191 2013 £500

Association – Hare, Julius Charles

Ramsay, Allan *The Ever Green.* Edinburgh: printed for Alexander Donaldson, 1761. 12mo., 2 volumes, frontispiece, contents leaf to volume II misbound at end of volume I, some slight dusting and foxing, generally very clean, rather tightly, in 19th century dark green cloth, gilt bands & lettering to spines, 19th century armorial bookplate of Julius Charles Hare 1795-1855, ownership label of Maurice Powell. Jarndyce Antiquarian Booksellers CCIV - 249 2013 £85

Association – Harmon, Ransom

Morrell, L. A. *The American Shepherd: being a History of the Sheep, with their Breeds, Management and Diseases.* New York: Harper and Bros., 1850. 8vo., illustrations, original cloth, minor chipping to ends of spine, foxed, this copy was awarded to Ransom Harmon for best black lambs by B. P. Janson, Rochester, NY 1857. M & S Rare Books, Inc. 95 - 340 2013 $100

Association – Harper, Lucius

Johnson, Jack *Johnson - In the Ring - and Out.* Chicago: National Sports Pub. Co., 1927. First edition, very near fine, lacking dust jacket, inscribed by Lucius C. Harper, editor of newspaper The Chicago Defender to Bettise Stalling. Between the Covers Rare Books, Inc. 165 - 17 2013 $850

Association – Harris, John Francis

Lamartine, Alphonse *Memoirs of Celebrated Characters.* London: Richard Bentley, 1858. Third edition, 187 x 12mm., most appealing 19th century light tan highly polished half calf, raised bands decorated with gilt floral roll, spines richly gilt in double ruled compartments with volute cornerpieces and central pomegranate surrounded by small tools, marbled sides and endpapers, bookplate of John Francis Harris in each volume, small handful of leaves lightly toned, corners just little rubbed, quite pretty set in nearly fine condition, text clean and fresh, attractive decorative binding scarce worn and especially lustrous.   Phillip J. Pirages   63 - 305   2013 $450

Association – Harrison, Henrietta

Briggs, John *The Remains of John Briggs...* Kirkby Lonsdale: printed and sold by Arthur Foster, 1825. First edition, old half calf gilt, neatly recased, original backstrip cracked but laid down, pages 408, half title and subscriber list, excellent copy, near contemporary inscription of Henrietta Harrison dated April 1826.   R. F. G. Hollett & Son Lake District & Cumbria - 176   2013   £395

Association – Harrison, Kathleen

Rattigan, Terence *The Winslow Boy.* London: Hamish Hamilton, 1946. First edition, 8vo. 109 pages, very good, signed by 10 f the 11 cast members of the first London production, including Kathleen Harrison, Emelyn Williams, Michael Newell, etc.   Second Life Books Inc.   183 - 330   2013 $350

Association – Harrison, Thomas

Byron, George Gordon Noel, 6th Baron   1788-1824 *English Bards and Scotch Reviewers.* London: printed for James Cawthorn and Sharpe and Hailes, 1811. Fourth edition, complete with half title, printed on stiff paper, watermarked 'J. Whatman/1805', 8vo., contemporary blue straight grained morocco, single gilt fillet on sides, spine gilt with lyre in each compartment, lettered gilt direct in one compartment, armorial bookplate of Thomas Harrison on top of what may be another bookplate on inside front cover, excellent, elegant copy.   Blackwell's Rare Books   B174 - 21   2013   £300

Association – Harrison, William

Clarke, Edward Daniel *The Life and Remains of the Rev. Edward Daniel Clarke, LLD.* London: printed for George Cowie and Co., 1824. First edition, 4to., some foxing to frontispiece, titlepage and subscriber list, contemporary sprinkled calf, gilt ruled border, attractive gilt decorated spine, red morocco label, expert repairs to hinges, corners and head and tail of spine, armorial bookplate of William Harrison.   Jarndyce Antiquarian Booksellers   CCIV - 94   2013   £380

Association – Hart, Gerald

Bagnold, Enid *The Loved and Envied.* London: Heinemann, 1951. First edition, 8vo., original black cloth, dust jacket, inscribed by author for Gerald Hart, near fine in slightly nicked dust jacket, rear inner flap price clipped.   Maggs Bros. Ltd.   1460 - 30   2013   £100

Association – Hart, J. N.

De La Mare, Walter   1873-1956 *On the Edge.* London: Faber and Faber, 1930. First edition, one of 300 numbered copies signed by author, this one additionally inscribed to J. N. Hart, tall 8vo., original red cloth, excellent copy, wood engravings by Elizabeth Rivers.   Maggs Bros. Ltd.   1460 - 213   2013   £150

Association – Hart, James

James, Henry   1843-1916 *The Reverberator.* London and New York: Macmillan and Co., 1888. Second edition, American issue, 184 x 127mm., 2 p.l., 229, (1) pages, publisher's original blue cloth with gilt titling and decoration, half title with ink ownership inscription "Kate D. Wilson, Jan. 26th 189(0)", bookplate inscribed "Capt. James Hart, Baltimore 26 Feb. (19)46", spine slightly rolled, tiny snag at top of backstrip and one at bottom, light rubbing to small portions of joints and extremities, still nearly fine, cloth and gilt especially bright, hinges solid, text with virtually no signs of use.   Phillip J. Pirages   63 - 263   2013 $250

Association – Hartmann, Hjalmar

Saxo Grammaticus *Danorum Regum Heroumque Historiae...* Paris: Jodocus Badius Ascensius, 1514. Rare first edition, folio, bound without final blank leaf, title printed in red within architectural woodcut border enclosing a woodcut of the Danish king at head of his army, fine woodcut crible initials, including several specially designed for the book incorporating a portrait of the King of Demark and the royal arms; early 18th century limp vellum with leather ties, spine lettered gilt on rose wash panel, edges stained blue, title border shaved at head, some minor mostly marginal worming, few marginal stains, early ink inscription of Christianus Torndallius, Helsing; Danorum (Elsinore) and another early ink inscription, bookplate of Hjalmar Hartmann, some scattered early ink marginalia and underlining, overall excellent copy.   Heritage Book Shop   50th Anniversary Catalogue - 86   2013 $20,000

Association – Harvey, Elizabeth

The Florence Miscellany. Florence: (privately) printed for G(aetano) Cam.(biagi)..., 1785. 224 pages, 3 leaves of engraved music within pagination, 8vo., some light foxing, mainly to prelims, bound in 20th century full light brown morocco in period style by Philip Dusel, gilt spine and dentelles, near contemporary signature of Eliz. Harvey. Jarndyce Antiquarian Booksellers CCIV - 230 2013 £2600

Association – Harvey, John

Rowntree, B. Seebohm *Poverty and Progress. A Second Social Survey of York.* London: Longmans, 1941. First edition, very good, original gilt lettered dark blue cloth, dust jacket little worn, inscribed 'a gift from Arnold Rowntree, Ernest Taylor, John Harvey, Oct. 1941'. Ken Spelman Books Ltd. 73 - 54 2013 £35

Association – Harvey, Margaret

Harvey, William Fryer *Midnight House and Other Tales.* London: Dent, 1910. First edition, title printed in red, prelims and final leaves lightly foxed, 16mo., original lime green boards, printed label and darkened backstrip little rubbed, free endpapers browned, untrimmed, good, inscribed with love of Margaret Harvey Xmas 1937. Blackwell's Rare Books B174 - 219 2013 £285

Association – Hathaway, Lowering

Cushing, Harvey Williams 1869-1939 *From a Surgeon's Journal 1915-1918.* Boston: Little Brown, 1936. First edition, deluxe issue signed by author, 8vo., frontispiece foxed, 34 illustrations, gilt stamped navy blue cloth, signed by previous owner Lowering Hathaway 1936, very good. Jeff Weber Rare Books 172 - 61 2013 $2000

Association – Hawkesbury

Hawkesbury, Lord *The Heraldry on the Gateway at Kirkham Abbey.* n.p.: 1902. 8vo., good copy, 8vo., contemporary half red calf, spine rubbed, bookplate of Hawkesbury. Ken Spelman Books Ltd. 73 - 112 2013 £25

Association – Hawkins, M. E.

Coleridge, Samuel Taylor 1772-1834 *Omniana; or Horae Otiosiores.* London: Longman &c., 1812. First edition, 2 volumes, odd spot, small tear from corner of leading f.e.p., contemporary full diced calf, excellent rebacked, slightly rubbed, booklabels of Kathleen Coburn, neat signatures of M. E. Hawkins. Jarndyce Antiquarian Booksellers CCIII - 524 2013 £200

Association – Hay, David

Blackmore, Richard 1654-1729 *A Treatise of Consumptions and Other Distempers Belonging to the Breast and Lungs.* London: John Pemberton, 1724. First edition, 8vo., original full polished calf, five raised spine bands, white spine library number, leather worn and discolored, spine ends chipped, top right front corner and lower spine edges torn, bookplate remnants, rear pastedown glue spots, bookplate of Dr. Morris Parker, formerly of Chicago Medical School, titlepage signature of David Hay(?), holograph table of contents at free endpaper, small recipe at rear free endpaper, very good, rare. Jeff Weber Rare Books 172 - 32 2013 $1850

Association – Hayden, Henri

Beckett, Samuel 1906-1989 *Fin de Partie Suivi de Acte sans Paroles.* Paris: Les Editions de Minuit, 1957. First edition, 8vo., original white wrappers, lettered black and blue, fore and bottom edges uncut, all over little browned, inscribed by author for Henri et Josette Hayden, very good. Maggs Bros. Ltd. 1442 - 15 2013 £1750

Beckett, Samuel 1906-1989 *Nouvelles et Textes pour Rien.* Paris: Les Editions de Minuit, 1955. One of 1000 numbered copies, first edition, 8vo., original white wrappers, lettered in black and blue, spine browned, fore and bottom edges uncut, inscribed by author for Henri et Josette Hayden, covers slightly browned, otherwise very good. Maggs Bros. Ltd. 1442 - 13 2013 £1000

Beckett, Samuel 1906-1989 *Watt. Roman.* Paris: Les Editions de Minuit, 1968. First French edition, 8vo., very good in original white wrappers, lettered in black and blue, spine little sunned, very good, inscribed by author for Henri et Josette (Hayden). Maggs Bros. Ltd. 1442 - 18 2013 £1000

Association – Hayden, Josette

Beckett, Samuel 1906-1989 *Fin de Partie Suivi de Acte sans Paroles.* Paris: Les Editions de Minuit, 1957. First edition, 8vo., original white wrappers, lettered black and blue, fore and bottom edges uncut, all over little browned, inscribed by author for Henri et Josette Hayden, very good. Maggs Bros. Ltd. 1442 - 15 2013 £1750

Beckett, Samuel 1906-1989 *Nouvelles et Textes pour Rien.* Paris: Les Editions de Minuit, 1955. One of 1000 numbered copies, first edition, 8vo., original white wrappers, lettered in black and blue, spine browned, fore and bottom edges uncut, inscribed by author for Henri et Josette Hayden, covers slightly browned, otherwise very good. Maggs Bros. Ltd. 1442 - 13 2013 £1000

Beckett, Samuel   1906-1989 *Watt. Roman.*   Paris: Les Editions de Minuit, 1968.   First French edition, 8vo., very good in original white wrappers, lettered in black and blue, spine little sunned, very good, inscribed by author for Henri et Josette (Hayden).   Maggs Bros. Ltd.   1442 - 18   2013   £1000

Association – Hayhurst, Thomas

Raddall, Thomas H. *Saga of the Rover.* Liverpool: Mersey Paper Co., 1931.   First edition, 2nd issue, without ad for paper company in front, limited to 250, small 8vo., decorated vellum boards and map endpapers, frontispiece plus 9 other plates, piece of vellum missing from top of spine and inner and outer hinge cracks and two small brown spots to front cover, obituary of Thomas W. Hayhurst attached to Raddall & Jones on back of titlepage.   Schooner Books Ltd.   104 - 103   2013 $200

Association – Hazard, J. B.

Facetiae Facetiarum hoc est Joco-Seriorum Fasciculus, Exhibens Varia Variorum Auctorum Scripta non tam Lectu Iucunda and Iocosa Amoena... Francofurti: ad Moenum, 1615.   16mo., contemporary calf with raised bands, gilt spine, edges stained red, titlepage printed in red and black, some mid-17th century listings of the book being offered for sale on front blank, from the library of J. B. Hazard, contemporary ownership signature.   Second Life Books Inc.   183 - 136   2013 $950

Association – Headfort, Marquess of

Colman, George   1732-1794 *Broad Grins...* London: T. Cadell & W. Davies, 1809.   Fourth edition, engraved title, woodcuts, contemporary full red grained calf, gilt spine and borders, little rubbed, and worn and slight worming at head of leading hinge, Marquess of Headfort's armorial bookplate, all edges gilt, good, sound.   Jarndyce Antiquarian Booksellers   CCIII - 662 2013   £40

Gamba, Peter *A Narrative of Lord Byron's Last Journey to Greece.* London: John Murray, 1825.   First edition, half title, 2 folding facsimiles, uncut in original pale blue boards, drab spine, paper label, corners bumped, spine little worn and chipped, with loss at tail, Marquess of Headfort's armorial bookplate, good plus.   Jarndyce Antiquarian Booksellers   CCIII - 386   2013   £220

Hoyle, Edmund *The Polite Gamester.* Dublin: printed by James Hoey, 1786.   12mo., slight browning, few corners little creased, full contemporary calf, raised bands, red morocco label of Marquess of Headfort, nice.   Jarndyce Antiquarian Booksellers   CCIV - 164   2013   £320

Hutcheson, Francis *An Essay on the Nature and conduct of the Passions and Affections.* London: printed for A. Ward, 1742.   Third edition, 8vo., full contemporary calf, raised bands, red morocco label, slight wear to upper hinge, small scratch to rear board, armorial bookplate of Marquess of Headfort, very good.   Jarndyce Antiquarian Booksellers   CCV - 143   2013   £380

La Calprenede, Gaultier De Cost, Seigneur De *Hymen's Praeludia; or Love's Master-Piece.* printed for Ralph Smith, 1698.   Title with double rules, occasional paper flaw, rust or other small holes with loss of odd letter, minor ink, wax of other stains, few leaves foxed, slightly browned in places, final ad leaf discarded, folio in 4's, near contemporary mottled calf rebacked, corners worn, inscription on flyleaf recording purchase of it on 3 Oct. 1699 for 18/6, few emendations to text in same early hand, 19th century bookplate of Marquess of Headfort, good.   Blackwell's Rare Books   B174 - 86   2013   £2000

Le Perouse, Jean Francois De Galaup, Comte De *A Voyage Round the World Which was Performed (sic) in the Years 1785 ...* Edinburgh: printed by J. Moir for T. Brown..., 1798.   folding engraved map, 3 engraved plates, bound without half title, map and plates and some pages bit browned, small 8vo., contemporary tree calf, spine gilt in compartments with ship in each, green lettering piece, black lettering piece in top compartment with crest and initials RT, slightly rubbed, head of spine chipped, Headfort armorial bookplate inside front cover, good.   Blackwell's Rare Books   B174 - 88   2013   £1500

Leigh, Edward *Select and Choice Observations Concerning All the Roman and Greek Emperors.* London: printed for J. Williams and are to be sold by Amos Curteyne Bookseller in Oxford, 1670.   Third edition, woodcut portraits, 8vo., very good, clean, contemporary unlettered calf, raised bands, leading hinge cracked at head but firm, slight wear to board edges, armorial bookplate of Marquess of Headfort & 19th century bookseller's label of W. A. Masson.   Jarndyce Antiquarian Booksellers   CCIV - 18   2013   £380

Maberly, Catherine Charlotte *The Love Match.* London: David Bryce, 1856.   New edition, contemporary half maroon calf, spine decorated n gilt, black leather label, spine and corners little rubbed, from the Headfort library, signed 'Bective 1854', good plus.   Jarndyce Antiquarian Booksellers   CCV - 182   2013   £45

Parry, William *The Last Days of Lord Byron, with His Lordship's Opinions on Various Subjects.* London: printed for Knight & Lacey, 1825.   First edition, frontispiece, 3 color aquatint plates, one or two gatherings slightly proud, contemporary half calf, gilt spine, maroon leather label, little dulled and rubbed, Marquess of Headfort's armorial bookplate.   Jarndyce Antiquarian Booksellers   CCIII - 428   2013   £320

Retz, Jean Francois Paul De Gondi, Cardinal De
Memoirs of the Cardinal de Retz... London: printed for Jacob Tonson, 1723. 4 volumes, 12mo., worming to lower inner margin volume I, disappearing to single hole by B4 of main text and also to outer blank margin of final five leaves of volume III, full contemporary panelled calf, raised bands, red morocco labels, little rubbed and worn, armorial bookplate of Marquess of Headfort, signature of Thomas Taylor dated 1756. Jarndyce Antiquarian Booksellers CCIV - 250 2013 £185

Vertot, Rene Aubert De *Revolutions de Portugal.* Paris: Chez les Libraires Associes, 1773. Small 8vo., frontispiece, folding genealogical plate, small 8vo., blank lower corner Ci torn, paper flaw to leading edge R1, otherwise fresh, clean copy, full contemporary mottled calf, triple gilt ruled borders, gilt spine, brown morocco label, little rubbed, all edges gilt, armorial bookplate of Marquess of Headfort. Jarndyce Antiquarian Booksellers CCIV - 301 2013 £150

Association – Headlam, John

Callwell, Charles *The History of the Royal Artillery from the Indian Mutiny to the Great War.* Woolwich: printed at the Royal Artillery Institution, 1931. First edition, 3 volumes plus portfolio of maps, very good, original gilt lettered blue cloth, spine of volume III little faded, although not inscribed, this came from the library of co-author John Headlam. Ken Spelman Books Ltd. 75 - 175 2013 £180

Ray, John *The Wisdom of God Manifested in the Works of the Creation.* Glasgow: printed by J. Bryce and D. Paterson, 1756. Thirteenth edition, 324 pages, 12mo., very good in full contemporary sprinkled calf, raised and gilt banded spine with red morocco label, some slight rubbing to spine and board edges, tiny amount of worming to front endpaper and foot of title, armorial bookplate of John Headlam, early signature of W. Milner. Ken Spelman Books Ltd. 75 - 21 2013 £120

Association – Headlam, T. E.

Brady, N. *A New Version of the Psalms of David, Fitted to the Tunes Used in the Churches.* Edinburgh: printed by Adrian Watkins, 1757. 8vo., with initial imprimatur leaf, full contemporary reverse calf with handsome red morocco label to upper board, "T. E. Headlam, Gateshead, 1770". Ken Spelman Books Ltd. 75 - 30 2013 £120

Association – Heaney, Seamus

Ledwidge, Francis *Selected Poems.* Dublin: New Island Books, 1992. First edition, 8vo., wrapper issue, near fine, from the library of Richard Murphy, inscribed for him by Seamus Heaney (provides introduction). Maggs Bros. Ltd. 1442 - 105 2013 £200

Association – Heap, J.

Warton, Thomas *The Union or Select Scots and English Poems.* London: printed for R. Baldwin, 1759. Second edition, small 8vo., browned and dusted throughout tear to B1 without loss, old wax seals on inner boards, contemporary calf, raised bands, red morocco label, boards rubbed, corners worn, early names of J. Heap, Brasenose Coll. and William Hutchinson on endpaper. Jarndyce Antiquarian Booksellers CCIV - 309 2013 £150

Association – Hearne, Thomas

Woodward, John *The State of Physick and of Diseases with an Inquiry into the Causes of the late Increase of them, but More Particularly of the Small-Pox.* London: printed for T. Horne, 1718. First edition, full contemporary calf gilt panelled spine, head of spine neatly repaired, author's presentation for Thomas Hearne. James Tait Goodrich 75 - 237 2013 $1500

Association – Heaston, Edward

How, William *Phytologia Britannica Natales Exhibens Indigenarum Stirpium Sponte Emergentium.* Richard Cotes for Octavian Pulleyn, 1650. First (only) edition, woodcut device on title, without initial leaf (blank except for signature A on recto), text printed in mixture of Roman, Italic and Black letter, 4 leaves with small holes affecting few letters (apparently not worming), small 8vo., contemporary calf, rebacked, corners worn, crackling of covers, contemporary signature at head of title of Edward Heaston, later indecipherable library stamp in outer margin of title, sound. Blackwell's Rare Books Sciences - 61 2013 £950

Association – Heckscher, William

Hugo, Herman *Pia Desideria....* Antwerp: Lucam de Potter, 1657. 12mo., 45 (of 46) engraved plates, slightly imperfect, having leaf G1 in early pen facsimile and lacking plate facing that leaf, old calf, worn at spine ends and corners, clasps lacking, occasional minor spotting and chips, good, tight copy, bookplate of William S. Heckscher. Joseph J. Felcone Inc. Books Printed before 1701 - 52 2013 $400

Association – Hefner, Hugh

The Playmate Book. Santa Monica: General Pub., 1996. First edition, this copy signed by Hugh Hefner, Gretchen Edgren and at least 7 of the playmates, fine in fine dust jacket. Ed Smith Books 75 - 58 2013 $300

Association – Hench, Philip

De Kruif, Paul *Life Among the Doctors.* New York: Harcourt Brace, 1949. 8vo., beige cloth, ownership signature of Philip S. Hench, Rochester, Minn., with his purchase slip, very good+. Jeff Weber Rare Books 172 - 75 2013 $50

Erichsen, Hugo *Medical Rhymes, a Collection of Rhymes of ye Anciente Time...* St. Louis: J. H. Cambers, 1884. 8vo., frontispiece, many fine illustrations, original brown publisher's blind and gilt stamped cloth, spine ends and corners worn, good, manuscript sheet written by Philip S. Hench and blank memo sheet with his printed name, with manuscript sheet where Hench has written out an anonymous poem. Jeff Weber Rare Books 172 - 88 2013 $95

Fishbein, Morris *The Medical Follies.* New York: Boni & Liveright, 1925. Fourth printing, 8vo., lacks front free endpaper, original reddish brown cloth, gilt, signed and inscribed by author, signed for Philip Hench by author, very good. Jeff Weber Rare Books 172 - 90 2013 $100

Association – Henderson, Winifred

Douglas, Norman 1868-1952 *Paneros. Some Words on Aphrodisiacs and the Like.* privately printed for subscribers by G. Orioli, Lungarno, Dec., 1930. First edition, out of series copy of the stated 250 numbered and signed copies, 8vo.,. original decorated and 'vermiculated' gold cloth boards, black leather spine label, inscribed by publisher Pino Orioli for Nancy Cunard, then passed on to her principal assistant Winifred Henderson by author, with Henderson's bookplate, extremities slightly rubbed, otherwise excellent. Maggs Bros. Ltd. 1460 - 242 2013 £750

Association – Henle, James

Shiel, M. P. *The Last Miracle.* London: Victor Gollancz, 1929. Reissue of 1906 title, modest edgewear, nice, very good, without dust jacket inscribed to head of his American publisher Vanguard, James Henle. Between the Covers Rare Books, Inc. Sci-Fi, Fantasy & Horror - 27817 2013 $850

Association – Henry, Francis

O'Conor, Matthew *The Irish Brigades; or Memoirs of the Most Eminent Irish Military Commanders Who Distinguished Themselves in the Elizabethan and Williamite Wars in their Own Country...* Dublin: 1855. First edition, 8vo., original cloth, subjected to amatuerish repairs, ex-library C. P. Curran (Francis Henry bookplate). C. P. Hyland 261 - 639 2013 £160

Association – Henry, Walter James

Bellamy, Edward *Looking Backward 2000-1887.* Boston: Houghton Mifflin, 1926. Riverside Library, 8vo., pages 337, very good in publisher's cloth, stain on hinge of rear endpaper, inscribed by author's wife, Emma for Walter James Henry, also inscribed by his daughter Marian Bellamy Ernshaw Oct. 24 1935, laid in is 9 x 6 inch handbill advertising talk given by Marion and Emma Bellamy at the Seattle Civic Auditorium, scarce. Second Life Books Inc. 183 - 21 2013 $300

Association – Hervey, Mary

Hervey, James *Meditations and Contemplations.* London: printed for John and James Rivington, 1749. Fifth edition, 2 volumes, frontispieces, one full page illustrations, old ink splash page 272 volume i and slight foxing traces of wax seals to inner board and lacking following endpaper volume i, full contemporary calf, gilt ruled borders, raised bands, red morocco labels, spines slightly chipped, leading hinges cracked but firm, inscribed by author to his sister Mary Hervey. Jarndyce Antiquarian Booksellers CCIV - 157 2013 £480

Association – Herz

Ludolf, H. *A New History of Ethiopia.* London: for Samuel Smith, 1682. First edition in English, folio, 8 engraved plates, engraved plate of Ethiopic alphabet, folding table, contemporary or early 18th century calf, front hinge cracked but held by cords, corners worn, some light browning, but very good, signatures of Edmund and Rufus Marsden, latter dated 1762, Herz booklabel. Joseph J. Felcone Inc. Books Printed before 1701 - 65 2013 $2200

Association – Hesketh, Thomas

Medicina Flagellata; or the Doctor Scarificed. printed for J. Bateman and J. Nicks, 1721. First edition, additional letterpress title with engraved vignette, 8vo., contemporary tree calf, flat spine gilt in compartments, red lettering piece, minor wear, top of upper joint snagged foot of spine chipped, contemporary signature at head of title of W. Beeson, engraved bookplate of Sir Thomas Hesketh, and Easton Neston Library shelf label, very good. Blackwell's Rare Books Sciences - 101 2013 £750

Association – Hesterberg, Bill

Bewick, Thomas 1753-1828 *Vignettes from Birds, Quadrupeds and Fables.* Chicago: Black Cat Press, 1971. Limited to 200 copies, 6.8 x 5.5 cm., leather, author's surname gilt stamped on spine, full name gilt stamped on front board, unpaginated, included is one of the actual Bewick wood blocks that was used to print illustration on page 8, also includes letter dated May 25 2004 from Bill Hesterberg of Hesterberg Press of Evanston to Donn Sanford, loose pages 5 and 8 of text laid in.   Oak Knoll Books   303 - 50   2013 $750

Association – Hewett, Thomas

Knox, Vicesimus 1752-1821 *Elegant Extracts; or Useful and Entertaining Pieces of Poetry.* (with) *Elegant Extracts; or Useful and Entertaining Passages in Prose.* (with) *Elegant Epistles.* London: printed for Charles Dilly, 1790. 1789? 1790. Respectively. Second edition of first work, new edition of second work, first work 4 parts in 2 volumes, 2 engraved titlepages, each with vignette, little foxing here and there; second work with engraved titlepage; third work half title discarded; royal 8vo., contemporary tree calf, gilt roll tooled Greek key borders on sides, spines gilt in compartments, red lettering piece and small circular black numbering pieces (on Poetry), slightly worn, head and tail caps of Prose particularly, ownership inscription of Thomas Hewett to blank endpapers, good.   Blackwell's Rare Books   B174 - 84   2013   £1200

Association – Hext, John

My Book of Noble Deeds. Blackie & Son, n.d circa, 1907. Large 8vo., original cloth backed glazed pictorial boards, little soiled, 4 color plates, other plates and illustrations, inscribed by Joan Ruskin for John Hext.   R. F. G. Hollett & Son   Children's Books - 71   2013   £75

True Stories of the Olden Days. Blackie & son, n.d. circa, 1907. Large 8vo., original cloth backed glazed pictorial boards, upper board little soiled, especially at one corner, 4 color plates, other plates and illustrations, inscribed by Joan Ruskin Severn for John Hext.   R. F. G. Hollett & Son   Children's Books - 72   2013   £65

Association – Hiatt, Charles

Miall, A. Bernard *Nocturns and Pastorals: a Book of Verse.* London: Leonard Smithers, 1896. First edition, rare first book, original dark blue cloth, chipping to spine ends and bumping to corners, otherwise very nice, offsetting to free endpapers and slight browning to page edges, but clean and tight, bookplates of W. MacDonald MacKay, Charles Hiatt (writer on art) and Barry Humphries (actor), illegible signature in ink, 109 pages.   The Kelmscott Bookshop   7 - 121   2013 $450

Association – Hibbard, Charles

Vergilius Maro, Publius *The Aeneid of Virgil.* London: printed for R. Dodsley, 1740. First complete edition, 2 volumes, 4to., contemporary paneled calf, rebacked with sheep at early date, corners worn, early leather labels, 1918 bookplate of John W. Thomson whose parents bought Fanny Kemble's Lenox Mass. residence, gift inscription from Charles L. Hibbard, prominent Pittsfield Mass. judge.   Howard S. Mott Inc.   262 - 119   2013 $1250

Association – Hibbert, James

Reid, Mayne 1818-1883 *The Young Yagers; or a Narrative of Hunting.* London: David Bogue, 1857. First edition, half title with ads on verso, frontispiece and plates, 4 pages ads, original purple brown morocco grained cloth, some slight rubbing, boards unevenly faded, long inscription on leading f.e.p. to 12 year old James Hibbert from his father Oct. 14 1857.   Jarndyce Antiquarian Booksellers   CCV - 228   2013   £150

Association – Hill, Aline

Martel, Yann *Life of Pi.* Canongate, 2002. First English edition, crown 8vo., original dark blue boards, backstrip blocked in silver, illustrated endpapers, rare first issue dust jacket with folds incorrectly aligned causing misalignment of backstrip panel, fine, titlepage inscribed by author to a member of Canongate's Export sales staff, Aline Hill.   Blackwell's Rare Books   172 - 217   2013   £300

Association – Hillary, William

Boerhaave, Hermann *Atrocis Nec Descripti Prius Morbi Historia* (bound with) *Atrocis, Rarissimique Morbi Historia Altera.* Leyden: Ex Officina Boutestentiana, 1724. Leyden: Apud Samulem Luchtmans & Theodorum Haak, 1728, Title skilfully laid down on old paper, top outer blank corner lacking, recent binding of quarter calf and marbled boards, clean, crisp copy, on first title is penned " E. Libris Gulilelmi Hillary" (William Hillary).   James Tait Goodrich   75 - 34   2013 $1950

Association – Hinckes, Theodosia

Coleridge, Sara *Phantasmion.* C. Whittingham for William Pickering, 1837. First edition, inscribed presentation from Mrs. H. N. Coleridge for Miss Theodosia Hinckes, , loosely inserted ALS by author to Mrs. Lonsdale, (pencil inscription "Given me by John Sparrow), 8vo., flyleaves little spotted, through setting slightly on to half title, few areas of minor spotting, contemporary pebble grained green morocco, double blind ruled borders on sides with corner ornaments, thick blind rules on either side of raised bands on spine, lettered direct in gilt, gilt edges by Hayday, mostly faded to brown, little rubbed, short split at head of lower joint, good.   Blackwell's Rare Books   172 - 43   2013   £3500

Association – Hindle, Winifred

Turgenev, Ivan Sergeevich 1818-1883 *A Month in the Country.* London: Heinemann, 1943. First English edition, 8vo., 94 pages, very good in dust jacket, bookplate of Hugh Beaumont on front endpaper, inscribed by Emlyn Williams for Beaumont, signed by 13 members of the opening night cast including Michael Redgrave, David Baxter, Winifred Hindle, etc.   Second Life Books Inc.   183 - 383   2013 $400

Association – Hinds, Mary

Campbell, Thomas 1777-1844 *Specimens of the British Poets: with Biographical and Critical Notices...* London: John Murray, 1845. New edition, half title, engraved frontispiece and title (1841), printed title (1845), uncut in original green cloth, lettered and decorated gilt, small repairs to inner hinges, ownership stamp of Mary M. Hinds, with unusual stamped coat of arms on leading pastedown, very good.   Jarndyce Antiquarian Booksellers   CCIII - 469   2013   £50

Association – Hinsch, L. L.

Faber, Basil *Thesaurus Eruditionis Scbolasticae; Sive Supellex Instructissima Dictionum, Verborum, Phrasium, Adagiorum...* Lipsae & Francofurti: Sumptibus Johannis Fritzschii, 1680. Early edition, folio in 6s, large copperplate engraved frontispiece, title with ownership signature of L. L. Hinsch, original full blindstamped vellum, joints repaired, recent front endleaves, very good.   Jeff Weber Rare Books   171 - 119   2013 $1500

Association – Hirschhorn, Clive

Sillitoe, Alan *The Loneliness of the Long-Distance Runner.* Allen, 1959. First edition, pages 176, foolscap 8vo., original grey green cloth, backstrip gilt lettered, free endpapers partly lightly browned as usual, dust jacket little frayed at head, very good, inscribed by author for film critic Clive Hirschhorn.   Blackwell's Rare Books   B174 - 299   2013   £525

Sillitoe, Alan *Saturday Night and Sunday Morning.* Allen, 1958. First edition, 216 pages, foolscap 8vo., original red boards, backstrip gilt lettered, faint staining to free endpaper edges, bookplate, dust jacket, faintly waterstained, good, inscribed by author to film critic Clive Hirschhorn.   Blackwell's Rare Books   B174 - 300   2013   £600

Association – Hirst, Walter

Gilchrist, Alexander *Life of William Blake.* London and Cambridge: Macmillan, 1863. First edition, 2 volumes, half titles, frontispieces, plates, illustrations, original maroon cloth by Burn & Co., blocked and lettered gilt, corners slightly worn, spines faded, booklabels of Walter Hirst very good, clean and attractive copy.   Jarndyce Antiquarian Booksellers   CCIII - 10   2013   £320

Association – Hislop, M. K.

Johnson, Samuel 1709-1784 *The Rambler.* London: F. C. and I. Rivington et al, 1820. 2 volumes, 12mo., frontispiece and titlepage to each volume, inscription removed from each half title, few pencil marks to volume I index, publisher's sugar paper covered boards, backed in very faded cloth, paper covering little torn, edges worn and corners fraying, uncut edges, somewhat dusted, ownership inscriptions of M. K. Hislop 1863, bookseller's notes in pencil to front pastedown of volume I.   Unsworths Antiquarian Booksellers   28 - 174   2013   £60

Association – Hoare, Hannah

Wordsworth, William 1770-1850 *Memorials of a Tour on the Continent, 1820.* London: Longman, Hurst, Rees, Orme and Brown, 1822. First edition, tall 8vo., 4 pages ads dated March 1822, untrimmed and bound with half title, contemporary boards, rebacked with later cloth and leather label, contemporary ownership signature of Hannah Hoare.   Second Life Books Inc.   183 - 431   2013 $1250

Association – Hodson, James

Campbell, Thomas 1777-1844 *Gertrude of Wyoming: a Pennsylvania Tale. And Other Poems.* London: Longman &c, 1814. Fifth edition, slightly spotted, 4 page catalog, contemporary full diced calf gilt spine and borders, black leather label, hinges little worn, armorial booklabel of James Hodson, label and signature of Charles Rossier, San Francisco 1942.   Jarndyce Antiquarian Booksellers   CCIII - 466   2013   £35

Association – Hoe, Arthur

Jameson, Anna Brownell Murphy 1794-1860 *The Communion of Labour: a Second Lecture on the Social Employments of Women.* London: Longman Brown, Green, Longmans & Roberts, 1856. First edition, small 8vo., small bookplate of Arthur Hoe, flexible cloth, stamped in gilt, cover little soiled, very good, tight copy.   Second Life Books Inc.   182 - 123   2013 $225

Association – Hofmann, Michael

Muller, Herta *The Land of Green Plums.* New York: Metropolitan/Holt, 1996. First American edition, awarded IMPAC prize, inscribed by author to Greg Gatenby, one of IMPAC judges, Muller has also drawn a caricature of Gatenby, as well as adding her address, phone and fax, also inscribed by translator, Michael Hofmann, stamp of the award on front flyleaf, hint of crown bump, fine in very near fine dust jacket with shallow vertical crease to spine, remarkable copy.   Ken Lopez Bookseller   159 - 143   2013 $1000

Association – Hole, M. Jane

Margoliouth, Moses *Curates of Riversdale: Recollections in the Life of a Clergyman.* London: Hurst and Blackett, 1860. First edition, 3 volumes, half dark blue calf, marbled boards, expertly and handsomely rebacked, inscription to leading f.e.p. volume from author for Mrs. Buckley, later signature of M. Jane Hole.   Jarndyce Antiquarian Booksellers   CCV - 190   2013   £750

Association – Holliday, R. G.

Kingsley, Charles 1819-1875 *Hereward the Wake. "Last of the English".* Macmillan and Co., 1893. 8vo., contemporary olive calf prize binding, spine gilt, red morocco lettering piece, front board with gilt stamp of Oxford High School, marbled edges and endpapers, little rubbed, spine slightly sunned, prize bookplate of R. G. Holliday for Divinity Form VI in the 1896 midsummer examination, very good.   Blackwell's Rare Books   172 - 82   2013   £25

Association – Holyoake, G. J.

Hennell, Mary *A Outline of the Various Social systems and Communities which Have Been Founded on the principle of Co-operation.* London: Longman, 1844. First edition, author's names added to title in pencil odd pencil annotation, signatuare of G. J. Holyoake on leading blank, additional later signature of J. J. Deakin, unsympathetic green marbled endpapers, 20th century half green crushed morocco, label on following endpaper of Midlands Workers' Library, very good.   Jarndyce Antiquarian Booksellers   CCV - 135   2013   £450

Association – Honeyman, H. L.

Headlam, Cuthbert *The Three Northern Counties of England.* Gateshead: Northumberland Press, 1939. Limited edition (500 copies), small 4to., original full dark blue levant morocco gilt, untrimmed, 23 plates, 8 maps and plans, few spots to half title and fore-edges, most attractive, loosely inserted are several letters relating to production of the book between H. L. Honeyman (one of the contributors) and publishers and others, with press cuttings.   R. F. G. Hollett & Son   Lake District and Cumbria - 244   2013   £120

Association – Hood, Viscount

Dallas, Robert Charles *Recollections of the Life of Lord Byron, from the Year 1808 to the end of 1814...* London: Charles Knight, 1824. First edition, contemporary half maroon calf, slightly rubbed, very good, bookplate of Viscount Hood, very good.   Jarndyce Antiquarian Booksellers   CCIII - 370   2013   £250

Association – Hooper, John

Hennessy, John Pope *Sir Walter Raleigh in Ireland.* 1883. First edition, 8vo., vellum binding, top edge gilt, fore-edge untrimmed, signed presentation to John Hooper, M.P. Cork, covers dull, text very good.   C. P. Hyland   261 - 740   2013   £150

Association – Hope

Young, Edward 1683-1765 *Night Thoughts on Life, Death and Immortality.* London: J. Walker, 1807. 140 x 75mm, very pretty contemporary red straight grain morocco, covers with gilt fillet border and blind tooled floral frame, upper cover with central medallion containing crest of Hope family surrounded by motto "At Spes Non Facta" and a wreath, raised bands, spine panels with cruciform centerpiece tooled in gilt and blind, gilt titling and turn-ins, all edges gilt, engraved frontispiece and pictorial title, front pastedown with booklabel of Abel Berland, spine bit darkened, joints just slightly rubbed, mild foxing to opening leaves, otherwise fine, clean and fresh internally and in solid, pleasing binding with little wear.   Phillip J. Pirages   63 - 506   2013 $150

Association – Hopton, Richard

Mathias, Thomas James *The Pursuit of Literature. (bound with) A Translation of the Passages from Greek, Latin, Italian and French Writers...* London: printed for T. Becket, 1799. 1798. Third edition, 2 volumes in 1, 8vo., lightly spotted, contemporary diced and polished tan calf spine divided by Greek key rolls and lettered gilt direct, other compartments with gilt centrepieces, marbled edges and endpapers, rubbed at extremities, spine sunned, armorial bookplate of Richard Hopton, signed binding by T. B. Watkins/Hereford with his ticket.   Unsworths Antiquarian Booksellers   28 - 113   2013   £150

Association – Horine, Emmet Field

Drake, Daniel *An Inaugural Discourse on Medical Education: Delivered at the Opening of the Medical College of Ohio in Cincinnati 11 Nov. 1820.* New York: Henry Schuman, 1951. First edition thus, reprint limited to 500 copies, now quite scarce, fine, signed and inscribed by Emmet Field Horine (provided introduction).   Leather Stalking Books   October 2013 - 2013 $100

Association – Hornbuckle, J. W.

Cottle, Joseph *Reminiscences of Samuel Taylor Coleridge and Robert Southey.* London: Houlston & Stoneman, 1847. First edition, half title, frontispiece, plates, bound without final ad leaf, plates slightly spotted, contemporary half calf, little rubbed, lacking title label, booklabel of J. W. Hornbuckle, good, sound copy.   Jarndyce Antiquarian Booksellers   CCIII - 581   2013 £125

Association – Hornby, R. Antony

Wilde, Oscar   1854-1900 *The Young King and Other Tales.* London: Ashendene Press, 1924. First edition, 8vo., original full brown morocco and printed on vellum, bound by W. H. Smith with his monogram under the direction of Douglas Cockerell, spine in six panels with raised bands, each panel with gilt border and dots at each corner, gilt lettering, double gilt borders on turn-ins pencilled ownership inscription of R. Antony Hornby, fine.   Maggs Bros. Ltd.   1442 - 324   2013   £16,500

Association – Hough, John

Day, Thomas   1748-1789 *The History of Sandford and Merton.* Whitehall: printed for William Young, Philadelphia, 1798. Seventh edition, 12mo., 3 volumes in 1, contemporary sheep, front hinge split, rear beginning to crack, gathering G foxed, scattered foxing elsewhere, small piece torn from blank margin of 2P5, just touching letter or two, contemporary signature of John Hough.   Joseph J. Felcone Inc.   English and American Literature to 1800 - 18   2013 $900

Association – Houghton, Lord

Cogniard, Hippolyte *Byron a l'Ecole d'Harrow, Episode Mele de Couplets...* Paris: J. Breaute, 1834. 24mo., contemporary full green marbled morocco, wheat sheaf device of Lord Houghton in gilt on upper board, armorial booklabel of Marquis of Crewe, all edges gilt, very good, attractive copy.   Jarndyce Antiquarian Booksellers   CCIII - 364   2013   £450

Association – Housman, A. E.

Barckley, Richard *A Discourse of the Felicitie of Man or His Summum Bonum.* London: William Ponsonby, 1598. First edition, small quarto, woodcut device on leaf facing title and on final leaf, old worn and mottled calf, rebacked and restored, later endpapers, morocco lettering piece, spine bit rubbed, tiny wormhole at gutter near center, neat marginal ink annotations, occasional pencil notes or underlining, bookplate of A. E. Housman, 19th century signatures to recto of first leaf, rare.   Heritage Book Shop   50th Anniversary Catalogue - 6   2013 $10,000

Association – How, John

Smollett, Tobias George   1721-1771 *Travels through France and Italy...* London: printed for R. Baldwin, 1766. Second edition, 2 volumes, 8vo., some slight foxing, endpapers replaced with laid paper, full contemporary sprinkled calf, raised and gilt banded spines, red morocco labels, corners little worn, contemporary signature of John How on half title and head of first page of text.   Jarndyce Antiquarian Booksellers   CCIV - 274   2013   £380

Association – Howard, Fannie May

Wordsworth, William   1770-1850 *The Complete Poetical Works.* Boston and New York: Houghton Mifflin, 1910-1911. Large paper edition, one of 500 copies, 10 volumes, 279 x 159mm., lovely dark olive brown three quarter crushed morocco, handsomely gilt, marbled sides and endpapers, raised bands, spine compartments, densely gilt with floral and foliate tools emanating from a large central rose, top edge gilt, other edges untrimmed, entirely unopened, vignette titlepage, map, 75 photogravure plates with letterpress tissue guards, including one hand colored plate at beginning with duplicates a black and white plate elsewhere in the volume, titlepage in red and black, each volume with tipped in bookplate of Fannie May Howard; in remarkably fine condition, essentially without any wear, virtually pristine internally and obviously used so little that volumes open unwillingly.   Phillip J. Pirages   63 - 503   2013 $3500

Association – Howell, W. G.

Derby, George H. *The Squibob Papers.* New York: Carleton, 1865. First edition, frontispiece 11 plates, 17 text illustrations, publisher's brown cloth, light wear and chipping to head of spine, corners slightly jammed, slight foxing, fading to spine, overall fine, internally fine with very little of the usual heavy foxing, original owner's dated signature W. G. Howell July 18 1865.   Argonaut Book Shop   Recent Acquisitions June 2013 - 88   2013 $150

Association – Howes, Barbara

Magloire-Saint-Aude, Clement *Veillee.* Port-au-Prince: Imprimerie Renelle, 1956. First edition, signed by author with full page inscription to poet Barbara Howes, stitching absent, staining to covers, good in wrappers, with wraparound band addressed to Howes in author's hand, excellent association.   Ken Lopez Bookseller   159 - 125   2013 $750

Association – Howson, Sarah

Fontenelle, Bernard Le Bovier De *The History of Oracles and Cheats of the Pagan Priests.* London: printed in the year, 1688. 8vo., small paper flaw to E4 touching several letters, blank margin of #6 and L3 repaired, some browning, contemporary calf, double gilt ruled borders, gilt panelled spine, red morocco label, expert rpeairs to hinges and corners, contemporary inscription "Ex-libris Sarah Howson (?)" struck through. Jarndyce Antiquarian Booksellers CCIV - 13   2013   £620

Association – Hudleston, C. Roy

Boumphrey, R. S. *Armorial for Westmorland and Lonsdale.* Lake District Museum Trust and CWAAS, 1975. Original crimson rexine gilt, frontispiece and 5 pages illustrations, inscribed by Roy Hudleston for his cousin Cayton Hall and dated Ambleside 1 Sept. 1976.   R. F. G. Hollett & Son   Lake District & Cumbria - 149   2013   £65

Cowper, Henry Swainson *Robert Kitchin, Mayor of Bristol: a Native of Kendal.* Kendal: Titus Wilson, 1920. Reprint, original wrappers, portrait, extending pedigree, presentation copy from author for C. R(oy) H(udleston).   R. F. G. Hollett & Son   Lake District & Cumbria - 323   2013   £30

Great Britain. Historical Manuscripts Commisssion *The Manuscripts of S. H. Le Fleming Esq. of Rydal Hall. Twelfth Report, Appendix Part VII.* London: HMSO, 1890. Tall 8vo., old binder's cloth, gilt, hinges little rubbed, some staining to final leaves, C. Roy Hudleston's copy.   R. F. G. Hollett & Son   Lake District and Cumbria - 261   2013   £95

Association – Hudson, John

Whitehead, William *The Historian's Pocket Companion; or Memory's Assistant.* Newcastle: printed by T. Angus..., 1777. 12mo., little soiled, foxed and browned, recent calf backed boards with original marbled paper covers laid down, ownership inscriptions on engraved title of John Hudson and Ruth Borrowman, sound, rare.   Blackwell's Rare Books   172 - 103   2013   £450

Association – Hughes, J.

Dixon, Joshua *The Literary Life of William Brownrigg...* London: Longman & Rees etc. and Whitehaven: A Dunn, 1801. First edition, original blue boards, paper spine label, very rubbed, very scarce, excellent, uncut, unsophisticated copy from the library of J. (Fred) Hughes of Kendal, local historian, with his label.   R. F. G. Hollett & Son   Lake District and Cumbria - 40   2013   £375

Association – Hughes, T. Arthur

Llewellyn, Richard *How Green Was My Valley.* New York: Macmillan, 1941. (1940). Later printing, round-robin, signed in fountain pen on location during making of the film on July 19 1941, gift copy from Freda Knill (niece of cast member Thomas A. Hughes) to her daughter, with autographs and inscriptions of Roddy McDowall, Maureen O'Hara, Walter Pidgeon, Donald Crisp, Barry Fitzgerald, Sara Allgood, Anna Lee, T. Arthur Hughes, Richard Fraser and Evan H. Evans; fair to good only, binding intact, shaken and with fraying to edges of cloth, in very good supplied dust jacket with some rubbing and light wear at extremities.   Ed Smith Books   75 - 39   2013 $1750

Association – Hughes, Ted

Plath, Sylvia 1932-1963 *Uncollected Poems.* Turret Books 1965, but published, 1966. First edition, one of 165 copies, double plate facsimile printed on pink paper, pages 20, foolscap 8vo., original plain white stapled card wrappers, stiff card dust jacket faded at spine and little soiled, good, superb association inscribed by Ted Hughes to fellow poet Richard Murphy.   Blackwell's Rare Books   B174 - 276   2013   £850

Association – Humphrey, Mr.

Manners, Janetta *Encouraging Experiences of Reading and Recreation Rooms; Aims of Gilds; Nottingham Social Gild...* Edinburgh: William Blackwood & Sons, 1886. Half titles, original pink paper wrappers, spine cracked with some slight loss, little dulled, presentation inscription from author for Mr. Humphreys.   Jarndyce Antiquarian Booksellers   CCV - 188   2013   £120

Association – Humphries

Kingston, William H. G. *Marmaduke Merry, the Midshipman.* London: Bemrose and Sons, circa, 1882. Fourth edition, 2 p.l., iv, 405 pages, very pleasing contemporary navy blue half morocco over royal blue cloth boards, raised bands, spine attractively gilt in double ruled compartments with scrolling cornerpieces and complex central fleuron, marbled endpapers, all edges gilt, originally highly decorative cloth covers and spine (as well as front free endpaper) bound in, titlepage vignette, charming headpieces, tailpieces, initials and vignettes in text, 7 engraved plates, including frontispiece, armorial bookplate of "Humphries" and gift inscriptions on original flyleaf dated 1882 and 1966; corners rather worn, otherwise fine in attractive binding, with only trivial internal imperfections.   Phillip J. Pirages   63 - 297   2013 $150

Association – Humphries, Barry

Miall, A. Bernard *Nocturns and Pastorals: a Book of Verse.* London: Leonard Smithers, 1896. First edition, rare first book, original dark blue cloth, chipping to spine ends and bumping to corners, otherwise very nice, offsetting to free endpapers and slight browning to page edges, but clean and tight, bookplates of W. MacDonald MacKay, Charles Hiatt (writer on art) and Barry Humphries (actor), illegible signature in ink, 109 pages.   The Kelmscott Bookshop   7 - 121   2013 $450

Association – Huntingdon, Margaret

Johnson, Samuel   1709-1784   *The Beauties of Johnson.* London: printed for G. Kearsley at no. 46 in Fleet Street, 1781. First edition, 8vo., bound in fours, marginal tears to Q2-3, some old waterstaining, contemporary sprinkled calf, rebacked rather plainly, but not recently, inner hinge strengthened, new pastedowns, ownership signature of Lt. Colonel Clayton, 1829, later bookplate of Margaret Huntingdon, several 19th century marginal annotations. Jarndyce Antiquarian Booksellers   CCIV - 171   2013   £125

Association – Huston, John

Bradbury, Ray   *Fahrenheit 451.*   New York: Ballantine Books, 1953. First edition, 8vo., original red cloth, browned on spine, otherwise excellent, inscribed by author for director John Huston Aug. 19 1953.   Maggs Bros. Ltd.   1460 - 131   2013   £2500

Association – Hutchins, Frederick

Robertson, William   1721-1793   *History of America.* London: printed by A. Strahan for A. Strahan, T. Cadell and W. Daiveson, 1800. Ninth edition, 218 x 130mm., pleasing contemporary tree calf, expertly and attractively rebacked with complementary modern calf, raised bands flanked by double gilt rules, red and black morocco labels, marbled endpapers, four large engraved folding maps and one folding plate, bookplate of Fred(eric)k L. Hutchins and engraved armorial bookplate of Frederick Edwin Eyre; corners very worn, boards with several small abrasions and patches of lost patina, opening and closing leaves bit foxed, faint offsetting in text, one map rather wrinkled and two small tears along folds, still appealing copy, text fresh and clean, well restored bindings quite solid and very attractive on shelf. Phillip J. Pirages   63 - 402   2013 $400

Association – Hutchinson, Joshua

Addison, Joseph   1672-1719   *The Works of.* Birmingham: printed by John Baskerville, 1761. 4 volumes, without the very scarce "Directions to the Binder" leaf in volume i (which carried instruction that it be cut out) but with 7 plates in volume ii (probably not printed by Baskerville, and sometimes missing), frontispiece and titlepage of volume I browned, little browning elsewhere, occasional foxing, mostly sparse but heavier on few gatherings, 4to., contemporary red morocco, single gilt fillet borders on sides, upper covers with arms of Joshua Hutchinson blocked in gilt at centre, gilt rules around raised bands on spines, gilt edges, lower edges of boards with waterstain of varying height (not affecting textblock), not exceeding 1 inch, engraved Hutchinson bookplate inside front cover, later bookplate opposite Henry J. B. Clements, good.   Blackwell's Rare Books   B174 - 2   2013   £1200

Association – Hutchinson, T.

Anderson, James   1739-1808   *Essays Relating to Agriculture and Rural Affairs.*   London: printed for G. G. and J. Robinson and for Bell and Bradfute (sic), Edinburgh (volume iii: Edinburgh: printed for Bell & Bradfute, 1796), 1797. Fourth edition, volume first (-third) editions, 3 engraved plates, page of woodcuts in volume i, 18 engraved plates and page of woodcuts in volume ii, and a page of woodcuts in volume iii, some foxing and browning, 8vo., contemporary tan calf, gilt rules on either side of raised bands on spine, red lettering pieces, bit worn, especially spine ends, of the raised bands on spine, red lettering pieces, bit worn, especially spine ends, ownership inscription T. Hutchinson in volumes i and iii, armorial bookplates in all volumes of William Hutchinson of Eggleston (Teesdale, Co. Durham) and above it the later bookplate of Seton of Mounie, sound. Blackwell's Rare Books   Sciences - 7   2013   £300

Association – Hutchinson, William

Anderson, James   1739-1808   *Essays Relating to Agriculture and Rural Affairs.*   London: printed for G. G. and J. Robinson and for Bell and Bradfute (sic), Edinburgh (volume iii: Edinburgh: printed for Bell & Bradfute, 1796), 1797. Fourth edition, volume first (-third) editions, 3 engraved plates, page of woodcuts in volume i, 18 engraved plates and page of woodcuts in volume ii, and a page of woodcuts in volume iii, some foxing and browning, 8vo., contemporary tan calf, gilt rules on either side of raised bands on spine, red lettering pieces, bit worn, especially spine ends, of the raised bands on spine, red lettering pieces, bit worn, especially spine ends, ownership inscription T. Hutchinson in volumes i and iii, armorial bookplates in all volumes of William Hutchinson of Eggleston (Teesdale, Co. Durham) and above it the later bookplate of Seton of Mounie, sound. Blackwell's Rare Books   Sciences - 7   2013   £300

Warton, Thomas *The Union or Select Scots and English Poems.* London: printed for R. Baldwin, 1759. Second edition, small 8vo., browned and dusted throughout tear to B1 without loss, old wax seals on inner boards, contemporary calf, raised bands, red morocco label, boards rubbed, corners worn, early names of J. Heap, Brasenose Coll. and William Hutchinson on endpaper.   Jarndyce Antiquarian Booksellers   CCIV - 309   2013   £150

Association – Huth, Edward

Wilkinson, John Gardner *Manners and Customs of the Ancient Eygptians, Including their Private Life, Government, Laws, Arts, Manufactures, Religion, Agriculture and Early History.* London: John Murray, 1847. Third edition, 5 volumes, 94 lithographed plates, some color, double page and or folding and over 500 woodcuts, 8vo., contemporary tree calf, rebacked, raised bands, red morocco title label, black morocco volume label, both in gilt, boards ruled and bordered gilt, edges ad turn-ins decorated with gilt dentelles, marbled endpapers, very good, extremities rubbed, one volume with top fore-corners bumped and worn, minor loss, labels with some chipped edges, owner's bookplate on front pastedowns, binding solid, contents fine, beautiful set, bookplates of Edward Huth.   Kaaterskill Books   16 - 90   2013 $950

Association – Hutton, Mary

Fournier, Edmund E. *An English Irish Dictionary & Phrase Book.* 1903. First edition, 8vo., cloth, needs recasing, owner inscribed by Mary Hutton, text clean.   C. P. Hyland   261 - 439   2013   £75

Salaman, M. C. *Modern Book Illustrators and their Work.* London: The Studio, 1914. First edition, owner inscription Mary Hutton, very good, 8vo., cloth.   C. P. Hyland   261 - 767   2013   £85

Association – Hyman, Trina Schart

Cushman, Karen *Midwife's Apprentice.* New York: Clarion, 1995. First edition, first printing, 8vo., cloth, as new in like dust jacket, with no award medal, color dust jacket by Trina Schart Hyman, warmly inscribed by author and Hyman as well, scarce edition and with both signatures.   Aleph-Bet Books, Inc.   104 - 137   2013 $450

Association – Ignatow, David

Lazer, Hank *On Equal Terms. Poems by Charles Bernstein, David Ignatow, Denise Levertov, Louis Simpson, Gerald Stern.* Tucscaloosa: Symposium Press, 1984. First edition, limited to 275 copies, although not called for, this copy signed by all contributors, one of the few copies we've seen signed by any of the poets, 4to., original green wrappers, as new.   James S. Jaffe Rare Books   Fall 2013 - 5   2013 $450

Association – Iles, Ellis

Pote, Joseph *The Foreigner's Guide; or a Necessary and Instructive Companion...* London: printed and sold by K. Kent, E. Comyns and Jo. Jollifee, 1752. Third edition, 12mo., contemporary sheep, 213 pages + 3 pages of publisher's terminal ads, ownership signature of Ellis Iles dated 1760 on front free endpaper, with price paid of 2/6, front hinge nearly detached, edges little rubbed, small tear in one leaf with minor loss, but not to sense, very good.   The Brick Row Book Shop   Miscellany Fifty-Nine - 46   2013 $1200

Association – Ingersoll, Robert

Traubel, Hoarce L. *In Re Walt Whitman.* Philadelphia: David McKay, 1893. First edition, 1 of 1000 copies, 8vo., recent half leather, marbled boards, inscribed by author Sept. 12 1893 for Robert G. Ingersoll.   M & S Rare Books, Inc.   95 - 370   2013 $950

Association – Ingleby

Martial, Marcus Valerius *The Epigrams of M. Val. Martial in Twelve Books.* London: printed by Baker and Galabin, 1782. First edition of Elphinston's complete translations, 4to., engraved frontispiece, some foxing and browning in places, final ad leaf discarded, contemporary diced Russia, spine divided by raised bands between gilt rules, black morocco label, marbled endpapers, edges yellow, joints and endcaps rubbed, Ingleby family heraldic crest and monogram gilt stamped in compartments 1 and 6 respectively.   Unsworths Antiquarian Booksellers   28 - 32   2013   £350

Association – Innes, George

Maggi, Girolamo *De Tintinnabulis Liber Postumus. (with, as issued) De Equleo Liber Postumus...* Amsterdam: Sumptibus Andreae Frisii, 1664. Enlarged edition, engraved half title and 5 engraved plates, numerous full page engravings within pagination, 12mo., 19th century biscuit calf, spine lettered in gilt, marbled edges and endpapers, bit rubbed and marked, bookplate of Rev. George Innes of the College, Warwick, good.   Blackwell's Rare Books   172 - 95   2013   £600

Association – Irby, William

Hamilton, William   1704-1754 *Poems on Several Occasions.* Edinburgh: printed for W. Gordon, Bookseller in the Parliament Close, 1760. 8vo., engraved frontispiece, lightly toned and spotted, contemporary cat's paw tan calf, spine gilt in compartments, red morocco label, bit rubbed at extremities, slight wear to headcap and front joint, ink inscription of Wm. Irby August 3rd out of 1769 Mr. Tompsons library at Gottingen" armorial bookplate of William Irby.   Unsworths Antiquarian Booksellers   28 - 105   2013   £200

Association – Ireland, S. F.

Day Lewis, Cecil *A Penknife in My Heart.* New York: Harper & Bros., 1958. First US edition, 8vo., original grey cloth, red spine, dust jacket, excellent copy, one small piercing to spine, dust jacket browned at spine, inscribed by author for S. F. Ireland. Maggs Bros. Ltd. 1460 - 207 2013 £200

Association – Irons, Arthur

Carnegie, Andrew *James Watt.* Edinburgh: Oliphant Anderson & Ferrier, n.d., First edition, original red cloth, spine faded on spine, otherwise near fine, inscribed by author to Arthur Irons. Maggs Bros. Ltd. 1460 - 162 2013 £350

Association – Isaacs, Peter

Penn, John *A Timely Appeal to the Common Sense of the People of Great Britain in General...* London: printed for J. Hatchard (second work) by W. Bulmer, 1798-1800. 2 works in 1 volume, first bound without half title or final ad leaf, the whole interleaved, titlepage of second slightly soiled and with reddish stain in fore-margin which persists for a few leaves, 8vo. (text) and 4to. (interleaves), contemporary calf, rebacked, corners worn, pencil notes on interleaves, some quite extensive, to first 42 pages, bookplate of Peter Isaacs, good. Blackwell's Rare Books B174 - 115 2013 £1200

Association – Ivory, James, Mrs.

Hales, William *The Inspector, or Select Literary Intelligence for the Vulgar A.D. 1798 but Correct A.D.1801 to the first Year of the XIXth Century.* printed for J. White and J. Wright, 1799. 8vo., library shelf mark in ink at head of titlepage, some foxing and browning, 19th century purple hard grained cloth, shelfmark in gilt on spine, spine slightly darkened, inscription "to Mrs. James Ivory from Mr. Baron Manres 1799", bookplate of Dundee Free Libraries inside front cover, good. Blackwell's Rare Books B174 - 65 2013 £500

Association – Jackson, Fred

Stearns, Samuel *The American Herbal or Materia Medica.* Walpole: David Carlise for Thomas & Thomas and the author, 1801. 12mo., 360 pages, full modern calf, gilt spine rules, red gilt stamp spine label, 19th century style, some browning as might be expected, small stamp on title verso, early ownership signatures of A. E. Bigelow MD (1893), J. Henry Jackson (1870) and Fred K. Jackson (1903), very good, rare. Jeff Weber Rare Books 169 - 426 2013 $3500

Association – Jackson, J. Henry

Stearns, Samuel *The American Herbal or Materia Medica.* Walpole: David Carlise for Thomas & Thomas and the author, 1801. 12mo., 360 pages, full modern calf, gilt spine rules, red gilt stamp spine label, 19th century style, some browning as might be expected, small stamp on title verso, early ownership signatures of A. E. Bigelow MD (1893), J. Henry Jackson (1870) and Fred K. Jackson (1903), very good, rare. Jeff Weber Rare Books 169 - 426 2013 $3500

Association – James, Eliza

Bingham, Frances Lydia *Short Poems, Religious and Sentimental.* Bolton-le-Moors: Henry Bradbury, 1848. Second edition, original red limp cloth wrappers, front wrapper lettered gilt, slightly marked, small repair to head of spine, contemporary owner's signature Eliza G. James, all edges gilt, good plus. Jarndyce Antiquarian Booksellers CCIII - 645 2013 £75

Association – James, Henry

Gosse, Edmund 1849-1928 *Ibsen. Literary Lives Series.* London: Hodder and Stoughton, 1907. First edition, 8vo., original blindstamped red cloth, inscribed by author for Henry James, very good, spine faded, marked and in one place pierced, cloth in general little soiled. Maggs Bros. Ltd. 1460 - 356 2013 £600

Association – James, Joseph

Coleridge, Samuel Taylor 1772-1834 *Notes and Lectures Upon Shakespeare and Some of the Old Poets and Dramatists with Other Literary Remains.* London: William Pickering, 1849. First edition, 2 volumes, original purple cloth, paper labels browned, spines fading to brown and slightly rubbed at heads and tails, armorial bookplates of Joseph James. Jarndyce Antiquarian Booksellers CCIII - 567 2013 £75

Association – James, William Rhodes

Grainger, James *The Sugar-Cane: a Poem.* London: printed and sold by the Booksellers, 1766. Second edition, half title, engraved frontispiece, 8vo., slight foxing to some pages, front endpaper little loose, contemporary mottled calf, gilt, borders and spine, hinges cracked, spine rubbed and chipped, lacking label, armorial bookplate of William Rhodes James. Jarndyce Antiquarian Booksellers CCIV - 148 2013 £280

Association – Janson, B. P.

Morrell, L. A. *The American Shepherd: being a History of the Sheep, with their Breeds, Management and Diseases.* New York: Harper and Bros., 1850. 8vo., illustrations, original cloth, minor chipping to ends of spine, foxed, this copy was awarded to Ransom Harmon for best black lambs by B. P. Janson, Rochester, NY 1857.   M & S Rare Books, Inc. 95 - 340   2013 $100

Association – Jefferson, Geoffrey

Kisch, Bruno *Forgotten Leaders in Modern Medicine.* Philadelphia: June, 1954. Large 4to., original brown printed wrappers, light wear, else very good, numerous illustrations, ex-libris from Sir Geoffrey Jefferson with his bookplate and signature.   James Tait Goodrich   S74 - 165 2013 $145

Association – Jocelyn, Mr.

Boyle, Robert 1627-1691 *An Essay of the Great Effects of Even Languid and Unheeded Motion.* London: By M. Flesher for Richard Davis, 1685. First edition with first state titlepage (without Boyle's name), 8vo., neat modern calf antique, retaining original front flyleaf with signature of Mr. Jocelyn, light dust soiling of first few leaves, else fine, clean copy.   Joseph J. Felcone Inc.   Books Printed before 1701 - 12   2013 $2800

Association – Johnson, Edward

Wakefield, P. *Mental Improvement or the Beauties and Wonders of Nature and Art.* Dublin: printed by T. Burnside for P. Wogan, H. Colbert and J. Gough, 1799. Rare first Dublin edition, 12mo., contemporary tree sheep, gilt ruled, compartments on spine, red lettering piece, crack at head of upper joints, ownership inscription "Edward Johnsons Book, Carrickfergus, July 20th 1811", good.   Blackwell's Rare Books   Sciences - 128   2013   £600

Association – Johnson, John

Allsop, Thomas *Letters Conversations and Recollections of S. T. Coleridge.* London: Edward Moxon, 1836. Second edition, half title, original dark green cloth by Westleys, spine little worn at head, booklabel of John Johnson.   Jarndyce Antiquarian Booksellers   CCIII - 558   2013   £40

Association – Johnson, Oliver

Garrison, William Lloyd *Sonnets and Other Poems.* Boston: Oliver Johnson, 1843. First edition, 16mo., 96 pages, original cloth, some browning, near fine, this copy inscribed in ink by publisher, to his sister.   M & S Rare Books, Inc.   95 - 120   2013 $600

Association – Johnson, Ronald

Eshleman, Clayton *The Chavin Illumination.* Lima: 1965. First edition, copy 50 of 100, very near fine in string tied wrappers, very good plus dust jacket with some creasing to top edge near spine, signed by Eshleman on limitation page, additionally inscribed by him for poet Ronald Johnson.   Jeff Hirsch Books   Fall 2013 - 129345   2013 $75

Association – Johnson, Thomas

Trevigar, Luke *Sectionum Conicarum Elementa Methodo Facillima (sic) Demonstrata.* Cambridge: University Press, 1731. First edition, 11 folding engraved plates, little browned in places, 4to., contemporary plain calf, red lettering piee, worn, contemporary ownership inscription on title of Tho. Johnson, Magd(alene College), sound.   Blackwell's Rare Books   Sciences - 122   2013   £350

Association – Johnstone, James

Morgagni, Giovanni Battista 1682-1771 *De Sedibus e Causis Morborum per Anatomen Indagatis.* Venice: Remondin, 1761. First edition, 2 volumes bound as one, first title printed in red and black, both titles with same engraved vignette, with engraved frontispiece, scattered foxing and browning, mainly mild, Birmingham Central Hospital Library stamp in numerous places but not overwhelming, some 150 pages manuscript at end, folio, 20th century calf, red lettering piece on spine "Birmingham medical Institute" in small gilt letters at foot of spine, crack at head of upper joint, Johnstone family bookplate inside front cover and a portion of the original front pastedown or flyleaf, recording book as being James Johnstone's and a further inscription by his grandson John dated 1834, good.   Blackwell's Rare Books   Sciences - 84   2013   £11,000

Association – Johnstone, John

Morgagni, Giovanni Battista 1682-1771 *De Sedibus e Causis Morborum per Anatomen Indagatis.* Venice: Remondin, 1761. First edition, 2 volumes bound as one, first title printed in red and black, both titles with same engraved vignette, with engraved frontispiece, scattered foxing and browning, mainly mild, Birmingham Central Hospital Library stamp in numerous places but not overwhelming, some 150 pages manuscript at end, folio, 20th century calf, red lettering piece on spine "Birmingham medical Institute" in small gilt letters at foot of spine, crack at head of upper joint, Johnstone family bookplate inside front cover and a portion of the original front pastedown or flyleaf, recording book as being James Johnstone's and a further inscription by his grandson John dated 1834, good.   Blackwell's Rare Books   Sciences - 84   2013   £11,000

Association – Johnstone, Richard Bempde

Ozanam, Jacques *Recreations Mathematical and Physical...* printed for R. Bonwick, W. Freeman, Tim Goodwin (and 7 others), 1708. First edition in English, 26 engraved plates, numerous woodcut diagrams and illustrations in text, some dampstaining and browning throughout and few leaves dust soiled, couple of glue spots on one plate have lifted a small amount of letterpress on opposite page (present on plate, whose engraved area is not affected), 8vo., late 18th century tree calf, flat spine gilt in compartments, black lettering piece, crack in upper joint, headcap defective, armorial bookplate inside front cover of Sr Richard Bempde Johnstone, sound.   Blackwell's Rare Books   Sciences - 91   2013   £700

Association – Joicey, Edward

Forster, Westgarth *A Treatise on a Section of the Strata, from Newcastle-upon-Tyne, to the Mountains of Cross Fell, in Cumberland.* Alston: printed for the author at the Geological Press and sold by John Pattinson, etc., 1821. 12mo., original boards, corners worn, attractively rebacked in pigskin with green lettering piece, uncut, 12 plates, mostly folding or extending and including 3 colored plates of sections, large folding table of superposition of strata, 12 hand colored pages of sections of strata and 8 further hand colored woodcuts, little scattered browning, excellent wide margined copy, rare, with 12mo. ad leaf, tipped in before title, text woodcuts are not usually found colored, armorial bookplates of William Henry Brockett and Edward Joicey of Whinney House.   R. F. G. Hollett & Son   Lake District and Cumbria - 136   2013   £650

Association – Jones, Charlotte Harriet

Cats, Jacob *Moral Emblems with Aphorisms, Adages and Proverbs of All Ages and Nations.* London: Longman, Green Longman and Roberts, 1860. First edition with these illustrations, 275 x 195mm., xvi, 239, (1) pages, allegorical frontispiece, 60 large tondo emblems and 60 tailpieces by John Leighton and others after Adriaen van de Venne; fine contemporary green straight grain morocco handsomely gilt, covers framed by multiple rules and wide, ornate dentelle, the whole enclosing detailed Greek urn centerpiece, raised bands, spine densely gilt in compartments featuring many small botanical and floral tools, gilt turn-ins, all edges gilt, presentation "Wilhelmina Colquhoun Jones/1863/with Charlotte Harriet Jones/love and best wishes", spine darkened to olive brown (as almost always with green morocco), just faintest hint of wear to joints, occasional minor foxing or staining, extremely attractive, very decorative contemporary binding bright and scarcely worn and text very fresh and showing no signs of use.   Phillip J. Pirages   63 - 315   2013 $750

Association – Jones, Edward

Sheraton, Thomas *The Cabinet Dictionary....* London: printed by W. Smith and sold by W. Row, Matthews, Vernon and Hood and M. Jones, 1803. First edition, 89 engraved plates, several folding, plates irregularly numbered and sometimes misbound, with a plate 81 not called for, last few leaves at either end stained from binding turn-ins, occasional browning or foxing, waterstain to front flyleaves, 8vo., contemporary mottled calf, skillfully rebacked, original green lettering piece, signature at head of introduction of Edward Jones, sound.   Blackwell's Rare Books   B174 - 138   2013   £750

Association – Jones, Horace

Beamish, C. T. M. *Beamish, a Genealogical Study of a Family in County Cork and Elsewhere.* 1950. First edition, 275 pages, ex-libris Horace E. Jones, with his informative annotations, cloth, very good.   C. P. Hyland   261 - 372   2013   £175

Pratt, John *Pratt Family Records.* for private circulation, 1931. 8vo., signed presentation to H. P. Gordon, added pencil notes from Horace E. Jones, very good.   C. P. Hyland   261 - 409   2013   £250

Association – Jones, James

Houghton, William *British Fresh-Water Fishes.* London: William MacKenzie, 1879. First edition, large 4to., 41 colored full page chromolithographs, 64 engraved vignettes, red and black titlepage, top edge gilt, modern dark brown quarter morocco over original cloth boards, raised bands, gilt stamped spine title, bookplate of James Jones, rare, fine.   Jeff Weber Rare Books   171 - 171   2013 $2200

Association – Jones, Joseph

Coleridge, Samuel Taylor 1772-1834 *Biographia Literaria; or Biographical Sketches of My Literary Life and Opinions.* London: William Pickering, 1847. Second edition, 2 volumes, half titles, preceded by 8 page catalog Jana. 1852 volume I, unopened in original brown cloth, spines chipped at head, armorial bookplates by Joseph Jones.   Jarndyce Antiquarian Booksellers   CCIII - 537   2013   £60

Colton, Charles Caleb *Lacon; or Many Things in Few Words; Addressed to Those Who Think. (with) Remarks Critical and Moral on Talents of Lord Byron and the Tendencies of Don Juan. With The Conflagration of Moscow: a Poem.* London: Longman, 1825. 1819. 1822. New edition, 4 volumes in 1, contemporary half red morocco, marbled boards, hinges and corners rubbed, armorial bookplate of Joseph Jones.   Jarndyce Antiquarian Booksellers   CCIII - 367   2013   £75

Association – Jones, R. D. G.

To-Night! or the Total Eclipse.   London: J. J. Stockdale, 1818.   Fifteenth edition, half title, 6 color plates by C. William bound together following title, uncut in original pink boards, marked, spine reinforced with later cream paper, ink title, bookplates of R. D. G. Jones and Renier.   Jarndyce Antiquarian Booksellers   CCIII - 630   2013   £60

Association – Jones, R. Maurice

Keill, John   *An Examination of Dr. Burnet's Theory of the Earth.*   Oxford: printed at the Theater, 1698.   First edition, 8vo., browned old ink strokes in margins, prelim blank leaf torn without loss, some old waterstaining to lower margins, full contemporary unlettered panelled calf, raised bands, armorial bookplate of Rd. Maurice Jones.   Jarndyce Antiquarian Booksellers CCIV - 17   2013   £225

Association – Jones, Wilhelmina Colquhoun

Cats, Jacob   *Moral Emblems with Aphorisms, Adages and Proverbs of All Ages and Nations.*   London: Longman, Green Longman and Roberts, 1860.   First edition with these illustrations, 275 x 195mm., xvi, 239, (1) pages, allegorical frontispiece, 60 large tondo emblems and 60 tailpieces by John Leighton and others after Adriaen van de Venne; fine contemporary green straight grain morocco handsomely gilt, covers framed by multiple rules and wide, ornate dentelle, the whole enclosing detailed Greek urn centerpiece, raised bands, spine densely gilt in compartments featuring many small botanical and floral tools, gilt turn-ins, all edges gilt, presentation "Wilhelmina Colquhoun Jones/1863/with Charlotte Harriet Jones/love and best wishes", spine darkened to olive brown (as almost always with green morocco), just faintest hint of wear to joints, occasional minor foxing or staining, extremely attractive, very decorative contemporary binding bright and scarcely worn and text very fresh and showing no signs of use. Phillip J. Pirages   63 - 315   2013 $750

Association – Joseph, E.

Taylor, Deems   *Walt Disney's Fantasia.*   New York: Simon and Schuster, 1940.   First edition, folio, profusely illustrated in color and black and white, including 16 tipped in color illustrations, titlepage printed in red, black and blue, bound by Zaehnsdorf, circa 1977 for E. Joseph, full brown crushed levant morocco, front cover and smooth spine lettered in gilt after original binding lettering, board edges ruled gilt, turn-ins decoratively tooled in gilt, pale gray watered silk doublures and liners, all edges gilt, very fine.   David Brass Rare Books, Inc.   Holiday 2012 Chapter One - DV00420   2013 $1800

Association – Joseph, Edward

Cosway, Richard   *Catalogue of a Collection of Miniatures by Richard Cosway...*   N.P.: for private circulation only, 1883.   Limited edition, limitation not stated, folio, (32)ff., frontispiece, 26 full page mounted original photographic plates, original half brown morocco, marbled boards, morocco corners, raised bands, gilt spine title, all edges gilt, bound by J. Leighton, Brewer St. (stamp on front flyleaf), inscribed "With Mr. Edward Joseph's Kindest regards New York 22 Dec. (18)83", bookplate of John Nolty, fine, rare.   Jeff Weber Rare Books   171 - 78   2013 $750

Association – Jowling, Thomas

Derham, William   1657-1735   *Astro-Theology; or a Demonstration of the Being and Attributes of God, from a Survey of the Heavens.*   London: printed for W. Innys, 1715.   8vo., 3 folding copper engraved plates, titlepage little dusted, first gathering slightly browned, full contemporary panelled calf, raised bands, red morocco label, small paper shelf number at head of spine, hinges cracked, head and tail of spine slightly rubbed, contemporary booklabel of Tho. Jowling, A.M. Rect de Alcester 19th century armorial bookplate of W. Wynne.   Jarndyce Antiquarian Booksellers CCIV - 111   2013   £280

Association – Judkins, J.

Bloomfield, Robert   *The Banks of the Wye: a Poem.*   London: printed for the author, Vernor, Hood & Sharpe &c, 1811.   First edition, engraved frontispiece, final ad leaf, uncut in original drab boards, fairly recently respined with tan calf, inscribed by author for Dr. J. Judkins.   Jarndyce Antiquarian Booksellers   CCIII - 26   2013   £185

Association – Kachline, Cliff

Riley, James A.   *The All-Time All-Stars of Black Baseball.*   Cocoa: TK Pub., 1983.   First edition, 306 pages, photos, fine in fine dust jacket with just touch of toning, inscribed by author for Cliff Kachline, scarce.   Between the Covers Rare Books, Inc.   165 - 17   2013 $850

Association – Kael, Pauline

Day, Wesley   *On to me Now.*   N.P.: self published, n.d., Quarto, near fine in claspbound wrappers, inscribed by author to Pauline Kael, former New Yorker film critic.   Ken Lopez Bookseller   159 - 174   2013 $200

Gershe, Leonard   *Butterflies are Free.*   New York: Random House, 1970.   First edition, review copy with review slip laid in, fine in fine dust jacket, from the library of film critic Pauline Kael.   Ken Lopez Bookseller   159 - 68   2013 $125

Association – Kahn, Bruce

Bear, Greg *Anvil of Stars.* London: Century a Legend Book, 1992. First edition, one of 200 copies, fine in illustrated boards and slipcase, signed by author, from the library of Bruce Kahn.   Between the Covers Rare Books, Inc.   Sci-Fi, Fantasy & Horror - 311553   2013 $80

Brett, Simon *The Detection Collection.* Gladestry: Scorpion Press, 2005. First edition, one of 16 lettered copies (this being C), fine in quarter leather with raised bands, marbled boards and fine acetate dust jacket, signed by editor, Claire Francis, Robert Goddard, John Harvey, Reginald Hill, P. D. James, H. R. F. Keatin, Michael Ridpath, Margaret Yorke, Robert Barnard, Lindsey Davis and Colin Dexter, includes signatures of Boris Akunin and Michael Johnson, from the library of Bruce Kahn.   Between the Covers Rare Books, Inc.   Mystery & Detective Fiction - 312104   2013 $400

Caldwell, Erskine Preston 1903-1987 *God's Little Acre.* New York: Viking, 1933. First edition, tiny books tore label to rear pastedown and small rectangle of offsetting to front flyleaf, still fine in fine dust jacket with just minuscule corner nicks, beautiful copy, from the Bruce Kahn collection.   Ken Lopez Bookseller   159 - 30   2013 $4500

Carver, Raymond *Will You Please Be quiet, Please?* New York: McGraw Hill, 1976. First edition, signed by author, trifling spotting to top stain, still fine in fine dust jacket, beautiful copy, from the Bruce Kahn collection.   Ken Lopez Bookseller   159 - 35   2013 $5000

Coel, Margaret *Day of Rest.* Clarkston: Mission Viejo: A.S.A.P., First edition, one of 26 lettered copies, signed by author, C. J. Box who wrote introduction and Phil Parks, the artist, fine in purple cloth with paper label and fine plastic slipcase, from the library of Bruce Kahn.   Between the Covers Rare Books, Inc.   Mystery & Detective Fiction - 312263   2013 $250

Faulkner, William Harrison 1897-1962 *The Hamlet.* New York: Random House, 1940. First issue, fine in very near fine, price clipped, first issue dust jacket with hint of rubbing to front spine fold and short closed tear on rear panel, beautiful copy, from the Bruce Kahn collection.   Ken Lopez Bookseller   159 - 59   2013 $7500

Gaines, Ernest J. *The Autobiography of Miss Jane Pittman.* New York: Dial Press, 1971. First edition, fine in fine dust jacket with tiny creased tear on front panel, nicely inscribed by author in year of publication, very nice, although not marked in any way, this copy from the collection of Bruce Kahn.   Between the Covers Rare Books, Inc.   165 - 303   2013 $600

Gieson, Judith Van *The Stole Blue: a Claire Reyneir Mystery.* Albuquerque: University of New Mexico Press, 2000. First edition, fine in fine dust jacket, signed by author, from the library of Bruce Kahn.   Between the Covers Rare Books, Inc.   Mystery & Detective Fiction - 304603   2013 $60

Kijewski, Karen *Katapult.* New York: St. Martin's Press, 1990. First edition, fine in fine dust jacket, signed by author, from the library of Bruce Kahn.   Between the Covers Rare Books, Inc.   Mystery & Detective Fiction - 201759   2013 $65

Nunn, Kem *Tapping the Source.* New York: Delacorte Press, 1984. First edition, fine in fine dust jacket, signed by author, from the library of Bruce Kahn.   Between the Covers Rare Books, Inc.   Mystery & Detective Fiction - 302254   2013 $350

Nunn, Kem *Tijuana Straits.* New York: Scribner, 2004. First edition, fine in fine dust jacket, signed by author, from the library of Bruce Kahn.   Between the Covers Rare Books, Inc. Mystery & Detective Fiction - 392223   2013 $65

O'Connell, Carol *Mallory's Oracle.* New York: G. P. Putnams Sons, 1994. First edition, fine in fine dust jacket, signed by author, from the library of Bruce Kahn.   Between the Covers Rare Books, Inc.   Mystery & Detective Fiction - 301912   2013 $65

O'Hara, John *Appointment in Samarra.* New York: Harcourt Brace, 1934. First edition, fine in fine, first issue dust jacket, errata slip present, from the Bruce Kahn collection.   Ken Lopez Bookseller   159 - 163   2013 $15,000

Palahniuk, Chuck *Fugitives and Refugees: a Walk in Portland, Oregon.* New York: Crown Journeys/Crown Publishers, 2003. First edition, fine in fine dust jacket, signed by author, from the library of Bruce Kahn.   Between the Covers Rare Books, Inc.   Mystery & Detective Fiction - 304849   2013 $200

Salinger, Jerome David *Raise High the Roof Beam, Carpenters and Seymour an Introduction.* New York: Little Brown, 1963. First edition, first issue, exceptionally scarce issue, fine in very near fine dust jacket with tiny closed catch to spine, from the Bruce Kahn collection.   Ken Lopez Bookseller   159 - 172   2013 $5000

Simmons, Dan *Worlds Enough and Time.* Burton: Subterranean Press, 2002. First edition, one of 26 lettered copies, signed by author, fine in fine dust jacket and fine gilt cloth clamshell slipcase; from the library of Bruce Kahn. Between the Covers Rare Books, Inc. Sci-Fi, Fantasy & Horror - 311781   2013 $600

Steinbeck, John Ernst   1902-1968 *In Dubious Battle.* New York: Covici Friede, 1936. First edition, tiny bookstore stamp lower rear pastedown, fine in fine dust jacket, custom clamshell box, from the Bruce Kahn collection, beautiful copy.   Ken Lopez Bookseller   159 - 181   2013 $8500

Association – Kalbfleisch, Charles

Jami *Salaman and Absal: an Allegory.* London: J. W. Parker and Son, 1856. First edition, 213 x 148mm., xvi, 84 pages, frontispiece; lovely early 20th century chestnut brown morocco handsomely gilt by Zaehnsdorf (stamp signed), covers with multiple-rule frame and central panel containing 25 gilt flowers in rows, each flower with long curving leafy stem, background accented with tiny gilt dots and crescents, raised bands, spine gilt in compartments featuring alternating gilt blossom and twining vines, gilt turn-ins, light brown silk endleaves, original blue paper wrappers bound in at rear, slightly rubbed brown morocco felt lined pull-off case with raised bands and gilt title, flyleaf with offset image of leather bookplate of bookplate of Charles Kalbfleisch, bookplate no longer present, trial marginal soiling or dots of foxing on handful of leaves, else especially fine, text fresh and smooth, margins considerably more than ample, glittering decorative binding unworn and especially lustrous.   Phillip J. Pirages   61 - 132   2013 $4500

Association – Kane, Robert

Courlander, Harold *The Fire on the Mountain and Other Ethiopian Stories.* New York: Henry Holt, 1950. First edition, fine in lightly soiled, very good dust jacket with pencilled number on front panel, faint sticker shadow on spine and light general wear, illustrations, nicely inscribed by author and artist, Robert Kane, to same recipient. Between the Covers Rare Books, Inc.   165 - 121   2013 $150

Association – Kasuboske, Kent

Hamady, Walter *Neopostmodernism or Gabberjab Number 6.* Mt. Horeb: Perishable Press, 1988. First edition, limited to 125 copies printed on various handmade papers, oblong small 8vo., illustrations, original boards, signed by binder, Marta Gomez, Hamady's assistant, Kent Kasuboske and especially inscribed by Hamady to collector, very fine.   James S. Jaffe Rare Books   Fall 2013 - 125   2013 $2500

Association – Keate, John

Lucretius Carus, Titus *De Rerum Natura Libri Sex.* London: in aedibus Ricardi Taylor et socii, 1824. 4to., printer's vignette to titlepage and at colophon, light foxing in places, contemporary tan calf, rebacked with old spine relaid, boards ruled in blind and gilt, slightly scratched, patches of surface-loss near bottom edge of lower board, corners worn, marbled edges and endpapers, prelims (only) creased and starting to loosen at gutter, gift inscription of Dr. Keate.   Unsworths Antiquarian Booksellers   28 - 28   2013   £150

Association – Keats, Mary

Hayley, William *The Triumphs of Temper.* Chichester: printed by J. Seagrave, for T. Cadell and W. Davies, London, 1803. Twelfth edition, 6 plates, few spots, bound without half title, later 'antique' panelled calf by V. A. Brown of Mildenborough, spine gilt in compartments, red and green leather labels, slightly rubbed, all edges gilt, nice, bright copy, signature of Mary Keats on titlepage, pencil notes in prelims by Grant Gration-Maxfield.   Jarndyce Antiquarian Booksellers   CCIII - 7   2013   £650

Association – Kekenick, E.

Norris, John *A Collection of Miscellanies; Consisting of Poems, Essays, Discourses and Letters, Occasionally Written. (bound with) The Theory and Regulation of Love.* Oxford: printed at the Theatre for John Crosley, 1687. Oxford: printed at the Theatre for Hen. Clements, 1688. First edition, engraved vignette on title, slightly browned and one or two spots; second work large or thick paper copy, 8vo., bound together in contemporary calf, blind ruled borders on sides, roll tooled border at inner edge repeated an inch out, spine gilt in compartments, red lettering piece, rebacked, preserving original spine, covers rubbed and with some craquelure, contemporary ownership inscription at head of dedication "S. Pendarves 89", few notes in his hand to text of Miscellanies, 18th century inscription of Eliz. Kekenick, Norris's Postscript, retracting the Considerations upon the nature of Sin, copied out apparently in her hand on verso of its sectional title, good.   Blackwell's Rare Books   B174 - 109   2013   £750

Association – Kelbs, Arnold

Vesalius, Andreas *De Humani Corporis Fabrica.* Basel: Oporinus, 1555. Second folio edition, folio, engraved frontispiece/title, early 17th century full speckled calf with gilt paneled spine, light wear to fore edges, joints just starting but firm, some peeling to leather on front board, very good showing some light wear, printing impressions of plates excellent, light staining and foxing, 2 inscriptions skilfully removed from title, rear flyleaf with rubber stamp of Arnold Kelbs, M.D.   James Tait Goodrich   75 - 210   2013 $79,500

Association – Kelley, Florence

Bynington, Margaret F. *Homestead: the Households of a Mill Town.* New York: Charities Publication Committee, 1910. First edition, 8vo., 292 pages, foldout photo frontispiece (panorama), green cloth (little dust soiled), very good tight copy, from the library of reformer Florence Kelley (1859-1932). Second Life Books Inc. 182 - 35 2013 $375

Clark, Sue Ainslie *Making both Ends Meet: The Income and Outlay of New York Working Girls.* New York: Macmillan, 1911. First edition, 8vo., 270 pages, nice, frontispiece photo, from the library of reformer Florence Kelley (1859-1932), inscribed by Edith Wyatt to Kelley. Second Life Books Inc. 182 - 41 2013 $65

Du Bois, W. E. B. *The Crises. A Record of the Darker Races. Volume 24 No. 4 Whole Number 142.* New York: NAACP August, 1922. 8vo., pages 147-190 + ads, original pictorial wrappers, front separate, lacking rear wrapper, some nicked and stained, good, rare, from the library of consumer advocate Florence Kelley, rare. Second Life Books Inc. 183 - 114 2013 $175

Goldmark, Josephine *Fatigue and Efficiency a Study in Industry.* New York: Charities Publication Committee, 1912. First edition, 8vo., 591 pages, little rubbed drab green cloth, hinges little tender, very good, from the library of reformer Florence Kelley (1859-1932) presentation copy from author to Kelley. Second Life Books Inc. 182 - 94 2013 $325

Graber, G. *Zurich and Environs.* Zurich: Official General Inquiry Office, 1917. Small 8vo., pages 80, illustrations by C. Conradin, large folded map, printed wrappers, from the library of reformer Florence Kelley (1859-1932) with her light signature and holograph notes, some staining, good. Second Life Books Inc. 182 - 137 2013 $75

Illinois. State Health Commission *Report of the Health Insurance Commission of the State of Illinois.* Springfield: Illinois State Journal May 1, 1919. First edition, 8vo., 647 pages, wrappers, lacks the front, some light marginal stain, consumer advocate Florence Kelley's copy, good. Second Life Books Inc. 183 - 335 2013 $65

Merriam, Charles C. *Report of the City Council Committee on Crime of the City of Chicago.* Chicago: H. G. Adair March 22, 1915. First edition, 8vo., pages 916, foldout-charts, printed wrappers (cover nearly separate, lacks rear), from the library of reformer Florence Kelley (1859-1932). Second Life Books Inc. 182 - 39 2013 $150

Nexo, Martin Andersen *Pelle the Conqueror.* New York: Holt, 1917. 2 volumes, 8vo., red cloth stamped in black, from the library of consumer advocate Florence Kelley with her ownership signature, covers scuffed, spotted and faded, volume I has front hinge tender, volume II has small tear top side of spine and rear hinge tender, very good. Second Life Books Inc. 183 - 290 2013 $65

Pankhurst, E. Sylvia *The Suffragette Movement, an Intimate Account of Persons and Ideals with Illustrations.* London: Longmans Green, 1931. First edition, 8vo., frontispiece, 631 pages, bookplate, small name sticker on endpaper, another removed from front blank otherwise fine, without dust jacket, scarce, from the library of reformer Florence Kelley (1859-1932). Second Life Books Inc. 182 - 186 2013 $175

Parker, Theodore *The Critical and Miscellaneous Writings of...* Boston: Munroe, 1843. First edition, 8vo., pages 360 plus ads, black cloth, partially unopened, from the library of consumer advocate Florence Kelley, front hinge tender, cover somewhat faded and little worn at corners and ends of spine, else very good, ownership signatures of Judge, abolitionist and Congressman, William D. Kelley. Second Life Books Inc. 183 - 311 2013 $85

Association – Kelley, William

Parker, Theodore *The Critical and Miscellaneous Writings of...* Boston: Munroe, 1843. First edition, 8vo., pages 360 plus ads, black cloth, partially unopened, from the library of consumer advocate Florence Kelley, front hinge tender, cover somewhat faded and little worn at corners and ends of spine, else very good, ownership signatures of Judge, abolitionist and Congressman, William D. Kelley. Second Life Books Inc. 183 - 311 2013 $85

Association – Kellogg, Jean

Jeffers, Robinson 1887-1962 *The Loving Shepherdess.* New York: Random House, 1956. Limited to 155 numbered copies (#64), 4to., quarter gilt stamped black cloth over white paper backed boards, black cloth slipcase by Silverlake Bindery, signed by author and artist, with original etchings by Jean Kellogg, additionally signed and inscribed from Kellogg to Dick McGraw, with prospectus, backing sheet and 3 ALS's laid in, fine. Jeff Weber Rare Books 171 - 192 2013 $2000

Association – Kelly, Henry

Longley, Michael *Ten Poems.* Belfast: Festival Publications, Queen's University, 1965. First edition, 8vo., original wrappers, slightly marked, otherwise excellent copy, ownership copy of Henry Kelly with his inscription. Maggs Bros. Ltd. 1442 - 178 2013 £350

Association – Kelly, J.

Smith, William 1813-1893 *Dictionary of Greek and Roman Biography and Mythology. (and) Dictionary of Greek and Roman Geography. (and) Dictionary of Greek and Roman Antiquities.* Boston: Charles C. Little and James Brown; Boston: Little Brown and Co., 1849-1859. Apparently first edition of the first two works, second edition of Antiquities, 230 x 149mm., 3 works in 6 volumes, pleasing half calf in tan, olive or black over buckram or marbled paper, raised bands flanked by thick and thin gilt rules, morocco labels, numerous woodcuts in text, titlepages with contemporary ink inscription "Ex Libris J. Kelly", joints and extremities with bit of rubbing, boards lightly chafed, but fine, fresh little used copies with only most trivial internal imperfections and in solid bindings that make attractive appearance on the shelf.   Phillip J. Pirages   63 - 442   2013 $2000

Association – Kendall, Henry

Karpinski, Louis C. *Bibliography of Mathematical Works Printed in America through 1850.* Ann Arbor & London: University of Michigan Press & Oxford University Press, 1940. First edition, inscribed by author to Henry P. Kendall, Burndy bookplate, 4to., illustrations, dark blue cloth, blind-stamped cover emblem, gilt stamped spine title, extremities lightly speckled, inner hinge cracked, very good.   Jeff Weber Rare Books   169 - 247   2013 $400

Association – Kenne, M.

Josephus, Flavius *The Works of Flavius Josephus.* London: printed for R. Sare, 1702. First L'Estrange edition, folio, many errors in pagination but collates complete, at page 196-7 a pin is visible which is holding gathering in place, p. 199 stained at fore-edge, pages 553-88 with little loss to top margin, page 591 remargined, occasional marginal notes, wax spots and short closed tears, tan Cambridge style calf, red morocco and gilt label to spine, edges sprinkled red, spine creased and scratched, loss to endcaps, joints cracked but cords holding, lower board scraped, corners frayed, prelim blanks loose, inscriptions of M. Kenne stating 'the gift of Rnd. Fortiscue' and Albert Victor Murray, Magdalen and Mansfield Colleges Oxford, May 11 1914, pink 'Cancelled' stamp to front pastedown.   Unsworths Antiquarian Booksellers   28 - 20   2013   £250

Association – Kent, W. Dawson

Clare, John 1754-1832 *The Village Minstrel and Other Poems. (with) Poems Descriptive of Rural Life and Scenery.* London: Taylor & Hessey, 1821. Stamford: E. Drury, 1821. First edition and fourth edition, uniformly bound as "Clare's Poems" in contemporary full purple panelled calf, gilt spines, small chip at head of leading hinge volume 1, hinges and edges little worn, fading to brown in places, contemporary ownership inscription of W. Dawson Kent and armorial bookplates of John A. G. Gere.   Jarndyce Antiquarian Booksellers   CCIII - 480   2013   £850

Association – Kerr, Alfred

Duhamel, Georges *Memorial de la Guerre Blanche.* Paris: Mercure de France, 1939. First edition, 8vo., original yellow wrappers preserved in folding cloth box, wrappers worn, hinges cracking, spine darkened, good copy, inscribed by author for Alfred Kerr.   Maggs Bros. Ltd.   1460 - 258   2013   £175

Association – Kerrigan, J. M.

Mercier, Vivian *The Irish Comic Tradition.* 1962. First edition, 8vo., cloth, dust jacket, some marks, owner inscribed by J. M. Kerrigan (actor), very good.   C. P. Hyland   261 - 603   2013   £50

Association – Kershaw, James

Bible. English - 1827 *The Comprehensive Bible containing the Old and New Testaments.* London: printed for Samuel Bagster, 1827. 330 x 250mm., excellent contemporary black pebble grain morocco, handsomely gilt, covers with floral frame enclosing central panel featuring scrolling cornerpiece compartments and, at center, intricate elongated ornament, wide raised bands with multiple gilt rules and floral endpieces, spine panels tooled gilt, floral and leaf ornaments, gilt titling and turn-ins, all edges gilt (neat older repairs to head and tail of joints); with bustling modern fore-edge painting by Martin Frost, showing flotilla of vessels on Thames with St. Paul's Cathedral in background; large gilt presentation bookplate "Tribute of Respect from Teachers of Mosely Street Sabbath School, Manchester, to their kind and generous friend James Kershaw, Esq. June 28 1838", joints little worn, corners and extremities bit rubbed, one tiny gouge to upper cover, otherwise fine, ornate binding entirely solid and generally well preserved and text exceptionally clean, fresh and smooth.   Phillip J. Pirages   61 - 56   2013 $3500

Association – Kesslere, G. Maillard

Rockwell, Donald S. *Women of Achievement.* New York: House of Field, 1940. First edition, Press numbered edition, number 206, 4to., 213 pages, white cloth, heavily embossed, stamped in gilt, cover worn at corners and ends of spine, spine split along part of its length, one hinge tender, some marginal chips to leaves, otherwise very good, signed by Rockwell and photographer, G. Maillard Kesslere.   Second Life Books Inc.   182 - 201   2013 $75

Association – Kettaneh, Francis

Keats, John 1795-1821 *Endymion: a Poetic Romance.* London: printed for Taylor and Hessey, 1818. First edition, 218 x 135mm., 6 p.l., 207 pages, bound without leaf of ads at back; sumptuous chocolate brown crushed morocco, elaborately gilt and inlaid by Zaehnsdorf (signed on front turn-in and with stamped oval, normally marking firm's best work), covers with gilt ruled and inlaid frames of ochre and maroon morocco, central panel intricately diapered with curving ochre acanthus leaves forming original compartments containing maroon fleuron, raised bands, maroon framed compartments with inlaid ochre and maroon centerpiece, brown morocco doublures and endleaves, doublures continuing use of maroon and ochre inlays to form a frame entwined with sinous leafy vine sprouting berries, all edges gilt, slightly frayed, grey cloth dust jacket with gilt titling, faint foxing on few leaves near back, otherwise only most trivial imperfections, extremely fine, text clean and mostly bright, beautiful binding in perfect condition, bookplate of Francis Kettaneh.   Phillip J. Pirages   61 - 133   2013 $9500

Association – Keynes, Quentin

Pound, Ezra Loomis 1885-1972 *Quia Pauper Amavi.* London: Egoist Ltd., 1919. First edition, number 30 of 100 copies signed by author, with ink correction by Pound of the misprint on line 24 of page 34, correcting "Wherefore" to "Wherefrom" (some copies were not corrected), printed on handmade paper, one short tear margin of page 21, five pages have very minor fox marks, back endpapers with very minor waterstain at lower margin, binding with very slight discoloration, overall very crisp, very good, from the Quentin Keynes collection.   Gemini Fine Books & Arts., Ltd.   Art Reference & Illustrated Books - 2013 $2400

Association – Kidd, Stewart

Rothenstein, William *Men and Memories.* New York: Coward McCann Inc., 1931-1932. First editions, 2 volumes, 244 x 159mml., striking black three quarter morocco by Whitman Bennett for Stewart Kidd (stamp signed), raised bands, spines gilt in compartments with centerpiece of artist's palette and brushes, geometrically patterned paper boards and endpapers, top edge gilt, other edges rough trimmed (second volume largely unopened), 96 collotype plates, just touch of wear to joints and extremities, paper boards, lightly chafed, paper clip impression to front free endpaper of volume I (also affecting pastedown and flyleaf), otherwise quite appealing set in fine condition, bindings especially lustrous and with only minor rubbing, text quite clean and fresh.   Phillip J. Pirages   63 - 408   2013 $225

Association – Killner, Sophia

Duck, Stephen *Poems on Several Occasions.* London: printed for W. Bickerton, 1737. Second edition, 8vo., engraved frontispiece, touch of minor spotting, contemporary sprinkled calf, unlettered spine divided by gilt rules, slight wear to headcap, boards scratched and rear board stained white, contemporary ink ownership inscription Thos. Packwood/E. Libris 1748 and later ink inscription 1811/ Sophia Killner her/Book. Southam Febry 19.   Unsworths Antiquarian Booksellers   28 - 90   2013   £250

Association – Kinal, Murl

Cushing, Harvey Williams 1869-1939 *Meningiomas: Their Classification, Regional Behavior, Life History and Surgical End Resutls.* Springfield: Charles C. Thomas, 1938. First edition, 8vo., frontispiece, illustrations, original navy blue cloth, gilt stamped spine, dust jacket, spine faded, jacket spine ends chipped, ownership signature of Dr. Murl E. Kinal, bookplate of Harry B. Friedman, very good in like dust jacket.   Jeff Weber Rare Books   172 - 67   2013 $1500

Association – Kindersley

Campbell, Thomas 1777-1844 *Gertrude of Wyoming: a Pennsylvania Tale. And Other Poems.* London: Longman, Hurst, Rees & Orme, 1809. First edition, 4to., errata slip, 16 page catalog (Dec. 1808), uncut 8vo. sheets bound in 4to., uncut in original blue boards, edges little rubbed, inner hinges cracking, signed "Kindersley" in contemporary hand, good plus.   Jarndyce Antiquarian Booksellers   CCIII - 463   2013   £150

Association – King, W.

Allsop, Thomas *Letters Conversations and Recollections of S. T. Coleridge.* London: Edward Moxon, 1836. First edition, 2 volumes, half titles, pencil notes in text volume I, original dark green cloth, paper label volume I chipped and missing entirely volume II, spines faded and slightly worn at heads and tails, inscribed to G. H. B. Coleridge by W. King. Mar 14 1944.   Jarndyce Antiquarian Booksellers   CCIII - 557   2013   £85

Association – Kingston, C. U.

Boaden, James *An Inquiry into the Authenticity of Various Pictures and Prints....* London: printed for Robert Triphook, 1824. First edition, scarce large paper copy, with 5 mounted India proofs, tipped in at end is copy of a printed letter from portrait painter Abraham to C. U. Kingston of Ashbourne, Birmingham, March 24th 1847, 4to., later half red morocco, marbled boards, front hinge repaired, spine gilt raised bands, half title, title, 5 plates, tipped in sheet, top edge gilt, fore and bottom edges uncut, fine.   Howard S. Mott Inc.   262 - 18   2013 $400

Association – Kirklees, Mrs.

Byron, George Gordon Noel, 6th Baron 1788-1824 *The Works.* London: John Murray, 1823-1825. 6 volumes, volume 1, slight spotting and browning in prelims, contemporary full dark blue grained calf, spine gilt in compartments, gilt borders and dentelles, occasional rubbing, fading to purple in places, each volume signed Mrs. Kirklees in contemporary hand, good plu.   Jarndyce Antiquarian Booksellers CCIII - 72   2013   £750

Association – Kirkup, John

Wiseman, Richard *Eight Chirurgical Treatises on the Following Heads...* London: Benjamin Tooke and Luke Meedith, 1696. Small folio, few short tears, faint dampstaining in few gatherings, wormtrack bottom margin of few gatherings touching a few letters, contemporary paneled calf with blind rulings, skillfully rebacked saving endpapers, raised bands, green gilt label bookplate of John Kirkup, Thomas Marsh, William Viger (ownership signature dated 1751), light marginalia.   James Tait Goodrich   S74 - 239 2013 $975

Wiseman, Richard *Several Chirurgicall Treatises.* London: E. Flesher and J. Macock for R. Royston, 1676. Half title, small folio, contemporary English panel calf with blind ruling on boards, which have been skilfully rebacked with minor repairs to corners, endpapers saved, small marginal loss in E2, occasional light soiling, staining and short tears in margins, final leaf with large loss in blank margin, touching two letters and laid down, early ownership signatures of William Taylor, from the library of John R. Kirkup with his bookplate.   James Tait Goodrich S74 - 238   2013 $2500

Association – Knight, Charles

Day, Thomas 1748-1789 *A History of Sandford and Merton.* London: F. and C. Rivington et al, 1815. Abridged edition, 8vo., frontispiece, lacks 12 pages of publisher's ads, very good internally, tan marbled sheep, somewhat worn, upper joint cracking, spine and edges rubbed, ownership inscription of Master Charles Knight dated Aug. 16th 1821, with scrap of paper (presumably part of the packaging in which he received it) addressed to same loosely inserted, frontispiece with inscription "C. H. Knight's present to his daughter Fanny. Leamington Jan. 7th 1850" and beneath this ownership inscription of Jack Marshall dated 1887.   Unsworths Antiquarian Booksellers 28 - 156   2013 £30

Association – Knight, Enoch

Book of Mormon *Book of Mormon: An Account Written by the Hand of Mormon...* Paljyra: E. B. Grandin, 1830. First edition, 588 pages, octavo, original brown calf boards with gilt rules on backstrip, completely unsophisticated copy, which has hand no repair or restoration work, contemporary name "Manchester" in ink on rear pastedown, label on backstrip missing, usual foxing, name "Enoch Knight" stamped in small ink twice on front free endsheet.   Ken Sanders Rare Books   45 - 17   2013 $90,000

Association – Knight, Fanny

Day, Thomas 1748-1789 *A History of Sandford and Merton.* London: F. and C. Rivington et al, 1815. Abridged edition, 8vo., frontispiece, lacks 12 pages of publisher's ads, very good internally, tan marbled sheep, somewhat worn, upper joint cracking, spine and edges rubbed, ownership inscription of Master Charles Knight dated Aug. 16th 1821, with scrap of paper (presumably part of the packaging in which he received it) addressed to same loosely inserted, frontispiece with inscription "C. H. Knight's present to his daughter Fanny. Leamington Jan. 7th 1850" and beneath this ownership inscription of Jack Marshall dated 1887.   Unsworths Antiquarian Booksellers 28 - 156   2013 £30

Association – Knight, Joseph

Plutarchus *Les Ouvvres Morales & Meslees du Plutarque.* Paris: De l'Impriemrie de Michel de Vascosan, 1572. First edition, title creased and slightly frayed at edges, short closed tear reinforced with tissue, some light spotting elsewhere, few sections toned, folio 18th century calf, scraped and worn at edges, rebacked, black morocco lettering piece, hinges relined, bookplate of drama critic Joseph Knight (1829-1907), sound.   Blackwell's Rare Books   172 - 116 2013   £3500

Association – Knill, Freda

Llewellyn, Richard *How Green Was My Valley.* New York: Macmillan, 1941. (1940). Later printing, round-robin, signed in fountain pen on location during making of the film on July 19 1941, gift copy from Freda Knill (niece of cast member Thomas A. Hughes) to her daughter, with autographs and inscriptions of Roddy McDowall, Maureen O'Hara, Walter Pidgeon, Donald Crisp, Barry Fitzgerald, Sara Allgood, Anna Lee, T. Arthur Hughes, Richard Fraser and Evan H. Evans; fair to good only, binding intact, shaken and with fraying to edges of cloth, in very good supplied dust jacket with some rubbing and light wear at extremities. Ed Smith Books   75 - 39   2013 $1750

Association – Knox, Richard

Holliday, Thomas *A Complete Treatise on Practical Land Surveying.* London: published by Whittaker and Co., 1838. First edition, 229 x 146mm., recent quite pleasing sympathetic quarter calf over contemporaneous paper boards, raised bands, red morocco label, numerous small illustrations and diagrams in text, 20 engraved plates, ownership inscription "Richard A. Knox July 1884", one leaf with few marginal manuscript calculations, isolated underscoring, lower corners bit rubbed, boards with few stains, upper corner of titlepage reinforced with fore edge of one leaf with neat paper repair, occasional minor soiling and isolated foxing, plates lightly offset onto adjacent leaves, otherwise very good internally, text well preserved and with no significant faults, in skillfully restored and attractive binding.   Phillip J. Pirages   63 - 457   2013 $375

Association – Kobler, John

Joyce, James 1882-1941 *Haveth Childers Everywhere. Fragment from work in Progress.* Paris: Henry Babou and Jack Kahane; New York: The Fountain Press, 1930. First edition, limited issue, one of 100 copies on iridescent handmade Japan, signed by author, this copy #24 (there were an additional 500 on paper and 85 writer's copies), original white paper covers with printed titling on front and spine, leaves untrimmed and unopened in original glassine protective wrapper, whole in original (slightly rubbed), three panel stiff card folder covered with gilt paper (without the original slipcase), title printed in green and black, initials and headlines printed in green, inside front cover of folder with bookplate of John Kobler; corners just slightly bumped, one small faint brown spot to tissue cover, outstanding copy, very fragile and always torn glassine entirely intact and text with no signs of use, most of it never having seen the light of day.   Phillip J. Pirages   63 - 282   2013 $18,000

Joyce, James 1882-1941 *A Portrait of the Artist as a Young Man.* New York: B. W. Huebsch, 1916. First edition, 193 x 125mm, 2 p.l., 299, (1) pages, publisher's blue cloth, blindstamped title on front cover, flat spine with gilt titling, bookplates of John Kobler and of "Porcaro", very slight chafing to joints and extremities, spine ends just little curled, otherwise fine, binding especially clean, spine gilt very bright and text virtually pristine.   Phillip J. Pirages   63 - 284   2013 $9500

Joyce, James 1882-1941 *Stephen Hero, Part of the First Draft of "A Portrait of the Artists as a Young Man".* London: 1944. First edition, 200 x 130mm., 210 pages, publisher's black cloth flat spine with gilt titling, original dust jacket, very nice black clamshell box, bookplate of John Kobler, touch of soil and hint of rumpling to white dust jacket, otherwise fine, volume itself mint.   Phillip J. Pirages   63 - 285   2013 $475

Association – Kolb, Emery

Kolb, E. L. *Through the Grand Canyon from Wyoming to Mexico.* New York: Macmillan, 1914. First edition, presentation inscription signed by author's brother, Emery Kolb and dated 1916, xx, 344 pages, plus publisher's catalog at end, color frontispiece and 7 plates, 103 photos by author and his brother, decorated dark blue cloth stamped in orange and gilt, color illustration pastedown to front cover, slight rubbing to corners of cover pastedown, but very fine.   Argonaut Book Shop   Recent Acquisitions June 2013 - 179   2013 $175

Association – Kreutzberger, Erica

Gordimer, Nadine *The Lying Days.* London: Victor Gollancz, 1953. Second impression, 8vo., original red cloth, excellent copy, spine slightly faded, inscribed by author for Erica Kreutzberger.   Maggs Bros. Ltd.   1460 - 530   2013   £100

Association – Kronenberger, Louis

Auden, Wystan Hugh 1907-1973 *The Dyer's Hand and Other Essays.* New York: Random House, 1962. First edition, 8vo., original green cloth, dust jacket, inscribed by author for Louis Kronenberger, excellent copy in slightly chipped dust jacket.   Maggs Bros. Ltd.   1460 - 27   2013   £375

Association – Kynnersley, Thomas Sneyd

Miller, Philip *The Practical Gardener Containing Plain and Familiar Instructions for Propagating and Improving the Different Kinds of Fruit Trees, Plants and Flowers...* printed by W. Day & Co. for M. Jones, 1805. First edition, 9 engraved plates, 2 folding, others tunred in, 1 frayed and dust soiled at fore-edge, not affecting engraved surface, 8vo., contemporary tree calf, backed marbled boards, ownership inscription of Thomas Sneyd dated 1807 and his armorial bookplate as Thomas Sneyd Kynnersley (of Loxley Park, Staffs, added Kynnersley to his name in 1815), very good.   Blackwell's Rare Books   Sciences - 83   2013   £120

Association – La Bedoyere, H., Comte De

Bonet, Honore *L'Apparition de Jehan de Meun ou le Songe Du Prieur De Salon.* Paris: Imprime par Crapelet pur la Societe des Bibliophiles Francais, 1845. One of 170 copies on vellum (this copy #7 printed for M. Le Comte e La Bedoyere, member of the Societe des Bibliophiles) (another 100 copies on issued on paper), recent fine white pigskin, decorated in blind to a Medieval style by Courtland Benson, housed in titled custom made morocco backed folding cloth box, 10 engraved plates, morocco bookplate of Comte H. De La Bedoyere and engraved bookplate of Marcellus Schlimovich, embossed library stamp of Dr. Detlef Mauss; half title with ink library stamp of Sociedad Hebraica Argentina, fine, especially clean and bright internally, only most trivial imperfections in new retrospective binding. Phillip J. Pirages   63 - 477   2013 $3500

Association – Labouisse, Harry

Eddy, William A. *F. D. R. Meets Ibn Saud.* New York: American Friends of the Middle East Inc., 1954. First edition, near fine, signed twice and inscribed to Harry (Henry R.) Labouisse American diplomat, very scarce.   Leather Stalking Books   October 2013 - 2013 $1500

Association – Lachaise, Gaston

Gallatin, A. E. *Gaston Lachaise. Sixteen Reproductions in Collotype of the Sculptor's Work.* New York: E. P. Dutton & Co., 1924. First edition, limited to 400 copies, 4to., photogravures from photos by Charles Sheeler, original cloth backed boards, printed labels, glassine dust jacket, very fine, unopened copy in somewhat worn and chipped glassine dust jacket, inscribed by Lachaise to friend and patron Scofield Thayer, with Thayer bookplate laid in.   James S. Jaffe Rare Books   Fall 2013 - 8   2013 $1750

Association – Lahr, Karl

Bates, Herbert Ernest   1905-1974 *A German Idyll.* Waltham St. Lawrence: The Golden Cockerel Press, 1932. First edition, number 218 of 307 copies signed by author, small 4to., original quarter red leather, patterned cloth, lettered gilt on spine, fine, inscribed by dedicatee, Karl (Charles) Lahr for F. G. Robinson, wood engravings by Lynton Lamb.   Maggs Bros. Ltd.   1460 - 48   2013   £300

Association – Lake, Atwill

Concanen, Matthew *The Flower-Piece.* London: printed for J. Walthoe, 1731. First edition, little browned in places, 2 leaves crinkled, 12mo., contemporary speckled calf, double gilt fillet borders on sides, spine gilt in compartments, red lettering piece spine worn at head and tail, slightly darkened, upper joint cracked but cords firm, 18th century armorial bookplate of Sir Atwill Lake, with that of Sr John J. Scott Douglas (engraved by Lizars) superimposed, good. Blackwell's Rare Books   B174 - 38   2013   £350

Association – Lamb, Pansy

Dunsany, Edward John Moreton Drax Plunkett   1878-1957 *The Old Folk of the Centuries.* London: Elkin Matthews, 1930. First edition, 8vo., original quarter cloth, marbled paper boards, number 861 of 1000 copies, this being one of 50 copies for presentation, boards scuffed, spine dusty, otherwise very good, inscribed by author for Pansy Longford who married Henry Lamb.   Maggs Bros. Ltd.   1460 - 259   2013   £500

Association – Lancaster, Oscar Ehrhardt

Moore, Thomas *Lalla Rookh, an Oriental Romance.* London: Longman, Hurst, Rees, Orme, Brown and Green, 1824. 218 x 136mm., 2 pl., 397, (1) pages, very pleasing contemporary midnight blue crushed morocco attractively gilt, covers with fillet borders and delicate inner frame, wide raised bands decorated with horizontal gilt fillets and floral tool terminations, spine gilt in compartments featuring unusual obliquely oriented quatrefoil ornament, gilt titling and turn-ins, all edges gilt, with fine later(?) fore-edge painting of an animated London street scene, bookplate of Oscar Ehrhardt Lancaster, touch of rubbing to joints and extremities (but this successfully masked with dye), chalky endpapers a bit blotchy from chemical reaction, slight separation and discoloration at hinge before title leaf, very few trivial marginal spots, still excellent copy, leaves quite clean, fresh and smooth, original decorative binding bright and without any significant wear and painting very well preserved. Phillip J. Pirages   61 - 53   2013 $1250

Association – Lancaster, Richard

Hedley, William *A Complete System of Practical Arithmetic and Three Forms of Bookkeeping...* Newcastle upon Tyne: T. Saint and J. Whitfield & Co., 1779. First and only edition, contemporary speckled sheep, upper joint cracking but firm, early names and scribbles on pastedowns (Richard Lancaster, Kirkby Stephen, Aug. 15th 1791), old inked erasures on title, occasional spots and lightly patched brown patches, rare.   R. F. G. Hollett & Son   Children's Books - 273   2013   £275

Association – Lane, John, Mrs.

France, Anatole *Honey-Bee.* London: John Lane/the Bodley Head, 1911. First edition, illustrations by Florence Lundburg, 4to., original pictorial red cloth blocked in gilt, black and brown, top edge gilt, others untrimmed, inscribed by author to his English translator, Mrs. John Lane, rear hinge cracked, otherwise excellent copy.   Maggs Bros. Ltd. 1460 - 298   2013   £350

Association – Langley, J.

Hobhouse, John Cam *Historical Illustrations of the Fourth Canto of Childe Harold...* London: John Murray, 1818. Second edition, contemporary full vellum, spine gilt in compartments, red label slightly marked, small split to leading hinge, ownership inscription "J. Langley 1829", very good. Jarndyce Antiquarian Booksellers CCIII - 150 2013 £110

Association – Latham, Richard Oskatel

Clare, John 1754-1832 *The Village Minstrel and Other Poems.* London: Taylor & Hessey, 1821. First edition, 2 volumes in 1, frontispiece volume 1, contemporary half calf, gilt spine carefully repaired ata head and hinges, maroon leather label, armorial bookplate of Richard Oskatel Latham. Jarndyce Antiquarian Booksellers CCIII - 482 2013 £450

Association – Lauderdale, Earl of

Fielding, Henry 1707-1754 *An Enquiry into the Causes of the Late Increase of Robbers, &c...* London: printed for A. Millar, 1751. First edition, 8vo., full brown calf by Whitman Bennett of NY, with shelfmark "Lauderdale Law" in contemporary hand, presumably Earl of Lauderdale. Howard S. Mott Inc. 262 - 49 2013 $750

Association – Lawson, Thomas

Pyne, William Henry 1769-1843 *The History of the Royal Residences of Windsor Castle, St. James's Palace, Carlton House, Kensington Palace, Hampton Court....* London: printed for A. Dry...., 1819. First edition, large paper copy, 3 volumes, 100 hand colored aquatint plates, plate of Frogmore Exterior supplied from smaller copy, full green morocco by Charles E. Lauriat Boston, USA, covers with ruled borders enclosing spandrels of leafy sprigs and flower beads, spines in six compartments, four similarly decorated and lettered gilt, dates at foot, silk endpapers, bookplate of Thomas W. Lawson. Marlborough Rare Books Ltd. 218 - 121 2013 £7500

Association – Layden, Elmer

Whittle, Glenn *1935 Supplement to the Intercollegiate Football 1869-1934.* St. Paul: Intercollegiate Football Association, 1935. Thin quarto, wrappers, slight wear and short tear top of spine, else very good, ownership stamp, facsimile of his signature of Elmer Layden on titlepage. Between the Covers Rare Books, Inc. Football Books - 83773 2013 $125

Association – Leay, Joseph

Cooper, Ambrose *The Complete Distiller.* printed for P. Vaillant, 1757. First edition, folding engraved plate, slight offsetting on plate, tendency to browning, 8vo., contemporary calf, rebacked preserving original spine, corners worn, ownership inscription on title of Joseph Leay, Feb. 26th 1822 on title, pencil scribblings on verso of half title in same hand, armorial bookplate of one of the Barons Caher, good. Blackwell's Rare Books Sciences - 36 2013 £950

Association – Lee, Anna

Llewellyn, Richard *How Green Was My Valley.* New York: Macmillan, 1941. (1940). Later printing, round-robin, signed in fountain pen on location during making of the film on July 19 1941, gift copy from Freda Knill (niece of cast member Thomas A. Hughes) to her daughter, with autographs and inscriptions of Roddy McDowall, Maureen O'Hara, Walter Pidgeon, Donald Crisp, Barry Fitzgerald, Sara Allgood, Anna Lee, T. Arthur Hughes, Richard Fraser and Evan H. Evans; fair to good only, binding intact, shaken and with fraying to edges of cloth, in very good supplied dust jacket with some rubbing and light wear at extremities. Ed Smith Books 75 - 39 2013 $1750

Association – Lee, Henry

Buckland, Francis Trevelyan *Log-Book of a Fisherman and Zoologist.* London: Chapman & Hall, 1875. First edition, wood engraved frontispiece, 3 plates, illustrations in text, some full page, endpapers through-set on to outside of flyleaves, 8vo., original green cloth, slightly darkened and worn, neat repair to front inner hinge and spine ends, inscribed by author to friend Henry Lee of the Brighton aquarium, good. Blackwell's Rare Books 172 - 37 2013 £300

Association – Lee, P. R.

Bigmore, E. C. *A Bibliography of Printing with Notes and Illustrations.* London: Bernard Quaritch, 1880-1886. small 4to., 3 volumes in 1, two color title (printed in red and black), illustrations, original brown leather (signed by Bennett, NY), professionally rebacked by Bruce Levy, gilt stamped spine title with raised spine bands, top edge gilt, some marginal checkmarks, bookplates of Marcus Crahan and the Zamorano Club (gift of Crahan), signature P. R. Lee Jr. (1939), near fine, choice copy. Jeff Weber Rare Books 171 - 31 2013 $750

Association – Lee, William

Burke, Edmund   1729-1797   *Reflections on the Revolution in France and on the Proceedings in Certain Societies in London Relative to that Event...*   London: printed for J. Dodsley, 1790.   First edition, first issue, 19th century half sheep over marbled boards, original bluish-gray drab wrappers bound in to front and back, some wear at corners and joints, spine bit scuffed, some occasional pale spotting along top edge, overall very nice, octavo, the copy of William Lee, Bart (presentation inscription) and of Archibald Philip Primrose, 5th Earl of Rosebery, ALS to Rosebery from John Morley tipped in, small Rosebery/Durdans blindstamp on titlepage and page 99, gift inscription, armorial bookplate.   Heritage Book Shop   50th Anniversary Catalogue - 16   2013 $15,000

Association – Legge, Georg

Newton, Isaac   1642-1727   *Opera Qua Extant Omnia.*   printed by John Nichols, 1779-1785.   First edition, diagrams in text, 33 engraved plates, some folding, half title to volume iv slightly soiled, very occasional spotting and little dampstaining in lower margin of volume v, contemporary mottled calf, all volumes sturdily rebacked preserving most all of the original spines, which are gilt in compartments, red lettering piece, numbering pieces absent, Snelston Hall bookplate in each volume, ink signature of ?George Legge erased in each volume, good.   Blackwell's Rare Books   Sciences - 88   2013   £6500

Association – Leigh, Theodosia

Tacitus, Cornelius   *The Works of...*   London: printed for G. G. J. and J. Robinson, 1793.   4 volumes, 4to., folding engraved maps, plates somewhat foxed, contemporary speckled calf, spines gilt in compartments, red and black morocco labels, rubbed, corners and endcaps worn, joints cracking, label from first two and partly lost from third volumes, stipple engraved booklabel of Theo. Leigh/Toft, ink ownership inscription 'Theodosia Leigh'.   Unsworths Antiquarian Booksellers   28 - 51   2013   £300

Association – Leighton, Frederic

Browning, Robert   1812-1889   *Poems.*   London: Chapman & Hall, 1849.   New edition, 8vo., original brown bevelled cloth, inscribed by author for Frederic Leighton Aug. 2 56, with Leighton's distinctive bookplate by Robert Anning Bell, worn at extremities, otherwise excellent set in quarter blue leather slipcase, lettered in gilt.   Maggs Bros. Ltd.   1460 - 146   2013   £3000

Association – Leighton, T. K.

Coleridge, Samuel Taylor   1772-1834   *Aids to Reflection in the Formation of a Manly Character on the Several Grounds of Prudence, Morality and Religion...*   London: William Pickering, 1839.   Fourth edition, Half title, contemporary plain maroon morocco by Hayday, slightly rubbed, signature of T. K. Leighton, 1842, all edges gilt.   Jarndyce Antiquarian Booksellers   CCIII - 547   2013   £50

Association – Leo, E. F.

Davenant, William   1606-1668   *The Works of Sr. William Davenant Kt...*   London: by T. N. for Henry Herringman, 1673.   First collected edition, folio, portrait, turn of the century red levant morocco, gilt arabesque centerpiece on covers, all edges gilt, by Riviere, very skillfully rebacked, though the new leather at joints and on cords has uniformly faded, unusually fine, fresh, wide margined copy with fine impression of the portrait, leather tipped fleece lined slipcase, edges rubbed, bookplates of Duke of Beaufort, E. F. Leo, A. E. Newton.   Joseph J. Felcone Inc.   English and American Literature to 1800 - 12   2013 $2200

Association – Leperly, Paul

Hardy, Thomas   1840-1928   *Jude the Obscure.*   Lakewood: printed for private circulation, 1917.   First edition, number 11 of 27 numbered copies, 12mo., original printed gray wrappers, stitched as issued, wrappers slightly browned, fine, the letter was owned by Paul Leperly who privately printed this limited edition, inscribed by Leperly, from the Gary Lepper Collection of Thomas Hardy.   The Brick Row Book Shop   Bulletin Nine - 61   2013 $650

Association – Lepper, Gary

Cox, J. Stevens   *Monographs on the Life of Thomas Hardy.*   Beaminster: Dorset & elsewhere: Stevens Cox, the Toucan Press, 1962-1971.   72 volumes, 12mo., original wrappers, stapled as issued, numerous illustrations, uniformly very good, from the Gary Lepper Collection of Thomas Hardy.   The Brick Row Book Shop   Bulletin Nine - 101   2013 $850

Ellis, Henry Havelock   1859-1939   *Concerning Jude the Obscure.*   London: Ulysses Bookshop, 1931.   First edition, number 14 of 185 numbered copies signed by Ellis, 4to., original gray cloth, salmon paper boards, printed in black on upper board, untrimmed, fine in original glassine wrapper, from the Gary Lepper Collection of Thomas Hardy.   The Brick Row Book Shop   Bulletin Nine - 91   2013 $125

ASSOCIATION COPIES

Griersn, Francis *Modern Mysticism and Other Essays.* London: George Allen, 1899. First edition, 12mo., original green cloth, gilt lettering, cloth waterstained, very good, from Thomas Hardy's library with his posthumous Max Gate bookplate and his signature, tipped to front free endpaper is printed presentation slip from publisher, George Allen, from the Gary Lepper Collection of Thomas Hardy. The Brick Row Book Shop Bulletin Nine - 43 2013 $750

Hardy, Thomas 1840-1928 *A Catalogue of the Library of Thomas Hardy...* London: Messrs. Hodgson, 1938. First edition, 55 pages, 309 lots, fine, original printed wrappers, 4to., from the Gary Lepper Collection of Thomas Hardy. The Brick Row Book Shop Bulletin Nine - 94 2013 $250

Hardy, Thomas 1840-1928 *A Changed Man, The Waiting Supper and Other Tales. Concluding with the Romantic Adventures of a Milkmaid.* London: Macmillan, 1913. First edition, colonial issue, 8vo., original decorated pale blue cloth, gilt lettered, frontispiece and double page map, 8 page publisher's catalog, cloth faded, somewhat worn, good copy, from the Gary Lepper Collection of Thomas Hardy. The Brick Row Book Shop Bulletin Nine - 54 2013 $450

Hardy, Thomas 1840-1928 *A Changed Man, The Waiting Supper and Other Tales. Concluding with the Romantic Adventures of a Milkmaid.* London: Macmillan, 1913. First edition, 8vo., original dark green cloth, gilt lettered, top edge gilt, frontispiece, double page map, 2 pages publisher's terminal ads, edges little worn, very good in like dust jacket (spine darkened, edges worn), from the Gary Lepper Collection of Thomas Hardy. The Brick Row Book Shop Bulletin Nine - 52 2013 $400

Hardy, Thomas 1840-1928 *Compassion: an Ode in Celebration of the Royal Society for the Prevention of Cruelty to Animals.* Dorchester: privately printed, 1924. First edition, number 8 of 25 numbered copies, initialed by Florence Emily Hardy on colophon page, 4to., original printed wrappers, stitched as issued, 6 pages, fine in chemise and quarter morocco slipcase, from the Gary Lepper Collection of Thomas Hardy. The Brick Row Book Shop Bulletin Nine - 69 2013 $3500

Hardy, Thomas 1840-1928 *The Duke's Reappearance: a Tradition.* New York: privately printed, 1927. First separate edition, number 30 of 89 numbered copies, 8vo., original yellow paper boards, printed paper label, boards slightly soiled, fine, from the Gary Lepper Collection of Thomas Hardy. The Brick Row Book Shop Bulletin Nine - 78 2013 $250

Hardy, Thomas 1840-1928 *The Dynasts: a Drama of the Napoleonic Wars in Three Parts, Nineteen Acts and One Hundred and Thirty Scenes.* London: Macmillan, 1903-1908. First edition, first issue volume one, second issue of volume two with titlepage a cancel, 3 volumes, 8vo., original olive-green cloth, gilt decoration and lettering, bookplate on front pastedown in volume one of Edward Joseph Dent, cloth little worn, hinges in volume one carefully repaired, very good in original printed dust jackets which have had skillful paper restoration to corners and spines, enclosed in chemise and morocco slipcase, from the Gary Lepper Collection of Thomas Hardy. The Brick Row Book Shop Bulletin Nine - 46 2013 $4500

Hardy, Thomas 1840-1928 *The Dynasts: a Drama of the Napoleonic Wars, in Three Parts, Nineteen Acts & One Hundred and Thirty Scenes.* New York and London: Macmillan, 1904-1906. First American edition of part one and first English edition of Part second, second state as issued, 2 volumes, 8vo., original dark green cloth, gilt decoration and lettering, fine, from the Gary Lepper Collection of Thomas Hardy. The Brick Row Book Shop Bulletin Nine - 47 2013 $750

Hardy, Thomas 1840-1928 *The Dynasts: an Epic Poems of the War with Napoleon.* London: Macmillan, 1910. First one volume edition, 8vo., original green cloth, gilt lettered, frontispiece, one leaf of publisher's ads, followed by 32 page publisher catalog, fine presentation copy inscribed by author for Miss Alice Balfour, 1912 with her stylized initials, cloth slightly worn, very good, enclosed in morocco clamshell box, from the Gary Lepper Collection of Thomas Hardy. The Brick Row Book Shop Bulletin Nine - 50 2013 $6000

Hardy, Florence *The Early Life of Thomas Hardy 1840-1891. (with) The Later Years of Thomas Hardy 1892-1928.* London: Macmillan, 1928-1930. First edition, 2 volumes, 8vo., original light green cloth, gilt lettering, top edge gilt, frontispiece in each volume and 25 plates, cloth slightly worn, fine copies in slightly worn dust jackets, from the Gary Lepper Collection of Thomas Hardy. The Brick Row Book Shop Bulletin Nine - 87 2013 $200

Hardy, Thomas 1840-1928 *Earth and Air and Rain: Ten Songs for Baritone and Piano. Words by Thomas Hardy. Music by Gerald Finzi.* Paris: London: New York: Sydney: Boosey & Hawkes, 1936. First edition, original orange down printed wrappers slightly worn, 15 pages, fine, from the Gary Lepper Collection of Thomas Hardy. The Brick Row Book Shop Bulletin Nine - 93 2013 $125

Hardy, Thomas   1840-1928   *The Famous Tragedy of the Queen of Cornwall at Tintagel in Lyonnesse.*   London: Macmillan, 1923.   First edition, 4to., original decorated green cloth, gilt lettering, frontispiece, one plate, fine in slightly worn and darkened dust jacket, from the Gary Lepper Collection of Thomas Hardy.   The Brick Row Book Shop   Bulletin Nine - 67   2013 $200

Hardy, Thomas   1840-1928   *The Famous Tragedy of the Queen of Cornwall. At Tintagel in Lyonnesse.*   Dorchester: 1923.   First edition, 4to., original blue wrappers, stitched as issued (8) pages, one illustration, 2 news clippings about performance tipped inside front wrappers, little browned at edges and slightly worn, very good, remaining portions of original envelope, from the Gary Lepper Collection of Thomas Hardy.   The Brick Row Book Shop   Bulletin Nine - 71   2013 $400

Hardy, Thomas   1840-1928   *Far from the Madding Crowd.*   New York: Henry Holt, 1874.   First American edition, small 8vo., original decorated white cloth, black lettering, publisher's ads on endpapers dated Nov. 17 1874, cloth somewhat soiled, good copy, from the Gary Lepper Collection of Thomas Hardy.   The Brick Row Book Shop   Bulletin Nine - 4   2013 $100

Hardy, Thomas   1840-1928   *The Greenwood Edition of the Novels and Stories of Thomas Hardy.*   London: New York: Macmillan, 1964.   Reprint, 18 volumes, 8vo., original blue cloth, gilt lettered, map of Wessex on endpapers, fine in somewhat worn dust jacket, from the Gary Lepper Collection of Thomas Hardy.   The Brick Row Book Shop   Bulletin Nine - 102   2013 $250

Hardy, Thomas   1840-1928   *A Group of Noble Dames.*   Melbourne: Sydney and Adelaide: E. A. Petherick; London: James R. Osgood, 1891.   First Australian edition, using sheets of London edition with new titlepage, 8vo., original blue-green cloth, gilt lettered, publisher's ads dated Aug. 1891, cloth little worn, front blank removed, very good, from the Gary Lepper Collection of Thomas Hardy.   The Brick Row Book Shop   Bulletin Nine - 24   2013 $650

Hardy, Thomas   1840-1928   *A Group of Noble Dames.*   New York: Harper and Brothers, 1891.   First American edition, 8vo., original decorated brown cloth, gilt lettering, frontispiece and five plates, 4 pages of publisher's terminal ads, printed on thick paper and spine decorations more elaborate than subsequent issues, prelims slightly soiled, fine, from the Gary Lepper Collection of Thomas Hardy.   The Brick Row Book Shop   Bulletin Nine - 22   2013 $375

Hardy, Thomas   1840-1928   *A Group of Noble Dames.*   New York: Harper and Brothers, 1891.   First American edition, 8vo., 4 pages publisher's terminal ads, original decorated brown cloth, gilt lettered, frontispiece and five plates, printed on thin paper and decorations on spine less elaborate, probably second of two states, edges little rubbed, good, from the Gary Lepper Collection of Thomas Hardy.   The Brick Row Book Shop   Bulletin Nine - 23   2013 $300

Hardy, Thomas   1840-1928   *The Hand of Ethelberta: a Comedy in Chapters.*   New York: Henry Holt, 1876.   First American edition, 8vo., original decorated white cloth, black lettering, publisher's ads on endpapers dated May 9 1876, earliest issue has May 9 1876 date on front free endpaper as here, cloth little soiled, very good, from the Gary Lepper Collection of Thomas Hardy.   The Brick Row Book Shop   Bulletin Nine - 5   2013 $500

Hardy, Thomas   1840-1928   *"How I Built Myself a House." in Chamber's Journal of Popular Literature, Science and Art...*   London & Edinburgh: W. & R. Chambers, 18 March, 1865.   Third Annual volume, consisting of 24 issues, large 8vo., contemporary brown quarter calf, marbled boards, black leather label, gilt lettering, edges little rubbed, very good, from the Gary Lepper Collection of Thomas Hardy.   The Brick Row Book Shop   Bulletin Nine - 1   2013 $275

Hardy, Thomas   1840-1928   *Jude the Obscrue.*   Lakewood: printed for private circulation, 1917.   First edition, number 11 of 27 numbered copies, 12mo., original printed gray wrappers, stitched as issued, wrappers slightly browned, fine, the letter was owned by Paul Leperly who privately printed this limited edition, inscribed by Leperly, from the Gary Lepper Collection of Thomas Hardy.   The Brick Row Book Shop   Bulletin Nine - 61   2013 $650

Hardy, Thomas   1840-1928   *Jude the Obscure.*   London: Osgood, McIlvaine, 1896.   First edition, 8vo., original dark green cloth, front blocked in gold with monogram medallion, top edge gilt, gilt lettering, fine, bright copy in original publisher's printed dust jacket (two very small chips at edges), enclosed in chemise and quarter morocco slipcase, from the Gary Lepper Collection of Thomas Hardy.   The Brick Row Book Shop   Bulletin Nine - 35   2013 $30,000

Hardy, Thomas   1840-1928   *Late Lyrics and Earlier with Many Other Verses.*   London: Macmillan, 1922.   First edition, 8vo., original olive green cloth, gilt decoration and lettering, neat signature on front free endpaper dated June 13 1922, scattered spots of foxing, fine in publisher's dust jacket (just slightly worn), from the Gary Lepper Collection of Thomas Hardy.   The Brick Row Book Shop   Bulletin Nine - 66   2013 $350

Hardy, Thomas 1840-1928 *Life's Little Ironies: a Set of Tales with Some Colloquial Sketches.* London and New York: Macmillan, 1894. First edition, colonial issue, 8vo., original printed wrappers, 301 pages, 7 pages publisher's ads dated July 20 1894, wrappers little soiled and worn, very good, from the Gary Lepper Collection of Thomas Hardy.   The Brick Row Book Shop   Bulletin Nine - 28   2013 $150

Hardy, Thomas 1840-1928 *The Mayor of Casterbridge. The Life and Death of a Man of Character.* London: Smith Elder, 1886. First edition, first binding, 2 volumes, 8vo., original decorated blue cloth, black and gilt lettering, 2 pages of publisher's terminal ads in volume one and four pages in volume two, cloth little worn and soiled, particularly at edges, some light foxing, very good, from the Gary Lepper Collection of Thomas Hardy.   The Brick Row Book Shop   Bulletin Nine - 16   2013 $7500

Hardy, Thomas 1840-1928 *The Mellstock Edition of the Works in Thirty-Seven Volumes.* London: Macmillan and Co., 1919-1920. First edition, one of 500 copies signed by author, 37 volumes, 8vo., original blue cloth, gilt decorated and lettered spines, untrimmed, frontispiece, map, fine, from the Gary Lepper Collection of Thomas Hardy.   The Brick Row Book Shop   Bulletin Nine - 62   2013 $12,500

Hardy, Thomas 1840-1928 *Old Mrs. Chundle: a Short Story.* New York: Crosby Gaige, 1929. First edition, number 117 of 700 numbered copies, 8vo., original green cloth spine, decorated boards, gilt lettering, untrimmed, vignette title, fine in publisher's glassine, wrapper, from the Gary Lepper Collection of Thomas Hardy.   The Brick Row Book Shop   Bulletin Nine - 90   2013 $75

Hardy, Thomas 1840-1928 *Our Exploits at West Poley by Thomas Hardy.* London: Oxford University Press, 1952. First edition, one of 1000 numbered copies, 8vo., original blue cloth, silver lettering, vignette title and two wood engravings by Lynton Lamb, fine in dust jacket, from the Gary Lepper Collection of Thomas Hardy.   The Brick Row Book Shop   Bulletin Nine - 100   2013 $75

Hardy, Thomas 1840-1928 *A Pair of Blue Eyes.* Philadelphia: Henry T. Coates, circa, 1897. Later American edition, 8vo., original decorated dark green cloth, gilt lettering, top edge gilt, uncommon, date taken from ink signature on front free endpaper dated Sept. 23 1897, fine, from the Gary Lepper Collection of Thomas Hardy.   The Brick Row Book Shop   Bulletin Nine - 39   2013 $1000

Hardy, Thomas 1840-1928 *The Return of the Native.* London: Smith Elder, 1878. First edition, 3 volumes, 8vo., original decorated brown cloth, gilt lettering, frontispiece, faint evidence of lending library labels on upper boards of each volume, bookplate of American collector Kenyon Starling on front pastedown, below which is the earlier bookplate of illustrator and connoisseur Pickford Waller, designed by Austin Osman Spare circa 1907, cloth little worn and soiled, some light foxing, particularly on prelims, very good, from the Gary Lepper Collection of Thomas Hardy.   The Brick Row Book Shop   Bulletin Nine - 6   2013 $10,000

Hardy, Thomas 1840-1928 *Romantic Adventures of a Milkmaid.* New York: John W. Lovell, 1883. One of several unauthorized American editions, 12mo., original pictorial wrappers, 91 pages, wrappers little stained and soiled, very good, from the Gary Lepper Collection of Thomas Hardy. The Brick Row Book Shop   Bulletin Nine - 14   2013 $125

Hardy, Thomas 1840-1928 *Selected Poems of...* London: Liverpool and Boston: the Medici Society, 1921. First Medici Society edition, number 313 of 1000 numbered copies, signed by Hardy with his holograph note, laid in is note sent Feb. 21 1928 from Florence Hardy to Lucy Chew of Bryn Mawr, PA, 8vo., original tan cloth spine, blue boards and printed paper labels, frontispiece, engraved titlepage, fine in original printed dust jacket, slightly faded and enclosed in chemise and quarter morocco slipcase, from the Gary Lepper Collection of Thomas Hardy.   The Brick Row Book Shop   Bulletin Nine - 67   2013 $3750

Hardy, Thomas 1840-1928 *The Sergant's Song (1803). Words by Thomas Hardy Music by Gustav Holst.* London: Edwin Ashdown, 1923. First edition, 4to., original printed self wrappers, fine, from the Gary Lepper Collection of Thomas Hardy.   The Brick Row Book Shop Bulletin Nine - 68   2013 $350

Hardy, Thomas 1840-1928 *The Short Stories of Thomas Hardy.* London: Macmillan, 1928. First edition, 8vo., original maroon cloth, gilt lettering, fine in very slightly worn dust jacket, from the Gary Lepper Collection of Thomas Hardy. The Brick Row Book Shop   Bulletin Nine - 86   2013 $150

Hardy, Thomas 1840-1928 *The Society for the Protection of Ancient Buildings. The General Meeting of the Society: Twenty-Ninth Annual Report of the Committee and Paper Read by Thomas Hardy Esq. June 1906.* London: 1906. First edition, 8vo., original printed pale blue wrappers, 98 pages, 2 plates, leaflet about the Society laid in, edges slightly foxed, fine, from the Gary Lepper Collection of Thomas Hardy.   The Brick Row Book Shop   Bulletin Nine - 48   2013 $150

Hardy, Thomas   1840-1928   *Tess of the D'Urbervilles. A Pure Woman.*   London: Osgood McIlvaine, 1895.   First Wessex Novels Edition, 8vo., original green cloth, gilt decoration and lettering, top edge gilt, etched frontispiece, one plate, map, from the library of English author A. E. Coppard, paper browning slightly in margins, very good, from the Gary Lepper Collection of Thomas Hardy.   The Brick Row Book Shop   Bulletin Nine - 33   2013 $250

Hardy, Thomas   1840-1928   *Tess of the D'Urbervilles: a Pure Woman.*   London: Osgood, McIlvaine, 1892.   First one volume edition, called the "fifth Edition", 8vo., original beige cloth, gilt decorations and brown lettering, frontispiece, later ink signature, cloth slightly soiled, very good, from the Gary Lepper Collection of Thomas Hardy.   The Brick Row Book Shop   Bulletin Nine - 26   2013 $500

Hardy, Thomas   1840-1928   *Tess of the D'Urbervilles: a Pure Woman.*   London: Macmillan and Co., 1926.   First edition thus, one of 325 large paper copies signed by author, royal 4to., original quarter velum, marbled paper sides, gilt lettering, frontispiece and engravings, fine in nearly fine dust jacket, few mended tears on verso, some slight creases, from the Gary Lepper Collection of Thomas Hardy.   The Brick Row Book Shop   Bulletin Nine - 74   2013 $3500

Hardy, Thomas   1840-1928   *Tess of the D'Urbervilles: a Pure Woman Faithfully Presented.*   London: Osgood McIlvaine, 1891.   First edition, 3 volumes, 8vo., sand colored cloth, gilt decorations and lettering after designs by Charles Ricketts, from the British Club Library at Malaga, Spain with their bookplate, from the Gary Lepper Collection of Thomas Hardy, LA Bookseller Maxwell Hunley sold to Estelle Doheny Dec. 3 1932, some foxing, few edges slightly bumped, three hinges skillfully repaired, fine, unusually bright copy, enclosed in chemise and quarter morocco slipcase.   The Brick Row Book Shop   Bulletin Nine - 25   2013 $17,500

Hardy, Thomas   1840-1928   *The Thieves Who Couldn't Help Sneezing...*   Waterville: Colby College Library, 1942.   First separate edition, number 78 of 100 numbered copies, 8vo., white linen spine, decorated boards, yellow lettering, from the Gary Lepper Collection of Thomas Hardy.   The Brick Row Book Shop   Bulletin Nine - 96   2013 $75

Hardy, Thomas   1840-1928   *The Three Wayfarers: a Play in One Act.*   Dorchester: printed by Henry Ling (for Florence Emily Hardy), 1935.   First English edition, one of 250 copies, 4to., original printed white wrappers, stitched as issued, wrappers slightly soiled and foxed, very good, from the Gary Lepper Collection of Thomas Hardy.   The Brick Row Book Shop   Bulletin Nine - 92   2013 $125

Hardy, Thomas   1840-1928   *The Trumpet Major. A Tale.*   London: Sampson Low Marston, Searle & Rivington, 1881.   Cheap edition, first one volume edition, 8vo., original decorated red cloth, gilt lettering, 32 page publisher's catalog dated Jan. 1881, cloth little soiled and worn, very good, morocco clamshell box, inscribed by author for Tindal Atkinson, with holograph note by Hardy on his Max Gate stationery to Atkinson, from the Gary Lepper Collection of Thomas Hardy.   The Brick Row Book Shop   Bulletin Nine - 10   2013 $4500

Hardy, Thomas   1840-1928   *The Trumpet Major: a Tale.*   London: Smith, Elder, 1880.   First edition in book form, 2nd issue binding, 3 volumes, 8vo., original pictorial red cloth, black and gilt lettering, faint evidence of lending library labels on upper boards, edges lightly foxed, minor wear to cloth, very nice in chemises and quarter morocco slipcase, from the Gary Lepper Collection of Thomas Hardy.   The Brick Row Book Shop   Bulletin Nine - 9   2013 $10,000

Hardy, Thomas   1840-1928   *Two on a Tower.*   New York: Henry Holt, 1882.   First American edition, small 8vo., original pictorial mustard yellow cloth, black and gilt lettering, publisher's ads on front and rear endpapers, fine, from the Gary Lepper Collection of Thomas Hardy.   The Brick Row Book Shop   Bulletin Nine - 12   2013 $400

Hardy, Thomas   1840-1928   *Two on a Tower.*   New York: John W. Lovell, circa, 1882.   Pirated American edition, 8vo., original decorated mustard yellow cloth, gilt lettering, 2 pages terminal ads, paper little browned, fine, from the Gary Lepper Collection of Thomas Hardy.   The Brick Row Book Shop   Bulletin Nine - 13   2013 $425

Hardy, Thomas   1840-1928   *Under the Greenwood Tree: a Rural Painting of the Dutch School.*   New York: Henry Holt, 1873.   First American edition, second issue with the Henry Holt imprint, small 8vo., original decorated yellow cloth, black lettering, cloth little worn, very good, enclosed in clamshell box, from the Gary Lepper Collection of Thomas Hardy.   The Brick Row Book Shop   Bulletin Nine - 2   2013 $600

Hardy, Thomas   1840-1928   *Under the Greenwood Tree: a Rural Painting of the Dutch School.*   New York: Hovendon Company, n.d. but circa, 1895.   Uncommon later American edition, 8vo., original decorated light green cloth, dark green lettering, cloth slightly worn, fine, from the Gary Lepper Collection of Thomas Hardy.   The Brick Row Book Shop   Bulletin Nine - 34   2013 $175

Hardy, Thomas 1840-1928 *Unos Ojos Azules. (A Pair of Blue Eyes).* Barcelona: Gustavo Gili, 1919. First edition in Spanish, 2 volumes, 8vo., original decorated brown pictorial cloth, gilt decorations and lettering, fine, presentation copy inscribed by author to George Douglas, from the Gary Lepper Collection of Thomas Hardy. The Brick Row Book Shop   Bulletin Nine - 63   2013 $4500

Hardy, Thomas 1840-1928 *The Variorum Edition of the Complete Poems of Thomas Hardy.* London: Macmillan, 1979. First edition, 2nd issue, 4to., original red cloth, gilt lettering, fine in fine dust jacket, signed by editor, John Gibson, from the Gary Lepper Collection of Thomas Hardy. The Brick Row Book Shop   Bulletin Nine - 104   2013   £100

Hardy, Thomas 1840-1928 *The Well-Beloved: a Sketch of Temperament.* New York: Harper & Brothers, 1897. First American edition, 8vo., original green cloth, gilt decorations and lettering, frontispiece and maps, cloth little spotted, fine in original printed dust jacket which is little browned and slightly stained, overall very good, from the Gary Lepper Collection of Thomas Hardy. The Brick Row Book Shop   Bulletin Nine - 40   2013 $1000

Hardy, Thomas 1840-1928 *Wessex Poems and other Verses.* Toronto: George N. Morang, 1899. First Canadian edition using sheets of American Harper & Brothers edition of same year, 8vo., original pictorial green cloth, gilt lettering, frontispiece and 29 illustrations, cloth little soiled and worn, very good, from the Gary Lepper Collection of Thomas Hardy. The Brick Row Book Shop   Bulletin Nine - 41   2013 $350

Hardy, Thomas 1840-1928 *Winter Words in Various Moods and Metres.* New York: Macmillan, 1928. First American edition, advance page proofs, oblong 4to., loose sheets, set up mostly two pages per sheet on rectos only, with few sheets halved, 184 pages, very good, enclosed in chemise and cloth slipcase, from the Gary Lepper Collection of Thomas Hardy. The Brick Row Book Shop   Bulletin Nine - 83   2013 $1500

Hardy, Thomas 1840-1928 *Winter Words: in Various Moods and Metres.* London: Macmillan, 1928. First edition, 8vo., original light green cloth, gilt decoration and lettering, fine in very good dust jacket, spine somewhat darkened, from the Gary Lepper Collection of Thomas Hardy. The Brick Row Book Shop   Bulletin Nine - 82   2013 $300

Hardy, Thomas 1840-1928 *The Woodlanders.* London and New York: Macmillan, 1887. First edition, 2nd binding, 3 volumes, 8vo., original dark green pebbled cloth, gilt lettering, few hinges repaired, edges lightly rubbed, fine, from the Gary Lepper Collection of Thomas Hardy. The Brick Row Book Shop   Bulletin Nine - 18   2013 $3500

Hardy, Thomas 1840-1928 *The Woodlanders...* London and New York: Macmillan, 1903. Later printing of 1895 Wessex Novels, 8vo., original blue cloth, gilt decoration and lettering, 10 pages of publisher's terminal ads, cloth slightly worn, very good. from the Gary Lepper Collection of Thomas Hardy. The Brick Row Book Shop   Bulletin Nine - 45   2013 $3000

Hardy, Thomas 1840-1928 *Yuletide in a Younger World.* New York: William Edwin Rudge, 1927. First American edition, one of only 27 copies, 12mo., original printed pale yellow wrappers stapled as issued, fine, from the Gary Lepper Collection of Thomas Hardy. The Brick Row Book Shop   Bulletin Nine - 77   2013 $450

Purdy, Richard L. *Thomas Hardy 1840-1928: Catalogue of a Memorial Exhibition of First Editions, Autograph Letters and Manuscripts.* New Haven: Yale University Library, 1928. First edition, one of 25 copies on rag paper, designed by Carl Purington, 8vo. original tan linen spine, blue boards, black lettering, untrimmed, presentation copy from Purdy to American Literature scholar and curator, Gilbert Troxell, with note and Hardy keepsake, also produced by Purdy laid in, fine, from the Gary Lepper Collection of Thomas Hardy. The Brick Row Book Shop   Bulletin Nine - 85   2013 $300

Weber, Carl J. *Hardy Music at Colby. A Check-List Compiled with an Introduction.* Waterville: Colby College Library, 1945. First edition, one of 200 copies, fine, 8vo. original salmon paper boards, printed paper label, from the Gary Lepper Collection of Thomas Hardy. The Brick Row Book Shop   Bulletin Nine - 99   2013 $85

Association – Lettsom, John Coakley

Ring, John *Reflections on the Surgeon's Bill: in Answer to Three Pamphlets.* printed for Hookham and Carpenter and J. Johnson, 1798. First edition, first few gatherings somewhat foxed, little browning and just staining elsewhere, 8vo., uncut in original boards, rebacked, inscribed on title "Dr. Granville with the author's best respects" and with Granville's stamp, inscribed "Dr. (John Coakley) Lettsom from the author" with Lettsom's booklabel inside front cover, sound, scarce.   Blackwell's Rare Books   Sciences - 105   2013   £1200

Association – Levenson, Roger

Petko, Edward *Fine Printing and the '80's.* Los Angeles: Columbian 415 Chappel, 1980. Limited to 100 numbered copies, this copy with presentation by author to Roger Levenson, 7.3 x 5.9cm., marbled cloth, label with title on spine, top edge cut, other edges uncut, from the collection of Donn W. Sanford.   Oak Knoll Books   303 - 99   2013 $150

Association – Leverson, Ada

Wilde, Oscar 1854-1900 *Ravenna.* Oxford: Thos. Shrimpton & Son, 1878. First edition, 8vo., slightly later half green morocco over marbled boards, ownership signature of Ada Leverson. Maggs Bros. Ltd. 1442 - 313 2013 £3500

Association – Levertov, Denise

Lazer, Hank *On Equal Terms. Poems by Charles Bernstein, David Ignatow, Denise Levertov, Louis Simpson, Gerald Stern.* Tucscaloosa: Symposium Press, 1984. First edition, limited to 275 copies, although not called for, this copy signed by all contributors, one of the few copies we've seen signed by any of the poets, 4to., original green wrappers, as new. James S. Jaffe Rare Books Fall 2013 - 5 2013 $450

Loy, Mina *Lunar Baedeker & Time-Tables. Selected Poems.* Highlands: Jonathan Williams, 1958. First edition, one of only 50 hardbound copies of an Author's Edition, numbered and signed by Loy, tall 8vo., titlepage illustration by Emerson Woelffer, original cloth, printed paper spine label, presentation copy inscribed by book's publisher, Jonathan Williams to Denise Levertov, who contributed one of the introductions, extremities lightly rubbed, few small faint spots near bottom edge of front cover, some barely perceptible offset from binding adhesive along endpaper gutters, otherwise near fine. James S. Jaffe Rare Books Fall 2013 - 93 2013 $2500

Association – Levitan, Kalman

Chandler, John Greene *The Remarkable History of Chicken Little.* Boston: A. & D. Bromer, 1979. Limited to 85 numbered copies of which 50 are for sale,, 3.1 x 2.5cm., marbled paper covered boards, paper cover label (24) pages, printed letterpress by Darrell Hyder with hand colored initial letter miniature bookplate of Kalman Levitan, from the collection of Donn W. Sanford. Oak Knoll Books 303 - 67 2013 $175

Association – Lewis, F. H.

Stock, Joseph *A Narrative of What Passed at Killalla, in the County of Mayo and the Parts Adjacent During the French Invasion in the Summer of 1798.* Dublin: printed by and for R. E. Mercier and Co., 1800. 8vo., bound with 2 final ad leaves, titlepage lightly foxed, some browning, small hole at blank head of H8, contemporary half red morocco, marbled boards, spine rubbed and dull, corners bumped, some abrasions to boards, presentation form author "F. H. Lewis given by the Bishop of Killala 1806", 19th century armorial bookplate of H. M. Williamson and pencil signature of Michael Foot. Jarndyce Antiquarian Booksellers CCIV - 284 2013 £480

Association – Lewis, Jim

Hall, Frederick Garrison *Book-Plates.* Boston: Troutsdale Press, 1905. 8vo., 24 black and/or red plates, original quarter white paper over gray paper backed boards, front cover tipped in gilt stamped title label, lightly rubbed, spine slightly soiled, bookplate of Jim Lewis, titlepage and first text page library blindstamps and rubber stamps, rear pastedown rubber stamp, very good, scarce. Jeff Weber Rare Books 171 - 156 2013 $75

Association – Leyel, Hilda

Le Sage, Alain Rene 1668-1747 *The Adventures of Gil Blas of Santillana.* Edinburgh: William Paterson, 1886. 3 volumes, 248 x 165mm., quite pleasing three quarter vellum over sturdy textured cloth boards by Tout (stamp signed), flat spines heavily gilt in compartments in antique style featuring large and intricate central fleuron, three brown morocco labels on each spine, marbled endpapers, gilt tops, title vignettes and 21 fine etched plates, including frontispiece by Adolphe Lalauze, large attractive bookplate of Hilda Leyel signed "A M H 1940" in each volume, top corners of volume 1 slightly bumped, turn-ins little spotted (trivial spots and superficial marks elsewhere to covers and spines, particularly to labels, otherwise excellent set, no significant wear, gilt still bright and attractive, slight offsetting from plates but very fine internally. Phillip J. Pirages 63 - 319 2013 $550

Association – Libby, Edward

Osler, William 1849-1919 *The Principles and Practice of Medicine.* New York: D. Appleton and Co., 1892. First edition, first state, large 8vo., original green cloth, some rubbed and bumped, rebacked with original spine laid down, first state with misspelling 'Georgias' for Gorgias' facing contents page and second set of ads dated Nov. 1891, holograph presentation by Dr. George B. Shattuck, Jan. 2 1897 with ownership signature of Edward N. Libby, small date stamp on top of titlepage, very good, clean, tight copy. Second Life Books Inc. 183 - 308 2013 $7500

Association – Liechtenstein, Prince of

Seneca, Lucius Annaeus *Tragoediae.* Florence: studio et impensa Philippi di Giunta, 1506. 8vo., final blank discarded, rather foxed in places, some soiling, intermittent stain in gutter, few early ink marks, early ownership inscription to second leaf, 8vo., later vellum, spine with four raised bands lettered in ink somewhat soiled and splayed, bookplates of Biblioteca Senequiana and the Prince of Liechtenstein, sound. Blackwell's Rare Books B174 - 133 2013 £950

Association – Liggett, Wallace

Jolas, Eugene *Transition. No. 22, 23, 25 and 26.* The Hague: Servire Press, 1932-1933. New York: 1936-1937. First editions, 4 separately issued volumes, original pictorial paper wrappers, numerous black and white photos, issue no 22 with original (somewhat chipped, but intact) yellow paper band reading "Revolutionary Romanticism", issue no. 25 with ink inscription "Wallace Liggett/April 18 1946" on rear cover, issue no. 26 with ink stamp of Messageries Dawson, Paris on rear cover, few tiny chips to edge of boards, little light soiling, No. 26 with short scratch and pencilled number on front cover, No. 25 with occasional small, faint stains to fore edge, few inevitable), corner creases, otherwise fine, clean, fresh, bright internally in very well preserved paper wrappers.   Phillip J. Pirages   63 - 289   2013 $1500

Association – Light, J. K.

Harris, William T. *Hegel's Doctrine of Reflection.* New York: D. Appleton, 1881. First edition, 24cmo., green publishers' cloth, contemporary name stamp of "J.K. Light" on endpapers and some text pages, scattered annotations in pencil, good, moderate rubbing, few spots of faint on board, corners bumped and modest wear at spine ends, scarce.   Between the Covers Rare Books, Inc.   Philosophy - 63985   2013 $185

Association – Lightfoot, William Burton

Lightfoot, John *Flora Scotica; or a Systematic Arrangement, in the Linnaean Method of the Native Plants of Scotland and the Hebrides.* printed for B. White, 1777. First edition, 2 volumes, additional engraved titles, including illustration and 35 engraved plates, some folding, small hole in one leaf touching 2 letters on verso, short tear in lower margin of one leaf, occasional mild foxing, letterpress impression faint in few places, 8vo., contemporary sprinkled calf, gilt rules on either side of raised bands on spine, green lettering pieces, numbered direct, slight wear ad cracking of joints but good and solid, ownership inscription on flyleaves of both volumes of Wm. Burton Lightfoot dated 1817 and of C. A. Pitowsky dated 1872, good.   Blackwell's Rare Books   Sciences - 75   2013   £900

Association – Lindberg, David

Grant, Edward *Mathematics and Its Applications to Science and Natural Philosophy in the Middle Ages...* Cambridge et al: Cambridge University Press, 1987. 8vo., xii, 337 pages, navy cloth, gilt stamped cover and spine titles, signature of David C. Lindberg (contributing author's copy), fine.   Jeff Weber Rare Books   169 - 70   2013 $125

Grant, Edward *Studies in Medieval Science and Natural Philosophy.* London: Variorum Reprints, 1981. 8vo., iv, 378 pages, blue cloth, gilt stamped cover and spine titles, presentation copy from author to David Lindberg, fine.   Jeff Weber Rare Books   169 - 170   2013 $100

Hessenbruch, Arne *Reader's Guide to the History of Science.* London & Chicago: Fitzroy Dearborn Pub., 2000. Thick 8vo., printed boards, signature of contributor David C. Lindberg, fine.   Jeff Weber Rare Books   169 - 203   2013 $85

Singer, Charles *A History of Technology.* London: Oxford University Press, 1954-1958. 4 volumes, reprints, large 8vo., thin paper issue, tables, illustrations, color frontispieces, plates, navy blue cloth, gilt stamped spines, dust jackets slightly torn especially at spine ends, spines faded, bookplates, ownership signatures of David C. Lindberg, near fine very good jackets.   Jeff Weber Rare Books   169 - 415   2013 $75

Association – Lindberg, Johanna Maria

Chapone, Hester *Letters on the Improvement of the Mind, Addressed to a Young Lady.* London: published for the proprietors and printed and sold by H. and G. Mozley, Market Place, Gainsboro, 1800. 12mo., signed in sixes, browned, tears to H3 and H4 without loss, contemporary sheep, double gilt banded spine, red morocco label, following hinge little cracked, wear to foot of spine and corners, contemporary signature of Johanna Maria Lindberg and underneath this Hannah Maria.   Jarndyce Antiquarian Booksellers   CCIV - 88   2013   £50

Association – Lindley, Caroline

Ellis, William *Philo-socrates. Part V. Among the Boys.* London: Smith, Elder & Co., 1863. Original light brown printed paper wrappers, hinges slightly splitting with some repair to head of leading hinge, inscription from author for Caroline Lindley.   Jarndyce Antiquarian Booksellers   CCV - 100   2013   £150

Association – Lindsay

Curry, Eugene *Cath Mhuighe Leana Or the Battle of Magh Leana. Together with Tocmarc Momera, or the Courtship of Momera.* Dublin: Celtic Society, 1855. First edition thus, 8vo., some foxing, mainly to prelims, publisher's olive cloth decorated in blind bit faded with bumping to corners and edges, nick to headcap, edges uncut, as issued and slightly dusty, bookplate of Bibliotheca Lindesiana, Irish Archaeological and Celtic Society leaflet loosely inserted.   Unsworths Antiquarian Booksellers   28 - 155   2013   £125

Association – Lingo, Jane

Hillman, William *Mr. President.* New York: Farrar, Straus and Young, 1952. First edition, inscribed by President Truman to Jane Lingo, April 10, 1952, laid in is 3 x 5 card is a note in young hand signed by Lingo asking the President to sign the book for her, quarter beige cloth with blue cloth covered boards and gilt title label to spine, toning to edges of boards and small bump along bottom edge of rear board, clean, bright interior with errata slip laid in, blue dust jacket with red title to spine and front panel, large open tear on front of jacket affecting title, few closed tears along edges, very good in good dust jacket, 253 pages.   The Kelmscott Bookshop   7 - 133   2013 $1500

Association – Lippincott, Jay B.

Staal, Marguerite Jeanne Baronne De *Memoirs of Madame de Staal de Launay.* London: Richard Bentley & Son, 1877. 8vo., 16 plates, cloth, extra illustrated edition, scattered foxing, mainly to prelims and edges of added plates, else fine, slipcase lightly worn at extremities, bookplate of Jay B. Lippincott.   Kaaterskill Books   16 - 80   2013 $300

Association – Lipsitz, Solly

Longley, Michael *Secret Marriages.* Didsbury: Phoenix Pamphlet Poets Press, 1968. Number 33 of 50 numbered copies, signed by author and additionally inscribed by him for friend Solly Lipsitz, near fine, small 8vo., original red cloth, dust jacket with minor loss at head of lower wrapper.   Maggs Bros. Ltd.   1442 - 168   2013   £600

Association – Lisburne Lord

Edwards, Thomas *Canons of Criticism and Glossary; the Trial of the Letter (Upsilon) alias Y, and Sonnets.* London: printed for C. Bathurst, 1758. 8vo. toned and bit spotted, contemporary speckled calf, spine gilt in compartments with raised bands, red morocco label, marbled edges and endpapers, rubbed, slight wear to headcap, contemporary ink inscription 'North Side/Case 7 Shelf 7 No. 10" on rectangular paper label on front pastedown, pencil annotation on first plain flyleaf states 'from the library of Lord Lisburne".   Unsworths Antiquarian Booksellers   28 - 94   2013   £95

Association – Liverpool, Cecil Foljambe, 1st Earl of

Buller, Walter Lawry *A History of the Birds of New Zealand.* London: John Van Voorst, 1873. First edition, frontispiece, 35 fine hand colored lithographs, 4to., half calf, spine gilt bookplate, lovely copy, the Foljambe copy bearing bookplate of Cecil Foljambe, first early of Liverpool.   Maggs Bros. Ltd.   1467 - 73   2013   £7500

Association – Livingston, Robert

Gregory, John *A Comparative View of the State and Faculties of Man with those of the Animal World.* London: printed for J. Dodsley, 1785. New edition, 8vo., contemporary tree calf, minor wear, leather label, half title, large armorial bookplate of Robert R. Livingston.   Howard S. Mott Inc.   262 - 68   2013 $200

Association – Lloyd, J. M.

Hayley, William *The Life, and Posthumous Writings of William Cowper...* Chichester: printed by J. Seagrave for J. Johnson, 1806. New edition, 4 volumes, half titles, frontispiece volume 1, contemporary full diced calf, spines ruled and lettered in gilt, devices in blind, spines and hinges slightly rubbed, armorial bookplates of J. M. Lloyd and later Lloyd family booklabels, nice.   Jarndyce Antiquarian Booksellers   CCIII - 616   2013   £120

Association – Locke, John

Tymme, Thomas *A Silver Watch Bell, the Sound Whereof is Able (by the Grace of God) to Win the Most Prophane Worldling and Careless Liver...* London: printed by John Haviland for Thomas Alchorn, 1638. Small octavo, lacking A2 (titlepage) and I2 (pages 115-116), text within double ruled border, with headline, page numbers and marginal glosses inside outer border, 16 headpieces, 14 ornamental initials and 2 tailpieces, contemporary marbled boards, rebacked (possibly in 1915, according to pencil note on front pastedown), with speckled calf, modern red and white paper spine label lettered in ink, plain endpapers, all edges speckled red, some trimmed close to headlines and in a few cases to marginal inscriptions, boards worn, hinges cracked, tiny rust or ink hole to top of front free endpaper, tiny wormhole to outer margin of beginning leaves, affecting a letter or two of marginal glosses, over opened at a few places, still very good, from the library of John Locke with ink inscriptions, signatures and marginal notations in at least five different hands, (John Locke, Ri. Yolland, Emmanual Bayhind, William Yoo and Riettell).   Heritage Book Shop   50th Anniversary Catalogue - 67   2013 $35,000

Association – Locock, Charles

Malton, Thomas *Views of Oxford.* London: White & Co.; Oxford: R. Smith, 1810. First complete edition, 411 x 315mm., appealing 19th century circa 1860s?), dark green half morocco over lighter green textured cloth by T. Aitken (stamp signed), upper cover with gilt titling, raised bands, spine gilt incompartments with elongated fleuron centerpiece and scrolling cornerpieces, gilt titling, marbled endpapers, all edges gilt (small, very expert repairs to upper outer corners and perhaps top of joints), mezzotint frontispiece after Gilbert Stuart, engraved title, 30 fine plates, 24 of then aquatints and 6 of them etched, armorial bookplates of Sir Mayson M. Beeton and Sir Richard Farrant, ink presentation inscription "Sir Charles Locock, Bart./ with Captn. Malton's kindest regards/Nov. 1860", subscription proposal for the work printed by T. Bensley and dated "London, May 30, 1301" (i.e. "1801"), laid in at front, couple of small smudges to boards, portrait faintly foxed and browned, isolated small stains (not affecting images), still fine, plates especially clean, fresh and smooth and pleasing binding with virtually no wear.   Phillip J. Pirages   63 - 327   2013 $9500

Association – Lodge, Henry Cabot

Queen, Ellery, Pseud. *The Roman Hat Mystery.* New York: Frederick A. Stokes, 1929. Fifth printing, very good, original endpapers missing, and one internal page is torn, however this is an interesting copy in that according to a "Property of" sticker, this book was donated to Beverly Library in 1933 by H. C. Lodge, Jr., U.S. Senator.   Leather Stalking Books   October 2013 - 2013 $100

Association – Lombard, J. N.

Six Lectures... before the Cork Young Men's Association... During ... 1851-2. Cork: Religious Tract & Book Society, 1852. 6mo., vii, 219 pages, original red cloth, hinges worn, gilt titling, inscribed by J. N. Lombard to his son, very good.   C. P. Hyland   261 - 253   2013   £75

Association – Long, Stephen Pitt Hatherell

Brooke, Frances *The Excursion, a Novel.* London: printed for T. Cadell, 1785. Second edition, rare, lightly spotted, occasional browning, 12mo., contemporary half green roan, marbled boards, spines lettered gilt and divided by gilt fillet, rubbed, backstrips darkened, bookplate of antiques dealer Stephen Pitt Hatherell Long and early ownership inscription of John Mansel, good.   Blackwell's Rare Books   172 - 35   2013   £600

Brooke, Henry *Juliet Grenville; or the History of the Human Heart.* printed for G. Robinson, 1774. First edition, lightly spotted, occasional browning, 12mo., contemporary half green roan, marbled boards, spines lettered in gilt, and divided by gilt fillet, (volume iii mistakenly labelled as volume i and vice versa), rubbed, backstrips darkened, slight wear to headcaps, bookplate of antiques dealer Stephen Pitt Hatherell Long and early ownership inscription of John Mansel, good.   Blackwell's Rare Books   172 - 36   2013   £900

Association – Longfield, Mary

Stawell, George D. *A Quantock Family: the Stawells of Somerton & Devonshire and the County Cork.* 1910. First edition, 53 plates, text illustrations, 14 folding pedigrees, very good, very scarce, signed presentation copy to Mary Longfield.   C. P. Hyland   261 - 412   2013   £400

Association – Lonsdale, Hugh Cecil, Earl of

Corner, Miss *Little Plays for Little People. Series the First.* Dean & Son, n.d., First edition, original blue cloth, gilt over bevelled boards with oval central chromolithograph on upper board, extremities little rubbed, all edges gilt, woodcut illustrations, upper joint cracked, few spots, armorial bookplate of Hugh Cecil, Earl of Lonsdale.   R. F. G. Hollett & Son Children's Books - 149   2013   £95

Association – Lonsdale, Mrs.

Coleridge, Sara *Phantasmion.* C. Whittingham for William Pickering, 1837. First edition, inscribed presentation from Mrs. H. N. Coleridge for Miss Theodosia Hinckes, , loosely inserted ALS by author to Mrs. Lonsdale, (pencil inscription "Given me by John Sparrow), 8vo., flyleaves little spotted, through setting slightly on to half title, few areas of minor spotting, contemporary pebble grained green morocco, double blind ruled borders on sides with corner ornaments, thick blind rules on either side of raised bands on spine, lettered direct in gilt, gilt edges by Hayday, mostly faded to brown, little rubbed, short split at head of lower joint, good.   Blackwell's Rare Books   172 - 43   2013   £3500

Association – Lott, Jeremiah

Sarjeant, Thomas *Elementary Principles of Arithmetic... (with) An Introduction to the Counting House...* Philadelphia: printed by Thomas Dobson..., 1788, i.e., 1789. First edition, 8vo., original tree calf, front hinge starting, leading edges gilt rolled, half title, rare, fine save for cracked front hinge, 4 ownership signatures of Jeremiah Lott.   Howard S. Mott Inc.   262 - 130   2013 $3500

Association – Lovat Fraser, Claude

The Mariner's Concert, Being a New Collection of the Most Favorite Sea Songs... printed by J. Evans, 1797. 4to., large woodcut vignette on title, poorly printed on cheap paper with bit of consequent browning, pages 8, early 20th century navy blue buckram lettered on upper cover, slightly worn, pencil note inside front cover, good, from the library of Lovat Fraser. Blackwell's Rare Books B174 - 132 2013 £375

Association – Lovett, Bob

MacLeish, Archibald *Einstein.* Paris: Black Sun Press, 1929. First edition, one of 100 numbered copies (of 150 copies), printed in black & red on Van Gelder handmade paper, this unnumbered being stamped H(ors) Commerce) and reserved for presentation purposes, frontispiece of MacLeish by Paul Emile Becat, tissue guard present, 4to., printed cream wrappers, untrimmed, tissue jacket, somewhat defective, fine, half title inscribed by author for Bob and Odile Lovett 12th Jan. 1930. Blackwell's Rare Books 172 - 269 2013 £500

Association – Lovett, Odile

MacLeish, Archibald *Einstein.* Paris: Black Sun Press, 1929. First edition, one of 100 numbered copies (of 150 copies), printed in black & red on Van Gelder handmade paper, this unnumbered being stamped H(ors) Commerce) and reserved for presentation purposes, frontispiece of MacLeish by Paul Emile Becat, tissue guard present, 4to., printed cream wrappers, untrimmed, tissue jacket, somewhat defective, fine, half title inscribed by author for Bob and Odile Lovett 12th Jan. 1930. Blackwell's Rare Books 172 - 269 2013 £500

Association – Low-Beer, John

Ford, Richard *A Piece of My Heart.* London: Collins Harvill, 1987. First British edition, inscribed by author to Irish memoirist Nuala O'Faolain and her partner John Low-Beer, couple of small, stray marks to edge of text block, still fine in fine dust jacket, good literary association. Ken Lopez Bookseller 159 - 64 2013 $250

Association – Lowdell, Stephen

Livius, Titus *Titi Livii Patavini Historiarum Libri Qui Extant.* Paris: apud Fredericum Leonard, 1679. 5 volumes bound as 6, 4to., engraved half title and 2 engraved maps, folding engraved plate and 1 other engraved plate, light toning and some spotting, contemporary Cambridge style panelled calf, spines darkened with stain and paneled gilt, red morocco labels, rubbed at joints and corners, joints cracked, endcaps worn, some labels lost, contemporary armorial bookplate of "Sr Robert Clayton of the City of London/Knight Alderman & Mayor thereof Ano. 1679", covered up by later plain endpapers (volume 4 excavated locally to reveal identity), early 19th century armorial bookplate of Stephen Lowdell. Unsworths Antiquarian Booksellers 28 - 24 2013 £450

Association – Lowe, Emily Lynch

Smith, Horace 1779-1849 *Brambletye House; or Cavaliers and Roundheads.* London: Henry Collins, 1826. Third edition, 3 volumes, 191 x 12mm., lavishly gilt contemporary olive green straight grain morocco, covers divided into three square panels at top and bottom of an elongated panel at right and left, these panels densely gilt with repeated versions of a large stamp formed by a floral cross radiating oak leaves, central panel with gilt rule frame featuring spiral cornerpieces decorated with acanthus leaves and flowers, raised bands, spine compartments heavily gilt repeating fleuron stamps used on covers, gilt turn-ins, marble endpapers, all edges gilt; each volume with handsome fore-edge painting of a picturesque location important to plot of the novel; engraved bookplate of Emily Lynch Lowe (NY artist), extremities and joints slightly rubbed (but well masked with dye), occasional minor foxing or stains, really excellent set, remarkably decorative bindings lustrous and most appealing, text clean and fresh, expert fore-edge paintings in fine condition. Phillip J. Pirages 61 - 55 2013 $3500

Association – Lucas, Tindall

Livingstone, David 1813-1873 *Missionary Travels and Researches in South Africa.* London: John Murray, 1857. First edition, original brown embossed cloth gilt, neatly recased with much of backstrip relaid, extending wood engraved frontispiece by J. W. Whymper, engraved portrait, 2 folding maps (1 in rear pocket), 22 full page woodcut plates, folding plan, text woodcuts, very nice, armorial bookplate of Tindall Lucas, later issue with woodcuts replacing tinted lithographs of first issue. R. F. G. Hollett & Son Africana - 127 2013 £275

Association – Luke, Elizabeth

Fitz-Florian's Alphabet; or Lyrical Fables for Children Grown Up. London: J. J. Stockdale, 1819. Second edition, full contemporary calf, gilt borders and dentelles, slightly marked and bit rubbed, contemporary gift inscription to Elizabeth Luke, Renier booklabel. Jarndyce Antiquarian Booksellers CCIII - 631 2013 £75

Association – Lunt, Alfred

Coward, Noel 1899-1973 *Quadrille.* London: Heinemann, 1952. First edition, 8vo., 116 pages, signed by 17 members of the English cast and producer Jack Wilson and by Lynn Fontanne and Alfred Lunt, inscribed by author to Dorothy Sands (Octavia in NY production). Second Life Books Inc.   183 - 83   2013 $500

Association – Luxmoore, C. T. C.

Sterne, Laurence 1713-1768 *A Sentimental Journey through France and Italy. (with) Yorick's Sentimental Journey...* London: T. Becket and P. A. De Hondt, 1770. New edition and second edition respectively, 12mo., 4 volumes, very good full contemporary calf, double gilt fillet borders, raised and gilt banded spines with simple volume numbers tooled directly onto spines, some slight chipping to head and tail of spines, strictly unsophisticated state, bookplate "C. T. C. Luxmoore", signature "Cha. Luxmore" in all volumes, pencilled note 'obit 1863' in volumes 3-4 'St John's Col. Camb'.   Ken Spelman Books Ltd.   75 - 32   2013   £395

Association – Lyman, Samuel

Sketch of a Railway Judiciously Constructed Between Desirable Points (in Pennsylvania). New York: Egbert Hedge, Railroad Journal Office, 1841. First edition, 8vo., 125 pages, 2 folding maps, contemporary finely ribbed cloth, title stamped in gilt on upper cover, edges and corners worn, spine effectively if artlessly backed with leather, library book plate and stamp on front pastedown with pocket in rear, shelf number neatly inked on margin of first page of text and stamp on blank verso of last page of text, boldly inscribed by Samuel Lyman for Archibald Maclay.   M & S Rare Books, Inc.   95 - 308   2013 $375

Association – Lymington, Viscount

Swift, Jonathan 1667-1845 *Travels in to Several Remote Nations of the World.* London: printed for Benj. Motte, 1726. First edition, Teerink's state A with 4 necessary points, frontispiece in second state, 4 maps, 2 plans, decorative woodcut and typographic head and tailpieces and initials, contemporary panelled calf, spines with raised bands, brown morocco gilt lettering labels, board edges decoratively tooled gilt, edges sprinkled red, joints just starting portion of rear free endpaper volume II torn away, short tear to lower gutter margin of c2, not affecting text, small waterstain to outer margin of 17-k4 in part II, few additional minor stains or soil marks, armorial bookplate of Rt. Hon. Lord Viscount Lymington in each volume, sensational copy, totally unsophisticated, chemised in quarter red morocco pull off case.   Heritage Book Shop   Holiday Catalogue 2012 - 148   2013 $125,000

Association – Lyon, Mary

Bage, Robert *Man As He Is.* London: printed for William Lane, at the Minerva Press, Leadenhall Street, 1792. First edition, 12mo., half titles, original paper flaw to leading edge volume III E2 not affecting text, old pen strokes volume IV, page 122, some foxing and occasional browning to text, contemporary quarter calf, marbled boards, vellum tips, gilt banded spines, red morocco labels, spines rubbed, each spine has faint shelf number blindstamped at head with contemporary ownership name of Mary Lyon.   Jarndyce Antiquarian Booksellers   CCIV - 53   2013   £2500

Association – Lyttleton, David

Raymond, Dora Neill *The Political Career of Lord Byron.* London: George Allen & Unwin, 1925. First English edition, original red cloth, slightly marked, spine slightly faded, booklabel of David A.. Lyttleton, from the library of Doris Langley Moore.   Jarndyce Antiquarian Booksellers   CCIII - 438   2013   £30

Association – Macaulay, Rose

Forster, Edward Morgan 1879-1970 *The Longest Journey.* London: Edward Arnold, 1937. Uniform edition, first reprint, 8vo., original red cloth, inscribed by author for Rose Macaulay, excellent copy.   Maggs Bros. Ltd.   1460 - 294   2013   £350

Association – Macauley, Ian

Clarke, Arthur C. *Astounding Days: a Science Fictional Autobiography.* London: Victor Gollancz, 1989. First edition, fine in fine dust jacket, signed by author, additionally inscribed by him on titlepage to his protege and one time secretary and longtime friend Ian Macauley, splendid association copy.   Between the Covers Rare Books, Inc.   Sci-Fi, Fantasy & Horror - 312490   2013 $850

Association – Macclesfield

Bethune, John Drinkwater 1762-1844 *A History of the Late Siege of Gibraltar.* London: 1786. Second edition, printed on thick paper, extra large folding frontispiece, 4 large folding engraved maps, engraved vignette to title and 6 fine folding engraved views printed in sepia, 4to., extremely fine contemporary tree calf, spine richly gilt in compartments with red morocco label and Macclesfield library plates, discreet Macclesfield crest blindstamped to title and maps, magnificent copy on thick paper.   Maggs Bros. Ltd.   1467 - 39   2013   £2250

Blundeville, Thomas *M. Blundeuile His Exercises, Containing Eight Treatises...* imprinted by William Stansby, 1613. Fourth edition, woodcuts on section titles, numerous woodcuts in text, some with volvelles, 4 folding tables (3 unattached), map, 2 diagrams cropped, one by about 5mm, the other just touched, one signature of gathering Q shaved, few rust holes with minor loss, square 8vo., early 17th century calf, blind ruled borders on sides, double blind fillets towards spines, spine gilt in compartments, red lettering piece, marbled edges, sides rubbed, spine defective at either end, loss of gilt, Macclesfield copy with bookplate and blindstamp. Blackwell's Rare Books Sciences - 13 2013 £5000

Euclides *Geometricorum Elementorum Libri XV.* Paris: Henri Estienne, 7 January, 1516-1517. Sixth edition, Roman types with numerous woodcut geometrical diagrams in margins, fine crible initials in a variety of styles and sizes, titlepage soiled and cut down and mounted on old paper, one diagram just cropped at its extreme outer corner, folio, 19th century half brown calf by Hatton of Manchester, marbled edges, original order for the binder loosely inserted (in fact calling for half Russia), the Macclesfield copy with bookplate but no blindstamps and annotated by John Collins, preserved in cloth folding box, good. Blackwell's Rare Books Sciences - 48 2013 £15,000

Hall, Joseph *Mundus alter et Idem sive Terra Australis...* Frankfurt: apud haeredes Ascanii de Rinialme, 1607? 8vo., first state engraved titlepage, 5 folding engraved plates (all first editions) text mixed edition, two gatherings from second printing), somewhat soiled and browned, few outer edges slightly frayed, title slightly abraded, some contemporary manuscript notes, ownership inscriptions to title and flyleaf and Macclesfield embossment to first two leaves, 8vo., original limp vellum, somewhat soiled, ties lost, stitching loosening, Shirburn Castle bookplate, preserved in clamshell morocco. Blackwell's Rare Books B174 - 66 2013 £5500

Newton, John *Trigonometria Britanica; or the Doctrine of Triangles, in Two Books.* printed by R. and W. Leybourn and are to be sold by George Hurlock, Joshuah Kirton, Thomas Pierrepont and William Fisher, 1658. First edition, 4 parts in one volume, sectional titles to last 3 parts, woodcut diagrams in text in first part, woodcut initials and headpieces, browned in places, titlepage ill attached to a later (rather stiff) flyleaf, last leaf folding with errata pasted to verso of flap, folio in 4s, contemporary panelled mottled calf, rebacked, preserving most of original spine, edges parti-colored, the 2 canones logarithmorum red, remainder marbled, the Macclesfield copy with blindstamps and bookplate, few annotations in the hand of John Collins, sound. Blackwell's Rare Books Sciences - 85 2013 £2000

Snell, Willebrord *Tiphys Batavus, sive Histioromice de Navium Cusribus et re Navali.* Leiden: Elzevier, 1624. First edition, woodcut printer's device on title, diagrams in text, 3 engraved plates, chart just shaved at for margin, trifle browned in plates minor dampstaining, 4to., contemporary deerskin, gilt and blind ruled borders on sides, spine gilt in compartments, lettered in gilt direct, in top compartment, blue edges, spine faded and defective at top and tail, ownership inscriptions and notes in French and Dutch on flyleaves, the Macclesfield copy with blindstamp and bookplate. Blackwell's Rare Books Sciences - 113 2013 £1500

Association – MacCon, Malcolm

Gallenga, Antonio *A Summer Tour in Russia.* London: Chapman & Hall, 1882. First edition, half title, folding map, final ad leaf, 2 lines of annotation in different hand, original dark olive green cloth, slight rubbing, lending library label on pastedown, contemporary signature of Malcolm McCon, nice. Jarndyce Antiquarian Booksellers CCV - 109 2013 £150

Association – MacDonald, Arch Deacon

Bowles, William Lisle *Hermes Britannicus.* London: J. B. Nichols & Son, 1828. First edition, disbound, inscribed on title Arch Deacon Macdonald, some corrections in ink, possibly authorial, few marginal notes in another hand. Jarndyce Antiquarian Booksellers CCIII - 37 2013 £125

Association – MacDonald, John D.

Hallday, Brett *Michael Shayne's 50th Case.* New York: Torquil/Dodd, Mead, 1964. First edition, very slightly cocked, else fine in fine, gilt foil dust jacket, inscribed by author to fellow mystery writer John D. MacDonald, outstanding association. Between the Covers Rare Books, Inc. Mystery & Detective Fiction - 97549 2013 $1250

Association – MacKay, D.

Lockhart, John Gibson 1794-1854 *The Life of Robert Burns.* Edinburgh: Constable & Co., 1828. First edition, portrait, contemporary half calf, spine with raised bands and devices in gilt, dark green leather label, hinges little rubbed, armorial stamp "DTM" contemporary ownership inscription of D. Mackay. Jarndyce Antiquarian Booksellers CCIII - 61 2013 £125

Association – MacKay, W. MacDonald

Miall, A. Bernard *Nocturns and Pastorals: a Book of Verse.* London: Leonard Smithers, 1896. First edition, rare first book, original dark blue cloth, chipping to spine ends and bumping to corners, otherwise very nice, offsetting to free endpapers and slight browning to page edges, but clean and tight, bookplates of W. MacDonald MacKay, Charles Hiatt (writer on art) and Barry Humphries (actor), illegible signature in ink, 109 pages.   The Kelmscott Bookshop   7 - 121   2013 $450

Association – MacKenzie, David

Dexter, Colin *The Remorseful Day.* London: Macmillan, 1999. Second impression, 8vo. original black cloth, dust jacket, near fine, inscribed by author to David MacKenzie.   Maggs Bros. Ltd.   1460 - 227   2013   £125

Association – MacKenzie, F. R. S. Murdoch

Ferguson, James   1710-1776 *Astronomy Explained Upon Sir Isaac Newton's Principles and made Easy to Those Who Have not Studied Mathematics.* London: printed for and sold by author, 1757. Second edition, small 4to., 283 pages + index, very good in full contemporary calf with gilt lettering on red leather spine label, complete with 13 folding copper plate engravings and folding frontispiece, from the library of F. R. S. Murdoch Mackenzie, with his signature, scuffs, edgewear to spine and covers, owner bookplate, scattered foxing and soil.   By the Book, L. C.   36 - 98   2013 $2000

Association – MacKenzie, Richard Charlton

Gibbon, Edward   1737-1794 *Gibbon's History of the Decline and Fall of the Roman Empire.* London: printed for G. Kearsley, 1789. First abridged edition, 2 volumes, 8vo., contemporary tree calf, rebacked and rehinged with new endpapers, old backs laid down, corners repaired, edges rubbed, leather labels, wanting half titles and terminal ad leaf in each volume, still very good, with 1941 ownership signature of Richard Charlton MacKenzie.   Howard S. Mott Inc.   262 - 61   2013 $750

Association – MacKintosh, Graham

Duncan, Robert *Medea at Kolchis. The Maiden Head.* Berkeley: Oyez, 1965. First edition, hardbound issue, one of 28 numbered copies, signed by author, out of a total edition of 500, although not called for, this copy also signed by Graham Mackintosh, book's designer and printer, 8vo., original unprinted linen over boards, dust jacket, the second dust jacket with same design (as first) but printed on white enameled stock, with design of first jacket embossed on front cover, covers slightly splayed, otherwise fine.   James S. Jaffe Rare Books   Fall 2013 - 43   2013 $1250

Association – Maclay, Archibald

Sketch of a Railway Judiciously Constructed Between Desirable Points (in Pennsylvania). New York: Egbert Hedge, Railroad Journal Office, 1841. First edition, 8vo., 125 pages, 2 folding maps, contemporary finely ribbed cloth, title stamped in gilt on upper cover, edges and corners worn, spine effectively if artlessly backed with leather, library book plate and stamp on front pastedown with pocket in rear, shelf number neatly inked on margin of first page of text and stamp on blank verso of last page of text, boldly inscribed by Samuel Lyman for Archibald Maclay.   M & S Rare Books, Inc.   95 - 308   2013 $375

Association – MacLean

Colquhoun, Patrick   1745-1820 *Treatise on Wealth, Power and Resources of the British Empire, in Every Quarter of the World, Including the East Indies.* London: printed for Joseph Mawman, 1815. Second edition, 4to., slight indentations to opening leaves, uncut in original brown paper boards, paper label, slightly rubbed in places, label with small repair, armorial bookplate of MacLean of Ardgour, signed on leading f.e.p. by Auls (?) MacLean, 1822, very nice in original binding, from the library of the clan of MacLean.   Jarndyce Antiquarian Booksellers CCV - 71   2013   £480

Association – Macleod, M. D.

Josephus, Flavius *Opera quae Exstant...* Geneva: Jacobum Crispinum, 1634. Third Geneva printing, folio, slightly toned, little marginal worming to first few quires, blot from hot wax to page 610 affecting a couple of words and slightly marking the preceding page, small marginal inkstain to several leaves at rear, tan calf, gilt spine and borders, rebacked retaining original spine, boards scratched with a little surface loss suggesting tape removal, few wormholes to upper board, edges and corners worn, upper hinge neatly repaired, ownership inscription of M. D. Macleod, the University Southampton, much older ink inscription to front pastedown.   Unsworths Antiquarian Booksellers   28 - 19   2013   £500

Association – MacNeice, Frederick

O'Brien, R. Barry *A Hundred Years of Irish History.* Pitman, 1911. Second edition, 184 pages + 24 page publisher's catalog, very good, owner inscribed by Frederick MacNeice.   C. P. Hyland   261 - 621   2013   £30

Association – Macy, Edith Carpenter

Darwin, Charles Robert 1809-1882 *Works.* New York: D. Appleton and Co., 1896. Authorized edition, 15 volumes, folding plates, illustrations, interior pages very clean, margins slightly browned, modern brown cloth, gilt titles to spines, many pages unopened, each volume with bookplate of Valentine Everit Macy and Edith Carpenter Macy, chairman of Girl Scouts, very good.   The Kelmscott Bookshop 7 - 131   2013 $1250

Association – Macy, Valentine Everit

Darwin, Charles Robert 1809-1882 *Works.* New York: D. Appleton and Co., 1896. Authorized edition, 15 volumes, folding plates, illustrations, interior pages very clean, margins slightly browned, modern brown cloth, gilt titles to spines, many pages unopened, each volume with bookplate of Valentine Everit Macy and Edith Carpenter Macy, chairman of Girl Scouts, very good.   The Kelmscott Bookshop 7 - 131   2013 $1250

Association – Majendie, E. A.

Milman, Henry Hart *The Fall of Jerusalem: a Dramatic Poem.* London: John Murray, 1820. New edition, 222 x 140mm., attractive contemporary crimson straight grain morocco, gilt covers with wide gilt dentelles comprising closely spaced palmettes, flat spine in gilt compartments formed by three thin rules and decorated in roman style, scrolling foliate cornerpieces and charming floral centerpiece incorporating morocco onlaid circle, turn-ins with gilt decoration echoing outer dentelles, all edges gilt, with very fine fore-edge painting of Monk Soham in Suffolk, titlepage with signature of E. A. Majendie, dated May 1839. corners quite worn, spine ends very slightly chipped, joints rather flaked, spine somewhat darkened, few marks on front board, binding still quite solid with bright covers, narrow faint dampstain along fore edge throughout (probably related to the process of painting), first half of text with variable foxing, but no major problems internally, leaves still fresh with ample margins.   Phillip J. Pirages 63 - 189   2013 $1250

Association – Makdougall, Henry Hay

Gomeldon, Jane *The Medley.* Newcastle: printed by J. White and T. Saint, 1766. 220 pages, frontispiece, 8vo., offsetting from frontispiece, occasional foxing, 19th century half calf, marbled boards, leading hinge cracked but firm, spine rubbed, bookplate of Sir Henry Hay Makdougall, Bart, of Makerstoun.   Jarndyce Antiquarian Booksellers CCIV - 146   2013   £520

Association – Malagodi, Olindo

Nesbit, Edith *The Rainbow and the Rose.* London: Longmans, Green & Co., 1905. First edition, rare presentation copy from author to Olindo Malagodi, July 1905, original green cloth with lovely floral and fleur-de-lis design in gilt on front cover along with author and title, light bumping and small light stain to top of rear cover, otherwise beautiful, front and rear endpapers foxed but interior pages bright and clean, each section preceded by blank page with flower illustration, each illustration is different color, 143 pages, 4 pages ads.   The Kelmscott Bookshop 7 - 123   2013 $2000

Association – Malahide Castle

The Tourist's Illustrated Handbook for Ireland.. London: John Cassell, 1853. Deluxe edition, gilt decorated calf with silk endpapers, all edges gilt, ex-Malahide Castle, text interleaved throughout with rice paper guards, sadly foldover of Plan of the Building has been torn-off from the crease.   C. P. Hyland 261 - 822   2013   £200

Association – Mallam, Ethel

Dodgson, Charles Lutwidge 1832-1898 *The Game of Logic.* London: Macmillan and Co., 1887. Second edition, 8vo., original scarlet cloth, gilt, frontispiece pattern, other plans, envelope containing printed plan, two grey and one red counter (from five and four respectively), browned on spine and slightly worn at head and tail of spine, otherwise excellent copy, as is envelope, inscribed by author Mar 20 1894 for Ethel Mallam.   Maggs Bros. Ltd. 1460 - 234   2013   £950

Association – Mandley, Gwen

Keating, H. R. F. *In Kensington Gardens Once...* Newcastle upon Tyne: Flambard Press, 1997. First edition, original wrappers, illustrations by Gwen Mandley, presentation copy from artist, inscribed.   R. F. G. Hollett & Son Children's Books - 318   2013   £25

Association – Mann, Arthur

Bell, John 1763-1820 *The Anatomy and Physiology of the Human Body.* New York: Collins, 1817-1822. Complete set, mixed set, volumes I and II third American edition, volume III fourth American edition, 3 volumes, small 4to., 35 engraved plates, foxed, browned, volume III heavily, occasional ink marginalia, volumes I and II, offsetting from plates and figures, occasional marginal waterstaining, original tree calf, gilt spine, brown leather spine labels, rebacked, preserving original spines, rubbed, ownership signatures of George Eagen, Cranford, Montgomery, New York, N.D. 1837 and William H. Mann, John Mann and Arthur H. Mann Jr., Baltimore, very good.   Jeff Weber Rare Books 172 - 23   2013 $750

Association – Mann, John

Bell, John 1763-1820 *The Anatomy and Physiology of the Human Body.* New York: Collins, 1817-1822. Complete set, mixed set, volumes I and II third American edition, volume III fourth American edition, 3 volumes, small 4to., 35 engraved plates, foxed, browned, volume III heavily, occasional ink marginalia, volumes I and II, offsetting from plates and figures, occasional marginal waterstaining, original tree calf, gilt spine, brown leather spine labels, rebacked, preserving original spines, rubbed, ownership signatures of George Eagen, Cranford, Montgomery, New York, N.D. 1837 and William H. Mann, John Mann and Arthur H. Mann Jr., Baltimore, very good.   Jeff Weber Rare Books   172 - 23   2013 $750

Association – Mann, Peter

Coleridge, Samuel Taylor 1772-1834 *Confessions of an Inquiring Spirit.* London: William Pickering, 1840. First edition, half title, contemporary half black morocco by Hayday, slightly rubbed, top edge gilt, signature and bookplate of Alexander W. Gillman and of Peter Mann 1951.   Jarndyce Antiquarian Booksellers   CCIII - 562   2013   £180

Coleridge, Samuel Taylor 1772-1834 *The Literary Remains.* London: William Pickering, 1836-1839. First edition, 4 volumes, half title volumes II, III and IV, errata slip volume II, occasional mark, small tear to volume I repaired on verso with tape, rebound in 20th century half maroon morocco, very good, signature of Peter Mann, London.   Jarndyce Antiquarian Booksellers   CCIII - 561   2013   £200

The Friend, a Series of Essays... London: William Pickering, 1837. Third edition, 3 volumes, half titles, 16 page catalog and final ad leaf volume I, pencil notes, original blue cloth, paper labels, spines and paper labels rubbed and little worn, Peter Mann's copy with his signature.   Jarndyce Antiquarian Booksellers   CCIII - 518   2013   £95

The Friend, a Series of Essays... London: Bell and Daldy, 1865. Half title obscured by booklabel, portrait, initial and final catalogs including endpapers, original uniform green cloth, two booklabels, one of C. J. Peacock, ownership inscription of Peter Mann, very good.   Jarndyce Antiquarian Booksellers   CCIII - 521   2013   £30

Association – Mann, William

Bell, John 1763-1820 *The Anatomy and Physiology of the Human Body.* New York: Collins, 1817-1822. Complete set, mixed set, volumes I and II third American edition, volume III fourth American edition, 3 volumes, small 4to., 35 engraved plates, foxed, browned, volume III heavily, occasional ink marginalia, volumes I and II, offsetting from plates and figures, occasional marginal waterstaining, original tree calf, gilt spine, brown leather spine labels, rebacked, preserving original spines, rubbed, ownership signatures of George Eagen, Cranford, Montgomery, New York, N.D. 1837 and William H. Mann, John Mann and Arthur H. Mann Jr., Baltimore, very good.   Jeff Weber Rare Books   172 - 23   2013 $750

Association – Manney, Richard

Bronte, Charlotte 1816-1855 *Jane Eyre.* London: Smith, Elder & Co., 1847. First edition, 3 volumes, octavo, with half titles as called for but without 32 page publisher catalog (dated Oct. 1847) in volume 1 and without inset catalog fly title dated June 1847 and the inset leaf on thicker paper advertising the Calcutta Review, many copies lack these two haphazardly inserted elements, the Richard Manney copy (Sotheby's NY 1991) and presentation copy of Pierpont Morgan Library, rebound in half blue morocco over blue cloth, spines ruled and lettered gilt, top edges gilt, marbled endpapers, 2 previous owner's bookplates to each volume, old bookseller description tipped in to front free endpaper volume I, some light foxing to blanks and half titles of each volume, also some light foxing to fore-edge of text block, bit of light marginal soiling, overall very nice, housed in slipcase.   Heritage Book Shop   Holiday Catalogue 2012 - 20   2013 $35,000

Association – Manning, Olivia

Green, Henry 1905-1973 *Nothing.* London: Hogarth Press, 1950. First edition, 8vo., original red cloth, near fine in dust jacket, chipped at extremities, inscribed by author for Olivia Manning.   Maggs Bros. Ltd.   1460 - 367   2013   £4000

Association – Manres, Baron

Hales, William *The Inspector, or Select Literary Intelligence for the Vulgar A.D. 1798 but Correct A.D.1801 to the first Year of the XIXth Century.* printed for J. White and J. Wright, 1799. 8vo., library shelf mark in ink at head of titlepage, some foxing and browning, 19th century purple hard grained cloth, shelfmark in gilt on spine, spine slightly darkened, inscription "to Mrs. James Ivory from Mr. Baron Manres 1799", bookplate of Dundee Free Libraries inside front cover, good.   Blackwell's Rare Books   B174 - 65   2013   £500

Association – Mansel, John

Brooke, Henry *Juliet Grenville; or the History of the Human Heart.* printed for G. Robinson, 1774. First edition, lightly spotted, occasional browning, 12mo., contemporary half green roan, marbled boards, spines lettered in gilt, and divided by gilt fillet, (volume iii mistakenly labelled as volume i and vice versa), rubbed, backstrips darkened, slight wear to headcaps, bookplate of antiques dealer Stephen Pitt Hatherell Long and early ownership inscription of John Mansel, good.   Blackwell's Rare Books   172 - 36   2013   £900

Brooke, Frances *The Excursion, a Novel.* London: printed for T. Cadell, 1785. Second edition, rare, lightly spotted, occasional browning, 12mo., contemporary half green roan, marbled boards, spines lettered gilt and divided by gilt fillet, rubbed, backstrips darkened, bookplate of antiques dealer Stephen Pitt Hatherell Long and early ownership inscription of John Mansel, good.   Blackwell's Rare Books   172 - 35   2013   £600

Association – Marceau, Robert

Doctor Comicus or the Frolics of Fortune. London: B. Blake, 1825? 210 x 133mm., without printed titlepage, very attractive light tan smooth calf by Sangorski & Sutcliffe/Zahensdorf (stamp signed), corners bordered with French fillet and fleuron cornerpieces, raised bands, spine gilt in compartments featuring decorative bands, scrolling cornerpieces, fleuron centerpiece and small tools, maroon morocco labels, gilt inner dentelles, marbled endpapers, all edges gilt, 12 plates, all colored by hand, bookplate of Robert Marceau, engraved title and two plates little foxed, 3 plates slightly trimmed at fore edge without apparent loss, few leaves with light marginal foxing or soiling, otherwise excellent copy, plates bright and well preserved, leaves clean and fresh, sympathetic binding mint.   Phillip J. Pirages   63 - 460   2013 $400

Association – Marchant, Nicolas

Galen *Epitome Galeni Pergame ni Opervm.* Basileae: apud Mich. Ifingrinium anno, 1551. Small folio, full rich contemporary calf skillfully rebacked with original spine tastefully laid down, from the library of Nicolas Marchant with his signature and stamp on title, some early signatures, gilt armorial crest on front board of two lions facing crowned staff, ruled boards, gilt emblems in each corner, raised tooled bands on spine, text with light marginal dampstaining, early underlining of text with contemporary marginalia throughout, early ownership signature of Rene Minault, 1702.   James Tait Goodrich   75 - 97   2013 $2950

Association – Marsden, Edmund

Ludolf, H. *A New History of Ethiopia.* London: for Samuel Smith, 1682. First edition in English, folio, 8 engraved plates, engraved plate of Ethiopic alphabet, folding table, contemporary or early 18th century calf, front hinge cracked but held by cords, corners worn, some light browning, but very good, signatures of Edmund and Rufus Marsden, latter dated 1762, Herz booklabel.   Joseph J. Felcone Inc. Books Printed before 1701 - 65   2013 $2200

Association – Marsden, Rufus

Ludolf, H. *A New History of Ethiopia.* London: for Samuel Smith, 1682. First edition in English, folio, 8 engraved plates, engraved plate of Ethiopic alphabet, folding table, contemporary or early 18th century calf, front hinge cracked but held by cords, corners worn, some light browning, but very good, signatures of Edmund and Rufus Marsden, latter dated 1762, Herz booklabel.   Joseph J. Felcone Inc. Books Printed before 1701 - 65   2013 $2200

Association – Marsh, Edward

Scott, Walter   1771-1832 *Marmion: a Tale of Flodden Field.* Edinburgh: Archibald Constable and Co., 1808. First edition first impression, 287 x 221mm., contemporary burgundy half morocco, two raised bands setting off elongated central spine panel, backstrip with gilt rules, botanical head and tailpiece and gilt titling, marbled boards, edges and endpapers, extra illustrated with engraved titlepage and 6 engraved plates by Richard Westall from 1809, large engraved bookplate and armorial bookplate with ink ownership inscriptions of Charles Leeson Prince, engraved bookplate of Edward S. Marsh dated 1909, flyleaf with armorial bookplate of Johnson Phillott, front joint and hinge cracked with slight bit of give to board, paper sides noticeably chafed, extremities and bands rather rubbed, significant offsetting from plates, half dozen leaves at front and back somewhat foxed, other minor imperfections with condition issues, still intact and internally fresh and clean as well as desirable for its added illustrations and special provenance. Phillip J. Pirages   63 - 428   2013 $250

Association – Marsh, Thomas

Wiseman, Richard *Eight Chirurgical Treatises on the Following Heads...* London: Benjamin Tooke and Luke Meedith, 1696. Small folio, few short tears, faint dampstaining in few gatherings, wormtrack bottom margin of few gatherings touching a few letters, contemporary paneled calf with blind rulings, skillfully rebacked saving endpapers, raised bands, green gilt label bookplate of John Kirkup, Thomas Marsh, William Viger (ownership signature dated 1751), light marginalia.   James Tait Goodrich   S74 - 239   2013 $975

Association – Marshall, Edmund Henry

Cowley, Abraham 1618-1667 *Poems: viz. I. Miscellanies. II. The Mistress, or Love Verses. III. Pindarique Odes. And IV. Davideis, or a Sacred Poem of the Troubles of David.* London: for Humphrey Moseley, 1656. First collected edition, contemporary panelled calf, edges gilt, very skillfully rebacked to style, later endpapers, occasional minor spots and repaired marginal tears, 3L2, soiled and with paper defect costing several letters, lovely, early signature of Edmund Henry Marshall, "Ex Libris George Bernard Shaw" on front endpaper. Joseph J. Felcone Inc. English and American Literature to 1800 - 11 2013 $2500

Association – Marshall, Evelyn

Thomson, James 1700-1748 *The Seasons, with His Life and a Complete Index and Glossary.* London: printed by and for J. Chapman, 1795. 8vo., 5 plates, further illustrations in text, bound without final ad leaf found in some copies, dark brown calf, gilt spine and borders, marbled endpapers, neatly rebacked, corners worn, front hinge repaired with marbled paper though just starting to crack, gift inscription to Henrietta Marshall from Evelyn Marshall Aug. 6 '07 to prelim blank. Unsworths Antiquarian Booksellers 28 - 135 2013 £80

Association – Marshall, Harry

Two Worlds. New York: Two Worlds Pub., September, 1925. September 1926, First editions, each one of 500 copies, issues 1-5, original printed paper wrappers, first four issues in original (somewhat worn) black cardboard slipcases, issue 5 with 8 full page illustrations and numerous illustrations in text, issue No. 3 with ink owner inscription of Harry Marshall, No. 4 with same signature inside front wrapper, paper wrapper of first issue coming loose from spine, wrappers bit darkened, spines slightly wrinkled, two spines with minor chips, isolated faint smudges, other trivial imperfections, otherwise in excellent condition, generally clean, fresh and bright. Phillip J. Pirages 63 - 290 2013 $500

Association – Marshall, Henrietta

Thomson, James 1700-1748 *The Seasons, with His Life and a Complete Index and Glossary.* London: printed by and for J. Chapman, 1795. 8vo., 5 plates, further illustrations in text, bound without final ad leaf found in some copies, dark brown calf, gilt spine and borders, marbled endpapers, neatly rebacked, corners worn, front hinge repaired with marbled paper though just starting to crack, gift inscription to Henrietta Marshall from Evelyn Marshall Aug. 6 '07 to prelim blank. Unsworths Antiquarian Booksellers 28 - 135 2013 £80

Association – Marshall, Jack

Day, Thomas 1748-1789 *A History of Sandford and Merton.* London: F. and C. Rivington et al, 1815. Abridged edition, 8vo., frontispiece, lacks 12 pages of publisher's ads, very good internally, tan marbled sheep, somewhat worn, upper joint cracking, spine and edges rubbed, ownership inscription of Master Charles Knight dated Aug. 16th 1821, with scrap of paper (presumably part of the packaging in which he received it) addressed to same loosely inserted, frontispiece with inscription "C. H. Knight's present to his daughter Fanny. Leamington Jan. 7th 1850" and beneath this ownership inscription of Jack Marshall dated 1887. Unsworths Antiquarian Booksellers 28 - 156 2013 £30

Association – Martin, H. Bradley

Burgess, Gelett 1866-1951 *Goops and How to Be Them.* New York: Frederick A. Stokes, 1900. First edition, 4to., original pictorial red cloth, excellent, Mildred Greenhill/H. Bradley Martin copy. Howard S. Mott Inc. 262 - 24 2013 $300

Clare, John 1754-1832 *The Shepherd's Calendar; with Village Stories, and Other Poems.* London: published for John Taylor, Waterloo Place by James Duncan, Paternoster Row and sold by J. A. Hessey 93 Fleet Street, 1827. First edition, 2 pages publisher's ads at back, presentation copy inscribed by author to Mrs. Bellairs, April 30 1827, spine perished, boards somewhat soiled, gatherings bit loose, otherwise good copy with rare inscription, Bradley Martin copy preserved in folding cloth box. James S. Jaffe Rare Books Fall 2013 - 32 2013 $8500

Stevenson, Robert Louis Balfour 1850-1894 *Treasure Island.* London: Cassell & Co., 1883. First edition, first issue, octavo, original olive green diagonal fine ribbed cloth, exceptionally fine, gilt on spine bright and fresh, the Bradley Martin copy with bookplate of Mildred Greenhill on front pastedown, chemised in quarter green morocco slipcase. David Brass Rare Books, Inc. Holiday 2012 Chapter Five - DB 00036 2013 $32,500

Association – Martineau, Anne

Blake, William 1757-1827 *Songs of Innocence and Experience.* London: Pickering, 1866. Vellum, gilt decorated, all edges gilt, monogram on front cover FAF, inscribed Eleanor Alicia O'Brien with Anne Martineau's afft. love Nov. 1866 and F. G. Arnold-Forster from R. V. O'Brien Aug. 1891, New Hall, and Flora Vere O'Brien Sept. 19, 1921, very good. C. P. Hyland 261 - 187 2013 £105

Association – Marton, Ralph Creyke

Brady, John *Clavis Calendaria, or a Compendious Analysis of the Calendar...* London: printed for the author and sold by Longman (and others), 1812. 8vo., wood engraved frontispiece, 7 engravings in text, few leaves, little dusted, some foxing to titlepages, contemporary half calf, marbled boards, gilt banded spine, red morocco labels, gilt volume numbers within circular flower head frames, hinges rubbed, spines little dry, one headcap slightly chipped, armorial bookplate of Ralph Creyke Marton. Jarndyce Antiquarian Booksellers CCIV - 72 2013 £125

Association – Martyn, Thomas

Parry, William Edward 1790-1855 *Journal of a Second Voyage for the Discovery of a North-West Passage from the Atlantic to the Pacific Performed n the Years 1821, 1822 and 1823 in His Majesty's Ships Fury and Hecla.* London: 1824. First edition, 40 engraved maps, charts, views, 4to, contemporary calf, expertly rebacked with contemporary style endpapers, inscribed by author for Thomas Martyn. Maggs Bros. Ltd. 1467 - 138 2013 £3250

Association – Masefield, John

Drinkwater, John 1882-1937 *The Storm.* published by author at the Birmingham Repertory Theatre, 1915. First edition, 12mo., original green wrappers, fine, inscribed by author for John Masefield, with Masefield's bookplate. Maggs Bros. Ltd. 1460 - 251 2013 £100

Association – Mason, H. T.

Sheridan, Thomas *The Life of the Rev. Swift, Dean of St. Patrick's, Dublin.* London: printed for C. Bathurst et al, 1784. First edition, 8vo, 2 engraved portrait plates, discoloration on page 24-5 (transfer from inserted envelope), speckled tan calf, rebacked, red and green morocco labels and gilt to spine, little worn, top edge dusty, bookplate of University of London Library, library ticket of same, small inkstamp to verso of titlepage and final page, letter from Prof. H. T. Mason to Dr. D. Nokes dated 3rd Oct. 1983 loosely inserted. Unsworths Antiquarian Booksellers 28 - 128 2013 £200

Association – Massingherd, Charles Langton

Coombe, William *The History of the Abbey Church of St. Peter's Westminster in Antiquities and Monuments.* London: printed for R. Ackermann by L. Harrison & J. C. Leigh, 1812. First edition, 2 volumes, folio, color frontispiece and plates, some offsetting and foxing, but largely nice, clean copy, full contemporary calf, tooled in blind and marbled edges, slightly rubbed and well rebacked with gilt raised bands, red and brown morocco labels, armorial bookplates of Charles Langton Massingherd. Jarndyce Antiquarian Booksellers CCV - 76 2013 £750

Association – Mathews, R. St. John

Chaucer, Geoffrey 1340-1400 *The Works.* London: printed for Bernard Lintot, 1721. First Urry edition, engraved frontispiece, fine portrait of Chaucer, title vignette and 27 excellent headpiece vignettes of pilgrims, just little light browning, folio, 19th century diced Russia, boards panelled and framed in blind, gilt roll tool border, neatly rebacked preserving original spine, decorated in gilt and blind, corners renewed, old leather somewhat scratched and rubbed around edges, bookplate of R. St. John Mathews and pencil inscription of J. Henry Stormont dated 1901 to endpapers good. Blackwell's Rare Books B174 - 31 2013 £1200

Association – Matthews, Carmen

Albee, Edward *A Delicate Balance.* New York: Atheneum, 1966. First edition, signed by author as well as six members of the original cast, Jessica Tandy, Hume Cronyn, Rosemary Murphy, Carmen Matthews, Henderson Forsythe and Marian Seldes, fine in nearly fine dust jacket. Ed Smith Books 78 - 3 2013 $750

Association – Matthews, Harry

Byron, George Gordon Noel, 6th Baron 1788-1824 *The Deformed Transformed. (bound with) The Island, or Christian and His Comrades.* London: printed for J. & H. L. Hunt, 1824. London: John Hunt, 1823. Second edition and third edition, 2 volumes in 1, half titles, contemporary half calf, gilt spine, rubbed, corners and spine little worn, booklabel ad signature of Alex Bridge, library label of Harry Matthews. Jarndyce Antiquarian Booksellers CCIII - 319 2013 £180

Association – Mauss, Detlef

Bonet, Honore *L'Apparition de Jehan de Meun ou le Songe Du Prieur De Salon.* Paris: Imprime par Crapelet pur la Societe des Bibliophiles Francais, 1845. One of 170 copies on vellum (this copy #7 printed for M. Le Comte e La Bedoyere, member of the Societe des Bibliophiles) (another 100 copies on issued on paper), recent fine white pigskin, decorated in blind to a Medieval style by Courtland Benson, housed in titled custom made morocco backed folding cloth box, 10 engraved plates, morocco bookplate of Comte H. De La Bedoyere and engraved bookplate of Marcellus Schlimovich, embossed library stamp of Dr. Detlef Mauss; half title with ink library stamp of Sociedad Hebraica Argentina, fine, especially clean and bright internally, only most trivial imperfections in new retrospective binding. Phillip J. Pirages 63 - 477 2013 $3500

Association – Maxwell, Robert

Cicero, Marcus Tullius *Opera Rhetorica.* Paris: Venundantur cu(m) Ceteris ab Ioanne Paruo & Iodoco Badio, 1511. Editio princeps, 4 volumes bound in 2, fine woodcut titlepages printed in red and black decorative initial letters, some worming just touching few letters and leading edge of titlepage to volume 1 frayed with slight loss, clean tear without loss to second titlepage, with some neat contemporary marginal notes, handsomely bound in 18th century full panelled calf, raised bands, black morocco labels, corners expertly repaired, armorial bookplate of Robert Maxwell of Finnebrogue on the verso of titlepages.   Ken Spelman Books Ltd.   75 - 1   2013   £950

Association – Maxwell, Vincent

Fisher, St. John *Sermon Against Luther.* Pepler & Sewell St. Dominic's Press, Ditchling, Sussex, 1935. One of 30 copies printed on handmade paper, small wood engraving of Luther by Edward Walters, after Holbien, 16mo., original quarter cream canvas, spine sunned, printed front cover label, pale grey boards with little handling soiling, corners rubbed, small glue stain left following bookplate removal, untrimmed, good, inscribed by Michael Sewell 23 March 1936 for Vincent Maxwell.   Blackwell's Rare Books   B174 - 379   2013   £120

Association – Maxwell, William

Shaw, George Bernard   1856-1950 *The Adventures of the Black Girl in Her Search for God.* 1932. First edition, 208 x 135mm., original black pictorial boards and endpapers, designed and engraved by John Farleigh, in custom made gilt titled black cloth folding box (slightly soiled), illustrated titlepage and 18 woodcut engravings by John Farleigh, with proofs of the cover, endpapers and 19 engravings (one a trial version of a scene), all signed in pencil by Fairleigh and numbered "3/9" the cover with Farleigh's inscription "This set was Specially printed for William Maxwell" (proofs contained in portfolio inside folding box), front flyleaf with inscription by Shaw for Maxwell, hint of rubbing to edges, couple of faint spots of foxing, proof copy of cover slightly wrinkled at edges, otherwise fine copy, fresh, bright and unworn.   Phillip J. Pirages   63 - 437   2013 $2500

Association – May, Richard

Byron, George Gordon Noel, 6th Baron   1788-1824 *The Prisoner of Chillon.* Lausanne: 1818. Disbound, ownership inscription of Richard May.   Jarndyce Antiquarian Booksellers   CCIII - 228   2013   £85

Association – May, Samuel Joseph

Walker, James *A Sermon Preached in Brooklyn, Connecticut at the Installation of Rev. Samuel Joseph May, Nov. 5 1823.* Boston: 1824. First edition, 8vo., 40 pages, sewn and uncut as issued, inscribed in ink on titlepage by May.   M & S Rare Books, Inc.   95 - 229   2013 $150

Association – Mayer, Bernadette

Berrigan, Ted *Memorial Day. A Collaboration by Ted Berrigan and Anne Waldman.* New York: Poetry Project, 1971. First edition, mimeographed, signed on first leaf of blue India paper by author with address and date "242 W 14th Fri. 8.30", presentation copy inscribed by author for Bernadette Mayer, fine.   James S. Jaffe Rare Books   Fall 2013 - 17   2013 $1500

Association – Mayfield, John

Dos Passos, John   1896-1970 *One Man's Initiation.* London: George, Allen & Unwin, 1920. First edition, 2nd state, with handwritten signed postcard from author laid in, in original envelope addressed to John S. Mayfield also laid in, very good in blue cloth boards, black title to spine and front board, fading to spine although title remains bright, offsetting to first and last couple of pages and remnants a sticker on rear pastedown, otherwise interior very clean, very good, 128 pages.   The Kelmscott Bookshop   7 - 107   2013 $1300

Association – Mazumdar, Bijay Chandra

Athale, Bhikadev Vasudev *A Marathi-English Dictionary.* Bombay: printed at the Asiatic Printing Press, 1871. Only edition, 12mo., modern cloth, 230 pages, ownership stamp on title B(ijay) C(handra) Mazumdar (1861-1942), title backed with loss of one letter, last leaf repaired at bottom with tape, with no loss.   Howard S. Mott Inc.   262 - 11   2013 $250

Association – McClintic, Guthrie

Howard, Sidney *Yellow Jack, a History by...* New York: Harcourt Brace, 1933. First edition, 8vo., 152 pages, full brown morocco by Brentanos, spine gilt in compartments, initials "G. McC" on first board, little scuffing, near fine, this copy was presented by author to director Guthrie McClintic and bears affectionate presentation for Howard and DeKruif.   Second Life Books Inc.   183 - 174   2013 $375

Association – McCord, Margaret

Burton, Richard Francis 1821-1890 *The Tale of Abu Kir and Abu Sir.* Belfast: Crannog Press, 1974. First edition, one of 100 numbered copies, large 8vo., original brown hessian wrappers, printed paper label, with four single page and one double page and 8 other line block and linocut illustrations by publisher Margaret McCord, fine. Maggs Bros. Ltd. 1442 - Crannog 2013 £75

Association – McCormick, Edith Rockefeller

Ruskin, John 1819-1900 *Deucalion Collected Studies of the Lapse of Waves and Life of Stones.* Orpington, Kent: George Allen, 1879-1880. 8 parts in 2 volumes, 212 x 141mm., 11 plates in form of drawings by Ruskin, two of them in several colors and two in blue; lovely chestnut brown morocco, handsomely gilt by Doves Bindery (turn-ins at back signed and dated '19 C-S 09'), covers with French fillet border enclosing two rectangular strapwork frames with semicircular interlacing at top and bottom, inner frame interlaced further with two strapwork triangles that form a six-sided star at center, each point of star surmounted with small open circles (and top and bottom point with additional three petalled floral design), star surrounding a garland composed of two leafy sprays, raised bands, spines gilt in compartments featuring concentric square frames enclosing prominent daisy within lozenge, turn-ins with rules and petalled floral cornerpieces, all edges gilt and with stippled gauffering, original front wrappers as well as extra titlepages, bound in at back of each volume, very dark blue full morocco pull-off suede-lined cases in the shape of a book (just slightly rubbed) with raised bands and gilt titling; pastedown of first volume with bookplate of Dr. Samuel L. Siegler, pastedown of second volume with bookplate of "E. R. McC." (Edith Rockefeller McCormick) and with vestige of removed Siegler bookplate, beautifully bound set in pristine condition, even original wrappers in perfect shape. Phillip J. Pirages 61 - 104 2013 $10,000

Ruskin, John 1819-1900 *The Queen's Gardens.* Manchester: printed in Aid of the St. Andrews Schools Fund, 1864. First printing, 221 x 144mm., 19, (1) pages, very fine dark blue morocco by Doves Bindery (signed and dated 1911), covers with gilt fillet border and central oval wreath of tudor roses and rose leaves, raised bands, spine with gilt fillet compartments containing vertical titling, gilt ruled turn-ins, all edges gilt, slightly scuffed felt lined tan morocco pull-off box by Riviere & Son, bookplate of Edith Rockefeller McCormick, usual minor offsetting to free endpapers from turn-ins, otherwise sparkling copy. Phillip J. Pirages 61 - 105 2013 $2500

Association – McCutcheon, George Barr

Garrett, Phineas *One Hundred Choice Selections...A Repository of Readings, Recitations and Declamations...* Philadelphia and Chicago: P. Garrett & Co., 1877. First edition, 8vo., original printed yellow wrappers, 180 pages + 10 pages of publisher's terminal ads, from the library of George Barr McCutcheon with his bookplate tipped in, wrappers little worn and stained, very good, enclosed in cloth slipcase. The Brick Row Book Shop Miscellany Fifty-Nine - 27 2013 $750

Association – McDaniel, David

Young, Al *Snakes.* New York: Holt Rinehart & Winston, 1970. First edition, bookplate of Earl David McDaniel, fine in fine dust jacket, signed by author, inscribed by author and additionally inscribed by him for David E. McDaniel. Between the Covers Rare Books, Inc. 165 - 297 2013 $100

Association – McDaniel, Earl

Young, Al *Snakes.* New York: Holt Rinehart & Winston, 1970. First edition, bookplate of Earl David McDaniel, fine in fine dust jacket, signed by author, inscribed by author and additionally inscribed by him for David E. McDaniel. Between the Covers Rare Books, Inc. 165 - 297 2013 $100

Association – McDowall, Roddy

Llewellyn, Richard *How Green Was My Valley.* New York: Macmillan, 1941. (1940). Later printing, round-robin, signed in fountain pen on location during making of the film on July 19 1941, gift copy from Freda Knill (niece of cast member Thomas A. Hughes) to her daughter, with autographs and inscriptions of Roddy McDowall, Maureen O'Hara, Walter Pidgeon, Donald Crisp, Barry Fitzgerald, Sara Allgood, Anna Lee, T. Arthur Hughes, Richard Fraser and Evan H. Evans; fair to good only, binding intact, shaken and with fraying to edges of cloth, in very good supplied dust jacket with some rubbing and light wear at extremities. Ed Smith Books 75 - 39 2013 $1750

Association – McGee, John

Bacon, Francis Viscount St. Albans 1561-1626 *The Works of Francis Bacon.* Boston: Brown and Taggard, 1861. 8vo., frontispieces, original triple ruled pebbled brown cloth, gilt stamped spines, mild edgewear, some spine heads torn, few inner hinges repaired, bookplates of John F. McGee, very good. Jeff Weber Rare Books 169 - 24 2013 $650

Association – McGowan, Lord

Singer, Charles *A History of Technology.* Oxford: Clarendon Press, 1958. 5 volumes, preferred issue (thicker paper stock), thick 8vo., maps, tables, illustrations, color frontispieces, pastedowns and free endpapers foxed, else text and plates clean, navy blue cloth, gilt stamped spines, dust jackets torn and foxed, volume V with slip reading "Spare copy returned by Lord McGowan. with Compliments of Imperial Chemical Industries Limited" laid in, very good in good jackets. Jeff Weber Rare Books 169 - 414 2013 $185

Association – McGraw, Dick

Jeffers, Robinson 1887-1962 *The Loving Shepherdess.* New York: Random House, 1956. Limited to 155 numbered copies (#64), 4to., quarter gilt stamped black cloth over white paper backed boards, black cloth slipcase by Silverlake Bindery, signed by author and artist, with original etchings by Jean Kellogg, additionally signed and inscribed from Kellogg to Dick McGraw, with prospectus, backing sheet and 3 ALS's laid in, fine. Jeff Weber Rare Books 171 - 192 2013 $2000

Association – McGrigor, Alexander

Leigh, Percival *The Comic English Grammar...* London: Richard Bentley, 1840. First edition, frontispiece plate, tailpiece and 48 illustrations after drawings by John Leech, very attractive polished calf, handsomely gilt by Riviere & Son (signed), covers bordered with gilt French fillet and small roundel cornerpieces, raised bands, spine gilt in compartments featuring elegant floral cornerpieces, sidepieces and centerpiece with surrounding small dots and stars, decorative bands at head and foot, red morocco label, gilt inner dentelles, marbled endpapers, top edge gilt, front joint very expertly repaired, original cloth bound in at end, morocco bookplate of Alexander McGrigor, very fine in especially pretty binding. Phillip J. Pirages 63 - 312 2013 $350

Leigh, Percival *The Comic Latin Grammar.* London: Charles Tilt, 1840. First edition, 197 x 127mm., very attractive polished calf, handsomely gilt by Riviere & Son (signed on verso of front endpaper), covers bordered with French fillet and small roundel cornerpieces, raised bands, spine gilt in compartments, featuring elegant floral cornerpieces, sidepieces, and centerpiece with surrounding small dots and stars, decorative bands at head and foot, red morocco label, gilt inner dentelles, marbled endpapers, top edge gilt, 54 illustrations in text and 8 engraved plates after drawings by John Leech, joints slightly flaked (front joint just beginning to crack at head and foot), one inch tear in fore edge of one leaf (well away from text), excellent copy in very pretty binding, covers quite lustrous and text smooth, fresh and clean, bookplate of Alexander McGrigor. Phillip J. Pirages 63 - 313 2013 $350

Association – McKeon, Robert

Pagel, Walter *William Harvey's Biological Ideas: Selected Aspects and Historical Background.* New York: S. Karger, 1967. 8vo., 394 pages, illustrations, light pencil marginalia, gilt stamped blue cloth, sunned, Burndy bookplate, formerly belonging to Robert M. McKeon, very good. Jeff Weber Rare Books 172 - 125 2013 $120

Association – McLean, Ruari

Daudet, Alphonse *Tartarin of Tarascon.* printed by Richard W. Ellis, The Georgian Press, 1930. 253/1500 sets, 2 volumes, signed by artist, several illustrations from sketches by W. A. Dwiggins, 16mo., original pale grey, black cloth backed boards, backstrips gilt lettered and decorated, boards with overall decorative pattern in green and pink untrimmed, dust soiled board slipcase with printed label, very good, Ruari McLean's copy with his booklabel. Blackwell's Rare Books B174 - 361 2013 £150

Association – McMurtry, Larry

Shakespeare, William 1564-1616 *Complete Works.* London: Oxford University Press, 1969. 8vo., 1166 pages, publisher's cloth, very good, tight copy, bookseller Larry McMurtry's copy with his 1969 ownership inscription and "Booked Up" card with 7 lines of holograph laid in, second slip of paper with 6 lines of holograph in laid in as well. Second Life Books Inc. 183 - 352 2013 $50

Association – Meier, Schuitema

Baker, Henry *Employment for the Microscope.* London: printed for R. and J. Dodsley, 1764. Second edition, folding engraved frontispiece, 17 folding three quarter, slightly browned, little offsetting from plates, 8vo., mid 20th century half green straight grained morocco, top edge gilt, otherwise uncut, bookplate of microscope collector Schuitema Meier, good. Blackwell's Rare Books Sciences - 10 2013 £500

Goring, C. R. *Micrographia: Containing Practical Essays on Reflecting, Solar, Oxy Hydrogen Gas Microscopies, Micrometers; Eye-pieces &c.* Whittaker and Co., 1837. First edition, folding engraved frontispiece, 2 engraved plates and one full page illustration, 8vo., original boards, surface cracks at joints, contemporary signature of Michael Carmichael at head of title and his arms stencilled inside front cover, bookplate of D. J. Schuitema Meier, very good. Blackwell's Rare Books Sciences - 52 2013 £400

Association – Melland, William

Valpy, Richard *Elements of Greek Grammar.* London: printed by A. J. Valpy, 1830. New edition, 8vo., 2 fold-out plates, very occasional pencil annotations, little soiled, particularly near front, tan half calf with brown label to spine and marbled boards, upper joint splitting, edges bit worn, boards rubbed, ownership inscription of William Melland. Unsworths Antiquarian Booksellers 28 - 55 2013 £30

Association – Menzies, J.

Marjoribanks, Alexander *Tour to the Loire and La Vendee in 1835...* London: Effingham Wilson, 1836. Second edition, frontispiece, original pink paper boards, green glazed cloth spine, paper label, spine slightly faded, signature of J. Menzies and library stamp of St. Mary's College, Blairs on leading pastedown, 'Eastern Division' stamp on title, very good. Jarndyce Antiquarian Booksellers CCV - 192 2013 £280

Association – Menzies, Jill Elizabeth Duncan

Betjeman, John 1906-1984 *Shropshire. A Shell Guide.* London: Faber and Faber, 1951. First edition, 4to., original yellow cloth, dust jacket, inscribed by Betjeman to his secretary Jill Elizabeth Duncan Menzies, very good, jacket reinforced with tape in such a way that jacket cannot be removed. Maggs Bros. Ltd. 1460 - 93 2013 £1250

Association – Metcalf, I.

Talfourd, Thomas Noon *Literary Sketches and Letter: Being the Final Memorials of Charles Lamb...* New York and Philadelphia: Appleton, 1849. Second edition, 8vo., black blindstamped cloth, spine stamped in gilt "I. Metcalf, Providence 1852" on flyleaf, very good, tight copy. Second Life Books Inc. 183 - 371 2013 $65

Association – Metcalf, Nancy

Williams, Jonathan *A Celestial Centennial Reverie for Mr. Charles Ives.* Highlands: Jonathan Williams Feb. 20-27, 1975. Produced on Xerox 4000, in an edition of 100 for friends, 4to., 24 pages, self wrappers, plastic binder, inscribed by author for Paul and Nancy Metcalf. Second Life Books Inc. 183 - 407 2013 $150

Williams, Jonathan *62 Climerikews to Amuse Mr. Lear.* Roswell/Denver: DBA/JCA Editions Christmas, 1983. #62 of 200 numbered copies, this signed for Paul and Nancy (Metcalf), 4to., printed wrappers, nice. Second Life Books Inc. 183 - 402 2013 $150

Williams, Jonathan *Homage, Umbrage Quibble & Chicane.* Roswell: DBA Editions, 1981. First edition, one of 120 copies, this #68, inscribed by author for Paul and Nancy Metcalf, 4to., 72 pages. Second Life Books Inc. 183 - 413 2013 $125

Williams, Jonathan *The Lucidities, Sixteen in Visionary Company.* London: Turret Books, 1967. First edition, 18 pages, bound in cloth with illustrations by John Furnival on foil, fine, of a total edition of 280 this is one of 250 for sale, inscribed by author for poet Paul Metcalf and his wife Nancy. Second Life Books Inc. 183 - 416 2013 $125

Williams, Jonathan *Untinears & Antennae for Maurice Ravel.* St. Paul: Truck Books, 1977. First edition, printed wrappers, very nice, inscribed by author for Paul and Nancy Metcalf. Second Life Books Inc. 183 - 422 2013 $50

Association – Metcalf, Paul

Williams, Jonathan *Affilati Attrezzi Per I Giardini Di Catullo.* Milano: Lerici Editori, 1966. First edition, 8vo., 121 pages, paper wrappers, English and Italian on facing pages, inscribed by author for Metcalf, very good, little soiled. Second Life Books Inc. 183 - 403 2013 $50

Williams, Jonathan *A Celestial Centennial Reverie for Mr. Charles Ives.* Highlands: Jonathan Williams Feb. 20-27, 1975. Produced on Xerox 4000, in an edition of 100 for friends, 4to., 24 pages, self wrappers, plastic binder, inscribed by author for Paul and Nancy Metcalf. Second Life Books Inc. 183 - 407 2013 $150

Williams, Jonathan *Glees Swarthy Monotonies Rince Cochon & Chozzerai for Simon.* Roswell: DBA Editions, 1980. First edition, 1/128 copies distributed for friends, not for sale, 4to., 94 pages, very good, inscribed by author for friend Paul Metcalf, #74 for Paul from the Colonel Highlands 1980", in addition author has circled in pen the statement on titlepage "May contain language that is offensive to children". Second Life Books Inc. 183 - 412 2013 $100

Williams, Jonathan *Homage, Umbrage Quibble & Chicane.* Roswell: DBA Editions, 1981. First edition, one of 120 copies, this #68, inscribed by author for Paul and Nancy Metcalf, 4to., 72 pages. Second Life Books Inc. 183 - 413 2013 $125

Williams, Jonathan *The Lucidities, Sixteen in Visionary Company.* London: Turret Books, 1967. First edition, 18 pages, bound in cloth with illustrations by John Furnival on foil, fine, of a total edition of 280 this is one of 250 for sale, inscribed by author for poet Paul Metcalf and his wife Nancy. Second Life Books Inc. 183 - 416 2013 $125

Williams, Jonathan *Lullabies Twisters Gibbers Drags.* Highlands: Nantahala Foundation, 1963. Oblong wrappers, very good, inscribed by author for Paul Metcalf. Second Life Books Inc. 183 - 417 2013 $75

Williams, Jonathan *62 Climerikews to Amuse Mr. Lear.* Roswell/Denver: DBA/JCA Editions Christmas, 1983. #62 of 200 numbered copies, this signed for Paul and Nancy (Metcalf), 4to., printed wrappers, nice. Second Life Books Inc. 183 - 402 2013 $150

Williams, Jonathan *Untinears & Antennae for Maurice Ravel.* St. Paul: Truck Books, 1977. First edition, printed wrappers, very nice, inscribed by author for Paul and Nancy Metcalf. Second Life Books Inc. 183 - 422 2013 $50

Association – Metcalfe, Christopher

Stillingfleet, Edward *The Unreasonableness of Separation; or an Impartial Account of the... Present Separation from the Communion of the Church of England.* London: T. N. for Henry Mortlock, 1681. First edition, 4to., some spotting and toning, first few leaves soiled, title a touch worn at fore edge, contemporary calf, marbled edges, rebacked and recornered by Chris Weston, old leather scratched and crackled early ink inscription Christopher Metcalfe, also printed booklabel Rev. Richard Gibbons Binnali, M.A. Unsworths Antiquarian Booksellers 28 - 133 2013 £275

Association – Meynell, Wilfrid

Blunden, Edmund *The Waggoner and Other Poems.* London: Sidgwick & Jackson, 1920. Second impression, 8vo., original burgundy cloth, printed paper label on spine inscribed in unknown pencilled hand "To a fine critic 28 June 1921. F.P." and inscribed below by author, recipient is Frederick Page, loosely inserted ALS to Page from Blunden and short ALS to Page from Wilfrid Meynell, faded on spine, label rubbed, otherwise excellent copy, enclosures in presentable order. Maggs Bros. Ltd. 1460 - 111 2013 £180

Association – Miles, Charles Popham

Liebig, Justus *Researches on the Chemistry of Food.* printed for Taylor and Walton, 1847. First edition, slightly foxed at either end, 8vo., original cloth with elaborate blind-stamped panel on sides, spine lettered gilt by Remnant and Edmonds, slightly worn at extremities, signature of Rev. Chas. Popham Miles, Glasgow 1848, inside front cover very good. Blackwell's Rare Books Sciences - 74 2013 £200

Association – Miles, Jeremiah

Lycophron *Alexandra (...) Accedunt Versiones, Variantes Lectiones, Emendationes, Annotationes, & Indices Necessarii.* Oxford: E Theatro Sheldoniano, 1697. 2 parts in 1 volume, folio, Greek and Latin text, full page engraved frontispiece, titlepage with engraved vignette, tiny burn hole to frontispiece, unobtrusive embossed Athenaeum Library stamp to titlepage, small tear to lower margin page 7 not affecting text, contemporary speckled calf, rebacked in sheep gilt Athenaeum Library stamps to spine not affecting text, contemporary speckled calf, rebacked in sheep, gilt Athenaeum Library stamps to spine and upper board, edges and pages worn, corners fraying, hinges repaired with cloth, armorial bookplate of Jeremiah Miles to front pastedown. Unsworths Antiquarian Booksellers 28 - 30 2013 £350

Association – Millar, J.

Smith, Adam 1723-1790 *The Theory of Moral Sentiments.* London: printed for A. Strahan and T. Cadell, 1790. Volume 1 (of two) only, presentation copy, inscribed by author for Professor Millar, octavo, half title, contemporary tree calf, neatly rebacked and recornered to style, covers decoratively bordered gilt, board edges tooled in blind, edges sprinkled blue, marbled endpapers, early ink signature of "J. Millar, Millheugh" and Milheugh bookplate, excellent copy, housed in custom green cloth slipcase. Heritage Book Shop 50th Anniversary Catalogue - 92 2013 $37,500

Association – Millard, Alice

Homerus *Opero (in Greek).* Florence: printer of Virgil C6061, probably Bartolommeo di Libri and Demetrius Damilas...9th December, 1488. but not before Jan. 1488/89 date of dedication. Editio princeps, 2 median folio volumes, unrubricated, early 19th century russia gilt, marbled endpapers and edges, volume II is about 15mm. shorter in its binding, bindings uniform height, inner margin of first leaf strengthened, slight worming at beginning of volume II, some foxing, from the collection of Dr. Charles Burney 1757-1817 whose collection was sold to British Museum (red library stamps), sold as duplicate in 1931 to Alice Millard; to Estelle Doheny. Heritage Book Shop 50th Anniversary Catalogue - 51 2013 $250,000

Association – Miller, De Witt

Andrews, William Loring *Sextodecimos et Infra.* New York: Charles Scribner's Sons, 1899. First edition, limited to 152 copies, this one of 140 printed on English handmade plate paper by Gilliss Press, 8vo., 27 illustrations of miniature books, 14 of which are in full color, stiff paper wrappers, outer dust jacket, extremely scarce, small tears along bottom and top of hinges of dust jacket, from the library of De Witt Miller with his ink inscription, also from the library of noted miniature collector Kathryn Rickard with her bookplate, with additional bookplate on front free endpaper, number in ink in corner of front free endpaper, paper slipcase not present, scarce; from the collection of Donn W. Sanford. Oak Knoll Books   303 - 7   2013 $450

Association – Miller, Henry

Rose, Billy *Wine, Women and Words.* New York: Simon and Schuster, 1948. First edition, limited to unspecified number of copies signed by author, this number 1451, octavo, illustrations by Salvador Dali, inscription from Henry Miller for Pierre Sicari, quarter gold cloth over pictorial boards, spine printed in black, top edge black, red endpapers, red silk placemarker, boards bit rubbed, edges with some light wear and corners bumped, small stain top of fore-edge, very good.   Heritage Book Shop   Holiday Catalogue 2012 - 34   2013 $1500

Association – Millikan, Michael

Wagner, Bruce *Force Majeure.* New York: Random House, 1991. First edition, inscribed by author to Michael Millikan, fine in fine dust jacket.   Ken Lopez Bookseller   159 - 209   2013 $150

Association – Millin, Sarah Gertrude

Eliot, Thomas Stearns   1888-1965 *Four Quartets.* London: Faber and Faber, 1944. First UK edition, 8vo., original tan cloth, near fine, slightly marked dust jacket with slight wear to extremities, preserved in folding box, inscribed by author for Sarah Gertrude Millin Jan. 1950.   Maggs Bros. Ltd.   1460 - 271   2013   £2500

Association – Mills, Mrs.

Winslow, Anna Green *Diary of Anna Green Winslow. A Boston Girl of 1771.* Cambridge: Boston and New York: Houghton Mifflin Co., Riverside Press, 1894. First edition, 8vo., canvas covered boards with ties in blue, red, green and black on front cover, half title, black and white frontispiece, facsimile and 5 black and white illustrations, spine darkened and inscription on first flyleaf "Mrs. Mills with compliments Nellie F. Booth 1895".   Schooner Books Ltd.   101 - 128   2013 $55

Association – Mills, Ralph

Heaney, Seamus *Wintering Owl.* New York: Oxford University Press, 1973. First American edition (500 copies), 8vo., original blue cloth bards, very fine in very slightly dust soiled jacket, scarce, poet and critic Ralph Mills Jr's copy with his ownership signature.   James S. Jaffe Rare Books   Fall 2013 - 64   2013 $1250

Association – Milne, George

Coleridge, Samuel Taylor   1772-1834 *Aids to Reflection...* London: William Pickering, 1848. Sixth edition, 2 volumes, half titles, slightly later full calf, gilt spines, borders, dentelles, red and green label, gilt monograms on front boards, booklabels of George Milne obscuring previous owner's bookplate, all edges gilt, very good, handsome.   Jarndyce Antiquarian Booksellers   CCIII - 548   2013   £75

Association – Milner, Charles

Procter, Bryan Waller *The Flood of Thessaly, The Girl of Provence and Other Poems.* London: Henry Colburn, 1823. First edition, half title, uncut in original drab boards, paper label, front board marked, head of spine slightly rubbed, bumped corners carefully strengthened, signed "Charles Milner", good plus.   Jarndyce Antiquarian Booksellers   CCIII - 607   2013   £85

Association – Milner, W.

Ray, John *The Wisdom of God Manifested in the Works of the Creation.* Glasgow: printed by J. Bryce and D. Paterson, 1756. Thirteenth edition, 324 pages, 12mo., very good in full contemporary sprinkled calf, raised and gilt banded spine with red morocco label, some slight rubbing to spine and board edges, tiny amount of worming to front endpaper and foot of title, armorial bookplate of John Headlam, early signature of W. Milner.   Ken Spelman Books Ltd.   75 - 21   2013   £120

Association – Milner, William Mordaunt Sturt, 4th Baronet

Marryat, Frederick   1792-1848 *Peter Simple.* London: Saunders & Otley, 1834. Third edition, 3 volumes, bound for the library of Nun-Appleton Hall in contemporary half green calf, gilt spines with family crest of a winged horse at head, maroon morocco labels, slight rubbing, but very good, attractive set, bookplate of Sir William Mordaunt Sturt Milner, 4th Baronet, Nun Appelton.   Jarndyce Antiquarian Booksellers   CCV - 193   2013   £150

Association – Minault, Rene

Galen *Epitome Galeni Pergame ni Opervm.* Basileae: apud Mich. Ifingrinium anno, 1551. Small folio, full rich contemporary calf skillfully rebacked with original spine tastefully laid down, from the library of Nicolas Marchant with his signature and stamp on title, some early signatures, gilt armorial crest on front board of two lions facing crowned staff, ruled boards, gilt emblems in each corner, raised tooled bands on spine, text with light marginal dampstaining, early underlining of text with contemporary marginalia throughout, early ownership signature of Rene Minault, 1702.   James Tait Goodrich   75 - 97   2013 $2950

Association – Mitchell, Frederick

Roberts, Brigham Henry *Life of John Taylor; third President of the Church of Jesus Christ of Latter-Day Saints.* Salt Lake City: George Q. Cannon & Sons, 1892. First edition, 468 pages, octavo, full leather, gilt stamped title on front board and backstrip, all edges gilt, 1 plates, fine, ex-libris Frederick A. Mitchell with his name in ink on front free endsheet.   Ken Sanders Rare Books   45 - 39   2013 $1000

Association – Mitchell, R.

Mitchell, J. Leslie *Three Go Back.* Indianapolis: Bobbs Merrill, 1932. First American edition, boards little soiled, top edge little darkened, very good or better in very good plus dust jacket with two scratches on spine and few tiny nicks and tears, laid in is ALS from author's widow (R. Mitchell) telling her correspondent that her husband died in 1932, letter has old, light glue stain on verso where it was presumably affixed in an album, else near fine.   Between the Covers Rare Books, Inc.   Sci-Fi, Fantasy & Horror - 84977   2013 $450

Association – Moffatt, George

Byron, George Gordon Noel, 6th Baron   1788-1824 *English Bards and Scotch Reviewers.* London: James Cawthorn, 1809. Second edition, half title, final ad leaf, contemporary half speckled calf, armorial bookplate of George Moffatt & later Nowell-Smith booklabels, very good.   Jarndyce Antiquarian Booksellers   CCIII - 119   2013   £200

Association – Molesworth, William

Vergilius Maro, Publius *Opera quae quidem Exstant Omnia.* Basilae: Sebastianum Henriepetri, 1613. Folio, little worming to fore-edge margins around columns 180 and 279, toning at very edge of margins to varying degrees, occasional discoloration around text especially to volumes 1079-1802 and 1901-1904, contemporary speckled tan calf, neatly rebacked and corners repaired, red morocco gilt spine label, boards heavily scratched, few dents, edges worn, armorial bookplate of Sir William Molesworth with ink inscription of Kenneth J. Cox, Dalton Hall Victoria Park, Manchester 14 added, old ink ownership inscription of Johannis Glover on titlepage, small contemporary (?) list of Latin names for various vegetables and herbs loosely inserted.   Unsworths Antiquarian Booksellers   28 - 57   2013   £500

Association – Mompesson, John

The Compleat Wizzard; Being a Collection of Authentic and Entertaining Narratives of the Real Existence and Appearance of Ghosts, Demons and Spectres... London: printed for T. Evans, 1770. 8vo., name or note roughly erased from foot of page 74 with some thinning to paper and one small hole shaving a letter, some browning in first four leaves, occasional foxing, slight old waterstaining to few lower margins, marginal notes on two pages in early hand, one noting an alias and letters IM and date added within decorative initial to account of John Mompesson, the Invisible Drummer, 19th century half calf, marbled boards, rebacked retaining original spine and label, corners worn, bookplate removed.   Jarndyce Antiquarian Booksellers   CCIV - 43   2013   £4800

Association – Monks, G. H.

Baas, J. H. *Outlines of the History of Medicine and the Medical Profession.* New York: Vail, 1889. First English edition, 1173 pages, original cloth, inner hinges just starting to split, light rubbing, otherwise good, tight copy, translator's presentation from H. E. Handerson to Dr. G. H. Monks.   James Tait Goodrich   75 - 14   2013 $495

Association – Monroe, Harriet

Pound, Ezra Loomis   1885-1972 *Cathay.* London: Elkin Mathews, 1915. First edition, limited to 1000 copies, small thin 8vo., original printed wrappers (somewhat dust soiled and rubbed, few faint stains on covers, otherwise very good), enclosed in half morocco slipcase, inscribed by author in month before publication for Harriet Monroe.   James S. Jaffe Rare Books   Fall 2013 - 131   2013 $17,5000

Association – Montague, Holland

Dwight, Theodore *The Father's Book; or Suggestions for the Government and Instruction of Young Children...* Springfield: Merriam, 1835. Second edition, 12mo., frontispiece, contemporary embossed cloth, covers faded, very good, tight, contemporary name on endpaper and titlepage of Granby Mass farmer and diarist Holland Montague. Second Life Books Inc. 183 - 118 2013 $150

Association – Monteith, Charles

Golding, William 1911-1993 *The Inheritors.* London: Faber and Faber, 1955. First edition, 8vo., original blue cloth, dust jacket, excellent copy in slightly browned dust jacket, worn at head and tail of spine, inscribed by author with ownership signature of Faber's publishing director, Charles Monteith above. Maggs Bros. Ltd. 1460 - 348 2013 £1500

Joyce, James 1882-1941 *Poems Penyeach and other Verses.* London: Faber and Faber, 1965. Uncorrected proof copy, new edition, small 8vo. original pink wrappers, Charles Monteith's copy with his book label loosely inserted and his name in non-authorial hand, on cover, near fine. Maggs Bros. Ltd. 1442 - 139 2013 £200

Larkin, Philip 1922-1985 *XX Poems.* N.P.: privately printed, 1951. First edition printed in an edition of 100 copies, 8vo., original printed white wrappers, presentation copy inscribed to his editor at Faber, Charles Monteith, beautiful copy, none of the discoloration typical of paper used to bind this publication, cloth folding box. James S. Jaffe Rare Books Fall 2013 - 85 2013 $15,000

Association – Montgomery, Bruce

Dickson, John Carr *Fear is the Same.* London: William Heinemann, 1956. First edition, some scuffing to boards, foxing to fore edge and edges of pages, near very good in attractive, near fine dust jacket, nicely inscribed by author to Bruce Montgomery, real name of mystery writer Edmund Crispin, nice association. Between the Covers Rare Books, Inc. Mystery & Detective Fiction - 94111 2013 $1500

Association – Montgomery, Field Marshal Lord

Van Der Post, Laurens *Journey into Russia.* London: Hogarth Press, 1964. Third impression, 8vo., folding map, original blue cloth, inscribed copy from author to Field Marshal Lord Montgomery. J. & S. L. Bonham Antiquariam Booksellers Europe - 9805 2013 £45

Association – Moore, Doris Langley

Austin, Alfred *A Vindication of Lord Byron.* London: Chapman & Hall, 1869. Second edition, disbound, inserted into dusted paper wrapper from parcel addressed to Doris Langley Moore, from the Bookshop, Wells, 9 pages. Jarndyce Antiquarian Booksellers CCIII - 352 2013 £60

Brydges, Egerton *Letters on the Character and Poetical Genius of Lord Byron.* London: Longman &c, 1824. First edition, unobtrusive tear on title repaired with archival tape on verso, contemporary half purple calf, black leather label, slight rubbing, spine faded to brown, armorial bookplate of Dr. Nathaniel Rogers and with "Dr. Rogers" stamped in gilt at tail of spine, Doris Langley Moore's copy with few pencil notes by her. Jarndyce Antiquarian Booksellers CCIII - 349 2013 £250

Byron, George Gordon Noel, 6th Baron 1788-1824 *Correspondence. Chiefly with Lady Melbourne, Mr. Hobhouse, The Hon. Douglas Kinnaird, and P. B. Shelley.* London: John Murray, 1922. Reprint, 2 volumes, half titles, frontispiece, plates, pastedowns strengthened at edges with tape, original dark green cloth, spines little dulled and slightly worn at head and tail, Doris Langley Moore's copy with her signature and bookplates and extensive annotations in her hand. Jarndyce Antiquarian Booksellers CCIII - 326 2013 £75

Byron, George Gordon Noel, 6th Baron 1788-1824 *His Very Self and Voice: Collected Covnersationsw of Lord Byron.* New York: Macmillan, 1954. First edition, half title, original maroon cloth, dusted and torn dust jacket, Doris Langley Moore's copy with her pencil notes. Jarndyce Antiquarian Booksellers CCIII - 106 2013 £30

Byron, George Gordon Noel, 6th Baron 1788-1824 *Letters and Journals of Lord Byron; With Notices of His Life.* London: John Murray, 1830. First edition, 2 volumes, large 4to., half title volume I, engraved frontispiece and errata leaf volume II, text slightly spotted, contemporary full calf, black leather labels, borders in blind, rubbed, corners worn, remains of sellotape on endpapers, some time rebacked, hinges volume 1 slightly weakening, from the library of Doris Langley Moore. Jarndyce Antiquarian Booksellers CCIII - 323 2013 £250

Byron Painted by His Compeers; or all About Lord Byron, from His Marriage to His Death as Given in the Various Newspapers of His Day... London: Samuel Palmer, 1869. Original dark green cloth, bevelled boards, front board lettered in gilt within attractive gilt roundel, very good, tight copy, Doris Langley Moore's copy with few pencil notes by her. Jarndyce Antiquarian Booksellers CCIII - 340 2013 £150

Chew, Samuel C. *Byron in England: His Fame and After-Fame.* London: John Murray, 1924. First edition, half title, frontispiece, 6 pages ads, original green cloth, repaired tears at head of spine, traces of cellophane wrappers attached to endpapers, bookplate of Doris Langley Moore and signature "Centenary week" April 1924.   Jarndyce Antiquarian Booksellers   CCIII - 359   2013   £60

Jeaffreson, John Cordy *The Real Lord Byron.* Leipzig: Bernhard Tauchnitz, 1883. (1896-1905). Copyright edition, 3 volumes, half titles, uncut, original printed cream wrappers, spine torn without loss, volume I little dusted, well preserved copy in clear protective wrappers, Doris Langley Moore's copy.   Jarndyce Antiquarian Booksellers   CCIII - 396   2013   £40

Lovelace, Ralph Milbanke, Earl of *Astarte; a Fragment of Truth Concerning George Gordon Byron...* London: printed at the Chiswick Press, 1905. First edition, half title, frontispiece slightly spotted, plates facsimiles, original blue boards, brown cloth spine, paper label slightly chipped, little dulled, Lord Rosebery's copy with letter from Lord Lovelace tipped in, Doris Langley Moore's copy with few pencil notes.   Jarndyce Antiquarian Booksellers   CCIII - 108   2013   £85

Lovell, Ernest James *Captain Medwin: Friend of Byron and Shelley.* Austin: University of Texas Press, 1962. First edition, half title, original blue cloth, very good in slightly worn dust jacket, Doris Langley Moore's copy, few pencil notes by her.   Jarndyce Antiquarian Booksellers   CCIII - 420   2013   £25

Mayne, Ethel Colburn *Byron.* London: Methuen & Co., 1912. 2 volumes, half titles, frontispiece portraits, plates, 31 page catalog in both volumes, original dark blue/green cloth, lettered gilt and blind, tiny nick in spine cloth volume II, otherwise very good, Doris Langley Moore's copy with occasional notes by her in text.   Jarndyce Antiquarian Booksellers   CCIII - 413   2013   £35

Pickering, Leslie P. *Lord Byron, Leigh Hunt and the "Liberal".* London: Drane's Ltd., 1925. Half title, frontispiece, original red cloth, bevelled boards, lettered gilt, spine little faded, small split at head, Doris Langley Moore's copy.   Jarndyce Antiquarian Booksellers   CCIII - 309   2013   £30

Raymond, Dora Neill *The Political Career of Lord Byron.* London: George Allen & Unwin, 1925. First English edition, original red cloth, slightly marked, spine slightly faded, booklabel of David A.. Lyttleton, from the library of Doris Langley Moore.   Jarndyce Antiquarian Booksellers   CCIII - 438   2013   £30

Association – Moore, Henry

Hedgecoe, John *Henry Moore. Energy in Space.* Greenwich: New York Graphic Society, 1973. First trade edition, 8vo., 83 pages, signed and inscribed by Henry Moore, near fine hardback, mild soil to edges, near fine dust jacket, price clipped.   By the Book, L. C.   36 - 21   2013 $400

Association – Moore, Marianne

Lancaster, Clay *Prospect Park Handbook.* New York: Walton H. Rawls, 1967. First edition, fine in fine original glassine dust jacket, signed by Lancaster and by Marianne Moore, provided foreword, beautiful copy.   Between the Covers Rare Books, Inc.   New York City - 99835   2013 $150

Association – Moore, Steven

Pychon, Thomas *Against the Day.* New York: Penguin Press, 2006. Advance reading copy, issued in limited quantities to sales reps and reviewers, sales rep's name on titlepage, some copies misprinted pages, this copy appears not to, this copy was given by sales rep to reviewer Steven Moore with note signed by Moore to that effect laid in, Moore has made several small pencilled check marks in margins (and noted few typos), bulky book, slightly cocked, near fine, with Moore's handwritten notes for review (4 pages), his typed review (2 pages) and copy of Washington Post Book World Nov. 19 2006 with his review.   Ken Lopez Bookseller   159 - 168   2013 $3500

Association – More, Peter

Pratchett, Terry *Sourcery.* London: Gollancz, 1988. First edition, 8vo., original bright yellow boards, backstrip gilt lettered, dust jacket, near fine, inscribed by author to Peter More.   Blackwell's Rare Books   172 - 232   2013   £200

Association – Morgan, Dale

Stucki, John Stettler *Family History Journal of John S. Stuckii: Handcart Pioneer of 1860.* Salt Lake City: Pyramind Press, 1931. First edition, 164 pages, 20cm., red marbled yapp wrappers with title and illustration on front panel, very good, extremities rubbed, more so at corners, faded notation on rear panel in ink, inscribed by author, ex-libris Dale Morgan, with his name in pencil.   Ken Sanders Rare Books   45 - 14   2013 $600

Association – Morgan, John

Vergilius Maro, Publius *The Nyne Fyrst Bookes of the Eneidos of Virgil Converted Into Englishe Verse by Thomas Phaer.* London: by Rouland Hall for Nicholas England, 1562. Rare early edition, 4to., (220) pages, woodcut on title, text in black letter, 19th century morocco, ruled in gilt, edges gilt, extremities lightly worn, minor scuffing, first quire washed and neatly extended at top edge, possibly supplied from another copy, few internal repairs, else very good, with excellent full margins, Rubislaw House bookplate of John Morgan. Joseph J. Felcone Inc. Books Printed before 1701 - 86 2013 $11,000

Association – Morgan, John Pierpont

Lefevre, Raoul *Le Recueil des Histoires de Troyes.* Bruges: William Caxton, 1473. First edition in French, small folio, Lettre batarde, lacking 32 printed leaves and two blanks, early 19th century brown straight grain morocco by Charles Lewis, gilt and blind ruled in geometric patterns, gilt inner dentelles, gilt edges, fine, unrestored, the missing leaves are internal and first and last printed leaves are present from the collection of the Duke of Roxburghe (sale 1812) of the third Earl Spencer (sale 1823), John Dent, with his notes (sale 1827), P. A. Hanrott (sale 1834) the Earl of Ashburnham (sale 1897); Richard Bennett with his bookplate and John Pierpont Morgan with his bookplate and shelfmark. Heritage Book Shop 50th Anniversary Catalogue - 62 2013 $950,000

Association – Morgan, William Forbes

Wilde, Oscar 1854-1900 *The Happy Prince and Other Tales.* London: David Nutt, 1888. First edition, 4to., illustrations by Crane and Hood, original cream paper boards printed in red and black, one of 1 thousand copies printed, spine browned and chipped at head, corners bumped, bookplate of William Forbes Morgan, otherwise very good. Maggs Bros. Ltd. 1442 - 317 2013 £600

Association – Morgerstern, Charles

Graves, Robert 1895-1985 *The Isles of Unwisdom.* Cassell, 1950. First English edition, double page map, foolscap 8vo., original black cloth, backstrip gilt lettered, light edge spotting, dust jacket with backstrip panel trifle sunned and with internal sellotape repair at head, very good, inscribed by author for Charles (Morgenstern). Blackwell's Rare Books 172 - 189 2013 £500

Association – Morison, R.

Roy, William *The Military Antiquities of the Romans in the North of Britain and Particularly, Their Ancient System of Castramentation...* London: pub. by order and expense of the Society of Antiquaries, 1793. Elephant folio, 51 plates of maps and plans, some double page or folding as called for, internally bright, only occasional very light spotting limited to text rather than plates, few finger smudges to title and half title, contemporary half dark brown morocco with marbled boards, gilt and blind tooling to spine, more recent red morocco label, somewhat worn, boards rubbed, endpapers flat with signs of previous creases, ownership inscription of R. Morison? Unsworths Antiquarian Booksellers 28 - 125 2013 £750

Association – Morison, Sam

Tweedsmuir, Susan Charlotte Buchan *John Buchan by His Wife and Friends.* London: Hodder and Stoughton Ltd., 1947. First edition, large 8vo., original black cloth, inscribed by Buchan's widow Susan Tweedsmuir to Sam Morison, below which is a pencilled note by recipient, inscribed photo of Lady Tweedsmuir, inscribed postcard and ALS from John Buchan to recipient, excellent copy with Morison's bookplate, now loose. Maggs Bros. Ltd. 1460 - 149 2013 £175

Association – Morley, John

Burke, Edmund 1729-1797 *Reflections on the Revolution in France and on the Proceedings in Certain Societies in London Relative to that Event...* London: printed for J. Dodsley, 1790. First edition, first issue, 19th century half sheep over marbled boards, original bluish-gray drab wrappers bound in to front and back, some wear at corners and joints, spine bit scuffed, some occasional pale spotting along top edge, overall very nice, octavo, the copy of William Lee, Bart (presentation inscription) and of Archibald Philip Primrose, 5th Earl of Rosebery, ALS to Rosebery from John Morley tipped in, small Rosebery/Durdans blindstamp on titlepage and page 99, gift inscription, armorial bookplate. Heritage Book Shop 50th Anniversary Catalogue - 16 2013 $15,000

Association – Morpugo, Jack

Blunden, Edmund *De Bello Germanico. A Fragment of Trench History.* Hawstead: G. A. Blunden, 1930. First edition, limited to 250 copies, 8vo., original grey boards, paper label on spine, paper label browned and nicked, otherwise excellent copy, enclosed within protective box, inscribed by author for Jack Morpugo 22 April 1953. Maggs Bros. Ltd. 1460 - 114 2013 £275

Association – Morrell, Ottoline

Rosenberg, Isaac *Poems.* London: William Heinemann, 1922. First edition, 8vo., original black cloth, lower and fore edges uncut, one long crease to front cover, otherwise excellent copy, inscribed by T. S. Eliot for Ottoline Morrell. Maggs Bros. Ltd.   1460 - 262   2013   £2500

Association – Morris, William

Cicero, Marcus Tullius *De Officis Paradoxa De Amicitia De Senectute; De Somno Scipionis...* Venice: Filippo di Pietro, 1480. Small folio, 90 leaves, including prelim blank, 36 lines in Roman type, some passages in Greek, first initial painted in blue with ornamental penwork, initials painted somewhat flamboyantly in red, rubricated; modern maroon morocco by Doves Binder Charles McLeish for William Morris, from the library of Morris, spine lettered gilt, five raised bands, gilt board edges and turn-ins, all edges gilt, few light spots and stains, numerous contemporary and 16th century marginalia, bookplates, overall very good, housed in brown cloth open ended slipcase.   Heritage Book Shop 50th Anniversary Catalogue - 23   2013 $15,000

Association – Morrison, G.

Palladio, Andrea *The Four Books of Andrea Palladio's Architecture.* London: published by Isaac Ware, 1755. Folio, 205 plates, contemporary calf, rebacked to style, spine in compartments, profusely decorated in gilt, brown label lettered in gilt, inscribed "G. Morrison given the Earl of Burlington 1746", armorial bookplate of G. Morrison. Marlborough Rare Books Ltd.   218 - 115   2013   £1250

Association – Morrow, Brad

Himes, Chester *A Case of Rape.* New York: Targ Editions, 1980. First American edition, one of 350 copies, signed by author, fine in quarter cloth and paper covered boards in near fine, unprinted glassine dust jacket with small tears at extremities warmly inscribed by publisher to novelist Brad Morrow.   Between the Covers Rare Books, Inc.   165 - 169   2013 $250

Association – Morrow, Grace

Forster, Edward Morgan   1879-1970 *Howards End.* London: Edward Arnold, 1929. Uniform edition, first reprint, 8vo., original red cloth, excellent copy, inscribed by author for Mrs. Grace Morrow 13-6-31.   Maggs Bros. Ltd. 1460 - 292   2013   £275

Association – Morrow, Virginia

Bernstein, Morey *The Search for Bridey Murphy.* Garden City: Doubleday and Co., 1965. Stated new edition, near fine in very good dust jacket with modest chip at crown, with rubbing and small tears, inscribed by subject of the book, Virginia Morrow as "Bridey".   Between the Covers Rare Books, Inc.   Psychology & Psychiatry - 394851   2013 $100

Association – Mowat, R. C.

Verney, Frances Parthenope *Memoirs of the Verney Family Volumes I-IV.* London: Longmans, Green and Co., 1892. 1892. 1894. 1899. First editions, 4 volumes, 8vo., 50 plates as called for, further woodcuts and illustrations to text, protective tissue removed from volume I frontispiece, brown cloth, gilt spine and armorial centerpiece, top edge gilt, fore-edges uncut, endcaps creased, pages and edges little worn, boards faded, minor dent to upper board volume I, upper hinge of volume II cracking but bindings sound, very good internally, armorial bookplate of Frances Fortescue Urquhart of Balliol College 1909 to each front pastedown and his ownership inscription, bookplate of R. C. Mowat, pencilled ownership of P. A. Slack.   Unsworths Antiquarian Booksellers   28 - 202   2013   £120

Association – Muir, Margaret

Birrell, Augustine *Obiter Dicta.* London: Elliott Stock, 1884. First edition, inscribed by author for friend Margaret Muir, very good, original green cloth with gilt title and small rectangle gilt design to front cover, spine faded and some bumping to spine and corners, interior pages clean with slight pulling away of rear hinge, nice, scarce, 234 pages. The Kelmscott Bookshop   7 - 97   2013 $350

Association – Muir, Percy

O'Flaherty, Liam   1897-1984 *The Fairy Goose and Two Other Stories.* New York: Faber and Gwynn/Crosby Gaige, 1927. First edition, 16mo., original quarter buckram, shamrock patterned boards, paper label, slight nicking to spine label, else fine, inscribed by author for Percy Muir.   Maggs Bros. Ltd.   1442 - 267   2013   £150

Association – Muirhead, Arnold

Pater, Walter   1839-1894 *Marius the Epicurean: His Sensations and Ideas.* London: Macmillan and Co., 1892. Sixth thousand, inscribed by author to Lady Brooke, Ranee of Sarawak, original dark blue cloth with gilt title and author to spine, some bumping and rubbing but in very good condition, hinges volume I tender and discoloration to endpapers, otherwise very good, booklabel of Arnold Muirhead affixed to front pastedown of each volume, 2 volumes, 165; 246 pages.   The Kelmscott Bookshop   7 - 126   2013 $875

Association – Mulholland, John

Cunningham, A B. *Death Rides a Sorrel Horse.* New York: E. P. Dutton, 1946. First edition, very slight sunning to boards, still about fine in fresh and attractive, near fine dust jacket with some modest wear, mostly at spine ends, inscribed by author to John Mulholland. Between the Covers Rare Books, Inc. Mystery & Detective Fiction - 65848   2013 $275

Association – Munn, George

Cox, George *Back Gowns & Red Coats, or Oxford in 1834.* London: James Ridgway & Sons, 1834. Part I first edition, pages II-VI second edition, Parts I-VI, half titles, contemporary half red morocco, slightly rubbed, armorial bookplate of George S. Munn, good plus. Jarndyce Antiquarian Booksellers   CCIII - 672   2013   £80

Association – Murphy, Bernadine

Benci, Spinello *Storia di Montepulciano... Dedicata al Sereniss. Principe Giovancarlo di Toscana...* Florence: Amador Massi, 1646. Second edition, 4to., engraved titlepage coat of arms, full page woodcut portrait, errata, woodcut initials, headpieces and tailpieces, light foxing to final 2 pages, 19th century quarter vellum over marbled paper backed boards, gilt stamped leather spine label, label worn, bookplate of Bernadine Murphy, booklabel at spine's foot, fine. Jeff Weber Rare Books   171 - 22   2013 $1000

Borghini, Vincenzio *Discorsi di Monsignore Don Vincenzio Borghini.* Florence: Filippo & Jacopo Giunti, 1584-1585. First edition, 2 volumes, 4to., 8 engraved plates on 7 sheets, 5 folding with blank Rr8 in volume I, added titlepage (volume II), some minor staining, light foxing, occasional browning, original full vellum with manuscript spine titles and additional inscriptions on both front covers, cover stain with some light wear, early ownership inscription (1597), bookplate of Bernadine Murphy, very good. Jeff Weber Rare Books   171 - 48   2013 $1600

Association – Murphy, Richard

Boland, Eavan *The War Horse.* London: Gollancz, 1975. First edition, 8vo. original wrappers, from the library of Richard Murphy, signed by him, excellent copy. Maggs Bros. Ltd.   1442 - 26   2013   £50

Bolger, Dermot *Never a Dull Moment.* Dublin: Raven Arts, 1978. First edition, slim 8vo., original wrappers, from the library of Richard Murphy, inscribed by author, covers slightly foxed, otherwise near fine. Maggs Bros. Ltd.   1442 - 29   2013   £125

Bolger, Dermot *No Waiting America.* Dublin: Raven Arts, 1982. First edition, 8vo., original wrappers, fading to spine, else near fine, from the library of Richard Murphy, inscribed by author. Maggs Bros. Ltd.   1442 - 30   2013   £100

Clarke, Austin   1896-1974 *Flight to Africa.* Dublin: Dolmen Press, 1963. Proof copy, original beige wrappers printed in brown, yapp edges slightly creased, otherwise near fine, form the library of Richard Murphy, signed by him. Maggs Bros. Ltd.   1442 - 38   2013   £125

Deane, Seamus *The Field Day Anthology of Irish Writing.* Derry: Field Day Pub., 1991. First editions, 4to., original blue cloth, lettered gilt, fine set in matching slipcase, from the library of Richard Murphy. Maggs Bros. Ltd.   1442 - 59   2013   £250

Deane, Seamus *Gradual Wars.* Shannon: Irish University Press, 1972. First edition, 8vo., original wrappers, from the library of Richard Murphy, signed by him, near fine. Maggs Bros. Ltd.   1442 - 56   2013   £100

Deane, Seamus *History Lessons.* Dublin: Gallery Press, 1983. First edition, 8vo., original black cloth, near fine in dust jacket, from the library of Richard Murphy, signed by him on front endpaper. Maggs Bros. Ltd.   1442 - 58   2013   £125

Durcan, Paul *O Westport in the Light of Asia Minor.* Dun Laoghaire: Anna Livia Books, 1975. First edition, 8vo., original wrappers, near fine, from the library of Richard Murphy, inscribed by author to Murphy. Maggs Bros. Ltd.   1442 - 74   2013   £450

Flanagan, Thomas *The Year of the French.* London: Macmillan, 1979. First UK edition, 8vo., original green cloth, dust jacket, near fine, jacket nicked and browned, from the library of Richard Murphy, inscribed by author for Murphy. Maggs Bros. Ltd.   1442 - 80   2013   £75

Gregory, Isabella Augusta Perse   1859-1932 *The Kiltartan Poetry Book.* Dundrum: Dun Emer Press, 1918. First edition, limited to 400 copies, 8vo., original linen backed boards, printed label on spine, covers marked and browned, very good, inscribed by Murphy "Richard Murphy I bought this book from Willie Figgis....Hodges Figgis & Co. in Dublin, c. 1946-47". Maggs Bros. Ltd.   1442 - 71   2013   £200

Hartnett, Michael *A Farewell to English and Other Poems.* Dublin: Gallery Press, 1975. First edition, 8vo., wrappers, near fine, from the library of Richard Murphy, signed by him. Maggs Bros. Ltd.   1442 - 86   2013   £60

Hayes, Maurice *The Flight Path.* Oldcastle: The Gallery Press for The American Ireand Fnd, 1996. First edition, one of 500 copies, large 8vo., original quarter burgundy cloth, mock vellum boards, shamrock device blocked in gilt on upper board, fine in matching slipcase, from the library of contributor Richard Murphy. Maggs Bros. Ltd. 1442 - 249 2013 £150

Heaney, Seamus *Laments.* London: Faber and Faber, 1995. First edition, 8vo., original black cloth, dust jacket, fine in slightly rubbed dust jacket, from the library of Richard Murphy. Maggs Bros. Ltd. 1442 - 107 2013 £75

Heaney, Seamus *North.* New York: Oxford University Press, 1976. First US edition, 8vo., original blue cloth, dust jacket, near fine, from the library of Richard Murphy. Maggs Bros. Ltd. 1442 - 90 2013 £600

Higgins, Aidan *Balcony of Europe.* London: Calder and Boyars, 1972. First edition, 8vo., original red cloth, dust jacket, from the library of Richard Murphy, signed by him, fine in dust jacket, slightly browned on spine. Maggs Bros. Ltd. 1442 - 129 2013 £50

Hutchinson, Pearse *Barnsley Main Seam.* Oldcastle: Gallery Press, 1995. First edition, 8vo., original black cloth, dust jacket, fine in dust jacket, from the library of Richard Murphy, inscribed for him by author. Maggs Bros. Ltd. 1442 - 131 2013 £60

Joyce, James 1882-1941 *Finnegans Wake.* London: Faber and Faber Ltd., 1939. First trade edition, 8vo., original crimson cloth, gilt, from the library of Richard Murphy, signed by him, some spotting to endpapers and dusty at page edges, otherwise excellent. Maggs Bros. Ltd. 1442 - 136 2013 £500

Kavanagh, Patrick *Collected Poems.* New York: Devin Adair, 1964. First US edition, tall 8vo., original quarter black cloth, burgundy boards, from the library of Richard Murphy, inscribed, nicked at head and tail of spine, otherwise excellent. Maggs Bros. Ltd. 1442 - 147 2013 £250

Kavanagh, Patrick *The Complete Poems of Patrick Kavanagh.* New York: Peter Kavanagh Hand Press, 1972. First edition, 8vo., original black cloth, dust jacket, from the library of Richard Murphy, signed by him on front free endpaper, very good in dust jacket, nicked at extremities and browned on spine. Maggs Bros. Ltd. 1442 - 149 2013 £250

Kennelly, Brendan *A Time for Voices.* Newcastle upon Tyne: Bloodaxe Books, 1990. First edition, 8vo., wrapper issue, fine, from the library of Richard Murphy, inscribed to him by author. Maggs Bros. Ltd. 1442 - 153 2013 £50

Kinsella, Thomas *Another September.* Dublin: Dolmen Press, 1958. First edition, 8vo., mustard cloth, dust jacket, from the library of Richard Murphy, inscribed by author, near fine, jacket inexorably browned and split on spine. Maggs Bros. Ltd. 1442 - 156 2013 £375

Kinsella, Thomas *Downstream.* Dublin: Dolmen Press, 1960. First edition, 8vo., original pale grey cloth, dust jacket, excellent copy, jacket slightly rubbed and nicked at extremities, inscribed by author for Richard Murphy. Maggs Bros. Ltd. 1442 - 158 2013 £250

Kinsella, Thomas *Finistere.* Dublin: Dolmen Press, 1972. First edition, limited to 250 numbered copies, signed by author, square 4to., original blindstamped green cloth, lettered gilt, top edge gilt, fine in acetate dust jacket, from the library of Richard Murphy, loosely inserted receipt for the book to Murphy on Dolmen Press printed invoice sheet. Maggs Bros. Ltd. 1442 - 165I 2013 £350

Kinsella, Thomas *Nightwalker.* Dublin: Dolmen Press, 1967. First edition, 8vo., original wrappers, fine, inscribed by author for Richard Murphy. Maggs Bros. Ltd. 1442 - 159 2013 £250

Kinsella, Thomas *Notes from the Land of the Dead.* Dublin: Cuala Press, 1972. First edition, 8vo., original quarter linen, grey boards, fine, from the library of Richard Murphy, inscribed by author for Murphy. Maggs Bros. Ltd. 1442 - 164 2013 £100

Kinsella, Thomas *One Fond Embrace.* Dublin: Peppercanister, 1988. First edition, original wrappers, from the library of Richard Murphy with his signature, inscribed to him by author, limited to 500 copies, near fine. Maggs Bros. Ltd. 1442 - 170 2013 £175

Lavin, Mary *The Patriot Son and other Stories.* London: Michael Joseph, 1956. First edition, 8vo. original black cloth, dust jacket, excellent copy, jacket rubbed and marked, most notably at spine, inscribed by author for Richard Murphy. Maggs Bros. Ltd. 1442 - 175 2013 £175

Ledwidge, Francis *Selected Poems.* Dublin: New Island Books, 1992. First edition, 8vo., wrapper issue, near fine, from the library of Richard Murphy, inscribed for him by Seamus Heaney (provides introduction). Maggs Bros. Ltd. 1442 - 105 2013 £200

Longley, Michael *Selected Poems.* London: Jonathan Cape, 1988. First edition, original red cloth, touch foxed on top edge, otherwise fine, dust jacket, inscribed by author for Richard Murphy. Maggs Bros. Ltd. 1442 - 181 2013 £120

Longley, Michael *Snow Water.* London: Jonathan Cape, 2004. First edition, original wrappers, 8vo., fine, inscribed by author for Richard Murphy. Maggs Bros. Ltd. 1442 - 183 2013 £100

MacNeill, Marie *The Festival of Lughnasa.* London: Oxford University Press, 1962. First edition, 8vo., original green cloth, near fine in slightly chipped and rubbed dust jacket, from the library of Richard Murphy, inscribed by author for Murphy. Maggs Bros. Ltd. 1442 - 208 2013 £250

McGahern, John *The Barracks.* London: Faber and Faber, 1963. First edition, 8vo., original red cloth, very good, dust jacket torn at head and tail of spine with small loss here and there and nicked extremities, from the library of Richard Murphy, signed by him. Maggs Bros. Ltd. 1442 - 214 2013 £600

McGahern, John *The Collected Stories.* London: Faber & Faber, 1990. First edition, 8vo., burgundy cloth, fine in slightly rubbed dust jacket, inscribed by author for Richard Murphy. Maggs Bros. Ltd. 1442 - 217 2013 £450

Montague, John *Drunken Sailor.* Oldcastle: Gallery Press, 1995. First edition, 8vo., original black cloth, dust jacket, bumped at head, otherwise near fine, inscribed by author for Richard Murphy. Maggs Bros. Ltd. 1442 - 230 2013 £175

Montague, John *Home Again.* Belfast: Festival Publications, Queen's University of Belfast, 1966. First edition, 8vo., original green wrappers lettered in black, fine, from the library of Richard Murphy, signed by him. Maggs Bros. Ltd. 1442 - 226 2013 £75

Montague, John *Hymn to the New Omagh Road.* Dublin: Dolmen Press, 1968. First edition, limited to 175 copies signed by author, large 8vo., original tan wrappers, hand stitched with red cotton, some uneven fading on covers, otherwise near fine, from the library of Richard Murphy. Maggs Bros. Ltd. 1442 - 227 2013 £225

O'Donoghue, Bernard *Poaching Rights.* Dublin: Gallery Press, 1986. First edition, 8vo., original black cloth, dust jacket, inscribed by author for Richard Murphy, fine in slightly rubbed dust jacket, uncommon. Maggs Bros. Ltd. 1442 - 258 2013 £125

O'Flaherty, Roderic *A Chorographical Description of West Or H-iar Connaught.* Dublin: for the Irish Archaeological Society, 1846. First edition, small square 4to., recent blue cloth, lettered gilt, excellent copy, from the library of Richard Murphy with his inscription, illustrations by James Hardiman. Maggs Bros. Ltd. 1442 - 269 2013 £175

O'Grady, Desmond *Reilly. Roma MCMLXI.* London: Phoenix Press, 1961. First edition, 4to., original black cloth, dust jacket stained and nicked, excellent copy, inscribed, but not signed, by author for Richard Murphy. Maggs Bros. Ltd. 1442 - 270 2013 £150

O'Nolan, Brian *Myles Away from Dublin.* London: Granada, 1985. First edition, 8vo., original orange cloth, dust jacket, from the library of Richard Murphy and inscribed to him by selector, Martin Green, fine in dust jacket. Maggs Bros. Ltd. 1442 - 275 2013 £125

Ormsby, Frank *A Northern Spring.* Dublin/London: Gallery Press/Secker & Warburg, 1986. First edition, 8vo., original black cloth, fine in dust jacket, slightly discolored, from the library of Richard Murphy, inscribed by author for Murphy. Maggs Bros. Ltd. 1442 - 276 2013 £40

Plath, Sylvia 1932-1963 *Uncollected Poems.* Turret Books 1965, but published, 1966. First edition, one of 165 copies, double plate facsimile printed on pink paper, pages 20, foolscap 8vo., original plain white stapled card wrappers, stiff card dust jacket faded at spine and little soiled, good, superb association inscribed by Ted Hughes to fellow poet Richard Murphy. Blackwell's Rare Books B174 - 276 2013 £850

Yeats, William Butler 1865-1939 *A Full Moon in March.* London: Macmillan, 1935. First edition, one of 2000 copies pub. Nov. 22nd 1935, 8vo., original green cloth, spine lettered gilt, dust jacket, very good in slight nicked and marked dust jacket, browned on spine and stained on rear panel, from the library of Richard Murphy, signed by him. Maggs Bros. Ltd. 1442 - 350 2013 £150

Association – Murphy, Rosemary

Albee, Edward *A Delicate Balance.* New York: Atheneum, 1966. First edition, signed by author as well as six members of the original cast, Jessica Tandy, Hume Cronyn, Rosemary Murphy, Carmen Matthews, Henderson Forsythe and Marian Seldes, fine in nearly fine dust jacket. Ed Smith Books 78 - 3 2013 $750

Association – Murray, Albert

Tuskegee Institute *The 1939 Tuskeana of Tuskegee Institute.* Tuskegee: Senior Class, 1939. Quarto, padded leatherette, several student inscriptions, some slight wear to spinal extremities, near fine, with author Albert Murray's inscription beneath his senior picture. Between the Covers Rare Books, Inc. 165 - 227 2013 $750

Association – Murray, Albert Victor

Josephus, Flavius *The Works of Flavius Josephus.* London: printed for R. Sare, 1702. First L'Estrange edition, folio, many errors in pagination but collates complete, at page 196-7 a pin is visible which is holding gathering in place, p. 199 stained at fore-edge, pages 553-88 with little loss to top margin, page 591 remargined, occasional marginal notes, wax spots and short closed tears, tan Cambridge style calf, red morocco and gilt label to spine, edges sprinkled red, spine creased and scratched, loss to endcaps, joints cracked but cords holding, lower board scraped, corners frayed, prelim blanks loose, inscriptions of M. Kenne stating 'the gift of Rnd. Fortiscue' and Albert Victor Murray, Magdalen and Mansfield Colleges Oxford, May 11 1914, pink 'Cancelled' stamp to front pastedown. Unsworths Antiquarian Booksellers 28 - 20 2013 £250

Association – Murray, Charles Fairfax

Erasmus, Desiderius 1466-1536 *Eloge De La Folie D'Erasme.* Paris: Librarie Des Bibliophiles, 1876. Third edition, number 266 of 500 copies on Holland paper, original wrappers sewn in, 83 black and white gravures, small 4to., three quarter red morocco over red marbled boards, raised bands, gilt titles, marbled endpapers, very good plus or better, tight, clean copy, just bit of wear at extremities, handsome copy, somewhat uncommon Charles Fairfax Murray bookplate. Kaaterskill Books 16 - 28 2013 $300

Lefevre, Raoul *Le Recueil des Hystoires Troyennes, ou est Comte nuc la Genealogie de Saturne (&) de Juipter...* Lyons: Jacques Sacon, 1510. Extremely rare, small folio, lacks final blank, Gothic type, 98 woodcuts, 6 full page cuts, large device of Saccon on titlepage, on reverse is full page cut of the Siege, divided horizontally into two compartments, this also on n6; on I3 is the full page "Troye la Grande" repeated on I6, another full page cut on I6 and The Stratagem of the Horse on F6, in text are 92 cuts with only few repeated, 19th century crimson morocco gilt extra, by A. Motte, gilt dentelles, morocco doublures, gilt interlacements, gilt edges and clean and fresh, nicely margined copy in fine binding, from the renowned Fairfax Murray collection of French Books. Heritage Book Shop 50th Anniversary Catalogue - 63 2013 $85,000

Association – Murray, David

Maxwell, John *True Reform; or Character a Qualification for the Franchise.* Edinburgh: Thomas Constable & Co., 1860. Half green calf, red label, slightly faded, presentation from the author with later signature and bookplate of David Murray, very good, 50 pages. Jarndyce Antiquarian Booksellers CCV - 197 2013 £50

Scotland's Opposition to the Popish Bill. Edinburgh: printed by David Paterson, 1780. 8vo., some browning in places, contemporary sprinkled sheep, flat spine divided by triple gilt fillet, red morocco lettering piece, some old scratches to boards, armorial bookplate of Brown of Waterhaughs and ownership inscription of David Murray, Glasgow, with few of his notes on endpapers, very good. Blackwell's Rare Books 172 - 118 2013 £425

Association – Murray, Dorothea

Anderson, George *The Art of Skating.* London: Horace Cox, 1880. Fourth edition, 191 x 127mm., original green cloth over thin flexible boards, upper cover with stylized gilt titling around central illustration of skates, flat unlettered spine, with 9 full page illustrations, 7 of them diagrams and the other two showing a very still figure gliding on the ice in top hat, as well as five diagrams in text, front free endleaf with ink ownership inscription of Dorothea L. S. Murray, Jan. 1887; lower corner of rear cover with faint diagonal crease, hinge open at page 66, but very fine of an insubstantial book, binding solid and with surprisingly few signs of wear, text very clean and fresh. Phillip J. Pirages 63 - 440 2013 $325

Association – Murray, Humphrey Desmond

Pasteur, Louis *Studies on Fermentation, the Diseases of Beer, Their Causes and the Means of Presenting Them.* London: Macmillan, 1879. First edition in English, 8vo., 12 plates, original black stamped dark grey-green cloth, gilt stamped spine, neatly repaired hinges, bookplate of H.D. (Humphrey Desmond) Murray, rubber stamps of Murray, Bull & Spencer, limited, canceled titlepage ownership signature "Union Brewery 1889". Jeff Weber Rare Books 169 - 342 2013 $375

Association – Musgrave, Frances

Moore, John 1729-1802 *A View of Society and Manners in Italy.* Dublin: printed for H. Chamberlaine, 1786. Third edition, 3 volumes, half titles in volumes I and II, prelim blank volume III, 12mo., very good, attractive set in full contemporary calf, gilt banded spines, red and olive green morocco labels, form the library of John Musgrave, with armorial bookplates and contemporary signatures of Frances Musgrave. Jarndyce Antiquarian Booksellers CCIV - 208 2013 £480

Association – Musgrave, John

Moore, John 1729-1802 *A View of Society and Manners in Italy.* Dublin: printed for H. Chamberlaine, 1786. Third edition, 3 volumes, half titles in volumes I and II, prelim blank volume III, 12mo., very good, attractive set in full contemporary calf, gilt banded spines, red and olive green morocco labels, form the library of John Musgrave, with armorial bookplates and contemporary signatures of Frances Musgrave. Jarndyce Antiquarian Booksellers CCIV - 208 2013 £480

Association – Musgrave, S.

Alden, W. L. *Among the Freaks.* London: Longmans Green & Co., 1896. Half title, frontispiece and illustrations, original decorated turquoise cloth, slightly rubbed, signature of S. Musgrave on half title. Jarndyce Antiquarian Booksellers CCV - 2 2013 £150

Association – Namien, Mr.

Wild, Charles *Twelve Perspective Views of the Exterior and Interior Parts of the Metropolitical Church of York...* London: W. Bulmer & Co., 1809. Folio, 14 plates, including 12 fine aquatints, very good, large uncut copy in original sugar paper boards, printed label on upper cover, neatly rebacked, corners and board edges rubbed, slightly worn, fresh contemporary front endpaper, inscribed John Lewis Wolfe, Oct. 1813 from Mr. Namien, scarce. Ken Spelman Books Ltd. 73 - 13 2013 £650

Association – Naranjo, Enrique

Barcia, Jose Fernandez *Sonatina Gijonesa.* Madrid: Talleres Espasa Calpe, 1929. First edition, small 8vo., paper wrappers worn, small chips to edges, some minor sunning, spine cocked, still very good, very scare, inscribed by author to Enrique Naranjo. Kaaterskill Books 16 - 79 2013 $500

Association – Newell, Michael

Rattigan, Terence *The Winslow Boy.* London: Hamish Hamilton, 1946. First edition, 8vo. 109 pages, very good, signed by 10 f the 11 cast members of the first London production, including Kathleen Harrison, Emelyn Williams, Michael Newell, etc. Second Life Books Inc. 183 - 330 2013 $350

Association – Newry, Viscount

Campbell, Thomas 1777-1844 *The Poetical Works.* London: Edward Moxon, 1854. Half title, frontispiece, illustrations, contemporary full green morocco, gilt spine borders and dentelles, slightly rubbed, spine little darkened, armorial booklabel of Viscount Newry and neat gift inscription "Newry from A. F. Birch. Eton Election 1858", all edges gilt, attractive copy. Jarndyce Antiquarian Booksellers CCIII - 454 2013 £45

Association – Newton, A. Edward

Davenant, William 1606-1668 *The Works of Sr. William Davenant Kt...* London: by T. N. for Henry Herringman, 1673. First collected edition, folio, portrait, turn of the century red levant morocco, gilt arabesque centerpiece on covers, all edges gilt, by Riviere, very skillfully rebacked, though the new leather at joints and on cords has uniformly faded, unusually fine, fresh, wide margined copy with fine impression of the portrait, leather tipped fleece lined slipcase, edges rubbed, bookplates of Duke of Beaufort, E. F. Leo, A. E. Newton. Joseph J. Felcone Inc. English and American Literature to 1800 - 12 2013 $2200

Johnstone, Charles *Chrysal; or the Adventures of a Guinea in America.* London: T. Becket, 1760. First edition, 2 volumes, large 12mo., 19th century antique mottled calf by Riviere, gilt, expertly rebacked, old backs laid down, leather labels, raised bands, inner gilt dentelles, fine, bookplates of John Leveson Douglas Stewart and A. Edward Newton, slipcase. Howard S. Mott Inc. 262 - 80 2013 $500

Lamb, Charles 1775-1834 *Poetry for Children.* London: The Leadenhall Press, 1892. One of 112 copies, signed by press founder, Andrew White Tuer (this copy #2), 157 x 99mm., 2 volumes, charming contemporary batik textured calf by Zaehnsdorf (stamp-signed in gilt on front turn-in), covers gilt with fillets and dogtooth roll border, upper cover with thick festooned garland of fruit and leaves, flat spines divided into panels by plain and decorative rules, densely gilt turn-ins, marbled endpapers, top edge gilt, each volume with engraved frontispiece, engraved bookplate of A. Edward Newton of Oak Knoll with (loose) bookplate of H. Marion Soliday, minor offsetting from frontispieces, just vaguest hint of rubbing to extremities, but very fine, bindings bright and scarcely worn, text with virtually no signs of use. Phillip J. Pirages 63 - 67 2013 $1500

Association – Newton, Eric

Betjeman, John 1906-1984 *Murray's Buckinghamshire Guide.* London: John Murray, 1948. First edition, 4to., original red cloth, dust jacket, rubbed, somewhat torn at extremities, with modicum of loss, excellent copy, inscribed by John Piper to Stella and Eric Newton. Maggs Bros. Ltd. 1460 - 92 2013 £250

Association – Newton, Stella

Betjeman, John 1906-1984 *Murray's Buckinghamshire Guide.* London: John Murray, 1948. First edition, 4to., original red cloth, dust jacket, rubbed, somewhat torn at extremities, with modicum of loss, excellent copy, inscribed by John Piper to Stella and Eric Newton.   Maggs Bros. Ltd.   1460 - 92   2013   £250

Association – Nichols, Susan

Freneau, Philip *Poems Written Between the Years 1768 & 1794...* Monmouth: printed at the presss of the author, at Mount Pleasant, near Middletown Point, 1795. Only edition, contemporary sheep, many gatherings variously foxed or browned, as always with this book, else unusually nice, contemporary signatures of Geo. J. Warner and slightly later Susan Nichols.   Joseph J. Felcone Inc.   English and American Literature to 1800 - 14   2013 $1200

Association – Nicholson, May

Dodgson, Charles Lutwidge 1832-1898 *Sylvie and Bruno.* London: Macmillan and Co., 1889. First edition, 8vo., 46 illustrations by Harry Furniss original scarlet cloth, gilt, edges gilt, spine faded and rebacked, frontispiece and Magic Locket engraving colored by previous owner, otherwise very good, inscribed by author for May Nicholson May 26 1896.   Maggs Bros. Ltd.   1460 - 235   2013   £750

Association – Nicholson, Nancy

Graves, Robert 1895-1985 *Treasure Box.* London: Chiswick Press, 1919. First edition, 8vo., original blue unprinted wrappers, excellent copy in protective oversized folding box, leather label, lettered in gilt, inscribed by author and Nancy Nicholson for Robert Graves, inherited by his son Alec Waugh who gave it to Cyril Connolly at Christmas 1967.   Maggs Bros. Ltd.   1460 - 359   2013   £1750

Association – Nicholsons, Norman

Griffin, A. Harry *The Roof of England.* Robert Hale, 1968. First edition, original cloth, gilt, dust jacket (title lettering on spine and trifle faded), 192 pages, illustrations, Norman Nicholson's copy with his bookplate, scarce.   R. F. G. Hollett & Son   Lake District and Cumbria - 215   2013   £45

Association – Nims, Bonnie Larkin

Bellow, Saul *Him with His Foot in His Mouth.* New York: Harper & Row, 1984. First edition, inscribed by author to Chicago author John Frederick Nims and his wife, Bonnie Larkin Nims, offsetting to rear endpages where two articles about Bellow were laid in, also laid in is copy of typed review of the book by Chicago bookseller Stuart Brent.   Ken Lopez Bookseller   159 - 19   2013 $500

Association – Nims, John Frederick

Bellow, Saul *Him with His Foot in His Mouth.* New York: Harper & Row, 1984. First edition, inscribed by author to Chicago author John Frederick Nims and his wife, Bonnie Larkin Nims, offsetting to rear endpages where two articles about Bellow were laid in, also laid in is copy of typed review of the book by Chicago bookseller Stuart Brent.   Ken Lopez Bookseller   159 - 19   2013 $500

Association – Nirenberg, Marshall

Watson, James D. *Molecular Biology of the Gene.* Menlo Park: Benjamin Cummings, 1977. Third edition, 2nd printing, 4to., signed and dated by Marshall Nirenberg, few pages dog eared, original color illustrated cloth, scarce association.   By the Book, L. C.   37 - 89   2013 $200

Association – Noble, L. H. G.

Coleridge, Mary Elizabeth *Fancy's Following.* Oxford: Daniel Press, 1896. First edition, number 88 of 125 copies, contemporary dark blue crushed morocco, blocked in gilt, signature of L. H. G. Noble on leading blank, top edge gilt, very good.   Jarndyce Antiquarian Booksellers   CCV - 64   2013   £250

Association – Nokes, D.

Sheridan, Thomas *The Life of the Rev. Swift, Dean of St. Patrick's, Dublin.* London: printed for C. Bathurst et al, 1784. First edition, 8vo, 2 engraved portrait plates, discoloration on page 24-5 (transfer from inserted envelope), speckled tan calf, rebacked, red and green morocco labels and gilt to spine, little worn, top edge dusty, bookplate of University of London Library, library ticket of same, small inkstamp to verso of titlepage and final page, letter from Prof. H. T. Mason to Dr. D. Nokes dated 3rd Oct. 1983 loosely inserted.   Unsworths Antiquarian Booksellers   28 - 128   2013   £200

Association – Nokes, David

Johnson, Samuel 1709-1784 *The Lives of the Most Eminent English Poets.* Oxford: Clarendon Press, 2006. First edition, boxed set of 4 volumes, no dust jackets issued, light wear and markings to slipcase, from the library of David Nokes with his occasional light pencil underlinings to text and review notes loosely inserted.   Unsworths Antiquarian Booksellers   28 - 176   2013   £300

Association – Nolty, John

Cosway, Richard *Catalogue of a Collection of Miniatures by Richard Cosway...* N.P.: for private circulation only, 1883. Limited edition, limitation not stated, folio, (32)ff., frontispiece, 26 full page mounted original photographic plates, original half brown morocco, marbled boards, morocco corners, raised bands, gilt spine title, all edges gilt, bound by J. Leighton, Brewer St. (stamp on front flyleaf), inscribed "With Mr. Edward Joseph's Kindest regards New York 22 Dec. (18)83", bookplate of John Nolty, fine, rare. Jeff Weber Rare Books   171 - 78   2013 $750

Association – Nomikos, Christopher

Cavafy, Constantine P. *Poiemata (1908-1914).* Alexandria: Kasimath & Iona (Print Shop), circa, 1920. First edition, tall 8vo., 29 numbered pages printed rectos only, table of contents, beige printed wrappers, very fine in half morocco folding box, presentation copy from author to Christopher Nomikos.   James S. Jaffe Rare Books   Fall 2013 - 30   2013 $25,000

Association – Norman, Haskell

Bright, Timothy *A Treatise of Melancholie.* London: imprinted...by Thomas Vautrollier, 1586. First edition, small octavo, this copy includes original leaf O8, which was intended to be canceled, woodcut printer's device on title, bound by Lakeside Bindery in full antique style calf, covers panelled in gilt, smooth spine decoratively tooled and lettered gilt, edges stained red, lower margin of title and following leaf renewed with some loss to few letters of imprint on title, title soiled slightly, bottom edge of lower margin frayed slightly in prelims, short internal tear to A4 crossing text, few other minor marginal flaws or repairs, some faint dampstaining, very good, extremely rare, from the library of Haskell Norman, with his bookplate.   Heritage Book Shop   50th Anniversary Catalogue - 13   2013 $25,000

Donders, Franciscus Cornelius *Astigmatisme en Cilindrische Glazen.* Amsterdam: C. C. Van der Post, 1862. First edition, 8vo., 15 figures, tables, light browning and spotting, modern half cloth, cloth corners, marbled boards, decorative endleaves, bookplate of Haskell Norman, very good.   Jeff Weber Rare Books   172 - 81   2013 $500

Gerhardt, Charles *Traite de Chimie Organique.* Paris: Fermin Didot Freres, 1853-1856. First edition, 4 volumes, 8vo., contemporary quarter green morocco, marbled boards, gilt spine, marbled endleaves, former owner added to volume 1 a carte de viste photographic portrait of Gerhardt (albumen print) taken by Ch. Winter of Strasbourg, also inserted is 2 page ALs dated Jan. 1883 from Gerhardt's son to unidentified correspondent, bookplates of Haskell Norman, fine.   Jeff Weber Rare Books   172 - 104   2013 $800

Graefe, Friedrich Wilhelm Ernst Albrecht Von *Symptomenlehre der Augnmuskellahmungen.* Berlin: Hermann Peters, 1867. First edition, 8vo., contemporary quarter black morocco, morocco corners, brown boards, gilt spine, gilt filigree covers, lightly rubbed, bookplate and rubber stamps of Bernard Samuels Library, NY Eye and Ear Infirmary, bookplate of Haskell Norman, another ownership signature, fine.   Jeff Weber Rare Books   172 - 110   2013 $1333

Association – Norman, Sylva

Blunden, Edmund *The Face of England. A Series of Occasional Sketches.* London: Longmans, Green and Co., 1932. First edition, small 8vo., original green cloth, dust jacket, fading to spine, otherwise excellent copy, inscribed by author for Sylva Norman, with pencilled correction in author's holograph on page 141.   Maggs Bros. Ltd.   1460 - 117   2013   £400

Blunden, Edmund *Poems of Many Years.* London: Collins, 1957. First edition, 8vo., original dark pink cloth, inscribed by author for Sylva, loosely inserted are clippings from news reviews of book, excellent copy in thoroughly browned dust jacket.   Maggs Bros. Ltd.   1460 - 120   2013   £300

Blunden, Edmund *A Selection of this Poetry and Prose.* London: Rupert Hart-Davis, 1950. First edition, 8vo., original green cloth, fine in dust jacket browned on spine, inscribed by author for Sylva 1 Nov. 1950.   Maggs Bros. Ltd.   1460 - 119   2013   £300

Association – Northesk

Pepys, Samuel 1633-1703 *Memoires Relating to the State of the Royal Navy of England.* London: printed Anno, 1690. First edition, issue for private distribution without commercial imprint on titlepage, 8vo., contemporary panelled calf, red morocco label, gilt decorations and lettering, frontispiece and folding table, early ink signature of "Northesk", which is probably that of John Carnegie, 7th Earl of Northesk, edges little rubbed, upper joints starting, but sound, fine.   The Brick Row Book Shop   Miscellany Fifty-Nine - 33   2013 $4500

Association – Nowell-Smith, Simon

Beddoes, Thomas Lovell 1803-1849 *The Bride's Tragedy.* London: F. C. & J. Rivington, 1822. First edition, 2 pages ads, nicely bound in later half vellum, dark green leather label, Nowell-Smith booklabels.   Jarndyce Antiquarian Booksellers   CCIII - 642   2013   £120

Brooke, Rupert 1887-1915 *Poems.* London: Sidgwick & Jackson, 1911. First edition, minimal faint foxing to prelims, pages viii, 88, foolscap 8vo., original dark blue cloth, printed label just touch chipped, Simon Nowell's copy with his booklabel, very good.   Blackwell's Rare Books   B174 - 178   2013   £550

Byron, George Gordon Noel, 6th Baron 1788-1824 *English Bards and Scotch Reviewers.* London: James Cawthorn, 1809. Second edition, half title, final ad leaf, contemporary half speckled calf, armorial bookplate of George Moffatt & later Nowell-Smith booklabels, very good.   Jarndyce Antiquarian Booksellers   CCIII - 119   2013   £200

Graves, Robert 1895-1985 *John Kemp's Wager; a Ballad Opera.* Oxford: Blackwell, 1925. First edition, 21/100 copies, printed on Kelmscott handmade paper and signed by author, 16mo., original white vellum backed cream boards with overall repeat pattern in green, backstrip gilt lettered, tail corners rubbed, book label of Simon Nowell-Smith, untrimmed and partly unopened, very good.   Blackwell's Rare Books   B174 - 212   2013   £500

Graves, Robert 1895-1985 *Mock Beggar Hall.* Hogarth Press, 1924. First edition, occasional faint foxing to prelim and final few leaves, 4to., original dark grey boards, imposing overall front cover design by William Nicholson and printed in black, Simon Nowell-Smith, untrimmed, fine.   Blackwell's Rare Books   B174 - 213   2013   £500

Graves, Robert 1895-1985 *Poems 1929.* Seizin Press, 1929. First edition, 76/225 copies, printed on Batchelor handmade paper and signed by author foolscap 8vo., original apple green buckram, faded backstrip gilt lettered, faint band of fading also to head of rear cover, browned free endpapers, booklabel of Simon Nowell-Smith and bookplate of Oliver Brett, First Viscount Esher, very good.   Blackwell's Rare Books   B174 - 214   2013   £300

Graves, Robert 1895-1985 *Ten Poems More.* Paris: Hours Press, 1930. First edition, 98/200 copies signed by author, small folio original green morocco backed boards, backstrip gilt lettered, illustrated monochrome boards reproducing a photographic montage by Len Lye, booklabel of Simon Nowell-Smith, untrimmed, fine.   Blackwell's Rare Books   B174 - 215   2013   £300

Wordsworth, William 1770-1850 *Poems, in Two Volumes.* London: printed for Longman Hurst Rees & Orme, 1807. First edition, 2 volumes, 8vo., original drab boards with pink paper covered spines as issued, one of 500 copies printed, with cancels D11-12 in volume I and B2 in volume II, Volume I has half title and erratum leaf H8, Volume II has half title, sectional half title B1 and first sheet F9 (i) volume 2, contemporary ownership inscription to Anne Watson in volume I with her pencil ownership signature on titlepage, bookplates of Simon Nowell-Smith and his wife, light foxing, covers slightly chipped and worn, but very good.   James S. Jaffe Rare Books   Fall 2013 - 152   2013 $27,500

Association – O'Brien, Eleanor Alicia

Blake, William 1757-1827 *Songs of Innocence and Experience.* London: Pickering, 1866. Vellum, gilt decorated, all edges gilt, monogram on front cover FAF, inscribed Eleanor Alicia O'Brien with Anne Martineau's afft. love Nov. 1866 and F. G. Arnold-Forster from R. V. O'Brien Aug. 1891, New Hall, and Flora Vere O'Brien Sept. 19, 1921, very good.   C. P. Hyland 261 - 187   2013   £105

Association – O'Brien, Flora Vere

Blake, William 1757-1827 *Songs of Innocence and Experience.* London: Pickering, 1866. Vellum, gilt decorated, all edges gilt, monogram on front cover FAF, inscribed Eleanor Alicia O'Brien with Anne Martineau's afft. love Nov. 1866 and F. G. Arnold-Forster from R. V. O'Brien Aug. 1891, New Hall, and Flora Vere O'Brien Sept. 19, 1921, very good.   C. P. Hyland 261 - 187   2013   £105

Association – O'Brien, R. V.

Blake, William 1757-1827 *Songs of Innocence and Experience.* London: Pickering, 1866. Vellum, gilt decorated, all edges gilt, monogram on front cover FAF, inscribed Eleanor Alicia O'Brien with Anne Martineau's afft. love Nov. 1866 and F. G. Arnold-Forster from R. V. O'Brien Aug. 1891, New Hall, and Flora Vere O'Brien Sept. 19, 1921, very good.   C. P. Hyland 261 - 187   2013   £105

Association – O'Brien, Thea

Cheyney, Peter *Sinister Errand.* London: Collins, 1945. First edition, 8vo., original yellow cloth, excellent copy, some light soiling to cloth, inscribed by author to Mrs. Thea O'Brien 14/11/45.   Maggs Bros. Ltd.   1460 - 168   2013   £50

Association – O'Callaghan, Thomas

Condon, T. *Gilla Hugh or the Patriot Monk.* Cork: 1864. First edition, cover dull, some foxing in text, else good, signed presentation from author to Thomas A. O'Callaghan, later Bishop of Cork April 7th 1864. C. P. Hyland 261 - 201 2013 £65

Association – O'Donoghue, D. J.

Geoghegan, A. G. *The Monks of Kilcea & Other Poems.* 1861. First edition, with 2 page ALS from poet to D J. O'Donoghue, dated 17 Dec. 1888, confirming authorship, 348 pages, original cloth, very good. C. P. Hyland 261 - 443 2013 £150

Association – O'Faolain, Nuala

Ford, Richard *A Piece of My Heart.* London: Collins Harvill, 1987. First British edition, inscribed by author to Irish memoirist Nuala O'Faolain and her partner John Low-Beer, couple of small, stray marks to edge of text block, still fine in fine dust jacket, good literary association. Ken Lopez Bookseller 159 - 64 2013 $250

Association – O'Faolain, Sean

Yeats, William Butler *1865-1939* *Shadowy Waters.* London: Hodder and Stoughton, 1900. First edition, 8vo., original dark blue cloth, backstrip and front cover gilt blocked, gilt lettered quarter dark blue morocco and cloth, book-form box fine, inscribed by author, this was originally Oliver St. John Gogarty's copy with his bookplate, subsequently, in ownership of Sean O'Faolain and inscribed by him, photo of Yeats tipped to front free endpaper. Blackwell's Rare Books 172 - 259 2013 £3250

Association – O'Farrell, Michael

Wolf, Hieronymus *Demosthenis et Aeschinis Principum Graeciae Oratorum Opera...* Francofurti: Apud Cladium Marnium & Haeredes Iohannis Aubrii, 1604. Second edition, folio, 3 engraved, head and tailpieces, initials, quarter bound alter morocco over marbled paper covered boards, Greek and Latin in parallel columns, scarce, 17 x 11cm. section of titlepage, which includes printer's device, has been excised, leaf neatly repaired, top edge lightly trimmed, boards and spine rubbed, scuffing to top edge, otherwise very clean with occasional cross references pencilled in margins, binding tight, very nice, institutional bookplate noting the book was a gift of Michael J. O'Farrell, first Bishop of the Diocese of Trenton. Kaaterskill Books 16 - 24 2013 $1000

Association – O'Hara, Maureen

Llewellyn, Richard *How Green Was My Valley.* New York: Macmillan, 1941. (1940). Later printing, round-robin, signed in fountain pen on location during making of the film on July 19 1941, gift copy from Freda Knill (niece of cast member Thomas A. Hughes) to her daughter, with autographs and inscriptions of Roddy McDowall, Maureen O'Hara, Walter Pidgeon, Donald Crisp, Barry Fitzgerald, Sara Allgood, Anna Lee, T. Arthur Hughes, Richard Fraser and Evan H. Evans; fair to good only, binding intact, shaken and with fraying to edges of cloth, in very good supplied dust jacket with some rubbing and light wear at extremities. Ed Smith Books 75 - 39 2013 $1750

Association – O'Keefe, Timothy

De Burca, Seamus *The Soldier's Song. The Story of Peadar Kearney.* Dublin: P. J. Bourke, 1957. First edition, small 8vo., original burgundy cloth, excellent copy in dust jacket slightly torn on front panel, inscribed by author to publisher Timothy O'Keefe. Maggs Bros. Ltd. 1442 - 357 2013 £150

Hewitt, John *Out of My Time.* Belfast: Blackstaff Press, 1974. First edition, 8vo., original wrappers, inserted are two ALS's from author to publisher Timothy O'Keefe, letters and book in excellent state. Maggs Bros. Ltd. 1442 - 359 2013 £350

Kavanagh, Patrick *Collected Poems.* London: MacGibbon & Kee, 1964. First edition, file copy of publisher, stamped "File copy Editorial and inscribed by editorial director Timothy O'Keefe, marked - return to T O K, with his minor marks on 6 pages, 8vo., original fawn cloth, dust jacket, near fine, jacket slightly nicked and worn at extremities. Maggs Bros. Ltd. 1442 - 360 2013 £650

Montague, John *Hymn to the New Omagh Road.* Dublin: Dolmen Press, 1968. First edition, limited to 175 copies, large 8vo., original wrappers, hand stitched with red cotton, rear cover and facing page marked with damp, else good, from the library of Timothy O'Keefe and inscribed by author. Maggs Bros. Ltd. 1442 - 362 2013 £125

Montague, John *Poisoned Lands.* London: MacGibbon & Kee, 1961. First edition, 8vo., original mottled grey cloth, dust jacket, book slightly dampstained at rear, else excellent copy in dust jacket, loosely inserted c. 90 word autographed postcard from author's Dublin address to publisher Timothy O'Keefe dated 2nd Jan. 1961 in English with some Gaelic, card in excellent state. Maggs Bros. Ltd. 1442 - 361 2013 £175

O'Brien, Darcy *A Way of Life, Like Any Other.* London: Martin Britain & O'Keefe, 1977. Proof copy, 8vo., original yellow wrappers, author's pencilled corrections sprinkled throughout, inscribed by publisher Timothy O'Keefe, excellent copy. Maggs Bros. Ltd. 1442 - 363 2013 £175

Plunkett, James *The Trusting and Maimed.* New York: Devon Adair Co., 1955. First edition, 8vo., original quarter blue cloth, dust jacket, inscribed by author, with name and address, from the library of publisher Timothy O'Keefe, bumped at extremities, otherwise very good, nicked and torn dust jacket. Maggs Bros. Ltd. 1442 - 364 2013 £200

Association – O'Looney, Bryan

Joyce, P. W. *On Spenser's Irish Rivers.* 1867. First edition, 13 pages, disbound, 8vo., note "presented to me by author 11th Oct. 1867 Bryan O'Looney". C. P. Hyland 261 - 790 2013 £45

Association – O'Mahony, Eoin

Ronayne, C. O'L. *History of the Earls of Desmond and Earl of Cork & Sir Walter Raleigh in Munster.* 1929. First edition, 8vo., cloth, very good, Eoin 'The Pope' O'Mahony's copy with his bookplate, very good. C. P. Hyland 261 - 410 2013 £150

Association – O'Neil, Buck

Wheelock, Sean D. *Buck O'Neil: a Baseball Legend.* Mattituck: American House, 1994. First edition, hardcover issue fine in boards, without dust jacket as issued, inscribed by Buck O'Neil, very uncommon. Between the Covers Rare Books, Inc. 165 - 76 2013 $250

Association – Oates, Robert Washington

Bloomfield, Robert *The Banks of the Wye: a Poem.* B. & B. Crosby & Co., 1813. Second edition, engraved frontispiece and plate, full contemporary calf, gilt borders and dentelles, spine rather worn, poor copy, armorial bookplate of Robert Washington Oates, Renier booklabel. Jarndyce Antiquarian Booksellers CCIII - 27 2013 £30

Byron, George Gordon Noel, 6th Baron 1788-1824 *Poems with His Memoirs.* London: Jones & Co., 1826. 32mo., frontispiece, 2 pages ads, original purple moire, patterned silk cloth, black paper label, slightly bumped, slight fading to spine Renier and Robert Washington Oates booklabels, all edges gilt, very good. Jarndyce Antiquarian Booksellers CCIII - 94 2013 £50

Association – Odenbaugh, A. G.

Evans, Nathaniel *Poems on Sever Occasions with some other Compositions.* Philadelphia: John Dunlap, 1772. First and only contemporary edition, contemporary calf, very skillfully rebacked in period style, usual foxing, nicest copy we have seen, late 19th century booklabel of A. G. Odenbaugh. Joseph J. Felcone Inc. English and American Literature to 1800 - 13 2013 $750

Association – Odets, Clifford

Fitzgerald, Francis Scott Key 1896-1940 *The Great Gatsby.* New York: Charles Scribner, 1925. First edition, 8vo., original black cloth, covers rubbed and edges bumped, otherwise very good, Clifford Odets' copy with his personal rubber stamp on front pastedown and name blindstamped on front free endpaper. Maggs Bros. Ltd. 1460 - 284 2013 £4500

Association – Oe, Kenzaburo

The Showa Anthology 2. Modern Japanese Short Stories 1961-1984. New York: Kodansha, 1985. Fine in fine dust jacket, Kenzaburo Oe's copy which he used as a reading copy at Toronto's Harbourfront International Festival of Authors in 1985, inscribed by Oe to Greg Gatenby, director of the festival, with Gatenby's signature. Ken Lopez Bookseller 159 - 161 2013 $1000

Association – Oldenburg, Claes

Rose, Barbara *Claes Oldenburg.* New York: Museum of Modern Art, 1970. First edition, oblong padded vinyl binding, checklist laid in, about very good with some offsetting to front panel and other slight wear, internally clean, signed and dated by Oldenburg in 1973 and additionally inscribed by Rose on titlepage. Jeff Hirsch Books Fall 2013 - 129137 2013 $500

Association – Olds, William

Ford, Worthington Chauncey *George Washington.* New York: Goupil & Co. and Charles Scribner's sons, 1900. One of 200 copies of "Edition de Luxe", 2 volumes, 267 x 203mm., 88 full page plates, as well as 32 tailpieces, chapter initials in black and red; attractive green crushed morocco, covers with two-line gilt frame, raised bands, gilt framed compartments and gilt titling, red morocco doublures surrounded by inch wide green morocco turn-ins with four gilt fillets, watered silk endleaves, top edges gilt, other edges untrimmed, large paper copy, hint of wear to joints and extremities, spines mildly faded to olive green, spine of second volume with just slightly irregular fading, still fine, bindings solid and pleasing, text and plates virtually pristine; bookplate of William P. Olds laid in at front of each volume. Phillip J. Pirages 63 - 487 2013 $1500

Association – Onahan, William

Keynes, John *A Rational, Compendious Way to Convince without any dispute, all Persons Whatsoever, Dissenting from the True Religion.* N.P.: London: printed in the year, 1674. First edition, 12mo., contemporary sheep, nearly fine, with final blank leaf, faint ownership stamp on front endpaper of William J. Onahan (1836-1919). Howard S. Mott Inc. 262 - 85 2013 $750

Association – Onslow, Nina Sturdee

Anouilh, Jean *Pieces Brillantes. L'Invitation au Chateau.* Paris: Les Editions de la Table Ronde, 1960. Later edition, 8vo., original cloth, pictorial label on upper cover, excellent copy, cloth unevenly browned with some pale soiling to tail of spine, inscribed by author for Lady Onslow (Nina Sturdee). Maggs Bros. Ltd. 1460 - 15 2013 £150

Association – Orioli, Pino

Douglas, Norman 1868-1952 *Paneros. Some Words on Aphrodisiacs and the Like.* privately printed for subscribers by G. Orioli, Lungarno, Dec., 1930. First edition, out of series copy of the stated 250 numbered and signed copies, 8vo,., original decorated and 'vermiculated' gold cloth boards, black leather spine label, inscribed by publisher Pino Orioli for Nancy Cunard, then passed on to her principal assistant Winifred Henderson by author, with Henderson's bookplate, extremities slightly rubbed, otherwise excellent. Maggs Bros. Ltd. 1460 - 242 2013 £750

Association – Orr, Charles W.

King, Martin Luther *Stride Toward Freedom.* New York: Harper & Bros., 1958. First edition, fine in very good dust jacket with two 1 1/2 inch tears on front panel, inscribed by author to Dr. Charles W. Orr. Between the Covers Rare Books, Inc. 165 - 1 2013 $10,000

Association – Orr, Robert

Clarke, Samuel 1675-1729 *A Collection of Papers, Which Passed Between the Late Learned Mr. Leibnitz and Dr. Clarke in the Years 1715 and 1716.* London: James Knapton, 1717. First edition, 8vo., headpieces, decorative initials, tailpieces, 2 figures, occasional spotting, contemporary paneled calf, raised bands, blindstamped spine title, outer hinge starting, early 19th century engraving of lady mounted on front pastedown, ownership signature of Robert Orr, very good. Jeff Weber Rare Books 169 - 68 2013 $1300

Association – Ossory, Godfrey

Day, J. G F. *The Cathedrals of the Church of Ireland.* 1932. First edition, illustrations, cloth, very good, signed presentation from Godfrey Ossory. C. P. Hyland 261 - 296 2013 £38

Association – Ostling, Helen R. C.

Dunbar, Paul Laurence *Lyrics of Lowly Life.* London: Chapman & Hall, 1897. First British edition, half title, frontispiece, occasional pencil underlining, original dark grey cloth, news clipping laid down on leading pastedown, inscription "Helen R. C. Ostling with love from Irene, Xmas 1905", all edges gilt, near fine. Jarndyce Antiquarian Booksellers CCV - 98 2013 £180

Association – Oswald, John Clyde

Goudy, Frederic W. *The Story of the Village Type by Its Designer.* New York: Press of the Woolly Whale, 1933. First edition, one of 450 copies on Arnold unbleached handmade paper for members of the AIGA, of an edition of 650, pencil ownership signature of John Clyde Oswald, fine in chipped glassine jacket and soiled slipcase, 8vo., original cloth backed boards, paper labels, uncut. Howard S. Mott Inc. 262 - 65 2013 $100

Association – Ouseley, Gore

Delille, Jacques *L'Homme des Champs ou les Georgiques Francoises... (with) Dithyrame sur l'Immoralitie de l'ame, Suivi du Passage du st. Gothard...* Basel: Chez Jacques Decker, 1800. Paris: chez giguet et Michaud, 1802. First editions, 4 plates, dampstaining throughout at tail of gutter margin, some browning; engraved frontispiece, 12mo., bound together in contemporary dark blue straight grain morocco, smooth backstrip divided by double gilt rules, second compartment gilt lettered direct, single gilt rule on sides, gilt ball roll on board edges and turn-ins, marbled endpapers, all edges gilt, touch of rubbing to joints, very good, bookplate of Sir Gore Ouseley, Baronet. Blackwell's Rare Books 172 - 49 2013 £150

Association – Outhwaite, Leonard

Puckett, Newbell Niels *Folk Beliefs of the Southern Negro.* Chapel Hill: The University of North Carolina Press, 1926. First edition, publisher's cloth, tears to cloth at crown and along joints, good copy without dust jacket, complimentary copy with handwritten presentation to Leonard Outhwaite with compliments of University of North Carolina Pres. Between the Covers Rare Books, Inc. 165 - 248 2013 $85

Association – Oxley-Brennan, C. G.

Blunden, Edmund *English Poems.* Thavies Inn: Richard Cobden Sanderson, 1925. First edition, tall 8vo., original red cloth, dust jacket, excellent copy in browned and slightly nicked dust jacket, enclosures in excellent state, inscribed by author Sep. 9 1926 for C. G. Oxley Brennan, and further APS c. 65 words. Maggs Bros. Ltd. 1460 - 112 2013 £175

Association – Packwood, Thomas

Duck, Stephen *Poems on Several Occasions.* London: printed for W. Bickerton, 1737. Second edition, 8vo., engraved frontispiece, touch of minor spotting, contemporary sprinkled calf, unlettered spine divided by gilt rules, slight wear to headcap, boards scratched and rear board stained white, contemporary ink ownership inscription Thos. Packwood/E. Libris 1748 and later ink inscription 1811/ Sophia Killner her/Book. Southam Febry 19. Unsworths Antiquarian Booksellers 28 - 90 2013 £250

Association – Paden, Irene

Moorman, Madison Berryman *The Journal of.... 1850-1851.* San Francisco: California Historical Society, 1948. First edition, frontispiece, folding map, gilt lettered dark green cloth, spine and edges faded as usual, offsetting to front ends from news clipping, very good, presentation inscription signed by editor, Irene Paden. Argonaut Book Shop Summer 2013 - 243 2013 $75

Association – Page, Frederick

Blunden, Edmund *The Waggoner and Other Poems.* London: Sidgwick & Jackson, 1920. Second impression, 8vo., original burgundy cloth, printed paper label on spine inscribed in unknown pencilled hand "To a fine critic 28 June 1921. F.P." and inscribed below by author, recipient is Frederick Page, loosely inserted ALS to Page from Blunden and short ALS to Page from Wilfrid Meynell, faded on spine, label rubbed, otherwise excellent copy, enclosures in presentable order. Maggs Bros. Ltd. 1460 - 111 2013 £180

Association – Page, Russell

Flanner, Janet *Men and Monuments.* New York: Harper and Brother, 1957. First edition, 8vo., original black cloth over boards, inscribed by author for Russell Page, excellent copy unevenly faded, lettering rubbed and faded. Maggs Bros. Ltd. 1460 - 285 2013 £150

Association – Palgrave, Francis Turner

Tennyson, Alfred Tennyson, 1st Baron 1809-1892 *Ballads and Other Poems.* London: C. Kegan Paul and Co., 1880. First edition, with 3 pages ads at back, 8vo., original green cloth panelled in blind, presentation copy, inscribed by author for F. T. Palgrave, spine panel slightly rubbed, few soft creases in front free endpaper, otherwise very good, preserved in cloth clamshell box. James S. Jaffe Rare Books Fall 2013 - 143 2013 $2500

Association – Palmer, Hugh

Lewis, Sinclair 1885-1951 *Main Street.* New York: Harcourt Brace and Howe, 1920. First edition, first issue (mixed issue?), with folio 54 unbattered but the 'y' in 'may' on page 387 imperfect, inscribed by author to Hugh Palmer, Aug. 20 1947, on front pastedown facing inscription is ownership inscription of Von Jagermann 1920, original dark blue cloth stamped in orange on front cover and spine, spine lightly sunned and edges of spine with small amount of wear, bit of light foxing to prelims, overall very good. Heritage Book Shop Holiday Catalogue 2012 - 88 2013 $2000

Association – Palmer, James Nelson

Maxwell, Colonel Montgomery *My Adventures.* London: Henry Colburn, 1845. First edition, 2 volumes, 200 x 126mm., special very attractive presentation binding of contemporary Oxblood pebble grain morocco, elaborately gilt, covers with blind ruled borders and complex gilt frame featuring shell head and tailpieces, scrolling corners and sides, many floral tools, raised bands, spine compartments gilt with flower basket centerpiece and leaf frond corners, blind tooled turn-ins, all edges gilt, frontispiece portraits, ink presentation inscription for Reginald Porter from friend, James Nelson Palmer on his leaving Eton Xmas 3rd 1846, spines slightly and uniformly sunned, gilt still bright, one board with little dulling because of leather preservative, otherwise very fine, clean, fresh, smooth internally in handsome binding with virtually no wear. Phillip J. Pirages 63 - 332 2013 $600

Association – Palmes, George

Newton, Isaac 1642-1727 *Opticks; or a Treatise of the Reflections, Refractions, Inflections and Colours of Light.* London: printed for William and John Innys, 1721. Third edition, 12 folding engraved plates, trifle browed in places, 1 plate bit dust soiled on verso, contemporary panelled calf, rebacked, few old scratches on covers, ownership at head of title "George Palmes 1796" (of Naburn in Yorkshire) and his armorial bookplate inside front cover. Blackwell's Rare Books Sciences - 86 2013 £3500

Association – Panton, Jane

Inchbald, Elizabeth *A Simple Story.* London: printed for G. G. J. and J. Robinson, 1791. Second edition, 4 volumes, half titles discarded, ownership inscription of Jane Panton on titlepages, touch of light soiling and browning, one leaf in volume 1 with small paper flaw to blank margin, one gathering in volume iii, rough at bottom edge (missed by binder's knife), 8vo., late 19th century half calf, sometime rebacked to style, dark brown morocco lettering pieces, marbled boards, edges and endpapers, slightly rubbed, corners bit worn, hinges neatly relined, good. Blackwell's Rare Books   B174 - 73   2013   £750

Association – Parker, Morris

Blackmore, Richard   1654-1729 *A Treatise of Consumptions and Other Distempers Belonging to the Breast and Lungs.* London: John Pemberton, 1724. First edition, 8vo., original full polished calf, five raised spine bands, white spine library number, leather worn and discolored, spine ends chipped, top right front corner and lower spine edges torn, bookplate remnants, rear pastedown glue spots, bookplate of Dr. Morris Parker, formerly of Chicago Medical School, titlepage signature of David Hay(?), holograph table of contents at free endpaper, small recipe at rear free endpaper, very good, rare.   Jeff Weber Rare Books   172 - 32 2013 $1850

Association – Parker, Willard

Dupuytren, Guillaume *Lecons Orales de Clinique Chirurgicale.* Paris: Germer Bailliere, 1839. 1839, 6 volumes, bound in later marbled boards, rebacked with plain brown linen, no labels, from the collection of Dr. Willard Parker and his signature on front fly of each volume, library stamp on titles, no external markings.   James Tait Goodrich   75 - 86   2013 $1495

Association – Parkin, Agness

Barnard, George *The Theory and Practice of of Landscape Painting in Water Colours.* London: William S. Orr, 1855. Large 8vo., 26 plates, 43 woodcuts, index, occasional light foxing, especially verso plates, decorative blindstamped brown cloth, gilt stamped front cover and spine extremities lightly worn, rare hinge cracked, bookplate of Agness A. Parkin, titlepage signature of John Dawson, very good.   Jeff Weber Rare Books   171 - 12   2013 $200

Association – Parnau, Franz Pollack

Knight, Ellis Cornelia   1757-1837 *Dinarbas: a Tale Being a Continuation of "Rasselas, Prince of Abissinia".* London: printed for Luke Hansard for T. Caldwell, Jun. and W. Davies, 1800. Fourth edition, 178 x 108mm., very attractive contemporary flamed calf, flat spine gilt in panels formed by double rules and decorative rolls and featuring an oval centerpiece encircling a four pointed star with roundel center, crimson morocco label, bookplate of Franz Pollack Parnau, extremities and joints bit flaked, occasional very minor foxing and offsetting, but excellent copy, attractive original binding completely sound with boards lustrous, especially clean, smooth and fresh internally.   Phillip J. Pirages   63 - 272   2013 $175

Association – Parrott, Frank

Bouch, C. M. L. *Prelates and People of the Lake Counties.* Kendal: Titus Wilson, 1948. First edition, original cloth, 9 illustrations and map, the copy of Frank Parrott, Kirkby Stephen historian with presentation card to him tipped to flyleaf.   R. F. G. Hollett & Son   Lake District & Cumbria - 153   2013   £50

Association – Parsons, Ian

Eberhart, Richard *Song and Idea.* London: Chatto & Windus, 1940. First edition, tall 8vo., original ochre cloth backed patterned boards, excellent copy, some fading to spine, inscribed by author for Trekkie and Ian Parsons. Maggs Bros. Ltd.   1460 - 261   2013   £150

Association – Parsons, Trekkie

Eberhart, Richard *Song and Idea.* London: Chatto & Windus, 1940. First edition, tall 8vo., original ochre cloth backed patterned boards, excellent copy, some fading to spine, inscribed by author for Trekkie and Ian Parsons. Maggs Bros. Ltd.   1460 - 261   2013   £150

Association – Pasley, Thomas

Great Britain. Royal Navy - 1790 *A List of the Flag-Offices of His Majesty's Fleet; with the Dates of their First Commissions, as Admirals, Vice-Admirals, Rear Admirals and Captains.* London: 1790. 8vo., original red morocco, gilt roll tooled borders on sides, flat spine gilt in compartments, lacking lettering piece, little worn and few abrasions, engraved armorial bookplate of Sir Thomas Pasley inside front cover, pencil signature of another Pasley on flyleaf, good.   Blackwell's Rare Books   B174 - 64   2013   £900

Association – Patchett, H.

Armengaud, Jacques Eugene *The Engineer and Machinist's Drawing-Book: a Complete Course of Instruction for the Practical Engineer...* Glasgow (printed): Edinburgh: London: and New York: Blackie and Son, 1855. With additional engraved title and 71 leaves of plates (2 pairs forming double-page plates, both pages numbered), one hand colored, 2 plates with clean tears, one browned, first two leaves creased, few minor stains, folio, contemporary half brown morocco little worn, cloth bubbled on upper cover, original owner's name in gilt at foot of spine (H. Patchett), sound.   Blackwell's Rare Books   172 - 14   2013   £170

Association – Patti, Adelina

Corelli, Marie *Vendetta! or the Story of One Forgotten.* London: Richard Bentley & Son, 1891. New edition, 8vo., original black cloth, inscribed by author to Italian opera singer Adelina Patti, excellent copy, head and tail of spine lightly rubbed.   Maggs Bros. Ltd.   1460 - 199   2013   £125

Association – Pattison, Mark

Phillips, Edward *Theatrum Poetarum Anglicanorum: Containing the Names and Characters of All the English Poets.* London: Canterbury, 1800. first printing of this enlarged updated edition, 203 x 120mm., appealing recent brown quarter morocco over linen boards, raised bands, red morocco label, front flyleaf with inscription "G. D./ Canonbury" (George Daniel), titlepage with small embossed stamp of "Mark Pattison, Lincoln College, Oxon", exceptionally fine.   Phillip J. Pirages   63 - 320   2013 $750

Association – Paulin, Gita

Friel, Brian *The Yalta Game.* Loughcrew: Gallery Press, 2001. First edition, 8vo., original black cloth, fine in dust jacket, inscribed by author Oct. '01 for Tom and Gita Paulin.   Maggs Bros. Ltd.   1460 - 309   2013   £300

Friel, Brian *Dancing at Lughnasa.* London: Faber & Faber, 1990. First edition, inscribed by author June '90 for Tom and Gita (Paulin), cheap paper slightly browned as usual, otherwise fine.   Maggs Bros. Ltd.   1460 - 302   2013   £450

Friel, Brian *Fathers and Sons.* London: Faber and Faber, 1987. First edition, 8vo., original wrappers, cheap paper slightly browned as usual, otherwise fine, inscribed by author Aug. 87 for Gita and Tom (Paulin).   Maggs Bros. Ltd.   1460 - 301   2013   £275

Friel, Brian *Give Me Your Answer, Do!* Loughcrew: Gallery Press, 1994. First edition, 8vo., original black cloth fine in dust jacket slightly faded on spine and bleeding on to lower cover, inscribed by author in month of publication March 97 for Tom and Gita Paulin.   Maggs Bros. Ltd.   1460 - 307   2013   £300

Friel, Brian *The Home Place.* Loughcrew: The Gallery Press, 2005. First edition, 8vo., original black cloth, fine in dust jacket, inscribed by author for Tom and Gita Paulin.   Maggs Bros. Ltd.   1460 - 312   2013   £300

Friel, Brian *Molly Sweeney.* Loughcrew: Gallery Press, 1994. First edition, 8vo., original black cloth, dust jacket, fine in dust jacket slightly nicked at head of spine with very minor fading to spine, inscribed by author 18 Aug 94 for Tom and Gita (Paulin).   Maggs Bros. Ltd.   1460 - 306   2013   £300

Friel, Brian *A Month in the Country. After Turgenev.* Loughcrew: Gallery Press, 1992. First edition, 8vo., original black cloth, fine in dust jacket, inscribed by author for Tom and Gita Paulin.   Maggs Bros. Ltd.   1460 - 304   2013   £300

Friel, Brian *Performances.* Loughcrew: The Gallery Press, 2003. First edition, 8vo., original black cloth, fine in dust jacket, inscribed by author for Tom and Gita Paulin Oct. '03.   Maggs Bros. Ltd.   1460 - 311   2013   £300

Friel, Brian *Selected Plays.* London: Faber and Faber, 1984. First edition, 8vo., original black cloth, dust jacket, inscribed by author to Tom Paulin and his wife Gita, cheap paper browning as usual and slightly faded on spine, otherwise near fine in dust jacket.   Maggs Bros. Ltd.   1460 - 300   2013   £375

Friel, Brian *Three Plays After. The Yalta Game. The Bear and Afterplay.* Loughcrew: The Gallery Press, 2002. First edition, 8vo., original black cloth, dust jacket, fine, jacket slightly nicked on upper cover, inscribed by author March '02 for Tom and Gita Paulin.   Maggs Bros. Ltd.   1460 - 310   2013   £300

Friel, Brian *Uncle Vanya.* Loughcrew: Gallery Press, 1998. First edition, 8vo., original black cloth, fine, dust jacket with slightest of fading on spine, inscribed by author Oct. 98 for Tom and Gita Paulin.   Maggs Bros. Ltd.   1460 - 308   2013   £300

Friel, Brian *Wonderful Tennessee.* Loughcrew: Gallery Press, 1993. First edition, 8vo., original black cloth, fine, dust jacket slightly nicked at head of spine and with very minor fading to spine, inscribed by author June 30 '93 for Tom and Gita (Paulin). Maggs Bros. Ltd. 1460 - 305 2013 £300

Association – Paulin, Tom

Friel, Brian *Dancing at Lughnasa.* London: Faber & Faber, 1990. First edition, inscribed by author June '90 for Tom and Gita (Paulin), cheap paper slightly browned as usual, otherwise fine. Maggs Bros. Ltd. 1460 - 302 2013 £450

Friel, Brian *Fathers and Sons.* London: Faber and Faber, 1987. First edition, 8vo., original wrappers, cheap paper slightly browned as usual, otherwise fine, inscribed by author Aug. 87 for Gita and Tom (Paulin). Maggs Bros. Ltd. 1460 - 301 2013 £275

Friel, Brian *Give Me Your Answer, Do!* Loughcrew: Gallery Press, 1994. First edition, 8vo., original black cloth fine in dust jacket slightly faded on spine and bleeding on to lower cover, inscribed by author in month of publication March 97 for Tom and Gita Paulin. Maggs Bros. Ltd. 1460 - 307 2013 £300

Friel, Brian *The Home Place.* Loughcrew: The Gallery Press, 2005. First edition, 8vo., original black cloth, fine in dust jacket, inscribed by author for Tom and Gita Paulin. Maggs Bros. Ltd. 1460 - 312 2013 £300

Friel, Brian *Molly Sweeney.* Loughcrew: Gallery Press, 1994. First edition, 8vo., original black cloth, dust jacket, fine in dust jacket slightly nicked at head of spine with very minor fading to spine, inscribed by author 18 Aug 94 for Tom and Gita (Paulin). Maggs Bros. Ltd. 1460 - 306 2013 £300

Friel, Brian *A Month in the Country. After Turgenev.* Loughcrew: Gallery Press, 1992. First edition, 8vo., original black cloth, fine in dust jacket, inscribed by author for Tom and Gita Paulin. Maggs Bros. Ltd. 1460 - 304 2013 £300

Friel, Brian *Performances.* Loughcrew: The Gallery Press, 2003. First edition, 8vo., original black cloth, fine in dust jacket, inscribed by author for Tom and Gita Paulin Oct. '03. Maggs Bros. Ltd. 1460 - 311 2013 £300

Friel, Brian *Selected Plays.* London: Faber and Faber, 1984. First edition, 8vo., original black cloth, dust jacket, inscribed by author to Tom Paulin and his wife Gita, cheap paper browning as usual and slightly faded on spine, otherwise near fine in dust jacket. Maggs Bros. Ltd. 1460 - 300 2013 £375

Friel, Brian *Three Plays After. The Yalta Game. The Bear and Afterplay.* Loughcrew: The Gallery Press, 2002. First edition, 8vo., original black cloth, dust jacket, fine, jacket slightly nicked on upper cover, inscribed by author March '02 for Tom and Gita Paulin. Maggs Bros. Ltd. 1460 - 310 2013 £300

Friel, Brian *Uncle Vanya.* Loughcrew: Gallery Press, 1998. First edition, 8vo., original black cloth, fine, dust jacket with slightest of fading on spine, inscribed by author Oct. 98 for Tom and Gita Paulin. Maggs Bros. Ltd. 1460 - 308 2013 £300

Friel, Brian *Wonderful Tennessee.* Loughcrew: Gallery Press, 1993. First edition, 8vo., original black cloth, fine, dust jacket slightly nicked at head of spine and with very minor fading to spine, inscribed by author June 30 '93 for Tom and Gita (Paulin). Maggs Bros. Ltd. 1460 - 305 2013 £300

Friel, Brian *The Yalta Game.* Loughcrew: Gallery Press, 2001. First edition, 8vo., original black cloth, fine in dust jacket, inscribed by author Oct. '01 for Tom and Gita Paulin. Maggs Bros. Ltd. 1460 - 309 2013 £300

Association – Payn, James

Blackmore, Richard Doddridge 1825-1900 *Lorna Doone.* London: Sampson Low, Son & Marston, 1869. First edition, one of only 500 printed, 3 small octavo volumes, bound circa 1960 by Bayntun-Riviere in full red morocco, few minor tears and some occasional minor foxing or soiling, laid in is ALS from author to James Payn, Teddington, Dec. 3rd 1877 thanking him for his assistance in publishing of his works, excellent copy. David Brass Rare Books, Inc. Holiday 2012 Chapter Five - DB 00726 2013 $6500

Association – Payne, Elwood

Dobie, Jame Frank 1888-1964 *Apache Gold & Yaqui Silver.* Boston: Little Brown, 1939. Reprint, 8vo., illustrations, first signature shaky, gilt stamped rust cloth, front cover Apache head pictorial, dust jacket chipped top front corner missing, signed and inscribed from author to Elwood Payne in ink, near fine in good jacket. Jeff Weber Rare Books 171 - 105 2013 $165

Association – Paz, Octavio

Octavio Paz: A Celebration. New York: Academy of American Poets and the Mexican Cultural Institute, 1994. First edition, 8vo., original wrappers, although not called for, this copy signed by Paz, Mark Strand, John Ashbery, Bei Dao and Charles Tomlinson.   James S. Jaffe Rare Books   Fall 2013 - 6   2013 $750

Association – Peacock, C. J.

The Friend, a Series of Essays... London: Bell and Daldy, 1865. Half title obscured by booklabel, portrait, initial and final catalogs including endpapers, original uniform green cloth, two booklabels, one of C. J. Peacock, ownership inscription of Peter Mann, very good.   Jarndyce Antiquarian Booksellers   CCIII - 521   2013   £30

Association – Pearson, S.

Jones, Robert   *Artificial Fireworks, Improved ot the Modern Practice from the Minutest to Hightest Branches.* Chelmsford: printed and sold by Meggy and Chalk, 1801. 210 x 136mm., very pleasing recent retrospective smooth calf, raised bands, red morocco label, edges entirely untrimmed, 20 copper engraved plates, inscription of Mr. S. Pearson, Steeton in 19th century hand, minor foxing and soiling here and there, generally text in excellent condition, unexpectedly clean and fresh, unworn sympathetic binding.   Phillip J. Pirages   63 - 374   2013 $1500

Association – Peltzer, G.

Marsden, Richard   *Cotton Waving: Its Development, principles and Practice.* Chiswick Press for George Bell and Sons, and Manchester: Marsden, 1895. First edition, oval inkstamp of G. Peltzer - Teacher - Manchester on title, 8vo., original cloth, good.   Blackwell's Rare Books   Sciences - 119   2013   £60

Association – Pembroke, G.

Conrad, Joseph 1857-1924   *Typhoon and Other Stories.* London: William Heinemann, 1903. First English edition, initial ad leaf, uncut in original grey cloth blocked and lettered in gilt, slight rubbing, inscription on leafing f.e.p. "G. Pembroke 17th June 1903", very good.   Jarndyce Antiquarian Booksellers   CCV - 74   2013   £380

Association – Pena, S.

Bates, Herbert Ernest 1905-1974   *The Seekers.* London: John and Edward Bumpus, 1926. First edition, 8vo., original grey paper boards, gilt, inscribed by author for S. Pena, near fine, remains of tissue dust jacket in rear.   Maggs Bros. Ltd.   1460 - 45   2013   £75

Association – Pendarves, S.

Norris, John   *A Collection of Miscellanies; Consisting of Poems, Essays, Discourses and Letters, Occasionally Written.* (bound with) *The Theory and Regulation of Love.* Oxford: printed at the Theatre for John Crosley, 1687. Oxford: printed at the Theatre for Hen. Clements, 1688. First edition, engraved vignette on title, slightly browned and one or two spots; second work large or thick paper copy, 8vo., bound together in contemporary calf, blind ruled borders on sides, roll tooled border at inner edge repeated an inch out, spine gilt in compartments, red lettering piece, rebacked, preserving original spine, covers rubbed and with some craquelure, contemporary ownership inscription at head of dedication "S. Pendarves 89", few notes in his hand to text of Miscellanies, 18th century inscription of Eliz. Kekenick, Norris's Postscript, retracting the Considerations upon the nature of Sin, copied out apparently in her hand on verso of its sectional title, good.   Blackwell's Rare Books   B174 - 109   2013   £750

Association – Pender, Seamus

Simington, Robert C.   *The Civil Survey AD 1654-6. County of Tipperary.* 1931. Volume I of 2, map, 8vo., cloth, very good, ex-libris Seamus Pender.   C. P. Hyland   261 - 504   2013   £90

Simington, Robert C.   *The Civil Survey AD 1654-6. Volume X Miscellanies.* 1962. large folding map in end-pocket, 8vo., cloth, very good, ex-libris Seamus Pender.   C. P. Hyland   261 - 506   2013   £90

White, Newport   *Extent of Irish Monastic Possessions 1540-1541.* 1943. First edition, 8vo., cloth, very good, ex-libris Seamus Pender.   C. P. Hyland   261 - 508   2013   £45

White, Newport   *Irish Monastic & Episcopal Deeds 1200-1600.* 1936. 512 copies printed, 8vo, cloth, very good, ex-libris Seamus Pender.   C. P. Hyland   261 - 509   2013   £100

Association – Penfold, Richard

White, Charles   *A Treatise on the Management of Pregnant and Lying-in Women and the Means of Curing, and More Especially of Preventing the Principal Disorders to which they are liable.* printed for Edward and Charles Dilly, 1773. First edition, 2 engraved plates, slight dampstaining around edges of titlepage, uniformly very lightly browned, 8vo., contemporary calf, red lettering piece on spine, slightly worn, ownership inscription "Rich. Penfold", good.   Blackwell's Rare Books   Sciences - 130   2013   £850

Association – Pepper, Frank

Galsworthy, John 1867-1933 *Loyalties. A Drama in three Acts.* London: Duckworth, 1930. First illustrated edition, one of 315 numbered and signed copies, 4to., original buff buckram, very good dust jacket with few nicks and closed tears at edges, word 'signed' handwritten in ink on spine, an excellent copy, spine browned, inscribed by author for Frank Pepper.   Maggs Bros. Ltd.   1460 - 321   2013   £75

Association – Perkins, Roger Griswold

Peterson, Frederick *A Text-Book of Legal Medicine and Toxicology.* Philadelphia: and London: W. B. Saunders & Co., 1903-1904. First edition, 2 volumes, 8vo., 23 plates, 1975 text figures, original olive cloth, gilt stamped spine titles, neatly rebacked preserving original spines, new endpapers, ink signature of Roger G. Perkins, 1904, Cleveland, fine, rare.   Jeff Weber Rare Books   172 - 197   2013 $450

Association – Perrot, James

Dodsley, Robert 1703-1764 *A Collection of Poems in Six Volumes.* London: for R. and J. Dodsley, 1763. 6 volume, 2 engraved plates, engraved title vignettes and headpieces, half titles present, contemporary mottled calf, spines gilt, red and black spine labels, bindings moderately rubbed at extremities, few hinges cracking but secure, very attractive set, armorial bookplates of James Perrot and Admiral Duff, latter dated 1858.   Joseph J. Felcone Inc.   English and American Literature to 1800 - 8   2013 $500

Association – Petersham, Miska

Petersham, Maud *An American ABC.* New York: MacMillan, Sept., 1941. First edition, 4to., cloth, fine in dust jacket, color lithographs, this copy signed by Maud and Miska Petersham.   Aleph-Bet Books, Inc.   104 - 418   2013 $450

Association – Petrus, Andreas

Cicero, Marcus Tullius (Opera). *Orationes, Epistolarum ad Atticum, Philosophicorum.* Strasbourg: Impensis Iosiae Rihelii & Iacobi Dupuys, 1581. 5 volumes only (form a 9 volume set of the works), 8vo., toned and sometimes spotted, fifth volume with staining to first half, third volume with occasional early ink notes, uniformly bound in contemporary pigskin dyed yellow, boards with blind rolled borders and central portrait stamp, all edges red and gauffered, intials 'APA' stamped in black to front board, ownership inscription of A. P. Alvin (1801) and Andreae Petri Aubogiensis (i. e. Andreas Petrus of Arboga in Sweden) dated 1591. Unsworths Antiquarian Booksellers   28 - 8   2013   £625

Association – Philips, Edmund

Skelton, John *The Poetical Works.* London: Thomas Rodd, 1843. 2 volumes, attractive contemporary polished calf, covers with double gilt fillet border, raised bands, spines gilt in compartments with quatrefoil centerpiece enclosed by rosettes and small tools as well as paisley cornerpieces, each spine with one black and one red label, marbled endpapers and edges, armorial bookplate of Edmund Philips, very slight rubbing to spines, joints and extremities, two covers with (naturally occurring?) tiny dark spots, second volume with handful of gatherings variably foxed, never serious, other trivial imperfections but excellent set, decorative bindings sound and still lustrous, text clean and fresh.   Phillip J. Pirages   63 - 441   2013 $375

Association – Philips, Ismay

Brown, Christy *My Left Foot.* London: Secker & Warburg, 1954. First edition, 8vo., original maroon cloth, dust jacket, excellent copy in dust jacket, little chipped at head and tail of spine, inscribed by author for Ismay Philips 30/5/56 and inscribed below this by his mother Bridget Brown, half title and rear endpaper contain 31 signatures of unknown personages.   Maggs Bros. Ltd.   1460 - 144   2013   £275

Association – Phillips, Freddy

Cheyney, Peter *Dark Hero.* London: Collins, 1946. First edition, one of 250 numbered copies, signed by author and additionally inscribed by him to Freddy Phillips? 8vo., original purple cloth, excellent copy, dust jacket little nicked and worn at extremities.   Maggs Bros. Ltd. 1460 - 169   2013   £75

Association – Phillips, George

Montaigne, Michel De 1533-1592 *The Complete Works of...* London: John Templeman, 1842. First edition, 2 volumes, large 8vo., engraved portrait, engraved titlepage in volume one, presentation by Ralph Waldo Emerson for George Phillips, July 1848, three quarter black morocco, raised bands, some rubbed and scuffed, very good set, some holograph notes on rear blank, probably by Phillips. Second Life Books Inc.   183 - 279   2013 $3500

Association – Phillips, William

Ferguson, R. S. *On a Massive Timber Platform of Early Date Uncovered at Carlisle and on Sundry Relics Found in Connection Therewith.* Archaeological Journal, 1892. Old plain wrappers, trifle chipped, 5 plates, 2 page ALS to author from William Phillips of Carlisle, loosely inserted.   R. F. G. Hollett & Son   Lake District and Cumbria - 103   2013   £25

Association – Phillott, Johnson

Scott, Walter 1771-1832 *Marmion: a Tale of Flodden Field.* Edinburgh: Archibald Constable and Co., 1808. First edition first impression, 287 x 221mm., contemporary burgundy half morocco, two raised bands setting off elongated central spine panel, backstrip with gilt rules, botanical head and tailpiece and gilt titling, marbled boards, edges and endpapers, extra illustrated with engraved titlepage and 6 engraved plates by Richard Westall from 1809, large engraved bookplate and armorial bookplate with ink ownership inscriptions of Charles Leeson Prince, engraved bookplate of Edward S. Marsh dated 1909, flyleaf with armorial bookplate of Johnson Phillott, front joint and hinge cracked with slight bit of give to board, paper sides noticeably chafed, extremities and bands rather rubbed, significant offsetting from plates, half dozen leaves at front and back somewhat foxed, other minor imperfections with condition issues, still intact and internally fresh and clean as well as desirable for its added illustrations and special provenance. Phillip J. Pirages 63 - 428 2013 $250

Association – Phillott, Sarah

Bacon, Francis Viscount St. Albans 1561-1626 *Essays, Moral, Economical and Political.* London: Printed for J. Johnson (and others), 1807. 8 woodcut plates, frontispiece, some offsetting from frontispiece, little marked, occasional light browning, full contemporary diced calf, double gilt ruled borders, gilt tooled spine, bookplate of Sarah Phillott, attractive. Jarndyce Antiquarian Booksellers CCIV - 51 2013 £75

Johnson, Samuel 1709-1784 *The History of Rasselas, Prince of Abyssinia.* London: printed by C. Whittingham for Longman et al, 1806. 163 x 100mm., viii, 1923 pages, very attractive contemporary diced calf, covers framed by three plain and decorative gilt rules, flat spine divided ito panels by wide black and thin gilt rules, 3 panels with gilt floral centerpiece, two with gilt titling, marbled endpapers, frontispiece, five engraved plates, armorial bookplate of Sarah Phillott, barely perceptible short crack top of front joint, hint of soil to covers, faint offsetting from plates, other trivial imperfections, quite excellent copy, binding lustrous and scarcely worn and text especially fresh, clean and bright. Phillip J. Pirages 63 - 268 2013 $250

Association – Pilcher, Cobb

Cushing, Harvey Williams 1869-1939 *The Medical Career and Other Papers.* Boston: Little Brown, 1940. First edition, 8vo., 302 pages, green cloth, printed paper labels, spine label slightly soiled, bookplate (foxed) of Cobb Pilcher (light offsetting), very good. Jeff Weber Rare Books 172 - 63 2013 $95

Association – Pinney, Anna Maria

Bowles, William Lisle *Sonnets with other Poems.* Bath: printed by R. Cruttwell and sold by C. Dilly, Poultry, London, 1794. Third edition, half title, contemporary full calf, gilt spine, border and dentelles, dark green leather label, bit rubbed, hinges little worn, one or two small splits, possibly author's copy with armorial bookplate "Revd. Mr. Bowles", also small booklabel of Charles Wells and gift inscription "Anna Maria Pinney 1835. From S. M. Booth", blindstamped and labels of Birkbeck College Library. Jarndyce Antiquarian Booksellers CCIII - 33 2013 £150

Association – Piorry, Pierre Adolph

Labarraque, Antoine Germain *De l'Emploi de Chlorures d'Oxide de Sodium et de Chaux.* Paris: Madame Huzard, 1825. First edition, 8vo., 48 pages, tears at page 47 repaired with only minor loss of text, some staining and spotting on various leaves, modern marbled wrappers, housed in cloth clam shell box, red gilt stamped leather label on spine of box, bookplate of Haskell Norman, inscribed by author for Pierre Adolph Piorry, very good, scarce. Jeff Weber Rare Books 172 - 177 2013 $1450

Association – Piper, John

Betjeman, John 1906-1984 *Murray's Buckinghamshire Guide.* London: John Murray, 1948. First edition, 4to., original red cloth, dust jacket, rubbed, somewhat torn at extremities, with modicum of loss, excellent copy, inscribed by John Piper to Stella and Eric Newton. Maggs Bros. Ltd. 1460 - 92 2013 £250

Betjeman, John 1906-1984 *Poems in the Porch.* London: SPCK, 1955. Later edition, 8vo., original cream illustrated wrappers, lettered in red, signed by artist, covers dusty and browning, otherwise near fine, illustrations by John Piper. Maggs Bros. Ltd. 1460 - 94 2013 £75

Association – Piraulx, Edward

Fraunce, Abraham *The Lawiers Logike...* London: by William How for Thomas Gubbin and T. Newman, 1588. First edition, 4to., folding table, title within type ornament border, woodcut initials, mixed black letter and roman, full red gilt panelled morocco, edges gilt by Bedford, first two leaves lightly washed, short closed tear on table, blank corner of 2K4 replaced, else fine clean copy, armorial bookplate of Sir Edwin Priaulx and booklabel of Abel E. Berland. Joseph J. Felcone Inc. Books Printed before 1701 - 40 2013 $8000

Association – Pirie, Robert

Donne, John   1571-1631   *Poems by J. Donne.*   London: printed by M. F(lesher) for John Marriot, 1633. First edition, small quarto, this copy contains page 273 in corrected state (with running title and 33 lines of text), and bound without first blank leaf, but retaining last, two inserted leaves bound immediately after titlepage, 18th century mottled calf, neatly rebacked to style, minimal wear to extremities, trimmed close, though not affecting text, very lightly browned, bookplate of Robert S. Pirie, excellent, very fresh copy, custom quarter morocco clamshell.   Heritage Book Shop   50th Anniversary Catalogue - 32   2013 $55,000

Association – Pitowsky, C. A.

Lightfoot, John   *Flora Scotica; or a Systematic Arrangement, in the Linnaean Method of the Native Plants of Scotland and the Hebrides.*   printed for B. White, 1777. First edition, 2 volumes, additional engraved titles, including illustration and 35 engraved plates, some folding, small hole in one leaf touching 2 letters on verso, short tear in lower margin of one leaf, occasional mild foxing, letterpress impression faint in few places, 8vo., contemporary sprinkled calf, gilt rules on either side of raised bands on spine, green lettering pieces, numbered direct, slight wear ad cracking of joints but good and solid, ownership inscription on flyleaves of both volumes of Wm. Burton Lightfoot dated 1817 and of C. A. Pitowsky dated 1872, good.   Blackwell's Rare Books   Sciences - 75   2013   £900

Association – Pitt, Anne

Cowley, Abraham   1618-1667   *The Works of Mr. Abraham.*   London: printed for J. Tonson, Charles Harper, 1710-1711. Ninth edition, 3 volumes, 8vo., frontispiece, 17 engraved plates, frontispiece, 9 engraved plates, frontispiece and 4 engraved plates, lightly browned, little minor spotting, contemporary calf, plain spine with red morocco labels, boards bordered in blind, edges sprinkled red, rubbed at extremities, neatly conserved by Chris Weston replacing original labels, f.f.e.p. removed from first volume, early ink ownership inscription "Anne Pitt and large armorial bookplate John Borthwick/Crookston".   Unsworths Antiquarian Booksellers   28 - 87   2013   £225

Association – Plath, Aurelia

Hughes, Ted   1930-1998   *"Roosting Hawk".*   Northampton: Grecourt Review, 1959. First separate edition, offprint, 8vo., original printed wrappers, offsetting from newspaper insert on inside front cover, otherwise fine, presentation copy, inscribed by poet to his mother in law, Aurelia Plath.   James S. Jaffe Rare Books   Fall 2013 - 71   2013 $8500

Association – Player, I. E.

Doyle, Arthur Conan   1859-1930   *The Great Boer War.*   London: Smith Elder and Co., 1903. Complete edition, 19th impression, 8vo., original blue cloth, very good, little faded on spine, endpapers foxed, inscribed by author for I. E. Player July 30th 1906, loosely inserted ALS to Player from author.   Maggs Bros. Ltd.   1460 - 246   2013   £450

Association – Politi, Leo

Clark, Ann Nolan   *Looking for Something.*   New York: Viking, 1952. First edition, 8vo., cloth, fine in slightly worn dust jacket, beautifully illustrated in color by Leo Politi, special copy with watercolor of burro and embellished inscription.   Aleph-Bet Books, Inc.   104 - 432   2013 $400

Association – Pope-Hennessy, James

Beaton, Cecil   *Far East.*   London: B. T. Batsford, 1945. First edition, large 8vo., original orange cloth, lettered in yellow, near fine, spine faded, inscribed by author for James Pope-Hennessy, neat bookplate of recipient.   Maggs Bros. Ltd.   1460 - 52   2013   £350

Association – Popper, Louise

Wood, John George   *Our Living World: an Artistic Edition of the Rev. J. G. Wood's Natural History of Animate Creation.*   New York: Selmar Hess circa, 1898. 332 x 249mm., 3 volumes, publisher's black half roan over burgundy buckram, gilt pictorial upper covers with ornate titling, raised bands, spine panels with gilt arabesque centerpiece, textured endpapers, all edges gilt, illustrated titlepage, numerous woodcuts, 84 full page woodcuts and 42 chromolithographic plates, original tissue guards, front flyleaf with pencilled ownership inscription of Rebecca and Louise Popper; joints and extremities somewhat rubbed, three inch crack in one joint, front board of volume I nearly detached, three boards with scattering of small white spots, occasional mild foxing or marginal stains, other minor imperfections, bindings obviously with condition issues, but internally excellent copy, richly colored plates and few signs of use. Phillip J. Pirages   63 - 499   2013 $450

Association – Popper, Rebecca

Wood, John George *Our Living World: an Artistic Edition of the Rev. J. G. Wood's Natural History of Animate Creation.* New York: Selmar Hess circa, 1898. 332 x 249mm., 3 volumes, publisher's black half roan over burgundy buckram, gilt pictorial upper covers with ornate titling, raised bands, spine panels with gilt arabesque centerpiece, textured endpapers, all edges gilt, illustrated titlepage, numerous woodcuts, 84 full page woodcuts and 42 chromolithographic plates, original tissue guards, front flyleaf with pencilled ownership inscription of Rebecca and Louise Popper; joints and extremities somewhat rubbed, three inch crack in one joint, front board of volume I nearly detached, three boards with scattering of small white spots, occasional mild foxing or marginal stains, other minor imperfections, bindings obviously with condition issues, but internally excellent copy, richly colored plates and few signs of use. Phillip J. Pirages 63 - 499 2013 $450

Association – Porcaro

Joyce, James 1882-1941 *A Portrait of the Artist as a Young Man.* New York: B. W. Huebsch, 1916. First edition, 193 x 125mm, 2 p.l., 299, (1) pages, publisher's blue cloth, blindstamped title on front cover, flat spine with gilt titling, bookplates of John Kobler and of "Porcaro", very slight chafing to joints and exremities, spine ends just little curled, otherwise fine, binding especially clean, spine gilt very bright and text virtually pristine. Phillip J. Pirages 63 - 284 2013 $9500

Association – Porter, John

Quarles, Francis *Enchiridion Miscellaneum.* reprinted for Charles Baldwyn, 1822. 12th impression, 2 volumes, frontispiece, contemporary full vellum, gilt borders, red leather labels, slightly marked, volume II little discolored, booklabels of John Porter, top edge gilt, very good, with unsigned inscription by Henry Nelson Coleridge, signed by Sara and Edith Coleridge. Jarndyce Antiquarian Booksellers CCIII - 597 2013 £350

Association – Porter, Reginald

Maxwell, Colonel Montgomery *My Adventures.* London: Henry Colburn, 1845. First edition, 2 volumes, 200 x 126mm., special very attractive presentation binding of contemporary Oxblood pebble grain morocco, elaborately gilt, covers with blind ruled borders and complex gilt frame featuring shell head and tailpieces, scrolling corners and sides, many floral tools, raised bands, spine compartments gilt with flower basket centerpiece and leaf frond corners, blind tooled turn-ins, all edges gilt, frontispiece portraits, ink presentation inscription for Reginald Porter from friend, James Nelson Palmer on his leaving Eton Xmas 3rd 1846, spines slightly and uniformly sunned, gilt still bright, one board with little dulling because of leather preservative, otherwise very fine, clean, fresh, smooth internally in handsome binding with virtually no wear. Phillip J. Pirages 63 - 332 2013 $600

Association – Porter, Robert

Blackwell, Elizabeth *The Laws of Life, With Special Reference to the Physical Education of Girls.* New York: George P. Putnam, 1852. First edition, first book by America's first female doctor, original grey-green blindstamped cloth, all edges stained red, spine sunned to green (as usual with this cloth), small professional repair at bottom of spine resulting in loss of part of "P" and all of "U" and "T" in publisher's name, original owner's name in pencil, "Robert Porter" dated 1852, name in pencil repeated on page 63, else fine, lovely copy, scarce. Priscilla Juvelis - Rare Books 55 - 3 2013 $15,000

Association – Postlethwaite, J.

Cumberland Association for the Advancement of Literature and Science *Transations No. VIII.* Carlisle: G. & T. Coward, 1883. Original wrappers, neatly rebacked and wrappers laid on to matching card, presentation copy from J. Postlethwaite to H. E. Quilter. R. F. G. Hollett & Son Lake District & Cumbria - 346 2013 £35

Association – Potts, Bert

Duke-Elder, Stewart *System of Ophthalmology.* St. Louis & London: C. V. Mosby Co. & Henry Kimpton, 1958-1976. Complete set, mixture of St. Louis and London issues, 19 volumes, 8vo., 250 color plates, 350 text figures, blue cloth (15 volumes) and red cloth (4 volumes), dust jackets (3 volumes), signatures and embossed stamps of Bert Potts, very good. Jeff Weber Rare Books 172 - 83 2013 $800

Association – Poulin, Arthur

Our Exagmination Round His Factification for Incamination of Work in Progress. Paris: Shakespeare and Co., 1929. First printing, one of 96 special copies in the limited edition (there was also a trade edition of 200 copies, original printed paper wrappers designed by Sylvia Beach, front flyleaf with ink ownership inscription of Arthur W. Poulin/November 1944/San Francisco", one inch tears at top of front and bottom of rear joint, spine little scuffed, covers with faint soiling, two small chips to fore edge of front cover, otherwise fragile wrappers in excellent condition, except for slight browning at edges because of paper stock, fine internally.   Phillip J. Pirages   63 - 293   2013 $5000

Association – Powell, Lawrece

Caulibus, Johannes De   *The Mirrour of the Blessed Lyf of Jesu Christ.*   Oxford: at the Clarendon Press, Henry Frowde, 1908.   Occasional fox spot, pencil note in margin of introduction, 4to., original quarter line, printed paper label, pale blue paper boards, couple of tiny marks and merest touch of wear to fore corners, prospectus (creased at top) loosely inserted very good, inscribed by editor, Lawrence Powell for Ethelywn Steane.   Blackwell's Rare Books   B174 - 27   2013   £100

Association – Powell, Maurice

Ramsay, Allan   *The Ever Green.*   Edinburgh: printed for Alexander Donaldson, 1761. 12mo., 2 volumes, frontispiece, contents leaf to volume II misbound at end of volume I, some slight dusting and foxing, generally very clean, rather tightly, in 19th century dark green cloth, gilt bands & lettering to spines, 19th century armorial bookplate of Julius Charles Hare 1795-1855, ownership label of Maurice Powell.   Jarndyce Antiquarian Booksellers   CCIV - 249   2013   £85

Association – Powers, David

Kennedy, John Fitzgerald   1917-1963   *As We Remember Joe.*   Cambridge: privately printed, 1945.   First edition, first issue, one of about 500 copies distributed to friends and family, with all points as described by Kennedy Library Head, David Powers, titlepage in two colors, with sunken panel on front cover, ivory colored paper and caption on page 64, octavo, 33 black and white photos, including frontispiece, publisher's original full burgundy cloth, front cover stamped in black and gilt on sunken panel, spine lettered in gilt, very small amount of rubbing to spine and back board, otherwise near fine, original glassine, with three ALS's from Powers to Dr. Moury Bromsen.   Heritage Book Shop   Holiday Catalogue 2012 - 92   2013 $3750

Association – Powers, Tim

Dick, Philip K.   *The Broken Bubble.*   New York: Ultramarine, 1988.   First edition, limited issue, one of 26 lettered copies bound by Denis Gouey (of a total edition of 150), signed by Tim Powers and James Blaylock, full morocco, fine, this is Tim Powers' copy designated "AC1" (for "Author's Copy #1" with letter from publisher laid in to Powers sending his copies.   Between the Covers Rare Books, Inc.   Sci-Fi, Fantasy & Horror - 88045   2013 $1850

Association – Preston, William

Shakespeare, William   1564-1616   *The Works of William Shakespeare.*   London: Bickers and Son, 1864.   4to., half title, engraved frontispiece, fine, superbly bound in full contemporary straight grain red morocco, wide gilt decorated borders, ornate gilt panelled spine decorated with thistles and floral motifs, all edges gilt, gilt dentelles, armorial bookplate of William Preston of Ellel Grange.   Ken Spelman Books Ltd.   75 - 132   2013   £320

Association – Price, Cecil

Byron, George Gordon Noel, 6th Baron   1788-1824   *The Prisoner of Chillon and Other Poems. (with) The Corsair, a Tale. (with) Beppo a Venetian Story. (with) Letter to **** ********.*   London: John Murray, 1816.   1815. 1818. 1821, 4 volumes in 1, contemporary half purple calf, gilt spine faded to brown, very good, ms. notes by Cecil Price loosely inserted.   Jarndyce Antiquarian Booksellers   CCIII - 88   2013   £125

Association – Price, Roberto Salinas

Darwin, Charles Robert   1809-1882   *On the Origin of Species by means of Natural Selection or the Preservation of Favoured Races in the Struggle for Life.*   London: John Murray, 1859.   First edition, first issue, octavo, one folding diagram, original green cloth decoratively stamped in blind on covers, hinges expertly repaired, spine decorated and lettered in gilt (Freeman variant 'a'), extremities and corners slightly rubbed, binder's ticket of Edmonds & Remnants of London on back pastedown, contemporary bookplate of John Clerk with his signature dated "Jun 1859" and Roberto Salinas Price bookplate, overall very good, housed in full green morocco clamshell case.   Heritage Book Shop   50th Anniversary Catalogue - 28   2013 $160,000

Association – Price, Thomas

Frere, John Hookham   *The Monks and the Giants.*   London: John Murray, 1821.   Fourth edition, half title, uncut, original blue boards, drab spine, paper label and spine chipped, inscribed to revd. Thomas Price by Henry Bartle Frere, brother of author.   Jarndyce Antiquarian Booksellers   CCIII - 382   2013   £65

Lucas, Richard *Enquiry After Happiness.* London: printed for R. Gosling; printed for W. Innys and R. Manby, 1734-1735. Parts I-II sixth edition Part III Fifth edition, 2 volumes, contemporary sprinkled calf, spines divided by gilt rules, red morocco labels, boards bordered with gilt rule, touch rubbed at extremities, few corners lightly worn, contemporary ink ownership inscription "Thomas Price 1740". Unsworths Antiquarian Booksellers   28 - 111   2013   £350

Wotton, Henry *Reliquiae Wottonianae; or a Collection of Lives, Letters, Poems.* London: by T. Roycroft for R. Marriott, 1672. Third edition, 8vo., portraits, 19th century red morocco, early signatures of J. Grien? 1725, Thomas Price and John Francis Cole, 1828, bookplates of J. J. Chapman and Molly Flagg Gibb, very good.   Joseph J. Felcone Inc.   English and American Literature to 1800 - 26   2013 $900

Association – Prince, Charles Leeson

Scott, Walter   1771-1832 *Marmion: a Tale of Flodden Field.* Edinburgh: Archibald Constable and Co., 1808. First edition first impression, 287 x 221mm., contemporary burgundy half morocco, two raised bands setting off elongated central spine panel, backstrip with gilt rules, botanical head and tailpiece and gilt titling, marbled boards, edges and endpapers, extra illustrated with engraved titlepage and 6 engraved plates by Richard Westall from 1809, large engraved bookplate and armorial bookplate with ink ownership inscriptions of Charles Leeson Prince, engraved bookplate of Edward S. Marsh dated 1909, flyleaf with armorial bookplate of Johnson Phillott, front joint and hinge cracked with slight bit of give to board, paper sides noticeably chafed, extremities and bands rather rubbed, significant offsetting from plates, half dozen leaves at front and back somewhat foxed, other minor imperfections with condition issues, still intact and internally fresh and clean as well as desirable for its added illustrations and special provenance. Phillip J. Pirages   63 - 428   2013 $250

Association – Prinknash Abbey

Lupi, Antonio Maria *Dissertatio et Animadversiones ad Nuper Inventum Severae Martyris Epitaphium.* Palermo: ex typographia Stephani Amato, 1734. First edition, small folio, 15 leaves of plates, additional woodcut illustrations, edges speckled red, occasional light soiling, small closed tear to blank margin of one folding plate, contemporary vellum boards, gilt to spine, soiled, touch of wear to tail of spine, 3 small spots of worming to pastedowns, ownership inscription of Geo. Errington and bookplate of library of Prinknash Abbey, few early marginal pen notes. Unsworths Antiquarian Booksellers   28 - 29   2013   £800

Association – Pritchett, Dorothy

Hellman, Lillian *Maybe.* London: Macmillan, 1980. First edition, inscribed by author to V. S. Pritchett and his wife Dorothy, with Pritchett's ownership label, shallow crease to front flyleaf, else fine in near fine, mildly spine faded and dusty dust jacket.   Ken Lopez Bookseller   159 - 79   2013 $200

Association – Pritchett, V. S.

Hellman, Lillian *Maybe.* London: Macmillan, 1980. First edition, inscribed by author to V. S. Pritchett and his wife Dorothy, with Pritchett's ownership label, shallow crease to front flyleaf, else fine in near fine, mildly spine faded and dusty dust jacket.   Ken Lopez Bookseller   159 - 79   2013 $200

Association – Putnam, A. K.

Coleridge, Samuel Taylor   1772-1834 *Biographia Literaria; or Biographical Sketches of My Literary Life and Opinions.* New York: Leavitt, Lord & Co.; Boston: Crocker & Brewster, 1834. Second American edition, 2 volumes in 1, as issued, in original pale blue boards, paper label, pink cloth spine faded and slightly rubbed, signature of A. K. Putnam.   Jarndyce Antiquarian Booksellers   CCIII - 536   2013   £110

Association – Puxley, Adeleine

Coleridge, Samuel Taylor   1772-1834 *Osorio: a Tragedy.* London: John Pearson, 1873. First edition, half title, contemporary full tan calf by Bickers & Son, gilt spine, borders and dentelles, maroon and green leather labels, spine slightly chipped at head, hinges rubbed, armorial bookplate of Adeleine Puxley, all edges gilt, fine binding using poor leather, good plus.   Jarndyce Antiquarian Booksellers   CCIII - 527   2013   £85

Association – Pym, Horace Noble

Bennett, Charles Henry *London People; Sketched from Life.* London: Smith, Elder and Co., 1863. 4to., half title, frontispiece and plates, some spotting, original blue cloth, bevelled boards, slightly rubbed and dulled, armorial bookplate of Horace Noble Pym, all edges gilt.   Jarndyce Antiquarian Booksellers   CCV - 19   2013   £150

Blake, William   1757-1827 *Songs of Innocence and Experience with other Poems.* London: Basil Montagu Pickering, Chiswick Press, 1866. Half title, uncut in original plain brown cloth, paper label slightly chipped, repairs to following hinge, armorial bookplate of Horace Pym. Jarndyce Antiquarian Booksellers   CCIII - 4   2013   £120

Association – Pynchon, Thomas

Munro, H. H. *The Novels and Plays of Saki.* New York: Viking Press, 1933. Stated "Second Omnibus" volume, rebound in blue half morocco gilt and paper covered boards, probably soon after publication, spine expertly preserved, otherwise nice, near fine, with two identical examples of the armorial bookplate of Thomas Ruggles Pynchon, presumably the bookplate of author's (Thomas Pynchon) father, also named Thomas Ruggles Pynchon. Between the Covers Rare Books, Inc. Sci-Fi, Fantasy & Horror - 86650 2013 $950

Association – Pytts, Sam

Catullus, Gaius Valerius *Catullus, Tibullus, Propertius Cum C. Galli Fragmentis.* Amstaeledami sic: Apud Isbrandum Haring, 1686. 16mo., engraved titlepage, paper flaw to lower outer corner P2 touching couple of letters, full contemporary panelled calf, blindstamped corner-piece decoration, raised bands, blind ruled spine, leading hinge cracked but firm, nice, early signature of Sam Pytts on prelim blank, later bookplate "Pytt's book Room at Kyre". Jarndyce Antiquarian Booksellers CCIV - 8 2013 £180

Association – Quayle, Eric

Milton, John 1608-1674 *... Pro Populo Anglicano defensio, contras Claudii Anonymi Alias.* London: i.e Gouda?: Typis du Gardianis, 1652. False imprint, probably from Gouda, 12mo., 192 pages, woodcut arms on title, modern calf, antique, one inch piece torn from titlepage margin, not affecting type and neatly repaired, else very good, Eric Quayle's copy with his bookplate. Joseph J. Felcone Inc. Books Printed before 1701 - 70 2013 $750

Association – Quilter, H. E.

Cumberland Association for the Advancement of Literature and Science *Transactions No. VIII.* Carlisle: G. & T. Coward, 1883. Original wrappers, neatly rebacked and wrappers laid on to matching card, presentation copy from J. Postlethwaite to H. E. Quilter. R. F. G. Hollett & Son Lake District & Cumbria - 346 2013 £35

Association – Quinn, John

Ellis, Henry Havelock 1859-1939 *Affirmations.* London: Constable and Co., 1915. Second edition with new preface, 8vo., original black cloth, gilt, spine faded, otherwise excellent copy, inscribed by author to the Ellis Club, with John Quinn's bookplate. Maggs Bros. Ltd. 1460 - 274 2013 £150

Joyce, James 1882-1941 *Exiles. A Play in three Acts.* New York: B. W. Huebsch, 1918. First edition, 199 x 128mm., publisher's gray paper boards backed with green buckram, title blindstamped on front cover, gilt titling on spine, original pale yellow dust jacket printed in black, bookplate of John Quinn, photo of Joyce tipped on, 3 short, brown marks to rear cover, otherwise volume very fine in somewhat soiled dust jacket that is slightly torn, chipped and frayed at edges (small hole in middle of spine). Phillip J. Pirages 63 - 280 2013 $2500

Association – Rackham, Arthur

Andersen, Hans Christian 1805-1875 *Fairy Tales.* London: Harrap, 1932. One of 25 copies, of a total limited edition of 525 copies (of which 500 were for sale), this marked presentation in Rackham's hand and signed by Rackham, with original drawing by Rackham on integral blank, 4to., publisher's special full green morocco with triple gilt fillet border and pictorial gold design on front cover after Rackham, spine slightly toned, else fine, 12 beautiful color plates, pictorial endpapers and 59 wonderful black and whites. Aleph-Bet Books, Inc. 105 - 491 2013 $22,000

Goldsmith, Oliver 1730-1774 *Vicar of Wakefield.* London: Harrap, 1929. First edition, 4to., gilt cloth, top edge gilt, endpaper foxed, light wear, very good+, illustrations by Arthur Rackham with cover design, pictorial endpapers, 12 color plates plus 22 black and whites, this copy has large half page drawing signed and dated Nov. 1929 by Rackham special copy. Aleph-Bet Books, Inc. 105 - 498 2013 $2200

Walton, Izaak 1593-1683 *The Compleat Angler or the Contemplative Man's Recreation.* London: Harrap, 1931. First Rackham edition, one of 775 numbered copies, this unnumbered, but inscribed by Arthur Rackham above his signature on limitation page 'Special Copy' and printed on Millbourn, handmade paper, 12 color printed plates, each with captioned tissue guard, 25 drawings and pictorial endpapers, all by Rackham, titlepage printed in black and green, 4to., original white buckram, backstrip and front cover gilt lettered and decorations and triple line border in gilt to a design by Rackham, top edge gilt, others untrimmed and partly unopened, near fine. Blackwell's Rare Books 172 - 233 2013 £875

Association – Radbill, Samuel

Brendel, Johann Philipp *Consilia Medica Celeberrimorum Quorundam Germaniae Medicorum.* Frankfurt am Main: ex Bibliopolio Palthenlano, 1615. 4to., early 17th century full calf, surface worming on front board, text browned, ex-libris of Samuel X. Radbill with his bookplate, bookstamp of Melk Benedictine Monastery. James Tait Goodrich S74 - 33 2013 $495

Association – Radford, C. H.

Honorius of Autun *Elucidarius Dvalogicus Theologie Tripertitus: Infinitarum Questionum Resolutiouus.* Landshut: Johann Weyssenburger 20 June, 1514. Scarce edition, title printed in red, and blow in five vignettes, four within circles and altogether surrounded by a square frame, inner margin of first leaf strengthened, few minor spots and stains, 4to. in sixes, early 20th century calf backed buckram, spine faded, blindstamped of C. H. Radford, good.   Blackwell's Rare Books   172 - 72   2013   £1500

Association – Radstock

Hayley, William *The Life and Posthumous Writings of William Cowper...* Chichester: printed by J. Seagrave for J. Johnson, 1803-1806. First edition, 4 volumes including supplementary pages, in three, with 6 plates by William Blake, first impressions of those in volumes i and ii (no second state for those in volume iii) and one plate engraved by Caroline Watson, bound without half titles, little browned in places, some worming in lower margins of volumes i and ii, 4to., contemporary calf, blind roll tooled borders on sides, flat backstrips tooled in blind and lettered gilt direct, gilt inner dentelles, bit rubbed and bumped, spines little darkened, crack at foot on one joint, contemporary ownership of Elizabeth? Cardigan, that of C. Waldegrave dated 1824 in two places and Radstock bookplate in each volume, good. Blackwell's Rare Books   172 - 70   2013   £450

Association – Rae, Mrs.

Dowden, Edward *Poems.* London: Henry S. King & Co., 1876. First edition, 8vo., original green cloth, decorated in gilt and black, excellent copy, extremities rubbed, inscribed by author for Mrs. Rae, inscription in another hand on front free endpaper has been effaced leaving only 'from A.M.'. Maggs Bros. Ltd.   1460 - 243   2013   £100

Association – Raeder, O. J.

Bernard, Claude *Lecons sur la Physiologie et la Pathologie de Systeme Nerveux.* Paris: J. B. Bailliere et Fils, 1858. First edition, 2 volumes, 8vo., lightly foxed, 12 figures, contemporary cloth backed marbled boards, cloth corners, gilt spine, rubbed, fore edge bumped on volume I, very good, ownership signature of O. J. Raeder.   Jeff Weber Rare Books   172 - 25   2013 $750

Association – Raid, Sigmund Maximilian

Guazzo, Stefano *De Civilii Conversatione Libri Quatuor.* Ambergae: M. Forster, 1598. 24mo., vellum over beveled boards, rules and flora embosses, boards scuffed, free endpapers loose, few wormholes at corners, more evident on pastedowns and endpapers at hinge, but rarely if ever affecting leaves, scattered mnor foxing, scattered underlining in red in fine hand with occasional marginalia former owner's name under date on titlepage and on front board though mainly rubbed away, title in like hand to spine also nearly faded, good copy, the copy of Sigmund Maximillan Raid, a 17th century Jena jurist with his name on titlepage and front board. Kaaterskill Books   16 - 41   2013 $500

Association – Raistrick, Arthur

Forder, John *Hill Shepherd.* Kendal: Frank Peters, 1989. First edition, oblong 4to., original pictorial boards, dust jacket, pages 157, illustrations in color, inscribed to Arthur (Raistrick) from authors.   R. F. G. Hollett & Son Lake District and Cumbria - 133   2013   £50

Association – Ralphaelson, Samson

Huggins, Nathan Irvin *Black Odyssey: The Afro-American Ordeal in Slavery.* New York: Pantheon, 1977. First edition, boards little soiled, extensive pencil notes by Samson Raphaelson on endpapers and in text, else very good in very good plus dust jacket with couple of short tears, inscribed by author to Mr. and Mrs. Raphaelson, Christmas 1977.   Between the Covers Rare Books, Inc.   165 - 309 2013 $200

Association – Ranney, George

Plutarchus *Plutarch's Lives (with) a Life of Plutarch.* London: printed by C. Baldwin for J. Mawman et al, 1819. Third printing of this edition, 6 volumes, pleasing contemporary diced russia skillfully rebacked to style (in early 20th century?), flat spines divided into panels by blind tooling and gilt rules, square panels at head and tail with gilt central floral arabesque and blindstamped flower cornerpieces, elongated central panel with gilt floral spray centerpiece inside blind tooled floral frame, each spine with one black and one reddish brown morocco label, marbled endpapers; frontispiece in volume I; bookplate of George and Nora Ranney, extremities somewhat rubbed, half corners worn through, boards little soiled and stained, two gatherings in volume V noticeably foxed, faint offsetting it text, still excellent set, clean and fresh internally, solidly restored bindings that look good on the shelf.   Phillip J. Pirages   63 - 368   2013 $650

Association – Ranney, Nora

Plutarchus *Plutarch's Lives (with) a Life of Plutarch.* London: printed by C. Baldwin for J. Mawman et al, 1819. Third printing of this edition, 6 volumes, pleasing contemporary diced russia skillfully rebacked to style (in early 20th century?), flat spines divided into panels by blind tooling and gilt rules, square panels at head and tail with gilt central floral arabesque and blindstamped flower cornerpieces, elongated central panel with gilt floral spray centerpiece inside blind tooled floral frame, each spine with one black and one reddish brown morocco label, marbled endpapers; frontispiece in volume I; bookplate of George and Nora Ranney, extremities somewhat rubbed, half corners worn through, boards little soiled and stained, two gatherings in volume V noticeably foxed, faint offsetting it text, still excellent set, clean and fresh internally, solidly restored bindings that look good on the shelf.   Phillip J. Pirages   63 - 368   2013 $650

Association – Rasdale, Ernest

De La Mare, Walter   1873-1956   *On the Edge.*   London: Faber and Faber, 1947. New edition, 8vo., original blue cloth, price clipped by publishers with new printed price, otherwise near fine in dust jacket, slightly nicked at head and tail of spine, inscribed by author for Ernest Rasdale.   Maggs Bros. Ltd.   1460 - 217   2013   £50

Association – Rattray, R. J.

The History of Ripon; with Descriptions of Studley-Royal, Fountains' Abbey, Newby, Hackfall &c &c.   Ripon: W. Farrer, 1806. Second edition, 314 pages, aquatint frontispiece and woodcuts in text, very good, contemporary half calf, marbled boards, raised gilt bands, blindstamped decoration in each compartment, foolscap 8vo., signature of John Hammond 24th August 1863, later bookplates of Chapman-Purchas and R. J. Rattray.   Ken Spelman Books Ltd.   73 - 142   2013   £120

Association – Rawnsley, Edith

Cook, Theodore Andrea   *The Water-Colour Drawings of J. M. W. Turner, R.A. in the National Gallery.*   London: Cassell and Co., 1904. Limited edition (No. 217 of 1200 copies), folio, original cloth gilt folder with line ties, 5 plates plus 88 color plates set into mounts, top edge gilt, all loose in folder as issued, scarce, presentation copy from Canon Hardwick Rawnsley for his wife Edith.   R. F. G. Hollett & Son   Lake District & Cumbria - 308   2013   £450

Association – Rawnsley, Hardwick

Cook, Theodore Andrea   *The Water-Colour Drawings of J. M. W. Turner, R.A. in the National Gallery.*   London: Cassell and Co., 1904. Limited edition (No. 217 of 1200 copies), folio, original cloth gilt folder with line ties, 5 plates plus 88 color plates set into mounts, top edge gilt, all loose in folder as issued, scarce, presentation copy from Canon Hardwick Rawnsley for his wife Edith.   R. F. G. Hollett & Son   Lake District & Cumbria - 308   2013   £450

Association – Rawson, Clayton

Fish, Robert L.   *The Bridge that Went Nowhere.*   New York: Putnam, 1968. First edition, fine in lightly worn, very good dust jacket with couple of nicks and short tears at extremities, inscribed by author to fellow mystery writer, Clayton and Kate Rawson, splendid association.   Between the Covers Rare Books, Inc.   Mystery & Detective Fiction - 34366   2013 $475

Association – Rawson, Kate

Fish, Robert L.   *The Bridge that Went Nowhere.*   New York: Putnam, 1968. First edition, fine in lightly worn, very good dust jacket with couple of nicks and short tears at extremities, inscribed by author to fellow mystery writer, Clayton and Kate Rawson, splendid association.   Between the Covers Rare Books, Inc.   Mystery & Detective Fiction - 34366   2013 $475

Association – Ray, James

Burke, Bill   *Portraits by Bill Burke.*   New York: Ecco Press, 1987. First edition, signed in full by Raymond Carver and inscribed by him for James and Norma Ray, June 1988, fine in near fine dust jacket.   Ed Smith Books   75 - 14   2013 $750

Association – Ray, Norma

Burke, Bill   *Portraits by Bill Burke.*   New York: Ecco Press, 1987. First edition, signed in full by Raymond Carver and inscribed by him for James and Norma Ray, June 1988, fine in near fine dust jacket.   Ed Smith Books   75 - 14   2013 $750

Association – Raymond, Alfred

Rousseau, Jean Jacques 1712-1778 *The Confessions.* Philadelphia: Gebbie and Co., 1902. One of 53 copies for sale (of a total of 56) of the Astral Edition, this #9, 12 parts in 6 volumes, 310 x 230mm., vignette on limitation page, title vignettes and vignette headpieces and tailpieces as well as 48 fine plates by Maurice Leloir, printed on fine Japon vellum, titles in red and black, striking reddish brown inlaid and gilt Spanish calf, covers with ornately framed gilt panel featuring prominent gray morocco inlaid fleur-de-lys in center and smaller inlays at corners, spines in compartments featuring inlaid fleur-de-lys of white and green morocco (four per spine), beautiful green morocco doublures panelled in gilt and featuring quite large and very striking spray of lilies in gilt and 7 inlays of red or white, ivory watered sik endleaves, top edges gilt, other edges untrimmed, this set especially designed and bound for Alfred Raymond, very fine, exceptionally attractive.   Phillip J. Pirages   61 - 117   2013 $7500

Association – Redgrave, Michael

Turgenev, Ivan Sergeevich 1818-1883 *A Month in the Country.* London: Heinemann, 1943. First English edition, 8vo., 94 pages, very good in dust jacket, bookplate of Hugh Beaumont on front endpaper, inscribed by Emlyn Williams for Beaumont, signed by 13 members of the opening night cast including Michael Redgrave, David Baxter, Winifred Hindle, etc.   Second Life Books Inc.   183 - 383   2013 $400

Association – Redmayne, Miss

Greenwood, W. *The Redmans of Levens and Harewood.* Kendal: Titus Wilson, 1905. First large paper issue, 4to., original crimson cloth gilt, little marked and neatly recased, 12 pedigrees and 30 plates, flyleaves rather spotted, presentation copy from author to Miss Redmayne, 7th March 1908.   R. F. G. Hollett & Son   Lake District and Cumbria - 206   2013   £275

Association – Reed, Howard Sprague

Blanco, Francisco Manuel *Flora de Filipinas.* Manila: Impr. de St. Thomas, 1837. First edition, 4to., lacking final leaf of errata (should be 2ff. last a blank), waterstains first and last leaves torn and repaired, last leaves loose (also with some loss), original gilt stamped brown tree calf with red and black calf spine labels, rubbed, good, rare on market, bookplate of Howard Sprague Reed and ownership inscription Jaime Barrachina y Almeda, Madrid 1929.   Jeff Weber Rare Books   172 - 33   2013 $1600

Association – Regs, R.

Selby, Thomas G. *As the Chinese See Us.* London: T. Fisher Unwin, 1901. First edition, 8vo., few pages unopened, very good+, inscribed "R. Regs. Esq. with author's compliments".   By the Book, L. C.   38 - 71   2013 $200

Association – Reik, Theodore

Linder, Robert *Explorations in Psychoanalysis: a Tribute to the Work of Theodor Reik.* New York: Julian Press, 1953. First edition, very good with light wear to spine ends, good only dust jacket with extensive wear to spine and along top edge, significant use of clear tape on spine, signed by Reik on frontispiece.   Between the Covers Rare Books, Inc.   Psychology & Psychiatry - 283263   2013 $200

Association – Reiss, G. F.

Spielmann, M. H. *Kate Greenaway.* London: A. & C. Black, 1905. Thick 8vo., original decorated cloth gilt, spine trifle faded, top edge gilt, 52 color plates, color endpapers, 3 monochrome plates, 90 text illustrations, slight creasing to corner of flyleaf, bookplate of G. F. Reiss.   R. F. G. Hollett & Son   Children's Books - 567   2013   £150

Association – Reisz, Karel

Fowles, John *Ourika.* Austin: W. Thomas Taylor, 1977. First edition, limited to 500 copies signed by author at foot of page 64, 4to., original quarter blue morocco, marbled paper boards, lettered in gilt, printed at the Bird and Bull Press on Green's Hayle paper, inscribed by author for Karel Reisz, near fine, spine little sunned.   Maggs Bros. Ltd.   1460 - 297   2013   £650

Association – Reitlinger, Gerald

Powell, Anthony *Agents and Patients.* London: Duckworth, 1936. First edition, faint foxing to prelims and final few leaves little to edges, foolscap 8vo., original pink cloth cocked, faded backstrip gilt lettered and with chafing to its head and tail, good, with friendly 2 page ALS from author loosely tucked into book, dated 29 Dec. 1945 and addressed to Gerald Reitlinger.   Blackwell's Rare Books   172 - 231   2013   £1000

Association – Relin, David

Mortenson, Greg *Three Cups of Tea.* New York: Viking, 2006. Advance reading copy, signed by author and by David Relin, fine in wrappers and custom clamshell case, scarce.   Ken Lopez Bookseller   159 - 142   2013 $750

Association – Renaudot, V. C. E.

Norden, John *A Mirror for the Multitude, or Glasse, Wherein Maie be Seene the Violence, the Error, the Weakness and Rash Content of the Multitude and the Dangerous Resolution of Such as Without Regard of the Truth...* London: printed by John Windet, 1586. First edition, 8vo., ornate border to titlepage, headpieces and some woodcut initials, printer's waste used as r.f.e.p., small marginal hole to titlepage, little dampstaining to bottom margin page 49 onwards, few spots and smudges, 17th century brown calf, small paper label to spine, blind tooled triple fillet to spine and borders, single gilt fillet to edges 'Edward Gwynn' in gilt to upper board and initials E.G. to lower board, joints little creased, upper inner hinge splitting a little but binding strong, endpapers soiled, small label pasted to bottom of titlepage reading "Ex Bibliotheca . Cl. Eusebii Renaudot quam Monasterio sancti Germani a Pratis legacvit anno Domini 1720", also to titlepage in ink, E. 1714 and old MS note opposite. Unsworths Antiquarian Booksellers 28 - 118 2013 £3000

Association – Renier, Anne

Agg, John *The General-Post Bag; or News!* London: J. Johnston, 1814. First edition, half title, uncut in original blue boards, little marked, drab spine defective, slight worming to endpapers and first four pages, Renier booklabel. Jarndyce Antiquarian Booksellers CCIII - 334 2013 £50

Bloomfield, Robert *The Banks of the Wye: a Poem.* B. & B. Crosby & Co., 1813. Second edition, engraved frontispiece and plate, full contemporary calf, gilt borders and dentelles, spine rather worn, poor copy, armorial bookplate of Robert Washington Oates, Renier booklabel. Jarndyce Antiquarian Booksellers CCIII - 27 2013 £30

Bloomfield, Robert *The Farmer's Boy: a Rural Poem.* London: Longman, 1827. Fifteenth edition, half title, engraved title and plates after R. Westall, some spotting, slightly later half calf, gilt bands, brown leather label, signed "Fanny Tetley" in contemporary hand, Renier booklabel, very good. Jarndyce Antiquarian Booksellers CCIII - 20 2013 £30

Bloomfield, Robert *Rural Tales, Ballads and Songs.* London: Longman &c., 1820. Ninth edition, illustrations, 4 neatly colored by previous owner, some internal marking, full contemporary green calf, gilt spine, gilt and blind borders, Renier booklabel, very good, school prize inscription Bromely Seminary 1826. Jarndyce Antiquarian Booksellers CCIII - 21 2013 £30

Bloomfield, Robert *Wild Flowers; or Pastoral and Local Poetry.* London: Longman &c, 1819. New edition, frontispiece and plates, uncut in original blue boards, drab spine titled in ink chipped, Renier booklabel. Jarndyce Antiquarian Booksellers CCIII - 23 2013 £35

Brown, Thomas *The Paradise of Coquettes, a Poem.* Edinburgh: printed by George Ramsay & Co. for Archibald Constable & co., 1817. Second edition, half title, final ad leaf, uncut in blue boards, spine chipped at head and tail, hinges and corners worn, Renier booklabel, good, solid copy. Jarndyce Antiquarian Booksellers CCIII - 648 2013 £40

Byron, George Gordon Noel, 6th Baron 1788-1824 *Correspondence of Lord Byron, with a Friend, Including His Letters to his Mother... in 1809, 1810 and 1811...* Paris: A. & W. Galignani, 1825. 2 volumes, half titles, browned, contemporary half dark green calf, slightly rubbed, Renier booklabels. Jarndyce Antiquarian Booksellers CCIII - 321 2013 £60

Byron, George Gordon Noel, 6th Baron 1788-1824 *English Bards and Scotch Reviewers, a Satire.* London: James Cawthorn, 1809. Spurious issue of first edition, 12mo., half title, uncut in original drab printed boards, slightly marked, hinges splitting, corners strengthened, good, Renier booklabel. Jarndyce Antiquarian Booksellers CCIII - 117 2013 £150

Byron, George Gordon Noel, 6th Baron 1788-1824 *Lara, a Tale. Jacqueline, a Tale.* London: printed for J. Murray by T. Davison, 1814. First edition, first variant, original half dark green sheep, spine chipped at head and tail, hinges and corners rubbed and worn, Renier booklabel, contemporary booklabel and signature of Marianne Ford, good, sound copy. Jarndyce Antiquarian Booksellers CCIII - 195 2013 £65

Byron, George Gordon Noel, 6th Baron 1788-1824 *Marino Faliero, Doge of Venice. The Prophecy of Dante, a Poem.* London: printed and published by W. Dugdale, 1826. Contemporary full calf, recently neatly rebacked leading f.e.p. replaced, Renier booklabel. Jarndyce Antiquarian Booksellers CCIII - 295 2013 £110

Byron, George Gordon Noel, 6th Baron 1788-1824 *Monody on the Death of the Right Honourable R. B. Sheridan...* London: John Murray, 1816. First edition, first issue, half title, disbound, little foxed, Renier signature. Jarndyce Antiquarian Booksellers CCIII - 231 2013 £180

Byron, George Gordon Noel, 6th Baron 1788-1824 *Poems with His Memoirs.* London: Jones & Co., 1826. 32mo., frontispiece, 2 pages ads, original purple moire, patterned silk cloth, black paper label, slightly bumped, slight fading to spine Renier and Robert Washington Oates booklabels, all edges gilt, very good. Jarndyce Antiquarian Booksellers CCIII - 94 2013 £50

Byron, George Gordon Noel, 6th Baron 1788-1824 *Sardanapalus.* London: John Murray, 1823. First separate edition, uncut in original blue boards, drab spine and paper label slightly chipped, hinges slightly cracked, armorial bookplate of Prof. W. Blair-Bell, Renier booklabel. Jarndyce Antiquarian Booksellers CCIII - 301 2013 £35

Clinton, George *Memoirs of the Life and Writings of Lord Byron.* London: James Robins & Co., 1828. Reprint, frontispiece, engraved title dated 1824 and plates with some browning and staining, marks in text, contemporary black straight grained morocco, decorated spine, dark green labels, slightly rubbed, signed "W.B. 1831", Renier and earlier booklabels. Jarndyce Antiquarian Booksellers CCIII - 362 2013 £80

Colton, Charles Caleb *Hypocrisy.* London: Taylor & Hessey, 1812. Later 2 pages ads (June 1823), uncut in original drab boards, paper label darkened, slightly rubbed at head of spine, stamped, " A. J. above coronet design at head of introduction", Renier booklabel, good plus. Jarndyce Antiquarian Booksellers CCIII - 668 2013 £120

Crowe, Catherine *Susan Hopley or the Adventures of a Maid Servant.* Edinburgh: William Tait &c, 1842. Half title, frontispiece, contemporary half brown calf, hinges slightly splitting, Renier booklabel, nice, clean copy. Jarndyce Antiquarian Booksellers CCV - 79 2013 £120

Dumont, Pierre Joseph *Narrative of Thirty-Four Years Slavery and Travels in Africa.* London: Sir Richard Phillips & Co., 1819. 42 pages, frontispiece, uncut, disbound, from the library of Anne and Fernand Renier. Jarndyce Antiquarian Booksellers CCV - 96 2013 £120

Fitz-Florian's Alphabet; or Lyrical Fables for Children Grown Up. London: J. J. Stockdale, 1819. Second edition, full contemporary calf, gilt borders and dentelles, slightly marked and bit rubbed, contemporary gift inscription to Elizabeth Luke, Renier booklabel. Jarndyce Antiquarian Booksellers CCIII - 631 2013 £75

Galt, John 1779-1839 *The Life of Lord Byron.* London: Henry Colburn, 1830. First edition, 2 pages ads preceding series title, engraved frontispiece and title, plate, slightly spotted, original glazed purple cloth faded to brown, black label, marked, Renier booklabel, good, sound. Jarndyce Antiquarian Booksellers CCIII - 384 2013 £125

Gordon, Cosmo *Life and Genius of Lord Byron.* London: Knight and Lacey, 1824. First edition, frontispiece very slightly browned, engraved title, odd internal mark, uncut in slightly later blue morocco by J. Larkins, spine slightly faded, Renier signature and booklabel. Jarndyce Antiquarian Booksellers CCIII - 387 2013 £220

Harral, Thomas *Anne Boleyn and Caroline of Brunswick Compared...* London: W. Wright, 1820. Portrait, disbound, odd spot, three small holes near inner title margin, from the Renier library. Jarndyce Antiquarian Booksellers CCV - 130 2013 £40

Iley, Matthew *The Life, Writings Opinions and Times of... Lord Byron...* London: Matthew Iley, 1825. First edition, 3 volumes, frontispiece volumes I & II, folding frontispiece volume III, frontispieces browned, text slightly spotted, contemporary half calf, gilt spines, dark green and maroon leather labels, slightly rubbed, Renier booklabels, very good. Jarndyce Antiquarian Booksellers CCIII - 393 2013 £280

Procter, Bryan Waller *Dramatic Scenes.* New York: D. Appleton & Co., 1857. Slightly spotted, illustrations, contemporary quarter black sheep, pink glazed boards, rubbed, some loss of glazed paper on following board, corners worn, Renier booklabel, good, sound copy. Jarndyce Antiquarian Booksellers CCIII - 601 2013 £30

Smith, Horace 1779-1849 *(Rejected Addresses). A Sequel to the "Rejected Addresses"; or the Theatrum Poetarum Minorum.* London: Sherwood, Neely & Jones, 1813. First edition, uncut in original drab boards, spine slightly chipped, paper label defective, Renier booklabel. Jarndyce Antiquarian Booksellers CCIII - 157 2013 £75

To-Night! or the Total Eclipse. London: J. J. Stockdale, 1818. Fifteenth edition, half title, 6 color plates by C. William bound together following title, uncut in original pink boards, marked, spine reinforced with later cream paper, ink title, bookplates of R. D. G. Jones and Renier. Jarndyce Antiquarian Booksellers CCIII - 630 2013 £60

Association – Renier, Fernand

Agg, John *The General-Post Bag; or News!* London: J. Johnston, 1814. First edition, half title, uncut in original blue boards, little marked, drab spine defective, slight worming to endpapers and first four pages, Renier booklabel. Jarndyce Antiquarian Booksellers CCIII - 334 2013 £50

Bloomfield, Robert *Rural Tales, Ballads and Songs.* London: Longman &c., 1820. Ninth edition, illustrations, 4 neatly colored by previous owner, some internal marking, full contemporary green calf, gilt spine, gilt and blind borders, Renier booklabel, very good, school prize inscription Bromely Seminary 1826. Jarndyce Antiquarian Booksellers CCIII - 21 2013 £30

Bloomfield, Robert *The Banks of the Wye: a Poem.* B. & B. Crosby & Co., 1813. Second edition, engraved frontispiece and plate, full contemporary calf, gilt borders and dentelles, spine rather worn, poor copy, armorial bookplate of Robert Washington Oates, Renier booklabel. Jarndyce Antiquarian Booksellers CCIII - 27 2013 £30

Bloomfield, Robert *The Farmer's Boy: a Rural Poem.* London: Longman, 1827. Fifteenth edition, half title, engraved title and plates after R. Westall, some spotting, slightly later half calf, gilt bands, brown leather label, signed "Fanny Tetley" in contemporary hand, Renier booklabel, very good. Jarndyce Antiquarian Booksellers CCIII - 20 2013 £30

Bloomfield, Robert *Wild Flowers; or Pastoral and Local Poetry.* London: Longman &c, 1819. New edition, frontispiece and plates, uncut in original blue boards, drab spine titled in ink chipped, Renier booklabel. Jarndyce Antiquarian Booksellers CCIII - 23 2013 £35

Brown, Thomas *The Paradise of Coquettes, a Poem.* Edinburgh: printed by George Ramsay & Co. for Archibald Constable & co., 1817. Second edition, half title, final ad leaf, uncut in blue boards, spine chipped at head and tail, hinges and corners worn, Renier booklabel, good, solid copy. Jarndyce Antiquarian Booksellers CCIII - 648 2013 £40

Byron, George Gordon Noel, 6th Baron   1788-1824 *Correspondence of Lord Byron, with a Friend, Including His Letters to his Mother... in 1809, 1810 and 1811...* Paris: A. & W. Galignani, 1825. 2 volumes, half titles, browned, contemporary half dark green calf, slightly rubbed, Renier booklabels. Jarndyce Antiquarian Booksellers CCIII - 321 2013 £60

Byron, George Gordon Noel, 6th Baron   1788-1824 *English Bards and Scotch Reviewers, a Satire.* London: James Cawthorn, 1809. Spurious issue of first edition, 12mo., half title, uncut in original drab printed boards, slightly marked, hinges splitting, corners strengthened, good, Renier booklabel. Jarndyce Antiquarian Booksellers CCIII - 117 2013 £150

Byron, George Gordon Noel, 6th Baron   1788-1824 *Lara, a Tale. Jacqueline, a Tale.* London: printed for J. Murray by T. Davison, 1814. First edition, first variant, original half dark green sheep, spine chipped at head and tail, hinges and corners rubbed and worn, Renier booklabel, contemporary booklabel and signature of Marianne Ford, good, sound copy. Jarndyce Antiquarian Booksellers CCIII - 195 2013 £65

Byron, George Gordon Noel, 6th Baron   1788-1824 *Marino Faliero, Doge of Venice. The Prophecy of Dante, a Poem.* London: printed and published by W. Dugdale, 1826. Contemporary full calf, recently neatly rebacked leading f.e.p. replaced, Renier booklabel. Jarndyce Antiquarian Booksellers CCIII - 295 2013 £110

Byron, George Gordon Noel, 6th Baron   1788-1824 *Monody on the Death of the Right Honourable R. B. Sheridan...* London: John Murray, 1816. First edition, first issue, half title, disbound, little foxed, Renier signature. Jarndyce Antiquarian Booksellers CCIII - 231 2013 £180

Byron, George Gordon Noel, 6th Baron   1788-1824 *Poems with His Memoirs.* London: Jones & Co., 1826. 32mo., frontispiece, 2 pages ads, original purple moire, patterned silk cloth, black paper label, slightly bumped, slight fading to spine Renier and Robert Washington Oates booklabels, all edges gilt, very good. Jarndyce Antiquarian Booksellers CCIII - 94 2013 £50

Byron, George Gordon Noel, 6th Baron   1788-1824 *Sardanapalus.* London: John Murray, 1823. First separate edition, uncut in original blue boards, drab spine and paper label slightly chipped, hinges slightly cracked, armorial bookplate of Prof. W. Blair-Bell, Renier booklabel. Jarndyce Antiquarian Booksellers CCIII - 301 2013 £35

Clinton, George *Memoirs of the Life and Writings of Lord Byron.* London: James Robins & Co., 1828. Reprint, frontispiece, engraved title dated 1824 and plates with some browning and staining, marks in text, contemporary black straight grained morocco, decorated spine, dark green labels, slightly rubbed, signed "W.B. 1831", Renier and earlier booklabels. Jarndyce Antiquarian Booksellers CCIII - 362 2013 £80

Colton, Charles Caleb *Hypocrisy.* London: Taylor & Hessey, 1812. Later 2 pages ads (June 1823), uncut in original drab boards, paper label darkened, slightly rubbed at head of spine, stamped, " A. J. above coronet design at head of introduction", Renier booklabel, good plus. Jarndyce Antiquarian Booksellers CCIII - 668 2013 £120

Crowe, Catherine *Susan Hopley or the Adventures of a Maid Servant.* Edinburgh: William Tait &c, 1842. Half title, frontispiece, contemporary half brown calf, hinges slightly splitting, Renier booklabel, nice, clean copy. Jarndyce Antiquarian Booksellers CCV - 79 2013 £120

Dumont, Pierre Joseph *Narrative of Thirty-Four Years Slavery and Travels in Africa.* London: Sir Richard Phillips & Co., 1819. 42 pages, frontispiece, uncut, disbound, from the library of Anne and Fernand Renier. Jarndyce Antiquarian Booksellers CCV - 96 2013 £120

Fitz-Florian's Alphabet; or Lyrical Fables for Children Grown Up. London: J. J. Stockdale, 1819. Second edition, full contemporary calf, gilt borders and dentelles, slightly marked and bit rubbed, contemporary gift inscription to Elizabeth Luke, Renier booklabel.   Jarndyce Antiquarian Booksellers   CCIII - 631   2013   £75

Galt, John   1779-1839   *The Life of Lord Byron.*   London: Henry Colburn, 1830. First edition, 2 pages ads preceding series title, engraved frontispiece and title, plate, slightly spotted, original glazed purple cloth faded to brown, black label, marked, Renier booklabel, good, sound.   Jarndyce Antiquarian Booksellers   CCIII - 384   2013   £125

Gordon, Cosmo   *Life and Genius of Lord Byron.*   London: Knight and Lacey, 1824. First edition, frontispiece very slightly browned, engraved title, odd internal mark, uncut in slightly later blue morocco by J. Larkins, spine slightly faded, Renier signature and booklabel.   Jarndyce Antiquarian Booksellers   CCIII - 387   2013   £220

Harral, Thomas   *Anne Boleyn and Caroline of Brunswick Compared...*   London: W. Wright, 1820. Portrait, disbound, odd spot, three small holes near inner title margin, from the Renier library.   Jarndyce Antiquarian Booksellers   CCV - 130   2013   £40

Iley, Matthew   *The Life, Writings Opinions and Times of... Lord Byron...*   London: Matthew Iley, 1825. First edition, 3 volumes, frontispiece volumes I & II, folding frontispiece volume III, frontispieces browned, text slightly spotted, contemporary half calf, gilt spines, dark green and maroon leather labels, slightly rubbed, Renier booklabels, very good.   Jarndyce Antiquarian Booksellers   CCIII - 393   2013   £280

Procter, Bryan Waller   *Dramatic Scenes.*   New York: D. Appleton & Co., 1857. Slightly spotted, illustrations, contemporary quarter black sheep, pink glazed boards, rubbed, some loss of glazed paper on following board, corners worn, Renier booklabel, good, sound copy.   Jarndyce Antiquarian Booksellers   CCIII - 601   2013   £30

Smith, Horace   1779-1849   *(Rejected Addresses). A Sequel to the "Rejected Addresses"; or the Theatrum Poetarum Minorum.*   London: Sherwood, Neely & Jones, 1813. First edition, uncut in original drab boards, spine slightly chipped, paper label defective, Renier booklabel.   Jarndyce Antiquarian Booksellers   CCIII - 157   2013   £75

To-Night! or the Total Eclipse.   London: J. J. Stockdale, 1818. Fifteenth edition, half title, 6 color plates by C. William bound together following title, uncut in original pink boards, marked, spine reinforced with later cream paper, ink title, bookplates of R. D. G. Jones and Renier.   Jarndyce Antiquarian Booksellers   CCIII - 630   2013   £60

Association – Rexroth, Kenneth

Stevens, Wallace   1879-1955   *Harmonium.*   New York: Alfred A. Knopf, 1923. First edition, 3rd printing, 8vo., 140 pages, original blue cloth, printed paper label, soiling of edges of binding and marginal chipping of title label, fellow poet, Kenneth Rexroth's copy with partially faint penciled signature.   M & S Rare Books, Inc.   95 - 354   2013 $1250

Association – Reynolds, John Taylor

Combe, William   1742-1823   *The Three Tours of Dr. Syntax: In Search of the Picturesque, In Search of Consolation, in Search of a Wife.*   London: R. Ackermann's Repository of Arts, 1812.   1820. 1821. First editions in book form, 3 separately published volumes, very handsome gilt decorated early 20th century dark blue crushed morocco by Riviere & Son (stamp signed), cover with French fillet border, spines lavishly and elegantly gilt in compartments with flower filled cornucopia centerpiece surrounded by small tools and volute cornerpieces, inner gilt dentelles, top edge gilt, other edges untrimmed, one woodcut illustration, one engraved tailpiece and 80 artfully hand colored aquatint plates by Thomas Rowlandson, engraved armorial bookplate of John Taylor Reynolds; spines uniformly more black than blue, four of the covers with just hint of soiling, most plates with variable offsetting (usually faint but noticeable in half dozen cases), other trivial imperfections, extremely desirable set, strong impressions and good coloring of first edition plates, spacious margins, lovely bindings, lustrous and virtually unworn.   Phillip J. Pirages   63 - 409   2013 $4500

Association – Rice, David

Hunter, John   1728-1793   *A Treatise on the Blood, Inflammation and Gun-shot Wounds.*   London: John Richardson for George Nicol, 1794. First edition, 4to., frontispiece, 9 plates foxed, occasional light scattered foxing throughout text, modern quarter gilt stamped calf over marbled paper backed boards, gilt stamped red leather spine label, corners faintly rubbed, inscribed by David Rice 8/25/1820 for W. Buxton, better than very good.   Jeff Weber Rare Books   172 - 145   2013 $6500

Association – Richardson

Eachard, John   *Mr. Hobb's State of Nature Considered... (bound with) The Grounds and Occasions of the Contempt of the Clergy and Religion... (bound with) Some Observations Upon the Answer to an Enquiry into the Grounds and Occasions of the Contempt of the Clergy.*   London: Printed for E. Blagrave, 1696. Fourth edition, 8vo., contemporary mottled calf, blind ruled borders, expertly rebacked in matching style, some browning, slight wear to foot of front endpaper, 19th century armorial bookplate of Richardson of Pitfour, Bart.   Jarndyce Antiquarian Booksellers   CCIV - 11   2013   £380

Association – Rickard, Kathryn

Andrews, William Loring *Sextodecimos et Infra.* New York: Charles Scribner's Sons, 1899. First edition, limited to 152 copies, this one of 140 printed on English handmade plate paper by Gilliss Press, 8vo., 27 illustrations of miniature books, 14 of which are in full color, stiff paper wrappers, outer dust jacket, extremely scarce, small tears along bottom and top of hinges of dust jacket, from the library of De Witt Miller with his ink inscription, also from the library of noted miniature collector Kathryn Rickard with her bookplate, with additional bookplate on front free endpaper, number in ink in corner of front free endpaper, paper slipcase not present, scarce; from the collection of Donn W. Sanford.   Oak Knoll Books   303 - 7   2013 $450

Bible. English - 1985 *The Song of Songs by Solomon.* Ultrecht: Catharijne Press, 1985. Limited to 167 copies, this one of 150 numbered trade copies, 6.2 x 4.3cm. paper coverd boards stamped in gilt, design and initials by Bram de Does, copperplate engraving by Bertril Schmull and binding and hand coloring by Luce Thurkow, engraving signed and numbered in pencil, large initial letters hand colored, miniature bookplate of Kathryn Rickard, from the collection of Donn W. Sanford.   Oak Knoll Books   303 - 88   2013 $125

Doyle, Arthur Conan 1859-1930 *A Case of Identity.* Kokie: Black Cat Press, 1984. Limited to 249 copies, signed by producer, 6.1 x 4.5 cm., leather, title gilt stamped on spine, decoration gilt stamped on front cover, marbled endpapers, miniature bookplate of Kathryn Rickard, from the collection of Donn W. Sanford.   Oak Knoll Books   303 - 52   2013 $125

Doyle, Arthur Conan 1859-1930 *A Case of Identity.* Sacramento: Press of Arden Park, 1987. Limited to 120 numbered copies signed by Budd Westreich, 5.8 x 7.2 cm., cloth, title gilt stamped on spine, dust jacket, illustrations in text and on endpapers, with miniature bookplate of Kathryn Rickard, from the collection of Donn W. Sanford.   Oak Knoll Books   303 - 34   2013 $100

Doyle, Arthur Conan 1859-1930 *A Scadal in Bohemia.* Skokie: Black Cat Press, 1984. Limited to 240 copies signed by producer, 6.1 x 4.5 cm., cloth, title stamped on spine, decoration gilt stamped on front cover, binding by Lariviere, miniature bookplate of Kathryn Rickard, from the collection of Donn W. Sanford.   Oak Knoll Books   303 - 53   2013 $125

Doyle, Arthur Conan 1859-1930 *The Red-Headed League.* Sacramento: Press of Arden Park, 1985. Limited to 120 copies signed by Budd Westreich, 5.8 x 7.2 cm., cloth, title gilt stamped on spine, dust jacket, illustrated endpapers, illustrations, from the collection of Donn W. Sanford, miniature bookplate of Kathryn Rickard.   Oak Knoll Books   303 - 35   2013 $100   **Freyer, Kurt** *Mikrobiblion: Das Buch Von Den Kleinen Buchern.* Berlin: Horodisch & Marx, 1929. Limited to 426 numbered copies, 10.5 x 7.3 cm., full parchment, title hand lettered on front board, fore-edge uncut, text in German, with miniature bookplate of Kathryn Rickard, from the collection of Donn W. Sanford.   Oak Knoll Books   303 - 15   2013 $550

H., B. *The Twelve Months by B. H.* Zuilichem: Catharijne Press, 1990. Limited to 165 copies, this one of the 150 numbered trade copies, bound by Gus Thurkow and hand coloring by Luc Thurkow, each month with hand colored scene, 4.5 x 6.2cm., paper covered boards with color illustration on front cover, miniature bookplate of Kathryn Rickard, from the collection of Donn W. Sanford.   Oak Knoll Books   303 - 90   2013 $125

Henderson, James D. *Miniature Books.* Leipzig: Tondeur & Sauberlich, 1930. Limited to 260 numbered copies, 16mo., limp leather, covers rubbed, miniature bookplate of Kathryn Rickard, from the collection of Donn W. Sanford. Oak Knoll Books   303 - 18   2013 $300

Irving, Washington 1783-1859 *Rip Van Winkle.* Utrecht: Catharijne Press, 1987. Limited to 165 copies, this one of 150 numbered copies, with 4 tipped in illustrations by Henk van der Haar, 6.5 x 4.5cm, pictorial paper covered boards, miniature bookplate of Kathryn Rickard, from the collection of Donn W. Sanford.   Oak Knoll Books   303 - 85   2013 $125

Poska, Valentine J. *Microbibliotrivia, a Curious Adventure in Miniature Books.* San Antonio: privately printed, 1984-1989. Issues 1-5, 4to., stiff paper wrappers, plastic comb binding, not paginated, miniature bookplate of Kathryn Rickard, 5th in the series signed by author, from the collection of Donn W. Sanford.   Oak Knoll Books   303 - 22   2013 $250

Stone, Wilbur Macey *The Thumb Bible of John Taylor.* Brookline: the LXIVMOS, 1928. Limited to 100 copies, 12mo., cloth backed boards, paper label, illustrations, rubbed along edges, miniature bookplate of Kathryn Rickard with acquisition date of 1990 added in ink beneath bookplate, pages 65-68 (one sheet) loose from not being sewn in, from the collection of Donn W. Sanford.   Oak Knoll Books   303 - 24   2013 $200

Weber, Francis J. *Smallpaxweber.* San Diego: Ash Ranch Press, 1989. Limited to 128 copies, 100 numbered, deluxe edition lettered A-Z and 2 state deluxe proofs, this is lettered copy, signed by author and publisher, Don Hildreth, Artwork by Isabel Piczek and Leo Politi, photo by Alphonse Antczak, color frontispiece, 4.6 x 6.1cm., quarter leather with raised bands, title gilt stamped on spine, decorated cloth boards, clamshell box with inset color illustration, 23, (3) pages, from the collection of Donn W. Sanford, miniature bookplate of Kathryn Rickard. Oak Knoll Books 303 - 41 2013 $200

White, Robert W. *A History of the Cadiz Short Line Railroad.* Chicago: Black Cat Press, 1966. Limited to 200 copies, 5.5 x 7.8 cm., black and white illustrations, leather, miniature bookplate of Kathryn Rickard, from the collection of Donn W. Sanford. Oak Knoll Books 303 - 59 2013 $200

Wilde, Oscar 1854-1900 *The House of Judgement.* Utrecht: Catharijne Press, 1986. Limited to 165 copies, this one of 150 numbered copies, 5 x 6.7cm., brown cloth with paper cover label, printed in four colors by Hans Hartzheim with calligraphed original by J. H. Moesman, colophon separately printed on four pages and loosely inserted in pocket in back, miniature bookplate of Kathryn Rickard, from the collection of Donn W. Sanford. Oak Knoll Books 303 - 91 2013 $150

Williams, Gordon *Ravens & Crows.* Los Angeles: William Cheney, 1966. 2.4 x 1.7cm., paper covered boards, miniature bookplate of Kathryn Rickard, from the collection of Donn W. Sanford. Oak Knoll Books 303 - 96 2013 $100

Association – Ridler, Anne

Eliot, Thomas Stearns 1888-1965 *The Dry Salvages.* London: Faber, 1941. First edition, pages 16, 8vo., original printed pale blue grey stapled wrappers, spine faded, untrimmed, good, Anne Ridler's copy gifted to her by Eliot. Blackwell's Rare Books B174 - 202 2013 £3500

Yeats, William Butler 1865-1939 *Wheels and Butterflies.* Macmillan, 1934. First edition, title vignette by Edmund Dulac repeated in gilt on front cover, flyleaves darkened in part, foolscap 8vo., original lime green cloth, backstrip lettering and front cover design all gilt blocked, faint free endpaper and edge foxing, rough trimmed, dust jacket chipped at head of darkened backstrip panel, very good, at one time Anne Ridler's copy with her address embossed on front free endpaper. Blackwell's Rare Books 172 - 260 2013 £150

Association – Ridler, Vivian

Delamotte, F. *A Primer of the Art of Illumination for the Use of Beginners...* Lockwood, 1874. Printed in black and red, 20 chromolithographed plates of initial letters, 20 plates of examples, small 4to., original bevel edged maroon cloth, plain backstrip faded, sides with blindstamped double line border and fleur-de-lys cornerpieces, upper side elaborately gilt blocked with title and passion flowers, yellow chalked endpapers, gilt edges, Vivian Ridler's copy with his embossed address on front free endpaper. Blackwell's Rare Books B174 - 45 2013 £200

Association – Rietteel

Tymme, Thomas *A Silver Watch Bell, the Sound Whereof is Able (by the Grace of God) to Win the Most Prophane Worldling and Careless Liver...* London: printed by John Haviland for Thomas Alchorn, 1638. Small octavo, lacking A2 (titlepage) and I2 (pages 115-116), text within double ruled border, with headline, page numbers and marginal glosses inside outer border, 16 headpieces, 14 ornamental initials and 2 tailpieces, contemporary marbled boards, rebacked (possibly in 1915, according to pencil note on front pastedown), with speckled calf, modern red and white paper spine label lettered in ink, plain endpapers, all edges speckled red, some trimmed close to headlines and in a few cases to marginal inscriptions, boards worn, hinges cracked, tiny rust or ink hole to top of front free endpaper, tiny wormhole to outer margin of beginning leaves, affecting a letter or two of marginal glosses, over opened at a few places, still very good, from the library of John Locke with ink inscriptions, signatures and marginal notations in at least five different hands, (John Locke, Ri. Yolland, Emmanual Bayhind, William Yoo and Riettell). Heritage Book Shop 50th Anniversary Catalogue - 67 2013 $35,000

Association – Riker, Richard

Colden, Cadwallader D. *Memoir... at the Celebration of the Completion of the New York Canals. (and) Appendix... (and) Narrative of the Festivities Observed in Honor of the Completion of the Grand Erie Canal...* New York: W. A. Davis, 1825. 1826. 1825. First edition, 4to., maps, lithographic plates, portraits, complete old marbled boards, rebacked, presentation inscription from Recorder of NY, Richard Riker. M & S Rare Books, Inc. 95 - 258 2013 $2250

Association – Ripley, Edwin

Butler, Frederick *The Farmer's Manual: Being a Plain Practical Treatise on the Art of Husbandry...* Weathersfield: published by the author, 1821. 8vo., text toned and foxed with some waterstaining, still clearly legible, original quarter brown calf over marbled paper backed boards, pieces missing at corners and spine head, front cover torn, binding heavily worn, ownership signature of Edwin B. Ripley, a Connecticut farmer, rare, as is. Jeff Weber Rare Books 169 - 50 2013 $75

Association – Rippiner, Samuel

Wolff, Christian *A Treatise of Algebra, with the Application of It to a Variety of Problems in Arithmetic, to Geometry, Trigonometry and Conic Sections.* printed for A. Bettersworth and C. Hitch, 1739. First edition in English, 8 folding engraved plates, one or two spots or stains, but crisp copy, 8vo. , contemporary unlettered polished calf, double gilt ruled borders on sides, gilt rules on either side of raised bands on backstrip, trifle worn, short crack at top of upper joint, two signatures inside front cover, earlier being that of Chas. Berkeley the other of Saml. Rippiner, Builder, Oundle May 1850, very good.   Blackwell's Rare Books   Sciences - 131   2013   £750

Association – Rizzoli, Hugh

Haymaker, Webb *The Founders of Neurology.* Springfield: Thomas, 1970. 616 pages, illustrations, original binding, worn dust jacket, copy shows some use, from the library of Hugh Rizzoli, M.D., neurosurgeon.   James Tait Goodrich   S74 - 145   2013 $125

Association – Robbins, Mary

Bowles, Paul *Their Heads Are Green Their Hands are Blue.* London: Peter Owen, 1985.   Second British edition, inscribed by author for Mary Robbins, fine in very near fine dust jacket with small nick to rear panel.   Ken Lopez Bookseller   159 - 22   2013 $175

Mrabet, Mohammed *The Lemon.* New York: McGraw Hill, 1972. First American edition, inscribed by author for Mary Robbins, Tangier 14/IV/90, fine in very near fine dust jacket with slight rubbing to spine colors.   Ken Lopez Bookseller   159 - 23   2013 $300

Association – Roberts, Morley

Friel, Brian *To Let.*   London: William Heinemann, 1921. First edition, 8vo., original pale green cloth, spine and upper cover lettered in gilt, spine darkened, pages browned, some very faint soiling to lower cover, otherwise very good, inscribed by author for Morley Roberts.   Maggs Bros. Ltd.   1460 - 316   2013   £50

Association – Roberts, Theodore

Prowse, D. W. *The Newfoundland Guide Book 1905...* London: Bradbury, Agnew & Co. Ltd., 1905. 8vo., beige cloth, frontispiece, folding map, numerous black and white photos, sketches, line drawings, interior very good, author's presentation to Theodore Roberts dated Jan. 1906.   Schooner Books Ltd.   101 - 60   2013 $175

Association – Robinson, F. G.

Bates, Herbert Ernest   1905-1974 *A German Idyll.* Waltham St. Lawrence: The Golden Cockerel Press, 1932. First edition, number 218 of 307 copies signed by author, small 4to., original quarter red leather, patterned cloth, lettered gilt on spine, fine, inscribed by dedicatee, Karl (Charles) Lahr for F. G. Robinson, wood engravings by Lynton Lamb.   Maggs Bros. Ltd.   1460 - 48   2013   £300

Association – Rodes, John

Haydock, Roger *A Collection of Christian Writings, Labours, Travels and Sufferings of that Faithful and Approved Minister...* London: by T. Sowle, 1700. First edition, contemporary calf, very worn, spine shabby, part of front free endpaper torn away, light foxing and occasional browning from the library of Sir John Rodes (1670-1743), with his signature.   Joseph J. Felcone Inc.   Books Printed before 1701 - 49   2013 $300

Association – Roebuck, Wilfred

Goldsmith, Oliver   1794-1861 *The Rising Village and Other Poems.*   Saint John: Mc'Millan, printed by Henry Chubb, Market Square, 1834. 12mo., original dark brow silk with gilt title to spine, spine has outer hinge cracks with small loss of silk cover and bottom of spine is loose, interior very good with half title, small bookplate of Nova Scotia collector Wilfred Roebuck, Truro, Nova Scotia, with small news clipping, book review, attached to first flyleaf.   Schooner Books Ltd.   101 - 11   2013 $1250

Association – Roethhe, Theodore

Char, Rene *Poemes et Prose Choisis de Rene Char.* Paris: Gallimard, 1957. First edition, 8vo., original wrappers, preserved in folding case, inscribed by author for Ted Roethke, wrappers slightly soiled, otherwise excellent. Maggs Bros. Ltd.   1460 - 165   2013   £450

Association – Roethke, Beatrice

Murphy, Richard *The Kick.*   London: Granta, 2002. First edition, 8vo., original black cloth, dust jacket, near fine, inscribed by author for Beatrice Roethke Lushington, the dedicatee was wife of poet Theodore Roethke.   Maggs Bros. Ltd.   1442 - 250   2013   £50

Skelton, Robin *A Valedictory Poem.*   Victoria: privately circulated, 1963. First edition, limited to 100 copies, 8vo., original wrappers, fine, inscribed by author for Beatrice Roethke.   Maggs Bros. Ltd.   1442 - 289   2013   £50

Association – Rogers, Bruce

Targ, William *The Making of the Bruce Rogers World Bible.* Cleveland: World Pub. Co., cop., 1949. First edition, signed by Rogers and A. Colish copy number 10, fine, without slipcase, 4to., illustrations, original red cloth. Howard S. Mott Inc.   262 - 122   2013 $100

Association – Rogers, Nathaniel

Brydges, Egerton *Letters on the Character and Poetical Genius of Lord Byron.* London: Longman &c, 1824. First edition, unobtrusive tear on title repaired with archival tape on verso, contemporary half purple calf, black leather label, slight rubbing, spine faded to brown, armorial bookplate of Dr. Nathaniel Rogers and with "Dr. Rogers" stamped in gilt at tail of spine, Doris Langley Moore's copy with few pencil notes by her.   Jarndyce Antiquarian Booksellers   CCIII - 349   2013   £250

Association – Rolle, Baron

Stevens, John *The History of Portugal...* London: W. Rogers, 1698. First edition, 8vo., table, contemporary brown speckled calf, covers scuffed, good copy, library label of Baron Rolle.   J. & S. L. Bonham Antiquariam Booksellers   Europe - 8419   2013   £500

Association – Roscoe, Will

Marino, Giambattista *L'Adone, Poems.* Amsterdam: 1651. 2 volumes, 12mo. bound in sixes, small marginal tear to V1 volume II, some light browning, few ink splashes but very good, most handsome early 19th century dark blue straight grain morocco, gilt ruled borders, attractive gilt panelled spines decorated with flower head, open circles and small gilt dots, pink endpapers and pastedowns, armorial bookplate of John Barron, early inscription of J. Stirling, alter 19th century bookplate of Alfred Coco of Middle Temple, ownership name of J. Stroud Read, London Nov. 1928, earlier hand notes "Will. Roscoe's Library", all edges gilt. Jarndyce Antiquarian Booksellers   CCV - 191   2013   £620

Association – Rose, E. B.

Scott, Walter   1771-1832 *Miscellaneous Poems.* Edinburgh: printed for Archibald Constable and Co., 1820. First edition, 2nd issue, 235 x 143mm., original publisher's drab paper boards with paper title label on spine, fore and tail edges untrimmed in (rather soiled, scuffed and faded), green linen covered slipcase with red morocco spine label, pencilled ownership inscription of E. B. Rose 62 Burton Crescent", front board detached parts of backstrip missing, spine label rather abraded (with considerable loss of letterpress), isolated spots of light foxing, otherwise fine internally text quite clean fresh and bright.   Phillip J. Pirages   63 - 429   2013 $75

Association – Rose, Gill

Davidoff, Leo *The Normal Encephalogram.* Philadelphia: Lea & Febiger, 1946. Second edition, 1155 engravings, 240 pages, original green cloth very clean tight copy, author's presentation to Gill Rose.   James Tait Goodrich   S74 - 73   2013 $175

Association – Rose, Henry John

Coleridge, Samuel Taylor   1772-1834 *On the Constitution of Church and State, According to the Idea of Each, with Aid Towards a Right Judgment on the Late Catholic Bill...* London: Hurst, Chance and Co., 1830. Second edition, contemporary full calf, gilt, little rubbed, very good, inscribed by author for Rev. (Hugh)James Rose, presentation to Henry John Rose by Coleridge.   Jarndyce Antiquarian Booksellers   CCIII - 553   2013   £2000

Association – Rose, Hugh James

Coleridge, Samuel Taylor   1772-1834 *On the Constitution of Church and State, According to the Idea of Each, with Aid Towards a Right Judgment on the Late Catholic Bill...* London: Hurst, Chance and Co., 1830. Second edition, contemporary full calf, gilt, little rubbed, very good, inscribed by author for Rev. (Hugh)James Rose, presentation to Henry John Rose by Coleridge.   Jarndyce Antiquarian Booksellers   CCIII - 553   2013   £2000

Association – Rosebery, Earl of

Burke, Edmund   1729-1797 *Reflections on the Revolution in France and on the Proceedings in Certain Societies in London Relative to that Event...* London: printed for J. Dodsley, 1790. First edition, first issue, 19th century half sheep over marbled boards, original bluish-gray drab wrappers bound in to front and back, some wear at corners and joints, spine bit scuffed, some occasional pale spotting along top edge, overall very nice, octavo, the copy of William Lee, Bart (presentation inscription) and of Archibald Philip Primrose, 5th Earl of Rosebery, ALS to Rosebery from John Morley tipped in, small Rosebery/Durdans blindstamp on titlepage and page 99, gift inscription, armorial bookplate.   Heritage Book Shop   50th Anniversary Catalogue - 16   2013 $15,000

Jeaffreson, John Cordy *The Real Lord Byron: New Views on the Poet's Life.* London: Hurst & Blackett, 1883. First edition, 2 volumes, half titles, 16 pages ads volume II, original brown cloth, spines lettered in gilt, Durdans bookplate of the Earl of Rosebery very good, attractive copy.   Jarndyce Antiquarian Booksellers   CCIII - 395   2013   £75

Lovelace, Ralph Milbanke, Earl of *Astarte; a Fragment of Truth Concerning George Gordon Byron...* London: printed at the Chiswick Press, 1905. First edition, half title, frontispiece slightly spotted, plates facsimiles, original blue boards, brown cloth spine, paper label slightly chipped, little dulled, Lord Rosebery's copy with letter from Lord Lovelace tipped in, Doris Langley Moore's copy with few pencil notes. Jarndyce Antiquarian Booksellers   CCIII - 108   2013   £85

Association – Rosin, Arnold

Behan, Brendan *The Quare Fellow.* London: Methuen, 1956. First edition, original black cloth, dust jacket slightly nicked and creased at head and tail of spine and at corners, near fine, inscribed by author to artist Arnold Rosin. Maggs Bros. Ltd.   1460 - 71   2013   £1800

Association – Rossier, Charles

Campbell, Thomas   1777-1844 *Gertrude of Wyoming: a Pennsylvania Tale. And Other Poems.* London: Longman &c, 1814. Fifth edition, slightly spotted, 4 page catalog, contemporary full diced calf gilt spine and borders, black leather label, hinges little worn, armorial booklabel of James Hodson, label and signature of Charles Rossier, San Francisco 1942.   Jarndyce Antiquarian Booksellers   CCIII - 466   2013   £35

Association – Rostrevor-Hamilton, George

Arlott, John *Clausentum.* London: Jonathan Cape, 1946. First edition, 8vo. original turquoise boards, dust jacket, excellent copy, jacket lightly browned and with slight wear towards edges, inscribed by author for George Rostrevor-Hamilton.   Maggs Bros. Ltd.   1460 - 18   2013   £125

Association – Rothenstein, William

Douglas, Lord Alfred *The City of the Soul.* London: Grant Richards, 1899. First edition, inscribed by author to artist, William Rothenstein, original vellum backed blue-grey boards with faded gilt title to spine, spine slightly darkened and boards show minor signs of handling, previous owner affixed something to corners of front and rear endpapers with tape and tape has left residue on those pages, tape mark slightly overlaps Rothenstein's name but does not affect its legibility, typical offsetting to endpapers, Rothenstien bookplate, very good, 110 pages, 2 pages ads. The Kelmscott Bookshop   7 - 105   2013 $3250

Association – Rothschild, Barbara

Eliot, Thomas Stearns   1888-1965 *For Lancelot Andrewes. Essays on Style and Order.* London: Faber & Gwyer, 1928. Second impression, 8vo., original blue cloth, printed paper label on spine, inscribed by author for Barbara Rothschild, excellent copy.   Maggs Bros. Ltd.   1460 - 263   2013   £600

Moore, George *Celibate Lives.* London: William Heinemann, 1927. First edition, large 8vo., original quarter brown cloth, printed paper label on spine, excellent copy, light shelfwear to upper cover, inscribed by Arnold and Dorothy Bennett to the future Lady Rothschild, Barbara Hutchinson.   Maggs Bros. Ltd.   1460 - 84   2013   £250

Association – Rouse, Ronald

Hemyng, Bracebridge *Money Marks; or the Sailor Highwayman.* London: George Vickers, circa, 1865. Dark brown binder's cloth, illustrations, from the collection of Ronald Rouse, Norwich, very good.   Jarndyce Antiquarian Booksellers   CCV - 134   2013   £125

Association – Rowe, Jerry

Barker, George *Calamiterror.* London: Faber and Faber, 1937. First edition, 8vo., original green cloth, dust jacket, near fine in slightly rubbed dust jacket, small closed tear at head of spine, inscribed by author for Jerry Rowe.   Maggs Bros. Ltd.   1460 - 36   2013   £50

Association – Rowntree, Arnold

Rowntree, B. Seebohm *Poverty and Progress. A Second Social Survey of York.* London: Longmans, 1941. First edition, very good, original gilt lettered dark blue cloth, dust jacket little worn, inscribed 'a gift from Arnold Rowntree, Ernest Taylor, John Harvey, Oct. 1941'.   Ken Spelman Books Ltd.   73 - 54   2013   £35

Association – Rowse, A. L.

Acton, Harold *Three Extraordinary Ambassadors.* London: Thames and Hudson, 1983. First edition, 8vo., original grey cloth, gilt, dust jacket, inscribed by author for A. L. Rowse, with occasional marginal stress marks, near fine in slightly marked dust jacket.   Maggs Bros. Ltd.   1460 - 6   2013   £150

Association – Roxburghe, Duke of

Lefevre, Raoul *Le Recueil des Histoires de Troyes.* Bruges: William Caxton, 1473. First edition in French, small folio, Lettre batarde, lacking 32 printed leaves and two blanks, early 19th century brown straight grain morocco by Charles Lewis, gilt and blind ruled in geometric patterns, gilt inner dentelles, gilt edges, fine, unrestored, the missing leaves are internal and first and last printed leaves are present from the collection of the Duke of Roxburghe (sale 1812) of the third Earl Spencer (sale 1823), John Dent, with his notes (sale 1827), P. A. Hanrott (sale 1834) the Earl of Ashburnham (sale 1897); Richard Bennett with his bookplate and John Pierpont Morgan with his bookplate and shelfmark.   Heritage Book Shop   50th Anniversary Catalogue - 62   2013 $950,000

Association – Roy, Ralph Lord

Shaw, J. Beverly F. *The Negro in the History of Methodism.* Nashville: Parthenon Press, 1954. First edition, small owner stamp bottom textblock and on copyright page, bookplate of author Ralph Lord Roy, else near fine in very good dust jacket with small chips at spine ends, scarce in this condition.   Between the Covers Rare Books, Inc. 165 - 261   2013 $200

Association – Royse, F.

Defoe, Daniel *The Life and Adventures of Robinson Crusoe.* printed for C. Cooke, 1793. First Cooke edition, 3 volumes, 6 engraved plates (3 each in volumes i and ii, none in iii), woodcut device on titlepages and woodcut tailpiece, last page of volume ii with two small sections of text adhering to flyleaf, 12mo., original tree sheep, gilt ruled compartments on spine, red lettering piece on volume iii, missing from i and ii, numbered gilt direct, joints cracked, corners worn, ownership inscription of F. Royse dated 1793, fair.   Blackwell's Rare Books   B174 - 44   2013   £250

Association – Rudmose-Brown

Scoresby, William *Journal of a Voyage to the Northern Whale Fishery...* Edinburgh: 1823. First edition, one large and one other folding map, 6 engraved plates, further illustrations in text, 8vo. contemporary half calf marbled boards, upper joint repaired, occasional very light browning as usual, with distinctive library stamp of Rudmose-Brown.   Maggs Bros. Ltd.   1467 - 139   2013   £850

Association – Rummler, Fritz

Le Carre, John 1931- *Call for the Dead.* London: Hodder & Stoughton, 1992. 8vo., pages 144, original black boards, backstrip gilt lettered, dust jacket, fine, inscribed by author for his secretary, Fritz Rummler. Blackwell's Rare Books   172 - 206   2013   £235

Le Carre, John 1931- *The Honourable Schoolboy.* London: Hodder & Stoughton, 1990. Lamplighter edition, 8vo., original black boards, backstrip gilt lettered, endpapers, final leaf of text and edges foxed, waterstaining faintly to tail of covers and interior of dust jacket, good, inscribed by author for his secretary Fritz Rummler.   Blackwell's Rare Books   172 - 207   2013   £200

Le Carre, John 1931- *A Small Town in Germany.* London: Hodder & Stoughton, 1991. Lamplighter edition, 8vo., original black boards, backstrip gilt lettered, foxing to edges, dust jacket, very good, inscribed by author for his secretary Fritz Rummler.   Blackwell's Rare Books   172 - 210   2013   £200

Association – Ruskin, John

Byron, George Gordon Noel, 6th Baron 1788-1824 *Letters and Journals of Lord Byron; With Notices of His Life.* London: John Murray, 1833. Third edition, 3 volumes, frontispiece volumes I and III, plates, volume II and III lacking titlepages, volume II lacking frontispiece, expertly recased in original sand grained purple cloth, spines lettered gilt, borders in blind, spines uniformly faded to brown, slightly marked, "From Hugh Walpole's library with his bookplate, formerly the copy of John Ruskin with his bookplate and marginal notes.   Jarndyce Antiquarian Booksellers   CCIII - 324   2013   £850

Association – Russell, Adah

Blunt, Wilfrid Scawen *The Poetical Works of Wilfrid Scawen Blunt.* London: Macmillan, 1914. 2 volumes, original dark blue cloth, excellent set, spine of second volume slightly faded, inscribed by author for Adah Russell, loosely inserted are two small photos of Blunt in Arab dress and manuscript poem in his hand dated Aug. 5 1900. Maggs Bros. Ltd.   1460 - 121   2013   £650

Association – Russell, Edward

Jayne, Caroline Furness *String Figures.* New York: Charles Scribner's Sons, 1906. First edition, small 4to., original blue cloth gilt, neatly recased, 867 figures, few marginal pencil lines to introduction, otherwise excellent copy, inscribed by author to Sir Edward Russell dated 1906.   R. F. G. Hollett & Son   Children's Books - 304   2013   £250

Association – Russell, Jean Stewart

Eliot, George, Pseud. 1819-1880 *Romola.* London: Smith Elder and Co., 1880. One of 1000 copies (this being #57), 2 volumes, 265 x 180mm., remarkable contemporary honey brown crushed morocco by Fazakerley (stamp signed on front turn-in), upper cover of one volume with ornate gilt monogram of "MMK", the other front cover with monogram of "NDK", spines with raised bands and gilt titling, splendid brown morocco doublures elaborately tooled in gilt featuring scalloped French fillet frame incorporating large floral cornerpieces and enclosing exuberantly swirling flowering vines emerging from a Greek urn at foot, brown watered silk endleaves, edges gilt and ornately gauffered in bold strapwork pattern on stippled ground, each volume with 3 lovely and delicate fore-edge paintings the ones at head and tail of each fore-edge being lozenge-shaped views (measuring approximately 25 x 30 mm across) and larger rectangular painting at center (measuring approximately 80 x 45mm), all depicting finely painted scenes from book; 24 engraved plates, mounted plates after Sir Frederick Leighton, plus 13 smaller engravings mounted in text as called for, flyleaf of each volume with lovely calligraphic manuscript inscription of quote from book, half title of volume 1 with ink ownership inscription of Jean Stewart Russell dated 1902; spine faintly and evenly sunned, plates bit spotted (from mounting glue?), otherwise superb copy, text clean, fresh and bright, margins especially ample, bindings lustrous and unworn, fore edges richly painted and glittering with particularly bright gold. Phillip J. Pirages 61 - 78 2013 $16,000

Association – Ruston-Harrison, C. W.

Cumbria Parish Registers *Stanwix: the Marriage Register of Stanwix.* W. P W. Phillimore & Co., n.d., 56 pages, original cloth, paper label, endpapers little spotted, inscribed on label "Transcriber's Copy" (C. W. Ruston-Harrison). R. F. G. Hollett & Son Lake District & Cumbria - 363 2013 £85

Association – Ruyters, Andre

Gheon, Henri *Jeux et Miracles pour la Peuple Fidele.* Paris: Editions de la revue des Jeunes, 1922. First edition, later cloth, red morocco label to spine, original wrappers bound in, cloth slightly spotted, otherwise excellent, inscribed by author for Andre Ruyters. Maggs Bros. Ltd. 1460 - 334 2013 £275

Association – Ryan, Marion

Golding, Louis *Magnolia Street.* London: Victor Gollancz, 1932. First edition, 8vo., original black cloth, excellent copy, dust jacket nicked and browned, inscribed by author for Marion Ryan. Maggs Bros. Ltd. 1460 - 347 2013 £175

Association – Rysbrooke, J. Wolus

Doherty, Hugh *The Discovery; or the Mysterious Separation of Hugh Doherty, Esq. and Ann His Wife.* London: sold at no. 12, Temple Place &c, 1807. Third edition, 12mo., illustrations, slight spotting and occasional small marginal tears, contemporary marbled boards, later tan calf spine, gilt ands and compartments, maroon morocco label, signature of author Hugh Doherty on title, very slightly trimmed through, additional signature of J. Wolus, Rysbrooke, 1878, recent bookplate of Peter Haining. Jarndyce Antiquarian Booksellers CCV - 93 2013 £580

Association – Sachs

Bacon, Francis Viscount St. Albans 1561-1626 *The Twoo Bookes of Francis Bacon, of the Proficience and Advancement of Learning, Divine and Humane.* London: for Henri Thomes, 1605. First edition, 4to., lacks final blank 3H2 and, as always, the rare two leaves of errata at end, late 18th century half calf and marbled boards, (extremities of boards worn), very skilfully and imperceptively rebacked retaining entire original spine, small worm trail in bottom margin of quires 2D-2F, occasional minor marginalia in early hand, else lovely copy, early signature of Row'd Weatherald and signature of Horatio Carlyon, 1861, Sachs bookplate and modern leather book label, calf backed clamshell box. Joseph J. Felcone Inc. Books Printed before 1701 - 5 2013 $7500

Association – Sackville-West, Victoria

Bonaparte, Napoleon *Maximes de Napoleon.* London: Arthur L. Humphreys, 1903. 164 x 127mm., appealing russet crushed morocco, covers with gilt rule border and blind tooled three leaf extensions from raised bands, spine gilt in compartments with either an "N" and coronet or bee centerpiece, turn-ins with multiple gilt rules, all edges gilt, engraved bookplate of Victoria Sackville West, just hint of rubbing to joints, scattered freckling, dark spots on boards, minor offsetting on free endpapers from turn-ins, isolated spots of foxing or faint marginal stains, otherwise excellent copy, clean, fresh , bright in binding with very few signs of wear. Phillip J. Pirages 63 - 418 2013 $200

Brassey, Thomas, Lord *Gleanings . I. A. Christmas Card for 1899.* Melbourne: printed for private circulation by Sands & McDougall Ltd., 1899. One volume only, of two, pleasing contemporary crimson crushed morocco for Hatchards of Piccadiilly (stamp signed), covers with gilt rule border, raised bands, spine compartments with central gilt lily, gilt ruled turn-ins, marbled endpapers, all edges gilt, bookplate of V(ictoria) Sackville West, hint of uniform darkening to spine just slightest wear to joints and extremities, several pages with marginal pencil markings, but never any words, otherwise fine, especially fresh and clean inside and out. Phillip J. Pirages 63 - 414 2013 $150

Bret, Antoine *Ninon De Lenclos.* London: Arthur L. Humphreys, 1904. 214 x 154mm., attractive contemporary russet morocco in Arts and Crafts style, covers with frame of plain gilt rules and oak leaves and dots at intersections of lines, gilt titling on upper cover, raised bands, spine gilt in double ruled compartments with three large gilt dots at each corner connected by lines of tiny dots, gilt ruled turn-ins, all edges gilt, engraved bookplate of Victoria Sackville West, with best wishes from Bob Capel Xmas 1904, black and white photo portrait of Ninon de Lenclos tipped onto verso of half title, with identifying inscription in Victoria Sackville-West's hand, spine bit sunned, little mild soiling at boards, extremities lightly rubbed, hint of moisture here and there to tail edge margin, otherwise excellent, binding sound, text unusually bright clean and fresh.   Phillip J. Pirages   63 - 417   2013 $250

Browning, Robert   1812-1889 *Poems.* London: George Bell & sons, 1904. 205 x 138mm., excellent contemporary brick red crushed morocco for Hatchards of Piccadilly (stamp signed), covers with unusual asymmetrical frame combining geometrical gilt rules with twisting black strapwork, central panel with two interlocked circles, one containing a "V", the other and "S", and both surmounted by a coronet, raised bands, spine with simple gilt ruled compartments, turn-ins with gilt fillets, marbled endpapers, top edge gilt, numerous head and tailpieces, vignettes in text, 21 full page wood engravings by Byam Shaw; bookplate of Victoria Sackville-West, black and white photo of Browning tipped onto verso of front free endpaper, labelled apparently in Lady Sackville's hand, slight wear to joints, just breath of foxing in couple of places, otherwise fresh and clean, inside and out.   Phillip J. Pirages   63 - 412   2013 $550

Christina, Queen of Sweden *Pensees De Christine, Reine de Suede.* Stockholm: P. A. Norstedt & Soners Forlag, 1906. One of 42 copies (this #42), 195 x 129mm., original dark blue calf, upper cover with elegant gilt floral frame, floral cornerpieces and royal arms at center lower cover with entwined "RS" , flat spine with gilt titling and coat of arms, gilt turn-ins, marbled endpapers, all edges gilt, front pastedown with engraved bookplate of Victoria Sackville, Knole, occasional pencilled underlinings, spine somewhat faded, joints and extemities rather rubbed, half a dozen small scratches to spine, top inch of rear board bit faded, once handsome binding still sound, very fine internally.   Phillip J. Pirages   63 - 415   2013 $400

Douglas, Robert *Sophie Arnould.* Paris: C. H. Carrington, 1898. One of 425 copies, this #8, 238 x 154mm., titlepage vignette, engraved vignettes at beginning and end of text, allegorical frontispiece and 3 full page plates by Adolphe Lalauze, very pretty contemporary tan crushed morocco, gilt and inlaid, covers with border of leafy tools and French fillets, central panel formed by a delicate frame of plain and dotted rules punctuated by leafy ornaments, cornerpieces of inlaid black morocco inside wreath of gilt leaves topped by tulip, central panel with palmette and garland cornerpieces accented with floral tools, upper cover with gilt titling at center, flat spine gilt in one long compartment with multiple ruled frame and central inlaid black morocco dot with floral extensions terminating at head and tail with ornate leaf design, lavishly gilt wide inner dentelles, marbled endpapers, all edges gilt, original slightly browned printed paper wrappers bound in, elaborate - apparently original - pen, ink and wash scenic bookplate of Victoria Sackville-West with handwritten note (by her?) tipped in at front stating bookplate design was based on Lalauze's frontispiece (as is apparent), thin cracks alongside top inch of joints, otherwise only trivial defects, very attractive, luxurious paper clean, fresh and bright, margins very wide, handsome binding lustrous and generally well preserved.   Phillip J. Pirages   61 - 110   2013 $1250

Doyle, Arthur Conan   1859-1930 *The Memoirs of Sherlock Holmes.* London: Smith, Elder & Co., 1912. New edition, 8vo., original red cloth lettered in gilt, bookplate of Victoria Sackville of Knole and neat inscription to her by author, excellent copy.   Maggs Bros. Ltd.   1460 - 245   2013   £750

Doyle, Arthur Conan   1859-1930 *The Stark Munro Letters.* London: Longmans Green and Co., 1909. New impression, 8vo., original brown cloth, frontispiece by Alice Barber Stephens, pictorial titlepage, excellent copy, spine slightly faded, inscribed by author to Lady Sackville, Victoria Sackville-West.   Maggs Bros. Ltd.   1460 - 247   2013   £850

Goncourt, Edmond *La Femme Ali Dix-Huitieme Siecle.* Paris: Bibliotheque-Charpentier, 1903. 183 x 116mm., pleasing contemporary green morocco, covers with double gilt rule border, upper over with gilt titling, spine gilt in compartments with central floral spring and curling floral vine cornerpieces, turn-ins densely gilt, snakeskin patterned green endpapers, all edges gilt, engraved bookplate of Victoria Sackville West, spine uniformly sunned to pleasing light brown, leaves somewhat browned because of inferior paper stock, few tear of no consequence, one repaired, otherwise excellent, few signs of use.   Phillip J. Pirages   63 - 416   2013 $175

Association – Sainthill

Sainthill, Richard *The Old Countess of Desmond: an Inquiry.* Private printing, 1861-1863. 2 volumes, 76 + 105 pages, 2 plates, 3 pedigrees, very good, 2 ALS's from Caulfield, 1 from Sainthill, many cuttings. C. P. Hyland 261 - 766 2013 £350

Association – Saintsbury, George

Prior, Matthew 1664-1721 *Selected Poems of Matthew Prior.* London: Kegan Paul, Trench & Co., 1889. 12mo., frontispiece, original burgundy cloth, very good, spine faded, some slight wear to head and tail of spine, inscribed by Austin Dobson to French scholar and wine writer George Saintsbury. Maggs Bros. Ltd. 1460 - 230 2013 £150

Association – Sala, George Augustus

Cervantes Saavedra, Miguel De 1547-1616 *Don Quixote De La Mancha.* London: Charles Daly, 1842. 8vo., 2 parts bound in single volume, frontispiece and engraved titlepage pus 30 engraved plates, all by Sir John Gilbert, full calf (rubbed and scuffed, front cover separate), nice, clean copy, this copy belonged to English journalist George Augustus Sala with his ownership signature at top of titlepage in his neat hand. Second Life Books Inc. 183 - 66 2013 $95

Association – Salomons, David

Uzanne, Octave *Son Altesse, La Femme.* Paris: A. Quantin, 1885. First edition, one of 100 special large paper copies on Japon, 292 x 216mm, vignette on title, small illustrations or vignettes on 50 text pages, 11 vignette borders or headpieces (3 of them in color, 10 of them in one or two extra states) and 10 color plates, each in two states (before and after letters), beautifully and elaborately gilt contemporary blue-gray crushed morocco by Zaehnsdorf (signed on front turn-in), covers framed with single rule around very broad and intricate floral border of many leaves, blossoms and tendrils enclosing central field of rows of alternating flower and small stars, raised bands, spine compartments similarly decorated, very handsome densely gilt inner dentelles, marbled endpapers, top edge gilt, other edges untrimmed, original paper and silk materials bound in; armorial bookplate of Sir David Salomons, spine slightly and uniformly faded, one inch cut in lower margin of one leaf, else extremely fine and beautifully bound set. Phillip J. Pirages 61 - 135 2013 $2500

Association – Sanderson, Emma

Massey, Gerald *Robert Burns: a Centenary Song and Other Lyrics.* London: W. Kent & Co. (late D. Bogue), 1859. First edition, 2 pages ads, contemporary full purple morocco blocked and lettered gilt, spine and edges rubbed and worn, initial blank signed Emma Sanderson June 1859, good, sound copy. Jarndyce Antiquarian Booksellers CCIII - 63 2013 £65

Association – Sandford, Elizabeth Anne

Austen, Jane 1775-1817 *Emma: a Novel.* London: John Murray, 1816. First edition, 3 volumes, 12mo., nick to upper margin of title, volume I, bound without half titles, contemporary half brown calf, gilt bands, compartments in blind, light brown morocco labels, some slight rubbing to extremities, but very nice, inscription "Elizabeth Anne Sandford with affectionate love from her Aunt, Anne Anderton, Wake Green Dec. 29, 1869". Jarndyce Antiquarian Booksellers CCV - 12 2013 £15,000

Association – Sands, Dorothy

Coward, Noel 1899-1973 *Quadrille.* London: Heinemann, 1952. First edition, 8vo., 116 pages, signed by 17 members of the English cast and producer Jack Wilson and by Lynn Fontann and Alfred Lunt, inscribed by author to Dorothy Sands (Octavia in NY production). Second Life Books Inc. 183 - 83 2013 $500

Association – Sanford, Donn

Adomeit, Ruth E. *Miniature Book Collector. Volume I Nos. 1-4; Volume 2, Nos. 1-4 Complete, plus index.* Worcester: Achille J. St. Onge, 1960-1963. Complete run, 10.1 x 8.5 cm., later full leather with original paper wrappers bound in, 16 16, 16, 16, 72, 40 pages, from the collection of Donn W. Sanford. Oak Knoll Books 303 - 3 2013 $350

Adomeit, Ruth E. *Three Centuries of Thumb Bibles: a Checklist.* New York: Garlard Publishing, 1980. First edition, 8vo., cloth, xl, 390 pages, from the collection of Donn W. Sanford. Oak Knoll Books 303 - 4 2013 $152

Albert Schloss's Bijou Almanacs 1839-1843. London: Nattali & Maurice, 1969. Limited to 150 numbered copies, 4to., 19, (33) pages with plate, 4to., quarter vellum, paper covered boards, title gilt stamped on spine, dust jacket, impressions tissue guard, dust jacket chipped along edges, from the collection of Donn W. Sanford. Oak Knoll Books 303 - 2 2013 $125

Albert Schloss's Bijou Almanacs 1839-1843. London: Nattali & Maurice, 1969. Limited to 150 numbered copies, one of 25 copies, nos. 1-25 include a full set of impressions direct from plates, of which this copy is such, 4to., quarter vellum, paper covered boards, title gilt stamped on spine, dust jacket, 19, (33) pages, with plates, impressions tissue guarded, dust jacket torn at front bottom along spine and along back bottom, pencilled notation on front pastedown about this special limited edition; from the collection of Donn W. Sanford.   Oak Knoll Books   303 - 1   2013 $325

Andrews, William Loring   *Sextodecimos et Infra.*   New York: Charles Scribner's Sons, 1899. First edition, limited to 152 copies, this one of 140 printed on English handmade plate paper by Gilliss Press, 8vo., 27 illustrations of miniature books, 14 of which are in full color, stiff paper wrappers, outer dust jacket, extremely scarce, small tears along bottom and top of hinges of dust jacket, from the library of De Witt Miller with his ink inscription, also from the library of noted miniature collector Kathryn Rickard with her bookplate, with additional bookplate on front free endpaper, number in ink in corner of front free endpaper, paper slipcase not present, scarce; from the collection of Donn W. Sanford. Oak Knoll Books   303 - 7   2013 $450

Arkwright His Counterblast to an Effusion Entitled: Pamflet on the Four Basic Dialects of Pig-Latin. Tujunga (Los Angeles): William M. Cheney, 1951.   7.7 x 5cm., stiff paper wrappers, label on front wrapper, from the collection of Donn W. Sanford.   Oak Knoll Books   303 - 94   2013 $150

Aungerville, Richard   1281-1345   *Philobiblon.*   Zuilichem: Catharijne Press, 1992. Experimental miniature book limited to only 25 unnumbered copies, 5.8 x 4.1 cm., stiff paper wrappers, 2 illustrations, from the collection of Donn W. Sanford.   Oak Knoll Books   303 - 77   2013 $150

Avery, Samuel P.   *A Short List of Microscopic Books in the Library of the Grolier Club Mostly Presented by Samuel P. Avery.*   New York: Grolier Club, 1911. First edition, 16mo., paper wrappers, well preserved, from the collection of Donn W. Sanford.   Oak Knoll Books   303 - 6   2013 $75

Baker, Piet D.   *The Young Stork's Baedeker, Travel Guide with Lexicon.* Zuilichem: Catharijne Press, 1998. Limited to 190 copies, this one of 15 lettered copies bound thus and has the second volume which is not in original edition, 6.7 x 4.2 cm., paper covered boards, slipcase, illustrations, including foldout map, bound by Luce Thurkow, from the collection of Donn W. Sanford.   Oak Knoll Books   303 - 75   2013 $275

Bewick, Thomas   1753-1828   *Vignettes from Birds, Quadrupeds and Fables.*   Chicago: Black Cat Press, 1971. Limited to 200 copies, 6.8 x 5.5 cm., leather, author's surname gilt stamped on spine, full name gilt stamped on front board, unpaginated, included is one of the actual Bewick wood blocks that was used to print illustration on page 8, also includes letter dated May 25 2004 from Bill Hesterberg of Hesterberg Press of Evanston to Donn Sanford, loose pages 5 and 8 of text laid in.   Oak Knoll Books   303 - 50   2013 $750

Bewick, Thomas   1753-1828   *Vignettes from Birds, Quadrupeds and Fables.*   Chicago: Black Cat Press, 1971. Limited to 200 copies, 6.8 x 5.5cm., full leather, author's surname gilt stamped on spine, full name gilt stamped on front board, unpaginated, illustrations printed from original woodblocks by R. Hunter Middleton, from the collection of Donn W. Sanford.   Oak Knoll Books   303 - 49   2013 $275

Bible. English - 1896   *The Holy Bible.*   Glasgow: David Bryce and Son, n.d, but, 1896. 4.5 x 3.3 cm., with frontispiece and illustrations, pocket on back pastedown for magnifying glass, no indication of that in this copy, original leather, title stamped on spine, frontispiece and titlepage folded, from the collection of Donn W. Sanford.   Oak Knoll Books   303 - 74   2013 $400

Bible. English - 1985   *The Song of Songs by Solomon.* Ultrecht: Catharijne Press, 1985. Limited to 167 copies, this one of 150 numbered trade copies, 6.2 x 4.3cm. paper covered boards stamped in gilt, design and initials by Bram de Does, copperplate engraving by Bertril Schmull and binding and hand coloring by Luce Thurkow, engraving signed and numbered in pencil, large initial letters hand colored, miniature bookplate of Kathryn Rickard, from the collection of Donn W. Sanford.   Oak Knoll Books   303 - 88   2013 $125

Blumenthal, Walter Hart   *Book Gluttons and Book Gourmets.*   Chicago: Black Cat Press, 1961.   Limited to 300 copies, 6.7 x 5.3cm., full leather, 84, (1) pages, from the collection of Donn W. Sanford.   Oak Knoll Books   303 - 51   2013 $150

Blumenthal, Walter Hart   *Formats and Foibles, a few Books Which Might Be Called Curious.* Worcester: Achille J. St. Onge, 1956. Limited to 300 copies, 6 x 4.9 cm., printed on Barcham Green's handmade paper, bound by Sangorski & Sutcliffe, full red morocco, all edges gilt, from the collection of Donn W. Sanford.   Oak Knoll Books   303 - 26   2013 $175

Bondy, Louis W. *Small is Beautiful.* Morro Bay: Miniature Book Society, 1987. Limited to 400 copies, printed at Tabula Rasa Press, 6.5 x 6 cm., cloth with gilt lettering on front cover and gilt design on spine, signed by author and by Francis Weber, from the collection of Donn W. Sanford. Oak Knoll Books   303 - 5   2013 $150

Bonnobergers, Ludwig *Betbuechlein.* Vienna: K. K. Hofibliothek, 1912. 32mo., bound in buff cloth with interwoven silver threads, edges gilt, with two indented circles on each edge housed in scooped out compartment at back of a parent volume, boards of miniature facsimile volume partly detached at spine, boards of larger volume lightly scuffed at edges, from the collection of Donn W. Sanford. Oak Knoll Books   303 - 63   2013 $850

Bradbury, Robert C. *Antique United States Miniature Books 1690-1900.* North Clarendon: Microbibliophile, 2001. Limited to 1000 copies, 8vo., 13 pages fo illustrations, cloth, dust jacket, from the collection of Donn W. Sanford. Oak Knoll Books   303 - 8   2013 $150

Carter, Yolanda *Amistad Courier, a Newsletter About Miniature Books.* Austin: Yolanda Carter of Amistad press, 1984. Reprint, contains all 24 issues, includes 9 supplements, 5 x 11 inch unbound sheets in 9.75 x 11.75 inch three ring notebook with plastic covered boards, from the collection of Donn W. Sanford. Oak Knoll Books   303 - 12   2013 $125

Cervantes Saavedra, Miguel De   1547-1616 *The Ingenious Gentleman Don Quixote De La Mancha Chapter VIII.* 's-Hertogenbosch: Catharijne Press, 2001. Limited to 170 copies, of which this is one of the 20 lettered copies bound thus with an extra wood engraving, printed in a different color, 7 x 4.2cm., paper covered boards, slipcase, illustrations on both covers, 47 pages, frontispiece numbered and signed by the artist Gerard Gaudaen, bound by Luce Thurkow, from the collection of Donn W. Sanford. Oak Knoll Books   303 - 76   2013 $300

Chandler, John Greene *The Remarkable History of Chicken Little.* Boston: A. & D. Bromer, 1979. Limited to 85 numbered copies of which 50 are for sale,, 3.1 x 2.5cm., marbled paper covered boards, paper cover label (24) pages, printed letterpress by Darrell Hyder with hand colored initial letter miniature bookplate of Kalman Levitan, from the collection of Donn W. Sanford. Oak Knoll Books   303 - 67   2013 $175

Classics Written by the Goddess of Mercy. Tokyo: National Treasure, n.d., 9.4 x 3.8cm., scroll, housed in wooden box bound with ribbon, unpaginated, from the collection of Donn W. Sanford. Oak Knoll Books   303 - 97   2013 $250

Clemens, Samuel Langhorne   1835-1910 *Mark Twain Compliments the President's Wife.* Boston: Anne & David Bromer, 1984. Limited to 200 numbered copies signed by printer, this one of 150 trade copies, 5. x 4.6 cm., brown cloth, paper cover label inset onto front cover, printed letterpress by Rez' Lignen at his Poote Press, from the collection of Donn W. Sanford. Oak Knoll Books   303 - 68   2013 $100

Clemens, Samuel Langhorne   1835-1910 *Nicodemus Dodge.* San Diego: Ash Ranch Press, 1989. Limited to 52 copies, 26 black bonded leather, gold stamped and numbered, deluxe edition of 26 bound in special printed and goldstamped paper over boards with blue bonded leather spine and slipcase, and matching endpapers, signed by publisher, Don Hildreth, this is a deluxe copy, from the collection of Donn W. Sanford. Oak Knoll Books   303 - 40   2013 $275

Codex Argenteus. Uppsala: Bibliothecae R. Univ. Upsaliensis, n.d. but, 1959. 3.5 x 3cm., silver case with clasps, text loosely inserted, unpaginated, from the collection of Donn W. Sanford. Oak Knoll Books   303 - 98   2013 $350

Doyle, Arthur Conan   1859-1930 *A Case of Identity.* Kokie: Black Cat Press, 1984. Limited to 249 copies, signed by producer, 6.1 x 4.5 cm., leather, title gilt stamped on spine, decoration gilt stamped on front cover, marbled endpapers, miniature bookplate of Kathryn Rickard, from the collection of Donn W. Sanford. Oak Knoll Books   303 - 52   2013 $125

Doyle, Arthur Conan   1859-1930 *A Case of Identity.* Sacramento: Press of Arden Park, 1987. Limited to 120 numbered copies signed by Budd Westreich, 5.8 x 7.2 cm., cloth, title gilt stamped on spine, dust jacket, illustrations in text and on endpapers, with miniature bookplate of Kathryn Rickard, from the collection of Donn W. Sanford. Oak Knoll Books   303 - 34   2013 $100

Doyle, Arthur Conan   1859-1930 *A Scadal in Bohemia.* Skokie: Black Cat Press, 1984. Limited to 240 copies signed by producer, 6.1 x 4.5 cm., cloth, title stamped on spine, decoration gilt stamped on front cover, binding by Lariviere, miniature bookplate of Kathryn Rickard, from the collection of Donn W. Sanford. Oak Knoll Books   303 - 53   2013 $125

Doyle, Arthur Conan   1859-1930 *The Red-Headed League.* Sacramento: Press of Arden Park, 1985. Limited to 120 copies signed by Budd Westreich, 5.8 x 7.2 cm., cloth, title gilt stamped on spine, dust jacket, illustrated endpapers, illustrations, from the collection of Donn W. Sanford, miniature bookplate of Kathryn Rickard. Oak Knoll Books   303 - 35   2013 $100

Dutch Windmills. Zuilichem: Catharijne Press, 1993. Limited to 199 copies, of which this is one of 175 numbered copies, 6 x 4.7 cm., brown paper covered boards, paper spine label, picture of a windmill mounted on front cover, illustrations, from the collection of Donn W. Sanford.   Oak Knoll Books   303 - 78   2013 $100

Edlefsen, David   *The Mystery of the Magic Box: an Open and Shut Case.*   Anchorage: Anchorage Museum of History and Art, n.d. but, 1995.   Square miniature, 8.5 x 8.5cm., text housed in paper covered box, laid in insert signed "Ed", color illustrations with descriptive text, from the collection of Donn W. Sanford.   Oak Knoll Books   303 - 33   2013 $125

Engelbreit, Mary   *Book.*   San Diego: Ash Ranch Press, 1990.   Limited to 100 copies, 24 with jewelled onlay on front board, of which this copy is one, 5 x 3 cm., leather, jewelled onlay on front board, title gilt stamped on spine, marbled endpapers, from the collection of Donn W. Sanford.   Oak Knoll Books   303 - 37   2013 $100

Favorsky, V.   *Miniature Woodcuts.*   Leningrad: Aurora Art Pub., 1979.   6 x 7 cm., cloth, title gilt stamped on spine, initial gilt stamped on front boards, slipcase, unpaginated, 3 volumes, illustrations in black and white, inscribed on dust jacket to Margaret and Ward Schori, bottom and top of slipcase missing, slipcase worn at edges, from the collection of Donn W. Sanford.   Oak Knoll Books   303 - 42   2013 $225

Florilegium, a Collection of Flower initials designed by Maurice Dubrene.   Utrecht: Catharijne Press, 1988. Limited to 168 copies,, this one of the 15 lettered copies bound thus and having initial heightened in gold, full color floral alphabet, 6.2 x 4 cm., full green suede with brown leather cover label, enclosed in slipcase with leather pull-off spine covering, not paginated, from the collection of Donn W. Sanford.   Oak Knoll Books   303 - 81   2013 $450

Forgue, Norman W.   *Bibliography of Miniature Books and Ephemera 1961-1977.* Chicago: Skokie: Black Cat Press, 1977.   Limited to 240 copies, 2 volumes, leather, title gilt stamped on spine, press mark gilt stamped on front board, decorated endpapers, marbled slipcase, from the collection of Donn W. Sanford.   Oak Knoll Books   303 - 54   2013 $125

Freyer, Kurt   *Mikrobiblion: Das Buch Von Den Kleinen Buchem.*   Berlin: Horodisch & Marx, 1929. Limited to 426 numbered copies, 10.5 x 7.3 cm., full parchment, title hand lettered on front board, fore-edge uncut, text in German, with miniature bookplate of Kathryn Rickard, from the collection of Donn W. Sanford.   Oak Knoll Books   303 - 15   2013 $550

Gorey, Edward   *Q. R. V.*   Boston: Anne & David Bromer, 1989.   Limited to 400 numbered copies signed by Gorey, 3.2 x 3.8 cm., decorated paper covered boards, paper cover label, 29 Gorey illustrations in black and white, bound by Barbara Blumenthal, from the collection of Donn W. Sanford.   Oak Knoll Books   303 - 69   2013 $725

H., B.   *The Twelve Months by B. H.*   Zuilichem: Catharijne Press, 1990.   Limited to 165 copies, this one of the 150 numbered trade copies, bound by Gus Thurkow and hand coloring by Luc Thurkow, each month with hand colored scene, 4.5 x 6.2cm., paper covered boards with color illustration on front cover, miniature bookplate of Kathryn Rickard, from the collection of Donn W. Sanford.   Oak Knoll Books   303 - 90   2013 $125

Hanson, Robert   *The Microbibliophile, a Bi-Monthly Review of Literature Concerning Miniature Books.* Mattituck/Venice: Robert F. Hanson, 1977-2005.   Small 4to. newsletter and small 8vo. magazine, self wrappers and stiff paper wrappers, 10-15 pages each, consecutive run of 162 issues, color photos tipped to cover of each issue in magazine format starting with volume 4, from the collection of Donn W. Sanford.   Oak Knoll Books   303 - 16   2013 $650

He is Nothing but a Little Boy.   Skokie: Black Cat Press, 1980.   Limited to 240 copies, 2 x 1.8 cm., cloth, title gilt stamped on spine, decoration gilt stamped on front cover, frontispiece, illustrations by Barbara Raheb, from the collection of Donn W. Sanford.   Oak Knoll Books   303 - 55   2013 $225

Henderson, James D.   *Lilliputian Newspapers.* Worcester: Achille J. St. Onge, 1936.   First edition, limited to 1000 copies. tall 12mo., 95 pages, cloth backed boards, leather spine label, top edge gilt, slipcase, number of facsimiles in pocket in back of book, very fine, from the collection of Donn W. Sanford.   Oak Knoll Books   303 - 17   2013 $275

Henderson, James D.   *Miniature Books.*   Leipzig: Tondeur & Sauberlich, 1930. Limited to 260 numbered copies, 16mo., limp leather, covers rubbed, miniature bookplate of Kathryn Rickard, from the collection of Donn W. Sanford.   Oak Knoll Books   303 - 18   2013 $300

Hildreth, Don   *Tiny Tome/Tomo Minisculo.*   San Diego: Ash Ranch Press, 1991. Limited to 126 copies, 26 lettered and signed, foldout illustration, 5 x 3.5 cm., leather, title gilt stamped on spine, mounted metal teddy bear on both boards, slipcase, 40 pages, from the collection of Donn W. Sanford.   Oak Knoll Books   303 - 38   2013 $200

Hines, Laurence *Mary, Queen of Scots.* San Diego: Ash Ranch Press, 1990. Limited to 33 copies, 26 lettered and 7 state proofs, all signed by author and printer on colophon, this is a lettered copy, frontispieces on both sides, leather, 5.7 x 8cm., brass hinges and studs, purple tinted edges, embossed boards, gilt slipcase with title gilt stamped on signed, included is prospectus limited to 225 copies, illustrations, stiff paper wrappers, front wrapper illustrated with gilt seal of Queen Mary, from the collection of Donn W. Sanford. Oak Knoll Books   303 - 39   2013 $300

Horatius Flaccus, Quintus *Carmina Sapphica.* Boston: Anne & David Bromer, 1983. Limited to 150 copies, printed by Linnea Gentry using original plates of Ashendene Press edition from 1923, c.5 x 2.6 cm., full morocco with gilt fillets, two raised bands, inserted in tray in larger cloth case with leather spine, which also holds prospectus, in specially made slipcase holding the miniature book, miniature bookplate of Kathryn rickard, binding by David Bourbeau, from the collection of Donn W. Sanford.   Oak Knoll Books   303 - 71   2013 $450

In Praise of the Virtuous Woman. Zuilichem: Catharijne Press, 1994. Limited to 193 copies, this one of 15 lettered copies, Hebrew characters heightened in gold, 6 x 4cm., white paper covered boards, stamped in gilt, frontispiece, binding by Luce Thurkow, from the collection of Donn W. Sanford.   Oak Knoll Books   303 - 82   2013 $250

Irving, Washington   1783-1859 *Rip Van Winkle.* Utrecht: Catharijne Press, 1987. Limited to 165 copies, this one of 150 numbered copies, with 4 tipped in illustrations by Henk van der Haar, 6.5 x 4.5cm, pictorial paper covered boards, miniature bookplate of Kathryn Rickard, from the collection of Donn W. Sanford.   Oak Knoll Books   303 - 85   2013 $125

Kavin, Mel *Catalog of the Thirty-three Miniature Designer Bindings You Can Judge a Book by Its Cover by Bernard C. Middleton.* Rivera: Kater-Crafts Bookbinders, 1998. Limited to 500 copies, signed by compiler, oblong 4to., cloth, title stamped on spine and cover, color illustrations, from the collection of Donn W. Sanford.   Oak Knoll Books   303 - 19   2013 $180

Kennedy, John Fitzgerald   1917-1963 *Inaugural Address.* Los Angeles: Bela Blau, 1965. Limited to 1000 numbered copies, one of the copies printed on vellum, 4 x 3.5 cm., full vellum stamped in gilt, vellum covered slipcase, handset, printed and bound by Blau, covers show age yellowing of vellum, from the collection of Donn W. Sanford. Oak Knoll Books   303 - 60   2013 $200

Kipling, Rudyard   1865-1936 *Just So Stories.* Mendocino: Attic Press, 1992. Limited to 75 copies, 3 volumes, 5.3 x 7.3 cm., quarter leather with gilt stamped title set on spine, marbled paper covered boards, paper label on front board, slipcase, from the collection of Donn W. Sanford.   Oak Knoll Books   303 - 43   2013 $225

Koch, Theodore Wesley *More Tales for Bibliophiles.* Chicago: Black Cat Press, 1966. First edition, printed in limited number, 5.8 x 4.3cm., full leather, slipcase, 3 volumes, from the collection of Donn W. Sanford.   Oak Knoll Books   303 - 56   2013 $250

Kok, Henri A. R. *The Diary of Anne Frank (1929-1945), a Biography.* Zuilichem: Catharijne Press, 1995. Limited to 190 copies, this one of 15 lettered copies bound thus, 6.5 x 4.2cm., full red leather with 14 ct. gold Star of David mounted on front cover, clamshell box with leather spine and marbled paper covered boards, mounted miniature of Frank as frontispiece, from the collection of Donn W. Sanford.   Oak Knoll Books   303 - 84   2013 $275

Lenier, Jules *A Midget Book of Mighty Mental Magic.* Fullerton: Baffles Press, 1994. Limited to 50 numbered copies, signed by author, 6.5 x 7.8 cm., cloth, slipcase with labels, from the collection of Donn W. Sanford.   Oak Knoll Books   303 - 44   2013 $350

A Little Black Book. Marcham: The Alembic Press, 1995. Limited to 100 numbered copies, 7.2 x 6 cm., sewn in 8 sections with a Coptic binding in heavy textured black boards, 63 pages, printed in black and red, from the collection of Donn W. Sanford.   Oak Knoll Books   303 - 30   2013 $125

Miniature Book News. St. Louis: n.p., 1965-2001. Small 8vo., nos. 1-108, complete run, self paper wrappers, variously paginated, illustrations, from the collection of Donn W. Sanford.   Oak Knoll Books   303 - 20   2013 $450

Miniature Book Society *Catalogue of the Miniature Book Competitions and Exhibitions.* N.P.: Miniature Book Society, 1988-2002. 14 volumes, excluding 1994, miniature books, various sizes, stiff paper wrappers, from the collection of Donn W. Sanford.   Oak Knoll Books   303 - 13   2013 $350

Morris, Henry *No. V-109, the Biography of a Printing Press.* N.P.: Anne and David Bromer, 1978. First edition, limited to 150 numbered copies, printed by hand by Henry Morris, very scarce, 6.1 x 4.7 cm., quarter leather over pastepaper covered boards, from the collection of Donn W. Sanford.   Oak Knoll Books   303 - 72   2013 $525

Nixon, Richard Milhous *The Inaugural Address of Richard Milhous Nixon, President of the United States.* Worcester: Achille J. St. Onge, n.d. circa, 1969. Limited to 1500 copies, 6.6 x 4.6cm., full leather, all edges gilt, tipped in frontispiece portrait, printed in Holland by Enschede on handmade Hayle paper made at the Hayle mill in England, this copy signed by Nixon beneath frontispiece portrait, from the collection of Donn W. Sanford.   Oak Knoll Books   303 - 27   2013 $750

Petko, Edward *Fine Printing and the '80's.* Los Angeles: Columbian 415 Chappel, 1980. Limited to 100 numbered copies, this copy with presentation by author to Roger Levenson, 7.3 x 5.9cm., marbled cloth, label with title on spine, top edge cut, other edges uncut, from the collection of Donn W. Sanford.   Oak Knoll Books   303 - 99   2013 $150

Poe, Edgar Allan   1809-1849 *Two Poems.* Utrecht: Catharijne Press, 1984. Limited to 100 numbered copies, each with signed and numbered photogravure by Johan de Zoete, 4 x 6.5cm., full leather, vellum cover label on set, bound by Luce Thurkow, from the collection of Donn W. Sanford.   Oak Knoll Books   303 - 87   2013 $200

Porter, William Sydney   1862-1910 *An O. Henry Gift from Henry, The Gift of the Magi.* North Hills: Bird & Bull Press, 1979. Limited to 250 copies, 2.125 x 50 inches (scroll), housed in protective "plastic pill box", this copy does not have a mailing label attached so it was probably one of those produced for booksellers, from the collection of Donn W. Sanford.   Oak Knoll Books   303 - 48   2013 $100

Poska, Valentine J. *Microbibliotrivia, a Curious Adventure in Miniature Books.* San Antonio: privately printed, 1984-1989. Issues 1-5, 4to., stiff paper wrappers, plastic comb binding, not paginated, miniature bookplate of Kathryn Rickard, 5th in the series signed by author, from the collection of Donn W. Sanford.   Oak Knoll Books   303 - 22   2013 $250

Powell, Lawrence Clark *Bookshops.* Los Angeles: 1965. No limitation given, but obviously very small, bound by Bela Blau, 6 x 4.3 cm., leather, presentation "W.T.'s. book from L.P.' 65", from the collection of Donn W. Sanford.   Oak Knoll Books   303 - 65   2013 $250

Roscoe, William *Butterfly's ball and Grasshopper's feast.* Boston: Anne & David Bromer, 1977. Limited to 150 copies, this one of 25 deluxe copies, bound in full leather by Gray Parrot and containing a pocket in back with extra prints of woodcut illustrations, printed letterpress by Sarah Chamberlain at her press, she has signed and lettered this copy, 6 x 5 cm., full green leather stamped in gilt, (24) pages, from the collection of Donn W. Sanford.   Oak Knoll Books   303 - 73   2013 $850

Six-Line Wood Letter Alphabets. Marcham: Alembic Press, 1995-1997. Limited to 100 numbered copies, 6 miniature books, 7 x 5 cm., sewn, stiff paper wrappers, paper covered slipcase, from the collection of Donn W. Sanford.   Oak Knoll Books   303 - 31   2013 $125

A Small Book of Fists. Oxford: Alembic Press, 1990. Limited to 100 numbered copies, 4 volume set, 4.3 x 6.2 cm., quarter cloth, marbled paper covered boards, marbled slipcase, 2 volumes with title gilt stamped on spine, two with label, from the collection of Donn W. Sanford.   Oak Knoll Books   303 - 32   2013 $250

A Typesticker's Tract on Typefaces What They Are & What He Thinks they Ought Not to Be; with a Review of the Opinions of Others on This. Los Angeles: W. M. Cheney, 1949. Labeled 'reading copy' on front board, 10.3 x 7.3 cm., paper covered boards, label on front, from the collection of Donn W. Sanford.   Oak Knoll Books   303 - 95   2013 $125

Snyder, Dee *The ABC's of Baker Street: a Guide to the Holmesian Habitat.* Skokie: Black Cat Press, 1983. Limited to 249 copies, 7.3 x 5.2 cm., cloth, title gilt stamped on spine and front cover, marbled endpapers, 97, (5) pages, illustrations, bound by Bela Blau, from the collection of Donn W. Sanford.   Oak Knoll Books   303 - 58   2013 $100

Spielmann, Percy Edwin *Catalogue of the Library of Miniature Books Collected by...* London: Edward Arnold, 1961. Limited to 500 numbered copies, 8vo., cloth backed patterned paper covered boards, dust jacket, chip out of dust jacket at top of spine, scarce, from the collection of Donn W. Sanford.   Oak Knoll Books   303 - 10   2013 $300

Stone, Wilbur Macey *The Thumb Bible of John Taylor.* Brookline: the LXIVMOS, 1928. Limited to 100 copies, 12mo., cloth backed boards, paper label, illustrations, rubbed along edges, miniature bookplate of Kathryn Rickard with acquisition date of 1990 added in ink beneath bookplate, pages 65-68 (one sheet) loose from not being sewn in, from the collection of Donn W. Sanford.   Oak Knoll Books   303 - 24   2013 $200

Swift, Jonathan   1667-1845 *Gulliver's Travels, a Voyag to Lilliput.* Zuilichem: Catharijne Press, 1995. Limited to 190 copies, this one of 15 lettered copies, bound thus and with extra suite of the illustrations, hand colored, under passe-partout and placed in a second volume, bound by Luce Thurkow, 6.7 x 4.2cm., paper covered boards, slipcase, from the collection of Donn W. Sanford.   Oak Knoll Books   303 - 89   2013 $275

The History of Reynard the Fox. Zuilichem: Catharijne Press, 1991. Limited to 190 copies, this one of 175 numbered trade copies, 6.6 x 5.1cm., cloth, paper cover label, wood engraving by Pam Reuter, binding by Luce Thurkow, wood engraved frontispiece signed and numbered in pencil, from the collection of Donn W. Sanford. Oak Knoll Books 303 - 83   2013 $125

Thoreau, Henry David   1817-1862 *Wild Apples.* Worcester: Achille J. St. Onge, 1956. Limited to 950 copies, 7.5 x 5.1 cm., full leather, gilt lettering on spine and both covers, designed by Bruce Rogers, from the collection of Donn W. Sanford.   Oak Knoll Books   303 - 28   2013 $200

Viger, Denis B. *The Year of the Maple.* N.P.: Margaret Challenger, 2000. Limited to 20 numbered copies, 7 x 5.8 cm., printed paper covered boards in maple leaf design, slipcase with paper cover label, bound accordion style, (14) leaves, with 2 Canadian 6 cent stamps and two Canadia 7 cent stamps tipped in, from the collection of Donn W. Sanford.   Oak Knoll Books   303 - 93   2013 $145

Walsdorf, John J. *Printers on Morris.* Beaverton: Beaverdam Press, 1981. Limited to 326 copies, this is one of 300 bound thus, 7.6 x 5.6 cm., leather spine, floral paper covered boards, (36) pages, frontispiece by Barry Moser, 4 page prospectus loosely inserted, from the collection of Donn W. Sanford.   Oak Knoll Books   303 - 47   2013 $125

Weber, Francis J. *Smallpaxweber.* San Diego: Ash Ranch Press, 1989. Limited to 128 copies, 100 numbered, deluxe edition lettered A-Z and 2 state deluxe proofs, this is lettered copy, signed by author and publisher, Don Hildreth, Artwork by Isabel Piczek and Leo Politi, photo by Alphonse Antczak, color frontispiece, 4.6 x 6.1cm., quarter leather with raised bands, title gilt stamped on spine, decorated cloth boards, clamshell box with inset color illustration, 23, (3) pages, from the collection of Donn W. Sanford, miniature bookplate of Kathryn Rickard. Oak Knoll Books   303 - 41   2013 $200

Weber, Francis J. *What Happened to Junipero Serra?* Los Angeles: Bela Blau, 1969. Limited to 1000 numbered copies, handset, printed and bound by Bela Blau, 3.5 x 5.2 cm., dark green leather stamped in gilt, patterned paper endpapers, from the collection of Donn W. Sanford.   Oak Knoll Books   303 - 62   2013 $150

Weber, Franics J. *Bela Blau Bookbinder 1914-1993.* Los Angeles: Privately printed for Mariana Blau, 1993. Limited to 150 copies, one of the numbered deluxe copies bound thus, bound and signed by Mariana Blau, 5.2 x 4 cm., full dark brown leather with inset full color photo of Bela Blau on front cover, slipcase, each contributor has signed their contribution, from the collection of Donn W. Sanford.   Oak Knoll Books   303 - 61   2013 $225

Webster, Daniel *On the Powers of Government Assigned to It by the Constitution from His Address in the United States Senate May 7, 1834.* Worcester: New Hampshire Historical Society, 1952. Limited to 100 copies, 8 x 5.5 cm., red cloth stamped in gilt, from the collection of Donn W. Sanford.   Oak Knoll Books   303 - 29   2013 $175

Welsh, Doris Varner *A Bibliography of Miniature Books (1470-1965).* New York: Kathryn I. Rickard, 1989. First edition, limited to 500 copies, 4to., cloth, dust jacket, signed by author, with presentation from publisher on facing page "Dear Mr. Sanford, Welcome to a new World. Kathryn V. Rickard 8.30.90", corner bumped, from the collection of Donn W. Sanford.   Oak Knoll Books   303 - 25   2013 $200

White, Robert W. *A History of the Cadiz Short Line Railroad.* Chicago: Black Cat Press, 1966. Limited to 200 copies, 5.5 x 7.8 cm., black and white illustrations, leather, miniature bookplate of Kathryn Rickard, from the collection of Donn W. Sanford.   Oak Knoll Books   303 - 59   2013 $200

Wilde, Oscar   1854-1900 *The House of Judgement.* Utrecht: Catharijne Press, 1986. Limited to 165 copies, this one of 150 numbered copies, 5 x 6.7cm., brown cloth with paper cover label, printed in four colors by Hans Hartzheim with calligraphed original by J. H. Moesman, colophon separately printed on four pages and loosely inserted in pocket in back, miniature bookplate of Kathryn Rickard, from the collection of Donn W. Sanford.   Oak Knoll Books 303 - 91   2013 $150

William Morris, Wallpapers. Zuilichem: Catharijne Press, 1997. Limited to 190 copies, of which this is one of the 15 lettered copies bound thus, and with a separate "wallpaper book" containing an extra suite of the plates in larger format, bound by Luce Thurkow, 11 specimens of wallpaper, 6.6 x 4.3cm., paper covered boards, paper cover label (1st volume); cloth ties (2nd volume), clam shell box covered with reproduction of Morris wallpaper, paper cover label, from the collection of Donn W. Sanford.   Oak Knoll Books   303 - 92   2013 $325

Williams, Gordon *Ravens & Crows.* Los Angeles: William Cheney, 1966. 2.4 x 1.7cm., paper covered boards, miniature bookplate of Kathryn Rickard, from the collection of Donn W. Sanford. Oak Knoll Books 303 - 96 2013 $100

XXIII Psalm: a Psalm of David. Canberra: Bookarts, 2001. Limited to 15 presentation copies and 150 numbered copies, this copy numbered and signed by publishers, John and Joy Tonkin, 7 x 4. cm., leather, brass clasp, 4 raised bands on spine, excess leather tied in topknot, marbled endpapers, in leather pouch unpaginated, from the collection of Donn W. Sanford. Oak Knoll Books 303 - 64 2013 $200

Association – Sarton, George

Holmes, Thomas *Cotton Mather: a Bibliography of His Works.* Cambridge: Harvard University Press, 1940. First edition, limited to 500 copies, 3 volumes, 8vo., decorative red title border, illustrations, original quarter dark brown levant over lighter brown cloth, top edge gilt, gilt stamped spine by Harcourt Bindery, Boston, fine, Burndy bookplate, beautiful set, George Sarton's copy (and Harvard University's) bookplate and ownership signature. Jeff Weber Rare Books 169 - 212 2013 $500

Association – Saunders, M. T.

Croly, George *Salathiel the Immortal: a History.* London: David Bryce, 1856. New edition, half title, contemporary signature of M. T. Saunders, Wilmington Hall, odd spot, original purple cloth, slightly marked, spine faded to brown, good plus. Jarndyce Antiquarian Booksellers CCIII - 673 2013 £35

Association – Saunders, William

Dickens, Charles 1812-1870 *Great Expectations.* London: Chapman and Hall, 1861. Volume I second impression, volume II fourth impression, volume 3 first impression, 3 volumes, later inserted half title volume I, engraved title and plates by Pailthorpe, occasional light browning in prelims, slightly later full brown crushed morocco by Riviere, spines gilt in compartments, gilt borders and dentelles, armorial bookplates of William H. R. Saunders, top edge gilt, very good, handsome. Jarndyce Antiquarian Booksellers CCV - 86 2013 £4500

Association – Saville, Elizabeth

The Polite Jester; or, Theatre for Wit. printed by and for J. Drew, 1796. First edition, engraved frontispiece, frontispiece trimmed at fore margin with slight loss of image and 3 letters of the legend (sense recoverable), 12mo., early pink card wrappers, paper spine, cracks on spine, with ownership inscription "Elizabeth Savil(le) May 1st 1809, a quatrain in pencil in early hand on verso of flyleaf in German and another, in English on recto of frontispiece, good. Blackwell's Rare Books B174 - 78 2013 £700

Association – Saxton, Nathalie

De La Mare, Walter 1873-1956 *Songs of Childhood.* London: Longmans, Green and Co., 1902. First edition, 8vo., frontispiece after Richard Doyle, original half parchment and pale blue linen over boards, top edge gilt, dust jacket, author's own copy, signed by poet and inscribed below to his nurse and companion of many years, Sister Nathalie Saxton, backstrip lightly rubbed along joints, otherwise fine in dust jacket with very small chip out of bottom spine panel and offsetting from two small old cello-tape repairs at bottom spine and bottom front flap fold, preserved in half morocco slipcase, booklabel of J. O. Edwards, beautiful and distinguished association copy, in extremely rare jacket. James S. Jaffe Rare Books Fall 2013 - 37 2013 $12,500

Association – Schaap, Dick

McConkey, Phil *Simms to McConkey: Blood, Sweat and Gatorade.* New York: Crown, 1987. First edition, fine in dust jacket, signed by Simms, McConkey and Schaap, scarce thus. Between the Covers Rare Books, Inc. Football Books - 29211 2013 $475

Association – Schanbel, Julian

Clearwater, Rudi Fuchs *Julian Schnabel. Versions of Chuck and Other Words.* Derneburg: 2007. First edition, 4to, 206 pages, fine, in fine dust jacket, inscribed and dated by Schanbel. By the Book, L. C. 36 - 22 2013 $400

Association – Schilpp, Arthur

Carnap, Rudolf *Philosophy and Logical Syntax.* London: Kegan Paul, Trench, Trubner, 1935. First edition, signed and inscribed by author for educator and philosopher, Arthur Schilpp, very good, red spine and cream colored printed boards, paper spine label Schilpp's bookplate, mild sun and scuff to spine, cover edges worn, 16mo., 100 pages. By the Book, L. C. 38 - 25 2013 $500

Association – Schlimovich, M.

Bonet, Honore *L'Apparition de Jehan de Meun ou le Songe Du Prieur De Salon.* Paris: Imprime par Crapelet pur la Societe des Bibliophiles Francais, 1845. One of 170 copies on velllum (this copy #7 printed for M. Le Comte e La Bedoyere, member of the Societe des Bibliophiles) (another 100 copies on issued on paper), recent fine white pigskin, decorated in blind to a Medieval style by Courtland Benson, housed in titled custom made morocco backed folding cloth box, 10 engraved plates, morocco bookplate of Comte H. De La Bedoyere and engraved bookplate of Marcellus Schlimovich, embossed library stamp of Dr. Detlef Mauss; half title with ink library stamp of Sociedad Hebraica Argentina, fine, especially clean and bright internally, only most trivial imperfections in new retrospective binding. Phillip J. Pirages   63 - 477   2013 $3500

Association – Schlimovich, Marcellus

Bonet, Honore *L'Apparition de Jehan de Meun ou le Songe Du Prieur De Salon.* Paris: Imprime par Crapelet pur la Societe des Bibliophiles Francais, 1845. One of 170 copies on vellum (this copy #7 printed for M. Le Comte e La Bedoyere, member of the Societe des Bibliophiles) (another 100 copies on issued on paper), recent fine white pigskin, decorated in blind to a Medieval style by Courtland Benson, housed in titled custom made morocco backed folding cloth box, 10 engraved plates, morocco bookplate of Comte H. De La Bedoyere and engraved bookplate of Marcellus Schlimovich, embossed library stamp of Dr. Detlef Mauss; half title with ink library stamp of Sociedad Hebraica Argentina, fine, especially clean and bright internally, only most trivial imperfections in new retrospective binding. Phillip J. Pirages   63 - 477   2013 $3500

Association – Schmidt, J. M.

Hudson, Ernest *Barton Records.* Penrith: St. Andrew's Press, 1951. First edition, original cloth, gilt trifle rubbed, 79 pages, illustrations, relevant cuttings on endpapers, presentation copy inscribed by author April 1951 for J. M. Schmidt.   R. F. G. Hollett & Son   Lake District and Cumbria - 306   2013   £25

Association – Schneider, H. W.

Graham, Henry *The New Coinage.* Civil Service Printing & Publishing Co., 1878. 152 pages, original black cloth gilt, rather bubbled and stained by damp, endpapers rather cockled and stained, presentation with author's compliments for Hy. W. Schneider Dec. 26th 1878.   R. F. G. Hollett & Son   Lake District and Cumbria - 185   2013   £75

Association – Schori, Margaret

Favorsky, V. *Miniature Woodcuts.* Leningrad: Aurora Art Pub., 1979. 6 x 7 cm., cloth, title gilt stamped on spine, initial gilt stamped on front boards, slipcase, unpaginated, 3 volumes, illustrations in black and white, inscribed on dust jacket to Margaret and Ward Schori, bottom and top of slipcase missing, slipcase worn at edges, from the collection of Donn W. Sanford.   Oak Knoll Books   303 - 42   2013 $225

Association – Schori, Ward

Favorsky, V. *Miniature Woodcuts.* Leningrad: Aurora Art Pub., 1979. 6 x 7 cm., cloth, title gilt stamped on spine, initial gilt stamped on front boards, slipcase, unpaginated, 3 volumes, illustrations in black and white, inscribed on dust jacket to Margaret and Ward Schori, bottom and top of slipcase missing, slipcase worn at edges, from the collection of Donn W. Sanford.   Oak Knoll Books   303 - 42   2013 $225

Association – Scotchler, J. B.

California. Insurance Commission *Second Annual Report of the Insurance Commissioner for the State of California (Year Ending Dec. 31, 1869).* Sacramento: D. W. Gelwicks, State Printer, 1870. First edition thus, 361 pages, plus index, handsomely bound in modern three quarter brown calf, marbled sides, original presentation label affixed to front cover, head of spine with slight wear, titlepage bit darkened, else fine, original presentation label affixed to front cover, printed in gold on black leather "J.B. Scotchler, President Merchants' Mutual Marine Ins. Co.". Argonaut Book Shop   Recent Acquisitions June 2013 - 52   2013 $150

Association – Scott, Laurence

Moore, Marianne 1887-1972 *The Pangolin and Other Verse.* London: Brendin Pub. Co., 1936. First edition, limited to 120 copies, 8vo., illustrations by George Plank, original decorated paper boards with printed label on front cover, presentation copy inscribed by author for Laurence Scott, extremely rare signed or inscribed, very fine.   James S. Jaffe Rare Books   Fall 2013 - 106   2013 $3500

Association – Scott, Robert Falcon

Bible. English - 1910 *The New Testament of Our Lord and Saviour Jesus Christ.* London: Oxford University Press, circa, 1910. 8vo., limp black morocco, 'Antarctic Expedition Terra Nova 1910' gilt to upper cover, inscribed by A. R. Falconer, Sailor's Missionary Dunedin, for Captain Robert Falcon Scott.   Maggs Bros. Ltd.   1467 - 141   2013   £6000

Association – Scott, Thomas

Thompson, George *A Sentimental Tour, Collected from a Variety of Occurrences from Newbiggin, near Penrith...* Penrith: printed by Anthony Soulby for the author, 1798. 12mo., old splash mark to H12, ink note at foot of p. 234, uncut, recent boards, paper spine label, contemporary ownership name of Thos. Scott at head of titlepage and under author's name is presentation inscription, presumably from author to J. H. Allinson from his preceptor.   Jarndyce Antiquarian Booksellers   CCIV - 295   2013   £380

Association – Scribner, Charles

English Lyrics. London: printed at the Chiswick Press for Kegan Paul, Trench & Co., 1883. First edition, one of 50 large paper copies, this #32, 206 x 130mm., fine turn-of-the-century Hazel brown crushed morocco, very elaborately gilt by Zaehnsdorf (stamp signed on front turn-in, oval blindstamp on rear pastedown), covers richly gilt with very wide floral border featuring many tendrils and small tools, border enclosing panel filled with alternating rows of floral sprigs and leaves (tiny stars in between), raised bands, spine compartments gilt with either floral bouquet or rows of leaves and flowers, densely gilt turn-ins, gray silk endleaves, top edge gilt, other edges untrimmed, armorial bookplate of Mary Louise Curtis Bok, half title with pencilled note "Wedding present to M.L.C./from Charles Scribner October 1896", (spine just slightly sunned toward a darker brown, front joint and very top and bottom of back joint little worn, with flaking and thin cracks, but no looseness), corners slightly rubbed, still especially attractive with lovely binding with glistening covers and beautifully printed text pristine.   Phillip J. Pirages   63 - 65   2013 $1250

Association – Sedgwick, Susan

Thorburn, Grant *Forty Years' Residence in America...* Boston: Russell, Odiorne & Metcalf, 1834. First edition, publisher's green pebble grain cloth, leather spine label, 264 pages, ownership signature of author Susan Anne Livingston Ridley Sedgwick, light scattered foxing, near fine,.   Between the Covers Rare Books, Inc.   New York City - 292192   2013 $400

Association – Sedgwick, William

Pollux, Julius *Onomaticum Graece & Latine.* Amstelaedami: ex Officina Wetsteniana, 1706. 2 volumes, folio, double page plate to volume II, additional engraved titlepage, engraved frontispiece, titlepage in red and black, Gathering 8N in volume I bound out of sequence, small hole to page 373 affecting a few letters, repair to corner of rear endpaper in volume I, tan Cambridge style calf with catspaw staining to frame, neatly rebacked with red morocco gilt spine labels, edges sprinkled red, boards scratched, some small areas of surface loss, corners worn, hinges relined, to each volume bookplate of Robert Edward Way, bookplate of William Sedgwick, Queens College Cambridge and inscription of Caroli Beaumont, another inscription beneath oval inkstamp of Queens College Library.   Unsworths Antiquarian Booksellers   28 - 43   2013   £750

Association – Seldes, Marian

Albee, Edward *A Delicate Balance.* New York: Atheneum, 1966. First edition, signed by author as well as six members of the original cast, Jessica Tandy, Hume Cronyn, Rosemary Murphy, Carmen Matthews, Henderson Forsythe and Marian Seldes, fine in nearly fine dust jacket.   Ed Smith Books   78 - 3   2013 $750

Association – Self, William

Dickens, Charles 1812-1870 *Dombey and Son.* London: Bradbury & Evans, 1848. First edition in book form, first state following all points in Smith, the Kenyon Starling - William Self copy, octavo, publisher's variant binding of moderate green fine diaper grain cloth, original pale yellow coated endpapers, spine very faded, corners very slightly bumped, just tiny amount of board show through, otherwise binding as fresh as one could possibly wish for, chemised in half green morocco slipcase, Self bookplate on chemise.   David Brass Rare Books, Inc.   Holiday 2012 Chapter Five - DB 01693   2013 $11,500

Association – Sendak, Maurice

Grimm, Wilhelm *Dear Mili.* New York: Farrar Straus & Giroux, 1988. Stated first edition, oblong 4to., cloth, as new in like dust jacket, magnificent, rich and detailed full page color illustrations by Maurice Sendak, this copy inscribed by Sendak.   Aleph-Bet Books, Inc.   104 - 514 2013 $125

Association – Seton

Alleyne, James *Every Man His Own Doctor; or a New English Dispensatory in four parts.* printed for Thomas Astley, 1733? First edition?, possibly lacking prelim ad leaf, little staining from use, piece torn from corner of first flyleaf at front, last gathering little proud, 8vo., contemporary calf, spine gilt ruled in compartments, red lettering piece, spine chipped at either end, corners slightly worn, armorial bookplate of Seton of Mounie, sound.   Blackwell's Rare Books   Sciences - 4   2013   £250

Anderson, James   1739-1808 *An Account of the Present State of the Hebrides and Western Coasts of Scotland...* Edinburgh: printed (by Mundell & Wilson) for G. Robinson, London and C. Elliot, Edinburgh, 1785. First edition, large folding map, 1 engraved plate and folding table, map torn an repaired with small patch missing from engraved text to right, split in folding table also neatly repaired, 8vo., contemporary tree calf, red lettering piece on spine, slightly worn, armorial bookplate inside front cover of Seton of Mounie, descendant of author, good.   Blackwell's Rare Books   Sciences - 6   2013   £400

Anderson, James   1739-1808 *Essays Relating to Agriculture and Rural Affairs.* London: printed for G. G. and J. Robinson and for Bell and Bradfute (sic), Edinburgh (volume iii: Edinburgh: printed for Bell & Bradfute, 1796), 1797. Fourth edition, volume first (-third) editions, 3 engraved plates, page of woodcuts in volume i, 18 engraved plates and page of woodcuts in volume ii, and a page of woodcuts in volume iii, some foxing and browning, 8vo., contemporary tan calf, gilt rules on either side of raised bands on spine, red lettering pieces, bit worn, especially spine ends, of the raised bands on spine, red lettering pieces, bit worn, especially spine ends, ownership inscription T. Hutchinson in volumes i and iii, armorial bookplates in all volumes of William Hutchinson of Eggleston (Teesdale, Co. Durham) and above it the later bookplate of Seton of Mounie, sound. Blackwell's Rare Books   Sciences - 7   2013   £300

Association – Seton, Alexander David

Dodd, James Solas *An Essay Towards a Natural History of the Herring.* London: printed for T. Vincent, 1752. First edition, 8vo., contemporary calf, double gilt fillet borders on sides, spine gilt ruled in compartments later green paper label, lettering in ink faded, slightly worn, contemporary ownership inscription of P. Bartley with note of the price (5s), armorial bookplate of Alexander David Seton of Mounie Castle, with pencil Mounie shelfmark inside front cover, good.   Blackwell's Rare Books   Sciences - 44   2013   £400

Anderson, James   1739-1808 *Works.* Edinburgh and London: various publishers, 1776-1800. Volumes II-IV, a total f 23 monographs, pamphlets, prospecti &c, manuscript titlepage in volume II, few plates, occasional minor foxing and browning, 3 leaves in volume II scorched with loss to outer margins (not affecting text), half Russia c. 1800 spines gilt and blind tooled with gilt wheatsheaf and pair of agricultural tools in each compartment, lettered direct "Anderson's Works", marbled edges, joints and corners skillfully repaired, first volume in volumes ii and iii with bookstamp of George Anderson designed by John Anderson, each volume with armorial bookplate of Alexander David Seton of Mounie, with pencil Mounie Castle shelfmark.   Blackwell's Rare Books   172 - 11   2013   £8500

Association – Seton-Karr, John

Jonson, Ben *The Workes of Benjamin Jonson. (with) The Workes of Benjamin Jonson. The second volume...* London: printed by William Stansby, 1616. 1640-1641. First folio edition, 3 volumes, bound in two, folio, volume II divided into 4 parts, originally issued in two volumes), volume 1 bound with rare initial blank leaf, engraved allegorical title by William Hole, volume 1 full contemporary brown paneled calf expertly rebacked to style, spine with red and green spine labels, lettered gilt, all edges gilt, former owner's signature on top of titlepage not affecting engraving, another signature on front pastedown, volume 2 full brown calf, ruled in blind, expertly rebacked and uniform with volume 1, with red and green spine labels, lettered gilt, previous owner's bookplate, Walter Scott Seton-Karr and John Seton Karr, together a very handsome set.   Heritage Book Shop   Holiday Catalogue 2012 - 82   2013 $35,000

Association – Seton-Karr, Walter Scott

Jonson, Ben *The Workes of Benjamin Jonson. (with) The Workes of Benjamin Jonson. The second volume...* London: printed by William Stansby, 1616. 1640-1641. First folio edition, 3 volumes, bound in two, folio, volume II divided into 4 parts, originally issued in two volumes), volume 1 bound with rare initial blank leaf, engraved allegorical title by William Hole, volume 1 full contemporary brown paneled calf expertly rebacked to style, spine with red and green spine labels, lettered gilt, all edges gilt, former owner's signature on top of titlepage not affecting engraving, another signature on front pastedown, volume 2 full brown calf, ruled in blind, expertly rebacked and uniform with volume 1, with red and green spine labels, lettered gilt, previous owner's bookplate, Walter Scott Seton-Karr and John Seton Karr, together a very handsome set.   Heritage Book Shop   Holiday Catalogue 2012 - 82   2013 $35,000

Association – Severn, Joan Ruskin

My Book of Noble Deeds. Blackie & Son, n.d circa, 1907. Large 8vo., original cloth backed glazed pictorial boards, little soiled, 4 color plates, other plates and illustrations, inscribed by Joan Ruskin for John Hext.   R. F. G. Hollett & Son   Children's Books - 71   2013   £75

True Stories of the Olden Days. Blackie & son, n.d. circa, 1907. Large 8vo., original cloth backed glazed pictorial boards, upper board little soiled, especially at one corner, 4 color plates, other plates and illustrations, inscribed by Joan Ruskin Severn for John Hext.   R. F. G. Hollett & Son   Children's Books - 72   2013   £65

Association – Sewell, Michael

Fisher, St. John   *Sermon Against Luther.*   Pepler & Sewell St. Dominic's Press, Ditchling, Sussex, 1935. One of 30 copies printed on handmade paper, small wood engraving of Luther by Edward Walters, after Holbein, 16mo., original quarter cream canvas, spine sunned, printed front cover label, pale grey boards with little handling soiling, corners rubbed, small glue stain left following bookplate removal, untrimmed, good, inscribed by Michael Sewell 23 March 1936 for Vincent Maxwell.   Blackwell's Rare Books   B174 - 379   2013   £120

Association – Seyferth, Larry

Glines, Carroll V.   *Doolitte's Tokyo Raiders.*   New York: Arno Press, 1980. Reprint, 8vo., illustrations, gilt stamped blue cloth, signed and inscribed by James Doolittle to Larry Seyferth in ink, near fine.   Jeff Weber Rare Books   171 - 107   2013 $75

Thomas, Lowell   *Doolittle: a Biography.*   Garden City: Doubleday, 1976. 8vo., 67 illustrations, quarter gilt stamped black cloth over maroon cloth, dust jacket rear slightly soiled, signed and inscribed from Doolittle to Larry Seyferth in ink, very good.   Jeff Weber Rare Books   171 - 108   2013 $200

Association – Sharpe, Catherine

Bloomfield, Robert   *May Day with the Muses.*   London: printed for the author &c. for Baldwin, Cradock & Joy, 1822. First edition, 12mo., illustrations, uncut in contemporary pale blue boards, drab spine, paper label, gift inscription to Catherine Sharpe 1822, later inscription in blue ink on leading f.e.p., very good.   Jarndyce Antiquarian Booksellers   CCIII - 28   2013   £125

Association – Shattuck, George

Osler, William   1849-1919   *The Principles and Practice of Medicine.*   New York: D. Appleton and Co., 1892. First edition, first state, large 8vo., original green cloth, some rubbed and bumped, rebacked with original spine laid down, first state with misspelling 'Georgias' for Gorgias' facing contents page and second set of ads dated Nov. 1891, holograph presentation by Dr. George B. Shattuck, Jan. 2 1897 with ownership signature of Edward N. Libby, small date stamp on top of titlepage, very good, clean, tight copy.   Second Life Books Inc.   183 - 308   2013 $7500

Association – Shaw, George Bernard

Cowley, Abraham   1618-1667   *Poems: viz. I. Miscellanies. II. The Mistress, or Love Verses. III. Pindarique Odes. And IV. Davideis, or a Sacred Poem of the Troubles of David.*   London: for Humphrey Moseley, 1656. First collected edition, contemporary panelled calf, edges gilt, very skillfully rebacked to style, later endpapers, occasional minor spots and repaired marginal tears, 3L2, soiled and with paper defect costing several letters, lovely, early signature of Edmund Henry Marshall, "Ex Libris George Bernard Shaw" on front endpaper.   Joseph J. Felcone Inc.   English and American Literature to 1800 - 11   2013 $2500

Association – Shea, Dorothy Jayne Pedrini

White, Henry Kirke   *The Poetical Works of Henry Kirke White.*   London: Charles Whittingham for William Pickering, 1853. 168 x 105mm., lviii, 252 pages, elegant contemporary dark green morocco inlaid, embossed and elaborately gilt, each cover with broad inlaid ochre morocco frame intricately gilt, large central mandorla of heavily embossed and gilt morocco of same color (both frame and centerpiece highlighted with red painted rules, raised bands, spine gilt in compartments framed by plain and decorative gilt rules, floral centerpiece and lancet cornerpieces richly gilt turn-ins, cream colored watered silk endleaves, all edges gilt, pleasing fore-edge painting of Nottingham Castle; engraved portrait and printer's anchor device on titlepage, pencilled inscription to Bessie Carey from Walter Shipper dated 13 October 1868, pastedown with morocco bookplate of Estelle Doheny, bookplate of Edward Laurence Doheny, bookplate of Carrie Estelle Doheny, bookplate of Dorothy Jayne Pedrini Shea; hint of wear to joints and corners, red paint bit rubbed with minor loss, minor foxing to portrait and titlepage, other trivial imperfections, but excellent copy, handsome binding solid and lustrous, text clean and fresh, fore-edge painting very well preserved.   Phillip J. Pirages   63 - 193   2013 $1100

Association – Shelton, Chuck

Ainsworth, Ed   *Painters of the Desert.*   Palm Desert: Desert Magazine, 1960. First edition, large quarto, 111 pages, reproductions form drawings, paintings, with portraits, orange cloth, very fine with dust jacket (some extremity rubbing and chipping to head of spine), long presentation inscription signed by author, also signed by Chuck Shelton, also signed by five of the thirteen artists.   Argonaut Book Shop   Recent Acquisitions June 2013 - 13   2013 $400

Association – Sherrington, Charles

Scultetus, Johann   *...Cheiroplotheke Armamentarium Chirurgicum...*   The Hague: ex officina Adriani Vlacq 1656, i.e., 1657. First octavo edition, contemporary calf, newly rebacked in calf, endpapers renewed, signed inscription of Sir Charles Sherrington.   James Tait Goodrich   75 - 188   2013 $2500

Association – Shiel, M. P.

Van Vechten, Carl 1880-1964 *Le Paradis des Negres. (Nigger Heaven).* New York: Alfred A. Knopf, 1927. Eleventh printing, little light foxing in text, else near fine, without dust jacket, inscribed by author for M. P. Shiel, July 4 1927.   Between the Covers Rare Books, Inc.   Sci-Fi, Fantasy & Horror - 273811   2013 $850

Association – Shipman, Samuel

Arlen, Michael *These Charming People: Being a Tapestry of the Fortunes, Follies, Adventures, Gallantries and General Activities...* New York: George H. Doran, 1924. First American edition, very near fine in very good dust jacket with some shallow chips and tears at upper extremities, nicely inscribed by author for Samuel Shipman.   Between the Covers Rare Books, Inc.   Sci-Fi, Fantasy & Horror - 94877   2013 $250

Association – Shipper, Walter

White, Henry Kirke *The Poetical Works of Henry Kirke White.* London: Charles Whittingham for William Pickering, 1853.   168 x 105mm., lviii, 252 pages, elegant contemporary dark green morocco inlaid, embossed and elaborately gilt, each cover with broad inlaid ochre morocco frame intricately gilt, large central mandorla of heavily embossed and gilt morocco of same color (both frame and centerpiece highlighted with red painted rules, raised bands, spine gilt in compartments framed by plain and decorative gilt rules, floral centerpiece and lancet cornerpieces richly gilt turn-ins, cream colored watered silk endleaves, all edges gilt, pleasing fore-edge painting of Nottingham Castle; engraved portrait and printer's anchor device on titlepage, pencilled inscription to Bessie Carey from Walter Shipper dated 13 October 1868, pastedown with morocco bookplate of Estelle Doheny, bookplate of Edward Laurence Doheny, bookplate of Carrie Estelle Doheny, bookplate of Dorothy Jayne Pedrini Shea; hint of wear to joints and corners, red paint bit rubbed with minor loss, minor foxing to portrait and titlepage, other trivial imperfections, but excellent copy, handsome binding solid and lustrous, text clean and fresh, fore-edge painting very well preserved.   Phillip J. Pirages 63 - 193   2013 $1100

Association – Shipton, John

Baldelli, Francesco *Di Polidoro Virgilio Da Vrbino de Gli Invetori Delle Cose, Libri Otto.* In Florenza: per Filippo Givnti, 1692.   4to., rebound by Bernard Middleton in contemporary style full panel English calf, endpapers renewed, first 8 leaves washed, title browned, text foxed in parts, overall very good, clean, crisp copy, Sir Kenelm Digby's copy with his gold signature and signature of John Shipton.   James Tait Goodrich   75 - 17   2013 $1495

Association – Shirburn Castle

Hall, Joseph *Mundus alter et Idem sive Terra Australis...* Frankfurt: apud haeredes Ascanii de Rinialme, 1607? 8vo., first state engraved titlepage, 5 folding engraved plates (all first editions) text mixed edition, two gatherings from second printing), somewhat soiled and browned, few outer edges slightly frayed, title slightly abraded, some contemporary manuscript notes, ownership inscriptions to title and flyleaf and Macclesfield embossment to first two leaves, 8vo., original limp vellum, somewhat soiled, ties lost, stitching loosening, Shirburn Castle bookplate, preserved in clamshell morocco.   Blackwell's Rare Books   B174 - 66   2013   £5500

Association – Shore, Mary

Olson, Charles *Projective Verse.* New York: Totem, 1959.   First separate edition, near fine in stapled wrappers, one spot to front cover, warmly inscribed by author to poet Vince Ferrini and his wife, Mary Shore.   Ken Lopez Bookseller   159 - 164   2013 $750

Association – Shuster, Paula

De La Mare, Walter 1873-1956 *Peacock Pie.* London: Constable, 1913.   Second impression, 8vo., original blue cloth, near fine inscribed by author for Paula Shuster.   Maggs Bros. Ltd.   1460 - 211   2013   £150

Association – Shute, Nevil

Sophocles *Quae Exstant Omnia cum Veterum Grammaticorum Scholiis.* Strasbourg: Apud Joannem Georgium Treuttel, 1786.   First Brunck edition, 2 volumes, bound without final leaf in volume ii (blank except for colophon on verso, often missing), few minor spots, small early manuscript date to volume i title, 4to., contemporary russia, boards bordered with gilt roll with torch tools at corners, spines divided by double gilt fillet, second and fourth compartments gilt lettered direct, rest with central gilt tool of mask and instruments, all edges gilt, marbled endpapers, front board of volume i with prize inscription lettered direct in gilt and enclosed on top and sides by gilt flower and pearl tools, old repair to spine ends in slightly different colour, some cracking to front of volume i, few old scratches and marks, bookplate of author Nevil Shute and lending label of the Sandford Press to front endpapers, good.   Blackwell's Rare Books   B174 - 144   2013   £900

Association – Shuttleworth, Phyllis

Forster, Edward Morgan 1879-1970 *Pharos and Pharillon.* Surrey: Leonard and Virginia Woolf at the Hogarth Press, 1923.   First edition, 8vo., original blue cloth backed patterned board boards, printed paper label on spine, extremities and spine label slightly browned, otherwise excellent, inscribed by author for Phyllis Shuttleworth 16-5-23.   Maggs Bros. Ltd.   1460 - 290   2013   £2500

Association – Sicari, Pierre

Rose, Billy *Wine, Women and Words.* New York: Simon and Schuster, 1948. First edition, limited to unspecified number of copies signed by author, this number 1451, octavo, illustrations by Salvador Dali, inscription from Henry Miller for Pierre Sicari, quarter gold cloth over pictorial boards, spine printed in black, top edge black, red endpapers, red silk placemarker, boards bit rubbed, edges with some light wear and corners bumped, small stain top of fore-edge, very good.   Heritage Book Shop   Holiday Catalogue 2012 - 34   2013 $1500

Laurents, Arthur *The Way We Were.* New York: Harper & Row, 1972. First edition, inscribed by author for Pierre Sicari, fine dust jacket, price clipped, would be fine but for blue line from old style glassine jacket protector.   Ed Smith Books 78 - 30   2013 $125

Association – Siegler, Samuel

Ruskin, John 1819-1900 *Deucalion Collected Studies of the Lapse of Waves and Life of Stones.* Orpington, Kent: George Allen, 1879-1880. 8 parts in 2 volumes, 212 x 141mm., 11 plates in form of drawings by Ruskin, two of them in several colors and two in blue; lovely chestnut brown morocco, handsomely gilt by Doves Bindery (turn-ins at back signed and dated '19 C-S 09'), covers with French fillet border enclosing two rectangular strapwork frames with semicircular interlacing at top and bottom, inner frame interlaced further with two strapwork triangles that form a six-sided star at center, each point of star surmounted with small open circles (and top and bottom point with additional three petalled floral design), star surrounding a garland composed of two leafy sprays, raised bands, spines gilt in compartments featuring concentric square frames enclosing prominent daisy within lozenge, turn-ins with rules and petalled floral cornerpieces, all edges gilt and with stippled gauffering, original front wrappers as well as extra titlepages, bound in at back of each volume, very dark blue full morocco pull-off suede-lined cases in the shape of a book (just slightly rubbed) with raised bands and gilt titling; pastedown of first volume with bookplate of Dr. Samuel L. Siegler, pastedown of second volume with bookplate of "E. R. McC." (Edith Rockefeller McCormick) and with vestige of removed Siegler bookplate, beautifully bound set in pristine condition, even original wrappers in perfect shape.   Phillip J. Pirages 61 - 104   2013 $10,000

Association – Simms, Phil

McConkey, Phil *Simms to McConkey: Blood, Sweat and Gatorade.* New York: Crown, 1987. First edition, fine in dust jacket, signed by Simms, McConkey and Schaap, scarce thus.   Between the Covers Rare Books, Inc. Football Books - 29211   2013 $475

Association – Simons, Ellen

Wood, Ellen 1814-1887 *East Lynne.* London: Richard Bentley & son, 1879. 96th thousand, half title, frontispiece, original dark green cloth, blocked in blind, lettered in gilt, signed "Ellen Simons" in contemporary hand, very good, bright.   Jarndyce Antiquarian Booksellers   CCV - 293   2013   £45

Association – Simpson, F.

Greene, Graham 1904-1981 *The Potting Shed.* London: William Heinemann, 1958. First edition, small 8vo., original blue cloth, inscribed by author for Fr. Simpson, near fine in dust jacket.   Maggs Bros. Ltd. 1460 - 374   2013   £750

Association – Simpson, Louis

Lazer, Hank *On Equal Terms. Poems by Charles Bernstein, David Ignatow, Denise Levertov, Louis Simpson, Gerald Stern.* Tuscaloosa: Symposium Press, 1984. First edition, limited to 275 copies, although not called for, this copy signed by all contributors, one of the few copies we've seen signed by any of the poets, 4to., original green wrappers, as new.   James S. Jaffe Rare Books   Fall 2013 - 5   2013 $450

Association – Simson, David

Andersson, Charles John *Notes on the Birds of Damara Land and the Adjacent Countries of South-West Africe.* John van Voorst, 1872. First edition, original green blind panelled cloth, gilt, spine slightly worn and scraped at head ad foot, frontispiece map, 4 lithographed plates, presentation from editor, J. H. Gurney to his friend Jules Verraux (1807-1873), engraved bookplates on endpapers of David Simson of Ickleford.   R. F. G. Hollett & Son   Africana - 2   2013   £450

Association – Sinclair, Olivia

Wilson, Daniel *Chatterton. A Biographical Study.* London: Macmillan, 1869. First edition, 8vo., original burgundy cloth, faded on spine and lower cover, otherwise excellent copy, inscribed by Thomas Carlyle for Miss Olivia Sinclair (The Henk, Lockaby), Jan. 7 1870, further inscription author author's compliments presumably to Carlyle.   Maggs Bros. Ltd. 1460 - 161   2013   £500

Association – Singer, Charles

Hewson, J. B. *A History of the Practice of Navigation.* Glasgow: Brown, Son & Ferguson, 1951. First edition, 8vo., viii, 270 pages, illustrations, dark blue cloth, gilt stamped cover and spine titles, dust jacket worn with pieces missing and tape repair, else very good, Burndy bookplate, rare in jacket, with Charles Singer's bookplate.   Jeff Weber Rare Books   169 - 205   2013 $125

Association – Siree, John Hamilton

Burke, Edmund   1729-1797   *A Philosophical Enquiry into the Origin of Our Ideas of the Sublime and Beautiful.* London: printed for R. and J. Dodsley, 1757. First edition, limited to 500 copies, octavo, bound without half title, contemporary calf, early ink inscription of John Digby Jr. and armorial bookplate of John Hamilton Siree, very good.   Heritage Book Shop   50th Anniversary Catalogue - 17   2013 $3500;

Association – Sitgreaves, Samuel

De Segur, Alexandre Joseph Pierre, Viscount   *Women their Condition and Influence in Society.*   London: printed by C. Whittingham for T. N. Longman, 1803. First English edition, 3 volumes, small 8vo., somewhat foxed, original boards, untrimmed, spines and fore tips chipped, lacks paper on spines, one board detached, very good set in original state, with ownership signature (last name only) in each volume of US diplomat and Congressman, Samuel Sitgreaves, scarce.   Second Life Books Inc.   182 - 51   2013 $1800

Association – Skipper, Jacobi

Keill, James   *The Anatomy of the Humane Body Abridg'd or a Short and full View of all the Parts of the Body.*   printed for William Keblewite, 1703. Second edition, little bit of light staining in margins, 12mo., contemporary Cambridge style panelled calf, attractive but slightly defective, red lettering piece on spine, extremities worn, joints cracked but cords firm, old pen scribble on titlepage, ownership inscription at top of flyleaf, ex-libris Jacobi Skipper Coll. Cor., i.e. Corpus Christi College 1706 and later armorial bookplate.   Blackwell's Rare Books   Sciences - 66   2013   £250

Association – Slack, P. A.

North, Thomas   *A Chronicle of the Church of S. Martin In Leicester During the Reigns of Henry VIII Edward VI Mary and Elizabeth with some Account of its Minor Altars and Ancient Guilds. (with) The Accounts of the Churchwardens of S. Martin's, Leicester 1489-1844.*   London: Bell and Daldy, Leicester: Crossley and Clarke, Leicester: Samuel Clarke, 1866. 1884, 2 volumes, 8vo., very slightly browned to edges, some spotting, not affecting text or illustrations, some staining to rear pastedown to volume I, bound uniformly in brown cloth, gilt lettering to spine, blindstamp decorations to both volumes, little bumped and worn to extremities in both volumes, but binding sound, volume I, author's inscription and ALS tipped to front pastedown, ownership signatures one of P. A. Slack, bookplate of antiquary John Edwin Cussans.   Unsworths Antiquarian Booksellers   28 - 189   2013   £80

Owen, H.   *The History of Shrewsbury. Parts V and VI.* London: printed for Harding, Mavor and Lepard, 1823. 1824, Folio, 5 plates, small repair to page 325, half green cloth with marbled paper boards, original paper wrappers with publisher's ads to rear retained inside binding, spine faded, board edges and corners worn, edges uncut and little discolored, some unopened, very good, ownership inscription of P. A. Slack April 1976 and initials BRH.   Unsworths Antiquarian Booksellers   28 - 190   2013   £90

Verney, Frances Parthenope   *Memoirs of the Verney Family Volumes I-IV.*   London: Longmans, Green and Co., 1892. 1892. 1894. 1899. First editions, 4 volumes, 8vo., 50 plates as called for, further woodcuts and illustrations to text, protective tissue removed from volume I frontispiece, brown cloth, gilt spine and armorial centerpiece, top edge gilt, foreedges uncut, endcaps creased, pages and edges little worn, boards faded, minor dent to upper board volume I, upper hinge of volume II cracking but bindings sound, very good internally, armorial bookplate of Frances Fortescue Urquhart of Balliol College 1909 to each front pastedown and his ownership inscription, bookplate of R. C. Mowat, pencilled ownership of P. A. Slack.   Unsworths Antiquarian Booksellers   28 - 202   2013   £120

Association – Sladen, Douglas

Sladen, Douglas Brooke Wheelton   *In Cornwall and Across the Sea...*   London: Griffith, Farran, Okeden & Welsh, 1885. Half title, 32 page catalog (1/85), partly unopened in original cream decorated cloth, dulled, slight cracking to front board leading to lifting of cloth, presentation inscription, Teddie Fiske from Douglas Sladen.   Jarndyce Antiquarian Booksellers CCV - 249   2013   £35

Association – Slater, T. W.

De La Mare, Walter 1873-1956 *The Fleeting and Other Poems.* London: Constable, 1933. First edition, 8vo., original green cloth, spine faded, otherwise excellent, inscribed by author to T. W. Slater.   Maggs Bros. Ltd.   1460 - 216   2013   £60

Association – Sloan, William Eyres

Piozzi, Hester Lynch Salusbury Thrale *Mrs. Thrale, afterwards Mrs. Piozzi, a Sketch of Her Life and Passages from Her Diaries, Letters & Other Writings.* London: Seeley and Co., 1891. 206 x 140mm., very attractive contemporary dark blue three quarter morocco by Tout (stamp signed), raised bands, spine lavishly gilt in compartments with central oval medallion containing a flora spray, medallion within a frame of entwined volutes, floral tools and stippling, marbled boards and endpapers, top edge gilt, frontispiece, 8 portraits, bookplate of William Eyres Sloan, very fine in especially pretty binding, only most trivial imperfections.   Phillip J. Pirages   63 - 367   2013 $450

Association – Slosberg, Helen

Maricain, Raissa *Chagall ou l'Orage Enchante.* Geneve/Paris: Editions des Trois Collines, 1948. Small quarto, half title, original color drawing and inscription by Marc Chagall for Samuel and Helen Slosberg, 8 full color plates tipped in with descriptions under the flaps, numerous black and white photographic plates and illustrations, many of which are full page, publisher's full green illustrated dust jacket wrapper, jacket illustrated and lettered in black ink, uncut and partially unopened, jacket with very slight amount of sunning to spine and minimal rubbing to spine extremities and edges, overall very good with beautiful original drawing.   Heritage Book Shop   Holiday Catalogue 2012 - 28   2013 $12,500

Association – Slosberg, Samuel

Maricain, Raissa *Chagall ou l'Orage Enchante.* Geneve/Paris: Editions des Trois Collines, 1948. Small quarto, half title, original color drawing and inscription by Marc Chagall for Samuel and Helen Slosberg, 8 full color plates tipped in with descriptions under the flaps, numerous black and white photographic plates and illustrations, many of which are full page, publisher's full green illustrated dust jacket wrapper, jacket illustrated and lettered in black ink, uncut and partially unopened, jacket with very slight amount of sunning to spine and minimal rubbing to spine extremities and edges, overall very good with beautiful original drawing.   Heritage Book Shop   Holiday Catalogue 2012 - 28   2013 $12,500

Association – Smith, Aileen

Smith, W. Eugene *Minamata.* New York: Holt, Rinehart & Winston, 1975. First edition, 4to., 192 pages, near fine, original printed wrappers, signed by Eugene and Aileen Smith.   By the Book, L. C.   36 - 25   2013 $350

Association – Smith, Albert

Paul, Doris A. *The Navajo Code Talkers.* Pittsburgh: Dorrance Pub., 1990. Seventh printing, 8vo., signed by fourteen Navajo code talkers, including Albert Smith (President 4th Mar. Div. 4th Sig. Co.), Paul Blatchford, Bill Toledo, Harold Foster, George Smith, Harold Evan and others, fine in near fine dust jacket.   By the Book, L. C.   38 - 38   2013 $900

Association – Smith, Beatrice

Goldsmith, Oliver 1730-1774 *The Vicar of Wakefield.* London/New York: Macmillan, 1922. Reprint, 8vo., finely bound by Riviere in brown leather with cottage motif on front cover and steaming bowl with clay pipe on rear cover, all edges gilt, gilt ruled turn-ins, spine creased at joints, generally clean and sound, fine etched bookplate for Beatrice E. Smith, signed by "H. Martyn", handsome copy, illustrations by Hugh Thomson.   Ed Smith Books   75 - 32   2013 $375

Association – Smith, Cecil Woodham

Guinness, Bryan *A Fugue of Cinderellas.* London: Heinemann, 1956. First edition, 8vo., original blue cloth, excellent copy in dust jacket, chipped at head of spine, inscribed by author for Cecil Woodham Smith Nov. 1963.   Maggs Bros. Ltd.   1460 - 385   2013   £50

Association – Smith, Cyril Stanley

Brock, Alan St. H. *A History of Fireworks.* London, et al: George G. Harrap, 1949. First edition, 8vo., 280 pages, 40 plates, including frontispiece, text illustrations, dark blue cloth, gilt stamped spine, dust jacket worn, Burndy bookplate, very good, signed by Cyril Stanley Smith.   Jeff Weber Rare Books   169 - 44   2013 $125

Association – Smith, E. G.

Cunn, Samuel *A New Treatise of the Construction and Use of the Sector.* printed for John Wilcox and Thomas Heath, Mathematical Instrument Maker, 1729. First edition, engraved frontispiece, large folding engraved plate, diagrams in text, bit browned, closed tear in folding plate, not affecting engraved surface, 8vo., contemporary panelled calf, rebacked, ownership inscription of E. G. Smith, Caius College Cambridge, 1814, sound.   Blackwell's Rare Books Sciences - 39   2013   £950

Association – Smith, George

Paul, Doris A. *The Navajo Code Talkers.* Pittsburgh: Dorrance Pub., 1990. Seventh printing, 8vo., signed by fourteen Navajo code talkers, including Albert Smith (President 4th Mar. Div. 4th Sig. Co.), Paul Blatchford, Bill Toledo, Harold Foster, George Smith, Harold Evan and others, fine in near fine dust jacket. By the Book, L. C. 38 - 38 2013 $900

Association – Smith, Robert

Creswick, Paul *The Turning Wheel.* London: Heath Cranton Ltd., 1928. First edition, bookstore stamp, couple of tiny spots and rubbed spots on boards, still near fine, in about very good dust jacket, with top edge of rear flap fold slightly eroded, nicely inscribed by author for Mr. and Mrs. Robert H. Smith July 22 1929, rare in jacket,. Between the Covers Rare Books, Inc. Sci-Fi, Fantasy & Horror - 84793 2013 $1500

Association – Smith, W.

Nicholson, Peter *The New Practical Builder and Workman's Companion.* London: Thomas Kelly, 1823. 1825. First edition, 4to., half title, frontispiece, plates, slightly foxed, full contemporary mottled calf, raised bands, gilt band, red and black morocco labels, expert repairs to hinges, boards slightly rubbed and marked, ownership label W. Smith 1829. Jarndyce Antiquarian Booksellers CCV - 213 2013 £520

Association – Snelston Hall

Newton, Isaac 1642-1727 *Opera Qua Extant Omnia.* printed by John Nichols, 1779-1785. First edition, diagrams in text, 33 engraved plates, some folding, half title to volume iv slightly soiled, very occasional spotting and little dampstaining in lower margin of volume v, contemporary mottled calf, all volumes sturdily rebacked preserving most all of the original spines, which are gilt in compartments, red lettering piece, numbering pieces absent, Snelston Hall bookplate in each volume, ink signature of ?George Legge erased in each volume, good. Blackwell's Rare Books Sciences - 88 2013 £6500

Association – Snyder, Dr.

Prince, David *Illustrations of Deformities and Their Treatment.* Jacksonville: printed at the Jacksonville Journal Office, 1866. First edition, 8vo., 32 pages, contents comprising 61 text figures, original printed wrappers, chipped with some loss, signature torn from one margin, some spotty foxing and faint stains internally, not quite very good, with second contemporary signature of Dr. Snyder. M & S Rare Books, Inc. 95 - 232 2013 $750

Association – Soames, Arthur

Lysons, Daniel *Magna Britannia...* London: printed for T. Cadell and W. Davies, 1806-1822. Large paper copy, 6 volumes bound in 10, 346 x 260mm., pleasing contemporary red hard-grain half morocco over marbled boards by J. Mackenzie & Son (stamp-signed), raised bands, spines attractively gilt in compartments with very large and complex central fleuron surrounded by small tools and volute corner-pieces, gilt titling, marbled endpapers, all edges gilt, 398 plates of maps, plans, views and architecture, 264 as called for, and extra illustrated with 134, the total, including 72 double page, 7 folding and 13 in color; armorial bookplate of Arthur G. Soames, signed and dated by plate by C. Helard (18)99, paper boards somewhat chafed, extremities (especially bottom edges of boards) rather rubbed, spines slightly (but uniformly) darkened, few of the leather corners abraded, small portions of morocco dulled from preservatives, but bindings completely solid - with no cracking to joints - and still impressive on shelf, handsomely decorated spines unmarked, majority of plates with variable foxing (usually minimal but perhaps two dozen noticeably foxed), number of engravings with small faint dampstains at very edge of top margin, but text itself in very fine condition, looking remarkably clean, fresh and smooth within its vast margins. Phillip J. Pirages 63 - 325 2013 $6500

Association – Soliday, H. Marion

Lamb, Charles 1775-1834 *Poetry for Children.* London: The Leadenhall Press, 1892. One of 112 copies, signed by press founder, Andrew White Tuer (this copy #2), 157 x 99mm., 2 volumes, charming contemporary batik textured calf by Zaehnsdorf (stamp-signed in gilt on front turn-in), covers gilt with fillets and dogtooth roll border, upper cover with thick festooned garland of fruit and leaves, flat spines divided into panels by plain and decorative rules, densely gilt turn-ins, marbled endpapers, top edge gilt, each volume with engraved frontispiece, engraved bookplate of A. Edward Newton of Oak Knoll with (loose) bookplate of H. Marion Soliday, minor offsetting from frontispieces, just vaguest hint of rubbing to extremities, but very fine, bindings bright and scarcely worn, text with virtually no signs of use. Phillip J. Pirages 63 - 67 2013 $1500

Association – Solme, E.

Burnet, Gilbert, Bp. of Salisbury 1643-1715 *A Relation of a Conference, Held about Religion at London the Third of April 1676.* London: printed and are to be sold by Moses Pitt, 1676. First edition, 8vo., prelim imprimatur leaf and final ad leaf, ink splashes to A4 recto of pages 12-13, one marginal note identifying an anonymous name in text, full contemporary calf, raised bands, rubbed, hinges cracked, head and tail of spine worn, early paper label chipped, handwritten shelf label flap, armorial bookplate of W. Wynne, signature of G. Wynne on title, Edw. Solme (?) struck through. Jarndyce Antiquarian Booksellers CCIV - 6 2013 £150

Association – Somerville, Edith

Pitman, Isaac *Manuscript Writing & Lettering.* 1921. Second edition, 8 plate, quarter cloth, some staining on boards, text very good, inscribed "Edith Somerville from BTS July 1926" in her own hand.   C. P. Hyland   261 - 786   2013   £35

Association – Somes, Daniel

New York. (City) *Manual of the Corporation of the City of New York for 1861.* New York: D. T. Valentine, 1861. 700 pages, duotones, color plates, engravings, many foldout maps and illustrations, original purple cloth decorated in blind and gilt, 3 bookplates, one of Samuel W. Galpin, another from a library (with minimal marking), spine little sunned, else very good plus, inscribed by Galpin to Maine Congressman Daniel Somes.   Between the Covers Rare Books, Inc.   New York City - 299888   2013 $450

Association – Sondheim, Norman

Hornby, Charles Harry St. John *A Descriptive Bibliography of the Books Printed at the Ashendene Press.* Chelsea: Shelley House, 1935. Limited to 390 numbered copies, this #186 printed on special paper made by Joseph Batchelor & sons, 4to., beautiful plates and woodcuts, some initial letters filled by hand by Graily Hewitt, errata slip tipped in, original gilt stamped maroon calf, five raised bands, spine bands, spine professionally rebacked to imitate original corners faintly rubbed, signed by printer Charles Harry St. John Hornby in ink at limitation page, prospectus for later printing laid in, bookplate of Norman J. Sondheim, near fine, gorgeous copy.   Jeff Weber Rare Books   171 - 9   2013 $2850

Sampson, John *XXI Welsh Gypsy Folk Tales.* Newtown, Powys: Gregynog Press, 1933. 216/235 copies (of an edition of 250), printed on Portal handmade paper, title vignette and 7 other exquisite wood engravings by Agnes Miller Parker, imperial 8vo., original mustard yellow bevel edged sheepskin, backstrip rubbed, more so at head and tail, edges and corners also with some fairly light rubbing, design of horizontal lines on front cover incorporating the title lettering and lettering on backstrip, all gilt blocked, usual offsetting for turn-ins and faint tape stains to free endpapers, bookplates of M. Weiss and Norman J. Sondheim, untrimmed, good.   Blackwell's Rare Books   172 - 293   2013   £1250

Association – Sotheby, William

Vergilius Maro, Publius *Georgica Publii Virgilii Maronis Hexaglotta.* E Typographeo Gulielmi Nicol, 1827. presentation copy from English translator and printer, half title inscribed "For the library of the Royal Institution from William Sotheby 12 Grosvenor Street Feby 19 1833", letter front printer presenting the volume tipped in, some light dust soiling, imperial 4to., contemporary half purple roan over marbled boards, edges untrimmed, spine divided by triple gilt fillets, second compartment gilt lettered direct, rubbed at extremities, worn, front hinge cracking after title, rear flyleaf removed 'withdrawn' stamp to front pastedown, good.   Blackwell's Rare Books   172 - 147   2013   £1400

Association – Southouse

Spence, Joseph 1699-1766 *Polymetis; or an Enquiry concerning the Agreement Between the Works of the Roman Poets adn the Remains of the Antient Artists.* London: printed for R. and J. Dodsley, 1755. Second edition, engraved frontispiece and 41 other engraved plates, some minor spotting, plates offset onto facing pages, folio, contemporary calf, neatly rebacked preserving original gilt spine, gilt now somewhat worn, new green morocco lettering piece to style, boards with elaborate stencilled frame dyed a lighter brown, marbled endpapers, some tidy repairs to corners, rubbed, bookplates of Strathallen and Southouse, good.   Blackwell's Rare Books   B174 - 145   2013   £650

Association – Spalding, John Tricks

Beck, Thomas Alcock *Annales Furnesienses. History and Antiquities of the Abbey of Furness.* London: Payne and Foss, M. A. Nattali; s. Soulby, 1844. First and only edition (250 copies), large 4to. contemporary full pebble grain morocco gilt by Murray's Nottingham Book Company with their ticket, monogram of JTS intertwined (John Tricks Spalding) in black and red leathers, decorated in gilt on upper board, all edges gilt, engraved title, printed title in red and black 3 lithographed facsimiles, 1 engraved plan, 18 fine tissue guarded steel engraved plates, 3 tinted lithographs, 11 text woodcuts, scattered foxing, mainly to flyleaves and half title.   R. F. G. Hollett & Son   Lake District & Cumbria - 93   2013   £595

Association – Sparkes, Stewart

Wiseman, Richard *Eight Chirurgical Treaties on these Following Heads Viz. 1. cf. Tumours. II. Cf. Ulcers. III. Cf. Diseases of the Anus. IV. Cf. the King's Evil. V. Cf. wounds. VI. Cf. Gun-Shot Wounds. VII. Cf. Fractures and Luxations. VIII Cf. the Lues Venerea.* London: for B. T. & L. M. and sold by W. Keblewhite and J. Jones, 1697. Third edition, folio, including half title A1, 18th century paneled calf, very skilfully rebacked retaining original gilt spine, period style label, tiny (half inch) repaired tear in lower margin of third leaf, else remarkably fine, fresh copy, contemporary ownership signature of Stewart Sparkes.   Joseph J. Felcone Inc.   Books Printed before 1701 - 68   2013 $3200

Association – Sparrow, John

Barton, Bernard *Selections from the Poems and Letters.* London: Hall, Virtue & Co., 1850. Second edition, frontispiece, plates, unopened in original light blue cloth, spine slightly faded, small booklabel of John Sparrow, very good. Jarndyce Antiquarian Booksellers CCIII - 638 2013 £40

Bowles, William Lisle *The Missionary: a Poems.* London: John Murray, 1813. Second edition, full contemporary dark blue morocco, gilt and blind spine and borders, gilt dentelles, spine slightly rubbed, slight wear to head small booklabel of John Sparrow, all edges gilt, inscribed "from the author..." Latin ownership and note, armorial bookplate of George Downing Bowles, of Fawley, Southampton. Jarndyce Antiquarian Booksellers CCIII - 34 2013 £150

Bowles, William Lisle *(Collection) Poems. (with) Sonnets and Other Poems.* London: T. Cadell Jun. and W. Davies, 1801. 1802. First edition, eighth edition, plates, frontispiece an plates, 2 volumes, attractively bound in slightly later full blue calf, gilt spines, borders and dentelles, maroon leather labels, author's name on spine, slightly rubbed and faded, small booklabels of John Sparrow, all edges gilt, handsome. Jarndyce Antiquarian Booksellers CCIII - 31 2013 £280

Brydges, Samuel Egerton *The Autobiography, Times, Opinions and Contemporares.* London: Cochrane & M'Crone, 1834. First edition, 2 volumes, half titles, frontispiece portraits little foxed, titles in red and black, contemporary half maroon morocco, gilt spines, marbled boards, edges and endpapers, slight rubbing, bookplates of John Sparrow with few pencil notes by him, very good. Jarndyce Antiquarian Booksellers CCIII - 43 2013 £150

Brydges, Samuel Egerton *Coningsby, a Tragic Tale.* Paris & Geneve: J. J. Paschoud; London: Rob. Triphook, 1819. First edition, half title, few marks in text, full contemporary maroon calf, gilt spine, slightly faded, gilt borders, old booklabel defaced, later booklabel of John Sparrow. Jarndyce Antiquarian Booksellers CCIII - 42 2013 £450

Coleridge, Sara *Phantasmion.* C. Whittingham for William Pickering, 1837. First edition, inscribed presentation from Mrs. H. N. Coleridge for Miss Theodosia Hinckes, , loosely inserted ALS by author to Mrs. Lonsdale, (pencil inscription "Given me by John Sparrow), 8vo., flyleaves little spotted, through setting slightly on to half title, few areas of minor spotting, contemporary pebble grained green morocco, double blind ruled borders on sides with corner ornaments, thick blind rules on either side of raised bands on spine, lettered direct in gilt, gilt edges by Hayday, mostly faded to brown, little rubbed, short split at head of lower joint, good. Blackwell's Rare Books 172 - 43 2013 £3500

Frere, John Hookham *The Monks and the Giants.* Bath: printed by H. E. Carrington, 1842. Half title, uncut in original brown wrappers, spine excellently rebacked, booklabel of John Sparrow, very good. Jarndyce Antiquarian Booksellers CCIII - 383 2013 £50

Rossetti, Christina 1830-1894 *The Prince's Progress and Other Poems.* London: Macmillan, 1866. First edition, half title, frontispiece, vignette title, additional printed title, untrimmed in original green glazed cloth by Burn & Kirby's decorated and lettered in gilt, John Sparrow's small booklabel, very good, bright copy. Jarndyce Antiquarian Booksellers CCV - 234 2013 £850

Spence, Joseph 1699-1766 *An Essay on Mr. Pope's Odyssey.* London: printed for S. Wilmot, Bookseller in Oxford, 1737. Second edition, 12mo., engraved frontispiece, toned and little bit spotted, contemporary sheep, later olive morocco label, joints cracking but strong, boards marked, little rubbed at extremities, ink ownership inscription " J. Filmer 1774" at upper forecorner of f.f.e.p. printed booklabel of John Sparrow. Unsworths Antiquarian Booksellers 28 - 131 2013 £175

Wilde, Oscar 1854-1900 *Letters to the Sphinx from Oscar Wild with Reminiscences of the author by Ada Leverson.* London: Duckworth, 1930. First edition, large 8vo., original blue cloth, lettered gilt on spine, number 64 of 275 copies signed by author, bookplate of John Sparrow, near fine. Maggs Bros. Ltd. 1442 - 325 2013 £275

Wheelwright, C. A. *Poems, Original and Translated...* A. J. Valpy, 1810. 8vo., uncut, original boards, worn, covers detached, Earl of Hardwicke's copy, later in the library of John Sparrow, with tipped-in printed slip requesting subscribers to pay for their copies on delivery. Ken Spelman Books Ltd. 75 - 66 2013 £35

Association – Spaulding, John

Walton, Izaak 1593-1683 *The Complete Angler.* London: D. Bogue, 1844. Sixth (titled fourth) John Major edition, 12 steel engravings, 74 woodcuts, early 20th century binding by Riviere & Son in full forest green levant morocco, fine, unique copy with four signed watercolors by John Absolon, from the renowned collection of John T. Spaulding. David Brass Rare Books, Inc. Holiday 2012 Chapter Five - DB 01876 2013 $3850

Association – Spencer, Earl of

Lefevre, Raoul *Le Recueil des Histoires de Troyes.* Bruges: William Caxton, 1473. First edition in French, small folio, Lettre batarde, lacking 32 printed leaves and two blanks, early 19th century brown straight grain morocco by Charles Lewis, gilt and blind ruled in geometric patterns, gilt inner dentelles, gilt edges, fine, unrestored, the missing leaves are internal and first and last printed leaves are present from the collection of the Duke of Roxburghe (sale 1812) of the third Earl Spencer (sale 1823), John Dent, with his notes (sale 1827), P. A. Hanrott (sale 1834) the Earl of Ashburnham (sale 1897); Richard Bennett with his bookplate and John Pierpont Morgan with his bookplate and shelfmark.   Heritage Book Shop   50th Anniversary Catalogue - 62   2013 $950,000

Association – Spiers, Graham

Bronowski, J. *The Ascent of Man.* London: BBC, 1973. First edition, 4to., original brown cloth, near fine in dust jacket, inscribed by author for Graham Spiers, 1 Nv. 1973, loosely inserted are two black and white photos of author and another depicting an artist's head and shoulders study of him, also inserted are programme for a tribute service, 2 obit clippings and invitation to the preview of BBC programme of the same name.   Maggs Bros. Ltd.   1460 - 141   2013   £75

Association – Spingarn, Arthur

Cartwright, William *Comedies, Tragi-Comedies with other Poems.* London: for Humphrey Moseley, 1651. 8vo., engraved portrait, 5 section titles, with duplicates leaves U1-3 as usual, blank f4 present, b2 folded an untrimmed to preserve shoulder notes, modern calf very skillfully executed in 17th century style, title and dedication leaf and few running heads slightly cropped by binder's knife, one note to binder cropped, very nice, Arthur Spingarn's copy, rebound, with his bookplate and collation notes laid in.   Joseph J. Felcone Inc.   English and American Literature to 1800 - 4   2013 $2400

Association – Spitaels, Albert

Tench, Watkin *Voyage a la Baie Botanique...* Paris: Letellier, 1789. First French edition, folding map, 8vo., original paste paper wrappers, uncut, slightly worn, inner joints mended with plain paper some time ago, and ms. label added to spine, old signature and stamp of Albert Spitaels (probably the Dutch banker), housed in black cloth box, with rare map "Carte de le Baye Botanique et Harvres Adjacens...".   Maggs Bros. Ltd.   1467 - 97   2013   £5000

Association – Spivak, John

Wexley, John *They Shall Not Die.* New York: Alfred A. Knopf, 1934. First edition, fine in fine dust jacket with very short rubbed tear on rear panel, warmly inscribed by author to journalist John Spivak.   Between the Covers Rare Books, Inc.   165 - 337   2013 $475

Association – Spon, Baron De

Ayres, Philip *Cupids Addresse to the Ladies.* London: Sold by R. Bently in Covent Garden, S. Tidmarch..., 1683. frontispiece, 44 emblematic plates and engraved verse in Latin, English, Italian and French, 8vo., several plates bound in incorrect order, some occasional browning mainly to fore-edges, 19th century tree calf, hinges repaired, new red morocco label, spine and board edges rubbed, corners little worn, bookplate of Baron de Spon.   Jarndyce Antiquarian Booksellers   CCIV - 2   2013   £2500

Association – Squires, Roy

Imagination!   Los Angeles: Los Angeles Science Fiction Society, 1937-1938. Complete run, 13 monthly issues from Volume 1 No. 1 in October 1937 to Anniversary Issue October 1938, remarkable set, mimeographed productions, in stapled covers, all issues fine, very scarce, the set has folder wrapping the first issue, with ownership name of Roy Squires II.   Ken Lopez Bookseller   159 - 176   2013 $7500

Association – Stacy, D.

Burns, Robert 1759-1796 *Poems, Chiefly in the Scottish Dialect.* London: printed for a. Strahan and T. Cadell,, in the Strand, and W. Creech Edinburgh, 1787. Third edition, frontispiece, bound without half title, contemporary half calf, marbled boards, spine with raised and gilt bands, red morocco label, very slightly rubbed, slight wear to marbled paper on edges of following board, very good, clean copy in attractive contemporary binding, this copy was bought for 6s by Mr. D. Stacy of Hackney, London who adds his name to subscriber list.   Jarndyce Antiquarian Booksellers   CCIII - 49   2013   £1600

Association – Staines, William

Derham, William 1657-1735 *Astro-Theology.* London: Printed for J. Richardson, 1758. Ninth edition, 8vo., 3 folding copper engraved plates, offset browning on endpapers and titlepage, one plate rather foxed, contemporary sprinkled calf, double gilt ruled borders, expertly rebacked, raised and gilt banded spine, red morocco labels, corners neatly repaired, early signature of Wm. J. Staines, ownership name of Walter Crouch, Wanstead.   Jarndyce Antiquarian Booksellers   CCIV - 112   2013   £250

Association – Stalling, Bettise

Johnson, Jack *Johnson - In the Ring - and Out.* Chicago: National Sports Pub. Co., 1927. First edition, very near fine, lacking dust jacket, inscribed by Lucius C. Harper, editor of newspaper The Chicago Defender to Bettise Stalling.   Between the Covers Rare Books, Inc. 165 - 17   2013 $850

Association – Stanell, William

Donne, John 1571-1631 *Poems, &c. With Elegies on the Author's Death.* London: printed by T. N. for Henry Herringman, 1669. Fifth edition, complete with initial and terminal blanks, some dampstaining in later half of volume, contemporary calf, double blind ruled borders on sides, ornamental corner pieces, binder's flyleaf at end of early 16th century text printed in red and black, bearing contemporary (1669), signature of William Stanell, rebacked, cover crackled, bookplate of archaeologist John William Brailsford. Blackwell's Rare Books   B174 - 50   2013   £3250

Association – Stanger, Joshua, Mrs.

Bush, James *The Choice; or Lines on the Beatitudes Square.* London: R. Saywell; Cockermouth: Bailey & Sons and Carlisle: C. Thurnam, 1841. First edition, square 8vo., full polished calf gilt, edges rubbed, pages 102, engraved frontispiece of Buttermere Chapel (foxed), scattered foxing in places, scarce, presentation copy inscribed by author to Mrs. Joshua Stanger. R. F. G. Hollett & Son   Lake District & Cumbria - 246   2013   £75

Association – Stanley, John Thomas

Fielding, Henry 1707-1754 *The Adventures of Joseph Andrews and His Friend Mr. Abraham Andrews...* London: printed for J. Murray... and J. Sibbald, Edinburgh, 1792. 8vo., 8 etched plates, contemporary calf with rope twist gilt borders, expertly rebacked retaining original gilt decorated spine and labels, spine rubbed, labels slightly chipped, armorial bookplate of John Thomas Stanley Esq. of Alderley. Jarndyce Antiquarian Booksellers   CCIV - 131   2013   £280

Association – Starer, Robert

Updike, John 1932- *Hugging the Shore.* New York: Knopf, 1983. First edition, inscribed by author for Robert Starer, book appears read, with some sagging to bulky text block and modest fading to covers, in very good to near fine dust jacket. Ken Lopez Bookseller   159 - 197   2013 $350

Association – Starling, Kenyon

Dickens, Charles 1812-1870 *Dombey and Son.* London: Bradbury & Evans, 1848. First edition in book form, first state following all points in Smith, the Kenyon Starling - William Self copy, octavo, publisher's variant binding of moderate green fine diaper grain cloth, original pale yellow coated endpapers, spine very faded, corners very slightly bumped, just tiny amount of board show through, otherwise binding as fresh as one could possibly wish for, chemised in half green morocco slipcase, Self bookplate on chemise. David Brass Rare Books, Inc. Holiday 2012 Chapter Five - DB 01693   2013 $11,500

Hardy, Thomas 1840-1928 *The Return of the Native.* London: Smith Elder, 1878. First edition, 3 volumes, 8vo., original decorated brown cloth, gilt lettering, frontispiece, faint evidence of lending library labels on upper boards of each volume, bookplate of American collector Kenyon Starling on front pastedown, below which is the earlier bookplate of illustrator and connoisseur Pickford Waller, designed by Austin Osman Spare circa 1907, cloth little worn and soiled, some light foxing, particularly on prelims, very good, from the Gary Lepper Collection of Thomas Hardy. The Brick Row Book Shop   Bulletin Nine - 6   2013 $10,000

Association – Starr, Harvey

Outland, Charles F. *Man-Made Disaster: the Story of the St. Francis Dam...* Glendale: Arthur H. Clark Co., 1963. First edition, 249 pages, illustrations, maps, portraits, brown cloth, bookplate, very fine, pictorial dust jacket, presentation inscription signed by author for friend Harvey Starr, extremely scarce. Argonaut Book Shop   Recent Acquisitions June 2013 - 220   2013 $500

Association – Steadman, Ralph

Dodgson, Charles Lutwidge 1832-1898 *The Hunting of the Snark.* London: Dempsey, 1975. Illustrations by Ralph Steadman, fine in near fine, price clipped dust jacket with some fading to edges and spine, signed by Steadman with drawing dated in year of publication. Ken Lopez Bookseller   159 - 180   2013 $150

Thompson, Hunter S. *The Curse of Lono.* New York: Bantam, 1983. First edition, illustrations by Ralph Steadman, signed by artist with original full page caricature by him of Thompson, only issued in wrappers, near fine. Ken Lopez Bookseller   159 - 183   2013 $350

Association – Steane, Ethelwyn

Caulibus, Johannes De *The Mirrour of the Blessed Lyf of Jesu Christ.* Oxford: at the Clarendon Press, Henry Frowde, 1908. Occasional fox spot, pencil note in margin of introduction, 4to., original quarter line, printed paper label, pale blue paper boards, couple of tiny marks and merest touch of wear to forecorners, prospectus (creased at top) loosely inserted very good, inscribed by editor, Lawrence Powell for Ethelywn Steane.   Blackwell's Rare Books B174 - 27   2013   £100

Association – Steele, C. H.

Carmichael, Richard *An Essay on Veneral Diseases and the Uses and Abuses of Mercury in their Treatment.* Philadelphia: Judah Dobson and A. Sherman, 1825. Second American edition, 4to., uncut, 5 color plates, modern green library buckram, gilt stamped spine title, ex-library bookplates, early signature of Ch. H. Steele (?), very good. Jeff Weber Rare Books   172 - 52   2013 $400

Association – Steepe, Ian

Deane, Seamus *Rumours.* Dublin: Dolmen Press, 1977. First edition, 8vo., original wrappers, inscribed by author on titlepage, for Ian Steepe, fine.   Maggs Bros. Ltd.   1442 - 57   2013   £90

Association – Stephens, Stephens Lyne

Hugo, Victor 1802-1865 *Notre Dame de Paris.* Bruxelles: Louis Hauman et Comp., 1834. Second Bruxelles edition, 3 volumes, 12mo., very pretty set, finely bound in near contemporary half calf, marbled boards, spines most ornately covered in geometric gilt lattice tooling with red and black gilt morocco labels, marbled edges and endpapers, armorial bookplate of Stephens Lyne Stephens, scarce.   Ken Spelman Books Ltd.   75 - 96   2013   £295

Association – Sterling, George

Sterling, George *The Caged Eagle and Other Poems.* San Francisco: A. M. Robertson, 1916. First edition, first issue with the two errors called for by Johnson on pages 34 and 162, olive green cloth, gilt lettered spine and front cover, inner front hinge with short crack, spine gilt slightly dulled, else fine, presentation inscription signed by author, for George Sterling, with corrections in Sterling's hand for the issue point errors (pages 34, 162) as well as corrections in his hand on page 161 for errors not noted by bibliographers. Argonaut Book Shop   Recent Acquisitions June 2013 - 271   2013 $350

Association – Stern, Gerald

Lazer, Hank *On Equal Terms. Poems by Charles Bernstein, David Ignatow, Denise Levertov, Louis Simpson, Gerald Stern.* Tuscaloosa: Symposium Press, 1984. First edition, limited to 275 copies, although not called for, this copy signed by all contributors, one of the few copies we've seen signed by any of the poets, 4to., original green wrappers, as new.   James S. Jaffe Rare Books   Fall 2013 - 5   2013 $450

Association – Sternfeld

Jeanneret-Oehl, Auguste *Souvenirs du Sejour d'un Horloger Neuchatelois en Chine.* Neuchatel: G. Guillaume Fils, 1866. 135 x 205mm., 136 pages, frontispiece, original mustard printed wrappers, few chips, spine paper taped, Sternfeld bookplate, very rare.   Jeff Weber Rare Books 169 - 239   2013 $365

Association – Stevens, F. E.

Dickens, Charles 1812-1870 *David Copperfield.* London: Bradbury & Evans, 1850. First edition, half title, frontispiece, vignette title, plates by Phiz, some plates browned, generally quite clean, contemporary half dark green calf, spine decorated in gilt, black leather label, bit rubbed, signed F. E. Stevens in contemporary hand on printed title, loose armorial bookplate of Arthur Earl of Castlestewart.   Jarndyce Antiquarian Booksellers   CCV - 85   2013   £450

Association – Steward, N.

Cushing, Harvey Williams 1869-1939 *Instruction in Operative Medicine.* Offprint from Johns Hopkins Hospital Bulletin, 1906. 2 diagram illustrations, plates, some soiling and foxing on front wrapper, early writing on first leaf, signed inscribed presentation copy from author for Prof. N. Steward.   James Tait Goodrich   S74 - 63   2013 $1750

Association – Stewart, John Levenson Douglas

Johnstone, Charles *Chrysal; or the Adventures of a Guinea in America.* London: T. Becket, 1760. First edition, 2 volumes, large 12mo., 19th century antique mottled calf by Riviere, gilt, expertly rebacked, old backs laid down, leather labels, raised bands, inner gilt dentelles, fine, bookplates of John Leveson Douglas Stewart and A. Edward Newton, slipcase.   Howard S. Mott Inc.   262 - 80   2013 $500

Association – Stirling, J.

Marino, Giambattista *L'Adone, Poems.* Amsterdam: 1651. 2 volumes, 12mo. bound in sixes, small marginal tear to V1 volume II, some light browning, few ink splashes but very good, most handsome early 19th century dark blue straight grain morocco, gilt ruled borders, attractive gilt panelled spines decorated with flower head, open circles and small gilt dots, pink endpapers and pastedowns, armorial bookplate of John Barron, early inscription of J. Stirling, alter 19th century bookplate of Alfred Coco of Middle Temple, ownership name of J. Stroud Read, London Nov. 1928, earlier hand notes "Will. Roscoe's Library", all edges gilt. Jarndyce Antiquarian Booksellers   CCV - 191   2013   £620

Association – Stockton, John

Morgan, John *A Discourse Upon the Institution of Medical Schools in America.* Philadelphia: William Bradford, 1765. 19th century full blond paneled calf, endpapers renewed, top edge gilt remargined along inner edge, text foxed, dampstaining affecting outer upper blank corner of pages, presentation copy to John Shaw Billings, from John Stockton, quite rare.   James Tait Goodrich   75 - 153   2013 $8995

Association – Stone, P. M.

Freeman, R. Austin *A Savant's Vendetta.* London: Arthur Pearson, 1920. First English edition, cheap paper browned, small spot on front board, very good or better, inscribed by author for P. M. Stone, scarce, very seldom found and never signed or inscribed.   Between the Covers Rare Books, Inc.   Mystery & Detective Fiction - 54833   2013 $2500

Association – Stopes, Marie

Ellis, Henry Havelock   1859-1939 *Little Essays of Love and Virtue.* London: A. & C. Black, 1922. First edition, 8vo., original green cloth, inscribed by author for Dr. Marie Stopes, with a number of her pencilled underlinings and emphases, with 3 textual holograph remarks, excellent copy. Maggs Bros. Ltd.   1460 - 275   2013   £500

Forster, Edward Morgan   1879-1970 *Virgina Woolf. The Rede Lecture 1941.* Cambridge: at the University Press, 1942. First edition, 8vo., original cream wrappers, near fine, inscribed by author for Marie Stopes, near fine. Maggs Bros. Ltd.   1460 - 295   2013   £950

Association – Stormont, J. Henry

Chaucer, Geoffrey   1340-1400 *The Works.* London: printed for Bernard Lintot, 1721. First Urry edition, engraved frontispiece, fine portrait of Chaucer, title vignette and 27 excellent headpiece vignettes of pilgrims, just little light browning, folio, 19th century diced Russia, boards panelled and framed in blind, gilt roll tool border, neatly rebacked preserving original spine, decorated in gilt and blind, corners renewed, old leather somewhat scratched and rubbed around edges, bookplate of R. St. John Mathews and pencil inscription of J. Henry Stormont dated 1901 to endpapers good.   Blackwell's Rare Books   B174 - 31   2013   £1200

Association – Strachey, Charles

Byron, George Gordon Noel, 6th Baron   1788-1824 *The Corsair, a Tale.* London: John Murray, 1814. Fourth edition, first issue, half title, 8 page catalog, later drab wrappers, spine with two small repaired tears, ink title, booklabel of Alex Bridge and ownership inscription of Charles Strachey, very good.   Jarndyce Antiquarian Booksellers   CCIII - 184   2013   £30

Association – Strachey, Lytton

Earle, John *Microcosmography or a Piece of the World Discover'd in Essays and Characters.* London: printed by E. Say, 1732. 12mo., top corner of titlepage excised (clear of text), lightly browned throughout, some light staining, contemporary sprinkled sheep, title lettered gilt to front board, sometime rebacked, later vertical red morocco label to spine, somewhat rubbed and scratched, fore edges bit worn, smaller bookplate of Lytton Strachey.   Unsworths Antiquarian Booksellers   28 - 93   2013   £200

Association – Stradbroke, A.

Coleridge, Samuel Taylor   1772-1834 *The Poetical Works.* London: Macmillan & Co., 1893. Half title, frontispiece uncut in original green cloth, following board slightly marked, spine very lightly dulled, signed "A Stradbroke 1894", very good.   Jarndyce Antiquarian Booksellers   CCIII - 499   2013   £30

Association – Strand, Mark

Brodsky, Joseph *Verses on the Winter Campaign 1980.* London: Anvil Press Poetry, 1981. First edition, one of 200 copies signed by Brodsky and by Translator, Alan Myers (out of a total edition of 500), 12mo., original unprinted wrappers, dust jacket, fine, presentation copy inscribed by author to poet Mark Strand, with Brodsky's corrections. James S. Jaffe Rare Books   Fall 2013 - 29   2013 $1250

Octavio Paz: A Celebration. New York: Academy of American Poets and the Mexican Cultural Institute, 1994. First edition, 8vo., original wrappers, although not called for, this copy signed by Paz, Mark Strand, John Ashbery, Bei Dao and Charles Tomlinson.   James S. Jaffe Rare Books   Fall 2013 - 6   2013 $750

Association – Strang, Agnes

Ashford, Daisy   *The Young Visiters, or Mr. Salteena's Plan.* London: Chatto & Windus, 1919. Reprint, 8vo., frontispiece and one facsimile, original marbled boards, black cloth, printed paper label, signed by author and inscribed by actress Edyth Goodall and one Agnes Strang, worn along edges of boards and lettering piece, otherwise very good.   Maggs Bros. Ltd. 1460 - 23   2013   £75

Association – Stratford, John

Boyle, Robert   1627-1691   *Experiments, Notes &c. about Mechanical Origine or Production of Divers Particular Qualities...*   E. Flesher for R. Davis, bookseller in Oxford, 1676. First edition, 2nd issue (same as the 1675 first issue apart from cancel title, remains of cancelled title visible), 11 parts in one volume, without blank leaf B8 but with the other three, closed tear to blank margin of second leaf, little dampstaining in margins of few leaves, tiny hole caused by paper fault in one leaf, not affecting text, little bit of spotting here and there, various paginations, small 8vo., contemporary calf, skillfully rebacked with original spine laid on, later spine label, contemporary signature of John Stratford, Balliol College, 1681.   Blackwell's Rare Books   Sciences - 15   2013   £4800

Association – Strathallen

Spence, Joseph   1699-1766   *Polymetis; or an Enquiry concerning the Agreement Between the Works of the Roman Poets adn the Remains of the Antient Artists.* London: printed for R. and J. Dodsley, 1755. Second edition, engraved frontispiece and 41 other engraved plates, some minor spotting, plates offset onto facing pages, folio, contemporary calf, neatly rebacked preserving original gilt spine, gilt now somewhat worn, new green morocco lettering piece to style, boards with elaborate stencilled frame dyed a lighter brown, marbled endpapers, some tidy repairs to corners, rubbed, bookplates of Strathallen and Southouse, good.   Blackwell's Rare Books   B174 - 145   2013   £650

Association – Street, William

Cabala; Sive Sacra. Myteries of State Government: in Letters of Illustrious Persons, and Great Agents; in the Reigns of Henry the Eighth, Queen Elizabeth, K. James and the Late King Charles...   London: printed for G. Bedel and T. Collins..., 1654. First edition, small 8vo., cloth, general titlepage and titlepage to part 2 in red and black, from the library of William R. Williams, NY 1856 and William R. Street, 1845; spine label scuffed, owner's name on top edge of first blank and title, first titlepage and last page of index mounted, rare marginalia, damp spotting to lower margin of last half of second part, few last leaves soiled at top edge, overall still solid.   Kaaterskill Books   16 - 4   2013 $475

Association – Streeter, Frank

Mechain, Pierre Francois Andre   *Base du Systeme Metrique Decimal, ou Mesure d l'arc du Meridien Compris entre les Paralleles de Dunkerque...*   Paris: Boudoin, 1806-1810. First edition, rare, 3 volumes, quarto, 28 folding engraved plates by C. Collin, numerous tables in text, contemporary French tree calf with gilt borders, smooth spines stamped and lettered gilt, red morocco spine labels, all edges marbled, marbled endpapers, lacking endpapers in volume 1, some insignificant pale marginal dampstaining, few small splits to joints, corners and boards bit rubbed, some staining to boards volumes I and III, bookplate of Frank Streeter, overall very nice.   Heritage Book Shop   Holiday Catalogue 2012 - 106   2013 $35,000

Association – Strong, Jane

Anderson, Robert   *Poetical Works...*   Carlisle: printed and sold by B. Scott, 1820. First edition, 2 volumes, uncut in original blue boards, carefully rebacked, dusted and little rubbed, signature of Jane Strong 1835, volume I.   Jarndyce Antiquarian Booksellers   CCIII - 628   2013   £350

Association – Sturt

King, Philip Parker   *Narrative of a Survey of the Intertropical and Western Colonies of Australia. Performed Between the Years 1818 and 1822.* London: 1827. First edition, 2nd issue, 2 volumes, engraved folding chart, 10 uncolored aquatint views, 8 woodcut engravings, plan, contemporary half calf over marbled boards, spines gilt and sound, slightly shelfworn, extremities rubbed, the Sturt family copy with Alington bookplate, lovely association.   Maggs Bros. Ltd. 1467 - 81   2013   £3750

Association – Suffield, Edward Lord

Koran *The Koran, Commonly called the Alcoran of Mohammed.* printed for C. Ackers, 1734. First sale edition, title printed in red and black, 5 engraved plates, including map of Arabia, variable moderate browning, 4to., contemporary panelled calf, blind tooling around central mottled panel, spine gilt in compartments, red lettering piece, gilt Suffield crest in 5th panel, rebacked preserving original spine, but raised bands of lighter new calf, engraved armorial bookplate of Edward Lord Suffield inside front cover, good, well above average copy. Blackwell's Rare Books 172 - 83   2013   £2500

Association – Sullivan, F. W.

Sullivan, Timothy Daniel *Speeches from the Dock or Protests of Irish Patriotism.* Dublin: Gill & Son, circa, 1910? 8vo., 160 pages, illustrations, puckered publisher's cloth, spine faded, signed on endpaper by F. M. Sullivan, very good. Second Life Books Inc.   183 - 366   2013 $75

Association – Summers, A. Montague

Pope, Alexander 1688-1744 *Selecta Poemata Italorum qui Latine Scripsersunt.* Londini: Impensis J. & P. Knapton, 1740. 2 volumes, 8vo., touch of foxing to titlepages, contemporary sprinkled calf, spines in six compartments with raised bands and morocco labels, numbered in gilt, rest with gilt decoration (much rubbed), joints and corners repaired spines bit darkened, ownership inscriptions to front endpaper of Geoffrey Woledge, Birmingham 1937 and A. Montague Summers (1899). Unsworths Antiquarian Booksellers   28 - 122   2013   £300

Association – Surtees, Robert

Paris, Matthew 1200-1259 *Flores Historiarum pr Matthaeum Westmonasteriensem Collecti, Praecipue de Rebus Britannicis ab Exordio Mundi Usque ad Annum Domini 1307.* Ex officina Thomae Marshii, 1570. Second printed edition, Folio, titlepage trimmed close to woodcut border, final blank leaf discarded, index bound at front of text, one leaf with original paper flaw affecting a few characters, first leaf of index with bottom margin folded over to preserve early ms. note, verso of title also filled with text in early ms. (trimmed at bottom), few short notes or marks later on, last dozen leaves showing faint but substantial dampmark, some soiling/minor staining elsewhere, touch of worming to blank fore-edge margin, two leaves remargined, gathering Ttt in earlier(?) state without (and not calling for) the additional unsigned singleton leaf, 18th century mottled calf, spine with five raised bands, red morocco lettering pieces in second and third compartment, rubbed, front joint cracking (but strong), little peeling to leather, light wear to endcaps, marbled endpapers, bookplates of Robert Surtees (1779-1834) and his Mainsforth Library, sound. Blackwell's Rare Books   172 - 109   2013   £1600

Association – Sutro, Gillian

Gautier, Jean Jacques *Une Femme Prisonniere.* Paris: Editions Bernard Grasset, 1968. First edition, original wrappers, fine, inscribed by author for Gillian Sutro. Maggs Bros. Ltd.   1460 - 327   2013   £350

Association – Swaffer, Hannen

Caine, Hall *Recollections of Rossetti.* London: Cassell and Co., 1928. First edition, 8vo., original red cloth gilt, inscribed by author to Hannen Swaffer, journalist, very good with some water damage to top corners, otherwise just little rubbed and darkened in places. Maggs Bros. Ltd.   1460 - 154   2013   £175

Association – Sweet, William

Cushing, Harvey Williams 1869-1939 *Selected Papers on Neurosurgery.* New Haven: 1969. 669 pages, near fine, in worn dust jacket, nice association, from the library of William Sweet, M.D. with his bookplate and name rubber-stamped on flyleaf. James Tait Goodrich   S74 - 68   2013 $175

Freeman, Walter *Psychsurgery. Intelligence Emotion and Social Behavior Following Prefrontal Lobotomy for Mental Conditions.* Springfield: Thomas, 1942. 337 pages, text illustrations, original cloth, dust jacket bit worn, else very good plus, presentation copy from James Watts for Bill Sweet. James Tait Goodrich   S74 - 117   2013 $350

Association – Swinbourn, Arthur

Bloomfield, Robert *Rural Tales, Ballads and Songs.* (bound with) *Wild Flowers; of Pastoral and Local Poetry.* (bound with) *The Farmer's Boy: a Rural Poem.* London: Vernor, Hood and Sharpe, Poultry, 1811. London: Longman etc., 1816. London: Longman &c. 1837. Seventh and fifteenth edition, 3 volumes in 1, contemporary half green calf, spine gilt in compartments, maroon leather label, armorial bookplate of Henry Hickman Barnes, with his name crossed through and that of Arthur Swinbourn added, Barnes' name has been struck through where present, very good. Jarndyce Antiquarian Booksellers   CCIII - 14   2013   £75

Association – Symmes, Minnehaha

Duncan, Robert *Poems 1948-49.* Berkeley: Miscellany Editions, 1949. First edition, second (expurgated) state, 8vo., original printed wrappers, usual, but in this instance very faint, discoloration to poor quality paper wrappers, still fine, presentation copy from author to his mother. James S. Jaffe Rare Books   Fall 2013 - 38   2013 $2500

Association – Symmonds, C. P.

Bailey, Percival *Tumors Arising from the Blood Vessels of the Brain.* London: Bailliere, Tindall & Cox, 1928. One of 1000 copies, first English edition, 219 pages, original red cloth, light wear, otherwise clean, tight copy, signature of "CP Symmonds".   James Tait Goodrich   S74 - 62   2013 $495

Association – Symons, Gunning

Byron, George Gordon Noel, 6th Baron   1788-1824 *The Poetical Works.* London: John Murray, 1854. Tall 8vo., frontispiece and engraved title, dedication leaf from John Murray to Sir Robert Peel, facsimiles, 32 page catalog (Jan. 1854), original pink cloth by Edmonds & Remnants, little marked, spine faded and with repairs to following hinge signed "Gunning Symons 1854" to leading f.e.p., fairly good copy.   Jarndyce Antiquarian Booksellers   CCIII - 81   2013   £45

Association – Tabori, Paul

Isherwood, Christopher *Prater Violet.* London: Methuen, 1946. First edition, foolscap 8vo., original purple cloth, backstrip blocked in green, dust jacket with backstrip panel and fore-edges darkened, small chip in front panel at head and tail, good, bookplate of Paul Tabori.   Blackwell's Rare Books   B174 - 239   2013   £100

Association – Talbot, Henry

Byron, George Gordon Noel, 6th Baron   1788-1824 *The Age of Bronze, or Carmen Secualre et Annus Haud Mirabilis.* London: printed for John Hunt, 1823. First edition, disbound, lacking half title, signature of Henry Talbot, very good.   Jarndyce Antiquarian Booksellers   CCIII - 310   2013   £120

Association – Talbot, Sarah Frances

Barbauld, Anna Laetitia   1743-1825 *Works.* London: Longman &c, 1825. First edition, 2 volumes, frontispiece volume I slightly spotted, contemporary half maroon calf largely faded to brown, spines lettered and with compartments in gilt, slight rubbing to corners and heads & tails of spines, signatures of Sarah Frances Talbot, 1840, good plus tight copy.   Jarndyce Antiquarian Booksellers   CCIII - 636   2013   £180

Association – Tandy, Jessica

Albee, Edward *A Delicate Balance.* New York: Atheneum, 1966. First edition, signed by author as well as six members of the original cast, Jessica Tandy, Hume Cronyn, Rosemary Murphy, Carmen Matthews, Henderson Forsythe and Marian Seldes, fine in nearly fine dust jacket.   Ed Smith Books   78 - 3   2013 $750

Association – Tate, Caroline

Ford, Ford Madox   1873-1939 *A Mirror to France.* London: Duckworth, 1926. First edition, 8vo., original green cloth, cloth little soiled, spine and edges faded, very good, inscribed to Caroline Tate (wife of Allen Tate), cloth little soiled, spine and edges faded, very good.   Maggs Bros. Ltd.   1460 - 286   2013   £750

Association – Tate, Mrs.

Binyon, Laurence   1859-1943 *The Winnowing Fan: Poems on the Great War.* London: Elkin Matthews, 1914. First edition, 8vo., original grey wrappers, uncut, inscribed by author to Mrs. Tate April 1915, covers unevenly browned, half title marked, otherwise excellent in protective folding box.   Maggs Bros. Ltd.   1460 - 105   2013   £75

Association – Taubman, P.

Homerus *The Iliad of Homer.* London: printed for Henry Lintot, 1743. 6 volumes, engraved portrait bust, folding map, 28 plates, , volume II bound without A2 (blank?), 12mo., contemporary calf, raised and gilt banded spines, heads and tails of 3 volumes little chipped, lacking 4 labels, corners bumped, ownership name on inner front boards of P. Taubman, 1798.   Jarndyce Antiquarian Booksellers   CCIV - 162   2013   £160

Association – Tayler, Alistair

Bennett, Arnold   1867-1931 *The Truth About an Author.* New York: George H. Doran, 1911. New edition, 8vo., original cream cloth, printed paper label on spine, inscribed by author for Duff (Alistair Tayler - sic), excellent copy, loosely inserted is ALS to Duff from John Drinkwater.   Maggs Bros. Ltd.   1460 - 80   2013   £350

Association – Taylor, A. J. P.

Deighton, Len *Twinkle, Twinkle Little Spy.* London: Jonathan Cape, 1976. First edition, 8vo., original black cloth, dust jacket, near fine, inscribed by author for Alan with A J. P. Taylor's bookplate.   Maggs Bros. Ltd.   1460 - 225   2013   £150

Association – Taylor, Ernest

Rowntree, B. Seebohm *Poverty and Progress. A Second Social Survey of York.* London: Longmans, 1941. First edition, very good, original gilt lettered dark blue cloth, dust jacket little worn, inscribed 'a gift from Arnold Rowntree, Ernest Taylor, John Harvey, Oct. 1941'.   Ken Spelman Books Ltd.   73 - 54   2013   £35

Association – Taylor, Francis Henry

Avery, C. Louise *Masterpieces of European Porcelain: a Catalogue of a Special Exhibition March 18- May 15 1949.* New York: printed by Marchbanks Press for The Metropolitan Museum of Art, 1949. One of 2000 copies, 290 x 222mm., attractive crimson crushed morocco by James MacDonald Co. of NY (stamp signed), covers with single gilt fillet border, upper cover with initials "F.W." in lower right corner, raised bands flanked by gilt rules, small gilt fleuron at head and tail of spine, vertical titling, densely gilt turn-ins, marbled endpapers; with 32 black and white photos; tipped to front pastedown is handwritten note to Mr. Wickes from Francis Henry Taylor, director of Metropolitan Museum, presenting this book in gratitude for Wickes' support of the Exhibition; couple of small marks to covers, but very fine with virtually no signs of use. Phillip J. Pirages 63 - 492   2013 $150

Association – Taylor, Peter

Gibson, Richard *Mirror for Magistrates.* London: Anthony Blond, 1958. First edition, octavo, 172 pages, very good, some age toning and scattered light stains to endpapers, else near fine in near fine dust jacket with some light soiling to top edge and light age toing to inside panel, inscribed by author for writer Peter Taylor. Between the Covers Rare Books, Inc. 165 - 157   2013 $650

Association – Taylor, R. G.

Cunningham, Allan *Paul Jones: a Romance.* Edinburgh: Oliver & Boyd, 1826. First edition, 3 volumes, half titles removed, slightly spotted, contemporary half calf, red leather labels, slightly rubbed, booklabels of R. G. Taylor. Jarndyce Antiquarian Booksellers   CCIII - 674   2013   £380

Association – Taylor, Thomas

Retz, Jean Francois Paul De Gondi, Cardinal De *Memoirs of the Cardinal de Retz...* London: printed for Jacob Tonson, 1723. 4 volumes, 12mo., worming to lower inner margin volume I, disappearing to single hole by B4 of main text and also to outer blank margin of final five leaves of volume III, full contemporary panelled calf, raised bands, red morocco labels, little rubbed and worn, armorial bookplate of Marquess of Headfort, signature of Thomas Taylor dated 1756. Jarndyce Antiquarian Booksellers   CCIV - 250   2013   £185

Association – Taylor, William

Wiseman, Richard *Several Chirurgicall Treatises.* London: E. Flesher and J. Macock for R. Royston, 1676. Half title, small folio, contemporary English panel calf with blind ruling on boards, which have been skilfully rebacked with minor repairs to corners, endpapers saved, small marginal loss in E2, occasional light soiling, staining and short tears in margins, final leaf with large loss in blank margin, touching two letters and laid down, early ownership signatures of William Taylor, from the library of John R. Kirkup with his bookplate. James Tait Goodrich S74 - 238   2013 $2500

Association – Tetley, Fanny

Bloomfield, Robert *The Farmer's Boy: a Rural Poem.* London: Longman, 1827. Fifteenth edition, half title, engraved title and plates after R. Westall, some spotting, slightly later half calf, gilt bands, brown leather label, signed "Fanny Tetley" in contemporary hand, Renier booklabel, very good. Jarndyce Antiquarian Booksellers   CCIII - 20   2013   £30

Association – Thackeray, William Makepeace

Homerus *Homeri Odyssea Cum Scholis Veteribus. Accedut Batrachomyomachia, Hymni, Fragmenta.* Oxonii: E Typographeo Clarendoniano, 1827. 228 x 138mm., 2 volumes, very attractive 19th century red pebble grain morocco, covers with multiple frames formed by plain and decorative gilt rules and Greek key roll as well as fleuron cornerpieces, raised bands, spine compartments with similar Greek key and gilt rule borders enclosing fleuron centerpiece, turn-ins gilt, marbled endpaper, all edges gilt, ink ownership inscription "W.M. Thackeray" dated "Arpil 1828", each titlepage with very small oval embossed stamp "W M T" at top, minimal foxing here and there, but especially fine, text very fresh, clean and bright, binding lustrous and virtually unworn. Phillip J. Pirages 63 - 464   2013 $3250

Association – Thayer, Scofield

Gallatin, A. E. *Gaston Lachaise. Sixteen Reproductions in Collotype of the Sculptor's Work.* New York: E. P. Dutton & Co., 1924. First edition, limited to 400 copies, 4to., photogravures from photos by Charles Sheeler, original cloth backed boards, printed labels, glassine dust jacket, very fine, unopened copy in somewhat worn and chipped glassine dust jacket, inscribed by Lachaise to friend and patron Scofield Thayer, with Thayer bookplate laid in. James S. Jaffe Rare Books   Fall 2013 - 8   2013 $1750

Association – Thom, D.

Thom, Robert *Wang Keaou Lwan Pih Neen Chang Han; or the Lasting Resentment of Miss Keaou Lwan Wang. A Chinese Tale.* Canton: Canton Press Office, 1839. First edition, one lithograph plate, small 4to., modern half calf, original front wrapper (worn and repaired) preserved and bound in, some wear throughout, margin of title stained and frayed, lower corner repaired, library stamp, title with presentation inscription from author's brothers "To the Manchester New College for D. Thom 1842".   Maggs Bros. Ltd.   1467 - 65   2013   £4200

Association – Thomas, G. D. P.

Mac Flogg'em, Peter, Pseud. *Aesculapian Secrets Revealed; or Friendly Hints and Admonitions Addressed to gentlemen of the Medical Profession...* printed (by W. Flint) for C. Chapple, 1813. First edition, fine hand colored folding aquatint frontispiece, signed, little spotting her and there, 12mo., uncut in original blue paper wrappers, contemporary ownership inscription of G. D. P. Thomas, very good. Blackwell's Rare Books   Sciences - 76   2013   £1200

Association – Thomas, William

Inchbald, Elizabeth *Nature and Art.* London: printed for G. G. and J. Robinson, 1796. First edition, half title in volume i, half title probably discarded from volume ii, some soiling and staining, hole in G8 in volume i touching couple of letters on recto, tear in one leaf entering text without loss, 8vo., uncut, contemporary marbled boards, worn at extremities, rebacked, label inside front cover of Rotherham's circulating Library, Coventry, signature of William Thomas in both volumes, one dated, 1857, sound.   Blackwell's Rare Books   B174 - 74   2013   £1200

Association – Thompson, Ellen

Goldsmith, Oliver 1730-1774 *The Vicar of Wakefield.* New York: printed by James Oram for Christian Brown, 1803. First American illustrated edition, first NY edition in any form, excellent copy, 2 volumes in 1, 12mo., contemporary tree calf, rebacked, old back laid down, corners rubbed, leather label, pages 252 + 4 wood engraved plates by Anderson, early oval hand decorated bookplate of Ellen Thompson, very good.   Howard S. Mott Inc.   262 - 62   2013 $650

Association – Thomson, E. G.

Trelawny, Edward John *Adventures of a Younger Son.* London: T. Fisher Unwin, 1890. New edition, half title, frontispiece, plates, original red cloth, dulled, minor damp marks, slight worming inner margin of upper board through half title, bookplates of E. G. Thomson.   Jarndyce Antiquarian Booksellers   CCIII - 444   2013   £30

Association – Thomson, John

Vergilius Maro, Publius *The Aeneid of Virgil.* London: printed for R. Dodsley, 1740. First complete edition, 2 volumes, 4to., contemporary paneled calf, rebacked with sheep at early date, corners worn, early leather labels, 1918 bookplate of John W. Thomson whose parents bought Fanny Kemble's Lenox Mass. residence, gift inscription from Charles L. Hibbard, prominent Pittsfield Mass. judge. Howard S. Mott Inc.   262 - 119   2013 $1250

Association – Thomson, Mrs.

Walker, Josiah *An Account of the Life and Character of Robert Burns.* Edinburgh: printed by John Moir, 1811. Few internal marks, contemporary full mottled calf, olive green leather label, leading hinge weakening, presentation inscription from author to Mrs. Thomson.   Jarndyce Antiquarian Booksellers   CCIII - 68   2013   £85

Association – Thomson, Virgil

James, William 1842-1910 *Pragmatism: a New Name for Some Old Ways of Thinking.* New York: Longmans, Green and Co., 1919. 22cm., green publisher's cloth with printed paper spine label, label bit worn and little light fraying at spine ends, else near fine, American composer Virgil Thomson's copy with his pencilled ownership signature, March 1920.   Between the Covers Rare Books, Inc. Philosophy - 326790   2013 $400

Association – Thorney, Catherine Neville

Cooper, John Gilbert *Letters Concerning Taste.* London: printed for R. and J. Dodsley, 1757. Third edition, half title, frontispiece by Grignion, very good in contemporary calf, expertly rebacked with corners repaired, some occasional browning and light foxing, ownership name of Catherine Nevile Thorney 1809.   Ken Spelman Books Ltd.   75 - 22 2013   £395

Association – Thurburn, Gwyneth

Eliot, Thomas Stearns 1888-1965 *The Rock.* London: Faber and Faber, 1934. Second impression, 8vo., original grey board, spine slightly browned, otherwise excellent copy, inscribed by author for Miss Gwyneth Thurburn.   Maggs Bros. Ltd.   1460 - 268   2013   £450

Association – Tice, Clara

ABC Dogs. New York: Wilfred Funk, 1940. First edition, folio, cloth backed pictorial boards, tips worn and few faint marks on cover, else very good+, illustrations in color on every page, this copy signed by Clara Tice with charming 3 inch drawing of Scottie dog.   Aleph-Bet Books, Inc.   104 - 5   2013 $1500

Association – Tillotson, Geoffrey

Hubert, Francis *The Life of Edward II. With the Fates of Gavestone and the Spencers.* London: printed for Tho. Harbin, 1721. Engraved frontispiece, titlepage printed in red and black, 12mo., outer leaves little dusted, later marbled paper wrappers, ownership signature of Geoffrey Tillotson, 1942. Jarndyce Antiquarian Booksellers CCIV - 165   2013   £120

Association – Tillou, Francis Redding

Irving, Washington   1783-1859 *Sketch Book of Geoffrey Crayon, Gent.* New York: printed By C. S. Van Winkel, 1819-1820. First edition, first printings of parts 1-6, second printing of part 7, 2 volumes, 8vo., 20th century crimson straight grained morocco, spine and inner dentelles gilt, all edges gilt, bound without wrappers as usual, 4 ownership signatures of Francis Redding Tillou (1795-1865), very minor occasional browning, fine, beautifully bound. Howard S. Mott Inc.   262 - 79   2013 $5000

Association – Tippett, Michael

Auden, Wystan Hugh   1907-1973 *New Year Letter.* London: Faber and Faber, 1941. First edition, 8vo., original cream cloth, one of 2000 copies, very good, cloth stained on back cover and tail of spine, inscribed by T. S. Eliot for Michael Tipett.   Maggs Bros. Ltd.   1460 - 269   2013   £750

Association – Todd, Albert May

Galilei, Galileo *Dialogo... Sopra i due Massimi Sistemi del Mondo Tolemaico e Copernicano...* Florence: Per Gio: Batista Landini, 1632. First edition, quarto, bound without final blank leaf, printed correction slip pasted in margin of versos of F6 (p. 92), engraved title, fourth state, with artist's signature present, sized and mounted (no loss whatsoever), woodcut diagrams in text, woodcut printer's device on title, late 18th century quarter dark red roan over marbled boards, vellum tips, smooth spine decoratively tooled and lettered gilt, some light foxing and browning to few gatherings, few marginal paper flaws, front joint starting, bookplate of Albert May Todd, with one other armorial bookplate, excellent and very tall copy, many leaves uncut, quarter red morocco clamshell, gilt stamped.   Heritage Book Shop 50th Anniversary Catalogue - 38   2013 $95,000

Association – Todd, Robert Bentley

Ballance, Charles *Some Points in the Surgery of the Brain and Its Membranes. (with) Essays on the Surgery of the Temporal Bones.* London: Macmillan, 1907. xv, 405 pages, illustrations, original cloth worn and rubbed, especially along fore-edges, internally very good, author's presentation with penned note in ink on front flyleaf, for R(obert) B(entley) Todd; xxiv, 223 pages, 75 plates, xiii, (255)-612 pages, 50 plates, partially colored, tall 4to., 2 volumes, original publishers green cloth, recased, new endpapers renewed, cloth bit rubbed, couple of signatures loosening, some marginalia from early owner.   James Tait Goodrich S74 - 19   2013 $3500

Association – Toledo, Bill

Paul, Doris A. *The Navajo Code Talkers.* Pittsburgh: Dorrance Pub., 1990. Seventh printing, 8vo., signed by fourteen Navajo code talkers, including Albert Smith (President 4th Mar. Div. 4th Sig. Co.), Paul Blatchford, Bill Toledo, Harold Foster, George Smith, Harold Evan and others, fine in near fine dust jacket.   By the Book, L. C.   38 - 38   2013 $900

Association – Tolnay, John

Harris, Walter *De Morbis Acutis Infantum.* Samuel Smith, 1689. First edition, final ad leaf, imprimatur leaf present but cut down, old front endpaper mostly clipped neatly leaving an old purchase note with price, little soiling, especially to final leaf, last 2 leaves with minor tear in gutter, ownership inscription to title margin (trimmed - of John Tolnay? Chirurg. 173-) and to initial blank of Richard Drinkwater, Jr. Surgeon 1753, errata corrected in old hand, 8vo., modern calf boards panelled in blind, backstrip with five raised bands, morocco label in second compartment with remainder with central floral blind tools, new endpapers, good.   Blackwell's Rare Books   Sciences - 57   2013   £2500

Association – Tomlinson, Charles

Octavio Paz: A Celebration. New York: Academy of American Poets and the Mexican Cultural Institute, 1994. First edition, 8vo., original wrappers, although not called for, this copy signed by Paz, Mark Strand, John Ashbery, Bei Dao and Charles Tomlinson.   James S. Jaffe Rare Books Fall 2013 - 6   2013 $750

Association – Tonnies, Ferdinand

Bacon, Francis Viscount St. Albans 1561-1626 *Sylva Sylvarum, sive Hist. Naturalis et Novus Atlas.* Amsterdam: Apud Ludovicum Elzevirium, 1648. Pocket edition, 12mo., engraved titlepage, some light browning, contemporary vellum boards, spine lettered ink, bit soiled, front flyleaf excised, old ownership inscription foot of titlepage (partially rubbed on), from the collection, but without any signs of ownership, of Ferdinand Tonnies (1855-1936).   Unsworths Antiquarian Booksellers   28 - 69   2013   £350

Petavius, Dionysius *Rationarium Temporum: in Quo Aetatum Omnium Sacra Profanaque Historia Chronolgoicis Probationibus Munita Summatim Traditur.* Leiden: Apud Theodorum Haak, 1724. 8vo., 3 parts in 1 volume, frontispiece, additional engraved titlepage and 6 plates, lightly toned, some minor spotting, contemporary vellum boards, spine lettered in ink, small gilt decoration to centre of boards, soiled and small tear to head of spine, ownership inscription of Mitford dated 1803 with a later paragraph long biographical note, from the collection (but without any signs of ownership) of Ferdinand Tonnies (1855-1936). Unsworths Antiquarian Booksellers   28 - 121   2013   £200

Association – Toppin, Aubrey

Cottingham, E. R. *Pedigree of Bowen of Court House.* 1927. First edition, large 4to., 36 pages, 2 folding pedigrees, cloth, very good, inscribed by Aubrey Toppin.   C. P. Hyland   261 - 374   2013   £75

Association – Torndallius, Christianius

Saxo Grammaticus *Danorum Regum Heroumque Historiae...* Paris: Jodocus Badius Ascensius, 1514. Rare first edition, folio, bound without final blank leaf, title printed in red within architectural woodcut border enclosing a woodcut of the Danish king at head of his army, fine woodcut crible initials, including several specially designed for the book incorporating a portrait of the King of Demark and the royal arms; early 18th century limp vellum with leather ties, spine lettered gilt on rose wash panel, edges stained blue, title border shaved at head, some minor mostly marginal worming, few marginal stains, early ink inscription of Christianus Torndallius, Helsing; Danorum (Elsinore) and another early ink inscription, bookplate of Hjalmar Hartmann, some scattered early ink marginalia and underlining, overall excellent copy.   Heritage Book Shop   50th Anniversary Catalogue - 86   2013 $20,000

Association – Towhouse, P

Dryden, John 1631-1700 *Fables Ancient and Modern.* London: printed for Jacob Tonson, 1700. First edition, folio, tiny burnhole in one leaf (clear of text), two pinprick wormholes in lower margin of first half (few times stretching slightly but never near text), some light browning in places, few tiny stains, contemporary Cambridge style panelled calf, rebacked in different shade, corners repaired, few old scratches to old leather, hinges neatly relined, beginnings of early manuscript index, early ownership inscriptions of John Weekes and P. Towhouse?   Unsworths Antiquarian Booksellers   28 - 89   2013   £500

Association – Towneley, Charles

Nannini, Remigio *Civill Considerations Upon Many and Sundrie Histories as well Ancient as Moderne...* London: by F(elix) K(ingston) for Matthew Lowndes, 1601. Folio, woodcut device on titlepage, woodcut head and tailpieces and initials with cancel bifolium C1.2, contemporary calf with 1603 Towneley arms of Richard Towneley of Towneley stamped (in blind?) on both covers, remains of green cloth ties, front blank A1 and rear blank 2A6 present and seemingly correct, binding very heavily worn and scuffed, early reinforcing to inner hinges, blank lower corner of G5 and O3 torn away, dampstain in upper left margin of first several leaves and reappearing toward rear of text, occasional spotting and soiling and browning but very nice internally, Richard Towneley's copy with armorial bookplate dated 1702, signature of Cha.. Towneley, probably Richard's father.   Joseph J. Felcone Inc.   Books Printed before 1701 - 71   2013 $3500

Association – Towneley, Richard

Nannini, Remigio *Civill Considerations Upon Many and Sundrie Histories as well Ancient as Moderne...* London: by F(elix) K(ingston) for Matthew Lowndes, 1601. Folio, woodcut device on titlepage, woodcut head and tailpieces and initials with cancel bifolium C1.2, contemporary calf with 1603 Towneley arms of Richard Towneley of Towneley stamped (in blind?) on both covers, remains of green cloth ties, front blank A1 and rear blank 2A6 present and seemingly correct, binding very heavily worn and scuffed, early reinforcing to inner hinges, blank lower corner of G5 and O3 torn away, dampstain in upper left margin of first several leaves and reappearing toward rear of text, occasional spotting and soiling and browning but very nice internally, Richard Towneley's copy with armorial bookplate dated 1702, signature of Cha.. Towneley, probably Richard's father.   Joseph J. Felcone Inc.   Books Printed before 1701 - 71   2013 $3500

Association – Tracy, E.

The Riot at New Haven Between the Students and the Town Boys on the Night of March 17, 1854. New Haven: Richardson's Book Magazine and Newspaper Depot, 1854. First edition, 12mo., 47 pages, original printed and pictorial wrappers, removed, worn along spine and gutter, short tear without loss in fore-edge of front wrapper and first leaf, two short side lines in ink, small shelf label on first leaf, withal very good, signature "E. Tracy".   M & S Rare Books, Inc.   95 - 109   2013 $225

Association – Traill, Thomas Stewart

Kirchmann, Johann   *De Annulis Liber Singularis.*   Leiden: Apud Hackios, 1672.   12mo., engraved fore-title, illustrations, early vellum (trifle soiled), light dampstain on upper part of number pages, very good bookplate of Thomas Stewart Traill, M.D.   Joseph J. Felcone Inc.   Books Printed before 1701 - 74   2013 $400

Association – Trapp, Joseph

Blount, Charles   *The Oracles of Reason... in Several Letters to Mr. Hobbs and Other Persons of Eminent Quality and Learning.*   London: printed, 1693.   First edition, 12mo., full modern calf, new endpapers, red leather label, gilt lettering, ink signature of Joseph Trapp dated 1724, paper browned, one signature trimmed little close in top margin, shaving some page numbers, front free endpaper, little stained from removal of pastedown bookseller's description, very good.   The Brick Row Book Shop   Miscellany Fifty-Nine - 13   2013 $1750

Association – Tredwell, Samuel

Bell, Charles   1774-1842   *The Anatomy and Physiology of the Human Body.*   New York: Collins, 1827.   Fifth American edition, 2 volumes, 4to., 9 plates, tables foxed, browned, original tree calf, gilt spine, red leather spine label, rubbed, ownership signature of Samuel Tredwell, very good.   Jeff Weber Rare Books   172 - 15   2013 $900

Association – Trefusis, Violet

Berners, Lord   *A Distant Prospect, a Sequel to First Childhood.*   London: Constable, 1945.   First edition, 8vo., original blue cloth, dust jacket, inscribed by author to Violet Trefusis, near fine in dust jacket.   Maggs Bros. Ltd.   1460 - 89   2013   £650

Cooper, Diana   *The Rainbow Comes and Goes; The Light of Common Day; Trumpets from the Steep.*   London: Rupert Hart-Davis, 1958-1960.   First editions, 3 volumes, 8vo., original cloth, dust jackets, inscribed by author to Violet Trefusis, excellent, jackets of first and last volumes show light signs of wear.   Maggs Bros. Ltd.   1460 - 197   2013   £250

Dinesen, Isak   1885-1962   *Last Tales.*   London: Putnam, 1957.   First edition, 8vo., original black cloth, spine lettered gilt, attractive dust jacket, few light marks to cloth, dust jacket little marked and slightly worn at head and tail of spine, inscribed by author for Violet Trefusis.   Maggs Bros. Ltd.   1460 - 229   2013   £1000

Association – Trevelyan, G. O.

Great Britain. Historical Manuscripts Commission - 1890   *The Manuscripts of S. H. Le Fleming Esq. of Rydal Hall. Twelfth Report. Part VII.*   London: HMSO, 1890.   Tall 8vo., contemporary binder's cloth, gilt, modern slipcase, pages iv, 474, signature of G. O. Trevelyan.   R. F. G. Hollett & Son   Lake District and Cumbria - 260   2013   £120

Association – Trevor-Robert, Hugh

Hume, David   1711-1776   *Essays on Suicide and the Immortality of the Soul, Ascribed to the Late David Hume, Esq.*   London: printed for M. Smith, 1783.   Second edition, despite what titlepage states, small octavo, iv, 107 pages, contemporary full mottled calf, covers ruled in gilt, spine covered in red morocco onlay, decorated with gilt urns and lyres, gilt board edges, marbled endpapers, front blank missing bit from upper corner, superb copy, from the collection of historian Hugh Trevor-Robert (with his bookplate on front pastedown),.   Heritage Book Shop   50th Anniversary Catalogue - 55   2013 $15,000

Association – Troxell, Gilbert

Purdy, Richard L.   *Thomas Hardy 1840-1928: Catalogue of a Memorial Exhibition of First Editions, Autograph Letters and Manuscripts.*   New Haven: Yale University Library, 1928.   First edition, one of 25 copies on rag paper, designed by Carl Purington, 8vo. original tan linen spine, blue boards, black lettering, untrimmed, presentation copy from Purdy to American Literature scholar and curator, Gilbert Troxell, with note and Hardy keepsake, also produced by Purdy laid in, fine, from the Gary Lepper Collection of Thomas Hardy.   The Brick Row Book Shop   Bulletin Nine - 85   2013 $300

Association – Truman, Harry

Hillman, William   *Mr. President.*   New York: Farrar, Straus and Young, 1952.   First edition, inscribed by President Truman to Jane Lingo, April 10, 1952, laid in is 3 x 5 card is a note in young hand signed by Lingo asking the President to sign the book for her, quarter beige cloth with blue cloth covered boards and gilt title label to spine, toning to edges of boards and small bump along bottom edge of rear board, clean, bright interior with errata slip laid in, blue dust jacket with red title to spine and front panel, large open tear on front of jacket affecting title, few closed tears along edges, very good in good dust jacket, 253 pages.   The Kelmscott Bookshop   7 - 133   2013 $1500

Association – Tucker, Edith Ellen

Yeats, William Butler 1865-1939 *Selected Poems. Lyrical and Narrative.* London: Macmillan, 1929. First edition, small 8vo., titlepage heliotype portrait by John Singer Sargent, original embossed blue cloth dust jacket, presentation copy inscribed by author for Edith Ellen "Nelly" Tucker, very fine in fine dust jacket, uncommon.   James S. Jaffe Rare Books   Fall 2013 - 159   2013 $17,500

Association – Turner, Decherd

Blake, William 1757-1827 *Poetical Sketches.* London: Ballantyne Press, 1899. Half title, illustrations, uncut, original pale blue boards, paper label on spine defective, spine little dulled and slightly chipped at head, booklabel of Decherd Turner.   Jarndyce Antiquarian Booksellers   CCIII - 3   2013   £85

Association – Tuttle, Donald

Sterne, Laurence 1713-1768 *A Sentimental Journey through France and Italy.* Dublin: printed for G. Faulkner, 1768. 2 volumes in 1, 12mo., half titles, very good, full contemporary calf, slight chip to head of spine and upper joint cracked but firm, old waterstain to corner of front endpaper and prelim blank, very slight tear to lower corner of 1, B1, not affecting text, in quarter bound solander box in red morocco with dark red cloth, gilt lettering, bookplate of Donald S. Tuttle.   Ken Spelman Books Ltd.   75 - 27   2013   £250

Association – Tyndall, Thomas

The Punishments of China.. London: printed for William Miller by W. Bulmer and Co., 1801. First edition, 357 x 267mm., (27) leaves, 22 hand colored stippled engravings, contemporary marbled boards and endpapers, rebacked and recornered to style, flat spine in panels with central gilt star tool, gilt titling; armorial bookplate of Thomas Tyndall Jr., paper boards bit chafed and darkened by glue near spine and corners, bit rubbed along top and bottom edges of boards, occasional thumbing or minor stains to very generous margins, otherwise excellent, binding scarcely worn, and internally clean, fresh and bright, without any of the usual offsetting from text to plates.   Phillip J. Pirages   63 - 331   2013 $2500

Association – Underwood, E. R.

Merton, Thomas 1915-1968 *Thirty Poems.* Norfolk: New Directions/Poets of the Year, 1944. First edition, scarce hardbound issue, signed by author, laid in is TLS 1 page April 5, 1945 to E. R. Underwood from the Abbot of Our Lady Gethsemani Monastery, spine ends trifle bumped, small bookseller's label on front pastedown, otherwise very fine and bright copy.   James S. Jaffe Rare Books   Fall 2013 - 99   2013 $3500

Association – Ure, Jim

Ruess, Everett *On Desert Trails with Everett Ruess.* El Centro: Desert Magazine Press, 1950. Second edition, Advance Readers copy? 80 pages, quarto, tan publisher's wrappers with title printed on front panel, very good, minor discoloring to spine and surrounding area of panel, prints and photos, warmly inscribed by author's brother, Waldo Ruess for Jim and Stephanie Ure.   Ken Sanders Rare Books   45 - 49   2013 $300

Association – Ure, Stephanie

Ruess, Everett *On Desert Trails with Everett Ruess.* El Centro: Desert Magazine Press, 1950. Second edition, Advance Readers copy? 80 pages, quarto, tan publisher's wrappers with title printed on front panel, very good, minor discoloring to spine and surrounding area of panel, prints and photos, warmly inscribed by author's brother, Waldo Ruess for Jim and Stephanie Ure.   Ken Sanders Rare Books   45 - 49   2013 $300

Association – Urquhart, Frances Fortescue

Verney, Frances Parthenope *Memoirs of the Verney Family Volumes I-IV.* London: Longmans, Green and Co., 1892. 1892. 1894. 1899. First editions, 4 volumes, 8vo., 50 plates as called for, further woodcuts and illustrations to text, protective tissue removed from volume I frontispiece, brown cloth, gilt spine and armorial centerpiece, top edge gilt, fore-edges uncut, endcaps creased, pages and edges little worn, boards faded, minor dent to upper board volume I, upper hinge of volume II cracking but bindings sound, very good internally, armorial bookplate of Frances Fortescue Urquhart of Balliol College 1909 to each front pastedown and his ownership inscription, bookplate of R. C. Mowat, pencilled ownership of P. A. Slack.   Unsworths Antiquarian Booksellers   28 - 202   2013   £120

Association – Van Doren, Dorothy

Berryman, John *Stephen Crane. The American Men of Letters Series.* New York: William Sloane Associates, 1950. First edition, 8vo., original cloth, dust jacket, inscribed by author to his teacher Mark Van Doren and Dorothy, fine, dust jacket neatly reinforced on verso of couple of places along flap folds.   James S. Jaffe Rare Books   Fall 2013 - 23   2013 $5000

Association – Van Doren, Irita

Ford, Ford Madox 1873-1939 *New York is Not America.* London: Duckworth, 1927. First edition, 8vo., original green cloth, dust jacket, excellent copy in slightly nicked dust jacket, inscribed by author for Irita van Doren, editor of NY Herald Tribune.   Maggs Bros. Ltd.   1460 - 287   2013   £750

Association – Van Doren, Mark

Berryman, John *Stephen Crane. The American Men of Letters Series.* New York: William Sloane Associates, 1950. First edition, 8vo., original cloth, dust jacket, inscribed by author to his teacher Mark Van Doren and Dorothy, fine, dust jacket neatly reinforced on verso of couple of places along flap folds.   James S. Jaffe Rare Books   Fall 2013 - 23   2013 $5000

Merton, Thomas   1915-1968 *The Pasternak Affair in Perspective.* New York: Thought, 1960. First separate edition, offprint, tall 8vo., original printed wrappers, presentation from author for Mark (Van Doren), wrappers partially faded at margins, front outer corners bumped, otherwise very good, rare.   James S. Jaffe Rare Books   Fall 2013 - 102   2013 $3500

Association – Van Hoytema, Theo

Andersen, Hans Christian   1805-1875 *Het Leelijke Jonge Eendje. (The Ugly Duckling).* Amsterdam: C. M. Van Gogh, 1893. Number 1 proof copy, inscribed by Hoytema, limitation page has 2 extra mounted color plates, limitation leaf and ownership leaf, both inscribed by Hoytema, 31 large color plates mounted on heavy paper by Theo Van Hoytema, cloth backed pictorial boards, covers soiled and edges rubbed, else very good+.   Aleph-Bet Books, Inc.   105 - 328   2013 $3500

Association – Vandermin, Doctor

Hardy, Florence *The Early Life of Thomas Hardy 1840-1891. (and) The Later Years of Thomas Hardy 1892-1928.* Macmillan, 1928-1933. First editions, 2 volumes, frontispiece portraits, plates and facsimiles, 8vo., original mid green cloth, lettering on backstrips and Hardy medallion on front covers all gilt blocked, faint endpaper foxing, small newspaper clipping pasted to rear free endpaper of volume ii, top edge gilt, dust jackets chipped and with short tears, very good, this was Doctor Vandermin's copy, quite possibly Florence Hardy's doctor with presentation inscription from Florence Hardy Nov. 1928.   Blackwell's Rare Books   172 - 191   2013   £550

Association – Vansittart, C. Arthur

Campbell, Thomas   1777-1844 *Theodric: a Domestic Tale, and Other Poems.* London: Longman, 1824. First edition, half title, text largely erased, lacking leading f.e.p., spotted, uncut in original drab boards, paper label chipped, spine worn with some old repairs, bookplate of C. Arthur Vansittart of Pontifical Zouaves, fairly good copy.   Jarndyce Antiquarian Booksellers   CCIII - 470   2013   £35

Association – Vaughan, Charles Richard

Anquetil, Louis Pierre *Compendio de la Historia de Espana.* Madrid: Imprenta real, 1806. Corrected edition, 8vo., 54 engravings, three quarter polished calf over marbled boards, five raised bands, 4 compartments decorated gilt, brown morocco labels, 3 of four boards detached, edges worn, rear board volume I worn through, otherwise contents quite clean, images sharp, gift from Pedro de Alcantara Alvarez de Toledo and Salm-Salm, to Sr Charles Richard Vaughan, with ALS from Alvarez de Toledo to Vaughan.   Kaaterskill Books   16 - 77   2013 $500

Association – Vaughan, Robert Chambre

Homerus *The Odyssey of Homer.* London: printed for T. Osborne (and others), 1763. 3 volumes, 12mo., C2 volume II torn with loss, tear to lower corner of K6 volume III, full contemporary sprinkled calf, raised and gilt banded spines, ownership name of Francisco Chalmer, 19th century armorial bookplate and signature of Robert Chambre Vaughan, Esq. of Burlton Hall Co. Salop.   Jarndyce Antiquarian Booksellers   CCIV - 163   2013   £200

Association – Veness, Jack

Bird, Will R. *The Two Jacks: the Amazing Adventures of Major Jack M. Veness and Major Jack L. Fairweather.* Toronto: Ryerson Press, 1954. First edition, green cloth with gilt to spine in dust jacket, half title, 22 black and white photo illustrations, 8vo., previous owner's bookplate on front endpaper, otherwise very good, dust jacket chipped and worn with small pieces missing form lower spine, signed by author and Jack Veness and Jack Fairweather.   Schooner Books Ltd.   105 - 56   2013 $75

Association – Verney, Margaret

Verney, Frances Parthenope *Memoirs of the Verney Family.* London: Longmans Green and Co., 1892. 1894. 1899. First edition, royal 8vo., 69 engravings, drawings and woodcuts, 2 foldouts, pebbled brown cloth, red and gilt edge bands, gilt titles and coat of arms, top edge gilt, inscribed by Margaret Verney, author of volume III, very good or better set with wear to extremities.   Kaaterskill Books   16 - 87   2013 $350

Association – Verraux, Jules

Andersson, Charles John *Notes on the Birds of Damara Land and the Adjacent Countries of South-West Africa.* John van Voorst, 1872. First edition, original green blind panelled cloth, gilt, spine slightly worn and scraped at head ad foot, frontispiece map, 4 lithographed plates, presentation from editor, J. H. Gurney to his friend Jules Verraux (1807-1873), engraved bookplates on endpapers of David Simson of Ickleford.   R. F. G. Hollett & Son   Africana - 2   2013   £450

Association – Vickery, Willis

Pervigilium Veneris. Doves Press, 1910. One of 150 copies (of an edition of 162), printed in black on handmade paper with title, initials and refrain at end of each verse, printed in red, 8vo., original russet morocco, backstrip gilt panelled between seven raised bands, second and third gilt lettered and with date 1910 at tail, single gilt rule border to sides, green leather booklabels of Willis Vickery and Cortland Bishop, with some offsetting to front free endpaper, gilt edges, by Doves Bindery, fine.   Blackwell's Rare Books 172 - 272   2013   £1500

Association – Viereck, George

Viereck, Peter   *Terror and Decorum Poems 1940-1948.* New York: Charles Scribner's Sons, 1948. First edition, 8vo., 120 pages, very good in nicked dust jacket, inscribed to his infamous father.   Second Life Books Inc.   183 - 389   2013 $250

Association – Viger, William

Wiseman, Richard   *Eight Chirurgical Treatises on the Following Heads...* London: Benjamin Tooke and Luke Meedith, 1696. Small folio, few short tears, faint dampstaining in few gatherings, wormtrack bottom margin of few gatherings touching a few letters, contemporary paneled calf with blind rulings, skillfully rebacked saving endpapers, raised bands, green gilt label bookplate of John Kirkup, Thomas Marsh, William Viger (ownership signature dated 1751), light marginalia.   James Tait Goodrich   S74 - 239   2013 $975

Association – Von Jagermann

Lewis, Sinclair   1885-1951   *Main Street.* New York: Harcourt Brace and Howe, 1920. First edition, first issue (mixed issue?), with folio 54 unbattered but the 'y' in 'may' on page 387 imperfect, inscribed by author to Hugh Palmer, Aug. 20 1947, on front pastedown facing inscription is ownership inscription of Von Jagermann 1920, original dark blue cloth stamped in orange on front cover and spine, spine lightly sunned and edges of spine with small amount of wear, bit of light foxing to prelims, overall very good.   Heritage Book Shop   Holiday Catalogue 2012 - 88   2013 $2000

Association – Waddington, Monsieur

Beaumont, Roberts   *Colour in Woven Design.* Chiswick Press for Whittaker and Co. and George Bell & sons, 1890. First edition, inscribed by author, 8vo., original cloth, very good, inscribed to Mons. Waddington, secretary of Jury in class 77 Paris Exhibition 1900 with author's compliments.   Blackwell's Rare Books   Sciences - 118   2013   £60

Association – Waddington, William

Bolingbroke, Henry St. John, 1st Viscount   1678-1751   *Letters on the Study and Use of History.*   London: printed for A. Millar, 1752. 2 volumes in 1, half titles, engraved portrait has been mounted to from a frontispiece, 8vo., clean copy, contemporary tree calf, spine attractively decorated in gilt, red morocco label, armorial bookplate of William Waddington with ownership inscription, contemporary ms. notes to margins of pages 182-183, slightly trimmed in binding.   Jarndyce Antiquarian Booksellers   CCIV - 64   2013   £250

Chaucer, Geoffrey   1340-1400   *The Canterbury Tales of Chaucer Modemis'd by Several Hands.*   London: printed for J. and R. Tonson, 1741. 3 volumes, 8vo., bound without frontispiece, full contemporary sprinkled calf, raised and gilt banded spines, red morocco labels, some wear to tail volume I and III, armorial bookplate of William Waddington, attractive set.   Jarndyce Antiquarian Booksellers   CCIV - 89   2013   £380

Swift, Jonathan   1667-1845   *The Poetical Works...* Edinburgh: at the Apollo Press by the Martins, 1772. 4 volumes in 2, frontispiece, additional engraved titlepage to each volume, general and divisional printed titlepages to each volume, 8mo., slight full contemporary tree calf, gilt decorated spines, twin red morocco labels, armorial bookplate of William Waddington.   Jarndyce Antiquarian Booksellers   CCIV - 288   2013   £150

Association – Wagstaffe, Agnes

Sterne, Laurence   1713-1768   *A Sentimental Journey through France and Italy.* P. Miller and J. White, 1774. Probably printed edition, 328 pages, five volumes in one, each with separate titlepage but continuous pagination, 328 pages, very good, 8vo., 19th century half calf, gilt panelled spine, signature of Agnes Wagstaffe 1777 on first titlepage.   Ken Spelman Books Ltd.   75 - 35   2013   £120

Association – Waithman, Arabella

Gaskell, Elizabeth Cleghorn   1810-1865   *Cranford.* London: Macmillan, 1891. First reprint, 8vo., original green cloth, excellent copy, cloth just little marked and scuffed, inscribed by Lady Augusta Gregory for Arabella Waithman, Dec. 25 1981.   Maggs Bros. Ltd.   1460 - 379   2013   £250

Association – Waldegrave, C.

Hayley, William *The Life and Posthumous Writings of William Cowper...* Chichester: printed by J. Seagrave for J. Johnson, 1803-1806. First edition, 4 volumes including supplementary pages, in three, with 6 plates by William Blake, first impressions of those in volumes i and ii (no second state for those in volume iii) and one plate engraved by Caroline Watson, bound without half titles, little browned in places, some worming in lower margins of volumes i and ii, 4to., contemporary calf, blind roll tooled borders on sides, flat backstrips tooled in blind and lettered gilt direct, gilt inner dentelles, bit rubbed and bumped, spines little darkened, crack at foot on one joint, contemporary ownership of Elizabeth? Cardigan, that of C. Waldegrave dated 1824 in two places and Radstock bookplate in each volume, good. Blackwell's Rare Books 172 - 70 2013 £450

Association – Walker, Aston

Euripides *Opera Omnia.* London: Richard Priestley, 1821. 9 volumes, 8vo., text in Greek with Latin footnotes, printer's list in volume vi, triangular closed tear to page ix in volume vii (no loss of text) sporadic foxing, occasional light pencil annotations, half vellum, marbled paper boards and endpapers, black morocco label to spine, edges red, boards rubbed, edges worn with occasional small bumps but still very good, armorial bookplate of Aston Walker to each front pastedown, various library tickets and inkstamps from London Borough of Southwark Special Collection to prelims, pencilled ownership inscription of M. R. Barker to half title. Unsworths Antiquarian Booksellers 28 - 13 2013 £300

Homerus (Opera). *Illias cum Brevi Annotatione; Odyssea cum Scholiis Veteribus; Batrachomyomachia; Hymni; Fragmetna.* Oxford: Clarendon Press, 1834. 1827, 4 volumes, text in Greek with footnotes in Latin, occasional trivial spotting, but generally very clean, half vellum, marbled paper boards and endpaper, spines gilt with black and red morocco labels, edges red, slight evidence of removed library stickers to darkened spines, boards rubbed, still very good, armorial bookplate of Aston Walker to each front pastedown, various library tickets and stamps from London Borough of Southwark Metropolitan Special Collection to prelims of each volume, tiny bookseller tickets of W. Winkley, Harrow on the Hill. Unsworths Antiquarian Booksellers 28 - 15 2013 £200

Association – Walker, M. M.

Campbell, Thomas 1777-1844 *The Poetical Works.* London: Edward Moxon, 1864. New edition, half title, frontispiece, contemporary half dark green calf, brown leather label, slightly rubbed, signature of M. M. Walker, 1860. Jarndyce Antiquarian Booksellers CCIII - 455 2013 £35

Association – Walker, T. M.

Sewell, Anna *Black Beauty.* London: J. M. Dent, 1915. Limited edition, signed, number 20 of 600 copies, large 4to., original green cloth gilt, large gilt embossed roundel of horses' heads on upper board, trifling wear to extreme corners, top edge gilt, uncut, 30 colored plates tipped on to fawn mounts, few scattered spots but lovely copy, inscribed "T. M. Walker, to myself Christmas 1915". R. F. G. Hollett & Son Children's Books - 322 2013 £795

Association – Walker, W.

Bucke, Charles *The Philosophy of Nature; or the Influence of Scenery on the Mind and Heart.* London: John Murray, 1813. First edition, 2 volumes, half titles, contemporary full maroon calf, gilt spines, borders and dentelles, slightly marked, spines faded and hinges, little rubbed, small repair at tail of spine volume I, contemporary signature of W. Walker, very good. Jarndyce Antiquarian Booksellers CCIII - 650 2013 £250

Association – Wallace, Abraham

Doyle, Arthur Conan 1859-1930 *Tales of Long Ago.* London: John Murray, 1922. First edition, small 8vo., later half red calf, some wear to extremities, otherwise excellent copy, inscribed by author for Abraham Wallace, with Doyle's visiting card loosely inserted. Maggs Bros. Ltd. 1460 - 249 2013 £750

Association – Waller, J. Wallett

Barrie, James Matthew 1860-1937 *Courage.* London: Hodder and Stoughton, 1922. First edition, large 8vo., original cream cloth, covers rubbed, rear endpaper damaged, otherwise very good, inscribed by author to J. Wallett Waller. Maggs Bros. Ltd. 1460 - 42 2013 £250

Association – Waller, Mrs.

Cobbe, Frances Power *Darwinism in Morals and Other Essays.* Williams & Norgate, 1872. First edition of this collection, slightly foxed at either end, 8vo., original smooth green cloth, spine gilt lettered, trifle worn at extremities, inner hinges strained, inscription "Mrs. Waller from Nora, Christmas 1872", good. Blackwell's Rare Books Sciences - 30 2013 £275

Association – Waller, Pickford

Hardy, Thomas   1840-1928   *The Return of the Native.* London: Smith Elder, 1878. First edition, 3 volumes, 8vo., original decorated brown cloth, gilt lettering, frontispiece, faint evidence of lending library labels on upper boards of each volume, bookplate of American collector Kenyon Starling on front pastedown, below which is the earlier bookplate of illustrator and connoisseur Pickford Waller, designed by Austin Osman Spare circa 1907, cloth little worn and soiled, some light foxing, particularly on prelims, very good, from the Gary Lepper Collection of Thomas Hardy.   The Brick Row Book Shop   Bulletin Nine - 6   2013 $10,000

Association – Walpole, Hugh

Bennett, Arnold   1867-1931   *The Old Wives' Tale.* London: Hodder & Stoughton, 1912. First edition, 8vo., original blue cloth, inscribed by author for Hugh Walpole, with his armorial bookplate, excellent copy.   Maggs Bros. Ltd.   1460 - 81   2013   £1200

Byron, George Gordon Noel, 6th Baron   1788-1824 *Letters and Journals of Lord Byron; With Notices of His Life.* London: John Murray, 1833. Third edition, 3 volumes, frontispiece volumes I and III, plates, volume II and III lacking titlepages, volume II lacking frontispiece, expertly recased in original sand grained purple cloth, spines lettered gilt, borders in blind, spines uniformly faded to brown, slightly marked, "From Hugh Walpole's library with his bookplate, formerly the copy of John Ruskin with his bookplate and marginal notes.   Jarndyce Antiquarian Booksellers   CCIII - 324   2013   £850

Association – Wanamaker, Rodman

Watts, Alaric   *Lyrics of the Heart: with Other Poems.* London: Longman, Brown, Green and Longmans, 1851. First edition, 211 x 132mm., superb late 19th century olive brown crushed morocco gilt and inlaid by Fazakerley (stamp signed on front turn-in), covers with frames of gilt rules, dots and inlaid tan morocco, central panel of upper cover with inlaid red morocco rectangle emblazoned with title gilt at head, below it a large topiary-shaped, symmetrical design in inlaid morocco and gilt tooling, incorporating 34 heart shaped green leaves on curling hairline stems as well as five lotus blossoms with lavender petals and inverted red heart centers (lower cover with smaller version of same inlaid elements inside plain ruled panel), raised bands, gilt spine compartments continuing same design (each with four inlaid leaf cornerpieces and central lotus flower), turn-ins with gilt and dot frames and lotus and leaf cornerpieces, ivory silk endleaves, marbled flyleaves, edges gilt and elaborately gauffered with deep gouging (in similar floral pattern), fore edge with three exquisitely painted scenes, within pointed frames, these vignettes taken from illustrations appearing within book, felt lined slipcase; with 41 engraved headpieces, as called for, engraved bookplate of Rodman Wanamaker, spine and front board sunned to pleasing uniform tan (as almost always with this color of morocco), occasional minor foxing, more prominent on first and last gatherings), still extremely fine, lovely, morocco lustrous and without perceptible wear, edges with particularly brilliant gilding, 3 painted fore-edge vignettes in perfect condition. Phillip J. Pirages   61 - 79   2013 $12,500

Association – Wandrei, Donald

Machen, Arthur   1863-1947   *The Terror.* London: Duckworth, 1917. First edition, pages browned as always, tiny chips from bottom corner of several pages and small spot on front board, still attractive, very good plus lacking dust jacket, label laid in indicating that this volume was from the library of Donald Wandrei.   Between the Covers Rare Books, Inc.   Sci-Fi, Fantasy & Horror - 43094   2013 $200

Association – Ward, Susan Hayes

Wharton, Edith   1862-1937   *The Decoration of Houses.* New York: Charles Scribner's Sons, 1897. First edition, 8vo., original marbled paper boards and printed paper label, 57 plates, from the library of poetry editor, Susan Hayes Ward, with her signature, boards somewhat rubbed, rear hinge repaired, tissue guard little foxed, very good.   The Brick Row Book Shop   Miscellany Fifty-Nine - 48   2013 $450

Association – Ware, J.

Warren, Edward   *Some Account of the Letheon; or Who is the Discoverer?* Boston: Dutton and Wentworth, 1847. Third edition, first issue, 88 pages, original printed publisher's wrappers, author's presentation to Dr. J. Ware.   James Tait Goodrich   S74 - 15   2013 $1750

Association – Warner, G. J.

Freneau, Philip *Poems Written Between the Years 1768 & 1794...* Monmouth: printed at the presss of the author, at Mount Plesant, near Middletown Point, 1795. Only edition, contemporary sheep, many gatherings variously foxed or browned, as always with this book, else unusually nice, contemporary signatures of Geo. J. Warner and slightly later Susan Nichols. Joseph J. Felcone Inc. English and American Literature to 1800 - 14 2013 $1200

Association – Warner, H. Lee

Excerpta Lyrica. Rugby: Crossley and Billington, 1866. First edition, 8vo., pages 16, Greek text, moderate foxing, original plain wrappers, foxed, worn with some loss to extremities, ownership inscription of H. Lee Warner and his light pencil notes to wrapper and few places in text, scarce. Unsworths Antiquarian Booksellers 28 - 2 2013 £30

Association – Waterman, E. D.

Stowe, Harriet Elizabeth Beecher 1811-1896 *Woman Sacred in History.* New York: J. B. Ford and Co. 1873 i.e., 1874? First complete edition, thick 4to., publisher's full brown Turkey morocco, title stamped in blind, gold border, inner gilt dentelles, coated moire silk doublures, 400 pages + frontispiece and 24 inserted plates, each with printed tissue, all edges gilt, nearly fine, all printed tissue guards present, although four have tear holes in blank areas, with no loss of print, spine title printed in gold with name "E. D. Waterman" stamped in gold at bottom, minor browning to top of some leaves,. Howard S. Mott Inc. 262 - 144 2013 $450

Association – Waterman, Lewis

New York. (City) *Manual of the Corporation of the City of New York for 1856.* New York: D. T. Valentine, 1856. Publisher's brown cloth stamped in blind and gilt, duotones, color plates and engravings, many foldout maps and facsimiles, small tears to one or two of the foldouts and few small tears to cloth, else fresh and near fine, bookplate of Lewis E. Waterman. Between the Covers Rare Books, Inc. New York City - 291609 2013 $750

Association – Watkins, Anne

Homes, Nathanael *An Essay Concerning the Sabbath.* London: printed for the author, 1673. 12mo., erratic pagination but complete, prelim erratum leaf, tear to G7 without loss, full contemporary sheep, blind ruled borders, spine worn with loss, early signatures of Anne and Jane Watkins, and Katherine. Jarndyce Antiquarian Booksellers CCIV - 15 2013 £85

Association – Watkins, Jane

Homes, Nathanael *An Essay Concerning the Sabbath.* London: printed for the author, 1673. 12mo., erratic pagination but complete, prelim erratum leaf, tear to G7 without loss, full contemporary sheep, blind ruled borders, spine worn with loss, early signatures of Anne and Jane Watkins, and Katherine. Jarndyce Antiquarian Booksellers CCIV - 15 2013 £85

Association – Watson, Anne

Wordsworth, William 1770-1850 *Poems, in Two Volumes.* London: printed for Longman Hurst Rees & Orme, 1807. First edition, 2 volumes, 8vo., original drab boards with pink paper covered spines as issued, one of 500 copies printed, with cancels D11-12 in volume I and B2 in volume II, Volume I has half title and erratum leaf H8, Volume II has half title, sectional half title B1 and first sheet F9 (i) volume 2, contemporary ownership inscription to Anne Watson in volume I with her pencil ownership signature on titlepage, bookplates of Simon Nowell-Smith and his wife, light foxing, covers slightly chipped and worn, but very good. James S. Jaffe Rare Books Fall 2013 - 152 2013 $27,500

Association – Watts, James

Freeman, Walter *Psychsurgery. Intelligence Emotion and Social Behavior Following Prefrontal Lobotomy for Mental Conditions.* Springfield: Thomas, 1942. 337 pages, text illustrations, original cloth, dust jacket bit worn, else very good plus, presentation copy from James Watts for Bill Sweet. James Tait Goodrich S74 - 117 2013 $350

Association – Watts-Dunton, Theodore

Morris, William 1834-1896 *A Dream of John Ball and a King's Lesson.* Kelmscott Press, 1892. (One of 300 copies) of an edition of 311, printed in Golden types on handmade paper, in black with shoulder notes and 2 small areas of text printed in red, wood engraved frontispiece by Edward Burne-Jones, wood engraved leaf border and wood engraved vine border to adjacent page of text designed by Morris, large and small wood engraved initial letters throughout, crown 8vo., original limp cream vellum, backstrip gilt lettered, front free endpaper, little darkened, green silk ties, untrimmed and unopened, recent maroon cloth, solander case with gilt lettered black leather labels, near fine, inscribed by Morris to friend Theodore Watts-Dunton. Blackwell's Rare Books B174 - 356 2013 £4000

Association – Waugh, Alec

Graves, Robert 1895-1985 *Treasure Box.* London: Chiswick Press, 1919. First edition, 8vo., original blue unprinted wrappers, excellent copy in protective oversized folding box, leather label, lettered in gilt, inscribed by author and Nancy Nicholson for Robert Graves, inherited by his son Alec Waugh who gave it to Cyril Connolly at Christmas 1967.   Maggs Bros. Ltd.   1460 - 359   2013   £1750

Association – Way, Robert Edward

Pollux, Julius *Onomaticum Graece & Latine.* Amstelaedami: ex Officina Wetsteniana, 1706. 2 volumes, folio, double page plate to volume II, additional engraved titlepage, engraved frontispiece, titlepage in red and black, Gathering 8N in volume I bound out of sequence, small hole to page 373 affecting a few letters, repair to corner of rear endpaper in volume I, tan Cambridge style calf with catspaw staining to frame, neatly rebacked with red morocco gilt spine labels, edges sprinkled red, boards scratched, some small areas of surface loss, corners worn, hinges relined, to each volume bookplate of Robert Edward Way, bookplate of William Sedgwick, Queens College Cambridge and inscription of Caroli Beaumont, another inscription beneath oval inkstamp of Queens College Library.   Unsworths Antiquarian Booksellers   28 - 43   2013   £750

Association – Weatherald, R.

Bacon, Francis Viscount St. Albans 1561-1626 *The Two Bookes of Francis Bacon, of the Proficience and Advancement of Learning, Divine and Humane.* London: for Henri Thomes, 1605. First edition, 4to., lacks final blank 3H2 and, as always, the rare two leaves of errata at end, late 18th century half calf and marbled boards, (extremities of boards worn), very skilfully and imperceptively rebacked retaining entire original spine, small worm trail in bottom margin of quires 2D-2F, occasional minor marginalia in early hand, else lovely copy, early signature of Row'd Weatherald and signature of Horatio Carlyon, 1861, Sachs bookplate and modern leather book label, calf backed clamshell box.   Joseph J. Felcone Inc.   Books Printed before 1701 - 5   2013 $7500

Association – Webb, Alan

Bond, Edward *The Sea.* London: Methuen, 1973. First edition, small 8vo., original black cloth, fine in dust jacket, inscribed by author to Alan Webb, the actor.   Maggs Bros. Ltd.   1460 - 124   2013   £200

Association – Webb, Thomas

Butler, Samuel 1612-1680 *Hudibras.* London: printed or C. Bathurst et al, 1772. Third edition, 2 volumes, 8vo., frontispiece ad 9 engraved plates after Hogarth, + 7 engraved plates after Hogarth, light toning, plates little foxed, contemporary sprinkled tan calf, spines gilt in compartments, red and green morocco labels, edges speckled, joints and corners repaired, old leather darkened, scratched at extremities, contemporary armorial bookplate of Thomas Webb/Hoston.   Unsworths Antiquarian Booksellers   28 - 78   2013   £120

Association – Webber, Philip

Locke, John 1632-1704 *Some Thoughts Concerning Education.* London: printed for A. and J. Churchill at the Black Swan in Pater Noster Row, 1693. First edition, octavo, contemporary calf, expertly rebacked at early date preserving original spine, covers bordered on three sides with double blind rule and with floriated blind border at joints, spine in six compartments with five raised bands, sprinkled edges, holograph ink title on front board "Education of Young Persons", early holograph notes on pastedown endpapers, signatures D-F with small wormtracks affecting approximately 12 leaves, manuscript ex-libris of Philip Webber on titlepage dated 1745 with another ink signature on verso of title, minor soiling in few places, very good.   Heritage Book Shop   50th Anniversary Catalogue - 66   2013 $9000

Association – Weber, Francis

Bondy, Louis W. *Small is Beautiful.* Morro Bay: Miniature Book Society, 1987. Limited to 400 copies, printed at Tabula Rasa Press, 6.5 x 6 cm., cloth with gilt lettering on front cover and gilt design on spine, signed by author and by Francis Weber, from the collection of Donn W. Sanford.   Oak Knoll Books   303 - 5   2013 $150

Association – Weber, Jeff

Francis, Edward William *Characters and Caricatures.* Charlottesville: John S. Francis, 2010. Limited to 42 copies, oblong 8vo., silver stamped black cloth, dust jacket, illustrations, TLS 10/24/2010 from author to rare book dealer Jeff Weber laid in, mint.   Jeff Weber Rare Books   171 - 123   2013 $75

Glaister, Geoffrey Ashall *Glossary of the Book.* London: George Allen and Unwin, 1960. First edition, signed letter from author to LA bookseller Jeff Weber, 8vo., frontispiece, plates, text illustrations, quarter maroon cloth with gray cloth sides, gilt stamped cover illustrations and spine title, dust jacket bit worn and spotted, very good.   Jeff Weber Rare Books   171 - 139   2013 $150

Princeton University *A Catalogue of the Cotsen Children's Library Volumes I and II.* Princeton: Princeton University Press, 2000-2003. 2 volumes, large folio, handsome color reproductions, decorative endpapers, gilt stamped pictorial green Japanese cloth, gilt stamped black leather spine label, fine, signed presentation inscription by collector Lloyd Cotsen to Jeff Weber in volume I.   Jeff Weber Rare Books   171 - 79   2013 $400

Association – Weber, Jonas Christian

Suetonius Tranquillus, Gaius *Caesarum XII Libri a Mendis ad Interpretum Sententiam & Vetustorum Exemplarium fidem Repeurgati...* Basel: per Henricum Petrum, 1537. First Gallus edition, touch of soiling to titlepage, institutional stamp and small paper shelfmark label at foot, earlier inscription at head, contemporary wooden boards backed in blindstamped pigskin, spine dyed black and with three raised bands, later paper labels in second and fourth compartments, two clasps (both lost), little bit rubbed, old inscriptions to front endpapers (one the purchase note of Jonas Christian Weber), very good.   Blackwell's Rare Books   172 - 136   2013   £1400

Association – Webling, A. F.

Blunden, Edmund *In Summer. The Rotunda of the Bishop of Derry.* London: privately printed for Terence Fytton Armstrong, 1931. First edition, 8vo., original grey boards, lettered in pale green, acetate dust jacket slightly torn, near fine, inscribed by author for A. F. Webling, rector of Stansfield in Suffolk.   Maggs Bros. Ltd.   1460 - 115   2013   £125

Association – Webster, Hedley

Webster, C. A. *St. Patrick's Lodge, No. 8 1808-1908.* Offprint JCHAS, 1909. 39 pages, many portraits, cloth, presentation copy from Hedley Webster.   C. P. Hyland   261 - 863   2013   £35

Association – Wedgwood, Hensleigh

Darwin, Charles Robert 1809-1882 *Narrative of the Surveying Voyages of His Majesty's Ships Adventure and Beagle, Between the Years 1826 and 1836.* London: Henry Colburn, 1839. First edition, first issue of volume III, 2 folding maps, half title, contemporary diced calf (probably a gift binding) neatly rebacked, marbled endpapers and edges, armorial bookplate of Hensleigh C. Wedgwood, inscribed by author to same (his brother-in-law), endpapers little foxed and soiled, otherwise exceptional association and attractive looking copy in custom full brown morocco clamshell case, gilt stamped.   Heritage Book Shop 50th Anniversary Catalogue - 27   2013 $100,000

Association – Wedgwood, Josiah

Richardson, Samuel 1689-1761 *The Works.* London: printed for William Miller and James Carpenter, 1811. 187 x 127mm., 19 volumes, very pleasing contemporary polished calf, handsomely gilt flat spines with panels formed by bands of multiple fillets, each spine with panel at top featuring lozenge centerpiece and three other panels diapered with azured and solid diagonals as well as with one red and two dark blue morocco labels (four spines with small repairs to paste down loose pieces of leather), engraved frontispiece in first volume, 19th century booklabel in each volume of Josiah Wedgwood; some joints bit flaked, extremities little rubbed, isolated abrasions on covers, other minor defects but very decorative original bindings without any major problems and generally very pleasing, unambitious worming in first few leaves of one volume two minor tears into text without loss, other trivial imperfections excellent copy internally, text uniformly clean and smooth.   Phillip J. Pirages   63 - 398   2013 $1800

Association – Weekes, John

Dryden, John 1631-1700 *Fables Ancient and Modern.* London: printed for Jacob Tonson, 1700. First edition, folio, tiny burnhole in one leaf (clear of text), two pinprick wormholes in lower margin of first half (few times stretching slightly but never near text), some light browning in places, few tiny stains, contemporary Cambridge style panelled calf, rebacked in different shade, corners repaired, few old scratches to old leather, hinges neatly relined, beginnings of early manuscript index, early ownership inscriptions of John Weekes and P. Towhouse?   Unsworths Antiquarian Booksellers   28 - 89   2013   £500

Association – Weinberg, Steven

Feynman, Richard *Elementary Particles and the Laws of Physics.* Cambridge: Cambridge University, 1987. First edition, small 8vo., x, 110 pages, signed by Steven Weinberg, small 8vo., x, 110 pages, fine in near fine dust jacket.   By the Book, L. C.   36 - 97   2013 $500

Association – Weir, J. L.

Colvil, Samuel *The Whigs Supplication or the Scotch-Hudibra.* Glasgow: printed by Robert Urie, 1751. 8vo., pages 164, lightly spotted and browned, recent dark brown half calf, marbled boards, spine with two raised bands, middle compartment lettered vertically in gilt, 18th century armorial bookplate of "Geo. Jas. Campbell Esqr./of Treesbank, relaid on front pastedown, above in the paper ex-libris of J. L. Weir.   Unsworths Antiquarian Booksellers   28 - 84   2013   £125

Association – Weiss, M.

Sampson, John *XXI Welsh Gypsy Folk Tales.* Newtown, Powys: Gregynog Press, 1933. 216/235 copies (of an edition of 250), printed on Portal handmade paper, title vignette and 7 other exquisite wood engravings by Agnes Miller Parker, imperial 8vo., original mustard yellow bevel edged sheepskin, backstrip rubbed, more so at head and tail, edges and corners also with some fairly light rubbing, design of horizontal lines on front cover incorporating the title lettering and lettering on backstrip, all gilt blocked, usual offsetting fro turn-ins and faint tape stains to free endpapers, bookplates of M. Weiss and Norman J. Sondheim, untrimmed, good.   Blackwell's Rare Books   172 - 293   2013   £1250

Association – Wells, Charles

Bowles, William Lisle *Sonnets with other Poems.* Bath: printed by R. Cruttwell and sold by C. Dilly, Poultry, London, 1794. Third edition, half title, contemporary full calf, gilt spine, border and dentelles, dark green leather label, bit rubbed, hinges little worn, one or two small splits, possibly author's copy with armorial bookplate "Revd. Mr. Bowles", also small booklabel of Charles Wells and gift inscription "Anna Maria Pinney 1835. From S. M. Booth", blindstamped and labels of Birkbeck College Library.   Jarndyce Antiquarian Booksellers   CCIII - 33   2013   £150

Association – Wells, John

Anacreon *Teiou Mele: Praefixo Commentario quo Poetae Genus...* Parma: Bodoni, 1791. One of 150 copies, 16mo. in 4's, 2 engraved portraits, text i Greek, commentaries in Latin, very occasional marginal foxing, small marginal tear to page 91, contemporary vellum, spine gilt with black morocco labels, all edges gilt, upper joint split but neatly repaired with vellum, lower joint starting, binding little soiled, particularly at spine, labels slightly chipped, armorial bookplate of John Wells Esq. to front pastedown, with small Greek inscription, armorial bookplate of Gul. D. Geddes.   Unsworths Antiquarian Booksellers   28 - 1   2013   £600

Association – Werner, Arno

Tate, Allen *The Hovering Fly and Other Essays.* Cummington: Cummington Press, 1949. First edition, one of only 12 copies on Van Gelder paper with original drawing and woodcuts hand colored, this copy specially bound and signed by author and artist, out of a total edition of 245 copies, 8vo., woodcuts by Wightman Williams, full russet morocco with inlaid hand colored panel on front cover by Arno Werner, this the binder's copy, signed by Werner "Arno Werner Bookbinder 1949", very fine, half morocco, folding box with Werners booklabel.   James S. Jaffe Rare Books   Fall 2013 - 36   2013 $15,000

Association – Weston, C.

Cotton, Robert *Cottoni Posthuma.* London: printed by Francis Leach, 1651. 8vo., slight browning, titlepage little dusted, one small rust hole, contemporary calf, neatly rebacked, not recently, corners slightly worn, inscription, ex-library Car. Weston 1761, earlier name at head of titlepage.   Jarndyce Antiquarian Booksellers   CCIV - 9   2013   £225

Association – Weston, Harris

Brown, Christy *Of Snails and Skylarks.* London: Secker & Warburg, 1977. First edition, original brown cloth, excellent copy in dust jacket, chipped and rubbed, inscribed by author for friend Harris Weston Jan. 1978, tipped in is TLS from author to same, recipient's bookplate.   Maggs Bros. Ltd.   1460 - 145   2013   £350

Association – Wetzel, Helen Janssen

Sherard, Robert Harborough *Oscar Wilde: the Story of an Unhappy Friendship.* London: privately printed at the Hermes Press, 1902. First edition, 254 x 198mm., 277, (1) pages, handsome contemporary olive green morocco lavishly gilt in Art Nouveau style by Stikeman (stamp-signed on rear turn-in), covers with multiple plain and decorative gilt rules enclosing large quatrefoil with very prominent floral cornerpieces and floral tool accents, central panel of that on upper cover containing coronet imposed upon crossed writing tools, raised bands, spine attractively gilt in compartments with large central lily framed by drawer hand tools, intricate gilt floral turn-ins, marbled endpapers, top edge gilt, original paper and cloth bound in, frontispiece photo of Wilde, five other portraits and two facsimiles of letters as called for, large paper copy, morocco bookplates of Helen Janssen Wetzel and Mary Pinkerton Carlisle, spine sunned to rich brown, just touch of rubbing to joints, usual offsetting to free endpapers from turn-ins, titlepage little browned from acidic(!) tissue guard (now removed), last page with faint darkening from bound-in cloth cover, handful of leaves with small, light brown stains along gutter (from binder's glue), other trivial imperfections but still excellent copy, leaves fresh, clean and bright, margins enormous and animated, glittering binding scarcely worn.   Phillip J. Pirages   61 - 126   2013 $1250

Association – Wharton, G. B.

Byron, George Gordon Noel, 6th Baron   1788-1824 *Marino Faliero, Doge of Venice. The Prophecy of Dante, a Poem.* London: John Murray, 1821. First edition, 2nd issue, variant A, half title, small repair, disbound, ownership inscription G. B. Wharton, 1821.   Jarndyce Antiquarian Booksellers   CCIII - 292   2013   £35

Association – Wheelock, John Hall

Harvard University *Harvard Class of 1908 Thirtieth Anniversary Report June 1938 (Seventh Report).* Norwood: privately printed for the Class by the Plimpton Press, 1938. Red cloth, gilt, fine, poet John Hall Wheelock's copy, signed by him by his statement. Between the Covers Rare Books, Inc. 165 - 202 2013 $200

Association – Whistler, Rex

Asquith, Cynthia *She Walks in Beauty.* London: William Heinemann, 1934. First edition, 8vo., original blue cloth, excellent copy, spine slightly faded, inscribed by author to Rex Whistler with pencil drawing, possibly by Whistler. Maggs Bros. Ltd. 1460 - 24 2013 £175

Association – White, Horace

La Valliere, Louise Francoise De La Baume Le Blanc, Duchess De *Lettres De Madame La Duchesse De La Valliere, Morte Religieuse Carmelite...* Paris: Antoine Boudet, 1767. 12mo., brown speckled boards, leather label, bookplate and signature of Horace White, Paris 1875. Second Life Books Inc. 182 - 151 2013 $225

Association – Whytehead, Thomas Bowman

A Description of the Grand Musical Festival, Held in the City of York, September the 23rd (-26th) 1823... York: Henry Cobb, 1823. 8vo., 4 engraved plates, half title, very good, uncut in original boards, neatly rebacked, handsome 19th century armorial bookplate of Thomas Bowman Whytehead, of Fulford York, later name at head and front endpaper, scarce. Ken Spelman Books Ltd. 73 - 196 2013 £160

Association – Wiater, Stanley

The Arkham Sampler. Sauk City: Arkham House, 1949. Four issues, Winter, Spring, Summer and Fall 1949, each issue with stamp of horror writer Stanley Wiater inside front cover, titles and dates handwritten on spines, Winter issue has chip to lower spine, all issues wearing at spine folds and have bit of bleedthrough at staples, still very good, each issue had print run of 1200 copies, scarce now. Ken Lopez Bookseller 159 - 8 2013 $200

Bradbury, Ray *The Halloween Tree.* Colorado Springs: Gauntlet Press, 2005. Limited edition, #507 of 750 numbered copies, assembled by Donn Albright, signed by author, bookplate of Stanley Wiater, fine in fine dust jacket. Ken Lopez Bookseller 159 - 26 2013 $450

Lansdale, Joe R. *Act of Love.* New York: Kensington/Zebra, 1981. Paperback original, signed by author, dated 11/1/86, stamp of recipient Stanley Wiater, spine creased, very good in wrappers, laid in is folded autograph note signed by author to Wiater. Ken Lopez Bookseller 159 - 98 2013 $150

Lansdale, Joe R. *Cold in July.* New York: Bantam, 1989. Publisher's copy, (indicated "P/C" on colophon) of limited edition, which was issued with numbered limitation of 100 copies, signed by author, colophon laid in, having detached as glue which is tipped in has dried, glue stains at hinge and light spine crease, ownership stamp of Stanley Wiater, very good in wrappers, uncommon issue of this paperback original. Ken Lopez Bookseller 159 - 101 2013 $100

Lansdale, Joe R. *The Drive-in 2.* New York: Bantam, 1989. Uncorrected proof, inscribed by author to Stanley Wiater, with his bookplate, edge sunned with small crown bump, near fine in wrappers. Ken Lopez Bookseller 159 - 102 2013 $75

Lansdale, Joe R. *Freezer Burn.* Holyoke: Crossroads Press, 1999. Uncorrected proof of this limited edition, signed by author, comb-bound with both printed and acetate covers, stamp of Stanley Wiater, near fine in wrappers. Ken Lopez Bookseller 159 - 105 2013 $150

Shepard, Lucius *The Jaguar Hunter.* Sauk City: Arkham House, 1987. First edition, review copy, inscribed by author to Stanley Wiater, one of 3194 copies, illustrations by J. K. Potter, with Wiater's Gahan Wilson designed bookplate, near fine in like dust jacket with review slip laid in. Ken Lopez Bookseller 159 - 177 2013 $350

Association – Wickes, Forsyth

Avery, C. Louise *Masterpieces of European Porcelain: a Catalogue of a Special Exhibition March 18- May 15 1949.* New York: printed by Marchbanks Press for The Metropolitan Museum of Art, 1949. One of 2000 copies, 290 x 222mm., attractive crimson crushed morocco by James MacDonald Co. of NY (stamp signed), covers with single gilt fillet border, upper cover with initials "F.W." in lower right corner, raised bands flanked by gilt rules, small gilt fleuron at head and tail of spine, vertical titling, densely gilt turn-ins, marbled endpapers; with 32 black and white photos; tipped to front pastedown is handwritten note to Mr. Wickes from Francis Henry Taylor, director of Metropolitan Museum, presenting this book in gratitude for Wickes' support of the Exhibition; couple of small marks to covers, but very fine with virtually no signs of use. Phillip J. Pirages 63 - 492 2013 $150

Association – Widnell, Mary Augusta

De Quincey, Thomas 1785-1859 *Autobiographical Sketches.* Edinburgh: James Hogg, 1853. First edition, inscribed by author for Mary Augusta Widnell, 8vo., crudely rebound in black morocco with recent gift inscription, excellent copy.   Maggs Bros. Ltd.   1460 - 221   2013   £600

Association – Williams, C.

Algarotti, Francesco *Sir Isaac Newton's Philosophy Explain'd for the Use of the Ladies.* London: printed for E. Cave at St. John's-gate and sold also by Messrs Bindley (and others), 1739. 2 volumes, 12mo., some even browning, old waterstaining to endpapers in volume 1, full contemporary mottled calf, double gilt ruled borders, gilt panelled spines, little rubbed, lacking labels, slight wear double gilt ruled borders, gilt panelled spines, little rubbed, lacking labels, slight wear to foot of spine volume II, early ownership name Cath: Williams on front endpapers.   Jarndyce Antiquarian Booksellers   CCIV - 216   2013   £580

Association – Williams, Carlos

Bedouin, Jean Louis *Andre Breton. Une etude par Jean-Louis Bedouin.* Paris: Editions Pierre Seghers, 1950. First edition, square 12mo., original wrappers, preserved in folding box, inscribed by author for Carlos Williams, very good, worn at extremities, spine faded.   Maggs Bros. Ltd.   1460 - 137   2013   £450

Association – Williams, E. H.

Byron, George Gordon Noel, 6th Baron 1788-1824 *The Works - Poetry - Letters & Journals.* London: John Murray, 1899-1904. 13 volumes, half titles, plates, uncut in original blue cloth, decorated and lettered gilt, boards creased in places, some spines little dulled, volume III with library stamps and shelf marks, volume VI with booklabel of E. H. Williams, top edge gilt, good plus, made up set.   Jarndyce Antiquarian Booksellers   CCIII - 83   2013   £250

Association – Williams, Emelyn

Rattigan, Terence *The Winslow Boy.* London: Hamish Hamilton, 1946. First edition, 8vo. 109 pages, very good, signed by 10 f the 11 cast members of the first London production, including Kathleen Harrison, Emelyn Williams, Michael Newell, etc.   Second Life Books Inc.   183 - 330   2013 $350

Association – Williams, Jonathan

Loy, Mina *Lunar Baedeker & Time-Tables. Selected Poems.* Highlands: Jonathan Williams, 1958. First edition, one of only 50 hardbound copies of an Author's Edition, numbered and signed by Loy, tall 8vo., titlepage illustration by Emerson Woelffer, original cloth, printed paper spine label, presentation copy inscribed by book's publisher, Jonathan Williams to Denise Levertov, who contributed one of the introductions, extremities lightly rubbed, few small faint spots near bottom edge of front cover, some barely perceptible offset from binding adhesive along endpaper gutters, otherwise near fine.   James S. Jaffe Rare Books   Fall 2013 - 93   2013 $2500

Niedecker, Lorine *My Friend Tree. Poems.* Edinburgh: Wild Hawthorn Press, 1961. First edition, oblong 8vo., original wrappers, dust jacket, extremely rare, fine association copy, inscribed by author for her publisher Jonathan Williams.   James S. Jaffe Rare Books   Fall 2013 - 108   2013 $7500

Association – Williams, Tennessee

Capote, Truman 1924-1985 *Music for Chameleons.* New York: Random House, 1980. First trade edition, signed by author and also signed by book's dedicatee, Tennessee Williams, marvelous association, foxing to top and front edges, else near fine in like dust jacket (price clipped).   Ed Smith Books   75 - 13   2013 $2500

Association – Williams, William

Cabala; Sive Sacra. Mysteries of State Government: in Letters of Illustrious Persons, and Great Agents; in the Reigns of Henry the Eighth, Queen Elizabeth, K. James and the Late King Charles... London: printed for G. Bedel and T. Collins..., 1654. First edition, small 8vo., cloth, general titlepage and titlepage to part 2 in red and black, from the library of William R. Williams, NY 1856 and William R. Street, 1845; spine label scuffed, owner's name on top edge of first blank and title, first titlepage and last page of index mounted, rare marginalia, damp spotting to lower margin of last half of second part, few last leaves soiled at top edge, overall still solid.   Kaaterskill Books   16 - 4   2013 $475

Association – Williamson, H. M.

Stock, Joseph *A Narrative of What Passed at Killalla, in the County of Mayo and the Parts Adjacent During the French Invasion in the Summer of 1798.* Dublin: printed by and for R. E. Mercier and Co., 1800. 8vo., bound with 2 final ad leaves, titlepage lightly foxed, some browning, small hole at blank head of H8, contemporary half red morocco, marbled boards, spine rubbed and dull, corners bumped, some abrasions to boards, presentation form author "F. H. Lewis given by the Bishop of Killala 1806", 19th century armorial bookplate of H. M. Williamson and pencil signature of Michael Foot.   Jarndyce Antiquarian Booksellers   CCIV - 284   2013   £480

Association – Willis, John Ralph

Burton, Richard Francis   1821-1890   *To the Gold Coast for Gold.*   London: 1883.   First edition, 2 volumes, octavo, 2 folding, colored maps in volume 1 and colored frontispiece in volume II, original red cloth, stamped in black and gilt on boards, spines lettered gilt and stamped in black, black coated endpapers, spines slightly rubbed and sunned, top edges bit foxed, minimal and invisible restoration to inner hinges, bookplate of John Ralph Willis, prominent collector of Rare Africana, each volume with previous owner's ink signature and date of 1888 on front free endpapers, on same page in same hand is written "Valley Forge Historical Society & Washington Memorial Library, Valley Forge", very good, handsome set.   Heritage Book Shop   Holiday Catalogue 2012 - 24   2013 $5500

Association – Wilson, Arch

Smollett, Tobias George   1721-1771   *The Expedition of Humphrey Clinker.*   London: W. Johnston and B. Collins in Salisbury, 1671, i.e., 1771.   First edition, 3 volumes, 12mo., contemporary calf (front hinge volume 1 cracked and slightly chipped at head of spine), leather titlepieces, raised bands, excellent copy, with all half titles, early ownership signature "Arch. Wilson/Dedham", old stamp of "W. C. Day" and bookplate of Chicago book collector Harold Greenhill (1893-1968) in each volume, morocco backed cloth folding case.   Howard S. Mott Inc.   262 - 139   2013 $1350

Association – Wilson, Bill

Alcoholics Anonymous. The Story of How Many Thousands of Men and Women Have Recovered from Alcoholism.   New York: Works Publ Inc., 1950.   First edition, 13th printing, 8vo., viii, 400 pages, signed, inscribed and dated by Bill Wilson using his full name, mild toning to endpapers mild sun to spine, near fine in very good++ original dust jacket (with mild scuffs, minimal edge wear, unobtrusive tape dust jacket verso, in custom cloth covered clamshell box gilt, gilt lettering on clamshell cover and spine labels.   By the Book, L. C.   36 - 79   2013 $8500

Association – Wilson, Carroll

Burgess, Gelett   1866-1951   *The Purple Cow!*   San Francisco: William Doxey, 1895.   First edition, first issue printed on both sides of each leaf on rough paper, 12mo., original pictorial self wrapper, 8 leaves (including wrappers), stapled, uncut as issued, folding case, signed by author, one short marginal slit in front wrapper, else fine, Carroll Wilson's copy.   Howard S. Mott Inc.   262 - 25   2013 $400

Association – Wilson, Jack

Coward, Noel   1899-1973   *Quadrille.*   London: Heinemann, 1952.   First edition, 8vo., 116 pages, signed by 17 members of the English cast and producer Jack Wilson and by Lynn Fontann and Alfred Lunt, inscribed by author to Dorothy Sands (Octavia in NY production).   Second Life Books Inc.   183 - 83   2013 $500

Association – Wilson, Kate

James, Henry   1843-1916   *The Reverberator.*   London and New York: Macmillan and Co., 1888.   Second edition, American issue, 184 x 127mm., 2 p.l., 229, (1) pages, publisher's original blue cloth with gilt titling and decoration, half title with ink ownership inscription "Kate D. Wilson, Jan. 26th 189(0)", bookplate inscribed "Capt. James Hart, Baltimore 26 Feb. (19)46", spine slightly rolled, tiny snag at top of backstrip and one at bottom, light rubbing to small portions of joints and extremities, still nearly fine, cloth and gilt especially bright, hinges solid, text with virtually no signs of use.   Phillip J. Pirages   63 - 263   2013 $250

Association – Wilson, Lois

D., Margaret   *Al-Anon's Favorite Forum Editorials.*   New York: Al-Anon Family Group, 1970.   Stated first edition, 8vo., xx, 268 pages; near fine with mild wear to cover edges and with inscriptions and signatures on endpapers, signed and inscribed by Margaret D. and signed by Lois (Wilson), and by other members of AA and Al-Anon, very good+ dust jacket with mild sun edgewear.   By the Book, L. C.   36 - 81   2013 $1500

Association – Wilson, Robin

Yeats, William Butler   1865-1939   *The Tables of the Law and Adoration of the Magi.*   Stratford upon Avon: Shakespeare Head Press, 1914.   Second published edition, 108 of 510 numbered copies, small 8vo., original mottled cloth, lettered on upper cloth, ownership copy of poet Robin Wilson, excellent copy.   Maggs Bros. Ltd.   1442 - 343   2013   £125

Association – Wilson, William

Davis, William *A Complete Treatise of Land Surveying by the Chain, Corss and Offset Staffs Only.* London: printed for the author, 1798. 8vo., 6 folding plates, numerous diagrams in text, slight foxing, mainly to leading edges and plates, contemporary half calf marbled boards, gilt morocco label, expert repairs to hinges and corners, spine repaired, contemporary signature of J. Brooke and of William Wilson, Tilsey.   Jarndyce Antiquarian Booksellers   CCIV - 105   2013   £320

Association – Windele, John

O'Brien, Henry *The Round Towers of Ireland; or the Mysteries of Freemasonry of Sabaism and of Budhism for the First Time Unveiled.* 1834. First edition, half calf, 4 plates, many text illustrations, quarter leather, not a pretty copy but it has owner inscription of the doyen of Cork antiquaries, John Windele, pasted to front loose leaf an appreciation of O'Brien from "A Gallery of Literary Characters No. LXIII" and on rear free endpaper some correspondence by Windele and another from the Southern Reporter.   C. P. Hyland   261 - 620   2013   £250

Association – Winnington-Ingram, A. R.

Boys, Edward *Narrative of a Captivity and Adventures in France and Flanders Between the Years 1803 and 1809.* London: printed for Richard Long, 1827. 8vo., frontispiece, folding colored lithograph plan, 3 lithograph plates, woodcut in text, 8vo., some foxing, later 19th century half roan, gilt banded and lettered spine, little rubbed, signature of A. R. Winngton-Ingram, 1885, few pencil underlinings in text.   Jarndyce Antiquarian Booksellers   CCIV - 71   2013   £150

Burke, Edmund   1729-1797 *A Philosophical Enquiry into the Origin of Our Ideas of the Sublime and Beautiful.* London: printed for J. Dodsley, 1767. 8vo., some occasional foxing and light browning, full contemporary calf, gilt panelled spine, red morocco label, leading hinge cracked but firm, slight insect damage, spine chipped at head, 18th century armorial bookplate of Rev. Chas. Bishop, with name A. R. Winnington-Ingram 1880 who has underlined many sections of text in pencil and added several marginal notes to his reading.   Jarndyce Antiquarian Booksellers   CCIV - 78   2013   £125

La Rochefoucauld, Francois, Duc De   1613-1680 *Maxims and Moral Reflections...* 1781. 12mo., late 19th or early 20th century ink annotations to text, contemporary quarter calf, marbled boards, vellum tips, gilt ruled spine, black morocco label, boards rubbed, ownership name of A. R. Winnington-Ingram, name erased from front endpaper.   Jarndyce Antiquarian Booksellers   CCIV - 181   2013   £85

Association – Wintzingerode, Ferdinand Von

Tahsin al-Din *The Loves of Camarupa and Camelata, an Ancient Indian Tale.* London: printed for T. Cadell, 1793. First edition of this translation, staining from turn-in affecting borders of few leaves at either end, cancelled library stamp on half title, 8vo., contemporary sheep, gilt rules on flat spine forming compartments, red lettering piece, upper hinge repaired, spine darkened and with vertical crack ascending little over half of the height, contemporary armorial bookplate (Ferdinand) Graf on Wintzingerode, sound.   Blackwell's Rare Books   B174 - 150   2013   £750

Association – Wise, T. J.

Byron, George Gordon Noel, 6th Baron   1788-1824 *Childe Harold's Pilgrimage. Canto the Third.* London: John Murray, 1816. First edition, 2nd issue, 2nd variant, half title, 4 pages ads (Dec. 1816), uncut in original drab wrappers, spine slightly chipped at tail, leading hinge splitting, good plus as originally issued in later blue cloth folder, armorial bookplate of Chadwyck-Healey, loosely inserted is letter dated 1930 in original envelope from T. J. Wise to Oliver Nowell Chadwyck-Healey.   Jarndyce Antiquarian Booksellers   CCIII - 144   2013   £350

A Vindication of Lady Byron. London: Richard Bentley & son, 1871. First edition, original brick brown cloth, inner hinges slightly cracking, slightly rubbed, spine little worn at head and tail, T. J. Wise's copy.   Jarndyce Antiquarian Booksellers   CCIII - 350   2013   £180

Association – Wismar, Cyril

Updike, John   1932- *Bech: a Book.* New York: Knopf, 1970. First edition, inscribed by author for Cyril and Sylvia Wismar, foxing to top edge of text block, else fine in near fine dust jacket foxed on verso and with couple of small edge chips.   Ken Lopez Bookseller   159 - 192   2013 $650

Updike, John   1932- *Bessere Verbaltnisse. (Rabbit is Rich).* Berlin: Verlag Volt und Welt, 1986. German language edition, inscribed by author for Cyril Wismar, mild age toning to acidic paper and foxing to top edge of text block, near fine in fine dust jacket.   Ken Lopez Bookseller   159 - 198   2013 $250

Updike, John   1932- *Buchanan Dying.* New York: Knopf, 1974. First edition, inscribed by author for Cyril Wismar, half dozen instances of underlining in as many pages, presumably by Wismar, foxing to fore edge, thus near fine in like dust jacket, price clipped.   Ken Lopez Bookseller   159 - 193   2013 $750

Updike, John 1932- *Five Poems.* Cleveland: Bits Press, 1980. Of a total edition of 185, this one of 135 numbered copies, signed by author, this #184, additionally inscribed by author for Sylvia and Cyril Wismar, some staining to fore edge of cover, bit of foxing to fore edge of text block, fine in saddle stitched wrappers. Ken Lopez Bookseller 159 - 195 2013 $375

Updike, John 1932- *Hawthorne's Creed.* New York: Targ, 1981. One of 250 signed by author, inscribed by author for Sylvia & Cyril Wismar, together with a deck of Pinochle playing cards inscribed on case "From John & Martha Updike" in unknown hand, cards and case near fine, book fine in near fine, unprinted dust jacket (mildly sunned). Ken Lopez Bookseller 159 - 196 2013 $550

Updike, John 1932- *Problems and Other Stories.* New York: Knopf, 1979. First edition, inscribed by author for Sylvia and Cyril Wismar, trace of fore edge foxing, else fine in very near fine dust jacket. Ken Lopez Bookseller 159 - 194 2013 $750

Updike, John 1932- *Thanatopses.* Cleveland: Bits Press, 1991. One of 237 copies, this copy inscribed by author for Cyril Wismar, fine in saddle stitched self wrappers. Ken Lopez Bookseller 159 - 199 2013 $250

Updike, John 1932- *Toward the End of Time.* New York: Knopf, 1997. First edition, fine in fine dust jacket, inscribed by author for Cyril Wismar. Ken Lopez Bookseller 159 - 200 2013 $250

Association – Wismar, Sylvia

Updike, John 1932- *Bech: a Book.* New York: Knopf, 1970. First edition, inscribed by author for Cyril and Sylvia Wismar, foxing to top edge of text block, else fine in near fine dust jacket foxed on verso and with couple of small edge chips. Ken Lopez Bookseller 159 - 192 2013 $650

Updike, John 1932- *Five Poems.* Cleveland: Bits Press, 1980. Of a total edition of 185, this one of 135 numbered copies, signed by author, this #184, additionally inscribed by author for Sylvia and Cyril Wismar, some staining to fore edge of cover, bit of foxing to fore edge of text block, fine in saddle stitched wrappers. Ken Lopez Bookseller 159 - 195 2013 $375

Updike, John 1932- *Hawthorne's Creed.* New York: Targ, 1981. One of 250 signed by author, inscribed by author for Sylvia & Cyril Wismar, together with a deck of Pinochle playing cards inscribed on case "From John & Martha Updike" in unknown hand, cards and case near fine, book fine in near fine, unprinted dust jacket (mildly sunned). Ken Lopez Bookseller 159 - 196 2013 $550

Updike, John 1932- *Problems and Other Stories.* New York: Knopf, 1979. First edition, inscribed by author for Sylvia and Cyril Wismar, trace of fore edge foxing, else fine in very near fine dust jacket. Ken Lopez Bookseller 159 - 194 2013 $750

Association – Woivodich, Simon

Jourdanet, Denis *Influence de la Pression de l'air sur la Vie de l'Homme Climats d'Altitude et Climats de Montagne.* Paris: G. Masson, 1875. First edition, 2 volumes, large 8vo., 39 engraved plates 3 chromolithographic plates, 8 color maps, figures, numerous tables, foxed and water-stained, text is clean, original reddish brown cloth, gilt stamped cover and spine titles, top edge gilt, extremities stained, ownership ink stamps of Simon D. Woivodich, very good. Jeff Weber Rare Books 172 - 161 2013 $500

Association – Woledge, Geoffrey

Pope, Alexander 1688-1744 *Selecta Poemata Italorum qui Latine Scripsersunt.* Londini: Impensis J. & P. Knapton, 1740. 2 volumes, 8vo., touch of foxing to titlepages, contemporary sprinkled calf, spines in six compartments with raised bands and morocco labels, numbered in gilt, rest with gilt decoration (much rubbed), joints and corners repaired spines bit darkened, ownership inscriptions to front endpaper of Geoffrey Woledge, Birmingham 1937 and A. Montague Summers (1899). Unsworths Antiquarian Booksellers 28 - 122 2013 £300

Association – Wolfe, John Lewis

Wild, Charles *Twelve Perspective Views of the Exterior and Interior Parts of the Metropolitical Church of York...* London: W. Bulmer & Co., 1809. Folio, 14 plates, including 12 fine aquatints, very good, large uncut copy in original sugar paper boards, printed label on upper cover, neatly rebacked, corners and board edges rubbed, slightly worn, fresh contemporary front endpaper, inscribed John Lewis Wolfe, Oct. 1813 from Mr. Namien, scarce. Ken Spelman Books Ltd. 73 - 13 2013 £650

Association – Wood, Harry

Wood, Ellen 1814-1887 *Oswald Cray.* Edinburgh: Adam and Charles Black, 1864. First edition, 3 volumes, half titles, original dark green morocco grained cloth boards, attractively blocked in blind, gilt spines, very good, presentation inscription from the author "For Harry, from Momma". Jarndyce Antiquarian Booksellers CCV - 294 2013 £1200

Association – Wood, Mark

Ellis, Mattie *Bell Ranch Wagon Work.* Conchas Dam: 1984. 76 pages, illustrations, folding map laid in, soft cover with light rubbing, else very good, photos, signed by both Ellis and co-author, Mark Wood, (although handwriting looks suspiciously similar), scarce.   Dumont Maps & Books of the West   122 - 57   2013 $65

Association – Wood, Mary

Coleridge, Samuel Taylor   1772-1834   *The Watchman. No. 1-10, Tuesday March 1 1796-Friday May 13 1796.* Bristol: published by author, pages 291/2 chipped at edges with some loss of text but carefully repaired with appropriate paper, contemporary half calf expertly rebacked, signatures and bookplate of Mary Wood, overall very good, scarce. Jarndyce Antiquarian Booksellers   CCIII - 502   2013   £3500

Milton, John   1608-1674   *Paradise Lost.* London: printed for Jacob Tonson, 1707. Eighth edition, engraved frontispiece dated 1670, 12 engraved plates, some browning and waterstaining, clean tears without loss to one plate and Gg3, small pencil dots in margin mark certain passages, full contemporary calf, ruled borders, smal thistle device in each corner, gilt panelled spine, red morocco label, expert repairs to hinges & head and tail of spine, early ownership signature of Martha Drew, 1748 and 19th century bookplate of Mary Wood, handsome copy.   Jarndyce Antiquarian Booksellers   CCV - 203   2013   £350

Association – Wood, May

Thomas, Frederick   *Humorous and Other Poetic Pictures, Legends and Stories of Devon.*   London: W. Kent & Co., 1883. First edition, Original red decorated cloth, slightly dulled and marked, inscription "May B. Wood - from Mother Ot. 1891".   Jarndyce Antiquarian Booksellers   CCV - 263   2013   £30

Association – Wood, Richard

Drake, Francis   1540-1596   *Eboracum; or the History and Antiquities of the City of York, from its Original to Present Times...*   London: W. Bowyer for the author, 1736. 60 engraved plates, 53 engravings in letterpress, very clean, large copy, contemporary sprinkled calf, gilt ruled borders, expertly rebacked in matching style, raised and gilt banded spine with handsome red morocco label, folio, inscribed "Richard Wood of Red Lyon Square and of Hollin Hall near Rippon in the County of York Esqr. 1778" with pen and ink crest beneath, later pencil note referencing a page in text that refers to the Wood family.   Ken Spelman Books Ltd.   73 - 2   2013   £850

Association – Woodford, John

Churchill, Winston   1620-1688   *Divi Britannici being a Remark Upon the Lives of all the Kings of This Isle...* London: printed by Tho. Roycroft, 1675. Folio, small wormhole in text from page 77 onwards, often touching a letter never affecting sense, gatherings e and d bound in reverse order, lightly browned, occasional spotting, watermark traced in pencil on verso of titlepage, contemporary speckled calf, crackled and rubbed, now rebacked and recornered with reverse calf, printed paper label to spine, new f.f.e.p., ownership inscriptions of Charlotte Bull (19th century) and John Woodford of Pembroke College, Oxford (18th century) to titlepage.   Unsworths Antiquarian Booksellers   28 - 83   2013   £750

Association – Woodruff, Robert

Williams, Tennessee   1911-1983   *I Rise in Flame, Cried the Phoenix.*   Norfolk: New Directions, 1951. First edition, one of 310 copies signed by Williams, this #243, 4to., very good original publisher's slipcase with label, near fine, bookplate of Robert W. Woodruff Library, Emory University stamped "withdrawn", bookplate of Merle Armitage, signed by him.   Ed Smith Books   78 - 77   2013 $300

Association – Woodward, Benjamin Duryea

Varcaresco, Helene   *The Bard of the Dimbovitza: Romanian Folk-Songs Second Series Collected from the Peasants.*   London: Osgood, McIlvaine, 1896. First edition, presentation copy from principal translator, Carmen Sylva (Pseud. of Elizabeth, Queen of Romania) to Benjamin Duryea Woodward, original brown cloth, gilt front cover and spine by Charles Ricketts, binding very good with some rubbing and fading, some foxing to endpapers but interior pages clean with edges untrimmed, 130 pages.   The Kelmscott Bookshop   7 - 128   2013 $500

Association – Woodwell, C. H.

Drake, Samuel G.   *Indian Captivities or Life in the Wigwam...*   Auburn: Derby and Miller, 1850. First edition, 200 x 125mm., 367, (5) pages, publisher's green buckram, flat spine with gilt titling and large indian stamped in gilt on lower half, frontispiece, 3 full page illustrations and 6 vignettes in text; front free endpaper with pencilled ownership signature of F. D. Woodwell and ink inscription of C. H. Woodwell; extremities rubbed, cloth bit faded (with gilt not as bright as it once was), titlepage somewhat foxed, occasional minor foxing elsewhere, one gathering little loose, otherwise excellent copy, clean and fresh in solid original binding.   Phillip J. Pirages   63 - 258   2013 $350

Association – Woodwell, F. D.

Drake, Samuel G. *Indian Captivities or Life in the Wigwam...* Auburn: Derby and Miller, 1850. First edition, 200 x 125mm., 367, (5) pages, publisher's green buckram, flat spine with gilt titling and large indian stamped in gilt on lower half, frontispiece, 3 full page illustrations and 6 vignettes in text; front free endpaper with pencilled ownership signature of F. D. Woodwell and ink inscription of C. H. Woodwell; extremities rubbed, cloth bit faded (with gilt not as bright as it once was), titlepage somewhat foxed, occasional minor foxing elsewhere, one gathering little loose, otherwise excellent copy, clean and fresh in solid original binding.   Phillip J. Pirages   63 - 258   2013 $350

Association – Wormley, Stanton

Brown, Sterling *The Negro in American Fiction.* Washington: Associates in Negro Folk Education, 1937. First edition, wrapper issue, 209 pages, very top of the paper at crown lacking, else near fine, inscribed by author for Stanton Wormley, who was president of Howard University.   Between the Covers Rare Books, Inc.   165 - 27   2013 $650

Association – Worsley, T. C.

Ackerley, J. R. *My Dog Tulip.* London: Secker & Warburg, 1956. First edition, 8vo., original brown cloth, dust jacket, loosely inserted 2 page ALS from author to T. C. Worsley dated 17/7/58, excellent copy in slightly rubbed and foxed dust jacket.   Maggs Bros. Ltd.   1460 - 4   2013   £500

Association – Wright, Arthur

Elze, Karl *Lord Byron, a Biography.* London: John Murray, 1872. First English edition, half title, frontispiece, folding facsimile, original brown cloth, rubbed, spine little darkened and slightly worn at head and tail, leading inner hinge slightly cracking, bookplate of Arthur Wright.   Jarndyce Antiquarian Booksellers   CCIII - 380   2013   £50

Association – Wright, Percival

Brown-Sequard, Charles Edouard *Notice sur les Travaux Originancx...* Paris: Victor Masson et Fils, 1863. First edition, 8vo., lightly foxed, original printed wrappers, soiled, extremities rubbed, inscribed by author for Dr. Percival Wright, very good.   Jeff Weber Rare Books   172 - 44   2013 $800

Association – Wyatt-Edgell, Edgell

Apuleius *Lucii Apulei Madaurensis Platonici Philosophi Opera Interpretatione et Notis Illustravit Julianus Floridus...* Parisiis: apud Fredericum Leonard, 1688. First edition edited by Julien Fleury, 2 volumes, 4to., elaborate engraved frontispiece, title vignette, woodcut coat of arms, engraving, woodcut diagram, original full rose vellum, rubbed but in excellent condition, printed library marks on titles, ownership signature of Rev. Edgell Wyatt Edgell, Rome 1854, very good.   Jeff Weber Rare Books   171 - 4   2013 $350

Association – Wyatt, Edith

Clark, Sue Ainslie *Making both Ends Meet: The Income and Outlay of New York Working Girls.* New York: Macmillan, 1911. First edition, 8vo., 270 pages, nice, frontispiece photo, from the library of reformer Florence Kelley (1859-1932), inscribed by Edith Wyatt to Kelley.   Second Life Books Inc.   182 - 41   2013 $65

Association – Wyeth, N. C.

Defoe, Daniel *Robinson Crusoe.* New York: Cosmopolitan, 1920. First edition, 4to., royal blue gilt cloth, pictorial paste-on, nearly as new, top edge plain not gilt illustrations by N. C. Wyeth, signed and dated by artist, great copy, very scarce with signature.   Aleph-Bet Books, Inc.   105 - 598   2013 $3500

Association – Wyndham, Richard

Betjeman, John 1906-1984 *An Oxford University Chest.* London: John Miles, 1938. First edition, 4to., original dark blue cloth, lettered gilt, marbled boards, top edge gilt, illustrations in line and half tone by L. Moholy-Nagy, Osbert Lancaster, Edward Bradley, et al, excellent copy, inscribed to the widow of the artist Richard Wyndham, Greta by author.   Maggs Bros. Ltd.   1460 - 90   2013   £350

Association – Wynne, G.

Burnet, Gilbert, Bp. of Salisbury 1643-1715 *A Relation of a Conference, Held about Religion at London the Third of April 1676.* London: printed and are to be sold by Moses Pitt, 1676. First edition, 8vo., prelim imprimatur leaf and final ad leaf, ink splashes to A4 recto of pages 12-13, one marginal note identifying an anonymous name in text, full contemporary calf, raised bands, rubbed, hinges cracked, head and tail of spine worn, early paper label chipped, handwritten shelf label flap, armorial bookplate of W. Wynne, signature of G. Wynne on title, Edw. Solme (?) struck through.   Jarndyce Antiquarian Booksellers   CCIV - 6   2013   £150

Association – Wynne, Maurice

Baker, Henry *The Microscope Made Easy.* London: printed for R. Dodsley, 1744. Third edition, 8vo., blank lower corner of E6 torn, light browning, contemporary calf, gilt ruled borders, raised bands, early paper spine label, hinges little cracked but firm, covers rather rubbed, some crazing to surface leather, foot of spine worn, small and unusual bookplate of Maurice Wynne. Jarndyce Antiquarian Booksellers CCIV - 55   2013   £220

Association – Wynne, W.

Burnet, Gilbert, Bp. of Salisbury   1643-1715 *A Relation of a Conference, Held about Religion at London the Third of April 1676.* London: printed and are to be sold by Moses Pitt, 1676. First edition, 8vo., prelim imprimatur leaf and final ad leaf, ink splashes to A4 recto of pages 12-13, one marginal note indentifying an anonymous name in text, full contemporary calf, raised bands, rubbed, hinges cracked, head and tail of spine worn, early paper label chipped, handwritten shelf label flap, armorial bookplate of W. Wynne, signature of G. Wynne on title, Edw. Solme (?) struck through. Jarndyce Antiquarian Booksellers   CCIV - 6   2013   £150

Derham, William   1657-1735 *Astro-Theology; or a Demonstration of the Being and Attributes of God, from a Survey of the Heavens.* London: printed for W. Innys, 1715. 8vo., 3 folding copper engraved plates, titlepage little dusted, first gathering slightly browned, full contemporary panelled calf, raised bands, red morocco label, small paper shelf number at head of spine, hinges cracked, head and tail of spine slightly rubbed, contemporary booklabel of Tho. Jowling, A.M. Rect de Alcester 19th century armorial bookplate of W. Wynne. Jarndyce Antiquarian Booksellers CCIV - 111   2013   £280

Association – Yarnold, Edwin

Burns, Robert   1759-1796 *An Address to the Deil.. with Explanatory Notes.* London: James Gilbert, 1832. 11 first rate engravings on wood, engraved frontispiece and title, plates, odd spot, original pink printed wrappers, slightly dusted, spine partly defective, contemporary plain booklabel of Edwin Yarnold, all edges gilt, good plus. Jarndyce Antiquarian Booksellers   CCIII - 53   2013   £65

Association – Yeats, Anne

Curtis, Edmund *A History of Ireland.* 1937. Third edition, 8vo., cloth, cover dull, text very good, ownership inscription by Anne Yeats.   C. P. Hyland   261 - 958   2013   £32

Association – Yolland, R.

Tymme, Thomas *A Silver Watch Bell, the Sound Whereof is Able (by the Grace of God) to Win the Most Prophane Worldling and Careless Liver...* London: printed by John Haviland for Thomas Alchorn, 1638. Small octavo, lacking A2 (titlepage) and I2 (pages 115-116), text within double ruled border, with headline, page numbers and marginal glosses inside outer border, 16 headpieces, 14 ornamental initials and 2 tailpieces, contemporary marbled boards, rebacked (possibly in 1915, according to pencil note on front pastedown), with speckled calf, modern red and white paper spine label lettered in ink, plain endpapers, all edges speckled red, some trimmed close to headlines and in a few cases to marginal inscriptions, boards worn, hinges cracked, tiny rust or ink hole to top of front free endpaper, tiny wormhole to outer margin of beginning leaves, affecting a letter or two of marginal glosses, over opened at a few places, still very good, from the library of John Locke with ink inscriptions, signatures and marginal notations in at least five different hands, (John Locke, Ri. Yolland, Emmanual Bayhind, William Yoo and Riettell).   Heritage Book Shop   50th Anniversary Catalogue - 67   2013 $35,000

Association – Yoo, William

Tymme, Thomas *A Silver Watch Bell, the Sound Whereof is Able (by the Grace of God) to Win the Most Prophane Worldling and Careless Liver...* London: printed by John Haviland for Thomas Alchorn, 1638. Small octavo, lacking A2 (titlepage) and I2 (pages 115-116), text within double ruled border, with headline, page numbers and marginal glosses inside outer border, 16 headpieces, 14 ornamental initials and 2 tailpieces, contemporary marbled boards, rebacked (possibly in 1915, according to pencil note on front pastedown), with speckled calf, modern red and white paper spine label lettered in ink, plain endpapers, all edges speckled red, some trimmed close to headlines and in a few cases to marginal inscriptions, boards worn, hinges cracked, tiny rust or ink hole to top of front free endpaper, tiny wormhole to outer margin of beginning leaves, affecting a letter or two of marginal glosses, over opened at a few places, still very good, from the library of John Locke with ink inscriptions, signatures and marginal notations in at least five different hands, (John Locke, Ri. Yolland, Emmanual Bayhind, William Yoo and Riettell).   Heritage Book Shop   50th Anniversary Catalogue - 67   2013 $35,000

Association – Young, George

Cobbett, William *Rural Rides in the Counties of Surrey, Kent.* London: William Cobbett, 1830. First edition, 12mo., plate, 12 pages ads, original brown drab boards, carefully rebacked in contemporary pebble grained blue cloth, neat new paper label, contemporary signature in brown ink of George Young of Staines. Jarndyce Antiquarian Booksellers   CCV - 62   2013   £850

Association – Zinn, Howard

Walker, Alice   1944-   *In Love & Trouble: Stories of Black Women.*   New York: Harcourt Brace Jovanovich, 1973. First edition, fine in fine dust jacket, very slightly rubbed, inscribed by author to Howard Zinn and his wife.   Between the Covers Rare Books, Inc.   165 - 276   2013 $950

Walker, Alice   1944-   *Revolutionary Petunias and Other Poems.*   New York: Harcourt Brace Jovanovich, 1973. First edition, trifle rubbed at base of spine, else fine in near fine dust jacket with minimal soiling, warmly inscribed by author to Howard Zinn and wife Roz, very scarce thus. Between the Covers Rare Books, Inc.   165 - 335   2013 $600

Association – Zinn, Roz

Walker, Alice   1944-   *In Love & Trouble: Stories of Black Women.*   New York: Harcourt Brace Jovanovich, 1973. First edition, fine in fine dust jacket, very slightly rubbed, inscribed by author to Howard Zinn and his wife.   Between the Covers Rare Books, Inc.   165 - 276   2013 $950

Walker, Alice   1944-   *Revolutionary Petunias and Other Poems.*   New York: Harcourt Brace Jovanovich, 1973. First edition, trifle rubbed at base of spine, else fine in near fine dust jacket with minimal soiling, warmly inscribed by author to Howard Zinn and wife Roz, very scarce thus. Between the Covers Rare Books, Inc.   165 - 335   2013 $600

Association – Zobell, Albert

Morgan, Dale L.   *Bibliography of the Church Of Jesus Christ.*   (28) pages, octavo, blue publisher's buckram, gilt stamped title on front board, tipped in frontispiece of facsimile titlepage of "The Ensign" by William Bickerton, fine, ex-libris Albert Zobell Jr. with his signature.   Ken Sanders Rare Books   45 - 26   2013 $200

Fine Bindings

Binding – 19th Century

Bible. English - 1827 *The Comprehensive Bible containing the Old and New Testaments.* London: printed for Samuel Bagster, 1827. 330 x 250mm., excellent contemporary black pebble grain morocco, handsomely gilt, covers with floral frame enclosing central panel featuring scrolling cornerpiece compartments and, at center, intricate elongated ornament, wide raised bands with multiple gilt rules and floral endpieces, spine panels tooled gilt, floral and leaf ornaments, gilt titling and turn-ins, all edges gilt (neat older repairs to head and tail of joints); with bustling modern fore-edge painting by Martin Frost, showing flotilla of vessels on Thames with St. Paul's Cathedral in background; large gilt presentation bookplate "Tribute of Respect from Teachers of Mosely Street Sabbath School, Manchester, to their kind and generous friend James Kershaw, Esq. June 28 1838", joints little worn, corners and extremities bit rubbed, one tiny gouge to upper cover, otherwise fine, ornate binding entirely solid and generally well preserved and text exceptionally clean, fresh and smooth.   Phillip J. Pirages   61 - 56   2013 $3500

Browning, Robert   1812-1889 *The Poetical Works.* London: Smith, Elder & Co., 1888-1894. First complete edition, one of 250 copies on handmade paper, 17 volumes, 235 x 159mm, excellent contemporary purple morocco (stamped "Knickerbocker Press" on rear turn-in), front covers with flourish or gilt monogram (perhaps "G") at center, wide raised bands, spine panels with gilt titling, very broad turn-ins with simple gilt ruling, violet watered silk pastedowns and free endleaves, morocco hinges, edges untrimmed and all but 3 volumes unopened, frontispiece in five volumes, large paper copy, spines uniformly faded to pleasing chestnut brown, shadow of a silk place marker on two pages, otherwise extremely fine set with almost no wear to bindings, text nearly pristine.   Phillip J. Pirages   61 - 96   2013 $3600

Douglas, Robert *Sophie Arnould.* Paris: C. H. Carrington, 1898. One of 425 copies, this #8, 238 x 154mm., titlepage vignette, engraved vignettes at beginning and end of text, allegorical frontispiece and 3 full page plates by Adolphe Lalauze, very pretty contemporary tan crushed morocco, gilt and inlaid, covers with border of leafy tools and French fillets, central panel formed by a delicate frame of plain and dotted rules punctuated by leafy ornaments, cornerpieces of inlaid black morocco inside wreath of gilt leaves topped by tulip, central panel with palmette and garland cornerpieces accented with floral tools, upper cover with gilt titling at center, flat spine gilt in one long compartment with multiple ruled frame and central inlaid black morocco dot with floral extensions terminating at head and tail with ornate leaf design, lavishly gilt wide inner dentelles, marbled endpapers, all edges gilt, original slightly browned printed paper wrappers bound in, elaborate - apparently original - pen, ink and wash scenic bookplate of Victoria Sackville-West with handwritten note (by her?) tipped in at front stating bookplate design was based on Lalauze's frontispiece (as is apparent), thin cracks alongside top inch of joints, otherwise only trivial defects, very attractive, luxurious paper clean, fresh and bright, margins very wide, handsome binding lustrous and generally well preserved.   Phillip J. Pirages   61 - 110   2013 $1250

Goethe, Johann Wolfgang Von   1749-1832 *Faust.* Stuttgart & Tubingen: J. G. Cotta, 1854-1858. 2 volumes in one, folio, 19 full page steel engravings, woodcuts, scattered foxing throughout some plates heavily foxed, original full morocco, with gorgeous gilt stamped decorations in style of Seibertz, initials "E.S." in stylized botanical decorations, professionally restored, marvelous original binding,.   Jeff Weber Rare Books   171 - 140   2013 $2000

Moore, Thomas *Lalla Rookh, an Oriental Romance.* London: Longman, Hurst, Rees, Orme, Brown and Green, 1824. 218 x 136mm., 2 pl., 397, (1) pages, very pleasing contemporary midnight blue crushed morocco attractively gilt, covers with fillet borders and delicate inner frame, wide raised bands decorated with horizontal gilt fillets and floral tool terminations, spine gilt in compartments featuring unusual obliquely oriented quatrefoil ornament, gilt titling and turn-ins, all edges gilt, with fine later(?) fore-edge painting of an animated London street scene, bookplate of Oscar Ehrhardt Lancaster, touch of rubbing to joints and extremities (but this successfully masked with dye), chalky endpapers a bit blotchy from chemical reaction, slight separation and discoloration at hinge before title leaf, very few trivial marginal spots, still excellent copy, leaves quite clean, fresh and smooth, original decorative binding bright and without any significant wear and painting very well preserved.   Phillip J. Pirages   61 - 53   2013 $1250

Moore, Thomas *Lalla Rookh, an Oriental Romance.* London: Longman, Rees Orme, Brown & Green, 1828. 165 x 99mm., 2 p.l., 376 pages, extra engraved titlepage with vignette and 3 engraved plates after designs by Richard Westall; quite attractive contemporary dark green straight grain morocco, ornately gilt covers with 13 gilt or blind (mostly gilt) rules and frames (including elegant palmette frame), tulip cornerpieces at board edges and scrolling foliate cornerpieces closer in, central panel with large and elaborate lyre, raised bands, spine gilt in compartments with foliate cornerpieces and central lyre surrounded by small tools, densely gilt turn-ins, all edges gilt, gauffered in diapered pattern; with fine fore-edge painting of an oriental landscape, very surprisingly hidden beneath gauffered edge; spine evenly sunned to softer green, just hint of wear to joints and extremities, minor offsetting from mild foxing to plates, otherwise fine, binding sound and pleasing, text quite clean, fresh and bright and fore-edge painting well preserved.   Phillip J. Pirages   61 - 57   2013 $1750

Smith, Horace   1779-1849 *Brambletye House; or Cavaliers and Roundheads.* London: Henry Collins, 1826. Third edition, 3 volumes, 191 x 12mm., lavishly gilt contemporary olive green straight grain morocco, covers divided into three square panels at top and bottom of an elongated panel at right and left, these panels densely gilt with repeated versions of a large stamp formed by a floral cross radiating oak leaves, central panel with gilt rule frame featuring spiral cornerpieces decorated with acanthus leaves and flowers, raised bands, spine compartments heavily gilt repeating fleuron stamps used on covers, gilt turn-ins, marble endpapers, all edges gilt; each volume with handsome fore-edge painting of a picturesque location important to plot of the novel; engraved bookplate of Emily Lynch Lowe (NY artist), extremities and joints slightly rubbed (but well masked with dye), occasional minor foxing or stains, really excellent set, remarkably decorative bindings lustrous and most appealing, text clean and fresh, expert fore-edge paintings in fine condition.   Phillip J. Pirages   61 - 55   2013 $3500

White, Henry Kirke *The Poetical Works of Henry Kirke White.* London: Charles Whittingham for William Pickering, 1853.   168 x 105mm., lviii, 252 pages, elegant contemporary dark green morocco inlaid, embossed and elaborately gilt, each cover with broad inlaid ochre morocco frame intricately gilt, large central mandorla of heavily embossed and gilt morocco of same color (both frame and centerpiece highlighted with red painted rules, raised bands, spine gilt in compartments framed by plain and decorative gilt rules, floral centerpiece and lancet cornerpieces richly gilt turn-ins, cream colored watered silk endleaves, all edges gilt, pleasing fore-edge painting of Nottingham Castle; engraved portrait and printer's anchor device on titlepage, pencilled inscription to Bessie Carey from Walter Shipper dated 13 October 1868, pastedown with morocco bookplate of Estelle Doheny, bookplate of Edward Laurence Doheny, bookplate of Carrie Estelle Doheny, bookplate of Dorothy Jayne Pedrini Shea; hint of wear to joints and corners, red paint bit rubbed with minor loss, minor foxing to portrait and titlepage, other trivial imperfections, but excellent copy, handsome binding solid and lustrous, text clean and fresh, fore-edge painting very well preserved.   Phillip J. Pirages   63 - 193   2013 $1100

Binding – 20th Century

Lockhart, John Gibson   1794-1854 *Memoirs of the Life of Sir Walter Scott.* Boston and New York: Houghton Mifflin and Co., 1902.   Cambridge edition, 213 x 149mm, 5 volumes, lovely contemporary red half morocco, beautifully gilt in style of Doves Bindery, raised bands, spines in fine gilt compartments featuring sprays of tulips, marbled boards and endpapers, top edge gilt, other edges untrimmed and (except for the prefatory material in the first volume), entirely unopened, frontispiece portraits, small portions of two spine bands, corners and just few joints with insignificant wear (the rubbing carefully refurbished), one leaf with jagged fore edge from rough opening, but lovely set in nearly fine condition, bindings unusually lustrous and text virtually pristine, because obviously unread.   Phillip J. Pirages   63 - 431   2013 $2400

Lowell, James Russell 1819-1891 *The Complete Writings.* Cambridge: Riverside Press, 1904. One of 1000 copies, 222 x 146mm, 16 volumes, Edition de luxe, 80 mounted photogravure illustrations on India paper, original tissue guards, very handsome dark green morocco, extravagantly gilt, covers with wavy gilt border and charming floral ornaments at corners, central panel (with square notched corners) formed by six parallel gilt lines, raised bands, spine compartments attractively gilt with scrolling flowers and foliate enclosing a floral fleuron centerpiece, wide turn-ins with elaborate gilt decoration featuring many large and small roses and leaves on stylized lattice work, turn-ins enclosing scarlet colored polished morocco doublures crimson watered silk free endleaves, top edge gilt, other edges rough trimmed, mostly unopened (six of the volumes entirely unopened, and all but one of the others largely so), front joint of first volume bit worn (wear joint little flaked), half dozen other joints with hint of rubbing, spines evenly sunned to attractive olive brown, one small cover scuff, two leaves roughly opened (no serious consequences), other isolated trivial imperfections, nearly fine, attractive binding, leather lustrous, (mostly unopened), text essentially undisturbed. Phillip J. Pirages   61 - 127   2013 $3000

Rousseau, Jean Jacques 1712-1778 *The Confessions.* Philadelphia: Gebbie and Co., 1902. One of 53 copies for sale (of a total of 56) of the Astral Edition, this #9, 12 parts in 6 volumes, 310 x 230mm., vignette on limitation page, title vignettes and vignette headpieces and tailpieces as well as 48 fine plates by Maurice Leloir, printed on fine Japon vellum, titles in red and black, striking reddish brown inlaid and gilt Spanish calf, covers with ornately framed gilt panel featuring prominent gray morocco inlaid fleur-de-lys in center and smaller inlays at corners, spines in compartments featuring inlaid fleur-de-lys of white and green morocco (four per spine), beautiful green morocco doublures panelled in gilt and featuring quite large and very striking spray of lilies in gilt and 7 inlays of red or white, ivory watered sik endleaves, top edges gilt, other edges untrimmed, this set especially designed and bound for Alfred Raymond, very fine, exceptionally attractive.   Phillip J. Pirages   61 - 117   2013 $7500

Binding – Aiken, Sydney

Heaney, Seamus *A Tribute to Michael McLaverty.* Belfast: Linen Hall Library, 2005. First edition, limited to 250 copies signed by author, narrow 8vo., original marbled paper wrappers, sewn with Barbour thread and hand bound by Sydney Aiken, fine in black four-fold card sleeve. Maggs Bros. Ltd.   1442 - 123   2013   £250

Binding – Aitken, T.

Malton, Thomas *Views of Oxford.* London: White & Co.; Oxford: R. Smith, 1810. First complete edition, 411 x 315mm., appealing 19th century circa 1860s?), dark green half morocco over lighter green textured cloth by T. Aitken (stamp signed), upper cover with gilt titling, raised bands, spine gilt incompartments with elongated fleuron centerpiece and scrolling cornerpieces, gilt titling, marbled endpapers, all edges gilt (small, very expert repairs to upper outer corners and perhaps top of joints), mezzotint frontispiece after Gilbert Stuart, engraved title, 30 fine plates, 24 of then aquatints and 6 of them etched, armorial bookplates of Sir Mayson M. Beeton and Sir Richard Farrant, ink presentation inscription "Sir Charles Locock, Bart./ with Captn. Malton's kindest regards/Nov. 1860", subscription proposal for the work printed by T. Bensley and dated "London, May 30, 1301" (i.e. "1801"), laid in at front, couple of small smudges to boards, portrait faintly foxed and browned, isolated small stains (not affecting images), still fine, plates especially clean, fresh and smooth and pleasing binding with virtually no wear.   Phillip J. Pirages   63 - 327   2013 $9500

Binding – Anthony, Bill

Hamady, Walter *Papermaking by Hand.* Minor Confluence Perry Township: Perishable Press, 1982. One of 200 copies, on a variety of contemporary handmade papers, 13 various Shadwells, Roma and Perusia from Miliani in Fabriano, Canterbury from Barcham Green in Maidstone, Kent (all three retain their watermarks), Barlow from HMP in Woodstock, Conn., Banana-sisal from Carriage House in Brookline, Mass., Yale (in wove and laid surfaces) for Twinrocker in Brookston, Indiana, bound by Bill Anthony & Associates in tan Irish linen over boards, housed in custom made black cloth clamshell box with leather label printed in gold gilt on spine, 56 pages surfaces in 7 signatures, 26 pages of text, 3 illustrations from Diderot and 12 linoleum cuts by Jim Lee, especially for this text, 2 titlepages, one by Hamady and one penned by Hermann Zapf.   Priscilla Juvelis - Rare Books   55 - 21   2013 $2500

Hamady, Walter *Papermaking by Hand. A Book of Suspicions.* Minor Confluence, Perry Township: Perishable Press, 1982. One of 200 copies on a variety of contemporary hand made papers, 13 various Shadwells, Roma & Perusia from Miliani in Fabriano, Canterbury from Barcham Green in Maidstone, Kent (all three retain their watermarks), Barlow from HMP in Woodstock, Connecticut, banana sisal from Carriage House in Brookline, Massachusetts, Yale (in wove and laid surfaces) from Twinrocker in Brookston, Indiana, laid in is original prospectus for book and original invoice from Perishable Press, bound by Bill Anthony & Associates tan Irish linen over boards, pages size 11 x 7 1/2 inches, 56 pages surfaces in 7 signatures, 26 pages of text, page size of prospectus 6 11/16 x 9 11/16 inches, page size of invoice 7 3/16 x 10 7/16 inches, custom made wood veneer clamshell box with brown leather spine banded in vellum, lined in buff felt, fine, 3 illustrations from Diderot and 12 linoleum cuts by Jim Lee especially for this text, there are 2 titlepage - one by Walter Hamady and one penned by Hermann Zapf who also designed typeface, Palatino, used for this text, type was handset and printed by Hamady, 50 of the pages printed in 88 press runs, in 5 basic colors, on 19 different colors of paper, beautiful book.   Priscilla Juvelis - Rare Books   56 - 24   2013 $3000

Petrakis, Harry Mark *Chapter Seven from the Hour of the Bell, a Novel Concerning the Greek War of Independence.* Mt. Horeb: Perishable Press, 1976. One of 150 copies, all on Frankfur and Frankfurt Cream paper signed by author, laid in is broadside prospectus for book printed Frankfurt Cream paper with titlepage illustration by Warrington Colescott reproduced in a reduced size, book page size 9 3/4 x 7 1/4 inches, 44 pages, 22 of which are printed, broadside size 16 3/4 x 11 1/2 inches, bound by Bill Anthony, hand marbled paper by Norma Rubovits over boards, each book with different patterned marbled paper, black blind-stamped oasis spine, fine in acetate jacket, reset monotype Jan Van Krimpen Spectrum (1955), titlepage illustration by Warrington Colescott which the printer calls his best to date'.   Priscilla Juvelis - Rare Books   56 - 25   2013 $275

Binding – Arts & Crafts

Barham, Richard Harris 1788-1845 *The Ingoldsby Legends or Mirth & Marvels.* London: J. M. Dent & Co., 1898. First Rackham edition, 200 x 137mm., frontispiece, titlepage with green ornamental border, numerous black and white illustrations and 13 color plates, all by Arthur Rackham, very attractive contemporary Arts & Crafts style binding of russet Niger goatskin, lavishly gilt, covers with central panel of gilt ruled squares within wide frame of flowers and foliage, raised bands, spine compartments densely gilt with tooling repeating cover frame design, gilt turn-ins, top edge gilt, other edges gilded on the rough, slight and even darkening to spine, covers with minor soiling, title and frontispiece rather foxed, text with hint of browning at edges, very attractive copy, animated gilt of binding still bright, leather with only insignificant wear, text almost entirely bright, clean and fresh.   Phillip J. Pirages   61 - 99 2013 $1500

Pater, Walter 1839-1894 *Marius the Epicurean.* London: Macmillan and Co., 1910. 224 x 140mm, 2 volumes, titlepage printed in red and black, excellent contemporary russet morocco, gracefully tooled in gilt and inlaid in Arts and Crafts style, covers delicately framed in gilt with cornerpieces of inlaid ivory flowers and gilt leaves, front covers with large central medallion composed of thin, linked gilt ovals accented with gilt dots and enclosing lozenge of inlaid ivory flowers and green leaves with green daisy at center (total of 90 floral or foliate inlays in all), raised bands, spine compartments with finely tooled flower centerpieces and gilt dots at corners, turn-ins with multiple gilt rules, all edges gilt, titlepage printed in red and black, very slight variations in color of leather (some of this due to fading?), one corner little bruised, leaves bit browned at edges because of paper stock quality (no doubt same as in all copies), first volume with occasional minor spotting, otherwise very appealing set, fresh internally and generally very well preserved with nothing approaching significant condition problem.   Phillip J. Pirages   61 - 98   2013 $1250

Binding – Asper, Rene

Scott, Walter 1771-1832 *Redgauntlet.* Edinburgh: printed for Archibald Constable and Co., 1824. First edition, first state with 1823 watermark and comma following title on titlepage of volumes I and II, 3 volumes, 203 x 129mm., without 2 leaves of ads at end of volume 3, pleasing 19th century brown quarter morocco over marbled boards by Rene Asper of Geneva (stamp signed), raised bands, gilt titling, edges untrimmed, hint of rubbing to joints, trivial scratch to one board, occasional minor foxing, other insignificant defects, still excellent set, text fresh and clean, bindings showing little wear.   Phillip J. Pirages   63 - 430   2013 $200

Binding – Asprey

Kipling, Rudyard 1865-1936 *The Jungle Book. (and) The Second Jungle Book.* New York: Century Co., 1903-1909. Later editions, octavo, 2 volumes, numerous illustrations, beautifully bound by Asprey in contemporary full green morocco, elaborately gilt decorated spine and covers, raised bands, brown, gray, burgundy and black morocco animal onlays on each of the four covers, marbled endpapers, all edges gilt, gilt dentelles, previous owner's bookplates on front pastedown of each volume, fine set, custom quarter morocco slipcase, with morocco edges. Heritage Book Shop Holiday Catalogue 2012 - 93   2013 $3000

Joyce, James 1882-1941 *Ulysses.* Paris: Shakespeare and Co., 1922. First edition, copy 811 of 750 copies numbered 250 to 1000, 4to., later blue half morocco by Bayntun, blue cloth sides, gilt rules and lettering, top edge gilt, others untrimmed, with half title, bound without printed wrappers, half title slightly smudged, fine.   The Brick Row Book Shop Miscellany Fifty-Nine - 29   2013 $20,000

Oliphant, Margaret Oliphant Wilson 1828-1897 *The Literary History of England in the End of the Eighteenth and Beginning of the Nineteenth Century.*   Macmillan and Co., 1882. First edition, Volumes I-III, extra illustrated by insertion of 112 portraits and views, some illustrations foxed, some of these offsetting into text, 8vo., mid 20th century dark brown morocco by Bayntun, French fillets on sides with arabesque corner ornaments, spines gilt, gilt edges, lower joint volume ii tender, spines slightly faded, one or two minor knocks, good.   Blackwell's Rare Books   B174 - 110 2013 £450

Binding – Bayntun-Riviere

A'Beckett, Gilbert Abbott *The Comic History of England. (and) The Comic History of Rome...*   London: Punch Office, 1847-1848. & London: Bradbury & Evans, 1852. First edition of first title and first edition in book form of second work, 3 volumes, 8vo., half green crushed levant morocco by Bayntun Riviere, gilt spines, raised bands, all edges gilt, 30 colored plates and 338 in-text woodcuts in all.   Howard S. Mott Inc.   262 - 1   2013 $500

Blackmore, Richard Doddridge 1825-1900 *Lorna Doone.* London: Sampson Low, Son & Marston, 1869. First edition, one of only 500 printed, 3 small octavo volumes, bound circa 1960 by Bayntun-Riviere in full red morocco, few minor tears and some occasional minor foxing or soiling, laid in is ALS from author to James Payn, Teddington, Dec. 3rd 1877 thanking him for his assistance in publishing of his works, excellent copy.   David Brass Rare Books, Inc. Holiday 2012 Chapter Five - DB 00726   2013 $6500

Haggard, Henry Rider 1856-1925 *King Solomon's Mines.* London: Cassell & Co., 1885. First edition, first issue, folding color map inserted as frontispiece, black and white map on page 27, original front cover cloth bound in at back, beautifully bound by Bayntun Riviere in full red morocco, boards ruled in gilt, spine printed and lettered gilt, gilt dentelles, all edges gilt, marbled endpapers, few professional repaired closed tears to folding map, about fine. Heritage Book Shop   Holiday Catalogue 2012 - 71   2013 $5000

Hardy, Thomas 1840-1928 *The Trumpet-Major.* London: 1880. First edition in book form, 3 volumes, octavo, volumes I and II without prelim blank, publisher's primary binding of volume I and secondary binding of volumes II and III all of red diagonal fine ribbed cloth, only difference being back covers stamped in blind with double rule (volume 1) or triple rule (volumes 2 and 3) border, front covers decoratively stamped in black with three panel design incorporating two vignettes, on encampment at top, a mill at bottom and lettering in center panel, spines decoratively stamped in gilt and black with standard sword and bugle and lettered in blind and gilt (with imprint at foot of spine, Smith, Elder & Co.), yellow coated endpapers, spines of all volumes bit darkened, cloth of all spines with some wrinkling as well as to cloth of back board of volume one, bit of soiling and rubbing to cloth, some light shelfwear to spines, previous owner's bookplate on front pastedown of each volume, occasional thumb soiling along fore-edges, volumes slightly skewed, overall good set housed in quarter morocco clamshell and chemise.   Heritage Book Shop   Holiday Catalogue 2012 - 72   2013 $7500

Omar Khayyam *The Rubaiyat of Omar Khayyam.* London: Hodder and Stoughton, n.d., 1909. First trade edition, large quarto, 20 color plates mounted on buff vellum-like paper with gilt over tan decorative borders, with descriptive tissue guards, text printed on rectos only within brown decorative border, bound in full red calf by Bayntun-Riviere, gorgeous copy, housed in red cloth slipcase. David Brass Rare Books, Inc.   Holiday 2012 Chapter One - DB 01778   2013 $1100

Binding – Bedford

Byron, George Gordon Noel, 6th Baron 1788-1824 *Hours of Idleness: a Series of Poems.*   Newark: S. & J. Ridge, 1807. First edition, first issue, half title, uncut in full calf by F. Bedford, expertly rebacked retaining gilt spine and dentelles, dark green morocco label, armorial booklabel of Cardiff Castle, top edge gilt, very good, handsome. Jarndyce Antiquarian Booksellers   CCIII - 109   2013   £1850

Fraunce, Abraham *The Lawiers Logike...*   London: by William How for Thomas Gubbin and T. Newman, 1588. First edition, 4to., folding table, title within type ornament border, woodcut initials, mixed black letter and roman, full red gilt panelled morocco, edges gilt by Bedford, first two leaves lightly washed, short closed tear on table, blank corner of 2K4 replaced, else fine clean copy, armorial bookplate of Sir Edwin Priaulx and booklabel of Abel E. Berland. Joseph J. Felcone Inc.   Books Printed before 1701 - 40   2013 $8000

Binding – Atelier Bindery

Hawthorne, Nathaniel 1804-1864 *The Scarlet Letter.* Boston: Ticknor, Reed and Fields, 1850. First edition, mixed issue with 'reduplicate' for 'repudiate' on page 21, line 20 and contents ending on page 'iv', without publisher's ads inserted, small octavo, titlepage printed in black and red, bound by Atelier Bindery in full blue morocco, boards ruled in gilt with leaf corner devices, front board with scarlet calf letter "A" outlined in gilt, inlaid in center, spine stamped and lettered in gilt, top edge gilt, gilt dentelles, marbled endpapers, original brown cloth bound in at back, slipcase with blue morocco edges, overall very good.   Heritage Book Shop   Holiday Catalogue 2012 - 75   2013 $2750

Binding – Bagguley

Irving, Washington 1783-1859 *The Alhambra.* London and New York: Macmillan and Co., 1896. One of 500 extra-illustrated copies, 264 x 194mm., xx, 436 pages, numerous illustrations in text and 12 inserted lithographs by Joseph Pennell, magnificent contemporary dark green crushed morocco, extravagantly gilt by Bagguley (signed with firm's ink 'Sutherland' patent stamp on verso of front endleaf), covers with borders of multiple plain and decorative gilt rules, lobed inner frame with fleuron cornerpieces, whole enclosing large and extremely intricate gilt lozenge, raised bands, spine lavishly gilt in double ruled compartments, gilt titling and turn-ins, beautiful vellum doublures elaborately tooled in diapered gilt, red and green Moorish pattern, green watered silk endleaves, top edge gilt, other edges rough trimmed, bookplate of Harold Douthit, boards with slight humpback posture(as often with vellum doublures), otherwise in beautiful condition inside and out, lovely binding with lustrous morocco, vellum and gilt, text virtually pristine.   Phillip J. Pirages   61 - 97   2013 $5500

Binding – Bain

Knight, Charles *Half Hours of English History from the Roman Period to the Death of Elizabeth.* London: Frederick Warne and Co., 1868. 222 x 146mm., 4 p.l., 687 pages, lavishly gilt contemporary black half calf by Bain (stamp signed on verso front free endpaper), raised bands, decorated with gilt roll, spines in six compartments, two of these with titling labels of red or black, the other four quite intricately gilt with large central filigree ornament framed by scrolling leafy cornerpieces, marbled boards, edges and endpapers, trivial wear to corners and top of spine, nearly fine in attractive binding, leather unusually lustrous and text very clean and fresh.   Phillip J. Pirages   63 - 300   2013 $175

Binding – Bartlett & Co.

Grimm, The Brothers *German Popular Stories.* London: published by C. Baldwyn, 1823. James Robbins and Co., London and Joseph Robins Junr. and Co., Dublin, 1826. First English edition, first issue without umlaut on the word "Marchen" on first pictorial titlepage, with half titles, but without final blank leaf in volume II, 2 volumes, full brown morocco by Bartlett & Co. Boston, 12 etched plates by George Cruikshank, printed in sepia, including pictorial title, 10 etched plates by Cruikshank, printed in black, including pictorial title, all edges gilt, fine, minor browning on few leaves, morocco backed slipcase.   Howard S. Mott Inc. 262 - 69   2013 $11,500

Binding – Bayntun

Berkeley, George, Bp. of Cloyne 1685-1793 *Three Dialogues Between Hylas and Philonous.* London: printed for William and John Innys, 1725. Second edition, without 4-leaf gathering of ads at end, washed, several corners repaired (notably last leaf), small contemporary inscription to titlepage, 8vo., modern (not new) half calf, yellow edges by Bayntun sound.   Blackwell's Rare Books   172 - 20   2013 £1200

Bronte, The Sisters *The Novels of...* Edinburgh: John Grant, 1907. 12 volumes, 8vo., titlepages printed in red and black, frontispiece portraits, numerous plates throughout, dark green three quarter calf and green cloth, spine gilt in compartments, top edge gilt, by Bayntun of Bath, hinge of volume little tender, fine.   Second Life Books Inc.   183 - 55   2013 $2000

De Lespinasse, Mlle. *Letters.* London: William Heinemann, 1903. 8vo., 342 pages, half title, frontispiece, very good in dark blue half morocco by Bayntun, top edge gilt, spine in 6 compartments with gilt floral device.   Ken Spelman Books Ltd.   75 - 155   2013   £50

Dickens, Charles 1812-1870 *The Posthumous Papers of the Pickwick Club.* London: Macmillan and Co., 1886. Jubilee Edition, 2 volumes, octavo, illustrations extra illustrated, 94 plates, stamped on rear flyleaves of each volume "Extra illustrated by A. W. Waters", bound circa 1925 by Bayntun of Bath in three quarter blue morocco, fine.   David Brass Rare Books, Inc.   Holiday 2012 Chapter Five - DB 00561   2013 $1800

Gay, John 1685-1732 *Fables by John Gay, with a Life of the Author...* London: by Darton & Harvey for E. & C. Rivington et al, 1793. xvi, 256 pages, plates, full calf, richly gilt, all edges gilt by Bayntun, hinges split but held by cords, else lovely copy, cloth slipcase.   Joseph J. Felcone Inc.   English and American Literature to 1800 - 15   2013 $250

Malory, Thomas *The Most Ancient and Famous History of the Renowned Prince Arthur King of Britainne.* London: printed by William Stansby for Jacob Bloome, 1634. Sixth edition, small quarto, 3 parts in 1 volume with separate titlepages each with facing woodcut of King Arthur and the Knights of the Round Table, black letter text, Roman and italic prelims, headlines, rubrics and proper names, first title skilfully repaired in inner and lower margins, frontispieces to parts I and II skilfully renewed in outer margins, that of 11 also restored at inner corner, with few letters supplied in facsimile, and just shaved at foot, E3 Part 1 mounted on guard, one catchword and headline at beginning of part II shaved, tiny rust hole in PP1 of Part II affecting one letter of headline, natural paper flaw affecting few letters in part III; bound by Bedford in 19th century brown morocco, ruled gilt on covers, decorated gilt on spine, all edges gilt, housed in custom brown cloth clamshell, very good, extremely rare. Heritage Book Shop 50th Anniversary Catalogue - 70 2013 $40,000

Shelley, Percy Bysshe 1792-1822 *Queen Mab, a Philsophical Poem with Notes.* London: printed by P. B. Shelley, 1813. First edition, 8vo., full green morocco by Bedford, gilt rules and lettering, gilt inner dentelles, top edge gilt, others untrimmed, edges slightly rubbed, fine. The Brick Row Book Shop Miscellany Fifty-Nine - 39 2013 $18,000

Binding – Bennett, Whitman

Bigmore, E. C. *A Bibliography of Printing with Notes and Illustrations.* London: Bernard Quaritch, 1880-1886. small 4to., 3 volumes in 1, two color title (printed in red and black), illustrations, original brown leather (signed by Bennett, NY), professionally rebacked by Bruce Levy, gilt stamped spine title with raised spine bands, top edge gilt, some marginal checkmarks, bookplates of Marcus Crahan and the Zamorano Club (gift of Crahan), signature P. R. Lee Jr. (1939), near fine, choice copy. Jeff Weber Rare Books 171 - 31 2013 $750

Dickens, Charles 1812-1870 *Posthumous Papers of the Pickwick Club.* New York: George D. Sproul, 1902. Autograph Variorum Edition, 6 volumes, signed original frontispiece, finely bound by Whitman Bennett, frontispiece and plates, descriptive tissue guards, frontispiece in volumes I, III and V on India paper mounted, signed by artist, Harry Furniss, three quarter burgundy leather and marbled boards, gilt ruled and spine divided into six compartments with "CD: cipher in third, gilt lettering ad design spines, top edges gilt, marbled endpapers, mild cover edgewear, owner name, small 4to. By the Book, L. C. 36 - 43 2013 $750

Fielding, Henry 1707-1754 *An Enquiry into the Causes of the Late Increase of Robbers, &c...* London: printed for A. Millar, 1751. First edition, 8vo., full brown calf by Whitman Bennett of NY, with shelfmark "Lauderdale Law" in contemporary hand, presumably Earl of Lauderdale. Howard S. Mott Inc. 262 - 49 2013 $750

Rothenstein, William *Men and Memories.* New York: Coward McCann Inc., 1931-1932. First editions, 2 volumes, 244 x 159mml., striking black three quarter morocco by Whitman Bennett for Stewart Kidd (stamp signed), raised bands, spines gilt in compartments with centerpiece of artist's palette and brushes, geometrically patterned paper boards and endpapers, top edge gilt, other edges rough trimmed (second volume largely unopened), 96 collotype plates, just touch of wear to joints and extremities, paper boards, lightly chafed, paper clip impression to front free endpaper of volume I (also affecting pastedown and flyleaf), otherwise quite appealing set in fine condition, bindings especially lustrous and with only minor rubbing, text quite clean and fresh. Phillip J. Pirages 63 - 408 2013 $225

Suetonius Tranquillus, Gaius *The Lives of the Twelve Caesars.* Chicago: Argus Book Shop, 1930. One of 2000 numbered copies, of which 1500 are for America and 500 for England (this copy #a9), 270 x 186mm., frontispiece, striking orange morocco by Bennett of NY (stamp signed), covers with gilt panelled frame containing 8 large gilt rosettes (at corners and middle of each side), rosettes radiating black dotted lines or fleurons, raised bands, spine compartments with similar design, deep blue morocco doublures framed by decorative gilt rolls, leather hinges, indigo watered silk endleaves, top edge gilt, other edges rough trimmed, with illustrated title, 23 figures in text, 16 full page illustrations, all with patterned tissue guards, binding lightly soiled, joints and extremities bit rubbed, otherwise excellent, unusual binding solid and without serious condition problems, immaculate internally. Phillip J. Pirages 63 - 455 2013 $175

Binding – Benson, Courtland

Bonet, Honore *L'Apparition de Jehan de Meun ou le Songe Du Prieur De Salon.* Paris: Imprime par Crapelet pur la Societe des Bibliophiles Francais, 1845. One of 170 copies on velllum (this copy #7 printed for M. Le Comte e La Bedoyere, member of the Societe des Bibliophiles) (another 100 copies on issued on paper), recent fine white pigskin, decorated in blind to a Medieval style by Courtland Benson, housed in titled custom made morocco backed folding cloth box, 10 engraved plates, morocco bookplate of Comte H. De La Bedoyere and engraved bookplate of Marcellus Schlimovich, embossed library stamp of Dr. Detlef Mauss; half title with ink library stamp of Sociedad Hebraica Argentina, fine, especially clean and bright internally, only most trivial imperfections in new retrospective binding. Phillip J. Pirages 63 - 477 2013 $3500

Binding – Bickers

Byron, George Gordon Noel, 6th Baron 1788-1824
Poetical Works. London: Henry Frowde, Oxford University Press, 1910. Oxford edition, half title, frontispiece, contemporary half tan crushed morocco by Bickers & Son, ruled in gilt, armorial bookplate of Cordell William Firebrace, top edge gilt, very good in fine binding.   Jarndyce Antiquarian Booksellers   CCIII - 84   2013   £120

Byron, George Gordon Noel, 6th Baron 1788-1824
Poetical Works. London: Oxford University Press, Humphrey Milford, 1935. Oxford edition, half title, frontispiece, contemporary half dark blue calf by Bickers & Son, front board blocked with school crest in gilt, spine slightly faded, Newcastle Grammar school prize label 1935-1936, top edge gilt, very good. Jarndyce Antiquarian Booksellers   CCIII - 85   2013   £35

Coleridge, Samuel Taylor 1772-1834 *Osorio: a Tragedy.* London: John Pearson, 1873. First edition, half title, contemporary full tan cal by Bickers & Son, gilt spine, borders and dentelles, maroon and green leather labels, spine slightly chipped at head, hinges rubbed, armorial bookplate of Adeleine Puxley, all edges gilt, fine binding using poor leather, good plus. Jarndyce Antiquarian Booksellers   CCIII - 527   2013   £85

Cottle, Joseph *Early Recollections, Chiefly Relating to the Late Samuel Coleridge, During His Long Residence in Bristol.* London: Longman, Rees & Co., 1837. First edition, 2 volumes, half titles, frontispieces, plates, contemporary full tan calf by Bickers & Son, gilt spines, borders and dentelles, maroon & brown leather labels, heads of spines chipped with some loss, hinges cracking, armorial booklabel of Adelaine Puxley, all edges gilt, fine binding using poor leather, good plus.   Jarndyce Antiquarian Booksellers   CCIII - 580   2013   £125

Hughes, Thomas 1822-1896 *David Livingstone; Charles George Gordon. Englishmen of Action Series.* Macmillan, 1897. Full calf gilt by Bickers, extremities little worn, top of spine frayed, 2 portraits and colored folding map.   R. F. G. Hollett & Son   Africana - 91   2013   £35

Irving, Washington 1783-1859 *A History of the Life and Voyages of Christopher Columbus.* London: John Murray, 1828. First edition, 8vo., 4 volumes, 2 large folding maps, bound into rear of volume IV, all 4 bound with half titles, full calf, stamped in gilt on spine, by Bickers & Son, some rubbed and nicked, very nice, clean set.   Second Life Books Inc.   183 - 186   2013 $950

McCarthy, Justin *Four Works: History of Our Own Times. The Four Georges & William IV. The French Revolution. The Regin of Queen Anne.* London: Chatto & Windus, 1884-1901. First editions of the last three works, 222 x 144mm., 15 volumes, pleasing contemporary dark blue three quarter morocco by Bickers & son (stamp signed), raised bands, spine gilt in single ruled compartments, marbled endpapers, top edges gilt, tiny chip to top of one spine, three joints with short cracks at head, minor dulling from leather preservative, first volume with hinge open at rear (but volume quite sound), one leaf with older tissue paper repair to head-edge tear into text, but legibility not lost), other trivial defects, but still quite attractive set in excellent condition, clean and fresh internally, bright, solid bindings showing little wear. Phillip J. Pirages   63 - 334   2013 $650

Binding – Birdsall

Eliot, George, Pseud. 1819-1880 *The Legend of Jubal and Other Poems.* Berlin: Albert Cohn, printed by Stephen Geibel & Co., Altenbourg, 1874. Contemporary half red sheep by Birdsall & Son, dark green leather label, ownership inscription June 1887.   Jarndyce Antiquarian Booksellers   CCV - 99   2013   £175

O'Brien, Edward *The Lawyer, His Character and Rule of Holy Life.* London: William Pickering, 1842. First edition, 167 x 105mm., pleasing contemporary rose colored pebble grain morocco by Birdsall & Son (stamp signed), covers with multiple blind rule frame, raised bands, spine compartments ruled in blind, gilt tooling, gilt ruled turn-ins, marbled endpapers, all edges gilt, decorative frame on titlepage, headpieces and tailpieces, spine somewhat faded, joints and extremities little rubbed, one opening with offsetting from old laid-in clipping, excellent copy, clean and fresh internally, sound, well executed binding.   Phillip J. Pirages   63 - 310   2013 $175

Binding – Blau, Bela

Powell, Lawrence Clark *Bookshops.* Los Angeles: 1965. No limitation given, but obviously very small, bound by Bela Blau, 6 x 4.3 cm., leather, presentation "W.T.'s. book from L.P.' 65", from the collection of Donn W. Sanford.   Oak Knoll Books   303 - 65   2013 $250

Snyder, Dee *The ABC's of Baker Street: a Guide to the Holmesian Habitat.* Skokie: Black Cat Press, 1983. Limited to 249 copies, 7.3 x 5.2 cm., cloth, title gilt stamped on spine and front cover, marbled endpapers, 97, (5) pages, illustrations, bound by Bela Blau, from the collection of Donn W. Sanford.   Oak Knoll Books   303 - 58   2013 $100

Weber, Francis J. *What Happened to Junipero Serra?* Los Angeles: Bela Blau, 1969. Limited to 1000 numbered copies, handset, printed and bound by Bela Blau, 3.5 x 5.2 cm., dark green leather stamped in gilt, patterned paper endpapers, from the collection of Donn W. Sanford.   Oak Knoll Books   303 - 62   2013 $150

Binding – Blau, Mariana

Weber, Franics J. *Bela Blau Bookbinder 1914-1993.* Los Angeles: Privately printed for Mariana Blau, 1993. Limited to 150 copies, one of the numbered deluxe copies bound thus, bound and signed by Mariana Blau, 5.2 x 4 cm., full dark brown leather with inset full color photo of Bela Blau on front cover, slipcase, each contributor has signed their contribution, from the collection of Donn W. Sanford.   Oak Knoll Books   303 - 61   2013 $225

Binding – Blumenthal, Barbara

Gorey, Edward *Q. R. V.* Boston: Anne & David Bromer, 1989. Limited to 400 numbered copies signed by Gorey, 3.2 x 3.8 cm., decorated paper covered boards, paper cover label, 29 Gorey illustrations in black and white, bound by Barbara Blumenthal, from the collection of Donn W. Sanford. Oak Knoll Books   303 - 69   2013 $725

Binding – Bone

Coleridge, Samuel Taylor   1772-1834 *Notes on the English Divines.* London: Edward Moxon, 1853. First edition, 2 volumes, half titles, mostly unopened in original bright green pebble grained cloth by Bone and Son, blocked in blind, spines lettered gilt, slightly rubbed, later booklabels, very good.   Jarndyce Antiquarian Booksellers   CCIII - 569   2013   £85

Mayhew, Augustus *Paved with Gold; or the Romance and Reality of the London Streets.* London: Chapman & Hall, 1858. First edition, illustrations by Phiz, frontispiece, added engraved title and plates, uncut in original dark green cloth by Bone & Son, bookseller's ticket of J. Philipson, North Shields on leading pastedown, very good, bright copy. Jarndyce Antiquarian Booksellers   CCV - 198   2013   £150

Binding – BookLab

Rumi, Jalaluddin Mohammad *Divan e Shams.* New York: Vincent FitzGerald & Co., 1996. Signed limited edition, one of 50 copies, all on handmade papers by Dieu Donne and BFK Rives, bound by Craig Jensen at BookLab in ivory linen in coptic style binding with brown and gray endpapers that are etchings of various leaves, housed in silver silk over boards custom made clamshell box, title in palladium on spine and engraved ornament on front panel of box, fine, extremely beautiful, with graphic works and one sculpture (glass laid in to back of custom made clamshell box) by 15 artists, some mounted, some on multiple or folded leaves, some on colored or translucent paper, most signed in pencil by respective artist.   Priscilla Juvelis - Rare Books   55 - 9   2013 $15,000

Binding – Bourbeau, David

Horatius Flaccus, Quintus *Carmina Sapphica.* Boston: Anne & David Bromer, 1983. Limited to 150 copies, printed by Linnea Gentry using original plates of Ashendene Press edition from 1923, c.5 x 2.6 cm., full morocco with gilt fillets, two raised bands, inserted in tray in larger cloth case with leather spine, which also holds prospectus, in specially made slipcase holding the miniature book, miniature bookplate of Kathryn rickard, binding by David Bourbeau, from the collection of Donn W. Sanford.   Oak Knoll Books   303 - 71   2013 $450

Joyce, James   1882-1941 *Brideship and Gulls.* New York: Vincent FitzGerald & Co., 1991. One of 25 copies, text on Apta Royale Laid Richard de Bas paper (made in 1938), images on Musee paper, backed on custom made papers by Paul Wong on Dieu Donne papermill, page size 16 x 26 inches, bound by Zahra Partovi in Coptic style mauve grey silk over boards, box by David Bourbeau, Thistle Bindery, fine, 6 original line etchings by Susan Weil hand painted in watercolor and gouache with gold leafing throughout, each mounted on museum board, images surround the 40 page text when sitting in the box and when lifted out become three dimensional paintings; there are also 2 original collages in text and on boards of cover, which is printed in 3 colors, box itself is piece of sculpture.   Priscilla Juvelis - Rare Books   55 - 8   2013 $10,000

Binding – Burlen, Robert, & Son

Garcia-Marquez, Gabriel   1928- *One Hundred Years of Solitude.* New York: Limited Editions Club, 1982. First edition, 1/2000 copies, large 8vo., 348 pages, with additional original lithograph, bound in natural straw colored Chinese silk with gilt stamped spine of top grain aniline leather, text and drawings printed at Stinehour Press, 8 oil paintings reproduced by Seaboard Lithograph Corp. in New York and original lithograph hand painted on Rives paper at Blackburn Studio, bound by Robert Burlen & Son, signed by Ferrer, Reid and Rabassa, fine in original slipcase, LEC Monthly Letter laid in.   Second Life Books Inc.   183 - 259   2013 $250

Binding – Burn

Coleridge, Samuel Taylor 1772-1834 *Seven Lectures on Shakespeare and Milton.* London: Chapman and Hall, 1856. First edition, half title, original purple pebble grained cloth by Burn, borders in blind, unevenly faded with slight wear at head of spine. Jarndyce Antiquarian Booksellers CCIII - 572 2013 £65

Gilchrist, Alexander *Life of William Blake.* London and Cambridge: Macmillan, 1863. First edition, 2 volumes, half titles, frontispieces, plates, illustrations, original maroon cloth by Burn & Co., blocked and lettered gilt, corners slightly worn, spines faded, booklabels of Walter Hirst very good, clean and attractive copy. Jarndyce Antiquarian Booksellers CCIII - 10 2013 £320

Hughes, Thomas 1822-1896 *Tom Brown's School Days.* London: Macmillan & Co., 1869. First illustrated edition, frontispiece, illustrated title, plates and illustrations, original decorated blue cloth by Burn & Co., bevelled boards, slight repair to upper front corner, otherwise fine, bright copy. Jarndyce Antiquarian Booksellers CCV - 141 2013 £250

Kingsley, Henry *Tales of Old Travel.* London: Macmillan and Co., 1869. First edition, half title, frontispiece, 56 page catalog (August 1869), original green decorated cloth by Burn & Co., hinges slightly cracking, W. H. Smith embossed stamp on leading f.e.p. very good, bright. Jarndyce Antiquarian Booksellers CCV - 156 2013 £45

Shorthouse, Joseph Henry *John Inglesant; a Romance.* Birmingham: Cornish Brothers, 1880. Only 100 copies printed, half title, original parchment by Burn and Co., lettered in red on front and spine, slightly rubbed and marked, minor repairs, leading inner hinge cracking, bookplate of Alex Bridge on front pastedown, overall very good, handsome custom made maroon cloth slipcase, black leather spine label, scarce. Jarndyce Antiquarian Booksellers CCV - 247 2013 £650

Binding – Burn & Kirby

Rossetti, Christina 1830-1894 *The Prince's Progress and Other Poems.* London: Macmillan, 1866. First edition, half title, frontispiece, vignette title, additional printed title, untrimmed in original green glazed cloth by Burn & Kirby's decorated and lettered in gilt, John Sparrow's small booklabel, very good, bright copy. Jarndyce Antiquarian Booksellers CCV - 234 2013 £850

Binding – Campbell-Logan

Updike, John 1932- *Jester's Dozen.* Northridge: Lord John Press, 1984. First edition, limited to 50 numbered copies, specially bound, this no. 13, 8vo., signed by author, fine, paper is Frankfurt White, the Spectrum type as handset by Denise Grimsman, binding by Campbell-Logan in quarter black cloth and patterned paper covered boards, printed paper spine label. By the Book, L. C. 38 - 103 2013 $400

Binding – Carss

Campbell, Thomas 1777-1844 *Gertrude of Wyoming: a Pennsylvania Tale. And Other Poems.* London: Longman, Hurst, Rees & Orme, 1809. First edition, 4to., contemporary half dark blue calf by J. Carss & Co. of Glasgow, spine gilt in compartments, maroon leather label, hinges and corners little rubbed, contemporary gift inscription, bookseller's ticket J. Carss & Co. Glasgow. Jarndyce Antiquarian Booksellers CCIII - 464 2013 £120

Binding – Chambolle-Duru

Lacroix, Paul *Ma Republique.* Paris: Librairie L. Conquet, 1902. One of 40 special copies with two extra states of the plates and inscribed by publisher to Monsieur L. Rattier, limited edition of 100 copies on Japan vellum (out of a total edition of 400 copies), 7 etchings, each in three states (for a total of 21 plates) by Edmond Adolphe Rudaux; very fine crimson morocco gilt and inlaid by Chambolle-Duru (stamp signed), covers with broad border comprised of seven gilt fillets, raised bands, spine compartments outlined with five concentric gilt rules, doublures of brown crushed morocco featuring stylized flowers of inlaid olive brown morocco, elegant arching gilt stems, cloth endleaves, marbled flyleaves, all edges gilt, original printed wrappers bound in, virtually mint. Phillip J. Pirages 61 - 114 2013 $3250

Binding – Charriere, Gerard

Mamet, David *The Frog Prince: a Play.* New York: Vincent FitzGerald & Co., 1984. One of 130 copies on rives paper, printed at Wild Carrot Letterpress by Karen with one original etching, signed and numbered in pencil by artist and 4 plates after drawing by Edward Koren. etching was pulled by Lynn Rogan of Printmaking Workshop, 4 additional illustrations printed on Misu paper at the Meriden Gravure Co., titlepage calligraphy by Jerry Kelly, all copies signed by Mamet and Korne, bound in orange cloth stamped in frog-green handmade endpapers by Gerard Charriere. Priscilla Juvelis - Rare Books 56 - 8 2013 $700

Binding – Christian

Levaillant, F. *Second Voyage Dans L'Interieure de 'Afrique...* Paris: chez J. Jansen et Compe, l'an 3 de La Republique, 1795. First edition, 3 volumes, early 20th century half crimson morocco gilt by Christian of Eastbourne, small label removed from foot of each spine, top edge gilt, uncut, 3 half titles, 22 engraved plates, labels removed from endpapers, small stamps of Bibliotheca Oatesiana and an earlier German library, otherwise excellent, clean, sound set. R. F. G. Hollett & Son   Africana - 122   2013   £850

Binding – Cleaver

Fearnside, William *Eight Picturesque Views on the Thames and Medway.* London: published by Tombleson & Comp. circa 1830's, 283 x 222mm., 2 p.l., iv, 84 pages, contemporary moss green moire cloth by Cleaver (binder's ticket), flat spine, original brown morocco label, engraved dedication, engraved title with vignette, folding panoramic map (frequently missing), 79 steel engravings, corners and head of spine little bumped, rear joint starting at head, label chipped at lower edge, two small water spots to front board, persistent minor foxing to plates, as usual (noticeable on four, but never offensive), otherwise excellent, fresh, strong plate-marks, ample margins and sound binding (map without usual extra creases and entirely smooth and clean).   Phillip J. Pirages   63 - 470   2013 $1250

Binding – Clulow, E.

Seward, Anna *Memoirs of the Life of Dr. Darwin, Chiefly During His Residence at Lichfield,...* London: Printed for J. Johnson by T. Bensley, 1804. First edition, occasional light foxing, 8vo., 19th century half calf by E. Clulow of Derby, slightly worn, neatly recased, titlepage inscribed "From the author", recipient's name erased, with number of pencil notes to text, good.   Blackwell's Rare Books   Sciences - 112   2013   £650

Binding – Cohen, Claudia

Mathews, Harry *Singular Pleasures.* New York: Grenfell Press, 1988. First edition, one of 26 deluxe copies printed on Japanese papers, 8vo., lithographs by Francesco Clemente, specially bound in original full black morocco, ruled in blind, with red morocco lettering strip by Claudia Cohen, in publisher's red morocco and paper over boards slipcase, specially bound with original signed watercolor by Clemente, signed by author and artist out of a total edition of 350, this copy unlettered and out-of-series, very fine. James S. Jaffe Rare Books   Fall 2013 - 96   2013 $2750

Binding – Copeland, Robert McCleary

Man, George Flagg *The Geranium Leaf.* Boston: Marsh, Capen, Lyon & Webb, 1840. First edition, fine, signed binding, 12mo., original gilt lettered and decorated green ribbon embossed cloth, blindstamped on both covers "Copeland Binder", signed by Robert McCleary Copeland, with 20th centry gift inscription.   Howard S. Mott Inc.   262 - 95   2013 $200

Binding – Cosway

Lee, Sidney *A Life of William Shakespeare.* London: Smith, Elder & Co., 1898. Second edition, octavo, 2 photogravure plates, and four additional plates, bound by Riviere & son (stamp signed gilt on front turn-in), full brown crushed levant morocco expertly and almost invisibly rebacked, original spine laid down, front cover set with large oval miniature scene on ivory under glass by Miss C.B. Currie (stamped in gilt on front doublure: "Miniatures by C. B. Currie") within elaborate gilt frame incorporating onlaid red morocco gilt roses, spine in 6 compartments with five raised bands, gilt lettered in two compartments, with gilt date at foot, remaining four compartments decoratively tooled in gilt in similar design with onlaid red morocco gilt roses, board edges ruled in gilt, turn-ins ruled in gilt with gilt floral ornaments with onlaid red morocco gilt roses, green watered silk doublures and liners, top edge gilt, signed in gilt on fore-edges of front and rear boards "Cosway Binding" and "Invented by J. H. Stonehouse", superb example, inserted certificate leaf signed by Stonehouse and Currie and numbered in ink identifies this as being copy "No. 804 of the Cosway Bindings invented by J. H. Stonehouse, with Miniatures on Ivory by Miss Currie".   Heritage Book Shop Holiday Catalogue 2012 - 32   2013 $13,500

Binding – Courteval

Labillardiere, Jacques Julien Houton De *Relation du Voyage a la Recherche de La Perouse, Fait par Ordre de l'Assemblee Constituante, Pendant les annes 1791, 1792...* Paris: Chez H. J. Jansen, An VIII de la Republique Francoise, 1799-1800. First edition, quarto issue, 2 volumes, quarto, atlas with engraved title, double page route map, 43 plates engraved by Copia after drawings by Piron, and botanical plates by Redoute, contemporary French mottled calf by Courteval, covers with borders of rope and disc design enclosed between gilt rules, smooth spines divided into sections using wide gilt bands stripped vertically, sections with large gilt designs, black morocco gilt lettering labels, gilt board edges turn-ins decorated gilt in gilt greek-key pattern, marbled endpapers, edges speckled yellow, atlas corners and caps expertly strengthened, old and scattered oxidation stains to pages 148-149 in volume II (text), plate 10 with old, opaque stain to lower corner (into plate margin but not affecting image), four other plates with browning to spots to lower blank margin, truly exceptional set, beautifully bound, very tall and very clean.   Heritage Book Shop   Holiday Catalogue 2012 - 97   2013 $15,000

Binding – Cox & Ogle

Kennedy, James *Conversations on Religion with Lord Byron and Others, Held in Cephalonia...* London: John Murray, 1830. First edition, half title, folding facsimile plate, 3 pages ads, attractively bound in slightly later half maroon calf by Cox & Ogle of Cambridge gilt spine, black leather label, slight rubbing, F. J. Sebley booklabel, very good. Jarndyce Antiquarian Booksellers CCIII - 397 2013 £180

Binding – Creuzevault, Henri

Regnier, Henri De *Les Rencontres de Mr. de Breot.* Paris: chez Sylvain Sauvage, 1927. First Sauvage edition, number 15 of 25 copies on Japon Imperial, from a total edition of 177; 46 original pochoir enhanced color woodcuts printed by Pierre Bouchet, 248 pages, superb Art Deco signed master binding by Henri Creuzevault, front panel with mosaic of stylized guitar with onlaid multi color leathers, spine with 4 raised bands, top edge gilt, doublures with fillets of gilt and morocco, framing moire fabric, fit in slipcase, overall size 11.5 x 10 inches, in excellent condition. Gemini Fine Books & Arts., Ltd. Art Reference & Illustrated Books - 2013 $2700

Binding – Currie, C. B.

Lee, Sidney *A Life of William Shakespeare.* London: Smith, Elder & Co., 1898. Second edition, octavo, 2 photogravure plates, and four additional plates, bound by Riviere & son (stamp signed gilt on front turn-in), full brown crushed levant morocco expertly and almost invisibly rebacked, original spine laid down, front cover set with large oval miniature scene on ivory under glass by Miss C.B. Currie (stamped in gilt on front doublure:"Miniatures by C. B. Currie") within elaborate gilt frame incorporating onlaid red morocco gilt roses, spine in 6 compartments with five raised bands, gilt lettered in two compartments, with gilt date at foot, remaining four compartments decoratively tooled in gilt in similar design with onlaid red morocco gilt roses, board edges ruled in gilt, turn-ins ruled in gilt with gilt floral ornaments with onlaid red morocco gilt roses, green watered silk doublures and liners, top edge gilt, signed in gilt on fore-edges of front and rear boards "Cosway Binding" and "Invented by J. H. Stonehouse", superb example, inserted certificate leaf signed by Stonehouse and Currie and numbered in ink identifies this as being copy "No. 804 of the Cosway Bindings invented by J. H. Stonehouse, with Miniatures on Ivory by Miss Currie". Heritage Book Shop Holiday Catalogue 2012 - 32 2013 $13,500

Binding – Davidson Laura

Davidson, Laura *Culinaria.* Boston: 2009. Artist's book, one of 10 copies only, all on magnani pecia paper, each signed and numbered by artist in pencil, page size 5 x 6 inches, 20 pages, bound by artist in stainless steel with red and green floral print retro fabric recalling vintage apron or kitchen curtains on spine, copper grommets with brass spatula ingeniously held on by magnets decorating front panel, endpapers are original linoleum prints in pink and white check, with forks, knives, spoons and measuring cups within checks, book comprised of 10 dry points with ink wash of well designed and useful kitchen tools, such as egg beater, strainer, scoop, whisk and masher, etc. Priscilla Juvelis - Rare Books 56 - 6 2013 $1250

Binding – Dawson & Lewis

Byron, George Gordon Noel, 6th Baron 1788-1824 *English Bards and Scotch Reviewers.* London: James Cawthorn, 1816. Fifth spurious fourth edition, bound without half title or final ad leaf, interspersed with leaves from unidentified edition of English Bards, bound in at corresponding pages and at end, profusely illustrated with 87 portraits and views, contemporary full green grained morocco by Dawson & Lewis of Soho, boards attractively blocked in gilt, spine gilt in compartments, gilt dentelles, leading hinge very slightly rubbed, armorial bookplate of Charles Tennant, all edges gilt, very good, handsome. Jarndyce Antiquarian Booksellers CCIII - 131 2013 £480

Binding – De Merrit, John

Lopez, Barry *The Mappist.* San Francisco: Pacific Editions, 2005. First edition thus, one of 48 copies, all on BFK Rives paper, signed by author and artist, Charles Hobson, in pencil and numbered by Hobson, page size 11 x 12 inches, original USGS maps for the concertina binding, which when opened creates its own vista of mountain and valleys representing the maps that figure prominently in the Lopez story, covers made of paper over boards, paper reproducing a 1911 map of Bogota, publisher's slipcase of wood grained paper over boards, with brass toned metal label holder attached to spine of box holding white paper label with title and author in black, all suggesting a map cabinet, further housed in tan corrugated paper board slipcase, slipcase and board covers made by John De Merrit with assistance of Kris Langan, new. Priscilla Juvelis - Rare Books 56 - 23 2013 $2100

Binding – De Vauchelle

Tocqueville, Alexis Charles Henri Maurice Clerel De 1805-1859 *De La Democratie en Amerique.* Paris: Librairie de Charles Gosselin, 1835-1840. First edition, 4 volumes, small octavo, hand colored folding lithograph map in volume 1, uniformly bound by De Vauchelle in modern antique-style quarter black calf over marbled boards, smooth spines ruled and decoratively tooled in gilt in compartments, red and olive green calf gilt lettering labels marbled endpapers, sprinkled edges, expertly clean, wonderful copy. Heritage Book Shop 50th Anniversary Catalogue - 191 2013 $40,000

Binding – Deighton

Mayhew, Henry *London Labour and the London Poor; the Condition an Earnings of Those that Will Work, Cannot Work and Will Not Work. (with) the Extra Volume: Those that Will Not Work.* London: Charles Griffin, 1864. 1862, 4 volumes, frontispieces in volumes 3 and 4, plates, illustrations, maps, tar with loss to following f.e.p. volume II, original maroon cloth by Deighton, volume I slightly damp marked, little rubbed, contemporary signature on title volume I. Jarndyce Antiquarian Booksellers CCV - 199 2013 £850

Binding – Dillon

Poetry of the Anti-Jacobin. London: printed for J. Wright, 1799. First edition, contemporary full dark blue morocco by Dillon of Chelsea, spine lettered and ruled gilt, slightly rubbed, all edges gilt, very good. Jarndyce Antiquarian Booksellers CCIII - 629 2013 £65

Binding – Doves Bindery

Bible. English - 1903 *The English Bible.* Hammersmith: Doves Press, 1903-1905. One of 500 copies, printed on handmade paper by T.J. Cobden-Sanderson and Emery Walker, five volumes, folio, printed in red and black, beautiful full blue morocco by Doves Bindery, boards with triple gilt rule, spines lettered and stamped in gilt, gilt dentelles with floral corner devices, all edges gilt, very minimal foxing and "Genesis" leaf very clean, small split to inner hinge of volume 1 when opened wide, bit of offsetting to endpapers from dentelles, previous owner's bookplate on front pastedown on each volume, near fine, housed in morocco tipped cloth slipcase. Heritage Book Shop Holiday Catalogue 2012 - 46 2013 $35,000

Cobden, Sanderson, Thomas James 1840-1922 *Credo.* London: printed at the Doves Press, 1908. One of 250 copies printed on paper, an additional 12 copies were printed on vellum, contemporary full crushed morocco by Doves Bindery, lettered in gilt on front board and spine, very slightly dulled, otherwise handsome copy, unidentified leather book-label on leading pastedown, small paper label printed with '63' on following f.e.p., all edges gilt. Jarndyce Antiquarian Booksellers CCV - 63 2013 £320

L'Empereur Constant *The Tale of the Emperor Coustans and of Over Sea.* Kelmscott Press, 1894. One of 545 copies (20 of which were on vellum), 142 x 106mm., 2 p.l., 130 pages, elegant crimson crushed morocco, handsomely gilt by Doves Bindery (stamp-signed and dated 1901 on rear turn-in), covers tooled gilt with French fillet frame punctuated with dots and with rose leaf cornerpieces, raised bands, spine beautifully gilt in compartments with Tudor rose centerpiece and rose leaves at corners, gold tooled turn-ins featuring mutiple fillets and leaf clusters at corners, all edges gilt with typical simple stippling, with white-vine borders of twining grape clusters and leaves on each of the two full page woodcuts as well as on first page of text of both stories, three line foliated woodcut initials, shoulder notes (in red) on every page, breath of rubbing to extremities, one very faint marginal smudge, outstanding copy, simply sparkling inside and out. Phillip J. Pirages 61 - 102 2013 $4500

Lamb, Charles 1775-1834 *(The Works).* London: Macmillan and Co., 1891-1898. 178 x 121mm., 7 volumes, fine honey brown crushed morocco handsomely gilt by Doves Bindery (stamp signed with bindery name and '18 C-S 98" on rear turn-in of each volume), raised bands, spines in extremely attractive gilt compartments featuring dense gouge work in the shape of stemmed hearts, along with open circles and circlets, turn-ins ruled in gilt with cornerpieces incorporating heart and tulip tools, all edges gilt, (stippled gauffering), frontispiece in volume V, joints of first volume little worn at juncture of raised bands, extremely slight wear to joints and extremities of other volumes, spines uniformly sunned to very pleasing lighter brown (minor irregular fading to small areas on covers), still most attractive set, beautifully designed bindings solid and with no significant wear, pristine internally. Phillip J. Pirages 61 - 103 2013 $8500

Pervigilium Veneris. Doves Press, 1910. One of 150 copies (of an edition of 162), printed in black on handmade paper with title, initials and refrain at end of each verse, printed in red, 8vo., original russet morocco, backstrip gilt panelled between seven raised bands, second and third gilt lettered and with date 1910 at tail, single gilt rule border to sides, green leather booklabels of Willis Vickery and Cortland Bishop, with some offsetting to front free endpaper, gilt edges, by Doves Bindery, fine. Blackwell's Rare Books 172 - 272 2013 £1500

Ruskin, John   1819-1900 *Deucalion Collected Studies of the Lapse of Waves and Life of Stones.*   Orpington, Kent: George Allen, 1879-1880.   8 parts in 2 volumes, 212 x 141mm., 11 plates in form of drawings by Ruskin, two of them in several colors and two in blue; lovely chestnut brown morocco, handsomely gilt by Doves Bindery (turn-ins at back signed and dated '19 C-S 09'), covers with French fillet border enclosing two rectangular strapwork frames with semicircular interlacing at top and bottom, inner frame interlaced further with two strapwork triangles that form a six-sided star at center, each point of star surmounted with small open circles (and top and bottom point with additional three petalled floral design), star surrounding a garland composed of two leafy sprays, raised bands, spines gilt in compartments featuring concentric square frames enclosing prominent daisy within lozenge, turn-ins with rules and petalled floral cornerpieces, all edges gilt and with stippled gauffering, original front wrappers as well as extra titlepages, bound in at back of each volume, very dark blue full morocco pull-off suede-lined cases in the shape of a book (just slightly rubbed) with raised bands and gilt titling; pastedown of first volume with bookplate of Dr. Samuel L. Siegler, pastedown of second volume with bookplate of "E. R. McC." (Edith Rockefeller McCormick) and with vestige of removed Siegler bookplate, beautifully bound set in pristine condition, even original wrappers in perfect shape.   Phillip J. Pirages   61 - 104   2013 $10,000

Ruskin, John   1819-1900 *The Queen's Gardens.* Manchester: printed in Aid of the St. Andrews Schools Fund, 1864.   First printing, 221 x 144mm., 19, (1) pages, very fine dark blue morocco by Doves Bindery (signed and dated 1911), covers with gilt fillet border and central oval wreath of tudor roses and rose leaves, raised bands, spine with gilt fillet compartments containing vertical titling, gilt ruled turn-ins, all edges gilt, slightly scuffed felt lined tan morocco pull-off box by Riviere & Son, bookplate of Edith Rockefeller McCormick, usual minor offsetting to free endpapers from turn-ins, otherwise sparkling copy.   Phillip J. Pirages   61 - 105   2013 $2500

Binding – Dusel, Philip

Braidwood, James *On the Construction of Fire-Engines and Apparatus...*   Edinburgh: sold by Bell & Bradfute and Oliver & Boyd, 1830.   First edition, double frontispiece tipped in on stub, folding plates, uncut in recent half brown calf by Philip Dusel, gilt spine signed M. Braidwood 1.2.22 on recto of front. additional inscription "City road 14.12.69" with signature of J. Grant in similar hand, handsome copy.   Jarndyce Antiquarian Booksellers   CCV - 28   2013   £2250

The Florence Miscellany.   Florence: (privately) printed for G(aetano) Cam.(biagi)..., 1785.   224 pages, 3 leaves of engraved music within pagination, 8vo., some light foxing, mainly to prelims, bound in 20th century full light brown morocco in period style by Philip Dusel, gilt spine and dentelles, near contemporary signature of Eliz. Harvey.   Jarndyce Antiquarian Booksellers   CCIV - 230   2013   £2600

Binding – Edmonds & Remnants

Byron, George Gordon Noel, 6th Baron   1788-1824 *Childe Harold's Pilgrimage.*   London: John Murray, 1855.   4to., half title, unopened in original glazed pale green printed boards by Edmonds & Remnants, pink cloth spine, corners little worn, otherwise, very good.   Jarndyce Antiquarian Booksellers   CCIII - 138   2013   £65

Byron, George Gordon Noel, 6th Baron   1788-1824 *The Poetical Works.*   London: John Murray, 1854.   Tall 8vo., frontispiece and engraved title, dedication leaf from John Murray to Sir Robert Peel, facsimiles, 32 page catalog (Jan. 1854), original pink cloth by Edmonds & Remnants, little marked, spine faded and with repairs to following hinge signed "Gunning Symons 1854" to leading f.e.p., fairly good copy.   Jarndyce Antiquarian Booksellers   CCIII - 81   2013   £45

Darwin, Charles Robert   1809-1882 *On the Various Contrivances by Which British and Foreign Orchids are Fertilised by Insects and on the Good Effects of Intercrossing.*   London: John Murray, 1862.   First edition, original plum cloth with vertical lines, Freeman variant 'a', ad dated Dec. 1861, bound by Edmonds & Remnants, with their ticket, publisher's blindstamp "Presented by Mr. Murray" on titlepage, this often indicated a copy sent on request of Darwin to a friend or colleague, volume rebacked with remnants of original sunned spine laid down, minimal cover edge wear, scuffs to front pastedown, scattered foxing, 8vo., very good.   By the Book, L. C.   37 - 22   2013 $2750

Darwin, Charles Robert   1809-1882 *The Origin of Species by Means of Natural Selection...*   London: John Murray, 1861.   Third edition, seventh thousand, folding chart, half title present, edges of text lightly browned, soiled at foot of titlepage, 8vo., original wavy grain green cloth by Edmonds & Remnants, with their ticket, extremities rubbed, backstrip gilt lettered direct, sides blind paneled with stamped border, chalked brown endpapers, hinges strengthened, neat repairs to head and tail of spine, good.   Blackwell's Rare Books   172 - 46   2013   £3850

Binding – Embroidered

Caulfeild, S. F. A. *Encyclopedia of Victorian Needlework.* New York: Dover Publications, 1972. First Dover edition, 2 volumes, quarto, extensively illustrated in black and white, original printed wrappers bound in full blue cloth over boards, covers elaborately decorated in multi-colored needlework, floral patterns in red, yellow, purple and green thread, spines and front boards lettered in gilt, original wrappers bound in, housed in red cloth slipcase.   Heritage Book Shop   Holiday Catalogue 2012 - 56   2013 $850

Binding – Fazakerley

Eliot, George, Pseud. 1819-1880 *Romola.* London: Smith Elder and Co., 1880.   One of 1000 copies (this being #57), 2 volumes, 265 x 180mm., remarkable contemporary honey brown crushed morocco by Fazakerley (stamp signed on front turn-in), upper cover of one volume with ornate gilt monogram of "MMK", the other front cover with monogram of "NDK", spines with raised bands and gilt titling, splendid brown morocco doublures elaborately tooled in gilt featuring scalloped French fillet frame incorporating large floral cornerpieces and enclosing exuberantly swirling flowering vines emerging from a Greek urn at foot, brown watered silk endleaves, edges gilt and ornately gauffered in bold strapwork pattern on stippled ground, each volume with 3 lovely and delicate fore-edge paintings the ones at head and tail of each fore-edge being lozenge-shaped views (measuring approximately 25 x 30 mm across) and larger rectangular painting at center (measuring approximately 80 x 45mm), all depicting finely painted scenes fromn book; 24 engraved plates, mounted plates after Sir Frederick Leighton, plus 13 smaller engravings mounted in text as called for, flyleaf of each volume with lovely calligraphic manuscript inscription of quote from book, half title of volume 1 with ink ownership inscription of Jean Stewart Russell dated 1902; spine faintly and evenly sunned, plates bit spotted (from mounting glue?), otherwise superb copy, text clean, fresh and bright, margins especially ample, bindings lustrous and unworn, fore edges richly painted and glittering with particularly bright gold.   Phillip J. Pirages   61 - 78   2013 $16,000

Watts, Alaric   *Lyrics of the Heart: with Other Poems.* London: Longman, Brown, Green and Longmans, 1851. First edition, 211 x 132mm., superb late 19th century olive brown crushed morocco gilt and inlaid by Fazakerley (stamp signed on front turn-in), covers with frames of gilt rules, dots and inlaid tan morocco, central panel of upper cover with inlaid red morocco rectangle emblazoned with title gilt at head, below it a large topiary-shaped, symmetrical design in inlaid morocco and gilt tooling, incorporating 34 heart shaped green leaves on curling hairline stems as well as five lotus blossoms with lavender petals and inverted red heart centers (lower cover with smaller version of same inlaid elements inside plain ruled panel), raised bands, gilt spine compartments continuing same design (each with four inlaid leaf cornerpieces and central lotus flower), turn-ins with gilt and dot frames and lotus and leaf cornerpieces, ivory silk endleaves, marbled flyleaves, edges gilt and elaborately gauffered with deep gouging (in similar floral pattern), fore edge with three exquisitely painted scenes, within pointed frames, these vignettes taken from illustrations appearing within book, felt lined slipcase; with 41 engraved headpieces, as called for, engraved bookplate of Rodman Wanamaker, spine and front board sunned to pleasing uniform tan (as almost always with this color of morocco), occasional minor foxing, more prominent on first and last gatherings), still extremely fine, lovely, morocco lustrous and without perceptible wear, edges with particularly brilliant gilding, 3 painted fore-edge vignettes in perfect condition. Phillip J. Pirages   61 - 79   2013 $12,500

Binding – Feaston

Galt, John   1779-1839   *Sir Andrew Wylie, of that Ilk.* Edinburgh: printed for William Blackwood, 1822. 3 volumes, 8vo., lightly browned, contemporary straight grained half green morocco with marbled boards, spine in compartments with central gilt tools, lettered and numbered in gilt direct, edges marbled, spines gently sunned, armorial bookplate of William, Duke of Bedford, Edinburgh, signed binding by Feaston, with his circular red ticket on front pastedown. Unsworths Antiquarian Booksellers   28 - 165   2013   £180

Binding – Ferrari, Julia

Carr, Daniel   *Gifts of the Leaves with Prints from the Ova Series by Julia Ferrari.*   Ashuelot: Trois Fontaines (Golgonooza Letter Foundry), 1997.   One of 80 regular copies, from a total issue of 109 (26 lettered copies, 80 numbered copies, 3 Artist's proof copies), all on Arches paper, each signed and numbered or lettered by author and type designer, punch cutter and printer, Dan Carr, and artist, Julia Ferrari, bound by Julia Ferrari, in green pastepaper over boards.   Priscilla Juvelis - Rare Books   56 - 13 2013 $1500

Carr, Daniel *Gifts of the Leaves with Prints from the Ova Series by Julia Ferrari.* Ashuelot: Trois Fontaines, Golgonooza Letter Foundry, 1997. One of 26 lettered 'de tete' copies, from a total issue of 109 (26 lettered copies, 80 numbered copies, 3 Artist's proof copies), all on Arches paper, each signed and numbered or lettered by author and type designer, punch cutter and printer, Dan Carr, and artist, Julia Ferrari, the lettered copy has unique colored monotype by Richard de Bas paper as the frontispiece of book, a copper strike from the hand cut punches bound into custom made clamshell box, housing book and 4 etchings, page size 12 1/2 x 9 1/4 inches, 74 pages, bound by Julia Ferrari, handmade tan/brown pastepaper over boards housed in black cloth clamshell box with copper strike from hand cut punches inlaid into inside, front panel of box, pastepaper spine label, new.   Priscilla Juvelis - Rare Books 56 - 12 2013 $3500

Binding – Fine Bindery

Banville, John *The Sea.* Oxford: Joe McCann, 2005. One of 46 numbered copies signed by author, 40 only for sale, from total edition of 56 (48 copies only for sale), 8vo., original blue Ratchford cloth, letterpress printed moulmade paper labels by the Evergreen Press, sewn by hand and bound by Fine Bindery, fine in clear acetate dust jacket.   Maggs Bros. Ltd.   1442 - 5   2013   £250

Barry, Sebastian *The Pinkening Boy.* Oxford: Joel McCann, 2004. First edition, limited to 65 copies signed by author, from a total edition of 85, 8vo., original brown cloth, printed paper labels on spine and upper cover, blue endpapers, hand bound by Fine Bindery in Northamptonshire, fine in clear acetate dust jacket.   Maggs Bros. Ltd.   1442 - 8   2013   £50

Barry, Sebastian *Tales of Ballycumber.* First edition, limited to 40 copies signed by author, from a total edition of 52, 8vo., original green cloth, 150gsm archival paper with paper labels on spine and upper cover with red endpapers reproducing the author's drawing of the stage design for the play, hand bound by Fine Book Bindery.   Maggs Bros. Ltd. 1442 - 9   2013   £75

Heaney, Seamus *The Testament of Cresseid.* London: Enitharmon Editions, 2004. Limited edition, signed by author and artist, 4to., original dark green cloth with paper label on spine and color image on upper board, printed on Arches Velin and bound by Fine Bindery, Wellingborough.   Maggs Bros. Ltd.   1442 - 119   2013   £300

O'Hagan, Andrew *Be Near Me.* Dublin: Tuskar Rock Press, 2006. First edition, number IX of 15 roman numeral copies in morocco (only 12 for sale), from a total edition of 75, fine in mid blue slipcase, as issued, 8vo., original full red morocco lettered gilt on spine, with red and yellow head and tail bands, bound by The Fine Bindery.   Maggs Bros. Ltd. 1442 - 272   2013   £225

Toibin, Colm *Brooklyn.* Dublin: Tuskar Rock Press, 2009. First edition, number VII of 25 roman numeral copies in morocco from total edition of 100, 8vo., original full yellow morocco lettered gilt on spine, red and yellow head and tail bands, cream laid paper endpapers, bound by Fine Bindery, fine in matching yellow slipcase.   Maggs Bros. Ltd.   1442 - 300   2013   £450

Toibin, Colm *Brooklyn.* Dublin: Tuskar Rock Press, 2009. First edition, number 46 of 75 numbered copies in cloth, form total edition of 110, 8vo., original yellow cloth, lettered gilt on spine, red and yellow head and tail bands, cream laid paper endpapers, bound by Fine Bindery, fine in matching yellow slipcase.   Maggs Bros. Ltd.   1442 - 301 2013   £175

Trevor, William 1928- *Men of Ireland.* Oundle: Oundle Festival of Literature, 2008. Number 18 of 120 copies signed by author, small 8vo., original patterned paper boards, printed on Somerset Laid mould-made paper and bound by Fine Book Bindery, Wellingborough.   Maggs Bros. Ltd.   1442 - 306   2013   £175

Binding – Fontanes, Simone

Audiberti, Jacques *Lagune Herissee.* Paris: Societe des Cent Une, 1958. First Carzou edition, number 44 of 145 copies (total edition) signed by Jean Carzou and President & VP of Societe on justification page, 20 origina color lithographs, including 16 full page, each with tissue guard, lithos and 169 text leaves printed on Arches a la Forme, handmade paper, each leaf watermarked 'Arches', except for front cover litho, which contains an extra suite of 20 full page lithos in tones of black and one refusee litho, with additional justification page for the suite, numbered 8/8 and signed by Jean Carzou in pen, lithos not signed, unique copy in signed Master binding by Simone Fontanes, full tan calf, beautiful mosaic design of gilt and black engraved lines with onlaid painted strips of leather, on both front and back panels, spine with lettering gilt and black, integrating covers' design, endleaves made of fine suede, all edges gilt, original wrappers preserved and bound in, contained in matching half leather chemise and leather trimmed slipcase, overall size 32.5 x 25.5 x 5.5. cm, very slight age toning to spine, otherwise in new condition, from the library of Jean Jacobs with his small bookplate.   Gemini Fine Books & Arts., Ltd. Art Reference & Illustrated Books - 2013 $1300

Binding – Frost, Brian

Schiller, Johann Christoph Friedrich Von 1759-1805 *The Piccolomini or the First Part of Wallenstein. (with) The Death of Wallenstein.* London: T. N. Longman & O. Rees, 1800. First edition translated by Samuel T. Coleridge, handsomely bound in full green morocco by Brian Frost and Co., gilt borders and dentelles, spine fading to brown, all edges gilt, very good.   Jarndyce Antiquarian Booksellers CCIII - 507   2013   £650

Binding – Galwey & Co.

Cuala Press *A Woman's Reliquary.* Churchtown: Cuala Press, 1916. One of 300 copies, 8vo., original quarter linen over pale cream boards, spine and upper board lettered in black, small rectangular ticket of binder "Galwey & Co. Eustace St. Dublin" at foot of front pastedown, offsetting to endpapers and boards slightly marked, otherwise near fine.   Maggs Bros. Ltd.   1442 - 42   2013   £250

Binding – Gardner, Anthony

Salmon, William *The Country Builder's Estimator, or the Architect's Companion.* printed for James Hodges at the Looking Glass on London Bridge, 1737. Second edition, few diagrams and illustrations in text, washed and repaired, 12mo., fairly modern (1954) tan Niger goatskin by Anthony Gardner, OBE, blind tooled borders on sides, lettered direct in gilt on spine, binder' Apologia penned inside front cover in sepia ink in accomplished calligraphic italic script, his detailed invoice-cum-letter to the then owner loosely inserted, very good.   Blackwell's Rare Books   Sciences - 109   2013   £1250

Binding – Gerard, Manuel

Miro, G. *Jan Gabriel Daragnes. Semaine Sainte.* Lyon: Societe les XXX, 1931. First edition, number 3 of 30 'exemplaires nominatifs', with 19 hand colored engravings, of which 7 are hors texte and an additional suite of 18 hand colored engravings, all hors texte by Daragnes, printed on velin d'Arches filigrane paper, circa 13 x 1 inches, page size 360 x 270mm., 61 pages, signed binding by Manuel Gerard, blue snakeskin with inlaid large geometric wood panels, plain spine with gilt lettering, dark blue painted endleaves, top edge gilt, original wrappers bound in, morocco trimmed matching slipcase, few faint fox marks, otherwise fine, rare. Gemini Fine Books & Arts., Ltd.   Art Reference & Illustrated Books - 2013 $1450

Binding – Gerlach, Gerhard

Hunter, Dard   1883-1966 *A Papermaking Pilgrimage to Japan, Korea and China.* New York: Pynson Printers, 1936. Limited to 370 signed copies, this #317, signed by Hunter and publisher, Elmer Adler on colophon page, 4to., plates, binding by Gerhard Gerlach, quarter black leather and patterned paper boards with gilt lettering and red design spine, mild foxing to few specimen pages, very good publisher's paper covered printed slipcase with wear and scuffs. By the Book, L. C.   38 - 64   2013 $3000

Binding – Gomez, Marta

Hamady, Walter *Neopostmodernism or Gabberjab Number 6.* Mt. Horeb: Perishable Press, 1988. First edition, limited to 125 copies printed on various handmade papers, oblong small 8vo., illustrations, original boards, signed by binder, Marta Gomez, Hamady's assistant, Kent Kasuboske and especially inscribed by Hamady to collector, very fine.   James S. Jaffe Rare Books   Fall 2013 - 125   2013 $2500

Binding – Grace-Bindings

Walton, Izaak   1593-1683 *The Lives of John Donne, Sir Henry Wotton, Mr. Richard Hooker, Mr. George Herbert and Dr. Robert Sanderson.* New York: privately printed (at the Chiswick Press) for the Scott-Thaw Co., 1904. One of 200 copies for sale, signed by publisher, this copy #88, 362 x 22mm., engraved titlepage and historiated initials by Dion Clayton Calthrop, printer's device in colophon and 6 engraved portraits, original tissue guards, printed in black and red on thick textured paper; simply decorated but quite elegant modern retrospective olive brown crushed morocco by Grace-Bindings (stamp signed), cover with slender chain gilt roll border, raised bands, spine panels with gilt titling and central 8 point sunburst lozenge, marbled endpapers, untrimmed, bottom edges, other edges rough trimmed, original paper spine label from publisher's cloth binding tipped in a rear of volume), four (of the 9) blank flyleaves vaguely browned, isolated trivial foxing, but very fine, excellent edition, binding unworn, text especially bright, fresh and clean. Phillip J. Pirages   63 - 486   2013 $950

Binding – Gray, Earle

Bukowski, Charles *Bone Palace Ballet: New Poems.* Santa Rosa: Black Sparrow Press, 1997. First edition, #131 of 426 numbered copies, pictorial boards by Earle Gray, with original color serigraph by author, fine in fine glassine dust jacket.   Charles Agvent   Charles Bukowski - 7   2013 $125

Bukowski, Charles *Bukowski Photographs 1977-1991.* Hollywood: Bukskin Press, 1993. First edition, folio, #22 of only 74 signed copies, signed by author and photographer, Michael Montfort, handbound by Earle Gray in white boards with color photo of Bukowski on front cover, tipped-in photos, fine.   Charles Agvent   Charles Bukowski - 38   2013 $1000

Bukowski, Charles *Horsemeat.* Santa Barbara: Black Sparrow Press, 1982. First edition, #76 of 125 copies signed by author and photographer on colophon page, folio handbound by Earle Gray in pictorial boards with color photo of Bukowski on front cover, tipped in color photos by Michael Montfort, fine.   Charles Agvent   Charles Bukowski - 39   2013 $1500

Bukowski, Charles *The Night Torn Mad with Footsteps: New Poems.* Santa Rosa: Black Sparrow Press, 2001. First edition, #57 of 526 numbered and lettered copies, handbound by Earle Gray in pictorial boards, and containing original serigraph print by Bukowski, in addition there were 100 hardcover copies and an unspecified edition in wrappers, fine in fine glassine dust jacket. Charles Agvent Charles Bukowski - 18   2013 $75

Bukowski, Charles *The Night Torn Mad with Footsteps.* Santa Rosa: Black Sparrow Press, 2001. First edition, #57 of 526 numbered and lettered copies handbound by Earle Gray and containing an original serigraph print by Bukowski, in addition there were 1000 hardcover copies and un unspecified edition in wrappers, fine in fine glassine dust jacket. Charles Agvent Charles Bukowski - 19   2013 $125

Bukowski, Charles *Open All Night: New Poems.* Santa Rosa: Black Sparrow Press, 2000. First edition, #195 of 426 numbered copies, hand bound in pictorial boards by Earle Gray, with original color serigraph by author, fine in fine glassine. Charles Agvent   Charles Bukowski - 21   2013 $125

Binding – Grieve, Andrew

Douglas, Gavin *The Poetical Works of...* Edinburgh: William Paterson, 1874. First edition, 4 volumes, 8vo., contemporary polished calf by Andrew Grieve of Edinburgh, sides gilt panelled with pairs of double fillets with fleurons in corners, spines gilt in compartments, twin red lettering pieces, top edge gilt, others uncut and unopened, spines trifle faded, fore edges lightly spotted, excellent, beautiful copy. Blackwell's Rare Books   B174 - 51   2013   £600

The Lives of Illustrious and Eminent Persons of Great Britain. London: printed for Longman, Hurst, Rees, Orme and Brown, 1820. First edition, 63 engraved portraits; quite pretty brown morocco gilt and inlaid in most animated design by Andrew Grieve of Edinburgh (stamp-signed), covers bordered by multiple plain and decorative gilt rules enclosing unusual gilt frame of baroque style flowers, leaves, volutes, swirls and quatrefoils, cornerpieces of inlaid red morocco quatrefoils outlined in gilt, central panel dominated by red morocco oval medallion adorned with gilt laurel wreath, oval with four red morocco petals from which spring gilt fronds and quatrefoils, these terminating at top and bottom of panel with ochre morocco outlined mandorlas containing gilt floral sprig, background of panel exuberantly decorated with many small gilt flowers, inlaid green morocco dots, ochre morocco half moons and assorted small tools, raised bands, spine elegantly gilt in compartments with central red morocco oval framed in gilt with oval branch cornerpieces, turn-ins with gilt frames formed by multiple decorative rules, marbled endpapers, all edges gilt, intermittent minor foxing, more prominent on first few leaves, one page with small inkspot obscuring a couple of letters, otherwise fine, text clean and fresh, binding lustrous and virtually unworn.   Phillip J. Pirages   61 - 111   2013 $1500

Maidment, James *A Book of Scottish Pasquils 1568-1715.* Edinburgh: William Paterson, 1868. One of 3 copies on vellum, (there were a limited but unspecified, number of copies, also printed on paper), 206 x 128mm., handsome contemporary crimson morocco, attractively gilt by Andrew Grieve (stamp signed), covers gilt with multiple plain and decorative rules enclosing a delicate dentelle frame, large intricate fleuron at center of each cover, spine gilt in double ruled compartments with complex fleuron centerpiece and scrolling floral cornerpieces, turn-ins decorated with plain and decorative gilt rules, patterned burgundy and gold silk endleaves, top edge gilt, slightly worn matching morocco lipped slipcase; woodcut titlepage illustration, numerous decorative tailpieces and occasional woodcut vignettes in text; armorial bookplate of H. D. Colvill-Scott, armorial bookplate of Clarence S. Bemens; tiny dark spot on spine, corners with just hint of rubbing, couple of leaves with slightly rumpled fore edge, still fine, text clean, smooth and bright, binding unusually lustrous and with virtually no wear. Phillip J. Pirages   63 - 479   2013 $4800

Shakespeare, William 1564-1616 *The Works.* London: Edward Moxon, 1857. First printing of this edition, 222 x 140mm., one gathering in third volume with leaves bound out of order, but complete, 6 volumes, frontispiece and one title leaf bit foxed, beautiful contemporary tree calf by Andrew Grieve of Edinburgh for William Paterson, Edinburgh bookseller (stamp-signed with both names on verso front free endpaper of each volume), covers with gilt double fillets and twining leaf border, raised bands, spines very attractively gilt in compartments with graceful floral cornerpieces and elaborate fleuron centerpiece, red and dark green morocco title labels, gilt rolled turn-ins, marbled endpapers and edges, isolated very minor foxing elsewhere, couple of very faint scratches to covers, exceptionally fine, lovely bindings lustrous and virtually unworn, text showing no signs of use.   Phillip J. Pirages   61 - 112   2013 $4800

Binding – Gruel

Duret, Theodore *(Henri de Toulouse)-Lautrec.* Paris: Bernheim Jeune, 1920. First edition, one of 100 deluxe copies, printed entirely on Japon paper (total edition 200), 124 pages, 38 full page heliogravure plates + 1 original etching, + 1 original color lithograph, both are strong impressions, very clean and bright, half calf janseniste binding by Gruel, signed by the Master binder, original wrappers bound in, top edge gilt, front hinge strengthened, otherwise in excellent condition.   Gemini Fine Books & Arts., Ltd.   Art Reference & Illustrated Books - 2013 $1500

Herriot, Edouard *Andre Mare.* Paris: Aux Editions de l'Estampe, 1927. First illustrated edition, from a total edition of 170, this number 86 of 105 copies on Arches wove paper, 40 original black and white lithographs , including 10 hors texte, and extra suite of the 40 lithos, printed in sanguine on Japon, 287 pages, very handsome signed Master binding by Gruel with engraved design of black and gilt geometric decorations on both covers and spine, on rich emerald snakeskin, raised bands, top edge gilt, beautifully designed internal endleaves, wrappers and backstrip well preserved and bound in, overall size 10.5 x 8.75 x 2 inches, spine sunned to nice gold brown, otherwise as new, very handsome binding.   Gemini Fine Books & Arts., Ltd.   Art Reference & Illustrated Books - 2013 $1300

Binding – Guild of Women Binders

Bible. English - 1897 *The Song of Solomon.* London: printed by William Clowes and Sons for Guild of Women Binders, circa, 1897. One of 100 copies on Japanese paper, this copy #13, 290 x 220mm., 1 p.l., 16 pages plus illustrations, with 12 pleasing plates by H. Granville Fell on Japanese paper, made from pencil drawings, as well as 4 different illustrated titles and vignette closing leaf, immaculate copy, superb contemporary dark blue morocco, elegantly gilt by Guild of Women Binders (stamp signed), covers tooled in Art Nouveau design featuring a large central anthemium of flowers rising on long stem from stippled base, this central ornament flanked by three long stemmed irises on either side, flat spine with vertical gilt titling, single fillet and small circles, matching blue morocco doublures tooled with with particularly attractive complex central oval ornament encompassing considerable stippling and 20 large stylized flowers on curvilinear stems, vellum free endleaves with gilt hearts at corners, top edge gilt, fine matching folding morocco box, lined with pale blue suede gilt titling on its spine.   Phillip J. Pirages   61 - 108   2013 $3500

Field, Michael, Pseud.   *Stephania: a Trialogue.* London: Elkin Mathews & John Lane, 1892. One of 250 copies, 197 x 146mm., 6 p.l., 100 pages, 4 leaves colophon and ads, titlepage with full woodcut border filled with intertwined pine branches and mistletoe, colophon with pine cone device, exceptionally attractive modelled goatskin by Mrs. Annie MacDonald of the Guild of Women Binders, front cover with large lobed frames, its upper corners enclosing binder's initial and date (1897), lower corners with daffodil blooms, large central panel showing an elaborately detailed scene featuring a woman with long, flowing hair entreating god mercury in his signature winged hat and sandals, two figures surmounted by imperial brown through which twines a sprig of mistletoe (design that appears in woodcut frame on titlepage), lower cover showing woman kneeling by man reclining on a couch, this scene enclosed in an oval beaded frame, flat spine with modelled title flanked by pine cone device at head and tail, green watered silk pastedowns, framed by unusual turn-ins decorated with gilt vines and calf circles painted green and blue, leather hinges, top edge gilt, others edges untrimmed, verso of front flyleaf with engraved bookplate of Charles Williston McAlpin, extra paper title labels tipped onto rear blank, 2 tiny red (ink?) marks to upper cover, inevitable offsetting from turn-ins to endpapers, once detached front flyleaf tipped onto front free endpaper, other trivial defects, still very attractive copy, binding lustrous and scarcely worn and leaves fresh and clean.   Phillip J. Pirages   61 - 106   2013 $4500

Rogers, Samuel *Italy, a Poem.* London: Edward Moxon, 1838. 297 x 213mm., 114 fine engraved plates, 54 of these with additional state, being proof 'before letters' along with one proof plate of engraved tailpiece and four proofs on India paper, large paper copy; very striking dark green morocco with extraordinarily elaborate gilt and inlaid decoration, for the Guild of Women Binders (stamp-signed), covers with exceptionally animated and complex design featuring central stippled cruciform radiating a controlled riot of gilt tooling and more than 600 inlays of red, moss green, gray and ochre morocco forming flowering vines and geometrical shapes, raised bands, spine panels each decorated with six inlaid flowers and multiple teardrop tools, second panel with gilt tooling, azure morocco doublures with attractive Art Nouveau frame featuring delicate gilt tooling and inlaid dark green sidepieces, orange dot accents, vellum endleaves with tiny gilt heart at each corner, all edges gilt, very fine velvet lined modern dark green morocco folding box, occasional faint foxing to margins and to about one-third of the plates, one plate with old repaired two inch tear to tail edge, in amazing condition, text fresh and bright, margins immense, plates richly impressed, unusually exuberant binding, especially lustrous and entirely unworn.   Phillip J. Pirages   61 - 107   2013 $24,000

Binding – Guy

Gibson, C. B. *The History of the County and City of Cork.* 1861. First edition, 2 volumes, map, signed presentation copy to his daughter, Dorinda, in Guy's special red morocco binding, gilt embossed, all edges gilt, lacks signature 31 (pages 72-89) of volume 2, else very good.   C. P. Hyland   261 - 447   2013   £750

Binding – Harcourt Bindery

Frank, Anne *Diary of a Young Girl.* West Hatfield: Pennyroyal Press with Jewish Heritage Pub., 1985. Limited to 350 numbered copies, signed by artist, Joseph Goldyne and designer Barry Moser, with additional suite of etchings, each signed in pencil by artist, folio, 10 color etchings by Joseph Goldyne, each signed in pencil by artist, plates with tissue guards, printed by Harold McGrath in gray and rose in Bembo on Mohawk Letterpress, etchings printed by R. C. Townsend Inc. on gray Arches, engraved tailpiece on endgrain boxwood, publisher's full gray morocco by Harcourt Bindery, front cover and spine ruled and lettered in blind, fine, with the additional suite of ten color etchings in quarter gray morocco portfolio, both items housed in publisher's linen slipcase, fine set.   Heritage Book Shop Holiday Catalogue 2012 - 114   2013 $2750

Holmes, Thomas *Cotton Mather: a Bibliography of His Works.* Cambridge: Harvard University Press, 1940. First edition, limited to 500 copies, 3 volumes, 8vo., decorative red title border, illustrations, original quarter dark brown levant over lighter brown cloth, top edge gilt, gilt stamped spine by Harcourt Bindery, Boston, fine, Burndy bookplate, beautiful set, George Sarton's copy (and Harvard University's) bookplate and ownership signature.   Jeff Weber Rare Books   169 - 212   2013 $500

Smollett, Tobias George   1721-1771   *The Adventures of Covnt Fathom.* London: Navarre Society Ltd. circa, 1902. One of 2000 copies, 181 114mm., 2 volumes, very fine burgundy morocco, handsome gilt and onlaid, by Harcourt Bindery of Boston (stamp-signed on front flyleaf), boards with triple fillet border, each cover with elaborate heraldic frame of gilt and onlaid green morocco around an empty oval, raised bands, very pretty gilt spine compartments, featuring looping tendril frame enclosed a charming flower centerpiece densely gilt turn-ins, marbled endpapers, top edge gilt, 2 frontispieces by G. Cruikshank, very fine, bindings especially bright, text with virtually no signs of use.   Phillip J. Pirages   63 - 443   2013 $400

Smollett, Tobias George   1721-1771   *The Adventures of Peregrine Pickle.* London: Navarre Society Ltd. circa., 1902. One of 2000 copies, 4 volumes, 181 x 114mm., very fine burgundy morocco, handsomely gilt and onlaid by Harcourt Bindery of Boston (stamp signed), boards with triple fillet border, each cover with elaborate heraldic frame of gilt and onlaid green morocco around an empty oval, raised bands, very pretty gilt spine compartments featuring looping tendril frame enclosing a charming flower centerpiece, densely gilt turn-ins, marbled endpapers, titlepage, 4 frontispiece drawings by George Cruikshank, very fine, bindings bright, text with virtually no signs of use.   Phillip J. Pirages   63 - 444   2013 $600

Smollett, Tobias George   1721-1771   *The Adventures of Roderick Random.* London: Navarre Society Ltd. circa, 1902. One of 2000 copies, 3 volumes, 181 x 114mm., very fine burgundy morocco, handsomely gilt onlaid by Harcourt Bindery of Boston (stamp signed), boards with triple fillet border, each cover with elaborate heraldic frame of gilt and onlaid green morocco around an empty oval, raised bands, very pretty gilt spine compartments featuring looping tendril frame enclosing a charming flower centerpiece, densely gilt turn-ins, marbled endpapers, top edge gilt, three frontispiece drawings by George Cruikshank, very fine, bindings especially bright and text virtually unused.   Phillip J. Pirages   63 - 445   2013 $550

Sterne, Laurence 1713-1768 *A Sentimental Journey through France and Italy.* London: Navarre Society, circa, 1926. One of 2000 copies, 181 x 114mm., frontispiece, very fine burgundy morocco, handsomely gilt and onlaid by Harcourt Bindery of Boston (stamp signed), boards with triple fillet border, reach cover with elaborate heraldic frame of gilt and onlaid green morocco around an empty oval, raised bands, very pretty gilt spine compartments, featuring looping tendril frame enclosing a charming flower centerpiece, densely gilt turn-ins, marbled endpapers, top edge gilt, very fine, bindings especially bright, text with virtually no signs of use. Phillip J. Pirages   63 - 450   2013 $375

Binding – Harrison

Browning, Robert 1812-1889 *The Ring and the Book.* London: Smith Elder, 1868-1869. First edition, 4 volumes, 8vo., occasional light scattered foxing to free endleaves, original black stamped green cloth, gilt stamped spines by Harrison in quarter gilt stamped calf over blue cloth slipcase, volume 3 rear hinge cracked with light front pastedown soiling, volumes 1 and 2 hinges cracked, Robert Browning's signature tipped in volume I opposite titlepage, ownership signatures of W. J. Settle, Sherborne, Dorset Feb. 21 1869 and F. Rowlandson, ownership signatures of E. M. Forster volume 2, attractive, very good copy. Jeff Weber Rare Books   171 - 53   2013 $4000

Binding – Hatchards

Beyle, Marie Henri 1783-1842 *Maxims of Love.* London: Arthur L. Humphreys, 1906. 167 x 130mm., 2 p.l., 201 pages, very attractive contemporary hunter green crushed morocco for Hatchards, stamp signed on front turn-in, covers with simple gilt Arts & Crafts style frame, gilt titling on upper cover, raised bands, spines gilt in double ruled compartments with gilt dot in each corner, titling in gilt, 3 compartments with gilt dot in each corner, titling gilt in three compartments, gilt ruled turn-ins, top edge gilt, text in French and English, bookplate of Victoria Sackville, occasional pencilled marginalia, spine uniformly a couple of shades darker, mild offsetting from turn-ins, otherwise fine, especially clean inside and out. Phillip J. Pirages   63 - 413   2013 $550

Walpole, Horace *The Letters.* London: Richard Bentley and Son, 1891. 9 volumes, 230 x 149mm., 43 engraved plates, protected by tissue guards; extremely pleasing polished calf for Hatchards (stamp signed), blind ruled triple frame on covers, raised bands, spine compartments of thick and thin gilt rules enclosing decorative frames with dotted sides and volute cornerpieces, each spine, two morocco labels, top edges gilt; one joint mostly and two joints partly, cracked (but nothing loose), faint hairline scratches on few covers, couple of volumes with slightest hint of wear to extremities, otherwise fine, attractive binding, looking handsome on the shelf, text entirely fresh and clean. Phillip J. Pirages   63 - 484   2013 $950

Binding – Hayday

Coleridge, Samuel Taylor 1772-1834 *Aids to Reflection in the Formation of a Manly Character on the Several Grounds of Prudence, Morality and Religion...* London: William Pickering, 1839. Fourth edition, Half title, contemporary plain maroon morocco by Hayday, slightly rubbed, signature of T. K. Leighton, 1842, all edges gilt. Jarndyce Antiquarian Booksellers   CCIII - 547   2013   £50

Coleridge, Samuel Taylor 1772-1834 *Confessions of an Inquiring Spirit.* London: William Pickering, 1840. First edition, half title, contemporary half black morocco by Hayday, slightly rubbed, top edge gilt, signature and bookplate of Alexander W. Gillman and of Peter Mann 1951. Jarndyce Antiquarian Booksellers   CCIII - 562   2013   £180

Coleridge, Sara *Phantasmion.* C. Whittingham for William Pickering, 1837. First edition, inscribed presentation from Mrs. H. N. Coleridge for Miss Theodosia Hinckes, , loosely inserted ALS by author to Mrs. Lonsdale, (pencil inscription "Given me by John Sparrow), 8vo., flyleaves little spotted, through setting slightly on to half title, few areas of minor spotting, contemporary pebble grained green morocco, double blind ruled borders on sides with corner ornaments, thick blind rules on either side of raised bands on spine, lettered direct in gilt, gilt edges by Hayday, mostly faded to brown, little rubbed, short split at head of lower joint, good. Blackwell's Rare Books   172 - 43   2013   £3500

Binding – Howell, Edward

Oliphant, Margaret Oliphant Wilson 1828-1897 *Makers of Modern Rome.* London and New York: Macmillan and Co., 1895. 222 x 154mm., handsome contemporary red crushed morocco gilt by Howell of Liverpool (stamp signed), covers with gilt fillet border and triple fillet framed central panel with ornate fleur-de-lys cornerpieces, raised bands, spine attractively gilt in compartments with fleur-de-lys centerpiece within lozenge of small tools and with scrolling cornerpieces, densely gilt turn-ins, all edges gilt, pleasing later fore-edge painting of the eternal city, signed with cypher formed by initials "A" and "V", with 25 full page illustrations and numerous illustrations in text, slight rubbing to joints, lower inner corner with faint arching dampstain extending into part of bottom four lines of text, very few tiny dots of foxing, otherwise fine, attractive decorative binding bright, text fresh and clean, painting very well preserved. Phillip J. Pirages   63 - 190   2013 $650

Prescott, William Hickling 1796-1859 *History of the Conquest of Mexico.* London: Swan Sonnenschein & Co., 1906. 8vo., 2 maps, one handwriting facsimile plate, 8vo., contemporary tree calf, boards with gilt roll border, spine in five compartments with raised bands, green morocco lettering piece, compartments with gilt floral centrepieces and corner vine sprays, marbled edges and endpapers, gilt prize stamp Cambridge Local Examinations Southport Centre, at front board and prize bookplate, inside binder's ticket of Edward Howell, Liverpool, spine gently sunned, near fine, awarded to W. T. Waterhouse for First Class Honors in History and Geography. Blackwell's Rare Books 172 - 119 2013 £95

Prescott, William Hickling 1796-1859 *History of the Conquest of Peru.* London: Swan Sonnenschein & Co., 1907. 8vo., contemporary tree calf boards with gilt roll border, spine in five compartments with raised bands, green morocco lettering piece, compartments with gilt floral centrepieces and corner vine sprays, marbled edges and endpapers, gilt prize stamp (Cambridge Local Examinations, Southport Centre) to front board and prize bookplate inside, binder's ticket of Edward Howell, Liverpool, spine gently sunned, awarded to W. T. Waterhouse for First Class Honours in English 1908. Blackwell's Rare Books 172 - 120 2013 £95

Binding – Jenkins, R.

Remarques Historique sur la Bastille, sa Demolition & Revolutions de Paris en Juillet 1789. Londres: 1789. Folding plan, without half title, 8vo., marginal paper flaw to d2 of second part, some old waterstaining towards end, titlepage foxed, 19th century half dark green calf by R. Jenkins with his ticket, marbled boards, hinges and corners rubbed, few marks to spine. Jarndyce Antiquarian Booksellers CCIV - 57 2013 £180

Binding – Jensen, Craig

Rumi, Jalaluddin Mohammad *Divan e Shams.* New York: Vincent FitzGerald & Co., 1996. Signed limited edition, one of 50 copies, all on handmade papers by Dieu Donne and BFK Rives, bound by Craig Jensen at BookLab in ivory linen in coptic style binding with brown and gray endpapers that are etchings of various leaves, housed in silver silk over boards custom made clamshell box, title in palladium on spine and engraved ornament on front panel of box, fine, extremely beautiful, with graphic works and one sculpture (glass laid in to back of custom made clamshell box) by 15 artists, some mounted, some on multiple or folded leaves, some on colored or translucent paper, most signed in pencil by respective artist. Priscilla Juvelis - Rare Books 55 - 9 2013 $15,000

Binding – Kieffer, Rene

Conrad, Joseph 1857-1924 *Heart of Darkness.* Paris: Editions d'Art Edouard Pelletan, 1910. First Steinlen edition, number 221 of 267 copies on wove Marais paper (total edition 340) signed by publisher in ink on justification page, 252 original black and white lithographs, by Theophile Alexandre Steinlen, 366 pages, bound by Rene Kieffer in exceptionally handsome Art Deco dark green full polished morocco with mosaic of inlaid maroon leathers and embossed gilt decorations on both covers and spine, latter with 4 embossed bands, dentelles, matching design, framing decorative silk centerpiece, matching front endleaf, additional endleaves of decorative green with silver and gilt paper, top edge gilt, original wrappers and backstrip preserved and bound in, contained in matching morocco trimmed slipcase, binding signed by Kieffer, publisher subscription ads bound in at end, overall size 27 x 21, pristine condition. Gemini Fine Books & Arts., Ltd. Art Reference & Illustrated Books - 2013 $2900

Heredia, Jose Maria De *Les Trophees.* Paris: Librairie des Amateurs, 1914. First Rochegrosse edition, number 40 of 75 deluxe copies on Grand Japon paper (total edition 512), initialled in pen by publisher, 33 original etchings, 25 hors texte by Georges Rochegrosse, engraved by Eugene Decisi, each of the etchings in 3 states, 2 of the states with artist's remarques (small proof etching printed on same plate, usually an image different from the larger one), all etchings signed in plate by Rochegrosse and Decisi, total number of etchings is 99, 81 of them hors-texte, in addition, book illustrated with numerous woodcut, over 300 leaves bound in very beautiful signed Master binding by Rene Kieffer, full burgundy backstrip bound in, top edge gilt, matching slipcase, overall size 33 x 24 cm., in excellent condition. Gemini Fine Books & Arts., Ltd. Art Reference & Illustrated Books - 2013 $3000

Binding – Lakeside Bindery

Bright, Timothy *A Treatise of Melancholie.* London: imprinted...by Thomas Vautrollier, 1586. First edition, small octavo, this copy includes original leaf O8, which was intended to be canceled, woodcut printer's device on title, bound by Lakeside Bindery in full antique style calf, covers panelled in gilt, smooth spine decoratively tooled and lettered gilt, edges stained red, lower margin of title and following leaf renewed with some loss to few letters of imprint on title, title soiled slightly, bottom edge of lower margin frayed slightly in prelims, short internal tear to A4 crossing text, few other minor marginal flaws or repairs, some faint dampstaining, very good, extremely rare, from the library of Haskell Norman, with his bookplate. Heritage Book Shop 50th Anniversary Catalogue - 13 2013 $25,000

Binding – Langan, Kris

Lopez, Barry *The Mappist.* San Francisco: Pacific Editions, 2005. First edition thus, one of 48 copies, all on BFK Rives paper, signed by author and artist, Charles Hobson, in pencil and numbered by Hobson, page size 11 x 12 inches, original USGS maps for the concertina binding, which when opened creates its own vista of mountain and valleys representing the maps that figure prominently in the Lopez story, covers made of paper over boards, paper reproducing a 1911 map of Bogota, publisher's slipcase of wood grained paper over boards, with brass toned metal label holder attached to spine of box holding white paper label with title and author in black, all suggesting a map cabinet, further housed in tan corrugated paper board slipcase, slipcase and board covers made by John De Merrit with assistance of Kris Langan, new. Priscilla Juvelis - Rare Books 56 - 23 2013 $2100

Binding – Lariviere

Doyle, Arthur Conan 1859-1930 *A Scadal in Bohemia.* Skokie: Black Cat Press, 1984. Limited to 240 copies signed by producer, 6.1 x 4.5 cm., cloth, title stamped on spine, decoration gilt stamped on front cover, binding by Lariviere, miniature bookplate of Kathryn Rickard, from the collection of Donn W. Sanford. Oak Knoll Books 303 - 53 2013 $125

Binding – Lauriat, Charles

Pyne, William Henry 1769-1843 *The History of the Royal Residences of Windsor Castle, St. James's Palace, Carlton House, Kensington Palace, Hampton Court....* London: printed for A. Dry...., 1819. First edition, large paper copy, 3 volumes, 100 hand colored aquatint plates, plate of Frogmore Exterior supplied from smaller copy, full green morocco by Charles E. Lauriat Boston, USA, covers with ruled borders enclosing spandrels of leafy sprigs and flower beads, spines in six compartments, four similarly decorated and lettered gilt, dates at foot, silk endpapers, bookplate of Thomas W. Lawson. Marlborough Rare Books Ltd. 218 - 121 2013 £7500

Rosenberg, Jakob *Rembrandt.* Cambridge: Harvard University Press, 1948. First edition, 2 volumes, attractive rose colored half morocco for Lauriat's of Boston (stamp signed), raised bands, spines gilt in compartments with central fleuron, top edge gilt, color frontispiece, 281 black and white plates by Rembrandt, spine slightly and uniformly darkened, mild soiling to cloth on one board, one corner little rubbed, otherwise fine set, signs of use to text or bindings. Phillip J. Pirages 63 - 397 2013 $150

Binding – Leighton, John

Cosway, Richard *Catalogue of a Collection of Miniatures by Richard Cosway...* N.P.: for private circulation only, 1883. Limited edition, limitation not stated, folio, (32)ff., frontispiece, 26 full page mounted original photographic plates, original half brown morocco, marbled boards, morocco corners, raised bands, gilt spine title, all edges gilt, bound by J. Leighton, Brewer St. (stamp on front flyleaf), inscribed "With Mr. Edward Joseph's Kindest regards New York 22 Dec. (18)83", bookplate of John Nolty, fine, rare. Jeff Weber Rare Books 171 - 78 2013 $750

Hort, Richard *The Embroidered Banner and Other Marvels.* London: John and Daniel A. Darling, 1850. First edition, color frontispiece and plates by Alfred Ashley, 8 pages catalog on smaller paper, 4 pages ads, original olive green cloth by Josiah Westley, gilt centerpiece "Libertad", spine decorated and lettered in gilt, signed JL (designed by John Leighton) some watermarking on front board. Jarndyce Antiquarian Booksellers CCV - 138 2013 £150

Binding – Lemardeley

Leconte de Lisle, C. R. M. *Les Erinnyes Tragedie Antique.* Paris: A. Romagnol Editeur, 1908. First edition, number 184 of 190 copies on Arches paper (total edition 301), 25 original etchings + 12 original woodcut decorations and wood engraved color frames on each page by Frank Kupka, 11.25 x 8 inches, 89 pages, very handsome lightly brown morocco, signed by by Lemardeley, front cover with inlaid original copper plate for one of the etchings, spine with 5 raised bands, gilt lettering, all edges gilt, beautifully designed dentelles, nicely designed double endleaves and edges of covers, housed in matching slipcase, very handsome in as new condition. Gemini Fine Books & Arts., Ltd. Art Reference & Illustrated Books - 2013 $2500

Binding – Lewis, Charles

Lefevre, Raoul *Le Recueil des Histoires de Troyes.* Bruges: William Caxton, 1473. First edition in French, small folio, Lettre batarde, lacking 32 printed leaves and two blanks, early 19th century brown straight grain morocco by Charles Lewis, gilt and blind ruled in geometric patterns, gilt inner dentelles, gilt edges, fine, unrestored, the missing leaves are internal and first and last printed leaves are present from the collection of the Duke of Roxburghe (sale 1812) of the third Earl Spencer (sale 1823), John Dent, with his notes (sale 1827), P. A. Hanrott (sale 1834) the Earl of Ashburnham (sale 1897); Richard Bennett with his bookplate and John Pierpont Morgan with his bookplate and shelfmark. Heritage Book Shop 50th Anniversary Catalogue - 62 2013 $950,000

Binding – Lobstein-Laurenchet

Cabet, Etienne *Voyage et Aventures de Lord Villiam Corisdall en Icorie.* Paris: Hippolyte Souverain, 1840. (1839). First edition, 2 volumes, modern half morocco, marbled sides, gilt lettering to spine by Lobstein-Laurenchet, repair to "Tables des Chapitres" of volume I, without loss of text. Heritage Book Shop 50th Anniversary Catalogue - 18 2013 $10,000

Binding – MacDonald, Annie

Field, Michael, Pseud. *Stephania: a Trialogue.* London: Elkin Mathews & John Lane, 1892. One of 250 copies, 197 x 146mm., 6 p.l., 100 pages, 4 leaves colophon and ads, titlepage with full woodcut border filled with intertwined pine branches and mistletoe, colophon with pine cone device, exceptionally attractive modelled goatskin by Mrs. Annie MacDonald of the Guild of Women Binders, front cover with large lobed frames, its upper corners enclosing binder's initial and date (1897), lower corners with daffodil blooms, large central panel showing an elaborately detailed scene featuring a woman with long, flowing hair entreating god mercury in his signature winged hat and sandals, two figures surmounted by imperial brown through which twines a sprig of mistletoe (design that appears in woodcut frame on titlepage), lower cover showing woman kneeling by man reclining on a couch, this scene enclosed in an oval beaded frame, flat spine with modelled title flanked by pine cone device at head and tail, green watered silk pastedowns, framed by unusual turn-ins decorated with gilt vines and calf circles painted green and blue, leather hinges, top edge gilt, others edges untrimmed, verso of front flyleaf with engraved bookplate of Charles Williston McAlpin, extra paper title labels tipped onto rear blank, 2 tiny red (ink?) marks to upper cover, inevitable offsetting from turn-ins to endpapers, once detached front flyleaf tipped onto front free endpaper, other trivial defects, still very attractive copy, binding lustrous and scarcely worn and leaves fresh and clean. Phillip J. Pirages 61 - 106 2013 $4500

Binding – MacDonald, James

Avery, C. Louise *Masterpieces of European Porcelain: a Catalogue of a Special Exhibition March 18- May 15 1949.* New York: printed by Marchbanks Press for The Metropolitan Museum of Art, 1949. One of 2000 copies, 290 x 222mm., attractive crimson crushed morocco by James MacDonald Co. of NY (stamp signed), covers with single gilt fillet border, upper cover with initials "F.W." in lower right corner, raised bands flanked by gilt rules, small gilt fleuron at head and tail of spine, vertical titling, densely gilt turn-ins, marbled endpapers; with 32 black and white photos; tipped to front pastedown is handwritten note to Mr. Wickes from Francis Henry Taylor, director of Metropolitan Museum, presenting this book in gratitude for Wickes' support of the Exhibition; couple of small marks to covers, but very fine with virtually no signs of use. Phillip J. Pirages 63 - 492 2013 $150

Binding – Maclehose

Campbell, Thomas 1777-1844 *The Poetical Works.* London: George Bell & Sons, 1875. Frontispiece, contemporary full olive brown morocco by Maclehose of Glasgow, corners and hinges very slightly rubbed, all edges gilt, very good, attractive copy. Jarndyce Antiquarian Booksellers CCIII - 458 2013 £120

Binding – Mason

The Sunday Scholars' Magazine and Juvenile Miscellany for 1847 and 1848. J. Bakewell, Methodist New Commission Book Room, 1847-1848. Volumes XXIV and XXV, 12mo., original half green sheep gilt by Mason of Thorne with his ticket, little rubbed, numerous woodcuts, scattered spotting, scarce. R. F. G. Hollett & Son Wesleyan Methodism - 51 2013 £65

Binding – May, G. H.

Byron, George Gordon Noel, 6th Baron 1788-1824 *(Hebrew Melodies) Fugitive Pieces and Reminiscences.* London: Whittaker, Treacher & Son, 1829. Half title, 12 page catalog, handsomely bound in later half tan calf by G. H. May of London, spine with raised bands and devices gilt, armorial bookplate of Gilbert Compton Elliot, top edge gilt, very good, handsome. Jarndyce Antiquarian Booksellers CCIII - 207 2013 £480

Byron, George Gordon Noel, 6th Baron 1788-1824 *Marino Faliero, Doge of Venice. The Prophecy of Dante, a Poem.* London: John Murray, 1821. First edition first issue, half title, final ad leaf, uncut in slightly later tan calf by G. H. May of London, spine with raised bands and gilt devices, armorial bookplate of Gilbert Compton Elliot, top edge gilt, very handsome, neatly tipped into prelims are 3 printed playbills, in excellent condition. Jarndyce Antiquarian Booksellers CCIII - 286 2013 £1800

Binding – McCarthy, Mary

McCarthy, Mary *Emily.* Boston: 2011. Artist's book, one of 20 copies from a total edition of 30, all on Lanaquarell 90lb hot pressed paper, each signed and numbered by artists, Mary McCarthy and Shirley Veenema, page size 5 x 7 inches, 56 pages, bound by McCarthy, white weave Asahi cloth on spine and Nasumi white Japanese paper over boards, title stamped in gold gilt on front panel, handmade pale green Thai Mango paper endpapers, custom made green suede open front box with button and silk tie close, box opens to book laid in on left side and an original collage used as the art which was scanned and bound with poems, text printed in 12 point imprint MT Shadow with Epson Stylus Pro 3800 printer, original images of mixed media and paper added to a single piece of Stonehenge paper were crafted by both artists responding to one another's work and to the verse, there are 25 images reproduced in with 12 of the 12 poems, bound book is laid in on one side of box and an original collage is laid in on the other side. Priscilla Juvelis - Rare Books 56 - 20 2013 $975

Binding – McKim, Alicia

McKim, Alicia *Greetings from California.* Denver: 2009. Artist's book, one of 50 copies, each containing five dioramas of three separate layers each of vintage postcards, printed on inkjet printer with pigmented ink on neutral pb paper, each copy numbered by author, page size 5 1/2 x 6 1/2 inches, carousel book, bound by the artist, paper over boards, blue cloth spine and blue ribbon ties, housed in publisher's stiff white board folding box. Priscilla Juvelis - Rare Books 56 - 21 2013 $500

Binding – Mercer, George

Trollope, Anthony 1815-1882 *Australia and New Zealand.* Melbourne: George Robertson, 1873. Second (First Australian) edition, 8vo., contemporary full polished calf by George Mercer, Geelong, Victoria, gilt arms of Geelong Anglican school within circle with motto, spine elaborately gilt, leather label, inner gilt dentelles, binder's ticket inside front cover. Howard S. Mott Inc. 262 - 152 2013 $275

Binding – Meunier, Charles

Pisan, Christine De *Poemes et Ballades du Temps Passe.* Paris: Imprime pour Charles Meunier "Maison du Livre", 1902. One of 115 copies, 100 of which were for sale (this #53), 320 x 233mm., with additional state of illustrated wrapper, woodcut tailpieces by Pierre Gusman and 50 large etchings by Albert Robida beginning each of the poems and ballads, and (bound in at back), extra suite of tailpieces on China paper as well as extra suite of etchings in two states (black and bistre) on China paper, (and tipped in at front), fine full page original signed pen and wash painting in sepia tones by Robida, text printed in red and black; remarkably attractive and animated 'Cuir-Cisele' binding of mahogany morocco over heavy bevelled boards by Charles Meunier (signed, with tiny inscription in leather at bottom of front cover, as well as stamp-signed gilt and dated 1904 on front turn-in), both covers with elaborately detailed sculpted scenes filling large brown calf panel, upper cover featuring golden sword hilt at top middle and skull at foot with swirling acanthus leaves emanating from each and framing head and foot of panel, large lyre at center acting as scabbard for sword and incorporating cartouche bearing title, and beneath that shield and troubadour's hat over crossed rifles and swords, all highlighted with silver or gold paint, this intricate frame laid down as whole on ground of sharkskin stippled in blind, lower cover with similar elements but very differently designed, featuring 'cuir-cisele' acanthus leaf cornerpieces and larger centerpiece medallion on much later ground of stippled sharkskin, centerpiece with shield over two crossed swords and lance, lute and horn hanging from latter these elements highlighted with silver or gold paint and encircled by laurel branch, raised bands, center spine panel with gilt titling, panels above and below it with simple gilt floral medallion, turn-ins consisting of light brown morocco punctuated with inlaid mahogany morocco overall, gold watered silk endleaves, marbled flyleaves, all edges gilt, original pictorial paper wrappers bound in, few trivial smudges, but very fine, impressive binding unusually lustrous and virtually unworn, text with almost no signs of use. Phillip J. Pirages 61 - 116 2013 $6500

Binding – Middleton, Bernard

Baldelli, Francesco *Di Polidoro Virgilio Da Vrbino de Gli Invetori Delle Cose, Libri Otto.* In Florenza: per Filippo Givnti, 1692. 4to., rebound by Bernard Middleton in contemporary style full panel English calf, endpapers renewed, first 8 leaves washed, title browned, text foxed in parts, overall very good, clean, crisp copy, Sir Kenelm Digby's copy with his gold signature and signature of John Shipton. James Tait Goodrich 75 - 17 2013 $1495

Cicero, Marcus Tullius *Here Begynneth the Prohemye Upon the Reducynge Both Out of Latyn as of Frensshe in to Our Englyssh Tongue of the Polytque Book....* Westminster: William Caxton, 1481. Editio princeps in English, 2 parts in one folio volume, complete but for two blanks 1 and 72 and retaining blank 11, complex and ornate Flemish lettre batarde for the text, bold English block letter for some proper names (type 3), rubricated, capitals painted red and red underscores and paragraph marks, 271 x 192, modern blind tooled reddish goatskin to antique style, clasps and catches by Bernard Middleton, old red edges, this copy is fine, presented to Sion College by Lord Berkeley, excellent copy. Heritage Book Shop   50th Anniversary Catalogue - 24   2013 $1,250,000

Martin, Benjamin *A Course of Lectures in Natural and Experimental Philosophy, Geography and Astronomy...* Reading: printed and sold by J. Newberry and C. Micklewright (and others in London and the provinces), 1743. First edition, 8 folding engraved plates, some browning and spotting, 4to., recent half calf by Bernard Middleton, early 20th century ownership inscription, sound. Blackwell's Rare Books   Sciences - 80   2013   £1500

Martin, Benjamin *Micrographia Nova; or a New Treatise n the Microscope and Microscopic Objects.* Reading: printed and sold by J. Newberry and C. Micklewright (and others in London),, 1742. First edition, 2 large folding engraved plates, both plates with long tears across middle repaired, some foxing, 4to., recent half calf by Bernard Middleton, sound. Blackwell's Rare Books   Sciences - 79   2013   £1800

Binding – Monsey, Therese

Bedier, Joseph *La Chanson de Roland.* Paris: Societe Ippocrate & Ses Amis, 1932. First Daragnes edition, number 49 of 135 examples, none were for sale, 29 original woodcuts with pochoir in very bright colors, printed on "Hollande" handmade paper, justification page signed in ink by artist and publisher, about 200 leaves, unique copy bound by master binder Therese Monsey signed by her, full red morocco with an Art Deco motif in gilt with onlaid mosaic of colored leathers, all edges gilt, handsome suede endleaves, original wrappers bound in, fit in chemise and slipcase by binder, overall 34 x 25cm., excellent condition. Gemini Fine Books & Arts., Ltd.   Art Reference & Illustrated Books - 2013 $2900

Binding – Morrell

Songs and Lyrics from the Dramatists 1533-1777. London: George Newnes; New York: Charles Scribner's Sons, 1905. 164 x 88mm., xiv, 242, (1) pages, 81 illustrations, decorative titlepage and head and tailpieces; excellent olive brown morocco by Morrell, heavily and flamboyantly decorated gilt in "Scottish Wheel" design, each cover with large central wheel of 20 compartments containing slender and elegant floral tools between two lines of dots radiating from central rosette, all contained within two scalloped concentric rings filled with dense and very regular stippling, wheel with tangent massed gilt circlets at top and bottom and then complex fleurons farther above and below featuring a very charming cherub, corners with triangular floral ornaments, other small tools surrounding central wheel, raised bands, spine compartments attractively gilt in playful scrolling manner with interwoven design including two shell ornaments, very wide turn-ins with intricate and complementary gilt decoration, pastedowns and free endpapers of bright crimson watered silk, all edges gilt, minor fading to leather, still lavish binding in very fine condition, internally with virtually no signs of use.   Phillip J. Pirages 61 - 119   2013 $750

Gleave, Tom *They Fell in the Battle A Roll of Honour of the Battle of Britain 10 July - 31 October 1940.* London: Royal Air Force Museum printed by Rampant Lions Press, 1980. First edition, limited to 80 signed copies, this #42, signed by Prince Philip, near fine in specially dyed goatskin binding with cross device stamped in gilt on front board and titles gilt on spine, top edge gilt, mild sun spine, printed on Arches Velin mould made paper, binding by Morrell in original blue cloth covered slipcase as issued, mildly sunned, folio.   By the Book, L. C.   36 - 2   2013 $1250

Herrick, Robert 1591-1674 *Hesperides or Works both Hvman and Divine by Robert Herrick. Together with His Noble Nvmbers or His Piouvs Pieces.* London: George Newnes Ltd., New York: Charles Scribner's Sons, 1902. 2 volumes, 165 x 110mm., 26 line drawings in black and white by Reginald Savage, as called for, leaf with printed copy of Robert Bridges poem "In a Volume of Herrick" tipped in at front, verso signed by Bridges and dated June 22, 1905; splendid burgundy morocco, lavishly and intricately gilt in "Scottish Wheel" design by Morrell (stamp-signed), covers with large central wheel of 20 compartments containing slender and elegant floral tools between two lines of dots radiating from central rosette, massed tiny circle tools at head and foot of wheel, triangle formed by small scalloped compartments and multiple tiny flowers above and below the centerpiece, large leaf frond tools at corners and many small tools accenting background, raised bands, interlocking floral garlands forming overall wreath in spine compartments, punctuated on either side by cluster of crescents and other small tools, elegantly and elaborately gilt turn-ins, ivory watered silk endleaves, all edges gilt; top of spine of second volume with barely perceptible loss of leather, silk endleaf in each volume with dampstain (no doubt from removal of bookplate), leaves little browned at edges because of quality of paper, else particularly attractive glittering bindings unusually lustrous. Phillip J. Pirages 61 - 120 2013 $1600

Macaulay, Thomas Babington Macaulay, 1st Baron 1800-1859 *Critical and Historical Essays, contributed to the Edinburgh Review.* London: Longman, Brown, Green, Longmans & Roberts, 1858. Ninth edition, 3 volumes, 229 x 152mm., extra illustrated with 122 engraved plates, primarily portraits, lovely contemporary honey brown crushed morocco, elegantly gilt, by Morrell (signed on front turn-in), covers with double gilt rule frame, raised bands, spine gilt in charming Arts and Crafts design of interlocking flowers and leaves gilt titling, turn-ins with gilt floral roll, top edges gilt, other edges rough trimmed, upper cover of third volume in one inch and two-three inch scratches (all shallow and well masked with dye), thin band of offsetting to free endpapers from gilt turn-ins (as usual), some plates with minor foxing and bit offset onto facing pages, otherwise quite handsome set in fine condition, text fresh and clean, bindings very lustrous and virtually no wear to joints or extremities. Phillip J. Pirages 61 - 121 2013 $850

Binding – Myers-Rich, Paulette

O'Driscoll, Dennis *All the Living.* Minnesota: Traffic Street Press, 2008. First edition, Letter H of 26 lettered copies (from a total edition of 49), initialled by printer and signed by author, large 8vo., original navy blue cloth, printed paper label on upper cover, printed letterpress and bound by Paulette Myers-Rich, etching by Niall Naessens inkjet printed in ultrachrome inks, fine in mustard and blue slipcase, printed paper label on spine. Maggs Bros. Ltd. 1442 - 259 2013 £250

O'Driscoll, Dennis *All the Living.* Minnesota: Traffic Street Press, 2008. Number 10 of 23 numbered copies (from total edition of 49) initialled by printer and signed by author, large 8vo., original blue decorative Japanese paper wrappers with printed paper label on upper cover, printed letterpress and bound by Paulette Myers-Rich, with etching by Nial Naessens, fine. Maggs Bros. Ltd. 1442 - 260 2013 £200

Binding – Noulhac

La Fontaine, Jean De 1621-1695 *Contes et Nouvelles en Vers.* Paris: De l'Imprimerie de P. Didot l'Aine, 1795. First printing of the Fragonard edition, 2 volumes, very fine honey brown crushed morocco, handsomely gilt by Noulhac (stamp-signed and dated 1902 on front turn-ins), covers with French fillet border and sawtooth edging with very elegant large floral ornaments in corners, raised bands, spines very attractively gilt in compartments formed by triple rules and featuring poppy centerpiece framed by leafy sprays wide and lovely turn-ins with gilt flowers linked by sprays and ribbons, marbled endpapers, all edges gilt, 3 full page portraits, one smaller portrait, one vignette, 20 very fine plates 'Before Letters" from the original edition, (16 of them after Fragonard), in addition 57 etchings "Before Letters) published in 1880 by Rouquette Based on Fragonard's 57 planned illustrations for the 1795 edition, along with 16 original sepia wash drawings done in 1869, slightest hint of foxing internally (perhaps half dozen leaves more foxed, but worst being just about negligible), perhaps 10 leaves expertly repaired short marginal tears (typically less than an inch and never anywhere near text), very special copy in beautiful condition, finely executed lovely bindings lustrous and virtually without wear, margins nothing short of vast, text and plates and inserted material all extraordinarily fresh and clean. Phillip J. Pirages 61 - 115 2013 $17,500

Binding – O'Mara, Allwyn

Richardson, Charles Leland *Selected Shore Plants of Southern California.* Pasadena: Weather Bird Press, 1992. Limited edition, one of 20 copies, rare deluxe edition, tall 8vo., 86 pages, 16 signed color pochoir prints, bound loose in separate case, original full cloth by Allwyn O'Mara printed paper spine labels, matching folding print case, housed within matching drop back box, fine, with the separate set of color plates, individually signed and numbered by Gerry, along with the original drawing of 'Sea Rocket', signed by author and Gerry. Jeff Weber Rare Books 171 - 134 2013 $2000

Binding – Parrot, Gray

Dodgson, Charles Lutwidge 1832-1898 *Through the Looking Glass and What Alice Found There.* West Hatfield: Pennyroyal Press, 1982. Limited to 350 copies signed by Barry Moser, illustrated by him with 92 wood engravings, including additional suite of illustrations, each one signed by Moser, printed on handmade paper in red and black, folio, publisher's half morocco lettered in gold and decorative paper boards, bound by Gray Parrot, fine, with additional suite of plates in cloth chemise, all housed in morocco backed and linen clamshell box (with slightest touch of fading). Aleph-Bet Books, Inc. 105 - 113 2013 $4000

Hecht, Anthony *Interior Skies: Late Poems from Liguria.* Camden: Two Ponds Press, 2011. Artist's book, 1 of 75 copies, all on paper made by Velke Losiny in Czech republic, each copy hand numbered, 38 pages, bound by Gray Parrot, his own teal blue pastepaper over boards with coral morocco spine, author and title in gold gilt stamped on spine, handsewn teal headbands housed in matching grey cloth clamshell box with title and author's initials stamped in gold gilt on coral morocco within rules, binder's ticket on lower inside turn-in, 2 engravings by Abigail Rorer printed on Zirkall paper by artist,. Priscilla Juvelis - Rare Books 55 - 25 2013 $950

Miller, Arthur *Death of a Salesman.* New York: Limited Editions Club, 1984. First edition, 1/500 copies, signed by author and artist, 4to., full brown morocco by Gray Parrot, fine in original slipcase, little worn, five etchings by Leonard Baskin. Second Life Books Inc. 183 - 275 2013 $750

Roscoe, William *Butterfly's ball and Grasshopper's feast.* Boston: Anne & David Bromer, 1977. Limited to 150 copies, this one of 25 deluxe copies, bound in full leather by Gray Parrot and containing a pocket in back with extra prints of woodcut illustrations, printed letterpress by Sarah Chamberlain at her press, she has signed and lettered this copy, 6 x 5 cm., full green leather stamped in gilt, (24) pages, from the collection of Donn W. Sanford. Oak Knoll Books 303 - 73 2013 $850

Binding – Partovi, Zahra

Rumi, Jalaluddin Mohammad *Letters.* New York: Vincent FitzGerald, 1987. One of 75 copies, each signed by artist, Agnes Murray and translator, Zahra Partovi, 3 colored lithographs each containing 12 plates, bound by Partovi accordion style, turquoise Japanese paper over boards with label on front panel on buff handmade paper with title printed in gold gilt, housed in salmon colored paper envelope with black silk tie and silver sealing wax, fine, calligraphy is by Jerry Kelly and printed by John Hutcheson, lithographs by Murray and editioned by Murray and Partovi at Bob Blackburn's Printmaking Workshop, page size is 9 1/3 x 6 1/2 inches, beautiful book. Priscilla Juvelis - Rare Books 56 - 9 2013 $700

Binding – Patron, Rene

Hugo, Victor 1802-1865 *The Hunchback of Notre Dame.* Philadelphia: Carey, Lea and Blanchard, 1834. First American edition, one of only 1000 copies, 2 volumes, octavo, original quarter blue cloth over drab boards, untrimmed, light toning and foxing throughout as expected, heavy crease to lower corner of front board of volume one, some other minor edgewear, remnants of printed paper labels on untouched cloth spines, original owner's dated (1835) signature on titlepages, very good, rarely found in original binding, chemised and housed within elegantly handsome modern ful blue goatskin, gilt decorated, two spine slipcase by Rene Patron. David Brass Rare Books, Inc. Holiday 2012 Chapter Five - DB 02091 2013 $3850

Binding – Pax, Ben

Vollmann, William T. *The Grave of Lost Stories.* Sacramento: CoTangent Press, 1993. Artist's book, one of 15 deluxe copies only, 13 of which are for sale, all on Johannot paper, each signed and numbered by artist/author and binder, from an edition of 200, 185 regular edition, bound by Ben Pax, steel and grey marble box (tomb) fitted to custom steel hinge by means of a copper sheet riveted to the steel and then crimped upward to form a pan, hinge is powder-coated black as is the interior, front cover incised with title, author's initials and Poe's dates, copy number appears in roman numeral on back cover, along foredge of box (tomb) 13 cow's teeth have been set in handmade silver bezels, inside covers each have four brass and copper rods (oxidized green), book itself is bound in boards with linen spine which are "leafed, and variegated and painted in metallic fungoid patterns over which the author has painted a female figure to represent one of the stories", gessoed boards are copper colored and female is in blue with onlays of four small white bones outlining skeleton, book lays into marble box (tomb), the four illustrations are hand colored by author who has also made a number of small revisions in text, titlepage printed in three colors, guards of black and gold gilt Japanese paper. Priscilla Juvelis - Rare Books 55 - 26 2013 $5000

Binding – Percival, George

Craighead, Meinrad *The Mother's Birds. Images for a Death and a Birth.* Worcester: Stanbrook Abbey Press, 1976. XXV/XXX special copies (of an edition of 235 copies), printed on Chatham handmade paper and signed by author and printer, 20 full page reproductions of charcoal drawings by author, 4to., original black morocco by George Percival, backstrip gilt lettered there is large circle blind tooled in front cover and correspondingly large square to rear cover, De Wint coffee mouldmade paper endpapers, untrimmed, boards slipcase, fine. Blackwell's Rare Books B174 - 386 2013 £285

Binding – Period Binders

Woodall, John *The Surgeons Mate or Military and Domestique Surgery...* London: Robert Young (J. Legate? and E. Purslowe) for Nicholas Bourne, 1639. Modern calf by Period bookbinders, blind tooling on boards, done in contemporary style, early signature of John Spence, some marginalia, Bath Medical Library with few marginal stamps. James Tait Goodrich   S74 - 240   2013 $3750

Binding – Petit

Beaumarchais, Pierre Augustin Caron De *Le Folle Journee, ou Le Mariage de Figaro.* Paris: Chez Ruault Librarie, Pres. le Theatre, 1785. First edition, first issue, octavo, five plates after Saint Quentin, half title present, 19th century full green morocco by Petit, triple gilt ruled borders, spine gilt in compartments and with central flower devices, gilt spine lettering, gilt board edges and turn-ins, densely gilt burgundy morocco doublures, marbled endpapers, all edges gilt, morocco edged slipcase, sumptuous presentation for this scarce title.   Heritage Book Shop   Holiday Catalogue 2012 - 10   2013 $2000

Binding – Poehlmann, Jo Anna

Poehlmann, Jo Anna *Escargot Under Glass. A Day in the Life of a Forest Snail.* Milwaukee: 2011. Artist's book, one of 35 copies on white stock, hand numbered by artist on verso of titlepage, page size 1 7/16 inches in diameter, 34 pages, bound by artist accordion fold with card stock as titlepage and endpage, housed in small metal circular box with glass lid showing cover of book, hand painted and lettered by Jo Anna Pohelmann, then copied and then hand colored by her, charming homage.   Priscilla Juvelis - Rare Books   56 - 29   2013 $140

Binding – Prat, May Rosina

Wilde, Oscar   1854-1900 *Essays, Criticisms and Reviews.* London: privately printed, 1901. First edition, one of 300 copies (ths #250), 258 x 188mm., unusual red and crimson morocco by May Rosina Prat (stamp signed in blind "M R I" and dated "1903" on rear doublure), covers tooled in black with three vertical rows of stylized tulips, each row within a panel formed by plain rules, these floral rows set against red morocco, but with undecorated vertically oriented panels of crimson in between red, raised bands, spine titling in black, red morocco doublures with black ruled frame and tulip cornerpieces, in a lightly worn matching morocco trimmed slipcase (almost certainly by the binder), first few and last few leaves with vague rumpling, otherwise especially fine, text quite clean and fresh, binding unworn.   Phillip J. Pirages   63 - 494   2013 $750

Binding – Pratt

A View of London and Westminster, or the Town Spy. (bound with) *A Second part of a View of London and Westminster.* London: sold by T. Warner and by the booksellers, 1728. London; sold by J. Isted... and by all booksellers, 1725. Fourth edition? and first edition, 2 parts in one volume, 8vo., pages (iv), 59, (1) blank; half title, folding engraved plate, (ii), 62, titlepage with repaired tear, no loss of surface and text unaffected, 19th century calf gilt by W. Pratt, spine sometime neatly repaired, very good.   Marlborough Rare Books Ltd.   218 - 95   2013   £3850

Salisbury, Robert Cecil *The Copies of a Letter to the Right Honourable, the Earl of Leycester, Lieutenant General of all Her Majesties Forces in the United Provinces of the Low Countreys...* London: Christopher Barker, 1586. 4to., without final blank leaf, woodcut arms on A, verso, facing titlepage, large woodcut initials, this copy is variant A, recto starting "Albeit with earnest...", bound by Pratt in 19th century brown crushed morocco with gilt arms on both covers, all edges gilt, bookplate of Fairfax of Cameron, fine copy.   Second Life Books Inc.   182 - 207   2013 $4000

Binding – Presentation

Armstrong, John   1709-1799 *The Art of Preserving Health.* London: printed for A. Millar, 1744. Rare first edition, Tall large paper copy, tall 4to., blue levant morocco with lavish gilt tooling and borders and centerpieces, spine gilt in compartments and red burgundy label, all edges gilt, fine presentation binding, previous owners bookplates, including W. N. Elliot, Graham Pollard,.   James Tait Goodrich   75 - 12   2013 $995

Maxwell, Colonel Montgomery *My Adventures.* London: Henry Colburn, 1845. First edition, 2 volumes, 200 x 126mm., special very attractive presentation binding of contemporary Oxblood pebble grain morocco, elaborately gilt, covers with blind ruled borders and complex gilt frame featuring shell head and tailpieces, scrolling corners and sides, many floral tools, raised bands, spine compartments gilt with flower basket centerpiece and leaf frond corners, blind tooled turn-ins, all edges gilt, frontispiece portraits, ink presentation inscription for Reginald Porter from friend, James Nelson Palmer on his leaving Eton Xmas 3rd 1846, spines slightly and uniformly sunned, gilt still bright, one board with little dulling because of leather preservative, otherwise very fine, clean, fresh, smooth internally in handsome binding with virtually no wear.   Phillip J. Pirages   63 - 332   2013 $600

Binding – Putnams

Cinderella *Cinderella.* London: William Heinemann: Philadelphia: J. B. Lippincott, 1919. One of 850 copies signed, this #417, one of 525 on English hand made paper, 286 x 229, illustrations by Arthur Rackham, very attractive red three quarter morocco (stamp signed "Putnams" along front turn-in), raised bands, spine handsomely gilt in compartments formed by plain and decorative rules, quatrefoil centerpiece surrounded by densely scrolling cornerpieces, sides and endleaves of rose colored linen, top edge gilt, with one color plates and silhouette illustrations, tiny portion of one spine band and of leather at head of spine worn away, very slight hints of wear to corners and joints, faint offsetting from illustrations (never severe, but more noticeable in those opening with facing illustrations, otherwise excellent copy. Phillip J. Pirages 63 - 377 2013 $1250

Goldsmith, Oliver 1730-1774 *The Vicar of Wakefield.* Philadelphia: David McKay Co., 1929. One of 775 copies signed by artist, including 575 for Engalnd (ours being #95 of 200 copies for America), 267 x 206mm., illustrations by Arthur Rackham, very attractive red three quarter morocco stamp signed "Putnams" along front turn-in, raised bands, spine handsomely gilt in compartments formed by plain and decorative rules, quatrefoil centerpiece surrounded by densely scrolling cornerpieces, sides and endleaves or rose colored linen, top edge gilt, other edges untrimmed and mostly unopened, 12 color plates by Rackham, front board with insignificant small, round spot to cloth, very fine, unusually bright and clean inside and out, almost no signs of use. Phillip J. Pirages 63 - 378 2013 $2900

Grimm, The Brothers *The Fairy Tales of the Brothers Grimm.* London: Constable and Co. Ltd., 1909. One of 750 copies signed by artist, Arthur Rackham, this #732, 292 x 235mm., very attractive red three quarter morocco (stamp signed Putnams), raised bands, spine handsomely gilt in compartments formed by plain and decorative rules, quatrefoil centerpiece surrounded by densely scrolling cornerpieces, sides and endleaves of rose colored linen, top edge gilt (front joint and headcap very expertly repaired by Courtland Benson), titlepage with pictorial frame, numerous black and white illustrations in text, 10 full page black and white illustrations, 40 color plates by Arthur Rackham, mounted on cream stock and protected by lettered tissue guards, cover with faint minor soiling, just hint of wear to corners, small corner tear to one plate, 2 tissue guards with minor creasing or chipped edges, otherwise fine, handsome binding, text and plates clean and fresh, bright. Phillip J. Pirages 63 - 379 2013 $4500

Keats, John 1795-1821 *Poems.* Vale Press, 1898. One of 217 copies, 232 x 145nn, 2 volumes, woodcut white-vine initials and intricate full borders on opening leaves by Charles Ricketts, handsome contemporary oxblood crushed morocco (signed "G. P. Putnam's sons" on front turn-ins), covers gilt with graceful leafy frame of twining veins accented with small floral tools and dots as well as intricate floral sprig cornerpieces, raised bands, double ruled spine compartments repeating floral sprig as centerpiece surrounded by small tools and leafy branch cornerpieces, French fillets on turn-ins, Japanese vellum endpapers, top edges gilt, matching felt lined morocco slipcase with slightly soiled paper sides and matching morocco pull-off protective spine cover with gilt tilting, hint of darkening at edges of free endpapers because of turn in glue (as usual), two pages with very minor soling perhaps during printing, but extremely fine set, text and lovely bindings virtually pristine. Phillip J. Pirages 61 - 109 2013 $4500

Some British Ballads. London: Constable & Co., 1919. One of 575 copies signed by artist, this #379, 286 x 229mm., very attractive red engraved plates morocco (stamp signed Putnams"), raised bands, spine handsomely gilt in compartments formed by plain and decorative rules, quartrefoil centerpiece, surrounded by densely scrolling cornerpieces, sides and endleaves of rose colored linen, top edge gilt, with titlepage, vignette, black and white illustrations in text and 17 color plates by Arthur Rackham, all tipped on and with letterpress guards, morocco bookplate of W. A. M. Burden; only most trivial signs of use externally, exceptionally fine inside and out, especially lustrous handsome gilt binding. Phillip J. Pirages 63 - 382 2013 $1500

Binding – Ramage

Santos, Francisco De Los *The Escurial; or a Description of that Wonder of the World for Architecture and Magnificence of Structure.* London: printed for T. Collins and J. Ford, 1671. First edition in English, small 4to., 19th century polished calf by Ramage, gilt decorations and lettering, all edges gilt, from the library of Hispanophile Richard Ford (1796-1858) with his bookplate and signature dated 1836, later small bookplate of Henry Huth with clipped description of this book from Sotheby's Huth Sale catalog laid in, some light foxing, margins trimmed little close in places, very good. The Brick Row Book Shop Miscellany Fifty-Nine - 37 2013 $3000

Binding – Relfe Brothers

Kingsley, Charles 1819-1875 *The Water Babies.* Macmillan, 1891. Full scarlet calf gilt prize binding by Relfe Brothers, few slight scratches, 100 woodcut illustrations by Linley Sambourne. R. F. G. Hollett & Son Children's Books - 324 2013 £50

Binding – Remnant & Edmonds

Byron, George Gordon Noel, 6th Baron 1788-1824 *The Poetical Works.* London: John Murray, 1855-1856. New edition, 6 volumes, half titles, frontispiece, 32 page catalog (Feb. 1871 volume VI, original pink cloth by Remnant & Edmonds, few slight marks, spines fading to brown, nice crisp set.   Jarndyce Antiquarian Booksellers   CCIII - 82   2013   £120

Liebig, Justus   *Researches on the Chemistry of Food.* printed for Taylor and Walton, 1847.   First edition, slightly foxed at either end, 8vo., original cloth with elaborate blind-stamped panel on sides, spine lettered gilt by Remnant and Edmonds, slightly worn at extremities, signature of Rev. Chas. Popham Miles, Glasgow 1848, inside front cover very good.   Blackwell's Rare Books   Sciences - 74   2013   £200

Binding – Riley, E., & Son

Tucker, Abraham   *Vocal Sounds by Edward Search, Esq.* London: printed by T. Jones and sold by T. Payne, 1773. First edition, small 8vo., 195h century half maroon morocco by E. Riley & Son, very good.   Blackwell's Rare Books 172 - 143   2013   £1500

Binding – Riser, Rudolf

Beckett, Samuel 1906-1989   *Fizzles/Foirades.* London: Petersburg Press, 1976.   First English edition, artist's book limited signed edition, one of 250 copies, each with 33 original etchings by Jasper Johns (26 lift-ground aquatints, most with etching, soft-ground-etching, drypoint, screenprint and/or photogravure), 5 etchings, 1 soft ground etching and 1 aquatint, 31 in black, 2 (endpapers) in color and 1 lithograph (box lining) in color, signed by author and artist, all on handmade paper by Richard de Bas, watermarked with initials of Beckett and signature of Johns, 62 unnumbered folios (including endpapers and excluding binding support leaves), bound by Rudolf Riser in Cologne, as issued, in paper wrappers, accordion fold around support leaves with colored etchings as endpapers, housed in tan cloth clamshell box with Johns' colored etchings in green, purple and orange laid down in inside trays with distinctive purple silk pull visible when box closed, set in 16pt. Caslon Old Face and handprinted by Frequent and Bawdier in Paris.   Priscilla Juvelis - Rare Books   55 - 12   2013 $35,000

Binding – Rivage

Legendre, Adrien Marie   *Essai sue la Theorie des Nombres.* Paris: Courcier, 1808-1825.   Second edition, with the two supplements, 3 parts in 1 volume, folding engraved plate to first supplement, occasional spotting, 1 gathering browned in first part, 4to., contemporary green speckled calf, gilt tooled borders on sides, stamp of College Royal de St. Louis, Universite de France, wreathed and crowned at centre of upper cover, flat spine gilt with twin red lettering pieces, marbled edges, matching pastedowns and front free endpapers, by Rivage with his ticket, spine and lower cover unevenly faded, head of spine little worn, good. Blackwell's Rare Books   Sciences - 70   2013   £500

Binding – Riviere

Alken, Henry   *Ideas, Accidental and Incidental to Hunting and Other Sports...* London: Thomas M'Lean, n.d., 1826-1830.   First edition, early issue, plates dated 1826-1830 and watermarked 1831-32, upright folio, letterpress title and 42 hand colored etchings, full forest green crushed morocco by Riviere or Sangorski & Sutcliffe (circa 1940), occasional mild spots to margins not affecting imagery, neat professional repair to closed margin tear on plate #6, otherwise beautiful copy.   David Brass Rare Books, Inc.   Holiday 2012 Chapter Two - DB 02149   2013 $16,500

Amory, Thomas   *The Life of John Bucle, Esq.* London: printed for T. Becket and P. A. Dehondt and T. Cadell, 1770. New edition, 4 volumes, 12mo., few minor spots, late 19th/early 20th century sprinkled and polished tan calf by Riviere, rebacked to style by Chris Weston, board edges slightly rubbed, ink ownership inscription 'B. Gaskell' with 'Thomas House' added in volume 4, armorial bookplate of Charles George Milnes Gaskell.   Unsworths Antiquarian Booksellers   28 - 62   2013   £300

Apperley, Charles James 1777-1843   *The Life of a Sportsman.* London: Rudolph Ackerman, 1842.   First edition, first issue, with plates at pages 13, 14, 15 and 55, mounted, fine, bound without 8 pages of ads at end, large 8vo., full red morocco, front hinge expertly and almost imperceptibly repaired, upper and lower covers gilt ruled, elaborately gilt decorated spine and inner dentelles, raised bands, top edge gilt by Riviere & Son, handsome copy, cloth slipcase.   Howard S. Mott Inc.   262 - 9   2013 $2650

Burns, Robert 1759-1796   *Poems, Chiefly in the Scottish Dialect.* Edinburgh: printed for the author and sold by William Creech, 1787.   Second edition, half title, frontispiece, uncut in later full scarlet rushed morocco by Riviere & Son, gilt spine, border and dentelles, top edge gilt, very good, close to fine.   Jarndyce Antiquarian Booksellers CCIII - 48   2013   £3800

Byron, George Gordon Noel, 6th Baron   1788-1824
Childe Harold's Pilgrimage. Canto the Fourth. London: John Murray, 1818. First edition, 4th issue, 12 page catalog preceding title, final ad leaf, uncut in original pale blue boards, paper label, small ink stain on front board, spine and hinges little worn, armorial bookplate of Chadwyck-Healey, good copy, custom made blue morocco and cloth slipcase by Riviere & son.   Jarndyce Antiquarian Booksellers   CCIII - 148   2013   £300

Byron, George Gordon Noel, 6th Baron   1788-1824
Ode to Napoleon Bonaparte. London: printed for John Murray by W. Bulmer and Co., 1814. First edition, retains often missing half title, final ad leaf, slight spotting to prelims, handsomely bound in full royal blue crushed morocco by Riviere & Son, gilt spine, borders and dentelles, armorial bookplate of Chadwyck-Healey, very good, attractive copy.   Jarndyce Antiquarian Booksellers   CCIII - 189   2013   £850

Chaucer, Geoffrey   1340-1400 *The Workes of Geoffrey Chaucer...* London: printed by Thomas Godfray, 1532. First collected edition, folio in sixes, black letter, 48 lines plus headline, double columns, several sets of decorated initials and lombards used as initials, few capital spaces with guides, 15 woodcuts in Canterbury Tales, handsomely bound by Riviere & Son, decoratively panelled in blind, spine in six, compartments with five raised bands, gilt lettered in two compartments and decoratively tooled in blind in remaining four, board edges and turn-ins ruled in blind, all edges gilt, few early ink annotations, house in custom full brown morocco clamshell.   Heritage Book Shop   50th Anniversary Catalogue - 21   2013 $100,000

Chaucer, Geoffrey   1340-1400 *The Workes of Geffrey Chaucer.* London: imprinted by John Kyngston for John Wight, 1561. Fifth collected edition, first issue, 22 woodblocks in "The Prologues" taken from blocks used by Caxton in his second edition of Canterbury Tales, folio, 22 woodcuts of Pilgrims in "the Prologues" and woodcut of a knight on a horse at head of "The Knightes Tale", large and small historiated and decorative initials and their ornaments, black letter, 56 lines, double columns; late 19th century crimson morocco by Riviere, covers with gilt and toll tool border enclosing a central olive wreath and elaborate cornerpieces composed of scroll work and spreading olive branches, remaining field seme with cinquefoils, spine in seven compartments with six raised bands, lettered in gilt in two compartments, rest decoratively tooled in gilt with repeated olive leaf motif, board edges and turn-ins decoratively tooled in gilt, all edges gilt, marbled endpapers, pastedowns with decorative gilt tooling, title creased and lightly soiled with small repair in outer blank margin, lower corner of second leaf renewed, affecting catchword on recto and two letters on verso, closed tear through lower half of divisional title to "Canterbury Tales", closed tear to A2 of "The Prologues" affecting 8 lines of text in first column and another closed tear at lower margin, F2 with small paper repair to margin and closed tear just touching text 2U2 with paper fault affecting one word in bottom line of text on recto and verso, few additional small marginal tears or repairs, not affecting text, occasional early ink underlining and markings, early ink signature of James Reo (faded) on title, wonderful copy, from the library of C. W . Dyson Perrins and William Foyle, with their bookplates.   Heritage Book Shop   50th Anniversary Catalogue - 22   2013 $65,000

Cleveland, John *The Idol of the Clownes or Insurrection of Wat the Tyler, with His Priests Baal and Straw...* London: printed in the year, 1654. Second edition, small 8vo., (12), 154 pages, full polished calf, spine gilt, edges gilt, by Riviere, without final blank L4, front cover cleanly detached, few very tiny repairs.   Joseph J. Felcone Inc.   English and American Literature to 1800 - 7   2013 $1200

Combe, William 1742-1823 *The Three Tours of Dr. Syntax: In Search of the Picturesque, In Search of Consolation, in Search of a Wife.* London: R. Ackermann's Repository of Arts, 1812. 1820. 1821. First editions in book form, 3 separately published volumes, very handsome gilt decorated early 20th century dark blue crushed morocco by Riviere & Son (stamp signed), cover with French fillet border, spines lavishly and elegantly gilt in compartments with flower filled cornucopia centerpiece surrounded by small tools and volute cornerpieces, inner gilt dentelles, top edge gilt, other edges untrimmed, one woodcut illustration, one engraved tailpiece and 80 artfully hand colored aquatint plates by Thomas Rowlandson, engraved armorial bookplate of John Taylor Reynolds; spines uniformly more black than blue, four of the covers with just hint of soiling, most plates with variable offsetting (usually faint but noticeable in half dozen cases), other trivial imperfections, extremely desirable set, strong impressions and good coloring of first edition plates, spacious margins, lovely bindings, lustrous and virtually unworn. Phillip J. Pirages 63 - 409 2013 $4500

Cruikshank, George *The Bachelor's Own Book.* London: D. Bogue, 1844. First edition, colored state, intermediate issue with misspelling "Persuit" on title corrected, but "Amusememt" not corrected, oblong 8vo., full crushed red morocco by Riviere & Son, original colored front wrapper bound in, spine gilt, inner gilt dentelles, title leaf + 24 colored etchings on 12 leaves, evidence of removed bookplate, else fine. Howard S. Mott Inc. 262 - 37 2013 $600

Davenant, William 1606-1668 *The Works of Sr. William Davenant...* London: by T. N. for Henry Herringman, 1673. First collected edition, folio, portrait, turn of the century red levant morocco, gilt arabesque centerpiece on covers, all edges gilt, by Riviere, very skillfully rebacked, though new leather at joints and on cords has uniformly faded, unusually fine, fresh, wide margined copy, with fine impression of the portrait, leather tipped fleece lined slipcase (edges rubbed), the Duke of Beaufort, E. F. Leo and A. E. Newton copy with their bookplates. Joseph J. Felcone Inc. Books Printed before 1701 - 27 2013 $2200

Davenant, William 1606-1668 *The Works of Sr. William Davenant Kt...* London: by T. N. for Henry Herringman, 1673. First collected edition, folio, portrait, turn of the century red levant morocco, gilt arabesque centerpiece on covers, all edges gilt, by Riviere, very skillfully rebacked, though the new leather at joints and on cords has uniformly faded, unusually fine, fresh, wide margined copy with fine impression of the portrait, leather tipped fleece lined slipcase, edges rubbed, bookplates of Duke of Beaufort, E. F. Leo, A. E. Newton. Joseph J. Felcone Inc. English and American Literature to 1800 - 12 2013 $2200

Defoe, Daniel *The Dyet of Poland, a Satyr.* printed at Dantzick, 1705. 4to. some light spotting and browning, few small expert paper repairs, bound by Riviere in full crushed red morocco, elaborate gilt borders and dentelles, raised bands, gilt compartments, armorial bookplate of William Henry Smith, Viscount Hambleden, all edges gilt, very good, handsome. Jarndyce Antiquarian Booksellers CCIV - 107 2013 £850

Dickens, Charles 1812-1870 *Great Expectations.* London: Chapman and Hall, 1861. Volume I second impression, volume II fourth impression, volume 3 first impression, 3 volumes, later inserted half title volume I, engraved title and plates by Pailthorpe, occasional light browning in prelims, slightly later full brown crushed morocco by Riviere, spines gilt in compartments, gilt borders and dentelles, armorial bookplates of William H. R. Saunders, top edge gilt, very good, handsome. Jarndyce Antiquarian Booksellers CCV - 86 2013 £4500

Dickens, Charles 1812-1870 *Nicholas Nickleby.* London: Chapman & Hall, 1839. First edition, half title, frontispiece, 39 plates by Phiz, uncut in later full olive green crushed morocco by Riviere & Son, gilt spine, borders and dentelles, front wrapper to part XIV bound in at end, armorial bookplate of John Nevill Cross, top edge gilt, very good, handsome copy. Jarndyce Antiquarian Booksellers CCV - 88 2013 £850

Dodgson, Charles Lutwdige 1832-1898 *Alice's Adventures in Wonderland.* London: Macmillan & co., 1866. First edition, 8vo., early full polished blue calf with triple gilt rules by Riviere with original covers and spine bound in at rear, spine has raised bands in 6 compartments with gold flower design, all edges gilt, gilt dentelles, fine, 42 illustrations by John Tenniel, remainder of the unacceptable first issue sheets were sent to New York and bound by Appleton, with new titlepage, tipped in to this copy is quirky 2 sided letter by author using his characteristic purple ink, dated Feb. 8 1888. Aleph-Bet Books, Inc. 104 - 113 2013 $12,500

Flatman, Thomas *Poems and Songs.* London: printed for Benjamin Tooke at the Ship in St. Paul's church-yard, 1682. 8vo., frontispiece, small mark to foot of frontispiece, minor tear to foot of titlepage, slight browning, bound without prelim blank but with two final errata and ad leaves, manuscript correction from errata on page 101, bound by Riviere and son in full dark red crushed morocco gilt, ruled border, elaborate gilt decorated spine, inner gilt cornerpiece decoration, marbled endpapers, slight rubbing to board edges, corners little bruised, contemporary signature at head of titlepage, bookplates of E. M. Cox and John Drinkwater, latter adding bibliographical pencil note to leading endpaper, all edges gilt, variant with M74 and the ad, in a different setting, beginning on verso. Jarndyce Antiquarian Booksellers CCV - 102 2013 £620

FINE BINDINGS

Goldsmith, Oliver   1730-1774   *The Vicar of Wakefield.*   London/New York: Macmillan, 1922.   Reprint, 8vo., finely bound by Riviere in brown leather with cottage motif on front cover and steaming bowl with clay pipe on rear cover, all edges gilt, gilt ruled turn-ins, spine creased at joints, generally clean and sound, fine etched bookplate for Beatrice E. Smith, signed by "H. Martyn", handsome copy, illustrations by Hugh Thomson.   Ed Smith Books   75 - 32   2013 $375

Johnstone, Charles   *Chrysal; or the Adventures of a Guinea in America.*   London: T. Becket, 1760.   First edition, 2 volumes, large 12mo., 19th century antique mottled calf by Riviere, gilt, expertly rebacked, old backs laid down, leather labels, raised bands, inner gilt dentelles, fine, bookplates of John Leveson Douglas Stewart and A. Edward Newton, slipcase.   Howard S. Mott Inc.   262 - 80   2013 $500

Lee, Sidney   *A Life of William Shakespeare.*   London: Smith, Elder & Co., 1898.   Second edition, octavo, 2 photogravure plates, and four additional plates, bound by Riviere & son (stamp signed gilt on front turn-in), full brown crushed levant morocco expertly and almost invisibly rebacked, original spine laid down, front cover set with large oval miniature scene on ivory under glass by Miss C.B. Currie (stamped in gilt on front doublure: "Miniatures by C. B. Currie") within elaborate gilt frame incorporating onlaid red morocco gilt roses, spine in 6 compartments with five raised bands, gilt lettered in two compartments, with gilt date at foot, remaining four compartments decoratively tooled in gilt in similar design with onlaid red morocco gilt roses, board edges ruled in gilt, turn-ins ruled in gilt with gilt floral ornaments with onlaid red morocco gilt roses, green watered silk doublures and liners, top edge gilt, signed in gilt on fore-edges of front and rear boards "Cosway Binding" and "Invented by J. H. Stonehouse", superb example, inserted certificate leaf signed by Stonehouse and Currie and numbered in ink identifies this as being copy "No. 804 of the Cosway Bindings invented by J. H. Stonehouse, with Miniatures on Ivory by Miss Currie".   Heritage Book Shop Holiday Catalogue 2012 - 32   2013 $13,500

Leigh, Percival   *The Comic English Grammar...*   London: Richard Bentley, 1840.   First edition, frontispiece plate, tailpiece and 48 illustrations after drawings by John Leech, very attractive polished calf, handsomely gilt by Riviere & Son (signed), covers bordered with gilt French fillet and small roundel cornerpieces, raised bands, spine gilt in compartments featuring elegant floral cornerpieces, sidepieces and centerpiece with surrounding small dots and stars, decorative bands at head and foot, red morocco label, gilt inner dentelles, marbled endpapers, top edge gilt, front joint very expertly repaired, original cloth bound in at end, morocco bookplate of Alexander McGrigor, very fine in especially pretty binding.   Phillip J. Pirages   63 - 312   2013 $350

Leigh, Percival   *The Comic Latin Grammar.*   London: Charles Tilt, 1840.   First edition, 197 x 127mm., very attractive polished calf, handsomely gilt by Riviere & Son (signed on verso of front endpaper), covers bordered with French fillet and small roundel cornerpieces, raised bands, spine gilt in compartments, featuring elegant floral cornerpieces, sidepieces, and centerpiece with surrounding small dots and stars, decorative bands at head and foot, red morocco label, gilt inner dentelles, marbled endpapers, top edge gilt, 54 illustrations in text and 8 engraved plates after drawings by John Leech, joints slightly flaked (front joint just beginning to crack at head and foot), one inch tear in fore edge of one leaf (well away from text), excellent copy in very pretty binding, covers quite lustrous and text smooth, fresh and clean, bookplate of Alexander McGrigor.   Phillip J. Pirages   63 - 313   2013 $350

More, Thomas   1478-1535   *The Debellacyon of Salem and Bizance.*   London: printed by W. Rastell, 1533.   First edition, 2 parts in one small octavo volume, bound without final blank leaf, this copy has leaf C8 in probable facsimile and lacks rare bifolium, Black Letter, title within woodcut border, woodcut historiated initials, early 20th century brown crushed levant morocco by Riviere and Son, covers ruled in gilt and blind with gilt corner ornaments, spine ruled in gilt and blind decoratively tooled and lettered gilt in compartments, board edges ruled in gilt, turn-ins ruled in gilt and blind, all edges gilt, marbled endpapers, washed prelims and few other leaves with slight discoloration at upper corners, leaf a4 with crease marks to covers and short tear at upper margin, final leaves slightly discolored, excellent copy of this extremely rare work, from the library of William Foyle with his bookplate, quarter brown morocco clamshell.   Heritage Book Shop   50th Anniversary Catalogue - 74   2013 $12,500

More, Thomas   1478-1535   *A Frutefull Pleasaunt & Wittie Worke...called Utopia.*   London: Abraham Vele, 1556.   Second edition in English second state with colophon on (S8), 12mo., 144 leaves, many misnumbered, full red morocco by Riviere and Sons, covers ruled in gilt, spine lettered gilt in compartments, cream endpapers, all edges gilt, former signature and bookplate of W. A. Foyle, title with some soiling, overall beautiful copy, elegantly bound, housed in custom black morocco clamshell, gilt stamped.   Heritage Book Shop   50th Anniversary Catalogue - 75   2013 $45,000

Morris, William   1834-1896   *The Earthly Paradise.*   London: Reeves and Turner, 1890.   Revised edition, octavo. titlepage vignette after design by Burne-Jones, bound by Riviere & Son in full green morocco with gilt central floral design and single gilt fillet border on covers, gilt title and floral design on spine, gilt fillet on turn-ins, top edges gilt, marbled endpapers rubbing to front joint, spine little toned, else near fine.   Between the Covers Rare Books, Inc. Philosophy - 337508   2013 $350

Palliser, Fanny Marryat 1805-1878 *History of Lace.* London: Sampson Low, Son & Marston, 1865. First edition, 209 x 140mm., iv, 460 pages, very attractive blue-gray crushed morocco by Riviere & Son (stamp signed), covers with blind and gilt rules enclosing wide gilt filigree frame, raised bands, spine panels gilt in similar intricate pattern, gilt inner dentelles, marbled endpapers, all edges gilt, original purple and gilt cloth bound in at rear, engraved frontispiece, more than 150 illustrations in text and 26 plates of lace patterns, small portions of joints and extremities very slightly rubbed (and carefully refurbished), spine sunned to a hazel brown (hint of fading to portions of boards as well), once very handsome binding, still quite impressive and almost none of the original appeal diminished, beautiful internally, text and illustrations especially clean, fresh and smooth. Phillip J. Pirages   63 - 303   2013 $375

Pepys, Samuel 1633-1703 *Everybody's Pepys: The Diary...* London: G. Bell & Sons, 1926. 195 x 133mm., attractive contemporary tree calf, gilt by Riviere & Son (stamp signed), covers with decorative gilt rule border, raised bands, spine gilt in compartments with intricate scrolling cornerpieces and side fleurons, two with anchor centerpiece, two with lyre, two tan morocco labels, densely gilt turn-ins, marbled endpapers (showing maps) bound in at rear, with 60 plates by E. H. Shepard; presentation inscription from Christmas in year of publication; lower cover with faint circular mark, very light wear to joints and extremities, but binding still solid and appealing, fine internally, text especially fresh and clean.   Phillip J. Pirages   63 - 362   2013 $125

Ruskin, John 1819-1900 *The Queen's Gardens.* Manchester: printed in Aid of the St. Andrews Schools Fund, 1864. First printing, 221 x 144mm., 19, (1) pages, very fine dark blue morocco by Doves Bindery (signed and dated 1911), covers with gilt fillet border and central oval wreath of tudor roses and rose leaves, raised bands, spine with gilt fillet compartments containing vertical titling, gilt ruled turn-ins, all edges gilt, slightly scuffed felt lined tan morocco pull-off box by Riviere & Son, bookplate of Edith Rockefeller McCormick, usual minor offsetting to free endpapers from turn-ins, otherwise sparkling copy.   Phillip J. Pirages   61 - 105   2013 $2500

Santorio, Santorio 1561-1636 *Medicina Statica.* London: W. & J. Newton, 1720. Second edition, Engraved frontispiece, folding chart, elegant gilt polish speckle calf by Riviere, gilt panel spine, gilt ruled edges and inner dentelles, all edges gilt, lower outer board with small gash in letter, otherwise fine binding, near fine copy.   James Tait Goodrich   S74 - 220   2013 $495

Spenser, Edmund 1552-1599 *The Faerie Queene Disposed into XII Bookes.* London: printed by H(umphrey) L(ownes) for Mathew Lownes, 1609. First folio and first complete edition, small folio in sixes, bound without final blank, as usual, woodcut printer's device, colophon and numerous head and tailpieces and initials, bound by Riviere & Son in antique style full sprinkled calf, covers bordered gilt, spine decoratively tooled in gilt in compartments, lettered gilt on brown morocco labels, marbled endpapers, all edges gilt, gilt turn-ins and gilt board edges, Lytton Strachey's copy with his bookplate, and that of Roger Senhouse, hinges slightly tender, minimal wear to spine, superb copy, fresh and clean, lovely copy.   Heritage Book Shop   50th Anniversary Catalogue - 83   2013 $10,000

Sterne, Laurence 1713-1768 *A Sentimental Journey through France and Italy.* London: for T. Becket and P. A. De Hondt, 1768. First edition, text variant 2 in volume 1 and text variant 1 in volume 2, as usual, 2 volumes, 8vo., engraved coat of arms, with half titles and list of subscribers' names, but, as usual, without rare inserted ad leaf, full sprinkled calf, fully gilt by Riviere, spines bit dry, hinges worn, small chip at crown of volume 2, Hobart F. Cole bookplate.   Joseph J. Felcone Inc.   English and American Literature to 1800 - 21   2013 $900

Stow, John *A Survey of the Cities of London.* London: W. Innys et al, 1754-1755. Sixth and best edition, 2 volumes, folio, titles printed in red and black, 132 engraved plates, neat early 20th century brown morocco, spines in seven compartments with raised bands, lettered and dated gilt, inner gilt dentelles, gilt edges by Riviere.   Marlborough Rare Books Ltd.   218 - 147   2013   £16,500

Thomson, James 1700-1748 *The Seasons.* London: P. W. Tomkins, 1797. Magnificent edition, imperial folio, frontispiece and dedication leaf, five full page engravings, 10 head and tailpieces and five vignettes, extra illustrated with four later engraved full page plates, each with vignette, beautifully bound by Riviere in full dark red levant morocco, boards ruled in gilt tooling, spine elaborately stamped and lettered in gilt, gilt dentelles, all edges gilt, marbled endpapers, previous owner's bookplate, some restoration to outer hinges, overall beautiful copy.   Heritage Book Shop Holiday Catalogue 2012 - 150   2013 $3500

Walton, Izaak 1593-1683 *The Complete Angler.* London: D. Bogue, 1844. Sixth (titled fourth) John Major edition, 12 steel engravings, 74 woodcuts, early 20th century binding by Riviere & Son in full forest green levant morocco, fine, unique copy with four signed watercolors by John Absolon, from the renowned collection of John T. Spaulding.   David Brass Rare Books, Inc.   Holiday 2012 Chapter Five - DB 01876   2013 $3850

Wraxall, Nathaniel William 1751-1831 *The Historical and the Posthumous Memoirs.* London: Bickers and Son, 1884. 5 volumes, 221 x 149mm., pleasing contemporary dark plum half morocco over marbled boards by Riviere & Son (stamp signed on verso of front free endpaper), raised bands, spines gilt in compartments with delicate fleuron centerpiece, gilt titling, marbled endpapers, top edge gilt, 14 engraved portraits, front pastedown with faint discoloration, apparently from bookplate removal, 2 joints with bit of rubbing, paper boards little chafed and with some light soiling, leaves faintly browned at right edges (because of quality of paper stock), otherwise quite excellent set, text fresh and clean with few signs of use, attactive bindings with no significant wear. Phillip J. Pirages 63 - 504 2013 $375

The Writs Magazine and Attic Miscellany. London: Thomas Tegg, 1818. First and only edition, 20 original parts in 2 volumes, 2 volumes, small octavo, 40 hand colored etchings, 16 by George Cruikshank and 24 by Thomas Rowlandson, elegantly bound circa 1900 by Riviere & Son, full blue crushed levant morocco, upper joint of volume one very slightly cracked but still sound, exceptionally fine, clean. David Brass Rare Books, Inc. Holiday 2012 Chapter Two - DB 02094 2013 $11,500

Binding – Robinson, John

Goodrich, Abraham *A River Claim. Letters from the California Gold Fields, 1857.* El Cajon: Nineteen Hundred Press, 2007. First edition, one of 115 numbered copies, 4 wood engravings by James Horton, map ends, bound by John Robinson at the Tortoise Press in half Nigerian goatskin, marbled boards, very fine. Argonaut Book Shop Recent Acquisitions June 2013 - 122 2013 $125

Binding – Robson & Kerslak

Swift, Jonathan 1667-1845 *Travels into Several Remote Nations of the World.* London: printed for Benj. Motte, 1726. Teerink's "B" edition, one of three 8vo. editions printed the same year the first "A" published, 2 volumes, 8vo., 19th century speckled calf by Robson & Kerslak (hinges repaired), leather labels, raised bands, inner gilt dentelles, marbled endpapers, frontispiece, 3 maps, 1 diagram, minor scattered foxing. Howard S. Mott Inc. 262 - 146 2013 $3500

Binding – Root

Scott, Walter 1771-1832 *Harold the Dauntless: a poem in six cantos.* Edinburgh: printed by James Ballantyne and Co. for Longman et al, 1817. First edition, 175 x 108mm., pleasing mid 19th century brown three quarter morocco over green marbled boards by Root and Son (stamp signed), raised bands, spine gilt in compartments with curling frame and large lozenge containing thistle centerpiece, gilt titling, marbled endpapers, top edge gilt, 2 engraved plates, engraved bookplate of John Waugh dated 1896; bit of carefully refurbished rubbing to corners and spine bands, about two thirds of leaves with thin brown stains, sustained before binding?, right at fore and tail edge and well away from text, additional trivial defects, otherwise excellent copy, text fresh and clean, ample margins and in binding solid and appealing. Phillip J. Pirages 63 - 427 2013 $200

Binding – Rotzcher, Klaus

Flaubert, Gustave 1821-1880 *Flaubert & Louise: Letters and Impressions.* San Francisco: Pacific Editions & Limestone Press, 1988. One of 18 copies only, each numbered and signed by artist/publisher, all on BFK Rives paper, 5 original monotypes by Charles Hobson, each presented with 5 letterpress printed texts, printed in Baskerville and Baskerville italic at Limestone Press, assembled in 18 portfolios, loose as issued in blue cloth with white labels on spine and front cover by Klaus Rotzcher, quite scarce. Priscilla Juvelis - Rare Books 55 - 20 2013 $3000

Binding – Rousselle, Emile

Mascarenhas, Jose Freire de Monterroyo *Relacam dos Progressos das Armas Portuguezas no Estado da India...* Lisbon: Pascoal de Sylva, 1715-1716. First edition, 4 parts in one volume, 4to., 20th century polished blue morocco by Emile Rouselle, gilt dentelles and spine, some very light staining to titlepage of second part, otherwise very clean, attractive volume. Maggs Bros. Ltd. 1467 - 55 2013 £3500

Binding – Rowse, A. L.

Betjeman, John 1906-1984 *Summoned by Bells.* London: John Murray, 1969. First reprint, 4to., original green cloth, dust jacket, inscribed by author for A. L. Rowse with holograph drawing of coat of arms with words "one & all 1975", with Rowse's familiar initials across the join of the front endpapers and his manuscript annotations throughout, excellent copy in price clipped and nicked dust jacket, faded to white on spine. Maggs Bros. Ltd. 1460 - 100 2013 £200

Binding – Royal

Beaufort, Jean De *Le Tresor des Tresors de France...* Paris?: 1615. First edition, extremely rare quarto format, this copy dedicated to King Louis XIII and specially bound for him in full vellum entirely covered with gilt stamped fleur-de-lys on both covers, gilt heart within larger central fleur-de-lys, triple fillet gilt borders, gilt floral corner ornaments, fleurs-de-lys on spine, housed in custom brown calf clamshell stamped with fleur de lys on front and back, gilt stamped on spine.   Heritage Book Shop   50th Anniversary Catalogue - 8   2013 $37,500

Binding – Sangorski & Sutcliffe

Ackermann, Rudolph *The History of the Colleges of Winchester, Eton and Westminster.* London: printed for and published by R. Ackermann, 1816. First edition, large quarto, 48 hand colored plates, text watermarked 1812, plates watermarked 1812 and 1816, bound circa 1950 (by Sangorski & Sutcliffe) for C. J. Sawyer in full red crushed levant morocco, decoratively tooled in gilt, occasional very light offsetting from plates to text, "Eton College" with small light stain to inner margin of recto of leaf G1 (page 41) and very slight browning to recto of leaf K1 (page 65), excellent copy with early watermarks, very attractive binding.   David Brass Rare Books, Inc.   Holiday 2012 Chapter Two - DB 00331   2013 $4500

Alken, Henry *Ideas, Accidental and Incidental to Hunting and Other Sports...* London: Thomas M'Lean, n.d., 1826-1830. First edition, early issue, plates dated 1826-1830 and watermarked 1831-32, upright folio, letterpress title and 42 hand colored etchings, full forest green crushed morocco by Riviere or Sangorski & Sutcliffe (circa 1940), occasional mild spots to margins not affecting imagery, neat professional repair to closed margin tear on plate #6, otherwise beautiful copy.   David Brass Rare Books, Inc.   Holiday 2012 Chapter Two - DB 02149   2013 $16,500

Battie, William *A Treatise on Madness.* London: printed for J. Whiston and B. White, 1758. vii, 99 pages, rebound in half calf by Sangorski & Sutcliffe, endpapers renewed with binding, text foxed in parts, lower right blank portion of leaf B4 missing.   James Tait Goodrich   75 - 19 2013 $2250

Blumenthal, Walter Hart *Formats and Foibles, a few Books Which Might Be Called Curious.* Worcester: Achille J. St. Onge, 1956. Limited to 300 copies, 6 x 4.9 cm., printed on Barcham Green's handmade paper, bound by Sangorski & Sutcliffe, full red morocco, all edges gilt, from the collection of Donn W. Sanford.   Oak Knoll Books   303 - 26   2013 $175

Browne, Thomas 1605-1682 *Urne Buriall and the Garden of Cyrus.* Cassell, 1932. 212/215 copies printed on Barcham Green handmade paper, 32 stencilled collotypes, by Paul Nash, small folio original cream vellum by Sangorski & Sutcliffe, backstrip gilt lettered, large dark brown crushed morocco, front cover inlay incorporating a Design by Paul Nash comprising two cream vellum inlays and interrelated gilt urn and lattice work design, rear cover repeating gilt front cover urn and lattice-work design and incorporates two dark brown crushed morocco inlays, gilt edges, brown cloth, slipcase, fine.   Blackwell's Rare Books   172 - 222   2013   £6000

Doctor Comicus or the Frolics of Fortune. London: B. Blake, 1825? 210 x 133mm., without printed titlepage, very attractive light tan smooth calf by Sangorski & Sutcliffe/ Zahensdorf (stamp signed), corners bordered with French fillet and fleuron cornerpieces, raised bands, spine gilt in compartments featuring decorative bands, scrolling cornerpieces, fleuron centerpiece and small tools, maroon morocco labels, gilt inner dentelles, marbled endpapers, all edges gilt, 12 plates, all colored by hand, bookplate of Robert Marceau, engraved title and two plates little foxed, 3 plates slightly trimmed at fore edge without apparent loss, few leaves with light marginal foxing or soiling, otherwise excellent copy, plates bright and well preserved, leaves clean and fresh, sympathetic binding mint.   Phillip J. Pirages   63 - 460   2013 $400

Joyce, James 1882-1941 *Ulysses.* London: John Lane, The Bodley Head, 1936. One of 100 copies signed by author, (there were also 900 unsigned copies), 265 x 195mm., 8 p.l., 765, (1) pages, original vellum, gilt titling on spine, large stylized gilt bow on each cover, top edge gilt, other edges untrimmed and mostly unopened, original (slightly worn but very solid), black and white patterned paper slipcase with paper label, housed in fine silk lined gray morocco clamshell box by Sangorski & Sutcliffe, title printed in blue and black, prospectus laid in at front, hint of smudging to vellum (or perhaps just a natural variation in color), but in any case, virtually mint, binding entirely unworn, especially bright and mostly unopened text pristine.   Phillip J. Pirages   63 - 288   2013 $50,000

Lowell, James Russell 1819-1891 *The Writings.* London: Macmillan and Co., 1890. Riverside edition, 10 volumes, 194 x 130mm., 3 of the volumes with portrait frontispiece, beautiful early 20th century olive green textured calf handsomely gilt by Sangorski & Sutcliffe (stamp signed), covers with double ruled gilt border and blindstamped in basket weave pattern, raised bands, spines lavishly gilt in compartments with central cruciform ornament framed by wide densely gilt cornerpieces filled with leaves, flowers and small tools, each spine with two maroon morocco labels, turn-ins gilt in lacy filigree, marbled endpapers, top edge gilt, other edges rough trimmed, light rubbing and flaking to one joint (only), spines uniformly sunned to a mellow olive brown, one leaf with triangular tear at upper right just into text (no loss), isolated very minor stains or foxing, otherwise beautiful set in fine condition, handsome bindings very lustrous and with no significant wear, text fresh, clean and bright.   Phillip J. Pirages   61 - 145   2013 $1750

Mitchell, Margaret *Gone with the Wind.* New York: Macmillan Co., 1936. First edition, first issue (with "published May, 1936" on copright page and no note of further printing), signed by author, 222 x 152mm., 4 p.l., 1037 pages, very pleasing gray crushed morocco by Sangorski & Sutcliffe (stamp signed on front turn-in), covers with single gilt rule border, raised bands, decorated with stippled rule and flanked by gilt rules, panels with intricate gilt fleuron centerpiece and gilt tilting, gilt ruled turn-ins, marbled endpapers, top edge gilt, upper right corner of back cover slightly soiled (with a series of short, thin, faint parallel lines about two of three inches in length descending from top edge), spine slightly and evenly sunned to pleasant light brownish gray, trivial internal imperfections, otherwise very fine.   Phillip J. Pirages   63 - 342   2013 $7500

Pepys, Samuel 1633-1703 *The Diary.* London: G. Bell and Sons Ltd., 1924. 8 volumes bound in 3, frontispiece, fine in contemporary terra cotta crushed morocco by Sangorski & Sutcliffe (signed on front turn-in), double gilt fillet border on covers, upper covers with gilt insignia incorporating initials "S P" crossed anchors and looping ropes with Pepys' (misspelled) motto in Latin on ribbon above it, raised bands, spines gilt in double ruled compartments with central ornament of either a crown, a sailor's knot, an anchor or crossed quills, turn-ins ruled in gilt, marbled endpapers, all edges gilt, spines lightly and uniformly sunned toward pink, otherwise extremely pleasing set in beautiful condition inside and out.   Phillip J. Pirages   61 - 146   2013 $1250

Tennyson, Alfred Tennyson, 1st Baron 1809-1892 *The Princess: a Medley.* London: Edward Moxon and Co., 1860. 218 x 147mm., 3 p.l., 188 pages, 26 illustrations engraved on wood by Dalziel, Green, Thomas and E. Williams from drawings by Daniel Maclise, R.A., sumptuous dark green morocco, very densely gilt intricately inlaid and adorned with jewels by Sangorski & Sutcliffe (stamp-signed), covers with diapered central panel enclosed by wide and ornate frame of inlaid brown and green strapwork on heavily stippled gilt ground accented with leafy fronds of gold, inner edge of frame punctuated at corners and on sides by dozen lotus blossoms of purple and green morocco, upper cover with large central medallion framed by green blue and brown strapwork with knots at head and foot, with a total of 6 cabochon sapphires and the frame inset set with 10 cabochon emeralds, medallion filled with swirling gilt vines, tiny red morocco berries and flowers on very densely stippled ground, whole with dramatically superimposed "A T" monogram of inlaid green morocco at center, lower cover with similar central medallion in which red dots of inlaid morocco take place of gemstones and centerpiece is gilt quatrefoil with inlaid circles of green morocco, raised bands, spine richly gilt in compartments with inlaid brown strapwork, gilt leaves, red morocco berries, much gilt stippling, chestnut brown morocco doublures inside wide green morocco frame decorated with plain dotted gilt rules and floral spray cornerpieces of inlaid lavender flowers, red hearts and gilt rose leaves, panel of front doublure with sunken scalloped oval medallion containing a portrait of poet on ivory under glass, this encircled by wide, thickly gilt collar with 10 cabochon turquoises, near doublure with similar sunken panel featuring a large floral spray of roses and tulips in gilt and inlaid morocco within inlaid strapwork frame, whole surrounded by wide band of heavy gilt, brown watered silk endleaves, edges gilt, gauffered and painted, in delicate diapered floral pattern, in matching straight grain morocco solander box lined with felt (slightly scuffed, with front joint expertly renewed), occasional mild foxing but dazzling copy in exceptionally fine condition.   Phillip J. Pirages   61 - 144   2013 $35,000

Whitman, Walt 1819-1892 *Two Rivulets.* Camden: 1876. First edition, first printing of only 100 copies, 8vo., signed and dated by author on frontispiece (albumen photo of author), near fine, in fine Sangorski & Sutcliffe/Zaehnsdorf green full morocco leather with gilt lettering and rules on spine which is in 6 compartments, custom marbled paper covered, lined slipcase.   By the Book, L. C.   36 - 61   2013 $6500

Binding – Schuberth Bookbindery

Jeffers, Robinson 1887-1962 *Granite & Cypress: Rubbings from the Rock...* University of California at Santa Cruz: Lime Kiln Press, 1975. Limited to 100 numbered copies, oblong folio, printed on English Hayle handmade paper, titlepage woodcut by William Prochnow, bound by Schuberth Bookbindery in German linen, open laced deerskin over Monterey Cypress spine, Japanese Uwa endpapers, custom slipcase made of Monterey Cypress inlaid with square 'window' of granite from Jeffers' stoneyard (drawn by the poet from the sea), built to stand erect on felt lined cypress stand, case with hair-line crack, else fine, signed by printer William Everson in ink at limitation page, prospectus signed by Everson and three proof sheets laid in, exceptionally rare.   Jeff Weber Rare Books   171 - 190   2013 $15,000

Kroeber, Theodora *The Inland Whale.* Covelo: Yolla Bolly Press, 1987. First edition thus, one of 115 copies on Rives BFK Cream each signed by artist, Karin Wilkstrom and numbered, page size 12 x 14 inches, 94 pages + colophon and sources, bound by Schuberth Bookbindery, tan Belgian linen over flexible boards, laced at spine with linen cord, black and white engraving on front panel, housed in publisher's slipcase of brown roma Fabriano paper, fine, the artist, Karin Wikstrom has hand colored wood engravings, hors texte as well as chapter headings and tailpieces, prints were hand colored in gouache paints applied from her own stencils, lovely book.   Priscilla Juvelis - Rare Books   55 - 27   2013 $600

Muir, John 1838-1914 *My First Summer in the Sierra.* Covelo: Yolla Bolly Press, 1988. First edition thus, limited edition, one of 125 bound in linen from a total edition of 150 copies, all on Incisioni cream, mould made paper at Magnani paper mill on Pescia, Italy, all signed by artist, Michael McCurdy, 162 pages, bound by Schuberth Bookbindery in tan linen handwoven at Myung Jin Fabricus with endsheets of handmade bark paper, housed in blue-grey publisher's slipcase with tan paper label with brown border printed with author and title in black, fine, 12 wood engravings by McCurdy, type is Jan Van Krimpen's Van Dijck and Caslon, was handset at Press and by Monotype at MacKenzie-Harris Corporation.   Priscilla Juvelis - Rare Books   55 - 29   2013 $900

Binding – Seacome, J.

Byron, George Gordon Noel, 6th Baron 1788-1824 *The Works.* London: John Murray, 1815. 4 volumes, some light foxing in prelims, slightly later half purple calf by J. Seacome of Chester, spines ruled gilt, black leather labels, spines uniformly faded, very slight rubbing, nice set.   Jarndyce Antiquarian Booksellers   CCIII - 69   2013   £420

Binding – Seidenberg, Caryl

Seidenberg, Caryl *Insomnia.* Winnetka: The Vixen Press, 2008. One of 12 copies, each signed an numbered by artist/author/printer, all on Somerset cover stock, page size 5 3/4 x 7 inches, 20 pages, bound by artist, black cover stock, exposed spine with three white ribbons printed by author woven behind wires that are affixed to each page with tape, ribbons extend on to front and back panels, front label with hand printed releif print in black that resembles a bid or open curtains (with eyes peering out), and a sleeping pill and the title "In somnia", text handset in Eusebius and printed on a number 4 Vandercook, images are hand painted relief prints as well as drawings translated to polymer plates, beautiful book.   Priscilla Juvelis - Rare Books   56 - 36   2013 $1200

Seidenberg, Caryl *Operation Rescue.* Winnetka: Vixen Press, 1980. Artist's book, one of 35 copies only, all on Arches paper, each signed and numbered by artist/author/printer/binder, Caryl Seidenberg, page size 6 x 8 1/8 inches, 16 pages, bound by artist, sewn, brown paper over boards, tan cloth spine, brown Fabriano endsheets, label printed in brown with title and artist on front panel, poem printed letterpress on Number 4 Vandercook in 18 pt. Caslon Openface, 12 pt. Bauer Bodoni Italic, 12 pt. Bodoni Book and 10 p.t Bauer Bodoni.   Priscilla Juvelis - Rare Books   56 - 37   2013 $500

Binding – Sellers, David

Rich, Adrienne *Letters Censored, Shredded, Returned to Sender or Judged Unfit to Send.* Hopewell: Pied Oxen Printers, 2009. First edition thus, one of 100 copies, 85 of which are for sale, all on Somerset Book wove paper, each signed by poet, by artist, Nancy Grossman on each of her two prints and by printer/designer, David Sellers, who has aso hand numbered each copy on colophon page, page size 16 5/8 x 12 7/8 inches, 22 pages, bound by David Sellers hand sewn in tan Belgian linen over boards, headbands, author and title printed in black on pastepaper with black rule inset on front panel, title printed on marbled paper on spine, fine, designed band bound by Sellers, printed by Sellers and his son Jonathan, book set in ATF Garamond 459 and 460 and printed on 1848 Hopkinson & Cope Albion Press, 2 intaglio prints drawn on copper plates by the artist, Nancy Grossman and etched, steel faced and printed by Marjorie Van Dye at Van Deb Editions.   Priscilla Juvelis - Rare Books   56 - 27   2013 $3500

Snyder, Gary *Sixteen T'ang Poems.* Hopewell: Pied Oxen Printers, 1993. First edition, one of 126, 100 of which were for sale all on Rives paper, each signed by poet and translator, Gary Snyder on author's Notes pages, and hand numbered on colophon, frontispiece Hanga woodcut by Bill Paden, on kizuki-kozo, sarashi paper made by Kazuo Yamaguchi is also signed and numbered, page size 8 1/4 x 11 1/2 inches, 26 pages, bound by printer/designer, David Sellers, handsewn in handmade paper from India over boards, stamped with Chinese characters in black on front panel, title in back type in contrasting red label on spine, fine. Priscilla Juvelis - Rare Books 56 - 28 2013 $950

Binding – Sickles

Turgenev, Ivan Sergeevich 1818-1883 *The Jew and Other Stories.* New York: Charles Scribner's Sons, 1904. 213 x 146mm., frontispiece lovely contemporary dark rose colored morocco, ornately gilt by Sickles (stamp signed), covers with border of double gilt rules enclosing an Art Nouveau style frame of wavy rules connecting large cornerpieces, these with small oval medallion onlaid black morocco enclosed by gilt drawer handle tools and leafy sprays, upper cover with circular stylized monogram "C E B" at center, raised bands, spines gilt in double ruled compartments decorated with drawer handles and circlets, wide turn-ins with gilt frame featuring pretty fleuron cornerpieces, ivory watered silk pastedowns and free endleaves, top edge gilt, spine evenly faded to soft rose, three leaves with uneven fore edges from rough opening, half a dozen leaves with corner creases, other trivial imperfections, but fine, text clean, fresh and bright and handsome binding, lustrous and virtually unworn. Phillip J. Pirages 63 - 472 2013 $375

Turgenev, Ivan Sergeevich 1818-1883 *Phantoms and Other Stories.* New York: Charles Scribner's Sons, 1904. 213 x 146mm., frontispiece, lovely contemporary dark rose colored morocco, ornately gilt by Sickles (stamp signed), covers with border of double gilt rules enclosing an Art Nouveau style frame of wavy rules connecting large cornerpieces, these with small oval medallion onlaid black morocco enclosed by gilt drawer handle tools and leafy sprays, upper cover with circular stylized monogram "C E B" at center, raised bands, spines gilt in double ruled compartments decorated with drawer handles and circlets, wide turn-ins with gilt frame featuring pretty fleuron cornerpieces, ivory watered silk pastedowns and free endleaves, top edge gilt, except for even fading of spine, very fine and very pretty copy. Phillip J. Pirages 63 - 473 2013 $350

Turgenev, Ivan Sergeevich 1818-1883 *A Reckless Character, and Other Studies.* New York: Charles Scribner's Sons, 1904. 213 x 146mm., frontispiece, lovely contemporary dark rose colored morocco, ornately gilt by Sickles (stamp signed), covers with border of double gilt rules enclosing an Art Nouveau style frame of wavy rules connecting large cornerpieces, these with small oval medallion onlaid black morocco enclosed by gilt drawer handle tools and leafy sprays, upper cover with circular stylized monogram "C E B" at center, raised bands, spines gilt in double ruled compartments decorated with drawer handles and circlets, wide turn-ins with gilt frame featuring pretty fleuron cornerpieces, ivory watered silk pastedowns and free endleaves, top edge gilt, spine evenly faded very small dark spot on upper cover, otherwise very attractive decorative binding in fine condition, first half of book with very faint dampstain in upper quarter of page (front endleaves with slightly larger and darker dampstain), four leaves with cellotape mends to short marginal tears (none touching text), one page with 3 marginal inkspots, otherwise excellent internally. Phillip J. Pirages 63 - 474 2013 $125

Binding – Sinclair

Davenport, W. *A Week in Holland.* London: Sinclair, Haymarket, 1905. volumes I and II, oblong 8vo., 2 calligraphic titles and 90 Platinum prints measuring from 48 x 72mm. to 75 x 104mm., some occasional foxing, contemporary crushed full ed morocco by Sinclair of Haymarket, London, ruled and lettered in gilt, inner dentelles, ornamented in gilt, all edges gilt, mottled red endpapers,. Marlborough Rare Books Ltd. 218 - 80 2013 £250

Binding – Smith, W. H.

Burne-Jones, Edward *The Flower Book.* Reproduced by Henri Piazza et Cie for the Fine Art Society, 1905. First edition, 221/300 copies, 38 color plates, half title, titlepage and prelim leaves printed in red and green, remainder of text printed in green except for the 4 page facsimile list of flowers made by Burne-Jones at rear which is printed in black, printed rectos only (except for half title/limitation leaf and facsimile list), very slight spotting, page bearing Plate X and verso of its title leaf opposite browned, large 4to., contemporary crushed dark green morocco in Cockerell style by W. H. Smith Bindery, flat spine divided by wide low raised bands, gilt lettered direct in second compartment and at foot, remaining compartments with gilt single line border and three gilt dots at corners, repeated on sides, upper spine gilt lettered, gilt single fillet on board edges, grey endpapers, top edge gilt, others uncut, one corner with small snag, preserved in its original fleece lined green cloth drop-down folding box with metal catch, lettered gilt on upper side, box rebacked and showing bit of wear and tear, but performing its function splendidly, good. Blackwell's Rare Books B174 - 18 2013 £7500

Thucydides *History of the Peloponnesian War.* Chelsea: printed at the Ashendene Press, 1930. One of 260 copies on paper (240 for sale), out of a total edition of 280 (257 for sale), folio, printed in black in Ptolemy type with 3 line initials at beginning of each chapter and larger initials and opening line of each of the 8 books designed by Graily Hewitt and printed in red, marginal chapter summaries also in red in Blado italic type, printer's mark D printed in black, publisher's white pigskin by W. H. Smith & Son Ltd., spine lettered gilt, raised bands, all edges gilt, spine very slightly darkened, overall very good.   Heritage Book Shop   Holiday Catalogue 2012 - 4   2013 $4000

Binding – Sotheran

Millais, John Guille *A Breath from the Veldt.* London: Henry Sotheran, 1895. Large paper signed limited edition, number 31 of 60 copies, folio, original half crimson morocco gilt by Sotheran with cream boards, upper board with vignettes of sable and kudu antelope, extremities little rubbed and boards trifle soiled in places, short soiled tear to cloth of upper panel, top edge gilt, untrimmed, etched frontispiece, 12 further full page electro etched plates, 12 full page plates and numerous text illustrations, little scattered foxing to plates, small Oatesiana roundel stamp to title, most handsome copy, armorial bookplates of William Edward Oates and Robert Washington Oates, presentation label of latter and printed label of Newton Library.   R. F. G. Hollett & Son   Africana - 145   2013   £1950

Neale, John Preston *Views of the Seats of Noblemen and Gentlemen in England, Wales, Scotland and Ireland.* London: Sherwood, Neely and Jones, 1820-1829. Large paper copy, 11 volumes, 4to., 11 engraved titles and 721 plates, all on india paper and marked 'proof, mounted, 7 wood engraved text vignettes, late 19th century purple half morocco by Sotheran & Co.   Marlborough Rare Books Ltd.   218 - 109   2013   £3000

Binding – Soudee

Carco, Francis *Auguste Brouet. Jesus-la-Caille.* Paris: Editions de l'Estampe, 1925. From a total edition of 272 copies, this example is from the edition of 50 copies on Madagascar handmade paper with 30 original etchings, 10 of them full page by Auguste Brouet, 11 x 8.5 inches, 225 pages, bound in outstanding Art Deco binding by Soudee, signed by the master binder, full dark blue morocco with geometric mosaic of silver, burgundy, brown and beige leather onlays, both covers, plain spine with burgundy onlay stamped in black, original wrappers preserved and bound in, top edge gilt, double endleaves of silk and hand painted heavy stock, housed in quarter morocco chemise with gilt on spine, matching slipcase, very handsome.   Gemini Fine Books & Arts., Ltd.   Art Reference & Illustrated Books - 2013 $2995

Binding – Staggemeier & Welcher

Mayer, Luigi *Views in Egypt, Palestine and Other Parts of the Ottoman Empire.* London: Thomas Bensley for R. Bowyer, 1801-1804. First editions in book form, 482 x 335mm., 3 separately published works bound in 1 volume, very fine contemporary russia, elaborately gilt by Staggemeier & Welcher (their ticket), covers gilt with frame of Greek-key rolls on either side of cresting roll, this frame enclosing another role of linked palmettes, raised bands, spine expertly rebacked retaining original backstrip, its compartments with unusual Egyptian hieroglyphic designs, turn-ins with gilt chain roll, marbled endpapers, all edges gilt; with engraved frontispiece and 96 fine hand colored aquatint views of near east; bookplate of Dayton Art Institute (but sold with their authorization at auction), corners slightly bumped, few small portions of the spine with vague crackles, occasional minor offsetting from plates, isolated faint marginal foxing, thumbing or rust spots, but still fine, especially clean and fresh internally, generous margins and richly colored plates, solidly restored, lustrous binding that retains virtually all of its original considerable appeal.   Phillip J. Pirages   63 - 333   2013 $18,500

Binding – Stikeman

Bible. Latin - 1921 *A Noble Fragment. Being a Leaf of the Gutenberg Bible 1450-1455.* New York: Gabriel Wells, 1921. Limited to 600 copies, folio, actual leaf 393 x 287mm., (6) pages text, titlepage and on initial letter printed in red, original unwatermarked paper leaf from Gutenberg Bible tipped in, black gothic letter, rubricated in red, headlines, chapter numbers and two large initial letters supplied in red and blue, original full black blindstamped morocco by Stikeman & Co., front cover lettered gilt, gilt turn-ins, grey endpapers, head and foot of spine very lightly worn, leaf in this copy very clean except for minor foxing at edges, ink still very black and crisp, remarkably fresh and lovely example.   Heritage Book Shop   50th Anniversary Catalogue - 10   2013 $100,000

Brough, Robert B. *The Life of Sir John Falstaff.* London: Longman, Brown, Green, Longmans and Roberts, 1858. First edition in book form, pages xx, 196 + 20 etched plates, including frontispiece and 1 in text illustration, tall 8vo., full crushed blue morocco (original pictorial gilt cloth, front cover bound in), upper and lower covers ruled, spine and dentelles elaborately gilt, raised bands by Stikeman & Co., cloth slipcase.   Howard S. Mott Inc.   262 - 19   2013 $275

Conrad, Joseph 1857-1924 *The Works.* Garden City: Doubleday Page & Co., 1920-1926. One of 735 copies signed by Conrad, 22 volumes, "Sun-dial edition", frontispiece, fine and especially flamboyant lilac morocco, elaborately gilt, by Stikeman, covers panelled with single, double gilt fillets and intricate scrolling foliate cornerpieces, raised bands, spine attractively gilt in ruled compartments with marine ornaments (seashell or anchor) as centerpiece and with scrolling cornerpieces, crimson morocco doublures, front doublures with central panel of blue morocco, wide turn-ins with alternating floral tools, doublures decorated with wavy gilt lines and (at corners) floral bouquets, blue central panels with large gilt sailing vessel at middle, watered silk endleaves, morocco hinges, all edges gilt; with APS signed by author tipped in, also signature of Richard Curle, written next to his printed name as dedicatee of volume 16, spines uniformly faded to even chestnut brown, hint of rubbing to handful of joints and corners (only), one opening in one volume with marginal spots, quite handsome set in fine condition, text virtually pristine, covers bright and wear to leather entirely minor. Phillip J. Pirages 61 - 122 2013 $15,000

James I, King of Scotland *The Kingis Quair.* Vale Press, 1903. One of 260 copies, (another 10 copies on vellum), 236 x 150mm., lv, (1) pages, printed in red and black, extremely pleasing midnight blue crushed morocco, intricately gilt by Stikeman, stamp signed, covers with gilt frame formed by three rows of tiny gilt circlets enclosing two intertwining veins that combined at 12 intervals to produce a trio of rose blossoms, raised bands, spine gilt in double ruled compartments containing tulip beneath a daisy, flowers surrounded by gilt circlets, inner gilt dentelles, marbled endpapers, top edge gilt, matching morocco backed flat lined solander box, morocco bookplate of Paul Chevalier, inevitable slight offsetting to free endpapers from turn-ins otherwise, most attractive copy in very fine condition, binding lustrous and unworn, text with no signs of use. Phillip J. Pirages 61 - 125 2013 $3500

Motley, John Lothrop 1766-1851 *Correspondence.* New York: Harper & Bros., 1889. First edition, 2 volumes, 251 x 175mm., attractive contemporary dark green half morocco over marbled boards by Stikeman (stamp signed), raised bands, spines gilt in compartments with tulip centerpiece and scrolling cornerpieces, gilt titling, marbled endpapers, top edge gilt, frontispiece in volume I, bookplate of W. M. Burden; little wear to joints and extremities (five corner tips worn through), spines uniformly darkened toward brown, otherwise fine, clean and fresh internally, in solid pleasing bindings. Phillip J. Pirages 63 - 350 2013 $150

Porter, William Sydney 1862-1910 *The Complete Writings of O. Henry.* Garden City: Doubleday Page and Co., 1917. One of 1075 copies, Memorial Edition and Edition deluxe, 229 x 152mm., 14 volumes, 90 plates (45 images, each in two states), including color frontispiece in each volume, one in volume 1 signed by artist), as well as engraved half title with vignette, signed by publishers, original tissue guards, prelim page of first volume with folding leaf of manuscript, apparently in Porter's hand, tipped in, titlepages and half titles in blue and black lovely dark blue crushed lavishly gilt by Stikeman, covers with very broad and animated gilt borders of swirling foliage, flowers and butterflies in style of Derome, raised bands, spine compartments attractively gilt with antique tools red morocco doublures, multiple rules and other gilt elaboration, watered silk free endleaves, top edge gilt, others untrimmed, entirely unopened, spines evenly sunned, one leaf with marginal tear at fore edge, otherwise extraordinarily beautiful set in virtually faultless condition. Phillip J. Pirages 61 - 124 2013 $11,500

Sherard, Robert Harborough *Oscar Wilde: the Story of an Unhappy Friendship.* London: privately printed at the Hermes Press, 1902. First edition, 254 x 198mm., 277, (1) pages, handsome contemporary olive green morocco lavishly gilt in Art Nouveau style by Stikeman (stamp-signed on rear turn-in), covers with multiple plain and decorative gilt rules enclosing large quatrefoil with very prominent floral cornerpieces and floral tool accents, central panel of that on upper cover containing coronet imposed upon crossed writing tools, raised bands, spine attractively gilt in compartments with large central lily framed by drawer hand tools, intricate gilt floral turn-ins, marbled endpapers, top edge gilt, original paper and cloth bound in, frontispiece photo of Wilde, five other portraits and two facsimiles of letters as called for, large paper copy, morocco bookplates of Helen Janssen Wetzel and Mary Pinkerton Carlisle, spine sunned to rich brown, just touch of rubbing to joints, usual offsetting to free endpapers from turn-ins, titlepage little browned from acidic(!) tissue guard (now removed), last page with faint darkening from bound-in cloth cover, handful of leaves with small, light brown stains along gutter (from binder's glue), other trivial imperfections but still excellent copy, leaves fresh, clean and bright, margins enormous and animated, glittering binding scarcely worn. Phillip J. Pirages 61 - 126 2013 $1250

Whittier, John Greenleaf 1807-1892 *The Literary Remains of John G(ardiner) C(alkis) Brainard with a Sketch of His Life.* Hartford: P. B. Goodsell, 1832. First edition, 8vo., later full calf, little rubbed along for edge and along hinges, top edge gilt, with gilt dentelles by Stikeman, bookplate of Charles B. Foote. Second Life Books Inc. 183 - 400 2013 $300

Binding – Stoakley

Bunyan, John   1628-1688   *A Book for Boys and Girls; or Country Rhymes for Children.*   London: Elliot Stock, 1889. 1889, Large paper copy, top edge gilt, untrimmed, handsome copy, large square 8vo., later quarter levant morocco gilt by Stoakley of Cambridge (but unsigned).   R. F. G. Hollett & Son   Children's Books - 94   2013   £120

Scott, Walter   1771-1832   *Rokeby.*   Edinburgh: printed for John Ballentyne and Co. by James Ballantyne and Co., 1813.   First edition, 4to., toned and somewhat spotted, early 20th century dark blue Niger morocco, spine divided by four broad flat raised bands, tooled in gilt, lettered gilt direct, top edge gilt with others uncut, scratched, front joint and ends of rear joint renewed, ink ownership inscription "C & Q A Head, from original endpaper archivally pasted at upper forecorner of pastedown, ex-libris heraldic bookplate of Vincent Henry Stanton, signed binding "Bound by Stoakley Late Hawes".   Unsworths Antiquarian Booksellers   28 - 197   2013   £50

Binding – Thistle Bindery

Joyce, James   1882-1941   *Brideship and Gulls.*   New York: Vincent FitzGerald & Co., 1991. One of 25 copies, text on Apta Royale Laid Richard de Bas paper (made in 1938), images on Musee paper, backed on custom made papers by Paul Wong on Dieu Donne papermill, page size 16 x 26 inches, bound by Zahra Partovi in Coptic style mauve grey silk over boards, box by David Bourbeau, Thistle Bindery, fine, 6 original line etchings by Susan Weil hand painted in watercolor and gouache with gold leafing throughout, each mounted on museum board, images surround the 40 page text when sitting in the box and when lifted out become three dimensional paintings; there are also 2 original collages in text and on boards of cover, which is printed in 3 colors, box itself is piece of sculpture.   Priscilla Juvelis - Rare Books   55 - 8   2013 $10,000

Binding – Thurkow, Gus

H., B.   *The Twelve Months by B. H.*   Zuilichem: Catharijne Press, 1990.   Limited to 165 copies, this one of the 150 numbered trade copies, bound by Gus Thurkow and hand coloring by Luc Thurkow, each month with hand colored scene, 4.5 x 6.2cm., paper covered boards with color illustration on front cover, miniature bookplate of Kathryn Rickard, from the collection of Donn W. Sanford.   Oak Knoll Books   303 - 90   2013 $125

Binding – Thurkow, Luce

Baker, Piet D.   *The Young Stork's Baedeker, Travel Guide with Lexicon.*   Zuilichem: Catharijne Press, 1998.   Limited to 190 copies, this one of 15 lettered copies bound thus and has the second volume which is not in original edition, 6.7 x 4.2 cm., paper covered boards, slipcase, illustrations, including foldout map, bound by Luce Thurkow, from the collection of Donn W. Sanford.   Oak Knoll Books   303 - 75   2013 $275

Cervantes Saavedra, Miguel De   1547-1616   *The Ingenious Gentleman Don Quixote De La Mancha Chapter VIII.*   's-Hertogenbosch: Catharijne Press, 2001.   Limited to 170 copies, of which this is one of the 20 lettered copies bound thus with an extra wood engraving, printed in a different color, 7 x 4.2cm., paper covered boards, slipcase, illustrations on both covers, 47 pages, frontispiece numbered and signed by the artist Gerard Gaudaen, bound by Luce Thurkow, from the collection of Donn W. Sanford.   Oak Knoll Books   303 - 76   2013 $300

The History of Reynard the Fox.   Zuilichem: Catharijne Press, 1991.   Limited to 190 copies, this one of 175 numbered trade copies, 6.6 x 5.1cm., cloth, paper cover label, wood engraving by Pam Reuter, binding by Luce Thurkow, wood engraved frontispiece signed and numbered in pencil, from the collection of Donn W. Sanford.   Oak Knoll Books   303 - 83   2013 $125

In Praise of the Virtuous Woman.   Zuilichem: Catharijne Press, 1994.   Limited to 193 copies, this one of 15 lettered copies, Hebrew characters heightened in gold, 6 x 4cm., white paper covered boards, stamped in gilt, frontispiece, binding by Luce Thurkow, from the collection of Donn W. Sanford.   Oak Knoll Books   303 - 82   2013 $250

Poe, Edgar Allan   1809-1849   *Two Poems.*   Utrecht: Catharijne Press, 1984.   Limited to 100 numbered copies, each with signed and numbered photogravure by Johan de Zoete, 4 x 6.5cm., full leather, vellum cover label on set, bound by Luce Thurkow, from the collection of Donn W. Sanford.   Oak Knoll Books   303 - 87   2013 $200

Swift, Jonathan   1667-1845   *Gulliver's Travels, a Voyage to Lilliput.*   Zuilichem: Catharijne Press, 1995.   Limited to 190 copies, this one of 15 lettered copies, bound thus and with extra suite of the illustrations, hand colored, under passe-partout and placed in a second volume, bound by Luce Thurkow, 6.7 x 4.2cm., paper covered boards, slipcase, from the collection of Donn W. Sanford.   Oak Knoll Books   303 - 89   2013 $275

William Morris, Wallpapers. Zuilichem: Catharijne Press, 1997. Limited to 190 copies, of which this is one of the 15 lettered copies bound thus, and with a separate "wallpaper book" containing an extra suite of the plates in larger format, bound by Luce Thurkow, 11 specimens of wallpaper, 6.6 x 4.3cm., paper covered boards, paper cover label (1st volume); cloth ties (2nd volume), clam shell box covered with reproduction of Morris wallpaper, paper cover label, from the collection of Donn W. Sanford. Oak Knoll Books 303 - 92 2013 $325

Binding – Toovey, James

Bray, Anna Eliza *Life of Thomas Stothard, R. A.* London: John Murray, 1851. First edition, 216 x 171mm., excellent contemporary dark green morocco, handsomely gilt by James Toovey (stamp signed), covers with French fillet border, raised bands, heavily gilt spine compartments featuring scrolling cornerpieces and large ad intricate floral centerpiece, turn-ins densely gilt with botanical tools, marbled endpapers, all edges gilt, frontispiece, engraved titlepage frame and more than 50 illustrations in text; spine evenly faded to pleasing olive brown, covers with just touch of fading and soiling, handful of pages with extensive freckled foxing, trivial to minor foxing in much of the rest of the text, still extremely fresh, scarcely worn and very attractive binding. Phillip J. Pirages 63 - 451 2013 $550

Binding – Tout

Byron, George Gordon Noel, 6th Baron 1788-1824 *Letters and Journals of Lord Byron with Notices of His Life.* London: John Murray, 1830. First edition, 4 volumes, large 4to., half titles, frontispiece, portraits, plates, additional titlepage volume I, occasional light spotting and offsetting, contemporary half red morocco by Tout, little rubbed, spine and corner of volumes III and IV slightly worn, very good, attractive. Jarndyce Antiquarian Booksellers CCIII - 322 2013 £580

Le Sage, Alain Rene 1668-1747 *The Adventures of Gil Blas of Santillana.* Edinburgh: William Paterson, 1886. 3 volumes, 248 x 165mm., quite pleasing three quarter vellum over sturdy textured cloth boards by Tout (stamp signed), flat spines heavily gilt in compartments in antique style featuring large and intricate central fleuron, three brown morocco labels on each spine, marbled endpapers, gilt tops, title vignettes and 21 fine etched plates, including frontispiece by Adolphe Lalauze, large attractive bookplate of Hilda Leyel signed "A M H 1940" in each volume, top corners of volume 1 slightly bumped, turn-ins little spotted (trivial spots and superficial marks elsewhere to covers and spines, particularly to labels, otherwise excellent set, no significant wear, gilt still bright and attractive, slight offsetting from plates but very fine internally. Phillip J. Pirages 63 - 319 2013 $550

Piozzi, Hester Lynch Salusbury Thrale *Mrs. Thrale, afterwards Mrs. Piozzi, a Sketch of Her Life and Passages from Her Diaries, Letters & Other Writings.* London: Seeley and Co., 1891. 206 x 140mm., very attractive contemporary dark blue three quarter morocco by Tout (stamp signed), raised bands, spine lavishly gilt in compartments with central oval medallion containing a flora spray, medallion within a frame of entwined volutes, floral tools and stippling, marbled boards and endpapers, top edge gilt, frontispiece, 8 portraits, bookplate of William Eyres Sloan, very fine in especially pretty binding, only most trivial imperfections. Phillip J. Pirages 63 - 367 2013 $450

Rogers, Samuel *Italy, a Poem. (and) Poems.* London: T. Cadell, 1830. 1834., 197 x 140mm. 2 separately published volumes (though often sold together), quite appealing light tan polished calf by Tout & Sons (stamp signed on verso of front free endpaper), covers with plain gilt rule frame, raised bands, spines richly gilt in compartments filled with fleurons and curls, each backstrip and two red morocco labels (title in second compartment and thin strip with publication information at bottom), gilt turn-ins, marbled endpapers, all edges gilt, 54 fine engraved vignettes, joints and extremities little rubbed, intermittent minor foxing to head margin, otherwise fine, especially clean, fresh and bright, solid, lustrous and attractive bindings. Phillip J. Pirages 63 - 405 2013 $200

Walpole, Horace *Horace Walpole and His Words: Select Passages from His Letters.* London: Seeley and Co. Ltd., 1892. Fourth edition, 206 x 140mm., frontispiece and 7 portraits, very attractive contemporary dark blue three quarter morocco by Tout (stamp signed), raised bands, spine lavishly gilt in compartments with central oval medallion containing a floral spray, medallion within frame of entwined volutes, floral tools and stippling, marbled boards and endpapers, top edge gilt, other edges rough trimmed; spine slightly and evenly sunned to pleasing dark blue green, otherwise very fine, no signs of use inside or out; bookplate of William Eyres Sloan. Phillip J. Pirages 63 - 485 2013 $375

Binding – Tuckett

Wordsworth, William 1770-1850 *Yarrow Revisited and Other Poems.* London: Longman, Rees, Orme, Brown, Green and Longman, 1835. First edition, presentation copy, inscribed by author to Eliza M. Hamilton as a token of affectionate esteem from W. M. Wordsworth on a slip of paper pasted to verso of title and with "From the Author" written on half title by publisher's clerk, erratum slip tipped in, ads discarded, 12mo., slightly later 19th century olive pebble grain morocco by Tuckett ('binder to the Queen'), backstrip panelled and ruled in gilt and infilled with volutes and other tools, lettered in gilt in second compartment, sides with triple gilt fillet borders, inner panel with cornerpieces and central panels of curving lines, all edges gilt, marbled endpapers, booklabel of J. O. Edwards, small scrape to upper board, extremities slightly rubbed, good. Blackwell's Rare Books B174 - 159 2013 £3500

Binding – Walters, Curtis

Poe, Edgar Allan 1809-1849 *Tales.* New York: Wiley and Putnam, 1845. First edition, third printing, octavo, half title, bound by Curtis Walters c. 1910-20 in full brown morocco, original green cloth preserved at rear, joints expert and almost invisible repair, near fine, internally fresh and clean, original chamois-lined leather edged slipcase. David Brass Rare Books, Inc. Holiday 2012 Chapter Five - DB 02101 2013 $9500

Binding – Watkins, T. B.

Mathias, Thomas James *The Pursuit of Literature. (bound with) A Translation of the Passages from Greek, Latin, Italian and French Writers...* London: printed for T. Becket, 1799. 1798. Third edition, 2 volumes in 1, 8vo., lightly spotted, contemporary diced and polished tan calf spine divided by Greek key rolls and lettered gilt direct, other compartments with gilt centrepieces, marbled edges and endpapers, rubbed at extremities, spine sunned, armorial bookplate of Richard Hopton, signed binding by T. B. Watkins/Hereford with his ticket. Unsworths Antiquarian Booksellers 28 - 113 2013 £150

Binding – Werner, Arno

Stevens, Wallace 1879-1955 *Three Academic Pieces. The Realm of Resemblance, Someone Puts a Pineapple Together, Of Ideal Time and Choice.* Cummington: Cummington Press, 1947. First edition, one of 102 copies printed on Worthy Dacian paper and bound thus by Arno Werner out of a total edition of 246 copies, small 8vo., original bright green paper covered hand decorated boards, plain unprinted dust jacket, fine, bright copy in rare dust jacket. James S. Jaffe Rare Books Fall 2013 - 140 2013 $2250

Tate, Allen *The Hovering Fly and Other Essays.* Cummington: Cummington Press, 1949. First edition, one of only 12 copies on Van Gelder paper with original drawing and woodcuts hand colored, this copy specially bound and signed by author and artist, out of a total edition of 245 copies, 8vo., woodcuts by Wightman Williams, full rsusset morocco with inlaid hand colored panel on front cover by Arno Werner, this the binder's copy, signed by Werner "Arno Werner Bookbinder 1949", very fine, half morocco, folding box with Werners booklabel. James S. Jaffe Rare Books Fall 2013 - 36 2013 $15,000

Binding – Western Mail Bindery

Jackson, Charles James *An Illustrated Histo... Plate, Ecclesiastical and Secular.* London: Cour... Limited and B. T. Batsford, 1911. First edition, 2... 343 x 279mm., original dark green half binding of fa... morocco by Western Mail Bindery in Cardiff (with the... et), cloth sides, spines with raised bands, gilt ruled co... ments, gilt titling, top edge gilt, etched frontispiece, 76 p... togravure plates and 1500 other illustrations, titles in red and black, text printed on coated stock, plates printed on high quality thick paper, bookplate of Dorothy Riley Brown in each volume, leather somewhat flaked from joints and extremities, few superficial marks to covers, hinges cracked before half title in each volume, bindings otherwise sound and not without appeal, fine set internally, only trivial defects. Phillip J. Pirages 63 - 439 2013 $175

Binding – Westley, Josiah

Hort, Richard *The Embroidered Banner and Other Marvels.* London: Johna and Daniel A. Darling, 1850. First edition, color frontispiece and plates by Alfred Ashley, 8 pages catalog on smaller paper, 4 pages ads, original olive green cloth by Josiah Westley, gilt centerpiece "Libertad", spine decorated and lettered in gilt, signed JL (designed by John Leighton) some watermarking on front board. Jarndyce Antiquarian Booksellers CCV - 138 2013 £150

Binding – Westleys

Allsop, Thomas *Letters Conversations and Recollections of S. T. Coleridge.* London: Edward Moxon, 1836. Second edition, half title, original dark green cloth by Westleys, spine little worn at head, booklabel of John Johnson. Jarndyce Antiquarian Booksellers CCIII - 558 2013 £40

Bronte, Charlotte 1816-1855 *Villette.* London: Smith, Elder and Co., 1853. First edition, 3 volumes, 12 page catalog (Jan. 1853) volume I, colophon leaf volume III, pale yellow endpapers, small marginal tear to pages 209.210 volume 1, and pages 79/80 and 196 volume II, original dark brown cloth by Westley's and Co., boards blocked in blind, spines blocked in blind and lettered in gilt, some small expert repairs to hinges and tail of volume 1, small pencil inscription of J. J. Brigg, very good. Jarndyce Antiquarian Booksellers CCV - 34 2013 £380

Watson, Joseph *Autumn Leaves.* London?: printed for private circulation, 1859. Half title, photo frontispiece and title vignette, original brown cloth by Westleys and Co., bevelled boards, borders and title in gilt, little rubbed with slight loss to head and tail of spine, all edges gilt, bookplate of Joshua Watson, presentation inscription for Watson from his niece Mary Spence Watson with uncle Fossy's best wishes, recent blue ink notes on leading f.e.p.'s. Jarndyce Antiquarian Booksellers CCV - 282 2013 £450

Binding – Weston, Chris

Bramston, James *The Art of Politicks.* London: printed for Lawton Gilliver, 1729. Variant issue of first edition, 8vo., frontispiece, few light spots, small abrasion to title affecting one letter of imprint, recent quarter calf by Chris Weston, paste paper boards red morocco label lettered vertically. Unsworths Antiquarian Booksellers 28 - 75 2013 £125

Burnet, Gilbert, Bp. of Salisbury 1643-1715 *A Exhortation to Peace and Union. A Sermon at St. Lawrence-Jury at the Election of Lord Mayor of London on the 29th of September 1681.* London: printed for Richard Chiswell, 1681. Small 4to., first and last leaves bit soiled, faint damp mark to upper cover, recent quarter calf by Chris Weston, paste paper boards, red morocco label lettered vertically, contemporary but not Burnet's ink inscription. Unsworths Antiquarian Booksellers 28 - 77 2013 £95

Waterland, Daniel *Scripture Vindicated; In Answer to Book Intituled Christianity as Old as the Creation. Part I-(II).* London: printed for W. Innys, Cambridge: printed for Cornelius Crownfield and John Crownfield, 1730. 2 parts bound as 1, with collective half title, 8vo., few minor spots, lower corner of first leaf worn, plain calf by Chris Weston. Unsworths Antiquarian Booksellers 28 - 138 2013 £150

Binding – Wofsey, Tammy

Wofsey, Tammy *The Pest.* New York: Plotzing Press at Bob Blackburn's Printmaking Workshop, 1998. Artist's book, one of 10 copies, all on Rives BFK paper, each signed and numbered by artist, page size 6 1/2 x 7 x 6.6 inches, 280 pages, 140 double page black and white linoleum cuts, bound by artist accordion fold with pages hinged with Gampi paper with two original linoleum cuts from book inset into green cloth over boards as the ends, housed in custom made black cloth over boards clamshell box (also made by artist), with title in small white paper square lettered in black in center of front panel, clamshell 8 x 8 x 8 inches; there are 10 pages of text printed letterpress starting with five pages at front, including titlepage "The Pest" set in 10 pt. Times New Roman with succeeding pages repeating the title in every increasing point size. Priscilla Juvelis - Rare Books 56 - 39 2013 $4000

Binding – Wood

Lennox, Sarah *The Life and Letters of Lady Sarah Lennox... also a Short Political Sketch of the Years 1760 to 1763 by Henry Fox, 1st Lord Holland.* London: John Murray, 1901. First edition, third printing, 2 volumes, especially attractive contemporary moss green three quarter morocco over lighter green linen by Wood of London (stamp signed), raised bands, spines handsomely gilt in compartments with large central fleuron within a lozenge of small tools and scrolling cornerpieces accented with gilt dots, marbled endpapers, top edge gilt, 30 photogravures of portraits, many by Sir Joshua Reynolds, engraved bookplate of F. Ambrose Clark, leather of spine and edges of boards darkened (as nearly always with green morocco) to olive-brown, offsetting to endpapers from bookplate and turn-in, fine set, the stiffly opening volumes with virtually no signs of use and handsome bindings lustrous and unworn. Phillip J. Pirages 63 - 317 2013 $375

Surtees, Robert Smith 1803-1884 *Jorrocks's Jaunts and Jollities.* London: Rudolph Ackermann Eclipse Sporting Gallery, 1843. Second edition, octavo, hand colored engraved vignette title and 14 hand colored aquatint plates, plates watermarked 1832, handsomely bound by Wood of London circa 1920, full red crushed levant morocco, contemporary covers and spine bound in at end, housed in red cloth slipcase. David Brass Rare Books, Inc. Holiday 2012 Chapter Two - DB 02169 2013 $1500

Binding – Worrall

Gatty, Margaret Scott 1809-1873 *The Book of Sun-Dials.* London: George Bell and Sons, 1900. Fourth edition, folio, frontispiece, additional 8 photographic and engraved plates, numerous black and white illustrations, plates with tissue guards, beautifully bound by Worrall Birmingham in full green morocco, boards double ruled in gilt, single ruled in blind with corner ornaments, spine elaborately stamped and lettered in gilt, gilt dentelles, marbled endpapers, top edge gilt, some toning to tissue guards, about fine. Heritage Book Shop Holiday Catalogue 2012 - 68 2013 $1250

Binding – Zaehnsdorf

The Aldine Poets. London: printed by Charles Whittingham for William Pickering, 1830-1845. Complete series, 53 volumes, 24 frontispiece portraits, especially pretty polished light brown calf, attractively gilt by Zaehnsdorf, stamp signed, covers with gilt double fillet border and gilt Aldine/Pickering anchor centerpiece, raised bands, spines gilt in compartments with scrolling foliate cornerpieces and loping stem centerpiece, surrounded by diamond frame of circlets and tiny stars, each spine with red and green titling label (at bottom) a red date label, elaborately gilt turn-ins, marbled endpapers, all edges gilt, spines uniformly faded to darker brown, a number of small nicks or tiny scuffs to backstrips, slight offsetting from engraved frontispieces, but fine and in many ways an amazing set, joints and remarkably bright covers almost entirely without wear and text pristine.
Phillip J. Pirages   61 - 134   2013 $7800

Barrie, James Matthew 1860-1937 *Peter Pan in Kensington Gardens.* London: Hodder & Stoughton, n.d., 1912. Deluxe edition, one of 50 (?) copies, large quarto, 50 mounted color plates by Arthur Rackham, finely bound by Zaehnsdorf in full red morocco pictorially stamped and lettered gilt to match, original 1906 cover stamping, excellent.
David Brass Rare Books, Inc.   Holiday 2012 Chapter One - Db 00581   2013 $3800

Browning, Robert 1812-1889 *Some Poems by Robert Browning.* Ergany Press, 1904. One of 215 copies on paper (an additional 11 copies printed on vellum), 210 x 134mm., 64 pages, (3) leaves, lovey wood engraved color frontispiece, large decorative initials and device at end, all by Lucien and Esther Pissarro, very fine handsomely gilt and inlaid cordovan crushed morocco by Zaehnsdorf (signed on front turn-in), covers ruled in gilt, inlaid olive green morocco frame decorated with gilt scrolling foliation and inlaid pink morocco roses, raised bands, spine compartments similarly decorated with gilt and inlays, turn-ins gilt with inner toothed roll, ruled borders and foliation, top edge gilt, original paper covers bound in rear, bookplate of John Whiting Friel and Helen Otillie Friel, area under frontispiece with ink inscription dated 1905, now very faded (presumably after an attempt to wash it out?), printed in black and red, very few leaves with quite minor foxing but (setting aside inscription on frontispiece), very fine in splendid binding, especially fresh, bright inside and out.   Phillip J. Pirages 61 - 130   2013 $3500

Clark, Robert *Poems on Golf.* Edinburgh: printed (by Robert Clark) for private circulation, 1867. First edition, 8vo., fine armorial binding of full dark green horizontal ribbed 19th century crushed morocco by Zaehnsdorf (original green cloth covers and spine bound in), gilt Lion rampant in center of both covers, around each of which are 24 gilt thistle badges, spine gilt, raised bands, light green silk moire endpapers and free halves of endpapers, large gilt stamped heraldic devices of Robert Tyndall Hamilton Bruce, all edges gilt, fine copies as here are rarely found.   Howard S. Mott Inc.   262 - 63   2013 $4000

Cooper, Elizabeth *The Muses Library; or a Series of English Poetry, from the Saxons to the reign of King Charles II.* London: printed for J. Wilcox, 1737. First edition, 216 x 140mm., xvi, 400 pages, titlepage with volume number obscured by early ink hatching, especially attractive caramel-colored morocco handsomely gilt by Zaehnsdorf (signed on front turn-in) covers framed in gilt with border and inner panel of French fillets as well as fleuron tool cornerpieces, raised bands, spine densely gilt in compartments with stippled scrolling cornerpieces, center panel with an ornament featuring 8 points and French fillet border as well as small floral centerpiece, elaborately gilt turn-ins, marbled endpapers, top edge gilt, other edges untrimmed, boards with hint of soiling, occasional very light foxing, two leaves at rear with faint dampstain in upper fore margin, one leaf with small, neatly repaired marginal tear, other trivial imperfections, excellent copy, untrimmed text bright, clean and fresh, handsome binding lustrous and generally very pleasing.
Phillip J. Pirages   61 - 129   2013 $1250

Doctor Comicus or the Frolics of Fortune. London: B. Blake, 1825? 210 x 133mm., without printed titlepage, very attractive light tan smooth calf by Sangorski & Sutcliffe/Zahensdorf (stamp signed), corners bordered with French fillet and fleuron cornerpieces, raised bands, spine gilt in compartments featuring decorative bands, scrolling cornerpieces, fleuron centerpiece and small tools, maroon morocco labels, gilt inner dentelles, marbled endpapers, all edges gilt, 12 plates, all colored by hand, bookplate of Robert Marceau, engraved title and two plates little foxed, 3 plates slightly trimmed at fore edge without apparent loss, few leaves with light marginal foxing or soiling, otherwise excellent copy, plates bright and well preserved, leaves clean and fresh, sympathetic binding mint.   Phillip J. Pirages   63 - 460   2013 $400

English Lyrics. London: printed at the Chiswick Press for Kegan Paul, Trench & Co., 1883. First edition, one of 50 large paper copies, this #32, 206 x 130mm., fine turn-of-the-century Hazel brown crushed morocco, very elaborately gilt by Zaehnsdorf (stamp signed on front turn-in, oval blindstamp on rear pastedown), covers richly gilt with very wide floral border featuring many tendrils and small tools, border enclosing panel filled with alternating rows of floral sprigs and leaves (tiny stars in between), raised bands, spine compartments gilt with either floral bouquet or rows of leaves and flowers, densely gilt turn-ins, gray silk endleaves, top edge gilt, other edges untrimmed, armorial bookplate of Mary Louise Curtis Bok, half title with pencilled note "Wedding present to M.L.C./from Charles Scribner October 1896", (spine just slightly sunned toward a darker brown, front joint and very top and bottom of back joint little worn, with flaking and thin cracks, but no looseness), corners slightly rubbed, still especially attractive with lovely binding with glistening covers and beautifully printed text pristine.
Phillip J. Pirages   63 - 65   2013 $1250

FINE BINDINGS

Estienne, Henri 1528-1598 *Traicte de la Conformite du Langage Francois avec le Grec, Divise en Trio Liures dont les Deux Premiers Traictent des Manieres de Parler Conformes le Troisieme...* Paris: Robert Estienne, 1569. First Paris edition, small 8vo., all edges gilt, Zaehnsdorf style full brown morocco, blind ruled covers and spine, gilt stamped ornaments, raised bands, gilt stamped title, gilt stamped turn-ins, 19th century leather armorial bookplate of Marigues de Champ-Repus, fine.   Jeff Weber Rare Books   171 - 118   2013 $2500

The Four Gospels of the Lord Jesus Christ According to the Authorized Version of King James I. Wellingborough: September Press, 1988. 14/80 copies of an edition of 600 printed on Saunders' mouldmade paper, afterword printed using monotype Gill Sans Light on Mohawk Superfine Smooth Softwhite paper, supplemented with reproductions of 4 photos, folio, original tan morocco by Zaehnsdorf, gilt lettered black morocco label, "Cockerel" press device blind-stamped on front, single gilt rule inner borders, top edge gilt, rough trimmed, felt lined black cloth, slipcase, fine. Blackwell's Rare Books   B174 - 337   2013   £1500

Gray, Thomas 1716-1771 *An Elegy Wrote in a Country Church Yard.* London: for R. Dodsley and sold by M. Cooper, 1751. First edition, 4to., 11 pages, full black crushed levant morocco by Zaehnsdorf (very lightly rubbed at extremities), fine with no loss of punched-through types, bookplates.   Joseph J. Felcone Inc.   English and American Literature to 1800 - 16   2013 $15,000

Gronow, Rees Howell *The Reminiscences and Recollections of Captain Gronow...* London: printed by Ballantyne and Co. for C. Nimmo, 1889. One of 870 copies printed for England and America with 25 plates in two states (this copy #22), 268 x 169mm., 2 volumes, 50 plates (comprising 25 images, each in two states; one proofs before letters done on plate paper, the other on Whatman paper titled and hand colored), as called for, a large paper copy; extremely handsome red crushed morocco, ornately gilt by Zaehnsdorf (stamp-signed on front turn-ins and with special oval gilt stamp on rear pastedowns), cover with wide filigree frame with massed densely scrolling fleurons, raised bands, unevenly spaced in the continental style, forming five compartments, second and two small bottom compartments with titling, top and elongated middle compartment decorated with intricate gilt in same way as boards, broad inner gilt dentelles, marbled endpapers (with thickly gilt lining between dentelles and pastedowns), top edge gilt, other edges untrimmed, engraved bookplate of John Raymond Danson, couple of very faint scratches on back cover volume II, just hint of rubbing at top and bottom of lower joint of same volume, especially fine in gloriously decorated morocco, text virtually pristine and bindings extremely lustrous and scarce worn.   Phillip J. Pirages   63 - 66   2013 $1900

Hamilton, Anthony 1646-1720 *Memoirs of Count Grammont.* London and Edinburgh: printed by Jas. Ballantyne & Co. for William Miller and James Carpenter, 1811. 2 volumes, 235 x 146mm., with a total of 143 engraved portraits, including 64 called for, and extra illustrated with 79 additional portraits apparently taken from 1793 edition of the work inserted specially in this copy, large paper copy, splendid crimson straight grain morocco, elegantly and attractively gilt by Zaehnsdorf (stamp signed and dated 1900 on front turn-ins), covers gilt with double ruled border enclosing fleurons and floral sprays, large fleuron cornerpieces accented with circlets and dots, broad raised bands adorned with six gilt rules, spine compartments with filigreen frames echoing the cover decoration, densely gilt filigree turn-ins, marbled endpapers, top edge gilt, other edges untrimmed, noticeable offsetting from portraits whenever there is a facing text page (as opposed to verso of another plate) and rather conspicuous in about half dozen cases, otherwise, extremely fine, text very fresh and clean, beautiful, unworn bindings, extraordinarily bright.   Phillip J. Pirages   61 - 131   2013 $1600

Hardy, Thomas 1840-1928 *The Works of Thomas Hardy in Prose and Verse.* London: Macmillan and Co., 1912-1913. 21 volumes, octavo, photogravure frontispieces and double page maps, bound by Zaehnsdorf in 1914, full purple calf, gilt triple border on covers, spines decoratively paneled in gilt, four red morocco floral onlays and purple calf, gilt triple rule, border on covers, spines decoratively paneled in gilt, four red morocco floral onlays and three brown morocco lettering labels, top edge gilt, marbled endpapers, gilt dentelles, bit of rubbing to some board edges and head and tail of few spines, overall near fine, very attractive.   Heritage Book Shop   Holiday Catalogue 2012 - 73   2013 $6000

Jami *Salaman and Absal: an Allegory.* London: J. W. Parker and Son, 1856. First edition, 213 x 148mm., xvi, 84 pages, frontispiece; lovely early 20th century chestnut brown morocco handsomely gilt by Zaehnsdorf (stamp signed), covers with multiple-rule frame and central panel containing 25 gilt flowers in rows, each flower with long curving leafy stem, background accented with tiny gilt dots and crescents, raised bands, spine gilt in compartments featuring alternating gilt blossom and twining vines, gilt turn-ins, light brown silk endleaves, original blue paper wrappers bound in at rear, slightly rubbed brown morocco felt lined pull-off case with raised bands and gilt title, flyleaf with offset image of leather bookplate of bookplate of Charles Kalbfleisch, bookplate no longer present, trial marginal soiling or dots of foxing on handful of leaves, else especially fine, text fresh and smooth, margins considerably more than ample, glittering decorative binding unworn and especially lustrous.   Phillip J. Pirages   61 - 132   2013 $4500

Joyce, James 1882-1941 *Ulysses.* London: John Lane, the Bodley Head, 1936. First English edition printed in England, one of 900 numbered copies, printed on Japon vellum, out of a total edition of 1000 copies, this being number 748, bound by Zaehnsdorf (stamp signed in gilt on front turn-in) in full green morocco, front cover decoratively stamped in gilt with a Homeric bow (matching original design), spine lettered gilt in compartments, board edges ruled in gilt, turn-ins decoratively tooled in gilt, top edge gilt, others uncut, marbled endpapers, fine. Heritage Book Shop Holiday Catalogue 2012 - 85 2013 $4000

Keats, John 1795-1821 *Endymion: a Poetic Romance.* London: printed for Taylor and Hessey, 1818. First edition, 218 x 135mm., 6 p.l., 207 pages, bound without leaf of ads at back; sumptuous chocolate brown crushed morocco, elaborately gilt and inlaid by Zaehnsdorf (signed on front turn-in and with stamped oval, normally marking firm's best work), covers with gilt ruled and inlaid frames of ochre and maroon morocco, central panel intricately diapered with curving ochre acanthus leaves forming original compartments containing maroon fleuron, raised bands, maroon framed compartments with inlaid ochre and maroon centerpiece, brown morocco doublures and endleaves, doublures continuing use of maroon and ochre inlays to form a frame entwined with sinous leafy vine sprouting berries, all edges gilt, slightly frayed, grey cloth dust jacket with gilt titling, faint foxing on few leaves near back, otherwise only most trivial imperfections, extremely fine, text clean and mostly bright, beautiful binding in perfect condition, bookplate of Francis Kettaneh. Phillip J. Pirages 61 - 133 2013 $9500

Lamb, Charles 1775-1834 *Poetry for Children.* London: The Leadenhall Press, 1892. One of 112 copies, signed by press founder, Andrew White Tuer (this copy #2), 157 x 99mm., 2 volumes, charming contemporary batik textured calf by Zaehnsdorf (stamp-signed in gilt on front turn-in), covers gilt with fillets and dogtooth roll border, upper cover with thick festooned garland of fruit and leaves, flat spines divided into panels by plain and decorative rules, densely gilt turn-ins, marbled endpapers, top edge gilt, each volume with engraved frontispiece, engraved bookplate of A. Edward Newton of Oak Knoll with (loose) bookplate of H. Marion Soliday, minor offsetting from frontispieces, just vaguest hint of rubbing to extremities, but very fine, bindings bright and scarcely worn, text with virtually no signs of use. Phillip J. Pirages 63 - 67 2013 $1500

Mortimer, Alfred *S(t.) Mark's Church Philadelphia and its Lady Chapel with an Account of Its History and Treasures.* New York: privately printed by the De Vinne Press, 1909. One of 400 copies, 300 x 235mm., 71 pages, 127 photo plates, 20 of these in color, all with captioned tissues, remarkably animated gothic style black morocco, very elaborately decorated gilt and blind by Zaehnsdorf (stamp signed on front turn-in), covers with ornate frames comprised of 16 compartments, 8 of these intricately gilt featuring repeating Maltese crosses, rose windows and flame design, other 8 with blindstamp of one of the four evangelists (at corners), or else the Salvator, frame enclosing large central panel stamp within gilt frame enclosing large central panel stamp within gilt frame, that on upper cover depicting St. Mark with his lion and that on lower cover showing Virgin Mary holding lily, raised bands, spine compartments with central blindstamped fleuron flanked by gilt rules and several small gilt stamps, turn-ins repeating gilt elements in cover frames, cream color watered silk endleaves, all edges gilt, just hint of rubbing to corners, otherwise choice copy. Phillip J. Pirages 63 - 68 2013 $1900

Rivers, John *Greuze and His Models.* London: Hutchinson & Co., 1912. First edition, 225 x 171mm., 9 p.l., including frontispiece, 282 pages, fine contemporary emerald green crushed morocco for Hatchards (done according to pencilled note at front, by Zaehnsdorf), covers gilt in Arts and Crafts design of interlocking plain rule frames with floral stamps at corners and gilt titling flanked by leaves and berries, raised bands, spine gilt in double ruled compartments with central floral sprig and three circles in each corner, gilt ruled turn-ins, gray endpapers, all edges gilt, extra engraved titlepage and 44 plates, 40 with tissue guards, spine faintly sunned to pleasing slightly darker green front free endpaper with two small very faint vestiges of tape, quite fine, handsomely bound in unworn, clean and fresh, bright inside and out. Phillip J. Pirages 63 - 69 2013 $400

Shakespeare, William 1564-1616 *The Works.* London: Macmillan And Co., 1902-1905. Cambridge Edition, 235 x 159mm., 9 volumes, very appealing olive brown half morocco over green linen by Zaehnsdorf (stamp-signed on verso of front free endpaper), raised bands, spines gilt in double ruled compartments with dotted inner frame and floral cornerpieces as well as large central ornament formed by crossed swords, a crown and a garland, marbled endpapers, top edges gilt, other rough trimmed, spines uniformly sunned to a pleasing honey brown, first volume with shallow chip at top of spine with one band little abraded, otherwise only trivial defects, bindings in all other ways showing only very minor signs of use and text quite clan and fresh. Phillip J. Pirages 63 - 435 2013 $2500

Taylor, Deems *Walt Disney's Fantasia.* New York: Simon and Schuster, 1940. First edition, folio, profusely illustrated in color and black and white, including 16 tipped in color illustrations, titlepage printed in red, black and blue, bound by Zaehnsdorf, circa 1977 for E. Joseph, full brown crushed levant morocco, front cover and smooth spine lettered in gilt after original binding lettering, board edges ruled gilt, turn-ins decoratively tooled in gilt, pale gray watered silk doublures and liners, all edges gilt, very fine.   David Brass Rare Books, Inc.   Holiday 2012 Chapter One - DV00420   2013 $1800

Tennyson, the Brothers *Poems by Two Brothers.* London: printed by R. and R. Clark; Edinburgh for Macmillan and Co., 1893. Large paper limited edition, 10 pages of facsimiles at end, royal 8vo., contemporary red morocco by Zaehnsdorf with their exhibition stamp, single gilt fillet borders on sides enclosing an inner border of leafy tendrils, interstices filled with gilt dots, area widening at foot and incorporating 3 onlaid flower heads in darker red, both covers lettered gilt in fancy 'Japanese' style, spine similarly decorated but conventionally lettered, gilt inner dentelles, top edge gilt, others uncut, short cracked at head of upper joint, very good.   Blackwell's Rare Books   B174 - 13   2013   £1500

Uzanne, Octave *Son Altesse, La Femme.* Paris: A. Quantin, 1885. First edition, one of 100 special large paper copies on Japon, 292 x 216mm, vignette on title, small illustrations or vignettes on 50 text pages, 11 vignette borders or headpieces (3 of them in color, 10 of them in one or two extra states) and 10 color plates, each in two states (before and after letters), beautifully and elaborately gilt contemporary blue-gray crushed morocco by Zaehnsdorf (signed on front turn-in), covers framed with single rule around very broad and intricate floral border of many leaves, blossoms and tendrils enclosing central field of rows of alternating flower and small stars, raised bands, spine compartments similarly decorated, very handsome densely gilt inner dentelles, marbled endpapers, top edge gilt, other edges untrimmed, original paper and silk materials bound in; armorial bookplate of Sir David Salomons, spine slightly and uniformly faded, one inch cut in lower margin of one leaf, else extremely fine and beautifully bound set.   Phillip J. Pirages   61 - 135   2013 $2500

Westall, William *Picturesque Tour of the Thames.* London: R. Ackermann, 1828. First edition, first issue plates, large paper copy, with two spots of discoloration in sky on Twickenham plate, folio, 24 hand colored aquatint plates, 2 aquatint vignettes and double page engraved map laid down on linen, elegantly bound by Zaehnsdorf in full crimson crushed morocco, internally pristine, very scarce in large paper format.   David Brass Rare Books, Inc. Holiday 2012 Chapter Two - DB 02070   2013 $12,500

Whitman, Walt 1819-1892 *Two Rivulets.* Camden: 1876. First edition, first printing of only 100 copies, 8vo., signed and dated by author on frontispiece (albumen photo of author), near fine, in fine Sangorski & Sutcliffe/Zaehnsdorf green full morocco leather with gilt lettering and rules on spine which is in 6 compartments, custom marbled paper covered, lined slipcase.   By the Book, L. C.   36 - 61   2013 $6500

Binding – Zahn, Otto

Stith, William *A History of the First Discovery and Settlement of Virginia.* Williamsburg: printed by William Parks, 1747. First edition, third issue possibly printed in 1753, 8vo., polished crimson morocco (finely rebacked, old back laid down), gilt ruled covers, spine elaborately gilt, wide inner gilt crimson borders, marbled endpapers, signed "Toof & Co./Zahn", fine copy in fine signed binding by Otto Zahn (1857-1928), signature on endpaper of Massachusetts politician Gaspar G. Bacon (1886-1947).   Howard S. Mott Inc.   262 - 142   2013 $8500

Fore-edge Paintings

Fore-edge – 1809

Vergilius Maro, Publius (Works). *P. Virgilius Maro: in Usum Scholarum/ Ad Novissimam Heynii Editionem Exactus.* Londini: Imprensis J. Johnson et al, 1809. 250 x 147mm., 2 p.l., 700 pages, handsome contemporary navy blue straight grain morocco, densely gilt, covers with thick and thin gilt rule border and large central laurel wreath, that on front with Latin motto "Honoris Causa", that on rear with name Thomas T. Churton and date 1817, raised bands, spine lavishly gilt in compartments filled with foliage and small tools emanating from a central fleuron gilt titling and turn-ins, all edges gilt, with splendid later painting of Mount Etna on the Fore Edge, recent plush lined folding cloth box with gilt spine titling, ink stamp of Bolton Public Library on verso of title and first page of text, corners slightly bumped, boards little faded, first two gatherings mildly foxed, isolated dust spots or faint freckled foxing, still especially attractive copy, handsome binding virtually unworn, text clean and smooth and unusual fore-edge painting, very well preserved. Phillip J. Pirages   63 - 192   2013 $2900

Fore-edge – 1810

Mason, James *Comelia and Alcestis: Two Operas.* London: printed for T. Payne, 1810. First edition, 195 x 125mm., harmless contemporary purple straight grain morocco, covers with gilt fillet border, raised bands flanked by plain gilt rules, gilt titling, all edges gilt, with excellent later fore-edge painting of Acropolis, joints bit rubbed and flaked, boards little stained and rather faded, rear board with two small abraded patches, otherwise excellent copy, clean and fresh internally in solid, inoffensive binding, with vividly colored painting in fine condition.   Phillip J. Pirages   63 - 188   2013 $1100

Scott, Walter   1771-1832 *Minstrelsy of the Scottish Border.* Edinburgh: printed by J. Ballantyne and Co., 1810. Fourth edition, second (Large Paper) impression, 240 x 145mm., pleasing contemporary black straight grain morocco, covers with gilt floral frame enclosing central panel with blindstamped thistle cornerpieces, raised bands, spines heavily gilt in compartments with much swirling foliate, gilt turn-ins, marbled endpapers, all edges gilt, volume I with attractive fore-edge painting of the Mercat Cross in Melrose, Roxburghshire; pastedown volumes II and III with engraved bookplate of W. J. Denison, volume I with evidence of bookplate removal, copy of engraving of Boston Church, Lancashire laid in at rear volume II, joints and extremities somewhat rubbed, boards bit marked and abraded, minor foxing here and there in text, 9 gatherings with faint overall browning due to poor quality paper, still excellent set, leaves clean, once quite dazzling bindings still sound and pleasing, fore edge painting well preserved.   Phillip J. Pirages   63 - 191   2013 $1250

Fore-edge – 1820

Milman, Henry Hart *The Fall of Jerusalem: a Dramatic Poem.* London: John Murray, 1820. New edition, 222 x 140mm., attractive contemporary crimson straight grain morocco, gilt covers with wide gilt dentelles comprising closely spaced palmettes, flat spine in gilt compartments formed by three thin rules and decorated in roman style, scrolling foliate cornerpieces and charming floral centerpiece incorporating morocco onlaid circle, turn-ins with gilt decoration echoing outer dentelles, all edges gilt, with very fine fore-edge painting of Monk Soham in Suffolk, titlepage with signature of E. A. Majendie, dated May 1839. corners quite worn, spine ends very slightly chipped, joints rather flaked, spine somewhat darkened, few marks on front board, binding still quite solid with bright covers, narrow faint dampstain along fore edge throughout (probably related to the process of painting), first half of text with variable foxing, but no major problems internally, leaves still fresh with ample margins.   Phillip J. Pirages   63 - 189   2013 $1250

Fore-edge – 1822

Scott, Walter   1771-1832 *The Lady in the Lake.* Edinburgh: printed for Arch. Constable and Co., 1822. 2 volumes (volumes IV and V of the Poetical Works of Sir Walter Scott), each volume with fore-edge painting, volume IV with fore-edge painting of Craigmiller Castle, and volume V with fore-edge painting of Loch Leven Castle; full navy blue straight grain morocco, boards stamped with vignette in gilt of a countryside scene and paneled in blind, spine stamped and lettered gilt, all edges gilt, blue drab endpapers bit of foxing and dampstaining, mainly to blank prelims and not affecting fore-edge, overall very good.   Heritage Book Shop   Holiday Catalogue 2012 - 64   2013 $1000

Fore-edge – 1824

Moore, Thomas *Lalla Rookh, an Oriental Romance.* London: Longman, Hurst, Rees, Orme, Brown and Green, 1824. 218 x 136mm., 2 pl., 397, (1) pages, very pleasing contemporary midnight blue crushed morocco attractively gilt, covers with fillet borders and delicate inner frame, wide raised bands decorated with horizontal gilt fillets and floral tool terminations, spine gilt in compartments featuring unusual obliquely oriented quatrefoil ornament, gilt titling and turn-ins, all edges gilt, with fine later(?) fore-edge painting of an animated London street scene, bookplate of Oscar Ehrhardt Lancaster, touch of rubbing to joints and extremities (but this successfully masked with dye), chalky endpapers a bit blotchy from chemical reaction, slight separation and discoloration at hinge before title leaf, very few trivial marginal spots, still excellent copy, leaves quite clean, fresh and smooth, original decorative binding bright and without any significant wear and painting very well preserved. Phillip J. Pirages   61 - 53   2013 $1250

Fore-edge – 1826

Smith, Horace   1779-1849 *Brambletye House; or Cavaliers and Roundheads.*   London: Henry Collins, 1826. Third edition, 3 volumes, 191 x 12mm., lavishly gilt contemporary olive green straight grain morocco, covers divided into three square panels at top and bottom of an elongated panel at right and left, these panels densely gilt with repeated versions of a large stamp formed by a floral cross radiating oak leaves, central panel with gilt rule frame featuring spiral cornerpieces decorated with acanthus leaves and flowers, raised bands, spine compartments heavily gilt repeating fleuron stamps used on covers, gilt turn-ins, marble endpapers, all edges gilt; each volume with handsome fore-edge painting of a picturesque location important to plot of the novel; engraved bookplate of Emily Lynch Lowe (NY artist), extremities and joints slightly rubbed (but well masked with dye), occasional minor foxing or stains, really excellent set, remarkably decorative bindings lustrous and most appealing, text clean and fresh, expert fore-edge paintings in fine condition.   Phillip J. Pirages   61 - 55   2013 $3500

Fore-edge – 1827

Bible. English - 1827 *The Comprehensive Bible containing the Old and New Testaments.*   London: printed for Samuel Bagster, 1827.   330 x 250mm., excellent contemporary black pebble grain morocco, handsomely gilt, covers with floral frame enclosing central panel featuring scrolling cornerpiece compartments and, at center, intricate elongated ornament, wide raised bands with multiple gilt rules and floral endpieces, spine panels tooled gilt, floral and leaf ornaments, gilt titling and turn-ins, all edges gilt (neat older repairs to head and tail of joints); with bustling modern fore-edge painting by Martin Frost, showing flotilla of vessels on Thames with St. Paul's Cathedral in background; large gilt presentation bookplate "Tribute of Respect from Teachers of Mosely Street Sabbath School, Manchester, to their kind and generous friend James Kershaw, Esq. June 28 1838", joints little worn, corners and extremities bit rubbed, one tiny gouge to upper cover, otherwise fine, ornate binding entirely solid and generally well preserved and text exceptionally clean, fresh and smooth.   Phillip J. Pirages   61 - 56   2013 $3500

Gilpin, Joshua *Twenty-One Discourses Delivered in the Parish Church of Wrockwardine, in the County of Salop.*   London: John Hatchard and Son, 1827.   First edition, 219 x 133mm., appealing contemporary red straight grain morocco, covers with gilt ruled border and small sunburst cornerpieces, raised bands flanked by plain and decorative gilt rules, turn-ins with decorative gilt roll, marbled endpapers, all edges gilt, front joint very expertly renewed, very accomplished fore-edge painting of West Gate, Canterbury, flyleaf facing titlepage with faint but readable offset of the (backward) text of a previously tipped in presentation letter from author, corners bit bruised, spine little dried, leather slightly marked and soiled, expertly repaired binding sound and attractive, lustrous covers, 2 inch horizontal tear to front endpaper, top edge gilt bit soiled, text remarkably clean, bright and fresh.   Phillip J. Pirages   63 - 187   2013 $1250

Fore-edge – 1828

Moore, Thomas *Lalla Rookh, an Oriental Romance.*   London: Longman, Rees Orme, Brown & Green, 1828. 165 x 99mm., 2 p.l., 376 pages, extra engraved titlepage with vignette and 3 engraved plates after designs by Richard Westall; quite attractive contemporary dark green straight grain morocco, ornately gilt covers with 13 gilt or blind (mostly gilt) rules and frames (including elegant palmette frame), tulip cornerpieces at board edges and scrolling foliate cornerpieces closer in, central panel with large and elaborate lyre, raised bands, spine gilt in compartments with foliate cornerpieces and central lyre surrounded by small tools, densely gilt turn-ins, all edges gilt, gauffered in diapered pattern; with fine fore-edge painting of an oriental landscape, very surprisingly hidden beneath gauffered edge; spine evenly sunned to softer green, just hint of wear to joints and extremities, minor offsetting from mild foxing to plates, otherwise fine, binding sound and pleasing, text quite clean, fresh and bright and fore-edge painting well preserved.   Phillip J. Pirages   61 - 57   2013 $1750

Fore-edge – 1851

Watts, Alaric *Lyrics of the Heart: with Other Poems.* London: Longman, Brown, Green and Longmans, 1851. First edition, 211 x 132mm., superb late 19th century olive brown crushed morocco gilt and inlaid by Fazakerley (stamp signed on front turn-in), covers with frames of gilt rules, dots and inlaid tan morocco, central panel of upper cover with inlaid red morocco rectangle emblazoned with title gilt at head, below it a large topiary-shaped, symmetrical design in inlaid morocco and gilt tooling, incorporating 34 heart shaped green leaves on curling hairline stems as well as five lotus blossoms with lavender petals and inverted red heart centers (lower cover with smaller version of same inlaid elements inside plain ruled panel), raised bands, gilt spine compartments continuing same design (each with four inlaid leaf cornerpieces and central lotus flower), turn-ins with gilt and dot frames and lotus and leaf cornerpieces, ivory silk endleaves, marbled flyleaves, edges gilt and elaborately gauffered with deep gouging (in similar floral pattern), fore edge with three exquisitely painted scenes, within pointed frames, these vignettes taken from illustrations appearing within book, felt lined slipcase; with 41 engraved headpieces, as called for, engraved bookplate of Rodman Wanamaker, spine and front board sunned to pleasing uniform tan (as almost always with this color of morocco), occasional minor foxing, more prominent on first and last gatherings), still extremely fine, lovely, morocco lustrous and without perceptible wear, edges with particularly brilliant gilding, 3 painted fore-edge vignettes in perfect condition. Phillip J. Pirages   61 - 79   2013 $12,500

Fore-edge – 1853

White, Henry Kirke *The Poetical Works of Henry Kirke White.* London: Charles Whittingham for William Pickering, 1853. 168 x 105mm., lviii, 252 pages, elegant contemporary dark green morocco inlaid, embossed and elaborately gilt, each cover with broad inlaid ochre morocco frame intricately gilt, large central mandorla of heavily embossed and gilt morocco of same color (both frame and centerpiece highlighted with red painted rules, raised bands, spine gilt in compartments framed by plain and decorative gilt rules, floral centerpiece and lancet cornerpieces richly gilt turn-ins, cream colored watered silk endleaves, all edges gilt, pleasing fore-edge painting of Nottingham Castle; engraved portrait and printer's anchor device on titlepage, pencilled inscription to Bessie Carey from Walter Shipper dated 13 October 1868, pastedown with morocco bookplate of Estelle Doheny, bookplate of Edward Laurence Doheny, bookplate of Carrie Estelle Doheny, bookplate of Dorothy Jayne Pedrini Shea; hint of wear to joints and corners, red paint bit rubbed with minor loss, minor foxing to portrait and titlepage, other trivial imperfections, but excellent copy, handsome binding solid and lustrous, text clean and fresh, fore-edge painting very well preserved.   Phillip J. Pirages   63 - 193   2013 $1100

Fore-edge – 1880

Eliot, George, Pseud. 1819-1880 *Romola.* London: Smith Elder and Co., 1880.   One of 1000 copies (this being #57), 2 volumes, 265 x 180mm., remarkable contemporary honey brown crushed morocco by Fazakerley (stamp signed on front turn-in), upper cover of one volume with ornate gilt monogram of "MMK", the other front cover with monogram of "NDK", spines with raised bands and gilt titling, splendid brown morocco doublures elaborately tooled in gilt featuring scalloped French fillet frame incorporating large floral cornerpieces and enclosing exuberantly swirling flowering vines emerging from a Greek urn at foot, brown watered silk endleaves, edges gilt and ornately gauffered in bold strapwork pattern on stippled ground, each volume with 3 lovely and delicate fore-edge paintings the ones at head and tail of each fore-edge being lozenge-shaped views (measuring approximately 25 x 30 mm across) and larger rectangular painting at center (measuring approximately 80 x 45mm), all depicting finely painted scenes from book; 24 engraved plates, mounted plates after Sir Frederick Leighton, plus 13 smaller engravings mounted in text as called for, flyleaf of each volume with lovely calligraphic manuscript inscription of quote from book, half title of volume 1 with ink ownership inscription of Jean Stewart Russell dated 1902; spine faintly and evenly sunned, plates bit spotted (from mounting glue?), otherwise superb copy, text clean, fresh and bright, margins especially ample, bindings lustrous and unworn, fore edges richly painted and glittering with particularly bright gold.   Phillip J. Pirages   61 - 78   2013 $16,000

Fore-edge – 1895

Oliphant, Margaret Oliphant Wilson 1828-1897 *Makers of Modern Rome.* London and New York: Macmillan and Co., 1895. 222 x 154mm., handsome contemporary red crushed morocco gilt by Howell of Liverpool (stamp signed), covers with gilt fillet border and triple fillet framed central panel with ornate fleur-de-lys cornerpieces, raised bands, spine attractively gilt in compartments with fleur-de-lys centerpiece within lozenge of small tools and with scrolling cornerpieces, densely gilt turn-ins, all edges gilt, pleasing later fore-edge painting of the eternal city, signed with cypher formed by initials "A" and "V", with 25 full page illustrations and numerous illustrations in text, slight rubbing to joints, lower inner corner with faint arching dampstain extending into part of bottom four lines of text, very few tiny dots of foxing, otherwise fine, attractive decorative binding bright, text fresh and clean, painting very well preserved.   Phillip J. Pirages   63 - 190   2013 $650

ISBN-13: 978-1-57302-853-0
ISBN-10: 1-57302-853-3